# ENVIRONMENTAL LAW AND POLICY: NATURE, LAW, AND SOCIETY

HEILMAN

Zygmunt J.B. Plater
*Boston College Law School*

Robert H. Abrams
*Wayne State University Law School*

William Goldfarb
*Rutgers University*

Robert L. Graham, Esq.
*Jenner & Block, Chicago*

AMERICAN CASEBOOK SERIES®

ST. PAUL, MINNESOTA

**Second Edition, 1998**

 TEXT PRINTED ON 10% POST
CONSUMER RECYCLED PAPER

This book was designed and produced by Michael Kitchen of PixelAntics, An Electronic
Design and Publication Studio, Ann Arbor, Michigan. The design and layouts were created
directly from the authors' word processing files; the entire book was created on personal
computers from start to finish, with camera-ready pages and artwork provided to the pub-
lisher from the designer's files. The book is set in the Trump Mediaeval type face.

## DEDICATION


To our families

and to all who act to protect this fragile planet.

# Foreword

*Joseph L. Sax*

In introducing a 1986 symposium on environmental law I observed that the subject, born perhaps twenty years earlier, had changed dramatically in that short span. Despite the predictions of some observers that the environmental movement and environmental law would be passing fads, the tide was racing the other way. I wrote that, far from fading away, environmental law had become institutionalized, an accepted and significant enterprise both for government and for attorneys.[1]

Now, a half-dozen years later, it seems more like a flood, challenging our ability to assimilate its force and volume. There is so much environmental law that few academics still try to focus on the entire field.

A survey of environmental law teachers[2] that I conducted in 1989 revealed that many of us feel that our broader goals as teachers are no longer being met in the basic environmental law course. Massive legislative interventions in the pollution control field have seemed to call forth an inordinate focus on statutory detail while broader perspectives on the subject recede. Rich and exciting cognate areas like natural resources management, land use, and international issues are shunted to the side or ignored totally.

*Environmental Law and Policy: Nature, Law, and Society* can be seen as the first "second generation" environmental law book. Its major teaching premise is that environmental law will continue to grow and evolve. By employing a legal process orientation, the book responds to the desire to teach broadly without sacrificing attention to regulatory detail. By breaking down statutes into categories that reflect their underlying regulatory technique, this book also makes teaching statutory analysis a more fruitful endeavor. Students are taught about the different ways in which statutes address environmental problems, including the strengths and weaknesses of each generic statutory type. Beyond simplifying the task of teaching the statutory portions of the course, this approach insures that the student's knowledge does not become obsolete as statutes and regulations are amended and altered.

This book captures the diversity that is a hallmark of contemporary environmental law. The staples are, of course, present, including materials on air and

---

Professor Sax is the James H. House and Hiram H. Hurd Professor of Environmental Regulation, University of California, Berkeley School of Law.

1. Sax, Introduction to Environmental Law Symposium, 19 J. Law Reform 797 (1986).
2. Sax, Environmental Law in the Law Schools: What We Teach and How We Feel About It, 19 ELR 10251 (1989).

water pollution control, toxic torts and other common law approaches, conflicts between private and public rights, and the procedures of the administrative state. Beyond that, the volume also addresses the "hot" topical areas of risk assessment, regulation of toxics, and hazardous materials. Still other important issues, like public trust law, economic incentives to environmental improvement, endangered species protection, alternative dispute resolution, and international law have their own chapters. The book seriously addresses the role citizens play in environmental decision making.

This is a challenging book designed in response to a challenging subject matter. I am confident that it will help make teaching environmental law as enjoyable and rewarding as it was in the early days.

# Summary Table of Contents

## PART ONE: THE LEGAL PROCESS OF ENVIRONMENTAL LAW

### Chapter 1
### ANALYTIC THEMES IN THE LEGAL PROCESS
### OF ENVIRONMENTAL LAW

### Chapter 2
### ECONOMICS AND RISK MANAGEMENT AS COMPONENTS OF
### ENVIRONMENTAL POLICY MAKING

### Chapter 3
### THE COMMON LAW IN MODERN ENVIRONMENTAL LAW:
### NON-STATUTORY CAUSES OF ACTION

# Table of Contents

## Chapter 4
## THE SPECIAL CHALLENGES OF TOXIC TORT LITIGATION

## Chapter 7
## THE ADMINISTRATIVE LAW OF ENVIRONMENTAL LAW

**PART FIVE: COMPLIANCE, ENFORCEMENT, AND DISPUTE RESOLUTION MECHANISMS**

## Chapter 20
### EVOLVING PATTERNS OF ENFORCEMENT AND COMPLIANCE

---

## REFERENCE

# AUTHORS' PREFACE

"When we try to pick out anything by itself, we find it hitched to everything else in the universe," John Muir, founder of the Sierra Club, once said.[1] Indeed, "Everything is connected to everything else" is the First Law of Ecology. This is depressing news for anyone designing a coursebook on environmental law. It means that it is impossible to capture in one book a field that ultimately takes on the entire planet as its subject matter.

So this is primarily a book about environmental law. Environmental law necessarily includes environmental science, environmental economics, and environmental policy as essential elements of its analysis. Even so, environmental law itself has become so extensive and complex that courses in the subject run the risk of bogging down, a danger that has encouraged us to use a different approach to organizing the field.

Professor Joseph Sax, a pioneer in the teaching of environmental law, described the exponential expansion of the environmental law field as a constant challenge to those who attempt to teach it. Sax reported his findings after polling more than one hundred colleagues.[2]

> The subject seems to have overwhelmed us. Virtually every law teacher — however broad his or her overlook — wants to introduce students to the specific materials in the field, and to provide some experience and familiarity with it. Yet, every such attempt is an encounter with statutes of numbing complexity and detail.... David Getches of the University of Colorado observes that we have more and more "environmental artillery": more lawyers working on problems that seem increasingly sophisticated, with ever greater economic stakes, and at the same time ever greater attenuation from the ultimate causes and concerns that gave rise to the field. "Lawyers in great numbers are finding jobs doing environmental law," he says. "But law, lawyers, law schools, and law students seem to have so little to do with *environment* as seen by knowledgeable people."

How then does this coursebook handle the numbing complexity and detail of modern environmental law? Using a legal process structure, the book tries to probe every nook and cranny of the legal system, exploring ways in which environmental attorneys in and out of government have attempted to understand the fascinating complexities of environmental problems in the real world — both human and ecological — and to use law imaginatively and competently to address them.

Environmental law is a relatively young subject. Courses were first introduced, and only in a few law schools, around 1970. Initially most environmental law materials were drawn from other well-established legal sub-disciplines such as land use, tort, criminal law, property, and constitutional law. The complex administrative subculture that now dominates pollution control was barely in its

---

1. J. Muir, My First Summer in the Sierra 211 (1911).
2. Sax, Environmental Law in the Law Schools: What We Teach and How We Feel About It, 19 ELR 10251 (1989).

formative stages. The innovative burden, especially in the first generation of environmental law, was to harness and adapt an array of legal tools originally designed for other societal purposes.

In past decades, environmental law itself has matured. Interest has grown to the point that environmental law is a standard offering at more than one hundred-fifty law schools. Environmental consciousness, the number of students trained in environmental science, and the number of statutes directed at pollution and other forms of environmental degradation have all grown dramatically. Industry has in large measure come to accept the legitimacy and permanence of environmental values which at first it fiercely resisted. The seriousness with which the bar takes environmental law today is reflected by the breadth of experience and specialization of corporate law practitioners like our new colleague on this edition, Robert Graham. The challenges facing environmental lawyers today include managing the remarkable bulk of both statutory and nonstatutory environmental protection law,[3] and making it work for our private and public clients and for the sustainable development of human society.

This coursebook has a relatively long history. It began as a collection of teaching materials developed for an experimental course taught to graduate and undergraduate students at the University of Michigan in 1971. Strongly influenced by Professor Sax and his advocacy of citizen involvement in environmental decision-making, the materials aim to prepare interested and concerned students to be active participants in the processes that shape their environmental future. In addition to teaching students about the substance of the laws pertaining to the environment, the course pursues a broader goal of teaching about how the legal system functions in an area of vital public concern.

In the face of the numbing mass and complexity of modern environmental law, this coursebook uses the variegated structure of the legal system as its organizing principle, selecting the best examples of how the process works — including an array of classic environmental cases — without specific regard for the type of pollution or policy involved. The way the legal system works, not the intricacy of some media-specific physical science area, is our primary concern.

In this edition of the coursebook, we have added several new chapters and have rearranged the text. The objective was to reinforce the approach of analyzing how various legal standards and mechanisms can be designed to integrate civic environmental values into the complexities of modern life, and how these systems continued to evolve after the first generation of environmental regulations. The book continues to offer students and teachers an array of chapters that can be organized and deployed in different alignments to suit different ways of approaching the subject.

This book aims to give students analytical skills and a solid doctrinal footing in environmental law, along with encouraging a taste for the pleasures of creative lawyering in meeting the challenges of human governance in the ecological

---

3. For example, the federal Environmental Protection Agency (EPA) today employs more than fifteen thousand people, with its major environmental statutes filling a book of more than 600 pages, and its regulations filling a dozen volumes and almost 10,000 pages of the Code of Federal Regulations. EPA's operating programs are funded at a level of more than $4 billion annually. See Reitze, Environmental Policy — It Is Time for a New Beginning, 14 Colum. J. Envtl. L. 111 (1988).

context. Ultimately we are guardedly optimistic that our society's environmental dilemmas can be resolved, and that law will be a sensitive part of the solution.

## NOTE ON EDITING CONVENTIONS USED IN THIS BOOK

In editing materials for this book we have tried to make the text as smooth as possible to the reader's eye, and to keep the amount of text as short as possible, while covering this dauntingly broad and expansive field. This has required quite a bit of editorial surgery on text and excerpted materials.

Within excerpts, many internal citations (especially string citations) are simply excised, with no indication by ellipsis, or are dropped to footnotes. (In some cases in the text itself, when discussing general scientific or other nonlegal data, only limited citations are supplied.) Footnotes in excerpted materials, when they remain, do not have their original numbers unless a footnote holds special importance to subsequent commentators. Judicial opinions are often drastically cut and edited, indicated only by simple ellipsis, and in a few cases portions of text are reordered to make the presentation flow more smoothly. As with most casebooks, if the reader wishes to delve into a particular case or text, the excerpts here should serve to get the inquiry started, but there is no substitute for going back to the original full text.

Various departures from literary convention and Blue Book style have been incorporated throughout the book to improve scansion (as in eliminating brackets on [i]nitial capitalization changes, or our simplified *infra* and *supra* references). Case opinion excerpts, however, usually retain the originating court's stylistic idiosyncrasies.

Swarms of acronyms have invaded environmental law — EISs, NIMBY, LULUs, PSD, SARA, ToSCA, TMDLs, ad infinitum — so to help the reader cope, the back reference pages (which contain all reference sections except the Tables of Contents), also include a GLOSSARY OF ACRONYMS AND ABBREVIATIONS.

Gender-sensitivity was a virtually unknown editing concept until the 'Sixties. Accordingly, many classic cases, and some modern texts as well, address all significant parties as male. In this book the pronouns "he" and "she" when used generically should be understood to refer inclusively to all persons regardless of gender (although in retrospect it seems most polluters still appear here as male).

## ACKNOWLEDGEMENTS

This book sometimes seems to have evolved with as much biodiversity of input as any marsh or rainforest. Dozens of people have helped shape and reshape it over the years. For all who know the work of Professor Joseph Sax, now teaching at Berkeley, the mark of his thinking and advice on our efforts will be discernible throughout these pages. In its earliest form the book derives from materials prepared by a committee of law students at the University of Michigan in the early 'Seventies, including two of the present authors, for a course called Nature, Law, and Society offered to graduate and undergraduate students. In that original group Peter W. Schroth served not only as a major contributor but also as administrator of the course, a thankless and demanding task; without his energetic work the whole project might well have died a-borning. The Nature, Law, and Society project was supported and advised by Joe Sax and Professor William Stapp of the School of Natural Resources; they served graciously and well as mentors and midwives. Prior to its first publication in 1992, this book went through repeated reincarnations at a succession of schools at which we taught — Boston College Law School, Harvard Law School, the University of Michigan Law School, Rutgers, the University of Tennessee College of Law, and Wayne State Law School. Before 1992 and since then we have greatly benefited from the suggestions and comments we have gratefully received from students and colleagues around the country. In this edition, helpful contributions came from John Butcher, Manning Gasch, Jr., Roy Hoagland, Matt Jamin, Gail deRita, and Steven Snyder, and from our colleagues Professors Glen Adelson, Harry Bader, John Dernbach, Lewis Grossman, Jeffrey Hanes, Casey Jarman, Ann Powers, Joel Trachtman, and David Wirth.

Among the many students who contributed to this edition, we want to thank especially Kurt Brauer, Scott Cernich, Lance Davis, Sarah Evans, Johns Hopkins, Jeffrey LaBine, Patrick Nickler, Adam Scoville, Jay Staunton, and the Boston College Law School Environmental Law Society.[4] For support and assistance at Boston College Law School, we warmly thank Dean Aviam Soifer, and at Wayne Law School, Dean James Robinson. The Boston College Law School Library reference staff repeatedly has provided indispensable detective work and support, receiving fiendish eleventh-hour requests and calmly coming through for us: Karen Beck, Irene Good, Ann MacDonald, John Nann, Connie Sellers, Mark Sullivan, Susan Sullivan, Joan Shear, and Jon Thomas. The Boston College Law School Word Processing Center ably and with smiles handled a variety of last-minute burdens, with special efforts made for us by Frances Piscatelli, Donna Gattoni, Susan Noonan, Linda Raute, Wenona Russ, and Ginette Blackburn, for which we express our thanks. As for the many authors and publishers who graciously granted us permission to reprint portions of their works, a complete listing follows immediately after the text.

We also owe a debt to the computers of the WESTLAW system and Reed Elsevier's LEXIS, and the people who built and provided us with those services, and also to the computers (and eyes and brains) of Michael Kitchen, for design and typesetting wizardry.

Ultimately, our greatest warm thanks and appreciation must be reserved for our families, who naïvely expressed pleasure when they first heard of this project.

Z.J.B.P.
R.H.A.
W.G.
R.L.G.

June, 1998

---

4. Tables of authorities were compiled under deadline pressures by the much-appreciated efforts of Boston College Environmental Law Society volunteers Joshua Bowman, Gale Chang, Eric Chodowski, Charles Glover, James Hunnicutt, Matthew Lawlor, David McKay, Monique McNeil, and Jennifer Neal.

# Introduction

*We travel together, passengers on a little space ship, dependent on its vulnerable resources of air and soil, all committed for our safety to its security and peace, preserved from annihilation only by the care, the work, and, I will say, the love we bestow on our fragile craft.*

— Adlai Stevenson, at the United Nations, 1965

## SPACESHIP EARTH[1]

David Brower, one of the founding elders of the 20th century American environmental movement, who held the title role in Encounters with the Archdruid, John McPhee's book about environmentalism in America,[2] was standing on a lakeshore talking to an environmental law class. White-haired and raw-boned with piercing blue eyes, Brower stretched out his arm, with thumb and forefinger held about two inches apart, and said:

> Imagine if you will our entire planet reduced to this, the size of an egg.... If the planet Earth were reduced to the size of an egg, what do you think, proportionally, all its air, its atmosphere, would be? And what would be the total volume of the water that, along with air and sunlight, sustains life on this Earth?... According to the computations I've seen, the sum total of atmosphere veiled around this egg planet Earth would be equivalent to no more than the volume of a little pea wrapped around the globe. And the water? That would be no more than a matchhead, a tiny volume spread thin enough to fill the oceans, rivers and lakes of the world.[3]

Looking at the students, Brower asked,

> Thinking of those limits, can you any longer not believe that our planet is a tremendously vulnerable little system, totally dependent on this fragile tissue of air and water, a thin fabric of life support made up of all the air and water the Earth will ever have?[4]

Like the astronauts who reported dramatic and startling personal reactions to their first glimpse down upon planet Earth from their position in outer space, the

---

1. See Kenneth Boulding, The Economics of Spaceship Earth, in Environmental Quality in a Growing Economy 3-14 (1971), arguing that the economy of the future will be like a space craft with closed-cycle limited resources.

2. McPhee, Encounters with the Archdruid (1971).

3. In fact, the relative scale of the mass of atmosphere and water to the planet Earth is apparently even more dramatic. According to Dr. Heinrich Holland of Harvard's geology department, taking the relative *masses* of Earth's air and water (as opposed to spatial volume which is a misleading construct), the atmosphere constitutes less than one-millionth of the planet's mass, and the water less than one-thousandth.

4. Brower was speaking on a beach on Mission Point Peninsula, Grand Traverse Bay, Michigan, October 1977.

images of Brower's egg and Stevenson's Spaceship Earth force us to recognize our interrelatedness with all other human and natural systems that make up the planet. The Earth is indeed one small, limited, totally self-contained entity, a single natural system (albeit made up of many interconnected and interdependent systems) containing great richness, diversity, and vulnerability.

As the First Law of Ecology says, everything is connected to everything else. Environmentalists tend to be conservative at least in this regard: out of utilitarian caution as well as ethical impulse they tend to value the dynamic natural systems that have evolved over millennia, and they distrust the wholesale human intrusions on these systems that have occurred particularly since the arrival of the industrial age. Every act of technology or human behavior is likely to have direct and indirect results, some quite drastic, unpredictable, and long-term in their effects. Who but environmentalists would have foreseen that the choice of coal-burning methods in the Midwest would hurt maple sugar producers in Vermont, and leach lead into the water supplies of eastern New England homes 700 miles away? Yet acid rain was a natural chemical reaction just waiting to be triggered. It is important, environmentalists say, to look wide and long before we leap.

Unfortunately, the "long view" looking out for long-term negative consequences, does not seem instinctive to the human brain. Quite the contrary. If it can, the human species will consistently overlook ecological repercussions and other long-term problems, and instead focus on the more upbeat realm of short-term payoffs. The supposition is that as problems start piling up one can ignore them, get around them, pass them off or away downstream and downwind, or one can move on to new frontiers. Brower's egg planet reminds us that there are no such frontiers left; everything goes somewhere and remains within the system in which we must continue to live.

Environmental law attempts to build foresight into the human decisional system, along with an awareness of costs and values that are typically invisible because, though real, they exist outside the formal market economy. Often environmental law works after the fact, attempting to force accountings for depredations that have already occurred, in hopes of deterring future repetitions. Environmental law has also developed elaborate doctrines attempting to anticipate and prevent environmental disruptions. The goal is to incorporate a process of fair, overall, comprehensive accounting of real societal costs, benefits, and alternatives into major public and private decisionmaking.

Over the past 30 years there has been a dramatic change in the stature of the field. It is no longer dismissable as the fad of a disgruntled minority. It is now the stuff of presidential campaigns and national public opinion poll majorities. There are now more environmental lawyers in the United States than there are labor lawyers. Given these toeholds and the reality of environmental problems, the field inevitably will continue to grow ever more intricate, challenging, and important.

## THE BOOK'S PERSPECTIVE

This book is designed to track through environmental law according to the structure of the legal process. It uses some of the classic cases and materials of environmental law as well as some of the most recent.

There are a few further necessary comments — our bias, for example. Every book has its bias, usually unacknowledged. If it isn't already, we wish to make this book's clear. We view most environmental problems as arising from a fundamental tension between short-term marketplace interests and the larger civic-societal public interest. In a dynamic human logic that has built the greatest economy the world has ever known, individual human actors behave rationally to maximize their own short-term best interests, without sufficient consideration or accounting of the natural and societal consequences of their actions. The ecological and civic-societal values affected by such human actions will be most efficiently addressed if they can be brought into the marketplace economy, but the altruism of market players cannot be relied upon to do that job. Environmental law therefore seeks to force these public values into the markets of daily life, in spite of the inevitable and powerful resistance of market forces. The powerful tension between marketplace dynamics and public civic values remains a consistent day-by-day reality within the legal process.

In large part the corporate marketplace, we believe, has come to accept and internalize public environmental values, not necessarily as a result of civic instincts but rather because of the credible prospect today of environmental enforcement by agencies and an active citizenry. This book therefore approaches many, though not all, environmental cases from the perspective of those who enforce environmental laws — citizens, public interest groups, and agencies. Our approach will often be "how can this problem be appropriately managed and corrected within the legal system?" presuming in most cases that the problem does exist.

This approach seems realistic and useful as well as defensible. To understand environmental law one must understand environmental plaintiffs, especially the individuals and increasingly professionalized groups who make up the active environmental "movement." (Environmental defendants generally do not offer similarly broad countervailing legal theories of environmental defense.[5]) So to get deeper into the forests of environmental law, in practical terms one must follow the environmental enforcement trail, which often means the efforts of active citizens. Whether readers ultimately view the field from the point of view of plaintiffs or defense, an understanding of the plaintiffs' perspective is indispensable to a recognition of what's going on, and how it could be done better.

---

5. Legal defenses typically amount to a series of attempts to avoid the issue — "the facts aren't sufficiently shown," "the plaintiffs don't have the right to be heard in this court," "the matter has continued for so long that the law is estopped from changing the status quo," "enforcement of the law would violate our constitutional rights," in short "the law should not be applied."

## STRUCTURE

The structure of this coursebook should be clear from the table of contents. It surveys environmental law issues throughout the vast range of the American legal process (with brief glimpses beyond into international environmental law, which is growing fast, often on the American model).

Most books on environmental law have fallen into an organization by physical science categories — air, water, toxics, wildlife, groundwater, energy, etc. — not by legal categories, which often leads them to duplicative legal analysis. This book contains material from each such area, but takes its organization from the elements of the legal system itself, building upon a base of common law and constitutional law, and continuing on to statutory and administrative law. We find that this approach is a faster and more efficient way of getting students into technical and structural questions of environmental law. In large part the aim is not to teach hyper-technical details of current law, like the regulatory parts-per-million hydrocarbon standards for automobile tailpipe emissions, and so on. We aim, rather, to show the structure and how it works. Environmental law changes daily. This book is used for the first, and often the student's only, course in environmental law, and we therefore feel obligated to leave students with a well-rounded legal overview. Not all professors design their course syllabus in similar layouts; this book, consistent with its legal process approach to organizing the large and unwieldy field, therefore offers teachers a menu of shorter chapters with which to design and build each individual course.

Part I of the book begins with an examination of major themes in modern environmental law analysis — an evolution of ecological science, legal techniques and mechanisms, environmental politics, economics, and risk assessment, and the growing (if sometimes reluctant) systemic acceptance of the legitimacy of environmental controls. It also introduces the public trust doctrine, which may be environmental law's single most dramatic contribution to the modern legal system. Based on this review and orientation, the book explores the traditional legal structures and remedies of the common law upon which environmental law doctrines originally developed and continue to flourish. The common law foundation also serves to underscore how individual citizens in a modern democrcy, here as environmental plaintiffs, can serve to integrate overlooked public values into the economic and political marketplace.

Part II explores basic Public Law, the development of statutory and regulatory law in the administrative state as an overlay on the common law. The chapters survey an array of statutes arising in toxics cases, setting out a system of "statutory taxonomies" illustrating the array of statutory and regulatory options that have been applied in the modern administrative state, followed by materials on fundamental structural questions raised in U.S. law by the complexities of federal-state relations, with a basic chapter on the Administrative Law of environmental law. Look under the surface of almost any significant environmental case and you will find yourself dealing with basic questions of democratic governance.

Part III's chapters examine one-by-one a variety of different statutory models that can be selected by legislatures and administrative agencies *to define* specific regulatory standards. These different standard-setting approaches, which have application in other statutory structures as well, are viewed here in the context of the major command-and-control industrial pollution regulatory systems: Harm-based ambient standards in the Clean Air Act, best-available-technology-based standards in the Clean Water Act, technology-forcing standards in automobile pollution and atmospheric chlorofluorocarbons, and novel new procedure-based negotiated standards.

Part IV's chapters examine the different designs and strategies of regulatory structures created by legislatures *to apply* environmental standards to the practical realities of the marketplace. These different implementation approaches — in addition to the classic command-and-control model for pollution control — include broad-brush procedural and substantive compliance statutes like the National Environmental Policy Act and the Endangered Species Act, a new generation of approaches that attempt to enlist market dynamics into the environmental protection process, and the special designs and strategies of modern toxics statutes.

In Part V the focus is on *compliance, enforcement, and dispute resolution* mechanisms, both civil and criminal, with enforcement initiatives coming from agencies, citizens, and, increasingly, from industries themselves. ADR (Alternative Dispute Resolution) methods provide a further evolving realm of nonmandatory mechanisms for environmental protection.

Part VI wrestles with conflicts between societal rights and responsibilities and private rights and responsibilities, leading off with the Public Trust doctrine and constitutional rights, public resource management and its special constraints and clienteles, and the political and legal tensions between public interests and private due process property rights.

Finally, Part VII acknowledges the accelerating globalization and convergence in international legal practice as well as in technology and commerce. A knowledge of comparative law techniques in understanding foreign nations' internal law is an increasingly necessary skill for attorneys carrying environmental law into the 21st century. The recent flowering of international environmental law has created a new field and has changed the way many economies do business, as well as modifying some governmental behaviors and providing some collective hopes for the future.

## GOING BEYOND THE BOOK

An environmental law course is broad in scope. The text and commentary in this book often incorporate analysis of source material, cases, and issues extending far beyond the excerpted textual material. The excerpted material often serves to supplement the text, rather than vice-versa as in most law course books. To provide more depth and familiarity with detail, students and professors have often added other components to the coursework. Some students take a concurrent nonlaw course, for example in field biology, toxicology, or environmental policy. Some take on projects or internships with active groups outside academe. Some classes have carried one chosen problem area through the course of the term, or kept track of an ongoing local controversy — a particular toxic disposal case, wildlife or park management issue, mining, dredging, or dam project. Others have assigned short individual research papers, class presentations, field visits, and so on, and each of these has been valuable in providing reinforcing feedback to the analyses and techniques of environmental law set out broadly in the book.

Some very fine loose-leaf services provide information updates on a regular, often weekly, basis: the Environmental Law Reporter (cases and analyses by The Environmental Law Institute); the BNA Environment Reporter (cases, statutes, and current developments by the Bureau of National Affairs); the BNA International Environmental Reporter; the BNA Chemical Regulation Reporter; the BNA Toxics Law Reporter; and the BNA Asbestos Abatement Reporter. Student subscriptions to activist newsletters are also available and valuable: The Amicus Journal, Natural Resources Defense Council, 122 E.42d St., Suite 4500, NYC 10168; Earth Island Institute's E.I. Journal, 300 Broadway, San Francisco CA 94133; Environmental Defense Fund's monthly EDF Letter, 257 Park Ave. S, NYC 10010; Not Man Apart, Friends of the Earth, 530 7th St. SE, Washington DC 20003; the National Wildlife Federation's Weekly News Report, 1416 P. St. NW, Washington DC 20036; RESOLVE, published by Center for Environmental Dispute Resolution, World Wildlife Fund and The Conservation Foundation, 1250 24th St. NW, Washington, DC 20037; and the Sierra Club National Newsletter, 320 Pennsylvania Ave. SE, Washington DC 20003. The National Wildlife Federation's Conservation Directory is a useful catalogue of hundreds of environmental organizations; the Federation also has a congressional hotline recording for legislative updates, at 202-797-6655. Many industry organizations also publish newsletters and are pleased to provide extensive materials in support of their positions.

A number of excellent law reviews specialize in environmental law, and WestLaw and the Index to Legal Periodicals offer effective access to their contents. A plethora of useful Websites has also developed and can be explored in virtually every part of the field. Background books on environmental analysis provide helpful orientation in this sprawling field. Worthwhile books include Eugene Odum's Fundamentals of Ecology, Rachel Carson's Silent Spring, Barry Commoner's The Closing Circle, and the fountainhead, Aldo Leopold's Sand County Almanac.

The best environmental law hornbook we know is Professor William Rodgers' Handbook on Environmental Law, and Professor Rodgers has also published a very helpful multivolume treatise. West Publishing Company produces a very useful annual statutory compilation, Selected Environmental Law Statutes. Joseph Sax's Defending the Environment (1971) continues to be a vivid introduction and guide to the use of law in resolving the pervasive social, economic, and ecological governance problems we call "environmental."

---

And don't be daunted by the "numbing complexity and detail" of some sectors of environmental law. Because everything is connected to everything else, if one just picks up a trail and follows it, it will lead to all there is to know.

# ENVIRONMENTAL LAW AND POLICY:
# NATURE, LAW, AND SOCIETY

# PART ONE

# THE LEGAL PROCESS OF ENVIRONMENTAL LAW

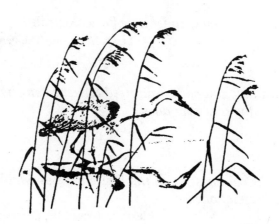

*All thinking worthy of the name must now be ecological.*
— Lewis Mumford, The Pentagon of Power, 1970.

*Never doubt that a small group of committed citizens can change the world;
indeed it's the only thing that ever does.*
— Margaret Mead

*There is hardly a political question in the United States which does not sooner
or later turn into a judicial one.*
— Alexis de Toqueville, Democracy in America, 1848.

# Chapter 1

# ANALYTIC THEMES IN THE LEGAL PROCESS OF ENVIRONMENTAL LAW

A. *The Environmental Perspective, the Commons, and a Salty Paradigm*
B. *Analytic Themes in a Classic Industrial Pollution Setting: Allied Chemical and* Kepone — *a Milestone 1970s Industrial Pollution Case*
C. *A Case-Study in Industrial Pollution Law at the Turn of the 21st Century: the* Smithfield *Litigation*
D. *Beyond Direct Threats to Human Health and Property: The Public Trust Doctrine*

## A. THE ENVIRONMENTAL PERSPECTIVE, THE COMMONS, AND A SALTY PARADIGM

The ecological future of the planet is being shaped by its geophysical past; by continuing natural forces of sun, rain, wind, water, seismics, vulcanism, and diversifying biological evolution; and by humans, corporations, and government. These last three are very recent arrivals and relatively trivial in mass. They have proved, however, to have a remarkable capacity for causing planetary effects, for good and ill, and environmental law focuses upon them in doing its work.

### Section 1. THE BREADTH AND SCOPE OF ENVIRONMENTAL LAW

Consider the amazing diversity of the field called environmental law. It includes...

- Chemical wastes buried in a suburban field.
- Seal puppies clubbed to death on floating ice packs in the Gulf of St. Lawrence.
- Uranium fuel rods shipped to nuclear power plants in India.
- Schools of fish dying from bacterial toxins triggered in coastal waters by upland hog and chicken farmers dumping wastes.
- Toxic gases spreading from chemical plants to poison surrounding low-income neighborhoods in Italy, India, and Kansas.
- A factory emitting smoke from its stacks and liquid wastes from its drainpipes.
- Sprawl development creating towns that resemble residential parking lots more than communities.

- A single-hulled oil tanker more than three football fields long, with an exhausted crew, running at high speed through icebergs in a narrow channel at night.
- The imminent extinction of an endangered snapdragon plant in Maine.
- A superhighway cutting through a park and low-income neighborhood in Memphis.
- Hairdressing salons in Yosemite National Park.
- A decision to put an incinerator for highly toxic wastes in the midst of an urban ethnic community.
- Carcinogenic chemical fire-retardants in infant sleepwear.
- The cutting of shade trees along rural roads.
- A Tennessee river and its fertile valley eliminated by a federal recreational dam.
- A centuries-old church bulldozed for a parking lot, and other historic preservation issues.
- Non-returnable bottles lying along highways and in urban trash.
- Disappearing rainforests, and desertification in the Third World.
- New Jersey's refusal to permit Philadelphia's garbage to be disposed of in New Jersey landfills.
- Children exposed to rat bites and lead poisoning in an urban slum.
- Redwood trees turned into tomato stakes; our remnant ancient forests cut for subsidized export.
- An internationally-known 10 million-year old paleontological fossil site in Colorado, being bulldozed for a resort subdivision.
- Asbestos dust in local elementary schools.
- The construction of a new federal prison breaking apart a cohesive low-income minority neighborhood in New York City.
- Chlorofluorocarbons thinning stratospheric ozone, causing increased ultraviolet radiation hazards on earth.
- A primitive tribe in Panama threatened by extension of the Pan-American Highway through their jungle territory.
- Global warming; and hazardous exposures to ultra-violet radiation caused by the thinning of stratospheric ozone by chlorofluorocarbons.
- And hundreds more.

Is this just *one* field of law? All of these widely diverse situations are labelled "environmental" issues, and activists called "environmentalists" have taken legal action on each of them (and hundreds of others) over the past few decades, with varying degrees of success. Each case involves a highly individualized set of scientific facts, economic and political issues, and social and natural consequences. Many of them have no obvious connection with others on the list, beyond their environmental label. (What do they have in common? The environmentalist

- A single-hulled oil tanker more than three football fields long, with an exhausted crew, running at high speed through icebergs in a narrow channel at night.
- The imminent extinction of an endangered snapdragon plant in Maine.
- A superhighway cutting through a park and low-income neighborhood in Memphis.
- Hairdressing salons in Yosemite National Park.
- A decision to put an incinerator for highly toxic wastes in the midst of an urban ethnic community.
- Carcinogenic chemical fire-retardants in infant sleepwear.
- The cutting of shade trees along rural roads.
- A Tennessee river and its fertile valley eliminated by a federal recreational dam.
- A centuries-old church bulldozed for a parking lot, and other historic preservation issues.
- Non-returnable bottles lying along highways and in urban trash.
- Disappearing rainforests, and desertification in the Third World.
- New Jersey's refusal to permit Philadelphia's garbage to be disposed of in New Jersey landfills.
- Children exposed to rat bites and lead poisoning in an urban slum.
- Redwood trees turned into tomato stakes; our remnant ancient forests cut for subsidized export.
- An internationally-known 10 million-year old paleontological fossil site in Colorado, being bulldozed for a resort subdivision.
- Asbestos dust in local elementary schools.
- The construction of a new federal prison breaking apart a cohesive low-income minority neighborhood in New York City.
- Chlorofluorocarbons thinning stratospheric ozone, causing increased ultraviolet radiation hazards on earth.
- A primitive tribe in Panama threatened by extension of the Pan-American Highway through their jungle territory.
- Global warming; and hazardous exposures to ultra-violet radiation caused by the thinning of stratospheric ozone by chlorofluorocarbons.
- And hundreds more.

Is this just *one* field of law? All of these widely diverse situations are labelled "environmental" issues, and activists called "environmentalists" have taken legal action on each of them (and hundreds of others) over the past few decades, with varying degrees of success. Each case involves a highly individualized set of scientific facts, economic and political issues, and social and natural consequences. Many of them have no obvious connection with others on the list, beyond their environmental label. (What do they have in common? The environmentalist

# Chapter 1

# ANALYTIC THEMES IN THE LEGAL PROCESS OF ENVIRONMENTAL LAW

A. *The Environmental Perspective, the Commons, and a Salty Paradigm*

B. *Analytic Themes in a Classic Industrial Pollution Setting: Allied Chemical and* Kepone *— a Milestone 1970s Industrial Pollution Case*

C. *A Case-Study in Industrial Pollution Law at the Turn of the 21st Century: the* Smithfield *Litigation*

D. *Beyond Direct Threats to Human Health and Property: The Public Trust Doctrine*

## A. THE ENVIRONMENTAL PERSPECTIVE, THE COMMONS, AND A SALTY PARADIGM

The ecological future of the planet is being shaped by its geophysical past; by continuing natural forces of sun, rain, wind, water, seismics, vulcanism, and diversifying biological evolution; and by humans, corporations, and government. These last three are very recent arrivals and relatively trivial in mass. They have proved, however, to have a remarkable capacity for causing planetary effects, for good and ill, and environmental law focuses upon them in doing its work.

### Section 1. THE BREADTH AND SCOPE OF ENVIRONMENTAL LAW

Consider the amazing diversity of the field called environmental law. It includes...

- Chemical wastes buried in a suburban field.
- Seal puppies clubbed to death on floating ice packs in the Gulf of St. Lawrence.
- Uranium fuel rods shipped to nuclear power plants in India.
- Schools of fish dying from bacterial toxins triggered in coastal waters by upland hog and chicken farmers dumping wastes.
- Toxic gases spreading from chemical plants to poison surrounding low-income neighborhoods in Italy, India, and Kansas.
- A factory emitting smoke from its stacks and liquid wastes from its drainpipes.
- Sprawl development creating towns that resemble residential parking lots more than communities.

### a. The science of Ecology (macro and micro)

Law draws many lessons and arguments from ecology and the other flourishing environmental sciences. Modern environmentalists have drawn inspiration and momentum from two giants in the field, Rachel Carson and Aldo Leopold. Here are two brief examples of their work:

### Aldo Leopold, A Sand County Almanac
### 214–220 (1948, 1968 ed.)

The image commonly employed in conservation education is "the balance of nature." For reasons too lengthy to detail here, this figure of speech fails to describe accurately what little we know about the land mechanism. A much truer image is the one employed in ecology: the biotic pyramid.... Plants absorb energy from the sun. This energy flows through a circuit called the biota, which may be represented by a pyramid consisting of layers. The bottom layer is the soil. A plant layer rests on the soil, an insect layer on the plants, a bird and rodent layer on the insects, and so on up through various animal groups to the apex layer, which consists of the larger carnivores....

In the beginning, the pyramid of life was low and squat; the food chains short and simple. Evolution has added layer after layer, link after link. Man is one of thousands of accretions to the height and complexity of the pyramid. Science has given us many doubts, but it has given us at least one certainty: the trend of evolution is to elaborate and diversify the biota. Land, then, is not merely soil; it is a fountain of energy flowing through soils, plants, and animals. Food chains are the living channels which conduct energy upward; death and decay return to the soil. The circuit is not closed; some energy is dissipated in decay, some is added by absorption from the air, some is stored in soils, peats, and long-lived forests; but it is a sustained circuit, like a slowly augmented revolving fund of life....

The velocity and character of the upward flow of energy depend on the complex structure of the plant and animal community, much as the upward flow of sap in a tree depends on its complex cellular organization. Without this complexity, normal circulation would presumably not occur. Structure means the characteristic numbers, as well as the characteristic kinds and functions, of the component species. This interdependence between the complex structure of the land and its smooth functioning as an energy unit is one of its basic attributes.

When a change occurs in one part of the circuit, many other parts must adjust themselves to it. Change does not necessarily obstruct or divert the flow of energy; evolution is a long series of self-induced changes, the net result of which has been to elaborate the flow mechanism and to lengthen the circuit. Evolutionary changes, however, are usually slow and local. Man's invention of tools has enabled him to make changes of unprecedented violence, rapidity, and scope.... The combined evidence of history and ecology seems to support one general deduction: the less violent the man-made changes, the greater the probability of successful readjustment in the pyramid.... This deduction runs counter to our current philosophy, which assumes that because a small increase in density enriched human life, that an indefinite increase will enrich it indefinitely. Ecology knows of no density relationship that holds for indefinitely wide limits. All gains from density are subject to a law of diminishing returns.

### Rachel Carson, Silent Spring
### 54–57, 61 (1962)

There are few studies more fascinating, and at the same time more neglected, than those of the teeming populations that exist in the dark realms of the soil. Perhaps the most essential organisms in the soil are the smallest — the invisible hosts of bacteria and threadlike fungi. Statistics of their abundance take us at once into astronomical figures. A teaspoonful of topsoil may contain billions of bacteria. In spite of their minute size, the total weight of this host of bacteria in the top foot of a single acre of fertile soil may be as much as a thousand pounds. Ray fungi, bacteria, [and] small green cells called algae, these make up the microscopic plant life of the soil [and are] the principal agents of decay, reducing plant and animal residues to their component minerals. The vast cyclic movements of chemical elements such as carbon and nitrogen through soil and air and living tissue could not proceed without these microplants. Without the nitrogen-fixing bacteria, for example, plants would starve for want of nitrogen, though surrounded by a sea of nitrogen-containing air. Other organisms form carbon dioxide, which, as carbonic acid, aids in dissolving rock. Still other soil microbes perform various oxidations and reductions by which minerals such as iron, manganese, and sulfur are transformed and made available to plants.

Also present in prodigious numbers are microscopic mites and primitive wingless insects called springtails. Despite their small size they play an important part in breaking down the residues of plants, aiding in the slow conversion of the litter of the forest floor to soil. The specialization of some of these minute creatures for their task is almost incredible. Several species of mites, for example, can begin life only within the fallen needles of a spruce tree. Sheltered here, they digest out the inner tissues of the needle. When the mites have completed their development only the outer layer of the cells remains. The truly staggering task of dealing with the tremendous amount of plant material in the annual leaf fall belongs to some of the small insects of the soil and the forest floor. They macerate and digest the leaves, and aid in mixing the decomposed matter with surface soil.

Besides all this horde of minute but ceaselessly toiling creatures there are of course many larger forms, for soil life runs the gamut from bacteria to mammals. Some are permanent residents of the dark subsurface layers; some hibernate or spend definite parts of their life cycles in underground chambers; some freely come and go between their burrows and the upper world. In general the effect of all this habitation of the soil is to aerate it and improve both its drainage and the penetration of water throughout the layers of plant growth.

Of all the larger inhabitants of the soil, probably none is more important than the earthworm. Over three quarters of a century ago, Charles Darwin...gave the world its first understanding of the fundamental role of earthworms as geologic agents for the transport of soil — a picture of surface rocks being gradually covered by fine soil brought up from below by the worms, in annual amounts running from many tons to the acre in most favorable areas.[2] At the same time, quantities of organic matter contained in leaves and grass (as much as 20 pounds to the square yard in six months) are drawn down into the burrows and incorporated in soil. Darwin's calculations showed that the toil of earthworms might add a layer of soil an inch to inch and a half thick in a ten-year period. And this is by no means all

---

2. C. Darwin, The Formation of Vegetable Mould, through the Action of Worms, with Observations on Their Habits (1897).

they do: their burrows aerate the soil, keep it well drained, and aid the penetration of plant roots.... The soil community, then, consists of a web of interwoven lives, each in some way related to the others — the living creatures depending on the soil, but the soil in turn a vital element of the earth only so long as this community within it flourishes.

The problem that concerns us here is one that has received little consideration: What happens to these incredibly numerous and vitally necessary inhabitants of soil when poisonous chemicals are carried down into their world, either introduced directly as soil "sterilants" or borne on the rain that has picked up a lethal contamination as it filters through the leaf canopy of forest and orchard cropland? Is it reasonable to suppose that we can apply a broad-spectrum insecticide to kill the burrowing larval stages of a crop-destroying insect, for example, without also killing the "good" insects whose function may be the essential one of breaking down matter? Or can we use a nonspecific fungicide without also killing the fungi that inhabit the roots of many trees in a beneficial association that aids the tree in extracting nutrients from the soil?...

Chemical control of insects seems to have proceeded on the assumption that the soil could and would sustain any amount of...poisons without striking back. The very nature of the world of the soil has been largely ignored.... A group of specialists who met to discuss the ecology of the soil...summed up the hazards of using such potent and little understood tools.... "A few false moves on the part of man may result in destruction of soil productivity, and the arthropods may well take over."

COMMENTARY AND QUESTIONS

1. **Leopold, ecology, and "natural equilibrium."** In the years since Aldo Leopold wrote Sand County Almanac, his observations of the things and interconnections he found in the Wisconsin countryside helped the new old science of ecology to flourish. The study of organisms as they actually live and interact in living networks over time offers important advantages over the reductionistic study of a creature or compound or its genetic building blocks isolated on a slide or lab table. The multifactored effects of industrial activities on the people and environments they impact are not realistically predictable through traditional scientific disciplines. For lawyers in the field, a survey course in ecology and environmental science techniques is a good investment of time. The University of Maryland's environmental law program is publishing a short course book on "Environmental Science for Lawyers." There are also useful books that can help to illustrate the breadth and depth of modern ecological sciences, and how to ask intelligent questions about them. See, e.g., Shrader-Frechette, K.S., and McCoy, E.D., Method in Ecology (1993).

As Leopold noted, the image commonly employed of "the balance of nature" fails to describe accurately what we now know about ecology. It now is generally conceded that the "balance of nature" or "natural equilibria" are dynamic ongoing systems, not static balances. There is no ideal historical natural balance from which today's environment came and to which natural communities can be returned, despite the classical rhetoric of some environmentalists. But the rate and character of evolving changes in natural systems around us have encountered rapid disruptions from human impacts in the past 100 years that are unprecedented in scale and reverberating disruptive consequences. See Symposium on Ecology and the Law, 25 IIT/Chic-Kent L.Rev. 847–985 (1994). Environmental law, of course, flourishes in the dynamics of human and ecological interconnections.

2. **The broad reverberations of Rachel Carson's microcosm.** Rachel Carson's perceptive observations revealed a systemic deficiency in the way mid-20th century humans made decisions, and changed the way many Americans viewed their world.[3] The way most people have planned projects or solved problems has typically been one-shot technology — insulated, narrow, and unidimensional —

"You got bugs? So get a pesticide." ... Zap.

"Now you've got what you wanted. Dead bugs. The end."

Similarly narrowed human thinking has been applied in cutting timber from fragile mountainsides, or discharging wastes from industrial factories. Carson showed, however, that the desired result is typically *not* all that happens. Predictable problems follow when official players, both corporate and governmental, make decisions in traditional terms, seeking short term benefits with a narrowed and insulated field of vision. There is no such thing as a simple one-shot technology. Everything has continuing long-term consequences. Pesticides don't just disappear after they have killed the target bugs. They linger on and on, blowing in the wind, leaching into groundwater, eliminating the rich, interconnected communities that had naturally evolved in the land to give it its fertility in the first place, moving up through ecological food chains.

The lessons Carson drew from DDT pesticides can readily be applied to many other settings as well — to other kinds of pollution, to resource management issues like timber and grazing, to highway and transportation planning, pharmaceuticals and health technology, and by extension to many other areas of national policy. Although humans may not take account of the real social and ecological costs of their actions, nature keeps a comprehensive tab and real consequences follow.

Western societies have traditionally tended to view human actors as the central players in the life of the planet, with nature as a subservient and pliant backdrop. Carson showed through the ecological realm that the natural backdrop to human activity may be far larger in scale and importance than the human figures pirouetting in the foreground. The earth's environment has developed richly diverse and dynamic interconnected natural systems, communities of communities spread around the planet providing services previously unrecognized, fulfilling important productive functions previously taken for granted, capable of causing broadly destructive systemic consequences when they are disrupted or destroyed, and intimately linked to the human communities that share the environment with them.

From this perspective an important utilitarian precautionary principle asserts itself: unless you collectively are pretty sure that the negative consequences will be foreseeable, minor, and mitigatable, or that the background foundational inter-

3. It is remarkable in retrospect how three books written at virtually the same historical moment so powerfully reshaped so much of modern American society's view of life: Jane Jacobs, The Death and Life of Great American Cities (1961); Rachel Carson, Silent Spring (1962); Betty Friedan, The Feminine Mystique (1963).

connections will not be disrupted, you had better be sure that what somebody proposes to do is worth the potential costs; it is safer not to risk casually the escalating domino consequences that may follow. In this regard Carson showed that moving from a human-centered master-of-nature perspective to the holistic human-species-as-constituent-part-of-nature view is not just an ethical idea — it is fundamentally practical and utilitarian as well.

---

### Thomas Sancton, What on Earth Are We Doing?
Time, 2 January 1989, 24–30

*One generation passeth away, and another generation cometh: but the earth abideth forever.*                                                    *— Ecclesiastes*

No, not forever. At the outside limit, the earth will probably last another 4 billion to 5 billion years. By that time, scientists predict, the sun will have burned up so much of its own hydrogen fuel that it will expand and incinerate the surrounding planets, including the earth. A nuclear cataclysm, on the other hand, could destroy the earth tomorrow. Somewhere within those extremes lies the life expectancy of this wondrous, swirling globe. How long it endures and the quality of life it can support do not depend alone on the immutable laws of physics. For man has reached a point in his evolution where he has the power to affect, for better or worse, the present and future state of the planet....

By 1800 there were 1 billion human beings bestriding the planet. That number had doubled by 1930 and doubled again by 1975. If current birthrates hold, the world's present population of 5.1 billion will double again in 40 more years.... 40,000 babies die of starvation each day in Third World countries.... Smokestacks have disgorged noxious gases into the atmosphere, factories have dumped toxic wastes into rivers and streams, automobiles have guzzled irreplaceable fossil fuels and fouled the air with their detritus in the name of progress, forests have been denuded, lakes poisoned with pesticides, underground aquifers pumped dry.... Changing weather patterns could make huge areas infertile or uninhabitable, touching off refugee movements unprecedented in history....

Whatever the validity of this or that theory, the earth will not remain as it is now. Says Harvard biologist E.O. Wilson: "The extinctions ongoing worldwide promise to be a least as great as the mass extinction that occurred at the end of the age of dinosaurs...." Increasingly, technology has come up against the law of unexpected consequences.... Advances in health care have lengthened life-spans, lowered infant mortality rates and, thus, aggravated the population problem. The use of pesticides increased crop yields but polluted water supplies. The invention of automobiles and jet planes revolutionized travel but sullied the atmosphere.... Let there be no illusions.... Both the causes and effects of the problems that threaten the earth are global, and they must be attacked globally....

### COMMENTARY AND QUESTIONS

1. **The depressing perspectives of global ecology, and the law.** To observers like Sancton, the global challenges can be met only through a basic change in attitudes toward use and preservation of natural resources that would dramatically change lifestyles in virtually all parts of the world. What role, if any, would law play in

that process? Laws can prohibit directly and indirectly some forms of environmental carnage, as with attempts to protect endangered species. The effectiveness of such attempts, however, remains an open question. Finding laws that seem capable of effecting larger behavioral changes, such as reducing global emissions of greenhouse gases produced by fossil fuel consumption and deforestation, remains more problematic. The law often adopts Abbie Hoffman's compromise advice to "think globally, act locally."

Arnold Reitze, in a penetrating article reviewing 20 years of environmental efforts,[4] dourly noted that virtually all global environmental degradation can be traced back to three major human phenomena — population, wasteful resource consumption, and pollution — all of which are out of control.[5] Of these, he said, the most devastating is population pressure. Relentless population growth undercuts the hopes of nationbuilders and those who try to apply industrial, social, economic, and legal technology to alleviate the ills of humankind and the planet. It may be that the world's population is in the process of levelling off by 2050 at 10 billion, twice the current total, but dehumanizing poverty, hunger, homelessness, and lack of opportunity are still increasing in both relative and absolute terms. Individuals and nations who can do so strive to increase their wealth and consumption, rather than ratcheting-down to allow the earth's resource base to carry more souls, so the numbers and problems of abject underclasses tend to grow rather than shrink. Society, instead of moving toward global cooperation, often seems to be degenerating into mutually antagonistic tribes. These human conditions can themselves be considered "environmental" problems. And they have the disastrous further consequence of reducing the terms of human decision-making to purely short-term coping and survival, so that long-term ecological rationality seems a wistful impossibility. Urban decay, children having children, desertification, desperate exploitation of resources — these are products of population pressures and it is far from clear what law can do about it. In fact, Reitze noted, governments find the problems of population and resource consumption so hard to handle that they tend to ignore them, and focus instead on pollution, which, though serious, is the least important of the major causes of environmental degradation.

This book, to some extent, incorporates that mistake. It is far easier to study legal remedies for controlling pollution than for controlling population and resource consumption patterns. This coursebook does look beyond pollution, however, and the legal process approaches examined here can be flexibly extended as far as environmental analysis can go. Law will be a participant in the mission to bring humankind and the planet into some dynamic equilibrium, even if that sometimes appears to be a quixotic quest.

---

4. Reitze, Environmental Policy — It is Time for a New Beginning, 14 Colum. J. Envtl. L. 111 (1989).

5. Observing where we are today, we might add that there are *four* systemic problems, "Four Horsemen of the Eco-palypse." (This egregious pun comes from Environmental Law as a Mirror of the Future, 23 B.C. Envtl. Aff. L. Rev 733 (1996).) The Fourth Horseman is the Gap between What We Know and What We Do. Despite a truly amazing expansion of ecological knowledge — about pollution, population, resource losses, and the interconnectedness of human and natural systems, and the ability to communicate that knowledge globally at the speed of light — it is distressing to observe the difference between knowledge and practice. Our capacity to implement what we know about these serious threats consistently falls short, and may even be falling further behind, because of political marketplace resistance.

**2. A need for integrated environmental management?** Reality exists in the holistic, integrated overview, but knowledge and the capacity to manage discrete problems build from the bottom, from a narrow, incisive, specialized focus. Several strategy reports prepared by the U.S. Environmental Protection Agency[6] begin with a fundamental declaration that EPA should take an overall "systems approach" that views the environment as an integrated whole, and should coordinate all protection strategies on that basis. The proposal has global implications, considered in the last chapter of this book. Perhaps ironically, however, the rest of the EPA report was organized on a medium-by-medium approach — air, water, toxics, noise, land use, and so on. Is it practically inevitable that bureaucrats, legislators, lawyers, litigants, and humans generally will focus on narrow slices of the environmental dilemma? In an increasingly specialized world, how do we keep our eyes open to the whole?

### b. Environmental ethics

### Aldo Leopold, A Sand County Almanac
### 129–130, 203, 224–225 (1948)

THINKING LIKE A MOUNTAIN... Only the mountain has lived long enough to listen objectively to the howl of a wolf.... My own conviction on this score dates from the day I saw a wolf die. We were eating lunch on a high rimrock, at the foot of which a turbulent river elbowed its way. We saw what we thought was a doe fording the torrent, her breast awash in white water. When she climbed the bank toward us and shook out her tail, we realized our error: it was a wolf. A half-dozen others, evidently grown pups, sprang from the willows and all joined in a welcoming mêlée of wagging tails and playful maulings. What was literally a pile of wolves writhed and tumbled in the center of an open flat at the foot of our rimrock.

In those days we had never heard of passing up a chance to kill a wolf. In a second we were pumping lead into the pack, but with more excitement than accuracy.... When our rifles were empty, the old wolf was down, and a pup was dragging a leg into impassable slide-rocks. We reached the old wolf in time to watch a fierce green fire dying in her eyes. I realized then, and have known ever since, that there was something new to me in those eyes — something known only to her and to the mountain. I was young then, and full of trigger-itch; I thought that because fewer wolves meant more deer, that no wolves would mean hunters' paradise. But after seeing the green fire die, I sensed that neither the wolf nor the mountain agreed with such a view....

THE LAND ETHIC... There is as yet no ethic dealing with man's relation to land and to the animals and plants which grow upon it.... The extension of ethics to this...element in human environment is, if I read the evidence correctly, an evolutionary possibility and an ecological necessity.... The "key-log" which must be moved to release the evolutionary process for an ethic is simply this: quit thinking about decent land-use as solely an economic problem. Examine each question in terms of what is ethically and esthetically right, as well as what is economically expedient. A thing is right when it tends to preserve the integrity, stability, and beauty of the biotic community. It is wrong when it tends otherwise.

---

6. L. Thomas, Environmental Progress and Challenges: EPA Update (1988).

**AN ENVIRONMENTAL ETHIC BEYOND UTILITARIANISM?...** Leopold's lyrical ecology has inspired generations of environmental scientists, and a vigorous ongoing ethical debate. Isn't the environment more than a commodity and medium for human designs? Shouldn't there be a recognized moral and ethical standard extending beyond pure human self-interest, recognizing the normative rights of the planet, of nature itself?

It is true, of course, that many environmentalists (like most chapters of this book) do indeed focus on utilitarian arguments for environmental quality: basic human self-interest, health and economics, should force society not to ignore ecological consequences. Even Leopold himself is ambiguous. He continues the wolf-killing story by showing how wolves are important in controlling populations of deer and other foraging animals that otherwise will strip the forests bare and turn cattle ranges to dustbowls. When he later criticizes current land use policy because "it assumes, falsely, I think, that the economic parts of the biotic clock will function without the uneconomic parts," he is again making a utilitarian argument.

But the fire dying in the she-wolf's eyes, that is something else.

Could it be that humans are not indeed the measure of all things? Are we instead only one part of a larger ecological community, with responsibilities accompanying our undoubted powers and rights? Is there, in other words, a moral-legal basis for environmentalism beyond utilitarianism? This question increasingly reappears in environmental law cases. When a project is stopped because it threatens extinction for some endangered insect, or a court considers awards of natural resource damages for ecosystems destroyed by oil spills, the law must reach beyond the normal justifications founded upon net human benefit.

Should we declare that the wolf herself has legal rights, rights that, although not absolute, must nevertheless be substantively weighed in the legal process? Impressive work has been devoted to animal rights and natural rights theories.[7] Nagging problems arise, however, in drawing lines. Is sentiency the litmus? If not, shouldn't plants, rocks, and hills as well be able to claim these rights?[8] Unless the broader view prevails, the ethic ignores the rights of ecosystems. If natural rights can be defined, moreover, who defines them and determines when and how they are to be applied and weighed against human rights and the rights of other entities in the system?

Taking another approach, can it be argued that a God commands ecological sensitivity? Many have criticized the Bible's call for humans to conquer nature:

> Be the terror and dread of all the wild beasts and all the birds of heaven, of everything that crawls on the ground and all the fish of the sea; they are handed over to you.... Teem over the earth and be lord of it. Genesis 9:1-2, 7.[9]

---

7. See Roderick Nash's Rights of Nature: A History of Environmental Ethics (1989); H. Rolston, Environmental Ethics: Duties to and Values in the Natural World (1988); R. Nozick, Anarchy, State and Utopia 35-42 (1975); and the active literature of environmental ethics including the journal Environmental Ethics.

8. See Christopher Stone, Should Trees Have Standing? (1972). Cf. the view from the self-styled "wise use" movement, noted further at the end of the next section: "Environmentalism is the new paganism, trees are worshipped and humans sacrificed at its altar.... It is evil...and we intend to destroy it." Ron Arnold, chairman of the Center for the Defense of Free Enterprise, Boston Globe, January 13, 1992.

9.Calvin and many other Christian theologians have argued that God "created all things for man's sake." Institutes of Religion 182; bk.1, ch. 14, 22 (Battles edition 1961); see generally J.A. Passmore, Man's Responsibility for Nature (1974)(Passmore).

But other strands in Judaeo-Christian theology and other religious cultures cast humans in a less domineering role. Primitive humans were probably animists. The mountains and rivers had spirits, and humans spoke with the trees and animals they were about to kill for their use. In many Eastern and Native American[10] cultures, gods are intimately linked with nature; humans are merely a part of the web, the Tao. Human disruption of nature is deplored as having destroyed "the age of perfect virtue, when men lived in common with birds and beasts, as forming one family."[11] The Dalai Lama, speaking of his Buddhism, said "We have always considered ourselves as part of our environment."[12] The great Jewish philosopher Maimonides dramatically recanted his early Greek-inspired view of human primacy: "It should *not* be believed that all things exist for the sake of the existence of man. On the contrary, all the other beings, too, have been intended for their own sakes and not for the sake of something else."[13]

Christianity, whose God became a human, has been more resistant to any diminution of human-centeredness. The Protestant ethic, when it appeared, fit nicely with the Industrial Revolution's conquest of nature. Fundamentalist Christians' resistance to the notion that humans evolved as part of the natural world demonstrates a continuing need to see humans as separate and distinct from nature. But others can now read the Old Testament, particularly the Noah story, as affirming the sanctity and uniqueness of every living species, and setting humans the task of preserving the earth's natural heritage. Some new Christian scholarship urges an active ethic of human "stewardship" over all Creation.[14] These theological debates between human-centered and more interrelational metaphysics have been paralleled in the dialogues of nonreligious philosophy as well.[15]

Without a clearly divine or natural source of a moral ethic for the environment, the ethic, if it is to exist, must come from humans. Much of any human-based environmental ethic will of course continue to be based on utilitarianism: if we want our species' descendants to survive on the planet we must take the sensitive cautious long view. But beyond self-interest, further distinctions can extend

---

10. "Human beings are not superior to the rest of creation. If human beings were to drop out of the cycle of life, the earth would heal itself and go on. But if any of the other elements would drop out — air, water, animal or plant life — human beings and the earth itself would end." Audrey Shenandoan, Onandaga tribe, NY. This echoes the "Gaia" hypothesis that the planet Earth itself is a living, self-regulating organism; disruptions will modify the system, and life as we know it may disappear, though the planet will ultimately strike a new balance. J. Lovelock, The Ages of Gaia, (1988); A. Miller, Gaia Connections (1991). In this sense, the planet Earth may not be so "fragile."

11. Chuang Tsu, 4th c. B.C., in Passmore at 7–8. "When humans interfere with the Tao, the sky becomes filthy, the equilibrium crumbles, creatures become extinct." Lao-tzu, Tao Te Ching (500 B.C.).

12. He continues, "Our scriptures speak of the container and the contained. The world is the container — our house — and we are the contained — the contents of the container.... As a boy studying Buddhism I was taught the importance of a caring attitude toward the environment. Our practice of nonviolence applies not just to human beings but to all sentient beings.... In Buddhist practice we get so used to this idea of nonviolence and the ending of all suffering that we become accustomed to not harming or destroying anything indiscriminately. Although we do not believe that trees or flowers have minds, we treat them also with respect. Thus we share a sense of universal responsibility for both mankind and nature." H.H. the 14th Dalai Lama, and G. Rowell, My Tibet 79–80 (1990).

13. See Passmore, at 12.

14. Fellows of the Calvin Center for Christian Scholarship, Earthkeeping: Christian Stewardship of Natural Resources (1980); P. Riesenberg, The Inalienability of Sovereignty in Medieval Political Thought (1956) explores medieval concepts of human (and royal) stewardship.

15. Goethe and Henry More were early outposts in the resistance to the human-centeredness of Bacon, Descartes, and even Kant. See generally Passmore, 16–23.

the ethic. We may indeed currently be the dominant species on the earth, possessing earth-changing knowledge, technology, and physical powers, but along with these powers may come ethical responsibilities. Perhaps these are responsibilities to past generations and to the future, to steward and pass on the extraordinary legacy we have received. A classic legal algorithm holds that for every power there is a countervailing responsibility. The ability to destroy surely does not carry with it the moral right to do so, tempered only by the limitations of self-interest against self-inflicted wounds. That would be too primitive a norm for a species that has been maturing for three million years.

From the fact of human intellectual development come other bases for an environmental ethic. On one hand are the arguments that proceed from our superiorities, like the claim for an ecological *noblesse oblige* — because humans uniquely have been able, in some settings at least, to move beyond the bare demands of food, shelter, and survival to build an abstract culture and to understand the effects of our actions upon the planet, our species has a high calling to protect the less powerful parts of the ecological community in which we live. Aesthetic principles, also a unique human development, likewise argue for an extended stewardship.

On the other hand lie the arguments from humility. The more one knows, the more one realizes one does not know. The greater the expansion of our knowledge and technology, the vaster the realm of the unknown. When we look into the she-wolf's eyes with Leopold, some of what we feel may be anthropomorphic sympathy. But the fire dying there may also spark a recognition that we will never know the world she knows, and that should make us hesitant to make ourselves the measure of it all. Ultimately humans may be impelled to honor an environmental ethic protecting the planet's ecology for the same reason that they are impelled to climb Mt. Everest: because it is there. The very existence — the "is-ness" — of the wolf and her rivers and mountains, separate from humans, makes the ethic fitting and proper for recognition.

When the question arises, as it continually does in legislatures and agencies, courts and saloons, 'Why protect such-and-such particular part of the environment?' environmentalists will undoubtedly continue to argue practically, "Because it may turn out to be important to us, or to hurt us if we lose it." But often, when the setting and the light are right, won't many also feel a further pull, coming from something more than the stark counsels of daily human utility?

### Section 3. ENVIRONMENTAL ANALYSIS — THE TRAGEDY OF THE COMMONS, AND ROAD SALT, A PROBLEM THAT HAS NOT YET FOUND A LEGAL FORUM

#### a. The commons

Life is not a cow pasture, nor a salty highway. These two images, however, present fundamental illustrations of how human beings act in ways that pose problems for the environment and for democratic governance. Unfortunately, much of the natural world is a commons — air, water, wildlife — which puts it on a collision course with dynamics of human behavior that are based on individually-based rational choices.

### Garrett Hardin, The Tragedy of the Commons
162 Science, 13 December 1968, 1243, 1243–1248

The tragedy of the commons develops this way. Picture a pasture open to all. It is to be expected that each herdsman will try to keep as many cattle as possible on the commons. Such an arrangement may work reasonably satisfactorily for centuries because tribal wars, poaching, and disease keep the numbers of both man and beast well below the carrying capacity of the land. Finally, however, comes the day of reckoning, that is, the day when the long-desired goal of social stability becomes a reality. At this point, the inherent logic of the commons remorselessly generates tragedy.

As a rational being, each herdsman seeks to maximize his gain. Explicitly or implicitly, more or less consciously, he asks, "What is the utility to me of adding one more animal to my herd?" This utility has one negative and one positive component:

> The positive component is a function of the increment of one animal. Since the herdsman receives all the proceeds from the sale of the additional animal, the positive utility is nearly +1.
>
> 2. The negative component is a function of the additional overgrazing created by one more animal. Since, however, the effects of overgrazing are shared by all the herdsmen, the negative utility for any particular decision-making herdsman is only a fraction of -1.

Adding together the component partial utilities, the rational herdsman concludes that the only sensible course for him to pursue is to add another animal to his herd. And another; and another.... But his is the conclusion reached by each and every rational herdsman sharing a commons. Therein is the tragedy. Each man is locked into a system that compels him to increase his herd without limit — in a world that is limited. Ruin is the destination toward which all men rush, each pursuing his own best interest in a society that believes in the freedom of the commons. Freedom in a commons brings ruin to all.

Some would say that this is a platitude. Would that it were! In a sense, it was learned thousands of years ago, but natural selection favors the forces of psychological denial. The individual benefits as an individual from his ability to deny the truth even though society as a whole, of which he is a part, suffers. Education can counteract the natural tendency to do the wrong thing, but the inexorable succession of generations requires that the basis for this knowledge be constantly refreshed....

In an approximate way, the logic of the commons has been understood for a long time, perhaps since the discovery of agriculture or the invention of private property in real estate. But it is understood mostly only in special cases which are not sufficiently generalized. Even at this late date, cattlemen leasing national land on the western ranges demonstrate no more than an ambivalent understanding, in constantly pressuring federal authorities to increase the head count to the point where overgrazing produces erosion and weed dominance. Likewise, the oceans of the world continue to suffer from the survival of the philosophy of the commons. Maritime nations still respond automatically to the shibboleth of the "freedom of the seas." Professing to believe in the "inexhaustible resources of the oceans," they bring species after species of fish and whales closer to extinction.

The National Parks present another instance of the working out of the tragedy of the commons. At present, they are open to all, without limit. The parks themselves are limited in extent — there is only one Yosemite Valley — whereas population seems to grow without limit. The values that visitors seek in the parks are steadily eroded. Plainly, we must soon cease to treat the parks as commons or they will be of no value to anyone.

What shall we do? We have several options. We might sell them off as private property. We might keep them as public property, but allocate the right to enter them. The allocation might be on the basis of wealth, by the use of an auction system. It might be on the basis of merit, as defined by some agreed-upon standards. It might be by lottery. Or it might be on a first-come, first-served basis, administered to long queues. These, I think, are all the reasonable possibilities. They are all objectionable. But we must choose — or acquiesce in the destruction of the commons that we call our National Parks.

POLLUTION... In a reverse way, the tragedy of the commons reappears in problems of pollution. Here it is not a question of taking something out of the commons, but of putting something in — sewage, or chemical, radioactive, and heat wastes into water; noxious and dangerous fumes into the air; and distracting and unpleasant advertising signs into the line of sight. The calculations of utility are much the same as before. The rational man finds that his share of the cost of the wastes he discharges into the commons is less than the cost of purifying his wastes before releasing them. Since this is true for everyone, we are locked into a system of "fouling our own nest," so long as we behave only as independent, rational, free-enterprisers.

The tragedy of the commons as a food basket is averted by private property, or something formally like it. But the air and waters surrounding us cannot readily be fenced, and so the tragedy of the commons as a cesspool must be prevented by different means, by coercive laws or taxing devices that make it cheaper for the polluter to treat his pollutants than to discharge them untreated. We have not progressed as far with the solution of this problem as we have with the first. Indeed, our particular concept of private property, which deters us from exhausting the positive resources of the earth, favors pollution. The owner of a factory on the bank of a stream — whose property extends to the middle of the stream — often has difficulty seeing why it is not his natural right to muddy the waters flowing past his door. The law, always behind the times, requires elaborate stitching and fitting to adapt it to this newly perceived aspect of the commons.

The pollution problem is a consequence of population. It did not much matter how a lonely American frontiersman disposed of his waste. "Flowing water purifies itself every 10 miles," my grandfather used to say, and the myth was near enough to the truth when he was a boy, for there were not too many people. But as population became denser, the natural chemical and biological recycling processes became overloaded, calling for a redefinition of property rights.

HOW TO LEGISLATE TEMPERANCE?... Analysis of the pollution problem as a function of population density uncovers a not generally recognized principle of morality, namely: the morality of an act is a function of the state of the system at the time it is performed....

The laws of our society follow a complex, crowded, changeable world. Our epicyclic solution is to augment statutory law with administrative law. Since it is practically impossible to spell out all the conditions under which it is safe to burn trash in the back yard or to run an automobile without smog-control, by law we delegate the details to [agencies]. The result is administrative law, which is rightly feared for an ancient reason — Quis custodiet ipsos custodes? — "Who shall watch the watchers themselves?"... Administrators, trying to evaluate the morality of acts in the total system, are singularly liable to corruption, producing a government by men, not laws.

Prohibition is easy to legislate (though not necessarily to enforce); but how do we legislate temperance? Experience indicates that it can be accomplished best through the mediation of administrative law.... The great challenge facing us now is to invent the corrective feedbacks that are needed to keep custodians honest. We must find ways to legitimate the needed authority of both the custodians and the corrective feedbacks.

PATHOGENIC EFFECTS OF CONSCIENCE... The long-term disadvantage of an appeal to conscience [as a means to mitigate the tragedy of the commons] should be enough to condemn it, but it has serious short-term disadvantages as well. If we ask a man who is exploiting a commons to desist "in the name of conscience," what are we saying to him?... Two communications, and they are contradictory: (i)(the intended communication) "If you don't do as we ask, we will openly condemn you for not acting like a responsible citizen"; (ii)(the unintended communication) "If you do behave as we ask, we will secretly condemn you for a simpleton who can be shamed into standing aside while the rest of us exploit the commons." Every man then is caught in what Bateson has called a "double bind."...

MUTUAL COERCION MUTUALLY AGREED UPON... "Responsibility...is the product of definite social arrangements." The social arrangements that produce responsibility are arrangements that create coercion, of some sort. Consider bank-robbing. The man who takes money from a bank acts as if the bank were a commons. How do we prevent such action? Certainly not by trying to control his behavior solely by a verbal appeal to his sense of responsibility. Rather than rely on propaganda we...insist that a bank is not a commons; we seek the definite social arrangements that will keep it from becoming a commons. That this would infringe on the freedom of would-be robbers we neither deny nor regret....

To say that we mutually agree to coercion is not to say that we are required to enjoy it, or even to pretend we enjoy it. Who enjoys taxes? We all grumble about them. But we accept compulsory taxes because we recognize that voluntary taxes would favor the conscienceless. We institute and (grumblingly) support taxes and other coercive devices to escape the horror of the commons.

An alternative to the commons need not be perfectly just to be preferable. With real estate and other material goods, the alternative we have chosen is the institution of private property coupled with legal inheritance. Is this system perfectly just? As a genetically trained biologist I deny that it is. It seems to me that, if there are to be differences in individual inheritance, legal action should be perfectly correlated with biological inheritance — that those who are biologically more fit to be the custodians of property and power should legally inherit more. But...an idiot can inherit millions, and a trust fund can keep his estate intact. We must admit that our legal system of private property plus inheritance is unjust — but we put up with it because we are not convinced, at the moment, that anyone has invented a better system....

But we can never do nothing. That which we have done for thousands of years is also action. It also produces evils. Once we are aware that the status quo is action, we can then compare its discoverable advantages and disadvantages with the predicted advantages and disadvantages of the proposed reform, discounting as best we can for our lack of experience. On the basis of such a comparison, we can make a rational decision which will not involve the unworkable assumption that only perfect systems are tolerable.

RECOGNITION OF NECESSITY... Perhaps the simplest summary of this analysis of man's population problems is this: the commons, if justifiable at all, is justifiable only under conditions of low-population density. As the human population has increased, the commons has had to be abandoned in one aspect after another.

First we abandoned the commons in food gathering, enclosing farm land and restricting pastures and hunting and fishing areas. These restrictions are still not complete throughout the world.

Somewhat later we saw that the commons as a place for waste disposal would also have to be abandoned. Restrictions on the disposal of domestic sewage are widely accepted in the Western world; we are still struggling to close the commons to pollution by automobiles, factories, insecticide sprayers, fertilizing operations, and atomic energy installations.

In a still more embryonic state is our recognition of the evils of the commons in matters of pleasure. There is almost no restriction on the propagation of sound waves in the public medium. The shopping public is assaulted with mindless music, without its consent.... Advertisers muddy the airwaves of radio and television and pollute the view of travelers. We are a long way from outlawing the commons in matters of pleasure....

Every new enclosure of the commons involves the infringement of somebody's personal liberty. Infringements made in the distant past are accepted because no contemporary person complains of a loss. It is the newly proposed infringements that we vigorously oppose; cries of "rights" and "freedom" fill the air. But what does "freedom" mean? When men mutually agreed to pass laws against robbing, mankind became more free, not less so. Individuals locked into the logic of the commons are free only to bring on universal ruin; once they see the necessity of mutual coercion, they become free to pursue other goals. I believe it was Hegel who said, "Freedom is the recognition of necessity."

COMMENTARY AND QUESTIONS

1. **Extrapolating to global scale.** Does Hardin's analysis apply beyond the cow pasture, to the continental air masses, or the oceans? Air, water, oceans, wildlife — these are parts of the planet's bounty that are open to use by all and not readily converted into private property. Other natural systems share characteristics of commons but are more easily reduced to ownership — forests, prairies, wetlands, hydrocarbons, and other resources — although something vital may ultimately be lost in the process. The uses of all these commons are so diverse and diffuse that it is often difficult to demonstrate who is causing what effects. Even here, although individual actions hurting the common resource are often invisible, diffuse or unaccountable, they can be cumulatively critical. The difficulty of the grand scale lies in discovering the true measure of public costs, and what controls may avert the logic of the tragedy, nowhere more difficult than in the area Hardin targeted, global population control. Environmental law addresses many different problems of cumulative effects in a wide variety of ways, at different scales. The basic logic of the tragedy of the commons, however, permeates virtually all environmental issues.

2. **A political philosophy of the tragedy of the commons: Locke, Coase, and Carson.** Under Lockean political theory, if we lived under Eden-like conditions of plenty

there would be no competition for resources, and property law would not be necessary because all desired items would be sufficiently abundant. With increasing populations and limited resources, however, a means for allocating available goods had to be found. To Locke, the institution of exclusive individual property fit nicely with his sense of the order of God's universe, and also responded to social needs.[16] Private property induces people to work by granting them ownership of all or some of the fruits of their labors. Non-exclusive rights to property would fail to produce work incentives. Like the rational choice theories of modern economics, Locke presumed that human actors generally act in their own rational self interest. For private property's relationship to a commons, this means that owners will do whatever will maximize their advantage in regard to their own property.

The Nobel laureate Ronald Coase popularized the further underpinning of Hardin's tragedy of the commons in his article The Problem of Social Cost, 3 J. Law & Econ. 1, 3-5, 42–44 (1960).

In the old days prior to 1960, individual enterprises lived in a version of the frontier myth, where each could operate independently on his own terrain, and the negative consequences that individual actions generated would disappear away into an all-absorbing tolerant vacuum.

Rachel Carson showed us, however, that this tendency is dominated by short term individualized thinking, and can be quite dysfunctional in overall terms. Humans, corporations, and disparate segments of the environment are not dissociated individual islands floating in a vacuum; they live in a web of direct and indirect interconnections. Externalized costs don't disappear, even if they are ignored. The "free" absorption of negatives by the commons, or the destruction of resources that do not in the commons have to be paid for, are not in reality "free goods" in terms of a societal accounting. These externalities have serious accumulated consequences that can end up dwarfing the short term logic that spawned them. Then and now, however, humans and their marketplace do not voluntarily rush to take into account the negative effects of what they do, so law is necessary and inevitable.

3. **The pessimism and optimism of the commons.** Does Hardin seem too optimistic about the chances for reforming the tragedy of the commons? Some who have considered the matter find Hardin's view — that necessity will induce us to accept protections based on "mutual coercion, mutually agreed upon"– grossly over-optimistic. See W. Ophuls, Ecology and the Politics of Scarcity 145–165 (1977). At the opposite pole are the "cornucopialists." Susan Cox, for example, argues that problems of the commons are not of the magnitude that Hardin fears, and humans will always find new resources and technologies to cope. In her assessment, society has adequately managed such problems through the ages, with the major lapses coming only in times of cultural shifts. See Cox, No Tragedy of the Commons, 7 Envtl. Ethics 49 (1985).

---

16. For a more thorough discussion of John Locke's view of private property, see Sanders, The Lockean Proviso, 10 Harv. J.L. & Pub. Pol'y 401 (1988).

4. **The commons and positive outcomes.** How do you decide what things should be maintained in common ownership rather than being reduced to a form of exclusive private property? Locke, Bentham, and Adam Smith all noted how private property ownership and the right to exclude others play a crucial role in motivating political and economic life. As Professor Carol Rose writes:

> The right to exclude others has often been cited as the most important characteristic of private property. This right, it is said, makes private property fruitful by enabling owners to capture the full value of their individual investments, thus encouraging everyone to put time and labor into the development of the resources. Moreover, exclusive control makes it possible for owners to identify other owners, and for all to exchange the fruits of their labors until these things arrive in the hands of those who value them most highly — to the great cumulative advantage of all.[17]

What kinds of things are better suited to public ownership and communal use? Rose cites public libraries and public highways as examples of successful commons. What of lakes and rivers? Forests? Antarctica? In most of the world, private land owners do not own resources beneath their land; the public retains the right to determine their use and development.

5. **Measuring sustainability.** Another fundamental problem with the commons is defining the level of sustainability. It isn't easy to define the point where cows exceed the sustainable carrying capacity of the commons. It is far harder to define the acceptable level of imposition on a common resource like air or water ("assimilative capacity") or an ocean fishery. Is anything less than purity a negative burden on the commons? What constitutes tolerable depreciation, and what constitutes Hardin's downward spiral to disaster? See the discussion of environmental standard setting in Chapters 8–11.

6. **Law as mutual coercion.** Assuming that much of the commons paradigm is relevant to analyzing environmental policy, note how Hardin sets up a critical role for the law but doesn't specify its operation. If nonmandatory policies or physical privatization are unlikely to work on a pollution commons (are they?), what kinds of legal intervention are likely to be effective and appropriate to avoiding the tragedy of the commons? Criminal sanctions, taxes, individual lawsuits, administrative bureaucracies? The choice is not easy. In practice, as this book repeatedly notes, environmental law has developed an amazing biodiversity of statutory design models, whether by accident or pragmatic plan — producing a wide range of legal approaches to environmental protection.

7. **On the other hand: A contrary view from the marketplace.** Juxtaposed against an environmental economics overview is the traditional view of nature as a resource base for dynamic human enterprise. The marketplace logic of industrial and development interests casts resource exploitation and pollution externalities in a far more upbeat light. Here is part of a manifesto from the self-styled "Wise Use" movement:

> Humans, like all organisms, must use natural resources to survive. This fundamental truth is never addressed by environmentalists.... If environmental-

17. Rose, The Comedy of the Commons, 53 U. Chi. L. Rev. 711, 711–12 (1986).

ism were to acknowledge our necessary use of the earth, its ideology would lose its meaning. To recognize the legitimacy of the human use of the earth would be to accept the unavoidable environmental damage that is the price of our survival. Once that price is acceptable, the moral framework of environmentalist ideology becomes irrelevant and the issues become technical and economic.... The earth and its life are tough and resilient, not fragile and delicate. Environmentalists tend to be catastrophists, believing that any human use of the earth is "damage" and massive human use of the earth is "a catastrophe." An environmentalist motto is "We all live downstream," the viewpoint of helpless or vengeful victims. Wise users, on the other hand, tend to be cornucopians.... A wise use motto is "We all live upstream," the viewpoint of responsible and concerned individuals....

The only way we humans can learn about our surroundings is through trial and error. Even the most sophisticated science is systematized trial and error. Environmental ideology fetishizes nature to the point that eco-activists will not permit others to make errors with the environment, dead-ending in no trials and no learning.... Our limitless imaginations can break through natural limits to make earthly goods and carrying capacity virtually infinite. Just as settled agriculture increased goods and carrying capacity vastly beyond hunting and gathering, so our imaginations can find ways to increase total productivity by superseding one level of technology after another.... Man's reworking of the earth is revolutionary, problematic and ultimately benevolent.... Ron Arnold, What Do We Believe?[18]

Where is the commons in this rhetorical context? The marketplace's optimistic focus on the ongoing achievements of human enterprise comes from a totally different way of seeing the world, a perspective from which most environmental regulations based on ecological and civic concepts of the commons appear dismally negativistic, unnecessary, and obstructive. Both perspectives cannot be right.

### b. Salting the earth

The prosaic environmental controversy that follows has as yet hardly been noticed by the legal system. It nevertheless illustrates a classic environmental law conundrum. Readers in Snow Belt states are living in the midst of this exercise. For readers in Sun Belt states, it offers a bemusing and instructive opportunity to observe from a distance. The contaminant is highway de-icing salt, which in its own ways can spread as widely as a toxic industrial chemical, with serious human effects including even death.

Like King Lear, one can learn much from salt. A few years ago the U.S. Environmental Protection Agency (EPA) prepared a major analysis of the effects of highway salt, based on more than 300 prior research projects and reports.[19] Dr. Charles Wurster, of the State University of New York's Marine Sciences Research Center, published the following summary (which in retrospect is even more sobering because virtually nothing has changed since he wrote it.)

---

18. Mr. Arnold is a principal spokesman of the "Wise Use" movement, and Chairman of the Center for the Defense of Free Enterprise, part of the marketplace coalition that attempted to roll back environmental regulation across the board in the 104th Congress; text from www.cdfe.org/wiseuse.html.

19. EPA Document 600/2-76-105 (May 1976).

**Wurster, Of Salt...**
New York Times, 4 March 1978, A21

The use of salt on roads for snow and ice removal has increased in the years [since the early 1960s]. About nine million tons, more than 10 percent of all salt produced in the world, are applied annually to American highways in snowy states.

The benefits of salt for road de-icing — and its costs — are rarely questioned. A recent report of the EPA, which weighed the costs and benefits of the practice, includes surprises.

The costs of salting begin with $200 million for the salt and its application. Roadside vegetation destroyed by salt, particularly shade trees, was estimated by EPA to add another $150 million. Underground water mains, telephone cables and electric lines are corroded by salt seepage, adding another $10 million in damages. The Consolidated Edison Company, which owns the world's largest underground electrical system, estimated that road salt did $5 million in damages during [a single] winter....

Salt finds its way into drinking-water supplies, especially ground-water aquifers, thereby becoming a health hazard. Recent research implicates salt intake as a causative factor in hypertension, heart disease and other circulatory problems, as well as various liver, kidney and metabolic disorders. It is estimated that at least 20 percent of Americans should restrict salt intake.

Individuals can control the salt that is added to foods, but salt in drinking water is harder to manage. About 27 percent of the drinking water supplies in Massachusetts are contaminated with road salt, and New Hampshire has a state-financed system for replacing contaminated wells. Long Island is especially vulnerable, since its sole drinking water is ground water recharged by precipitation, including highway runoff.

The EPA estimated that 25 percent of the population in the Snow Belt drinks water contaminated with road salt. The cost of providing pure water for these people was put at $150 million, but no objective cost was ascribed to health damage.

Salt damages bridges and other highway structures, best exemplified by the deterioration and collapse of New York City's West Side Highway. Corrosion by salt is believed to have been a major cause of the failure. The EPA estimated the national annual cost of damage to highway structures by salt at $500 million.

But the largest and most obvious cost of road salt is automobile corrosion, estimated by the EPA at $2 billion annually, or an average of about $34 per car per year in the Snow Belt. Heavy salting of highways hastens auto depreciation by about 20 percent. Telephone company vehicles last twice as long in the South as they do in New England.

Although they are usually assumed without question, the benefits of road salting have proven elusive to substantiate. At temperatures near or slightly below freezing, salt hastens melting and increases traction. But at lower temperatures, salt makes dry snow shiny and more slippery, and causes it to stick on windshields hampering vision. Salt also prolongs street wetness, reducing the friction.

Solid evidence of increased safety is lacking, because inadequate studies have been confounded by too many variables. The effects of salting are often inseparable from the effects of plowing and sanding. A Michigan study found fewer accidents during years when salt was used, but the number of storms and quantity of snowfall were ignored. Other studies showed no effects on accident rates.

Salt usually permits faster driving which would benefit emergency vehicles but is a mixed blessing for others. In snow, people tend to drive slowly and have "fender benders," but after salt applications they tend to drive faster and have more serious accidents.

The benefits of salt in preventing accidents, if any, are small. Not surprisingly, this conclusion is disputed by the salt industry, which claims great benefits from its use.

An interesting benefit-cost analysis results. Whereas benefits are uncertain but apparently small (except to the salt and automobile industries), costs total nearly $3 billion per year. Only a small amount of the cost is the salt itself, 93 percent consisting of indirect costs, borne especially by owners of motor vehicles.

Road salting should be re-examined. Reduced salting, combined with increased plowing, tire modifications, and driver education in snow driving might yield better results at lower costs.

---

The EPA report summarized by Dr. Wurster contains many other fascinating details:

- The state of Alaska manages to maintain its highways without any use of road salt.

- The citizens of Michigan, leading the world in auto production, also lead in auto corrosion, losing $198,630,000 each year in salt-caused depreciation, which almost matches the total cost of salt application in the nation.

- Urban shade trees are vulnerable to salt, and have substantial monetizable values[20] (a 15" diameter tree was valued at $1,767; if a tree starts showing leaf damage from salt it is beyond saving).

- So much salt has spilled into the Great Lakes that parts of the Lake Michigan depths now have a marine salt water ecology, including marine fish like flounder.

- Salt infiltrates through concrete and sets up a powerful pressure reaction with reinforcing steel bars, causing potholes and overpass damage.

- All things being equal, people favor the "bare pavement" look of salted roads because the visual impression is misleadingly clearer than that of a scraped and sanded roadway.

- Salt intake is a critical factor in many health afflictions including hypertension, cardiovascular diseases, renal and liver diseases and metabolic disorders, with likely linkages to increased mortalities, but no studies have focused on the widespread effects of highway salt on drinking water supplies.

- The report also notes that highway salt can be harmful to fish and wildlife, but doesn't pursue these costs.

- The report makes extensive cost comparisons with a "scrape, sand, and

---

20. The words "monetized" and "marketized" are used in the text in the informal sense of "having been attributed a market value," not in the technical economics sense of converting to legal obligation.

selective salting" alternative model. (The net cost of the unlimited salting model was almost twice that of the restricted model.)

- The report doesn't review any of the available salt substitutes for de-icing like organic CMA (calcium magnesium acetate).

**EVALUATING THE BENEFITS, COSTS, AND ALTERNATIVES TO SALTING...** Is salt an "environmental" problem? Although it involves potential damages to public health, vegetation, fish, and wildlife, these are precisely the areas that are least covered in the report, although they are potentially quite significant in terms of tangible costs. They lie at the end of an indirect chain of causation, and are the hardest to prove and least quantifiable in money terms. The presence of these interconnected human and natural effects, and the narrowed basis upon which the salt decision is made, make it an issue typical of the environmental realm.

Salting is a classic example of how humans typically think in terms of "one-shot" technology. Who wants to bother with thinking about where the salt goes after the zap? Out of sight, out of mind. Environmental science, however, reminds us that everything goes somewhere and has residual consequences. We will live in a natural system with those residuals long after the ice and snow are gone.

Dr. Wurster's article demonstrates the elements of a classic environmental policy analysis, likewise applicable to a polluting factory or a federal agency's dam-building project. Note the decision as it is actually made: road commissions decide to put salt on roads because, for them, it is a logical benefit-cost-alternatives decision; they get the *benefits* of bare roads for $200 million a year. But then note that this market decision ignores at least 93 percent of the true *costs* as seen by environmentalists, and some far better *alternatives*.

**COSTS, ECONOMIC AND NATURAL...** Environmentalists typically argue that the costs of a proposal are far greater than the limited costs considered by those who make the decision. Here are the conservative EPA estimates of some of the total yearly costs of road salting that can be monetized:[21]

| ITEM | ESTIMATED YEARLY COST |
|---|---|
| Water Supplies | $ 150 million |
| Vegetation | 50 million |
| Highway Structures | 500 million |
| Vehicles | 2,000 million |
| Utilities | 10 million |
| Salt Purchase & Application | 200 million |
| **TOTAL:** | **$2.91 BILLION** |

This set of costs is, of course, not complete. Remarkably, the analyzed costs completely excluded health costs, beyond a factor based on substitute drinking water supply, and do not include any fish and wildlife or other environmental

21. All salt figures in the EPA Report and the text discussion are given in 1976 dollars.

values. They also ignore the costs that occur at the source of the salt, such as harms caused by mining, which typically include local water pollution from mine run-off and leachate.

As is usually the case in environmental matters, most of these costs are indirect and borne in small amounts by a large, dispersed class of adversely affected individuals. In many cases, however, the majority of costs are not so easily marketizable. In the case of seal pups slaughtered on the ice, what cost is attributable to human revulsion at the inhumanity of the massacre, not to mention to the seals themselves? Benefit-cost analysis is a rational process only to the degree that it incorporates full consideration of real costs and benefits, whether or not they are marketizable. This requires conceptual weighing as well as monetary weighing, a very tough assignment. Resource economists often assert that a properly conducted benefit-cost analysis must weigh concepts even if there is no numerical figure for their worth:

For any real world choice, there will always be some considerations that cannot easily be enumerated or valued, where the analysis becomes quite conjectural. Benefit-cost analysis does not, and should not, try to hide this uncertainty. The sensible way to deal with uncertainty about some aspects of a benefit or cost is to quantify what can be quantified, to array and rank non-quantifiable factors, and to proceed as far as possible. E. Gramlich, A Guide to Benefit-Cost Analysis 5 (2d ed., 1990).

One of the difficulties in achieving practical acceptance of the environmental perspective and its comprehensive benefit-cost-alternatives analysis is that many public and private decision-makers are responsive only to data that reckons the costs *they* must bear in relation to the project. There is an understandable inclination to ignore costs that are either indirect, externalized or unmonetized. A federal pork barrel dam project tends to ignore the values of free-flowing rivers, disrupted communities, and loss of farmland. A polluting factory tends to ignore the far-flung health, property, ecological, and aesthetic damages caused by the hazardous liquids and fumes it emits. Environmentalists spurred by a normative preference for ecosystem protection (and those seeking an accurate benefit-cost analysis) will note that establishing a major new factory will not only cause costs associated with air and water pollution. They will also point out that the project requires the construction of roads and schools, police and fire protection, and the like. These are all costs that ought to be counted in the decision whether or not to go forward with a plant, but these are not often costs borne by the plant as part of its cost of construction or maintenance, and these costs may be overlooked by governmental regulators (even assuming that there is a governmental agency empowered to block the project because of an unfavorable benefit-cost analysis).

The point is, of course, that most of these kinds of costs are hidden from direct public view, and not chargeable to the persons who decide to impose them. Returning to the salt problem, how many of the salt costs listed above, for example, will have to be paid by the road commissions that choose to use salt?

BENEFITS... The classic environmental response to a proposal's claimed benefits is to doubt them. The decision-makers in the official marketplace have decided to go ahead for their direct market reasons, but why is a supersonic transport plane needed? Will this new factory bring in as much local revenue as claimed? Does this area need another recreational reservoir? Are coats made of baby seal skins really necessary?

In the case of highway salt, this argument focuses on the lack of proof of benefits from the "bare pavement" model. What is the value of a road that appears to be clear, especially if it retains a film of icy slush? What is the value of faster-moving traffic, especially in light of the evidence that accidents on salted road systems are more likely to be fatal than the scrape-and-sand model's "fender-benders"? The environmentalist would admit the benefits of time saved and disruptions avoided by highway salting, but would argue that these benefits are illusory, or insubstantial, when offset by costs. In practice, on the other hand, the operative valuation of salt's benefits is based on intuitive judgments made by highway commissioners that insofar as they are concerned the "bare-pavement" result of salting is worth more than the yearly $200 million cost of buying and applying salt, and that is the only calculus that they consider. And in this as in other cases where valuation is difficult, one is tempted to leave the benefit calculus to administrative discretion and the marketplace.

**AVAILABLE ALTERNATIVES: CMA?...** The analysis of a proposal's benefits and costs is meaningless unless it is linked to a comparison of alternatives. Environmentalists can accurately be regarded as narrow-minded negativists if they merely attack proposals, without reviewing alternative courses of action. One alternative in every case, of course, is the "no-action" alternative. When developers planned to build a dam that would flood part of the Grand Canyon for power and water supply, environmentalists were able to show that those benefits were not needed at that time and place, in light of the social costs. The better option was to do nothing.

Often the analysis of alternatives turns upon whether the action can better take place with a different design, location, timing, process, etc. A particular factory might be a better neighbor, for example, if it installed pollution-control mechanisms, used a higher temperature process, or located itself downwind. Beverage bottles would cause less litter and save energy and raw materials if they were returnable. In the Memphis highway case, the citizens argued for location and construction designs that were feasible and prudent alternatives to going through the middle of their park.

In the case of salt, the purpose of the proposed action — removal of snow from the highways so as to allow traffic to move — is clearly necessary. Only the most troglodytic environmentalist would argue that traffic should come to a halt when the snow falls. Rather, the analysis should turn to a comparison of realistic alternatives. Installation of infra-red electric melting devices in highway pavements might be effective and avoid all the indirect costs of salting, but the direct costs would be outrageous.

Excellent alternatives to salt exist, however — salt substitutes with the same snow melting characteristics as salt yet lacking its destructive characteristics. CMA (calcium magnesium acetate), invented by Chevron, is a prime example.

It can be made from readily available materials including recycled milk whey, it has none of the destructive effects of salt, and in fact it actually rebuilds salt-damaged soils by replacing stripped magnesium and calcium.[22] In 1994 the state of Oregon made a generic switch to using de-icing chemicals including CMA, based on an overall analysis of direct and indirect costs, with special consideration of corrosion effects and environmental effects, particularly to the state's protected salmon runs.[23] Even ignoring the public health costs that were not accounted for in the EPA study, it appears reasonable that non-salt alternatives like CMA might realize savings of almost $2 billion per year when compared with continued use of salt. This would be true even if the direct costs for de-icing increased fivefold, from $200 million to $1 billion. The actual overall public costs would still drop more than $1.9 billion.

CMA, however, costs $300–600 per ton to the highway officials who budget for roads, as opposed to salt's $20–$70. "The problem," says Chevron's Dan Walter, "is that the benefit of CMA does not go back to the governmental agency that pays for de-icers, typically state maintenance departments. If a bridge on an interstate highway must be replaced, the federal government will pay 80% of the cost. Therefore the highway department cannot justify paying $600 per ton for CMA."[24] The way the commercial-political marketplace is set up, no one and no forum is in a position to bring the overall public economics to bear upon the operative decisions.

So assume that a careful study did conclusively prove that the United States was losing a net $2 billion annually, unnecessarily, to road salt. In all probability, what would occur? Probably not much.

THE HEART OF THE MATTER — HUMAN NATURE, CONTENDING FORCES, AND THE ROLE OF NONGOVERNMENTAL ORGANIZATIONS... Even though modern environmental law has carried environmental analysis into the heart of the governmental process, so far as can be determined the 1976 EPA salt study has not produced any changes in law or practice. This might well be so even if it had conclusively established annual net losses of more than $2 billion. Why?

Look at the participants in the process. Road salt manufacturers (in the U.S., primarily deep-mining companies) have expanded their production enormously over the past thirty years. Because of the growth of the road salt market, their payrolls and capital investments have increased. Because of their financial position, the salt producers and associated industries have a strong incentive and capacity to encourage the sale of salt. They have little or no financial accountability for the consequences of salt use; these costs are therefore irrelevant or "external" to their business decisions. Accordingly the salt industry organizes to increase production and promote the sale of road salt through advertising and trade publications that stress the low initial cost and high effectiveness of intensive salt use. To promote

22. See R. Horner and M. Brenner, Environmental Evaluation of Calcium Magnesium Acetate for Highway Deicing Applications, 7 Resources, Conservation and Recycling 213–237, 219 (1992).
23. See D. Keep and D. Parker, Tests Clear Snow, Path for Use of Liquid Anti-icing in Northwest, Roads & Bridges (Aug. 1995); the state reports significant overall savings (including cleanup costs).
24. U.S. Water News, Jan. 1990 at 11. If a road commission simply could not find the cash to pay for a 100% switch to CMA, 20–60% CMA-to-salt blends are available that buffer much of the salt's negatives, but still cost two to three times as much as salt.

its position nationally, the industry formed the American Salt Institute, a lobbying and trade association located in the Washington D.C. area.

Which leads to government: At the operative level, it is government agencies that actually spread salt on highways. Local and state highway commissions, however, are in the same narrowed decisional situation as the salt industry itself. They want the most removal punch for the money, and have virtually no accountability or concern for the cost consequences of salt beyond their initial expenditures to get the job done. Accordingly they turn to intensive use of salt. The officials of the highway agencies also have their national associations, which have ties to the Highway Users Federation (the trade coalition that represents and lobbies for the many players in the highway industry) which in turn has ties to the Salt Institute. Nor does the Federal Highway Administration in the U.S. Department of Transportation demonstrate much incentive to challenge the salting procedures. It has traditionally been linked in interest to the corporate highway lobby.

In another corner of the legal system, however, the state and federal governments do have resource protection agencies that are designed to regulate and protect against the kinds of danger involved here. What will they do? The EPA did take action — it wrote the study. But it did nothing more. The environmental regulatory agencies, especially in recent years, have been constrained in their financial and political resources. It is often difficult for them, internally and externally, to oppose ongoing business decisions. With the negative effects of salting so diffused, indirect, and hard to quantify in cumulative form, it has been difficult to do anything about highway salting. In the absence of a political push, the environmental and health agencies have done nothing, with the exception of a few inquiries about local well water contamination.

What about the legislatures? It would of course be possible for a local or state legislative body or Congress to pass a law in response to the problem. (Some local communities have in fact adopted no-salt policies.) But merely pointing out a factual case to a legislative committee does not get the job done. Environmental groups learned early that legislatures and politicians generally respond to pressures, rather than out of some vague loyalty to the "public interest." Government is a process of contending forces. Several state legislators have unsuccessfully proposed salt-limitation bills. As soon as proposals surface in governmental agencies or legislatures, industry lobbyists (often backed by local highway commissions) apply pressure throughout the governmental process — in committee rooms, in offices and bureaus, in the corridors, and in the expense-account restaurants — emphasizing the direct cost savings in doing things consistent with their own market interests.[25] Given the nature of the problem, and the immense resources of

---

25. The authors received the following letter from Richard L. Hanneman, President of the Salt Institute, touting a study released in January, 1992, by the Transportation Research Board, an arm of the National Research Council, concluding that CMA was not — or at least not yet — a sufficiently economical substitute for highway de-icing to justify a switch away from rock salt. Mr. Hanneman concluded that —

> there is a strong relationship between the application of de-icing salt and the prevention of about 80 percent of the fatalities and serious injuries that would otherwise occur on untreated highways....
> Using highway de-icing salt may prevent huge numbers of tort recoveries, but it still (sic) might be of interest to aspiring attorneys.

Upon examination, the report actually found that external costs of salting exceeded $2 billion by an

the market players, a rational overview analysis of the public interest is likely to be lost, no matter how compelling the facts.

Until the 1960s, there was generally no contest at all. The governmental process was essentially bi-polar, composed of market forces and regulatory government.[26] Until the late 1800s, the private marketplace was the dominant "government" of the United States. (In some senses it still is, for, in a society that is basically structured by the private corporate market, the vast majority of daily actions and personal incentives are shaped by private economic decisions.) In the trust-busting era of the 1890s, however, the laissez-faire theory of governance began to be supplemented by selective government regulation. Left to itself, the market ignores major external considerations that a society must deal with. Government intervention was necessary in order to impose certain non-market values upon the market, through laws on child labor, antitrust, worker safety, consumer fraud, and so on. The bi-polar system of government — with government agencies acting to correct failures of the marketplace to protect the public interest — was never clearer than in the 1930s New Deal. But over time, government agencies tend to come ever closer to the corporate entities they regulate, as demonstrated by the highway commissions and highway-related industries. Given the dominant position of the market in everyday lives, this so-called "capture" phenomenon really doesn't come as a surprise, nor does the well-funded persuasive force of the marketplace in the legislatures. Many of the lions of the past — the ICC, SEC, FCC, CAB, FTC and others — have subsequently become lambs.

The comfortable bi-polar structure of government, however, has been wedged open in the last twenty years by an energetic multi-centricism — through the active participation of many different civic interest groupings, notably the strident presence of non-market NGOs (non-governmental organizations). Public-interest citizen groups, with environmentalists in the vanguard, have re-invigorated a process of active pluralistic democracy, and have been the dominant enforcers of many environmental statutes. This book repeatedly emphasizes the central role played by citizen activists in the creation and continuing development of modern environmental law. The legal system would have much dimmer prospects in its efforts at conserving the planet without the informed participation of citizen environmentalists.

---

undetermined amount. The report concluded, however, that the preponderate advantage of CMA could not yet be proved. There were some serious exclusions from the research. In comparing salt and CMA the committee used an overall economic accounting approach and monetary estimations. The quantification, however, excluded certain public costs that may indeed be significant from their calculus — notably human health problems, particularly those from salt infiltration into drinking water supplies, and "environmental damages" — both of potentially large magnitude and both excluded on grounds of "insufficient information." As to safety statistics, moreover, it would appear that untreated highways were not the appropriate comparison to salted highways. The citation for the report is: Transportation Research Board, Highway De-icing: Comparing Salt and Calcium Magnesium Acetate (Special Report 235, 1991).

26. The bipolar system described by Professor Lon Fuller — where the public interest is defended by government agencies, which correct "market failure" by regulating public harms caused by the marketplace — has become too narrow a basis for rational societal governance. To many modern observers, rational governance now requires pluralistic "multipolarity" — with active roles for government entities, for industry and other market players, and also for the remarkably diverse spectrum of citizen outsiders who are impacted by official decisions and uniquely in the American system have been able to influence outcomes within the legal and political process.

Who are the environmentalists? At one pole they include the ecoguerrillas of the EarthFirst! movement, and the "Greens" and "deep ecologists" dedicated to iconoclastic political action, then ranging rightward across a wide spectrum of groups and programs all the way to the silkstockinged salons of Brahmin conservationists. Environmentalism today includes citizens from a wide range of income levels and racial backgrounds.[27] At every point across the spectrum stand environmental lawyers and legal advocacy groups. Environmentalists are often volunteers, unfunded by the market or official government, attempting to bring their concerns into government processes that so often seem to ignore them. Ultimately environmentalists of all stripes are saying that the society cannot afford to make its decisions in a manner that leaves so many real values and consequences out of its calculus. Someone has to be in a place to say that the Emperor is not wearing clothes.

**THE STRATEGIES OF AN ENVIRONMENTAL LAW CASE...** Back to the annual $2 billion in net salt damage: Assuming that no official players are likely to take action, and that citizens could prove the facts of destructive, unnecessary waste, how could nonofficial players marshal sufficient force to interpose their arguments into the process?

**MARKETPLACE REMEDIES...** Theoretically, they can work within the private marketplace, either buying out the salt producers, mobilizing boycotts, or advertising salt's harms sufficiently to dry up the market. A moment's reflection on costs in the modern marketplace and the environmentalists' volunteer status will reveal the limits of this approach. And then there is ADR (Alternative Dispute Resolution), negotiation, mediation, and the like. Avoiding the battlefield mode of dispute resolution is a growing and desirable trend, and probably 90 percent of legal controversies are ultimately settled out of court. The problem is that, without the portent of legal battle, it is highly unlikely that the market players would willingly sit down to negotiate any compromises.

**PUBLIC LAW REMEDIES: PETITIONING THE AGENCIES...** The argument can be taken to the administrative agencies, through rulemaking petitions and requests for administrative hearings. As previously noted, however, the highway commissions' dominating constraint of direct budgetary costs is likely to prevent serious rethinking of the policy, and the environmental protection agencies probably lack the political momentum to undertake such a crusade. Imagine the lot of the administrative official who did decide to take on the problem. After presentation of petitions, public testimony, and a scattering of news stories, the citizens go home, leaving the official to face the constant presence and pressure of the salt industry and its allies who respond against threats to their interests.

**PETITIONING THE LEGISLATURE...** Prospects are somewhat brighter on the legislative side. Particularly at the local level, petitions and testimony may represent

---

27. The early predominance of white upper-middle-income activists has been changing due to outreach by national environmental organizations, and grassroots efforts of groups like Highlander Center, New Market, Tennessee; Citizens for a Better America, Halifax, Virginia; Native Americans for a Clean Environment, Tahlequah, Oklahoma; Tools for Change, San Francisco; and ACE: Alternatives for Community and Environment in Boston.

sufficient potential votes to command attention. Even if a local government passes an ordinance notwithstanding the pressures of the market forces and its own highway commission, however, the environmental analysis still runs into strategic problems of scale. There are tens of thousands of local governments in the Frost Belt, each of which would have to be educated and pushed to take action, because the salt problem spreads so widely. Even if one town were to halt the practice, its citizens' cars and even water supplies would pick up the problem from elsewhere. State or federal legislation is less likely, because the issue and its active constituency, relatively speaking, are minor in scale. To get legislative attention, the environmentalists would need an altruistic legislative crusader, a vivid crisis, or a blockbusting TV exposé.

**THE MEDIA...** The media have often and accurately been called a branch of government. Media attention on an issue can be extremely effective. It makes politicians respond for reasons that lie in the theatrical nature of the governing process as well as in the quest for votes. But media coverage is often just "info-tainment," hard to mobilize and keep focused. An effective media strategy is highly contingent upon citizens' ability to interest the media in the issue, to transmit sufficient detail to reporters (and note how complex most environmental analyses are, in comparison to straightforward market arguments, that "salt clears roads," etc.), to focus coverage on the relevant governmental target, and perhaps hardest, to keep the media on the story as long as required.

**SUE THEM...** Notice that all of the prior strategies focus upon rational persuasion. As such they are appealing, for one likes to think that human society has the capacity to respond to logic, analysis, and concerned debate. Realistically, however, many environmental cases must turn to the force of law to give practical effect to their arguments — the threat of legal action to force negotiated consideration of public environmental values, or the actuality of legal action when threats are not enough.

If a fundamental problem of our economic system is that decision-makers won't take account of many of the real costs they impose unless they themselves have to pay for them,[28] then environmental law fundamentally is the art of presenting the bill for environmental social costs, most often by litigation.

The legal weaponry available to environmental activists in the United States is remarkably broad. Most of the available legal actions are based on actions in court. Although there are often useful opportunities to intervene directly in agency proceedings, most such interventions are backed up by the litigation option. In this country courts have their fingers in the widest array of pies.

Here are some available lawsuits, all of which have possible applications to the salt problem:

• *Tort actions*: Property owners can sue for injury to their homes, farms, cars; representatives of the public can sue against salt as a public nuisance. Salt could be

---

28. This is the basic "cost-externalization" syndrome studied in the next section. The managers of a factory, for example, will often try to pass on to others ("externalize") as much of the costs of their operations as they can, while holding onto, or "internalizing," maximum benefits, i.e., income, analyzed further in Chapter Two.

the basis of several creative tort law suits, posing interesting procedural problems but offering the potential of money damages or injunctions, in individual or class actions. To date only a very few such cases have been reported.[29]

• *Constitutional claims*: Particular actions by government officials may run afoul of the federal or state constitution by violating due process rights, taking property without compensation, unlawfully restricting interstate commerce, etc. Salt might be the subject of an inverse condemnation claim.

• *Public trust theories*: The public trust is a resurrected ancient remedy for protecting the public's common resource base inherited from the past, for the sake of future generations. Salt use might violate public trust duties of government to protect water quality, natural resources and other resources.

• *Statutorily-based actions*: There are a host of statutes that could be the basis of citizen enforcement, some clearly not so intended by their originating legislators. Highway salt, for instance, might be classified as "point-source" pollution under the Clean Water Act when the salt is foreseeably discharged from highway drains into roadside watercourses, which then would require road commissions to get permits and use best available techologies.[30] Salt dust may give rise to sanctions under the Clean Air Act. No such suits have yet been tried, but the creativity of statutes is that they are applied and developed at the initiative of suing parties, and evolve over time.

• *Administrative law litigation*: Administrative law offers two major formats: the approach of pressuring regulatory agencies to take action against a problem (e.g., mandamus to obtain EPA enforcement of the Clean Water Act), and suit against those agencies that are the direct cause of problems (for example, a suit against state highway commissions for the "arbitrary and capricious" irrationality of their decision to salt).

• *International law*: This field covers international treaties and conventions, and transboundary pollution cases. In the latter case, it is clearly possible that Canadian waters would be injured by cumulative salt infiltration into the Great Lakes drainage system, with possible arbitral and litigative remedies.

The list goes on, each avenue raising a sequence of technical and procedural problems as well — standing to sue, class actions, estoppel, how to finance these suits, and so on. Some litigation approaches would be quite limited in their direct effects, and some quite far-reaching (depending on class actions or the effect of precedent for broadening their impact).

Ultimately it is necessary to remind ourselves that the genius of the Anglo-

---

29. See Morash v. Commonwealth, 296 N.E.2d 461 (Mass. 1973); Mueller v. Brunn, 313 N.W.2d 790 (Wis. 1982).

30. This possibility will also be affected by future implementation of Clean Water Act amendments which classify highway runoffs as stormwater discharges. EPA's proposed general permit for stormwater discharges has been integrated into some state regulations. As a result of a pair of California lawsuits brought by the Natural Resources Defense Council against several cities and the state Department of Transportation for failure to comply with general permits issued by state Water Quality Boards, the court required comprehensive stormwater control systems to control runoff, a precedent that could be applied in the salting setting as well. See 25 BNA Env. Reptr. Curr. Dev. 1492 (1994).

EPA missed the October 1, 1994 statutory deadline to promulgate Phase II municipal stormwater regulations, covering governmental units with separate storm sewers serving populations of over 50,000 people. NRDC has reached a settlement with EPA to implement the Phase II permitting program within six years.

American system of law is that it is always in flux, though the process remains the same. Creative use of legal theories has shaped today's environmental law and will continue to do so. Perhaps some day environmental mediation and consensus negotiation will resolve the pressing questions of the day. For now, however, sweet reason and facts alone have insufficient force in the system. They require the support of credible legal leverages, mobilized to make their point in a vastly complex confrontational system. To give effect to values and analyses, one must know the full array of ways to play the game.

**OVERVIEW...** It is important to put the efforts of environmentalists in strategic perspective. If one accepts the premise that in most cases environmentalists are defending real public values that are being ignored, and doing so as volunteers, not for profit — and that on the other side market decisions are being made by persons who will have a direct, narrow profit or power stake in the proposed actions — then it seems that *a priori* the broader values should be dominant.

They are not. Environmentalists lose most battles, the complaints of business to the contrary notwithstanding. Try to name a dozen major government projects or programs that have been permanently stopped or ameliorated by environmentalists. Pollution continues in air, water, toxic wastes, noise, land abuse.... Anyone who has watched a state legislative hearing, an agency proceeding on regulation of an industry, or a court enforcement action against a large polluter, knows the heavy guns that the marketplace can bring to bear against "the do-gooders." The relative weakness of environmentalists in absolute terms would be justified if their concerns were trivial, or their input not sufficiently expert. (Often volunteer environmentalists *don't* do their homework well enough to compete with well-funded market opposition.) But the environmental accounting approach is not trivial, and environmentalists have necessarily become more expert in science, economics, politics, and law. Of the vast array of challengeable projects, only a tiny handful can be contested, so only the worst, in economic and ecological terms, can be challenged. Of these, most will survive environmental attacks anyway. It would not be so if the environmental side of the debate were funded in any rough parity with the marketplace, but that has never been the case.

Yet if the problems posed by greenhouse gases, for example, are more important than private and governmental market decision-makers consider them to be, it is critical that the environmental position be heard effectively. If acid rain in the Northeast is eroding the lead from urban pipes into water supplies, wiping out life in mountain lakes and fragile water-based vegetation systems, then it is critical that upwind state governments and industries do not make the narrow "free market" decisions on how much air pollution is "economically reasonable."

It should come as little surprise that "environmentalism" is a task as broad as government itself, highly frustrating, burdensome, never permanently successful or satisfying, altruistic, necessary.

Most environmentalists will tell you that they lose more cases than they win. For what it's worth, before the 1970s, environmentalists were almost never successful in being heard, and that has clearly changed. Perhaps the success of environmental efforts should be measured in the (unmeasurable) numbers of bad projects, programs or polluting plants that nowadays are not proposed, for fear of "those damned environmentalists."

...And the salt goes on.

## SOME ANALYTIC THEMES

Some basic analytic themes in the legal process of environmental law should be emerging here. Rachel Carson, Ronald Coase, Garrett Hardin, and EPA's analysis of highway salting each present fundamental logical and ecological perceptions that underlie environmental analysis and environmental law. To begin a catalog of crosscutting analytic concepts in environmental law, here are some of the basic themes —

▪ **UNCERTAINTY, SCIENTIFIC COMPLEXITY, AND RISK** are endemic problems in environmental policy. Often both the presence and the effects of a harmful human impact are invisible until too late. When chemicals leach through the subsoil killing communities of microscopic soilbuilding organisms, or highway salt poisons the root systems of trees, neither cause nor effect will be seen until the soil's productivity crashes, or the trees begin to die. When pollution is spread widely through an air or water commons, its concentrations are so diffused that the pollution is not noticed until huge volumes have been discharged. When human health begins to show signs of illness and injury from widespread exposures to environmental toxins — sometimes 30 years after the exposure — the individual pathways of contamination and proof of causation are typically so scientifically complicated as to be practically impossible to pin down.

And trying to ascertain and handle "Risk," the statistical likelihood of particular perils in particular settings, confronts even greater scientific complexities and subjectivities, as well as psychological and political barriers. Tradeoffs do occur on risks, and between short-term material welfare and long-term ecological integrity: Some toxic residues can be tolerated in foods in order to have the benefit of crops that are not destroyed by pests; some continuing risks like global warming are accepted in the short term for the sake of developing economies and consumption desires. Environmentalists, however, continually argue against false tradeoff choices when rational alternatives are available. Is it really true that "You have to choose — either economic progress, or environmental quality, you can't have both"? To most modern environmental analysts that universal cliché sounds like the classic false tradeoff. In the long term both are inseparable; in the short term they can and must at the least be reconcilable.

Science and Law continually work together, but they are essentially different worlds. In the complex business of proving "causation," for example — that exposure to chemical X can be identified as causing malady Y — science requires a certainty level of 95% (a margin of error of no more than 5%), the criminal law requires a super majority ("beyond a reasonable doubt," perhaps somewhat less than 95%), the common law requires only 50% plus one ("probable"), and statutory law (which in many cases only needs to be "not arbitrary") can regulate with even less certain proof of causation.[31] This often produces confusion. Navigating the cross-channels of science and law is a continuing subtle challenge.

---

31. Regulatory law often deals with risk situations where government must protect against unproved or unquantified threats, as when it controls releases of genetically-altered organisms into the environment. Sometimes these include "zero-infinity" problems, where public law attempts to control the risks of harms that are close to zero in likelihood of happening, but which would be catastrophic in scale of harm if they ever were to occur.

■ **HUMAN NATURE AND THE EXTERNALIZATION OF SOCIAL COSTS.** Hardin's tragedy of the commons and Coase's descriptions of cost externalization illustrated how individual human actors are powerfully motivated to maximize their own gains at the expense of the public and the commons. Humans tend to make decisions in relatively short-term horizons, in insulated, self-referential terms. We tend to try to maximize our personal pleasures and profits, we strenuously avoid and ignore burdensome liabilities if we can, and we may hope or pretend that negative consequences will disappear and not accumulate to the detriment of others. Coase the economist showed us how this process of cost externalization is a strong and logical tendency in individualized human behavior. When we are involved in any activity, the economists say, we resolutely display an inclination to pass wide the costs onto others who will not be able to hold us accountable, and to hold close the profits and benefits, focusing on the short term. It is a fundamentally rational strategy in individual terms, at least for the short term in which most of us live.

As a consequence there is a powerful inherent pressure within corporate management and market forces generally, and government agencies as well, to externalize pollution and other social costs into the environment. These drives produced the biggest marketplace economy the world has known, with all the blessings that follow it, and all the forlorn consequences that arise from not planning for and dealing with the realities of costs that are externalized onto nature and the public.

■ **ENVIRONMENTAL LAW ATTEMPTS TO "INTERNALIZE" SOCIAL COSTS.** Since Carson's Silent Spring provided an ecological context for the economists' concept of social costs, it has become impossible to maintain the 'out-of-sight, out-of-mind' illusion that externalities can be ignored. In effect, Rachel Carson spread a broad intellectual catch-basket beneath the welfare economists' universe of benefit-maximizing individual actors, so as to collect and take overall account of their jettisoned "externalized" social costs, even if they are indirect and unmarketized. Her work has helped make it painfully obvious that we all must ultimately live together, interconnected, in an essentially closed system. Pollution, risk, and resource depletion are real social costs that have far-reaching consequences that modern science has learned to track and measure, and modern policy has been forced to address as a high utilitarian priority. For a society to hope to survive and prosper into the indefinite future, it must learn how to integrate an environmental accounting — both natural costs and public costs — into social governance.

That has been the role of environmental law — to attempt through common law, state and federal statutory and regulatory systems, and even constitutional theories, to force externalized environmental and social costs back into the politics and economics of the marketplace. Wistfully, many economists think that externalities will be readily marketized and privately ordered, so that overall optimal results can be brokered by the marketplace without requiring the artifices of governmental control. But "market failure" — the marketplace's inability to cure its own excesses and to internalize certain public values — has in practice been the dominant reality and the reason why law and regulatory government are necessary.

■**BIODIVERSITY... OF NATURE AND LAW.** From ecological science comes the proposition that natural systems that evolve and maintain a wider diversity of living things are more likely to be successful in the long run. A rich natural biodiversity means that ecosystems are likely to have more interlocking practical mechanisms and more available adaptive options for coping with ongoing changes.[32] Law too has its biodiversity.

---

32. See discussion of biodiversity in Chapter 14.

The American legal system has always had as one of its special strengths that it combines statutory, regulatory, constitutional, and common law mechanisms within a single system, and has a rich variety of different approaches and remedies within each of these. Environmental law evolves opportunistically in each of these areas of the law, attempting to adapt and integrate changing environmental knowledge and values into the structures of law, a process that continues throughout this book and environmental law practice.

■**THE GOAL OF ENVIRONMENTAL LAW (AND DEMOCRATIC GOVERNANCE)?** What is the ultimate goal of environmental law? Some environmentalists would say preservation of the natural economy is the core value: Nature has a sense about it of ageless truth, evolving over hundreds of millions of years, with the human market economy appearing only in the latest tiny historical moment. Humans are a recent addition to the planetary web of life, only one species, with volatile propensities, so a wary conservatism argues for a norm of ecological preservation.

We suggest, however, that for most of us the ultimate perspective must center upon human society, both in terms of survivability and the quality of human life. Since the quality of a human society's existence has meaning beyond the size or duration of our collective bank balances, the marketplace must be considered a major component but not a complete definition of societal success.

Long term survivability and success in maintaining civic and social quality of life for present and future human generations is thus an appropriate goal for a society. Careful consideration and stewardship of natural systems typically contributes to that goal. Because of our human natural history, our species' ethical perceptions, the remarkable qualities of life that flow from contact with natural processes, or the stark utilitarian necessity of not betraying the natural systems that support and nourish us, nature is important. The cultural richness of human experience over time must likewise be part of the mix. A sensitive ongoing balance between the dynamics of daily life and the past, present, and future richness of human existence, in its complex natural context, will define the successes that environmental law strives to achieve.

■**SUSTAINABLE DEVELOPMENT AND INTERGENERATIONAL EQUITY.** Perhaps the phrase that best captures the goal of environmental law and policy is "sustainable development." It was the leitmotif of the Rio Conference on the Environment of 1992, where more than 100 presidents and kings, and hundreds of delegations from around the world, agreed that the momentum and practices of the status quo threaten our common global future, and that coherent international planning and action are necessary. "Sustainable development" means many things to different people, but its gravamen seems to be that our societies and legal systems owe it to ourselves and our posterity to live within available resources, and not to destroy the environmental birthright of future generations for the needs and profits of today, a theme echoed in the public trust doctrine later in this chapter. Development must not be based upon an erosive diminution of global assets, but rather on systems of indefinitely extendable human sustenance and life quality, in balance with the resource capacity of the planet's environments.

## B.  ANALYTIC THEMES FROM A CLASSIC INDUSTRIAL POLLUTION SETTING: ALLIED CHEMICAL AND *KEPONE* — A MILESTONE 1970s INDUSTRIAL POLLUTION CASE

The following narrative presents a famous pollution case from the first generation of modern environmental law in the 1970s. The Allied Chemical Kepone in Hopewell set off a media avalanche that galvanized public and regulatory attention, and subsequently helped push Congress into major overhauls of federal environmental statutes.[33] The case illustrates many of the classic determinants of industrial market behavior that made environmental law necessary in the first place. The various cases that followed the Kepone disaster, however, did not result in court decisions that told the story of what had happened. (Most cases were settled by the company before they went to a verdict.) The following narrative of the Kepone case was gathered from a wide variety of field and archival sources. As you read it, note the different kinds of serious negative externalities — to occupational health conditions within the factories, to air, water and environmental quality outside the plants, and to ultimate consumers exposed to pesticides — and consider how the corporate and legal systems should or could have taken account of them.

### William Goldfarb, Kepone: A Case Study
8 Environmental Law 645 (1978)

Hopewell (population approximately 24,000) is an industrial city located on the banks of the James River in southern Virginia. Calling itself "the Chemical Capital of the South," Hopewell has actively recruited large chemical manufacturers. Consequently, Firestone, Hercules, Continental Can, and Allied Chemical (now known as Allied-Signal, with $3 billion in annual sales in the 1970s) located chemical plants in Hopewell.

Allied Chemical opened its Hopewell plant in 1928, the first industrial plant capable of utilizing atmospheric nitrogen for the production of ammonia and nitrogen fertilizer. Eventually Allied's Hopewell plant became the Hopewell "complex," which in 1975 was Hopewell's largest employer with 4,000 workers.

The initial batch of 500 pounds of a pesticide named Kepone was produced by Allied in 1949. Two patents for the process were awarded to it in 1952. Allied did not consider Kepone to be a major pesticide. With less than $200,000 in annual sales over a 16 year period, Kepone production never exceeded 0.1 percent of America's total pesticide production. Kepone was intended primarily for export to Europe for use against the Colorado Potato Beetle, and to South America to control the Banana Root Borer.

---

33. A major retrospective symposium on the Kepone incident appears in 29 U.Richmond L.Rev. 493ff. (1995). Portions of this text incorporate material from Goldfarb, Changes in the Clean Water Act since Kepone, 29 U. Richmond L.Rev. 603 (1995). See also the 1992 tax court opinion, Allied-Signal v. Commissioner of Internal Revenue, Docket Nos. 9662-89, 17584-89, 1992 WL 67399 (Tax Court), 63 T.C.M. (CCH) 2672, T.C.M. (P-H) 92,204 (April 6, 1992), aff'd without opinion, 54 F.3d 767 (3d Cir. 1995); Zim, Allied Chemical's $20-Million Ordeal with Kepone, FORTUNE, Sept. 11, 1978, at 82; Christopher D. Stone, A Slap on the Wrist for the Kepone Mob, 22 Business & Society Review 4-11, Summer 1977, reprinted in Corporate Violence 121 (Stuart L. Hills ed., 1977); Morton Mintz & Daniel Klaidman, Creative Settlement or Improper Deal?, Legal Times, May 11, 1992, at 1; and Facing a Time of Counter-Revolution — The Kepone Incident and a Review of First Principles, 29 U. Rich. L. Rev. 657 (1995).

Before moving to commercial production, Allied subjected Kepone to an extensive series of toxicity tests. Such tests were necessary in order to obtain registration under the federal pesticide laws.[34] The results of this research revealed Kepone to be highly toxic to all species tested: it caused cancer, liver damage, reproductive system failure, and inhibition of growth and muscular coordination in fish, mammals, and birds. Upon being presented with the test results, Allied voluntarily withdrew its petition to the Food and Drug Administration for the establishment of Kepone residue tolerances for agricultural products.

Kepone is a chlorinated hydrocarbon pesticide, a chemical relative of DDT, Aldrin/Dieldrin, and Mirex (all of which have been banned by the EPA). As such, Kepone is a contact poison, capable of being absorbed through the skin or cuticle; it is lipophilic (fat soluble), but insoluble in water: it is persistent in the environment; and it will bioaccumulate in the fatty tissues of the body. The exact mechanism by which chlorinated hydrocarbons kill target pests is uncertain. What is known is that they are nerve poisons, interfering with the transmission of electrical impulses along nerve channels. The results of contact with Kepone are loss of control over muscular coordination, convulsions, DDT-like tremors and eventually death.

Despite the unfavorable toxicity test results, Allied deemed Kepone ready for commercial production, and contracted with the Nease Chemical Company of State College, Pennsylvania, to produce it for them. The relationship between Allied and Nease lasted from 1958 through 1960. Allied entered into a similar arrangement with Hooker Chemical during the early 60's.

By 1966 even more negative test results had been associated with Kepone, but Allied nevertheless decided to manufacture Kepone on an increased basis in its own Semi-Works facility in Hopewell. In preparation for production, an area supervisor of the Semi-Works was asked to develop a production manual. This manual was to contain operating and safety instructions for the production process. The supervisor naturally consulted available toxicity research results, and his recommended precautions reflect the test findings. At Allied, Kepone spills and dust were closely controlled, and workers wore safety glasses, rubber boots and gloves. Allied's Kepone operations were directed by William Moore until 1968, and thereafter by Virgil Hundtofte.

Prior to preparation of the production manual, there had been no recorded case of human exposure of Kepone to the level of acute poisoning. Allied apparently discounted such a possibility, regardless of the documented adverse effects of Kepone on animals. However, a witness for the United States at the trial testified that Allied should have suspected "that the same symptomology would be induced in man if exposed to Kepone."

In 1970, the Federal government resurrected the Refuse Act Permit Program, which required all industries discharging wastes into navigable waters to obtain permits from the U.S. Army Corps of Engineers.[35] The Allied complex at Hopewell had three pipes discharging directly into a stream called Gravelly Run, a tributary of the James River. One of these pipes originated at the Semi-Works where Kepone was manufactured. The Refuse Act Permit application was discussed by Allied's

34. Eds.: The Federal Insecticide, Fungicide, and Rodenticide Act (FIFRA) (now codified at 7 U.S.C.A. §§135 — 136 (1976)) is the applicable statute, considered below in Chapter 15.

35. The Refuse Act is a subsection of the 1899 Rivers and Harbors Appropriation Act, 30 Stat. §1151 (1899), 33 USCA §407, noted further at the start of Chapter 19. For a time it was the most effective federal water pollution law; it still has enforceable effect in a number of settings.

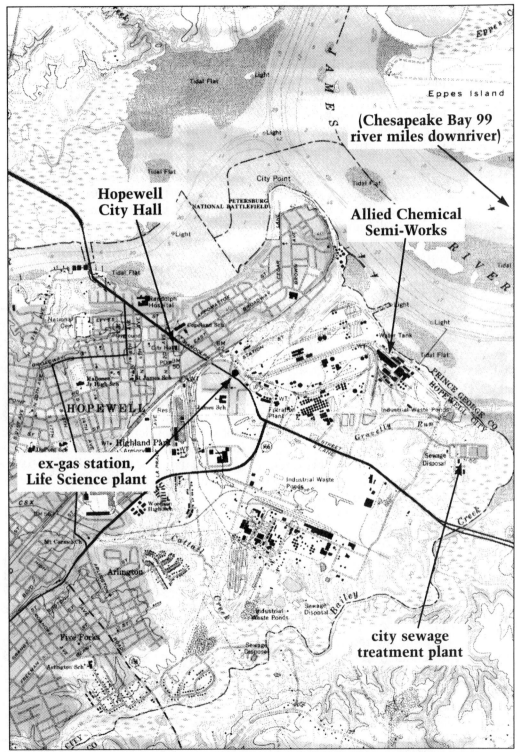

ADAPTED FROM USGS MAP NO. 37077-C3-TF-024 HOPEWELL QUADRANGLE

*Schematic overview of the Allied Chemical Semi-Works and Life Science Products Co. in Hopewell, Virginia, site of the Kepone pesticide waste contamination controversy.*

plant managers and their assistants, who found themselves on the horns of a dilemma. Allied was discharging Kepone process wastes without treatment of any kind, and the installation of pollution control equipment would be expensive. Moreover, planning was being conducted for the construction of a regional sewage treatment plant which would treat the wastes of all industries in Hopewell, but the municipal treatment plant would not be completed before 1975. What should Allied do during the construction period?

Allied decided to list the Semi-Works discharge as a temporary phenomenon which would be discontinued within two years. In such cases a short form Refuse Act application required only that the discharge be identified as a "temporary discharge." (Allied gratuitously added that it was unmetered and unsampled.) Thus, neither Kepone nor two plastics products (TAIC and THEIC) also manufactured at the Semi-Works were listed by Allied on its Refuse Act application, even though Allied quite clearly did not intend to terminate production at Hopewell.

In 1972 the Refuse Act expired, but a new permit program had been enacted — the National Pollutant Discharge Elimination System (NPDES) permit program under the Federal Water Pollution Control Act Amendments of 1972 (FWPCA). The NPDES permit program was to be administered by EPA in Washington D.C. until such time as EPA certified delegation of the federal program to a state's regulatory agencies.[36]

EPA requested data on the nature, volume, and strength of Allied's discharges, and again the dilemma manifested itself. One of Hundtofte's assistants prepared an option memorandum, outlining three strategies which Allied might follow: (1) to do nothing and hope for a lack of enforcement by EPA; (2) to divert the Semi-Works effluent to another outfall pipe for which a permit had been obtained; or (3) to slowly improve the Semi-Works effluent so as to "buy time" until completion of the municipal system. None of these last options was selected, and, as in 1970, Allied submitted data to the federal government describing the Semi-Works discharges as unmetered, unsampled, temporary outfalls. As a result, between 1966 and 1974 Allied discharged untreated Kepone and plastics wastes into Gravelly Run without revealing the nature of its discharges to the Federal government.

In 1973 Allied underwent a corporate reorganization, during which control of the Semi-Works facility was transferred from the Agricultural Division to the Plastics Division. The transfer took place in expectation of the Agriculture Division's impending move to new facilities in Baton Rouge, Louisiana. Virgil Hundtofte, plant manager of Allied's Agricultural Division at Hopewell, and William Moore, Research Director, made plans to retire from the company rather than relocate. (Hundtofte had been with Allied in Hopewell since 1965, and Moore since 1948.)

One effect of the reorganization was a reorientation of production priorities among the products manufactured at the Semi-Works. Kepone production had decreased steadily, but THEIC, which had been manufactured in small quantities for eighteen years, suddenly found a lucrative market calling for a doubling of production. THEIC and Kepone shared certain production equipment, and with the surge in demand for THEIC a decision was made in 1973 to "toll" Kepone production. Tolling is a common arrangement in the chemical industry whereby another company performs processing work for a fee or "toll" and then returns the final

---

36. 33 U.S.C.A. §§1251-1376 (Supp. V 1973); §1342(a)(1)(Supp. V 1975). The federal Clean Water Act is studied in Chapter Nine.

product. The keynote of a tolling arrangement is that during the processing period legal title to the materials and product remains in the supplier, in this case Allied. (More recently, many U.S. companies have entered into tolling agreements with "maquiladora" companies they have set up across the border in Mexico to take advantage of looser environmental standards and labor rights.)

In January, 1973, when the decision to toll Kepone was divulged, William Moore saw his opportunity to remain in Virginia and continue in the Kepone manufacturing business. He immediately contacted Hundtofte, who had recently resigned from Allied and gone to work for a fuel oil distributor. Moore and Hundtofte agreed to form a corporation and bid for the Kepone tolling contract. On November 9, 1973, Life Science Products Company (LSP) was incorporated under the laws of the Commonwealth of Virginia. Moore and Hundtofte were the only shareholders, directors, and officers of LSP. Less than a month later, the tolling agreement between Allied and LSP was signed. Allied had solicited bids from Hooker Chemical, Nease Chemical, Velsicol and LSP, but LSP's bid was by far the lowest: 54 cents per pound for 500,000 pounds of Kepone. Nease Chemical (which, it may be recalled, manufactured Kepone for Allied from 1958 through 1960) declined to bid, but responded that if it chose to bid on the contract it would cost Nease 30 cents per pound for waste disposal alone. Hooker (Nease's successor) bid $3.00 per pound.

The details of the tolling agreement are important because the question of Allied's responsibility for LSP's illegal acts loomed large at the criminal trial. The contract provided that Allied would supply — at its own expense — all of the raw materials for Kepone production, with the title to remain in Allied. Within certain broad limits, Allied would determine the monthly production rate of Kepone, which would be packed in Allied containers and transported in Allied trucks. Allied also agreed to pay LSP's taxes, other than corporate income taxes. LSP was to receive between 32 and 38 cents per pound for 650,000 pounds or more of Kepone. Through a capital surcharge arrangement, Allied was to pay for all of LSP's approved capital expenditures, whether for production or pollution control, except for land and building. If LSP was closed for pollution violations during the first year of the contract, Allied had the option to purchase LSP's assets for $25,000. And if the contract was terminated by either party for any reason, LSP agreed to refrain from producing Kepone for anyone else.

The relationship between Allied and LSP was only partially defined by the tolling agreement. Moore and Hundtofte promised Allied that they would not dispose of their shares in LSP without Allied's consent. Moreover, Allied assisted LSP in many ways — in obtaining equipment and loans (including the mortgage to buy the gas station in which Kepone would be made) from outside sources, in meeting temporary cash deficits, in augmenting fuel supplies during the oil embargo, and in attaining greater efficiency by the use of Allied facilities. Most importantly, LSP's effluent was sampled and analyzed by Allied personnel after Virginia ordered such testing. Before that (up to October 1974), LSP had tested its effluent only by a visual check — if the effluent was cloudy, the presence of suspended Kepone was indicated.

Allied officials regularly toured the LSP plant, and were informed by mail of the waste disposal problems which LSP faced almost from its inception. Allied had discharged the residues of its Kepone production process directly into tributaries of the James River. LSP at first discharged into a disposal pit on Allied's property, as well as tank-trucking some wastes to the Hopewell landfill. As the possibility of legal enforcement increased, it was decided that LSP would discharge into the Hopewell sewer system, despite the fact that the treatment plant was still under construction. By this means, LSP could avoid having to apply for an NPDES permit, which is not required of "indirect dischargers" (dischargers into publicly-owned treatment works — POTWs).[37] Having made the decision to "plug in" to the Hopewell system, LSP contacted C.L. Jones, Director of Hopewell's Department of Public Works, for permission. At the time, Hopewell possessed a primary waste treatment plant — a series of filters and settling tanks without biological or chemical treatment other than disinfection and sludge digestion. Such a rudimentary system would not degrade Kepone, but would merely divide Kepone effluent between outfall pipe and sludge. Jones, who had been Plant Manager of Allied's Hopewell Semi-Works prior to Hundtofte, recommended to Hopewell's City Manager that LSP be permitted to discharge. Permission was granted in November of 1973. (LSP was asked by Hopewell to meet a pretreatment standard of three parts per million of Kepone.) Thus, LSP became the only industry in Hopewell allowed to discharge into the municipal sewerage system. Allied Chemical's attorneys participated in these negotiations and agreed to pay for the pollution control equipment that Life Science would require in order to meet the pretreatment standard.

Problems developed as soon as LSP began diverting Kepone wastes into Hopewell's treatment plant. In October 1974 a state inspector discovered that the sludge digester at the plant was inoperative, and his investigation revealed LSP to be the source of contamination. Prior to the plant breakdown, the State was apparently unaware that Kepone was being discharged into the Hopewell system because Hopewell's application for an NPDES permit for its treatment plant (filed a month before plug-in permission was granted to LSP) made no mention of any industrial discharge into the municipal system.[38] When the State brought the situation to the attention of LSP and Hopewell officials, LSP's discharges were not halted even though the pretreatment standard was being violated. Instead, a study was commenced to determine a "safe" effluent limit for Kepone.

In March, 1975 the EPA accepted the Commonwealth of Virginia's application for certification to take over by delegation the role of issuing and enforcing NPDES permits governing the discharge of pollutants into navigable waters within the Commonwealth. In June of 1975, a pretreatment standard was imposed on LSP (.5 parts per billion) that was weaker than EPA had wished but stricter than prior standards. EPA, which had been informed of the situation, agreed to this compromise. In order to meet this standard LSP was supposed to further pretreat its wastes and hold its discharges in "equalization" tanks until such time as discharge would not violate the pretreatment standard (i.e. to even-out the flow). Allied had participated in the negotiations among LSP, Hopewell, Virginia, and EPA, and Allied opted to pay for the necessary pollution control equipment. Allied and LSP then began to discuss the capital costs of expanding Kepone production to 2,500,000 pounds per year in order to meet an increasing demand in the European market. (From the inception of LSP, Allied had constantly requested increased Kepone production.) However, even after the new equipment was installed, the pretreatment standard

---

37. 33 U.S.C.A. §1317(b)(Supp. V 1975) as amended by Clean Water Act of 1977. Pub. L. No. 95 — 217, 33 U.S.C.A. §1317(b)(West Supp. 1977); 49 C.F.R. §125.4(a)(1977).

38. The Virginia State Water Control Board was by this time administering the NPDES program pending formal delegation by EPA, 33 U.S.C.A. §1342(b)(Supp. V 1975) provides that the states may administer the NPDES program.

was violated in nineteen out of twenty-one samplings, though local and state officials appear to have taken no action on the violations.

The most horrific manifestation of the pollution was the physical poisoning of workers at the site. As a chlorinated hydrocarbon, Kepone can be absorbed through the skin as well as breathed in or swallowed. As it accumulates in the body it generates neurological symptoms, including eye tremors, hand tremors, and serious liver dysfunction, and apparently has effects on the reproductive system as well. Conditions within the LSP workplace "might have shocked Charles Dickens," Kepone dust was "flying through the air...saturating the workers' clothing, getting...into sandwiches they munched...."[39] Workers were "virtually swimming in the stuff," were not required to wear protective equipment, even when it was available, and no warning signs were posted.

On July 7, 1975, as LSP was preparing for increased Kepone production, one of its employees visited Dr. Chou, a Hopewell internist, complaining of tremors, weight loss, quickened pulse rate, unusual eye movements, and a tender, enlarged liver. Such symptoms were not unusual among LSP employees, but were generally dismissed as a necessary price to be paid for the $5.00 per hour wage they received. Although about twenty physicians had been consulted during the sixteen months of LSP's existence, only Dr. Chou suspected a connection between the ailments and the workplace environment. After questioning his patient and taking a blood sample, Dr. Chou forwarded the sample to the Center for Disease Control in Atlanta, where an analysis for Kepone could be performed. The tests disclosed that the blood sample contained 7.5 parts per million of Kepone, an astounding concentration to be found in human blood. Federal doctors then contacted the Virginia State Epidemiologist, Dr. Robert Jackson, who quickly arranged a meeting with Hundtofte and Moore.[40]

When Jackson toured the plant he was appalled: "Kepone was everywhere"; conditions were "incredible." Seven out of ten production workers present had "the shakes" so severely that they required immediate hospitalization.[41] On July 25, 1975, LSP voluntarily closed out its operations under threat of a closure order by the Virginia Department of Health. Further investigation divulged seventy-five cases of acute Kepone poisoning among LSP workers and high levels of Kepone in the blood of some of their family members. Some workers showed dramatically lowered sperm counts and low sperm motility. Moreover, there was found to be massive contamination of air, soil, and especially water in the vicinity of the plant.

---

39. See Harvard Business School, "Allied Chemical Corporation Case" 5 (1979, written by Joseph L. Bodaracco). Interestingly, the HBS case study essentially ignores the role of Allied managers in the Kepone affair, treating contamination as the result of isolated renegade acts of the Life Sciences company, which was identified only as a small Allied "supplier," thereby finessing the point that the tolling contract was a carefully considered corporate externalization by Allied itself.

40. Meetings had previously been requested by the Virginia State Department of Labor and Industry, but LSP had been successful in postponing them. Even though a former LSP worker had filed a complaint with the United States Occupational Safety and Health Administration (a branch of the United States Department of Labor), that agency had also failed to inspect the LSP factory. Only one Federal official, an EPA pesticide inspector, visited LSP before 1973; but he was not authorized to enter the production area. Other media under EPA jurisdiction — air and water pollution — had been delegated to State and local officials. At various times representatives of the Virginia Air Pollution Control Board, Water Pollution Control Board, and State Health Department had all visited LSP, but they were not responsible for inspecting LSP's working conditions.

41. In late 1974, the federal Occupational Safety and Health Agency (OSHA) had received a complaint from an LSP worker who claimed to have been fired for refusing to work in the Kepone-laden work setting. OSHA merely sent a written inquiry to LSP, and after receiving a mollifying response closed the file without even making an on-site inspection.

As a result, the State of Virginia closed one hundred miles of the James River and portions of Chesapeake Bay to fishing. (Parts of the river and Bay remained closed to fishing until 1980.)

The operations of Life Science and the Allied Semi-Works discharges into James River tributaries resulted in Kepone contamination of the atmosphere, soil, and waterways.[42] EPA confirmed that the James River and its local tributaries had unacceptable levels of Kepone, as did shellfish and finfish taken from the river and bay. EPA reported Kepone particulates in the atmosphere as far away as Richmond, and Kepone contamination of the Life Science plant, a neighboring building, the soil at the plant site, a section of the Hopewell landfill, and a lagoon adjacent to the Hopewell waste treatment facility.... In January 1976, the National Cancer Institute released a report implicating Kepone as a possible carcinogen in humans. The local and national press laid the blame for the Kepone incident on Allied. Life Science became insolvent when the plant was closed, and was financially incapable of remedying the consequences of the Kepone incident. Some news reports and editorials charged that Life Science had been used by Allied as a front for Kepone manufacture, while others ignored Life Science's role altogether, laying full responsibility upon Allied. On December 14, 1975, the CBS program "60 Minutes" sharply criticized Allied for the Kepone incident.

In an early attempt to address the unfavorable publicity that Allied had suffered as a result of its involvement in the Kepone incident, Allied decided to implement an advertising campaign that would portray it as a good and concerned corporate citizen. However, because of persistent negative stories on Allied's alleged role in the Kepone incident which dominated the media, as well as the prospect of significant litigation, Allied decided to postpone implementation of the advertising campaign. Allied's board of directors maintained a high level of interest in senior management's responses to the Kepone incident and to the negative publicity and litigation that Allied faced. At its February 1976 meeting, the board was informed that Allied's outside auditors had identified the Kepone incident as having a potentially significant impact on Allied's financial statements. The auditors' opinion with respect to Allied's financial statements for 1976 was "qualified" because of the inability to predict what additional costs from pending lawsuits and other exposure Allied would incur as a result of the Kepone incident....

As a result of the Kepone incident, hundreds of personal injury and other damage claims were filed against Allied. Approximately 10,500 persons alleging to have been harmed by the Kepone incident sought to recover damages in excess of $25 billion from Allied. Claims by Life Science employees, their families, and others aggregated approximately $85 million. Approximately 400 fishermen, alleging that their livelihood was impaired by the closing of the James River and Chesapeake Bay, filed claims against Allied aggregating $24 million. In addition, a class action suit was brought against Allied on behalf of some 10,000 fishermen and other members of the Bay-area seafood industry, claiming damages of $25 billion. The Virginia Water Control Board brought suit against Allied for $3.5 million in civil penalties. Allied was also informed that the Commonwealth of Virginia, the City of Hopewell, the EPA, the Army Corps of Engineers, and other govern-

---

42. This and following paragraphs are taken from the 1992 tax court opinion, Allied-Signal v. Commissioner of Internal Revenue, 1992 WL 67399 (Tax Court), 63 T.C.M. (CCH) 2672, T.C.M. (P-H) 92,204 (April 6, 1992), aff'd without opinion, 54 F.3d 767 (3d Cir. 1995). This decision was written 16 years after the Kepone case ended, and resulted from the happenstance of the industry's attempt to write off $8 million dollars of criminal penalties as tax-deductible business expenses.

mental agencies involved in the investigation of the Kepone incident and its subsequent cleanup would demand reimbursement from Allied for expenses incurred
or expected to be incurred in the cleanup. In the aggregate, these cleanup expenses
could have exceeded $20 million.

EPA referred criminal charges in the case to the United States Attorney for the
Northern District of Virginia, who in early 1976 obtained grand jury criminal
indictments against Allied, LSP, Hundtofte, Moore, and the City of Hopewell
under the federal water pollution act and the Refuse Act. In the summer of 1976,
Judge Robert Mehrige presided over in a criminal trial given so much passionate
public attention that it had to be moved to West Virginia. [The Kepone criminal
case is discussed in Chapter 19.]

In January 1976, the Senate Committee on Environment and Public Works
held hearings focusing on the Kepone incident that ultimately led to the Clean
Water Act of 1977 (CWA), an important component of current federal water pollution law.

COMMENTARY AND QUESTIONS

1. **A first-generation regulatory setting.** The Allied Kepone case illustrated an early
stage in the modern history of environmental regulation. Initially, at the time
Allied began manufacturing Kepone in Hopewell in 1966, it was regulated only
under the State of Virginia's water pollution statute, which was a permissive
1940s-style law that apparently imposed no significant constraint on the industry's
behavior until it was too late. The federal Refuse Act, a 1890s criminal law redis-
covered in the late 1960s that coincidentally fit the needs of environmentalists,
appears to have been the first statute to require significant modification in corporate behavior.[43] The Refuse Act provisions were relatively primitive, however,
requiring only a simple permit from the Corps, and the statutory standards for
issuing permits were unclear.

Then in 1972, because water quality was chronically underprotected by the states
(who were often locked into a "Race to the Bottom," a competition of laxity
between states vying to attract industry), Congress passed a comprehensively
amended Federal Water Pollution Control Act.[44] FWPCA absorbed much of the
Refuse Act coverage and tied factories into a more complex federal regulatory
scheme. Each industrial discharge "point source" now required a National
Pollution Discharge permit (NPDES) based on best available technology standards,
and behind that lay a further water quality standard based on fishable, swimmable
uses whenever attainable. (Under federal water law, "non-point sources" like agricultural runoff and erosion, which constitute huge environmental problems, are
not required to have permits and are largely unregulated.) In the Kepone years, the
setting of point source standards was just getting started. In the early years the

---

43. The strict, simple terms of the Refuse Act's criminal provisions are noted in Chapter 19.
44. 33 USCA §1251 ff. The new law set federal minimum standards without which, it is thought, an
intense interstate competition for jobs and revenues powerfully induces states to lower their environmental standards. States that enforce environmental protections tend to lose their industries to states
that require less. Pollution, moreover, is an interstate problem. More than 20 states receive more
than 50% of their water pollution from other states, and an additional 15 states receive between 25
and 50%.

federal EPA often carried the burden of defining and applying the pollution standards. Most states, including Virginia, moved to take over implementation of the federal program, after receiving EPA approval. (Virginia was reportedly eager to take over the program in order to moderate the strictness anticipated under the federal program. In 1973 the state added a few amendments to its old law and was certified.) In the Kepone case, no citizen actions were filed to enforce the state and federal laws. In subsequent years, however, citizen enforcement became a major force in shaping and applying water quality standards. At first it was not clear how workable and credible the federal water program would be. Within a few years, in part because of citizen enforcement, it became an accepted regulatory reality.

Each regulatory statute, in other words, begins its life as an unfinished product — it is not initially clear how it will actually work in practice, and it is shaped and evolves over time according to the quality of the enforcement, compliance, political support and resistance it encounters. The first generation of a statute's implementation may look very different from the later stages of the statute's evolution.

2. **Legal repercussions of the Kepone disaster.** As noted, one of the consequences of Kepone was legislative action in Congress. The legislative debates leading to the 1977 CWA repeatedly invoked the disaster, and four major provisions in the new act derived from specific reactions against the Kepone incident.[45] There were regulatory responses too, as federal and state agencies were prompted by the Kepone case's notoriety to tighten reporting and enforcement practices under state and federal pollution acts. The agencies also entered into administrative negotiations with Allied to force cleanups of contaminated areas. During the latter half of 1975, Allied Chemical voluntarily decontaminated the Life Science plant site at a cost of nearly one million dollars. Allied Chemical also sponsored health tests for former Life Science workers and conducted intensive research on methods of retrieving Kepone from the James River and incinerating Kepone residuals. In early 1976, Allied Chemical donated $88,000 to the Medical College of Virginia for monitoring and treating former Life Science employees who had been severely affected by Kepone. (As a result of these studies, the College's medical team perfected a technique for accelerating elimination of Kepone from the human body, thereby speeding the recovery of those persons who had suffered from Kepone poisoning.)

In a criminal trial, before Judge Robert Merhige, Moore and Hundtofte were both convicted of conspiracy to furnish false information to the Federal government, conspiracy relating to LSP's discharge of Kepone, and 79 counts under the Federal Water Pollution Control Act for Kepone discharges into the Hopewell sewer system, for which they were fined $25,000 each. Hopewell was fined $10,000 because, as Judge Merhige stated, "heavy fines would serve no purpose, [taking] money from one pocket of the taxpayer to another." Allied pleaded "nolo contendere," was convicted of 940 counts of violating of FWPCA, and was fined $13.3 million. Following up on an indirect suggestion by Judge Merhige, Allied then proposed to set up an $8 million fund for a "Virginia Environmental Endowment," a nonprofit corporation which would perform research and implement programs to

---

45. See Goldfarb, The CWA since Kepone, 29 U.Richmond L.Rev. at 612-615, describing Kepone's explicit role in Congress's "mid-course corrections" of water pollution law.

mitigate the environmental effects of Kepone, for which Allied received a penalty reduction down to $5 million. [Allied's attempt to write off this $8 million as a tax exempt business expense is noted in Chapter 19]. No one got jail time in the Kepone incident.[46]

As to civil litigation, the sum total of Allied's ultimate liability is not known because of confidential sealed settlements. We do know how much the state and local governments collected: $5,250,000 (in addition to the nearly one million dollars spent in cleaning up the Life Science plant site). For this sum, Allied settled all of the claims of the Commonwealth of Virginia and the City of Hopewell for Kepone-related costs that these governmental entities had incurred, as well as administrative penalties assessed by the Virginia Water Control Board. There were no federal civil recoveries, the federal toxic cleanup statutes not yet having become law.

As to civil litigation filed by individual plaintiffs for personal injuries, little was officially reported about the cases or the amounts of damages paid out to private victims of the toxic exposures. After several cases had proceeded through initial stages of tort litigation (in which the most effective cause of action surprisingly turned out to be *product liability*-based claims — see excerpt from Complaint in Civ. Action 75-0469), Allied adopted a policy of settling all suits out of court, each with a stipulation that no information ever be provided on the amount of payments.[47] According to one insider, the personal injury settlements totalled about $5 million.

The only civil damage action to go to verdict, a suit filed by ten classes of fishermen and other users of Chesapeake Bay who suffered economic losses, resulted in damages awarded to two of the plaintiff classes likewise in the neighborhood of $5 million. (That opinion, Pruitt et al. v. Allied Chemical, is noted in Chapter Three.)

For the Kepone event as a whole, Allied's total outlay was reported by a company attorney to have approached $30 million.

What about natural resources damages? The judge acknowledged in the *Pruitt* fishing case that "the costs...of Kepone pollution...were borne most directly by the *wildlife* of Chesapeake Bay," but no natural resources damages or restoration orders were ever issued in a Kepone case.

To what extent did Allied have to account for the *totality* of the costs its decisions had caused? Are there other legal accountings that could have occurred in this

---

46. Early in the trial Judge Merhige commented "nobody is going to jail in this case," thereby dampening the prosecutors' attempts to persuade some defendants to turn state's evidence. The criminal case was Crim. Act. No. 76-0129-R , U.S. District Court for the Eastern District of Virginia, Richmond Div. (1977, unreported).

47. In most legal settlement agreements, a standard provision decrees that no details of the settlement are ever to be revealed on pain of forfeiting the cash; some also require plaintiff's attorney to refrain from such representations in the future. The facts of settled cases, however, including investigative research, could be important in warning other injured persons and helping to pursue legal remedies. As a matter of social policy, should such information be open? See Twomey, "Breaking the Silence: Examining the Enforceability of Private Settlements which Conceal Environmental Hazards," 4 New Eng. Envtl Law Forum 109 (1997); Gibeaut, Secret Justice, ABA Journal, April 1998 at 50 (reporter fined $500 thousand for revealing $36 million settlement amount in pollution class action suit against Conoco Inc.).

UNITED STATES DISTRICT COURT
EASTERN DISTRICT OF VIRGINIA
Richmond Division

DALE F. GILBERT, DELBERT R. WHITE,
EVERETTE L. MESSER, NICKEY F. SHOWN,
JAMES O. ROGERS, JR., JOHN EDWARD COX,          CIVIL ACTION NO. CA-75-0469-R
MELVIN L. RUSSELL, ROBERT W. NEWMAN,            **FILED** : Sep 19 1973
FRANK M. ARRIGO
                    Plaintiffs,
              v.
ALLIED CHEMICAL CORPORATION,
a New York corporation,...
                    Defendants

**COUNT 1**                          COMPLAINT

  1. Plaintiffs are all citizens of the Commonwealth of Virginia. Defendant, Allied Chemical Corporation, hereinafter referred to as "Allied", is a New York corporation and has its principal place of business in the State of New Jersey;... The matter in controversy..., exclusive of interest and costs, exceeds the sum of Ten Thousand Dollars ($10,000.00).

  **2. That defendants...beginning in about March, 1974, furnished, sold or supplied certain chemicals to Life Science Products Company of Hopewell, Virginia...which were used by Life Science in the manufacture or production of a chemical substance sold under the Allied trade name of Kepone; that defendants knew or should have known that the said chemicals are imminently and inherently dangerous to life or property, yet defendants negligently supplied said chemicals to Life Science without notice or warning of the defect or danger to the plaintiffs who were users of said chemicals; that defendants failed to exercise a high degree of care and vigilance in dealing with these dangerous chemicals; that it was reasonably foreseeable to the defendants that their failure to warn, explain, instruct and apprise the plaintiffs of the dangers involved would result in serious injuries to them.**

  **3. As a proximate result of the defendants' negligent failure to warn and/or to adequately warn the plaintiffs of the dangers involved, the plaintiffs have suffered severe and permanent injuries** to their health, bodies and minds, including, but not limited to, tremors, opisclonus, memory deficits, pleuritic and joint pains, liver damage, cataracts, and injuries to their reproductive systems, and did suffer and will suffer in the future, loses due to being prevented from following their usual course of affairs and the expenditure of large sums of money for medical treatment in an effort to be cured....

  **COUNT 2...**

  ...WHEREFOR, plaintiffs demand judgment against Allied...in the sums opposite their respective names, together with costs and interest from date of injury:

| | |
|---|---|
| Gilbert, Three Million Dollars | $3,000,000.00 |
| White, Three Million Dollars | $3,000,000.00 |
| Messer, Two Million Five Hundred Thousand Dollars | $2,500,000.00 |
| Shown, Three Million Dollars | $3,000,000.00 |
| Rogers, Two Million Five Hundred Thousand Dollars | $2,500,000.00 |
| Cox, Two Million Three Hundred Thousand Dollars | $2,300,000.00 |
| Price, Two Million Three Hundred Thousand Dollars | $2,300,000.00 |
| Russell, Two Million Three Hundred Thousand Dollars | $2,300,000.00 |
| Newman, Two Million Dollars | $2,000,000.00 |
| Arrigo, Two Million Dollars | $2,000,000.00 |

TRIAL BY JURY IS DEMANDED.     By:_____, Counsel
                               Edward W. Taylor, James D. Hundley
                               HUNDLEY, TAYLOR & GLASS
                               P.O. Box 518, Richmond, Virginia 23204

*Excerpt from a personal injury Complaint filed in the aftermath of the Kepone incident. Three other counts replicated the factual allegations of Count 1, adding claims for negligent supervision of Life Sciences, strict liability personal injury, and strict liability failure to warn. All such private complaints were settled prior to trial.*

process? The public trust materials at the end of this chapter address some further possibilities.

3. **Why did it happen? A system breakdown?** Why hadn't responsive action been taken by somebody within the company or in the external community earlier on? The chronology of the Kepone story in the years following Allied's 1949 invention of the compound involved dozens of management decisions, many of them inevitably involving corporate attorneys. It seems unlikely that the corporate players were ignorant of the hazardous externalities in the workplace, in the surrounding environment, and to human consumers overseas. To what extent did the corporate and legal systems incline them toward ignoring those externalized costs? Consider the Allied attorneys working sequentially on the patents, franchise agreements, the withdrawn domestic pesticide application, export permits, occupational health regulations, disposal practices, Refuse Act applications, and other critical actions. Could they have raised the hazards issues?

Environmental cases continually present true moral dilemmas and tough questions of legal ethics. What is the attorney's role and duty upon discovering a significant environmental hazard created by a client, that the client refuses to report or correct?

> Despite the threat of harm, the rules of ethics bind you to remain silent if the danger arises from negligence rather than a criminal act.... Which duty should predominate — the duty to maintain the confidences of the client or the duty to avert a danger to the community?... The applicable rule of ethics [Rule 1.6 of the ABA Model Rules of Professional Conduct in its currently diluted form] appears to allow an attorney to remain silent despite significant danger to the public or an individual.... Society has a critical interest in the balance struck between these conflicting duties and in encouraging lawyers to assess environmental dangers rather than blindly adhering to an ethic of silence.[48] Russell, Cries and Whispers: Environmental Hazards, Model Rule 1.6, and the Attorney's Conflicting duties to Clients and Others, 72 Wash. L.Rev.409, 411–415 (1997).

For Allied's executives in the 1970s, passing the costs of toxic wastes into the environment was probably a normal matter-of-fact business decision, that went sour when Life Science's pollution became a dramatic flash point. But in ignoring the foreseeable costs to human health, water quality, fisheries resources, and the like, were Allied and LSP being irrational, shortsighted, evil? Most industries, at least before the mid-1970s, regarded pollution as a normal industrial by-product. "Pollution is the price of progress." "That smoke smells like money." Still today, the basic logic of cost externalization — the inherent incentive to avoid paying for anything that doesn't return private benefits — means that, in the absence of some public reckoning system like environmental law, industry will understandably tend to try to pass its waste disposal costs and consequences into the public commons.

In the Kepone era the prospect of legal accountability was quite unlikely. Who could be expected to keep a close eye on Kepone production? The federal agencies? The local city government? The Commonwealth of Virginia? No one acted until a

---

48. In her extended analysis of this dilemma, Professor Russell also notes that there is a growing countervailing risk of tort liability to victims for attorneys who fail to warn nonclients of such dangers.

foreign-born doctor blew the whistle. This suggests that then, as now, a law's enforceability and its institutional follow-through within the legal system are as vital as its substantive standards.

**4. Kepone as a problem of the commons.** To what extent was Kepone a tragedy of the commons? The waters of the James River and Chesapeake Bay, and the air in Hopewell, are commons in the sense that they are resources that can be used by all and are owned by none, and these commons undoubtedly were polluted by the actions of Allied and Life Science. So far as we know, however, neither company had to face internal production problems from polluted air or water supplies, so the "comes-back-around" feature of Hardin's tragedy was missing. Unlike overfishing a marine commons, which destroys the industry itself, the physical consequences of chemical pollution do not ultimately come back to burden the polluters, and any legal accounting depends on the initiatives of others. Kepone and other pollution and resource depletion situations typically do reflect the tragedy of Hardin's cowpasture commons through the entrepreneurial tendency to pass diffuse harms into the commons to avoid facing their full cost, and the pollution settings also illustrate the strong pressures in the competitive marketplace to continue doing so. The commons metaphor emphasizes basic drives in human nature that produce externalized costs, and significant differences between the management dynamics of privately-owned property and the pressures on a common resource.

**5. Kepone and Environmental Justice.** Looking at the map of Hopewell, it perhaps should not be surprising to discover that the residential areas most directly exposed to air and water toxics from the plants that produced Kepone were poor minority neighborhoods. "Poor people and people of color bear the brunt of environmental dangers, from pesticides to air pollution to toxics to occupational hazards. At the same time, poor people and people of color also have the fewest resources to cope with these dangers, legally, medically or politically."[49] The Hopewell neighbors appear to have had only a passive role in the story.

Issues of environmental justice — the way race, low income, and political disenfranchisement can be reflected in environmental impacts — appear in a number of places in this coursebook. The text does not regularly note the income and political character of plaintiff groups or their racial composition. Yet it is increasingly clear that many environmental burdens are especially likely to be visited upon communities of color or communities marked by low-level incomes and limited political clout. The burdens range from loss of critical urban amenities and quality of life issues to rat bites and pollution exposure effects.[50] In the ongoing

49. Luke Cole, Empowerment as a Key to Environmental Protection: The Need for Environmental Poverty Law, 19 Ecology L. Q. 619 (1992).

50. Among the current catalogue of environmental justice settings:

- The physical location of hazardous-waste treatment, storage and disposal facilities
- Physical taking of low-income and/or minority communities through eminent domain such as the *Poletown* and *Overton Park* cases
- The effects of pesticides on migrant workers in the California grape-growing regions
- Disproportionate environmental exportation of toxic and other wastes to Third World countries for disposal
- Discrimination against the indigenous peoples of an area, such as the HydroQuebec Power Project in James Bay, PQ.
- The frequency of heavy industrial facilities located in or near low-income/racial minority neighborhoods
- Accusations of racism within the environmental movement, including predominantly white, middle and upper class membership in environmental organizations, hiring biases within environmental agencies and organizations, and claims that the environmental movement is a movement out of touch with the people it should be working with and for on a daily basis.

discourse about environmental justice (or "environmental racism"), it is toxics exposure that has provided the focusing images of the phenomenon: it seems that many hazardous substance facilities tend to be sited where the neighboring communities are poor or of color, or both.

Over the past decade many people began to see a pattern in the distribution of toxic harms and the characteristics of the people who were most often exposed to them. The correlation was first highlighted in Charles Lee's 1987 study "Toxic Wastes and Race in the United States," sponsored by the United Church of Christ Commission for Racial Justice, followed by Dr. Robert Bullard's Dumping in Dixie: Race, Class & Environmental Quality (1990). In these and subsequent studies, racial minorities' and low-income groups' risk of exposure to environmental hazards appeared to be both quantitatively and qualitatively greater than that of the general public.

Recognition of disproportionate exposure patterns has produced a number of serious attempts to mobilize the tools of environmental law to rectify the phenomenon of environmental injustice. Lawsuits have attempted to prove intentional discrimination on the basis of race and poverty in pollution management decisions, tracking an Equal Protection analysis. Whether because of the times or the circumstances, however, this approach has not been highly successful in court,[51] leading to other approaches, including increasing attempts to use Title VI of the 1964 Civil Rights Act. See EPA Guidance on Title VI, pages 477–482 below.[52]

Environmental justice issues are often quite ambiguous, however. As in the Kepone case, and in Chapter 25's materials on siting, the decision to locate hazardous waste activities is not clearly motivated by invidious discriminatory intent. Land in poor areas is cheaper, and effective political opposition less likely, so straightforward economic and political marketplace considerations favor such siting. Professor Vicki Been has argued that even if the original decision for siting toxic facilities were totally free of discrimination, with the site placed in a well-off white area, it is altogether likely that normal market effects would soon shift the surrounding neighborhood toward a population of color and lower income.[53] Siting thus is only one problem of many.

In addition to increasingly active environmental citizens groups,[54] environmental justice has received federal government attention, including President Clinton's

51. See East Bibb Twiggs Nbhd. Assoc. v. Macon-Bibb County Planning & Zoning Comm., 706 F.Supp. 880 (M.D. Ga. 1989); Bean v. Southwestern Waste Management Corp., 482 F. Supp. 673 (S.D. Tex. 1979).

52. See also Chester Residents v. Pennsylvania DEP, 132 F.3d 925 (3rd. Cir. 1997).

53. Been, Locally Undesirable Land Uses in Minority Neighborhoods: Disproportionate Siting or Market Dynamics? 103 Yale L.J. 1383 (1994)

54. Environmental justice activism started in local citizen groups, some of which have allied with law school programs, including ACE, Alternatives for Community and Environment at Boston College Law School, and environmental justice clinics at Berkeley and Georgetown. Pointed criticism of established national environmental groups as lily-white middle class enterprises have prompted serious soul-searching and extensive efforts to integrate more minority and low-income individuals and groups into the mainstream environmental organizations and alliances that built the successes of environmentalism in the U.S., the "Group of Ten" (the Sierra Club, Earth Justice Legal Defense Fund, Friends of the Earth, Wilderness Society, National Audubon Society, Natural Resources Defense Council, Environmental Defense Fund, National Wildlife Federation, Izaak Walton League, and National Parks and Conservation Association).

1994 Executive Order 12898, "Federal Actions to Address Environmental Justice in Minority Populations and Low-Income Populations." The Clinton EPA issued a guidance document as well as Title VI regulations to permit the integration of environmental justice issues into the agency's implementation of a variety of statutes.[55] Addressing the distributional inequities in different communities' differing levels of environmental quality is becoming a civic and social necessity for a society attempting to achieve long term sustainability.

6. **The legal skill of comparative law.** Part of the art of modern environmental law is the contextual analysis skill of comparative law, noted in Chapter 26. For an attorney approaching any environmental case — Love Canal, the Kepone incident at Hopewell in 1976, an oil syndication in the North Sea, a disaster like Bhopal in 1984 or Chernobyl in 1986 or the Exxon Valdez spill in 1989 — an initial step is to survey not only physical facts and causation, but also the legal culture of the locale. How does the law on the books actually work in practice? This requires a "culturally-relative" and incisive analysis of the regulatory systems existing at the time of the incident, politics, and public and private law remedies available to respond to what happened. In the Kepone case this analysis would also have to take into account the differing (sometimes reluctant) regulatory abilities of state and federal agencies before and after the disaster, and the different avenues of statutory and nonstatutory liability and remedies that could be tried. An analysis of these practicalities, and of the differing types of relationship between agencies, citizens, and courts, provides a more competent basis for planning a party's legal course of action.[56] The same comparative process recurs, to varying degrees, whenever attorneys deal with situations outside their home jurisdiction.

## SOME ANALYTIC THEMES, after Kepone

■ **Common law and public law.** Our legal system is formed of two interlocking systems of legal standards and mechanisms, each playing a range of potential roles in an incident like the Kepone poisoning. The structures of the modern administrative state — public law agencies, statutes, and regulations, at local, state, and federal levels — are built as supplements upon the flexible and evolving foundation structures of common law that over of the past 800 years were largely responsible for producing today's Anglo-American legal system. Environmental attorneys often find it necessary to use both systems, sometimes simultaneously.

Then-existing public law devices essentially failed to prevent the Kepone disaster from happening (could they have?) The common law might also have played an anticipatory role, as we will see, and did not. After the Kepone debacle was discovered, both systems were invoked to provide partial remedies. The interplay between common law and public law is a continuing prospect in most environmental settings.

---

55. An excellent periodical resource on issues of environmental justice is "Race, Poverty & the Environment," a quarterly newsletter published by the California Rural Legal Assistance Foundation and the Earth Island Institute Urban Habitat Program, 300 Broadway, San Francisco.

56. The comparative overview also allows one to gauge larger societal themes, noting in the Bhopal case, for example, how a holistic ideology like that in Hindu India subordinates the individual to society, while an individualistic ideology of the sort that often characterizes the Christian West tends to subordinate society to the individual in its emphasis on personal initiative and autonomy.

■ **LAISSEZ-FAIRE: how well does it work for longterm societal and environmental concerns?** Allied's problems in Hopewell would seem to confirm Hardin's skepticism about market players' ability to avoid externalizing social costs. There is an instinct in most humans' nature to maximize individual profits and avoid thinking of diffused public detriments. If nonstatutory law cannot effectively protect the public interests impacted by the market economy, government regulation of some sort will be necessary to bring civic concerns into the daily life of business.

■ **ENVIRONMENTAL JUSTICE.** In the *Kepone* case, as in many other modern pollution settings, note which areas are likely to get the most risky, polluting, industrial installations. Whether from managers' desires to save money and site operations where they will be least likely to face effective environmental opposition, or from the self-condescension of poorer communities or communities of color exhibited in uncritical eagerness to attract jobs at any price, or as result of simple discrimination, the ultimate location of many potentially dangerous facilities often turns out to be these least empowered populations.

■ **THE RACE TO THE BOTTOM: state and federal jurisdictions.** A basic pressure within environmental law comes from a tendency of states to compete with each other for industrial payrolls by lowering regulatory standards. This "Race to the Bottom" is a political kind of tragedy of the commons, which in the *Kepone* case may explain why Virginia and local officials did not apply meaningful limits upon Allied and Life Sciences, in order to attract industry and keep it from moving to some laxer state.[57] This powerful erosive tendency appears throughout environmental regulation. Federal statutes thus are often conceived as a way to provide federal minimum floors to counter the race to the bottom with national level standards (though on the other hand federal agencies may not understand local conditions). Environmental law repeatedly serves as a battleground for economic conflicts playing out the basic allocation of roles between federal and state governments in "federalism" debates.

■ **THE ROLE OF CITIZEN-INITIATED ACTIONS IN THE LEGAL SYSTEM.** To a limited extent, private citizens played critical roles in the legal process of Kepone: it was Dr. Chou who triggered federal agency attention by reporting his patients' blood toxin levels to the federal Center for Disease Control; it was private plaintiffs who ultimately forced an accounting in damages from Allied of the toxic human exposures from Kepone.[58] But in the Kepone incident there were no citizen enforcement actions against violations of state or federal statutes and regulations. Over subsequent years, one of the dominant characteristics of U.S. environmental law has been the legal standing provisions allowing "private attorneys-general" to enforce environmental statutes. Citizen enforcement has been an important strategic element in the evolution of most areas of modern environmental practice.

■ **THE STRATEGIC ROLE OF THE MEDIA.** A critical part of the Kepone narrative, as with many or most significant environmental issues, is the amount and kind of media coverage it received. The Kepone story got a lot of press. It just happened to break at a time

---

57. The concept of race to the bottom is subject to ongoing debate, explored further in Chapter Five.

58. In many countries, it would be up to a government agency to recover such damages for injured citizens. After 2500 people were killed by methyl-isocyanate in Bhopal India in 1984, it was the Government of India that sued Union Carbide, recovering $14,500 per death; after the Seveso dioxin incident in Italy in 1976, the settlement negotiated by the government ended the liability claims. After the Exxon Valdez oilspill disaster in Alaska in 1989, the state government briefly considered

when the news media did not have any other big stories going on. It was mediagenic and engaging, with sympathetic victims and a large toxic corporate wrongdoer. But note that on another day this case of contaminated industrial workers might have generated little notice, which would probably have meant that the waters of the James and the Chesapeake Bay would not have been tested and fishing not closed down.

Media climate is often critically important in making an environmental case effective. It builds the momentum of citizen organizations, and appears to be particularly helpful in making public law mechanisms responsive. Regulatory agencies tend to devote their resources to enforcement of public interest issues where there is most public attention. Sluggishness and inertia tend to characterize their efforts when issues lack press coverage, especially where potent industrial entities are the alleged violators. The effective public communication of information thus plays a significant role in social governance.

And media coverage often impels corporate acknowledgment of public concerns.[59]

■ **THE SYSTEMIC ROLES OF "OUTRAGE."** There is a tension between outrage-driven controversies and cool-headed analysis. Environmentalists often find that they must cast their public arguments in terms of outrage and extremes. Lacking revenues and political power, it is often difficult to enlist volunteers and allies on important but complex issues, or to obtain press coverage and political credibility, unless issues can be cast in terms of good and bad. Especially in the first generation of any field of regulation, when civic advocates attempt to launch a new environmental protection initiatives, they will try to demonstrate the outrageous conduct and great public risks posed by existing market practices. But industries like Allied Chemical often feel that they are at the mercy of crude emotionalism, unscientific uninformed civic criticisms, and would prefer more rational and subdued debates and more respectful forums like the corridors of the bureaucracy. Outrage can skew the subtleties of an issue; it can also focus necessary attention on issues the public cares about, whereas cool, less passionate discussions may end up missing the public reality.

■ **REMEDY AND ENFORCEMENT CHOICES.** Both private parties and public agencies generally have a wide choice of potential legal remedies, and make selections based upon the character of acts and actors, the scope of harms, the parties' own agendas, the climate of public reaction, and more. In the Kepone case private citizens apparently sought only damages for injuries to health. As we will see, the common law offered them other remedies as well — other forms of damages and a number of creative injunctive remedies. For public agencies' law enforcement efforts there are similar ranges of remedies, plus the possibility of criminal punishments. In Kepone the state and local governments decided to negotiate civil compensation agreements with Allied; the federal government pursued criminal penalties. The administrative options for civil and criminal remedies, or combinations thereof, add a further level of tactical analysis to the complexities of environmental enforcement. See Chapters 19–20.

■ **THE "THREE ECONOMIES."** A fundamental theme and force in virtually every environmental case, as in most of modern life, is Economics. In trying to understand the economic processes of environmental and landuse issues, Professor Joseph Sax has argued

---

59. As the tax court observed, "The local and national press laid the blame for the Kepone incident on Allied...[as] a 'corporate mugger.' After the criminal trials, Allied undertook [an] advertising campaign that would portray petitioner as a good and concerned corporate citizen...including the creation of...a foundation or trust to engage in research for the purpose of developing methods to eradicate Kepone from the environment."

that we should recognize not one but two economic systems — an economics of the natural economy as well as of the marketplace.[60]

It seems to us, however, that a comprehensive analytic structure for understanding the dynamics of modern life requires recognition of three different intersecting economies — comprised not only of marketplace economics and natural systems economics, but also of a civic-societal economics incorporating the society's overall cumulative well-being. This three-economies construct provides a useful way to talk about an array of long-established concepts of environmental law (and public policy generally), integrating an analysis of societal necessities and ecological realities with the powerful machinery of market dynamics.[61]

Example: A developer planning a lucrative project building a restaurant, shop, or fancy vacation residence wants to fill in an acre of coastal wetlands. Wetlands provide rich habitats for wildlife and fish including commercial fisheries spawning areas, climatic stability, groundwater recharge functions, flood retention and storm-buffering functions, and more. To protect the natural and civic values of wetlands, federal, state, and local regulations are written to limit wetland development. As soon as government interposes civic restrictions on private enterprise, however, the marketplace understandably begins to try to subvert them. Governmental conservation agencies are so involved with marketplace political pressures that they often hesitate to enforce the laws. Real estate lobbies write legislation overriding wetland conservation rules or requiring taxpayers to buy out propertyowners if regulations lower market values by 25% or more; market-oriented judges insert the same logic into constitutional takings tests, as in Lucas v. South Carolina Coastal Commission;[62] and so on. This situation cannot be realistically analyzed in terms of just one economy. It needs three.

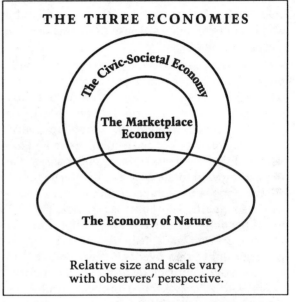

THE THREE ECONOMIES

The Civic-Societal Economy

The Marketplace Economy

The Economy of Nature

Relative size and scale vary with observers' perspective.

---

60. Sax, Property Rights and the Economy of Nature, 45 Stanford L. Rev. 1433 (1993). See also Mark Sagoff, The Economy of the Earth (1988), and the work of a respected consultant on fisheries management policy based in Sequim, Washington, James Lichatowich: "A New Vision for Pacific Salmon," Oregon Business Council, (November 1996), and Lichatowich, "It's the Economies, Mr. President," 34 TROUT No. 3 at 22-23 (Summer 1993). Sax uses the phrase "transformative economy" for marketplace uses of land; Lichatowich uses "industrial economy."

61. See The Three Economies, 25 Ecol. L.Q. No. 3 (1998). All three can be called "economies" because each is a complex system of interconnecting subsystems processing inputs and outputs, causes and effects, and uses of resources over time. No other modern word captures the concept of a dynamic system of systems quite so well.

62. Several states have passed such automatic compensation laws, e.g., Tex. Gov't Code Ann. §2007.001 et seq. (1995); the House of Representatives has several times passed them, e.g., 104 HR 925 (20/50%, passed March 3, 1995), though as yet Congress has not; Justice Scalia's opinion in Lucas, 505 U.S. 1003 (1992), seemed directly calculated to make market values dominant. Other examples of the relevance of all three economies include CFCs/ozone depletion; global warming; pesticide and fertilizer runoffs in the Great Lakes drainage area; BLM mining and grazing permits; and so on down to the local auto body shop throwing solvents in the creek. Most environmental cases involve at least two of the three economies....

**THE MARKETPLACE ECONOMY** is the well-known mechanism of everyday economic and political behavior. It sits at the center — the dynamic, driving force of human society, dynamically churning out economic and political power, interlocking networks of motivations and institutions, property rights, production, politics, and wastes. It dominates daily life, and is undoubtedly the most intricate and sophisticated social mechanism ever devised to manage the extraordinary onrolling complexity of human society. The marketplace economy, however, is systematically blind to many important elements of reality; for the most part it deals only with things and services which can be bought and sold. It takes for granted many natural and public values that are priceless. It generates waste and externalities. These problems are massive and real, and need to be part of a societal accounting.

**THE NATURAL ECONOMY,** as noted by Sax and others, is what happens in the natural physical world, the intricate system of living and geophysical systems that sustain dynamic planetary processes. It partly overlaps the two human economies, supplying vital resources and services to both, but in part lies outside them. The economy of nature processes everything, adapts to everything, (though often with altered and diminished qualities of ecosystem health and diversity), absorbs wastes and other externalities from the marketplace, and passes the effects of many of these externality impacts onward to the civic economy. The teemingly fertile lifeforms of Carson's subsoil evolve along with changing conditions, but suffer harm if hit with persistent pesticides, as do songbirds, and humans. Leopold's wolf lives in an ancient life pattern that balances habitat, predator, and prey until the arrival of gunmen and trappers. Hardin's commons — grazing lands, fisheries, waters, and land masses — can maintain a productive diversity until users overload the resource and drive it downward. Wurster's salt can upset the dynamic ecology of a wetland, roadside forest, or even the depths of the Great Lakes. And Allied's Kepone production ultimately contaminated the waters, fish, and other living systems of the Bay. Human interventions with the commons of nature — with chemicals, bulldozers, or whatever — can create widespread residual cumulative consequences, mostly in disruptive directions reaching as far as extinction.

Recognition of a natural "economics" forces us to recognize that nature is not just a charming sidenote to human life, but a complex and utilitarian system in its own right, superbly integrated, diversified, and efficient in processing and recycling energy and nutrients, integrating millions of ongoing and evolving life cycles, adapting to natural change, ultimately important to humans (which links it to the civic societal economy), and vulnerable.

**THE CIVIC-SOCIETAL ECONOMY** is the ultimate "economic" forum in human terms. It incorporates the dynamic marketplace economy, but its terms and elements extend much further beyond just those things that can be bought and sold. Societal economics are the comprehensive reality of the full actual social costs, benefits, resources, energy, inputs, outputs, values, qualities and consequences, over time that carry the life and welfare of a human society from day to day and into the future, whether the marketplace acknowledges them or not. Where do externalities go? Costs externalized by marketplace enterprises — by factories, porkbarrel government agency projects and programs, or undertakings combining private and public entrepreneurs — exit the marketplace economy, but they do not thereby drop into oblivion: by the laws of physics, ecology, and logic *they are internalized into one or both of the other economies,* into the fabric of the natural and societal economics in which we and our society will continue to live. Widespread pesticide use, or overgrazing, or dumping pollutants like Kepone wastes, or highway salting, or massive layoffs of corporate workers, or a host of other cost externalizations may make powerfully good sense to market players in the narrow market terms of individual gains, but be quite irrational in societal economics terms. Regulatory agencies have mandates designed to serve the civic economy, but they spend most if not all of their daily political lives dominated by the pressures and constraints of marketplace politics. The natural economy's complex elements are often directly and substantially linked to the utilitarian concerns of societal economics. Healthy societal economic systems are founded upon healthy and sustainable ecological system cycles of soil, water, air, and living communities. When a resource system is derogated or destroyed, some enterprises may prosper greatly, but the society is likely to be far less well off. The societal public economy needs the market economy, but for the sake of its own short and long term interests a society must somehow contrive to value and incorporate into its governance important elements of civic economic reality that the daily dominant marketplace resists.

---

The theoretical importance of a comprehensive accounting for externalized costs[63] has long been acknowledged by academic economists, but gets overlooked in the day to day economic and political pressures of the marketplace. Economic analyses that ignore civic societal economics, or the impacts of natural economics on society, however, are naïvely or disingenuously narrow, ignoring substantial realities that inevitably will be felt by the society. The analytical construct of three economies facilitates this overall economic and legal accounting.

Environmental law directs itself toward all three economies. Its instrumental focus is almost always upon the marketplace economy — attempting to integrate appropriate external constraints and values into the marketplace in three separate settings:

a. where marketplace externalities directly impact upon human welfare in the civic-societal economy — as in direct human toxic exposures, urban transit, historic preservation, and the like — without reference to the economy of nature,

b. where marketplace externalities impinge upon natural systems so as to cause consequential harms to human welfare in the civic-societal economy — as with global warming, Forest Service clearcutting sales, toxic discharges into the nation's waters, and the like, and

c. (most problematically) where environmental law protections target marketplace externalities purely for the sake of the economy of nature itself, where there are few or no material consequences upon human welfare — as in those cases of endangered species protection where no substantial human utility is served, in humane treatment cases, in ecological preservation for moral, religious, aesthetic, or intellectual purposes, and the like.

---

63. Since the dawn of environmental law, it has been evident that most environmental problems derive from human actions driven by the dynamic logical calculus of marketplace economics. Human nature and the corporate processes that reflect it resolutely focus upon internalizing benefits and externalizing costs. The result is that a vast array of real social costs — like the totality of what happens when a mountain is stripmined or a river polluted — are diffused into the public and natural commons. Only with great difficulty, and against the resistance of marketplace politics, do environmental costs and other unmarketized civic concerns get acknowledged and accounted for in the governance process.

The economy of nature often impacts critically upon the civic-societal economy. In positive terms the civic-societal economy receives the values and benefits humans derive from natural systems, like the multi-trillion-dollar "natural capital" values that resource economists say we annually receive "free" from nature, values unacknowledged by the marketplace economy.[64] The civic-societal economy also absorbs negatives from the economy of nature's disruptions from market economy impacts. Some marketplace externalities may only affect natural systems, with no human consequences, but many others pass through the environment into the human welfare context of civic-societal economics. Thus toxic spills into watercourses, global warming, lost fisheries, eroded soils, wetlands destruction, pesticide loading, and a host of other environmental issues demonstrate important linkages between all three economies. The logical connection between natural systems and societal interests provides the compelling utilitarian linkage that should force hardnosed economics-based legal and policy analyses to integrate environmental considerations.

Both natural and societal economics, however, are often ignored and overwhelmed by the marketplace economy's narrowed perspectives and power. Scratch an environmental law controversy anywhere in the world and you are likely to find a natural value or a public value being destructively disregarded by the market's political and entrepreneurial forces. Nevertheless the three economies are interdependent, and the competent practice of environmental law, and rational democratic governance, implicitly incorporate and require an understanding of the reality of all three economies.

## C. A CASE-STUDY IN INDUSTRIAL POLLUTION LAW AT THE TURN OF THE 21ST CENTURY: THE *SMITHFIELD* LITIGATION

The Kepone incident typified the first generation of modern pollution law cases, when meaningful regulatory laws were just beginning to supplement the common law in applying public controls to corporate pollution. Now, at the turn of the new century, a significant line of water pollution cases, also coming from Virginia, typifies a second or third stage of pollution law. The *Smithfield* cases have many shared characteristics with the Kepone case, as well as very illuminating differences. For years the jointly-owned Gwaltney and Smithfield Packing factories discharged large amounts of hog-processing wastes through two outfall pipes into Virginia's Pagan River (ceasing only in 1997, when they finally connected to a public water treatment facility — HRSD, the Hampton Roads Sanitation District). The cases involve decisions by the same judge as in Kepone, with industrial operations dumping into a tributary of the same James River, with large volumes of contaminants similarly diffused into the river environment, their harms continuing downriver into the Chesapeake Bay.

As you read through a chronology of *Gwaltney* and *Smithfield* decisions, which spend a great deal of time on civil penalty discussions, note legal similarities and differences between this litigation and the first generation cases of the Kepone era.

---

64. As noted in Chapter Two: see R. Costanza et al., The Value of the World's Ecosystem Services and Natural Capital, 387 Science 253 (15 May 1997); Costanza & Daly, Natural Capital and Sustainable Development, 6 Conservation Biology 37–46 (1992).

## Chesapeake Bay Foundation v. Gwaltney of Smithfield, Ltd.
United States District Court for the Eastern District of
Virginia, Richmond Division, 1984
611 F. Supp. 1542

[In 1983 the Natural Resources Defense Council (NRDC), one of the nation's most noted public interest environmental law firms, decided to launch a national Clean Water Project to seek out and file high profile citizen enforcement actions against polluters, in order to improve the level of public and administrative attention being paid to the problems of water pollution. The Chesapeake Bay was one target area. NRDC and the Chesapeake Bay Foundation (CBF), its regional partner, prowled through the tributaries of the Bay and the files of the Virginia State Water Control Board (SWCB, a division of the state DEQ, Department of Environmental Quality, which had been certified to administer the federal water program) looking for deserving cases. What they found, according to Professor Ann Powers who was counsel for CBF, was that state enforcement was extremely lax, but also that state discharge permits were set so permissively that many dischargers were not clearly in violation. "So when CBF and NRDC found Smithfield with so many state violations on the records, that meant it was really excessive." As one citizen said, "There's a lot of pig in the Pagan." In February 1984 the groups filed 60-day citizen-enforcement jurisdictional notices under CWA §505 against the two Smithfield plants, Smithfield Packing Co. and Gwaltney of Smithfield, based on the company's own pollution reports. On June 15, 1984 the citizens filed a federal court enforcement action against Gwaltney. (As to Smithfield Packing, for a time the citizens' initiative was preempted by a state enforcement action, in which CBF intervened, that led in 1985 to state civil penalties of $50,000.)]

ROBERT MERHIGE, DISTRICT JUDGE. This suit is a citizen enforcement action — a "citizen suit" — authorized by Section 505 of the Clean Water Act, 33 U.S.C.A. §1365. Plaintiffs are two non-profit corporations dedicated to protecting natural resources: the Chesapeake Bay Foundation, a regional environmental group with over 19,000 members residing in the Chesapeake Bay area, including Virginia, and the Natural Resources Defense Council, an environmental group with members throughout the nation, including over 800 members in Virginia. Defendant Gwaltney of Smithfield, Ltd., is in the business of processing and packing pork products. It is a subsidiary of Smithfield Foods, Inc. Gwaltney's plant, the operation of which is the subject of this lawsuit, is situated on the Pagan River near Smithfield, Virginia. In the course of its production, the plant discharges wastewater into that river.

At all times material hereto, Gwaltney was allowed to discharge various pollutants from that plant into the river within certain limits, as set out in a National Pollution Discharge Elimination System (NPDES) permit issued by the Virginia State Water Control Board...pursuant to procedures and regulations under the federal Clean Water Act.

From October 27, 1981 until May 15, 1984, Gwaltney's plant exceeded its discharge limitation for a variety of pollutants on a number of occasions.[65] Gwaltney

---

65. Those pollutants are: (i) fecal coliform; (ii) chlorine (Cl2); (iii) total suspended solids (TSS); (iv) total Kjeldahl nitrogen (TKN)[ a nitrogen compound that can degrade a river by depleting its oxygen supply. Natural chemical and biological processes involving TKN and bacteria in the river transpire after TKN is added to a river. Those processes consume the dissolved oxygen in a river, to the detriment of many forms of river life.]; and (v) oil and grease.

itself reported these violations in its discharge monitoring reports (DMRs), as required by law....[66] The plant repeatedly exceeded a number of its NPDES discharge limitations. Gwaltney acknowledges that it was aware...of non-compliance.... Where a permittee is in violation of an NPDES discharge limitation, it is also "in violation of...an effluent standard or limitation under [the Act]," §505(a)(1), which makes the permittee subject to citizen suits. For citizen suits under the Clean Water Act, Congress has authorized the district courts to assess appropriate civil penalties...as high as "$10,000 per day of such violation."...

Plaintiffs filed a citizen suit under Section 505 alleging violations of the pollutant effluent limits contained in Gwaltney's state-issued National Pollutant Discharge Elimination System permit, issued pursuant to Section 402 of the federal Act, 33 U.S.C. §1342....

STANDING... The Court must dispose of defendant's contention that plaintiffs have no standing under either the Act or Article III of the Constitution. Gwaltney contends that plaintiffs' allegations are insufficient to establish standing for CBF and NRDC to sue in their own right [or] on behalf of some of their members.... Plaintiffs...argue that they have established standing to sue both in their own right and on behalf of their members.

It is clear that, at least under the Clean Water Act, a citizen enforcer can only establish standing if it meets the requirements of "injury in fact" set forth in Sierra Club v. Morton, 405 U.S. 727 (1972). An organizational plaintiff, such as CBF or NRDC, can establish "injury in fact" through injury to their members as well as through injury to the organization itself. 405 U.S. at 739.

The Court need not consider the dispute over whether plaintiffs have established standing to sue in their own right, because it concludes that they have established standing to sue on behalf of their members. They established such standing when the Court granted their motion for summary judgment on the issue of liability. In support of that motion, plaintiffs included an affidavit of one of their counsel stating:

> Members of CBF reside in Virginia, in the vicinity of the Pagan River, and recreate in, on, or near, and otherwise use or enjoy the Pagan River and the water system of which it is a part.... The interests of CBF and of CBF's members have been, are being, and will be adversely affected by [Gwaltney's] failure to comply with its NPDES permit requirements.

The affidavit included an identical paragraph about members of NRDC. Defendant failed to dispute this in any way at the summary judgment hearing....

JURISDICTION... Gwaltney also argues that the Court has no jurisdiction over this suit because Gwaltney was not in violation of its NPDES permit when the complaint was filed, or subsequently. Gwaltney contends that the Clean Water Act's citizen suit provision only confers jurisdiction where the polluter is engaged in an ongoing violation; where the violation occurred entirely in the past, Gwaltney urges that there is no jurisdiction. Plaintiffs contend, on the contrary, that citizens can sue regardless of whether the polluter's unlawful conduct was continuing at the time the suit was filed.

---

66. Section 1318(a)(3)(A) of Title 33 mandates, among other things, that the Administrator of the Environmental Protection Agency "require the owner or operator of any point source" to establish and maintain such records of effluent discharges and to make such reports as the Administrator may "reasonably require." Currently, permittees under the Clean Water Act must submit DMRs. See 40 C.F.R. § 122.41(1)(4) (1984). Such reports are public information, by statute. See 33 U.S.C. § 1318(b)(2).

The dispute is one of statutory construction. Gwaltney's argument centers around the portion of the Clean Water Act's citizen suit provision that reads, in pertinent part:

...any citizen may commence a civil action on his own behalf —

(1) against any person...who is alleged to be *in violation of* (A) an effluent standard or limitation under this chapter.... 33 U.S.C. § 1365(a)(1) (emphasis added).

Gwaltney points out that the statute does not include the words "to have violated," and argues that the statute therefore only authorizes citizen suits against polluters whose unlawful conduct is occurring at the time the suit is filed.

The words "to be in violation" may reasonably be read as comprehending unlawful conduct that occurred solely prior to the filing of the lawsuit as well as unlawful conduct that continues into the present. For example, a person who under-pays taxes one year remains "in violation" of the relevant tax laws, even though that person pays the proper amount of taxes for the following year. Similarly, a polluter that exceeds various discharge limitations in its NPDES permit, such as Gwaltney, arguably remains "in violation" with respect to those excesses [until they are penalized], even though in subsequent years it brings itself into compliance. Indeed, its discharge violations remain on the records, and the effects of the excess discharges may linger well after they occur....

These sorts of citizen suits — in which a citizen can obtain an injunction but cannot obtain money damages for himself — are a very useful additional tool in enforcing environmental protection laws.... A reading of the citizen-suit provision that would authorize suits for civil penalties against polluters for past unlawful conduct regardless of their compliance status when the suit is filed is also consistent with one of the primary policy objectives inherent in the concept of citizen suits: deterrence of violations. Indeed, unless citizens may sue for civil penalties in such circumstances, citizen suits would provide little, if any, additional incentive for polluters to comply with their discharge limitations until a citizen suit is actually commenced.[67]

The problem of determining whether a violation is a "continuing" one is highlighted well in this case. Plaintiffs filed this suit in mid-June of 1984. With a history of violations of its TKN limitations in the wintertime, Gwaltney had just experienced another winter of repeated violations of its TKN violations, despite the changes it had implemented in its wastewater treatment system to address the problem. At the time of trial in December of 1984, one of Gwaltney's own witnesses — Mr. Sneed — expressed doubt as to whether Gwaltney would meet its TKN limitations.... Thus, plaintiffs' allegation in the complaint, that Gwaltney was continuing to violate its NPDES permit when plaintiffs filed suit appears to have been made fully in good faith.... In light of the language of the Clean Water Act's citizen suit provision, its legislative history, and its underlying policy goals, the Court concludes that the Clean Water Act authorizes citizen suits for civil penalties for violations of the Act, regardless of whether the polluter is engaged in unlawful conduct at the time the suit is filed or afterward....

---

67. The legislative history provides direct support, as well as by implication, for the view that the Clean Water Act authorizes citizen suits based on unlawful conduct that occurred in the past regardless of whether the conduct continues through the time the complaint is filed. Senator Muskie, the manager in the Senate of the bill...stated: "...a citizen has a right under Section 505 to bring an action for an appropriate remedy in the case of any person who is alleged to be, *or to have been*, in violation, whether the violation be a continuous one, or an occasional or sporadic one." 118 Cong. Rec. 33,700, reprinted in 1 A Legislative History of the Water Pollution Control Act Amendments of 1972 at 179 (1973) (emphasis added).

The number of days during which a polluter violates a limitation in its permit sets the polluter's maximum liability in civil penalties:...

> Any person who violates...any permit condition or limitation...shall be subject to a civil penalty not to exceed $10,000 per day of such violation. 33 U.S.C. A. § 1319(d)....

Determining the number of days involved in a given violation is thus an important aspect of assessing civil penalties....

VIOLATING A MONTHLY AVERAGE. Gwaltney has violated its "monthly average" permit limitations for several substances on a number of occasions. The monthly average for the pollutants at issue in this case is roughly half of the maximum daily amount allowed.[68]Gwaltney argues that a violation of a monthly average constitutes a single day of violation. Part of Gwaltney's argument is based on the suggestion that no real harm is being done where maximum daily limitations are not violated. But the mere fact that a daily maximum is not violated does not mean that the polluter's discharges are harmless. .... When a polluter violates a monthly average, every day of its discharges contributes to the violation....

MULTIPLE VIOLATIONS WITHIN A DAY. In some instances, Gwaltney violated discharge limitations for several substances on the same day. Gwaltney argues that the Clean Water Act limits its liability to $10,000 per day, regardless of the number of its violations on a given day. Plaintiffs, on the other hand, argue that the Act only limits a permittee's liability to $10,000 per day per violation of the discharge limitations on a given substance.... The Court concludes that...Section 1319(d) authorizes a maximum of $10,000 per day in civil penalties for violations that are enumerated therein, even where the defendant has violated discharge limitations for several substances during the same day....

The Court now faces the task of determining the actual penalty, within the statutory limits, that Gwaltney shall be assessed. The parties differ markedly on this point. Plaintiffs urge the Court to impose the statutory maximum: here, as the Court has discussed, over $6,000,000. Gwaltney argues that a far smaller amount ought to be assessed: somewhere between $12,000 and $20,000....

> EPA's civil penalty policy is...useful here in light of the...total absence of guidance Congress has provided in assessing penalties.... The policy aims at two general goals: (i) deterrence; and (ii) "fair and equitable treatment of the regulated community."

> For deterrence...of future violations by the violator (specific deterrence) and by other regulated firms (general deterrence),... the policy recommends a penalty that includes two components. First, it should include the *"economic benefit of non-compliance...."* Second, the penalty should include...a *"gravity component"* [reflecting] the seriousness of the violation....

> Once an appropriate penalty for deterrence purposes has been estimated, the policy recommends that [it] be adjusted to ensure that *the regulated community is fairly treated....*

---

68. The average and maximum permit limitations for four of the pollutants at issue in this case read as follows: (i) for TSS: 228.000 KG/D (daily average over a month), 455.000 KG/D (daily maximum); (ii) for fecal coliform: 200.0000 N/CML (daily average over a month), 400.000 N/CML (daily maximum); (iii) for TKN: 109.0000 KG/D (daily average over a month), 219.0000 KG/D (daily maximum); (iv) for oil and grease: 78.0000 KG/D (daily average over a month), 156.0000 KG/D (daily maximum). For chlorine, (C12), there was no average limitation: rather, a daily minimum (1.5000 MG/L) and maximum (2.5000 MG/L) were set.

GWALTNEY'S VIOLATIONS. The Court shall consider two distinct compliance problems in arriving at Gwaltney's penalty, [fecal coliform-chlorine violations and TKN biological contaminants]....

FECAL COLIFORM-CHLORINE. From November, 1981 to October, 1982, Gwaltney...chronically violated its permit limits for fecal coliform and chlorine. These violations were due to both insufficient and excessive exposure of Gwaltney's wastewater to chlorine.... Fecal coliform, a type of microbe associated with human and animal feces, is a good indicator of the safety of water for drinking, swimming, and shellfish harvesting. Gwaltney's permit includes both monthly average and daily maximum limitations on its discharges of fecal coliform....[69]

ECONOMIC BENEFIT. The Court feels compelled to ensure that Gwaltney receives no economic benefit whatever from its delay in having a properly operating chlorination system.... Determining with precision a firm's economic benefit from noncompliance is not a simple matter. As EPA's penalty policy points out, there are at least three distinct types of economic benefits that a violator may enjoy as a result of its violation. First, by delaying the expenditure of funds on compliance, a violator obtains the use of the money for other purposes in the meantime. Second, a violator may also avoid some costs altogether — for example, the costs of maintaining and operating the pollution control system until it is implemented. Third, a violator may, in addition, obtain a competitive advantage as a result of its violation — for example, it may be able to offer goods at a lower price, thereby possibly increasing its sales and profits. While these different types of benefit are not difficult to understand in the abstract, determining their amounts is more complicated....

GRAVITY COMPONENT. Gwaltney argues that there is no reason to impose a penalty with an adjusted gravity component of more than $4,900.... Gwaltney trivializes the seriousness of its fecal coliform violations.... Increased levels of fecal coliform in waters used for recreational swimming and shellfish harvesting pose health hazards to human beings, and act as a medium of disease transmission for a variety of diseases. In light of this, the Court finds Gwaltney's characterization of its violations as posing "no threat whatever to the public health" to be nothing less than offensive....

ADJUSTMENTS. Of course, liability under §1319(d) is strict. But...under EPA's civil penalty policy, a violator's willfulness or negligence is nevertheless relevant to the amount of penalty. Gwaltney argues...that it had no "absolute statutory obligation" to close its plant or slow its production, absent "imminent and substantial endangerment to health or welfare." Gwaltney's premise...reflects a certain degree of willfulness.... Gwaltney dealt with its chlorination problems in an exceedingly unconcerned manner [that] borders on benign neglect.

In light of Gwaltney's economic benefit, the gravity component, and appropriate adjustments, Gwaltney's total penalty for the violations arising out of its chlorination problems is $995,500.

---

69. In the subsequent *Smithfield Packing* case, the court noted that "Defendants' effluent included fecal matter from hogs, as well as humans namely the approximately 3,000 employees working at the plants each day.... Combined flows from Outfalls 001 and 002 averaged over 2.5 million gallons per day, while the flows of the Town of Smithfield averaged less than .5 million gallons per day."

BIOLOGICAL TREATMENT SYSTEM [TKN]... Gwaltney's second source of compliance problems was its biological treatment system. Inadequacies in that system led to repeated violations of Gwaltney's TKN limitations during the winter months early in 1982 and the winter months of 1982-83.... TKN is a nitrogen compound that can degrade a river by depleting its oxygen supply. Natural chemical and biological processes, involving TKN and bacteria in the river, transpire after TKN is added to a river. Those processes consume the dissolved oxygen in a river, to the detriment of many forms of river life....

[The judge then went through the same analytic steps as for fecal coliform, with the same skepticism of Gwaltney's arguments, and concluded]... Gwaltney's penalty for the problems stemming from its biological treatment system is $289,822.

CONCLUSION... Having determined that Gwaltney shall be assessed a civil penalty of $289,822 for violations arising out of the problems with its biological treatment system, as well as $995,500 for violations arising out of its chlorination system, the Court shall impose upon Gwaltney a total civil penalty of $1,285,322. An appropriate order will issue.

---

### Chesapeake Bay Foundation, Natural Resources Defense Council v. Gwaltney of Smithfield, Ltd.
#### Supreme Court of the United States, 1987
#### 484 U.S. 49

[The Supreme Court accepted the trial court's finding of extensive violations, but sent the case back , holding that the Clean Water Act only gave citizen groups jurisdiction to enforce against violations that were ongoing or likely to recur....]

MARSHALL, J. ...It is little questioned that the EPA Administrator may bring enforcement actions to recover civil penalties for wholly past violations.... [As to citizens, the lower courts concluded] that §505 authorizes citizens to bring enforcement actions on the basis of wholly past violations....

We now vacate the Fourth Circuit's opinion and remand the case.... The most natural reading [of §505]...is a requirement that citizen-plaintiffs allege a state of either *continuous or intermittent* violation — that is, a reasonable likelihood that a past polluter will continue to pollute in the future.... The interest of the citizen-plaintiff is primarily forward-looking....

Our conclusion that §505 does not permit citizen suits for wholly past violations does not necessarily dispose of this lawsuit.... The District Court found persuasive the fact that "[the citizens'] allegation in the complaint, that Gwaltney was continuing to violate its NPDES permit when plaintiffs filed suit, appears to have been made fully in good faith."...

Because we agree that §505 confers jurisdiction over citizen suits when the citizen-plaintiffs make a good-faith allegation of continuous or intermittent violation, we remand the case to the Court of Appeals for further consideration.... In the remand to the district court, the citizen-plaintiffs can prove an ongoing violation either (1) by proving actual violations that continue on or after the date the complaint is filed, or (2) by adducing evidence from which a reasonable trier of fact could find a continuing likelihood of a recurrence in intermittent or sporadic violations. Intermittent or sporadic violations do not cease to be ongoing until the date when there is no real likelihood of repetition.... Vacated and remanded. [Scalia, J., wrote separately, joined by O'Connor and Stevens, arguing that citizens should not be able to enforce the Act, at least not without *proof* of continuing violations, not just allegations.]

---

### Chesapeake Bay Foundation and Natural Resources Defense Council v. Gwaltney of Smithfield, Ltd.

United States District Court for the Eastern District of Virginia,
Richmond Division, 1988
688 F. Supp. 1078

[On remand to the trial court, Judge Merhige again finds that the citizens had sufficient standing, and as to the jurisdictional issue of ongoing violations holds as follows:]

MERHIGE, D.J. ...Having found that the evidence adduced at trial shows a reasonable continuing likelihood of a recurrence of intermittent violations at the time the action was filed, the Court FINDS that plaintiffs proved an ongoing violation. The original judgment of the Court imposing upon Gwaltney a total civil penalty of $ 1,285,322 shall be reinstated.

---

### Chesapeake Bay Foundation and Natural Resources Defense Council v. Gwaltney of Smithfield, Ltd.

United States Court of Appeals for the Fourth Circuit, 1989
890 F.2d 690

[The Court of Appeal supported the trial judge's jurisdictional finding, but modified the civil damages amount downward under a theory that damages could be apportioned, chlorine-fecal coliform violations having ended, and TKN contaminants not:]

PER CURIAM ...We think that "a reasonable trier of fact could find a continuing likelihood of a recurrence in intermittent or sporadic violations." We therefore affirm the district court in so finding....

At the remand hearing, Gwaltney urged that the court should make separate determinations for the TKN and chlorine violations. The trial court, interpreting our remand quite strictly, deemed it was permitted only to determine whether there was an ongoing violation; finding that there was, the court then reinstated the original judgment, which was based on both TKN and chlorine violations. We reverse....

We...hold that the district court had no jurisdiction to impose penalties for Gwaltney's wholly past chlorine violations; [only the TKN violations were likely to continue at the time of complaint.] We vacate the judgment for $1,285,322 and remand for the court to enter judgment against Gwaltney in the amount of $289,822 — the amount attributable to TKN violations — with interest....

[The parties subsequently settled for a payment to the U.S. Treasury in the amount of $289,822, plus reimbursement to the citizens of approximately $200,000 under CWA §505(d) for expert witness and attorneys fees from their six-year enforcement effort. EPA, which under the Supreme Court's holding had not lost its capacity to sue for past violations, was by this time barred from recovering the rest of the $1,285,322 penalty by the 5-year statute of limitations.]

---

**U.S. v. Smithfield Foods, Smithfield Packing Co., and
Gwaltney of Smithfield, Ltd. (the *Smithfield Packing* case)**
United States District Court for the Eastern District of Virginia,
May 30, 1997; August 8, 1997
965 F. Supp. 769; 972 F. Supp. 338

[Smithfield's pollution problems on the Pagan River did not end with the final *Gwaltney* decision. Like the Gwaltney plant, Smithfield Packing, the second plant in the Smithfield industrial complex on the Pagan River, faced an array of problems involving discharges of phosphorus, cyanide, grease, TKN, acidity pH, carbonaceous biological oxygen demand ("CBOD"), and ammonia-nitrogen. The state filed a penalty action in the mid1980s to preempt a citizen suit concurrent with *Gwaltney*, but thereafter basically ignored the plant's violations. The citizen groups led by CBF again played a role. The Commonwealth of Virginia's pollution control agency granted a series of requested extensions of noncompliance. In 1990 Smithfield made a deal with the state that it could continue discharges into the Pagan, subject to certain conditions, until such time as the HRSD treatment plant was built and could be connected to the pig factories. In 1991 Smithfield felt sufficiently secure under state "special orders" and extensions that it ceased cutting back on production when overload violations threatened; it opposed tightening phosphorus standards in 1993 by threatening to move to North Carolina; it cut costs by leaving its wastewater treatment plant unsupervised for one shift a day. On July 21, 1994 Smithfield's discharge records covering the period up to December 1993 were destroyed by Gwaltney's wastewater plant manager. Meanwhile the state amended its rules further to prevent citizen enforcement and other elements required by federal law. Starting in 1990 the citizens pushed EPA to take over enforcement, and to decertify the state's NPDES program. EPA did three de-certification reviews. In late August 1996 EPA announced that it would itself sue Smithfield for past violations. Immediately the Virginia SWCB attempted to "pre-file" a state enforcement action to preempt federal enforcement, but EPA went ahead, obtaining the following decision:]

REBECCA BEACH SMITH, DISTRICT JUDGE.... The Virginia State Water Control Board issued Permit No. VA0059005 to Smithfield on May 13, 1986. The Permit placed various restrictions on...the amount and concentration of certain pollutants in the wastewater [and] required Smithfield to monitor the wastewater discharged from the outfalls, submit Discharge Monitoring Reports reporting the results of wastewater sampling and analysis, submit the results of annual toxicity testing, and retain all sampling and analysis data for three years.... Because Smithfield challenged the schedule of compliance for the phosphorus limitations...as unreasonable and not practicable of attainment, the Board agreed "to defer commencement of the schedule...until December 1, 1990."

[The court opinion then explored in great detail the extensive back-and-forth conversations over a six-year period between the Smithfield company and the

Virginia water board, postponing the date the plants would have to come into compliance with various parameters of the Permit.]

Under the NPDES enforcement program administered by the EPA, point source facilities that are not complying with their NPDES permit are listed in the EPA's Quarterly Noncompliance Report ("QNCR").... Defendants' violations of Permit No. VA0059005 did not appear on the QNCR until the third quarter of the 1994 fiscal year, because Smithfield falsely and inaccurately reported its discharges, and because the Commonwealth of Virginia issued consent orders ["special orders"] allowing defendants to exceed the limits established in the Permit....

If a state does not achieve compliance, the EPA steps in and initiates its own enforcement action to ensure compliance. Once defendants' violations of Permit No. VA0059005 appeared on the QNCR in 1994, the EPA tracked the Commonwealth's attempts to get Smithfield into compliance.[70]

On April 8, 1996, the Commonwealth's Department of Environmental Quality ("DEQ") notified Smithfield that it had evidence of numerous violations of the Permit and Special Orders, including violations of effluent limits, sampling and analysis methods, recording of results, records retention, reporting requirements, operator requirements, treatment works operation, quality control requirements, and unauthorized discharge of pollutants.... At their May 22, 1996 meeting, however, the Board instead voted to "reaffirm their March 21, 1996...Special Order [further suspending compliance pending a future sewer hookup]...and direct [its] staff not to take enforcement action against Smithfield, Inc. for violations of their 1991 Consent Special Order...."

When it became apparent that the Commonwealth's actions were not resulting in compliance, and the Commonwealth did not intend to seek a civil penalty for the violations, the EPA initiated its own enforcement action. On August 27, 1996, the EPA informed the Commonwealth that it had referred a case against defendants to the United States Department of Justice for an enforcement action, and invited the Commonwealth to join the federal action.... The Commonwealth declined the EPA's invitation to join the federal action. Although the Commonwealth never mentioned its plan to file its own enforcement action to the EPA, on August 30, 1996, the Commonwealth filed an action against Smithfield in the [state] circuit court.... The United States filed this action on December 16, 1996, seeking permanent injunctive relief and civil penalties....

Defendants argue that they agreed to connect to the HRSD system to achieve compliance with the Permit, but were unable to connect earlier due to circumstances and delays beyond their control.... The Clean Water Act is a strict liability statute, intended to protect the public from environmental damage.... Accordingly it is defendants, and not the public, who should pay the price for the damage to the environment caused by their permit violations and the delay in the HRSD connection.... Defendants committed thousands of days of violations of the Clean Water Act by discharging pollutants into the Pagan River....

Defendants assert that [federal enforcement] is barred under §309 because the state has "commenced and is diligently prosecuting" an administrative action against Smithfield under Virginia law. [The judge then discussed this allegation thoroughly and found that the state law does not contain provisions comparable to CWA requirements on penalties, agency enforcement, and citizen enforcement....]

---

70. [Ed. note: This EPA effort was initially prompted and subsequently given investigative support by the CBF citizen group's enforcement initiative.]

CIVIL PENALTIES. [As in *Gwaltney*, the court totalled up an inventory of violations.] At trial, it was established that defendants' records covering the period up to December, 1993, were destroyed on or around July 21, 1994, by Terry Rettig, chief operator of defendants' wastewater treatment plants. Thereafter, defendants... were in violation [for] 884 days, until December 31, 1996.

Defendants argued they should only be assessed one day of violation for the record-keeping requirement violations. They claim the records were...only destroyed on a single day in July, 1994, by Rettig.... The court finds 884 days of violation.... Treating destruction of records as a single violation would create a terrible incentive to destroy records covering a certain time period to get one single day of violation, rather than submitting records which might reflect a larger number of days of violation....

During the entire trial, defendants' approach to their Permit violations was rather cavalier. They repeatedly argued there was no real harm caused by their numerous violations, and that the Pagan River would still be environmentally damaged and unsafe for swimming and shellfish harvesting, even if defendants complied with their permit. Such arguments miss the mark.... A violator cannot escape liability or penalties for permit violations simply by pointing to the violations of others. Each must do its part to clean up the environment....

Based on the credible testimony and evidence, most of defendants' violations were severe.... On average, defendants' discharges accounted for approximately 10% of the freshwater flow into the Pagan River, and as much as 50% of freshwater flow during low flow periods.... Excessive nutrient loadings, or nutrient enrichment, in the Pagan River cause eutrophication and are a primary cause of the absence of submerged aquatic vegetation ("SAV") in the Pagan River. Eutrophication is the overstimulation or overproduction of organic carbon in an estuary. Excessive nutrient loadings stimulate productivity of algae, which decreases sunlight to plants, and causes increased algae growth on plants and increased turbidity. Eutrophication is likely to cause changes in phytoplankton, zooplankton, and benthos, which can affect fish.... Nutrient loadings discharged into the Pagan River contribute to nutrient loadings in the James River, and ultimately the Chesapeake Bay....

CONCLUSION... Most of defendants' permit discharge exceedances clearly had a severe and significant impact on the water quality of the Pagan River, in light of their frequency and severity. The harm to the environment and the risk to human health caused by defendants' numerous effluent limit violations are serious.... Accordingly, the court finds that the appropriate civil penalty for defendants' permit violations is $12,600,000.... Further, plaintiff shall submit to the court, within 30 days, a proposal for the allocation of this penalty, with a specific focus on the feasibility of directing all, or part of, the penalty toward the restoration of the Chesapeake Bay and its tributaries, namely the James and the Pagan Rivers. It is so ordered.

COMMENTARY AND QUESTIONS

1. **Aftermath of Judge Smith's decision.** Smithfield's owner, Mr. Joe Luter, made it clear that he would appeal Judge Smith's decision. Beyond the kind of arguments on the amount of penalties that had substantially reduced his penalties on appeal in the prior *Gwaltney of Smithfield* cases (the *Smithfield Packing* case, for

instance, clearly raises the question whether multiple violations on one day equal more than one violation), Luter would also argue that the Virginia state agency's "pre-filing" of an enforcement action preempted federal EPA enforcement, and the EPA "over-filing" of the action in Judge Smith's court hence was void despite her contrary holding. As to any SEP ("supplemental environmental project") remedy for restoration of the Chesapeake Bay and its tributaries, as proposed to the court by the Chesapeake Bay Foundation, Mr. Luter was quoted as saying that Hell would freeze over before he paid any penalties that might benefit an environmental citizens group.

Three months after her decision, Judge Smith, in an unpublished memo opinion, held that penalties, once they have been assessed, must be paid into the Treasury under the federal Miscellaneous Receipts Act and cannot be diverted into SEP remedial projects. Several pending bills in Congress would amend the law to permit such restoration funds.

2. **Generational differences.** What's going on in these cases? Much has changed since the *Kepone* generation. Don't these cases mostly deal with computation of environmental penalties, not arguments about wrongful causation of harm? As both Judge Merhige and Judge Smith noted, today's Clean Water Act, like many environmental statutes, is essentially a strict liability system: fault need not be proved in order to assess penalties for pollution. More than two decades after Kepone and the first generation of major pollution law enforcement actions, pollution cases are now more numerous than in the 1970s, but often are quite different in character, turning on subtleties of administrative implementation of the statutes and regulations.

> The challenges we confront today — atmospheric buildup of carbon dioxide and other greenhouse gases, the potential environmental impacts of genetically modified organisms, and the risk of exposure to trace residues of pesticides that might disrupt endocrine cycles within a human body — were not even contemplated by first-generation environmental laws....
>
> Since the time of Earth Day in 1970, we have cleaned up thousands of the "big dirties" through the use of pioneering federal legislation designed to take direct action against these threats to air, water, and land. Now, a generation later, we must confront environmental problems that are subtler, less visible, and more difficult to address: fertilizer runoff from thousands of farms and millions of yards; emissions from gas stations, bakeries, and dry cleaners; and smog produced by tens of millions of motor vehicles. Like nature itself, the size and shape of environmental problems constantly evolve; so too must the strategies, approaches, institutions, and tools chosen to address them. Chertow & Esty, Environmental Policy: The Next Generation, Issues in Sci. & Tech., Fall 1997 at 73.[71]

Industry has generally come to accept the inevitability of environmental regula-

---

71. Marian Chertow & Daniel Esty are the editors of Thinking Ecologically: The Next Generation of Environmental Policy (Yale University Press, 1997).

tion. Expectations of serious environmental enforcement mean that the cost of violating laws is generally perceived in a hard-nosed business planning sense as likely to be a greater risk than the cost of complying. There is little rhetoric and outrage here from any quarter. Instead there is seemingly a new attitude of acceptance, and internalization of many environmental requirements into daily business practice.

> Environmental protection cannot be boiled down to a struggle between the "good guys" (environmental activists) and the "bad guys" (big industry). The corporate world is not monolithic with regard to environmental performance. Some companies take environmental stewardship very seriously, wheras others pollute with abandon. The next generation of environmental policy must recognize shades of gray, create positive incentives for the leaders, and still hold the laggards accountable. Id.

There are also unsubtle differences between the first generation of environmental law and now. In *Kepone*, no one went to jail. In the *Smithfield* cases, Gwaltney's Terry Rettig went to prison, sentenced to 30 months, based in part on statutory changes strengthening criminal penalties after the Kepone incident. Chapter 19 reviews the rising numbers of criminal prosecutions.

Note also the increased sophistication and specificity of the scientific standards that have been set by the regulations. Along with new laws (more than two dozen new federal environmental statutes by the end of the 1970s), the federal and state environmental agency structures and their regulations and guidelines, like the EPA Penalty Policy (BNA Env't Rep. 41:2991, June 1, 1984), have proliferated since the early 1970s into a quantum of public law that is now far more complex and voluminous than the Internal Revenue Code and its rules.

Regulatory standards and court enforcement today, moreover, are not just preoccupied with preventing human disasters, but look farther to the diffused ecological effects of pollution. The *Smithfield Packing* decision ends with a reminder of effects on vegetation, zooplankton, and fish, as well as effects on humans, because today the linkage is clear: disruptions of the natural economy can have serious effects within the societal economy as well. As a recent example, hog processing wastes in North Carolina's Neuse River triggered the first serious outbreak of a toxic aquatic bacterium, *Pfisteria piscicida* ['fishkiller'] in 1995, killing more than five million fish. In 1997 the same *Pfisteria* appeared along the eastern Chesapeake coastline, home to poultry factories with more than 62 million resident chickens, and the Pagan River seems ripe for the same kind of outbreak.[72]

The ultimate pollution cleanup of the Smithfield companies came by hooking up their discharges to a publicly-owned treatment works (POTW), the Hampton Roads

---

72. *Pfisteria* , which produces bi-level toxins that first stun the fish and then make lesions to invade their flesh, apparently has been around at low levels for thousands of years. Its modern explosion appears traceable to abnormally high nutrient loading. The Delmarva Peninsula's chicken factories now produce more than 1.5 million tons of raw waste annually, containing 24,000 tons of nitrogen and 13 million pounds of phosphorus. Tens of thousands of commercial fish died in the fish kills of 1997, and there were two dozen cases of skin and organic injury to exposed fishermen. Fish with lesions have been reported in the lower James River on the Pagan side of the Bay. The Pagan is nutrient-rich and sluggish, conditions prime for bacterial outbreaks. See Trout, Winter 1998 at 39–41. Fall Newsletter, Univ. of Md. Center for Environmental Science.

Sanitation District. To achieve centralized economies of scale and public subsidies, and to avoid separate NPDES permits, many industries today seek to connect to POTWs, and if pretreatment standards are implemented well this is often a salutary arrangement. It is noted further in Chapter Nine.

Another change over 20 years: Hasn't the courts' scientific and legal sophistication in reviewing environmental cases apparently increased as well? Not to mention their handling of a host of strange new acronyms — NPDES, CBOD, TKN, QNCRs, POTWs, DMRs....?[73]

3. **The "Why me? It's not only my fault" defense.** Smithfield Packing's attorneys argued in defense that "If you took ours out, it wouldn't make any difference," pointing to the pollution violations of others that contributed to the river's low overall water quality. The court simply rebuffed that argument, saying "each must do its part to clean up the environment." This simple response masks a far more complicated issue of regulatory policy.

First, Gwaltney's argument implies that, when an agency is faced with a Tragedy of the Commons problem, the only proper response is to regulate all polluters or none at all. As a matter of logic and practicality, is that true? Regulating a few of the largest violators might be sufficient to solve the problem and would save scarce enforcement resources. Even if selective enforcement were workable and necessary, however, is it fair? Gwaltney's deliberate noncompliance undercuts the fairness objection, but even absent fault the general view of the law (in all fields, not just environmental law) allows for selective enforcement and partial cures for social problems. What the law forbids is discriminatory enforcement based on illegitimate classifications (violating equal protection), or excessive and unfair burdens on otherwise legitimate uses of property (like regulatory takings of property).

Gwaltney's argument against selective enforcement also bumps into Hardin's tragedy of the commons. Hardin suggests a rationale for why later-in-time developers can be subjected to "mutual coercion" when he notes that the morality of an act is a function of the state of the system in which it occurs. The tragedy occurs through the serial acts of many actors, which in combination ultimately exceed the common's carrying capacity, a "nibbling" phenomenon (for example, filling wetlands for development in incremental chunks over time) where ultimately the cumulative effects are fatal to an entire ecosystem.

4. **Statutory evolution since Kepone.** Kepone stimulated amendments to the Clean Water Act in 1977, and this evolution has continued, making it highly improbable that massive, long-term, but relatively localized, pollution of the ambient environment like the Kepone situation could take place today in the United States.

Amendments in 1987 tightened (1) control of toxic pollutants, (2) industrial stormwater management, (3) industrial pretreatment, (4) sewage sludge disposal, (5) "placed-based" environmental protection (also called "ecosystem management," "watershed management," or "bioregionalism," which the Act applied with special emphasis on Chesapeake Bay), and (6) expanding and strengthening

---

73. For a Glossary of the acronyms that facilitate and plague environmental law, see the Reference Materials at the back of this book.

the CWA's criminal enforcement mechanisms. Judges now possess stronger criminal sanctions with which to punish knowing violators of the CWA: "knowing endangerment" which "places another person in imminent danger of death or serious bodily injury" can lead to fines of $250,000 or 15 years imprisonment, doubled for second convictions. 33 U.S.C. A. §1319. (It was under these enhanced federal charges that Smithfield's Terry Rettig was sentenced on eight counts of destroying records and rendering false information, and began serving a 30-month prison term in January 1997.)

Potential federal and state criminal prosecution is a continuing part of environmental practice, with no sign of any decrease in its importance as a deterrent motivating compliance. The battery of state and federal statutory and regulatory law, moreover, continues to grow in sophistication and bulk, although almost 40% of the nation's waters are still not "fishable or swimmable."

Regulatory technique is also evolving. Chapters 8–18 study a variety of regulation approaches, each going through stages of development, reflecting an ongoing evolution in the role of government:

> It is difficult to be simultaneously referee and quarterback. Under the current regulatory scheme, government sets the rules, which is necessary and appropriate, but also tries to dictate exactly which plays to use.... This approach [can be] stifling to innovation, does not account for differences across industries and ecosystems, and creates incentives to try to get around the law. Another approach [is] to continue to use the existing regulatory system as a minimum benchmark but try, at the same time, to increase opportunities at all levels of implementation to improve environmental performance through other than narrowly prescribed regulatory means. In other words, the government should still command [through performance standards], but it does not need to control [i.e. by design standards] exactly how regulated parties should achieve compliance with established goals. The regulated community should be empowered to design its own enforceable alternative compliance methods, provided they achieve equivalent or better environmental performance....
>
> Four central recommendations for ecological policy are: Do not focus only on EPA and the government but on the critical roles of other actors and sectors, move from heavy reliance on command-and-control approaches to include more flexible tools, recognize the potential of the market as an ecological model that is dynamic and flexible, and adopt systems approaches such as industrial ecology and ecosystem management that foster an examination of context and address interconnections rather than singular phenomena. Chertow & Esty, at 77–78.

5. **A biodiversity of public laws, and an introduction to statutory taxonomy.** In addition to evolving common law remedies, an amazing number of public laws have developed and evolved since the early 1970s. The list below identifies 16 of the major federal statutes potentially applied in modern environmental pollution cases, each of which typically also has a state or local counterpart regulation. In the setting of the *Smithfield cases*, the first dozen would be most likely to apply. The Kepone case would today trigger virtually every federal statute on the main list and many of their state corollaries:

1. **CWA:** the federal **Clean Water Act**,[74] administered by U.S. EPA, a federal-state partnership where the EPA sets permissible levels of discharge for different industrial categories, based on the performance of the best available technology (BAT); states issue National Pollution Discharge Elimination System (NPDES) permits based on the federal standards, backed up by on-site ambient water quality requirements; state enforcement of permits is backed up by the federal EPA.

2. **CWA §404:** the federal dredge-and-fill regulation program also falls under CWA, restricting the elimination of wetlands, and, in cooperation with the U.S. Army Corps of Engineers' administration of the Refuse Act,[75] also requiring permits for installing in-stream structures like Smithfield's sewerage outfalls.

3. **CAA:** the federal **Clean Air Act**,[76] administered by EPA, like the CWA a federal-state partnership, requires enforcement of "state implementation plans" (SIPs) to prevent overall ambient levels of pollution from exceeding federal "primary standards" set according to harm-based safety criteria; the CAA also has special provisions regulating hazardous air pollutants, and holds new air pollution sources to the cleanliness levels of the best available technology (BAT).

4. **FDCA:** the federal **Food, Drug, and Cosmetics Act**,[77] administered by EPA and HHS, provides, among others, protections for food quality by setting permissible tolerances for chemical residues like pesticides in food products, and monitoring compliance; this obviously would be a significant regulatory constraint for Smithfield's ham processing.

5. **EPCRA:** the federal **Emergency Planning and Community Right-To-Know Act**,[78] passed after the Bhopal disaster, administered by EPA, requires mandatory public reporting by industry of the nature and characteristics of certain hazardous materials, and requires states to establish state-wide and local emergency response plans.

6. **RCRA:** the federal **Resource Conservation and Recovery Act**,[79] an update of the Solid Waste Disposal Act (SWDA) administered by EPA, regulates waste disposal in general and certain hazardous wastes (via Subtitle C) in particular, tracking the wastes (not the original chemicals), beginning with their generation and ending with their treatment, storage, or disposal (somewhat imprecisely dubbed "cradle to grave" regulation); RCRA also authorizes EPA to take corrective actions to prevent or remedy contamination; special provisions apply to leaking underground storage tanks and medical wastes.

7. **CERCLA:** the federal **Comprehensive Environmental Response, Compensation and Liability Act**, or "Superfund" Act,[80] provides for EPA investigations and supervised cleanups of hazardous contaminated sites, paid for by the parties who own or contaminated the sites, with backup funding from a federal fund combining taxes from chemical production, penalties, and taxpayer dollars.

---

74. 33 USCA 1365 (1972, 1977).

75. The Refuse Act, 30 Stat. §1151 (1899), 33 USCA §407, as noted above, is an old statute that was part of the Rivers and Harbors Act of 1899; some of its provisions, like structural alterations in watercourses alongside CWA §404, remain effective alongside §9, remain effective alongside CWA §404.

76. 42 USCA §7401 et seq. (1970).

77. 21 USCA §346 et seq. (1954, as amended).

78. 42 USCA §11001 et seq. (1986).

79. 42 USCA §6901 et seq. (1976).

80. 42 USCA §9601 et seq. (1980) as amended by SARA, the Superfund Amendments and Reauthorization Act of 1986.

8. **SDWA:** the federal **Safe Drinking Water Act**,[81] administered by EPA, fixes water quality standards for drinking water suppliers and protection of underground drinking water sources; it regulates the deep well injection of wastes, a common industrial practice of pumping chemicals into old wells and drill holes as a method of disposal.

9. **OSHA:** the federal **Occupational Safety and Health Act**,[82] administered by the Occupational Health and Safety Administration [likewise called "OSHA"], OSHA addresses safety conditions within industrial workplaces and other work settings. The agency sets general industry standards, and tries to monitor and enforce them through agency inspections.

10. **CZMA:** the federal **Coastal Zone Management Act**,[83] administered by the National Oceanic and Atmospheric Administration (NOAA) in the Department of Commerce, applying comprehensive state planning and siting controls in coastal and tidal regions (reaching 100 miles inland up the James River watershed) with federal reinforcement.

11. **NEPA:** the **National Environmental Policy Act**,[84] a generic procedural statute administered by the President's Council on Environmental Quality, that does not stipulate any pollution control measures, nor any direct regulation of any private industry, but levies the significant, litigatable requirement that all federal agencies must prepare an environmental impact statement (EIS) before taking any "major federal action significantly affecting the human environment"; many agency permits, like the permits for Smithfield's sewerage outfall pipes, thus have to go through the EIS process.

12: **PPA:** the federal **Pollution Prevention Act**,[85] administered by EPA, is mainly an exhortation to industry to reduce, recycle, or prevent pollution through internal planning, design, and technology adaptations; EPA has the power, however, to impose PPA requirements as permit conditions or as part of violation penalty orders.

13. **ESA:** the federal **Endangered Species Act**,[86] administered by the Department of Interior Fish and Wildlife Service (FWS), and the National Oceanic and Atmospheric Administration (NOAA) in the Department of Commerce, prohibiting harms to endangered and threatened species; if a listed species is present in an ecosystem, pollution discharge permits and construction projects can be forced to go through significant modification procedures, or be blocked.

14. **ToSCA:** the federal **Toxic Substances Control Act**,[87] administered by EPA, is a "market access" regulation authorizing the agency to require manufacturers to test chemical substances for hazards to human health and the environment before they are permitted to be manufactured and sold; failure of EPA to act to restrict use of a substance acts like a grant of a permit; a ban on use functions like a permit denial.

15. **FIFRA:** the **Federal Insecticide, Fungicide, and Rodenticide Act**,[88] administered by EPA, requires persons distributing, selling, offering, or receiving any pesticide to register the poison with the EPA after testing for "unreasonable

---

81. 15 U.S.C.A. §1261 et seq. (1974, as amended).

82. 29 USCA §651 et seq. (1970).

83. 33 USCA §1251 et seq. (1970).

84. 42 USCA §4331 et seq. (1970).

85. 42 USCA §13101 et seq. (1990).

86. 16 USCA §1531 et seq. (1973, as amended).

87. 15 USCA §2601 et seq. (1976).

88. 7 USCA §136 et seq. (1975).

risks to humans and the environment, taking into account the economic, social, and environmental costs and benefits of the pesticide's intended use"; the "market access" registration, once granted with practicable tolerance levels, is akin to a perpetual license to market the product, though registrations can be canceled or suspended.

16. **HMTA:** the federal **Hazardous Materials Transportation Act,**[89] administered by the U.S. Department of Transportation, provides for extensive regulation of hazardous substances in transit, with requirements for spill control and prevention, and central reporting in the event of spills of toxic or hazardous substances, and invites concurrent state regulation.

There are further federal statutes that can be applied in environmental cases, including a long list of natural resources management statutes, statutes limiting ocean dumping and export of hazardous or contaminated products, laws protecting parks and marine sanctuaries, historic preservation regulations, transportation planning, the market disclosure requirements of the SEC and the FTC, significant IRS tax code provisions, and so on.

Add to these the state corollaries of these federal laws, and also an array of state laws in areas not covered by federal statutes: land use controls and siting, groundwater protection, recycling and noise regulations, landfill regulations beyond toxics and industrial wastes, toxic product standards, land sale disclosure laws, and more.[90] There is a lot of law here. For a fuller description of significant state and federal environmental statutes and their operation, see the **Statutory Capsule Appendix** in the reference section at the back of the book.

**STATE AND LOCAL REGULATION...** The following chart shows state and local permits that might be required in setting up a plant like Smithfield Packing Co.:

| AGENCY: | REGULATORY REQUIREMENT: |
|---|---|
| State air, water, natural resources commissions | [More than a dozen permits directly analogous to the federal regulatory systems noted above] |
| *plus* | |
| State Department of Labor | Permit for boiler installation |
| State Department of Labor | Permit for any elevators involved in a plant |
| State Department of Natural Resources | Permit for dredging and filling as required on site |
| State Water Resources Commission | Permit for alteration of channels or floodplains, or any drains |
| State Department of Natural Resources | Permit for construction in zone close to major bodies of water |
| State Department of Health | Approval of sanitary sewer system |
| State Police | Approval for above-ground storage of flammable liquids |
| County Road Commission | Permit for altering or temporary closing of highways for construction |
| County Health Commission | Permit for alteration of any drains |
| County Health Commission | Approval of sewer system |

CONTINUED...

---

89. 49 USCA §1801 et seq. (1980).

90. A number of these state laws are noted in the Statutory Capsule Appendix, including California's Proposition 65 toxic product labelling, New Jersey's land transfer disclosure requirements, and waste minimization laws.

...CONTINUED

| AGENCY: | REGULATORY REQUIREMENT: |
|---|---|
| State air, water, natural resources commissions | [More than a dozen permits directly analogous to the federal regulatory systems noted above] |
| *plus* | |
| Local Township | Building, electrical, and plumbing permits |
| Local Township | Permits for water use and sewerage |
| State Air Pollution Commission | Permit for boilers and diesel generators |
| State Department of Aeronautics | Permit for construction of high smokestacks |
| State Water Resource Commission | Permit for use of water during plant construction, operation, and sewage treatment (in addition to state water pollution control, or NPDES permit) |
| State Department of Natural Resources | Soil erosion and sedimentation permit |
| State Department of Natural Resources | Inland streams alteration permit |
| State Public Utilities Commission | Permit for construction of high voltage electric transmission lines |
| State Public Utilities Commission | Permission for connection to high voltage electric transmission lines |
| State Department of Highways | Permit for alteration of highway access |
| State Public Utilities Commission | Railroad spur construction, alteration, and connection to existing railroad spurs |
| State Public Utilities Commission | Permits for building grade crossings across railroad tracks |
| State Public Utilities Commission | Construction permit for operation of electrical substation |
| County, and Local Municipality | Zoning permits |

A "taxonomy" analysis can help in the task of processing all these many public laws; as with biologists who analyze different creatures according to their elements, a legal taxonomy can usefully clarify the different statutory options:

There are a variety of different statutory types, structural designs, and standard-setting approaches that can be seen in these laws, and that can be considered in choosing how future laws should be constructed. Some statutes focus on the threshold, like the point of market access, others on the production process, others at the back end of production with waste disposal regulation. Some require permits, others require inspections, reactive enforcement, or just planning procedures. Some set regulatory standards based on best available technology, others on harm to humans and nature, or on politically-desired technology-forcing, or on participant negotiations, or on industry self-regulatory standards. Some statutes avoid command regulation in favor of the carrot of subsidies, or market-enlisting procedures like pollution credit trading. Given the complexity of modern environmental public law, this book looks at statutes from the perspective of these descriptive elements, in order to organize, simplify, and deepen the regulatory analysis.

6. **Are the *Smithfields* typical of modern pollution cases?** Given the huge diversity of modern environmental practice, there probably is no such thing as a typical case, but the *Smithfields* have most of the elements of modern enforcement litigation. (The least typical element in the *Smithfields* may be the latent obstructive momentum of Joe Luter, Smithfield's owner, who appears never to have accepted

the basic legitimacy of environmental regulation, and tried relentlessly to oppose the enforcement of federal law against his companies. Most industry players, except for the brief cataclysm when they attempted to repeal many environmental laws during the Contract with America Congress, have basically come to accept these laws' existence.)

The *Smithfield* cases are also typical in the strategic role played by citizen environmental groups, and the tactical importance of potential citizen enforcement.

**7. Citizen enforcement as part of modern environmental law.** On closer inspection, aren't the *Smithfield* cases really about *Enforcement*? The *Smithfield Packing* suit turned on whether the EPA, once it was persuaded by citizens to enforce the law, could take the case to court over the head of the state agency. The citizen enforcement suit in *Gwaltney* was filed *after* the Gwaltney plant had come into compliance with the amounts of discharge allowed under its state permits, so the implicit question was whether the suit was even necessary.

Why did the citizens bother in either case? There are several reasons, and they focus on how and whether the law, in reality, would actually be enforced.

In the years after Kepone (in which, remember, there was no citizen enforcement of statutes) the fact of citizen participation in environmental public law has completely permeated the system, both in litigation and in informal and formal participation in agency practice.[91] As noted further in Chapter Seven, every major federal environmental law since 1970 has included an authorization for citizen enforcement, and recoupment of enforcement costs. Citizen litigation has subsequently shaped every part of the public law structure. Agencies, it turns out, often lack the resources to enforce statutes, or are not inclined to constrain industry. In a lesson that has begun to spread to the rest of the world, American practice has shown that if you really want to have a public law enforced, it is sensible to provide, at least, for supplemental private enforcement by those who are personally affected and hence have a personal incentive to do so. This not only enlists the efforts of "private attorneys-general"; it also means that in many cases the mere looming potential for citizen enforcement will push agencies themselves into enforcement that otherwise would be stalled by political inertia. So citizen groups in general have tended to take on the same kind of enforcement actions that government agencies are authorized to undertake (CWA authorized agencies to penalize violations past or present, and when *Gwaltney* was filed nobody distinguished between citizen and agency enforcement[92]).

Moreover the citizens' enforcement action in *Gwaltney* and their pressure on EPA in *Smithfield Packing* were clearly motivated by the conviction that the Virginia pollution agencies were not very interested in enforcement, both generally and with specific regard to Smithfield. If the state Water Control Board would not use

91. As for instance the citizens' groups were instrumental in the later *Smithfield* case in motivating and supporting the EPA's enforcement action.
92. As CBF's current counsel Roy Hoagland noted, only one case, Hamter v. Diamond Shamrock Chemical Co., 756 F.2d 392 (5th Cir. 1985), had previously made a distinction between citizen and government enforcement actions, holding that citizens were limited to suing for ongoing violations. The Supreme Court holding thus came somewhat as a surprise.

Smithfield's DMRs in compliance proceedings, then CBF would try to persuade EPA to do it, or would do it themselves. If the state agency was systematically undercutting the national water pollution control system, then it would be the citizens who had to push EPA (which obviously does not relish the task of taking over state pollution controls) to consider decertifying the delegation of federal pollution control powers to the state.

The dynamics of this citizen enforcement logic are not limited to Virginia, and obviously continue. Citizen intervention has been the major element in shifting social governance in environmental law from the old bi-polar model — where a government agency held the sole responsibility for counterbalancing the excesses of the corporate marketplace — to a Jeffersonian multicentric pluralism where a diversity of affected interests can be actively involved in the legal process to assure that public and individual values do not get lost in the tangles of the political-economic marketplace. In terms of the three economies, citizen enforcement is often the strategic force pushing implementation of public interest statutes through the snarls and blandishments of marketplace politics into practical service to the civic economy.

**8. Biodiversity of law: the common law's continuing roles.** A major sector of legal response in the Kepone case was common law tort. In the *Smithfield* controversy there was none, at least so far as reported. It is true that modern public law remedies, based on state and nation-wide regulatory systems, do have advantages in scale (broad-scale comprehensiveness) and applicability (e.g. requiring no proof of causation of unreasonable harms).

The common law, however, continues to be a fundamentally important part of modern environmental law. Public law remedies build upon and supplement the common law, but common law remains the foundational underpinning of the legal system. It is a traditionally open legal forum for affected individuals, and often is more flexible and creative in integrating public civic values into new and significant settings.

Consider Alaska's Exxon-Valdez oilspill, for example. In that extraordinary case of negligence by the Alyeska pipeline consortium and Exxon Corporation, a cataclysmic contamination poured out over one of the nation's richest ecosystems, threatening billions of dollars of commercial fisheries, not to mention priceless natural and cultural resources not valued by the market economy. See Chapter Three. After the wreck of the Exxon-Valdez in 1989, the majority of legal claims filed by the state of Alaska and thousands of individuals hurt by the spill proceeded on common law theories of public and private nuisance and marine tort, not public law.

The numerical majority of environmental cases each year probably continue to be common law cases, where neighborhoods face or suffer harm from a local polluter, or individuals are exposed to environmental contamination. When public agencies are not responsive, or the machinery of statutory enforcement is too complex, hampered by administrative discretion, or too static to respond to novel problems, many environmental controversies will continue to turn to the classic and evolving remedies of the common law.

Common law litigation imposes potentially heavy costs and burdens on its participants, although the availability of damages and counterclaims provides funding in some settings. Because of its costs and occasional crudeness, the common law is often a backup to public law, but in some settings it can provide necessary legal remedies to be found nowhere else.

9. **A state tendency toward laxity?** In Kepone, the state's administrative inattention to pollution problems contributed to the scope and severity of contamination. The unexpressed story of the *Smithfield* cases is the Commonwealth of Virginia's attempts to shield Smithfield from liability. It was this inertia that ultimately motivated the citizen groups to step forward and seek enforcement of federal penalties. In general, Virginia's government structures — legislature, agencies, and courts — have often been strongly industry-oriented, reflected in their hesitancy to enforce environmental standards. The state's water pollution statute and regulations, for example, were among the weakest in the NPDES system, and several times were amended further to reduce their enforceability. Eliminating citizen enforcement provisions (when CBF and the University of Richmond Law School's Environmental Law Center were seeking to enforce existing law) was just one such instance. In the *Smithfields*, moreover, there were specific potential suasions that tended to undercut the integrity of state efforts. Mr. Joe Luter, Smithfield's owner, has been a vociferous and generous supporter of efforts to undercut governmental regulations. Luter was reported to have donated $125,000 to the political war chest of George Allen, the likeminded Governor of the state. When Luter fought the original *Gwaltney* verdict, he hired and was represented by Anthony Troy, who had just ended his term as Virginia's Attorney-General. Governor Allen orchestrated what has been described as "a decimation of what little enforcement activity the Board had been doing." In the 1996, for example, the sum total of civil penalties collected statewide for violations was $4000. When CBF and other citizens sought to cooperate in state enforcement they were treated as critics rather than allies. To ward off federal enforcement, the Virginia pollution control agency tried to pre-file its own state complaint. In *Smithfield Packing* it complained against federal EPA "over-filing" on the state's regulatory turf.

The laxity of the Virginia agencies seems to reflect the same inter-state competition for industry and jobs that originally prompted Hopewell to advertise itself as "the Chemical Capital of the South." That pressure to compete for jobs undercuts the vigilance of local and state officials. The "race to the bottom" continues to be a powerful competitive tendency within the political marketplace at all levels, nibbling away at state regulations as well as the federal laws that attempt to provide a national floor. In most areas of the field one continues to see arguments of federalism and devolution to the states as a recurring theme of industrial politics.

10. **On the other hand: the state's perspective on the *Smithfield* cases.** State officials caution that implications of state agency lassitude in this story are unfair. Virginia had a 1946 state water pollution law, long before the federal government had any such law. The state agency had been told by its technical people that there was no provable effect on river quality from the packing plant discharges, at least as far as was then known. Smithfield and the state had made a reasonable 1991

agreement that the discharges would go to zero as soon as HRSD was built, and the Pagan River would have absolutely no remaining point sources. Smithfield kept its 1991 deal, so the state just was riding herd on compliance with the agreement. (In contrast, the agency shut down harmful polluters cold, like a rayon plant in Front Royal, probably the worst polluter in the state.) It was the state that turned up the Rettig violations and sent them to prosecution, not EPA investigators.

Some agency staffers thought the *Smithfield Packing* federal case was pure politics. EPA had previously asked the state to stop a civil enforcement suit, and so the state did, then in another administration the Department of Justice restarted the case. The feds did not inform the state prior to the day they filed suit in December 1996, and based their federal suit mainly on phosphorus violations, which the state did not have grounds to sue on because of the 1991 agreement. The federal case was sloppy, utilizing only a few thousand files, whereas there had been 22,500 files in the state complaint. The bottom line is that since 1997 there have not been any point source discharges into the entire Pagan River, thanks to the state agency's 1991 deal. EPA's review whether to withdraw Virginia's NPDES certification ended with a decision not to decertify.

11. **Deference to administrative agencies' discretion.** In the modern administrative state there is a general tendency in the public and in the courts to defer to government agencies for the specialized handling of public problems. Agencies have specialized authority, expertise, public funding, and structures for implementing the laws.

Agencies, however, reflect the full diversity of a society's pressures and thus can be less than vigilant, neutral enforcers of public laws. Consider the diffidence of Virginia's water pollution board, for instance, in regulating Allied Chemical and Smithfield, and the hesitancy of EPA to undertake prompt enforcement, at the very least reflecting that each agency has a limited budget in terms of personnel, funding, and political capital.

Courts too typically tend to defer to agencies' discretionary actions, as the federal courts here deferred to EPA's guidelines in *Gwaltney* and deferred to EPA's enforcement expertise in *Smithfield Packing*.

What if, for example, the Virginia SWCB had appeared in the citizens' *Gwaltney* suit, stating that the agency believed that enforcement procedures had not been properly followed, or that standards had been improperly interpreted, or were not clearly violated? Most courts tend to defer to such agency presentations unless citizens can show a stark clearcut statutory violation, or bring in a more impressive agency (perhaps EPA) willing to state a contrary position. Consider also what might have happened if the state and federal agencies had clashed in *Smithfield Packing*.

Administrative process, both law and tactics, forms a major sector of modern environmental law, and the tendency to defer to agency discretion is one of its most necessary, but often problematic, features.

12. **Contending forces: the three economies, and Market Backlash.** Human nature has not changed over the past decades, and that means that the fundamental

behavioral logic and market dynamics that produced the Kepone crisis still shape the way market forces tend to act, and still requires a civic system that will induce the players to take account of broader societal interests. The same market forces that make civic regulation necessary attempt to resist, moderate, and undercut that regulation. For most environmental statutes, however, particularly the pollution and toxics laws, with only occasional exceptions, the marketplace has generally come to accept the basic validity and permanence of regulation.[93]

A latent contest of contending societal forces nevertheless inevitably lies at the heart of environmental law and modern democracy. Consider the way an economic entity naturally tends to resist cost internalization, then multiply this by tens of thousands of economic entities, and one finds a broad concurrent tendency permeating the governance process. Every meaningful regulatory provision feels that pressure, as the marketplace economy impinges upon the public concerns of the natural economy and civic-societal economics. Like flowing water, market forces and the behavioral realities that drive them, inherently resist any artificial barriers that curtail their externalizations of social costs. To place a single sandbag into the current is difficult and not likely to have significant effect. As other sandbags are added with great effort, the inherent pressures of the market economy still pour around them. When finally a working accumulation of sandbags is secured, the waters may mostly turn to the path of less resistance, but do not stop trying to infiltrate and undercut the obstacles blocking their maximum satisfaction. Across the entire face of the environmental law dike the pressures are felt. Lobbyists, lawyers, media managers, PACs, and a host of political players apply subtle, comprehensive pressure within all three branches of government. When citizens attempt to get around the phenomenon of agency capture[94] by bringing private enforcement actions in the courts, the forces of the marketplace try to undercut citizen standing and judicial remedies. Often the tension between the market economy and civic regulations is not subtle.

The self-styled populist "Wise Use" movement is one very visible marketplace alliance against regulation. Started in the late 1980s in the West, funded by mining, timber, grazing, and other environment-related industries, Wise Users create coalitions of local and regional groups loudly opposing environmental regulation.[95] At the national level, particularly for media consumption, the leaders of the Wise Use movement voice the message that humans, nature, and commerce can live together in productive harmony. In other settings their message sounds more like an assertion of an inherent human right to exploit nature without regard to environmental cost, with an added conspiratorial tone blaming environmental élitists and big government for sacrificing the economic interests of ordinary people on the

---

93. Endangered species laws are a major exception. See The Embattled Social Utilities of the Endangered Species Act, 27 Envtl. L. 845 (1997).

94. On the classic political science phenomenon of "agency capture," see Chapter Seven.

95. "Wise use" is the conservation slogan developed by the eminent conservationist Gifford Pinchot, father of the Forest Service, who used the phrase to emphasize the necessity of tighter sustainability restrictions on resource use. The marketplace sponsorship of the movement, with a long lineup of mining companies, is noted in Montana State AFL-CIO, Corporate Funding of People for the West (1993).

altar of environmental purity.[96]

The 104th Congress's "Contract with America" provided more examples of marketplace backlash. In the early 1990s more than 300 industry groups gathered together to create "Project Relief," a lobbying movement to roll back and repeal governmental regulation across a wide swath of American society. They represented industrial lobbies including chemical manufacturers (including Allied-Signal), automobile lobbyists, insurance companies, oil and timber companies, the food and farm industries (it is not clear whether Smithfield's Joe Luter contributed), the "Wise Users," and more.[97] They poured $19 million into the 1994 congressional campaigns. After that year's Contract with America election, the marketplace's long-simmering resistance to various public regulation suddenly found itself with enthusiastic congressional majorities, and proceeded to generate a parade of bills attempting to change America and environmental law. The 104th Congress's majorities produced a remarkable "first hundred days," and a flood of bills, riders, and low-profile technical amendments attempting to roll back environmental law:[98]

- suspending all substantive regulations retroactive to the election and freezing all ongoing major rulemaking in a year-long moratorium;
- drastically cutting protective agencies' budgets and specifically forbidding enforcement against various industrial lobbyists' clients;
- overriding all laws applicable to forestry conservation by mandating an increase in the subsidized clearcutting of public forests;
- repealing the 1990 Clean Air Act Amendments;
- cutting back on dozens of provisions in the Clean Water Act;
- reducing the Endangered Species Act to a symbolic minimum;
- decommissioning national parks or opening them to commercial uses;
- drilling the Arctic National Wildlife Refuge;
- requiring rigorous and time-consuming cost-benefit procedures when agencies protect resources, but not when they issue permits to exploit them;
- forcing government to compensate industry for regulatory burdens on asset market value;
- shifting regulatory responsibilities toward state governments, which are traditionally more vulnerable to market forces, and also overriding state common law provisions burdensome to industry;
- eliminating the citizen enforcement provisions that have built much of American environmental law;[99]... and dozens more.

---

96. A political analysis sponsored by the Wilderness Society canvasses the structure and philosophy of the Wise Use Movement and the extent of its activities. See MacWilliams Cosgrove Snider, The Wise Use Movement: Strategic Analysis & Fifty State Review (revised edition, March, 1993).

The Wise Use movement's appropriation of Pinchot's phrase is ironic. Grazing, mining, and lumbering interests on western public lands bitterly opposed Pinchot's pioneering efforts, backed by President Teddy Roosevelt, to manage federal lands on a sustainable basis. When William Howard Taft succeeded Roosevelt in 1909, Pinchot's days were numbered. In 1910, at the annual national meeting of wool growers at Ogden, Utah, Idaho's Senator Heyburn beamed as he announced to the gathering:

When the sun rolled over the eastern mountains this morning, it marked a new epoch in the history of the West. Czar Pinchot has been dethroned! The western stockman is now free!

The heirs of the same special interest lobbies appropriated Pinchot's words in the 1990s for their Wise Use movement. See Behnke, Going Home Again, Winter 1998 Trout magazine at 56.

97. Prior to the 104th Congress, the most visible front line of the political opposition to environmentalism was made up of the National Association of Manufacturers, the Business Roundtable, the National Chamber of Commerce, the Heritage Foundation, and the Wise Users, who peddled anecdotes of ordinary citizens – small time ranchers, logging families, "Mom and Pop" businesses — hurt by "Kafkaesque" regulations.

98. For citations and further descriptions, see 23 Envt'l Aff. L. Rev. 733, 742–762 (1996). See also Walker, Environment: License to Pollute, Guardian, Sept. 6, 1995, at A2; Cook, Laws for Sale; Congress Let Lobbyists Write Laws, Wash. Monthly, July 1995, at 44.

A number of these bills passed one or both chambers of Congress; a few of the bills became law. Industry lobbyists were openly given the role of authoring legislative drafts, and conducting congressional briefings on their antienvironmental bills. The Contract bills reflected a heavy-handed industrial lobbying process driven by the same pressures that necessitated federal statutes in the first place.Ultimately most of these frontal attacks were halted in the Senate or by veto, assisted by a belated pragmatic recognition that voters did not want to see environmental law overturned. Most Contract supporters pulled back sharply in the second session in order to get reelected. For environmental law, the lesson of the 104th Congress was that in the ongoing process of contending forces, future marketplace resistance to environmental protections in legislatures, agencies, media, and judicial politics will continue, though probably with more subtlety.

13. **Biodiversity in today's marketplace economy.** Today, thanks to the federal statutes of the 1970s, there has arisen a small but dynamic and growing secondary industry bloc in the marketplace, the environmental control technology industry. This industry's enterprises include innovative cleanup and prevention technology companies with a growing global market, consulting firms, creators of control software and hardware, and more. In the *Smithfield* setting, for example, there were a significant number of firms with different sophisticated control technologies available for installation within the industrial process, that simply did not exist at the time of the Kepone disaster. The regional HRSD treatment plant has multimillion dollar innovative technologies representing a significant new national infrastructure investment. When nationally the 104th Congress tilted toward gutting environmental laws, in concert with primary industry lobbyists, the nation's new secondary industries stood with the citizen groups to try to protect the market the laws had created for them.

14. **"Market enlistment" legal techniques.** Regulatory commands are not the only way that public values are imposed on polluters. Another longstanding approach is to enlist the market in the process of implementing public objectives. Today several notable experiments seek to set up market-trading systems for pollution cleanup credits. A much older example is subsidies. The Smithfield plants ultimately plugged into the HRSD plant, and thus took advantage of a considerable public subsidy. Originally, an industrial user of a POTW was required to repay a portion of the federal grant corresponding to its percentage use of the system's total capacity. "Industrial cost recovery" was intended to provide funds for reconstruction and repair, and to encourage an industry to choose the most cost-effective solution to its waste treatment problems, whether it was indirect or direct discharge. After prolonged and concerted opposition from municipalities and sewerage authorities, industrial cost recovery was first suspended, then limited to large indirect dischargers, and finally repealed entirely. Thus, as the CWA now stands, there is a major federal subsidy for industries that "plug in" to POTWs, because they pay only user charges (to cover operation and maintenance) and therefore save on construction costs. Goldfarb, Water Law 199–200 (2d ed. 1988).

15. **New science, new remedies: SEPs.** In the *Kepone* cases very little data on the off-site poisoning effects of Kepone were ever collected, much less a comprehensive quantification of natural resources damages. Since then, however, environ-

99. The critical role of citizen suits in enforcing federal pollution laws is studied in Chapters 7 and 20. Initiatives against citizen enforcement can be observed in the courts as well as in political lobbying, as narrow majorities in the Supreme Court have narrowed the grounds for citizen standing and jurisdiction, as in the *Gwaltney* case and the 1998 *Steel Company* case discussed in later chapters.

mental sciences and assessment technologies have expanded dramatically. It is now possible to measure a wide range of ecological disruptions, tracing their interconnections through different natural systems, and in many cases to craft remedies that can help injured resources to recover.

Under natural resources damage provisions of the federal Clean Water Act and other statutes, and under innovative new common law theories of restoration and the public trust, water pollution violations like Smithfield's can be assessed damages beyond permit penalties to provide funding for resource remediation.

One such innovative remedy is the SEP: Supplemental Environmental Projects. Notice that at the end of Judge Smith's opinion she invites legal arguments regarding her ability to condition the penalty "toward the restoration of the Chesapeake Bay and its tributaries." The citizens proposed creation of a SEP fund — remarkably like the remedy created by Judge Merhige from penalties in the Kepone criminal case — to carry out a range of sophisticated protective measures in the Bay's waterways. Despite the judge's rejection of the *Smithfield* SEP proposal,[100] in the future timely motions for supplemental environmental restoration projects are likely to become increasingly common. In this and other remedy innovations environmental law will continue to be at the cutting edge.

16. **Have we already done enough?** Has modern environmental law reached the limit of reasonable returns? A number of media voices have echoed the traditional marketplace plaint that the environmental pendulum has swung too far. In his 1995 book A Moment on the Earth, Gregg Easterbrook argues that environmentalists "are surely on the right side of history, but increasingly on the wrong side of the present, risking their credibility by proclaiming emergencies that do not exist." He advocates that we declare victory domestically and cease tightening pollution standards, and focus instead on the large-scale environmental problems of the Third World. Besides attracting criticisms of their use of scientific fact,[101] such arguments are often accused of missing the point:

> At first blush, many people might conclude from the visible improvements to the environment that we have done our work well and that, except for maintenance, the...government should move on to other pressing priorities. Others would prefer to see a rollback of environmental legislation, as was proposed in the 104th Congress, in the belief that we have simply gone too far. [Others] might feel that the enormous problems of maintaining clean water and air in the world's developing megacities or habitat destruction in Asia or South

---

100. The problem in *Smithfield Packing* was that the judge fixed penalties before the SEP motion had been made, and under the federal Miscellaneous Receipts Act all awarded penalties must be paid into the general Treasury. Judges, however, could characterize SEPs as CWA natural resources damages, or as an equitable adjunct of securing compliance with their decisions, or as an element of remittitur on civil penalties, thereby achieving a targeted local linkage between violations and remediation, and avoiding the siphoning of environmental penalties into the generic vaults of the faroff federal government.

101. See L. Haimson, B. Goodman, eds., A Moment of Truth: Correcting the Scientific Errors in Gregg Easterbrook's A Moment on the Earth (1996). The authors scrutinize dozens of allegations and conclude that Easterbrook's account of environmental issues "is replete with errors and misinterpretations of the scientific evidence. This is especially notable in regard to the four chapters that deal with habitat loss, global warming, ozone depletion, and species extinction, probably the four most serious threats to the natural environment according to a recent report by the Science Advisory Board of the U.S. Environmental Protection Agency."

America are now more important than reforming environmental protection in the United States.... These assessments overlook some important facts. First, many once "quiet" issues are emerging as population densities increase. Second, our understanding of ecological and public health threats continues to change. Substances that were beneficial in direct application, such as chlorofluorocarbons, turn out to be harmful long after they have served their local function. Third, the environmental advances of recent years are not evenly distributed among urban and suburban areas, rich and poor neighborhoods, and geographical regions. Fourth, we are just beginning to appreciate how deeply the environment is intertwined with many other issues such as human health, energy and food production, and international trade. Thus, rather than retrench, we must renew our commitment to environmental protection. Chertow & Esty, at 73–74.

17. **A view to the future.** Trying to find common ground, a group of 80 brainstormers from business, government, and citizen environmental groups put together a consensus prescription for future environmental protection:

A VISION FOR THE FUTURE

1. Maintain basic standards of environmental protection, and effectively and efficiently prevent and control threats to human health and the environment;

2. Ensure that all environmental laws and regulations are fairly and consistently enforced;

3. Distribute costs and benefits fairly, accounting for impacts on both present and future generations, and address disproportionate impacts on any group in society, especially low-income individuals, people of color, or other disadvantaged groups;

4. Set and pursue clear environmental goals and milestones for the nation, states, localities, and tribes, and use understandable indicators to measure progress;

5. Adapt and adjust policies, strategies, and systems based on experience and new information;

6. Generate, disseminate, and rely on the best available scientific and economic information;

7. Offer flexibility of means coupled with clarity of responsibility, accountability for performance, and transparency of results;

8. Rely on a broad set of policy tools, including:

- economic incentives that are aligned with environmental goals, reward superior environmental performance, and stimulate technological innovation,

- incentives for changes in individual behavior, and

- disclosure of consistent and accurate source-level performance information;

9. Place authority, responsibility, and accountability at the appropriate level of government;

10. Promote collaborative problem solving and integrated policy making by all branches and levels of government;

11. Promote high levels of environmental stewardship and continuous improvement in environmental performance; and

12. Create decision processes that meaningfully involve affected stakeholders and engage all citizens in protecting the environment. Ruckelshaus, Stepping Stones, Envt'l Forum March 1998 at 31.

Though such matrices often fall prey to their vague generality, this prescription charts a potentially useful course.

## ANALYTIC THEMES, after the *Smithfield* cases

■ **ENVIRONMENTAL STATUTES EVOLVE.** Statutes change over time, for better and worse, in the same way as living species evolve, according to the pressures, experience, and changing contexts they encounter.

■ **THE POLLUTER-PAYS PRINCIPLE.** As the strict liability character of today's Clean Water Act shows, a basic premise of most modern regulation here and abroad is that absorbing environmental costs is a responsibility of marketplace industries, not a cost to be absorbed by public subsidies paying for prevention and cleanups, nor by the unpaid subsidy of public toleration of pollution (even if it were more "efficient" to pay industry to end pollution).

■ **ADMINISTRATIVE PROCESS.** The delegation of pervasive administrative powers to government agencies is a vital part of modern legal process, and part of the perplex of environmental law. Deference to administrative agencies is obviously important in order to allow implementation of public law in a complex world. On the other hand, agencies are vulnerable to the suasions of politics. The skills of managing the administrative process are technically challenging, and also raise fundamental questions about democratic governance in modern industrial societies.

■ **CITIZEN ENFORCEMENT, MULTI-CENTRIC PLURALISM.** A fundamentally important element of the U.S. legal system, increasingly being adopted abroad, is the legal and practical opportunity for participation in regulation and enforcement by directly affected citizens, a multi-centric process that alters the legal dynamic of the old bipolar regulation by pluralizing the participants.

■ **CONTINUING RESISTANCE TO FORCED INTERNALIZATION OF PUBLIC VALUES.** The daily life of environmental lawyers duelling over details of environmental protections, and the dramatic history of the Contract Congress, demonstrate a continuing natural market resistance to the imposition of unprofitable public values. This is unsurprising, indeed inevitable, given human nature, and will continue to be a fundamental part of the process of societal governance, discernible in calls for de-regulation or self-regulation, in pervasive pressures to modify standards and procedures, in the pitch for "Free Market Environmentalism" urging that society rely on the marketplace for voluntary environmental protection efforts, and so on.

■ **A REACTION AGAINST PLURALISM.** Given that citizen participation and enforcement have been strategically important in achieving compliance with laws constraining the marketplace, it is likewise unsurprising that a major continuing theme of daily politics has been to limit the role of citizens and to return to the past's more insulated relationship between agencies and industries. This market resistance against the pluralization of the American legal system, beginning in the Nixon years, can be seen daily in the regulatory process, in legislative attempts to rescind citizen enforcement provisions, and in some federal courts' ongoing attempts to cut back on citizen standing and judicial scrutiny of agency decisionmaking.

■ **THE VARIETY OF AVAILABLE PUBLIC LAW OPTIONS.** A consistent reality in environmental practice is the multiplicity of public law statutes and regulations — not to mention potential common law liabilities — that can come to bear in a particular environmental case. Until such time as a consolidated, integrated regulatory scheme is created (if that is a good idea) the wide biodiversity of environmental laws will ensure that there is a need for professionals who can cope with complexity.

■ **RISK, AND COST-BENEFIT ANALYSES.** Part of the ongoing debates about enhancing or decreasing environmental protections will continue to be the relativity questions. Given the costs and uncertainties of trying to achieve high degrees of protection, and alternative demands on precious public and private resources of time and money, it is consistently important to gauge the balance of costs, benefits and alternatives, though the perspectives of the marketplace economy and the civic economy will cast the balance in very different terms.

■ **INTERNATIONAL CONVERGENCES.** Just as problems of environmental pollution and resource depletion spread across international boundaries, so too will the responsive mechanisms of environmental law, through international conventions and evolving principles of responsibility for sustainability. There are corresponding escalations in marketplace dynamics as well. If Allied, or Smithfield, or other domestic companies are held to higher standards they can point to overseas competitors who thereby gain advantages. The threat of corporate flight into a global business commons replays a version of Hardin's tragedy and the interstate race to the bottom, and has often operated to undercut protective standards. To hold to higher standards is to redistribute monetary wealth to lower standard nations; the premise, however, is that if environmental law is done right, the societies that accomodate to its guidances will in the short and long run be stronger and healthier in real terms.

---

## D. BEYOND DIRECT THREATS TO HUMAN HEALTH AND PROPERTY: THE PUBLIC TRUST DOCTRINE

*By the law of nature, these things are common to mankind: the air, running water, the sea, and consequently the shores of the sea....*

— Institutes of Justinian, 2.1.1 (529 A.D.)

*I do not believe that there is either a moral or any other claim upon me to postpone the use of what nature has given me, so that the next generation or generations yet unborn may have an opportunity to get what I myself ought to get.*

— Colorado Senator Henry M. Keller

*We do not inherit the earth from our fathers. We borrow it from our children.*

— David Brower

The rediscovery of the Public Trust Doctrine is environmental law's unique contribution to the modern legal system, and the trust's continuing background presence can be discerned throughout the field.

At its heart, environmental law has come to incorporate a set of principles representing and accounting for natural and civic values, for present and future, that lie beyond the daily marketplace and current events. It may be only in environmental law that the legal system directly incorporates issues of long-term societal needs into today's operative norms and doctrinal provisions. The "sustainable development" principle of domestic and global natural resources management is a prime example. As studied later in Chapter 22, the public trust doctrine embodies this perspective and goes further, incorporating societal protections that go beyond strict human utility.

Most environmental cases, of course, are built upon the ultimate social utility of environmental protection. By keeping Smithfield's slaughterhouse wastes out of the river and Bay, human and economic health are protected along with natural resources.[102] We protect birds from pesticides in part to protect human genetics as well. We protect stratospheric ozone and the carbon dioxide functions of global forests on behalf of long term human and planetary health.

The concerns of environmental law, however, extend beyond physical survival and threats to human health and property, and there too you will find the public trust doctrine.

Why is it, for instance, that environmental law protects groundwater aquifers from pollution *even if they may never be used by anyone*, and are not connected to other water bodies? Why do we protect endangered species even if we are virtually certain they will never have any human or ecosystem usefulness? Why do we protect clean environments against minor lowering of air or water quality when some polluting development projects could generate huge economic profits and still come nowhere near the legal levels of harm to health or property?[103] Why do we try to make stripminers in the mountains of Appalachia restore hillsides to premining conditions, when the cost of remediation is ten times the market value of the land per acre before or after the restoration? Protecting a pristine waterfall, an endangered species, a unique prairieland, or a wilderness virgin grove of trees in the face of commercial development apparently serves some further societal objectives.

How and why may the law attempt to achieve abstract "legacy" values in addition to utilitarian environmental goals that protect human welfare? The answer in American law, and in emerging international law doctrines like "inter-generational equity" and the "common heritage of humankind," lies in the public trust doctrine.

———

Here are some further illustrations of the concept of the public trust (continued later in Chapter 22):

**THE METHUSALEH TREE.** What is lost when an ancient forest is gone, or an ancient tree? A few years ago a geography professor set off on a summer grant project to

102. As noted above, nutrient runoffs from chicken-processing plants in the Chesapeake Bay watershed, and hog wastes in North Carolina rivers, triggered outbreaks of the toxic *Pfisteria piscicida* organism that not only caused the death of hundreds of thousands of fish, but also caused human skin lesions and illness. See Environmental Law at Maryland, Summer 1997 at 1.
103. PSD rules have been instituted in a number of areas for the "prevention of significant deterioration."

find the oldest living thing on the face of the earth. What would that be? Not a great whale, not a giant redwood. It seems the oldest living things on earth are bristle-cone pine trees. Bristle-cone pines are not majestic monoliths, but rather small scraggly survivors, more than 3000 years old, twisted and gnarled with the winds of time, surviving icestorms, droughts, and wildfires, clinging to a ridge in a federal forest reserve in a remote region of eastern Nevada.

The professor, however, did not have a modern microscopic coring tool for dating trees; the only method he had available to determine a tree's age was to cut it down and count the cross-section rings. So with the approval of the government official in charge of the forest, he found the oldest living thing on the face of the earth, and dated it the only way he knew. It was 4990 years old. To be certain he had found the real Methuselah tree, moreover, he also killed and dated the next two oldest living things.

What did we lose by the death of those trees? Since another bristle-cone pine was automatically made the oldest living thing by the professor's actions, what difference did it make? If you feel something move in the pit of your stomach from the death of the Methusaleh tree, however, it may be the public trust doctrine. If the matter could have been brought to a court in time, seeking to stop the cutting, there would have to be a cause of action in order for an injunction to issue. Analytically the cause of action would probably be, expressly or implicitly, the legal theory of public trust.

**SELLING LAKE MICHIGAN.** A classic public trust case arose from a scandalous case of political corruption in the 1890s, when the Illinois state legislature was induced by railroad lawyers to pass a statute selling two square miles of submerged lands along the Chicago waterfront, at a very cheap price, to the Illinois Central Railroad Company which planned to fill and develop the submerged lands for a multimillion dollar profit. When a subsequent presumably-cleaner legislature tried to rescind the statute, it faced the prospect of paying huge compensation awards to get the waterfront back. In Illinois Central RR. v. Illinois,[104] the Supreme Court had to figure out how to avoid the takings claim without spreading on the public record the unseemly story of how the state had made the deal in the first place. The Court seized upon the unwritten ancient public trust doctrine: the state never had the unbridled authority to give away such trust lands in the first place, the Court explained, so the sale and the statute were void, and Lake Michigan remained a public trust resource owned by all.

**THE IDAHO SHOSHONE COUNTY RIVER OIL-SHEEN CASE.** Can a state require a million-dollar restoration effort to remove a slight oil sheen from a river, if there is no proof and no likelihood of any harm to humans or the ecosystem? In the mid-1990s it was discovered that a small amount of petroleum was leaching underground from an old railroad switching area into Idaho's St. Joe River, causing a rainbow effect on the downstream water surface. The successors of the railroad argued that the sheen did not come from a regulatable "point source" and was

---

104. 146 U.S. 387 (1892). A virtually identical more recent case is Lake Michigan Federation v. U.S. Army Corps of Engineers, 742 F.Supp 441 (N.D. Ill. 1990).

totally insignificant. What did it matter that viewed from one angle the water looked a little different, if no other invidious effects could be shown?[105] The state of Idaho, however, prepared a lawsuit "as the trustee of the natural resources within the state...entrusted with the management and protection of said natural resources... and as *parens patriae* [likewise a trusteeship sounding in public trust] on behalf of all residents of the state," alleging injury to, among other things, "ecological" and "aesthetic qualities." Faced with the public trust claim for broad affirmative injunctive relief as well as natural resource damages, the companies ultimately settled, agreeing to fund and carry out a long term treatment protocol under state oversight.

**NATURAL RESOURCES DAMAGES:** *STEUART TRANSPORTATION.* The public trust has frequently surfaced, expressly or implicitly, in the blossoming area of natural resources damages. In one typical case, a badly-maintained oil barge foundered while being towed, dumping thousands of gallons of crude oil into coastal marshes of the Chesapeake Bay, killing or injuring wildlife and habitat:

> Approximately 30,000 migratory birds allegedly were destroyed as a result of the oil spill.... Steuart contends that...to recover money damages for the loss of property one must establish an ownership interest, and...neither the state nor the federal Government has an ownership interest in migratory waterfowl.... The Commonwealth and the United States, on the other hand, maintain...their right to recover for the loss of migratory waterfowl...upon the sovereign right to protect the public interest in preserving wildlife resources. This sovereign right derives from...the public trust doctrine and the doctrine of parens patriae....

> This Court is of the opinion that both of these doctrines are viable and support the State and the Federal claims for the waterfowl.... Under the public trust doctrine, the State of Virginia and the United States have the right and the duty to protect and preserve the public's interest in natural wildlife resources. Such right does not derive from ownership of the resources but from a duty owing to the people.... Clarke, J., In Re Steuart Transportation Company, Owner of the Tank Barge STC-101, 495 F. Supp. 38, 40 (E.D. Va. 1980).

Similar natural resources damages were claimed on common law public trust principles after the Exxon-Valdez oilspill in Alaska, and in a host of cases under resource damage provisions of several federal pollution statutes.

**THREE LEGAL PUBLIC TRUST SETTINGS:** Public trust law comes from constitutional and statutory sources as well as nonstatutory judicial holdings;[106] cases occur in a wide range of natural settings but can be categorized into three basic legal settings. One category, represented in all but one of the preceding examples, might be called "resource-defense" or "derogation" cases, often seen in the water pollution setting but including land-based cases like the bristle-cone pines, where human actors threaten to pollute or destroy trust assets. Another public trust setting is the "alienation" situation, restricting government attempts to sell public trust assets

---

105. In fact it seems to the authors who are troutfishers that entomologists could have been found to demonstrate a lethal effect on subimago stages of certain aquatic insect species, which would impact the river's food chain.

106. See Calif. Const. Art. XV §§2, 3; Penn. Const. Art. I §27; Massachusetts Const. Art. IX §1; Mich. Comp. Laws §§691–1201; Mass. Gen. Laws Ch. 214 §7A; Tenn. Code Ann. §70.324.

to a private party, which was the basis of the *Illinois Central* Chicago waterfront case. A third category, of "diversion" cases, limits government agency attempts to divert ownership and use of public trust assets from one public use like parkland to other more exploitive uses like construction sites, dumps, or parking lots.

What the public trust doctrine contributes to each setting is an abstract societal interest in present and future legacy terms. Its extent is particularly significant, however, in its unique representation of the social and cultural values of natural conditions, going beyond traditional definitions of harm.

The trust's primary remedies are equitable — prohibitory or affirmative restoration injunctions and other orders — but can include monetary damages for remediation or natural resources losses as well.

The public trust's ancient lineage and essential societal role do not mean that it is uncontroversial. For instance, just as environmental conditions do not stop at international borders, note that sometimes, as in the following milestone case, the public trust doctrine does not shy away from private property boundaries:

### Marks v. Whitney
Supreme Court of California, 1971
6 Cal. 3d 251, 491 P.2d 374, 98 Cal.Rptr. 790

McCOMB, Justice. This is a quiet title action.... A part of Marks' property on the westerly side of Tomales Bay in Marin County is tidelands acquired under an 1874 patent issued pursuant to the Act of March 28, 1868.... A small [strip] of these tidelands adjoins almost the entire shoreline of Whitney's upland property. Marks asserted complete ownership of the tidelands and the right to fill and develop them. Whitney opposed on the ground that this would cut off his rights as a littoral owner and as a member of the public.... He requested a declaration in the decree that Marks' title was burdened with a public trust easement.... The trial court...held that Whitney had no standing to raise the public trust issue and refused to make a finding as to whether the tidelands are so burdened....

This land was patented as tidelands to Marks' predecessor in title [on] May 15, 1874...by the Governor of California "by virtue of authority in me vested" pursuant to "statutes...for the Sale and Conveyance of the Tide Lands belonging to the State by virtue of her sovereignty...."

Regardless of the issue of Whitney's standing to raise this issue the court may take judicial notice of public trust burdens in quieting title to tidelands. This matter is of great public importance, particularly in view of population pressures, demands for recreational property, and the increasing development of seashore and waterfront property....

The title of Marks in these tidelands is burdened with a public easement.... The trial court found that the portion of Marks' lands here under consideration constitutes a part of the tidelands of Tomales Bay.... Tidelands...extend from the Oregon line to Mexico and include the shores of bays and navigable streams as far up as tide water goes and until it meets the lands made swampy by the overflow and seepage of fresh water streams.... The state holds tidelands in trust for public purposes, traditionally delineated in terms of navigation, commerce and fisheries.... They are, therefore, subject to a reserved easement in the state for trust purposes.... Our opinion is that the buyer of land [via] statutes receives the title to the soil, the *jus privatum*, subject to the public right of navigation, and in subordination to the right of the state to take possession and use and improve it for that purpose, as it may deem necessary....

Public trust easements are traditionally defined in terms of navigation, commerce and fisheries. They have been held to include the right to fish, hunt, bathe, swim, to use for boating and general recreation purposes the navigable waters of the state, and to use the bottom of the navigable waters for anchoring, standing, or other purposes. The public has the same rights in and to tidelands.

The public uses to which tidelands are subject are sufficiently flexible to encompass changing public needs. In administering the trust the state is not burdened with an outmoded classification favoring one mode of utilization over another. There is a growing public recognition that one of the most important public uses of the tidelands — a use encompassed within the tidelands trust is the preservation of those lands in their natural state, so that they may serve as ecological units for scientific study, as open space, and as environments which provide food and habitat for birds and marine life, and which favorably affect the scenery and climate of the area. It is not necessary to here define precisely all the public uses which encumber tidelands....

The power of the state to control, regulate and utilize its navigable waterways and the lands lying beneath them, when acting within the terms of the trust, is absolute, except as limited by the paramount supervisory power of the federal government over navigable waters. We are not here presented with any action by the state or the federal government modifying, terminating, altering or relinquishing the *jus publicum* in these tidelands or in the navigable waters covering them. Neither sovereignty is a party to this action. This court takes judicial notice, however, that there has been no official act of either sovereignty to modify or extinguish the public trust servitude upon Marks' tidelands.... In the absence of state or federal action the court may not bar members of the public from lawfully asserting or exercising public trust rights on this privately owned tidelands.

There is absolutely no merit in Marks' contention that as the owner of the *jus privatum* under this patent he may fill and develop his property, whether for navigational purposes or not; nor in his contention that his past and present plan for development of these tidelands as a marina have caused the extinguishment of the public easement. Reclamation with or without prior authorization from the state does not *ipso facto* terminate the public trust nor render the issue moot....

The relief sought by Marks resulted in taking away from Whitney rights to which he is entitled as a member of the general public....

Members of the public have been permitted to bring an action to enforce a public right to use a beach access route, to bring an action to quiet title to private and public easements in a public beach, and to bring an action to restrain improper filling of a bay and secure a general declaration of the rights of the people to the waterways and wildlife areas of the bay. Members of the public have been allowed to defend a quiet title action by asserting the right to use a public right of way through private property. They have been allowed to assert the public trust easement for hunting, fishing and navigation in privately owned tidelands as a defense in an action to enjoin such use, and to navigate on shallow navigable waters in small boats....

Whitney had standing to raise this issue. The court could have raised this issue on its own.... Where the interest concerned is one that, as here, constitutes a public burden upon [private] land,... that servitude should be explicitly declared.

## COMMENTARY AND QUESTIONS

1. **The evolving public trust.** Note how the court matter-of-factly states that "the public uses to which tidelands are subject are sufficiently flexible to encompass changing public needs." As in other states, the definition of public trust resources and rights is not static, but evolves with changing societal concepts of what resources, uses, and values constitute such legacy commons. As constitutional jurisprudence constantly demonstrates, the definition of any significant basic doctrine capable of evolution in ongoing societal contexts is bound to be fascinating and controversial.

2. **How is the public trust a trust?** As studied later in Chapter 22, the public trust doctrine comes into the legal system as a corollary to the familiar field of private trust law. In both cases there must be a "corpus" of the trust, resources or assets owned and managed under the trust framework. In Anglo-American law trustees legally "own" the resources, with a right to manage, sell, lease, develop, etc., but only insofar as a careful fiduciary would and could so as to protect the assets and achieve the purposes of the trust. The equitable owners of a trust, however, are its designated "beneficiaries," for whom ultimately the trust is to be managed. The "terms" of a trust, however, differ from trust to trust and are critically important. The public trust, as it has developed, construes governments as the trustees of public commons, rights, and resources, with a duty to protect the trust in a balanced fiduciary fashion, with only a qualified right to sell, develop, or permit exploitation. The terms of the public trust thus generally reflect a presumption in favor of preservation of the natural and cultural legacy received from past generations, to be passed to the future. The beneficiaries, it then might be said, are all the citizens of the jurisdiction — of the present, the future, and even the past.

3. **Public trust and private property.** Can a public trust lie latent within private property rights? Apparently so, and that means political passions will be stirred. Marks v. Whitney held precisely that there was an inherent public right in privately-owned tidelands, so that the private property owner could be completely restricted unless the government as public trustee gave the private rights owner permission to develop them. Once the public trust genie has been released from the bottle, it is likely to cast its shadow over situations previously unknown. What if you owned the oldest burr oak tree in Illinois, or the house in which Benjamin Franklin was born, or the land on which the state's oldest church was located, and in each case you wanted to bulldoze the property to make a profitable parking lot? Might the public trust doctrine apply with force and litigatability to your land? What standards would apply?

4. **The public trust: how far does it go?** The public trust doctrine captures part of a deep cultural and philosophical conviction that human life, individual and societal, is made up of more than the dictates of a cash register.

Does it cover human-created cultural resources, too? If as noted above a person owns the house in which Benjamin Franklin was born, or a rock outcrop with 10,000 year old rock painting "petroglyphs," or an archaeological treasure from ancient India, there is some question under the public trust — and similar emerging international law doctrines like intergenerational equity and common heritage of humankind — that the law can prevent their being destroyed at the whim of an owner.

The trust doctrine is not absolute. Private property rights obvious must be weighed in the trust balance, and the balance struck in the Florissant Fossil Beds case in Chapter 22 (enjoining destruction until Congress had a chance to buy the paleontological site) appears to be an appropriate balance. But in some cases the conflict between public rights and private property will produce bitter political confrontations: how far can the system go in regulating private business decisions in favor of protecting cultural and natural values where nobody is going to be hurt except for fossils, or antelope, or a historic battlefield, or ... where does it stop?

Public trust law, then, lies in the deep background of most environmental cases, and at the cutting edge of many. If, as some leaders of the American Bar Association said after the original Earth Day, "Environmental Law is what will give the legal profession a soul," it will probably be the public trust doctrine that supplies the conceptual and spiritual compass.

## ANALYTIC THEMES, from the Public Trust

▪ **A BIODIVERSITY OF LAW AS WELL AS OF NATURE.** The public trust doctrine is a further reminder that there are many different kinds of law that can be brought to bear on important social issues. Is the public trust doctrine common law? quasi-statutory law? quasi-constitutional law? Perhaps it has the force of constitutional principle, because it can be used in some settings, like the *Illinois Central* litigation, to override statutes. It is at the very least an intriguing legal principle that plays a significant role in defining core concepts of law and society.

▪ **CULTURAL VALUES BEYOND MARKET VALUES.** The ultimate measure of a society would seem to be based upon more than just the essential physical needs for survival — to this should be added the full quality of its people's life, and the legacy of ideas, accomplishments, and potentials it seeks to pass on to successor generations. The public trust, whether incorporated in statutes or existing within our nonstatutory jurisprudence, represents and gives legal force to many of the unmarketized present and future social values that often get overlooked in the immediacy of daily life but are part of the ultimate measure.

▪ **STEWARDSHIP, INTERGENERATIONAL EQUITY, & SUSTAINABILITY.** The public trust embodies fundamentally conservative principles. If a society is to survive and advance over time, like species competing in the Darwinian process of replicating and prolonging their genetic identity over succeeding generations, it must incorporate present realities and the needs of future generations into its present legal norms. Ethical concepts of environmental stewardship described by eco-philosophers evoke concepts of legacy — nations, like most non-dysfunctional families, honoring what they have received from the past, and trying to pass it on, enhanced, to their posterity. The ancient public trust doctrine thus fits well with principles and technologies of sustainability.

*By conducting ourselves ethically toward all creatures, we enter into a spiritual relationship with the universe.*

— Albert Schweitzer

# Chapter 2

# ECONOMICS AND RISK MANAGEMENT AS COMPONENTS OF ENVIRONMENTAL POLICY MAKING

A. *Using the Tools of Economics to Craft Environmental Law and Policy*

B. *Risk Reduction, Risk Management, and Environmental Law*

---

In the creation and evolution of environmental law, two of the most compelling policy concerns are economics and risk management. Economic concerns play a vital role in setting policy in an industrialized democracy like the United States. The well-being of the citizenry, to a significant extent, is linked to economic performance and, increasingly, prospective courses of action are evaluated by reference to their economic consequences. Risk management is an extension of economics, bringing variegated calculations about human health effects and environmental outcomes into the mix of decisional concerns, representing profound questions of policy choice under conditions of great uncertainty.

As noted in Chapter One's discussion of "three economies," marketplace economics dominate most economic discussions, but the evolution of environmental law and policy have helped to frame a broader and more sophisticated scope for economic analysis. Innovative economists have begun to question the narrowed terms in which economic analyses have traditionally been made — like "gross domestic product" (GDP) which fails to offset for social debits,[1] deflated project discount rates, and even the definition of capital which is being expanded to include "natural capital."[2] If economic analysis and policy debates are expanded to include the three economies — linking the marketplace economy with wider societal economics and effects within the economy of nature — the resulting policymaking and legal processes become more reliable and realistic.

---

## A. USING THE TOOLS OF ECONOMICS TO CRAFT ENVIRONMENTAL LAW AND POLICY

Environmental law often is portrayed as counterpoised against economic development and productive activity. If environmental laws result in blocking con-

---

1. See Cobb, Kalstead, and Rowe, If the GDP is Up, Why Is America Down? Atlantic Monthly, October 1995 at 59–78.
2. See the work of Robert Costanza, Herman Daly, and others on "natural capital," estimating that natural systems if undisrupted contribute on average $33 trillion per year to human economics, 38 Science 253, 15 May 1997, noted below.

struction of a large dam and reservoir project, for example, certain forms of economic development associated with the project will not occur. Similarly, stringent
air pollution control laws that result in cleaner air and improved public health do
so by requiring "dirty" plants to cease operation, or by imposing costs on manufacturers who must install pollution control devices. These added costs may make
products sufficiently more expensive that consumers no longer buy as many units,
and production levels and jobs in the production sector must be scaled back. Some
might allege these as examples of an inherent conflict between environmental concerns and economic well-being, and call for the curtailment of environmental protection in order to increase material welfare. A more reflective approach is to treat
them as evidence that neither environmental protection nor economic activity
should be viewed in isolation — they are part of three intersecting economies.

The economist, like the environmentalist, should want to know what effects,
negative as well as positive, would occur from construction of a dam and reservoir
or from allowing manufacturers to avoid pollution controls. There are, for example, potential hidden economic costs to fisheries that depend on free flowing
streams, or to health and welfare among those exposed to high concentrations of
pollution near factory sites. In each case, informed economic judgment, like
informed environmental judgment, has to consider the totality of effects, some of
which are immediate and local, but some which may reach into the future and far
away. It was with that broad perspective in mind that Barber Conable, then
President of the World Bank concluded that, "Good ecology is good economics."[3]

In the dam and factory examples, and in environmental controversies more
generally, there are two fundamental questions that need to be addressed — (1)
"What decision is to be taken?" and (2) "How is that decision to be implemented?"
— echoing the different roles of environmental policy-making and environmental
law. Economics provides tools that both assist in policy analysis, and also aid in
effective implementation. Some policymakers would urge further that economic
analysis can be used normatively to select what courses of action ought to be pursued. Some legal theorists urge that law ought to be the handmaiden of economics, assigning legal rights in ways that make the market system more effective as
an engine for allocating resources. The following materials first explore the theory
and tools of economic analysis before turning to more controversial possibilities.

### Section 1. THE BEHAVIORAL ASSUMPTIONS AND DESCRIPTIVE POWER OF ECONOMIC ANALYSIS

#### a. From the rational maximizer to the externalization of costs and their control

Essentially, modern economics is predicated on assumptions about human
behavior that comport with general notions of what constitutes the decisionmaking approach of a rational human actor. Stated more technically, one commentator
on the influence of economics on law put it this way:

> Partly, it is because economics is seen today as comprising much more than
> the narrow attempt to model general equilibrium or the decision-making of

---

3. Conable, Address to the World Resources Institute, May 5, 1987.

firms and households. To understand those topics, economists postulate a type of human agent who seeks rationally to maximize the satisfaction of his own wants in a context where others are engaged in a similar enterprise, against a finite stock of resources. That simple image of agent-as-maximizer proved remarkably fertile as economists were able to model interactions among very large numbers of people using the most modest assumptions, and to generate abstract results that were in fact quite powerful and interesting when applied to the messier reality of commerce, consumption and production in modern capitalist societies. Given that success, it was natural to try to extend these models of human choice and interaction into other fields and to apply them to other problems. Waldron, Criticizing Economic Analysis of Law, 99 Yale L.J. 1441 (1990).

The explanatory power of the rational maximizer and the economic theories built upon it is evident in environmental controversies. Environmental degradation, on a very simple level, appears to be explained by the traditional tools and assumptions of economic analysis. In the absence of legal rules forbidding pollution or requiring polluters to pay for harms caused to others, a rational maximizing factoryowner will make no expenditures for pollution control, because to do so will increase costs and thereby reduce profits. Historically, experience confirms this thesis. In response to non-existent or lax pollution control laws, pollution of air and water as a low-cost means of disposing of unwanted waste products was a prevalent practice.

Economic analysis of pollution does not stop with merely identifying an incentive that leads an individual rational actor to engage in polluting activity. Economists also consider aggregate social welfare, which is generally treated as the sum of the welfare of all individuals. For this reason, economists look at the effects of pollution on others, on people downwind or downstream from the plant who are made worse off by the pollution. The harm to these individuals (and their activities) is a cost to them, and the sum of those costs is a cost of the polluting activity to society as a whole. Thus, economists, like environmentalists, are interested in the costs that pollution thrusts upon its victims. The comprehensive comparison of aggregate benefits and costs is called, not surprisingly, "benefit-cost analysis." The resulting comparison often is expressed as a B/C ratio. When benefits in a ratio are in excess of 1.0, that means that total benefits exceed total costs.

The benefit side of that calculation is made simpler by the presence of a functioning market system. Economists typically measure the benefits of the activity on the basis of willingness to pay in the market. Thus, under economic analysis, the total receipts earned through the sale of the product measure the benefits of its production. The cost side of the equation begins in the same way, that is, all of the firm's costs of production are totaled. The essentials of production, things such as materials and labor, are purchased in a market system. They, too, are easy to value. The total social cost calculation, however, is much more problematic because of the lack of markets in which the cost of harms suffered by pollution victims is valued, or pollution effects are freely traded.[4] Nevertheless, if the totality of bene-

---

4. Some of the more difficult valuation issues, monetizing subjective non-market values and accommodating the interests of future generations, are considered in the following section, and continued in the market-enlisting devices of Chapter 16.

fits and costs can be estimated in one way or another, economic analysis provides a valuable datum to policymakers.

Assume next that policymakers, whether because of a low benefit cost ratio or otherwise, decide that the polluting action being studied should be forbidden or limited. Here too, the tools of economic analysis aid those who seek to alter polluter behavior. Presumably, excessive air and water pollution will continue unless or until rational maximizers find it less profitable to pollute than to make other arrangements for disposal of unwanted by-products. Rational choice theory predicts that making pollution more expensive to the polluter than other environmentally less harmful methods of disposal will effect a reduction in pollution with a corresponding improvement in environmental quality. Law intersects with this simple economic analysis because the devices that change the calculus facing polluters are imposed by the legal system. Common law or statutory liability rules allow polluters to be sued for harms caused to others by the release of pollution. Recoveries by plaintiffs in those suits add to the costs of pollution and make continuation of the polluting practice less likely to be preferred from the firms' internal benefit/cost perspective. Alternatively, the law may, under threat of costly penalties, prescribe installation of pollution control equipment, or mandate reductions in emissions. A third legal control mechanism is to enact a tax on effluents so that polluters must pay a specified charge for each unit of pollution discharged into the environment. Regardless of the legal means adopted, belief in rational choice theory undergirds the strategy: those making laws expect that regulated parties (i.e., polluters), will reduce pollution if the benefits of doing so exceed the costs.

### b. Economic approaches to the problem of a finite commons

American law is predicated on a variety of unarticulated as well as explicit assumptions about the relationship of the government to the governed, and about the institutions comprising that relationship, especially the ownership of private property. Under Lockean political theory, property law would not be necessary under Eden-like conditions of plenty, with no competition for resources, because all desired items would be abundant. With increasing population and limited goods, however, a way to allocate available goods has to be created. To Locke, the institution of exclusive property fit nicely with a sense of the order of God's universe, and also responded to social needs when goods were no longer abundant in relation to demand. Private property would induce people to act to improve their lot by assuring them the fruits of their labors in gathering nature's bounty or refining the products of nature to make human life more comfortable.[5] Non-exclusive rights to property would fail to produce incentives for engaging in productive work. Like the tenets of modern economics, Locke's theory subscribes to rational choice theory: human actors are assumed to act in their own rational self interest. Owners will do whatever will maximize their advantage in regard to the private property.

Fortunately or unfortunately, much of the natural world is, as Garrett Hardin pointed out, a commons. Air, water, oceans, wildlife — these are parts of the

5. For a more thorough discussion of John Locke's view of private property, see Sanders, The Lockean Proviso, 10 Harv. J.L. & Pub. Pol'y 401 (1988).

planet's bounty open to use by all. When coupled with the dynamics of human behavior, unlimited shared use of a commons can generate environmental tragedy. Hardin argues that if such problems are not to be resolved by converting resources into private property, then regulatory "mutual coercion, mutually agreed upon" must respond to the tragedy of the commons. Economists agree, though they might characterize the problem, more technically, as the divergence between conduct that maximizes individual welfare and conduct that maximizes the aggregate social welfare. More importantly, economics has its own way of responding to commons problems, treating them as a subset of the more general problem of externalized costs, or, more simply, "externalities."

The disjunctions between social good and private good raised by the road salt and Kepone scenarios of Chapter One result in externalities. Humans tend not to respond to costs that they do not personally bear. Corporations, in this sense, are even more responsive: they are resolutely driven by self interest, responding to the equations of profit maximization with (understandably) no inherent charitable impulse to take on costs when not required to do so.

The process of identifying externalized costs, and then inserting them into some form of legal accounting so that they will be internalized within market and government decisions, constitutes one of the basic strategies of environmental law. In his book, Intermediate Microeconomics, Professor Hal Varian defined both negative and positive consumption and production externalities:

> We say that an economic situation involves a consumption externality if one consumer cares directly about another agent's production or consumption. For example, I have definite preferences about my neighbor playing loud music at 3 in the morning, or the person next to me in a restaurant smoking a cheap cigar, or the amount of pollution produced by local automobiles. These are all examples of negative consumption externalities. On the other hand, I may get pleasure from observing my neighbor's flower garden — this is an example of a positive consumption externality.

> Similarly, a production externality arises when the production possibilities of one firm are influenced by the choices of another firm or consumer.... A fishery cares about the amount of pollutants dumped into its fishing area, since this will negatively influence its catch.

> The crucial feature of externalities is that there are goods people care about that are not sold on markets. There is no market for loud music at 3:00 in the morning, or drifting smoke from cheap cigars, or a neighbor who keeps a beautiful flower garden. It is this lack of markets for externalities that causes problems....

> The market mechanism is capable of achieving Pareto efficient[6] allocations when externalities are not present. If externalities are present, the market will not necessarily result in a Pareto efficient provision of resources. However, there are other social institutions such as the legal system, or government intervention, that can "mimic" the market mechanism to some degree and thereby achieve Pareto efficiency. H. Varian, Intermediate Microeconomics 542–43 (1987).

---

6. Eds.: Efficiency as a technical economic term is discussed later in this chapter. For now, treat efficiency, as used in this context, as a measure of whether the action is a step along the path toward an optimal outcome.

Economists generally prefer to correct the injurious effects of externalities through the creation of functioning markets, positing systems of legal entitlements that will allow the market to correct externalizations. One way is through "privatizing" the commons economically. Professor Varian, for example, ascribes the absence of functioning markets, in part, to a failure of law to provide sufficiently well-defined and transferable legal rights. To demonstrate his point, he posits two roommates, each having a certain amount of money and each having a different attitude toward smoke in the shared room. If the legal entitlement to clean air were certain and were considered to be a property right of the non-smoker, Varian describes how the two roommates would engage in a Pareto efficient trade whereby the non-smoker might trade some of the entitlement to smoke-free air for some of the smoker's money.[7] A trade will take place if the non-smoker values having additional money more than the surrender of some portion of the right to clean air and the smoker values the ability to smoke by the agreed amount more than the money that must be paid. The precise amount of smoke and clean air would be determined, not by a rulemaker who can only guess at how much the affected parties value their clean air and smoke, but by the parties themselves in a way that maximizes utility. If a trade is mutually satisfactory to both participants, it is by definition Pareto efficient.

Professor Varian's materials on externalities not only probe the use of markets as a means to eliminate the inefficiencies associated with externalities, but also discuss how cost internalization techniques allow efficient levels of production to be calculated in the absence of functioning markets. Take a steel producer whose discharge of effluents adversely impacts a fishery: the production function of the steel firm, reflecting a lack of pollution control law, treats the current cost of discharging effluents as zero. Nevertheless, the steel firm has knowledge of how much expense would be incurred for installation of various levels of effluent control. The production function for the fishery is affected by pollution and reflects the effluent discharges of the steel company. As pollution increases, so does the cost of fishing. To measure the degree of effluent reduction that would be optimal, a simple theoretical expedient is employed: the two firms are treated as if they were merged. At that point, there is no longer any "external" cost at all. An efficient outcome can be calculated by figuring out what will maximize the "merged" firm's welfare, for at that point the private costs of the merged firm will account for (some) social costs (the commercial harm to the fishery) that had previously been ignored by the steelmaker in its decisional process.

COMMENTARY AND QUESTIONS

1. **Poorly-defined property rights as an impediment to efficient trading.** In the steel mill/fishery hypothetical, if either the merger of the two firms or a voluntary trade between them will lead to an optimal result, why doesn't that behavior take place?

---

7. Likewise, in the opposite case of legal entitlement, the smoker would be better off by selling some of the unlimited right to smoke. In fact, any legal rule, as long as it is sufficiently precise in defining the property rights of the two roommates, will permit them to bargain for an efficient outcome. See H. Varian, Intermediate Microeconomics, 546–47 (1987).

Looking at merger, it ought to be plain that it is in the interests of both firms to merge and internalize the externality because, as Varian points out, "if the joint profits of the two firms with coordination exceed the sum of the profits without coordination, then the current owners could each be bought out for an amount equal to the present value of the stream of profits for their firm, the two firms could be coordinated, and the buyer could retain the excess profits." Varian, Intermediate Microeconomics, at 557. In answer to why the coordinating merger doesn't take place, Varian asserts that, in many cases, it does. He then says that inefficiency-producing externalities do arise in cases of poorly defined property rights. In particular, he analyzes the Tragedy of the Commons, using Hardin's cow grazing example as an archetype of poorly defined property rights.

2. **Can all costs be made part of the calculus, even with well-defined property rights?** As noted in Chapter One, standard economic analysis is not sufficiently inclusive to address many significant real impacts that occur beyond the confines of the marketplace economy. In the steel plant/fishery example, only those costs reflected in the marketplace will be counted. Costs that are natural, societal, diffuse, and hard to measure, cannot be accurately accounted for by market forces, nor will even the most exacting conventional definitions of property rights make these costs cognizable in the marketplace economy. For the market to respond to costs of that sort, a process wholly external to market economics must take place. Public concerns about costs in the "natural economy" and the "civic societal economy" lead to policy-making initiatives, regulation, and/or mechanisms (such as the creation of a comprehensive tradeable emission credits system) that allow the marketplace economy to play a role in regulating the problem.

3. **Externalities and moral fault.** Economists do not view negative externalities as inherently bad. For them, the goal is not the elimination of externalities as much as it is elimination of the distortions that externalities impose on resource allocation. Is there, nevertheless, moral fault involved in the production of negative externalities? It is difficult to read about the *Kepone* case without feeling dismayed by the conduct of Allied, LSP, and the individuals involved. Is the same moral condemnation of polluters for imposing external costs on their neighbors always valid? For example, is burning coal to generate the electricity that supports vital human activities immoral because it emits combustion by-products into the atmosphere? Is the perceived "fault" involved in the coal-burning example legal in origin, stemming from invasion of the legal right (also the initial economic endowment) of the plant's neighbors to be free from pollution?

4. **Law as entitlement, and the welfare effects of market transfers.** Efficient market exchanges, as contemplated in the smoker/non-smoker situation, have an effect on wealth distribution. Those who must pay for change are less well-off, in absolute terms, than they would have been if the original distribution of entitlements had been more favorable to them. What role, if any, should welfare consequences play in shaping environmental law rules? What role, if any, should the relative cost-bearing abilities of the parties have in selecting the rule of entitlements? For example, should the potential welfare distribution effects of efficiency-seeking influence the assignment of initial endowments, such as a right to pollute versus a right to

be free of pollution, in a controversy pitting a large, well-capitalized industrial polluter against its neighbors? This raises issues of environmental justice.

5. **The Coase theorem.** A central theme of the economists' strategy stresses the
need for law to create property rights that are capable of being traded via market
exchange. A famous article by Nobel laureate Ronald Coase argues that, through
bargaining starting from a clear legal rule of entitlement, the same outcome will be
reached irrespective of which of two different parties holds the legal entitlement.
See The Problem of Social Cost, 3 J.L. & Econ. 1 (1960). Coase's demonstration
relies on assumptions about equal resources, equal access of all participants to
information, and the absence of transaction costs. Perhaps efficiency-maximizing
bargaining seems likely to occur in a simple model such as the smoker/non-smoker
hypothetical, or in a dispute between a neighboring rancher and farmer over fencing (Coase's hypothetical). Is bargaining toward an efficient solution likely to be
easy when a large number of parties are joint holders of a legal right, as would be
the case if a generalized right to clean air were acknowledged? The difficulties of
organizing groups of victims of pollution to bargain as one (a form of "transaction
costs") poses one problem. Would the bargaining go better if the initial legal right
were assigned to the polluter? If that is the case, might some members of the group
refuse to participate, in the belief that they will be able to reap the shared benefit
without active participation? This is a version of the "free rider" problem.

6. **Taxes as an alternative to markets.** Besides merger, what other solutions to the
steel mill/fishery externality can be employed? The microeconomics texts offer
two. One is the creation of a market like that of the smoker/non-smoker hypothetical. The second is to place a tax (called a Pigouvian tax) on the production of
pollution. The difficulty with the Pigouvian tax is in knowing how high to set the
tax: too high and the steel firm's lost profit due to output restriction will exceed
the fishery firm's increased profit due to improved environmental conditions; too
low and the steel company's savings on pollution control still will be outweighed
by the loss in fishery.

7. **Economic analysis and automobile emissions.** If, for example, automobile emissions are an externality, would a Pigouvian tax avert (or at least limit) the "tragedy
of the commons" effect? Such a tax would provide an incentive to drive less, to use
cleaner fuels and to develop engines that emit less pollutants. Could the same
behavioral changes be mandated by legislative fiat rather than by a tax? Is it practicable to fashion a market for automobile emissions trading, or to merge all of the
entities whose actions affect and are affected by the commons? The principal legal
approach to automobile emissions is considered in Chapter Ten, and efforts to
adopt a market-oriented regulatory approach are studied in Chapter 16.

## Section 2. GETTING THE NUMBERS "RIGHT" IN BENEFIT-COST ANALYSIS
### a. Measuring costs and benefits

It is important to be able to make an accounting of the benefits, costs, and
alternatives of any given project or proposal. There is at least as much a need in
the realm of public policy as in the private sector to assess the potential benefits
and costs of proposed courses of action.

Historically, benefit-cost analysis has long been associated with governmental public works construction projects. The recognition of environmental values by benefit-cost accountants as part of their work does not ensure that benefit-cost analysis will fully consider environmental concerns. Paralleling the corporate tendency to externalize environmental costs is a bureaucratic tendency to overstate project benefits and understate project costs in an effort to allow the "pork barrel" of governmental spending on projects having questionable real benefits to roll on. Despite an emerging set of cost accounting principles designed to address the natural resource effects of projects, environmental costs remain prominent among the classes of costs most readily subject to manipulation.

The thrust of benefit-cost analysis is to facilitate the ready comparison of alternative courses of action, especially when one of the options is to do nothing other than continue the status quo. As one expert in the field says, "Benefit-cost analysis is beguiling in its simplicity and seems to have very wide ramifications. In evaluating any choice, just add up the benefits, subtract the costs, and choose the alternative that maximizes the net benefits."[8] As we have seen from the start with Chapter One's highway salting example, when benefit-cost analysis is performed with thoroughness and careful consideration of environmental impacts and alternatives, it is a strong ally of the environmental perspective. When done in a superficial manner, however, relying primarily on easily-quantified market impacts, benefit-cost analysis too easily becomes a means of obscuring environmental costs in order to cast proposed projects in an overly favorable light.

Benefit-cost analysis relies heavily on concepts and methodologies developed by economists. Whenever a benefit-cost analysis is performed, the choice that will emerge as the best by that test will be the choice that maximizes net social benefits. This is the language of economics and is very little removed from the idea of efficiency. Measuring the values to be toted up as benefits and costs is both a science and an art. The tools of measurement include sophisticated supply and demand functions, discount rates, equilibrium models, distributional coefficients, and glorified intuition.

Environmental lawyers need not be economists to recognize the difference between a well done benefit-cost analysis and one that bears the hallmarks of an *ex post facto* rationalization for an insular decision. Nevertheless, when a legal or policy debate has focused on the benefits and costs of a project, the expertise of an economist or public policy analyst is as indispensable as the counsel of an expert toxicologist on matters of toxicology, or a hydrogeologist on matters of the movement of contaminants in groundwater. As in other areas, lawyers need not be experts, but must have a general understanding of the expert's processes of analysis, and familiarity with terms that are likely to be encountered.

Within the study of benefit-cost analysis, some analytical classifications have been developed for grouping types of projects and proposals. Of particular interest for environmental law is the analysis of "physical investment" cases, because a large number of environmental cases fall into that category. In lay terms, the generic physical investment case is one that produces some valuable resource such

---

8. E. Gramlich, A Guide to Benefit-Cost Analysis 2 (2d ed. 1990).

as oil, or flood control. In his text on benefit-cost analysis, Professor Gramlich observes that physical investment cases raise standard problems regarding valuation of resources, uncertainty, discounting, and dealing with the gains and losses of different groups, but these cases frequently have a unique character as well:

> Unlike many other benefit-cost issues, where it might sometimes seem that the stakes are rather small, environmental issues can often attain significant proportions [in physical investment cases]. When deciding to build a dam that will kill an endangered species or a power plant that will generate long-lived nuclear contaminants, public sector decision-makers are often being asked to make very fundamental choices. To a large degree, these choices may not be the stuff of economics, that marginalist discipline. But as with questions of valuing human lives and assessing distributional changes, there are some techniques and styles of reasoning that can still help focus analysis on the fundamentals.... Gramlich, 134–135 (2d ed. 1990).

The various devices he describes tend toward complex, formula-ridden microeconomics. The difficulties in estimating environmental costs of physical projects include opportunity cost valuation — for example, the lost benefits of the Alaska National Wildlife Refuge if oil drilling is approved;[9] there is no obvious means to decide how much a refuge is worth. The second difficulty is evaluating residual costs. Gramlich gives the example of estimating the long-term cost of disposing of nuclear wastes, discounting future costs down to present value, and uncertainty about the range of costs that may be incurred. The valuation of natural resource damages is studied further in the next chapter and Chapter 18.

From the environmental perspective, indeed, from almost any perspective, both market pricing and nonmarket "shadow pricing" is likely to omit significant public values.

### COMMENTARY AND QUESTIONS

1. **Replacement value and mitigation cost.** An alternative to quantifying environmental damage costs in their own right is to consider the cost of either replacing the damaged environmental resource or the cost of altering the proposed project in a way that will not harm resources. If a wetland is to be destroyed, replacement cost could be measured as the cost of purchasing similar property and dedicating it to use as a wetland. If a wetland is going to be dewatered by construction of a road that blocks the natural inflow of water, mitigation costs would be measured by the additional expenditure needed to assure the wetland of a continued water supply. Are these means of measuring environmental costs more accurate than the previously-discussed methods? Can replacement value and mitigation costs be used in benefit-cost analysis and later ignored when the project is constructed? Plainly, the answer is yes. Benefit-cost analysis is intended to evaluate a project's desirability. The considerations that go into actually building a project are governed by the applicable policies that have been incorporated into the substantive governing law.

---

9. Exploration alone has some environmental costs that would adversely affect the refuge, but the greater disruption of production would destroy the essential characteristics of the area and eliminate its value as a refuge.

This duality between informed judgment and physical action is reflected most starkly in some National Environmental Policy Act cases in which agencies propose mitigation efforts to justify a project, but later decline to implement them. See Chapter 13.

2. **Environmental benefits of reduced pollution.** The benefits of environmental improvements are equally hard to evaluate. A reduction of air pollution in Los Angeles can be achieved through major alterations in transportation practices. How great are the potential benefits? Without question, the benefits include a reduction of pollution-induced death and illness. Is the value of those improvements adequately measured in terms of salary income earned by people who live longer and of the reduction in health care costs for pollution-induced illness? The real benefits also include productivity gains from a workforce that has less eye irritation and suffers fewer headaches from breathing polluted air. Is it arbitrary to say, as did one recent benefit-cost analysis of the subject, that each avoided headache is worth a specific dollar amount? Is it even more arbitrary to ignore those benefits altogether?

3. **Cost externalization in the bureaucratic sector.** Government officials in public works agencies have internal agency incentives to inflate project benefits and understate project costs. Their "production" is measured in cubic yards of concrete poured, or miles of roadway built, or acres of waterway drained, dug, or dammed. Their "profit" is measured in terms of jobs gained for the agency and its contractors, renewed federal appropriations from the public purse, dollars passed through local public works constituencies, and political capital gained at federal, state, and local levels. Internal "costs" are measured in terms of political capital expended, hassles, and opportunity costs. Dollars, supplied by the taxpayers, are often only indirectly felt as determinative costs. With their project promotion orientation, most public works agencies would rather not consider or internalize broader assessments of project costs. The fact is that many public works projects cannot be justified by their real benefit-cost merits. The internal reckoning that drives many such projects is an agency's need to keep its agenda full and appropriations flowing: a rolling stone gathers momentum. The survival and perpetuation of the organization is a basic loyalty and a compelling managerial responsibility. Accurate accounting of costs and benefits does not necessarily serve the pork barrel agenda. Bureaucratic instinct is to maintain the flow of direct internal organizational benefits, not to serve some nebulous public good concept of net benefit-cost accounting. These pressures often affect the benefit-cost assessment process.

### b. Intergenerational justice and the discount rate

Physical investment projects that disrupt the environment are typically long-lived. Their benefits will be enjoyed, and at least some of their costs will be borne, a number of years into the future. Benefit-cost analysis, to be effective, must include a way to compare those future pluses and minuses with more immediate items, such as the costs incurred at the outset on mortar and concrete. In effect, there must be a common denominator in order for a meaningful comparison to take place, and that common denominator is to discount future benefits and costs down to present value.

The formal means by which analysts discount benefits and costs to present value may be unfamiliar, but the concept is an intuitively familiar one. The familiar adage that a bird in the hand is worth two in the bush suggests that the uncertainty of what will come to pass makes the present value of a benefit greater than its future value. An even more explicit recognition of the reduced value of future benefits is the charging of interest for the extension of credit, even where borrowers are certain to repay, so that risk is not a part of the "cost" of credit. The bank will make a student loan today on condition that the full amount lent be paid back plus something more at a specified time in the future. The "something more" covers not only the cost of initiating the loan and the risk of default,[10] but also reflects the fact that our society values present consumption more than future consumption. As another example, the fact that banks will pay five percent interest on a fully insured savings deposit for a year means that a dollar placed in the account will be worth $1.05 one year hence. This shows that the present value of the benefit of being paid $1.05 in one year is no more than $1.00. Another way to describe the reason for discounting is to say that devoting current assets to production of future benefits incurs an "opportunity cost," that is, a loss of the alternative present benefits that could have been obtained.

Economists and others acknowledge that future value is less than present value. There are highly competitive markets that offer a fairly reliable indication of just how much society as a whole discounts future values, and that indicator is called a discount rate — usually the prevailing interest rate for a sound, safe investment. Once a discount rate is adopted, a formula can be used to calculate future values, not just a year from now, but also any number of years into the future. The present value of a future benefit depends critically upon the discount rate chosen.[11] If a one percent rate is used, a $1 million benefit ten years hence has a present value of $905,287. If, instead, the rate is ten percent, the present value of future benefits falls sharply to only $385,543; at fifteen percent the present value is a mere $247,185.

Government pork barrel projects have been notorious over the years for using an unrealistically low discount rate. As the figures just set forth reveal, this tends to inflate the value of future benefits, thus making the good aspects of the project, such as electric generation and flood control, look better. Simultaneously, the unrealistically low discount rate tends to inflate future costs, including the costs of adverse environmental effects. Although this might appear to be even-handed, it almost assuredly is not. Benefits are often unrealistically inflated. As to costs, the most easily quantified environmental harms accrue in the near term — items such as fish kills when a free flowing stream is first impounded. More important, long-term environmental costs tend to be underestimated due to the difficulty of quantification. The question of how a discount rate is selected remains important.

---

10. Were the loan "guaranteed" by the national government, as many are, a lower, but still more than 0 percent, rate of interest would be charged, making it clear that the cost of credit reflects more than risk-taking alone.

11. The formula for discounted present value of a future benefit is Bt /(1+r)t, where B is the dollar value of the future benefit to be obtained, t is the number of years in the future when the benefit will be obtained and r is the discount rate.

One high visibility environmental law debate that illustrates this question is the promotion of nuclear electric generation that will burden future generations with potentially significant costs for long-term waste disposal and/or treatment. See Baltimore Gas & Electric Co. v. Natural Resources Defense Council, 462 U.S. 87 (1983); Pacific Gas & Electric Co. v. California State Energy Resources Comm., 461 U.S. 190 (1983), cases considered in Chapters Six and Seven.

COMMENTARY AND QUESTIONS

1. **Does discounting miss the point?** Some observers resist the very idea of applying market discount approaches to issues of planetary ecological management. Economist Peter Brown argues:

> There are some things that are not, and should not be, discounted. No one asks, "What is the optimal rate of shredding for the U.S. Constitution?" On the contrary, we assume that we should preserve the historic document for posterity. This is precisely analogous to what many people think we should do with respect to these issues; but all this response demonstrates is that [market accounting] doesn't tell us what the discount rate with respect to these issues should be, or even whether there should be one. [Moreover,] in any situation where there is a long-term asymmetry between costs and benefits, as is the case with global warming, discounting imperils the future by undervaluing it. Although the costs of averting the greenhouse effect are paid in the present, the benefits accrue in the distant future. The discounted value of harms that occur a century from now are insignificant when compared with the present costs of avoiding them. As D'Arge, Schulze, and Brookshire argue in Carbon Dioxide and Intergenerational Choice, "a complete loss of the world's GNP a hundred years from now would be worth about one million dollars today if discounted by the present prime rate." Brown, Greenhouse Economics: Think Before You Count, a Report from the Institute for Philosophy & Public Policy 10, 11 (1991).

2. **Discounting for uncertainty.** How should benefit-cost analysis evaluate events that are not certain to occur? Is there a difference in evaluating the costs of a decision that will increase toxic exposure-induced cancer deaths by two persons per thousand and a decision that might not increase cancer deaths at all, or might increase them by four persons per thousand exposures? The problem of valuing loss of human life is common to the two situations, but the number of lives at stake is uncertain in the second example. Studies demonstrate that there is "consumer preference" for certainty. Alternatively stated, there is consumer aversion to certain forms of risk-taking. To reflect this, benefit-cost analysis has developed methods for figuring in the disutility of uncertainty. The crux of the adjustment is to discount the value of uncertain benefits, and attach a premium to disfavored uncertain costs. Part B of this chapter explores in greater depth the issues surrounding uncertainty and risk in environmental law settings.

### Section 3. BENEFIT-COST ANALYSIS AS A DIRECT LAWMAKING STANDARD?

It is possible to go a step further and use economic analysis prescriptively as the determinant of what policy choices are to be made?

Relying on benefit/cost ratios as the exclusive policy making tool glosses over numerous concerns raised in the context of Chapter One's three economies. First is the market's shortcomings in estimating dollar values of goods and "bads."[12] Second, the reliance on markets takes the pre-existing distribution of wealth as a given. However, not all individuals or organizations have the same amount of money available to them to compete in the purchase of goods and services. Third, just as the poor are to some extent disenfranchised by markets, the interests of the future are likewise under-represented when decisions are made solely on the basis of the present preferences of current "consumers." The unborn generations who will inherit nuclear wastes generated in this century have no say in today's marketplace beyond the altruistic impulses of the earth's present inhabitants. Economic analysis addresses this third issue by trying to evaluate future benefits and costs and to calculate their present value.[13] Finally, exclusive reliance on markets is an entirely homocentric means of evaluating outcomes. Trees and fish do not buy and sell goods and bads.[14] Consider, in this context, a bill passed by the House of Representatives in the "Contract with America" Congress that was brought to the Senate by Senator Dole and others in May of 1995:

### Comprehensive Regulatory Reform Act of 1995
104th CONGRESS, 1st Session
S. 343[15]

A BILL to reform the regulatory process, and for other purposes....

## 2. ANALYSIS OF AGENCY PROPOSALS.

### Sec. 621. Definitions
(4)(A) the term "major rule" means —

(i) a rule or a group of closely related rules that the agency proposing the rule or the President reasonably determines is likely to have a gross annual effect on the economy of $50,000,000 or more in reasonably quantifiable increased direct and indirect costs, or has a significant impact on a sector of the economy....

### Sec. 622. Rulemaking cost-benefit analysis

(a)(1) Prior to publishing notice of a proposed rulemaking for any rule (or, in the case of a notice of a proposed rulemaking that has been published on or before the date of enactment of this subchapter, not later than 30 days after such date of enactment), each agency shall determine whether the rule is or is not a major rule....

(c)(1)(A) When the agency publishes a notice of proposed rulemaking for a major rule, the agency shall issue and place in the rulemaking record a draft cost-benefit analysis, and shall include a summary of such analysis in the notice of proposed rulemaking.

---

12. A "bad" here is intended to include the price one might need to pay someone to endure something unpleasant. In the pollution example, what is really at issue is the choice by affected parties to accept money, and the goods and services that money can buy, for the loss of health and amenity value.

13. As discussed more fully later in this chapter, this effort is not wholly successful.

14. Economists might claim that humans' market preferences are affected by their knowledge of ecological consequences, but that does not sufficiently include the non-human impacts in the decisional mix.

15. As reported to the Senate, May 26, 1995; H.R. 1022, a similar bill, had passed the House on March 3, 1995. The 104th Congress ultimately did not pass the proposed law, although similar attempts continue.

(B)(i) When the President has published a determination or designation that a rule is a major rule after the publication of the notice of proposed rulemaking for the rule, the agency shall promptly issue and place in the rulemaking file a draft cost-benefit analysis for the rule and shall publish in the Federal Register a summary of such analysis.

(ii) Following the issuance of a draft cost-benefit analysis under clause (i), the agency shall give interested persons an opportunity to comment pursuant to §553 of this title in the same manner as if the draft cost-benefit analysis had been issued with the notice of proposed rulemaking.

(2) Each draft cost-benefit analysis shall contain—

(A) an analysis of the benefit of the proposed rule, and an explanation of how the agency anticipates each benefit will be achieved by the proposed rule;

(B) an analysis of the costs of the proposed rule, and an explanation of how the agency anticipates each such cost will result from the proposed rule;

(C) an identification (including an analysis of the costs and benefits) of reasonable alternatives for achieving the identified benefits of the proposed rule, including alternatives that—

(i) require no Government action;

(ii) will accommodate differences among geographic regions and among persons with differing levels of resources with which to comply; and

(iii) employ performance or other market-based standards that permit the greatest flexibility in achieving the identified benefits of the proposed rule...

(D) an assessment of the feasibility of establishing a regulatory program that operates through the application of market-based mechanisms;

(E) in any case in which the proposed rule is based on one or more scientific evaluations or information or is subject to risk assessment requirements..., a description of actions undertaken by the agency to verify the quality, reliability, and relevance of such scientific evaluations or scientific information in accordance with the risk assessment requirements of subchapter III;

(F) an assessment of the aggregate effect of the rule on small businesses with fewer than 100 employees, including an assessment of the net employment effect of the rule; and

(G) an analysis of whether the identified benefits of the proposed rule are likely to exceed the identified costs of the proposed rule, and an analysis of whether the proposed rule will provide greater net benefits to society than any of the alternatives to the proposed rule, including alternatives identified in accordance with subparagraph (C).

(d)(1) When the agency publishes a final major rule, the agency shall also issue and place in the rulemaking record a final cost-benefit analysis, and shall include a summary of the analysis in the statement of basis and purpose.

(2) Each final cost-benefit analysis shall contain—

(A) a description and comparison of the benefits and costs of the rule and of the reasonable alternatives to the rule described in the rulemaking, including the market-based mechanisms identified pursuant to subsection (c)(2)(D); and

(B) an analysis, based upon the rulemaking record considered as a whole, of—

(i) whether the benefits of the rule outweigh the costs of the rule; and

(ii) whether the rule will provide greater net benefits to society than any of the alternatives described in the rulemaking, including the market- based incentives identified pursuant to subsection (c)(2)(D).

### Sec. 623. Decisional criteria

(a) No final rule subject to this subchapter shall be promulgated unless the agency finds that—

(1) the potential benefits to society from the rule outweigh the potential costs of the rule to society, as determined by the analysis required by §622(d)(2)(B); and

(2) the rule will provide greater net benefits to society than any of the reasonable alternatives identified pursuant to §622(c)(2)(C), including the market-based mechanisms identified pursuant to §622(c)(2)(D).

### Sec. 624. Judicial review....

(d) Each court with jurisdiction to review final agency action under the statute granting the agency authority to conduct the rulemaking shall have jurisdiction to review findings by any agency under this subchapter and shall set aside agency action that fails to satisfy the decisional criteria of §623. The court shall apply the same standards of judicial review that apply to the review of agency findings under the statute granting the agency authority to conduct the rulemaking.

COMMENTARY AND QUESTIONS

1. **The literal rationality of S. 343.** S. 343 would have targeted federal governmental agencies in their implementation of regulatory laws passed by Congress. Rulemaking is the process by which agencies promulgate most of their regulations, regulations that have the force of law. Chapter Seven will delve more deeply into administrative law. S. 343 would have required agencies to publish draft benefit-cost analyses as part of each proposed rulemaking at an unprecedented level of detail. What impact does that requirement have? As to rules determined by the agency to be major, based on the extent of the rule's anticipated impact, §622(c) forces the agency to include in the proposed rule a detailed draft benefit-cost analysis.§623 requires that the benefit-cost ratio be greater than 1:1, and that there is no more beneficial alternative action that could have been taken. Is it irrational of Congress to require selection by the agency of the most beneficial alternative?

2. **Substituting B/C analysis for policy-making.** Is it really irrational to select something other than the most beneficial alternative as measured by a B/C ratio? The problem of relying on the decisional criteria of §623 lies in the way it defines preferable choices exclusively by reference to the common denominator of benefit-cost ratios. Those ratios rely heavily on monetization of both costs and benefits, which the prior materials have demonstrated may tend to understate many environmental and conservation values while overstating, or at least emphasizing, commercial values. Good policy-making looks further, and not only at the aggregate but also at distributional consequences. If the budding awareness of environmental justice issues does nothing else, it will validate inquiries into distributive effects of regulatory action, effects that go unrecognized in a traditional by-the-

numbers benefit-cost analysis.

An extraordinary consortium of think-tank scholars that adhere to quite differing political philosophies has weighed in on the feasibility of using B/C analysis as a direct lawmaking criterion. The executive summary of the Report of an impressive collection of America's leading economists states:

> Benefit-cost analysis can play a very important role in legislative and regulatory policy debates on improving the environment, health, and safety. It can help illustrate the tradeoffs that are inherent in public policymaking as well as make those tradeoffs more transparent. It can also help regulatory agencies set regulatory priorities.

> Benefit-cost analysis should be used to help decisionmakers reach a decision. Contrary to the views of some, benefit-cost analysis is neither necessary nor sufficient for designing sensible public policy. If properly done, it can be very helpful to agencies in the decisionmaking process....

> Benefit-cost analysis should be required for all major regulatory decisions, but agency heads should not be bound by a strict benefit-cost test. Instead, they should be required to consider available benefit-cost analyses and to justify the reasons for their decisions in the event that the expected costs of a regulation far exceed the expected benefits. K. Arrow, M. Cropper, G Eads, R. Hahn, L. Lave, R. Noll, P. Portney, M. Russell, R. Schmalensee, V. Smith, & R. Stavins, Benefit-Cost Analysis in Environmental, Health, and Safety Regulation: A Statement of Principles 3 (1996).

3. **The practical agenda of "regulatory reform" — paralysis by analysis.** Many observers are critical of proposed laws like S. 343 for their potential diversion of vast amounts of agency resources into building the extensive and detailed evidentiary records that would have to accompany proposed rules. Beyond that, the law would allow regulated interests to slow proposed regulations by holding them hostage to litigation on the benefit-cost issue. S. 343's §625 literally invited wholesale reconsideration of every existing major regulatory rule; it declared —

> Any person subject to a major rule may petition the relevant agency or the President to perform a cost-benefit analysis under this subchapter for the major rule, including a major rule in effect on the date of enactment of this subchapter for which a cost-benefit analysis pursuant to such subchapter has not been performed, regardless of whether a cost-benefit analysis was previously performed to meet requirements imposed before the date of enactment of this subchapter.

Under other portions of that provision, the agency must act on such petitions within 180-days or else the petition is deemed granted and the rule's operation is suspended. In the event the agency denies the petition, the denial is subject to immediate judicial review.

### Section 4. USING ECONOMIC CONCEPTIONS TO FASHION ENVIRONMENTAL POLICY AND LEGAL RULES

Economists, in their own domain, do rely on economic analysis normatively, i.e., to select among alternative courses of action. Specifically, economic analysis has developed criteria to evaluate alternative courses of action as either better, or best. The umbrella term that is associated with these attempts to evaluate actions is "efficiency." In general, an allocation or use of resources is described as "efficient" when the greatest total net benefits have been derived from the employment of the resources.[16] In far more colloquial terms, the rough goal is to "make the most of what you've got."

Once again, the environmental perspective and the pursuit of economic efficiency share common ground. Efforts at resource conservation, a mainstay of the environmental movement, are often attempts to make better use of resources. If, for example, changing over to water-saving plumbing fixtures and increasing the use of xerophytic landscaping allows a thirsty city like Los Angeles to serve its population's water needs with 20 percent less water, an array of unattractive adverse ecological consequences are avoided. Less water can be withdrawn from natural systems such as Mono Lake or the Sacramento and San Joachin River deltas. This is efficient. The changes in lifestyle are neither expensive in terms of the investment required, nor do they significantly reduce the Angelenos' enjoyment of life. Water conservation, in this setting, allows a lesser amount of water to provide benefits almost identical to those obtained from a larger amount of water in the past, while incurring decreased total social and environmental costs.

### a. The Law and Economics Movement

There is room for a more extensive reliance on economic analysis in the service of public policy. Of particular importance for the study of environmental law is the strain of legal scholarship associated with the "Chicago School" of economics, often labeled "economic analysis of law." Scholars in this camp see the promotion of economic efficiency as a major function of law:

> Rights are to be assigned in a way that promotes the efficient use of resources. In some cases this assignment will be the natural result of parties' dealings with one another: if a right is not already assigned to the person who can use it most productively, he should be in a position to purchase it from someone making a less productive use and still be in a position to derive advantage from the purchase. However, in cases where such dealings are impeded by transaction costs, it is the task of a court to determine how the rights would have been transferred apart from those costs and to assign them accordingly. Waldron, 99 Yale L.J. at 1442.

Assuming, *arguendo*, that law ought to promote efficiency, the assessment of what is efficient in environmental cases is at times difficult to determine. Economic analysis of law appears to approach the choice of a rule of law in a way

---

16. Economists have developed a number of definitions of efficiency that are both technical and precise. These tests tend to be linked to rational choice theory because they often look to the position of individuals in regard to the maximization of their individual welfare. The most familiar and widely accepted efficiency criterion is the one developed by Vilfredo Pareto that bears his name. A trade or transfer of resources satisfies the Pareto criterion if, as a result, no one is harmed and some people are better off. Other efficiency criteria, associated with the work of Nicholas Kaldor and Tibor Scitovsky, test whether a change in policy is an improvement by inquiring if the people who gain from the change evaluate their gains at a higher dollar figure than the dollar figure that losers attach to their losses. Abram Bergson offers yet another approach by measuring the desirability of changes with reference to an explicit social welfare function. See E. Mansfield, Microeconomics: Theory and Applications 460, 482–83 (5th ed. 1985).

that is largely unrelated to the real questions of societal judgment that must under-lie the issue. As an example of normative economic analysis of law, take the issue of air pollution and ask, "Ought there be a right of manufacturers freely to dis-charge pollutants into the air?" In selecting a legal rule for pollution rights, a pro-ponent of economic analysis of law would first assess whether market mechanisms exist that result in efficient use of the affected resources (air, health, materials and labor needed to construct, install, and maintain pollution control devices, etc.). Legal intervention would be warranted only if market failure appeared likely. Here, market failure is likely because the harms of pollution are widely dispersed and fall on individuals and resource complexes that are not likely to be able to bargain with the polluter: transaction costs will impede the efficient allocation of the resource by market mechanisms alone.[17]

If market mechanisms are unsuccessful in achieving accurate accommodation of competing interests, the second phase of economic analysis of pollution rights law tries to assess what outcome is efficient and adopt a legal rule leading to that outcome. Economic analysis of law as a basis for prescription of rules is a less useful analytical device at this stage, especially from an ecological perspective. Efficiency is not a criterion that is concerned with natural systems as much as it is concerned with the material satisfaction of human desires. Even when the desires of ecologically sensitive individuals are taken into account, reliance on most measures of efficiency invites efforts at quantification in dollar terms as a means of facilitating comparisons. These efforts at monetization are highly impre-cise and are skewed in a way that disfavors environmental interests because they tend to minimize the value of subjectively measured satisfactions. Furthermore, they too heavily discount future values, such as preserving a natural patrimony for future generations.

Apart from giving insufficient weight to ecological values in making inter-personal welfare comparisons, considering only efficiency in adopting rules of law neglects common notions of responsibility for one's acts that are captured in the "polluter pays" principle. Similarly, the inquiry has little, if any, concern for the undemocratic power that may be granted to the polluting entity to impose its choice about the use of resources on a large class of neighbors without their con-sent. In this way, rote reliance on normative economic analysis arguably ignores traditional American democratic norms and ideals. Professor Waldron put it this way:

> [Economic analysis of law] raises but does not settle a number of important questions. Why is the promotion of efficiency to be taken as the aim of the legal process? Why not justice or the maximization of utility or some other value that requires us to go beyond efficiency (however that is understood)? 99 Yale L.J. at 1442.

---

17. Cases in which meaningful bargaining can take place between polluter and pollution victim will usually reach an "efficient" outcome without regard to the legal rule adopted. This may seem coun-terintuitive, but the basis for this claim is explored in detail later in this chapter. The choice of legal rule will affect welfare, and the level of pollution that is found to be efficient usually will be influ-enced somewhat by the initial entitlement either to pollute or to enjoy clean air.

It is possible to make too much of the potential antipathy between the environmental perspective and the reliance of economic analysis of law on efficiency as a norm for choosing rules of law. Environmental law as it exists today is a complex and variegated field. It is emphatically not an area of law that is dominated by one particular mode of analysis. For that reason, what remains most important about the interaction of environmental law and economics is the light that the tools of economic analysis can shed on problems of environmental law. The following material takes this cue and focuses on how economic science illuminates the character of environmental controversies, and, at times, contributes to their rational solution.

### b. Efficient regulation

A major portion of this book analyzes several types of regulation that are applied to the governance of environmental problems. This is substance of what Garrett Hardin had in mind when he called for "mutual coercion, mutually agreed upon." It should come as no surprise that economists have studied the types of regulation that are applied, and concluded that some forms of regulation are preferable to others.

Adherents of economic analysis prefer regulatory actions that achieve the same improvement in environmental quality but impose lower total social costs than other possible regulatory strategies. Put most simply, achieving the same result at a lower cost is more efficient. For example, assume that a given degree of effluent reductions is desired and the regulatory question is whether to require emission controls (devices that clean the effluent stream as it leaves the plant) or process changes (changes in production methods that reduce the amount of untreated effluent being produced).

To make the example more concrete, assume that the desired environmental improvement is reduction of $SO_2$ (sulfur dioxide) emissions from a factory that burns coal as a source of energy for its production processes: the plant currently emits 50 tons per year and the goal is to reduce emissions to 20 tons per year. The plant may reduce its emissions by cleansing the effluent stream — it can install filters or an electrostatic precipitator, or other devices that remove the $SO_2$ from the waste stream prior to emission into the atmosphere. Alternatively, the plant could change the type of coal it burns to coal that is naturally low in sulfur and reduce its $SO_2$ emissions in that way. If both methods can achieve the 30 ton per year reduction, the choice between them ought to be the one that involves the lowest total social costs.

How is the regulator to know which approach, emission controls, or process changes achieves the result at lowest cost? At this point, adherents of economic analysis offer the suggestion that the regulator need not make that calculation because the affected plant operator, acting out of self interest, will choose the least cost method of achieving the 30 ton per year reduction in emissions. Moreover, it is possible that, in a world containing hundreds or thousands of $SO_2$ emitters, all of whom are to be regulated, the least cost solution for achieving $SO_2$ reductions of any given magnitude may vary from plant to plant, so that some ought to install emissions controls and others ought to change production processes. The most efficient regulatory solution, therefore, is not to command and control the specific decisions of the polluters. Instead, it is more efficient to create a system of performance standards, setting the end result that must be achieved, relying on the market-based decisions of the individual firms to fill in the details of how to achieve compliance. After all, each firm knows far more about its own particular processes and abilities to change than does the governmental regulator. The cost of regulation itself also is reduced because the regulator need not invest time and effort in learning a great deal about the ins and outs of the production cycle of each regulated entity.

Once the hypothetical is expanded to include the polluting activities of many firms rather than a single firm, the argument of the adherents of economic analysis goes a step further than merely allowing each affected firm to choose between emission control and process changes. The overall least-cost pollution control effort might be obtained only if some firms (those for whom any form of pollution reduction is expensive) continue to pollute at present levels (or even expanded levels), while other firms (those for whom pollution control is relatively inexpensive) cut their emissions by more than a proportionate amount. The job of the regulator in this setting is merely to fix the overall limits on allowable pollution, and then to create a market system that allows the regulated firms to trade allowances to pollute among themselves. The predicted result is that pollution will be reduced in the desired amount by the firms for which pollution avoidance is less expensive, and the allowable pollution will be emitted by those firms for which the cost of avoiding pollution is higher. In that way, the desired emission reductions will be achieved and the total amount of scarce resources devoted to pollution control will be minimized. More pointedly, the total social cost of the desired environmental improvement will be much less than if every firm is subjected to command and control regulations that make mandatory a particular form or degree of emission reductions or the implementation of certain process changes.

Plainly, the adherents of economic analysis are not alone in their preference for minimizing the cost of effective pollution control, for it would be wasteful to devote more of society's scarce resources than necessary to accomplish any given result, environmental or otherwise. The point at which the adherents of economic analysis and others part company has more to do with the degree of confidence they place in market-based systems to achieve the desired outcomes in the real world. The use of economic incentives as a part of the regulatory system is discussed in Chapter 16.

1. **An economist's approach to equitable distribution of wealth.** The discussion of the role of economics in environmental quality issues frequently focuses on efficiency. Efficiency, no matter how desirable in a rationalist world, is not the only value that a society should pursue. Economics recognizes a need to account for the distributive consequences of using market allocation as a principal engine of social organization. If market allocations result in unfair distribution of social benefits, that too, just like malfunctioning markets, is a justification for governmental intervention in the market system to readjust the distribution of benefits. In assessing what constitutes fairness in this distributional context, economists have no special credibility, nor do they suffer any inherent disabilities — they are as sensitive and compassionate as individual conscience and world view may dictate.

When it comes to forms of intervention into the functioning of free markets in the name of equity, however, adherents of market allocations do have preferences. In general, they find it preferable to give cash stipends to individuals who have too small a share of the benefits pie, and then let those individuals maximize their own welfare by selecting and purchasing the precise mix of benefits they most desire given their improved financial position.

Consider in this light the question of environmental improvement of polluted inner city neighborhoods populated by citizens who are economically disadvantaged. Environmental improvement will increase their welfare, by improving living conditions and reducing some health risks caused by exposure to the existing pollution. Assume that society is willing to devote a fixed sum of money, $X, to improve the lot of this group of people. Which will generate greater benefits for the affected group, a government-financed program of environmental improvement or a direct grant of funds to those same inhabitants?

2. **Beyond the horizons of economic efficiency and equity.** Mark Sagoff has argued that efficiency and equity should not be the principal driving forces of "social regulation," a broad category of governmental actions that includes regulation of environmental quality. Instead, in his notable book on environmental economics, he advocates including ethical, aesthetic, and cultural goals in the process:

> The positive thesis...is that social regulation expresses what we believe, what we are, what we stand for as a nation, not simply what we want to buy as individuals. Social regulation reflects public values we choose collectively, and these may conflict with wants and interests we pursue individually. M. Sagoff, The Economy of the Earth 16 (1989).

3. **Contending forces, "Free Market Environmentalism," and other attempts to limit modern resource economics.** As noted in Chapter One, a number of national alliances have been formed to resist government regulation of pollution and other incursions on the commons, including the "Wise Use" movement, Project Relief, and other marketplace coalitions. A number of market-oriented lobbying groups have sought to promote the proposition that the environment is best protected by "voluntary cooperation," privatization of public natural resources to achieve managerial efficiencies through corporate ownership, emphasis on "secure property rights and the market process in the efficient and sensitive use of natural

resources," with compensation to be paid for regulatory restrictions upon private enterprise. Funded by right-wing foundations and natural resource industries, these groups sponsor junket seminars and speakers arguing that the marketplace should be the primary forum in which appropriate degrees of environmental protections should be determined.[18] They resist the "Polluter Pays" principle, modern resource economics' quantifications of externalities and "natural capital," and civic regulatory constraints on the marketplace.[19]

**4. Revisionist attempts to reform corporate power.** Plainly, not all environmental regulation of corporate behavior is good. Equally plainly, modern corporate structures still powerfully externalize social costs and resist attempts to apply civic controls. It is interesting to note a growing revisionist discussion contemplating minor or major overthrows of the corporation as a dominant entity in modern society. This initiative includes attempts to force more accurate accounting of public costs, attempts to require tighter interpretations of corporate charters, and attempts to change the constitutional status of corporations, which since 1886 have been allowed to claim most of the constitutionally-protected rights of natural persons.[20] See Ralph Estes, The Public Cost of Private Corporations, 6 Advances in Pub. Int. Accounting 329–351 (1995); and articles prepared by the Program on Corporations, Law, and Democracy (POCLAD) in Cambridge, Massachusetts, as part of the "Ending Corporate Dominance Alliance." While these initiatives may be regarded as quixotic, it should be noted that they have had increasing populist echoes in election campaign and talk show rhetoric, both left and right.

---

18. See Terry Lee Anderson and Donald Leal, Free Market Environmentalism (1990). The "Wise Use" movement, and groups like the "Discovery Institute" and the "Foundation for Research on Economics and the Environment" (FREE), apparently receive support from a catalog of manufacturing and resource-depletion industries and industry-oriented foundations. FREE, in Bozeman, Montana, offers free getaways for judges as well as professors, journalists, and others thought to shape public policy. In 1997 alone, FREE says, *"eight percent of the entire federal judiciary attended one of our four seminars"* in week-long all-expenses-paid holidays in Montana where they learned about the excessiveness of protections given endangered species, and a neo-retrograde resource economics emphasizing the necessity of compensating private corporations for restrictions protecting public environmental values. "Conference and travel expenses are paid and time is provided for cycling, fishing, golfing, hiking and horseback riding." See also Marcus, Issues Groups Fund Seminars for Judges, Washington Post Thursday, April 9, 1998, page A01.

19. Although some of the "free market environmentalists" criticize public subsidies, many in their alignment do not. FREE was founded in large part by oil money. Three major off-road vehicle (ORV) manufacturers are major contributors to the Wise Use Movement, whose leaders lobbied hard for legislation that funded $30 million in trails for ORVs on public lands; (see the case study of public lands ORV use in Chapter 24). Mining companies, which are given mining rights on federal lands for pennies on the dollar and no royalty payments to the public, are the largest contributors to several Wise Use groups.

20. One of the most important Supreme Court decisions shaping American society was also one of the most casual. In Santa Clara County v. Southern Pacific Railroad Company, 118 U.S. 394 (1886), a railroad wished to challenge its property tax assessments on equal protection grounds. To do so it had to assert that a corporation could demand the same civil rights as a natural person. Although arguments on this issue — "[whether] Corporations are persons within the meaning of the Fourteenth Amendment to the Constitution of the United States" — had been extensively prepared by the parties, before the Supreme Court argument could begin Chief Justice Waite announced: "The court does not wish to hear argument on the question whether the provision in the Fourteenth Amendment to the Constitution, which forbids a State to deny to any person within its jurisdiction the equal protection of the laws, applies to these corporations. We are all of opinion that it does." 118 U.S. at 394–95. Thus occurred a major milestone in the evolution of constitutional doctrine, consolidating the presence of marketplace structures within the public law.

Section 5. GREEN ECONOMICS, AND "NATURAL CAPITAL"

Traditional economists overlook an important facet of the environmental perspective, the public, societal economics that inhere within the economy of nature. The tools of classical economics are not attuned to measuring and accounting for long-term impacts on the environment. Some economists, however, have recently begun developing alternate modes of analysis that explicitly account for environmental quality. This "green" school of economics voices a new perspective on national and international economic policy:

### Passell, Rebel Economists Add Ecological Cost to Price of Progress
New York Times, November 27, 1990, C1

Could biologists, ecologists and other natural scientists have more to say about the economics of the environment than economists themselves?... Ecological economists are challenging traditional economics on its own turf, accusing economists of mismeasuring development, underestimating the intangible costs of pollution and ignoring society's responsibilities to future generations....

[The] International Society of Ecological Economists, [seek to] persuade governments to give the "sustainability" of natural "life support systems" priority over conventionally measured economic growth. That could mean radical changes in policy, sharply reducing efforts to improve living standards through investments in land-intensive agriculture and resource extraction.

But succeed or fail, they will almost certainly force economists to face up to the issue that traditional analysis tends to undervalue environmental resources. And they may kindle public debate on some very uncomfortable questions, everything from the need for population control to the compensation owed by the present generation to those who will inherit radioactive reactor wastes in the year 3000....

CALCULATING DEPRECIATION... Robert Repetto and his colleagues at the World Resources Institute have been widely applauded for an attempt to correct a common distortion introduced by conventional economics practices: the failure to include natural resource depletion in national income accounts. When economists measure a nation's net output, they subtract capital depreciation, the loss of machines, vehicles and buildings in the ongoing production process. But they rarely account for gains or losses of less tangible forms of capital, like human skills. Equally important, they neglect changes in reserves of natural resources, which are typically large (and negative) in poor countries.

The Repetto team used the example of Indonesia to show how important this omission can be in gauging national development. Losses from soil erosion, they calculated, reduce the net value of crop production by about 40 percent. And net losses of forest resources actually exceed timber harvests. Moreover, from 1980 to 1984 depletion of oil fields reduced the value of Indonesia's reserves base by about $10 billion annually, roughly 15 percent of national income. In industrialized countries, where total output is much larger relative to natural resources depletion, similar extensions of conventional accounting methods have been used to calculate the impact of environmental degradation. Japan, Germany, and France all have ambitious projects under way. And the United Nations Statistical Office is working on a general framework for environment and natural resource accounting.

SEEKING A NEW FRAMEWORK... What economics needs, they argue, is a whole new framework, one that fits economic production into ecological systems, rather than the other way around. To Herman Daly at the World Bank, David Pearce at the University of London, and Paul Ehrlich at Stanford University, the key goal is the achievement of "sustainability" — adjusting economic activity so it does not damage the natural systems that underpin all functioning economies. Too many economists, they argue, simply assume that the biosphere can roll with any economic punch and bounce back for more....

Mr. Daly...constructed an "index of sustainable economic welfare," adjusting conventionally measured output for environmental damage, resource depletion, the availability of leisure, even the degree of income equality. The index suggests that Americans' sustainable welfare peaked more than a decade ago, that "economic development" as contrasted with economic growth has stopped....

At the heart of the sustainability question, William Nordhaus argues, is the issue of endowing future generations with at least as much productive capacity as this generation inherited. Current levels of economic activity may deplete valuable resources and degrade ecological systems in irreversible ways, he acknowledges. But this generation will also pass on precious new technologies, cures for fatal diseases, incredibly efficient means for processing information, for example. Who is to judge whether our resource-stripping, environmentally stressful ways will more than offset this technological bounty?

TECHNOLOGICAL PESSIMISTS... Robert Hahn, an economist at the American Enterprise Institute, offers another way of parsing the question. Traditional economics implicitly assumes that as a practical matter no wasting asset, whether it be oil or the atmospheric ozone layer, is absolutely critical to economic growth or human welfare. Ecological economists, by contrast, are technological pessimists: if nations are not careful, they will make the planet uninhabitable.

No one really knows who is right.... It makes sense, Hahn argues, to err on the side of caution where the penalty in output forgone is not high. The ecological economists thus score most tellingly, Mr. Hahn suggests, in their criticism of traditional economists' live-and-let-live approach to population issues.... For any given living standard, it is virtually certain that more people mean more damage to ecological systems, whose carrying capacities are poorly understood....

It is not yet clear whether the ecologists will establish a beachhead in the economists' carefully constructed intellectual empire. What they have already demonstrated, though, is that environmental economics is too important to be left by default to economists....

### COMMENTARY AND QUESTIONS

1. **Measuring national product.** The standard measure of national economic activity currently in use is gross national product (GNP). In measuring GNP, no account is taken of the costs imposed by pollution or by a nation's dwindling stock of natural resources. These omissions constitute a fundamental inconsistency, because the output measured to make up GNP does take account of the depletion of other capital resources, such as the depreciation of plant and equipment. Is there any plausible reason for these omissions? Would a concept of net national product be more conducive to making the environmental costs of economic activity more highly visible? "Conventional measures of output...cannot be used as accurate measures of true changes in economic welfare...." Seneca and Taussig, Environmental Economics 325–27 (1974). See also the German Federal Statistical Office's Gross Ecological Product project, cited in Hinrichsen, Economists' Shining Lie, 13 Amicus J. 3 (Spring 1991).

2. **Population and more Tragedy of the Commons.** Hardin's brief article, excerpted in Chapter One, is undoubtedly one of the most influential environmental essays ever written. Do you hear strains of the tragedy of the commons in virtually every position expressed by the economists cited in the newspaper article? Even Robert Hahn, a champion of market solutions to environmental problems, sounds a Hardin-like caution on issues of population control. What is the relationship between sustainability and population? At a simplistic level, the argument is one of human welfare — if the Earth's sustainable bounty is likened to a pie, everyone can have a larger piece if there are fewer with whom to share. The more intractable issues arise in trying to calculate or predict whether the additional stress that greater population puts on the earth's resources will exceed sustainability, either temporarily or irreversibly. The revisionist view — that we need more people on earth, not less — seems to treat the net per capita benefit of individuals as if most are still needed and can be employed in low-tech manual farming. See Crossette, How to Fix a Crowded World: Add People, New York Times, Nov. 2, 1997 at 4-1.

3. **The idea of natural capital.** Would the typical policy supporting tools of economics, benefit-cost analysis and efficiency, be more accurate in their assessment of the relative desirability of courses of action if they did a better job of accounting for the economic value provided by the natural world? To justify a different mode of valuing natural resources, Robert Costanza, among others, has argued for the concept of valuing the services produced by the world's stock of "natural capital." If his premises and figures are correct, a great deal of the world's output of goods and services is not being accounted for by traditional measures.

> The services of ecological systems and the natural capital stocks that produce them are critical to the functioning of the Earth's life-support system. They contribute to human welfare, both directly and indirectly, and therefore represent part of the total economic value of the planet. We have estimated the current economic value of 17 ecosystem services for 16 biomes, based on published studies and a few original calculations. For the entire biosphere, the value (most of which is outside the market) is estimated to be in the range of US\$16–54 trillion ($10^{12}$) per year, with an average of US\$33 trillion per year. Because of the nature of the uncertainties, this must be considered a minimum estimate. Global gross national product total is around US\$18 trillion per year.[21]

Businessman-turned-author Paul Hawken describes the concept of natural capital in more intuitive terms. He says:

> "Natural capital"...comprises the resources we use, both nonrenewable (oil, coal, metal ore) and renewable (forests, fisheries, grasslands). Although we usu-

---

21. R. Costanza, R. d'Arge, R. de Groot, S. Farber, M. Grasso, B. Hannon, K. Limburg, S. Naeem, R. O'Neill, J. Paruelo. R. Raskin, P. Sutton, & M. van den Belt, The Value of the World's Ecosystem Services and Natural Capital, 387 Science 253 (15 May 1997). See also Robert Costanza & Herman Daly, Natural Capital and Sustainable Development, 6 Conservation Biology 37–46 (1992); Paul Hawken, Amory Lovins, Hunter Lovins, Natural Capitalism: The Coming Efficiency Revolution (1998).

Note also the idea of "social capital" — Robert Putnam, Bowling Alone: America's Declining Social Capital, 6 Journal of Democracy 66–77 (1995) ("social capital" one of a nation's important asssets, is threatened by the deterioration of "civic engagement" between people, and communities, given the stress of modern living).

ally think of renewable resources in terms of desired materials, such as wood, their most important value lies in the services they provide. These services are related to, but distinct from, the resources themselves. They are not pulpwood but forest cover, not food but topsoil, Living systems feed us, protect us, heal us, clean the nest, let us breathe. They are the "income" derived from a healthy environment: clean air and water, climate stabilization, rainfall, ocean productivity, fertile soil, watersheds, and the less-appreciated functions of the environment, such as processing waste — both natural and industrial. Hawken, Natural Capitalism, Mother Jones 40 (Mar/Apr. 1997).

Where does all of this new economics lead? Critics on the right seem to think it is a smoke-and-mirrors effort to reach an ideologically preferred result by injecting unsupportable numbers into the environmental cost side of the economic analysis. Critics on the left view it even more cynically, as an effort to forestall radical change of a materialistic capitalist economy that is destined to self-destruct. See S. Cooper, The Myth of Capitalist Sustainability: An Answer to the New Green Economics, Socialist Organizer Review 7 (Fall 1997). If natural resources were considered to be a form of scarce capital, and valued as such, however, it would routinely be the case that economic evaluations of actions that threatened serious environmental damage would have to be assigned larger costs than they do under present, more conventional, economic standards.

4. **Herman Daly's prescription.** The World Bank is an influential player in the financing of developing nations, and Herman Daly was its senior economist from 1988 to 1994. Upon his departure from the Bank, he offered a number of environmentally oriented suggestions for the Bank and its client nations, here summarized:

**The first remedy:** Stop counting the consumption of natural capital as income. When the Phillipines permits its forests to be carried off as logs to Japan, its balance of payments looks good, for several years. When Indonesia sells off its oil and when the United States fishes its great cod populations down to remnants, those economies boom until the resource is gone. That kind of behavior breaks the most time-honored economic law, which is to take this year only what will leave intact the capacity to produce the same amount next year. Don't spend down your capital. Every economist knows that. But economists have never counted soils, forests, clean water, clean air, mines, oil wells, or other species as capital. These resources are income-producing; indeed without them there would be no income. But we have no accounting systems to keep track of natural capital.

**Two:** Tax labor and income less; tax "throughput" more. Throughput means flows of energy and materials from the earth through the economy, and back as waste to the earth. It makes no sense ... to tax what you want (income, capital gains) instead of what you want less (depletion, pollution). The North should take this step first. The major weakness of the World Bank's ability to foster environmentally sustainable development is that it only has leverage on the south.

**Three:** Maximize the productivity of natural capital and invest in increasing it. Economists don't have to be told that the smartest way to invest is to find the most limiting factor in an economy or economic process, and find a way to use that factor more efficiently. What economists do have to be told is that the limiting factor is no longer labor or manmade capital. It is natural capital. "The fish catch is limited not by the number of fishing boats, but by the remaining fish in the sea. Cut timber is limited not by the number of sawmills, but by the standing forests." That realization is slow to come because of inadequate accounting, and because so many economists haven't yet adjusted to a world where nature is suddenly very limiting.

**Fourth suggestion:** Move away from the ideology of free trade and free capital mobility and toward national production for internal markets. "The royal road to development...is thought to be the unrelenting conquest of each nation's market by all other nations.... Take it as a prediction: ten years from now the buzzwords will be 'renationalization of capital' and 'community rooting of capital.'"[22]

## B. RISK REDUCTION, RISK MANAGEMENT, AND ENVIRONMENTAL LAW

In the Introduction to his intensive case study of the Northern Spotted Owl controversy (see Chapter 14), Professor Steven Yaffee finds lessons from the owl for broader environmental and natural resource policy issues:

> The owl dispute is like most present-day environmental controversies, in that it involves: [1] a multiplicity of interests and subissues in what often appear to be fairly simple issues, [2] a significant amount of technical uncertainty and complexity, and [3] a decisionmaking environment that is often portrayed as "zero sum," pitting those arguing for fairly intangible concerns against advocates of more tangible ones. The conflict also affects a large amount of geographic and intellectual landscape, requiring transboundary, integrative solutions from a political and administrative system that is inherently fragmented. It requires us to make choices that balance short-term costs against long-term benefits, and bind ourselves to a state of affairs that is probably rational in the long run, but may be hard to justify in the short term. Implicitly, the controversy also defines our society's obligations to future generations of humans and other life, and affects their quality of life many years down the line. Yaffee, The Wisdom of the Spotted Owl (1994).

Although the passage does not adopt the terms "risk management" or "risk reduction," those concerns are a common thread woven into the characteristics that distinguish Yaffee's environmental disputes from more conventional policy problems.

### Section 1. WHAT IS "RISK"?

"Risk" often is defined as a measure of (1) the probability that a particular act will cause damage to human health and the environment, and (2) the severity of any damage that may occur. That is where most technical definitions of risk end, but there is another dimension to "risk," involving public perceptions and outrage.

### Peter Sandman, Risk Communication: Facing Public Outrage
#### EPA Journal 21–22, November 1987

If you make a list of environmental risks in order of how many people they kill each year, then list them again in order of how alarming they are to the general public, the two lists will be very different. The first list will also be very debatable, of course; we don't really know how many deaths are attributable to, say, geologi-

---

22. From Donella Meadows, Daly Medicine, Amicus Journal 11 (Summer 1994).

cal radon or toxic wastes. But we do know enough to be nearly certain that radon kills more Americans each year than all our Superfund sites combined. Yet...millions who choose not to test their homes for radon are deeply worried about toxic wastes. The conclusion is inescapable: the risks that kill you are not necessarily the risks that anger and frighten you....

The core problem is one of definition. To the experts, risk means expected annual mortality. But to the public (and even to the experts when they go home at night), risk means much more than that. Let's redefine terms. Call the death rate (what the experts mean by risk) "hazard." Call all the other factors, collectively, "outrage." Risk, then, is the sum of hazard and outrage. The public pays too little attention to hazard; the experts pay absolutely no attention to outrage. Not surprisingly, they rank risks differently.

Risk perception scholars have identified more than 20 "outrage factors." Here are a few of the main ones:

*Voluntariness:* A voluntary risk is much more acceptable to people than a coerced risk, because it generates no outrage. Consider the difference between getting pushed down a mountain on slippery sticks and deciding to go skiing.

*Control:* Almost everybody feels safer driving than riding shotgun. When prevention and mitigation are in the individual's hands, the risk (though not the hazard) is much lower than when they are in the hands of a government agency.

*Fairness:* People who must endure greater risks than their neighbors, without access to greater benefits, are naturally outraged — especially if the rationale for so burdening them looks more like politics than science. Greater outrage, of course, means greater risk.

*Process:* Does the agency come across as trustworthy or dishonest, concerned or arrogant? Does it tell the community what's going on before the real decisions are made? Does it listen and respond to community concerns?

*Morality:* American society has decided over the last two decades that pollution isn't just harmful — it's evil. But talking about cost-risk tradeoffs sounds very callous when the risk is morally relevant. Imagine a police chief insisting that an occasional child-molester is an "acceptable risk."

*Familiarity:* Exotic, high-tech facilities provoke more outrage than familiar risks (your home, your car, your jar of peanut butter).

*Memorability:* A memorable incident — Love Canal, Bhopal, Times Beach — makes the risk easier to imagine, and thus (as we have defined the term) more risky. A potent symbol — the 55-gallon drum — can do the same thing.

*Dread:* Some illnesses are more dreaded than others; compare AIDS and cancer with, say, emphysema. The long latency of most cancers and the undetectability of most carcinogens add to the dread.

*Diffusion in time and space:* Hazard A kills 50 anonymous people a year across the country. Hazard B has one chance in 10 of wiping out its neighborhood of 5,000 people sometime in the next decade. Risk assessment tells us the two have the same expected annual mortality: 50. "Outrage assessment" tells us A is probably acceptable and B is certainly not.

These "outrage factors" are not distortions in the public's perception of risk. They explain why people worry more about Superfund sites than geological radon, more about industrial emissions of dimethylmeatloaf than aflatoxin peanut butter.

There is a peculiar paradox here. Many risk experts resist the pressure to consider outrage in making risk management decisions; they insist that "the data" alone, not the "irrational" public, should determine policy. But we have two decades of data indicating that voluntariness, control, fairness, and the rest are important components of our society's definition of risk. When a risk manager continues to ignore these factors — and continues to be surprised by the public's response of outrage — it is worth asking whose behavior is irrational.

## COMMENTARY AND QUESTIONS

1. **Reactions to the outrage.** Commentators who accept the legitimacy of outrage as an element of risk generally recommend two strategies for reconciling the discordances between "expert" and "public" definitions of risk: 1) better "risk communication," the two-way process of information exchange between governmental risk managers and the general public; and 2) involvement of "stakeholders," the parties that are affected by the risk management problem, during all stages of the risk definition and management process. See, e.g., Presidential/Congressional Commission on Risk Assessment and Risk Management, Final Report (hereinafter "Commission Report"), Volume 2, Chaps. 1–3 (1997). Others more skeptical of outrage as a genuine element of risk belittle these approaches. See Cross, The Public Role in Risk Control, 24 Env. L. 887 (1994) ("A variety of measures could be taken to facilitate the government's use of scientifically accurate measures of risk rather than mistaken public perceptions. Foremost is the reduction in opportunities for public participation in decisionmaking." Id. at 950.).

2. **How EPA considers risk in environmental protection.** Risk assessment is a burgeoning field in the realm of environmental regulation. For a summary of the methods of analysis used by the United States Environmental Protection Agency in performing risk assessment, see C. Coperland & M. Simpson, Considering Risk in Environmental Protection, 8 Congressional Research Service Review (No. 10) at 7-9 (1987). That article describes the risk quantification procedure that the federal government uses to evaluate health risks of hazardous substances. The two-fold inquiry first identifies the hazard, usually relying on epidemiologic studies, animal bioassays, short-term bioassays and chemical structure-activity studies. The second prong of the inquiry attempts to look at the exposure side of the problem, considering the magnitude (frequency and intensity) of the exposure to the substance that will be suffered by the populace and then trying to make an assessment of the likely response of exposed individuals to the exposure. This latter effort is fraught with scientific uncertainty primarily attributable to (1) the unknown physical mechanism that is at work and (2) imperfections in the measurement of the exposure. Each of these inquiries is fraught with uncertainties, such as the unknown physical mechanism by which exposure results in cancer. The results of studies tend to have unusual variability, possibly as a result of the imprecision of the measurements of most human exposure data.

3. **The law and outrage.** Should legal institutions take outrage into account? Is a court better equipped to do so than a politically responsible actor, such as a legislator or an executive branch administrative official? In the following case and in the other materials in this coursebook, observe whether the legal system ignores, represses, assuages (symbolically or authentically), channels into socially productive pathways, or is misdirected by public outrage. In that study also try to identify whose risk management decision is under review, that of a government regulator or that of a private project proponent.

### Village of Wilsonville v. SCA Services, Inc.
Supreme Court of Illinois, 1981
86 Ill. 2d 1, 426 N.E.2d 824

CLARK, J. On April 18, 1977, the plaintiff village of Wilsonville (the village) filed a complaint seeking injunctive relief in the circuit court of Macoupin County. Plaintiffs Macoupin County and the Macoupin County Farm Bureau were granted leave to intervene.... The gravamen of the complaints was that the operation of the defendant's chemical-waste-disposal site presents a public nuisance and a hazard to the health of the citizens of the village, the county and the State. The Attorney General of Illinois filed a complaint on May 26, 1977, seeking an injunction pursuant to the Environmental Protection Act (Ill. Rev. Stat. 1975, ch. 111½).... [The two actions were consolidated for trial and disposition.] Trial began on June 7, 1978, consumed 104 days, and resulted in judgment for the plaintiffs on August 28, 1978. The trial court's judgment order concluded that the site constitutes a nuisance and enjoined the defendant from operating its hazardous-chemical waste landfill in Wilsonville. It ordered the defendant to remove all toxic waste buried there, along with all contaminated soil found at the disposal site as a result of the operation of the landfill. Further, the court ordered the defendant to restore and reclaim the site. The defendant appealed....

The defendant has operated a chemical waste landfill since 1977. The site comprises approximately 130 acres, 90 of which are within the village limits of the plaintiff village. The remaining 40 acres are adjacent to the village. The defendant enters into agreements with generators of toxic chemical waste to haul the waste away from the generators' locations. The defendant then delivers it to the Wilsonville site, tests random samples of chemical waste, and then deposits the waste in trenches. There are seven trenches at the site. Each one is approximately 15 feet deep, 50 feet wide, and 250 to 350 feet long. Approximately 95 percent of the waste materials were buried in 55-gallon steel drums, and the remainder is contained in double-wall paper bags. After the materials are deposited in the trenches, uncompacted clay is placed between groups of containers and a minimum of one foot of clay is placed between the top drum and the top clay level of the trench.

The site is bordered on the east, west, and south by farmland and on the north by the village. The entire site, the village, and much of the surrounding area is located above the abandoned Superior Coal Mine No. 4, which operated from 1917 to 1954. The No. 6 seam of the mine was exploited in this area at a depth of 312 feet. The mining method used to extract coal was the room-and-panel method, whereby about 50 percent of the coal is left in pillars which provide some support for the earth above the mine. There was testimony at trial by Dr. Nolan Augenbaugh, chairman of the Department of Mining, Petroleum and Geological

Engineering at the University of Missouri at Rolla, that pillar failure can occur in any mine where there is a readjustment of stress. Also on the defendant's site is a 30-to 40-feet-high pile of "gob," or mine spoil of coal, shale, and clay, which was accumulated over the time the mine was operated. Acid drainage from the mine has seeped into the ground and contaminated three surface drainage channels at the site. The defendant has attempted to remedy this situation by covering the surface of the "gob pile" with excess soil from the trenches.

There are 14 monitoring wells along the perimeter of the site. They are designed to detect liquids which seep through the soil and into the wells. They are not designed to contain liquids, however. In fact, monitoring wells Nos. 5 and 6 are 650 feet apart, which would allow many materials to pass between those two wells and not be discovered. The wells are sampled quarterly by a private laboratory, and test results are submitted to the Illinois Environmental Protection Agency (IEPA). Additional water samples are taken from three surface channels and are tested and reported in the same manner as samples taken from the wells. The surface drainage and the ground-water drainage from the site are to the south, away from the village and toward farmland.

The village has no sewage-treatment plant and no municipally owned sewage system. Most homes are served by septic tanks, and some homes and businesses are connected to private sewers. The water-distribution system is centralized, and water is purchased from Gillespie, Illinois. The system was built in 1952 after the village tried unsuccessfully to find sufficient water by drilling municipal wells in the area. There are still 73 water wells in the village, some of which are used to water gardens or wash cars. At least one well is used to water pets, and another is used for drinking water. South of defendant's site, approximately one-half mile from the gob pile, is the Vassi Spring, the owner of which intends to use it as his water supply when he builds his home. Further south are four more springs used to water livestock.

On February 11, 1976, the defendant applied to the IEPA for a permit to develop and operate the hazardous-waste landfill. A developmental permit was issued by the IEPA on May 19, 1976. After a preoperation inspection was conducted by the IEPA, an operational permit was issued to the defendant on September 28, 1976. Each delivery of waste material to the site must be accompanied by a supplemental permit issued by the IEPA. A supplemental permit specifies the chemical nature and quantity of the waste to be deposited at the sites. Between November 12, 1976, and June 7, 1977, the first day of trial, the defendant had obtained 185 such permits.

The materials deposited at the site include polychlorinated biphenyls (PCBs), a neurotoxic, possibly carcinogenic chemical which it has been illegal to produce in this country since 1979. Due to the extensive use of PCBs in electrical equipment such as transformers, capacitors, and heat-transfer systems, and in hydraulic systems, any PCBs that were produced legally now have to be disposed of when they are no longer in use. PCBs have been stored at the site in liquid, solid and semisolid form. Additionally, there are a number of now-empty drums which had once contained PCBs, which are also buried at the site. Other materials buried at the site in large quantities are solid cyanide, a substance known as C5, 6, paint sludge, asbestos, pesticides, mercury, and arsenic. Considerable evidence was adduced to show that these and other substances deposited at the site are extremely toxic to human beings. Some of the adverse reactions which could result from exposure to these materials are pulmonary diseases, cancer, brain damage, and birth defects.

The general geologic profile of the site shows a surface layer of about 10 feet of loess (wind-blown silt and clay material), under which lies 40 to 65 feet of glacial till. In the till material there is a thin sand layer of a few inches to approximately two feet. Some ground water has been found in the sand layer. All trenches dug at the site have between 10 to 15 feet of glacial till below them. The glacial till is reported to be very dense and is not very permeable. Thus liquids do not travel through it quickly....

Subsidence of the earth underneath the site is another contention raised by the plaintiffs to support their thesis that the site is unsafe and is therefore an enjoinable nuisance. Dr. Nolan Augenbaugh testified extensively at trial. Dr. Augenbaugh took pictures of the area from an airplane as well as at ground level. During his testimony, he pointed out where subsidence occurred in the pictures he had taken. Dr. Augenbaugh stated that he had observed subsidence in a wheat field on the Wilbur Sawyer farm on June 17, 1977. Dr. Augenbaugh also testified that a subsidence basin lies to the northeast of the disposal site. The pictures also indicate, according to Dr. Augenbaugh, fractures in the ground. One picture depicts a fault, which, Dr. Augenbaugh explained, is a "fracture where there's been differential movement of the two blocks. One block has been moved more than the other block." Sawyer, the farmer, told Dr. Augenbaugh the cracks had begun to appear approximately two months before, which would have been spring 1977. Several of these subsidences and fractures are located approximately one-half mile from the western boundary of the lower part of the disposal site. Dr. Augenbaugh testified that, in his opinion, subsidence can and will occur at the disposal site. Further, that ruptures in the earth would occur which, like an open pipe, would act as conduits for artesian water to reach the trenches, thereby contaminating the water.

Dr. Augenbaugh...testified that on March 22, 1978, he...had a trench dug across the subsidence cracks which he had observed earlier. When the digging was completed, there was a trench nine feet long and approximately three feet wide, with a maximum depth of a little over eight feet. Photographs were taken and slides prepared of the operation at the site. As the trench was being dug, water began to seep into the trench at a depth of approximately 4 feet. Dr. Augenbaugh testified that the water flowed from subsidence fractures which were below the surface of the ground. Dr. Augenbaugh then poured some green dye into a surface fracture which was located approximately 10 feet away from the trench. The green dye entered the trench through two openings within 25 minutes. Thomas O. Glover, a mining engineer and liaison officer with the United States Bureau of Mining, Department of the Interior, also testified regarding subsidence. Glover defined subsidence as the settling of the ground, due to the diminution of the underground support structure, and either the pillars pushing into the fine clay bottom below the coal system, or the roof fracturing immediately above the coal seam and continuing to the surface. He stated that subsidence normally can be expected to appear, on the average, 40 years after a mine has closed down. Glover never visited the instant disposal site, but he had examined the information relative to Superior Mine No. 4 and he had witnessed subsidences many times in the field over the course of 27 years as a mining engineer. Glover offered the opinion that there is a possibility of subsidence wherever coal is mined and underground support is removed.

Several of the defendant's expert witnesses, James Douglas Andrews, the designer of the site and a consulting engineer for the defendant, John A. Mathes, an engineer, Steven Hunt, a geologist with the Illinois State Geological Survey (ISGS), and Paul B. DuMontelle, an engineering geologist with ISGS and coordinator of environmental geology for the Survey, testified in summary that there would be subsidence at the site, but that it would not be deep, would close in a short time, and could be repaired by means of engineering techniques.

Another of plaintiffs' witnesses, Dr. Arthur Zahalsky, offered the opinion that an "explosive interaction," resulting in chemical explosions, fires, or emissions of poisonous gases, will occur at the site. Dr. Zahalsky is a professor of biochemistry and head of the laboratory of biochemical parasitology at Southern Illinois University at Edwardsville. He testified in essence that if sufficient oxygen could reach the buried chemicals, and he believed it could, then an explosive interaction of unknown date of occurrence, magnitude, and duration is likely. Moreover, Dr. Zahalsky testified that it is unknown what interactions might occur when the waste materials combine after the deterioration of the steel containers and paper bags.

The defendant challenged Dr. Zahalsky's opinion during cross-examination and requested him to diagram the precise chemical formula which would result in an explosive interaction. Dr. Zahalsky testified that a precise formula could not be diagrammed. He stated that the defendant's trench logs indicate that several of the chemical wastes have flash points less than 80 degrees Fahrenheit. Zahalsky reviewed the trench logs and gave examples of chemicals, such as paranitroaniline, which is a strong oxidizing agent and may be explosive, and also paint sludge, which has a flash point of less than 80 degrees Fahrenheit, which could result in a chemical fire. Dr. Zahalsky offered one scenario in which acidic chlorinated degreasers would interact with waste phenolics, releasing the phenolics so that the flash point would be achieved, thereby setting off the paint sludges which, in turn, would set off paint wastes, which would achieve the temperature sufficient for the ignition and combustion of liquid PCBs. All of these materials are deposited together in trench No. 3.

Finally, considerable testimony was adduced, much of it conflicting, as to dust, odors, and spills of chemical waste which have occurred in the village. Various residents testified that dust emanating from the site blew toward their houses. Also, odors which caused burning eyes, running noses, headaches, nausea, and shortness of breath were mentioned in testimony. The odors themselves were said to resemble, among other things, fertilizer, insecticide, and burning rubber. There was further testimony that the dust and odors interfered with the witnesses' ability to use their yards for gardening or other recreational uses. The defendant presented witnesses who denied that the disposal site was the source of any odors, and that the odors resulted from the local practices of openly burning refuse and dumping sewage into a nearby creek.

There was testimony that trucks carrying the waste materials to the disposal site via Wilson Avenue, the main street of the village, sometimes spilled toxic liquids onto the street. The evidence is undisputed, both from the defendant's receiving reports and testimony from IEPA inspectors, that many drums arrived on the site leaking waste materials....

The defendant has raised several issues on appeal: (1) whether the finding of the circuit and appellate courts that the waste-disposal site is a prospective nuisance is contrary to the manifest weight of the evidence; (2) whether those courts applied the wrong legal standard in finding that the waste-disposal site constitutes a prospective nuisance; (3) whether the circuit and appellate courts erred in failing to balance the equities, either in finding a prospective nuisance or in fashioning relief; (4) whether the courts erred in failing to defer to, or to otherwise weight, the role of the IEPA, the United States Environmental Protection Agency (USEPA), and the Illinois State Geological Survey (PCB); (5) whether the courts erred in finding that plaintiffs have no adequate remedy at law; (6) whether the courts erred in ordering a mandatory injunction; and, finally, (7) whether the courts' decisions constituted a taking of property without due process of law.

We conclude that the evidence in this case sufficiently establishes by a preponderance of the evidence that the chemical-waste-disposal site is a nuisance both presently and prospectively....

The defendant points out three areas where, it argues, the trial court made erroneous findings of fact. The defendant refers to: (1) Dr. Arthur Zahalsky's opinion testimony concerning an explosive interaction and Dr. Stephen Hall's testimony which concurred in that opinion; (2) evidence concerning soil permeability; and, (3) infiltration of water into the trenches, and of migration out of the defendant's trenches of chemical waste either through the "bathtub effect" or subsidence.

We have reviewed the extensive record compiled in this case. While it is true that the defendant vigorously challenged the evidence concerning an explosive interaction, permeability, and infiltration and migration due to subsidence, the defendant has not overcome the natural and logical conclusions which could be drawn from the evidence. Findings of fact made by the trial court will not be set aside unless they are contrary to the manifest weight of the evidence....

The defendant [to refute the conclusions of Drs. Zahalsky and Hall] particularly relies upon the opinion of Dr. Raymond D. Harbison, a professor of pharmacology at Vanderbilt University, a toxicologist and consultant to the USEPA on toxic-waste handling. Dr. Harbison offered the opinion that the instant site is the most advanced scientific landfill in this country, and that the inventory system and the "absolute confinement" of the materials to the site render the interaction of the chemicals an impossibility.

At bottom, Dr. Harbison's opinion is premised upon his belief that the materials at the site will be sufficiently confined so that they will not pose a threat to the health or lives of the residents of the village. Dr. Harbison's opinions were discounted by the trial court, however, due to the substantial evidence which shows that the soil is more permeable than originally thought; that there is migration of water out of the trenches; and that there is subsidence in the area. Moreover, Dr. Harbison's opinion must be further discounted due to his erroneous statement that the waste materials will be sufficiently confined since "there is no ground water to be contaminated anyway below the particular site." Dr. Harbison later amended that statement to say there was no "usable water supply below the site" in terms of volume. This statement is also erroneous and also ignores evidence that the ground water would flow from beneath the site, thereby transporting any contamination into Cahokia Creek and could eventually flow into the Mississippi River. Thus we will not overturn the trial court's findings on this issue. They are amply supported by the manifest weight of the evidence....

The defendant also contends that the trial court's finding that subsidence warrants closing of the site is erroneous. The defendant argues that, assuming arguendo that subsidence would occur at the site, it could be counteracted by engineering techniques. This issue becomes complicated by the fact that the IEPA adopted a regulation providing that Class I disposal sites (i.e., chemical-waste-disposal sites), must be secure without engineering. The USEPA, however, has recently adopted regulations to require all landfill sites to establish containment-engineering systems to detect and prevent migration of chemicals. Moreover, the General Assembly has, since the inception of this suit, passed a statute prohibiting the placement of a hazardous-waste-disposal site above a shaft or tunneled mine.... The instant disposal site is above an inactive tunneled mine lying partly within the corporate limits of the village of Wilsonville. Without an express statutory provision stating an act is to have retroactive effect, it can only be applied prospectively. Thus, the defendant cannot be thought to be in violation of the foregoing provision. The fact remains, however, that the instant site, which is intended to be permanent, is located above an inactive tunneled mine.

Moreover, Dr. Nolan Augenbaugh testified at great length, supported by many photographs, of the considerable subsidence which has already occurred near the site. In Dr. Augenbaugh's opinion, subsidence will occur at the site itself. The defendant's experts testified that any subsidence would be negligible and shallow and would not present a threat to health or life. Dr. Augenbaugh refuted this testimony. He stated that subsidence would permit chemical-waste materials to seep into the ground water. In addition, Dr. Augenbaugh testified that subsidence would create a "bathtub effect" by permitting water to get into the trenches, eventually rise to the surface, overflow, and contaminate the ground around the site. We think the circuit court was fully justified in giving more weight to Dr. Augenbaugh's well-documented opinion than to the opinions of defendant's experts. We will not disturb that finding.... [A long discussion about the nature of Illinois nuisance law follows.]

Moreover, the trial court did engage in a balancing process.... The Court understands as does counsel that there is a need for disposal of industrial hazardous wastes. However, where disposal of wastes creates a nuisance said disposal site may be closed through legal action. Whether or not a business is useful or necessary or whether or not it contributes to the welfare and/or prosperity of the community are elements to be considered in a serious manner but said elements are not determinative as to whether or not the operation is a nuisance. The importance of an industry to the wealth and prosperity of an area does not as a matter of law give to it rights superior to the primary or natural rights of citizens who live nearby. However, such matters may be considered and have been in this case....

The defendant's next contention is that the courts below were in error when they failed to require a showing of a substantial risk of certain and extreme future harm before enjoining operation of the defendant's site. We deem it necessary to explain that a prospective nuisance is a fit candidate for injunctive relief. Prosser states: "Both public and private nuisances require some substantial interference with the interest involved. Since nuisance is a common subject of equity jurisdiction, the damage against which an injunction is asked is often merely threatened or potential; but even in such cases, there must be at least a threat of a substantial invasion of the plaintiff's interests." (Prosser, Torts §87, at 577 (4th ed. 1971).) The defendant does not dispute this proposition; it does, however, argue that the trial court did not follow the proper standard for determining when a prospective nuisance may be enjoined. The defendant argues that the proper standard to be used is that an injunction is proper only if there is a "dangerous probability" that the threatened or potential injury will occur. (See Restatement (Second) of Torts §933(1), at 561, comment b (1979).) The defendant further argues that the appellate court looked only at the potential consequences of not enjoining the operation of the site as a nuisance and not at the likelihood of whether harm would occur....

In this case there can be no doubt but that it is highly probable that the chemical-waste-disposal site will bring about a substantial injury. Without again reviewing the extensive evidence adduced at trial, we think it is sufficiently clear that it is highly probable that the instant site will constitute a public nuisance if, through either an explosive interaction, migration, subsidence, or the "bathtub effect," the highly toxic chemical wastes deposited at the site escape and contaminate the air, water, or ground around the site. That such an event will occur was positively attested to by several expert witnesses. A court does not have to wait for it to happen before it can enjoin such a result. Additionally, the fact is that the condition of a nuisance is already present at the site due to the location of the site and the manner in which it has been operated. Thus, it is only the damage which is prospective. Under these circumstances, if a court can prevent any damage from occurring, it should do so....

The next issue we consider is whether the trial court erroneously granted a permanent injunction.... Defendant cites Harrison v. Indiana Auto Shredders Co., 528 F.2d 1107 (7th Cir. 1975), for the proposition that the court must balance the relative harm and benefit to the plaintiff and defendant before a court may enjoin a nuisance....

In *Harrison*, an auto shredder operated its business in a residential neighborhood in Indianapolis.... The court concluded in *Harrison* that since the defendant was not in violation of any relevant zoning standards, and since the shredder did not pose an imminent hazard to the public health, the defendant should not be prevented from continuing to operate. The court then ordered that the defendant be permitted a reasonable time to "launder its objectionable features."

This case is readily distinguishable for the reason that the gist of this case is that the defendant is engaged in an extremely hazardous undertaking at an unsuitable location, which seriously and imminently poses a threat to the public health. We are acutely aware that the service provided by the defendant is a valuable and necessary one. We also know that it is preferable to have chemical-waste-disposal sites than to have illegal dumping in rivers, streams, and deserted areas. But a site such as defendant's, if it is to do the job it is intended to do, must be located in a secure place, where it will pose no threat to health or life, now, or in the future. This site was intended to be a permanent disposal site for the deposit of extremely hazardous chemical-waste materials. Yet this site is located above an abandoned tunneled mine where subsidence is occurring several years ahead of when it was anticipated. Also, the permeability-coefficient samples taken by defendant's experts, though not conclusive alone, indicate that the soil is more permeable at the site than expected. Moreover, the spillage, odors, and dust caused by the presence of the disposal site indicate why it was inadvisable to locate the site so near the plaintiff village.

Therefore, we conclude that in fashioning relief in this case the trial court did balance relative hardship to be caused to the plaintiffs and defendant, and did fashion reasonable relief when it ordered the exhumation of all material from the site and the reclamation of the surrounding area. The instant site is akin to Mr. Justice Sutherland's observation that "Nuisance may be merely a right thing in a wrong place — like a pig in the parlor instead of the barnyard." Village of Euclid v. Ambler Realty Co., 272 U.S. 365, 388 (1926).

We are also cognizant of amicus USEPA's suggestion in its brief and affidavits filed with the appellate court which urge that we remand to the circuit court so that alternatives to closure of the site and exhumation of the waste materials may be considered. The USEPA states: "Heavy equipment may damage drums, releasing wastes and possibly causing gaseous emissions, fires, and explosions. Repackaging and transporting damaged drums also risks releasing wastes. Workers performing the exhumation face dangers from contact with or inhalation of wastes; these risks cannot be completely eliminated with protective clothing and breathing apparatus. Nearby residents may also be endangered." It is ironic that the host of horribles mentioned by the USEPA in support of keeping the site open includes some of the same hazards which the plaintiffs have raised as reasons in favor of closing the site....

Accordingly, for all the reasons stated, the judgments of the circuit and appellate courts are affirmed and the cause is remanded to the circuit court to enable it to retain jurisdiction to supervise the enforcement of its order. Affirmed and remanded.

RYAN, J., concurring: While I agree with both the result reached by the majority and the reasoning employed supporting the opinion, I wish to add a brief comment.... Any injunction is, by its very nature, the product of a court's balancing of competing interests, with a result equitably obtained. Prosser, in discussing the law of nuisance...states:" If the possibility [of harm] is merely uncertain or contingent [the plaintiff] may be left to his remedy after the nuisance has occurred." Prosser, Torts §90, at 603 (4th ed. 1971).

Prosser thus recognizes that there are cases in which the possibility of inflicting harm is slight and where the plaintiff may be left to his remedy at law. However, I believe that there are situations where the harm that is potential is so devastating that equity should afford relief even though the possibility of the harmful result occurring is uncertain or contingent. The Restatement's position applicable to preventative injunctive relief in general is that "the more serious the impending harm, the less justification there is for taking the chances that are involved in pronouncing the harm too remote." Restatement (2d) of Torts §933, at 561, comment b (1979). If the harm that may result is severe, a lesser possibility of it occurring should be required to support injunctive relief. Conversely, if the potential harm is less severe, a greater possibility that it will happen should be required. Also, in the balancing of competing interests, a court may find a situation where the potential harm is such that a plaintiff will be left to his remedy at law if the possibility of it occurring is slight. This balancing test allows the court to consider a wider range of factors and avoids the anomalous result possible under a more restrictive alternative where a person engaged in an ultrahazardous activity with potentially catastrophic results would be allowed to continue until he has driven an entire community to the brink of certain disaster. A court of equity need not wait so long to provide relief.

Although the "dangerous probability" test has certainly been met in this case, I would be willing to enjoin the activity on a showing of probability of occurrence substantially less than that which the facts presented to this court reveal, due to the extremely hazardous nature of the chemicals being dumped and the potentially catastrophic results.

COMMENTARY AND QUESTIONS

1. *Wilsonville* **and outrage.** At the start, the citizens and officials of Wilsonville had apparently been told that no hazardous wastes would be disposed of in their village, and the landfill was going to be a park. The citizenry was so outraged by the discovery that the wastes were toxic that, before the case came to trial, armed vigilante groups had blockaded the main streets of the village against waste transport vehicles. The Illinois courts assuaged this citizen outrage by ordering the site closed, thoroughly cleaned up (with wastes and contaminated soil to be removed and shipped elsewhere), and restored. Was this an optimum result from a public policy standpoint? Should the courts have given more credence to USEPA's suggestion that exhumation and removal would pose a greater risk of explosion, among other things, than "containing" the site (e.g., laying a cement cap over the site to prevent further infiltration, building an underground slurry wall around the site, and installing leachate monitoring systems and "pump and treat" technology in case leaching of toxics into the groundwater did occur)? Should the courts have considered the comparative economic costs of both alternatives? In fact, it took one year and cost five million dollars—in 1981 dollars—to perform the court-ordered remediation. What about the risks of transporting the wastes offsite and depositing them in another landfill that might pose even greater risks than the Wilsonville site? The Resource Conservation and Recovery Act (RCRA), a federal law requiring that hazardous waste landfills be upgraded in order to protect the environment, had been enacted in 1976, but had not yet been fully implemented with regard to existing sites.[23] To what extent are common law courts capable of determining the overall public interest in the context of lawsuits between specific litigants? The Illinois Supreme court in *Wilsonville* accepts the challenge. Compare to this case the approach of the New York Court of Appeals in Boomer v. Atlantic Cement, a classic case in the next chapter.

2. **Administrative agencies as risk managers.** Presumably, expert administrators should be better risk managers than outraged litigants or inexpert judges and juries. What, then, explains the lackluster performance of the state and federal agencies in the *Wilsonville* case? In the space of just a few years IEPA granted 185 permits to the SCA facility, and USEPA, although it was aware of the problems at the site, did not intervene or otherwise oversee IEPA action, despite possessing clear legal authority to do so. What explains the willingness of those public agencies to support, through the grant of so many permits and other favorable actions, a project that they later came to view as fundamentally flawed, sufficiently so that the State of Illinois filed suit against SCA on their behalf?

3. **Private parties as risk promoters.** The underlying idea and impetus to site the toxic disposal facility in Wilsonville came from SCA Services. In an earlier, less regulation-bound era, SCA's private decision regarding the facility might have been dispositive, in the sense that no governmental pre-approval would have been needed. What factors motivated SCA's decision to select the Wilsonville site as a repository for wastes generated primarily in the nearby St. Louis metropolitan

---

23. RCRA is considered more fully in Chapter 17.

area? Most obvious are economic factors, such as low rural land costs, and acceptable transportation costs based on reasonable proximity. Are those factors the same ones that ought to be considered by the IEPA and USEPA (or the courts) in their roles as risk managers?

4. **Risk, scientific uncertainty, and expert testimony.** Professor Yaffee has indicated (see above) that pervasive scientific uncertainty is a prominent feature of environmental disputes. Scientific uncertainty makes the assessment and management of risk exceptionally difficult. Common law courts resolve questions of fact, in areas where scientific data is absent or inconclusive, by considering testimony presented by experts retained by the parties in light of appropriate burdens of proof. In the *Wilsonville* case, why were plaintiffs' experts believed rather than defendants' experts? Whose witnesses were better prepared to testify regarding the actual possibilities of release of materials from the Wilsonville site? In the ordinary case where individual citizens sue a large corporate defendant, whom would you expect to present the better qualified and prepared expert witnesses? Did the joinder of the Illinois Attorney General on the plaintiffs' side in this case alter the usual imbalance of resources? The standards of admissibility for testimony by expert witness is, quite evidently, a vital concern in environmental litigation that involves complex scientific issues. That topic is addressed in Chapter Four.

5. *Wilsonville* **as environmental injustice.** Apart from the previously identified economic motivation facing SCA Services, are there other factors that might have influenced a decision to site a hazardous waste landfill at this geologically dubious location: is this a case of environmental injustice? Wilsonville, a poor rural community whose residents included many unemployed ex-miners, had little political leverage compared to that of defendant, its clients (some of whom were highly capitalized hazardous waste generators), and state and federal agencies. The wonder is that the state's Attorney General was persuaded to change sides, and support the town's call for abatement. Most environmental justice cases do not end like this one. Would a state hazardous waste disposal facility siting statute have prevented this flawed siting decision? (See Chapter 25.)

## Section 2. ENVIRONMENTAL RISK AND PUBLIC RISK

In a classic early article on environmental risk management, Talbot Page recommended that the legal system manage risks caused by pollution and resource depletion based on where a particular risk falls on a continuum between what he terms "Classical Pollution" and "Environmental Risk." The former presents the more humdrum problem of dealing with relatively well understood and innocuous effluent streams and their effects on the environment. The latter is more complex. Page defines "Environmental Risk" in terms of nine characteristics, four dealing with the uncertainties surrounding environmental decisionmaking, and five bearing on institutional problems encountered in environmental management. Environmental problems differ as to how intensely they exhibit these characteristics. The first four characteristics of "Environmental Risk" are

(1) ignorance of mechanism (i.e., scientific uncertainty as to the generation and transmission of hazards, as well as their environmental impacts),

(2) relatively modest benefits,

(3) potentially catastrophic costs, and

(4) relatively low probability of occurrence of catastrophic outcomes.

Hazards manifesting these characteristics often present the "Zero-Infinity Dilemma"—a virtually zero probability of occurrence of a virtually infinite catastrophe. The remaining characteristics are

(5) internal benefits,

(6) external costs,

(7) collective risk,

(8) latency (e.g., carcinogenic effects may not manifest themselves until twenty or thirty years after exposure), and

(9) irreversibility of effects.

Page makes the following further observations:

### Talbot Page, A Generic View of Toxic Chemicals and Similar Risks
7 Ecology Law Quarterly 207 (1978)

...RELATIVE COSTS: FALSE NEGATIVES AND FALSE POSITIVES

By definition, the potential costs of environmental risks are great and the benefits are generally modest. Correspondingly, there is asymmetry in the costs of making wrong decisions. For classical pollutants, the asymmetry of potential costs and benefits, and hence the potential costs of wrong decisions, are likely to be less pronounced than for environmental risk problems.

The concept of false negatives and false positives helps to illustrate this distinction. In criminal law, two basic kinds of mistakes can occur: the jury (or judge) can find a guilty man innocent or an innocent man guilty. Testing chemicals for toxicity presents the same problem. Test results may indicate that a toxic chemical is not toxic or that a non-toxic chemical is toxic. The former type of error is called a false negative and the latter a false positive....

[In environmental risk situations] the cost of a false negative — deciding that the benign hypothesis is true when it is not — is much higher than the cost of a false positive — deciding that the catastrophic hypothesis is true when it is not.... Catastrophic results more than offset the modest benefits of erroneously accepting the benign hypothesis....

DIFFICULTIES IN THE MANAGEMENT OF ENVIRONMENTAL RISK...

1. ACCEPTABLE RISK... Even if the probability of an environmental risk were well defined, our legal, regulatory, and economic institutions must still decide what degree of risk is acceptable. Although there are several approaches for defining acceptable risk, there is little agreement on what is the best approach. This ambiguity presents a major difficulty in managing environmental risk. A few of the approaches are discussed below....

2. LIMITING FALSE POSITIVES [Limiting false positives], the most common approach for risks subject to governmental regulation and court proceedings, starts with the assumption that there is no risk and requires that a hazard be proved beyond some standard. Under this approach, by definition, if the standard of proof is not met, then the risk is acceptable. The burden of proof is placed on those seeking precautionary action.... However, the approach of limiting false positives, although often effective in defining acceptable risk for classical problems, has questionable value for the management of environmental risk....

3. LIMITING FALSE NEGATIVES Limiting false positives is the guiding principle of criminal law. The objective is to limit the chance of a false conviction. The common-sense justification for this objective is that it is better to free a hundred guilty men than to convict one innocent one....

A comparison of criminal law with environmental risk, however, suggests an important difference. The costs of false negatives and false positives are asymmetric for environmental risk as well, but the asymmetry is in reverse order. For environmental risk, the asymmetrically high cost arises from a false negative; in criminal law from a false positive. Similarly, just as a primary good, liberty, is an important concern in criminal law, so another primary good, health, is an important concern in environmental risk management, but again the roles are reversed. Typically, public health is adversely affected under a false negative for environmental risk, while liberty is adversely affected under a false positive for criminal law.

The analogy between criminal law and environmental risk requires that the roles of negatives and positives be reversed. If the emphasis on limiting false positives for criminal law is sensible and based on the asymmetry of costs of wrong decisions and the possible deprivation of a public good, then the implication is that a decision procedure based on limiting false negatives is more appropriate for environmental risk than one based on limiting false positives....

Focusing more attention on the need to limit false negatives brings us back to the importance of modeling the risks and hypotheses, including "credible" worst case modeling. It is clearly infeasible to take precautionary action for each conceivable environmental risk; there would be too many. Requiring some sort of model of the risk provides an entrance barrier against the flood of conceivable risks for which precautionary action should be evaluated. Because of the nature of environmental risk it is senseless to require proof of actual harm; the barrier should be no more than a reasonable basis within the context of the model for believing that there is a risk of harm. The risk itself may be small.

4. BALANCING FALSE POSITIVES AND FALSE NEGATIVES [Page then recommends a decision-making mechanism, which he calls "the expected value approach," that balances the cost of a false negative, weighted by its probability of occurrence, against the cost of a false positive, weighted by its probability of occurrence, and chooses the alternative with the lower weighted cost.[24] Page recognizes the importance and intransigence of "outrage" factors in risk management.]

The hard part is to uncover a social consensus on the appropriate amount of risk aversion and then to build this amount into the institutions which manage environmental risks.

The expected value approach does not require that each environmental risk be regulated, or not regulated, on the sole basis of a detailed and quantified cost-benefit analysis. For example, the internal transfer of benefits tends to be associated with a sharply focused group of proponents of the environmental risk taking, while the external transfer of the potential costs, both spatially and temporally, is associated with a broader but less focused group of opponents.[25] This imbalance in interests, for and against, is likely to lead to an imbalance in decision making, even for an ostensibly neutral cost-benefit analysis, unless the imbalance in interests is

24. Eds: Once the concepts of "minimizing false negatives" and "minimizing false positives" have been learned, it might be simpler to refer to them as the "proactive" and "reactive" approaches to risk management. The proactive approach is also linked to the "Precautionary Principle."
25. Eds.: This is one of the central tenets of "Public Choice Theory."

recognized and offset by the design of the decision making institutions. Alternatively, in order to come closer to a minimum expected cost of wrong decisions, it is necessary to adjust the rules of the decision process—the standards and burdens of proof, the rules of liability, the incentives for the generation and valuation of information, and so on. For instance, when the potential adverse effects of an environmental risk are many times greater than the potential benefits, a proper standard of proof of danger under the expected cost minimization criterion may be that there is only "at least a reasonable doubt" that the adverse effect will occur, rather than requiring a greater probability, such as "more likely than not," that the effect will occur.

COMMENTARY AND QUESTIONS

1. **Environmental risk and environmental justice.** Since Dr. Page wrote this article, environmental justice has emerged as a matter of concern. With that in mind, distributional inequality might qualify as a tenth characteristic of environmental risk. Environmental risks are imposed disproportionately on the least politically powerful members of our society — minorities, the poor, children, and the sick and disabled. The toxic effects of pesticides, for example, are most intensely experienced by farm workers. Most hazardous waste disposal facilities have been located in neighborhoods occupied by disadvantaged groups. Is that form of environmental injustice a form of racism?

2. **Species eradication as a catastrophic ecological cost.** The importance of biodiversity, both as a necessity for human survival and as an end in itself, is better understood today than it was even a generation ago. Managing environmental risks entails factoring ecological effects of human behavior into environmental decisionmaking. Extinction is the most profoundly irreversible phenomenon on this planet. How should risks of species extinction be managed? The Endangered Species Act is studied in Chapter 14.

3. **External cost transfers and political power.** Note how heavily Page, in his definition of environmental risk, relies on the theory of externalities. Internalization of economic benefits among a focused, knowledgeable, and politically powerful group of producers and consumers leads to concentrated political power that tends to outweigh the weaker political influence exercised by a diffuse, disorganized, unaware, and often politically powerless class of polluted public (which, in theory, includes future generations, which cannot directly participate in the political process). Furthermore, it is difficult to organize members of the general public to oppose the imposition of a collective risk because of the "transaction costs" (e.g., time and money) of participation and the "free rider problem" (i.e., the human tendency to believe that someone else will solve the problem). This political asymmetry is another reason for minimizing false negatives. It also explains the need for politically strong environmental groups to counterbalance the influence of powerful producer and consumer constituencies.

4. **Burdens of proof and liability rules in environmental risk management decision making.** Page clearly recognizes the importance of burdens of proof (burdens of going forward and burdens of ultimate persuasion) and liability rules in the legal

system's management of environmental risk. As cases studied in Chapter Four demonstrate, legal rules regarding burdens of proof and liability have been modified to some degree to accommodate legal claims made by victims of pollution. Of particular relevance to the management of environmental risk, courts are divided regarding the burden of proof in toxic exposure cases. Some courts require plaintiff to prove only that exposure to a toxic substance was a "substantial factor" causing her damage, whereas other courts adhere to a standard more nearly like the usual standard in civil cases that requires plaintiff to prove it is more likely than not that her injury would not have occurred "but for" the exposure.

5. *Wilsonville* **and the zero-infinity problem.** Was the *Wilsonville* case an example of the zero-infinity problem? That appears to be what Judge Ryan was discussing in his concurring opinion. Would Page agree with the court's decision in *Wilsonville*? The answer to this question must take into account the point in time to which it refers. Avoiding a false negative before SCA brought wastes to the site might justify an injunction. Once the waste is on-site, exhuming it and transporting it may exacerbate the very risks that militated in favor of an injunction at an earlier stage.

6. **Risk assessment and risk management.** Regulators typically have divided environmental risk analysis into "Risk Assessment" and "Risk Management" phases: risk assessment is seen as scientific, objective, and quantitative, whereas risk management considers the social, economic, and political factors involved in determining acceptable risk. The accuracy and utility of this distinction have been questioned by several commentators. In fact, because of the profound scientific uncertainties and measurement variabilities involved in determining environmental risk, assessors rely on conservative "default assumptions," combinations of science and policy that are sometimes referred to as "trans-science." For example, with regard to most carcinogenic substances, there is not certain knowledge that threshold dose levels exist (i.e., levels of exposure), below which an exposed individual would not contract cancer. Thus, to protect public health, cancer risk assessors assume that "one hit" of a carcinogenic substance can cause cancer. (Would Page agree with this approach?) For a useful review of the literature on risk assessment, as well as the methodology of cancer risk assessment, see Shere, The Myth of Meaningful Environmental Risk Assessment, 19 Harv. Env. L. Rev. 409 (1995). Commentators differ, however, about the importance of the trans-scientific elements of risk assessment. Contrast Shere ("the hard fact is that quantitative risk assessment generates numbers that are meaningless") with the Commission Report, noted above (risk assessments are useful for setting upper-bound estimates of risk and setting priorities for environmental regulation).

7. **The classic *Reserve Mining* case.** Reserve Mining v. EPA, 514 F.2d 492 (8th Cir. 1975) is a classic early risk-management case. Reserve was mining low-grade iron ore (taconite) in Minnesota and processing it into iron-rich pellets at facilities bordering on Lake Superior. The residues of this process were the discharge of taconite tailings into Lake Superior, and the emission of taconite particles into the air near several Minnesota towns. (It was proven at the trial that taconite is structurally identical to amosite asbestos.) In light of seemingly dramatic risks to public health,

but also of the profound uncertainties in the epidemiological and toxicological evidence regarding the toxicity of taconite, the court ordered Reserve to cease its water discharge "within a reasonable time," and to "promptly...use such available technology as will reduce the asbestos fiber count in the ambient air...below a medically significant level." Asbestos, however, is a zero-tolerance carcinogen — one exposure can trigger mortal disease — so the court's risk standard is ambiguous. Reserve moved to land disposal of tailings in 1980, and closed down several years later, not because of burdensome pollution control requirements but because of the general decline of the U.S. steel industry in the face of foreign competition.

Reserve is also a classic case of corporate intransigence on pollution control. For ten years, Reserve was able to frustrate federal, state, and citizen efforts to abate its dischargers. An entire legal process course could be taught out of the *Reserve Mining* case, which involved federal and state statutory and common law; federal, state, and private plaintiffs against corporate defendants and their labor and municipal supporters; carcinogenic pollutants and the esthetics of a pristine Great Lake; air and water pollution; convoluted industrial economics and much chemistry and technological debate.[26]

8. **Is Page overreacting to "public risk"?** In the terms of the following essay, does Page exhibit a systematic bias against "public risk"?

### Peter Huber, Safety and the Second Best: The Hazards of Public Risk Management in the Courts
85 Columbia Law Review 277, 277–81, 301–07, 329–37 (1985).

The devastating chemical plant tragedy in Bhopal, India will do little to reassure skeptics about the advantages of technological innovation and development. Those who already view the chemical, nuclear, pharmaceutical, and other high-tech industries with profound suspicion and fear can now point to the 2200 dead of Bhopal as martyrs to unbridled technological tyranny. And Bhopal will henceforth serve as the shrine of Nemesis for those who would defend the value of high technology.

But Bhopal is only one painfully vivid example in a much larger, longstanding legal debate in this country. The debate reflects a deep division among legal commentators regarding the role of mass production and technological change in the

---

26. Reserve Mining required nine trips to the federal district court (one hearing lasting nine months), two to the state courts, four to the Eighth Circuit, one to the Supreme Court in an unsuccessful petition to revoke a stay; injunctions, stays, modified injunctions, mandamus orders (also stayed, and reinstated); an elaborate permit and standard-setting administrative system; counterclaims by industry for tort damages owing to "negligently-issued permits"; a federal statute which, after 60 years of dormancy, suddenly imposed new prohibitions through a twist of statutory interpretation; plus an appellate order forcing the district judge to recuse himself for bias formed in the course of trial. See Reserve Mining Co. v. Minnesota Pollution Control Agency, 434 F. Supp. 1191 (D. Minn. 1976); United States v. Reserve Mining Co., 417 F. Supp. 791 (D. Minn. 1976); 417 F. Supp. 789 (D. Minn.), aff'd, 543 F.2d 1210 (8th Cir. 1976); 412 F. Supp. 705 (D. Minn. 1976); 408 F. Supp. 1212 (D. Minn. 1976); 394 F. Supp. 233 (D. Minn. 1974), modified sub nom. Reserve Mining Co. v. EPA, 514 F.2d 492 (8th Cir. 1975), modified en banc sub nom. Reserve Mining Co. v. Lord, 529 F.2d 181 (8th Cir. 1976) (recusal order); 380 F. Supp. 11 (D. Minn.), stayed, 498 F.2d 1073 (8th Cir.), motion to vacate stay denied, 418 U.S. 911, motion to vacate or modify stay denied, 419 U.S. 802 (1974) (Douglas, J., dissenting). See also Reserve Mining Co. v. Herbst, 256 N.W.2d 808 (Minn. 1977); Reserve Mining Co. v. Minnesota Pollution Control Agency, 294 Minn. 300, 200 N.W.2d 142 (1972); see N.Y. Times, Apr. 25, 1982, at 31, col.1; Bartlett, The Reserve Mining Controversy (1980); and Farber, Risk Regulation in Perspective: *Reserve Mining* Revisited, 21 Envtl L. 1321 (1991).

improvement of social welfare. Long before Bhopal, the standard diagnosis in many judicial opinions and in much of our scholarly legal literature has been that our society produces too much "public" risk, through its excessive or unwise use of dangerous new technology and the tools of mass production. The standard prescription has been for lawyers to do something about it. This article argues that the diagnosis is probably wrong, and that the prescription should certainly be rejected.

The legal debate about risks is very much a debate about "public" risks. These are threats to human health or safety that are centrally or mass-produced, broadly distributed, and largely outside the individual risk bearer's direct understanding and control. Public risks usually derive from new or especially complex technology — they are the hazards of large-scale electric power plants, air transport in jumbo jets, mass-produced vaccines, chemical additives and contaminants in food, or recombinant-DNA technology. For many lawyers, "advancements" such as these arouse deep suspicion and concern. "Private risks," by contrast, are discretely produced, localized, personally controlled, or of natural origin. They are the risks of cottage industries, wood stoves, transportation by car, or exposure to natural toxins or pathogens. Typically, private risks arouse little anxiety among legal commentators.

The legal system's almost obsessive preoccupation with public risks is, in my view, entirely misguided.[27] I wish to develop this argument soberly; there can be no technological arrogance in the shadow of Bhopal. But the facts and the regulatory arguments seem plain nonetheless. First, public risks are progressive — they improve the overall state of our risk environment — whenever the incremental risk created is smaller than the quantum of existing privately-created risk that is displaced. The point may seem obvious, but the fact that a large number of judges and legal commentators ignore it suggests otherwise.

Second, the judicial system is, for a variety of reasons, incapable of engaging in the aggregative calculus of risk created and risk averted that progressive public-risk management requires. While it is not my goal to replace an absolutist's aversion to public risk with an absolutist's embrace of it, I will argue that the judicial role sought (and achieved) by many commentators is imprudently biased against many progressive, risk-reducing (though still risky) technologies. This bias significantly hinders our progress towards a healthier, safer environment.

My arguments grow out of a single paradox of the risk economy: greater private safety is often to be found in the greater acceptance of public risk....

THE ATTACK ON THE WINDMILL... How much public risk is too much? And who shall decide how much is too much? Most of the legal debate revolves around these two questions. For many legal scholars and judges, the answer to the first question is almost self-evident: we currently bear more public risk than we should, because we have been too ready to accept the hazards of new or mass-production technology. Answers to the second question tend to be longer and more varied, but most have the same general thrust: lawyers and judges are well positioned to assess the problem and supply the additional deterrence that is so plainly needed. It is this pair of answers (both of which are, in my view, quite wrong) that this Part describes....

27. Eds. — Particularly at the outset, Huber is responding to the work of commentators who argued that public risk is being over-produced. Two articles in particular provoked Huber's attacks: Yellin, High Technology and the Courts: Nuclear Power and the Need for Institutional Reform, 94 Harv. L. Rev. 489 (1981) and Rosenberg, The Causal Connection in Mass Exposure Cases: A Public Law Vision of the Tort System, 97 Harv. L. Rev. 851 (1984).

EXCESS PUBLIC RISK... Life is already unacceptably hazardous, and likely to grow more so as the result of excessively rapid and overwhelming technological change. This is the common starting point in much of the legal commentary. How is the point to be proved? First, by referring to the public's aversion to public risks. Second, by reciting the myriad public terrors already in our midst. Third, by developing the microeconomic and philosophical underpinnings of a case against means of production that entail public hazards.

Lawyers opposed to public risks are in good company. The public consensus, if there is one, seems to be that risk-taking, like abortion, religion, travel, or marriage, should be a private affair. Indeed, consumer hostility to public risk is matched only by consumer affection for private risk. Illustrations of this division of preferences abound. The aerial spraying of malathion in a California program to combat the Mediterranean fruit fly provokes passionate opposition, but consumers eagerly spray tens of thousands of gallons of the same pesticide in their own, private gardens. A proposal to vent small amounts of radioactive gas and water from the damaged nuclear reactor at Three Mile Island in the course of cleaning up that facility — a comparatively minuscule investment in public risk with clear risk-reducing benefits — causes panic. But a proposal to ban saccharin — a proposal to curtail, as these things go, a fairly substantial investment in comparatively "private" patterns of risk taking — precipitates what was described in the New York Times as panic buying of the sweetener. Mass aircraft accidents arouse great concern, and the mandatory use of seat belts in planes is accepted without a murmur. But in the much more hazardous private-risk environment of automobile travel, seat belt interlock systems or mandatory seat belt laws encounter vociferous consumer opposition. Mandatory vaccination programs are vigorously attacked in the courts, but individuals also come to court to insist on their right to be treated with medical quackery of every description, apricot pits providing a recent and much-publicized example.

Panic, protest, and organized resistance thus greet almost every venture that entails new public risk. Meanwhile, efforts to restrain private risk-taking are denounced as grave attacks on personal freedom. Some litigants have seriously maintained — and some courts have agreed — that the Constitution itself enshrines both the right to bear a private risk and the right not to be exposed to a public one. In short, shared risks, like shared goods, are thought to be almost un-American — a collectivist affront to individual autonomy and self-reliance.

The layperson's aversion to public risks is shared by much of the legal community. Lawyers, for the most part, are convinced that there is too much public risk out there, and they generally begin their indictment of public risks by citing some that they especially dislike. Professor Yellin, for example, uses as his paradigm case the hazards of generating nuclear power, but he also points to chemical pesticides, air and water pollution, occupational hazards, and "complex environmental decisions" of every description — the "ominous, not yet fully understood risks to public health [that] involve decisions that may seriously alter our physical environment." Professor Rosenberg's concern centers on similar targets: the risks accompanying "the production, distribution, marketing, consumption, and disposal of toxic agents." He lists as examples "asbestos, Agent Orange and Agent White, Three-Mile Island, dioxin, and a string of acronyms — DES, PCB, PBB and IUD," drugs, and aircraft disasters. Numerous other commentators have similar lists of concerns, and all supply citations to cases in which judges and juries have echoed these fears.

It is easy enough to clothe a visceral aversion to public risk in the robes of market efficiency or social justice. So easy, in fact, that the exercise has become quite reflexive and mechanical in much of the legal literature.

To the lawyer qua economist, risk is a cost — the cost of confining, disposing of, or simply coexisting with hazardous matter or energy. The cost can, of course, vary enormously, depending on how wisely a particular hazard is managed. It is nevertheless ascertainable. As with all other costs, the lawyer-economist will contend, the creator of a risk must shoulder it if markets are to operate "efficiently." A producer of risk who is not held strictly accountable for the unconsented-to consequences of that risk will generate risk in socially undesirable amounts. The result will be a market failure. Or so the story goes.

The lawyer qua philosopher may reach similar conclusions about public risks on somewhat different grounds. Our libertarian, individualistic, political ideal forbids one person from imposing unconsented-to burdens on another. Burdens that take the form of external threats to health or safety are especially objectionable intrusions on the risk bearer's private space and personal autonomy. Like the lawyer-economist, the lawyer-philosopher is therefore opposed to external risk. The mass producer of a dangerous good, or the operator of a hazardous power plant, acts antisocially. Her conduct is worse than economically inefficient — it is morally wrong. Or so the story goes.

Arguments along these lines are wheeled out, with pedestrian regularity, by those opposed to everything from nuclear power to synthetic sweeteners. Absent the risk bearer's individual, fully informed, and entirely free consent, any activity that creates public risk is, pro tanto, both a threat to market efficiency and an infringement on the just entitlements of the risk bearer. Public risks are an absolute bad. We want as few of them as possible.

THE JUDICIAL ROLE... Though there is somewhat less unanimity about precisely why it is that a nation with a large and powerful government, fifty autonomous state governments, and 650,000 lawyers, has apparently allowed public-risk technology to run so wild, the consensus is that the existing, agency-centered system of risk regulation inadequately deters the production of public risk. Help from the legal community is therefore in order. It may come before the accident, or after it, but in either event its thrust should be to discourage new dangerous technologies and the instrumentalities of mass-produced risks. Professor Yellin's and Professor Rosenberg's proposals typify the two larger schools of thought.

Professor Yellin urges the courts to improve pre-accident decision-making. He advocates closer judicial scrutiny of "broad new regulatory departures." When an agency approves a novel technological venture that entails new public risk, the courts, suitably advised by "a committee of scientists, engineers, and lawyers to act as standing masters," should supply a "second" (read "final") opinion.

Professor Rosenberg, for his part, suggests a greater degree of judicial intervention after the public risk has been approved and is in place. The courts, again advised by "court-appointed experts, special masters, and blue-ribbon juries," should impose tort liability on public risk creators sooner, more often, and in larger amount. To this end, the cost of risk itself, rather than consummated injury, is to be made compensable — when, and only when, it is a "public" or "mass exposure" risk. Questions of legal causation are to be resolved under a relaxed "proportionality" rule, that will hold risk creators liable for the proportion of total injuries attributable to their activities, even when no single plaintiff can accurately claim that her injury was, more likely than not, caused by the defendant's conduct.

The Yellin and Rosenberg prescriptions are complementary in their intended effect on activities that create public risks. More before-the-accident review and stricter after-the-accident liability are mutually reinforcing responses to the same perceived problem — the excess creation of public risks. At first blush, it is hard to think of any reason not to applaud. Indeed, many do, by citation to or by development of Yellin's and Rosenberg's proposals.

[Major portions of the article are omitted here, including a segment in which Huber presents a case study of how vaccine development and use has been greatly over-deterred by the cost of paying damage awards to injured victims of the vaccine. Also omitted is a segment that argues against treating damage awards against public risk producers as desirable cost internalization. To internalize those costs, Huber argues, in the absence of imposing corresponding costs against natural risk producers, such as disease, leads to a distortion of risk consumption. He invokes the theory of second best in favor of non-internalization of public risks stating, "patchy, erratic risk internalization may impose greater costs on the safer substitutes within particular markets, and so may encourage a shift in consumption to the more hazardous." Huber claims that the morality of public risks also must be judged with reference to the private risks they retire, not merely on the basis of harms they may inflict. To prove that changes in lifestyle associated with public risk creating behaviors have made life safer in the aggregate, Huber invokes evidence of decreasing mortality and increases in life expectancy in the last several centuries. He then argues more narrowly that the degree of capitalization and expertise surrounding most public risk ventures are likely to make them more safe than the private risk counterparts that they displace.]

On close, objective examination one almost invariably discovers that public risk alternatives provide goods and services with less risk (per unit of good) than the private-supply substitutes. The reasons are not difficult to discover. Large, centralized, capital-intensive production facilities are easier to operate safely than their small, distributed, labor-intensive alternatives. The very characteristics of mass production and distribution that make public risks possible in the first place also make mass production inherently safer than the private-production alternative. The central– or mass-producers can and do deliver goods and services with much less attendant risk than distributed– or discrete-producers (including Nature) possibly could....

THE JUDICIAL ROLE IN MANAGING PUBLIC RISKS... The second large question in the public risk debate follows naturally from the first; who should decide how much public risk is enough? Since some measure of public risk is not only inevitable but desirable, some institution must be directed to define the measure and specify its ingredients....

Public control of public risks is therefore necessary, both to prevent the excess generation of public risk and to make possible the acceptance of as much public risk as is socially desirable. The government regulator, a single, central decision-maker, acts as the consumers' collective "broker" in a particular risk market. The regulator — whoever it may be — must perform at least two tasks. One, of course, is to reject unfavorable investments in public risk. The regulator has the resources to proceed against creators of unacceptable public risks. Here we have the more familiar regulator, government, saying "no," placing limits on the risks individuals may create.

But the regulator's second function is to acquiesce in risk creation. To represent his principal effectively, a broker in a risk market, like a broker in any other setting, must be able to buy as well as to sell. A centralized risk-regulatory system must not only reject bad public risk choices but also supply the public's consent to good ones. This is most clearly illustrated in comprehensively regulated industries such as those producing electric power, drugs, pesticides, and many other products of modern technology. In these areas, risk creators start with no freedom to do anything at all until they receive express regulatory permission. The nay-saying regulatory role then effectively disappears; the regulator's task is to serve as a retail deregulator, giving case-by-case consent to new ventures that entail public risks.

The administrative agencies are, of course, the more familiar regulators, wielding authority over public risks of every variety. But the courts are also vigorous regulators, and it is their role that most concerns me here. The courts are pivotal actors in the prospective approval of new technological ventures. They possess considerable authority to review agency approvals of new sources of risk, whether the risk involves a new vaccine, power plant, pesticide, or food additive. And in areas not subject to comprehensive administrative regulation the courts can use injunctions to act as first-tier gatekeepers of the risk environment. The courts are also heavily engaged in the retrospective regulation of public risks. Damage actions sounding in nuisance, negligence, strict liability, and absolute liability are powerful instruments of regulation. Indeed, the legal community invented the "emission fee" for dealing with hazards such as pollution long before the economists had much to say about it. Every risk creator and every risk bearer knows that the damage action, and most particularly an action seeking punitive damages, is potent medicine for regulating public risks.... [Huber's specific attacks on the judicial system as regulator are omitted.]

PRIVATE INJURY AND PUBLIC SAFETY: THE COURTS AND THE AGENCIES... My discussion in the previous Part brings me to two conclusions. First, governmental control of public risks is both necessary and useful. Many public risks should be excluded if they are not yet a part of our environment, or controlled if they already are. Government regulation, moreover, is also needed to fulfill the second half of the regulatory function — to supply our collective consent to public risks that are judged to be good risk investments. Second, the courts are institutionally predisposed to favor regressive public risk choices. The courts systematically prefer old risks to new ones and discretely produced or natural hazards to mass-produced substitutes, and have neither the inclination nor the expertise to distinguish sources of truly "excess" risk from their risky yet risk-reducing counterparts.

Who then should decide how much public risk we will accept and in what areas? The answer is painfully obvious to almost everyone outside the legal community: expert administrative agencies, not lawyers. To make life safer, faster, we need not more scientists in the legal process, but fewer lawyers in the scientific one. The legal system has no special competence to assess and compare public risks, and the legal process is not designed or equipped to conduct the broad-ranging, aggregative inquiries on which sensible public-risk choices are built. Expert administrative agencies, troubled and erratic though they may be, remain best able to regulate public risks in a manner calculated to advance the public health and welfare....

COMMENTARY AND QUESTIONS

1. **The benefits of public risk.** Huber is surely correct that credit should be given in the evaluation of public risks for the risks, private or public, that they displace. This is simply good accounting, just like the good accounting that the environmental perspective demands when ecosystem benefits are advanced in support of some regulatory activity, such as wetlands preservation. Does this mean that Page is wrong when he argues that environmental risk situations display the potential for catastrophic costs weighed against relatively modest benefits? Page uses nuclear power generation as a prototypical example of an environmental risk, with regard to which we should minimize false negatives. How might Huber champion nuclear power in preference to fossil fuel generation of electricity? Nuclear power reduces the risk of ecosystem harms due to the emission of sulfur oxides from coal-fired power plants, a major cause of acid precipitation. Likewise, nuclear energy reduces the risk of massive ecological harms that would accompany the global warming threatened by the production of greenhouse gases. Are courts in a position to measure the trade-offs? Huber, in his mocking comparison of wood stoves to nuclear power plants, conveniently omits elaborate discussion about the back end of the nuclear fuel cycle, the extreme difficulties of nuclear waste disposal, but even putting all the factors on the table, is it certain that nuclear power generation is a bad choice? Is one subject that Huber should address (but doesn't) the problems of risk assessment in high uncertainty (sometimes zero-infinity) situations? How do you suppose that Huber would analyze a technology that provided many calculable benefits but also posed a slight chance of destroying a significant part of the world? Should Huber also take public outrage seriously? At present, the American public appears to be unalterably opposed to expanding reliance upon nuclear power, regardless of rational cost-benefit accounting. Would Huber agree with the decision in *Wilsonville*?

2. **The opportunity costs of proactive regulation.** A point that Huber did not make, but well could have, is that risk management, by minimizing false negatives, may also adversely affect public health:

> Current risk assessment practice is also one-sided in failing to consider the potential negative health effects that may follow from regulatory costs themselves. Economic studies suggest that regulatory costs may impair public health, a point that has been picked up by some judges. Under this view, every dollar that goes to regulatory costs is unavailable for things that tend to promote health, such as extra medical exams, better neighborhoods, safer cars, shorter work hours, or basic nutrition. Moreover, investigators report that mortality data show a correlation between health and wealth. They suggest from this data that each $3 million to $7 million spent on regulatory costs may lead to one additional premature death. Shere, The Myth of Meaningful Environmental Risk Assessment, 19 Harv. Env. L. Rev. 409, 472 (1995).

Is this an effective argument? Are these costs commensurable?

3. **Breaking the Vicious Circle and other risk reformers.** Huber argued that (1) courts over-deter investment in public risk, and (2) reliance on administrative agencies is more likely to achieve acceptance of the optimal amount of public risk. Justice Stephen Breyer, in a book published shortly before his appointment to the

United States Supreme Court — Breaking the Vicious Circle: Toward Effective Risk Regulation (1993) — makes similar arguments and recommends the creation of a centralized federal administrative group that would develop, coordinate, and supervise federal risk regulation through a decisional structure similar to an agency of experts on a military command model.

Justice Breyer noted that there was no "detailed federal government list that prioritizes health or safety risk problems so as to create a rational, overall agenda." He decried the "tunnel vision" occurring when an agency "effectively carries single-minded pursuit of a single goal too far," thereby doing more harm than good. He pointed to the EPA ban on asbestos pipe featured in the *Corrosion Proof Fittings* case, 947 F.2d. 1201, or Chapter Twelve, pg. 595, which allegedly imposed extra costs of $200–300 million in order to save seven or eight lives over 13 years, while in the same period twice as many deaths could be expected from ingested toothpicks! Breyer proposed the development of a system by which regulatory resources could be shifted from areas of minimal risk to fields in which they "could buy the largest amount of safety per dollar."

Such calls for risk-based regulation have been echoed in radio talk shows, the 104th Congress, and a popular collection of anecdotes castigating government regulations as intemperate and disproportionate, like Philip Howard's The Death of Common Sense: How Law Is Suffocating America (1994),[28] calling, like Justice Breyer's book, for a body of statistical risk experts to reform regulatory practice. Analyzing this debate, two scholars recently wrote:

> The "cures" proposed by the ["Contract with America"] Congress...and by Breyer and Howard... —both of them "tyrannies of the rational" —are themselves risky and may very likely be worse than the "disease." Although it may not seem terribly exciting, the best solution may be for the public to demand more rational regulation through existing channels. The give-and-take among the branches of government and with the public may be a necessary, even desirable, characteristic of risk regulation. Democracy and cost-effective, rational regulation are not incompatible....
>
> Pending legislative proposals quite obviously would exacerbate the less desirable aspects of the current system rather than ameliorate them. In context, it is difficult to characterize the use of risk assessment in the legislative vehicles currently proposed as anything other than an abuse of that methodology, designed not to promote regulatory reform but to impede desirable or necessary regulatory activity. David A. Wirth and Ellen K. Silbergeld, Risky Reform, 95 Colum. L. Rev. 1857, 1895 (1995).

Professor Hornstein, after canvassing the virtues of comparative risk analysis, provided an array of arguments against uncritical reliance on comparative risk analysis as anything more than a useful datum in setting environmental protection priorities and policies. See Donald Hornstein, Reclaiming Environmental Law: A

---

28. More measured analyses are reflected in National Research Council, Science and Judgment in Risk Assessment (1994) and Adam M. Finkel and Dominic Golding, eds., Worst Things First? The Debate Over Risk-Based National Environmental Priorities (1994). Cf. Silbergeld, The Risks of Comparing Risks, 3 N.Y.U. Envtl. L. J. 405, 406 (1994) (arguing that comparative risk assessment proposals will not promote efficient government because of difficulty of meeting methodological and data requirements); and Victor Flatt, Should the Circle Be Unbroken?: A Review of The Hon. Stephen Breyer's Breaking The Vicious Circle, 24 Envtl. L. 1707 (1994).

Normative Critique of Comparative Risk Analysis, 92 Colum. L. Rev. 562 (1992). The article, marshaling arguments developed in social sciences literature, asserted that (like "efficiency") the comparative risk analysis process is sufficiently problematic that it should not be adopted uncritically as a normative touchstone.

4. **Attacking Huber's assessment of institutional competence.** Professors Clayton Gillette and James Krier, in their article entitled Risk, Courts, and Agencies, 138 U. Pa. L. Rev. 1027 (1990), directly attack Huber's arguments. They propose a method for deciding whether courts are being too generous or too stingy toward plaintiffs who challenge activities involving public risks. There are two lines of inquiry, one into process bias and one into access bias:

> Process bias arises from the interplay of legal doctrine and adjudicative decision-makers. It concerns the ways in which judges and juries interpret and apply the law that defines the rights and liabilities of the parties before them. Access bias, on the other hand, arises from the interplay of legal doctrine, the structure of litigation, and the nature of public risk. It concerns the ways in which victims decide whether (given prevailing doctrine, among other things) litigation is worthwhile, and the ability of victims to initiate claims. Access is anterior to process; only when obstacles to access are overcome, so that claims are actually filed and prosecuted, can process bias come into play. 138 U. Pa. L. Rev. at 1045.

They then focus on the failings of professional risk assessment (i.e., hazard alone) to account for the multi-dimensional character of the layperson's perception of risk:

> Whatever its motivations, the experts' approach to risk is obviously not senseless. Yet neither is the public's approach. This is why...the problem comes down to one of competing rationalities. Admit this, and it unarguably follows that the choice of approach is an ethical and political one that technical experts have neither the knowledge nor the authority to dictate, because the issue transcends technocratic expertise. Were we to defer to agencies simply on the basis of their technical proficiency, the ethical-political question would be begged entirely. Agencies could be expected to resort to methods the use of which denies the very values at stake (it is, after all, the claim of methodological proficiency that grounds the argument for deference in the first place). And, to return to the idea with which we began this section, methodological proclivities would bias agency risk processing in the direction of too much public risk — as viewed from the public's perspective.

Gillette and Krier also conclude that access bias unduly restricts the number of public risk cases heard by the courts, and that access bias skews the administrative process in favor of over-acceptance of public risks.

5. **Administrative agencies and judicial review of their risk management decisions.** As explored in greater detail throughout this book, courts decide cases having risk management implications in many contexts. Such issues may arise in common law actions, such as *Wilsonville*, or in judicial review of agency decisions on matters that have risk management implications. In the latter context, courts tend to be deferential to agencies. In part this recognizes the presumed expertise of the agency and the fact that the legislature has given the agency its mandate to protect public health. Courts, in most settings, can only overturn agency decisions where they have been found to be "arbitrary and capricious." See Chapter 7. When the

scientific uncertainty and potential danger are both great, reviewing courts tend to show even greater deference, and accept administrative records that they would reject under other circumstances. In Ethyl Corp. v. EPA, 541 F.2d 1 (D.C.Cir. 1976), the court upheld EPA's regulations phasing out lead in gasoline where the scientific knowledge regarding the effects of lead on urban children was highly uncertain:

> From extensive and often conflicting evidence, the Secretary in this case made numerous factual determinations.... But some of the questions involved in the promulgation of these standards are on the frontiers of scientific knowledge, and consequently as to them insufficient data is presently available to make a fully informed factual determination. Decision making must in that circumstance depend to a greater extent upon policy judgments and less upon purely factual analysis.... We note that many of the issues in this case do not involve "historical" facts subject to the ordinary means of judicial resolution. Indeed, a number of the disputes involve conflicting theories and experimental results, about which it would be judicially presumptuous to offer conclusive findings. In such circumstances, the finder of fact must accept certain areas of uncertainty, and the findings themselves cannot extent further than attempting go assess or characterize the strengths and weaknesses of the opposing arguments....
>
> Where a statute is precautionary in nature, the evidence difficult to come by, uncertain, or conflicting because it is on the frontiers of scientific knowledge, the regulations designed to protect public health, and the decision that of an expert administrator, we will not demand rigorous step-by-step proof of cause and effect. Of course, we are not suggesting that the Administrator has the power to act on hunches or wild guesses. His conclusions must be rationally justified. However, we do hold that in such cases the Administrator may assess risks.... He may apply his expertise to draw conclusions from suspected, but not completely substantiated, relationships between facts, from trends among facts, from theoretical projections from imperfect data, from probative preliminary data not yet certifiable as "fact," and the like.... Operating within the prescribed [statutory] guidelines, he must consider all the information available to him. Some of the information will be factual, but much of it will be more speculative scientific estimates and "guesstimates" of probable harm, hypotheses based on still-developing data, etc. 541 F.2d, at 26–29.

Assuming that the *Ethyl* case view is typical, isn't that exactly the degree of deference that Huber is advocating? Is it possible that an agency could rely on "bad science," yet still be acting rationally as the *Ethyl* court would require? If so, is that a warrant for more intrusive judicial review? See, Sierra Club v. Marita, discussed in Chapter Four.

### Section 3. RISK RANKING AS RISK MANAGEMENT POLICY

The number and scope of environmental concerns have burgeoned in recent years, with the result that they cannot all be addressed simultaneously. As Page recognizes, even if there were agreement that all environmental problems are worthy of action, to take on all of the perceived problems at once would demand more resources, human and fiscal, than society is willing to commit to the task. Inevitably, priorities must be set that select some problems for more immediate attention while postponing action on others. Setting those priorities is a vital form of policy-making. Setting priorities in addressing environmental problems may not be as simple as it appears:

- Which problem is in greater need of remediation, indoor or outdoor air pollution?
- How would $1,000,000 be better spent, cleaning up contaminated ground-water in Wichita, Kansas, or removing lead-based paint from aging single family homes in Detroit, Michigan?
- Which is a more urgent problem, species eradication resulting from urban sprawl in Southern California, or reduction of air toxics emissions from smelters?

There does not seem to be a ready common denominator for making such policy decisions, but to some extent, relative risk reduction fills that void. At least when the risks involved relate to human health, it seems that setting priorities that maximize risk reduction offers a form of cross-medium comparison. The greatest amount of risk reduction means, in effect, that the aggregate environmental hazard has been reduced by the greatest amount. EPA, in response to demands for consistency and rationality in priority setting, began to embrace risk reduction as a priority-setting mechanism in the late 1980s. In 1987 it published Unfinished Business: A Comparative Assessment of Environmental Problems that attempted to make relative risk reduction a part of EPA's policy-making process. William Reilly, then EPA Administrator, wrote, "To the extent permitted by our statutory mandates, sound science can help us set priorities based on risk. Indeed, the rigorous analysis of risk is fundamental to all of EPA's regulatory programs. Without some way of determining relative levels of risk, we would quickly become mired in a regulatory swamp, wherein all problems were equally important; all risks would have to be addressed with equal urgency; and accordingly, nothing would get done."[29] A more substantial EPA document soon followed, a portion of which is excerpted below.

### EPA, Reducing Risk: Setting Priorities and Strategies for Environmental Protection
### Report of the Science Advisory Board:
### Relative Risk Reduction Strategies Committee (RRRSC)
Science Advisory Board A101, SAB-EC 90-021, September, 1990

RELATIVELY HIGH RISKS TO HUMAN HEALTH... On reviewing the rankings...the Human Health Subcommittee of the Relative Risk Reduction Strategies Committee (RRRSC) identified those problems that represented major types of human exposure known to be associated with significant impacts on human health. In four such instances, relatively high-risk rankings were supported more firmly by the available data than they were for other health problems. The Subcommittee also noted that the development of better methodologies and more complete data could lead to a different approach to the assessment of human health risks, and that such an approach would involve the selection of specific environmental toxicants that warranted detailed assessment and major risk reduction efforts.

• Ambient Air Pollutants
Stationary and more mobile sources emit a range of different air pollutants to which large populations are exposed. Some have toxic and/or carcinogenic effects

---

29. William Reilly, Taking Aim Toward 2000: Rethinking the Nation's Environmental Agenda, 21 Envtl. Law 1359, 1361 (1991).

following direct inhalation exposure (e.g., carbon monoxide and benzene). Others, such as lead and arsenic, reach humans by a variety of pathways including direct inhalation, inhalation of re-suspended dust, and ingestion of dust deposited on food products. Still others are important precursors that can lead to compounds such as ozone, acid aerosols, and carcinogenic hydrocarbons that form in the atmosphere over large areas of North America.

• Worker Exposure to Chemicals in Industry and Agriculture
Industrial and agricultural workers are exposed to many toxic substances in the workplace. Such exposures can cause cancer and a wide range of non-cancer health effects. Due to the large population of workers directly exposed to a range of highly toxic chemicals, this problem poses relatively high human health risks.

• Pollution Indoors
Building occupants may be exposed to radon and its decay products as well as to many airborne combustion products, including nitrogen dioxide and environmental tobacco smoke. Indoor exposures to toxic agents in consumer products (e.g., solvents, pesticides, formaldehyde) also can cause cancer and a range of non-cancer health effects. Due to the large population directly exposed to a number of agents, some of which are highly toxic, this problem poses relatively high human health risks.

• Pollutants in Drinking Water
Drinking water, as delivered at the tap, may contain agents such as lead, chloroform, and disease-causing microorganisms. Exposures to such pollutants in drinking water can cause cancer and a range of non-cancer health effects. This problem poses relatively high human health risks, because large populations are exposed directly to various agents, some of which are highly toxic.

Other problem areas also involve potentially significant exposure of large populations to toxic chemicals, e.g., pesticide residues on food and toxic chemicals in consumer products. However, the data bases to support those concerns are not as robust as they are for the four areas listed above.

RELATIVELY HIGH RISKS TO ENVIRONMENT... The RRRSC not only reviewed the risk rankings contained in [the 1987 EPA study], but it also identified several environmental problems as relatively high-risk, based on available scientific data and technical understanding. This effort was challenging for a number of reasons. Ecological, health, and welfare risks can be manifested in a number of different end points; it is difficult to compare risks with widely different time scales and spatial dimensions; because of data gaps and methodological inadequacies, it is rarely feasible to quantify total risk....

Consequently, the RRRSC...grouped environmental problems into high-, medium-, and low-risk areas...[cautioning] that their assessments are based on incomplete and often inadequate knowledge about (1) the extent of human and ecological exposures to pollutants and (2) exposure-response relationships....

The four environmental problems that it considered high-risk...were selected because the geographic scale of all four is very large (regional to global), and because the time that could be required to mitigate all four is very long, and some effects are irreversible.

RELATIVELY HIGH-RISK ENVIRONMENTAL PROBLEMS
    • Habitat Alteration and Destruction: Humans are altering and destroying

natural habitats in many places worldwide, e.g., by the draining and degradation of wetlands, soil erosion, and the deforestation of tropical and temperate rain forests.

• Species Extinction and Overall Loss of Biological Diversity
Many human activities are causing species extinction and depletion and the overall loss of biological diversity, including the genetic diversity of surviving species.

• Stratospheric Ozone Depletion
Because releases of chlorofluorocarbons and other ozone-depleting gases are thinning the earth's stratospheric ozone layer, more ultraviolet radiation is reaching the earth's surface, thus stressing many kinds of organisms.

• Global Climate Change
Emissions of carbon dioxide, methane, and other greenhouse gases are altering the chemistry of the atmosphere, threatening to change the global climate.

RELATIVELY MEDIUM-RISK PROBLEMS
  • Herbicides/Pesticides
  • Toxics, Nutrients, Biochemical Oxygen Demand, and Turbidity in Surface Waters
  • Acid Deposition
  • Airborne Toxics

RELATIVELY LOW-RISK PROBLEMS
  • Oil Spills
  • Groundwater Pollution
  • Radionuclides
  • Acid Runoff to Surface Waters
  • Thermal Pollution

THE TEN RECOMMENDATIONS:
  1. EPA should target its environmental protection efforts on the basis of opportunities for the greatest risk reduction. Since this country already has taken the most obvious actions to address the most obvious environmental problems, EPA needs to set priorities for future actions so the Agency takes advantage of the best opportunities for reducing the most serious remaining risks.
  2. EPA should attach as much importance to reducing ecological risk as it does to reducing human health risk. Because productive natural ecosystems are essential to human health and to sustainable, long-term economic growth, and because they are intrinsically valuable in their own right, EPA should be as concerned about protecting ecosystems as it is about protecting human health.
  3. EPA should improve the data and analytical methodologies that support the assessment, comparison, and reduction of different environmental risks. Although setting priorities for national environmental protection efforts always will involve subjective judgments and uncertainty, EPA should work continually to improve the scientific data and analytical methodologies that underpin those judgments and help reduce their uncertainty.
  4. EPA should reflect risk-based priorities in its strategic planning processes. The Agency's long-range plans should be driven not so much by past risk reduction efforts or by existing programmatic structures, but by ongoing assessments of remaining environmental risks, the explicit comparison of those risks, and the analysis of opportunities available for reducing risk.
  5. EPA should reflect risk-based priorities in its budget process. Although EPA's

budget priorities are determined to a large extent by the different environmental laws that the Agency implements, it should use whatever discretion it has to focus budget resources at those environmental problems that pose the most serious risks.

6. EPA — and the nation as a whole — should make greater use of all the tools available to reduce risk. Although the nation has had substantial success in reducing environmental risks through the use of government-mandated end-of-pipe controls, the extent and complexity of future risks will necessitate the use of a much broader array of tools, including market incentives and information.

7. EPA should emphasize pollution prevention as the preferred option for reducing risk. By encouraging actions that prevent pollution from being generated in the first place, EPA will help reduce the costs, intermedia transfers of pollution, and residual risks so often associated with end-of-pipe controls.

8. EPA should increase its efforts to integrate environmental considerations into broader aspects of public policy in as fundamental a manner as are economic concerns. Other Federal agencies often affect the quality of the environment, e.g., through the implementation of tax, energy, agricultural, and international policy, and EPA should work to ensure that environmental considerations are integrated, where appropriate, into the policy deliberations of such agencies.

9. EPA should work to improve public understanding of environmental risks and train a professional workforce to help reduce them. The improved environmental literacy of the general public, together with an expanded and better-trained technical workforce, will be essential to the nation's success at reducing environmental risks in the future.

10. EPA should develop improved analytical methods to value natural resources and to account for long-term environmental effects in its economic analyses. Because traditional methods of economic analysis tend to undervalue ecological resources and fail to treat adequately questions of intergenerational equity, EPA should develop and implement innovative approaches to economic analysis that will address these shortcomings.

## COMMENTARY & QUESTIONS

1. **EPA's steps toward risk analysis.** EPA's general approach to quantitative risk assessment got a blue-ribbon stamp of approval in early 1994, when the National Academy of Sciences' Committee on Risk Assessment of Hazardous Air Pollutants released a 600-page report that found EPA's approach to be sound. Despite this endorsement, the report went on to offer 70 recommendations for changes in EPA's risk assessment practices. The report, Science and Judgment in Risk Assessment, was mandated by §112(o) of the 1990 Clean Air Act Amendments. Overall, the report advocates use of a range of approaches for evaluating risks of hazardous air pollutants, as is mandated under the Clean Air Act. The most elaborate evaluative methods would be used for chemicals shown by relatively inexpensive techniques to possess the most significant health risks. Additional stress was urged for chemical risks that arise through multiple exposure pathways or exposures to multiple chemicals.

2. **EPA's two-track use of relative risk as a policy making tool.** How far does EPA seem willing to go in the direction of using relative risk as a unified policy-making

tool? When activities create commensurate risks, such as human health dangers, recommendation 1, 4, and 5 indicate that EPA wants to increase the role of relative risk in setting its priorities. Likewise, several of the recommendations apply to ecological risk issues somewhat apart from health risk. However, EPA seems unwilling to try to mesh "ecological risk" with "human health risk" in a single, all-encompassing calculus. Instead, EPA seems to have made a qualitative decision that ecological risks are also quite important, and then seeks to improve ecological risk assessment tools so that relative risk analysis can be used to set priorities among those risks. In this fashion, EPA seems to have avoided the problem of trying to compare ecosystem harms with human health harms.

3. **Competing proposals for setting environmental priorities.** Resources for the Future sponsored a national Worst Things First conference on potential uses of risk-based analysis in setting the federal regulatory agenda. Several competing paradigms emerged from that conference.[30] Barry Commoner, director of the Center for the Biology of Natural Systems at Queens College, offered a pollution prevention-based approach to setting priorities. He proposed that the general public should set U.S. environmental priorities, based on what it decides are the most important opportunities to transform industries from polluting to non-polluting. John Graham, professor of health policy at Harvard University, argued that pollution prevention and comparative risk assessment-based approaches are complementary. Robert Bullard, professor of sociology at University of California-Riverside, argued that environmental protection is not a privilege to be doled out but is a right for all individuals. He argued that a strictly risk-based priority system may perpetuate the failure to identify and remediate "hot spots" of environmental risk that exist in communities with significant minority populations. Instead, EPA's priority should be to clean up hazardous waste sites in communities where minorities and the poor face multiple risks from multiple sites, and to limit imposition of new risks in these areas. A third alternative, "directed innovation," which focuses on evaluating the causes of environmental problems, was urged by Nicholas Ashford, a professor of technology policy at MIT. He argued that strict regulation, properly designed, can trigger technological innovation, allowing for more risk reduction at equal or lower costs. This view was contested by James Wilson of Monsanto, who argued that individual companies do not always know when a particular innovation will succeed, and thus it's folly to believe that the federal government can reliably choose targets for directed innovation. Chapter Ten discusses this problem in the context of technology-forcing.

Many economists, including participants at the Worst Things First conference, apparently believe in the value of risk assessment and are developing ever more sophisticated tools to measure potential harms and uncertainties. Even so, their comments indicate that they do not advocate risk assessment as a mechanical process for setting public policy. "Risk assessment does not provide answers," said one conference participant. "It only helps define considerations that should be part of the public political debate."

---

30. Finkel and Golding, eds., Worst Things First? The Debate Over Risk-Based National Environmental Priorities (1994); see also K. Arrow, et al., Benefit-Cost Analysis in Environmental, Health, and Safety Regulation: A Statement of Principles 3 (1996).

*They were careless people...they smashed up things and creatures and then retreated back into their money or their vast carelessness...and let other people clean up the mess they had made....*

— F. Scott Fitzgerald, The Great Gatsby (1925)

*Environmentalists are like misers. They are hard to live with, but make great ancestors.*

— The India Times

# Chapter 3

# THE COMMON LAW IN MODERN ENVIRONMENTAL LAW: NON-STATUTORY CAUSES OF ACTION

A. *Private Nuisance, Intentional Tort, and the Classic Boomer Case*

B. *Defenses in Environmental Tort Suits*

C. *A Compendium of Tort Causes of Action and Special Issues They Raise*

D. *Remedies in Environmental Litigation*

F. *Environmental Uses of Other Non-Statutory Causes of Action*

---

This chapter begins with the classic case of Oscar Boomer and the Atlantic Cement Company. Many students have already encountered the case in a torts or property class, so some aspects of the *Boomer* legal analysis may already be familiar. In this coursebook, however, *Boomer* serves as a case study of private intentional nuisance torts, strategies, defenses, the wide range of available environmental remedies, and some new twists in environmental litigation. It can simultaneously be a vehicle for developing the ecological, economic, and political accounting that underlies every environmental case. The chapter proceeds from *Boomer* to a more general study of how torts and other nonstatutory causes of action have been adapted to fit environmental cases, leading to Chapter Four and some special lessons to be drawn from modern toxic chemical cases.

Each year many environmental cases involving localized pollution are filed under common law theories. These local cases undoubtedly make up the numerical majority of environmental cases generally. Even so, when an oil tanker disaster strikes the waters and shores of a coastal state, or a chemical factory's dump-site poisons land and groundwater, the major remedies litigated by injured parties are likewise based almost entirely on common law. After the wreck of the Exxon-Valdez, for example, the majority of legal claims filed by the State of Alaska and its citizens primarily relied on tort and public trust theories to respond to that vast catastrophe.[1] The common law is a fertile hunting ground for environmental lawyers trying to get a handle on some of the most modern ecological problems, and underscores the critical role played by private litigation in U.S. environmental law.

The common law also provides the conceptual underpinning for most statutes and regulations. Legislatures and agencies rely on the continued existence of

---

1. See below. The largest damage awards resulting from the oilspill were based on common law. Government claims were also filed under criminal and civil provisions of state and federal water laws, and the penalties paid to the governments combined both common law and statutory claims.

common law to fill gaps in public law and to guide courts and agencies in their interpretation of statutes and rules. Statutes may come and go, but the common law generally rolls on.

Many fundamental issues raised in environmental law, moreover, will continue to be raised first in the common law realm. Questions of proof, uncertainty, balances of risk, fault, and other liability issues, foreseeability, standards of care, technological feasibility, causation, long-term residual injuries, remedies, practical deterrence, enforceability, and so on — all these are found first in the common law. Despite the existence of innumerable federal and state environmental statutes, and reams of administrative regulations, the common law of environmental protections remains vigorous and important.

## A. PRIVATE NUISANCE, INTENTIONAL TORT, AND THE CLASSIC BOOMER CASE

### Section 1. Seeking A Remedy For A Typical Pollution Problem

The *Boomer* case was brought as a common law tort action, based on a complaint by the victims of air pollution against the factory whose emissions were causing an injury to plaintiffs' property. The case sounds in intentional private nuisance,[2] the doctrine which serves as the basis for suit in the majority of today's non-statutory environmental law cases.

Tort law in general, and nuisance in particular, offer an aggrieved plaintiff the possibility of monetary recoveries and a variety of injunctive remedies. With its roots in everyday tort law, private nuisance is a familiar claim to judges and lawyers alike. Just as in the typical negligence lawsuit for damages based on injuries suffered in an automobile accident, the plaintiff in a nuisance action must carry the burden of proving that she has suffered harm, that the defendant's conduct is the cause of that harm, and that defendant's conduct is of a type for which the law affords a remedy.

As you read through *Boomer*, picture the practicalities of litigating the case, and the environmental benefit-cost-alternatives analysis that might be applied to the controversy between Mr. Boomer and his industrial neighbor.

### Boomer et al. v. Atlantic Cement Company
New York Court of Appeals, 1970
26 N.Y.2d 219, 257 N.E.2d 870, 309 N.Y.S.2d 312

BERGAN, J. Defendant operates a large cement plant near Albany. These are actions for injunction and damages by neighboring land owners alleging injury to property

---

2. As later discussed in greater detail, there are two different nuisance theories, public and private, each of which can be litigated on three culpability bases: intentional conduct, negligence, or strict liability. Both theories of nuisance draw upon the old maxim "sic utere tuo ut alienum non laedas," or "one should use her own property in such a manner as not to injure the interests of others." Private nuisance, the first to be discussed here, is concerned with individual private property rights in land. Public nuisance stems from the violation of a range of public interests in the maintenance of health, safety, and morals. The dramatic differences between them, and between intentional and negligent theories of culpability, will soon be apparent.

from dirt, smoke and vibration emanating from the plant. A nuisance has been found after trial, temporary damages have been allowed; but an injunction has been denied.

The public concern with air pollution arising from many sources in industry and in transportation is currently accorded ever wider recognition accompanied by a growing sense of responsibility in State and Federal Governments to control it. Cement plants are obvious sources of air pollution in the neighborhoods where they operate.

But there is now before the court private litigation in which individual property owners have sought specific relief from a single plant operation. The threshold question raised by the division of view on this appeal is whether the court should resolve the litigation between the parties now before it as equitably as seems possible; or whether, seeking promotion of the general public welfare, it should channel private litigation into broad public objectives.

A court performs its essential function when it decides the rights of parties before it. Its decision of private controversies may sometimes greatly affect public issues. Large questions of law are often resolved by the manner in which private litigation is decided. But this is normally an incident to the court's main function to settle controversy. It is a rare exercise of judicial power to use a decision in private litigation as a purposeful mechanism to achieve direct public objectives greatly beyond the rights and interests before the court....

It seems apparent that the amelioration of air pollution will depend on technical research in great depth; on a carefully balanced consideration of the economic impact of close regulation; and of the actual effect on public health. It is likely to require massive public expenditure and to demand more than any local community can accomplish and to depend on regional and interstate controls. A court should not try to do this on its own as a by-product of private litigation and it seems manifest that the judicial establishment is neither equipped in the limited nature of any judgment it can pronounce nor prepared to lay down and implement an effective policy for the elimination of air pollution. This is an area beyond the circumference of one private lawsuit. It is a direct responsibility for government and should not thus be undertaken as an incident to solving a dispute between property owners and a single cement plant — one of many — in the Hudson River valley.

The cement making operations of defendant have been found by the court of Special Term to have damaged the nearby properties of plaintiffs in these two actions. That court, as it has been noted, accordingly found defendant maintained a nuisance and this has been affirmed at the Appellate Division. The trial judge had made a simple, direct finding that "the discharge of large quantities of dust upon each of the properties and excessive vibration from blasting deprived each party of the reasonable use of his property and thereby prevented his enjoyment of life and liberty therein." The judge continued, however: "I have given careful consideration to the plea of plaintiffs that an injunction should issue in this action. Although the Supreme Court has the power to grant and enforce an injunction, equity forbids its employment in this instance. The defendant's immense investment in the Hudson River Valley, its contribution to the Capital District's economy and its immediate help to the education of children in the Town of Coeymans through the payment of substantial sums in school and property taxes leads me to the conclusion that an injunction would produce great public...hardship." The total damage to plaintiffs' properties is, however, relatively small in comparison with the value of defendant's operation and with the consequences of the injunction which plaintiffs seek.

The ground for the denial of injunction, notwithstanding the finding both that there is a nuisance and that plaintiffs have been damaged substantially, is the large disparity in economic consequences of the nuisance and of the injunction. This theory cannot, however, be sustained without overruling a doctrine which has been consistently reaffirmed in several leading cases in this court and which has never been disavowed here, namely that where a nuisance has been found and where there has been any substantial damage shown by the party complaining an injunction will be granted.

The rule in New York has been that such a nuisance will be enjoined although marked disparity be shown in economic consequence between the effect of the injunction and the effect of the nuisance. The problem of disparity in economic consequence was sharply in focus in Whalen v. Union Bag & Paper Co., 101 N.E. 805. A pulp mill entailing an investment of more than a million dollars polluted a stream in which plaintiff, who owned a farm, was "a lower riparian owner." The economic loss to plaintiff from this pollution was small. This court...reinstated the injunction [despite] the argument of the mill owner that in view of "the slight advantage to plaintiff and the great loss that will be inflicted on defendant" an injunction should not be granted.... "Although the damage to the plaintiff may be slight as compared with the defendant's expense of abating the condition, that is not a good reason for refusing an injunction."... The rule laid down in that case, then, is that whenever the damage resulting from a nuisance is found not "unsubstantial," viz., $100 a year, injunction would follow....

Although the court [at trial in this case] held that an injunction should be denied, it found that plaintiffs had been damaged in various specific amounts up to the time of the trial and damages to the respective plaintiffs were awarded for those amounts. The effect of this was, injunction having been denied, plaintiffs could maintain successive actions at law for damages thereafter as further damage was incurred. The court also found the amount of permanent damage attributable to each plaintiff, for the guidance of the parties in the event both sides stipulated to the payment and acceptance of such permanent damage as a settlement of all the controversies among the parties. The total of permanent damages to all plaintiffs thus found was $185,000. This basis of adjustment has not resulted in any stipulation by the parties.

This [refusal to enjoin] is a departure from a rule that has become settled; but to follow the rule literally in these cases would be to close down the plant at once. This court is fully agreed to avoid that immediately drastic remedy; the difference in view is how best to avoid it.[3]

One alternative is to grant the injunction but postpone its effect to a specified future date to give opportunity for technical advances to permit defendant to eliminate the nuisance; another is to grant the injunction conditioned on the payment of permanent damages to plaintiffs which would compensate them for the total economic loss to their property present and future caused by defendant's operations. For reasons which will be developed the court chooses the latter alternative. If the injunction were to be granted unless within a short period — e.g., 18 months — the nuisance be abated by improved methods, there would be no assurance that any significant technical improvement would occur.

---

3. Respondent's investment in the plant is in excess of $45,000,000. There are over 300 people employed there.

The parties could settle this private litigation at any time if defendant paid enough money and the imminent threat of closing the plant would build up the pressure on defendant. If there were no improved techniques found, there would inevitably be applications to the court at Special Term for extensions of time to perform on showing of good faith efforts to find such techniques.

Moreover, techniques to eliminate dust and other annoying by-products of cement making are unlikely to be developed by any research the defendant can undertake within any short period, but will depend on the total resources of the cement industry nationwide and throughout the world. The problem is universal wherever cement is made. For obvious reasons the rate of the research is beyond control of defendant. If at the end of 18 months the whole industry has not found a technical solution a court would be hard put to close down this one cement plant if due regard be given to equitable principles.

On the other hand, to grant the injunction unless defendant pays plaintiffs such permanent damages as may be fixed by the court seems to do justice between the contending parties. All of the attributions of economic loss to the properties on which plaintiffs' complaints are based will have been redressed.

The nuisance complained of by these plaintiffs may have other public or private consequences, but these particular parties are the only ones who have sought remedies and the judgment proposed will fully redress them. The limitation of relief granted is a limitation only within the four corners of these actions and does not foreclose public health or other public agencies from seeking proper relief in a proper court.

It seems reasonable to think that the risk of being required to pay permanent damages to injured property owners by cement plant owners would itself be a reasonable effective spur to research for improved techniques to minimize nuisance....

The damage base here suggested is consistent with the general rule in those nuisance cases where damages are allowed. "Where a nuisance is of such a permanent and unabatable character that a single recovery can be had, including the whole damage past and future resulting therefrom, there can be but one recovery" (66 C.J.S. Nuisances §140, 947). It has been said that permanent damages are allowed where the loss recoverable would obviously be small as compared with the cost of removal of the nuisance (Kentucky-Ohio Gas Co. v. Bowling, 95 S.W.2d 1)…. Equity will give full relief in one action and prevent a multiplicity of suits….

Thus it seems fair to both sides to grant permanent damages to plaintiffs which will terminate this private litigation. The theory of damage is the "servitude on land" of plaintiffs imposed by defendant's nuisance. (See United States v. Causby, 328 U.S. 256, 261, 262, 267, where the term "servitude" addressed to the land was used by Justice Douglas relating to the effect of airplane noise on property near an airport.) The judgment, by allowance of permanent damages imposing a servitude on land, which is the basis of the actions, would preclude future recovery by plaintiffs or their grantees. This should be placed beyond debate by a provision of the judgment that the payment by defendant and the acceptance by plaintiffs of permanent damages found by the court shall be in compensation for a servitude on the land.

Although the Trial Term has found permanent damages as a possible basis of settlement of the litigation, on remission the court should be entirely free to examine this subject. It may again find the permanent damage already found, or make new findings.

The orders should be reversed, without costs, and the cases remitted to

Supreme Court, Albany County to grant an injunction which shall be vacated upon payment by defendant of such amounts of permanent damage to the respective plaintiffs as shall for this purpose be determined by the court.

JASEN, J., DISSENTING.... To now change the rule to permit the cement company to continue polluting the air indefinitely upon the payment of permanent damages is, in my opinion, compounding the magnitude of a very serious problem in our State and Nation today.... The harmful nature and widespread occurrence of air pollution have been extensively documented. Congressional hearings have revealed that air pollution causes substantial property damage, as well as being a contributing factor to a rising incidence of lung cancer, emphysema, bronchitis and asthma.

The specific problem faced here is known as particulate contamination because of the fine dust particles emanating from defendant's cement plant. The particular type of nuisance is not new, having appeared in many cases for at least the past 60 years. (See Hulbert v. California Portland Cement Co., 118 P. 928 (Cal. 1911).) It is interesting to note that cement production has recently been identified as a significant source of particulate contamination in the Hudson Valley. This type of pollution, wherein very small particles escape and stay in the atmosphere, has been denominated as the type of air pollution which produces the greatest hazard to human health. We have thus a nuisance which not only is damaging to the plaintiffs, but also is decidedly harmful to the general public....

The majority is, in effect, licensing a continuing wrong. It is the same as saying to the cement company, you may continue to do harm to your neighbors so long as you pay a fee for it. Furthermore, once such permanent damages are assessed and paid, the incentive to alleviate the wrong would be eliminated, thereby continuing air pollution of an area without abatement.... It is clearly established that the cement company is creating a continuing air pollution nuisance primarily for its own private interest with no public benefit. This kind of inverse condemnation may not be invoked by a private person or corporation for private gain or advantage. Inverse condemnation should only be permitted when the public is primarily served in the taking or impairment of property. The promotion of the interests of the polluting cement company has, in my opinion, no public use or benefit. Nor is it constitutionally permissible to impose a servitude on land, without consent of the owner, by payment of permanent damages where the continuing impairment of the land is for a private use....

I would enjoin the defendant cement company from continuing the discharge of dust particles upon its neighbors' properties unless, within 18 months, the cement company abated this nuisance.[4]

It is not my intention to cause the removal of the cement plant from the Albany area, but to recognize the urgency of the problem stemming from this stationary source of air pollution, and to allow the company a specified period of time to develop a means to alleviate this nuisance.

I am aware that the trial court found that the most modern dust control devices available have been installed in defendant's plant, but, I submit, this does not mean that better and more effective dust control devices could not be devel-

---

4. The issuance of an injunction to become effective in the future is not an entirely new concept. For instance, in Schwarzenbach v. Oneonta Light & Power Co., 100 N.E. 1134, an injunction against the maintenance of a dam spilling water on plaintiff's property was issued to become effective one year hence.

oped within the time allowed to abate the pollution. Moreover, I believe it is incumbent upon the defendant to develop such devices, since the cement company, at the time the plant commenced production (1962), was well aware of the plaintiffs' presence in the area, as well as the probable consequences of its contemplated operation. Yet, it still chose to build and operate the plant at this site.

In a day when there is a growing concern for clean air, highly developed industry should not expect acquiescence by the courts, but should, instead, plan its operations to eliminate contamination of our air and damage to its neighbors. Accordingly [I would] grant an injunction to take effect 18 months hence, unless the nuisance is abated by improved techniques prior to said date.

### COMMENTARY AND QUESTIONS

1. **Boomer as an environmental case.** Do you think that Oscar Boomer regarded himself as an environmentalist? Mr. Boomer clearly wanted to stop the cement dust falling on him and get compensation, but he may have considered environmentalists to be a bunch of birdwatchers and tree huggers. Note that although there were undoubtedly a number of ecological consequences to natural resources in the area polluted by cement dust, the case is totally silent about these, focusing instead upon injury to plaintiffs' personal and real property. Injury to human health and property remains the primary focus of much environmental litigation; human quality of life is an important part of environmental concern. The law, however, is slowly growing conscious of the tangible importance of ecological natural resource harms as well.

2. **Boomer and the cement company's "cost externalization."** Besides its interesting holdings on permanent damages and balancing, many aspects of the Boomer case reflect classic environmental perceptions. The case involved a typical industrial setting, with the cement company doing its own internal benefit-cost analysis that made discharging waste dust into the commons the rational disposal option. Absent successful legal action, the company would have had to account for almost none of the pollution's cost, even if the total of actual costs to natural systems, human health, and property in the affected area, extending downwind many miles, were actually greater than the cost of installing better control equipment (or might even have exceeded total net benefits to the company).

The problem is that costs to the natural and societal economies are typically spread so far and wide, or are so hard to take account of and quantify in monetary terms, that the overall accounting is rarely done.

3. **The "cost internalizing" effect of the Boomer lawsuit.** To the extent that common law litigation like Boomer forces a factory to provide relief to plaintiffs, to that same extent the company is forced to internalize some of the negative effects of its pollution as a cost of doing business, to be passed on to its consumers. How much gets internalized here? The Boomer decision resulted in internalizing some of the private property damage suffered by the Boomers and their neighbors. What Boomer does not even attempt to do is to trace more carefully all of the negative consumption externalities caused by the pollution. Why not? Does the difficulty lie in cost accounting? Recall from the discussions in Chapter Two how

difficult it would be to provide an accurate measure of the harms to affected natural resources (forests, wildlife, etc.) or the low-level adverse human health effects of particulate pollution. Oscar Boomer may or may not care deeply about the environment, but it is probably not in his self-interest to spend vast amounts of effort and energy trying to marshal evidence on damages to the commons beyond his own private property. Even if such evidence could be assembled and litigated, it might not be worthwhile, or efficient, to do so.

Do we have the time or luxury, on the other hand, to consider all the diverse external costs of each industrial operation? The cacophony of voices raised by a host of far-off pollution victims in such efforts might mean that nothing gets done. Some pollution is necessary to progress, say the Chicago School pragmatists. It has to occur somewhere. The market's accounting dictates that it occur here, in a rural area where only a few relatively low income people will be affected. There is no complaint about health effects in *Boomer*, so the effects of cement dust pollution may be relatively slight. The benefits of cement are clearly substantial. Does the rough accounting reached in *Boomer* thus suffice? Does society have the luxury of performing an endless analysis of the benefits and costs of every enterprise like the Atlantic Cement Company, or should such scrutiny be reserved for cases of more dramatic environmental impact?

Class actions offer a vehicle for expanded internalization and dramatically increase defendants' incentives to clean up. *Boomer* was not filed as a class action case, although it could have been. Would that have achieved more rational results? See Wright, The Cost-Internalization Case for Class Actions, 21 Stan. L. Rev. 383 (1969), on environmental use of class actions. It could have been filed as a public nuisance, which would also have changed the dynamics of the case as noted later in this chapter.

4. **Tactics, politics, and the urge to litigate.** If the cement dust pollution was so obvious in this case, why didn't Boomer and his lawyer go straight to the state air pollution agency? Albany, the state capital, was close by, and the official state pollution control agency possessed statutory authority, extensive regulations, public funding appropriated for enforcement, and expertise. What practical advantages in getting relief persuade pollution victims to take on the burdens of litigating in common law courts, rather than trusting to the official public law system?

The United States is an unusually litigious society. For that reason, it may seem natural that when the Boomers felt themselves aggrieved by the action of their cement plant neighbor, they resorted to a lawsuit in an effort to obtain redress. Speculating about the reasons for that choice by the Boomers reveals a great deal about the attraction of the common law as a system for environmental governance in American society.

The avenues of potential redress for the Boomers other than a lawsuit were not particularly promising because of the Boomers' lack of access and influence in decisional processes. In the private corporate decision, of course, the Boomers' interests were not likely to be of great concern. But the public law, both state and local, might have been expected to be different.

The construction of a major facility like a cement plant is usually the subject of local governmental land use regulations, most often zoning. If the project was consistent with existing local zoning classifications, there was no opportunity for Boomer to oppose the project in the zoning board forum; if, however, the use was one not initially allowed by the zoning, the project proponents would have had to seek a zoning change in order to construct the plant. Even if the project were consistent with existing zoning, some communities require permits for either the siting or the construction of large facilities.

Are the various local regulatory systems likely to provide people like the Boomers a sympathetic local forum in which to oppose the plant before it is built? The $45 million in equities weigh heavily in the balance. Today, as communities prostrate themselves in efforts to attract the economic benefits that come with major industrial facilities, the pressures to grant needed permits are substantial. Except for immediate neighbors of the plant who may suffer, like the Boomers, most of the community will find its immediate self-interest aligned with having the plant built.

What about the state pollution control system? As studied later, beginning in Chapter Five, the regulatory statutes are highly complex and primarily concerned with the general business of pollution control, not with providing discrete local remedies for relatively small individual claims. The statutes are primarily tools for governmental regulation of polluters, and opportunities for individual citizens to play a significant role in that process are few. The regulators are seldom eager to expand their dialogue with regulated parties into a multi-dimensional process in which citizens seek results that are often at odds with the agency's own view of proper outcome. This is not to say that seeking the aid of public authorities charged with control of pollution is always unavailing, but merely that it is a process over which the private citizen has little control.

Compare the official public law processes to an ordinary common law tort suit. Plaintiffs can hire a lawyer, probably on a contingent fee basis, who seeks relief at the local courthouse where the opportunity to win damages and injunctions provides a strong self-interest incentive to prosecute the case, a flexible scope of remedies, and broad, familiar theories for the judge to apply, without any need for entering the quagmire of administrative proceedings where the outcome can be so heavily influenced by politics and regional economics. Plaintiffs can exercise a measure of control over the litigation, selecting the lawyer, perhaps helping to develop the evidence, and the litigation process can to some extent equalize the parties to the controversy. And unlike the agency regulatory process, of course, the common law can provide damage recoveries for the plaintiff's injuries. There is, moreover, a growing literature in the civil procedure area addressing the psychological benefits of the litigation process. In addition to its various participatory characteristics, litigation usually leads to a definitive end, sometimes providing a personal sense of vindication, and always at least providing closure, itself an important benefit.

5. **Environmental tort remedies.** Tort actions illustrate other advantages of common law remedies in environmental cases. Tort law typically looks to com-

munity standards of appropriateness; it provides jury trials, so that the actual decision-makers on whether community standards have been met are local citizens themselves. As a means of seeking redress, tort cases demystify the technicalities of environmental cases, reverting to shared community understandings about what is right and what is wrong.

When plaintiffs successfully establish defendant's liability under an environmental tort cause of action, one remedy is automatic: the award of compensatory damages for tort injuries suffered. The well-established checklist of compensatory damage categories includes recoveries for health and property damage, lost profits and earnings, pain and suffering, and the like. Environmental cases occasionally add new remedy theories, noted later. The *Boomer* case concerned only property damages, but added the relatively novel permanent damage approach in lieu of an injunction.

After a court awards compensatory damages, typically for past rather than permanent injuries, courts then move to the further question of whether an injunction will be issued. Mirroring *Boomer*, the grant of an injunction in virtually all modern courts is never automatic, but depends upon a balancing of the equities. Accepting that principle, does an environmental perspective on the *Boomer* case reveal any problems with the court's balance? Would you mention the cement dust's more general public effects? Following Judge Jasen's lead, would you have proposed alternative forms of injunction? These and other issues are developed below in subchapter D below, on remedies.

### Section 2. THE PRIMA FACIE ENVIRONMENTAL PRIVATE NUISANCE CASE

**THE ELEMENTS OF THE CAUSE OF ACTION...** Nuisance can roughly be described as use of property by one party so as to (a) interfere substantially with the reasonable use, enjoyment or value of another's property, (b) injure life or health, (c) offend the senses or violate principles of decency, or (d) obstruct free passage or use of highways, navigable streams, public parks and beaches, and other public rights.

Nuisance is divided into two distinctive branches: Private nuisance is based on interference with individual plaintiffs' private property rights in land, ((a) and (b) above), while public nuisance stems from violations of "public rights" of varying descriptions (primarily (c) and (d)). Public nuisance, although it can provide extremely useful and creative remedies for environmental problems, poses some special practical difficulties for private plaintiffs, noted later in this chapter. Until recently, almost all environmental nuisance actions have been brought in private nuisance.

The elements of a prima facie case of private nuisance, when it is brought as an "intentional" tort action like *Boomer*, merely require plaintiffs to prove that:

(1) they have suffered substantial unreasonable interference with property use,

(2) the interference was caused by defendant's use of its land, and

(3) that the defendant acted "intentionally."

What kind of evidence would be necessary to establish these elements in a case like *Boomer*? An effective plaintiffs' attorney might want to learn something about the effect of alkaline cement dust on paint, metal, gardens, and peoples' health; dust sampling techniques; the industry's prior knowledge of cement dust problems; citizen complaints; and so on.

After the plaintiff presents credible evidence on these three elements, the burden then shifts to the corporate defendant to raise its defenses, many of which pose interesting environmental issues. At the first line of defense — when defendant attempts to deny the truth of plaintiff's various factual allegations — denials of causation often enmesh environmental litigation in scientific quandaries. Then, even if the alleged facts of a prima facie case are proved, an array of affirmative defenses apply, noted in this chapter's subpart B *infra*.

If the plaintiff successfully avoids the defenses and proves the tort's elements at trial, liability is established and compensatory damages, at least, will be awarded. In *Boomer* the damages sought for past injuries were straightforward property claims, but modern cases present a parade of other damage claims — for physical illnesses, aesthetics, risk, fear of cancer, as well as for punitive damages. *Boomer* also raises further remedy issues of permanent damages and the wide powers of equitable relief. All these are noted later.

**INTENTION AND NEGLIGENCE...** Both public and private nuisance are usually brought as "intentional" rather than negligence-based tort actions. Environmental law gives new importance to this distinction. In most tort causes of action, plaintiffs can choose to base their case on one or more of the three basic theories of tort culpability. As one court set out the range of choices:

> An action to redress a private nuisance can be maintained upon allegations that the defendant's conduct is (1) intentional...(2) negligent or reckless, or (3) actionable under the rules governing [strict] liability for abnormally dangerous conditions or activities. State of New York v. Schenectady Chemicals, Inc., 459 N.Y.S.2d 971, 976 (1983).

How do you determine which basis for private nuisance Oscar Boomer's lawyer chose? In the cement dust setting he probably could not have based his action on strict liability, but could have used either or both of the other theories, intentional tort and negligence. As in most nuisance cases, the *Boomer* litigation never states which private nuisance theory is being applied.

Although intentional torts are not given much attention in the standard law school curriculum, environmental law early on discovered the dramatic advantages of intentional tort theories.

The *Boomer* case, viewed analytically, was brought as an intentional tort, not under a negligence theory, because it based liability on findings of plaintiffs' injuries without further findings on the defendant's unreasonableness that would be required in order to establish negligence. In intentional tort cases plaintiffs must show that the defendant acted knowing that such injuries were substantially certain to occur. This "civil intent" is quite different from criminal intent, amounting merely to substantial foreseeability. Plaintiffs are aided in proving intent by a legal presumption that an actor intends the natural consequences of an act. Once the plaintiff has shown that the defendant knew or should have known that the pollution was substantially certain to cause negative effects to persons like the plaintiff, the inquiry shifts to the seriousness of plaintiff's injury — was plaintiff suffering an unreasonable burden? — and proof that it was actually the defendant that caused the harm. Liability based on intent is quite direct and decisive. Where is the element of *fault*, or breach of a duty of care? It's not there.

Compare intentional private nuisance to the elements of nuisance liability under a negligence theory. In negligence cases, plaintiffs must show that injury was caused by the defendant's breach of a duty of care owed to them; defendant's conduct must be shown to be unreasonable in all the circumstances. If, instead of merely showing an unreasonable burden on themselves and defendant's civil intent, plaintiffs like Boomer had to prove that defendant's conduct itself was "unreasonable" in order to make a prima facie case, they would quickly run into serious problems establishing liability, with a host of additional negligence requirements and defenses. What exactly was the defendant's duty of care, was it breached, did the breach directly cause the plaintiffs' injuries, did the plaintiff miss an opportunity to prevent or mitigate? The defendant might also avoid negligence liability by showing that it is only doing what all other such factories are doing, that further pollution controls would be too expensive, that plaintiffs were contributorily negligent, or even that its production is socially more important than plaintiffs' injuries.

Notice what a difference this makes in plaintiffs' attempts to obtain a pollution accounting. If the court applies a negligence theory, the plaintiffs must show that the defendant corporation was acting unreasonable in so acting, considering all circumstances, which is no easy task; if they don't succeed they will recover nothing. If, on the other hand, the case is pleaded and proved under intentional tort, "fault" is not an issue, and the question of whether the defendant was unreasonable, and the balance of defendant's economic importance and utility, are wholly irrelevant, at least to the question of liability. The focus is upon the unreasonableness of burdens suffered by plaintiffs, which is a very different question from whether defendant acted unreasonably.

If plaintiffs are shown to be suffering an unreasonable burden in intentional tort, liability follows and defendant's payment of damages for neighborhood pollution becomes a straightforward cost of doing business. Modern environmental intentional torts therefore serve as matter-of-fact cost internalizers, and the concept of fault is increasingly irrelevant, either bypassed or diluted by the concept of civil intent.

Over the years many courts have confused the issues of what constitutes liability in nuisance with choice of remedy. Thus there have been some nuisance cases in which courts denied relief, finding defendants' conduct reasonable under the circumstances, as when major industrial facilities inflicted substantial damage on nearby houses. In doing so those courts replicated the over-simplification of an old English dictum, "Le utility del chose excusera le noisomeness del stink."[5]

5. Roughly, "The usefulness of the thing will excuse the pollution." The Legal French appears to be a version of Ranketts case: "Si home fait Candells deins un vill, per que il caufe un noyfom fent al Inhabitants, uncore ceo neft alcun Nusans, car le needfulnefs de eux difpenfera ove le noifomnefs del fmell." P. 3 Ja.B.R. Rolle's Abridgement, Nusans, 139 (1684).

Negligence is far more familiar than intentional tort to most attorneys and judges. Many appear not to know there is a difference, which may explain why courts sometimes apply negligence concepts in intentional tort cases. Environmental lawyers filing nuisance actions often bear the burden of clarifying the difference in the course of litigation. It is worth the effort. But if a court allows the decision on tort liability itself (not just the decision whether to enjoin the defendant) to depend on the comparative importance of the parties' activities, it creates an all or nothing contest. Such negligence-type balances inevitably favor industry and by definition completely ignore the negative burdens suffered by the losers. An early American pollution case, Madison v. Ducktown Sulfur, Copper & Iron Co., 83 S.W. 658 (Tenn. 1904), clearly rejected this mistaken version of intentional tort. Faced with farmers whose lands were being destroyed by the belching acid emissions of a primitive but important copper smelting factory, the *Ducktown* court held that a comparison of public importance and reasonableness was not relevant to establishing nuisance liability; rather, the comparative "balancing of equities" goes to the subsequent question of whether an injunction will be issued in addition to payment of compensatory damages. This is precisely the approach followed by the *Boomer* court. These remedy issues are discussed at length later in this chapter.

**POLLUTION AS AN INTERFERENCE WITH PLAINTIFFS' PROPERTY RIGHTS...** To prevent the intentional private nuisance action from becoming too disruptive, the law requires plaintiffs to prove that the interference with their rights is substantial and unreasonable; mere annoyance is not nuisance. By using the word "unreasonable," however, the possibility of confusion arises because that term is universally applied in the negligence equation. Courts in intentional nuisance cases may mistakenly import a question of the "unreasonableness of defendant's conduct" into their determinations of liability, instead of simply addressing the question of whether plaintiffs have suffered an unreasonable burden.

Where does mere annoyance end and substantial interference with the use and enjoyment of land begin? This is a typical legal problem of line drawing, where there are easy cases at the extremes: from the continuous emission of noxious solvent fumes from a paint factory, which would quite clearly be a nuisance, to a neighbor's occasional cooking of brussels sprouts, the smell of which is merely unpleasant and not legally a nuisance. These examples suggest, first, that the question is one of fact, not of law, and second, that the standard is an objective community standard rather than the subjective standard of the affected individual. Should that be so?

Environmental litigators must often look for the cheapest available probative evidence to make their cases. In *Boomer*, for example, corroded gutters, soiled wash from the clothesline, or cement dust-coated vegetables might be effective exhibits for proving the unreasonable burden on plaintiffs, because they graphically demonstrate that defendant's conduct materially interfered with plaintiffs' ordinary activities. What other physical evidence of pollution damage is likely to be persuasive? Can testimonial evidence of inconvenience, such as the need to dust windowsills, be equally effective? An aggrieved householder may be a vivid witness, able to express anger at defendant's unwarranted intrusions. Or would it be preferable to present third-party testimony, such as that of a real estate agent who observed the grit and dust and could correlate those phenomena with estimates of reduced market value of the parcel, or a doctor or occupational safety specialist who could testify about the health threat of airborne particulates while also describing the conditions at the plaintiff's house? Does the utility of such evidence vary depending on whether the case is being tried to a jury rather than to a judge sitting alone? (As in other common law torts, of course, in nuisance cases where damages are sought either party has the right to demand a jury.)

**THE QUALITATIVE CONDUCT OF THE POLLUTER...** What did the Atlantic Cement Company do that was "wrong"? The trial judge found that the cement plant had "installed at great expense the most efficient devices available to prevent the discharge of dust and polluted air into the atmosphere." Must the plaintiff prove "fault," as in a negligence case, showing that defendant's conduct was careless or unreasonable in some way? If that were so, then the case would be actionable in negligence, and the doctrine of intentional nuisance would be redundant.

In proving an intentional tort, must the plaintiffs show that the defendant's conduct was undertaken with malice aforethought, or was intended to harm the plaintiff? Not at all. Those are questions typically raised by the criminal law, under which the mental state of the actor is of great concern. In general, however, the tort of private nuisance imposes only the modest requirement that the defendant know with substantial certainty that such an injury was likely to occur to someone. In *Boomer*, the cement company had ignored the neighbors' repeated complaints and petitions, which virtually proves the civil intent element. In most pollution cases, the obvious likelihood that pollutants will travel into neighboring areas answers most quibbles on this point.

**CAUSATION...** In the *Boomer* case there was little dispute that the damages alleged by plaintiffs were caused by the Atlantic Cement Company, a new major industrial facility located in an area previously devoted to rural uses. In many environmental cases, however, proof of defendant's causation of plaintiffs' harm is extremely difficult. In a heavily industrialized area, for example, how do plaintiffs prove which of several factories is (are) the culprit(s) and to what degree? Prevailing wind charts and chemical or microscopic analysis of the invasive material may point to one installation rather than another, but the job of proof can be technically demanding. In appropriate cases, plaintiffs may try to establish joint and several liability between several polluters joined as defendants, all of whom may have contributed to the nuisance. If plaintiffs prevail, the burden shifts to the several defendants to apportion the loss among themselves. Joint and several liability will be studied with the toxics cases in the next chapter. The toxics cases also raise further tough causation problems, as, for example, when plaintiffs try to prove the etiology of long-latent diseases deriving from past chemical exposures. If Mr. Boomer had contracted chronic bronchial asthma, how easy would it be to recover health damages from Atlantic? See Chapter Four.

## B.  DEFENSES IN ENVIRONMENTAL TORT SUITS

There are two principal ways to defend a torts case: the defendant can deny and refute a critical element of the plaintiffs' prima facie case, or else can try to raise and prove an affirmative defense. As to affirmative defenses, a laundry list of the most common ones can be found in Fed. R. Civ. P. Rule 8(c). A quick review of that list shows only a few — discharge in bankruptcy, estoppel, laches, and res judicata — that might have a bearing on a typical nuisance lawsuit.

Apart from the standard affirmative defenses, environmental lawsuits confront a number of more specialized defenses. In a recent New York chemical dump case, the court reviewed an array of defenses:

### State of New York v. Schenectady Chemical Co.
N.Y. Supreme Court, Rensselaer County, 1983
117 Misc.2d 960, 459 N.Y.S.2d 971.

[The court first heard the defendant manufacturer's arguments that the elements of a common-law cause of action did not exist, and that cleanup costs at its Loeffel site were not recoverable under common law. Finding that these arguments lacked merit, the court turned to an illustrative laundry list composed mostly of affirmative defenses:]

The defendant has raised many additional objections.... It is argued that the action is untimely. The limitation applicable to a nuisance cause of action is the three-year period provided in N.Y. Civ. Prac. L. & R. 214. The rule with respect to an ongoing nuisance, as here alleged, is that the action continually accrues anew upon each day of the wrong although the recovery of money damages is limited to the three-year period immediately prior to suit. Defendant's contention that the limitation period should accrue upon the last day of dumping lacks merit since the law has long been settled that, "the right to maintain an action for...nuisance continues as long as the nuisance exists...."

The argument that [the governmental plaintiff] lacks standing to maintain the action because the waters are private rather than public cannot withstand scrutiny. The amended complaint alleges that the waste has migrated from the Loeffel site into neighboring surface and ground water, including two streams. By statute, "waters" is defined to include "all other bodies of surface or underground water... public or private (except those private waters which do not combine or effect a junction with natural surface or underground waters)...."

[As to an attempted constitutional prescriptive rights defense, the state high court has] rejected [the] claim that protecting water from pollution somehow violated a due process property right, stating that the argument was "untenable since such rights do not attach to water itself and in any event are required to yield to public health and public safety."

Defendant's next contention is that the complaint must be dismissed since the requested relief is speculative and to some degree not authorized or appropriate. A complaint will not be dismissed due to a prayer for inappropriate relief so long as some right to recover is demonstrated.

The court will dismiss the demand for attorney's fees since that relief is not available in the absence of a statute or contract authorizing same.[6]

The objection that the complaint is improperly set forth as eight separate and distinct causes of action instead of one is not a basis for relief. While better pled as a single nuisance cause of action, the method employed here does not constitute improper splitting since all claims are contained in a single action.

As to the request for dismissal for failure to join necessary parties, i.e., other alleged tortfeasors guilty of dumping at the site, the rule is that those contributing to a nuisance are liable jointly and severally and "it is fundamental that a plaintiff...is free to choose his defendant." If defendant feels that others may have contributed to plaintiff's damage it should commence the appropriate third-party practice.

The argument that plaintiff has released [co-defendants] General Electric Company and Bendix and thus defendant is released, must fail. First of all the...purported releases have not been furnished, lending credence to plaintiff's assertion that they do not yet exist. More importantly, plaintiff has averred that the language of the proposed releases will specifically reserve its rights against defendant; thus, [defendant] will not be discharged.

The defenses of res judicata and collateral estoppel due to the order and judgment of March 4, 1968 in Ingraham v. Loeffels Oil Removal & Serv. Co. are not available since this action involves different parties upon different causes of action, and defendant's responsibility, if any, was never addressed in the prior action.

Likewise, dismissal is not warranted under N.Y. Civ. Prac. L. & R. 3211 due to "another action pending between the same parties for the same cause of action," since the pending case of Thornton v. General Electric does not involve the identical parties and causes of action.

The defense that the statutory scheme of the Environmental Conservation Law is exclusive and bars common law actions is directly contradicted by §17-1101 of that law....

Likewise, the complaint cannot be dismissed upon defendant's "state of the art" defenses.... The fact that a manufacturer may have complied with the latest industry standards is no defense to an action to abate a nuisance since, as stated earlier with respect to public nuisances and inherently dangerous activities, fault is not an issue, the inquiry being limited to whether the condition created, not the conduct creating it, is causing damage to the public.

The final argument for dismissal worthy of discussion is the contention that by hiring a private contractor licensed to dispose of chemical wastes the defendant has met its legal duty and cannot be held liable for the contractor's wrongdoing. Defendant [however, can] be found liable for Loeffel's acts if: (1) it was negligent in retaining an incompetent contractor; (2) it failed, with knowledge thereof, to remedy or prevent an unlawful act; (3) the work itself was illegal; (4) the work itself

---

6. [Eds. This is not necessarily true. A traditional rule of equity is that — although the American rule, unlike the English, is that in the absence of contrary statute each party bears its own legal expenses — courts can order "fee-shifting" where the loser pays the prevailing party's expert witness and attorney fees when there is a showing of defendant's "bad faith," a "common fund" of value accrued by the defendant, or the court decides that plaintiffs have acted as private attorneys-general. This last exception sounds well-suited to environmental cases, and remains applicable in many state courts, though it was gutted in federal court practice by the Nixon Supreme Court in the *Alyeska Pipeline Company* case, 421 U..S. 240 (1975).

was inherently dangerous; or (5) the work involved the creation of a nuisance....

[The opinion on the merits in *Schenectady Chemical* appears later in this chapter.]

### COMMENTARY AND QUESTIONS

1. **Evaluating *Schenectady Chemical's* defenses.** Consider each of the foregoing defensive arguments made by the chemical company. Which of them deserve legitimate attention when such environmental cases go to trial? Although the company's lawyers raised a welter of attempted defenses, there are more:

2. **The permit defense.** One common line of defense in environmental cases, the "permit defense," is a form of pre-emption argument based on defendant's assertion that the polluting activity is being conducted under the terms of a valid government permit. (A number of pollution permit systems are explored *infra* in Chapters Five and thereafter.) This defense is consistently rejected in intentional nuisance cases, unless the statute creating the permit system has expressly repealed the availability of common law remedies in the field. Because environmental activists are keenly aware of this issue, virtually all pollution statutes have specifically rejected industry lobbyists' attempts to pre-empt common law by making statutory permit enforcement the exclusive pollution remedy. Where a case is argued as a negligence-based nuisance, on the other hand, courts have been readier to take notice of permit compliance as one element of defining defendant's duty of reasonable care and its breach. In policy terms, why shouldn't permit compliance always be a good defense?

The Alaska legislature, prompted by papermill lobbyists concerned with citizen tort suits, passed a bill in 1994 that prohibits lawsuits for common law nuisance law if defendant corporations are in compliance with state permits. Alaska Statutes §09.45.230. The statute, basing its regulation on statewide emission standards, thus tries to preempt common law, which traditionally tailors its protections according to particular local effects on neighbors (although it appears to contain some inadvertent loopholes). Such permit defense statutes raise the fascinating question: does repeal of traditional common law protections of private property constitute an invalid regulatory taking? See Hasselman, Alaska's Nuisance Statute Revisited: Federal Substantive Due Process Limits to Common Law Abrogation, 24 B.C. Envtl Aff. L.Rev. 347 (1997), and Chapter 23.

3. **Primary jurisdiction.** The "primary jurisdiction" defense is less dramatic but equally disliked by environmental plaintiffs. Under this defense, the defendant urges the judge to suspend the common law suit, in order to await enforcement by the government agency with jurisdiction over the matter. The argument is not that common law remedies do not co-exist with the public law remedy, but rather that courts should initially defer to the expertise, official appropriateness, and uniformity function represented by the statutory regulators. Environmental plaintiffs bemoan such remands to the agencies. Why? The fact that polluters want to be sent to the official agencies gives some indication of which forum is more likely to provide effective remedies against them (as well as giving an ironic twist to

familiar corporate arguments denouncing the bureaucratic state). Plaintiffs try to resist the primary jurisdiction defense by arguing that the reasons for deference to agencies don't apply in their case, that only a court can offer them damage remedies, that unlike the public law system the common law is designed to deal with localized controversies, and so on.[7] Primary jurisdiction is not a well-understood nor widely litigated defense. It invites interesting environmental arguments on both sides of the question.

4. **Statutory preemptions of common law?** Marketplace lobbyists often attempt to insert a seemingly innocuous phrase into drafts of environmental regulatory statutes: "The provisions of this title shall constitute the exclusive remedy for the subject matter it covers." What would be the consequence of this provision on pollution torts, for example, if it slipped into law? And note how this reflects the marketplace's healthy appreciation of how effective common law remedies can be. In some cases, however, defendants can argue that statutory preemptions of common law are implicit in strict federal regulatory schemes:

> This case requires us to determine whether a state [common law] award of punitive damages arising out of the escape of plutonium from a federally-licensed nuclear facility is pre-empted either because it falls within that forbidden field or because it conflicts with some other aspect of the Atomic Energy Act. Karen Silkwood was a laboratory analyst for Kerr-McGee at its Cimmaron plant near Crescent, Oklahoma. The plant fabricated plutonium fuel pins for use as reactor fuel in nuclear power plants. Accordingly, the plant was subject to licensing and regulation by the Nuclear Regulatory Commission (NRC) pursuant to the Atomic Energy Act. During a three-day period of November 1974, Silkwood was contaminated by plutonium from the Cimmaron plant. Karen's father brought the present diversity action...based on common law tort principles under Oklahoma law...to recover for the contamination injuries...
>
> Congress' decision to prohibit the states from regulating the safety aspects of nuclear development was premised on its belief that the Commission was more qualified to determine what type of safety standards should be enacted in this complex area.... Congress assumed that traditional principles of state tort law would apply with full force unless they were expressly supplanted. Thus, it is Kerr-McGee's burden to show that Congress intended to preclude such awards. Yet, the company is unable to point to anything in the legislative history.... We do not suggest that there could never be an instance in which the federal law would pre-empt the recovery of damages based on state law. But insofar as damages for radiation injuries are concerned, pre-emption should not be judged on the basis that the federal government has so completely occupied the field of safety that state remedies are foreclosed but on whether there is an irreconcilable conflict between the federal and state standards or whether the imposition of a state standard in a damages action would frustrate the objectives of the federal law. We perceive no such conflict or frustration in the circumstances of this case. White, J., in Silkwood v. Kerr-Mcgee Corporation, 464 U.S. 238 (1984).

If punitive damages are not preempted, clearly compensatory damages are available. What about injunctions?

---

7. See Comment, Primary Jurisdiction in Environmental Cases, 48 Indiana L.J. 676 (1973).

5. **Industry practice and custom.** Can a defendant prevail by proving that her conduct was "normal and customary industry practice," reasonable and accepted within that industry? This can be a useful defense in negligence actions, although in some cases courts find that the industry practice is negligent. But the *Ducktown* precedent, confronting this defense, shows why there is a strategic difference between intentional and negligent tort: Proof that defendant is doing things as well as others in her industry does not rebut the fact that, even using those methods, the pollution is substantially certain to occur. As with contributory negligence and other negligence-oriented defenses, the intentional tort finesses the defense. In the *Boomer* case, as in the *Schenectady Chemical* excerpt above, the defense made was even stronger, alleging that the defendant's plant was "state-of-the-art." If indeed the defendant can prove that there is no cleaner pollution control technology available, a consequent finding of the reasonableness of defendant's conduct is likely to defeat a negligence liability claim. Why shouldn't that be a good defense against intentional tort claims?

5. **Statutes of limitation and other time bars.** Can statutes of limitations provide a good defense for operators of longstanding nuisances? What if a state has a three-year general torts statute of limitation, and an offending plant commenced operations five years before the suit is brought? Not all state courts have treated the question alike, but the majority position seems to be like *Schenectady Chemical's*, that if the pollution is a "continuing nuisance," each day is a separate injury, so that a lawsuit can recapture all losses within the period of the statute of limitations. When, however, a nuisance is of a "permanent" nature (loosely defined as a nuisance plainly intended from the first to continue to operate for many years in exactly the same way, like a major electric generation facility), the defendant may use the tort statute of limitations to bar untimely suits. In such cases, the statute begins to run from the time at which the cause of action first accrues to the plaintiff. See Goldstein v. Potomac Electric Power Co., 404 A.2d 1064 (Md. 1979). Do you see that the two different scenarios are not always clearly distinguishable?[8]

Even where a lawsuit is brought within the statute of limitations, a defendant may claim to have acquired a prescriptive private right to pollute, the prescriptive period usually in the ten-to-twenty year range. Other estoppel arguments are also available against injunction suits under the equitable defense of laches. As in *Schenectady*, however, public rights usually override such private defenses. As to when limitations start to run.

6. **Coming to the nuisance.** A few states still recognize a special defense (a form of estoppel defense) called "coming to the nuisance." As the name suggests, the thrust of the claim is that the defendant had become established in the area before the plaintiff arrived, so the injury to plaintiff was, in effect, self-inflicted. Would a coming to the nuisance defense have prevailed in *Boomer*? As indicated by its lack of widespread recognition, the defense of coming to the nuisance is flawed analytically. Although the defendant may have begun operations that did no palpable harm to neighboring landowners at the time, with the advent of the injury to plain-

---

8. For more on toxic tort statute of limitations issues, see Chapter Four.

tiff the question is who enjoys the better right — plaintiff to the quiet enjoyment of her land, or defendant to continue the operation of its factory in the same fashion? To say, as a defendant does in raising this defense, that plaintiff could have avoided the conflict by settling elsewhere, begs the question whether defendant had any legal right to insist that plaintiff do so. In the last analysis, defendant is seeking to use another's land as its disposal site without ever having purchased that privilege from its neighbor. Most modern courts do not seem fully to understand the defense's internal flaws. Instead they most frequently point to the existence of tight housing markets, or zoning ordinances, to affirm the primacy of residential uses. The defense accordingly may still be applied in some rural areas.

7. **The best defense is a good offense?** One interesting environmental defense tactic is the filing of "SLAPPs" — strategic lawsuits against public participation. When public-interest citizen activists bring actions to enforce the common law or statutory law against polluters, developers, public utilities, and ranchers or other entrepreneurs using federal lands, in at least one hundred recent cases defendants have sued or countersued for damages averaging $7,400,000.[9] To get around the First Amendment's petition protection, defense lawyers argue in tort: plaintiffs' allegations amount to libel, slander, defamation, interference with business advantage, and abuse of judicial process.

On their merits, SLAPP suits are overwhelmingly thrown out of court if plaintiffs persevere in resisting them. The fear and burden on volunteer activists of defending against these intimidation suits, however, in practice has resulted in the collapse of many citizen initiatives. Well-heeled defendants can justify spending time and money on SLAPP suits as tax-deductible business expenses, knowing that the citizen plaintiffs are likely to be greatly hindered, or halted, in their efforts regardless of the SLAPP suit's minimal merits. Given the disparate status of the players and the courts' current lack of rigor against attorneys bringing such suits, environmental plaintiffs' ability to obtain sanctions (as allowed under FRCP Rule 11) against SLAPP attorneys remains largely theoretical. Note, however, that federal Rule 11 does not impose limits on the amount the judge may award.[10]

"SLAPP-back" suits, countersuing SLAPPers for damages, are increasing. See

---

9. SLAPPS have also issued in response to the filing of petitions and testimony by activists in legislative and executive proceedings. See generally Canan & Pring, Studying Strategic Lawsuits Against Public Participation, 22 Law & Soc'y Rev. 385 (1988:2); Pring, Intimidation Suits Against Citizens: A Risk for Public Policy Advocates, 7 Nat. L.J. 16 (1985); Comment, Counterclaim and Countersuit Harassment of Private Environmental Plaintiffs, 74 Mich. L. Rev. 106 (1975).

10. Should courts hold SLAPP plaintiffs to a heightened standard of pleading where litigation chills citizens' 1st Amendment right to petition government? In Florida Fern Growers Assoc., Inc. et al. v. Concerned Citizens of Putnam County, 616 So. 2d 562 (Fla. App. 1993), growers charged citizens with "intentional and malicious interference with business relationships" for challenging the issuance of consumptive water permits, but the court held that this did not justify requiring heightened pleadings, and sent the case for trial. Given the limited monetary sanctions that can be awarded under many states' procedural rules for instigating frivolous litigation, it is important to public interest groups to have SLAPP suits dismissed as early as possible.

For further reading on SLAPP suits, see Note, "Silencing SLAPPS: An Examination of Proposed Legislative Remedies and a Solution for Florida," 20 Fla. St. U. L. Rev. 487 (1992); Note, "SLAPP Suits: Weakness in First Amendment Law and In the Courts' Response to Frivolous Litigation," 39 U.C.L.A L. Rev. 979 (1992); Tobias, "Environmental Litigation and Rule 11," 33 Wm. & Mary L. Rev. 429 (1992).

Gordon v. Marrone, 590 N.Y.S. 2d 649 (1992) (Nature Conservancy recovers $10,000 for developer's harassing lawsuit challenging its tax exemption). For more on SLAPP-backs, see the California anti-SLAPP statute, 1991 Cal. S.B. 341 § 425/66(a), Leonardini v. Shell Oil, 216 Cal. App. 3d 547 (1989), Wegis v. J.G. Boswell Co., 1991 Lexis 4641 (1991), and the article by the father of SLAPP jurisprudence, Professor George "Rock" Pring, in 7 Pace Envtl. L. Rev. 3 (1989), in a symposium on SLAPPs.

8. **The strategies of environmental defendants.** Environmental defenses are predominantly directed toward blocking plaintiffs' claims from going to trial. Where plaintiffs can prove the factual elements of an intentional tort claim, there is no general substantive theory of environmental defense available to polluters for avoiding payment of environmental damages as a cost of doing business. As you go through environmental case law, keep an eye on the various defense strategies that are mobilized. Understandably, they are often attempts to duck the merits, or to switch them into forums that are more politically and economically sensitive to defendants' interests.

## C. A COMPENDIUM OF TORT CAUSES OF ACTION AND SPECIAL ISSUES THEY RAISE

A variety of common law theories beyond private nuisance can provide a basis for environmental lawsuits, each with particular requirements and utility. In each case a plaintiff must fit the defendant's conduct into a theory on which liability can be based, and must prove damage and causation. In general, damage and causation elements are the same for all torts; the principal difference among the torts lies in the definition of the other elements of each theory.

Modern tort law to some extent still reflects the old English common law courts' formulaic writ system. Under that arcane and rigid system, a plaintiff would have to select a single writ, such as trespass on the case (the writ that has grown into the typical modern day negligence cause of action), and then prove facts that precisely "fit the writ."

In the adaptation of tort law to environmental cases, the importance of the old writ system is greatly reduced by modern civil procedure's lenient fact pleading, eliminating the traps of hypertechnical writ allegations, and the procedure of pleading in the alternative. Today, an environmental plaintiff can allege the facts of pollution, and in a single lawsuit claim that defendant is maintaining a private nuisance and a public nuisance, committing a trespass, and causing personal injuries, and allege separate claims for recovery in each tort (except trespass) based on negligence, intentional conduct, and strict liability. The old writ system has produced differences that give the torts different tactical and strategic advantages, and sometimes continues to have confusing effects like mixing negligence and intention theories.

In analyzing each of the tort theories here, consider the different demands they place upon plaintiffs and defendants, and the different advantages they offer for capturing and bringing environmental values into the legal balance.

## Section 1. PUBLIC NUISANCE

Public nuisance, quite unlike private nuisance, is descended from criminal offenses against the public peace. Over time public nuisance became a civil action as well, providing remedies for violations of public rights. Traditionally it has applied to cases like the blocking of public rights of way, or offenses against public sensitivities and decency, like boisterous saloons and bawdy houses or, in modern times, pornography shops. In typical public nuisance actions, public prosecutors bring lawsuits seeking injunctions to force cessation of nuisances (often preferring the tort approach even where statutory remedies apply). Public nuisance is usually litigated as an intentional tort. In some circumstances public nuisance actions can be brought by private plaintiffs, and public nuisances can simultaneously be private nuisances. In analyzing the following cases, consider the tactical advantages public nuisance offers prosecutors and private plaintiffs.

### State of New York v. Schenectady Chemical Co.
N.Y. Supreme Court, Rensselaer County, 1983
117 Misc.2d 960, 459 N.Y.S.2d 971.

[The portion of the opinion dealing with defenses appears above.]

The court must decide if the State, either by statute or common law, can maintain an action to compel a chemical company to pay the costs of cleaning up a dump site so as to prevent pollution of surface and ground water when the dumping took place between 15 to 30 years ago at a site owned by an independent contractor hired by the chemical company to dispose of the waste material....

The amended complaint contains the following factual assertions. The action is brought by the State in its role as guardian of the environment against Schenectady Chemicals, Inc. with respect to a chemical dump site located on Mead Road, Rensselaer County, New York (the Loeffel site). Since 1906 Schenectady Chemicals has manufactured paints, alkyl phenols and other chemical products, a byproduct of which is waste, including but not limited to phenol, benzene, toluene, xylene, formaldehyde, vinyl chloride, chlorobenzene, 1,2 dichlorobenzene, 1,4 dichlorobenzene, trichloroethylene, chloroform, ethyl benzene, ethylene chloride, 1,1 dichloroethane, 1,2 dichloroethane, trans-1,2 dichloroethylene, lead, copper, chromium, selenium, and arsenic. These chemical wastes are dangerous to human, animal and plant life, and the defendant was so aware. During the 1950s until the mid-1960s the defendant disposed of its chemical wastes by way of contract with Dewey Loeffel, or one of Mr. Loeffel's corporations. Mr. Loeffel made pick-ups at the defendant's manufacturing plants and disposed of the material by dumping directly into lagoons at the Loeffel site, and in some instances by burying the wastes. It is alleged that with knowledge of the danger of environmental contamination if its wastes were not properly disposed, and knowing of Loeffel's methods, Schenectady Chemicals: (1) hired an incompetent independent contractor to dispose of the wastes; and (2) failed to fully advise Loeffel of the dangerous nature of the waste material and recommend proper disposal methods.

It is alleged that the Loeffel site is approximately 13 acres of low-lying swamp land located in a residential-agricultural area in Rensselaer County with surface soil consisting mainly of gravel and sand. The ground water beneath the site is part of an aquifer which serves as the sole source of water for thousands of area residents and domestic animals. The site drains into two surface streams, one a tributary of the Valatie Kill, and the other a tributary of Nassau Lake. During the period in question approximately 46,300 tons of chemical wastes were deposited at the Loeffel site, of which 17.8 percent, or 8,250 tons, came from defendant. The other material was generated by General Electric Company and Bendix Corporation and has been so inextricably mixed with defendant's as to become indistinguishable....

The complaint alleges that over the years the chemical wastes have migrated into the surrounding air, surface and ground water contaminating at least one area drinking well and so polluting, or threatening to pollute, the area surface and ground water as to constitute an unreasonable threat to the public well-being and a continuing public nuisance. As a result, the Department of Environmental Conservation (DEC) developed a plan to prevent further migration of chemical wastes from the site, and General Electric and Bendix have agreed to pay 82.2 percent of the costs thereof. Defendant's refusal to pay its portion of the clean-up costs gives rise to this suit.

The fourth through eighth causes of action rely upon a nuisance theory. The "term nuisance, which in itself means no more than harm, injury, inconvenience, or annoyance...arises from a series of historical accidents covering the invasion of different kinds of interests and referring to various kinds of conduct on the part of defendants." Nuisances are classified as either private or public. In *Copart*, the Court of Appeals described a public nuisance as:

> A public, or as sometimes termed a common, nuisance is an offense against the State and is subject to abatement or prosecution on application of the proper governmental agency. It consists of conduct or omissions which offend, interfere with or cause damage to the public in the exercise of rights common to all in a manner such as to offend public morals, interfere with use by the public of a public place or endanger or injure the property, health, safety or comfort of a considerable number of persons. 362 N.E.2d at 968....

[The court permitted the public nuisance to be litigated based on both intentional and strict liability theories.] While ordinarily nuisance is an action pursued against the owner of land for some wrongful activity conducted thereon, "everyone who creates a nuisance or participates in the creation or maintenance of a nuisance are liable jointly and severally for the wrong and injury done thereby" Even a non-landowner can be liable for taking part in the creation of a nuisance upon the property of another. Thus, in Hine v. Air-Don Co., 250 N.Y.S. 75, the Third Department held that it was for the jury to decide if the defendant had taken part in the creation of a nuisance so as to render it liable to the injured plaintiff through the act of leaving the unassembled parts of a furnace in a pile upon a public sidewalk. In Caso v. District Council, 350 N.Y.S.2d 173, the defendant, a union of employees working for municipal sewage treatment plants, engaged in an illegal strike resulting in one billion gallons of raw sewage being emitted into the East River. The plaintiffs, officials of Nassau County and affected towns on Long Island, sued on behalf of their governmental units seeking compensatory and punitive damages for injury done to their water and beaches. The union moved to dismiss the complaint, alleging that no such cause of action existed.... The Second Department stated, "A common law cause of action in nuisance would appear to be the appropriate remedy in the instant case." 350 N.Y.S.2d 177.

The common law is not static. Society has repeatedly been confronted with new inventions and products that, through foreseen and unforeseen events, have imposed dangers upon society (explosives are an example). The courts have reacted by expanding the common law to meet the challenge, in some instances imposing absolute liability upon the party who, either through manufacture or use, has sought to profit from marketing a new invention or product. The modern chemical industry, and the problems engendered through the disposal of its byproducts, is, to a large extent, a creature of the twentieth century. Since the Second World War hundreds of previously unknown chemicals have been created. The wastes produced have been dumped, sometimes openly and sometimes surreptitiously, at thousands of sites across the country. Belatedly it has been discovered that the waste products are polluting the air and water and pose a consequent threat to all life forms. Someone must pay to correct the problem, and the determination of who is essentially a political question to be decided in the legislative arena. As Judge Bergan noted in Boomer v. Atlantic Cement Co., resolution of the issues raised in society's attempt to ameliorate pollution are to a large extent beyond the ken of the judicial branch. Nonetheless, courts must resolve the issues raised by litigants and, in that vein, this court holds that the fourth through seventh causes of action of the amended complaint state viable causes of action sounding in nuisance.

[In subsequent proceedings, the case was settled out of court, with no admission of liability. There was, however, a consent judgment whereby the defendant paid $498,500 in damages. Additionally, the defendant was not excused from paying for future damages if pollution migrated off the site. –Eds.]

### COMMENTARY AND QUESTIONS

1. **Why public nuisance?** Why did the government prosecutors in this case use common law instead of the elaborate federal and state statutory provisions that were available for decontamination of toxic sites? Does public nuisance provide greater efficiency in establishing liability and obtaining effective remedies? This case may also illustrate how liberal the concept of "intentional" tort can be. How did the court determine civil intent? What did the defendant know was substantially certain to happen? In a public nuisance action brought by the appropriate public official, is the remedial calculus regarding grant of an injunction, including a balancing of the equities, the same as in *Boomer*? The public plaintiff is clothed with a presumptive authority to speak for the common good. Does that mean that the interests represented by the public official presumptively outweigh the costs to a private nuisance-maker when equities are balanced, or does it merely mean that (unlike in *Boomer*) the public values are allowed onto the scale?

2. **Vicarious liability.** Did Schenectady Chemical create the nuisance in this case or did Loeffel? Here Loeffel and his various companies are independent contractors. One who hires an independent contractor will usually not be vicariously liable for the contractor's acts.[11] Do you think Loeffel's creation of a nuisance should be imputed to Schenectady in any event? Is your answer based on the law of independent contractors or on a sense that the court is not about to let a large chemical concern hide behind a small (probably bankrupt) disposal firm?

---

11. Employers will typically be liable for the acts of an independent contractor only where they colluded in wrongful acts, or where strict liability can be proved. Some environmental attorneys have gotten around this bar by suing employers for their "negligent choice of independent contractor."

3. **Aquifers attract toxics.** Note the horrendous siting of this toxic dump, in a low-lying wetland with sub-strata of gravel and sand, precisely the kind of geology that carries groundwater and acts as an aquifer recharge area. Perversely, many dumpers over the years have chosen marshes and gravel quarries as the most convenient dumping spots — out of sight, out of mind. Once within an aquifer, a toxic plume spreads widely, and decontamination of the subsoil is grossly expensive and time-consuming if not impossible.

The following public nuisance case is best known for its strange remedy, but the environmental implications of its cause of action are likewise notable:

### Spur Industries, Inc. v. Del Webb Development Co.
Supreme Court of Arizona, 1972
108 Ariz. 178, 494 P.2d 700

CAMERON, J. The area in question is located in Maricopa County, Arizona, some 14 to 15 miles west of the urban area of Phoenix, on the Phoenix-Wickenburg Highway, also known as Grand Avenue. About two miles south of Grand Avenue is Olive Avenue which runs east and west. 111th Avenue runs north and south as does the Agua Fria River immediately to the west.

Farming started in this area about 1911. In 1929, with the completion of the Carl Pleasant Dam, gravity flow water became available to the property. By 1950, the only urban areas in the vicinity were the agriculturally related communities of Peoria, El Mirage, and Surprise located along Grand Avenue. Along 111th Avenue approximately one mile south of Grand Avenue and 1½ miles north of Olive Avenue, the community of Youngtown was commenced in 1954. Youngtown is a retirement community appealing primarily to senior citizens.

In 1956, Spur's predecessors in interest, H. Marion Welborn and the Northside Hay Mill and Trading Company, developed feedlots about one-half mile south of Olive Avenue. The area is well suited for cattle feeding and in 1959, there were 25 cattle feeding pens or dairy operations within a 7 mile radius of the location.... In April and May of 1959, the Northside Hay Mill was feeding between 6,000 and 7,000 head of cattle and Welborn approximately 1,500 head on a combined area of 35 acres.

In May of 1959, Del Webb began to plan the development of an urban area to be known as Sun City. For this purpose, the Marinette and Santa Fe Ranches, some 20,000 acres of farmland, were purchased for $15,000,000 or $750.00 per acre. This price was considerably less than the price of land located near the urban area of Phoenix, and along with the success of Youngtown was a factor influencing the decision to purchase the property in question.

By September 1959, Del Webb had started construction of a golf course south of Grand Avenue and Spur's predecessors had started to level ground for more feed-lot area. In 1960, Spur purchased the property... and began a rebuilding and expansion program extending both to the north and south of the original facilities. By 1962 Spur's expansion program was completed and had expanded from approximately 35 acres to 114 acres.

Accompanied by an extensive advertising campaign, homes were first offered by Del Webb in January 1960 and the first unit to be completed was south of Grand Avenue and approximately two and a half miles north of Spur. By May 2, 1960, there were 450 to 500 houses completed or under construction. At this time, Del Webb did not consider odors from the Spur feed pens a problem. [In 1963 Webb's

*Inset map from* Spur *decision, 494 P.2d 702, and two views of feedlot operations like those involved in* Spur. *Rather than grazing, the cattle have feed and water brought to them. Densities sometimes reach 400+ per acre, with predictable liquid and solid waste and animal health consequences. Note the manure runoff in lower photograph; in some feed-lots the wastes do not drain off but accumulate where the cattle stand. (Under a recent EPA regulation, concentrated animal feedlots can now be designated as regulated "point sources" under the CWA. 40 C. F. R. § 122.1(b)(2).)*

staff knew of the potential conflict, but decided to continue its southward development.] By December 1967, Del Webb's property had extended south to Olive Avenue and Spur was within 500 feet of Olive Avenue to the north.... Del Webb continued to develop in a southerly direction until sales resistance became so great that the parcels were difficult if not impossible to sell.... Del Webb filed its original complaint alleging that in excess of 1,300 lots in the southwest portion were unfit for development for sale as residential lots because of the operation of the Spur feedlot.

Del Webb's suit complained that the Spur feeding operation was a public nuisance because of the flies and the odor which were drifting or being blown by the prevailing south to north wind over the southern portion of Sun City. At the time of the suit, Spur was feeding between 20,000 and 30,000 head of cattle, and the facts amply support the finding of the trial court that the pens had become a nuisance to the people who resided in the southern part of Del Webb's development. The testimony indicated that cattle in a commercial feedlot will produce 35 to 40 pounds of wet manure per day, per head, or over a million pounds of wet manure per day for 30,000 head of cattle, and that despite the admittedly good feedlot management and good housekeeping practices by Spur, the resulting odor and flies produced an annoying if not unhealthy situation as far as the senior citizens of southern Sun City were concerned. There is no doubt that some of the citizens of Sun City were unable to enjoy the outdoor living which Del Webb had advertised and that Del Webb was faced with sales resistance from prospective purchasers as well as strong and persistent complaints from the people who had purchased homes in that area....

It is noted, however, that neither the citizens of Sun City nor Youngtown are represented in this lawsuit and the suit is solely between Del Webb Development Company and Spur Industries.... It is clear that as to the citizens of Sun City, the operation of Spur's feedlot was both a public and a private nuisance. They could have successfully maintained an action to abate the nuisance. Del Webb, having shown a special injury in the loss of sales, has a standing to bring suit to enjoin the nuisance. The judgment of the trial court permanently enjoining the operation of the feedlot is affirmed.

A suit to enjoin a nuisance sounds in equity and the courts have long recognized a special responsibility to the public when acting as a court of equity: Courts of equity may, and frequently do, go much further both to give and withhold relief in furtherance of the public interest than they are accustomed to go when only private interests are involved. Accordingly, the granting or withholding of relief may properly be dependent upon considerations of public interest.... 27 Am. Jur. 2d, Equity, §104, 626.

In addition to protecting the public interest, however, courts of equity are concerned with protecting the operator of a lawful, albeit noxious, business from the result of a knowing and willful encroachment by others near his business.

In the so-called "coming to the nuisance" cases, the courts have held that the residential landowner may not have relief if he knowingly came into a neighborhood reserved for industrial or agricultural endeavors and has been damaged thereby:

> Plaintiffs chose to live in an area uncontrolled by zoning laws or restrictive covenants and remote from urban development. In such an area plaintiffs cannot complain that legitimate agricultural pursuits are being carried on in the vicinity, nor can plaintiffs, having chosen to build in an agricultural area,

complain that the agricultural pursuits carried on in the area depreciate the value of their homes....

Were Webb the only party injured, we would feel justified in holding that the doctrine of "coming to the nuisance" would have been a bar to the relief asked by Webb, and, on the other hand, had Spur located the feedlot near the outskirts of a city and had the city grown toward the feedlot, Spur would have to suffer the cost of abating the nuisance as to those people locating within the growth pattern of the expanding city....

There was no indication in the instant case at the time Spur and its predecessors located in western Maricopa County that a new city would spring up, full blown, alongside the feeding operations and that the developer of that city would ask the court to order Spur to move because of the new city. Spur is required to move not because of any wrongdoing on the part of Spur, but because of a proper and legitimate regard of the courts for the rights and interests of the public.

Del Webb, on the other hand, is entitled to the relief prayed for (a permanent injunction), not because Webb is blameless, but because of the damage to the people who have been encouraged to purchase homes in Sun City. It does not equitably or legally follow, however, that Webb, being entitled to the injunction, is then free of any liability to Spur if Webb has in fact been the cause of the damage Spur has sustained. It does not seem harsh to require a developer, who has taken advantage of the lesser land values in a rural area as well as the availability of large tracts of land on which to build and develop a new town or city in the area, to indemnify those who are forced to leave as a result.

Having brought people to the nuisance to the foreseeable detriment of Spur, Webb must indemnify Spur for a reasonable amount of the cost of moving or shutting down. It should be noted that this relief to Spur is limited to a case wherein a developer has, with foreseeability, brought into a previously agricultural or industrial area the population which makes necessary the granting of an injunction against a lawful business and for which the business has no adequate relief.

It is therefore the decision of this court that the matter be remanded to the trial court for a hearing upon the damages sustained by the defendant Spur as a reasonable and direct result of the granting of the permanent injunction. Since the result of the appeal may appear novel and both sides have obtained a measure of relief, it is ordered that each side will bear its own costs.

COMMENTARY AND QUESTIONS

1. **The twist in *Spur*.** On remand, Webb settled, reportedly paying Spur more than $1 million in moving costs. In a subsequent case, the Arizona court also allowed Spur to sue for indemnity, so that Webb would have to reimburse the feedlot for tort damages Spur might have to pay to individual homeowners. Spur v. Superior Court, 505 P.2d 1377 (Ariz. 1973). The unusual feature of the *Spur* case is not its public nuisance theory, but its remedy, conditioning the injunction on plaintiff's payment of moving costs. Is this a case about comparative fault? The court seems to consider that it was the developer's fault that caused the conflict. Is Spur's nuisance therefore based on some kind of no-fault liability? What if the only suit for injunction and damages had been brought by homeowners, not Webb? What if Webb lacked funds to pay Spur? Doesn't this get the court into judicial land use decisions, as noted below?

On a larger scale, it is useful to note that agricultural pollution cases generally can only be litigated under common law theories, because the farm lobbies' political strength has successfully inserted blanket exemptions for agriculture into all significant federal and state pollution statutes. But farmers clearly need protection against tort suits filed by hypersensitive newcomers in rural areas. Since *Spur*, common law courts have not evolved a satisfactory balancing process for protecting rural farming from nuisance suits, but more than 40 states have enacted "right-to-farm" tort exemption statutes for rural areas.

2. **The tactical advantages of public nuisance.** What advantages did Webb get from suing in public nuisance? Part of his strategy was to get around the coming-to-the-nuisance defense. Did Webb also get a broader basis for nuisance claims than he would have under private nuisance, even class action private nuisance? The court unhesitatingly balanced the overall public interest against Spur. Note, moreover, that there was no proof of personal injury or property damage in *Spur*. The court said that "the odor and flies produced an annoying if *not unhealthy* situation," and seemed to focus on the aesthetics and quality of life of the community of Sun City. Would Oscar Boomer have gained from filing his case in public nuisance? Aesthetic nuisance litigation, applied to billboards, junkyards, and the like, is typically based on public nuisance.

Public nuisance also opens up otherwise impossible liability claims, like predecessor liability for land contamination. In most states, a buyer has no action against a seller who has sold property that turns out to be spoiled or hazardous. Caveat emptor. In several cases of contaminated land, however, the courts, though refusing to allow private nuisance claims because the parties did not own different parcels, allowed public nuisance claims. In Nashua Corp. v. Norton Co., 45 ERC 1013 (D.C.N.D.N.Y.1997),[12] public nuisance applied because groundwater pollution from the parcel threatened the general public. The plaintiff's response costs and alleged stigma damages qualified as special damages.

3. **A widening role for environmental public nuisance?** Public nuisance has traditionally been applied against actions which injure life or health; offend the senses; violate principles of decency; obstruct free passage or use of highways, navigable streams, public parks, and beaches; and otherwise disrupt public rights. These definitions obviously possess great potential to expand with contemporary sensibilities to incorporate a wide range of environmental values. How far into novel environmental settings can public nuisance be extended? The aesthetic enjoyment of low-tech visitors to a Walden Pond, a desert park, or a wilderness river can be disturbed by just a few individuals with boom-boxes or all-terrain vehicles. Are these public nuisances? Is smoking in public becoming litigatable as public nuisance? Destruction of historic monuments? Could public nuisance injunctions, if the facts had been known, have blocked the importation of alien species like gypsy moths, poisonous walking catfish, carp, and starlings into the U.S.? Can public nuisance be used where consequences are potentially disastrous but probabilities are uncertain, as with recombinant DNA genetic engineering experimentation out-

---

12. Plaintiff also filed under CERCLA and RCRA's private cleanup remedies, but the nuisance claims were filed in order to recover "stigma" damages, unrecoverable under statutory causes of action.

side the laboratory? For an ancient doctrine, the flexibility and scope of public nuisance give it remarkable evolutionary potential.

**4. Public nuisance/private plaintiffs.** Public nuisance, deriving from criminal law, is in the first instance supposed to be litigated by public prosecutors, but local and state governments often are not enthusiastic about litigation and are sometimes themselves the defendants in public nuisance actions. Private plaintiffs have thus played a major role in the expansion of public nuisance. Private standing, however, has traditionally posed a procedural barrier: in order to sue in public nuisance, private plaintiffs have to show "special injury" different in kind, and not just in degree, from the public as a whole. In *Spur*, for example, Webb's "sales resistance" is special injury. A homeowner in the neighborhood might or might not be granted special injury standing. A disgusted county resident with no health or property damage traditionally would have no hope of suing in public nuisance. Isn't it somewhat paradoxical that in order to represent public values in public nuisance, which offers wide attractions to environmental plaintiffs, they must prove that they are substantially different from the public? Recent amendments to the Restatement 2d of Torts §421c attempt to extend standing in public nuisance, for injunctive relief only, to any person "having standing to sue as a representative of the general public, as a citizen in a citizen suit, or class representative in a class action." Many courts have continued to follow the old special injury rule, although a number of states hold that any bodily injury is *per se* special. Note that public nuisance actions usually seek equitable relief only; private plaintiffs typically cannot recover public nuisance damages (unless special damages as in the *Nashua Corp.* case above), and public plaintiffs normally do not seek damages.[13]

**5. Judicial zoning under public nuisance?** Given the Arizona court's holding in *Spur*, would it have issued an injunction against Webb's southward development if Spur had timely brought such an action in 1962? The court clearly considered the natural and appropriate use for the area to be agricultural rather than urban. In a number of fascinating cases, courts have issued injunctions against, for instance, funeral parlors and gas stations in unzoned residential areas, judicially recognizing their primarily residential character. Powell v. Taylor, 263 S.W.2d 906 (Ark. 1954) (funeral parlor); State v. Feezell, 400 S.W.2d 716 (Tenn. 1966) (crematorium). In Harrison v. Indiana Auto Shredders, 528 F.2d 1102 (7th Cir. 1975), however, the court permitted a noisy, smelly, gas-and-dust emitting automobile shredding and recycling operation to locate in a low-income neighborhood, merely awarding damages, evidently classifying the neighborhood as less deserving of equitable protection. In Bove v. Donner-Hanna Coke Corp., 258 N.Y.S. 229, 233 (1932), the court denied even damages to a woman whose home was polluted by installation of a smelly coke oven, saying that "it is true that...when the plaintiff built her house, the land on which these coke ovens now stand was a hickory grove. But...this region was never fitted for a residential district; for years it has been peculiarly adapted for factory sites." Recognizing the environmental potential for incorporat-

---

13. There appears to be no reason limiting public plaintiffs from seeking to recover public nuisance damages, as was done in *Schenectady Chemical* and cases cited therein. In appropriate cases private plaintiffs might do the same, perhaps requesting that damages be placed in a common trust fund.

ing evolving public sensibilities into public nuisance, do you nevertheless feel uncomfortable with the role that judges can play in dictating appropriate uses for particular parcels of land?

## Section 2. TRESPASS

### Borland v. Sanders Lead Company, Inc.
Supreme Court of Alabama, 1979
369 So. 2d 523

JONES, J. This appeal involves the right of a property owner, in an action for trespass, to recover damages for pollution of his property.... J.H. Borland, Sr., and Sarah M. Borland, Appellants, own approximately 159 acres of land, located just south of Troy, Alabama, on Henderson Road. On this property, Appellants raise cattle, grow several different crops, and have a large pecan orchard.

In 1968, the Appellee, Sanders Lead Company, started an operation for the recovery of lead from used automobile batteries...just east of the Borlands' property.... The Appellee's smelter was placed on the west edge of their property, that part nearest to the Appellants' property. The smelter is used to reduce the plates from used automobile batteries. It is alleged by Appellants that the smelting process results in the emission of lead particulates and sulfoxide gases....

Appellee installed a filter system, commonly known as a "bag house," to intercept these lead particulates which otherwise would be emitted into the atmosphere. The "bag house" is a building containing fiber bags. The smoke emitting from the furnace is passed through two cooling systems before passing through the "bag house" so that the fiber bags will not catch fire. If properly installed and used, an efficient "bag house" will recover over 99 percent of the lead emitted. On two occasions, the cooling system at Appellee's smeltering plant has failed to function properly, resulting in the "bag house's" catching fire on both occasions.... Appellants allege that, because of the problems with the "bag house," their property has been damaged by a dangerous accumulation of lead particulates and sulfoxide deposits on their property....

The trial Court was under the mistaken impression that compliance with the Alabama Air Pollution Control Act shielded the Defendant from liability for damages caused by pollutants emitting from its smelter. This is not the law in this State.... Furthermore, the trial Court incorrectly applied the law of this State in concluding that, because there was evidence showing that the Plaintiffs' farm had increased in value as industrial property, due to its proximity to the lead plant, Plaintiffs could not recover of the Defendant. Such a rule, in effect, would permit private condemnation, which, unquestionably, is impermissible...[and] overlooks the fact that the appreciation factor is totally unrelated to the wrongful acts complained of....

Alabama law clearly provides an appropriate remedy for Plaintiffs who have been directly injured by the deleterious effects of pollutants created by another party's acts.... A trespass need not be inflicted directly on another's realty, but may be committed by discharging foreign polluting matter at a point beyond the boundary of such realty.... Restatement, 2d, Torts, §158 recites:

> In order that there may be a trespass under the rule stated in this Section, it is not necessary that the foreign matter should be thrown directly and immediately upon the other's land. It is enough that an act is done with knowledge that it will to a substantial certainty result in entry of foreign matters.

In Martin v. Reynolds Metals Co., 342 P.2d 790 (Or. 1959), a case remarkably similar to the present case, the Plaintiffs sought recovery...for trespass [alleging] that the operation by Defendants of an aluminum reduction plant caused certain fluoride compounds in the form of gases and particulates, invisible to the naked eye, to become airborne and settle on Plaintiffs' property, rendering it unfit for raising livestock. Plaintiffs in the present case allege that the operation of Defendant's lead reduction plant causes an emission of lead particulates, and $SO_2$, invisible to the naked eye, which emissions have settled on their property, making it unsuitable for raising cattle or growing crops.

The Defendants in *Martin* contended that there had not been a sufficient invasion of Plaintiffs' property to constitute trespass, but, at most, Defendant's acts constituted a nuisance. This would have allowed the Defendants to set up Oregon's two-year statute of limitations applicable to non-possessory injuries to land rather than Oregon's six-year statute for trespass to land. The *Martin* Court pointed out that trespass and nuisance are separate torts for the protection of different interests invaded — trespass protecting the possessor's interest in exclusive possession of property and nuisance protecting the interest in use and enjoyment. The Court noted, and we agree, that the same conduct on the part of defendant may, and often does, result in the actionable invasion of both interests....

The modern action for trespass to land stemmed inexorably from the common law action for trespass which lay when the injury was both direct and substantial. Nuisance, on the other hand, would lie when injuries were indirect and less substantial. A fictitious "dimensional" test arose, which obviated the necessity of determining whether the intrusion was "direct" and "substantial." If the intruding agent could be seen by the naked eye, the intrusion was considered a trespass. If the agent could not be seen, it was considered indirect and less substantial, hence, a nuisance.... The *Martin* Court rejected the dimensional test and substituted in its place a force and energy test, stating:

> The view recognizing a trespassory invasion where there is no "thing" which can be seen with the naked eye undoubtedly runs counter to the definition of trespass expressed in some quarters. It is quite possible that in an earlier day when science had not yet peered into the molecular and atomic world of small particles, the courts could not fit an invasion through unseen physical instrumentalities into the requirement that a trespass can result only from a direct invasion. But in this atomic age even the uneducated know the great and awful force contained in the atom and what it can do to a man's property if it is released. In fact, the now famous equation $E=mc^2$ has taught us that mass and energy are equivalents and that our concept of 'things' must be reframed. If these observations on science in relation to the law of trespass should appear theoretical and unreal in the abstract, they become very practical and real to the possessor of land when the unseen force cracks the foundation of his house. The force is just as real if it is chemical in nature.... Viewed in this way we may define trespass as an intrusion which invades the possessor's protected interest in exclusive possession, whether that intrusion is by visible or invisible pieces of matter or by energy which can be measured only by the mathematical language of the physicist. We are of the opinion, therefore, that the intrusion of the fluoride particulates in the present case constituted a trespass.

It might appear, at first blush, from our holding today that every property owner in this State would have a cause of action against any neighboring industry which emitted particulate matter into the atmosphere, or even a passing motorist, whose exhaust emissions come to rest upon another's property. But we hasten to point out that there is a point where the entry is so lacking in substance that the law will refuse to recognize it, applying the maxim de minimis non curat lex — the law does not concern itself with trifles. In the present case, however, we are not faced with a trifling complaint. The Plaintiffs in this case have suffered, if the evidence is believed, a real and substantial invasion of a protected interest.... If the intrusion is direct, then, under our present law, actual damages need not be shown; nominal damages may be awarded and this will support punitive damages....

Under the modern theory of trespass, the law presently allows an action to be maintained in trespass for invasions that, at one time, were considered indirect and, hence, only a nuisance. In order to recover in trespass for this type of invasion (i.e., the asphalt piled in such a way as to run onto plaintiff's property, or the pollution emitting from a defendant's smoke stack, such as in the present case), a plaintiff must show (1) an invasion affecting an interest in the exclusive possession of his property; (2) an intentional doing of the act which results in the invasion; (3) reasonable foreseeability that the act done could result in an invasion of plaintiff's possessory interest; and (4) substantial damages to the res [i.e., unlike direct trespasses which need not show substantial damages]....

If, as a result of the defendant's operation, the polluting substance is deposited upon the plaintiff's property, thus interfering with his exclusive possessory interest by causing substantial damage to the res, then the plaintiff may seek his remedy in trespass, though his alternative remedy in nuisance may co-exist.... Reversed and remanded.

### COMMENTARY AND QUESTIONS

1. **Trespass and tactics.** As the *Borland* and *Martin* courts both noted, pollution may be simultaneously both a trespass and a nuisance, and be litigated as either or both. Why do plaintiffs sue in trespass instead of nuisance? Trespass carries a number of internal restrictions, including those noted by the court and the fact that in most states it cannot be based on mere negligence liability. The statute of limitations for trespass, however, often extends back further in time than nuisance, as it did in *Martin*; damages are available for all consequential injuries throughout the actual chain of causation, not only those foreseeable; and trespass actions seem to encourage the grant of injunctions by emphasizing the fact of an unconsented invasion, penetration, or incursion onto private property. Even judges quite unattuned to environmental issues have acknowledged that "a man's home is his castle," and issued injunctions.

2. **How far can trespass go?** After *Borland*, Alabama apparently requires actual and substantial injury for an "indirect" trespass like a pollution case. Most other states, however, do not. If courts apply $E=mc^2$ to determine whether there has been "physical invasion" of plaintiff's property, is there any limit to how far the trespass action may apply? Noise? Light photons? Low-frequency electromagnetic radiation from high voltage transmission facilities? An ugly view? Has the distinction between trespass and nuisance become purely semantic; does it any longer make sense?

3. **Defenses in *Borland*.** Note the defendant's attempt to use the "permit defense." The court's reasoning reflects a distinction between the remedial purposes of the

common law and the regulatory purposes of the pollution control statutes — the former is concerned with redress for local injuries, the latter is concerned with minimum public health and welfare standards. Defendant also raised as a partial defense to the assessment of damages the argument that it had caused no loss to the plaintiff because the land had appreciated in value due to its value as commercial property which derived from its proximity to defendant's lead plant. The appellate court rejected the defense. If change in property value is not the measure of damage, what is? Is it possible to base the measure of damages on the change in value of the land as used for purposes desired by the plaintiff?

## Section 3. NEGLIGENT NUISANCE AND NEGLIGENCE

Negligence has seldom been the sole theory of recovery in successful environmental cases. The apparent reason for the relatively rare use of the negligence cause of action is that in cases involving injury to property, like most of those studied thus far, the intentional nuisance or trespass theories (or strict liability, considered in the following section) are easier to prove than negligence. The principal domain of the negligence cause of action is the traditional lawsuit by an injured victim to recover for bodily injuries caused by the defendant's negligence. Personal injury cases do arise in the environmental setting, and are occasionally litigated on negligence theories, see Greyhound v. Blakely, 262 F.2d 401 (9th Cir. 1958), but more typically are litigated under strict liability.

The following case illustrates some of the reasons why there are not many modern negligent nuisance actions.

### Dillon v. Acme Oil Company
New York Supreme Court, General Term, 1888
49 Hun 565, 18 N.Y. St. Rep. 477, 2 N.Y.S. 289

HAIGHT, J. The evidence tends to show that the plaintiff's wells were contaminated with oil and rendered unfit for use. The evidence also tends to show that there has been occasional leakage and spilling of oil and the refuse thereof upon the ground at the refinery where the crude is manufactured into refined oil; that the earth had become saturated with it around the refinery.... The plaintiff's premises...are twenty rods away. There is a public street and a railroad, with several tracks, intervening between the plaintiff's and defendant's premises. Taking into consideration the character of the surface soil, it hardly seems possible or probable that the oil upon the ground, at the defendant's refinery, would soak or percolate through the ground collaterally upon the surface so great a distance as to contaminate the plaintiff's wells from the surface. It appeared, upon the trial, that some feet under the surface there was a stratum of gravel, and the more rational and probable theory, to our minds, is that the oil at the refinery had percolated through the earth downward until some subterranean water vein was reached, probably in the stratum of gravel, from which it was conveyed into the wells. And this theory appears to have been the one upon which the case was tried. The court found, as a fact, that the works of the defendant were constructed and operated as well as such works could be, having reference to the location and nature of the business. The question is, therefore, presented as to whether there could be a recovery for contaminating a subterranean water stream or vein when the defendant is pursuing a legitimate business with works constructed and operated as well as they could be. It is said to be a legal maxim, that every man must so use his own property as not to injure that of another, but this maxim is not to be construed so as to deprive a party from using that which he owns for legitimate purposes, provided, in so doing, he exercise proper care and skill to prevent unnecessary injury to others....

It is only in exceptional cases that the channels of subterranean streams are known and their courses defined; it is only in such exceptional cases that the owner can know beforehand that his works will affect his neighbor's wells or supply of water, and we are, therefore, of the opinion that in the absence of negligence and of knowledge as to the existence of such subterranean water-courses, when the business is legitimate and conducted with care and skill, there can be no liability if such subterranean courses become contaminated....

### COMMENTARY AND QUESTIONS

1. **Negligence defenses.** The *Dillon* court based its holding in part on lack of foreseeability, an element that would equally have undercut intentional tort liability. (Was it indeed not foreseeable that oil spilled on the ground would contaminate the groundwater?) But the weight accorded defendant's "legitimate business conducted with care and skill," and its implicit balance of utilities, provided a virtually unbeatable defense under the negligent nuisance theory.

In a case where a coal processing operation's burning refuse piles released clouds of hydrogen sulfide gas that stunk up an entire neighborhood and caused housepaint to turn black, the Pennsylvania Supreme Court also used negligence theories to deny liability. The Court noted that the defendants "used every known means to prevent damage or injury to adjoining properties," but, unfortunately, "there is no known method by which such fires can be extinguished." Quoting two lower court opinions in similar cases, the Court continued:

> The plaintiffs are subject to annoyance [but] it is probable that upon reflection they will...still conclude that, after all, one's bread is more important than landscape or clear skies. Without smoke, Pittsburgh would have remained a very pretty *village*....

> The general rule that one must use his own land so as not to injure that of another — otherwise he is liable in damages — is subject to the exception that every man has the right to the natural use and enjoyment of his own property, and if while lawfully in such use and enjoyment, without negligence or malice on his part, an unavoidable loss occurs to his neighbor, it is *damnum absque injuria*, for the rightful use of one's own land may cause damage to another, without any legal wrong. Waschak v. Moffat, 109 A.2d 310, 316–17 (Pa. 1954) (emphasis in original).

Given the defensive effects of such negligence principles, it is unsurprising that most experienced plaintiff's attorneys in pollution cases avoid reliance on negligence theories, and try to clarify for trial judges the significant differences between negligent and intentional torts.

2. **The uses of negligence.** A few environmental suits not based on personal injuries are decided on negligence theories. See Rotella v. McGovern, 288 A.2d 258 (R.I.

1972) (negligent sewer maintenance produced sewage flood in basement).

In Hagy v. Allied Chemical, the chemical company was operating a plant in Los Angeles that produced large amounts of acidic smokestack emissions (on days of thermal inversion, the emissions, including amounts of sulphuric acid, would pour down the side of the stack as well as casting a pall over the neighborhood). Allied had instructed its employees to don gas masks during inversions, and to ignore telephone calls from gassed neighbors. The Hagys were gassed while driving by, sued for negligent personal injury instead of public nuisance, and won substantial damages. 265 P.2d 86 (Cal. App. 1953).

One of the advantages of negligence to plaintiffs, beyond its familiarity to bench and bar, is the extensive array of damage theories developed in negligence case law, including pain and suffering, offering opportunities for "running up" damage awards. Another is that tort claims acts waiving sovereign immunity may only cover negligence. Under some insurance policies, moreover, defendants will only be covered for accidental discharges, not for "intentional" pollution, so a negligence judgment is more likely to be paid. See, e.g., Technicon Electronic Corp. v. American Home Assurance Co., 542 N.E.2d 1048 (N.Y. 1989). Where violations of environmental laws and regulations are proved, plaintiffs' job of proving defendants' negligence may be greatly facilitated. As a tactical matter, even in intentional tort cases it may be to plaintiffs' advantage to present evidence of what the defendant could have done more carefully.

3. **The deterrence value of negligence actions.** Does the threat of negligence verdicts deter would-be polluters? There is no necessary relationship between the amount awarded to plaintiff and either the costs of avoiding the pollution or the culpability of defendant's conduct. Given the reputation of some negligence litigators, the possibility of large negligence damage awards would surely catch defendants' attention. Most cases, however, continue to proceed on non-negligence theories.

### Section 4. STRICT LIABILITY

(1) One who carries on an abnormally dangerous activity is subject to liability for harm to the person, land or chattels of another resulting from the activity, although he has exercised the utmost care to prevent such harm.

(2) Such strict liability is limited to the kind of harm, the risk of which makes the activity abnormally dangerous. Restatement 2d of Torts, §519.

In determining what constitutes an abnormally dangerous activity, under Restatement §520, the following factors are to be considered:

(a) Whether the activity involves a high degree of risk of some harm to the person, land, or chattels of others;

(b) Whether the gravity of the harm which may result from it is likely to be great;

(c) Whether the risk cannot be eliminated by the exercise of reasonable care;

(d) Whether the activity is not a matter of common usage;

(e) Whether the activity is inappropriate to the place where it is carried on; and

(f) The value of the activity to the community.

## Branch v. Western Petroleum, Inc.
Supreme Court of Utah, 1982
657 P.2d 267

STEWART, J. The Branches, the plaintiff property owners, sued for damages for the pollution of their culinary water wells caused by percolation of defendant Western Petroleum's formation waters into the subterranean water system that feeds the wells....

In December 1975, Western purchased forty acres of land in a rural area north of Roosevelt, Utah, which had previously been used as a gravel pit. Western used the property solely for the disposal of formation water, a waste water produced by oil wells while drilling for oil. Formation water contains oil, gas and high concentrations of salt and chemicals, making it unfit for culinary or agricultural uses. The formation water was transported by truck from various oil-producing sites and emptied into the disposal pit with the intent that the toxic water would dissipate through evaporation into the air and percolation into the ground. Alternative sites for disposing of the water were available to Western, but at a greater expense.

In 1976, the Branches purchased a parcel of property immediately adjacent to, and at an elevation of approximately 200 to 300 feet lower than Western's property. The twenty-one acre parcel had on it a "diligence" well, which had been in existence since 1929, some outbuildings, and a home. After acquiring the property, the Branches made some $60,000 worth of improvements to the home and premises. Prior owners of the property used the water from the well for a grade A dairy and later a grade B dairy. Both dairy operations required that the water be approved for fitness and purity by appropriate state agencies. The Branches, as had all prior owners since 1929, used water from the diligence well for culinary purposes. The water from the diligence well was described as being sweet to the taste and of a high quality until December of 1976.

Two months after purchasing the property, the Branches noticed that the well water began to take on a peculiar taste and had the distinctive smell of petroleum products. Soap added to the water would no longer form suds. They observed that polluted water from Western's disposal pit was running onto the surface of the Branches' property and, on one occasion, reached their basement, causing damage to food stored there. After testing the diligence well water and finding it unfit for human consumption, and after their rabbits and one hundred chickens had died, apparently from the polluted water, the Branches began trucking water to their property from outside sources. In November, 1977, the Branches dug an additional well south of their home. Water from the new well was tested and found safe for culinary purposes. But after a few months, the new well also ceased producing potable water, and on advice of the State Health Department, the Branches ceased using the new well for culinary purposes and hauled water to their property almost until the time of trial.

The Branches requested Western to cease dumping formation water in the disposal pit, but Western refused unless the Branches would post a bond to cover the costs....

At trial the major issue was whether and how Western's formation waters caused the pollution of the Branches' wells.... The Branches' expert, Mr. Montgomery, a state geologist who had spent nine years working for the Utah

Division of Water Resources, [said] that the subsurface waters consist of shallow groundwater and a deeper aquifer known as the Duchesne Formation.... Water in the disposal pit was percolating into the subsurface waters....

The major substantive dispute is whether the trial court erred in entering judgment against Western on the basis of strict liability for pollution of the Branches' wells. Western argues that other states have based liability for pollution of subterranean waters on either negligence, [intentional] nuisance, or trespass, and that since the Branches failed to allege nuisance or trespass, "the only accepted theory upon which this case could be based is negligence." Therefore, according to Western, the trial court erred in entering judgment on the basis of strict liability. Western further submits that since the court did not instruct the jury on proximate cause and comparative negligence, the judgment cannot stand. The Branches, on the other hand, take the position that Western created an abnormally dangerous condition by collecting contaminated water on its land for the purpose of having it seep or percolate into the groundwater and that, therefore, the law of strict liability controls....

In England under the common law, percolating water was considered part of the freehold and subject to private ownership. In American law it is generally recognized that a landowner has no absolute right to pollute percolating waters. In this state, a landowner has no such absolute right because percolating waters belong to the people of the state. For that reason, and because percolating waters are migratory and the rights of the landowners to those waters are correlative, such waters are subject to the maxim that one may not use his land so as to pollute percolating waters to the injury of another.

As Utah is one of the most arid states in the union, the protection of the purity of the water is of critical importance, and the Legislature has enacted laws for the protection of both surface and subterranean waters....

The landmark case of Rylands v. Fletcher, 3 H. & C. 774, 159 Eng. Rep. 737 (1865), rev'd in Fletcher v. Rylands, L.R. 1 Ex. 265 (1866), aff'd in Rylands v. Fletcher, L.R. 3 H.L. 330 (1868), held that one who uses his land in an unnatural way and thereby creates a dangerous condition or engages in an abnormal activity may be strictly liable for injuries resulting from that condition or activity. Whether a condition or activity is considered abnormal is defined in terms of whether the condition or activity is unduly dangerous or inappropriate to the place where it is maintained. That doctrine was the genesis of §519 of the Restatement of Torts (1939), which, however, limited strict liability to "ultrahazardous activities."

Although Rylands v. Fletcher was initially rejected by a number of states, its influence has been substantial in the United States. According to the latest edition of Dean Prosser's treatise on torts, only seven American jurisdictions have rejected the rule of that case, while some thirty jurisdictions have essentially approved the rule. Indeed, the strict liability rule of the Restatement of Torts was broadened in §519 of the Restatement 2d of Torts by making it applicable to "abnormally dangerous activities."

There are two separate, although somewhat related, grounds for holding Western strictly liable for the pollution of the Branches' wells. First, the facts of the case support application of the rule of strict liability because the ponding of the toxic formation water in an area adjacent to the Branches' wells constituted an abnormally dangerous and inappropriate use of the land[14] in light of its proximity to the Branches' property and was unduly dangerous to the Branches' use of their well water.[15]

[Second],...the common law rules of tort liability in pollution cases should be in conformity with the public policy of this state as declared by the Legislature,...[and an] industrial polluter can and should assume the costs of pollution as a cost of doing business rather than charge the loss to a wholly innocent party:

> We know of no acceptable rule of jurisprudence which permits those engaged in important and desirable enterprises to injure with impunity those who are engaged in enterprises of lesser economic significance. The costs of injuries resulting from pollution must be internalized by industry as a cost of production and borne by consumers or shareholders, or both, and not by the injured individual. *Atlas Chemical*, 514 S.W.2d 309.

---

14. Several cases on comparable facts have applied strict liability due to the abnormal danger of polluting activity. For example, Mowrer v. Ashland Oil & Refining Co., 518 F.2d 659 (7th Cir. 1975), applied strict liability to the leakage of crude oil and salt water into a fresh water well; Yommer v. McKenzie, 257 A.2d 138 (Md. 1969), applied the same rule to the seepage of gasoline from an underground tank into an adjoining landowner's well; Cities Service Co. v. Florida, 312 So. 2d 799 (Fla. 1975), applied strict liability to the escape of phosphate slime into a creek and river. See also Bumbarger v. Walker, 164 A.2d 144 (Pa. 1960) (strict liability for well pollution caused by defendant's mine blasting). See generally Clark-Aiken Co. v. Cromwell-Wright Co., 323 N.E.2d 876 (Mass. 1975)(strict liability applied to escape of impounded water); Indiana Harbor Belt Railroad Co. v. American Cyanamid Co., 517 F. Supp. 314 (N.D. Ill. 1981) (strict liability applied to spillage of toxic chemical that resulted in property damage and pollution of water supply); W. Prosser, Torts §78 at 512-13 and cases there cited. See also Atlas Chemical Industries, Inc. v. Anderson, 514 S.W.2d 309 (Tex. Civ. App. 6 Dist., 1974), aff'd 524 S.W.2d 681 (1975), where the Texas court, distinguishing a case relied upon by Western, Turner v. Big Lake Oil Co., 96 S.W.2d 221 (Tex. 1936), held the defendant strictly liable for polluting surface streams with industrial wastes. The strict liability rule of Rylands v. Fletcher was held to apply to pollution cases "in which the defendant has set the substance in motion for escape, such as the discharge of the harmful effluent or the emission of a harmful gas or substance."*Atlas Chemical*, 514 S.W.2d at 314.

15. Even if Western did not know that the formation water would enter the aquifer and cause damage to plaintiffs' wells, it could have determined the likelihood of that consequence. As Professor Davis has stated:

> A polluter should not be absolved from liability just because he may not be able to anticipate the movement of the polluted groundwater he created. This defense should not be recognized for several reasons. First, the hydrology of groundwater movement is much better understood now than it was when many of the early groundwater pollution cases were decided. Even though precise mapping of groundwater movement in any particular location is still expensive, it is within the reach of any major waste producer which proposes to inject wastes underground. Disposal wells need porous formations for successful waste injection and the appropriate hydrologic tests would insure a successful injection well. Therefore, persons deliberately disposing of wastes underground ought to be required to act in accordance with the information gained by such testing regarding the movement of the injected wastes and their probable effects on neighboring groundwater uses. If they do not make such tests, they should be charged with the information they would have gained had they made them. Second, it is generally known now that liquids placed on the ground will seep into the soil and may enter the body of groundwater percolating beneath the surface. Persons causing groundwater pollution, in ways other than by deliberate underground disposal, should be charged with such knowledge and should not be insulated from liability for groundwater pollution by claiming that they know nothing more about groundwater movement than was known in 1843 when Acton v. Blundell was decided. Although a particular polluter might still legitimately claim he could not predict particular injurious consequences of his activity, he can no longer claim legitimately that the polluting material vanished from the earth once it seeped beneath the surface. He knows it will go somewhere. Such a defense to nuisance liability is not recognized in surface watercourse and air pollution cases. Groundwater pollution cases should not recognize it either. Davis, Groundwater Pollution: Case Law Theories for Relief, 39 Mo. L. Rev. 117, 145–46 (1974). See also Wood v. Picillo, 443 A.2d 1244, 1249 (R.I. 1982). [This is note 6 in the original.]

We think these reasons adequately support application of the rule of strict liability in this case. In sum, the trial court properly ruled that Western was strictly liable for the damage which it caused the Branches....

COMMENTARY AND QUESTIONS

1. **Why strict liability?** Analytically, the *Branch* case is a private nuisance action, based on strict liability grounds rather than negligence or intent. What advantages does strict liability offer plaintiffs? Beyond shortcutting various foreseeability elements, and defenses like contributory negligence and others raised in *Schenectady Chemical*, strict liability also automatically extends liability to pollution sources despite their use of independent contractors as intermediaries. In *Branch*, strict liability sidesteps the need to prove foreseeability, basing liability on proof of harm caused.

2. **"Abnormally dangerous."** In *Branch*, what is found to be ultrahazardous or abnormally dangerous under the terms of Restatement §519–520? Is oil really an abnormally dangerous material? Or is storage of oil-drilling wastewater an abnormally dangerous activity? On the facts of *Branch*, the closest analogy to *Rylands* is disposing of formation waters by placing them in an impoundment near a property line or recharge area for local wells. Is that enough?

3. **Foreseeability.** Did Western know that the formation water would reach the wells? It appears that they did not foresee such an occurrence, and even after the fact disputed its occurrence through the testimony of their expert witness. To what degree is foreseeability relevant? In its footnote 6, the court relies on Professor Davis' argument to reject the importance of defendant's foreknowledge of events. What is Davis' argument? It first simply charges highly-capitalized waste disposers with foreseeing whatever testing would have revealed; it second simply recognizes that liquids tend to percolate down into aquifers, and it charges defendants with that knowledge, something that the law refused to do in an earlier era when less was known about hydrogeology. So stated, would there be sufficient evidence of foreseeability in *Branch* to reflect intent? In many settings these cases could just as well be litigated under intentional public or private nuisance.

4. **Strict liability for what harms?** The court points out the nonchalance of Western in its attitude toward the Branch's rights and its lack of inquiry into the pollution laws of Utah. Why is this relevant in a strict liability case? The answer lies with a claim for punitive damages, discussed in the following section on remedies.

In Langan v. Valicopters, 567 P.2d 218 (Wash. 1977), an aerial crop-dusting service had allowed its pesticide sprays to drift onto an organic farm. No crops were killed. The plaintiffs' injury claim was based purely on their crops' loss of "organic" certification caused by the spray. The court went step by step through Restatement §§519 and 520 and applied strict liability. Looking at §519(2), would you? If pesticide spraying is indeed an abnormally dangerous activity, what kinds of ecological harms can be recouped, by whom? Was Allied Chemical's making and dumping of Kepone an abnormally dangerous activity? If so, is damage to the environment the kind of hazard that made it dangerous, or is strict liability limited to personal injuries?

5. **Environmental applications of other tort theories.** Beyond the preceding commonly encountered torts, environmental cases filed by creative plaintiffs can be based on theories of "battery" (where pollution is characterized as unconsented intentional physical contact with plaintiffs' bodies), Martin v. National Steel, 607 F. Supp. 1430 (S.D. Ill. 1985); "waste" to land (where degradation of rented land, life estates, or a defeasible fee injures the reversion), U.S. v. Denver RGR Co., 190 F. 825 (D. Colo. 1911); water-based violations of "reasonable use" (impacting riparian property rights), Thompson v. Enz, 154 N.W.2d 473 (Mich. 1967), and other flexible applications of existing doctrine, each presenting different litigation requirements and potential benefits. Environmental plaintiffs are continually exploring and rethinking old tort options in order to develop new litigation approaches and tactics.

## D. REMEDIES IN ENVIRONMENTAL LITIGATION

Many novel issues arise in the context of environmental law remedies. The following sections explore equitable remedies, damages, restoration remedies, and natural resources remedies. Criminal penalties are considered in Chapter 19, and administrative sanctions in Chapter 7 and 20.

### Section 1. EQUITY AND INJUNCTIONS

#### Plater, Statutory Violations and Equitable Discretion
#### 70 California Law Review 524, 545–546, 533–544 (1982)

The exercise of equitable jurisdiction, particularly the availability of injunctions, has increased over the years. The anachronistic requirement of a property interest in order to invoke equity has been scrapped of necessity, and other impediments have been removed. Despite regular protestations to the contrary, the status of the injunction has become a common, widely used judicial remedy precisely because of its ability to fine-tune the requirements of private conduct in a complex, modern society. Its development parallels the expansion of cases [in environmental law and] in civil rights and other constitutional areas, where damage remedies are insufficient or miss the point....

When equity's application in traditional common law cases is subjected to careful analysis, some basic clarifications emerge. Analytically, it can be argued that the umbrella terms "balancing the equities" and "equitable discretion" obscure what are really three separate areas of balancing, three different functions fulfilled by three different types of equitable relativism. The three areas are:

1. *Threshold balancing*, based in both law and equity, tests whether plaintiffs can maintain their actions. This stage includes questions of laches, clean hands, other estoppels, the lack of an adequate remedy at law, proof of irreparable harm, and similar issues.

2. *Determination of contending conducts* ascertains which conduct will be permitted to continue and which will be subordinated. It often involves the question of abatement, a separate issue from the question of liability for past injuries to protected interests.

3. *Discretion in fashioning remedies* involves a process of tailoring remedies to implement the second stage determination of contending conducts.

Consider, for example, the relatively simple field of private nuisance torts where equity has traditionally played an active role. The classic *Ducktown Sulphur* case demonstrates all three of equity's distinctly different roles. In that turn-of-the-century case, 83 S.W. 658 (Tenn. 1904), the court had to deal with an early example of an environmental tradeoff. The smelting industry was getting underway in the foothills of southeastern Tennessee and northern Georgia. It was likely to provide sizable revenues for the entrepreneurs of Atlanta and Chattanooga, jobs for local residents, and copper and other materials for the nation's industrial economy. The copper ore was mined in nearby hills, then smelted in large open-air piles layered with firewood and coal. This firing process, however, produced acidic "sulphurectic" air emissions that eventually turned nearly a hundred square miles of hills into a remarkably stark, denuded desert, its topsoil slowly washing away down sterile, chemical-laden streams. The plaintiffs were farmers whose fields and orchards began to die as the smelting got underway.

The Tennessee high court held that the smelting was a continuing private nuisance, but after long and careful deliberation allowed the defendant industries to continue operations despite their drastic impact upon the plaintiffs' land and livelihood. The court required only that the mills compensate the plaintiffs for their losses. In common parlance, it awarded legal compensatory damages but denied any injunctive remedy, based on a balancing of equities. The *Ducktown* court certainly balanced the equities. Analytically, however, it did so not once but thrice:

*Threshold Balancing.* The first type of balancing addresses threshold questions which plaintiffs must survive if a cause of action is to be heard. Some issues appear in the guise of affirmative legal defenses: laches and coming to the nuisance, for example, are legal defenses grounded in principles of equitable estoppel. Other issues — clean hands, additional estoppel principles, proof of irreparable harm, and the inadequacy of legal remedies — are more specifically equitable, brought to bear only where the plaintiff seeks equitable remedies. Each of these threshold issues involves comparisons and balances that are part of the longstanding discretionary processes of equity. The *Ducktown* court made several such determinations, excluding some plaintiffs on laches grounds as to certain defendants, confirming their rights to sue as to others, and noting injuries to land that analytically made equitable remedies potentially available on grounds of irreparability.

*The Determination of Contending Conducts.* After plaintiffs survive equity's threshold gauntlet, nonstatutory litigation moves to the application of rules of conduct. The major discretionary function of the equity court at this second stage is the determination of whether the defendant's conduct will be permitted to continue. To reach this abatement determination, however, courts must first consider issues of liability....

The initial question is whether defendants are liable at all, whether their conduct is "illegal" under the common law.... Plaintiffs in private nuisance cases and in other common law areas seek equitable remedies — particularly injunctions — as well as damages. In such cases, once tort liability is found, the court turns to the different question of whether defendant's conduct will be abated....

The *Ducktown* abatement question focused on the desirability and consequences of the competing forms of conduct, considering relative hardship between the parties, the balance of comparative social utility between the two competing conducts, and the public interest (which usually amounts to the same thing). The court declared:

> A judgment for damages in this class of cases is a matter of absolute right, where injury is shown. A decree for an injunction is a matter of sound legal discretion, to be granted or withheld as that discretion shall dictate, after a full and careful considerations of every element appertaining to the injury.

Citing a series of equity cases in which the utility of defendant's enterprises weighed against injunctions, the court's "careful consideration" began with a question that virtually answered itself:

> Shall the complainants be granted, by way of damages, the full measure of relief to which their injuries entitle them or shall we go further, and grant their request to blot out two great mining and manufacturing enterprises, destroy half of the taxable values of a country, and drive more than 10,000 people from their homes?...

The tort debts owed by one party to the other might be decided by uniformly applicable substantive tort principles, but questions of the life and death of farms and smelting plants — of who must stop and who may go on — were left to the flexible hands and heart of equity. In short, courts have used equity to define and exercise a separate judicial role, grounded upon a rational discretion and working beyond the rigid rules of the law.

*Tailoring the Remedies....* At this point in a lawsuit, law and equity have determined all the substantive issues, and only the equitable function of implementation remains. If the court had decided in the second stage balance that defendant's conduct may continue, the award of legal damages for past injuries ends the question of remedy. In that situation no equitable remedy is necessary unless required to enforce payment of damages.

When the court determines that defendant's conduct may not continue, on the other hand, a full array of equitable options exists. If defendants agree to abate their activity voluntarily, the court has the option of not issuing any formal equitable remedy at all. This point...is taken for granted in the common law setting: an injunction need not issue if the court finds that the abatement decision will be implemented without it, but will usually issue where there is any doubt on the matter. Between these two extremes lies the declaratory judgment, a remedy slightly more formal and more assertive than the no-injunction option but similarly unenforceable through contempt proceedings. Yet in the case of good faith defendants, a declaratory judgment or less may be all that is necessary to implement the court's abatement decision.

The strength and flexibility of injunctions, however, makes them attractive as the remedy of choice in many cases. Equity courts shape injunctions in multifarious forms: injunctions to halt an enterprise completely, to shut down a particular component activity, to scale down overall activity by a certain percentage, to halt a specific offensive effect, to abate after a lapse of a specific term if certain performance standards are not achieved — these are but a few. Injunctions also serve different tactical ends. They can be wielded to drag a rambunctiously recalcitrant defendant into compliance, to tighten the reins on slipshod defendants whose compliance efforts may be sloppy, or merely to add a final reassuring level of certainty to a good faith defendant's compliance. In short, "the plastic remedies of the chancery are moulded to the needs of justice."

COMMENTARY AND QUESTIONS

1. **A range of equitable remedies.** The last paragraph offers a reminder that injunctions can be far more subtly crafted than mere cease-and-desist prohibitions. When Oscar Boomer went to his lawyer's office, he undoubtedly wanted to stop that cursed cement dust, and the remedy he instinctively favored for the factory was to shut it down. When most attorneys consider remedies beyond damages they are equally unsubtle; the only injunction they conceive of is an order halting the defendants in their tracks. Environmental attorneys can increase the force and effect of their litigation efforts, however, by considering a range of appropriate, innovative equitable remedies and proposing them to the court. Consider each of the following equity options available as remedies in settings ranging from localized pollution like *Boomer* to massive episodes like coastal oil spills:

- decrees encouraging technological innovation, like Judge Jasen's proposed order in Boomer, postponing shutdowns for a set term, to be effective thereafter unless clean technology can be applied;
- decrees ordering, say, a 30 percent cutback in production until cleaner technology is achieved;
- decrees restricting defendant's activity during times when weather conditions are particularly likely to cause pollution damage;
- decrees requiring ongoing corporate monitoring of offsite pollution;
- decrees requiring defendants actively clean up their externalized pollution;
- decrees ordering installation of particular specified control technology;
- decrees ordering restitution of profits gained from avoidance of pollution controls;
- decrees requiring periodic reporting to the court;
- decrees ordering "restoration" of trees, soil, personal property, and natural resources;
- appointment of equitable trial masters under Fed. R. Civ. P. 53 for managing complex factual and procedural issues prior to judgment;
- appointment of post-decree monitors to oversee defendants' compliance with court orders, backed by subpoena powers and reporting to the courts;[16]
- environmental receiverships, so that where defendant firms can't or won't comply with environmental requirements, courts will take over and run them through appointed equitable receiverships; and other creative applications of this remarkable judicial power.

Injunctions decree whatever a court chooses to prescribe, and their prescriptive capabilities are given extra credibility by the criminal contempt-of-court penalties they carry with them.

---

16. See Stuart Feldman, Post-Decree Judicial Agents in Environmental Litigation, 18 Envt'l. Aff. L. Rev. 809 (1991). The classic *Ducktown* case applied a court-appointed monitor remedy in order to police emissions limits, with the monitor guaranteed full access to defendant's operations. See *Tennessee Copper*, 237 U.S. at 478, and 240 U.S. 650.

When an injunction commands a halt to a polluting activity, it acts like a decisive statutory prohibition. Is that cost internalization? The more subtle equitable orders noted above can clearly improve the internalization process. In the Oregon aluminum factory cases cited in *Borland*, the courts prescribed precisely which pollution control devices defendants had to install, setting strict schedules. What about cleanup or restoration orders? There is no doctrinal reason why equity cannot take sensitive account of the natural resource consequences of wrongful acts, and remedy them in accord with modern public policy. Defendants' realization that they may have to pay restitution of profits, or to clean or replace soil, trees, or other property, drastically changes the economic calculus of industrial waste disposal, and raises ecological consciousness.

2. **The balance of equities.** The *Boomer* case is perhaps most famous for its rejection of the traditional New York common law rule that an injunction would routinely issue to shut down a continuing nuisance, in favor of the more flexible balancing the equities doctrine. Was the court undercutting environmental protection and sound policy when it reversed the automatic rule? In legal history terms, would you be surprised to find that for 50 years after the tough *Whalen* rule shut down a papermill, the tendency of trial courts in New York had been to find no nuisance at all, knowing that any finding of nuisance liability would automatically trigger a complete shutdown of industrial operations?

A fundamental canon of equity law is that an equitable decree must do equity. That means it must be sensitive to public as well as private consequences of proposed restrictions. Under the *Ducktown* principle, it was surely fitting and relevant that the *Boomer* court considered public interests weighing in favor of continued plant operation. But what items were allowed into the balance of equities in *Boomer*? Do they appear to include all relevant information for a full-scale balancing? The court weighed items of both public and private concern affirmatively in favor of the defendant, against the proposed injunction. What did it weigh in favor of the injunction for plaintiffs? A more evenhanded approach might have allowed plaintiffs to present evidence of the cement plant's adverse impacts on the community at large. Why does the majority explicitly remove public health issues from its consideration? In light of the public interest element in equitable balancing, which he himself applied in favor of the defendant, doesn't Justice Bergan's refusal to intrude "broad public objectives" into a simple suit between "individual property owners and a single cement plant" ring hollow? How would you have argued the point?

Would the equities of the case have been different if the Boomers, well before construction of the cement plant, had repeatedly told Atlantic Cement Company that they feared the dust would escape and injure them, only to receive assurances that there would be no problem? See Smith v. Staso Milling Co., 18 F.2d 736 (2d Cir. 1927) (opinion by Learned Hand granting an injunction in such circumstances, under Vermont nuisance law).

Note that when courts balance the equities to determine what kind of order to issue, they are not restricted to facts and values incorporated in the elements of the cause of action, nor even to the evidence adduced on the trial record. This means that in appropriate cases the equitable balancing can include consideration of a broad range of public environmental concerns that could not be directly litigated, including a community's quality of life, ecological consequences to natural resources, and declared public policies of local, state, and federal governments.

3. **Constraints on equitable remedies.** In addition to equity's particular threshold and balancing requirements noted in the equitable discretion article excerpt, equity law presents other constraints to environmental litigants. One of the most interesting is the defense of "prospective" or "anticipatory nuisance" seen in Chapter Two's *Wilsonville* case. The traditional rule was that in order to get an injunction against proposed actions, one had to prove the probability of serious injury or that it was a "nuisance per se"; otherwise the law would "wait and see." But in environmental litigation plaintiffs are often attempting to stop activities that have no legal track record. In Wallace v. Andersonville Docks, 489 S.W.2d 532 (Tenn. 1972), for example, a court refused on those grounds to halt a cross-country motorcycle race through a state reserve. Or a case may pose a "zero-infinity" problem — release of a particular chemical or gene-altered organism may have only a small possibility of negative effects, but if they occur they may be catastrophic. As a result the common law abdicated all such issues to the tender mercies of public authorities. There are signs, as in Judge Ryan's concurrence in *Wilsonville*, that the situation is changing. See Sharp, Rehabilitating the Anticipatory Nuisance Doctrine, 15 Envtl. Aff. L. Rev. 627 (1988).

4. **Other equitable actions.** The present focus on equitable remedies should not obscure the fact that although equity is usually employed to supply remedies for common law or statutory causes of action, there are some causes of action which are themselves based on the traditional equity jurisdiction. Substantive equitable claims thus may have environmental importance in cases involving fraud, bankruptcy, and trust law. Does equity embody a creative free-floating cause of action? In other words, can a judge issue an injunction whenever she is convinced that a wrong is occurring? Conventional wisdom holds rather that plaintiffs must show injury to a legal right.

5. **Restoration remedies.** Modern environmental cases have brought new and expanded currency to the old remedy of restoration. The restoration concept has great environmental utility, but raises some knotty problems. When and for what kind of case are injunctions or damages based on restoration justified and desirable? Note the potency of the restoration remedy in *Schenectady Chemical, supra*, and *Wilsonville* in Chapter Two where defendants were forced to remove polluted soils and restore the land. In the right settings, restoration can serve not only to restore the "status quo ante"[17] but also to protect human and ecological safety, and powerfully to deter. In deterrent terms, defendants face the prospect that ill-gotten profits can quickly be dwarfed by the costs of restoration. In a Michigan case a neighbor, when the plaintiff refused to sell him part of her rural land for a subdivision project, "accidentally" destroyed plaintiff's private arboretum, clearcutting

---

17. One of the traditional aims of legal damages and equitable orders has always been to return innocent plaintiffs to the position they had before the wrongdoing.

five acres of exotic imported trees. The defendant admitted the wrongful act, but argued that damages were purely nominal, since he had actually *improved* the plaintiff's development-based market value (a similar claim was made in *Borland*). Though the case never resulted in a reported decision, consider the abrupt change in defendant's position that occurs when a court allows consideration of restoration remedies, for example a restoration order requiring replanting equivalent mature trees. See Verdiccio, Environmental Restoration Orders, 12 Envtl. Aff. L. Rev. 171 (1985).

Equitable restoration orders tend to rehabilitate natural values that would be excluded from the usual monetary interests balanced in legal actions. Consider the effect of an order requiring Allied to cleanse the polluted sediments of the James River and Chesapeake Bay, or Atlantic Cement to reclaim its cement dust. Restoration provides a compelling deterrent in a variety of environmental settings, like the killing of fish in a river, the wrongful partial demolition of an historic building lacking market value, and so on. The prospect of forced restoration is a powerful deterrent to discharge of toxics: thousands of dollars can initially be made or saved by disposing of hazardous wastes carelessly, but the subsequent cost of retrieving and removing those toxics from soil and water can be geometrically more expensive, running into hundreds of thousands or millions of dollars. If you might be caught, it is far cheaper to treat and dispose of chemicals properly at the outset, when you have them in one place, than to recapture them after they have dispersed and percolated through a mile or more of underground gravel aquifer.

Restoration, however, may be impossible, or so grossly expensive that it makes no sense. How does a court decide when to order restoration? In a Louisiana case a court noted that the polluted property was a swamp, subject to overflowing by the Mississippi River, used seasonally for grazing, hunting and fishing....

> Its value was set at $375 per acre, or slightly over $200,000 for the 550 acres affected.... The restoration of the property, according to plaintiff's witness, would take about seven years, involve the use of 100 trucks running continuously during that time and would cost $170 million. Ewell v. Petro Processors, 364 So. 2d 604, 608 (La. App. 1978).

The *Ewell* court understandably denied the restoration, instead merely awarding the difference in market value, a remedy that left all the toxins in the ground and groundwater. The judge may have suspected that plaintiffs were using a restoration injunction claim to extort a hefty cash payoff from the defendants, or, if restoration damages were granted, might not actually spend them on restoration. Some case law makes likelihood of actual restoration a consideration in the decision. Puerto Rico v. S.S. Zoe Colocotroni, 628 F.2d 652, 676 (1st Cir. 1980). Should courts presume that market value ($375 per acre in *Ewell*) sets an appropriate maximum remedy?

The Restatement of Torts 2d §929 prescribes, as to measure of damages...

> for harm to land resulting from a past invasion and not amounting to a total destruction of value, the damages include compensation for (a) the difference between the value of the land before the harm and the value after the harm, *or at plaintiff's election in an appropriate case, the cost of restoration that has*

*been or may be reasonably incurred....*§929(1)(a) [emphasis added].

In Escamilla v. Asarco, a restoration case lying in the grey area between equitable remedies and damages, the court ordered a remediation of the top 15 inches of soil in Globeville, a low-income working class ethnic minority community in northern Denver contaminated with arsenic and cadmium, even though the cost of restoration was far in excess of market value losses. Applying Restatement §929, the court held —

> If the damage is reparable, and the costs, although greater than original value, are not wholly unreasonable in relation to that value, and if the evidence demonstrates that payment of market value likely will not adequately compensate the property owner for some personal or other special reason, we conclude that the selection of the cost of restoration as the proper measure of damages would be within the limits of a trial court's discretion.... It is precisely because the market value measure may not adequately compensate land owners that the remediation measure may come into play.

> It was undisputed that full use of the property can be restored simply by removing and replacing the contaminated topsoil.... The jury found that it would cost $20,125,000 to remediate Plaintiffs' properties. The jury found that Plaintiffs' properties suffered a diminution in market value of $4,159,000,...the jury found the uncontaminated market value of Plaintiffs' properties to be approximately $17.5 million, and the contaminated value to be approximately $13.4 million. Thus, the remediation costs exceed not only the diminution in market value, but also both the pre-and post-tort market values themselves.... This excess does not necessarily preclude remediation, but does require me to consider carefully whether the remediation costs are "wholly unreasonable" in relation to the properties' market values.... Relative to the total uncontaminated market value..., the excess represents only 13 percent of the total market value,...only $4,600 per class family.... Under all of the circumstances of this case, I cannot say that the remediation costs are "wholly unreasonable" in relation to the market value.

> Considering all the factors..., and with due regard for the overarching principles of full and just compensation on the one hand, but no windfalls on the other, I find and conclude: that the losses which Plaintiff class members have suffered to their residences as a result of Defendant's negligence are remediable; that the cost of that remediation, as found by the jury, is not wholly unreasonable in relation to the uncontaminated or "pre-tort" market value of the Plaintiff class members' residences; that the market value measure will not adequately compensate Plaintiff class members for the damage to their residences; that there is no significant risk that the Plaintiff class will be overcompensated by a remediation award,...or that such an award will encourage wasteful expenditures by Plaintiff class members; and therefore that the jury's remediation award is the more appropriate measure of damages to compensate Plaintiff class members for their property losses.... Robert and Margaret Escamilla, et al. v. Asarco, Inc., (D.C. Denver, Colorado No. 91 CV 5716, 23 April 1993).[18]

When should restoration be ordered? Neither the *Escamilla* court or the Restatement require a showing of special circumstances, but some special show-

---

18. After this decision the Asarco company decided to settle. In the settlement the plaintiffs agreed to allow the defendant itself to do most of the supervised remediation (i.e. the equivalent of an injunction to restore), reducing the defendant's cost to as little as $11 million; (the jury's award of $8 million for "discomfort" was raised to $11 million).

ing seems appropriate. A Florida wetlands case set out some guidelines for restoration orders: To establish that restoration is appropriate, "the selected plan must: (1) confer maximum environmental benefits, (2) be achievable as a practical matter, and (3) bear an equitable relationship to the degree and kind of wrong which it is intended to remedy."[19]

It would seem important to consider the proportionality between potential land uses and the costs of "Cadillac cleanups," to avoid over-reactions in excessive remedies, while acknowledging the array of values beyond market values that restoration can incorporate — protecting community integrity, protecting individual autonomy, recreating natural economy values as well as human, punishing malicious actions, vindicating the innocence of victimized plaintiffs by restoring them as much as possible to their status quo ante in a manner that market value compensation does not achieve.[20] Standards for when and how restoration is to be adopted as a remedy will undoubtedly continue to evolve in environmental law.

## Section 2. DAMAGES

### a. Compensatory damage remedies — past damages

The typical tort plaintiff seeks an award of compensatory damages for past injuries, whether or not an injunction is also being sought. Unlike injunctive relief, compensatory damages follow automatically upon a finding of defendant's liability. Compensatory damages can include sums awarded for all forms of property damage, injuries to the plaintiff's health, loss of consortium, etc. In *Boomer*, there was little dispute about the amount of damages awarded for past harms. Damages included injury to stored automobiles and other personal property, and, as to real property, the "loss of rental value or loss of usable value," averaging $60 per plaintiff per month. Imputed rental value attempts to gauge the burden imposed by pollution upon the lives of the plaintiffs, assuming that the amount of rent that people would be willing to pay adequately captures the sum total of life-quality values involved. Does it?

Compare the elements of damage allowed in *Boomer* to those found in the typical personal injury lawsuit. In the latter, the plaintiff's recovery is generally made up of two broad categories: (1) compensation for monetary losses such as lost

---

19. U.S. v. Weissmann, 489 F.Supp. 1331 (M.D. Fla 1980); the court included an extensive analysis of the values of wetlands. Because the Corps was plaintiff, no showing of plaintiff's circumstances was relevant; *Escamilla* merely had required a showing that land had been used personally by the plaintiff.

20. The Florida Supreme Court found that damages measured by diminution in value were inappropriate to compensate the municipality for the loss of 5 of its 6 water wells. The court stated that, in this instance, public policy supported restoration costs as the measure of damages because the court was "dealing with the single most necessary substance for the continuation of life.... Any danger to that primary necessity is ecologically and humanly unacceptable." Indicating that it thought it was diverging from the general rule on damages for wrongful injury, the court stated that extending damages beyond the loss of value of the property was further justified in this case because neither overcompensation nor overlapping of recoveries was likely. Davey Compressor Co. v. Delray Beach, 7 Toxic Law Reporter 97 (Fla., March 3,1994).

The *Esacamilla* court declined to consider punishment as a reason for a restoration remedy, but because punitive and deterrent considerations issues traditionally can be weighed in equitable balancing, they would seem to be appropriate here as well.

wages, medical expenses, and automobile repair costs; and (2) compensation for intangibles, especially pain and suffering, but also anxiety and emotional trauma. The *Boomer* damages were limited to the first category. Is there any reason to ignore intangible elements of damage? What if Oscar and June Boomer had long been planning on this farm as their idyllic retreat from the sights and sounds of urban America? "Hedonic damages" offer an interesting new remedy theory. Traditional recoveries compensate for injuries and pain sustained, and look to the future only in terms of lost profits or earnings. Hedonics compensate for losses of future quality of life, a broader concept that has obvious applicability in environmental law. See Sherrod v. Berry, 629 F. Supp 155 (N.D. Ill. 1985), affirmed 827 F.2d 195 (7th Cir. 1987), rev'd on rehearing 856 F.2d 802 (7th Cir. 1988).[21]

Note, however, that most damage awards make provision only for injuries to human plaintiffs. Possibilities for getting natural resource damages are noted in Section 3 *infra*.

### b. Permanent damages

Here is part of the trial court's original opinion in *Boomer*, 287 N.Y.S.2d 112 (1967), in which Judge Herzberg denied an injunction and calculated the proposed alternative of permanent damages:

> After reviewing the evidence in this action, I find that an injunction would produce great public hardship.... I find that the reasonable market value of each property as of September 1, 1962 (the date of the commencement of operations by Atlantic), the reasonable market value as of June 1, 1967 (the time of trial), and the permanent loss to each plaintiff, are as follows:

|  | REASONABLE MARKET VALUE | | PERMANENT DAMAGES |
|---|---|---|---|
|  | 9/1/62 | 6/1/67 | |
| Oscar H. Boomer and June C. Boomer | 25,000 | 12,500 | 12,500 |
| Theodore J. Richard and Miriam W. Richard | 30,000 | 12,000 | 18,000 |
| Avie Kinley, Martha Kinley and Mary Kinley | 140,000 | 70,000 | 70,000 |
| Kenneth Livengood and Delores Livengood | 18,000 | 7,000 | 11,000 |
| Floyd W. Millious and Barbara A. Millious | 20,000 | 8,000 | 12,000 |
| Joseph L. Ventura and Carrie Ventura | 25,000 | 12,500 | 12,500 |
| James W. McCall | 22,000 | 11,000 | 11,000 |
| Charles J. Meilak and Angelina Meilak | 26,000 | 12,000 | 14,000 |
|  |  | **Total** | **$185,000** |

---

21. Though the Seventh Circuit vacated and remanded the lower court's opinion, it did so on other grounds. The Seventh Circuit's prior approval of the hedonic damages, described as testimony that was "invaluable to the jury," 827 F.2d at 206, was not expressly overturned; subsequently, other courts have awarded hedonic damages. See also McClurg, It's a Wonderful Life: The Case for Hedonic Damages in Wrongful Death Cases, 66 Notre Dame L. Rev. 57 (1990).

COMMENTARY AND QUESTIONS

1. **The measure of permanent damages.** Permanent damages are supposed to account for all the named plaintiffs' private property rights lost to cement dust. In theory, these damages ought to be equal in value to the relief that would have been obtained from the denied injunction. Are they? Market values do capture the current best estimate of what the land's future profitable economic uses will be, discounted back into present dollars, in terms of what a willing buyer would pay a willing seller. According to Judge Herzberg's formula, however, what would be the permanent damages if in the years between 1962 and 1967 Boomer's property value, as polluted, had appreciated, along with general land values, back to $24,999?

Even if the accounting is accurately done (subtracting *present* value as polluted from *present* value as it would be without pollution) the net result of the refusal of an injunction and award of permanent damages is to force Boomer unwillingly to sell Atlantic Cement Company an easement to pollute at its market value. Can the court assess an extra amount to account for his unwillingness to sell? On remand, the trial court found the actual loss of market value to be $140,000, and then added a further $35,000, while admitting that it really couldn't define why: "If analogy is found in Newton's experiment with prisms showing that white light is composed of all the colors of the spectrum, each lending its own characteristics to a degree when passed through a prism, all the approaches to valuation entering into the informed mind and sensitive conscience of the court lend to an appropriate degree in the resulting decision." 340 N.Y.S.2d 97, 2d at 108 (1972). See also Hiley, Involuntary Sale Damages In Permanent Nuisance Cases: A Bigger Bang From *Boomer*, 14 Envtl. Aff. L. Rev. 61, 86-91 (1986). How is the court to choose between a forced sale of rights and the possibility that plaintiffs will use defendant's large sunk capital investment to "extort" a grossly exaggerated price for surrender of their rights?

2. **Do permanent damages create private expropriation?** Dissenting Judge Jasen in *Boomer* and some commentators have argued that permanent damages are unconstitutional because they amount to private exercise of the condemnation power, "which, unquestionably, is impermissible," said the *Borland* court. But is it? Defendants in cases like *Boomer* are using common law rather than the police power. There are other precedents for private forced purchases — to get access easements to landlocked parcels, to transport water over neighboring lands, or to build milldams — each justified by theories of public necessity. Are such forced sales justified by theories of efficient use of scarce resources? The right to deposit pollution on neighbors, however, is quite a different kind of claimed "necessity."

3. **The decision to award permanent damages.** Traditionally courts did not award permanent damages, instead permitting the plaintiff to return to court over time to prove a new case. What institutional factors relating to the court system workload and judicial competence militate for and against the old approach? As a litigant in a case like *Boomer*, how valuable to you is the sense of closure that accompanies the award of permanent damages?

**4. The future of permanent damages.** Despite much discussion in the literature, the *Boomer* decision's permanent damage remedy has not often been applied by subsequent courts. Is it a remedy that deserves more attention, assuming that standards for measuring the damages can be defined, or is there something organically wrong in a remedy that displaces permanent injunctions and is based on discounted future values? Do permanent damages imply that pollution is acceptable as long as polluters pay?

### c. Punitive damages

Punitive damages are extraordinary in a variety of ways. Law in general is conservative about intervening in the private ordering of affairs. Even when an injury that befalls one member of society can be said to have been caused by another member of society, the first impulse of the legal system is to erect relatively high barriers before the power of the state, acting through its courts, will redistribute the loss away from the victim. These barriers are, of course, the various elements of tort, contract, or other causes of action that the plaintiff must be able to prove by a preponderance of the evidence. In tort, the non-strict liability branches all involve culpable conduct. Even strict liability torts involve conduct that has been singled out for special loss-shifting treatment because (in most cases and especially in toxic tort cases) the defendants knowingly engaged in conduct involving great dangers. And even when these barriers are scaled, all that is awarded is compensation designed to make plaintiff whole, restoring the status quo before the defendant's act injured the plaintiff. Permanent damages and past compensatory damages are both pegged to determinations of actual damages suffered.

Punitive damages are based on the egregious wrongfulness of the defendant's conduct. When available, they add a new dimension to damage remedies, serving functions quite different from compensation — retributive punishment and deterrence. Thus in some cases plaintiffs may get $5,000 in compensatory damages, and $100,000 or more in punitives. Punitive damages find justification in the fact that, as the name implies, they are intended to *punish* fault, or reckless disregard for others, even in cases where fault is not an element of the tort. The forty or so states permitting awards of punitive damages typically prescribe them for cases where the defendant's conduct was found to be "willful," "wanton," "malicious," or "reckless." Because it is the wrongful character of defendant's conduct that is the issue, there need be no proportionality between the amount of punitive damages and the actual harm inflicted.

Punitive damages may also serve other purposes, including camouflaged compensation. To some environmental attorneys punitive awards are readily justifiable, not only to force defendants to confront the seriousness of environmental concerns, but more practically as a means of capturing and internalizing some of the unrecovered intangible costs, like ecological injuries to natural resources and property damages to persons downwind for whom injuries were real but insufficient to justify litigation. In the latter cases, punitives are forms of extended compensation for externalities. Further, punitive awards serve as a bounty incentive for private citizen enforcement of environmental standards, acknowledging that public officials are often unable to do so. Injured plaintiffs may also be especially deserving, having suffered disproportionately. To some observers, punitives raise serious concerns because of their absence of standards for quantification, their potential for duplication in multiple lawsuits, and their lack of direct nexus to the externalities imposed by the defendants.

## Branch v. Western Petroleum, Inc.
Supreme Court of Utah, 1982
657 P.2d 267, 277–78

[After discussing strict liability in its opinion excerpted above, the court went on to discuss punitive damages for the oil company's failure to protect groundwater:]

Western's final contention on its appeal challenges the award of punitive damages. It argues that punitive damages are appropriate only when willful and malicious conduct is shown and that the court erred in including the phrase "reckless indifference and disregard" in its instruction on punitive damages. However, punitive damages may be awarded when one acts with reckless indifference and disregard of the law and his fellow citizens:

> This presumed malice or malice in law does not consist of personal hate or ill will of one person towards another but rather refers to that state of mind which is reckless of law and of the legal rights of the citizen in a person's conduct toward that citizen.... In such cases malice in law will be implied from unjustifiable conduct which causes the injury complained of or from a wrongful act intentionally done without cause or excuse. Terry v. Zions Cooperative, 605 P.2d 314, 327 (Utah, 1979).

The evidence in this case meets that standard. Western discharged the waste water into the disposal pit intending that it seep into and percolate through the soil. Thus, the pollution of the percolating waters was willful and carried out in disregard of the rights of the Branches. Moreover, Western compounded the Branches' problems by its trespass on their land, the spraying of waste water over their land and the failure to comply with state law. In addition, Western continued its dumping activities even after notice of the pollution of the diligence well. The punitive damage award was adequately supported by evidence of reckless indifference toward, and disregard of, the Branches' rights.

Furthermore, there is no merit to Western's contention that the award of punitive damages was excessive and influenced by passion or prejudice rather than reason. The jury was properly instructed that the purpose of exemplary damages is to deter defendant and others from engaging in similar conduct....

## Fischer v. Johns-Manville Corp.
Supreme Court of New Jersey, 1986
103 N.J. 643, 512 A.2d 466.

[Plaintiff in this case was awarded punitive damages for lung injuries caused by exposure to asbestos more than forty years earlier. The defendant challenged the award on a number of grounds. Only a small excerpt of the court's discussion is reprinted.]

CLIFFORD, J. ..."Manufacturer misconduct" [justifying punitives has been typed] into five categories: (1) fraudulent-type, affirmative conduct designed to mislead the public, (2) knowing violations of safety standards, (3) inadequate testing and quality-control, manufacturing procedures, (4) failure to warn of known dangers, and (5) post-marketing failures to remedy known dangers. Owen, Punitive Damages in Products Liability Litigation, 74 Mich. L. Rev. at 1329–61 (1976).

We...view [this case] as falling within Professor Owen's categories one and four.... We cannot imagine that the conduct proven in this case would have been viewed as any less egregious in the 1940s, when the exposure commenced, than it is today. In this connection we share the Appellate Division's reaction to defendant's "knowingly and deliberately...subjecting (James Fischer) as an asbestos worker to serious health hazards with utter and reckless disregard of his safety and well-being."

It is indeed appalling to us that Johns-Manville had so much information on the hazards to asbestos workers as early as the mid-1930s and that it not only failed to use that information to protect these workers but, more egregiously, that it also attempted to withhold this information from the public. It is also clear that even though Johns-Manville may have taken some remedial steps decades ago to protect its own employees, it apparently did nothing to warn and protect those who, like plaintiff, were employed by Johns-Manville customers engaged in the manufacture and fabrication of asbestos products....

The corporate personnel who made the decisions at the time of the exposure are no longer with the defendant company, possibly no longer alive. From this fact it is argued that punitive damages are inappropriate because they will not punish the true wrongdoers. But as many courts have observed, this contention ignores the nature of a corporation as a separate legal entity. Although the responsible management personnel may escape punishment, the corporation itself will not.... A primary goal of punitive damages is general deterrence — that is, the deterrence of others from engaging in similar conduct. That purpose is, of course, well served regardless of changes in personnel within the offending corporation.

A related argument, which similarly ignores the legal nature of corporations, is that punitive damages unfairly punish innocent shareholders. This argument has been rejected repeatedly. It is the corporation, not the individual shareholders, that is recognized as an ongoing legal entity engaged in manufacturing and distributing products.... Also, we would not consider it harmful were shareholders to be encouraged by decisions such as this to give close scrutiny to corporate practices in making investment decisions.

Another characteristic of asbestos litigation is found in the startling numbers that reflect the massive amount of litigation generated by exposure to asbestos. Although we are mindful of the fact that the case before us involves one worker, whose exposure to asbestos caused legally compensable injury to him and his wife — it is not a class action, not a "mass" case — nevertheless we would be remiss were we to ignore the society-wide nature of the asbestos problem....

Studies show that between eleven million and thirteen million workers have been exposed to asbestos. More than 30,000 lawsuits have been filed already for damages caused by that exposure, with no indication that there are no more victims who will seek redress. Of the multitude of lawsuits that are faced by asbestos defendants as a group, Johns-Manville alone has been named in more than 11,000 cases. New claims are stayed because Johns-Manville is attempting reorganization under federal bankruptcy law.

Defendant argues that the amount of *compensatory* damages assessed and to be assessed is so great that it will effectively serve the functions of punitive damages — that is, defendants are more than sufficiently punished and deterred. We are not at all satisfied, however, that compensatory damages effectively serve the same functions as punitive damages, even when they amount to staggering sums. Compensatory damages are often foreseeable as to amount.... Anticipation of these damages will allow potential defendants, aware of dangers of a product, to factor those anticipated damages into a cost-benefit analysis and to decide whether to market a particular product. The risk and amount of such damages can, and in some cases will, be reflected in the cost of a product, in which event the product will be marketed in its dangerous condition.

Without punitive damages a manufacturer who is aware of a dangerous feature of its product but nevertheless knowingly chooses to market it in that condition, willfully concealing from the public information regarding the dangers of the product, would be far better off than an innocent manufacturer who markets a product later discovered to be dangerous — this, because both will be subjected to the same compensatory damages, but the innocent manufacturer, unable to anticipate those damages, will not have incorporated the cost of those damages into the cost of the product. All else being equal, the law should not place the innocent manufacturer in a worse position than that of a knowing wrongdoer. Punitive damages tend to meet this need.[22]

Defendant argues further that the cumulative effect of punitive damages in mass-tort litigation is "potentially catastrophic." The Johns-Manville bankruptcy is offered as proof of this effect. We fail to see the distinction, in the case of Johns-Manville, between the effect of compensatory damages and that of punitive damages....

Heretofore the typical setting for punitive damage claims has been the two-party lawsuit in which, more often than not, a punitive damages award was supported by a showing of some element of malice or intentional wrongdoing, directed by a defendant to the specific plaintiff. Even if the actual object of the malicious conduct was unknown to defendant, the conduct nevertheless was directed at a single person or a very limited group of potential plaintiffs.

Punishable conduct in a products liability action, on the other hand, will often affect countless potential plaintiffs whose identities are unknown to defendant at the time of the culpable conduct. We agree with the Illinois court that the mere fact that a defendant, "through outrageous misconduct...manage(s) to seriously injure a large number of persons" should not relieve it of liability for punitive damages. Froud v. Celotex Corp., 437 N.E.2d 910, 913 (1982).

Of greater concern to us is the possibility that asbestos defendants' assets may become so depleted by early awards that the defendants will no longer be in existence and able to pay compensatory damages to later plaintiffs. Again, it is difficult if not impossible to ascertain the additional impact of punitive damages as compared to the impact of mass compensatory damages alone.

Many of the policy arguments against punitive damages in mass tort litigation cases can be traced to Roginsky v. Richardson-Merrell, Inc., 378 F.2d 832 (2d Cir. 1967). The Roginsky court denied punitive damages to a plaintiff who suffered cataracts caused by MER/29, an anti-cholesterol drug. Although the denial of punitive damages rested on a determination that the evidence was insufficient to send the matter to the jury, the court expressed several concerns over allowing punitive damages for injuries to multiple plaintiffs. The fear that punitive damages would lead to "overkill" turned out to be unfounded in the MER/29 litigation.

---

22. In addition, it is questionable how much punishment is effected by compensatory damages alone, which are generally covered by liability insurance [unlike punitives].

Approximately 1,500 claims were made, of which only eleven were tried to a jury verdict. Punitive damages were awarded in only three of those cases, one of which was reversed on appeal. While we do not discount entirely the possibility of punitive damage "overkill" in asbestos litigation, we do recognize that the vast majority of cases settle without trial.

Accepting the possibility of punitive damage "overkill," we turn to means of addressing that problem. Because the problem is nationwide, several possible remedial steps can be effective only on a nationwide basis, and hence are beyond our reach. One such solution is the setting of a cap on total punitive damages against each defendant. Such a cap would be ineffective unless applied uniformly. To adopt such a cap in New Jersey would be to deprive our citizens of punitive damages without the concomitant benefit of assuring the availability of compensatory damages for later plaintiffs. This we decline to do....

At the state court level we are powerless to implement solutions to the nationwide problems created by asbestos exposure and litigation arising from that exposure. That does not mean, however, that we cannot institute some controls over runaway punitive damages. When a defendant manufacturer engages in conduct warranting the imposition of punitive damages, the harm caused may run to countless plaintiffs. Each individual plaintiff can fairly charge that the manufacturer's conduct was egregious as to him and that punitive damages should be assessed in his lawsuit.... Nonetheless, there should be some limits placed on the total punishment exacted from a culpable defendant. We conclude that a reasonable imposition of those limits would permit a defendant to introduce evidence of other punitive damage awards already assessed against and paid by it, as well as evidence of its own financial status and the effect a punitive award would have....

We realize that defendants may be reluctant to alert juries to the fact that other courts or juries have assessed punitive damages for conduct similar to that being considered by the jury in a given case. Although the evidence may convince a jury that a defendant has been sufficiently punished, the same evidence could nudge a jury closer to a determination that punishment is warranted. That is a risk of jury trial. The willingness to accept that risk is a matter of strategy for defendant and its counsel, no different from other strategy choices facing trial lawyers every day.

When evidence of other punitive awards is introduced, trial courts should instruct juries to consider whether the defendant has been sufficiently punished, keeping in mind that punitive damages are meant to punish and deter defendants for the benefit of society, not to compensate individual plaintiffs.

A further protection may be afforded defendants by the judicious exercise of remittitur. Should a trial court determine that an award is "manifestly outrageous" or "grossly excessive," it may reduce that award or order a new trial on punitive damages. In evaluating the excessiveness of challenged punitive damage awards, trial courts are expressly authorized to consider prior punitive damage awards....

### COMMENTARY AND QUESTIONS

1. **Do all intentional torts deserve punitive damages?** Could Oscar Boomer have gotten punitive damages against Atlantic Cement? Boomer proved that the cement dust pollution was an intentional tort; so wasn't it "willful," justifying punitives? In McElwain v. Georgia Pacific Corp., a pulp mill air pollution case, the court

majority allowed punitive damages in a case very much like *Boomer*:

> The intentional disregard of the interest of another is the equivalent of legal malice, and justifies punitive damages for trespass. Where there is proof of an intentional, unjustifiable infliction of harm with deliberate disregard of the social consequences, the question of award of punitive damages is for the jury.

> It is abundantly clear from the record that defendant knew when it decided to construct its [paper] mill in Toledo, that there was danger, if not a probability, that the mill would cause damage to adjoining property.... The jury could have found that during the period involved in this action the defendant had not done everything reasonably possible to eliminate or minimize the damage to adjoining properties by its mill. 421 P.2d 957, 958 (Or. 1966).

The dissenting justice in *McElwain* strongly disagreed, arguing that actual malice was a necessary and desirable requirement for award of punitive damages. Which is right? These and related questions resurface in the toxic tort cases.

2. **The availability and measure of punitives.** Analyzing *Branch*, *McElwain*, and *Fischer*, is the availability of punitive damages restricted to situations where defendants' conduct is extreme and anti-social? What is the proper measure of punitive damages? What checks are imposed? In a jury case, the process by which punitive damages are awarded most often begins with plaintiffs' closing argument urging the jury, in accordance with the judge's charge, to award punitives because the defendant's conduct has been shown to "merit" such an award. Thereafter, a jury instruction will be given to the effect that the prevailing plaintiffs are also entitled to punitive damages if the standard for disregard or indifference to the rights of others is met. Rather less is said in the jury charge about how those awards are to be calculated. Are juries free to vent their spleen?

Caps on punitives have been increasingly proposed. The 104th Congress failed to pass several bills containing caps. (see, e.g., 104 H.R. 956, §201(e).) Texas Gov. George Bush signed bill S.B. 25 in April 1996 capping punitive damages claims at two times economic damages, plus no more than $750,000 in non-economic damages or $200,000 whichever is greater. The bill requires a plaintiff to prove fraud or malice and changes the burden of proof from a preponderance of the evidence to clear and convincing evidence.

3. **Proving punitives**. What kind of proof is likely to incite a jury to award punitives? In a book on the asbestos litigation, Paul Brodeur chronicled the industry's 40 year-long "conspiracy of silence" in failing to warn workers or consumers about the fatal dangers of asbestos exposure that it had known about at least since the 1940s. Brodeur quotes a company memo written by Dr. Kenneth W. Smith, Johns-Manville's medical director, after a 1949 study showed that of 708 asbestos workers like Fischer, only four did not have asbestosis:

> It must be remembered that although these men have the X-ray evidence of asbestosis, they are working today and definitely are not disabled.... They have not been told of this diagnosis for it is felt that as long as the man feels well, is happy at home and at work, and his physical condition remains good, nothing should be said. When he becomes disabled and sick, then the diagnosis should be made and the claim submitted by the Company. The fibrosis of this disease is irreversible and permanent so that eventually compensation will be paid to each of these men. But as long as the man is not disabled it is felt that

he should not be told of his condition so that he can live and work in peace and the Company can benefit by his many years of experience. Should the man be told of his condition today there is a very definite possibility that he would become mentally and physically ill, simply through the knowledge that he has asbestosis.

Another memo from a later year revealed a conversation about a 52-year old man:

"Advanced pneumoconiosis," Dr. Smith declared after looking at the patient's medical file.

"Should we change him?" inquired Sheckler [a safety and health supervisor for the company, who wanted to know if a transfer to a non-dusty area was in order].

"Won't make any difference," Smith replied.

"If he hits sixty-five, I will be surprised," Dr. DuBow [a plant physician] said.

On the basis of such advice, Sheckler decided to take no action other than to watch the patient carefully and retire him on disability, if, as he put it, it became "necessary." And as to a woman testing positive for advanced asbestosis, "If she is called in, she will get hysterical, and I am sure you'll have a claim on your hands," so nothing was done. See P. Brodeur, Outrageous Misconduct: The Asbestos Industry on Trial 102–03, 145–46 (1985).

And so contaminated workers were not informed, nor were new employees entering the plant's work force in succeeding years told of the fatal hazard. Analyze why these items of evidence might have an effect on punitive damages (and why, as in the *Kepone case*, the system couldn't rely upon the medical profession for warnings and correction).

4. **Punitive problems in mass cases.** The *Fischer* case, involving a single plaintiff, raises many of the problems that have impelled some state legislatures to yield to industry lobbyists and prohibit punitive damages altogether, or to restrict their availability to special cases of malice, or to cap maximum awards. Are you satisfied with the *Fischer* court's rejoinders to these arguments? The facts of environmental cases often arouse anger and outrage in juries. If a defendant has limited funds, or if juries in sequential cases award duplicative punitive damages for a single mass exposure, there is at least the possibility of unfairness to defendants and other potential plaintiffs. If there are restraints imposed on later duplicative punitive awards, doesn't that prompt a race to court? In the 180 Exxon-Valdez cases, proposals were made for mandatory certification of one all-inclusive punitive damage claim. Should there be a national clearinghouse coordinating punitive damage claims filed against mass tortfeasors? Or is the risk of an avalanche of punitive-minded juries just part of the game?

5. **Constitutional checks on the award of punitive damages?** The United States Supreme Court has decided several cases considering whether due process limitations apply to the award of punitive damages. In Pacific Mut. Life Ins. Co. v. Haslip, 111 S.Ct. 1032 (1991), the Court acknowledged that awards of punitive damages could in some cases violate due process. The jury verdict of $800,000 in *Haslip*, more than four times the compensatory damages in the case, was upheld because the Alabama courts had applied seven test criteria in reviewing the punitives award: (1) the reasonable relationship between the amount awarded and the

harm caused or threatened by defendant's action; (2) the reprehensibility, duration, frequency, and consciousness of defendant's conduct; (3) the profitability of the action; (4) the defendant's financial position; (5) the costs of litigation; (6) whether criminal sanctions had been imposed (which would mitigate the punitives award); and (7) whether defendant had had to pay other civil awards.[23] The first Supreme Court decision actually to *strike down* a punitive damages award as a violation of 14th Amendment due process was Honda Motors v. Oberg, 517 U.S. 1219 (1996). Justice Stevens held that judicial review of the size of punitive damages awards is a necessary due process safeguard against excessive awards, and that a state's common law or statutory law must provide a set of standards for the size of a punitive award, providing for possible remission of punitive damages along the lines of the seven tests in *Haslip*. In BMW v. Gore, 116 S.Ct. 1589 (U.S. 1996), the Court held that "the Due Process Clause of the Fourteenth Amendment prohibits a State from imposing a 'grossly excessive' punishment on a tortfeasor," applying the same factors as in the *Haslip* case. The relevance of due process limits to environmental cases was made clear by the Court's decision in Combustion Engineering v. Johansen, 116 S.Ct. 1843 (U.S. 1996) where the Supreme Court remanded the $15 million punitive damages award in a Georgia strip mine acid drainage case for review of its due process proportionality.

6. **Remittitur.** As the above cases show, appellate (and even trial court) judges can and do at times order a rollback of punitive damage verdicts that they consider excessive, but there are virtually no generally agreed-upon common law judicial standards for remittitur. The Alabama courts' tests in *Haslip* are just a start. How would they tend to apply in environmental cases? Can uncompensated ecological damages be considered? See Garcia, Remittitur in Environmental Cases, 16 Envtl. Aff. L. Rev. 119 (1988).

7. **Punitive damages and insurance.** Under the typical corporate insurance policy's pollution exclusion clauses, punitive damages are usually not covered. An award to a harmed plaintiff is only as good as the defendant's ability to pay. Some states, however, like California, prohibit insurance coverage for willful or malicious acts on public policy grounds. For other examples of the intricacies of pollution-exclusion clauses, see Freedom Gravel Products v. Michigan Mutual Insurance, 819 F.Supp. 275, (WD NY 1993).

8. **Creative accounting in damage remedies: illgotten gains and punitive damages.** An intriguing potential for a new theory of damages is presented by 18 U.S.C.A. §3571 in the criminal law field:

> **Alternative fine based on gain or loss.** If any person derives pecuniary gain from the offense, or if the offense results in pecuniary loss to a person other than the defendant, the defendant may be fined not more than the greater of twice the gross gain or twice the gross loss, unless the imposition of a fine under this subsection would unduly complicate or prolong the sentencing process.

If, for example, a factory has avoided a million dollars in waste treatment expenses by violating pollution discharge limits, energetic application of this provision can

---

23. Substantially followed in In TXO v. Alliance Resources, 113 Sup. Ct. 2711 (1994).

provide a measure of equitable divestment of illgotten gains, a dramatically enhanced deterrent to future evasions, and, especially if the public is deemed an injured "person," a more accurate internalization of environmental harm losses to the commons.

To what extent can this same rationale be applied in civil cases under the common law? In a Georgia strip mine acid drainage case the jury awarded $15 million in punitive damages, in large part on an ill-gotten gains basis, to 24 plaintiffs whose 1100 acres of land had suffered $47,000 in damages from a strip mining operation. The punitive award's disproportion was justified in part by the fact that over the span of eleven years of unheeded warnings to correct its waste treatment, defendant had saved a great deal of money by not cleaning up — a saving of six million dollars in the last four years of operation alone — echoing the *Haslip* test of "profitability of the action." See Combustion Engineering v. Johansen, 98 F.3d 1351 (11th Cir. 1996).[24] The ill-gotten gains recoupment theory of punitive damage awards is likely to find increasingly active use.

A further theory for disgorgement can be based on the quasi-contract theories of "restitution" of ill-gotten gains or "unjust enrichment." So far the courts have not quite bought the theory: Evans v. Johnstown 410 N.Y.S.2d 199 (1978) (municipal sewage treatment plant), County Line Investment Co. v. Tinney, 933 F.2d 1508 (10th Cir. 1991) (suit against predecessor for landfill remediation by a successor).

### d. Remoteness, and indirect economic damages

The element of causation in tort has two distinct facets, termed cause-in-fact and proximate cause. Cause-in-fact refers to the everyday notion of cause and effect, like the row of dominoes linking the act that precipitates the fall of the first to the fall of the last. The usual linguistic test of cause-in-fact is "but for" — the plaintiff must show that but for the act of defendant, the plaintiff's injury would not have occurred. As will be seen in later cases where all that can be proved is that defendant increased the probability of the harm that befell plaintiffs, strict adherence to but-for causation would unfairly doom these cases to failure.

Proximate causation is concerned with the problem of remoteness. At times, but-for causation extends to great distances, perhaps linking defendant's conduct to losses that are beyond the scope of responsibility that defendant should bear. If a highway oil spill negligently caused by defendant's tanker truck causes a traffic jam that delays the delivery van that was carrying a needed part to fix the machine that was to make the widget that the plaintiff had contracted to supply to a customer who had to have it by today, and the cash from the sale was needed to pay the bill to ward off repossession of... etc., somewhere along the line it may be appropriate to limit the availability of remedies for the far-off consequences of wrongful acts, especially where injuries are purely economic. Where do you draw that line?

---

24. Johansen v. Combustion Engineering, S.D. Ga., No. CV-191-178 (June 1993); remitted 98 F.3d 1351 (11th Cir. 1996).The Supreme Court sent the verdict back for reconsideration under the due process remittitur theories of the 1997 *BMW* case. 116 S.Ct. 1843 (U.S. 1996).

The following is an excerpt from the only reported civil case decision arising from the Kepone debacle. It raises questions about how far down the chain of causation liability can be extended. Plaintiffs in this case are not alleging physical injuries to themselves or their property. (Allied quickly settled any and all local physical injury claims.) This is a case of long distance *economic* harms.

### Pruitt v. Allied Chemical Corp.
United States District Court, Eastern District of Virginia, 1981
523 F. Supp. 975

MERHIGE, D.J. Plaintiffs bring the instant action against Allied Chemical Corporation ("Allied") for Allied's alleged pollution of the James River and Chesapeake Bay with the chemical agent commonly known as Kepone....

Plaintiffs allegedly engage in a variety of different businesses and professions related to the harvesting and sale of marine life from the Chesapeake Bay. All claim to have suffered economic harm from defendant's alleged discharges of Kepone into the James River and thence into the Bay. Plaintiffs assert their right to compensation under each of the dozen counts to their complaint [including claims in negligence and strict liability]....

The general rule both in admiralty and at common law has been that a plaintiff cannot recover for indirect economic harm. The logical basis for this rule is obscure. Although Courts have frequently stated that economic losses are "not foreseeable" or "too remote," these explanations alone are rarely apposite. As one well-respected commentator has noted, "the loss to plaintiff in each case...would be readily recoverable if the test of duty — or remoteness – usually associated with the law of negligence were applied...."[25]

Given the conflicting case law from other jurisdictions, together with the fact that there exists no Virginia law on indirect, economic damages, the Court has considered more theoretical sources in order to find a principled basis for its decision.... Scholars in the field rely on Judge Learned Hand's classic statement of negligence...that a principal purpose of tort law is to maximize social utility: where the costs of accidents exceed the costs of preventing them, the law will impose liability.

The difficulty in the present case is how to measure the cost of Kepone pollution. In the instant action, those costs were borne most directly by the wildlife of the Chesapeake Bay. The fact that no one individual claims property rights to the Bay's wildlife could arguably preclude liability. The Court doubts, however, whether such a result would be just. Nor would a denial of liability serve social utility: many citizens, both directly and indirectly, derive benefit from the Bay and its marine life. Destruction of the Bay's wildlife should not be a costless activity....

Commercial fishermen are entitled to compensation for any loss of profits they may prove to have been caused by defendant's negligence. The entitlement given these fishermen presumably arises from what might be called a constructive property interest in the Bay's harvestable species...within a category established in Union Oil Co. v. Oppen, 501 F.2d 558 (9th Cir. 1974) (the Santa Barbara oil spill case): they "lawfully and directly make use of a resource of the sea."

25. James, Limitations of Liability for Economic Loss Caused by Negligence: A Pragmatic Appraisal, 25 Vand. L. Rev. 43 (1972). Prof. James has gone on to state that "the prevailing distinction between indirect economic loss and physical damage is probably a crude and unreliable one that may need reexamination if a limitation on liability for pragmatic reasons is to be retained." Id. at 50–51.

The use that marina and charterboat owners make of the water, though hardly less legal, is...less direct.... Still less direct, but far from nonexistent, is the link between the Bay and the seafood dealers, restaurants, and tackle shops that seek relief (as do the employees of these establishments).

One meaningful distinction to be made among the various categories of plaintiffs here arises from a desire to avoid double-counting in calculating damages. Any seafood harvested by the commercial fishermen here would have been bought and sold several times before finally being purchased for consumption. Considerations both of equity and social utility suggest that just as defendant should not be able to escape liability for destruction of publicly owned marine life entirely, it should not be caused to pay repeatedly for the same damage. The Court notes, however, that allowance for recovery of plaintiffs' lost profits here would not in all cases result in double-counting of damages. Plaintiff...seafood wholesalers, retailers, processors, distributors and restaurateurs...allegedly lost profits when deprived of supplies of seafood. Those profits represented a return on the investment of each of the plaintiffs in material and labor in their businesses, and thus the independent loss to each would not amount to double-counting.... Employees undoubtedly lost wages and faced a less favorable job market than they would have, but for defendant's acts, and they have thus been harmed by defendant. What is more, the number of parties with a potential cause of action against defendant is hardly exhausted in plaintiffs' complaint. In theory, parties who bought and sold to and from the plaintiffs named here also suffered losses in business, as did their employees. In short, the set of potential plaintiffs seems almost infinite.

Perhaps because of the large set of potential plaintiffs,...some limitation to liability, even when damages are foreseeable, is advisable.... The Court thus finds itself with a perceived need to limit liability, without any articulated reason for excluding any particular set of plaintiffs. Other courts have had to make similar decisions.[26] The Court concludes that [commercial fishermen can recover for their lost profits, but the categories of] plaintiffs who purchased and marketed seafood from commercial fishermen suffered damages that are not legally cognizable, because insufficiently direct.... The Court holds that plaintiff...boat, marina, and tackle and bait shop owners have suffered legally cognizable damages.... Only if some set of surrogate plaintiffs is entitled to press its own claims which flow from the damage to the Bay's sportfishing industry will the proper balance of social forces be preserved.... The Court's conclusion results from consideration of all these factors, and an attempt to tailor justice to the facts of the instant case....

## COMMENTARY AND QUESTIONS

1. **The rationale for barring indirect damages.** Is there any compelling reason for the traditional tort law rule that forbade recovery of indirect economic losses in the absence of physical injury? Could the reason be institutional, seeking to limit the number of cases in which courts were called upon to make necessarily speculative

---

26. See e.g., Judge Kaufmann's opinion in Petition of Kinsman Transit Co., 388 F.2d 821, 824–25 (2d Cir. 1968), where the court noted that "in the final analysis the circumlocution whether posed in terms of 'foreseeability,' 'duty,' 'proximate cause,' 'remoteness,' etc. seems unavoidable," and then turned to Judge Andrews well-known statement in Palsgraf v. Long Island R.R. Co., 162 N.E. 99, 104 (N.Y. 1928): "It is all a question of expediency...of fair judgment, always keeping in mind the fact that we endeavor to make a rule in each case that will be practical and in keeping with the general understanding of mankind."

determinations about the course of future events? Could the reason instead represent an inductive overgeneralization, that in a substantial majority of cases lacking physical damage there is likewise no credible economic damage? The bar against indirect recoveries has been widely applied in maritime tort cases under the rule of *Robins Drydock*, 275 U.S. 303 (1927), and has attracted criticism as a major barrier to oil spill plaintiffs in cases like the Exxon-Valdez spill, although statutory exceptions sometimes apply. See Mulhern, Marine Pollution: A Tort Recovery Standard for Pure Economic Losses, 18 Envtl. Aff. L. Rev. 85 (1990).

2. **Of double-counting and foreseeable losses.** What is the double-counting danger that is raised by defendants? The judge is correct in saying that the sum of the lost profits of the several categories of victims, by definition a net figure, is inherently free of double counting problems. Is it correct to limit the award to "replacement value of a plaintiff's actual investment"? What if a plaintiff bought a going fishing business at an unreasonably low price. Is there any reason to allow defendant to deprive that victim of the anticipated net income the wise investment would have generated?

The judge draws the line at the water's edge. Is that fair to inland plaintiffs who are foreseeable victims of massive contamination of the Bay? How does a recovery by the commercial fishermen in any way protect the interests of the owners and employees of a cannery that can no longer process fish from the Bay? And are you satisfied with the allowance of sport fishery industry recoveries as a proxy for natural resource damage?

Surveying the range of legal actions so far noted in the Kepone case, how complete an accounting did Allied Chemical face from private litigation?

## Section 3. NATURAL RESOURCES REMEDIES

Because the vast majority of environmental litigation is directed at recouping losses to humans and their property, one tends to lose sight of ecological reality: that human injuries are not necessarily the major consequences of disruptions of the natural equilibrium. As Judge Mehrige said in *Pruitt*, "Kepone pollution...costs were borne most directly by the wildlife of the Chesapeake Bay." When a wrongdoer destroys or injures natural resources, the law can do an adequate enough job establishing fault or equivalent basis for liability. The riddle is how to define and apply remedies for injuries beyond damages to humans. Over the past decade, environmental law has, in a variety of ways, committed itself to answering that question.

The public trust doctrine, as noted in Chapter One, offers a foundation for equitable restoration remedies and government economic recoveries for natural resources damage (NRD).[27] Public nuisance actions also have supplied authority for NRD remedies, as well as a number of state and federal statutes. The Clean Water Act, CERCLA, and other federal acts require the federal government to "identify the best available procedures to determine natural resources damages, including

---

27. Note that the field of NRD incorporates both equitable remedies and economic damages.

both direct and indirect injury, destruction or loss."[28] The evolution of NRD liability theories, evaluation methods, and remedies is occurring concurrently in both common law and public law settings.

The Exxon-Valdez oil spill provides a classic example of NRD accounting.

Shortly after midnight on March 24, 1989, the single-hulled supertanker Exxon-Valdez sliced into the submerged granite of Bligh Reef in Alaska's Prince William Sound. Pushed by northeasterly winds, the eleven million gallons of crude oil that spewed from the wreck spread out over 1,000 miles of coastal waters.[29] The ecosystem hit by the Exxon-Valdez spill was extraordinarily rich. Affected species included herring, black cod, cutthroat trout, dolly varden, shark, halibut, rock fish, shell fish, fin fish, several species of salmon, sea otters, fur seals, steller's sea lions, harbor porpoises, dall porpoises, killer whales, hump-back whales, minke whales, fin whales, blue whales, gray whales, deer, fox, coyotes, black bears, brown bears, bald eagles, several species of gulls, hundreds of thousands of sea birds, such as kittiwakes, puffins, hawks, guillemots, murres, murrelets, loons, grebes, diving ducks, dungeness crabs, pot shrimp, trawl shrimp...and these were just the upper layers of the ecological pyramid. The waters and wildlife of the Gulf of Alaska were among the most fertile coastal communities on earth, built upon a confluence of ocean currents rich in micro-organisms, zooplankton and phytoplankton.

In the aftermath of the Exxon-Valdez oil spill, more than one hundred and eighty civil suits were filed, almost all by people claiming injury to their economic interests. Some of those economic claims are relatively uninteresting — claims for direct property losses and diminution of market value. Others raise some of the questions noted in the preceding section about how far economic recoveries can extend along a chain of "indirect" causation, from commercial fishers, to processors, distributors, ship owners, outfitters, and restauranteurs, none of whom sustained actual physical damage.

The State of Alaska's lawsuit included many predictable economic claims — loss of tourism and recreation; reimbursement for out-of-pocket cleanup efforts by towns, native American tribes, and the State; emotional distress and disruption of citizens' lives; and so on — but the State also asked the trial court to award damages and injunctions that would capture a broader swath of values, based on natural resources losses. As you read the following brief excerpts from the State's 40-page complaint, note the problems faced in defining and separating human and ecological remedies:

---

28. CWA, 33 U.S.C.A. §1321(f)(4)(5); CERCLA, 42 U.S.C.A. §9651(C)(2). The other federal statutes that authorize NRD are: OPA90, 33 U.S.C.A. §2701, 2702(b)(2)(A); Trans-Alaska Pipeline Auth. Act, 43 U.S.C.A. §1653, (1973, 1988); Deepwater Port Act, 33 U.S.C.A. §1501 (1974, 1988); Outer Continental Shelf Lands Act Amdts of 1978, 43 U.S.C.A. §§1331-56 (1978, 1988); Marine Protection, Research, and Sanctuaries Act of 1988, 16 U.S.C.A. §1443; National Parks Systems Authority Act, 16 U.S.C.A. §19ii (Supp. V 1993). The doctrines of NRD liability and valuation methods are being actively debated and shaped in judicial review of federal agency NRD regulations. See Chapter 18.

29. As to fault, the wreck was an accident waiting to happen, attributable to cost-cutting and complacency within the oil industry, abetted by lassitude within the U.S. Coast Guard and state and federal regulatory agencies. See State of Alaska Oil Spill Commission, Spill: The Wreck of the Exxon-Valdez: Lessons for the Safe Transportation of Oil (1990). Disclosure notice: one of the authors worked for the State of Alaska and for the Oil Spill Commission itself on legal responses to the Exxon-Valdez spill.

# IN THE SUPERIOR COURT FOR THE STATE OF ALASKA
## THIRD JUDICIAL DISTRICT

THE STATE OF ALASKA, on its own behalf,    )
and as public trustee and as *parens patriae* for )
the citizens of the State, Plaintiff,           )      Case No. 3AN8906852CIV
                 vs.                   )
EXXON CORPORATION, a New Jersey    )
corporation; EXXON PIPELINE COMPANY, a    )
Delaware corporation; EXXON SHIPPING    )
COMPANY, a Delaware corporation;    )
ALYESKA PIPELINE SERVICE COMPANY,    )
   a Delaware corporation; et al.              )
                 Defendants.        )

COMPLAINTS FOR COMPENSATORY AND PUNITIVE DAMAGES, CIVIL
PENALTIES AND INJUNCTIVE RELIEF
...20. "Environmental damages" includes, but is not limited to, one or more types
of damages to use and enjoyment values derived from State lands, waters, and
resources:

(1) Use values, including consumptive and nonconsumptive uses;

(2) Nonuse values, including existence, intrinsic, option, bequest, temporal, and
quasi-option values;

(3) Values derived from the existence of management options and the expertise and
data to exercise and support same;

(4) Values associated with the necessity or desirability of restoration, replacement,
assessment or monitoring;

(5) Other ecosystem existing values....

DAMAGES TO PLAINTIFF
...61. As a result of the oil spill from the EXXON-VALDEZ, over a thousand square
miles of State lands, waters, and resources have suffered severe environmental
damage. A growing number of coastal and inland sounds and bays, beaches, tidelands, tidal pools, wetlands, estuaries, and other sensitive elements of the ecosystems have been devastated; thousands of mammals, fowl, and fish have been killed
or injured; anadromous streams, near shore environments and other fish and
wildlife critical habitats have been contaminated; aesthetics and scenic quality
have been destroyed or impaired, together with attendant opportunities for recreational experiences; air quality has deteriorated through the escape of evaporating
pollutants; commercial fisheries have been sharply curtailed, with adverse biological and economic consequences; the greater ecosystem in the spill area has been
deprived of its pristine condition with attendant damage to the condition of, and
interrelationship among, living creatures comprising the system; and the management opportunities available through the knowledge and data base generated from
prior experience with the ecosystem have been compromised....

RELIEF SOUGHT

WHEREFORE, plaintiff prays that this Court:

...Award all compensatory and punitive damages authorized under the common law, including, but not limited to, environmental and economic damages.

Award all compensatory and punitive damages authorized under the general maritime law.

Order that the defendants be permanently enjoined to remove all spilled oil and to restore the surface and subsurface lands, wildlife, waters, fisheries, shellfish and associated marine resources, air and other State lands, waters and resources affected directly or indirectly by the spill;

Order immediate and continuing environmental monitoring and assessment of the conditions of the air, waters and subsurface and surface lands, fisheries, shellfish and the associated marine resources and other natural resources... [and]

...Award such other and further relief as this Court deems just and proper.

DATED this 15th day of August, 1989.

Douglas B. Baily

Attorney General

COMMENTARY AND QUESTIONS

1. **Non-marketplace human-based remedies**. Assuming first that the numerical loss of living resources can be accurately established,[30] natural resources remedies then go beyond the mere commodity-pricing approach of the marketplace. As the appellate court wrote when Ohio challenged the Clean Water Act and Superfund natural resource regulations:

It is the incompleteness of market processes that give rise to the need for [non-market valuation].... While it is not irrational to look to market price as one factor in determining the use value of a resource, it is unreasonable to view market price as the *exclusive* factor, or even the predominant one. From the bald eagle to the blue whale and snail darter, natural resources have values that are not fully captured by the market system.... Option and existence values may represent 'passive' use, they nonetheless reflect utility derived by humans from a resource, and thus prima facie ought to be included in a damage assessment. Ohio v. U.S. Dept. of Interior, 880 F.2d 432, at 462–464 (D.C. Cir. 1989).[31]

Note how the court returns to humans. Likewise, although the Alaska complaint begins its narration of damages with environmental losses, even within the definition of "environmental damages" many if not all of the contentions are for *human*-based economic recovery.[32] The term "use value," for instance, seeks to

30. Measuring transient living resources that previously came to a particular place and now are absent is often a challenging scientific process. For one of the most awful judicial opinions on this point and generally, see Hampton v. North Carolina Pulp Co., 49 F.Supp. 625 (N.C. 1943), thankfully rev'd, 139 F.2d 840 (4th Cir. 1943).

31. Emphasis in original. The Supreme Court subsequently denied certorari.

32. Beyond the realm of natural resources, the Alaska complaint also raises environmental questions regarding remedies for the dramatic disruptions to the Alaska Native communities along the coast, where the prior-existing complex and stable subsistence culture may never recover from the onslaughts of oil and oilspill cleanup salaries. The complaint also seeks remedies for non-economic human losses in psychological stresses suffered by many non-Native Alaskans whose lives were severely impacted by the spill.

capture values for things that don't actually trade in the marketplace, but uses an attributed market value. "Consumptive value" attributes a value to lost resource uses of sportsmen and tourists who would have taken wildlife in hunting or fishing pursuits. "Non-consumptive" uses include the ecosystem's value to photographers, bird watchers, and the like. Some "non-use" values are based on attributed human value: what it means to people just to know the resource is there, even if they never actively use it; it is "option value" if they may use it. "Bequest value" reflects the resource as a legacy passed by the present generation to its children. "Temporal" and "quasi-option" values assess unknown future values foreclosed. There is a wide range of economic methods for estimating or "shadow pricing" some of these values, including travel cost (the amount that people are willing to spend to travel to such places); "hedonic" value, using market activity preferences; implied speculative rent values; and contingent valuation methods (CVM) based on public opinion surveys about willingness to pay (as in a hypothetical tax).[33]

Fundamentally, each of these approaches creates a hypothetical human market for resources, an approach which requires that the component fish, wildlife, bugs, and micro-organisms of an ecosystem be made sufficiently recognizable and attractive to a human audience to deserve monetary recognition.

2. **Natural resources' own intrinsic value?** None of the preceding remedies pretends to assess the value of the resources in and of themselves. It seems presumptuous, however, to argue that humans are the sole measure of what has been lost in an ecological catastrophe (although only humans, of course, are in a position to raise the intrinsic ethical claims). If courts can look beyond human-based values, as both law and ethics may currently be inviting them to do, serious questions arise. Can you talk intelligently about the lost wildlife's value to itself? First, it's dead; second, it's wildlife, not human. The flora and fauna and their ecosystem leave no probate estates for wrongful death recoveries. Who can sue, for what purpose, and for what measure of relief?

Who can sue? Given our legal system, it would be vastly easier to sue for the loss of resources if they were citizens, or someone owned them. In the absence of either, the state of Alaska can file its claims for remedies based on its "parens patriae" and public trustee roles, and environmentalists can sue as public trust beneficiaries (see Chapter 22), but the nature and extent of standing to recover for intrinsic natural resources losses are not self-evident.

What is the purpose of seeking natural resources damages? The dead wildlife cannot be brought back to life. In ordinary tort law the purpose of damages is a delicate mix of restoring plaintiffs to their prior position and taxing wrongdoers for their wrongdoing. "Destruction of the Bay's wildlife should not be a costless activity," said the judge in the *Pruitt* Kepone case in this chapter. To this extent the punitive damages sought in the Alaska complaint may be an attempt to capture unquantifiable intrinsic losses, and deter future wrongful actions.

---

33. See Cross, Natural Resource Damage Valuation, 42 Vand. L. Rev. 269 (1989); Cicchetti & Peck, Assessing Natural Resource Damages: The Case Against Contingent Value Survey Methods, 4 Natural Resources & the Environment 6 (Spring 1989).

But what is the measure of loss? The wildlife and their ecological pyramid had an "existence value" that is gone. The fact that they used to be there, and no longer are, reflects the disruption of an evolved ecological community that didn't just happen to be there, but had adapted and developed over thousands and millions of years. What is the value of the components of that system, especially the vast numbers of small rather prosaic protozoans, sea slugs, and the like?[34]

The fundamental problem of damage valuation for the *per se* loss of wildlife is that the intrinsic worth of natural resources does not conveniently fit the terms of economic accountability.

3. **Ecological restoration remedies**. The shortcomings in human-based valuations, and the perplexities of awarding intrinsic value natural resources damages, propel the law increasingly toward performance-based relief — restoration or mitigation remedies.

Restoration, as an in-kind ecological remedy, represents two different rationales: first, the aim to put things back as they were before defendants' wrongdoing occurred, a satisfying and understandable objective; second, to provide a performance standard as a proxy for the otherwise difficult task of valuing what has been lost. The court cuts through the riddles of natural resources valuation by ordering that the wrong be undone. If a piece of forest was wrongfully clear-cut, how fitting to order soil restoration and replanting of mature trees, shrubs, and undergrowth. As with human-based restoration remedies, natural resources remediation is a way to capture widespread values within judicial relief and raise potent deterrent examples for prospective wrongdoers. Restoration presents serious questions, however, not least the definition of what restoration means.

What does Alaska's complaint mean when it demands restoration? As requested, it is clearly impossible. It is technically and economically infeasible to recapture more than about 20 percent of any major oil spill. Most is now lodged deep within ocean bottom sediments, travelling in solution through ocean currents, or located within the tissues of coastal and marine wildlife, the strata of coastal beaches, etc. What would the cost of a partial restoration undertaking be, if it could be done? And might not the removal of oil, through solvents or organic methods, cause more destruction than the oil itself?

In fact, a natural restoration process begins as soon as an oil spill catastrophe occurs. Volatiles evaporate into the air and are diffused; hydrocarbons begin a very slow process of breaking down and becoming ever-more diluted components of the ecosystem. With the action of wind, waves, sun, and time, within 50 years the Gulf of Alaska is likely to be very similar to its condition prior to the oil spill (although several species may be gone). If that is the case, then what is meant by a legally-mandated restoration? Various ecosystem components can indeed be added imme-

---

34. In some cases, courts have tried to value the wildlife itself in terms of what it would bring at a meat market or pet store. In a case where millions of baby striped bass were sucked into the cooling intakes of a power plant, the court awarded the per pound price of striped bass in the fish market; zoos may have set a special market value by buying animals like sea otters, sometimes for tens of thousands of dollars; sea slugs have a value as delicacies in Japanese restaurants. Does this sound like an appropriate approach for estimating the intrinsic value of ecological losses?

diately by human actions: hatcheries can be created to propagate fish, birds, even mayflies and plankton, and those efforts, although they risk a sort of suburban homogenizing of the naturally diverse gene pool, nevertheless can serve a useful function. But if one begins with the curve of natural restoration, apparently the primary rationale of legal restoration remedies is to accelerate, artificially, the rate of natural recovery, a somewhat ambiguous undertaking even if it is feasible.

Restoration can arguably be vastly more expensive than it is worthwhile, which guarantees that it will attract strong resistance. The Clean Water and Superfund Acts both provide for "the restoration or replacement of natural resources damaged or destroyed as a result of discharge of oil or a hazardous substance.... Sums recovered shall be used to restore, rehabilitate, or acquire the equivalent of such natural resources[35] by the appropriate agencies. As issued by Secretary James Watt, however, the required regulations on natural resources remedies provided that the measure of damages should be "the *lesser* of restoration or replacement costs, or diminution of use values." The *Ohio* court struck down the regulations, declaring that "the Department of Interior erred by establishing a strong presumption in favor of market price,"[36] and emphasized the preferability of restoration. The NOAA regulations, with more inclusive NRD accounting, have been upheld as noted in Chapter 18.

But cost must play some part in the balance. An army of biologists can be deployed, sopping up oil with sponges, and propagating myriad tiny organisms and higher lifeforms to rebuild shattered food chains; sands and mud can be imported; floating filtration plants can be installed. The costs would be astronomical, however, and the results uncertain. In a case arising from a Puerto Rican oil spill, the First Circuit had to balance the feasibility and cost of restoration against a statutory restoration mandate. Puerto Rico had asked for removal and replacement of oil-soaked bottom sediments, and replanting of thousands of poisoned mangroves, at a cost of $7 million, or alternatively an award of "replacement value" based on a biologist's estimate that 92 million creatures had been destroyed, and a guesstimate that they averaged a replacement value or cost of $.06 each, totaling $5,526,583.20. The court decided that "the appropriate primary standard for determining damages in a case such as this, is the cost reasonably to be incurred by the sovereign or its designated agency to restore or rehabilitate the environment in the affected area to its pre-existing condition, or as close thereto as is feasible *without grossly disproportionate expenditures*...with attention to such factors as technical feasibility, harmful side effects, compatibility with or duplication of such regeneration as is naturally to be expected, and the extent to which efforts beyond a certain point would become either redundant or disproportionately expensive." The court rejected the government's $7 million remedy as "impractical, inordinately expensive, and unjustifiably dangerous to the healthy mangroves and marine animals still present in the area to be restored," and the second, replacement value theory on the ground that the government was not actually proposing to replace the 92 million creatures into the contaminated bay "which, being contaminated

---

35 33 U.S.C.A. §1321(f)(4)(5), echoed in Superfund, 42 U.S.C.A. §9651(C)(2).

36. Ohio v. U.S. Department of Interior, 880 F.2d 432, 464 (D.C. Cir. 1989) (emphasis added).

with oil, would hardly support them...."[37] Was this a judgment based on a finding that the cost was "grossly disproportionate," or that actual restoration was infeasible in the circumstances? If restoration is feasible, how does one weigh the cost of natural resources restoration?

**4. Must restoration awards be used to restore?** If Alaska recovers $500 million in damages based on the cost of feasible restoration, could Governor Wally Hickel then take the money and use it to build roads through the wilderness, which, he said, were a more worthwhile project? His road project failed, but approximately $55 million of NRD recovery was put into a Sea Life tourist attraction. Under the law of the case, or the public trust doctrine examined in Chapters One and 22, it would seem that restoration awards are impressed with a trust for restorative purposes, but it is not clearly so.

**5. NRD precedents from the Alaska oilspill.** The Exxon-Valdez spill was a milestone event in national environmental policy debates. See J. S. Picou et al., The Exxon Valdez Disaster: Readings on a Modern Social Problem (1997). In NRD terms, by 1992 Exxon was told it could stop further cleanup on the beaches of Prince William Sound because it had reached a point of diminishing returns.[38] The state and federal governments negotiated a settlement agreement with Exxon for a $125 million criminal penalty, $12 million of which went to the North American Wetlands Conservation Fund, and civil penalties of $900 million to be paid over ten years into a fund administered by a state-federal Trustee Council.[39]

The Trustees' management of the $900 million Exxon-Valdez fund constitutes a precedent-setting NRD experiment. The governmental civil penalties were the largest NRD recovery ever. The massive Gulf of Alaska program offers a superb opportunity for comprehensive analysis of NRD remediation. Unfortunately the Trustees' program, launched by the immediacy of the spill, has not produced a clear or comprehensive analysis of the legal regime of NRD. Ensuing study will be needed to analyze the full range of NRD options, methodologies, and requirements. At this point the authority and legal obligations of the Trustees are not clear to themselves as well as observers. Are they trustees under the public trust doctrine generally, as well as creatures of particular statutes, subject to judicial supervision of their trusteeship upon citizen petition?[40] What are the standards that bind them? The legal history of the Alaska NRD Trusteeship will be instructive. The Trustees have undertaken extensive scientific studies of harms done to the impacted envi-

---

37. Puerto Rico v. S.S. Zoe Colocotroni, 628 F.2d 652, 676, 677 (1st Cir. 1980) (emphasis added).

38. In fact it is questionable whether from the beginning the solvents used to produce clean beaches for the visitor's eye did not do more harm than good, contaminating the microecology of the beaches far down into the substrates. Oil stil remains within the subsurface layers.

Despite a golden opportunity, no other remedies in the nature of equitable relief were obtained.

39. The federal trustees are the Secretaries of Agriculture, Commerce, and Interior; state trustees are the Attorney-General and the Commissioners of the Alaska Department of Fish and Game and Department of Environmental Conservation. The Trustees' legal status and enforceable duties are basically unclear. 33 U.S.C.A. §3121(f)5; 42 U.S.C.A. §9607(f); 33 U.S.C.A. §2706(b); Executive Order 12580, 52 Fed. Reg. 2923 (1987).

40. This question was raised in regard to whether the Trustees were a federal agency, obliged to release their post-settlement scientific studies under the Freedom of Information Act, a question that ultimately was not clearly answered.

ronment, potentially consuming more than half the NRD recovery. Somewhat less than half of the fund has been targeted toward mitigation and restoration expenditures noted below.

(Private litigation for economic harms from the Alaska oilspill have resulted in verdicts exceeding five billion dollars, raising issues that will take a decade to be worked out in the courts. Virtually all such recoveries are for human economic losses, however, not NRD.)

6. **Mitigation and substituted resources.** An early common law suit filed by environmentalists in the Alaska oil spill case, analogizing to CWA provisions, requested the establishment of a fund or foundation for "the acquisition of equivalent [and additional] natural resources" as an alternative remedy where restoration was ecologically or economically infeasible.[41] Is such mitigation-by-acquisition a satisfactory natural resources remedy? In effect it merely secures (as a park or reserve) existing resources that otherwise might face destruction by economic development. Does it add or replace anything beyond what existed in the aftermath of an ecological catastrophe? Anticipatory mitigation was the approach taken in Alaska's Prince William Sound. The Trustees obligated almost $500 million of oilspill NRD to buy up forests surrounding the Sound to prevent the drastic clearcutting that otherwise, laws or no laws, would have choked spawning streams with erosion and débris, and altered stream flows and water quality throughout the area.

7. **Prospects.** Ultimately, natural resources remedies are not a neatly quantifiable concept, as they would be if they merely paralleled marketplace assessments. Natural resources remedies are an evolving part of the common law and have been written into statutes, so the evolution of NRD remedies, with their ambiguities and opportunities, will continue in judicial proceedings and administrative agency processes.

## E. ENVIRONMENTAL USES OF OTHER NON-STATUTORY CAUSES OF ACTION

Environmental law is where you find it. The dramatic evolution of environmental tort law demonstrates the ability of the legal system to find flexible solutions for modern problems in old doctrines creatively applied and litigated. But tort law is not the only source of this adaptive legal technology. Other nonstatutory fields can be drawn into environmental law cases: trust law in the environmental public trust doctrine, property law, contract law, corporate law (see Chapter 20), and a variety of other areas of practice. This provides a reminder to modern lawyers facing the challenges of a dynamically evolving field always to scope out broad possibilities within the common law, as well as within specific statutes and regulations on point.

---

41. National Wildlife Fed. et al. v. Exxon Corp., Alyeska Pipeline Service Co. et al., Super. Ct., 3d Dist. Alaska, 3 AN-89-2533 civ (1989).

Here is one of many examples:

Strip-mining is a highly emotional modern controversy of the "energy v. environment" variety, and a classic environmental problem in terms of overview benefit-cost accounting. The market's optimum production method in mountain terrain, "strip and augering,"[42] tends to externalize and thus ignore the serious costs it imposes on neighboring communities and the environment, unless an adequate statute is passed and enforced, which is difficult,[43] or unless plaintiffs can find a relevant nonstatutory cause of action.

Tort law, however, may not apply in this setting because in many places stripmine companies own subsurface coal rights under "broad form deeds" and claim the right to destroy the surface to get at it:

> [This deed] grants and conveys property, rights and privileges, in, of, to, on, under, concerning...all the coal, minerals and mineral products,...and such of the standing timber as may be by the Grantee, its successors, or assigns be deemed necessary for mining purposes.... Grantee may use and operate the same and surface thereof...in any and every manner that may be deemed necessary or convenient for mining, and therefrom removing minerals,...and in the use of said land and surface thereof by the Grantee, his heirs, successors and assigns, shall be free from, and are, hereby released from liability or claim of damage to the said Grantor, their representatives, heirs and assigns.... There is reserved to the Grantor all the timber upon the said land, except that necessary for mining, and the free use of land for agricultural purposes, so far as such use is consistent with the property, rights and privileges hereby bargained, sold, granted or conveyed to Grantee.[44]

Attempts to assert tort law protections in the face of this deed raise a basic questions of contract or deed interpretation — what was conveyed by the document?

> The only feasible and economical way to mine the coal in question is by the strip and auger method of mining.... Appellant contends that since all of the coal was conveyed it may be mined by any method, and the appellees' surface

---

42. Mountains in parts of Appalachia stand like multi-layered pyramidal chocolate cakes in which coal seams one to eight feet thick lie flat, one above the other, separated by five to a hundred feet of shale and earth, covered with mountainside ecosystems. Significant amounts of coal can be gotten cheaply with dynamite and bulldozers by carving benches around the sides of the mountains atop the coal outcroppings, pushing the trees and soil "overburden" over the side, clearing the way for front-end loaders to shovel up the coal and drive it away. After an outcrop coal seam has been stripped to the high walls (the point where the overhang of the excavated slope is too unstably high to be cut further inward), and the seams have been augered-drilled sideways further into the hill to salvage as much readily-reachable coal as possible, the mountain is so unstable that underground mining is impossible and 70% of a mountain's coal may be permanently unreachable thereafter, at least under today's technology. The mountain is often left a tortured moonscape, descending in ragged steps to the valley below, with sulfuric shale, runoff water, and the rubble of soil and trees sliding down the hillside, filling the valley below, poisoning the streams, covering the bottomland agricultural fields of the mountain communities that remain, and swelling seasonal floods.

43. Both state and federal governments have passed stripmining controls. At the state level, many regulatory systems have been dominated by the industry. At the federal level, regulation under the Surface Mining Control and Reclamation Act (SMCRA) has had a similarly checkered history, being almost completely diluted during the Reagan years under Interior Secretary James Watt. To many non-Kentucky environmental lawyers, at least, common law remedies often appear to be more practical than public law. In 1974 the Kentucky legislature actually passed a statute requiring stripmining consent by all who owned any interest in land, but the high court quickly declared it an unconstitutional taking. DNR v. No. 8 Limited, 528 S.W.2d 684 (Ky. 1975).

44. From a fee simple coal deed in Buchanan v. Watson, 290 S.W.2d 40 (Ky.,1956) dated May 19, 1903, from Miles Cole and wife to a land company agent, covering 129.47 acres of land in Magoffin County, for less than $3.00 per acre; similar language exists in some mineral easements and leases.

ZBP

*A stripmine in the Cumberland Mountains near the Kentucky-Tennessee border. Note the results of the primitive blast and scrape method, and its consequences in erosion, mudslides, and disruption of natural water flows. Photograph is taken from the unstable edge of an excavated seam higher up on the mountain. When trees start to lean, it means that the surface of the mountain is beginning to "creep" or slide. Mines on the mountains in the distance extract coal from the same horizontal seams.*

rights are subordinate to the rights of the appellant.... The deed by express language did not exclude or include this method of mining, and the proof shows
that such mining methods were known and had been used prior to the date of
the deed. It seems clear that the parties intended the conveyance of the coal.
To deny the right to remove it by the only feasible method is to defeat the principal purpose of the deed....

Two fundamental rules for construction of deeds [govern]: that a deed which
grants land and certain specific rights and privileges, there being no ambiguity
in the instrument, will be construed according to its terms, and enforced
strictly according to its terms, and where there is ambiguity or uncertainty in
the deed, it will be construed most strongly against the grantor and in favor of
the grantee.... Buchanan v. Watson, 290 S.W. 2d 40.

Here is the contrary argument based on contract and deed interpretation grounds:

There has been a long line of cases holding that grantees under "broad form"
deeds have a right to use the surface for any purpose "deemed necessary or convenient" by the grantee. However, all those cases involved deep-mining methods, which was the method of mining contemplated by the parties in 1905.
Even where a drastic technology was in theory known to exist on the date of
execution of a lease, courts should be guided by the implied intention of the
parties that minerals should be extracted in the customary manner that prevailed when the lease was executed. The parties to this deed had not contemplated the strip and auger method of mining nor did they contemplate that any
portion of the surface of the land would be destroyed or rendered valueless for
agricultural purposes or growing timber. Modern courts moreover should not
ignore and disregard the rights of the surface owner. Many courts have held
that the owner of the coal must leave pillars of coal to support the surface. To
permit stripmining in many of these areas would be to allow the dominant
estate to destroy the servient estate completely, and that diabolical devastation
and destruction could not have been the parties' intent or understanding.[45]

COMMENTARY AND QUESTIONS

1. **Interpretation of stripmine broadform deeds.** In applying the canons of interpretation against the grantor of a broadform deed, should courts consider the fact that
most such deeds were prepared by *grantees*, and that many grantors signed with an
"X"? If the terms of a document are clear, to what extent should courts look to the
intention of the parties, given that in the statutory interpretation setting, the clear
words govern? Does the subdivision of a parcel of land into two separate estates,
surface and subsurface, necessarily imply that a party who owns just one estate
cannot destroy the existence of the other? What do you make of the fact that many
original subsurface deeds were purchased for $3.00 an acre, which was often *more*
than the full assessed value of a full fee simple?

2. **The broad reach of private land controls.** Looking beyond review of deeds, note
that other private land use concepts — restrictive covenants, conservation
easements, and other private land interests — can be given strong environmental

---

45. This argument is paraphrased from Judge Hill's opinion in Martin v. Kentucky Oak Mining Co.,
429 S.W.2d 395 (Ky., 1968), a dissent (but reflecting majority holdings in all stripmining states
except Kentucky). The attorney for appellants in *Martin* was the late Harry Caudill, who wrote
Night Comes to the Cumberlands (1963) and three other anguishing chronicles of Appalachia and
stripmining.

applications, incorporating whatever terms and values the private parties want, far beyond the range of governmental regulations. Private land controls can create nonprofit wildlife preserves perpetually excluded from development, dictate the kinds of trees to be maintained, the preservation of buildings, control of developments' style, density and appearance, the total non-development of some developable areas, and so on. There is no clear legal basis, however, upon which to distinguish desirable private land use planning and controls from capricious restraints on future use of scarce resources.

3. **Prescriptive easements.** "Easements by prescription" can be acquired by using land without permission for a statutory term (typically 5 to 10 years), paralleling doctrines of squatters' rights to title in adverse possession of land. In some cases prescriptive easements can be used affirmatively to assert environmental rights, as in establishing public rights of access to beaches. In other cases they can set up environmental challenges: A "right to dump" can be an easement, so some polluters have claimed an "easement to pollute" particular streams into which they have discharged waste over the years, thus claiming immunity from private nuisance suits. In the absence of a statute, how do private plaintiffs overcome such polluters' "right to dump"? Prescriptive easements are usually defined fairly strictly in terms of the quantity and quality of use established over the prescriptive term, and squatters' rights are generally not recognized where they are in competition with public rights. See Anneberg v. Kurtz, 28 S.E.2d 769, 773 (Ga. 1944).

4. **Equitable restrictions.** On Shady Mountain in Tennessee, a land developer from Chattanooga had sold ten lots to families who moved in and, pursuant to covenants in their deeds, built single-family homes. Thereafter she stopped sales for a while, and later leased lots #11–18 to a coal stripmining company which had just moved onto the land and was ready to bulldoze and blast. The government control agencies provided no effective constraint on the stripmining. Some activist law students stopped the strip-mine operation for the families by a property law action based on a negative reciprocal covenant (sometimes confusingly called an "equitable servitude"). When a seller subdivides lots and begins to sell them with a similar or uniform set of restrictions, there is an enforceable implied equitable promise that all lots will similarly be held to the earlier restrictions.

5. **Toxic breach of implied warranty of title.** What happens if a buyer discovers toxic contaminants on the land between the day the contract to purchase was made and the date set for the transfer of title? The law creates an implied warranty that sellers will provide good marketable title at the closing. Will the mere presence of toxics on the land create a "cloud on the title" allowing purchasers to rescind contracts based upon violation of the warranty? The consequences of such a rule would be drastic. Because it would threaten marketability of any affected parcel, it would practically compel environmental assessment audits of all major land purchases. It is not yet clear how pollution per se affects the implied warranty of marketable title (unless the government has slapped a lien on the title). Should buyers be able to rescind in such cases? Note that, having notice, they probably could not claim the "innocent landowner" exception from Superfund liability. (In practice, most residential cases contracts are made contingent on buyers obtaining

financing, so all the buyer has to do in such cases is tell the bank about the chemicals and her financing will be withdrawn, triggering the contract release clause.)

6. **Breach of warranty — products liability.** The Uniform Commercial Code's §2314, the implied warranty of merchantability warranting that products are fit for ordinary use, also has a potential use in environmental cases. Strangely enough, in the Allied Kepone case studied in Chapter One it was reportedly the products liability cause of action that was most successful in the pre-trial process that led to damage settlements. Using warranty theories and strict tort liability defective products cases, plaintiffs have sought remedies for harms from formaldehyde insulation pollution inside mobile homes, for radiation effects from products using radium, for the deleterious effects of cigarettes, and for other environmental situations, with varying results. Brummett v. Skyline Corp., No. C-81-0103-L(B), slip opinion (W.D. Ky. June 3, 1985) (formaldehyde); Allen v. U.S. Radium Corp., No. L-013851-84, slip opinion (N.J. Super. 1984) (radium radiation); Cipollone v. Liggett Group, Inc., 505 U.S. 504 (1992) (cigarettes, action based on claim of express warranty); Wingo v. Celotex Corp., et al., 834 F.2d 375 (4th Cir. 1987) (asbestos). In other cases, express warranty claims are possible where manufacturers have incorrectly alleged that products are safe or environmentally benign. Contract-based warranty actions, with their opportunity for consequential damages under UCC §2714, may in some cases offer advantages over tort theories that are worth exploring.

7. **Environmental breach of federal contract.** Most government-supply contracts made by corporations — and these run into the billions of dollars each year — contain a standard clause agreeing that suppliers will comply with all relevant statutes and regulations, including environmental protection laws. When a supplier is discovered in violation of such laws, there are potential remedies for breach of contract and misrepresentation. These remedies gain special impetus from the fact that citizens are granted standing under the Federal False Claims Act, 31 U.S.C.A. §3729, to bring such actions even if the official parties aren't interested in doing so; treble damages are available, with a 25% bounty thereof payable to the individual plaintiffs. Does this bear further investigation?

8. **Other horizons for environmental law.** There are undoubtedly dozens of other situations in which environmental issues can be raised using statutory or non-statutory legal doctrines drawn from areas of modern practice that have rarely or never before been so applied — from labor law, tax, equity, antitrust, public utilities, consumer protection, banking, admiralty, and so on, as well as corporate law, property, trusts, and contract.

The point is, environmental law is where you find it.

# Chapter 4

# THE SPECIAL CHALLENGES OF TOXIC TORT LITIGATION

A. *Remedies for Victims of Toxic Contamination*

B. *Proof of Complex Causation*

C. *Law and Science in the Toxic Tort Context*

D. *Litigating Toxic Tort Cases*

E. *Relationships between Toxic Tort and Public Law*

## INTRODUCTION: LESSONS FROM THE WOBURN TOXICS CIVIL ACTION

Nowhere is the continued vitality, flexibility, and relevance of the common law more evident in modern environmental law than in the raucous field of toxic torts. The case reporters reflect this active field, as do the increasing numbers of law schools that offer specialized toxic tort courses.

Toxic tort case settings may be as localized as a single grease pit in a rural junkyard, or regional or even nationwide in scope, as in asbestos exposure litigation. The mass tort exposure cases present especially complex legal issues in establishing environmental liability, including fiendishly complex issues of civil procedure, but even smaller scale toxic exposure cases present challenging scientific and litigation issues. Potentially devastating harms to human health are the primary focus of toxic torts. In a modern world containing so many different exposures to so many different kinds of risk, voluntary as well as involuntary, common law toxics cases often face a virtual impossibility in proving that a particular harm was caused by a particular exposure. Proof of causation is difficult not only because of the attenuated pathways by which toxics may travel and combine in a course of exposure, but also by the long term latencies of environmental illnesses. A chemical may accumulate or lie latent in human bodies over decades before its serious or fatal effects are revealed. The character of toxic threats — typically moving invisibly and undetectably, occurring almost anywhere, and potentially so harmful — has created energetic social reactions against toxic contaminations.

Given the nature of the modern technological marketplace, toxic exposures present a dilemma. Chemicals, including very powerful compounds, are woven into the fabric of our production and consumption economy. Virtually the entire population is exposed to a lifelong interacting melange of at least small amounts of potentially harmful compounds (and some harmless compounds that become harmful when synergistically combined). Avoiding exposures is impossible. Remedying the horrors of some exposures is impossible. The amounts in damages that could be assessed against the industries that generated toxins over the past 50 years, if ever the "true" epidemiological causes of all exposure illnesses could be proved, would be astronomical.

To people like Peter Huber (in Chapter Two), the issue of toxic exposures is a fundamental problem of modern societal governance that should be handled by public law processes, not common law tort. Until the legislatures discover a scientifically, politically, and constitutionally feasible regime to take over the field, however, people who believe they have been or will be harmed by particular toxic events will continue to plunk down their filing fees in court, putting the force of the common law, evolving over seven centuries, to work on toxic torts.

This chapter uses the Woburn toxics case, a noted case of toxic contamination of groundwater, to introduce the array of elements in modern toxic tort law. The following account, written by the plaintiffs' attorney, gives one view of Anderson et al. v. W.R. Grace Co. and Beatrice Foods,[1] and conveys a sense of some of the tasks facing plaintiffs trying to prove causation in complex toxics cases. Many readers will have encountered the story in much greater detail in Jonathan Harr's bestselling book, A Civil Action (1995) and the movie made from it. This chapter addresses some legal issues not raised in the book. The elaborate civil procedure history of the case can be traced in Lewis Grossman and Robert Vaughn, A Civil Action: A Documentary Companion (Foundation, 1999).

## Jan Schlichtmann, Eight Families Sue W.R. Grace and Beatrice Foods for Poisoning City Wells with Solvents, Causing Leukemia, Disease, and Death
### (1987)

The Woburn case began with a mother's horror that her child had leukemia. Anne Anderson had moved to Woburn, Massachusetts, a small city 13 miles north of Boston, with her husband and daughter in 1965. Over the next few years she gave birth to two more children. Although all of the children seemed to have more than their fair share of colds, sore throats, and infections, James, the youngest, seemed to get sick more than the others and recovered slower. In the winter of 1971, when Jimmy did not get over the latest round of flu, the family doctor referred Ms. Anderson to a specialist at Massachusetts General Hospital in Boston. The specialist told Anne that Jimmy had cancer in his bone marrow. Treatment would be long and painful.

Anne Anderson's distress soon gave way to the realization that she was not the only mother in Woburn with a child suffering from leukemia. There were other

---

1. Anderson v. W.R. Grace, U.S.D.C. Mass. C.A. No. 82-1672-S (May, 1982); Anderson v. W.R. Grace, 628 F. Supp. 1219 (D.C. Mass. 1986) (summary judgment rulings); Anderson v. Cryovac, Inc., 805 F.2d 1 (1st Cir. 1986) (Gag order reversed); Anderson v. Beatrice Foods Co., 862 F.2d 910 (1st Cir. 1988); Anderson v. Beatrice Foods Co., 127 F.R.D. 1 (D. Mass. July, 1989) and 129 F.R.D. 394 (D. Mass. Dec., 1989); Anderson v. Beatrice Foods Co., 900 F.2d 388 (1st Cir. 1990), cert. denied, 111 S.Ct. 233 (1990).

The narrative is drawn from an article in ATLA Report: The Woburn Case: Stricken Families Take On a Chemical Giant and Win (Sept. 1987). See Jn. Harr, A Civil Action (1995), and the movie of the same title; L. Grossman and R. Vaughan, A Civil Action: A Civil Procedure Supplement (Foundation, 1999); an earlier version of the story was P. Brown and E. Mikkelson, No Safe Place (1990).

(Disclosure notice: one of this casebook's authors and his students worked with plaintiffs on the case.)

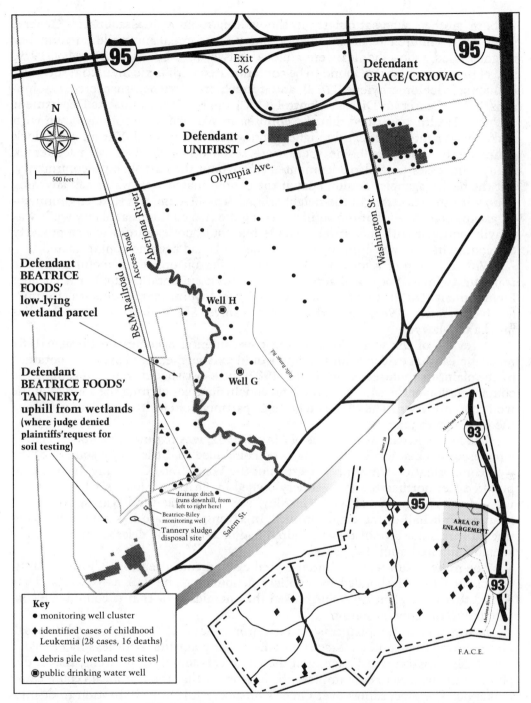

**Key**
- monitoring well cluster
- ◆ identified cases of childhood Leukemia (28 cases, 16 deaths)
- ▲ debris pile (wetland test sites)
- ◉ public drinking water well

SMALL MAP (lower right) shows the entire area in Woburn Massachusetts served by Wells G & H, and the 28 identified childhood leukemia cases (16 fatal) that occurred there between the time the wells were opened in 1964 and the time of trial. The ENLARGED MAP shows the properties involved in the lawsuit, Wells G & H, with defendant Grace Cryovac on an upward slope to the Northeast of the wells, defendant Beatrice's tannery atop a rise to the Southwest, from which a ditch leads downward to the low-lying wetland parcel that was filled with contaminants, and the Aberjona River, a creek wending through the middle of the area.

Woburn mothers who sat quietly in the waiting room at Massachusetts General while their children received chemotherapy — women and children from her neighborhood, whose homes were a block or two from her own.... In May, 1979, two of the city wells were found to be contaminated with toxic industrial solvents, including trichloroethylene (TCE) and tetrachloroethylene, suspected carcinogens.... The Center for Disease Control (CDC) and the Massachusetts Department of Public Health confirmed that the children in Woburn were coming down with leukemia at a rate significantly higher than would be expected. Within a six block radius of the Anderson home there were seven other children with leukemia. Many other cases were also documented throughout the East Woburn community. But the health agencies couldn't say if the contaminated well water had anything to do with the leukemia in the neighborhood. The EPA and the state environmental agency confirmed that the aquifer feeding the two contaminated city wells was heavily polluted with industrial solvents but could not say from whose property the contamination was coming or when the wells had become contaminated.

With the help of a local minister, Ms. Anderson organized members of the community into a vocal and active citizens' environmental group, For A Cleaner Environment (FACE), to monitor and prod the governmental agencies. Jimmy's death in January, 1981, strengthened her resolve. She and seven other families hired a tort lawyer.

A review of the work done by the governmental agencies up through 1981 made it clear that evidence for the case would in large measure have to be obtained by the plaintiffs themselves. In March, 1982, the EPA issued its report regarding the contamination of the aquifer. It drew no conclusions concerning the sources of the well contamination. The CDC and State Department of Health were still unsure of the next step to take.

The EPA field data available as of March, 1982, was reviewed by Robert Harris, a professor of chemical engineering, who concluded that the likely sources of the well contamination were the properties of the W.R. Grace Company, twenty-four hundred feet northeast, and a tannery owned by Beatrice Foods, six hundred feet west of the contaminated wells. In May, 1982, suit was filed against Grace and Beatrice on behalf of the eight families. In seven of the families a child had contracted leukemia. Five of those children had died from the disease. In one family an adult suffered from the disease.

The filing of suit received intense public and media attention. The defendants, especially Grace, responded by publicly denouncing the suit as baseless. They denied that their plant in Woburn used the chemicals, or that it could have contributed to the contamination.

In response to the plaintiffs' interrogatories as to chemical use and disposal, Grace moved to dismiss.... Grace contended that plaintiffs' attorneys had no good faith basis to assert that Grace used the chemicals found in the wells, that it disposed of them so as to contaminate the aquifer, or that the chemicals could cause leukemia. The proceedings over Grace's unsuccessful Rule 11[2] motion to dismiss consumed the entire first year of litigation.

Thereafter, in February, 1983, Grace was forced to answer plaintiffs' interrogatories. In its answers, Grace admitted that it had used the same type of chemicals found in the wells, and had disposed of "small quantities" of the chemicals on the

---

2. Since its original promulgation, FRCP Rule 11 has provided for the striking of pleadings and the imposition of disciplinary sanctions on the attorney, the client, or both to check abuses in pleadings and litigation.

ground to the rear of the plant building, as well as burying several drums in a pit. The grudging revelations by Grace of its chemical use and disposal practices sharply contrasted with information Grace had previously provided the EPA during that agency's investigation the year before. The EPA subsequently ordered Grace, Beatrice, and another company, Unifirst, to conduct on-site investigations of their properties to determine if their properties were contributing to the pollution of the aquifer. EPA lethargy over the next two years, however, prompted plaintiffs to conduct their own on-site investigations.

In January, 1984, a year after Grace was ordered to investigate its property and after its consultant's report documented contamination at the site, Grace moved for summary judgment on the basis that plaintiffs could not prove that the contaminated water caused the children's leukemia. In support of its motion, Grace submitted the affidavits of two hematologists, Drs. Maloney and Jandl, who asserted that there was no scientific basis for an opinion that the chemicals found in the contaminated wells could cause leukemia.

In the fall of 1983, plaintiffs had retained Dr. Allen S. Levin, an immuno-pathologist, who had a great deal of clinical experience treating people exposed to toxic substances. Dr. Levin was very knowledgeable regarding the effects of toxic exposure on the body's immune system. The plaintiffs' medical records, which had been systematically collected, were reviewed by Dr. Levin. In addition, he ordered blood tests of the surviving family members which were conducted at the Massachusetts General Hospital immuno-pathology lab. The review of the families' medical records revealed a pattern of infection, skin disorders, gastrointestinal problems, genito-urinary problems, and cardiac problems as well as cancer. The blood tests which looked at the absolute numbers and ratios of "T-cells," which are the specialized cells of the immune system, demonstrated striking abnormalities in many of the family members. Also, Harvard scientists examining health survey data from Woburn had concluded that there was an association between certain childhood disorders including leukemia and availability of water from the contaminated wells. This marked the first time that such an association had been shown.[3]

In his affidavit opposing summary judgment, Dr. Levin outlined the scientific methodology he followed in concluding that exposure to the contaminated water caused leukemia in the families. In so doing, he illustrated how a clinician makes use of epidemiological data, like the Harvard health study, not to prove causation in an individual case, but in conjunction with clinical data, history, examination and tests, to assist in forming opinions as to the likely etiology of a patient's disease.

Levin began by discussing the scientific knowledge regarding the capacity of the solvents found in the water to harm the building blocks of the body's cells, DNA and its constituents, making them potentially cancerous. He outlined how solvent exposure can damage the immune system, the role of which is to remove these cancerous elements. By both creating opportunities for cancer and awakening the body's ability to remove it, he explained how solvent exposure can increase a host's susceptibility to cancer. Further, Dr. Levin pointed to scientific studies of animals and human populations showing a statistical relation between solvent exposure and cancer. After establishing the toxic nature of the chemicals, and the

3. [This Harvard study was the fortuitous product of a student-faculty field project at the Harvard School of Public Health, which was launched when students looking for a fieldwork opportunity heard an informal presentation by several mothers and Schlichtmann. To have paid for the massive door-to-door survey would have been impossible for plaintiffs.–Eds.]

mechanism of harm, Dr. Levin turned his attention to the Woburn population exposed to the solvent-contaminated water. The government health studies done in Woburn showed that the community was suffering from an increased incidence of childhood leukemia. The Harvard health study demonstrated that this increased incidence of leukemia and other childhood disorders was associated with exposure to the contaminated water. Their relationship indicated that exposure to the contaminated well water had affected the population's ability to fight disease and cancer. Finally, Dr. Levin discussed the medical histories and test results of individual family members. The histories were consistent with people suffering from chemical exposure, and the blood tests demonstrated that this group of people had been resisting a carcinogen on a chronic basis. For these reasons he concluded that in all probability the exposure to the solvents in the water "substantially contributed" to the family members succumbing to leukemia.

Plaintiffs argued that to overcome Grace's motion for summary judgment it was their burden merely to show that there was factual dispute on the issue of causation. The court's role was not to determine which expert's opinion was more persuasive, but rather whether reasonable experts could disagree about whether the exposure to the contaminated water caused the plaintiffs' leukemias. If the court was satisfied that the expert's conclusion regarding the etiology of plaintiffs' disease was based on sound scientific methodology and principles, then the expert's conclusion, even if considered controversial, was sufficient to sustain plaintiffs' burden. The court in a brief opinion determined that the issue of medical causation as to leukemia was "hotly contested" and denied the defendant's motion for summary judgment in an unpublished opinion, July, 1984.

Over the next year and a half plaintiffs' medical condition was extensively examined. In an effort to establish a basis for proving a connection between exposure to the water and leukemia, the impact of toxic exposure on the health of the surviving plaintiffs was brought into sharper focus. The theory of cancer causation based on the toxic effects of the solvents on the body's immune system led to the examination of other organ systems which were known to be affected by solvents, namely the nerves and heart. Complete health histories, examinations, and tests were performed by experts in immunology and internal medicine to establish the overall health and condition of the plaintiffs, and to rule out other causes for their health problems. The plaintiffs were also extensively examined by experts in neurology, neuropsychology, and cardiology. The detailed testing in these specialties provided objective evidence that the surviving plaintiffs had indeed suffered significant damage to these organ systems. In addition, psychiatric examination revealed the interplay between the impact of the exposure on the body and the knowledge of it on the mind.

Because a domestic population had never before been examined and tested so extensively to determine the effects of exposure to solvents contaminating a drinking water supply, the unique findings of the clinicians studying the Woburn population was further supplemented and supported by work of scientists in toxicology, genetics, and epidemiology. The scientific effort included the establishment for the first time of control groups and scientific benchmarks for study of populations exposed to contaminated drinking water....

## COMMENTARY AND QUESTIONS

1. **Background notes.** The contamination of Wells G&H was originally discovered by happenstance. In May 1979 a midnight dumper dropped leaking barrels of waste

along the B&M RR access road, which scared city officials into testing the wells, at which point they found the four contaminants (none of which had been in the dumped barrels). The case would probably never have been a lawsuit, only a low-profile long term government cleanup case, had it not been for the extraordinary group-organizing efforts of the mothers of the affected children. They begged and dragooned Schlichtmann into taking the case against the advice of his colleagues, and suit was filed in May of 1982. Schlichtmann was a charismatic young attorney with tactical plans and enthusiasm for litigative battling far greater than his limited resources. Harr's book chronicles the lawsuit's wing-and-a-prayer character, not uncommon in contingent fee toxic tort cases. Defendants Grace and Beatrice appear to have been surprised by the allegations. Grace's dumping had apparently been done by low-level workers for casual convenience. Beatrice Foods had bought the tannery parcels after most of the dumping , which had occurred while the tannery was a small local operation owned by John Riley. Defendants had virtually unlimited resources, and, as Harr's book shows, superb attorneys.

2. **Causes of action.** Remarkably little mention is made here or anywhere of the causes of action in the Woburn case. The case's theories of liability were personal injury and public and private nuisance based on negligence, intentional tort, and strict liability. The judge did not distinguish clearly between these theories, usually treating the liability claims in negligence terms. This set up two important legal problems not treated in the Harr book. First was the question of foreseeability under the negligence or intentional culpability theories. The judge was surprised to learn that groundwater could travel under a creek to get from the tannery to the wells, and so made a negligence-style ruling on grounds of unforeseeability. He said Beatrice could not be held liable for contamination that left the tannery property prior to the date that engineering reports of the flow to the wells were received.[4] Shouldn't any dumper know, however, that it is extremely likely that toxics dumped on the ground will enter the groundwater, and travel along with the groundwater, thence to some public well? Whether the underground toxic plume ultimately moves toward Well G, H, or some other well is irrelevant.

If the strict liability theory had been examined, it might have revealed an interesting defense for the tannery. Since it was hard to prove the tannery's own dumping, plaintiffs tried to base their claim on the tannery's ownership of the lowlying parcel where a great deal of toxics had been discharged by "persons unknown." Assuming that toxics in the ground are abnormally dangerous, can owners who know of the toxics but cannot be proved to have dumped them or taken any other active role, nevertheless be held *strictly* liable for the results of the hazards?[5]

---

4. This ultimately meant that the jury did not have enough specific evidence of groundwater flow within the narrowed time window to find liablity. The unreported ruling was made under Restatement 2d §435(2), discussed below.

5. In some public law statutes there is an "innocent landowner" or "act of third party" defense, but the common law may allow passive strict liability. In the Woburn case, the plaintiffs found an old Massachusetts case holding that a defendant who owned a stone-walled house that burned out, and passively left it standing there, was strictly liable when later the walls toppled on a passerby. That case, however, seems to have based its "strict" liability on an act of omission, based on a duty to warn or duty to mitigate, both of which sound in negligence.

Strict liability is frequently the basis of toxic tort litigation, but the intentional and negligent nuisance and personal injury causes of action are often effective in these cases as well.

---

## A.  REMEDIES FOR VICTIMS OF TOXIC CONTAMINATION

One recent defense-oriented article began with the following introduction:

> The sphere of injuries for which plaintiffs may seek compensation in toxic tort cases is, it seems, bounded only by the ingenuity of counsel and by the human capacity to feel wronged.... To meet these more exotic toxic injury claims, the defense counsel in toxic tort cases must counter ingenious allegations with equally ingenious defenses.[6]

Toxic tort cases present special problems in the scope of liability for damages, including unique claims based on increased risk of contracting an exposure-induced disease, seeking present compensation for future damages that may or may not come to pass. In many cases, as in Anderson v. W.R. Grace, plaintiffs also make claims for fear and emotional distress in the toxic tort setting.

These are hotly contested issues. The stakes are high. Toxic exposures often create mass torts. Potential damages are multiplied by potentially large number of victims. The types of damage in dispute are significant items such as increased medical expenses and damages caused by catastrophic diseases. Many of the losses are either uninsured or uninsurable and become major unexpected costs for whoever ends up bearing them. The intensity with which the cases are litigated, coupled with the fact that plaintiffs have been pressing for novel extensions of tort liability, has led to friction between lawyers representing plaintiffs and those representing defendants.

In the Woburn case a typically broad array of claims for damages were made, although the damages issue was never finally adjudicated. Below is one preliminary skirmish, testing the availability of various emotional distress and risk-of-future-illness damage theories:

**Anderson v. W.R. Grace & Co., Beatrice Foods Co., et al.**
United States District Court for the District of Massachusetts, 1986
628 F. Supp. 1219

MEMORANDUM AND ORDER ON DEFENDANTS' JOINT MOTION FOR PARTIAL SUMMARY JUDGMENT

SKINNER, D.J. This case arises out of the defendants' alleged contamination of the groundwater in certain areas of Woburn, Massachusetts, with chemicals, including trichloroethylene and tetrachloroethylene. Plaintiffs allege that two of Woburn's water wells, Wells G and H, drew upon the contaminated water until the wells were closed in 1979 and that exposure to this contaminated water caused them to suffer severe injuries.

Of the 33 plaintiffs in this action, five are the administrators of minors who died of leukemia allegedly caused by exposure to the chemicals. They bring suit for

---

6. Pagliaro & Lynch, No Pain, No Gain: Current Trends in Determining Compensable Injury in Toxic Tort Cases, 4 BNA Toxics L. Rep. 271 (1989).

wrongful death and conscious pain and suffering. Sixteen of the 28 living plaintiffs are members of the decedents' immediate families. These plaintiffs seek to recover for the emotional distress caused by witnessing the decedents' deaths. Three of the living plaintiffs also contracted leukemia and currently are either in remission or treatment for the disease. The 25 non-leukemic plaintiffs allege that exposure to the contaminated water caused a variety of illnesses and damaged their bodily systems. All of the living plaintiffs seek to recover for their illnesses and other damage, increased risk of developing future illness, and emotional distress.... W.R. Grace & Co. and Beatrice Foods Co. (collectively "defendants"), have jointly moved for partial summary judgment on...plaintiffs' claims [of emotional distress and risk of future illness]....

CLAIMS FOR EMOTIONAL DISTRESS... Defendants move for summary judgment on plaintiffs' claims of emotional distress on the grounds that the non-leukemic plaintiffs' distress was not caused by any physical injury. They also move for summary judgment on the emotional distress claims of plaintiffs who witnessed a family member die of leukemia, arguing that Massachusetts law does not recognize such a claim....

(1) PHYSICAL INJURY... In seeking summary judgment on the non-leukemic plaintiffs' claims for emotional distress, defendants rely on Payton v. Abbott Labs, 437 N.E.2d 171 (Mass. 1982). In *Payton*, the Supreme Judicial Court answered a certified question as follows:

> In order for...plaintiffs to recover for negligently inflicted emotional distress, [they] must allege and prove [they] suffered physical harm as a result of the conduct which caused the emotional distress. We answer, further, that a plaintiff's physical harm must either cause or be caused by the emotional distress alleged, and that the physical harm must be manifested by objective symptomatology and substantiated by expert medical testimony. (437 N.E.2d at 181.)

Defendants attack plaintiffs' claims of emotional distress at three points: they argue that plaintiffs did not suffer physical harm as a result of defendants' allegedly negligent conduct; that, if the plaintiffs did suffer any harm, it was not "manifested by objective symptomatology"; and that any manifest physical harm did not cause the claimed emotional distress....

Each plaintiff states that exposure to contaminants in the water drawn from Wells G and H "affected my body's ability to fight disease, [and] caused harm to my body's organ systems, including my respiratory, immunological, blood, central nervous, gastro-intestinal, urinary-renal systems...." This alleged harm is sufficient to maintain plaintiffs' claims for emotional distress under *Payton*. As used in that opinion, the term "physical harm" denotes "harm to the bodies of the plaintiffs." 437 N.E.2d at 175 n.4. In requiring physical harm rather than mere "injury" as an element of proof in a claim for emotional distress, the court required that a plaintiff show some actual physical damage as a predicate to suit.

Defendants argue that plaintiffs' alleged harm is "subcellular" and therefore not the type of harm required to support a claim for emotional distress under *Payton*. I disagree. The Supreme Judicial Court requires that plaintiffs' physical harm be "manifested by objective symptomatology and substantiated by expert medical testimony." 437 N.E.2d at 181. In setting forth this requirement, the court did not distinguish between gross and subcellular harm. Instead, the court drew a line between harm which can be proven to exist through expert medical testimony based on objective evidence and harm which is merely speculative or based solely on a plaintiff's unsupported assertions. Upon review of the pleadings and the affidavits of plaintiffs' expert, I cannot say as a matter of law that this standard will not be met at trial.

The alleged damages to plaintiffs' bodily systems is manifested by the many ailments which plaintiffs claim to have suffered as a result of exposure to the contaminated water. Dr. Levin apparently will testify to the existence of changes in plaintiffs' bodies caused by exposure to the contaminated water. He will base his testimony on objective evidence of these changes, including the maladies listed.... Dr. Levin explicitly states that the changes in plaintiffs' systems have "produced illnesses related to these systems." Although the affidavit does not specifically identify the illnesses suffered by each plaintiff as a result of the changes, nor state that plaintiffs suffered more ailments than the average person would have over the same time span, it is sufficient evidence of harm to support the existence of a factual dispute and bar summary judgment.

Under *Payton*, of course, injury is not sufficient. The harm allegedly caused by defendants' conduct must either have caused or been caused by the emotional distress.... However, certain elements of plaintiffs' emotional distress stem from the physical harm to their immune systems allegedly caused by defendants' conduct and [these] are compensable. Plaintiffs have stated that the illnesses contributed to by exposure to the contaminated water have caused them anxiety and pain. The excerpts from plaintiffs' depositions appended to defendants' motion indicate that plaintiffs are also worried over the increased susceptibility to disease which results from the alleged harm to their immune systems and exposure to carcinogens. As these elements of emotional distress arise out of plaintiffs' injuries, plaintiffs may seek to recover for them.

Defendants contend that plaintiffs' physical harm did not "cause" plaintiffs' distress over their increased susceptibility to disease. They argue that the fear arose out of discussions between plaintiffs and their expert witness, Dr. Levin, in which the expert informed plaintiffs of their suppressed immune systems. Assuming, as I must for purposes of the motion, that Dr. Levin is telling the truth, this argument is frivolous.

Plaintiffs can recover "only for that degree of emotional distress which a reasonable person normally would have experienced under [the] circumstances." 437 N.E.2d at 181. The Supreme Judicial Court has explicitly stated that the reasonableness of a claim for emotional distress is to be determined by the trier of fact. Accordingly, defendants' motion for summary judgment on the non-leukemic plaintiffs' claims for emotional distress is DENIED.

(2) WITNESSING DEATH OF A FAMILY MEMBER... The second issue raised by defendants' motions is whether Massachusetts recognizes a claim for emotional distress for witnessing a family member die of a disease allegedly caused by defendants' conduct. This differs from the question considered in the preceding section because the concern now is whether the plaintiffs can recover for distress caused by witnessing the injuries of others, not by their own condition. The plaintiffs do not claim any physical harm resulted from this emotional distress.

The plaintiffs proceed on alternative theories: (1) that they were in the "zone of danger," Restatement 2d of Torts §313(2), and (2) that they themselves were the victims of an "impact" from the same tortious conduct that caused the death of the children.... The Supreme Judicial Court has [held that] damages may be recovered for emotional distress over injury to a child or spouse when the plaintiff suffers contemporaneous physical injury from the same tortious conduct that caused the injury to the close relative. Cimino v. Milford Keg, Inc., 431 N.E.2d 920, 927 (Mass. 1982)....

Plaintiffs would be entitled to go forward on the basis of *Cimino,* if it were not for three further prudential limitations on recovery of a bystander for emotional distress resulting from injuries to another. These are the requirements of physical proximity to the accident, temporal proximity to the negligent act, and familial proximity to the victim. The plaintiffs in this case were present during the illness and death of the children, and at least 16 of them...are immediate family members of the decedents, but they do not meet the [temporal proximity] test....

For emotional distress to be compensable under Massachusetts law...the distress must result from immediate apprehension of the defendant's negligence or its consequences. In each of the cases in which recovery for the emotional distress of a bystander has been allowed, there has been a dramatic traumatic shock causing immediate emotional distress. Such is not the case here. There is no indication in the Massachusetts cases that liability would be extended to a family member's emotional distress which built over time during the prolonged illness of a child.

Imposition of liability in that case, while logically indistinguishable from the trauma situation, would violate the Massachusetts court's demonstrated prudential inclination to keep the scope of liability within manageable bounds....

CLAIMS FOR INCREASED RISK OF FUTURE ILLNESS... Plaintiffs seek to recover damages for the increased risk of serious illness they claim resulted from consumption of and exposure to contaminated water.... In Massachusetts,

> a plaintiff is entitled to compensation for all damages that reasonably are to be expected to follow, but not to those that possibly may follow, the injury which he has suffered. He is not restricted to compensation for suffering and expense which by a fair preponderance of the evidence he has proved will inevitably follow. He is entitled to compensation for suffering and expense which by a fair preponderance of the evidence he has satisfied the jury reasonably are to be expected to follow, so far as human knowledge can foretell. Pullen v. Boston Elevated Ry. Co., 94 N.E. 469, 471 (Mass. 1911).

In addition, when there is a "reasonable probability" that future expenses will be required to remedy the consequences of a defendant's negligence, the jury may consider the expense in awarding damages. Menard v. Collins, 9 N.E.2d 387 (Mass. 1937). Plaintiffs argue that these cases indicate that Massachusetts accepts the general rule of tort law that "[o]ne injured by the tort of another is entitled to recover damages for all harm, past, present and prospective, legally caused by the tort." Restatement 2d of Torts §910. I agree, subject to two caveats. First, as is indicated by *Pullen* and *Menard,* when an injured person seeks to recover for harms that may result in the future, recovery depends on establishing a "reasonable probability" that the harm will occur. See Restatement 2d of Torts §912. Second, recovery for future harm in an action assumes that a cause of action for that harm has accrued at the time recovery is sought. See Restatement 2d of Torts §910....

Defendants argue that the cause of action for any future serious illness, including leukemia and other cancers, has not yet accrued because the injury has not yet occurred.[7] This is the rationale of the discovery rule applied to latent disease cases

---

7. The weight of authority would deny plaintiffs a cause of action solely for increased risk because no "injury" has occurred.

in Massachusetts under which the injury is equated with the manifestation of the disease. The question thus becomes whether, upon the manifestation of one or more diseases, a cause of action accrues for all prospective diseases so that a plaintiff may seek to recover for physically distinct and separate diseases which may develop in the future.

The answer to this question depends on the connection between the illnesses plaintiffs have suffered and fear they will suffer in the future. Unfortunately, the nature of plaintiffs' claim for increased risk of future illness is unclear on two counts. Nothing in the present record indicates the magnitude of the increased risk, or the diseases which plaintiffs may suffer....

A further reason for denying plaintiffs' damages for the increased risk of future harm in this action is the inevitable inequity which would result if recovery were allowed. To award damages based on a mere mathematical probability would significantly undercompensate those who actually develop cancer and would be a windfall to those who do not. In addition, if plaintiffs could show that they were more likely than not to suffer cancer or other future illness, full recovery would be allowed for all plaintiffs, even though only some number more than half would actually develop the illness. In such a case, the defendant would overcompensate the injured class.

Accordingly, action on plaintiffs' claims for the increased risk of serious future illness, including cancer, must be delayed....

### COMMENTARY AND QUESTIONS

1. **Physical harm/emotional distress.** What is the relevance of physical harm in a claim for emotional distress? Is it possible that an individual could be greatly distressed without suffering any injury whatever? The usual rationale for a physical harm requirement is the desire to prevent fictitious claims. It may be underinclusive in those genuine cases where a victim suffers emotionally without physical damage, and it may be overinclusive in allowing claims of emotional distress by unprincipled plaintiffs who suffer no distress at all.

In *Anderson*, satisfaction of the physical harm requirement by subcellular T-cell effects seems to be a needless formality.[8] Are the physical damage requirement and the required causal link between physical injury and emotional distress intended to substitute for a policy debate about whether the defendant's conduct should, as a matter of law and policy, result in liability for this type of injury? Recall that one of the functions of the proximate cause inquiry is to limit the extent of liability that could be imposed using but-for causation carried to extreme lengths. Pruitt v. Allied Chemical Co., in Chapter Three, however, shows that proximate cause analyses may also resort to arbitrary rules to guide their application.

Even if you are hostile to attempts to limit emotional distress claims for those personally victimized by contamination, is the argument for prudential limitations stronger in the case of those who suffer by witnessing the suffering of others? These claims are no less real to their victims, nor are they any less credible, in the

8. The defendants and the court could entertain no real doubt about the plaintiffs' sufferings. The defendants may think that the plaintiffs are suffering needlessly, i.e., that nothing will come of the exposures, but it is hard to believe that they discredit the claims of fear and anxiety.

context of watching an immediate family member die an agonizing and unnecessary death, than are first party claims for infliction of emotional distress. Is it simply too expensive to compensate these non-economic losses and still maintain affordable prices for goods that produce hazardous materials as by-products of their manufacture?

2. **Damages for increased risk of future illness.** It is undeniably true that certain exposures to toxics, by their effects including damage to the immune system, increase the likelihood that a person will suffer serious future illness and earlier death. Can exposed persons sue against identifiable sources of the contamination prior to the onset of disease, not for the disease but for the increased risk? Such damages could be claimed by a very broad swath of plaintiffs, many of whom in statistical terms surely would never get the illnesses, and would presumably not foreclose future recoveries by those who later actually got sick. Most courts have been extremely reluctant to grant relief for increased risk, but the court in Ayers v. Jackson Township, below, fashioned an ingenious remedy to address at least part of the issue of risk of future illness:

### Ayers v. Township of Jackson
Supreme Court of New Jersey, 1987
106 N.J. 557, 525 A.2d 287

STEIN, J. The litigation involves claims for damages sustained because plaintiffs' well water was contaminated by toxic pollutants leaching...from a landfill established and operated by Jackson Township. After an extensive trial, the jury found that the township had created a "nuisance" and a "dangerous condition" by virtue of its operation of the landfill, that its conduct was "palpably unreasonable" [a prerequisite to recovery under N.J.'s sovereign immunity tort claims waiver], and that it was the proximate cause of the contamination of plaintiffs' water supply. The jury verdict resulted in an aggregate judgment of $15,854,392.78, to be divided among the plaintiffs in varying amounts. The jury returned individual awards for each of the plaintiffs that varied in accordance with such factors as proximity to the landfill, duration and extent of the exposure to contaminants, and the age of the claimant.

The verdict provided compensation for three distinct claims of injury: $2,056,480 was awarded for emotional distress caused by the knowledge that they had ingested water contaminated by toxic chemicals for up to six years; $5,396,940 was awarded for the deterioration of their quality of life during the twenty months when they were deprived of running water; and $8,204,500 was awarded to cover the future cost of annual medical surveillance that plaintiffs' expert testified would be necessary because of plaintiffs' increased susceptibility to cancer and other diseases.

...The chemical contamination of their wells was caused by the township's improper operation of the landfill [resulting in infiltration into the wells by] acetone; benzene; chlorobenzene; chloroform; dichlorofluoromethane; ethylbenzene; methylene chloride; methyl isobutyl ketone; 1,1,2,2-tetrachloroethane; tetrahydrofuran; 1,1,1-trichloroethane; and trichloroethylene....

An expert in the diagnosis and treatment of diseases caused by exposure to toxic substances testified that the plaintiffs required annual medical examinations to afford the earliest possible diagnosis of chemically induced illnesses. Her opinion was that a program of regular medical surveillance for plaintiffs would improve prospects for cure, treatment, prolongation of life, and minimization of pain and disability.

A substantial number — more than 150 — of the plaintiffs gave testimony with respect to damages, describing in detail the impairment of their quality of life during the period that they were without running water, and the emotional distress they suffered. With regard to the emotional distress claims, the plaintiffs' testimony detailed their emotional reactions to the chemical contamination of their wells and the deprivation of their water supply, as well as their fears for the health of their family members. Expert psychological testimony was offered to document plaintiffs' claims that they had sustained compensable psychological damage as a result of the contamination of their wells.

QUALITY OF LIFE... Residents in need of water tied a white cloth on their mailbox and received a 40 gallon barrel containing a plastic liner filled with water. The filled barrels weighed in excess of 100 pounds.... One witness, who suffered from arthritis, testified to hauling her water for drinking, cooking and bathing up nine steps because, as she said, [t]here was no way that I could get the water upstairs except by hauling pot after pot out of the containers...which was a considerable amount of hauling everyday just to use for drinking and bathing the children and cooking....Plaintiffs' households...for nearly two years were compelled to obtain water in this primitive manner.

The trial court charged the jury that plaintiffs' claim for "quality of life" damages encompassed "inconveniences, aggravation, and unnecessary expenditure of time and effort related to the use of the water hauled to their homes, as well as to other disruption in their lives, including disharmony in the family unit."...

EMOTIONAL DISTRESS... Many of the plaintiffs testified about their emotional reactions to the knowledge that their well-water was contaminated.... Typically, their testimony did not indicate that the emotional distress resulted in physical symptoms or required medical treatment.... Nevertheless, the consistent thrust of the testimony offered by numerous witnesses was that they suffered anxiety, stress, fear, and depression, and that these feelings were directly and causally related to the knowledge that they and members of their family had ingested and been exposed to contaminated water for a substantial time period.

Plaintiffs also presented testimony from an experienced clinical psychologist, Dr. Margaret Gibbs...[who] testified that the sample of 88 plaintiffs she tested manifested abnormally high levels of stress, depression, health concerns, and psychological problems.... The township contended that plaintiffs had not proved that the emotional distress experienced by them was manifested by any discernible physical symptoms or injuries, arguing that proof of related physical symptoms was a prerequisite to recovery.... Our cases no longer require proof of causally-related physical impact to sustain a recovery for emotional distress.... [The N.J. sovereign immunity statute, however, bars emotional injury recoveries.]

CLAIMS FOR ENHANCED RISK, AND MEDICAL SURVEILLANCE... We concur with the Appellate Division's refusal to recognize plaintiffs' damage claim based on enhanced risk... We disagree with its conclusion that an award for medical surveillance damages cannot be supported by this record.

Our evaluation of the enhanced risk and medical surveillance claims requires that we focus on a critical issue in the management of toxic tort litigation: at what

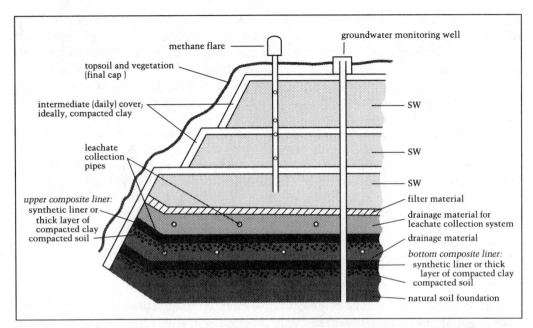

*Schematic cutaway diagram of the corner of a state-of-the-art solid waste landfill, showing protective liner layers, water-repelling capping, and internal drainage and monitoring systems. As in the Ayers case, solid waste landfill operations in practice are often much less fastidious about design and maintenance; moreover, as one state official said, the basic rule of liners is that they all eventually leak.*

stage in the evolution of a toxic injury should tort law intercede by requiring the responsible party to pay damages?... In the absence of statutory or administrative mechanisms for processing injury claims resulting from environmental contamination, courts have struggled to accommodate common-law tort doctrines to the peculiar characteristics of toxic-tort litigation....

Among the recent toxic tort cases rejecting liability for damages based on enhanced risk is Anderson v. W.R. Grace & Co.... We observe that the overwhelming weight of the scholarship on this issue favors a right of recovery for tortious conduct that causes a significantly enhanced risk of injury.... It is the highly contingent and speculative quality of an unquantified claim based on enhanced risk that renders it novel and difficult to manage and resolve.... On the other hand, denial of the enhanced-risk cause of action may mean that some of these plaintiffs will be unable to obtain compensation for their injury. Those who contract diseases in the future because of their exposure to chemicals in their well water may be unable to prove a causal relationship between such exposure and their disease...because of the difficulty of proving that injuries manifested in the future were not the product of intervening events or causes.... In our view, the speculative nature of an unquantified enhanced risk claim, the difficulties inherent in adjudicating such claims, and the policies underlying the Tort Claims Act argue persuasively against the recognition of this cause of action...for the unquantified enhanced risk of disease.

The claim for medical surveillance expenses stands on a different footing from the claim based on enhanced risk. It seeks to recover the cost of periodic medical examinations intended to monitor plaintiffs' health and facilitate early diagnosis and treatment of disease caused by plaintiffs' exposure to toxic chemicals.... An application of tort law that allows post-injury, pre-symptom recovery in toxic tort litigation for reasonable medical surveillance costs is manifestly consistent with the public interest in early detection and treatment of disease,...to deter polluters, [and] preventing or mitigating serious future illnesses [where an exposed person would otherwise be] unable to pay his own expenses when medical intervention is clearly reasonable and necessary....

Accordingly, we hold that the cost of medical surveillance is a compensable item of damages where the proofs demonstrate, through reliable expert testimony predicated upon the significance and extent of exposure to chemicals, the toxicity of the chemicals, the seriousness of the diseases for which individuals are at risk, the relative increase in the chance of onset of disease in those exposed, and the value of early diagnosis, that such surveillance to monitor the effect of exposure to toxic chemicals is reasonable and necessary...notwithstanding the fact that the extent of plaintiffs' impaired health is unquantified....

### COMMENTARY AND QUESTIONS

1. **The medical surveillance remedy and latency compensation.** The surveillance monitoring fund remedy invented by the attorneys in *Ayers* has been picked up in several other states as a response to the problems of long-term toxic torts' latency. It seems like an appropriate and measured response to the feeling of vulnerability and burden felt by wrongfully exposed persons who otherwise might not be able to provide themselves rigorous medical attention, while not breaking the bank. Subsequent courts, including New Jersey's, have amended the medical surveillance remedy by setting up a fund rather than awarding a lump sum.... "The indeterminate nature of damage claims in toxic-tort litigation suggests...the use of court-supervised funds to pay medical-surveillance claims as they accrue, rather than lump-sum verdicts." *Ayers*. Would the *Anderson* court have allowed medical surveillance, although it foreclosed recovery for risk?

Pre-illness claims are inherently enigmatic. On one hand, compensation can mulct defendants of damages even in cases where illness never occurs. This results in a form of systematic over-compensation. On the other hand, to refuse compensation is to ignore the goal of complete compensation because defendant's conduct has made plaintiffs less well-off. Consider whether an individual would voluntarily choose to drink contaminated water for several years. See R. Posner, Economic Analysis of Law 149 (2d ed., 1977). Likewise, consider what a prudent insurer of health risks would do if it discovered that an applicant for insurance had suffered a major toxic exposure, as had the plaintiffs in *Ayers*. Are there persuasive rebuttals to these assertions of over- and under-compensation? Is there a further argument that compensation for enhanced risk systematically undercompensates those victims who actually contract the feared disease?

To what extent is it necessary to know whether subsequent lawsuits (when diseases actually appear) will be barred by the statute of limitations or by doctrines of res judicata? As a policy matter, the majority in *Ayers* tried to indicate in dicta that New Jersey courts should be receptive to later suits. The court coupled that assurance with its perception that courts are facing only the beginning of a flood of toxic tort litigation, to justify its conservative wait-and-see, wait-and-sue approach to enhanced risk.

2. **The medical monitoring remedy since Ayers.** Since the invention of the medical monitoring remedy in *Ayers*, a number of states have adopted it.[9] In the Paoli Railroad Yard PCB Litigation, the 3rd Circuit set out a four part test for medical monitoring: courts should grant the medical monitoring remedy if plaintiffs demonstrate that (1) they were significantly exposed to hazardous materials as a result of the negligence of the defendant; (2) as a proximate result of their exposure, they suffer a significantly increased risk of contracting a serious latent disease; (3) the increased risk makes regular medical monitoring and treatment reasonably necessary; and (4) the monitoring and treatment make early detection and/or prevention of the disease possible. In several cases courts, including the Supreme Court, have indicated a willingness to apply the remedy though declining to do so in the particular case at hand. In an asbestos exposure case, Metro-North Commuter RR. v. Buckley, 117 S. Ct. 2113 (1997), the Supreme Court declined to award medical monitoring under the Federal Employers' Liability Act (FELA). Though the Court endorsed the *Paoli* tests in principle, it suggested that asymptomatic plaintiffs should be restricted to court-supervised monitoring funds rather than "full-blown lump sum recoveries," and clearly was worried that "tens of millions of individuals may have suffered exposure to substances that might justify some form of substance-exposure-related medical monitoring."

3. **"Cancerphobia."** A growing number of cases which have, in various degrees, accepted the concept of recovery for "cancerphobia," post-exposure emotional distress in reaction to exposure to carcinogenic chemicals. Some courts have allowed recovery for fear of cancer risk even though they have denied recovery for the risk itself. See Sterling v. Velsicol, 855 F.2d 1188 (6th Cir. 1988). The reluctance of courts to open a floodgate of cases based on fear with no attendant physical injury has led to a high standard in some states. In New Jersey, for instance, the *Ironbound* cases held that the neighbors of an Agent Orange production facility who had been contaminated by that defoliant could not recover for cancerphobia because their distress was not sufficiently "severe and substantial." Ironbound Health Rights Advisory Commission v. Diamond Shamrock Chemicals Co., 578 A.2d 1248 (N.J. Super. 1990); see also Gale and Goyer, Recovery for Cancerphobia and Increased Rick of Cancer, 15 Cumb. L. Rev. 734 (1985).

Part of the courts' hesitancy in the cancerphobia cases, and in other mass tort environmental cases, is that the theories of common law liability prove too much. The reasonable fears of chemical contamination are so serious and so widespread that a defendant who pollutes a community might readily face a billion dollars in jury verdicts, and the American economy cannot stand the imposition of such tort liability. When courts raise the threshold barriers to tort recovery in mass toxic tort cases, are they making a social policy judgment that for reasons of social utility the

---

9. In re Paoli Railroad Yard PCB Litigation, 916 F.2d 829, 852 (3d Cir.1990), cert. denied 499 U.S. 961 (1991); Hansen v. Mountain Fuel Supply Co., 858 P.2d 970 (Utah 1993); Potter, v. Firestone Tire & Rubber Co., 6 Cal. 4th 965, 863 P.2d 795 (1993); Burns v. Jaquays Mining Corp., 156 Ariz. 375, 752 P.2d 28 (Ct. App. 1987).

damages for non-physical injuries must remain where they lie? Is that policy judgment analytically different from the judicial role in enforcing the ordinary private nuisance requirement that the interference with plaintiff's quiet enjoyment be "unreasonable"?

4. **Hedonic "quality of life" damages.** What items of damage seem to have been included in the *Ayers* "quality of life" recovery? Hedonic damages, noted in Chapter Three, are recent arrivals in toxic tort law and will require judicial elaboration. Is there any recognition of the stigma of living in a contaminated community? Is there any argument that separates toxic tort cases from ordinary tort cases when it comes to compensation for subjective intangibles? The mass exposure aspect of toxic tort cases implies that defendant's financial exposure may be great. Under what circumstances will that justify modification of the ordinary substantive rules?

5. **Stigma and the new tort of "ToxiProx."** Owners of land situated in close proximity to hazardous materials sites frequently find that the market value of their land has been adversely affected as a result of the nearby presence of the hazardous materials. This is particularly true in the case of sites at which toxic materials have been released into the environment, but is true to a lesser extent where a nearby facility is used for the proper treatment or disposal of hazardous materials, or even where the facility is simply one at which hazardous materials are known to be in use. Would-be-buyers discount the value of the parcel in consequence of the proximity of the hazardous materials, often without reference to whether those materials pose even a scintilla of risk of harm to the parcel being offered for sale Compensation increasingly is being sought for losses that are consequent upon toxic proximity alone. Consider the following cases that are in the process of working their way through the courts —

> A New Jersey trial court judge has certified a class action lawsuit brought by owners of parcels located in close proximity to an infamous hazardous waste site. The principal claim of the suit is that the affected homes are either unsaleable or seriously devalued by their proximity to the contaminated site.[10]

New York's highest court, in determining how much compensation is due to owners of property condemned for high voltage lines, has recognized a compensable interest in favor of property owners who can prove that fear of EMF (electromagnetic field) emissions from high voltage power lines will cause a reduction in the value of their real property, and contemporary cases involving parcel valuation for tax assessment purposes are also beginning to take toxic contamination and its

---

10. See In re GEMS Landfill Superior Court Litigation, N.J. Super. Ct., Camden County, No. L-068199-85 (Feb. 2, 1994) as reported at 8 Toxics Law Reporter 1035-36 (Feb. 16, 1994).11 See also, Exxon Corp. v. Yarema, 516 A2d. 990 (Md. 1986) (allowing recovery for decreased property value caused by groundwater contamination that did not reach the affected parcel); but see, Adkins v. Thomas Solvent, 440 Mich. 293, 487 N.W.2d 715 (1992) holding that diminished property values caused by negative publicity affecting parcels proximate to, but not themselves subject to, hazardous waste contamination, is a loss without legal injury. A California jury awarded $826,500 to a property owner for post-cleanup stigmatization of the property, and $400,000 in lost rents. Bixby Ranch Co. v. Spectrol Electronic Corp., Cal. Super. Ct., Los Angeles County, No. BC052566 (Dec. 13, 1993) (8 Toxics Law Reporter 955–56, Jan. 26, 1994).

effect on market price into account in valuing the subject parcel.[11] In Strawn v. Incollingo, N.J. Super. Ct. App. Div., No. A-4764-91T3 (Feb. 22, 1994) purchasers of homes in a new development were held to have a cause of action against the builder and brokers who sold them houses without disclosing the proximity to a closed landfill suspected of containing toxic waste.

What is the legal theory supporting recovery in these cases? As these claims proliferate and more judicial opinions address the issue, it will be possible to determine whether these cases comprise a new unique toxic tort cause of action or are instead an additional element of damage (similar to fear of cancer claims) being asserted under existing rubrics of negligence, nuisance and/or strict liability.

6. **Distinguishing "community fears" from "rational fears."** In her article Arguing Public Policy as a Defense to Environmental Toxic Tort Claims, 8 Toxics Law Reporter 505 (1993), Martha Churchill[12] contrasts a community fear standard that relies on "popular anxiety, and even hysteria," with a rationally based fear standard that requires a plaintiff to "prove some objective danger which serves as a basis for the fear." She proposes this distinction as a means to prevent recovery in many fear-of-cancer cases. She views the extent of available compensation to be a matter of policy, and as an initial matter she castigates the legislative branch for not settling the dispute by enacting legislation requiring a rationally-based fear standard.

As for the judicial branch, acting in a vacuum of legislative inaction, she suggests that the toxic fear and stigma (toxiprox) cases decided thus far can be grouped into two camps according to which of those two standards a court adopts. The danger, in her view, of using the community fear standard to judge the reasonableness of a claimed toxic fear is that "a community exhibiting irrational or hysterical behavior may be considered "reasonable" simply on the grounds that its phobia is widely shared. Churchill argues that the better public policy is for courts to insist that the fears be rationally based. She states that it is wrong for courts to allow "the reality of the market place [to prevail] over the reality in the groundwater." From the affected owners' point of view, the loss in the market place is still a very real loss even if the groundwater is still clean. Is there any compelling reason why this externality should be treated differently than most?

7. **Fear and risk together.** In Potter v. Firestone Tire and Rubber Co., 6 Cal. 4th 965, 25 Cal. Rptr. 2d 550 (1993), the Supreme Court of California allowed recovery for emotional distress caused by exposure to a carcinogen, in the absence of physical injury. The court accepted as a general rule that —

> in the absence of a present physical injury or illness, recovery of damages for fear of cancer in a negligence action should be allowed only if the plaintiff pleads and proves that the fear stems from a knowledge, corroborated by reliable medical and scientific opinion, *that it is more likely than not that the feared cancer will develop* in the future due to the toxic exposure....

---

11. See, Criscuola v. Power Authority of the State of New York, 81 N.Y.2d 649, 621 N.E.2d 1195, 602 N.Y.S.2d 588 (1993); Westling v. County of Mille Lacs, 512 N.W.2d 863 (1994) (assessment included a deduction for the claimed stigma attached to the property because of the pollution).

12. In a note Ms. Churchill is described as being the president of Mid-America Legal Foundation, "a non-profit advocacy center devoted to products liability and environmental issues which affect the economy." See Houck, With Charity for All, 93 Yale L.J. 1415 (1984).

> [We admit that] a reasonable person who has consumed, cooked with, and bathed in water that has been contaminated by toxic waste is likely to sustain serious emotional distress relating to fear of developing a serious illness in the future, not only when the person's chances of developing an illness is more than 50 percent, but also when his or her chance of developing the illness is considerably lower, for example, "only" 25 or 30 percent.

But the court was not willing to go beyond probability. The court, however, did define "an exception to this general rule...if the toxic exposure that has resulted in the fear of cancer was caused by conduct amounting to 'oppression, fraud, or malice,'" and applied the exception to allow recovery in *Potter* for fears based on less than 50 percent probability. The *Potter* dissent would have allowed recovery for negligently inflicted emotional distress in toxic exposure cases even more liberally, where in addition to proof of serious emotional distress the plaintiff also proves that (1) the level of toxic substances to which he or she was exposed posed a significant risk that the plaintiff will develop the feared disease or illness (i.e., a risk that is sufficiently substantial that it would result in serious emotional distress in a reasonable, rather than an unusually sensitive, person), and (2) the defendant's negligence substantially increased plaintiff's risk of contracting the disease or illness (so that the plaintiff's serious emotional distress is a condition for which the defendant appropriately should be held responsible.) 6 Cal 4th at 1025, 25 Cal. Rptr.2d at 591.

**8. Statutes of limitation —"I wasted time, and now doth time waste me."**[13] Toxic tort cases raise a number of difficult statute of limitations problems. As an initial matter, the discovery by plaintiffs that they are victims of a tort is seldom concurrent with the defendant's tortious conduct. In both *Ayers* and *Anderson* the groundwater contamination and plaintiffs' exposure to it began long before plaintiffs learned that contamination had occurred, and years before plaintiffs suffered physical injury.

The courts have adopted two devices for dealing with statutes of limitations problems. The first doctrine, intended to protect courts from the burden of adjudicating unripe controversies, turns on the definition of when a cause of action accrues. Accrual occurs only when all of the elements necessary for successful prosecution of the claim have occurred. A lawsuit cannot be brought by a plaintiff before the basic facts required for a cause of action have happened, and a central element of any tort claim is the injury to the plaintiff. To hold otherwise defies logic, asking plaintiff to act on a legal right not yet in existence.

The second major concept in limitation of actions, offering particular protection to plaintiffs in toxic tort cases, is the so-called "discovery rule." It, too, helps to define when a cause of action accrues. In a portion of the *Anderson* opinion addressing the effect of the statute of limitations on wrongful death claims, the court stated the general discovery rule:

> The discovery rule is a method of defining when a cause of action accrues. The principle behind the rule is that "a plaintiff should be put on notice before his or her claim is barred by the passage of time." The notice required by the rule

---

13. Richard II, Act V, Scene V.

includes knowledge of both the injury and its cause — that plaintiff "has been harmed as a result of defendant's conduct." 628 F. Supp. at 1224.

This particular form of the discovery rule, requiring that the plaintiff must be on actual or constructive notice of the fact of injury, and who caused it, before the statute starts running, is not a majority rule although it appears to be gaining. Other states toll the statute of limitations in these toxic tort cases only until discovery of the injury. See Development in the Law — Toxic Waste Litigation, 99 Harv. L. Rev. 1458, 1906–07 (1986).

"Statutes of repose" — additional statutes of limitations that expressly disallow the operation of the discovery rule — have been enacted in some states.[14] These statutes appear to be motivated by marketplace concerns for the burdens placed on present-day operators of businesses by large judgments for "ancient torts." "Let sleeping dogs lie." Unfortunately many illnesses caused by wrongful exposures to environmental toxics lie latent for years before surfacing. Marketplace lobbyists argue that often the wrongful acts were committed by officers and employees who have no present relation to the defendant. Statutes of repose are likely to receive pointed attention in future toxic tort cases.

The discovery rule addresses the problem of long latency periods intervening between tortious exposure and the onset of disease. If the statute of limitations does not begin to run until the disease is manifest, then plaintiffs will have ample opportunity to bring suit after the onset of the disease. There may be some proof difficulties in reconstructing the events surrounding exposure, but these are the lesser of evils. The principal alternatives to the discovery rule are requiring defendants to compensate *all* exposure victims as if they have developed the disease, or abandoning the discovery rule, thereby limiting tort recoveries to just those harms that became manifest within a short time after exposure. *Ayers* recognizes another potential discovery rule problem, the operation of the rules of res judicata (in particular merger and bar) that the New Jersey court labels "the single controversy rule." In most instances, in order to avoid duplicative and inefficient litigation of a case, all claims must be joined in a single suit. To the extent that claims have been omitted and not placed in issue, the single controversy rule deems them extinguished and "merged" into the original judgment. In cases like *Ayers* the pitfall of the single controversy rule is that later-initiated claims for matured illness would be allowed by the discovery rule, but barred by merger. The New Jersey answer to this problem is to recognize that the policies of the discovery rule would

---

14. See Mass. Gen. L. Ch. 260 §2B(–6 years); Ill. Rev. Stat. Ch. 110 §13-213(6)(–12 years); Va. Code Ann. §8.01-250 (–5 years).

> An action of tort for damages arising out of any deficiency or neglect in the design, planning, construction or general administration of an improvement to real property...shall be commenced only within three years next after the cause of action accrues; *provided, however,* that in no event such actions be commenced more than six years after the earlier of the dates of: (1) the opening of the improvement to use; or (2) substantial completion of the improvement and the taking of possession for occupancy by the owner. Mass. Gen. L. Ch. 260 §2B.

Courts have reached different conclusions about the defense's applicability in long term latency environmental contamination cases. Pitney-Bowes v. Baker Industries, 649 A.2d 1325 (N.J. App. 1994); Weymouth v. Welch Co., 18 Mass. L. Rptr. 6 (Mass. App. 1996); Norfolk v. U.S. Gypsum, 360 S.E. 2d 325 (Va. 1987);Rowan County v. U.S. Gypsum, 418 S.E. 2d 648 (N.C. 1992).

be set at naught if merger and bar were applied. The court pointed out that merger and bar only apply to claims that could have been brought at the time of the first suit, and here, technically speaking, the cause of action for bodily injury would not yet have come into existence.

9. **Sovereign immunity.** Most sovereigns in history have not encouraged their citizens (or anyone else, for that matter) to sue them in the sovereign's own courts. The idea of sovereign immunity has long been a powerful part of the American law. In the nineteenth and twentieth centuries, however, numerous attacks on the unfairness and irrationality of immunity were mounted and, eventually, took their toll. In an era where government is acknowledged to have many similarities to other corporate entities, why, for example, should a pedestrian negligently run down by a government-owned vehicle find her suit barred by governmental immunity when no such bar would encumber a suit against a private company? In the *Ayers* case, for example, why should Jackson Township be any less responsible for harms caused by its dump operations than a private landfill operator?

Over time, the courts, and to a lesser extent legislatures, responded to arguments favoring a partial abolition of governmental immunity. On the common law front, a popular innovation is to distinguish between cases in which the governmental defendant is performing a governmental function, and those in which it is engaging in a mere proprietary function.[15] For example, setting the standard for airborne lead pollution would be governmental in character, and would be immune from suit even if the government did it negligently; running a hot dog stand at the public beach, or emitting excess pollutants from a furnace at a state-owned office building, would be proprietary in character and subject to suit. In between these two examples lie many gray areas. Another popular judicial device for limiting immunity is to grant official immunity for acts that are clothed with discretion (again, standard-setting is a good example), but to hold officials liable for negligence or intentional torts in the performance of mere "ministerial" functions.[16] Some legislatures have taken similar initiatives, while a larger number have codified what the courts have done, sometimes modifying the scope of the judicial abrogation of immunity, other times not.

In recent years, with the advent of widely publicized tort recoveries and a manifold increase in governmental liability insurance costs, a reaction to the liberalized abrogation of immunity has taken place. The statute construed in *Ayers* had reasserted a broader concept of governmental immunity in that state, though creating an exception to that immunity under statutorily-defined circumstances. Even in cases where the New Jersey statute allows governmental immunity, however, the statute expressly denies damages for pain and suffering and similar intangible items of damage.

---

15. "Proprietary" implies there is no functional difference from a privately-owned profitmaking enterprise; "governmental" implies a function carried on in satisfaction of a public duty.

16. "Ministerial" implies that the public employee is simply executing explicitlly required governmental duties; "discretionary" acts are based on broader, less constrained grants of delegated authority to act.

## B.  PROOF OF COMPLEX CAUSATION

In almost every toxic tort case, proof of causation of harm is a difficult litiga-tion hurdle for plaintiffs. (The exception is cases of mesothelioma, asbestosis or similar forms of cancer caused only by asbestos exposure, in settings where plain-tiffs have been exposed to only one clearly identifiable source.) In the Woburn toxics case the obstacle of proving causation was immense. No prior evidence was known of cancer being caused by the subject chemicals. Defendants steadfastly denied any such dumping. The victims, like most Americans, were exposed to lit-erally hundreds of possible carcinogens in daily life. The Aberjona creek itself car-ried the four toxics, though in smaller concentrations than the wellwater.[17] Leukemia has long been linked to radioactivity exposures, and Woburn had several radium watch-dial factories in the old days. (It took serious investigation to exclude the possibility that victims had been exposed to these long-defunct com-panies' wastes.) When plaintiffs filed (eight days before the three-year statute of limitations was set to expire) the best evidence they had was the EPA field memo from the time the wells were closed, saying that from agency groundwater sam-ples, Grace, Beatrice, and Unifirst were PRPs (potentially responsible parties, under CERCLA, or Superfund, studied in Chapter 18).[18] The Centers for Disease Control added their statistical conclusion that the leukemias were caused by abnormal exposure, and the Harvard public health students added evidence that some corre-lation existed between wellwater and illness, but neither of these data came close to establishing causation by the defendants' chemicals. Even the plaintiffs' discov-ery of Al Love, a Grace employee who lived near the Andersons and decided to reveal the solvent-dumping practices at the plant, did little to tie the defendants specifically to the plaintiffs' illnesses. Plaintiff's attorney Schlichtmann neverthe-less was confident he could do so at trial.

Conventional tort law doctrine places the burden of establishing causation on the plaintiff, requiring that the plaintiff be able to prove it is more likely than not that the defendant's tortious conduct is the "but for" cause of plaintiff's injury. The nature of the linkage between toxic exposure and the subsequent onset of disease makes this proof different in kind from that encountered in conventional bodily injury cases seeking recovery for injuries that are the obvious result of an automo-bile collision or other physical impact.

To carry the burden of proof in a toxic tort bodily injury case, the plaintiff eventually must prove (1) the linkage between exposure and the disease, (2) that defendant is the source of the exposure, and (3) that the exposure was of a magni-tude (concentration) sufficient to be consistent with the plaintiff's proof of linkage. None of those three inquiries is simple. The first requires delving deeply into the science of epidemiology. The second can be complicated by the fungible nature of toxic products (such as asbestos insulation) or the number of possible sources of

---

17. If concentrations are greater in groundwater than in an adjoining surface stream, that means the stream cannot be the source of contamination. Materials imported into groundwater do not become more concentrated in groundwater solution; if anything they diffuse. This basic logic never got incor-porated into trial findings.

18. The 1979 EPA memo was paradoxically the trigger that started the statute of limitations running.

the contaminants having the same toxic properties. Plaintiff's case becomes more difficult whenever the defendant(s) may not be responsible for all of the relevant exposures. The third requires proof of facts regarding plaintiff's exposure to the toxic substance when, in almost all cases, the plaintiff was unaware that the exposure was occurring and in historic contexts where the extent of the exposure was not being measured. This part of the chapter delves into these problem areas and also provides material on joint and several liability.

## Section 1. LINKING TOXIC EXPOSURES TO INJURIES

### Chevron Chemical Company v. Ferebee
United States Court of Appeals for the District of Columbia, 1984
736 F.2d 1529

[Richard Ferebee was a worker at the federal government's Beltsville Agricultural Research Center. He was exposed to the insecticide Paraquat, made by Chevron, on a number of occasions over a three year period, and once even collapsed after having walked behind a tractor spraying the pesticide. Ferebee developed severe lung fibrosis. In a wrongful death action brought by his family after his death, the jury awarded extensive damages against the pesticide manufacturer.]

MIKVA, C.J. This is an appeal by Chevron Chemical Company from a judgment rendered against it after a jury trial in a suit brought by the minor children and the estate of Richard Ferebee....

Even before 1977, Mr. Ferebee was not a picture of perfect health. He was overweight, suffered from high blood pressure, and had a life-long sinus problem. Nonetheless, in late 1977, according to Mr. Ferebee's testimony, he began to notice a marked change in his physical condition, most notably increasing shortness of breath. Over the next several years, Mr. Ferebee's condition progressively deteriorated. In November of 1979 he checked into Capitol Hill Hospital, where Dr. Muhammad Yusuf, a pulmonary specialist, diagnosed Ferebee's disease as pulmonary fibrosis. Dr. Yusuf referred Mr. Ferebee to the National Institutes of Health, where he was treated during 1981 and 1982 by Dr. Ronald G. Crystal, Chief of the Pulmonary Branch of the Heart, Lung, and Blood Institute. After several consultations and tests, both Drs. Yusuf and Crystal concluded that Ferebee's pulmonary fibrosis was caused by paraquat poisoning. Mr. Ferebee's lung condition continued to degenerate, and on March 18, 1982, he died.

In the legal action prosecuted by Ferebee's estate and minor children, appellees presented both of Mr. Ferebee's treating physicians as expert witnesses. Both Dr. Yusuf and Dr. Crystal testified that, in their opinion, paraquat had caused Mr. Ferebee's pulmonary fibrosis. To support this view, they relied not only upon their own observation of Mr. Ferebee and the medical tests performed on him, but also upon medical studies which, they asserted, suggested that dermal absorption of paraquat can lead to chronic lung abnormalities of the sort characterized as pulmonary fibrosis. Appellees then argued to the jury that Chevron had not adequately labelled paraquat to warn against the possibility that chronic skin exposure could lead to lung disease and death and that this failure was a proximate cause of Mr. Ferebee's illness and death.

An appellate court's function in reviewing the denial of a judgment notwithstanding the verdict is very limited.... The appellate court does not assess witness credibility nor weigh the evidence, but rather seeks to verify only that fair-minded jurors could reach the verdict rendered.... Judges, both trial and appellate, have no special competence to resolve the complex and refractory causal issues raised by the attempt to link low-level [long-term] exposure to toxic chemicals with human disease. On questions such as these, which stand at the frontier of current medical and epidemiological inquiry, if experts are willing to testify that such a link exists, it is for the jury to decide whether to credit the testimony....

Chevron first argues that the jury was obligated to reject appellee's theory that long-term exposure to paraquat caused Ferebee's illness and death. Chevron acknowledges that paraquat is known to be toxic, but argues that it is only acutely toxic — that is, that any injuries resulting from exposure to paraquat occur within a very short time of exposure, such as days or weeks, and that when exposure ceases, so too does the injury. In this case, Ferebee did not experience any of the symptoms of pulmonary fibrosis until late 1978, at which point it had been ten months since he last sprayed paraquat, and his chronic inflammatory lung disease continued to worsen long after his final use of paraquat in August of 1979. Plaintiffs' theory of recovery was thus that paraquat, when absorbed through the skin, can attack the lungs in such a way as to cause chronic and self-perpetuating inflammation. Chevron argues that there has never been any evidence nor any suggestion that paraquat can cause chronic injury of this sort and that, in any event, Ferebee could not have been exposed to enough paraquat to injure him in this fashion.

The short answer to Chevron's argument is that two expert witnesses refuted it and that the jury was entitled to believe those experts. Both Drs. Crystal and Yusuf, who are eminent specialists in pulmonary medicine and who were Ferebee's treating physicians, testified that paraquat poisoning was the cause of Ferebee's illness and death. Both admitted that cases like Ferebee's were rare, but Dr. Crystal identified three other cases he felt were similar to that of Mr. Ferebee. Chevron argues that these cases can be distinguished from Mr. Ferebee's, but it is not our role to decide the merits of Chevron's attempted distinctions; Dr. Crystal thought the cases were similar, and the jury was entitled to believe him. Chevron of course introduced its own experts who were of the view that Ferebee's illness was not caused by paraquat, but the testimony of those witnesses, who did not treat Mr. Ferebee or examine him, can hardly be deemed so substantial that the jury had no choice but to accept it. The experts on both sides relied on essentially the same diagnostic methodology; they differed solely on the conclusions they drew from the test results and other information. The case was thus a classic battle of the experts, a battle in which the jury must decide the victor....

Finally, Chevron argues that its expert, Dr. Fisher, proved that it was physically impossible for Ferebee to have been exposed to enough paraquat to cause him any injury. Dr. Fisher's testimony, however, went only to the amount of paraquat necessary to cause the short-term illnesses that have long been recognized to follow from paraquat exposure. Accepting Dr. Fisher's testimony as true, as plaintiffs did not at trial, it still would not necessarily follow that the same amount is needed to trigger a chronic disease like that which Ferebee allegedly contacted. The jury could therefore have concluded that Ferebee had been exposed to sufficient amounts of paraquat to cause the chronic disease from which he suffered — even if that exposure was not substantial enough to produce acute symptoms. The dose-response relationship at low levels of exposure for admittedly toxic chemicals like paraquat is one of the most sharply contested questions currently being debated in the medical community, see generally Leape, Quantitative Risk Assessment in Regulation of Environmental Carcinogens, 4 Harv. Envtl. L. Rev. 86, 100–103 (1980); surely it would be rash for a court to declare as a matter of law that, below a certain threshold level of exposure, dermal absorption of paraquat has no detrimental effect. We therefore conclude that there was sufficient evidence of causation to justify submission of that issue to the jury...and allow the jury's verdict to stand.

COMMENTARY AND QUESTIONS

1. **A quick torts review of strict liability for failure to warn.** Ferebee's lawsuit arises under state tort law, in this case, Maryland products liability law that requires warnings to consumers of a product's known dangers. On a failure to warn theory, the plaintiff must prove all of the causal links from exposure to injury, i.e., that "paraquat proximately caused Mr. Ferebee's illness and death" and also that "the inadequacy of the warning proximately caused Mr. Ferebee's illness and death." Warnings were on the package, but they did not refer to dermal absorption and lung disease. The warnings, which included the language "CAN KILL IF SWALLOWED, HARMFUL TO THE EYES AND SKIN" certainly indicated that paraquat isn't an appropriate skin lotion, but the warning did not specifically mention adverse consequences of dermal contact other than skin irritation. This failure in the warning to disclose consequences of exposure known to Chevron was deemed sufficient to support the jury finding.

2. **Causation: the jury as medical factfinders.** Chevron attacked causation in two ways, challenging the course of Ferebee's illness as inconsistent with any form of lung illness known to be caused by paraquat and claiming that acute paraquat poisoning required far higher levels of exposure than Ferebee encountered. The jury, at least implicitly, rejected those attacks. Is it appropriate that juries, skilled in neither law nor science, be given so vital a role in determining such a technical issue? What other possibilities exist? In making those determinations the jury relies on the testimony of experts, a topic that is considered more fully in Subchapter C.

3. **Other potential causes.** Mr. Ferebee worked at the Agricultural Research Center for more than 13 years, during which time he was exposed to a number of different insecticides, pesticides, and herbicides. Why was this case litigated only against Chevron? It may well be that substantial exposure to paraquat could be proven, and only paraquat had any scientific linkage to lung fibrosis. Would it be relevant to the case if Mr. Ferebee had been a three-pack-a-day chain smoker?

4. **Burden of proof on the issue of causation.** The *Ferebee* court makes no mention of the specific standard as to how certain it must be that Chevron caused the illness. The court applied the usual "more likely than not" standard. Will the plaintiffs in most toxic tort cases be able to carry the burden of proof on the issue of causation in fact if that is the standard? Consider that question after reading the case that follows.

## Landrigan v. Celotex Corp.
### Supreme Court of New Jersey, 1992
### 127 N.J. 404, 605 A.2d 1079

POLLACK, J. Plaintiff, Angelina Landrigan, sued defendants Owens-Corning Fiberglass Corporation and Owens Illinois, Inc. for the personal injuries and death of her husband, Thomas Landrigan, claiming that exposure to defendants' asbestos had caused his death from colon cancer....

Decedent worked as a maintenance man and pipe insulator at the Bayonne Terminal Warehouse from 1956 until December 1981, when he was diagnosed as suffering from colon cancer. From 1956 until 1972, he allegedly worked with insulation containing asbestos supplied by defendants. In January 1982, he underwent surgery but the cancer spread, and he died in December 1982. The cause of his death was adenocarcinoma, "a malignant adenoma arising from a glandular organ," the most common type of colon cancer. Generally speaking, colorectal cancer is the second most common cancer in the United States, striking 140,000 persons and causing 60,000 deaths annually. In 1984, plaintiff filed this survivorship and wrongful death action, asserting that exposure to asbestos had caused decedent's death.

At the trial in 1989, plaintiff relied on two experts, Dr. Joseph Sokolowski, Jr., a physician who is board certified in both internal medicine and pulmonary medicine, and Dr. Joseph K. Wagoner, an epidemiologist and biostatistician but not a physician. Dr. Sokolowski never treated or examined decedent. He based his conclusions on a review of decedent's history of exposure to asbestos, the absence of other risk factors in decedent's history, and on various epidemiological, animal, and in vitro studies. Stating that physicians regularly rely on epidemiological studies, Dr. Sokolowski testified that asbestos can cause colon cancer in humans. He also described the path asbestos fibers take from inhalation to the gastrointestinal tract. Dr. Sokolowski testified that exposure to asbestos was the cause of decedent's colon cancer...[and] further that decedent would not have contracted colon cancer if he had not been exposed to asbestos.

Plaintiff also offered Dr. Wagoner to testify that asbestos exposure had caused decedent's colon cancer. After conducting a hearing pursuant to Evidence Rule 8, the trial court ruled that as an epidemiologist and not a physician, Dr. Wagoner was not qualified to testify that asbestos had caused decedent's cancer. The court, however, permitted the witness to testify about epidemiological methods and studies linking colon cancer to asbestos exposure. It also allowed Dr. Wagoner to state his opinion that asbestos causes colon cancer in humans.... At the close of plaintiff's case, the trial court granted defendants' motions for a directed verdict.

In recent years, we have sought to accommodate the requirements for the admission of expert testimony with the need for that testimony. Nowhere is that accommodation more compelling than on the issue of causation in toxic-tort litigation concerning diseases of indeterminate origin. Many such injuries remain latent for years, are associated with diverse risk factors, and occur without any apparent cause. Steve Gold, Note, Causation in Toxic Torts: Burdens of Proof, Standards of Persuasion, and Statistical Evidence, 96 Yale L.J. 376, 376 (1986) (hereinafter Gold). In that context, proof that a defendant's conduct caused decedent's injuries is more subtle and sophisticated than proof in cases concerned with more traditional torts....

Traditionally, plaintiffs have established a connection between tortious conduct and personal injuries through the testimony of medical experts who testify that the defendant's specific conduct was the cause of the plaintiff's injuries. Toxic torts, however, do not readily lend themselves to proof that is so particularized. Developments in the Law-Toxic Waste Litigation, 99 Harv.L.Rev. 1458, 1620 (1986). Plaintiffs in such cases may be compelled to resort to more general evidence, such as that provided by epidemiological studies. A basic understanding of some fundamentals of epidemiology is essential for an assessment of the admissibility of such evidence.

Simply defined, epidemiology is "the study of disease occurrence in human populations." Gary D. Friedman, Primer of Epidemiology 1 (3d ed. 1987) (hereinafter Friedman). Epidemiology studies the relationship between a disease and a factor suspected of causing the disease, using statistical methods to determine the likelihood of causation. Bert Black & David E. Lilienfeld, Epidemiologic Proof in Toxic Tort Litigation, 52 Fordham L. Review 732, 750 (1984) (hereinafter Black & Lilienfeld). By comparison to the clinical health sciences, which are directly concerned with diseases in particular patients, epidemiology is concerned with the statistical analysis of disease in groups of patients. The statistical associations may become so compelling, as they did in establishing the correlation between asbestos exposure and mesothelioma, that they raise a legitimate implication of causation. "Statistical associations," however, "do not necessarily imply causation.... It is important, therefore, to have some basis for deciding whether a statistical association derived from an observational study represents a cause-and-effect relationship." Friedman, supra, at 182–83. See Austin B. Hill, The Environment and Disease: Association or Causation?, 58 Proc. Royal Soc. Med. 295 (1965) (criteria to assess likelihood of causal relationship from statistical associations).

At oral argument, defendants, for example, stressed two criteria, among others, that are crucial in determining whether a statistical association will give rise to an inference that a particular substance causes a certain disease in people who are exposed to it. The two criteria are the strength of the association and the consistency of any such association with other knowledge. The argument is sound. As Professor Friedman explains:

> In general, the stronger the association, the more likely it represents a cause-and-effect relationship. Weak associations often turn out to be spurious and explainable by some known, or as yet unknown, confounding variable.... Strength of an association is usually measured by the relative risk or the ratio of the disease rate in those with the factor to the rate in those without. The relative risk of lung cancer in cigarette smokers as compared to nonsmokers is on the order of 10:1, whereas the relative risk of pancreatic cancer is about 2:1. The difference suggests that cigarette smoking is more likely to be a causal factor for lung cancer than for pancreatic cancer.

> If the association makes sense in terms of known biological mechanisms or other epidemiologic knowledge, it becomes more plausible as a cause-and-effect relationship. Part of the attractiveness of the hypothesis that a high-saturated fat, high-cholesterol diet predisposes to atherosclerosis is the fact that a biologic mechanism can be invoked. Such a diet increases blood lipids, which may in turn be deposited in arterial walls. A correlation between the number of telephone poles in a country and its coronary heart disease mortality rate lacks plausibility as a cause-and-effect relationship partly because it is difficult to imagine a biologic mechanism whereby telephone poles result in atherosclerosis. [Friedman, supra, at 183–84]

The "attributable risk," by comparison, is the proportion of the disease that is statistically attributable to the factor. Black & Lilienfeld, supra, 52 Fordham L. Review at 761. It "is a composite measure that takes into account both the relative risk of disease if exposed and the proportion of the population so exposed." Ibid....

Turning to the experts in this case, plaintiff's medical expert was Dr. Sokolowski. Initially, he explained that he had examined certain literature on colon cancer, including the landmark study by Dr. Irving Selikoff. See Irving Selikoff, et al., Mortality Experience of Insulation Workers in the United States and Canada, 330 Annals N.Y. Acad. Sci. 91 (1979). The study indicated a relative risk of colon cancer from the exposure to asbestos of 1.55. The attributable risk, which would vary according to the extent and intensity of the exposure, was approximately thirty-five percent. Thus, assuming a causal relationship, the Selikoff study indicates that thirty-five percent of the cases of colon cancer in the population exposed to asbestos can be attributed to that exposure.

Dr. Sokolowski had never treated or examined decedent, but he had reviewed decedent's medical records and plaintiff's answers to interrogatories. Those materials indicated that decedent had been exposed to asbestos in his work. They also indicated the absence of other risk factors such as a family history of colon cancer, a high-fat diet, and the undue consumption of alcohol. Dr. Sokolowski acknowledged that "many studies...show no statistically significant increase in colon cancer in workers exposed to asbestos." Finally, he relied on the results of animal and in vitro studies.

The trial court rejected Dr. Sokolowski's testimony as a "net opinion" unsupported by any facts. Specifically, the court stated that "epidemiological evidence can only be used to show that a defendant's conduct increased a plaintiff's risk of injury to some measurable extent but it cannot be used to answer the critical question did the asbestos cause Mr. Landrigan's colon cancer."

The Appellate Division agreed with that assessment, explaining that Dr. Sokolowski had failed to account for other factors that may have caused decedent's cancer. Although it accepted the validity of the Selikoff study, the court stated that the 1.55 relative risk was insufficient to support Dr. Sokolowski's opinion that decedent's exposure had caused the cancer. Without expressly adopting a specific standard, the court cited with approval several cases that adopted a requirement that an epidemiological study show a relative risk in excess of 2.0 to prove that causation in a specific individual was more probable than not. The significance of a relative risk greater than 2.0 representing a true causal relationship is that the ratio evidences an attributable risk of more than fifty percent, which means that more than half of the cases of the studied disease in a comparable population exposed to the substance are attributable to that exposure. This finding could support an inference that the exposure was the probable cause of the disease in a specific member of the exposed population.

Defense counsel urges that the Appellate Division opinion may be read as requiring that an expert may not rely on an epidemiological study to support a finding of individual causation unless the relative risk is greater than 2.0. At oral argument before us, they agreed that such a requirement may be unnecessary. Counsel acknowledged that under certain circumstances a study with a relative risk of less than 2.0 could support a finding of specific causation. Those circumstances would include, for example, individual clinical data, such as asbestos in or near the tumor or a documented history of extensive asbestos exposure. So viewed, a relative risk of 2.0 is not so much a password to a finding of causation as one piece of evidence, among others, for the court to consider in determining whether the expert has employed a sound methodology in reaching his or her conclusion....

The court must also examine the manner in which experts reason from the studies and other information to a conclusion. As previously indicated, that conclusion must derive from a sound methodology that is supported by some consensus of experts in the field.

In the present case, Dr. Sokolowski began by reviewing the scientific literature to establish both the ability of asbestos to cause colon cancer and the magnitude of the risk that it would cause that result. Next, he assumed that decedent was exposed to asbestos and that his exposure, in both intensity and duration, was comparable to that of the study populations described in the literature. He then assumed that other known risk factors for colon cancer did not apply to decedent. After considering decedent's exposure and the absence of those factors, Dr. Sokolowski concluded that decedent's exposure more likely than not had been the cause of his colon cancer.

Without limiting the trial court on remand, its assessment of Dr. Sokolowski's testimony should include an evaluation of the validity both of the studies on which he relied and of his assumption that the decedent's asbestos exposure was like that of the members of the study populations. The court should also verify Dr. Sokolowski's assumption concerning the absence of other risk factors. Finally, the court should ascertain if the relevant scientific community accepts the process by which Dr. Sokolowski reasoned to the conclusion that the decedent's asbestos exposure had caused his cancer. Thus, to determine the admissibility of the witness's opinion, the court, without substituting its judgment for that of the expert, should examine each step in Dr. Sokolowski's reasoning.

Our decision does not necessarily mean that on remand the trial court must reach a different result. Although the diagnosis of decedent's disease and the cause of his death are not in dispute, the parties vigorously contest the probability that decedent's colon cancer was caused by asbestos exposure. The issue posed to both Dr. Wagoner and Dr. Sokolowski was the likelihood that decedent's colon cancer was caused by asbestos exposure. Dr. Wagoner did not rely exclusively on epidemiological studies in addressing that issue. In addition to relying on such studies, he, like Dr. Sokolowski, reviewed specific evidence about decedent's medical and occupational histories. Both witnesses also excluded certain known risk factors for colon cancer, such as excessive alcohol consumption, a high-fat diet, and a positive family history. From statistical population studies to the conclusion of causation in an individual, however, is a broad leap, particularly for a witness whose training, unlike that of a physician, is oriented toward the study of groups and not of individuals. Nonetheless, proof of causation in toxic-tort cases depends largely on inferences derived from statistics about groups. Gold, *supra*, 96 Yale L.J. at 401....[Reversed and remanded.]

COMMENTARY AND QUESTIONS

1. **Relative risk and attributable risk.** Although the *Landrigan* opinion is not very explicit on this point, relative risk (RR) and attributable risk (AR) are, in a sense, reciprocal measures. When the relative risk is 2.0 (sometimes expressed as 2:1), the attributable risk is 50 percent (.5). What this relative risk of 2.0 or 2:1 means in

popular parlance is that a person with that risk factor is twice as likely as someone without the factor to have the correlated harm occur. The precise equation
that relates the two values is RR-1/RR=AR. So, for example, in the cigarette smoking to lung cancer example, where the relative risk is 10, the attributable risk is 90
percent (.9), i.e., nine of the ten lung cancers that befall smokers are attributable to
smoking cigarettes rather than other factors. In the Selikoff study, the relative risk
is 1.55 so the attributable risk is (1.55-1)/1.55=.35, or 35 percent.

**2. Legal causation and statistical proof: comparing apples and pears.** What makes a
relative risk value of 2.0 appear to be particularly important in the legal arena? A
relative risk value in excess of 2.0 makes it appear more likely than not that the
risk factor is the operative cause of the injury. This linguistic formulation tracks
the standard that the plaintiff must meet to carry the burden of proof on the issue
of causation-in-fact. That is, the plaintiff has the burden of persuading the trier of
fact that defendant's action is more likely than not the cause of plaintiff's injury.
Using the term attributable risk makes this linguistically even clearer, when the
risk attributable to defendant is more than half (>50%) of the total risk it is easy
to conclude that the defendant's act is more likely than not the cause of the plaintiff's injury.

The court in *Landrigan*, makes it very clear that failure to establish a relative risk
value in excess of 2.0 is not fatal to a plaintiff's case. Why shouldn't it be? The
court's answer is that other factors could be proved in the case that would make it
more likely that in this particular case that the risk factor for which the defendant
is responsible is the operative cause of the particular plaintiff's injury. Examples
include specific clinical evidence, or proof of extraordinary exposures. What about
the flip side of the issue — will proof of a relative risk in excess of 2.0 always result
in a decision in plaintiff's favor on the issue of cause-in-fact? It should be obvious
that the same type of individualized proof that can allow a plaintiff to win despite
a relative risk that does not exceed 2.0, can also allow a defendant to prevail in a
case of relative risk higher than 2.0.

**3. Legal causation and statistical significance: comparing apples and pear melba.**
When the term significant appears in legal discourse, it usually has its lay mean-
ings that speak to the importance of a factor, or that contrast the central with the
peripheral. In relation to scientific studies that find a correlation significant (as
between an exposure and the subsequent onset of disease), the word "significant"
is a term of art that describes the reliability of the linkage. To be more precise, the
significance of a correlation is the likelihood that the data observed are not the
product of mere random chance. In a case of radiation exposure, one judge
explained statistical significance in the following way:

> Where there is an increase of observed cases of a particular cancer or leukemia
> over the number statistically "expected" to normally appear, the question
> arises whether it may be rationally inferred that the increase is causally con-
> nected to specific human activity. The scientific papers and reports will often
> speak of whether a deviation from the expected numbers of cases is "statisti-
> cally significant," supporting a hypothesis of causation, or whether the per-
> ceived increase is attributable to random variation in the studied population,
> i.e., to chance. The mathematical tests of significance commonly used in

research tend to be stringent; for an increase to be considered "statistically significant," the probability that it can be attributed to random chance usually
must be five percent or less (p=.05). In other words, if the level of significance
chosen by the researcher is p=.05, than an observed correlation is "significant"
if there is 1 chance in 20 — or less — that the increase resulted from chance.
In scientific practice, levels of significance of .01 or .001 are used providing an
even more stringent test of a chosen hypothetical relationship. Allen v. United
States, 588 F.Supp. 247, 416 (D. Utah 1984).

Accordingly, a causal hypothesis that narrowly fails to satisfy a .05 level of statistical significance is not, from the legal viewpoint, insignificant. For instance, data
for which there is only a 1 in 19 chance of its being random fails a .05 significance
test, but nevertheless evidences a relationship for which "the probability is 94.73
percent or 18 chances out of 19 that the observed relationship is not a random
event...[and] the certainty that the observed increase is related to its hypothetical
cause rather than mere chance is still far more likely than not." Id.

What does all this mean for the trial of toxic tort cases? First, even causal hypotheses that are not statistically significant at traditional p-values used in scientific
research may be significant proof that helps establish legal causation.

4. **The plaintiff's dilemma.** Under the Landrigan standard for proving causation,
how often can plaintiffs win exposure-induced cancer cases where the epidemiological studies do not evidence a relative risk value in excess of 2.0? What will be
the usual impact on available proof of the long latency periods between exposure
and the onset of disease? Most likely, the delay will make it difficult for plaintiffs
to obtain reliable proof of exposure levels and introduce, in the course of living,
many confounding variables, such as other exposures, or life-style choices, thereby
reducing the chance of making the individualizing proofs the Landrigan court
views as so important.

5. **The pitfalls of probabilistic proof.** A hot debate in the legal literature surrounds
the advisability of allowing proof of probabilities to establish causation in fact.
There are numerous good articles on this subject, two of the classics are Lawrence
Tribe, Trial by Mathematics: Precision and Ritual in the Legal Process, 84 Harv. L.
Rev. 1329 (1971) and Charles Nesson, Agent Orange Meets the Blue Bus:
Factfinding at the Frontier of Knowledge, 66 B.U. L.Rev. 521 (1986).

Consider the following hypotheticals:[19] Following exposure to defendant's toxic
waste that leached into an aquifer, the cancer rate in a community rises from 10
per year to 19 per year (hypo 1) or 21 per year (hypo 2) and all other possible causes
have been ruled out by undisputed expert testimony. If probability is translated
uncritically into plaintiffs' failure or success in carrying the burden of proof on the
cause in fact issue, then in hypo 1 defendant goes free of liability to any of the 19
victims and in hypo 2 defendant must compensate all 21 victims. Is such a result
absurd? Do the hypotheticals make it clear why the Landrigan court is chary of
making a relative risk of 2.0 a litmus for recovery?

---

19. The hypotheticals are adapted from Richard Delgado, Beyond Sindell, 70 Calif. L. Rev. 881, 885
(1982).

Should plaintiffs be relieved of their usual burden of proof because of these proof problems? In Allen v. United States, noted above for its discussion of statistical significance, the court fashioned a more lenient standard that adapts the substantial factor doctrine that was developed in the joint and several liability context to allow for proof of cause-in-fact in toxic exposure cases. *Allen* involved very compelling facts: the unannounced atmospheric testing of atomic weapons that resulted in mass exposure of the general public to ionizing radiation from the fallout released by the test. The government's lack of warning and haphazard monitoring of fallout levels made it impossible for citizens to avoid the exposure and, likewise, impossible for them to reliably prove their level of exposure. Still, the relative risk levels (a term not used in the *Allen* litigation) were far lower than 2.0. Although its precise ruling is elusive and not easy to summarize, the court allowed the plaintiffs to shift the burden of proof on the cause-in-fact issue (which the *Allen* court prefers to refer to as the factual connection issue) to the defendant by proving that the defendant's conduct was a substantial risk increasing factor. Once plaintiff makes that showing, the defendant is to come forward with evidence that tries to weaken the factual connection between its acts and the plaintiff's injuries. In the end, no fixed rule is announced: "Whether any of these factual connections will lead to liability is, as Professor Thode reminds us, 'an issue involving *the scope of the legal system's protection afforded to plaintiff* and not an issue of factual causation.' Thode, Tort Analysis: Duty-Risk v. Proximate Cause and the Rational Allocation of Functions Between Judge and Jury, 1977 Utah L. Rev. 1, 6." (emphasis by the court.) In short, the key issue becomes one of policy regarding the extent of protection offered by the legal system, the very essence of the proximate cause inquiry.

Are there other ways of relaxing the plaintiff's burden on cause in fact that are not fraught with unfairness to defendants? Professor Delgado suggests allowing full recovery for the harms caused by defendant (9 in hypo 1, 11 in hypo 2) to be shared by the entire class of 20 plaintiffs. This forces defendant to bear its costs and "Probabilities are not used...to establish a causal link between conduct of a certain type and a particular injury." Richard Delgado, Beyond *Sindell*, 70 Calif. L. Rev. 881, 905 (1982).

### Section 2. MULTIPLE DEFENDANTS AND THE DOCTRINE OF JOINT AND SEVERAL LIABILITY

The traditional analysis of causation in tort is more difficult when more than one defendant is involved in the case. First, the but-for problem rears its head again. When the acts of several parties converge to effect a result that injures plaintiff, tort law must find a way to allocate the loss. Traditionally, the plaintiff had to show which of several actors was responsible for the damage and to what extent, or all recovery would be denied. If there were six independent upwind industrial polluters all using coal for their boiler fuel, the plaintiff would be hard pressed to segregate the emissions of any of them as responsible for the injuries. Gradually the doctrine of joint and several liability developed to allow the plaintiff to obtain full compensation more easily in such circumstances by making them all liable to the plaintiff for the full amount of the injury and, in effect, allowing the plaintiff to select which defendant or defendants to pursue in court. Once judgment is obtained on that basis, the common law allows the plaintiff to collect the full judgment from any one of the jointly liable defendants ( who then can turn for contribution to other defendants ). In an earlier era, the common law forbade that defendant from shifting a portion of the loss to co-tortfeasors. Modern tort law recoiled at that unfairness and now allows loss shifting and spreading among the tortfeasors in contribution actions, but the problem of loss apportionment in hazardous waste toxic tort cases remains a major area of litigation.[20] The following case explores the imposition of joint and several liability, ostensibly in a conventional pollution setting. The doctrine, however, is of even greater importance in the toxic tort area because of the difficulties plaintiffs often face in specifically identifying which of several sources of toxic exposure is the cause on the injury.

## Velsicol Chemical Corporation v. Rowe
### Supreme Court of Tennessee, 1976
### 543 S.W.2d 337

[The original plaintiffs, residents and homeowners in the Alton Park area of Chattanooga, sued Velsicol Chemical for damages allegedly caused them by pollutants emitted from its chemical manufacturing plant. The complaint alleged that Velsicol's emissions contaminated the air and water, creating a nuisance and a trespass in depositing quantities of chemicals and other pollutants upon plaintiffs' properties. Because plaintiffs alleged that Velsicol had intentionally disregarded past injunctions, they also asked for punitive damages. Velsicol, however, argued that there were five other chemical polluters in the Alton Park area who could have caused or contributed to plaintiffs' injuries. This raised the question, first, whether plaintiffs could choose to proceed only against Velsicol, and second, if they prevailed, whether Velsicol could then turn and sue the five for contribution in paying damages.]

BROCK, J.... It has been suggested that joint torts be divided into four basic categories, viz., (1) the actors knowingly join in the performance of the tortious act or acts; (2) the actors fail to perform a common duty owed to the plaintiff; (3) there is a special relationship between the parties (e.g., master and servant or joint entrepreneurs); and (4) although there is no concert of action, nevertheless, the independent acts of several actors concur to produce indivisible harmful consequences. 1 Harper & James, Law of Torts, §10.1. While acknowledging that the last category, which may be termed independent, concurring torts, may not fall within the traditional definition of "joint torts," the authors note an increasing tendency in judicial decisions and among legal commentators to impose joint and several liability for such wrongs and thus to establish such torts as "joint" in their practical or legal effect.

The primary concern in dealing with independent, concurring torts is the proper extent of the liability of such wrongdoers, i.e., when should tortfeasors who do not act in concert, but whose acts combine to produce injury to the plaintiff, be

---

20. For the most part, the question of intra-defendant allocation of loss will be studied in conjunction with the statutory materials relating to the management of hazardous waste sites and their clean-ups. See Chapter 18.

held individually liable for the entire damage? It has been suggested that the proper approach should be to look to the combined effect of the several acts:

> If the acts result in separate and distinct injuries, then each wrongdoer is liable only for the damage caused by his acts. However, if the combined result is a single and indivisible injury, the liability should be entire. Thus the distinction to be made is between injuries which are divisible and those which are indivisible. Jackson, Joint Torts & Several Liability, 17 Tex. L. Rev. 399, 406 (1939).

The requirement of "indivisibility" can mean either that the harm is not even theoretically divisible, as death or total destruction of a building, or that the harm, while theoretically divisible, is single in a practical sense in that the plaintiff is not able to apportion it among the wrongdoers with reasonable certainty, as where a stream is polluted as the result of refuse from several factories.

In Landers v. East Texas Salt Water Disposal Co., 248 S.W.2d 731 (Tex. 1952), the plaintiff sued the defendant salt water disposal company and an oil company jointly and severally for the damage resulting when they independently deposited salt water in his lake. The court, apparently assuming that neither defendant acting alone would have caused the entire damage, extended the liability of such wrongdoers by holding them, in effect, to be jointly and severally liable, with the reservation that any one defendant could reduce his liability by showing the amount of damage caused by his acts only, or the amount that was caused by other defendants. The Texas court said:

> Where the tortious acts of two or more wrongdoers join to produce an indivisible injury, that is, an injury which cannot be apportioned with reasonable certainty to the individual wrongdoers, all of the wrongdoers will be held jointly and severally liable for the entire damages and the injured party may proceed to judgment against any one separately or against all in one suit. 248 S.W.2d at 734.

More recently, in Michie v. Great Lakes Steel, 495 F.2d 213 (6th Cir. 1974), residents of LaSalle, Ontario, brought a nuisance action in federal court, claiming that air pollutants from defendants' manufacturing plants across the Detroit River caused diminution of the value of their property, impairment of their health, and interference with the use and enjoyment of their land. Each plaintiff claimed at least $11,000 joint damage against these defendants, charging that the defendants were jointly and severally liable.

Relying upon Michigan automobile cases involving successive collisions, the Court reasoned that in any claim for relief there was a manifest unfairness in "putting on the injured party the impossible burden of proving the specific shares of harm done by each [defendant]," quoting Landers. The Court concluded that the Michigan Supreme Court would extend the principle of the automobile collision cases to the Michie facts and held that joint and several liability is applicable in nuisance actions. It is our conclusion that the rule stated and applied in the Landers and Michie cases is...consonant with modern legal thought and pragmatic concepts of justice....

After filing an answer generally denying the plaintiffs' allegations, Velsicol filed a third-party complaint against five third-party defendants, alleging that each of them operated a plant in the Alton Park area, that during the period alleged in the original complaint each of them emitted pollutants of the air and water, and that by reason of these facts the third-party defendants are liable to Velsicol for "whatever amount of recovery is made by said plaintiffs."...

The common law rule was that there could be no contribution between those who were regarded as "joint tortfeasors," when one had discharged the claim of the injured plaintiff.... Prosser, §50 and n. 38. The rule was originally adopted by the English courts in Merryweather v. Nixon, 101 Eng. Rep. (K.B. 1799). Apparently, the basis of the rule was the unwillingness of the court to allow anyone to found a cause of action upon his own deliberate wrong, an aspect of the "unclean hands" doctrine. When, in the United States, the codes of civil procedure permitted joinder of defendants who were merely negligent, such defendants came to be called "joint tortfeasors," and the reason for the rule against contribution was lost to sight. The great majority of American jurisdictions applied the rule of no-contribution to all situations, even those in which independent, but concurrent, acts of negligence had contributed to a single resulting injury. A small minority of states — including Tennessee — eventually came to a contrary conclusion, allowing contribution among joint tortfeasors without the aid of legislation. Davis v. Broad St. Garage, 232 S.W.2d 355 (1950); Huggins v. Graves, 210 F. Supp. 98 (E.D. Tenn. 1962).... In *Huggins*, the federal district judge concluded that:

> The right of contribution exists under Tennessee law as between joint tortfeasors in a negligence action in the absence of willful or wanton negligence upon the part of the party seeking contribution. Moreover, this result accords with reason and, as stated by the Tennessee Supreme Court in the Davis case, "justice, right, and equity demand this conclusion." 210 F. Supp. at 103.

Any remaining uncertainty regarding the extent of the right of contribution among joint tortfeasors in Tennessee was dispelled by the 1968 enactment of the Tennessee Uniform Contribution Among Tortfeasors Act. TCA 23-3104, 3105 (1975). Excluding intentional tortfeasors, the Tennessee Uniform Act provides that the right to contribution arises upon the satisfaction of two general conditions. First, there must be "two (2) or more persons...jointly or severally liable in tort for the same injury to person or property...." Secondly, one of those jointly or severally liable must have paid more than his pro rata share of the common liability.

Obviously, the meaning of the phrase "jointly or severally liable" is of primary importance in determining the right of contribution under our law. An early Tennessee case, Swain v. Tennessee Copper Co., 78 S.W. 93 (1903), stated that the test of joint liability is "whether each of the parties is liable for the entire injury done." It would appear that the Court was begging the question:

> If they [the defendants] are joint tortfeasors, each one is responsible for the damage resulting from the acts of all the wrongdoers, and they may all be sued severally or jointly; but, if they are not joint tortfeasors, each is liable only for the injury contributed by him, and can only be sued in a separate action therefor. 78 S.W. at 94.

The factual situation presented in the *Swain* case was markedly similar to that in the instant case. The plaintiff-landowners brought suit against two neighboring copper smelting plants, alleging that the noxious fumes emitted from their respective hearths became "indistinguishably mingled," creating "a great nuisance." The Court, however, refused to acknowledge that the harm done to the plaintiffs' land was indivisible. Rather, the Court said:

> Proof of the extent and capacity of the several plants causing the damages complained of, the tonnage of ores treated by each of them, the time each has been in operation, their comparative proximity or distance from the plaintiff's lands, the usual condition of the air currents in that locality, and many other facts

and circumstances, will show with substantial certainty the extent of the injury inflicted by each of the defendants.... Id. at 99.

Apparently, the Court was not troubled by the fact that it would be extremely difficult, if not impossible, for the plaintiff to apportion his damages among the defendants. The rationale of the *Swain* decision is shown:

> If it were otherwise...one defendant, however little he might have contributed to the injury, would be liable for all the damages caused by the wrongful acts of all the other defendants, and he would have no remedy against the latter, because no contribution could be enforced by the tortfeasors. Id. at 97, quoting Miller v. Highland Ditch Co., 25 P. 550 (Cal.1891).

Such was the state of our law regarding contribution among tortfeasors at the time *Swain* was decided. Since that time, however, as above indicated, we have developed not only a common law right of contribution among tortfeasors but the legislature has passed a uniform act specifically granting such a right. Thus, the no-contribution rationale of the *Swain* case has collapsed, so that we look elsewhere for the import of the phrase "jointly or severally liable."

In Waller v. Skelton, 212 S.W.2d 690 (1948), it was no defense for a defendant, who drove over the crest of a hill on the wrong side of the road in the face of congested oncoming traffic and collided with the oncoming car in which plaintiff was riding, that a motorist who was driving behind plaintiff's car negligently collided with plaintiff's car, contributing to the plaintiff's injuries. Since the following motorist's negligence was concurrent with the defendant's negligence, the Court reasoned, each would be jointly and severally liable for all of plaintiff's injury. Relying upon various legal authorities, the Court said:

> A defendant's negligent act, in order to be the proximate or legal cause of plaintiff's injuries, need not have been the whole cause or the only factor in bringing them about. It was enough if such act was a substantial factor in causing them. 212 S.W.2d at 696.

While not relying on the "single, indivisible injury" theory, the Court did decide that where successive impacts with different negligently operated vehicles contributed to or combined to cause the aggregate harm suffered, the plaintiff is entitled to a joint and several recovery against both tortfeasors....

We depart from *Swain*...and adopt the rule of *Landers* and *Michie* for determining joint and several liability when an indivisible injury has been caused by the concurrent, but independent, wrongful acts or omissions of two or more wrongdoers, whether the case be one of negligence or nuisance. We hold that the third-party complaint may stand as a claim for contribution by one tortfeasor from other alleged joint tortfeasors....

### COMMENTARY AND QUESTIONS

1. **Problems of joint liability.** In *Rowe*, and the *Landers* and *Michie* cases it discusses, is it clear that the plaintiffs have suffered a single harm from the air or water pollution? The plaintiffs have suffered a single type of harm in each of the three instances, but no single defendant is the cause-in-fact of the entire extent of the harm suffered. What justifies "extending" the liability of each potential defendant? Is the extension effectively offset by the availability of an action for contribution?

In each of those cases, the court presumes that the injuries were probably caused by multiple defendants, each of whom contributed a part. What if it had been a "single bullet" injury, however? Take the example of a landfill with a thousand toxic barrels in it, all unmarked, and just one unidentifiable barrel escapes in a flood to poison a city's drinking water. Even if one knows all seven companies that dumped there, it is clear that only one unidentifiable defendant caused the poisoning. Unless one company dumped more than 50 percent of the barrels, each defendant can say that it is statistically unlikely that it caused the pollution (therefore arguing that it is unreasonable or unconstitutional to assess liability), yet together it is clear that one of them did it. This is a Summers v. Tice problem, 199 P.2d 1 (Cal. 1948), similar to the DES market-share liability cases (e.g., Sindell v. Abbot Laboratories, 607 P.2d 924 (Cal. 1980), where recovery, however, was limited to each defendant's *pro rata* share.) Can it be answered by the concert of action principles with which the *Rowe* excerpt begins? The answer that seems to be evolving in toxic tort law is a blend of strict liability, concert of action, and enterprise liability, permitting courts to shift the impossible burden of proving which defendant caused the harm from innocent plaintiffs to the class of defendants, all of whom may have been careless or risky in dumping toxic barrels, but all but one of whom is innocent in such a case.

A further extension is the "Blue Bus" theory: if plaintiff was injured by a fast-moving hit and run bus on a dark and lonely road one night, can you use the fact that 70 percent of the buses on that route belong to the Blue Bus Company to assess full (or 70 percent) liability against that defendant? Nesson, Agent Orange Meets the Blue Bus: Factfinding at the Frontier of Knowledge, 66 B.U. L.Rev. 521 (1986).

2. **Contribution and indemnity.** Traditionally, contribution and indemnity were independent causes of action that became available only after a tortfeasor had paid more than its appropriate share of a judgment for the plaintiff. With the rise of more liberal joinder rules, in particular FRCP 14 and its state court counterparts, defendants who are sued alone may join potential contributors and indemnitors in the original action. This encourages efficiency by joining more of the issues in a single lawsuit, but it does not alter the plaintiff's option to enforce the ensuing judgment *in toto* against a single defendant. When is that option important?

Under the common law, the Uniform Contribution Among Tortfeasors Act (UCATA), and Uniform Comparative Fault Act (UCFA), contribution is usually *pro rata* unless there is some other provable basis on which to apportion the injury. The emergence and growth of comparative negligence in recent years has led to apportionment in accordance with the respective percentages of negligence. In cases founded on intentional nuisance, trespass and strict liability, comparative fault would seem to be irrelevant, but there too some courts nevertheless divide responsibility according to the Acts' comparative fault principles. Dole v. Dow Chemical, 282 N.E.2d 288 (N.Y. 1972). See Phillips, Contribution and Indemnity in Products Liability, 42 Tenn. L. Rev. 85 (1974). What avenues might a polluter in *Rowe* consider in trying to pay less than a *pro rata* amount?

3. **Predecessor landowners' liability.** Can the prior owner of a contaminated parcel of land be held liable for common law damages when the toxics are subsequently discovered? Some forms of predecessor liability are straightforwardly available — within the constraints of statutes of limitation, prior owners who polluted the land

will be liable to injured neighbors who sue in tort; federal and state cleanup statutes generally extend regulatory liability to prior owners (see Chapter 18), but other areas can be more problematic.

What about suits by private individuals who purchase contaminated land? The traditional property doctrine is *caveat emptor*, buyer beware. Unlike the case of contracts for the sale of goods, sellers of land are held to no implied warranty that the land will be fit for use. While awaiting the development of such an implied warranty, can landowners sue predecessor owners (particularly those who can be shown to have known about the toxics, not to mention those who actually dumped them) under nuisance theories? In Philadelphia Electric Co. v. Hercules, 762 F.2d 303 (3d Cir. 1985), the court held that private nuisance was unavailable, because that tort was designed for suits between owners of different parcels of land. It dismissed the public nuisance claims on standing grounds. If plaintiffs can show special injury, might public nuisance claims work? Does a claim of abnormally dangerous activity improve the situation by adding strict liability to the equation? See T&E Industries v. Safety Light Corp., 587 A.2d 1249 (N.J. 1991) (court allows strict liability in favor of landowner against predecessor in title).

The question of liability against and between predecessor and successor corporations is more fully developed, with liability typically cutting through changes in corporate form. See Civins, Environmental Law Concerns in Real Estate Transactions, 43 Sw. L. J. 819 (1990).

## C. LAW AND SCIENCE IN THE TOXIC TORT CONTEXT

In a very real sense, law and science are contrasting modes of ascertaining different varieties of truth:

• *Functional Differences.* The major function of the legal system is to resolve disputes efficiently, effectively, and equitably. The major function of science is to make accurate, empirically verifiable predictions about the physical world.

• *Conclusiveness vs. Tentativeness.* Because the primary function of private law (and to a lesser extent public law) is to finally resolve disputes so that they do not fester and threaten social cohesiveness, the legal system places a substantial value on the finality of decisions. Doctrines such as res judicata, collateral estoppel, double jeopardy, statutes of limitations, and the presumption against non-retroactivity of legislation support the need for finality of legal decisions. Science, with a goal of accurate prediction, can afford to wait. It proceeds by way of tentative (and sometimes conflicting) hypotheses that lead to data collection through empirical experiments that seek to verify these hypothesis through replicable tests.

• *Moralistic vs. Value-Free Approaches.* Law is unabashedly moralistic. Although law and morality are not always congruent, law is the formalized, enforceable embodiment of public morality. In its heavily prescriptive endeavors, law deals with concepts such as deterrence, compensation, motive, intent, rights, punishment, and environmental justice. Legal decision-makers seek to implement "average morality" through principles such as the "reasonable person" standard of tort law and institutions such as the jury system. Science, on the other hand, attempts to banish value preferences from application of the scientific method because the goal of science is the objective prediction of physical phenomena. Values and politics are, of course, rife within the scientific community, but every effort is made to exclude them from scientific method. Science itself — as distinguished from the politics of science or the role of scientists in politics — is descriptive rather than prescriptive.

• *Adversarial vs. Cooperative Mechanisms.* Legal process in general, and private law in particular, is institutionalized combat. Scientists are profoundly uncomfortable when they appear in the legal arena (as expert witnesses or otherwise) because scientists view the pursuit of scientific knowledge as a cooperative effort among members of the scientific community. There is sometimes acrimonious conflict among scientists regarding the reliability of data or the importance of particular research, but the ultimate arbiter of scientific disputes is the independent verifiability of empirical experiments, the results of which are disseminated by publications accessible to other scientists working in the field. Scientists tend to resolve scientific disputes through cooperation among peer researchers at symposia or in committees of scientific bodies, not in courts or administrative proceedings. The legal system possesses no counterpart of the scientific community.

• *Geographic Variability vs. Universality.* Because law is institutionalized morality, and morality is often contextual (situational), legal rules frequently differ among jurisdictions. Scientists find it difficult to deal with this variability because science ("good science" at least) is universal, in the sense that it is non-valuational, non-contextual, and empirically verifiable within the limits of scientific method.

• *Disparate Rates of Change.* Because law is generated by human beings in order to resolve policy issues that are perceived to be important to societies, legal rules can change relatively quickly in response to fluctuations in public opinion. The phenomenal growth of Environmental Law after 1970 is a prime example of how rapidly legal "paradigm shifts" can occur. Scientists can be uncomfortable with the comparative volatility of the legal system because, in contrast, the pace of fundamental change in scientific theory is glacial.

• *Deductive vs. Inductive Approaches.* Both deductive and inductive patterns of analysis are important in both law and science. Deduction allows the investigator to compare a new set of facts or circumstances against a known body of laws to arrive at a conclusion, whereas induction allows the investigator to expand the current body of knowledge based on a set of observations. On the whole, deduction is more significant in legal reasoning than induction. Scientific method, in contrast, places heavier emphasis on induction rather than deduction.

• *Different Conceptions of Causation.* Science accepts statistical evidence (e.g., cigarette smokers contract lung cancer at a rate ten times higher than non-smokers) as proof of general scientific propositions (e.g., cigarettes cause lung cancer) that facilitate predictability. The common law, with its emphasis on resolving individual disputes in conformance with prevailing social morality, requires particularized proof of causation (e.g., the defendant's cigarettes, in fact, caused plaintiff's cancer).[21] For many years, courts did not accept statistical epidemiological or toxicological data as evidence of individual causation. Nowadays, courts in many jurisdictions accept statistical evidence, but only where plaintiff has also produced individualized evidence of causation (e.g., clinical evidence or negative life-style factors). Thus, the legal system, in the context of common law tort actions and administrative decisionmaking, may refuse to accept fully general conclusions that are accepted in the scientific community. Conversely, a common law court or administrative agency, compelled to resolve a dispute with the best evidence available, may accept evidence that is not generally accepted in the scientific community. Scientific method requires that "good science" be validated by a 95% confidence level (that might be analogized to the same level of confidence as the law requires for criminal convictions when the standard of proof is "beyond a reasonable doubt"), whereas common law courts only require that plaintiff prove causation by a preponderance of the evidence (a roughly 51% confidence level), and administrative law only requires that administrative decisions pass a "fundamental rationality" test (i.e., they not be "arbitrary and capricious").

The *Daubert* case that follows is the United States Supreme Court's most important decision in decades bearing on the relationship between law and science. It addresses in an oblique way the difficulties that cases such as *Ferebee* and *Landrigan* pose regarding the distinction between legal and scientific proof. The dilemma confronting courts arises because cases involving claims of toxic exposure-caused injury must frequently be decided before the scientific community has accumulated sufficient data to establish scientific causation. If courts adopt a scientific standard of causation, then plaintiffs will invariably lose where the cases involve matters "at the frontier of current medical and epidemiological inquiry." If, on the other hand, courts impose no limits on plaintiffs' ability to place a particular theory of causation before the trier of fact (almost always a lay jury in toxic tort cases), then quackery, coincidence, or the sympathy of jurors with injured parties could lead to findings of causation where the preponderance of credible evidence favors the defendant.

Courts have responded to this dilemma by developing rules governing the admissibility of evidence. In matters of a scientific or technical nature, for example, virtually all courts require that testimony be given only by experts having appropriate qualifications. Although this requirement provides a safeguard of sorts, plaintiffs' and defendants' bars both have developed cadres of qualified expert witnesses skilled in presenting their respective opposing views on toxic injury causation. A growing number of courts are demanding more than mere expertise, and are increasingly sophisticated about the difference between legal and scientific proof.

*Daubert* speaks to the appropriate standard of admissibility for expert scientific evidence. A 1991 decision by the U.S. Court of Appeals for the Ninth Circuit (951 F.2d 1128) had affirmed summary judgment against two families who had alleged the morning sickness drug Bendectin caused their children's limb reduction birth defects. The Ninth Circuit opinion had ruled that the plaintiffs' expert

---

21. Causation in the legal arena also has a policy element subsumed in the proximate cause inquiry that limits the consequential reach of cause and effect chains.

proof was inadmissible because it was not based on methodologies generally accepted in the relevant scientific communities. Without peer-reviewed epidemiological evidence, the court said, the plaintiffs could not prove causation. This position is generally referred to as the *Frye* rule. It derives from an old criminal prosecution for murder in which the defendant attempted to have an expert witness testify to the results of a systolic blood pressure deception (lie detector) test, at that time a relatively novel scientific test. Frye v. United States, 293 F. 1013 (D.C. Cir. 1923). The *Frye* court said:

> Just when a scientific principle or discovery crosses the line between the experimental and demonstrable stages is difficult to define. Somewhere in this twilight zone the evidential force of the principle must be recognized, and while courts will go a long way in admitting expert testimony deduced from a well-recognized scientific principle or discovery, the thing from which the deduction is made must be sufficiently established to have gained general acceptance in the particular field in which it belongs. We think the systolic blood pressure deception test has not yet gained such standing and scientific recognition among physiological and psychological authorities as would justify the courts in admitting expert testimony deduced from the discovery, development, and experiments thus far made. *Frye*, 293 S. 1013 at 1014.

*Frye* has come under attack on a number of grounds, some having to do with the problem of scientific advancement. Expert testimony founded on new, but not yet recognized general principles is not admissible under *Frye*. As the argument goes, this either stymies science, or at least those who deserve the right to have their cases considered on the basis of new lines of scientific inquiry. By the time of *Daubert*, a third of jurisdictions, federal and state, had repudiated or recanted *Frye*. See, Edward Imwinkelreid, *Science Takes the Stand: The Growing Misuse of Expert Testimony*, The Sciences 20, 22 (Nov./Dec. 1986).

In *Daubert*, the plaintiffs (petitioners) claimed that the Federal Rules of Evidence controlled the case and would permit their evidence on causation to be heard. As you will see, the Supreme Court agreed, and then went on to offer some indication of how it viewed the meaning of the governing evidentiary rules. The relevant Rules of Evidence are:

> RULE 702. TESTIMONY BY EXPERTS... If scientific, technical, or other specialized knowledge will assist the trier of fact to understand the evidence or to determine a fact in issue, a witness qualified as an expert by knowledge, skill, experience, training, or education, may testify thereto in the form of an opinion or otherwise.

> RULE 703. BASES OF OPINION TESTIMONY BY EXPERTS... The facts or data in the particular case upon which an expert bases an opinion or inference may be those perceived by or made known to the expert at or before the hearing. If of a type reasonably relied upon by experts in the particular field in forming opinions or inferences upon the subject, the facts or data need not be admissible in evidence.

## Daubert v. Merrell Dow Pharmaceuticals, Inc.
### United States Supreme Court
### 509 U.S. 579; 113 S.Ct. 2786 (1993)

BLACKMUN, J. In this case we are called upon to determine the standard for admitting expert scientific testimony in a federal trial.

Petitioners Jason Daubert and Eric Schuller are minor children born with serious birth defects. They and their parents sued respondent in California state court, alleging that the birth defects had been caused by the mothers' ingestion of Bendectin, a prescription anti-nausea drug marketed by respondent. Respondent removed the suits to federal court on diversity grounds.

After extensive discovery, respondent moved for summary judgment, contending that Bendectin does not cause birth defects in humans and that petitioners would be unable to come forward with any admissible evidence that it does. In support of its motion, respondent submitted an affidavit of Steven H. Lamm, physician and epidemiologist, who is a well-credentialed expert on the risks from exposure to various chemical substances. Doctor Lamm stated that he had reviewed all the literature on Bendectin and human birth defects — more than 30 published studies involving over 130,000 patients. No study had found Bendectin to be a human teratogen (i.e., a substance capable of causing malformations in fetuses). On the basis of this review, Doctor Lamm concluded that maternal use of Bendectin during the first trimester of pregnancy has not been shown to be a risk factor for human birth defects.

Petitioners did not (and do not) contest this characterization of the published record regarding Bendectin. Instead, they responded to respondent's motion with the testimony of eight experts of their own, each of whom also possessed impressive credentials. These experts had concluded that Bendectin can cause birth defects. Their conclusions were based upon "in vitro" (test tube) and "in vivo" (live) animal studies that found a link between Bendectin and malformations; pharmacological studies of the chemical structure of Bendectin that purported to show similarities between the structure of the drug and that of other substances known to cause birth defects; and the "reanalysis" of previously published epidemiological (human statistical) studies.

The District Court granted respondent's motion for summary judgment. The court stated that scientific evidence is admissible only if the principle upon which it is based is " 'sufficiently established to have general acceptance in the field to which it belongs.' " The court concluded that petitioners' evidence did not meet this standard. Given the vast body of epidemiological data concerning Bendectin, the court held, expert opinion which is not based on epidemiological evidence is not admissible to establish causation. Thus, the animal-cell studies, live-animal studies, and chemical-structure analyses on which petitioners had relied could not raise by themselves a reasonably disputable jury issue regarding causation. Petitioners' epidemiological analyses, based as they were on recalculations of data in previously published studies that had found no causal link between the drug and birth defects, were ruled to be inadmissible because they had not been published or subjected to peer review....[Citing Frye v. United States, the United States Court of Appeals for the Ninth Circuit affirmed.]

The Court of Appeals emphasized that other Courts of Appeals considering the risks of Bendectin had refused to admit reanalyses of epidemiological studies that had been neither published nor subjected to peer review. Those courts had found unpublished reanalyses "particularly problematic in light of the massive weight of the original published studies supporting [respondent's] position, all of which had undergone full scrutiny from the scientific community." Contending that reanalysis is generally accepted by the scientific community only when it is subjected to verification and scrutiny by others in the field, the Court of Appeals rejected petitioners' reanalyses as "unpublished, not subjected to the normal peer review process and generated solely for use in litigation." The court concluded that petitioners' evidence provided an insufficient foundation to allow admission of expert testimony that Bendectin caused their injuries and, accordingly, that petitioners could not satisfy their burden of proving causation at trial. ...

In the 70 years since its formulation in the *Frye* case, the "general acceptance" test has been the dominant standard for determining the admissibility of novel scientific evidence at trial. Although under increasing attack of late, the rule continues to be followed by a majority of courts, including the Ninth Circuit. ...

The merits of the *Frye* test have been much debated, and scholarship on its proper scope and application is legion. Petitioners' primary attack, however, is not on the content but on the continuing authority of the rule. They contend that the *Frye* test was superseded by the adoption of the Federal Rules of Evidence. We agree.

We interpret the legislatively-enacted Federal Rules of Evidence as we would any statute. Rule 402 provides the baseline: "All relevant evidence is admissible, except as otherwise provided by the Constitution of the United States, by Act of Congress, by these rules, or by other rules prescribed by the Supreme Court pursuant to statutory authority. Evidence which is not relevant is not admissible." "Relevant evidence" is defined as that which has "any tendency to make the existence of any fact that is of consequence to the determination of the action more probable or less probable than it would be without the evidence." Rule 401. The Rule's basic standard of relevance thus is a liberal one. ...

Here there is a specific Rule [702] that speaks to the contested issue. [See text above]. Nothing in the text of this Rule establishes "general acceptance" as an absolute prerequisite to admissibility. Nor does respondent present any clear indication that Rule 702 or the Rules as a whole were intended to incorporate a "general acceptance" standard. The drafting history makes no mention of *Frye*, and a rigid "general acceptance" requirement would be at odds with the "liberal thrust" of the Federal Rules and their "general approach of relaxing the traditional barriers to 'opinion' testimony." Given the Rules' permissive backdrop and their inclusion of a specific rule on expert testimony that does not mention "general acceptance," the assertion that the Rules somehow assimilated *Frye* is unconvincing. *Frye* made 'general acceptance' the exclusive test for admitting expert scientific testimony. That austere standard, absent from and incompatible with the Federal Rules of Evidence, should not be applied in federal trials.

That the *Frye* test was displaced by the Rules of Evidence does not mean, however, that the Rules themselves place no limits on the admissibility of purportedly scientific evidence. Nor is the trial judge disabled from screening such evidence. To the contrary, under the Rules the trial judge must ensure that any and all scientific testimony or evidence admitted is not only relevant, but reliable.

The primary locus of this obligation is Rule 702, which clearly contemplates some degree of regulation of the subjects and theories about which an expert may testify. "If scientific, technical, or other specialized knowledge will assist the trier of fact to understand the evidence or to determine a fact in issue," an expert "may testify thereto." The subject of an expert's testimony must be "scientific...knowledge." The adjective "scientific" implies a grounding in the methods and procedures of science. Similarly, the word "knowledge" connotes more than subjective belief or unsupported speculation. The term "applies to any body of known facts or to any body of ideas inferred from such facts or accepted as truths on good grounds." Webster's Third New International Dictionary 1252 (1986). Of course, it would be unreasonable to conclude that the subject of scientific testimony must be "known" to a certainty; arguably, there are no certainties in science. But, in order to qualify as "scientific knowledge," an inference or assertion must be derived by the scientific method. Proposed testimony must be supported by appropriate validation — i.e., "good grounds," based on what is known. In short, the requirement that an expert's testimony pertain to "scientific knowledge" establishes a standard of evidentiary reliability.

Rule 702 further requires that the evidence or testimony "assist the trier of fact to understand the evidence or to determine a fact in issue." This condition goes primarily to relevance....

That these requirements are embodied in Rule 702 is not surprising. Unlike an ordinary witness an expert is permitted wide latitude to offer opinions, including those that are not based on first-hand knowledge or observation. Presumably, this relaxation of the usual requirement of first-hand knowledge — a rule which represents "a 'most pervasive manifestation' of the common law insistence upon 'the most reliable sources of information,' " Advisory Committee's Notes on Fed.Rule Evid. 602 — is premised on an assumption that the expert's opinion will have a reliable basis in the knowledge and experience of his discipline.

Faced with a proffer of expert scientific testimony, then, the trial judge must determine at the outset, pursuant to Rule 104(a), whether the expert is proposing to testify to (1) scientific knowledge that (2) will assist the trier of fact to understand or determine a fact in issue. This entails a preliminary assessment of whether the reasoning or methodology underlying the testimony is scientifically valid and of whether that reasoning or methodology properly can be applied to the facts in issue. We are confident that federal judges possess the capacity to undertake this review. Many factors will bear on the inquiry, and we do not presume to set out a definitive checklist or test. But some general observations are appropriate.

Ordinarily, a key question to be answered in determining whether a theory or technique is scientific knowledge that will assist the trier of fact will be whether it can be (and has been) tested. "Scientific methodology today is based on generating hypotheses and testing them to see if they can be falsified; indeed, this methodology is what distinguishes science from other fields of human inquiry."

Another pertinent consideration is whether the theory or technique has been subjected to peer review and publication. Publication (which is but one element of peer review) is not a *sine qua non* of admissibility; it does not necessarily correlate with reliability, and in some instances well-grounded but innovative theories will not have been published. Some propositions, moreover, are too particular, too new, or of too limited interest to be published. But submission to the scrutiny of the scientific community is a component of "good science," in part because it increases the likelihood that substantive flaws in methodology will be detected. The fact of publication (or lack thereof) in a peer-reviewed journal thus will be a relevant, though not dispositive, consideration in assessing the scientific validity of a particular technique or methodology on which an opinion is premised.

Additionally, in the case of a particular scientific technique, the court ordinarily should consider the known or potential rate of error, and the existence and maintenance of standards controlling the technique's operation.

Finally, "general acceptance" can yet have a bearing on the inquiry. A "reliability assessment does not require, although it does permit, explicit identification of a relevant scientific community and an express determination of a particular degree of acceptance within that community." Widespread acceptance can be an important factor in ruling particular evidence admissible, and "a known technique that has been able to attract only minimal support within the community," may properly be viewed with skepticism.

The inquiry envisioned by Rule 702 is, we emphasize, a flexible one. Its overarching subject is the scientific validity — and thus the evidentiary relevance and reliability — of the principles that underlie a proposed submission. The focus, of course, must be solely on principles and methodology, not on the conclusions that they generate.

Throughout, a judge assessing a proffer of expert scientific testimony under Rule 702 should also be mindful of other applicable rules. Rule 703 provides that expert opinions based on otherwise inadmissible hearsay are to be admitted only if the facts or data are "of a type reasonably relied upon by experts in the particular field in forming opinions or inferences upon the subject." Rule 706 allows the court at its discretion to procure the assistance of an expert of its own choosing. Finally, Rule 403 permits the exclusion of relevant evidence "if its probative value is substantially outweighed by the danger of unfair prejudice, confusion of the issues, or misleading the jury...." Judge Weinstein has explained: "Expert evidence can be both powerful and quite misleading because of the difficulty in evaluating it. Because of this risk, the judge in weighing possible prejudice against probative force under Rule 403 of the present rules exercises more control over experts than over lay witnesses."

We conclude by briefly addressing what appear to be two underlying concerns of the parties and amici in this case. Respondent expresses apprehension that abandonment of "general acceptance" as the exclusive requirement for admission will result in a "free-for-all" in which befuddled juries are confounded by absurd and irrational pseudoscientific assertions. In this regard respondent seems to us to be overly pessimistic about the capabilities of the jury, and of the adversary system generally. Vigorous cross-examination, presentation of contrary evidence, and careful instruction on the burden of proof are the traditional and appropriate means of attacking shaky but admissible evidence....These conventional devices, rather than wholesale exclusion under an uncompromising "general acceptance" test, are the appropriate safeguards where the basis of scientific testimony meets the standards of Rule 702.

Petitioners and, to a greater extent, their amici exhibit a different concern. They suggest that recognition of a screening role for the judge that allows for the exclusion of "invalid" evidence will sanction a stifling and repressive scientific orthodoxy and will be inimical to the search for truth. It is true that open debate is an essential part of both legal and scientific analyses. Yet there are important differences between the quest for truth in the courtroom and the quest for truth in the laboratory. Scientific conclusions are subject to perpetual revision. Law, on the other hand, must resolve disputes finally and quickly. The scientific project is advanced by broad and wide-ranging consideration of a multitude of hypotheses, for those that are incorrect will eventually be shown to be so, and that in itself is an advance. Conjectures that are probably wrong are of little use, however, in the project of reaching a quick, final, and binding legal judgment — often of great consequence — about a particular set of events in the past. We recognize that in practice, a gatekeeping role for the judge, no matter how flexible, inevitably on occasion will prevent the jury from learning of authentic insights and innovations. That, nevertheless, is the balance that is struck by Rules of Evidence designed not for the exhaustive search for cosmic understanding but for the particularized resolution of legal disputes.

To summarize: "general acceptance" is not a necessary precondition to the admissibility of scientific evidence under the Federal Rules of Evidence, but the Rules of Evidence — especially Rule 702 — do assign to the trial judge the task of ensuring that an expert's testimony both rests on a reliable foundation and is relevant to the task at hand. Pertinent evidence based on scientifically valid principles will satisfy those demands.

The inquiries of the District Court and the Court of Appeals focused almost exclusively on "general acceptance," as gauged by publication and the decisions of other courts. Accordingly, the judgment of the Court of Appeals is vacated and the case is remanded for further proceedings consistent with this opinion. It is so ordered.

## COMMENTARY & QUESTIONS

1. **What did *Daubert* decide?** Apart from holding that *Frye* is not controlling in the wake of Evidence Rule 702, can you isolate the meaning of *Daubert*? What seems to emerge is a requirement that the judge must employ discretion to insure that scientific evidence is sufficiently reliable, and that there are a number of non-exclusive factors to be considered in making that decision, but the factors, including general acceptance, certainly do resemble the *Frye* rule. *Daubert* does not confront the basic problem that civil suits are based on preponderance and science is based on something very different — resembling criminal law's "beyond a reasonable doubt."

2. **Is *Daubert* a plaintiff's victory?** On remand, what outcome would you predict? The plaintiffs' eight experts were characterized by the Supreme Court as being possessed of "impressive credentials," yet their reanalysis of the epidemiological data was unpublished and did not fit the orthodox interpretation given to that data by the defendant's expert and the literature in the field. Even if the remand does not result in admission of the proffered testimony in *Daubert*, isn't it fairly clear that toxic tort plaintiffs, in general, are far better off having the *Frye* "generally accepted" test declared dead and buried, at least in litigation conducted in federal court? To answer this question, it is good to recall the role played by summary judgment in the litigation process.

The standard for the grant of summary judgment requires that there be no genuine issue of material fact and that the party seeking summary judgment is entitled to judgment as a matter of law. See generally, Federal Rule of Civil Procedure 56. The basic idea is that cases presenting no honestly debatable issue of fact should not be tried. Berry v. Armstrong Rubber Co., discussed in the next note, fits this mold. In that case plaintiffs' experts' testimony was ruled inadmissible. As a result, there remained no credible evidence to support plaintiffs' affirmative case on causation and damage, so the court ruled that there was no genuine issue of material fact that could be tried to a jury, and granted the motion for summary judgment, thereby preventing a jury from hearing the case at all.

Preventing jury consideration is widely thought to have a major influence on outcomes. Tactically, once a toxic tort case is permitted to be decided by the jury, (i.e., where the judge allows the jury to hear and evaluate the weight of the testimony offered by the plaintiffs' experts on the liability and causation issues) the frequently sympathetic nature of the cases (innocent and badly injured victim suing a deep pocket corporate defendant), makes defending the case very problematic for the defendant and ripe for settlement.

3. **Daubert and bad expert testimony.** Will *Daubert* change the result in cases where the testimony of plaintiffs' experts is unconvincing? Cases that rely on bad expert testimony should, and do, and probably will continue to lose. One recent example of this is Berry v. Armstrong Rubber Co., 989 F.2d 822 (5th Cir. 1993). In consolidated cases plaintiffs sought recoveries for reduced property values traceable to defendant's long term waste disposal practices as well as for personal injuries caused by exposure to contaminated drinking water. The Fifth Circuit upheld defendant's summary judgment because of the inadequacy of plaintiff's expert testimony. More specifically, the exclusion of expert testimony under Federal Rule of Evidence 703 was held proper where the experts testified in areas in which they were not qualified, offering opinions that were not based on tests that they had performed, or using data and methodology that were not recognized by other experts in the field. For example, significant portions of the testimony were based on data developed at locations other than the plaintiffs' property; the plaintiffs' property was not itself tested. Another expert's testimony (that of Nolan Augenbaugh of the *Wilsonville* case) was held properly rejected because it rested on an assumption that groundwater flowed toward plaintiffs' land, despite the lack of any testing by plaintiffs to substantiate that claim and the presence of EPA testing that showed the groundwater flowed in the opposite direction. Correspondingly, medical experts' testimony that relied on Augenbaugh's conclusions about the level of contaminants present at the plaintiffs' property, were likewise unfounded. For a recent United States Supreme Court decision reemphasizing the trial court's function as gatekeeper with regard to the reliability of scientific evidence, see General Electric Co. v. Joiner, 118 S.Ct. 512 (1997)(reversing circuit court and upholding district court's exclusion of questionable toxicological and epidemiological evidence).

4. **Distinguishing innovative explanations of causation from junk science.** Peter Huber, whose excerpt in Chapter Two advocated increased acceptance of public risk, has also written a major article on this subject, Medical Experts and the Ghost of Galileo, 54 Law & Contemporary Problems 119 (1991). In that article, he argues

that there are virtually no "Galileos" serving as experts in toxic tort and product liability litigation. The credible scientific discoveries, the ones that identify "real risks," were not ones made and brought to light in the crucible of litigation. Rather, Huber traces the history of scientific evidence that supported liability in regard to asbestos, the Ford Pinto, the Dalkon Shield, Rely tampons, DES, and thalidomide to typical sources within the accepted scientific community — traditional epidemiological research and inquiries prompted and followed up on by administrative agencies concerned with public safety. In contrast, Huber tells the story of incorrect conclusions reached by researchers into traumatic cancer (claims that traumatic injury causes cancer) and cerebral palsy, as cautionary vignettes. He uses these examples to urge the legal system to be wary of the "post hoc fallacy" that arises when researchers seek to identify causes after first observing the result. He criticizes the effort of researchers who observed cancers and thereafter linked them to histories of trauma. He makes his point by repeating one scientist's pithy observation, "Because toads appear after a rain it is not necessary to assume that it has rained toads."[22] Surely, this criticism cuts too broadly, but it should sound a cautionary note. Is Huber correct in asserting that the legal system functions best when it follows scientific discovery rather than getting out ahead of it?

5. **The complex but necessary interplay between science and the courts.** In her significant book Science at the Bar: Law, Science, and Technology in America (1995), Professor Sheila Jasanoff argues that science and the legal process are inextricably interconnected:

> The central argument regarding toxic torts is that legally compelling knowledge about toxic properties of chemicals arises not from science alone but through complex interactions between adjudication and scientific activity. Mainstream science does not exist in a pure cognitive domain that courts can reach into at will. Like all other human knowledge, mainstream science is made, and it is made in part through the incremental efforts of the legal system to acquire relevant knowledge. However, to admit this is not to deny that there are defects in the traditional approach to litigating scientific uncertainty: the sometimes gross mismatch between scientific and judicial appraisals of credibility, the often ill-motivated efforts to fit scientific claims to legal concepts of causation, and the discrepant and idiosyncratic results reached in science-intensive litigation in different jurisdictions.

> The belief that mainstream science can dispel most of the legal system's problems in handling sociotechnical conflicts rests upon two fundamental misconceptions about the links between scientific and legal decisionmaking. First, good science is not a commodity that courts can conveniently shop for in some extrasocietal marketplace of pure knowledge. Second, scientific closure and legal controversy do not stand in a predictably linear chronological relationship. Disagreement is endemic in science, and knowledge claims as often as not remain open-ended within the scientific community at times when they must be subjected to further testing in court. Jasanoff, at pages 137, 207.

In the wake of *Daubert*, Professor Jasanoff recommends "educat[ing] judges, lawyers, and scientific experts in each other's modes of reasoning and discourse" (p. 68).

---

22. 54 Law & Contemp. Probs. at 160, quoting Fred W. Stewart, Occupational and Post-Traumatic Cancer, 23 Bull. New York Academy of Medicine 145 (1947).

6. **Administrative agencies and "good science."** Professor Jasanoff's insight that good science is not always readily identifiable is exemplified by the case of Sierra Club v. Marita, 46 F.3d 606 (7th Cir. 1995). Plaintiff conservation groups sued the United States Forest Service, seeking to enjoin timber harvesting, road construction, and the creation of wildlife openings in two national forests in northern Wisconsin. In effect, plaintiffs argued that the Forest Service had violated the National Forest Management Act and the National Environmental Policy Act[23] by utilizing "bad science" in developing its Land and Resource Management Plans for the forests. Plaintiffs alleged that the Forest Service had used scientifically unsupported techniques to address biodiversity concerns in its management plans, and had arbitrarily disregarded certain principles of conservation biology in developing those plans. In particular, the Forest Service's approach allegedly generated a plan that tended to allow extensive fragmentation of the forests into small patches, in contravention of the "large block" approach of conservation biology. The court affirmed the district court's granting of summary judgment to defendant Forest Service:

> The Service is entitled to use its own methodology, unless it is irrational.... The Service developed an appropriate method of analyzing diversity. The Sierra Club is correct that the Service did not employ conservation biology in its final analysis. However, the Service appropriately considered conservation biology and ultimately determined that science to be uncertain in application.... We cannot conclude from the record that the Service acted irrationally.

> In supporting the Sierra Club's allegation that the Service used "bad" science, amici Society for Conservation Biology and the American Institute of Biological Sciences have suggested that we borrow the Supreme Court's test for admissibility of scientific expert testimony as set forth in [Daubert] as a way of determining whether the Service's scientific assertions are owed any deference under NEPA. We decline the suggestion. While such a proposal might assure better documentation of an agency's scientific decisions, we think that forcing an agency to make such a showing as a general rule is intrusive, undeferential, and not required. An EIS is designed to ensure open and honest debate of the environmental consequences of an agency action, not to prove admissibility of testimony in a court of law. Marita, 46 F.3d at 621.

Clearly, the "arbitrary and capricious" doctrine of administrative law (see Chapter Seven), and the judicial deference to agency decisions that it symbolizes, gives a reviewing court a much less significant "gatekeeper" role, with regard to scientific information, than that performed by a common law court in a toxic tort case.

7. ***Daubert*'s progeny.** Approximately half of the state court systems still follow the *Frye* rule, instead of adopting the United States Supreme Court's rule in *Daubert*. With regard to the federal courts, one commentator describes the aftermath of *Daubert* as follows:

> An examination of post-*Daubert* cases reveals mixed results regarding the ability of trial judges to cope with *Daubert*. In a positive trend, *Daubert*'s mandate to focus on the underlying methodology employed by experts is clearly getting through to the lower courts. Expert opinion testimony that is entirely unsub-

---

23. The National Environmental Policy Act (NEPA) requires a federal agency proposing to undertake a major action that might have a significant impact on the human environment to prepare and circulate an Environmental Impact Statement before proceeding to implement its proposal. See Chapter 13.

stantiated by relevant scientific research has been excluded as being essentially per se inadmissible by most federal courts. Likewise, when an expert's methodology is generally accepted by the relevant scientific community for a particular purpose, courts have admitted the testimony. When a scientific claim is not unsubstantiated and there are a few, not easily reconcilable scientific studies, the disputes in the scientific literature are also played out in court. Judges are thus forced to apply the gatekeeper factors and review the expert's methodology, and the results are less encouraging. Courts have taken one of two approaches in this situation. Some courts perform a gatekeeping analysis and at times reach conflicting conclusions about the admissibility of similar sorts of evidence. But some courts simply duck the first prong of Daubert and exclude the evidence as being unhelpful or insufficient....

It is clear that trial judges do not enjoy their assignments under *Daubert*. Courts employ a gamut of proxies and distinctions to get around the first prong of *Daubert*. Some of the common ones are: classifying scientific evidence as not being novel to circumvent *Daubert*; finding scientific evidence to be insufficient without addressing admissibility; reclassifying expert testimony as not relating to a science; and declaring proferred expert testimony to be lay opinion. In addition, courts continue to rely on other judicial opinions without ascertaining whether those opinions were based on a *Daubert*-like admissibility inquiry.... Theoretically, *Daubert* is an eclectic solution to expert testimony on scientific matters. Practically, however, by replacing *Frye* with *Daubert*, the Court traded one set of problems for another.... Perhaps in the future we might even decide that *Daubert* is unworkable and revert to a well-defined substantial or general acceptance standard. But the need of the hour is greater consistency and guidance in the application of *Daubert*. Kesan, An Autopsy of Scientific Evidence in a post-*Daubert* World, 84 Geo. L. J. 1985, 2007–2008, 2040 (1996).

## D. LITIGATING TOXIC TORT CASES

The common law put down its roots in an age where its rigid formal procedures could be applied in lawsuits that might be described as simple binary litigation: one plaintiff, one defendant. The litigation was also bi-polar, having two clearly defined sides on the pivotal issue. Outcomes were likewise all-or-nothing; the plaintiff would either recover fully, or not at all. Traditionally, the rigid formalities of English law required the parties to select a single form of action (such as trespass), and thereafter reduce their dispute to a single contested issue (such as whether the emissions of the defendant were the cause-in-fact of the plaintiff's injury). Through intricate and bewildering pleading devices, all other issues were removed from the lawsuit. The rigidity was not a problem in most cases because in a simpler era most tort victims were injured in discrete events, involving clear direct injury to at most a few people at a time. Toxic torts, however, are often mass torts of staggering complexity, often with multiple defendants and involving large classes of victims. Examples include asbestos exposure as in the *Fischer* case in Chapter Three or the *Landrigan* case above, where literally millions of people may have suffered serious harm; pesticide and herbicide spraying as in the Agent Orange cases;[24] atmospheric nuclear testing in Nevada (Allen v. United States); and

---

24. See P. Schuck, Agent Orange on Trial: Mass Toxic Disasters in the Courts (1988).

all persons who drank water from contaminated public wells (Anderson v. W. R. Grace & Co. and Ayers v. Jackson Township). With their multiplicity of claims and proof of remote causation for long-latent disease, those cases present serious questions about the transaction costs of extended litigation, about defendants' ability to pay, and about the fairness of compensating victims far removed from defendant's action.

Courts have responded to the challenges of complex litigation through procedural innovation. In the environmental law context, the impact of changes in procedure has been absolutely essential to the emergence of meaningful common law remedies for injuries caused by both conventional and toxic tort. The complexity of many environmental cases as to matters of fact, issues of causation, measurement of damage, etc., would have been virtually impossible to litigate in a meaningful fashion without a procedural system that allowed for the concurrent pleading and proof of many theories and issues. Additionally, the advent of procedural devices allowing joinder of claims and joinder of parties has allowed a would-be plaintiff in a case involving great legal difficulty and expense to pool resources with other plaintiffs facing the same problem.[25]

When a toxic substance has entered the environment and when large numbers of potential plaintiffs have been exposed to it, sometimes on a nationwide scale, serious logistical problems confront the legal system. Many of the issues of liability, defenses, and proof will be exactly the same in hundreds and thousands of cases; to litigate them separately or even state by state would be wastefully redundant. Other issues may, however, be highly particular to individual plaintiffs. Litigation costs to plaintiffs and defendants alike become astronomical, and themselves become part of the tactical setting.

Compare an air pollution nuisance case of the *Boomer* variety. In that case as litigated, only a small number of individuals sued, each claiming a number of thousands of dollars in damages. They were all aided in their efforts to force the cement company to pay for their damage by the fact that their individual cost of seeking a remedy was reduced by the sharing of litigation expenses with their co-plaintiffs. As litigated, however, the *Boomer* case probably did not go as far in this direction as possible. There were numerous individuals owning land at a slightly greater remove from the cement plant who suffered lesser degrees of intrusion with their quiet enjoyment of their property. While the law of nuisance at some point says insubstantial loss of quiet enjoyment is not a violation of legal rights because the degree of interference is not unreasonable, it remains quite likely that many people suffering unreasonable interference with quiet enjoyment did not sue because the amount of their individual recovery would not justify the expense and hassle of pursuing the litigation. These people may choose to sue later,[26] but they may not.

---

25. In the American legal system, usually, absent special equitable considerations or legislation, each party must pay its own attorneys fees and expert witness fees.

26. Subsequent plaintiffs in some cases will benefit by the *Boomer* court's findings. This will depend on their ability to invoke the doctrine of collateral estoppel without mutuality of estoppel. Such parties are "free riders" on Boomer's efforts, but their recovery extends the sum of costs internalized by legal action.

Institutionally for the court system, efficiency would be better served if there is only one lawsuit on behalf of all of the victims of the pollution, rather than in multiple lawsuits. In joined or class actions, the court's workload is reduced because the basic underlying facts have to be resolved only once. Economic efficiency is also served because composite lawsuits internalize a greater portion of the costs of the pollution. See Wright, The Cost-Internalization Case for Class Actions, 21 Stan. L. Rev. 383 (1969).

Toxic torts are frequently ideal candidates for joined litigation because they are often mass torts: large numbers of individuals injured through the same pattern of events. One generic pattern involves a toxic release (or a series of releases) that exposes a community to hazardous materials. To some degree, that was the backdrop of the *Kepone* case. Two cases considered in this chapter, Anderson v. W.R. Grace & Co. and Ayers v. Jackson Township, also fit that pattern. In these cases, the impetus to group litigation lies both in the commonality of the questions presented for legal resolution and in the economies of scale obtained by pooling resources for litigation.

Modern procedure offers the class action device as an opportunity for bringing all pollution or toxic tort victims into a single lawsuit. In class actions, a large class of persons who are similarly situated in regard to the dispute being litigated are represented in litigation by a single member of the class or by a small group drawn from the class. The procedural rules governing class actions go to considerable lengths to insure full and fair representation of the members of the class. Rule 23 of the Federal Rules of Civil Procedure is the most prominent of the class action rules, operative in all federal court litigation, and serving as a model for the procedural rules of many of the states.

Most environmental class actions are litigated under the following two provisions of Rule 23:

> (b)(2) the party opposing the class has acted or refused to act on grounds generally applicable to the class, thereby making appropriate final injunctive relief or corresponding declaratory relief with respect to the class as a whole; or

> (b)(3) the court finds that the questions of law or fact common to the members of the class predominate over any questions affecting only individual members, and that a class action is superior to other available methods for the fair and efficient adjudication of the controversy.

The court exercises considerable control over cases that are maintained as a class action. The court decides whether the class action device is appropriate and must consider factors such as the ability of the class representative fully and fairly to represent the class, the interest of individual class member plaintiffs in controlling the prosecution of their own claims, the desirability of concentrating the litigation in a single court and, perhaps most importantly for mass toxic tort cases, "the difficulties likely to be encountered in the management of a class action."

Imagine, for example, the difficulty of a trial that seeks to present all of the health related claims arising from the widespread use of asbestos as insulating material in this country.[27] Who are the plaintiffs? Looking narrowly, the group still includes millions of construction workers, some who have contracted forms of cancer, others who have not, but who are now at far greater risk of developing cancer in the future. Who are the defendants? This second group, again looking narrowly, includes the hundreds (perhaps thousands) of companies that produced and distributed asbestos. Some of these companies were long aware of the harmful nature of contact with the product and concealed that fact, others may have been unaware. And what are the damages? And who is responsible for what share of the damages? And which particular defendant's product caused which particular plaintiff's injury when so much of the material was of a generic type that might be impossible to identify many years after the exposure to the asbestos?

The inescapable conclusion, considering that manageability is an element in class action suitability, is that no one class action can possibly take on so massive a problem, and that class action treatment may be inappropriate generally. Attempts to set up an alternative system with a special fund and arbitrational tribunal for asbestos claims (the "Wellington Agreement") have not succeeded either. While the asbestos problem is close to unique in its scale, it is not unique in displaying horrific manageability problems.

Environmental lawyers have become inventive and adaptive in using various procedural devices to overcome the manageability problems incident to the multiparty nature of many toxic tort cases. Where class actions are likely to be unmanageable, for example, the plaintiffs have in some cases opted to select "flagship" plaintiffs. These plaintiffs are similar to those who would have been selected as class representatives — their claims are among the most typical. If they win, the understanding, made clear to the defendant, is that other claims will follow.[28] At times, courts will require these later lawsuits to relitigate the disputed issues from scratch; other courts will allow later cases to make collateral use of determinations that were squarely faced in the earlier lawsuit.[29]

---

27. See, e.g., Jenkins v. Raymark Industries, 782 F.2d 468 (5th Cir. 1986). In *Jenkins*, the Court of Appeals approved trial court certification of a district-wide class action (the judicial district covered a part of Texas) to determine certain issues of liability against thirteen defendant asbestos manufacturers. The class, at the time of certification, included over 1,000 plaintiffs and continued to grow as asbestos-related disease manifested itself in additional exposed victims. Of course, if trial of an asbestos case like *Jenkins* appears daunting, consider the alternative of having that same trial 1,000+ times over! The total number of American workers exposed to asbestos was estimated by the *Jenkins* court to be "at least 21 million."

28. An interesting decision has just come out of the Fifth Circuit involving case mangement in complex toxic tort litigation. In Re Chevron U.S.A. Inc., 44 ERC 1890 (1997), the court discussed the differences between "non-elastic" and "elastic" mass torts in the context of deciding how to choose "bellwether" (flagship) plaintiffs in a mass groundwater pollution suit.

29. The use of the results in prior litigation to foreclose relitigation of claims or issues — res judicata — is subdivided into two branches, one that prevents the relitigation of entire claims (merger and bar) and another that prevents the relitigation of previously decided issues (collateral estoppel). In the successful flagship plaintiff toxic tort setting, later plaintiffs who were not parties of record in the first lawsuit would seek issue-preclusion against defendant on issues such as causation, or liability for the toxic release. The term that describes this use of the results of prior litigation by a second plaintiff against the common defendant is "offensive use of collateral estoppel without mutuality of estoppel." The leading federal case on the subject is Parklane Hosiery Co. v. Shore, 439 U.S. 322 (1979).

### COMMENTARY AND QUESTIONS

1. **Multiparty litigation as a cure for access bias.** Recall the concept of access bias raised by Professors Gillette and Krier in Chapter Two. In their view, deserving cases challenging defendants who create public risks are often deterred from even entering the judicial system by barriers to entry. Class actions and flagship lawsuits are among the tools that reduce access bias against those who seek to internalize costs that are externalized by public risk creators. Leaving a more particularized answer for courses in complex litigation, do class actions and other forms of representative litigation seem likely to overcome the problem of access bias in the toxic tort setting?

2. **The multiplier effect of multiparty litigation.** To a defendant, what is the impact of procedural devices that result in the joinder of multiple similar claims into a single lawsuit? One obvious result is that the amount at risk in the event of an award of damages may increase manyfold. In the toxic tort area, where the injuries are often serious, this may turn many cases into a "you bet your company" scenario. Is there anything unfair in this? In general, plaintiffs can be expected to meet any such claims by defendants by pointing out that the case arose only because the defendant's actions touched the lives of so many people. Can an individual plaintiff with a marginal case, by turning to a multiparty device, "extort" a handsome settlement of the case? Here it seems more plausible that defendants can make credible claims of unfairness. In this context the cost of responding to (or settling) marginal claims is a cost faced by virtually all enterprises, not just toxic tort defendants. What may be different in toxic tort cases is the cost, complexity, and uncertainty of maintaining a successful defense.

3. **The benefits of using multiparty devices.** There are ways in which the resort to multiparty litigation can make outcomes more just. Initially, to the extent that multiparty litigation reduces the need for repetitive litigation, the cost savings to the parties on both sides make the process preferable. There are at least two other settings in which having all of the claims joined in a single lawsuit holds a potential for making outcomes more just. On the plaintiffs' side, consider what happens when total liability exceeds a defendant's assets. If the litigation occurs in a piecemeal fashion, the early winners will collect their full damages, and later winners may find the defendant bankrupt and unable to pay any part of their claims. If the litigation all takes place in a single lawsuit, the proceeds can be placed in a common fund that is allocated in proportion to the individual entitlements of every deserving party. On the defendants' side, consider punitive damages. Assume that the conduct involved is such that punitive damages are awarded. If the litigation is piecemeal, punitive damages may be imposed numerous times, by numerous juries, each failing to take full account of what other punitive damages have been imposed. If only a single lawsuit is involved, a one-time-for-all award would more accurately measure the extent of punishment that should be imposed on the defendant. As Judge Clifford noted later in the *Fischer* asbestos case, "Perhaps the most likely solution to the problem of cumulative punitive damages lies in the use of a class action for those damages."

4. **Settlements.** In settling class action litigation, the judge has a special responsibility under FRCP 23(e) to insure that the settlement is fair to the non-party class members. For a case in which that power was used to reject a settlement, with the result that the parties reached a "fairer" result, see Shults v. Champion International Corp., 821 F.Supp. 520 (E.D. Tenn. 1993).

5. **Discovery issues.** The judge in the Woburn case repeatedly refused to allow plaintiffs to test for contamination on the site of the tannery itself and in its disposal lagoons, restricting testing to the wetland parcel downhill from the tannery. It is not clear why this ruling was made. Initially Beatrice's attorneys appeared to resist tannery investigation on the ground that the tannery had been reconveyed back to John Riley and was no longer owned by them. Later the rationale appears to have been that plaintiffs had based their case primarily on the wetland parcel, which they knew to be contaminated, not the tannery for which they had little information. One valid purpose of discovery, however, is to allow plaintiffs to investigate sources of contamination (that they have good faith reason to believe are sources, such as the lagoons behind the tannery, see map) in order to build a case. In the event, Beatrice took advantage of the exclusion to excavate and clean up the tannery site, including the lagoon areas.[30] Later the judge appears to have relented, if plaintiffs would use an expert of his choosing, but plaintiffs rejected that belated compromise. In other toxic tort cases discovery has been complex and inventive, including the use of physical experimentation on defendants' land, tracing of smokestack emissions via isotopes, or dye markers in groundwater as in Chapter Two's *Wilsonville* case, and the like. For plaintiffs the trick often has been to find probative evidence that can be obtained without great cost.

6. **Novel civil procedure: "polyfurcation."** The major issues of the Woburn toxics case in *Anderson* never went to trial, because the judge in February, 1986, split the case into four sequential phases. Under FRCP 42(b), a judge may phase a trial in the interests of efficiency, so basic questions, like liability, are raised and litigated first in a separate trial; then consequential issues, like remedies, are litigated as necessary. The Woburn judge, however, split the liability issue itself three ways. He set Phase 1 to determine whether defendants' contaminants ever reached the public wells, Phase 2 on causation of leukemia, Phase 3 on causation of other injuries to other family members, and Phase 4 on damages. Only the first phase ever went to trial, limited to the question of liability for groundwater flow. Plaintiffs' attorneys generally oppose such multiple phasing because it "cuts the heart out" of the continuity of the story they are trying to present to the jury. The Woburn jury nevertheless came in with a verdict against defendant Grace in Phase 1, and Grace quickly settled for $8 million. Does that outcome reinforce the rationale for phasing, or support the plaintiffs' fear of dilution? See Bedecarré, Polyfurcation of

---

30. The closest plaintiffs came to testing on the tannery site, according to plaintiffs' attorney, was the day Schlichtmann played Ivahoe: when a phone call from a neighbor told him the tannery land was being bulldozed, he raced off to a hardware store, bought a long piece of half-inch conduit pipe and drove to the site holding the pipe out the window of his girlfriend's Dodge like a knight charging with a lance. Thrusting the pipe through the security fence into a pile of excavated sludge, he was able to retrieve a plug of material from the site before a guard came rushing to intercept him. Although the sample proved to contain traces of the solvents, he was not able to introduce it at trial. This scene, inexplicably, didn't make it into book or movie.

Liability Issues in Environmental Tort Cases, 17 Envtl. Aff. L. Rev. 123 (1989), and Smith, Polyfurcation...in the Woburn case, 25 Envtl. Aff. L. Rev 649 (1998).

7. **Special jury questions.** The Woburn plaintiffs' case encountered another tactical disadvantage when the judge required the jury in the Phase 1 trial, instead of simply bringing in a simple verdict on whether the defendants' contamination reached the wells or not, to specify the particular time at which each of four chemicals reached the wells. The questions were so complex that even the jury verdict against Grace was internally inconsistent, and jury members confessed their extreme confusion about the highly technical subquestions they were required to answer. See Pacelle, Contaminated Verdict, The American Lawyer 75 (Dec. 1986); cf. Brodin, Accuracy, Efficiency, and Accountability in the Litigation Process: The Case for the Fact Verdict, 59 U. Cin. L. Rev. 15 (1990). (Confronted with the inconsistencies in the Woburn jury's answers, the judge overturned the verdict and ordered a new trial. Grace's decision, after weighing its options, to settle for $8 million, came the same day despite the overturned verdict.)

8. **The "highly extraordinary" defense, and its evidentiary consequences.** A critical legal ruling, not noted in the Woburn case's popular chronicles, was an application of Restatement 2d Torts §435(2)'s "highly extraordinary" excuse. Section 435(2) allows a judge to excuse liability where "looking back from the harm to the actor's negligent conduct, it appears to the court highly extraordinary that it should have brought about the harm." This grant of discretion to the trial judge was designed to nullify liability where the chains of causation are extremely improbable in statistical terms, as in the classic case of Palsgraf v. Long Island R. Co., 162 N.E. 99 (N.Y. 1928). Under Restatement §435, foreseeability is not the issue; rather it is a response to very unlikely Palsgrafian combinations of coincidence in a chain of causation. In the Woburn case, however, the judge used §435(2) to excuse the Beatrice tannery on foreseeability grounds from any liability prior to the time when it was told by an engineer that the groundwater under its property flowed laterally 800 feet, under the Aberjona stream, to the public wells. The judge said it was extraordinary to him that groundwater can flow laterally under a stream. How does this square with Professor Davis' analysis in footnote 6 in the Branch, in Chapter Three, which implies that long distance groundwater pollution flow is in fact not extraordinary? Scientifically, it is axiomatic under the laws of physics that pollutants would be drawn, along with the groundwater, under the creek and to the wells from a broad radius including the tannery's lowland parcel. The evidentiary effects of this ruling were dramatic. Although there was extensive evidence that contaminants came to the wells from Beatrice's property in the same way as from Grace, a point echoed in government assessments of cleanup liability against both, the judge told the jury that it had to ignore prior passage of contaminants from Beatrice's land. Beatrice could be held liable only for flows after the engineer's notice. The jury decided that with the evidence thus restricted it could not make the required specialized timing findings for chemical exposure in Beatrice's narrowed window of liability, and the case against Beatrice collapsed.

9. **Woburn's other evidentiary rulings.** The judge in *Anderson* made several other evidentiary rulings that were perplexing. At one point he substituted his own

observations for the testimony of chemists who had found tannery compounds in waste piles on the wetlands parcel: "I compared samples of this material with samples of tannery sludge both at the trial and during the recent hearings and found them totally different in color, consistency and odor." 127 F.R.D. 1 (1989). At the end of the trial he made another surprising finding in light of the established fact of groundwater flows to the wells: "In response to plaintiffs' post-verdict objection to the ambiguous form of the interrogatories, I made a finding of fact under FRCP 49(a): plaintiffs had not proven by a preponderance of the evidence that the complaint chemicals migrated to wells G and H." 129 F.R.D. 394 (1989) (This perhaps meant to say "within the time horizon I had set for liability under Restatement §435(2).")

10. **FRCP Rule 11 in the Woburn toxics case.** FRCP Rule 11, generally designed to police attorneys' ethical practice, waxes and wanes over the years. In toxic tort cases, including the Woburn case, Rule 11 motions often are made by defendants to challenge plaintiffs for proceeding without traditional proof of causation, when plaintiffs propose to prove their case based on statistical or circumstantial logic, or theories on the frontiers of science. In the *Anderson* case's first Rule 11 hearing, Judge Skinner ruled that plaintiffs had enough of a case on causation to proceed in good faith.

A second Rule 11 hearing, not noted in the movie, was more remarkable, putting the entire civil action into wry context. Shortly after losing the case against Beatrice, Schlictmann discovered by accident that although during discovery he had requested all data on tannery site contamination and had been told there was none, in fact two such reports existed. Known to the tannery attorneys, groundwater studies done in 1983 and 1985 showed the presence of several of the contaminants on the tannery site proper. Plaintiffs eagerly requested a retrial, arguing that these reports would have triggered greater scrutiny of the tannery, perhaps convincing the judge to allow them to test the tannery site and its lagoons. The judge's refusal to reopen the case was reversed and remanded by the First Circuit. Anderson v. Beatrice Foods Co., 862 F.2d 910 (1st Cir. 1988). On remand the judge made a finding of "deliberate misconduct" against Mr. Riley and his attorney (although refusing to allow Riley's counsel to introduce evidence implicating Beatrice's attorney in the coverup[31]).

Plaintiffs' expectations of a retrial against Beatrice, in which they hoped to overturn the key ruling under Restatement §435(2) narrowing the timeframe of the tannery's liability, were immediately dashed, however, by the judge's ruling sua sponte that plaintiffs, too, had committed an offsetting Rule 11 violation, so no new trial would be ordered:

---

31. "[Riley's attorney] came forward…with an affidavit asserting communications with defendant's attorneys never before revealed, said to be supported by no less than forty-one documents contradicting defendant's attorneys in several respects. No rule of due process that I know of permits an attorney…to withhold information until such time as it is to her advantage to reveal it…. Such a rule would put a premium on strategic concealment." 129 F.R.D. 394, 409. Plaintiffs, of course, were exasperated that this evidence of defendants' concealment would thus remain concealed, weakening plaintiffs' case for a retrial.

> The honors for sanctionable conduct are about evenly divided.... At least by the close of his investigation and discovery,...plaintiffs' counsel knew that there was no...basis in fact for the assertion that the defendant disposed of the complaint chemicals at the tannery site or on the 15 acres. 129 F.R.D. at 403.

After reviewing plaintiffs' investigative manual, the judge had decided that plaintiffs did not have enough evidence to proceed with the claim that the tannery had itself dumped contaminants. Offsetting Rule 11 sanctions meant that defendants won and plaintiffs lost. Schlictmann was apoplectic. The judge had discounted all the evidence of tannery-like wastes as insufficient to go to a jury. A jury, Schlichtmann believed, could easily have found direct tannery liability based on wastes in the ditch leading down from the tannery, and tannery wastes laced with solvents in the wetland. Moreover, the reason that plaintiffs had not gotten direct evidence of the tannery contamination was because defendants had unethically withheld the relevant reports, and because the judge had not permitted plaintiffs to go onto the tannery site with its old lagoon areas for investigation before the sites were cleaned up by defendants. Catch 22, said Schlichtmann: "I know the joy of a madman. He says *I* should be sanctioned!" The First Circuit declined to get back into this thicket, and a petition for certiorari to the Supreme Court was denied, 111 S. Ct. 233 (1990). See D'Imperio, An Analysis of the Rule 11 Sanction: Anderson v. Beatrice..., 25 Envtl. Aff. L. Rev. 619 (1998).

---

At the end of the Woburn tort case, one should ask whether the *Anderson* civil action shows the continued relevance and efficacy of tort law in toxic contamination situations, or the opposite. The plaintiffs recovered eight million dollars from Grace, and nothing from Beatrice. The trial cost plaintiffs more than two million dollars and defendants more than twice that amount. The actual determinations of fact in the litigation process were partial and some of them almost certainly were inaccurate. The government, as noted later in this chapter, had much more effective remedies available, and levied penalties of almost $70 million against the defendants. If there were no toxic tort actions available in the legal system in this case, or in general, would society be better off, or worse?

Does the account of the Woburn case give some indication of the enormous burdens imposed on plaintiffs trying to use the common law to redress their injuries in complex circumstances? As with all litigation, students must be reminded that a case does not develop and prove itself at trial. Each step of the litigation involves guesses and gambles, rationing of time and resources, choices made and viable options foregone. The actions of judges, not to mention attorneys and juries, are not necessarily predictable. Facts and procedural rulings can be slippery. Because of the burdens and complexities of the process, opportunities for appeal may offer no effective redress for mistakes. What ultimately emerges is a potpourri of happenstance that may or may not accord with one's sense of justice.

## E.  RELATIONSHIPS BETWEEN TOXIC TORT AND PUBLIC LAW

The common law's private remedies, of course, do not stand alone. Public law — governmental regulatory action — plays an even larger role in environmental law. Like many environmental issues, the mass toxic tort problem is simply too large for adequate control by after-the-fact damage suits and the rare injunction based on prospective nuisance.

The public law statute most readily applicable to the Woburn case was the Comprehensive Environmental Response, Compensation, and Liability Act (CERCLA, popularly known as Superfund), passed in 1980; a second major statute of potential applicability is RCRA, the Resource Conservation and Recovery Act. These are examined in Chapters 18 and 17 respectively. Both laws work to achieve cleanups of contaminated parcels. Neither grants private remedies for bodily injury or compensation for property damage, although CERCLA creates a private cause of action to obtain reimbursement for cleanup costs. On the governmental enforcement side, both laws allow the federal government to issue administrative orders requiring responsible parties to undertake cleanup, and CERCLA requires responsible parties in appropriate cases to pay damages to government for natural resource damages. RCRA also has elaborate requirements that seek to prevent releases of hazardous wastes into the environment in the first place, but events had moved far past that at Woburn by the time RCRA was enacted in 1976.

In the *Anderson* wellwater contamination case, as in many toxic tort controversies, both private law and public law ultimately played extensive roles. Private law and public law tend to be two different and uncoordinated worlds, both absorbing huge amounts of time and resources, and imposing major legal constraints on the industrial marketplace. Given the complex economic, political, and technical context, it is not surprising that systemic questions are constantly being raised whether the two legal régimes are redundant, and ought to be rationalized, most often by proposals for limiting or eliminating toxic tort litigation.

The Woburn case offers an opportunity to consider larger questions about the systemic role of tort civil actions against the backdrop of state and federal statutes and regulatory agencies. What observations can be drawn from the following partial chronology of the parallel processes in the Woburn case's public and private law? —

1979: Government agencies (the federal EPA, the state environmental agency, and the local health board) take the first legal actions after testing groundwater around the wellfield: they close the wells, fence the site, and identify potentially responsible parties (PRPs). In late 1981 the future plaintiffs ask CDC to study the seeming leukemia cluster.

1980: EPA began the Superfund process, doing site investigation and analysis of the need and method for remediation, under §§106 and 107 of CERCLA (a cleanup process that averages 12 years; see Chapter 18).

1980–81: Robbie Robbins, Jimmie Anderson, and Jarrod Aufiero died.

1981: Federal CDC affirms that leukemia cluster is extraordinary.

1982: Lawsuit filed; discovery and other extensive trial preparations begin; Schlichtmann and plaintiffs give presentation at Harvard School of Public

Health that prompts school to do a volunteer field study project.

1983–85: Plaintiffs' intensive investigation into medical causation of leukemias.

1984: CERCLA implementation process continues; Grace and Riley tell EPA they never used subject chemicals; Harvard Public Health Study published showing local health anomalies.

1985: Plaintiffs discover Al Love who reveals Grace's disposal practices. Plaintiffs' onsite testing accompanied by government investigators.

1986: Trial on exposure phase begins in February, verdict at end of July: plaintiffs proved Grace contaminated wells; cannot prove Beatrice's contamination. September: Grace settles for $8 million.

1987: Plaintiffs discover Yankee Report in EPA files in September, showing tannery contamination in test results.

1987–90: Plaintiffs appeal Beatrice verdict, and attempt to get a new trial to prove Beatrice's contamination. First Circuit refuses, cert. denied.

1988: EPA uses plaintiffs' evidence from Al Love to impose criminal perjury penalties on Grace.

1991: EPA and state agency settle with Beatrice and Grace for $69.5 million in cleanup costs, most of which is assessed against Beatrice. Remediation will take "several years."

1997: State Dept. of Public Health releases study concluding that the contaminated wellwater was the cause of increased likelihood of childhood leukemia in the plaintiffs' Woburn neighborhood.[32]

2000: Date of final remediation of contaminated land; groundwater not to be safe until 2020+....

## COMMENTARY AND QUESTIONS

1. **Did public law contribute to the private law civil action? and vice versa?** Looking at this chronology, one can ask, "to what degree, if any, did the parallel processes facilitate one another?" Were they at all coordinated, or were they moving on two quite separate tracks?

It is clear that EPA's initial studies helped to target plaintiffs' efforts, and the CDC's study confirmed the likelihood of wrongful causation of the leukemias. Governmental findings of cleanup liability might have helped prove some of the elements of tort liability, especially Beatrice's contamination of the wells, and improved the plaintiffs' momentum, but they were not finalized until five years after trial.[33] The state epidemiology study might have helped prove causation, but it was not completed until ten years after trial. During the tort litigation, as is so often the case, government staffers were hesitant to provide active aid to plaintiffs, who only by chance found the 1983 Yankee Report in EPA files.

Did the private litigation aid the government's efforts? Without the plaintiffs, the government agencies would probably never have discovered Al Love, whose testi-

---

32. Mass. Dept. Pub. Health, Bur. of Envtl Health assessment, Woburn Childhood Leukemia Follow-up Study (July 1997).

33. Tort plaintiffs often seek to go to trial after government has successfully prosecuted the same defendants for the same acts, riding the coattails of governmental findings of administrative liability or criminal penalties. A conviction or administrative penalty substantially aids private claims, but given uncoordinated statutes of limitations, the timing is often difficult.

mony about Grace's dumping produced criminal fines for perjury against the company. Government field investigators on several occasions lacked sufficient funds to do ongoing field studies, and requested permission to come along when plaintiffs hired backhoes to dig for evidence of contamination. Without the dramatic tort case, it is altogether likely the land and water would still ultimately reach the same level of remediation by EPA. Some government staffers said that the media climate around the case made it easier to negotiate with the corporations, and pushed the file with greater internal momentum within the agency. Others denied this. Plaintiffs' evidence tending to show active contamination by the tannery was of no special assistance to the government because in the Woburn defendants' context, the toxic cleanup statutes made mere ownership of contaminated land a basis for strict liability.

2. **Comparative advantages of public law.** For the people of Woburn the public law's cleanup mechanisms for contaminated land and groundwater presented some substantial advantages over private law. Emergency protective actions can be ordered instantaneously, as with the well closings. Sophisticated land remediation techniques are applied under expert agency supervision, at no expense to the neighborhood, paid for by the responsible corporations. Proof in a public law case can be far easier than in tort law. Unlike private plaintiffs, administrative agencies engaged in environmental protection are not required to prove causation by a preponderance of the evidence. Plaintiffs recovered zero from Beatrice's contamination of wellwater, while EPA got a large part of $69.5 million.[34] The agencies presumed expertise and authority to protect public health entitle their decisions to great deference from reviewing courts. Courts can only overturn agency decisions where they have been found to be "arbitrary and capricious" or the equivalent. See Chapter Seven. When scientific uncertainty and potential danger are both great, reviewing courts will show even greater deference, and accept administrative records that they would reject under other circumstances. When EPA issued its regulations prohibiting lead in gasoline (suspected to pose particular risks to urban children), for example, the agency admitted that scientific knowledge regarding the harmful effects of lead was highly uncertain. The evidence would never have supported tort liability. In Ethyl Corp. v. EPA, 541 F.2d 1 (D.C.Cir. 1976), however, the court upheld the public law prohibition:

> From extensive and often conflicting evidence, the EPA in this case made numerous factual determinations.... Some of the questions involved in the promulgation of these standards are on the frontiers of scientific knowledge, and consequently as to them insufficient data is presently available to make a fully informed factual determination. Decision making must in that circumstance depend to a greater extent upon policy judgments and less upon purely factual analysis.... We note that many of the issues in this case do not involve "historical" facts subject to the ordinary means of judicial resolution. Indeed, a number of the disputes involve conflicting theories and experimen-

---

34. Under the settlement, the companies agreed to pay $58.4 million to clean up polluted soil and groundwater, $5.8 million to fund EPA oversight of the cleanup, $2.7 million to the government for its previous work at the site and $2.6 million for further studies and cleanup costs. EPA assessed Beatrice for the majority of these costs, based on the EPA's determination that Beatrice had been responsible for the majority of the contamination.

tal results, about which it would be judicially presumptuous to offer conclusive findings. In such circumstances, the finder of fact must accept certain
areas of uncertainty, and the findings themselves cannot extent further than
attempting to assess or characterize the strengths and weaknesses of the
opposing arguments....

Where a statute is precautionary in nature, the evidence difficult to come by,
uncertain, or conflicting because it is on the frontiers of scientific knowledge,
the regulations designed to protect public health, and the decision that of an
expert administrator, we will not demand rigorous step-by-step proof of cause
and effect. Of course, we are not suggesting that the Administrator has the
power to act on hunches or wild guesses. His conclusions must be rationally
justified. However, we do hold that in such cases the Administrator may assess
risks.... He may apply his expertise to draw conclusions from suspected, but
not completely substantiated, relationships between facts, from trends among
facts, from theoretical projections from imperfect data, from probative preliminary data not yet certifiable as "fact," and the like.... Operating within the
prescribed [statutory] guidelines, he must consider all the information available to him. Some of the information will be factual, but much of it will be
more speculative scientific estimates and "guesstimates" of probable harm,
hypotheses based on still-developing data, etc. *Ethyl*, 541 F.2d at pages 26–29.

This process of imposing public law liability, needless to say, is totally different
from the process of proving legal liability in a tort case like the Woburn setting. As
studied later, in Chapters 17 and 18, government hazardous waste remedies have
no need to prove specific causation of harm, the scientifically subjective task that
overturns most tort plaintiffs. Agencies merely have to show that a PRP owned the
site, or transported, dumped, or arranged for anything to do with the disposal of
toxics at the site. The burden of proof in public law is effectively on the PRP, not
the prosecuting agency. It may take an average of 12 years to clean contaminated
sites, but government eventually gets the job done.

3. **Comparative advantages of private law.** But private law offers major utilities as
well. Public law remedies depend on official decisionmaking, which in some settings can be held back by politics or inertia. At common law, however, if a plaintiff pays the filing fee and has competent proof on point, a court has to hear the
case, and if the facts are there, a remedy is likely to issue. Public law produces no
compensation for injured citizens. Common law damages are a driving force
behind many private law actions against toxic industrial cost externalizations. The
self-interest of affected citizens, as in Boomer, is often a better motivator to bring
important issues into the law.[35] Courts in tort actions, moreover, as noted in this
and the preceding chapter, also have a variety of equitable remedies to tailor outcomes to public and private needs, a flexibility in available remedies that few agencies know to exercise. (Tort remedies, however, especially punitive damages, may
have no necessary proportionality in the burdens they impose. Public remedies,
which are developed in standardized administrative procedures, may have greater
uniformity and circumspection.) Tort remedies, evolved over centuries and familiar to judges, can sometimes be mobilized more readily and applied more flexibly,
without attenuated technical procedures, than public regulatory law.

---

35. Thus many pollution statutes add authorizations for citizen enforcement to supplement official
agency efforts. See Chapters 7 & 20.

Note in the Woburn toxics case a further societal utility of private law: in public law, there is little or no legal obligation of official agencies to investigate and remedy public health threats. The vigilance and perseverance of official agencies in investigating and defending against public toxic exposures depends on a variety of logistical and political conditions. A charged-up media climate is often necessary to attract official response to a diffuse health threat like a possible leukemia cluster. Private law tort actions can bring health considerations into the central focus of the legal forum, and serve to mobilize governmental attention. Public and private law thus operate in two different realms, serving quite different functions.

Do the two realms conflict with one another? On the ground they seem at most to supplement one another. To marketplace industries, however, the two forms of liability understandably seem like duplicative overkill — you can comply with CERCLA and still get sued by the neighbors for an even more stringent common law cleanup order[36] — which leads to calls for "tort reform" relief.

4. **The "tort reform" efficiency debate.** Does the Woburn toxics case throw any light on arguments (reflected in the Huber essay in Chapter Two) that complex cases involving scientific subtleties and public risk should in the future be handled by government agencies under public laws rather than by private litigation in courts?

Over the years there have been recurring calls (from many academics as well as defense attorneys) for tort reform, based not only on perceptions of the growing size of tort recoveries (the radio talkshows' favorite example probably is the plaintiff who recovered $2 million for burns from spilled coffee) but also on perceptions of the common law's limitations in coping with the problems of mass tort and toxics cases. The plaintiffs' bar responds that the average recovery in tort cases has not increased disproportionately, and that the insurance industry, in decrying the need to raise premiums, focuses on tort payments to the exclusion of its own internal investment policies. That debate is likely to be noisy and continuing.

In recent years, environmental tort cases have regularly provided some of the nation's largest damage recoveries.[37] As to mass toxic torts there is a substantial body of scholarship arguing that toxic exposure cases are too massive and complex to be left to the common law. The nature of epidemiology, the size of exposed plaintiff classes, the emotional and economic repercussions of litigation, and the problems of latency all combine to recommend statutory and administrative overrides of the tort law. See Trauberman, Statutory Reform of "Toxic Torts," 7 Harv. Envtl. L. Rev. 177, 188–202 (1983). Some scholars thus recommend statutory or administrative mechanisms that would permit compensation to be awarded on the basis of exposure and significant risk of disease, without the necessity of proving the existence of present injury. The size and arcane bureaucratic complexity of proposed public law remedies for mass torts, however, and their alleged vulnerability

---

36. That in fact was exactly the situation in Chapter Three's *Escamilla* case.

37. The Exxon-Valdez civil damage verdicts, totalling more than $5 billion in suits brought by harmed users of the Gulf of Alaska, takes a prize, but asbestos recoveries often have major price tags as well. Coyne and McCoubrey v. Celotex, (settled) (Wall St. J. 9 Feb. 1990, B1) ($76 million for each of two workers exposed to asbestos).

to political pressure from industry defendants, combine to raise substantial doubts about any such preemption of common law. What is the verdict on tort reform to be drawn from Woburn's Civil Action?

Tort law is a known commodity that carries its own internal incentives to prosecution of claims. Public law management cannot easily replicate the tort law's claims-processing mechanisms. For the time being, the legal situation is likely to continue with common law as an active and tangible element in most toxic exposure cases, with supplementary overlays from the public law system. Or is it vice versa?

*Environmentalists should make good urbanists, since they understand systems, diversity, connectivity and interdependence.*

— Caryl Terrell

*There are two types of environmentalists: those who understand that the city is part of the environment and those who do not.*

— Paul Soglin, Mayor of Madison, Wisconsin

# PART TWO

# ADMINISTRATIVE AGENCIES AND THE REGULATION OF THE ENVIRONMENT

*Why all this talk about efficiency? The last thing the "Founding Fathers" were after was efficiency. They were after freedom. And they understood that freedom implied a certain tolerance for messy conflict.*

— John Culver, quoted in N.Y. Times Mag., 12 March '89, at 101

# Chapter 5

# ENVIRONMENTAL REGULATORY STATUTES IN PERSPECTIVE

A. *The Evolution of the Environmental Regulatory Process*
B. *The Conceptual Building Blocks of Regulation*

Although common law provides the foundation of modern environmental law, and continues to be a powerful and important sector of environmental practice, the job of imposing civic values and policies on marketplace behavior — what Garrett Hardin termed "mutual coercion, mutually agreed upon" — today draws on techniques of regulatory public law even more than on common law.

Public law is built up of thousands of statutes and regulations at three (or more) levels of government, typically designed to implement public values in a manner that avoids many of the limitations of common law. While the forms and methods by which public law attempts to achieve various civic objectives are diverse, almost all approaches are built upon broadly applicable regulatory techniques. These public law regulatory programs have marked contrasts with private law remedies, in the presumption of validity of agency actions, easier proof of causation and liability, wide-scale applicability and effects, and so on.

Environmental regulation actually has a centuries-old history. London had smoke ordinances in the 1600s. Environmental regulation was neither varied nor sophisticated, however, until the last third of the twentieth century. Since 1970 environmental regulation has broadened its reach in terms of subjects addressed, and has developed a rich amalgam of types of regulatory approaches. This chapter briefly reviews that history of regulation and lays a foundation for analyzing the current spectrum of regulatory approaches, both as they exist today and as they are likely to evolve in the future. After the first part of the chapter explores the evolution of environmental regulation, Part B briefly introduces a theoretical framework for categorizing different regulatory systems and analyzing their structure and details. The section introduces a variety of generic regulatory models, the structures and elements of which can be assembled in a variety of configurations to regulate environmental quality. Understanding the legislative choices is important, and analysis from one regulatory context is often usefully applicable in another.

## A. THE EVOLUTION OF THE ENVIRONMENTAL REGULATORY PROCESS

### Section 1. EARLY EFFORTS AND THEIR LEGACY

#### Laitos, Legal Institutions and Pollution:
#### Some Intersections between Law and History
15 Natural Resources Journal 423 (1975)

Prior to 1880 the dominant social and economic institution which both affected and implemented choices was the market.... Beginning around 1880, America's legal, political, and economic institutions had to concern themselves with the general organization and effects of power concentrations. The rapid settlement of cities, the growth of urban living, and a large increase in population had led to social configurations that overshadowed individual lives. The startling pace of the industrial revolution had stimulated the growth of factories; men lived in the midst of machinery, mines, railroads, and automobiles....

By the turn of the century changes in America's social and economic condition forced closer attention to the social costs of reckless, unregulated natural resource use. First, the frontier had finally been pushed to the Pacific Ocean. With its disappearance had ended the nineteenth-century [1800 to 1880] assumption of inexhaustible natural resources.... Second, due in part to some of the worst decades of agricultural depression in our nation's history and in part to an unparalleled wave of immigration from Europe, there had been a sudden convergence of people upon America's cities. Water supply and sewage disposal lagged far behind the needs of mushrooming city populations.... Policy makers at last began to acknowledge the existence of social costs.... Due to the natural proclivity of injured parties to seek immediate relief through litigation, the courts were first to respond to twentieth century [1880 to 1930] air pollution.... In the case of air pollution the first legislative bodies to take affirmative action were the common councils of large industrial municipalities. It is not surprising that it was the city, and not the state or federal government, which first responded to air pollution. People saw dirty air as a local problem, not a regional or national concern....

Air pollution ordinances enacted by these late nineteenth century metropolitan common councils typically fell into three categories. Most common were the ordinances that simply declared (1) that the emission of dense smoke from any chimney or smokestack within the city was a public nuisance, and (2) that those who caused the emission of this smoke were liable to a fine, usually not exceeding $100.[1] A second type of ordinance did not merely declare the escape of dense smoke illegal; these more sophisticated laws placed an affirmative duty on polluters, requiring them not only to remove all ashes and cinders from their shops, but also to construct their furnaces "so as to consume smoke arising therefrom...."[2] These ordinances flatly prohibited the importation, sale, use or consumption of any coal containing more than 12 percent ash or 2 percent sulphur....[3]

Although the ordinance typically declared that the emission of thick, dense

---

1. Such ordinances are occasionally still enforced against air polluters, although maximum fines typically have been increased [eds].

2. Eds: This is an early example of a harm-based performance standard. See Chapter Eight.

3. Eds.: This is a "roadblock" device. See Chapter 14.

smoke was a public nuisance, no public official was empowered either to locate or abate these nuisances....[4] Unfortunately, whatever advantage there was in having dense smoke recognized as a nuisance per se was outweighed by the fact that such a narrowly focused prohibition ignored the more harmful invisible pollutants present in the smoke. Moreover, lawmakers and administrators failed to investigate whether more than just smoke affected the ambient air, and made no effort to define more precisely the acceptable and unacceptable density limits of smoke plumes....

### COMMENTARY AND QUESTIONS

1. **Why this system failed.** Local health commissions were the first stage of pollution regulation, supplementing common law tort actions, but, for a number of reasons, these attempts largely failed. (1) The industries that externalized their costs in the form of pollution continued to grow in both size and political influence, ultimately coming to dominate local governments (through their control over jobs and municipal tax bases) as well as common law courts (through their enhanced access to information, legal assistance, and scientific experts). (2) There was comparatively little scientific evidence to tie pollution (especially toxic pollution) to specific public health threats. (3) Attempts to control pollution through municipal ordinances and judicial decrees were primitive and ineffectual, incapable of adequately dealing with transboundary impacts, multiple polluter situations, and intransigent polluters.

2. **Scaling upward...first, a shift from municipal to state level.** As the scope, persistence, and intensity of pollution grew, and the environmental movement became a potent political force in the 1960s, major pollution control statutes began to emerge from state legislatures. State regulatory systems developed because of persistent and pervasive failure of the marketplace, common law courts, and local governments to deal adequately with the problem of air pollution. The political dynamics of the shift from the local to the state level of government, and later from state to federal, were exceedingly complex. See, e.g., Elliott et al., Toward a Theory of Statutory Evolution, 1 J.L. Econ. & Org. 313 (1985). Taking water pollution control as an example, during the 1940s and 1950s, local and later state boards of health had the primary role, mostly in constructing and operating sewage treatment plants. The federal presence mainly consisted of federal grants to sewerage authorities. Only later did the federal government move into an active regulatory role.

### Section 2. FROM THE GREAT DEPRESSION TO EARTH DAY

### A CASE STUDY:
### MICHIGAN'S MID-CENTURY WATER POLLUTION STATUTE, AND ADMINISTRATIVE AGENCY ENFORCEMENT AT UTILEX, INC.

In the evolution of environmental law through the middle of the twentieth century, as the primary forum shifted from the municipal level to the state level, the state regulatory experience was often not encouraging. The Michigan Water

---

4. Eds.: Weak or nonexistent enforcement is one variety of "symbolic assurance."

Resources Commission Act, as it stood from 1949 to the early 1970s,[5] was a typical example of a mid-century pollution control statute. The basic regulatory design can be described as "review-and-permit." Derived from an older public health statute, the Michigan statute established a seven-member, part-time Water Resources Commission (WRC),[6] "to prohibit the pollution of any waters of the state."[7]

> The commission shall protect and conserve the water resources of the state and shall have control of the pollution of surface or underground waters of the state and the Great Lakes which are or may be affected by waste disposal.... The commission shall enforce this act and shall promulgate rules as considered necessary to carry out its duties under this act. MCLA§323.2(1).

To go along with its broad mandate, the WRC was given investigatory power and the power to bring actions at law and in equity.[8] The legislation in general terms prohibited discharges that harmed public health or destroyed fish life in the water,[9] and granted the WRC the power to regulate discharges into the state's waters by setting and enforcing pollution standards, in terms common to other review-and-permit programs:

> The commission shall establish such pollution standards for lakes, rivers, streams and other waters of the state in relation to the public use to which they are or may be put, as it shall deem necessary.... It shall have the authority to make rules and orders [i.e. permits] restricting the polluting content of any waste material or polluting substance discharged or sought to be discharged into any lake, river, stream or other waters of the state. It shall have the authority to take all appropriate steps to prevent any pollution which is deemed by the commission to be unreasonable and against public interest in view of the existing conditions in any lake, river, stream or other waters of the state. MCLA§323.5.

With the broad authority to implement a review and permit process thus set, the statute also addressed some of the more critical details. Since the first enactment of the statutory plan, the WRC had enjoyed the power to make orders (permits) that would limit discharges. As of 1949, what might be called the "burden of initiation" of action under the WRC Act became explicit. As to existing facilities, the WRC had the burden of initiating standard-setting and permitting procedures. If it did not make standards and apply them to specific polluters, there was no need for the polluters to seek WRC approval of their practices. As to new or increased discharges only, a mandatory review and permit process was added:

> It shall be the duty of any person...requiring a new or substantial increase over and above the present use now made of the waters of the state for sewage or

---

5. The Act has since been amended to satisfy the rigorous requirements for state laws imposed by the federal Clean Water Act. See Act 293 of Pub. Acts of 1972, Mich. Comp. Laws §16.357.

6. The composition of the commission, as spelled out in the legislation in 1949, comprised the director of the state department of natural resources, the director of the state department of public health, the director of the state department of highways, the director of the state department of agriculture, and three citizens of the state to be appointed by the governor, by and with the advice and consent of the state senate, one from groups representative of industrial management, one from groups representative of municipalities, and one citizen from a group "representative of conservation associations or interests." The composition of the Commission tells a story, discussed further in Chapter 11.

7. Mich. P. A. 1929, No. 245, as amended.

8. MCLA§323.3-4.

9. MCLA§323.6.

waste disposal purposes, to file with the commission a written statement setting forth the nature of the enterprise or development contemplated, the amount of water required to be used, its source, the proposed point of discharge of said wastes into the waters of the state, the estimated amount so to be discharged, and a fair statement setting forth the expected bacterial, physical, chemical and other known characteristics of said wastes. Within 60 days of receipt of said statement, it shall be the duty of the commission to make an order stating such minimum restrictions as in the judgment of the commission may be necessary to guard adequately against such unlawful uses of the public waters.... MCLA§323.8(b).

### COMMENTARY AND QUESTIONS

1. **The 1949 mandatory permit system.** Why did the legislature decide to require a mandatory new and enlarged source permit system in 1949? One explanation was that the cumulative effects of pollution on aquatic ecosystems were then becoming a concern, as was the economic impact of deteriorating water quality on all forms of water use. Section 323.6 was expanded from a concern with pollution that endangered public health and fish kills to include pollution that would harm "any fish or migratory bird life or any wild animal or aquatic life." The language formerly addressed to public health alone was expanded to prohibit any water use "which is injurious to the public health or to the conducting of any industrial enterprise or other lawful occupation." Why was the 1949 mandatory permit process imposed only on new and increased sources? Plainly, this is not a trivial loophole, given that by 1949 existing pollution already was severe enough to be causing readily identifiable undesirable effects. It seems irrational to exclude all existing sources from the permit system; some countervailing political force probably explains that compromise.

2. **The standards to be applied by the WRC.** The 1949 statutory review-and-permit process calls for the polluter (the applicant) to furnish information about its anticipated discharge (the application); the WRC then must evaluate the application (review) and issue an order [permit] that includes restrictions on the discharge. The permit process is subject to subsequent judicial review. What standards must the WRC apply in acting on permit applications? Under §323.6 as it stood in 1949, pollution could not be permitted if it would injure public health and welfare or the aquatic ecosystem. In addition, "any pollution which is deemed by the commission to be unreasonable and against public interest" was prohibited under §323.5. Are these standards likely to obtain effective protection of water quality?

The standards' generality poses two different obstacles to preventing pollution. The first obstacle is interpretive — to the extent that the standards are vague (e.g., "injurious to public health or the conducting of any industrial enterprise"), the WRC had to provide more precise definitions. Recalling that the WRC was not a politically powerful agency — and by its very composition was somewhat sympathetic to industrial and commercial interests — suggests that it would tend not to interpret those terms stringently. Only the clearest cases of injury would be defined by the WRC as violating the threshold of harm that triggered its regulatory powers.

The second obstacle lies in the steps required in going from a case of probable unlawful discharge (i.e., a finding that the application, if granted without conditions, would result in an unlawful discharge) to the regulatory application of adequate permit conditions to prevent the proscribed harm from occurring. The WRC, for political reasons already described, was hesitant to deny permit applications outright. In general, the WRC could be expected to insert permit conditions that would allow the discharger to go forward with the overall project, but require that the effluent be treated in some manner before discharge. Here, the WRC's lack of staff and technical expertise was a major barrier to effective operation. Industrial applicants for permits have engineering expertise and use it well in negotiating permit conditions. The WRC, and most similar agencies or commissions, were, in the period under discussion, simply overmatched in that process.[10]

The third strike against the WRC Act was its under-enforcement:

### UTILEX: A WATER POLLUTION CASE STUDY

As part of a project undertaken by the University of Michigan Environmental Law Society in the early 1970s, law students examined a typical case file on one particular WRC permit, issued to the Utilex Company of Fowlerville, Michigan, an electroplating shop. (The file has been revisited to update the study.) The partial chronology that follows tells its own story.

### Michigan Department of Natural Resources Enforcement File # MI 0003727
### UTILEX-HOOVER BALL BEARING

[Digest of file entries:]

| | |
|---|---|
| December, 1952: | Utilex Company requests "new use" permit to allow dumping of cyanide, copper, zinc, nickel and other matter, in connection with new plating operations, into the adjoining Looking Glass River. |
| January, 1953: | WRC makes order granting permit, attaching [weak] standards for water quality. |
| July, 1953: | Staff field report: effluent violates permit standards. |
| September, 1953: | Staff field report: effluent violates permit standards. |
| September, 1954: | Staff field report: effluent violates permit standards. |
| March, 1955: | Staff field report: effluent violates permit standards. Staff writes letter to company suggesting new control equipment. |
| March, 1956: | Staff field report: effluent violates permit standards. |
| November, 1956: | Staff field report: effluent violates permit standards. |
| June, 1957: | Violation noted for nickel only. |
| June, 1959: | Staff field report: effluent violates permit standards in all categories. |
| January, 1960: | Staff field report: effluent violates permit standards in all categories. |
| October, 1960: | Staff field report: effluent violates permit standards in all categories. |

---

10. Despite the many shortcomings of the Michigan Water Resources Commission Act, it was in some ways a remarkably enlightened piece of legislation. One noteworthy feature is that it applied to both ground water and surface water. Few pollution control laws, either past or present (and most notably the Clean Water Act), take on ground water contamination. Second, the law addressed water quantity concerns in the environmental effects of diminished stream flow as well as pollution issues. This, too, was extraordinary.

| | |
|---|---|
| May, 1961: | Staff field report: effluent violates permit standards in all categories. Biological test shows long-term toxic effect; fifteen river miles required for recovery of water quality in river. |
| June, 1963: | Staff field report: effluent violates permit standards. |
| September, 1963: | Staff field report: effluent violates permit standards. |
| January, 1964: | Biological test shows no sign of life to three and one-half miles downstream; near-lethal cyanide levels. |
| October, 1964: | WRC writes company that controls would be "most desirable." |
| November, 1965: | Staff field report: concentrations exceeding standards 9.3 miles downstream. |
| September, 1966: | Citizen complaints [others have apparently been received, but are not copied in file] lead to staff field report: effluent violates permit standards. |
| November, 1966: | University biological test shows complete eradication of life to 4.7 miles downstream. |
| March, 1968: | Staff field report: excess effluents in all categories. |
| May, 1968: | In response to public environmental concern, WRC asks company for stipulation of new standards; company accepts, "prefers to have voluntary stipulation"; no mention of previous violations of permit. |
| December, 1968: | Excess effluents; company submits plans for control equipment to meet new standards by April, 1969. |
| July, 1969: | Company fails to install equipment by promised date due to "changed engineering plans." WRC sets new due date: April, 1970. |
| February, 1970: | Staff field report: effluent violates both old and new standards. |
| April, 1970: | Staff field report: effluent violates both old and new standards; no equipment installed by due date. |
| June, 1970: | Company requests postponement of due date; WRC notes the company "is moving expeditiously." |
| September, 1970: | Equipment installed. |
| October, 1970: | Staff field report: excess heavy metals in violation of 1953 standards. |
| December, 1970: | Staff field report: effluent violates permit standards. |
| Spring, 1971: | Environmental Law Society has been investigating WRC files; at next meeting WRC passes resolution limiting citizen access to its files. |
| March, 1972: | Staff field report: effluents exceed standards up to two miles downstream. Company writes letter explaining difficulty of cleaning up. Effluents do not meet 1953 permit standards. |
| [October 1972]: | [Congress passes Clean Water Act, requiring states in the National Pollution Discharge Elimination System (NPDES) program to upgrade their state pollution regulatory systems.] |
| February 28, 1974: | NPDES discharge permit issued; includes stricter standards. |
| August 9, 1974: | NPDES discharge permit issued on 02/28/74 found to be in error. |
| January 8, 1976: | Monitoring requirements are revised. Verification that cadmium was no longer present in detectable quantities; cadmium monitoring requirement could be deleted. |

January 20, 1977:      New NPDES permit is issued to Utilex on nickel and chromium discharges.

January 28, 1977:      Utilex receives a "I" rating for inadequate permit compliance; effluent violates NPDES permit.

February 7, 1977:      A waste water treatment construction project is begun at Utilex.

June 22, 1977:         A sulfuric acid spill occurs at Utilex.

June 30, 1977:         Revised draft permit for Utilex. Standards of original NPDES permit based on Michigan Waste Criteria were more stringent than EPA guidelines. WRC agrees to loosen standards.

July 11, 1977:         Completion of waste water treatment system at Utilex.

July 13, 1977:         A letter from Utilex explaining corrective actions taken in response to the acid spill of 06/22/77. Utilex installed a lining for a retaining wall and replaced storage tanks.

July 29, 1977:         Completion of water waste treatment project is confirmed.

September 13, 1977:    Field waste water survey done; shows violations of NPDES permit.

October 4, 1977:       Notice of non-compliance and Order to Comply sent to Utilex. Utilex found to have exceeded both its chromium and oil & grease maximums during July. Letter of explanation requested.

October 12, 1977:      Utilex writes that the parameters set forth by the permit have been attained.

November 8, 1977:      Utilex exceeds permit limits on ph acidity, zinc, and copper.

November 9, 1977:      Utilex writes that DNR limits for chrome, acid, and nickel had been exceeded due to a crack in a pipe sustained during demolition and replacement of roof.

December 6, 1977:      Letter from Water Quality Division stating that waste water survey of 09/13/77 indicated that limits on NPDES permit had been exceeded. A letter of explanation is requested.

December 22, 1977:     Notice of non-compliance with permit issued on 01/20/77. Chromium and nickel levels exceeded limits during the period from 10/14 to 10/25/77.

1978:                  Utilex closes, still in violation of standards.


COMMENTARY AND QUESTIONS

1. **The administrative explanation.** When asked about the Utilex file in 1972, the WRC Executive Director complained that he "didn't have sufficient manpower and budget to enforce the law" and that his agency also lacked sufficient legal authority. The manpower and budget complaints were, in large measure, well-founded. By 1972, the WRC was administering thousands of permits with a mere handful of staff, although there had been enough staff to do almost 20 years of violation reports. The claim of insufficient legal authority seems to be contradicted by the broad grant of enforcement authority set forth in the WRC Act. The WRC, however, had no legal counsel on its own staff, and its only method of seeking enforcement was to refer cases to the offices of the attorney general or local county prosecutors for action. Perhaps ironically, a number of cases like Utilex were not referred for

prosecution because the WRC staff had the erroneous belief that legally they had to be able to prove fish kills to mount a prosecution, and, as one field inspector said, "all of the fish were poisoned out of there in the 1950s."

**2. Improving the system — standard-setting.** The WRC case study and the Utilex file are paradigms of why enforcement of pollution control laws was problematic during the pre-1970 years of traditional "review and permit" statutes. A number of changes in regulatory approach had to be made if pollution control was to improve significantly, for example a move toward more definite standards. Chapters 8 to 11 are organized as a study of how various standard-setting methods are effectuated and made a part of regulatory regimes.

**3. Improving the system — changing the bipolar paradigm.** The traditional review and permit statutes function on a "bipolar" basis — a dialogue between the regulated corporation and the administrative agency. The only gesture to other constituencies was in the representative composition of the WRC itself. How could the regulatory process be changed to incorporate a broader "multi-polar" conception of the public interest? This question is addressed in later chapters, beginning with the discussion of modern administrative agencies in Chapter Seven.

**4. Improving the system — intra-agency changes.** The agencies that administered the mid-century permit systems were the forerunners of modern environmental protection agencies, and they pioneered changes in the bureaucratic landscape. In the case of Michigan and the WRC, the agency added in-house technical expertise. The WRC staff originally was drawn from the Department of Natural Resources (DNR), which historically was concerned with fish and game management, not pollution control. Over time, DNR and similar agencies throughout the nation added staff with environmental and pollution control expertise. These agencies, by introducing a new technocratic class into the regulatory process, heralded a new era in which regulatory agencies possess their own environmental and technical expertise. The commission composition and the Act's cumbersome procedures, however, hampered effective regulation.

Section 3. **THE "RACE OF LAXITY" AND THE FEDERALIZATION OF ENVIRONMENTAL LAW**

A role for the federal government began to take shape in the 1960s, as the mid-century primacy of state governments — operating 50+ independent review-and-permit systems — increasingly revealed its shortcomings. Some of the shortcomings were technical, and some lay in the "race of laxity," a problematic interstate rivalry for economic development that tended to hold down state environmental standards and enforcement.

Technical problems were posed by the geographic scope and complexity of pollution. The type of environmental problem that most frequently had driven the enactment of state environmental laws was what might be called a non-integrated "hot spots" phenomenon. Awareness and public arousal regarding environmental quality in this era was initially focused on dramatic local events, such as fish kills near a factory's outfall, or fumes and smoke invading a neighborhood, or raw sewage polluting beaches, and so on. Broader public health issues began to surface, indicating that pollution was not just in isolated hot spots, but affected large areas of the United States. Data from many cities began to show increased incidence of respiratory disease linked to increased air pollution. Fish populations were in decline almost everywhere.

No one city or state was in a position to collect or process the overall data, which could best be done and funded on a national level. In the aftermath of World War II, the national government had begun its first steps in the field. In 1948, Congress had enacted the Federal Water Pollution Control Act (FWPCA),[11] establishing funding for basic water pollution research and starting to fund some cleanup programs.[12] On the air side, the same evolution was taking place. In 1955, the federal Department of Health Education and Welfare (HEW) was assigned a major research role into the effects of air pollution.[13] Federal studies of automobile pollution began a few years later,[14] and in the 1963 version of the Clean Air Act,[15] HEW was directed to publish advisory national air quality criteria. These "criteria" documents based on epidemiological and other research that correlate levels of air quality with effects on health, later became federal air quality standards.[16] In 1956, the states successfully pushed the federal government into larger subsidies for sewage treatment, singled out for federal funding because of the interstate flow of many rivers.[17] Even in today's era of federal fiscal stringency, Congress still funds a portion of the construction costs of most Publicly Owned [sewage] Treatment Works (POTWs). Federal expertise and funding were clearly necessary, but a need for federal regulation also was becoming obvious.

Nor did state-by-state control of pollution address cross-border spillover effects. Downwind and downstream states had no power, other than persuasion and invocation of the doctrine of comity (voluntary respect by one state for the interests of a sister state), by which to protect themselves from transboundary pollution. The upwind and upstream states had little incentive to use scarce political capital to regulate their near-border polluters whose waste streams would have little or no effect on the state's own citizens. These scenarios also supported a more extensive federal role in environmental regulation.

By the late 1960s it was also becoming clear that many state programs could not or would not regulate pollution adequately, for *political* reasons. State review-and-permit systems varied greatly in structure, standards, and enforcement, in part

---

11. Act of June 30, 1948, ch. 758, 62 Stat. 1155.

12. FWPCA's one foray into providing substantive remedies was to establish a convoluted common law public nuisance cause of action that could conceivably be enforced by federal officials as a means for combating interstate water pollution, but wasn't.

13. Act of July 14, 1955, ch. 360, 69 Stat. 322.

14. Act of June 8, 1960, Pub. L. No. 86-493, 74 Stat. 162.

15. The Clean Air Act of 1963, Pub. L. 88-206, 77 Stat. 392.

16. The role of HEW was expanded to include the delineation of air quality control regions in the Air Quality Act of 1967 §108, 81 Stat. 490-97. Also included in that statute was an upgrading of the criteria documents from being merely "advisory" to a status as air quality standards. Three years later, in 1970, these standards became the federal government's nationwide mandatory minimum standards. See Chapter Eight.

17. The logic of that argument should make it plain that states as well as private firms externalize the costs of their pollution, using the environment as a pollution sink.

attributable to regional and local physical differences of climate and topography, and differences in the amount of existing industrial activity. Some of the states' inadequacies could be ascribed to the generic difficulty of pushing marketplace economic powers to respect public needs for environmental quality. To the minds of many, however, the low levels of many state-mandated pollution controls had an even more sinister aspect that argued then and now for *federal* minimum standards — the "race of laxity," also called the "race to the bottom," or "the Mississippi syndrome" after the industrial recruitment strategy of the poorest state in the Union.

The race of laxity appeared to be a major part of what was undercutting the nation's state-based pollution control efforts, manifested in an interstate lowering of standards as a key element in the competition to attract new industries. To be sure, environmental laws were but one of several components in the effort to woo industry, along with hospitable tax rates, labor costs, corporate law, and more. Nevertheless, a failure to join in the race of laxity in environmental regulation posed a major threat of lost economic prosperity to those states enforcing more burdensome environmental regulation than that enacted by their sister states.

By the beginning of the 1970s, the conviction that states were being pressured into keeping down their standards by an invidious race of laxity competition for marketplace economics prompted Congress to start a dramatic federal takeover of the job of setting nationwide minimum standards.

There is, not surprisingly, relatively little direct evidence to support the race of laxity's existence.[18] Whether there was an intentional race of laxity in the mid-century period is largely beside the point. Standards did vary, and state officials thought and reacted with the presumption that other states were doing it. It is unimaginable that a sophisticated firm considering major plant investment would not at least consider costs of environmental compliance in its decisional process. Most important, many members of Congress from the more populous and more industrialized states worried about interstate competition over pollution. For instance, in debates over the Clean Air Act of 1970, which imposed national standards, Rep. Vanik of Ohio declared:

> To date, the States have been left to establish their own air quality standards. In all too many areas, there has been delay and foot dragging — and ridiculously low standards set to accommodate local industries and interests. The establishment of national standards will ensure action throughout the Nation on a rapid basis.... National standards of pollution control would prevent another State from attracting any industries because of a greater pollution tolerance. Such competition is unfair and against the public interest.[19]

---

18. A recent governmental report provided evidence demonstrating a continuing race of laxity despite current federal floors designed to prevent it. See USGAO, Differences Among the States in Issuing Permits Limiting the Discharge of Pollutants 9 (1996), and Professor Engel's study in the Commentary notes below. Anecdotal evidence is abundantly available. In 1965, for example, Governor Ross Barnett of Mississippi gave a speech at Princeton University (attended by one of this book's authors) in which he lauded the state's lax environmental laws, low tax rates, and weak labor protections to a group of students whom he believed might become future corporate decisionmakers bringing new factories to Mississippi.

19. 116 Cong. Rec. 19,218.

By virtue of their voting strength in Congress, the senators and representatives from populous industrialized states that perceived the race of laxity as a threat could enact laws of nationwide scope that limited the race. Thus arrived the federal laws that marked the end of the mid-century review and permit era.

COMMENTARY AND QUESTIONS

1. **What is controversial about the federal role in pollution control and what is not.** Professor John Dwyer puts it this way:

> The usual justifications for a dominant federal role in environmental regulation are to take advantage of economies of scale with regard to research and data collection, to regulate interstate pollution, and to replace unduly weak state regulation. The first two arguments are not controversial, but they also do not justify an intrusive federal pollution program. The third argument — unduly weak state programs — is more controversial, but if persuasive would justify a more intrusive federal program. John Dwyer, The Practice of Federalism Under the Clean Air Act, 54 Maryland Law Review 1183, 1219–20 (1995).

2. **Federal law, the race of laxity, and modern devolutionism.** As noted, fear of a race of laxity among the states motivated Congress to give the federal government a dominant role in environmental regulation, rather than confining it to research, funding, and policing interstate pollution externalizations. The race of laxity apparently played a role in bringing an end to the era of variable state-designed review-and-permit systems.

Recently a revisionist academic and political debate has arisen over the question of whether such a race ever existed, or, beyond that, whether it leads to bad results. Professor Richard Revesz is the leading revisionist voice; see Revesz, Rehabilitating Interstate Competition: Rethinking the "Race-to-the-bottom" Rationale for Federal Environmental Regulation, 67 N.Y.U. Law Review 1210 (1992):

> Contrary to prevailing assumption, competition among the states for industry should not be expected to lead to a race that decreases social welfare; indeed, as in other areas, such competition can be expected to produce an efficient allocation of industrial activity among the states. It shows, moreover, that federal regulation aimed at dealing with the asserted race to the bottom, far from correcting evils of interstate competition, is likely to produce results that are undesirable. 67 N.Y.U. Law Review at 1211–12.

The argument is important for contemporary environmental policy making. If one agrees with the Revesz analysis, the modern federal role in environmental regulation should be scaled back and returned to the states, changing much of what will be studied in this book (and in all other current environmental law texts) about environmental standard setting and policy making, shifting it into 50 different systems. This is the "Devolution" agenda which has seized upon Revesz's theoretical inquiry. It is instructive to note that regulated industries have been throwing their weight on the side of state autonomy.[20]

As is often the case with important conceptual articles, players in the political marketplace often pick up ideas selectively, with less-than-full accuracy in noting the original authors' caveats and underlying assumptions. Revesz appends a cautious disclaimer:

> One should not overstate the nature of my claim against the race-to-the-bottom justifications for environmental regulation. The fact that there are no models consistent with race-to-the-bottom claims does not rule out the possibility that further research will yield such models. Modeling, by necessity, involves making strong sets of assumptions.... A theoretical literature evolves as assumptions are relaxed.... Rethinking the "Race-to-the-Bottom"..., 67 N.Y.U. Law Review at 1211–1212, 1244.

3. **Responding to Revesz.** An extensive reply and counter argument to Revesz and others questioning the race to the bottom is made in Kristin H. Engel, State Environmental Standard-Setting: Is There a "Race" and Is It "to the Bottom?" 48 Hastings Law Journal 271 (1997).[21] Professor Engel's article challenges Revesz' revisionist theory by suggesting that there are already well-established theoretical economic models that do predict a race-to-the-bottom. Her principal criticism of Revesz' theory attacks its reliance on neoclassical economic assumptions of purely competitive behavior, rather than the strategic behavior illustrated by game theory. She argues:

> The argument that interstate competition leads to a race-to-the-bottom and the revisionists' argument that it does not are both based on long-standing theoretical traditions. A principal argument for the existence of a race-to-the-bottom is based upon game theory, of which the classic Prisoner's Dilemma model is a simple but frequently cited example. According to this model, competition among a small number of players makes each player worse off than if he or she had not been a player in a game. The argument that interstate competition leads to socially-optimal environmental standards, on the other hand, is based upon competitive neoclassical economics, according to which competition among market participants leads to efficient outcomes for society as a whole.... Despite revisionist claims to the contrary, the argument that interstate competition in environmental standard-setting triggers a race-to-the-bottom is based upon a detailed theoretical literature. The Prisoner's Dilemma was...applied specifically to environmental problems in 1968 by

---

20. For example, in the failed effort to promote and obtain passage of H.R. 961 in the 104th Congress (a bill popularly referred to as the "Dirty Water Act") the two groups that drafted and pushed the bill through the House — "Project Relief" and the "Alliance for Reasonable Regulation" — designed the bill to undercut pollution controls primarily by shifting ultimate standard-setting and enforcement to the states. The corporations making up those groups include more than 500 of the nation's largest dischargers of water pollutants.

21. Revesz' article has gathered a number of critics in addition to Professor Engel. See, e.g., Daniel Esty, Revitalizing Environmental Federalism, 95 Mich. L. Rev. 570 (1996); Joshua Sarnoff, The Continuing Imperative (But Only from a National Perspective) for Environmental Protection, 7 Duke Envtl. L. & Policy Forum 225 (1997); Peter Swire, The Race to Laxity and the Race to Undesirability: Explaining Failures in Competition Among Jurisdictions in Environmental Law, 14 Yale J. on Regulation 67 (1996). See Revesz in reply, The Race to the Bottom and Federal Environmental Regulation: A Response to Critics, 82 Minn L. Rev. 535 (1997). The devolution debate will continue into the millennium.

Garrett Hardin. Many scholars have used a game-theoretic approach to model a race-to-the-bottom in interstate competition.... The rejection of game theory in favor of neoclassical competitive economic models as the theoretical foundation for interstate competition contains a deeper irony, however. Game theory was invented fifty years ago to address shortcomings in traditional neoclassical economics, which could not handle situations in which market participants interacted strategically. Thus, the revisionists' return to the neoclassical economic framework to understand interstate competition, a problem many theorists were already solving through the application of game theory, is, historically speaking, a conceptual step backward. 48 Hastings L.J. at 297–98 (1997).

Professor Engel did an empirical survey analysis of state officials and corporate executives. Somewhat surprisingly she found that many corporate executives said that environmental laxity was *not* a major inducement to their location decisions, but that nevertheless some state officials apparently acted in the assumption that it was. "A substantial minority of officials influential in the state environmental standard-setting process concede that their state has relaxed its standards and permit procedures in order to attract or retain industrial firms." 48 Hastings Law J. at 351–52 (1997).

Environmental attorneys who represent firms in regulatory settings confirm that their clients are very sensitive to the possibility of obtaining less stringent regulation from state regulators and will press those regulators to act in that fashion. The race to the bottom often seems visible even within today's federal Clean Water and Clean Air Act enforcement. Note the tension between the Virginia water pollution agency and EPA in Chapter One's *Smithfield* cases when Smithfield threatened to move to North Carolina. In the air pollution setting, a routine strategy of firms that realize they have violations that may be pursued by either state agencies or EPA, is to urge the state to file and then negotiate a settlement, on the belief that the state will be more lenient than EPA. Even more pointedly, when EPA files a complaint first, the polluter will often complain that EPA has deliberately "over-charged" them in the case. The polluter then will enlist the state agency to (1) file its own case and, thereafter, (2) to work on the polluter's behalf in getting EPA to dismiss its filing in deference to the state filing. The object of those efforts is to reduce the cost of regulatory compliance by being allowed to satisfy a lower standard.

Why should state agencies be willing to assist polluters in the effort to remove the federal agency and its more stringent demands from the case? One series of reasons relate to jurisdictional and institutional jealousy. EPA intervention is perceived as an insult to state agency performance and an intrusion on state prerogatives. Similarly, state agencies believe that they are better able than EPA to judge what is best in relation to the localized particulars of the situation. Finally, states do take polluters seriously when they threaten facility shutdowns or relocations, or other forms of economic disinvestment in the state.

4. **Racing to the bottom via lax enforcement.** Thus far the focus has been on a race to the bottom in standard setting because the conceptual question is being posed in relation to the need for national levels of assured environmental protection. To a considerable extent "federal floors" in standard setting limit the contemporary

race of laxity, but states eager to run in the race to the environmental bottom have other opportunities, particularly in enforcement. See Victor B. Flatt, A Dirty River Runs Through It (the Failure of Enforcement in the Clean Water Act), 25 B.C.J. Env. Affairs 1 (1997). Professor Flatt supports his assertion of a race to the bottom resulting from differential enforcement by comparing the Clean Water Act enforcement activities of the states of Georgia and Washington. One easily discerned strategy of the states in these cases is to take weak administrative action or to seek too lenient consent decrees in enforcement action, preventing more rigorous enforcement of the national standards either by EPA, or more often by citizen enforcers. Compare, e.g., Knee Deep Cattle Co. v. Bindnana Investment Co., Ltd., 94 F.3d 514 (9th Cir. 1996) (the state did not diligently prosecute a pending state law action for pollution in violation of NPDES permit, so citizen enforcement was allowed under federal law), with Arkansas Wildlife Federation v. ICI Americas, Inc., 29 F.3d 376 (8th Cir. 1994) (a state administrative penalty proceeding was sufficiently prosecuted to bar citizen suit for violation of NPDES permit). This topic is discussed more fully in Chapter 20.

5. **Inverting the race of laxity.** Is it possible that states could invert the race of laxity into a race for enhanced environmental quality? For that to happen, states raising their environmental standards would have to provide some offsetting benefits to firms, that would more than outweigh the increased cost of doing business there. Is the value of a cleaner, healthier environment a sufficient lure? To some executive decisionmakers who themselves would be living in the preferred setting, higher environmental standards might be a plus, and perhaps those same benefits would be useful in personnel recruitment. A more likely path by which states can raise environmental standards is market power, such as that enjoyed by California. California's economy is so large, that if it were an independent nation, its economy would be among the ten largest in the world. Most large firms doing business in the United States will act in ways that accommodate California if the alternative is to limit their access to California's market. In the environmental field, that market power has occasionally allowed California to invert the race of laxity to suit its will. For example, California developed its own higher-than-national standards for automobile emissions and had the both the market power to force the automakers to manufacture to California standards and the political power to keep Congress from preempting those standards in the Clean Air Act. Even more of an inversion of the race of laxity has occurred in the wake of California's Proposition 65 regulation of hazardous chemicals. Many producers serving the California market have chosen to adapt their products to meet California's most stringent in the nation regulation, and made the decision to market the identical products nationwide. The economic logic is built upon economies of scale in having to manufacture and distribute a unitary line of products, rather than separate (but similar) products designed to meet both higher and lower regulatory standards. There are not many states with market power like California. Moreover, as touched upon in Chapter Six, groups of states cannot act in concert in regulatory matters absent congressional approval under the Compact Clause of Article I, §10 of the United States Constitution.

## Section 4. THE MODERN RESULT — MEDIA-SPECIFIC REGULATION ENFORCED BY A FEDERAL-STATE PARTNERSHIP

In the late 'Sixties, public opinion against environmental degradation began to swell dramatically, and Congress responded, cranking out a remarkable parade of bills, more than two dozen major statutes between 1968 and 1974.[22] These statutes directed federal agencies, especially EPA, to engage in a gamut of regulatory activities, including the promulgation of reams of rules and guidance documents. This outpouring of regulatory statutes rivals or surpasses the New Deal's.

Public opinion fundamentally shaped the nature of the legislation that was enacted (including, because of the short-term, crisis-driven nature of public media outcrys, the somewhat fragmented pattern of modern environmental regulation).

After more than three decades of evolution of regulatory structures, the modern process of environmental regulation reflects a dramatic shift in power from the states to the national government in defining overall goals and methods of environmental regulation, while the states retain a major role in the operational side of the program. The resulting amalgamation of federal and state power is usually called "cooperative federalism," or a "federal-state partnership." In essence, cooperative federalism seeks to build upon the perceived strengths of the federal and state governments in combating pollution and resource depletion. The federal government can far better provide the technical and scientific expertise that is germane in standard setting. Likewise, because of its national perspective, if questions of environmental policy are questions of national import (and because of spillover effects and the race to the bottom, there is good reason to think this is so), the federal government ought to be the one setting that policy. As to implementation, however, the states are probably better situated.

Cooperative federalism begins with the federal government (almost invariably EPA) performing preliminary planning by conducting an assessment of the environmental quality of the medium in question, then comparing current environmental conditions to the goals enunciated by Congress, and then setting environmental protection standards based on one or more of the statutory standard-setting philosophies discussed later in this chapter. These federal standards are uniform throughout the United States, in order to discourage states from competing for polluting industry in the race to the bottom. These uniform national pollution control standards are a "federal floor." Based on these standards, EPA can conduct permitting, monitoring, surveillance, regulation, and enforcement.

Cooperative federalism, however, allows states to take over the federal program by delegation from EPA when it can demonstrate that it possesses the necessary legal authority, financial capability, and political will to administer the

---

22. The Wild and Scenic Rivers Act (1968); National Environmental Policy Act and Noise Pollution and Abatement Act (1969); the Clean Air Act, the Occupational Safety and Health Act, and Environmental Protection Agency Act (1970); the Fish and Wildlife Coordination Act, Noise Control Act, and Lead-Based Paint Poisoning Prevention Act (1971); Clean Water Act, Consumer Product Safety Act, Marine Mammal Protection Act, Noise Control Act, Coastal Zone Management Act, and Marine Protection, Research and Sanctuaries Act (1972); the Endangered Species Act and Oil Pollution Act (1973); Archeological and Historic Preservation Act, Environmental Education Act, Safe Drinking Water Act (1974); and at least a dozen more.

regulatory program effectively and efficiently. Once a state has succeeded in making this showing, EPA delegates "primacy" to the state, meaning that the state will thenceforth administer the permit program and perform primary monitoring, surveillance, and enforcement. States are authorized to impose stricter standards on industries within their jurisdictions, though state standards cannot be less strict than federal standards.

EPA retains carrots and sticks to encourage states to seek primacy and ensure that states, having been granted primacy, will not shirk their delegated responsibilities. The "carrots" available to EPA are state program grants and technical assistance. The "sticks" wielded by EPA include (1) cutoff of program grants, (2) backup EPA monitoring, surveillance, and enforcement authority, (3) EPA authority to veto individual state permits if a state violates the enabling federal statute, and (4) EPA cancellation of primacy if a state is systematically remiss in its administration of the program. These sticks are somewhat less fearsome than they appear. First, Congress has reduced funding for state program grants, rendering the carrot smaller and less juicy. Second, EPA does not possess the financial and personnel resources to exercise the oversight, concurrent regulation, permit veto, or primacy cancellation remedies on anything more than a sporadic basis.

Cooperative federalism has critics on all sides. On one end of the spectrum are those who criticize the delegation option, believing that states with primacy will try to engage in a "race to the bottom" because EPA is economically and politically incapable of exercising its oversight responsibilities. On the other end of the spectrum, supporters of full program "devolution" to states argue that states are both willing and able to protect the environment without "interference" by the federal government. They would continue federal program grants to states, but discontinue "unnecessary bureaucracy and paperwork" in the form of federal oversight over state pollution control activities. Sensitive to the strength of the devolution philosophy in Congress, EPA has attempted to delegate as many program responsibilities to states as possible, while retaining some measure of control over states that are clearly recalcitrant with regard to permitting, monitoring, surveillance, and enforcement.

## B. THE CONCEPTUAL BUILDING BLOCKS OF REGULATION

Most governmental environmental protection efforts are regulatory.[23] The overt goal of all environmental regulation, of course, is to create effective systems for minimizing environmental damage while satisfying political imperatives, and cost and technological constraints. The task is broad and open-ended because there are so many environmental problems to be addressed, and so many nuanced forms that regulation can take. The universe of environmental regulation, however, can be broken down into a manageable number of approaches or regulatory strategies, an approach which carries through this coursebook. To understand how a strategy

---

23. A non-regulatory environmental policy might be a proviso requiring governmental purchases of recycled materials whenever possible.

operates in one context is generally to understand how that strategy will operate in another context. A second strand in this book's coverage of regulation is the belief that one can see fairly consistent patterns in the evolution of different pieces of regulation, given the range of choices available for the original regulatory design, and continuing from first enactment through subsequent stages of change and maturation. In this section, the goal is to introduce, in capsule form, the pattern and the strategies, so that they can serve as framework for more detailed subsequent explorations of the regulatory regimes that dominate so much of modern environmental law.

### Section 1. THE STRUCTURES AND PROCESSES THAT COMPRISE ENVIRONMENTAL REGULATION

Modern environmental legislation initially was designed on a medium-by-medium basis, often targeting only a single phase of the process that affects the environment. In the pollution regulation lexicon, a "medium" is the carrying or receiving element — air, water, etc. Surface freshwater, ground water, marine and estuarine water, wetlands, air, and land are all environmental media.

Adopting a media-specific approach, Congress has enacted major (and fundamentally different) regulatory statutes at different times to control surface freshwater pollution (the Clean Water Act),[24] marine water pollution (the Oil Pollution Act of 1990, the Marine Protection, Research, and Sanctuaries Act), wetlands degradation (§404 of the Clean Water Act), air pollution (the Clean Air Act), and land pollution (RCRA and CERCLA). These statutes utilize different terminology for essentially the same things (e.g., a water "discharge," an air "emission," and a "release" to land). Each has a different list of hazardous or toxic substances that must be controlled, and each statute is based on an idiosyncratic combination of philosophies and methodologies of pollution control.

The targeted "phase" of marketplace behavior also varies — for instance, at what point in the chronology from creation to disposal of an environmental pollutant will regulatory controls be applied? Some federal statutes attempt to be "proactive" (preventive) by regulating the introduction of new chemicals into commerce. These are the "market access" and "product regulation" statutes (the Federal Insecticide, Fungicide, and Rodenticide Act, and the Toxic Substances Control Act). Federal "cleanup" statutes (the Comprehensive Environmental Response, Cleanup, and Liability Act (CERCLA) and RCRA, for example) are reactive and take effect at the back end of the waste disposal process. The Safe Drinking Water Act regulates the quality of drinking water, as distinguished from the Clean Water Act, which regulates the quality of water used for recreational and ecological purposes. The Emergency Planning and Community Right-To-Know Act governs public notification of toxic substance releases and development of emergency response mechanisms. The Clean Water Act, Clean Air Act, and RCRA impose permit requirements on dischargers (emitters, generators, releasers) of specified substances.

---

24. Groundwater pollution, except for deep well injection, is still not directly federally regulated. RCRA, particularly in regard to leaking underground tanks, attempts to protect groundwater quality in an indirect fashion.

Whatever their unique characteristics, however, all regulatory systems under environmental statutes include a series of common elements:

- *Planning* — the regulatory enterprise is coordinated by a governmental agency's oversight management and planning, often with public participation;

- *Standard-Setting* — is based on one or a combination of standard-setting philosophies (such as harm-based, technology-based, or technology-forcing) and methods of balancing environmental risks and economic costs;

- *Permitting* — general standards are translated into specific legal obligations of individuals and corporations;

- *Monitoring and Surveillance* — in order to determine whether permittees are complying with the terms of statutes and their permits, ongoing empirical review is maintained by permittees, agencies, and occasionally the public;

- *Enforcement* — against violators to insure compliance; and

- *Feedback from implementation* — a continuing reevaluation process, with ongoing adjustments in rules, procedures, and practices, sometimes expressed in terms of requirements for periodic legislative reauthorization.

Particular regulatory statutes emphasize one or a number of these elements, and place lesser emphasis on others. For example, under the Clean Water Act, each state must administer an elaborate continuing planning process to review water quality standards and implementation efforts. In other environmental statutes, such as the Federal Insecticide, Fungicide, and Rodenticide Act (FIFRA), planning may consist only of ad hoc advisory committees to comment on narrowly circumscribed issues. With regard to permitting, discharge permits, under the Clean Water Act and grazing permits under the Federal Lands, Policy, and Management Act are long and highly detailed documents that comprehensively spell out the obligations and liabilities of dischargers into public waterbodies and private ranchers grazing their cattle on federal lands. On the other hand, there is no formal permit under the Toxic Substances Control Act; if EPA does not, within a certain time after being informed of impending sale by a manufacturer of a new chemical, promulgate a rule requiring further testing of the environmental effects of that chemical, the manufacturer can simply proceed with its sales campaign without a formal authorization (permit) from EPA. As far as monitoring and surveillance is concerned, some regulatory statutes, like the Clean Water and Clean Air Acts, require permittees to perform elaborate self-monitoring activities — even to the point of installing particular monitoring technology — and quickly report all exceedances (violations of effluent or emissions limitations) to governmental agencies. In contrast, no self-monitoring is required of regulated parties under the Endangered Species Act; when an endangered species has been "taken," enforcement is entirely dependent on timely and effective governmental surveillance. Finally, as described in Chapters 19 and 20, enforcement devices vary widely, from criminal enforcement under certain environmental statutes to weak, symbolic enforcement remedies under others.

"The three Es" are the hallmarks of regulation, guiding judgments about how to design and evaluate alternative regulatory options. A regulatory system should be (1) effective, (2) efficient, and (3) equitable. In judging effectiveness one must consider whether a statute will really work in the real world, or whether it provides mere "symbolic assurance." Efficiency involves subjective benefit-cost analysis, cost effectiveness (whether equal or better results can be obtained at a lower cost), and technical feasibility. Evaluating the "equitableness" of a statute requires a careful comparative analysis of impacts and benefits.

## Section 2. REGULATORY STRATEGIES

In addition to the structural and process elements of a regulatory program listed above, most regulatory regimes subscribe to one of a number of regulatory strategies. Characterizing and delineating strategies is, perhaps, a more open-ended, subjective endeavor than analyzing structure and process. Nevertheless, even a tentative partial list of regulatory strategies can help to suggest the value of thinking in such terms. Consider the following list:

- Prescribing specific effluent limitations (a strategy that is referred to by many as "command and control");

- Creating economic incentives and otherwise using market mechanisms to encourage environmentally less damaging behavior;

- Prohibiting actions (a practice that will later be referred to as involving "roadblocks");

- Requiring environmental assessment and consideration as a precondition to action;

- Conditioning access to consumer markets on environmental or safety assessments;

- Requiring that costs of environmental damage be internalized via remedial expenditures or in other ways; and

- Requiring identification and disclosure of environmental liabilities and risks.

While not exhaustive, the list describes the operative strategies at work in most "modern" regulatory efforts.[25] If that is the case, and the structure and process analysis is apt, the "numbing complexity and detail" that plagues teaching the regulatory side of environmental law need not be the focus of study. What matters is understanding how the various strategies can be implemented using the structures and processes. Knowledge gained in one regulatory context will be transferable to another. Thus, weaknesses that can be identified in the current design of the air emissions acid deposition trading program are likely pitfalls that need to be avoided in structuring a trading program to reduce ozone emissions in the Los

---

25. A single statute may use more than one strategy. Regulation of stationary sources of air pollution under the Clean Air Act is one of the premiere examples of the first strategy, prescribing specific effluent limitations. Its acid deposition emissions trading program is simultaneously both a roadblock and a leading example of enlisting market mechanisms to foster efficiency in pollution control expenditures.

Angeles airshed, or a lead phase-out trading program for gasoline.[26] Similarly, understanding why Congress was able to impose the technology-forcing that led to the acceptance and utilization of the catalytic converter, could help in drafting a future regulatory program that seeks to force adoption of new technologies, such as bioremediation, that can reduce the cost of ground water decontamination.

## COMMENTARY AND QUESTIONS

1. **Different options for standard-setting.** Standard-setting is one stage in the progression of stages comprising the regulatory process. Standard-setting also reflects regulatory design strategies, with the different choices of how to set standards producing very different results. The four primary standard-setting methods — for harm-based, technology-based, technology-forcing, and process standards — are given separate treatment in Chapters 8–11, drawn from several different command-and-control pollution statutes.

2. **Some roadmapping.** Analysis of the design strategies, structures, and implementation processes of environmental regulation form the conceptual backbone of about two-thirds of the rest of this book. The next two chapters explore some federalism issues and administrative law. Part Three of the book then takes up a survey of *standard-setting methods*, including the important techniques of setting effluent limitations within the comprehensive permit-based "command and control" strategies. Part Four focuses on the full spectrum of *regulatory design strategies*, and Part Five returns to *implementation processes*, with an examination of the post-permit stages of monitoring and enforcement. The feedback loop in the evolution of regulatory statutes recurs in these chapters because most of the statutes used to illustrate standard-setting options and regulatory design strategies continually undergo modification over the years. For a fuller road-mapping, see the overview text at Part Three below, page 439–440.

---

26. This hypothetical is inverted in time. The trading program for the phase-out of lead in gasoline was an operational success before the Clean Air Act Amendments of 1990 created the acid deposition trading program. Several of the central features of the gasoline trading program were replicated in the air program. For example, both programs operated among a small number of homogenous trading entities (refiners and large power generators), known to one another so that transaction costs could be minimized.

# Chapter 6

# POWER RELATIONSHIPS BETWEEN FEDERAL AND STATE GOVERNMENT IN ENVIRONMENTAL REGULATION

A. *Constitutional Federalism and Environmental Law Controversies*

B. *Preemption of State Law*

C. *The Dormant Commerce Clause and Natural Resources*

D. *Limitations on Federal Power*

## A. CONSTITUTIONAL FEDERALISM AND ENVIRONMENTAL LAW CONTROVERSIES

The historical overview of environmental regulation in Chapter Five noted the distinct and evolving roles of the national and state governments. Those roles are not, of course, derived through happenstance, logic, or necessity alone. Instead, those roles, despite their variation over time, are rooted deeply in the defining elements of American democracy, the Constitution itself, and the concept of federalism. Owing to those origins, particularly those of constitutional dimension, the federal government and the states are subject to legally binding limitations that constrain their power. This chapter examines the constitutional structure of federal-state power relations as that topic relates to environmental law.

The material in this chapter that delineates the respective spheres of authority of the federal and state governments has a somewhat ethereal quality. At stake are momentous principles of American constitutional federalism more comfortably studied as part of a constitutional law course. The doctrines and case law that undergird contemporary decisions were crafted to resolve disputes involving subjects as remote as Revolutionary War debts, nineteenth century steamboat monopolies, and early twentieth century immigration issues. Although none of this would seem to have much practical importance for the modern environmental lawyer, that is emphatically not the case.

### Section 1. THE ROLES OF FEDERALISM IN DETERMINING ENVIRONMENTAL OUTCOMES

Consider, as a first example, the nuclear power industry. Without certain aspects of the American constitutional division of power between the federal government and the states, the industry likely would not exist. As Chapter Two noted briefly, nuclear generation is a public risk-laden enterprise. Moreover, if a major accident ever happens, the losses will be astronomical and will present a source of tort liability that would bankrupt virtually any private entity. It is also an industry that faces immense costs of facility construction and operation as a further barrier to entry for anyone seeking to become a commercial nuclear generator of electricity. To encourage commercial nuclear generation in the face of those risks and barriers to entry, a government has to be able to create a legal environment in which those risks can be managed efficiently. That is, before anyone will be bold enough to risk that much money in the industry, there has to be a predictable legal regime that makes possible economies of scale. If every single facility has to "reinvent the wheel" to be licensed and built, that wastes too many resources — it sacrifices too many economies of scale. If all fifty states are free to regulate the industry, the chances are great that their fifty sets of regulations (each influenced by local concerns, such as the in-state coal producers in one state, or a strong antinuclear lobby in another) will read like a crazy quilt that forestalls creation of the industry. It is economically more prudent, under that scenario, to invest in fossil fuel generation or some other means to supply electricity. But American federalism created a way out of that scenario by giving the national government the power to preempt the states from acting. With respect to nuclear power, the national government exercised that power in two ways. First, in 1957, in the Price-Anderson Act,[1] Congress used its affirmative authority to limit the total liability for a nuclear accident to $560 million (peanuts in the post-Exxon Valdez punitive damages world) and, because of the Supremacy Clause of the United States Constitution, no state law can provide otherwise. Second, it allowed the industry to realize the economies of scale offered by unitary regulation of reactors, expressly forbidding state regulation of facility design and safety.[2]

In other environmental controversies, American federalism may play a different, but still critical, role. What if a state, through geologic fortuity, is home to the nation's single best and largest hazardous waste disposal site. The site has been developed for just that purpose by the nation's largest and most experienced hazardous materials handling firm. The firm was able to do so at a relatively low cost because the site is so geologically favorable. Concurrently, due to the fear of more Love Canals, the NIMBY ("not in my back yard") phenomenon is at fever pitch, making it very hard for any other sites to obtain licenses, and driving up disposal prices due to the scarcity of disposal sites. As a result of all this, the site is both the safest site in the nation and, by a wide margin, the most economical site in the nation. Can the state withhold from out-of-state generators of hazardous wastes the benefit of using the site for disposal? Far more shrewdly, can the state allow its own citizens to use the site for a low cost by barely taxing disposal of in-state wastes, while capturing much of the profit of allowing disposal of out-of-state wastes by charging those wastes a large tax, but one that still makes it profitable

---

1. Pub.L. 85-256, Sept. 2, 1957, 71 Stat. 576.

2. Atomic Energy Act of 1954, 42 U.S.C. §§2011 et seq., especially §2074. See Northern States Power Co. v. Minnesota, 447 F.2d 1143 (8th Cir. 1971), aff'd, 405 U.S. 1035 (1972).

for the site operator to accept the out-of-state waste?[3] The answer to this legal question, and many more like it, again turns on the intricate division of power between the states and national government — Federalism.

As if the environmental disputes that are controlled by the preemption cases and interstate commerce cases are not enough, federalism has even more facets of importance for environmental laws. Not only does our federalism include doctrines that subordinate state power to that of the central government, but there are also whole lines of cases that curtail national power in favor of state power. Even more bewildering, the norm in most areas of environmental regulation is that the controversies — from pollution and licensing of miners to management of wild burros on the public lands — are regulated by both the national government and the states. Add to that the uneven efforts of the two governments to work cooperatively, and the possible complexity seems endless.

Rather than decrying that state of affairs, many lawyers find in the complexity and subtlety of federalism an opportunity for making interesting tactical choices. Some of the tactics are fairly straightforward: if the law of the one sovereign is anathema to the client, try to have it invalidated as being in contravention of the constitutional division of authority. In the nuclear and hazardous waste disposal hypotheticals above, the effort was to knock out state law, but the arguments can run the other way. For example, a lawyer representing a would-be land developer whose project was going to be blocked by federal wetland regulation of isolated inland wetlands argued (unsuccessfully) that the law being used was not supported by the grant to Congress of power to regulate interstate commerce.[4]

More subtle tactical maneuvering occurs in cases in which state and federal regulation overlap. Here, federalism has altered the way in which practicing lawyers represent their clients by raising the possibility of what might be called "forum shopping." A lawyer may try to influence the law's impact on a client by deliberately seeking to have the particular issue handled in one system or the other, either state or federal, depending upon which system is more favorable to the client's interests.

Imagine representing a client who owns a brownfields[5] parcel and wants to clean up the existing contamination and redevelop the parcel for light commercial use. As explored more fully in Chapter 18, there are concurrent federal and state

---

3. Perhaps unfairly impugning the motives of the State of Alabama, this hypothetical bears a more than passing resemblance to the facts presented by Hunt v. Chemical Waste Management, 504 U.S. 334 (1992), in which Alabama attempted to attach an "Additional Fee" of $72 per ton to out-of-state wastes. The fee proved that there was some price elasticity in the market. In the year after the fee went into effect the tonnage accepted at the facility was cut more than in half, from 791,000 tons in the last full, pre-fee year, to 290,000 tons in the first full post-fee year. Roughly 90% of the waste disposed of at the facility came from out-of-state. Thus, the "additional fee" "earned" Alabama about $19,000,000 in that first year, while depriving Chemical Waste Management of far more than that if it had been allowed to set its price for out-of-state waste with only a small state tax in place.

4. United State v. Riverside Bayview Homes, Inc., 474 U.S. 121 (1985).

5. "Brownfields" is the term given to urban land that has been used in the past and become environmentally degraded, as through the presence of contaminants. Nevertheless, for reasons of location and sound urban policy, many brownfields sites now are being considered for redevelopment. The usual competing option is "greenfields" land, that is, land that lies beyond the urban area in the as-yet-undeveloped surrounding farmland and open space.

regulations that might apply to the cleanup, imposing standards of how clean the parcel needs to be at the end of the process and the means by which the cleanup is effected. As a strategic matter, the lawyer will consider whether there is a practical advantage to the client that might favor seeking to have the cleanup governed by one sovereign or the other. The advantages might be, for example, a difference in the expected cost or duration of the process. As it turns out, because of the efforts and institutional need of the federal government to work cooperatively with the states in this field (and others), the affected party (i.e., the client) may be able to steer the case into one system or the other. In this way, the federalism superstructure that favors concurrency of regulatory authority becomes a fertile ground for tactical maneuvering by lawyers.

The bottom line for these federalism doctrines and structures is that they strongly affect outcomes in the real world. Even that may not be enough to make all of what follows scintillating.

## Section 2. BASIC FEDERALISM PRECEPTS

To begin at the most fundamental level, in a constitutional democracy, as a matter of elementary political theory, whatever is enshrined in the Constitution takes precedence over "mere" legislation or other efforts to alter constitutionally established norms. In the United States, the judiciary is the branch of government that serves as the guardian of constitutional norms. Exercising judicial review, the courts will invalidate laws and regulations that are inconsistent with constitutional requirements. Judicial review relies heavily on discerning the intent of the framers of the Constitution in interpreting and applying its doctrines to specific cases.

In regard to federal-state relations, the intent of the framers of the United States Constitution is well understood at a general level. The framers were keenly aware of the potential for conflict between the central government and the states. The document itself established a division of authority that has remained largely intact for two centuries, altered only by a few duly ratified amendments. The core concept is that the federal government is not given general powers, but only specific enumerated powers. If this principle was not made sufficiently clear by a carefully drawn list of powers granted to the central government, the Tenth Amendment, ratified almost as the ink was drying on the original document, stated:

> The powers not delegated to the United States by the Constitution, nor prohibited by it to the States, are reserved to the States respectively, or to the people.

On a structural level, this arrangement reflected the political reality. Although they had need of forming a union to secure their independence from England, at the time of forming the nation, the states were a group of independent sovereigns. For the states, the controlling premise in forming the union was continuation of their sovereignty to the fullest extent, with only a limited cession of power to the newly created national entity. The Tenth Amendment made this explicit; the states ceded only those powers expressly given to the national government and those that were specifically forbidden to the states in the Constitution.[6]

Despite leaving a great deal of power in the states, the constitutional power granted to the federal government is substantial. To avoid a narrow view of the enumerated powers from being an impediment that hamstrung the newly formed entity, the Framers included the "Necessary and Proper Clause," supplementing the enumerated powers with such lesser powers as are needed to effectuate the specifically granted ones. Even more significant to federal-state relations is the Supremacy Clause of Article VI, which provides:

> This Constitution, and the Laws of the United States which shall be made in Pursuance thereof; and all Treaties made, or which shall be made, under the authority of the United States, shall be the supreme Law of the Land; and the Judges in every State shall be bound thereby, any Thing in the Constitution or Laws of any State to the Contrary notwithstanding.

The potential supremacy of federal law is of considerable importance for environmental regulation and creates the possibility of tension between the national government and the states. Assume as a starting point, for now, the proposition that environmental regulation fits within the federal government's interstate commerce power.[7] From this alone, because of the Supremacy Clause, Congress is empowered to enact regulation and have that regulation take precedence over state regulation of the same conduct. Recall, however, (1) the retention of as much sovereignty as possible by the states, and (2) the fact that environmental regulation was traditionally a state function at the core of the state police power to regulate for health, safety, and welfare.

The potentially antagonistic concepts of federal supremacy and the continuing sovereignty of the states, can be, and often are, reconciled by creating a presumption in favor of the validity of concurrent regulation by both the federal and state governments.[8] The presumption of concurrency means, most simply, that state regulation is permitted absent additional indications that the federal government intends to employ its supremacy to block concurrent state activity.[9] This presumption does not do violence to the constitutional division of power. Indeed, especially in the environmental field, it would be odd to expect that the mere fact that Congress does some regulating, absent something more, would be enough to completely displace the ability of the states to exercise their traditional police

---

6. This latter concept is less familiar. A well-known prohibition of that latter type forbids the states from coining money. See U.S. Const., Art. I, §10, cl. 1. Another such prohibition forbids the states from entering into compacts (agreements to work together) unless Congress ratifies the action. See, U. S. Const., Art. I, §10, cl. 3. This prohibition prevents states from combining with one another to the detriment of other states or the nation. In the environmental and natural resources area, compacts often are made with Congress' blessing regarding the allocation of interstate resources, such as rivers.

7. The scope of the federal commerce power has varied over time. Some recent cases noted below raise questions concerning the limits of that federal power.

8. Local governments are created by the states. For the purposes of the federalism discussion in this chapter, local regulations and ordinances are a form of state regulation.

9. The one generic setting in which additional factors need not be present in finding a denial to the states of concurrent regulatory power is in the judge-made "dormant commerce clause" doctrine. For environmental law, the dormant commerce clause doctrine affects natural resources and the movement of solid waste.

power authority over the same subject. Also, it is only a presumption of concurrency, one that is subject to revision by Congress in the legislative process.

Over time, two lines of cases have emerged that delineate the extent to which federal laws and regulation displace state authority because of federal supremacy. The more general line of cases addresses the subject in terms of "federal preemption." The narrower line of cases applies to state efforts that directly affect the interstate movement of goods and services and is described as involving the "dormant commerce clause."

As a doctrinal matter affecting environmental law, there is more to federalism than just preemption and dormant commerce clause cases. There are two more pieces to the "power puzzle": (1) defining what falls within the enumerated powers of the United States (and what is beyond those powers) and (2) mapping out the very complex issue of state sovereign immunity in cases that are litigated in the courts of the federal sovereign. These last two topics are addressed more fully at the end of the chapter.

## B. PREEMPTION OF STATE LAW

Establishing concurrent regulation as the norm does not negate the power of supremacy. Thus, for example, if Congress expressly says that there shall be only federal law on an environmental topic, state laws to the contrary are not permitted. Congressional action of this type is called "express preemption." In the environmental field (as in almost all fields), express preemption is seldom used, but there are a few examples, the most prominent of which is express federal preemption of state regulation of nuclear safety.[10]

Express preemption is not the only way in which the effect of the Supremacy Clause can lead to the invalidation of state environmental regulation. A second branch of federal preemption is called "field occupancy." For there to be field occupancy preemption, the congressional legislation on a topic usually must be so extensive as to support the inference that Congress intends whatever parts of the topic it does not regulate be left unregulated. A third category of preemptive displacement of state law occurs when there is a conflict between state law and federal law. Even though Congress has not manifested an intent, either expressly or through field occupancy, to preempt the entire field, the simple command of the Supremacy Clause forbids state enactments incompatible with federal law, so the conflicting state regulatory effort must fall.

Cases of implied, nonexplicit "conflict" preemption range from very simple to very subtle. Simple cases, for example, might involve a federal specification of a design standard for supertankers that the state wishes to make more stringent in an effort to prevent oil spills.[11] Subtle cases more often involve claims that state

---

10. See, Atomic Energy Act of 1954 §§271 & 274(k), codified at 42 U.S.C. §§2018 & 2021(k).

11. See Ray v. Atlantic Richfield Co., 435 U.S. 151 (1978). Conflict preemption cases of this type are sometimes called "impossibility of dual compliance" cases. That label is underinclusive because there are some cases in which dual compliance is physically possible, but courts nevertheless find that an additional and more burdensome state requirement creates a conflict with the federal requirement.

regulation of an activity is contrary to federal policy. For example, consider the position of the holder of a federal license to operate a hydropower dam. The license was issued by the Federal Energy Regulatory Commission (FERC), which is authorized by Congress to grant such licenses as part of its authority to regulate power generation in the national interest. Moreover, FERC is required by statute to consider water quality and environmental issues in its licensing procedures. The state in which the dam is being built, unsatisfied with the environmental protection afforded by the terms of the FERC operating license of the project, requires that the applicant maintain larger instream flows than those required by FERC. Does the state regulation "[stand] as an obstacle to the full accomplishment and execution of the full purposes and objectives of Congress"when it delegated to FERC the implementation of the federal energy policy?[12]

The United States Supreme Court, in a case involving pesticide regulation, summarized the general framework of preemption analysis as follows:

> Under the Supremacy Clause, U.S. Const., Art. VI, cl. 2, state laws that "interfere with, or are contrary to the laws of Congress, made in pursuance of the constitution" are invalid. Gibbons v. Ogden, 9 Wheat. 1, 211 (1824) (Marshall, C.J.). The ways in which federal law may preempt state law are well established and in the first instance turn on congressional intent. Congress' intent to supplant state authority in a particular field may be express in the terms of the statute. Absent explicit preemptive language, Congress' intent to supersede state law in a given area may nonetheless be implicit if a scheme of federal regulation is "so pervasive as to make reasonable the inference that Congress left no room for the States to supplement it," if "the Act of Congress...touch[es] a field in which the federal interest is so dominant that the federal system will be assumed to preclude enforcement of state laws on the same subject," or if the goals "sought to be obtained" and the "obligations imposed" reveal a purpose to preclude state authority. Rice v. Santa Fe Elevator Corp., 331 U.S. 218, 230 (1947). See Pacific Gas & Electric Co. v. State Energy Resources Conservation and Development Commission, 461 U.S. 190, 203-204 (1983). When considering preemption, "we start with the assumption that the historic police powers of the States were not to be superseded by the Federal Act unless that was the clear and manifest purpose of Congress." Rice, supra, 331 U.S. at 230.

Even when Congress has not chosen to occupy a particular field, preemption may occur to the extent that state and federal law actually conflict. Such a conflict arises when "compliance with both federal and state regulations is a physical impossibility," Florida Lime & Avocado Growers, Inc. v. Paul, 373 U.S. 132, 142–143 (1963), or when a state law "stands as an obstacle to the accomplishment and execution of the full purposes and objectives of Congress." Hines v. Davidowitz, 312 U.S. 52 (1941).

> It is, finally, axiomatic that "for the purposes of the Supremacy Clause, the constitutionality of local ordinances is analyzed in the same way as that of statewide laws." Hillsborough v. Automated Medical Laboratories, Inc., 471 U.S. 707, 713 (1985).[13]

---

12 . Hines v. Davidowitz, 312 U.S. 52, 67 (1941). See California v. FERC, 495 U.S. 490 (1990) (holding the state regulation invalid). This example is more fully discussed in section 2 below.

13. Wisconsin Public Intervenor v. Mortier, 501 U.S. 597, 605 (1991).

### Section 1. PURPOSE REVIEW:
### ALLOWING THE STATES GREATER REGULATORY LEEWAY

While general statements of the law of federal preemption appear succinct and, perhaps, easily understood, the cases themselves frequently are difficult to understand and turn on very subtle distinctions. In the environmental area, the case of Huron Portland Cement Co. v. Detroit, 362 U.S. 440 (1960) marks the emergence of a very distinctive trend in environmental preemption litigation. That case upheld a local Detroit smoke abatement ordinance that was applied to ships that docked at Detroit. The cement company owned and operated ships whose boilers had to remain fired while in port in order to operate the deck equipment for loading and unloading. The particular boilers in question had operational characteristics that caused them to violate Detroit's Smoke Abatement Code. Those same boilers were regulated by federal law; they were inspected by the Coast Guard and found to meet all applicable federal requirements. In regard to the relevant legislation, the Court stated:

> 46 U.S.C.A. §392(c) make[s] clear that inspection of boilers and related equipment is for the purpose of seeing to it that the equipment "may be safely employed in the service proposed."... By contrast, the sole aim of the Detroit ordinance is the elimination of air pollution to protect the health and enhance the cleanliness of the local community. 362 U.S. at 445.

The "different purposes" test, as it might be called, does not sit easily alongside the line of cases that invalidate state regulations because of the difficulty or impossibility of dual compliance. In *Huron Portland Cement*, it was conceded that "structural alterations" of the vessels would be required for them to comply with the Detroit ordinance (i.e., the boilers could not easily be retrofitted to meet the Detroit standards and might have to be replaced). In considering the remainder of the materials on federal preemption of state environmental regulation, try to discern why the courts are so willing to adopt a very narrow view of what constitutes a direct conflict with federal law.

### Pacific Gas and Electric v. California Energy Resources Conservation & Development Commission
United States Supreme Court, 1983
461 U.S. 190, 103 S.Ct. 1713, 75 L.Ed. 752

WHITE, J. The turning of swords into plowshares has symbolized the transformation of atomic power into a source of energy in American society. To facilitate this development the Federal Government relaxed its monopoly over fissionable materials and nuclear technology, and in its place, erected a complex scheme to promote the civilian development of nuclear energy, while seeking to safeguard the public and the environment from the unpredictable risks of a new technology. Early on, it was decided that the States would continue their traditional role in the regulation of electricity production. The interrelationship of federal and state authority in the nuclear energy field has not been simple; the federal regulatory structure has been frequently amended to optimize the partnership.

This case emerges from the intersection of the Federal Government's efforts to ensure that nuclear power is safe with the exercise of the historic state authority over the generation and sale of electricity. At issue is whether provisions in the

1976 amendments to California's Warren-Alquist Act, Cal. Pub. Res. Code Ann. §25524[14] (c). As used in this section, "technology or means for the disposal of high-level nuclear waste" means a method for the permanent and terminal disposition of high-level nuclear waste. It shall not necessarily require that facilities for the application of such technology and/or means be available at the time the commission makes its findings. Such disposition shall not necessarily preclude the possibility of an approved process for retrieval of such waste. which condition the construction of nuclear plants on findings by the State Energy Resources Conservation and Development Commission that adequate storage facilities and means of disposal are available for nuclear waste, are preempted by the Atomic Energy Act of 1954, 42 U.S.C. §2011 et seq.

A nuclear reactor must be periodically refueled and the "spent fuel" removed. This spent fuel is intensely radioactive and must be carefully stored. The general practice is to store the fuel in a water-filled pool at the reactor site. For many years, it was assumed that this fuel would be reprocessed; accordingly, the storage pools were designed as short-term holding facilities with limited storage capacities. As expectations for reprocessing remained unfulfilled, the spent fuel accumulated in the storage pools, creating the risk that nuclear reactors would have to be shut down. This could occur if there were insufficient room in the pool to store spent fuel and also if there were not enough space to hold the entire fuel core when certain inspections or emergencies required unloading of the reactor. In recent years, the problem has taken on special urgency. Some 8,000 metric tons of spent nuclear fuel have already accumulated, and it is projected that by the year 2000 there will be some 72,000 metric tons of spent fuel. Government studies indicate that a number of reactors could be forced to shut down in the near future due to the inability to store spent fuel.

There is a second dimension to the problem. Even with water-pools adequate to store safely all the spent fuel produced during the working lifetime of the reactor, permanent disposal is needed because the wastes will remain radioactive for thousands of years. A number of long-term nuclear waste management strategies have been extensively examined. These range from sinking the wastes in stable deep seabeds, to placing the wastes beneath ice sheets in Greenland and Antarctica, to ejecting the wastes into space by rocket. The greatest attention has been focused on disposing of the wastes in subsurface geologic repositories such as

14. In relevant part the statute provides:

**California Civil Code §25524.2. Disposal of high-level nuclear waste; conditions for plant certification and land use; findings; resolution of disaffirmance; vested rights**

No nuclear fission thermal powerplant, including any to which the provisions of this chapter do not otherwise apply, but excepting those exempted herein, shall be permitted land use in the state, or where applicable, be certified by the [State Energy Resources Conservation and Development] commission until both conditions (a) and (b) have been met:

(a) The commission finds that there has been developed and that the United States through its authorized agency has approved and there exists a demonstrated technology or means for the disposal of high-level nuclear waste.

(b) The commission has reported its findings and the reasons therefor pursuant to paragraph (a) to the Legislature. Such reports of findings shall be assigned to appropriate policy committees for review. The commission may proceed to certify nuclear fission thermal powerplants 100 legislative days after reporting its findings unless within those 100 legislative days either house of the Legislature adopts by a majority vote of its members a resolution disaffirming the findings of the commission made pursuant to paragraph (a)....
[Footnote supplied by the editors]

salt deposits. Problems of how and where to store nuclear wastes have engendered considerable scientific, political, and public debate. There are both safety and economic aspects to the nuclear waste issue: first, if not properly stored, nuclear wastes might leak and endanger both the environment and human health; second, the lack of a long-term disposal option increases the risk that the insufficiency of interim storage space for spent fuel will lead to reactor shutdowns, rendering nuclear energy an unpredictable and uneconomical adventure....

The Act requires that a utility seeking to build in California any electric power generating plant, including a nuclear powerplant must apply for certification to the State Energy Resources Conservation and Development Commission....

Section 25524.2 deals with the long-term solution to nuclear wastes. This section imposes a moratorium on the certification of new nuclear plants until the Energy Commission "finds that there has been developed and that the United States through its authorized agency has approved and there exists a demonstrated technology or means for the disposal of high-level nuclear waste...." §§25524.2(a), (c). Such a finding must be reported to the state legislature, which may nullify it.

In 1978, petitioners Pacific Gas & Electric Co. and Southern California Edison Co. filed this action in the United States District Court, requesting a declaration that numerous provisions of the Warren-Alquist Act, including the two sections challenged here, are invalid under the Supremacy Clause because they are preempted by the Atomic Energy Act. The District Court held...that the two provisions are void because they are preempted by and in conflict with the Atomic Energy Act. 489 F. Supp. 699 (E.D. Cal. 1980). The Court of Appeals for the Ninth Circuit...held that the nuclear moratorium provisions of §25524.2 were not preempted because §§271 and 274(k) of the Atomic Energy Act, 42 U.S.C.A. §§2018 and 2021(k), constitute a congressional authorization for States to regulate nuclear powerplants "for purposes other than protection against radiation hazards." The court held that §25524.2 was not designed to provide protection against radiation hazards, but was adopted because "uncertainties in the nuclear fuel cycle make nuclear power an uneconomical and uncertain source of energy." 659 F.2d 903, at 925 (1981). Nor was the provision invalid as a barrier to fulfillment of the federal goal of encouraging the development of atomic energy. The granting of state authority in §§271 and 274(k), combined with recent federal enactments, demonstrated that Congress did not intend that nuclear power be developed "at all costs," but only that it proceed consistent with other priorities and subject to controls traditionally exercised by the States and expressly preserved by the federal statute....

It is well established that within constitutional limits, Congress may preempt state authority by so stating in express terms. Absent explicit preemptive language, Congress' intent to supersede state law altogether may be found from a "'scheme of federal regulation...so pervasive as to make reasonable the inference that Congress left no room for the States to supplement it,' because the 'Act of Congress may touch a field in which the federal interest is so dominant that the federal system will be assumed to preclude enforcement of state laws on the same subject,' or because 'the object sought to be obtained by the federal law and the character of obligations imposed by it may reveal the same purpose.'" Even where Congress has not entirely displaced state regulation in a specific area, state law is preempted to the extent that it actually conflicts with federal law. Such a conflict arises when "compliance with both federal and state regulations is a physical impossibility," or where state law "stands as an obstacle to the accomplishment and execution of the full purposes and objectives of Congress."

Petitioners, the United States, and supporting amici, present three major lines of argument as to why §25524.2 is preempted. First, they submit that the statute — because it regulates construction of nuclear plants and because it is allegedly predicated on safety concerns — ignores the division between federal and state authority created by the Atomic Energy Act, and falls within the field that the Federal Government has preserved for its own exclusive control. Second, the statute, and the judgments that underlie it, conflict with decisions concerning the nuclear waste disposal issue made by Congress and the Nuclear Regulatory Commission. Third, the California statute frustrates the federal goal of developing nuclear technology as a source of energy. We consider each of these contentions in turn.

Even a brief perusal of the Atomic Energy Act reveals that, despite its comprehensiveness, it does not at any point expressly require the States to construct or authorize nuclear powerplants or prohibit the States from deciding, as an absolute or conditional matter, not to permit the construction of any further reactors. Instead, petitioners argue that the Act is intended to preserve the Federal Government as the sole regulator of all matters nuclear, and that §25524.2 falls within the scope of this impliedly preempted field. But as we view the issue, Congress, in passing the 1954 Act and in subsequently amending it, intended that the federal government should regulate the radiological safety aspects involved in the construction and operation of a nuclear plant, but that the States retain their traditional responsibility in the field of regulating electrical utilities for determining questions of need, reliability, cost, and other related state concerns. Need for new power facilities, their economic feasibility, and rates and services, are areas that have been characteristically governed by the States....

So we start with the assumption that the historic police powers of the States were not to be superseded by the Federal Act "unless that was the clear and manifest purpose of Congress...."

[F]rom the passage of the Atomic Energy Act in 1954, through several revisions, and to the present day, Congress has preserved the dual regulation of nuclear-powered electricity generation: the Federal Government maintains complete control of the safety and "nuclear" aspects of energy generation; the States exercise their traditional authority over the need for additional generating capacity, the type of generating facilities to be licensed, land use, ratemaking, and the like.

The above is not particularly controversial. But deciding how §25524.2 is to be construed and classified is a more difficult proposition. At the outset, we emphasize that the statute does not seek to regulate the construction or operation of a nuclear powerplant. It would clearly be impermissible for California to attempt to do so, for such regulation, even if enacted out of non-safety concerns, would nevertheless directly conflict with the NRC's exclusive authority over plant construction and operation. Respondents appear to concede as much. Respondents do broadly argue, however, that although safety regulation of nuclear plants by States is forbidden, a State may completely prohibit new construction until its safety concerns are satisfied by the Federal Government. We reject this line of reasoning. State safety regulation is not preempted only when it conflicts with federal law. Rather, the Federal Government has occupied the entire field of nuclear safety concerns, except the limited powers expressly ceded to the States. When the Federal Government completely occupies a given field or an identifiable portion of it, as it has done here, the test of preemption is whether "the matter on which the State asserts the right to act is in any way regulated by the Federal Act." Rice v. Santa Fe Elevator Corp., 331 U.S. at 236. A state moratorium on nuclear construction grounded in safety concerns falls squarely within the prohibited field. Moreover, a state judgment that nuclear power is not safe enough to be further developed would conflict directly with the countervailing judgment of the NRC that nuclear construction may proceed notwithstanding extant uncertainties as to waste disposal. A state prohibition on nuclear construction for safety reasons would also be in the teeth of the Atomic Energy Act's objective to insure that nuclear technology be safe enough for widespread development and use — and would be preempted for that reason.

That being the case, it is necessary to determine whether there is a non-safety rationale for §25524.2. California has maintained, and the Court of Appeals agreed, that §25524.2 was aimed at economic problems, not radiation hazards....

Without a permanent means of disposal, the nuclear waste problem could become critical, leading to unpredictably high costs to contain the problem, or worse, shutdowns in reactors. "Waste disposal safety," the Reassessment Reports notes, "is not directly addressed by the bills, which ask only that a method [of waste disposal] be chosen and accepted by the federal government."

The Court of Appeals adopted this reading of §25524.2. Relying on the Reassessment Report, the court concluded:

[S]ection 25524.2 is directed towards purposes other than protection against radiation hazards. While Proposition 15 would have required California to judge the safety of a proposed method of waste disposal, section 25524.2 leaves that judgment to the federal government. California is concerned not with the adequacy of the method, but rather with its existence. 659 F.2d at 925.

Our general practice is to place considerable confidence in the interpretations of state law reached by the federal courts of appeals.

Although these specific indicia of California's intent in enacting §25524.2 are subject to varying interpretation, there are two further reasons why we should not become embroiled in attempting to ascertain California's true motive. First, inquiry into legislative motive is often an unsatisfactory venture. What motivates one legislator to vote for a statute is not necessarily what motivates scores of others to enact it. Second, it would be particularly pointless for us to engage in such inquiry here when it is clear that the States have been allowed to retain authority over the need for electrical generating facilities easily sufficient to permit a State so inclined to halt the construction of new nuclear plants by refusing on economic grounds to issue certificates of public convenience in individual proceedings. In these circumstances, it should be up to Congress to determine whether a State has misused the authority left in its hands.

Therefore, we accept California's avowed economic purpose as the rationale for enacting §25524.2. Accordingly, the statute lies outside the occupied field of nuclear safety regulation.

Petitioners' second major argument concerns federal regulation aimed at the nuclear waste disposal problem itself. It is contended that §25524.2 conflicts with federal regulation of nuclear waste disposal, with the NRC's decision that it is permissible to continue to license reactors, notwithstanding uncertainty surrounding the waste disposal problem, and with Congress' recent passage of legislation directed at that problem....

California [has not, however] sought through §25524.2 to impose its own standards on nuclear waste disposal. The statute accepts that it is federal responsibility to develop and license such technology. As there is no attempt on California's part to enter this field, one which is occupied by the Federal Government, we do not find §25524.2 preempted any more by the NRC's obligations in the waste disposal field than by its licensing power over the plants themselves....

Finally, it is strongly contended that §25524.2 frustrates the Atomic Energy Act's purpose to develop the commercial use of nuclear power. It is well established that state law is preempted if it "stands as an obstacle to the accomplishment and execution of the full purposes and objectives of Congress."

There is little doubt that a primary purpose of the Atomic Energy Act was, and continues to be, the promotion of nuclear power. The Act itself states that it is a program "to encourage widespread participation in the development and utilization of atomic energy for peaceful purposes to the maximum extent consistent with the common defense and security and with the health and safety of the public." 42 U.S.C. §2013(d). The House and Senate Reports confirmed that it was a "major policy goal of the United States" that the involvement of private industry would "speed the further development of the peaceful uses of atomic energy...."

The Court of Appeals' suggestion that legislation since 1974 has indicated a "change in congressional outlook" is unconvincing. The court observed that Congress reorganized the Atomic Energy Commission in 1974 by dividing the promotional and safety responsibilities of the AEC, giving the former to the Energy Research and Development Administration (ERDA) and the latter to the NRC. Energy Reorganization Act of 1974, 88 Stat. 1233, 42 U.S.C. §5801 et seq. The evident desire of Congress to prevent safety from being compromised by promotional concerns does not translate into an abandonment of the objective of promoting nuclear power. The legislation was carefully drafted, in fact, to avoid any antinuclear sentiment....

The Court of Appeals is right, however, that the promotion of nuclear power is not to be accomplished "at all costs." The elaborate licensing and safety provisions and the continued preservation of state regulation in traditional areas belie that. Moreover, Congress has allowed the States to determine — as a matter of economics — whether a nuclear plant vis-a-vis a fossil fuel plant should be built. The decision of California to exercise that authority does not, in itself, constitute a basis for preemption. Therefore, while the argument of petitioners and the United States has considerable force, the legal reality remains that Congress has left sufficient authority in the States to allow the development of nuclear power to be slowed or even stopped for economic reasons. Given this statutory scheme, it is for Congress to rethink the division of regulatory authority in light of its possible exercise by the States to undercut a federal objective. The courts should not assume the role which our system assigns to Congress.

The judgment of the Court of Appeals is affirmed.

### COMMENTARY AND QUESTIONS

1. **The concurring, even less preemptive view in** *Pacific Gas.* Justice Blackmun, joined by Justice Stevens, wrote separately, taking issue with the portion of the majority opinion arguing that a state could not prohibit nuclear power totally if it were motivated by safety. The first ground of disagreement was that the majority

had overstated the scope of the field expressly occupied by Congress: it was not the broad field of nuclear safety concerns that Congress had addressed; it was only the narrower field "of how a nuclear power plant should be constructed and operated to protect against radiation hazards." The concurrence also viewed the promotion of nuclear power as only intending to make that option an available energy source, not a mandatory one. This difference in view would deflect a challenge based on policy contradiction preemption when a state imposed extremely rigorous standards, or declined to have nuclear power for whatever reason.

2. **Congressional intent to preempt nuclear state safety standards.** Congress pretty clearly intended to preempt nuclear radiation safety issues from state and local control. Whatever one's views about the nuclear establishment and the national decision to add nuclear power to America's energy policy, a strong case can be made for uniform national nuclear radiation standards. The technical details of plant design and licensing are dictated by both applicable safety standards and available nuclear technology. If states set radiological emission standards different from federal standards, plants in different locations would be forced to employ different design and radiation control techniques. This variation would require expensive, unique designs for each such plant, making the cost of nuclear generation all the more expensive. Still, despite the logic in support of uniform standards, many state governments feel that health, safety, and welfare are quintessentially state concerns. Many would like to require safer, lower levels of radiation emissions into their receiving air and water, based on state-of-the-art scientific research. Several states tried to do so, but were quashed on federal preemption grounds. See Northern States Power , 447 F.2d 1143 (8th Cir. 1971), aff'd 405 U.S. 1035 (1972).

3. **The "different purpose" test of preemption.** The California legislation is but one of many examples that opposition to nuclear power plants has continued unabated since the advent of commercial reactors. The California legislation, in effect, placed a moratorium on nuclear development in the state. Do you suppose that fiscal responsibility was truly the driving purpose behind the state legislation and the popular referendum that preceded it?

Justice White declared that "the test of preemption is whether 'the matter on which the State asserts the right to act is in any way regulated by the Federal Act.'" He decided that it was not, mainly on the basis that California had a different purported purpose than safety when it regulated. In a federal system like that of the United States, with its many checks and balances, the Supreme Court should not readily ignore a state's declarations about its legislative purpose. Can the Court better evaluate for itself whether the state regulation effectively determines matters that the federal government is supposed to decide? For example, in *Pacific Gas*, it would seem that the Court can ascertain whether California is in fact regulating questions of nuclear plant construction and design. On the facts given, it is clear that California is not regulating those preempted areas within the nuclear field. What would Justice White do in the event that the NRC approves a technology for spent fuel reprocessing and the California Energy Commission or the

Legislature still refuses to certify a nuclear power plant? Does it matter how expensive the reprocessing method is?

4. **Beyond purpose: conflicting policies.** Perhaps *Pacific Gas* and other preemption cases can be better understood as judicial recognition that many areas of modern life involve a wide array of important governmental policies — economic, social, environmental, health, and safety — and that none of these policies, even nuclear promotion, is so predominant as to override all other legitimate governmental concerns. At one level, the resolution of this problem is semantic. The Court notes that if a field is "pervasively regulated" by the federal government, the state cannot enter it at all. The pervaded field might have been defined as anything affecting in any way the design and operation of nuclear plants, which would have precluded California's regulation. But the definition of pervasively regulated fields tends to be narrower, as with nuclear plant safety in *Pacific Gas*. If the courts decide that not everything remotely touching "nuclear design or safety" is preempted, the way is open to permit a variety of governmental policies, state as well as federal, to be applied. One may thus read *Pacific Gas* as an avenue toward democratic pluralism. Congress, if it finds federal interests being eclipsed, can always pass preemptive legislation to reassert its policy choices and protect them from interference.

5. **Federal preemption of tort remedies.** In Silkwood v. Kerr-McGee, 464 U.S. 238 (1984) sizeable awards of state common law damages, both compensatory and punitive, were upheld against a claim of federal preemption of nuclear safety issues. After *Silkwood*, how likely is it that federal preemption of any state common law tort recoveries for injuries caused by a federally regulated activity will be found in the absence of express congressional language to that effect?

In English v. General Electric Company, 496 U.S. 72 (1990), the Court revisited the subject of preemption of tort remedies in another case involving a nuclear materials processor as defendant. In that case, the plaintiff reported workplace safety violations and eventually was fired by her employer. She sought a statutory remedy under a whistleblower's provision of the federal Energy Reorganization Act of 1974, but was denied relief on procedural grounds. She subsequently filed a state common law tort suit for intentional infliction of emotional distress and was met with the claim of federal preemption. A unanimous Supreme Court rejected the preemption argument. The Court stated:

> Although the decision in *Silkwood* was based in substantial part on legislative history suggesting that Congress did not intend to include in the preempted field state tort remedies for radiation-based injuries, we think it would be odd, if not irrational, to conclude that Congress intended to include tort actions stemming from retaliation against whistleblowers in the preempted field but intended not to include tort actions stemming from radiation damage suffered as a result of actual safety violations. 496 U.S. at 85.

The court also rejected the narrower argument that the enactment of a federal whistleblower remedy precluded the availability of additional state law-based remedies that served a similar purpose.

6. **Other environmental preemptions.** preemption issues have arisen in a variety of other environmental controversies, in which regulated interests have attempted to

use federal law to trump state or local regulations (or state law to trump local regulations). The cases include efforts to prevent local town governments from passing ordinances requiring stricter standards of herbicide and pesticide applicators, as in *Mortier*, to industry efforts to prevent states from requiring broader public availability of information on toxics in the workplace than federal OSHA standards provide. See e.g., CSX Transp. v. Public Util. Comm. of Ohio, 901 F.2d 497 (6th Cir. 1990) (federal rail safety act preempted most of the state hazardous material transport law); Assoc. Industries of Mass. v. Dep't of Labor, 898 F.2d 274 (1st Cir. 1990) (state asbestos abatement statute generally not preempted by OSHA); Ohio Manuf. Assoc. v. City of Akron, 801 F.2d 824 (6th Cir. 1984) (local "right to know" ordinance preempted by federal statute).

Section 2. **PREEMPTING STATE INTERFERENCE
WITH FEDERAL RESOURCE PROGRAMS**

Beginning in the latter half of the 19th century with the federal mining acts and the creation of the National Forest system on the federal public lands, Congress established numerous federal resource management programs designed to promote a variety of declared national interests. When states try to regulate the environmental impacts of federal programs and their licensees, thorny preemption issues arise.

Generically, these cases most often raise claims that the state law interferes with the accomplishment of federal objectives. In broad terms, the argument goes like this: the federal agency, by licensing the private activity as part of its resource management program, has affirmatively authorized the activity; state laws that bar or burden the activity therefore conflict with federal law. The counter-argument rests on the view that federal licenses or permits are not intended to divest states of their traditional police power authority, including environmental quality regulation. Cases like *Huron Portland Cement* and the general judicial reluctance to find preemption, in the absence of additional facts, tend to support the validity of concurrent state regulation.

Frequently, however, cases are complicated by the fact that many federal licensing programs also include their own environmental standards and reviews. If a federal agency imposes environmentally protective conditions on its licensees, the preemption argument against additional state environmental regulation is strengthened. At that point, the additional state environmental review may be redundant and, more tellingly, inconsistent with federal determination of the proper balance between environmental quality and other national programmatic objectives. In this situation, concurrent state regulation arguably constitutes an interference with the federal program.

The Supreme Court decided two such cases in 1987 and 1990, one involving minimum streamflow requirements imposed on a federally-licensed hydropower facility and the other involving federally-permitted mining on National Forest lands. In California v. Federal Energy Regulatory Commission, 495 U.S. 490 (1990) (Rock Creek, a proposed hydroelectric facility on Rock Creek, a tributary of the American River in California, threatened to reduce stream flows in a way that would adversely affect fisheries. FERC, as part of its licensing process and pursuant to congressional directives,[15] reviewed information on these issues and granted the applicant a license that prescribed specified minimum stream flows. FERC's minimum flow standard allowed stream flows to decline to less than a third of the state's proposed minimum requirements. The Supreme Court held that FERC's minimal standards governed;[16] Faced with the seemingly clear intent of Congress to preserve state water regulatory powers, the *First Iowa* decision narrowed the clause's meaning, holding that its preservation of state jurisdiction is "confined to rights of the same nature as those relating to the use of water in irrigation or for municipal purposes." 328 U.S. at 175–176. California could not impose its own more environmentally protective stream flow requirements.[17]

California Coastal Commission v. Granite Rock Co., 480 U.S. 572 (1987), presented a similarly subtle preemption problem. Granite Rock had obtained a permit from the U.S. Forest Service to mine for pharmaceutical grade white limestone in a portion of the Los Padres National Forest near Big Sur (California). Due to the land's proximity to the Pacific Coast, the area was also within the jurisdiction of the California Coastal Commission (CCC), a state agency having extensive land use planning and environmental protection powers. Despite the existence of the federal permit, CCC directed Granite Rock to apply to it for an additional permit, a request that was met with a lawsuit claiming that the CCC's authority had been preempted.

The Ninth Circuit Court of Appeals decided in favor of Granite Rock's preemption argument, because the Forest Service, through its permit regulations, applied state environmental standards as the basis for its own permitting decisions.[18] Accordingly, the Ninth Circuit held there was no remaining function for the state agency to perform. The Supreme Court reversed, requiring Granite Rock to submit to the state permit proceeding. One key to the ruling lay in the language of the Forest Service regulations, several of which called for federal licensees to comply with applicable state environmental quality standards; one regulation

---

15. The Electric Consumers Protection Act of 1986, Pub. L. 99–495, codified as part of the Federal Power Act at 16 U.S.C.A. §797(e) and §803(a), requires FERC to consider fish and wildlife effects in making its licensure determinations, although in practice the statutory standards are neither substantively nor procedurally rigorous.

16. The Court applied the arguments of its 1946 decision in First Iowa Hydro-Electric Cooperative v. FPC, 328 U.S. 152, interpreting §27 of the FPA, which provides:

Nothing contained in this chapter shall be construed as affecting or intending to affect or in any way to interfere with the laws of the respective States relating to the control, appropriation, use, or distribution of water used in irrigation or for municipal or other uses, or any vested right acquired therein. 16 U.S.C.A. §821.

17. In Nugget Hydroelectric C. v. SWRCB, Civs-90-0203 EJG/EM (E.D. Cal. July 9, 1991), the pre-emptive effect of *Rock Creek* was extended to divest the California State Water Resource Control Board (SWRCB) of the authority to require the FERC licensee to submit information to the state on issues other than the availability of water. The SWRCB had required Nugget to provide more thorough analyses of the instream impacts of its project than those provided to FERC, at which point Nugget withdrew its application for a SWRCB permit and went to federal court seeking a preemption-based order to save it from having to "jump through a never-ending series of hoops [that] relate to matters already reviewed by FERC," adding that "the delay and cost impose a tremendous hardship on plaintiff [Nugget]." The court pre-empted the SWRCB efforts.

18. 768 F.2d 1077, 1083 (1985).

specifically mentioned state permits' usefulness for proving such compliance with state regulations. See 36 C.F.R. §§228.5 (b), 228.8 (a–c, h).

The licensee's second major contention in the Supreme Court was that the CCC's actions were a thinly-veiled effort to reverse the Forest Service's choices under its land use planning mandate, contained in the National Forest Management Act of 1976, 16 U.S.C.A. §§1600–1614. Granite Rock claimed that CCC was trying to prohibit mining in an area that the Forest Service had determined was appropriate for mining. The majority found this challenge speculative; CCC had not acted to impose any conditions or requirements on Granite Rock prior to the filing of the lawsuit.

Justice O'Connor's majority opinion also drew a rather fine semantic distinction between land use planning and environmental protection:

> The California Coastal Commission alleges that it will use its permit requirement to impose reasonable environmental regulation.... Federal land use statutes and regulations, while arguably expressing an intent to preempt state land use planning, distinguish environmental regulation from land use planning. 480 U.S. at 593.

### COMMENTARY AND QUESTIONS

1. **The case for finding preemption.** *Granite Rock* presents a strong case for displacement of state authority. The parallel state authority that is to be exercised affects lands in federal ownership that are part of the National Forest system and that are being managed under an articulated "multiple use" mandate that establishes federal policies regarding the administration of National Forest tracts. See Chapter 24. To whatever extent the California Coastal Commission (CCC) might thwart a federally approved project, there is both an intrusion upon federal government planning and *de facto* imposition of state land use controls on federal land. These points motivated a dissent by Justice Powell (joined by Justice Stevens) and a dissent by Justice Scalia (joined by Justice White). Even so, a majority of the Court was willing to support concurrent regulatory control as long as there was no concrete conflict of regulations. What can the CCC now impose by way of conditions that would not be in conflict with the Forest Service plan? Would erosion and dust emission control requirements that forced Granite Rock to keep excavated materials covered during mining operations, or a strict post-mining reclamation requirement, be allowed? Does it matter how much compliance with such requirements would cost? What if, for example, the increased cost made the proposed mining project more expensive than other feasible alternative sites?

2. **Local expertise and pluralism.** What makes concurrent levels of regulatory authority so attractive? Concurrency almost surely is less efficient, adding costs for dual filings, studies, and processing, constantly posing opportunities for delay. Does concurrency sustain the traditional view of the states as primary regulators of environmental matters? In an era of massive federal statutory intervention in the environmental field, it sometimes seems hard to resist the conclusion that Congress and the federal bureaucratic army have become the primary regulatory system. Is local expertise at issue here? Is there any indication that the CCC is

better apprized of the environmental consequences of the proposed action than the federal District Ranger? A different justification for concurrency lies in the desire to respect the sovereignty of the states. Making concurrency the norm arguably does not undercut federal authority; it simply places the burden on the federal government to announce its intentions to exercise unilateral control. It would appear that the environmental perspective is benefited by concurrency. The theory is that two forums are better than one. The public environmental perspective may receive a more hospitable reception in one place rather than the other, and a potentially destructive project must survive the rigors of both tests.

3. **State regulation of the federal public lands.** As an historical matter in the public lands area, it is only recently that the property clause of the United States Constitution has been recognized as supporting active federal management authority over federal lands. Nineteenth century cases frequently regarded that clause merely as an authority to own on the same basis as any other landholder, i.e., subject to state regulation. For an excellent discussion of this topic and many others relating to the federal public lands, see Cowart & Fairfax, Public Lands Federalism: Judicial Theory and Administrative Reality, 15 Ecol. L. Q. 375, 439–476 (1988). Cowart and Fairfax criticize the majority opinion in *Granite Rock*:

> The majority opinion fails to clarify either general preemption doctrine or its application to the public lands. Instead, the decision turns on a presumed fine-grained distinction between land use planning and environmental regulation. That distinction is unclear, unsupported by the public lands statutes and not at all helpful to state and federal legislators and administrators seeking to manage complex intermixed resources. [Id. at 463.]

Are these criticisms well taken? The distinction is indeed a fine one, but *Pacific Gas* and *Huron Portland Cement* similarly draw distinctions based on the purposes of statutes. It is unfortunate that no clear guide was announced, but is it really within the power of the Court rather than Congress to unravel the complexities of concurrency?

4. **Is preemption analysis better applied on a local or a national level?** Consider the following criticism of the *Granite Rock* approach:

> The Court focused on the preemptive effect of the governing federal statutes and nationwide regulations. Some vehicle was needed, it rightly assumed, to avoid giving the states a veto over federal land uses. But the Court could better have addressed the issue by instead considering the preemption of state law at the lowest level - the preemption that occurs when a federal agency at the local level lawfully acts in a way that causes conflict with a state or local law. So long as federal action preempts at that level, preemption at a higher level is unneeded and, in this setting at least, undesirable. From an institutional perspective, preemption at the lowest level can best foster cooperative land planning on the scene. For a variety of reasons, preemption should occur only when a federal agency concludes, in a site-specific determination made in the course of statutory land-planning processes, that a particular federal use should override contrary state and local rules. Freyfogle, Granite Rock: Institutional Competence and the State Role in Federal Land Planning, 59 U. Colo. L. Rev. 475, 477 (1988).

5. **State regulation of federal facilities.** To what extent can states and local governments apply their environmental regulations to federal facilities in their territory?

The question has recurred over the years, as Army posts allow toxics to leach into groundwater, federal hospitals violate air pollution standards, federal authorities authorize the construction of mammoth power transmission towers or radio transmission towers in historic zones, and so on. The simplest answer seems to be that the federal action trumps state and local regulations unless the basic federal statute accepts state jurisdiction, or unless the federal government has voluntarily agreed to accommodate state and local restraints.

6. **Requirements for federal-state coordination.** Given the numerous opportunities for overlapping federal-state jurisdictions over projects, activities, and regulatory programs, there are obvious advantages to coordinating actions. The federal government often has subscribed to the rhetoric of federal-state coordination and has implemented a succession of formal procedural requirements aimed toward that end. For many years, Circular A-95, issued by the federal Office of Management and Budget (OMB) in 1968, directed federal agencies to provide opportunities for advance consultation with state agencies whenever a federal proposal might affect state interests. If a state was about to be chosen as the site of a federal bombing range, waste dump, or penitentiary, the Governor's office was supposed to get early warning of it through A-95 procedures. Executive Order 12,372, "Intergovernmental Review of Federal Programs" (July 14, 1982), issued early in the Reagan Presidency, supplanted A-95 and sought to establish a more responsive process. Supplementing the Intergovernmental Cooperation Act of 1968, 42 U.S.C.A. §4231(a), E.O. 12,372 states that, "federal agencies shall provide opportunities for consultation by elected officials of those State and local governments that would provide the non-Federal funds for, or that would be directly affected by, proposed Federal financial assistance or direct Federal development." Section 2(a) of the order encouraged states to develop a process for formulating a position to be communicated to the relevant federal agency, and directed that federal agency to "utilize the State process to determine official views of State and local elected officials."

Executive Order 12,372 seems to have failed to live up to its potential. It has done little to improve avenues of federal consultation with states and appears to be largely ignored by federal agencies. There have been no comprehensive studies by OMB or the congressional General Accounting Office of its impact, but the informally expressed opinion of one expert in intergovernmental relations was that the order has resulted in "a debilitation of the [prior] consultative process." The few cases that raise E.O. 12,372 arguments seem to provide a basis for using the order to insist on consultation. In Azzolina v. United States Postal Service, 602 F. Supp. 859, 863 (D.N.J. 1985), for example, a case involving siting of a post office, the court affirmed that "federal agencies are to provide opportunities for consultation and communication and to make efforts to accommodate state and local concerns." The court went on to note that federal agencies also have an obligation to develop a reviewable record in cases where they choose to act in disharmony with local planning objectives. The commentators are divided on the effect of the executive order. Compare Bell & Johnson, State Water Laws & Federal Water Uses: The History of Conflict, The Prospects for Accommodation, 21 Envtl. L. 1, 68–70 (1991) (the order is ineffectual), with Mandelker, Controlling Non-Point Source Water

Pollution: Can It Be Done?, 65 Chicago-Kent L. Rev. 479, 490-91 (1989) (noting greater federal responsiveness to state planning concerns).

**7. Preemption by non-compliance with federal law.** Assume that a federal statute establishes requirements for conducting activity in a particular area that is pre-emptive of state regulation of that area. Assume further that the regulated party fails to comply with the federally mandated requirements. Is a state law suit based on that conduct still preempted by the federal law despite the non-compliance of the regulated party? Talbott v. C. R. Bard, Inc., 63 F.3d 25 (1st Cir. 1995) is such a case in which the plaintiff sued on a state law defective products theory against a catheter manufacturer whose product was preemptively regulated under the Medical Device Amendments of 1976 to the Federal Food, Drug, and Cosmetic Act, 21 U.S.C. §360k(a).

*Talbott* upholds the defendant's preemption defense. How does the decision in *Talbott* square with traditional tort evidentiary doctrines that allow proof of viola-tion of federal safety standards as relevant to non-preempted state law tort actions? One view is that the very nature of preemption, the displacement of state law in its entirety, renders the federal law the only operative regulatory regime, and if there is non-compliance with that law, remedies must be found under the federal law itself. A competing view is that allowing state remedies where there is viola-tion of the preemptive federal scheme adds a further incentive to obedience by the regulated party. There are additional positions. One of particular interest to envi-ronmental law is a fraud-on-the-agency theory in disclosure-based permitting statutes. In this regard, the Medical Device Amendments (MDA) at issue in *Talbott* is like the Toxic Substances Control Act and the Federal Insecticide, Fungicide, and Rodenticide Act, discussed in Chapter 15, mandating disclosure to the regulatory agency of test data as a prerequisite to obtaining agency approval to market the product. The thrust of this position is captured succinctly in a California MDA pre-emption case, Evraets v. Intermedic Intraocular Inc., 29 Cal. App. 4th 779, 790–91, 34 Cal. Rptr. 2d 852, 858 (2d Dist. 1999) in which the court states:

> It is fair to say that for a medical device manufacturer to claim the shield of preemption, the manufacturer must 'play by the rules.' If the manufacturer subverts the rules and obtains approval to market its products by misrepre-senting the risks involved [to the relevant agency], knowing that this disinfor-mation will ultimately harm patients, the injured party should be entitled to sue.

This position is squarely rejected in *Talbott* on the ground of the broad expressly preemptive language of the MDA, and also on the basis of a more process-oriented analysis of the law that views the Congress, through preemption, as having appointed the enforcing agency as the sole arbiter of how best to effectuate the statutory regime. As to the plight of victims, the court observes that Congress was free to create a federal private party remedy had it wanted to add that form of addi-tional compliance promotion to the MDA. Interestingly, in *Talbott*, the United States, as amicus, urged allowance of an exception to preemption where the rele-vant agency has made a determination of non-compliance as was done in relation to Bard. Presumably, such an agency finding would limit the possibility of private actions at variance with agency policy. Likewise, allowing private suits might allow the agency to devote its scarce resources to other tasks. But see Kenneth S. Geller and Alan E. Untereiner, Is There a 'Noncompliance' Exception to Federal Preemption?, 10 Toxics Law Reporter 1006 (1996) (approving the *Talbott* result and rejecting noncompliance exceptions to preemption).

8. **Preemption of local municipal laws, etc.** The preemption arguments between federal and state governments are echoed in many cases where local municipal ordinances are challenged, sometimes for double preemption, i.e., by conflict with both the federal law in violation of the supremacy clause, and state law, despite Home Rule. The caselaw tends to track the same analysis as federal/state preemption arguments. For some attorneys, preemption is one of the best fallback issues; if there appear to be no credible arguments on one's side, look for a preemption claim.

---

## C. DORMANT COMMERCE CLAUSE PROTECTION OF THE FREE MOVEMENT OF NATURAL RESOURCES

All of the federal preemption of state law cases described above begin with an affirmative act by Congress. Before the states, the traditional full-purpose sovereigns in the American federal system, can be displaced, the limited federal government must act using its enumerated powers.[19] That is, the mere fact that the Constitution permits federal action does not, alone, preempt state action. There is one major exception to this precept as it applies to the interstate commerce power, and it is an exception that has application in the environmental and natural resources area.

One of the important goals of the Constitution was to permit the development of a national economy. A common practice in the late 18th century (and thereafter) was for nations to erect a variety of barriers to trade with other nations, be it in the form of tariffs, prohibitions on the movement of goods of certain types, pilotage requirements, or other like devices. The states, in the pre-Constitutional period and to the present, have engaged in such trade-restrictive efforts, usually with the aim of protecting local industries from outside competition, requiring outside entities to make use of local goods and services, or to insure that certain natural resources or other natural advantages remained at home. Even without the passage of federal legislation in furtherance of the interstate and international commerce power, these myriad of state and local efforts at economic protectionism work at cross purposes to a constitutionally established national policy.

Recognizing that state and local laws that burden interstate commerce are contrary to constitutional policy is the first step toward allowing courts to declare such laws unconstitutional. The second step, which is seldom stated explicitly in judicial opinions, is more pragmatic: if Congress does not have enough time or resources to pass federal statutes overriding state or local laws whenever the

---

19. As noted above, there are a small number of areas as to which the Tenth Amendment recognizes that the Constitution itself may forbid power to the states.

federal interest in commerce requires it, the federal courts can take on the job. When the commerce clause has not been applied actively in legislation, its power still exists, lying "dormant" until the courts apply it to strike down laws with commerce-burdening effects. The judicial tests of the dormant commerce clause validity of state and local laws closely resembles the tests of regulatory takings (see Chapter 23): The state or local law must have a proper public purpose, not an improper one (e.g., like protectionism, favoring local businesses); its design must be reasonably related to achieving that purpose; and the burden on interstate commerce must not be excessive when balanced against the public purposes. Applying these standards is often a subjective process.

Natural resource cases have been a staple of dormant commerce clause jurisprudence for at least a century. Beginning with a famous opinion by Justice Oliver Wendell Holmes that allowed Connecticut to restrict the export of wild fowl captured by hunters,[20] the law in this area is now fairly well settled and permits states very little latitude in attempting to block the interstate movement of goods and services. That has not, however, kept the states from trying, especially in regard to the movement of solid and hazardous waste.

### Section 1. EVENHANDEDNESS AND THE RULE OF VIRTUAL 'PER SE' INVALIDITY OF DISCRIMINATORY STATE LAWS

For contemporary purposes, for almost fifteen years the leading Supreme Court decision in the dormant commerce clause area has been City of Philadelphia v. New Jersey, 437 U.S. 617 (1978). In that case, which follows, an effort by New Jersey to forbid out-of-state garbage from its landfill sites was struck down as unconstitutional. Philadelphia v. New Jersey was the first of many such cases involving the interstate movement of solid waste. Parochial legislation that seeks to block waste at the state border is easy to enact. Legislated preferences that provide local benefits at the expense of out-of-state third parties are popular and offer no viable political recourse to those who bear the brunt of the law (but who are not part of the in-state voting electorate). In a post-Love Canal, NIMBY[21] world, moreover, limiting in-state waste disposal to a minimum is a very popular position.[22] As one waste disposal official said in a federal hearing on the subject, "Everyone wants us to pick up the trash, but no one wants us to put it down."

### City of Philadelphia v. New Jersey
United States Supreme Court, 1978
437 U.S. 617, 98 S. Ct. 2531, 57 L. Ed. 2d 475

STEWART, J. A New Jersey law prohibits the importation of most "solid or liquid waste which originated or was collected outside the territorial limits of the State..." In this case we are required to decide whether this statutory prohibition violates the Commerce Clause of the United States Constitution.

---

20. See Geer v. Connecticut, 161 U.S. 519 (1896), overruled in Hughes v. Oklahoma, 441 U.S. 322 (1979).
21. "Not in my back yard!"
22. But see C & A Carbone, Inc. v. Town of Clarkston, 511 U.S. 383 (1994), and the flow control cases involving efforts to require that waste remain in-state to provide raw material for trash-to-energy facilities or other economic advantages. These efforts also are constitutionally suspect on dormant commerce clause grounds.

The statutory provision in question is Chapter 363 of 1973 N.J. Laws, which took effect in early 1974. In pertinent part it provides:

> No person shall bring into this State any solid or liquid waste which originated or was collected outside the territorial limits of the State, except garbage to be fed to swine in the State of New Jersey, until the commissioner [of the State Department of Environmental Protection] shall determine that such action can be permitted without endangering the public health, safety and welfare and has promulgated regulations permitting and regulating the treatment and disposal of such waste in this State. N.J. Stat. Ann. §13:1I–10.

As authorized by Ch. 363, the Commissioner promulgated regulations permitting four categories of waste to enter the State. Apart from these narrow exceptions, however, New Jersey closed its borders to all waste from other States.

Immediately affected by these developments were the operators of private landfills in New Jersey, and several cities in other States that had agreements with these operators for waste disposal....

Although the Constitution gives Congress the power to regulate commerce among the States, many subjects of potential federal regulation under that power inevitably escape congressional attention "because of their local character and their number and diversity." South Carolina State Highway Dept. v. Barnwell Bros., Inc., 303 U.S. 177, 185. In the absence of federal legislation, these subjects are open to control by the States so long as they act within the restraints imposed by the Commerce Clause itself. The bounds of these restraints appear nowhere in the words of the Commerce Clause, but have emerged gradually in the decisions of this Court giving effect to its basic purpose. That broad purpose was well expressed by Mr. Justice Jackson in his opinion for the Court in H.P. Hood & Sons, Inc. v. Du Mond, 336 U.S. 525, 537–538:

> This principle that our economic unit is the Nation, which alone has the gamut of powers necessary to control of the economy, including the vital power of erecting customs barriers against foreign competition, has as its corollary that the states are not separable economic units. As the Court said in Baldwin v. Seelig, 294 U.S. 511, 527, "What is ultimate is the principle that one state in its dealings with another may not place itself in a position of economic isolation."

The opinions of the Court through the years have reflected an alertness to the evils of "economic isolation" and protectionism, while at the same time recognizing that incidental burdens on interstate commerce may be unavoidable when a State legislates to safeguard the health and safety of its people. Thus, where simple economic protectionism is effected by state legislation, a virtually per se rule of invalidity has been erected. The clearest example of such legislation is a law that overtly blocks the flow of interstate commerce at a State's borders. But where other legislative objectives are credibly advanced and there is no patent discrimination against interstate trade, the Court has adopted a much more flexible approach, the general contours of which were outlined in Pike v. Bruce Church, Inc., 397 U.S. 137, 142:

> Where the statute regulates evenhandedly to effectuate a legitimate local public interest, and its effects on interstate commerce are only incidental, it will be upheld unless the burden imposed on such commerce is clearly excessive in relation to the putative local benefits.... If a legitimate local purpose is found, then the question becomes one of degree. And the extent of the burden

that will be tolerated will of course depend on the nature of the local interest involved, and on whether it could be promoted as well with a lesser impact on interstate activities....

The crucial inquiry, therefore, must be directed to determining whether Ch. 363 is basically a protectionist measure, or whether it can fairly be viewed as a law directed to legitimate local concerns, with effects upon interstate commerce that are only incidental.

The purpose of Ch. 363 is set out in the statute itself as follows:

The Legislature finds and determines that...the volume of solid and liquid waste continues to rapidly increase, that the treatment and disposal of these wastes continues to pose an even greater threat to the quality of the environment of New Jersey, that the available and appropriate land fill sites within the State are being diminished, that the environment continues to be threatened by the treatment and disposal of waste which originated or was collected outside the State, and that the public health, safety and welfare require that the treatment and disposal within this State of all wastes generated outside of the State be prohibited.

The New Jersey Supreme Court accepted this statement of the state legislature's purpose. The state court additionally found that New Jersey's existing landfill sites will be exhausted within a few years; that to go on using these sites or to develop new ones will take a heavy environmental toll, both from pollution and from loss of scarce open lands; that new techniques to divert waste from landfills to other methods of disposal and resource recovery processes are under development, but that these changes will require time; and finally, that "the extension of the lifespan of existing landfills, resulting from the exclusion of out-of-state waste, may be of crucial importance in preventing further virgin wetlands or other undeveloped lands from being devoted to landfill purposes." 348 A.2d at 509–512. Based on these findings, the court concluded that Ch. 363 was designed to protect, not the State's economy, but its environment, and that its substantial benefits outweigh its "slight" burden on interstate commerce. 348 A.2d at 515–519.

The appellants strenuously contend that Ch. 363, "while outwardly cloaked 'in the currently fashionable garb of environmental protection,'...is actually no more than a legislative effort to suppress competition and stabilize the cost of solid waste disposal for New Jersey residents...." The appellees, on the other hand, deny that Ch. 363 was motivated by financial concerns or economic protectionism....

This dispute about ultimate legislative purpose need not be resolved, because its resolution would not be relevant to the constitutional issue to be decided in this case. Contrary to the evident assumption of the state court and the parties, the evil of protectionism can reside in legislative means as well as legislative ends. Thus, it does not matter whether the ultimate aim of Ch. 363 is to reduce the waste disposal costs of New Jersey residents or to save remaining open lands from pollution, for we assume New Jersey has every right to protect its residents' pocketbooks as well as their environment. And it may be assumed as well that New Jersey may pursue those ends by slowing the flow of all waste into the State's remaining landfills, even though interstate commerce may incidentally be affected. But whatever New Jersey's ultimate purpose, it may not be accomplished by discriminating against articles of commerce coming from outside the State unless there is some reason, apart from their origin, to treat them differently. Both on its face and in its plain effect, Ch. 363 violates this principle of nondiscrimination.

The Court has consistently found parochial legislation of this kind to be constitutionally invalid, whether the ultimate aim of the legislation was to assure a steady supply of milk by erecting barriers to allegedly ruinous outside competition, or to create jobs by keeping industry within the State, or to preserve the State's financial resources from depletion by fencing out indigent immigrants. In each of these cases, a presumably legitimate goal was sought to be achieved by the illegitimate means of isolating the State from the national economy.

Also relevant here are the Court's decisions holding that a State may not accord its own inhabitants a preferred right of access over consumers in other States to natural resources located within its borders. These cases stand for the basic principle that a "State is without power to prevent privately owned articles of trade from being shipped and sold in interstate commerce on the ground that they are required to satisfy local demands or because they are needed by the people of the State." Foster-Fountain Packing Co. v. Haydel, 278 U.S. 1, 10.

The New Jersey law at issue in this case falls squarely within the area that the Commerce Clause puts off limits to state regulation. On its face, it imposes on out-of-state commercial interests the full burden of conserving the State's remaining landfill space. It is true that in our previous cases the scarce natural resource was itself the article of commerce, whereas here the scarce resource and the article of commerce are distinct. But that difference is without consequence. In both instances, the State has overtly moved to slow or freeze the flow of commerce for protectionist reasons. It does not matter that the State has shut the article of commerce inside the State in one case and outside the State in the other. What is crucial is the attempt by one State to isolate itself from a problem common to many by erecting a barrier against the movement of interstate trade....

Today, cities in Pennsylvania and New York find it expedient or necessary to send their waste into New Jersey for disposal, and New Jersey claims the right to close its borders to such traffic. Tomorrow, cities in New Jersey may find it expedient or necessary to send their waste into Pennsylvania or New York for disposal, and those States might then claim the right to close their borders. The Commerce Clause will protect New Jersey in the future, just as it protects her neighbors now, from efforts by one State to isolate itself in the stream of interstate commerce from a problem shared by all. The judgment is reversed.

### COMMENTARY & QUESTIONS

1. **Beyond facial import and export bans.** Recognizing that simple bans on out-of-state waste were legally doomed, states and local governments became more inventive in their efforts to prevent waste importation. A commonly chosen method was to charge differential tipping fees[23] that discouraged disposal of out-of-state wastes at in-state facilities by charging them far higher prices than those charged for in-state wastes. States claimed the differential was justified to offset the costs imposed by the presence of the waste, i.e., the potential environmental

---

23. A tipping fee is paid by a waste disposer seeking to dump at a disposal facility. Usually these fees are levied on a per ton basis. Calling them fees is a bit of a misnomer in this context, for the charges under constitutional scrutiny are more akin to taxes — they are legislatively imposed and inure to the benefit of the government as an addition to the amounts received by the facility operator for disposal.

harms and cost of remediation if the disposal site did have problems in the future. Put differently, the higher fees allegedly were established as an effort to internalize the costs of long-term waste management that were otherwise likely to be borne by the receiving state and its citizens. In Chemical Waste Management. Inc. v. Hunt, 504 U.S. 334 (1992), and again in Oregon Waste Systems, Inc. v. Oregon Department of Environmental Quality, 511 U.S. 93 (1994), differential tipping fees were held unconstitutional. In both instances, the Court treated the regulations as "discriminatory" and therefore prohibited under *Philadelphia's* virtual per se rule of invalidity. Undeterred, states attempted to erect other barriers to the entry of out-of-state wastes. Michigan, for example, erected a comprehensive statewide waste management system that gave local officials an optional veto power over non-local wastes. This was invalidated by the Supreme Court in Fort Gratiot Sanitary Landfill Inc. v. Michigan Department of Natural Resources, 504 U.S. 353 (1992). The Supreme Court quoted *Philadelphia* in stating that, "the evil of protection can reside in the legislative means as well as the legislative ends." 504 U.S. at 360.

2. **Mixed motives and discerning discriminatory legislative purpose.** In dormant commerce clause cases, the court decides whether a legislature has a discriminatory purpose on what might be called an "effects speak louder than words" basis. Contrast that approach with the classic preemption cases, such as *Huron Portland Cement* and *Pacific Gas & Electric* in which legislatures were taken at their word in regard to purposes. Moreover, in the preemption cases, laws motivated in part by a desire to enter the forbidden field could be saved by being mixed with a non-preempted motive. Why is the judicial attitude so much less lenient in dormant commerce clause cases?

3. **Presumptions of invalidity and Congressional authorization of discrimination.** An interesting way to characterize the contrast between the two sets of cases is to say that the presumption of concurrency is reversed. In preemption cases, the presumption is that the state law is to coexist with the federal interest; in dormant commerce clause cases the presumption is that the state law is to be invalidated if it overtly adversely affects the national interest. In the former case, courts defer to state efforts if there is any basis on which to avoid preemption, and Congress has to step in to alter that outcome if it wishes to do so. In dormant commerce clause cases, courts do not defer to state efforts if they discriminate against interstate commerce, and Congress has to step in to alter that outcome if it wishes to do so. Congress occasionally does act to authorize state laws that otherwise would be invalid as violative of the dormant commerce clause. The power to do so is inherent in Congress' plenary control over interstate commerce. The authorization claim is occasionally made in environmental dormant commerce clause cases but usually fails. See, e.g., South-Central Timber Development Co. v. Wunnicke, 467 U.S. 82 (1984) (rejecting claim that ban on export of raw timber was authorized by Congress).

4. **Even-handed legislation, the *Pike* test, and burden weighing.** Regulation that is not deemed discriminatory against interstate commerce is subjected to the test set forth in the quotation from Pike v. Bruce Church, Inc. that appeared in the

*Philadelphia* case. The purpose of the legislation must be legitimate (in furtherance of local public interest), and the burden on interstate commerce must be only
"incidental." Even then, the burden on interstate commerce must be weighed
against local benefits in a fairly complex calculus that seeks to account for the
importance of the local benefit and the extent of the burden on interstate commerce. In Minnesota v. Clover Leaf Creamery Co., 449 U.S. 456 (1981), an attack
on State legislation contended that it was prompted by mixed environmental and
protectionist motives. The Minnesota statute restricting certain types of milk containers arguably favored pulpwood manufacturers (a major Minnesota industry)
and disfavored plastics manufacturers (a non-Minnesota industry). The Court
found that the statute was not discriminatory, and proceeded to measure the burdens on interstate commerce under the *Pike* test, eventually concluding that "even
granting that the out-of-state plastics industry is burdened...we find that this
burden is not 'clearly excessive' in light of the substantial state interest in promoting conservation of energy and other natural resources and easing solid waste
disposal problems...."

The process of balancing is as subjective as it is important to determining validity.
The case of Procter & Gamble v. Chicago, 509 F.2d 69 (7th Cir. 1975), tested
whether Chicago could ban the sale in the city of all phosphate detergents in order
to protect water quality. After a long and detailed balancing process, the court
upheld the city ordinance:

> The burden is so slight compared to the important and properly local objective
> that the presumption [of validity]...should apply. We will accept the City's
> determination that this phosphate ban is a reasonable means of achieving the
> elimination and prevention of nuisance algae unless we find that the plaintiffs
> have presented clear and convincing proof to the contrary [and they haven't].

5. **"A barrier is a barrier is a barrier," or is it sometimes a quarantine?** Does it make
any difference for dormant commerce clause purposes whether Philadelphia v. New
Jersey is an import ban (blocking the import of waste), or an export ban (blocking
the export of landfill space)? In a word, the simple answer would seem to be, "No."
State efforts to exclude undesirable items and to hoard valuable ones equally interfere with treating the nation as "one economic unit." Even so, the Court in
*Philadelphia* was careful to distinguish the situation there from what it viewed as
valid state quarantine laws. The Court found the two situations different because
quarantine laws "did not discriminate against interstate commerce as such, but
simply prevented traffic in noxious articles, whatever their origin." 437 U.S. at 617.
The states have not experienced success in limiting waste movement on quarantine
theories. See, Government Suppliers Consolidating Services v. Bayh, 753 F.Supp.
739 (S.D.Ind. 1990). The case in the following note permits an import ban preventing the interstate movement of baitfish. It has many hallmarks of a quarantine. The
result was exceptional when the case was decided and remains so today.

6. **When is a barrier a legitimate quarantine?** In protecting public health and welfare states are allowed to ban the import of disease-ridden cattle, Med-fly bearing
produce, and other items that require quarantine. One environmental embargo
case, Maine v. Taylor, 477 U.S. 131 (1986) was sustained on that line of reasoning.

The case has not served as a widespread precedent because its holding that sustaining a naked import ban on out-of-state seined baitfish rested on very favorable fact finding that will be difficult to replicate in other cases. The trial court found, and the Supreme Court accepted the finding that the import ban was necessary to prevent introduction of non-native parasites into the Maine ecosystem. The Court majority stated:

> The evidentiary hearing on which the District Court based its conclusions was one before a magistrate. Three scientific experts testified for the prosecution and one for the defense. The prosecution experts testified that live baitfish imported into the State posed two significant threats to Maine's unique and fragile fisheries. First, Maine's population of wild fish — including its own indigenous golden shiners — would be placed at risk by three types of parasites prevalent in out-of-state baitfish, but not common to wild fish in Maine. Second, non-native species inadvertently included in shipments of live baitfish could disturb Maine's aquatic ecology to an unpredictable extent by competing with native fish for food or habitat, by preying on native species, or by disrupting the environment in more subtle ways. Maine v. Taylor, 477 U.S., 140–141.

The prosecution experts further testified that there was no satisfactory way to inspect shipments of live baitfish for parasites or commingled species. According to their testimony, the small size of baitfish and the large quantities in which they are shipped made inspection for commingled species "a physical impossibility." Parasite inspection posed a separate set of difficulties because the examination procedure required destruction of the fish. Although statistical sampling and inspection techniques had been developed for salmonids (i.e., salmon and trout), so that a shipment could be certified parasite-free based on a standardized examination of only some of the fish, no scientifically accepted procedures of this sort were available for baitfish.[24]

> Appellee's expert denied that any scientific justification supported Maine's total ban on the importation of baitfish. He testified that none of the three parasites discussed by the prosecution witnesses posed any significant threat to fish in the wild and that sampling techniques had not been developed for baitfish precisely because there was no need for them. He further testified that professional baitfish farmers raise their fish in ponds that have been freshly drained to ensure that no other species is inadvertently collected.

> Weighing all the testimony, the magistrate concluded that both prongs of the Hughes test were satisfied, and accordingly appellee's motion to dismiss the indictment should be denied. Maine v. Taylor, 477 U.S. at 142.

Maine's ban on the importation of baitfish in *Taylor* seems to exemplify the most blatantly discriminatory kind of legislation: a total ban on the interstate movement of a product that would compete with locally produced goods in the local market. The dissent argued that the traditional approach would mean that Maine would carry a very substantial burden of justification, one that seldom can be met. Did Maine's evidence in favor of its position meet that standard?

---

24. According to the prosecution testimony...the physical layout of baitfarms makes inspection at the source of shipment particularly difficult, and...border inspections are not feasible because the baitfish would die in the time it takes to complete the tests.

7. **Insisting on cleaner, leaner garbage.** Pike v. Bruce Church's more relaxed scrutiny of evenhanded state regulation, and allowing justification for discrimination such as that approved in Maine v. Taylor open the door to state laws that have the effect of discriminating against out-of-state interests. Can these "exceptions" to the pattern of invalidation of commerce-restricting state laws be adapted to aid the states in their "garbage wars" efforts to enforce differential tipping fees or otherwise disfavor out-of-state waste? There is, of course, very little that distinguishes an in-state pile of garbage from an out-of-state pile of garbage unless something has been done to the in-state garbage that makes it either safer or more economical to manage. Suppose a state, by statute, requires pre-disposal treatment of waste as a precondition to disposal or as a basis for obtaining a lower tipping fee. Pre-treatment could include mandatory recycling (to reduce volume), or segregation of waste streams to eliminate the presence of small volume hazardous materials such as household batteries and non-commercial volumes of paints and solvents. Are such laws even-handed? Do they remain even-handed if the state also makes pre-treatment mandatory within its borders? The leading case on point, National Solid Waste Management Association v. Meyer, 63 F.3d 652 (7th Cir. 1995), squarely considered a provision requiring mandatory recycling as a precondition to Wisconsin disposal of solid waste and invalidated it on a variety of grounds. The key flaw, in the court's view, inheres in the fact that if any waste in an out-of-state community is Wisconsin-bound, all of the waste in that community must be pre-treated to satisfy the Wisconsin law. 63 F.3d at 658. That amounts to impermissible extra-territorial regulation.[25] Turning to more familiar dormant commerce clause jurisprudence, the court found the law discriminatory against out-of-state waste hauler, "simply because [their waste] comes from a community whose ways are not Wisconsin's ways." 63 F.3d at 662. Finally, even under a non-discriminatory *Pike* analysis, the court found that Wisconsin had available to it less commerce-burdensome alternatives, such as having non-recycled out-of-state wastes subject to disposal after first being taken to a recycling facility. *Id.*

### Section 2. THE MARKET PARTICIPANT DOCTRINE AND LEGISLATED OVERCHARGES TO THE CITIZENRY

While the persistent efforts of the states to impede the interstate flow of waste have had little success, there is one line of cases that does allow states and localities to disadvantage interstate competitors. It is called the market participant doctrine.

### Swin Resource Systems Inc. v. Lycoming County [Pennsylvania]
United States Circuit Court of Appeals for the Third Circuit 1989
883 F.2d 245, certiorari denied, 110 S.Ct. 1127

[The operator of a solid waste processing facility brought suit against a county that operated a landfill, challenging on dormant commerce clause grounds regulations giving the county residents preference in use of the landfill.]

---

25. This ground of commerce clause scrutiny is of relatively recent origin and has its roots in state efforts to regulate prices charged to in-state wholesalers of alcoholic beverages. See Healy v. Beer Institute, 491 U.S. 324 (1989).

BECKER, Circuit Judge... Swin contends that Lycoming's attempt to preserve its landfill's capacity for local residents by charging a higher price to dispose of distant waste in the landfill (and limiting the volume of distant waste accepted by the landfill) constitutes an impermissible interference with and discrimination against interstate commerce in violation of the commerce clause. The district court granted the defendants' motion to dismiss the commerce clause claim on the ground that Lycoming had acted as a "market participant." Under the market participant doctrine, a state or state subdivision that acts as a market participant rather than a market regulator "is not subject to the restraints of the Commerce Clause." White v. Massachusetts Council of Construction Employers, Inc., 460 U.S. 204, 208 (1983).

For the reasons explained below, we hold that Lycoming County acted as a market participant rather than a market regulator in deciding the conditions under which Swin could use its landfill. It is useful to begin our analysis with a review of the four principal market participant cases.

In Alexandria Scrap Corp. v. Hughes, 426 U.S. 794 (1976) the Supreme Court upheld Maryland's statutory scheme to rid the state of derelict automobiles, even though the scheme entailed two types of discrimination: (1) Maryland paid bounties to in-state scrap auto hulk processors while refusing to pay bounties to out-of-state processors on the same terms; and (2) Maryland paid bounties only for vehicles formerly titled in Maryland. The Court held that the statutory scheme was consistent with the commerce clause on the ground that Maryland was participating in the market rather than regulating it. As the majority put it, "[n]othing in the purposes animating the Commerce Clause prohibits a State, in the absence of congressional action, from participating in the market and exercising the right to favor its own citizens over others." 426 U.S. at 810.

In Reeves, Inc. v. Stake, 447 U.S. 429 (1980), the Court upheld a South Dakota policy of confining the sale of cement by a state-operated cement plant to residents of South Dakota in order to meet their demand during a "serious cement shortage." The Court affirmed "[t]he basic distinction drawn in Alexandria Scrap between States as market participants and States as market regulators" and concluded that "South Dakota, as a seller of cement, unquestionably fits the 'market participant' label." 447 U.S. at 436. The Court upheld the South Dakota policy even though Reeves, a Wyoming corporation that had purchased about 95% of its cement from South Dakota's state-operated plant for over twenty years, was forced to cut production by over 75% as a result of the policy.

In White, the Court, deeming the case "well within the scope of Alexandria Scrap and Reeves," upheld an executive order of the Mayor of Boston requiring all construction projects funded in whole or in part either by city funds or city-administered federal funds to be performed by a work force of at least 50% city residents. 460 U.S. at 211 n.7.

In South-Central Timber Development Co. v. Wunnicke, 467 U.S. 82 (1984), however, a plurality struck down Alaska's requirement that timber taken from state lands be processed in-state prior to export. Adhering to the distinction suggested in White, the plurality held that "[t]he limit of the market-participant doctrine must be that it allows a State to impose burdens on commerce within the market in which it is a participant, but [does not] allow it to impose conditions, whether by statute, regulation, or contract, that have a substantial regulatory effect outside of that particular market." 467 U.S. at 97. The Alaska policy crossed the line distinguishing participation from regulation because the conditions it attached to its timber sales amounted to "downstream regulation of the timber-processing market in which it is not a participant." 467 U.S. at 99.

No court, to our knowledge, has ever suggested that the commerce clause requires city-operated garbage trucks to cross state lines in order to pick up the garbage generated by residents of other states. If a city may constitutionally limit its trucks to collecting garbage generated by city residents, we see no constitutional reason why a city cannot also limit a city-operated dump to garbage generated by city residents. With respect to municipal garbage trucks and municipal garbage dumps, application of the market participant doctrine enables "the people [acting through their local government] to determine as conditions demand what services and functions the public welfare requires." *Reeves*, 447 U.S. at 438 n.11. The residents who reside within the jurisdiction of a county or municipality are unlikely to pay for local government services if they must bear the cost but the entire nation may receive the benefit.

DOES A "NATURAL RESOURCE" EXCEPTION APPLY HERE?... Swin's vigorous argument that Lycoming has attempted to harbor a scarce natural resource for its own residents brings us to the potential caveat we mentioned. While the harboring of a scarce manufactured product or human service does not preclude the invocation of the market participant doctrine because it is scarce (in *Reeves* the Supreme Court applied the doctrine to South Dakota's effort to harbor cement for its own residents despite a serious cement shortage), it may be that there is some special rule to be applied to a state's effort to harbor a scarce natural resource. Unlike a manufactured product or the provision of a human service, a state does not have the ability to develop a natural resource if it has not had the fortuity to be favored with such a resource. While it may seem fair for South Dakota to favor its citizens in the sale of cement from a state-owned cement plant, for a state to favor its own citizens in selling right to mine coal or limestone on state-owned lands, for example, or in selling state-owned coal or limestone, would seem less fair, especially if the state happened to be endowed with the bulk of our nation's coal or limestone reserves and the other states were dependent upon it.

Whether there is a natural resource exception to the market participation doctrine is a difficult question, but, fortunately, one which we need not answer at this level of abstraction. First, land, the natural resource at issue here, cannot be used for a landfill without the expenditure of at least some money to prepare it for that purpose. The Lycoming landfill is therefore "not simply happenstance," Sporhase v. Nebraska, 458 U.S. 941, 957 (1982), but is at least to some extent like South Dakota's cement plant in that government funds were needed to construct it. Moreover, since the land upon which the landfill was constructed has to be leased in this case, the land, even prior to development, bore some resemblance to South Dakota's cement plant in that is devotion to public use required the disbursement or promise of future disbursement of government resources.... Affirmed.

COMMENTARY & QUESTIONS

1. **The dissent in *Swin*.** The majority opinion in *Swin* raised a vigorous dissent by Chief Judge Gibbons. He argued that the market participant doctrine is premised on economic unreality:

> The present appeal provides a typical case in point. However much their market might be regulated, private landfill operators still desire to turn a

profit. Few, if any, would give a second thought to the origin of the waste filling the space sold. Nor is it likely that any would long stay in business even assuming some highly unusual public commitment to the preservation of that space by locals. Under any realistic view, the Lycoming landfill in private hands would never have hindered its ability to sell space to the highest bidder by erecting a differential rate structure that discriminated against waste the further its point of origin. If anything, it would have created a fee structure that did precisely the opposite. A vendor of landfill space hoping to attract business, as do genuine market participants, would logically attempt to lure large volume purchasers concerned with transportation costs through a discount, especially when it appeared that customers dealing in local waste could not themselves provide sufficient business. As an exercise toward the political end of saving space for county waste, Lycoming County's price structure makes good regulatory sense. As an essay in market participation, it is aberrant and the majority's application of the label "market participant" to Lycoming County is an economic jest. 883 F.2d at 262.

2. **When economic unreality resembles indirect taxation.** There can be little doubt that Chief Judge Gibbons has correctly analyzed the economically irrational nature of the local preference aspect of Lycoming County's fee schedule, but is the market participant doctrine bottomed on the expectation that governmental entities will act in an economically rational fashion? Is a more plausible basis for the doctrine captured in the phrase that the state has "put its money where its mouth is." That is, the state has entered the market to buy the privilege of running a business irrationally. The state, when it spends its money, has not merely commanded via regulation that someone else, whose assets the state did not purchase in the marketplace, run her business in an irrational way that favors the state's residents and discriminates against interstate commerce.

3. **Flow control that keeps garbage at home.** As unlikely as it may once have sounded, in many states the compass has spun 180 degrees and keeping local trash at home is the object of numerous laws and regulations. The reason for the changed posture is, in most cases, the shift from landfilling trash to incinerating it. Trash is transformed from a "bad" subject to NIMBY, to a "good" that is the raw material that makes incinerators profitable, or at least, less expensive. One typical scenario is presented by the case of C. A. Carbone, Inc. v. Town of Clarkstown, 511 U.S. 383 (1994). In that case the old landfill was in violation of state law and had to be closed. To replace the local dump, the town opted for an incinerator that it did not want to finance using its own tax dollars. To induce a private operator to build the incinerator and, after five years, deed it over to the town, Clarkstown passed an ordinance having two principal features. First, the ordinance required all Clarkstown trash be taken to the incinerator (thereby generating a predictable volume) and, second, the ordinance specified an above market rate of $81 per ton as the tipping fee to be paid at the facility. In that way, the private facility operator would be guaranteed of profits sufficient to justify a $1.4 million investment and the town would cure its violation of state law and end up with a paid-for facility. Carbone, a Clarkstown-based recycler who imported trash for elsewhere, was required to send its waste to the facility and pay the above-market rate. Carbone challenged the ordinance on dormant commerce clause grounds. By a 6–3 vote, the

United States Supreme Court invalidated the ordinance, finding flow control indistinguishable from the trash embargo laws and differential tipping fees that it had previously struck down. Justice Souter's dissent argued that the case should be analyzed as a market participant case because the ordinance conveyed a privilege on the municipal government alone in its role as a market participant providing services to its citizens. Cases in which flow control is practiced by a municipality that owns and operates its trash facility have survived constitutional challenge. See, e.g., SSC Corp. v. Town of Smithtown, 66 F.3d 502 (2nd Cir. 1995), cert. den., 116 S.Ct. 911 (1996), red. den. 116 S.Ct. 1453 (1996).

---

## D. LIMITATIONS ON FEDERAL POWER

In the same way that the Constitution prescribes enforceable limitations on state authority, it also imposes limits on federal authority. In this latter regard, two doctrinal lines exist. The first grows from the fundamental precept that the federal government is one of limited powers, and powers not granted are withheld. This doctrinal line is often associated with the Tenth Amendment, which makes that limitation explicit, although it is certainly implicit in the body of the Constitution. A related development in this area is a newly increased willingness on the part of the United States Supreme Court and lower federal courts to find that the actions of Congress, purportedly taken pursuant to the enumerated power over interstate commerce, in fact exceed Congress' authority. The second doctrinal line also is associated with an amendment to the Constitution, in this case the Eleventh Amendment, that enacts a limitation on the federal judicial power that is bound up with the larger question of how much sovereign immunity was surrendered by the states when they entered into the Union.

### Section 1. THE TENTH AMENDMENT AND THE DECREASING BREADTH OF THE COMMERCE CLAUSE

There has long been debate as to whether the Tenth Amendment to the United States Constitution alters, in any way, the power relation between the states and the federal government established by the supremacy clause. The Tenth Amendment, in relevant part, declares that "powers not delegated to the United States by the Constitution, nor prohibited by it to the States, are reserved to the States...." The claim made for giving the Tenth Amendment some bite in the matter of federal-state relations, is that somehow the amendment erects an area of inviolate state sovereignty that cannot be encroached upon by the federal government.

The conventional wisdom and the vast majority of cases reject that claim. The rejection is captured in a phrase, often repeated in cases raising the issue:" [the tenth amendment] states but a truism that all is retained which has not been surrendered." United States v. Darby, 312 U.S. 100, 124 (1941). The "truism" confirms federal supremacy (within the sphere of the federal government's enumerated powers) and some abdication of state sovereignty as being surrendered on nationhood, but notes the fact that the remainder of state sovereignty was unaffected.

Nevertheless, the idea of state sovereignty is an important one in the federal system, and there are occasional cases in which the Supreme Court has been willing to restrict the federal government's encroachment on the states, even when the federal government is pursuing national objectives that are within its sphere of constitutional competence. Importantly for the study of environmental law, the tenth amendment argument is, at times, made in environmental cases.

In one recent case, the Tenth Amendment argument was successful in limiting one facet of the Low-Level Radioactive Waste Policy Amendments Act of 1985, Pub.L. 99–240, 99 Stat. 1842, 42 U.S.C. 2021b et seq. That litigation grew out of Congress' attempt to respond to the declining number of low-level radioactive waste disposal sites nationwide and the threat of a total absence of such sites in the future. Congress sought to spur the siting by the states of low-level radioactive waste facilities, preferably on a collaborative basis, where several states would send their waste to a regional facility. To ensure action by the states, Congress used a mix of incentives and penalties, three of which were challenged by the State of New York on Tenth Amendment and other grounds. The challenged provisions included what the Court characterized as "monetary incentives," "access incentives," and the "take title provision." The monetary incentives revolved around a series of federal disposal surcharges on wastes generated outside of the disposal state. The surcharges would create a fund that would be used to reward states that achieved specific milestones in the process of establishing disposal facilities. The access incentives potentially limited disposal to wastes generated in states participating in the programs that Congress sought to encourage. Finally, the take title provision, as a sort of last resort, required states that were not participating in the programs to take title to the waste involved.

## New York v. United States
### United States Supreme Court
### 505 U.S. 144, 112 S.Ct. 2408, 120 L.Ed.2d 120 (1992)

O'CONNOR, J. This case implicates one of our Nation's newest problems of public policy and perhaps our oldest question of constitutional law. The public policy issue involves the disposal of radioactive waste.... The constitutional question is as old as the Constitution: it consists of discerning the proper division of authority between the Federal Government and the States. We conclude that while Congress has substantial power under the Constitution to encourage the States to provide for the disposal of the radioactive waste generated within their borders, the Constitution does not confer upon Congress the ability simply to compel the States to do so.

These questions [of state and federal authority] can be viewed in either of two ways. In some cases the Court has inquired whether an Act of Congress is authorized by one of the powers delegated to Congress in Article I of the Constitution. In other cases the Court has sought to determine whether an Act of Congress invades the province of state sovereignty reserved by the Tenth Amendment. In a case like this one, involving the division of authority between federal and state governments, the two inquiries are mirror images of each other. If a power is delegated to Congress in the Constitution, the Tenth Amendment expressly disclaims any reservation of that power to the States; if a power is an attribute of state sovereignty reserved by the Tenth Amendment, it is necessarily a power the Constitution has not conferred on Congress.

It is in this sense that the Tenth Amendment "states but a truism that all is retained which has not been surrendered." As Justice Story put it, "[t]his amendment is a mere affirmation of what, upon any just reasoning, is a necessary rule of interpreting the constitution. Being an instrument of limited and enumerated powers, it follows irresistibly, that what is not conferred, is withheld, and belongs to the state authorities." J. Story, 3 Commentaries on the Constitution of the United States 752 (1833). This has been the Court's consistent understanding: "The States unquestionably do retai[n] a significant measure of sovereign authority to the extent that the Constitution has not divested them of their original powers and transferred those powers to the Federal Government."

Congress exercises its conferred powers subject to the limitations contained in the Constitution. Thus, for example, under the Commerce Clause Congress may regulate publishers engaged in interstate commerce, but Congress is constrained in the exercise of that power by the First Amendment. The Tenth Amendment likewise restrains the power of Congress, but this limit is not derived from the text of the Tenth Amendment itself, which, as we have discussed, is essentially a tautology. Instead, the Tenth Amendment confirms that the power of the Federal Government is subject to limits that may, in a given instance, reserve power to the States. The Tenth Amendment thus directs us to determine, as in this case, whether an incident of state sovereignty is protected by a limitation on an Article I power.

Petitioners do not contend that Congress lacks the power to regulate the disposal of low level radioactive waste. Space in radioactive waste disposal sites is frequently sold by residents of one State to residents of another. Regulation of the resulting interstate market in waste disposal is therefore well within Congress' authority under the Commerce Clause. Petitioners likewise do not dispute that under the Supremacy Clause Congress could, if it wished, preempt state radioactive waste regulation. Petitioners contend only that the Tenth Amendment limits the power of Congress to regulate in the way it has chosen. Rather than addressing the problem of waste disposal by directly regulating the generators and disposers of waste, petitioners argue, Congress has impermissibly directed the States to regulate in this field.

As an initial matter, Congress may not simply "commandee[r] the legislative processes of the States by directly compelling them to enact and enforce a federal regulatory program." Hodel v. Virginia Surface Mining & Reclamation Assn., Inc., 452 U.S. 264, 288, 101 S.Ct. 2352, 2366, 69 L.Ed.2d 1 (1981). In *Hodel*, the Court upheld the Surface Mining Control and Reclamation Act of 1977 precisely because it did not "commandeer" the States into regulating mining. The Court found that "the States are not compelled to enforce the steep-slope standards, to expend any state funds, or to participate in the federal regulatory program in any manner whatsoever. If a State does not wish to submit a proposed permanent program that complies with the Act and implementing regulations, the full regulatory burden will be borne by the Federal Government."

This is not to say that Congress lacks the ability to encourage a State to regulate in a particular way, or that Congress may not hold out incentives to the States as a method of influencing a State's policy choices. Our cases have identified a variety of methods, short of outright coercion, by which Congress may urge a State to adopt a legislative program consistent with federal interests. Two of these methods are of particular relevance here.

First, under Congress' spending power, "Congress may attach conditions on the receipt of federal funds." Second, where Congress has the authority to regulate private activity under the Commerce Clause, we have recognized Congress' power to offer States the choice of regulating that activity according to federal standards or having state law preempted by federal regulation.

With these principles in mind, we turn to the three challenged provisions of the Low-Level Radioactive Waste Policy Amendments Act of 1985.

[The opinion had little difficulty in concluding that monetary and access incentives in the legislation passed muster as rather straightforward examples of the federal power to tax and spend and the direct regulation of interstate commerce.]

The take title provision is of a different character. This third so-called "incentive" offers States, as an alternative to regulating pursuant to Congress' direction, the option of taking title to and possession of the low level radioactive waste generated within their borders and becoming liable for all damages waste generators suffer as a result of the States' failure to do so promptly. In this provision, Congress has crossed the line distinguishing encouragement from coercion.

The take title provision offers state governments a "choice" of either accepting ownership of waste or regulating according to the instructions of Congress. Respondents do not claim that the Constitution would authorize Congress to impose either option as a freestanding requirement. On one hand, the Constitution would not permit Congress simply to transfer radioactive waste from generators to state governments. Such a forced transfer, standing alone, would in principle be no different than a congressionally compelled subsidy from state governments to radioactive waste producers. The same is true of the provision requiring the States to become liable for the generators' damages. Standing alone, this provision would be indistinguishable from an Act of Congress directing the States to assume the liabilities of certain state residents. Either type of federal action would "commandeer" state governments into the service of federal regulatory purposes, and would for this reason be inconsistent with the Constitution's division of authority between federal and state governments. On the other hand, the second alternative held out to state governments - regulating pursuant to Congress' direction - would, standing alone, present a simple command to state governments to implement legislation enacted by Congress. As we have seen, the Constitution does not empower Congress to subject state governments to this type of instruction.

Because an instruction to state governments to take title to waste, standing alone, would be beyond the authority of Congress, and because a direct order to regulate, standing alone, would also be beyond the authority of Congress, it follows that Congress lacks the power to offer the States a choice between the two.

States are not mere political subdivisions of the United States. State governments are neither regional offices nor administrative agencies of the Federal Government. The positions occupied by state officials appear nowhere on the Federal Government's most detailed organizational chart. The Constitution instead "leaves to the several States a residuary and inviolable sovereignty," The Federalist No. 39, p. 245 (C. Rossiter ed. 1961), reserved explicitly to the States by the Tenth Amendment.

Whatever the outer limits of that sovereignty may be, one thing is clear: The Federal Government may not compel the States to enact or administer a federal regulatory program. The Constitution permits both the Federal Government and the States to enact legislation regarding the disposal of low level radioactive waste.

The Constitution enables the Federal Government to preempt state regulation contrary to federal interests, and it permits the Federal Government to hold out incentives to the States as a means of encouraging them to adopt suggested regulatory schemes. It does not, however, authorize Congress simply to direct the States to provide for the disposal of the radioactive waste generated within their borders. While there may be many constitutional methods of achieving regional self-sufficiency in radioactive waste disposal, the method Congress has chosen is not one of them. The judgment of the Court of Appeals is accordingly affirmed in part and reversed in part.

COMMENTARY & QUESTIONS

1. **The lines of dissent.** Justices White, Blackmun, and Stevens dissented from the invalidation of the take title provision. The thrust of their objection was based on estoppel (New York had reaped the benefits of the law) and the view that the precedents cited by the majority did not establish so great a limitation on congressional choice of means.

2. **The new "truism."** Has the old "truism" taken on a new meaning? Historically, the issue in Tenth Amendment cases was that of federal competence: was the action within federal power? Chief Justice Rehnquist and others have been advocating a concept of independent limitation of federal power derived from a notion of inviolable state sovereignty that survived the framing of the United States Constitution. A phrase associated with this idea is that the federal government is disabled from legislation that sought to regulate the "states qua states." To what extent is that view established as a general principle in the opinion and then applied to strike down the take title provision?

3. **Incentives and the dormant commerce clause.** Interestingly, for federalism purposes, among the incentives that Congress used (and the Court upheld) to spur the siting of regional facilities was granting those facilities the right to exclude waste from states not a party to the agreement governing the regional facility and allowing those facilities to charge differential waste disposal fees for out-of-state waste. The power of exclusion and charging differential fees for disposal, absent congressional authorization, would violate the dormant commerce clause.

4. **Commanding state execution of federal law.** Can Congress require the states, or state officials, to take action in furtherance of federal law? In a post-*New York* case involving the Brady Handgun Violence Prevention Act, a closely divided Supreme Court held unconstitutional a requirement that state law enforcement officers maintain files and do background checks on applicants for gun licenses as directed by that federal statute. See Printz v. United States, 117 S.Ct. 2365 (1997). Justice Scalia's majority opinion in *Printz* observed that there is no constitutional provision that specifically addresses the structural question of Congress' ability to direct state officers to execute federal laws. He found, further, that despite long-standing patterns and practices of Congress calling on state judges to enforce federal law, the imposition of federal tasks on other state officials was accomplished by implied consent. Finally, he concluded that the system of "dual sovereignty" that ensures the states a residuary and inviolable sovereignty, controls the issue,

making the involuntary imposition of federal duties on state officials unconstitutional. The *Printz* logic may affect a number of environmental laws. For example, the Emergency Community Planning and Right-to-Know Act (see Chapter 13) requires states and localities to promulgate various emergency plans. On what basis could challenge to that planning requirement be differentiated from requirements struck down in *Printz*?

5. **Curbing congressionally mandated environmental remedial programs.** To what extent do New York v. United States and *Printz* limit the ability of Congress to require the states to take action to abate environmental hazards? In 1988, Congress enacted the Lead Contamination Control Act (LCCA), 42 U.S.C.A. §300j-21 to 300j-26, as an amendment to the federal Safe Drinking Water Act, a law that sets health protective standards for drinking water supplies. Pursuant to §300j-24(d), the states are required to establish remedial action programs for the removal of lead contaminants from school drinking water systems within a period of months following the statute's effective date in 1988. In ACORN v. Edwards, 81 F.3d 1387 (5th Cir. 1996), a citizens group sued Louisiana for violation of the federal requirement and the state claimed the law violated the Tenth Amendment. The court stated:

> Few Congressional enactments fall as squarely within the ambit of New York as does §300j-24(d). Section 300j-24(d) requires each State to "establish a program, consistent with this section," to assist local educational agencies, schools, and day care centers in remedying potential lead contamination in their drinking water systems. Failure or refusal to establish the mandated program subjects the States to civil enforcement proceedings. 42 U.S.C. §300j-8(a). The States thus face a choice between succumbing to Congressional direction and regulating according to Congressional instruction, or being forced to do so through civil action in the federal courts. In actuality, this "is no choice at all." The LCCA gives the States no alternative but to enact the federal regulatory plan as prescribed in §300j-24(d), and such Congressional conscription of state legislative functions is clearly prohibited under New York's interpretation of the limits imposed upon Congress by the Tenth Amendment.
>
> Congress is free, pursuant to its Commerce Clause power, to combat lead contamination in drinking water by regulating drinking water coolers that move in interstate commerce. Such regulation, however, must operate directly upon the people, and not the States as conduits to the people. "The allocation of power contained in the Commerce Clause...authorizes Congress to regulate interstate commerce directly; it does not authorize Congress to regulate state governments' regulation of interstate commerce." New York, 505 U.S. at 165, 112 S.Ct. at 2423. Section 300j-24(d) is an attempt by Congress to force States to regulate according to Congressional direction. As the New York Court explained, the Constitution does not permit Congress to so control the States' legislative processes.
>
> ACORN and the United States argue §300j-24(d) is a valid exercise of Congress' Commerce Clause power because it affords the States complete discretion to determine the means employed in achieving the LCCA's goals. The New York Court addressed an identical argument and rejected it stating: "This line of reasoning...only underscores the critical alternative a State lacks: A State may not decline to administer the federal program. No matter which path the State chooses, it must follow the direction of Congress." New York, 505 U.S. at 177, 112 S.Ct. at 2429. Because §300j-24(d) deprives States of the option to decline regulating non-lead free drinking water coolers, we likewise find no merit to

this argument and conclude that §300j-24(d) is an unconstitutional intrusion upon the States' sovereign prerogative to legislate as it sees fit. ACORN v. Edwards, 81 F.3d 1387.

6. **The Unfunded Mandates Act.** The Unfunded Mandates Reform Act of 1995, P.L. 104-4, 109 Stat. 48, codified principally at 2 U.S.C.A. §§658 and 1501 et seq., is an amendment to general laws regarding federal spending. If the amounts involved are large enough, in most instances 50 million for a mandate affecting state, local, and tribal governments, $100 million for a mandate affecting the private sector, the act's more specific provisions apply. The Act defines a mandate as —

> any provision in legislation, statute, or regulation that...would impose an enforceable duty upon State, local, or tribal governments...or the private sector...or would place caps upon, or otherwise decrease, the Federal Government's responsibility to provide funding to State, local, or tribal governments under a program. §101.

In Congress itself, unfunded mandates can be the subject of a point of order, which means that any member of Congress can, as a parliamentary procedure, seek to have discussion of a bill containing an unfunded mandate deemed out of order if that legislation does not provide new budget authority to defray or cover the cost. See §101(a)(2). Somewhat more onerously, agencies issuing regulations of any sort must prepare an unfunded mandates report detailing "the future compliance costs of the Federal mandate" that include "disproportionate budgetary effects" on governments or the private sector, "estimates by the agency of the effect on the national economy," and, if the agency finds those effects "relevant and material," the agency must also describe its "prior consultation" with affected governments See §202(A)(3). For agency regulations that meet the relevant monetary thresholds:

> the agency shall identify and consider a reasonable number of regulatory alternatives, and from those alternatives select the least costly, most cost-effective, or least burdensome alternative that achieves the objectives of the rule. *Id.*

As sanctions for failure to obey the Act, a court may, as a remedy, compel an agency to prepare the written statement required by the Act. §401(a)(2)(B). There are, however, limitations on seeking judicial review that state that:

> ...no provision of this Act shall be construed to create any right or benefit, substantive or procedural, enforceable by any person in any administrative or judicial action. §401(b)(2).

Where does that leave the Act — is it a potent limitation on Congress and the federal agencies, or just an unenforceable gesture? Plainly, the Act expresses a congressional sentiment about agency rulemaking, and agencies that do not abide the terms of the Act risk losing favor with Congress, which controls their appropriations.

7. **Circumventing *Printz* and the Unfunded Mandates Act for federal environmental statutes?** If federal statutes cannot just require state governments to do certain things, because of *Printz* or the Unfunded Mandates Act, can Congress validly accomplish the same ends by offering states a choice: saying they theoretically can choose not to do what the federal statute requests, but if so they will lose federal funding for various or all programs? If, for instance, a federal statute says a state

will lose all federal highway funds if it refuses to set up a state water pollution control system under the CWA's NPDES, or a hazardous materials inventory and emergency planning council under EPCRA, the statute arguably is not "mandatory" on the state. (The Unfunded Mandates Act does not consider it a "mandate" where compliance is only a condition of federal funding.) Some courts, however, have hinted that there is a difference between mere inducements and what constitutes excessive compulsion.[26]

---

American federalism, because it is so intimately bound to the Constitution, is often given meaning by the judicial branch in its exercise of judicial review. This fact makes the legal rules in this area subject to a unique degree of reconsideration when changes in judicial philosophy occur. The period beginning in 1992, when the Supreme Court decided New York v. United States, is a period in which reconsideration is taking place.

A bit of background may be helpful in understanding these developments: Coming out of the Great Depression, a major shift in judicial philosophy established that the breadth of the commerce power was sufficient to support the New Deal legislation then being passed by Congress. That view rejected an earlier prevailing view that had led to invalidation of numerous efforts at federal regulation of economic practices. With that shift, constitutionally permissible federal legislation, at times, reached deep into the states, regulating what were arguably local transactions. For example, the Agricultural Adjustment Act of 1938 sought to protect against actions that would depress commodity prices. One feature of the law limited the acreage a farmer could plant. That limitation on planting was challenged in Wickard v. Fillburn as being in excess of the interstate commerce power. That case involved an Ohio farmer who was forbidden from producing crops on his own farm that would be consumed by his own farm animals without ever entering the stream of commerce. The law was sustained as a valid commerce power enactment because, in the aggregate, on-farm consumption of the crops reduced demand for the products moving in interstate commerce. In later decades, when Congress turned its attention to other national issues such as civil rights and the environment, the commerce power was the principal ground upon which Congress based its regulatory authority. While the basic precepts and precedents that establish the broad reach of the commerce power are not under attack, the case that follows has opened the possibility that some federal environmental laws, in specific applications, can exceed the limits of the commerce power.

---

26. Although it turned on a different constitutional point, a D.C. case held that a total appropriations cutoff of $3.7 billion would go too far, because it would cause —

> complete shut-down of municipal services in the District — from public hospitals and public schools, to garbage collection, law enforcement and virtually all other services essential to the health, safety and welfare of the District's residents. As the Government concedes, the severity of these consequences makes the Armstrong Amendment a "mandate" that the Council members "cannot...ignore." U.S. v. Clarke, 886 F. 2d 404 (D.C. Cir. 1989).

## Lopez v. United States
### United States Supreme Court
### 514 U.S. 549 (1995)

REHNQUIST, C.J.,

[This case involves a federal law making it a crime "for any individual know-ingly to possess a firearm at a place that the individual knows, or has reasonable cause to believe, is a school zone." Defendant Lopez was convicted under that statute, the Gun-Free School Zones Act of 1990, 18 U.S.C. §922(q)(1)(A) (1988 ed., Supp. V). The Court reviewed his constitutional challenge to the law in which Lopez claimed that Congress had exceeded the limits of the interstate commerce power in enacting a law that regulated intrastate activity that did not affect com-merce.]

Consistent with [the constitutional] structure, we have identified three broad categories of activity that Congress may regulate under its commerce power. First, Congress may regulate the use of the channels of interstate commerce. Second, Congress is empowered to regulate and protect the instrumentalities of interstate commerce, or persons or things in interstate commerce, even though the threat may come only from intrastate activities. Finally, Congress' commerce authority includes the power to regulate those activities having a substantial relation to inter-state commerce, those activities that substantially affect interstate commerce.

Within this final category, admittedly, our case law has not been clear whether an activity must "affect" or "substantially affect" interstate commerce in order to be within Congress' power to regulate it under the Commerce Clause. We con-clude, consistent with the great weight of our case law, that the proper test requires an analysis of whether the regulated activity "substantially affects" interstate commerce.

We now turn to consider the power of Congress, in the light of this framework, to enact §922(q). The first two categories of authority may be quickly disposed of: §922(q) is not a regulation of the use of the channels of interstate commerce, nor is it an attempt to prohibit the interstate transportation of a commodity through the channels of commerce; nor can §922(q) be justified as a regulation by which Congress has sought to protect an instrumentality of interstate commerce or a thing in interstate commerce. Thus, if §922(q) is to be sustained, it must be under the third category as a regulation of an activity that substantially affects interstate commerce.

First, we have upheld a wide variety of congressional Acts regulating intrastate economic activity where we have concluded that the activity substantially affected interstate commerce. Examples include the regulation of intrastate coal mining, intrastate extortionate credit transactions, restaurants utilizing substan-tial interstate supplies, inns and hotels catering to interstate guests, and produc-tion and consumption of home-grown wheat. These examples are by no means exhaustive, but the pattern is clear. Where economic activity substantially affects interstate commerce, legislation regulating that activity will be sustained....

Section 922(q) is a criminal statute that by its terms has nothing to do with "commerce" or any sort of economic enterprise, however broadly one might define those terms.[27] Section 922(q) is not an essential part of a larger regulation of

---

27. Under our federal system, the "States possess primary authority for defining and enforcing the criminal law."

economic activity, in which the regulatory scheme could be undercut unless the intrastate activity were regulated. It cannot, therefore, be sustained under our cases upholding regulations of activities that arise out of or are connected with a commercial transaction, which viewed in the aggregate, substantially affects interstate commerce.

To uphold the Government's contentions here, we would have to pile inference upon inference in a manner that would bid fair to convert congressional authority under the Commerce Clause to a general police power of the sort retained by the States. Admittedly, some of our prior cases have taken long steps down that road, giving great deference to congressional action. The broad language in these opinions has suggested the possibility of additional expansion, but we decline here to proceed any further. To do so would require us to conclude that the Constitution's enumeration of powers does not presuppose something not enumerated, and that there never will be a distinction between what is truly national and what is truly local. This we are unwilling to do.

[Lopez' federal conviction was reversed.]

COMMENTARY AND QUESTIONS

1. **The limited relevance of *Lopez* to environmental law.** The vast majority of federal environmental legislation, from the major laws such as the Clean Air Act and Clean Water Act, to lesser known statutes such as the Safe Drinking Water Act, is enacted pursuant to the commerce power, as was the Gun-Free School Zones Act of 1990. Does *Lopez* raise any serious doubt as to the constitutionality of those environmental laws? By characterizing environmental laws as intended to protect public health and safety, the analogy to *Lopez* gains some force. Just as the criminal law area at issue in *Lopez* is one in which the states possess primary authority, so too, the fields of public health and safety are at the core of the traditional state police power. The analogy, nevertheless, is flawed and misleading because, unlike the attenuated linkage between interstate commerce and the crime of knowingly possessing a firearm near a school, environmental laws typically bear a much clearer linkage to the national economy. Consider here the majority's "three broad categories of activity that Congress may regulate under its commerce power." Initially, it is more than a mere debaters' game to try to cast the nation's waters and airsheds in the first or second categories of "channels" or "instrumentalities" of commerce. Historically, water was the principal medium for interstate commerce. The earliest pollution control legislation, the Rivers and Harbors Act of 1899, had as a concern the impacts of pollution on commercial navigation. Environmental legislation such as the Toxic Substances Control Act and the Federal Insecticide, Fungicide, and Rodenticide Act, directly affect the marketing of products in the national economy. Support for an even broader array of federal environmental legislation lies in the third prong, "activities having a substantial relation to interstate commerce." At bedrock, much of the regulation in the Clean Water Act and Clean Air Act is directed toward the interstate economics of pollution control. The so-called race of laxity is a worry solely because states with lax regulation would provide a comparative economic benefit to firms that locate there. Finally, even the majority in *Lopez* cites with approval Hodel v. Virginia

Surface Mining & Reclamation Assn., Inc., 452 U.S. 264 (1981), a case involving commerce power-based regulation of intrastate strip mining activities. Likewise, the *Lopez* majority did not renounce the aggregation principle of Wickard v. Filburn — that the cumulative interstate economic effect of numerous local actions can support regulation of local activities. In this way, federal regulation of even small polluters remains well within the Court's vision of permissible commerce clause regulation.

2. **The legal process question in *Lopez*.** Which branch of government ought to decide whether federal legislation affects commerce? The Supreme Court, at least since the famous case of Marbury v. Madison in 1803, has the responsibility to exercise judicial review to ascertain whether Congress' enactments are within constitutional bounds, including whether the statutes are passed in pursuance of an enumerated power. Congress' view of its own actions, however, is entitled to considerable deference, for, as the majority opinion concedes, "as part of our independent evaluation of constitutionality under the Commerce Clause we of course consider legislative findings, and indeed even congressional committee findings, regarding the effect on interstate commerce...." Justice Breyer's dissent made even more of the deference argument, as did Justice Souter's dissent, which cited the *Hodel* strip mining case mentioned above: "In reviewing congressional legislation under the Commerce Clause, we defer to what is often a merely implicit congressional judgment that its regulation addresses a subject substantially affecting interstate commerce if there is any rational basis for such a finding." 452 U.S. at 276. In light of the deference that all members of the Court profess for congressional findings on this issue, most environmental legislation that has readily cognizable economic impacts seems safe from invalidation. Most likely, the lesson of *Lopez* is that the linkage to interstate commerce cannot be too attenuated, an issue that invites differences in view, much like the issue of proximate causation in tort.

3. **Environmental laws subject to attack on *Lopez* grounds.** At least three federal environmental laws already have been subjected to *Lopez*-based constitutional challenges. None of the cases challenge the entire statute, instead, the cases challenge only particular applications having local impacts that are, arguably, isolated and remote from interstate commerce.

*Superfund* — The first of these cases is United States v. Olin Corp., 107 F.3d 1506 (11th Cir. 1997). Olin owned a contaminated parcel of land in Alabama as to which EPA sought to obtain a cleanup order and reimbursement for funds it (EPA) had already expended at the site. The governing law providing EPA with those claims is the Comprehensive Environmental Response, Cleanup, and Liability Act (CERCLA). At the trial court level Olin was successful in having the statute invalidated on several constitutional grounds, including a *Lopez*-based commerce clause argument. See United States v. Olin Corp., 927 F.Supp. 1502 (S.D.Ala. 1996). The thrust of the claim was that the contamination was limited to soil and groundwater that would not migrate far enough to affect any areas beyond the immediate Alabama locale. Despite those findings, the Court of Appeals reversed, and in relevant part said:

This determination [of sufficient relationship to interstate commerce] turns on whether the statute constitutes "an essential part of a larger regulation of economic activity, in which the regulatory scheme could be undercut unless the intrastate activity were regulated." Lopez v. United States, 115 S.Ct. at 1631. A court's focus, thus, cannot be excessively narrow; if the statute regulates a "class of activities...and that class is within the reach of the federal power, the courts have no power 'to excise, as trivial, individual instances' of the class." '[W]here a general regulatory statute bears a substantial relation to commerce, the de minimis character of individual instances arising under that statute is of no consequence.'"

In light of [the] understanding [that the narrowest class of activities that CERCLA regulates is the on-site disposal of hazardous waste], we must assess whether on-site waste disposal substantially affects interstate commerce. Because the legislative history of CERCLA documents how the unregulated management of hazardous substances, even strictly within individual states, significantly impacts interstate commerce, we conclude the statute can be applied constitutionally under the circumstances of this case.

When the Senate considered S. 1480, a bill containing cleanup liability provisions later substantially incorporated into CERCLA, its Committee on Environment and Public Works ("the Committee") took notice of many facts that show a nexus between all forms of improper waste disposal and interstate commerce. First, the Committee noted the growth of the chemical industry and the concomitant costs of handling its waste. See S.Rep. No. 96-848, 96th Cong., 2d Sess. 2 (1980), reprinted in 1 Legislative History of the Comprehensive Environmental Response, Compensation and Liability Act of 1980, at 309 (1983). It also cited a 1980 report by the Office of Technology Assessment which gauged agricultural losses from chemical contamination in six states at $283 million. Id. at 310. The Committee reported that the commercial damages resulting from unregulated waste management were not attributable solely to interstate trafficking in hazardous materials for disposal, but also arose from accidents associated with purely intrastate, on-site disposal activities, such as improper waste storage in tanks, lagoons and chemical plants. Id. at 312. Thus, CERCLA reflects Congress's recognition that both on-site and off-site disposal of hazardous waste threaten interstate commerce.

Is the reasoning persuasive? Are there more direct interstate economic effects that the court could cite? Liability for its former operations at the site clearly affects Olin's current fiscal position. In this regard, it is interesting to advert to some of the furor surrounding the legislative efforts to change the liability scheme in CERCLA, which will be detailed in Chapter 18. One group strongly opposed to eliminating retroactive liability is composed of parties who have cleaned sites and "paid the price" under CERCLA. This group is afraid that their competitors who have not yet done so will escape liability and gain a competitive advantage in (plainly interstate) commerce.

**Endangered Species** — The second post-Lopez case of note is National Association of Home Builders v. Babbitt, 130 F.3d 1041 (D.C.Cir. 1997). In Home Builders, a builders' association and others including local governments challenged the Endangered Species Act (ESA) as it affected certain lands located solely in California. The land involved was designated as critical habitat of the Delhi Sands Flower-Loving Fly, a fly whose known habitat is restricted to a few hundred

square miles in the San Bernadino, California area. Section 9 of the Endangered
Species Act prohibits actions that "take" a listed endangered species (see Chapter
14) and in this case it had the effect of severely curtailing development possibilities. In response to the constitutional claim, the court stated:

> It is clear that, in this instance, section 9(a)(1) of the ESA is not a regulation of
> the instrumentalities of interstate commerce or of persons or things in inter-
> state commerce. As a result, only the first and the third categories of activity
> discussed in *Lopez* will be examined. In evaluating whether ESA section 9(a)(1)
> is a regulation of the use of the channels of interstate commerce or of activity
> that substantially affects interstate commerce, we may look not only to the
> effect of the extinction of the individual endangered species at issue in this
> case, but also to the aggregate effect of the extinction of all similarly situated
> endangered species. As the *Lopez* Court explained, "'where a general regula-
> tory statute bears a substantial relation to commerce, the de minimis charac-
> ter of individual instances arising under the statute is of no consequence.'"
> *Lopez*, 514 U.S. at 558. If a statute regulates "a class of activities...within reach
> of the federal power," the courts have "no power 'to excise, as trivial, individ-
> ual instances' of the class," *id*. Because section 9(a)(1) of the ESA regulates a
> class of activities — takings of endangered species — that is within Congress'
> Commerce Clause power under both the first and third *Lopez* categories, appli-
> cation of section 9(a)(1) to the Fly is constitutional.

***Wetlands regulation*** — Under §404 of the Clean Water Act, it is illegal to discharge fill material into a wetlands without first obtaining a federal permit from
Army Corps of Engineers. In United States v. Wilson, 45 E.R.C. 1801, 1997 WL
785530 (4th Cir. 1997), the defendants "were convicted of felony violations of the
Clean Water Act for knowingly discharging fill and excavated material into wetlands of the United States without a permit." On appeal, the defendants raised several challenges to their convictions,[28] including a *Lopez* challenge. The case
involved a very large development, approximately 9,100 acres in size, located in
the Chesapeake Bay area of Maryland. To complete portions of the project, the
defendants needed to drain several areas and did so by digging trenches and placing the removed dirt alongside, a process known as "sidecasting." The defendants
also placed fill on the parcels. The Court of Appeals began its discussion of the
*Lopez* issue by tracing the history of federal water regulation up to the Clean Water
Act, noting that, "the Supreme Court has indicated that in defining 'navigable
waters' as 'waters of the United States,' Congress intended 'to exercise its powers
under the Commerce Clause to regulate at least some waters that would not be
deemed 'navigable' under the classical understanding of that term.' United States
v. Riverside Bayview Homes, Inc., 474 U.S. 121 (1985)." *Riverside* had also
involved wetlands, but there the wetlands were adjacent to an international, interstate waterway.[29] The opinion continued:

---

28. Along with the *Lopez* challenge discussed here, the defendants also prevailed on a challenge that
the trial court erred in failing to attach a mens rea requirement to each element of the crime. That
subject is considered in Chapter 19.

29. Here, the wetlands were more than six miles from the Potomac River and more than ten miles
from Chesapeake Bay, although the parcels involved did abut streams that flowed into those major
water bodies. In a separate discussion later in the opinion, the principal opinion found error in a portion of the jury charge that was based on a very broad interpretation of *Riverside* (including within
the scope of Clean Water Act, wetlands "without a direct or even indirect surface connection to other
waters of the United States"). 1997 WL 785530 at 6. Only two judges addressed that issue, and they
split on the proper conclusion.

Presumably, Congress may also regulate the discharge of pollutants into non-navigable waters to the extent necessary to protect the use or potential use of navigable waters as channels or instrumentalities of interstate commerce, although the extent of that power is not entirely clear. Finally, it is arguable that Congress has the power to regulate the discharge of pollutants into any waters that themselves flow across state lines, or connect to waters that do so, regardless of whether such waters are navigable in fact, merely because of the interstate nature of such waters, although the existence of such a far reaching power could be drawn into question by the Court's recent federalism jurisprudence. See, e.g., Printz v. United States, 117 S.Ct. 2365, (1997); Seminole Tribe v. Florida, 517 U.S. 44 (1996); Lopez, 514 U.S. 549 (1995); New York v. United States, 505 U.S. 144 (1992).

However, we need not resolve these difficult questions about the extent and limits of congressional power to regulate nonnavigable waters to resolve the issue before us. The regulation challenged here, 33 C.F.R. §328.3(a)(3) (1993), defines "waters of the United States" to include:

> All other waters such as *intrastate* lakes, rivers, streams (including intermittent streams), mud flats, sand flats, wetlands, sloughs, prairie potholes, wet meadows, playa lakes, or natural ponds, the use, degradation or destruction of which *could* affect interstate or foreign commerce.... (Emphasis added by court).

This regulation purports to extend the coverage of the Clean Water Act to a variety of waters that are intrastate, nonnavigable, or both, solely on the basis that the use, degradation, or destruction of such waters could affect interstate commerce. The regulation requires neither that the regulated activity have a substantial affect on interstate commerce, nor that the covered waters have any sort of nexus with navigable, or even interstate, waters. Were this regulation a statute, duly enacted by Congress, it would present serious constitutional difficulties, because, at least at first blush, it would appear to exceed congressional authority under the Commerce Clause. This regulation is not, however, a statute. Absent a clear indication to the contrary, we should not lightly presume that merely by defining "navigable waters" as "the waters of the United States," 33 U.S.C. §1362(7), Congress authorized the Army Corps of Engineers to assert its jurisdiction in such a sweeping and constitutionally troubling manner....

Accordingly, we believe that in promulgating 33 C.F.R. §328.3(a)(3) (1993), the Army Corps of Engineers exceeded its congressional authorization under the Clean Water Act, and that, for this reason, 33 C.F.R. §328.3(a)(3) is invalid. For the same reason, the district court's instruction based upon this regulation is also erroneous. U.S. v. Wilson, 1997 WL 785530 at 4–5.

Even on its own terms, *Wilson* is a very difficult case to assess. Only two of the three judges agreed to the excerpted portions of the opinion. Read carefully, *Wilson* is not a *Lopez* case at all because it avoids the *Lopez* issue by concluding that the Corps, by choosing so broad a scope for its regulation, went beyond the limits Congress set. That is not a constitutional holding at all, it is one of statutory interpretation. Congress could, via new (and politically unpalatable) legislation, extend authority to the Corps that would allow the Corps to promulgate the challenged regulation. Likewise, Congress could by statute enact a definition of "waters of the United States" that tracks the language of 33 C.F.R. §328.3(a)(3).

Then, and only then, would the "hard" *Lopez* question be ripe for decision in the Fourth Circuit.[30]

When it is finally presented, how will the *Lopez* attack on federal wetlands regulation fare? What is the best analogy to *Olin* and *Home Builders* for the government to stress? Wetlands loss impacts commercially important species, including migratory wildfowl that are also subject to federal treaty protection. As another possibility, nothing in *Wilson* addresses the immense commercial importance of the wetlands-affecting developments themselves, or the aggregate costs that they externalize when they are allowed to disrupt wetlands.

### Section 2. SEMINOLE AND THE ELEVENTH AMENDMENT THICKET

In a 1996 decision, Seminole Tribe v. Florida, 517 U.S. 44 (1996), Justice Rehnquist reopened a cantankerous debate with environmental consequences over the meaning and effect of the Eleventh Amendment, which provides:

> The Judicial power of the United States shall not be construed to extend to any suit in law or equity, commenced or prosecuted against one of the United States by Citizens of another State, or by Citizens or Subjects of any Foreign State.

By its terms, the Amendment would seem to be a relatively narrow limitation on the judicial jurisdiction of the federal courts when one of the several states is sued by a party fitting the description given in the amendment. Through a series of arcane decisions the Amendment has not been limited to its terms.[31] The Amendment now describes a broader principle of state sovereign immunity to suit in federal court, playing a role in a resurgent debate about federalism in this country.

The relevance of the Eleventh Amendment to environmental law was, before *Seminole*, quite modest. The sole major environmental case raising a serious Eleventh Amendment issue was Pennsylvania v. Union Gas, 491 U.S. 1 (1989). There, the Court, by a 5–4 vote that produced no majority opinion, just a majority result, upheld the creation by Congress (using its commerce power to enact CERCLA) of a right for private parties to recover monetary relief in federal court from states found to be liable for cleanup costs under federal law. With *Union Gas* on the books, Congress had a relatively free hand in authorizing remedies against states that violated federal law. For example, as noted in the next chapter, many federal environmental laws expressly authorize citizen suits as a supplement to governmental enforcement. Under those laws, a state or local government that operated a polluting facility could be sued in federal court on the same basis as any

---

30. The division of the federal courts into circuits and restrictions on the doctrine of estoppel in its application to government agencies, leave the federal government free to employ 33 C.F.R. §328.3(a)(3) in locales outside of the Fourth Circuit. Thus, it is possible that another wetlands case may arise in a different locale that raises the *Lopez* issue for decision. Given the reversal of the convictions in *Wilson*, it is a safe bet to assume that little time will elapse before another wetlands case presents the constitutional issue for decision.

31. In Hans v. Louisiana, 134 U.S. 1 (1890), the scope of the Eleventh Amendment was expanded from its literal language interpreting suits brought by citizens of other states or foreign nations to include citizens of the defendant state as well.

other potential defendant. Likewise, Congress could permit a private suit against a state in federal court to compel the state to perform obligations it had undertaken in relation to environmental regulation.

*Seminole* — involving Indian casinos, not environmental laws, expressly overruled *Union Gas* and employed broad reasoning in doing so:

> We have understood the Eleventh Amendment to stand not so much for what it says, but for the presupposition...which it confirms. That presupposition...has two parts: first, that each State is a sovereign entity in our federal system; and second, that it is inherent in the nature of sovereignty not to be amenable to the suit of an individual without its consent....

> [In this statute] Congress clearly intended to abrogate the States' sovereign immunity.... In overruling *Union Gas* today, we reconfirm...the background principle of state sovereign immunity embodied in the Eleventh Amendment.... Even when the Constitution vests in Congress complete law-making authority over a particular area, the Eleventh Amendment prevents congressional authorization of suits by private parties against unconsenting States. The Eleventh Amendment restricts the judicial power under Article III, and Article I cannot be used to circumvent the constitutional limitations placed upon federal jurisdiction. Petitioner's suit against the State of Florida must be dismissed for a lack of jurisdiction. 517 U.S. at 72–73 (1996).

With *Union Gas* overruled, the effect is to prevent private enforcement suits, limiting enforcement to agencies in the political process. Congress loses the ability to enlist private federal court enforcement as a deterrent to state violations of federal environmental law. (The federal government can still bring its own lawsuits against the states in federal court because those are pretty clearly not affected by the Eleventh Amendment.) *Seminole* takes what might be described as a strict chronological approach to parsing out the federal-state power relationship in this area. Justice Rehnquist's opinion, which commanded five votes, took the position that the Eleventh Amendment creates a right of states to be free from private citizens' suits in federal court to recover monetary relief. Congress is not, despite the Supremacy clause, free to change this under most of its enumerated powers because these powers were granted *before* the ratification of the Eleventh Amendment.[32] The exception to this general rule would be legislation passed pursuant to the enumerated powers granted to Congress by the post-Civil War Amendments, because they came after the Eleventh Amendment and, therefore, are not subject to Eleventh Amendment limitation.

### COMMENTARY & QUESTIONS

1. **A short, simplified view of Eleventh Amendment jurisprudence for those who really want to know.** Almost since its enactment, meaning of the 11th Amendment has been shrouded in uncertainty. There is a fair amount of agreement that the amendment was designed to overrule Chisholm v. Georgia, 2 Dall. 419 (1793). In that case, a South Carolina citizen brought a federal lawsuit to

---

32. The federal law involved in *Seminole* was enacted pursuant to the commerce power as it applies to Native American tribes.

recover money owed on a debt incurred by the State of Georgia as part of its Revolutionary War effort. The Court held that Congress could authorize such suits against states by foreigners or citizens of other states. *Chisholm* prompted fears that British nationals and American Tories would file federal lawsuits seeking to collect Revolutionary War debts of the states, and claims of wartime expropriation... The new 11th Amendment therefore removed Congress's power to authorize such claims from the federal Article III judicial power.

  Things got murkier after the 1890 case of Hans v. Louisiana, 134 U.S. 1. In *Hans* the Court extended the 11th Amendment, with no textual support whatever, to suits brought by citizens of a state against that state, stating that to do otherwise would be "anomalous." Professor Irwin Chemerinsky notes the three very different views that followed — One theory is that the 11th Amendment puts a general limitation on the power of the federal courts. This view relies on *Hans* as demonstrating the greater breadth of the amendment and "affirms that the fundamental principle of [state] sovereign immunity limits the grant of [federal] judicial authority in Article III." The second major view of the 11th Amendment is that it reinstates the common law sovereign immunity of the states. This plays out into three general sub-principles that can be used to understand the array of decisions that have since followed: (a) states are free to consent to suit and, therefore, can waive their immunity; (b) Congress is free to authorize federal jurisdiction in suits against states (which may then opt to waive their immunity); and (c) because the immunity is grounded in common law, Congress can abrogate that immunity via statute. The third view is that the 11th Amendment restricts the diversity jurisdiction of the federal courts, when the basis for jurisdiction is the different citizenship of the parties to the lawsuit. On this view, Congress is unfettered in authorizing suits and abrogating the immunity of the states when the case is one based on federal law (or any jurisdictional basis other than diversity of citizenship). Chemerinsky, Federal Jurisdiction 2d ed., at §7.3.(1994).

Other issues have been tacked onto the 11th Amendment. Federalism arguments have produced theories of statutory construction requiring explicit congressional intent to allow suit against the state in the first place, to require clear intent to abrogate state immunity. Second are cases like Ex Parte Young, 209 U.S. 123 (1908) that bypass the 11th Amendment by saying that a suits against a state "may be brought in federal court by naming the state officer as the defendant." Chemerinsky, at §7.5. The continuing convoluted legal and political nuances of 11th Amendment caselaw will be quite relevant to environmental law. See Coates v. Strahan, Strahan v. Coxe, 127 F.3d 155 (1st Cir. 1997), on cert., No. 97-1485 (state sued for licensing fishing gear that kills endangered whales claims that federal government cannot require it to protect whales).

2. *Seminole*'s **holding in its Eleventh Amendment context.** *Seminole's* five member majority is comprised of the four *Union Gas* dissenters plus Justice Thomas. The majority opts for the first of the three visions of the Eleventh Amendment described in the previous note, that the Amendment limits the subject matter jurisdiction of the federal courts (except for cases arising under legislation passed pursuant to the later-in-time Fourteenth Amendment). In this way, *Seminole* has the effect of preventing Congress from abrogating state immunity, even when it legislates pursuant to an enumerated power. Particularly when the

majority's ex parte Young discussion is added in, the *Seminole* majority has painted with a very broad brush. In an effort to blunt criticism that the majority was disregarding precedent in overruling *Union Gas*, Justice Rehnquist observed that the principle of stare decisis has never been slavishly followed by the Supreme Court in areas were the controlling precedents were "unworkable." He then adds, "Our willingness to reconsider our earlier decisions has been "particularly true in constitutional cases, because in such cases 'correction through legislative action is practically impossible.'" This latter addition is ironic. Before *Seminole*, Congress, the political and electorally responsible branch, by ordinary legislation, controlled the extent and degree of state sovereign immunity to suits in federal court that redressed violations of federal law. Congress was "aided" in being sensitive to state sovereignty by the numerous interpretive doctrines that the Court had established that, in effect, disfavored the abrogation of state immunity. After *Seminole*, and the non-literal, textually unsupported view of the Eleventh Amendment that it contains, only constitutional amendment can alter its allocation of power between the Congress and the states.

3. ***Seminole*'s holding in its environmental law context.** The *Seminole* decision addresses only cases in which federal suit is brought against a state by a private party. This leaves unaffected federal court enforcement of federal law in suits brought by the United States. The dissenters are quite explicit in making this point and the majority also, although it is less directly stated, subscribes to that view as well. This can be inferred from the cases that the majority opinion uses to support its position. For example, in a key passage, Justice Rehnquist quotes a phrase from the Federalist, No. 81, that had been quoted in a previous Eleventh amendment case: "[i]t is inherent in the nature of sovereignty not to be amenable to the suit of an *individual* without its consent." (Emphasis added by editor.) As another example, in discussing the breadth of the Eleventh Amendment bar to federal suit as not being a function of the remedy sought in a particular case, the majority says, "The Eleventh Amendment does not exist solely in order to "preven[t] federal court judgments that must be paid out of a State's treasury," it also serves to "avoid the indignity of subjecting a State to the coercive process of federal judicial tribunals at the instance of *private parties*." (Emphasis added by editor, the Court quoting (for the second part) Puerto Rico Aqueduct and Sewer Authority v. Metcalf & Eddy, Inc., 506 U.S. 139, 146 (1993).)

The impact of *Seminole* on environmental law may be significant. Potentially, *Seminole* applies to all private efforts to enforce federal law-based environmental obligations in federal court against states, state entities, and state officers. Such suits are common, if not ubiquitous. For example, states operate large numbers of facilities that are regulated by the Clean air Act or the Clean Water Act. Violations of permits required by those federal acts (and others) can be raised by private parties under the statutes' citizen suit provisions. More generally, many of those same laws impose requirements on the states as regulators who can be sued by citizens to spur enforcement. Private party suits in federal court against non-consenting states are precluded by *Seminole*.

4. **Getting around *Seminole* by going to state court.** There is nothing in *Seminole* that limits the ability of private suits against states in state court. There are, however, hurdles to such suits that the states can erect under their law of sovereign

immunity. The law on this subject is too varied for treatment here. Consider the policy implications of requiring private suits against states for environmental violations to be brought in the state courts. Is it a good idea? State court judges are, often, elected locally; federal court judges are life-tenured. Might that difference affect a state court jurist's willingness to impose an expensive remedy that must be financed by a tax hike? Are state courts as well equipped to handle technical issues as federal court? Are state courts as proficient at interpreting federal legislation as are federal courts? In the wake of *Seminole*, there may be evidence with which to answer these questions.

5. **Getting around *Seminole* in federal court.** *Seminole* does not apply if the state involved in a particular case waives its immunity. Politically, states wishing to project a favorable image on environmental issues may be willing to be sued in these cases. Alternatively, Congress may be able to induce the states to waive their immunity, although this avenue around *Seminole* is complicated by the twists and turns of pre-*Seminole* Eleventh Amendment doctrine. One early way around the amendment was thought to be "constructive waiver." The idea here was that if a state entered into a field that Congress had regulated and in which Congress had prescribed federal judicial remedies, the state by entering the field, "consented" to be sued. See Parden v. Terminal Railway of Alabama State Docks Dept., 377 U.S. 184 (1964). That case, and with it the concept of constructive waiver, was eroded and eventually overruled. See Welch v. Texas Department of Highways and Public Transportation, 483 U.S. 468 (1987). At most, constructive waiver is now no more than a theoretical possibility in cases in which "[T]he congressional desire to make states liable must be in 'unmistakable language in the statute itself' and it must also be an area where the state realistically could choose not to engage in the activity." Chemerinsky, supra at §7.6 (footnotes omitted). What remains possible is where states expressly waive their Eleventh Amendment immunity. Congress, in the wake of *Seminole*, may well begin to require such express waivers as a condition precedent to the receipt of federal funds. For example, a waiver of immunity could be a pre-condition to receipt of federal funds for the construction of POTWs, mass-transit systems, highways, etc. The problem with this approach is twofold. First, it requires some lead time for Congress to act. In the interim, the environment may suffer. Second, it requires some political will on the part of Congress. It is important to remember that one facet of federal environmental law remains unchanged in all this: under the wording of the Eleventh Amendment the federal government remains free to bring suits in its own name to enforce federal environmental laws against states. The only limits on this power are a function of federal enforcement resources and the will to use them.

*The fight against adequate government control and supervision of...corporate wealth engaged in interstate business is chiefly done undercover, and especially under the cover of an appeal to state's rights.*

— Teddy Roosevelt (quoted by Prof. Kathleen Sullivan, New York Times Magazine, August 18, 1986 at 36, from Arthur Schlesinger, Cycles of American History and Capitals at 236).

# Chapter 7

# THE ADMINISTRATIVE LAW OF ENVIRONMENTAL LAW

A. *The Evolution of the Administrative Process*

B. *Administrative Law in a Nutshell*

C. Overton Park — *an Administrative Law Paradigm*

D. *Citizen Enforcement and Judicial Review*

E. *Statutory Interpretation: How, by Whom?*

F. *Administrative Process — Proposed Improvements*

## A. THE EVOLUTION OF THE ADMINISTRATIVE PROCESS

If one looks back over the history of the administrative process in America, it can be divided analytically into at least six different stages.[1]

• **The passive era.** The first stage would begin at the birth of the republic, or earlier, before the Revolution, when, it can be argued, the private marketplace economy was in fact the predominant "government" of America. Many historians argue that the Revolution was more an economic than a political phenomenon. The colonies matured "like ripe fruit" and dropped away from Great Britain when they had become self-sufficient market entities. State, federal, and local governments initially merely attended to minor governmental chores, and their major early role was to facilitate the private marketplace. Government agencies built roads, canals, and a postal system, and protected national and international trade.

• **1880+** The second stage, the advent of regulatory agencies, can be traced to the 1880s, when federal and state governments reacted to the perceived evils of an unregulated marketplace, including child labor, railroad gouging of farmers and shippers, and the like. Society discovered that there was a civic realm beyond the structures of the marketplace economy. Regulatory agencies were invented to correct "market failures," by imposing a bipolar theory of social governance: the marketplace on one hand would supply economic strength, and government on the other would protect its citizens and society from the excesses of the marketplace in specific regulated areas. Reaction against governmental regulation was immediate and passionate in the 1890s, and continues in much the same rhetorical terms today. From the beginning, however, private regulated interests in the marketplace

---

1. This historical analysis builds upon ideas in Stewart, The Reformation of American Administrative Law, 88 Harv. L. Rev. 1669 (1975).

did not merely oppose governmental regulatory agencies; they also moved to co-opt them. As the Attorney General wrote to the president of a railroad in 1892 in response to the latter's plea for abolition of the Interstate Commerce Commission as a "socialistic" federal regulatory agency:

> The Commission...is or can be made of great use to the railroads. It satisfies the popular clamor for government supervision of railroads, at the same time that the supervision is almost entirely nominal. Further, the older such a commission gets to be, the more inclined it would be found to take the business and railroad view of things. It thus becomes a sort of barrier between the railroad corporations and the people, and a sort of protection against hasty and crude legislation hostile to railroad interests.... The part of wisdom is not to destroy the Commission, but to utilize it.[2]

In any event, in this era government involvement in the economy remained the exception, not the rule.

• **1930+** The third stage, in the 1930s, marked a shift from regulatory agencies as mere occasional correctives, to the theory that agencies can be given a primary directive role in the economy, at least during national traumas like the Great Depression and the Second World War. The New Deal produced a host of agencies that were managers as well as regulators. It was at this point that the "administrative state" became a tangible entity. The powers of government reached into areas never before regulated. (This is not to say that the process was systematically rational or even that government became the dominant factor in American society. The relatively-unfettered private economy remained the pre-eminent force in the daily life of the nation.)

• **1946+** In 1946 a reaction against regulatory agency high-handedness resulted in the passage of the federal Administrative Procedures Act (APA),[3] copied in many states. There had always been a reaction against governmental interference with the marketplace, because so much human energy and passion is invested in private property and income-generating activities, and government tends to get in the way. The APA's clear and dominating purpose was to prevent the exercise of agency peremptory power through required procedures and judicial control of the agency process.

Nevertheless the United States, faced with all the postwar complexities of life as a great power, melting pot, social experiment, and economic dynamo, continued to develop its administrative substructure at every level of government. By 1968 the federal agencies comprised more than one hundred thirty agencies and two million civil servants.

• **1960s+** The next phase in the evolution of administrative law is quite closely linked to the growth of environmentalism: it was a 1960s shift from the bipolar model — regulatory agency versus regulated industry — to a far more realistic pluralistic, multi-centric model. Citizen outsiders began to use the legal tools created by industry for challenging government agency powers, but deployed them against

---

2. Letter from Attorney General Richard Olney to Charles Perkins, in Jaffe, The Effective Limits of the Administrative Process, 67 Harv. L. Rev. 1105, 1009 (1954).

3. 5 U.S.C.A. §501 et seq. (1946).

defendants who now were often agencies and industries working together (the "Establishment" that was targeted by 1960s activists). Beginning in 1966, the federal courts in particular began to be much more open to citizens — to environmentalists, consumers, civil rights activists, and so on — and the administrative process, responding to the courts, began to follow suit. From that pluralistic opening-up of the administrative law system came many of the significant social changes of the second half of the 20th century.

• **1976+** The year 1976, however, provided early steps in an initiative of retrenchment against pluralistic democratic involvement in the administrative process. The *Vermont Yankee* case later in this chapter was a major contribution to this trend. The Supreme Court has since moved in a variety of ways to limit opportunities for citizens to involve themselves in judicial challenges of agencies and regulated interests, themes echoed in occasional post-1980 campaigns for deregulation.

These stages in the evolution of administrative law overlap one another, so that in modern society one can still simultaneously see a tendency to turn to governmental agencies to handle newly identified societal problems, a reaction against governmental agencies, a pluralistic tendency toward a continuing democratization of the administrative process, and counter-tendencies attempting to limit outsider citizen participation.

From this quick excursion through history one can get a sense of how environmental law, which has consistently been shaped by private citizens' activist efforts, reflects major cross-currents in the development of American government. The administrative state, built upon a foundation of common law, forces environmentalists to deal with all the varied advantages and disadvantages of the government process.

Because environmentalism has been so ready to rock the boat — persistently trying to force an evasive status quo to confront a broad range of important concerns in the civic-societal economy, about pollution, chemical exposures, and dwindling resources — environmental law has tended to be on the cutting edge of a wide range of fields, including equity, tort, civil procedure, and others already encountered. Administrative law is a prime example on this list. A modern administrative law course could be taught using environmental cases exclusively.

This chapter, however, does not purport to be a course in administrative law. It is a glimpse at the field, to inform subsequent consideration of various environmental regulatory programs in later chapters.

## B.  ADMINISTRATIVE LAW IN A NUTSHELL

Practical questions of administrative law boil down to three broad areas of inquiry, analyzing —

- the process by which government agencies (at all levels — local, state, federal, and perhaps even international) receive the powers that they apply in their various regulatory settings.

- the methods by which they exercise their powers in particular cases, and
- how such agency exercises of power can be mobilized, demobilized, directed, overturned, or circumvented (usually by judicial review litigation second-guessing particular agency decisions, but also including the pressuring process in the legislative or executive branches of government, before or after decisions are made.)

**THE SOURCE OF POWER: DELEGATION...** Agencies are just that: agents. Their only reason for existence, since they are not provided for in the federal Constitution or most state constitutions, is that the constitutionally-created branches of government had too much detailed work to do than they could conveniently do themselves. The constitutionally-created branches accordingly delegated some of their powers to standing agents in order to spread the workload and drudgery of performing investigations, day-to-day oversight, and the hands-on administrative tasks of running a society.

This reality reflects the utilitarian assumption, common to all modern nations, that government has to take an active part in running a modern society. The market and various social relationships are incapable of managing the full scope and complexity of modern life. Without the external imposition of governmental powers into the market system, some important needs and values would not be adequately addressed. Without government, there would not be adequate machinery for defending our borders against enemies and building roads and schools for all. Without government, factories might well still be using the labor of children (which in localized market terms made compelling good sense), and disposing of pollution by dumping it willy-nilly.

Most government programs, therefore, originate in recognition of market failure, when the marketplace and processes of social accommodation have failed to do a job that a politically significant number of people think need doing. But virtually all such tasks turn out to be too much for the constitutionally-established officials (a couple thousand or so legislators and judges in the federal government, and a handful of executives) to handle. So they create agents. (And then, of course, more can be done, so then even more new tasks can be undertaken by government, so then more agents have to be created, and then... but that's another issue.)

Agencies can be created by each branch of government, acting alone. Courts can set up "special masters" to handle administrative tasks; legislatures can set up their own budget-analysis and investigatory offices (CBO, GAO, OTA); chief executives can set up councils of economic advisors, security advisors, budget advisors, and environmental advisors. But in the vast majority of cases where an agency is set up to manage affairs that directly affect people outside of government, including most agencies affecting the environment, the agency will be created by an act of the legislature signed into law by the chief executive, and will be placed more or less into the bailiwick of the executive branch.

The powers and duties of most agencies, therefore, must be derived from the statutes that create them (their respective "organic acts") and that delegate various powers to them. The agencies hold only subsidiary powers; they can make only

subsidiary rules. Their actions must be authorized by and conform to the requirements of the statutes (and, beyond the statutes, to the Constitution).

The requirements of the "delegation doctrine" provide some of the basic
inquiries by which agency actions are tested. Did a statute give the agency the particular power it is attempting to exercise? Do the legislature and the chief executive have the right to delegate a particular role or power to an agent? Is the
legislature's delegating language too broad or vague to give adequate definition and
limitation to the agency's actions? In some cases delegations to agencies have been
voided under the separation of powers theory: the statute has impermissibly delegated legislative or judicial power to an agent that is a nonlegislature or noncourt.
In some few cases agency actions have been struck down under the ultra vires
["beyond the powers"] theory: the delegating statute did not grant a power specifically enough or extend it broadly enough to cover the particular kind of thing that
the agency is attempting to do. In the vast majority of federal cases, however, the
delegation doctrine is only a background constraint on agency action.[4]

**THE EXERCISE OF AGENCY POWERS...** An administrative agency is itself an ongoing, functioning organism. As such it exercises a variety of powers, both internally,
within the agency, and externally, impacting upon people outside the agency. The
external powers include the power to investigate, require submission of information, etc. and these can be important. Day in and day out, however, the primary
exercises of an agency's external powers occur in two ways — rulemaking (the
issuance of regulations), and adjudication (the process of making operative agency
decisions by applying legal standards set out in statutes or regulations to the facts
of particular cases). Most agencies are delegated the power to act in both ways,
often according to their own choice of how best to proceed.

The life of the administrative state can be tracked through millions of reams
of paper each year. The RCRA statute, which is 96 pages long, for instance, has been
arduously articulated through more than 150 pages of regulations. Each rulemaking reflects hundreds of hours of agency process and disputation. Adjudications —
applying statutes and rules to tens of thousands of cases each year — multiply the
scope of the process geometrically. And a large number of these agency processes
are controversial, which makes their details important to lawyers. The federal
Administrative Procedure Act ("APA"), 5 U.S.C.A. §501 et seq. (1946, as amended),
is the blueprint of modern federal administrative law, and is used almost universally as a model by the states as well. It sets out many (although not all) of the basic
definitions and prescriptions for how an agency is to run itself — how to promulgate rules, how to give notice to the public, how hearings examiners (administrative law judges) are to proceed, and so on. Chapter 7 of the APA prescribes the basis
for judicial review of challenged agency actions. 5 U.S.C.A. §§701–706.

Both rulemaking and adjudication can be accomplished "formally," that is,
they can be done with full trial-type process, discovery, motions, production of evi-

---

4. A few federal judges have made occasional forays, trying to use the delegation doctrine to cut down
agency programs and decisions they dislike. Industrial Union Dept., AFL-CIO v. American Petroleum
Institute, 448 U.S. 607 (1980) (Rehnquist, J., concurring opinion); American Textile Manuf. Inst. v.
Donovan, 452 U.S. 490 (1981) (dissent); and these initiatives continue. What would happen if courts
held legislatures to a strict rule that the terms of all statutes must be "as precise as feasible"?

dence, cross-examination, stenographic record, and a decision-maker bound to decide in a reasoned judgment only on the basis of the record produced.

Both can also be undertaken "informally," through less than formal procedures, without full trial-type process. They also can be "hybrid," part trial-type process and part informal procedure. Hybrid procedures are not prescribed in the APA; they are applied when required by some other particular statute, by the voluntary decision of the agency itself, or in some cases by court order.

The following sections of the APA set out partial prescriptions for how these functions will be exercised; state codes have similar provisions:

|  | RULEMAKING | ADJUDICATION |
|---|---|---|
| Informal | §553 | (no prescribed process) |
| (hybrid, in-between) | §553, plus selected parts of | §§556–557 (no prescribed process) |
| Formal | §553, plus full §§556–557 | |
| | (trial-type procedures, "TTP") | §554, plus full §§556–557 |
| | | (trial-type procedures, "TTP") |

Section 553 says that informal rulemaking, when it affects parties outside government, must at a minimum provide for public notice and opportunity to comment prior to publication of a rule in the Federal Register.[5] Sections 556 and 557 are the add-ons for formal trial-type process — discovery, cross examination, a reasoned decision on the full record, etc. — that can be added-on to *either* adjudication or rulemaking. Section 554 is the prescription for formal adjudication, which always triggers the formal trial-type processes of §§556–557. There is no required process for informal adjudications, even though these are certainly the vast majority of agency actions. Where an agency, for example, says "Yes, you may build a house," or "No, you may not drain a swamp," or "Yes, you may treat pollution abatement as a tax-deductible business expense," or "No, you may not file a late application" — all these are typically informal adjudications, applying law to facts without trial-type procedures.

Battles are often fought between agencies and regulated parties, or intervening parties, about which kind of process the agency should follow, since often there is no express statutory requirement that an agency act through formal or informal rulemaking or adjudication. Sometimes parties want rulemaking rather than adjudication (because then an agency directive can only be prospective). More often parties try to get more formalized trial-type procedures, regardless of whether the agency is proceeding in rulemaking or adjudication. (Attorneys apparently consider

---

5. Rulemaking typically moves through a series of public notice stages before a regulation becomes law. After having been developed within a labyrinth of internal agency procedures, a draft rule is finally published in the Federal Register in a Notice of Proposed Rulemaking, with an explanation of what formal or informal procedures will be applied. At minimum the public has the opportunity to send in comments by mail. After at least 30 days, the agency can process the comments received and publish a Notice of Final Rulemaking in the Federal Register, along with its summarized reactions to public comments received. Every year or so, regulations are codified into CFR, the Code of Federal Regulations (a woefully poorly organized compilation; thankfully, regulations can now be searched through WestLaw and Lexis).

that the more procedure they get, the better the ultimate deal they'll get for their clients.)

The arguments for more procedure usually come down to one of a couple constitutional issues. Procedural due process is the prime argument, though it is not easy to force an agency to give procedure it doesn't want to give.[6] The other constitutional argument is grounded upon the basic judicial review jurisdiction of Article III of the federal Constitution: courts should require more procedure in a given case for the sake of the integrity of their own reviewing role, in order to produce a sufficient body of data (on a formal or informal agency record) to permit a court exercising judicial review to make an adequately incisive, though deferential, review of the agency action.

**PRESSURING AGENCY ACTION...** Since agencies wield such broad-ranging powers in modern society, pressuring them in one direction or another has become a fundamental task of hundreds of thousands of attorneys and other citizens. There are very few significant legal or economic issues that do not turn in substantial part upon the decisions of governmental agencies — local, state, or federal.

Pressure can be applied before or after a particular agency decision in a variety of forums. Agencies respond to lobbying, to the media, to internal or external politicking, and of course to the legislature that created them and annually can cut them down through the budget process, oversight hearings, and amendments to agencies' statutory authority.

**JUDICIAL REVIEW...** Judicial review, however, is the most visible consistent constraint on agency freedom of action. Disgruntled persons can in most cases easily obtain judicial review of particular agency actions, and judicial review can operate to cramp an agency's style even if ultimate reversal of the agency decision is not usually likely.

Judicial review of federal agency action operates under Chapter 7 of the APA, 5 U.S.C.A. §701 et seq. The challenging party must show standing' and reviewability under §702, and fulfill a few other judge-made requirements (ripeness for review, exhaustion of agency remedies, etc.). Section 706 then sets out a catalogue of challenges on the merits:[7] the "arbitrary, capricious, or abuse of discretion" test

---

6. The basic three-point balancing argument comes from Mathews v. Eldridge, 424 U.S. 319 (1976) — a court reviewing how much procedure an agency must constitutionally give a claimant should weigh (1) the hardship to the claimant in not receiving additional process, (2) the hardship to the government in having to provide additional process, and (3) the risk of error in not having particular additional procedures apply.

7. §706... To the extent necessary to decision and when presented, the reviewing court shall decide all relevant questions of law, interpret constitutional and statutory provisions, and determine the meaning or applicability of the terms of an agency action. The reviewing court shall —
(1) compel agency action unlawfully withheld or unreasonably delayed; and
(2) hold unlawful and set aside agency action, findings, and conclusions found to be –
  (A) arbitrary, capricious, an abuse of discretion, or otherwise not in accordance with law;
  (B) contrary to constitutional right, power, privilege, or immunity;
  (C) in excess of statutory jurisdiction, authority, or limitations, or short of statutory right;
  (D) without observance of procedure required by law;
  (E) unsupported by substantial evidence in a case subject to sections 556 and 557 of this title or otherwise reviewed on the record of an agency hearing provided by statute; or
  (F) unwarranted by the facts to the extent that the facts are subject to trial de novo by the reviewing court.
In making the foregoing determinations, the court shall review the whole record or those parts of it cited by a party, and due account shall be taken of the rule of prejudicial error.

(for informal rulemaking or adjudication) or the requirement of "substantial evidence" supporting the decision (in the case of most formal proceedings).

Most substantive challenges of agency decisions turn on the latter two standards, reviewing the rather subjective question of whether the agency's decision was reasonable in the circumstances. In some environmental cases, to be sure, challenges to agency action come down to straightforward application and interpretation of statutes: did the agency violate a provision of some particular law? In far more cases, however, the question is not so easy, instead turning on the assertion that the agency has exercised bad judgment. Courts understandably do not usually like to second-guess agencies, instead preferring to defer to agency discretion and expertise. But their Article III judicial mandate requires them to review cases presented.

**DEGREES OF DEFERENCE...** Issues constantly arise about what "standard of review" should be applied. In challenges to agency findings of fact, the judicial scrutiny can range from the rather minimal "arbitrary" test all the way to judicial takeover of the question (trial de novo). How deeply will the court pry into the particulars of a decision, especially when it realizes that the closer it looks, the more it is second-guessing and taking over the agency's decisional process? In all but the de novo cases, the question usually comes down to the same judicial determination: could a reasonable agency official have reached this decision on this record of facts? The practical difference between various standards of judicial review comes down to differences in degrees and moods of deference to agencies in each case, reflecting different sensitivities to separation of powers issues. In the minuet of contending powers, moreover, courts can use the choice of different standards of review — arbitrary for loose review, substantial evidence for tougher — to effectuate a result that they personally prefer. Politics and ideology in this way insinuate themselves into judicial review of agency action.

In challenges to agency interpretations of law, the same sort of scale applies, although a bit less predictably. Judges don't seem quite so inclined to defer to agencies' decisions of law (the agencies' interpretation of what a statute or regulation requires) as they do to agencies' decisions about questions of fact.

Issues also arise on "scope of review" — how broadly will the court look in scrutinizing the agency action, how much data and "record" will it require, will it allow new evidence to be introduced in court proceedings that was not brought before the agency? Normally the scope of judicial review is limited to the record of whatever was compiled and presented in the challenged agency proceedings. In some cases a court may say that its necessary scope of review requires more evidence to be prepared and presented.

**REMEDIES...** Finally there are questions of remedies. If the agency action was faulty, what sanction should the reviewing court apply — injunction, declaratory judgment, damages, criminal penalties,[8] remand to the agency, or something else?

---

8. One of the authors once briefly researched the possibility of convicting an agency head on a statutory felony charge. Some of the legal reasons, beyond politics, why such attempts are quixotic are set out in Smith, Shields for the King's Men: Official Immunity and Other Obstacles to Effective Prosecution of Federal Officials for Environmental Crimes, 16 Colum. J. Envtl. Law 1 (1991).

**SUMMARY...** As this quick excursion should make clear, administrative law and administrative process make up a separate legal ecosystem that is intricately intertwined with hundreds of important environmental issues, and differs in many regards from the standard litigation model that dominates the law school curriculum.

Whatever substantive area of practice a case arises in, it should by now be evident that a familiarity with underlying administrative law problems is a basic requirement of legal literacy. In no area is this truer than environmental law.

## C. *OVERTON PARK* — AN ADMINISTRATIVE LAW PARADIGM: CITIZEN SUITS AND JUDICIAL REVIEW

The administrative agencies are intimately woven into the power fabric of the nation, and accordingly are linked to most of the environmental issues discovered and decried over the past few decades by environmentalists. Within themselves, agencies mirror many of the forces, procedures, and vested interests that cause environmental problems. It therefore comes as no surprise that environmentalists often find themselves launching challenges against agency actions at all three levels of government, federal, state, and local. Because of their political context, citizen interventions often get short shrift in the agency process,[9] so citizen activists end up going to court.

In administrative law lawsuits, environmental plaintiffs are usually not asking the court to take over the matter and make the "right" decision itself. Rather, when a court is asked to look at an agency decision in most cases it is only applying judicial *review*, and that limitation has consequences. Judicial review of agency actions differs from review of decisions made by lower court judges or juries. An agency is a creature of a different branch of government, so more deference is required. Too much deference, however, would mean that courts abdicate their judicial role. So the critical question of administrative law is how, and how much, the court will scrutinize what an official agency has done.

Environmental plaintiffs must first successfully pass all the threshold obstacles to getting judicial review of administrative action — standing, reviewability, ripeness, exhaustion, and others. The reviewing court then turns to scrutiny of the procedural and substantive merits of the government actions being challenged.

### Section 1. **THE OVERTON PARK CASE**

In the following case, note the plaintiffs' array of arguments: that they did not receive adequate procedures, that the agency decision was substantively wrong, and that the Court should extend the most probing, least deferential, level of scrutiny to the agency's factfinding and decisions of law. They lost virtually all of these battle points, but won their war.

---

9. In the *Pigeon River* case, for instance, the citizens were rebuffed by the agency, which considered itself the rightful public representative in deciding whether the forest reserve should be drilled for oil, and they had to face the agency standing alongside the oil company when they went to court. West Mich. Env. Action Council v. NRC, 275 N.W.2d 538 (Mich. 1979).

## A Road

*I think that I have never knowed, a sight as lovely as a road.*

*A road upon whose concrete tops, the flow of traffic never stops;*

*A road that costs a lot to build, just as the City Council willed;*

*A road the planners say we need, to get the cars to greater speed;*

*We've let the contracts so dig in, and let the chopping now begin;*

*Somebody else can make a tree, but roads are made by guys like me.*

— Mike Royko[10]

### Citizens to Preserve Overton Park, Inc. v. John Volpe, Secretary of Transportation
United States Supreme Court, 1971
401 U.S. 402, 91 S. Ct. 814, 28 L. Ed. 2d 136

[The "Parkland Act," §4(f) of the Department of Transportation Act of 1966 and Section 138 of the Federal Aid to Highways Act of 1968,[11] provides as follows:]

Section 4(f)... It is hereby declared to be the national policy that special effort should be made to preserve the natural beauty of the countryside and public park and recreation lands, wildlife and waterfowl refuges, and historic sites. The Secretary of Transportation shall cooperate and consult with the Secretaries of the Interior, Housing and Urban Development, and Agriculture, and with the States in developing transportation plans and programs that include measures to maintain or enhance the natural beauty of the lands traversed. After the effective date of the Federal-Aid Highway Act of 1968, the Secretary shall not approve any program or project which requires the use of any publicly owned land from a public park, recreation area, or wildlife and waterfowl refuge of national, State, or local significance as determined by the Federal, State, or local officials having jurisdiction thereof, or any land from an historic site of national, State, or local significance as so determined by such officials unless (1) there is no feasible and prudent alternative to the use of such land, and (2) such program includes all possible planning to minimize harm to such park, recreational area, wildlife and waterfowl refuge, or historic site resulting from such use.

MARSHALL, J. The growing public concern about the quality of our natural environment has prompted Congress in recent years to enact legislation designed to curb the accelerating destruction of our county's natural beauty. We are concerned in this case with §4(f) of the Department of Transportation Act of 1966, as amended, and [§138] of the Federal-Aid Highway Act of 1968.

Petitioners, private citizens as well as local and national conservation organizations, contend that the Secretary has violated these statutes by authorizing the expenditure of federal funds for the construction of a six-lane interstate highway through a public park in Memphis, Tennessee....

Overton Park is a 342-acre city park located near the center of Memphis. The park contains a zoo, a nine-hole municipal golf course, an outdoor theater, nature

---

10. For further evidence of the inspirational qualities of trees, and the artistic tendencies of West Publishing Co., see Fisher v. Lowe, 333 N.W.2d 67 (Mich. App. 1983).

11. 49 U.S.C.A. §1653(f), and 23 U.S.C.A. §138. The two sections embody exactly the same language.

trails, a bridle path, an art academy, picnic areas, and 170 acres of forest. The proposed highway, which is to be a six-lane, high-speed, expressway, will sever the zoo from the rest of the park. Although the roadway will be depressed below ground level except where it crosses a small creek, 26 acres of the park will be destroyed. The highway is to be a segment of Interstate Highway I-40, part of the National System of Interstate and Defense Highways. I-40 will provide Memphis with a major east-west expressway which will allow easier access to downtown Memphis from the residential areas on the eastern edge of the city.

Although the route through the park was approved by the Bureau of Public Roads in 1956 and by the Federal Highways Administrator in 1966, the enactment of §4(f) of the Department of Transportation Act prevented distribution of federal funds for the section of the highway designated to go through Overton Park until the Secretary of Transportation determined whether the requirements of §4(f) had been met. Federal funding for the rest of the project was, however, available, and the state acquired a right-of-way on both sides of the park. In April 1968, the Secretary announced that he concurred in the judgment of local officials that I-40 should be built through the park. And in September 1969 the State acquired the right-of-way inside Overton Park from the city. Final approval for the project — the route as well as the design — was not announced until November 1969, after Congress had reiterated in §138 of the Federal-Aid Highway Act that highway construction through public parks was to be restricted. Neither announcement approving the route and design of I-40 was accompanied by a statement of the Secretary's factual findings. He did not indicate why he believed there were no feasible and prudent alternative routes or why design changes could not be made to reduce the harm to the park.

Petitioners contend that the Secretary's action is invalid without such formal findings and that the Secretary did not make an independent determination but merely relied on the judgment of the Memphis City Council. They also contend that it would be "feasible and prudent" to route I-40 around Overton Park either to the north or to the south. And they argue that if these alternative routes are not "feasible and prudent," the present plan does not include "all possible" methods for reducing harm to the park. Petitioners claim that I-40 could be built under the park by using either of two possible tunneling methods,[12] and the claim that, at a minimum, by using advanced drainage techniques the expressway could be depressed below ground level along the entire route through the park including the section that crosses the small creek.

Respondents argue that it was unnecessary for the Secretary to make formal findings, and that he did, in fact, exercise his own independent judgment which was supported by the facts. In the District Court, respondents introduced affidavits, prepared specifically for this litigation, which indicated that the Secretary had made the decision and that the decision was supportable....

We agree that formal findings were not required. But we do not believe that in this case judicial review based solely on litigation affidavits was adequate.

A threshold question — whether petitioners are entitled to any judicial review — is easily answered. Section 701 of the Administrative Procedure Act, 5 U.S.C. §701 provides that the action of "each authority of the Government of the United

---

12. Petitioners argue that either a bored tunnel or a cut-and-cover tunnel, which is a fully depressed route covered after construction, could be built. Respondents contend that the construction of a tunnel by either method would greatly increase the cost of the project, would create safety hazards, and because of increase in air pollution would not reduce harm to the park.

States," which includes the Department of Transportation, is subject to judicial review except where there is a statutory prohibition on review or where "agency action is committed to agency discretion by law." In this case, there is no indication that Congress sought to prohibit judicial review and there is most certainly no "showing of 'clear and convincing evidence' of a...legislative intent" to restrict access to judicial review. Abbott Laboratories v. Gardner, 387 U.S. 136, 141 (1967).

Similarly, the Secretary's decision here does not fall within the exception for action "committed to agency discretion." This is a very narrow exception. The legislative history of the Administrative Procedure Act indicates that it is applicable in those rare instances where "statutes are drawn in such broad terms that in a given case there is no law to apply." S. Rep. No. 752, 79th Cong., 1st Sess., 26 (1945).

Section 4 (f) of the Department of Transportation Act and §138 of the Federal-Aid Highway Act are clear and specific directives. Both the Department of Transportation Act and the Federal-Aid Highway Act provide that the Secretary "shall not approve any program or project" that requires the use of any public parkland "unless (1) there is no feasible and prudent alternative to the use of such land, and (2) such program includes all possible planning to minimize harm to such park...." This language is a plain and explicit bar to the use of federal funds for construction of highways through parks — only the most unusual situations are exempted.

Despite the clarity of the statutory language, respondents argue that the Secretary has wide discretion. They recognize that the requirement that there be no "feasible" alternative route admits of little administrative discretion. For this exemption to apply the Secretary must find that as a matter of sound engineering it would not be feasible to build the highway along any other route. Respondents argue, however, that the requirement that there be no other "prudent" route requires the Secretary to engage in a wide-ranging balancing of competing interests. They contend that the Secretary should weigh the detriment resulting from the destruction of parkland against the cost of other routes, safety considerations, and other factors, and determine on the basis of the importance that he attaches to these other factors whether, on balance, alternative feasible routes would be "prudent."

But no such wide-ranging endeavor was intended. It is obvious that in most cases considerations of cost, directness of route, and community disruption will indicate that parkland should be used for highway construction whenever possible. Although it may be necessary to transfer funds from one jurisdiction to another, there will always be a smaller outlay required from the public purse when parkland is used since the public already owns the land and there will be no need to pay for right-of-way. And since people do not live or work in parks, if a highway is built on parkland no one will have to leave his home or give up his business. Such factors are common to substantially all highway construction. Thus, if Congress intended these factors to be on an equal footing with preservation of parkland there would have been no need for the statutes.

Congress clearly did not intend that cost and disruption of the community were to be ignored by the Secretary. But the very existence of the statute indicates that protection of parkland was to be given paramount importance. The few green havens that are public parks were not to be lost unless there were truly unusual factors present in a particular case or the cost or community disruption resulting from alternative routes reached extraordinary magnitudes. If the statutes are to have any meaning, the Secretary cannot approve the destruction of parkland unless he finds that alternative routes present unique problems.

Plainly, there is "law to apply" and thus the exemption for action "committed to agency discretion" is inapplicable. But the existence of judicial review is only the start: the standard for review must also be determined. For that we must look to §706, which provides that a "reviewing court shall...hold unlawful and set aside agency action, findings, and conclusions found" not to meet six separate standards. In all cases agency action must be set aside if the action was "arbitrary, capricious, an abuse of discretion, or otherwise not in accordance with law," or if the action failed to meet statutory, procedural, or constitutional requirements. In certain narrow, specifically limited situations, the agency action is to be set aside if the action was not supported by "substantial evidence." And in other equally narrow circumstances the reviewing court is to engage in a *de novo* review of the action and set it aside if it was "unwarranted by the facts."

Petitioners argue that the Secretary's approval of the construction of I-40 through Overton Park is subject to one or the other of these later two standards of limited applicability.... Neither of these standards is, however, applicable.

Review under the substantial-evidence test is authorized only when the agency action is... based on a [trial-type] hearing. See 5 U.S.C. §§556, 557. The Secretary's decision to allow the expenditure of federal funds to build I-40 through Overton Park was plainly not an exercise of a rulemaking function. And the only hearing that is required by either the Administrative Procedure Act or the statutes regulating the distribution of federal funds for highway construction is a public hearing conducted by local officials for the purpose of informing the community about the proposed project and eliciting community views on the design and route. 23 U.S.C. §128. The hearing is nonadjudicatory, quasi-legislative in nature. It is not designed to produce a record that is to be the basis of agency action — the basic requirement for substantial-evidence review.

Petitioners' alternative argument also fails. *De novo* review of whether the Secretary's decision was "unwarranted by the facts" is authorized by §706(2)(F) in only two circumstances. First, such *de novo* review is authorized when the action is adjudicatory in nature and the agency factfinding procedures are inadequate. And, there may be independent judicial factfinding when issues that were not before the agency are raised in a proceeding to enforce nonadjudicatory agency action. Neither situation exists here.

Even though there is no *de novo* review in this case and the Secretary's approval of the route of I-40 does not have ultimately to meet the substantial-evidence test, the generally applicable standards of §706 require the reviewing court to engage in a substantial inquiry. Certainly, the Secretary's decision is entitled to a presumption of regularity. But that presumption is not to shield his action from a thorough, probing, in-depth review.

The court is first required to decide whether the Secretary acted within the scope of his authority. This determination naturally begins with a delineation of the scope of the Secretary's authority and discretion. As has been shown, Congress has specified only a small range of choices that the Secretary can make. Also involved in this initial inquiry is a determination of whether on the facts the Secretary's decision can reasonably be said to be within that range. The reviewing court must consider whether the Secretary properly construed his authority to approve the use of parkland as limited to situations where there are no feasible alternative routes or where feasible alternative routes involve uniquely difficult problems. And the reviewing court must be able to find that the Secretary could have reasonably believed that in this case there are no feasible alternatives or that alternatives...involve unique problems.

Scrutiny of the facts does not end, however, with the determination that the Secretary has acted within the scope of his statutory authority. Section 706(2)(A) requires a finding that the actual choice made was not "arbitrary, capricious, an abuse of discretion, or otherwise not in accordance with law." To make this finding the court must consider whether the decision was based on a consideration of the relevant factors and whether there has been a clear error of judgment. Although this inquiry into the facts is to be searching and careful, the ultimate standard of review is a narrow one. The court is not empowered to substitute its judgment for that of the agency.

The final inquiry is whether the Secretary's action followed the necessary procedural requirements. Here the only procedural error alleged is the failure of the Secretary to make formal findings and state his reason for allowing the highway to be built through the park.

Undoubtedly, review of the Secretary's action is hampered by his failure to make such findings, but the absence of formal findings does not necessarily require that the case be remanded to the Secretary. Neither the Department of Transportation Act nor the Federal-Aid Highway Act requires such formal findings. Moreover, the Administrative Procedure Act requirements that there be formal findings in certain rulemaking and adjudicatory proceedings do not apply to the Secretary's action here. See 5 U.S.C. §§ 553(a)(2), 554(a). And, although formal findings may be required in some cases in the absence of statutory directives when the nature of the agency action is ambiguous, those situations are rare. Plainly, there is no ambiguity here; the Secretary has approved the construction of I-40 through Overton Park and has approved a specific design for the project.

Petitioners contend that although there may not be a statutory requirement that the Secretary make formal findings and even though this may not be a case for the reviewing court to impose a requirement that findings be made, Department of Transportation regulations require them. This argument is based on DOT Order 5610.1, which requires the Secretary to make formal findings when he approves the use of parkland for highway construction but which was issued after the route for I-40 was approved. Petitioners argue that even though the order was not intended to have retrospective effect the order represents the law at the time of this Court's decision and under Thorpe v. Housing Authority, 393 U.S. 268, 281–282 (1969), should be applied to this case.... The general rule is "that an appellate court must apply the law in effect at the time it renders its decision." 393 U.S. at 281. While we do not question that DOT Order 5610.1 constitutes the law in effect at the time of our decision, we do not believe that *Thorpe* compels us to remand for the Secretary to make formal findings. Here, unlike the situation in *Thorpe*, there has been a change in circumstances — additional right-of-way has been cleared and the 26-acre right-of-way inside Overton Park has been purchased by the State. Moreover, there is an administrative record that allows the full, prompt review of the Secretary's action...without additional delay which would result from having a remand to the Secretary.

That administrative record is not, however, before us. The lower courts based their review on the litigation affidavits that were presented. These affidavits were merely "post hoc" rationalizations, which have traditionally been found to be an inadequate basis for review. Burlington Truck Lines v. United States, 371 U.S.

156, 168–69 (1962). And they clearly do not constitute the "whole record" compiled by the agency: the basis for review required by §706 of the Administrative Procedure Act.

Thus it is necessary to remand this case to the District Court for plenary review of the Secretary's decision. That review is to be based on the full administrative record that was before the Secretary at the time he made his decision. But since the bare record may not disclose the factors that were considered or the Secretary's construction of the evidence it may be necessary for the District Court to require some explanation in order to determine if the Secretary acted within the scope of his authority and if the Secretary's action was justifiable under the applicable standard.

The court may require the administrative officials who participated in the decision to give testimony explaining their action. Of course, such inquiry into the mental processes of administrative decision-makers is usually to be avoided. United States v. Morgan, 313 U.S. 409, 422 (1941). And where there are administrative findings that were made at the same time as the decision, as was the case in *Morgan*, there must be a strong showing of bad faith or improper behavior before such inquiry may be made. But here there are no such formal findings and it may be that the only way there can be effective judicial review is by examining the decision-makers themselves. See Shaughnessy v. Accardi, 349 U.S. 280 (1955).

The District Court is not, however, required to make such an inquiry. It may be that the Secretary can prepare formal findings including the information required by DOT Order 5610.1 that will provide an adequate explanation for his action. Such an explanation will, to some extent, be a "post hoc rationalization" and thus must be viewed critically. If the District Court decides that additional explanation is necessary, that court should consider which method will prove the most expeditious so that full review may be had as soon as possible. Reversed and remanded.

BLACK, J., joined by BRENNAN, J., concurring separately... I agree with the Court that the judgment of the Court of Appeals is wrong and that its action should be reversed. I do not agree that the whole matter should be remanded to the District Court. I think the case should be sent back to the Secretary of Transportation. It is apparent from the Court's opinion today that the Secretary of Transportation completely failed to comply with the duty imposed upon him by Congress not to permit a federally financed public highway to run through a public park "unless (1) there is no feasible and prudent alternative to the use of such land, and (2) such program includes all possible planning to minimize harm to such park...." That congressional command should not be taken lightly by the Secretary or by this Court. It represents a solemn determination of the highest law-making body of this Nation that the beauty and health-giving facilities of our parks are not to be taken away for public roads without hearings, factfindings, and policy determinations under the supervision of a Cabinet officer — the Secretary of Transportation....
I regret that I am compelled to conclude for myself that, except for some too-late formulations, apparently coming from the Solicitor General's office, this record contains not one word to indicate that the Secretary raised even a finger to comply with the command of Congress. It is our duty, I believe, to remand this whole matter back to the Secretary of Transportation for him to give this matter the hearing it deserves in full good-faith obedience to the Act of Congress. That Act was obviously passed to protect our public parks from forays by road builders except in

the most extraordinary and imperative circumstances. This record does not demonstrate the existence of such circumstances. I dissent from the Court's failure to send the case back to the Secretary, whose duty has not yet been performed.

BLACKMUN, J., concurring. I fully join the Court in its opinion and in its judgment. I merely wish to state the obvious: (1) The case comes to this Court as the end product of more than a decade of endeavor to solve the interstate highway problem at Memphis. (2) The administrative decisions under attack here are not those of a single Secretary; some were made by the present Secretary's predecessor and, before him, by the Department of Commerce's Bureau of Public Roads. (3) The 1966 Act and the 1968 Act have cut across former methods and here have imposed new standards and conditions upon a situation that already was largely developed. This undoubtedly is why the record is sketchy and less than one would expect if the project were one which had been instituted after the passage of the 1966 Act....

MR. JUSTICE DOUGLAS took no part in the consideration or decision of this case.

### COMMENTARY AND QUESTIONS

1. **Threshold administrative law issues in citizen suits.** Before plaintiffs can get to the merits of challenges to agency decisions, they must pass through threshold tests:

*Reviewability.* When challenged by citizen suits, agency attorneys often (as in the *Overton Park* case) initially argue that their challenged agency decisions are unreviewable because they contain discretionary elements. The courts, however, have demonstrated extreme hesitation in finding nonreviewability, often citing the words of *Abbott Laboratories*:

The enactment of the Administrative Procedures Act...embodies the basic presumption of judicial review to one "suffering legal wrong because of agency action...." The legislative material...manifests a congressional intention that it cover a broad spectrum of administrative actions, and this Court has echoed that theme by noting that the...Act's "generous review provision" must be given a "hospitable" interpretation.... Only upon a showing of "clear and convincing evidence" of a contrary legislative intent should the courts restrict access to judicial review. Abbott Laboratories v. Gardner, 387 U.S. 136, 141 (1967)

Sovereign immunity barriers to reviewability of federal agency actions were specifically removed in 1976 by amendments to APA §702.

*Standing.* In Overton Park, as in many environmental cases, there is no problem with standing. Some or all of the Tennessee plaintiffs would be directly affected by the consequences of the agency decision. It has long been established that plaintiffs' "injury in fact" necessitated by Article III's case-or-controversy requirement does not have to be economic or legal, but can extend to recreational, aesthetic, and other injuries.[13] If particular persons are not injured, or are injured only to the same extent as millions of other citizens, the courts may deny standing.

---

13. Sierra Club v. Morton, 405 U.S. 727, 734 (1972).

Occasionally, however, in part to allow troublesome environmental questions to be debated, the Supreme Court has allowed fairly broad standing to sue.[14]

*Exhaustion of remedies, and Ripeness.* In *Overton Park*, the legal issues were clearly ready for review when plaintiffs went to court. In some environmental cases it is argued that citizens should exhaust internal remedies within the agency before going to court; in other cases the argument is that an agency decision, though it has been made, is not yet ripe for judicial review because it has not actually been applied or is not yet completely final. These arguments have not generally been successful defenses against environmental litigation. Courts often seem to reflect the legal system's interest in resolving important legal questions at an efficient early stage, before major investments and commitments of resources are wasted. But not always. Does it seem likely that the *Overton Park* plaintiffs could have succeeded in getting an injunction against the *earlier* highway activities — the condemnation of land and highway construction up to the edge of the Park[15] — as a violation of §4(f)? Probably not. The defense would have been that the issue was not yet ripe, the law not yet violated.[16]

2. **The administrative law of *Overton Park*: tactics, and results.** Note how easily the Court in *Overton Park* accepts the plaintiffs' threshold showings allowing them to get into court. As to procedure, however, the plaintiffs did not succeed in their request for formal findings, nor did they get hearings before the Secretary. Both of these procedures would obviously have been helpful in sharpening their case against the highway through the park and obtaining closer judicial review of the subsequent decision. (The Supreme Court opinion, like many lawyers, seems to consider that all agency "adjudications" are formal adjudications, when in fact informal adjudications constitute the vast majority of government agency decisions.)

As to the substantive standard of review to be applied to the agency's factual decision, the plaintiffs didn't get de novo review, the toughest standard, nor even the substantial evidence test. They only got review; under the arbitrary and capricious test, and they never got a judicial ruling that the Secretary had indeed been arbitrary and capricious in approving the parkland route.

So why didn't the Department of Transportation win? While the Court says that "the ultimate standard of review is a narrow one," thus adopting a continued deference to the agency's expertise on fact-finding, it nevertheless recognizes that judges need to see enough facts to "be able to find that the Secretary could reasonably have believed that in this case there are no feasible alternatives...."

---

14. See, e.g., United States v. SCRAP, 412 U.S. 669 (1973); Duke Power v. Carolina Environmental Study Group, 438 U.S. 59 (1978).

15. Just as the *Overton Park* plaintiffs were able to bootstrap an injunction against the highway based on the thinness of the agency record, the defendants and their allies had attempted physical bootstrapping: prior to the filing of the case, the citizens had attempted to argue for alternative routes north and south of Overton Park. The highway authorities, however, proceeded to condemn homes, bulldoze them, and build the highway right-of-way right up to the boundary of the Park. They also built a multimillion dollar bridge across the Mississippi River on the Park highway alignment. It was only then that they turned to the Secretary to ask approval for the Park route on the grounds that there was no longer any feasible and prudent alternative.

16. A NEPA suit might offer better prospects (see Chapter 13).

If environmental lawyers can convince reviewing judges that the factual evidence considered by an agency would not be enough to allow the judges themselves to make intelligent decisions on critical points, then the judges are likely to send the case back to the agency, even if they are not ready to declare that the agency decision was indeed arbitrary. This invites environmental attorneys to search out points of decision that do not appear to be adequately supported by the agency's formal or informal record, and to leverage these thin areas into an argument for remand. In the tactics of lawyering, a remand on technical points is not as good as a substantive victory, but is far from a hollow victory. The challenger is perceived to have beaten the agency in court, an accomplishment in itself. Additionally, the challenger now gets another bite at the bureaucratic apple, presenting an opportunity for bringing political and public opinion pressures to bear.

3. **Interpreting the statutory language: who does it, and how** to have applied an incorrect interpretation of the statutory words "feasible and prudent." Are you satisfied with the Court's interpretation of the statutory language? Shouldn't judges defer to expert agencies in its interpretation of law to the same extent they do on fact-finding? In part it may be that judges consider themselves the experts in interpretation of law, and if a statute's meaning seems obvious to the judges, that is the interpretation the court will require. The "plain meaning" rule is an old maxim of statutory interpretation founded upon the assumption that in some cases the words of a statute are unambiguously clear and hence must be effectuated, whatever their results, because each word of a statute (as opposed to common law terms) is binding law. Ambiguity, however, is the norm. See the *Chevron* discussion in subchapter E, below. Could it also be, as Justice Black implies, that courts will defer less to those agencies that demonstrate institutional resistance to statutory requirements?

4. **"Arbitrary and capricious"?** Like many courts that decide to overturn a particular agency decision, the *Overton Park* court did not want to declare the Secretary's decision arbitrary and capricious, and so it remanded the case for development of a better record supporting the decision. Could it have found the decision "arbitrary"?

The answer depends on what the term "arbitrary" means. The courts have applied the term to a confusingly wide range of substantive and procedural holdings.[17] Applied as a test of the substantive merits of a decision, it is best defined in terms of rationality: "does the agency decision have rational support on the record reviewed by the court?" or "could a rational official have reached that decision on this record?"[18]

Even limited to application as a test of substantive rationality, analytically the arbitrary and capricious test can be applied in at least five different settings:

(a) where the agency has no legal standard to apply to the evidence, or uses an incorrect standard;

17. See Plater and Norine, Through the Looking Glass of Eminent Domain: Exploring the "Arbitrary and Capricious" Test and Substantive Rationality Review of Governmental Decisions, 16 Envt'l. Aff. L. Rev. 661, 712–722 (1989).

18. Thus, viewed conceptually, the arbitrary and capricious test and the stricter-sounding "substantial evidence" test come down to the same thing; the latter may just require a greater quantum of evidence to prove the point. Id. at pages 716–718.

(b) where the agency may have had enough evidence back home in its files to support a decision, but just didn't show it to the court;

(c) where the agency did not have enough evidence to support its decision; and

(d) where the agency had enough evidence to support its decision rationally, if it were accurate, but plaintiffs prove that the evidence is wrong.

(e) where the agency failed to consider the "relevant factors" set by the statute, or based its decision on irrelevant factors.

In Motor Vehicles Mfrs. Ass'n v. State Farm Mutual Life Ins. Co., 463 U.S. 29 (1983), for instance, the Supreme Court declared a Department of Transportation reversal of the prior administration's seat belt and air bag rule arbitrary and capricious because the agency hadn't considered, and failed to present to the Court, evidence supporting the need for a new rule. This would seem to fit the (b) or (c) definitions of arbitrary. Which would have applied to *Overton Park*? The Court could probably have used one or more of the first three of these tests. In other cases, after examining the record basis of agency decisions, plaintiffs can sometimes prove the fourth.[19]

Challenging agency actions under the arbitrary and capricious test, however, is no easy task because judges consider it such a deferential standard of review. In practical terms, in most cases, when a court begins reviewing an agency action under the arbitrary and capricious test, that means that the agency decision is shortly going to be upheld. Even if their case convinces the court, attorneys can reasonably expect that the agency, instead of being declared arbitrary, will receive the kind of face-saving remand that defendants got in *Overton Park* (although that proved to be enough for plaintiffs).

5. **"Feasible and prudent" as a public trust standard.** The "feasible and prudent" standard captures well the idea of a strong presumption in favor of protection, to be factored into decisions about how parkland public trust resources should be developed. By extension it can be read into the public trust generally. But what does it mean? Does it mean that questions of cost are not to be considered at all? Presumably there is always an alternative, if cost is no object. But "prudent" implies some attention to money factors.[20] If money is to be considered, how is it to be weighed against intangible natural values? Money tends to be an all-or-nothing factor. If you consider cost, going through parks will virtually always be the preferable option, and a test that incorporates the prudence of cost saving negates the protective purpose and effect. The Court suggests that only an "extraordinary magnitude" of expense would justify going through the Park. What would that mean? Is part of the balance of feasible and prudent the question whether the project should be built at all? Might a decision *not* to build an interstate highway through Memphis be a feasible and prudent alternative?

6. **The subsequent history of Overton Park.** After the Supreme Court's ruling, the case bounced around in the lower courts for a few more years. Finally, after new

---

19. See Motor Veh. Mfrs. Ass'n of U.S. v. EPA, 768 F.2d 385 (D.C. Cir. 1985) (by granting a methanol use permit based on a failed test, and tests of three dissimilar gas additives, EPA acted arbitrarily).

20. Note that the standard is *feasible* as well as prudent; agencies thus would want to argue that this includes economic feasibility, in order to expand their range of discretion.

hearings and an environmental impact statement, Secretary Volpe announced in January, 1973 that he could not find that there was no feasible and prudent alternative to going through the park. The Tennessee Department of Transportation thereupon challenged his decision, demanding that he tell them what the feasible and prudent alternative was, but the Sixth Circuit upheld the Secretary's ruling as it stood and the Supreme Court denied certiorari.[21] Congress has not disturbed the judicial results, so I-40 will apparently never be built through Overton Park. Today the original interstate highway corridor comes to an ignominious, disruptive halt at the edge of the Park. A loop bypass to the north now carries I-40's through traffic.

7. **Tradeoffs.** Memphis had already purchased 160 acres of private land in the northern part of the city to be made into parks to replace the 26 acres of Overton Park used for the highway, and indicated that it would probably acquire still more. Doesn't this mean there would have been a lot more parkland with the highway project through the Park than without it? Should that have ended the question?

## D.  CITIZEN ENFORCEMENT AND JUDICIAL REVIEW

### Section 1. THE IMPORTANCE OF CITIZEN ENFORCEMENT

In the Overton Park setting, who would have enforced the federal statute if a bunch of low-income citizens had not rallied to carry the case up through the federal courts? The Federal Highway Administration? The Governor of Tennessee? The Congress that had passed the Parklands Act? No.[22]

Woven through much of this book are examples of the central role of citizen activism (often resisted at each step by public and private entities) in creating and shaping environmental law, whether through common law strategies or the kind of pressuring for public law that produced the wetlands protection statutes, the Chicago phosphate ordinance in *Procter & Gamble*, or broad statutes like the Michigan environmental protection act.

Within the administrative processes that constitute the bulk of positive law in the administrative state, citizen efforts have likewise been critically important, although less visible.

Environmentalists operate within the administrative process in two basic ways — by "intervention," formal or informal, in ongoing agency procedures, and by bringing agency actions to court for judicial review. Once a state wetlands act, for instance, is passed on the strength of citizen lobbying, it can be neutered, or strengthened, depending on the regulations and administrative implementation given to it by the administering agency. Agency officials hear persistently and pow-

---

21. Citizens to Preserve Overton Park v. Brinegar, 494 F.2d 1212 (6th Cir. 1974), cert. denied, Citizens to Preserve Overton Park v. Smith, 421 U.S. 991 (1975).

22. The point is that enforcement of public law provisions by the official organs of government is often highly unlikely. Perhaps the Sierra Club, NRDC, or another national group could have picked up the immense burdens of litigating the case (and in fact national environmental groups did help in the later stages of the litigation), but these organizations' capabilities are severely limited. They litigate only a fraction of the deserving cases referred to them each year. That means that most cases deserving judicial attention either never get launched, or founder along the way.

erfully from regulated vested interests. Within the day-to-day administrative process, agencies now often also hear a great deal from concerned citizen activists. If rigorous, enforceable wetlands regulations are produced, it is altogether likely that citizen expertise and political pressure helped produce them. If environmental groups think agency regulations subvert the legislative mandate, they can sue, seeking to hold the agency to the original terms of the statute.

Likewise in the federal arena. The federal air and water acts studied in Chapters Eight & Nine, for example, were not only created through extraordinary citizen pressures on Congress, spearheaded by a few notable congressional leaders, but their voluminous subsequent anti-pollution regulatory programs have also been fundamentally shaped by citizen groups, through extensive interventions and litigation.[23]

**KNOWING THE PLAYERS...** In order to understand any administrative process litigation, one has to figure out the respective roles and status of the various competing participants.

The plaintiffs in the *Overton Park* case were exceptional, in that they were a small group of disgruntled neighbors who were able to hold the case together all the way to the Supreme Court of the United States. Far more typical are national environmental citizen organizations designed for sophisticated advocacy in courts, agencies, and the legislature.

Faced with resistance from industry lobbyists and hesitancy on the part of federal regulators, a "shadow government" has sprung up, including notably the Natural Resources Defense Council, the Environmental Defense Fund, the National Wildlife Federation, National Audubon Society, Friends of the Earth, and the Sierra Club Legal Defense Fund[24] — national public interest law groups that commit themselves to monitor, negotiate, litigate, and lobby for rigorous, enforceable regulatory programs. Beginning in 1970, a few young law graduates, many from Yale Law School, laid the foundations for such groups, attempting to hold federal government agencies to the terms of the environmental statutes so painfully won in the halls of Congress. The groups evolved to enroll thousands of subscribing members, with legal staffs and budgets of sufficient depth and strength to allow them to play an oversight role in many important administrative programs. The critical role these organizations have played in the securing of environmental protection in the United States is impressive, and their example is now being followed around the world, as the international environmental law movement begins to develop twenty years behind the American lead.

---

23. For instance, in the early stages of the Clean Air Act, the federal Environmental Protection Agency (EPA) decided over environmental protests to write rules allowing polluting industry to comply with the CAA by moving to clean air states like Wyoming and Idaho that had pristine air quality, thereby spreading pollution around but not abating it. It was only because of citizen litigation and negotiation that a nationwide "non-deterioration" policy was established. Sierra Club v. Ruckelshaus, 344 F. Supp. 253 (D.D.C. 1973), aff'd 412 U.S. 541. (Note in this controversy the interstate replay of a scene from the Tragedy of the Commons.)
24. This list covers most of the most frequent environmental litigation groups; there are other significant groups as well.

As to defendants, note how in many of these environmental cases there is no clear distinction between the regulatory agency entrusted with the environmental protection mandate and the industry and regulated interests which it is assigned to supervise. In the atomic energy field, for instance, the alignment of the Atomic Energy Commission (AEC) with the nuclear industry was so incestuous that Congress ultimately split the agency into two parts, the promotional Energy Research and Development Agency (ERDA), and the protective Nuclear Regulatory Commission (NRC). The environmental community does not necessarily believe that such organizational splits end the affinity of regulator and regulatee. In any event, it is noteworthy that the original bipolar design of the regulatory state — with regulated industries on one hand and the public interest defended by government on the other — has now evolved, under pressure from citizen activists, into a highly articulated and energetic pluralistic democracy, where courts and many agencies are open to a wide variety of differing points of view from a potpourri of citizen intervenors.

**OF THE IRON TRIANGLE, THE PORKBARREL, AND THE ESTABLISHMENT...** The *Overton Park* case reminds environmental observers that environmental quality initiatives, even when they are backed by statutory provisions, run into the opposition of vested interests, public as well as private. Some environmentalists call it the "Porkbarrel," others the "Iron Triangle" — in either case referring to the interlocking structure and political process linking private construction and industrial interests, government agencies that service the industry, and congressional delegations from areas like Memphis that want to attract particular public expenditures into their backyards. The momentum of that combination makes the porkbarrel one of the most consistently powerful and resistant forces of environmental alteration. Environmentalists are often underfinanced, politically powerless neighborhood agitators who come along late in the game seeking to stop the momentum of the good ol' boys' lucrative establishment steamroller.

In the Overton Park setting, for example, it was not only that interstate highways required just 10 percent contribution from state and local government, while 90 percent of costs would be tapped directly from federal taxpayers and the federal Highway Trust Fund. The attraction of parklands to the highway establishment is even more seductive: parklands are already owned by government. If Tennessee contributes 26 acres of parkland to the highway project, it gets to value that parkland as if it were a cash contribution based on its fair market value, the value of 26 acres of downtown urban land. For this reason, parks attract their own destruction, and it is for precisely that reason that environmentalists had found it so necessary to fight to put §4(f) into the highway legislation.[25]

By successfully, against the odds, putting the Parklands Act onto the federal books, environmentalists did not automatically succeed in enlisting the United States Government as a whole on the side of parkland preservation. Quite the contrary; federal program agencies often adopt a recalcitrant posture toward statutes

---

25. Thus the official argument in *Overton Park* for overriding §4(f), based on "prudent" limiting of acquisition costs, replayed the problem that required §4(f) in the first place.

that limit their standard operating procedures. Agencies that measure their success in terms of accomplishing their mission in pouring concrete and building road mileage understandably treat conservation legislation as a technicality, an annoyance, and often as a frustrating and contradictory obstacle that must be overridden in order to do their jobs.

The need to observe and identify the roles, powers and predilections of the contesting parties, needless to say, is a recurring reality in analyses of environmental controversies under both public and private law.

THE "CAPTURE" PHENOMENON... Environmentalists repeatedly identify the problem of governmental agencies' "capture" by market forces as a disturbing backdrop to many administrative process cases. A regulatory agency created in the fervor of a popular movement to regulate some designated problem may begin its life energetically pursuing the overall public interest, but over time its initiative may gradually be eroded into narrower views, intimately linked with the industry and problems it was intended to solve.

### Stewart, The Reformation of American Administrative Law
#### 88 Harvard Law Review 1669, 1684–1687 (1975)

Critics have repeatedly asserted...that in carrying out broad legislative directives, agencies unduly favor organized interests, especially the interests of regulated or client business firms and other organized groups at the expense of diffuse, comparatively unorganized interests such as consumers, environmentalists, and the poor. In the midst of a "growing sense of disillusion with the role which regulatory agencies play," many legislators, judges, and legal and economic commentators have accepted the thesis of persistent bias in agency policies. At its crudest, this thesis is based on the "capture" scenario, in which administrations are systematically controlled, sometimes corruptly, by the business firms within their orbit of responsibility, whether regulatory or promotional. But there are more subtle explanations of industry orientation, which include the following:

*First* The division of responsibility between the regulated firms, which retain primary control over their own affairs, and the administrator, whose power is essentially negative and who is dependent on industry cooperation in order to achieve his objectives, places the administrator in an inherently weak position. The administrator will, nonetheless, be held responsible if the industry suffers serious economic dislocation. For both of these reason, he may pursue conservative policies.

*Second* The regulatory bureaucracy becomes "regulation minded." It seeks to elaborate and perfect the controls it exercises over the regulated industry. The effect of this tendency, particularly in a regime of limited entry, is to eliminate actual and potential competition and buttress the position of the established firms.

*Third* The resources — in terms of money, personnel, and political influence — of the regulatory agency are limited in comparison to those of regulated firms. Unremitting maintenance of an adversary posture would quickly dissipate agency resources. Hence, the agency must compromise with the regulated industry if it is to accomplish anything of significance.

*Fourth* Limited agency resources imply that agencies must depend on outside sources of information, policy development, and political support. This outside input comes primarily from organized interests, such as regulated firms, that have a substantial stake in the substance of agency policy and the resources to provide such input. By contrast, the personal stake in agency policy of an individual member of an unorganized interest, such as a consumer, is normally too small to justify such representation. Effective representation of unorganized interests might be possible if a means of pooling resources to share the costs of underwriting collective representation were available. But this seems unlikely since the transaction costs of creating an organization of interest group members increase disproportionately as the size of the group increases. Moreover, if membership in such an organization is voluntary, individuals will not have a strong incentive to join, since if others represent the interests involved, the benefits will accrue not only to those participating in the representation, but to nonparticipants as well, who can, therefore, enjoy the benefits without incurring any of the costs (the free rider effect). As a somewhat disillusioned James Landis wrote in 1960, the result is industry dominance in representation, which has a "daily machine-gun like impact on both [an] agency and its staff" that tends to create an industry bias in the agency's outlook.

These various theses of systematic bias in agency policy are not universally valid. Political pressures and judicial controls may force continuing agency adherence to policies demonstrably inimical to the interests of the regulated industry.... Moreover, the fact that agency policies may tend to favor regulated interests does not in itself demonstrate that such policies are unfair or unjustified, since protection of regulated interests may be implicit in the regulatory scheme established by Congress. Nonetheless, the critique of agency discretion as unduly favorable to organized interests — particularly regulated or client firms — has sufficient power and verisimilitude to have achieved widespread contemporary acceptance.

## Section 2. STANDING, AND THE INSTITUTIONALIZATION OF CITIZEN ENFORCEMENT

Standing, one of the threshold constitutional and statutory tests citizens have to meet in order to obtain judicial review, is ultimately a judicial doctrine. It is courts that determine when citizens can claim standing and when they cannot, even under statutory grants of standing. In most cases the plaintiffs' premise in environmental standing cases is that the government agency is not eager to enforce the law, or itself has violated the law, and so there will be no enforcement unless the courts support the citizens' standing to sue. The practical motivation of anti-standing advocates seems to reflect precisely the same premise as its intended result. Standing principles can be broadened to permit litigation on issues for which judges want to have dispositive determinations, and conversely can be narrowed to nip off challenges that courts would rather not have to decide.

The law of standing in recent years has often been made through environmental cases. In all standing cases, plaintiffs' standing to sue will be tested under:

- Article III's case or controversy clause, (primarily a claim of injury, but also whatever other elements the Court holds to be constitutionally required); *plus*

- "prudential limitations" invented by the Supreme Court to restrict standing based on judicial discretion, not applicable if a statute overrides them (prudential principles included "no standing to enforce rights of third parties," a requirement of "imminent" injury, the likelihood of "redress-ability" of plaintiff's harm by judicial order, etc., but new ones continue to be added, and the Rehnquist Court has converted some to "constitutional" Art. III status so that statutory grants of standing cannot override them); *and either*

- statutory requirements for judicial review in the specific statute being applied, like "aggrieved" under §313(b) of the Federal Power Act in *Scenic Hudson* below, (typically no more than the Art. III requirements) — or special citizen-enforcement authorizations for "any person" who files a 60-day notice (included in many environmental statutes as noted below, they are far more liberal than the Art. III 'injury' requirement, and override prudential limitations); or

- the general statutory requirements for standing under definitions of APA §702's "person adversely affected or aggrieved...within the meaning of a relevant statute" (much the same as Art. III, but subject to prudential principles).

**A STANDING CHRONOLOGY...** The law of standing for citizens, in courts and agencies, lies at the heart of the evolution of environmental law, and is often the target for latterday marketplace reactions against environmental protections. A condensed chronology of standing cases reflects the changing context of the field:

**THE *STORM KING* CASE...** The first major milestone for environmental citizens' participation in administrative law and process — involving citizen enforcement of federal statutes, and citizen standing in agency proceedings as well as in subsequent judicial review of agency decisions — occurred in the mid-1960s in the shadow of Storm King Mountain, on the shores of New York's Hudson River. The Consolidated Edison Company and the Federal Power Commission (FPC) had been planning Con Ed's construction of a "pumped storage" hydroelectric project, cutting a crater reservoir out of the top of Storm King Mountain so that water could be pumped up in hours of slack electricity use, to be released through generator turbines (as "peaking power") when energy needs were greatest. Disturbed by the prospect, a group of local citizens formed the Scenic Hudson Preservation Conference, and began to question the utility company and the agency about the project's negative effects — loss of a beautiful mountain, scour, sedimentation, and other impacts on fish and the river when huge volumes of water were sucked up and down through turbines. Neither Con Ed nor the Federal agency wanted the citizens to participate in the various permit procedures required to license the Storm King project. The agency reluctantly allowed the citizens to enter a limited intervention, but excluded several studies on the project's negative consequences from the agency record.

When the Storm King license was granted, the citizens went to court. In a remarkable Second Circuit opinion, Judge Hays had to weigh the project's troubling facts against the agency's demand for deference. As a threshold matter he first had to consider arguments that the citizens had no right to judicial review, because they were not aggrieved parties in terms either of Article III's case or controversy clause, nor under the relevant statutory requirements for judicial review.

## Scenic Hudson Preservation Conference v. Federal Power Commission
### United States Court of Appeals for the Second Circuit, 1965
### 354 F.2d 608, cert. denied 384 U.S. 941 (1966)

HAYS, J....The Storm King project is to be located in an area of unique beauty and major historical significance. The highlands and gorge of the Hudson offer one of the finest pieces of river scenery in the world.... Respondents argue that "petitioners do not have standing to obtain review" because they make no claim of any personal economic injury resulting from the Commission's action...." [but only aesthetic injuries and thus are not "aggrieved" within the meaning of administrative law standing requirements.] The Commission takes a narrow view of the meaning of "aggrieved party."... The Supreme Court has observed that the law of standing is a "complicated specialty of Federal jurisdiction, the solution of whose problems is in any event more or less determined by the specific circumstances of individual situations...." The "case or controversy" requirement of Article III §2 of the Constitution does not require that an "aggrieved" or "adversely effected" party have a personal economic interest.... In order to insure that the Federal Power Commission will adequately protect the public interest in the aesthetic, conservational, and recreational aspects of power development, those who by their activities and conduct have exhibited a special interest in such areas must be held to be included in the class of "aggrieved" parties under §313(b) [of the Federal Power Act]....

We see no justification for the Commission's fear that our determination will encourage "literally thousands" to intervene and seek review in future proceedings. We rejected a similar contention in Associated Industries v. Ickes, 134 F.2d 694, 707 (1943), noting that "no such horrendous possibilities" exist. Our experience with public actions confirms the view that the expense and vexation of legal proceedings [are] not lightly undertaken.... [The citizens were acting as "private attorneys-general," enforcing the terms of statute in partnership with the agency, and thus should have been given a hospitable reception in the agency.]

A party acting as a "private attorney-general" can raise issues that are not personal to it.... Especially in a case of this type, where public interest and concern is so great, the Commission refusal to receive the [citizens' power study] testimony, as well as proffered information on fish protection devices and underground transmission facilities exhibits a disregard of the statute and of judicial mandates instructing the Commission to probe all feasible alternatives....

In this case as in many others the Commission has claimed to be the representative of the public interest. This role does not permit it to act as an umpire blandly calling balls and strikes for adversary groups appearing before it; the right of the public must receive active and affirmative protection at the hands of the Commission.

[Reasoning that the agency decision was not rationally supported on the record — absent full citizen participation and agency follow-up on the citizens' substantiated concerns — the court set aside the license and remanded the Storm King project to the district court and the Commission, where it died.[26]]

---

26. A number of books and law review articles have commented on *Scenic Hudson*. See, e.g. A. Talbot, Power Along the Hudson: The Storm King Case & the Birth of Environmentalism (1972). The full case deserves reading by anyone interested in the history of environmental law. For a scathing criticism of the case in terms of its putative anti-democratic élitism see W. Tucker, Environmentalism and the Leisure Class, 255 Harpers Magazine 49–56, 73–80 (Dec. 1977).

*MINERAL KING...* The first major Supreme Court case encouraging citizen participation through expanded judicial standing was Sierra Club v. Morton, 405 U.S. 727 (1972) (basing the standing question only on the Article III and APA "aggrieved" standard, with no specific grants of standing and no mention of prudential limitations). The Walt Disney Corporation sought to develop ski runs, lodges, and a winter resort on national forest public lands at Mineral King Mountain in the California Sierras. The environmental plaintiffs, trying to enforce federal conservation statutes, asked to be heard based only on their general interest in environmental protection, with no claim of individual injury.[27] Previously the Supreme Court had extended standing only to persons who had a clearly defined economic injury or a "legal interest" specifically protected by statute or constitution. Justice Stewart wrote for the Court:

> The complaint alleged that the development "would destroy or otherwise adversely affect the scenery, natural and historic objects and wildlife of the park and would impair the enjoyment of the park for future generations." We do not question that this type of harm may amount to an "injury in fact" sufficient to lay the basis for standing.... The trend of cases arising under the APA and other statutes authorizing judicial review of federal agency action has been toward recognizing that injuries other than economic harm are sufficient to bring a person within the meaning of the statutory language, and toward discarding the notion that an injury that is widely shared is *ipso facto* not an injury sufficient to provide the basis for judicial review.... The interest alleged to have been injured "may reflect aesthetic, conservational, and recreational, as well as economic values...." Aesthetic and environmental well-being, like economic well-being, are important ingredients of the quality of life in our society, and the fact that particular environmental interests are shared by the many rather than the few does not make them less deserving of legal protection through the judicial process. *Mineral King*, 405 U.S. at 734, 738.[28]

The *Mineral King* Court, however, declined to adopt the broadest definition of private attorneys-general set out in *Scenic Hudson*, instead requiring the Sierra Club to allege member injuries from the proposed government action, which on remand it quickly did.[29] Defining the Article III constitutional requirements for standing, the *Mineral King* Court nevertheless greatly extended the constitutionally-cognizable injuries that could be the basis of citizen lawsuits. The decision firmly estab

27. This broad commitment to environmental protection had been part of the Scenic Hudson group's successful argument for generalized standing, based on the environmentalists' "activities and conduct [exhibiting] a special interest in such areas." One of the more intriguing issues raised in environmental law has been the attempt to extend standing to non-living things. Could the plaintiffs have filed the lawsuit in the name of the Park itself? In a ringing dissent in the *Mineral King* case, Justice Douglas urged the adoption of Professor Chris Stone's argument that standing should be granted to organizations that speak knowingly and will commit resources in defense of inanimate trees, mountains, or wildlife. C. Stone, Should Trees Have Standing? (1974). Why might the Sierra Club have wanted to have the mountain itself as the plaintiff? To some extent such attempts may reflect a philosophical stance, an attempt to focus attention on the real long-term issues. In part such a claim might reflect the fact that members do not always live or hike in areas where citizen enforcement efforts are necessary, as in Arctic tundra threatened by oil drilling, or in outer space where some energy planners suggest dumping radioactive wastes.

28. Citing dicta in Assoc. of Data Processing Services v. Camp, 397 U.S. 150, 154 (1970). The Court did not buy Prof. Chris Stone's argument that "trees should have standing," see 45 S.Cal. L.Rev. 450 (1972), and so human plaintiffs need not prove human injury to represent claims of nature, as guardians or next-friends.

29. On remand the Club quickly supplied available evidence of direct use of the mountain by its members, and got standing. Were the original pleadings badly designed, or a grab for the brass ring?

lished that citizens no longer needed to show either economic injury or violation of a constitutional right.

*SCRAP...* Several years later, a group of law students in Washington D.C. decided to challenge Interstate Commerce Commission rate-making decisions that discouraged use of recycled materials by assigning lower transport tariffs to raw materials. U.S. v. Students Challenging Regulatory Agency Procedures (SCRAP), 412 U.S. 669 (1973). The Court, in another Stewart opinion, found that SCRAP had alleged sufficient individual harm to get standing:

> The challenged agency action in this case is applicable to substantially all of the Nation's railroads.... All persons who utilize the scenic resources of the country, and indeed all who breathe its air, could claim harm similar to that alleged by the environmental groups here. But we have already made it clear that standing is not to be denied simply because many people suffer the same injury.... To deny standing to persons who are in fact injured simply because many others are also injured would mean that the most injurious and widespread Government actions could be questioned by nobody. We cannot accept that conclusion.

> But the injury alleged here is [not] direct and perceptible.... Here, the court was asked to follow a far more attenuated line of causation to the eventual injury of which the appellees complained — a general rate increase would allegedly cause increased use of nonrecyclable commodities as compared to recyclable goods, thus resulting in the need to use more natural resources to produce such goods,... resulting in more refuse that might be discarded [along hiking trails used by the students] in national parks in the Washington area....

> Of course, pleadings must be something more than an ingenious academic exercise in the conceivable. A plaintiff must allege that he has been or will in fact be perceptibly harmed by the challenged agency action, not that he can imagine circumstances in which he could be affected by the agency's action. And it is equally clear that the allegations must be true and capable of proof at trial.... If proved, [however, plaintiffs' allegations] would place them squarely among those persons injured in fact by the Commission's action. *SCRAP*, 412 U.S. at 687–690. [Standing was granted.]

Understandably, *SCRAP* was viewed as an expansion of citizens' rights to sue against governmental abuses. Potential harms to plaintiffs had to be alleged, but the linkage of such harms to challenged agency actions could be quite indirect. Plaintiffs did not have to prove that they were "within the zone of interests" of a relevant statute,[30] nor did plaintiffs have to show a likelihood that the court's orders would "redress" the harms. Citizens could go to court to enforce statutes and the public values they embodied even where official enforcement agencies had been rendered quiescent by the politics of the marketplace. Citizen standing, and

---

30. The "zone of interests" test is drawn from words in APA §702, not from Article III constitutional grounds, and has generally been liberally interpreted:

> The [APA] should be construed "not grudgingly but as serving a broad remedial purpose."...
> The "zone of interest" formula [originally mentioned in *Data Processing*, 397 U.S. 153 (1970)] has not proved self-explanatory, but significant guidance can be drawn from that opinion. First, the Court interpreted the phrase "a relevant statute" in §702 quite broadly (indeed even using a different statute from the one sued under).... Second, the Court approved the "trend...toward [the] enlargement of the class of people who may protest administrative action."... The test is not meant to be especially demanding; in particular there need be no indication of congressional purpose to benefit the would-be plaintiff. Clarke v. Securities Industry Ass'n, 479 U.S. 388 at 395–400 (1987).

the pluralistic democracy it represented, provided a powerful mechanism for protecting civic and environmental interests, counteracting the marketplace's neutralizing pressures upon regulatory programs. In the absence of citizen action, many government agencies could not or would not do a sufficient job of enforcing federal law.

**CONGRESSIONAL GRANTS OF CITIZEN STANDING...** In more than a dozen environmental statutes, beginning in the early 1970s, Congress specifically authorized citizen standing,[31] acknowledging the importance of citizen enforcement where citizens can step in and take on the task of enforcing federal statutes when official agencies fail to do so. In the legal systems of other industrial nations it would be quite astonishing to find similar provisions. In the federal Clean Water Act's §505, a fairly typical provision noted in the *Smithfield* litigation in Chapter One, Congress provided that —

> §505(a) ...Any citizen may commence a civil action on his own behalf — (A)...(1) against any person (including (i) the United States, and (ii) any other government instrumentality or agency...) who is alleged to be in violation of (A) an effluent standard or limitation under this chapter or (B) an order issued by the Administrator or State with respect to such a standard or limitation, or (2) against the Administrator where there is alleged a failure of the Administrator to perform any act or duty under this chapter which is not discretionary with the Administrator....

> §505(b) No action may be commenced — (1)... (A) prior to sixty days after the plaintiff has given notice of the alleged violation (i) to the Administrator, (ii) to the State in which the alleged violation occurs, and (iii) to any alleged violator of the standard, limitation, or order,[32] or (B) if the Administrator or State has commenced and is diligently prosecuting a civil or criminal action in a court of the United States or a State to require compliance with the standard, limitation, or order, but in any such action in a court of the United States any citizen may intervene as a matter of right.... 33 U.S.C.A. §1365 (1972).

The federal courts have been quite attentive to these citizen suit provisions, generally acknowledging the strength of the congressional intent to encourage citizen enforcement as a parallel national strategy for achieving implementation of federal

---

31. See Toxic Substances Control Act §§19(d), 20(c)(2), 15 U.S.C.A. §2618(d), §2619; Endangered Species Act of 1973 §11(g)(4), 16 U.S.C.A. §1540(g)(4); Surface Mining Control and Reclamation Act of 1977, 30 U.S.C.A. §1270(d); Deep Seabed Hard Mineral Resources Act §117(c), 30 U.S.C.A. §1427(c); Clean Water Act (Federal Water Pollution Control Act Amendments of 1972 §505), 33 U.S.C.A. §1365(d); Marine Protection, Research, and Sanctuaries Act, 33 U.S.C.A. §1415(g)(4); Deepwater Port Act of 1974, 33 U.S.C.A. §1515(d); Safe Drinking Water Act §1449(d), 42 U.S.C.A. §300j-8(d); Noise Control Act of 1972 §12(d), 42 U.S.C.A. §4911(d); Energy Sources Development Act, 42 U.S.C.A. §5851(e)(2); Energy Policy and Conservation Act, 42 U.S.C.A. §6305(d); Solid Waste Disposal Act, 42 U.S.C.A. §6972(e); Clean Air Act §304, 42 U.S.C.A. §§7604, 7607(f); Powerplant and Industrial Fuel Act, 42 U.S.C.A. §8435(d); Ocean Thermal Energy Conservation Act, 42 U.S.C.A. §9124(d); Outer Continental Shelf Lands Act, 43 U.S.C.A. §1349(a)(5). Most of these also provide for attorney and expert witness fee awards if plaintiffs prevail. See Chapter 20.

32. The sixty day waiting period does not apply in cases of toxic and pre-treatment standards, or national performance standards. Environmentalists have argued that waivers to the sixty-day waiting period should also be granted or liberalized in other settings where the public interest and congressional policy require it. Irvin, When Survival is at Stake: a Proposal for Expanding the Emergency Exception to the Sixty-Day Notice Requirement of the Endangered Species Act's Citizen Suit Provision, 14 Harv. Env. L. Rev. 343 (1990)(the article presents interesting examples of the necessity for citizen enforcement where industry and government remain passive).

regulatory programs.[33] Starting in the late 1970s, however, Supreme Court decisions have inclined toward rolling back citizen enforcement, retreating to the narrowed industry/agency terms of traditional administrative process.[34]

**RETRENCHMENT IN THE REHNQUIST COURT...** In the years immediately following *SCRAP*, standing doctrine initially shifted toward *SCRAP's* less strict terms, and then the Court began a steady retrenchment against citizen enforcement.[35] The Court has followed several strategies — applying broadened prudential limitations where Congress has not granted specific standing rights,[36] holding statutory grants of citizen standing to their narrowest terms,[37] and adding more restrictive principles as constitutional requirements so as to overrride statutory grants and tighten standing generally.[38]

**THE 1990s: THE *LUJAN* CASES...** In *"Lujan I,"* Lujan v. National Wildlife Federation, 497 U.S. 871 (1990), the Court tightened definitions of standing to require environmentalists challenging agency actions to allege highly particularized injuries while resisting suits against alleged programmatic violations. In denying plaintiffs' standing in a suit (based on the APA, not on a specific statutory grant of standing) against Interior Sec. James Watt's agency-marketplace program to open Western public lands to grazing, timber, and mining operations, Justice Scalia scrutinized plaintiffs' claimed injuries closely:

> In its complaint, respondent averred generally that the reclassification of some withdrawn lands and the return of others to the public domain would open the lands up to mining activities, thereby destroying their natural beauty.... To support the [district court's standing ruling] the Court of Appeals pointed to the affidavits of two of respondent's members, Peggy Kay Peterson and Richard Erman, which claimed use of land "in the vicinity" of the land covered by two

---

33. "[Where the] only public entities that might have brought suit...[are] named as defendants...and vigorously [oppose] plaintiffs,...only private citizens can be expected to guard the guardians." La Raza Unida v. Volpe, 57 F.R.D. 94, 101 (N.D. Cal. 1972). The nation's "regrettably slow progress in controlling air pollution is blamed on [both] the scarcity of skilled personnel available to enforce control measures and on a lack of aggressiveness by EPA's predecessor agency.... The public suit seems particularly instrumental in the statutory scheme [in cases forcing agency compliance], for only the public – certainly not the polluter – has the incentive to complain if the EPA falls short...." NRDC v. EPA, 484 F.2d 1331 (1st Cir. 1973).

34. Hallstrom v. Tillamook County, 493 U.S. 20 (1989); Gwaltney of Smithfield v. Chesapeake Bay Found., 484 U.S. 49 (1987). *Gwaltney's* holding – that citizen suits can be filed only where an ongoing violation continues when the lawsuit is filed, but not for past violations – was specifically overridden by Congress as to the Clean Air Act. The 1990 CAA amendments provided for citizen lawsuits upon evidence that past violations have been repeated. Pub. L. 101–549, §707(g)(amending §304(a) of the Clean Air Act, 42 U.S.C.A. 7410).

35. Sometimes generous standing rulings, as in Duke Power v. Carolina Environmental Study Group, 438 U.S. 59 (1978), have reflected the Supreme Court's apparent desire to hear an environmental argument so as to dispose of it permanently in order to remove uncertainty from the marketplace. 438 U.S. at 78.

36. E.g., The proposition that plaintiffs cannot claim injury from harm to third parties was launched in Warth v. Seldin, 422 U.S. 490 (1975).

37. See *Gwaltney*, 484 U.S. 49, 52 (1987), and The Steel Company v. Citizens for a Better Environment, 118 S. Ct. 1003 (1998).

38. "The constitutional component of standing doctrine incorporates concepts concededly not susceptible of precise definition. The injury alleged must be, for example, "distinct and palpable," and not "abstract" or "conjectural" or "hypothetical." The injury must be "fairly" traceable to the challenged action, and relief from the injury ["redressability"] must be "likely" to follow from a favorable decision." Allen v. Wright, 468 U.S. 737 (1984). *SCRAP*, in other words, is history. By calling these tests constitutional rather than prudential, the Court can use them to limit congressional standing grants.

of the listed actions. Thus, the Court of Appeals concluded, there was "concrete indication that [respondent's] members use specific lands covered by the agency's Program and will be adversely affected by the agency's actions."... The Peterson affidavit averred:

"My recreational use and aesthetic enjoyment of federal lands, particularly those in the vicinity of South Pass–Green Mountain, Wyoming have been and continue to be adversely affected in fact by the unlawful actions of the Bureau and the Department. In particular, the South Pass–Green Mountain area of Wyoming has been opened to the staking of mining claims and oil and gas leasing, an action which threatens the aesthetic beauty and wildlife habitat potential of these lands...."

There is no showing that Peterson's recreational use and enjoyment extends to the particular 4500 acres covered by the decision to terminate classification....

Erman's affidavit was substantially the same.... The magnitude of Erman's claimed injury stretches the imagination.... The Arizona Strip consists of all lands in Arizona north and west of the Colorado River on approximately 5.5 million acres, an area one-eighth the size of the State of Arizona....

Respondent alleges that violation of the law is rampant within this program — failure to revise land use plans in proper fashion, failure to submit certain recommendations to Congress, failure to consider multiple use, inordinate focus upon mineral exploitation, failure to provide adequate environmental impact statements. Perhaps so. But respondent cannot seek *wholesale* improvement of this program by court decree, rather than in the offices of the Department or the halls of Congress, where programmatic improvements are normally made....

In the present case, the individual actions of the BLM identified in the six affidavits can be regarded as...announcing, with respect to vast expanses of territory that they cover, the agency's intent to grant requisite permission for certain activities, to decline to interfere with other activities, and to take other particular action if requested. It may well be, then, that even those individual actions will not be ripe for challenge until some further agency action or inaction more immediately harming the plaintiff occurs. But it is at least entirely certain that the flaws in the entire "program" — consisting principally of the many individual actions referenced in the complaint, and presumably actions yet to be taken as well — cannot be laid before the courts for wholesale correction under the APA, simply because one of them that is ripe for review adversely affects one of respondent's members. Respondent must seek such programmatic improvements from the BLM or Congress. Lujan v. National Wildlife Federation, 497 U.S. 871 (1990) (*Lujan I*).

**LUJAN II...** In "*Lujan II*," Justice Scalia extended his particularized injury rule of Article III standing even to cases where Congress had specifically authorized citizen standing. Environmentalists were trying to apply the protections of the federal Endangered Species Act to overseas projects of U.S. agencies that ignore ecological issues and endanger species. The Act's §7 forbids agencies to jeopardize species or destroy their habitat, (see Chapter 14) and requires formal consultations when there is a risk. ESA §11 authorizes "any person" to enforce the Act in court. In 1986 the Reagan Administration reversed a Carter Administration regulation that had applied §7(a)(2) to agency projects in other countries....

Shortly thereafter respondents, organizations dedicated to wildlife conservation and other environmental causes, filed this action against the Secretary of the Interior, seeking a declaratory judgment that the new regulation is in error as to the geographic scope of §7....

We think the...respondents had not made the requisite demonstration of (at least) injury and redressability.

Respondents' claim to injury is that [non-application of ESA] "increas[es] the rate of extinction of endangered and threatened species." Of course, the desire to use or observe an animal species, even for purely aesthetic purposes, is undeniably a cognizable interest for purpose of standing. But the "injury in fact" test requires more than an injury to a cognizable interest.... Respondents had to submit affidavits or other evidence showing, through specific facts, not only that listed species were in fact being threatened by funded activities abroad, but also that one or more of respondents' members would thereby be "directly" affected apart from their "special interest in the subject."...

The Court of Appeals focused on the affidavits of two Defenders' members — Joyce Kelly and Amy Skilbred. Ms. Kelly stated that she traveled to Egypt in 1986 and "observed the traditional habitat of the endangered Nile crocodile there and intend[s] to do so again, and hopes to observe the crocodile directly," and that she "will suffer harm in fact as a result of the American [agency]...role...in overseeing the rehabilitation of the Aswan High Dam on the Nile...and in developing...Egypt's...Master Water Plan." Ms. Skilbred averred that she traveled to Sri Lanka in 1981 and "observed th[e] habitat" of "endangered species such as the Asian elephant and the leopard" at what is now the site of the Mahaweli Project funded by the Agency for International Development (AID), although she "was unable to see any of the endangered species"; "this development project," she continued, "will seriously reduce endangered, threatened, and endemic species habitat including areas that I visited...[, which] may severely shorten the future of these species;" that threat, she concluded, harmed her because she "intend[s] to return to Sri Lanka in the future and hope[s] to be more fortunate in spotting at least the endangered elephant and leopard." When Ms. Skilbred was asked at a subsequent deposition if and when she had any plans to return to Sri Lanka, she reiterated that "I intend to go back to Sri Lanka," but confessed that she had no current plans: "I don't know when. There is a civil war going on right now."...

These affidavits...contain no facts...showing how damage to the species will produce "imminent" injury to Mss. Kelly and Skilbred.... "Some day" intentions — without any description of concrete plans, or indeed even any specification of when the some day will be — do not support a finding of the "actual or imminent" injury that our cases require.

Besides relying upon the Kelly and Skilbred affidavits, respondents propose a series of novel standing theories. The first, inelegantly styled "ecosystem nexus," proposes that any person who uses any part of a "contiguous ecosystem" adversely affected by a funded activity has standing even if the activity is located a great distance away. This approach, as the Court of Appeals correctly observed, is inconsistent with our opinion in *National Wildlife Federation*....

Respondents' other theories are called, alas, the "animal nexus" approach, whereby anyone who has an interest in studying or seeing the endangered animals anywhere on the globe has standing; and the "vocational nexus" approach, under which anyone with a professional interest in such animals can sue. Under these theories, anyone who goes to see Asian elephants in the Bronx Zoo, and anyone who is a keeper of Asian elephants in the Bronx Zoo, has standing to sue because the Director of AID did not consult with the Secretary regarding the AID-funded project in Sri Lanka. This is beyond all reason... It is clear that the person who observes or works with a particular animal threatened by a federal decision is facing perceptible harm, since the very subject of his interest will no longer exist. It is even plausible — though it goes to the outermost limit of plausibility — to think that a person who observes or works with animals of a particular species in the very area of the world where that species is threatened by a federal decision is facing such harm, since some animals that might have been the subject of his interest will no longer exist, see Japan Whaling Assn. v. American Cetacean Soc., 478 U.S. 221, 231, n. 4 (1986). It goes beyond the limit, however, and into pure speculation and fantasy, to say that anyone who observes or works with an endangered species, anywhere in the world, is appreciably harmed by a single project affecting some portion of that species with which he has no more specific connection.

Besides failing to show injury, respondents failed to demonstrate redressability....39 Since the agencies funding the projects were not parties to the case, the District Court could accord relief only against the Secretary: He could be ordered to revise his regulation to require consultation for foreign projects. But this would not remedy respondents' alleged injury unless the funding agencies were bound by the Secretary's regulation, which is very much an open question...

The Court of Appeals found that respondents had standing for an additional reason: because they had suffered a "procedural injury." The so-called "citizen-suit" provision of the ESA provides, in pertinent part, that "any person may commence a civil suit...to enjoin any person, including...any...governmental instrumentality or agency...who is alleged to be in violation."...

This is not a case where plaintiffs are seeking to enforce a procedural requirement the disregard of which could impair a separate concrete interest of theirs.... Nor...is it the unusual case in which Congress has created a concrete private interest in the outcome of a suit against a private party for the government's benefit, by providing a cash bounty for the victorious plaintiff. Rather, the court held that the injury-in-fact requirement had been satisfied by congressional conferral upon all persons of an abstract, self-contained, noninstrumental "right" to have the Executive observe the procedures required by law.

We reject this view.... [If] courts were to act...at the invitation of Congress, in ignoring the concrete injury requirement described in our cases, they would be discarding a principle...that identifies those "Cases" and "Controversies" that are the business of the courts rather than of the political branches.... Vindicating the public interest (including the public interest in government observance of the Constitution and laws) is the function of Congress and the Chief Executive. The question presented here is whether the public interest in proper administration of the laws (specifically, in agencies' observance of a particular, statutorily prescribed procedure) can be converted into an individual right by a statute that denominates it as such, and that permits all citizens (or, for that matter, a subclass of citizens who suffer no distinctive concrete harm) to sue. If the concrete injury requirement has the separation-of-powers significance we have always said, the answer must be obvious: To permit Congress to convert the undifferentiated public interest in executive officers' compliance with the law into an "individual right" vindicable in the courts is to permit Congress to transfer from the President to the courts the Chief Executive's most important constitutional duty, to "take Care that the Laws be faithfully executed." It would enable the courts, with the permission of

---

39. [eds.– This paragraph is from segment IIIB of the opinion, which draws only four votes — Scalia, Rehnquist, White, and Thomas. The redressability concept had been launched in Simon v. E. Ky. Welfare Rights Org., 426 U.S. 26, at 38, 41 (1976).]

Congress, "to assume a position of authority over the governmental acts of another and co-equal department."... Article III...established courts to adjudicate cases and controversies as to claims of infringement of individual rights...."Individual rights"...do not mean public rights that have been legislatively pronounced to belong to each individual who forms part of the public....

It is clear that in suits against the government, at least, the concrete injury requirement must remain. We hold that respondents lack standing to bring this action. Lujan v. Defenders of Wildlife, 504 U.S. 555 (1992) (*Lujan II*).

The *Lujan II* decision has been strongly criticized for undercutting the Court's previous acceptance of congressional definitions of generalized injury as a base of citizen standing.[40] Justice Blackmun, joined by Justice O'Connor, dissented, saying "I cannot join the Court on what amounts to a slash-and-burn expedition through the law of environmental standing."

*BENNETT v. SPEAR*... In a 1997 case the Court was handed an ambiguous opportunity. Two ranchers, fearing losses of their federal water supply, wished to attack the Department of Interior's rules under the Endangered Species Act (by now a favorite target of marketplace politics) protecting endangered fish in the Klamath River. The district court denied standing on a strict reading of the zone of interests test, saying that citizens opposing species protections were not in the zone of the ESA. The Court, in an opinion by Justice Scalia, allowed the ranchers standing:

The complaint asserts that there is no...available evidence indicating that the restrictions on lake levels imposed in the Biological Opinion will have any beneficial effect on the...populations of [endangered] suckers [and thus the] imposition of minimum water levels violated §7 of the ESA...and that the imposition of minimum water elevations constituted an implicit determination of critical habitat for the suckers, which violated §4 of the ESA because it failed to take into consideration the designation's economic impact [on ranchers]....

Petitioners' complaint alleges an injury in fact that is fairly traceable to the Biological Opinion and redressable by a favorable judicial ruling and, thus, meets Article III standing requirements.... [The Court held that where suit was brought under a citizen suit provision, the zone of interests test did not apply:] The ESA's citizen-suit provision, set forth in pertinent part in the margin, negates the zone-of-interests test (or, perhaps more accurately, expands the zone of interests).... The first operative portion of the provision says that "any person may commence a civil suit" — an authorization of remarkable breadth....

[Claims not covered under the citizen suit provision *did* have to met the zone test, and did so:] That economic consequences are an explicit concern of the Act is evidenced by §7(h) [the extraordinary God Committee procedure], which provides exemption from §7's no-jeopardy mandate where there are no reasonable and prudent alternatives to the agency action and the benefits of the agency action clearly outweigh the benefits of any alternatives. We believe the "best scientific and commercial data" provision is similarly intended, at least in part, to prevent uneconomic (because erroneous) jeopardy determinations. Petitioners' claim that they are victims of such a mistake is plainly within the zone of interests that the provision protects. Bennett v. Spear, 117 S. Ct. 1154 (1997).

---

40. Sunstein, What's Standing after *Lujan*? 91 Mich. L.Rev. 163 (1992); Nichol, Justice Scalia, Standing, and Public Law Litigation, 42 Duke L.J. 1141 (1993); Pierce, Lujan v. Defenders, 42 Duke L.J. 1170 (1993). See Buzbee, Expanding the Zone...after Bennett v. Spear, 49 Adm. L.Rev. 793 (1997).

The zone of interests test, though it is not generally applied to replicate the old tests where plaintiffs had to have a "legal interest" in order to sue, nevertheless remains a potential weapon against citizen suits. See Air Courier Conference v. Am. Postal Workers Union, 498 U.S. 517 (1991) (Rehnquist, J., denying standing).

**PORTENTS: *MAGNESIUM ELEKTRON*...** The possibilities for even more retrenchment against citizen enforcement is illustrated by a 1997 Third Circuit case, *Magnesium Elektron*, setting a strict standard for proof that violations harm plaintiffs:

> Public Interest Research Group and Friends of the Earth have sued Magnesium Elektron, Inc. for violating the terms of its [water pollution] permit.... MEI's discharge violations involved three types of effluent violations: temperature, sodium, and total organic carbon (TOC).... At the penalty phase of the litigation, the district court...found that MEI's permit violations had caused no harm and posed no threat to the Wickecheoke Creek, the waterway into which MEI discharged its effluent....
>
> [Plaintiffs] must show: (1) injury in fact, an invasion of a legally protected interest which is concrete and particularized and actual or imminent; (2) a causal link between the defendant's conduct and the injury, such that the conduct is "fairly traceable" to that conduct; and (3) the likelihood that judicial relief will redress the plaintiff 's injury. See Lujan, 504 U.S. at 560....
>
> PIRG cites the general-purpose section of the Clean Water Act, which states that Congress' intention was, "to restore and maintain the chemical, physical, and biological integrity of the Nation's waters." Focusing on this language, PIRG reasons that organizations and individuals may sue to protect waterways even if the waterways have not yet been polluted. "Even if the Delaware River and Delaware and Raritan Canal were pristine, PIRG would have standing to sue in order to maintain that pristine state."... We are...unwilling to hold that the Clean Water Act creates a cause of action to maintain waterways in their "pristine state" absent at least a plausible threat of imminent injury.... Significantly, PIRG's members do not allege in their complaint or affidavits any injury to the Delaware River. They have not cited any increases in the River's salinity, or a decrease in the number of fish, or any other negative change in the River's ecosystem.... PIRG's members have shown only that they reduced certain of their recreational activities near the Delaware River. They have not shown that the river suffers from particular types of pollution.... The district court credited this reduced activity as evidence of injury. But the reduction in a person's recreational activity cannot support the injury prong of standing when a court also concludes that a polluter's violation of an effluent standard has not harmed the affected waterway and that it, in fact, poses no threat to that waterway.... The only way PIRG could have met its injury requirement was to show that MEI's discharge violations posed a threat of injury to the members' recreational interests in the Delaware River.... We conclude that...neither PIRG nor its members can show any actual injury or credible threat of injury to the Delaware River. Consequently, they lack standing.... Even if PIRG's members can show that they "may be adversely affected" by MEI's pollution into the Wickecheoke Creek, they must also demonstrate that their threat of injury is imminent.... See Lujan, 504 U.S. at 564. Public Interest Research Group of New Jersey, and Friends of the Earth v. Magnesium Elektron, Inc., 123 F.3d 111 (3d Cir. 1997).

**THE STEEL COMPANY...** Later in the *Magnesium Elektron* decision, the court suggested that monitoring-reporting violations could only be prosecuted by government agencies, saying that "few courts have considered whether a plaintiff 's standing to pursue a polluter's monitoring and reporting violations can exist absent...injury or threat of injury.... We must conclude...that PIRG's members have failed to...allege a specific and concrete injury arising from a defendant's failure to monitor and report its effluent discharges...."

In 1998 the Supreme Court considered that possibility in The Steel Company v. Citizens for a Better Environment, 118 S. Ct. 1003 (1998), noted later in Chapter 20, but did not decide it: "Respondent asserts petitioner's failure to provide EPCRA information in a timely fashion, and the lingering effects of that failure, as the injury in fact to itself and its members. We have not had occasion to decide whether being deprived of information that is supposed to be disclosed under EPCRA — or at least being deprived of it when one has a particular plan for its use — is a concrete injury in fact that satisfies Article III. We need not reach that question in the present case." *Steel Company*, 118 S. Ct. 1003 (deciding the citizens' injury would not be redressed by an order).

### COMMENTARY AND QUESTIONS

1. **What's going on here?** Looking over this undulating line of decisions, does it seem that the variations in standing are the result of evolving doctrinal interpretation or organic decisionmaking? Is the *Bennett* case a sign that the Supreme Court is again interpreting standing liberally? Not likely, for the decision seems to turn more upon which team is at bat than upon precedent. There are discernable parallels between the changing political agendas of the Court and standing holdings over the years, because in tactical terms standing is a gatekeeper issue.[41] As Professors Davis and Pierce say,

> Why does the Court sometimes use a...test that is impossible to meet? What distinguishes these cases from the many cases in which the Court uses a logical and pragmatic test for determining [standing]? Those questions seem easy to answer, though the answer bears no logical relationship to standing. The Court uses standing...to preclude federal courts from intervening in disputes [a majority] considers inappropriate for federal judicial intervention. K.C. Davis and R. Pierce, Administrative Law Treatise §16.5 at 38–39 (1994).

2. **After *Lujan v. Defenders*, how much harm is needed to find sufficient injury for standing, a $5 bounty?** The Scalia opinion in *Lujan II* apparently would have held that if the two individual plaintiffs had plane tickets in hand, they would have had actionable injuries. Is the difference between having and not having plane tickets a serious distinction or a ridiculous technicality when determining standing?

The majority also says that constitutional standing would exist "[where] Congress has created a concrete private interest in the outcome of a suit[42]...for the govern-

---

41. Is the Rehnquist-Scalia line of restrictive holdings "conservative"? Note that they insulate big government agencies from judicial review. The insulation admittedly is not against marketplace players but against citizens, without whom there is no practical likelihood that actions supported by agency-industry coalitions — like the exploitation of Western lands in *Mineral King* and *Lujan I*, or destructive public works projects in *Scenic Hudson*, *Lujan II*, and many other cases — will ever be held accountable for ongoing violations of law.

42. The quote says "a suit against a private party," but it is difficult to see any Art. III difference between suits against private and public defendants.

ment's benefit, by providing a cash bounty for the victorious plaintiff." So if Congress authorized payment of a $5 pecuniary reward for successful law enforcement, even Scalia would admit there was standing — which makes the Court's test seem rather superficial and disingenuous.

If a small money bounty would be sufficient to give a citizen Art. III standing in the *Lujan* terms, then why not likewise the authorizations for attorneys and expert witness fees for prevailing parties, see coursebook at 571, which already exist on the books in the statutory standing provisions? Especially where plaintiffs are public interest attorneys groups, the prospect of recovering tens of thousand dollars for their labors enforcing the law would seem to be a tangible interest.

And here's an analytic braintickler: We all assume that when Congress passes a statute and gives an independent federal agency the authority to prosecute it — e.g. the FTC is given authority to prosecute antitrust violations — the agency has Art. III standing. Why? What's the FTC's constitutional injury or interest,[43] if it is not the enforcement standing created by Congress' delegation to the agency? If Congress can delegate statutory enforcement authority to the FTC, then why can't it also delegate that authority to private organizations similarly dedicated to enforcing public law? (In administrative law there is no bar preventing delegations to private parties, so that is not the distinction.) Could Scalia be wrong in asserting that a congressionally-created procedural interest is not sufficient for standing, especially if he admits that a paltry bounty would support standing?

3. **Changing the definition of injury.** Injury to whom or what? Could the constitutional test of plaintiff's injury in a pollution case also require a showing of harm to the natural resources protected by the statute? The *Magnesium Elektron* court says that "injury to the members' recreational interests" requires a showing of "injury to the Delaware River" — plaintiffs' recreational use interests can be harmed only if the river crosses some threshold of ecological ill-health. What if the violation was a discharge of a gross-colored or fetid-smelling dye that was proved to harm absolutely nothing in the river ecosystem, nor cause any human health problems?

4. **Redressability.** Redressability — considering whether the harms claimed by plaintiffs as a basis for standing are likely to be resolved by a judicial remedy — was previously considered a court-made "prudential principle" subject to being overridden by congressional mandates expanding standing, not an Article III requirement that must be met even if a statute purports to grant standing without it. When injunctions are sought, "Equity will not order a vain thing." Declaratory judgments, however, are thought to guide defendants generally, and particularly where in *Lujan II* the defendants were federal agencies, isn't it likely that the court's rulings would be followed? Is redressability an invitation to political science predictions?

---

43. The FTC is an independent agency, and thus would seem not to have constitutional standing as an executive subordinate of the President who has the Article II duty to see that the laws are faithfully executed.

**5. Ongoing scrutiny of standing law theory.** One of the best explorations of standing doctrine stimulated by the Supreme Court's recent efforts to constrain standing has been Professor Cass Sunstein's article "What's Standing after *Lujan?* — Of Citizen Suits, 'Injuries,' and Article III," 91 Mich. L. Rev. 163 (1992). Sunstein reviews the history and foundational logic of the Art. III case or controversy requirement. He calls into question recent Supreme Court caselaw establishing "injury" as the necessary and sufficient threshold test for standing and coupling it with further "prudential principles" like requirements for showing a causal nexus and a showing of redressability. "At least in general," the article concludes, "standing depends on whether any source of law has created a cause of action." If Congress can create new causes of action, it would seem that it generally could also "create standing [for enforcing them] as it chooses and...deny standing when it likes."

6. **A Catch-22?** Underlying the *Lujan I* case on the merits, apparently, was the fact that the Department of Interior had no plan guiding its releases of public lands as the statute required, nor a programmatic environmental impact statement (see Chapter 14). The Court was able to prevent scrutiny of the program by asserting that (absent such a plan, or programmatic EIS), the land reclassifications were not a program, but hundreds of small cases for which challengers have to plead individual injury related to each specific parcel in order to gain standing. Thus NWF would never be able to litigate the statutory question whether the land release program was a single programmatic action for purposes of FLPMA and NEPA. The court decided it was not, based on the pleadings, instead of letting it go to trial under FRCP 56(e), as the dissent noted. Could plaintiffs have broken out of the *Lujan I* conundrum by filing a class action as representatives of the class of all other specific users of all other past and future reclassified parcels of Western public lands? And is the Court right that legal "flaws in [an] entire "program"...cannot be laid before the courts for wholesale correction under the APA. Respondent must seek such programmatic improvements from the BLM or Congress."? This echoes a common judicial theme, reminiscent of Judge Bergan's preface to the *Boomer* majority opinion, that courts are not the proper forum for contesting broad public policies. Doesn't the assessment of standing in such cases depend on whether you consider it a situation requiring legislative oversight, administrative discretion, or statutory enforcement?

Do environmental groups have legal standing to challenge government management plans for a national forest if the plan does not yet authorize any ground-disturbing activity? In Ohio Forestry Association v. Sierra Club, cert. granted 1997, 97–16, the Sixth Circuit Court of Appeals said yes. The appeals court said environmentalists who contend the planning process was improperly biased toward clear-cutting timber need not wait to challenge a specific project. On the merits of their lawsuit, the court ruled that the plan was adopted improperly because the U.S. Forest Service discounted the forest's recreational value.

7. **Standing for citizen intervention in *agency* proceedings.** Section 6 of the Administrative Procedures Act, 5 U.S.C.A. §555(b), provides that "so far as the orderly conduct of the public business permits, an interested person may appear

before an agency or its responsible employees for the presentation, adjustment, or determination, request, or controversy in [any] proceeding." Section 555(b), however, has not been extensively developed, at least in non-formal, trial-type proceedings. What does the "orderly conduct of public business" limitation mean, and who is legally an "interested" party? *Scenic Hudson* presumed the validity of citizen participation in FPC proceedings. Since *Scenic Hudson*, permission for citizen intervention in agency proceedings seems to have become the norm, if only because agencies realize that judicial review standing has expanded, so that if intervention is denied within agency procedures, court review will nevertheless occur, and be tougher.[44] Some agencies, nevertheless, are known for their resistance to citizen intervention. See In the Matter of Edlow International Co., 3 NRC 563 (Nuclear Regulatory Commission, 1976) (dismissed as moot, NRDC v. NRC, 580 F.2d 698 (D.C. Cir. 1987)).

Intervention is a vital part of citizen involvement in the administrative process, allowing a pluralist debate to begin early in the process rather than later in retrospective judicial review. The future development of APA §555(b) will reflect the evolution of intervention in informal as well as formal proceedings. The arguments of environmentalists to be allowed to intervene in ongoing agency proceedings will continue to be reinforced by the fact that courts in subsequent review often consider that a record made without active participation is not sufficiently comprehensive, and does not cover certain critical features sufficiently to support the agency action in judicial review.

8. **Standing in courts and agencies.** In a notable case expanding citizens' rights to intervene in agency proceedings, then-Judge Warren Burger wrote that "all parties seem to consider that the same standards are applicable to determining standing before the Commission and standing to appeal a Commission decision to this court. We have, therefore, used the cases dealing with standing in the two tribunals interchangeably."[45] Judge Burger took note of the expanding law of standing in federal courts, and required expanded intervention standing in the agency. Analytically are the two tribunals the same? They are doing two very different tasks. A citizen's right to intervene in an agency, under 5 APA §555(b) or otherwise, is arguably broader than standing for judicial review, because administrative agency process is not constitutionally limited by Article III's "case or controversy" requirement.

9. **The role of an agency when citizens intervene.** Note that in the *Scenic Hudson* opinion the court criticized the agency for treating citizen intervention, not as a helpful contribution, but as a resented disruption; the commission had stepped back and acted like "an umpire blandly calling balls and strikes" between the industry and the small ad hoc group of citizen intervenors. Responding to the same

---

44. As a noted administrative law practitioner observed "today, at least in my experience, intervention is seldom denied.... In light of the role that the courts have carved out for intervenors, and the risks inherent in denying interested citizens the right to be heard, intervention has assumed the proportions of a right, even where the applicable statute or rules are phrased permissively." Butzel, Intervention and Class Actions Before the Agencies and the Courts, 25 Admin. L. Rev. 135, 136 (1973).

45. Office of Communication, United Church of Christ v. FCC, 359 F.2d 994, 1000 (D.C. Cir. 1966).

problem in the case noted in the preceding comment, Judge Burger roundly criticized the agency proceedings that had followed his prior order on remand:

> The examiner seems to have regarded [the citizen] appellants as "plaintiffs" and the licensee as "defendant," with burdens of proof allocated accordingly.... We did not intend that intervenors representing a public interest be treated as interlopers. Rather...a "public intervenor" is seeking no license or private right and is, in this context, more nearly like a complaining witness who presents evidence to police or a prosecutor whose duty it is to conduct an affirmative and objective investigation.... In our view the entire hearing was permeated by...the pervasive impatience — if not hostility — of the examiner...which made fair and impartial consideration impossible.... The public intervenors, who were performing a public service under a mandate of this court, were entitled to a more hospitable reception in the performance of that function. As we view the record the examiner tended to impede the exploration of the very issues which we would reasonably expect the Commission itself would have initiated; an ally was regarded as an opponent.... The administrative conduct reflected in this record is beyond repair. [The agency decision was revoked and the proceedings remanded to the agency.] Office of Communication of United Church of Christ v. FCC, 425 F.2d 543, 546-550 (D.C. Cir. 1969).

10. **Citizens' access to information: FOIA.** Information is power, or, at least, it is clear that without basic specific information, interested parties and intervenors will not be effective. In 1966 Congress dramatically reversed the prior widespread agency presumption that government information should be withheld unless there was specific legal authority for its release. The Freedom of Information Act (FOIA), 5 U.S.C.A. §552, provides that —

> each agency upon any request for records which...reasonably describes such records and [follows certain simple procedures] *shall make the records promptly available* to any person. §552(a)(3).

FOIA restricts permissible withholding to nine fairly narrow exceptions. §552(b)(1-9). Environmentalists have often found FOIA critically helpful in obtaining agency information through formal requests or, perhaps even more usefully, in prompting informal release of information. Federal courts have applied the Act with stringency in a number of environmental cases,[46] although the development of the Act's disclosure mandate, and its provisions for waiving data retrieval fees for requests "primarily benefiting the public interest,"[47] are still evolving.

11. **"Internalizing costs" through public law?** In approaching pollution and other environmental harms caused by private individuals and industries, environmental law often follows the strategy of cost internalization, attempting to force private decision-makers to account for environmental costs in their economic market behavior. Is there an equivalent accounting strategy in the public law setting, where decision-makers are not involved in a market enterprise?

---

46. See Soucie v. David, 448 F. 2d. 1067 (D.C. Cir. 1971)(negative reports on the predicted effects of a supersonic transport plane must be released); cf. Nat'l Parks & Conservation Ass'n v. Morton, 498 F. 2d 765 (D.C. Cir. 1974)(financial data from national park concessionaires need not be released).

47. §552(a)(4)(A). The Act's serious intent to compel an open governmental process is underscored by its provisions for advancing FOIA cases to the top of federal court dockets, §552(a)(4)(D); for award of attorney's fees against the agencies, §552(a)(4)(E); and for personal accountability, see next note.

To an extent, government decision-makers often seem to share the functional frame of reference of private corporate entrepreneurs. To the minds of promoters, whether private or public, accounting for negative external consequences is dysfunctional, hence to be avoided, because it gets in the way of the enterprise's mission. Development agencies, however, may tend to be institutionally less sensitive to cost-accounting. Their projects are paid for with taxpayer dollars.

How are agency officials practically induced to consider consequential public costs in their internal calculus? One approach is political. The currency of the bureaucratic marketplace is politics — who has power, who has momentum, who is under fire. Agencies can foresee that if they attract severe media criticism, or legislative committee oversight hearings, or negative reactions from an executive office, they will feel the heat, and so they act accordingly. Another internalizing approach is personal accountability, a rarity in government except at the highest levels. FOIA's §552(a) provides that —

> Whenever the court orders the production of any agency records improperly withheld from the complainant...and...issues a written finding that the circumstances surrounding the withholding raise questions whether agency personnel acted arbitrarily...with respect to the withholding, the Special Counsel [of the Civil Service merit system review process] shall promptly initiate a proceeding to determine whether disciplinary action is warranted.... §552(a)(4)(F).

Such personal sanctions catch and hold bureaucratic attention, but are infrequent. Ultimately it is legal constraints — in practical terms this means legal constraints that will be enforced against agencies, in many cases only by citizen efforts — that constitute the backbone of administrative accountability.

12. **Ripeness, exhaustion, financing, and other barriers to citizen enforcement.** The extended analysis of standing issues here should not obscure the fact that virtually every tactical issue in administrative law plays a frequent role in environmental litigation. "Ripeness" is a prime example — the question whether the agency has made a sufficiently final decision to be reviewed. See the Supreme Court's ripeness decision in Ohio Forestry v. Sierra Club, 118 S.Ct. 1665 (1998), noted below at page 1133. "Exhaustion of remedies" is another, asking whether citizens should seek all appropriate remedies in an agency before trying to pull the issues into court.[48] As to the tactics of financing litigation, when citizens embark as "private attorneys-general" attempting to enforce existing law in agencies and courts, they often face substantial administrative and financial burdens, against opponents who are either public officials or well-financed corporate entities writing off expenses against revenues. Expert witnesses and attorneys cost money. For plaintiff groups like the citizens in *Overton Park*, this often means having to raise funds through bake sales, raffles, selling logo tee-shirts, or passing the hat. In Chapter 20, which discusses practical issues of statutory enforcement, there is an extended analysis of awards of attorney fees and other practical issues in the logistics of litigation.

---

48. See EDF v. Hardin, where both issues arose in an environmental group's attempt to get an agency to curtail DDT as a pesticide. 428 F.2d 1093 (D.C. Cir. 1970).

### Section 3. POLITICAL RESISTANCE TO CITIZEN ENFORCEMENT: REMOVING COURTS' ABILITY TO GRANT RELIEF TO CITIZENS.

## Department of Interior and Related Agencies Appropriations Act, 1990
### Public Law 101–121 (1989)

§318(g)...[N]o restraining order or preliminary injunction shall be issued by any court of the United States with respect to any decision to prepare, advertise, offer, award, or operate...timber sales in fiscal year 1990 from the thirteen national forests in Oregon and Washington and Bureau of Land Management lands in Western Oregon known to contain northern spotted owls. The provisions of 5 U.S.C.A. §705 [authorizing courts to stay agency actions] shall not apply to any challenge to such a timber sale. *Provided,* that the courts shall have authority to [issue permanent injunctions for timber sales found to be] arbitrary, capricious, or otherwise not in accordance with law....

[Other provisions of this appropriations rider required the agencies to sell off increased annual quotas of timber; restricted the cutting of certain "ecologically significant old growth forest stands" except as necessary to meet the sales quotas; directed the Forest Service to prepare a new spotted owl plan and have it in place by September 30, 1990; insulated from judicial review Forest Service and Bureau of Land Management (BLM) decisions shown to be based on outdated information; and made quasi-judicial findings to reverse two injunctions against timbercutting.[49]]

### COMMENTARY AND QUESTIONS

1. **The spotted owl appropriations rider.** What's going on here? The preceding language was inserted into the Department of Interior 1990 appropriations bill in reaction to environmentalists' successes, under a variety of environmental statutes, in protecting the northern spotted owl, an endangered species threatened by clearcutting operations in various old-growth Forest Service public lands in the Pacific Northwest that plaintiffs had demonstrated were in violation of law. The appropriations rider was intended to end the citizens' disruption of ongoing practices.

What is the theory of such appropriations riders? They do not repeal or amend laws that stand in the way of promoters' enterprises. (Repeals or amendments are straightforward legislative alternatives available to Congress, and have been used in various settings over the years.) Instead it merely removes the citizens' ability to get preliminary injunctions (and forecloses permanent injunctions except in extraordinary cases where citizens are able to prove on the restricted merits that agency action was arbitrary, capricious, etc.)[50] Such appropriations riders are effec-

---

49. See §§314, 318(b)(6), 103 Stat. at 743, 747. In practice these timber sales typically auction off the public forests at below-cost subsidized prices. Section 318's quasi-judicial findings were held unconstitutional on separation of powers grounds, Seattle Audubon v. Robertson, 914 F.2d 1311 (9th Cir. 1990); cert. granted, 111 S.Ct. 2886 (1991).

Section 318 is a "rider" because it was tacked onto the on-rolling spending bill. In fact, attaching such substantive law provisions onto appropriations bills violates House Rule 23 and Senate Rule 16, but through parliamentary manoeuvres the rules were not applied.

50. In the timing of such citizen efforts, practically speaking, preliminary injunctions are the entire battle. If preliminary relief staying the agency action is not ordered, the forest is stripped bare before plaintiffs can get to trial on the permanent injunctions.

tive federal law for only one fiscal year, although when lobbyists successfully add them to an appropriations bill for one year, they tend to reappear thereafter.[51]

Isn't the rider's approach quite revealing? Its obvious rationale is that — absent citizen enforcement — neither the private industry logging the lands nor the two federal agencies supervising the logging will comply with federal laws. In order to nullify the laws, one doesn't have to repeal them (and they didn't have the votes to do that), but needs only to eliminate the citizen enforcers.

Why was this done by appropriations rider rather than by normal congressional legislation? The legislative standing committees with jurisdiction over forests and wildlife generally oppose any such overrides of judicial review. Senators Hatfield and Adams of Washington, Packwood of Oregon, and their timber industry backers went to the appropriations committees instead. Appropriations committees are often thought to be much more closely aligned to vested interests; they wield extraordinary power through the fact that they and they alone hold annual hearings and pass funding legislation for virtually every federal agency program. Once a rider has been attached to a bill by the appropriations committees, there are so many public spending projects linked to them that the bills become almost impregnable, and "veto-proof."

As a sign of the times, in the brief period when the 104th Congress was trying to give the marketplace economy its desired repeal of many environmental laws, a so-called "Timber Salvage" amendment was made law that directly overrode virtually all laws that constrained the timber industry's environmental practices. Timber lobbyists tacked the rider onto the Oklahoma bombing disaster relief bill, and it stayed in force for 18 months before dying in ill repute.[52]

Beyond the question of legislating on appropriations bills, is there any constitutional limit to the ability of special interest riders to foreclose judicial review of targeted agency practices? After a broad-ranging review of such provisions overriding judicial review, a recent study ended its constitutional and statutory analysis with the plaint that "it is crucial that courts apply a heightened standard of review in examining measures that limit judicial review.... Judicial review is fundamental to the 'very essence of liberty' [citing Marbury v. Madison, 5 U.S. 137, 163 (1803)]. The Supreme Court has held that any 'statutory preclusion of judicial review must be demonstrated clearly and convincingly.'"[53]

---

51. After 458 law professors from 61 schools in 41 states and the District of Columbia sent a letter to leaders of the House and Senate protesting §318 as a "dangerous precedent" for undermining protective federal laws, however, §318 was not re-promulgated for fiscal year 1991. The fight was successfully led by Senators Baucus and Chaffee, who not coincidentally were the ranking members of the standing committees bypassed by the appropriations stratagem, and by the Sierra Club Legal Defense Fund.

52. Emergency Supplemental Appropriations for Additional Disaster Assistance, for Anti-Terrorism Initiatives, for Assistance in the Recovery from the Tragedy that Occurred at Oklahoma City, and Rescissions Act, 1995, Pub. L. No. 104–19, 109 Stat. 194, 240 (1995). See Oregon Natural Resources Council v. Jack Ward Thomas, 92 F.3d 792 (9th Cir. 1996); Northwest Forest Resource Council, 82 F.3d 825 (9th Cir. 1996).

53. Sher and Hunting, Eroding the Landscape, Eroding the Laws: Congressional Exemptions from Judicial Review of Environmental Laws, 15 Harv. Envtl L. Rev. 435, 481 (1991) (citing NLRB v. United Food & Comm'l Wkrs. Union, 484 U.S. 112, 131 (1987)).

The Supreme Court upheld §318 against a challenge claiming it interfered with ongoing litigation. The Court noted on one hand that if Congress attempts to direct a particular judicial decision without changing the statute, it may not do so, because that is the role of the courts, but if Congress changes the terms of a statute, then the court must follow. Robertson v. Seattle Audubon Society, 503 U.S. 429 (1992). But what about the hidden issue that lies between? If Congress doesn't change the law, but removes judicial jurisdiction to consider violations in whole or in part, does that violate the Article III judicial power and the separation of powers doctrine? Absent a clear constitutional barrier to such legislative short-cuts, special interest attempts to foreclose citizen enforcement will undoubtedly continue, pressuring Congress to write specific exemptions from judicial review so that statutes will go unenforced.

## Section 4. ENVIRONMENTALISTS' ATTEMPTS TO EXPAND AGENCY PROCEDURES

In *Overton Park*, the plaintiffs were unsuccessful in persuading the courts to grant extended procedural opportunities to challenge the highway project within the agency or to require formal findings. In subsequent years many federal courts, led by the D.C. Circuit, began to expand the procedures owed to citizen challengers — sometimes on claims of individual due process, especially in matters of "Great Public Import," and sometimes based on the review needs of courts. The following case involved both. Note the tone of the Supreme Court opinion, the political alignments among the various parties, and how the citizen environmentalists focused their arguments on procedural claims as much as, or more than, attacking the substantive agency decision.

### Vermont Yankee Nuclear Power Corp. v. Natural Resources Defense Council
United States Supreme Court, 1978
435 U.S. 519, 98 S. Ct. 1197, 55 L. Ed. 2d 460

REHNQUIST, J. In 1946, Congress enacted the Administrative Procedure Act, which as we have noted elsewhere was not only "a new, basic and comprehensive regulation of procedures in many agencies," Wong Yang Sung v. McGrath, 339 U.S. 33 (1950), but was also a legislative enactment which settled "long-continued and hard-fought contentions, and enacts a formula upon which opposing social and political forces have come to rest."... Interpreting [§4 of the Act, now codified as §553] in United States v. Allegheny-Ludlum Steel Corp., 406 U.S. 742 (1972), and United States v. Florida East Coast Ry. Co., 410 U.S. 224 (1973), we held that generally speaking this section of the Act established the maximum procedural requirements which Congress was willing to have the courts impose upon agencies in conducting rulemaking procedures. Agencies are free to grant additional procedural rights in the exercise of their discretion, but reviewing courts are generally not free to impose them if the agencies have not chosen to grant them. This is not to say necessarily that there are no circumstances which would ever justify a court in overturning agency action because of a failure to employ procedures beyond those required by the statute. But such circumstances, if they exist, are extremely rare....

It is in the light of this background of statutory and decisional law that we granted certiorari to review [a judgment] of the Court of Appeals for the District of Columbia Circuit because of our concern that [the court] had seriously misread or misapplied this statutory and decisional law cautioning reviewing courts against engrafting their own notions of proper procedures upon agencies entrusted with substantive functions by Congress. We conclude that the Court of Appeals has done just that...and we therefore remand [the case] to it for further proceedings....

Under the Atomic Energy Act of 1954, as amended, 42 U.S.C.A. §2011 et seq., the Atomic Energy Commission was given broad regulatory authority over the development of nuclear energy. Under the terms of the act, a utility seeking to construct and operate a nuclear power plant must obtain a separate permit or license at both the construction and the operation stage of the project. In order to obtain the construction permit, the utility must file a preliminary safety analysis report, an environmental report, and certain information regarding the antitrust implications of the proposed project. This application then undergoes exhaustive review by the Commission's staff and by the Advisory Committee on Reactor Safe-guards (ACRS), a group of distinguished experts in the field of atomic energy. Both groups submit to the Commission their own evaluations, which then become part of the record of the utility's application. The Commission staff also undertakes the review required by the National Environmental Policy Act of 1969 (NEPA), 42 U.S.C.A. §4321 et seq., and prepares a draft environmental impact statement, which, after being circulated for comment, is revised and becomes a final environmental impact statement. Thereupon a three-member Atomic Safety and Licensing Board conducts a public adjudicatory hearing, and reaches a decision which can be appealed to the Atomic Safety and Licensing Appeal Board, and currently, in the Commission's discretion, to the Commission itself. The final agency decision may be appealed to the courts of appeals. The same sort of process occurs when the utility applies for a license to operate the plant, except that a hearing need only be held in contested cases and may be limited to the matters in controversy....

In December 1967, after the mandatory adjudicatory hearing and necessary review, the Commission granted petitioner Vermont Yankee a permit to build a nuclear power plant in Vernon, Vt. Thereafter, Vermont Yankee applied for an operating license. Respondent Natural Resources Defense Council (NRDC) objected to the granting of a license, however, and therefore a hearing on the application commenced on August 10, 1971. Excluded from consideration at the hearings, over NRDC's objection, was the issue of the environmental effects of operations to reprocess fuel or dispose of wastes resulting from the reprocessing operations. This ruling was affirmed by the Appeal Board in June 1972.

In November 1972, however, the Commission, making specific reference to the Appeal Board's decision with respect to the Vermont Yankee License, instituted rulemaking proceedings "that would specifically deal with the question of consideration of environmental effects associated with the uranium fuel cycle in the individual cost-benefit analyses for light water cooled nuclear power reactors." The notice of proposed rulemaking offered two alternatives, both predicated on a report prepared by the commission's staff entitled Environmental Survey of the Nuclear Fuel Cycle. The first would have required no quantitative evaluation of the environmental hazards of fuel reprocessing or disposal because the Environmental Survey had found them to be slight. The second would have specified numerical values for the environmental impact of this part of the fuel cycle, which values would then be incorporated into a table, along with the other relevant factors, to determine the overall cost-benefit balance for each operating license.

Much of the controversy in this case revolves around the procedures used in the rulemaking hearing which commenced in February 1973. In a supplemental notice of hearing the Commission indicated that while discovery or cross-examination would not be utilized, the Environmental Survey would be available to the public before the hearing along with the extensive background documents cited therein. All participants would be given a reasonable opportunity to present their position and could be represented by counsel if they so desired. Written and, time permitting, oral statements would be received and incorporated into the record. All persons giving oral statements would be subject to questioning by the Commission. At the conclusion of the hearing, a transcript would be made available to the public and the record would remain open for 30 days to allow the filing of supplemental written statements. More than 40 individuals and organizations representing a wide variety of interests submitted written comments. On January 17, 1973, the Licensing Board held a planning session to schedule the appearance of witnesses and to discuss methods for compiling a record. The hearing was held on February 1 and 2, with participation by a number of groups, including the Commission's staff, the United States Environmental Protection Agency, a manufacturer of reactor equipment, a trade association from the nuclear industry, a group of electric utility companies, and a group called Consolidated National Intervenors which represented 79 groups and individuals including respondent NRDC....

The Licensing Board forwarded its report to the Commission without rendering any decision. The Licensing Board identified as the principal procedural question the propriety of declining to use full formal adjudicatory procedures. The major substantive issue was the technical adequacy of the Environmental Survey.

In April 1974, the Commission issued a rule which adopted the second of the two proposed alternatives described above. The Commission also approved the procedures used at the hearing, and indicated that the record, including the Environmental Survey, provided an "adequate data base for the regulation adopted."... Respondents appealed from both the Commission's adoption of the rule and its decision to grant Vermont Yankee's license to the Court of Appeals for the District of Columbia Circuit.

With respect to the challenge of Vermont Yankee's license, the court first ruled that in the absence of effective rulemaking proceedings, the Commission must deal with the environmental impact of fuel reprocessing and disposal in individual licensing proceedings. The court then examined the rulemaking proceedings and, despite the fact that it appeared that the agency employed all the procedures required by 5 U.S.C.A. §553 and more, the court determined the proceedings to be inadequate and overturned the rule. Accordingly, the Commission's determination with respect to Vermont Yankee's license was... remanded for further proceedings.

Petitioner Vermont Yankee first argues that the Commission should grant a license to operate a nuclear reactor without any consideration of waste disposal and fuel reprocessing. We find, however, that this issue is no longer presented by the record in this case.... Vermont Yankee will produce annually well over 100 pounds of radioactive wastes, some of which will be highly toxic.... Many of these substances must be isolated for anywhere from 600 to hundreds of thousands of years. It is hard to argue that these wastes do not constitute "adverse environmental effects which cannot be avoided should the proposal be implemented," or that by operating nuclear power plants we are not making "irreversible and irretrievable commitments of resources." [Ed. note: these are requirements from NEPA §102].... For these reasons we hold that the Commission acted well within its statutory authority when it considered the back end of the fuel cycle in individual licensing proceedings.

We next turn to the invalidation of the fuel cycle rule. But before determining whether the Court of Appeals reached a permissible result, we must determine exactly what result it did reach, and in this case that is no mean feat. Vermont Yankee argues that the court invalidated the rule because of the inadequacy of the procedures employed in the proceedings. Respondents, on the other hand, labeling petitioner's view of the decision a "straw man," argue to this Court that the court merely held that the record was inadequate to enable the reviewing court to determine whether the agency had fulfilled its statutory obligation....

After a thorough examination of the opinion itself, we conclude that while the matter is not entirely free from doubt, the majority of the Court of Appeals struck down the rule because of the perceived inadequacies of the procedures employed in the rulemaking proceedings. The court first determined the intervenors' primary argument to be "that the decision to preclude 'discovery or cross-examination' denied them a meaningful opportunity to participate in the proceedings as guaranteed by due process." The court then went on to frame the issue for decision thus: "Thus, we are called upon to decide whether the procedures provided by the agency were sufficient to ventilate the issues." The court conceded that absent extraordinary circumstances it is improper for a reviewing court to prescribe the procedural format an agency must follow, but it likewise clearly thought it entirely appropriate to "scrutinize the record as a whole to insure that genuine opportunities to participate in a meaningful way were provided...." The court also refrained from actually ordering the agency to follow any specific procedures, but there is little doubt in our minds that the ineluctable mandate of the court's decision is that the procedures afforded during the hearings were inadequate. This conclusion is particularly buttressed by the fact that after the court examined the record, particularly the testimony of Dr. Pittman, and declared it insufficient, the court proceeded to discuss at some length the necessity for further procedural devices or a more "sensitive" application of those devices employed during the proceedings. The exploration of the record and the statement regarding its insufficiency might initially lead one to conclude that the court was only examining the sufficiency of the evidence, but the remaining portions of the opinion dispel any doubt that this was certainly not the sole or even the principal basis of the decision. Accordingly, we feel compelled to address the opinion on its own terms, and we conclude that it was wrong.

In prior opinions we have intimated that even in a rulemaking proceeding when an agency is making a "quasi-judicial" determination by which a very small number of persons are "'exceptionally affected, in each case upon individual grounds,'" in some circumstances additional [trial-type] procedures may be required in order to afford the aggrieved individuals due process. United States v. Florida East Coast R. Co., 410 U.S. at 242, 245 (quoting from Bi-Metallic Investment Co. v. State Board of Equalization, 239 U.S. 441, 446 (1915)). It might also be true, although we do not think the issue is presented in this case and accordingly do not decide it, that a totally unjustified departure from well-settled agency procedures of long standing might require judicial correction.

But this much is absolutely clear. Absent constitutional constraints or extremely compelling circumstances the "administrative agencies 'should be free to fashion their own rules of procedure and to pursue methods of inquiry capable of permitting them to discharge their multitudinous duties.'" FCC v. Schreiber, 381 U.S. 279, 290 (1965).

We have continually repeated this theme through the years.... [I]n determining the proper scope of judicial review of agency action under the Natural Gas Act, we held that while a court may have occasion to remand an agency decision because of the inadequacy of the record, the agency should normally be allowed to "exercise its administrative discretion in deciding how, in light of internal organization considerations, it may best proceed to develop the needed evidence and how its prior decision should be modified in light of such evidence as develops." We went on to emphasize: "At least in the absence of substantial justification for doing otherwise, a reviewing court may not, after determining that additional evidence is requisite for adequate review, proceed by dictating to the agency the methods, procedures, and time dimension of the needed inquiry and ordering the results to be reported to the court without opportunity for further consideration on the basis of the new evidence by the agency. Such a procedure clearly runs the risk of 'propel[ling] the court into the domain which Congress has set aside exclusively for the administrative agency.' SEC v. Chenery Corp., 332 U.S. 194, 196 (1947)."

Respondent NRDC argues that §[553] of the Administrative Procedure Act merely establishes lower procedural bounds and that a court may routinely require more than the minimum when an agency's proposed rule addresses complex or technical factual issues or "Issues of great Public Import." We have, however, previously shown that our decisions reject this view.... We also think the legislative history, even the part which it cites, does not bear out its contention. The Senate Report explains what eventually became §[553] thus: "This subsection states...the minimum requirements of public rule making procedure short of statutory hearing. Under it agencies might in addition confer with industry advisory committees, consult organizations, hold informal 'hearings,' and the like. Considerations of practicality, necessity, and public interest...will naturally govern the agency's determination of the extent to which public proceedings should go. Matters of great import, or those where the public submission of facts will be either useful to the agency or a protection to the public, should naturally be accorded more elaborate public procedures." S.Rep. No. 752, 79th Cong., 1st Sess., 14–15 (1945)....

The House Report is in complete accord: "The bill is an outline of minimum essential rights and procedures.... It affords private parties a means of knowing what their rights are and how they may protect them.... [The bill contains] the essentials of the different forms of administrative proceedings...." H.R.Rep. No. 1980, 79th Cong., 2d Sess., 9, 16–17 (1946). And the Attorney General's Manual on the Administrative Procedure Act 31, 35 (1947), a contemporaneous interpretation previously given some deference by this Court because of the role played by the Department of Justice in drafting the legislation, further confirms that view. In short, all of this leaves little doubt that Congress intended that the discretion of the *agencies* and not that of the courts be exercised in determining when extra procedural devices should be employed.

There are compelling reasons for construing §[553] in this manner. In the first place, if courts continually review agency proceedings to determine whether the agency employed procedures which were, in the court's opinion, perfectly tailored to reach what the court perceives to be the "best" or "correct" result, judicial review would be totally unpredictable. And the agencies, operating under this vague injunction to employ the "best" procedures and facing the threat of reversal if they did not, would undoubtedly adopt full adjudicatory procedures in every instance. Not only would this totally disrupt the statutory scheme, through which Congress enacted "a formula upon which opposing social and political forces have come to rest," Wong Yang Sung v. McGrath, 339 U.S. at 40, but all the inherent advantages of informal rulemaking would be totally lost.

Secondly, it is obvious that the court in these cases reviewed the agency's choice of procedures on the basis of the record actually produced at the hearing, and not on the basis of the information available to the agency when it made the decision to structure the proceedings in a certain way. This sort of Monday morning quarterbacking not only encourages but almost compels the agency to conduct all rulemaking proceedings with the full panoply of procedural devices normally associated only with adjudicatory hearings.

Finally, and perhaps most importantly, this sort of review fundamentally misconceives the nature of the standard for judicial review of an agency rule. The court below uncritically assumed that additional procedures will automatically result in a more adequate record because it will give interested parties more of an opportunity to participate and contribute to the proceedings. But informal rulemaking need not be based solely on the transcript of a hearing held before an agency. Indeed, the agency need not even hold a formal hearing. See 5 U.S.C.A. §553(c). Thus, the adequacy of the "record" in this type of proceeding is not correlated directly to the type of procedural devices employed, but rather turns on whether the agency has followed the statutory mandate of the Administrative Procedure Act or other relevant statutes. If the agency is compelled to support the rule which it ultimately adopts with the type of record produced only after a full adjudicatory hearing, it simply will have no choice but to conduct a full adjudicatory hearing prior to promulgating every rule. In sum, this sort of unwarranted judicial examination of perceived procedural shortcomings of a rulemaking proceeding can do nothing but seriously interfere with that process prescribed by Congress....

In short, nothing in the APA,...the circumstances of this case, the nature of the issues being considered, past agency practice, or the statutory mandate under which the Commission operates, permitted the court to review and overturn the rulemaking proceeding on the basis of the procedural devices employed (or not employed) by the Commission so long as the Commission employed at least the statutory *minima*, a matter about which there is no doubt in this case.

There remains, of course, the question of whether the challenged rule finds sufficient justification in the administrative proceedings that it should be upheld by the reviewing court. Judge Tamm, concurring in the result reached by the majority of the Court of Appeals, thought that it did not. There are also intimations in the majority opinion which suggest that the judges who joined it likewise may have thought the administrative proceedings an insufficient basis upon which to predicate the rule in question. We accordingly remand so that the Court of Appeals may review the rule as the Administrative Procedure Act provides. We have made it abundantly clear before that when there is a contemporaneous explanation of the agency decision, the validity of that action must "stand or fall on the propriety of that finding, judged, of course, by the appropriate standard of review. If that finding is not sustainable on the administrative record made, then the Comptroller's decision must be vacated and the matter remanded to him for further consideration." Camp v. Pitts, 411 U.S. 138, 143 (1973). The court should engage in this kind of review and not stray beyond the judicial province to explore the procedural format or to impose upon the agency its own notion of which procedures are "best" or most likely to further some vague, undefined public good....

[The procedural obstacles posed by the court of appeals] border on the Kafkaesque. Nuclear energy may some day be a cheap, safe source of power or it may not. But Congress has made a choice to at least try nuclear energy, establishing a reasonable review process in which courts are to play only a limited role. The fundamental policy questions appropriately resolved in Congress and in the state legislatures are not subject to reexamination in the federal courts under the guise of judicial review of agency action. Time may prove wrong the decision to develop nuclear energy,[54] but it is Congress or the States within their appropriate agencies which must eventually make that judgment. Reversed and remanded.

## COMMENTARY AND QUESTIONS

1. **Tactics.** In procedural terms, what was the NRC attempting to do in *Vermont Yankee*? By shifting the safety and radiation waste disposal questions into an informal rulemaking proceeding, thereafter to be published as a regulation that could be simply incorporated by reference, the agency would avoid having to face questioning and cross-examination on the issue in all future licensing adjudications. If the question remained in the contested cases, it would be subject to all the trial type procedures: full notice, full discovery, full cross examination, full right to present contrary evidence. In the rule-making proceeding itself, the agency did give hybrid procedures, more than mere notice and comment rule-making, but it prohibited discovery and much cross-examination. Would those really have made much difference to the agency's ultimate decision? After the *Vermont Yankee* decision, can agencies push environmental intervenors back into the closet, or do the continuing requirements of judicial review keep the intervenors as active players despite Justice Rehnquist's opinion?

2. **What was the holding of *Vermont Yankee?*** *Vermont Yankee* is a ringing denunciation of the Court of Appeal's requirements of agency procedures to benefit citizen environmental intervenors. Justice Rehnquist successfully argued that the APA's procedural minimum requirements for agencies were now also the maximum procedures that courts could require. Ironically, in doing so he relied on cases like *Wong Yang Sung*, in which the Court had actually granted extended process far beyond statutory requirements in order to protect individuals against agency procedures. What narrow exceptions to the new rule against court-expanded procedures would the Rehnquist opinion allow? He notes several situations in which courts may force agencies to grant more process.[55] But note the penultimate paragraph in the *Vermont Yankee* excerpt. The entire case was sent back for further review on the adequacy of the factual record: whether the NRC had shown enough facts so that a court could determine that reasonable NRC officials could or could

---

54. [Eds.: What does this latter clause imply? Cf. Chapter 6 on pre-emption of state nuclear regulations.]

55. One he doesn't note is the entire sector of agency adjudications. Since the APA provides no standards for less-than-formal adjudications, courts are not limited by the Vermont *Yankee* rationale in their ability to require that various procedures be added to agencies' informal adjudications.

not have decided as they did. This is a second kind of procedural argument — that for the *courts'* own sake, rather than for citizens, agencies must produce a sufficient formal or informal review record to permit judges to apply whatever standard of substantive review applies to the decision. The needs of judicial reviewers thus can still become the tail that wags the dog (as in *Overton Park*).

3. **The substantive question on the *Vermont Yankee* record.** The factual issue that triggered the *Vermont Yankee* remand appears to have been the shakiness of the report by Dr. Pittman, which was the basis of the NRC decision. Dr. Pittman had devoted most of his report to proposed federal repositories for above-ground storage of wastes, and less than two pages to the problem of geologic waste disposal. The NRC subsequently abandoned above-ground storage, and turned to geologic disposal solutions (although these have also been almost impossible to site). The further problem was that the Pittman report, upon which the NRC rule was based, had been produced without an extensive research effort. Might cross examination, if it had been available, have usefully focused on the thinness of this particular piece of evidence?

4. **Vermont Yankee, remand and back.** What ultimately happened with the nuclear waste rule? The NRC prepared a protocol rule with further documentation and research, reasserting its determination of an extremely low risk factor, based on an assumption that nuclear wastes would not be released into the environment. The Court upheld this optimistic determination against skeptical citizen challenge—

> The zero-release assumption — a policy judgment concerning one line in a conservative Table designed for the limited purpose of individual licensing decisions — is within the bounds of reasoned decisionmaking. It is not our task to determine what decision we, as Commissioners, would have reached. Our only task is to determine whether the Commission has considered the relevant factors and articulated a rational connection between the facts found and the choice made. Under this standard, we think the Commission's zero-release assumption, within the context of Table S-3 as a whole, was not arbitrary and capricious. Baltimore Gas & Electric v. NRDC, 462 U.S. 87 (1983).

5. **The "hard look" doctrine.** Prior to *Vermont Yankee*, and subsequent to the decision as well, federal courts have enunciated what is called the "hard look" doctrine: when Congress has set a statutory standard for agencies to apply, courts must see enough evidence on the record to be satisfied that the agency itself took a "hard look" at all relevant facts and the statutory standards that applied to them. The "hard look" determination is obviously subjective. Does *Vermont Yankee* do anything to dampen the courts' scrutiny of an agency's hard look?

6. **Rulemaking/adjudication: tactical considerations.** Other settings illustrate other tactical uses of the rulemaking/adjudication distinction. In some cases, unlike the NRC in *Vermont Yankee*, an agency will seek to proceed by adjudication, rather than rule-making, because subsequent courts do not hold agencies to the terms of their adjudicative precedents as strictly as they do to published rules. Conversely, regulated parties sometimes want to have rule-making on a matter because, unlike adjudication, rule-making is prospective and cannot penalize past activities. Regulated parties, on the other hand, sometimes prefer adjudication,

because of the formal trial-type procedures that normally accompany agency adjudicative processes.

Yet another twist shows judicial use of the rulemaking/adjudication distinction. In New York v. Thomas, 802 F.2d 1443 (D.C. Cir. 1986), then-Judge Scalia used the argument of mandatory rulemaking to nullify an environmental injunction on acid rain. According to §115 of the Clean Air Act (the result of a strenuous compromise between environmentalists and polluters), once EPA makes a formal determination that transboundary international air pollution is occurring, and that the foreign country (i.e., Canada) grants reciprocal standing to injured Americans, then the EPA must ensure that state air pollution plans take account of such acid precipitation and restrict it. Section 115 was used by Ontario and several downwind states, including New York and Massachusetts, to try to abate acid rain coming from Midwestern states. Just before he left office, President Carter's EPA administrator Douglas Costle made a formal finding under §115, dubbed the "Costle hand grenade," requiring certain states to clean up their acid rain emissions. Judge Scalia overturned the trial court's injunction on the ground that what Costle had done was "rulemaking" (because, like a rule under the APA definition, it had "future effect"), and therefore was void because EPA had not gone through notice and comment rulemaking before acting.[56] Would this unprecedented argument overrule *Overton Park*? There the Secretary's §4(f) decision clearly had future force and effect. If the *Thomas* opinion were followed more broadly, it would be a potent administrative law weapon for environmentalists and polluters alike, requiring any administrative decision that has future effect to go through notice and comment rulemaking, a possibility that would effectively bring most government to a halt. It was probably just an anomoly.

The distinctions between rulemaking and adjudication, and their tactical consequences, emphasize that administrative law is surprisingly young and evolving. Interesting administrative law issues arise in many areas of environmental law and will be repeatedly encountered in later chapters.[57]

*The simple plan: That they should take, who have the power, and they should keep, who can.*

— Meeker v. City of East Orange, 74 A. 379, 385 (N.J. 1909)

---

56. The Supreme Court has never specified when an agency must proceed by rulemaking as opposed to adjudication. The Scalia opinion found little precedent, and directed most of its analysis to a question not presented, whether policy rulemaking could be done without notice and comment, an argument that presumed the principal question.

57. Chapter 14, for instance, considers whether, when citizen environmentalists have proved a statutory violation, courts may permit violations to continue, based on traditional common law balancing of the equities (i.e. which party's interests and which policy considerations are more important). The Supreme Court, with one dissent, has said that judges can override legislation they consider to be outweighed by other judicial considerations.

# E. STATUTORY INTERPRETATION: HOW, BY WHOM?

## Section 1. JUDICIAL REVIEW OF AGENCY INTERPRETATIONS OF LAW

### Chevron U.S.A., Inc. v. Natural Resources Defense Council
United States Supreme Court, 1984
467 U.S. 837

[Section 111 of the Clean Air Act,[58] requires that tougher permit standards, based on "best available technology" (see Chapters Eight & Nine), must be applied to any "new source" of pollution in areas that violate existing air quality standards. A "source" was defined in the statute as "any building, structure, facility, or installation which emits or may emit any air pollutant." In 1980, the latter statutory phrase had been interpreted by the EPA to mean that every new sub-unit or smokestack of a factory was a source that had to meet those higher standards. In 1981, however, the agency changed its definition, applying a regulatory "bubble"[59] concept: the new regulation defined the statutory term "source" to mean "all of the pollutant-emitting activities which belong to the same industrial grouping, are located on one or more contiguous or adjacent properties, and are under the control of the same person or persons." The result was that the EPA could now view an entire industrial site as a single source. If a company could offset new emissions within a plant by closing old dirtier units, there would be no *net* increase of pollutants coming from within the bubble, so new construction did not count as a new source and did not have to meet the tougher standards. The Natural Resources Defense Council sued.]

STEVENS, J. The question presented by this case is whether EPA's decision to allow states to treat all of the pollution-emitting devices within the same industrial grouping as though they were encased within a single "bubble" is based on a reasonable construction of the statutory term "stationary source."

When a court reviews an agency's construction of the statute which it administers, it is confronted with two questions.

First, always, is the question whether Congress has directly spoken to the precise question at issue. If the intent of Congress is clear, that is the end of the matter; for the court, as well as the agency, must give effect to the unambiguously expressed intent of Congress.[60]

If, however, the court determines Congress has not directly addressed the precise question at issue, the court does not simply impose its own construction on the statute, as would be necessary in the absence of an administrative interpretation. Rather, if the statute is silent or ambiguous with respect to this specific issue, the question for the court is whether the agency's answer is based on a permissible construction of the statute.[61] "The power of an administrative agency to

58. 42 U.S.C.A. §7411, as amended in 1977 and 1990.

59. Air pollution "bubbles" are considered in the next chapter.

60. The judiciary is the final authority on issues of statutory construction and must recheck administrative constructions which are contrary to clear congressional intent. If a court, employing traditional tools of statutory construction, ascertains that Congress had an intention on the precise question at issue, that intention is the law and must be given effect [as a matter of the judges' own statutory interpretation]. [This is footnote 9 in the original opinion.]

61. The Court need not conclude that the agency construction was the only one it permissibly could have adopted to uphold the construction, or even the reading the court would have reached if the question had initially arisen in a judicial proceeding.

administer a congressionally created...program necessarily requires the formula-tion of policy in the making of rules to fill any gap left, implicitly or explicitly, by Congress."

The principle of deference to administrative interpretations has been consis-tently followed by this Court whenever decision as to the meaning or reach of the statute has involved reconciling conflicting policies, and a full understanding of the force of the statutory policy on the given situation has depended upon more than ordinary knowledge respecting the matters subjected to agency regulations. *Hearst Publications*, 322 U.S. 111 (1944).... "If this choice represents accommoda-tion of conflicting policies that were committed to the agency's care by the statute, we should not disturb it unless it appears from the statute or its a legislative his-tory that the accommodation is not one that Congress would have sanctioned...." United States. v. Shimer, 367 U.S. 374, 382 (1961).

Our review of the EPA's varying interpretations of the word "source" — both before and after the 1977 amendments — convinces us that the agency primarily responsible for administering this important legislation has consistently inter-preted it flexibly — not in a sterile textual vacuum, but in the context of imple-menting policy decisions in a technical and complex arena.... When a challenge to an agency construction of a statutory provision, fairly conceptualized, really cen-ters on the wisdom of the agency's policy, rather than whether it is a reasonable choice within a gap left open by Congress, the challenge must fail. In such a case, federal judges — who have no constituency — have the duty to respect legitimate policy choices made by those who do. Responsibilities for assessing the wisdom of such policy choices and resolving the struggle between competing views of the public interests are not judicial ones: "Our Constitution vests such responsibilities in the political branches." TVA v. Hill, 437 U.S. 153, 195 (1978). Reversed.

### COMMENTARY AND QUESTIONS

1. **The strategics of definitions.** Note how critical differences can often turn on agency interpretations of key statutory terms, "source" in *Chevron*, "feasible and prudent" in *Overton Park*, "aggrieved" in *Scenic Hudson*, "point source" in the CWA, and so on. In one famous example, the Reagan administration's EPA simul-taneously improved the average gas mileage of the Chrysler Corporation's "pas-senger vehicle" and "light truck" fleets by re-interpreting mini-vans as the latter, not the former, thereby shifting them from embarassment in one category to enhancement of another. Independent judicial scrutiny of these interpretations obviously can make significant differences for good and ill.

In *Chevron*, the interpretation of the term "source" as incorporating air pollution "bubbles" had immediate and far-reaching effects on American industry and air quality. The agency had strong arguments in favor of the bubble interpretation. Do you see how a bubble might result in cleaner air, despite allowing lower standards? If an industry considering upgrading its physical facilities knows it will be held to the highest standards, how might that affect its ongoing plant investment deci-sions? The question in every case is whether the agency's interpretation is to be second-guessed by the courts, or be deferred to.

2. **Judicial deference to agency interpretations of law, in *Chevron*.** Does *Chevron* set out a principle of general deference to agency interpretations of statutes, or just

for agency gap-filling? The Court holds that the agency can so interpret the term "source," "making...rules to fill any gap left, implicitly or explicitly, by Congress," because EPA is following Congress's overall statutory mandate to clean up the air and there is no evidence of any congressional intention on the particular question of bubbling. The *Chevron* rule has spread far beyond gap-filling, however, and is often used as a general deference rule.

The standard analysis drawn from *Chevron* has two steps, with a great deal of potential fudge in each:

- Step One: Given the statutory language, is *the intent of Congress* (in the eyes of the reviewing court) *clear*? If so, the court will declare that interpretation, whether the agency agrees or not.

- Step Two: If the court decides the meaning is not clear, then the court must review the agency's interpretation deferentially, upholding it if the agency's answer is based on "a permissible construction of the statute."

In Step One, great flexibility lies in the judicial determination whether or not Congress has "directly spoken" to the "precise question at issue" or "unambiguously expressed" its intent. There is even more flexibility in what courts will look at in deciding whether the congressional intent is clear or ambiguous: will a court look only at the specific words of the challenged statutory provision standing alone, or also at other relevant language in the statute, or at the provision in the full context of the statute, or at the legislative history of the provision in Congress, or at congressional policy on point, or is it open to all the other contextual analysis tools used in statutory interpretation? If courts close their eyes to anything but the specific words, they are in an irrational vacuum, but if they open their eyes to all that is relevant to determining intent, deference is quite diluted.

In Step Two, the question "whether the agency's answer is based on a permissible construction of the statute," likewise incorporates highly subjective weighing. Courts tend to go through all the traditional elements anyway, replicating a full judicial interpretation process, in order to see if the agency's interpretation is "permissible."[62] Judges tend to believe that courts are always competent to interpret statutes. They tend to find more than one interpretation "permissible" when they don't have a strong opinion of what the correct meaning is. Deference is decided case-by-case by the deferrers themselves. And what of the widely varying relationships between particular agencies and particular statutes? In his post-*Chevron* analysis, Professor Colin Diver noted that still "the decision to grant deference

---

62. That in fact was what was done in the leading administrative law case declaring deference to agency interpretations of statutes, Hearst v. NLRB, 322 U.S. 111 (1944), and in a recent such case, Holly Farms v. NLRB, 517 U.S. 392 (1996). In *Holly Farms* the Court said "Administrators and reviewing courts must take care to assure that exemptions...are not so expansively interpreted as to deny protection...the Act was designed to reach." Note that this implies that if the agency *broadened* the exemptions, courts could appropriately, on a *policy* analysis, defer much less to the agency interpretations. The Court also said "courts...must respect the judgment of the agency empowered to apply the law to varying fact patterns, even if the issue 'with nearly equal reason [might] be resolved one way rather than another.'" The word "even" missed the point. Can courts *decline* to defer when the interpretations are *not* "nearly equal"? In this labor case, at least, Justices Rehnquist, Scalia, O'Connor, and Thomas declared in dissent that "the deference owed to an expert tribunal cannot be allowed to slip into a judicial inertia...."

depends on various attributes of the agency's legal authority and functions, and of the administrative interpretation at issue."[63] Should courts defer to interpretations of the Federal Highway Administration, as in *Overton Park*, where the §4(f) parkland environmental protection provision was an unwelcome burr under the agency's bureaucratic saddle, to the same degree as they defer to EPA on toxicity definitions? Even after *Chevron*, would it not be a permissible argument against judicial deference to an agency interpretation that waters down a statutory provision, to show the court that the same agency, disliking that particular provision's strictness, had originally testified *against* its passage?

3. **Judicial deference to agency interpretations of law, after *Chevron*.** *Chevron* is the leading case cited by courts when they wish to defer broadly to agency interpretations of law. The contrary position is that, in many cases, courts will find that a statutory meaning is sufficiently clear that the court can determine on its own whether the agency interpretation of law is correct. Since *Chevron*, the Supreme Court has repeatedly demonstrated that it will dictate its own interpretation of statutory meaning, and will not defer to an agency's interpretation if it believes that standard norms of statutory construction, as interpreted by the court, would lead to a different answer. See INS v. Cardoza-Fonseca, 480 U.S. 421 (1987). The line between deference and judicial takeover of the fundamental decision can thus get quite hazy.

Deference to agencies' legal interpretations is most likely where a legislative scheme seems highly technical, with a wide range of details delegated to the agency's special expertise. *Chevron*, with its intricate air pollution act technicalities, was a particularly apt subject for deference to the agency on legal as well as factual matters. The less daunting the legal provisions faced by the courts, the less likely they are to be deferential on questions of law. Within judicial chambers the tendency is to apply the familiar judicial methods to reach an interpretation, then to consider whether the agency's interpretation agrees with the judge's view of the term's meaning, plain or fancy.[64]

4. **The "plain meaning" finesse.** It is interesting to see how courts since *Chevron* can avoid deferring to agency interpretations of law when they disagree with them. One of the approaches is the "plain meaning" theory — that if the legal meaning of a term is clear to a court on the face of a statute or regulation, then the court will apply that interpretation regardless of the expert agency's differing opinion.[65] A CERCLA case example of this dealt with §120(h) of the 1986 Superfund Amendments and Reauthorization Act (SARA), which imposed notice and covenant requirements on federal agencies that transfer real property contaminated by hazardous substances. Section 120(h)(1) provides in relevant part that —

> the head of such department, agency, or instrumentality shall include in such contract *notice of the type and quantity of such hazardous substance and*

---

63. Colin Diver, Statutory Interpretation in the Administrative State, 133 U. Penn. L. Rev. 549, 562 (1985).

64. On this point, also, see Diver, 133 U. Penn. L. Rev. 549, 562.

65. See Murphy, Old Maxims Never Die: The Plain Meaning Rule and Statutory Interpretation in Modern Federal Courts, 75 Colum. L.Rev. 1299 (1975).

*notice of the time at which such storage, release or disposal took place,* to the extent such information is available on the basis of a complete search of agency files.

In its regulations, however, EPA applied the notice requirements of §120(h)(1) only to real property on which hazardous substances were stored, released, or disposed of "during the time the property was owned by the United States." The EPA believed Congress was primarily concerned with federal facilities (chiefly military bases and nuclear weapons facilities) whose own operations involved the storage, release, or disposal of hazardous substances, and that §120(h) therefore was not intended to apply where contamination occurred prior to the government's acquisition of the property. This interpretation, it concluded, was "more appropriate..." and would avoid imposing unfair and unmanageable obligations on federal agencies that had no role in the storage, release or disposal of hazardous substances. The reviewing court held differently —

> By its terms, §120(h) requires agencies to disclose *all* information of the kind specified (namely, the "type and quantity" of hazardous substances on the property and "the time at which [the] storage, release or disposal took place") to the extent the information is contained in the agency's files, and the plain meaning of Congress's words thus extends the government's notice obligations to properties [contaminated] by prior owners.... Where, as here, the statute's language is plain, "the sole function of the courts is to enforce it according to its terms." We therefore need not look beyond the words of the statute to the legislative history for guidance. Hercules v. EPA, 938 F.2d 276, 280, 281 (D.C. Cir. 1991).

To get the "plain meaning," the *Hercules* court nevertheless reviewed legislative history, contextual analysis, policy analysis of congressional intent in the Act, the statute's broad remedial purposes, the limited agency burdens that would be imposed by the notice requirement, and the legislative purpose of dealing fairly with subsequent purchasers. This typical exercise in statutory interpretation demonstrates how ready courts are to embark on the familiar task of interpreting legal language, going far beyond plain meaning.

5. **Organic decisionmaking?** The *Chevron* tests can operate to insulate government agencies' interpretations of key statutory provisions from judicial scrutiny. If judges incline toward overriding an agency interpretation, on the other hand, under *Chevron* they can find a "plain meaning" for the statutory term that differs from the agency's, and override. The process of finding that "plain meaning," moreover, apparently does not have to take place on the face of the text, but can be based on the full range of judicial statutory interpretation techniques.

Flexibility exists, moreover, beyond the terms of *Chevron* analysis. If a court dislikes an agency position on an ambiguous term, but cannot say that an agency's interpretation is not a "permissible" reading of the statute, the court can utilize the old "delegation doctrine" restriction on agency actions. See Justice Rehnquist's arguments in the OSHA benzene and cotton-dust cases, attempting to reject OSHA's definition of "unsafe" environmental exposures on delegation grounds —

that Congress had not given the agency sufficient details on how to regulate — in effect rejecting the agency's gapfilling function.[66]

## F.  ADMINISTRATIVE PROCESS — PROPOSED IMPROVEMENTS

Regulatory reforms are repeatedly proposed, from all corners of the political compass and from government itself. In the 1990s environmental regulation faced frontal assaults by marketplace forces in the 104th Congress, a Clinton Administration program of "Re-inventing Government," continued experiments in negotiated rulemaking, market-enlisting economic incentive programs to change the traditional command-and-control regulatory model, and a number of agency initiatives to simplify regulatory procedures.

The 104th Congress, as noted in Chapters One and Two, produced a flurry of industry-inspired assaults on environmental regulation, some quite specific, targeting the Clean Water and Endangered Species Acts, and some quite generic. The House of Representatives, for instance, passed a "regulatory moratorium" drafted by Gordon Gooch, a Project Relief lobbyist for the petrochemical industry, which included as its major provision a freeze and rollback of almost all federal regulations proposed after November 1994.[67] The moratorium was an example of a crude blunt "reform" initiative. Its scope was breathtaking; in fact it suspended a host of rules without knowing what they were.[68] "Regulatory Reform Act" bills, like S.343 in Chapter Two, would set up an intricate series of procedural and analytical roadblocks before agencies could put forward environmentally-protective regulations, although the 104th Congress bills nhad fast-track exemptions for pesticide approvals and similar market-permissive rules.[69] The intent of these bills appears to be regulatory "paralysis by analysis." "Property rights" bills have provided that regulatory agencies would have to compensate regulated interests if any portion of their property was reduced in value by twenty percent or more; if the agency did not pay, regulations would be unenforceable.[70] The Unfunded Mandates Reform

---

66. Industrial Union Dept., AFL-CIO v. American Petroleum Institute, 448 U.S. 607 (1980)(Rehnquist, J., concurring opinion); American Textile Manuf. Inst. v. Donovan, 452 U.S. 490 (1981)(Rehnquist, dissent); (both opinions arguing that the agency had too much leeway filling gaps in the regulatory definition. For delegation arguments from the opposite pole, see Schoenbrod, The Delegation Doctrine: Could the Court Give It Substance? 83 Mich. L.Rev. 1223 (1985).

67. H.R. 450, 104th Cong., 1st Sess. (1995); passed the House on Feb. 24, 1995 with a vote of 276 to 146. 141 CONG. REC. D239–01 (daily ed. Feb. 24, 1995). Senate Bill 219, S. 219, 104th Cong., 1st Sess. (1995), a similar but more limited measure, passed the Senate on March 29, 1995. See 141 CONG. REC. S4758 (daily ed. Mar. 29, 1995). It also sought to create a process giving Congress 45 days to review and reject all regulations before they took effect.

68. The bill required the President to inform Congress within 30 days how many and which rules it had thus suspended. H.R. 450, 104th Cong., 1st Sess §3(b)(1995). Estimates put the number of regulations that would have been suspended by the Senate bill at 900, and by the House bill at 4300.

69. H.R. 1022, 104th Cong., 1st Sess. (1995) (passed by House Mar. 3, 1995);S. 343,; H.R. 2586, 104th Cong., 1st Sess. Title III (1995).

70. S. 605, 104th Cong., 1st Sess. §403 (1995). The bills would also have greatly expanded the jurisdiction of the regulation-averse Court of Federal Claims. On that court's aggressive compensation bent, see generally Thomas Hanley, *A Developer's Dream: The United States Claims Court's New Analysis of Section 404 Takings Challenges*, 19 B.C. ENVTL. AFF. L. REV. 317 (1991).

Act burdens federal-state regulatory systems of "cooperative federalism" by placing procedural hurdles before Congress can delegate regulatory roles to the states.[71]

These political initiatives to change regulatory practices to date have come to very little, as legislators have discovered that attacks on environmental regulation, once the media covers them, became political hot potatoes, ready to burn anyone who pick them up. With the exception of the unfunded mandates law, marketplace attempts to undercut the regulatory process are either in remission or keeping a lower profile.

Other reform attempts have come from within the executive branch itself — the "Reinventing Government" Executive Order on Regulatory Planning and Review,[72] the EPA's Regulatory Unified Agenda implementations of the Reinventing Government Executive Order,[73] EPA's Project XL Multimedia Permitting;[74] and various Advisory Councils established by EPA under the Federal Advisory Committee Act, PL 92463, including the Common Sense Initiative program, the National Environmental Justice Advisory Council, the Federal Facilities Environmental Restoration Dialogue Committee, and the National Advisory Council for Environmental Policy and Technology (NACEPT).[75]

**PROJECT XL: "MULTIMEDIA" PERMITTING...** In an attempt to reduce the expensive and lengthy permit process, the EPA has initiated the program known as "Project XL" — a multipurpose environmental permit designed to replace the extreme complexities of some existing procedures. Under the program the agency issues a single master permit — simplifying the regulatory process by combining or eliminating the need for separate permits in areas such as air, water, and hazardous wastes. The purpose of Project XL is to allow companies freedom to take innovative approaches to pollution control by allowing them to skirt certain regulatory requirements in exchange for setting up an alternative plan that will produce superior overall environmental results. The "multimedia" permit is a single, performance-based plan which considers a facility's total net impact on the environment rather than attempting to regulate individual technologies used. The danger, of course, is that in such master permit processes some of the substantive requirements of public and environmental health and safety get compromised If erosion of norms can be avoided, however, the rationality of the approach militates in favor of the experiment.

---

71. Pub. L. No. 104–4; 109 Stat. 48 (1996). In practice the Unfunded Mandates Act has generally been honored in the breach. The initiative is echoed in Scalia, J.'s *Printz* decision, 117 S.Ct. 2365 (1997). On the general principle, see David Dana, the Case for Unfunded Mandates, 69 USC L.R. 1 (1995).

72. Executive Order 12866, 58 FR 51735 (September 30, 1993).

73. See for example 60 FR 59658 and 60 FR 60604 (Nov. 28, 1995).

74. See for example Regulatory Reinvention (XL) Pilot Projects, 62 FR 19872 (April 23, 1997); EPA Permits Improvement Team Concept Paper on Environmental Permitting and Task Force Recommendations, 61 FR 41252 (Aug. 7, 1996).

75. See 61 FR 21856 (May 10, 1996); NACEPT provides advice and recommendations to the Administrator of EPA on a broad range of environmental policy issues. The Administrator has asked NACEPT to concentrate on regulatory incentives that could be used to promote a community-based approach (CBEP) to environmental management, assess whether EPA's information systems are designed to support CBEP and various new approaches to environmental protection relative to partnerships with states and regulated entities, and identify criteria and recommend a framework that the Agency can use to measure regulatory success. 61 FR 41606 (August 9, 1996).

**EPA'S INDUSTRY-SPECIFIC "COMMON SENSE INITIATIVE"**[76]... EPA announced in 1994 that it would begin an experiment in cooperation with industry groups to rationalize regulatory approaches where it appeared that equal or greater pollution abatements could be achieved by alternative lower-cost abatement strategies. Targeting the auto, petroleum refining, iron and steel, metal finishing and plating, computer and electronics, and printing industries, the approach presumes that in many cases industry expertise and self-interest will identify protective measures of greater efficiency and oversell net savings. One example is benzene emissions at oil refining facilities. The industry identified the loading stage — the point at which refined petroleum products were being nozzled into tankers or other transport facilities — as generating more ambient benzene emissions than the refining facilities themselves, and these emissions from loading were abatable at far lower cost. EPA proposes to allow that industry to comply with benzene standards by rolling back loading stage emissions rather than requiring the far more difficult and expensive refining process emission cutbacks.

This "common sense initiative" has the potential to improve both the tone and the overall results of our massive command and control regulatory systems, but obviously must take account of the opposing tensions inherent in regulation of economic forces. EPA acceptance of such tradeoffs requires full, comparative, accurate information before and after each tradeoff, and careful implementation and monitoring. A fear on the industry side is that there is no EPA estoppel: the accomplishment of net gains by an industry-suggested alternative does not prevent EPA from coming back later for further incremental improvements under the bypassed restrictions.

**NEGOTIATED RULEMAKING**... A number of regulatory experiments with negotiated rulemaking — "reg-neg" — have taken place in the environmental setting, particularly in EPA and the Department of Interior, as noted later in Chapter 21, under the terms of the Administrative Dispute Resolution Act (P.L. 101-552) and the Negotiated Rulemaking Act (P.L. 101-648), passed as amendments to the adjudication section of the Administrative Procedure Act.

**A REGULATORY EXPERIMENT — "OMNIBUS," OR CONSOLIDATED, GENERIC RULEMAKING**... Another example of a regulatory agency's procedural innovation occurred when the Occupational Health and Safety Administration (OSHA) desperately decided to forego the traditional unending treadmill of regulating contaminants in the workplace one-by-one — a process by which the agency was constantly falling farther and farther behind — and instead make an omnibus rule that would simultaneously regulate more than 400 substances. The experiment went to court in a consolidated appeal, in a lawsuit filed for different reasons by both industrial management and labor:

---

76. On EPA's CSI, see for example: Common Sense Initiative Council Federal Advisory Committee, 59 FR 55117 (Nov. 3, 1994), and Introduction to The Regulatory Plan and the Unified Agenda of Federal Regulatory and Deregulatory Actions, 62 FR 57003 (Oct. 29, 1997).

## AFL-CIO, et al. v. OSHA
United States Court of Appeal for the 11th Circuit, 1992
965 F.2d 962

FAY, C.J. On June 7, 1988, OSHA published a Notice of Proposed Rulemaking for its Air Contaminants Standard. 53 Fed. Reg. 20960-21393. In this single rulemaking, OSHA proposed to issue new or revised PELs (Permittable Exposure Limits) for over 400 substances.

Unlike most of the OSHA standards previously reviewed by the courts, the Air Contaminants Standard regulates not a single toxic substance, but 428 different substances. The agency explained its decision to issue such an omnibus standard in its Notice of Proposed Rulemaking:

> OSHA has issued only 24 substance-specific health regulations since its creation It has not been able to review the many thousands of currently unregulated chemicals in the workplace nor to keep up with reviewing the several thousand new chemicals introduced since its creation. It has not been able to fully review the literature to determine if lower limits are needed for many of the approximately 400 substances it now regulates.

> Using past approaches and practices, OSHA could continue to regulate a small number of the high priority substances and those of greatest public interest. However, it would take decades to review currently used chemicals and OSHA would never be able to keep up with the many chemicals which will be newly introduced in the future. 53 Fed.Reg. at 20963.

For this reason, OSHA "determined that it was necessary to modify this approach through the use of *generic* rulemaking, which would simultaneously cover many substances." 54 Fed. Reg. at 2333. "Generic" means something "common to or characteristic of a whole group or class...." Previous "generic" rulemakings by OSHA have all dealt with requirements that, once promulgated, could be applied to numerous different situations.[77]... By contrast, the new Air Contaminants Standard is an amalgamation of 428 unrelated substance exposure limits. There is little common to this group of diverse substances except the fact that OSHA considers them toxic and in need of regulation. In fact, this rulemaking is the antithesis of a "generic" rulemaking; it is a set of 428 specific and individual substance exposure limits. Therefore, OSHA's characterization of this as a "generic" rulemaking is somewhat misleading.

Nonetheless we find nothing in the OSH Act that would prevent OSHA from addressing multiple substances in a single rulemaking. Moreover, because the statute leaves this point open, [however,] and because OSHA's interpretation of the statute is reasonable, it is appropriate for us to defer to OSHA's interpretation. See *Chevron....*

However, we believe the PEL for each substance must be able to stand independently, i.e., that each PEL must be supported by substantial evidence in the record considered as a whole and accompanied by adequate explanation. OSHA may not, by using such multi-substance rulemaking, ignore the requirements of the OSH Act. Both the industry petitioners and the union argue that such disregard was what, in essence, occurred. Regretfully, we agree....

---

77. The three "generic" rulemakings were Cancer Policy, 29 C.F.R. Part 1990; Access to Employee Exposure and Medical Records Regulation, 29 C.F.R. §1910.20; Hazard Communication Standard, 29 C.F.R. §1910.1200.

[The Court held that:

(1) the evidence presented by OSHA failed to establish that the prior-existing exposure limits for the workplace presented significant risks of material health impairment, or that the new proposed standards eliminated or substantially lessened the risk;

(2) OSHA did not sufficiently establish that the new PELs were economically or technologically feasible; and

(3) OSHA had not sufficiently explained why it had allowed an across-the-board four-year delay before implementation of the new rule was required.

The rule was remanded to OSHA to try again, leaving open the practical question whether such omnibus rulemaking experiments offer a feasible prescription for resolving regulatory gridlock. ]

COMMENTARY AND QUESTIONS

1. **The quest for efficiency.** EPA's Project XL and Common Sense Initiative have faced problems with the battleground setting of interest-representation regulatory politics. OSHA's attempt to cope with the vast number of rulemakings Congress had required of it foundered on the rocks of judicial review, when the court's requirement of voluminous individual data bases for each proposed new standard proved quite simply to be impossible.

One of the dirty little secrets of American government is that legislatures do not give agencies the economic or political capital needed to enforce all the laws on the books. But a will to enforce, coupled with innovative administrative planning can improve upon the situation. EPA continues to try to make the administrative process "more transparent" so that citizen participation can enter into the bargaining process of regulation. Based on informal communications with OSHA, the agency is giving up the attempt to do consolidated rulemaking. EPA, on the other hand, is reportedly proceeding with major new "cluster rulemaking" under the Clean Water Act, treating classes of industry in the same business in an omnibus process. (EPA's job is easier than OSHA's because its statutory standards under the CWA are based on industry-wide "best available technology" rather than the individual safety of each substance standard as with OSHA.)

2. **Other reforms: Citizen oversight councils.** Citizen councils, built into governmental regulatory processes, offer an interesting innovations for environmental administrative law. (Chapter 11 reviews such councils in the rangeland setting.) Other notable examples of citizen councils were created in the aftermath of the Exxon-Valdez oilspill, bringing citizens most directly threatened by environmental hazards into the official public law process. Faced with the conclusion that official regulatory oversight and enforcement before the Alaska oil spill had been lax and complacent in the face of industry corner-cutting, three models of citizen oversight councils were initiated — a council formed in citizen negotiations with industry, a state-legislated citizens council, chaired by Professor Harry Bader who had helped conceptualize it, and a federal model of citizens council written into law in OPA '90. The first model was incorporated into the third. The state council, after its research began to produce embarrassing evidence of state non-enforcement of pollution laws, was defunded and shut down through the efforts of industry

lobbyists in the legislature. The terms of this innovative administrative experiment are interesting and potentially important far beyond the waters of the Gulf of Alaska. See Oil Pollution Act of 1994, 33 U.S.C.A. §2732; Alaska Stat. §24.20.160 et seq. (1990). These citizen councils offer valuable advantages in quality control efforts of both private and governmental resource protection activities, and are designed to be relatively immune from co-optation. These experiments bear continuing study as examples of utilitarian pluralism in government.

3. **"Collaborative governance."** From her study of environmental regulation at OSHA and EPA, Professor Jody Freeman has advocated experiments with "collaborative governance" to respond to the litany of criticisms about the quality, implementability, and legitimacy of rulemaking by agency establishments and cohorts of lobbyists. Collaborative governance would reorient regulatory reform toward joint problem solving and away from controlling discretion. Collaborative governance requires improved mechanisms for problem solving, broad participation, provisional solutions, the sharing of regulatory responsibility across the public-private divide, and flexible, engaged agencies:

> Recent experiments with multi-stakeholder decision-making processes, such as regulatory negotiation and Project XL, which offer parties more direct access to, and responsibility for, all stages of the administrative process are promising alternatives to discretion-constraining instruments. They have some potential to facilitate problem solving, produce better-quality rules, and create mechanisms of accountability that take advantage of the capacities of nongovernmental groups. They are not, however, without limitations.... All administrative law reform proposals must cope with the "structural embeddedness" of agencies.... It is still unclear whether a collaborative model that remains dependent upon interest groups can overcome the pathologies of interest-representation, including its strategic-bargaining orientation and its tendency to exclude less-organized interests. Moreover, the potential for a problem-oriented, deliberative dynamic to emerge in the administrative process may be undermined by the reality that "repeat players"...pursue their interests in a wide variety of settings beyond rule making and implementation.... Parties' interactions in the legislative process, litigation, election campaigns, and state and local regulation can hinder collaboration.... Freeman, Collaborative Governance in the Administrative State, 45 UCLA L.Rev. 1 (1997).

Nevertheless Professor Freeman concludes that the destructive and convoluted process of modern lobbyist-dominated interest-representation regulatory politics deserves to be rethought in a more transparent and articulated participatory decisionmaking system.

4. **Sunsets.** Sunsetting provisions are a regulatory reform device with mixed reviews. Much recent public interest legislation has been freighted with a provision suspending funds, authority, or both after a period of years, often five years, thereafter requiring renewal. This approach was touted as making agencies justify their work periodically in a democratic forum. In practice it has typically been attached to laws that do not have sustained marketplace political momentum, like the Endangered Species Act, and effectively guarantees that environmental protections passed into law have to be defended against assault every five years. Mining, lumbering, and grazing programs on public lands, Corps of Engineers draining and

damming programs, and the like, never seem to have sunsets attached to them. Administrative law, like the rest of life, is not consistently dominated by civic values or neutral principles, but rather is a continuing reflection of the convoluted tendencies of power coupled with human nature.

*I was always taught as I was growing up that democracy is not something you believe in, not something you hang your hat on. Democracy is something you do.*

— Abbie Hoffman, closing argument to jury, in Commonwealth v. Hoffman, et al.,
Amherst Mass. 1988

# PART THREE

# DIFFERENT MODES OF REGULATORY STANDARD-SETTING

## AN INTRODUCTION TO THE NEXT FOURTEEN CHAPTERS' "TAXONOMY" OF ENVIRONMENTAL STATUTORY DESIGNS

The next three Parts of this coursebook, in fourteen chapters, examine the intriguing analytical structure and details of modern environmental law regulatory systems, which are remarkable for their number and diversity. (The Statutory Capsule Appendix at the back of this book catalogues fifty major statutes, and there are many more that can be of significance in particular cases.) No one book can cover all environmental statutes — the Clean Air Act, Clean Water Act, or Superfund could each more than fill an entire semester of readings. The compromise chosen here is to study selected models — analyzing their structures, process, and enforcement mechanisms, their successes and failures. Each chapter focuses on one specific legislative approach, with most chapters focusing on one primary statutory example. By understanding a "taxonomy" of different statutory types, environmental lawyers can improve the depth, breadth, and speed of their analysis of any regulatory field. The categories set out in the taxonomy used here are not air-tight. Statutes overlap, and can contain multiple approaches.

Here is a brief digest of the fourteen chapters that follow, in three Parts, illustrating the "taxonomic" categories:

## PART III. DIFFERENT MODES OF REGULATORY STANDARD-SETTING

Part Three examines four basic statutory models, using several of the major command-and-control regulatory systems, showing how different laws go about the setting of regulatory standards. Major practical differences follow from the legislatures' different choices of approach in drawing the legal lines in each regulatory system between permissible pollution discharges and punishable violations.

**CHAPTER 8. HARM-BASED STANDARDS.** This chapter examines the way the Clean Air Act of 1970 provides for the definition of nationwide federal air quality emissions standards, primarily based on a complex process of measuring potential harm to human health from different levels of ambient air pollution, then generalizing to set federal baselines for safe levels of emissions, to be applied by complex regulatory structures in every state.

**CHAPTER 9. TECHNOLOGY-BASED STANDARD-SETTING.** The Clean Water Act of 1972 is the primary example of a sophisticated regulatory system in which the basic federal standards, to be applied nationwide, are defined by an EPA review of each category of industry that discharges pollution, in order to determine which pollution control technologies are both available and economically achievable. Performance standards, based on the results of adopting those best technologies, are then set for each category of dischargers and included in discharge permits.

**CHAPTER 10. TECHNOLOGY-FORCING STANDARD-SETTING.** In cases where pollution threats are imminent and serious, legislatures sometimes set standards at levels so stringent that they cannot be achieved with available technology. Target polluters must develop new control technology or prevent pollution by product reformulation or process changes. The Clean Air Act's auto pollution control provisions and the international phaseout of chloroflourocarbons are illustrations.

**CHAPTER 11. PROCESS-DRIVEN STANDARD-SETTING.** Standards can also be set as the outcome of procedures, rather than with reference to objective criteria like harm to human health or available technology. This chapter reviews some of the strengths and weaknesses of standards that are set in more or less political processes without objective substantive standards.

## PART IV. CHOICES OF STATUTORY DESIGNS AND STRATEGIES

**Chapter 12. COMMAND-AND-CONTROL AND THE ARRAY OF ALTERNATIVES,** reviews the classic regulatory model, and introduces market-enlisting alternatives that respond to erratic Congressional policy on command-and-control, and to issues of regulatory overkill.

**Chapter 13. DISCLOSURE STRATEGIES: NEPA'S STOP-AND-THINK LOGIC, AND THE POWER OF INFORMATION.** The National Environmental Policy Act, the Emergency Planning and Community Right-To-Know Act, and California's "Proposition 65" embody different types of disclosure strategies. "Information is power" in environmental law as well as in business. Mandatory disclosure of information raises the political and economic visibility of environmentally degrading activities, leading to improved protection processes.

**Chapter 14. ROADBLOCK STRATEGIES: STARK PROHIBITIONS AND THEIR VIABILITY.** Statutory roadblocks, like the Delaney Clause for carcinogens and the Endangered Species Act's stark bans on activities that harm listed species, can be necessary tools to enforce public values, but require careful implementation. When and how roadblocks get bypassed are key questions.

**Chapter 15. PRODUCT REGULATION & MARKET-ACCESS STRATEGIES.** Product regulation is an efficient means of regulating large manufacturers. Governmental approval before potentially dangerous products can be sold can proactively protect human health and the environment. But product regulation and restrictions on market access are resisted by the marketplace economy. Two laws that have a market-access/product regulation strategy — the Toxic Substances Control Act and Federal Insecticide, Fungicide, and Rodenticide Act — reflect these tensions.

**Chapter 16. MARKET-ENLISTING STATUTORY STRATEGIES: ACHIEVING ENVIRONMENTAL PROTECTIONS THROUGH ECONOMIC INCENTIVES, TAXES, AND TRADING.** Market-enlisting mechanisms are becoming increasingly important in environmental regulation as supplements and alternatives to command and control. Taxes, subsidies, preferential governmental purchasing, trading, and other market mechanisms — and the Clean Air Act's program of tradeable sulphur dioxide emissions rights — illustrate the possibilities.

**Chapter 17. LIFE-CYCLE WASTE CONTROL STRATEGIES: RCRA'S "CRADLE-TO-GRAVE" REGULATION.** The Resource Conservation and Recovery act regulates hazardous wastes from creation to ultimate disposal. It is also a composite of all the statutory taxonomy strategies presented in these fourteen chapters. Special issues include RCRA's criteria for determining whether waste is "hazardous," and its roadblock "land ban" against landfill disposal unless waste is treated to technology-based standards.

**Chapter 18. REMEDIAL LIABILITY STRATEGIES: CLEANUPS AND THEIR FUNDING UNDER CERCLA AND STATE PROGRAMS.** Cleanup statutes constitute a deterrent to pollution, as well as ensuring that contaminated sites will be remediated so as not to threaten current and future generations. Cleanup statutes like the Comprehensive Environmental Response, Compensation, and Liability Act raise difficult policy questions on liability, cost-allocation, funding, implementation, and goals.

## PART V. COMPLIANCE, ENFORCEMENT, AND DISPUTE RESOLUTION MECHANISMS

**Chapter 19. CRIMINAL PROSECUTION.** Many environmental statutes include criminal punishment as their ultimate enforcement weapon. Effective criminal enforcement, however, faces strong constitutional and statutory protections of individual rights, difficult issues of "criminal intent," and judicial sentencing variabilities.

**Chapter 20. CIVIL ENFORCEMENT.** Civil enforcement is the most common type of environmental enforcement. The government civil enforcement process contains a variety of options. Citizen enforcement is a strategic aspect of environmental law, as a backstop to government enforcement. Corporate voluntary compliance is increasingly common in the American business community, and various methods of encouraging voluntary compliance exist. The chapter concludes with a case study of corporate environmental ethics, in the context of possible self-enforcement strategies.

**Chapter 21. ADR — ALTERNATIVE DISPUTE RESOLUTION,** opens new possibilities for improving regulatory systems by avoiding the crudities of purely adversarial approaches.

# Chapter 8

# HARM-BASED AMBIENT STANDARDS: THE CENTRAL FEATURE OF THE CLEAN AIR ACT'S STATIONARY SOURCE REGULATION

This Chapter focuses on the use of pollution standards that govern ambient air quality.[1] The concepts addressed in this chapter can be applied, and are, to the pursuit of improved water quality, or with some adaptation, to the regulation of any commons.

The process involved in relying on ambient standards entails two major components. First, as a policy matter, a choice must be made regarding the level of ambient quality that is to be selected for the standard. Thereafter, regulation strategically allocates allowable emissions to the commons in a fashion that limits those emissions sufficiently that the end result is attainment of the desired ambient quality. It sounds simple, but, most assuredly, it is not.

The leading example of this regulatory technique is the federal Clean Air Act (CAA), 42 U.S.C.A. §7401 et seq., in its regulation of conventional air pollution for sulfur dioxide, nitrogen dioxide,[2] suspended particulates, carbon monoxide, ozone and lead. The CAA establishes National Ambient Air Quality Standards (NAAQSs) applicable on a nationwide basis. The standards are called "harm-based" here because the mandated quality levels are set by reference to ambient levels of pollutants that would limit harm to human health and the environment to acceptable levels.

---

1. The CAA does not address indoor air quality, a health hazard that is now considered to be quite substantial.

2 . In regard to sulfur dioxide and nitrogen dioxide, the ambient quality approach described in this chapter has been supplemented by the 1990 CAA amendments to include a tradeable emissions credit program intended to reduce long-range acid deposition problems. This alternative regulatory approach is considered in detail in Chapter 16.

## A. THE CLEAN AIR ACT: INTEGRATING ITS PIECES

At the outset, it is important to recognize that the harm-based ambient standards regulation of conventional air pollutants emitted by stationary sources in the Clean Air Act is a part of a larger undertaking: the overall effort to regulate air quality in the United States. This broader regulatory framework for protecting air quality is found in the Clean Air Act of 1970, as originally enacted, and significantly amended in 1977 and 1990.[3] Before tracing the Clean Air Act's evolution, it is helpful to make it clear that the Act embodies a combination of four distinct statutory techniques:

- Title I, §107, §108, §109, and §110, taken together created the broad basic workhorse regulatory system for control of the most commonly-produced and significant air pollutants by stationary (as opposed to mobile) sources. These sections apply a harm-based ambient quality regulatory approach which constitutes this chapter's primary focus.

- Title II, discussed in Chapter 10's analysis of technology-forcing standards, set specific strict congressional standards for across-the-board rollbacks of automobile and truck tailpipe emissions.[4]

- Section 111, which applies to "new [stationary] sources" of air pollution, establishes a system of "best-technology" emissions requirements, following a technology-based standard-setting approach. The technology-based regulatory technique is explored more fully in Chapter 9 using the Clean Water Act as its principal example.

- Section 112 originally called for uniform harm-based national emission standards for hazardous air pollutants. This effort, based on attempts to weigh relative hazards to health, proved unsatisfactory. In 1990 Congress shifted §112 to a technology-based strategy for regulating hazardous air pollutants.

***Stage 1 — 1970.*** Begin with the assumption that some particular air pollutant is in need of reduction by some quantified amount. The logical starting place in fashioning a pollution control strategy is to look at the sources emitting that pollutant into the atmosphere and measure the magnitude of their respective emissions. As an example, consider carbon monoxide (CO), a significant combustion by-product that is frequently found in harmful concentrations in many of the nation's urban areas. The survey of its sources finds that automobiles are emitting 64.2 million pounds per year nationally, and that large stationary sources of pollution that rely on fossil fuel combustion, such as power plants, foundries, etc., are also major contributors to the problem. Fortunately, the problem is thought to be largely a local one, for unlike some problem pollutants, such as ozone in the lower atmosphere, CO does not tend to travel long distances after its emission.

---

3. More technically, the legislation now known as the Clean Air Act was actually the Clean Air Act Amendments of 1970. The prior federal statute had relied almost exclusively on voluntary state efforts to control air pollution. 69 Stat. 322 (1955). The 1970 legislation amended it beyond recognition. Pub.L. 91-604 (1970). The 1970 statute continues to be the basis for the current law. The major amendments have been Pub.L. 95-95 (1977) and Pub.L. 101–549 (1990).

4 . The automobile pollution standards were based, to some degree, on the percentage rollback in tailpipe emissions thought necessary (at the time) to prevent smog in the worst urban air quality areas, such as Los Angeles. In this sense they are "harm-based" uniform national (i.e. not local ambient) standards. In another sense, the auto emissions limits were "politics-based" standards.

Having identified the major components of the CO emissions problem, the quest begins for a regulatory strategy that will reduce emissions sufficiently to achieve acceptable air quality. An array of strategies are possible, every source of emissions can be required to reduce emissions by the same percentage (a "roll-back" strategy) until the desired results are achieved, some sources can make all the reductions while others go unchanged, etc. There is also a question regarding which level of government should establish the regulation. Federal regulation that is uniformly applicable nationwide is one possibility, state-by-state regulation that addresses polluters on a localized, more particularized basis, is also a possibility. Further, the regulatory strategy need not be monolithic — any mix and match of uniform or localized, federal or state regulation is OK, as long as it works. The goal, hopefully, is to come up with a mix that works, and does so in a generally fair and efficient manner.

In regard to conventional air pollutants, one major strategic decision made by Congress was that of deciding on how clean the air should be. In 1970 Congress chose a "harm-based" approach to this question. For a series of pollutants of special concern, those widely emitted and posing dangers to public health and welfare (the so-called "criteria pollutants," one of which is CO), national ambient air quality standards (NAAQSs) were to be established by the EPA.[5] The primary concern was that the NAAQSs be strict enough "to protect the public health" after "allowing an adequate margin of safety." A secondary, more protective, NAAQS was also called for, with the goal of protecting public welfare.

Looking at the 1970 Clean Air Act, Congress made a number of additional fundamental strategy decisions by dividing the universe of sources of pollution into two major categories, mobile sources and stationary sources, with the former subject to direct federal regulation that applied nationwide and the latter subject to state-by-state control. In some ways the dichotomy is an obvious one. Even though there are millions of mobile sources, there are only a handful of producers of motor vehicles and the design of a car or truck calls for an integrated pollution control system that is best built into every vehicle at the time of manufacture. Moreover, there are tremendous economies of scale in the mass production of motor vehicles and to allow each of the fifty states (or smaller governmental units within the states) to each set their own standards for motor vehicles threatened to play havoc with that industry. With an exception for California, where the control of motor vehicle pollution was already underway and was recognized as requiring more stringent regulation than elsewhere in the nation, there was to be a single national standard for motor vehicle emissions. California could adopt a second, more stringent standard.

Stationary sources, on the other hand, are often custom built installations, and a one-regulation-fits-all approach promised tremendous inefficiencies. For example, a nationwide 20% CO emissions rollback for stationary sources would leave plants that could easily trim a far greater proportion of their CO pollution with no

---

5. Hazardous air pollutants were the subject of separate regulation in §112 that is discussed briefly in this chapter and in Chapter 12. In the wake of the 1990 amendments, a change in direction was taken by Congress that switched hazardous air pollutants to a technology-based system.

need or incentive to do so. Contrastingly, plants that could reduce CO pollution only by drastic and expensive measures would be forced to undertake such measures. Here, the Clean Air Act made a different choice, let the states, who are in far better touch with the economic and pollution control realities of their stationary sources, make the choice about how to get the needed reductions in emissions. The statutory mechanism that Congress chose was to require the states to adopt state implementation plans (SIPs) that were, in effect, a prescription for how the state would regulate its stationary sources in order to control pollution sufficiently to attain the NAAQSs. The federal government, working through the EPA, would superintend the process. EPA would review each SIP, for each of the criteria pollutants, to determine if the SIP would work. If EPA disapproved of a SIP, the state would have to redraft it until EPA approved. If the states refused to draft an adequate SIP, EPA was authorized to impose a federal implementation plan (FIP), a fate most of the states felt would be the worst of all possible regulatory worlds. Apart from reflexive opposition to yielding control to the national government, the states feared that EPA would be insensitive to the particular problems of their industries and ways of life.

In yet another aspect of the original Clean Air Act, Congress did make one national rule for stationary sources, it adopted a third distinctive approach for new pollution sources. These new source performance standards (NSPSs) required all new stationary sources to employ the best available technology for a facility of its kind.[6] In this way, Congress eliminated some facets of the race of laxity (of air pollution control) as a means by which relatively clean air areas could seek to attract new plants to locate there rather than in another state that would be forced to impose more costly air pollution control requirements to ensure attainment of the air quality called for by the NAAQS.

With the NAAQS mandating certain levels of ambient air quality and this bifurcated design of federal mobile source regulation and state stationary source regulation and the congressional choice of a quality target, the basic outline of the beast, the Clean Air Act of 1970, comes into focus. Congress decided that the air must be safe to breathe and, toward that end, directly regulated car and truck emissions, leaving the states to do the rest under the watchful eye of EPA, which would insure that the states faithfully did their part.

This particular division of regulation has a profound effect on the states' efforts to draw up their plans for attainment of the mandated ambient air quality. Three of the criteria pollutants CO, NOx, and ozone[7] are by-products of motor vehicle use and emitted by vehicles in substantial quantities. (Lead was in that category in 1970, but with the elimination of lead from gasoline, motor vehicles have ceased

---

6. Technology-based standards are explored in the next chapter, using the Clean Water Act as the primary example. Over time the Clean Air Act has increasingly employed technology-based forms of regulation, beginning in 1970 with the NSPS, expanding with technology based controls for non-attainment and PSD areas in 1977, and switching, in 1990, to technology-based controls as the primary approach to hazardous air pollutants.

7. Ozone is, to be more accurate, not itself part of automobile emissions. Rather, NOx and volatile organic compounds (VOCs), two components of automobile emissions, are ozone precursors, meaning that they undergo chemical changes after their emission and become ozone.

having an effect on lead air emissions.) Under the current division of authority, however, the contribution to ambient pollution from mobile sources is, to some significant degree, beyond state control. Much of the allowable emission of those pollutants will inevitably result from the operation of motor vehicles, whose emission characteristics the states are forbidden from regulating. Even under the 1970 law, states could influence the amount that vehicles are used by regulating transportation, encouraging car pooling and mass transit; insisting that the federally required pollution controls installed on mobile sources be inspected and properly maintained (I&M), and so on. These types of controls were seldom employed voluntarily because of their extreme unpopularity with the citizenry. Additionally, California was given authority in 1970 to require the sales of motor vehicles that were even lower in emissions than required by the federal mobile source standards.

The fact of the matter remains that most mobile source pollution remains beyond state control, requiring that states regulate their stationary sources all the more stringently. Especially in urbanized air quality control regions (AQCRs),[8] where the number and concentration of automobiles is high, coming up with a state plan that will attain the mandated air quality for CO, NOx, and ozone, is difficult. States have had little choice but to impose unpopular and expensive burdens on the industries whose stationary source emissions are being regulated.

*Stage 2 — 1977 Amendments.* After seven years experience with the Clean Air Act, several of its operative characteristics had become evident. The most important for understanding the basic building blocks of the regulatory system was that some AQCRs were unable to satisfy the NAAQSs and would be unable to do so in the short term without totally crippling the industrial (stationary source) economy of the region. A second major concern was that there was not sufficient regulation to protect clean air areas against degradation of air quality to the lowest legally mandated common denominator, air as dirty as the NAAQS allows. Both of these realizations prompted major additions to the Clean Air Act, one addressing the special concerns of non-attainment areas and one addressing the special concerns of prevention of significant deterioration (PSD) areas.

For non-attainment areas, which included most of the nation's industrial centers, their political power made it possible to force a retreat from the NAAQSs as a rigid short-term requirement, to the NAAQSs as a goal toward which "reasonable further progress" was required. This relaxation is significant, but because the NAAQSs represent the point at which public health is at stake, even the economic imperatives of allowing economic development to occur in non-attainment areas was kept in check by increased requirements for stationary sources and inspection and maintenance of automobiles. All sources were subjected to a technology-based requirement, that they employ "reasonable available control technologies" (RACT). All major new sources were held to a process-based technology standard called "lowest achievable emissions rate" (LAER), and to assure further progress toward attainment of the NAAQSs, major new sources had to "offset" their new

---

8. Most states have chosen to subdivide their regulatory effort into a series of smaller geographic divisions, each of which must meet the NAAQS. There are, in addition, some interstate AQCRs, mostly in metropolitan regions.

pollution by an even greater reduction of old pollution.[9]

In PSD areas, the key regulatory initiative was the imposition of a lower ceiling for allowable pollution that, in effect, superseded the NAAQSs as the federally mandated quality level. The new ceiling was calculated by measuring current air quality as a baseline, and then allowing only a relatively small incremental amount of pollution.

*Stage 3 — 1990 Amendments.* For more than a decade, the Clean Air Act seemed to muddle through in its 1977 configuration, making relatively little further progress toward attainment in non-attainment areas, and virtually no progress in the regulation of hazardous air pollutants. Additionally, the well-known, but largely unregulated, problem of long range transport of pollutants was attracting attention, particularly in regard both to ozone and to acid deposition that was poisoning the lakes of the northeastern states. The statute was being criticized on all fronts, some claimed it was too expensive in achieving the results it did obtain, others claimed it was inadequate because the air in hundreds of localities inhabited by tens of millions of people was not yet safe, let alone clean.

Congress took extraordinary action, making major revisions on all of these fronts. As to the basic NAAQS attainment issue, Congress became far more insistent on compliance by a time certain and far more directive in regard to what states would be required to include in their SIPs. It also gave states burdened by persistent excessive automotive emissions the option of requiring the sale of low emission vehicles (LEVs), essentially on the same basis as California. As to hazardous air pollutants, Congress abandoned the harm-based approach in favor of a technology based approach that called for the installation of the maximum available control technology (MACT). In regard to long range deposition, Congress put in place new devices to limit ozone transport. More radically, Congress established an elaborate emissions trading scheme (see Chapter 16) that promises to reduce $SO_2$ emissions by 10 million tons in a decade, thereby almost halving the most important precursor emissions of acid rain. Title IV, in a less-well known section (§407, 42 U.S.C.A. §7651f,) also mandated imposition of additional stringent command and control regulations to control NOx emissions.[10]

## B.  AMBIENT STANDARDS, THE COMMONS AND AMERICAN FEDERALISM

Both air and water are sometimes referred to as "pollution sinks," implying that airsheds and water bodies are like large vats into which pollutants can be thrown as a form of disposal. It is possible, perhaps even probable, that both air and water have an ability to assimilate some man-induced pollution without significant detriment to the natural systems of which the air and water are a part. Whether

---

9. Offsets, together with bubbles and allied concepts that allow some emissions trading among sources, were the first forays of the Clean Air Act into the use of market devices and trading as a regulatory strategy. These concepts are studied in greater detail in Chapter 16.

10. The NOx regulations have been promulgated by EPA and, in the main, survived judicial review. See Appalachian States Power Co. v. EPA, 135 F.3d 791 (D.C.Cir. 1998).

taking "advantage" of this assimilative capacity is a good idea, is a subject unto itself, but in the regulation of the criteria pollutants under the Clean Air Act Congress made a pragmatic choice to "use" that assimilative capacity up to the limit of damage to human health and the environment.

The fulcrum on which a system of permissible levels of pollution rests is the concept of ambient receiving body quality standards. These standards do not exist in a vacuum — they are a function of the purposes for which the resource base is to be used. Although the bulk of the material in this Chapter focuses on the use of ambient standards in the Clean Air Act, the link between ambient quality standards and intended use of the resource complex is more easily grasped by an example involving water as the pollution sink. Water in a receiving body can be used for a variety of purposes, such as drinking, bathing, supporting aquatic life, pleasure boating, industrial process source water, commercial navigation, effluent transport and so on. The quality of the water necessary to support the aforementioned uses varies greatly and, therefore, the ambient receiving body water quality standards that would be erected as necessary to support a particular use would also vary greatly. Such standards are harm-based. Water used for drinking that causes illness or death if ingested causes harm to the intended user. A harm-based ambient quality standard, therefore, will be set at a level that is sufficient to avoid the harm that would ensue to the intended use or user.

The resort to ambient receiving body quality standards can be understood as a form of response to the tragedy of the commons. Here, imagine that the commons is a receiving body, such as a lake surrounded by several industrial facilities that emit effluents into the lake. To any one industrialist, the cost of avoiding pollution of the lake creates an incentive to pollute the lake. To forego pollution might avoid costs of reduced receiving body quality, such as the need to treat water drawn from that source for industrial use, but the common pool nature of the receiving body vitiates that possible benefit of avoiding pollution. In the absence of regulatory intervention or comprehensive private agreement, there is no guarantee that the benefit of cleaner water will be obtained by any one of the firms because other the firms bordering the lake still may elect to dump their wastes into the commons.

Setting and maintaining ambient quality levels attacks the commons problem by outlawing the untoward result of unacceptable (harmful) deterioration in quality. In this way, an ambient standards approach initially addresses the problem of the commons at a collective level — it defers the intractable problem of translating a prescription about collective results into a series of controls on the behavior of individuals. It is important to emphasize that the choice of means for controlling the individual contributions to ambient quality is wholly independent of adopting an ambient standards approach. From an environmental quality standpoint, as long as the desired ambient quality level is achieved, the choice between a rule that requires zero discharge by all polluters born under the sign of Gemini as opposed to a rule requiring 15 percent reductions in emissions by all emitters is irrelevant. More realistically, however, the choice among possible means of individual control is important because of the economic and political ramifications of that choice.

COMMENTARY AND QUESTIONS

1. **Air, water and what else?** Would harm-based ambient standards be a valuable regulatory technique in fields other than air and water pollution? Harm-based standards are ubiquitous in other fields of regulation involving, for example, product safety for consumer goods and drugs, but there is no commons involved and therefore no concern with ambient standards. Noise regulation, if it relies on setting maximum allowable levels, is another possible example of a harm-based ambient standard.

2. **The federal-state partnership under the Clean Air Act stationary source program.** The principal sections of the Clean Air Act that erect the harm-based ambient standards program are §§107–110, 42 U.S.C.A §§7407–7410. Section 107(a) admirably summarizes the overall concept:

> §107(a)... Each State shall have the primary responsibility for assuring air quality within the entire geographic area comprising such State by submitting an implementation plan for such State which will specify the manner in which national primary and secondary standards will be achieved and maintained within each air quality control region in such State.

Harm-based ambient standards are perfectly matched to the vision of cooperative federalism. The federal government could set the goal with reference to relatively objective criteria — what level of pollution causes harm to human health (the NAAQS primary standards) and what level of pollution causes harm to welfare and the environment (the NAAQS secondary standards). The states, more familiar with their own needs and the capabilities of the polluters within their borders, would have the freedom and the responsibility to make the difficult and multi-faceted determinations about how to limit pollution to the allowable upper bound. The national need is served because unacceptable harm to health and welfare is eliminated. The states retain their sovereign prerogatives in managing and accommodating the competing interests of their constituents.

3. **State primacy.** Why should "primary responsibility" for air quality be lodged with the states? Does the national interest in the solution of the problem of air pollution end with the attainment of acceptable ambient quality? It would seem that the national interest might be affected by the ways in which the states choose to achieve and maintain air quality. A decision by an upwind state to require tall smokestacks and location of polluting facilities near the downwind state line might result in satisfactory ambient air quality in the upwind state, but it hardly seems consistent with sound national policy. The national interest can be protected in this sort of a case by the power of the federal government to reject that sort of an implementation plan as inadequate. Section 110(a)(2)(D) requires SIPs to:

> contain adequate provisions (i) prohibiting...any source or other type of emissions activity within the State from emitting any air pollutant in amounts which will (I) contribute significantly to nonattainment in, or interfere with maintenance by, any other State with respect to any such national primary or secondary ambient air quality standard, or (II) interfere with...the applicable implementation plan for any other State...to prevent significant deterioration of air quality.

Despite the statutory language regarding state primacy, who is really in control, the states or the federal government? Recalling the concept of federal supremacy, this is a game that the states have no choice but to play. The third prong of the federal role, taking over for states that do not undertake conforming regulation, is anathema to the states. No state would want the federal bureaucracy making decisions that may have calamitous economic repercussions in their states, such as forcing major manufacturing facilities to shut down or relocate due to the imposition of stringent pollution control requirements. Moreover, the federal government, through its power to refuse to approve SIPs and through funding cutoffs, can influence how any SIP is drawn.

4. **Ambient air quality standards and the race of laxity.** Do harm-based ambient standards eliminate the race of laxity among the states? Areas with cleaner-than-required air can still run in the race and attract new industry with lax pollution control programs. Their race, however, will be a short one, and their victory may be Phyrric. The NAAQS limit how long the race can be run, and Congress in 1977 supplemented that limitation on the race of laxity with the prevention of significant deterioration program, which effectively shortened the race still further by setting ceilings on incremental increases in pollution in areas that enjoy especially clean air. See CAA §§160-169B.

---

## C. HARM AS THE THRESHOLD OF REGULATION

### Section 1. SELECTING THE POLLUTANTS TO REGULATE AND THE HARM TO BE AVOIDED

In the absence of identifiable or threatened harm, there is no warrant for regulating conduct under most contemporary theories of social and political organization. In general, there is no social benefit to be had in the regulation of such conduct and it bears a cost in terms of both loss of individual autonomy and whatever resources are devoted to enforcement of, and compliance with, regulation. There is also little disagreement that government is authorized to act to prevent widespread harms caused by the activities of its citizens — to apply Garrett Hardin's "mutual coercion, mutually agreed upon." In between those poles, there are at least three controversial threshold decisions that must be made in adopting harm-based ambient standards: (1) determining what harms are sufficiently serious and widespread to justify the burden of regulation, (2) determining how great a burden is justified for any particular amount of harm avoidance, and (3) determining how strong a correlation between cause and effect must be established between a particular ambient quality level and avoidance of harm.

In regard to setting harm-based ambient standards for a medium like air or water, the fact that the common resource is a composite substance that can contain many things adds additional difficulty. There is no single litmus of what classifies air or water as benign or harmful. As previously mentioned, the Clean Air Act has approached the multiplicity of harmful agents that might be present in the air by regulating a small number of pollutants that are labeled "criteria pollutants" and an additional series of pollutants that are defined as hazardous air pollutants. Much goes unregulated.[11]

The term "criteria pollutants" is traceable to the halting pre-1970 federal air pollution control legislation. A series of statutes mandated federal study of the causes of air pollution and its health effects. One of those enactments assigned to the Secretary of Health, Education and Welfare the responsibility to "compile and publish *criteria* reflecting accurately the latest scientific knowledge useful in indicating the kind and extent of [harm] which may be expected from the presence of [an] air pollution agent (or combination of agents) in the air in varying quantities."[12] The term "criteria" is used in distinction to the term standards. Criteria are scientific data-oriented matters, concerned with the causal nexus between ambient concentrations and harmful effects. Standards are set with reference to the information adduced by the criteria studies, but standard-setting may also include consideration of technical and economic issues. The choice of members for the set of criteria pollutants thus reflected the patterns that had evolved in scientific studies of the harms caused by air pollution. Not surprisingly, the criteria pollutants included many of the most common and widely generated pollutants, principally those emitted by the combustion of fossil fuels.

Congress, in addition to the criteria pollutants, also left an avenue for additional regulation under the harm-based ambient standards regime. Section 108(a)(1) described in generic terms what types of pollutants should be regulated The law states:

> The Administrator [of EPA] shall publish, and shall from time to time thereafter revise, a list, which includes each air pollutant (A) emissions of which, in his judgment, cause or contribute to air pollution which may reasonably be anticipated to endanger public health or welfare; (B) the presence of which in the ambient air results from numerous or diverse mobile or stationary sources; and (C) for which air quality criteria had not been issued before December 31, 1970, but for which he plans to issue air quality criteria under this section.

Air quality criteria were already promulgated for several pollutants at the time the CAA was enacted in 1970. As to those pollutants §109(a)(1)(A) required the Administrator to convert them into NAAQSs.

### Natural Resources Defense Council v. Train
#### United States Circuit Court for the Second Circuit, 1976
#### 545 F.2d 320

SMITH, J. The Environmental Protection Agency and its Administrator, Russell Train, appeal from an order of the United States District Court for the Southern District of New York...requiring the Administrator of the EPA, within thirty days, to place lead on a list of air pollutants under §108(a)(1) of the Clean Air Act. We affirm the order of the district court.

The EPA concedes that lead meets the conditions of §§108(a)(1)(A) and (B) — that it has an adverse effect on public health and welfare, and that the presence of lead in the ambient air results from numerous or diverse mobile or stationary

---

11. The same is true in regard to water pollution as demonstrated quite dramatically by the *Atlantic States* case that appears in the next chapter.

12 . Pub.L. 88-206, §3(c)(2)(1963) (emphasis supplied).

sources. The EPA maintains, however, that under §108(a)(1)(C) of the Act, the Administrator retains discretion whether to list a pollutant, even though the pollutant meets the criteria of §§108(a)(1)(A) and (B). The Agency regards the listing of lead under §108(a)(1) and the issuance of ambient air quality standards as one of numerous alternative control strategies for lead available to it. Listing of substances is mandatory, the EPA argues, only for those pollutants for which the Administrator "plans to issue air quality criteria." He may, it is contended, choose not to issue, i.e., not "plan to issue" such criteria, and decide to control lead solely by regulating emission at the source, regardless of the total concentration of lead in the ambient air. The Administrator argues that if he chooses to control lead (or other pollutants) under §211, he is not required to list the pollutant under §108(a)(1) or to set air quality standards.

The EPA advances three reasons for the position that the Administrator has discretion whether to list a pollutant even when the conditions of §§108(a)(1)(A) and (B) have been met: the plain meaning of §108(a)(1)(C); the structure of the Clean Air Act as a whole; and the legislative history of the Act.

The issue is one of statutory construction. We agree with the district court and with appellees that the interpretation of the Clean Air Act advanced by the EPA is contrary to the structure of the Act as a whole, and that if accepted, it would vitiate the public policy underlying the enactment of the 1970 Amendments as set forth in the Act and in its legislative history.

Section 108(a)(1) contains mandatory language. It provides that "the Administrator *shall*...publish...a list..." (emphasis added). If the EPA interpretation were accepted and listing were mandatory only for substances "for which [the Administrator] plans to issue air quality criteria...", then the mandatory language of §108(a)(1)(A) would become mere surplusage. The determination to list a pollutant and to issue air quality criteria would remain discretionary with the Administrator, and the rigid deadlines of §108(a)(2), §109, and §110 for attaining air quality standards could be bypassed by him at will. If Congress had enacted §211 [relating to regulation of fuel additives, such as lead] as an alternative to, rather than as a supplement to, §§108-110, then one would expect a similar fixed timetable for implementation of the fuel control section. The absence of such a timetable for the enforcement of §211 lends support to the view that fuel controls were intended by Congress as a means for attaining primary air quality standards rather than as an alternative to the promulgation of such standards....

When a specific provision of a total statutory scheme may be construed to be in conflict with the congressional purpose expressed in an act, it becomes necessary to examine the act's legislative history to determine whether the specific provision is reconcilable with the intent of Congress. Because state planning and implementation under the Air Quality Act of 1967 had made little progress by 1970, Congress reacted by "taking a stick to the States in the form of the Clean Air Amendments of 1970...." Train v. NRDC, 421 U.S. 60, 64 (1975). It enacted §108(a)(1) which provides that the Administrator of the Environmental Protection Agency "shall" publish a list which includes each air pollutant which is harmful to health and originates from specified sources. Once a pollutant is listed under §108(a)(1), §§109 and 110 are to be automatically invoked, and promulgation of national air quality standards and implementation thereof by the states within a limited, fixed time schedule becomes mandatory.

The EPA contention that the language of §108(a)(1)(C) "for which [the Administrator] plans to issue air quality criteria" is a separate and third criterion to be met before §108 requires listing lead and issuing air quality standards, thereby leaving the decision to list lead within the discretion of the Administrator, finds no support in the legislative history of the 1970 Amendments to the Act. The summary of the provisions of the conference agreement furnished the Senate by Senator Muskie contained the following language:

> The agreement requires issuance of remaining air quality criteria for major pollutants within 13 months of date of enactment.... Within the 13-month deadline, the Congress expects criteria to be issued for nitrogen oxides, fluorides, lead, polynuclear organic matter, and odors, though others may be necessary.[13]

While the literal language of §108(a)(1)(C) is somewhat ambiguous, this ambiguity is resolved when this section is placed in the context of the Act as a whole and in its legislative history. The deliberate inclusion of a specific timetable for the attainment of ambient air quality standards incorporated by Congress in §§108-110 would become an exercise in futility if the Administrator could avoid listing pollutants simply by choosing not to issue air quality criteria. The discretion given to the Administrator under the Act pertains to the review of state implementation plans under §110, and to §211 which authorizes but does not mandate the regulation of fuel or fuel additives. It does not extend to the issuance of air quality standards for substances derived from specified sources which the Administrator had already adjudged injurious to health....

The structure of the Clean Air Act as amended in 1970, its legislative history, and the judicial gloss placed upon the Act leave no room for an interpretation which makes the issuance of air quality standards for lead under §108 discretionary. The Congress sought to eliminate, not perpetuate, opportunity for administrative foot-dragging. Once the conditions of §§108(a)(1)(A) and (B) have been met, the listing of lead and the issuance of air quality standards for lead become mandatory. The order of the district court is affirmed.

### COMMENTARY AND QUESTIONS

1. **The criteria pollutants.** There are currently six criteria pollutants under the Clean Air Act: sulfur dioxide, nitrogen dioxide, suspended particulates, carbon monoxide, ozone, and lead. In light of the generic statutory definition and the mandatory nature of EPA's obligation to add new criteria pollutants, does the brevity of the list surprise you? In part the small number reflects the fact that hazardous air pollutants are regulated separately by §112 of the Act, 42 U.S.C.A. §7412.

2. **EPA's better way to control lead emissions.** EPA raised two types of arguments against the addition of lead as a criteria pollutant, arguments that vested EPA with general discretion in the selection of criteria pollutants and what might be termed "lead-specific" arguments. The claims for a general discretion may have seemed a bit lame, but EPA had what it felt were strong reasons in support of its lead-specific argument. EPA studies had shown that almost 90 percent of lead emissions into the environment were traceable to motor vehicles, an air pollution source that EPA was empowered to regulate both directly and through the regulation of fuel additives. EPA felt the most effective means for limiting lead emissions to safe levels was to force the removal of lead from gasoline. Might EPA's position make good sense, but still be a violation of the statutory command?

13 . Legislative History, Clean Air Amendments, Vol. 1 at 430, 432 (1974).

3. **Setting the standard for standards.** The Clean Air Act requires EPA to follow the listing of a criteria pollutant with the promulgation of both primary and secondary NAAQSs. The Act, in §109(b)(1-2), defines the qualitative effect that adherence to the standards will have:

§109(b)(1)... National primary ambient air quality standards...shall be [ones] the attainment and maintenance of which in the judgment of the Administrator [of EPA], based on such criteria and allowing an adequate margin of safety, are required to protect the public health.

(2) Any national secondary ambient air quality standard...shall specify a level of air quality the attainment and maintenance of which in the judgment of the Administrator [of EPA], based on such criteria, is requisite to protect the public welfare from any known or anticipated adverse effects associated with the presence of such air pollutant in the ambient air.

4. **Setting the lead standards with less than perfect knowledge.** Standard-setting requires judgments about the causal effects of exposure to varying concentrations of pollutants. In a footnote not included in the text excerpt above, the court recognized that EPA may have to act despite uncertainty:

It is irrelevant that the current state of scientific knowledge may make it difficult to set an ambient air quality standard. The Administrator must proceed in spite of such difficulties [as the legislative history makes clear]:

"The Committee is aware that there are many gaps in the available scientific knowledge of the welfare and other environmental effects of air pollution.... A great deal of basic research will be needed to determine the long-term air quality goals which are required to protect the public health and welfare from any potential effects of air pollution. In the meantime, *the Secretary will be expected to establish such national goals on the basis of the best information available to him.* (emphasis added). S. Rep. No. 91-1196 on S. 4358." National Quality Standards Act of 1970, "Report of the Committee on Public Works, United States Senate," 91st Cong., 2d Sess. at 11; A Legislative History of the Clean Air Amendments of 1970, Vol. I at 411 (1974). 545 F.2d 320, at 324, note 5.

The one aspect of the Clean Air Act in which the problems of scientific uncertainty eventually gained the upper hand on the harm-based approach was in regard to the regulation of hazardous air pollutants. In that realm, the difficulties of standard setting totally compromised the program and in 1990, after 20-years of regulatory failure, Congress repealed the old §112 National Emission System for Hazardous Air Pollutants (NESHAPs), and replaced it with a technology-based system. The regulatory failure of the NESHSAPs program is commented on further in Chapter 12.

5. **Cost and feasibility.** The addition of lead as a criteria pollutant was followed by promulgation of primary and secondary ambient standards. The issue was contentious because the standards promulgated would require expensive pollution controls for a segment of the metals industry. A court challenge to those standards ensued and failed, see Lead Industries Association v. Environmental Protection Agency, 647 F.2d 1130 (D.C.Cir 1980), cert. denied 449 U.S. 1042 (1980). A number of issues were contested by the plaintiffs who attacked the EPA standards. One key ruling in upholding the stringency of the standards was the court's conclusion that EPA was to set the standards without regard to cost or technologic feasibility:

Where Congress intended the Administrator to be concerned about economic and technological feasibility, it expressly so provided. For example, Section 111 of the Act directs the Administrator to consider economic and technological feasibility in establishing standards of performance for new stationary sources of air pollution based on the best available control technology. S. Rep. No. 91-1196, 91st Cong. 2d Sess. 416 (1970). In contrast, §109(b) speaks only of protecting the public health and welfare. Nothing in its language suggests that the Administrator is to consider economic or technological feasibility in setting ambient air quality standards.

The legislative history of the Act also shows the Administrator may not consider economic and technological feasibility in setting air quality standards; the absence of any provision requiring consideration of these factors was no accident; it was the result of a deliberate decision by Congress to subordinate such concerns to the achievement of health goals. Exasperated by the lack of significant progress toward dealing with the problem of air pollution under the Air Quality Act of 1967, 81 Stat. 485, and prior legislation, Congress abandoned the approach of offering suggestions and setting goals in favor of "taking a stick to the States in the form of the Clean Air Amendments of 1970..." Train v. NRDC, Inc. 421 U.S. 60, 64 (1975); see Union Electric Co. v. EPA, 427 U.S. 246, 256-257 (1976). Congress was well aware that, together with Sections 108 and 110, Section 109 imposes requirements of a "technology-forcing" character.

It may well be that underlying St. Joe's argument is its feeling that Congress could not or should not have intended this result, and that this court should supply relief by grafting a requirement of economic or technological feasibility onto the statute. The Supreme Court confronted a similar suggestion in the Tellico Dam case. TVA v. Hill, 437 U.S. 153 (1978). There TVA argued that the Endangered Species Act should not be construed to prevent operation of the dam since it had already been completed at a cost of approximately $100 million, Congress had appropriated funds for the dam even after the Act was passed, and the species at risk — the snail darter — was relatively unimportant and ways might ultimately be found to save it. The Court rejected the invitation to "view the...Act 'reasonably,' and hence shape a remedy that 'accords with some modicum of common sense and the public weal.'" Lead Industries Association (LIA) v. EPA, 647 F.2d at 1150–51.

6. **Protectiveness.** On the health-protectiveness issues, the court rejected attacks that EPA was forbidden from considering mere "sub-clinical effects" rather than the onset of disease as the threshold of relevant harm, and that EPA could not base its regulation on achieving levels that would protect the health of the most sensitive population, urban children. The court also addressed the problem of EPA's need to act under conditions of scientific uncertainty:

It may be...LIA's [one of the plaintiffs in the case] view that the Administrator must show that there is a "medical consensus that [the effects on which the standards were based] are harmful..." If so, LIA is seriously mistaken. This court has previously noted that some uncertainty about the health effects of air pollution is inevitable. And we pointed out that "[a]waiting certainty will often allow for only reactive, not preventive regulat[ory action]." Ethyl Corp. v. EPA, 541 F.2d 1, 25 (D.C. Cir. 1976). Congress apparently shares this view; it specifically directed the Administrator to allow an adequate margin of safety to protect against effects which have not yet been uncovered by research and effects whose medical significance is a matter of disagreement. This court has previously acknowledged the role of the margin of safety requirement. In EDF v.

EPA, 598 F.2d 62, 81 (D.C. Cir. 1978), we pointed out that "[i]f administrative responsibility to protect against unknown dangers presents a difficult task, indeed, a veritable paradox...calling as it does for knowledge of that which is unknown...then, the term 'margin of safety' is Congress' directive that means be found to carry out the task and to reconcile the paradox." Moreover, it is significant that Congress has recently acknowledged that more often than not the "margins of safety" that are incorporated into air quality standards turn out to be very modest or nonexistent, as new information reveals adverse health effects at pollution levels once thought to be harmless. See H.R. Rep. No. 95-294 at 103–117. Congress' directive to the Administrator to allow an "adequate margin of safety" alone plainly refutes any suggestion that the Administrator is only authorized to set primary air quality standards which are designed to protect against health effects that are known to be clearly harmful....

As we read the statutory provisions and the legislative history, Congress directed the Administrator to err on the side of caution in making the necessary decisions. We see no reason why this court should put a gloss on Congress' scheme by requiring the Administrator to show that there is a medical consensus that the effects on which the lead standards were based are "clearly harmful to health." All that is required by the statutory scheme is evidence in the record which substantiates his conclusions about the health effects on which the standards were based. Accordingly, we reject LIA's claim that the Administrator exceeded his statutory authority. *LIA*, 647 F.2d at 1154–56.

## Section 2. TIGHTENING STANDARDS, MID-COURSE

Once the standards are established governing allowable, "safe" exposures to pollutants, the regulatory process goes to work and emitters must alter their behavior to insure that the standards are met. For many emitters, making any change in the method of operation in regard to pollution requires substantial investment in some form of pollution control equipment or process change. Evolving, or even occasionally changing standards, therefore, are inefficient because they place emitters who have made investment in meeting one standard, adjust all over again. For some it may be an easy thing to do, but for others, the new standard starts a new round of major investment. Both Congress and EPA understand that dynamic and are reluctant to change standards.[14] A powerful counterweight to that reluctance in the portion of the Clean Air Act here under study arises when new data shows that the currently established NAAQS levels are not safe enough.

In the main, Congress and EPA have been exceedingly cautious about raising standards. Few revisions have ever been proposed despite the NAAQSs' venerable (for environmental standards) age. In late 1996, EPA announced two major proposals for revision of the NAAQSs, a 50% reduction in the acute ozone exposure standard from 0.12 parts per million (ppm) to 0.08 ppm, and an entirely new standard in the area of particulate matter (PM) for fine particulates of 2.5 micrometers or less in diameter, the old standard had only regulated coarser particles of 10 micro-

---

14. Congress, at times, will even give assurances that new standards limiting emissions will not present a (rapidly) moving target. For example, in the 1990 Amendments that erected a level of emission limitation performance for hazardous air pollutants, firms meeting that standard are given a period during which they are assured that there will be no increase in their regulatory burdens. See §112(j)(6), see also, Clean Water Act §306(d).

meters or less. The new proposed PM2.5 standard included an annual average concentration limit of 15 micrograms per cubic meter of air and an acute one-hour standard of 50 micrograms per cubic meter. Industry's howls of anguish and a lengthy and vituperative comment period took its toll, but did not stop the change altogether. In 1997, EPA promulgated the new standards: for ozone the acute standard is now 0.08 ppm averaged over an 8-hour period; the PM2.5 standard is 65 micrograms per cubic meter on a 24-hour average and 15 micrograms per cubic meter annual average.

Despite EPA's efforts to brook the criticism, the politically significant opponents, including a solid phalanx of major industries and large numbers of anti-regulation members of Congress, won a reprieve. Bills were introduced to rescind the new regulations, and the political balance seemed to be tipping in favor of recission or relaxation by Congress. At that point, on July 16, 1997, President Clinton entered the fray with an open memorandum to the Administrator of EPA by which he stated:

> I also want to ensure that these new standards are implemented in a common sense, cost-effective manner. It is critically important that these standards be implemented in the most flexible, reasonable, and least burdensome manner, and that the Federal Government work with State and local governments and other interested parties to this end.

The memorandum then listed four points, three of which repeated the general policy concerns noted above, but one of which effectively reopened the scientific debate on the PM2.5 standard and delayed its effective date for five years:

> Implementation shall ensure that the EPA completes its next periodic review of particulate matter, including review by the Clean Air Scientific Advisory Committee, within five years of issuance of the new standards, as contemplated by the Clean Air Act. Thus, by July 2002, the EPA will have determined, based on data available from its review, whether to revise or maintain the standards. This determination will have been made before any areas have been designated as "nonattainment" under the PM2.5 standards and before imposition of any new controls related to the PM2.5 standards.

### COMMENTARY & QUESTIONS

1. **Regulatory benefits and costs.** Even with the stricter proposed standards, EPA's benefit-cost figures were quite favorable: approximately $120 billion per year in benefits as against only $6.5 to $8.5 billion per year in costs. Those large benefit number were generated because large numbers of people are affected. EPA "estimated the revised standards would result in 20,000 fewer premature deaths from air pollution, 250,000 fewer cases of aggravated asthma, 250,000 fewer incidences of acute childhood respiratory problems, 60,000 fewer cases of bronchitis, 9,000 fewer hospital admissions, and 1.5 million fewer cases of significant breathing problems." 27 BNA Env. Rep. 1571 (Nov. 29, 1996). EPA drew its support from almost 185 health studies involving ozone exposure and 86 such studies regarding PM. The impact of the changes was going to be widely dispersed. EPA estimated that the new standards would result in far more nonattainment. For ozone the

number of counties out of attainment was predicted to increase from 106 to 335; for PM the numbers were 41 and 167 respectively.

**2. Executive overreaching or executive acumen?** President Clinton included in his memorandum the following, "This memorandum is for the purposes of internal Administration management only, and is not judicially reviewable." He thus placed Carol Browner, the Administrator of EPA, with little choice but to delay the standards that she had determined were necessary to prevent pollution that she had found "may reasonably be anticipated to endanger public health." §108(a)(1)(A). Politically, the action had its intended effect, the threat of congressional action receded, but so too did the day of reckoning as to whether the PM2.5 standards would ever go into effect.

**3. Emergency powers to combat imminent and substantial endangerments.** Despite considerable pressure from the American Lung Association to promulgate a "high-level burst" exposure NAAQS for sulfur dioxide, EPA refused to do so. In litigation, EPA was generally upheld, see American Lung Association v. EPA, 134 F.3d 388 (D.C.Cir. 1998). Instead, EPA responded to the problems by resort to §303 of the Clean Air Act, entitled "Emergency Powers." That section authorizes EPA "upon receipt of evidence that a pollution source or combination of sources (including moving sources) is presenting an imminent and substantial endangerment to public health or welfare, or the environment" to take one of several courses of action. These include bringing a lawsuit seeking an injunction against the polluters, or issuing an administrative order if the lawsuit is "not [a] practicable [means] to assure prompt protection." The orders cannot remain in effect for more than 60 days, unless a lawsuit is thereafter filed and a court extends the effective span of the order. What kind of situation does that provision address? Legally speaking, can EPA found a program on §303 that has many of the same characteristics as a "high-level burst" five-minute exposure standard for sulfur dioxide, a criteria pollutant?

EPA has attempted to do so, invoking §303, but also invoking §301(a)(1), which is a general grant of power that states. "The Administrator is authorized to prescribe such regulations as are necessary to carry out his functions under this chapter."[15] The action taken is a proposed rule that establishes "Proposed Implementation Requirements for Reduction of Sulfur Oxide (Sulfur Dioxide) Emissions." 62 F.R. 210 (Jan. 2, 1997). The proposal stressed case-by-case- responses and flexibility as key principles. The proposal did not erect specific requirements, it set expectations in regard to what states and tribes would do in response to pollution episodes that exceeded the burst endangerment level. The proposal also seemed to hint at EPA action under §303 if the states and tribes did not take satisfactory steps in the face of exceedances.

---

15. "Chapter" is a term of art, that refers to all of Chapter 85 of Title 42 of the U.S.C.A., thereby including all of the Clean Air Act.

## D. MOVING FROM AVOIDING HARM TO REGULATING POLLUTERS: THE IMPLEMENTATION PLAN PROCESS

### Section 1. BROKERING EMISSIONS REDUCTIONS

The *Lead Industries* case was emphatic in ruling that economic feasibility had no role to play in the standard-setting process under a harm-based ambient quality approach. That position was supported by the statute's language and structure. Once the court has identified the approach as harm-based, it has no authority to inject the pragmatic concerns that economic and technologic feasibility embody. The reason for this limit on the court is simultaneously simple and politically sophisticated — because Congress said so. Considered as a matter of pure logic the irrelevance of cost and feasibility is even more clear: the scientific question of how stringent the standard must be to avoid harm has nothing at all to do with whether the standard is achievable or cost-effective.

As a pragmatic, political matter, however, it is patently incredible to believe that Congress could bar all consideration of cost and feasibility from the system used to regulate the most commonly produced air emissions. Those considerations, or others that are similar, must have a home somewhere in the Clean Air Act. The following case explains where.

### Union Electric Company v. Environmental Protection Agency
United States Supreme Court, 1976
427 U.S. 246

[Shortly after passage of the CAA, Missouri, like all of the states, was required to adopt a State Implementation Plan (SIP). SIPs address the means by which the states will limit emissions (especially stationary source emissions) within their borders to insure that the air quality meets the NAAQSs. Under the Missouri SIP, three plants operated by Union Electric Company were made subject to regulations that Union claimed to be impossible to meet on technical and/or financial grounds. Union pressed that objection in its negotiations with Missouri to no avail. Missouri presented the SIP to EPA for approval and approval was granted on May 31, 1972. Union took no action at that time to challenge the Missouri SIP. Instead, Union sought, and Missouri issued, variances for each of the three plants as allowed by the CAA, granting Union additional time to reduce their emissions to the limits specified in the Missouri SIP. In 1974, after two of the three variances had expired and Union had done nothing to reduce its emissions, EPA gave notice to Union that Union was in violation of the sulfur dioxide limitations for it contained in the Missouri SIP. Union sued EPA, and despite Union's having chosen a wrong procedural avenue for raising its claims of economic and technologic infeasibility, the Supreme Court addressed the merits of those claims.]

MARSHALL, J. Since a reviewing court regardless of when the petition for review is filed may consider claims of economic and technological infeasibility only if the Administrator may consider such claims in approving or rejecting a state implementation plan, we must address ourselves to the scope of the Administrator's responsibility. The Administrator's position is that he has no power whatsoever to reject a state implementation plan on the ground that it is economically or technologically infeasible, and we have previously accorded great deference to the

Administrator's construction of the Clean Air Act. See Train v. NRDC, 421 U.S., at 75. After surveying the relevant provisions of the Clean Air Amendments of 1970 and their legislative history, we agree that Congress intended claims of economic and technological infeasibility to be wholly foreign to the Administrator's consideration of a state implementation plan.

As we have previously recognized, the 1970 Amendments to the Clean Air Act were a drastic remedy to what was perceived as a serious and otherwise uncheckable problem of air pollution. The Amendments place the primary responsibility for formulating pollution control strategies on the States, but nonetheless subject the States to strict minimum compliance requirements. These requirements are of a "technology-forcing character" and are expressly designed to force regulated sources to develop pollution control devices that might at the time appear to be economically or technologically infeasible.

This approach is apparent on the face of §110(a)(2). The provision sets out eight criteria that an implementation plan must satisfy, and provides that if these criteria are met and if the plan was adopted after reasonable notice and hearing, the Administrator "shall approve" the proposed state plan. The mandatory "shall" makes it quite clear that the Administrator is not to be concerned with factors other than those specified and none of the eight factors appears to permit consideration of technological or economic infeasibility.[16] Nonetheless, if a basis is to be found for allowing the Administrator to consider such claims, it must be among the eight criteria, and so it is here that the argument is focused.

It is suggested that consideration of claims of technological and economic infeasibility is required by the first criterion that the primary air quality standards be met "as expeditiously as practicable but...in no case later than three years" and that the secondary air quality standards be met within a "reasonable time." §110(a)(2)(A). The argument is that what is "practicable" or "reasonable" cannot be determined without assessing whether what is proposed is possible. This argument does not survive analysis.

Section 110(a)(2)(A)'s three-year deadline for achieving primary air quality standards is central to the Amendments' regulatory scheme and, as both the language and the legislative history of the requirement make clear, it leaves no room for claims of technological or economic infeasibility. The 1970 congressional debate on the Amendments centered on whether technology forcing was necessary and desirable in framing and attaining air quality standards sufficient to protect the public health, standards later termed primary standards. The House version of the Amendments was quite moderate in approach, requiring only that health-related standards be met "within a reasonable time." H.R. 17255, 91st Cong., 2d Sess., §108(c)(1)(C)(i)(1970). The Senate bill, on the other hand, flatly required that, possible or not, health-related standards be met "within three years." S. 4358, 91st Cong., 2d Sess., §111(a)(2)(A)(1970).

The Senate's stiff requirement was intended to foreclose the claims of emission sources that it would be economically or technologically infeasible for them to achieve emission limitations sufficient to protect the public health within the

---

16. Comparison of the eight criteria of §110(a)(2) with other provisions of the Amendments bolsters this conclusion. Where Congress intended the Administrator to be concerned about economic and technological infeasibility, it expressly so provided. Thus, §§110(a), 110(f), 111(a)(1), 202(a), 211(c)(2)(A), and 231(b) of the Amendments all expressly permit consideration, e.g., "of the requisite technology, giving appropriate consideration to the cost of compliance." Section 110(a)(2) contains no such language.

specified time. As Senator Muskie, manager of the Senate bill, explained to his chamber:

> The first responsibility of Congress is not the making of technological or economic judgments or even to be limited by what is or appears to be technologically or economically feasible. Our responsibility is to establish what the public interest requires to protect the health of persons. This may mean that people and industries will be asked to do what seems to be impossible at the present time. 116 Cong. Rec. 32901-32902 (1970).

This position reflected that of the Senate committee:

> In the Committee discussions, considerable concern was expressed regarding the use of the concept of technical feasibility as the basis of ambient air standards. The Committee determined that 1) the health of people is more important than the question of whether the early achievement of ambient air quality standards protective of health is technically feasible; and 2) the growth of pollution load in many areas, even with application of available technology, would still be deleterious to public health.

Therefore, the Committee determined that existing sources of pollutants either should "meet the standard of the law or be closed down...." S.Rep. No. 91-1196, pp. 2–3 (1970).

The Conference Committee and, ultimately, the entire Congress accepted the Senate's three-year mandate for the achievement of primary air quality standards, and the clear import of that decision is that the Administrator must approve a plan that provides for attainment of the primary standards in three years even if attainment does not appear feasible.

Secondary air quality standards, those necessary to protect the public welfare, were subject to far less legislative debate than the primary standards. The House version of the Amendments treated welfare-related standards together with health-related standards, and required both to be met "within a reasonable time." The Senate bill, on the other hand, treated health and welfare-related standards separately and did not require that welfare-related standards be met in any particular time at all, although the Committee Report expressed the desire that they be met "as rapidly as possible." The final Amendments also separated welfare-related standards from health-related standards, labeled them secondary air quality standards, and adopted the House's requirement that they be met within a "reasonable time." §§109(b), 110(a)(2)(A). Thus, technology-forcing is not expressly required in achieving standards to protect the public welfare.

It does not necessarily follow, however, that the Administrator may consider claims of impossibility in assessing a state plan for achieving secondary standards. As with plans designed to achieve primary standards in less than three years, the scope of the Administrator's power to reject a plan depends on whether the State itself may decide to engage in technology forcing and adopt a plan more stringent than federal law demands.

[The Court then addressed the claim that the power to engage in technology-forcing is available to the states under the CAA. Here the utility's argument was that the second criterion for plan approval allowed plans to contain only such control devices as "may be necessary."]

We read the "as may be necessary" requirement of §110(a)(2)(B) to demand only that the implementation plan submitted by the State meet the "minimum conditions" of the Amendments.[17] Beyond that, if a State makes the legislative determination that it desires a particular air quality by a certain date and that it is willing to force technology to attain it or lose a certain industry if attainment is not possible such a determination is fully consistent with the structure and purpose of the Amendments, and §110(a)(2)(B) provides no basis for the EPA Administrator to object to the determination on the ground of infeasibility.[18]

In sum, we have concluded that claims of economic or technological infeasibility may not be considered by the Administrator in evaluating a state requirement that primary ambient air quality standards be met in the mandatory three years. And, since we further conclude that the States may submit implementation plans more stringent than federal law requires and that the Administrator must approve such plans if they meet the minimum requirements of §110(a)(2), it follows that the language of §110(a)(2)(B) provides no basis for the Administrator ever to reject a state implementation plan on the ground that it is economically or technologically infeasible. Accordingly, a court of appeals reviewing an approved plan under §307(b)(1) cannot set it aside on those grounds, no matter when they are raised.

Perhaps the most important forum for consideration of claims of economic and technological infeasibility is before the state agency formulating the implementation plan. So long as the national standards are met, the State may select whatever mix of control devices it desires and industries with particular economic or technological problems may seek special treatment in the plan itself. Moreover, if the industry is not exempted from, or accommodated by, the original plan, it may obtain a variance, as petitioner did in this case; and the variance, if granted after notice and a hearing, may be submitted to the EPA as a revision of the plan. §110(a)(3)(A), 42 U.S.C. §1857c-5(a)(3)(A)(1970 ed., Supp. IV). Lastly, an industry denied an exemption from the implementation plan, or denied a subsequent variance, may be able to take its claims of economic or technological infeasibility to the state courts.

While the State has virtually absolute power in allocating emission limitations so long as the national standards are met, if the state plan cannot meet the national standards, the EPA is implicated in any postponement procedure. There are two ways that a State can secure relief from the EPA for individual emission sources, or classes of sources, that cannot meet the national standards. [The opinion here identifies two explicit statutory methods for obtaining short extensions of the date for compliance by an affected emitter, such as Union.]

In short, the Amendments offer ample opportunity for consideration of claims of technological and economic infeasibility. Always, however, care is taken that consideration of such claims will not interfere substantially with the primary goal of prompt attainment of the national standards. Allowing such claims to be raised

---

17. Economic and technological factors may be relevant in determining whether the minimum conditions are met. Thus, the Administrator may consider whether it is economically or technologically possible for the state plan to require more rapid progress than it does. If he determines that it is, he may reject the plan as not meeting the requirement that primary standards be achieved "as expeditiously as practicable" or as failing to provide for attaining secondary standards within "a reasonable time."

18. In a literal sense, of course, no plan is infeasible since offending sources always have the option of shutting down if they cannot otherwise comply with the standard of the law. Thus, there is no need for the Administrator to reject an economically or technologically "infeasible" state plan on the ground that anticipated noncompliance will cause the State to fall short of the national standards. Sources objecting to such a state scheme must seek their relief from the State.

by appealing the Administrator's approval of an implementation plan, as petitioner suggests, would frustrate congressional intent. It would permit a proposed plan to be struck down as infeasible before it is given a chance to work, even though Congress clearly contemplated that some plans would be infeasible when proposed. And it would permit the Administrator or a federal court to reject a State's legislative choices in regulating air pollution, even though Congress plainly left with the States, so long as the national standards were met, the power to determine which sources would be burdened by regulation and to what extent. Technology forcing is a concept somewhat new to our national experience and it necessarily entails certain risks. But Congress considered those risks in passing the 1970 Amendments and decided that the dangers posed by uncontrolled air pollution made them worth taking. Petitioner's theory would render that considered legislative judgment a nullity, and that is a result we refuse to reach. Affirmed.

COMMENTARY AND QUESTIONS

1. **EPA review of SIPs that do consider economic and technologic feasibility.** In this case, the Court said EPA cannot disapprove a SIP that does not take economic and technologic feasibility into account. Can EPA disapprove of a SIP that does take feasibility into account? Although the Court doesn't say so in those precise words, it is clear that EPA can approve of SIPs that allow some industries relief on feasibility grounds so long as the allowance of feasibility in allocating plant-specific emissions limitations in one economic sector does not prevent attainment of the mandated ambient air quality. In fact, the Court virtually invites the states, as a part of SIP formulation, to take feasibility into account when it points to the state SIP formulation process as the principal forum for feasibility arguments.

Must the EPA approve SIPs that allow feasibility to be taken into account as long as those SIPs will result in timely attainment of the relevant NAAQS? Technically, the answer is, "No." EPA has discretion to reject feasibility allowances in SIPs if, in EPA's judgment, the SIPs do not achieve attainment as quickly as would still be practicable with less allowance for feasibility. Realistically, EPA will not refuse approval of a SIP on that basis. As a matter of federalism, to do so would seem to intrude on the primacy of the state that is envisioned in the SIP process.

2. **States as pollution allocation brokers.** What happens when states take advantage of their ability to consider economic and technologic feasibility in SIP formulation? Arguably, they open themselves up to horrific lobbying pressure from their most influential industries, all of whom can probably make a colorable claim that imposing stringent pollution control requirements on them exceeds their financial or technological abilities. Is there anything wrong with this? One argument is that the political allocation of pollution control burdens will almost certainly be suboptimal in terms of achieving attainment in a least-cost manner. Viewing the grant of dispensations based on feasibility as a sort of political patronage gives rise to the likelihood that political allocation will tend to result in SIPs that try to achieve attainment by the smallest margin possible. After all, what politician would not dole out as much patronage as possible. How cogent are these criticisms if EPA still insists on NAAQS attainment? Does EPA's watchdog role become more difficult when the states are trying to draw SIPs that are as close to painless as possible?

## Section 2. REVERSE ENGINEERING FROM STANDARDS TO ALLOCATIONS

Although the setting of harm-based ambient standards calls for difficult scientific judgments, an equally difficult problem attends the decisions that must be made in order to write a prescription for attainment of the standards. Under the Clean Air Act these latter decisions are made in the SIP process. As to stationary sources, the SIP requirements usually are put in the form of a permit that dictates how the plant may operate in regard to emitting pollution. The stationary source permits work together with the other parts of the SIP. Those might include transportation planning, vehicle M&I, mandatory installation of hoods or vapor recovery systems at gasoline stations, ozone action alerts recommending that citizens refrain from vehicle refueling vehicles or using lawnmowers on days having particular climatic conditions, and so on. Together, all of the parts of the plan must produce a net effect that allows all of the NAAQSs to be met at virtually all times[19] in all of the state's AQCRs. If a SIP will not have that result, EPA cannot approve it. If the state is unable or unwilling to propose a SIP that EPA approves, EPA must take over the process and write a Federal Implementation Plan (FIP). As the following case demonstrates, there is a good deal of both science and art involved in determining whether a proposed implementation plan will result in satisfactory ambient air quality.

Despite the many variables that must be considered in writing a SIP or FIP, there is little or no magic to the SIP process. The SIP writing process is nothing more than a form of reverse engineering from a desired result to a plan for attaining the result. The simplicity, however ends there. First, the standards that must be attained are themselves detailed. Note the chart reproduced here that was included by the court in the *Cleveland Electric* case summarizing the NAAQSs as they stood at the time of the case.[20] Beyond the specificity of the standards, the movement of emitted pollutants in the airshed must be predicted. This is done by creating computer-based airshed models. That is a monumental task because the dispersion of pollutants is affected by local topographic, climatic, and atmospheric conditions and the predictions have to be made for both long-term average concentrations of pollutants and ambient pollution levels under short-term extraordinary conditions. A substantial degree of precision is required, both to be able to confidently predict that a particular set of allowed emissions will satisfy ambient quality standards, and to identify a set of pollution controls that is not more stringent (and therefore more costly) than necessary. The airshed modeling is hotly contested because the choice of the model and the assumptions made in modeling directly affect the amount of emissions allowed under the SIP and the pollution control costs that various firms will be forced to incur. The battle lines are numerous. The affected states usually are at odds with EPA, seeking a model that will allow a higher level of emissions. Individual polluters within the airshed have interests adverse to one another

19. The NAAQSs, as to some short-term acute exposure standards, allow one or two annual exceedances.
20. The NAAQSs are to be reviewed on a regular basis for possible revision. In 1997 EPA proposed a tightening of ozone standards and the introduction of a standard for even finer particulate matter, having a diameter of 2.5 microns.

## TABLE 1.—EFFECTS THRESHOLD, BEST CHOICE SIGNIFICANT RISK LEVELS AND SAFETY MARGINS CONTAINED IN PRIMARY AMBIENT AIR QUALITY STANDARDS

| Pollutant | Lowest best judgment estimate for effects threshold and best choice for significant risk levels | | Adverse health effect | U.S. primary air quality standard | Margin of safety* (percent) |
| --- | --- | --- | --- | --- | --- |
| | Concentration | Averaging time | | | |
| Sulfur dioxide | 300 to 400 ug/m$^3$ | 24 hour | Mortality increase | 365 ug/m$^3$ | None |
| | 91 ug/m$^3$ | Annual | Increased frequency of acute respiratory disease | 80 ug/m$^3$ | 14 |
| Total suspended particulates | 250 to 300 ug/m$^3$ | 24 hour | Mortality increase | 260 ug/m$^3$ | None |
| | 70 to 250 ug/m$^3$ | do | Aggravation of respiratory disease | 260 ug/m$^3$ | None |
| | 100 ug/m$^3$ | Annual | Increased frequency of chronic bronchitis | 75 ug/m$^3$ | 33 |
| Suspended sulfates | 10 ug/m$^3$ | 24 hour | Increased infections in asthmatics | None | None |
| | 15 ug/m$^3$ | Annual | Increased lower respiratory infections in children | None | None |
| Nitrogen dioxide | 140 ug/m$^3$ | do | Increased severity of acute respiratory illness in children | 100 ug/m$^3$ | 40 |
| Carbon monoxide | 23 ug/m$^3$ | 8 hour | Diminished exercise tolerance in heart patients | 10 ug/m$^3$ | **130 |
| | 73 ug/m$^3$ | 1 hour | Diminished exercise tolerance in heart patients | 40 ug/m$^3$ | **82 |
| Photochemical oxidants | 200 ug/m$^3$ | do | Increased susceptibility to infection | 160 ug/m$^3$ | 25 |

* Safety margin equals effects threshold minus standard divided by standard X 100.
** Safety margins based upon carboxyhemoglobin levels would be 100 percent for the 8 hour standard and 67 percent for the 1 hour standard.

## TABLE 2.—THRESHOLD AND ILLUSTRATIVE HEALTH RISKS FOR SELECTED AMBIANT LEVELS OF SUSPENDED SULFATES

| Adverse health effect | Threshold concentration and exposure duration | Definition | Illustrative health risk | |
| --- | --- | --- | --- | --- |
| | | | Level | Sulfur dioxide equivalent |
| Increase in daily mortality | 25 ug/m$^3$ for 24 hr or longer | 2½ percent increase in daily mortality | 38 ug/m$^3$ for 24 hr | 600 ug/m$^3$ for 24 hr. |
| Aggravation of heart and lung disease in the elderly | 9 ug/m$^3$ for 24 hr or longer | 50 per cent increase in symptom aggravation | 48 ug/m$^3$ for 24 hr | 750 ug/m$^3$ for 24 hr. |
| Aggravation of asthma | 6 to 10 ug/m$^3$ for 24 hr | 75 percent increase in frequency of asthma attacks | 30 ug/m$^3$ for 24 hr | 450 ug/m$^3$ for 24 hr. |
| Excess acute lower respiratory disease in children | 13 ug/m$^3$ for several yr | 50 percent increase in frequency | 20 ug/m$^3$ annual average | 100 to 250 ug/m$^3$ annual average. |
| Excess risk for chronic bronchitis | 10 to 15 ug/m$^3$ for up to 10 yr | 50 percent increase in risk | 15 to 20 ug/m$^3$ annual average | 100 to 250 ug/m$^3$ annual average. |

*Tables from the Cleveland Electric case, showing the primary NAAQSs (national ambient air quality standards) for criteria air pollutants as they existed at the time of the case. The standards today would contain lead levels and several other additions. Note that the tables, as is typically the case, totally ignore the nonmandatory secondary air standards.*

because their allowable emissions will often vary depending on what model is used and what assumptions are made in modeling.

Procedurally, the contours of the SIP process are fixed by the Clean Air Act itself. A good summary of the statutory deadlines and the process by which EPA oversees the states appears in NRDC v. Train, 545 F.2d 320 (2d Cir. 1976). The key element is a fixed time line from the time a pollutant is added to the list of criteria pollutants to the time at which a state must have in place a successful program for limiting emissions of that pollutant sufficiently to attain the primary ambient air quality standard. The "hammer" that gives EPA an ability to insist that the states go forward is the threat that EPA itself will adopt a plan should the state fail to meet the statutory requirements. Under that threat, most states have managed to draft SIPs that have garnered EPA approval. The case that follows is an example of where a state failed to do so, whereupon EPA was forced to draft a FIP to control sulfur dioxide emissions in the State of Ohio.[21]

### Cleveland Electric Illuminating Co. v. Environmental Protection Agency
United States Circuit Court of Appeals for the Sixth Circuit, 1978
572 F.2d 1150

EDWARDS, Cir.J. This court now has before it 23 petitions involving 32 companies filed against the United States Environmental Protection Agency which levy a variety of complaints against the federal agency's imposition of a sulfur dioxide ($SO_2$) pollution control plan for industrial discharges into Ohio's ambient air. The issues, which have been extensively briefed and argued, divide into general legal and procedural complaints which might be applicable to any one of the petitioners and a wider variety of specific complaints about the application of the EPA controls to particular power-generating or industrial plants.

The major issues dealt with in this opinion are: 1) intervenor, the State of Ohio, claims that this court should disapprove the federal plan as irrational and arbitrary and rely upon Ohio to come forward with a more rational plan sometime in the future; 2) petitioners claim that the EPA $SO_2$ plan should be remanded for hearings because the informal rulemaking hearings employed by EPA under 5 U.S.C. §553 (1970 & Supp. V 1975) were inadequate; and 3) petitioners claim that the major model employed by the United States Environmental Protection Agency in establishing specific emission limitations for particular plants is invalid both intrinsically and as applied. This model is termed the "Real-Time Air-Quality-Simulator Model" (hereinafter RAM).[22]

National air quality standards for sulfur dioxide, one of the most important pollutants of the ambient air, were set by EPA in 1973 as follows:

**40 CFR §50.4 — National primary ambient air-quality standards for sulfur oxides (sulfur dioxide).** The national primary ambient air quality standards for sulfur oxides measured as sulfur dioxide by the reference method described in Appendix A to this part, or by an equivalent method, are: (a) 80 micrograms per cubic meter (0.03 p.p.m.) — annual arithmetic mean; (b) 365 micrograms per

---

21. The case has an extensive prior history of litigation concerning sulfur dioxide emission controls in Ohio. See Buckeye Power, Inc. v. EPA, 481 F.2d 162 (6th Cir. 1973) (*Buckeye Power I*) and Buckeye Power, Inc. v. EPA, 525 F.2d 80 (6th Cir. 1975) (*Buckeye Power II*).

22. Eds: A further issue was an attack on EPA's failure to adopt a separate implementation plan for secondary air quality standards. That attack failed.

cubic meter (0.14 p.p.m.) — Maximum 24-hour concentration not to be exceeded more than once per year.

Acute episodes of high pollution have clearly resulted in mortality and morbidity. Often the effects of high pollutant concentrations in these episodes have been combined with other environmental features such as low temperatures or epidemic diseases (influenza) which may in themselves have serious or fatal consequences. This has sometimes made it difficult to determine to what extent pollution and temperature extremes are responsible for the effects. Nevertheless, there is now no longer any doubt that high levels of pollution sustained for periods of days can kill. Those aged 45 and over with chronic diseases, particularly of the lungs or heart, seem to be predominantly affected. In addition to these acute episodes, pollutants can attain daily levels which have been shown to have serious consequences to city dwellers.

There is a large and increasing body of evidence that significant health effects are produced by long-term exposures to air pollutants. Acute respiratory infections in children, chronic respiratory diseases in adults, and decreased levels of ventilatory lung function in both children and adults have been found to be related to concentrations of $SO_2$ and particulates, after apparently sufficient allowance has been made for such confounding variables as smoking and socioeconomic circumstances. Rall, Review of the Health Effects of Sulfur Oxides, 8 Envt'l Health Perspectives 97, 99 (1974).

It appears that present national air quality standards have been set with little or no margin of safety. Adverse health effects are set forth in the NAAQS chart in this section, in which the scanty margins of safety are set out.

The major sources of sulfur dioxide pollution of the ambient air are coal-fired plants — exemplified by power plants operated by some of the petitioners in this case.

THE STATE OF OHIO'S PETITION... On July 13, 1977, the State of Ohio belatedly moved for leave to intervene in this proceeding. Its motion attacked the EPA sulfur dioxide emission control plan as having an adverse impact on the Ohio coal industry, and the Ohio economy as a whole. The motion also asserted that the State was developing a sulfur dioxide plan which would eliminate excessive abatement requirements which Ohio perceived to exist in the federal regulations. This court granted the motion for leave to intervene and has considered the brief and the reply brief filed by Ohio. Under this first disposition heading we consider only Ohio's suggestion that this court reject the United States Environmental Protection Agency's sulfur dioxide control plan and rely upon Ohio's implied promise to promulgate a state sulfur dioxide plan sometime in the future.

We reject this suggestion on the basis of a record of delay and default which has left Ohio in the position of being the only major industrialized state lacking an enforceable plan for control of sulfur dioxide. It was clearly the intention of Congress to have a plan for control of sulfur dioxide emissions in place in all states in need of such control by the year 1972. Clean Air Act §§109(a), 110(a). It was equally clearly the intention of Congress that the preferred mechanism for establishment of such a plan was through the establishment and operation of a state environmental agency. Section 107(a). [Here the court summarized the sorry history of Ohio's efforts to adopt a sulfur dioxide SIP.] Clearly, the State of Ohio has failed to submit an implementation plan for sulfur dioxide for which a national ambient air quality primary standard has been prescribed. Equally clearly, five years have now elapsed beyond the date when such an implementation plan was called for under the Clean Air Act. Under these circumstances, we find no warrant, consistent with the purposes of the federal legislation, for giving heed to Ohio's petition for further delay....[23]

THE "RAM" MODEL... The petitioners in these cases center most of their criticisms upon the United States EPA's use of the Real-Time Air-Quality-Simulation Model ("RAM") which was employed by the agency in preparation of the Ohio sulfur dioxide control plan. RAM is a dispersion model which evaluates the interaction of a variety of facts in order to make predictions concerning the contribution to the pollution of the ambient air by specific plants. Its formula takes into account the capacity of each plant on a stack-by-stack basis and adds thereto smokestack height, surrounding terrain, and weather conditions. The model is operated on the assumption that the plants concerned operate 24 hours a day at full capacity and predictions are made for every day of the year. The ultimate standards are set according to the predicted second-worst day in terms of pollution results shown.

In comparison to all other prior methods of controlling pollution, RAM starts with a solid, ascertainable data base. This is the established design capacity of the power plants in question related to the sulfur content of the fuel used by each. From these factors the "emissions data" for each plant are developed.

When stack height, wind, weather, terrain, land use, etc., are figured in, the RAM model has the additional value of allowing its user to predict with considerable accuracy the relative contributions of specific power plant stacks to the points of maximum concentration of pollution of the ambient air.

The RAM model was actually developed as a result of the United States EPA's public hearings on the proposed plan for Ohio after five days of hearings on said proposed plan in Columbus, Cleveland, Cincinnati, and Steubenville at which petitioners involved in this current litigation were given an opportunity (which most accepted) to appear, testify, or submit comments. At those hearings the major source of criticism from industries, including some of the present petitioners, was that the plan then under consideration did not determine limitations by individual stacks to a sufficient degree. EPA in its brief in this case compares the "rollback" model employed in the preparation of the first Ohio plan to dispersion models like RAM, which is now the source of present controversy.

Unlike the rollback model, the dispersion models used in developing the promulgated plan allow a determination of the cause-effect relationship between the $SO_2$ emissions of the pollution sources in an area and the resulting ambient air quality. Therefore, it is possible to determine the proportion by which each source must reduce emissions to meet ambient standards. With the use of the rollback model, in contrast, each source's emissions in the region, whether or not they contributed to a pollution problem, were required to be reduced. Through dispersion modeling, emission limitations can now be set with increased precision. Overcontrol is minimized, so that the plan will still insure attainment and maintenance of the air quality standards, but at a much reduced cost to the sources. This is most clearly demonstrated by comparing emission limitations for power plants under the various plans. Power plants account for approximately 80 percent of the sulfur dioxide emissions in the State.

However, achievement of this added precision requires a massive analytical task. Tremendous amounts of data are required for each source analyzed. In addi-

23. Eds.: The claim of inadequate hearing procedures was rejected by the court.

tion to the emissions data for each source, dispersion modeling requires detailed information on all the factors that affect the dispersion of emissions. These include the height of the source's stack (or usually stacks), the spatial orientation of the sources to each other, the topography of the area and the effects it will have on dispersion, and, of crucial importance, detailed weather data for the area.

All this information is needed so that the computer analysis reflects actual conditions. For example, a gaseous pollutant emitted over a grassy field will disperse much differently than if the pollutant is emitted over a large urban area. There the dispersion will be affected not only by the local weather conditions but also by the greater turbulence caused by the different types of surface areas and heat sources throughout a city.

EPA goes on to point out that there are more than 1,000 point sources in the State of Ohio and more than 2,000 area sources,[24] and that in relation to emission data, United States EPA utilized (among other sources) the data base on sulfur dioxide required to be reported to the State of Ohio under Ohio Rev. Code Ann. §§3704.03(I), 3704.05(C) (Page 1971 & 1976 Supp.).

It is, of course, no part of the responsibility of this court to determine whether the RAM model represents the best possible approach to determining standards or the control of sulfur dioxide emissions. Our standard of review of the actions of United States EPA is whether or not the action of the agency is "arbitrary, capricious, an abuse of discretion, or otherwise not in accordance with law." Thus, we are required to affirm if there is a rational basis for the agency action and we are not "empowered to substitute [our] judgment for that of the agency." Citizens to Preserve Overton Park v. Volpe, 401 U.S. 402 (1971).

Our review of this record convinces us that we cannot properly hold that United States EPA's adoption of the RAM model for predicting sulfur dioxide emissions and for fixing maximum levels of sulfur dioxide emissions by specific sources was arbitrary and capricious or beyond the agency's authority under the Clean Air Act. The factors cited below support EPA's argument that the RAM model is supported by sufficient evidence so that EPA's adoption cannot be held arbitrary and capricious:

1) United States EPA's use of the "rollback" model — the principal basis of its first plan on which five days of public hearings were conducted in Ohio — was strenuously objected to by representatives of many of the present petitioners because it was not source-specific and, as a consequence, tended to require more stringent sulfur dioxide controls than would be required if plant capacity, fuel, population, smokestack height, wind and climate were all taken into account. Thus John R. Martin, of Smith & Singer Meteorologists, Inc., commented on behalf of Ohio utilities on the first United States EPA plan as follows:

> More sophisticated modeling is necessary in all seven of the urban counties that use the proportional rollback. In this way, the Federal air quality standards can be attained without unnecessary $SO_2$ emission restrictions being imposed upon sources that do not contribute to $SO_2$ problem... We recommended that new strategies be tested which will more fairly identify and control $SO_2$ sources that create $SO_2$ problems.

---

24. An area source is a small source of emissions that is not a large industrial facility. Examples include dry cleaning establishments, gasoline stations, wood-burning stoves and, most relevant in this case, small combustion units.

Similarly, Dr. Howard M. Ellis, of Enviroplan, Inc., said on behalf of Ohio power plants:

> In developing an $SO_2$ control program for this plant, Region V did not consider economically efficient alternatives to constant uniform emission standards — alternatives such as utilizing a supplementary control system to achieve air quality standards or using separate $SO_2$ emission standards by stack in accordance with each stack's contribution to ground-level $SO_2$ concentrations. Separate emission standards by stack can reduce considerably the cost of achieving air quality standards.

2) EPA responded to these arguments favorably by devising and adopting the RAM model which did employ all of these source-specific factors.

3) Further, as shown on [charts that are not reprinted here], the United States EPA 1976-1977 $SO_2$ control plan (principally based upon the RAM and MAX-24 models) shows less stringent regulation on a county-by-county basis when compared to the Ohio $SO_2$ control plans originally promulgated in 1972 and 1974. In addition, when the comparison is limited to petitioners involved in this litigation, but including all of their facilities which were subjected to RAM modeling (and which are identified in this record), we find the plan slightly less strict than the Ohio 1974 plan by a count of 23 to 20.

These comparisons do not, of course, necessarily demonstrate RAM's accuracy. Rather, the comparison with Ohio's previous plans (based upon the earlier rollback model which was used and accepted nationwide) tends simply to show that the choice of RAM modeling lay within administrative discretion.

4) While this court has currently before it some 32 petitioners protesting the United States EPA's plan for $SO_2$ emission control for Ohio, it must be remembered that Ohio is estimated to have over 1,000 point sources and over 2,000 area sources of $SO_2$ pollution.

5) The RAM model is a general formula which can be applied to many individual sources of pollution to derive specific estimates of $SO_2$ emission rates for each. It employs a wider, more complete and more accurate data base than any prior model yet employed in devising a sulfur dioxide control strategy for a state or county. The crucial data with which the RAM model starts are the design capacity figure, plus the fuel sulfur content, from which is computed the $SO_2$ emission rate for each of the heating or power plants sought to be controlled. Thus at the outset the RAM model starts with ascertainable specific figures for each source where disputes can be resolved by inspection of the equipment or fuel concerned. Many of the additional components such as stack height, wind direction, physical relationship of sources to each other, and topography of the area are similarly ascertainable as matters of fact. With the enormous financial stakes involved in this litigation, every effort to avoid disputes about the accuracy of the data base should be made. This record shows that United States EPA's design of the RAM model was brought about at least in large part by Ohio industry's requests for greater specificity and hence lower costs of compliance with National Air Quality Standards.

6) While there may yet be developed (and hopefully will be) a better method of establishing a control strategy for sulfur dioxide emissions than the RAM model, no one has yet come forward with such....

7) We recognize that this record does not present positive proofs of the accuracy of RAM's predictions. Thus far technology has not developed foolproof methods for validating predictions concerning pollution of the ambient air absent years of collection of monitoring data with far more monitors and far more personnel

than have thus far been available....

[The court here compared predicted and actual monitor readings for a small number of monitoring sites in Dayton, Ohio:]

| SITE NO. | 2D HIGHSET 24-HR RAM-PREDICTED CONCENTRATION IN UG PER M/3 | 1972 | 1973 | 1974 | 1975 | 1976 |
|---|---|---|---|---|---|---|
| 1 | 195 | * | * | 219 | * | * |
| 2 | 201 | 73 | 438 | 181 | 163 | 81 |
| 3 | 83 | * | * | 117 | 62 | 57 |
| 4 | 109 | * | * | 151 | 109 | 17 |
| 5 | 161 | 57 | 198 | * | 68 | 41 |
| 6 | 207 | * | 13 | 66 | 110 | 73 |

Our analysis of these data shows that the yearly second-highest concentration of $SO_2$ pollution (for a 24-hour average) actually recorded on available monitors exceeded the RAM model prediction for each location once in a five-year period at five out of six locations. This analysis certainly falls short of showing RAM's predictive perfection. But it certainly tends to show that the EPA's use of RAM, if conservative, cannot be held to be arbitrary and capricious.

8) Finally, as we pointed out at the beginning of this opinion, $SO_2$ emissions have a direct impact upon the health and the lives of the population of Ohio — particularly its young people, its sick people, and its old people. If the RAM model did overpredict emission rates, such a conservative approach in protection of health and life was apparently contemplated by Congress in requiring that EPA plans contain "emission limitations.... necessary to *insure* attainment and maintenance" of national ambient air standards. 42 U.S.C.A. §1857c-5(a)(2)(B)(1970). (Emphasis added.)

In summary, we hold that United States EPA's adoption and employment of the RAM model as its general working tool was based upon informal rulemaking which satisfied the requirements of both the Clean Air Act and the Administrative Procedure Act, and the due process requirements of the United States Constitution. Further, the record indicates that the Administrator's control regulations for Ohio through use of the RAM model was a rational choice which was well within the discretion committed to him and his agency. We decline petitioners' requests to set the disputed orders aside on the ground that they are arbitrary and capricious.

OTHER ISSUES. Somewhat half-heartedly the leading brief for the utilities attacks the United States EPA plan for $SO_2$ controls in Ohio as excessively costly and asserts that the satisfactory operation of Flue Gas Desulfurization machine ("scrubbers") has not been demonstrated. We note that the United States EPA control strategy for Ohio does not rely heavily upon Flue Gas Desulfurization. (EPA estimates — and petitioners do not dispute — that only six utilities will choose this compliance route.) Alternatives to installation of "scrubbers" are the purchasing and use of low sulfur coals or the employment of coal cleaning or blending techniques. There is no doubt, of course, that $SO_2$ controls will indeed be costly. EPA estimates capital costs for Ohio industry of well over half a billion dollars and annual costs of 171 million dollars. It also projects these costs as requiring a 3 percent increase in annual electric bills for the consumers who will ultimately pay them — and who will also breathe the less polluted air. Basically the choice of economic burden versus continued deterioration of the air we breathe was made by Congress. In this litigation no issue is raised concerning Congress' power to do so.

We have genuine doubt that this court has the power to review what we regard as petitioners' slightly disguised economic and technological infeasibility arguments. See generally Union Electric Co. v. EPA, 427 U.S. 246 (1976). Since this issue does not appear to be definitely resolved as to a United States EPA-designed implementation plan (such as we deal with here), we observe that if we did have such power, we would conclude that the technical record compiled in the agency proceeding provides ample support for the economic and technological feasibility of the $SO_2$ control strategies which United States EPA has promulgated for Ohio.

### COMMENTARY AND QUESTIONS

1. **Technical complexity and the competence of courts.** Does a case like *Cleveland Electric* prove that the technical complexity of airshed modeling is so great that a judicial forum is inappropriate? Should there instead be a technological decision-making body? Justice Breyer of the Supreme Court has advocated such a tribunal. Under current practice, the abuse of discretion standard of review provides a significant safeguard that matters of technical expertise will be decided by an expert decisionmaker, subject only to review that no gross misjudgments have been made. Is there any indication that the court is over-matched by the technical matters involved in this case? Is there any reason to believe that a specialized court would do a better job with the science than EPA?

2. **Does deference include the right to be very wrong?** How much stronger would the petitioners' case have been if the chart correlating RAM-predicted pollution concentrations had exceeded actual observed results in every year at every monitoring station? At some degree of error, model failure becomes coextensive with model irrationality.

3. **Amending the emissions limitations later.** Assume post-implementation monitor readings demonstrate that the RAM over-predicted pollution levels by a significant degree and that EPA is willing to adjust the RAM model to make its predictive capacity more accurate, and revise upward allowable emissions from many of the regulated polluters. Is that a satisfactory method of proceeding? Why will the regulated petitioners claim that is an inadequate remedy? What becomes of their investment in pollution control equipment that is no longer necessary, or their lost profits due to higher operating costs in the interim? The amount of "over-investment" in pollution control might be significant. The opinion pointed out that large sums of money were involved in meeting the EPA-imposed limitations. As a general rule, the cost of emissions reduction is not a linear function. The first few units of reduction are usually inexpensive to achieve, but additional improvements are ever more expensive. Is Ohio harmed in the same way? In the interim its citizens have enjoyed cleaner air and, if it elects to continue emissions controls

at their existing levels of stringency on the polluters, it is in a position to introduce new sources of emissions without forcing new cutbacks by the current polluters.

**4. Overriding state sovereignty and state resentment of federally imposed plans.** The court's opinion is sharply critical of Ohio's foot-dragging in implementing $SO_2$ standards. In the absence of the federal mandate provided by §110, is it likely that the court's attitude would have been the same? Can Ohio fairly claim that the federal act has usurped too much of its traditional power to control local matters? *Cleveland Electric* offers an indication of why the states feel threatened by FIPs. Due to the economic burdens to be placed on Ohio industries (especially its coal mining and electric generating industries) Ohio seems opposed to any $SO_2$ control without regard to whose plan it is. That degree of opposition may be aberrational. The usual state fear of EPA-imposed plans is that EPA might impose the burdens of pollution control in ways that are politically unpopular. For example, EPA has frequently tried to insist that SIPs include regional transportation plans that discourage the use of automobiles by commuters, or reduce emissions by the vehicles that are in service. Limits on available parking spaces, carpool lanes, increased spending on mass transit and mandatory motor vehicle emissions testing and maintenance are all tools in this approach. These programs have proven violently unpopular and their imposition, even though ordered by EPA, have sometimes been the death knell of local political careers. There is a kindred fear that EPA may seek reductions in a way that is insensitive to the needs and ability to pay of local polluting firms.

**5. Using tall stacks and intermittent controls to meet NAAQS requirements.** In an effort to limit their costs of compliance with the SIP that would eventually emerge, the Ohio utilities were urging Ohio to allow the use of tall smokestacks and intermittent pollution control devices as part of the older (pre-1977) versions of the Ohio SIP. Tall stacks are among the least cost solutions to meeting ambient air quality standards. They operate in two ways to help attain or maintain NAAQS compliance. First, they lead to wider dispersion of the pollutants they emit which means that the concentrations of the pollutant are lower than they would be in areas near the emitting facility if shorter stacks were employed. In effect, the use of taller stack leads to more diluted emissions that cover a wider geographic area. Second, the use of tall stacks makes possible the export of pollution beyond the boundary of the AQCR, turning the pollution into someone else's problem.

Intermittent controls are also a lower cost method of meeting the national standards because they are less expensive than comparable continuous controls. Intermittent controls are employed when receiving body air quality is at or near the allowable NAAQS and these controls are not used when receiving body conditions are favorable, i.e., when there is a low concentration of pollutants in the receiving ambient air. A very simple example of an intermittent control would be a plan that called for turning off an electrostatic precipitator that traps emissions in the stack when the local air is clean. The savings to the firm of this practice result from reduced operating and maintenance costs (because large energy costs are avoided during periods when the precipitator is not needed and the device itself will require less maintenance if it is used less often) and reduced capital costs (because the useful life of the device will be extended). An even more dramatic form of intermittent control is to cease production when receiving body conditions are unfavorable and operate with no controls when receiving body conditions permit. Using intermittent controls as opposed to continuous controls results in an increase in total emissions by allowing greater emissions when conditions permit.

What is objectionable about SIPs that rely on tall stacks and intermittent controls to meet the NAAQS? The export of pollution (externalizing the cost) to another state or AQCR is obviously antithetical to notions of equity and responsibility for one's own deeds. The devices embedded in the CAA to deter export of pollution are discussed below. The second objection to tall stacks and intermittent controls turns on the fact that they increase the aggregate amount of pollution that can be emitted without violating the NAAQS. Is that bad? If the NAAQSs are set at levels that are sufficiently protective of health, welfare and the environment, the criticism loses part of its force.

The Clean Air Act Amendments of 1977 specifically addressed tall stacks and intermittent controls and limited their attractiveness as control devices. Section §123 explicitly allows firms to increase stack heights and to employ "other dispersion technique[s]" (defined to include intermittent controls), but the degree of emission control attributable to the excessive height of the stack or the use of dispersion techniques does not count toward meeting emission control limitations set by the relevant SIP. For a discussion of this provision and the motivation of Congress in passing it, see Sierra Club v. EPA, 719 F.2d 436, 440-41 (D.C.Cir. 1983). The crux of the arguments for limiting dispersion centered on export and the unreliability and lack of enforceability of intermittent controls.

6. **Must SIPs reverse engineer from airshed models?** Congress not only gave the states primacy in determining how the NAAQSs were to be met, it also gave the states great latitude in how to do it. As made explicit in the 1990 Amendments, §110(a)(2)(A), SIPS, "shall include enforceable emission limitations and other control measures, means, or techniques (including economic incentives such as fees, marketable permits, and auctions of emissions rights), as well as schedules and timetables for compliance, as may be necessary or appropriate to meet the applicable requirements of this chapter." Under that invitation, a state might be able to avoid reliance on a detailed airshed model by imposing a regulatory regime that relied on economic incentives. Evaluating the likelihood that such a system would result in adequate air quality requires a more thorough understanding of how economic incentives systems work. That is taken up in Chapter 16.

## Section 3. TRANSLATING STATUTORY OBLIGATIONS INTO PERMITS

Permits are a recurrent fact of life in studying environmental regulation. They have already figured prominently in cases and case studies such as the Gwaltney/Smithfield materials, Wilsonville, and the Utilex saga. Permits are critically important in the next chapter's study of the Clean Water Act, and in numerous places throughout the materials on regulation and enforcement. It is appropriate, therefore, and worthwhile, to isolate permits here for brief treatment.

In the 1990 Amendments to the Clean Air Act, Congress added an entire Title V devoted to permits as a subject unto themselves. That section is closely modeled on the National Pollution Discharge Elimination System (NPDES) permits of the Clean Water Act. In describing NPDES, the United States Supreme Court outlined the function of all permits to discharge waste materials into the environment:

> Under NPDES, it is unlawful for any person to discharge a pollutant without obtaining a permit and complying with its terms. A NPDES permit serves to transform generally applicable effluent limitations and other standards — including those based on water quality — into the obligations (including a timetable for compliance) of the individual discharger, and the [Clean Water Act] provide[s] for direct administrative and judicial enforcement of permits. With few exceptions, for enforcement purposes a discharger in compliance with the terms and conditions of an NPDES permit is deemed to be in compliance with those sections of the [statute] on which permit conditions are based. In short, the permit defines, and facilitates compliance with and enforcement of, a preponderance of a discharger's obligations under the [statute]. EPA v. California, 426 U.S. 200, 205, (1976).

There are two types of permits — individual and general permits. The individual permit process begins with an application, in which the applicant must give the permitting authority basic information. For example, the information presented by an air permit application will include such things as the product manufactured, the raw materials, the fuels used, the manufacturing process utilized, the locations of stacks, the predicted contents of air emissions, the type and effectiveness of current or planned air pollution control devices, information on current plant equipment, and details of the applicant's current monitoring regime. Once a permit application is complete, the permitting authority must decide whether to deny the permit or to prepare a draft permit. A draft permit must be accompanied by a fact sheet and a public notice that specifies how comments can be made and how a public hearing can be obtained if there is sufficient public interest. If a state is the permitting authority, the draft permit must be sent to EPA for comments or potential veto. Once a decision is made to issue a permit, the permitting agency must issue a final written decision that responds to comments. Interested persons who have filed comments may take an administrative appeal if they are dissatisfied with the terms of the final permit. Unlike the public hearing, this administrative hearing is "on the record"; that is, limited cross-examination is permitted and a formal record of the proceedings is kept. Further appeals may be taken to the head of the relevant permitting agency and to state or federal courts, depending on whether the permitting authority is EPA or a state.

Environmental waste discharge permits contain three major sections: (1) discharge standards; (2) compliance schedules; and (3) monitoring and reporting requirements.

- Discharge standards are detailed, quantified, descriptions of allowable emissions.
- Compliance schedules set interim requirements to assure that the ultimate compliance date is met. Each interim step is independently enforceable. Interim requirements may include retaining a consultant, contracting for installation of equipment, installing equipment on schedule, and attaining interim standards.

- Self-monitoring and reporting requirements are the key aspects of enforcing environmental discharge permits. A permittee is required to monitor its releases with the monitoring technology and at the frequencies set out in the permit. All violations of permit standards (called "excursions" or "exceedances") must immediately be reported to the permitting authority. A permittee must also submit periodic reports, signed, under oath, by a senior plant official, to the permitting authority. These reports must contain all monitoring and sampling data, and must include a list of excursions. Monitoring data is public information and cannot be retained as trade secrets. False or inadequate reporting will expose responsible corporate officials to potential criminal enforcement.

Permits may also contain clauses relating to "variances" or "planning." For example, air or water discharge permits frequently include variances or exceptions for "upsets" (temporary noncompliance because of factors beyond the control of the permittee, such as an unpredictable, catastrophic storm), or "bypasses" (e.g., shutting down pollution control equipment for unanticipated repairs). A water permit might allow excursions due to intake water variations (permittees are only responsible for pollutants that they add to intake water). Planning requirements may include written preparations for dealing with accidental spills of pollutants at the plant.

With regard to the permittee, a permit operates as both a "sword" and a "shield." Because a permittee is required to monitor in accordance with permit conditions and report its own permit violations, the permit is a sharp sword in the hands of the permitting authority in an enforcement proceeding, or a member of the public bringing a citizen suit. There are virtually no defenses — except for the variances included in the permit — to permit enforcement actions based on the permittee's self-monitoring and excursion reports. These will be treated as records kept by the permittee in the ordinary course of business, and can support a grant of summary judgment in the liability phase of a typical enforcement action. On the other hand, the permit can be used to shield the permittee from enforcement of alleged obligations that are not included in the permit. For example, if an applicant for a water discharger permit accurately discloses, in its permit application, all of its wastewater discharges, and the permitting authority does not see fit to include discharge standards for one of these substances in the permit, then no enforcement action can be brought against the permittee based upon an alleged unpermitted discharge of that substance. See Atlantic States Legal Foundation v. Eastman Kodak, excerpted in Chapter 9.

Permits are issued for periods of time set by statute. For example, Clean Water Act discharge permits may be issued for a maximum of five years. Before a permit expires, the permittee must apply for renewal, specifying whether any changes in production or wastewater discharge have occurred since filing the original permit application. The old permit remains in effect until the renewal is granted. Once a new permit is issued, a discharger is bound by its terms, even if the discharger is contesting these conditions in the permitting agency or in court. Permits may be modified or revoked and reissued during the permit period. Common grounds for modification or revocation and reissuance are alterations to permitted facilities, new information, supervening federal regulations (this is generally contained in a

"Reopener Clause" in a permit), unforeseen events, or procurement of a variance. Permits may also be terminated before the expiration date because of nondisclosure or noncompliance.

General permits, also referred to as "permits-by-rule," are conspicuous elements of some environmental regulatory programs, such as the program requiring a permit to deposit dredged or fill material in waters of the United States, under §404 of the Clean Water Act. See Chapter 25. This permit program is administered by the U.S. Army Corps of Engineers (COE). The statute provides for delegation of primacy to states, but few states have expressed a desire to administer this highly controversial program. In carrying out the 404 program, the COE utilizes both individual and general permits (called Nationwide Permits, or NWPs).

### COMMENTARY AND QUESTIONS

1. **Does more formal permitting make the system work better?** Operationally, is a more formal permit system likely to help or hinder the effectiveness of a pollution control system? Cumbersome and confusing processes and shifting demands for information as part of the application process will grind its gears.

2. **Using permits as enforcement mechanisms.** Using lessons learned from the Clean Water Act, Title V of the Clean Air Act, employs the permit process as the key to enforcement. Before the passage of Title V, enforcing the Clean Air Act was difficult. The idea is really quite simple: establish specific emission limits in the permit, require monitoring in the permit, require reporting of the monitoring, and then allow both agency and citizen lawsuits that rely on the comparison of the reports to the permitted limits. See, David T. Buente, Citizen Suits and the Clean Air Act Amendments of 1990: Closing the Enforcement Loop, 21 Environmental Law 2233 (1991).

3. **Blurring the nice distinctions: the CAM rules.** Do not take too seriously the boundaries of categorization used to describe permits, such as distinguishing "compliance" from "monitoring." Administratively, EPA is actively attempting to meld them. For example, a significant innovation under Title V of the Clean Air Act is the Compliance Assurance Monitoring (CAM) Rule. First published on August 13, 1996, the CAM rule replaced a proposed "enhanced-monitoring rule." The functionality of the proposed CAM rule was described as follows:

> In contrast to the proposed enhanced-monitoring rule, which was designed to use monitoring as a method for directly determining continuous compliance with applicable requirements, the CAM rule takes the indirect approach of considering the operation of emission-control measures at a facility. These control measures include air-pollution control devices, process modifications, and operating limitations. The CAM rule essentially requires a facility that employs control measures: to evaluate and document that the control measures are continuously operating within specific performance ranges that have been designed to assure compliance with applicable requirements; to indicate any excursions from these ranges; and to adequately respond to the data so that the excursions are corrected. George Van Cleve & Keith W. Hamilton, Promise and Reality in the Enforcement of the Amended Clean Air Act Part I: EPA's

"Any Credible Evidence" and "Compliance Assurance Monitoring" Rules, 27 ELR 10097, 10110 (1997).

## Section 4. ADDING ENVIRONMENTAL JUSTICE CONCERNS TO THE PERMIT PROGRAM

### Interim Guidance[25] for Investigating Title VI Administrative Complaints Challenging Permits
EPA Office of Enforcement and Compliance Assurance, February 1998

*No person in the United States shall, on the ground of race, color, or national origin, be excluded from participation in, be denied the benefits of, or be subjected to discrimination under any program or activity receiving Federal financial assistance. — Title VI*

This interim guidance is intended to provide a framework for the processing by EPA's Office of Civil Rights (OCR) of complaints filed under Title VI of the Civil Rights Act of 1964, as amended, 42 U.S.C. §§2000d to 2000d-7, alleging discriminatory effects resulting from the issuance of pollution control permits by state and local governmental agencies that receive EPA funding.

In the past, the Title VI complaints filed with EPA typically alleged discrimination in access to public water and sewerage systems or in employment practices. This interim guidance is intended to update the Agency's procedural and policy framework to accommodate the increasing number of Title VI complaints that allege discrimination in the environmental permitting context.

As reflected in this guidance, Title VI environmental permitting cases may have implications for a diversity of interests, including those of the recipient, the affected community, and the permit applicant or permittee. EPA believes that robust stakeholder input is an invaluable tool for fully addressing Title VI issues during the permitting process and informally resolving Title VI complaints when they arise.

BACKGROUND... On February 11, 1994, President Clinton issued Executive Order 12,898, "Federal Actions To Address Environmental Justice in Minority Populations and Low-Income Populations."[26] The Presidential memorandum accompanying that Order directs Federal agencies to ensure compliance with the nondiscrimination requirements of Title VI for all Federally-funded programs and activities that affect human health or the environment. While Title VI is inapplicable to EPA actions, including EPA's issuance of permits, Section 2-2 of Executive Order 12,898 is designed to ensure that Federal actions substantially affecting human health or the environment do not have discriminatory effects based on race, color, or national origin. Accordingly, EPA is committed to a policy of nondiscrimination in its own permitting programs.

Title VI itself prohibits intentional discrimination. The Supreme Court has ruled, however, that Title VI authorizes Federal agencies, including EPA, to adopt implementing regulations that prohibit discriminatory *effects*. Frequently,

---

25. The statements in this document are intended solely as guidance. This document is not intended, nor can it be relied upon, to create any rights enforceable by any party in litigation with the United States. EPA may decide to follow the guidance provided in this document, or to act at variance with the guidance, based on its analysis of the specific facts presented. This guidance may be revised without public notice to reflect changes in EPA's approach to implementing the Small Business Regulatory Enforcement Fairness Act or the Regulatory Flexibility Act, or to clarify and update text.

26. Executive Order 12,898, 3 CFR 859 (Feb. 11, 1994), reprinted at 42 U.S.C.A §4321 (note).

discrimination results from policies and practices that are neutral on their face, but have the *effect* of discriminating. Facially-neutral policies or practices that result in discriminatory effects violate EPA's Title VI regulations unless it is shown that they are justified and that there is no less discriminatory alternative.

In the event that EPA finds discrimination in a recipient's permitting program, and the recipient is not able to come into compliance voluntarily, EPA is required by its Title VI regulations to initiate procedures to deny, annul, suspend, or terminate EPA funding. EPA also may use any other means authorized by law to obtain compliance, including referring the matter to the Department of Justice (DOJ) for litigation. In appropriate cases, DOJ may file suit seeking injunctive relief. Moreover, individuals may file a private right of action in court to enforce the nondiscrimination requirements in Title VI or EPA's implementing regulations without exhausting administrative remedies....

OVERVIEW OF FRAMEWORK FOR PROCESSING COMPLAINTS...

...**2. Investigation/Disparate Impact Assessment.** Once a complaint is accepted for processing, OCR will conduct a factual investigation to determine whether the permit(s) at issue will create a disparate impact, or add to an existing disparate impact, on a racial or ethnic population. If, based on its investigation, OCR concludes that there is no disparate impact, the complaint will be dismissed. If OCR makes an initial finding of a disparate impact, it will notify the recipient and the complainant and seek a response from the recipient within a specified time period. Under appropriate circumstances, OCR may seek comment from the recipient, permittee, and/or complainant(s) on preliminary data analyses before making an initial finding concerning disparate impacts.

**3. Rebuttal/Mitigation.** The notice of initial finding of a disparate impact will provide the recipient the opportunity to rebut OCR's finding, propose a plan for mitigating the disparate impact, or to "justify" the disparate impact (see step 4 below regarding justification). If the recipient successfully rebuts OCR's finding, or, if the recipient elects to submit a plan for mitigating the disparate impact, and, based on its review, EPA agrees that the disparate impact will be mitigated sufficiently pursuant to the plan, the parties will be so notified. Assuming that assurances are provided regarding implementation of such a mitigation plan, no further action on the complaint will be required.

**4. Justification.** If the recipient can neither rebut the initial finding of disparate impact nor develop an acceptable mitigation plan, then the recipient may seek to demonstrate that it has a substantial, legitimate interest that justifies the decision to proceed with the permit notwithstanding the disparate impact. Even where a substantial, legitimate justification is proffered, OCR will need to consider whether it can be shown that there is an alternative that would satisfy the stated interest while eliminating or mitigating the disparate impact....

**8. Informal Resolution.** EPA's Title VI regulations call for OCR to pursue informal resolution of administrative complaints wherever practicable. 40 C.F.R. §7.120(d)(2). Therefore, OCR will discuss, at any point during the process outlined above, offers by recipients to reach informal resolution, and will, to the extent appropriate, endeavor to facilitate the informal resolution process and involvement of affected stakeholders....

PERMIT MODIFICATIONS... Permit modifications that result in a net increase of pollution impacts, however, may provide a basis for an adverse disparate impact finding, and, accordingly, OCR will not reject or dismiss complaints associated with permit modifications without an examination of the circumstances to determine the nature of the modification. In the permit modification context (as opposed to permit renewals), the matter under consideration by the recipient is the modified operation. Accordingly, the complaint must allege, and, to establish a disparate impact OCR must find, adverse impacts specifically associated with the modification.

INVESTIGATIONS OF ALLEGEDLY DISCRIMINATORY PERMIT RENEWALS... Generally, permit renewals should be treated and analyzed as if they were new facility permits, since permit renewal is, by definition, an occasion to review the overall operations of a permitted facility and make any necessary changes. Generally, permit renewals are not issued without public notice and an opportunity for the public to challenge the propriety of granting a renewal under the relevant environmental laws and regulations.

IMPACTS AND THE DISPARATE IMPACT ANALYSIS... Evaluations of disparate impact allegations should be based upon the facts and totality of the circumstances that each case presents. Rather than use a single technique for analyzing and evaluating disparate impact allegations, OCR will use several techniques within a broad framework. Any method of evaluation chosen within that framework must be a reasonably reliable indicator of disparity.

In terms of the types of impacts that are actionable under Title VI in the permitting context, OCR will, until further notice, consider impacts cognizable under the recipient's permitting program in determining whether a disparate impact within the meaning of Title VI has occurred. Thus, OCR will accept for processing only those Title VI complaints that include at least an allegation of a disparate impact concerning the types of impacts that are relevant under the recipient's permitting program.[27]

The general framework for determining whether a disparate impact exists has five basic steps.

**Step 1: Identifying the Affected Population.** The first step is to identify the population affected by the permit that triggered the complaint. The affected population is that which suffers the adverse impacts of the permitted activity. The impacts investigated must result from the permit(s) at issue.

The adverse impacts from permitted facilities are rarely distributed in a predictable and uniform manner. However, proximity to a facility will often be a reasonable indicator of where impacts are concentrated. Accordingly, where more precise information is not available, OCR will generally use proximity to a facility to identify adversely affected populations. The proximity analysis should reflect the environmental medium and impact of concern in the case.

---

27. Even where a recipient's authority to regulate is unclear concerning cumulative burden or discriminatory permitting pattern scenarios (see step 3 below), OCR will nonetheless consider impacts measured in these terms because Title VI is a Federal cross-cutting statute that imposes independent, nondiscrimination requirements on recipients of Federal funds. As such, Title VI, separate from and in addition to the strictures of state and local law, both authorizes and requires recipients to manage their programs in a way that avoids discriminatory cumulative burdens and distributional patterns. Thus, while Title VI does not alter the substantive requirements of a recipient's permitting program, it obligates recipients to implement those requirements in a nondiscriminatory manner as a condition of receiving Federal funds.

**Step 2: Determining the Demographics of the Affected Population.** The second step is to determine the racial and/or ethnic composition of the affected population for the permitted facility at issue in the complaint. To do so, OCR uses demographic mapping technology, such as Geographic Information Systems (GIS). In conducting a typical analysis to determine the affected population, OCR generates data estimating the race and/or ethnicity and density of populations within a certain proximity from a facility or within the distribution pattern for a release/impact based on scientific models. OCR then identifies and characterizes the affected population for the facility at issue. If the affected population for the permit at issue is of the alleged racial or ethnic group(s) named in the complaint, then the demographic analysis is repeated for each facility in the chosen universe(s) of facilities discussed below.

**Step 3: Determining the Universe(s) of Facilities and Total Affected Population(s).** The third step is to identify which other permitted facilities, if any, are to be included in the analysis and to determine the racial or ethnic composition of the populations affected by those permits....Ordinarily, OCR will entertain cases only in which the permitted facility at issue is one of several facilities, which together present a cumulative burden or which reflect a pattern of disparate impact. EPA recognizes the potential for disparate outcomes in this area because most permits *control* pollution rather than prevent it altogether. Consequently, permits that satisfy the base public health and environmental protections contemplated under EPA's programs nonetheless bear the potential for discriminatory effects where residual pollution and other cognizable impacts are distributed disproportionately to communities with particular racial or ethnic characteristics. Based on its experience to date, the Agency believes that this is most likely to be true either where an individual permit contributes to or compounds a preexisting burden being shouldered by a neighboring community, such that the community's cumulative burden is disproportionate when compared with other communities; or where an individual permit is part of a broader pattern pursuant to which it has become more likely that certain types of operations, with their accompanying burdens, will be permitted in a community with particular racial or ethnic characteristics.

**Step 4: Conducting a Disparate Impact Analysis.** The fourth step is to conduct a disparate impact analysis that, at a minimum, includes comparing the racial or ethnic characteristics within the affected population. It will also likely include comparing the racial characteristics of the affected population to the non-affected population. This approach can show whether persons protected under Title VI are being impacted at a disparate rate. EPA generally would expect the rates of impact for the affected population and comparison populations to be relatively comparable under properly implemented programs. Since there is no one formula or analysis to be applied, OCR may identify on a case-by-case basis other comparisons to determine disparate impact.

**Step 5: Determining the Significance of the Disparity.** The final phase of the analysis is to use arithmetic or statistical analyses to determine whether the disparity is significant under Title VI. OCR will use trained statisticians to evaluate disparity calculations done by investigators. After calculations are informed by expert opinion, OCR may make a prima facie disparate impact finding, subject to the recipient's opportunity to rebut.

MITIGATION...EPA expects mitigation to be an important focus in the Title VI process, given the typical interest of recipients in avoiding more draconian outcomes and the difficulty that many recipients will encounter in justifying an "unmitigated," but nonetheless disparate, impact. In some circumstances, it may be possible for the recipient to mitigate public health and environmental considerations sufficiently to address the disparate impact. The sufficiency of such mitigation should be evaluated in consultation with experts in the EPA program at issue. OCR may also consult with complainants. Where it is not possible or practicable to mitigate sufficiently the public health or environmental impacts of a challenged permit, EPA will consider "supplemental mitigation projects" (SMPs), which, when taken together with other mitigation efforts, may be viewed by EPA as sufficient to address the disparate impact. An SMP can, for example, respond to concerns associated with the permitting of the facility raised by the complainant that cannot otherwise be redressed under Title VI (i.e., because they are outside those considerations ordinarily entertained by the permitting authority).

JUSTIFICATION... If a preliminary finding of noncompliance has not been successfully rebutted and the disparate impact cannot successfully be mitigated, the recipient will have the opportunity to "justify" the decision to issue the permit notwithstanding the disparate impact, based on the substantial, legitimate interests of the recipient. While determining what constitutes a sufficient justification will necessarily turn on the facts of the case at hand, OCR would expect that, given the considerations described above, merely demonstrating that the permit complies with applicable environmental regulations will not ordinarily be considered a substantial, legitimate justification.... While the sufficiency of the justification will necessarily depend on the facts of the case at hand, the types of factors that may bear consideration in assessing sufficiency can include, but are not limited to, the seriousness of the disparate impact, whether the permit at issue is a renewal (with demonstrated benefits) or for a new facility (with more speculative benefits), and whether any of the articulated benefits associated with a permit can be expected to benefit the particular community that is the subject of the Title VI complaint.

Importantly, a justification offered will not be considered acceptable if it is shown that a less discriminatory alternative exists. If a less discriminatory alternative is practicable, then the recipient must implement it to avoid a finding of noncompliance with the regulations.

COMMENTARY AND QUESTIONS

1. **The Interim Guidance as a paradigm shift.** To what situations does the guidance apply and in what way does that contrast with past practice? EPA recognizes that attaching Title VI concerns to permitting greatly expands the federal involvement in environmental justice from a relatively narrow set of contexts (access to public water and sewer facilities and employment) to the heart of the pollution control process. The guidance applies not only to the issuance of new permits, but to permit modifications and permit renewals, taking advantage of the special leverage that can be had in the renewal context. In that latter context, the permit holder has already completed their investment in the facility and is, usually, protecting a productive asset that cannot continue to function if the renewal process results in loss of the permit. Given the prominence of cumulative impacts of multiple emitting facilities on minority communities, the ability to obtain pollution control

improvements in the renewal context is potentially at least as important as is the new facility siting context.

**2. Casting a federal shadow on a traditional state prerogative.** The Title VI guidance to the permit process federalizes to some degree what had previously been a state controlled area, that of facility siting. There are relatively few facilities that would pose significant environmental justice issues that can be sited without need of some sort of environmental permit. Under the guidance, state and local agencies receiving federal funds (i.e., virtually all state and local pollution control agencies, and many other governmental entities) are at risk of losing that funding. In many cases, that funding (and the threat of its loss) will persuade them to participate in the negotiation process described in the guidance. Contrast with the federal process envisioned here, the variety of state siting laws described in Chapter 25.

**3. Are the standards too muddy?** After reading the excerpts from the guidance, can the elements of a successful complaint be listed? Taking a different perspective, do permitting agencies and permit seekers know what is in store for them if their actions can be shown to have a disparate impact on a minority group? The subject matter does not lend itself to precision, so it would be unfair to treat EPA's effort too harshly. Reconsider the standards (or lack thereof) after reading Chapter 12.

**4. Using this guidance document to seek enforceable legal rights and remedies.** Where does the authority to promulgate the guidance come from and how much legal force should it have? Consider first how remote the guidance is from the relevant legislation. Congress, specifically empowered by §5 of the Fourteenth Amendment, passed general anti-discrimination legislation that included Title VI, but does not apply to EPA. Thereafter, the President issued Executive Order 12,898 that states in §6-609:

> This order is intended only to improve the internal management of the executive branch and is not intended to, nor does it create any right, benefit, or trust responsibility, substantive or procedural, enforceable at law or equity by a party against the United States, its agencies, its officers, or any person. This order shall not be construed to create any right to judicial review involving the compliance or noncompliance of the United States, its agencies, its officers, or any other person with this order.

That Executive Order provided the predicate for EPA issuance of the guidance. As a concluding statement in the guidance, EPA reiterates the non-binding nature of the guidance that appeared in the initial footnote. Nevertheless, this guidance purports to create a privately actionable and enforceable administrative remedy for permit actions having discriminatory effects of permit decisions that is itself subject to judicial review. Can it? In a more certain context, that of private suits to enforce federal administrative *regulations* implementing Title VI and *applying them to states* receiving funds from federal programs, courts have found that private rights are enforceable. See Chester Residents Concerned for the Quality of Living v. Seif, Secretary of the Pennsylvania Department of Environmental Protection, 132 F.3d 925 (1997) and cases cited therein. Based on the *Chester* case and others like it, the guidance will indirectly support a cause of action once EPA issues implementing regulations.

5. **The Shintech case.** Almost as prelude to the guidance, EPA on September 10, 1997, granted for the first time, a citizen petition opposing issuance of an operating permit for an industrial facility, basing the decision, at least in part, on environmental justice grounds. The facility involved is a $70 million chemical plant, proposed for construction in Convent, Louisiana. The population within a one-mile radius of the plant is 98% African-American, of whom half have annual incomes below $15,000. The case has gained national media attention because of its environmental justice aspects. While it remains far from resolution, it may set a very important precedent once it plays out. EPA regulations addressing Title VI appear at 40 C.F.R. §§7.120-7.130.

## E.  ASSURING ATTAINMENT OF DESIRED QUALITY LEVELS

The Clean Air Act has been in place since 1970 and ambient air quality now meets the NAAQS primary standards in many air quality control regions. and the secondary standards in numerous instances as well. There remain, however, a considerable number of areas where even the primary NAAQS remains unmet for one or more of the criteria pollutants. These areas are, quite appropriately, termed non-attainment areas and Congress has addressed special attention to them in post-1970 amendments to the Clean Air Act.[28]

A typical non-attainment area profile includes a densely populated, urbanized area, having industrial concentrations and substantial automobile use. Some of the most severe non-attainment areas, Los Angeles and Denver, for example, have unique topographic-meteorologic factors that exacerbate their problems. In these non-attainment areas, even stringent air pollution reduction efforts have failed to reduce sufficiently the concentration of the relevant criteria pollutant(s). As noted before, SIP-required efforts to control pollution need not be limited to direct emission controls, such as smokestack flue gas scrubbers. Additional requirements may include fuel switching to cleaner fuels, other process changes, transportation controls to limit the number and type of vehicles, and special limitations on new development.

As a matter of policy, Congress has not treated non-attainment areas too severely. Congress could, if it desired, order a total ban on all new development as a means of avoiding additional pollution of already unsafe air. So too, Congress could force the discontinuation of existing activities in an effort to provide the desired health benefits. The polluters refrain that was repeated so many times in the Clean Air Act cases, calling for someone to consider economic and technological feasibility, is answered in the political arena. Politically, choices that forbid development, or force closure of too many existing firms, are unpalatable because

---

28. After the 1990 Amendments the non-attainment provisions are codified at 42 U.S.C.A. §§7501-7515. N.B. — The 1990 Amendments, in rewriting the 1977 provisions, as well as making substantive changes, made a number of small readjustments in the order and organization of the material. As a result, some section numbers references that appear in cases and articles addressing this topic refer to the law as it stood from 1970 to 1990 and, therefore, no longer point to the correct location for the material.

of their economic and social consequences. Still, as the non-attainment area legislation makes clear, Congress has compromised, but not forsaken, its interest in the promotion of environmental quality and the protection of public health and welfare.

The signal content of the 1977 non-attainment areas legislation was the insistence that non-attainment areas make "reasonable further progress" toward attainment. This requirement is so well established and familiar, that in the 1990 amendments to the CAA, §172(c)(2), the provision requiring non-attainment SIPs to "require reasonable further progress" toward attainment, is entitled only "RFP." The statute defines RFP as "such annual incremental reductions in emissions of the applicable air pollutant as are required by this part [of the CAA] or may reasonably be required by the Administrator for the purpose of ensuring attainment of the applicable national ambient air quality standard by the applicable date." §171(1). The 1990 amendments set general requirements (§§171–180), and a series of very specific requirements as to compliance dates and incremental improvements for the various criteria pollutants (ozone, §181–185B; carbon monoxide, §§186–187; particulate matter, §§188–190; sulfur oxides, nitrogen dioxide and lead, §§191–192).

The backbone of the regulatory framework remains the SIP process, but for non-attainment areas, the 1977 Amendments required EPA to measure SIPs against a series of eleven explicit statutory requirements. The 1990 Amendments shortened the list to nine, §171(c)(1-9). In the criteria for non-attainment area SIPs, Congress moves away from harm-based ambient standards toward a technique and technology-based approach. For example, subsection (c)(1) states that the SIP must "... provide for the implementation of all reasonably available control measures as expeditiously as practicable (including such reductions in emissions from existing sources in the areas as may be obtained through the adoption, at a minimum, of reasonably available control technology [RACT])... ." New major sources of pollution must "comply with the lowest achievable emission rate [LAER][29]..." §173(2).

## Section 1. LOCATING NEW SOURCES IN TOO-DIRTY AIR AREAS

Under the 1977 Amendments, and still more emphatically after the 1990 Amendments, new major sources not only must avoid increasing pollution, their introduction of new emissions must be accompanied by more than offsetting reductions in existing emissions from other sources. A permit to operate a new major pollution source can be granted only if "by the time the source is to commence operation, sufficient offsetting emissions reductions have been obtained, such that total allowable emissions from existing sources in the region, from new or modified sources which are not major emitting facilities, and from the proposed source will be sufficiently less than total emissions from existing sources...prior to the application...so as to represent...reasonable further progress [toward attainment]. §173(a)(1)(A). Historically, as the following case demonstrates, the means for calculating offsets can at times frustrate the spirit of the non-attainment provisions.

---

29. LAER is considered to be an even more stringent technological command than is the employment of best available technology (BAT). BAT is discussed *infra* in Chapter Nine.

## Citizens Against the Refinery's Effects v. EPA
United States Circuit Court of Appeals for the Fourth Circuit, 1981
643 F.2d 183

HALL, Circuit Judge... Citizens Against the Refinery's Effects (CARE) appeals from a final ruling by the Administrator of the Environmental Protection Agency (EPA) approving the Virginia State Implementation Plan (SIP) for reducing hydrocarbon pollutants. The plan requires the Virginia Highway Department to decrease usage of a certain type of asphalt, thereby reducing hydrocarbon pollution by more than enough to offset expected pollution from the Hampton Roads Energy Company's (HREC) proposed refinery. We affirm the action of the administrator in approving the state plan....

[Before the 1977 amendments][t]he Clean Air Act created a no-growth environment in areas where the clean air requirements had not been attained. EPA recognized the need to develop a program that encouraged attainment of clean air standards without discouraging economic growth. Thus the agency proposed an Interpretive Ruling in 1976 which allowed the states to develop an "offset program" within the State Implementation Plans. 41 Fed. Reg. 55524 (1976). The offset program, later codified by Congress in the 1977 Amendments to the Clean Air Act, permits the states to develop plans which allow construction of new pollution sources where accompanied by a corresponding reduction in an existing pollution source. 42 U.S.C. §7502(b)(6) and §7503.[30] In effect, a new emitting facility can be built if an existing pollution source decreases its emissions or ceases operations as long as a positive net air quality benefit occurs.

If the proposed factory will emit carbon monoxide, sulfur dioxide, or particulates, the EPA requires that the offsetting pollution source be within the immediate vicinity of the new plant. The other two pollutants, hydrocarbons and nitrogen oxide, are less "site-specific," and thus the ruling permits the offsetting source to locate anywhere within a broad vicinity of the new source.

The offset program has two other important requirements. First, a base time period must be determined in which to calculate how much reduction is needed in existing pollutants to offset the new source. This base period is defined as the first year of the SIP or, where the state has not yet developed a SIP, as the year in which a construction permit application is filed. Second, the offset program requires that the new source adopt the Lowest Achievable Emissions Rate (LAER) using the most modern technology available in the industry.

HREC proposes to build a petroleum refinery and off-loading facility in Portsmouth, Virginia. Portsmouth has been unable to reduce air pollution enough to attain the national standard for one pollutant, photochemical oxidants, which is created when hydrocarbons are released into the atmosphere and react with other substances. Since a refinery is a major source of hydrocarbons, the Clean Air Act prevents construction of the HREC plant until the area attains the national standard.

In 1975, HREC applied to the Virginia State Air Pollution Control Board (VSAPCB) for a refinery construction permit. The permit was issued by the VSAPCB on October 8, 1975, extended and reissued on October 5, 1977 after a full public hearing, modified on August 8, 1978, and extended again on September 27, 1979. The VSAPCB, in an effort to help HREC meet the clean air requirements, proposed to use the offset ruling to comply with the Clean Air Act.

---

30. Eds.: After the 1990 Amendments, §§172(b)(4) and 173(a)(1) & (c) are the relevant provisions.

On November 28, 1977, the VSAPCB submitted a State Implementation Plan to EPA which included the HREC permit. The Virginia Board proposed to offset the new HREC hydrocarbon pollution by reducing the amount of cutback asphalt[31] used for road paving operations in three highway districts by the Virginia Department of Highways.[32] By switching from "cutback" to "emulsified" asphalt, the state can reduce hydrocarbon pollutants by the amount necessary to offset the pollutants from the proposed refinery.... [The plan was eventually approved by EPA.]

CARE raises four issues regarding the state plan. First, they argue that the geographic area used as the base for the offset was arbitrarily determined and that the area as defined violates the regulations. Second, CARE contends that EPA should have used 1975 instead of 1977 as the base year to compare usage of cutback asphalt. Third, CARE insists that the offset plan should have been disapproved since the state is voluntarily reducing usage of cutback asphalt anyway. Fourth, CARE questions the approval of the plan without definite Lowest Achievable Emissions Rates (LAER) as required by the statute. We reject the CARE challenges to the state plan....

CARE contends that the state plan should not have been approved by EPA since the three highway-district area where cutback usage will be reduced to offset refinery emissions was artificially developed by the state. The ruling permits a broad area (usually within one AQCR) to be used as the offset basis....

The agency action in approving the use of three highway districts was neither arbitrary, capricious, nor outside the statute. First, Congress intended that the states and the EPA be given flexibility in designing and implementing SIPs. Such flexibility allows the states to make reasoned choices as to which areas may be used to offset new pollution and how the plan is to be implemented. Second, the offset program was initiated to encourage economic growth in the state. Thus a state plan designed to reduce highway department pollution in order to attract another industry is a reasonable contribution to economic growth without a corresponding increase in pollution. Third, to be sensibly administered the offset plan had to be divided into districts which could be monitored by the highway department. Use of any areas other than highway districts would be unwieldy and difficult to administer. Fourth, the scientific understanding of ozone pollution is not advanced to the point where exact air transport may be predicted. Designation of the broad area in which hydrocarbons may be transported is well within the discretion and expertise of the agency.

Asphalt consumption varies greatly from year to year, depending upon weather and road conditions. Yet EPA must accurately determine the volume of hydrocarbon emissions from cutback asphalt. Only then can the agency determine whether the reduction in cutback usage will result in an offset great enough to account for the new refinery pollution. To calculate consumption of a material where it constantly varies, a base year must be selected. In this case, EPA's Interpretive Ruling establishes the base year as the year in which the permit application is made. EPA decided that 1977 was an acceptable base year. CARE argues that EPA illegally chose 1977 instead of 1975.

---

31. "Cutback" asphalt has a petroleum base which gives off great amounts of hydrocarbons. "Emulsified" asphalt uses a water base which evaporates, giving off no hydrocarbons.

32. The three highway districts so designated comprise almost the entire eastern one-third of the state. The area cuts across four of the seven Virginia Air Quality Control Regions (AQCR).

Considering all of the circumstances, including the unusually high asphalt consumption in 1977, the selection by EPA of that as the base year was within the discretion of the agency. Since the EPA Interpretive Ruling allowing the offset was not issued until 1976, 1977 was the first year after the offset ruling and the logical base year in which to calculate the offset. Also, the permit issued by the VSAPCB was reissued in 1977 with extensive additions and revisions after a full hearing. Under these circumstances, 1977 appears to be a logical choice of a base year.

For several years, Virginia has pursued a policy of shifting from cutback asphalt to the less expensive emulsified asphalt in road-paving operations. The policy was initiated in an effort to save money, and was totally unrelated to a State Implementation Plan. Because of this policy, CARE argues that hydrocarbon emissions were decreasing independent of this SIP and therefore are not a proper offset against the refinery. They argue that there is not, in effect, an actual reduction in pollution.

The Virginia voluntary plan is not enforceable and therefore is not in compliance with the 1976 Interpretive Ruling which requires that the offset program be enforceable. 41 Fed. Reg. 55526 (1976). The EPA, in approving the state plan, obtained a letter from the Deputy Attorney General of Virginia in which he stated that the requisites had been satisfied for establishing and enforcing the plan with the Department of Highways. Without such authority, no decrease in asphalt-produced pollution is guaranteed. In contrast to the voluntary plan, the offset plan guarantees a reduction in pollution resulting from road paving operations.

LOWEST ACHIEVABLE EMISSIONS RATE... Finally, CARE argues that the Offset Plan does not provide adequate Lowest Achievable Emission Rates (LAER) as required by the 1976 Interpretive Ruling because the plan contains only a 90 percent vapor recovery requirement, places an excessive 176.5 ton limitation on hydrocarbon emissions, and does not require specific removal techniques at the terminal. EPA takes the position that the best technique available for marine terminals provides only a 90 percent recovery and that the 176.5 ton limit may be reduced by the agency after the final product mix at the terminal is determined.

Since the record shows no evidence of arbitrary or capricious action in approving the HREC emissions equipment, the agency determination of these technical matters must be upheld.

In approving the state plan, EPA thoroughly examined the data, requested changes in the plan, and approved the plan only after the changes were made. There is no indication that the agency acted in an arbitrary or capricious manner or that it stepped beyond the bounds of the Clean Air Act. We affirm the decision of the administrator in approving the state plan.

## COMMENTARY AND QUESTIONS

1. **Insisting on "reasonable further progress."** Was EPA too permissive with Virginia in this case, so permissive that it violated the statutory "reasonable further progress" requirement? Couldn't EPA have gotten both the switch to the less polluting asphalt plus additional offsets if it has wanted to take a more aggressive stance regarding what is reasonable progress for Virginia under the circumstances?

2. **"Reasonably available control measures" (RACM) requirements.** The CAA §172(c)(1) requires that non-attainment SIPs apply RACM[33] to all sources in non-attainment areas as expeditiously as possible. Plainly that language authorizes EPA to refuse to approve SIPs or SIP revisions for non-attainment areas when those plans do not include RACT or RACM. For example, in Navistar International Transportation Co. v. EPA, 941 F.2d 1339 (6th Cir. 1991), the EPA disapproved a proposed Ohio non-attainment VOC SIP revision that would have relaxed VOC emission requirements at the truck manufacturer's plant. One ground EPA advanced (and the court approved) in support of its decision was that the relaxation would violate the requirement of implementing RACT as expeditiously as possible. Note that the *Navistar* case is not inconsistent with *CARE*. In *Navistar* EPA was claiming that Ohio was seeking to employ less than RACT, in *CARE* EPA was supporting Virginia's claim that it was making reasonable further progress. Deferential standards of review allow each decision of the agency to be upheld. Even so, if *CARE*'s litigation strategy had been to argue specifically that the asphalt switch was RACT, it seems possible that a court could have found an abuse of discretion in the failure to switch to the less polluting product while saving money at the same time.

When "weasel words" such as "reasonably available" are conjoined with a deferential standard of review, courts are very unlikely to reverse the agency determination. For example, EPA issued a rule regarding Transportation Control Measures (TCMs). This was a topic that Congress had addressed in the 1990 Amendments by requiring transportation planning and requiring EPA to provide information on TCMs, which were listed in §108(f). Many of the TCMs in the legislation are non-technical and site-independent, such as ride sharing, employer programs for flexible commuting, etc. The old EPA position had been that TCMs were RACMs. In 1992, however, EPA decided that TCMs are not RACMs for all non-attainment areas. 57 Fed. Reg. 13498 (April 16, 1992). That rule was upheld in Ober v. EPA, 84 F.3d 304 (9th Cir. 1996). Generalizations in this area are dangerous. Other 1990 Amendments regarding non-attainment area provisions have been held to impose mandatory duties on EPA, especially those involving deadlines. In Sierra Club v. EPA, 129 F.3d 137 (D.C.Cir. 1997), EPA was held to lack authority to provide a 12-month grace period during which transportation activities in non-attainment areas would be exempt from the transportation conformity requirements of §176(c). The "conformity requirements" insist that transportation activities in the AQCR must be consistent with the non-attainment SIP.

3. **Offsets pro and con.** Are offsets a good method of accommodating further development while still seeking improvement of ambient air quality in non-attainment areas? In the absence of state intervention in aid of the new source, either like that given in the *CARE* case, or in the form of placing tighter controls on existing sources, which emissions reductions will be realized first? Presumably, the operator of the new source will have to purchase the retirement of pollution sources. The least expensive retirements will involve taking marginally profitable enter-

---

33. RACM by its express language includes RACT when it comes to pollution control devices that might be prescribed for stationary sources.

prises out of production, or paying for pollution control improvements at those sites where the least expenditure produces the greatest reduction. To the extent that practice mirrors the prediction of theory, offsets obtain an apparently optimal result of reducing pollution at the lowest possible cost. Are there social costs that have been overlooked in that assessment? What about the dislocation of workers who lose their jobs when the marginal firms are bought out and closed? It is arguable that for many of them, their firm's survival was unlikely in any event.

4. **Bubbles and their similarity to offsets.** "Bubbles," in Clean Air Act parlance, are the device of treating all of the emitting sources at a single facility as a single point source for the purpose of regulation. For example, a factory having several buildings and multiple smokestacks could be treated as either a series of sources, each having an individual emissions limitation, or as a single entity having a total emissions limitation. The term bubble describes the latter method that treats the group of emitting sources as if all of the emissions occurred in a single bubble and then are released into the atmosphere.

Offsets are a cousin technique to bubbles. The relationship of bubbles to offsets is most evident in cases where the operator of the facility wants to change operations within the bubble. If increases in emission from one smokestack can be offset by reductions in emission from another stack, there would be no net change in total emissions. If the bubble concept is not employed, increases in emissions from one smokestack would require modification of that stack's permit. Suffice it to say that modification of a permit for a major source in a non-attainment area is a major headache. Likewise, if the firm replaces an old part of the facility with a new, less polluting one on the same site, under the bubble concept, no change in the permit would be required. If that new component is considered a major new source, in non-attainment areas it is required to employ LAER, and in attainment areas, pursuant to §111, it must employ BAT. In both instances, the applicability of the technology-based standards will usually increase the cost of the improvement. Bubbling can avoid these requirements. The need for administrative action on permit modifications or new permits will cause delays, as well as substantial expense. These topics are explored in more detail in Chapter 16.

5. **NSPS as a "protection" of non-attainment area economic growth potential.** Congress clearly recognized as a national concern the hardship that would be imposed on dirty air areas if they were subjected to a total ban on initiating new industrial activity. To allow those areas to compete for industrial growth and development, as demonstrated in the *CARE* case, the non-attainment area provisions allow new sources to obtain permits so long as they employ LAER (the most demanding technology-based standard) and obtain offsets so that "reasonable further progress" toward attainment is maintained. At the same time as it made the location of major new sources in non-attainment areas possible, Congress also took steps that lessened the comparative attractiveness of locating a major emitting facility in a clean air area. Congress imposed technology-based standards for pollution controls on all new major emitting sources, wherever they are located

through the New Source Performance Standards (NSPS) requirements.[34]

The NSPS program is mandated by §111 of the Act, 42 U.S.C.A. §7411. In general, the NSPS provisions require that all new or modified emitting sources employ the best adequately demonstrated pollution control technology (BADT) for their type of facility. This standard is defined in the Act and commands EPA to take "into consideration the cost of achieving such emission reduction." By requiring a uniform technology based performance standard to be employed nationwide, the potential for a race of laxity in permitting new sources is greatly reduced, although not entirely eliminated. Major new sources that emit more than a specified tonnage of pollutants are regulated even more tightly, using technology-based standards. In PSD areas (described in Part F below) major new emitting sources must employ the best available control technology (BACT) (42 U.S.C.A. §7475(a)(4)).

### Section 2. PRESCRIBING THE PATH TO ATTAINMENT

In 1990, after a decade of halting improvement under the 1977 non-attainment provisions, the situation on the ground (or, more aptly, in the ambient air) was better, but still unacceptable. Congress found that EPA had been too willing to approve non-attainment SIPs that moved too slowly toward attainment. Public health was perceived as seriously at risk, when almost one hundred metropolitan areas were still unable to meet the primary NAAQS ozone standard and roughly forty areas still failed to meet the primary carbon monoxide standard. Congress took the political initiative and the political heat, and passed legislation that promises to be more effective. Congress, in effect, took an inventory of non-attainment areas, then subdivided them according to how far out of attainment they were. Congress then set realistic, firm dates for achieving attainment for each level of non-attainment. It did this on a pollutant-by-pollutant basis giving longer lead times for solving more serious problems of non-attainment. Congress even required that, where necessary, more difficult non-attainment problems be addressed through transportation programs that would make reduction of aggregate mobile source emissions part of the solution. Beyond that, the legislation spelled out specific sanctions, cutoffs of federal highway funds and other federally bestowed benefits, for states that did not comply with the new timetables, and required promulgation of a federal implementation plan (FIP) within two years of a state's failure to submit an adequate SIP.

In regard to the most pressing problem, ozone non-attainment, Congress has differentiated five degrees of non-attainment, calling them marginal, moderate, serious, severe, and extreme.[35] The amendments set increasingly distant dates for compliance, ranging from three years for marginal areas up to twenty years for extreme areas. See §181(a), 42 U.S.C.A. §7511(a). Correlatively, Congress has

---

34. Additionally, as will be more fully described below, Congress enacted an affirmative prevention of significant deterioration (PSD) program that is designed to keep clean air areas from becoming as dirty as the NAAQSs alone would otherwise allow. The PSD program shortens the race of laxity by limiting the ability of clean air areas to offer lax pollution control as an inducement to attract new firms to locate there.

35. A similar, but far simpler two-track system of moderate and serious non-attainment is employed in relation to carbon monoxide and particulates and attainment deadlines are set for all of the remaining criteria pollutants. See CAA §§186-192, 42 U.S.C.A. §§7512-7514a.

mandated that SIPs for those areas include an increasingly stringent set of requirements. See §182(a-e), 42 U.S.C.A. §7511a(a-e). Some samples of these requirements include the following: in marginal areas SIPs must include the use of reasonably available control technologies (RACT), vehicle maintenance and inspection programs, and offsets must be obtained in a ratio of at least 1.1 to 1; in moderate areas, mandatory gasoline vapor recovery is added and the offset requirement increases to 1.15 to 1; in serious areas general transportation plans are required and clean-fuel vehicles must be considered as an option, and the offset ratio must be at least 1.2 to 1; in severe areas there must be an enforceable offset for any growth in the number of vehicle miles travelled and mandatory carpool and other vehicle use requirements must be imposed, the offset ratio increases to 1.3 to 1; and in extreme areas major sources are redefined to include much smaller units (10 tons/year of volatile organic compound emissions), switching to cleaner fuels such as natural gas is required for large emitting sources, high polluting vehicles cannot be used during rush hours, and the general offset requirement is 1.5 to 1. To insure that the severe and extreme areas do eventually meet their attainment deadlines, the amendments provide specific enforcement measures that call for penalties of $5,000/ton/yr for excess emissions from major sources if timely attainment does not occur. CAA §185, 42 U.S.C.A. §7511d.[36]

Coupled with the host of specific nonattainment prescriptions, Congress, by 1990, had a very keen sense of EPA capabilities in implementing programs and built numerous deadlines into the nonattainment amendments in hopes of keeping EPA and the states on track and on time. Frequently in its administration of programs, missed deadlines had landed EPA in court. In most cases the results were consent decrees pursuant to which EPA agreed to take actions according to judicially approved timetables. With the nonattainment amendments, Congress set deadlines for EPA in its relationship to the states and the SIP process. This has engendered a slightly different dynamic.

Under the new amendments, EPA and the states have, at least in part, a mutual interest in easing the process of complying with the new law. There are numerous instances where both the states and EPA prefer to delay making the changes required by the non-attainment SIP process. Of necessity, the required provisions of those SIPs will alter the status quo, which generates resistance. Moreover, experience has proved that many of the congressionally required elements of non-attainment SIPs are decidedly unpopular, such as transportation controls, or vehicle I&M programs. EPA's efforts to soften the transition to the new regime have often taken the form of EPA using its interpretive power to grant more time to the states. These efforts have met with mixed results when challenged in court. For example, in NRDC v. Browner, 57 F. 3d 1122 (1995) the court upheld EPA's interpretation of how the §110(m) sanctions clock was to be measured when states revised SIP proposals were judged to be incomplete. EPA, in effect, reset the clock at zero whenever a revised proposal was submitted, even if that proposal was ulti-

---

36. These special sanctions are in addition to the more general power of the Administrator to impose SIP requirements on states that fail to reach timely attainment and the power to withhold federal highway funds. See generally CAA §179, 42 U.S.C.A. §7509.

mately rejected by EPA. In contrast, in Sierra Club v. EPA, 129 F. 3d 137 (D.C.Cir. 1997), the court invalidated part of a rule[37] that created a 12-month grace period during which transportation activities in designated non-attainment areas would be exempt from transportation conformity requirements[38] established by §176(c).[39] As before, when EPA misses deadlines for the promulgation of non-attainment regulations, courts have not been hesitant to rebuke EPA.[40] Another provision as to which the courts have required more stringent implementation is §110(k)(4), which has to do with SIP deadlines:

> First, the NRDC challenges the EPA's use of a "conditional approval" procedure, under §110(k)(4) to permit states to comply with statutory SIP deadlines by submitting "committal" SIPs that contain no specific remedial measures but merely promise to adopt such measures within a year. The NRDC contends this procedure is contrary to congressional intent and has impermissibly postponed the statutory deadlines for the affected SIP submittals. To remedy the delay caused by the EPA's conditional approval procedure, the NRDC asks that we require prompt submission and review of all overdue SIPs and immediate imposition of statutory sanctions on states that have not submitted adequate SIPs as of July 15, 1994. [We] hold that the EPA misconstrued and misapplied §110(k)(4).... NRDC v. EPA, 22 F.3d 1125 (D.C.Cir. 1994).

### COMMENTARY AND QUESTIONS

1. **The 1990 Amendments and their host of regulatory strategies.** As will become evident in the coming chapters, environmental regulation is not all of one form and method. Rather, that regulation is best described as employing a number of techniques. By the time 1990 rolled around, Congress had learned to employ several techniques in combination to address complex issues, such as ending non-attainment. RACT (for all existing sources) and LAER (for major new sources locating in non-attainment areas) are technology-based standards, mandatory fuel and vehicle switching are forms of legislated pollution control standards akin to technology-forcing. Bans on the use of high-polluting vehicles during periods of heavy traffic volume are in the roadblock category, the per-ton fines are market incentives, and so on. Is the application of these other statutory types to address the problem of non-attainment proof that harm-based ambient controls do not work? That view gives too little credit for the majority of instances in which

37. See 60 Fed.Reg. 57,179 (1995), see also 40 C.F.R. §51.394(d) (1996).
38. "Conformity" in this context is a term of art that describes Congress' requirement that the federal government "conform" its actions to the requirements of implementation plans and to fostering state compliance with the CAA and its SIP process. See generally, James T. Lang, Clean Air Act Section 176 General Conformity Program, 2 The Environmental Lawyer 353 (1996).
39. The provision at issue in that case demonstrates that Congress knows how to select language that affords agencies no wiggle room, "No department, agency, or instrumentality of the Federal government shall engage in, support in any way or provide financial assistance for, license or permit, or approve, any activity which does not conform to an implementation plan after it has been approved or promulgated under section 7410 of this title."
40. See, e.g., NRDC v. EPA 797 F.Supp. 194 (E.D.N.Y. 1992) (missed deadline for I & M program regulations). Most significantly, EPA, once it has disapproved a state plan, does not have discretion to decline to issue or delay the issuance of the dreaded FIP beyond the statutory deadline. See Coalition for Clean Air v. EPA, 971 F.2d 219 (9th Cir. 1992).

NAAQSs are being met, but it is indicative of the fact that harm-based systems are vulnerable to failure and therefore need the support of additional regulatory reinforcement.

## F. TRANSBOUNDARY AIRFLOWS AND PROTECTING STATE, INTERSTATE, AND NATIONAL CONCERNS IN A NATIONWIDE AMBIENT STANDARDS PROGRAM

The implementation of a national harm-based ambient standards approach to protect public health from the dangers of conventional air pollutants requires more than the mere establishment of standards and implementation plans. In a system that relies on *state* implementation plans to achieve the desired results, some special steps need to be taken to insure that national objectives are not sacrificed to the more parochial concerns of the states who play so large a role in drawing most SIPs. First, as just set out, there is the need to protect the economic growth potential of the dirty air states. Even the relatively dirty air areas of the nation need to be able to remain competitive with clean air areas in attracting new economic activity (and therefore additional pollution sources) into their borders. Second, for aesthetic as well as environmental reasons, preserving the cleanliness of existing clean air regions is a significant benefit, even when this increases the cost of pollution control in those regions above what it would cost if NAAQS attainment were the only requirement. Finally, and perhaps most obviously, some form of protection must be erected against efforts to control local pollution within a single state by the inexpensive expedient of building tall smokestacks or siting polluting enterprises near the state line and letting the wind blow the pollution problem into another state. Historically, the Clean Air Act as first passed in 1970, addressed less than all of these problems. With the 1977 and 1990 Amendments all of these concerns are addressed.

### Section 1. PREVENTION OF SIGNIFICANT DETERIORATION (PSD)

This consideration received its most careful attention in that portion of the 1977 Amendments that are now codified at 42 U.S.C.A. §§7470-7491. Although the particularity of the Congressional requirements for the PSD program makes the statute seem incredibly complex, the basic design is rather pedestrian and amounts to little more than limitations on the incremental amount of pollution that is allowed in clean air areas, with smaller increments allowed in areas where there are special national or state interests served by limiting increases in pollution.

The PSD process begins by classifying all attainment air quality control regions (AQCRs), or parts thereof, into three categories. Under the 1977 Amendments Class I areas include international and national parks, wilderness areas, and national memorial parks that exceed a prescribed acreage.[41] Class II areas are, in

---

41. There were additional areas that were classified as Class I under the pre-1977 law. These areas continued as Class I areas, but, if they are not required to be designated Class I by the 1977 Amendments, they are subject to redesignation downward under §7474.

essence, all remaining attainment areas.[42] No Class III areas are established by the legislation, but the states have the ability to redesignate areas according to a process set out in §7474. With classification comes an allowable increment, that is, a statutorily or administratively set upper limit on the amount of increase in ambient concentrations of pollutants that can be added to the region's air. As an example the Class I, II, and III allowable increments in the annual geometric mean of particulate contamination are 5, 19, and 37 micrograms per cubic meter respectively.[43] This pattern of relative stringency in §7473 is repeated as to other contsaminants. The Class I increments are usually a very small percentage of the NAAQS. This aspect of the PSD program and its legislative history are thoroughly reviewed in a case successfully challenging EPA's setting of the nitrogen oxides PSD increments. See EDF v. EPA, 898 F.2d 183 (D.C.Cir. 1990).

The next step in the PSD process is to establish the baseline upon which the allowable increment can be added. Conceptually, this would seem to be no more difficult than getting an accurate measure of the current concentration of pollutants. In practice, that measure is not readily available in many locations and due to the difficulty in establishing an accurate baseline, no effort to do so is made until the need arises. Usually this occurs at the time an application for a permit is received from a new major source of emissions. Thereafter, new ambient air quality standards are calculated for the AQCR. In many cases, the new standards are the sum of the baseline concentrations plus allowable increments that are fixed by statute for particulates and sulfur dioxide and by EPA regulation for other criteria pollutants. Particularly in Class III areas, however, the possibility exists that the sum of the baseline concentration plus the increment will exceed the allowable NAAQS limit. In that case, of course, the NAAQS continues as the maximum allowable level of ambient pollution and the AQCR is not allowed to "use" the full amount of the increment.

To provide additional protection for national parks and other areas that obtain Class I designation because of the presence of a federal enclave to which visibility is essential, there are special visibility protection requirements that are even more stringent than the basic PSD provisions. The visibility protection provision even requires the reduction of existing emissions if they interfere with Congressionally announced visibility goals. See §169A, 42 U.S.C.A. §7491.

The PSD provisions are sensitive to the desire of the states to have a substantial degree of control over their own environmental and economic growth policy. As a result, redesignations by states of AQCRs from one classification to another is expressly authorized by the statute. Federal interests are protected in this process by forbidding downward reclassifications of areas of federal concern — the parks, wilderness and other areas of special scenic and recreational significance. The statute also gives Indian tribes authority over the classification of reservation airsheds. Thereafter, however, the states are allowed to reclassify to satisfy state policies. Carte blanche is given to reclassifications upward to Class I. State decisions

---

42. See 42 U.S.C.A. §7472(b).

43. The primary standard for annual mean concentration of particulates is 100 micrograms per cubic meter. Thus, the PSD increments are, respectively, 5 percent, 19 percent and 37 percent.

to promote and preserve higher air quality are encouraged in this fashion. Even downward reclassifications are largely a matter of state choice. EPA approval of such redesignations is required, but may be withheld only if specified procedures are not followed or if statutorily protected interests are adversely affected. For the most part, these are the statutory designations protective of federal land management prerogatives laid out in the classification system itself, but §7474(a)(2)(B) also requires that redesignations "not cause, or contribute to, concentrations of any air pollutant which exceed any maximum allowable increase or maximum allowable concentration...."

### COMMENTARY AND QUESTIONS

1. **Federalism and PSD.** The very nature of the PSD program takes a degree of autonomy away from the states. The level of allowable growth in Class I areas is limited by the stringent PSD increments and the option of redesignation is limited by the presence of various types of federal lands. Should the federal sites of importance, the Yosemites and Grand Canyons, be insulated against loss of amenity value that is at times obtained at the expense of economic development in the host state? Even more generally, the PSD program restricts development in less-developed or later developing states by taking away the potential advantage of less expensive pollution control requirements.

2. **Exceeding the federal requirements.** The Clean Air Act, although less explicitly than the Clean Water Act's §510, 33 U.S.C.A. §1370, gives the states latitude to do more to limit air pollution than the minimum required by federal law. This is manifest in the PSD reclassification program that allows states to designate all areas other than Indian reservations as Class I areas. Likewise, states in their SIPs and permitting of polluting facilities (except for mobile sources like cars and planes) are free to be as stringent as they like. EPA review will insure only that the SIPs and permits granted thereunder do not fail to meet the NAAQS.

### Section 2. INTERSTATE TRANSPORT OF POLLUTION

Exporting pollution as a means of meeting ambient standard requirements properly can be thought of as both a race of laxity problem and an externality problem. As originally enacted in 1970, the Clean Air Act addresses this problem most frontally in 42 U.S.C.A. §§7426 and 7410(a)(2)(D)(i-ii). Notice must be given by the upwind state to the downwind state of new and proposed major sources that will have an effect on the downwind state's ability to meet the NAAQSs or will interfere with the downwind state's PSD program. The adversely affected state may protest to EPA, with EPA becoming the arbiter of the interstate clash of interests. The statute is drawn using language that seems to favor the downwind states. To be approved, an upwind state's SIP must:

> contain adequate provisions (i) prohibiting...any source or other type of emissions activity within the State from emitting any air pollutant in amounts which will (I) contribute significantly to nonattainment in, or interfere with maintenance by, any other State with respect to any such national primary or secondary ambient air quality standard, or (II) interfere with measures

required to be included in the applicable [PSD] implementation plan for any other State....

In practice, under the language as it stood prior to the 1990 Amendments,[44] the downwind states won very few concessions from upwind states through the appeal to EPA process. As in virtually all aspects of Clean Air Act administration, those same states have an even worse record in seeking judicial invalidation of upwind activities that have received EPA approval.

Air Pollution Control District v. EPA, 739 F.2d 1071 (6th Cir. 1984), an early leading case in this area, gives a flavor of the difficulty downwind states have experienced. The case involves sulfur dioxide contributions to the Louisville, Kentucky airshed of a coal-fired power plant located just across the Ohio River in Indiana. For a few months after Indiana and Kentucky had their initial SIPs approved under the then-new Clean Air Act of 1970, the Kentucky and Indiana SIPs required identical sulfur dioxide control efforts for coal fired power plants, an emission limitation of 1.2 pounds of $SO_2$ per million British thermal units of heat input (MBTU). Indiana almost immediately won EPA approval for a revised SIP that allowed unregulated $SO_2$ emissions from coal-fired electric generating facilities.[45] Kentucky, on the other side of the river, held firm to the 1.2 lb./MBTU standard and eventually forced Louisville Gas & Electric (LG&E), the primary Kentucky $SO_2$ producer in the AQCR, to meet that standard. The court described the contrast in an understated way:

> It can therefore be seen that a significant disparity exists between the permissible emission limits of power plants in Jefferson County, Kentucky and the Gallagher plant in Floyd County, Indiana. LG&E, the primary producer of SO2 in Jefferson County, spent approximately $138 million installing scrubbers to remove SO2 from its emissions, while just across the river, Gallagher's SO2 emissions were completely uncontrolled.[46]

Despite Kentucky's $SO_2$ control efforts in the Louisville AQCR, it remained a non-attainment area even after LG&E had completed installation of all of the needed emission controls. A petition was lodged with the EPA, seeking relief against the interstate effects of $SO_2$ pollution from the nearby Indiana plant. EPA's record of findings based on its modelling of the airshed concluded that only 3 percent of the Jefferson County, Kentucky $SO_2$ concentrations that resulted in violations of the NAAQS were attributable to the Gallagher plant. Those same findings also noted, however, that the Gallagher plant contributed large concentrations of $SO_2$ that were not part of predicted violations of the NAAQS. In particular, Gallagher contributed significantly to the highest second-highest 24-hour and 3-hour predicted concentrations in Kentucky, the amounts being 34.5 percent of the NAAQS primary 24-hour standard and 47 percent of the NAAQS secondary 3-hour standard. EPA's own study of the data observed these impacts have "a far more serious potential for limiting growth in Kentucky..." EPA even stated that by 1985,

---

44. The 1990 Amendments to the section made substantive changes further favoring downwind states by enlarging the classes of upwind sources to be considered.

45. The standard was later revised to 6 lb $SO_2$/MBTU, but that level of emissions was the same rate as uncontrolled emissions for the plant involved in this case.

46. 739 F.2d at 1077.

when controls at the LG&E plant would be fully on line, the Gallagher plant "will be the predominate [sic] influence upon air quality in Louisville, Kentucky."

EPA denied Kentucky's petition and judicial review in the federal court followed. The two central issues in the case were the affirmance of EPA's interpretation of the relevant legislation as (1) prohibiting only interstate pollution that "significantly contributes" to present violations of the NAAQS or an already established PSD program,[47] and (2) meaning that interference with potential growth in the downwind state is not a ground on which relief can be granted in the absence of interference with an established PSD plan or program. It is hard to be too critical of the EPA position on the first issue. Given the fugitive nature of emissions into the common airshed, it is unlikely in the extreme that Congress meant to forbid all interstate pollution. The statutory language of §7426 suggests as much when it requires notice to downwind states of new sources in the upwind state that "may significantly contribute" to air quality problems in the downwind state. With the EPA data attributing only 3 percent of the non-attainment problem to emissions from the Gallagher plant, EPA's position seems quite reasonable.

The proper accommodation of interstate interests on the margin for growth question presents a more subtle and difficult issue. To grasp the competing positions of Kentucky and the EPA more clearly, imagine what would be the course of events if the Kentucky AQCR involved in the litigation, through additional reductions in emissions, remedies the excessive concentrations of $SO_2$ in all locations and becomes an attainment area. At that point, Kentucky would be able to adopt a new PSD SIP that allows some new pollution to be introduced if continued compliance with the NAAQS can be maintained. As the facts set forth above showed, EPA's model of the airshed indicated that there are some parts of the AQCR where, but for the Indiana emissions from the Gallagher plant, there would be substantial room for incremental $SO_2$ emissions without exceeding the NAAQS. On this basis, Kentucky claims that Indiana has "stolen its PSD increment" through the failure to limit Gallagher emissions.

In the case as it was litigated, Kentucky made this argument. EPA's response was formalistic and, in light of its own findings in the case, a bit disingenuous. EPA said there could be no present stealing of a PSD increment, because no PSD baseline could be set in advance of becoming an attainment area. When attainment occurred, the Kentucky concentrations attributable to the Gallagher plant would not then constitute stealing the increment because those concentrations would be part of the baseline. In this way, regardless of terminology, EPA allows Indiana to dispose of significant $SO_2$ emissions at Kentucky's expense.[48]

---

47. Here, because the relevant Kentucky AQCR was still a non-attainment area, no PSD plan was in place.

48. The position of EPA in this case is not an isolated event. In Connecticut v. EPA, 696 F.2d 147 (2d Cir. 1982), EPA allowed (and the court affirmed) the same sort of outcome in a case where New York emissions were raising ambient concentrations in the Connecticut airshed prior to Connecticut's setting of a PSD baseline. There too, it appeared that when the baseline was set there would be no allowable increment left for growth in emissions because the baseline would be so close to the NAAQS, in part as a result of the New York emissions that were challenged by Connecticut under the interstate pollution provisions of the Clean Air Act.

While the EPA position seems palpably unfair to Kentucky, it has the administrative advantage of limiting the need to exercise discretion. It avoids the pitfalls of some vague equity-based approach that would inevitably embroil EPA in bitter interstate disputes involving protracted evidentiary matters concerning the precise extent of interstate pollution. The EPA approach also maintains ambient standards as its central technique, whereas an alternative rule that called for equal pollution control efforts on both sides of the state line would rely more on a mandated technology approach. Although these observations hardly amount to a ringing defense of the EPA position, they give it sufficient rationality to be sustained by a reviewing court applying a deferential standard of review.

COMMENTARY AND QUESTIONS

1. **EPA's dilemma.** Do not be too quick to criticize EPA for failing to be more aggressive in these cases. On what principled basis can EPA determine how much pollution can cross state boundaries without constituting an injury to the downwind state? The general movement of air masses and the pollutants they carry is an uncontrollable natural event. For that reason, a zero transboundary emission limit is unattainable and undesirable. To meet that goal, emissions limits in the upwind state would have to be excessively restrictive. Remember that the way the NAAQSs are set, with some of the standards being short-term standards and the variability of wind and other atmospheric conditions, virtually all states are both importers and exporters of pollution.

Once EPA is committed to allowing a reasonable amount of pollution to move from a source state to another state, the almost inevitable focus of comparison will be in the relative stringency of regulation of the emissions in the source and recipient state. On that score, the disparity between the uncontrolled emissions at the Gallagher plant and the need to use scrubbers at the LG&E plant may seem to embarrass EPA. Should it? It is possible to argue that EPA is only carrying out the will of Congress. This is a case being resolved using the ambient standards approach that Congress chose for the regulation of conventional air pollutants. The key questions for EPA are whether Indiana is meeting the NAAQS (without need of regulating Gallagher more stringently) and whether Kentucky is being prevented from meeting the NAAQS by Indiana emissions. On the record in the case, there is no warrant for EPA to act because the lax Indiana controls are not undermining the operation of the harm-based ambient standards approach. If Congress had intended EPA to insist on an equivalency of interstate effort in emission control, it could have chosen a technology-based approach, or a system that relied on uniform emissions control efforts nationwide.

2. **Non-federal remedies.** When sections 110 and 126 fail, downwind areas can resort to state law remedies. In Her Majesty the Queen v. City of Detroit, 874 F.2d 332 (6th Cir. 1989) Canada had obtained no satisfaction in a §126 effort to block the construction of a large trash-to-energy incinerator in Detroit, upwind of Windsor, Ontario. Canada, in the name of the Queen, filed an action based on Michigan's Environmental Protection Act. The case was allowed to go forward on

that basis. Before a final disposition on the merits, the incinerator was retrofitted to further reduce its emissions.

3. **Interstate transport commissions.** As a partial response to the unhappy experience of downwind states with their attempts to use §§110 and 126 to block out-of-state pollution, the 1990 Amendments create a new institution called interstate transport commissions. See CAA §176A, 42 U.S.C.A. §7506a. These commissions can be formed at EPA's discretion on EPA's own initiative or following a request from an affected state whenever EPA finds there is a significant interstate transport of air pollutants that significantly contribute to an NAAQS violation. If formed, a commission is comprised of two members from each of the interested states and two EPA officials. The commission then assesses the degree of interstate pollution transport and the strategies for mitigating that pollution and makes recommendations to EPA for SIP provisions that will satisfy the interstate control obligations of §7410(a)(2)(D). The 1990 Amendments also created a multistate entity called the Ozone Transport Commission (OTC) and gave EPA the authority to establish a larger entity, the Ozone Transport Advisory Group (OTAG) to consider the movement of NOx and other ozone precursors. For an extended consideration of interstate ozone transport, see Geoffrey L. Wilcox, New England and the Challenge of Interstate Ozone Pollution under the Clean Air Act of 1990, 24 Boston College Environmental Affairs Law Review 1 (1996).

*When humans interfere with the Tao,*
*the sky becomes filthy,*
*the equilibrium crumbles,*
*creatures become extinct.*

— Lao-tzu, Tao Te Ching, 500 B.C.E.

*These must be the years when America pays its debts to the past by reclaiming the purity of its air, its water and our living environment. It is literally now or never.*

— Richard Nixon, 1970

# Chapter 9

# ADMINISTRATIVE STANDARDS BASED ON "AVAILABLE TECHNOLOGY": THE FEDERAL CLEAN WATER ACT

A. *An Overview of the Clean Water Act*

B. *The Origin and Evolution of TBELs*

C. *Implementing TBELs Through the NPDES Process*

D. *Water Quality-based Permitting Under the CWA*

E. *Controlling Nonpoint Source Pollution Without Regulation*

F. *A Complex Hypothetical: the Average River*

---

## A. AN OVERVIEW OF THE CLEAN WATER ACT

The Clean Water Act (CWA), 33 U.S.C.A. §1251 et seq., already encountered in Chapter One's *Kepone, Gwaltney,* and *Smithfield Packing* cases, derives from the old Federal Water Pollution Control Act, and was given its modern form in its major amendments of 1972. Like the CAA, the CWA imposes national baseline pollution standards. For the CWA, however, Congress chose a converse approach to the standard-setting methods of the CAA. The CAA primarily employs a strategy of harm-based standard-setting, although it has gradually been moving in the direction of technology-based standard-setting. The CWA, on the other hand, is fundamentally premised on technology-based standard-setting, but in recent years has increasingly included elements of harm-based standard-setting.

The basic federal "floor" standards under the CWA are effluent limitations based on "Best Available Technology Economically Achievable" (commonly referred to as "BAT"), or one of its sister standards, "Best Conventional Pollutant Control Technology" ("BCT") or "Best Available Demonstrated Control Technology" ("BDT"). Under the CWA's National Pollutant Discharge Elimination System ("NPDES," noted in Chapter One) all "point source" dischargers of pollutants[1] (e.g., outfall pipes from factories, municipal sewage treatment plants,

---

1. As noted in Chapter 1, the distinction between "point" and "nonpoint" source discharges is a critical one, and will be thoroughly explored below. In general, point source discharges are regulated by the CWA, but nonpoint source discharges are not. The CWA's regulatory mechanism applies to the "discharge of a pollutant," which is defined as "any addition of any pollutant to navigable waters from any point source." §502(12). A "point source" discharges through a discrete and confined conveyance, such as a pipe, ditch, or channel. A "nonpoint source" produces a diffuse and unconfined discharge, such as overland runoff from a farm or paved surface.

vessels) are assigned EPA-promulgated performance standards based on the best water pollution control technology that has been found to be both available and economically achievable industry-by-industry among dischargers performing similar economic activities or using similar mechanical processes.[2] The resulting "technology-based effluent limitations" are frequently called "TBELs." In many cases, compliance with TBELs by point source dischargers located on a particular waterbody has enabled the public to utilize those waters for fishing and swimming, which is the CWA's goal. Waterbodies that can attain the fishable-swimmable criterion through the operation of TBELs alone are called "effluent-limited" regulated waterbodies.

Situations arise where compliance with TBELs by point source dischargers does not produce "fishable-swimmable" water quality, and additional limits must be applied. These "water quality-limited" stretches may occur where high concentrations of factories or municipal treatment plants overtax the assimilative capacities of receiving waters, where past pollution has heavily contaminated the sediments and water column, or where unregulated nonpoint sources, such as large agricultural or silvicultural activities, cause heavy pollutant loadings to nearby waterbodies. Point source dischargers on water quality-limited stretches must meet, in addition to TBELs, more stringent *harm-based* effluent limitations based on achieving fishable-swimmable water quality, where that is attainable. These "Better-Than-Best" effluent limitations are customarily referred to as water quality-based effluent limitations, or WQBELs.

From 1972 to 1987 the major preoccupation of CWA administration was the implementation of TBELs for all point source dischargers. This stage has, for the most part, been reached. Although TBEL implementation remains a high priority for water pollution control agencies, the major focus of water pollution control programs is shifting to WQBEL-setting and implementation. This chapter first analyzes the traditional standard-setting mechanism of the CWA — TBELs — and then addresses the comparatively recent developments associated with WQBELs. The chapter concludes with a discussion of nonpoint source pollution control.

The Clean Water Act's basic strategy of technology-based standard-setting has made a monumental contribution to cleaning up America's surface waterbodies. Major waterbodies that, in the 1960s, were virtual open sewers are now fit for fishing and swimming.[3] The infamous lower Cuyahoga River, which in 1969 was declared a fire hazard and actually caught fire (for the third time) as surface oil and grease was ignited by a spill of hot slag, is now sufficiently safe and attractive (though not yet fishable-swimmable) that the Cleveland Flats area at the river's mouth has been transformed from a foetid industrial zone into a waterside entertainment district lined with nightclubs and bistros, with tables on decks at river-

2. "Performance standard" means that the law will require a certain *result*, without dictating *how* a person must meet it (which would be a "design standard"). Thus although the CWA sets limits for how much of a pollutant can be discharged in a water effluent by figuring out what the best technology would achieve, it is a performance standard because it does not require you to use that technology if you can reach the same result another way, say by cutting down the total volume of discharge.

3. These waterbodies include major stretches of the Delaware, Connecticut, Potomac, and Tennessee Rivers, Lake Erie, New York City's East River, and Puget Sound.

side and tie-ups for pleasure boaters. According to EPA estimates, about 60% of the nation's rivers, lakes, and estuaries are now fishable-swimmable, compared with approximately 36% in 1972. This nationwide improvement in water quality has resulted from the elimination, by roughly 90%, of point source discharges. Despite clear and often dramatic progress in cleaning up America's surface waterbodies, the bad news is that a large percentage of America's waterbodies still do not meet the CWA's fishable-swimmable goal, and non-point sources are still largely unregulated.

The following excerpt serves as an introduction to the range of contaminants that degrade water quality, and the typical sources of those pollutants.

### United States Environmental Protection Agency
### National Water Quality Inventory: 1994 Report to Congress
Executive Summary, 7-15

LOW DISSOLVED OXYGEN... Dissolved oxygen is a basic requirement for a healthy aquatic ecosystem. Most fish and beneficial aquatic insects "breathe" oxygen dissolved in the water column. Some fish and aquatic organisms (such as carp and sludge worms) are adapted to low oxygen conditions, but the most desirable fish species (such as trout and salmon) suffer if dissolved oxygen concentrations fall below 3 to 4 mg/L (3 to 4 milligrams of oxygen dissolved in 1 liter of water, or 3 to 4 parts of oxygen per million parts of water). Larvae and juvenile fish are more sensitive and require even higher concentrations of oxygen.

Many fish and other aquatic organisms can recover from short periods of low dissolved oxygen availability. However, prolonged episodes of depressed dissolved oxygen concentrations of 2 mg/L or less can result in "dead" waterbodies. Prolonged exposure to low dissolved oxygen conditions can suffocate adult fish or reduce their reproductive survival by suffocating sensitive eggs and larvae or can starve fish by killing aquatic insect larvae and other prey. Low dissolved oxygen concentrations also favor anaerobic bacteria activity that produces noxious gases or foul odors often associated with polluted waterbodies.

Oxygen concentrations in the water column fluctuate under normal conditions, but severe oxygen depletion usually results from human activities that introduce large quantities of biodegradable organic materials into surface waters [measured in terms of Biochemical Oxygen Demand ("BOD")]. Biodegradable organic materials contain plant, fish, or animal matter. Leaves, lawn clippings, sewage, manure, shellfish processing waste, milk solids, and other food processing wastes are examples of oxygen-depleting organic materials that enter our surface waters.[4]

In both pristine and polluted waters, beneficial bacteria use oxygen to break apart (or decompose) organic matrials. Pollution-containing organic wastes provide a continuous glut of food for the bacteria, which accelerates bacterial activity and population growth. In polluted waters, bacterial consumption of oxygen can rapidly outpace oxygen replenishment from the atmosphere and photosynthesis performed by algae and aquatic plants. The result is a net decline in oxygen concentrations in the water.

---

4. The hog processing wastewaters from the Gwaltney and Smithfield Packing plants, discussed in Chapter 1, were oxygen-demanding discharges [Eds.].

Toxic pollutants can indirectly lower oxygen concentrations by killing algae, aquatic weeds, or fish, which provides an abundance of food for oxygen-consuming bacteria. Oxygen depletion can also result from chemical reactions that do not involve bacteria. Some pollutants trigger chemical reactions that place a chemical oxygen demand [COD] on receiving waters.

Other factors (such as temperature and salinity) influence that amount of oxygen dissolved in water. Prolonged hot weather will depress oxygen concentrations and may cause fish kills even in clean waters because warm water cannot hold as much oxygen as cold water. Warm conditions further aggravate oxygen depletion by stimulating bacterial activity and respiration in fish, which consumes oxygen....

NUTRIENTS... Nutrients are essential building blocks for healthy aquatic communities, but excess nutrients (especially nitrogen and phosphorus compounds) overstimulate the growth of aquatic weeds and algae.[5] Excessive nutrient discharges are also suspected of creating the conditions under which the *pfisteria piscicida* bacteria has proliferated and killed hundreds of thousands of fish in Chesapeake Bay and the Pamlico River, North Carolina [Eds.]. Excessive growth of these organisms, in turn, can clog navigable waters, interfere with swimming and boating, outcompete submerged aquatic vegetation, and lead to oxygen depletion.

Oxygen concentrations can fluctuate daily during algal blooms, rising during the day as algae perform photosynthesis, and falling at night as algae continue to respire, which consumes oxygen. Beneficial bacteria also consume oxygen as they decompose the abundant organic food supply in dying algae cells.

Lawn and crop fertilizers, sewage, manure, and detergents contain nitrogen and phosphorus, the nutrients most responsible for water quality degradation. Rural areas are vulnerable to ground water contamination from nitrates (a compound containing nitrogen) found in fertilizer and manure. Very high concentrations of nitrate (more than 10 mg/L) in drinking water cause methemoglobinemia, or blue baby syndrome, an inability to fix oxygen in the blood....

SEDIMENT AND SILTATION... In a water quality context, sediment usually refers to soil particles that enter the water column from eroding land. Sediment consists of particles of all sizes, including fine clay particles, silt, sand, and gravel. Water quality managers use term "siltation" to describe the suspension and deposition of small particles in waterbodies.

Sediment and siltation can severely alter aquatic communities. Sediment may clog and abrade fish gills, suffocate eggs and aquatic insect larvae on the bottom, and fill in the pore spaces where fish lay eggs. Silt and sediment interfere with recreational activities and aesthetic enjoyment of waterbodies by reducing water clarity and filling in waterbodies. Nutrients and toxic chemicals may attach to sediment particles and ride the particles into surface waters where the pollutants may settle with the sediment or detach and become soluble in the water column.

Rain washes silt and other soil particles off of plowed fields, construction sites, logging sites, urban areas, and strip-mined lands into waterbodies....

BACTERIA AND PATHOGENS... Some waterborne bacteria, viruses, and protozoa cause human illnesses that range from typhoid and dysentery to minor respiratory

5. This process is called "eutrophication," or the premature aging of a waterbody.

and skin diseases. These organisms may enter waters through a number of routes, including inadequately treated sewage, stormwater drains, septic systems, and sewage dumped overboard from recreational boats. Because it is impossible to test waters for every possible disease-causing organism, States and other jurisdictions usually measure indicator bacteria that are found in great numbers in the stomachs and intestines of warm-blooded animals and people. The presence of indicator bacteria suggests that the waterbody may be contaminated with untreated sewage and that other, more dangerous organisms may be present....[6]

TOXIC ORGANIC CHEMICALS AND METALS... Toxic organic chemicals are synthetic compounds that contain carbon, such as polychlorinated biphenyls (PCBs), dioxins, and the pesticide DDT. These synthesized compounds often persist and accumulate in the environment because they do not readily break down in natural ecosystems. Many of these compounds cause cancer in people and birth defects in other predators near the top of the food chain, such as birds and fish.

Metals occur naturally in the environment, but human activities (such as industrial processes and mining) have altered the distribution of metals in the environment. In most reported cases of metals contamination, high concentrations of metals appear in fish tissues rather than the water column because the metals accumulate in greater concentrations in predators near the top of the food chain.[7]

ACIDITY/ALKALINITY pH... Acidity, the concentration of hydrogen ions, drives many chemical reactions in living organisms. The standard measure of acidity is pH, and a pH value of 7 represents a neutral condition. A low pH value (less than 5) indicates acidic conditions; a high pH (greater than 9) indicates alkaline conditions. Many biological processes, such as reproduction, cannot function in acidic or alkaline waters. Acidic conditions also aggravate toxic contamination problems because sediments release toxicants in acidic waters. Common sources of acidity include mine drainage, runoff from mine tailings, and atmospheric deposition.

HABITAT MODIFICATION/HYDROLOGIC MODIFICATION... Habitat modifications include activities in the landscape, on shore, and in waterbodies that alter the physical structure of aquatic ecosystems and have adverse impacts on aquatic life. Examples of habitat modifications include: 1) removal of streamside vegetation that stabilizes the shoreline and provides shade, which moderates instream temperatures; 2) excavation of cobbles from a stream bed that provide nesting habitat for fish; 3) stream burial or destruction; and 4) excessive suburban sprawl that alters the natural drainage patterns by increasing the intensity, magnitude, and energy of runoff waters. Hydrologic modifications alter the flow of water. Examples include channelization, dewatering, damming, and dredging.

OTHER POLLUTANTS... These include salts and oil and grease. Fresh waters may become unfit for aquatic life and some human uses when they become contaminated by salts. Sources of salinity include irrigation runoff, brine used in oil extraction, road deicing operations, and the intrusion of sea water into ground and

---

6. The most common bacterial indicator is the E-Coli bacteria. An overabundance of these organisms in a waterbody can trigger beach closings and shutdowns of shellfish beds to harvesting [Eds.].

7. Excessive concentrations of toxic pollutants frequently result in fish consumption advisory warnings in affected waterbodies [Eds.].

surface water in coastal areas. Crude oil and processed petroleum products may be spilled during extraction, processing, or transport or leaked from underground storage tanks.

THE LEADING CAUSES OF WATER QUALITY IMPAIRMENT... The five leading causes of water quality impairment, ranked by the arial (sic) extent of waterbodies affected,[8] are illustrated in Table 1:

| TABLE 1: Five Leading Causes of Water Quality Impairment | | | |
|---|---|---|---|
| **RANK** | **RIVERS** | **LAKES** | **ESTUARIES** |
| 1 | Bacteria | Nutrients | Nutrients |
| 2 | Siltation | Siltation | Bacteria |
| 3 | Nutrients | Oxygen-depleting substances | Oxygen-depleting substances |
| 4 | Oxygen-depleting substances | Metals | Habitat alterations |
| 5 | Metals | Suspended Solids | Oil and grease |

WHERE DOES THIS POLLUTION COME FROM?... Of the Nation's 615,806 surveyed river miles, 64% have good water quality. Of these waters, 57% fully support their designated uses, and an additional 7% support uses but are threatened and may become impaired if pollution control actions are not taken.

Some form of pollution or habitat degradation prevents the remaining 36% (224,236 miles) of surveyed river miles from fully supporting a healthy aquatic community or human activities all year round. Twenty-two percent of the surveyed river miles have fair water quality that partially supports designated uses. Most of the time, these waters provide adequate habitat for aquatic organisms and support human activities, but periodic pollution interferes with these activities and/or stresses aquatic life. Fourteen percent of the surveyed river miles have poor water quality that consistently stresses aquatic life and/or prevents people from using the river for activities such as fishing and swimming.

Bacteria pollute 76,397 river miles (which equals 34% of the impaired river miles). Siltation impairs 75,792 river miles (which equals another 34% of the impaired river miles). In addition to siltation and bacteria, nutrients, oxygen-depleting substances, metals, and habitat alterations impact more miles of rivers and streams than other pollutants and processes. Often, several pollutants and processes impact a single river segment. For example, a process, such as removal of shoreline vegetation, may accelerate erosion of sediment and nutrients into a stream.

Agriculture is the most widespread source of pollution in the Nation's surveyed rivers. Agriculture generates pollutants that degrade aquatic life or interfere with public use of 134,557 river miles (which equals 60% of the impaired river miles) in 49 jurisdictions. [There have been] declines in pollution from sewage

---

8. Note that pollution by toxic metals is not among the top-ranked problems, in terms of miles or acres of waterbodies impacted. However, toxic metals may directly and adversely affect human health, especially the health of urban low-income and minority fishers who catch and eat fish from the urban waters that are listed as "toxic hot spots" (see below).

treatment plants and industrial discharges as a result of sewage treatment plant construction and upgrades and permit controls on industrial discharges. Despite the improvements, municipal sewage treatment plants remain the second most common source of pollution in rivers (impairing 37,443 miles) because population growth increases the burden on our municipal facilities. Urban runoff and storm sewers impair 26,862 river miles (12% of the impaired rivers), resource extraction impairs 24,059 river miles (11% of the impaired rivers), and removal of streamside vegetation impairs 21,706 river miles (10% of the impaired rivers). Hydrologic modifications and habitat alterations are a growing concern. "Natural" sources, such as low flow and soils with arsenic deposits, can prevent waters from supporting uses in the absence of human activities.

Agriculture is [also] the most widespread source of pollution in the Nation's surveyed lakes. Agriculture generates pollutants that degrade aquatic life or interfere with public use of 3.3 million lake acres (which equals 50% of the impaired lake acres). Municipal sewage treatment plants pollute 1.3 million lake acres (19% of the impaired lake acres), urban runoff and storm sewers pollute 1.2 million lake acres (18% of the surveyed lake acres), hydrologic modifications and habitat alterations degrade 832,000 lake acres (12% of the impaired lake acres), and industrial point sources pollute 759,000 lake acres (11% of the impaired lake acres).

Most of the Great Lakes shoreline is polluted by toxic organic chemicals — primarily PCBs — that are often found in fish tissue samples. Toxic organic chemicals impact 98% of the impaired Great Lakes shoreline miles. Other leading causes of impairment include pesticides, affecting 21%; other organic chemicals, affecting 20%; nutrients, affecting 6%; and metals, affecting 6%.

Urban runoff and storm sewers are the most widespread source of pollution in the Nation's surveyed estuarine waters. [These sources] degrade aquatic life or interfere with public use of 4,508 square miles of estuarine waters (which equals 46% of the impaired estuarine waters). Municipal sewage treatment plants pollute 3,827 square miles of estuarine waters (39% of the impaired estuarine waters), agriculture pollutes 3,321 square miles of estuarine waters (34% of the impaired estuarine waters), and industrial discharges pollute 2,609 square miles (27% of the impaired estuarine waters). Urban sources contribute more to the degradation of estuarine waters than agriculture because urban centers are located adjacent to most major estuaries.

COMMENTARY AND QUESTIONS

1. **A regulatory paradox.** With most point source industrial and municipal pollution having been cleaned up since 1972, today agriculture is clearly the major source of water pollution in most rivers and lakes, and a significant source of pollution in estuaries. Almost all agricultural operations are classified as nonpoint sources of pollution, however, and are thus outside the regulatory scope of the CWA. One of the most contentious issues raised during the debates on reauthorization of the CWA has been whether agriculture should finally be subject to regulation.

2. **Of goals and policies.** Professor Robert Adler cautions that the statistics included in the EPA Report above are suspect and may overstate the good news, because only 17% of all river miles and 42% of all lake acres have actually been surveyed, and current surveys and assessments do not necessarily include chemical monitoring.

Adler, et al., The Clean Water Act 20 Years Later, chap. 2 (1993). Even assuming the accuracy of EPA's statistics, the CWA's statutory goals have not been completely met, or its policies thoroughly implemented. The CWA declares —

> The objective of this chapter is to restore and maintain the chemical, physical, and biological integrity of the Nation's waters. In order to achieve this objective it is hereby declared that, consistent with the provisions of this chapter —
>
> (1) it is the national goal that the discharge of pollutants into the navigable waters be eliminated by 1985;
>
> (2) it is the national goal that wherever attainable, an interim goal of water quality which provides for the protection and propagation of fish, shellfish, and wildlife and provides for recreation in and on the water be achieved by July 1, 1983;
>
> (3) it is the national policy that the discharge of toxic pollutants in toxic amounts be prohibited....
>
> (7) it is the national policy that programs for the control of nonpoint sources of pollution be developed and implemented in an expeditious manner....
> 33 U.S.C.A. §1251

By "integrity of the Nation's waters" Congress meant their ecological stability, not the revival of a dehumanized state of primeval purity. The "Zero-Discharge Goal" of subsection (1) is not an enforceable requirement of the CWA, but a rebuttable presumption that all discharges are environmentally deleterious and a declaration that pollution prevention is the most desirable form of pollution control. The CWA's enforceable requirements are derived from the "interim goal" of subsection (2).

According to Adler et al., the national effort to attain these goals and implement these policies has become stalled because of (1) flaws and loopholes in the CWA's regulation of industrial discharges, allowing hundreds of millions of pounds of toxics to be released annually into surface waters and causing numerous fish consumption bans or advisories, especially in the Great Lakes area, (2) inadequate controls on municipal sewage discharges, resulting in frequent beach and shellfish bed closures, (3) inadequate controls on habitat loss and other forms of biological impairment, leading to the disproportionately high incidence of aquatic species on endangered and threatened species lists, and (4) the CWA's failure to regulate agriculture, leading to well-documented environmental degradation and damage to human users.

## B. THE ORIGIN AND EVOLUTION OF TBELs

### Environmental Protection Agency v. California
United States Supreme Court, 1976
426 U.S. 200, 96 S. Ct. 2022, 48 L. Ed. 2d 578

[In this opinion explaining the mechanics of the CWA, the Court held that federal facilities were not required to obtain NPDES permits from states with approved programs, a decision later overridden by Congress in the Clean Water Act amendments of 1977.]

WHITE, J. Before it was amended in 1972, the Federal Water Pollution Control Act employed ambient water quality standards specifying the acceptable levels of pollution in a State's interstate navigable waters as the primary mechanism in its program for the control of water pollution. This program based on water quality standards, which were to serve both to guide performance by polluters and to trigger legal action to abate pollution, proved ineffective. The problems stemmed from the character of the standards themselves, which focused on the tolerable effects rather than the preventable causes of water pollution, from the awkwardly shared federal and state responsibility for promulgating such standards, and from the cumbrous enforcement procedures. These combined to make it very difficult to develop and enforce standards to govern the conduct of individual polluters.

Some States developed water quality standards and plans to implement and enforce them, and some relied on discharge permit systems for enforcement. Others did not, and to strengthen the abatement system federal officials revived the Refuse Act of 1899, which prohibits the discharge of any matter into the Nation's navigable waters except with a federal permit. Although this direct approach to water pollution abatement proved helpful, it also was deficient in several respects: the goal of the discharge permit conditions was to achieve water quality standards rather than to require individual polluters to minimize effluent discharge, the permit program was applied only to industrial polluters, some dischargers were required to obtain both federal and state permits, and federal permit authority was shared by two federal agencies.

In 1972, prompted by the conclusion of the Senate Committee on Public Works that "the Federal water pollution control program...has been inadequate in every vital aspect," Congress enacted the Amendments, declaring "the national goal that the discharge of pollutants into the navigable waters be eliminated by 1985." For present purposes the Amendments introduced two major changes in the methods to set and enforce standards to abate and control water pollution. First, the Amendments are aimed at achieving maximum "effluent limitations on point sources," as well as achieving acceptable water quality standards. A point source is "any discernible, confined and discrete conveyance...from which pollutants are or may be discharged." An "effluent limitation" in turn is "any restriction established by a State or the Administrator [of EPA] on quantities, rates, and concentrations of chemical, physical, biological or other constituents which are discharged from point sources...including schedules of compliance." Such direct restrictions on discharges facilitate enforcement by making it unnecessary to work backward from an overpolluted body of water to determine which point sources are responsible and which must be abated. In addition, a discharger's performance is now measured against strict technology-based effluent limitations — specified levels of treatment — to which it must conform, rather than against limitations derived from water quality standards to which it and other polluters must collectively conform. Water quality standards are retained as a supplementary basis for effluent limitations, however, so that numerous point sources, despite individual compliance with [technology-based] effluent limitations, may be further regulated to prevent water quality from falling below acceptable levels.

Second, the Amendments establish the NPDES as a means of achieving and enforcing the effluent limitations. Under NPDES, it is unlawful for any person to discharge a pollutant without obtaining a permit and complying with its terms. A NPDES permit serves to transform generally applicable effluent limitations and other standards — including those based on water quality — into the obligations (including a timetable for compliance) of the individual discharger, and the Amendments provide for direct administrative and judicial enforcement of permits. With few exceptions, for enforcement purposes a discharger in compliance with the terms and conditions of an NPDES permit is deemed to be in compliance with those sections of the Amendments on which the permit conditions are based. In short, the permit defines, and facilitates compliance with and enforcement of, a preponderance of a discharger's obligations under the Amendments.

NPDES permits are secured, in the first instance, from EPA.... Consonant with its policy "to recognize, preserve, and protect the primary responsibilities and rights of the States to prevent, reduce, and eliminate pollution," Congress also provided that a State may issue NPDES permits "for discharges into navigable waters within its jurisdiction," but only upon EPA approval of the State's proposal to administer its own program. EPA may require modification or revision of a submitted program but when a plan is in compliance with EPA's guidelines...EPA shall approve the program and "suspend the issuance of permits...as to those navigable waters subject to such program."

The EPA retains authority to review operation of a State's permit program. Unless the EPA waives review for particular classes of point sources or for a particular permit application, a State is to forward a copy of each permit application to EPA for review, and no permit may issue if EPA objects that issuance of the permit would be "outside the guidelines and requirements" of the amendments. In addition to this review authority, after notice and opportunity to take action, EPA may withdraw approval of a state permit program which is not being administered in compliance with the [Act as amended]....

COMMENTARY AND QUESTIONS

1. **Ineffectuality of prior law.** Before 1972, under the old federal water statute, in more than two decades only one water pollution violation was successfully prosecuted, and in that case — which involved hog processing wastes, similar to the pollution from the Gwaltney and Smithfield Packing plants detailed in Chapter One — more than four years elapsed between the initial enforcement conference and the final consent decree. In those benighted days, desired uses were set by individual states, which classified waterways in categories ranging from Class A (swimming) to Class D (agricultural and industrial use). If a state was satisfied that a particular river need only be aesthetically tolerable and fit for commercial navigation, the law did not afford relief unless the river stank or corroded hulls of ships. The Cuyahoga River was not considered legally objectionable until it caught fire, because the state-designated use of that river was waste disposal. See generally, Congressional Research Service, Library of Congress, A Legislative History of the Federal Water Pollution Control Act Amendments of 1972 (1973).

If the harm-based prior law had failed so miserably, why did Congress, in the 1972 CWA, adopt both technology-based and harm-based controls, superimposing water quality-based controls on a fundamental level of technology-based controls? The answer has to do with congressional politics. The Senate favored replacing the water quality-based approach with progressively stricter technology-based effluent limitations, leading to the ultimate cessation of all discharges. The House, however, believed that a water quality-based approach was still viable. The resulting compromise entails a dual approach, with a harm-based system applicable only where necessary. Several analysts believe that the CWA's many ambiguities can be traced to this original, unsuccessful compromise.

Why did Congress move to a primarily technology-based standard-setting methodology in 1972, when it had embraced an almost totally harm-based strategy in the Clean Air Act only two years earlier? The Clean Air Act was, in effect, a statute of the 1960s because it extended and strengthened the harm-based Air Quality Act of 1967, which, ironically, followed the ambient standard approach earlier established in the 1965 Federal Water Pollution Control Act. Between late 1970, when the Clean Air Act was being finalized, and the summer of 1971, when the Senate Air and Water Pollution Subcommittee released its technology-based clean water bill (drawn from the new source performance standard section of the 1970 Clean Air Act §111), the burgeoning environmental movement had inspired dissatisfaction with the harm-based approach and its philosophy that there exists a right to discharge up to the assimilative capacity of the environment.

2. **Pros and cons of technology-based controls.** Critics of the technology-based approach argue that it is (1) economically inefficient because it frequently demands "redundant treatment" (i.e., greater treatment than necessary to maintain desired uses for waterbodies); and (2) insufficiently technology-stimulating, because it does not encourage industry to develop innovative technology (and in fact may be an example of a "perverse incentive" prompting industries to stifle cleaner technology). As for the first charge, defenders of the CWA respond that (1) the harm-based system has not effectively controlled pollution; (2) BAT standards are significantly simpler and less expensive to administer than harm-based standards; (3) the economic costs of BAT have been exaggerated, and its public health benefits undervalued; and (4) normatively, producers should do the best they can to protect human lives.

3. **Frozen technology?** In fact, water quality-based effluent limitations themselves freeze current technology, at least until water quality standards have been violated. To some extent, the charge that BAT standards create perverse incentives by freezing current technology is based on a misunderstanding of the manner in which technology-based standards are implemented in the CWA. There are two types of BAT standards: (1) equipment and design specification standards; and (2) performance standards. The former specifies the precise type of technology that a regulated party must install, whereas the latter establishes a performance standard, based on the technology utilized by the best performers in a particular industrial category, but allows the regulated party to meet that standard either by installing the base technology or in any other least-cost way, including using different technology or achieving pollution prevention. As the *Rybachek* opinion excerpted later in this chapter points out, the CWA relies on BAT-based performance standards, not equipment and design specification standards. Equipment and design specification standards are typically imposed where technology has

become standardized and pollutants are difficult to measure, as in drinking water treatment. Several of the CWA's detractors, however, have not recognized the fact that the CWA relies upon performance standards, rather than equipment and design specification standards.[9]

The CWA's technology-based approach, as originally conceived, can circumvent the perverse incentive to freeze current technology by encouraging the development of innovative technology by entrepreneurial ventures outside the regulated industrial sector. Although technology-based effluent limitations are based on available technology, EPA must review promulgated effluent limitations every five years, with a view toward tightening them to reflect the existence of improved pollution control devices. CWA §301(d). Improved BAT should be reflected in stricter TBELs that are included in five-year permit renewals.[10] In other words, build a better pollutant trap and the regulated dischargers must either beat a path to your door or find some other way to meet the performance standard. Unfortunately, EPA has been so preoccupied with developing its initial technology-based standards that it has only recently begun its five-year reviews of technology-based effluent limitations, partially as a result of Congressional prodding through §304(m) of the CWA, added by the Water Quality Act Amendments of 1987, setting deadlines for EPA promulgation of effluent guidelines.

There is evidence that the CWA's strategy of progressively tightening technology-based standards so as to ultimately achieve either significant pollutant reductions or zero-discharge has been realized as to some discharge categories. EPA's final effluent limitation guideline regulations for the pesticide formulating, packaging, and repackaging industry allows dischargers to choose between zero-discharge limits or a pollution prevention alternative. In 1993, EPA proposed a set of "Cluster Rules" for the pulp and paper industry (combining effluent and emissions limitations for both water and air pollution control — counteracting the inefficiencies of the media-specific approach).The water pollution control element of this proposal was based on oxygen delignification, a process that substitutes oxygen for chlorine in the bleaching of paper, thus eliminating the discharge of dioxin, a highly toxic by-product of chlorine bleaching. Goaded by the high cost of complying with this proposed BAT standard, several paper companies began substituting chlorine dioxide for chlorine, which reduced dioxin discharges by approximately 96% at substantially lower cost than oxygen delignification. In 1996, EPA reproposed these regulations and requested comments on both process changes as potential BAT. Finally, in 1997, EPA promulgated BAT standards based on the chlorine dioxide

---

9. See, e.g., Hahn, Getting More Environmental Protection for Less Money: A Practitioner's Guide, 9 Oxford Review of Economic Policy 112, 116 (1993)("the technology-based standard, which specifies a particular technology a firm must use to comply with the law,...is used frequently in both air and water regulation in the United States."); and Derzko, Using Intellectual Property Law and Regulatory Processes to Foster the Innovation and Diffusion of Environmental Technologies, 20 Harv. Env. L. Rev. 3, 18-19 ("Technology standards require polluting firms to reduce pollution using a certain prescribed technology;...[the Clean Air Act and Clean Water Act] still operate using technology standards.").

10. Discharge permits have a maximum duration of five years, but, once a renewal application is filed, the original permit remains in effect until renewal. The discharge permit renewal process has traditionally been plagued by severe backlogs, and many dischargers are operating under expired permits.

bleaching process. The virtually zero-discharge option was foregone in favor of a slightly less effective alternative that will be less costly to industry. In contrast to these apparent success stories, EPA has resisted realistic opportunities to implement zero-discharge as to other industrial categories.

4. **Navigable waters.** In the CWA, "discharge of a pollutant" means "any addition of any pollutant to navigable waters from any point source." §502(12). "Navigable waters" is generally defined as "waters of the United States." §502(7). It is well-settled that, as far as surface waters are concerned, "waters of the United States" transcends traditional definitions of navigability and is coterminous with the limits of the federal government's commerce clause jurisdiction. U.S. v. Ashland Oil, 504 F.2d 1317 (6th Cir. 1974). Thus, wetlands, drainage ditches, mosquito canals, and even intermittent streams are considered waters of the United States.

A major unresolved question with regard to the CWA is whether its provisions apply to point source discharges to groundwater. EPA has waffled on this issue, and the courts have split as to whether "tributary groundwater" (groundwater that is hydrologically connected to surface water) is covered by the Act. Contrast Exxon v. Train, 554 F.2d 1310 (5th Cir. 1977) (no groundwater is covered by the CWA), with U.S. Steel v. Train, 556 F.2d 822 (7th Cir. 1977) (groundwater is covered if it is hydrologically connected to surface water). Relying on CWA §510's express authority for states to adopt stricter standards and limitations than those imposed by EPA, a number of states, for example California and New Jersey, require discharge permits for point source dischargers to groundwater. California Water Code §10350(3); N.J.S.A. 58:10A-3.

5. **Point and nonpoint sources.** A "point source" is "any discernible, confined and discrete conveyance, including but not limited to any pipe, ditch, channel, tunnel, conduit, well, discrete fissure, container, rolling stock, concentrated animal feeding operation, or vessel or other floating craft from which pollutants are or may be discharged. This term does not include agricultural stormwater discharges and return flows from irrigated agriculture." §502(14). A "nonpoint source" is any man-made source, discharging to surface waters, that is not a point source. In general, a nonpoint source is a diffuse, intermittent source of pollutants that does not discharge at a single location but whose pollutants are carried over or through the soil by way of stormflow processes. Nonpoint source pollution generally results from land runoff, atmospheric deposition,[11] drainage, or seepage of contaminants. Major sources of nonpoint pollution include agricultural and silvicultural runoff and runoff from urban areas. In contrast to the high-level technological controls that are most often used to prevent point source pollution, nonpoint sources are best controlled by low-technology Best Management Practices (BMPs) — methods, measures, or practices consisting of structural or nonstructural controls and operation-and-maintenance procedures. BMPs generally involve comparatively inexpensive land-use controls and land-management practices. They are selected based on site-specific conditions that reflect natural background as well as politi-

---

11. 76 to 89 percent of PCBs in Lake Superior and up to 40 percent of nitrogen loadings to Chesapeake Bay are estimated to come from air pollution. EPA, Deposition of Air Pollution to the Great Waters: Report to Congress (1994).

cal, social, economic, and technical feasibility. For example, a set of BMPs to reduce runoff of nutrients, herbicides, and pesticides from a farm into a river might include diminished and staggered applications of these substances, contour plowing, and maintenance of vegetated stream buffers. BMPs are technology-based performance standards, rather than equipment and design specification standards, because nonpoint source control programs offer the discharger a choice from among a menu of BMPs, such as those available to the farmer in the preceding example.

The CWA regulates only point source pollution. In 1972, Congress excluded nonpoint sources from the regulatory ambit of the CWA because (1) point sources were perceived as the primary causes of water pollution, and little was then known about the deleterious impacts of nonpoint source runoff, (2) the BMPs to control nonpoint source pollution call for land-use and land-management restrictions that are generally implemented by local governments, and (3) nonpoint source pollution being diffuse and sporadic, it is more difficult to ascertain the dischargers and environmental effects of nonpoint source pollution than it is with regard to point sources.

The term "point source" is liberally construed, and has been held to include earth-moving equipment in a wetland and ponded mine drainage that erodes a channel to a river. Dams, which often cause adverse water quality impacts downstream, are treated as nonpoint rather than point sources. In a criminal case involving a co-owner of a blood-testing laboratory who threw vials containing blood contaminated with hepatitis-B virus into the Hudson River, the Second Circuit Court of Appeals held that an individual human being is not a point source within the meaning of the CWA. U. S. v. Plaza Health Laboratories, 3 F.3d 643 (1993), *cert. denied* 114 S.Ct. 2764 (1994).

The Second Circuit has also decided a case that, if followed by other circuits, may facilitate the regulation of some agricultural pollution under the CWA. Concerned Area Residents For the Environment (CARE) v. Southview Farms, 34 F.3d 114 (1994), *cert. denied* 115 S.Ct. 1793 (1995), was a citizen suit contesting the unpermitted liquid manure-spreading operation of a large dairy farm in western New York State. Southview Farms owned 1,100 acres and a herd of over 2,000 cows. Unlike older dairy farms, the cows were not pastured but remained in their barns, except during milking. The massive quantities of manure generated by these cows was first pumped into a separator, which drained off the liquid and compressed the solids. The solids were transported to a landfill, while the liquid residue was piped to a four-acre manure storage lagoon and thence to smaller lagoons. The liquid stored in these lagoons was spread over Southview's fields by (1) a center pivot irrigation system, (2) hose systems, and (3) manure spreaders pulled by tractors. Some of the runoff from the manure spreading operations drained into a natural swale, then into a man-made tile drain leading under a stone wall, and finally into a natural ditch that drained into a river. Reversing the district court, which had found the operation to be a nonpoint source, the circuit court held that the manure runoff was a point source because: (1) the swale/tile drain/ditch drainage system was a point source; (2) the manure spreading vehicles were point sources; and (3) the defendant was operating a concentrated animal feeding operation ("CAFO"), which is statutorily defined as a point source. In response to defendant's argument that its manure runoff fell within the CWA's "agricultural stormwater discharge" exemption, the court stated that

> ...there can be no escape from liability for agricultural pollution simply because it occurs on rainy days.... We think the real issue is not whether the discharges occurred during rainfall or were mixed with rain water run-off, but rather whether the discharges were the result of precipitation. Of course, all discharges eventually mix with precipitation run-off in ditches or steams or navigable waters so the fact that the discharge might have been mixed with run-off cannot be determinative.... We think the jury could properly find that the run-off was primarily caused by over-saturation of the fields rather than the rain and that sufficient quantities of manure were present so that run-off could not be classified as "stormwater." 34 F.3d, at page 120.

The court's finding that the drainage system was a point source is potentially the most important for future cases. Pure sheet-flow runoff is comparatively rare. Most runoff over unpaved surfaces ultimately finds its way to, or creates, gullies or swales that discharge into surface waterbodies.

If these are indeed point sources, then agricultural activities that do not comply with Best Management Practices (e.g., for manure spreading or pesticide applications) may be subject to regulation under the CWA because they are not included in the "agricultural stormwater discharge" exemption.

6. **Types of point source dischargers.** Point source dischargers may be either municipal, industrial, or stormwater dischargers. Municipal point source dischargers are known as Publicly-Owned Treatment Works or "POTWs." Industrial point source dischargers are either direct dischargers, which discharge directly into waterbodies, or indirect dischargers, which discharge into sewers that lead to POTWs, which then discharge into waterbodies. As will be discussed below, the types of pollutants discharged by an industrial discharger, as well as whether it is an existing or new source of water pollution, will determine the technology-based standards that it will be required to meet. Stormwater dischargers either channel stormwater runoff into a waterbody, or discharge into a municipal storm sewer, which itself discharges into a waterway.

7. **The federal-state partnership.** Forty states have been delegated primacy to administer their own counterparts of the NPDES permit program. The EPA is authorized by §518 to treat a Native American tribe as a State for purposes of administering the CWA, and a number of tribes have achieved primacy. In the remaining states, EPA regional offices are administering the program. Do you think that the CWA's safeguards, as described in the EPA v. California opinion, are adequate to prevent a state from treating dischargers leniently in order to attract and retain industry? In particular, given EPA's lack of resources, can EPA effectively review draft state permits? Would an EPA threat to withdraw state program authorization be credible?[12] Can EPA meaningfully exercise its backup enforcement

---

12. Professor Victor B. Flatt concludes that "the possibility of program revocation is now almost non-existent." A Dirty River Runs Through It (The Failure of Enforcement in the Clean Water Act), 25 B.C. Env. Aff. L. Rev., 1, 16 (1997). But note the pending EPA rescission review of Virginia's program, after *Smithfield Packing* in Chapter One C above.

authority under §309 of the CWA? Can state pollution control agencies be significantly influenced by EPA's diminishing ability to award program grants, conduct research, and perform technical assistance activities?

## C. IMPLEMENTING TBELS THROUGH THE NPDES PROCESS

Because environmental issues arise from competing demands on natural resources, environmental lawyers learn to work closely with scientists, engineers, natural resource managers, planners, policy analysts, and social scientists in formulating multidisciplinary, holistic environmental protection strategies for presentation to courts, legislatures, administrative agencies, private corporations, and the general public. The following case is unusual among CWA effluent limitation cases in that it involves a relatively simple technology and is thus intelligible to readers who lack a background in environmental science or chemical engineering, while showing some of the legal complexities:

### Rybachek v. EPA
United States Circuit Court for the Ninth Circuit, 1990
904 F.2d 1276

O'SCANNLAIN, J.... Placer mining is one of the four basic methods of mining metal ores; it involves the mining of alluvial or glacial deposits of loose gravel, sand, soil, clay, or mud called "placers." These placers often contain particles of gold and other heavy minerals. Placer miners excavate the gold-bearing material (paydirt) from the placer deposit after removing the surface vegetation and non-gold-bearing gravel (overburden). The gold is then separated from the other materials in the paydirt by a gravity-separation process known as "sluicing."

In the sluicing process, a miner places the ore in an on-site washing plant (usually a sluice box) which has small submerged dams (riffles) attached to its bottom. He causes water to be run over the paydirt in the sluice box; when the heavier materials (including gold) fall, they are caught by the riffles. The lighter sand, dirt, and clay particles are left suspended in the wastewater released from the sluice box.

Placer mining typically is conducted directly in streambeds or on adjacent property. The water usually enters the sluice box through gravity, but may sometimes also enter through the use of pumping equipment. At some point after the process described above, the water in the sluice box is discharged. The discharges from placer mining can have aesthetic and water-quality impacts on waters both in the immediate vicinity and downstream. Toxic metals, including arsenic, cadmium, lead, zinc, and copper, have been found in higher concentration in streams where mining occurs than in non-mining streams.

It is the treatment of the sluice-box discharge water before it re-enters a natural water course that is at the heart of this case.

STATUTORY FRAMEWORK... Congress enacted the Clean Water Act to "restore and maintain the chemical, physical, and biological integrity of the Nation's waters." Under the Act, the EPA must impose and enforce technology-based effluent limitations and standards through individual NPDES permits. These permits contain specific terms and conditions as well as numerical discharge limitations, which govern the activities of pollutant dischargers. Through the Clean Water Act,

Congress has directed the EPA to incorporate into the permits increasingly stringent technology-based effluent limitations.

Congress specified a number of means for the EPA to impose and to enforce these limitations in NPDES permits. For instance, it requires the Agency to establish effluent limitations requiring dischargers to use the "best practicable control technology currently available" ("BPT") within an industry. These limits are to represent "the average of the best" treatment technology performance in an industrial category. See EPA v. National Crushed Stone Ass'n., 449 U.S. 64 (1980). The EPA is further required to promulgate limitations both for the discharge of toxic pollutants by mandating that an industry use the "best available technology economically achievable" ("BAT") and for discharge of conventional pollutants by requiring the use of the "best conventional pollution control technology" ("BCT"); the congressionally imposed deadline for promulgation of these limitations was March 31, 1989....

In addition, new pollution sources in an industry must meet a separate set of standards, called new-source performance standards ("NSPS"). These standards limit the discharge of pollutants by new sources based on the "best available demonstrated control technology" ("BDT"). Finally, the EPA is authorized to establish best management practices ("BMPs") "to control plant site runoff, spillage or leaks, sludge or waste disposal, and drainage from raw material storage" in order to diminish the amount of toxic pollutants flowing into the receiving waters.

RULEMAKING HISTORY... On November 20, 1985, proceeding under the Clean Water Act, the EPA proposed regulations for placer mining. For most mines processing fewer than 500 cubic yards of ore per day ("yd3/day"), the EPA proposed BPT effluent limitations of 0.2 millilitres per litre ("ml/l") of discharge for settleable solids and 2,000 milligrams per litre ("mg/l") for total suspended solids. For mines processing more than 500 yd3/day of ore, the EPA proposed more stringent BCT and BAT limitations as well as new-source performance standards (NSPS) prohibiting the discharge of processed wastewater. Twice during the rulemaking process, the Agency published notices of new information and requested public comment on additional financial and technical data.

As a result of its studies, the comments received during the review-and-comment periods, and new studies undertaken in response to the submitted comments, the EPA promulgated final effluent-limitation guidelines and standards on May 24, 1988. The EPA established a BPT limitation, based on simple-settling technology, for settleable solids of 0.2 ml/l for virtually all mines. The final rule also established BAT limitations and NSPS based on recirculation technology, restricting the flow of processed wastewater that could be discharged. In addition, the EPA promulgated five BMPs to control discharges due to mine drainage and infiltration. These regulations were to become effective on July 7, 1988....

The Alaska Miners Association ("AMA") and Stanley and Rosalie Rybachek timely petitioned this court for review of the EPA's regulations. We ordered the petitions consolidated....

THE FINAL RULE... Petitioners make a host of arguments about the content of the final rule. For instance, they attack the EPA's setting of BPT and BAT limitations. They also allege various errors by the EPA in its promulgation of BMPs and its enunciation of new-source criteria....

MERITS OF THE LIMITATIONS... Petitioners challenge the merits of the EPA's regulations on a number of grounds; indeed, virtually every aspect of the regulations is attacked. To the extent the regulations may be divided into component parts (e.g., the BPT limitations, the BAT limitations, and new-source criteria), we address petitioner's arguments along those lines.

DETERMINATION OF BPT... We turn first to petitioners' argument that the EPA erred in its determination that settling ponds are the best practicable control technology currently available (BPT) within the placer mining industry. There is no dispute that settling ponds are currently available pollution control technology; in fact, the AMA concedes that they are now used by almost all miners. Rather, petitioners contend that the EPA failed to use a "cost-benefit analysis" in determining that settling ponds were BPT for placer mining. They also argue that the EPA failed to consider costs when it set forth BPT limitations governing settleable solids for small mines.

The Clean Water Act controls when and how the EPA should require BPT. Under 33 U.S.C. §1311(b)(1)(A), the Act requires "effluent limitations for point sources...which shall require the application of best practicable control technology currently available [BPT]." Under this section, the EPA is to determine whether a technology is BPT; the factors it considers "shall include...total cost of" the technology "in relation to effluent benefits to be achieved" from it, the age of equipment, engineering aspects, "non-water quality environmental impact...and such other factors as the Administrator deems appropriate."

From this statutory language, it is "plain that, as a general rule, the EPA is required to consider the costs and benefits of proposed technology in its inquiry to determine the BPT." Association of Pacific Fisheries v. EPA, 615 F.2d 794 (9th Cir. 1980). The EPA has broad discretion in weighing these competing factors. It may determine that a technology is not BPT on the basis of this cost-benefit analysis only when the costs are "wholly disproportionate" to the potential effluent-reduction benefits.

We look first to whether the EPA properly considered the costs of BPT and second to whether it properly weighed these costs against the benefits.

First, the record shows that the EPA properly considered costs in conducting the analysis which led to the determination that settling ponds are BPT and to the establishment of BPT effluent limitations for settleable solids. The EPA used a model-mine analysis to estimate the costs to mines of installing settling ponds. The Agency developed several model mines to represent the typical operating and compliance costs that open-cut mines and dredges of various sizes would incur. Commenters attempted to insure that the model-mine analysis reflected actual industry conditions, and the EPA accordingly modified the analysis when it thought it appropriate during the rulemaking. The EPA then determined, for each of its model mines, the incremental costs that would be incurred to construct and operate settling ponds to retain wastewater long enough to achieve a certain settleable solids level. It proceeded to conduct a detailed and complex assessment of the effect of the compliance costs on the mining industry's profits.

The EPA then properly weighed these costs against the benefits of settling ponds. Its data indicated that placer mine wastewater contained high levels of solids and metals that were reduced substantially by simple settling. The upshot of the EPA's analysis was its estimation that installation of settling ponds by open-cut mines industry-wide would remove over four million pounds of solids at a cost

of approximately $2.2 million — a removal cost of less than $1 per pound of solids.
We would uphold the EPA's determination of BPT.

DETERMINATION OF BAT: ANALYSIS OF COSTS... We next confront the AMA's
challenge to the EPA's determination that recirculation of process wastewater is
the best available technology economically achievable (BAT) in the placer mining
industry. By definition, BAT limitations must be both technologically available and
economically achievable. We conclude that the EPA's BAT limitations were both
and therefore uphold them.

The technological availability of recirculating process wastewater is not in dispute; in fact, placer mines commonly practice it. It is recirculation's economic
achievability that petitioner's challenge.

In determining the economic achievability of technology, the EPA must consider the "cost" of meeting BAT limitations, but need not compare such cost with
the benefits of effluent reduction. The Agency measures costs on a "reasonableness standard"; it has considerable discretion in weighing the technology's costs,
which are less-important factors than in setting BPT limitations.

The record demonstrates that the EPA weighed the costs that recirculation
would impose on gold placer mining....

TOTAL SUSPENDED SOLIDS LIMITATIONS... We come to petitioner's claim that the
EPA has impermissibly established BAT standards to regulate the discharge of total
suspended solids. Petitioners argue that total suspended solids are conventional
pollutants and therefore subject to BCT (best conventional pollution control technology), rather than BAT, standards. EPA's adoption of recirculation as BAT to control total suspended solids was arbitrary, petitioners contend, because recirculation
could not pass the cost-reasonableness test required in determining BCT.

The EPA declined to establish BCT for total suspended solids because test
results indicated that settling technology could not consistently control the level
of total suspended solids. Moreover, recirculation failed the BCT cost-reasonableness test.

Petitioners are incorrect in contending that the EPA instead adopted BAT to regulate the level of total suspended solids. The EPA's discussion of BAT in the final
rule makes no reference to controlling total suspended solids. Instead, EPA set BAT
standards to control the discharge of toxic pollutants — a category which, the parties agree, does not encompass total suspended solids. We therefore reject the contention that the EPA was arbitrary in establishing BAT standards.

SETTLEABLE SOLIDS LIMITATIONS... Petitioners also claim that settleable solids
are a component of total suspended solids and that the EPA should have classified
settleable solids as a conventional pollutant rather than a nonconventional pollutant. Petitioners contend that the BAT-based effluent limitations are therefore
inappropriate for settleable solids. We disagree.

In the Clean Water Act, Congress classified suspended solids as a conventional
pollutant. Congress did not classify settleable solids. We must determine, therefore, whether the EPA's classification of settleable solids as a nonconventional pollutant "is based on a permissible construction of the [Clean Water Act]." Chevron
U.S.A., Inc. v. EPA, 467 U.S. at 843. This court may not substitute its own construction of the Act if the EPA's interpretation is reasonable.

The EPA argues that because settleable solids were not designated by Congress as either a conventional or a toxic pollutant, they should be considered a nonconventional pollutant under 33 U.S.C.A. §1311(b)(2)(F). This argument is buttressed by the fact that EPA has subjected settleable solids to BAT-level controls in other regulatory areas. And even if settleable solids should more properly be considered a conventional pollutant, we note that the EPA has determined that settleable solids in placer mining effluent are a toxic pollutant indicator and thus may be subject to BAT-level limitations. We find, therefore, that the EPA's decision to treat settleable solids as a nonconventional pollutant and thus subject to BAT standards was both reasonable and permissible....

MANDATING OF TECHNOLOGY... The AMA next claims that by forbidding the discharge of any process wastewater, the EPA is mandating that placer miners use recirculation technology. According to the AMA, the EPA's action violates Congress' intent to avoid dictating technologies and to encourage innovation. While admitting that the wastewater flow standards are currently achievable only through certain technology, the EPA responds that the regulations only prescribe limitations reflecting actually achieved wastewater reduction. We agree with the EPA....

The EPA has not mandated use of a particular technology. The Agency first determined that recirculation is BAT for the control of discharges by placer mines of toxic metals and settleable solids. Based on this determination, the EPA established that Zero discharge of process wastewater is achievable and should be the BAT limitation and new-source performance standard. That the standards and limitations are stringent and currently may be achievable only through certain technology is true. However, nothing in the EPA's regulations specifies the use of any particular technology to meet the BAT limitations and new-source performance standards achievable through recirculation. In fact, the EPA has encouraged miners to employ innovative technologies and to seek compliance extensions and alternative BAT limitations under §301(k) of the Act. We find that the EPA's setting of zero-discharge limitations based on recirculation results was within its mandate under the Clean Water Act.

AVAILABILITY OF VARIANCES... Petitioners claim that EPA has contravened Congress' intent by failing to allow miners to obtain variances for site-specific conditions. We first note that this assertion is flatly contradicted by the final rule's express language allowing miners to apply for fundamentally different factor ("FDF") variances for both the BPT and BAT limitations....

Petitioners argue that the EPA's classification of settleable solids as a toxic pollutant indicator will prevent miners from obtaining a variance. Normally, BAT limitations for nonconventional pollutants (here, settleable solids) are subject to modification under §§301(c) and (g) of the Clean Water Act. In this instance, modifications for settleable solids under these provisions are unavailable because settleable solids are considered an indicator of toxic pollutants. This does not mean, however, that no variance in the BAT limitations for settleable solids is available; miners may still apply for an FDF variance under §301(n) of the Act....

TIME FOR COMPLIANCE... The AMA contends that Alaskan miners were not given sufficient time to comply with the EPA's regulations.... Congress mandated that the BCT and BAT limitations must be achieved no later than March 31, 1989. The EPA does not have discretion to extend this deadline. This does not mean, however, that the EPA must be inflexible in enforcing the regulations.

"Section 309 of the Act provides that, if a discharger fails to comply with a 'final deadline' the [EPA] shall schedule a 'reasonable' time for compliance 'taking into account the seriousness of the violation and any good faith efforts to comply with applicable requirements.'" Chemical Manufacturers Ass'n v. EPA, 870 F.2d 177, 242 (5th Cir. 1989), cert. denied, 110 S. Ct. 1936 (1990). It was "Congress' intention that good faith compliance [in appropriate instances] would be accommodated by the EPA's post-deadline enforcement policy." *Id.* Thus, while we acknowledge the miner's concerns, we do not think that as a general matter enforcement of the new regulations for the 1989 mining season was unreasonable.

### COMMENTARY AND QUESTIONS

1. **Evolution of categorical technology-based limitations.** When the CWA was enacted in 1972, it contained two phases of technology-based limitations. In the first phase, existing industrial point source dischargers were required to meet effluent limitations based on Best Practicable Control Technology Currently Available ("BPT") by 1977. During the second phase, dischargers were to meet stricter effluent limitations based on Best Available Technology Economically Achievable ("BAT") by 1983. BPT was intended to be primarily "end of pipe" treatment, with process changes required only if they were normal practice within an industry. The factors to be considered in setting BAT limitations were similar to those relied upon in setting BPT-based limitations (and described in the *Rybachek* opinion), except that (1) BAT was based on the single best performer within an industry, rather than on an average of "exemplary plants," (2) BAT was based on process changes adopted within the industry or reasonably transferable from another industry, and (3) BAT involved a consideration only of the cost of achieving such reduction (cost effectiveness), not comparative benefits and costs, unless costs were "wholly disproportionate" to water quality benefits. Congress realized that some facilities would be forced to cut back production or even close down as a result of these BAT-based limitations.

EPA adopted a "categorical" approach to setting technology-based effluent limitations. Industries were divided into categories, based on products manufactured, and subcategories, based on processes or raw materials utilized in producing the products (e.g., the dredge-mining subcategory of the placer mining category). Then the BPT and BAT criteria were applied to these categories and subcategories, not to individual plants. EPA's effluent limitation regulations for each industrial subcategory contained maximum daily and monthly average limitations on relevant "parameters" (pollutants) expressed in terms of maximum volume of wastewater, or concentration of parameters in wastewater, per unit of production or other measure of output. These "single number" effluent limitations were uniform for existing plants in a particular subcategory, wherever they were located. EPA cannot establish a subcategory based solely on geographical location. Hundreds of lawsuits by industry, and numerous divergences among circuit courts of appeals, were resolved in Dupont v. Train, 430 U.S. 12 (1977), in which the Supreme Court upheld EPA's categorical approach, but stipulated that EPA must devise a variance for plants that do not fit within an industrial subcategory. This procedure, known as the

Fundamentally Different Factors ("FDF") variance, was later codified as §301(n) of the CWA. For dischargers receiving an FDF variance (e.g., a placer miner that does not have adequate space for a settling pond), and dischargers for which effluent limitation regulations have not yet been promulgated, effluent limitations are set using Best Professional Judgment ("BPJ") in light of the statutory criteria. The water quality of the receiving body of water cannot be considered in setting technology-based effluent limitations. Can a discharger dilute its effluent in order to meet effluent limitations? Weyerhaeuser v. Costle, 590 F.2d 1011 (D.C. Cir. 1978) and other cases make it clear that in-plant dilution is not an acceptable solution to pollution under the CWA. Developers of new sources possess the advantage of being able to build pollution control mechanisms into their original plant designs. Consequently, new sources are required to immediately comply with New Source Performance Standards ("NSPS") based on Best Available Demonstrated Control Technology ("BDT"), or zero-discharge where practicable. As in *Rybachek*, NSPS are most often equivalent to BAT. However, having met the relevant NSPS, a new source cannot be required to meet stricter technology-based standards for ten years or the facility's amortization period, whichever comes first. §306.[13]

2. **The mid-course corrections of 1977.** Between 1972 and 1977, the installation of BPT by industry, and the decrease in pollution from POTWs, had significantly reduced the loadings of so-called "conventional pollutants" (BOD, TSS, pH, fecal coliform, and oil and grease) to America's waterbodies. At the same time, Congress had come to the realization that toxic pollutants were far more of a problem than had initially been envisioned. Thus, a mid-course correction was made in 1977 with regard to conventionals and toxics.

In 1977, convinced that the cost of moving to BAT for conventionals was too high, Congress devised a new standard — Best Conventional Pollutant Control Technology ("BCT") — for them. §301(b)(2)(E). BCT includes two cost tests: (1) a comparison between the costs of reducing discharges of conventionals and the resulting water quality benefits; and (2) a comparison between industrial and municipal costs for treating conventionals. §304 (b)(2)(B). The congressional supporters of BCT felt that it would produce effluent limitations falling between BPT and BAT, but in practice BCT is identical to BPT.

The CWA's original toxic pollutant control mechanism was a cumbersome pollutant-by-pollutant, harm-based system — modeled after §112 of the Clean Air Act — that resulted in little control of toxic water pollutants. Rejecting this exercise in futility, EPA decided to regulate toxic pollutants primarily through BAT-based effluent limitations. EPA's decision was upheld by the famous "Consent Decree of 1976." NRDC v. Train, 8 ERC 2120 (often called the "Flannery Decree" after the trial court judge). This decree established timetables for EPA to promulgate effluent limitations, based on BAT, for many industrial categories covering 65 families

---

13. Stricter new source performance standards are sometimes criticized as counterproductive, in that they allegedly discourage new plant construction and delay the phaseout of inefficient, polluting older facilities. There is little evidence that this has occurred in the water pollution control area. Competitive pressures militate against the perpetuation of inefficient facilities simply to save on pollution control costs. A greater danger is the offshore migration of dischargers.

of compounds, which EPA has broken down into 126 "priority pollutants."[14] EPA is authorized to add toxic pollutants to this list by regulation, but has not done so. In 1977, Congress codified this methodology for regulating toxics. §§301(b)(2)(C) and 307(a)(1) and (2). As *Rybachek* illustrates, non-toxic pollutants that indicate the presence of toxics ("indicator" or "surrogate" parameters) may be regulated as toxics themselves. 40 CFR §122.44(e)(2)(ii).

In addition to conventional and toxic pollutants, Congress in 1977 created a third class of pollutants called "nonconventional" (or "nonconventional/non-toxic") pollutants. §301(b)(2)(F). Ammonia, chlorine, color, iron, and total phenols are some of the designated nonconventional pollutants. Dischargers of nonconventionals are entitled to apply for two variances, the cost-based §301(c) variance and the harm-based §301(g) variance. In *Rybachek*, petitioners unsuccessfully contested EPA's classification of settleable solids, ordinarily a nonconventional pollutant, as a toxic pollutant indicator because such classification rendered the nonconventional pollutant variances unavailable to them. Dischargers of toxics, like dischargers of conventionals, may only apply for FDF variances and §301(k) variances for innovative technology.

Table 2 illustrates the classes of water pollutants with their appropriate technology-based effluent limitations, compliance dates, and available variances:[15] *Train v. Colorado Public Interest Research Group*, 426 U.S. 1 (1976). States can, however, control the siting of nuclear power plants through their traditional powers over the need for, and the economic costs of, electrical power. See Chapter Six.

## TABLE 2: TBELs — Technology-Based Effluent Limitations

| POLLUTANT TYPE | EFFLUENT LIMITATION | COMPLIANCE DATE | VARIANCES? |
|---|---|---|---|
| **Conventional Pollutants** (BOD, TSS, etc.) | BCT | 3 years from promulgation | FDF: Fundamentally Different Factors variances |
| **Non-Conventionals Non-Toxics** (Ammonia, color, etc.) | BAT | same | FDF: §301(c) and (g) variances based on economics and receiving water quality |
| **Toxics** | BAT | same | FDF: §301(k) 2-year extension for adoption of innovative/alternative technology |
| **Heat** | BAT | same | §316(a) |
| **New Source Discharges** | BDT | upon construction | none 10-year grace period |

14. The time limits in the consent decree were frequently delayed, and it was not until 1987 that EPA promulgated the last of these effluent limitations. The consent decree covered both direct and indirect dischargers of toxics. EPA estimates that BAT-based effluent limitations imposed under this program have reduced discharges of priority pollutants by 99%, but heavy discharges of priority and hazardous nonpriority pollutants still continue from point and nonpoint sources.

15. Neither EPA nor a state has the authority to regulate discharges of radioactive materials, which are within the exclusive jurisdiction of the Nuclear Regulatory Commission.

3. **Stormwater discharges.** When the *Rybachek* discharge permit was issued, there was only one nonpoint source of industrial stormwater that could be directly regulated under the CWA. §304(e) authorizes EPA to establish best management practices (BMPs) "to control plant site runoff, spillage or leaks, sludge or waste disposal, and drainage from raw material storage" in order to diminish the amount of toxic pollutants flowing into receiving waters. In *Rybachek*, EPA had promulgated five BMPs to control discharges due to mine drainage and infiltration.

In the 1987 CWA amendments, Congress expanded EPA's jurisdiction to issue discharge permits for stormwater discharges that (1) are associated with industrial activity, (2) emanate from municipal separate storm sewers serving a population of 100,000 or more,[16] and (3) contribute to violations of water quality standards or are significant contributors of water pollution. Phase I of EPA's stormwater program, covering municipalities of over 100,000 people and construction sites of over five acres, has already been implemented. Phase II, covering smaller communities and construction sites, will soon become effective. Both the industrial and municipal stormwater permit programs emphasize the promulgation of general permits containing BMPs to prevent pollutants from entering municipal stormwater systems. EPA's industrial stormwater control program has been one of the most exciting developments in water pollution control. It is a model of regulatory efficiency, and might serve as a template for an agricultural nonpoint source control program. An industrial discharger of stormwater must comply with the terms of a general permit for its industrial category. Each general permit requires the development and implementation of Stormwater Prevention Plans ("SPPs") incorporating BMPs such as planning, reporting, personnel training, preventive maintenance, and good housekeeping. For example, a discharger that experiences runoff from an uncovered outdoor pile of raw materials might either (1) build an enclosure for the pile, or (2) move it indoors. SPPs must be reviewed and certified by a Registered Professional Engineer.

4. **Municipal dischargers.** POTWs must also possess NPDES permits containing technology-based effluent limitations. They were required to have met effluent limitations based on "Secondary Treatment" (generally defined as a biological process that achieves 85 percent removal of conventional pollutants) by 1988. §301(b)(B) and 40 CFR §133. Waivers from secondary treatment are available to POTWs that discharge into deep ocean waters. §301(h). Since 1972, federal monetary subsidies have been available for the construction and upgrading of POTWs and their sewerage systems. These federal incentives were first administered as the "Construction Grants Program" (CWA Title II), which provided almost $60 billion to municipalities and sewerage authorities in 55 percent to 85 percent matching grants for construction and land acquisition. In 1989, the Construction Grants Program was replaced by federal capitalization grants to State Revolving Loan Funds ("SRFs"). CWA Title VI. Approximately another $20 billion has been granted to the states under this program. However, there is an unmet need for

---

16. In older urban centers, a single sewerage system may carry stormwater as well as domestic and industrial wastewater. These "combined sewers" may overflow during storm events. Combined Sewer Overflow (CSO) is discussed below.

approximately an additional $140 billion in investment for POTW and sewerage infrastructure upgrades. There is a growing trend toward privatization of POTWs in order to allow for badly-needed improvements to municipal wastewater infrastructure that government is increasingly unable to fund.

Combined sewer overflows are a major source of urban water pollution, in general, and, in particular, beach closings and swimming advisories due to high concentrations of pathogens (bacteria and viruses) from untreated municipal sewage. Nationwide, there are approximately 1,100 combined sewer systems, serving about 43 million people. In order to protect sewerage systems and POTWs from flooding during large storm events, sewage overflow points were built into combined sewer systems. See generally, Northwest Environmental Advocate v. Portland, 56 F.3d 979 (9th Cir. 1995), *cert. denied* 116 S.Ct. 2550 (1996). During heavy rainstorms, mixed stormwater and domestic and industrial wastewater back up into residential basements or overflow into municipal storm sewers or directly into waterways. Although CSOs are significant point sources of pollution, the CWA does not specifically address them. EPA has elected to issue its CSO Control Policy as unenforceable guidance. 59 Fed. Reg. 18688. Because separation of combined sewer systems and technological CSO controls are prohibitively expensive, the CSO Control Policy focuses on BMPs and the development of long-term CSO control plans targeting environmentally sensitive receiving waters.

5. **Indirect dischargers and biosolids disposal**. Toxic and hazardous materials discharged into sanitary and combined sewers compose a substantial percentage of toxic pollutant loadings to waterways:

> A large number of industrial facilities, ranging from pesticide manufacturers to small local electroplaters, discharge toxic wastes to the nation's sewage treatment plants. A 1986 EPA study identified approximately 160,000 industrial and commercial facilities discharging wastes with hazardous constituents to public sewers, representing about 12 percent of the total flow to POTWs.... Secondary treatment alone does not remove these pollutants. While some fraction of organic hazardous constituents is degraded incidentally in the POTW's conventional treatment process, many of these substances evaporate during the treatment (or from the sewer pipes themselves) or wind up in the water or the sludge. None of the metals that go to a treatment plant are degraded: toxic metals pass through the plant into receiving waters or into the sludge generated by the treatment process. Adler, et al., 144–145.

Section 307 of the CWA requires EPA to promulgate "pretreatment standards" for indirect discharges that interfere with POTW operations, contaminate sludge, or pass untreated through the POTW, causing the POTW to violate its discharge permit. The CWA does not compel indirect dischargers to procure discharge permits, although some states require Significant Industrial Users ("SIUs") to obtain permits.

There are two types of national pretreatment standards: "prohibited discharge standards" and "categorical pretreatment standards." 40 CFR §403. Prohibited discharge standards require that pollutants introduced into a POTW not inhibit the POTW's performance. Categorical pretreatment standards set out national discharge limits based on BAT, similar to TBELs for direct dischargers. Categorical pretreatment standards may be supplemented by stricter state or local standards where necessary to enable a POTW to comply with the effluent limitations in its own discharge permit or with an element of its CSO control plan.

Pretreatment standards are primarily enforced by the POTWs themselves — through local sewer connection permits or user agreements — with the states and EPA retaining backup enforcement authority. This system creates a "fox-in-the-henhouse" situation, because POTWs are reluctant to enforce against their own customers unless (1) the indirect discharge disrupts the plant's operations, or (2) the POTW's discharge permit contains effluent limitations for toxics, the permit is being violated, and enforcement action is being taken against the POTW — a rare conjunction of circumstances. Not only has indirect discharge been a significant loophole in the CWA, but it has also been exacerbated by RCRA's exclusion of indirect discharges from its regulatory ambit. See Chapter 17. In Chapter One, the Gwaltney and Smithfield Packing plants, as well as the LSP plant that discharged Kepone, ultimately opted for indirect discharge into the local POTWs.

EPA reports that although toxic loadings to POTWs have decreased by up to 75% through pretreatment, approximately 54% of SIUs are in significant noncompliance with pretreatment standards (compared with a 6% noncompliance rate for direct dischargers), and 39% of POTWs are failing to implement at least one major component of their approved pretreatment programs. These statistics are indicative of problems that have plagued the pretreatment program since 1972. In response, EPA has increased its enforcement efforts against POTWs that are not implementing their approved pretreatment programs.

Biosolids (previously called "sewage sludge," but euphemistically renamed by EPA) are the final residual of the municipal sewage treatment process. Biosolids may be heavily contaminated due to inadequate pretreatment, uncontrolled flushing of household toxics (e.g., drain cleaners and pesticides), toxics entering sewers from road runoff into combined sewers or leaky sanitary sewers, and illegal hazardous waste dumping into municipal sewerage systems. Biosolids contaminated with heavy metals can preclude beneficial use as a soil conditioner on farmland, which EPA now favors as an alternative to disposal in landfills or incineration. CWA §405 establishes a permit system for biosolids disposal, and requires EPA to promulgate regulations setting guidelines for biosolids disposal and reuse. EPA's biosolids disposal and reuse regulations have been highly controversial, and have thus been subject to extraordinary slippage. Farmers are understandably reluctant to accept biosolids for land application, because compliance with EPA standards will not insulate a farmer from common law actions brought by neighbors for abnormally dangerous activities resulting in groundwater contamination. See the *Branch* case in Chapter Three.

6. **Drinking water protection.** Ambient water quality and tap water quality are regulated by different federal statutes. Under the Safe Drinking Water Act, 42 U.S.C.A. §§300f et seq., EPA is required to promulgate national primary and secondary drinking water regulations applicable to "public water systems," defined as systems that have at least 15 service connections or regularly serve at least 25 individuals at least 60 days per year. Primary drinking water regulations identify

potential toxic contaminants, and for each contaminant set a maximum contaminant level (MCL) if the contaminant can feasibly be measured or a treatment technique if it cannot. Secondary drinking water regulations set MCLs for nontoxic contaminants that affect other parameters, for example, color and taste.

The Safe Drinking Water Act, like the Clean Water Act, relies on technology-based standards. EPA first promulgates Maximum Contaminant Level Goals ("MCLGs"), which are nonenforceable health goals for public water systems. MCLGs are to be set at levels at which "no known or anticipated adverse effects on the health of persons occur and which allows an adequate margin of safety." Then, EPA promulgates enforceable primary drinking water regulations, including MCLs and monitoring and reporting requirements for dangerous contaminants. MCLs must be set as close to MCLGs as is "feasible," which means "with the use of the best technology, treatment techniques, and other means, which the Administrator finds are generally available (taking costs into consideration)." The Safe Drinking Water Act also authorizes federal contributions to state revolving loan funds — modeled on the State Revolving Loan Funds under the CWA — for the construction and upgrade of water purification facilities.

7. **Critiques of BAT under the CWA.** Although he believes that "BAT under the Clean Water Act has probably been the most effective pollution control program in the world in terms of producing identifiable abatement," Professor Oliver Houck concludes that EPA's technology-based effluent limitation program is faltering with regard to toxic pollutants. Regulation of Toxic Pollutants Under the Clean Water Act, 21 ELR 10528 (1991). EPA has not added any priority pollutants or industrial categories to its lists since the consent decree of 1976. According to Houck, "a greater number of individual industries remain unregulated than regulated, and a growing list of toxics have escaped scrutiny and standards."[17] Moreover, in Houck's view,

> ...discharge standards have emerged unevenly, with a heavy "zero discharge" hand on such unfortunates as seafood canners and placer mine operators, and a remarkably blind eye to available closed-cycle systems for some of the nation's highest volume dischargers of broad-spectrum toxins [like petroleum refiners, and certain organic chemical producers]. The disparities in these standards reflect nothing more starkly than a disparity in clout. 21 ELR, at 10539.

Skeptical of the water quality-based approach, Professor Houck recommends that Congress either (1) establish specific deadlines for EPA to promulgate new technology-based effluent limitations, with a zero-discharge "hammer" similar to RCRA's land ban (see Chapter 17), or (2) fix timetables, based on relative risk and reasonable lead times, for the elimination of toxic discharges. What are the potential disadvantages of so closely involving Congress in the intricacies of standard-setting? An argument can be made that since Congress possesses a minimum of expertise in the technical aspects of water pollution control, its decisions will be either hopelessly unrealistic or even more politically motivated than EPA's. Under

---

17. A recent report by the Comptroller General of the United States supports Professor Houck's conclusion. The GAO found that 77% of the discharge of all toxic pollutants across its sample (the vast majority of which were nonpriority pollutants) was uncontrolled. USGAO, Poor Quality Assurance and Limited Pollutant Coverage Undermine EPA's Control of Toxic Substances (1994).

some political scenarios, Professor Houck might be better off with EPA than with Congress.

Adler et al. observe that TBELs, as currently administered, enable dischargers to "game" the system by exaggerating production figures and mixing waste streams in-plant so as to achieve dilution. More importantly, "the Environmental Protection Agency's effluent guidelines program reflects an end-of-pipe focus, that is, an exaltation of treatment systems that reduce pollutants *after* they are generated over methods to eliminate the creation of pollutants in the first place." Adler, et al., 143. These authors recommend that the CWA be amended to allow EPA to ban ("to 'sunset'") particularly dangerous chemicals in the shortest feasible time.

The *Atlantic States* case that follows illustrates the problem of controlling non-priority toxic pollutants in the context of administering TBELs through the discharge permit of a large, multifaceted industrial operation. The industrial discharge of Kodak and the complexity of the permit in *Atlantic States* case is more representative of the ordinary discharge permitting context than *Rybachek*. Notice how many pieces of the puzzle that have been studied thus far (e.g., CWA regulations, discharge permits, cooperative federalism, and deferential judicial review) combine to generate the law of water pollution control. Notice also that this litigation arose by way of a citizen suit, one of the over 1200 CWA citizen suits that have been filed since 1972.

### Atlantic States Legal Foundation, Inc. v. Eastman Kodak Company
United States Court of Appeals for the Second Circuit, 1993
12 F.3d 353, cert. den., 513 U.S. 811 (1994)

WINTER, Circuit Judge: This appeal raises the issue of whether private groups may bring a citizen suit pursuant to §505 of the Clean Water Act to stop the discharge of pollutants not listed in a valid permit issued pursuant to CWA §402. We hold that the discharge of unlisted pollutants is not unlawful under the CWA. We also hold that private groups may not bring such a suit to enforce New York State environmental regulations.

Appellee Eastman Kodak Company ("Kodak") operates an industrial facility in Rochester, New York that discharges wastewater into the Genesee River and Paddy Hill Creek under a State Pollutant Discharge Elimination System ("SPDES") permit issued pursuant to CWA §402. Appellant Atlantic States Legal Foundation, Inc. is a not-for-profit environmental group based in Syracuse, New York.

Kodak operates a wastewater treatment plant at its Rochester facility to purify waste produced in the manufacture of photographic supplies and other laboratory chemicals. The purification plant employs a variety of technical processes to filter harmful pollutants before discharge into the Genesee River at the King's Landing discharge point (designated Outfall 001) pursuant to its SPDES permit.

Kodak first received a federal permit in 1975. At that time, the pertinent regulatory scheme was the NPDES administered directly by the federal Environmental Protection Agency. Subsequently, CWA §402(b-c) delegated authority to the states to establish their own programs in place of the EPA's. As a result, Kodak applied in July 1979 to renew its permit to the New York State Department of Environmental Conservation ("DEC"). The DEC declined to act on Kodak's renewal application, and Kodak's NPDES permit remained in effect. As part of the pending application for a SPDES permit, in April 1982, Kodak provided the DEC with a Form 2C describing estimated discharges of 164 substances from each of its outfalls. Kodak also submitted an Industrial Chemical Survey ("ICS") disclosing the amounts of certain chemicals used in Kodak's facility and whether they might appear in the plant's wastewater. Although the ICS originally requested information on 144 substances, including some broad classes such as "unspecified metals," the DEC restricted the inquiry to chemicals used in excess of specified minimum levels.

On the basis of these disclosures, DEC issued Kodak a SPDES permit, number 000-1643, effective November 1, 1984, establishing specific effluent limitations for approximately 25 pollutants.[18] The permit also included "action levels"[19] for five other pollutants as well as for three of the pollutants for which it had established effluent limits. DEC further required Kodak to conduct a semi-annual scan of "EPA Volatile, Acid and Base/Neutral Fractions and PCB's priority pollutants on a 24-hr. composite sample." In May 1989, Kodak applied to renew the SPDES permit submitting a new Form 2C and ICS, but the 1984 permit will continue to remain in effect until DEC issues a final determination.

On November 14, 1991, Atlantic States filed the complaint in the instant matter. The complaint alleged that Kodak had violated CWA §§301 and 402 by discharging large quantities of pollutants not listed in its SPDES permit.[20] After discovery, Atlantic States moved for partial summary judgment as to Kodak's liability in relation to the post-April 1, 1990 discharge of one or more of 16 of the 27 pollutants listed in the complaint.[21] The 16 pollutants are all listed as toxic chemicals under §313(c) of the Emergency Planning and Community Right-to-Know Act, 42 U.S.C. §11023(c). Atlantic States argued that General Provision 1(b) of the SPDES permit and §301 of the CWA prohibit absolutely the discharge of any pollutant not specifically authorized under Kodak's SPDES permit. Kodak made a cross-motion for summary judgment on the ground that neither the CWA nor the federal regulations implementing it prohibit discharge of pollutants not specifically assigned effluent limitations in an NPDES or SPDES permit.

---

18. UOD, TKN, Ammonia, BOD sub5, oil & grease, phosphorus, cyanide, cadmium, chromium, copper, iron, lead, nickel, silver (total and ionic), zinc, mercury, chloroform, 4-Chloro-3, 5-dimethylphenol, 1,2-Dichloroethane, 1,2-Dichloropropane, N,N-Dimethylaniline, Dichloromethane, Pyridine, and Xylene.

19. If the action level is exceeded, the permittee must undertake a "short-term, high-intensity monitoring program." If levels higher than the action levels are confirmed, the permit is reopened for consideration of revised action levels or effluent limits.

20. Specifically, the complaint alleged that Kodak had discharged "282,744 pounds of unpermitted pollutants in 1987, 308,537 pounds in 1988, 321,456 pounds in 1989, and 290,121 pounds in 1990," and that Atlantic States believed that Kodak continued to discharge such pollutants. The 27 substances Atlantic States alleged that Kodak discharged were acetonitrile, acetone, carbon tetrachloride, catechol, cyclohexane, dibutyl phthalate, diethanolamine, ethylene glycol, glycol ethers, formaldehyde, hydroquinone, manganese, methanol, methyl ethyl ketone, methyl isobutyl ketone, n-butyl alcohol, nitrobenzene, 1,1,1-trichloroethane, 1,1,2-trichloroethane, 1,4- dioxane, 2-ethoxyethanol, 2-methoxyethanol, tert-butyl alcohol, toluene, and trichloroethylene.

21. [Original footnote 7] Atlantic States' contentions regarding the number and amount of pollutants discharged are not material given our disposition of this matter. Of the 16 substances on which Atlantic States moved for partial summary judgment, seven were listed by Kodak in its permit application, Form 2C, or ICS, or were specifically mentioned in the DEC's 1988 Notice Letter: dibutyl phthalate, ethylene glycol, manganese, 1,4-dioxane, 1,1,1- trichloroethane, 1,1,2-trichloroethane, and toluene. These substances received specific regulatory inquiry. The remaining nine substances appeared on Kodak's Form R's, the source of Atlantic States' information. Kodak must file annual Form Rs, a Toxic Chemical Release Inventory Reporting Form, with both EPA and DEC, pursuant to 42 U.S.C. §11023. Although not listed in Kodak's SPDES permit, these substances were subject to DEC regulation. Even had there been no regulation of the particular substances, Atlantic States would still not have standing to sue unless it could show violations of established regulatory limits.

Atlantic States argues first that the plain language of §301 of the CWA prohibits the discharge of any pollutants not expressly permitted. Section 301(a) reads: "Except as in compliance with this section and §§1312, 1316, 1317, 1328, 1342, and 1344 of this title, the discharge of any pollutant by any person shall be unlawful." This prohibition is tempered, however, by a self-referential host of exceptions that allow the discharge of many pollutants once a polluter has complied with the regulatory program of the CWA. The exception relevant to the instant matter is contained in §402, which outlines the NPDES, and specifies the requirements for suspending the national system with the submission of an approved state program, CWA §402(b-c). Section 402(k) contains the so-called "shield provision" which defines compliance with a NPDES or SPDES permit as compliance with §301 for the purposes of the CWA's enforcement provisions. The Supreme Court has noted that: "The purpose of [§402(k) ] seems to be...to relieve [permit holders] of having to litigate in an enforcement action the question whether their permits are sufficiently strict." E.I. du Pont de Nemours & Co. v. Train, 430 U.S. 112, 138 n.28 (1977).

Atlantic States' view of the regulatory framework stands that scheme on its head. Atlantic States treats permits as establishing limited permission for the discharge of identified pollutants and a prohibition on the discharge of unidentified pollutants. Viewing the regulatory scheme as a whole, however, it is clear that the permit is intended to identify and limit the most harmful pollutants while leaving the control of the vast number of other pollutants to disclosure requirements. Once within the NPDES or SPDES scheme, therefore, polluters may discharge pollutants not specifically listed in their permits so long as they comply with the appropriate reporting requirements and abide by any new limitations when imposed on such pollutants.

The EPA lists tens of thousands of different chemical substances in the Toxic Substances Control Act Chemical Substance Inventory pursuant to 15 U.S.C. §2607(b). However, the EPA does not demand even information regarding each of the many thousand chemical substances potentially present in a manufacturer's wastewater because "it is impossible to identify and rationally limit every chemical or compound present in a discharge of pollutants." Memorandum from EPA Deputy Assistant Administrator for Water Enforcement Jeffrey G. Miller to Regional Enforcement Director, Region V, at 2 (Apr. 28, 1976). "Compliance with such a permit would be impossible and anybody seeking to harass a permittee need only analyze that permittee's discharge until determining the presence of a substance not identified in the permit." Indeed, at oral argument Atlantic States could provide no principled reason why water itself, which is conceded to be a chemical, would not be considered a "pollutant" under its view of the Act.

The EPA has never acted in any way to suggest that Atlantic States' absolutist and wholly impractical view of the legal effect of a permit is valid. In fact, the EPA's actions and policy statements have frequently contemplated discharges of pollutants not listed under a NPDES or SPDES permit. It has addressed such discharges by amending the permit to list and limit a pollutant when necessary to safeguard the environment without considering pre-amendment discharges to be violations calling for enforcement under the CWA. The EPA thus stated in its comments on proposed 40 C.F.R. §122.68(a), which applied the "application-based" limits approach to implementation of the CWA reporting scheme:

There is still some possibility...that a [NPDES or SPDES] permittee may discharge a large amount of a pollutant not limited in its permit, and EPA will not be able to take enforcement action against the permittee as long as the permittee complies with the notification requirements [pursuant to the CWA]. 45 Fed. Reg. 33516, 33523 (1980).

The EPA's statement went on to note that this possibility constituted a "regulatory gap," and that, "the final regulations control discharges only of the pollutants listed in the [NPDES or SPDES] permit application, which consist primarily of the listed toxic pollutants and designated hazardous substances." [The opinion went on to uphold EPA's statutory interpretation using the deferential Chevron v. NRDC, 467 U.S. 837 (1984) standard of review. The decision in favor of Kodak was affirmed.]

## COMMENTARY & QUESTIONS

1. **CWA §402(k) and the NPDES permit shield defense.** Is compliance with an NPDES permit a complete defense to *all* claims related to the discharge of pollutants through the regulated outfall? The statutory language of §402(k) only links the permit compliance defense to claims asserting violation of the CWA's effluent limitation provisions. Common law actions (primarily nuisance) survive despite permit compliance, as do state law-based statutory actions that go beyond the CWA.

2. **Regulating unlisted discharges.** Is it clear that Kodak's unlisted discharges will later be subjected to regulation? Federal law requires that states taking primacy, such as New York in this case, can at any time terminate or modify the permit. CWA §402(b)(1)(C)(iii). More routinely, the revision could be accomplished as part of the five-year periodic renewal process contemplated by §402(b)(1)(B). Even after a state takes primacy, EPA, under §402(i), retains residual enforcement power. Having established that DEC or EPA can force a change in Kodak's discharges, the real question is whether DEC or EPA must act to do so. General administrative law doctrines give the agency a good deal of latitude in enforcement matters. In *Atlantic States*, the court and the agencies seem resigned to allowing the shocking amounts of unlisted toxic discharge because of the impossibility of regulating all of the chemicals admittedly present in Kodak's effluent stream.

3. **The effluent limitations — BAT and BPJ.** In its ongoing implementation of the CWA, EPA has identified BAT for all 126 toxic pollutants on its priority list, although it has yet to promulgate those limits for all categories of dischargers. As to non-priority toxic pollutants, regulation of their discharge is to be based on Best Professional Judgment (BPJ).[22] A slightly more comforting view of events in *Atlantic States* can be gleaned from the fact that TBELs are applied to 25 substances, including BAT-level treatments for the priority toxic chemicals, and BPJ for a number of non-priority toxics. According to experts in the field, the treatments required (whether based on BAT or BPJ) for the toxic chemicals expressly regulated by a complex permit, such as the Kodak permit, will be identical, in a some cases, to the treatments that are appropriate for some of the additional chemicals also

---

22. BPJ is set on the same basis as BAT, but is implemented in the case-by-case context of writing specific permits. In that context, it is easy to imagine that a state permit writer could more easily be persuaded to give greater consideration to the "economically achievable" strand of the BAT standard than might EPA when it establishes its categorical BAT standards. Thus, BPJ may tend to demand less stringent controls than those that would obtain if the substance were a priority pollutant regulated by EPA.

present in the discharge, but not regulated by the permit. Put differently, chemicals listed in the permits sometimes serve as regulatory surrogates for other chemicals. The matter, however, requires careful case-by-case scrutiny. The toxic combinations may require additional treatments, or, worse, present treatment antagonisms rather than treatment synergies.

4. **What did the permit writers know, and when did they know it?** The facts of the case are a bit hard to follow: the complaint alleged unpermitted discharge of 27 pollutants, but the motion for summary judgment limited itself to 16 substances that are all on the EPCRA (Emergency Planning and Community Right-to-Know Act) list of toxic substances. The court observes (in original footnote 7) that seven of the unlisted 16 substances were included by Kodak on its permit application documents or raised for discussion by DEC. As to those substances, the court is on firm ground in saying the agency knew of them and opted not to regulate them, thereby placing them behind the permit shield. The remaining nine substances, however, appeared only on the EPCRA Form R. That form is a routine, annual report, that is filed with a different department within the state agency. The fact that the Form Rs were filed with DEC is not, without more, a very solid basis for concluding that the permit writers took cognizance of what those forms disclosed.[23]

5. **CWA federalism, devolution, stricter state standards, and citizen suits.** In *Atlantic States* there is a transfer from federal to state primacy, exactly as envisioned by Congress. In portions of the case that were not excerpted here, the plaintiffs argued that linguistic nuances in the New York statutes establishing the SPDES program resulted in SPDES permits having a different impact than federal NPDES permits in regard to unlisted pollutants. States can indeed regulate more stringently than the "federal floor" set by the CWA. Section 510 of the CWA, entitled "State Authority," somewhat elliptically provides:

> ...nothing in this chapter shall (1) preclude or deny the right of any State or political subdivision thereof or interstate agency to adopt or enforce (A) any standard or limitation respecting discharges of pollutants, or (B) any requirement respecting control or abatement of pollution; except if [the state regulation] is less stringent than [the federal regulation imposed by the CWA].

In *Atlantic States*, the court, in dicta, found that the New York SPDES system was not more stringent in limiting the permit shield defense than the NPDES system in this regard. The actual holding on this point is more technical, but quite important. The court ruled that a CWA §505 citizen suit cannot be used to enforce claims that are based on those stricter state laws (if the state has indeed enacted stricter-than-federal regulation). As will be detailed in Chapter 20, this ruling carries significance because under the CWA, in §505(d), the court "may award costs of litigation (including reasonable attorney and expert witness fees) to any prevailing,

---

23. Judge Winter adds, at the end of his footnote 7, an even more enigmatic limitation on Atlantic States' ability to bring suit. He asserts that there is no standing to bring suit in regard to discharges of chemicals not revealed to the agency in any fashion unless Atlantic States can also "show violations of established regulatory levels." Recalling the way in which non-priority toxic pollutants are regulated by the *ad hoc* generation of BPJ standards, there are no *established* standards for those chemicals. Their discharge would be insulated from attack in a citizen suit if the footnote is correct on this point.

or substantially prevailing party, whenever the court determines such award is appropriate." This fee shifting is not generally available under state law.

6. **What had gone before.** Like many environmental cases, this one has a somewhat extended prior history. Atlantic States first informed Kodak and DEC of its intent to sue over Kodak's excessive discharges in April of 1989, at a time when Kodak was not complying with the limitations for several of the pollutants listed and regulated by the permit. When no DEC action against Kodak was filed after 60 days (see CWA §505(b)(1) in Chapter Seven) a citizen suit was filed. A few months later, Kodak entered into negotiations with DEC regarding the violations. In April of 1990, the negotiations resulted in an extensive consent decree and a criminal plea agreement covering Kodak's violations that called for more than $2 million in penalties, and operational changes related to monitoring, reporting, disclosure of information, and other measures intended to improve public relations in regard to plant operations. Those agreements were then used as a basis to secure dismissal of the pending citizen suit. Atlantic States appealed that dismissal. On appeal the Second Circuit remanded because the record was unclear as to whether there were sufficient allegations of ongoing violations to survive the test laid down by the Supreme Court's *Gwaltney* opinion discussed in Chapter One. 933 F.2d 124 (2d Cir. 1991). On remand the case was dismissed on *Gwaltney* grounds, whereupon the instant case was filed. On that first appeal, Atlantic States did win a vital point regarding their ability to collect attorney's fees as a prevailing plaintiff:

> Plaintiff may seek an award of expenses and attorneys' fees. Although the case may be subject to dismissal, the function of the citizen suit — the cessation of violations of the Clean Water Act — will have been served. We believe that when the polluter's settlement with state authorities follows the proper commencement of a citizen suit, one can, absent contrary evidence, infer that the existence of the citizen suit was a motive for the polluter's settlement and that the citizen suit plaintiff is therefore a prevailing party. 933 F.2d at 128.

## D. WATER QUALITY-BASED PERMITTING UNDER THE CWA

In the 1990s, with the TBEL process a mature and reasonably successful program, WQBELs, which had been on the back burner for 15 years, progressively became the most visible and contentious aspect of point source control under the CWA. Professor Houck has pointed out the irony of this trend:

> At the bottom of these developments is an approach to pollution control — regulating dischargers by their impact on receiving water quality — that never really worked in the first place and is back for another try.... No step in the process worked: use determinations were highly variable, leaving protective states at a distinct disadvantage, and a race-to-the bottom; information on those biological conditions necessary to support aquatic life was spotty and insufficient; impact assessment was equally imprecise, and the chore of tracing impacts from multiple-dischargers was overwhelming; and abatement in the face of these uncertainties was ephemeral and rarely achieved.... One could have legitimate doubts about it this time as well. It is no small irony that the reason the Clean Water Act retained this approach, and directed its use for the upgrade of polluted waters, is that both the states and pollution dischargers

insisted on it.... Houck, TMDLs: The Resurrection of Water Quality Standards-Based Regulation under the Clean Water Act, 27 ELR 10329, 10330 (1997).

The major Clean Water Act provision governing the WQBEL process is §303 (d), 33 U.S.C.A. §1313 (d):

§303(d)(1)(A) Each State shall identify those waters within its boundaries for which [TBELs] are not stringent enough to implement any water quality standard applicable to such waters. The State shall establish a priority ranking for such waters, taking into account the severity of the pollution and the uses to be made of such waters....

(C) Each State shall establish for the waters identified in paragraph (1)(A) of this subsection, and in accordance with the priority ranking, the total maximum daily load ["TMDL"] for those pollutants which the Administrator identifies...as suitable for such calculation. Such load shall be established at a level necessary to implement the applicable water quality standards with seasonal variations and a margin of safety which takes into account any lack of knowledge concerning the relationship between effluent limitations and water quality....

(D)(2) Each State shall submit to the Administrator from time to time, with the first such submission not later than one hundred and eighty days after the date of publication of the first [EPA] identification of pollutants [suitable for calculation], for his approval the waters identified and the loads established under...this subsection. The Administrator shall either approve or disapprove such identification and load not later than thirty days after date of submission. If the Administrator approves such identification and load, such State shall incorporate them into its current plan under subsection (e) of this section. If the Administrator disapproves such identification and load, he shall not later than thirty days after the date of such disapproval identify such waters in such State and establish such loads for such waters as he determines necessary to implement the water quality standards applicable to such waters and upon identification and establishment the State shall incorporate them into its current plan under [its continuing planning process]....

Section 303(d) is silent with regard to implementation of TMDLs, beyond requiring that states include them in their continuing planning processes. The implication is that states will convert TMDLs to Wasteload Allocations ("WLAs")[24] and Load Allocations ("LAs"),[25] with WLAs becoming WQBELs in discharge permits and LAs enabling states to control nonpoint sources of pollution. But implications are not legally enforceable requirements. Professor Houck has explored the problems inherent in §303(d) implementation:

Section 303(e) proceeds to require a "continuing planning process" (CPP) with plans that "include" §303(d)'s TMDLs. While these sections authorize EPA to approve or disapprove a CPP on the basis, *inter alia*, of TMDLs, they do not authorize the Agency to implement them. The question is, at this point, has the statute run its string? Does all the work of TMDLs and their load allocations wind up as references in state plans, implemented if and as the states may wish? Or does the TMDL itself have to include the means of its own

---

24. A WLA is "(t)he portion of a receiving water's loading capacity that is allocated to one of its existing or future point sources of pollution." 40 CFR §130.2(h).

25. An LA is "(t)he portion of a receiving water's loading capacity that is attributed either to one of its existing or future nonpoint sources of pollution or to natural background sources." Id., §130(g).

implementation in order to receive EPA approval? EPA's authority to review and reject TMDLs may succeed in securing the inclusion of those steps and commitments necessary to implement them, retaining some meaningful outcome for the process. Further, if these measures are inadequate, EPA may reject a TMDL and may then promulgate measures of its own in a federal TMDL. But then what? For point sources, the Agency may ensure that those additional limitations imposed by a TMDL are actually implemented through its supervision of discharge permits under the NPDES program. But for nonpoint sources, here is the rub: there are no federal controls over nonpoint sources under the Clean Water Act. For those sources, the §303(d) program leads, ultimately, to a state prerogative.... Houck, Are We There Yet?: The Long Road Toward Water Quality-Based Regulation under the Clean Water Act, 27 ELR 10391, 10397 (1997).

Moreover, §303(d) ignores the economic and technological consequences of setting "Better-Than-Best" WQBELs; and it also lacks lead times for compliance with WQBELs.[26] In light of these prospective implementation horrors, and also given EPA's preoccupation with developing and implementing TBELs, as well as the failure of WQBELs to control water pollution prior to 1972, it is understandable that EPA "backburnered" §303(d) between 1972 and 1987.

As the following case indicates, in 1987 Congress revived the languishing WQBEL process with regard to so-called "toxic hot spots":

**Natural Resources Defense Council v. Environmental Protection Agency**
United States Court of Appeals for the Ninth Circuit, 1990
915 F.2d 1314

FLETCHER, J.... Congress, in passing the Clean Water Act [in 1972], shifted the focus of the water pollution control laws away from the enforcement of water quality standards and toward the enforcement of technological standards. But Congress recognized that even if all the firms discharging pollutants into a certain stream segment were using the best available technology, the stream still might not be clean enough to meet the water quality standards set by the states. To deal with this problem, Congress supplemented the "technology-based" limitations with "water quality-based limitations."

The water quality standard for a particular stream segment was to be determined in the following manner. First, the state in which the stream segment was located was to designate the uses to which it wished to put the segment. The designations that the states had made prior to the 1972 Clean Water Act were deemed to be the initial designations under that Act; however, states were thereafter to review their designations at least once every three years. Pursuant to the statute's policy that the designation of uses "enhance" the quality of water, EPA enacted regulations setting limits on the states' ability to downgrade previously designated uses. If a state wished to redesignate a use so that the new use did not require water clean enough to meet the statutory goal of fishable, swimmable water, it had to conduct a "use attainability analysis" as a condition to federal approval of the

26. In Ackels v. EPA, 7 F.3d 862 (9th Cir. 1993), Alaska placer miners (including the Rybacheks) sued EPA, which is the permit-issuing authority in Alaska, to contest water quality-based effluent limitations for arsenic and turbidity. In response to the plaintiffs' arguments that further controls were economically and technologically unavailable, the court responded that "the economic and technological constraints are not a valid consideration" (7 F.3d, at page 866).

redesignated use. CWA §303(c)(3), 40 CFR §§131.10(j), 131.3(g) (1989). If the result of the "use attainability analysis" was that it was feasible to attain fishable, swimmable waters, EPA would reject the redesignated use.

Second, the state was to determine the "criteria" for each segment — the maximum concentrations of pollutants that could occur without jeopardizing the use. These criteria could be either numerical (e.g., 5 milligrams per liter) or narrative (e.g., no toxics in toxic amounts). The criteria, like the uses, were subject to federal review. The EPA was to reject criteria that did not protect the designated use or that were not based on a "sound scientific rationale." 40 CFR §131.11 (1989).

Under §§301(b)(1)(C) and 402(a)(1), NPDES permit writers were to impose, along with the technology-based limitations, any more stringent limitations on discharges necessary to meet the water quality standards. Although ostensibly they were supposed to impose these more stringent limitations, in practice they often did not.

One explanation for this failure is that the criteria listed by the states, particularly for toxic pollutants, were often vague narrative or descriptive criteria as opposed to specific numerical criteria. These descriptive criteria were difficult to translate into enforceable limits on discharges from individual polluters. As one commentator put it:

> The descriptive criteria, in particular, call for both expert testimony and a receptive forum to transform, let us say, a general obligation to maintain "recreational" uses into a specific obligation to reduce loadings of phosphorus or nitrogen from a particular source. The decision requires, among other things, judgments about the degree of algal bloom that interferes with "recreational" uses such as swimming or boating, estimates of loadings from all contributing point and nonpoint sources, assumptions about degrees of control elsewhere, and predictions of how a water segment will respond to a hoped-for change of parameters. Rodgers, 2 Environmental Law §4.16 at 250–251 (1986).

The Clean Water Act dealt with the difficulty of these decisions and judgments in various ways, for example by calling for the publication by the EPA of criteria documents spelling out causes and effects of various pollutant loads, see CWA §304(a), and by requiring states to set total maximum daily loads for certain pollutants (but, notably, not for toxic pollutants) CWA §303(d)(1). However, the complexity of these decisions and judgments led many a permit writer to avoid making them altogether. Rodgers, §4.18 at 283-284.[27]

In 1987, Congress reexamined the water pollution laws. It found that the requirement that individual polluters use the best available technology was not sufficient to solve the pollution problem, particularly the problem of toxic pollutants; a renewed emphasis on water quality-based standards was necessary. Congress enacted a number of new provisions. Three are relevant for our purposes.

CWA §319 requires states to submit for federal approval nonpoint source reports and management programs by August 4, 1988, identifying specific nonpoint sources of pollution and setting forth a plan for implementing the "best management practices" to control such sources by 1992. Section 319 does not require states to penalize nonpoint source polluters who fail to adopt best management practices; rather it provides for grants to encourage the adoption of such practices.

---

27. Eds.: State permit writers also did not typically include WQBELs in discharge permits because EPA was not pushing them to do so.

CWA §303(c)(2)(B), requires states to adopt "specific numerical criteria" for toxics for which the EPA has published criteria pursuant to §304(a). Those criteria are to be adopted when the state first reviews its water quality standards following the enactment of the 1987 amendments. The requirement of numerical criteria for toxics makes it easier for permit writers to incorporate the water quality standards into individual permits. Permit writers thus no longer have an excuse for failing to impose water quality-based limitations on permit holders.

In addition to requiring the adoption of numerical criteria, Congress enacted new CWA §304(l), which provides:

§304(l) State List of Navigable Waters and Development of Strategies. Not later than 2 years after the date of the enactment of this subsection [February 4, 1987], each State shall submit to the Administrator for review, approval, and implementation under this subsection —

(A) a list of those waters within the state which after the application of effluent limitations required under §301(b)(2) of this Act cannot reasonably be anticipated to attain or maintain (i) water quality standards for such waters reviewed, revised, or adopted in accordance with §303(c)(2)(B) of this Act, due to toxic pollutants, or (ii) that water quality which shall assure protection of public health, public water supplies, agricultural and industrial uses, and the protection and propagation of a balanced population of shellfish, fish, and wildlife, and allow recreational activities in and on the water.

(B) a list of all navigable waters in such state for which the State does not expect the applicable standard under §303 of this Act will be achieved after the [application of technology-based effluent limitations], due entirely or substantially to discharges from point sources of any toxic pollutant listed pursuant to §307(a);

(C) for each segment of the navigable waters included on such lists, a determination of the specific point sources discharging any such toxic pollutant which is believed to be preventing or impairing such water quality and the amount of such toxic pollutant discharged by each such source; and

(D) for each such segment, an individual control strategy which the state determines will produce a reduction in the discharge of toxic pollutants from point sources identified by the State under this paragraph through the establishment of effluent limitations...and water quality standards..., which reduction is sufficient, in combination with existing controls on point and nonpoint sources of pollution, to achieve the applicable water quality standard as soon as possible, but not later than 3 years after the date of establishment of such strategy.

(2) Approval or Disapproval. Not later than 120 days after the last day of the 2-year period referred to in paragraph (1), the Administrator shall approve or disapprove the control strategies submitted under paragraph (1) by any State.

(3) Administrator's Action. If a State fails to submit control strategies in accordance with paragraph (1) or the Administrator does not approve the control strategies submitted by such State in accordance with paragraph (1), then, not later than 1 year after the last day of the period referred to in paragraph (2), the Administrator, in cooperation with such State and after notice and opportunity for public comment, shall implement the requirements of paragraph (1) in such State....

Section 304(l) requires the preparation of three lists. The list required by §304(l)(1)(B) (hereinafter the "B list") is the narrowest of the three lists. It consists only of the waters that are not expected to meet water quality standards, even after the application of the technology-based limitations, due entirely or substantially to toxic pollution from *point sources*. The list required by §304 (l)(1)(A)(i) (hereinafter the "A(i) list") is broader; it includes most of the waters on the B list plus waters expected not to meet water quality standards due to pollution attributable entirely or almost entirely to toxic pollution from *nonpoint sources*. The list required by §304 (l)(1)(A)(ii) (hereinafter the "A(ii) list") is the broadest. It includes all the waters on the other two lists plus any waters which, after the implementation of technology-based controls, are not expected to meet the water quality goals of the Act; since the goals of the Act are sometimes higher than the state standards, the A(ii) list includes even some waters expected to comply fully with applicable water quality standards.

The effect of the individual control strategies is simply to expedite the imposition of water quality-based limitations on polluters — limitations which otherwise would have had to be imposed when the polluters' NPDES permits expired. NPDES permits are issued for periods of no more than five years, although administrative delays can extend de facto the duration of the permits....

[The holding in the case overturned EPA's interpretation that, under subsection (C), states were only required to identify point source dischargers to waters on the B list. The court also invited EPA to reconsider its position that only dischargers to B list waters are subject to the Individual Control Strategy (ICS) requirement, but the Agency refused to accept the invitation and reaffirmed its original position.]

COMMENTARY & QUESTIONS

1. **EPA's interpretations of §304(l).** Why did EPA go to such great lengths to attempt to limit the identification of point sources, under §304's subsection (C), and the number of point sources subject to ICS requirements, under subsection (D), to waters on the B list that are entirely or substantially polluted by point source dischargers of toxics? EPA went as far as arguing that Congress had committed a drafting error in subsection (C): the plural noun *lists* should have been singular, relating only to the B list. Perhaps EPA wanted to avoid the palpable inequity of requiring an industrial discharger of a toxic pollutant to install Better-Than-BAT on a segment that is substantially polluted by that same toxic pollutant discharged by an uncontrolled agribusiness operation located upriver. On a national level, §304(l) is inequitable enough as it is. The entire burden of further controlling toxic water pollution falls upon point source dischargers that have only recently installed BAT, while agricultural operations that could reduce toxic runoff by adopting cost-effective BMPs remain uncontrolled.

2. **Setting WQBELs.** The first step in the process of setting WQBELs is the establishment of water quality standards (WQS) by a state, or by EPA if the state does not. As the NRDC v. EPA court explains, water quality standards consist primarily of two aspects — designated uses and criteria, either numerical or narrative, for attaining those uses. Water quality standards also contain an antidegradation policy, which is discussed below. Most often, the designated use is "fishable-swimmable" waters, but this statutory minimum use can take many forms. "States may adopt sub-categories of a use and set the appropriate criteria to reflect varying needs of such sub-categories of uses, for instance, to differentiate between cold

water and warm water fisheries." 40 CFR §131.10(c). States may also adopt seasonal uses, based on water temperature, flow regimes, and types of aquatic biota present. Under §303(c)(B), states must adopt numeric criteria for relevant toxic pollutants, and EPA must publish guidance containing recommended criteria for toxics, but states can adopt less stringent criteria for toxics if they are scientifically defensible.[28] In translating narrative criteria, such as "no toxics in toxic amounts," to numerical criteria, states may utilize "the EPA recommended numeric water quality criteria, but only on a 'case by case basis' and 'supplemented where necessary by other relevant [site-specific] information.'" American Paper Institute v. EPA, 996 F.2d 346, 350 (D.C. Cir. 1993) (upholding 40 CFR §122.44(d)(1)(vi)). Thus, water quality standards for particular parameters may differ widely from state to state and from waterbody to waterbody.

States also differ with regard to methods employed to translate WQS to WQBELs (WLAs) for particular point source dischargers. States have adopted different policies with regard to the water quality models used to translate WQS to WLAs, as well as with regard to mixing zones,[29] measurement of high and low flow conditions, reserves for margins of safety and economic growth, and background concentrations.[30] Many states offer site-specific variances from WQBELs. 40 CFR §131.13. Unlike TBELs, WQBELs are not uniform from state to state, or waterbody to waterbody. The USGAO found that WQBELs for mercury, a persistent and bioaccumulative pollutant, were 775 times greater at one facility than at a similar facility in another state. Once again, the race of laxity is rearing its ugly head:

> In 1995, an industrial facility in Pennsylvania challenged a discharge limit for arsenic because Pennsylvania's numerical criterion was 2,500 times more stringent than that used by the neighboring state of New York, into which the discharge flowed. (Pennsylvania had updated its water quality standards on the basis of current information on health effects published by EPA.... New York continued to rely on earlier guidance....) Among other things, the discharger argued that having to comply with the more stringent criterion created an economic disadvantage for the company. Eventually, Pennsylvania agreed to reis-

---

28 . See NRDC v. EPA, 16 F.3d 1395 (4th Cir. 1993)(Virginia adoption of dioxin criterion weaker than EPA guidance upheld as scientifically defensible). Given the scientific uncertainties involved in ascertaining the impacts of pollutants on human health and aquatic life, scientific defensibility, in this area at least, covers a great deal of ground. For example, some states base numeric criteria on a risk level of one excess cancer case per one million people, while others base their criteria on a risk level of one excess cancer case per 100,000 people. See USGAO, Differences Among the States in Issuing Permits Limiting the Discharge of Pollutants (1996), 12.

29. WQBELs are not measured at the outfall pipe, as are TBELs, but at the outer limits of a mixing zone, within which at least chronic impacts on aquatic life are permitted. Some states have established Zones of Initial Dilution ("ZIDs"), within mixing zones, where acute effects are also tolerated. Adler, et al., question the application of dilution factors, such as mixing zones, where persistent or bioaccumulative pollutants are concerned. For judicial discussions of mixing zones, see American Iron and Steel Institute v. EPA, 115 F.3d 979 (D.C.Cir. 1997)(EPA's prohibition of mixing zones for toxics in the Great Lakes system remanded for consideration of economic impacts), and Granite City Division of National Steel Company v. Illinois Pollution Control Board, 155 Ill.2d 149, 613 N.E.2d 719 (Ill.Sup.Ct. 1993)(state mixing zone and ZID regulations upheld).

30. Background concentrations are the level of pollutants already present in the receiving waters as a result of naturally occurring pollutants, permitted discharges from upstream, spills, unregulated discharges, etc. "Connecticut, for example, assumes background concentrations of zero in deriving [WQBELs], while Colorado uses actual data. All other things being equal, the discharge limits established by Connecticut will be less stringent than those set by Colorado whenever the actual background concentration is greater than zero." USGAO Report, 1996, 13.

sue the permit with a monitoring requirement for arsenic instead of a discharge limit. The state has also revised its water quality standards using the
less stringent criterion. USGAO, Differences Among the States in Issuing
Permits Limiting the Discharge of Pollutants 9 (1996).

As with the Clean Air Act's criteria pollutants control program, state allocation of
assimilative capacity, in the form of WQBELs, to dischargers of water pollutants
can be a highly political brokerage exercise.

3. **Whole Effluent Testing ("WET") as an alternative.** Water quality-based standard-
setting is obviously problematic. Setting WQS and establishing TMDLs based on
them involves enormous scientific and political complexity. Additionally, current
EPA criteria for toxic pollutants require updating, and many criteria for nonpriority pollutants are needed. Finally, EPA's water quality criteria are narrowly focused
on the water column. The Agency has made little progress in developing criteria
oriented towards sediment, wildlife, aquatic life habitat, and biodiversity protection. A promising development for setting both WQS and WQBELs has been the
emergence of biomonitoring procedures. Biomonitoring (also known as "whole
effluent testing" or "bioassay") is essentially a laboratory simulation of the effects
of ambient water quality, or a particular waste stream, on indigenous aquatic biota
used as an indicator of the desired quality of an actual waterbody. In conducting a
bioassay, a representative aquatic organism is subjected, either for a shorter ("acute
bioassay") or longer ("chronic bioassay") period of time, to a waste stream diluted
in a manner that attempts to reproduce existing ambient conditions. The WQS or
WQBEL is then set at a certain percentage (providing a margin of safety) of the concentration of the waste stream that causes adverse effects on the organism (e.g., for
an acute bioassay, 30 percent of the concentration that kills 50 percent of the
organisms over a 96-hour period). Under most state Individual Control Strategies
("ICSs") for toxic hot spots, if a discharger exceeds its bioassay-based effluent limitation more than twice during a particular period, it must conduct a Toxicity
Reduction Evaluation ("TRE"), and the results of the TRE are included as conditions of its discharge permit. Biomonitoring furnishes a useful alternative to a
chemical-by-chemical approach to dealing with mixed waste streams. It also provides some indication of how certain levels of water quality will affect ecosystems.
However, there is concern that the science of biomonitoring, especially with
regard to chronic bioassays, is not sufficiently well developed to support a regulatory program. EPA is reportedly prepared to propose regulations requiring all major
dischargers to comply with WET-based effluent limitations in addition to chemical-specific ones, but the Agency's current enforcement policy is that no enforcement action will be taken for a single violation of a WET-based limitation. There
is also concern that biomonitoring is "better suited to assuring protection of
aquatic life than human health." American Paper Institute v. EPA, 995 F.2d 346,
350 (D.C. Cir. 1993).[31]

4. **Antidegradation and attainability.** The NRDC v. EPA decision, excerpted above,

---

31. EPA's administration of the CWA has been criticized for providing insufficient protection against
bioaccumulative substances. See Williamson, et al., Gathering Danger: The Urgent Need To Regulate
Toxic Substances That Can Bioaccumulate, 20 Ecol. L. Q. 605 (1994).

briefly mentioned the issues of antidegredation and attainability. Section 101 of the CWA declares a policy to "restore and maintain" clean water, and antidegradation policies have traditionally been a feature of water pollution control law. Although antidegradation under the CWA is less well developed than its counterpart in the Clean Air Act (Prevention of Significant Deterioration, or "PSD"), Congress in 1987 recognized for the first time that antidegradation is an essential part of the Act. §303(d)(4)(B). But the statutory reference to antidegradation is cryptic; it does not clarify what Congress meant by antidegradation, or how this policy is to be implemented.

In 1983, EPA promulgated a set of regulations intended to explicate the antidegradation policy. 40 CFR §131.12. These regulations rest on a distinction between "water quality" and "water uses." Each state must adopt an antidegradation policy and identify methods of applying it where waterbodies are of better quality than fishable-swimmable, for example if trout can propagate there. The antidegradation policy is divided into three general levels of protection. "Tier I" establishes the minimum level of fishable-swimmable water quality that must be maintained in every body of water, wherever attainable. "Tier II" applies to waters whose quality already exceeds the level "necessary to support propagation of fish, shellfish, and wildlife and recreation in and on the water," and only allows a reduction in quality when "necessary to accommodate important economic or social development." For certain exceptionally high quality bodies of water (e.g., waters in parks, wildlife refuges, and other "waters of exceptional recreational and ecological significance"), "Tier III" prohibits any degradation of existing water quality, except on a temporary basis. Waters falling into Tier III are designated Outstanding National Resource Waters ("ONRWs"). Existing water uses are the antidegradation baseline, and thus must always be preserved. In effect, these regulations establish a rebuttable presumption that existing water quality, outside of ONRWs, must be maintained, and an irrebuttable presumption that existing water quality in ONRWs, as well as all existing water uses in other waterbodies, must be maintained.

Most states have adopted antidegradation policies, but few have meaningful implementation measures. In the first place, many waterbodies that are subject to antidegradation are threatened by nonpoint source pollution that EPA does not possess the authority to regulate. In the second place, EPA's antidegradation regulations leave implementation almost entirely to the states, which may want to attract development with the inducement of unpolluted segments that will be classified as "effluent limited" (i.e., where water quality standards can be met by the imposition of TBELs), thus avoiding the imposition of more stringent WQBELs. EPA can sue a state that has not adopted an acceptable antidegradation policy, but it is doubtful whether EPA can enforce antidegradation in a state that has not adopted such an antidegradation policy or is not enforcing its adopted policy. States have a relatively free hand even as to designating and protecting ONRWs. National Wildlife Federation v. EPA, 127 F.3d 1126 (D.C. Cir. 1997). EPA can object to a state discharge permit that allegedly violates the state antidegradation policy, but this rarely occurs. However, suits can be brought, in state courts, to invalidate discharge permits that violate state antidegradation policies. See Columbus &

Franklin County District v. Ohio EPA, 65 Ohio St.3d 86, 600 N.E.2d 1042 (Ohio Sup.Ct. 1993) (state agency violated antidegradation policy in issuing discharge permit to a POTW).

Section 101 of the CWA establishes a "national goal that wherever attainable, an interim goal of water quality which provides for the protection and propagation of fish, shellfish, and wildlife and provides for recreation in and on the water be achieved by July 1, 1983." What does "wherever attainable" mean? In contrast to antidegradation, attainability applies where a waterbody is of worse quality than the CWA's minimum fishable-swimmable condition. Under EPA regulations (40 CFR §131.10), a use is attainable if it is already being attained. Thus, where existing water quality standards specify designated uses of a lesser nature than those that are presently being attained, the state must revise its standards to reflect the current uses. Second, a use is attainable if it can be achieved by the imposition of technology-based effluent limitations for point sources "and cost-effective and reasonable best management practices for nonpoint source control." Third, a use is deemed attainable unless the state, after a "use attainability analysis," can demonstrate that attaining the fishable-swimmable use is not feasible because of specified natural or intractable man-induced conditions, or that "(c)ontrols more stringent than [the CWA's technology-based effluent limitations] would result in substantial and widespread economic and social impact."[32] How can a definition of attainability be based upon control of nonpoint sources of pollution, when EPA has no authority to regulate them or to compel a state to do so? What is "substantial and widespread economic and social impact"? Few states have found it necessary to petition EPA for the removal of fishable-swimmable uses because of the virtually infinite state flexibility in setting WQS and implementing WQBELs.

5. **A spate of §303(d) lawsuits.** After twenty years on the backburner, §303(d) has become a boiling cauldron. Dozens of lawsuits have been brought against EPA for failing to set TMDLs for states that have not done so. See e.g., Idaho Sportsmen's Coalition v. EPA, 951 F. Supp. 962 (D.C.W.D.Wash.1996) (EPA ordered to submit a five-year schedule for developing TMDLs for water quality-limited stretches in Idaho; case dismissed when Idaho agreed to develop TMDLs within eight years). EPA has issued a policy statement giving states between eight and thirteen years to complete the task of setting TMDLs for appropriate waterbodies. Realistically, however, the job might take as much as twenty-five years.

Is it wise for environmental groups to bring lawsuits to enforce the CWA's water quality-based standard-setting provisions? Might TMDL suits stimulate a backlash against the CWA by point source dischargers that are unfairly being required to install Better-Than-BAT in order to clean up water pollution that is, in reality, being caused by nonpoint sources? Will TMDLs be set but not converted into enforceable WQBELs? Will the TMDL process result in a diversion of scarce state

---

32. After failing to invalidate their TBELs, and then failing to overturn the more stringent WQBELs in their discharge permit, the Rybacheks petitioned the Alaska Department of Environmental Conservation to downgrade ("remove") the water use classifications of streams into which they discharged. The Department, after conducting a use attainability analysis, decided not to remove the use classifications applicable to the Rybacheks, and the Alaska Supreme Court upheld the Department. Alaska Department of Environmental Conservation v. Rybachek, 912 P.2d 536 (1996).

and federal resources from successful programs such as TBEL-implementation, permitting, and enforcement? Will this spate of TMDL lawsuits stimulate a political coalition between environmentalists and point source dischargers that will finally result in meaningful controls on nonpoint source pollution? Or, on the other hand, should Congress repudiate the CWA's water quality-based standard-setting provisions, and strengthen EPA's application of TBELs to both point and nonpoint sources? See Goldfarb, Water Law, 2d ed., chap. 2 (1988), arguing that CWA §303 should be repealed.

6. **Interstate water pollution.** Interstate water pollution can be severe, especially in the Mississippi River basin. More than 40% of the phosphorus present in the waterbodies of 16 states in the Mississippi River basin originates in other states. Section 402(d) of the CWA deals with interstate water pollution in the context of issuing discharge permits. In effect, EPA acts as an arbitrator of interstate disputes. This process was described by the United States Supreme Court in International Paper Company v. Ouellette, 497 U.S. 481 (1987):

> While source States have a strong voice in regulating their own pollution, the CWA contemplates a much lesser role for States that share an interstate waterway with the source (the affected States). Even though it may be harmed by the discharges, an affected state only has an advisory role in regulating pollution that originates beyond its borders. Before a federal permit may be issued, each affected State is given notice and the opportunity to object to the proposed standards at a public hearing. An affected State has similar rights to be consulted before the source State issues its own permit; the source State must send notification, and must consider the objections and recommendations submitted by other States before taking action. Significantly, however, an affected State does not have the authority to block the issuance of the permit if it is dissatisfied with the proposed standards. An affected State's only recourse is to apply to the EPA Administrator, who then has the discretion to disapprove the permit if he concludes that the discharges will have an undue impact on interstate waters.... Thus, the Act makes it clear that the affected States occupy a subordinate position to source States in the federal regulatory program. 479 U.S. 481, at pages 490–491.[33]

When an impasse develops between EPA and a source state with an approved permit program, EPA can retake jurisdiction and issue its own permit. Affected states are given additional power over discharges in source states by an EPA regulation that prohibits the issuance of a discharge permit "(w)hen the imposition of conditions cannot ensure compliance with the applicable water quality standards [including antidegradation policies] of all affected states." 40 CFR §122.4(d). In Arkansas v. Oklahoma, 112 S.Ct. 1046 (1992), the United States Supreme Court upheld this regulation on the ground that federally-approved water quality standards become federal law that preempts conflicting state regulations. Referring to CWA §402(d), the Court stated that "(l)imits on an affected State's direct participation in a permitting decision, however, do not in any way constrain the EPA's

---

33. *Ouellette* involved interstate pollution of Lake Champlain. The Vermont plaintiffs eventually prevailed to the extent that their state law nuisance claims were not preempted by the CWA, nor was International Paper allowed to erect a permit defense. The Supreme Court did require, however, that source state nuisance law be applied to the case.

authority to require a point source to comply with downstream water quality standards." 112 S.Ct. 1046, at page 1057. Since Native American Tribes are treated as States by the CWA, if a tribe has been delegated primacy, and has established water quality standards that have received EPA approval, upstream discharges must comply with the tribal standards. Albuquerque v. EPA, 97 F.3d 415 (10th Cir. 1997), *cert. denied* 117 S.Ct. 410 (1997). A second attempt to curtail interstate conflicts over water pollution is CWA §118, added in 1987, which requires EPA to promulgate uniform Water Quality Guidance regulations for the Great Lakes States with regard to water quality standards, antidegradation policies, and implementation procedures. It is noteworthy that the increase in litigation and legislation relating to interstate water pollution has primarily occurred because of the resurgence of water quality-based standard-setting and permitting under the CWA.

7. **State water quality certification.** CWA §401 provides that

> Any applicant for a Federal license or permit to conduct any activity...which may result in any discharge into the navigable waters, shall provide the licensing or permitting agency a certification from the State in which the discharge originates or will originate...that any such discharge will comply with [applicable State water quality standards]. No license or permit shall be granted until the certification required by this section has been obtained or has been waived.... No license or permit shall be granted if certification has been denied by the State.... Any certification provided under this section...shall become a condition on any Federal license or permit subject to the provisions of this section.

Section 401 allows states to veto, or place conditions on, federal permits that causes discharges to navigable waters, such as U.S. Army Corps of Engineers permits to discharge dredged and fill material, hydroelectric licenses under the Federal Power Act, discharge permits where EPA is the permitting authority, and perhaps even federal grazing permits.

In Public Utility District No 1 of Jefferson County and City of Tacoma v. Washington Department of Ecology, 114 S.Ct. 1900 (1994), petitioners wanted to build a hydroelectric project on a river possessing exceptionally high water quality. The project would have appreciably reduced the river's flow, and thus would have interfered with the excellent fishery in the river. In order to protect the fishery, respondent state environmental agency included a minimum flow requirement in its §401 certification to the Federal Energy Regulatory Commission, the federal agency that licenses hydroelectric works under the Federal Power Act. The Supreme Court, in a 7-2 decision, affirmed the Washington Supreme Court's finding that FERC had to honor the minimum flow certification. Justice O'Connor, writing for the majority, reasoned that the state agency had a legal right to protect its water quality standards, which included a strong antidegradation requirement for the particular segment involved. In response to petitioners' argument that the CWA is only concerned with water "quality," not water "quantity," Justice O'Connor responded:

> This is an artificial distinction. In many cases, water quantity is closely related to water quality; a sufficient lowering of the water quantity in a body of water could destroy all of its designated uses, be it for drinking water, recreation,

navigation, or, as here, as a fishery. In any event, there is recognition in the Clean Water Act itself that reduced stream flow...can constitute water pollution. 114 S.Ct. 1900, at pages 1912–1913.

## E. CONTROLLING NONPOINT SOURCE POLLUTION WITHOUT REGULATION

The NRDC v. EPA court mentioned §319 of the CWA, relating to nonpoint source control planning. Section 319, like its predecessor §208, established an essentially voluntary program run by the states:

> States would prepare reports to (1) identify waters polluted by nonpoint sources, (2) identify nonpoint sources to these waters, (3) identify management practices applicable to these sources, and (4) prepare a management program for EPA approval.... The nonpoint management plans could include regulatory or nonregulatory methods such as training, demonstration projects, and financial assistance. There were no standards or performance criteria; no abatement had to happen. There were, further, no consequences if no management planning happened at all. Unlike TMDLs and ICSs, the federal government would not step in. This was the epitome of a voluntary program, and it produced about the same results as its predecessor had in 1972; a volume of studies, a number of voluntary programs, and little noticeable cleanup of nonpoint source pollution. Houck, TMDLs: The Resurrection of Water Quality Standards-Based Regulation Under the Clean Water Act, 27 ELR 10327, 10342 (1997).

In 1990, as an amendment to the Coastal Zone Management Act, Congress enacted a coastal runoff program that required coastal states to submit Coastal Nonpoint Pollution Control Programs for EPA approval. 16 U.S.C.A. §1455b. Ostensibly going further than §319, coastal state programs had to "provide for the implementation, at a minimum, of management measures in conformity with [EPA] guidelines to protect coastal waters...." But the "hammer" over state performance — loss of federal funding under the CZMA and §319 — has been disarmed by sporadic and relatively meager Congressional funding of these sections. Furthermore, the hammer can only fall if the coastal state "has failed to submit an approvable program"; there is no mention of the possibility that the state might submit an approvable program and then fail to enforce it.

In the end, the fact remains that that agriculture is the major source of water pollution in the United States. With regard to agricultural nonpoint source pollution, "the federal role [has been] indirect, almost passive, and largely ineffective."[34] A number of provisions of the 1985, 1990, and 1996 Farm Bills addressed nonpoint source pollution. The "sodbuster" provision of the 1985 Farm Bill is an example of a "cross-compliance" legislative strategy, where existing subsidies are manipulated to achieve compliance with new requirements. A "sodbuster" — one who farms on highly erodible land not previously in agricultural use — is ineligible for crop subsidies unless she implements a soil conservation plan containing BMPs to

34. Gould, Agriculture, Nonpoint Source Pollution, and Federal Law, 23 U.C. Davis L. Rev. 461, 474 (1990).

control erosion. 16 U.S.C.A. §§3811-3812. Under the Conservation Reserve Program ("CRP"), 16 U.S.C.A. §§3831-3836, the United States Department of Agriculture pays producers to temporarily retire environmentally sensitive lands from production. Producers sign ten-year CRP contracts and agree to convert their enrolled acres to approved conservation uses (e.g., vegetated stream buffer strips), receiving rental payments in return. After the contracts expire, producers can return these lands to agriculture. The Wetlands Reserve Program ("WRP") is a voluntary USDA program in which willing sellers receive fair market value to permanently retire wetland acres from farm production. Thirty-year easements can also be purchased under this program. Another aspect of the WRP involves cost-sharing with landowners who agree to restore wetlands on cropland.

Reorientation of subsidies and payments to farmers may be marginally helpful in reducing nonpoint source pollution, but they can only scratch the surface of the agricultural nonpoint source pollution problem. Professor Gould believes that antipollution subsidies are appropriate in the agricultural sector because "(g)overnment has played a major role in the structure of the farm economy, and government programs have indirectly encouraged some of the agricultural practices responsible for agricultural pollution (p. 488)." But subsidies and cost-sharing mechanisms cannot be the entire answer because (1) they are dependent upon the vagaries of funding, (2) they pay only part of the cost of pollution control, and (3) " most of the agricultural nonpoint source pollution effects occur off-farm...substantial voluntary efforts by farmers to control this pollution are unlikely (Gould, p. 489)." Professor Gould concludes that, in most respects, agricultural nonpoint source pollution is a traditional externality, and there is a need for a stronger federal presence if we expect to significantly reduce it. Adler, et al., recommend that Congress enact strict mandatory programs requiring that (1) states create priority lists of watersheds degraded by nonpoint source pollution, and agree to restore those watersheds "on a reasonable timetable," and (2) landowners or operators contributing to nonpoint pollution loadings in a target watershed develop site-specific water quality plans and implement them within three-to-five-year time frames. Professor Houck goes even further: "At this juncture, the only safe observation from the fact and scale of nonpoint source pollution and its effect on achieving water quality standards is that, unless TMDLs include quantified restrictions on nonpoint sources, they are wasting everyone's time." Houck, Are We There Yet?: The Long Road Toward Water Quality-Based Regulation Under the Clean Water Act, 27 ELR 10391, 10401 (1997).

A promising mechanism for reducing nonpoint source pollution, while at the same time counteracting the "Better-Than-Best" problem, is point-nonpoint source pollution trading. In a recent example, the Rahr Malting Co., of Shakopee Minnesota, wanted to build a plant to treat wastewater from expanded malt production facilities, but the entire nutrient TMDLs for the potential receiving segment of the Minnesota River had been allocated to regional POTWs. The Minnesota Pollution Control Agency (MPCA) arranged a point/nonpoint source trading framework whereby Rahr will fund relatively low-cost BMPs on upstream farmland, leading to reductions in nutrient loadings which will be offset against Rahr's point source discharge of nutrients.

Point/nonpoint source pollution trading may be one element of watershed management, a variety of "place-based" environmental protection. EPA's watershed management program involves awarding federal grant funds for coordinating resource management activities — including CWA water quality-based standard-setting and permitting — within watershed or aquifer recharge area boundaries. This is a "bottom-up" process, involving the participation of watershed stakeholders and the formation of partnerships among federal, state, and local agencies, and non-governmental organizations with interests in the watershed. The stakeholders and partners identify environmental objectives, taking into account the condition of the ecological resource and the economic and social needs of the watershed's population. After a consensual management plan has been developed, the governmental partners then coordinate planning, standard-setting, permitting, monitoring and surveillance, and enforcement in accordance with the watershed plan. The most significant watershed management efforts are being conducted with regard to the Gulf of Mexico, Long Island Sound, the Great Lakes Basin, Chesapeake Bay, Lake Champlain, 28 estuaries in the National Estuary Program, and a number of large lakes in the Clean Lakes Program. CWA §§1267–1270, 1324, 1330. Smaller watershed management processes, focusing primarily on nonpoint source control, are being conducted throughout the nation, under the joint auspices of EPA and USDA. Adler, et al., recommend that (1) current watershed management programs be strengthened by raising funding levels and mandating planning deadlines and implementation schedules, and 2) watershed planning and management be instituted for every major watershed in the United States. However, past attempts to establish effective programs based on boundaries other than political ones have not fared particularly well in the United States. See Goldfarb, Watershed Management: Slogan or Solution? 21 B.C. Env. Aff. L. Rev. 483 (1994), for an analysis of the historical development of watershed management and a critique of recent proposals.

State nonpoint pollution control laws differ widely with regard to strategy, coverage, institutional structure, enforceability, variances and exemptions, funding, and effectiveness. As one might expect,

> Agriculture is the most problematic area for enforceable mechanisms. Many laws of general applicability...have exceptions for agriculture. Where state laws exist, they often defer to incentives, cost-sharing, and voluntary programs. Nevertheless, about a fifth of the states have some statewide sediment requirements applicable to agriculture, often administered by local governments or soil and water conservation districts. Even more states (about a fourth) authorize individual soil and water conservation districts, as a matter of local option, to adopt enforceable "land use regulations" for the control of erosion and sedimentation. But most of these require approval of landowner referendum, with approval requiring a super-majority (ranging from 66 to 90 percent) in order for such regulations to become effective. Environmental Law Institute, Enforceable State Mechanisms for the Control of Nonpoint Source Water Pollution (1997), iii.

One can only wonder how enthusiastically local governments and soil and water conservation districts, in agricultural areas, will regulate agricultural nonpoint sources.

The debate over nonpoint source pollution control, and especially control of runoff from agricultural operations, dominates the CWA reauthorization process. Should Congress legislate a statutory goal for achieving NPS control (e.g., 20 years for agricultural pollution), leaving states to adopt a mix of strategies to meet these goals? How long should the compliance period be? Should EPA play a "backstop role," stepping in as the enforcement authority when a state has not shown progress toward meeting its goal? Or is a federal regulatory program necessary in the first instance? Would the most effective regulatory program rely on numerical performance standards, as in the BAT approach to point source regulation? Or are numerical limits inappropriate to diffuse and diverse nonpoint sources, which might be more amenable to a mandatory choice among a "menu" of site-specific BMPs? Should nonpoint source controls be required nationwide or only on water quality-limited segments? Should agricultural nonpoint source control programs be administered by EPA or USDA? What should be the role of subsidies in controlling nonpoint source pollution? These and other contentious policy questions relating to agricultural nonpoint source pollution control assure that this issue will continue in the forefront of the national clean water debate.

### COMMENTARY AND QUESTIONS

1. **CWA reauthorization.** The CWA is presently being funded under annual continuing reauthorizations. Congress' last attempt at a general reauthorization, in 1995, became a heated political struggle from which no major interest group emerged unscathed. The House passed a bill (H.R. 961, dubbed the Dirty Water Act) that undercut broad swaths of the CWA, but it was stopped in the Senate. Some of the major issues in this failed reauthorization were marketplace lobbyists' attempts (1) to require EPA to perform risk assessment before issuing TBELs and water quality criteria, (2) to override the *Southview Farms* and *Pub. Utility Dist. #1 of Jefferson County* decisions, noted earlier, that extended controls to agricultural runoffs and harmful low-flows, (3) to exclude stormwater from the CWA's "point source" definition, (4) to repeal EPA's stormwater permitting program, (5) requiring that if WQBELs are necessary, they should include cost-benefit analyses, (6) rebutting WET-based effluent limitations by field bio-assessments, (7) requiring EPA to update water quality criteria every five years, (8) to set special conditions for ephemeral and effluent-dependent streams (mostly in the West), (9) to exempt dischargers in watersheds covered by approved state watershed management plans from WQBELs, and (10) to authorize variances from categorical BAT-based pretreatment standards applicable to indirect dischargers for POTWs with approved pretreatment programs, that are in compliance with standards. Given the highly controversial nature of most of these issues, it is not surprising that Congress is not eager to resume the CWA reauthorization battle. Instead, Congress might either continue to fund the CWA by continuing reauthorization, or else might enact a so-called "CWA Lite," which would codify some of the relatively uncontroversial provisions of H.R. 961, such as funding State Revolving Funds, explicitly authorizing both pollution prevention as a potential TBEL and also effluent trading (with either point or nonpoint sources), requiring water quality standards for toxic

pollutants to take bioaccumulation potential into account, and extending the maximum term of discharge permits from five to ten years.

**2. CWA Evaluation.** Americans should be proud of the progress in waterway cleanup that has been made since 1972. Overall, the CWA has been successful. Major water pollution problems remain, however. Some of these — especially those involving the continued presence of toxic substances in our waterways — are the result of inadequate implementation of the CWA. Others, such as groundwater pollution and agricultural nonpoint source pollution, arise from gaps in the CWA's coverage. Solving these remaining water pollution problems will require considerable political and financial commitment, vigilance, imagination, and expertise. The CWA's qualified success in cleaning up America's surface waterbodies is symbolized by the following quip, attributed to a former EPA Administrator: "The Cuyahoga River may not be fishable and swimmable, but it is no longer flammable."

## F.   A COMPLEX HYPOTHETICAL: THE AVERAGE RIVER

Here is a cumulative watershed problem that illustrates many of the CWA's complexities and offers a vehicle for understanding the Act's different sections:

The Average River is just that, a hypothetical typical river system. It arises on the slopes of Magic Mountain and flows into the Pedantic Ocean. As shown on the accompanying map, the Average River is also subject to typical threats to its water quality: (1) a second home development, "Fox Ridge," with each home serviced by its own on-site septic system, is planned for the lower slopes of Magic Mountain, threatening to degrade the currently pristine water quality found in Riverview State Park (2); (3) Purview Farms, downstream from the park, is a large, multifaceted agricultural operation that causes fertilizer, pesticide, and manure residues to flow overland into the river during storm events, and also causes groundwater contamination by leaching these pollutants into groundwater; (4) the Dratt Chemical Co., Inc., discharges BOD, toxic organic chemicals, and phenols from its plant's production and sanitation facilities directly into the river, causing a violation of state-established water quality standards — based on fishable-swimmable water quality — downstream of the plant; Dratt also collects its stormwater, which is contaminated by runoff from uncovered raw materials storage piles, and discharges it through a drainage ditch into the river; (5) the Tribal Council of the Unpoll-Ute Indian Nation, which owns a reservation located just below Dratt's discharge points, has approved, and submitted to EPA, water quality criteria based on a "None Detectable" standard for the parameters discharged by Purview and Dratt; (6) across the river from the reservation is a wetland area, in which another residential subdivision ("Heron's Harbor") is planned; (7) The City of Grossville, population 500,000, is serviced by a POTW that utilizes secondary treatment, but is connected to a combined sewer system that contains 100 "overflow points," which discharge raw sewage mixed with stormwater into the ocean when storm flows exceed the capacity of the sewerage system; (8) Grossville's CSO and sewage treatment problems are exacerbated by the Nurd Auto Co., Inc.'s discharges of heavy metals into the Grossville sewers, and these heavy metals also contaminate

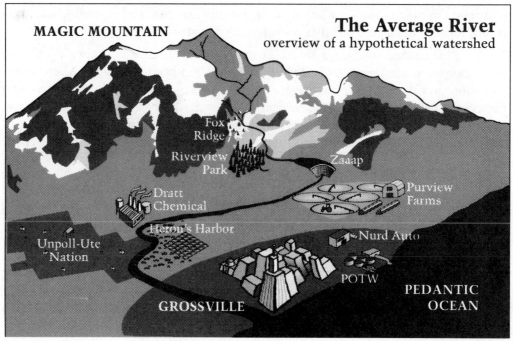

The Average River
overview of a hypothetical watershed

MAGIC MOUNTAIN

Fox Ridge

Riverview Park

Zaaap

Dratt Chemical

Purview Farms

Heron's Harbor

Nurd Auto

Unpoll-Ute Nation

POTW

GROSSVILLE

PEDANTIC OCEAN

GRAPHIC BY ADAM SCOVILLE

*Here's a cumulative water shed problem with a series of hypothetical uses (named as only a law professor could name them).*

the POTW's sewage sludge ("biosolids"), which is currently being stored in concrete silos at the POTW because ocean dumping — which the POTW once used to dispose of sludge — has been prohibited by federal law and the high heavy metal levels in the sludge preclude incineration, land application or landfilling; (9) The Zaaapp Power Company has applied to the Federal Energy Regulatory Commission for a license to construct a hydroelectic power dam on the river between Riverview State Park and Purview Farms; if constructed, this facility will add to existing pollution problems by raising water temperatures (depressing dissolved oxygen levels) and causing eutrophication in the reservoir behind the dam, and also by decreasing water flows (providing less dilution) and dissolved oxygen levels below the dam.

How might the Clean Water Act apply to each and all of these activities in the Average River watershed? If government does not act effectively to protect the river in these settings, can citizens?

# Chapter 10

# TECHNOLOGY-FORCING STANDARDS

    A. *Reducing Auto Emissions Through Technology-Forcing*
    B. *International Technology-Forcing: The Phaseout of Ozone-Depleting Substances*

Any of the regulatory strategies analyzed in this coursebook, if sufficiently stringent, might operate drastically to force the development of new technology. This chapter focuses on standards set by legislatures with the direct intent to force the development of new technology — either limiting releases of a target substance to lower amounts than can be achieved with currently available technology, or else by banning some or all uses of a substance to force the invention of substitutes. Insofar as government seeks to achieve technology-forcing through a complete prohibition on manufacture or use (sometimes referred to as "sunsetting" a dangerous substance), technology-forcing simultaneously acts as a "roadblock" to continuation of the commercial activity (see Chapter 14), while encouraging the development of new alternatives. Like roadblock statutes, product bans are crude, blunt instruments that frequently contain mitigating devices in order to gain acceptance by the regulated public. Some of these flexibility mechanisms are lead times for product phaseout, waivers, hardship variances, and sympathetic enforcement. In addition, market-based approaches noted in Chapter 16, such as the use of marketable permits, excise taxes, and governmental purchasing power, can effectively support technology-forcing.

Because the American legal system discourages potential curtailment of economic activity, technology-forcing is often a last regulatory resort. Judge Jasen's recommendation in *Boomer* that the defendant be forced to develop and adopt new pollution control technology, was rejected by the majority. The following statement by the Fifth Circuit Court of Appeals in Corrosion Proof Fittings v. Environmental Protection Agency, 947 F.2d 1201 (1991),[1] typifies the prevailing judicial skepticism regarding technology-forcing:

> As a general matter we agree with the EPA that a product ban can lead to great innovation, and it is true that an agency [under the Toxic Substances Control Act] as under other regulatory statutes, "is empowered to issue safety standards which require improvements in existing technology or which require the development of new technology. As even the EPA acknowledges, however,

---

1. In this case, the court overturned EPA's ban on the use of asbestos in almost all products.

when no adequate substitutes currently exist, the EPA cannot fail to consider this lack when formulating its own guidelines. Under ToSCA, therefore, the EPA must present a stronger case to justify the ban, as opposed to regulation, of products with no substitutes. 947 F.2d, at page 1221.

It would appear that administrative technology-forcing will be judicially condoned only where a regulatory agency has exhausted all other regulatory alternatives for controlling a demonstrably intolerable material. See Ethyl Corp. v. EPA, 541 F.2d 1 (D.C. Cir. 1976) (upholding EPA's phaseout of lead in gasoline).

In the relatively few situations where technology-forcing has been attempted, industry has been successful in developing innovative technology that has significantly reduced the environmental threat. In addition to the auto emissions reduction and CFC phaseout case studies presented below, the following regulatory efforts are examples of effective technology-forcing: EPA's prohibition of the commercial distribution and manufacture of PCBs (see Chapter 15); EPA's phased reduction leading to a prohibition on the use of lead in gasoline (see Ethyl Corp. v. EPA, above.); OSHA's drastic reduction in the occupational exposure standard for lead; and the prohibition of phosphate detergents by many state and local governments.[2] It may be that technology-forcing has generally been successful because legislatures and regulatory agencies "hedge their bets" when forcing technology. For example, when Congress enacted the strict 1970 reductions in permissible tailpipe emissions, it was aware that the catalytic converter technology had been developed and subjected to limited testing.

## A. REDUCING AUTO EMISSIONS THROUGH TECHNOLOGY-FORCING

The most ambitious and controversial use of technology-forcing as a regulatory strategy to achieve environmental protection goals was the 1970 CAA's Title II, a remarkable example of a drastic, direct, numerical regulatory standard stipulated by the legislature itself, declaring that —

> emissions of carbon monoxide and hydrocarbons from light duty vehicles...manufactured during or after model year 1975 shall...require a reduction of at least 90 per centum from emissions allowable...in model year 1970.[3] CAA §202(b)(1)(a) (1970).

### International Harvester v. Ruckelshaus
United States Circuit Court of Appeals
for the District of Columbia Circuit, 1973
478 F.2d 615

LEVENTHAL, Circuit Judge... These consolidated petitions of International Harvester and the three major auto companies, Ford, General Motors, and Chrysler, seek review of a decision by the Administrator [of EPA] denying peti-

2. See, e.g., Proctor & Gamble Corp. v. Chicago, 509 F.2d 69 (7th. Cir. 1975), cert. denied, 421 U.S. 978 (1976) (upholding Chicago's phosphate detergent ban against a dormant commerce clause challenge).
3. The Act applied the same specific rollback to oxides of nitrogen starting in the 1976 model year.

tioners' applications...for one year suspensions of the 1975 emissions standards prescribed under the statute for light duty vehicles....

The tension of forces presented by the controversy over automobile emission standards may be focused by two central observations: (1) the automobile is an essential pillar of the American economy. Some 28 percent of the nonfarm workforce draws its livelihood from the automobile and its products; (2) The automobile has had a devastating impact on the American environment. As of 1970, authoritative voices stated that "automotive pollution constitutes in excess of 60% of our national air pollution problem" and more than 80 percent of the air pollutants in concentrated urban areas.

Congressional concern over the problem of automotive emissions dates back to the 1950s, but it was not until the passage of the Clean Air Act in 1965 that Congress established the principle of Federal standards for auto emissions. Under the 1965 act and its successor, the Air Quality Act of 1967, the [Federal authorities] were authorized to promulgate emission limitations commensurate with existing technological feasibility.

The development of emission control technology proceeded haltingly. The Secretary of Health, Education, and Welfare testified in 1967 that "the state of the art has tended to meander along until some sort of regulation took it by the hand and gave it a good pull.... There has been a long period of waiting for it, and it hasn't worked very well."

The legislative background must also take into account the fact that in 1969 the Department of Justice brought suit against the four largest automobile manufacturers on the grounds that they had conspired to delay the development of emission control devices.

On December 31, 1970, Congress grasped the nettle and amended the Clean Air Act to set a statutory standard for required reductions in levels of hydrocarbons (HC) and carbon monoxide (CO) which must be achieved for 1975 models of light duty vehicles. Section 202(b) of the Act...provides that, beginning with the 1975 model year, exhaust emission of HC and CO from light duty vehicles must be reduced at least 90 per cent from the permissible emission levels in the 1970 year. In accordance with the Congressional directives, the Administrator...promulgated regulations limiting HC and CO emissions from 1975 model light duty vehicles to .41 and 3.4 grams per mile respectively....[4]

Congress was aware that these 1975 standards were "drastic medicine" designed to "force the state of the art." There was, naturally, concern whether the manufacturers would be able to achieve this goal. Therefore, Congress provided...a "realistic escape hatch": the manufacturers could petition the EPA for a one-year suspension of the 1975 requirements, and Congress took the precaution of directing the National Academy of Sciences to undertake an ongoing study of the feasibility of compliance with the emission standards. The "escape hatch" provision addressed itself to the possibility that the NAS study or other evidence might indicate that the standards would be unachievable despite all good faith efforts at compliance.[5] This provision was limited to a one-year suspension....

---

4. This was a default standard; some car models that were cleaner had even tougher standards. The same regulation also prescribed an interim 3.0 grams per mile 1975 standard for nitrogen oxides (NOx). HC and NOx combine with sunlight to produce photochemical oxidants (ozone), also known as "smog" [Eds.].

5. The suspension provision also included a criterion that the suspension must be "essential to the public interest or the public health and welfare of the United States" [Eds.].

*A modern urban scene with air pollution caused by automobile emissions. This could be any one of the more than four dozen American cities that are consistently in violation of federal air quality standards due to hydrocarbons, nitrogen oxides, and carbon mmonoxide produced by automobiles.*

[The EPA Administrator rejected petitioners' applications for suspensions on the ground that petitioners had not established the unavailability of control technology that could meet the stricter standards. The NAS Report concluded that the necessary control technology was not available.]

Two principal considerations compete for our attention. On the one hand, if suspension is not granted, and the prediction of the EPA that effective technology will be available is proven incorrect, grave economic consequences could ensue.... On the other hand, if suspension is granted, and it later be shown that the Administrator's prediction of feasibility was achievable in 1975 there may be irretrievable ecological costs. It is to this second possibility to which we first turn.

The most authoritative estimate in the record of the ecological costs of a one-year suspension is that of the NAS Report. [The NAS concluded]

...the effect on total emissions of a one-year suspension with no additional interim standards appears to be small. The effect is not more significant because the emission reduction now required of model year 1974 vehicles, as compared with uncontrolled vehicles (80 percent for HC and 69 percent for CO), is already so substantial.

[The court added that because the technology being tested to meet the 1975 standards would cause fuel economy, acceleration, and "driveability" problems, while adding significantly to the cost of new motor vehicles, "a drop-off in purchase of 1975 cars will result in a prolonged use of older cars with *less* efficient pollution control devices.... It might even come to pass that total actual emissions (of all cars in use) would be greater under the 1975 than the 1974 standards."]

We also note that it is the belief of many experts — both in and out of the automobile industry — that air pollution cannot be effectively checked until the industry finds a substitute for the conventional automotive power plant — the reciprocating internal combustion (i.e., "piston") engine. According to this view, the conventional unit is a "dirty" engine. While emissions from such a motor can be "cleaned" by various thermal and catalytic converter devices, these devices do nothing to decrease the production of emissions in the engine's combustion chambers. The automobile industry has a multi-billion-dollar investment in the conventional engine, and it has been reluctant to introduce new power plants or undertake major modifications of the conventional one. Thus the bulk of the industry's work on emission control has focused narrowly on converter devices. It is clear from the legislative history that Congress expected the Clean Air Act Amendments to force the industry to broaden the scope of its research — to study new types of engines and new control systems. Perhaps even a one-year suspension does not give the industry sufficient time to develop a new approach to emission control and still meet the absolute deadline of 1976. If so, there will be ample time for the EPA and Congress, between now and 1976 to reflect on changing the statutory approach. This kind of cooperation, a unique three-way partnership between the legislature, executive, and judiciary, was contemplated by the Congress and is apparent in the provisions of the Act....

If the automobiles of Ford, General Motors and Chrysler cannot meet the 1975 standards..., the Administrator of EPA has the theoretical authority...to shut down the auto industry, as was clearly recognized in the Congressional debate. We cannot put blinders on the facts before us so as to omit awareness of reality that this authority would undoubtedly never be exercised, in light of the fact that approximately 1 out of every 7 jobs in this country is dependent on the production of the automobile. Senator Muskie, the principal sponsor of the bill, stated quite clearly in the debate on the Act that he envisioned the Congress acting if an auto industry shutdown were in sight....

This case is haunted by the irony that what seems to be Ford's technological lead may operate to its grievous detriment, assuming the relaxation-if-necessary [of the standards]. If...any one of the three major companies cannot meet the 1975 standards, it is a likelihood that standards will be set to permit the higher level of emission control achievable by the laggard. This will be the case whether or not the leader has or has not achieved compliance with the 1975 standards. Even if the relaxation is later made industry-wide, the Government's action, in first imposing a standard not generally achievable and then relaxing it, is likely to be detrimental to the leader who has tooled up to meet a higher standard than will ultimately be required.

In some contexts high achievement bestows the advantage that rightly belongs to the leader, of high quality. In this context before us, however, the high achievement in emission control results, under systems presently available, in lessened car performance — an inverse correlation. The competitive disadvantage to the ecological leader presents a forbidding outcome...for which we see no remedy....

[The court remanded the case to EPA for reconsideration of its denial of suspension.]

COMMENTARY AND QUESTIONS

1. **Was this really technology-forcing?** Is technology-forcing legislation credible when the bill's sponsor assures his colleagues that the "hammer" (shutdown of large auto manufacturers) will never be allowed to fall? Is it any wonder that the auto industry did not take the threat seriously, instead continuing to tinker with add-on devices that would require little modification of existing automobiles and could later be abandoned if Congress changed its mind? In fact, the "three-way partnership" among the legislature, executive branch, and judiciary acted to postpone compliance far beyond the one-year suspension. On remand, EPA granted the extension for both the HC and the CO standards, but promulgated interim standards for 1975 of 1.4 and 15 gpms respectively.

EPA granted a one-year suspension of the 1976 NOx [nitrogen oxides] standard of 0.2 gpms, and set an interim standard of 2 gpms. Through a combination of Congressional extensions and Congressionally-authorized EPA suspensions, the HC and CO standards, based on a 90 percent rollback, were not finally met until 1980 and 1983 respectively. Congress abandoned the 0.2 gpm NOx standard in 1977, and, in its place, imposed a 1 gpm standard to be met in 1984. By the mid-1980s, the auto industry was willing to accept the standards because market demand was moving toward smaller, less-polluting, and more fuel-efficient vehicles.

Was this an example of successful technology-forcing? Or was the final attainment of the 1975 and 1976 standards merely accidental?[6] Was attainment "too little, too late"?

2. **Why the denial?** Why did EPA deny the one-year suspension, knowing that its decision was in conflict with the prestigious NAS Report and sensing the lack of Congressional support for strict deadlines and draconic enforcement? EPA must have realized that its denial would be overturned by a court, or Congress, (or both, as it turned out). Is it possible that EPA wanted to censure the auto industry for its failure to make a genuine effort to consider new technology, and its alleged conspiracy to suppress new technology, but that it would have been politically inexpedient for the EPA to try to prove that the auto industry had violated the requirement of making "all good faith efforts" to meet the standards?

3. **Rewarding the laggard and the risks of leading the way.** Was the court correct in its assumption that a company making good faith efforts to comply with the standards would inevitably be disadvantaged by a standard relaxation dictated by the overall public interest? Whenever standards are set and then reset at different levels, parties that comply quickly may suffer unintended penalties. What if standards are tightened after a company has invested in new technology in order to meet the first change in the standard? What if a rollback approach is taken after one firm has already reduced its emissions? Both situations pose serious inter-polluter equity problems that a regulatory scheme should address. (Another approach to this problem can be found in §306(d) of the Clean Water Act, which provides that a new source of water pollution that has achieved its New Source

---

6. One serendipitous result of the standards was the EPA phaseout of leaded gasoline; lead poisons the catalytic converter.

Performance Standards cannot be subject to stricter standards for ten years, or the depreciation or amortization period of the facility, whichever ends first.) What about using incentives such as tax deductions or preferential governmental purchasing to add inducements to early compliance?

4. **The court's balancing test.** Note that the court's cost-benefit analysis followed the recommendation of Talbot Page (see Chapter Two) that the costs of false negatives be weighed against the costs of false positives in making environmental regulatory decisions. In this case, as analyzed by the court, the cost of a false negative (not granting the suspension when it should have been granted) was relatively high in economic terms, while the cost of a false positive (granting the suspension when it should not have been) was relatively low in environmental terms. Given the broad "public interest" test articulated by Congress, balancing the costs of potential erroneous decisions appears to have been justified. But did the court conduct the balance fairly, in light of the fact that the one-year extension was not a firm one, making further "slippage" predictable?

5. **Types of technology-forcing mechanisms.** Note that, in the case of auto emission controls, Congress itself set the standards based on technology-forcing, instead of delegating standard-setting to the experts at EPA. With regard to the phaseout of lead in gasoline, on the other hand, Congress generally delegated to EPA the authority to control or prohibit fuel additives (42 U.S.C.A. §7545(c)), and EPA did the rest. Why did Congress retain direct control of auto emission standard-setting? Because it wanted to ensure that the standards could be modified quickly if they proved to be unachievable? Because it was afraid that EPA would be unable to resist the political power of the auto industry? Because it wanted to take primary credit for responding to this important issue?

6. **The 1990 Clean Air Act Amendments, technology-forcing, and auto pollution.** By 1987, emissions of HC, CO, and lead from new cars had dropped by over 95% from uncontrolled levels, and emissions of NOx by over 75%, but increases in automobile use caused ambient air quality standards for ozone to be exceeded in many urban areas. With the lessons of its 1970 technology-forcing effort firmly in mind, Congress, in 1990, adopted a more sophisticated but still aggressive technology-forcing strategy to cope with ozone nonattainment problems:

### Henry Waxman, Gregory Wetstone, and Phillip Barnett, Cars, Fuels and Clean Air: A Review of Title II of the Clean Air Act Amendments of 1990
21 Environmental Law 1947, 1991–2004 (1991)

A major innovation in Title II is the clean-fuel vehicle program, contained in new part C. This program requires the use of a new generation of "clean fuel vehicles" in the most heavily polluted cities. These vehicles, which must meet emission standards eighty percent below today's standards, will often run on clean alternative fuels, such as natural gas, ethanol, or even electricity....

The clean-fuel requirements for light-duty vehicles and light-duty trucks in the final legislation have three central components. First, new sections 242 through 245 establish special emission standards for clean-fuel vehicles. Second, new §246 establishes a program to require the use of clean-fuel vehicles in centrally fueled fleets in polluted cities. Finally, new §249 establishes a large-scale program to introduce clean-fuel vehicles to the passenger car market in California.

Section 242 of the Act requires EPA to set emission standards for clean-fuel vehicles in two years. These standards...mandate a [sixty and later an] eighty percent reduction in exhaust emissions of organic gasses and NOx from today's already controlled levels. They are intended to develop a new generation of clean vehicles, in a fuel-neutral manner. The most heavily polluted cities must reduce aggregate emissions of VOCS [volatile organics] and NOx by sixty to eighty percent from today's levels — and keep them there notwithstanding future economic and population growth — to attain the federal health standard for ozone. This is an immense undertaking, made more immense by the fact that most polluted cities have already adopted most of the obvious control measures. It cannot be accomplished unless vehicle emissions are cut drastically. Indeed, Los Angeles, the most polluted city in the country, cannot achieve attainment by 2010 without the widespread use of zero-emission, electric vehicles.

The standards for clean-fuel vehicles reflect this imperative.... In percent terms, this [eighty percent reduction] is equivalent to the level of technology-forcing required by the 1970 amendments. Under the new clean-fuel standards, organic gas and NOx emissions will be reduced ninety-eight percent below uncontrolled levels.

Meeting these standards will necessitate major advances in vehicles and fuels. Unlike any standards previously established, the final standards appear unachievable by vehicles running on conventional gasoline. They probably can be met by vehicles that use reformulated gasoline, but only if manufacturers develop an additional "preheated" catalyst to capture the emissions that occur during the first seconds of operation. Vehicles built to run on alternative fuels like natural gas, ethanol, or methanol are also likely to meet the standards....

The 1990 amendments establish two programs to require the use of clean-fuel vehicles meeting the [emissions] standards.... One is for fleet vehicles and one is for passenger cars in California.

The fleet program...requires clean-fuel vehicles to be used by the owners of centrally fueled fleets of ten or more vehicles in serious, severe, and extreme ozone nonattainment areas. Examples of centrally fueled fleets are fleets of delivery vans, taxicabs, or school buses that regularly refuel at a common location. When the program is fully phased in, it is expected to cover 250,000 vehicles per year.... By model year 2000, seventy percent of the new vehicles purchased by covered fleet operators must be clean-fuel vehicles.... To ensure that the clean-fuel vehicles run on the clean fuels for which they are designed, the [fleet owners must] fuel the vehicles exclusively with clean fuels....

Ultimately, clean-fuel vehicles must penetrate the passenger-car market to achieve major reductions in air pollution. For this reason, the second clean-fuel program in part C establishes a mandatory pilot program in California that will introduce clean-fuel vehicles to the passenger-car market....

Developing a successful alternative fuels program is often said to pose a "chicken and egg" problem. Car makers argue that they should not be forced to make clean-fuel vehicles until clean fuels are widely available. Oil companies argue the converse: they should not be forced to make clean fuels until clean-fuel vehicles are widely available. Both sides argue that even if the vehicles and fuels are available, there is no guarantee that the consumer will buy them.

The fleet program...tackles this problem through a demand-side approach: it requires fleet operators to buy clean-fuel vehicles and to refuel them with clean fuels. These requirements create a built-in demand that overcomes the "chicken and egg" issue. In the case of the passenger car market, however, it is not practical to mandate that a certain percentage of consumers buy only clean-fuel vehicles. Instead, the California pilot program takes a supply-side approach to ensuring the use of both clean-fuel vehicles and clean fuels.

The California pilot program mandates that vehicle manufacturers produce and sell minimum volumes of clean-fuel vehicles in California. [The California Air Resources Board has determined that 2 percent of the cars offered for sale in the 1998 model year must be electric, rising to 5 percent in 2001 and 10 percent in 2003.]

The "production mandate" in the California program makes it the obligation of the vehicle manufacturer to ensure that the vehicles find their way into the consumer's garage. The program thus capitalizes on the enormous capacity of manufacturers to influence vehicle purchases. Car companies control the most important factors that affect consumer purchases: they determine how well the vehicle will perform, what its styling will look like, how the vehicle is advertised, and at what price the vehicle will sell. The production mandate forces manufacturers to develop and market a vehicle that consumers will want to buy — which is exactly the incentive that is needed to make the clean-fuel program a success.

### COMMENTARY AND QUESTIONS

1. **Auto emissions control since 1990.** Once again, implementation of technology-forcing legislation in the auto emissions control area has not gone smoothly. The Clean Air Act preempts state regulation of emissions from new automobiles except for California — the only "extreme" ozone nonattainment area — which can petition EPA for a preemption waiver. Other states may "piggyback" on the California standards under certain conditions.[7] Most of the administrative and political activity in this area has involved the attempt by several of the twelve Northeastern states and the District of Columbia, organized as the Ozone Transport Commission ("OTC"), to adopt the California standards in whole or part. As indicated above, the California Air Resources Board ("CARB") initially determined that 2 percent of the cars offered for sale in California in the 1998 model year must be Zero Emission Vehicles ("ZEVs") powered by electricity, rising to 5 percent in 2001 and 10 percent in 2003. New York and Massachusetts adopted this program (called California-Low-Emission Vehicle, or "CAL-LEV") virtually intact. In 1996, however, CARB, accepting the arguments of the automobile manufacturers that advanced battery technology for practicably fueling electric vehicles is currently unavailable, repealed the 1998 and 2001 requirements, while retaining the requirement that the manufacturers include ZEVs as 10 percent of their California sales in 2003. In return, the manufacturers agreed to report to CARB on their ZEV product plans, and also to introduce National Low-Emission Vehicles ("NLEVs," a "49-state car") in the Northeast in 1999, and in the rest of the country in 2001, two years before an EPA-proposed deadline.

---

7. The California preemption waiver and other state "piggyback" provisions can be found at 42 U.S.C.A. §§7543 and 7589. See also Motor Vehicle Manufacturers Association of the United States v. New York State Department of Conservation, 15 F.3d 521 (2nd Cir. 1993) (substantially upholding New York's adoption of the California program).

The auto manufacturers have stated that their voluntary NLEV Program is contingent upon the acceptance of all of the OTC jurisdictions. But at least four of these (New York, Vermont, Massachusetts, and Maine) have opted for CAL-LEV. Has the California preemption waiver created a chaotic implementation climate with regard to the technology-forcing strategies in the 1990 CAA Amendments? Or will the confusing demands caused by this "moving target" finally convince the manufacturers to perform serious research on alternative fuel sources? Exciting developments in fuel cell technologies promise major breakthroughs in auto emission control, but uncertainty about the resolve of federal and state governments to force technology is retarding research and development.

2. **Technology-forcing: the auto verdict?** The congressionally-dictated 90% rollbacks in auto emissions certainly caused major disruptions in the automobile industry, derailing ongoing investment planning, rewarding laggards, forcing the companies into expensive last-minute attempts to retool the old design engines rather than being able to take the time to design new ones, and costing as much as $18 billion.[8] On balance, was it a good idea? What would the air in traffic jams probably look like today had Congress imposed a more typical harm-based or technology-based review-and-permit standard? Michael Walsh, former EPA Director of Motor Vehicle Emissions Regulation has said that "Title II was blunt, but it was the only thing that would work.... Forcing technological development through a 'regulatory hammer' has been and continues to be the only demonstrated way to succeed." Telephone interview, Oct. 16, 1991.

## B. INTERNATIONAL TECHNOLOGY-FORCING: THE PHASEOUT OF OZONE-DEPLETING SUBSTANCES.

The auto emissions case study shows that technology-forcing, which is inherently problematic as a regulatory strategy, becomes increasingly difficult when multiple jurisdictions are involved in setting and implementing standards. If this has been true in the United States, where Congress can preempt state legislation, it is almost inconceivable that technology-forcing could be effective in the international arena, where there is no universal legislature (see Chapter 26). The improbability of successful international technology-forcing, therefore, underscores the magnificent diplomatic and legal accomplishments of those individuals and nations that negotiated the Montreal Protocol on Substances that Deplete the Ozone Layer:

### Steven Shimberg, Stratospheric Ozone and Climate Protection: Domestic Legislation and the International Process
21 Environmental Law 2175 (1991)

In accordance with Article 2, §2 of the U.S. Constitution, the international negotiations that led to the September 1987 signing of the Montreal Protocol on Substances that Deplete the Ozone Layer (the Protocol) and the June 1990 agreement in London to strengthen the Protocol were conducted by the Executive

8. L. White, The Regulation of Air Pollutant Emissions from Motor Vehicles 64 (1982).

Branch of the United States Government. Throughout the negotiations, however, the U.S. Congress was proceeding on a parallel track with domestic legislative proposals designed to protect the stratospheric ozone layer — the thin atmospheric shield that safeguards life on Earth from dangerous ultraviolet radiation.

The legislative effort that culminated with the enactment of title VI of the Clean Air Act Amendments of 1990 (1990 Amendments), which addresses stratospheric ozone and global climate protection, began in October 1986. The timing of this legislative effort was selected to predate, by several weeks, the first session of renewed international negotiations to protect the stratospheric ozone layer. These negotiations led to the signing of the Protocol on September 16, 1987. The legislative proposals under consideration were more stringent than the proposed Protocol provisions that were being supported by the U.S. delegation to the international negotiations, and were designed to accomplish several objectives: first, to encourage the U.S. delegation to support a more stringent Protocol than it was otherwise prepared to support by creating a serious, viable threat of congressional enactment of more stringent domestic legislation;[9] second, to encourage the delegations of other nations to support a more stringent protocol...by creating a...threat of [U.S.] trade sanctions; third, to eliminate the disproportionately large U.S. contribution to the problems of ozone depletion and global climate change that are created by emissions of chloroflorocarbons (CFCs) and other ozone-destroying compounds and reestablish the United States as a world leader in matters relating to environmental protection; and finally, to force domestic industries to develop safe alternatives more quickly than would be required under the terms of the protocol.

The signing of the Protocol on September 16, 1987 was an historic event.[10] It was, however, only "a major half-step forward." Even after the international agreement to strengthen the Protocol was reached at the Second Meeting of the Parties to the Montreal Protocol in London on June 29, 1990, the U.S. Congress proceeded to enact more stringent domestic legislation....

Throughout the effort to enact domestic legislation, opponents of unilateral action argued that such action would do nothing to help the environment; would put domestic industries at a competitive disadvantage; and would tie the hands of the U.S. government [negotiators].... These arguments were soundly rejected when the [U.S. Congress]...passed the 1990 [Clean Air Act] Amendments, and on November 15, 1990 President Bush signed the bill that became Public Law 101-549....

Ozone is a toxic compound consisting of three oxygen atoms. It is also the only gas in the atmosphere that prevents harmful solar ultraviolet radiation from reaching the surface of the Earth. In the region of the atmosphere extending from ground level to approximately six miles above the Earth, known as the troposphere, ozone is a primary component of smog and is responsible for numerous health and environmental problems. Under the Clean Air Act Title I, ozone is recognized as one of the six criteria pollutants, and activities that result in emissions of ozone precursors are subject to stringent regulations.

Most of the Earth's atmosphere resides in the stratosphere — the region extending from approximately six miles to thirty miles above the Earth's surface.

---

9. The Reagan Administration was consistently opposed to a strong Protocol [Eds.].

10. This was the first time that the international community had banned the production and consumption of a product [Eds.].

It is this stratospheric ozone layer that serves as Earth's main shield against harmful solar radiation. A decrease in stratospheric ozone produces an increase in the amount of ultraviolet radiation that reaches the Earth. Increased exposure to solar radiation results in increased incidence of skin cancer,[11] cataracts, and may cause suppression of the immune system. Increased ultraviolet radiation has also been shown to damage crops and marine resources.

Prior to anthropogenic influences, the destruction and creation of stratospheric ozone occurred as part of a natural continuing process that maintained a relatively constant amount of ozone in the stratosphere. The introduction of CFCs and similar manufactured substances, however, upset the natural balance of nature. These persistent, stable compounds are not destroyed in the troposphere but survive and rise up into the atmosphere, where the sun's radiation breaks them apart, releasing the chlorine atoms that are integral parts of the molecules. The released chlorine then reacts with ozone to form chlorine monoxide and oxygen, and in the process, destroys ozone molecules.

In addition to the role CFCs play in destroying the stratospheric ozone layer, CFCs are also connected to the global climate change that is predicted to occur as a result of an intensified greenhouse effect.... CFCs are estimated to account for a substantial portion of the problem —from fifteen to twenty percent....

In 1974, Drs. Sherwood Rowland and Mario Molina, from the University of California, published a paper demonstrating how CFCs destroy ozone in the atmosphere.[12] In this country, the original scientific theory prompted Congress to include, in the Clean Air Act Amendments of 1977, a provision authorizing the Administrator of EPA to regulate "any substance...which in his judgment may reasonably be anticipated to affect the stratosphere, especially ozone in the stratosphere, and such effect may reasonably be anticipated to endanger public health or welfare." In 1978, the EPA and the Food and Drug Administration promulgated a ban on the use of CFCs in most aerosols [e.g., in cans of hair spray or deodorant]. There were [then] no measurements of actual ozone loss, just the scientific theory.

Recognizing the problem, industry began to look for safe substitutes. Progress was being made when, in the early 1980s, Ronald Reagan became President of the United States; the threat of further government regulation subsided; the search for substitutes came to a virtual standstill; and worldwide use of CFCs continued to grow. Despite the aerosol ban in the United States, nonaerosol uses of CFCs in this country [e.g., in refrigerators and automobile air-conditioners] grew to record high levels and per capita use of CFCs in the United States reached levels that were among the highest in the world. By the middle of the 1980s, the United States was producing approximately 700 million pounds of CFCs each year, roughly one-third of the world total.

In 1985, scientists discovered a significant loss of stratospheric ozone over a large portion of the southern hemisphere. The affected area was approximately the size of North America. This collapse of the stratospheric ozone layer was not predicted by any of the scientific theories or models. Measurements of what had become a seasonal phenomenon revealed losses of greater than fifty percent in the total column of stratospheric and tropospheric ozone and greater than ninety-five percent in stratospheric ozone between an altitude of fifteen to twenty kilo-

---

11. Each five-percent decrease in ozone causes an increase of approximately 40,000 skin cancers in the United States [Eds.]

12. Drs. Molina and Rowland received the 1995 Nobel Prize for this research [Eds.].

meters — nine to twelve miles. The discovery of this "hole" in the stratospheric ozone layer over Antarctica gave renewed impetus to international and domestic efforts to understand and protect the ozone layer.

Congressional interest and concern was triggered by this shocking and graphic, albeit inconclusive, evidence that the Rowland and Molina theory of ozone destruction was correct. For more than eight years, EPA [had] failed to exercise its authority under the CAA to address the threat presented by continued production and use of CFCs. The Agency had been working unsuccessfully for more than a decade to produce an international agreement to reduce emissions of CFCs. These failures suggested to some members of Congress that it was time "to reassert our role as national decisionmakers...."

A new round of international negotiations was scheduled to begin in December 1986.... On February 19, 1987, legislation was introduced in the Senate to impose unilateral controls on the production and use of CFCs and related compounds such as methyl chloroform, carbon tetrachloride, and hydrocholoroflorocarbons (HCFCs). Trade restrictions were included in the bill as a means of forcing other nations to adopt comparable programs to curb CFCs and to avoid placing the domestic industries that would be subject to controls at a competitive disadvantage in the world marketplace.

As the international negotiations progressed through the spring and summer of 1987, congressional pressure and the attention of the national news media remained focused on the activities of the U.S. delegation. At a May 1987 congressional hearing, the U.S. negotiators were reminded that they were being watched carefully, encouraged to resist efforts to weaken the U.S. negotiating position, and urged to continue to press for virtual elimination of CFCs. At that hearing, representatives of EPA reviewed the results of a six volume risk assessment that had been prepared by the Agency. They also presented the results of recent studies that showed the overwhelming positive cost-benefit ratio associated with elimination of CFCs and related compounds.

The date of May 29, 1987 represents a watershed for proponents of stringent CFC controls. On that day, the news media published reports of recent efforts by Secretary of the Interior Donald Hodel to revoke the authority of the U.S. delegation to negotiate significant reductions in the production and use of ozone-destroying compounds. The Washington Post's front page headline read: "Administration Ozone Policy May Favor Sunglasses, Hats; Support for Chemical Cutbacks Reconsidered."... The public outcry was prompt and furious. The opponents of mandated reductions in the production and use of ozone destroying compounds had created a backlash that virtually guaranteed the imposition of stringent controls.

On September 16, 1987, more than two dozen nations concluded negotiations and signed the Montreal Protocol on Substances that Deplete the Ozone Layer.[13] Signatories to the Protocol, including the United States, agreed to respond to the threat of global ozone depletion by imposing limits on consumption — defined as production plus imports minus exports of bulk quantities — of CFCs....

Within two weeks after the Protocol was negotiated and signed..., the causal link between CFCs and the Antarctic ozone "hole" was substantiated. Efforts to

---

13. There are currently over 150 signatories to the Protocol. The 1987 Montreal Protocol obliged each signatory nation to halve its consumption of CFCs by the year 2000. The 1990 Protocol amendment requires the parties to achieve a total phase-out by that date [Eds.].

reopen the negotiations and strengthen the terms of the agreement began almost immediately. These efforts, and efforts to impose stringent unilateral controls, received an additional push just one day after the Senate voted to approve ratification of the Protocol. On March 15, 1988, the Ozone Trends Panel, a group of more than one hundred scientists from around the world, released an international study on global ozone trends. The Panel's report demonstrated that destruction of the ozone layer was not limited to remote uninhabited portions of Antarctica. Scientists observed and measured losses of ozone on a global scale, including significant losses over densely populated portions of the northern hemisphere. This and similar scientific reports created a new sense of urgency and highlighted the need for controls that went beyond those agreed to as part of the original Protocol.

The Protocol was ratified by a sufficient number of countries to enter into force on the scheduled date of January 1, 1989. Momentum for an international agreement to eliminate CFCs began to build during the spring of 1989. Several nations, including the United States, pledged to support a rapid international phase-out of CFCs.[14] At the same time, momentum was building for the imposition of more stringent unilateral domestic controls.[15]...

In preparation for a diplomatic conference scheduled to be held in London at the end of June 1990, international negotiations to strengthen the Protocol were initiated in the summer of 1989. At the June 1990 diplomatic conference, the second meeting of the parties to the Protocol, an international agreement to strengthen the Protocol was reached.... Despite the new international agreement, Congress proceeded to enact domestic legislation that was more stringent than the newly strengthened Protocol.

The 1990 Amendments include provisions that are more stringent than the Protocol in three major areas: first, the Amendments include an accelerated phase-out schedule for CFCs, halons, and methyl chloroform; second, the new law includes provisions to control and ultimately eliminate production and use of HCFCs;[16] and third, it includes provisions to eliminate emissions of ozone-destroying compounds and substitute compounds....

The 1990 Amendments [declared] the following four major objectives: first, domestic production of the compounds that pose the greatest threat to the ozone layer — fully halogenated CFCs, halons, carbon tetrachloride, and methyl chloroform — will be eliminated as soon as possible and no later than January 1, 2002; second, the production of other, less potent, ozone-destroying chemicals, such as HCFCs, will be controlled and ultimately eliminated; third unnecessary emissions of all ozone-depleting chemicals and some greenhouse gasses will be eliminated by implementation of a new recapture, recycling, and safe disposal program; and finally, options for reducing emissions of methane, a powerful greenhouse gas, will be developed and presented to Congress by EPA.

---

14. By this time, the Reagan Administration had been replaced by that of George Bush, which was more receptive to a ban on CFCs [Eds.].

15. In March 1989, the Federal Republic of Germany's Bundestag unanimously decided to proceed with unilateral action and adopted legislation mandating a 95% reduction in production and use of CFCs by no later than 1995. [This is footnote 59 in the original.]

16. Some of the compounds that are being promoted as substitutes for CFCs, such as hydroflorocarbons, may be safe for the ozone layer due to lack of a chlorine molecule, but due to radiative forcing properties, are expected to contribute to an intensified greenhouse effect.... [This is footnote 72 in the original.]

The new Title VI includes four main elements. First, the Administrator of EPA (the Administrator) is required to implement a phase-out schedule more aggressive than the schedule set forth in [Title VI] if information suggests that it may be necessary to protect human health and the environment; based on the availability of substitutes, an accelerated schedule is attainable; or the Protocol is modified to include a more aggressive schedule. Second, subject to acceleration by the Administrator, [Title VI] place[s] CFCs, halons, carbon tetrachloride and methyl chloroform on phase-out schedules that are more stringent than those required by the current version of the Protocol. Third, where the Montreal Protocol will allow unlimited production and use of other, less potent ozone-depleting chemicals such as HCFCs and by doing so, continue the threat to the ozone layer, under [Title VI], domestic production of HCFCs will be limited as of January 1, 2015 and eliminated by January 1, 2030. In addition, specific use limitations will take effect on January 1, 2015. Finally, as a supplement to production phase-outs, the law provides for significant reductions in...emissions.... To achieve this fourth objective the 1990 Amendments developed [schedules for EPA to promulgate regulations[17] (1) requiring the recapture, recycling, and safe disposal of ozone-depleting substances, (2) prohibiting the practice of venting ozone-depleting refrigerant gases during appliance service, repair, and disposal, (3) requiring the use of certified recycling equipment when servicing motor vehicle air conditioners, (4) banning the sale and distribution of nonessential consumer products containing CFCs and other substances, (5) imposing labeling requirements, (6) instituting a safe alternatives policy to promote the transition to safe substitutes, (7) requiring federal agencies to purchase safe substitutes; (8) prohibiting the export of technologies that produce Class I substances[18] and on investments to produce Class I or Class II substances in nations that are not parties to the Protocol, and (9) authorizing a U.S. contribution to the international fund that has been established by the Protocol to assist developing nations in complying with its provisions.]

It is not expected that there will be a need to authorize production of methyl chloroform beyond December 31, 2001. Safe substitutes already exist for the vast majority of uses and should be available for all uses by the year 2000. In the unlikely event that safe substitutes have not been developed for some uses by that time, if a particular use is determined by the Administrator to be essential, production of a limited amount of methyl chloroform may be authorized by the Administrator for that use....

As with Class I substances, the Administrator is directed to promulgate regulations to control and eliminate consumption of Class II substances, and on a conditional basis, is authorized to grant limited exemptions for use [of Class I and II substances] in medical devices and for export to developing countries in accordance with the Protocol....

The Administrator is directed to promulgate regulations that will authorize interpollutant transfers and trading of production allowances among producers. As an example of an interpollutant transfer, a producer may decide to reduce production of CFC-11 by an amount greater than is required in a given year, and in the same year, be authorized to produce a greater amount of CFC-113 than would

---

17. EPA's regulations regarding ozone-depleting substances are codified at 40 C.F.R. §82 et seq.

18. Class I substances, such as CFCs, present a serious risk to the ozone layer; Class II substances, such as HCFCs, pose a less serious current threat, and may, in the short term, act as interim replacements for Class I substances, but must ultimately be phased-out [Eds.].

otherwise be allowed. Interpollutant transfers are limited, however, to transfers among substances listed in the same group....

The Administrator is directed to promulgate regulations prohibiting the replacement of any Class I or Class II substance with a substitute that the Administrator determines may present adverse effects to human health or the environment if an alternative that reduces the overall risk...has been identified.... The Administrator is also directed to require that any person who produces a chemical substitute for a Class I substance (1) provide the Administrator with health and safety studies on the substitute...and (2) notify the Administrator not less than ninety days before new or existing chemicals are introduced into inter-state commerce for significant new uses as a Class I substitute....

### COMMENTARY AND QUESTIONS

1. **The delicate interplay between international treaty-making and domestic legislation.** Throughout this case study, Congress was seen as favoring stricter controls on ozone-depleting substances than the Reagan Administration. International agreements, in and of themselves, are not binding on signatory nations; they must be implemented by domestic legislation (see Chapter 26). The Constitution of the United States places the responsibility for negotiating treaties in the Executive Branch, but requires ratification by a two-thirds vote of the Senate before a treaty can have the full force and effect of domestic law. In this case, the Senate first rat-ified the Montreal Protocol and then Congress passed strengthening legislation, which was subsequently signed by a more sympathetic President, George Bush. One might also imagine a converse situation — like the global warming conven-tions of the late 1990s — where an administration was more favorably inclined toward a particular treaty than the sitting Congress. In that case, the Senate might refuse to ratify an entire treaty, or else might ratify part of it and reject the rest. Congress might then enact weaker legislation to replace the rejected aspects of the treaty, but the President might veto the bill. Implementing treaties adds another level of complexity to our already elaborate system of checks and balances.

2. **EPA's ambivalent position.** EPA found itself caught between the President and Congress. EPA, along with the FDA, had banned the use of CFCs in consumer aerosol products, but it had not otherwise carried out the broad regulatory author-ity over ozone-depleting substances given to it by Congress in the 1977 Clean Air Act Amendments. Most of EPA's efforts in this area had gone into supporting the Executive Branch team attempting to negotiate a Protocol. But, as the scientific evidence supporting the Rowland-Molina thesis mounted, and as Congress and the media began to criticize the Reagan Administration for its timidity regarding ozone-destroying substances, EPA took another tack. At a 1987 congressional hear-ing, Agency officials testified that the benefits of eliminating CFCs and related compounds would clearly outweigh the costs.

3. **Green technologies and technology-forcing.** To some extent, Congress' position was enhanced by Germany's decision, in 1989, to virtually "sunset" all CFCs by 1995. (In 1992, the United States and the remainder of the European Economic Community announced that they would advance their phaseout deadlines to the

end of 1995.) In fact, Germany and Japan have utilized technology-forcing to compel the development of "green technologies" that will both prevent domestic pollution and also satisfy a growing international demand for minimally polluting industrial processes. See Moore, Green Revolution in the Making, Sierra, January/February 1995, 50. A number of American companies, e.g., Robinair and Trane Company, have also increased their profits by exporting substitutes for CFCs. There has been some discussion in the United States about encouraging technological innovation for pollution prevention through a national "Industrial Policy," but no comprehensive legislation has been enacted on this subject.

4. **Supervising the development of substitutes.** Notice that Congress did not leave the development of substitutes entirely to industry. EPA is authorized to certify acceptable substitutes and to prohibit unacceptable ones. Also, industries developing substitutes for banned ozone-depleting substances must notify EPA before introducing substitutes into commerce, and also furnish EPA with health and safety data on the substitutes. These notice and reporting requirements were based on provisions in the Federal Insecticide, Fungicide, and Rodenticide Act and the Toxic Substances Control Act (see Chapter 15).

5. **Federal procurement as an incentive.** The federal government is a major consumer of a variety of products, from automobiles to ashtrays. The Clean Air Act requires federal agencies to revise their procurement regulations to further the policies of Title VI. Another section of the Clear Air Act provides incentives to federal agencies to purchase clean fuel vehicles for their fleets, even if clean fuel vehicles are more expensive than ordinary vehicles (42 U.S.C.A. §7588). The Resource Conservation and Recovery Act (see Chapter 17) requires federal agencies to procure items composed of the highest percentage of recovered materials practicable, or explain why this has not been done (42 U.S.C.A. §6962). With regard to ozone-depleting chemicals, the United States Department of Defense revised its procurement "specs" to first allow, and then require, use of alternatives to CFC-113 cleaning solvents. See Wexler, New Marching Orders, in Cook, Ed., Ozone Protection in the United States (1996).

6. **The judicious use of variances and exemptions.** Note how Congress authorized EPA to grant variances and exemptions to temper the harsh effects of technology-forcing in worthwhile cases, e.g., with regard to essential applications of methyl chloroform where no substitutes are available, and to allow the production of limited quantities of Class I and II substances for use in medical devices and for export to developing countries that are parties to the Montreal Protocol.

Wherever a variance or exemption is authorized, however, it is closely circumscribed as to both the maximum amounts that can be produced for this purpose, as well as the duration of the variance or exemption.

7. **Interpollutant trading and a CFC tax.** The above excerpt describes Title VI's provision for interpollutant trading in order to achieve reductions of ozone-depleting substances in a least-cost manner. In addition, Congress has imposed an excise tax on these substances, graduated according to the destructive potential of the substance (26 U.S.C.A. §4682 et seq.). Pollutant trading and pollution taxes are

discussed in Chapter 16. The operation of the interpollutant trading system has helped U.S. companies to meet Protocol requirements without major economic disruptions and at a lower cost than anticipated. Along with environmental benefits, the excise tax has brought in some $2.9 billion in federal revenue in its first five years.

8. **Industry's reaction to technology-forcing.** At first, the Alliance for Responsible CFC Policy, the industrial trade association representing CFC manufacturers and users, argued strongly against a CFC phaseout. But the Alliance reversed its stand after the "ozone hole" was substantiated, and then actually supported the Montreal Protocol. A Texas Instruments plant in McKinney Texas, which had used CFCs as a solvent to clean lead solder from its circuit boards, achieved compliance with the phaseout by "borrowing" a new soldering process that had been used extensively in Europe, but had not yet been adopted in the United States. Using the phaseout as an opportunity to evaluate and install the new technology, the TI engineers found that the new process would leave the circuit boards clean, thus obviating both CFC use and also the disposal of lead-contaminated hazardous wastes. TI's turning of a technology-forcing mandate into a pollution prevention opportunity was facilitated by a unique industry-government coordinating committed entitled the International Cooperative for Ozone Layer Protection ("ICOLP"). Initiated by EPA, ICOLP's mission was to "promote and coordinate the worldwide exchange of non-proprietary information on alternative technologies, processes, and substances for ozone-depleting solvents." With ICOLP's assistance, other large companies such as Digital Equipment Corporation, The Ford Motor Company, and IBM were able to phase out their use of CFCs at a relatively modest cost. See Hinrichsen, Fixing the Ozone Hole Is a Work In Progress, The Amicus Journal, Fall 1996, 35.

E.I. Du Pont de Nemours and Company (Du Pont) discovered the CFC group of chemicals in 1928, and, under the trade name Freon, was its largest manufacturer. Du Pont earned $600 million in revenues from its Freon business in 1987. At the height of its Freon operations, Du Pont maintained eleven Freon plants, including six in Europe, Japan, and Latin America, and five in the United States. After the 1978 ban on CFC use in consumer aerosols, Du Pont lost one-third of its CFC business and closed several of its Freon manufacturing plants. During the late 1970s, after the publication of Rowland and Molina's findings, Du Pont devoted three to four million dollars per year to attempts to identify substitutes. However, in the first Reagan Administration years (1980–1984), Du Pont's expenditures for research into Freon substitutes fell to virtually nothing. Since the signing of the Montreal Protocol, DuPont has reversed course and invested steadily increasing amounts in this area. For example, in 1988 Du Pont spent more than $30 million on research into potential Freon substitutes. Also during that year, Du Pont announced that it would phase out CFC production by 1997. Much of Du Pont's research has focused on HCFCs, which are less stable than — and only two percent as destructive to the ozone layer as — CFCs. But the above excerpt reveals that the United States has elected to phase out HCFCs by 2030; and in 1995, following the United States' lead, the parties to the Protocol agreed that the developed world would phase out HCFC production by 2020 and the developing world by 2040. There are currently no economically achievable substitutes available for HCFCs, but it is widely believed that Du Pont is feverishly conducting research in order to recapture this potentially massive market. See Buchholz et al., Managing Environmental Issues (1992), 261.

Notice the fundamental difference between the cooperative approach to technology-sharing exemplified by ICOLP, and the proprietary search for patents illustrated by Du Pont. Both strategies must be pursued if the search for alternatives to ozone-depleting substances is to be successful.

9. **Where do we stand?** On the one hand, the widespread phaseout of CFCs has been a major environmental success story, and a triumph of international cooperation for environmental protection. In under a decade, a group of chemicals that is stable, non-flammable, non-toxic, cheap to manufacture, and easy to store; that was an essential component of over $100 billion worth of equipment, including refrigerators, air conditioners in buildings and automobiles, and factories producing products from solvents, to insulation, to medical instruments; and for which no acceptable alternative was readily available, is no longer being used in many nations of the world.[19] On the other hand, the CFC phaseout has been incomplete.

> The biggest challenge of all may lie in the developing world and Russia. Most of th[e] remaining production of CFCs is being used in Russia and the newly independent states of the former Soviet Union — in violation of their treaty obligations. Third World Countries, which account for a smaller share, have another decade to phase out CFCs. And their use is predicted to grow enormously as countries like China continue to develop toward a consumer-oriented industrial economy; expanding in population size all the while. Household appliance companies in both China and India, for instance, are planning to produce millions of refrigerators and freezers using CFCs, as well as HCFCs, over the next few decades....

> The problem in both regions is lack of resources to make the transition. ICOLP, of course, is sharing its technological breakthroughs with developing countries. But despite the multiple advantages and relatively short payback periods of many of these advances, eliminating CFCs requires some hefty upfront investments....

> Many companies in developing countries cannot raise that kind of capital in the span of a few years. In theory, there is a mechanism in place to help them do it.... One of the provisions hammered out during the [Montreal Protocol negotiating sessions] was a special Multilateral Fund, to be paid for by the industrialized world, which would help poorer countries offset the costs of the phaseout.

> To date, the Fund has financed more than 1,000 projects at a total cost of $440 million. These projects, which are already in place and working, will eliminate 30 percent of all ozone depleters used in the Third World by the turn of the century. Much of the investment has been used to finance suitable alternatives to CFCs, especially as coolants, solvents, and degreasers. "In 1995, we approved $205 million worth of projects to phase out 22,000 metric tons of

---

19. According to reliable estimates, global production of CFCs declined from more than one million tons in 1986 to about 250,000 tons in 1995; and production of halons decreased from about 200,000 tons in 1986 to about 40,000 tons in 1995; but production of HCFCs rose sharply during that period. 28 BNA Env. Rptr. Curr. Dev. 837-838 (1997).

these chemicals in Third World countries," says Omar El-Arini, head of the fund. "If we kept that up, we could replace all the chemicals the developing countries are committed to phase out by 2010, if they continue their current rate of consumption."

That last qualification, however, is a big one. It is virtually a given that developing countries will increase their rate of consumption, and that they will need even more help than the framers of the Montreal Protocol originally envisioned. But as the ozone emergency has dropped off the front pages and out of the public's consciousness, the resolve of the signatories has wavered. The multilateral Fund has been receiving about 20 percent less money than was pledged for 1966. Hinrichsen, Fixing the Ozone Hole Is a Work In Progress, The Amicus Journal, Fall 1996, 38.

Assuming that the international phaseout proceeds according to plan, what will be the ultimate effect on the ozone layer?

Because it can take up to a decade for a CFC molecule to reach the stratosphere, the ozone that is being destroyed today is very probably, in part, being destroyed by CFCs put into the atmosphere before the first ozone hole was discovered. As a result, CFC concentrations in the stratosphere are expected to double from 1989 to 2000, and decades will pass before we feel effects of the resultant five to twenty percent increase in u.v. radiation. Another source claims that half of the total amount of CFCs produced since 1930 will be produced from now until the phaseout is complete, and yet another source predicts increasing ozone destruction for some 20 years and a return to pre-ozone layer hole concentrations around 2050.... One of the most worrisome aspects of the ozone-hole problem is that the worst is yet to come.... We simply do not know how much damage we have done (or will do) to ourselves, to other species, and to the natural balance among the forces that control the biosphere. We know that some destruction will happen, indeed is happening, but the effects are presently impossible to calculate. Newton and Dillingham, Watersheds (1994), 155, 165, 167.

And finally, the most commonly utilized substitutes for CFCs — HCFCs — are themselves ozone-destroying substances, as well as "Greenhouse Gases."

10. **Enforcing technology-forcing.** Technology-forcing creates economic opportunities not only for enterprising entrepreneurs, but for unscrupulous criminals as well. Smuggling illegal CFCs into the United States has become a lucrative business because 90 percent of automobiles in the U.S. have air-conditioning, compared to about 10 percent in Europe. Since the late 1980s, new automobiles have utilized an HCFC substitute for CFCs in their air-conditioning systems, but over 50 million older automobile air-conditioning systems still rely on CFCs, which are becoming scarce and thus expensive. Also, there is a network of small users, such as garages, among which controls on ozone depleting substances are difficult to promote, monitor and enforce. In addition, the U.S. excise tax on CFCs has created an incentive for tax avoidance. It has been widely reported that contraband CFCs are the second largest smuggling problem — next to drugs — for U.S. customs agents along the Mexican border.[20]

---

20. On August 29, 1997, a Florida company was fined $37 million by a federal court for smuggling 4,000 tons of CFCs into the United States. Jail sentences were also imposed on three company officials. 28 BNA Env. Rptr. Curr. Dev. 839 (1997). At the Ninth Meeting of the Parties to the Montreal Protocol, the Parties agreed on a new international licensing system to track trade in CFCs.

11. **Other technology-forcing issues.** Governmental decision-makers are seriously considering proposals to "sunset" the use of chlorine in paper mills in order to eliminate discharges of dioxin, and to ban discharges of persistent toxic pollutants, such as mercury, in the Great Lakes Watershed. Which factors are critical to instigating these decisions? How should these decisions be made (e.g., through Congressional action, regulation, or alternative dispute resolution)? Which devices can be utilized to tailor bans to the legitimate needs of industry and the general public? The Minnesota experience provides some instructive answers. In 1991, the Minnesota legislature enacted a statute prohibiting the sale or use, after 1998, of inks, pigments, paints, or fungicides, containing certain heavy metals at concentrations over 100 parts per million, without regard to economic consequences. After complaints by Minnesota industries that were unable to find substitutes for the banned materials, the blanket toxics ban was repealed, and replaced by a toxics advisory council that will examine products containing toxic substances and, after consideration of available substitutes and the economic and environmental impacts of potential chemical bans, make nonbinding recommendations to the Minnesota Pollution Control Agency. See 28 BNA Env. Rptr. Curr. Dev. 387 (1997). Has this statutory amendment established a reasonable process for analyzing the feasibility of chemical bans, or, on the other hand, has it gone from the draconic to the symbolically assuring?

12. **Technology-forcing reconsidered.** Technology-forcing can be a viable mechanism for coping with environmental threats if some or all of the following are features of the problem context or regulatory strategy:

- A substantial, and comparatively clear, environmental threat, and especially a direct threat to public health.
- A credible "hammer" limiting the use of, or banning, a dangerous substance.
- Substitutes that are at least theoretically recognized, and also comparable with regard to costs.
- Variance and exemption procedures that are flexible, fair, limited, predictable, and enforceable.
- Effective market-enlisting mechanisms, such as tax incentives or disincentives, trading systems, preferential governmental purchasing, and opportunities for private industry.
- Clear standards without opt-out possibilities, such as the California preemption waiver.
- Supervision of the introduction of substitutes, in order to avoid adverse unintended consequences.
- Adequate enforcement at all stages of the process.
- Agreement between the Executive and Legislative branches with regard to the need for, and the structure of, the technology-forcing system finally adopted.
- Adequate lead time for compliance.

- On the international level, differential standards for developed and developing nations, technology-sharing and funding assistance by developed nations for the benefit of developing nations, and effective trade restrictions to track and prevent smuggling.

*When you come to a fork in the road, take it.*

— Yogi Berra

# Chapter 11

# PROCESS-DRIVEN
# STANDARD-SETTING

A. *The Process Element in Standard-Setting*

B. *Vague Delegations to an Implicit Interest-Representation Process*

C. *Agency Standard-Setting Shaped by Procedures or Stakeholder Negotiation Processes*

D. *Incorporations of External, Nongovernmental Standard-Setting Processes*

## A. THE PROCESS ELEMENT IN STANDARD-SETTING

The environmental statutes studied up to this point rely primarily on standard-setting based on empirically-defined criteria: "available technology," "harm to human health," or legislatively-dictated regulatory requirements (stipulated numerical standards, rollbacks, phase-outs, and the like) that force technological improvement. To a considerable extent these are "derived standards," where the legislative intent and the parameters by which the standards are to be set are sufficiently clear that the process of generating standards leads, through a series of administrative steps, toward a predictable result (a result, moreover, that can be challenged and reviewed in citizen litigation).

This chapter explores a different type of standard-setting element: in practice, under the delegation of power in many other statutes, the principal formative element in agency standard-setting, explicitly or implicitly, is the *process* by which the standard is generated rather than a specific legislated norm. Standards of this latter sort can be described by the phrase "process-driven standards."

What is a process-driven standard? An almost-pure example (drawn from the field of labor law because there is no equally pure environmental example), is provided by the national labor relations statutes. Under those statutes, the operative standards of labor-management relations in the U.S. are established in procedural controls and a process of collective bargaining between the parties, sometimes on an industry-wide basis, with the potential or actual participation of federal mediators. Apart from minimal objective regulatory requirements — the federal minimum wage and worker safety rules under OSHA — the statutes merely set procedural standards: that the substantive contract terms for labor be worked out in a process of good faith bargaining, without "unfair labor practices." Congress set out no civic norm that labor contracts must live up to, and even though the public is very significantly affected by particular outcomes, civic interests are unrepresented in the labor regulatory process. This standard-setting by procedure has nevertheless established an accepted national framework for setting terms and conditions of labor.

There are two different categories of environmental process-driven standard-setting. Under the first approach — represented in this chapter by the midcentury state water pollution commissions and current federal forestry regulations — agencies are given broad and undefined discretion. The statutory delegation often amounts to little more than an invitation to turn standard-setting over to a protracted administrative process with extensive opportunities for numerous affected parties to participate and influence the eventual outcome according to their political power. The only statutory directives given are vague directions to regulate "in the public interest," or the like.

The second process-driven approach involves delegations with similarly vague legislative directives, but where the legislature chooses to remit the making of standards to a process that relies upon specific procedures and/ or particularly constituted entities. (Resembling the labor law model, this category includes, as noted below, historical landmark commissions, the Department of Interior's reliance on the use of rangeland advisory councils, and negotiated rulemaking). By selecting participants according to civic criteria or to achieve comprehensive stakeholder representation, a legislature can steer regulatory standardmaking beyond the daily pressures of the marketplace.

There is not, in the real world, a sharp divide between derived and process-driven standards. Although the major modern pollution regulation statutes' derived standards do represent empirically-definable criteria, they also inevitably come to include process pressures in their standard-setting. Analyzed in terms of Chapter One's three economies, environmental statutes are created to protect the interests of the civic, societal economy from marketplace failures to account for externalized social costs. Harm-based, technology-based, and tech-forcing environmental standards, like other regulatory approaches, attempt to operate for the public good beyond the dictates of the marketplace economy. But extremely tangible market pressures persistently intrude upon the process of virtually all regulatory standard-setting. As a result, few regulatory standards are ever simply determined by objective facts. Marketplace pressures find their way into the administrative processes in which the standards are set. Even legislation that leaves the implementing agency with minimal discretion in the standard setting realm, is still subject to some process-driven effects as the agency does its work.

Process-driven elements in standard-setting can serve useful adaptive ends if appropriately implemented, and on the other hand can be extremely problematic, undercutting public policies and values if the process is narrowed or diverted from civic goals. The process-driven environmental settings noted later in this chapter vary according to a series of different dimensions:

**Specificity of statutory standard.** Statutes vary according to the specificity and objective or empirical criteria that are the guides to administrative standard-setting. Some laws offer little or no substantive guidance, as in the labor setting, delegating broadly to "protect the public interest." In contrast, some laws have very limited process elements, setting detailed numerical standards, as in

CAA's Title II 90% rollback of tailpipe emissions for CAA exhaust standards (in Chapter 10). The more specific a statutory standard, the less likely will be process-driven variability (and the more likely it will be that citizens can enforce it if agencies do not).

**Degree of process formality.** Process-driven elements of standard-setting vary in terms of formality and informality. The labor-management negotiation forum, or the environmental standard-setting by rangeland councils or historic preservation commissions noted below, are formalized processes. The realities of modern daily bureaucratic life, however, guarantee that an intensive volume of informal process pressures, e.g. a parade of lobbying inputs, will be brought to bear on even such "objective" determinations as that 90% rollback measurement of each particular car model's exhaust by the EPA mobile source lab. The process of political balancing is consistently a component of regulatory standard-setting.

**Who gets to play?** The character of process-driven standard-setting also depends on who gets to play a meaningful part in the process. The legislature's prescription for the composition of a commission is a way to shape the process and the resulting standards. A commission of experts who are focused on the agency's mission mandate will operate quite differently from a panel dominated by regulated industry representatives. With or without a commission, moreover, agency standard-setting is exposed to an ongoing process of lobbying inputs and persuasions, and depending upon which interest representatives are allowed into the process and listened to, process outcomes will differ dramatically.

**Transparency.** The transparency of a standard-setting process affects its character. Where the decision will be made in an open forum on an open record, in straightforward evaluation of facts and principles, with media scrutiny and without backroom deals, the process is likely to show greater integrity and less propensity toward hidden agendas and skewed results. One of the notable attributes of ADR techniques like mediation and "reg-neg" negotiated rule-making[1] is that they bring the merits of a matter out on the table, in a process which by its nature encourages discussion in terms of the civic standards to be served. When process takes place between insiders behind closed doors, agency decisionmakers are far less likely to be guided by their putative public interest mandate.

**Operative norms.** The norms that in practice guide decisional processes are not always the civic standards for which a regulatory statute was created. In the 1980s, for instance, decisions on occupational environmental exposures under OSHA were being made by agency executives who announced that they believed OSHA unnecessary, and hoped to disband the agency. Rangeland grazing and forest timber cutting decisions were being made by officials who considered economic returns to industry predominant over the statutory norm of sustainability. The degree to which civic norms characterize the decisionmakers' approach to standard-setting varies. Regulators may be guided in everything they do by the statute's civic goals. On the other hand they may sometimes, or consistently, be driven by the values, pressures, and blandishments of regulated interests in the political and economic marketplace economy. Whichever operative normative context prevails obviously will determine what kind of regulatory criteria will be produced in the process.

**Methodological assumptions.** Environmental regulatory standard-setting is inevitably preceded by risk-assessment and benefit-cost analysis. Agency risk-

---

1. See Chapter 21.

assessment processes contain policy-driven assumptions to guide regulators in deciding whether to regulate or not, and if regulation is chosen, how strict it should be. For example, substantive regulatory actions, aimed at minimizing excess cancer cases, will vary dramatically depending on whether a "one shot" exposure or "threshold" exposure model of cancer causation is adopted. See Chapter Two's discussions of risk-assessment and benefit-cost analysis.

**Complexity.** The complexity of a matter likewise shapes the process of standard-setting, and makes process investigation, balancing, negotiation, and fine-tuning necessary. When subject matter is complex — as with toxics and pollution regulation, community disruptions, global effects, and the like — the process of inputting data into agency decisions, and institutional dynamics generally, become more prone to variable pressures. Especially where data is sparse, agencies may be hesitant in asserting their mandate. Process can become a ponderous, politically entangled regulatory mechanism instead of a problem-solving procedural design.

Elements of process-driven standard-setting are inevitable in environmental regulatory practice, and can present both advantages and disadvantages in crafting appropriate civic regulations for protecting environmental quality. Given the difficulties of objective legislative prescriptions, process elements are often a necessary coping strategy for complex regulatory line-drawing, in spite of the potential for equivocations.

## B. PROCESS ELEMENTS WHEN AGENCIES ARE DELEGATED UNBRIDLED DISCRETION

### Section 1. The Midcentury Michigan State Water Resources Commission

The old state pollution control commissions noted earlier are a particularly uninspiring example of process-driven standard-setting, showing what can happen with legislative delegations of pollution regulatory power to politically-constituted committees without meaningful statutory criteria for how standards are to be set.

In the Michigan Water Resources Commission statute studied in Chapter Five, for example, the commission had been set up as a "mini-legislature" of establishment interests — one member from industry, one representing municipalities (which in volume discharge the majority of water pollution in the state), four members representing government agencies (including the departments of agriculture and highways, public health and natural resources), and one representative of the public drawn from "conservation associations" (in the early 1970s this person was a chemist employed by the Dow Chemical Company who was the head of the state rod-and-gun club). Note further how broad and vague the legislative delegation to the WRC was:

> The commission shall establish such pollution standards...as it shall deem necessary...to prevent any pollution which is deemed to be unreasonable and against public interest.... MCLA §323.5

This delegation has two notable process-focused characteristics: the limited spectrum of represented interests comprising the standard-setting body (in this case dominated by players in the political marketplace), and the permissive vagueness of the legislative directive. Whenever a statute delegates great latitude to an agency in deciding whether and how to set standards, not to mention unfettered discretion in enforcement,[2] it is an invitation to draw regulatory lines according to the particular interests of whichever of the commission's various members constitute a majority. Such delegations too easily can end up as political football games serving the interests of insiders, representing no coherent civic norm of environmental quality, and providing no objective statutory terms as a foundation for citizens to seek judicial scrutiny of the standards that emerge from the process. This amorphousness, in such a subjective multifactored regulatory definition process, has allowed many state and federal agencies to mold standards according to the short term pressures of market forces.

### Section 2. Forestry Standards under the National Forest Management Act

Given the dynamics of the political marketplace, regulatory statutes that do not set up standard-setting commissions representing marketplace interests likewise experience the intrusion of active interest-representation into the process.

During the late 1960s, a bitter controversy arose over clearcutting in the national forests. See generally, Wilkinson, Crossing The Next Meridian (1992). The Izaac Walton League, a conservation group active in anti-clearcutting campaigns, was particularly opposed to the extensive clearcutting in West Virginia's Monongahela National Forest. In 1974, the League brought a lawsuit to enjoin clearcutting in the Monongahela on the grounds that clearcutting violated provisions of the 1897 Forest Service Organic Act that authorized the Forest Service (USFS) to sell only "dead, matured, or large growth of trees" that had been "marked and designated" before sale. These restrictions had indeed been intended to prevent the large timber companies, early in the twentieth century, from practicing "cut and run" forestry in the national forests. Ignoring the Organic Act's legislative history, the Forest Service argued that "mature" meant economic — not physical — maturity, and that it was unnecessary to mark and designate individual trees as long as entire stands were identified for cutting.

In West Virginia Div. of Izaak Walton League of America, Inc. v. Butz, 522 F.2d 945 (4th Cir. 1975), the court rejected the Forest Service's arguments and granted the injunction. At the end of its opinion, the court made the following observations

> It is apparent that the heart of this controversy is the change in the role of the Forest Service which has taken place over the past thirty years. For nearly half a century following its creation in 1905, the National Forest System provided

---

2. This state delegation of standard-setting power is no broader than those in many federal agencies' organic statutes, where the agency is merely directed to write its regulations "in the public interest." See e.g. the Federal Trade Commission's Organic Act, which authorized the FTC to issue rules, orders, and judicial complaints against "unfair methods of competition," the Interstate Commerce Commission which was to regulate carriers "in the public interest," the Federal Communications Commission which was directed to issue radio station licenses "as the public convenience, interest, or necessity requires." Despite continuing calls for stricter terms of regulatory delegations, in many cases no doubt such broad discretion will continue to be deemed an expedient legislative necessity.

Even with highly·specific standards, of course, agency lassitude in enforcement can undercut the entire program, as seen in Chapter One's Virginia case studies.

only a fraction of the national timber supply with almost ninety-five per cent coming from privately owned forests. During this period the Forest Service regarded itself as a custodian and protector of the forests rather than a prime producer, and consistent with this role the Service faithfully carried out the provisions of the Organic Act with respect to selective timber cutting. In 1940, however, with private timber reserves badly depleted, World War II created an enormous demand for lumber and this was followed by the post-war building boom. As a result the posture of the Forest Service quickly changed from custodian to a production agency. It was in this new role that the Service initiated the policy of even-aged management [i.e. clearcutting] in the national forests, first in the West and ultimately in the Eastern forests. The [USFS and timber industry] appellants urge that this change of policy was in the public interest and that the courts should not permit a literal reading of the 1897 Act to frustrate the modern science of silviculture and forest management presently practiced by the Forest Service to meet the nation's current timber demands. Economic exigencies, however, do not grant the courts a license to rewrite a statute no matter how desirable the purpose or result might be.... 522 F.2d, at pages 954–955 [injunction issued].

Western courts followed the Fourth Circuit's precedent, and clearcutting in the national forests came to a grinding halt. Congress was in an unenviable bind. The construction industry, financial community, and potential homebuyers were demanding a resumption of wood supplies from the national forests, subject only to the silvicultural judgment of local Forest Rangers, and quick amendment of the Organic Act to legalize clearcutting. Conservationists viewed clearcutting as anathema, and the public, influenced by the burgeoning environmental movement, generally shared that view. In the context of this intractable political issue, Congress enacted the National Forest Management Act of 1976 (NFMA), 16 U.S.C.A. §1600 et seq. Ostensibly, NFMA dealt with the major subissues embedded in the clearcutting controversy by setting standards for: (1) maintenance of biodiversity; (2) reforestation of cutover areas; (3) pesticide use in the National Forests; (4) limitations on timber harvesting, in general, and clearcutting in particular; (5) cutting on frail lands; (6) maturity of timber stands; (7) the definition of "sustained yield"; and (8) below-cost timber sales. The following excerpts from NFMA exemplify the nebulous standard-setting strategy that Congress adopted in order to escape from its political trap:

> §1601(d)(1) It is the policy of Congress that all forested lands in the National Forest System shall be maintained in appropriate forest cover with species of trees, degree of stocking, rate of growth, and conditions of stand designed to secure the maximum benefits of multiple use sustained yield management in accordance with land management plans....

> (e) The Secretary shall submit an annual report to the Congress on the amounts, types, and uses of herbicides and pesticides used in the National Forest System, including the beneficial or adverse effects of such uses....

> §1604(g) [The Secretary shall promulgate regulations] that set out the process for the development and revision of the land management plans, and the guidelines and standards [for that planning process]. The regulations shall include, but not be limited to...specifying guidelines which...

(3)(B) provide for diversity of plant and animal communities based on the suitability and capability of the specific land area in order to meet overall multiple-use objectives, and within the multiple-use objectives of a land management plan adopted pursuant to this section, provide, where appropriate, to the degree practicable, for steps to be taken to preserve the diversity of tree species similar to that existing in the region controlled by the plan:

(F) insure that [cutting methods] designed to regenerate an even-aged stand of timber will be used as a cutting method on National Forest lands only where —

(i) for clearcutting, it is determined to be the optimum method...

(iii) cut blocks, patches, or strips are shaped and blended to the extent practicable with the natural terrain;

(iv) there are established according to geographic areas, forest types, or other suitable classifications the maximum size limits for areas to be cut in one harvest operation, including provision to exceed the established limits after appropriate public notice and review by the responsible Forest Service officer....

In these NFMA provisions, Congress set facially attractive, but essentially meaningless, standards. The effect of NFMA was to create a process in which the Forest Service, widely regarded as captured by the forest products industry, had a free hand. This broad discretion in effect invited process-based weakening of the statute's conservation principles. It produced (1) rampant ambiguity (e.g., "appropriate forest cover"); (2) procrastination of decision making until the Land and Resource Management Planning process; (3) ubiquitous and stacked exceptions and variances (e.g., "where appropriate, to the degree practicable, for steps to be taken," etc.); (4) "paralysis by analysis" (e.g., the pesticide study); and (5) taking refuge in dubious mechanisms such as salvage sales.

The portentous but essentially empty provisions of NFMA symbolically assured the general public that home construction would continue with safeguards that would adequately protect the national forests. The conservationists were symbolically assured that Congress had finally recognized the problem and established a viable framework for "multiple-use, sustained-yield" forest management. Meanwhile, the clearcutting, road construction, and environmental damage continued unabated in the national forests. Twenty years later, these problems are still unresolved. The "multiple-use, sustained-yield" NFMA statutory standard has been widely criticized as an unenforceable "succotash syndrome." (See Chapters Seven, 14, and 24 on national forest clearcutting controversies.)

Some active negotiation and interest-representation in the standard-setting process is clearly necessary and useful. To the extent that a process permits a dominant role for marketplace players, however, and underrepresents the interests of nonconsumptive users and the civic, societal interests of the public at large, the tendency to shift toward subjective process balances can tend to undercut long term environmental protections.

## C. AGENCY STANDARD-SETTING SHAPED BY PROCEDURES OR STAKEHOLDER NEGOTIATION PROCESSES

### Section 1. The New York City Landmarks Preservation Commission

Explicit delegations of process-driven standard-setting continue to occur in modern environmental practice. An interesting example, in which agency discretion is guided by procedures, as well as the selected composition of the decisional body, arises in the field of historic preservation. The New York City Landmarks Law creates an eleven-member Landmarks Preservation Commission with the authority to designate landmarks and historic districts. Its membership is chosen by the mayor for three year terms with limited statutory direction — it must comprise at least three architects, one historian, one city planner or landscape architect, and one realtor — and in practice has generally represented a composition that is inclined toward the civic goal of historic preservation. The law defines the term "landmark" to include structures at least thirty years old that have "a special character or special historical or aesthetic interest or value" to the city. This statutory directive, needless to say, is not an objective empirical standard. The standard of what constitutes "special historical or aesthetic interest" is formulated entirely within the commission's deliberative decisional process, and applied case by case. Once a landmark is designated, it becomes unlawful for any person to "alter, reconstruct or demolish" the landmark unless the Commission issues either a certificate of no effect on protected architectural features, a certificate of appropriateness, or a notice to proceed....

A look inside the landmarking process was provided in Shubert Organization, Inc. v. Landmarks Preservation Commission, 570 NYS2d 504 (App. Div. 1991). Following the highly publicized and lamented demolition of two theaters in the Times Square area, the Commission "calendared public hearings to consider the designation of forty-five Broadway theaters." The hearings were scheduled "to allow preparation of reports on the historical, cultural, and architectural significance of the individual theatres"; the concerned property owners "received individual notice and offered testimony" and were also permitted to submit "additional comments and [their own architectural] report, analyzing the listed theatres."... The Commission had received a large amount of material from various sources regarding the unique qualities of each subject theatre. The Commission received staff reports describing each theater's cultural, historical, architectural, and aesthetic importance. In turn, the Commission prepared a detailed designation report for each. The Commission also addressed each proposed designation in public sessions that the theatre owners attended....

The appellate division agreed with the trial court that "the administrative determination was based on substantial evidence, was not arbitrary and capricious and did not violate the law." The court noted that given "the wealth of analyses and reports, as well as anecdotal testimony provided...prior to the subject designations," it was "beyond serious challenge that a reasonable basis existed for the designations as to each theatre, upon a consideration of the statutory criteria [viz. 'special character,...interest or value']." The owners were also afforded a fair opportunity to present their case. Because the court "was not empowered to substitute its own judgment for that of the administrative body," the question "was whether the record...supported the voting procedure and the determination." It did. Nivala, Saving the Spirit of Our Places: A View on Our Built Environment, 15 UCLA J. Envtl. L. & Policy at 47 (1996).

The historic landmark designation process indicates how an agency's statutory and self-imposed procedures, if they are appropriately detailed, transparent, and give regulated parties sufficient process, can be effective and survive judicial scrutiny, though the agency is given virtually no substantive statutory guidance on where to draw its lines.

### Section 2. Federal rangeland resource advisory councils (RACs)

Another interesting example comes from the Department of Interior's management of federal grazing lands in western states. Interior has used the Federal Land Policy and Management Act (FLPMA), 43 U.S.C.A. §1739, to accelerate the creation of Resource Advisory Councils (RACs) that guide Interior's Bureau of Land Management (BLM), on land planning and management issues.

The councils are to be composed not only of ranchers, but also of environmentalists and representatives of other stakeholder groups interested in the public lands, and resemble the "Reg-Neg" negotiated rulemaking models encouraged under the federal Negotiated Rulemaking Act, 5 U.S.C.A. §§561-70 App. A (1990) (See Chapter 21).

> §1739(a) The Secretary shall establish advisory councils of not less than ten and not more than fifteen members appointed by him from among persons who are representative of the various major citizens' interests concerning the problems relating to land use planning or the management of the public lands located within the area for which an advisory council is established....
>
> (d) An advisory council may furnish advice to the Secretary with respect to the land use planning, classification, retention, management, and disposal of the public lands within the area for which the advisory council is established and such other matters as may be referred to it by the Secretary.
>
> (e) In exercising his authorities under this Act, the Secretary, by regulation, shall establish procedures, including public hearings where appropriate, to give the Federal, State, and local governments and the public...opportunity...to participate in the preparation and execution of plans and programs for, and the management of, the public lands.

The regulations which authorized RACs became effective on August 21, 1995. Under the new rules, RACs, appointed by the Secretary of the Interior and the state Governor, comprise:

> • five members representing commercial uses or users such as livestock grazing, timber production, mining, oil and gas, realty/rights-of-ways, off-highway vehicle groups and commercial recreation such as guides and outfitters,
>
> • five members representing environmental organizations, historic/cultural interests, wildlife and other conservation organizations, wild horse and burro interests and dispersed/general recreation users, and
>
> • five members representing elected officials, state or other governmental agencies, tribes, academic institutions, and the public-at-large.

RACs can and do provide advice and recommendations to BLM on the entire spectrum of resources and uses on the public lands, guided by no particular statutory standard. RACs can choose to set up two kinds of further process negotiation committees, "technical review teams" and five-person "rangeland resource teams" comprising two resident permittees, a community representative, a environmental representative, and a wildlife/recreation representative. The RACs and their subcommittees operate on the principle of collaborative decision making and strive for consensus before making official recommendations to BLM. Formal recommendations to the BLM must have agreement from a majority of members in each interest category. The council can request review by the Secretary of the Interior if BLM does not abide by RAC recommendations.

Note that this is an advisory process. RACs do not promulgate mandatory federal standards. In practice, however, the decisions of the RACs — deciding allotments, range sectors to be opened and closed to grazing, and setting grazing levels — are typically adopted and enforced by the Department as federal law.

Here following are summaries of some of the process-driven rangeland standards, substantially shortened, that have resulted from the RAC process; (for more on public lands grazing issues see Chapter 24).

**Standards for Public Land Health** [drafted by RACs in Colorado, 1997, published by BLM]

**Standard 1:** Upland soils will exhibit infiltration and permeability rates that are appropriate to soil type, climate, land form, and geologic processes....
*Indicators:* Evidence of actively-eroding gullies is minimal.... Diversity of plant species....

**Standard 2:** Riparian systems associated with both running and standing water will function properly and have the ability to recover from major disturbance such as fire, severe grazing, or 100-year floods....
*Indicators:* Streambank vegetation is present and is comprised of species and communities that have root systems capable of withstanding high streamflow events....

**Standard 3:** Healthy, productive plant and animal communities of native and other desirable species will be maintained at viable population levels....
*Indicators:* Noxious weeds and undesirable species are minimal....

**Standard 4:** Special status, threatened and endangered species (federal and state), and other plants and animals officially designated by the BLM, and their habitats will be maintained or enhanced....
*Indicators:* Stable and increasing populations of endemic and protected species in suitable habitat....

**Standard 5:** The water quality of all water bodies, including ground water...will achieve or exceed the Water Quality Standards....
*Indicators:* Appropriate populations of macroinvertebrates, vertebrates, and algae are present....

Pursuant to these Standards, the RAC and Interior have also promulgated Guidelines to shape the definition of "best management practices" to be applied to achieve these standards, most notably an elaborate set of performance standards as Guidelines for Livestock Grazing Management. These standards are applied by members of the RACs in proposing particular allotments, grazing levels, and range closings.

Are the standards produced by this process an improvement on the prior agency-industry collaboration? Johanna Wald, an attorney with the Natural Resources Defense Council, fears that the advisory groups will still be dominated by ranchers and their backers. BLM's erosive stewardship of public lands in past years has been attributed to its vague legislative mandate and its operational closeness to the grazing, mining, and timber industries. Judged by the substance and tone of some of the RAC rangeland standards, however, the RAC process results to date seem promising. Similar stakeholder processes have been instituted for parties involved with river corridors, under the statutory terms of §10 of the Wild and Scenic Rivers Act, 16 U.S.C.A. §1282, and for "reasonable use" conferences for determining water allocations under the authority of California's Water Code §179.6.

## D. INCORPORATIONS OF EXTERNAL, NONGOVERNMENTAL STANDARD-SETTING PROCESSES

It should also be noted that some police power regulations are authorized to incorporate guidelines created completely outside the realm of government. Some state statutes, for instance, set consumer health or safety standards based on codes or standards defined by private associations — by the Underwriters Laboratory (UL standards), American Society for Testing Materials (ASTM standards), the restaurant industry's National Sanitary Institute (NSI standards), the Society of Automotive Engineers (SAE standards), Int'l Standards Organization (ISO 14000 standards) and the like. Courts have generally held that such incorporations are not a violation of delegation doctrines unless they are arbitrary or seriously biased.[3]

### COMMENTARY AND QUESTIONS

1. **Process-driven standards as an inevitable regulatory element, for better or worse.** Given that legislatures are rarely able to draft statutes that do not require subtle interpretation and implementation, some administrative process involving multi-factor interest representations inevitably intrudes into the standard-setting process. The broader and more ambiguous the standard, the more important it becomes that the participants in the process meaningfully reflect the civic interests that the statute was intended to protect, as well as the entities that were to be regulated.

---

3. An early delegation of regulatory standard-setting under the National Industrial Recovery Act to code-drafting committees made up of representatives of industries to be regulated was struck down by the Supreme Court in Schechter Poultry Corp. v. U.S., 295 U.S. 495 (1935), but since the Court's subsequent "switch in time that saved nine" supporting New Deal legislation, such delegations are upheld so long as they reflect general indicia of fairness, including self-imposed procedural due process.

Considering the list of variables noted at the outset of this chapter, note how the differing structure of each example of process-driven standard-setting set out in the chapter produces differing practical expectations for its regulatory results. Note also how a specific regulatory context — like the landmarks commission — operates differently according to the particular and variable compositions of the decisional body.

2. **Citizen enforcement as a variable.** Citizen enforcement has been critically important to the development and implementation of environmental regulation, as has been noted regularly since the *Smithfield* cases in Chapter One. When statutory standard-setting criteria are substantively specific, citizens are able to enforce them through litigation. To the extent that standard-setting is process-driven, however, there may not be sufficient statutory specificity for meaningful judicial review. If citizens are sufficiently included within standard-setting processes, on the other hand, and process decisions require consensus or something close to it, then the pluralistic advantages of citizen participation can be retained.

The process element in regulatory standard-setting — an element that is flexibly adaptive to variable contexts but vulnerable to undue influence from the regulated forces it was intended to constrain — offers yet another illustration of how environmental law continually presents basic theoretical questions about the details of democratic governance in a modern industrial economy.

*Nobody made a greater mistake than he who did nothing because he could only do a little.*

— Edmund Burke

# PART FOUR

# CHOICES OF STATUTORY DESIGN

The preceding four chapters have compared a variety of ways in which the standards incorporated into several of the major environmental statutes are set. Statutory "design," the way in which the parts of a statute are structured and work together to accomplish the legislative goals, is often intimately linked to the way standards are set. The linkage is illustrated by the different designs required to implement technology-based performance standards and harm-based ambient standards.

What the preceding chapters did not emphasize is the fact that there is often room for choice among statutory designs in environmental protection and improvement of environmental quality. For example, as studied in Chapter 16, well-designed market mechanisms can under appropriate conditions provide a substitute for Technology-Based Effluent Limitations or an alternative to the plant-specific emissions permits created by the State Implementation Plan process in a harm-based regime, without compromising environmental quality.

Not all forms of environmental regulation rely heavily on standards of performance like standards in the Clean Air and Clean Water Acts. Instead, some statutes utilize a wholly different apparatus, where the regulatory design is chosen for its own special properties — like the mandatory disclosure statutes NEPA, EPCRA, and others in the next chapter — and the application of regulatory standards is secondary.

The following chapters stress the different choices available for the design of regulatory systems. There is a wide range of design categories — disclosure statutes, prohibition of specific acts beyond pollution, regulation of products and product market access, using market forces to control pollution, regulating on a life-cycle basis, or imposing remedial liability to obtain cleanups of contamination and deter future releases.

*In the seconds it takes you to read this sentence, 24 people will be added to the Earth's population.*

*In six minutes, 1100. Within an hour, 11,000. By day's end 260,000.*

*Before you go to bed two nights from now, the net growth in human numbers will be enough to fill a city the size of San Francisco.*

*It took four million years for humanity to reach the two-billion mark. Only 30 years to add a third billion. And now we're increasing by 95 million every single year.*

*No wonder they call it the human race.*

— Zero Population Growth, 1995

# Chapter 12

# COMMAND-AND-CONTROL, AND THE ARRAY OF ALTERNATIVES

A. *Regulatory Shortcomings at the Legislative Level*
B. *Regulatory Shortcomings at the Implementation Level*

Ultimately what counts most about regulatory efforts can be boiled down to a few essentials:

- Does the statute work and, if not, what can be done to correct its flaws?
- Are the statute's economic and lifestyle burdens tolerable?
- Are there better ways to accomplish the same result?

"Command-and-control" regulatory systems for decades have been the classic default design for governmental regulation of environmental quality (and many other civic concerns). Command-and-control systems are generally programs of centralized regulatory commands issued in excruciating detail via permits to pollution dischargers throughout a jurisdiction in order to implement environmental goals. Clean Air and Clean Water Act permits issued by state agencies and EPA are archetypical command-and-control mechanisms, defining pollution standards in general and in very specific terms, and seeing that they are applied discharge by discharge.

But command-and-control systems can be expensive, rigid, and wasteful, so accordingly there has been a longrunning debate over whether the command-and-control regulatory paradigm should be abandoned in favor of nonregulation, self-regulation, or alternative methods of applying public values and needs. There has been enough experience in the years since 1970, when forceful environmental regulation exploded onto the scene, to begin to address these questions.

## A. REGULATORY SHORTCOMINGS AT THE LEGISLATIVE LEVEL

While it is not always easy to agree on what constitutes regulatory success, failures are usually self-evident. Statutes may fail to work for a number of reasons. The material that follows focuses primarily on the failure of Congress's promise to protect the public from toxic air emissions by putting health before questions of cost and feasibility. Toxic pollutants place heavy pressures on environmental policy-makers, presenting the question of "what works, and what doesn't?" and simultaneously underscoring the costs of failure.

## John P. Dwyer, The Pathology of Symbolic Legislation
### 17 Ecology Law Quarterly 233 (1990)

Most regulatory statutes instruct agencies to balance competing concerns in setting standards. Some regulatory statutes, however, impose short deadlines and stringent standard-setting criteria that are designed to address a single, overriding concern to the exclusion of other factors. Typically addressed to exotic and particularly dreaded health threats, this type of legislation reflects the public's urgent desire to avoid such risks. Well known examples include the Delaney Clause in the Food, Drug and Cosmetic Act (food additives, color additives, and animal drug residues), the original §307 of the Clean Water Act (toxic pollutants), and §112 of the Clean Air Act (hazardous air pollutants).

The programs mandated by such legislation are more symbolic than functional. Frequently, the legislature has failed to address the administrative and political constraints that will block implementation of the statute. By enacting this type of statute, legislators reap the political benefits of voting for "health and the environment" and against "trading lives for dollars," and successfully sidestep the difficult policy choices that must be made in regulating public health and the environment. Thus, while the statute, literally read, promises a risk-free environment, the hard issues involved in defining acceptable risk are passed on to the regulatory agency or to the courts. The actual regulatory program takes shape only after additional legislative, administrative, or judicial developments that transform symbolic guarantees into enforceable standards.

The enactment of symbolic legislation reflects a breakdown of the legislative policymaking machinery, a system that all too frequently addresses real social problems in an unrealistic fashion. It also creates a dilemma for regulators and judges. While they generally are reluctant to usurp the legislature's policymaking prerogatives by substituting their own version of appropriate public policy, they also are loath to implement and enforce a statute whose costs are grossly disproportionate to its benefits. The critical issue, then, is whether and how the agency or court should take the initiative to transform symbolic legislation into a functional regulatory program.

Believing that it would be irresponsible and politically mad to interpret and implement symbolic statutory provisions literally, the agency's usual response is to resist implementation. Although an agency may experiment with interpretations that moderate the stringent statutory standard-setting criteria, it will implement its reformulation slowly in order to delay judicial review. As a result, the agency adopts very few standards.[1]

The most significant problem with symbolic legislation, however, is not delay; it is the resulting distortions in the regulatory process. Symbolic legislation hobbles the regulatory process by polarizing public discussion in agency proceedings and legislative hearings. Environmental groups take the legislation's promise of a

---

1. Even if the agency were to adopt the stringent standards required by the symbolic legislation, it would not vigorously enforce such standards. Polluters, as well as the legislature, the agency, and many public interest groups, understand that the commands in such statutes are "aspirational" and thus are "accompanied by a number of unstated, but very real and necessary qualifications — e.g., without unnecessary or unreasonable dislocation costs." Henderson & Pearson, Implementing Federal Environmental Policies: The Limits of Aspirational Commands, 78 Colum. L. Rev. 1429, 1451 (1978). Although supporters may argue that the statutory criteria are morally required or are necessary to "force" the development of technology, such standards are ultimately viewed by all as requiring the industrial firms' "best efforts."

risk-free environment at face value and tend to refuse to compromise the "rights" inherent in such promises. Industry fears that regulators will implement the statute literally and, consequently, vigorously opposes the regulatory process at every stage. By making promises that cannot be kept, and by leaving no middle ground for accommodation, the legislature makes it more difficult to reach a political compromise (either in the agency or the legislature) that would produce a functional regulatory program.

The problems inherent in symbolic legislation can be seen by taking a detailed look at the legislative, regulatory, and judicial history of the hazardous air pollutant program under §112 of the Clean Air Act.[2] Under §112, Congress requires the Environmental Protection Agency (EPA) to set "health-based" emission standards for hazardous air pollutants, but prohibits the Agency from considering evidence of implementation costs and technological feasibility in setting a "safe" or "acceptable" emission standard. EPA maintains that health-based standards are unrealistically stringent because most industrial facilities could not meet such standards without closing their doors.[3]

SECTION 112 AS SYMBOLIC LEGISLATION... The statutory language creating the federal hazardous air pollutant program is uncomplicated, but its very simplicity conceals a range of policy issues. The key provision requires EPA to set emission limits for "hazardous air pollutants" "at the level which in [the Administrator's] judgment provides an ample margin of safety to protect the public health." Section 112 does not explicitly mention technological feasibility or economic costs to industry as factors to be considered in setting standards. This omission contrasts sharply with other provisions in the Act, such as §111, that explicitly require EPA to consider costs and technological feasibility in setting emission standards for new sources of nonhazardous pollution. As Congress emphasized in the Clean Air Act Amendments of 1977, the statutory language manifested "the predominant value of protection of public health" and the "precautionary or preventive purpose of the act."

The most striking features of §112 are its extremely short deadlines and its substantive criteria for emission standards. §112 required the EPA Administrator to publish a list of hazardous air pollutants within ninety days of the effective date of the statute, to issue proposed emission standards 180 days later, and to issue final emission standards 180 days after that. Significantly, the statute provides no timetable for listing additional chemicals for regulation under §112. That is, even though EPA is under strict deadlines to adopt emission standards for listed hazardous air pollutants, the Agency has broad discretion to decide whether to designate a chemical as a hazardous air pollutant in the first place.

The short statutory deadlines implicitly, and incorrectly, assumed the

---

2. 42 U.S.C. §7412 (1982). There are, of course, important limitations to this approach. The circumstances studied may not be representative of most symbolic legislation. Agency and legislative behavior are the product of numerous factors, including environmental crises, presidential and congressional elections, shifts of power within the legislature, and court decisions. As a result, precise predictions of agency and legislative responses to symbolic legislation would be unjustified. This Article, however, does not attempt to reach definitive conclusions about the behavior of political institutions. Rather, it uses the empirical material to identify the range of possible agency and legislative responses to symbolic legislation and suggests how agencies and courts should deal with symbolic legislation.

3. National Emission Standards for Hazardous Air Pollutants; Policy and Procedures for Identifying, Assessing, and Regulating Airborne Substances Posing a Risk of Cancer, 44 Fed. Reg. 58,642, 58,657 (1979) (proposed rulemaking)].

existence of adequate and reliable scientific data on the amount and geographic distribution of hazardous emissions, the extent of human exposure to hazardous air pollutants, and the size and distribution of health risks from such exposures. But because there often is no clear scientific information correlating current exposures with health risks, EPA must spend time evaluating studies, weighing scientific evidence, and developing policies to set standards. EPA has estimated that before beginning the standard-setting process, it must spend at least three years to prepare a technical health assessment document for a single chemical. The entire process can last as long as seven years. Although EPA probably is exaggerating the time needed to issue final emission standards, it is indisputable that the one-year deadline is grossly insufficient.

The strict deadlines in §112 were matched by tough-sounding substantive criteria for setting emission standards. Not only does §112 require EPA to set standards at levels that "protect the public health" with "an ample margin of safety," it precludes EPA from considering technological and economic factors in adopting emission standards. That is, EPA must set standards that protect public health, regardless of their cost or feasibility.

[In omitted material, Dwyer traces the politics that led Senator Muskie, President Nixon, and others to become advocates for stringent legislation, positions far-divergent from where they had started.] The stringent provisions in the 1970 Clean Air Act, at least in part, were the product of this competitive "policy escalation." By the end of the legislative process, the "symbolic benefits [of the Clean Air Act had become] overwhelmingly important, whereas costs of all sorts were far less significant." The particular form that §112 finally took was a product of that process.

Other legislators were not subject to the identical pressures that Muskie faced. Nevertheless, both houses voted overwhelmingly in favor of the 1970 Act. Like Muskie, other legislators sensed a widespread and deeply felt public concern about the health risks from air pollution, and they realized the political risks of opposing strong environmental controls as well as the potential benefits of championing those controls. Although Love Canal and Bhopal were not yet symbols of the dangers created by modern chemical technologies and irresponsible corporate and government officials, even in 1970 proponents of the Clean Air Act portrayed human health and the environment as endangered by corporate greed and irresponsibility.

The political risks and benefits associated with taking a position on environmental issues are magnified when hazardous chemicals are involved because the regulation of hazardous chemicals raises "deeply disturbing questions about national attitudes toward life and death, [and] about the appropriate claims which proponents of environmentally secure surroundings can make against other socially advantageous goals and norms." With so much potentially at stake in the regulation of hazardous pollutants, there is a tendency for interest groups to be strongly polarized on basic policy issues. Public consensus is not easily achieved.

In such a volatile policy area, even legislators who understand that complete safety is unattainable avoid positions that can be characterized as trading lives for dollars. It is safer politically to vote "for" safety — or better yet, an "ample margin of safety" — and to let the agency or the courts deal with the unresolved legal, ethical, and political questions. Requiring health-based standards allows legislators to assert that society can have a virtually risk-free environment without significant social or economic costs, while avoiding difficult choices and the accompanying political costs.

Legislating in this fashion may not be responsible, but neither is it unusual or surprising. Legislators want to enact sound public policies, but they also have personal goals, which may include acquiring wealth, gaining prestige or power within the legislature, being reelected, or being elected to another office. Viewing congressional behavior as fundamentally strategic reveals a deeper pathology of lawmaking in a representative democracy. Rational behavior by individual legislators may produce irrational public policy. Thus, in anticipating the next election, some legislators will propose or support symbolic legislation, such as §112, because it minimizes political costs and maximizes political credit.

To characterize some statutory provisions, such as §112, as being symbolic, however, is not to deny their instrumental value. Section 112 probably reflects the concern that absent an unequivocal (if somewhat idealistic) national policy to eliminate risks from air-borne hazardous pollutants, the compromises characteristic of rulemaking and enforcement would undermine the goal of protecting public health. Supporters may have believed that whenever regulators explicitly consider tradeoffs, such as implementation costs and technical feasibility, the resulting emission standards do not protect public health as well as when the Agency has public health protection as its only mission. As Senator Muskie argued, "[W]e have learned that tests of economic and technological feasibility...compromise the health of our people and lead to inadequate standards."

The argument is not just that cost-sensitive standards are inherently weaker than health-based standards, but that explicit consideration of costs overemphasizes costs and underemphasizes health concerns. Implementation costs seem quantifiable and their impact is felt immediately, while public health risks are difficult to quantify, statistical, and remote. Because of these differences, political pressure may be greater from, and the agency may be more sensitive to, constituencies that feel immediate regulatory costs. In addition, industry generally has the best information about the costs and feasibility of pollution controls, and thus it is able to present data supporting predictions of dire economic consequences if strict standards are adopted.

AGENCY RESISTANCE TO SYMBOLIC LEGISLATION... Symbolic legislation does not suppress the conflicts that arise in designing and implementing a regulatory scheme; instead, it transfers those conflicts to agencies, and at times to courts, for resolution. Not only must the agency resolve the policy and technical disputes that the legislature so deftly avoided, it also must frame its resolution in terms of statutory interpretation. Confronted with this challenge, an agency has three options. It can implement and enforce the legislation literally. Alternatively, it can use the rulemaking process to "rewrite" the legislation to a form more compatible with the agency's policy goals or its notions of practicability. This rewrite may be done openly with the agency announcing its intentions and consulting with Congress, or it may be done silently if the political costs or the risk of judicial reversal are too high. Finally, the agency can use the time-honored bureaucratic tactic of delay in the hope that either Congress or the courts will rescue it.

Agencies view literal implementation of symbolic legislation as politically and professionally unsound. They do not want to bear the political consequences that inevitably flow from adopting excessively stringent standards, and they do not believe that regulatory consequences should be ignored. Moreover, the professional values of regulators generally demand that regulatory decisions be made in light of costs.

Rewriting the statute and delaying implementation are not exclusive of each other. In practice, agencies resist by degrees — rewriting a little here, delaying a little there — to achieve their goals. An agency's response to the legislative mandate will reflect its evaluation of...: the intensity and durability of political support for the statute, and the risks of judicial reversal or legislative revision. Delay, for example, could be a politically costly strategy if Congress becomes sufficiently irritated with the agency. But delay may be a more practical approach than revision if the agency believes the courts would reject its construction of the statute.

EPA has adopted both strategies in implementing §112. Although EPA initially denied that it based the §112 standards partly on economic factors, it later candidly informed Congress and the public that its standard-setting criteria included implementation costs and technological feasibility. Stating openly that §112 demands impossibly strict standards, EPA has refused steadfastly to implement the provision literally. At the same time, EPA moved slowly in adopting emission standards, apparently fearing judicial reversal. When reversal finally came, EPA proposed a standard-setting procedure that masks its reliance on the factors that Congress excluded in §112.

THE COSTS OF SYMBOLIC LEGISLATION... Despite congressional rhetoric to the contrary, it is not possible in an industrialized society to implement and enforce health-based standards for hazardous pollutants. Because the economic and social costs of such standards would be staggering, EPA will not adopt, much less enforce, such standards.

To maintain this position in the face of explicit statutory language to the contrary, however, the Agency must distort the regulatory process. As the regulatory history of §112 suggests, one significant distortion is the delay in standard setting. Lengthy delays create not only greater health risks than are permissible under the statutory health-based standards, but higher risks than would be allowed under the more lenient cost-sensitive standards that EPA prefers.

A statute requiring EPA to do the impossible also undermines the integrity of the rulemaking process and forces the Agency to misrepresent its decisionmaking process to the public and to the courts. When decisionmaking is driven underground, rationality and genuine public participation are sacrificed and public confidence in government is eroded.

### COMMENTARY & QUESTIONS

1. **For more on this, read the book.** The Dwyer text excerpted above conveys a great deal of useful information about §112 and how it failed, serving only as symbolic legislation. The excerpt does not, however, retain the litany of important details surrounding such topics as the basis for properly interpreting the section as indifferent to cost, the politics of its gestation and passage in its final form, EPA's efforts to mold it via delay and misinterpretation, or Dwyer's own reflections on what can be salvaged from the experience.

2. **The impossible dream of absence of risk without consideration of cost.** Section 112, as a political response to public outcries for strong environmental protection, promised an unrealistic bargain. The force of its focus on health protection, divorced from practical concerns for cost and feasibility, made §112 anathema to the regulated community. Even so, is it clear why EPA appeared unwilling to go for-

ward aggressively under the shield of "Congress made us do it"? Dwyer asserts that a combination of political and professional judgments made aggressive enforcement abhorrent to the agency. If not, what would have happened?

3. **Other paths to the same paralysis.** Dwyer asserts that the agency was left in the impossible position of trying to make the political decision balancing protectiveness and cost without any legislative guidance regarding how the balance was to be struck. The over-broad delegations that typified mid-century review and permit statutes presented the same predicament. Are the situations meaningfully different? Both frequently have the same poor results. Can laws also fail by requiring too much administrative study and justification of standards chosen?

4. **Congress and subjectivity.** It is easy to criticize the settings in which Congress has acted symbolically, unless one first considers alternatives available. In the materials studied so far, one ready example of a subjective balance is the BAT standard of the Clean Water Act, in reality a balanced "BATEA" — best available technology economically achievable.

A more elaborate example of congressional balancing is ToSCA's §6:

### Toxic Substances Control Act of 1976 (ToSCA), §6(a)
### 15 U.S.C.A.§§2605(a)

[ToSCA is one of the principal regulatory attempts to control health risks created by toxic exposure. ToSCA attempts to manage toxic risks associated with the use of toxic substances by regulating the ability of firms that produce them to market the substances. The specifics of ToSCA's statutory design are explored in Chapter 15.]

**§6. Regulation of hazardous chemical substances and mixtures**
(a) Scope of regulation.

If the Administrator finds that there is a reasonable basis to conclude that the manufacture, processing, distribution in commerce, use, or disposal of a chemical substance or mixture, or that any combination of such activities, presents or will present an unreasonable risk of injury to health or the environment, the Administrator shall by rule apply one or more of the following requirements to such substance or mixture to the extent necessary to protect adequately against such risk using the least burdensome requirements:

(1) A requirement (A) prohibiting the manufacturing, processing, or distribution in commerce of such substance or mixture, or (B) limiting the amount of such substance or mixture which may be manufactured, processed, or distributed in commerce.

(2) A requirement (A) prohibiting the manufacture, processing, or distribution in commerce of such substance or mixture for (i) a particular use or (ii) a particular use in a concentration in excess of a level specified by the Administrator in the rule imposing the requirement, or (B) limiting the amount of such substance or mixture which may be manufactured, processed, or distributed in commerce for (i) a particular use or (ii) a particular use in a concentration in excess of a level specified by the Administrator in the rule imposing the requirement.

(3) A requirement that such substance or mixture or any article containing such substance or mixture be marked with or accompanied by clear and adequate warnings and instructions with respect to its use, distribution in commerce, or disposal or with respect to any combination of such activities. The

form and content of such warnings and instructions shall be prescribed by the Administrator.

(4) A requirement that manufacturers and processors of such substance or mixture make and retain records of the processes used to manufacture or process such substance or mixture and monitor or conduct tests which are reasonable and necessary to assure compliance with the requirements of any rule applicable under this subsection.

(5) A requirement prohibiting or otherwise regulating any manner or method of commercial use of such substance or mixture.

(6)(A) A requirement prohibiting or otherwise regulating any manner or method of disposal of such substance or mixture, or of any article containing such substance or mixture, by its manufacturer or processor or by any other person who uses, or disposes of, it for commercial purposes. (B) A requirement under subparagraph (A) may not require any person to take any action which would be in violation of any law or requirement of, or in effect for, a State or political subdivision, and shall require each person subject to it to notify each State and political subdivision in which a required disposal may occur of such disposal.

(7) A requirement directing manufacturers or processors of such substance or mixture (A) to give notice of such unreasonable risk of injury to distributors in commerce of such substance or mixture and, to the extent reasonably ascertainable, to other persons in possession of such substance or mixture or exposed to such substance or mixture, (B) to give public notice of such risk of injury, and (C) to replace or repurchase such substance or mixture as elected by the person to which the requirement is directed.

Any requirement (or combination of requirements) imposed under this subsection may be limited in application to specified geographic areas.

### COMMENTARY AND QUESTIONS

1. **"Using the least burdensome requirements."** Is this the phrase in §6 that makes ToSCA workable for both the agency and the reviewing court (not to mention the regulated entities)? In what way does this legislated preference for regulatory restraint avoid the perils that doomed the NESHAPs program of Clean Air Act §112 and the broad delegation statutes? A fuller view of ToSCA is afforded in Chapter 15, from which it may appear that Congress made ToCSA unworkable in other ways, by placing impossibly short time limits and higher than normal burdens of justification on the agency.

2. **Can agencies undermine a workable statute?** Even without examples at hand, the answer would seem obviously to be "Yes." An agency can delay or distort implementation, although a court may order action, as in the old NESHAPs program. The case excerpted below is one in which EPA appears to have tried to remove much of the balancing that Congress put into ToSCA §6 and remake the risk management decision reflected in the statute.

## Corrosion Proof Fittings v. Environmental Protection Agency
United States Court of Appeals for the Fifth Circuit, 1991
947 F.2d 1201

[EPA, after an elaborate seven-year review of the scientific evidence of asbestos carcinogenicity, concluded in 1986 that asbestos exposure "poses an unreasonable risk to human health." It proposed a series of regulatory options for asbestos usage and, for two more years collected more data and received comments on its regulatory proposals. In 1989, EPA announced its final rule, imposing a staged ban on most commercial uses of asbestos. A number of affected firms challenged the rule as violative of ToSCA §6.]

SMITH, J. The Environmental Protection Agency (EPA) issued a final rule under §6 of the Toxic Substances Control Act (ToSCA) to prohibit the future manufacture, importation, processing, and distribution of asbestos in almost all products. Petitioners claim that EPA's rulemaking procedure was flawed and that the rule was not promulgated on the basis of substantial evidence.

Asbestos is a naturally occurring fibrous material that resists fire and most solvents. Its major uses include heat-resistant insulators, cements, building materials, fireproof gloves and clothing, and motor vehicle brake linings. Asbestos is a toxic material, and occupational exposure to asbestos dust can result in mesothelioma, asbestosis, and lung cancer.

ToSCA §6(a) was quoted at this point in the opinion.] Congress did not enact ToSCA as a zero-risk statute. The EPA, rather, was required to consider both alternatives to a ban and the costs of any proposed actions and "to carry out this chapter in a reasonable and prudent manner [after considering] the environmental, economic, and social impact of any action."

We conclude that EPA has presented insufficient evidence to justify its asbestos ban. We base this conclusion upon two grounds: the failure of the EPA to consider all necessary evidence and its failure to give adequate weight to statutory language requiring it to promulgate the least burdensome, reasonable regulation required to protect the environment adequately. Because the EPA failed to address these concerns, and because the EPA is required to articulate a "reasoned basis" for its rules, we are compelled to return the regulation to the agency for reconsideration.

LEAST BURDENSOME AND REASONABLE... ToSCA requires that EPA use the least burdensome regulation to achieve its goals of minimum reasonable risk. This statutory requirement can create problems in evaluating just what is a "reasonable risk." Congress' rejection of a no-risk policy, however, also means that in certain cases, the least burdensome yet still adequate solution may entail somewhat more risk than other, known regulations that are far more burdensome on the industry and the economy. The very language of ToSCA requires that the EPA, once it has determined what an acceptable level of non-zero risk is, choose the least burdensome method of reaching that level.

In this case, the EPA banned, for all practical purposes, all present and future uses of asbestos — a position the petitioners characterize as the "death penalty alternative," as this is the most burdensome of all possible alternatives listed as open to EPA under ToSCA. ToSCA not only provides the EPA with a list of alternative actions, but also provides those alternatives in order of how burdensome they are. The regulations thus provide for EPA regulation ranging from labeling the least toxic chemicals to limiting the total amount of chemicals an industry may use. Total bans head the list as the most burdensome regulatory option.

By choosing the harshest remedy given to it under ToSCA, the EPA assigned to itself the toughest burden in satisfying ToSCA's requirement that its alternative be the least burdensome of those offered to it. Since both by definition and by the terms of ToSCA the complete ban of manufacturing is the most burdensome alternative — for even stringent regulation at least allows a manufacturer the chance to invest and meet the new, higher standard — the EPA regulation cannot stand if there is any other regulation that would achieve an acceptable level of risk as mandated by ToSCA....

The EPA considered, and rejected, such options as labeling asbestos products, thereby warning users and worker involved in the manufacture of asbestos-containing products of the chemical's dangers, and stricter workplace rules. EPA also rejected controlled use of asbestos in the workplace and deferral to other government agencies charged with workplace and consumer exposure to industrial and product hazards such as OSHA, the [Consumer Product Safety Commission], and the Mine Safety and Health Administration. The EPA determined that deferral to these other agencies was inappropriate because no one other authority could address all the risks posed "throughout the life cycle" by asbestos, and any action by one or more of the other agencies still would leave an unacceptable residual risk.

Much of the EPA's analysis is correct, and the EPA's basic decision to use ToSCA as a comprehensive statute designed to fight a multi-industry problem was a proper one that we uphold today on review. What concerns us, however, is the manner in which the EPA conducted some of its analysis. ToSCA requires the EPA to consider, along with the effects of toxic substances on human health and the environment, "the benefits of such substances or mixtures for various uses and the availability of substitutes for such uses," as well as "the reasonably ascertainable economic consequences of the rule, after consideration for the effect on the national economy, small business, technological innovation, the environment, and public health."

[The court then reviewed EPA's methodology and calculation of the benefits and costs of the regulatory options. It found a number of problems. One had to do with discounting to present value the future costs to industry of the regulation but not always discounting the benefits of lives saved at future dates. The court indicated that both costs and benefits must be discounted to preserve an "apples-to-apples" comparison. Even when it did discount the benefits of its proposed regulation, EPA used the time of exposure instead of the time of injury as the point in time from which to discount. Beyond that, EPA declined to compute benefits and costs beyond the year 2000, but listed lives saved after that point in time as "unquantified benefits."]

Of more concern to us is the failure of the EPA to compute the costs and benefits of its proposed rule past the year 2,000.... In performing its calculus, the EPA only included the number of lives saved over the next thirteen years, and counted any additional lives saved as simply "unquantified benefits." The EPA and interveners now seek to use these unquantified lives saved to justify calculations as to which the benefits seem far outweighed by the astronomical costs. For example, the EPA plans to save about three lives with its ban of asbestos pipe, at a cost of $128–227 million (i.e., approximately $43–76 million per life saved). Although the EPA admits that the price tag is high, it claims that the lives saved past the year 2000 justify the price.

Such calculations not only lessen the value of the EPA's cost analysis, but also make any meaningful judicial review impossible. While ToSCA contemplates a useful place for unquantified benefits beyond the EPA's calculation, unquantified benefits never were intended as a trump card allowing the EPA to justify any cost calculus, no matter how high.

The concept of unquantified benefits, rather, is intended to allow the EPA to provide a rightful place for any remaining benefits that are impossible to quantify after the EPA's best attempt, but which still are of some concern. But the allowance for unquantified costs is not intended to allow the EPA to perform its calculations over an arbitrarily short period so as to preserve a large unquantified portion.

Unquantified benefits can, at times, permissibly tip the balance in close cases. They cannot, however, be used to effect a wholesale shift on the balance beam. Such a use makes a mockery of the requirement of ToSCA that the EPA weight the costs of its actions before it chooses the least burdensome alternative....

REASONABLE BASIS... Most problematical to us is the EPA's ban of products for which no substitutes presently are available. In these cases, the EPA bears a tough burden indeed to show that under ToSCA a ban is the least burdensome alternative, as ToSCA explicitly instructs the EPA to consider "the benefits of such substance or mixture for various uses and the availability of substitutes for such uses." These words are particularly appropriate where the EPA actually has decided to ban a product, rather than simply restrict its use, for it is in these cases that the lack of an adequate substitute is most troubling under ToSCA.

As the EPA itself states, "when no information is available for a product indicating that cost-effective substitutes exist, the estimated cost of a product ban is very high." Because of this, the EPA did not ban certain uses of asbestos, such as its use in rocket engines and battery separators. The EPA, however, in several other instances, ignores its own arguments and attempts to justify its ban by stating that the ban itself will cause the development of low-cost, adequate substitute products.

As a general matter, we agree with the EPA that a product ban can lead to great innovation, and it is true that an agency under ToSCA, as under other regulatory statutes, "is empowered to issue safety standards which require improvements in existing technology or which require the development of new technology." Chrysler Corp. v. Department of Transportation, 472 F.2d 659, 673 (6th Cir. 1972). As even the EPA acknowledges, however, when no adequate substitutes currently exist, the EPA cannot fail to consider this lack when formulating its own guidelines. Under ToSCA, therefore, the EPA must present a stronger case to justify the ban, as opposed to regulation, of products with no substitutes.

[The court then concluded that EPA's ban waiver provision for industries where the hoped-for substitutes failed to materialize in time did not relieve the agency of its heavy burden of justifying a total ban, in the face of inadequate substitutes, by shifting the burden to the waiver proponent.]

We are also concerned with the EPA's evaluation of substitutes even in those instances in which the record shows that they are available. The EPA explicitly rejects considering the harm that may flow from the increased use of products designed to substitute for asbestos, even where the probable substitutes themselves [such as PVC pipe] are known carcinogens. The EPA justifies this by stating that it has "more concern about the continued use and exposure to asbestos than it has for the future replacement of asbestos in the products subject to this rule with other fibrous substitutes." The agency thus concludes that any "regulatory decisions about asbestos which poses well-recognized, serious risks should not be delayed until the risk of all replacement materials are fully quantified."

This presents two problems. First, ToSCA instructs the EPA to consider the relative merits of its ban, as compared to the economic effects of its actions. The EPA cannot make this calculation if it fails to consider the effects that alternate substitutes will pose after a ban. Second, the EPA cannot say with any assurance that its regulation will increase workplace safety when it refuses to evaluate the harm that will result from the increased use of substitute products. While the EPA may be correct in its conclusion that the alternate materials pose less risk than asbestos, we cannot say with any more assurance than that flowing from an educated guess that this conclusion is true....

In short, a death is a death, whether occasioned by asbestos or a toxic substitute product, and the EPA's decision not to evaluate the toxicity of known carcinogenic substitutes is not a reasonable action under ToSCA. Once an interested party brings forth credible evidence suggesting the toxicity of the probable or only alternatives to a substance, the EPA must consider the comparative toxic costs of each. Its failure to do so in this case thus deprived its regulation of a reasonable basis, at least in regard to those products as to which petitioners introduced credible evidence of the dangers of the likely substitutes.[4]

UNREASONABLE RISK OF INJURY... Even taking all of the EPA's figures as true, and evaluating them in the light most favorable to the agency's decision (non-discounted benefits, discounted costs...), the agency's analysis results in figures as high as $74 million per life saved. For example, the EPA states that its ban of asbestos pipe will save three lives over the next thirteen years, at a cost of $128–227 million ($43–76 million per life saved), depending on the price of substitutes; that its ban of asbestos shingles will cost $23–34 million to save 0.32 statistical lives ($72–106 million per life saved); that its ban of asbestos coatings will cost $46–181 million to save 3.33 lives ($14–54 million per life saved); and that its ban of asbestos paper products will save 0.60 lives at a cost of $4–5 million ($7–8 million per life saved)....

While we do not sit as a regulatory agency that must make the difficult decision as to what an appropriate expenditure is to prevent someone from incurring the risk of an asbestos-related death, we do note that the EPA, in its zeal to ban any and all asbestos products, basically ignored the cost side of the ToSCA equation. The EPA would have this court believe that Congress, when it enacted its requirement that the EPA consider the economic impacts of its regulations, thought that spending $200–300 million to save approximately seven lives (approximately $30–40 million per life) over thirteen years is reasonable.

The EPA's willingness to argue that spending $23.7 million to save less than one-third of a life reveals that its economic view of its regulations, as required by ToSCA, was meaningless. As the petitioner's brief and our review of EPA case law reveals, such high costs are rarely, if ever, used to support a safety regulation. If we were to allow such cavalier treatment of the EPA's duty to consider the economic effects of its decisions, we would have to excise entire sections and phrases from the language of ToSCA. Because were are judges, not surgeons, we decline to do so.[5]

---

4. We note that at least part of the EPA's arguments rest on the assumption that regulation will not work because the federal government will not adequately enforce any workplace standards that EPA might promulgate. This is an improper assumption. The EPA should assume reasonable efforts by the government to implement its own regulations. A governmental agency cannot point to how poorly the government will implement regulations as a reason to reject regulation. Rather, the solution to poor enforcement is better enforcement, not more burdensome alternative solutions under ToSCA.

5. As the petitioners point out, EPA regularly rejects as unjustified, regulations that would save more lives at less cost. For example, over the next 13 years we can expect more than a dozen deaths from ingested toothpicks — a death toll more than twice what the EPA predicts will flow from the quarter billion dollar bans of asbestos pipe, shingles, and roof coatings.

COMMENTARY AND QUESTIONS

**1. Who is in charge, and what about the *Chevron* argument?** Who is the appropriate decision maker in this case? The four candidates are: the entities who manufacture and use asbestos, Congress, the EPA, and the reviewing court. The political theory answer is that Congress has made the policy choice to protect against unreasonable health risks and authorized EPA to act in that regard by circumscribing the untrammeled freedom of action of the asbestos-using community, subject to judicial review (at the behest of aggrieved parties such as the asbestos users) to ensure that EPA's action conforms to congressional policy as set forth in ToSCA. How well did the actors play their roles? How would Peter Huber and Talbot Page, the commentators on risk management studied in Chapter Two, react to EPA's performance and the court's review of it in this case?

One way to think about the *Corrosion Proof Fittings* case is in terms of how §6 of ToSCA sets out a methodology and process of risk assessment and risk management. In the end, both are assigned to EPA, but there is a substantial question of what latitude EPA has in acting to fulfill those mandates, particularly the management function. Does *Chevron* require the court to defer to EPA's interpretation of how the law is supposed to work? Must a court defer if EPA claims that Congress intended ToSCA to work in a very open-ended way, pointing to phrases such as "reasonable basis," "unreasonable risk of injury to health or the environment," and "to protect adequately against such risk"? Even if courts defer on the interpretive issue, pursuant to ToSCA §19(c)(1)(B), in order to be upheld a rule promulgated under §6 must be supported by "substantial evidence in the rulemaking record."

**2. Non-enforcement of other laws as a factor.** Was EPA's reliance on government's chronic non-enforcement of OSHA regulations as one factor justifying an absolute prohibition on asbestos as silly as the court makes it sound? OSHA has some of the hallmarks of a symbolic assurance law, but more pragmatically, it has a sorry track record in regard to consistent enforcement. Does that help to explain EPA's preference for an absolute prohibition, such as the asbestos ban sought here? Flat prohibitions do avoid many of the implementation difficulties inherent in more sophisticated statutory designs and can thus avoid becoming mere symbolic assurances. See the discussion of roadblock statutes in Chapter 14.

**3. Reviewing benefit-cost calculations: the value of a life.** Is the court correct in treating the avoidance of cancers like any other economic benefit, i.e., the benefits accrue at various points in time and should be quantified in dollar terms and discounted to present value? Once quantified, the value of lives saved can be plugged into a benefit-cost analysis and compared to the costs that must be expended to attain the reduction in mortality. Can a benefit-cost analysis in a situation like this ever be an "apples-to-apples" comparison, or does this approach so debase the dignity of human life as to be offensive? The benefits calculus is notably incomplete because it omits placing a monetary value on the avoided pain and suffering and health care costs of those who never become victims and it also takes no account of costs associated with those who are made ill but who do not die. The court is both critical and skeptical of EPA's reliance on "unquantified benefits" that will accrue in the more distant future. The court refers to a proper role for unquantified benefits: what is that role?

**4. Reviewing risk management: how safe is safe enough in dealing with cancer risks?** The regulatory zeal of EPA in *Corrosion Proof Fittings* appears to be unusually stringent, at least in regard to the thirteen year period for which EPA quantifies both benefits and costs. Investigators have found that federal agencies are relatively consistent in defining "acceptable risk." More often than not, if a substance is expected to increase the number of cancer cases by more than four in 1,000 over a lifetime of exposure, federal agencies decide to regulate that substance to reduce the risk below that level. If a substance is expected to increase the number of cases by less than one in a million, the chemical is rarely regulated. Between these extremes, federal decision-makers conduct cost-effectiveness analyses, which weigh the cost of the regulation against the number of lives that regulation is likely to save. If the cost falls below $2 million per life saved, the substance is regulated. Travis, Richter, Crouch, Wilson & Klema, Cancer Risk Management, 21 Envtl. Sci. Tech. 15 (1987). The mere fact that the average agency enforcement behavior has been more lenient is not in itself proof that the more lenient approach is appropriate, but it is solid evidence of how risk managers have responded to "life and death" choices in the past.

## B. REGULATORY SHORTCOMINGS AT THE IMPLEMENTATION LEVEL

Assume that the legislature has done its job on the policymaking level, avoiding the pitfalls of "symbolic assurance" laws, over-broad delegations, and impossible or unworkable administrative burdens. In short, the law "is workable." That alone is no guarantee of effectiveness. In the realm of statutory design, a different set of trade-offs come to the fore.

### Howard Latin, Ideal versus Real Regulatory Efficiency: Implementation of Uniform Standards and "Fine Tuning" Regulatory Reforms
37 Stanford Law Review 1267, 1267–1273 (1985)[6]

Many environmental, public health, and safety statutes place primary emphasis on the implementation of uniform regulatory standards. In return for benefits that are often difficult to assess, "command-and-control" standards promulgated under such statutes as the Clean Air Act, Occupational Safety and Health Act, and Clean Air Act impose billions of dollars in annual compliance costs on society and also entail significant indirect costs including decreases in productivity, technological innovation, and market competition. As these costs have become increasingly evident, prominent legal scholars such as Bruce Ackerman, Steven Breyer, and Richard Stewart have concluded that command-and-control regulation is inefficient and should be replaced by more flexible strategies. Their principal criticisms may be summarized as follows: Uniform standards do not reflect the

6. Copyright © 1985 by the Board of Trustees of Leland Stanford, Junior University. Reprinted by permission of the copyright holder, the author, and Fred B. Rothman Co.

opportunity costs of environmental protection,[7] the concept of "opportunity cost" is essential for any comparison of regulatory systems and for any analysis of public policy issues. It means that the real cost of any resource allocation must be measured not by its financial expense alone, but by the value of incompatible resource uses that must be foregone. they disregard the individual circumstances of diverse conflicts,[8] they do not achieve environmental protection on a "lowest-cost" basis,[9] and they fail to provide adequate incentives for improved performance.

In response to these alleged deficiencies in the present system, advocates of "regulatory reform" argue that environmental controls should be tailored to particularized ecological and economic circumstances, regulatory benefits weighed against the costs of environmental protection, and increased reliance placed on economic incentive mechanisms, such as taxes on environmentally destructive activities or transferable pollution rights. Professor Stewart, for example, recently advocated "a more individualized or 'fine-tuning' approach to regulation." Critics of command-and-control standards differ on suggested 'fine-tuning' prescriptions, but there is widespread agreement that some alternative must be preferable to the current regulatory system....

The academic literature on "regulatory reform" reflects an excessive preoccupation with theoretical efficiency, while it places inadequate emphasis on actual decisionmaking costs and implementation constraints. Any system for environmental regulation must function despite the presence of pervasive uncertainty, high decisionmaking costs,[10] and manipulative strategic behavior resulting from conflicting private and public interests. Under these conditions, the indisputable fact that uniform standards are inefficient does not prove that any other approach would necessarily perform better. In a "second-best" world, the critical issue is not which regulatory system aspires to ideal "efficiency" but which is most likely to prove effective.[11]

---

7. Command-and-control standards often place an absolute priority on environmental protection, with little consideration of competing resource uses that will be foreclosed. Critics of the current approach usually attribute the resulting inefficiencies to public and governmental ignorance about the true social costs of environmental regulation or to the political pressure of extremist special-interest groups. See e.g., B. Ackerman, S. Rose-Ackerman, J. Sawyer & D. Henderson, The Uncertain Search for Environmental Quality 165-207 (1974); M. Douglas & A. Wildavsky, Risk and Culture (1982).

8. Regulatory standards impose uniform requirements on broad categories of activities. Yet ecological conditions, environmental impacts of human actions, and potential resource uses vary widely at different times and in different locations. The inflexibility of uniform standards leads to "too much" environmental protection in some contexts and "too little" in others....

9. Some regulated parties...will have lower than average abatement costs because of the technological characteristics of their operations or the ecological characteristics of their facility sites. Uniform standards do not discriminate between the differing control capabilities and cost functions of particular polluters, and therefore cannot achieve any given level of environmental protection at the lowest possible cost....

10. Decisionmaking costs are typically high for each environmental conflict because ecological systems are complex, interactions are subtle and may require many years to become evident, people or biospecies are exposed to many potentially harmful agents, relative costs and benefits are difficult to assess, and sharply conflicting values and priorities are the norm rather than the exception. Moreover, many thousands of environmental resource conflicts must be resolved each year; thus, the cumulative costs of environmental decisionmaking would be high even if the cost of each regulatory decision were not. See e.g., A. Kneese & C. Schultze, Pollution, Prices and Public Policy 19, 81, 117 (1975).

11. There are numerous formal economic definitions of efficiency. See, e.g., Coleman, Efficiency, Exchange, and Auction: Philosophic Aspects of the Economic Approach to Law, 68 Calif. L. Rev. 221 (1980); Latin, Environmental Deregulation and Consumer Decisionmaking Under Uncertainty, 6 Harv. Envt'l. L. Rev. 187, 191 n.26 (1982). For purposes of this article, the important contrast is between an emphasis on ideal or optimal decisionmaking, which is denoted below by the label "efficiency," and an emphasis on "effective" decisionmaking, which means the achievement of a reasonable congruence between regulatory accomplishments and desired legislative objectives.

In recognition of severe implementation constraints on environmental regulation there are numerous advantages of uniform standards in comparison with more particularized and flexible regulatory strategies. These advantages include decreased information collection and evaluation costs, greater consistency and predictability of results, greater accessibility of decisions to public scrutiny and participation, increased likelihood that regulations will withstand judicial review, reduced opportunities for manipulative behavior by agencies in response to political or bureaucratic pressures, reduced opportunities for obstructive behavior by regulated parties, and decreased likelihood of social dislocation and "forum shopping" resulting from competitive disadvantages between geographical regions or between firms in regulated industries. A realistic implementation analysis indicates that "fine-tuning" would prove infeasible in many important environmental contexts; indeed, the effectiveness of environmental regulation could often be improved by reducing even the degree of "fine-tuning" that is currently attempted.

There is more at stake here than academic disagreement and the possible miseducation of a generation of students. When the Reagan Administration took office, it was explicit about its desire for widespread deregulation. After Congress proved generally unwilling to repeal regulatory legislation, the Administration changed its approach and argued that environmental control programs should be made more "efficient." In a letter to the New York Times, for example, an EPA Assistant Administrator claimed that the agency was committed to "clean water," but that the EPA intended to improve regulatory efficiency by: (1) expanding reliance on "cost/benefit analysis"; (2) basing standards on "scientific evidence and not on rumor and soothsaying"; (3) employing "site-specific data"; (4) providing "more flexibility to local governments"; and (5) not imposing regulatory costs unless "a designated [water quality] use is attainable." These are all proposals for increased "fine-tuning." The letter mentioned nothing about Administration initiatives that reduced EPA budgets and manpower, or about information scarcity and "site-specific" collection costs, or about inadequate scientific understanding of many water quality-related problems. Well-intentioned scholars often recommend "fine-tuning" because they focus on ideal efficiency, while Administration officials may advocate "fine-tuning" precisely because they believe it will seldom work in practice and would therefore accomplish sub rosa deregulation. Intemperate academic criticisms of command-and-control standards combined with support of unrealistic "fine-tuning" strategies may lend an aura of intellectual credibility to political initiatives designed to achieve less regulation, not better regulation....

Comparison between the demonstrated inefficiencies of uniform standards and the theoretical advantages of "fine-tuning" cannot lead to the development of a wise regulatory policy.... Uncertainty, high decisionmaking costs, and varying strategic behavior for different regulatory approaches all affect regulatory effectiveness. These constraints would degrade the performance of any environmental protection program, but competing strategies are not all subject to the same kinds of imponderables, expenses, and manipulation, nor are they all vulnerable to the same degree.... The most "efficient" strategies in theory will frequently be the least effective in practice. Moreover, many commentators espouse variations of approaches that have already been tried and found unsatisfactory.... The implementation problems which subverted these approaches in the past remain essentially unchanged, and consequently...most "fine-tuning" proposals reflect wishful thinking rather than a realistic appraisal of present environmental knowledge and regulatory capabilities. Despite its imperfections, command-and-control regulation has fostered significant improvements in environmental quality at a societal cost that has not proved prohibitive.[12] Critics of uniform standards should therefore be required to demonstrate with reasonable assurance that "fine-tuning" approaches can be successfully implemented, and will actually perform better, before the current regulatory system is "reformed."

### Bruce Ackerman & Richard Stewart, Reforming Environmental Law
### 37 Stanford Law Review 1333, 1333-1340 (1985)[13]

In 1971, Ezra Mishan brilliantly satirized the views of a Dr. Pangloss, who argued that a world of largely unregulated pollution was "optimal" because cleanup would involve enormous transaction costs. Less than 15 years later, Professor Latin uses the same Panglossian argument to rationalize the current regulatory status quo. He not only accepts but endorses our extraordinarily crude, costly, litigious and counterproductive system of technology-based environmental controls. Like Mishan's Pangloss, he seems to believe that if it were possible to have a better world, it would exist. Since it does not, the transaction costs involved in regulatory improvement must exceed the benefits. Proposals for basic change accordingly are dismissed as naive utopianism.

What explains this celebration of the regulatory status quo? As critics of the present system, we believe this question to be of more than academic interest. The present regulatory system wastes tens of billions of dollars every year, misdirects resources, stifles innovation, and spawns massive and often counterproductive litigation. There is a variety of fundamental but practical changes that could be made to improve its environmental and economic performance. Why have such changes not been adopted? Powerful organized interests have a vested stake in the status quo. The congressional committees, government bureaucracies, and industry and environmental groups that have helped to shape the present system want to see it perpetuated. But the current system is also bolstered by an often inarticulate sense that, however cumbersome, it "works," and that complexity and limited information make major improvements infeasible.

Professor Latin has performed an important service in providing an articulate, informed, and sophisticated exposition of this view. By developing and making transparent the arguments that might justify the status quo, he has made it easier to assess their merits. If, as we believe, those arguments lack merit, his sophisticated defense of the status quo may ultimately serve to hasten its demise.

We will not respond to all of the groundless charges that Professor Latin levels at the critics of the current system, ourselves included. We focus instead on the major flaws in his defense of existing law and policy. First, Latin's view is based on a Panglossian interpretation of the status quo. The current system does not in fact "work" and its malfunctions, like those of Soviet-style central planning, will

---

12. See Costle, Environmental Regulation and Regulatory Reform, 57 Wash. L. Rev. 409, 416 (1982) (estimating that pollution control requirements imposed regulatory costs of about 3.3% of GNP and about 3.1% of total industry expenditures on plants and equipment in 1981; Costle does admit, however, that "the effects [of environmental costs] on specific industries can be substantial"). Critics of command-and-control regulation contend that current programs "waste" billions of dollars, not that society is incapable of absorbing the aggregate costs if necessary. See, e.g., A. Kneese & C. Schultze, Pollution, Prices and Public Policy (1975); Stewart, Regulation, Innovation, and Administrative Law: A Conceptual Framework, 69 Calif. L. Rev. 1256, 1367–68 (1981).

13. Copyright © 1985 by the Board of Trustees of Leland Stanford, Junior University. Reprinted by permission of the copyright holder, the author, and Fred B. Rothman Co.

become progressively more serious as the economy grows and changes and our knowledge of environmental problems develops. Second, Latin mistakenly treats economic incentive systems as a form of regulatory "fine-tuning," rather than recognizing them as fundamental alternatives to our current reliance on centralized regulatory commands to implement environmental goals. Moreover, he completely ignores experience showing that economic incentive systems are feasible and effective. Third, Latin ignores the increasingly urgent need to improve the process by which Congress, the agencies, and the courts set environmental goals. He is mesmerized by decisionmaking costs, ignoring the great social benefits flowing from a more intelligent and democratically accountable dialogue on environmental policy. We deal with each of these points in turn.

**THE EXISTING SYSTEM...** The existing system of pollution regulation, which is the focus of Latin's defense, is primarily based on a Best Available Technology (BAT) strategy. If an industrial process or product generates some non-trivial risk, the responsible plant or industry must install whatever technology is available to reduce or eliminate this risk, so long as the costs of doing so will not cause a shutdown of the plant or industry. BAT requirements are largely determined through uniform federal regulations. Under the Clean Water Act's BAT strategy, the EPA adapts nationally uniform effluent limitations for some 500 different industries. A similar BAT strategy is deployed under the Clean Air Act for new industrial sources of air pollution, new automobiles, and industrial sources of toxic air pollutants. BAT strategies are also widely used in many fields of environmental regulation other than air and water pollution, which are the focus of Latin's analysis.

BAT was embraced by Congress and administrators in the early 1970s in order to impose immediate, readily enforceable federal controls on a relatively few widespread pollutants, while avoiding widespread industrial shutdowns. Subsequent experience and analysis has demonstrated:

1. Uniform BAT requirements waste many billions of dollars annually by ignoring variations among plants and industries in the cost of reducing pollution and by ignoring geographic variations in pollution effects. A more cost-effective strategy of risk reduction could free enormous resources for additional pollution reduction or other purposes.

2. BAT controls, and the litigation they provoke, impose disproportionate penalties on new products and processes. A BAT strategy typically imposes far more stringent controls on new sources because there is no risk of shutdown. Also, new plants and products must run the gauntlet of lengthy regulatory and legal proceedings to win approval; the resulting uncertainty and delay discourage new investment. By contrast, existing sources can use the delays and costs of the legal process to burden regulators and postpone or "water-down" compliance. BAT strategies also impose disproportionate burdens on more productive and profitable industries because these industries can "afford" more stringent controls. This "soak the rich" approach penalizes growth and international competitiveness.

3. BAT controls can ensure that established control technologies are installed. They do not, however, provide strong incentives for the development of new, environmentally superior strategies, and may actually discourage their development. Such innovations are essential for maintaining

long-term economic growth without simultaneously increasing pollution and other forms of environmental degradation.

4. BAT involves the centralized determination of complex scientific, engineering, and economic issues regarding the feasibility of controls on hundreds of thousands of pollution sources. Such determinations impose massive information-gathering burdens on administrators, and provide a fertile ground for complex litigation in the form of massive adversary rule-making proceedings and protracted judicial review. Given the high costs of regulatory compliance and the potential gains from litigation brought to defeat or delay regulatory requirements, it is often more cost-effective for industry to "invest" in such litigation rather than to comply.

5. A BAT strategy is inconsistent with intelligent priority setting. Simply regulating to the hilt whatever pollutants happen to get on the regulatory agenda may preclude an agency from dealing adequately with more serious problems that come to scientific attention later. BAT also tends to reinforce regulatory inertia. Foreseeing that "all or nothing" regulation of a given substance under BAT will involve large administrative and compliance costs, and recognizing that resources are limited, agencies often seek to limit sharply the number of substances on the agenda for regulatory action.

This indictment is not idle speculation, but the product of years of patient study by lawyers, economists, and political scientists. There are, for example, no fewer than 15 careful efforts to estimate the extra cost burden generated by a wide range of traditional legalistic BAT systems used to control a variety of air and water pollutants in different parts of the country. Of the twelve studies of different air pollutants — ranging from particulates to chlorofluorocarbons — seven indicated that traditional forms of regulation were more than 400 percent more expensive than the least-cost solution; four revealed that they were about 75 percent more expensive; one suggested a modest cost-overrun of 7 percent. Three studies of water pollution control in five different watersheds also indicate the serious inefficiency of traditional forms of command-and-control regulation. These careful studies of selected problems cannot be used to estimate precisely the total amount traditional forms of regulation are annually costing the American people. Nonetheless, very large magnitudes are at stake. Even if a reformed system could cut costs by "only" one-third, it could save more than $15 billion a year from the nation's annual expenditure of $50 billion on air and water pollution control alone.

While Latin entirely fails to address this evidence, he does not seriously contest the economic wastefulness of the current system's excessive compliance costs and penalties on new investment. He simply ignores the last three points in our indictment, even though they have been well developed in the literature. Instead, Latin spends all his time castigating all reform proposals as unrealistic. In his view, reformers characteristically propose utopian efforts at administrative "fine-tuning" that would in practice lead to a bureaucratic nightmare, making the present system seem benign by comparison.

We do not accept this despairing view. To explain why, however, we must correct an analytic deficiency in Latin's critique. The various reforms rejected in his article have little in common with one another — except that they all represent departures from BAT. Indeed, it is a sign of Latin's deep commitment to the status quo that, simply because they depart from BAT, he thinks of them as if they were all variations on the problem of "fine-tuning" that he decries. But "fine-tuning" is much too diffuse a notion on which to base an analysis of the reform agenda. Some of our proposals involve reform of the criteria and procedures which Congress, agencies, and the courts use in setting environmental goals; others involve reform of the means by which the goals (whatever they may be) are implemented in the real world. Latin's indiscriminate condemnation of "fine-tuning" fails to distinguish systematically between these two types of proposals. In this, as in so much else, his critique is faithful to the BAT system, which also conflates means and ends, preventing the intelligent assessment of either. If, however, we are to move beyond the status quo, it is best to treat these two different kinds of structural reform separately, beginning with the implementation problem and concluding with the question of goal-setting.

### COMMENTARY AND QUESTIONS

1. **Defining command-and-control.** What kinds of statutes fit within the description, "command-and-control"? For example, it is abundantly clear that the foremost target of the Ackerman and Stewart attacks is reliance on uniform performance standards such as the Clean Water Act's categorical source performance standards. Consider their list of additional culprits: the Clean Air Act's New (stationary) Source Performance Standards; the congressionally-required 90% automobile emission rollbacks of the Clean Air Act; the Clean Air Act's then-current NESHAPS program that relied on conservatively set harm-based performance standards; and BAT as used "in many fields of environmental regulation other than air and water pollution...." Recalling the chapters of Part III, the list is not homogeneous from a standard-setting point of view. What are the identifying characteristics that define a regulatory system as belonging to the "command and control" family? As a first approximation, all of the schemes involve coercion that requires the regulated entity to perform to a *governmentally* set level of performance. Would that mean a technology-based standard erected through a reg-neg process is any less command-and-control?

2. **What is wrong with command-and-control and what are the alternatives?** Identify the criticisms raised against command-and-control statutes by Ackerman and Stewart. Do the arguments raised against BAT-based standards apply with equal force to harm-based systems? Some, such as the claim that categorical BAT standards "waste many billions" by ignoring the variation of plant and receiving body characteristics are plainly inapposite, given the particularized nature of the SIP process, for example. There are some criticisms raised in the excerpt and elsewhere, however, that seem to be more generic, such as claims of huge transaction costs and information burdens, stifled creativity, or greater cost of achieving equivalent results. The common denominator of many of the criticisms is that reliance on market mechanisms could do the same job for less money. The two principal types of market mechanisms are effluent taxes and tradeable emission credits. Those alternatives, and other regulatory designs that use market enlisting mechanisms, are studied at length in Chapter 16.

3. **Separating goals from implementation.** Ackerman and Stewart distinguish between environmental goals and the methods suited to accomplish them. What

would you expect Ackerman and Stewart (and other proponents of economic analysis) to say about environmental goal setting? They first argue that the goals for environmental regulation ought to be expressed in terms of how much pollution reduction is desirable (e.g. a percentage reduction figure) within a given time frame. Perhaps surprisingly, Ackerman and Stewart feel that these are not economic questions to be determined by benefit-cost analysis. Rather, they describe these matters as "the quintessentially political question that should be answered by the legislative process." Why should such concrete goals be set politically? What is likely to be wrong, in their view, with having an administrative agency collect data and determine appropriate goals on that basis? Their second proposal in the area of goal-setting, operative in the longer run, is for regional and local differentiation of goals to reflect the differences in the underlying natural systems that are affected by the regulation. This may include especially stringent regulation for pristine areas, or laxer regulation in areas of great waste assimilative capacity. Could it also include a decision to commit some areas to service as pollution havens or national sacrifice areas? The third and final goal-oriented change is to set priorities in the regulatory agenda in a cost-effective way so that the largest gains in environmental quality are realized sooner, rather than later. For a measured criticism of the Ackerman-Stewart prescription, and particularly of the longer-term items, see Mintz, Economic Reform of Environmental Protection: A Brief Comment on a Recent Debate, 15 Harv. Envt'l L. Rev. 149, 160–162 (1991).

4. **Non-debatable theory: skepticism regarding implementation and motives.** The Latin excerpt does not take issue with the claim that there are, *in theory*, obtainable benefits *if* the legislated standards could be met in a lower cost or least-cost fashion. For Latin, that is a big "if." He lists several reasons for thinking that the claimed efficiencies might be offset by greater costs in operating the system advocated by Ackerman and Stewart. The reasons to expect dissipation of the theoretical fine-tuning benefits include increased information collection and evaluation costs, lack of predictability of regulatory endpoints as costs to the affected firms, greater costs in transmitting information to the public and in judicial review of the resultant controls, greater opportunities for strategic behavior by the regulated community in ways that drive up regulatory costs for other affected interests, foregone social benefits related to inter-firm equity, and increased likelihood of significant social dislocations.

A second avenue of attack posed by Latin (elsewhere in the article) controverts the Ackerman and Stewart position at a more fundamental level. Latin sincerely doubts that the fine-tuning theory can be made operational without sacrificing the overriding goal of having a cleaner, healthier environment. How well did a decentralized, individualized, case-by-case emission limitation system perform in the mid-century period? Latin also suggests that the Ackerman-Stewart position is being used as a cover by marketplace players who Latin accuses of wanting to dismantle environmental regulation altogether. This echoes the devolution-deregulation debates about the race-to-the-bottom chronicled in Chapter Five.

5. **Non-debatable practice: environmental improvement as measured by the numbers.** From their inception to the present, the Clean Air Act and Clean Water Act,

the leading embodiments of command and control strategies, have made immense contributions to environmental quality in the United States. Consider the following data compiled by EPA.

| **TABLE 1: Clean Air Act and Clean Water Act Contributions to Quality** | | |
|---|---|---|
| CRITERIA POLLUTANT | AIR QUALITY CONCENTRATION % CHANGE 1977–1996 | EMISSIONS % CHANGE 1970–1996 |
| Carbon monoxide | -61% | -31% |
| Lead | -97% | -98% |
| Nitrogen Dioxide and NOx (1988–1996 data) | -27% | increased 8% |
| Ozone | -30% | -38% (VOC) |
| PM10 | Data not available | -73% (includes only direct emissions, not secondary formation from SOx and NOx |
| Sulfur dioxide | -58% | -39% |

Source: U.S. EPA, 1996 National Air Quality and Emission Trends Report, R-97-013, January 1998, Table 1-2.

These gains were achieved in the face of considerable growth in population and economic activity:

Since 1970, total U. S. population increased 29%, vehicle miles traveled increased 121%, and the gross domestic product (GDP) increased 104%. During that same period, notable reductions in air quality concentrations and emissions took place. Aggregate criteria pollutant emissions decreased 32%." *Id.* at page 1-2.

Latin adverted to the improvements in air and water quality achieved by 1985, when he was writing, as one justification for resisting tampering with the system. Given the unenviable pre-1970 history of American pollution control, wouldn't any serious regulatory effort have made huge initial gains? A better measure of the value of the command-and-control regimes might look to their performance over a longer period to make sure that there is more than a period of initial improvement.

Air quality data for the criteria air pollutants for the period 1987–1996 showed continued improvement:

ı

| TABLE 2: Air Quality Data 1987–1996 | | |
|---|---|---|
| CRITERIA POLLUTANT | AIR QUALITY CONCENTRATION | EMISSIONS |
| Carbon monoxide | -37% | -18% |
| Lead | -75% | -50% |
| Nitrogen Dioxide and NOx (1988–1996 data) | -10% | + 3% |
| Ozone | -15% | -18% (VOC) |
| PM10 | -25% | -12% (includes only direct emissions, not secondary formation from SOx and NOx |
| Sulfur dioxide | -37% | -14% |

Source: U. S. EPA, 1996 National Air Quality and Emission Trends Report, R-97-013, January 1998, Table 1-1.

6. **Has the debate had a winner on the ground?** The superficial answer is that Latin's views have prevailed insofar as Congress has resisted efforts at repeal or wholesale reworking of either the Clean Air Act or Clean Water Act, the two major embodiments of command-and-control laws. That said, however, a closer look at events shows a remarkable degree to which the Ackerman-Stewart side of the debate has also made its mark without wholesale abandonment of command and control. Important examples of moves toward the Ackerman-Stewart side are readily seen in both the Clean Water Act and the Clean Air Act contexts. On the water side, consider the 1977 change in the standard for conventional pollutants discharged by point sources — from BAT to BCT. That change was prompted by a critical assessment of the benefit-cost issues. Additionally, the §301(h) deep water ocean discharge variance procedure is precisely the kind of fine-tuning that Ackerman and Stewart applauded. What departs from their vision is the fact that Congress made the adjustments, and because of the nature of the political process the changes came about, more slowly and with greater political effort than had the agency been tasked with far broader discretion from the outset. On the CAA side, some of the fine-tuning and flexibility has been in the statute from its inception. The SIP process, for all its difficulty, is not villainous command-and-control; it is the essence of fine-tuning. Additionally EPA had, and exercised, its interpretive power under the *Chevron* rule to allow a degree of emissions trading in the form of bubbles, netting, and offset banking. See Chapter 16. Finally, in 1990, Congress greatly expanded the use of trading in regard to sulfur dioxide emissions, mandating a so-far successful system of tradeable emissions credits. See Chapter 16.

The way events have unfolded reveals a significant dynamism of the sort described in Chapter Five, where the regulatory process has a cyclical character that proceeds through a series of stages — Planning, Standard-Setting, Permitting, Monitoring and Surveillance, Enforcement, and a Feedback loop from implementation.

Given the various amendments and add-on programs encountered by the Clean Water Act, the Clean Air Act, and other environmental statutes, the feedback loop can result in extensive continuing changes in the regulatory regime.

7. **Three postulates of sound environmental legislation.** In a field so complex as environmental law, it is easy to lose sight of basic principles. What are the basic requirements for framing effective environmental laws? First, the legislature should set the policy and not leave that burden to the agency. Dwyer's article points out the dangers that beset a law when the legislature had abdicated that responsibility. Second, the agency should not deliberately distort the policy choices made by the legislature. The *Corrosion Proof* case exemplifies the untoward results when, for example, an agency decides to disregard the policy set down by Congress regarding the balance between cost and hazard reduction. See also Chapter 17 where, instead of being overzealous as in the *Corrosion Proof* case, EPA attempted to downplay the congressional mandate by systematic non-implementation of RCRA. Finally, in the implementation phase of the legislation, whether it be a statutory choice of Congress or an administrative choice by the agency, the framer of the statutory design should consider command-and-control strategies, market enlistment strategies, and a variety of other approaches in an effort to seek effective operational results. There is no foreordained winner in such debates, and there will always be room for improvement in statutory design.

---

*I have no quarrel with...what I believe to be the intent of NEPA.... I do have a quarrel with those who, ever since its enactment, have used NEPA to obstruct the orderly progress of obtaining the power supply this region must have if we are to continue to provide for a reasonable lifestyle for ourselves, our children, and the generations to come.... The anti-producers who are abusing the National Environmental Policy Act by using it as a sword have an avowed purpose — to stop growth in our society. They say "Write an environmental impact statement or we'll take you to court." If we write the Environmental Impact Statement, then they claim it is inadequate and take us to court anyway. If they lose, they appeal. In the meantime, the "development based on planned growth"...is delayed, and thereby the full benefit of the planning is lost.*

— "The Prophets of Shortage," Speech by Don Hodel, past Administrator of the Bonneville Power Administration who presided over utility over-building that brought about the WPPSS default, and later was a high-ranking member of the Reagan administration, Portland Oregon City Club, July 11, 1975.

# Chapter 13

# DISCLOSURE STRATEGIES: NEPA'S STOP-AND-THINK LOGIC, AND THE POWER OF INFORMATION

A. *NEPA, the National Environmental Policy Act*

B. *NEPA in Court; the first generation*

C. *NEPA in the courts since* Kleppe

D. *Federal Community Right-to-Know Statutes*

---

This chapter focuses on the broadest, most coherent, and best known statutory model of an environmental disclosure statute — the National Environmental Policy Act (NEPA) — which tries to induce agencies to stop-and-think before launching projects that harm the environment, and enforces that objective with environmental impact statements (EISs) — information-disclosure procedures that have been repeatedly enforced by citizen litigation.

NEPA is by no means the only environmental statute to have an information-disclosure element, although it is more central in NEPA than in many others. Much of environmental law is concerned with obtaining information, organizing it, and directing it to where it can do the most legal and political good. Information is power in environmental policy-making, because if the media and the public have critical information on the negatives of a dubious proposal, the public inclinations toward environmental protection often will produce a corrective decision in court or in the political arena. Getting strategic information into open public debate is often more than half the battle, especially where the availability of direct citizen enforcement mechanisms can make information regarding environmental threats actionable by members of the public, without the intervention of governmental agencies.

Thus information disclosure components can be found in many environmental statutes, especially federal. The biological assessment mechanism of §7 of the Endangered Species Act pressures federal wildlife agencies to examine and publish the factual biological vulnerabilities of endangered species populations, forcing many potential conflicts into the open which otherwise would be lost in bureaucratic bogs. Pollution statutes often are linked to public information, requiring submission of data to governmental agencies with a strong presumption in favor of public availability.[1] Product regulation and market access statutes typically

---

1. See, e.g., CWA §308(a), 33 U.S.C.A. §1318(a).

require the intensive development and production of information regarding product safety as a core regulatory element. Market-enlisting statutes can succeeed or fail depending on the availability of good data on the physical conditions to be addressed as well as the economic and financial impacts of taxes and incentives. Effective enforcement and informal dispute resolution demand reliable data of all varieties. The public trust doctrine in part operates to discourage low-visibility decision-making by requiring public ventilation of information and consideration of it by responsible political or legal institutions. And international law often operates far more by information generation and production than by mandate.

Following the NEPA analysis, the chapter studies several "community right-to-know" statutes, including the federal Emergency Planning And Community Right-to-Know Act (EPCRA), and an influential state disclosure law, California's "Proposition 65."

## A. NEPA, THE NATIONAL ENVIRONMENTAL POLICY ACT

NEPA, the National Environmental Policy Act,[2] is a statute that provokes a wide diversity of reactions. To some it is a paper tiger, of awesome but toothless aspect. To others, it is a ringing statutory declaration of environmental protection and rational human governance, setting a precedent of international significance. To some it is an unproductive attempt to intrude on productive public-private enterprises. To others, it is a legislative accident (whether fortunate or unfortunate) that was created and continues to evolve by happenstance. As usual, there is probably some truth in each of these perspectives.

Ultimately, NEPA's successes may be impossible to measure, in part because its effectiveness includes the anonymous thousands of destructive federal projects that are withdrawn, or never proposed in the first place, in anticipation of NEPA scrutiny.

In taxonomic form, a distinct new model of statutory regulation can be discerned within NEPA's provisions: NEPA is a broad stop-and-think, disclose-to-the-public administrative law. It is general in its statutory commands — a broad, simple set of directives that apply across the board to all federal agencies. Its operative terms require agencies to contemplate the context and consequences of their actions before acting, in effect mandating a particularized process of program planning, intended to begin early in the genesis of agency decisions. Public disclosure is NEPA's complementary mandate: agencies must produce a publicly reviewable physical document reflecting the required internal project analysis. Preparation of this document is supposed to ensure that the agency has given "good faith consideration" to the environmental consequences of its proposed action and its reasonable alternatives, but, in practice, this assumption is frequently false.

The rationality of this requirement — requiring documented formal consideration of negatives and alternatives as well as benefits before acting — may be obvious, but NEPA was its pioneer. Its logic has subsequently been adopted in many

---

2. 42 U.S.C.A. §4321 et seq., Pub. L. 91-190 (1970).

international and domestic systems. The potent nonenvironmental forces that NEPA attempts to control, however, have kept up a running resistance to its statutory mandates, with some successes over the years.

Here is the text of NEPA, as it was signed into law by Richard Nixon on January 1, 1970. As you read it, note its terms, its style, its poetry, and the regulatory approaches it consciously or unconsciously incorporated:

## Public Law 91-190 (1970)

AN ACT: To establish a national policy for the environment, to provide for the establishment of a Council on Environmental Quality, and for other purposes.

Be it enacted by the Senate and House of Representatives of the United States of America in Congress assembled, that this Act may be cited as the "National Environmental Policy Act of 1969."

### Title I. Declaration of National Environmental Policy

Sec. 101 (a) The Congress, recognizing the profound impact of man's activity on the interrelations of all components of the natural environment, particularly the profound influences of population growth, high-density urbanization, industrial expansion, resource exploitation, and new and expanding technological advances and recognizing further the critical importance of restoring and maintaining environmental quality to the overall welfare and development of man, declares that it is the continuing policy of the Federal Government, in cooperation with State and local governments, and other concerned public and private organizations, to use all practicable means and measures, including financial and technological assistance, in a manner calculated to foster and promote the general welfare, to create and maintain conditions under which man and nature can exist in productive harmony, and fulfill the social, economic, and other requirements of present and future generations of Americans.

(b) In order to carry out the policy set forth in this Act, it is the continuing responsibility of the Federal Government to use all practicable means, consistent with other essential considerations of national policy, to improve and coordinate Federal plans, functions, programs, and resources to the end that the Nation may —

(1) fulfill the responsibilities of each generation as trustee of the environment for succeeding generations; (2) assure for all Americans safe, healthful, productive, and esthetically and culturally pleasing surroundings; (3) attain the widest range of beneficial uses of the environment without degradation, risk to health or safety, or other undesirable and unintended consequences; (4) preserve important historic, cultural, and natural aspects of our national heritage, and maintain, wherever possible, an environment which supports diversity and variety of individual choice; (5) achieve a balance between population and resource use which will permit high standards of living and a wide sharing of life's amenities; and (6) enhance the quality of renewable resources and approach the maximum attainable recycling of depletable resources.

(c) The Congress recognizes that each person should enjoy a healthful environment and that each person has a responsibility to contribute to the preservation and enhancement of the environment.

Sec. 102. The Congress authorizes and directs that, to the fullest extent possible:

(1) The policies, regulations, and public laws of the United States shall be interpreted and administered in accordance with the policies set forth in this Act, and

(2) all agencies of the Federal Government shall —

(A) utilize a systematic, interdisciplinary approach which will insure the integrated use of the natural and social sciences and the environmental design arts in planning and in decisionmaking which may have an impact on man's environment;

(B) identify and develop methods and procedures, in consultation with the Council on Environmental Quality established by title II of this Act, which will insure that presently unquantified environmental amenities and values may be given appropriate consideration in decision-making along with economic and technical considerations;

(C) include in every recommendation or report on proposals for legislation and other major Federal actions significantly affecting the quality of the human environment, a detailed statement by the responsible official on —

(i)   the environmental impact of the proposed action,

(ii)  any adverse environmental effects which cannot be avoided should the proposal be implemented,

(iii) alternatives to the proposed action,

(iv)  the relationship between local short-term uses of man's environment and the maintenance and enhancement of long-term productivity, and

(v)   any irreversible and irretrievable commitments of resources which would be involved in the proposed action should it be implemented.

Prior to making any detailed statement, the responsible Federal official shall consult with and obtain the comments of any Federal agency which has jurisdiction by law or special expertise with respect to any environmental impact involved. Copies of such statement and the comments and views of the appropriate Federal, State, and local agencies, which are authorized to develop and enforce environmental standards shall be made available to the President, the Council on Environmental Quality and to the public as provided by section 552 of Title 5, United States Code, and shall accompany the proposal through the existing agency review processes;

(D) study, develop, and describe appropriate alternatives to recommended courses of action in any proposal which involves unresolved conflicts concerning alternative uses of available resources;

(E) recognize the worldwide and long-range character of environmental problems and, where consistent with the foreign policy of the United States, lend appropriate support to initiatives, resolutions, and programs designed to maximize international cooperation in anticipating and preventing a decline in the quality of mankind's world environment;

(F) make available to States, counties, municipalities, institutions, and individuals, advice and information useful in restoring, maintaining, and enhancing the quality of the environment;

(G) initiate and utilize ecological information in the planning and development of resource-oriented projects; and

(H) assist the Council on Environmental Quality established by Title II of this Act.

Sec. 103. All agencies of the Federal Government shall review their present statutory authority, administrative regulations, and current polices and procedures for the purpose of determining whether there are any deficiencies or inconsistencies therein which prohibit full compliance with the purposes and provisions of this Act....

Sec. 104. Nothing in Section 102 or 103 shall in any way affect the specific statutory obligations of any Federal agency (1) to comply with criteria or standards of environmental quality, (2) to coordinate or consult with any other Federal or State agency, or (3) to act, or refrain from acting contingent upon the recommendations or certification of any other Federal or State agency.

Sec. 105. The policies and goals set forth in this Act are supplementary to those set forth in existing authorizations of Federal agencies.

[Title II establishes the President's Council on Environmental Quality (CEQ), which gathers information and conducts studies on environmental trends and conditions, reviews federal government programs in light of NEPA's substantive goals, and recommends national policies for environmental improvement. By executive order, the CEQ issues regulations for coordinating federal agency compliance with NEPA. E.O. 11514 (1970) as amended by E.O. 11991 (1977).[3]]

### COMMENTARY AND QUESTIONS

1. **NEPA as paper tiger.** Note that NEPA, as finally passed, contains a great deal of poetic language and precious little that is mandatory. There are ringing hortatory declarations of policy, and wistful commitments to processes of scientific rationality, especially in §101, and in most of §102. Does all this amount to anything? Is there anything in §101, purportedly the primary section of NEPA, that has any legal effect? There is, of course, the small matter of §102(2)(C). Note that even that subsection is filled with vague verbiage; the instrumental words are limited to a couple of dozen out of two hundred. If you parse it carefully, however, §102(2)(C) levies a sole, narrow, statutory requirement: an EIS shall be prepared for all major federal actions significantly affecting the quality of the human environment. That deceptively simple requirement has produced virtually all NEPA caselaw. Nevertheless, even though there may be an enforceable EIS requirement, it seems merely procedural and does not purport to dictate substantive results. In other words, NEPA provides a right to information, not to particular programmatic actions. Observing the course of application of NEPA to the intricate internal mechanisms of federal agencies, and the market forces with which they are linked, many observers have said that this procedural restraint is relatively meaningless. As Professor Sax wrote about NEPA, "I think the emphasis on the redemptive quality of procedural reform is about nine parts myth and one part coconut oil...."[4] A sustained process in some federal courts, and many federal agencies over the years, has held NEPA to procedural terms and minimal formal compliance.

Continuing through these NEPA materials, therefore, one should note that they may chronicle a statutory program that some consider a symbolic assurance sham, not worth the extensive time and energies invested in it.

---

3. 40 CFR §§1500-1508. These regulations are the most complete guide to the interpretation of NEPA; when an important NEPA court decision is handed down, it is customarily codified here.
4. Sax, The (Unhappy) Truth about NEPA, 26 Okla. L.R. 239 (1973).

2. **NEPA as international milestone and state model.** NEPA can also be categorized as a remarkable, internationally-pioneering declaration of a national policy of environmental sensitivity. Beyond the high principle of its declaration of policy, moreover, NEPA's environmental impact statement requirement is a novel strategic assertion of an all-too-obvious truth: Government agencies, like all other human actors, are prone to tunnel vision. The realities of a complex world require an institutionalized comprehensive stop-and-think review process within the governmental system itself. The NEPA model has been emulated by more than 25 states and over 80 countries around the world, and serves as a model for environmental impact assessments for such global institutions as the World Bank.[5] In following the NEPA model, these other governmental entities have treated the impact statement process as an apt mechanism for achieving practical enforcement of the broad declarations of environmental policy that accompany it, and as a caveat to the administrative state that it look before it leaps.

3. **NEPA as accidental legislation.** The political reality underlying NEPA's legislative history was an extraordinary post-Silent Spring late-1960s groundswell of popular attention to problems of environmental quality. Facing upcoming by-elections, Congress and President Nixon hastened to adjust to the issue. "The 1970s must be the years that America pays its debts to the past by reclaiming the purity of its air, its water, and our living environment. It is literally now or never," said Nixon. A number of legislative details, however, reveal the moderate intent of the President and Congress. As the various draft bills that became NEPA moved through the legislature in 1969 (as S.1075 and H.R.12549, 91st Congress), they initially were quite innocuous. Section 101 read then much as it does now. §102 merely called for governmental funding for environmental studies. Where teeth seemed to exist, they were pulled. Section 101(c) originally read: "The Congress recognizes that each person has a fundamental and inalienable right to a healthful environment..." and that was changed. Rep. Wayne Aspinall of Colorado, a stalwart friend of the mining and lumber industries, was able to insert a provision into the House bill that "Nothing in this act shall increase, decrease, or change any responsibility or authority of any federal official or agency created by other provision of law...." What would have been the effect of this provision? (It was changed in conference committee to read as in §§103-105, over Aspinall's objection.) And what does the actual title of the act tell you?

On April 16, 1969, however, in one of a seemingly endless series of small committee hearings, Professor Lynton Caldwell, a political scientist from Indiana University, mentioned in testimony before Senator Jackson's Interior Committee that he "would urge that in the shaping of such policy it have an action-forcing, operational aspect...." Chairman Jackson, to the surprise of his staff, picked up on this: "I agree with you that realistically what is needed in restructuring the governmental side of this problem is to legislatively create those situations that will

5. Council on Environmental Quality, The National Environmental Policy Act: A Study of its Effectiveness After Twenty-five Years (1997)(hereafter "CEQ Study"). See Nicholas A. Robinson, International Trends in Environmental Impact Assessment, 19 B.C. Env. Aff. L. Rev. 591 (1991), and Nicholas A. Robinson, SEQRA's Siblings: Precedents from Little NEPA's in the Sister States, 46 Alb. L. Rev. 1155 (1982)(state EIS development in the dozen years after NEPA).

bring about an action-forcing procedure that departments must comply with. Otherwise these lofty declarations are nothing more than that.... I am wondering if I may broaden the policy provision in the bill so as to lay down a general requirement that would be applicable to all agencies...."[6] Based on this brief interchange, Caldwell sat down with a couple of staffers and drafted the text of the present §102. The underlying mood of Congress continued to be felt, however. Jackson accepted an amendment inserting the phrase "to the fullest extent possible" into §102, a clause apparently intended to modify the otherwise strict command of its first sentence. In §102(2)(C), Jackson's language originally read that there had to be an environmental *finding* by the responsible official, a term that was amended to read "statement," apparently to avoid the implication that there might be required findings of fact that would be judicially reviewable.[7]

Imagine the shock of Richard Nixon and many members of Congress when, early in 1970, they discovered that these apparently innocuous words of §102 could be the basis of very real lawsuits. Section 102, like a snake in the grass, carried the hidden but potent impact statement requirement. There have subsequently been hundreds of NEPA lawsuits, affecting federal projects and programs running into billions of dollars. Why didn't Congress recognize this potential? If Congress didn't recognize NEPA's potential, can courts nevertheless enforce the statute to give it precisely the judicial effect that Congress had tried to eliminate?

In the years immediately following NEPA's passage almost two hundred bills were introduced to weaken or repeal it. None passed. This indicates that, once passed, a "motherhood" statute is no less sacred for having been unintended. Isn't it likely, however, that Congress would have passed almost any proposed environmental statute, and that it was only an accident of the legislative process that produced a statute with some teeth? What does that say about the process?

**4. NEPA's de facto statutory strategy.** Despite NEPA's unintended, rather serendipitous legislative history, one can still analyze the provisions that emerged from Congress as embodying a novel de facto statutory strategy, as noted earlier.

First, whatever NEPA requires is government-wide, not a series of directives specifically tailored to particular governmental agencies. This umbrella approach provides strengths as well as weaknesses.

Second, NEPA asserts a strong general declaration of policy that might be made relevant to a wide range of substantive interpretations and applications of various statutes, although this has not noticeably been the case.

Third, the impact statement procedure requires an internal process of overview accounting, specifying a detailed analysis of agency proposals. It pins down this required process with the EIS, a specific workproduct that provides tangible reviewable evidence of the agency's compliance. The notion, moreover, that the EIS will

---

6. National Environmental Policy Act, 1969: Hearings on S.1075, S. 233, and S.1752 before the Senate Committee on Interior and Insular Affairs, 91st Cong., 1st Sess. 116-117 (1969)(statement of Lynton Caldwell, Professor of Government, University of Indiana).

7. For a complete history of NEPA's legislative genesis, see R.N.L. Andrews, Environmental Policy and Administrative Change (1976).

accompany proposals through the decisional process may impose a practical timing requirement bringing environmental impact accounting into the earlier project stages.

There is no enforcement mechanism on the face of NEPA. Caldwell and the committee staff presumed that NEPA would be actively enforced by the President, acting through OMB and CEQ, and by Congress. In reality, as we shall soon see, enforcement, if it was to come, had to come from somewhere else.

Nevertheless, the statutory framework can be viewed as incorporating a coherent and quite novel regulatory logic. Through its provisions, even low-visibility agency decisions that might significantly impact the environment would have to be "ventilated" within and outside the agency, and made accessible in published form to the President, Congress, and the public for their review and response.

5. **The political science of NEPA.** Note that the only legally-specific section of NEPA targeted its environmental protection efforts upon the federal agencies, not upon the corporate polluters who previously had been the primary focus of public attention. Federal agencies, however, happen to be intimately involved with a host of major production and development activities across the face of the economy and the territory of the United States. Federal agencies are involved in the logging of national forests, in water resources, minerals and mining, the construction of highways and airports, urban redevelopment, the oil industry and offshore oil development, and the like. As the extent of potential NEPA litigation has become more obvious, the targeting of NEPA on federal agencies has provided a broad handle on a very broad range of environmental problems. NEPA applies not only to federal construction activities, but also to federal regulations, leases, contracts, permits, purchases, and other proposed actions that might have a significant impact on the human environment.

6. **The role of citizens.** The history of each statute is unique. NEPA was written in broad terms, achieved support, and passed through Congress, as a product of its unique times. It is impossible to overestimate the importance of public opinion in pushing NEPA into law. NEPA would never have moved beyond its first drafts without the environmental fervor of hundreds of thousands of citizens in the late 1960s.

Even more than most statutes, however, NEPA was only an incipient force when it was signed in January 1970. Its growth and development once again depended upon citizens' efforts, this time in the courts. Turning to NEPA in the courts, it is important to remember a basic irony: when the terms of a statute require interpretation, courts put their primary reliance upon the intention of the legislature, but in the case of NEPA's §102, there really *wasn't* any.

## B. NEPA IN COURT — THE FIRST GENERATION

Whenever a new statute is legislated, an elaborate series of further questions must be answered. Has it created a new cause of action? If so, who can file lawsuits? Against what defendants? What is the statute of limitations? What actions can be attacked? What are potential defendants required to do under the Act? What do plaintiffs have to show in their complaint and at trial? What defenses are available? What remedies are provided for? The evolving answers to these questions create a common law of the statute. Depending upon how they are answered in court, a statute can flourish or wither on the vine.

NEPA litigation has, from the beginning, focused upon the one clear requirement of the Act — a major federal action significantly affecting the environment must have an EIS. Tracing some of the issues raised in the cases over the years not only clarifies the law of NEPA, but also illuminates the process by which courts shape the flight of the statutory "missile" after the legislature launches it. In the case of NEPA's environmental impact statement requirement, the fact that Congress pretty clearly did not intend to create any new cause of action has had remarkably little effect on the growth of the statute in court cases over time.

### Section 1. NEPA IN THE JUDICIAL PROCESS: THE CHICOD CREEK CONTROVERSY — A CHRONOLOGICAL ANALYSIS OF A CLASSIC NEPA CASE

No case can be a "typical" NEPA case, because of the remarkable diversity of NEPA lawsuits over the years. The legal and practical elements of the *Chicod Creek* decisions, however, offer a broadly instructive blueprint of NEPA litigation generally, as well as a fascinating example of how NEPA, which was not intended to be litigable, quickly became a highly functional cause of action when plaintiffs dragged it before federal judges.

### Natural Resources Defense Council v. Grant (*Chicod Creek*)
U.S. District Court, Eastern District of North Carolina, 1972
341 F. Supp. 356

LARKINS, District Judge...Chicod Creek Watershed, located in mideastern North Carolina, covers an area of 35,100 acres of which 29,625 acres are in Pitt County and 5,475 acres in Beaufort County. Plans for solving flooding, water management, and other resources problems have been prepared with the concurrence of local sponsors and with federal assistance under the the provisions of P.L. 566. The sponsoring local organizations are the Pitt Soil and Water Conservation District, Beaufort Soil and Water Conservation District, Pitt County Board of Commissioners, and Pitt County Drainage District Number Nine. Under the Chicod Creek Watershed Work Plan and Supplements, the local organizations assume all local responsibilities for the installation, operation and maintenance of planned structural works.

The topography of the watershed is nearly level to gently sloping. The outer perimeter is flat and well drained and the flood plains are broad swamps. Land use in the watershed consists of 15,600 acres of cropland; 15,550 acres of woodland; 350 acres of grassland; and 3,600 acres of miscellaneous uses. Approximately 10,000 acres of crop and pasture land are subject to flooding.... A loss of at least 50 percent is sustained on the crops grown on land subject to flooding about once each five years. [Such flooding] causes interrupted traffic, blocked school bus and mail delivery routes, interrupted feeding schedules of farm animals, and additional maintenance and repair on the roads. Excessive rainfall and flooding create a health hazard. Septic tanks, nitrification lines, and approved pit-privies overflow to the surface of the soil after excessive rainfall. Poor drainage often results in low quality crops and high unit cost of production.

The population of the watershed is approximately 3,000 people. The entire population is classified as rural with 25 percent being non-farm. Agriculture is the principal enterprise in the watershed. The chief cash crops are tobacco, corn, soybeans, and cotton. Livestock production, consisting of beef cattle and swine, make up ten percent of the cash farm receipts. Value of farm products sold was under $10,000 for 77.6 percent of the 250 farms in the watershed. Fifty-five percent of the families make less than $3,000 income per year.

Chicod Creek originates about 6 miles south of Grimesland and flows generally (about 10 miles) north to its confluence with the Tar River. Cow Swamp and Juniper Branch are the two largest tributaries and they enter Chicod Creek from the west. Chicod Creek and the surrounding area has significant value for numerous waterfowl, fur bearers and other wetland wildlife species. The streams have substantial resident fish population and support a significant spawning run of herring during the spring.

The project was developed for the purposes of flood prevention, drainage, and conservation, development, and improvement of agricultural tracts of land. These objects are to be achieved by land treatment measures and structural measures. The land treatment measures will include conservation cropping systems, cover crops, crop residue use, minimum tillage, grasses and legumes, and tile and open drains. Also, 300 acres of open land will be reforested, while 1,350 acres of land will be subject to thinning and removal of trees. Structural improvements will consist of approximately 66 miles (comprising the main stream and all the various tributaries) of channel enlargement or "stream channelization." Mitigation measures to reduce the adverse effects on fish and wildlife resources are (1) 73 acres of wildlife wetland preservation area, (2) a 12 acre warm-water impoundment area, (3) 11 channel pools, and (4) 30 swamp drainage control structures. These mitigation measures are designed to mitigate for the disruption to the fish caused by the construction of the channels and to offset the wildlife habitat destroyed by the channels and spoil areas. Certain groups feel that these mitigation measures do not sufficiently lessen the adverse effects of the project on the environment. A letter [from] the Fish and Wildlife Service, dated September 10, 1971, reflects such an opinion:

> It is the opinion of the Service that the original mitigation measures plus the additional measures do not significantly lessen the adverse effects of the project on the ecosystem of the watershed.

The Watershed Work Plan and an agreement for the implementation thereof were executed on behalf of [the local] Soil and Water Conservation District... organizations, who are parties to the agreement and plan, and before execution by the Soil Conservation Service, the plan was reviewed by the Corps of Engineers of the United States Department of the Army and the United States Department of the Interior, and other federal agencies...and approved by the Committees on Agriculture [both House and Senate]....

Pursuant to the provisions of the National Environmental Policy Act and the Council on Environmental Quality [regulations], the Administrator of the Soil Conservation Service, through the issuance of Environment Memorandum 1 and Watersheds Memorandum 108, the Chicod Creek Watershed project was placed in Group 2, i.e., those projects having some adverse effect which can be eliminated by minor project modification..... After consideration of environmental concerns, including the unfavorable comments of the Fish and Wildlife Service, officials of the Soil and Conservation Service determined that the project as modified was not a major federal action significantly affecting the quality of human environment and that the project should proceed.

The present action was instituted to enjoin the defendants from financing and participating in the construction of the Chicod Creek Watershed Project. The total installation cost of the project is estimated to be $1,503,831. Public Law 566 funds are to pay $706,684 and other funds will provide $797,147. There has been extensive preparation by the defendants and the intervenors for this project. The landowners have incurred approximately $13,000 of debts to create the drainage district. Easements and rights-of-way have been obtained on 282 tracts of land involving 230 landowners. The local sponsors have procured a Farmers Home Administration loan. The Soil Conservation Service has incurred substantial expenses on the project, having expended $50,000 for planning and $159,176 for engineering, design, and land treatment. The Soil Conservation Service will suffer expenses as a result of the delay caused by this action. The projected cost of delay amounts to $7,650 per month, representing salaries and increased construction costs. The cost of preparing impact statements is approximately $7,500 per project....

### COMMENTARY AND QUESTIONS (ON CHICOD CREEK UP TO THIS POINT)

1. **The factual setting.** Can you figure out what is going on here? Physically, these Soil Conservation Service (SCS) channelization projects involve cutting a swath of trees (here about 10 percent of the area's woodland) along a watercourse, then, using power-scoopers called "draglines," cutting a wide open-banked canal in a straight line through the watershed. The natural meandering stream is thus replaced by a broad ditch. The judge does not seem particularly aware of what "adverse effects" might result. What kind of ecological evidence would you have brought to the hearing on a preliminary injunction to demonstrate the facts?

What were the purposes of the project? "Flood prevention" clearly does not mean protection of lives and property from rampaging floodwaters. Rather, the flood problem appears to be drainage, and the purpose of the project is largely to promote agriculture (although traffic and sanitation consequences are mentioned). By channelizing the watershed and adding open ditches and tile drains, the project would not only have reduced seasonal drainage problems but also have created new arable land out of "useless marshes." About 17 percent of the benefited acreage was owned by the Weyerhaeuser Lumber Company.

Economically, it is Public Law 566, the Watershed Protection Act, 16 U.S.C.A. §§1001 et seq. (1970) that pushes the project along. The court notes that $706,684 out of the $1,503,831 total cost is to be contributed by federal taxpayers under P.L. 566. The "local" contribution is typically not wholly paid in dollars. By donating land rights (i.e., easements of access for the dragline, rights-of-way for ditches), landowners are credited with economic contributions toward the local share. The remainder is made up by assessments in the drainage district. As a result, local agriculture gets a construction project subsidy five to ten times its own dollar outlay (the federal contribution rate varies depending upon how much can be called "flood protection" (75 percent) rather than drainage (50 percent)). Does the

KARL SCHURR

*Stream channelization involves bulldozing or draglining the natural contours and mean-*
*ders of a stream into straight-line trapezoidal cross-section ditches. The trees and shrubs*
*naturally clustered along the streambanks are stripped away and burned or left in spoil*
*piles. Water flows change dramatically from natural flows in terms of temperature,*
*volume, velocity, erosion, and water quality. The pre-existing populations of fish and other*
*aquatic life typically decline severely. In this photograph, the dragline is re-dredging a*
*silted-in channelization done approximately five years prior.*

fact that the private market does not build these projects on its own show that they
are not cost-effective without federal subsidies?

2. **The political setting.** The political organization of SCS projects is part of the
NEPA story. Originally the SCS was an erosion-control agency whose motto was
"stop the raindrop where it falls" through contour plowing and other methods. The
agency was so successful that it worked itself out of a job. Accordingly, the SCS
shifted its focus to carrying water away from the land, an about-face that naturally
brought it into the business of managing small streams, as the Corps had carved
out its jurisdiction over rivers. Annually, huge sums of federal money are appropriated by the congressional agricultural appropriations subcommittees for distribution around the nation to SCS projects. At the local level, agribusiness and
individual farmers, who will ultimately benefit from the subsidies, are organized
into Drainage Districts through the efforts of the county or regional agent who
administers the local-level SCS Soil Conservation District. The drainage districts
are basically state-chartered quasi-governmental units with the power to contract
for construction, and to assess fees. A project is proposed by one of the participants
(often the local SCS agent, whose career advancement typically is linked to success
in getting such projects underway). A majority of affected landowners (measured
by acreage rather than per capita) must approve the project; if approved, all must
subsequently contribute. The project is then transmitted by the SCS's "State

Conservationist" to Washington where it is "authorized" for construction by the SCS and the FHA, and the Secretary of Agriculture. (The SCS and the TVA are rare examples of agencies that have been given extraordinary powers to self-authorize projects without a congressional vote). Appropriated money is then released to the District for sequential planning, design, and construction. Low interest loans, moreover, are granted to finance part of the local share. The participants, throughout this process, are linked in an identity of interests. The SCS owes its existence to the continuation of the drainage function; the Congressional appropriations committees derive their political power from the ability to deliver dollars throughout the country; the Department of Agriculture and its subdepartments likewise; state and local government officials may be incorporated into the District funding process; and private individuals receive direct financial benefits, some from the project's subsidized land modifications, others from the award of construction contracts. The various private and public participants have their nationwide organizations, with annual conventions, newsletters, and Washington-based lobbyists, all to assure the system's smooth functioning.

Outside the network of drainage-oriented interests are other public and private bodies. The state Wildlife Commission had received a report from its expert, George Burdick, noting the drastic ecological effects of channelization, and had tried to persuade the SCS to terminate the program. The SCS told the state agency that Chicod Creek was being pushed by local landowners and was beyond SCS control. ("Meantime," said one state official, "the SCS agents were whooping it up with the local people telling them what they wanted where.") In controversial matters like this, a state agency will usually not sue to achieve its objectives, nor even complain administratively over the SCS officer's head. The state commission did not insist on its position, but did take part in some planning "at a time when the SCS had already established the design"; it did follow the litigation closely, however, and participated in subsequent negotiations. The federal Fish and Wildlife Service volunteered the letter cited, noting adverse effects. But the FWS had no legal basis to participate in the decision even if it had wanted to interfere with a sister agency. In sum, from top to bottom, no governmental body existed to defend environmental interests. This gap left things up to the local sporting and conservation groups, which happened to find out about the project and got organized in time to persuade the National Resources Defense Council, a private entity, to take on the expensive task of litigating this, out of hundreds of other potential cases.

3. **Judicial attitudes towards NEPA challenges.** How do you interpret the mood of Judge Larkins at this stage of the case? Do you notice the inevitability implied in the phrasing (so common in NEPA cases) that "1350 acres of land will be [deforested]," etc.?

4. **Financial commitments and delay costs.** The judge notes the amounts of money committed to date and the cost of delay if an injunction were granted. This information is regularly emphasized by environmental defendants to show that too much project expenditure has occurred before trial to permit the project reasonably to be stopped. Has the $130,000 been *spent*? Were easements paid for? Can the FHA

loan be returned? Do any of the SCS expenditures, for "land treatment," etc., have value irrespective of project completion? How much of this financial commitment took place after NEPA became law in January 1970? As to delay, is it relevant that the majority of costs that would inflate over the course of the suit would ultimately be paid in federal tax dollars that have likewise inflated in revenue terms? In light of the $7,500 cost of an SCS environmental impact statement, what relevance do all these numbers seem to have for the judge?

### NRDC v. Grant, 341 F. Supp. 356, continued...

CONCLUSIONS OF LAW: JURISDICTION... This Court has jurisdiction of this matter pursuant to 28 U.S.C.A. §1331 (federal question) and 5 U.S.C.A. §702 (Administrative Procedure Act).

The National Environmental Policy Act of 1969, 42 U.S.C.A. §4321 et seq., requires all federal agencies, in performing their respective functions, to be responsive to possible environmental consequences of their actions. The Act makes it the "continuing" responsibility of the federal government to "use all practicable means and measures" to carry out the national policy of restoring and maintaining a quality environment....

RETROACTIVITY... [Judge Larkin, as most other judges in the early development of NEPA, held that NEPA was applicable to ongoing projects, like the Chicod Creek channelization, on which substantial actions remained to be taken.[8]]

REQUIREMENTS OF §102(2)C OF NEPA... Section102(2)(C) directs all agencies of the federal government to prepare an environmental impact statement for every major federal action significantly affecting the environment. The defendants contend that even though they have not filed an environmental impact statement, "a particular form," that in substance they have fulfilled all of the requirements of §102(2)(C). In support they assert that a detailed statement has been prepared and circulated; that the environmental impact has been considered by the Soil Conservation Service and agencies of both state and federal government; that adverse effects which cannot be avoided have been considered and weighed against the total benefit of going on with the project; that alternatives have been considered and some have been adopted; that there have been consultations with other federal agencies and with state and local agencies; and that the project has been open to and has received public comment. According to the record and the testimony received at the motion hearing on January 5, 1972, this cannot be disputed. But the fact remains that an environmental impact statement has not been prepared and filed for the Chicod Creek Watershed Project. Mr. Hollis Williams, Deputy Administrator of Watersheds, Soil Conservation Service at the motion hearing testified to the effect: "We had the belief and still do, that an environmental impact statement is not needed in the Chicod Creek Project." An environmental impact statement must be filed for every major federal action significantly affecting the quality of the human environment. The District of Columbia Circuit noted in Calvert Cliffs v. AEC, 449 F.2d 1109 (D.C. Cir. 1971) that "...the §102 duties are not inherently flexible. They must be complied with to the fullest

---

8. But see Oregon Natural Resources Council v. Bureau of Reclamation, 49 F.3d 1441 (9th Cir. 1994) (agency's lowering water levels and applying aquatic herbicides in a federal impoundment is not a "major federal action" because these activities were ongoing in 1970).

extent, unless there is a conflict of statutory authority. Considerations of administrative difficulty, delay or economic cost will not suffice to strip the section of its fundamental importance...."

ADMINISTRATIVE DISCRETION... It is contended that the determination of whether a project is (1) "a major Federal action" and (2) "significantly affecting the quality of the human environment" is within the discretion of the Administrator of the Soil Conservation Service, and that an administrative determination should not be reversed by this Court in the absence of a strong showing that it was arbitrary, capricious, or clearly erroneous. In the case at bar the administrator, with the advice of scientists and specialists, made the determination that the project as modified could not significantly affect the quality of the human environment within the meaning and intent of NEPA, and as such "going forward with the project as modified" was in compliance with the requirements of NEPA. Certainly, an administrative agency like the Soil Conservation Service may make a decision that a particular project is not major, or that it does not significantly affect the quality of the human environment, and, that, therefore, the agency is not required to file an impact statement. However, when the failure to file an impact statement is challenged, it is the court that must construe the statutory standards of "major federal action" and "significantly affecting the quality of the human environment," and having construed them, then apply them to the particular project, and decide whether the agency's failure violates the Congressional command.

STATUTORY STANDARDS... A "major federal action" is federal action that requires substantial planning, time, resources, or expenditure. The Chicod Creed Watershed Project is a "major federal action." This project calls for sixty-six miles of channelization and the expenditure of $1,503,831, $706,684 of which is to be federally funded. The project has been in the planning and preparation stages for several years. Many persons and agencies have become involved and concerned with this project, and the construction of this project will require a substantial amount of time and labor. Certainly this can be considered to be a "major federal action."

The standard "significantly affecting the quality of the human environment" can be construed as having an important or meaningful effect, direct or indirect, upon a broad range of aspects of the human environment. The cumulative impact with other projects must be considered. Any action that substantially affects, beneficially or detrimentally, the depth or course of streams, plant life, wildlife habitats, fish and wildlife, and the soil and air "significantly affects the quality of the human environment." This project will require sixty-six miles of stream channelization. As a result of such channelization there will be a substantial reduction (ninety percent) in the fish population. As a result of drainage and the clearing of right of ways, there will be significant lossage [sic] in wetland habitat which is vital to waterfowl and forest game. The Chicod Creek Watershed Project as presently proposed will have a cumulative effect upon the environment in the eastern plains of North Carolina. There are a total of forty Soil Conservation projects either authorized for construction, under construction, or completed, representing 1,562 miles of stream channelization, affecting over 100,000 acres of wetlands, and having very serious repercussions upon fish and wildlife in the Coastal Plains of North Carolina. The Chicod Creek Watershed Project "significantly affects the quality of the human environment."

It is interesting to note that one of the Soil Conservation Service's own biologists, prior to the implementation of any mitigation, concluded that this project would have significant effects upon the environment. Also noteworthy is the fact that subsequent to Watersheds Memorandum 108, the Soil Conservation Service placed this project in Group 2, a category established by the Watersheds Memorandum indicating that projects placed in this group could have some adverse effect upon the environment. After certain mitigation measures were implemented, this project was placed in Group 1, signifying minor or no known adverse effect upon the environment. It is the opinion of this Court that an environmental impact statement should have been issued when this project was placed in Group 2.

STANDING... It is contended that the plaintiffs lack standing to pursue this action on the grounds that they have not suffered a legal wrong and have not been adversely affected by agency action.... The plaintiffs have standing to maintain this action as they have alleged injury to conservational interests and that such interests are within the zone of interests protected by NEPA.

LACHES... The mere lapse of time does not constitute laches. Laches is determined in light of all the existing circumstances and requires all delay to be unreasonable and cause prejudice to the adversary. This project has been in the planning and preliminary stages for several years. However, NEPA became effective only on January 1, 1970. The plaintiffs instituted this action on November 30, 1971. At that date no construction contract had been let nor had any construction on the installation of the project taken place. Therefore, it appears to this Court that there was no unreasonable delay in the commencement of this action, and even assuming such, there does not appear to be any prejudice to the defendants or intervenors as construction of the project has yet to begin.

INJUNCTION... The plaintiffs seek a preliminary injunction to enjoin construction of the Chicod Creek Watershed Project on the grounds that an environmental impact statement has not been issued as required by NEPA. The tests for granting such relief were recently restated by the Fourth Circuit:

> In the exercise of its discretion (to issue a preliminary injunction) it is sufficient if a court is satisfied that there is a probable right and a probable danger and that the right may be defeated, unless the injunction is issued, and considerable weight is given to the need of protection to the plaintiff as contrasted with the probable injury to the defendant.... W. Virginia Highlands Conservancy v. Island Creek Coal, 441 F. 2d 232, 235 (4th Cir. 1971).

In summary, the movants are entitled to preliminary injunctive relief if they demonstrate (a) a substantial likelihood that they will prevail on the merits, and (b) that a balancing of the equities favors the granting of such relief. Here, the plaintiffs have shown more than a substantial likelihood that they will prevail on the merits upon final determination of their NEPA environmental impact statement claim as NEPA requires that an environmental impact statement be filed for "major federal actions significantly affecting the quality of the human environment." The plaintiffs have shown that this project is a "major federal action significantly affecting the quality of the human environment," and that an impact statement has not been filed.

The question as to the balancing of the equities gravely concerns this Court. Basically, there are three different interests represented in this action: the conservationists, the Soil Conservation Service, and the landowners. In considering the various interests the public interest is a relevant consideration. This project was designed to enable the landowners to control severe drainage problems and to increase farm productivity. These farmers have spent much time, effort, and money in preparation for this project with the expectation of federal aid. This has been no easy task for farmers in an area in which fifty-five percent of the families make less than $3,000 income per year. These farmers have given up much in expectation of innumerable benefits resulting from the project.... It was only when the preparations had been made and construction ready to begin that this action was initiated to enjoin the project. The Soil Conservation Service's... primary concern in this action seems to be that if it has to issue an impact statement for this project, it will have to do the same for many other ongoing projects. This will cause delay and, in many cases, duplicity [sic]. The projected cost per project for issuing an impact statement is approximately $7,500. This cost is minute indeed in comparison to the equity of the farmers and the effect that this project will have on the environment. The conservationists are organizations dedicated to the laudable cause of conservation and preservation of our environment. They have shown that this project will have a significant effect on the environment. It is to the public's welfare that any project significantly affecting the environment comply with the procedures established by NEPA so there can be assurance that the environmental aspects have been fully considered. It would constitute irreparable damage for this project to proceed without the environmental aspects being properly considered as required by NEPA. Therefore, the equitable considerations favor the environment, the public, and the plaintiffs and require that the construction of the Chicod Creek Watershed Project be enjoined until the requirements of NEPA are satisfied.

The defendants shall have thirty days within which to prepare and file a "full disclosure" environmental impact statement. The preliminary injunction shall remain in effect thereafter until all of the procedures of NEPA have been complied with. The plaintiffs shall file a bond for the payment of costs and damages as may be suffered by any party who is found to have been wrongfully restrained herein. The amount of bond shall be commensurate to the possible damages incurred by the defendants and the intervenors as a result of the injunction. Over $200,000 has already been expended on this project by the Soil Conservation Service and $130,000 of debt has been incurred by the intervenors. The projected cost of delay to the Soil Conservation Service resulting from the institution of this suit is approximately $7,650 per month. Taking into consideration the amounts that have been expended, the costs of delay, and that other amounts are obligated, this Court sets the bond at $75,000.

NOW THEREFORE, in accordance with the foregoing, it is ORDERED, that the defendants and their agents, employees, and persons in active concert and participation with them who receive actual notice hereof, be and the same are hereby restrained and enjoined from taking any further steps to authorize, finance, or commence construction or installation of the Chicod Creek Watershed Project until an environmental impact statement is filed and circulated according to the requirements of the National Environmental Policy Act; and,

FURTHER ORDERED, that the defendants prepare and file a "full disclosure" environmental impact statement within thirty (30) days from the filing of this Order; and,

FURTHER ORDERED, that plaintiffs file a bond for the payment of costs and damages as may be suffered by any party who is found to have been wrongfully or unlawfully restrained herein, in the amount of, or security equivalent to, $75,000.... Let this Order be entered forthwith.

### COMMENTARY AND QUESTIONS

1. **Standing.** Note how little trouble the court has in finding standing to challenge agency action, despite the fact that NEPA had not given citizens such a right. However, in Lujan v. National Wildlife Federation, 497 U.S. 871 (1990), the Supreme Court denied NEPA standing to an environmental group whose members alleged that they used federal lands "in the vicinity" of the ones whose reclassification for mining purposes were being contested. Purely economic interests have consistently been held not to provide standing under NEPA. See, e.g., Region 8 Forest Service Timber Purchasers Council v. Alcock, 993 F.2d 800 (11th Cir. 1993).

2. **A cause of action?** The court presumes, with the other courts that encountered NEPA, that §102 must be actionable, because it plainly set up a legal duty — all agencies shall prepare statements — that sounds enforceable, and if Congress had not meant that as a requirement, surely it would not have said that. This amounts to the principle of statutory interpretation that "the Emperor must be wearing clothes."

3. **Laches.** Owing to its casual congressional history, NEPA had no statute of limitations; the equitable doctrine of laches will prevent injunction suits that are "unreasonably delayed." Here, would the judge have decided differently if a construction contract had been let? Should the doctrine of laches be waived for public interest plaintiffs?

4. **The bureaucratic temptation to minimize.** NEPA's enforceability was initially unclear, and some construction agencies tended to minimize its requirements. The following is reportedly the text, in its entirety, of an impact statement as it was first published by the Bureau of Reclamation in satisfaction of NEPA:

> Palmetto Bend Project, Jackson County, Tex. Proposed construction of a 12.3-mile long, 64-foot high earthfill dam on the Navidad River. The purpose of the project is the supply of industrial and municipal water. Approximately 18,400 acres (11,300 of which will be inundated) will be committed to the project; 40 miles of free-flowing stream will be inundated; nine families will be displaced; fresh water inflow to the Matagorda estuary will be altered; fish and shellfish nursery areas will be impaired; habitat for such endangered species as the Texas red wolf, the American alligator, the Southern bald eagle, the Peregrine falcon, and the Attwater prairie chicken will be lost.

(The Bureau subsequently was persuaded that more was required, and the project was ultimately subjected to a full formal EIS preparation and review process.)

5. **The classic Calvert Cliffs case.** Part of the legal backdrop to Judge Larkins' review of the Chicod Creek case was a forceful decision from the District of Columbia Court of Appeals that became the most important of all early NEPA cases. Calvert Cliffs Coordinating Committee v. AEC, 449 F.2d 1109 (D.C. Cir. 1971), confronted the Atomic Energy Commission's ingenious refusals to consider environmental

issues in its nuclear power plant construction program until after the projects were under construction. In his admonitory and ironic majority opinion, excerpts from which are reproduced below, Judge Skelley Wright "took a stick to the federal agencies" and served notice that NEPA would have to be taken seriously:

> In these cases, we must for the first time interpret the broadest and most important of the recent [environmental] statutes: the National Environmental Policy Act. We must assess claims that one of the agencies charged with its administration has failed to live up to the congressional mandate. Our duty, in short, is to see that important legislative purposes, heralded in the halls of Congress, are not lost or misdirected in the vast hallways of the federal bureaucracy.... The Commission contends that the vagueness of the NEPA mandate and delegation leaves much room for discretion.... We find the policies embodied in NEPA to be a good deal clearer and more demanding than does the Commission. We conclude that the Commission's procedural rules do not comply with the congressional policy. Hence we remand these cases for further rulemaking....
>
> Of course, all of the §102 duties are qualified by the phrase "to the fullest extent possible." We must stress as forcefully as possible that this language does not provide an escape hatch for footdragging agencies; it does not make NEPA's procedural requirements somehow "discretionary." Congress did not intend the Act to be such a paper tiger. Indeed, the requirement of environmental consideration "to the fullest extent possible" sets a high standard for the agency, a standard which must be rigorously enforced by the reviewing courts....
>
> NEPA makes only one specific reference to consideration of environmental values in agency review processes. Section 102(2)(c) provides that copies of the staff's "detailed statement" and comments thereon "shall accompany the proposal through the existing agency review process."... The question here is whether the Commission is correct in thinking that its NEPA responsibilities may "be carried out in toto outside the hearing process" — whether it is enough that environmental data and evaluations merely "accompany" an application through the review process, but receive no consideration whatever from the hearing board. We believe that the Commission's crabbed interpretation of NEPA makes a mockery of the Act. What possible purpose could there be in the requirement...if "accompany" means no more than physical proximity — mandating no more than the physical act of passing certain folders and papers, unopened, to reviewing officials along with other folders and papers? What possible purpose could there be in requiring the "detailed statement" to be before hearing boards, if the boards are entitled to ignore entirely the contents of the statement? NEPA was meant to do more than regulate the flow of papers in the federal bureaucracy. The word "accompany" must not be read so narrowly as to make the Act ludicrous. It must, rather, be read to indicate a congressional intent that environmental factors, as compiled in the "detailed statement," be considered through agency review processes.
>
> The rationale of the Commission's limitation of environmental issues to hearings in which parties affirmatively raise those issues may have been one of economy. It may have been supposed that, whenever there are serious environmental costs overlooked or uncorrected by the staff, some party will intervene to bring those costs to the hearing board's attention.... NEPA establishes environmental protection as an integral part of the Atomic Energy Commission's basic mandate. The primary responsibility for fulfilling that mandate lies with the Commission. Its responsibility is not simply to sit back,

like an umpire, and resolve adversary contentions at the hearing stage. Rather, it must itself take the initiative of considering environmental values at every distinctive and comprehensive stage of the process beyond the staff's evaluation and recommendation.

[As to the AEC's dilatory and grudging intepretation of NEPA], strangely, the Commission has principally relied on...pragmatic arguments. It seems an unfortunate affliction of large organizations to resist new procedures and to envision massive roadblocks to their adoption.... The introduction of environmental matters cannot have presented a radically unsettling problem. And, in any event, the obvious sense of urgency on the part of Congress should make clear that a transition, however "orderly," must proceed at a pace faster than a funeral procession.

As to [multiple statutory mandates, NEPA] clearly requires obedience to standards set by other [statutes]. But obedience does not imply total abdication.... It does not suggest that other "specific statutory obligations" will entirely replace NEPA....

We hold that...the Commission must revise its rules governing consideration of environmental issues. We do not impose a harsh burden on the Commission. For we require only an exercise of substantive discretion which will protect the environment "to the fullest extent possible." No less is required if the grand congressional purposes underlying NEPA are to become a reality. *Calvert Cliffs*, 449 F.2d, at pages 1111–1124.

6. **What is a "major federal action"?** Is the Chicod Creek channelization project federal? The entire project is to be undertaken by the local District. Yet federal dollars are being spent and "many persons and agencies have become involved." Does that mean that every expenditure of federal revenue-sharing funds requires an EIS?

Note the following excerpt from the CEQ regulations, 40 CFR §§1501 et seq., on the meaning and implementation of NEPA —

§1508.18 Major Federal Action. "Major Federal action" includes actions with effects that may be major and which are potentially subject to Federal control and responsibility. Major reinforces but does not have a meaning independent of significantly (§1508.27). Actions include the circumstance where the responsible officials fail to act and that failure to act is reviewable by courts or administrative tribunals under the Administrative Procedure Act or other applicable law as agency action.

(a) Actions include new and continuing activities, including projects and programs entirely or partly financed, assisted, conducted, regulated, or approved by federal agencies; new or revised agency rules, regulations, plans, policies, or procedures; and legislative proposals. Actions do not include funding assistance solely in the form of general revenue sharing funds, distributed under the State and Local Fiscal Assistance Act of 1972, 31 U.S.C.A. §1221 et seq., with no Federal agency control over the subsequent use of such funds. Actions do not include bringing judicial or administrative civil or criminal enforcement actions.

In addition, §1508.18 explains that federal actions tend to involve the adoption of official policy, formal plans, or programs, or the approval of specific projects. Courts also have held federal permits, licenses, contracts, or leases given to private parties to be federal actions.

As to whether it is a "major" action, isn't the Chicod Creek project's $706,684 cost a trifling amount in the federal context? Conceptual rather than financial definitions obviously are part of the decision, which depends on an analysis of surrounding circumstances. Is an armed forces plan to launch an amphibious practice assault on a beach in Marine's Acadia National Park a "major" action? What about the installation of an incinerator on a federal hospital? The courts answered "no" and "yes," respectively, perhaps making a distinction based upon short-term versus long-term actions. If Chicod Creek were only 4 miles long, would the project be "major"? Can you take notice of *cumulative* effects in order to judge whether an action is "major" or of significant effect? See §1508.27, *infra*, at (b)(7).

7. **The "small handle" problem.** Consider this not-so-hypothetical: several Japanese and Korean corporations plan to open seventeen woodchipping installations throughout the southeastern United States, designed to process trees and vegetation stripped from hundreds of thousands of acres of private forests, and ship the chips by barge and freighter to the Far East, as raw material for paper and laminates. This activity would affect the biological and climatalogical character of major portions of six southern states. Assume that the only federal permit required is a Corps of Engineers wharf-building permit for the barge-loading facilities. With that federal permit, the operation will take place; without it, it will not. The corporate proponents and the Corps can argue, however, that a barge wharf is too minor a structure to require an EIS.

This is the small handle problem. Courts disagree on whether, in such cases, the NEPA EIS requirement is triggered by the entire factual consequences of a federal action or focuses exclusively on the effects of the federal component of the project. In Winnebago Tribe v. REA, 621 F.2d 269 (8th Cir. 1980), the court held that a federal river-crossing permit necessary for construction of a 67-mile high-tension power line was not sufficient federal involvement to require an EIS. Some courts have been more willing to note the actual effect of federal actions. Colorado River Indian Tribes v. Marsh, 605 F. Supp. 1425 (C.D.Cal. 1985), held that a Corps permit for riverbank reinforcement (a practical precondition for a proposed large rural commercial and residential development) required an EIS covering the entire actual impact deriving from the federal action. NEPA, the court held, implicitly incorporates reasonable forecasting of consequential and environmental effects. In a Maine case, where construction of a major oil terminal on Sears Island depended upon grant of a Corps permit for an access road causeway, the court required an EIS covering the entire development, taking into account the "reasonably foreseeable indirect effects" of consequential industrial development, because the causeway was a necessary part of the larger plan. Sierra Club v. Marsh, 769 F.2d 868, 877 (1st Cir. 1985). See Fitzgerald, Small Handles, Big Impact…, 23 Envtl. Aff. L. Rev. 437 (1996).

8. **"Significantly affecting the human environment."** This standard echoes the preceding issues. "Significance" similarly varies according to context. What if the project allegedly has net beneficial effects? One SCS official argued that this was so in stream channelization cases, adding that "Conservation is our middle name!" NEPA is clearly aimed at adverse environmental effects (and the present CEQ regulations so direct the EIS procedure); if adverse effects exist, the courts have gen-

erally not permitted the counterbalancing of alleged benefits to avoid NEPA.[9] The CEQ regulations describe "significantly" in terms of "context" and "intensity:"

§1508.27 "Significantly." "Significantly" as used in NEPA requires considerations of both context and intensity:

(a) *Context.* This means that the significance of an action must be analyzed in several contexts such as society as a whole (human, national), the affected region, the affected interests, and the locality. Significance varies with the setting of the proposed action. For instance, in the case of a site-specific action, significance would usually depend upon the effects in the locale rather than in the world as a whole. Both short- and long-term effects are relevant.

(b) *Intensity.* This refers to the severity of impact. Responsible officials must bear in mind that more than one agency may make decisions about partial aspects of a major action. The following should be considered in evaluating intensity:

(1) Impacts that may be both beneficial and adverse. A significant effect may exist even if the Federal agency believes that on balance the effect will be beneficial.

(2) The degree to which the proposed action affects public health or safety.

(3) Unique characteristics of the geographic area such as proximity to historic or cultural resources, park lands, prime farmlands, wetlands, wild and scenic rivers, or ecologically critical areas.

(4) The degree to which the effects on the quality of the human environment are likely to be highly controversial.

(5) The degree to which the possible effects on the human environment are highly uncertain or involve unique or unknown risks.

(6) The degree to which the action may establish a precedent for future actions with significant effects or represents a decision in principle about a future consideration.

(7) Whether the action is related to other actions with individually insignificant but cumulatively significant impacts. Significance exists if it is reasonable to anticipate a cumulatively significant impact on the environment. Significance cannot be avoided by terming an action temporary or by breaking it down into small component parts.

(8) The degree to which the action may adversely affect districts, sites, highways, structures, or objects listed in or eligible for listing in the National Register of Historic Places or may cause loss or destruction of significant scientific, cultural, or historical resources.

(9) The degree to which the action may adversely affect an endangered or threatened species or its habitat that has been determined to be critical under the Endangered Species Act of 1973.

(10) Whether the action threatens a violation of Federal, State, or local law or requirements imposed for the protection of the environment.

**9. FONSIs and mitigation.** The *Chicod Creek* case offers an example of another tack: The SCS Administrator made a "negative declaration" or "FONSI" ("finding of no significant impact"), a declaration that the project would cause no significant environmental effect. A FONSI must be based upon an initial Environmental Assessment, or "EA," in which the agency briefly discusses the need for the

---

9. After an agency has complied with NEPA, issuing an adequate EIS, it may still decide to proceed based on a balance of environmental and nonenvironmental issues (unless going forward can be shown to be "arbitrary").

proposal as well as the environmental impacts of, and alternatives to, the proposal." The CEQ defines the FONSI and EA as follows:

> §1508.9 Environmental Assessment. "Environmental assessment" (a) means a concise public document for which a Federal agency is responsible that serves to: (1) briefly provide sufficient evidence and analysis for determining whether to prepare an environmental impact statement or a finding of no significant impact. (2) aid an agency's compliance with the Act when no environmental impact statement is necessary. (3) facilitate preparation of a statement when one is necessary. (b) shall include brief discussions of the need for the proposal, of alternatives..., of the environmental impacts of the proposed action and alternatives, and a listing of agencies and persons consulted.
>
> §1508.13 Finding of no significant impact. "Finding of no significant impact" means a document by a Federal agency briefly presenting the reasons why an action...will not have a significant effect on the human environment and for which an environmental impact statement therefore will not be prepared. It shall include the environmental assessment or a summary of it and shall note any other environmental documents related to it....

An EA is a threshold document, and is held to a lower degree of analysis than an EIS. Judge Larkin rejected the SCS's argument that its decision to prepare an EA and FONSI, instead of a full-scale EIS, had to be upheld unless it was arbitrary and capricious. After many years of division among the federal circuit courts on this issue, the United States Supreme Court settled the matter in Marsh v. Oregon Natural Resources Council, 490 U.S. 360 (1989) (reviewing courts must apply the "arbitrary and capricious" standard in reviewing agency decisions on "significance"). FONSIs are tactically attractive to many federal agencies because they permit the agency to circumvent EIS requirements.

The SCS, in *Chicod Creek*, claimed that its mitigation measures obviated a full EIS — an argument that Judge Larkin did not accept. In fact, according to the CEQ's study, "The National Environmental Policy Act: A Study of its Effectiveness After Twenty-five Years" (1997) (hereafter "CEQ Study") the "mitigated FONSI" has become the primary means of agency procedure under NEPA:

> Since NEPA was passed, the role of the EA has evolved to the point where it is the predominant way agencies conduct NEPA analyses. Conceived as a brief analysis to determine the significance of environmental effects, the EA today increasingly includes mitigation measures that reduce adverse effects below significant levels. With the increased use of EAs, often to the overall benefit of the environment, comes the danger than public involvement will be diminished and that individually minor actions will have major cumulative effects.... There is a great deal of confusion about what public involvement is required, appropriate, or allowed in the preparation of EAs, because NEPA regulations and guidance are primarily oriented to the preparation of EISs.... Some states, citizen groups, and businesses believe that certain EAs are prepared to avoid public involvement.... The preparation of an EA, rather than an EIS, is the most common source of conflict under NEPA....

All signs point to a significant increase in EAs and a decrease in EISs. The annual number of draft, revised, supplemental, and final EISs prepared has declined from approximately 2,000 in 1973 to 608 in 1995, averaging 508 annually between 1990–1995. By 1993, a CEQ survey of federal agencies estimated that about 50,000 EAs were being prepared annually. That survey also found that five federal agencies — the U.S. Forest Service, the Bureau of Land Management, the Department of Housing and Urban Development, the U.S. Army Corps of Engineers, and the Federal Highly Administration — produce more than 80% of the EAs. While some federal agencies...provide for a public comment period on EAs, many do not.

Another significant trend is that of agencies increasingly identifying and proposing measures to mitigate adverse effects of proposed actions during the preparation of EAs.... If an agency finds that such mitigation will prevent a project from having significant impacts on the environment, the agency can conclude the NEPA process by issuing a FONSI, rather than preparing an EIS. The result is a "mitigated FONSI." While mitigated FONSIs are a good way to integrate NEPA into planning..., not all EAs resulting in mitigated FONSIs are meeting the spirit and intent of NEPA. When the EIS process is viewed as merely a compliance requirement rather than a tool to improve decision-making, mitigated FONSIs may be used simply to prevent the expense and time of the more in-depth analysis required by an EIS. The result is likely to be less rigorous scientific analysis, little or no public involvement, and consideration of fewer alternatives, all of which are at the very core of NEPA's strengths. Moreover, not all agencies that commit to mitigation monitor to determine whether the mitigation was actually implemented or whether it was effective.[10] CEQ Study at 19–20.

Nevertheless, EAs must also take a "hard look" at a reasonable range of alternatives and their environmental consequences. See Sierra Club v. Department of Energy, below.

10. **Formal compliance vs. "functional equivalence."** The judge scarcely listened to the SCS's claim that even though it had not filed a formally-prepared EIS, it had substantially complied with the various requirements of an EIS; yet Congress appears to have drafted the phrase "statement" instead of "formal finding" precisely in order to avoid formal requirements. This court simply says, however, that "an environmental impact statement has not been prepared and filed for the Chicod Creek Watershed Project."

In several early NEPA cases, polluters tried to use the statute against EPA itself, and courts began to develop an exception for environmental protection agencies whose procedures provide the "functional equivalent" of NEPA. "[The courts have seen] little need in requiring a NEPA statement from an agency whose raison d'etre is the protection of the environment and whose decision...is necessarily infused with the environmental considerations so pertinent to Congress in designing the statutory framework. To require a 'statement,' in addition to a decision setting forth the same considerations, would be a legalism carried to the extreme." International Harvester Co. v. Ruckelshaus, 478 F. 2d 615, 650 n. 130 (D.C. Cir. 1973); Texas Committee on Natural Resources v. Bergland, 573 F.2d 201, 207 (5th Cir. 1979). How similar to the EPA procedures do other agency procedures need to be in order to be deemed "functionally equivalent" to NEPA? Agencies such as the Forest Service and the Bureau of Land Management, which consider environmental

---

10. Although the CEQ Regulations require that mitigation measures be implemented (§1505.3), the United States Supreme Court has held that NEPA does not require an agency to either include a mitigation plan in an EA or EIS, or to actually implement identified implementation measures. Robertson v. Director of U.S. Forest Service, 490 U.S. 332 (1989).

protection along with other multiple-use criteria, are not exempt from NEPA under the "functional equivalent" doctrine; but federal circuit courts have split about whether designations of critical habitat under the Endangered Species Act are the functional equivalent of NEPA. Contrast Douglas County v. Babbitt, 48 F.3d 1495 (9th Cir. 1994) (ESA procedures are the functional equivalent of NEPA), with Catron County Board of Commissioners v. U.S. Fish and Wildlife Service, 75 F.3d 1429 (10th Cir. 1996) (ESA and NEPA serve different purposes). What are the consequences of this judge-made doctrine?

In State of Alabama ex rel. Siegelman v. EPA, 911 F. 2d 499 (11th Cir. 1990), the EPA issued a permit to allow the ChemWaste company to open the nation's largest hazardous waste disposal facility at Emelle, Alabama, a low income community of color, without preparing an EIS. The court held that the RCRA permit process was the functional equivalent of an EIS.

Does the "functional equivalence" doctrine adequately address the role of public involvement and comment in the EIS procedure under NEPA? The procedures mapped out in the CEQ's NEPA regulations include extensive provisions requiring agencies to make diligent efforts to solicit information from the public and from other agencies with relevant expertise, to provide adequate notice of NEPA-related hearings, and to respond to comments in the final EIS. Were the SCS procedures in *Chicod Creek* the functional equivalent of NEPA?

11. **Conflicting statutory mandates.** Courts have recognized a narrow exception to NEPA's EIS requirement where compliance with NEPA would result in a "clear and fundamental conflict of statutory duty." Flint Ridge Dev. Co. v. Scenic Rivers Ass'n., 426 U.S. 776, 791 (1976). In *Flint Ridge*, the court held that the Secretary of HUD was not required to prepare an EIS before allowing disclosure notices for large-scale rural subdivisions to be filed, even if the developments would significantly affect the environment. Because the Interstate Land Sales Full Disclosure Act required the Secretary to allow accurate and complete notices to go into effect within 30 days of filing, the Court found that it would be impossible simultaneously to prepare an EIS and to respond adequately to comments. While acknowledging that NEPA requires that agencies comply "to the fullest extent possible," the Court reasoned that NEPA was not intended to "repeal by implication any other statute." The Court also, however, quoted statements from House Conferees involved in drafting §102, providing that "no agency shall utilize an excessively narrow construction of its existing statutory authorization to avoid compliance [with NEPA]."

Courts have been unwilling to apply the *Flint Ridge* exception liberally. In Jones v. Gordon, 621 F. Supp. 7 (D. Alaska 1985), the district court held that the National Marine Fisheries Service (NMFS) could not issue a permit for the taking of up to 100 Orca whales without preparing an EIS. The court rejected the argument that the 90-day time limit for issuing such permits under the Marine Mammal Protection Act rendered NMFS compliance with NEPA impossible. Instead, the court held that "in the rare cases where an EIS may be required, the NMFS can create time in the application process by delaying initial publication of the notice of the application in the Federal Register." The court found the conflict between statutes in this case to be minor and ultimately reconcilable. But an irreconcilable conflict was found in Westlands Water District v. NRDC, 43 F.3d 457 (9th Cir. 1994) (Congress dictated that conservation releases from federal dams take place "upon enactment").

12. **Emergency exemptions from NEPA.** To what extent can agencies ignore NEPA in situations that they deem to be "emergencies" (recognizing that such a loophole could invite self-serving agency evasions of their mandates)? 40 CFR §1506.11 provides that the requirements of NEPA can be bypassed in emergencies. In Crosby v. Young, 512 F.Supp 1363 (E.D.Mich.1981), a district court upheld the claim that Detroit's use of federal funds to raze the Poletown community in order to build a Cadillac plant (see Chapter 23) was an emergency precluding the application of NEPA. The same result occurred in Hester v. Nat'l Audubon Soc., 801 F.2d 405 (9th Cir. 1986), where the U.S. Fish and Wildlife Service was granted leave, without an EIS, to capture the last 26 surviving California Condors for zoo propagation. Although common sense indicates that in some situations the requirements of NEPA must be inapplicable, how do courts or the CEQ fashion such exceptions to a clear legislative mandate?

13. **NEPA and national security.** NEPA does not provide for a national security exception. The Supreme Court, however, has refused to review Defense Department compliance with NEPA where to do so inevitably would result in the disclosure of confidential matters regarding national security. Weinberger v. Catholic Action of Hawaii, 454 U.S. 139 (1981) involved a NEPA challenge to the Navy's construction of nuclear weapon storage structures. The Navy's regulations prohibited it from either admitting or denying that nuclear weapons were actually stored at the facility. The complaint claimed that the Navy's determination that no significant environmental hazards were present failed to take into account the enhanced risks of a nuclear accident and the potential effects of radiation from the storage of nuclear weapons in a populated location. The Court held that the Navy could not be made to disclose the military secret regarding whether or not it proposed to store nuclear weapons on Hawaii, even in confidential judicial chambers *ex parte*, and thus the entire matter was beyond judicial scrutiny.

Subsequent cases have held that some NEPA claims involving national security are justiciable. In NO GWEN Alliance of Lane County, Inc. v. Aldridge, 841 F.2d 946 (9th Cir. 1988), the appeals court held that a lawsuit claiming that the Air Force did not discuss environmental impacts of installing radio towers designed to send war messages to U.S. strategic forces in the event of nuclear war raised justiciable questions. See also Romer v. Carlucci, 847 F.2d 463 (8th Cir. 1988) (review of EIS for compliance with NEPA is justiciable under political question doctrine, in connection with proposed deployment and peacetime operations of MX missiles in minuteman silos). While both the eighth and ninth circuits pointed out that there is no national security exemption from NEPA, the *Carlucci* court refused to require the Army EIS to discuss alternative basing modes or alternative weapons systems, as such strategic considerations would "involve review of intricate and sensitive defense policy information." In addition, the *NO GWEN* court ultimately did not require the Air Force to prepare an EIS on the grounds that its EA adequately addressed non-nuclear effects and that the nexus between constructing the radio towers and nuclear war was too attenuated to trigger NEPA requirements of discussing environmental effects of nuclear war.

**14. The "human environment"?** What does this phrase mean? Chicod Creek is not human, but without much questioning courts have interpreted the phrase to cover natural environmental qualities that affect humans. What about an Army decision to close down a military depot, which will have major socio-economic dislocation impacts on humans? See Breckinridge v. Rumsfeld, 537 F.2d 864 (6th Cir. 1976) (no compliance necessary because closure is a secondary, socioeconomic impact without a primary physical impact on the environment).

The Supreme Court confronted the question about NEPA's application to the human environment in Metropolitan Edison v. PANE, 460 U.S. 766 (1983). The worst nuclear accident Americans have yet experienced occurred on March 28, 1979, at Three Mile Island, south of Harrisburg, Pennsylvania. After the accident, the two nuclear reactors at the plant were shut down. Only one of them, however, had been damaged in the accident. After a lengthy investigation and public hearings, the NRC decided to allow restart of the undamaged reactor (TMI-1). During the hearings, the commission consistently refused to consider neighboring residents' claims that NEPA requires it to study the psychological distress that would allegedly accompany the restart. People Against Nuclear Energy (PANE), a group composed primarily of neighbors of TMI, sought judicial review.

Note the definition of "Human Environment" articulated in the CEQ regulations:

> §1508.14 Human environment. Human environment shall be interpreted comprehensively to include the natural and physical environment and the relationship of people with that environment.... This means that economic or social effects are not intended by themselves to require preparation of an environmental impact statement. When an environmental impact statement is prepared and economic or social and natural or physical environmental effects are interrelated, then the environmental impact statement will discuss all of these effects on the human environment.

The NRC argued that NEPA requires only that effects on the "natural environment" must be studied. Psychological stress in this case is a product of area residents' fear of a second accident at Three Mile Island, and is not a product of physical changes in the environment. "Peoples' anxiety has very little to do with the environment," the NRC said. Did the psychological effects of restarting the reactor mean that it would be an "action significantly affecting the human environment?"

Justice Rehnquist's opinion held that the NRC need not consider PANE's contentions.

> First, §102(2)(C) does not require an agency to assess every impact or effect of its proposed action, but only impacts or effects on the environment. The statute's context shows that Congress was talking about the physical environment. Although NEPA states its goals in sweeping terms of human health and welfare, these goals are ends that Congress has chosen to pursue by means of protecting the physical environment.
>
> Second, NEPA does not require agencies to evaluate the effects of risk *qua* risk. The terms "environmental effects" and "environmental impact" in §102(2)(C) should be read to include a requirement of a reasonably close causal relation-

ship between a change in the physical environment and the effect at issue. Here, the federal action that affects the environment is permitting renewed operation of TMI-1. The direct effects of this action include release of low-level radiation, increased fog, and the release of warm water into the Susquehanna River, all of which are effects the NRC has considered. The NRC has also considered the risk of a nuclear accident, but a risk of an accident is not an effect on the physical environment. In a causal chain from renewed operation of TMI-1 to psychological health damage, the element of risk and its perception by PANE's members are necessary middle links. That element of risk lengthens the causal chain beyond NEPA's reach. Regardless of the gravity of the harm alleged by PANE, if a harm does not have a sufficiently close connection to the physical environment, NEPA does not apply.

Finally, the fact that PANE's claim was made in the wake of the accident at TMI-2 is irrelevant. NEPA is not directed at the effects of past accidents and does not create a remedial scheme for past federal actions. [PANE syllabus]

Are these conclusions self-evident? What happened to the word "human" in the phrase "human environment"? Is the opinion nevertheless correct in holding that there must be some limits upon NEPA coverage of effects that occur far down a chain of indirect causation? Or does the gravity of potential harms, or NEPA's logic in general, argue for consideration of all real consequential effects? Compare the *Pruitt* case's consideration of long-distance liability in the Kepone affair, in Chapter Three.

15. **The injunction.** Quite simply, the Chicod Creek project had no EIS, so NEPA was violated. Note, however, that injunctive relief was not automatic; the court traditionally balances the equities before deciding to issue an injunction. How does the judge weigh the value of NEPA compliance against the financial costs involved? In some NEPA cases, judges have permitted the agency to continue construction while preparing an EIS on the question of whether the project should be built. EDF v. Ellis Armstrong, 487 F.2d 814 (9th Cir. 1973) (New Melones Dam). How does a court determine whether an injunction is justified for an ongoing project that does not have an EIS? In another context, the Supreme Court has said that, once having found a statutory violation, it had no discretion but to see that the law was complied with. TVA v. Hill, 437 U.S. 153 (1978). As to NEPA violations, however, the Court has appeared less ready to hold defendants strictly to compliance. Amoco Prod. Co. v. Village of Gambell, 480 U.S. 531 (1987); cf. Sierra Club v. Marsh, 872 F.2d 497, 500 (1st Cir. 1989). Does failure to consider environmental consequences in agency decisionmaking constitute irreparable harm?

16. **A bond requirement?** Finally, having won everything at issue, the citizens unexpectedly were faced with Judge Larkins' requirement of a $75,000 bond. Such bonds are common in commercial litigation. Why not here?

### NRDC v. Grant
U.S. Court of Appeals for the Fourth Circuit, 1972
(unreported ORDER) 2 ELR 20,555 (Sept. 5, 1972) (No. Misc. 979)

HAYNSWORTH, J. In this ecology case, the District Judge issued a preliminary injunction because no environmental impact statement had been filed. It was conditioned, however, upon the filing by the plaintiffs of a bond in the amount of

$75,000. The bond was not filed, and the District Judge withdrew the preliminary injunction on that account. Meanwhile, however, an environmental impact statement had been filed, substantially changing the posture of the case.

The controversy is far from ended. The plaintiffs intend to attack the adequacy of the environmental impact statement and they seek a continuing injunction against commencement of the project until that question is determined. That is a question initially for the District Court, not for us, but the plaintiffs, organizations interested in conservation and having no financial interest in this controversy, are fearful that any further injunctive order will again be conditioned upon their posting a large bond.

Thus, they seek to prosecute an appeal and have requested a stay of the order dissolving the injunction. The defendants have countered with a suggestion of mootness.

Under all the circumstances, we think an immediate remand of this case to the District Court appropriate.

Any further preliminary injunctive order should not be issued unless the District Judge, after examination of the environmental impact statement, is of the opinion that it is probably deficient, and that the plaintiffs more likely than not will prevail. If he satisfies himself on that score, there seems little or no reason for requiring more than a nominal bond of these plaintiffs, who are acting much as private attorneys general. If he finds no apparent deficiencies in the statement and little probability that the plaintiffs will ultimately prevail, he should deny all interim relief and await the conclusion of the hearing on the merits.

### COMMENTARY AND QUESTION

1. **The bond.** Note the court's discussion of the only point the citizens care about, the possibility of another $75,000 bond. Does Judge Haynsworth's opinion reflect economic reality? On the other hand, what would be the result of a blanket requirement that environmental plaintiffs seeking to enforce federal laws must post bonds sufficient to cover potential damages to defendants wrongfully restrained?[11]

---

The case then went back to Judge Larkins' court for review of the SCS's newly-prepared EIS. The citizen plaintiffs again sued for a preliminary injunction, alleging that even though there now was an EIS, it was inadequate under the terms of NEPA.

### NRDC v. Grant
U.S. District Court, Eastern District of North Carolina, 1973
355 F. Supp. 280

LARKINS, District Judge:

*"The River...is the living symbol of all the life it sustains or nourishes — fish, aquatic insects, water ouzels, otter, fisher, deer, elk, bear, and all other animals, including man, who are dependent upon it or who enjoy it for its sight, its sound or its life." Justice William O. Douglas, dissenting in Sierra Club v. Morton, 405 U.S. 727 (1972)....*

---

11. See Calderon, Bond Requirements Under FRCP 65(c): an Emerging Equitable Exemption for Public Interest Litigants, 13 B.C. Envt'l Aff. L. Rev. 125 (1985).

FINDINGS OF FACT AND CONCLUSIONS OF LAW... There is a substantial probability that the provisions of NEPA are not satisfied by the Chicod Creek Watershed environmental impact statement.

A. SCOPE OF JUDICIAL REVIEW OF THE ENVIRONMENTAL IMPACT STATEMENT
As the Court views this case, the ultimate decisions must not be made by the judiciary but by the executive and legislative branches of our government. This court does not intend to substitute its judgment as to what would be the best use of Chicod Creek and its environs for that of the Congress or those administrative departments of the executive branch which are charged by the Congress with the duty of carrying out its mandate. The Court's function is to determine whether the environmental effects of the proposed action and reasonable alternatives are sufficiently disclosed, discussed, and that conclusions are substantiated by supportive opinion and data.

B. REQUIREMENTS OF NEPA Section 102(2)(C) of NEPA requires, first, that federal agencies make full and accurate disclosure of the environmental effects of proposed action and alternatives to such action; and, second, that the agencies give full and meaningful consideration to these effects and alternatives in their decision-making. "At the very least, NEPA is an environmental full disclosure law...intended to make...decision-making more responsive and responsible. The 'detailed statement' required by 102(2)(C) should, at a minimum, contain such information as will alert the President, the Council on Environmental Quality, the public, and indeed, the Congress to all known possible consequences of proposed agency action."

But NEPA requires more than full disclosure of environmental consequences and project alternatives. NEPA requires full consideration of the same in agency decision making. Calvert Cliffs Coordinating Committee v. Atomic Energy Commission, 449 F.2d 1109 (D.C. Cir. 1971). The environmental impact statement "must be written in language that is understandable to the nontechnical minds and yet contains enough scientific reasoning to alert specialists to particular problems within the field of their expertise."

C. THE FINAL STATEMENT OMITS AND MISREPRESENTS A NUMBER OF IMPORTANT ENVIRONMENTAL EFFECTS OF THE PROJECT.
*(1) The Statement Misrepresents the Adverse Environmental Effects of the Project upon Fish Habitat*
The final Statement concedes that the Project will greatly increase the quantities of sediment carried downstream from the project area into the lower reaches of Chicod Creek and the Tar River. Immediately after construction, annual sediment deposit in the lower Chicod will be 11,670 tons. Sediment yield at the confluence of the Tar River is expected to be 730 tons annually. On the assumption that the banks will stabilize in two years, sedimentation will still be increased to 4,010 tons deposited annually in Chicod Creek and 250 tons in the Tar River.... While disclosing the fact of this increase in sediment load, the statement contains no discussion of its downstream effects. The statement merely concludes, without supportive scientific data and opinion that "No significant reduction in quality of the waters of the Tar River, Pamlico River, and Pamlico Sound is expected." Credible evidence suggests the opposite conclusion. Having conceded a massive increase in sedimentation, the Statement disposes of its environmental effects in

one conclusory statement unsupported by empirical or experimental data, scientific authorities or explanatory information of any kind....

*(2) The Statement Misrepresents the Effect of the Project upon Fish Resources*

The Statement is not at all clear on the effect of the Project on the fishery resources in Chicod Creek. It suggests that there will be effects upon the resident and anadromous fish in Chicod Creek, but the Statement does not define the effects. Yet the Statement without any supportive data declares "Most of the fishery resources within the watershed will not be affected by the project's works of improvement or will be mitigated." This falls far short of the standards of NEPA.

*(3) The Statement Ignores the Effect of the Project on Potential Eutrophication Problems in the Tar-Pamlico Estuary*

Eutrophication problems occur in waterways which accumulate an excess of nutrients such as nitrogen and phosphorous. Nutrients may be introduced in the waterways from several sources including agricultural runoff and swamp drainage. At the present time the nearby Chowan River is suffering from a very serious eutrophication problem.... Eutrophication is a problem that needs extensive study and research. Yet the Statement is silent on eutrophication. This is a violation of the "full disclosure" requirements of NEPA.

*(4) The Statement Fails to Disclose the Maintenance History of P.L. 566 Projects*

...Evidence indicated that local sponsors have failed to adequately perform their maintenance responsibilities in the past.... The Statement should disclose the history of success and failure of similar projects.

*(5) The Statement Ignores the Serious Environmental Consequences of the Proposed Use of Kudzu*

Although one may not know what it is called, a person does not have to be a scientist to recognize kudzu..... It can be seen growing on banks, stretching over shrubs and underbrush, engulfing trees, small and large, short and tall, slowly destroying and snuffing out the life of its unwilling host. Even manmade structures are susceptible to the vine — the tall slender green tree may be your telephone pole. However, if controlled, kudzu may have erosion preventing value. The defendants propose to plant one row of kudzu at the top edge of the channel slope in cultivated areas — along 23.5 miles of the new channels. As to the use of kudzu, the Statement merely discloses; "one row of kudzu will be planted at the very top edge of the channel slope through cultivated areas. The growth of kudzu will be controlled by mechanical methods." The Statement fails to disclose *how* the growth of kudzu can be controlled by mechanical or any other methods and in this respect fails to satisfy the requirements of NEPA.

*(6) The Statement Misrepresents and Fails to Disclose Other Important Environmental Effects of the Project*

The Statement fails to disclose that over 17 percent of the acreage to be benefited by the Project is held by the Weyerhaeuser Company, a large lumber company. The Statement does not contain an adequate discussion of the possible adverse effects of the Project upon downstream flooding.

D. THE STATEMENT DOES NOT DISCLOSE OR DISCUSS THE CUMULATIVE EFFECTS OF THE PROJECT. ...The [Regulations] of the Council of Environmental Quality focus attention upon the "overall cumulative impact of the action proposed (and further actions contemplated)," since the effect of decision about a project or a complex of projects "can be individually limited but cumulatively considerable." Yet, the Defendants have failed to consider fully in the final Statement the cumulative impact of the Chicod Creek Watershed Project and other channelization projects on the environmental and economic resources of Eastern North Carolina.... The cumulative effect of sedimentation is ignored in the Statement. There is no discussion of the potential adverse effects of long-term accumulation of nutrients caused by this and other channelization projects in the Tar-Pamlico River Basin. There is no discussion of the cumulative impact of drainage projects upon hardwood timber or groundwater resources.... Such effects should be assessed and disclosed in the environmental impact statement.

E. THE STATEMENT DOES NOT FULLY DISCLOSE OR ADEQUATELY DISCUSS ALTERNATIVES TO THE PROJECT. The "full disclosure" impact statement required by NEPA must contain a full and objective discussion of (1) reasonable alternatives to the proposed project and (2) the environmental impacts of each alternative. The Statement falls far short of satisfying these important and essential standards. Several critical reasonable alternatives are not discussed at all in the Statement. The recommendation of the Bureau of Sport Fisheries and Wildlife that seven miles of channelization be deleted from the most productive portion of the Chicod ecosystem is not discussed as an alternative to the Project. The Statement fails to discuss the alternative of deferral of the Project. Deferral is particularly appropriate in view of differing opinions about the environmental effects of the Project and §102(2)(A) of NEPA which "makes the completion of an adequate research program a prerequisite to agency action." Many of the conclusions in the Statement as to the potential adverse effects of the Project are not supported by references to scientific or other sources. The Statement omits any discussion of the recommendation of the North Carolina Department of Natural and Economic Resources that vertical drainage and water level control structures be discussed in the alternatives section, specifically as they mitigate any adverse ground water effects of the proposed project.

Alternatives are discussed only superficially, and nowhere are the environmental impacts of the alternatives discussed. The Statement thus does not provide "information sufficient to permit a reasoned choice of alternatives so far as environmental aspects are concerned." Natural Resources Defense Council v. Morton, *supra*. It is not the "full disclosure" statement required by NEPA.

F. CONCLUSIONS. This Court finds as a fact that the final Chicod Creek Watershed Environmental Statement does not fully and adequately disclose the adverse environmental effects of the Chicod Creek Watershed Project; nor does the Statement adequately disclose or discuss reasonable alternatives to the Project; and, therefore, there is a substantial probability that the Plaintiffs will be able to demonstrate at trial on the merits that the final Statement is not the "full disclosure" statement required by this Court's Order of March 16, 1972, and NEPA. A preliminary injunction barring further action on the Project pending a full hearing on the merits is thus appropriate....

### COMMENTARY AND QUESTIONS

1. **Agencies and EISs — a shotgun marriage?** What apparently was the nature and tone of the Chicod Creek EIS? Most agencies have an understandable inclination to build their projects as conveniently as possible, and EISs do not serve this end.

The central problem of the §102 EIS requirement is that it presents federal agencies (especially "construction" agencies and regulatory agencies with a high level of market involvement like the Nuclear Regulatory Commission, the Department of Agriculture, etc.) with conflicting mandates. On one hand, they have specific statutory missions, backed by the elaborate reward structure of supportive congressional committees, money, and the support of the related private industries and organizations with which they work. On the other hand, they have the vague, generalized values and directives of NEPA, for which there is no affirmative administrative reward system (beyond the satisfaction of a job well done in environmental terms). At the end of a year, agency officials tend to measure their accomplishments in terms of how many miles of river were dammed or channelized, or how many reactors licensed — it must be harder to measure institutional success in terms of how many wetlands have not been disrupted, or how many rivers left as they are. Yet EISs, by illuminating facts and concerns that previously had no legal place in the institutional decisionmaking process, now can show, in some cases, that the country would be better off without the agency's projects. A straightforward EIS may militate against building the project at all, or may indicate a less destructive way of constructing it, for the sake of newly-declared ecological values that do not square with the agency's own specific mandate.

Little wonder, then, that there is a marked tendency to write EISs in a manner that is consistent with agencies' program missions. Pick up any recent environmental impact statement, review its content and prose, and you will probably be confronted with the predictable agency reaction to contradictory statutory mandates.

So the temptation is great to make the EIS a "post hoc rationalization" which is supportive of the decision the agency has already effectively made. Sometimes, project benefits are stressed, negative effects are briefly noted and rated "manageable," "mitigation" is discussed, and alternatives are cursorily noted and dismissed. Other times, the agency's strategy is to prepare an excessively long, hypertechnical, and unreadable EIS that is calculated to prevent public scrutiny. The CEQ Regulations require that EISs be prepared using an interdisciplinary approach (§1502.6), that they not exceed approximate page limitations (§1502.7), and that they be written in "plain language" (§1502.8); but these commands are rarely followed and never enforced. The CEQ itself has admitted that

> frequently NEPA takes too long and costs too much, agencies make decisions before hearing from the public, documents are too long and technical for many people to use, and training for agency officials, particularly senior leadership, is inadequate. The EIS process is still frequently viewed as merely a compliance requirement rather than as a tool to effect better decision-making. Because of this, millions of dollars, years of time, and tons of paper have been spent on documents that have little effect on decision-making. CEQ Study, 7.

Courts rarely mention the reality of this administrative inclination to write self-justifying impact statements, but in the Chicod Creek case the court seems skeptical of the SCS's sincerity. In judicial review of agency decisions under NEPA and other environmental laws, can environmental lawyers ask judges to take account of political science and be less deferential, where applicable laws were designed to constrain the agencies' singlemindedness? Do they already do so implicitly?

2. **Judicial psychology.** Do you detect a change in Judge Larkins' tone? What happened? There is no mention now of the alleged project benefits to small farmers; rather the opinion is a catalog of the project's negative effects. Can you discern which pieces of evidence at trial got through to the judge most dramatically? How sophisticated would the various pieces of plaintiff's evidence have to be on eutrophication, sedimentation, fisheries, and kudzu? What about Weyerhaeuser's ownership? Problems of past maintenance? How do environmental plaintiffs get around a judge's natural inclination to defer to official expertise?

3. **Epilogue to *Chicod Creek*.** What did finally happen in our North Carolina case? As one state official put it, "Old John Larkins saw he was going to make some enemies either way he decided this thing, so he called in the attorneys for both sides and said 'Boys, we've gone through this stuff long enough now, why don't you go settle it between yourselves?' And because the handwriting was on the wall, the SCS agreed to a compromise." [Confidential interview, February 1981]. No channelizing, channel straightening, or major treecutting was allowed; silt removal was permitted in the upper stretches. The lower six to seven miles of the creek were cleaned of snags and silt, but no draglines were permitted. As a result, the stream and its tributaries were, to a great degree, returned to the quality of the days before intensive agriculture, with a meandering wooded course and restored swimming holes. The redesigned project was so successful that the North Carolina legislature passed a Stream Restoration Act in 1979, mandating consultation with the State Wildlife Resources Commission for all such projects. Is this a success story? What about the poor families that Judge Larkins wrote of in his first opinion? No new subsidized farmland was created. Is this another example of élite conservationism oppressing poor folks?

### Section 2. THE JUDICIAL AND ADMINISTRATIVE DEVELOPMENT OF NEPA

Especially when a statute is written in such general and enigmatic terms as NEPA, and passed with so little relevant legislative history, it is inevitable that a parade of questions will have to be answered before the statute's shape and substance become clear in practice. The position to which NEPA has evolved over the years, almost entirely as a function of citizen litigation, was certainly not preordained. As the *Chicod Creek* case demonstrated, NEPA could have become merely a footnote of judicial deference to agency action, but didn't. With few exceptions, the federal courts took NEPA seriously. NEPA could also have become a superstatute, imposing strict court-enforced substantive controls on the administrative process. That didn't happen either.

The following materials review some of the basic questions raised in the judicial and administrative implementation of NEPA. In the course of this development, NEPA became what it is today — a useful, mixed proposition, a milestone statute in the emerging evolution of national (and international) environmental policy.

### a. Issues in implementing the impact statement requirement

**THE EIS: WHAT MUST IT CONTAIN?...** Note the array of requirements for the preparation of EISs set out in §102 as it was drafted by Professor Caldwell. Is there any real difference between (i) "environmental impacts," (ii) "adverse environmental effects which cannot be avoided," (iii) "the relationship between short-term uses and maintenance of long-term productivity(?)"; and (iv) "irretrievable commitments of resources"? Some EISs dutifully separate out multiple sections to cover each of these, but analytically it seems that §102 just requires a statement of *effects*, (§102(2)(C) i , ii, iv, & v), and *alternatives* (C(ii) and D), prepared in consultation with other relevant agencies.

Judge Larkins' opinion follows this approach — it looks at only two categories, effects and alternatives. Note the kinds of effects that were left out, insufficiently disclosed, or, worse, "misrepresented" in the EIS. What effects must be discussed, and to what extent, in order to comply with whatever it is that §102 is supposed to do? Effects on human sport? The aesthetics of a scraped-off linear canal? Slight thermal changes in the local micro-climate? Is a short description of sedimentation enough to disclose the existence of a problem to whomever is intended by NEPA to read the EIS? Judge Larkins requires the EIS to consider cumulative effects of this and other projects. Is this supported by the implied intention of NEPA? What if the plaintiffs claim that the project will have an effect that is not clearly provable, like increasing the likelihood of earthquakes? The courts have generally held that if the alleged adverse effect is not purely speculative or minimal, and is supported by some responsible scientist's opinion, then the EIS must deal with it.

But this presents a paradox: in order to convince a court of substantial doubts attending an agency project, plaintiffs must find out in advance much of the information they are asking the agency to develop in an EIS. This requires private plaintiffs to come up with a lot of expensive expert testimony, and to some extent mixes up the players' roles.

To what extent must environmental effects be analyzed and discussed in the EIS? The Chicod Creek EIS discussed eutrophication, for example, but not extensively enough for Judge Larkins. If, as some courts have said, the purpose is to bring the project's consequences to the attention of the agency decision-maker, mere disclosure may be enough. If, on the other hand, the EIS is intended to demonstrate to a court that the agency gave "full consideration" to the impact, *Calvert Cliffs*, 449 F.2d at 1128, then more analysis must be reflected in the EIS itself. A middle ground definition was given by the Ninth Circuit: "reasonably thorough discussion of the significant aspects of the probable environmental consequences is all that is required by an EIS," said the court in Trout Unlimited v. Morton, 509 F.2d 1276, 1283 (1974)(the decision that allowed the construction of the Teton Dam in spite of environmentalists' safety warnings; the dam collapsed, killing more than 100 people). This is one manifestation of the "rule of reason," that courts apply in interpreting most aspects of NEPA.

**ALTERNATIVES...** Alternatives have been part of our environmental analysis from the beginning of this book, and are a critical part of NEPA's EIS requirement. In some SCS EISs, and those of other agencies, the agency refused to consider the "do-nothing," "no-action," or "zero" alternative. Why? Other agencies refused to consider any alternatives that they themselves could not build or manage. NRDC v. Morton, 458 F.2d 827 (D.C. Cir. 1972) set those arguments to rest: the Interior Department had to consider all practical alternative sources of energy, regardless of whether they were within the agency's control, before deciding to lease offshore oil deposits. Note the relationship between discussions of alternatives and of environmental consequences required by the CEQ regulations:

§1502.14 Alternatives including the proposed action. This section is the heart of the environmental impact statement...[I]t should present the environmental impacts of the proposal and the alternatives in comparative form, thus sharply defining the issues and providing a clear basis of choice among options by the decision maker and the public. In this section agencies shall:

(a) Rigorously explore and objectively evaluate all reasonable alternatives and for alternatives which were eliminated from detailed study, briefly discuss the reasons for their having been eliminated.

(b) Devote substantial treatment to each alternative considered in detail including the proposed action so that reviewers may evaluate their comparative merits.

(c) Include reasonable alternatives not within the jurisdiction of the lead agency.

(d) Include the alternative of no action....

§1502.16 Environmental consequences.... The discussion will include the environmental impacts of the alternatives including the proposed action, any adverse environmental effects which cannot be avoided...and any irreversible or irretrievable commitments of resources which would be involved in the proposal should it be implemented....

Section 1502.16 also provides that the EIS will include discussions of direct and indirect effects and their significance; possible conflicts between the proposed action and the objectives of land use plans, policies, and controls for the area concerned; and the energy and resource requirements and conservation potential of the various alternatives. An EIS also must address urban quality, historic and cultural resources, and measures to mitigate adverse environmental impacts.

If courts did not require consideration of rational alternatives, the stop-and-think process would be neutralized. In Citizens Against Burlington v. Busey, for instance, 938 F.2d 190 (D.C. Cir. 1991) cert. denied 112 S.Ct. 616 (1991) an air freight carrier wanted permission to shift its operations 80 miles from Fort Wayne to a Toledo air field, increasing night traffic there from 400 to more than 11,700 flights per year, in order to save operating expenses. The Federal Aviation Administration's EIS considered only the two options advanced by the corporation — the proposed facility, or nothing — ignoring the citizens' evidence that operations could be improved at the original facility. Writing for the D.C. Circuit, Judge Clarence Thomas permitted this circumscribing of EIS alternatives.[12] Writing in dissent, Judge James Buckley, a conservative Reagan appointee, complained that

---

12. The Court also declined to require noise mitigation measures required under §509(b)(5) of the Airport & Aviation Import Act (AAIA), 494 U.S.C.A. §2298(b)(5).

the Thomas opinion allowed nonfederal parties "to define the limits of the EIS inquiry and thus to frustrate one of the principal safeguards of the NEPA process, the mandatory consideration of reasonable alternatives." 938 F.2d at 209.

**SEGMENTATION...** One agency strategy for avoiding the effect of NEPA has been segmentation. If an entire project raises major environmental questions, divide it into smaller segments, and build the least destructive segment first, with an EIS (or less, an EA with a FONSI) limited to that segment. Then the later segments will draw momentum from the approval and construction of the first. Some courts have rejected these EISs, on the grounds that the segmentation did not have "independent utility" or, implicitly, that this was an attempt to evade NEPA through coercive construction "bootstrapping." Other courts have allowed the strategy. Swan v. Brinegar, 542 F.2d 364 (7th Cir. 1976); Sierra Club v. Callaway (Wallisville Dam), 499 F.2d 982 (5th Cir. 1974); Indian Lookout Alliance v. Volpe, 484 F.2d 11 (8th Cir. 1973).

Would it be legal for the builders of a highway to take one portion of the project that is environmentally destructive — say the portion of the highway that runs through a wetlands — and have the state road department build that without federal dollars, thereby trying to "defederalize" the wetlands stretch of road, avoiding an EIS that would reveal major negative impacts? See Village of Los Ranchos de Albuquerque v. Barnhart, 906 F.2d 1477 (10th Cir. 1990), where the court permitted segmentation by defederalization.

**NEPA AND SCIENTIFIC UNCERTAINTY...** One of the recurring themes of environmental law and policy is how to make policy decisions under conditions of pervasive scientific uncertainty. Before 1986, the CEQ Regulations required a "worst case analysis" in such situations, but, during the Reagan Administration, these Regulations were amended to read as follows:

§1502.22 Incomplete or unavailable information. When an agency is evaluating reasonably foreseeable significant adverse effects on the human environment...and there is incomplete or unavailable information, the agency shall always make clear that such information is lacking.

(a) If the incomplete information...is essential to a reasonable choice among alternatives and the overall costs of obtaining it are not exorbitant, the agency shall include the information in the environmental impact statement.

(b) If the information...cannot be obtained because the overall costs of obtaining it are exorbitant, or the means to obtain it are not known, the agency shall include within the environmental impact statement:

(1) A statement that such information is incomplete or unavailable; (2) a statement of the relevance of the incomplete or unavailable information...; (3) a summary of existing credible scientific evidence...; and (4) the agency's evaluation of such impacts based upon theoretical approaches or research methods generally accepted in the scientific community. For the purposes of this section, "reasonably foreseeable" includes impacts which have catastrophic consequences, even if their probability of occurrence is low, provided that the analysis of the impacts is supported by credible scientific evidence, and is within the rule of reason.

In Robertson v. Methow Valley Citizens' Council, 490 U.S. 332 (1989), discussed below, the United States Supreme Court upheld the CEQ's abandonment of the "worst case analysis" requirement.

Who determines whether information is incomplete, unavailable, or only available at "exorbitant" cost? Since NEPA is a full-disclosure statute, should judges give less deference to agency decisions regarding uncertainty than would be entailed by the "arbitrary and capricious" standard of judicial review? Should agency analysis be limited to "theoretical approaches or research methods generally accepted in the scientific community"? (See Chapter Four). What is "credible scientific evidence"? The CEQ's insistence that the impacts analysis should be consistent with the "rule of reason," and not based on "pure conjecture," is consistent with judicial interpretations of NEPA.

Where relevant new information becomes available after the EIS is adopted, the lead agency may be required to prepare and circulate a "supplemental environmental impact statement" (SEIS)(40 CFR §1502.9(c)). A SEIS may also be required when substantial changes are made in the project after original NEPA compliance. (See the Carmel-by-the Sea case, below, holding that an SEIS is necessary to consider additional alternatives in light of recent project changes). An agency decision whether or not to prepare an SEIS is reviewable under the "arbitrary and capricious" standard. Marsh v. Oregon Natural Resources Council, 490 U.S. 360 (1989).

**INTERAGENCY CONSULTATION...** Section 102(2)(C) does not merely require EIS preparation; it also requires that, in this case, the SCS "consult with and obtain the comments of any Federal agency [involved relevant to environmental issues]," and those comments must "accompany the proposal through existing agency review processes." This requirement may have tactical importance, e.g. if the Department of Interior's Fish and Wildlife Service wants to raise serious questions about habitat destruction, but has no direct power over its sister agency, what can plaintiffs make of the fact that this EIS does not reflect much of an interagency consultation process? If the SCS tried to solicit comments of other agencies, but received none, can the plaintiffs demand an injunction until such consultation does occur? In fact, a consulted federal agency has no duty to comment: it may reply with a "no comment" (40 CFR §1503.2). In other cases, as in *Chicod Creek*, environmental plaintiffs may alterted to information that they could not produce themselves by the comments of other federal agencies and state agencies, that also must be invited to comment (§1503.1(2)).

**WHO REALLY PREPARES THE EIS?...** Who prepares the EIS? NEPA says "the responsible official," and in a number of early cases the courts had to deal with EISs that were drafted at the local level by state officials or other project proponents and merely adopted by the relevant federal agencies. Citizen plaintiffs successfully urged the courts to require the EISs to be prepared by the federal agencies themselves, on the ground that NEPA was designed to inform the federal decision as it was being made. Greene County Planning Board v. FPC, 455 F.2d 412 (2d Cir. 1972), *cert. denied*, 409 U.S. 849 (1972). What premises are reflected in such lawsuits about the relative bias within and outside the federal agency? Congress amended NEPA in 1975 to permit preparation of the EIS by state agencies that receive federal grants for particular projects. In practice today many agencies hire consultant firms to prepare "winning" EISs for them, which may set up yet another bias problem. If several federal agencies are involved in a proposal, NEPA compliance is the primary responsibility of a "lead agency," with the assistance of "cooperating agencies." The CEQ resolves disputes among federal agencies over which will be the lead agency (§§1501.5, 1501.6).

**ARE AGENCY PROMISES IN AN EIS ENFORCEABLE?...** What if an agency prepares an EA or EIS that promises extensive mitigation work (setting up new wetland reserves, wildlife enchancement, etc.) to offset negative project effects, defeats a citizen lawsuit on this basis, and then announces that it will not undertake the promised work (because it has insufficient funds or whatever)? In Robertson v. Methow Valley Citizens' Council, 490 U.S. 332 (1989), the Supreme Court made it clear that courts cannot agencies to implement mitigation measures discussed in EISs. The lower courts have uniformly said that the citizens have no remedy if promises made (or implied) in an EISs are not kept. NOE v. Metro. Atlanta Transit Auth., 485 F. Supp. 501 (N.D. Ga. 1980); Ogunquit Village Corp. v. Davis, 553 F. 2d 243 (1st Cir. 1977). Even if the plaintiffs prove agency bad faith, a court will weigh the value of the requested compliance against the costs. EDF v. Marsh, 651 F. 2d 983 (5th Cir. 1981).

**RATIONAL DECISIONMAKING AND NEPA'S SUBSTANTIVE EFFECT?...** The earliest chapters of this book set out the analytical basis of questions now raised by NEPA: a sound, rational decision requires consideration of all the significant effects of a proposal, and of its *alternatives*, as well as its real benefits. When these have finally been disclosed in an adequate EIS, however, can a court force the agency to make its substantive decision consistent with the EIS? Could Judge Larkins, for example, forbid the Chicod Creek project if the final EIS showed major sedimentation, eutrophication, wildlife and drainage disruption, and showed that the countervailing benefits to farming were estimated at less than $100 per acre?

Put another way, does NEPA have an enforceable substantive requirement — i.e., that agency decisions must be environmentally sound — as well as the bare procedural requirement that an EIS be prepared and circulated? If it is only the latter, then NEPA appears superficial, allowing an agency to go ahead with major destructive projects if only it first accurately catalogs the destructive effects in an EIS document. If, on the other hand, courts can enforce a substantive application of NEPA's broad principles upon an unwilling agency, what limit is there to the judicial power? Suppose Judge Larkins was deeply convinced, at the end of the trial on the merits, that the Chicod Creek case was ludicrously negative on an overall balance of effects. What could he do? Justice Rehnquist, writing for the Supreme Court in Vermont Yankee Nuclear Power Corp v. Natural Resources Defense Council, 435 U.S. 519, 558 (1978), stated that while NEPA "establishes significant substantive goals for the Nation," its actual requirements for the agencies are "essentially procedural." The Supreme Court reiterated its view that NEPA does not demand particular subtantive results in Marsh v. Oregon Natural Resources Council, 490 U.S. 360 (1989) ("NEPA merely prohibits uninformed — rather than unwise — agency decisions"), and Robertson v. Methow Valley Citizens' Council, 490 U. S. 332 (1989). In its Record of Decision, at the conclusion of the NEPA process, an agency must identify the environmentally preferable alternative, but it does not have to choose this alternative (§1505.2).

## JUDICIAL REVIEW: THE ARBITRARY AND CAPRICIOUS TEST?

Even if courts do not have a direct substantive review power under NEPA, they have some ability to review the decisions of federal agencies under the Administrative Procedures Act's §706, which prohibits actions that are "arbitrary, capricious, or an abuse of discretion" (studied further in Chapter Seven). What does this test mean? There have been several interpretations in NEPA cases:

> The test is whether the balance of cost and benefits that was struck was arbitrary or clearly gave insufficient weight to environmental values. *Calvert Cliffs*, 449 F.2d at 1115;

> Our review will perforce be a narrow one, limited to ensuring that the Commission has adequately explained the fact and policy concerns it relied on [and that these] considerations could by themselves lead a reasonable person to make the judgment that the Agency has made. NRDC v. SEC, 606 F.2d 1031, 1053 (D.C. Cir. 1979);

> [The role of the court is to assure that] the agency made a good faith balancing of environmental benefits and costs. EDF v. TVA, 339 F. Supp. at 810 (1972);

> [The reviewing court must insure that] the agency has taken a "hard look" at environmental consequences. Kleppe v. Sierra Club, 427 U.S. 390, 410 n. 21 (1976).

Each of these tests permits a court to review the agency's substantive decision to some degree. Strycker's Bay Neighborhood Council v. Karlen, 444 U.S. 223 (1980), however, considerably clouded the issue. A low-income housing unit that was determined to have serious environmental consequences (including social and economic ghettoization — urban NEPA issues?) was proposed for a site in Manhattan. The EIS showed alternative sites available, which did not have such adverse environmental effects, but each alternative would have required a two-year delay to shift the project. The agency chose to build as planned in order to save time. The Court of Appeals for the Second Circuit said that in light of NEPA's policy, the two-year time factor could not be treated as "an overriding factor"; "environmental factors...should be given determinable [sic] weight." 590 F.2d at 44. The Supreme Court reversed, saying "once an agency has made a decision subject to NEPA's procedural requirements, the only role for a court is to insure that the agency has *considered* the environmental consequences." What then is the test? The Court cannot mean that an agency can ignore the environmental evidence after considering it. Even the defendant agency in *Strycker's Bay* conceded that its decision would be arbitrary if it gave little or no decisional weight to environmental factors. Because of the high court's opinion, however, the lower court could no longer give superior weight to environmental factors. So how about equal weight? Does that simplify the question? If the costs of a two-year delay closely balance the negative environmental effects, the agency can be expected to tilt in favor of its original plans, and that decision will not be "arbitrary." But who is to say the opposing factors (apples and oranges?) are or are not closely balanced? If the courts can do so, are they necessarily making part of the substantive decision? This is an enduring problem in NEPA, where an adequate EIS is presumptive evidence of "good faith consideration" by the proposing agency. Ironically, a legally adequate EIS generally insulates the agency from judicial review on the basis of not having considered relevant factors, not explaining its decision satisfactorily, or not having provided a reviewable record.

### b. The EIS process: questions of timing and scope

INTERNAL AGENCY TIMING... The CEQ regulations prescribe basic time parameters for the preparation of an EIS. These timing requirements are minimal, however, reflecting CEQ's view that comprehensive agency scheduling requirements would be too inflexible.

The standard course of the EIS's production as a public document follows the APA rulemaking model: the agency prepares a Draft EIS ("DEIS," analogous to a notice of proposed rulemaking); the DEIS is opened for public comment; the agency prepares the Final EIS ("FEIS," analogous to a final rulemaking) with an appendix of comments received on the draft and the agency's responses thereto. 40 CFR §1506. (Note that there is no requirement that agencies hold hearings on draft or final EISs.) Finally, the agency prepares and distributes a Record of Decision, stating the alternatives considered, including the environmentally preferable alternative, the non-environmental factors that the agency balanced against environmental factors, and "whether all praticable means to avoid or minimize harm from the alternative selected have been adopted, and if not, why they were not." 40 CFR §1505.2.

Once EPA has published notice that an EIS has been filed, an agency cannot make a decision sooner than 90 days after publication, for a draft EIS, or 30 days after publication, for a final EIS. If the periods overlap, the later of the two cut-off dates applies. Agencies must allow at least 45 days for comments on draft statements. 40 CFR §1506.11. The lead agency may set time limits consistent with these parameters. In setting such time limits, the regulations suggest that the agency consider factors such as the scope of the action, the potential environmental risks, the consequences of delay, and the degree to which the proposed action is controversial. Are these time parameters realistic, given the long lead time customarily involved in planning agency projects, not to mention the length and complexity of modern EIS preparation? Do members of the public have sufficient time to verify the information included in the EIS, or uncover information that the agency may have omitted?

The CEQ regulations suggest that the EIS should indeed be a decision-making tool:

> §1502. 1 Purpose. The primary purpose of an environmental impact statement is to serve as an action-forcing device to insure that the policies and goals defined in [NEPA] are infused into the ongoing programs and actions of the Federal Government.... *An environmental impact statement is more than a disclosure document. It shall be used by Federal officials in conjunction with other relevant material to plan actions and make decisions.* (emphasis added)

> §1505.1 Agency decisionmaking procedures. Agencies shall adopt procedures to ensure that decisions are made in accordance with the policies and purposes of the Act. Such procedures shall include... (d) Requiring that relevant environmental documents, comments, and responses accompany the proposal

through existing agency review processes *so that agency officials use the statement in making decisions.* (emphasis added)

§1502.2 Implementation.... (f) Agencies shall not commit resources prejudicing selection of alternatives before making a final decision.

§1502.5 Timing. The [EIS] shall be prepared early enough so that it can serve practically as an important contribution to the decision making process and will not be used to rationalize or justify decisions already made.[13]

SCOPING... The NEPA regulations also introduce the process of "scoping." 40 CFR §1501.7 At an early stage in the decisional process an agency must review the breadth of project effects and alternatives, invite comments from the public and other governmental agencies, and prepare a comprehensive plan for addressing all significant issues. The intent is clearly to facilitate EIS preparation. What would its effect have been on the Chicod Creek EIS? The CEQ, however, points out that scoping cannot be expected to change an agency's preconceptions:

> Citizens are frustrated when they are treated as adversaries rather than welcome participants in the NEPA process. When they are invited to a formal scoping meeting to discuss a well-developed project about which they have heard little, they may feel that they have been invited too late in the process. In addition, public "hearings" at times are seen as parties "talking past each other," with very little listening. Some citizens complain that their time and effort spent providing good ideas is not reflected in changes to proposals or satisfying explanations for why suggestions were not incorporated.... Citizens report that they often feel overwhelmed by the resources available to proponents and agencies. As a consequence, litigation can be seen as the only means to affect environmental decisions significantly. CEQ Study, 18.

When in a project's life history should the EIS be prepared? The *SIPI* case, Scientists Institute for Public Information v. Atomic Energy Commission, 481 F.2d 1079 (D.C. Cir. 1973), presented a demand for an EIS for the federal fast breeder reactor research program, a sequentially evolving enterprise with millions of dollars in present expenditures, leading to billions in future expenditures, with great potential environmental costs. The question of when in this process an EIS must be presented was poignantly put in the trial judge's question:

> There comes a time, we start with $E=MC^2$, we both agree you don't have to have the impact statement then. Then there comes a time when there are a thousand of these breeder plants in existence all over the country. Sometime before that, surely...there has to be an impact statement, and a long time before that, actually. But the question is, exactly where in this chain do we have to have an impact statement? 481 F.2d at 1093.

The appeals court set up a four-factor balancing test, designed to require an EIS at the point where binding decisions are being made. The factors were: (1) the program's likelihood of practical feasibility, and how soon; (2) the availability of data

---

13. In the *Chicod Creek* case the EIS was drafted after the SCS had decided exactly what it wanted to do. Should Judge Larkins have ordered the SCS to *reopen* the entire question while the EIS was being drafted? If NEPA is interpreted as a directive to include environmental concerns in the actual decision-making process, that question necessarily arises. If NEPA is primarily considered a disclosure requirement (to whom? Congress, the President, the public, the courts?) then courts need not pretend that it will change the minds of agencies, but rather can insist on full EISs for reasons external to the agency process.

on the technology and its alternatives, and their effects; (3) the likelihood that irretrievable commitments are being made and options foreclosed as the program continues; and (4) the potential seriousness of environmental effects. Based on these criteria, the Court of Appeals required an EIS, which exposed the issues of plutonium radiation hazards and runaway costs, and led to Congress' deauthorization of the reactor. What was *SIPI's* premise? That if an EIS is truly to inform governmental decision-making, it has to occur sufficiently early in the process to make a meaningful difference, rather than as a last-step afterthought. As §102(2)(c) says, the draft EIS "shall accompany the proposal through the existing agency review [decision-making?] process."

**PROGRAMMATIC IMPACT STATEMENTS...** The reality of agency behavior is that individual projects are often part of broad ongoing programs. The CEQ regulations provide two rationales underlying the requirement that agencies prepare "programmatic" EISs where appropriate. §1502.4, 1502.20. For the agency, preparation of a programmatic EIS can greatly streamline the EIS process for all of the subsequent specific projects that derive from it. A programmatic EIS on nuclear waste disposal, for example, can be done once and for all, and then merely incorporated by reference in subsequent nuclear powerplant EIS proceedings. For environmentalists, a timely programmatic EIS can raise fundamental issues and shape basic agency decisions at a sufficiently early stage to improve or block a program before it is cast in bureaucratic stone.

The Supreme Court later, in a very different setting, had the opportunity to consider both questions — of programmatic EISs and the timing of EISs in evolving agency processes.

### Kleppe v. Sierra Club
United States Supreme Court, 1976
427 U.S. 390, 96 S.Ct. 2718, 49 L.Ed.2d 576

POWELL, J.... Respondents, several organizations concerned with the environment, brought this suit in July 1973 in the United States District Court for the District of Columbia. The defendants in the suit, petitioners here, were the officials of the Department [of Interior] and other federal agencies responsible for issuing coal leases, approving mining plans, granting rights-of-way and taking...other actions necessary to enable private companies and public utilities to develop coal reserves on land owned or controlled by the Federal Government. Citing widespread interest in the reserves of a region identified as the "Northern Great Plains region," and an alleged threat from coal-related operations to their members' enjoyment of the region's environment, respondents claimed that the federal officials could not allow further development without preparing a "comprehensive environmental impact statement" under §102(2)(C) on the entire region.... [Plaintiffs lost in the District Court, but the Court of Appeals reversed and granted an injunction.]

The "Northern Great Plains region" identified in respondents' complaint encompasses portions of four States — northeastern Wyoming, eastern Montana, western North Dakota and western South Dakota. There is no dispute about its richness in coal, nor about the waxing interest in developing that coal, nor about the critical role the federal petitioners will play due to the significant percentage of the coal to which they control access. The Department has initiated, in this decade, three studies in areas either inclusive of or included within this region....

While the record does not reveal the degree of concern with environmental matters in the first two studies, it is clear that the NGPRP [Northern Great Plains Resources Program] was devoted entirely to the environment. It was carried out by an interagency federal-state task force with public participation, and was designed "to assess the potential, economic and environmental impacts" from resource development in five States — Montana, Wyoming, South Dakota, North Dakota, and Nebraska....

In addition, since 1973 the Department has engaged in a complete review of its coal leasing program for the entire Nation.... The purpose of the program review was to study the environmental impact of the Department's entire range of coal-related activities and to develop a planning system to guide the national leasing program. The impact statement, known as the "Coal Programmatic EIS," went through several drafts before issuing in final form on September 19, 1975 — shortly before the petition for certiorari was filed in this case....

The major issue remains the one with which the suit began: whether NEPA requires petitioners to prepare an environmental impact statement on the entire Northern Great Plains region. Petitioners, arguing the negative, rely squarely on the facts of the case and the language of §102(2)(C) of NEPA. We find their reliance well placed....

Respondents can prevail only if there has been a report or recommendation on a proposal for major federal action with respect to the Northern Great Plains region. Our statement of the relevant facts shows there has been none; instead, all proposals are for actions of either local or national scope....

The Court of Appeals, in reversing the District Court, did not find that there was a regional plan or program for development of the Northern Great Plains region. It accepted all of the District Court's findings of fact, but concluded nevertheless that the petitioners "contemplated" a regional plan or program....

Even had the record justified a finding that a regional program was contemplated by the petitioners, the legal conclusion drawn by the Court of Appeals cannot be squared with the Act. The Court recognized that the mere "contemplation" of certain action is not sufficient to require an impact statement. But it believed the statute nevertheless empowers a court to require the preparation of an impact statement to begin at some point prior to the formal recommendation or report on a proposal. The Court of Appeals accordingly devised its own four-part "balancing test" for determining when, during the contemplation of a plan or other type of federal action, an agency must begin a statement. The factors to be considered were [based on SIPI:] the likelihood and imminence of the program's coming to fruition, the extent to which information is available on the effects of implementing the expected program and on alternatives thereto, the extent to which irretrievable commitments are being made and options precluded "as refinement of the proposal progresses," and the severity of the environmental effects should the action be implemented....

The Court's reasoning and action find no support in the language or legislative history of NEPA. The statute clearly states when an impact statement is required, and mentions nothing about a balancing of factors. Rather...the moment at which an agency must have a final statement ready "is the time at which it makes a recommendation or report on a *proposal* for federal action." The procedural duty imposed upon agencies by this section is quite precise and the role of the courts in enforcing that duty is similarly precise. A court has no authority to depart from the statutory language and, by a balancing of court-devised factors, determine a point during the germination process of a potential proposal at which an impact statement *should be prepared*. Such an assertion of judicial authority would leave the agencies uncertain as to their procedural duties under NEPA, would invite judicial involvement in the day-to-day decision making process of the agencies, and would invite litigation....

Respondents [further] insist that, even without a comprehensive federal plan for the development of the Northern Great Plains, a "regional" impact statement nevertheless is required on all coal-related projects in the region because they are intimately related....

We begin by stating our general agreement with respondents' basis premise that §102(2)(C) may require a comprehensive impact statement in certain situations where several proposed actions are pending at the same time.... Thus, when several proposals for coal-related actions that will have a cumulative or synergistic environmental impact upon a region are pending concurrently before an agency, their environmental consequences must be considered together[14]....

Respondents conceded at oral argument that to prevail they must show that petitioners have acted arbitrarily in refusing to prepare one comprehensive statement on this entire region, and we agree. The determination of the region, if any, with respect to which a comprehensive statement is necessary requires the weighting of a number of factors, including the extent of the interrelationship among proposed actions and practical considerations of feasibility. Resolving those issues requires a high level of technical expertise and is properly left to the informed discretion of the responsible federal agencies. Absent a showing of arbitrary action, we must assume that the agencies have exercised this discretion appropriately. Respondents have made no showing to the contrary.

MARSHALL, J., concurring in part and dissenting in part.

While I agree with much of the Court's opinion, I must dissent from [that part] which holds that the federal courts may not remedy violations of [NEPA] — no matter how blatant — until too late for an adequate remedy to be formulated. As the Court today recognizes, NEPA contemplates agency consideration of environmental factors throughout the decisionmaking process. Since NEPA's enactment, however, litigation has been brought primarily at the end of that process — challenging agency decisions to act made without adequate environmental impact statements or without any statements at all. In such situations, the courts have had to content themselves with the largely unsatisfactory remedy of enjoining the proposed federal action and ordering the preparation of an adequate impact statement. This remedy is insufficient because, except by deterrence, it does nothing to further early consideration of environmental factors. And, as with all after-the-fact remedies, a remand for the preparation of an impact statement after the basic decision to act has been made invites *post hoc* rationalizations, rather than the candid

---

14. At some points in their brief respondents appear to seek a comprehensive ["programmatic"] impact statement covering contemplated projects in the region as well as those that already have been proposed. The statute, however, speaks solely in terms of *proposed* actions; it does not require an agency to consider the possible environmemntal impacts of less imminent actions when preparing the impact statement on proposed actions. Should contemplated actions later reach the stage of actual proposals, impact statements on them will take into account the effect of their approval upon the existing environment; and the condition of that environment presumably will reflect earlier proposed actions and their effects.

and balanced environmental assessments envisioned by NEPA. Moreover, the remedy is wasteful of resources and time, causing fully developed plans for action to be laid aside while an impact statement is prepared.

Nevertheless, until this lawsuit, such belated remedies were all the federal courts had had the opportunity to impose under NEPA. In this case, confronted with a situation in which, according to respondents' allegations, federal agencies were violating NEPA prior to their basic decision to act, the Court of Appeals...seized the opportunity to devise a different and effective remedy....

The Court begins its rejection of the [Court of Appeals'] four-part test by announcing that the procedural duty imposed on the agencies by §102(2)(C) is "quite precise" and leaves a court "no authority to depart from the statutory language." Given the history and wording of NEPA's impact statement requirement, this statement is baffling. A statute that imposes a complicated procedural requirement on all "proposals" for "major federal actions significantly affecting the quality of the human environment" and then assiduously avoids giving any hint, either expressly or by way of legislative history, of what is meant by a proposal for a "major federal action" can hardly be termed precise. In fact, this vaguely worded statute seems designed to serve as no more than a catalyst for development of a "common law" of NEPA. To date, the courts have responded in just that manner and have created such a "common law." Indeed, that development is the source of NEPA's success. Of course, the Court is correct that the courts may not depart from NEPA's language. They must, however, give meaning to that language if there is to be anything in NEPA to enforce at all.

### COMMENTARY AND QUESTIONS

1. **Tiering of EISs.** Plaintiffs-respondents wanted a full complement of impact statements on the federal coal-leasing program: a national (programmatic, or generic) EIS; a regional EIS; and impact documents for each local coal lease and right-of-way granted by the Department. This hierarchy of impact documents is called "tiering." See CEQ regulations, §1508.28. How informative could the national EIS and the local impact statements be without a regional EIS integrating them? Regional, or "ecosystem," planning is currently seen the most efficient and effective prelude to intelligent environmental management:

> An ecosystem, or place-based approach to strategic planning through NEPA can provide a framework for evaluating the environmental status quo and the combined cumulative impacts of individual projects. Analyzing similar but individual projects on a watershed basis, for example, can be very efficient, reducing the number of analyses and documents, and allowing agencies to focus on cumulative impacts within a geographic area. *CEQ Study*, 14.

Was the Court suggesting that the NGPRP was the "functional equivalent" of a regional EIS?

2. **To plan or not to plan.** Is the *Kleppe* decision a disincentive to comprehensive planning? After all, from the standpoint of a federal agency, if you don't plan, you then don't have to go public with an EIS, thus avoiding public controversy until the action has become a self-fulfilling prophecy. If this is so, doesn't *Kleppe* contradict NEPA's emphasis on early planning in order to forestall irretrievable commitments of resources to environmentally damaging projects?

3. **When is there a proposal?** *Kleppe* stands for the rule that a proposal only comes into existence when the agency declares it, unless the agency has been arbitrary and capricious in not making a proposal. The CEQ regulations (§1508.23) state that a proposal may exist in fact even if it is not explicitly made. Should CEQ or the Court have the the last word in interpreting NEPA? On one hand, courts should defer to an agency's interpretation of its own enabling act, but this presumption does not apply where the agency interpretation violates the plain language of the statute. Do you agree with Justice Powell or Justice Marshall about how strictly the language of NEPA should be interpreted?

In effect, the *Kleppe* Court holds that the agency itself must determine when a "proposal" is being made, and a court should only overturn this decision if it is arbitrary. Under the *Kleppe* ruling, environmental plaintiffs find it difficult to establish the existence of "de facto proposals." (cf. CEQ regulation §1508.23) Is the *Kleppe* interpretation consistent with NEPA's goal of factoring environmental analysis into federal agency planning at the earliest possible time? What could the NRC now do in a *SIPI* situation if it wanted to begin a breeder reactor research program with minimal public scrutiny?

How successful do you think you would be in contending in court that an agency has been arbitrary and capricious because it hasn't done something that you claim it should have done?

See Defenders of Wildlife v. Andrus, 627 F.2d 1238 (D.C. Cir. 1980) (NEPA compliance unnecessary where the Secretary of the Interior did not act to prevent the State of Alaska from killing wolves on federal lands).

4. **Cumulative impacts and NEPA.** Do you agree with the Court that the cumulative impacts of potential activities in the surrounding area cannot be considered in impact documents until the activities have actually been proposed? Doesn't this lead to fragmented, reactive planning? Even if you only consider the impacts of proposed projects, how helpful is it to consider them in each local, site-specific impact document? Once again, the CEQ regulations appear to conflict with the Supreme Court's interpretation of NEPA. (see §1508.28).

5. **Hard cases make bad law.** Should the Sierra Club have decided not to file this action under this set of facts? After all, it's not as if the Department hadn't done any planning for utilization of the Northern Great Plains coal reserves. The Sierra Club simply disagreed with Interior about what the relevant planning area should have been.

6. **NEPA as post-hoc rationalization.** Is Justice Marshall correct when he charges that a NEPA lawsuit usually comes too late in the agency decision-making process to be effective? Has the agency already invested too much money and political capital to change its plans? Or, on the other hand, does the spectre of a NEPA suit that would expose substantial waste and shoddy planning inspire agency officials to give prudent consideration to environmental problems early in the process? Is Justice Marshall's reservation about NEPA answered by the CEQ's "scoping" suggestions? (§1501.7.) Note that if the agency doesn't scope, its failure to do so can't be raised until after the final EIS has been released.

7. **Applying NEPA to federal agencies' international actions.** In United States Trade Representative v. Public Citizen, et al., 5 F.3d 549 (D.C. Cir. 1993) NEPA was held inapplicable to the North American Free Trade Agreement (NAFTA) on the following grounds: 1) NAFTA was not a final agency action because it remained to be finalized by the President and Congress; 2) it was not a final agency action because it was to be submitted to Congress by the President, who is not an "agency"; and 3) it was not reviewable, under the APA, because it was not an action that "directly affected" the plaintiff. Isn't NEPA's mandate of EISs on "agency...proposals for legislation" quite nullified by this logic? Could any agency proposal for legislation ever be subject to judicial review, or are the terms of NEPA now left up to voluntary enforcement by the executive branch and Congress, which have not enforced NEPA in the past? The "direct effect" element of this decision sounds like a heightened standing inquiry — plaintiffs have to claim a direct injury deriving from the challenged action. If this *USTR* case means that an agency gets a good defense against NEPA suits by saying that other actors will have to act before the harm can occur, that would open up a large loophole indeed.

In Environmental Defense Fund v. Massey, 986 F.2d 528 (D.C. Cir. 1993), the court held that NEPA applied to the National Science Foundation's plans to build an incinerator at NSF's McMurdo Station research facility in Antarctica because: 1) the administrative action would occur primarily, if not exclusively, within the United States; 2) the alleged extraterritorial effect of NEPA would be felt in a place without a sovereign; and 3) it would be felt in an area over which the United States has a great measure of legislative control. If all three of these criteria are necessary in order to imply extraterritorial effect for a statute that does not clearly assert it, won't the rule of this case be limited to federal actions that play themselves out on the high seas, or at the other Pole, or in outer space? If only the first of these criteria must be satisfied, a wide range of United States activities with international repercussions might be covered by NEPA. Especially where a statute is procedural, like NEPA, U.S. regulation of agency decisionmaking procedures is less likely to create a contradiction with the laws of a foreign nation. This is doubly true in cases where statutes are being applied to regulate federal agencies that are spending U.S. funds in a foreign country, instead of directly regulating conduct. It would seem less controversial to put strings on spending projects of, for example, U.S.A.I.D., the federal Agency for International Development.

8. **Where is NEPA's overview?** Observing the scene that has followed the *Kleppe* decision, Professor Oliver Houck comments that

> NEPA is missing the point. It is producing lots of little statements on highway segments, timber sales, and other foregone conclusions; it isn't even present, much less effective, when the major decisions on a national energy policy and a national transportation policy are made. On the most pivotal development questions of our time, NEPA comes in late in the fourth quarter, in time to help tidy up.[15]

---

15. Letter to Michael Deland, Chairman, CEQ, 19 Feb. 1991. Houck urges that CEQ not focus on making each EIS "a 'succinct review for a single project'...[but] rather, to make NEPA work for legislative proposals and for programs that all but conclusively determine what the subsequent projects will be."

The CEQ has recently repeated this critique:

> The NEPA process is often triggered too late to be fully effective. Generally, agency and private sector planning processes begin long before the NEPA process. By the time an environmental impact analysis is started, alternatives and strategic choices are foreclosed. Congress envisioned that federal agencies would use NEPA as a planning tool to integrate environmental, social, and economic concerns directly into projects and programs. However, during the 25 years of NEPA, application has focused on decisions related to site-specific construction, development, or resource extraction projects. NEPA is virtually ignored in formulating specific policies and often is skirted in developing programs, usually because agencies believe that NEPA cannot applied within the time available or without a detailed proposal. Instead, agencies tend to examine project-level environmental effects in microscopic detail. The reluctance to apply NEPA analysis to programs and policies reflects the fear that microscopic detail will be expected, even when such depth of analysis is not possible that early in the project development stage. CEQ Study, 12.

Do you think that federal agencies really do not employ NEPA as a long-range, programmatic planning tool because they are afraid of being compelled to divulge too much detail too early? Or do agencies find it difficult to resist making low-visibility decisions that may be more responsive to political influences?

---

## C. NEPA IN THE COURTS SINCE *KLEPPE*

The *Kleppe* decision ushered in a period of relatively unfriendly handling of NEPA claims by the Rehnquist Supreme Court. Through *Strycker's Bay* (1980), *PANE* (1983), and two cases decided in 1989, Marsh v. Oregon Natural Resources Council, 490 U.S. 360, and Robertson v. Methow Valley Citizens' Council, 490 U.S. 332, the Court has consistently narrowed NEPA's coverage.

**MARSH v. OREGON NATURAL RESOURCES COUNCIL...** *Marsh* involved construction, by the Corps of Engineers, of the third dam of a three-dam grouping in the Rogue River watershed in Oregon, a famous fishing area. The original EIS was completed in 1971. After acquiring 26,000 acres of land and relocating residents and utilities, the Corps acknowledged incomplete information about the water quality impacts of the dam, and began further studies centered on the dam's effects on stream turbidity. A Final Supplemental EIS ("FEISS") was completed in 1980. After reviewing the FEISS, the Corps decided to proceed with the project and, in 1985, Congress appropriated funds for the construction of the dam project, now one-third completed. Plaintiffs sued, claiming that the Corps had violated NEPA by, among other things, failing to prepare a second SEIS to review two documents developed after 1980 — one prepared by the Oregon Department of Fish and Wildlife, and the other by the United States Fish and Wildlife Service — indicating that the downstream water quality impacts of the dam would be greater than suggested in the FEISS. The Court of Appeals, reversing the District Court, held that the Corps should prepare another SEIS because the two documents brought to light important new information, which the Corps had not adequately considered. The Supreme Court reversed the Circuit Court and upheld the Corps' decision:

> The parties are in essential agreement concerning the standard that governs an agency's decision to prepare a supplemental EIS... [The] cases make clear that

an agency need not supplement an EIS every time new information comes to light after the EIS is finalized. To require otherwise would render agency decisionmaking intractable, always awaiting updated information only to find the new information outdated by the time a decision is made. On the other hand, as the Government concedes, NEPA does require that agencies take a "hard look" at the environmental effects of their planned action, even after a proposal has received initial approval. Application of the "rule of reason" thus turns on the value of the new information to the still pending decisionmaking process. In this respect the decision whether to prepare a supplemental EIS is similar to the decision whether to prepare an EIS in the first instance: If there remains "major federal action" to occur, and if the new information is sufficient to show that the remaining action will "affect the quality of the human environment" in a significant manner or to a significant extent not already considered, a supplemental EIS must be prepared....

The parties disagree, however, on the standard that should be applied by a court that is asked to review the agency's decision.... Respondents contend that the determination of whether the new information suffices to establish a "significant" effect is either a question of law or, at a minimum, a question of ultimate fact and, as such "deserves no deference" on review.... We disagree.... The question presented for review in this case is a classic example of a factual dispute the resolution of which implicates substantial agency expertise. Respondent's claim...rests on the contentions that the new information undermines conclusions contained in the FEISS, that the conclusions contained in the ODFW memorandum and the SCS survey are accurate, and that the Corps' expert review of the new information was incomplete, inconclusive, or inaccurate. The dispute does not turn on the meaning of the term "significant" or on an application of this legal standard to settled facts. Rather, resolution of this dispute involves primarily issues of fact.... Accordingly, as long as the Corps' decision not to supplement the FEISS was not "arbitrary or capricious," it should not be set aside. Marsh v. Oregon Natural Resources Council, 490 U.S. 360, 372–377.

The Court then held that the Corps' decision not to prepare another SEIS was not a clear error of judgment.

**ROBERTSON v. METHOW VALLEY CITIZENS' COUNCIL...** In the *Robertson* case, plaintiffs contested the United States Forest Service's EIS on a proposed permit to construct a ski resort in the Okanogan National Forest in Washington. Plaintiffs claimed that the EIS was defective because it did not include a "worst case analysis" of the effects of the resort on the resident mule deer herd or a mitigation plan to reduce the project's impacts on the herd and local air quality. The Court of Appeals agreed with both of plaintiffs' arguments. The Supreme Court reversed, holding that (1) a worst case analysis was no longer necessary (see above discussion), and (2) a mitigation plan was not required by NEPA:

The sweeping policy goals announced in §101 of NEPA are...realized through a set of "action forcing" procedures that require that agencies take a "hard look" at environmental consequences, and that provide for broad dissemination of relevant environmental information. Although these procedures are almost certain to affect the agency's substantive decision, it is now well settled that NEPA itself does not mandate particular results, but simply prescribes the necessary process. If the adverse environmental effects of the proposed action are adequately identified and evaluated, the agency is not constrained by NEPA from deciding that other values outweigh the environmental costs. In this case, for example, it would not have violated NEPA if the Forest Service, after complying with the Act's procedural prerequisites, had decided that the benefits to be derived from downhill skiing...justified the issuance of a special use permit, notwithstanding the loss of 15 percent, 50 percent, or even 100 percent of the mule deer herd. Other statutes may impose substantive environmental obligations on federal agencies, but NEPA merely prohibits uninformed — rather than unwise — agency action.

To be sure, one important ingredient of an EIS is the discussion of steps that can be taken to mitigate adverse environmental consequences.... Without such a discussion, neither the agency nor other interested groups and inviduals can properly evaluate the severity of the adverse impacts. An adverse effect that can be remedied by, for example, an inconsequential public expenditure is certainly not as serious as a similar effect that can only be modestly ameliorated through the commitment of vast public and private resources.... There is a fundamental distinction, however, between a requirement that mitigation be discussed in sufficient detail to ensure that environmental consequences have been fairly evaluated, on the one hand, and a substantive requirement that a complete mitigation plan be actually formulated and adopted, on the other. In this case, the off-site effects on air quality and on the mule deer herd cannot be mitigated unless nonfederal government agencies take appropriate action. Since it is those state and local governmental bodies that have jurisdiction over the area in which the adverse effects need to be addressed and since they have the authority to mitigate them, it would be incongrous to conclude that the Forest Service has no power to act until the local agencies have reached a final conclusion on what mitigating measures they consider necessary. Even more significantly, it would be inconsistent with NEPA's reliance on procedural mechanisms — as opposed to substantive, result-based standards — to demand the presence of a fully developed plan that will mitigate environmental harm before an agency can act. Robertson v. Methow Valley Citizens' Council, 490 U.S. 332, 350–352.

Do you agree with the Court that NEPA's procedural requirements "are almost certain to affect [an] agency's substantive decision"? If the Forest Service concludes that significant environmental impacts of the resort could be mitigated by state and local activities, should USFS be permitted to issue the permit before it has received reasonable assurances that those steps will actually be taken?

---

Although the United States Supreme Court has, in recent years, been unreceptive to NEPA claims, the lower federal courts are continuing to enforce the statute. The following case illustrates NEPA's continuing deterrent impact on environmentally problematic federal actions:

### Sierra Club v. Department of Energy
### District Court for the District of Columbia
### 808 F.Supp. 852 (1991)

LAMBERTH, J. Five years ago, the Department of Energy attempted to import spent nuclear fuel rods from Taiwan through a West Coast port without filing the documentation required by NEPA. Once they were caught by an environmental group and enjoined by a prior lawsuit, the Department shifted its plans to an East Coast Port and filed an EA which did not consider real alternatives. The Department filed a second EA in 1988 that similarly did not consider real alternatives. The

Department was sued once again and the plaintiff specifically identified a variety of perceived flaws in the EA. In 1991, the Department again filed an EA, correcting some, but not all of the problems. For the reasons stated [below], this EA is almost adequate, but not quite. While none of the parties and especially not this court wish to waste government time and resources, the Department must make another attempt to comply with the law. It is not this court's order, but rather it is the Department's failure to follow the requirements of NEPA that has forced this duplication of effort.

While the risks are small in absolute terms, the relative risks reveal that there are significant differences in the risk of a port accident as population density varies.... These differences are particularly important in a situation involving nuclear material where the worst case scenario is catastrophic, if highly unlikely, and the subject of great public concern. Even the Department's least likely credible accident would result in the exposure of hundreds of thousands of people over a 379 sq. km area to excess radiation. Further casting doubt on the Department's decision making process is its change in policy that led the Department to bring the fuel rods in through Hampton Roads rather than through a West Coast port as was originally planned. After two years of unsuccessful litigation, the Department decided to try the East Coast which does indeed provide a safer route to the Savannah [Ga.] site. All of the Department's plans have involved transit of the nuclear fuel rods to the Savannah River processing site. The 1991 EA states that the Idaho processing site "does not handle uranium products." It has never been clear to the court whether this facility cannot process such uranium or whether some modification would be required or whether the government simply prefers the Savannah site based on economic or other considerations. The only evidence that has been presented indicates that the Idaho facility is actually more sophisticated than the Savannah site because it can extract krypton gas from spent fuel products.... The court does not (and cannot) say that the Department must use the Idaho site, but the Department has never clearly explained why this is not a feasible and sensible alternative.... Here the court does not believe that the Department took a "hard look" at a reasonable range of alternatives when it prepared its 1991 EA and selected the port of Hampton Roads....

Although the court holds that the Department need not file a programmatic EIS, the court nonetheless does not believe that the Department can ignore the fact that, by continuing to bring spent fuel through a single port, a narrow range of the population bears the entire risk.... In its new EA, the Department should calculate [the] cumulative dose, explaining the amount of radiation, the number of people it might involve, and its potential health effects.... The court does not impose this requirement[16] to arouse public furor that Hampton Roads appears to be the port of choice for nuclear fuel shipments, but rather to insure that, as the court assumes the Department's calculations will reveal, those along the transportation route know that exposure to multiple incident-free doses has a very minimal health effect on them.... Admittedly these doses are below those permissible by law and cannot by themselves serve as a basis for an injunction; the Department has not, however, calculated the risk from repeated exposure to such doses to those along the transportation route. Further, permitting the importation of the nuclear fuel

---

16. The amount of time and resources spent defending this lawsuit dwarfs the effort that would have been expended had the Department simply analyzed all eleven ports suggested by the plaintiff and examined the full range of risks.

rods will unquestionably create a risk of greater environmental harm (through an accident), which...cannot at this time be said to be insignificant. Requiring an adequate environmental assessment will ensure that the risk is sufficiently minimal that the Department would choose to proceed with its program through Hampton Roads or perhaps would reveal that another more safe port is a preferable port of entry. The court finds that the public interest will be served both by the simple enforcement of NEPA and by insuring that an appropriate risk analysis is completed before the shipment is completed....

### COMMENTARY AND QUESTIONS

1. **NEPA is alive and well?** Another example of the fact that NEPA is alive and well in the lower federal courts is City of Carmel-by-the-Sea v. U.S. Department of Transportation, 95 F.3d 892 (9th Cir. 1996). In *Carmel* the City challenged the adequacy of the EIS/EIR for a proposed road project under applicable provisions of NEPA and the California Environmental Quality Act ("CEQA"). The court held that "the EIS/R failed to consider adequately the effects [of the proposed project] on wetlands, failed to analyze adequately the project's cumulative impacts, and failed to consider reasonable alternatives, in light of the statement of purpose and need articulated in the final EIS/R." The major problem that the court found with the EIS/R was that there had been a material change in the statement of purpose between the Draft and the Final EIS/R. However, this change in the statement of purpose was not accompanied by a consideration of additional alternatives that satisfied the requirements of the revised statement of purpose. The stated purpose of the Draft EIS/R was "to improve the capacity of Highway 1 and reduce crossing and turning conflicts." The Final EIS/R, on the other hand, changed the stated purpose to the requirement of "a specific traffic flow Level of Service."

> Defendants materially altered the statement of purpose and need between the Draft and Final EIS/R by adding a specific requirement of attaining Level of Service C. They did not, however, update the list of alternatives under consideration to reflect the more specific goals of the Final EIS/R's statement of purpose and need. All of the alternatives except the one chosen fail to even come close to satisfying the new goals.... The issues under NEPA and CEQA are whether, once the Level of Service C goal was added, a reasonable range of alternatives was considered. By materially changing the goal of the EIS/R without also considering an acceptable range of alternatives designed to meet the changed purpose, Defendants failed to consider a range of alternatives which were "dictated by the nature and scope of the proposed action, and sufficient to permit a reasoned choice." Where, as here, a range of alternatives is developed in conjunction with one statement of purpose and need, and the statement of purpose and need is subsequently changed to eliminate all but one of the initial range of alternatives, there has been an abuse of discretion.... The Federal Highway Administration and CALTRANS should have either prepared appropriate new alternatives in light of the new statement of purpose and need, or else retained the original statement of purpose and need and provided a reasonable analysis of all relevant factors. Carmel-by-the-Sea, 95 F.3d, at 903, 908.

Another recent federal circuit court of appeals decision that falls into the "NEPA is alive and well" category is Simmons v. U.S. Army Corps of Engineers, 120 F.3d 664 (7th Cir. 1997).

Like *Sierra Club* and *Carmel-by-the-Sea*, the *Simmons* case involved an artificial narrowing of alternatives by the lead federal agency, the Corps of Engineers. In *Simmons*, the Corps proposed to dam a scenic and recreationally important river in southern Illinois in order to provide water supply for neighboring towns. Throughout the gestation of the proposal, local conservationists and landowners had opposed the project, instead advocating either expansion of an existing pipeline from another lake or construction of several smaller dams on various rivers. The Corps first prepared an EA and FONSI, considering only the single-dam alternative. The EA and FONSI were invalidated by the district court as arbitrary and capricious because they did not consider other apparently viable alternatives. The Corps then prepared a full EIS, which also ignored alternatives other than the proposed single dam. The circuit court struck down the EIS for the same reason:

> Eight years have elapsed since the City of Marion, Illinois, first proposed building a new water reservoir in the southernmost tip of Illinois. In those eight years a tale has unfolded that is all too familiar. Lawsuits have stopped the project short; and Marion is still no closer to a new water supply. As is routine in American administrative law, the litigation has little to do with what anybody really cares about. One side wants a dam built and a new lake created, and the other does not. Instead, the dispute, now in and out of federal court for five years, has centered on procedures — whether the [Corps] fulfilled its procedural obligations under federal environmental law. All this is true. But the case provides a textbook vindication of the wisdom of Congress in insisting that agencies follow those procedures in the first place....
>
> When a federal agency prepares an [EIS], it must consider "all reasonable alternatives" in depth. No decision is more important than delimiting what those "reasonable alternatives" are. That choice, and the ensuing analysis, forms "the heart of the environmental impact statement." 40 CFR §1502.14. To make that decision, the first thing an agency must define is the project's purpose. The broader the purpose, the wider the range of alternatives; and vice versa. The "purpose" of a project is a slippery concept, susceptible of no hard-and-fast definition. One obvious way for an agency to slip past the strictures of NEPA is to contrive a purpose so slender as to define competing "reasonable alternatives" out of consideration (and even out of existence). The federal courts cannot condone an agency's frustration of congressional will. If the agency constricts the definition of the project's purpose and thereby excludes what truly are reasonable alternatives, the EIS cannot fulfill its role. Nor can the agency satisfy the Act. We are confronted here with an example of this defining-away of alternatives.... At no time has the Corps studied whether this single-source idea is the best one — or even a good one. *Simmons v. Corps*, 120 F.3d 664, at 665–667.

**2. Has NEPA been worth the effort?** In The (Unhappy) Truth about NEPA, 26 Okla. L. R. 239 (1973), where he concluded that NEPA's procedural reform is "nine parts myth and one part coconut oil," Joseph Sax argued that the Act was unlikely to change decisionmaking. Here are his five basic rules of the game:

1. Don't expect hired experts to undermine their employers.

2. Don't expect people to believe legislative declarations of policy. The practical working rule is legislatures' true policy is what they choose to *fund*.

3. Don't expect agencies to abandon their traditional friends.

4. Expect agencies to back up their subordinates and professional colleagues.

5. Expect agencies to go for the least risky options (even where risk means performing their missions).

Consider, however, the latent effect of NEPA that is likely to affect virtually all agency actions that faced citizen challenge after the *Chicod Creek* case. Ultimately, for instance, it was the potential disclosure process of NEPA that prevented construction of the environmentally threatening, excessively expensive nuclear fast breeder reactor. The CEQ quotes a former Secretary of Energy as having remarked, regarding his decision to defer selection of a tritium production technology, "Thank God for NEPA, because there were so many pressures to make a selection for a technology that might have been forced upon us and that would have been wrong for the country." *CEQ Study*, 13.

In fact, information has a power of its own, even in the absence of substantive review mechanisms. Human beings and their institutions are averse to being embarassed by public exposure of their nonconformity with generally accepted behavioral norms. The fundamental currency of politics is not money, but "image." International law is the clearest example of this phenomenon. International agreements can be effective, because they threaten sanctions by central enforcement authorities, but because they require parties to produce compliance information, witholding or clear distortion of which will hold the offending party up to obloquy among its international peers. See chapter 26.

## D. COMMUNITY RIGHT-TO-KNOW STATUTES

There are many significant legal mechanisms by which the public may be able to enforce the public availability of important information, including the Freedom of Information Act (FOIA, 50 S.C.A. §552) noted earlier, in Chapter Seven. Community right-to-know statutes reflect this strategy, requiring that users of toxic or hazardous materials compile specific information about processes or products and disclose these data to the general public.

This statutory strategy attempts to stimulate pollution prevention by (1) forcing companies to audit their processes and emissions systematically, thus revealing opportunities to prevent pollution and probably save money by doing so, (2) providing information to that increasing segment of the American public that practices "green consumerism," and giving a company that achieves pollution prevention a competitive public relations advantage, and (3) informing corporate shareholders, who use their votes to stimulate their companies to improve their environmental performance. Where companies fail to prevent their pollution, governmental agencies utilize these data to design and implement enforcement programs. Citizen activists utilize the information to (1) lobby legislatures and agencies for stricter pollution control requirements, (2) supervise compliance with emissions permits and bring citizen suits where violations are occurring, and (3) perform "environmental justice" analysis to determine whether members of racial, ethnic, or economic minority groups are being disproportionately exposed to toxic chemicals.

Section 1. **THE EMERGENCY PLANNING**
**AND COMMUNITY**
**RIGHT-TO-KNOW ACT (EPCRA)**[17]

Section 313 of EPCRA establishes the Toxic Release Inventory (TRI), which applies to manufacturing facilities that employ ten or more full-time workers.[18] These facilities must file annual reports with EPA that identify their use and release of one or more of approximately 650 listed toxic chemicals above yearly threshold amounts. See generally Clay, The EPA's Proposed Phase-III Expansion of the Toxic Release Inventory (TRI) Reporting Requirements: Everything *and* the Kitchen Sink, 15 Pace Env. L. Rev. 293 (1997). A facility submits its TRI information on a so-called "Form R," which must include the following information:

> (i) Whether the toxic chemical at the facility is manufactured, processed, or otherwise used, and the general category or categories of use of the chemical. (ii) An estimate of the maximum amounts (in ranges) of the toxic chemical present at the facility at any time during the preceding calendar year. (iii) For each waste stream, the waste treatment or disposal methods employed, and an estimate of the treatment efficiency typically achieved by such methods for that waste stream. (iv) The annual quantity of the toxic chemical entering each environmental medium. EPCRA, §313(g).

Facilities must also report offsite transfers of TRI chemicals (e.g., to sewage treatment plants or hazardous waste treatment, storage or disposal facilities), as well as source reduction, recycling, and waste minimization efforts. More than 20,000 American facilities file Form Rs annually. EPA's compilation of the Form Rs is made available to the general public through published reports and an on-line database system (TOXNET) that is available via the Internet.[19] Published TRI information is organized by total releases and transfers, chronological trends, geographic distributions, and industry-by-industry comparisons. There is a two-year lag between submission of Form Rs and EPA's published TRI report.

EPCRA was enacted, in 1986, in response to a tragic series of toxic chemical releases, especially the methyl isocyanate release in Bhopal, India, that killed 2,000 people. In addition to the functions of community right-to-know statutes listed above, Congress explicitly intended EPCRA to make citizens aware of health and safety risks in their communities in order to facilitate emergency planning and notification procedures to cope with potential chemical releases. Consequently, local police, fire, public health officials, and citizen participants, organized into local emergency planning committees, are significant users of TRI material. Local citizen groups also utilize TRI data to establish cooperative relationships with local industries so as to promote pollution prevention, obtain limited community surveillance and inspection of facilities, and improve community warning systems.

---

17. 42 U.S.C.A. §11,023.

18. The subject facilities are identified by Standard Industrial Classification (SIC) codes numbered 20–39.

19. TOXNET can be accessed from EPA's TRI home page — <http://www.epa.gov/opptintr>.

## COMMENTARY AND QUESTIONS

1. **An evaluation of EPCRA.** EPCRA has been substantially successful in reducing emissions of toxic chemicals without resort to a full-fledged command-and-control regulatory system. Reported toxic chemical emissions have decreased over 40% since 1988. While some of this decrease has been caused by more accurate reporting and stringent regulation, there is broad agreement among industry and environmentalists that most of the reduction is due to EPCRA and other disclosure laws. On the negative side, EPCRA, like NEPA, is plagued by the major flaw in all mandatory disclosure strategies: disclosure is required of entities that have an incentive either not to disclose, or else to disclose inaccurate or misleading information. Enforcement of TRI reporting requirements is difficult because agencies and citizen groups seldom know enough about facility operations to form a basis for asserting with confidence that the mandated disclosures are missing or incomplete. Violations of TRI reporting obligations are reportedly widespread. Limitations on citizen suits, such as the need to allege "continuing violations," have hampered citizen efforts to enforce EPCRA.[20]

2. **Should "materials accounting" data be reported?** On October 1, 1996, EPA issued an Advance Notice of Proposed Rulemaking (ANPR), announcing its intention to expand the TRI requirements to include "materials accounting" (MA) data. 61 Fed. Reg. 51,322. Materials accounting would involve a complete throughput analysis of toxic chemicals: (1) the amounts of TRI chemicals coming into the facility; (2) the amounts transformed into products and wastes; and (3) amounts leaving the facility as products, releases, and offsite transfers. The States of New Jersey and Massachusetts require MA data under their state community right-to-know statutes.[21]

Is disclosure of MA data necessary to further identify opportunities for pollution prevention and protect against nondisclosure and inaccurate disclosure? Or is it a superflous, statutorily unauthorized intrusion on a facility's confidential business information? Clay argues that "the collection of MA data is an unjustified, fundamental change in the TRI program that is not in harmony with the intent or purpose of EPCRA." EPA has received over 40,000 responses to its ANPR, and the MA issue is unlikely to be resolved quickly.

3. **Does the TRI convey misleading data?** Critics of EPCRA argue that the disclosure of toxic release data, in terms of total amounts of chemicals released, can lead to media campaigns that distort the actual public risks caused by these releases. As an example, they point to the National Wildlife Federation's "Toxic 500 List," which identifies the 500 "worst" polluters in the United States. On the other hand, it could be argued that EPA has corroborated the toxicity of these chemicals by listing them, and their reportable quantities, for TRI reporting, and thus "more" is certainly not "better."

---

20. See the discussion in the *Gwaltney* case in Chapter One, and Citizens for a Better Environment v. Steel Co., noted in Chapter Seven, holding that environmental plaintiffs must allege continuing violations of EPCRA reporting requirements in order to bring citizen suits.

21. Mass. Gen. Laws Ann. ch. 211 §§1-23, and N.J. Stat. Ann. §§34:5A-1 to 31.

### Section 2. CALIFORNIA'S "PROPOSITION 65"

During the same year that EPCRA was enacted, 1986, California voters approved the Safe Drinking Water and Toxic Enforcement Act of 1986[22], an initiative popularly known as Proposition 65. See generally Rechtschaffen, The Warning Game: Evaluating Warnings Under California's Proposition 65, 23 Ecol. L. Q. 303 (1996). Unlike EPCRA, which mandates disclosure to toxic chemical releases and transfers, Proposition 65 requires that companies provide warnings with regard to consumer product exposures, occupational exposures, and environmental exposures to toxic chemicals.

Proposition 65 coverage extends to over 650 listed carcinogens and reproductive toxicants.[23]

Like EPCRA, Proposition 65 applies to private businesses with ten or more employees, but its ambit is considerably broader than EPCRA's because all businesses are covered, not just certain manufacturing facilities. Proposition 65 contains exceptions for carcinogens that pose "no significant risk" of contracting cancer (administratively defined as less than one excess cancer case per 100,000 persons exposed for a lifetime) and reproductive toxicants below 1/1000th of the No Observable Effect Level (NOEL) for that chemical.

The text of Proposition 65 only specified that warnings be "clear and reasonable"; it did not explicitly designate the form of consumer product, occupational, and environmental exposure warnings. Even legible, conspicuous, clear, and informative warnings might be unsuccessful in alerting recipients to the risks associated with the products or activities to which the warnings refer. Professor Rechtschaffen points out that

> (c)onsumers may lack the time or interest to seek out information. Many may have difficulty understanding certain information, especially information about risks. In particular, less educated and limited-English speaking individuals are less likely to be able to read, understand, and use warning information. Even when individuals read and comprehend warnings, they often do not change their behavior in response to the information they receive. Workers, for instance, may disregard the seriousness of the risks to which they are exposed when they perceive the risks as involuntary or out of their control.... Moreover, persons exposed to chemicals in the environment have no traditional "market" in which they can express their preferences. Additionally, conveying information about environmental exposures is much more difficult because there is no single point of purchase, as with consumer products, or even a single point of exposure as in the workplace. Despite these limitations...only a small number of motivated persons — e.g., attentive, information-seeking consumers, unions, or environmental organizations — actually needs to use infor-

---

22. Cal. Health & Safety Code §§25249.5-.13.

23. Here we have yet another list of toxic or hazardous materials that creates legal obligations. Other such lists exist under EPCRA, the CWA, the CAA, RCRA, and other state laws. These lists are not uniform and are frequently inconsistent, leading to regulatory inefficiencies and a "toxic shell game," where a pollutant is discharged to the medium of least regulatory supervision. See Dernbach, The Unfocussed Regulation of Toxic and Hazardous Pollutants, 21 Harv. Env. L. Rev. 1 (1997). Professor Dernbach recommends that Congress or the EPA adopt a common list of the most toxic substances, based on the EPCRA list, that would become the basis of a facility-wide and cross-media pollution prevention program.

mation to accomplish some of the desire benefits of information disclosure laws. 23 Ecol. L. Q. at pages 316–318.

In fact, a significant percentage of Proposition 65 warnings have been inconspicuous, uninformative, misleading, and confusing. For example, consumer product warnings have been placed on the backs of product labels or in small print on the fronts of already crowded labels, on the underside or inside lids of product containers, or in insignificant signs on store shelves or checkout counters. Warnings state that the product "contains" a toxic chemical, not that the product will "expose" the consumer to that chemical. Disclaimers frequently counteract or minimize the warning language. Environmental warnings can be found in small signs placed on the grounds of polluting facilities, or buried in the "Legal Notices" sections of local newspapers.

Ironically, Proposition 65 appears to have achieved its purposes in spite of the inadequacies of many warnings:

> Proposition 65's warning requirement has stimulated significant consumer-product reformulation, due to a combination of industry concerns about [tort] liability and consumer reaction to warnings. In some instances, the reformulations have been close to industry-wide, reflecting the competitive pressures that arise once a portion of the industry alters its products. Almost all reformulated products are sold nationwide, giving the statute national effect. Moreoever, the reported product reformulations probably represent only a portion of the private businesses' actions. As one business columnist suggests, "most of the good arising from Proposition 65 remains hidden, in the form of companies that quietly assess what they're doing, and presumably clean up their act to avoid the brouhaha that might arise from having to tell all the neighbors they're being poisoned.... Enforcement actions have triggered many product reformulations.... [With regard to environmental exposure warnings], enforcement actions have stimulated some of the most notable reductions, as prosecuting parties have traded large penalties in exchange for emissions cutbacks.... 23 Ecol. L. Q., at pages 341, 348.

### COMMENTARY AND QUESTIONS

1. **The interstate effects of state product regulation.** When California enacted Proposition 65, businesses began to include informational warnings on products sold throughout the United States. By and large, industry cannot afford to sell different forms of the same product, or the same product in different packaging, in different jurisdictions. When the City of Chicago and several other cities, counties, and states enacted bans on the sale of phosphate detergents within their boundaries, detergent manufacturers reformulated their products to eliminate phosphates. Automobile manufacturers are lobbying hard for a National Low-Emissions Vehicle (NLEV), rather than sell "California Cars" in some states and different low-emission vehicles in other states. See Chapter Ten. Industry's need for national uniformity in the marketplace gives enhanced importance to state laws that affect consumer products.

2. **Are mandatory disclosure laws "self executing"?** This category of statutes does avoid some of the typical accoutrements of command-and-control regulation, such as permitting. But mandatory disclosure laws are far from self-executing. Lists of

toxic substances must be prepared, and standards and reportable quantities established. Governmental agencies must perform monitoring and surveillance to ensure that regulated parties are complying with the law. And enforcement programs must be effective, efficient, predictable, and credible if voluntary compliance is to be achieved among a majority of the regulated community. The success of Proposition 65, in spite of the manifold inadequacies of the warning mechanism, can partly be attributed to vigorous enforcement by governmental and private plaintiffs.

3. **The Federal Trade Commission's "Green Guides."** Another variety of mandatory disclosure statute prevents the communication of false and deceptive environmental marketing claims. "Green marketing" has become so lucrative that some unscrupulous businesspersons invent environmental advatanges for their products in order to appeal to green consumers who cannot readily determine whether the products possess the advertised attributes. How, for example, can a consumer verify whether an aerosol spray she uses will deplete the ozone layer or contribute to smog? The Federal Trade Commission enforces Sction 5 of the FTC Act, 15 U.S.C.A. §57a., which generally prohibits "unfair or deceptive acts of practices," including advertising or labeling that is false or misleading. Sporadic state legislation in the area of false environmental advertising has been effectively replaced by the FTC's Guides for the Use of Environmental Marketing Claims (1992), commonly known as the "Green Guides." These guides were issued as policy interpretations, not promulgated as regulations, but industry treats them as authoritative because the FTC uses them as a basis for its enforcement actions. (When dealing with green consumers, who are adept at formal and informal product boycotts, public exposure for disseminating specious environmental claims can be commercially disastrous.) The Green Guides specify that all express and implied claims about objective product attributes must be substantiated by competent and reliable scientific evidence before they are made. For example, a manufacturer of coffee filters included the phrase "recycled paper" on the side of the box, which could, to a reasonable consumer, mean that both the cardboard box and the coffee filters were made from recycled content. One of the settlements negotiated by the FTC arose from its allegation that it was deceptive to fail to indicate whether the claim referred to the product or the package, because, although the box was made of recycled materials, the filters were not. The Green Guides identify the types of substantiation required, and the standard disclaimers that should be included, when using terms such as "environmentally safe," "environmentally friendly," "degradable," "recyclable," "source reduction," and "ozone friendly." They also cover alleged third-party certification claims, such as environmental seals of approval and "green globe" logos. From all indications, industry is voluntary complying with the Green Guides, and the number of deceptive environmental claims has been reduced.

---

*I know of no safe repository of the ultimate powers of the society but the people themselves; and if we think them not enlightened enough to exercise their discretion, the remedy is not to take it from them, but to inform their discretion.*

— Thos. Jefferson to William Charles Jarvis, 28 September 1820

# Chapter 14

# ROADBLOCK STRATEGIES: STARK PROHIBITIONS AND THEIR VIABILITY

A. *The Endangered Species Act §§7 & 9*

B. *The Endangered Species Act and Pressures for Flexibility Compromises*

C. *The Delaney Clause as a Contrasting Example of the Roadblock Approach*

## INTRODUCTION: ROADBLOCK STATUTES

There are times when a problem is so complex, so incapable of careful measurement and fine tuning, so emotional, or so politically difficult to approach in piecemeal fashion, that a stark flat prohibition provision provides particular effectiveness. There are a number of such roadblock statutes in the environmental realm — the "Delaney Clause" in the Food and Drug Act, prohibiting sale for human consumption of any compound that causes cancer in test animals, 21 U.S.C.A. §348(c)(3)(A) — and other prohibitions that contain very limited exceptions like *Overton Park's* federal highway act §4(f) provision in Chapter Seven, Title II of the Clean Air Act prohibiting auto emissions beyond 10 percent of 1970 levels in Chapter Ten, and the like.

As such examples demonstrate, "roadblock" prohibition statutes have great potential force because of the directness of their prohibitions and their lack of ambiguity. Where would parkland protection be without the roadblock of §4(f), or auto emissions without the stark 90% rollback? For the same reason, however, they may be especially subject to the problems of the unguided missile. The trade-off for decisiveness is the risk that they may hit too hard, in not exactly the right place, or with disruptive or disproportionate consequences that weren't predicted.

Section 7 of the 1973 Endangered Species Act (ESA), which begins this chapter, contained a strict roadblock (although, like NEPA's §102, its authorization of environmental lawsuits challenging a variety of federal agency actions had not been noticed by most legislators). Unlike NEPA, however, §7's provisions were substantive, specific, and mandatory, providing a useful case study of the strengths and drawbacks of the roadblock approach. Endangered species protections confront strong marketplace resistance because they get in the way of land development, and are politically less secure because they don't have overt human importance. Without tough legal standards, the law could be expected to be honored in the breach. When §7's roadblock was strictly enforced by the Supreme Court, endangered species conservation began to be taken seriously. The ESA's §9 presents yet another roadblock, and it too received strong judicial support. Faced with a perceived need for flexibility, Congress passed compromising exemption amendments for §7 in 1978 and for §9 in 1982, considered later in subchapter B. The chapter ends with a consideration of the Delaney Clause, another classic roadblock presenting the dilemma of strict standards.

## A. THE ENDANGERED SPECIES ACT AS A ROADBLOCK STATUTE

*The militant environmentalist movement in America today is a new homosocialism, communism. What these people are is against private property rights. They are trying to attack capitalism and corporate America in the form of going after timber companies. And they're trying to say that we must preserve these virgin trees because the spotted owl and the rat kangaroo and whatever live in them, and it's the only place they can live, the snail darter and whatever it is.*

— Rush Limbaugh, The Rush Limbaugh Show, Dec. 7, 1993

### Section 1. SNAIL DARTERS AND A FEDERAL DAM

The Endangered Species Act of 1973[1] was a revolutionary legal document. It was the first major piece of legislation in any legal system that sought to put teeth into the protection of endangered species domestically and internationally, and has been a model for subsequent wildlife conservation efforts throughout the world. The Act has a triple approach to the problem of conserving species threatened with extinction.

First, it provides a partial answer to the threats posed by the worldwide market in endangered wildlife by closing down the United States market for endangered species. The free market fails to protect endangered species that have market value, such as leopards, turtles, rare birds for feathers, elephants for ivory, cacti, and the like. Indeed, the market encourages the complete destruction of any endangered species that has market value by *raising* the value of each animal as it approaches extinction. As the market price per skin or rhino horn skyrockets, exploitation of the endangered species becomes almost impossible to stop. Either the Third World countries of origin cannot afford to halt the lucrative trade, or high prices create poaching pressures that can subvert any local enforcement efforts. The only way to prevent the elimination of the species is by shutting down the market in developed countries. The United States was a major market for such endangered species. To the extent that it has closed down that market, the ESA eliminated some pressure on animals hunted to provide fur coats and other luxuries for the American fashion world's cosmopolitan tastes.

---

1. 16 U.S.C.A. §1531 et seq. (1973, as amended). The text is adapted in part from an article, Plater, In The Wake of the Snail Darter: An Environmental Law Paradigm and its Consequences, 19 J. Law Ref. 805 (1986).

The ESA's §9 seemed to be a straightforward prohibition against "taking" any endangered species, a prohibition that attaches heavy criminal sanctions to the act of killing or capturing endangered animals. The taking provision was further strengthened by a Fish and Wildlife Service interpretive rule defining *habitat modification or degradation* as a "harm" that could amount to an illegal "take."[2] This makes ecological sense. Habitat alteration is probably the major cause of extinction of species on the face of the earth, a far more important threat than hunting and killing. As a result of the broad agency definition of "harm," however, the ESA became a potential roadblock against private development, arousing a volcano of political opposition.

Section 7 of the ESA contains a direct congressional prohibition against federal agency projects and programs that harm endangered species. (The ESA's §9, also studied below, on its terms seemed a straightforward prohibition against "taking" any endangered species, but when the agency interpreted "take" to include the "harm" of habitat destruction, the ESA became a potential roadblock against private development, creating a firestorm of marketplace backlash.) Section 7 was likewise surreptitious. Simply labeled "Interagency cooperation," §7 lay camouflaged, but when parsed carefully its words absolutely prohibit certain harmful federal agency actions. As you read through the following words of §7 (while noting the prose style that made it unlikely that many members of Congress knew what they were passing), underline the series of phrases which, added together, create a substantive mandate and several causes of action for citizen lawsuits.

### Section 7 of the Endangered Species Act of 1973
16 U.S.C.A. §1536 (the original version prior to 1978 amendments)

§7. INTERAGENCY COOPERATION. The Secretary [of Interior] shall review other programs administered by him and utilize such programs in furtherance of the purposes of this chapter. All other Federal departments and agencies shall, in consultation with and with the assistance of the Secretary, utilize their authorities in furtherance of the purposes of this chapter while carrying out programs for the conservation of endangered species and threatened species listed pursuant to section 1533 of this title and by taking such action necessary to insure that actions authorized, funded, or carried out by them do not jeopardize the continued existence of such endangered species and threatened species or result in the destruction or modification of habitat of such species which is determined by the Secretary, after consultation as appropriate with the affected States, to be critical.

The strategic resemblance between ESA §7 and NEPA's §102 is remarkable. Both provisions got their leverage from targeting the actions of federal agencies. Both contained teeth that subsequently emerged to the surprise of most members of Congress who had voted for them. NEPA, however, only requires procedural compliance; §7 contained a flat substantive prohibition. The ESA, moreover, specifically authorizes enforcement by citizens acting as private attorneys-general, §1540.

**RATIONALES FOR ENDANGERED SPECIES PROTECTION...** Why might a nation consider it sufficiently important to pass a statute with such patent and latent

---

2. 16 U.S.C.A. §§1532(19); 1538(a)-(b)(1982); 50 CFR §17.3 (1985).

strengths in an abstract area of natural science? The question is made all the more pointed by the fact that protection of endangered species inevitably causes a head-on confrontation with marketplace politics.

It is easiest to say that the ESA of 1973 was passed to satisfy a vague popular clamor, beginning in the 1960s, to conserve natural resources. Endangered species had the good fortune to be represented by such mediagenic figures as the bald eagle, the polar bear, whales, and whooping cranes, all of which were sentimentally appealing, fairly remote from market considerations affecting most people, and dramatic or beautiful. Further, there were international conventions ratified by the United States which in broad, hortatory terms expressed an international intention to conserve such species and all endangered and threatened wildlife. Part of the impetus came from the well-organized nationally-based conservation groups that have long made the United States a leader in international conservation.

But political pressure and aesthetics alone do not represent a sufficient explanation for why the ESA of 1973 became domestic law. The argument for protection of endangered species represented not only protection of the aesthetic beauties of certain species, but also ecological and philosophical principles asserting the value of the survival of the widest possible number of species, some of them quite homely, in the context of the continuing loss each year of hundreds of species worldwide. In utilitarian terms, preserving endangered species can in some way be directly or indirectly important for the continued survival of human beings. An endangered species may possess chemical or medical properties that will never be discovered if the creatures are rendered extinct. We preserve species because of lessons they may teach us in the future; at some point, "they may reveal a cure for cancer." Another argument is that the more diversity that exists in the natural world, the more adaptable that world is to continuing stresses. This argument reflects a fundamental law of ecology that the more diverse a gene pool or ecosystem, the greater the natural bank of adaptive diversity upon which society can draw.

Unfortunately, as repeatedly demonstrated in subsequent hearings on the Act, it is very difficult to show the utility of many species, especially species previously unknown that happen to confront a specific valuable development project. Therefore, beyond the strict utility argument, endangered species protection often draws upon a variety of quasi-religious principles emphasizing the sanctity of life. This latter philosophical principle was the most difficult to articulate amidst congressional hearings or agency proceedings, but it reflects an important thread running through the endangered species cases — humans are stewards of their natural environment and ultimately are only constituent members of the community of life of the globe. The ESA, which made no distinction between species that have a commercial value or direct human utility and those that do not, affirmed a variety of abstract interests in protecting species because they were endangered. The statute gave legal value to an abstraction. The survival of species, insofar as possible, was declared a valid and important national goal.

**THE SNAIL DARTER AND THE TELLICO DAM CASE...** The Tennessee Valley Authority's (TVA) Tellico Dam case was a classic environmental conflict between a citizens group, including farmers, sportsmen, archaeologists, and the Cherokee Indians on one hand, and on the other a porkbarrel group comprising a federal construction agency allied with private business interests, primarily real estate. The case started in the early 1960s and decided the fate of the last remaining undammed segment of the Little Tennessee River.[3]

As reported during the 1970s, the story consistently came down to a simple caricature: the snail darter, a two-inch minnow, discovered at the last possible moment and misused by extremist environmentalists, halts completion of a massive $150,000,000 hydroelectric dam. On the factual record virtually every element of that story was wrong. The Tellico Dam was small with no generators, and was only a fractional part of a quixotic federal land development project that subsequently fell of its own weight. The river valley itself, without the dam, held the potential to produce more public profits than the project. And far from discovering the snail darter at the last moment, TVA knew about the endangered fish in 1973, but ignored the law and spent most of its budget after 1973 in an accelerated effort to foreclose alternatives to the reservoir. The perceived media reality, however, had an immutable force of its own, possessing more importance than the facts on the record. In that irony lies one of the important lessons to be drawn from the case.

**THE LITTLE TENNESSEE VALLEY AND ITS LEGAL HISTORY...** The valley of the Little Tennessee River (the "Little T"), where it flows out of the Great Smoky Mountains, was settled more than 10,000 years ago. The river's waters ran cool, highly oxygenated, fertile, and filled with fish. The valley lands were rich beyond belief, high-grade topsoil to a depth of twenty feet or more. The Cherokees became a people here over the last millennium. Their most sacred places and Chota, their holy city of refuge, were located here. The first Anglo colonists entered the valley in the 18th century, building Fort Loudon as their southwestern-most redoubt to protect them and their Cherokee allies from the French and other Indian tribes. In the 1830s, responding to the land demands of the white settlers, Andrew Jackson drove the Cherokees off their lands in the Little T Valley in a forced emigration, which culminated in the Trail of Tears to Oklahoma. The white settlers immediately moved in to take over the vacated Cherokee lands. Fort Loudon and many of those early families were still there 200 years later when the TVA arrived and began building dams.

The TVA first hypothesized the Tellico Dam in a 1936 compilation of all dammable sites in the Tennessee Valley system. The Authority gave the site, located at the mouth of the Little Tennessee River where it flows into the Big Tennessee, lowest priority on a list of approximately 70 dam sites because of its marginal cost justification. It remained only a hypothetical site over the years while the TVA built hydroelectric dams and flood control structures elsewhere throughout the river system. All dams justifiable in terms of flood control, navigation, and power — more than 40 — had been built by 1950. The Authority continued building dams, however, stretching to justify each on grounds such as "economic development demonstrations." By 1960, more than 60 dams had been built, and the TVA finally turned to the few remaining sites, including Tellico. By then what had always been a treasure had also become unique. The remnant 33-mile stretch of the Little T, flowing with all its ancient qualities of richness and clarity, was the last such stretch of river left.

Congress at first refused to permit the dam to be built, but, faced with repeated TVA requests, in 1966 the House Appropriations Committee finally passed an appropriations bill providing funds for the project. Its primary stated purposes were

---

3. The case background, because it occupied six years of efforts by one of the authors from 1974 to 1980, is set out here with more detail than usual.

not hydroelectric. They were (1) to provide recreation and (2) to promote industrial development through the sale of large blocks of condemned farmlands. To support the benefit-cost justification claims, the TVA projected extraordinary net recreation increases, although by this time the Little T was the last remaining stretch of high-quality recreational flowing river, with 24 other reservoirs within a 50-mile radius. TVA hypothesized extensive shoreland development based on a model industrial city to be called "Timberlake," which theoretically would be attracted to the project area, with a series of factories requiring hundreds of acres for industrial development.

But more than 300 farm families then lived in the valley; hundreds of fishermen and canoeists loved it as the last, best remaining stretch of clean flowing river in the region; and the valley of the Little T was sacred to the Cherokees, whose most revered places would be destroyed by a reservoir. A rough citizen coalition, "The Association for the Preservation of the Little Tennessee River," was formed in 1964, and attempted to resist the project in Congress and through local political opposition. Faced with a solid linkage between the TVA, the pork-barrel congressional committees, local politicians, and land speculators, however, the citizens had no realistic chance, legally or on the merits, to stop the project during the 1960s. The concrete part of the dam structure was built in 1968, costing somewhat less than $5 million, that would not impound any part of the river until later, with the construction of earthen dikes. In 1970, however, NEPA gave the citizens a new lease on life, and they filed suits to stop the project.

Litigation under NEPA produced an injunction, which held for two years but ultimately was dissolved in 1973 when the Authority produced an adequate statement of the project's negative consequences. In the same year, Dr. David Etnier, a University of Tennessee ichthyologist, discovered a small endangered perch living in the midst of the Tellico project area, and a new round of litigation began. Section 7 of the ESA apparently prohibited federal agencies from taking any action that jeopardized the existence of an endangered species or modified a critical habitat. The Tellico project would do both. The fish was endangered and required the clean flowing river habitat that the dam would destroy. No federal statutes permitted a straightforward challenge to the dam project; the snail darter and §7 offered a "handle" to raise the challenge indirectly. Armed with the clear statutory violation, the dam's citizen opponents formed an ad hoc litigation group, filed administrative petitions in 1974 under the terms of the Endangered Species Act, and began court proceedings in 1975. TVA, meanwhile, began working three shifts, night and day, to moot the case before an injunction could issue.

**TELLICO'S "ENVIRONMENTAL" CASE...** In the case of the Tellico Dam, the project's environmental opponents had determined early that they would have to do more than merely oppose the dam and reservoir using §7's roadblock terms. Instead, as so often occurs in environmental cases, to have a realistic chance of prevailing in the long run, they had to back up their legal argument with a rational benefit-cost-alternatives accounting. On one hand, the Tellico citizens group reviewed the purported benefits of the reservoir — recreation, industrial development on condemned lands, and various vestigial benefits in water supply, flood control, and hydroelectric capacity — and found that on the objective record, viewed in businesslike terms, the economic case for the dam project was a fantasy. They then looked at the purported costs of the project, arguing that the *true* costs extended beyond the Authority's costs for cement, fill dirt, land condemnation,

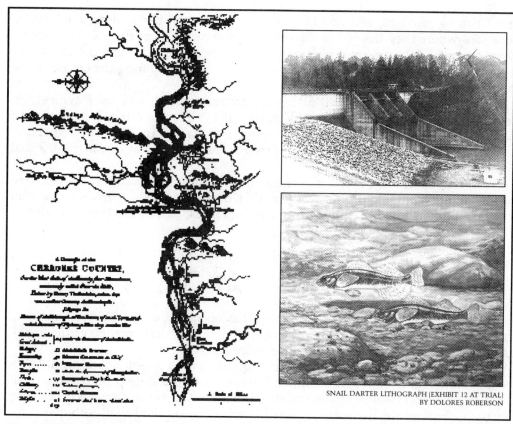

SNAIL DARTER LITHOGRAPH (EXHIBIT 12 AT TRIAL)
BY DOLORES ROBERSON

*The Little Tennessee River Valley, the dam, and the snail darter. The river and valley were sacred to the Cherokee, whose towns and sanctuaries appear on the 1762 colonial map. Prior to the Tellico case, TVA had dammed all of the river beyond and through the Enemy (Smoky) Mountains. Tellico Dam, located 14 miles downriver from the bottom of the map, eliminated all of the remaining free-flowing river. The dam structure, as shown, is small (note size of adjacent trees), costing less than $5 million. The darters lived on a broad shallow shoal below the Great Island.*

and roads and bridges. A realistic accounting of the true social costs would have to include the loss of all the special qualities of the river valley that had made it a treasure over the centuries. The river was a major recreational resource on its own terms, even before it had been rendered a virtually unique resource by the impoundment of 2500 linear miles of river in the surrounding region. The agricultural soils of the valley were of great economic value, the historic resources held great public value in their own right and could be capitalized monetarily in a tourist-based development if the valley's central portion was not flooded, and a major parcel of upriver project lands had particular potential for use as an access and overflow management area for the Great Smoky Mountains National Park. The citizens' benefit-cost accounting thus included extensive consideration of development alternatives. With increasing sophistication over the years they argued for a comprehensive river-based development project, allowing displaced families to go back onto most of the rich agricultural lands of the valley, developing a tourist highway through the valley to the Park, developing recreation to promote canoe float trips and other water-based sports, improving access to the superb trout fishing resource, and providing for two industrial parks along the river at locations where they would not disturb the other qualities of the valley. The citizens' analysis of the project consistently proved more accurate than the TVA's projections in every subsequent expert review that took place during the course of the controversy.

The availability of the snail darter, the citizens argued, was not a cynical fortuity. The precarious existence of the endangered fish in the Little T constituted a barometer of endangered human and economic values in this last remaining stretch of high quality river. The snail darter in the Little T was a "canary in a coal mine."[4]

The trial court judge found that the dam would destroy the canary but declined to issue an injunction. The Sixth Circuit Court of Appeals corrected the trial judge's omission, and the case went to the Supreme Court of the United States.[5]

### Tennessee Valley Authority v. Hiram Hill, et al.
United States Supreme Court, 1978
437 U.S. 153, 98 S. Ct. 2279, 57 L. Ed. 2d 117

BURGER, C.J. We begin with the premise that operation of the Tellico Dam will either eradicate the known population of snail darters or destroy their critical habitat. Petitioner does not now seriously dispute this fact.

Starting from the above premise, two questions are presented: (a) would TVA be in violation of the Act if it completed and operated the Tellico Dam as planned? (b) if TVA's actions would offend the Act, is an injunction the appropriate remedy for the violation? For the reasons stated hereinafter, we hold that both questions must be answered in the affirmative.

It may seem curious to some that the survival of a relatively small number of three-inch fish among all the countless millions of species extant would require the permanent halting of a virtually completed dam for which Congress has expended more than $100 million....

One would be hard pressed to find a statutory provision whose terms were any plainer than those in §7 of the Endangered Species Act. Its very words affirmatively command all federal agencies "to insure that actions authorized, funded, or carried out by them do not jeopardize the continued existence" of an endangered species or "result in the destruction or modification of habitat of such species...." This language admits of no exception. Accepting the Secretary's determinations, as we must, it is clear that TVA's proposed operation of the dam will have precisely the opposite effect, namely the eradication of an endangered species.

Concededly, this view of the Act will produce results requiring the sacrifice of the anticipated benefits of the project and of many millions of dollars in public funds, but close examination of the language, history, and structure of the

4. The "canary in the coal mine" function reflects the old days when canaries were carried by miners because when the sensitive little species began to show harm from odorless methane coal gas, it gave warning of serious threats to human health. Like the canaries, an endangered species can show by its presence that habitat qualities are in jeopardy, with human welfare consequences that may follow. DDT's threat to human metabolic systems was first identified via reproductive disasters visited upon endangered birds, whose metabolic cumulation of diphenyls passed through ovarian tissues and disrupted egg-laying. In other settings, like the snail darter's, the barometer function of endangered species serves to protect human interests including public economics and threatened social values.
5. Hill v. TVA, 419 F. Supp. 753 (E.D. Tenn. 1976), 549 F.2d 1064 (6th Cir. 1977).

legislation under review here indicates beyond doubt that Congress intended endangered species to be afforded the highest of priorities.

"The dominant theme pervading all Congressional discussion of the proposed [ESA] was the overriding need to devote whatever effort and resources were necessary to avoid further diminution of national and worldwide wildlife resources. Much of the testimony at the hearings and much debate was devoted to the biological problem of extinction. Senators and Congressmen uniformly deplored the irreplaceable loss to aesthetics, science, ecology, and the national heritage should more species disappear." Coggins, Conserving Wildlife Resources: An Overview of the Endangered Species Act of 1973, 51 N.D.L. Rev. 315, 321 (1975).

The legislative proceedings in 1973 are, in fact, replete with expressions of concern over the risk that might lie in the loss of any endangered species. Typifying these sentiments is the Report of the House Committee on Merchant Marine and Fisheries on HR 37, a bill which contained the essential features of the subsequently enacted Act of 1973; in explaining the need for the legislation, the Report stated:

> As we homogenize the habitats in which these plants and animals evolved, and as we increase the pressure for products that they are in a position to supply (usually unwillingly) we threaten their and our own genetic heritage. The value of this genetic heritage is, quite literally, incalculable. From the most narrow possible point of view, it is in the best interests of mankind to minimize the losses of genetic variations. The reason is simple: they are potential resources. They are keys to puzzles which we cannot solve, and may provide answers to questions which we have not yet learned to ask. To take a homely, but apt, example: one of the critical chemicals in the regulation of ovulations in humans was found in a common plant. Once discovered, and analyzed, humans could duplicate it synthetically, but had it never existed — or had it been driven out of existence before we knew its potentialities — we would never have tried to analyze it in the first place. Who knows, or can say, what potential cures for cancer or other scourges, present or future, may lie locked up in the structures of plants which may yet be undiscovered, much less analyzed?.... Sheer self-interest impels us to be cautious. The institutionalization of that caution lies at the heart of HR 37.... HR Rep. No. 93–412.

As the examples cited here demonstrate, Congress was concerned about the unknown uses that endangered species might have and about the unforeseeable place such creatures may have in the chain of life on this planet.

In shaping legislation to deal with the problem thus presented, Congress started from the finding that "[t]he two major causes of extinction are hunting, and destruction of natural habitat." Sen. Rep. No. 93-307,2 (1973). Of these twin threats, Congress was informed that the greatest was destruction of natural habitats.

It is not for us to speculate, much less act, on whether Congress would have altered its stance had the specific events of this case been anticipated. In any event, we discern no hint in the deliberations of Congress relating to the 1973 Act that would compel a different result than we reach here.

One might dispute the applicability of these examples to the Tellico Dam by saying that in this case the burden on the public through the loss of millions of unrecoverable dollars would greatly outweigh the loss of the snail darter. But neither the Endangered Species Act nor Article III of the Constitution provides federal courts with authority to make such fine utilitarian calculations. On the contrary, the plain language of the Act, buttressed by its legislative history, shows clearly that Congress viewed the value of endangered species as "incalculable." Quite obviously, it would be difficult for a court to balance the loss of a sum certain — even $100 million — against a congressionally declared "incalculable" value, even assuming we had the power to engage in such a weighing process, which we emphatically do not.

Having determined that there is an irreconcilable conflict between operation of the Tellico Dam and the explicit provisions of §7 of the Endangered Species Act, we must now consider what remedy, if any, is appropriate. It is correct, of course, that a federal judge sitting as a chancellor is not mechanically obligated to grant an injunction for every violation of law.

Once Congress, exercising its delegated powers, has decided the order of priorities in a given area, it is for the Executive to administer the laws and for the courts to enforce them when enforcement is sought.

Here we are urged to view the Endangered Species Act "reasonably," and hence shape a remedy "that accords with some modicum of common sense and the public weal." But is that our function? We have no expert knowledge on the subject of endangered species, much less do we have a mandate from the people to strike a balance of equities on the side of the Tellico Dam. Congress has spoken in the plainest of words, making it abundantly clear that the balance has been struck in favor of affording endangered species the highest of priorities, hereby adopting a policy which it described as "institutionalized caution."

Our individual appraisal of the wisdom or unwisdom of a particular course consciously selected by the Congress is to be put aside in the process of interpreting a statute. Once the meaning of an enactment is discerned and its constitutionality determined, the judicial process comes to an end. We do not sit as a committee of review, nor are we vested with the power of veto. The lines ascribed to Sir Thomas More by Robert Bolt are not without relevance here:

> The law, Roper, the law. I know what's legal, not what's right. And I'll stick to what's legal.... I'm not God. The currents and eddies of right and wrong, which you find such plain-sailing, I can't navigate. I'm no voyager. But in the thickets of the law, oh there I'm a forester.... What would you do? Cut a great road through the law to get after the Devil?.... And when the last law was down, and the Devil turned round on you, where would you hide, Roper, the laws all being flat?.... This country's planted thick with laws from coast to coast — Man's laws, not God's — and if you cut them down...d'you really think you could stand upright in the winds that would blow then? Yes, I'd give the Devil benefit of law, for my own safety's sake. R. Bolt, A Man for All Seasons, Act I, 147 (Heinemann ed. 1967).

We agree with the Court of Appeals that in our constitutional system the commitment to the separation of powers is too fundamental for us to pre-empt congressional action by judicially decreeing what accords with "common sense and the public weal." Our Constitution vests such responsibilities in the political branches.

Affirmed. POWELL, J., joined by BLACKMUN, J., and REHNQUIST, J., wrote separate opinions.

### COMMENTARY AND QUESTIONS

1. **An "environmental" opinion?** Much of the snail darter majority opinion looks at the Endangered Species Act only to determine, via statutory construction, the bald question of whether it applied to the dam, and whether a court had to obey the statute. The court does not mention any of the plaintiffs' evidence on overall environmental-economic balancing, or on rational development alternatives. Justice Burger does echo congressional declarations of the high purposes of endangered species preservation, and "institutionalized caution," a critical environmental principle, but in his oral presentation of the decision he invited Congress to repeal protection for the fish. And the media predictably chorused the "little fish bites dam" theme, casting the case and plaintiffs in damaging terms of extreme environmentalism. On balance, did the snail darter litigation aid the cause of conservation, or undercut it?

2. **A tactical footnote on ESA legislative history.** Would it change your view of §7 of the 1973 ESA if you were told that it had been consciously drafted by a legislative aide and an ardent wildlife advocate in a form that would avoid its being recognized as a substantive roadblock statute? If §7, which has become one of the landmark environmental protections in federal law, would never have been passed without a virtually impenetrable verbal camouflage, what does that say about Congress and the legislative process? What does it say about the ethics of the drafters of the provision who successfully slipped it into federal law? It is not a satisfactory excuse, for many environmentalists, that the opponents of environmental protection regularly slip exceptions and destructive undercutting amendments into ongoing legislation.

The tactical questions that arise when environmentalists actively participate in the legislative process continually force thoughtful people to reconsider their philosophy of government, of public interest advocacy, and ethics.

And the text virtually admits that the plaintiffs used the snail darter as a convenient "handle" to raise public issues about farmland, historic values, river recreation, and economics. Isn't this a misuse of the law, one that, moreover, selfishly risked the destruction of the ESA itself?

3. **The clash between stark roadblocks and pressures for flexibility.** Stark "roadblock" prohibitions clearly have a potent ability to effectuate their terms. Section 7 helped make the ESA a high-profile and credible governmental protective program. But strict prohibitions are not always rational when applied in the realities of a complex world. Inevitably there will be circumstances in which they may require modification. In every case there will be regulated and affected parties who argue strongly for eliminating the roadblock, or opening it up with a variety of discretionary or bureaucratic flexibility devices. How can and should flexibility be considered?

4. **Flexibility: statutory violations and equitable balancing.** One way for a roadblock to gain flexibility is if appellate courts say that it need not be enforced if violated. Justice Burger's opinion, however, declared a ringing endorsement of the environmentalists' proposition (and the basis of their empowerment strategy) that

if citizens are able to prove a statutory violation, the court must enforce the law without equitable balancing, and transfer the debate to the legislative forum. This was a fairly conservative, non-activist theory of judicial review. It distinguished the traditional three areas of equitable balancing,[6] and argued that where statutory violations are concerned, the scope of equitable balancing is restricted to threshold questions (of laches, clean hands, etc.) and to the question of which remedy is necessary to effectuate the legislature's substantive prohibition. It does not extend to second-guessing what actions should be prohibited.

Justice Rehnquist wrote a scathing dissent in *Hill* arguing that trial judges, as in this case, should have equitable discretion to override statutory violations, allowing projects to go on. This activist argument raises a basic question about roadblock statutes. When they are violated, who should be able to grant the necessary flexibility, a trial judge "balancing the equities," or the Congress? The plaintiffs argued throughout the case that it was perfectly proper for Congress to consider such exemptions. In that way citizens might win the opportunity to have full, rational legislative hearings on the issue, based on the tactical leverage of the injunction.[7] The courts' narrow role, the citizens successfully argued, if a violation existed, was to apply their discretion so as to see that the law was obeyed.[8]

The basic question in the snail darter case — whether courts are bound to enforce statutes when citizens prove violations — continues. Weinberger v. Romero-Barcelo, 456 U.S. 305 (1982) (violation of CWA not so critical as ESA in *Hill*, so no injunction); Amoco Prod. Co. v. Village of Gambell, 480 U.S. 531 (1987) (Court implies some judicial flexibility not to enforce laws);[9] cf. Sierra Club v. Marsh, 872 F.2d 497, 500 (1st Cir. 1989) (court could not override statutory violation).

5. **Flexibility through statutory interpretation?** The Supreme Court's opinion in TVA v. Hill also included an extensive analysis rejecting the agency's arguments that the statute should be interpreted not to cover the snail darter and the dam — primarily arguments based on retroactivity, implied amendment, and "common sense."

The retroactivity argument urged that since the concrete part of the dam, worth $5 million of the $150 million total, had been built before the Endangered Species Act was passed, the project could continue even if it would eliminate the endangered

---

6. Noted earlier in Chapter Three's consideration of equitable remedies: a threshold balance to show equitable standing, a balance of what action would to permitted and what proscribed, and a balance to tailor appropriate remedies.

7. See Plater, Statutory Violations and Equitable Discretion, 70 Cal. L. Rev. 524, 583-588 (1982).

8. The citizens argued that, under Hecht Co. v. Bowles, 321 U.S. 321 (1944),. the leading statutory equity case, 9 courts remained free to deny injunctions or modify injunctions as necessary so long as they accomplished whatever the statute required or prohibited. The second balance, however, as to whether the defendant's activity should in fact be prohibited, was pre-empted by statute. In *Hecht*, the Supreme Court had made a much-quoted declaration of a court's continuing power to balance the equities when confronted with a petition for an injunction. But in that case it had been established that the defendant would no longer violate the statutory price-fixing prohibition. The injunction was not necessary because the legislature's wish was being obeyed.

9. *Gambell* holds that a court may balance the equities so as to allow a violation to continue, although it includes language that:

> Environmental injury, by its nature, can seldom be adequately remedied by money damages and is often permanent or at least of long duration, i.e., irreparable. If such injury is sufficiently likely, therefore, the balance of harms will usually favor the issuance of an injunction to protect the environment. 480 U.S. at 545.

species. The Court upheld the citizens' argument that a statute should be applied if it prohibits actions which would cause, as in Justice Holmes's dictum, "the evils that the legislature intended to address." Further, governmental agencies have no civil right or vested right to proceed with favorite projects in spite of subsequent federal legislation (see *Thorpe*, noted in the *Overton Park* case).

TVA had continued to receive funding for the dam project from the porkbarrel appropriations committees year after year despite the committee's knowledge of the endangered species statutory violation. The agency and appropriations committees also added phrases to the annual funding bills stating the committees' opinion that the Act did not apply, that the Act was frivolous in this setting, and that the importance of the project so exceeded the importance of the endangered species that the project should continue irrespective of any possible statutory violation. TVA argued that continued funding, plus this legislative intent, constituted an implied amendment, implied repealer, or implied statutory exception to the Act. The Supreme Court disagreed, noting a long line of cases declaring that repeals by implication are suspect, particularly if they are found in appropriations bills, which typically deal with budgetary and financial matters rather than substantive law.

As to common sense in statutory interpretation, at many stages during the course of the litigation, and in the halls of Congress and the agencies, it was argued that a statute should not be applied if it would lead to what the particular observer considered an "absurd" or "extreme" result. As Justice Powell said —

> In my view §7 cannot reasonably be interpreted as applying to a project that is completed or substantially completed when its threat to an endangered species is discovered. Nor can I believe that Congress could have intended this Act to produce the "absurd result" — in the words of the District Court — of this case. 437 U.S. at 196.

The Supreme Court held, however, that even when a statute led to what a court might think was an absurd result, if the facts fit the law, the statute was to be applied as it was written.

6. **Flexibility: remand to Congress.** Throughout the Tellico Dam case, the environmentalists had argued that courts should merely enforce the statute, and the matter then would necessarily be transferred to the legislature, where for the first time they could obtain public review of the controversy on the factual and economic merits.

The case by no means ended with the Supreme Court decision, given the cantankerousness of the contending parties. Congress responded with three series of hearings in the relevant substantive committees, considering whether this extreme application of the law should be reversed. Three times the committees were convinced, much to their surprise, that preservation of the river was not an example of environmental irrationality; and no Tellico amendment was passed. The media, however, remained fixed upon its "fish bites dam" characterization of the case.

7. **The God Committee Amendments and the snail darter.** Ultimately, as noted in Subchapter B below, Congress was persuaded in late 1978 to create a new statutory flexibility device to calm the avalanche of criticism levied against the "extrem-

ism" of the Act revealed by the snail darter decision. An exemption procedure was added to §7, providing that a Cabinet-level review board (dubbed the God Committee) could authorize the removal of protections, hence allowing extinction of a species, if an agency satisfactorily proved a stringent set of criteria. The statute stipulated that the Tellico project would be one of the first two reviewed by the God Committee for exemption. (This was the plaintiffs' first chance to argue their full case before a legal forum that would, unlike the courts, have to make a comprehensive judgment on the full project merits.)

The God Committee unanimously denied an exemption for Tellico, on economic as well as ecological grounds.[10] "I hate to see the snail darter get the credit for stopping a project that was ill-conceived and uneconomic in the first place," said Chairman Andrus. As Charles Schultze, then-Chairman of the Council of Economic Advisers and a member of the Committee said, "Here is a project that is 95 percent complete, and if one takes just the cost of finishing it against the [total project] benefits, and does it properly, it doesn't pay,... which says something about the original design." The river defenders had to make their arguments on the basis of tangible economic values rather than "intangible" ecological values. The river's non-dam development alternatives, with a host of nonquantifiable social values, were largely ignored in the governmental process and the media. Despite the expenditure of millions of dollars, the non-dam alternatives still compared favorably to the dam plan.

The citizens had been vindicated on the merits in every element of their long-running campaign against the project. The possibility lay open for an innovative redevelopment of the valley and its river resource, demonstrating to the nation what could be done with coordinated management of prime agricultural lands and a valley's historic, recreational, touristic, and ecological assets.

8. **Denouement for the snail darter.** For the next four and a half months after the God Committee decision, the citizens worked desperately to begin implementation of alternative planning for the river and the valley. Despite some reforms in TVA's stonewalling behavior, however, the agency declined to talk with the farmers or environmentalists, and nothing happened. Into the vacuum, on June 18, 1979, stepped Senator Howard Baker and John Duncan, a local Tennessee congressman. Through a parliamentary maneuver engineered by the porkbarrel appropriations committee, Duncan, in 42 seconds, slipped a rider onto the ongoing House appropriations bill explicitly overriding the Supreme Court decision and all other federal or state protective laws as they applied to Tellico and ordering the reservoir's immediate completion. Because the amendment was not read in the empty chamber, none of the few congressmen on the floor other than the committee members knew what was being done. Ultimately the rider passed through the Senate with Baker's decisive help. President Jimmy Carter threatened to veto, then signed the bill with an abject telephone call apology to plaintiffs on October 4, 1979.

The Cherokees filed another lawsuit based upon the constitutional rights that would be infringed if their most sacred places were destroyed by the reservoir. (Was

---

10. Decision of Endangered Species Committee, January 23, 1979 (remarkably this is unreported).

this an "environmental" suit?) The case died in the courts when an injunction was denied on grounds that the Indians could not assert religious rights on land they did not own, and TVA closed the gates to start flooding the valley on November 28, 1979. Ammoneta Sequoyah v. TVA, 480 F. Supp. 608 (E.D. Tenn. 1979), 620 F.2d 1159 (6th Cir. 1980), cert. denied, 449 U.S. 953 (1980).

Of the last major population, 25,000 darters that had lived in the Little Tennessee prior to dam construction, none has survived. Small relict populations have been discovered in several sites downstream, and at two other sites, and the Department of Interior has downlisted the darter to "threatened" status.[11] The condemned valley lands produced no model industrial city, and little economic development.[12]

9. **ESA procedures: consultation.** The §7 roadblock provision in its original form contained a bare requirement for endangered species "consultation" between Interior and other agencies. When it became clear that §7 was strictly enforceable, the consultation process evolved quickly in agency practice to mediate conflicting interests. By 1979, Department of Interior records showed that more than 4500 potential conflicts between endangered species and federal projects had arisen, and in all but four cases[13] the agencies were able to adjust project design, timing, or location to accommodate the ESA protections.

When §7's strict prohibition was modified to include the God Committee exemption possibility, the consultation process was further articulated by statute and rule. 50 C.F.R. Pt. 402; 16 U.S.C.A. §1536(b)(3)(1978). If agencies or concerned citizens believe that a possible species problem exists, they may ask the Department of Interior to do a Biological Assessment to ascertain if it is so. If the BA finds there is a threat to endangered species, the project agency requests "consultation" which triggers a strict time schedule. FWS undertakes active consultation, and must issue a "biological opinion," analyzing the conflict and suggesting alternatives, if necessary, within 90 days. The consultation process and biological opinions are held to good faith and best available data.[14]

---

11. A side note: both Hiram Hill, the student-plaintiff who discovered the potential for this endangered species litigation while writing an environmental law term paper, and the Senate aide who drafted the tough "clearly outweighs" God Committee test noted in subchapter B below, had studied environmental law using an earlier version of this coursebook.

12. TVA strove to sell the condemned lands for development, but without much success. The first major development proposal after two years of stagnation was to create regional toxic waste landfills on the valley lands; the citizens quashed it. Subsequently a small industrial park (smaller than the industrial park included as part of the citizens' non-dam alternative plan) attracted several small businesses. To achieve more development, TVA then transferred a substantial portion of the valley, on a subsidized basis, to a second-home vacation housing developer.

13. The exceptions were, according to Interior testimony, attributable to agency intransigence rather than irresolvability — TVA's Tellico Dam, the FHWA's insistence on putting Interstate-10 through a sandhill crane habitat, the Corps of Engineers' Meramec Dam, and the Corps and REA's Greyrocks Dam. See Endangered Species Oversight Hearings, Senate Committee on Environment and Public Works, No. 95-H33, 62-75, 79-91 (1977). Of these, all but Tellico were settled through negotiation after citizen litigation. Greyrocks' settlement was incorporated into a God Committee ruling under the 1978 ESA amendments. The Administration's data for the hearings was compiled by Mardi Hatcher and Deborah Labelle, working in the federal archives as student volunteers from the Wayne Environmental Law Society.

14. Bob Marshall Alliance v. Hodel, 852 F.2d 1223 (9th Cir. 1988); Village of False Pass v. Watt, 733 F.2d 605 (9th Cir. 1984); Roosevelt Campobello Int'l Park v. EPA, 684 F.2d 1041 (1st Cir. 1982).

10. **Critical habitat.** In the snail darter case, designation of critical habitat was pro forma. In subsequent cases, however, critical habitat listing has been hotly contested, in part because it automatically requires at least minimal review of any federal actions within the habitat areas. Public and private project proponents often view it in more drastic terms, as a "power grab" (as when Interior considers listing broad geographical areas[15]), and a nefarious part of protectionists' "agenda to lock up all public lands as de facto wilderness."[16]

The Interior Department is often diffident about declaring critical habitat. Only half of listed endangered species have critical habitat listings.[17] Critical habitat protection lawsuits are accordingly rare.

11. **Agencies' affirmative conservation duties?** Section 7's vague hortatory provision urging agencies to "carry...out programs for the conservation of endangered species" may become a litigable requirement. In Carson-Truckee Water Conservancy District v. Clark,[18] for example, the court held that the Department of Interior was required not only to protect existing habitats and endangered species, but also to "use programs administered by [the Department] to further the conservation purposes of [the Endangered Species Act]." The Department must "conserve threatened and endangered species to the extent that they are no longer threatened" and "halt *and reverse* the trend toward species extinction, whatever the cost." 741 F.2d at 262 (the emphasis is the court's).

## Section 2. SPOTTED OWLS AND ANCIENT FORESTS

### Seattle Audubon Society v. John L. Evans (U.S. Forest Service) and Washington Contract Loggers Assoc.
United States District Court, Western District of Washington, 1991
771 F. Supp. 1081[19]

DWYER, J. ...Plaintiffs Seattle Audubon Society, et al. have moved for a permanent injunction prohibiting the sale of logging rights in northern spotted owl [strix occidentalis caurina] habitat areas.... The national forests are managed by the Forest Service.... Regulations promulgated under [NFMA, the National Forest Management Act, and the ESA] provide that fish and wildlife shall be managed to maintain viable populations of existing native and desired non-native vertebrate species.... A viable population is "one which has the estimated numbers and distribution of reproductive individuals to insure its continued existence is well distributed in the planning area." To insure viability, habitat must be provided to

---

15. This is especially so when Interior proposes designating habitat in ranchland or other developed areas where a predator endangered species has been exterminated but may be re-introduced.

16. Murray, The Act Will Work — If They Let It, 7 Envt'l Forum 32 (July 1990).

17. Illustrating this diffidence, the regulations provide for habitat listing "to the maximum extent *prudent* and *determinable*." (emphasis added). Those mitigating adjectives are complemented by a requirement that FWS "tak[e] into consideration the probable economic and other impacts...," 50 C.F.R. §424.12, and "exclude any...area from the critical habitat if the benefits of such exclusion outweigh the benefits of [inclusion]." §424.19.

18. 741 F.2d 257 (9th Cir. 1984), cert. denied 105 S. Ct. 1842 (1985).

19. On remand from the Ninth Circuit., 914 F.2d 1311 (9th Cir. 1991); cert. granted, 111 S. Ct. 2886 (1991).

© 1988 GARY BRAASCH

*The winged blur in the center right of this ancient forest clearing is a rare daylight image of the northern spotted owl (Strix occidentalis caurina), perhaps about to strike a red-backed vole. The background shows a fallen "nurse log" which opens a hole in the canopy for sunlight to reach the forest floor, allowing new trees to grow up from the nurse log's decomposing organic matter. The lushness of the decomposition and growth processes in the natural old-growth forests of the Pacific Northwest is supported by rhizoform fungus nodules in the forest's root systems. The fungi provide nutrients and water retention to balance forest moisture throughout the low-precipitation summer season. Red-backed voles live in the nurse logs and specialize in eating the subsoil fungal truffles. The owls eat the voles. The fungi are then transplanted through the forests in owl pellet droppings. Without the owl, the forest's balances of life and water are disrupted.*

support at least a minimum number of reproductive individuals.... Since not every species can be monitored, "indicator species" are observed as signs of general wildlife viability. The northern spotted owl is an indicator species....

In recent years logging and development have steadily reduced wildlife habitat in the Pacific Northwest. At the same time many local mills have experienced log shortages. The result is an intensified struggle over the future of the national forests.... In June 1990, the Fish and Wildlife Service...listed the owl as a threatened species under the Endangered Species Act....On February 26, 1991, Judge Zilly ruled that the FWS had again failed to comply with the law, stating:

> Upon the record presented, this Court finds the Service has failed to discharge its obligations under the Endangered Species Act and its own administrative regulations. Specifically, the Service, acting on behalf of the Secretary of the Interior, abused its discretion when it determined not to designate critical habitat concurrently with the listing of the northern spotted owl, or to explain any basis for concluding that the critical habitat was not determinable. These

actions were arbitrary and capricious, and contrary to law. Northern Spotted Owl v. Lujan, 758 F. Supp. 621, 629 (W.D. Wash. 1991).

[In September 1990, without notice, hearing, environmental impact statement, or other rule-making procedures, the Forest Service announced that it was proceeding with the timber sales, and this court issued a preliminary injunction.]...

The fate of the spotted owl has become a battleground largely because the species is a symbol of the remaining old growth forest. As stated in the Interagency Scientific Committee (ISC) Report:[20]

Why all the fuss about the status and welfare of this particular bird? The numbers, distribution, and welfare of spotted owls are widely believed to be inextricably tied to mature and old-growth forests. Such forests have been significantly reduced since 1850 (mostly since 1950) by clearing for agriculture, urban development, natural events such as fire and windstorms, and most significantly, by logging in recent decades. Nearly all old growth has been removed on private lands. Most of the remainder is under the management of the BLM, FS, and NPS on Federal lands. As its habitat has declined, the owl has virtually disappeared from some areas and its numbers are decreasing in others.

An old growth forest consists not just of ancient standing trees, but of fallen trees, snags, massive decaying vegetation, and numerous resident plant and animal species, many of which live nowhere else. A great conifer forest originally covered the western parts of Washington, Oregon, and Northern California, from the Cascade and Coast mountains to the sea. Perhaps ten percent of it remains. The spaces protected as parks or wilderness areas are not enough for the survival of the northern spotted owl. The old growth forest sustains a biological community far richer than those of managed forests or tree farms. As testified by Dr. William Ferrell, a forest ecologist:

The most significant implication from our new knowledge regarding old-growth forest ecology is that logging these forests destroys not just trees, but a complex, distinctive, and unique ecosystem.

The remaining old growth stands are valued also for their effects on climate, air, and migratory fish runs, and for their beauty. A 1984 Forest Service document summed up the controversy:

There are at least three main reasons cited for maintaining old growth: wildlife and plant habitat, ecosystem diversity, and preservation of aesthetic qualities. Those opposed to the retention of old growth are primarily concerned with economic factors and urge rapid conversion of the existing old growth to managed forests of productive, young age classes. Forest Service, Regional Guide for Pacific Northwest Region 3-40 (May 1984).

Through most of the country's history there was little or no logging in the national forests. Intensive logging began with World War II and has accelerated.... Despite increasing concern over the environment, logging sales by the Forest Service have continued on a large scale....

The records of this case...show a remarkable series of violations of the environmental laws.... In the fall of 1990 the Forest Service admitted that [its protocol for logging old growth national forests] was inadequate after all — that it would fail to preserve the northern spotted owl. In seeking a stay of proceedings in this court

---

20. [The ISC, chaired by Jack Ward Thomas of the Forest Service, recommended setting aside 20-30 percent of the available old growth in public forests to protect the owls.].

in 1989 the Forest Service announced its intent to adopt temporary guidelines within thirty days. It did not do that within thirty days, or ever. When directed by Congress to have a revised ROD [record of decision] in place by September 30, 1990, the Forest Service did not even attempt to comply....

The reasons for this pattern of behavior were made clear at the evidentiary hearing. [A Forest Service wildlife biologist testified that the agency process had been diluted] —

> because in every instance there was a considerable — I would emphasize considerable — amount of political pressure to create a plan which was an absolute minimum. That is, which had a very low probability of success and which had a minimum impact on timber harvest.... [Other testimony showed repeated political amendments to the spotted owl plan made in executive offices in Washington.]...

The agency...has the benefit of an [endangered species consultation] opinion letter from the FWS...commenting at length on the ISC strategy and giving recommendations. With the knowledge at hand, there is no reason for the Forest Service to fail to develop quickly a plan to ensure the viability of the spotted owl in the national forests. The northern spotted owl is now threatened with extinction. The ISC Report states:

> We have concluded that the owl is imperiled over significant portions of its range because of continuing losses of habitat from logging and natural disturbances. Current management strategies are inadequate to ensure its viability. Moreover, in some portions of the owl's range, few options for managing habitat remain open, and available alternatives are steadily declining throughout the bird's range....

The population of northern spotted owls continues to decline. "We're going to have to arrest that decline and reverse it," as Dr. Thomas testified. "Spotted owl habitat," also called "suitable habitat," is defined as follows by FWS:

> Suitable owl habitat has moderate to high canopy closure (60 to 80 percent); a multi-layered, multi-species canopy dominated by large (> 30 inches in diameter at breast height (dbh)) overstory trees; a high incidence of large trees with various deformities (e.g., large cavities, broken tops, dwarf-mistletoe infections, and other evidence of decadence); numerous large snags; large accumulations of fallen trees and other woody debris on the ground; and sufficient open space below the canopy for owls to fly.

The Forest Service estimates that an additional 66,000 acres of spotted owl habitat would be destroyed if logging went forward to the extent permitted by the ISC Report over the next sixteen months. That would be in addition to about 400,000 acres of habitat logged in the seven years since the agency began preparing these guidelines, all without having a lawful plan or EIS for the owl's management in place....

Over the past decade many timber jobs have been lost and mills closed in the Pacific Northwest. The main reasons have been modernization of physical plants, changes in product demand, and competition from elsewhere. Supply shortages have also played a part. Those least able to adapt and modernize, and those who have not gained alternative supplies, have been hardest hit by the changes....

Job losses in the wood products industry will continue regardless of whether the northern spotted owl is protected.... The timber industry no longer drives the Pacific Northwest's economy.... The wood products industry now employs about four percent of all workers in Western Oregon, two percent in Western

Washington, and six percent in Northern California. Even if some jobs in wood products were affected by protecting owl habitat in the short-term, any effect on the regional economy probably would be small.

The remaining wilderness contributes to the desirability of this region as a site for new industries and their employees. The resulting economic gains, while hard to measure, are genuine and substantial. The FWS has recently noted that preservation of old growth brings economic benefits and amenities "of extremely high value." The court must weigh and consider the public interest in deciding whether to issue an injunction in an environmental case. ...The public interest and the balance of equities require the issuance of an injunction directing the Forest Service to comply with the requirements of NFMA by March 5, 1992, and preventing it from selling additional logging rights in spotted owl habitat until it complies with the law.

## COMMENTARY AND QUESTIONS

1. **The ESA and the owl.** Note that *Seattle Audubon* is not a pure Endangered Species Act case. The endangered species issues — primarily raised in parallel lawsuits in the Oregon and Washington district courts[21] — provided the backdrop for *Seattle Audubon's* NFMA injunction. Judge Dwyer's excerpted opinion reveals the conflicting pressures within the federal agencies about the listing of the owl and its critical habitat.

According to the data of the ISC Report, the spotted owl's survival would probably *not* have been threatened by cutting the 4 billion board feet of timber already sold, but probably would be by further cutting thereafter. Thus §7's prohibitions will kick in only when the owl's habitat is knowingly brought to the brink of endangerment. Do §7's affirmative conservation provisions provide for earlier anticipatory protective efforts?

Facing the inevitability of a §7 injunction action, Interior Secretary Lujan called for a God Committee exemption process, the first since the snail darter's Tellico Dam and its companion case, in which 13 timber contracts received partial exemptions.[22]

2. **Owl politics.** *Seattle Audubon* describes much of the political backdrop of the spotted owl controversy. The privately-owned old growth forests have long since been largely eliminated, replaced with monoculture (single species) tree farms that are less productive in terms of biomass and have not served to maintain the industry (as well as drastically reducing plant and wildlife ecosystem diversity). Timber companies have thus turned to the remaining old growth public forests to maintain their prosperity, in large part through exports of raw timber to Japan and Korea.

---

21. Lane County Audubon v. Jamison, No. 91-6123 (D. Ore. Sept. 11, 1991, Jones, J.); Northern Spotted Owl v. Hodel and Northern Spotted Owl v. Lujan, 716 F.Supp. 478, amd'd 758 F.Supp. 621 (W.D. Wash. 1988 and 1991, Zilly, J.). Judge Dwyer lifted the injunction in the excerpted case in early June 1994 after the federal agency had complied with statutory procedures.

22. See subchapter B below. In exemption process proceedings, the detail in which the factfinding review process examines overall economics is critical. The spotted owl decision focused narrowly on the benefits of proposed logging, with little consideration of alternatives, and was marked by politicization. See Portland Audubon Society v. Endangered Species Committee, 984 F.2d 1534 (9th Cir. 1992).

The coalition against the owl is led by the forests products industry's national associations, with its public positions vocally presented in the media by loggers whose jobs appear threatened.[23] The spotted owl issue is often portrayed in the media as a "jobs vs. owls" conflict, but the actual tradeoff is more subtle: the historical backdrop is the timber industry's past broad-scale cutting of private lands, and more than two-thirds of the marketable public forests, with inadequate reforestation.

The economic reality of the conflict, moreover, is a massive program of latent federal subsidies. Federal taxpayers subsidize the timber industry in four major ways. The Forest Service (in ascending order):

- sells timber from national forests below regular market price;[24]
- spends several hundred million dollars per year on building and maintaining logging roads in rugged terrain (to date the Service has built 7 times more road mileage than the entire Interstate highway system) and providing other free services to the industry. Thus the timber itself is even sold in many cases below the Government's own out-of-pocket cash flow costs. During the 1980s, the Service sold 124 billion board feet at a loss of $3.5 billion; for fiscal 1997 above the net loss was more than $2.2 billion;[25]
- pays 25 percent of its gross timber receipts to local communities as payments in lieu of property taxes;[26]
- and, fourth, the largest subsidy (unaccounted for in economic analyses) is the ecological subsidy — the permanent sacrifice of thousands of acres of diverse natural forests, often on fragile, high-elevation steep slopes — that otherwise would be available for multiple non-logging public uses. The logging of old-growth forests leads to severe erosion, wildlife losses, water quality degradation, a ten-fold drop in the ecosystem's diversity of species, and other serious long-term effects.[27]

23. The Northwest's loggers have taken a yellow ribbon tied to the truck antenna as their totem, arguing forcefully against environmental accounting and cuts in public subsidies, and informally advocating extermination of the spotted owl. With mass gatherings of logging trucks on the roads and in the capitals of the Northwest, the yellow-ribbon timbercutters have forcefully argued their special perspective on timbering, "Shoot an owl, save a job." "I love spotted owls... *fried.*" "If it comes down to my family or that bird, that bird's going to suffer." Time, 25 June 1990 at 60. See Plater, Political Tribalism in Natural Resources Management, 11 Pub. Land L.Rev. 1, 11 (1990).

24. The Forest Service sets its auction base price with reference to the *average* potential buyer, rather than the normal appraisal standard of the price that would be paid by a willing buyer to a willing private market seller. See Wolf, National Forest Timber Sales and the Legacy of Gifford Pinchot: Managing a Forest and Making it Pay, 60 Univ. of Colo. L. Rev. 1037 (1989); and Wolf's resource analyses prepared at the request of the House Governmental Operations Subcommittee on Environment, Energy, and Natural Resources, 102d Cong., 1st Sess., Fall 1991.

25. If interest is figured in, the 1980s' number is a loss of $6.3 billion. Other services besides providing logging roads include surveying and inventorying timberlands, fire protection, staff personnel and structures, mapmaking, and disease control. Under cost-accounting analysis, most of the 122 national forests have never earned a penny on timber; in 1990 only 15 showed a cash flow profit. Wolf, preceding note; Knize, The Mismanagement of the National Forests, 268; The Atlantic Monthly Oct. 1991 at 98–101. 1990s net losses averaged over $2 billion per year. See 14 Different Drummer (Spring 1998) at Supp. 1–4.

26. In 1990 this amounted to $327 million. The theory of these payments is that the federal government ought to contribute because it is exempt from state and local property taxation. The Service does not reckon these and many other public costs against revenues in figuring net revenues. Id.

27. See Young, Tree Slaughter: Your Taxes at Work, Wash. Post, Aug. 13, 1989, at B3; Barlow, Evolution of the NFMA, 8 Envt'l Law 539 (1978).

3. **Protecting biodiversity.** The spotted owl is an indicator of the declining health of the old-growth ecosystem, which is characterized by unparalleled biodiversity. If we want to preserve biodiversity, why don't we simply set aside bioreserves[28] instead of indirectly attempting to preserve ecosystems through endangered species protection? The ESA, perhaps mistakenly, wasn't primarily intended to preserve habitat, although habitat loss is the major cause of species extinction. Are we being fair, not only to ourselves, but to the spotted owls and snail darters of the world, when we use indicator species as legal "handles" to preserve critical ecosystems? Or does our political system, which functions to muddle through and "satisfice" conflicting demands, militate against attacking the habitat issue directly? Is the ESA only a stopgap measure while we build a political constituency for bioreserve protection?

4. **Canaries in a coal mine: the practical utility of endangered species.** The "roadblock" character of ESA §7 was important because tough marketplace confrontations would have made a looser standard politically unenforceable. Whatever the moral and philosophical arguments for species protection, it is clear that the everyday logic of the political process responds far more readily to practical economic self-interest than to abstract principle; endangered species are generally considered to reflect the latter more than the former. During the Tellico Dam oral argument Justice Powell skeptically inquired: "Apart from biological interest, which I do not challenge, *what purpose is served*, if any, by those little darters? Are they used for food?... Are they suitable for bait?"[29]

Many advocates defending strong endangered species protections therefore try to stress human utilitarian reasons for doing so.[30] In the spotted owl debates enviros emphasize the useful function played by the owl in maintaining the ecological and water-cycle balance in the Northwest forests.[31] They tell how the Pacific yew tree (Taxis brevifolia), a slow-growing endangered plant living under the ancient forest canopy, is the only known source of taxol, a promising new drug for treating ovarian and breast cancer. Protection of endangered species' habitat protects the critical sources of useful medicines and other products, some of which will remain unknown until future scientists find them, if the trees survive.

But most endangered species will not cure cancer, so utilitarian arguments must range further. One important rationale is the "indicator function" of endangered species. Like the canaries that were carried into coal mines (because the birds were sensitive to odorless coal gas, so that when they began to asphyxiate, it was time for miners to flee) endangered species can be vivid living indicators of important human concerns. Endangered birdlife revealed the danger of DDT and other pesticides to humans. In the snail darter case, when Justices, reporters, or TVA's

---

28. This is the approach taken by a bill in the 102d Congress, The National Biological Diversity Conservation and Environmental Research Act, H.R. 2082 and S. 58, authored by Rep. Gerry Studds and Sen. Daniel Moynihan.

29. Transcript of Oral Argument, April 18, 1976, pages 43–44.

30. Why do we protect endangered species even in cases in which they cannot conceivably help human prosperity?

31. D. Kelly and G. Braasch, Secrets of the Old Growth Forest 32 (1988). The owl's droppings spread critically important water-storing fungus spores to root systems throughout its habitat.

minions asked, "What good is the snail darter?" the citizens responded that it was a sensitive physical and legal barometer of the highly specific qualities of its habitat — the Southeast's last cool, clean, highly-oxygenated big river, flowing through a rich, unpolluted valley. The little fish was endangered because all other portions of its prior range, 2500 linear miles of river valley, had been destroyed by muddy reservoirs, so that this was the last such place left in the Southeast for humans as well. Although the answer seemed too complex for many questioners, the endangered species' barometer function is often an applicable rationale in endangered species cases.[32]

5. **ESA implementation.** The courts since TVA v. Hill have generally been more attentive to the Act's requirements than the national administration.[33] In most cases courts have strictly interpreted the Endangered Species Act to the detriment of powerful market forces. Oil well leases have been delayed, a major East Coast refinery was scuttled in part because of endangered species problems, western water reclamation allocations have been changed to favor species protection over industrial and municipal use, and the courts have written these opinions without reference to the "significance" of the species concerned. How strong would the courts have been in these cases had not the Supreme Court held such a strong line in a highly publicized case poising an "insignificant" species against a purported multimillion dollar project? Judicial experience to date thus offers indications that future cases will be held to a high level of species protection. The snail darter itself may be subject to continued disparagement, and ultimately did not fare well in congressional porkbarrel politics, but its precedential position seems to have secured protections to its comrades throughout the natural world. Endangered species protection seems likely to be with us for a long time.

6. **The "roadblock" statutory approach.** In terms of statutory taxonomy, what do you think of the wisdom of absolute roadblocks? The original §7 permitted no flexibility. Proof of potential jeopardy to a species raised an absolute bar to continuation of federal projects. Was this extreme? naïve? necessary? Flexibility, of course, can always be imposed upon strict roadblock statutes by taking them back to Congress for specific amendments, as ultimately occurred in the darter case. If extinction is to be decreed, perhaps it is most appropriate that this be done in the nation's most democratic forum, after debate by elected officials, considering all factors and balancing all tradeoffs. Or is the legislature *not* such an ideal forum for micro-management? Are statutory adjustments via legislative amendments not certain to be made in an atmosphere of thoughtful trusteeship? Are the protective standards of an environmental statute better entrusted to a system of flexible adjustment by courts, or administrative agencies, with a more or less formal

---

32. See The Embattled Social Utilities of the Endangered Species Act — a Noah Presumption, and a Caution against Putting Gas Masks on the Canaries in the Coal Mine, 27 Envt'l Law 845 (1997).

33. During the 1980s the Administration was unenthusiastic about endangered species protection. When he was Vice President, George Bush initially made the endangered species regulatory process a target of the anti-regulation commission he headed. Subsequently, unable to convince Congress to back away from the terms of the Act, the Administration resorted to an administrative slowdown, drastically curtailing the rate at which new species were listed and species protection programs funded in the field. In the later 1980s, however, implementation improved somewhat.

agency process for definition, investigation, application, and enforcement, subject as always to some judicial review?

**7. Endangered species in national governance.** It will be interesting to see in the controversies ahead how much we have learned from the whooping crane, the snail darter, and the spotted owl. Will endangered species be listened to as early warning devices serving to identify larger governance issues at stake, or will they be cast in the narrowed caricature of localized tradeoffs — "what do you want, owls or jobs?" When the pumps that divert water from northern California's Sacramento River to farms and cities in California's arid south threaten to eliminate the delta smelt (Hypomesus transpacificus),[34] will the question be cast as another "worthless little minnow" versus jobs and progress, or an occasion to raise sensible questions about where most of the water now goes — to massive fiscal and water subsidies for inappropriate agriculture. One such basic question: "Why should we be subsidizing California farmers to grow rice and other water-intensive crops in the middle of the desert?"

Like so much of environmental law, endangered species protections can serve as triggering opportunities for reviewing long-term necessities of rational social governance, or can be overwhelmed by the concentrated forces of short-term self-aggrandizement.[35] If the decisional processes ultimately turn on the merits rather than political ploys, endangered species will continue to play their socially useful role — as well as continuing to be prime symbols of a national environmental ethic.

### Section 3. ESA §9 AND THE "NO TAKE" PROVISION

The ESA had another lurking roadblock provision, this one potentially even more politically explosive because it potentially hits private land as well as federal agencies.

### Bruce Babbitt, Sec. of Interior v. Sweet Home Chapter of Communities for a Great Oregon
Supreme Court of the United States, June 29, 1995
115 S.Ct. 2407

STEVENS, J. The Endangered Species Act of 1973 contains a variety of protections designed to save from extinction species that the Secretary of the Interior designates as endangered or threatened....

Section 9(a)(1) of the Endangered Species Act provides the following protection for endangered species:[36]

---

34. See Gross, A Dying Fish May Force California to Break Its Water Habits, N.Y. Times, Oct. 27, 1991 A16.

35. Illustrating such obstacles, a May 1, 1990 Forest Service - Bureau of Reclamation study indicating that management of Northwest forests to protect the spotted owl could actually create more than 15,000 new jobs for former timber workers was suppressed and recalled by the Administration. Leaked copies available: Assoc. of Forest Service Employees for Environmental Ethics (AFSEEE), POB 111615, Eugene, OR 97440.

36. The Act defines the term "endangered species" to mean "any species which is in danger of extinction throughout all or a significant portion of its range other than a species of the Class Insecta determined by the Secretary to constitute a pest whose protection under the provisions of this chapter would present an overwhelming and overriding risk to man." 16 USCA §1532(6). §9 generally does not apply to plants.

...With respect to any endangered species of fish or wildlife listed pursuant to section 1533 of this title it is unlawful for any person subject to the jurisdiction of the United States to... "(B) take any such species within the United States or the territorial sea of the United States. 16 U. S. C. §1538(a)(1).

Section 3(19) of the Act defines the statutory term "take":

The term "take" means to harass, harm, pursue, hunt, shoot, wound, kill, trap, capture, or collect, or to attempt to engage in any such conduct. 16 U. S. C. §1532(19).

The Act does not further define the terms it uses to define "take." The Interior Department regulations that implement the statute, however, define the statutory term "harm":

"Harm" in the definition of "take" in the Act means an act which actually kills or injures wildlife. Such act may include significant habitat modification or degradation where it actually kills or injures wildlife by significantly impairing essential behavioral patterns, including breeding, feeding, or sheltering. 50 CFR §17.3....

Respondents in this action are small landowners, logging companies, and families dependent on the forest products industries in the Pacific Northwest and in the Southeast, and organizations that represent their interests. They brought this declaratory judgment action against petitioners...to challenge the statutory validity of the Secretary's regulation defining "harm," particularly the inclusion of habitat modification and degradation in the definition.... Their complaint alleged that application of the "harm" regulation to the red-cockaded woodpecker, an endangered species, and the northern spotted owl, a threatened species, had injured them economically...

We assume respondents have no desire to harm either the red-cockaded woodpecker or the spotted owl; they merely wish to continue logging activities that would be entirely proper if not prohibited by the ESA. On the other hand, we must assume arguendo that those activities will have the effect, even though unintended, of detrimentally changing the natural habitat of both listed species and that, as a consequence, members of those species will be killed or injured. Under respondents' view of the law, the Secretary's only means of forestalling that grave result — even when the actor knows it is certain to occur — is to use his §5 authority to purchase the lands on which the survival of the species depends....

The text of the Act provides three reasons for concluding that the Secretary's interpretation is reasonable.... The dictionary definition of the verb form of "harm" is "to cause hurt or damage; to injure." In the context of the ESA, that definition naturally encompasses habitat modification that results in actual injury or death to members of an endangered or threatened species.... The dictionary definition does not include the word "directly" or suggest in any way that only direct or willful action that leads to injury constitutes "harm." ...

Second, the broad purpose of the ESA supports the Secretary's decision to extend protection against activities that cause the precise harms Congress enacted the statute to avoid. In TVA v. Hill, 437 U. S. 153 (1978), we described the Act as "the most comprehensive legislation for the preservation of endangered species ever enacted by any nation"..., among its central purposes is "to provide a means whereby the ecosystems upon which endangered species and threatened species depend may be conserved." "The plain intent of Congress in enacting this statute," we recognized, "was to halt and reverse the trend toward species extinction, whatever the cost. This is reflected not only in the stated policies of the Act, but in literally every section of the statute." Although the §9 "take" prohibition was not at issue in *Hill*, we took note of that prohibition, placing particular emphasis on the Secretary's inclusion of habitat modification in his definition of "harm."... Respondents...ask us to invalidate the Secretary's understanding of "harm" in every circumstance, even when an actor knows that an activity, such as draining a pond, would actually result in the extinction of a listed species by destroying its habitat....

Third, the fact that Congress in 1982 authorized the Secretary to issue permits for takings that §9(a)(1)(B) would otherwise prohibit, "if such taking is incidental to, and not the purpose of, the carrying out of an otherwise lawful activity," 16 U. S. C. §1539(a)(1)(B), strongly suggests that Congress understood §9(a)(1)(B) to prohibit indirect as well as deliberate takings.... Several of the words that accompany "harm" in the §3 definition of "take," especially "harass," "pursue," "wound," and "kill," refer to actions or effects that do not require direct applications of force.... The statutory context of "harm" suggests that Congress meant that term to serve a particular function in the ESA, consistent with but distinct from the functions of the other verbs used to define "take."...

Our conclusion that the Secretary's definition of "harm" rests on a permissible construction of the ESA gains further support from the legislative history of the statute. The Committee Reports accompanying the bills that became the ESA do not specifically discuss the meaning of "harm," but they make clear that Congress intended "take" to apply broadly to cover indirect as well as purposeful actions. The Senate Report stressed that "'take' is defined...in the broadest possible manner to include every conceivable way in which a person can 'take' or attempt to 'take' any fish or wildlife." The House Report stated that "the broadest possible terms" were used to define restrictions on takings. The House Report underscored the breadth of the "take" definition by noting that it included "harassment, whether intentional or not.... When Congress has entrusted the Secretary with broad discretion, we are especially reluctant to substitute our views of wise policy for his. See *Chevron*. In this case, that reluctance accords with our conclusion, based on the text, structure, and legislative history of the ESA, that the Secretary reasonably construed the intent of Congress when he defined "harm" to include "significant habitat modification or degradation that actually kills or injures wildlife." ... Reversed.

O'CONNOR, concurring.... The challenged regulation is limited to significant habitat modification that causes actual, as opposed to hypothetical or speculative, death or injury to identifiable protected animals.... I do not find it as easy as Justice Scalia does to dismiss the notion that significant impairment of breeding injures living creatures. To raze the last remaining ground on which the piping plover currently breeds, thereby making it impossible for any piping plovers to reproduce, would obviously injure the population (causing the species' extinction in a generation). But by completely preventing breeding, it would also injure the individual living bird, in the same way that sterilizing the creature injures the individual living bird. To "injure" is, among other things, "to impair."... To make it impossible for an animal to reproduce is to impair its most essential physical functions and to render that animal, and its genetic material, biologically obsolete. This, in my view, is actual injury....

JUSTICE SCALIA, joined by REHNQUIST and THOMAS, dissenting. I think it unmistakably clear that the legislation at issue here (1) forbade the hunting and killing of endangered animals, and (2) provided federal lands and federal funds for the acquisition of private lands, to preserve the habitat of endangered animals. The Court's holding that the hunting and killing prohibition incidentally preserves habitat on private lands imposes unfairness to the point of financial ruin — not just upon the rich, but upon the simplest farmer who finds his land conscripted to national zoological use.... To "take," when applied to wild animals, means to reduce those animals, by killing or capturing, to human control..., a class of acts (not omissions) done directly and intentionally (not indirectly and by accident) to particular animals (not populations of animals).... "Harm" is merely one of 10 prohibitory words...and the other 9 fit the ordinary meaning of "take" perfectly. To "harass, pursue, hunt, shoot, wound, kill, trap, capture, or collect" are all affirmative acts...which are directed immediately and intentionally against a particular animal....

The regulation...produces a result that no legislature could reasonably be thought to have intended: A large number of routine private activities — farming, for example, ranching, road building, construction and logging — are subjected to strict-liability penalties when they fortuitously injure protected wildlife, no matter how remote the chain of causation....

[eds. — Justice Scalia, who traditionally is (justifiably) skeptical about excessive reliance upon legislative history, then dismisses the majority's use of congressional committee reports asserting that "take" should be defined in "the broadest possible manner" as an "empty flourish." He focuses on the removal of a habitat destruction ban from one bill, and land acquisition as the "as the Act's only response to habitat modification by private landowners."]

Habitat modification can constitute a "taking," but only if it results in the killing or harming of individual animals, and only if that consequence is the direct result of the modification. This means that the destruction of privately owned habitat that is essential, not for the feeding or nesting, but for the breeding, of butterflies, would not violate the Act, since it would not harm or kill any living butterfly.... Only action directed at living animals constitutes a "take."... I respectfully dissent.

## COMMENTARY AND QUESTIONS

1. **What's going on here?** Is this a seminar on statutory interpretation? An administrative law exercise deciding whether to defer to an agency's interpretive regulation? It should be remembered that *Sweet Home* reflects one pitched battle in the ongoing war between, on one hand, Western Wise Use local sovereignists, resource exploitation corporations, and private property rights activists, and on the other hand the federal government, environmental preservationists, and others who have found that endangered species law often provides the only effective forum for obtaining an overall public accounting of challenged activities. The defenders won this round, but Justice O'Connor noted, "Congress may, of course, see fit to revisit this issue. And nothing the Court says today prevents the agency itself from narrowing the scope of its regulation at a later date."

A fervent political backlash was inevitable. The potential consequences of the *Sweet Home* decision are dramatic. Land development, which traditionally has been one of the most unregulated, politically-charged economic ventures, can come under federal government scrutiny forcing intense review of the particular facts of a development site and plan, subject to heavy civil and criminal penalties. The definition of "harm" is subjective and potentially extremely broadranging, and property that is determined important to endangered species may in effect be frozen.

2. **Statutory interpretation games.** The question is about the meaning of one of ten words: the meaning of "harm" in the statutory definition of "take" as to "harass, harm, pursue, hunt, shoot, wound, kill, trap, capture, or collect." Is this another example of legislative legerdemain — "harm," an environmentally protective phrase, being slipped into a statute by indirection, in this case on the Senate floor after "habitat destruction" had been stricken from the bill in committee? Or is it fairly within the central mandate of the Act?

And what of conflicting canons of interpretation? *Noscitur a sociis* is one canon, which the majority used to establish an interpretive context — a word "gathers meaning from the words around it." 367 U. S. 303, 307 (1961). On the other hand, Sweet Home's narrow-interpretationists had in mind the stricter *ejusdem generis* — "a word should be defined like the others in the same series, without independent meaning." Given the way lawyers in legislatures write statutes, which canonic interpretation should govern?

3. **Foreseeability and proximate cause.** In order to be subject to the Act's criminal penalties or the more severe of its civil penalties, one must "knowingly violate" the Act or its implementing regulations. 16 USCA §1540(a)(1),(b)(1). Congress added "knowingly" in place of "willfully" in 1978 to make "criminal violations of the act a general rather than a specific intent crime." As noted in Chapter 19 on environmental crimes, the courts have imputed scienter requirements to criminal statutes that impose sanctions without expressly requiring scienter. The *Sweet Home* majority said that they "do not agree with the dissent that the regulation covers results that are not 'even foreseeable...no matter how long the chain of causality between modification and injury.' Respondents have suggested no reason why either the 'knowingly violates' or the 'otherwise violates' provision of the statute — or the 'harm' regulation itself — should not be read to incorporate ordinary requirements of proximate causation and foreseeability." Given this constraint, how far in practice can the regulatory definition stretch to burden private parties?

4. **Administrative law — *Chevron*.** The *Sweet Home* majority and dissenting opinions treat the *Chevron* precedent differently. The majority said that "our conclusions that Congress did not unambiguously manifest its intent to adopt respondents' view, and that the Secretary's interpretation is reasonable, suffice to decide this case. *Chevron.* The latitude the ESA gives the Secretary in enforcing the statute, together with the degree of regulatory expertise necessary to its enforcement, establishes that we owe some degree of deference to the Secretary's reasonable interpretation," citing Breyer, Judicial Review of Questions of Law and Policy, 38 Admin. L. Rev. 363, 373 (1986). In dissent, on the other hand, Justice Scalia who has been a consistent supporter of broad *Chevron* deference to agencies, argued that here the Secretary's decision need not be deferred to because "the

regulation...dispense[s] with a [necessary] proximate-cause requirement.... This Court...may not uphold a regulation by adding to it even the most reasonable of elements it does not contain." Justice Scalia implied that he could ignore *Chevron* deference because he would find either that the agency interpretation was unreasonable or that it violated an express congressional mandate. Coupled with *Chevron* deference, however, the agency's interpretation created a strong statutory roadblock.

## B. THE ENDANGERED SPECIES ACT AND PRESSURES FOR FLEXIBILITY COMPROMISES

### Section 1. A RANGE OF FLEXIBILITY DEVICES

Thus, as upheld by the Supreme Court, both §7 and §9 of the ESA on their original terms created stark statutory roadblock prohibitions. This sets up a classic dilemma of democratic process. Any stark rule is likely to be a crude blunt instrument that in many circumstances will fall short of perfect rationality, yet without the strength of such a strict clear rule the pressures of marketplace politics will often neutralize the non-market based civic values that the law seeks to protect.

What would happen, for example, if the statutory language had merely said that "protection of endangered species must be strongly weighed" in agency dredging or dambuilding projects, in developers' plans to drain wetlands to build upscale subdivisions, or in agency decisions to grant mining, clearcutting, or grazing permits in endangered species habitats? Given the hard realities of marketplace politics within regulatory agency bureaucracies — which necessitated the roadblock approach in the first place — not only would such a discretionary legal standard invite superficial agency and judicial balancing of species protection, but the prospect of citizen enforcement lawsuits would be effectively neutralized by the hard-to-litigate, indeterminate standard as well.

Strict rules, however, reasonably lead to calls for flexibility exemption procedures, often backed by examples of extreme statutory overkill. Should the law be enforced as written if a whole city's water system will be preempted by an endangered spider? Should a hospital being built to serve a poor community be stopped because it might endanger a listed species of mouse? Should an expensive 90% rollback of auto emissions be required for cars in Idaho where the air is unpolluted? Should a substance which may cause one in a billion to die of cancer be banned from foods while far more dangerous noncarcinogenic additives are tolerated?

Sometimes a rule must be adhered to in particular hard cases so as not to undermine the general principle.[37] More often it is not truly an either-or choice. If the legal standard is taken seriously, not considered easily-avoidable, there are almost always feasible accommodations of location, timing, design, technology,

---

37. A prosaic example from the ESA are the "look-alike" import bans, where a non-endangered species' fur pelt is excluded from the U.S. on the ground that it so resembles a listed endangered species that customs enforcement and market deterrence would be hindered by allowing its entry and sale. 50 C.F.R. 17.50-.52.

and the like which can accommodate both general initiatives (though often not on the agency or private entrepreneur's own desired terms, nor without added costs in planning and implementation). In cases where a private firm is told to go elsewhere — as in an Alabama coastal dune site where attempts to halt expensive condos were argued in terms of threats to a beach mouse rather than to human health, safety, and property damage[38] — strict rules protecting relatively new civic values understandably attract all the artillery of constitutional regulatory takings challenges, and the national anti-regulatory campaign that accompanies it.

In many situations there clearly must be some flexibility mechanisms in order to prevent one particular civic value from unreasonable preemption of other socially-important enterprises. The trick is how to set a standard for when to allow balancing, who is to do it, and how a process can be designed so as to avoid undercutting the civic principle. Balancing procedures that would operate rationally in the setting of a seminar room or the open air of a public forum are likely to operate quite differently in the less visible, heavily-lobbied daily political reality of agency process.

The realities of legal process have led to a variety of explicit and implicit flexibility mechanisms that may or may not be applied to strict roadblock standards, each embodying the perils and potentialities of variances from a clear rule. Balancing accommodations can be made —

- by private ordering: When private parties — prompted by idealism, business judgment, public or media pressure, or apprehension about the costs of contesting a civic standard—decide to accept it, they are often able to construct practical and beneficial accommodations to eliminate the conflict.

- by agency conflict-resolving procedures: Interior, for example, has successfully resolved hundreds of potential conflicts through formal or informal ESA§7 interagency "consultation" processes,[39] pushing project agencies to alter harmful elements of their plans to adjust to the needs of species protection; there have been hundreds of similar negotiations with private parties under §9.

- by administrative interpretations of legal terms or facts: Agencies can in practice make or break a statute in the vast number of decisions that are made in the daily process of implementation — including how they define the terms of a statute or regulation, like "harm" in Sweet Home, or by findings of fact that acknowledge, or evade, critical elements of the statutory mandate. The degree of transparency of the internal agency process can make a great difference in outcomes.

- by judicial interpretations of legal terms or facts: As with agency decisions, the role of courts in enforcement actions and judicial review can vary the strictness given to a roadblock. In the Tellico Dam case Judges

---

38. Fort Morgan Civic Assoc. v. Babbitt, Civ. No. 97-00773 (D.D.C., filed May 20, 1997, subsequently transferred to D. Ala.).

39. The §7 roadblock provision contained a requirement for endangered species "consultation" between Interior and other agencies. After the snail darter injunction was ordered by the Supreme Court, the consultation process developed quickly as a serious part of federal agency practice, now codified in 16 U.S.C.A. §1536(a)-(d).

Rehnquist and Powelll were clearly ready to take on the legislative balancing act themselves. Courts grants or denials of standing, reviewability, deference, narrow scope of review, and equitable relief can operate *sub rosa* to strengthen or weaken roadblocks.

- *by violation or non-feasance that is not challenged:* In many cases the logistics and politics of particular cases are such that neither an agency nor a citizen enforcement action is likely to be brought. Thus the practical setting, or else "prosecutorial discretion" not to enforce, in effect reflect a rough balancing choice on whether the roadblock will be applied.

- *by legislative amendments that eliminate the roadblock provision:* Faced with roadblocks, affected interests often seek to repeal the obstruction. Thus numerous environmental provisions that blocked industry practices, including wetlands and endangered species protections, were targeted for repeal in the 104th Congress, though unsuccessfully. Marketplace lobbying in the legislatures and agency rulemaking likewise try to rescind the procedures that implement a roadblock (as in Chapter Seven's §318, selectively eliminating citizen enforcement of the ESA and forestry laws), or to override laws as applied to particular cases (as ultimately in the appropriations rider repealing the ESA insofar as it prevented TVA from building the Tellico Dam).

- *by legislative amendments that incorporate more or less rigorous balancing mechanisms:* As noted below, the ESA offers prime examples, in the 1978 §7 God Committee exemption amendments, and the 1982 "incidental take" amendments to §9. Private property interests further pushed campaigns at the end of the 1990s to expand the incidental take exemptions to incorporate substantial "habitat conservation plan" bargaining into ESA enforcement, allowing moderate harms to endangered species. If balancing is consigned to agency discretion, the species protection process is likely to be narrowed if not undercut.

In each and every case, of course, the rigor of the balance can vary widely, and opportunities for fudging in each direction are constantly presented. For this reason no flexibility mechanism can be meaningfully evaluated without realistic consideration of its political context.

## Section 2. THE ESA §7 GOD COMMITTEE AMENDMENTS

After the Tellico Dam case, the 1978 ESA amendments brought statutory flexibility into §7.[40] The extraordinary Endangered Species Committee (the "God Committee" or "God Squad"), comprised of the Administrators of EPA and NOAA, the Chair of the Council of Economic Advisors, a state representative, and the Secretaries of Army, Agriculture, and Interior, can permit species extinctions:

§1536 (h) ...The Committee shall grant an exemption...if, by a vote of not less than five of its [seven] members voting in person —

(A) it determines on the record [after a full hearing] that —

(i)    there are no reasonable and prudent alternatives to the agency action;

---

40. See 16 U.S.C.A. §1536 (e)-(o).

(ii) the benefits of such action clearly outweigh the benefits of alternative courses of action consistent with conserving the species or its critical habitat, and such action is in the public interest;

(iii) the action is of regional or national significance; and

(iv) neither the federal agency concerned nor the exemption applicant made [, with notice of the species,] any irreversible or irretrievable commitment of resources; and

(B) it establishes such reasonable mitigation and enhancement measures, including, but not limited to, live propagation, transplantation, and habitat acquisition and improvement, as are necessary and appropriate to minimize the adverse effects of the agency action upon the endangered species, threatened species, or critical habitat concerned.


### COMMENTARY AND QUESTIONS

1. **Evaluating the amendment of the §7 roadblock.** Does this amendment mean that the original roadblock in §7 was misguided? Is the amendment ultimately a tragic watering-down of the ESA? Or is it a consolidation of the roadblock's strengths? Is it likely that the stringencies of the God Committee amendments would have been achievable legislatively if there had never been a roadblock in the original 1973 act, establishing a strong legal beachhead against federal projects that threaten extinction? The statute's political vulnerability, given the belittling press coverage of the snail darter case, meant that the whole statute might have been repealed if the statute had *not* received such a flexibility mechanism in 1978. Instead it may be that the God Committee procedure secured §7's protections subject to an exemption process so rigorous that agencies have only rarely been willing to undertake the difficulties of obtaining one. The net result is more than a pragmatic compromise. It leaves the United States with the strongest enforceable legal provisions protecting endangered species that exist anywhere today.

2. **The God Committee in practice.** In the Carter Administration two dam cases went to the God Committee, Tellico and the Greyrocks Dam in North Dakota which threatened the flyway resting areas of the whooping crane. The Committee unanimously refused an exemption on Tellico, and granted an exemption on Greyrocks conditioned on river-flow management rules protecting the cranes.[41]

On petition by the Bureau of Land Management, the Committee during the Bush Administration exempted 13 timber sales in spotted owl habitat from the ESA, subject to some mitigation and enhancement measures to be undertaken by the BLM. The God Committee decision did not immediately lead to reopened timber cutting in the owl's prime habitat because timber sales were still under a variety of injunctions under other statutes, and serious questions were raised about the vote. The political pressures of the Committee process were revealed in Portland Audubon Society v. Endangered Species Committee, 984 F.2d 1534 (9th Cir. 1992).[42]

---

41. Decision of Federal Endangered Species Committee, Jan. 23, 1979.

42. For example, one Cabinet official who had voted for the exemption commented that he had felt politically obliged by White House pressure to override ESA protections, although the elements of the exemption had not in his judgment been met.

The fact that so few cases have been brought to the Committee raises question whether the elements of the flexibility mechanism are too inflexible to be of practical use, or whether the law is perceived as sufficiently strong that accommodations are sought instead in compliance or in less demanding forms of roadblock evasion.

**3. Securing a balance: avoiding sunk cost tactics.** Mechanisms for statutory balancing like the God Committee can easily become politicized tactical battlegrounds. One congressional response to this problem was the ESA §7(d) amendment, reflected in the fourth exemption test above. With the *Tellico Dam* and a host of other major cases, especially those dealing with public works projects like Chapter Seven's *Overton Park* case, defendants have tried to accelerate construction in the face of potential statutory constraints, pouring so much concrete or cutting so many trees before a citizen group can finally get to a court hearing that they can then argue that the balance now tips decisively in their favor, or that species preservation and statutory compliance have regrettably become moot. ESA §7(d) was amended to prevent just such disingenuity —

> §1536(d) After initiation of consultation...the Federal agency and the permit or license applicant shall not make any irreversible or irretrievable commitment of resources with respect to...agency action which has the effect of foreclosing the formulation or implementation of any reasonable or prudent alternative measures....

This provision is intended to undercut the sunk cost strategy, and to that extent protect the bona fides of the balancing process. It is not well understood, however. See Kopf, Steamrolling §7(d) of the ESA: How Sunk Costs Undermine Environmental Regulations, 23 B.C. Envt'l Aff. L.Rev. 393 (1996), and Houck, The "Institutionalization of Caution" under §7 of the Endangered Species Act: What Do You Do When You Don't Know? 12 ELR 15001 (1982).

### Section 3. ESA §10 "INCIDENTAL TAKE" EXEMPTIONS TO THE §9 PROHIBITION

As part of the reaction to the marketplace caricature of the snail darter case as proof of the ESA's irrational extremism, Congress was pushed to pass further exemption balance mechanisms to shield certain private propertyowners from the §9 roadblock. The 1982 amendments created a new §10[43] providing that:

> §1539(a)(1). The Secretary may permit, under such terms and conditions as he shall prescribe —
>
> (B) any taking otherwise prohibited by §9 if such taking is incidental to, and not the purpose of, the carrying out of an otherwise lawful activity.
>
> (2)(A) No permit may be issued by the Secretary authorizing any taking referred to in paragraph (1)(B) unless the applicant therefor submits to the Secretary a conservation plan [universally referred to as an "HCP": habitat conservation plan] that specifies —
>
> (i)   the impact which will likely result from such taking;

---

43. Pub. L. 95-632 (1982). The amendments also created a simpler incidental take exemption process for federal agencies, who can apply for and receive an immunity letter without doing a conservation plan. §1536(b)(4)(B-C).

(ii) what steps the applicant will take to minimize and mitigate such impacts, and the funding that will be available to implement such steps;

(iii) what alternative actions to such taking the applicant considered and the reasons why such alternatives are not being utilized; and

(iv) such other measures that the Secretary may require as being necessary or appropriate for purposes of the plan.

(B) If the Secretary finds, after opportunity for public comment, with respect to a permit application and the related conservation plan that —

(i) the taking will be incidental;

(ii) the applicant will, to the maximum extent practicable, minimize and mitigate the impacts of such taking;

(iii) the applicant will ensure that adequate funding for the plan will be provided;

(iv) the taking will not appreciably reduce the likelihood of the survival and recovery of the species in the wild; and

(v) the measures, if any, required under subparagraph (A)(iv) will be met; and he has received such other assurances as he may require that the plan will be implemented, the Secretary shall issue the permit. The permit *shall* contain such terms and conditions as the Secretary deems necessary or appropriate to carry out the purposes of this paragraph....

This incidental take exemption provision theoretically allows the Secretary to modify unnecessary burdens placed on propertyowners by §9, but it also reflects many of the potential risks that lie in retrenchments from roadblocks. Note the elements that may be quite permissive. Virtually all harm to species from habitat destruction is "incidental," because virtually no market projects set out purposefully to harm species. The standard that impacts on species must be minimized "to the maximum extent practicable" could be interpreted to allow the developer's own practicalities to dominate the balance. The element requiring that "the taking...not appreciably reduce the likelihood of survival and recovery" retreats from the statutory goal of improving the chances for recovery and uses "not appreciably," an indeterminate measure. Ultimately the rationality of such balances depends completely upon the Secretary. If he or she wishes to hold applicants to high standards for HCPs, strict terms for maximum mitigations, and is stringent in setting "such other measures that the Secretary may require as being necessary and appropriate," then the balance is likely to be sufficiently protective of species. If an Administration doesn't like the Act, however, the process in practice can eviscerate §9. The decisions, moreover, are effectively immune from citizen suits, so the amendment rolls the law back to the old bi-polar system where the public interest depends totally upon bureaucratic enforcement.[44]

44. The elements of the exemption are determined by relatively unreviewable agency discretion, HCPs are designed to exclude citizen enforceability (the FWS itself expressly proposes that the public not be granted the status of 3d party beneficiaries; see HCP Handbook App. 9 Template Agreement §14.8.), and the most citizens can do is try to prove that particular exemption shortcomings "jeopardize the existence" of endangered species, a tough burden. The legal opponents are likewise tough: The propertyowners who take advantage of §10 are unlikely to be the little guys who can least bear the burdens of ESA restrictions and whose limited property holdings have limited impacts. It takes a lot of time, money, biologists, and lawyers to negotiate a §10 exemption, and those who do so will fight to defend their permits.

For a decade after the "incidental take" amendments to the §9 roadblock, surprisingly few permits were granted — less than 20 from 1982 to 1994 — but beginning in 1993 the Clinton Administration dramatically accelerated the volume of §10 HCP exemptions, with more than 450 approved in the following five years and 200 pending. Prior to 1996, most of the HCPs which were approved covered areas of less than 1,000 acres. In pending §10 applications after 1996, 25 exceeded 10,000 acres in size, 25 exceeded 100,000 acres, and 18 exceeded 500,000 acres. The volume and character of permits means that it is extremely difficult to gauge how rationally the balancing process works in practice.[45] Some HCPs and §10 permits appear to be biologically sophisticated and carefully balanced to protect the species while accommodating human uses.[46] Others appear to be hapless political capitulations.[47]

> A group of scientists funded by the National Science Foundation released the results of the first comprehensive study of HCPs [in late 1997].... Among the more disturbing findings of the study are these: over three-quarters of the plans lacked such basic information as the population size of species and whether it was growing or shrinking; a third of the plans did not know the life spans of the species at issue; over half did not have adequate monitoring, without which, of course, there is no way to tell whether the measures are working or not; of the 44 plans studied in depth, many prescribed mitigation measures that would do more harm than good. Patrick Parenteau, letter to New England Senators, March 3, 1998.

Nevertheless a number of committed environmental leaders have urged further amendments to the ESA. Some wish to strengthen protections by encouraging multi-species and ecosystem-wide protections rather than species-by-species regulation.[48] Ecosystem and biodiversity concepts[49] are far more realistic measures of

45. See Hood, Frayed Safety Nets: Conservation Planning under the ESA (1998); Symposium on HCPs, 27 Envt'l law 755-1323 (1997). A number of studies have concluded that because of political pressures and other constraints, the federal agencies with jurisdiction over endangered species, Interior's Fish and Wildlife Service and Commerce's National Oceanic and Atmospheric Administration, are under-protecting species in their recovery planning under the ESA. Tear et al., Status and Prospects for Success of the Endangered Species Act: A Look at Recovery Plans, Science, November 1993 at 976. Cf. Friends of Endangered Species v. Jantzen, 760 F.2d 976 (9th Cir. 1985) (court upholds §10 permit against challenge). This was the case of California's Mission Blue butterfly, an interesting confrontation where an incidental take permit was issued after extensive biological study and mitigation, and was the model for subsequent HCP regulations. The court upheld the HCP and permit against challenge, though local citizens remain bitterly critical.

46. The authors have been impressed, for instance, by the Atlantic Coast Piping Plover HCP and Massachusetts' three-year experimental permit allowing restricted dune buggy use of the plover's beach habitat.

47. HCPs and permits allowing large timber companies to cut down nest trees of red-cockaded woodpeckers after waiting 60 days for them to find alternative homes seem to verge on the cynical.

48. This idea has generic rationality: "By overemphasizing the role of single chemicals, and single media in pollution policy, and of single species in land management policy, we underestimate the interactive effects of chemicals, the cross-media effects of emissions, and the interdependence of habitats." Chertow & Esty, Environmental Policy: The Next Generation, Issues in Sci. & Techn., Fall 1997 at 74. The ecosystem proposals, however, run the practical risk of magnifying what already are very difficult scientific requirements for proposing and defending species protections. Strengthening amendments in any event face daunting opposition.

49. "Biodiversity" as a regulatory concept can be difficult to define. It means something more than merely having larger numbers of species: if a road is cut through a wilderness rainforest or tundra, it may actually *increase* the net number of species, but extirpate unique native indicator species. Conservation biologists prefer a concept of "native biodiversity" or "continuum biodiversity" to capture the goal of diverse natural communities evolving as much as possible without anthropogenic extirpations and disturbances, but the regulatory complexities that would be required have militated against legislative initiatives in that direction. See D. Perlman & G. Adelson, Biodiversity: Exploring Values and Priorities in Conservation (1997).

natural habitat qualities than are single-species indicators, but their subtleties make them less feasible as legal concepts. Other environmentalists, traumatized by the close call the ESA barely survived in the 104th Congress, and noting that Interior is barely enforcing the politically explosive "take" prohibitions, urge further preemptive modification of the strictness of §9. Given the dramatic goals of the ESA and the widespread human-based character of species endangerment, it is inevitable that major political conflicts arise in ESA enforcement. It is probably equally inevitable that some agency officials will tend to avoid strong enforcement of their statutory mandate in order to avoid exacerbating the political context. Is this a problem or a solution?

COMMENTARY AND QUESTIONS

1. **The political context.** Especially after the *Sweet Home* decision, above at page 694, loud cries were increasingly heard for a rolling-back of the ESA's stringencies. Every five years the ESA must go to Congress for reauthorization, which virtually guarantees its awkward status as a political football.[50] Is the Endangered Species Act so much more embattled than other federal environmental statutes? With only occasional exceptions, the marketplace has generally come to accept the validity and permanence of pollution and toxics statutes. Only the ESA is still regularly subjected to plenary denunciations on the floor of Congress; only the ESA faces serious non-reauthorization initiatives; only the ESA was hit by a sweeping one-year listing moratorium;[51] it was the spotted owl that got hit by the so-called Timber Salvage rider cynically attached to the Oklahoma bombing relief bill;[52] it is the ESA that has sustained amendments undermining its fundamental goal, species recovery; and if things go awry it is the ESA that could be undercut instead of reinforced by the HCP strategy.

Why is it that the Endangered Species Act suffers from this particular precariousness? Pollution and toxics statutes have come to be accepted by agencies and industry, primarily because their direct human utility is intrinsically obvious to public opinion. The societal rationale for endangered species conservation, on the other hand, is generally characterized in terms of philosophy, emotions, and aesthetics — often regarded as heartfelt but not so substantially significant when weighed against the "practical" world of production, payrolls, and profits.

The ESA would clearly gain political strength if it were publicly recognized to fulfill significant *utilitarian* functions as well. Utility arguments can made far beyond

---

50. From 1992-98 the Act was not reauthorized, surviving on one-year continuing resolutions.

51. Senator Kay Bailey Hutchinson, R-TX, fronted the successful marketplace campaign for an ESA moratorium, Pub. L. 104-6. Emergency Supplemental Appropriations and Rescissions for the Department of Defense to Preserve and Enhance Military Readiness Act of 1995..., Pub. L. 104-6, ch. 4, 109 Stat 73, 86 (1995).

52. See Chapter Seven discussion. Pub. L. 104-19, §2001 (1995) The same tactic was narrowly avoided when Rep. Richard Pombo, R-CA, attempted to attach a rider to a Northwest flood relief bill exempting thousands of water-related public works nationwide from the ESA. H.R. 478 105th Cong. (1997); 143 Cong. Rec. H2283-H2313.

the physical or medicinal use of individual species.[53] The overwhelmingly dominant cause of endangered species is not hunting or trapping or market harvesting — rather it is the alteration and destruction of habitat. Because of the logic of this causation, endangered species often play a role serving human utility by identifying and triggering protections for habitat areas and conditions that hold threatened human values as well.

The "canary in the coal mine" indicator role is not necessarily the primary nor an omnipresent function of the ESA, but it deserves recognition as a tangible and systemically important function lying within the logic of endangered species protection generally, that is at least potentially relevant in every case. The ESA's provisions are likely to wax or wane in its current political gauntlets depending on how the various utilities of species protection are or are not publicly perceived.

2. **"No surprises" and other amendments.** In the limbo between reauthorizations, coalitions formed for and against further HCP amendments of the ESA, echoing the perennial question of how the strict terms of a roadblock should be tempered. The Environmental Defense Fund led the initiative, advocating a legislative codification of Interior's "no surprises" and other policies for expanding §10 exemptions.[54] "No surprises" agreements provide landowners who get a §10 permit that upon completion of an HCP they will face no further obligations toward any covered species. If approved actions turn out to harm species, the applicant will face no further restrictions, and any necessary adjustments will be paid for by the agency.[55]

Environmental opponents argue that such amendments amount to preemptive capitulation to political threats:

> This is a reckless policy based on bad science, bad logic, and bad policy,... a recovery strategy that is doomed to fail.... Codifying "no surprises" will mean "no recovery" for many species. Whatever certainty "no surprises" may give to some developers, i.e., those lucky enough to cut their deals early, it will almost certainly take away from others when the plans fail, individually and in the aggregate, to achieve recovery and the covered species continue to decline, to be joined perhaps by other species dependent on the same shrinking habitat base.... A more effective way to address landowner concerns is to provide meaningful economic incentives for habitat conservation...including

---

53. "Traditionally, endangered species protection is not viewed as pollution control. It is, however, in a larger sense, exactly that. Endangered species are useful, though incomplete, indicators of the health of their ecosystems and of the earth we share. While the best indicators may often be mollusks, plants, and lower life forms, the decline of the bald eagle from the effects of chlorinated hydrocarbons is a good indication of the impact of those chemicals on human life. As water quality becomes inadequate to protect the delta smelt, it will also become inadequate for human uses." Oliver A. Houck, Why do we Protect Endangered Species, and What Does That Say About Whether Restrictions on Private Property to Protect Them Constitute "Takings"?, 80 Iowa L. Rev. 297, 327–328 (1995).

54. See Wilcove, et al., Rebuilding the Ark, Toward a More Effective Endangered Species Act for Private Land (1996).

55. Other modifications include Candidate Conservation Agreements ("CCAs") by which the agency agrees not to list a listable species so long as certain promises are made (thereby leaving implementation up to the agency and blocking potential citizen enforcement); "safe harbors," when landowners agree to improve habitat quality and the agency guarantees that there will be no added obligations if other species are attracted to the new habitat, and no liability if the habitat is later returned back to a minimum baseline; and "low-effect" HCPs, like EAs under NEPA are determined by the agency to require lesser levels of protection.

tax credits and financial and technical assistance. Parenteau, letter to New Eng. Senators, Mar. 3, 1998.

> The statute is moving away from a system of regulation by citizen enforcement toward a system of largely closed-door negotiations between agencies and regulated interests, with little meaningful public involvement.... HCP initiatives have seriously weakened safeguards for listed species that were a key feature of the 1982 amendments. John Kostyack, Surprise, Envt'l Forum, March 1998 at 19.

3. **Anti-ESA agitation, "Noah's Choice," and the future of the ESA.** An impressive marketplace campaign to modify the protections of the ESA was organized through the 1990s,[56] moving at low levels of "wise use" rhetoric as well as through academic think tanks — from discredited but incessant stories of how protections for kangaroo rats resulted in propertyowners' inability to save their homes from wildfires, to sophisticated arguments about "bad science" imprecisions in ESA enforcement.

Part of the anti-ESA campaign was a beautifully-written 1995 book, Noah's Choice,[57] ostensibly seeking to set out a rational overall policy assessment of the Act. The book argued that we get very limited tangible benefits from the ESA,[58] and noted "perverse incentives" the Act creates for private property interests to subvert its protections. The authors' main argument, as the book's title indicates, is that endangered species pose an inescapable loaded choice: If we as a society want to save species for whatever their charms, we have to ratchet back living standards and pay trillions of dollars; otherwise we must regretfully override endangered species according to whatever course of action is dictated by the marketplace.

> It is easy to say that society should extract money from developers and give it to black-capped vireos that need protection. But it is not possible to do this and simultaneously ensure that good housing is available and affordable to everyone. Or good health care, for that matter, or a good education. Embracing the goal of saving biodiversity and the goals of providing housing, health care, and education, as well as the many other goals we have taken up during the past two hundred years, makes our choices difficult.... To borrow from Freud, what do we humans want? Noah's Choice at 26, 213.

The book, in other words, was seductively written to frame a version of the classic false tradeoff — the allegedly unavoidable all-or-nothing choice between ecology and economics.[59]

---

56. NESARC, the Nat'l End. Species Reform Council, a coalition of anti-ESA industries, many of whom had participated in the 104th Congress's anti-regulatory jihad, was formed to coordinate a broad front initiative in the ongoing battles of ESA reauthorization.

57. Charles Mann and Mark Plummer, Noah's Choice: The Future of Endangered Species (1995). See critical discussion in Gasmasks on the Canaries, 27 Envt'l Law 845, 862-65 (1997).

58. "Mann and Plummer's case against the Act is based...on anecdotes and cursory evaluation of evidence of the Act's benefits.... Their mission is accomplished once they reach the conclusion that the Act has no benefits." Rachlinski, Noah by the Numbers: an Empirical Evaluation of the Endangered Species Act, Book Review, 82 Cornell L.R. 356, 357, 359, 365 (1997). Rachlinski undertakes an extended statistical analysis, essentially refuting the book's premise. 82 Cornell L.R. at 379-386.

59. Doubts about the book's integrity come from its use of history, including the Tellico case, as well as its authors' linkages to the ESA's industrial opposition. In the book's Chapter 6, "The Awful Beast is Back," the authors frame the snail darter as a prime example of diseconomic effects of the Act, and ignore the case's net economic utilities, although they had been briefed at length on the economic data from the God Committee review.

The measure of the ESA as a roadblock with bypasses will be taken in continuing debates over reauthorization. The degree to which full scientific and economic merits are brought to bear in these debates will be critical to the Act's future.

## C. THE DELANEY CLAUSE AS A CONTRASTING EXAMPLE OF THE ROADBLOCK APPROACH

As seen in the ESA's protections for endangered species, the relative inflexibility of stark statutory roadblocks can be both an asset and a liability for effective enforcement of national policy. The following case was an historical milepost in the national debates about risk assessment, the practical virtues of a clear unambiguous draconian statutory standard, and political distrust of agencies' ability to stand up to regulated interests.

### Kathleen Les et al. v. William K. Reilly
United States Court of Appeals for the Ninth Circuit, 1992
968 F.2d 985

SCHROEDER, C.J. Petitioners [including the environmental groups NRDC and Public Citizen] challenge the final order...of the Environmental Protection Agency permitting the use of four pesticides as food additives...on the ground that it violates the provisions of the Delaney clause, 21 U.S.C. §348(c)(3), which prohibits the use of any food additive that is found to induce cancer.... In 1988, the EPA found these pesticides to be carcinogens. Notwithstanding the Delaney clause, the EPA refused to revoke [their registrations], reasoning that, although the chemicals posed a measurable risk of causing cancer, that risk was *de minimis.*

We set aside the EPA's order because we agree with the petitioners that the language of the Delaney clause, its history and purpose all reflect that Congress intended the EPA to prohibit all additives that are carcinogens, regardless of the degree of risk involved.

The Federal Food, Drug, and Cosmetic Act (FFDCA), 21 U.S.C. §§301-394 , is designed to ensure the safety of the food we eat.... The Delaney clause, FFDCA §409, prescribes that —

21 U.S.C. §348(c)(3). No additive shall be deemed to be safe if it is found to induce cancer when ingested by man or animal, or if it is found, after tests which are appropriate for the evaluation of the safety of food additives, to induce cancer in man or animal....

The FFDCA also contains special provisions which regulate the occurrence of pesticide residues on raw agricultural commodities.... When a tolerance or an exemption has been established for use of a pesticide on a raw agricultural commodity, the FFDCA allows for the "flow-through" of such pesticide residue to processed foods, even when the pesticide may be a carcinogen. This flow- through is allowed, however, only to the extent that the concentration of the pesticide in the processed food does not exceed the concentration allowed in the raw food.... It is undisputed that the EPA regulations at issue in this case allow for the concentration of cancer-causing pesticides during processing to levels in excess of those permitted in the raw foods....

In October 1988 when the EPA published a list of substances, including these pesticides, that were found to induce cancer,...EPA simultaneously announced a new interpretation of the Delaney clause: the EPA proposed to permit concentrations of cancer-causing pesticide residues greater than that tolerated for raw foods so long as the particular substances posed only a *"de minimis"* risk of actually causing cancer. 53 Fed. Reg. at 41,110.... The Agency announced that it would not immediately revoke its previous regulations authorizing use of these substances as food additives....

The issue before us is whether the EPA has violated the Delaney clause by permitting the use of carcinogenic food additives which it finds to present only a *de minimis* or negligible risk of causing cancer. The Agency acknowledges that its interpretation of the law is a new and changed one.... The EPA also acknowledges that the language of the statute itself appears, at first glance, to be clear on its face....

The language is clear and mandatory. The Delaney clause provides that no additive shall be deemed safe if it induces cancer. The EPA states in its final order that appropriate tests have established that the pesticides at issue here induce cancer in humans or animals. 56 Fed. Reg. at 7774–75. The statute provides that once the finding of carcinogenicity is made, the EPA has no discretion....

The legislative history, too, reflects that Congress intended the very rigidity that the language it chose commands. The food additive Delaney clause was enacted in response to increasing public concern about cancer.... The scientific witnesses who testified before Congress stressed that because current scientific techniques could not determine a safe level for carcinogens, all carcinogens should be prohibited....

EPA argues that a *de minimis* exception to the Delaney clause is necessary in order to bring about a more sensible application of the regulatory scheme. It relies particularly on a recent study suggesting that the criterion of concentration level in processed foods may bear little or no relation to actual risk of cancer, and that some pesticides might be barred by rigid enforcement of the Delaney clause while others, with greater cancer-causing risk, may be permitted through the flow-through provisions because they do not concentrate in processed foods. See National Academy of Sciences, Regulating Pesticides in Food: The Delaney Paradox (1987).[60] The EPA in effect asks us to approve what it deems to be a more enlightened system than that which Congress established.... Revising the existing statutory scheme, however, is neither our function nor the function of the EPA. There are currently bills pending before the House and the Senate which would amend the food additive provision to allow the Secretary to establish tolerance levels for carcinogens, including pesticide residues in processed foods, which impose a negligible risk. H.R. 2342, 102d Cong., 1st Sess. (1991); S. 1074, 102d Cong., 1st Sess. (1991). If there is to be a change, it is for Congress to direct.

---

Les v. Reilly stimulated renewed debate about the "absolutism" of the Delaney clause, which ultimately produced congressional exemptions. The first excerpt below speaks for the EPA, the second for the NRDC.

---

60. See also Merrill, FDA's Implementation of the Delaney Clause: Repudiation of Congressional Choice or Reasoned Adaptation to Scientific Progress?, 5 Yale J. on Reg. 1, 87 (1988) (concluding that the Delaney clause is both unambiguous and unwise: "at once an explicit and imprudent expression of legislative will").

## Victor J. Kimm, The Delaney Clause Dilemma[61]
### EPA Journal, 39–41 (Jan. 1993)

Les v. Really has unfortunate implications for pesticide decision-making and food-safety policy in the United States.... EPA believes the court's recent [strict] interpretation of the Delaney clause could adversely affect the nation's food supply by making it difficult for farmers to use the safest pesticides on their crops.

The court acknowledged that EPA's interpretation of the FFDCA's statutory structure — namely its policy of applying a negligible risk standard across the board to all potentially carcinogenic pesticides — might produce a more "enlightened" scheme than does a literal interpretation of the Delaney clause...[but its] interpretation precludes any risk/benefit analysis where even the tiniest risk of cancer is involved....

The court's interpretation will produce some strange results. For example, because the Delaney clause does not affect FFDCA §408, a pesticide carrying a negligible risk of cancer can be used on crops that will be consumed raw, such as apples and tomatoes. And [under] the "flow-through" provision, pesticide residues carrying a negligible risk of cancer can appear in processed food — as long as the residue level does not exceed the tolerance limit for the raw commodity. Thus a grocery store could legally sell raw apples containing Pesticide X residues that carry a negligible risk of cancer, and the store could also sell applesauce containing residues of Pesticide X, as long as the residues in the sauce were not higher than the tolerance for residues in the raw apples (calculated in both cases as the parts per million of residue in the food).

But if the residues of Pesticide X in applesauce happen to exceed the residues in the raw apples, the Delaney clause would prohibit sale of the applesauce. The applesauce would be legally "unsafe" even if the carcinogenic risk presented by the residues in the applesauce were less than the risk in the raw apples. This is an entirely plausible scenario because *risks* from pesticide residues in processed food may be less than from the same pesticide in raw foods. The reason is the magnitude of risk depends on both the *level* of residue and the *amount* of food consumed....

Our goal must be to bring U.S. pesticide regulation into conformity with current science and ensure that the nation's pesticide safety laws provide the best available protection to consumers.... The current framework is illogical in that it results in opposite outcomes for pesticides having similar risks, benefits, costs, and efficacy. The situation becomes even more troublesome when the anomalies in the law result in the elimination of safer pesticides in favor of more risky pesticides.

Thus, the appeal court's ruling that the Delaney clause contains no implicit exception for negligible or *de minimis* carcinogenic risks...highlights the need for all parties to begin a working dialogue to resolve the controversy. The goal should be to come to an agreement on how to proceed to ensure that the nation's pesticide safety laws provide the best available protection to consumers.[62]

---

61. Mr. Kimm was head of EPA's pesticide bureau.

62. An attorney representing the National Food Processors Association added more in this vein:
     EPA has acknowledged that more than 30, and probably more than 60, food-use pesticides may be required to be banned.... The reduced number of effective pesticides will disrupt agricultural production, diminish food quality, increase food costs, and reduce the availability of nutritious fruit, vegetable, and grain products.... The risk to the public will be increased by forcing EPA to ban beneficial pesticides that pose *de minimis* cancer risks and requiring the substitution of pesticides posing greater health risks which are not associated with cancer.... EPA prohibition of pesticides approved and used in other countries which export food products to the United States will have an adverse impact on international trade. Clausen Ely, The Delaney Clause: an Obscure EPA Policy is to Blame, EPA Journal, 44–45 (Jan. 1993).

**Al Meyerhoff, Let's Reform a Failed Food Safety Regime**
EPA Journal, 42–43 (Jan. 1993)

The essential premise of the Delaney clause of the Food, Drug and Cosmetic Act is as simple as it is powerful: What we understand best about carcinogens is the limited extent of our knowledge. Accordingly, the famous clause is grounded in a policy of prevention: prohibiting the addition of carcinogens in the food supply to prevent avoidable cancers in humans. This approach was deemed necessary by Congress since the entire nation's population would otherwise be routinely exposed to carcinogens in their daily diet. More than three decades after the Delaney clause was enacted in 1958, the public policy issue now presented is whether science has evolved to the point where this premise is no longer valid.... Unfortunately, but demonstrably, the answer remains no.

Agencies like EPA risk losing the integrity of the science and objectivity they need from it by continuing to suggest that risk assessments are better than they are, and that cancer risk can be so clearly dismissed as *de minimis* solely on a scientific basis....

The reality of life is that we are exposed to a multiplicity of toxic substances.... For this reason, ultimately, the overall policy underlying the Delaney clause — that we should avoid unnecessary and involuntary exposure to cancer-causing agents — remains as valid today as when enacted... During the Reagan administration, in describing dietary risk, the former Director of EPA's Pesticide Program said, "Pesticides dwarf the other environmental risks the Agency deals with. Toxic waste dumps [on which EPA spends a major portion of its budget, merely] may affect a few thousand people who live around them."... Yet, to date, EPA's consistent approach to carcinogens in food has been to ignore or evade the Delaney clause.... Since the Delaney clause became law, much new scientific knowledge has been developed. Yet we still do not know whether humans are more or less sensitive than experimental animals to various carcinogens. We don't know how to assess the contribution of one carcinogen in relation to the impacts of exposures to other carcinogens. We don't know the *cumulative* impact of dozens of carcinogens now permitted in the food supply. We should, therefore, follow Rachel Carson's advice three decades ago: "The ultimate answer is to use less toxic chemicals, [rejecting] this system of deliberately poisoning our food and then policing the result."[63]

**COMMENTARY AND QUESTIONS**

1. **Tactical views of crude blunt roadblocks.** Here's the further dilemma that the NRDC attorney does not talk about: Assume that a stark statutory provision like the Delaney clause has been on the books since 1958, and it starts to look a bit outdated in the minds of many fair-minded observers. Or assume that a new environmental protection provision is being proposed that would be a decisive, readily-enforceable crude blunt instrument, but in a number of cases its terms would be overinclusive, and undersensitive to the rational public policy sensitivities of the issue. Assume further that an environmental advocacy group knows that the agency in charge of enforcing a more subjective, flexible, discretionary

63. Mr. Meyerhoff was lead attorney for the NRDC in *Les.*

standard would be extremely vulnerable to political pressure from the regulated industry — as for instance with the Forest Service and the timber industry, the Federal Highway Administration and the highway construction industry.

What is an environmental group to do then, especially in cases like the chemical risk field where many rational policy analysts and resource economists outside the industry establishment affirm that a stark prohibition may be logically inconsistent and poor public policy, and that a measured balancing process would be a far better way to set standards? An intricate, complex, expert balancing process for setting standards for a wide array of substances, however, cannot be done case-by-case in Congress. Such standard setting inevitably must be delegated to an administrative agency, and there the whole statutory mandate can be lost to the cupidity of the political marketplace within the agency process.

This is a dilemma regularly faced by public interest groups, including the NRDC, which brought the *Les* case. On one hand are arguments for striving to achieve optimal balanced rational policies, with legal standards that accurately reflect the complex subtleties of an issue. On the other is the political reality that subtle protective standards can turn out to be no standards at all in agency practice. It is a dilemma between optimal substantive theory and tactical realities, and its resolution requires acknowledgment that often both sides are right.

2. **A congressional bypass for the Delaney Clause roadblock.** As the judge in *Les* anticipated, Congress broke the pesticide policy logjam, choosing to overrride Delaney and incorporate a "reasonable risk" risk assessment approach in the Food Quality Protection Act of 1996.[64] In a much-debated bargain, environmental groups like NRDC agreed to give up the strict enforceability of the Delaney clause insofar as pesticide residues are concerned, to be replaced with a standard of "reasonable certainty that no harm will result from aggregate exposure." This eliminated the "Delaney Paradox" of prior law, where pesticide residues on raw food were governed by the basic tolerance provisions of the FFDCA, while pesticide residues on processed foods were additionally regulated by the Delaney clause if they concentrated during processing. "Aggregate exposure" includes dietary exposures and all other non-occupational exposures for which there is reliable information. The health of children is established as the baseline against which the "reasonable certainty of no harm" standard is to be applied. The Delaney clause remains in effect with regard to other food additives. The FQPA bargain also established a Consumer Right To Know Program. Worries about whether the amendments would permit erosions of strict health standards were reinforced by subsequent executive policy declarations that some of the amended act's health-based equirements were discretionary rather than mandatory.

Does the history of the Delaney clause and ESA roadblocks imply that ultimately all roadblocks will be amended to incorporate flexibility provisions?

3. **What's an agency to do?** Is an agency ever justified in not reading a clear statutory mandate literally? The Delaney clause, enacted in 1958, is a crude regulatory device that makes a number of questionable toxicological assumptions, including

64. Pub. L. No. 104-170, 110 Stat. 1489 (1996).

(1) that high-dose, relatively small group animals tests can accurately predict low-dose, large group human responses, and (2) that substances causing cancer in animals also invariably cause cancer in human beings. The atmosphere in Congress during hearings on the Delaney clause was one of pervasive "cancerphobia." But isn't an unambiguous legislative directive to be followed to the letter, regardless of its scientific or policy merits? Sometimes the whole point of a stark statutory command is to avoid the delay, dilution, and political vulnerability of the normal administrative process where agencies study conditions, make and remake tentative draft standards, negotiate with every squeaking wheel about adjusting terms, defend the final standards in court challenges, and then undertake a similar odyssey in designing and applying an enforcement scheme. A clear statutory command efficiently sidesteps much of this administrative process morass.

The same dilemma arises in this area as in the case of the ESA. Clear stark statutory commands don't leave much wiggle room, and subject the agencies and regulatees to a tougher level of judicial superintendence. For that reason, such commands are more likely to be obeyed by regulatees and regulators alike. The agency that considers whether to inject a little flexibility or slack into statutory enforcement — recognizing that strict enforcement of all statutes is practically impossible, politically problematic, or irrational — runs the risk of overstepping its constitutional role, being accused of abdicating its public service obligations, and sabotaging declared national policy, as indeed it may be. Perhaps that is why so many important administrative issues are ultimately shifted to courts and Congress.

*Sixty percent of all mammals are nocturnal.*
> — The Book Arts Press, Thoughts for Valentine's Day, 1975

*Animals are not brethren, they are not underlings. They are other nations, caught with ourselves in the net of life and time.*
> — Henry Beston

*I've known rivers ancient as the world and older than the flow of human blood in human veins. My soul has grown deep like the rivers....*
> — Langston Hughes

# Chapter 15

# PRODUCT REGULATION AND MARKET-ACCESS CONTROL STRATEGIES: PESTICIDES AND TOXICS

A. *Pesticides: the Federal Insecticide, Fungicide, and Rodenticide Act*
B. *Regulating Market Access of Toxics: the Toxic Substances Control Act*

Environmental protection in the United States is in transition. For many years, regulatory strategies were oriented towards pollution cleanup. More recently, however, regulatory strategies have targeted pollution prevention as well as pollution control.

At one end of the continuum are regulatory strategies dominated by a desire to minimize "false positives" — regulating only after environmental problems have already appeared. See Chapter Two. These strategies have resulted in serious and widespread damage to human health and the environment. Good examples of the damage caused by these strategies are our abandoned hazardous waste sites, which can only be cleaned up at a cost running into many billions of dollars.

At the other end of the continuum are regulatory strategies based on the minimization of "false negatives" — regulating only in anticipation of environmental problems which have not yet appeared. These strategies, when they are strictly preventive in nature, emphasize stringent precautionary control of a chemical's market access. They would prohibit the introduction of new products, or the further sales of existing products, where products might conceivably be hazardous to human health or the environment. Such broad denials of market access, based exclusively on speculative environmental damage, can have a disabling effect on our system of market enterprise, especially in light of increasing foreign competition. There are many products, moreover, whose palpable economic, health, or environmental benefits outweigh their uncertain environmental costs.

With one exception, federal environmental protection statutes adopting a product regulation strategy have attempted to achieve a balance between the environmental benefits and economic costs of denying market access to a particular product. The single exception was the so-called "Delaney Clause" of the Federal Food, Drug, and Cosmetic Act, which provided, in pertinent part, that:

> ...no [food] additive shall be deemed to be safe if it is found to induce cancer when ingested by man or animal....[1]

---

1. 21 U.S.C.A. §348(c)(3)(A.) The "Delaney Clause," first enacted in 1958, was such a crude regulatory device that the Food and Drug Administration ("FDA") only applied it in a limited number of situations where certain explicit toxicological criteria had been satisfied, e.g., an increased risk of fatality of "one in a million."

Prodded by the Courts, Congress finally undertook a further review of the Delaney Clause in 1996. In Les v. Reilly, 968 F.2d 985 (9th Cir. 1992), the Ninth Circuit ruled that, consistent with the Delaney Clause, EPA had no discretion to permit the use of food additives, including pesticides, if those additives were known to be carcinogenic. Requiring EPA to interpret the Delaney Clause's prohibition literally, the Ninth Circuit held that "once the finding of carcinogenicity is made, the EPA has no discretion." See Chapter 14. Four years after Les v. Reilly, Congress finally addressed the Delaney Clause again. Specifically, Congress passed, and President Clinton signed into law, the Food Quality Protection Act of 1996 , Pub. L. No. 104-170, 110 Stat. 1489, which significantly amended both FIFRA and the Federal Food, Drug, and Cosmetic Act ("FFDCA".) Congress did not comprehensively repeal the Delaney Clause, but did remove pesticide residues from its ambit by amending the FFDCA's definition of "food additive" (the Delaney Clause applies only to food additives) to exclude pesticide chemical residues on raw or processed foods. (The Delaney Clause remains in effect regarding other food additives.) In particular, Congress determined that a pesticide residue on such foods is only to be considered unsafe if the EPA has set a tolerance level for the substance and the residue fails to satisfy that level. The EPA is now allowed to grant a tolerance and register a pesticide upon a finding of safety. As defined in §405 of the amendments, "safe" means that "there is a reasonable certainty that no harm will result from the aggregate exposure to the pesticide chemical residue," including both dietary and non-dietary total exposure. Thus, the "zero risk" approach of the former Delaney Clause has been repealed insofar as pesticide residues are concerned, in favor of a standard of "reasonable certainty" that no harm will come from aggregate exposure.[2]

The two most important federal environmental product regulation statutes are the Federal Insecticide, Fungicide, and Rodenticide Act (FIFRA)[3] and the Toxic Substances Control Act (TSCA, or ToSCA.)[4] Although these statutes take a similar approach to environmental regulation of toxics, they present instructive differences in practice resulting from their disparate approaches to the triggering mechanisms for regulation and enforcement.

Assume that a manufacturer has invented a potentially useful chemical which can serve as an effective pesticide but which has never before been used. In connection with bringing this new chemical to market, the manufacturer would need to consider the regulatory effect of both FIFRA and ToSCA. Under FIFRA, Congress established the basic framework for pesticide regulation, including the registration of pesticides and the process by which EPA may ban unreasonably dangerous pesticides. Under ToSCA, Congress provided EPA with comprehensive authority to regulate or prohibit the manufacture, distribution, or use of chemicals that pose

---

2. As a result of the 1996 amendments, there has been a lively debate over the extent to which the Delaney Clause was rendered obsolete by Congress' action. See Turner, Delaney Lives! Reports of Delaney's Death Are Greatly Exaggerated, 28 ELR 10003 (Jan., 1998) (concluding that the 1996 amendments neither remove the protections provided by the Delaney Clause prohibition against adding cancer causing additives to food nor reflect a public policy rationale or political consensus to do so.)

3. 7 U.S.C.A. §135 et seq.

4. 15 U.S.C.A. §2601 et seq.

unreasonable risks, including the authority to require premanufacture notification to EPA for new chemicals or significant new uses of existing chemicals.

To a great extent, FIFRA places the burden of going forward — collecting data, establishing testing protocols, testing, and proving safety — on the manufacturer itself under threat of potentially severe legal sanctions. By placing the burden of going forward and proving safety on the manufacturer, FIFRA attempts to provide a comprehensive approach to the pesticide regulation process which regulates environmental toxics from the very outset. By contrast, ToSCA largely places the burden on EPA, not the manufacturer. ToSCA requires the EPA to establish, by substantial evidence, that chemical testing is necessary and then to set testing protocols. Under ToSCA, EPA uses its statutory authority for "gap-filling," focusing primarily on environmental toxics not otherwise caught up in the regulatory net.

As you consider these laws, analyze which approach is more likely to be effective. For example, consider whether it is the government or the manufacturer which is in the best position to collect data, to engage in chemical testing, or to establish testing protocols. Consider whether it is more efficient for government to regulate a product during the manufacturing process or to wait until after the product has reached the market. Are there phases in the manufacturing process when an industry is more likely to be receptive to and cooperative with governmental regulation than at other times? If so, how can government most efficiently take advantage of a manufacturer's profit motive to induce greater cooperation and more effective regulation?

## A. PESTICIDES: THE FEDERAL INSECTICIDE, FUNGICIDE, AND RODENTICIDE ACT

### M. Miller, Federal Regulation of Pesticides, Environmental Law Handbook (14th Ed.)[5]
### 284–301 (1997)

The benefits of pesticides, herbicides, rodenticides, and other economic poisons[6] are well known. They have done much to spare us from the ravages of disease, crop infestations, noxious animals, and choking weeds. Over the past two decades, however, beginning with Rachel Carson's Silent Spring in 1962, there has been a growing awareness of the hazards, as well as the benefits of these chemicals, which may be harmful to man and the balance of nature.

The ability to balance these often conflicting effects is hampered by continuing scientific uncertainties. We still lack full understanding of environmental side effects, the sub-cellular mechanism of human carcinogens, and a host of other factors that are important for a proper evaluation of pesticide suitability. Yet scientific progress, especially in the genetic area, has been so rapid over the past decade or two that we are now realizing that many of our previous assumptions have been

---

5. Mr. Miller is a partner in the Washington, D.C. firm of Baise and Miller.

6. Ed. note: The term "economic poisons" has been applied to pesticides since the 1940s. It reflects the "necessary evil" character of these substances, which FIFRA expresses in its weighing of benefits against costs. As "economic poisons", pesticides can cause adverse effects beyond their target species, thereby resulting in "collateral damage" which must be weighed against the benefits of pesticidal use.

wrong, or at least over-simplified. The best scientific knowledge is now critical for the agency as it attempts to conduct accelerated reviews of hundreds of chemicals that had been registered earlier under less strict standards.

Public concern regarding pesticides was a principal cause for the rise of the environmental movement in the United States in the late sixties and early seventies, and therefore was probably the single most important reason for the creation of the EPA. While public attention since then has shifted to various other environmental media, the pesticide issue — with its implications for the safety of food supply and of people in the agricultural area — is still central to the public's notion of environmental protection. Indeed, the fluctuation of interest in this topic is often an accurate barometer of public distrust in the official environmental agencies.

In the last few years this distrust has taken a new and different form. EPA is now being criticized not only by the environmentalists for not doing enough, but also by others for ordering unnecessarily costly or extreme measures. At the heart of both views is the belief that the agency's actions are not always firmly based on good science — a skepticism that is of course by no means limited to EPA's pesticide program.

Chemical pesticides have been subject to some degree of federal control since the Insecticide Act of 1910. This Act was primarily concerned with protecting consumers, usually farmers, from ineffective products and deceptive labeling, and it contained neither a federal registration requirement nor any significant safety standards. The relatively insignificant usage of pesticides before World War II made regulation a matter of low priority.

The resulting effects on public health and farm production made pesticides a virtual necessity. The agricultural chemical industry became an influential sector of the economy. In 1947, Congress enacted a more comprehensive statute, the Federal Insecticide, Fungicide, and Rodenticide Act ("FIFRA".) This law required that pesticides distributed in interstate commerce be registered with the United States Department of Agriculture ("USDA".) It also established rudimentary labeling requirements. This Act, like its predecessor, was mostly concerned with product effectiveness; the statute did, however, declare pesticides "misbranded" if they were necessarily harmful to man, animals, or vegetation (except weeds) even when properly used.

Three major defects in the new law soon became evident. First, the registration process was largely an empty formality since the Secretary of Agriculture could not refuse registration even to a chemical he deemed highly dangerous. He could register "under protest," but this had no legal effect on the registrant's ability to manufacture or distribute the product. Second, there was no regulatory control over the use of a pesticide contrary to its label, as long as the label itself complied with statutory requirements. Third, the Secretary's only remedy against a hazardous product was a legal action for misbranding or adulteration, and — this was crucial — the difficult burden of proof was on the government....

In 1964 the USDA persuaded Congress to remedy two of these three defects: the registration system was revised to permit the secretary to refuse to register a new product or to cancel an existing registration, and the burden of proof for safety and effectiveness was placed on the registrant. Those changes considerably strengthened the act, in theory, but made little difference in practice. The Pesticide Registration Division, a section of USDA's Agricultural Research Service, was understaffed...and the division was buried deep in a bureaucracy primarily concerned with promoting agriculture and facilitating the registration of pesticides. The cancellation procedure was seldom if ever used, and there was still no legal sanction against a consumer's applying the chemical for a delisted use.

The growth of the environmental movement in the late 1960s, with its concern about the widespread use of agricultural chemicals, overwhelmed the meager resources of the Pesticide Division. Environmental groups filed a barrage of lawsuits demanding the cancellation or suspension of a host of major pesticides such as DDT, Aldrin-Dieldrin, Mirex, and the herbicide 2,4,5-T. This demanding situation demanded a new approach to pesticide regulations.

On December 2, 1970, President Nixon signed Reorganization Order No. 3 creating the Environmental Protection Agency. This Order assigned to EPA the functions and many of the personnel previously under Interior, Agriculture, and other government departments. EPA inherited from USDA not only the Pesticides Division but also the environmental lawsuits against the Secretary of Agriculture....

The Federal Insecticide, Fungicide, and Rodenticide Act (FIFRA), as amended by the Federal Environmental Pesticide Control Act (FEPCA) of October 1972 and the FIFRA amendments of 1975, 1978, 1980, 1988, and 1996, is a complex statute. Terms sometimes have a meaning different from, or even directly contrary to, normal English usage. For example, the term "suspension" really means an immediate ban on a pesticide, while the harsher-sounding term "cancellation" indicates only the initiation of administrative proceedings which can drag on for many years....

All new pesticide products used in the United States, with minor exceptions, must first be registered with EPA. This involves the submittal of the complete formula, a proposed label, and "full description of the tests made and the results thereof upon which the claims are based." The registration is very specific; it is not valid for all formulations or uses of a particular chemical. That is, separate registrations are required for each specific crops and insects on which the pesticide product may be applied, and each use must be supported by research data on safety and efficacy....

The Administrator must approve the registration if the following conditions are met:

(1) Its composition is such as to warrant the proposed claim for it;

(2) Its labeling and other materials required to be submitted comply with the requirements of this act;

(3) It will perform its intended function without unreasonable adverse effects on the environment; and

(4) When used in accordance with widespread and commonly recognized practice it will not generally cause unreasonable adverse effects on the environment.

The operative phrase in the above criteria is "unreasonable adverse effects on the environment," which was added to the act in 1972. This phrase is defined elsewhere in FIFRA as meaning "any unreasonable risk to man or the environment, taking into account the economic, social, and environmental costs and benefits of the use of the pesticide."...

Registrations are for a limited, five-year period; thereafter, they automatically expire unless an interested party petitions for renewal and, if requested by EPA, provides additional data indicating the safety of the product. For the past few years, pre-EPA registrations have been coming up for renewal under much stricter standards than when originally issued....

Until the 1972 reforms, the government had no control over the actual use of a pesticide once it had left a manufacturer or distributor properly labeled. Thus, for example, a chemical which would be perfectly safe for use on a dry field might be environmentally hazardous if applied in a marshy area, and a chemical acceptable for use on one crop might leave dangerous residues on another. EPA's only recourse...was to cancel the entire registration — obviously too unwieldy a weapon to constitute a normal means of enforcement. A second problem was that a...chemical might be too dangerous for general use but could be used safely by trained personnel. There was, however, no legal mechanism for limiting its use only to qualified individuals.

Because of these problems, both environmentalists and the industry agreed that EPA should be given more flexibility than merely the choice between cancelling or approving a pesticide. Congress therefore provided for the classification of pesticides into general and restricted categories, with the latter group available only to Certified Applicators....

While the registration process may be the heart of FIFRA, cancellation represents the cutting edge of the law and attracts the most public attention. Cancellation is used to initiate review of a substance suspected of posing a "substantial question of safety" to man or the environment.

Contrary to the public assumptions, during the pendency of the proceedings the product may be freely manufactured and shipped in commerce. A cancellation order, although final if not challenged within thirty days, usually leads to a public hearing or scientific review committee, or both, and can be quite protracted; this can last a matter of months or years. A recommended decision from the agency hearing examiner (now called the administrative law judge) goes to the Administrator or his delegated representative, the chief agency judicial officer, for a final determination on the cancellation....

A suspension order, despite its misleading name, is an immediate ban on the production and distribution of a pesticide. It is mandated when a product constitutes an "imminent hazard" to man or the environment, and may be invoked at any stage of the cancellation proceeding or even before a cancellation procedure has been initiated....

The purpose of an ordinary suspension is to prevent an imminent hazard during the time required for cancellation or change in classification proceedings. An ordinary suspension proceeding is initiated when the Administrator issues notice to the registrant that he is suspending use of the pesticide and includes the requisite findings as to imminent hazard. The registrant may request an expedited hearing within five days of receipt of the Administrator's notice. If no hearing is requested, the suspension order can take effect immediately thereafter and the order is not reviewable by a court....

The emergency suspension is the strongest action EPA can take under FIFRA. It immediately halts all uses, sales, and distribution of the pesticide. An emergency suspension differs from an ordinary suspension in that it is *ex parte*. The registrant is not given notice or the opportunity for an expedited hearing prior to the suspension order taking effect. The registrant is, however, entitled to an expedited hearing to determine the propriety of the emergency suspension. The Administrator can only use this procedure when he determines that an emergency exists which does not allow him to hold a hearing before suspending use of a pesticide. This authority has only rarely been invoked....

### Environmental Defense Fund v. Environmental Protection Agency
United States Court of Appeals for the District of Columbia Circuit, 1972
465 F.2d 528

LEVENTHAL, C.J. On December 3, 1970, petitioner Environmental Defense Fund (EDF), a non-profit New York Corporation, petitioned the Environmental Protection Agency under the Federal Insecticide, Fungicide, and Rodenticide Act, for the immediate suspension and ultimate cancellation of all registered uses of aldrin and dieldrin, two chemically similar chlorinated hydrocarbon pesticides. On March 18, 1971, the Administrator of the EPA announced the issuance of "notices of cancellation" for aldrin and dieldrin because of "a substantial question as to the safety of the registered products which has not been effectively countered by the registrant." He declined to order the interim remedy of suspension, pending final decision on cancellation after completion of the pertinent administrative procedure, in light of his decision that "present uses [of aldrin and dieldrin] do not pose an imminent threat to the public such as to require immediate action." EDF filed this petition to review the EPA's failure to suspend the registration....

The EPA's Statement points out that whereas a notice of cancellation is appropriate whenever there is "a substantial question as to the safety of a product," immediate suspension is authorized only in order to prevent an "imminent hazard to the public," and to protect the public by prohibiting shipment of an economic poison "so dangerous that its continued use should not be tolerated during the pendency of the administrative process." The EPA describes its general criteria for suspension as follows:

> This agency will find that an imminent hazard to the public exists when the evidence is sufficient to show that continued registration of an economic poison poses a significant threat of danger to health, or otherwise creates a hazardous situation to the public, that should be corrected immediately to prevent serious injury, and which cannot be permitted to continue during the pendency of administrative proceedings. An "imminent hazard" may be declared at any point in a chain of events which may ultimately result in harm to the public. It is not necessary that the final anticipated injury actually have occurred prior to a determination that an "imminent hazard" exists. In this connection, significant injury or potential injury to plants or animals alone could justify a finding of imminent hazard to the public from the use of an economic poison. The type, extent, probability and duration of potential or actual injury to man, plants, and animals will be measured in light of the positive benefits accruing from, for example, use of the responsible economic poison in human or animal disease control or food production.

Part II of the Statement of Reasons, captioned "Formulation of Standards," begins with the general standards deemed pertinent to the administration of FIFRA.

EPA points out that, in general, economic poisons, including those under present consideration, are "ecologically crude" — that is, by reason of technology limitations, [they] are toxic to non-target organisms as well as to pest life. Thus continued registration for particular ecologically crude pesticides "are acceptable only to the extent that the benefits accruing from use of a particular economic poison outweigh" the adverse results of effects on non-target species. EPA cites "dramatic steps in disease control" and the gradual amelioration of "the chronic problem of world hunger" as examples of the kind of beneficial effect to be looked for in balancing benefits against harm for specific substances. But it cautions that "triumphs of public health achieved in the past" will not be permitted to justify future registrations, recognizing that fundamentally different considerations are at work in evaluating use of a dangerous pesticide in a developed country such as the United States rather than in a developing non-industrial nation....

Laboratory tests with some substances have raised serious questions regarding carcinogenicity that "deserve particular searching" because carcinogenic effects are generally cumulative and irreversible when discovered. Threats presented by individual substances vary not only as to observed persistence in the environment but also as to environmental mobility — which in turn depends in part on how a particular pesticide is introduced into the environment either by ground insertion or by dispersal directly into the ambient air or water.

Based on the discussion of these general considerations, the EPA concludes that individual decisions on initial or continued registration must depend on a complex administrative calculus, in which the "nature and magnitude of the foreseeable hazards associated with use of a particular product" is weighed against the "nature of the benefit conferred" by its use....

The EDF's main argument [is that] while the Statement of Reasons sets forth, as a matter of EPA policy, that suspension decisions would be made only after the Administrator makes a preliminary assessment of immanency of hazard that includes a balancing of benefit and harm, yet when the EPA discussed aldrin and dieldrin, it inconsistently failed to identify any offsetting benefits, and limited itself to the reference to certain hazards.

The EPA concedes that the "thrust" of the Administrator's analysis related to the absence of any short run major hazards. But it parries that he "did refer to the purposes for which aldrin and dieldrin are used."

In light of his findings with respect to the absence of any foreseeable hazard, there was little need for the Administrator to go into detail in considering — as he had indicated he would do in suspension decisions... — "the positive benefits."

We are not clear that the FIFRA requires separate analysis of benefits at the suspension stage. We are clear that the statute empowers the Administrator to take account of benefits or their absence as affecting imminency of hazard. The Administrator's general decision to follow that course cannot be assailed as unreasonable. The suspension procedures of this agency, though in the abstract designed for emergency situations, seem to us to resemble more closely the judicial proceedings on a contested motion for a preliminary injunction, to prevail during the pendency of the litigation on the merits, rather than proceedings on an ex parte application for an emergency temporary restraining order. The suspension decision is not ordinarily one to be made in a matter of moments, or even hours or days. The statute contemplates at least the kind of ventilation of issues commonly had prior to decisions by courts that govern the relationships of parties pendente lite, during trial on the merits.

Judicial doctrine teaches that a court must consider the possibility of success on the merits, the nature and extent of the damage to each of the parties from the granting or denial of the injunction, and where the public interest lies. It was not inappropriate for the Administrator to have chosen a general approach to suspension that permits analysis of similar factors. By definition, a substantial question of safety exists when notices of cancellation issue. If there is no offsetting claim of any benefit to the public, then the EPA has the burden of showing that the substantial safety question does not pose an "imminent hazard" to the public.

EDF is on sound ground in noting that while the EPA's general approach contemplates a decision as to suspension based on a balance of benefit and harm, the later discussion of aldrin and dieldrin relates only to harm.

The Administrator's mere mention of these products' major uses, emphasized by the EPA, cannot suffice as a discussion of benefits, even though the data before him...reflected the view that aldrin-dieldrin pesticides are the only control presently available for some twenty insects which attack corn and for one pest which poses a real danger to citrus orchards....

The interests at stake here are too important to permit the decision to be sustained on the basis of speculative inference as to what the Administrator's findings and conclusions might have been regarding benefits....

Our conclusion that a mere recitation of a pesticide's uses does not suffice as an analysis of benefits is fortified where, as here, there was a submission, by EDF, that alternative pest control mechanisms are available for such use. The analysis of benefit requires some consideration of whether such proposed alternatives are available or feasible, or whether such availability is in doubt.

The importance of an EPA analysis of benefits is underscored by the Administrator's flexibility, in both final decisions and suspension orders, to differentiate between uses of the product. Aldrin and dieldrin are apparently not viewed by the EPA as uniform in their benefit characteristics for all their uses. The Administrator had previously stopped certain uses of the pesticides in question in house paints, and in water use. These actions presumably reflected some evaluation of comparative benefits and hazards. The Administrator's reliance on the "pattern of declining gross use" itself indicates that for some purposes aldrin and dieldrin are or will soon become non-essential. Even assuming the essentiality of aldrin and dieldrin, and of the lack of feasible alternative control mechanisms for certain uses, there may be no corresponding benefit for other uses, which may be curtailed during the suspension period....

We do not say there is an absolute need for analysis of benefits. It might have been possible for EPA to say that although there were no significant benefits from aldrin-dieldrin, the possibility of harm — though substantial enough to present a long-run danger to the public warranting cancellation proceedings — did not present a serious short-run danger that constituted an imminent hazard. EPA's counsel offers this as a justification for its action.

If this is to be said, it must be said clearly, so that it may be reviewed carefully. Logically, there is room for the concept. But we must caution against any approach to the [statutory] term "imminent hazard"...that restricts it to a concept of crisis. It is enough if there is substantial likelihood that serious harm will be experienced during the year or two required in any realistic projection of the administrative process. It is not good practice for an agency to defend an order on the hypothesis that it is valid even assuming there are no benefits, when the reality is that some conclusion of benefits was visualized by the agency. This kind of abstraction pushes argument — and judicial review — to the wall of extremes, when realism calls for an awareness of middle ground.

### COMMENTARY AND QUESTIONS

1. **The subsequent suspension of aldrin and dieldrin.** The court remanded the matter to EPA for further study. After considering the Advisory Committee Report and further public comments, EPA affirmed its previous decisions to cancel without interim suspension. Twelve months into the cancellation proceeding, the Administrator issued a notice of intent to suspend, and the suspension became

final on October 1, 1974. EPA's suspension decision was substantially upheld in EDF v. EPA, 510 F.2d 1292 (D.C. Cir. 1975), where Judge Leventhal, emphasizing that "the responsibility to demonstrate that the benefits outweigh the risks is upon the proponents of continued registration," upheld EPA's finding that alternatives to aldrin-dieldrin were currently available. See also EDF v. EPA, 548 F.2d 998 (D.C. Cir. 1976) (heptachlor and chlordane.)

2. **Emergency suspension.** The aldrin-dieldrin case was an ordinary suspension rather than an emergency suspension. EPA first used the emergency suspension procedure in 1979 when it suspended many uses of 2,4,5-T and Silvex. Emergency suspension is the most potent action available to EPA under FIFRA, because it immediately stops all uses, sales, and distribution of the pesticide. In Dow Chemical Co. v. Blum, 469 F. Supp. 892 (E.D. Mich. 1979), a federal district court, upholding EPA's emergency suspension, concluded that whereas an ordinary suspension proceeding is similar to a motion for a preliminary injunction during a lawsuit, the emergency suspension proceeding is similar to an application for a temporary restraining order. An emergency suspension order will be upheld if there is "minimal evidence in the record to support EPA's decision." But see Love v. EPA, 838 F.2d 1059 (9th Cir. 1988), where the emergency suspension of dinoseb in the Northwest was overturned because "EPA's evaluation of the relevant factors under FIFRA was incomplete and rushed and...simply not adequate to justify the emergency suspension...." Registration of dinoseb was later cancelled, but existing stocks were permitted to be used for limited purposes. See Northwest Food Processors Ass'n. v. EPA, 886 F.2d 1075 (9th Cir. 1989.) Should a reviewing court be more or less deferential to an EPA decision on an ordinary suspension because of the existence of the emergency suspension device? Does the emergency suspension device provide reassurance to courts that EPA can act quickly if further information indicates that suspension is desirable? If so, does the existence of the emergency suspension device affect judges' views pertaining to whether to overturn an ordinary suspension?

Section 102 of the Food Quality Protection Act of 1996 amended FIFRA to make a material change in the emergency suspension process, by allowing a suspension for no more than 90 days without a simultaneous notice of intent to cancel. What concerns was Congress addressing in making this change?

3. **Imminent hazards.** FIFRA operates as a threshold preventive, in that it applies "up front" before a potentially dangerous pesticide is introduced into commerce. On the other hand, FIFRA's standards are not purely safety criteria because the economic benefits and costs of regulation are weighed at the registration, cancellation, and suspension stages. Does the "imminent hazard" standard serve as a margin of safety where economic benefits are tangible, and potential environmental harms are uncertain? EPA's interpretive statement on "imminent hazard" is highly precautionary, justifying action whenever there is "significant injury or potential injury to plants or animals alone...." Another administrative mechanism for erring on the side of safety is EPA's Special Review process (formerly called Rebuttable Presumption Against Registration, or "RPAR"), in which evidence developed by EPA or a third party that a pesticide exceeds specified "risk criteria" will raise a pre-

sumption against registration or in favor of cancellation or suspension. 40 CFR Part 154. Moreover, the EDF v. EPA court adds that once a notice of cancellation is issued — if there is no offsetting claim of benefits — then "EPA has the burden of showing that the substantial safety question does not pose an 'imminent hazard' to the public." It seems clear, as the court points out, that "imminent hazard" does not mean "crisis." Operationally it means that the greater the amount of credible evidence EPA has about potential dangers posed by a registered pesticide, the more quickly and easily its use can be discontinued, and the more pronounced benefits must be in order to justify its continued use. Recalling the Huber excerpt in Chapter Two, would Huber approve of a regulatory scheme that allows a product to be marketed, but makes quick protective withdrawal possible once negative evidence appears? How is negative evidence to be measured or quantified, particularly when scientific uncertainty factors affect benefit-cost analysis? Is it easier for EPA to suspend a pesticide under a "significant threat" standard then under a "crisis" standard of "imminence"?

"Imminent hazard" is one of those all-important statutory terms that defy precise analysis but facilitate administrative and judicial determinations regarding uncertainty and burdens of proof, creating the "common law" of particular statutes. The "imminent hazard" phrase serves a similar function in RCRA (see Chapter 17) and CERCLA (see Chapter 18.) Another such term is "endanger." See Ethyl Corp. v. EPA, 541 F.2d 1 (D.C. Cir. 1976.)

4. **The role of benefits in a suspension proceeding.** Must benefits be analyzed in a suspension proceeding? Judge Leventhal's opinion is not consistent on this point. Does it depend on whether evidence of available alternatives has been introduced? If there is no short-term danger, why bother analyzing benefits at all? In order to analyze benefits, must they be quantifiable? If not, how do we measure them? Is it possible to distinguish clearly between short and long-term hazards?

5. **Non-registration of exports.** Whereas imported pesticides are subject to FIFRA registration requirements, exports are excluded from the regulatory provisions of the Act; e.g., in Chapter One, Kepone was unregulated because it was not intended for domestic use. Should DDT be permitted to be exported to a developing nation where malaria is a serious problem, if DDT is the only affordable malaria-control alternative? To what extent should the transboundary character of pollution from persistent pesticides be considered in such judgments? Are risk-benefit calculations, as applied to challenged pesticides in the United States, applicable to conditions faced abroad? If the United States unilaterally regulates pesticide exportation, will other pesticide producing nations gain an unfair competitive advantage? One of Ronald Reagan's first actions as President was to rescind the Carter Administration's ban on export of dangerous pesticides and contaminated pharmaceuticals.

6. **Paying for suspension.** A controversial provision of the 1972 amendments required EPA to indemnify registrants, formulators, and end users of cancelled or suspended pesticides for remaining stocks that were not permitted to be exhausted. Needless to say, this provision had a chilling effect on cancellations and suspensions. In the 1988 FIFRA amendments, the indemnity requirement was

deleted except for end users (farmers and applicators.)[7]

**7. FIFRA and pre-emption.** There are several issues involved here. First, do FIFRA's labeling requirements pre-empt private common law tort suits filed in state court based on inadequate labeling ("failure to warn")? Courts are split on this issue, although the general rule is that a license or permit will not insulate a defendant from obligations imposed by common law or other statutes. Thus, FIFRA registration is ordinarily no defense to a tort action or to an action demanding compliance with NEPA.[8] The second issue is whether states can impose labeling and packaging requirements stricter than those imposed by EPA under FIFRA. Thus far, courts have upheld more restrictive state pesticide registration requirements.[9] In 1992, in Cipollone v. Liggett Group, 505 U.S. 504 (1992), the Supreme Court decided a pre-emption case involving health warnings on cigarette packs, addressing the extent to which federal law preempts state common law damages claims brought against cigarette manufacturers. Subsequently, when the FIFRA preemption case of Papas v. Zoecon Corporation, 112 S. Ct. 3020 (1992), reached the Supreme Court, the Court remanded the case to the Eleventh Circuit to decide in light of Cipollone. Since that time, however, although a number of federal appellate courts have ruled that FIFRA expressly preempts state law on the issue of labeling,[10] the appellate courts have continued to disagree on the extent to which they will uphold pre-emption on matters pertaining to product defects, warranties, and product testing.[11] In light of this disagreement among the federal appellate courts, why did Congress choose not to clarify these issues in its latest 1996 amendments to FIFRA?

Finally, can municipalities ban or limit the use of pesticides registered under FIFRA? The Supreme Court resolved a conflict among the federal circuits by unanimously holding, in Wisc. Public Intervenor v. Mortier, 501 U.S. 597 (1991), noted in Chapter Six, that municipalities are not pre-empted by FIFRA from controlling pesticide use:

> FIFRA nowhere seeks to establish an affirmative permit scheme for the actual use of pesticides. It certainly does not equate registration and labeling requirements with a general approval to apply pesticides throughout the Nation without regard to regional and local factors like climate, population, geography, and water supply. Whatever else FIFRA may supplant, it does not occupy the field of pesticide regulation in general or the area of local use permitting in particular. 501 U.S. at 613.

---

7. Pub. L. 100-532 §501.

8. Compare *Ferebee*, Chapter 4 (state suit not pre-empted) with Papas v. Upjohn, 926 F.2d 1019 (11th Cir. 1991)(state suit pre-empted); Save Our Ecosystems v. Clark, 747 F.2d 1240 (9th Cir. 1984)(FIFRA does not avoid duty to comply with NEPA.) See also Howarth, Pre-emption And Punitive Damages: The Conflict Continues Under FIFRA, 136 U. Pa. L. Rev. 1301 (1988) (favoring pre-emption.)

9. See Nat'l Agric. Chem. Ass'n. v. Rominger, 500 F. Supp 465 (E.D. Cal. 1980) and N.Y. State Pesticide Coalition v. Jorling, 874 F.2d 115 (2d Cir. 1989); see also Stever, Law of Chemical Regulation and Hazardous Waste §3.08 (1991) for an interesting discussion of this question.

10. The majority of courts since *Cipollone* have held that common law actions based on inadequate labeling or failure to warn are preempted by FIFRA. See the thorough discussion of this issue by the Kansas Supreme Court in Jenkins v. Amchem Products, 256 Kan. 602, 886 P.2d 869 (1994.)

11. See, e.g., Arkansas-Platte & Gulf Partnership v. Van Waters & Rogers, Inc., 981 F. 2nd 1177 (10th Cir. 1993); Papas v. Upjohn Co., 985 F.2d 516 (11th Cir. 1993); Lowe v. Sporicidin International, 47 F.3d 124 (4th Cir. 1995); Worm v. America Cyanamid, 5 F.3d 744 (4th Cir. 1993); King v. E.I. Dupont De Nemours & Co., 996 F.2d 1346 (1st Cir. 1993); Shaw v. Dow Brands, Inc., 994 F.2d 364 (7th Cir. 1993); Bice v. Leslie's Poolmart, Inc., 39 F.3d 887 (8th Cir. 1994.)

Although the local ordinance upheld in the *Mortier* case involved the legality of a permit requirement for aerial spraying on private lands, the opinion appears to condone local pesticide bans as well.

**8. FIFRA as a licensing statute.** As commentators have noted, FIFRA creates a unique form of licensing system. See The Perils of Unreasonable Risk: Information, Regulatory Policy, and Toxic Substances Control, 91 Colum. L. Rev. 261 (1991) (hereafter "Applegate"). Professor Applegate has written:

> If as a general rule manufacturers can develop toxicology information more cheaply than EPA, or if the cost is more efficiently or equitably borne by them and their customers, then it makes sense to assign the burden of proof to the manufacturer. In regulatory systems, shifting the burden of proof from the government to industry is typically accomplished by enacting a licensing or screening system. In the case of toxic substances, chemical producers would have to demonstrate the safety of their products before these products could be introduced into commerce. Licensing, therefore, not only provides an incentive to development of new information; it also shifts the cost of development away from government to a group that in theory has the capacity to absorb and spread the loss.

> Of the toxics statutes, only FIFRA has a true licensing scheme. Before pesticides can be sold, they must be registered and EPA must determine that they do not present an unreasonable risk. The registrant has the initial and continuing burden of demonstrating safety, though EPA has an initial burden of production in a cancellation proceeding and must ultimately be able to support its conclusions by substantial evidence. By placing the burden on the registrant, EPA is able to obtain whatever information it deems necessary to assess whether the chemical poses an unreasonable risk through the simple expedient of specifying data requirements for registration. EPA needs only the most general justification for these requirements, given the breadth of factors relevant to the unreasonable risk determination. Furthermore, the data requirements apply to all pesticides, eliminating the need to demand data on a chemical-by-chemical basis. This technique obviously brings the full profit motive to bear in developing adequate data in an expeditious manner. (Id. 308–309.)

Nevertheless, FIFRA, like all licensing statutes, has two major disadvantages:

> First, the premarket phase of product development is the time when the least information is known about a chemical's long-term effects. Without indications of chronic toxicity, it is hard to justify lengthy, expensive bioassays. Second, a licensing scheme intercepts only new or prospective risks. Since older chemicals are likely to be less well-tested relative to more recently licensed chemicals, the lack of data on existing chemicals constitutes a major gap in an information generation system. This problem can be resolved by a retroactive licensing arrangement like FIFRA's re-registration process.... Recognizing that licensing fails to generate any information for existing chemicals or post-license information for new ones, FIFRA established a five-year registration period after which reconsideration is necessary. This provision has not generated large amounts of data, however, because EPA has never used the five-year period aggressively for this purpose. Indeed, EPA has lacked sufficient resources to do much more than keep current on new registrations and cancellations. (Id., 312–313.)

These drawbacks in the FIFRA licensing system further emphasize the importance of the cancellation and suspension mechanisms. Ultimately, the best way to prevent pesticide pollution may be Integrated Pest Management (IPM) — placing primary reliance on biological and management controls, with limited applications of pesticides permitted only when absolutely necessary and where least likely to cause environmental damage. Genetic engineering also shows promise in redesigning plants for immunity to traditional pests.

**9. The trouble with FIFRA.** Although FIFRA creates a unique form of licensing, FIFRA has nonetheless come under attack for not effectively protecting public health and the environment against the adverse effects of toxic pesticides. The underlying problem of pesticide policy, manifested in FIFRA, has been to implement a defensible standard of "reasonable risk" that effectively places the burden of proof on pesticide registrants to show that their products' risks are acceptable under FIFRA's cost-benefit framework.

Well over one billion pounds of pesticides are applied annually in the United States, at least 50 million pounds in the Great Lakes Watershed alone. USGAO, Issues Concerning Pesticides Used in the Great Lakes Watershed (June, 1993). Pesticides have been shown to cause significant environmental impacts, such as acute or chronic health effects among workers in the manufacturing process, on third parties due to accidents in manufacturing or transport, among applicators and farmworkers, and among consumers due to residues on food; contamination of groundwater due to leaching; contamination of surface waters from farm run-off; poisoning of wildlife; and contamination of the environment due to improper disposal of unused pesticides and their containers. Hornstein, Lessons from Federal Pesticide Regulation on the Paradigms and Politics of Environmental Law Reform, 10 Yale J. Reg. 369, 394–95 (1993). Pesticide contamination of groundwater, for example, is a potent threat to human health because nearly 50 percent of all Americans derive their potable water from groundwater. Many of these are home-owners on private wells who drink untreated groundwater directly from aquifers.

In 1991, the United States General Accounting Office evaluated EPA's efforts to deal with the problem of groundwater contamination by pesticides. Pesticides: EPA Could Do More to Minimize Groundwater Contamination (April, 1991). In testimony based on that study, a USGAO official concluded that

> EPA needs to take more initiative in ensuring that groundwater contamination by pesticides is minimized. Efforts are needed in three areas. First, EPA has been slow in reviewing the scientific studies needed to assess pesticides' potential to leach into groundwater. Therefore, detailed information on the factors that contribute to leaching is not available to pesticide applicators and the pace of reassessing older pesticides has been slowed. Second, while EPA has used the regulatory tools available[12] in some cases, the agency could do more to help prevent groundwater contamination from worsening. Third, when EPA assesses risks from pesticide residues in food — in order to set residue limits known as tolerances — the agency is not routinely considering the additional exposure that can result from pesticide-contaminated groundwater. As a result, the agency lacks assurance that tolerances for pesticides that leach into groundwater are set low enough to protect public health.

---

12. Such as prominent advisories on pesticide labels, prohibitions on use within a specified distance of wells (i.e., well setbacks), prohibitions on use in designated geographic areas, and restricting pesticides' use to certified applicators. [Eds.]

Professor Hornstein attributes these problems, in great measure, to the centrality of risk assessment under FIFRA:

> Risk analysis...serves as a procedural device that favors pesticide-using political constituencies in three ways. First, because EPA has no independent method of developing data, risk analysis makes EPA dependent on the data generated by pesticide manufacturers — raising opportunities for various types of bias. Information bias is not limited to cases of data falsification.... The more intractable problems are foot-dragging in submitting data to [EPA] and the ability of industry to shade the way data is presented (without falsification) simply by emphasizing the subtle but genuinely contestable "inference options" on which risk assessments depend. In the mid-70s, an internal EPA audit on the data underlying twenty-three randomly selected pesticides found that "all but one of the tests reviewed were unreliable and inadequate to demonstrate safety" — a level of unreliability that, by 1992, continued for at least some pesticides.... In short, the risk assessment enterprise is so information intensive that it creates strategic incentives to avoid a serious scientific examination of "true" levels of public health and environmental risk.

> Second, despite the burden of proof ostensibly shouldered by pesticide manufacturers under FIFRA, the informational demands of risk analysis doom the regulatory process to a perpetual state of slow motion. The General Accounting Office (GAO) reported in March 1992 that, "After some 20 years collecting data to reevaluate the health and environmental effects of 19,000 older pesticides, EPA...had reregistered only 2 products. Despite a congressional deadline of 1997 recently set for reregistration, GAO confirms EPA's own projections that the reregistration effort will extend "until early in the next century." Even when EPA chooses to act, the risk analyses required for Special Reviews or cancellation proceedings effectively inoculate manufacturers against timely action. Special Reviews, which were introduced in the mid-1970s to accelerate the cancellation process which then took an average of two years, now themselves average over seven years.... As a practical matter, the burdensomeness of risk analysis has tempered FIFRA's success in shifting the burden of proof to manufacturers.

> Third, risk analysis offers the conceptual umbrella of "science" under which numerous non-scientific values can take shelter from public scrutiny and yet prolong the longevity of pesticides that may be neither desirable nor needed....[13]

Thus FIFRA, although it facially requires a manufacturer to bear a more demanding burden of proof than ToSCA, has failed because, in practice, political pressures have caused the same "information bias" in FIFRA that has virtually disabled ToSCA.[14]

Are proactive market access statutes inherently ineffectual in a nation that presumes the beneficence of an unregulated market system? Professor Hornstein does not directly ask this question, but he appears to imply a positive answer to it when

13. Hornstein, Lessons From Federal Pesticide Regulation on the Paradigms and Politics of Environmental Law Reform, 10 Yale J. Reg. 369, 436-38 (1993) (hereinafter "Hornstein".)

14. Of particular interest to the observation that market access statutes are handicapped by a persistent "information bias" is a line of cases holding that a manufacturer that withholds information from a federal agency is estopped from asserting preemption of packaging and labeling claims. See Roberson v. DuPont, 863 F. Supp. 929 (W. D. Ark. 1994); Burke v. Dow Chem. Co., 797 F. Supp. 1128, 1141 (E.D.N.Y. 1992) (recognizing that allowing preemption would "permit a manufacturer that was...aware of dangers to refrain from informing EPA of needed changes in its product's label and then to hide behind the very label it knew to be inadequate."); and Hurley v. Lederle Lab. Div. of American Cyanamid, 863 F.2d 1173 (5th Cir. 1988.)

he argues that FIFRA has "[been] one of the most colossal regulatory failures in Washington" because it does not get at the root causes of excessive pesticide use. American pesticide law "is not a body of law that addresses in any strategic way the underlying prevalence of pesticides in American agriculture, nor is it a body of law designed to minimize pesticide use."[15] He recommends a cause-based approach to pesticide regulation that would emphasize pest control technologies to limit pesticide use without significantly decreasing crop yields or growers' profitability and that would address existing economic incentive structures that lead growers to bypass improved technologies in favor of pesticide use which exceeds economically optimal levels. Professor Hornstein advocates the exploration of various policy options, such as pesticide risk taxes and enhanced "extension" programs, to encourage low-input agriculture.

There is evidence that EPA is beginning to use its authority to prevent pesticide pollution of groundwater. For the first time, EPA has registered a pesticide (acetochlor) only on condition that it not be detected in groundwater. Production of acetochlor must immediately be suspended if it is detected in groundwater. The acetochlor registration also includes a ten-year "sunset" (termination of registration) provision.

## B. REGULATING MARKET ACCESS OF TOXICS: THE TOXIC SUBSTANCES CONTROL ACT

The Toxic Substances Control Act of 1976 (ToSCA) extended the product regulation concept to most new and existing chemicals. Both environmental and industry groups lobbied heavily during congressional deliberations over ToSCA. The result is perhaps the most complex, confusing, and ineffective of all our federal environmental protection statutes.

### R. Druley and G. Ordway, The Toxic Substances Control Act, 1-4 (1977)

As summarized by the House Interstate and Foreign Commerce Committee Report, the major provisions of the Act:

- Require manufacturers and processors of potentially harmful chemical substances and mixtures to test the substances or mixtures, as required by rules issued by the Administrator of [EPA], so that their effect on health and the environment may be evaluated.
- Require manufacturers of new chemical substances and manufacturers and processors of existing chemical substances for significant new uses to notify the Administrator ninety days in advance of commercial production.
- Authorize delays or restrictions on the manufacture of a new chemical substance if there is inadequate information to evaluate the health or environmental effects of the substance and if in the absence of such information, the substance may cause or significantly contribute to an unreasonable risk to health or the environment.

---

15. Hornstein, 392.

- Authorize the Administrator to adopt rules to prohibit the manufacture, processing, or distribution of a chemical substance or mixture, to require labeling, or to regulate the manner of disposal of a chemical substance or mixture for which there is a reasonable basis to conclude that it causes or significantly contributes to an unreasonable risk to health or the environment.

- Authorize the Administrator to obtain injunctive relief from a United States district court to protect the public and the environment from an imminently hazardous chemical substance or mixture.

- Authorize the Administrator to require manufacturers and processors to submit reports and maintain records respecting their commercially produced chemical substances and mixtures, to maintain records respecting adverse health or environmental effects of such substances and mixtures, and to provide available health and safety data on them.

- Require manufacturers and processors of chemical substances and mixtures to immediately notify the Administrator of information indicating that one of their substances or mixtures causes or contributes to a substantial risk to health or the environment.

- Permit administrative inspections to enforce the bill and authorize court actions for seizures of chemical substances and mixtures which have been manufactured or distributed in violation of the requirements of the bill or of rules and orders promulgated under it.

- Permit citizens to bring suits to obtain compliance with the bill.

- Permit federal district courts to order the Administrator to initiate rule-making proceedings in response to citizen petitions.

- Set up procedural mechanisms to insure that all interested persons have an opportunity to participate in the agency rulemaking proceedings.

- Provide protection for employees who cooperate in the enforcement of the bill.

- Provide for evaluation on a continuing basis of the effects on employment of actions taken under the bill....

TESTING AND PREMARKET NOTIFICATION... Under the Act, EPA cannot require testing of every chemical. The Act does not regulate all chemicals which pose a risk, but only those which the EPA finds present an "unreasonable" risk of harm to human health or the environment. Accordingly, EPA must first find that there may be a risk or that there may be extensive human or environmental exposure and that information is lacking and testing is necessary. Given these findings, EPA must issue a rule requiring a manufacturer to perform testing and specifying the actual form of testing.

EPA is to issue its testing rules with the advice of an inter-agency committee, which will recommend testing priorities. Although the committee's advice is not binding, EPA is required to publish reasons for not requiring testing of certain specially designated compounds given high priority by the committee.

One of the key provisions of the Act is the section requiring manufacturers to provide EPA with data in advance of marketing. Chemical manufacturers must provide at least a 90-day notice before starting the manufacture of a new chemical or marketing a chemical for a new use as prescribed by EPA.

In order to determine what constitutes a new chemical that must be reported to EPA, EPA must publish an inventory list of chemicals known to be manufactured in the U.S. If a substance is not listed, it is to be considered a new chemical, and its planned production must be reported.

Under certain circumstances EPA can block the marketing of a chemical product pending the completion of testing. If a test order has been issued, test data must be submitted at the same time as the pre-market notification. Because testing may often require several years, this is a much more stringent requirement than simple 90-day notification.

EPA may also publish a hazardous substance list and can even do so by generic names. A manufacturer planning to market a substance included in the list must submit data to show that it is not a hazard for health or the environment.

Finally, if EPA determines upon notification that it has insufficient data on which to base a safety judgment, it may issue a proposed order to block production until testing is completed. The manufacturer may protest this order, and in this case EPA must apply to a federal district court for an injunction in order to block production.

Experimental and research chemicals produced in small quantities are exempt from the premarket notification requirements of the Act.

[ToSCA also does not apply to the following products regulated under other federal laws: firearms and ammunition; food, food additives, and drugs and cosmetics; meat and meat products; eggs and egg products; poultry and poultry products; pesticides; tobacco or tobacco products; and nuclear materials.]

### Chemical Manufacturers Association v. Environmental Protection Agency
United States Circuit Court of Appeals for the D.C. Circuit (1988)
859 F.2d 977

WALD, C.J. Petitioners, Chemical Manufacturers Association and four companies that manufacture chemicals (collectively "CMA"), seek to set aside a rule promulgated by the Environmental Protection Agency. This Final Test Rule was promulgated under §4 of the Toxic Substances Control Act. The final test rule required toxicological testing to determine the health effects of the chemical 2-ethylhexanoic acid ("EHA")....

We uphold EPA's interpretation of TSCA as empowering the Agency to issue a test rule on health grounds where it finds a more-than-theoretical basis for suspecting that the chemical substance in question presents an "unreasonable risk of injury to health." This, in turn, requires the Agency to find a more-than-theoretical basis for concluding that the substance is sufficiently toxic, and human exposure to it is sufficient in amount, to generate an "unreasonable risk of injury to health." We hold, further, that EPA can establish the existence and amount of human exposure on the basis of inferences drawn from the circumstances under which the substance is manufactured and used. EPA must rebut industry-supplied evidence attacking those inferences only if the industry evidence succeeds in rendering the probability of exposure in the amount found by EPA no more than theoretical or speculative. The probability of infrequent or even one-time exposure to individuals can warrant a test rule, so long as there is a more-than-theoretical basis for determining that exposure in such doses presents an "unreasonable risk of injury to health." Finally, we hold that the Agency correctly applied these standards in this case and that its findings are supported by substantial evidence.

Consequently, we affirm the Final Test Rule.

TSCA provides for a two-tier system for evaluating and regulating chemical substances to protect against unreasonable risks to human health and the environment. Section 6 of the Act permits EPA to regulate a substance that the Agency has found "presents or will present an unreasonable risk of injury to health or the environment." Section 4 of the Act empowers EPA to require testing of a suspect substance in order to obtain the toxicological data necessary to make a decision whether or not to regulate the substance under §6. The Act provides, not surprisingly, that the level of certainty of risk warranting a §4 test rule is lower than that warranting a §6 regulatory rule. EPA is empowered to require testing where it finds that the manufacture, distribution, processing, use or disposal of a particular chemical substance "may present an unreasonable risk of injury to human health or the environment." The Agency's interpretation of this statutory standard for testing is the central issue in this case.

One of the chief policies underlying the Act is that adequate data should be developed with respect to the effect of chemical substances and mixtures on health and the environment and that the development of such data should be the responsibility of those who manufacture and those who process such chemical substances and mixtures.

The statute establishes an Interagency Testing Committee, comprised of scientists from various federal agencies, to recommend that EPA give certain chemicals "priority consideration" for testing. Under §4, the Agency "shall by rule require that testing [of a particular chemical] be conducted" if three factors are present: (i) activities involving the chemical "may present an unreasonable risk of injury to health or the environment"; (ii) "insufficient data and experience" exist upon which to determine the effects of the chemical on health or environment; and (iii) testing is necessary to develop such data. The companies that manufacture and process the substance are to conduct the tests and submit the data to the Agency. Costs of the testing are to be shared among the companies, either by agreement or by EPA order in the absence of agreement.

A test rule promulgated under §4 is subject to judicial review in a court of appeals.... A test rule may be set aside if it is not "supported by substantial evidence in the rulemaking record...taken as a whole."

EHA is a colorless liquid with a mild odor. It is used exclusively as a chemical intermediate or reactant in the production of metal soaps, peroxyesters and other products used in industrial settings. EHA itself is totally consumed during the manufacture of these products; as a result, no products offered for sale to industry or to consumers contain EHA.

The Interagency Testing Committee first designated EHA for priority consideration for health effects tests on May 29, 1984. The Committee based its recommendation in part on the structural similarity of EHA to chemicals known to cause cancer in test animals and on its finding that insufficient information existed concerning the chronic health effects of EHA. Subsequently, EPA held two public meetings on EHA. During these meetings, in which persons representing the petitioners made appearances, EPA sought information on a variety of issues relating to EHA uses, production and human exposure.

EPA issued a proposed test rule on May 17, 1985. The rule proposed a series of tests to ascertain the health risks of EHA, and it set out proposed standards for the conduct of those tests. EPA based the Proposed Test Rule on a finding that EHA "may present an unreasonable risk" of subchronic toxicity (harm to bodily organs from repeated exposure over a limited period of time), oncogenicity (tumor formation) and developmental toxicity (harm to the fetus.) As to subchronic toxicity, EPA cited studies suggesting that both EHA and chemicals structurally similar to it cause harm to the livers of test animals. As to oncogenicity, EPA cited studies suggesting that chemicals structurally analogous to EHA cause cancer in laboratory animals. As to developmental toxicity, EPA cited studies indicating that both EHA and its chemical analogues have produced fetal malformations in test animals.

The Proposed Test Rule also addressed the question of whether humans are exposed to EHA, a question of critical importance to this case. The Agency acknowledged that, since no finished products contain EHA, consumer exposure is not a concern. It likewise discounted the dangers of worker exposure to EHA vapors. The Agency based its Proposed Test Rule solely on the potential danger that EHA will come in contact with the skin of workers. As evidence of potential dermal exposure, the Agency noted that approximately 400 workers are engaged in the manufacture, transfer, storage and processing of 20 to 25 million pounds of EHA per year. Further, rebutting claims by industry representatives that gloves are routinely worn during these activities, EPA noted that worker hygiene procedures "can vary widely throughout the industry," that workers are not required by existing federal regulations to wear gloves, and that the industry had not monitored work sites for exposure to EHA.

A public comment period commenced with the publication of the Proposed Test Rule and ended on July 16, 1985. EPA held a public meeting on October 8, 1985, to discuss issues related to the Proposed Test Rule. Industry representatives submitted extensive comments on July 15, 1985, and January 17, 1986. Before publication of the Final Test Rule, EPA received notice of a new study purporting to present further evidence of the potential developmental toxicity of EHA....

EPA published the Final Test Rule for EHA on November 6, 1986. The Rule required a 90-day subchronic toxicity test, a developmental toxicity test, and a pharmacokinetics test....The pharmacokinetics study required by the rule entailed the oral and dermal administration of EHA to experimental animals at low and high doses. The subchronic toxicity study involved administering EHA to animals in graduated daily doses over a period of 90 days. The developmental toxicity tests entailed administering EHA orally in various doses during the pregnancy of experimental animals. All studies were to be conducted in accordance with EPA standards. Results were to be submitted by certain deadlines, the last of which was 18 months after the effective date of the Final Test Rule....

The Toxic Substances Control Act requires EPA to promulgate a test rule under §4 if a chemical substance, *inter alia*, "may present an unreasonable risk of injury to health or the environment." The parties both accept the proposition that the degree to which a particular substance presents a risk to health is a function of two factors: (a) human exposure to the substance, and (b) the toxicity of the substance. See Ausimont U.S.A., Inc. v. EPA, 838 F.2d 93, 96 (3d. Cir.1988.) They also agree that EPA must make some sort of threshold finding as to the existence of an "unreasonable risk of injury to health." The parties differ, however, as to the manner in which this finding must be made. Specifically, three issues are presented.

The first issue is whether, under §4 of TSCA, EPA must first find that the existence of an "unreasonable risk of injury to health" is more probable than not in order to issue a test rule. CMA argues that the statute requires a more-probable-than-not finding. EPA disagrees, contending that the statute is satisfied where the existence of an "unreasonable risk of injury to health" is a substantial probability — that is, a probability that is more than merely theoretical, speculative, or conjectural.

The second issue is whether, once industry has presented evidence tending to show an absence of human exposure, EPA must rebut it by producing direct evidence of exposure. CMA claims that, when industry evidence casts doubt on the existence of exposure, the burden of production shifts back to EPA, which must produce direct evidence documenting actual instances in which exposure has taken place. EPA, on the other hand, argues that it can make the requisite finding of exposure based solely on inferences drawn from the circumstances under which a chemical substance is manufactured and used.

The third issue is whether the Agency has authority to issue a test rule where any individual's exposure to a substance is an isolated, non-recurrent event. CMA argues that, even if EPA presents direct evidence of exposure, the Act precludes issuance of a test rule where exposure consists only of rare instances involving brief exposure. EPA contends, on the other hand, that the Act does not require in all circumstances a risk of recurrent exposure....

As to the first issue in this case,...[b]oth the wording and structure of TSCA reveal that Congress did not expect that EPA would have to document to a certainty the existence of an "unreasonable risk" before it could require testing. This is evident from the two-tier structure of the Act. In order for EPA to be empowered to regulate a chemical substance, the Agency must find that the substance "presents or will present an unreasonable risk of injury to health or the environment." The testing provision at issue here, by contrast, empowers EPA to act at a lower threshold of certainty than that required for regulation. Specifically, testing is warranted if the substance "*may* present an unreasonable risk of injury to health or the environment." Thus, the language of §4 signals that EPA is to make a probabilistic determination of the presence of "unreasonable risk."

The legislative history of TSCA compels a further conclusion. It not only shows that "unreasonable risk" need not be a matter of absolute certainty; it shows the reasonableness of EPA's conclusion that "unreasonable risk" need not be established to a more-probable-than-not degree.

A House Report on the version of the bill that eventually became TSCA underscores the distinction between the §6 standard and the §4 standard. To issue a test rule, EPA need not find that a substance actually does cause or present an "unreasonable risk."

> Such a finding requirement would defeat the purpose of the section, for if the Administrator is able to make such a determination, regulatory action to protect against the risk, not additional testing, is called for. H.R. Rep. No.1341, 94th Cong., 2d Sess.

The House Report also contains signals indicating that Congress expected EPA to act even when evidence of "unreasonable risk" was less than conclusive. According to that report, the word "may" in §4 was intended to focus the Agency's attention on chemical substances "*about which there is a basis for concern, but about which there is inadequate* information to reasonably predict or determine the effects of the substance or mixture on health or the environment." Id. at 17 (emphasis added.) The Conference Committee Report re-emphasized that the statutory language focused the Agency's attention on substances "about which there is a basis for concern." H.R. Conf. Rep. No. 1679, 94th Cong., 2d Sess. 61 (1976.)

These indications of congressional intent illustrate that EPA's reading of TSCA is a permissible one. Congress intended to authorize testing where the existence of an "unreasonable risk" could not yet be "reasonably predicted." The Agency's determination that it is empowered to act where the existence of an "unreasonable risk" cannot yet be said to be more probable than not is entirely consistent with that expression of intent. The EPA interpretation is likewise consistent with the level of certainty suggested by the phrase "basis for concern." To accept the CMA's position would require the Agency to gather "adequate" information to make a reasonable prediction or determination of risk before issuing a test rule. To say the least, this is not mandated by the statutory history, which indicates Congress's desire that EPA act on the basis of rational concern even in the absence of "adequate" information that an unreasonable risk existed. Section 4 may permissibly be read to authorize issuance of a test rule on the basis of less than more-probable-than-not evidence about a potentially unreasonable risk to health.

This conclusion is further bolstered by the legislative history underlying §6. If CMA were correct that EPA must make a more-probable-than-not finding of risk under §4's "may present" language, then it would logically follow that §6 — which contains the term "presents or will present an unreasonable risk" — must require an even stronger than more-probable-than-not demonstration of "unreasonable risk." Yet neither §6 nor its legislative history indicate any such super-requirement of certainty. Indeed, §6 states expressly that the Agency need only find a "reasonable basis" to conclude that an "unreasonable risk" exists. A "reasonable basis" requirement is certainly no more demanding than a more-probable-than-not requirement; indeed the phrase suggests a less demanding standard. This interpretation is confirmed by the House Report, which states that an EPA finding of "unreasonable risk" under §6 is not expected to be supported by the same quantum of evidence as is customary in administrative proceedings.... In sum, the standard Congress set for §6 regulation, that the chemical "will present an unreasonable risk," is no more rigorous (and arguably is less rigorous) than a more-probable-than-not finding. It follows as a matter of course that §4's "may present" language demands even less.

Of course, it is also evident from the legislative history that Congress did not intend to authorize EPA to issue test rules on the basis of mere hunches. The House Report states:

> The term "may"...does not permit the Administrator to make a finding respecting probability of a risk on the basis of mere conjecture or speculation, i.e., [that] it may or may not cause a risk. H.R. Rep. No.1341, at 18.

Congress obviously intended §4 to empower EPA to issue a test rule only after it had found a solid "basis for concern" by accumulating enough information to demonstrate a more-than-theoretical basis for suspecting that an "unreasonable risk" was involved in the use of the chemical....

[Relying on the "more-than-theoretical-basis" test, the court then rejected CMA's other two arguments regarding use of inferences versus direct evidence of exposure and rare versus recurrent exposure. Finally, the court analyzed the evidence submitted by EPA for the Final Test Rule and held that the Agency had produced substantial evidence to demonstrate not fact, but doubt and uncertainty."]

## COMMENTARY AND QUESTIONS

1. **An exceptional case.** *Chemical Manufacturers* is an unusual example of ToSCA working smoothly with regard to the promulgation of test rules for existing chemicals. When ToSCA was enacted, some commentators predicted that the statute would be unenforceable because it had been so compromised during the legislative process. Unfortunately, these dire predictions have often been borne out. ToSCA's requirements that EPA promulgate test rules through notice and comment rule-making and support them by substantial evidence, combined with the inadequacy of EPA's budget for ToSCA implementation and intense lobbying by industry, have militated against EPA promulgation of test rules. "By the end of fiscal year 1989, EPA had received full test data for only six chemicals and had not completed review of the data for any."[16] EPA did not perform its mandatory duty to respond to Interagency Testing Committee ("ITC") recommendations until compelled to do so by court order. NRDC v. Costle, 14 ERC 1858, 10 E.L.R. 20274, 11 E.L.R. 20202 (1980.) Moreover,

> EPA has historically rarely imposed a testing rule.... The agency has more often found reasons for declining to follow the ITC's testing recommendations. In addition, EPA has followed an administrative practice of entering into Negotiated Testing Agreements (NTAs) with industry trade associations in lieu of issuing test rules, wherever possible. Stever, The Law Of Chemical Regulation And Hazardous Waste 2-8 (1991).

The NTA program was struck down in NRDC v. EPA, 595 F. Supp 1255 (S.D. N.Y. 1984), partly because it excluded public interest groups. A new process called "testing consent agreements," which provides for public participation, is currently in effect. But ToSCA's cumbersome test rule procedures give EPA and the public little leverage in negotiations with industry.

2. **ToSCA and new chemicals.** ToSCA is no more effective with regard to the introduction of new chemicals into commerce. EPA cannot require the testing of all new chemicals under ToSCA. Unless a test rule is in effect for a component of a new chemical compound, or that component is included on EPA's §5(b)(4) "suspect list," a manufacturer need not submit health and environmental test data unless it has independently developed these data or they are generally available elsewhere. Thus, ToSCA does not require a set of premarket data on a new chemical. Consequently, only half of all premarket notifications (PMNs) submitted under ToSCA contain any toxicity information at all, and less than twenty percent include data on long-term toxicity.[17] Does ToSCA actually discourage premarket testing and encourage concealment of information? Or would a manufacturer most likely test a substance prior to manufacture in order to forestall tort liability? For a negative answer to the latter question, see Applegate at 299 ("industry has real incentives to avoid either creating toxic risk data or disclosing the data it already has"), and Lyndon, Information Economics and Chemical Toxicity: Designing Laws to Produce and Use Data, 87 Mich. L. Rev. 1795 (1989).

---

16. Applegate, at 319, citing USGAO, EPA's Chemical Testing Program Has Made Little Progress (April, 1990.)

17. Applegate, at 303, citing Office of Technology Assessment, The Information Content of Premanufacture Notices (1983.)

If EPA does not act to require testing before the expiration of the 90-day PMN period plus an optional additional 90 days, the manufacturer may commence manufacture or distribution. On the other hand, if after receipt of a PMN EPA finds that it has insufficient information on which to base an evaluation of the chemical substance, it may propose a test rule or, after making findings similar to those in §4, it may issue a proposed order to prohibit or limit the production of the substance. If the manufacturer formally objects to the proposed order, EPA must seek an injunction in federal district court under §5(e.) The strictness of these time constraints and the necessity of resorting to judicial action if a test rule cannot be proposed in time virtually guarantees agency inaction.

3. **FIFRA and ToSCA.** In the congressional proceedings leading to the passage of ToSCA, the Senate preferred a licensing system similar to FIFRA, while the House favored allowing new chemicals to be marketed without notification or registration unless the chemicals or their components appeared on EPA's "suspect list." The emergent ToSCA compromise was based on notification and discretionary intervention by EPA. According to Professor Lyndon, the FIFRA presumption that a substance is unsafe unless the manufacturer proves safety has, in ToSCA, been transformed into a presumption that a substance is safe unless EPA can prove that it is unsafe:

> TSCA's requirement that the EPA issue a rule before requiring testing distinguishes it from food, drug, and pesticide regulations, which mandate production of safety data prior to marketing. The TSCA standard essentially establishes a presumption of safety, which the agency must overcome before it may require further testing of a chemical. Thus, the TSCA's use of strict rule-making standards inhibits the very information production the statute was written to encourage.[18]

There is a fundamental ToSCA paradox or "Catch-22" in regulatory information-gathering. Where is EPA to procure the information that it needs to require manufacturers — who have every incentive to suppress information — to produce health and safety data regarding new and existing chemicals? Does EPA have to know already what it needs to know in order to ask for information about it?

4. **Regulation and the common law.** CMA's arguments in opposition to the Final Test Rule were based on common law analogues: (1) the more-probable-than-not test is similar to the "preponderance of the evidence" standard in common law civil litigation; (2) the criticism of EPA's inferences regarding modes of EHA use reflects the burden placed on a common law plaintiff to prove causation-in-fact by a preponderance of the evidence; and (3) the objection to EPA's regulating non-recurrent exposures echoes a common law defendant's argument that an injunction should not be granted because there is an adequate remedy at law (damages) if the event is unlikely to recur. Administrative agencies, however, are not limited by these common law constraints, as the court reaffirmed in its rejection of CMA's arguments.

5. **The more-than-theoretical-basis test.** Could this standard be used to support a test rule where EPA has not yet explored the toxicity of a chemical, but suspects,

---

18. Lyndon, 87 Mich. L. Rev. at 1824.

based on an educated guess, that the substance may be toxic? The more-than-the-oretical-basis test could probably not be extended this far, but another section of ToSCA might cover such a situation. Section 4(a)(1)(B) provides that EPA may require testing where

> a chemical substance or mixture is or will be produced in substantial quanti-ties, and (i) it enters or may reasonably be anticipated to enter the environment in substantial quantities or (ii) there is or may be significant or substantial human exposure to such substance or mixture.

In Chemical Manufacturers Association v. EPA, 899 F.2d 344 (5th Cir. 1990)(fre-quently referred to as *Chemical Manufacturers II*), EPA contended that

> while there is a need to show a potential for exposure in order to make a §4(a)(1)(A) finding ["may present an unreasonable risk of injury to health or the environment"], the exposure threshold is much lower than that under §4(a)(1)(B.) This is because the former...finding was intended to focus on those instances where EPA has a scientific basis for suspecting potential toxicity and reflects that the potential for risk to humans may be significant even when the potential for exposure seems small, as, for example, when the chemical is dis-covered to be hazardous at very low levels. In contrast, the §4(a)(1)(B) finding was intended to allow EPA to require testing, not because of suspicions about the chemical's safety, but because there may be a substantial or significant human exposure to a chemical whose hazards have not been explored. 899 F.2d at 358, n. 20.

The language of §4(a)(1)(B), however, is so ambiguous that this section is of doubt-ful utility. In *Chemical Manufacturers II*, the Court remanded the test rule to EPA to explain what it meant by "substantial" quantities and human exposure.

6. **The role of economics.** All ToSCA regulatory decision-making must balance eco-nomic costs against environmental benefits under the "unreasonable risk" stan-dard imported from FIFRA. In addition, §2(c) provides that EPA "shall consider the environmental, economic, and social impact of any action" taken by it under ToSCA. Section 2(b) declares a policy that "authority over chemical substances...be exercised...so as not to impede unduly or create unnecessary economic barriers to technological innovation." Pursuant to §4(b), in specifying tests to be carried out, the EPA shall consider "the relative costs of the various test protocols and the methodologies which may be required." Is it fair to balance tangible and pre-dictable economic costs against intangible and uncertain environmental benefits? The human mind naturally prefers the certain to the uncertain, leading to a "fal-lacy of numeration." Should the "unreasonable risk" balance be weighted on the side of the environment? Going even further, Professor Applegate recommends that the "unreasonable risk" standard be eliminated from §4:

> Unreasonable risk should be replaced in the §4 context by a more readily sat-isfied, less complex standard — something, in short, with less baggage. The term "unreasonable" should be dropped. The appropriate level (as opposed to existence) of risk is a policy question and more suitable in the standard-setting stage than in data collection. Under §4, EPA should be exploring policy options, not setting policy. Reasonable restraint by EPA can be assured by the existing provision requiring cost-effective testing and by the usual under-standing that the term "risk" standing alone does not include de minimis risks. Applegate, at 320.

But is it likely that Congress will repudiate "unreasonable risk," even as to data collection? Congress often prefers standards such as "unreasonable risk," which leave the difficult policy decisions to administrative agencies and courts. Although many critics recommend that Congress allow agencies flexibility in areas of technical expertise and administrative procedure, and the Supreme Court has acknowledged that agencies should be allowed flexibility in setting their own procedures, the trend in Congress is often towards selective "micro-management" of deadlines and other goals. In many cases, the result has been agency paralysis, missed deadlines, and bureaucratic frustration.

**7. ToSCA §6.** Under §6 of ToSCA, EPA has authority to regulate existing chemicals that present unreasonable risks to health or the environment. EPA may place controls and restrictions, including outright bans if necessary, upon the manufacture, use, processing, disposal, or distribution of such chemicals. As discussed in *Chemical Manufacturers*, "if the Administrator finds that there is a reasonable basis to conclude that the manufacture, processing, distribution in commerce, use, or disposal of a chemical substance or mixture, or that any combination of such activities presents or will present an unreasonable risk of injury to health or the environment, the Administrator shall by rule" impose one of the following measures: a prohibition or limitation on the manufacture, processing, or distribution of a substance in general or for specific uses, or an imposition of concentration limits; a requirement as to labeling, public warning, recall, or recordkeeping; or a ban or limitation on a particular form of use or disposal. All other things being equal, however, EPA must regulate under another statute rather than ToSCA §9(b.) Although §6, like §4, has not been utilized very often,[19] it does represent a "catchall" or residuary pollution control statute, providing authority to regulate substances or uses that cannot be controlled under other federal pollution control statutes. EPA, for example, initially moved to regulate leaking underground storage tanks under ToSCA §6 until Congress enacted the 1984 RCRA amendments. See Chapter 17. EPA has also relied on §6 to set soil concentration limits for land application of dioxin-containing pulp and paper sludge. See 56 Fed. Reg. 21802 (May 10, 1991.)

**8. The EPA's Attempted Asbestos Ban.** Asbestos is a naturally occurring fibrous material that resists fire and most solvents. For years, it was used as a heat resistant insulator, in building materials, in fireproof gloves and clothing, and in motor vehicle brake linings. Asbestos, however, is also a toxic material. Occupational exposure to asbestos dust can cause cancer.

In 1989, after years of review of scientific evidence of asbestos carcinogenity, the EPA promulgated a final rule imposing a staged ban on most commercial uses of asbestos. Invoking §6 of ToSCA, EPA concluded that asbestos exposure "poses an unreasonable risk to human health."

In its 1991 decision in Corrosion Proof Fittings v. EPA (see Chapter 12), the Fifth Circuit held that the EPA had presented insufficient evidence to justify the asbestos ban. The Fifth Circuit concluded that EPA had failed to consider all necessary evidence and had failed to give adequate weight to the statutory language in

---

19. USGAO, Toxic Substances: Effectiveness of Unreasonable Risk Standards Unclear, 1-2 (1990.)

§6, which requires EPA to promulgate the least burdensome, reasonable regulation necessary to protect the environment adequately.

Corrosion Proof Fittings highlights the constraints on EPA in assessing risk and in engaging in risk management under §6 of ToSCA. Although EPA has the duty under ToSCA to assess and manage the risk posed by products like asbestos, Congress has imposed statutory limitations upon EPA in carrying out those functions. How is EPA to determine what is the least burdensome, reasonable regulation necessary to protect the environment? How should EPA engage in a cost-benefit risk balancing under §6? Would EPA's attempted asbestos ban have had more likelihood of success if §6 were more like the stark prohibition provisions of the former Delaney Clause?

9. **The PCB Mega Rule.** Polychlorinated biphenyls ("PCBs") are a class of compounds that were widely used in electrical equipment because of their low flammability, heat capacity, and dielectric properties. Transformers, cooling systems, hydraulic systems, electromagnets, switches, and voltage regulators were the primary types of equipment that contained PCBs.

When Congress enacted ToSCA, it was aware that PCBs were potentially carcinogenic and very persistent in the environment (they decomposed slowly.) Congress also was aware that PCBs can accumulate in plants, animals, and human tissue, and that PCBs have adverse effects on fish and wildlife. As a result, in §6(e) of ToSCA, Congress determined that PCBs presented an unreasonable risk to human health and the environment and banned the manufacture, processing, and distribution of PCBs, with certain exemptions. Congress directed EPA to promulgate regulations concerning the use, storage, and disposal of PCBs. EPA issued its first PCB regulations in 1979. See EDF v. EPA, 636 F.2d 1267 (D.C.Cir. 1980) (EPA's PCB regulations overturned and remanded.)

In the years since EPA began regulating PCBs, a number of issues have arisen that EPA and industry did not originally anticipate. Rather than address these issues on a piecemeal basis, EPA proposed a comprehensive overhaul of its PCB regulations on December 6, 1994 (59 Fed. Reg. 62787.) EPA's proposal, which is more commonly known as the "PCB Mega Rule," would amend the existing PCB regulations in several significant ways.

One of the most important changes under the proposed Rule is EPA's reinterpretation of the so-called "anti-dilution" rule. The anti-dilution rule states that no PCB regulation specifying a concentration can be avoided through dilution. In the past, EPA has applied the rule to all cases where dilution has occurred, even if the dilution was accidental.

For example, when liquids containing PCBs greater than 50 ppm are accidentally spilled onto soil or other material, the past interpretation of the anti-dilution rule required that all of the contaminated material be considered to contain the same PCB concentration as the original liquid (i.e., greater than 50 ppm.) This contaminated material was to be disposed of in an incinerator or in a RCRA-approved chemical waste landfill, even though its actual concentration might otherwise have allowed the material (but for the rule) to be disposed of in municipal or industrial solid waste landfills (at significantly less cost.) Under the proposed Rule, EPA will now allow PCBs to be disposed of according to the actual PCB concentration at the time of disposal, thereby reducing disposal costs for large volumes of soil contaminated with low concentrations of PCBs.

The proposed PCB Mega Rule also substantially revises EPA's PCB Spill Cleanup Policy (the "Spill Policy"). The Spill Policy establishes the criteria used by EPA to determine the adequacy of spill cleanups resulting from the release of materials containing PCBs. The Spill Policy requires the cleanup of PCBs to certain levels depending upon the spill location, the potential for exposure to residual PCBs remaining after cleanup, the concentration of PCBs initially spilled (high concentration or low), and the nature and size of the population at risk of exposure to residual PCBs. Under the Proposed Mega Rule, the EPA is now proposing to address the problem of PCBs in the environment through a single, flexible process. PCBs released into the environment prior to April 18, 1978 will now be considered disposed of in a manner that does not present a risk of exposure. No further disposal of non-landfilled material will be required unless EPA makes a finding that the released material presents a risk of exposure. If such a finding is made, EPA will then require remediation based on the degree of risk posed by the spill.

For spills or releases occurring after April 18, 1978, the PCB Mega Rule proposes three different methods for remediating the PCB-contamination: (1) remediation in accordance with specific parameters identified in the PCB Mega Rule itself; (2) remediation under a work plan meeting specified performance criteria approved by EPA; and (3) remediation utilizing a risk assessment, under which EPA would approve a cleanup consistent with the specific risks posed to the human health and the environment. Remediation under the parameters laid out in the PCB Mega Rule itself requires a 30-day notice to the regulatory authorities prior to implementation. Both the performance-based and risk-based categories require the submittal of an application to the appropriate regulatory parties followed by an approval before remediation can begin.

EPA is also proposing cleanup standards and procedures for PCB "non-remediation" waste. PCB non-remediation waste includes non-liquid bulk wastes such as debris from the demolition of buildings and "fluff" from the shredding of automobiles, household and industrial appliances. PCB non-remediation wastes must be disposed of in a TOSCA-approved incinerator or chemical waste landfill if the PCB concentration in the waste is above 50 ppm or in a municipal or industrial solid waste facility if the concentration is less than 50 ppm.

Industry is expected to save millions annually in disposal costs under the PCB Mega Rule. Is the Rule a form of deregulation for high volume, low PCB-concentration wastes?

10. **Market access statutes and confidentiality.** Given industry's desire to protect trade secrets from competitors, and potential tort plaintiffs' eagerness for access to health and safety testing data, both FIFRA and TOSCA contain extensive provisions regarding confidentiality of information disclosed to EPA. With regard to FIFRA, see Ruckelshaus v. Monsanto, 467 U.S. 986 (1984); as to TOSCA, see McGarity and

Shapiro, The Trade Secret Status of Health and Safety Testing Information: Reforming Agency Disclosure Policies, 93 Harv. L. Rev. 837 (1980), and Chevron v. Costle, 443 F. Supp 1024 (N.D. Cal.1978.)

11. **The future of ToSCA.** Although ToSCA is currently in eclipse, several commentators agree that it has tremendous potential for achieving environmental protection. Professor Guruswamy sees §3(5) of ToSCA, which defines the term "environment" to include "water, air, land, and the interrelationship which exists among and between water, air, and land and all living things," as the statutory lever for integrating our fragmented, media-specific pollution control statutes. Guruswamy, Integrating Thoughtways: Re-Opening of the Environmental Mind?, 1989 Wis. L. Rev. 463, 523-525 (1989.) Professor Applegate envisions an amended ToSCA as the key to coordinating and enhancing federal information-acquisition regarding toxic substances. In a gloomier vein, Professor Flournoy condemns the basic approaches of all agency decision making with regard to environmental protection, and recommends that Congress enact a more sophisticated structure. Flournoy, Legislating Inaction: Asking the Wrong Questions in Protective Environmental Decisionmaking, 15 Harv. Envtl. L. Rev. 327, 382–391 (1991.)

Statutes like ToSCA fail because there is an insufficient political consensus (1) to include provisions that are sufficiently clear and mandatory to be enforceable, and (2) if statutes are indeed clear and enforceable, to fund and enforce them once enacted. Congress is adept at enacting compromise legislation that appears to decide disputes between contending interest groups but does little to change the status quo. Agencies are adept at taking refuge in nonenforcement or "moderated" enforcement of statutes. ToSCA has failed for both reasons. Thus the real problem with ToSCA is not so much a legal one, as some commentators appear to suggest, as a political one. The dilemma that besets ToSCA has not changed since its congressional evolution during the 1970s: as a nation we have been, and still are, unwilling to institutionalize a fully preventive approach to pollution control in the face of the pervasive uncertainty that characterizes environmental decisionmaking. This dilemma recurs in discussions of recent policy shifts toward "pollution prevention." See Pollution Prevention Act of 1990, 42 U.S.C.A. §13101 et seq.

*For a successful technology, reality must take precedence over public relations, for nature cannot be fooled.*

— Richard Feynman

*No one ever went broke underestimating the taste of the American public.*

— H.L. Mencken

*Ready or not, we're all about to embark on one of the greatest adventures in industrial history.*

— Amory Lovins

# Chapter 16

# MARKET-ENLISTING STRATEGIES: ENVIRONMENTAL PROTECTIONS VIA EMISSIONS TRADING & OTHER ECONOMIC INCENTIVES

A. *Bubbles, Netting, Offsets, and Banking: the Initial Clean Air Act Trading Devices*

B. *Using Emissions Trading to Reduce Acid Deposition[1]*

C. *Using Emissions Trading to Slow Global Climate Change*

---

Market incentives and market-based regulatory strategies have found a new and somewhat unexpected medium for expression in environmental regulation. This is not a new idea in environmental regulation, although conscious use of market incentives to influence polluting behavior has played only a very small role until recently. Effluent taxes, such as disposal fees at landfills, have a considerable history and have had the effect of reducing the flow of landfill wastes. Bounties, beverage container deposit laws for example, affect polluting behavior, as do subsidies, a staple of the Clean Water Act's application to POTWs since its inception. In recent years, however, the use of emissions trading systems and other forms of economic strategies has become a major regulatory option in combating serious environmental problems at state and local levels, and, pushed by American enthusiasm, is now going global.

The appeal of market incentives is easy to understand: they seem to promise a form of regulation that works more effectively at lower total social cost and without extensive governmental oversight and bureaucracy.

There is a very simple matrix of behavioral assumptions underlying virtually all of the market incentives-based approaches to environmental regulation. As introduced in Chapter Two, these behavioral assumptions assume that firms and individuals are rational profit maximizers reacting to conditions set by relevant regulations. In the absence of regulation, waste disposal into the commons is a near costless activity, and is therefore the disposal method of choice. If costs are added to disposal, firms will react. The two predominant market regulatory devices that are used to internalize disposal costs are effluent taxes and marketable trading systems.[2] The behavioral assumptions are elementary —

---

1. Title IV contains both the sulfur dioxide trading program highlighted here and a nitrogen oxides control program that relies on traditional command and control performance techniques. See 42 U.S.C.A. §7651f.

2. After-the-fact cost internalization, as might be obtained using the common law, or CERCLA, is a slightly more attenuated form of effluent tax. The imposition of the cost (liability for damages) is less certain (suit might not be brought, a defense might succeed, etc.), but the expected results of such cases should influence polluting behavior. If the cost of controlling pollution is less than the expected cost of polluting and paying damages, firms will choose not to pollute.

## Table 1: Behavioral Assumptions

| FIRM CHARACTERISTICS | EFFLUENT TAXES | EMISSIONS TRADING SYSTEMS |
|---|---|---|
| High-cost pollution avoider | Will pay the tax and continue to pollute | Will purchase credits in the market and continue to pollute |
| Low-cost pollution avoider | Will avoid the tax and reduce pollution | Will sell credits in the market and reduce pollution |

The expansion in the use of market enlisting regulatory regimes, particularly emissions trading, is nothing short of revolutionary. In 1990, Congress enacted Title IV of the Clean Air Act, a market trading program that is intended to reduce sulfur dioxide emission in the United States by 50% as part of the Clean Air Act Amendments' effort to combat acid rain. By December 1997, emissions trading had emerged at the Kyoto conference on global climate change as the central strategy for managing greenhouse gases on a global scale. During those same few years, emissions trading also has been tried or suggested to manage local air pollution in the Los Angeles area and in other AQCRs, to reduce otherwise unregulated upstream non-point source agricultural discharges into rivers, to cap total metals deposition into POTWs so that the resulting sewage sludge is less hazardous, and more.

Given the apparent simplicity of using market incentives to affect polluter behavior, it almost strains credulity to realize that there has been so little use of them in the history of pollution control in the United States. First, and more importantly for present purposes, designing market incentive systems that implement any particular degree of environmental protection is not so simple to do as it appears. Second, the history of environmental regulation (See Chapter Five), beginning as it did with small-scale decentralized efforts to solve isolated congestion of the commons problems, then growing into broad delegations to administrative agencies, and so on, simply did not lend itself to "discovering" the elegance of market incentives as a regulatory device until relatively late in the game. This chapter emphasizes air pollution emissions trading since 1970, addressing other media, older developments, and effluent taxes only secondarily.

## A. BUBBLES, NETTING, OFFSETS, AND BANKING: THE INITIAL CLEAN AIR ACT TRADING DEVICES

Bubbles, netting, offsets and banking are four terms that describe different parts of the emissions trading programs that came into use during the first twenty years of the Clean Air Act's existence. It is important to understand that these emissions trading devices, as they have been employed to date, have been used as an adjunct to the Clean Air Act's stationary source emissions control strategies for the criteria pollutants. This means that firms engaged in emissions trading are large emitters operating with permits written under state implementation plans (SIPs). As discussed in Chapter Eight, even before 1990 these permits fixed, with considerable precision, allowable maximum emissions limits for each of the criteria pollutants from each stationary source.

Bubbles, netting, and offsets are related activities: each allows a reduction in presently authorized emissions of pollutants to excuse some increase in permitted emissions. Banking, as the name suggests, allows for reductions in pollution to be stored in an "account" which is later drawn upon as part of a bubble, netting, or offset transaction. The central device for emissions trading is the recognition of credit for reducing pollution below the allowable (permitted) levels previously established by the Clean Air Act:

> EPA's emissions trading program extends, rather than replaces, the system for regulating emissions of air pollutants established under the Clean Air Act. Emissions trading allows the exchange of emission rights, both externally (between firms) and internally (within a single firm). The commodities exchanged in emissions trading are emission reduction credits (ERCs), which are property rights to emit air pollutants. A firm creates ERCs by reducing its emissions of a specific pollutant below the baseline level allowed by its permit, thereby creating surplus reductions. EPA regulations specify that these reductions must be surplus, enforceable, permanent, and quantifiable in order to qualify as ERCs.[3]

Conceptually, there is very little difference among the three operative programs — bubbles, netting, and offsets. All involve trading reductions in presently allowable pollution in exchange for rights to increase other emissions. As the following excerpt explains, the most vital distinctions among the devices lie in the contexts in which they are applicable and, consequently, the regulatory command and control requirements that can at times be avoided by the use of the emissions trades.

### Robert Hahn & Gordon Hester, Marketable Permits: Lessons for Theory and Practice
16 Ecology Law Quarterly 361, 370–372 (1989)

To understand why different elements of emissions trading vary widely in their performance, it is important to have a working knowledge of what they enable firms to do. As the following summary reveals, the four elements [netting, offsets, bubbles, and banking] differ dramatically: they vary in their provision for external trades, in the types of sources that can participate, and in the locus of administrative control.

Netting allows a modified source to avoid the most stringent emission limits that would be applied to the modification by reducing emissions from another source within the same plant.[4] Thus, netting necessarily involves internal trading only. This reduces the net emission increase to a level below that which is considered significant — hence the term, netting. Netting can result in small net increases in emissions because the cutoff level for treating an emission increase as significant is greater than zero. Netting is controlled at the state level and — subject to individual state restrictions — may be used in attainment and nonattainment areas.[5]

Offsets are used by new and modified sources in nonattainment areas and by certain specified sources in attainment areas. The Clean Air Act specifies that no

---

3. Hahn & Hester, Where Did All the Markets Go? An Analysis of EPA's Emissions Trading Program, 6 Yale J. on Reg. 109, 114 (1989). In support of the passage, Hahn and Hester cite EPA, Emission Trading Policy Statement, General Principles for Creation, Banking and Use of Emission Reduction Credits, Final Policy, 51 Fed. Reg. 43,831 (1986).

4. EPA, Prevention of Significant Air Quality Deterioration, 39 Fed. Reg. 42,510 (1974) (final rule).

5. EPA, Emissions Trading Policy Statement, 51 Fed. Reg. 43,814 (1986) (final policy).

## Table 1: Relation of Emission Limits, by Source Type and Area Class, to Emissions Trading

| SOURCE TYPE | AREA CLASS | EMISSIONS TRADING OPTIONS | OPTIONAL OR MANDATORY | APPLICABLE EMISSION LIMIT[1] | CAN LIMIT BE AVOIDED BY TRADING? |
|---|---|---|---|---|---|
| New | Attainment | Offsets | Optional | BACT | No |
| New | Non-Attainment | Offsets | Mandatory | LAER | No |
| Modified | Attainment | Netting | Optional | BACT | Yes |
| Modified | Non-Attainment | Netting | Optional | LAER | Yes |
| Modified | | Offsets[2] | Mandatory | LAER | No |
| Existing | Attainment | Bubbles | Optional | State Limits[3] | Yes |
| Existing | | Banking[4] | Optional | State Limits[3] | Not Applicable[4] |
| Existing | Non-Attainment | Bubbles | Optional | RACT | Yes |
| Existing | | Banking[4] | Optional | RACT | Not Applicable[4] |

**NOTES FOR TABLE 2:**

1. Of these limits, LAER (Lowest Achievable Emission Rate) is the most stringent, Clean Air Act §171(3), 42 U.S.C.A. §7501(3); BACT (Best Available Control Technology) is the next most stringent, id. §169(3), 42 U.S.C.A. §7479(3); and RACT (Reasonably Available Control Technology) is the least stringent, id. §172(3), 42 U.S.C.A. §7502(3). Modified sources that use netting are exempted from BACT or LAER, but may be subject to other limits called NSPS (New Source Performance Standards) that are typically approximately equivalent to BACT. For stringency of state limits, see note 3 below.

2. Offsets are mandatory in nonattainment areas for modified sources that do not use netting. EPA, Emissions Trading Policy Statement, 51 Fed. Reg. 43,830 (1986).

3. There are no specific federally defined emission limits that states must apply to existing sources in attainment areas. States, however, are required to institute measures that assure the maintenance of air quality in attainment areas. Clean Air Act §107(a), 42 U.S.C.A. §7407(a). To do so, states usually employ a permit system as they do in nonattainment areas and impose emission limits on existing sources through that system. While the resulting state limits can vary widely, they are typically no more stringent than RACT, and may be less stringent.

4. Applicable emission limits are used to calculate emission credits for banking, but the use of banking does not, in itself, enable firms to avoid emission limits. See EPA, Emissions Trading Policy Statement, 51 Fed. Reg. 43,835 (1986). The use of their banked credits in other emissions trading activities may enable firms to avoid applicable emission limits, however. [Eds: banked emissions credits can be used for offsets or for netting.]

new emission sources would be allowed in areas that did not meet the original 1975 air quality deadlines. Concern that this provision would stifle economic growth prompted EPA to institute the offset rule in 1976.[6] This rule requires new and modified emission sources in these areas to obtain emission credits from sources in the same area to offset their new emissions.[7] The sources are still subject to the most stringent emission limits.[8] Offsets may be obtained through internal or external trades.[9] Like netting, offset transactions are controlled at the state level.

Bubbles, first allowed in 1979,[10] are used by existing sources in attainment or nonattainment areas. The name derives from the concept of placing an imaginary bubble over a multi-source plant. The levels of emission controls applied to different sources in a bubble may be adjusted to reduce control costs so long as the aggregate limit is not exceeded. In effect, emission credits are created by some sources within the plant and used by others. Originally, all bubbles had to be submitted by the states to EPA for approval. In 1981 EPA began to approve "generic bubble rules" that enabled states to approve bubbles.[11] Several states now have such rules.

Banking, which was first allowed in 1979, provides a mechanism for firms to save emission credits for future use. EPA has established guidelines for banking programs, but states must set up and administer the rules governing banking.

As the third column in Table 1 shows, different types of sources, classified according to type and location, have different emissions trading options available to them. New sources have the fewest options; the only activity they may engage in is offsets, and the use of offsets is mandatory in nonattainment areas. The stringent emission limits that apply to these sources cannot be avoided thorough trading. Modified sources are faced with similar requirements, except that they may use netting, thus avoiding the most stringent emission limits. Existing sources in nonattainment areas may use bubbles or banking; the former can be used to avoid emission limits that otherwise would apply to individual sources.

These differences in options are crucial to understanding the performance of emissions trading. New and modified sources have the greatest incentive to use emissions trading since they are subject to the most stringent emission limits; however, under the program only modified sources can avoid the stringent emission requirements by doing so. Existing sources enjoy the most flexibility in using emissions trading but have less incentive to do so since they are subject to less stringent emission limits.

---

6. EPA, Emission Offset Interpretive Ruling of Dec. 21, 1976, 41 Fed. Reg. 55,524-25 (1976).

7. 44 Fed. Reg. 3284 (1979).

8. Clean Air Act §§171, 173(2), 42 U.S.C. §§7501, 7503(2)(1982); see also EPA, Emission Offset Interpretive Ruling, supra, at 55,526.

9. See EPA Emission Offset Interpretive Ruling, 44 Fed. Reg. 3,274-76 (1979)(final rule modifying EPA, Emission Offset Interpretive Ruling, supra).

10. EPA, Recommendation for Alternative Emission Reduction Options within State Implementation Plans, 44 Fed. Reg. 3,740-42 (1979)(proposed policy statement); id. at 71,780-88 (final policy statement).

11. EPA, Recommendation for Alternative Emission Reduction Options within State Implementation Plans, 44 Fed. Reg. 3,740-42 (1979); Proposed Revision to the New Jersey State Implementation Plan, 45 Fed. Reg. 77,459-60 (1980)(proposed rule and amendment to policy statement)(codified at 40 C.F.R. §52.06 (1987)).

### COMMENTARY AND QUESTIONS

1. **What trades get made?** Hahn and Hester have been the most vigorous students of emissions trading under the Clean Air Act and they have collected considerable empirical evidence about the extent to which trades have taken place. They recount much of that material in Hahn & Hester, Where Did All the Markets Go? An Analysis of EPA's Emissions Trading Program, 6 Yale J. on Reg. 109, 114, 119–32 (1989). As the title suggests, trading has not flourished. Offsets, the only mandatory trading device, were used approximately 2,000 times nationwide in the ten-year period from 1977 to 1986. By 1986, only 42 bubbles had been approved, with a little more than twice that number pending or proposed. Netting has been far and away the most common type of trading, with a probable number of 8,000 instances in the decade from 1974 to 1984. Quite significantly, most of the bubbles, and by definition all netting, are internal to the firm. Likewise, many offsets were also internal rather than external trades among firms. Not surprisingly (given the low volume of interfirm trades), there was very little evidence of active banking. What explains the low level of interfirm trading? Is it the higher transaction cost of locating an external trading partner in comparison to making internal (intrafirm) changes? Is it the novelty of emissions trading? Is it the lack of true markets in which ERCs are freely bought and sold? Does the EPA requirement that trades involve only emission reductions that are surplus, enforceable, permanent, and quantifiable set too high a threshold for most trades to take place?

2. **The extraordinary attraction of netting.** Netting is popular with firms for good reason. One major attraction of netting is its ability to allow firms to avoid the command and control technology-based standards for modified sources in both attainment and non-attainment areas. Firms realize additional savings by avoiding the costs and delays associated with the permitting process. A review of the quantitative data that attempts to calculate the magnitude of the cost savings of netting appears in Hahn & Hester, Where Did All the Markets Go? An Analysis of EPA's Emissions Trading Program, 6 Yale J. on Reg. 109, 114, 132–136 (1989). They conclude that the average savings on emissions control when a technology-based standard (such as BACT or LAER) is avoided range from $100,000 to $1 million. The savings attributed to avoidance of the permit process is estimated to range from $5,000 to $25,000.

3. **The history of bubbles.** Bubbles, and the emissions trading program more generally, were not clearly addressed by the original 1970 Clean Air Act. The programs were introduced administratively by the EPA. Emissions trading was controversial because it permitted what environmental groups saw as a form of backsliding from the commands of the Clean Air Act, especially when trading could be used to avoid the technology-based requirements for new sources wherever located, or modified sources in non-attainment areas. The pivotal legal issue in the bubble controversy became the interpretation given to the statutory term "stationary source." A plant-wide definition (or larger) would allow bubbles; if the definition was restricted to a single smokestack, bubbling would not be allowed. EPA's determination to adopt the wider definition (for many, but not all circumstances) was upheld by the Supreme Court in Chevron U.S.A., Inc., v. NRDC, 467 U.S. 837 (1984).

4. **Trading emissions rights in non-attainment areas.** Recalling that non-attainment areas are, by definition, areas where the air is not clean enough to protect health (primary NAAQS), is it sensible to allow any ERCs to be traded as "surplus"

when the air itself is still too dirty? Congress, in the 1977 amendments, took this into account by requiring that offsets exceed new emissions by an amount sufficient to constitute "reasonable further progress" toward attainment. In this way a degree of continued growth was allowed in those regions while overall air quality improved. Even in the absence of net reductions in air emissions, trading in non-attainment areas can be defended as efficient: trades make a bad air quality situation no worse, while at least reducing the total social cost of creating the problem. Is this second argument flawed because the fact of non-attainment is an indication that the current level of permitted pollution is too high?

5. **Offsets pro and con.** Try to predict which stationary source emissions reductions in a non-attainment area will be the ones obtained as required offsets by a new source locating in the area. Presumably, in purchasing the retirement of pollution sources, the least expensive retirements will involve taking marginally profitable enterprises out of production, or paying for pollution control improvements at those sites where the least expenditure produces the greatest reduction. To the extent that practice mirrors the prediction of theory, offsets obtain an apparently optimal result of reducing pollution at the lowest possible cost. Are there social costs that are overlooked in that assessment? What about the dislocation of workers who lose their jobs when marginal firms are bought out and closed? Perhaps it could be argued, for many of them, that the firm's survival was unlikely in any event. Is there a sense in which those reductions, much like the switch to water-based asphalt in the *CARE* case excerpted in Chapter Eight, should already have been required under a non-attainment SIP that is making reasonable further progress toward attainment?

6. **The strange aversion to effluent taxes.** Effluent taxes as such are not used on a large scale in American pollution control. The closest thing to effluent taxes that can be found is the high cost of heavily-regulated, legal disposal of hazardous waste imposed by RCRA. The cost of legal disposal has led to waste reduction. See Chapter 17. Perhaps counterintuitively, imposing effluent taxes to achieve the desired amount of pollution reduction is a very difficult task. Choosing the amount of the tax is the most problematic issue. The amount chosen "dictates" the amount of pollution reduction that the market incentive will induce, but it will require a good deal of information about the cost of reducing pollution of each of the affected emitters to have any clear advance idea about the amount of reduction that will be achieved. Likewise, physically measuring emissions to serve as a basis for collecting the tax requires considerable effort and expense (whether in real-time measurement or source-by-source modeling). Still, those difficulties alone do not explain the virtual non-use of effluent taxes in the United States. To what extent are these difficulties equally applicable to emissions trading systems?

7. **Subsidies.** Just as imposing a charge on environmentally damaging behavior is a form of economic regulation, paying a bounty for environmentally favorable behavior creates an economic incentive that leads to improved environmental outcomes. Subsidies can take a number of forms. The most obvious, and therefore the politically most sensitive, are direct payments to the subsidized entities. Less obviously, government offers subsidies when it provides goods or services to entities at below-cost prices. Perhaps least obvious, government extends a subsidy when it provides special tax treatment to an activity. Subsidies falling into this last category are at times called "tax expenditures." A subsidy that helps corporations pur-

chase pollution control equipment, for example, alters the cost function of the firm and makes the installation of that equipment a more likely choice,[12] especially when there are costs associated with continuing pollution at previous levels. Congress has also created rather subtle subsidies in legislation. For example, the federal government can pay a premium for low polluting vehicles, see 42 U.S.C.A. §7588, or must seek to use products containing the highest practicable percentage of recycled materials. See 42 U.S.C.A. §6962(c).

## B. USING EMISSIONS TRADING TO REDUCE ACID DEPOSITION[13]

The Clean Air Act Amendments of 1990 revamped the Clean Air Act in many ways. Among the most novel is the establishment of a system of tradeable emissions allowances designed to achieve a 10 million ton per year reduction in $SO_2$ emissions by the year 2000. This represents more than a 50% reduction in the emission of $SO_2$ for sources so regulated in comparison with 1980 levels. The principal purpose of the wholesale reduction is to combat downwind acid rain and other forms of deposition.

### EPA, Title IV Acid Deposition Program, in ABA, Implementing the 1990 Clean Air Act: EPA Speaks 51–57
#### February 21, 1991

***$SO_2$ Allowances —Basic Program.*** The legislation seeks $SO_2$ emissions reductions from electric utility plants through the use of a market based system of emission allowances. Under this system, "affected units" (essentially all utility boilers that serve generators larger than 25 megawatts (MW)) are allocated allowances in an amount which is based on their past fossil fuel consumption and the emissions rate required by the legislation. An allowance is defined as an authorization allocated to an affected unit, to emit, during or after a specified calendar year, one ton of $SO_2$. Any new utility units which commence operation after December 31, 1995 are not allocated allowances and must obtain allowances sufficient to cover their emission by January 1, 2000 and thereafter. Industrial sources may also become affected sources by electing to opt-in to the allowance system.

***Allowance Holding Requirement.*** Affected sources are required to hold sufficient allowances to cover their level of emissions. Allowances may not be used prior to the calendar year for which they are allocated. Sources may not exceed emission limitations provided in the law unless the owner or operator obtains and holds additional allowances to emit excess tons of $SO_2$. However, the fact that an affected source holds excess allowances does not entitle it to exceed the National Ambient Air Quality Standard limits.

---

12. A subtle point: not all subsidies that seem to promote environmentally favorable outcomes are economic incentives as that term is used in this chapter. Subsidies that support behavior that is already required are not being used as economic incentives, they are simply wealth transfers that benefit the subsidized party. For example, when the Internal Revenue Service issued its June, 1994 ruling that CERCLA cleanup costs were tax deductible as a business expense (rather than capital improvements to the underlying land), it reduced the cost of cleanups to profitable corporate PRP's. The PRP's still paid the same amount for the cleanup, but their taxable profits were reduced by the amount of the cleanup expense and, therefore, they paid less tax. The estimate of the cost to the United States Treasury of this reduction in tax revenue was estimated to be as much as $50 billion. Because there was already an enforceable obligation to clean up, however, the subsidy was not required to induce cleanup behavior.

13. Title IV contains both the sulfur dioxide trading program highlighted here and a nitrogen oxides control program that relies on traditional command and control performance techniques. See 42 U.S.C.A. §7651f.

*Penalties for Non-Compliance.* Sources whose emissions exceed allowances held will be required to pay $2000 per excess ton, and will be required to offset excess tons the following year.

*Allowance Usage.* Once allocated, allowances can be used by affected sources to cover emissions, banked for future use, or sold to others. Allowances transferred to others are not effective until a written certification of transfer from the parties involved is received and recorded by EPA. No permit alteration is required.

*Allowance Tracking.* EPA will develop a system for issuing, recording and tracking allowances.

*Cap on SO$_2$ Emissions/Allowances Allocated.* Beginning in 2000, the total number of allowances issued by EPA to utility units is, with limited exceptions, not to exceed 8.9 million allowances. This effectively caps emissions and ensures maintenance of the 10 million ton SO$_2$ reduction.

*SO$_2$ Reduction Program.* SO$_2$ reductions are obtained in two phases. Phase I Reductions. Phase I reductions are required by January 1, 1995 from 111 plants listed in the legislation. These plants have large units — 100 MWs or more — and have high emission rates — 2.5 lbs/mmBtu or more.[14] There will be approximately 265 affected units in these Phase I plants. Phase I plants are located in 21 eastern and midwestern states.

*Phase I Allowance Allocations.* Phase I affected units will be issued allowances as reflected in the legislation. The allocation was based on a 2.5 lbs/mmBtu emission rate, multiplied by their "baseline," the average fossil fuel consumed during the years 1985, 1986, and 1987.

*Phase II Reductions.* In Phase II, which begins on January 1, 2000, the emissions limits imposed on Phase I plants are tightened, and emissions limits are imposed on smaller, cleaner plants as well. In general, all utility plants emitting at a rate above 1.2 lbs/mmBtu will have to reduce their emissions to a level equal to 1.2 lbs/mmBtu multiplied by their baseline.

*Special Reserve for EPA Allowance Sales and Auctions.* EPA is to create an allowance reserve by tapping each affected source's allocation 2.8% during 1995–99, and 2.8% of the basic Phase II allocation for each year beginning in 2000. These allowances are to be set aside for EPA allowance sales and auctions.

*Allowance Sales.* A portion of the allowances in the reserve established above are to be put in a direct sale subaccount and sold by EPA in accordance with EPA regulations. The proceeds of the allowance sales are to be returned to the affected units on a pro rata basis.... Unsold allowances are to be transferred to the auction subaccount (discussed below).

*EPA Direct Allowance Sales.* EPA will offer for sale allowances...[in accordance with a schedule[15]]. They shall be offered at a price of $1500 per allowance (CPI adjusted). Sales are to be made on a first come first served basis subject to the priority for Independent Power Producers.

*Allowance Auctions.* EPA is to establish a subaccount in the allowance reserve for auctions.... Auctions will be open to any person, and will be carried out by sealed bid, with sales based on bid price. No minimum bid will be established. Auction

---

14. Eds: The emission rates are measured in pounds of SO$_2$ emitted per million British thermal units of heat produced (mmBtu). It is widely conceded that fossil fuel fired power plants can, using widely available techniques and technologies, meet a standard of 1.2 lbs/mmBtu. Some plants using both controls and low sulfur fuel achieve rates as low as .3 lbs/mmBtu.

15. Eds: The schedule calls for advance sale of 25,000 allowances per year for each year beginning in 1993 and spot sales of an additional 25,000 allowances in 2000 and each year thereafter. Spot sale allowances must be used in the year of the sale unless banked. Advance sale allowances may be used only in the 7th year (or after) following the sale unless banked.

proceeds will be transferred to affected units contributing to the reserve on a pro rata basis, and allowances held for auction which were not sold at the auction will be returned to contributing affected units on a pro rata basis.[16]

## COMMENTARY AND QUESTIONS

1. **Key steps in the acid deposition program.** What goes into establishing a trading system? There are at least four vital building blocks in EPA's Title IV efforts to create a market in tradeable emissions allowances for $SO_2$. They are (1) the allowances, (2) the means by which EPA limits their total number, (3) the initial distribution of the allowances and, (4) the means by which allowances are redistributed.

2. **Making the reductions of emissions certain to occur.** The allowance system appears likely to reduce $SO_2$ emissions substantially. The penalties for excess emissions ($2,000 per ton) may be inconsequential to a large entity such as a power plant, but the offset requirement for the following year means that the offending firm must obtain allowances and apply them against the previous year's excess emissions in addition to paying the fine. Even if this cost is modest, applying the allowances to "retire" the excess means that the total multi-year pollution remains limited to the number of allowances.

3. **Knowing the goal.** Trading reduces emissions, but does it end acid rain? Whether the 10 million ton reduction will be sufficient to alleviate the acid deposition problem remains an open question. A 1995 EPA report entitled "Acid Rain Program, Update No. 2," was optimistic about the program, but its evidence consisted solely of data about reductions of emissions, not quantitative or qualitative measures of environmental quality. Definitive data on that score will not be available for many years. In Title IV, the goal is clearly to end acid rain and the trading program is understood to be a means to that end. That is not always going to be the case. As one commentator puts it, "Market mechanisms will not set our goals for us and may even disguise their absence." William Pedersen, Jr., The Limits of Market-Based Approaches to Environmental Protection, 24 Env. Law Rep. 10173 (1994).

### A. Denny Ellerman, Richard Schmalensee, Paul L. Joskow, Jaun Pablo Montero, Elizabeth M. Bailey, Emissions Trading Under the U.S. Acid Rain Program: Evaluation of Compliance Costs and Allowance Market Performance (1997)
Massachusetts Institute of Technology, excerpts from pages 5–8

Title IV of the 1990 Clean Air Act Amendments introduced the world's first large-scale, public policy experiment in the use of tradeable permits to achieve an environmental goal. The major part of the reduction, which concerns $SO_2$, is to be achieved entirely by marketable emission permits. The initial limitation of $SO_2$ emissions took effect in 1995, when major generating units with relatively high emission levels were issued permits, or "allowances," requiring an intermediate

---

16. Eds: There is also a schedule for the number of allowances to be offered at auction. Like the direct sales schedule it is bifurcated between spot auction of current year allowances and advance auction of allowances good in the 7th year after the auction. In general, 150,000 allowances are offered in the spot auction in each year beginning in 1995 and 100,000 allowances are offered in the advance auction.

aggregate reduction of emissions during a five-year "Phase I" period. The full reduction will be implemented in Phase II: in the year 2000, all electricity-generating units will be issued allowances limiting SO$_2$ emissions nationally to about 9 million tons — roughly 50% of their 1980 emissions.

This "cap and trade" approach to emissions control establishes an aggregate emissions limit, distributes to individual sources a number of permits equal to this limit according to certain criteria, and allows individual sources to trade permits with other parties or to bank unused permits for later use. No further emission or technology requirements are imposed; sources are required only to have a valid permit for each ton of SO$_2$ emitted.

The year Title IV took effect was marked by significant overcompliance. A total 8.70 million allowances were issued to 72 operating utilities to cover emissions at 445 electricity-generating units having a total capacity of 130 GWe. These units had emitted 10.68 million tons of SO$_2$ in 1985; their 1995 emissions, however, were only 5.30 million tons — about 3.9 million less than would have been expected without Title IV, and 3.4 million below the "cap." The 1995 emissions reduction is the more remarkable in that the cap required only a slight reduction beyond that achieved through 1994, because emissions had already declined significantly prior to 1995 — largely due to railroad deregulation's effects on the competitiveness of western low-sulfur coal in the midwest, where local high-sulfur coal had traditionally been used. The 1995 reduction in SO$_2$ emissions was achieved about equally by retrofitting equipment (e.g., installing "scrubbers") to desulfurize flue gas, and by switching to lower-sulfur coal. Despite fears that "hot spots" would result from emissions permit trading, significant 1995 emissions reductions occurred in the upper Ohio River Valley, where emissions from high sulfur coal use have caused particular concern.

A viable market for allowances has developed despite considerable early doubt, providing current information on the value of additional abatements as well as more opportunities to reduce compliance costs. In the first years after allowances were issued, few allowances were traded outside of a mandated EPA auction; in 1994, however, the volume of private trades increased notably, and various indicators of market price converged to a relatively tight range of values for allowances. Furthermore, derivative instruments — options, swaps, forwards, and futures — have emerged and are being used increasingly.

The total cost of achieving the 3.9-million-ton reduction in SO$_2$ emissions in 1995 was at the lower bound of earlier predictions. We estimate the appropriately annualized total cost to have been approximately $725 million, in 1995 dollars - an average total cost of $187 or $210 per ton of SO$_2$ removed, depending on whether 425,000 tons of apparently costless emissions reductions are included.

On a total-cost basis, scrubbing (though its cost has been much lower than predicted) has proved to be a more expensive means of compliance than switching fuel. On average, retrofitted scrubbers achieved emissions reductions in 1995 at an average cost of $265/ton SO$_2$, compared to $153/ton for fuel switching — in marked contrast to earlier studies that estimated average total costs for scrubbing to be $450 — 500/ton. Most of the difference between predicted and actual scrubbing costs has been due to lower-than-predicted operating costs and to greater-than-expected utilization rates of scrubbers that spread the initial fixed cost over more tons of SO$_2$ removed. While the average total cost of achieving Title IV's mandated reduction in SO$_2$ emissions has been at the low end of early estimates, the price of allowances, at about $100 (equivalently, $100 per ton of SO$_2$ removed), has been well below earlier predictions of Phase I allowance prices, which ranged from $250 to $400. The explanation for this disparity is two-fold: first, the price of allowances reflects short-run, marginal cost — not necessarily long-run, average total emission control cost; and, second, mistaken expectations concerning the value of allowances led to overinvestment in compliance during Phase I. Most decisions to invest in scrubbers were made early — before the first EPA auction, when expected allowance prices were well above the values that later materialized — or in response to explicit incentives in Title IV and state regulations to encourage such investment during Phase I.

Estimation of 1995 cost savings from emissions trading is fraught with conceptual and empirical difficulties that prevent us from offering a firm figure. For one thing, the hypothetical alternative program from which savings are to be calculated is not obvious. Our rough estimate of the cost savings attributable to emissions trading in 1995 lies between $225 and $375 million, in current dollars, which implies that the cost of compliance with Title IV would have been one-third to one-half again as costly had electric utilities simply reduced emissions without taking advantage of the emissions-trading provisions.

COMMENTARY & QUESTIONS

1. **Cost of compliance success.** Nothing in the apparent early success of Title IV is more vital than the estimates of cost saving as compared to other alternative emissions reduction strategies that accomplish the same results. Theorists and EPA had all predicted this sort of success,[17] but as the excerpt's opening sentence makes clear, Title IV is the first major test of this theory in the world. See, e.g., Regulatory Reforms of Title IV Responsible for Lowering Cost of $SO_2$ Emission Reduction, 26 BNA Env. Rep. 1038 (Oct. 13, 1995); $SO_2$ Allowance Trading Program Successful Despite Certain Criticism's, Economist Says, 26 BNA Env, Rep. 1757 (Jan. 19, 1996). Who are the cost bearers? While the obvious answer is electric consumers, the choice of allocation methodologies importantly influences who pays how much. Under Title IV, as in much of pollution control history, the costs will fall disproportionately on new sources of pollution (and thereafter on their customers). New sources coming on line before the turn of the century will receive allowances based on a .3 lbs/mmBtu basis and will be granted allowances for only 65% of their designed capacity. Accordingly, new units will immediately be seeking to purchase some allowances. Plants coming on line after the year 2000 will be granted no allowances whatever and will have to seek them in the marketplace.

2. **Emission reduction success.** There never was any doubt that Title IV would obtain the mandated reductions in emissions, not just in Phase I, but over the life of the program. If "cap and trade" programs are enforceable, they will reduce emis-

---

17. The Congressional Budget Office estimated in 1986 that achieving the mandated 10 million ton reduction in electric utility $SO_2$ reductions would increase annual electric costs by $3.2 to 4.7 billion. Congressional Budget Office, Curbing Acid Rain: Cost, Budget, and Coal-Market Effects 7 (1986). As a national average, this amounts to an increase in electric costs of between 2 percent and 5 percent. In some Midwestern states, however, the average increase in electric cost would be as much as 10 percent. Congressional Office of Technology Assessment, Acid Rain and Transported Air Pollutants: Implications for Public Policy 14 (1984). The early returns suggest that trading will approximately halve that cost.

sions. This particular cap and trade program was almost certain to work easily. The 50% rollback of 10 million tons per year reduction in SO$_2$ sounds like a monumental improvement, but that level of reductions is not nearly what is achievable at an affordable level of effort. In 1990, the known and in-use technology (including fuel switching to low sulfur coal, and the use of scrubbers for high sulfur coal) was capable of achieving required rates (1.2 lb/MMBtu), and some plants were already operating at rates four times lower than that. As a result, Title IV required no technology forcing. See Chapter 10. All Title IV needed was a small amount of gamesmanship on the part of highly capitalized firms who could choose how best to minimize their long-term costs. Expectations of far higher cost were based on data provided by (guess who) the regulated entities who had two decades of experience fighting against air pollution regulation. The only surprise of note to the economists was as follows:

> Judging from the 1995 results, utilities did take advantage of of the cost-saving flexibility provided by emissions trading — to a surprising extent, given the conservative nature of the electric utility industry and uniformly low expectations for emissions trading among the analysts." Ellerman, et al., at 8.

3. **What to do with excess credits that are selling for far less than their expected worth?** At least one utility located in an acid deposition importing area chose to give away 5,000 credits valued at $480,000 away to obtain a public relations benefit. See, N.Y. Utility Donates Pollution Credits to Environmental Group to Stop Acid Rain, 27 BNA Env. Rep. 2343 (Apr. 4, 1997). Other holders of credits have either traded them or are holding them as a hedge against the stricter Phase II limits. A substantial fear of the acid deposition importing states was that the utilities in the Midwest would buy emissions credits and continue to pollute. In the early years of Title IV, New York went so far as to sue to enjoin a trade by one of its firms to an Ohio Valley power plant. See Matthew Wald, Suit Attacks Swap Plan on Pollution, New York Times, March 14, 1993, at 35. In 1995, an EPA economist told a conference that there was not hoarding of emissions credits by upwind Midwestern utilities. See, Midwest Utilities Not Buying Up Supply of SO$_2$ Allowances, Agency Analysis Finds, 27 BNA Env. Rep. 350 (June 16, 1995). The data compiled by Ellerman, et al., *id.* at 36, appear to differ from that of the EPA in regard to which states are the most active in the market, but with the exception of Pennsylvania, none of the principal upwind states was a heavy net buyer in the credits market. The last word on this topic will be written in the future as firms continue to revise their strategies. See, Increased Use of High-Sulfur Coal Spurs Debate Over Environmental Consequences, 28 BNA Env. Rep. 2102 (Feb. 13, 1998).

4. **Title IV as prototype.** If tradeable emissions allowances work to solve (or reduce) the acid deposition problem, will the same sort of system work with equal facility to reduce the emission of pollutants other than SO$_2$? There are many ways in which the SO$_2$ situation is unique. First, the class of major SO$_2$ emitters regulated by Phase I numbers only 111 and all are in the same business, burning fossil fuels to produce electricity. It is an industry that has been extensively studied and the technological options for emission reduction are all quite well-known and widely available, and as noted above, economically achievable. EPA's most successful

emissions trading program in the 1980s was its lead trading program that allowed gasoline refiners "greater flexibility in meeting emissions standards during a period when the amount of lead in gasoline was being reduced significantly." Hahn & Stavins, Incentive-Based Environmental Regulation: A New Era from an Old Idea?, 18 Ecol. L.Q. 1, 17 (1991). By producing gasoline with lower lead content than required, refiners earned credits which they could use at a later date for their own products that might exceed the then-current standard, or sell to other refiners. Over half of the nation's refineries participated in the trading program, at an estimated 20% savings over costs that would have been incurred without the trading program.[18] To what extent is Title IV of the 1990 Clean Air Act Amendments similar to this lead credit system? First, there is clear definition of the class of potential traders. Second, the credits available for trading can be precisely quantified. Third, there is free transferability of credits without reference to the situs of origin of the credits or their situs of use. The long-term stability of regulatory climate is also important, supporting traders' confidence in their assessment of the value of credits.

5. **Accountability and measurement.** Measurement of emissions is a necessary element of a workable system. Without accurate measures of emissions, no trading system can be assured that all of the players have in hand the needed credits to cover their emissions. For large, technologically sophisticated, highly capitalized plants, the cost of monitoring is likely to be a small fraction of the cost of the operation. Is that true for small scale emitters? What would the cost be of monitoring a wood burning stove as a percentage of the cost of the stove and its wood? How expensive would it be to monitor the hydrocarbon emissions of a dry cleaning establishment, or a farmer's on-farm gas tank? When does leaving the small entities out of the trading system undermine the overall program?

6. **Emissions trading and the NAAQS.** What is the relationship of Title IV trading of sulfur dioxide credits to attainment of the NAAQS harm-based ambient standard for sulfur dioxide? It may overstate the case to deny all relationship, but the two regimes are both independent of one another, serving quite distinct purposes, both of which must be met. There is no warrant to allow a utility to economize on its emissions control expenditures by purchasing credits and increasing its local $SO_2$ emissions if to do so puts the area in violation of the NAAQS (or other relevant ambient air quality standard, such as a PSD standard). Indeed, local $SO_2$ problems have led some utilities to invest heavily in controls, making them sellers in the emissions credits market. See, Tight Limits in Wisconsin Acid Rain Program May Yield Glut of Allowances, EPA Official Says, 22 BNA Env. Rep. 2665 (Apr. 3, 1992).

7. **Hot spots and market operations.** What would happen in an emissions trading system if a single immense polluter with a very high cost of pollution avoidance were to buy a huge number of emissions credits and emit an overwhelming amount of pollution from a single location? Despite the lack of verisimilitude of the hypothetical, the "hot spots" problem is a real one. Trading programs, to be most effective, seek to be location-independent to obtain the largest possible uni-

---

18. *Id.*, citing EPA, Costs and Benefits of Reducing Lead in Gasoline, Final Regulatory Impact Analysis VIII-31 (1985).

verse of traders and the fewest constraints on trades. Nevertheless, total indifference to the location of emissions can result in excessive local concentrations of pollutants. In at least one prominent trading system, the South Coast Air Quality Management District's Regional Clean Air Incentives Market (RECLAIM), VOC credits purchased to support refinery operations were challenged by a nearby neighborhood group as threatening violation of the NAAQS and on environmental justice grounds. Can a market operate when local impacts create uncertainty as to the legality of a purchase? Perhaps *caveat emptor* can protect the seller, but the uncertainty of being able to apply the credits to avoid emission reductions may deter buyers and thereby scuttle the market.

8. **Going generic: EPA's once (and future?) "Open Market Trading Rule."** States have been eager to adopt trading programs as part of their SIPs, but have found the process of SIP revision too cumbersome. The desirability of such a rule may be obvious, but doing it in a way that responds to legitimate concerns is difficult:

> To succeed, a market-based system must be sufficiently flexible to accommodate the rapid flux of commercial transactions. It must also assure that the public interest in achieving healthful air quality is protected. The latter consideration raises a host of subissues — appropriate "baselines," proper definition of the airshed within which the trading may take place, proper accounting for emission credits, how to assure the system is enforceable, and how to divide the benefits of trading between emitters and the public. It comes as no surprise, therefore, that implementing market-based systems that deliver on their promise is proving to be a difficult task. Richard E. Ayres, Developing A Market in Emission Credits Incrementally: An "Open Market" Paradigm for Market-Based Pollution Control, 25 BNA Env. Rep. 1522, 1522 (Dec. 2, 1994).

Ayres, who has worn many hats, ranging from attorney and co-founder of the NRDC to representing industry in air regulation issues, urged EPA to promulgate a generic rule. Despite concern over the chemical and region specific nature of the problem, EPA, basking in the glow of its SO$_2$ success, initially tried to craft a "model" open market emissions trading rule that states could add to their SIPs without going through the SIP revision process. See 60 Fed. Reg. 39668 (Aug, 3, 1995). When EPA recognized that a generic rule would require extensive localization in every case, it switched routes, providing instead a guidance to states that could facilitate SIP revisions adopting trading. Eventually, this retreat on EPA's part came in for a roundhouse of criticism from Rep. Thomas Bliley (R-Va), chair of one of the committees with jurisdiction over EPA. See, House Commerce Chair Seeks Answers on Fate of EPA Open Market Trading Rule, 28 BNA Env. Rep. 2290 (Feb. 27, 1998).

Is the agency wrong? Is there a happy medium that maximizes trading freedom but maintains public health and welfare? Surveying possible trading programs and their inherent uniqueness suggests the EPA may be acting prudently. For global climate change, where the sink is the entire atmosphere, the time frame is long, and the mixing characteristics are such that the resulting concentrations are truly "average" concentrations, location indifference is acceptable. For ground level ozone where local topographic conditions vary and in some cases trap pollutants in the region (e.g., Los Angeles and Denver's periodic air mass inversions), or where upwind sources are concentrated (e.g., the high concentration of upwind NOx emitters), or the local sources are simply too numerous and their control is too costly on a polluter-by-polluter basis, trading rules will have to be quite particularized to be a helpful tool in obtaining lower-cost improved environmental quality. Don't forget, even with trading, the resultant air quality matters: purchasing unbreathably unsafe air, albeit efficiently, is not an acceptable outcome.

9. **From emissions credits to free market environmentalism.** In a book that is a self-described "Berlitz course in free market environmentalism," a series of anecdotal episodes of market incentives leading to positive environmental outcomes is offered as evidence that "voluntary exchange of property rights between consenting owners...promotes cooperation and compromise...[and] offers an alternative that channels the heightened environmental consciousness into win-win solutions that can sustain economic growth, enhance environmental quality and promote harmony." T. Anderson & D. Leal, Free Market Environmentalism 8 (1991).

At least one commentator thinks that...

> Decision-making in environmental markets must [necessarily] be inefficient because decentralized market actors ordinarily lack the environmental information necessary to make choices in line with their preferences. Thus the remedy for inefficient environmental regulation will generally be better government, not a reversion to primary reliance on market transactions. Latin, Environmental Deregulation and Consumer Decisionmaking Under Uncertainty, 6 Harv. Envt'l L. Rev. 187, 190 (1982).

Considering the material in Chapter Two on economics, and in this chapter on the use of market incentives, is the pollution market approach a blanket cure-all for all future environmental concerns? If not, what areas of environmental law seem best suited for free market approaches?

10. **Market incentives in the natural resource setting.** The market incentive systems studied in this chapter focus on pollution control. Do they have a place in resource management? During James Watt's tenure at Interior, numerous efforts were made to allow market decisionmaking to replace federal resource management planning: proposals for wholesale transfer of parts of the public domain into private ownership, plans to give a freer hand to concessionaires in the National Park system, etc. Although these initiatives were blunted, they were not unprecedented. The federal government has long believed in "privatizing" resources, giving them away or transferring them at rates below market value: mining rights, grazing leases, oil exploration leases, timber rights, and park concessions. In these programs the government is typically driven by non-market political incentives, and as a consequence may be accused even in economic terms of managing the resources in a sub-optimal way. What if "true" market prices were charged? Would that improve resource management?

## C. USING EMISSIONS TRADING TO SLOW GLOBAL CLIMATE CHANGE

A marked enthusiasn for emissions trading in this country has become a cornerstone of U.S. environmental foreign policy, and trading is now going global. On December 10, 1997, the United States became a signatory, along with more than 150 other nations, of the Kyoto Protocol to the United Nations Framework Convention on Climate Change.[19] The protocol targets a reduction of greenhouse gas emissions from 1990 levels by 5% between 2008 and 2012. Signatory nations are required to reduce their emissions from 1990 levels by differing amounts, determined as a function of economic profiles and individual circumstances. For the most industrialized nations, the protocol calls for the European Union (EU), the United States, and Japan respectively to reduce their emissions by 8%, 7%, and 6%. Developing nations are encouraged to set voluntary reduction targets.[20] The emission reductions are a compromise between President Clinton's proposal to stabilize emissions at 1990 levels, and the EU's position that emissions should be cut by 15% below 1990 levels.

The protocol does not commit the signatories to a particular regulatory regime, but the United States advocated and won adoption of the following provision:

> **Article 16.** ...The Conference of the Parties shall define the relevant principles, modalities, rules and guidelines, in particular for verification, reporting and accountability for emissions trading. The Parties included in Annex B may participate in emissions trading for the purposes of fulfilling their commitments under Article 3 of this Protocol. Any such trading shall be supplemental to domestic actions for the purpose of meeting quantified emission limitation and reduction commitments under that Article.

Complementing the general acceptability of trading is commitment to work out a "clean development mechanism" that will allow firms in developed countries to transfer energy-efficient technologies and non-polluting forms of energy production to developing nations in exchange for emission reduction credits.

### Michael McElroy, Clean Machines
The New Republic, May 4, 1998 at 24

The Kyoto treaty on global warming calls upon the United States to reduce its carbon dioxide emissions by seven percent in just over ten years' time.... While the most straight-forward solution — a tax on carbon — is politically impossible (or at least deemed so by most political professionals), a system of tradeable pollution permits could also do the trick....

[Let] the government set a limit on emissions over the next several years (say, to an annual average of one billion tons of carbon) and then allocate permits to fossil fuel producers in proportion to their average consumption over the past several years. Firms would then be free to trade these permits: an oil company looking to increase its sales could purchase emission rights from a coal producer.

---

19. The Protocol can be downloaded from the Climate Change Secretariat at www.unfccc.de.

20. This aspect of the protocol is a political flash point in the United States. The Senate had, by a 95–0 vote, passed a resolution in advance of the Kyoto meetings warning that it would not ratify an agreement committing the United States to specific greenhouse gas limitations unless that agreement also places specific limitations on developing nations.

A utility needing coal to fuel its coal-fired boilers would have to pay a premium. Overall, investing in cleaner-burning fuels would become more attractive financially — and, although the economic impact would be about the same, it would be more politically viable than a straightforward tax.

Conceivably, this approach could...work in an international context — in other words, countries could agree to issue permits and then allow firms or individuals to trade the permits across national borders. But this would add complications as well. Consider, for example, a country like Russia. Its emissions are already well below the 1990 level the Kyoto treaty set as the standard. In a system of globally traded permits, Russia could probably afford to sell its permits without actually decreasing its pollution further. Meanwhile, a relatively wealthy nation like the U.S. could probably purchase Russia's permits and, in so doing, avoid having to reduce its emissions. The total amount of pollution in the world would thus remain unchanged. This is why a system of globally traded permits could only work after countries had reached a more equal footing when it comes to pollution.

### COMMENTARY AND QUESTIONS

1. **"The Devil is in the details."** Just what emissions trading scheme will emerge from Kyoto (assuming that the framework itself hangs together over time) is anyone's guess. What does seem clear is that the general outlines of the agreement will require significant emissions reductions in the United States, and there is every reason to expect that trading will be a key means of limiting the cost of meeting those requirements. Two types of trades seem to be on the horizon. One might be described as domestic reduction trading. There are going to have to be cuts in domestic emissions, and a trading system will play a role in decreasing the cost of obtaining those reductions and in determining which firms do the actual reducing of emissions. The second types of trades are going to involve lesser developed nations via trades of technology from the United States and other industrialized nations to developing nations in exchange for some portion of the reductions that technology allows the developing nation to make in meeting its energy needs.

2. **A good subject matter for trading?** Global warming seems to have many of the characteristics that make trading a likely success, but also some pitfalls that will need to be avoided. Try to list them. The good side of the ledger includes the fungibility of emissions and, almost ironically, the large number and surprising volume of sources of greenhouse gasses. The pitfalls lay in the difficulty of enforcing limits, both as a simple technical matter of monitoring, but also as a matter of lack of a credible enforcement authority against firms in nations that might adopt weak enforcement as a domestic policy.

# Chapter 17

# LIFE-CYCLE WASTE CONTROL STRATEGIES: RCRA'S "CRADLE TO GRAVE" REGULATION

A. *Tracking and Controlling the Life Cycle of Hazardous Waste Materials*
B. *The "Land Ban" and the Use of "Hammers" to Control Agency Action*
C. *RCRA Citizen Suits to Obtain Cleanup and Potential Cost Recovery*

Dangerous substances — including PCBs, mercury, arsenic, various petroleum distillates, and a host of others — play vital, even indispensable, roles in producing the material benefits of modern life. They aid in the production of paper, plastics, and other goods; the transmission of electricity; and the powering of motor vehicles. When properly confined, these materials cause little mischief. If released into the environment, however, they pose threats of serious harm to humans, as well as to plants, animals, and natural systems that make up the ecosphere.

As noted in Chapter One, a number of significant statutes play a role in regulating various aspects of the production, use, and disposal of hazardous materials. In connection with hazardous waste contamination and control, however, two federal statutes are key — the Comprehensive Environmental Response, Compensation, and Liability Act (CERCLA or Superfund ), 42 U.S.C.A. §9601 et seq., and the Resource Conservation and Recovery Act (RCRA), 42 U.S.C.A. §6001 et seq. Although these statutes both address the handling and disposal of wastes, they represent disparate, albeit complementary, approaches. CERCLA, studied in Chapter 18, establishes the authority to remediate contamination from past waste disposal practices that now endanger, or threaten to endanger, public health or the environment. CERCLA does so primarily by imposing strict liability on those parties responsible for the release of "hazardous substances" and by creating a "Superfund" to finance actions to clean up such releases. By contrast, RCRA establishes a regulatory program designed to track and control the life cycle of "hazardous wastes" from the time of their initial generation (i.e., the "cradle") to the time of their ultimate disposal (i.e., the "grave"). Rather than focus on past disposal practices, RCRA's "cradle to grave" regulation seeks to eliminate the threats of harm from present and future waste disposal.[1] The principal goal of RCRA is to

---

1. Note that the standard "cradle-to-grave" metaphor for RCRA does *not* mean that RCRA tracks all hazardous *materials* from creation to disposal. It only means that covered chemical and other waste materials are tracked from the time they become *wastes*. Other statutes, like ToSCA, regulate commercial chemicals and other hazardous materials at the stages of manufacture and use (i.e. before they become waste). In terms of the cradle-to-grave life-cycle of *wastes*, these prior regulations are forms of pre-natal care.

prevent future Superfund sites.

Because monumental difficulties surround the cleanup of hazardous materials once those materials have already been released into the environment, the life cycle waste control strategies of RCRA — focusing on preventing or limiting the release of hazardous wastes in the first instance — deserve a very high regulatory priority. RCRA establishes a comprehensive, complex, and detailed scheme for regulating hazardous waste management activities, that governs the day-to-day operations and waste handling activities of literally hundreds of thousands of corporations and individuals. By regulating all those who (1) generate, (2) transport, or (3) treat, store, or dispose of hazardous wastes, RCRA creates a three stage regulatory approach which is pervasive and comprehensive. RCRA's broad scope, in fact, was a major factor in the growth of the environmental regulatory community beginning in the early 1980's, as the requirements of RCRA created a demand for environmental consultants, engineers, and lawyers. In its comprehensive approach, RCRA utilizes a variety of regulatory devices, reviewed in preceding chapters, to meet its specific regulatory needs. This chapter seeks to explore the substantive content of RCRA, while simultaneously reviewing a variety of statutory approaches considered earlier.

It is important to note that this perspective on RCRA inevitably de-emphasizes two important matters. First, although the chapter focuses on hazardous wastes, RCRA as a statute covers much more, including regulation of solid waste generally (a category dominated by non-hazardous industrial waste and municipal waste), underground storage tanks, medical waste, and other categories. Second, although the coverage here focuses solely on the requirements set by federal law, much RCRA enforcement and regulation takes place at the state level. RCRA, like many federal environmental statutes, encourages the states to take primary authority.[2]

## A. TRACKING AND CONTROLLING THE LIFE CYCLE OF HAZARDOUS WASTE MATERIALS

RCRA's Subtitle C, regulating hazardous waste, 42 U.S.C.A. §6926 et seq., is organized around a pragmatic strategy that can be reduced to the simplest of terms: "If I know where hazardous waste material is, and I know the place is secure, I also know that the material is not loose in the environment causing problems."

In addition to tracking wastes, RCRA and its implementing regulations prescribe waste handling and treatment standards and practices intended to reduce the possibility of escape. This involves equipment, procedure, and design specifications for all parties that play a role in the life cycle of hazardous wastes. In this fashion, generators of waste are regulated, as are transporters and operators of treatment, storage, and disposal ("TSD") facilities. RCRA even tries to assure that waste handlers are responsible people who can be trusted with a dangerous assignment,

---

2. RCRA §3009, 42 U.S.C.A. §6929. The statute also directs the EPA's Administrator to "give a high priority to assisting and cooperating with States in obtaining full authorization of State programs" under Subtitle C. 42 U.S.C.A. § 6902 (a)(7).

and whose long-term stability can be demonstrated. Administrative effort under RCRA, moreover, has increasingly encouraged policies of "waste minimization," under the assumption that there will be fewer releases if there is less hazardous waste to control.[3]

## Section 1. RCRA'S ENACTMENT AND INITIAL IMPLEMENTATION

RCRA was described by one judge called upon to interpret it as a statute of "mind-numbing" complexity.[4] Many forces contributed to its complexity, but EPA's early failure to implement RCRA is surely among the most prominent.

In the years shortly before RCRA's appearance in 1976 (in the form of amendments to the ineffectual Solid Waste Disposal Act), both the Clean Air Act (see Chapter 8) and the Clean Water Act (see Chapter 9) established major new programs that protected the nation's air and water, by mandating the capture and removal of hazardous materials before they were released and allowed to pollute these two environmental media. However, the new air and water programs also served to exacerbate an already existing problem — specifically, the improper disposal of the hazardous materials extracted from industrial smokestacks and wastewater systems. The disposal and extraction of these hazardous materials was soon determined to be an increasing cause of pollution to other environmental media, in particular the soil and groundwater. Reacting to the need to protect these other environmental media, Congress passed RCRA in an effort to close the circle of environmental regulation.[5]

Although Congress instructed EPA to promulgate regulations promptly, the Carter Administration treated RCRA as a low EPA priority, channeling funds and energy into other issues. Successful citizen suits eventually forced EPA to issue regulations just as the Reagan Administration was taking office. The incoming administration, however, made the environmental area one of the prime targets of its deregulation philosophy, and further delayed the promulgation of implementing regulations and the creation of an effective enforcement program. The foot-dragging of EPA in regard to RCRA, coupled with scandals regarding the administration of CERCLA, eroded Congressional confidence in EPA. This led, in 1984, to a major legislative effort requiring more vigorous administration of hazardous waste law, under the Hazardous and Solid Waste Amendments of 1984 (HSWA), Pub. L. No. 98-616 (1984). HSWA represented a key turning point in the

---

3. The waste reduction strategy also seeks to limit the need for (1) long-term storage of materials for which treatment methods are not yet available, and (2) disposal of the by-products of treatment that may themselves be hazardous materials (such as ash from incineration.) See 42 U.S.C.A. §6902(a)(6)(b.) The Pollution Prevention Act of 1990, 42 U.S.C.A. §13101 et seq., confirms and generalizes the waste minimization strategy, applying it to all types of pollution. RCRA also contributes to hazardous waste minimization by making the treatment, storage and disposal of such wastes far more costly, creating a market incentive to waste reduction.

4. American Mining Congress v. EPA, 824 F.2d 1177, 1189 (D.C. Cir. 1987) (Starr, J., writing for the majority.)

5. The environmentalist Barry Commoner has admonished that "Everything goes somewhere," in recognition of the fact that every waste treatment process creates a residual which, because it is more concentrated, may be more toxic than the corresponding waste inputs. In passing RCRA, Congress was concerned with the residual hazardous wastes left over from waste treatment under the Clean Air Act and the Clean Water Act.

congressional relationship with EPA. Rather than relying on the EPA to set regulatory parameters and to exercise its discretion in setting and enforcing requirements, Congress became extraordinarily prescriptive and detailed in HSWA, utilizing statutory "hammers" (i.e., the land ban considered later in this chapter) to establish deadlines and limit EPA's discretion. The following article recounts the political climate that surrounded the initial implementation of RCRA:

### James Florio, Congress as Reluctant Regulator: Hazardous Waste Policy in the 1980's
### 3 Yale J. on Reg. 351, 353-376 (1986)[6]

....Congress passed the Resource Conservation and Recovery Act , the first federal effort to control the disposal of hazardous waste, in 1976, before the extent and danger of hazardous waste disposal problems became widely known. RCRA created a "cradle to grave" regulatory system for hazardous waste, requiring generators, transporters, and disposers to maintain written records of waste transfers, and establishing standards, procedures, and permit requirements for disposal.

As in most other federal regulatory statutes, including other environmental laws, Congress (in 1976) prescribed goals in broad terms only: what was to be achieved by EPA and when. For example, EPA was directed to develop standards within eighteen months for facilities disposing of hazardous waste and to include provisions for record-keeping; treatment, storage, and disposal methods; requirements for location, design, and construction; contingency plans for accidents; and financial responsibility requirements. The only substantive direction was a requirement that the EPA regulations protect "health and the environment."

Although the task given to EPA was enormously complex — perhaps more complex than anyone, including Congress, understood at the time — the delegation of enormous discretion to EPA was sensible. Prescribing standards for hazardous waste disposal required careful analysis of scientific and economic data and a thorough understanding of the commercial system for hazardous waste disposal. In 1976, the information and analysis necessary for sound formulation of the regulatory details were simply not available to Congress, although enough was known to indicate that considerable hazards did exist.

In our scheme of government, the role of an environmental regulatory agency is to act as the scientific and technical expert in filling in the details of the environmental protection policy enunciated by Congress. Only an executive branch agency possessing sufficient technical expertise, administrative skills, and bureaucratic resources can administer a nationwide regimen for controlling the disposal of hazardous waste. Soon after the enactment of RCRA, EPA learned that the development of hazardous waste regulations would be an enormously difficult task. The complexity of the technical issues involved in determining disposal methods appropriate to the thousands of different chemicals and other wastes, each presenting different dangers, was compounded by the enormous economic impact of controlling the high volume of hazardous waste produced in this country. In the developmental stage of this regulatory system, EPA, like any bureaucracy in a similar situation, moved slowly....

---

6. In 1986, when Mr. Florio authored this article, he was a member of the House of Representatives from New Jersey and Chairman of the House Subcommittee on Commerce, Transportation, and Tourism, which had jurisdiction over hazardous waste issues.

Implementation of the RCRA program began during the Carter Administration. The delays and false starts inherent in the initial implementation of most regulatory efforts were commonplace: EPA quickly fell behind schedule in efforts to issue regulations for permits and standards by the statutory deadlines as it discovered the complexity of the problem and the decisions it faced. EPA's pace under Carter prompted criticism, but its underlying commitment to implementing the statute was not challenged.

In 1981, the situation changed. EPA's nominal efforts to implement the protective provisions of RCRA clearly reflected the Reagan Administration's antipathy for regulation by the federal government and its concern for selection of the least expensive means to dispose of hazardous waste. Indeed, the test at EPA was not whether a regulatory system met the statutory prescription to protect the environment, but rather whether it met the Administration's ideological regulatory standard. Congress fully expects agencies to exercise delegated discretion in a manner consistent with the Executive's political ideology. Tension between legislative intent and regulatory implementation is inevitable and expected. This tension is usually resolved through a series of small compromises and skirmishes between the legislative and executive branches, often effectuated through Congressional oversight. In the case of EPA and RCRA, however, the Administration's philosophy was more fundamentally at odds with the statute. EPA's implementation of the Administration's philosophy actually subverted the statutory goals by delaying statutorily required action and ignoring technical and scientific information that indicated a need for additional requirements.

In the early 1980's, evidence of the seriousness and scope of the hazardous waste problem mounted while EPA stalled. Congress grew increasingly frustrated with the obvious manipulation practiced by the political appointees at the Agency, as well as with the substantive environmental policy the Agency pursued.

In 1983, five and one-half years after the mandatory deadline for promulgation of RCRA standards and permits, the 98th Congress began a reauthorization process for RCRA. There was still no enforceable system for regulating the disposal of hazardous waste and little prospect for one soon. The problems recognized in 1976 had become common knowledge and, by 1983, evidence of the dangers was even more compelling. Not surprisingly, Congress made clear that it would not allow the delays to continue. Any confidence that EPA could be trusted to act expeditiously had long since evaporated. Witnesses at Congressional hearings urged a legislative solution requiring that disposal firms obtain a permit and meet the federal operating standards.

Congress responded by reauthorizing RCRA with a maze of new deadlines and statutory requirements... Congressional reluctance to rely on EPA judgments was not limited to technological standards, but extended into all areas of the RCRA program....

In the area of hazardous waste regulation during the 1980's,...the traditional reliance on delegated responsibility...collapsed, with profound implications for the overall regulatory structure. The wide discrepancy between the public's desire for vigorous environmental protection and the Reagan Administration's ideological preference for regulatory relief...forced Congress to produce a new regulatory system that significantly reduces agency discretion.

COMMENTARY AND QUESTION

1. **The tension between Congress and the Executive Branch**. One axiom of regulatory design is that the implementing agency should not distort or disrupt the policy established by Congress in its enabling legislation (see Chapter 12). This axiom was apparently violated by EPA in its early approach toward implementing RCRA. Congress' response was to attempt to "micromanage" RCRA implementation. The advantages and disadvantages of legislative micromanagement will be discussed below.

### Section 2. RCRA'S ADMINISTRATIVE THICKET: DEFINING HAZARDOUS WASTES

A significant threshold issue under RCRA is defining what materials are to be statutorily regulated as "solid waste," and, further, what solid waste is to be considered "hazardous waste." Congress defined "solid waste" as:

> any garbage, refuse, sludge from a waste treatment plant, water supply treatment plant, or air pollution control facility and other discarded material, including solid, liquid, semisolid, or contained gaseous material resulting from industrial, commercial, mining, and agricultural operations, and from community activities, but does not include solid or dissolved material in domestic sewage, or solid or dissolved materials in irrigation return flows or industrial discharges which are point sources subject to permits under §402 of the Federal Water Pollution Control Act [33 U.S.C.A. §1342], or source, special nuclear, or byproduct material as defined by the Atomic Energy Act of 1954 [42 U.S.C.A. §2011 et seq.]42 U.S.C.A. §6903(27).

Under this portion of the statute, as illustrated in Figure 1 below, EPA has promulgated a definition of solid waste that includes abandoned, recycled, and inherently waste-like materials. See 40 CFR §261.2(a)(2). Abandoned materials are those that have been disposed of, burned, incinerated, or accumulated or stored in lieu of being disposed of, burned, or incinerated. See 40 CFR §261.2(b). Recycled materials include sludges, by-products, some commercial chemicals, and scrap metals that have been recycled in various ways. See 40 CFR §261(c). Recycled materials include sludges, by-products, some commercial chemicals, and scrap metals that have been recycled in various ways (1-4). The "inherently waste-like" category is a catch-all that includes materials that are usually treated like waste in that they are usually disposed of, burned, or incinerated. Materials are also classified as inherently waste-like if they contain EPA-listed toxic constituents (See 40 CFR §261, Appendix VIII) that are not ordinarily found in the raw materials for which the toxic-bearing materials is being used as a substitute. See 40 CFR §261.2(d)(2). Further, materials like dioxin, that may pose a substantial hazard to human health and the environment when recycled, are likewise defined as inherently waste-like. *Id.*

Certain categories of waste have been exempted from RCRA by Congress or EPA by excluding them from the definition of solid waste. These exclusions can have significant environmental consequences, because the wastes removed from the RCRA regulatory program include whole categories of hazardous materials whose disposal is largely unregulated. As Figure 1 shows, the most important

---

7. As reflected in Figure 1, the exclusions are listed in 40 CFR § 261.4(a).

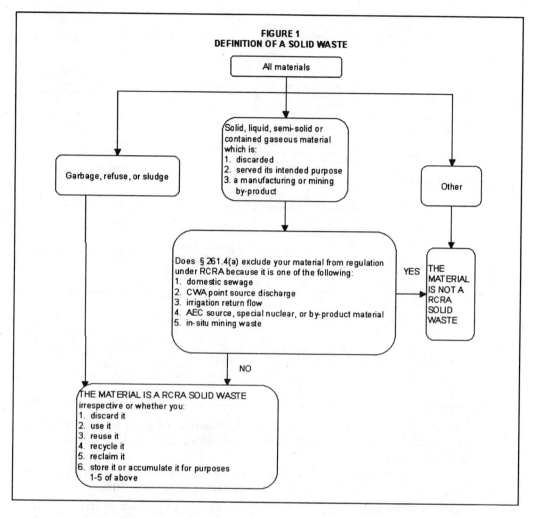

FIGURE 1
DEFINITION OF A SOLID WASTE

exclusions from the solid waste definition[7] include domestic sewage — alone or in combination with other waste material — that passes through publicly owned treatment works, legal point source discharges, irrigation return flows, and material regulated by the Atomic Energy Act of 1954. In addition, EPA regulations also exempt a number of solid wastes from being considered hazardous wastes. The principal exemptions of this type are household wastes (i.e., the garbage generated at home) and fertilizer used in agricultural operations.[8]

Once material is found to be solid waste, it must further be defined as hazardous waste before the more stringent segments of RCRA Subtitle C are applicable. The statute defines "hazardous waste" as:

---

8. Still further exemptions from Subtitle C were established by Congress with regard to five categories of "special wastes." In general, these wastes are high-volume, low-toxicity material, including certain mining materials that remain largely in place throughout the mining process, cement kiln dust, and certain coal and fuel combustion by-products such as fly ash. For each category of special waste, EPA is required to study the matter and determine whether the exemption from Subtitle C should be made permanent. Pending that determination, special wastes are subject to RCRA regulation on the same basis as most non-hazardous solid waste. RCRA § 3001(b)(2)-(3), 42 U.S.C.A. § 6921(b)(2)-(3.)

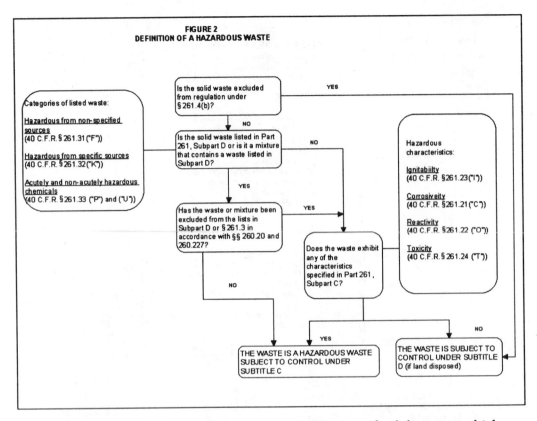

FIGURE 2
DEFINITION OF A HAZARDOUS WASTE

42 U.S.C.A. §6903(5).... a solid waste, or combination of solid wastes, which because of its quantity, concentration, or physical, chemical, or infectious characteristics may —

(A) cause, or significantly contribute to an increase in mortality or an increase in serious irreversible, or incapacitating reversible, illness; or

(B) pose a substantial present or potential hazard to human health or the environment when improperly treated, stored, transported, or disposed of, or otherwise managed.

A separate section of RCRA, 42 U.S.C.A. §6921(a), directs that EPA promulgate regulations for hazardous wastes taking into account (1) toxicity, persistence, and degradability, (2) the potential of the material to bioaccumulate in plants and animals, and (3) flammability, corrosiveness, and other hazardous characteristics. EPA responded with a dual approach, one that defined material as hazardous waste due to its generic characteristics, and the other listing specifically identified materials or waste streams as hazardous. The characteristics approach relies on four criteria: ignitability, corrosivity, reactivity, and toxicity.[9] See 40 CFR §§261.21–.24. Under

---

9. To assess toxicity, EPA utilizes a test method called the "TCLP" (Toxicity Characteristic Leaching Procedure). TCLP is a testing procedure that extracts the toxic constituents from a waste in a manner that EPA believes simulates the leaching action that occurs in landfills. See 40 C.F.R. § 261.24, as amended, 55 Fed. Reg. 11862 (March 29, 1990). Under TCLP, solid waste exhibits the characteristic of toxicity if, using the test methods prescribed, the extract from a representative sample of the waste contains contaminants at levels of regulatory concern. The TCLP tests for 25 organic chemicals, 8 inorganics, and 6 insecticides/herbicides. The levels that trigger the toxicity characteristic reflect health-based concentration thresholds and a factor for dilution and attenuation that was developed using modeling of the subsurface fate and transport of contaminants in groundwater.

the specific listing approach, EPA produced three lists, one identifying specific materials that are hazardous without regard to source (See 40 CFR §261.31), another listing materials that are hazardous due to their generation as part of a particular waste stream (e.g., waste from the inorganic chemical industry) (See 40 CFR §261.32), and a third for a variety of discarded materials that are acutely hazardous or toxic. See 40 CFR §261.33.

Figure 2 illustrates graphically the dual approach undertaken by EPA in determining whether solid waste is "hazardous." If a solid waste is not exempted or excluded from Subtitle C regulation,[10] a determination as to whether a solid waste is hazardous depends upon whether it exhibits one of the four hazardous characteristics ("characteristic wastes") or is specifically listed as a hazardous waste in EPA regulations ("listed wastes").

As Figure 2 shows, waste streams can be specifically listed as hazardous if EPA determines that they routinely contain hazardous constituents or exhibit hazardous characteristics. As further specified in Figure 2, EPA has established several general categories of listed wastes (e.g., the "F", "K", "P", and "U" lists.)[11]

In order to prevent generators from evading hazardous waste regulations by diluting or otherwise changing the composition of listed waste streams, EPA has also adopted two important rules, which are also illustrated in Figure 2: the "mixture rule" and the "derived from" rule. Under the "mixture rule," any mixture of a listed waste with another solid waste is deemed to be a hazardous waste. Characteristic wastes are not covered by the mixture rule; they cease to be hazardous wastes once they have been mixed or treated so as to remove the hazardous characteristic. Under the "derived from" rule, any waste derived from the treatment, storage, or disposal of a listed waste (e.g., ash residue from the burning of a listed waste) is deemed to be a hazardous waste. As Figure 2 illustrates, wastes falling under either the "mixture" or "derived from" rules are also considered by EPA to fall within the definition of a hazardous waste.

In summary, as Figure 2 shows, EPA considers a solid waste to be "hazardous" when

- the waste exhibits a hazardous characteristic,
- the waste meets the description of a listed waste,
- the waste is mixed with a listed waste, or
- the waste is derived from the storage, treatment, or disposal of a hazardous waste.

To avoid the hazardous waste regulatory system, as Figure 2 illustrates, the waste must be wholly or partially exempted or the hazardous waste status must be terminated.[12]

---

10. The disposal of exempted materials is subject to the much more lenient provisions of RCRA Subtitle D. 40 CFR § 261.4(b).

11. The key categories of "listed wastes" list wastes that are (1) hazardous from nonspecific sources (40 CFR § 261.31) ("F"), (2) hazardous from specific sources (40 CFR § 261.32) ("K"), and (3) acutely hazardous chemical products (40 CFR § 261.33) ("P"), or (4) non-acutely hazardous chemical products (40 CFR § 261.33(f)) ("U"). By the end of 1990, EPA had listed over 760 types of wastes as hazardous by placing them in one of these four categories.

12. Wastes that have been listed as hazardous must be managed under Subtitle C, unless EPA grants a petition to delist a waste generated at a particular site under § 3001(f) of RCRA.

As the following case illustrates, a decision by EPA identifying particular solid wastes as "hazardous" is often controversial and the subject of litigation, due to the significant consequences that arise from such identification.

## Dithiocarbamate Task Force v. Environmental Protection Agency
### United States Court of Appeals for the District of Columbia Circuit, 1996
### 98 F.3d 1394

WILLIAMS, C.J. This consolidated case concerns four classes of carbamate compounds — carbamates proper, carbamoyl oximes, thiocarbamates and dithiocarbamates (collectively "carbamates") — whose similar names reflect similarities in their chemical origins and structures. All are derivatives of carbamic acid. Carbamates and derivative products are used as pesticides, herbicides and fungicides; they are also used in various ways by the rubber, wood and textile industries. In the rulemaking giving rise to this lawsuit the Environmental Protection Agency listed many of these carbamate-based products, as well as waste streams generated in carbamate-based production processes, as hazardous wastes under the Resource Conservation and Recovery Act, 42 U.S.C. §6901-6992k ("RCRA") (1994.) Petitioners, the Dithiocarbamate Task force (treated collectively with intervenor Uniroyal Chemical Co. as "DTF" or the "Task Force"), Zeneca Inc., and Troy Chemical Corp., are (or represent) manufacturers who make various carbamate-based products or use carbamates in their production processes. They challenge a portion of these listings as arbitrary and capricious.

Because we find that in promulgating some of the challenged rules EPA failed to meet the minimum standard required of it by the Administrative Procedure Act, Sec 5 U.S.C. §706(2)(A) (1994), we vacate in part and affirm in part....

*Statutory and Regulatory Authority*: RCRA, enacted in 1976, directs the EPA to promulgate criteria for identifying and listing hazardous wastes, "taking into account toxicity, persistence, and degradability in nature, potential for accumulation in tissue, and other related factors such as flammability, corrosiveness, and other hazardous characteristics." 42 U.S.C. §6921(a). In 1980 EPA issued rules for identifying hazardous wastes, along with its first list of wastes subject to RCRA....Those rules remain in force today, with minor adjustments.

These rules lay out three different routes to listing a substance as a hazardous waste, of which the third is of primary relevance here. Under it a waste can be listed as hazardous if it satisfies two conditions:

[1] It contains any of the toxic constituents listed in appendix VIII [to 40 CFR Part 261] and [2] after considering the following factors [listed below], the Administrator concludes that the waste is capable of posing a substantial present or potential hazard to human health or the environment when improperly treated, stored, transported or disposed of or otherwise managed....

The first step in the process, adding chemicals to appendix VIII, is to occur "only if [the chemicals] have been shown in scientific studies to have toxic, carcinogenic, mutagenic or teratogenic effects on humans or other life forms." In the second step, the Administrator is to consider the following factors:

(i) The nature of the toxicity presented by the constituent.

(ii) The concentration of the constituent in the waste.

(iii) The potential of the constituent or any toxic degradation product of the constituent to migrate from the waste into the environment under the types of improper management considered in paragraph (a)(3)(vii) of this section.

(iv) The persistence of the constituent or any toxic degradation product of the constituent.

(v) The potential for the constituent or any toxic degradation product of the constituent to degrade into non-harmful constituents and the rate of degradation.

(vi) the degree to which the constituent or any degradation product of the constituent bioaccumulates in ecosystems.

(vii) The plausible types of improper management to which the waste could be subjected.

(viii) The quantities of the waste generated at individual generation sites or on a regional or national basis.

(ix) The nature and severity of the human health and environmental damage that has occurred as a result of the improper management of wastes containing the constituent.

(x) Action taken by other governmental agencies or regulatory programs based on the health or environmental hazard posed by the waste or waste constituent.

(xi) Such other factors as may be appropriate.

Once the EPA decides to list a waste as hazardous, the substance is assigned a particular code and included in the appropriate lists in Subpart D of Part 261. Wastes generated by manufacturing processes are listed in K wastes. Chemical products or manufacturing chemical intermediates that are hazardous if they are discarded or intended to be discarded are listed as P or U wastes, the P designation being reserved for "acute hazardous wastes" of this type. (EPA made 18 P listings in this rulemaking but none is disputed here.)[13]

Listing has significant consequences. Any hazardous waste is subject to precisely prescribed rules on disposal,...record-keeping (covering both makers and users),...and transport.... In addition, hazardous wastes listed under RCRA or exhibiting one or more of the characteristics of a listed RCRA hazardous waste are considered hazardous substances under the regulatory scheme set up by the Comprehensive Environmental Response, Compensation, and Liability Act ("CERCLA").... CERCLA requires that every release of a hazardous substance above a specified level, known as the reportable quantity ("RQ"), be reported to the National Response Center and to state and local authorities. The EPA set the RQ for all the hazardous wastes we consider here at one pound, the statutory fallback level...pending further study.

*The Present Rulemaking*: Invoking its authority under 40 CFR §261.11(a)(3), EPA proposed to list six K wastes and 70 P and U wastes, running the gamut of the carbamate industry. In addition, the agency proposed to list four generic U wastes that would cover any substance that could be classified as one of the four kinds of carbamates. The Agency also proposed to add to Appendix VIII of Part 261 each of the chemical constituents that were the basis of the proposed listings, which in the case of the P and U listings were the products or manufacturing chemical intermediates themselves. Proposed Rule: Carbamate Production Identification and Listing of Hazardous Waste, 59 Fed.Reg. 9808 (March 1, 1994).

The final rule differed from the proposal only slightly. In response to comments, the EPA said it would not list the four generic U wastes. It also decided not to make 12 of the proposed U listings because of insufficient toxicity data. Based on a re-analysis of the toxicity data it did have, EPA moved four chemicals from the P listings for acutely hazardous substances to the U listings. The K listings, aside from some tinkering with special exemptions not at issue here, remained

---

13. No "F" wastes, or hazardous wastes from non-specific sources, were involved in this case. [Eds.]

essentially unchanged. The result was that 40 carbamate industry products received U listings, 18 received P listings and all 58 were listed on Appendix VIII. In addition, manufacturers involved in each of the four classes of carbamates had at least one production waste stream listed as a K waste. Final Rule: Carbamate Production Identification and Listing of Hazardous Waste, 60 Fed.Reg. 7824, 7825–7827 (Feb. 9, 1995)....

*The U Listings*: Of the 40 products listed as U wastes, DTF challenges the listing of 17 dithiocarbamates, Zeneca the listing of six of its thiocarbamate products, and Troy the listing of its product, IPBC, U375, a carbamate proper.

Petitioners' first line of attack is on the EPA's adding items to Appendix VIII and listing them pursuant to the 40 CFR §261.11(a)(3), all in one rulemaking rather than two. They do not, however, point to any language in §261.11(a)(3) suggesting any requirement of sequential listing. Nor do they identify any way in which the EPA's consolidated process might jeopardize their rights or increase the risk of error. Petitioners also claim that it is unreasonable for EPA to consider aquatic toxicity data, or the harm caused to aquatic environments, in making Appendix VIII listings or the actual hazardous waste listings we consider below. But they point to nothing in the regulations or the statute that prevents EPA from considering the harm to organisms other than mammals or land-based creatures.

Second, petitioners argue that in making the determination necessary in the second step of a §261.11(a)(3) listing — determining "that the waste is capable of posing a substantial present or potential hazard to human health or the environment when improperly treated, stored, transported or disposed of or otherwise managed" — EPA did not consider all of the 11 specified factors. (There are really only ten, since the final factor is a catch-all allowing the Administrator to consider any other factor she finds relevant.) EPA argues both that §261.11(a)(3) does not require the Administrator to consider all ten factors, and that in any event she did consider them.

The theory that §261.11(a)(3) does not require consideration of the ten factors defies the language of the rule, which we have already quoted. Its structure is simple. Given an Appendix VIII listing, the Administrator is to make a determination about "hazard to human health or the environment," and is to do so "after considering" the named factors. EPA, indeed, makes no effort to parse the language to yield a different result. It cites *NRDC v. EPA*, 25 F.3d. 1063 (D.C. Cir. 1994), in support of its reading, but *NRDC* merely upheld EPA's discretion to "emphasize or de-emphasize particular factors," *id.* at 1071, and carefully noted that petitioners there did "not contend that the Administrator failed to consider the relevant factors...."*Id.*

Moreover, the structure of 40 CFR §261.11(a) forbids EPA's reading. Section 261.11(a)(2), the second of three routes to listing a substance as hazardous, states specific toxicity criteria; if a substance exceeds the specified levels, it is to be listed pure and simple. If EPA were able to list substances that exhibited toxicity *below* the §261.11(a)(2) thresholds without examining the ten factors and making an overall assessment of the hazards posed by improper management (or doing so only as whimsy moved the agency), the brightline sense of §261.11(a)(2) would be completely undercut. In fact, this rulemaking underscores the structural point. EPA calculated the aquatic toxicity levels for most of the chemicals it listed and found those levels — which were high, but not within the criteria stated in §261.11(a)(2) — to be the most significant factor in its decision to make the listings. See 60 Fed.Reg. at 7838/1.

EPA points to prior statements that §261.11(a)(3) requires it to consider only "appropriate factors," see Identification and Listing of Hazardous Waste, 55 Fed.Reg. 18,726 (May 4, 1990) (technical amendment to 40 CFR §261.11(a)(3)), or "relevant factors," see Identification and Listing of Hazardous Waste, 57 Fed.Reg. 12, 14 (Jan. 2, 1992) (final rule), arguing that these reflect a past practice that is consonant with, and vindicates, the interpretation it asserts here. But neither of these statements adopts the position we understand EPA to argue before us, namely, that it may simply disregard a factor without a word as to *why* it is irrelevant or unimportant.

Accordingly, despite the great deference we owe an agency in the interpretation of its own regulations,...we must apply the regulation's specific language over the agency's current interpretation. If EPA finds a factor to be irrelevant or unimportant in a particular listing, of course, that finding would be subject to very deferential review. But with no such finding, the court has no reason to suppose that the agency considered each factor, as required by its own regulation.

Almost as an afterthought, EPA argues in its brief that it did consider all the factors in §261.11(a)(3). At oral argument, counsel for EPA acknowledged that EPA did not consider each factor for each of the products listed, but at most considered them in the aggregate, for each of the four classes of chemicals. Where it is reasonable to consider the factors in relation to a class of chemicals, EPA may do so....[T]hat means essentially that if the known similarities of members of a class are such that it is reasonable to infer the presence of a disputed characteristic throughout the class (not just among members for which it has been shown), the EPA is free to draw that inference. Thus, if the agency is considering a class A$i$-$n$, and members A$i$-$iv$ exhibit a specific attribute, and there is reason to believe that they do so because of some trait shared by the whole class, then the agency may draw the inference that all the members of the class exhibit the attribute....

To summarize: EPA's discussion of the quantities of waste is slight and oblique, but we need not consider whether such an inadequacy would require us to vacate the rule. Where EPA falls down completely is on the interlocked topics of other regulatory controls (factor (x)) and mismanagement (factor (vii)). It is tempting to say that the toxicity of these chemicals alone marks them as hazardous, and, of course, in one of the purely colloquial senses of the word, they are. But 40 CFR §261.11(a)(2) gives explicit toxicity benchmarks that are not satisfied here. That relationship underscores what would be true anyway — that a failure on the EPA's part to give serious consideration to the "softer" variables of §261.11(a)(3) tends to turn its application of that section into an exercise in totally standardless discretion. Accordingly, we vacate the challenged U listings as arbitrary and capricious....

### COMMENTARY AND QUESTIONS

1. **EPA's choice of listing criteria.** RCRA §3001, 42 U.S.C.A. §6921, requires EPA to establish criteria for identifying and listing hazardous waste "taking into account toxicity, persistence, and degradability in nature, potential for accumulation in tissue, and other related factors, such as flammability, corrosiveness, and other hazardous characteristics." The actual listing process, which formed the basis of this lawsuit, was promulgated by EPA as a regulation in 1980. 40 CFR §261.11(a)(3), which EPA relied on in listing the carbamate wastes, established a complex two-

step listing process by which EPA must (1) determine whether the waste contains any of the toxic constituents listed in Appendix VIII; and, if it does, (2) find "that the waste is capable of posing a substantial present or potential hazard to human health or the environment when improperly treated, stored, transported, or disposed of or otherwise managed" after consideration of the ten factors listed in 40 CFR §261.11(a)(3). The court correctly held that EPA had been arbitrary and capricious in not explicitly considering two of the ten factors. Is §261.11(a)(3) more demanding than Congress required? Is it more complex than necessary? Why, for example, should a waste not be automatically listed as hazardous if it contains one of the toxic constituents contained in Appendix VIII? Should EPA withdraw §261.11 and repropose it, including a less exacting set of listing criteria? Does it matter if §261.11 is well-established (i.e., firms have conformed their business practices to its current operation), or would accounting for such actions tend to ossify environmental regulation? Plainly, if EPA enjoys the authority to promulgate the rule in the first place (which it surely does), EPA enjoys the same authority to alter the rule, but EPA may lack the political will to do so.

### Section 3. REGULATING PARTICIPANTS IN THE HAZARDOUS WASTE LIFE CYCLE

As noted previously, RCRA divides the universe of persons in the hazardous waste life cycle into three categories: (1) generators of waste; (2) transporters of waste; and (3) owners and operators of treatment, storage, and disposal ("TSD") facilities. Of the three groups, only TSD facilities require RCRA permits to operate, but for each of these groups RCRA sets statutory duties that are liberally supplemented by administrative regulation. In general, the very demanding requirements for TSD licensure have limited the number of TSD sites and greatly increased the cost of lawful disposal of hazardous waste.[14]

Although RCRA divides the universe of persons into these three categories, RCRA also links these categories together through the use of a manifest system. The Uniform Hazardous Waste Manifest (the manifest) is the paper trail linking the generator, the transporter, and the TSD for every shipment of hazardous waste from the point of its generation to the point of its ultimate treatment, storage, or disposal. Each time the waste is transferred (e.g., from one transporter to another, or from a transporter to a designated facility), the manifest must be signed to acknowledge the receipt of the waste. A copy of the manifest is retained by each link in the transportation chain, and provides verification that waste was delivered where designated or, alternatively, that the waste was not delivered and its whereabouts must be determined.

The EPA's manifest form is reproduced in Figure 3. Both the use of the manifest, and the linkage which it provides among the three discrete sets of participants

14. To avoid the possibility that generators will seek to avoid the cost of disposal by storing waste on-site, EPA requires that all but a small portion of a generator's hazardous waste must be consigned for delivery to a TSD facility within 90 days after the date of generation. 40 CFR § 262.34 (the "90 day accumulation rule"). A small number of generators have obtained on-site RCRA permits, but the burdens of RCRA regulation and economies of scale have made off-site treatment, storage, and disposal the norm. Small quantity generators of between 100 kilograms per month and 1,000 kilograms per month may store hazardous wastes on site for longer periods than prescribed in the 90-day accumulation rule but must comply with RCRA in virtually all other respects. See 40 C.F.R. § 262.34(d)(i).

*[Uniform Hazardous Waste Manifest form — Michigan Department of Natural Resources, EPA Form 8700-22 (Rev. 9/88)]*

PLEASE TYPE OR PRINT CLEARLY USING BALL POINT PEN — PRESS HARD. PLEASE DO NOT FOLD DOCUMENT.

READ INSTRUCTIONS ON BACK OF MANIFEST

**DNR**
MICHIGAN DEPARTMENT
OF NATURAL RESOURCES

DO NOT WRITE IN THIS SPACE
ATT. ☐   DIS. ☐   REJ. ☐   PR. ☐

**UNIFORM HAZARDOUS WASTE MANIFEST**

1. Generator's US EPA ID No.
Manifest Document No.
2. Page 1 of — Information in the shaded areas is not required by Federal law.

A. State Manifest Document Number   MI 3695833
B. State Generator's ID

3. Generator's Name and Mailing Address
4. Generator's Phone ( )
5. Transporter 1 Company Name   6. US EPA ID Number
C. State Transporter's ID
D. Transporter's Phone
7. Transporter 2 Company Name   8. US EPA ID Number
E. State Transporter's ID
F. Transporter's Phone
9. Designated Facility Name and Site Address   10. US EPA ID Number
G. State Facility's ID
H. Facility's Phone

11. US DOT Description (including Proper Shipping Name, Hazard Class, and ID NUMBER)
12. Containers — No., Type
13. Total Quantity
14. Unit Wt/Vol
I. Waste No.

a.
b.
c.
d.

J. Additional Descriptions for Materials Listed Above
K. Handling Codes for Wastes Listed Above
a/ /
b/ /
c/ /
d/ /

15. Special Handling Instructions and Additional Information

16. GENERATOR'S CERTIFICATION: I hereby declare that the contents of this consignment are fully and accurately described above by proper shipping name and are classified, packed, marked, and labeled, and are in all respects in proper condition for transport by highway according to applicable international and national government regulations.

If I am a large quantity generator, I certify that I have a program in place to reduce the volume and toxicity of waste generated to the degree I have determined to be economically practicable and that I have selected the practicable method of treatment, storage, or disposal currently available to me which minimizes the present and future threat to human health and the environment; OR, if I am a small quantity generator, I have made a good faith effort to minimize my waste generation and select the best waste management method that is available to me and that I can afford.

Printed/Typed Name   Signature   Date Month Day Year

17. Transporter 1 Acknowledgement of Receipt of Materials
Printed/Typed Name   Signature   Date Month Day Year

18. Transporter 2 Acknowledgement of Receipt of Materials
Printed/Typed Name   Signature   Date Month Day Year

19. Discrepancy Indication Space

20. Facility Owner or Operator: Certification of receipt of hazardous materials covered by this manifest except as noted in Item 19
Printed/Typed Name   Signature   Date Month Day Year

EPA Form 8700-22 (Rev. 9/88)   To be mailed by Generator to: Michigan DNR, Box 30038, Lansing, MI 48909

in the hazardous waste life cycle, are key to the controlled tracking system which is at the heart of RCRA —

*1. Generators.* Generators of hazardous waste are subject to obligations that begin with "recordkeeping practices that accurately identify the quantities...constituents...and the disposition of such wastes." 42 U.S.C.A. §6922(a)(1). RCRA, and its attendant EPA regulation (40 CFR §262), also require generators to use specific types of containers for hazardous wastes, to label those wastes in a particular fashion, to provide information about the wastes and their characteristics, and to employ the manifest system to track the whereabouts of material until its delivery to a permitted TSD facility. As a review of the manifest form illustrates, the information that must appear on the manifest includes just what you might expect — the name, address, telephone number, and EPA hazardous waste number of the generator, the transporter, and the TSD facility; a carefully quantified description of the materials and the number and types of containers involved; and a series of descriptive names and codes that identify the waste and its hazards in accordance with EPA regulations. The generator must also certify the accuracy of the manifest and that the material was properly prepared for shipment in addition to signing a certificate that states:

> I have a program in place to reduce the volume and toxicity of waste generated to the degree I have determined to be economically practicable and I have selected the method of treatment, storage, or disposal currently available to me which minimizes the present and future threat to human health and the environment. 40 CFR §262, Appendix.

The administrative burden of the proper functioning of the manifest system is largely on the generator, who must obtain from the transporter and TSD facility endorsed copies of the manifest that document proper delivery of the material to the TSD facility within 35 days of the time that the material was consigned for delivery. If successful delivery is not documented within 45 days, the generator must file a report with EPA (or the state where the state program is authorized) advising it of that failure and detailing the generator's efforts to locate the waste. See 40 CFR §262.42.

*2. Transporters.* Transporters are the least heavily regulated actors in the RCRA hazardous waste life cycle.[15] Their basic obligations under RCRA are to facilitate the operation of the manifest system by making sure (as far as possible) that the manifests are accurate and delivering the material in accordance with the manifests. In the event of a spill, transporters come under additional obligations to minimize the spill's effects and to notify local and federal spill response authorities. Transporters can, if they mix dissimilar wastes for shipment in a single container, or accept wastes from sources outside of the country, become liable as generators of wastes for RCRA purposes. Likewise, transporters who store wastes beyond regulatory limits or alter the characteristics of the wastes can become subject to regulation as TSD facilities.

*3. Treatment, storage and disposal facility owners or operators.* TSD facilities are the most extensively regulated parties in the RCRA hazardous waste life cycle. The three components of TSD are defined broadly.

Treatment includes:

> any method, technique, or process, including neutralization, designed to change the physical, chemical, or biological character or composition of any hazardous waste so as to neutralize such waste, or so as to recover energy or material resources from the waste, or so as to render such waste non-hazardous, or less hazardous, safer to transport, store, or dispose of, or amenable for recovery, amenable for storage, or reduced in volume. 40 CFR §260.10.

Storage includes:

> the holding of hazardous waste for a temporary period, at the end of which the hazardous waste is treated, disposed of, or stored elsewhere. *Id.*

---

15. Transporters are, however, regulated separately by the United States Department of Transportation (DOT) pursuant to the Hazardous Materials Transportation Act, 49 U.S.C.A. §§1801–1812. DOT has promulgated extensive equipment and materials-handling specifications under this statute.

Disposal includes:

> the discharge, deposit, injection, dumping, spilling, leaking, or placing of any solid waste or hazardous waste into or on any land or water so that such solid waste or hazardous waste or any constituent thereof may enter the environment or be emitted into the air or discharged into any waters, including ground waters. *Id.*

The obligations of TSD facilities are again predictable. RCRA requires that TSD facilities:

> (1) treat, store, and dispose of wastes in a manner consistent with EPA directives and standards; (2) maintain records of the wastes treated, stored, or disposed of; (3) comply with the requirements of the manifest system; (4) be built to meet certain EPA specified design and siting requirements that seek to ensure safety, such as not being located in flood plains or along earthquake faults; (5) monitor the site for releases of hazardous materials; and (6) take corrective action in the event of a release or threatened release of hazardous materials.[16] Going further, EPA has set standards for continuity of operations, training personnel, and eventual closure of the facility.

RCRA also requires that TSD operators meet qualifications that touch on issues of financial responsibility, past record of regulatory compliance, and freedom from criminal activity. The financial responsibility standards are intended to avoid the dangers associated with "orphan" sites that have been a major problem in the past. The worry is that a presently solvent and viable TSD operation may become insolvent, leaving behind a potential toxic time bomb that becomes a burden on public resources. The good character and compliance record requirements are aimed at excluding organized crime organizations from the industry and also limiting the class of TSD operators to persons and companies having a good history of regulatory compliance.

EPA labels the phases of the TSD facility life cycle as operational, closure, and post-closure. In the operational stage, the site is able to accept wastes, for which fees are charged and from which an income stream is generated. Closure is a six-month period that begins when wastes are no longer accepted at the facility, during which time treatment and disposal operations are completed on all wastes that are not going to be relocated to other operating TSD facilities. Closure also includes dismantling and decontaminating equipment and making needed site improvements, such as applying clay capping over hazardous materials that are to be disposed of on-site. Post-closure is a 30-year period following closure during which the TSD facility operator has continuing monitoring, maintenance, and remediation responsibilities.

Both closure and post-closure costs, including costs for relocation of waste, are substantial and pose a special problem that must be addressed by the financial responsibility regulations. By definition, those costs occur at a time when no additional waste is being accepted at the site and, hence, there is no longer a positive

---

16. See generally RCRA § 3004, 42 U.S.C.A. § 6924. Especially in the early years of RCRA operation, TSD licensing proceeded on a dual track that allowed facilities to obtain "interim" licenses by meeting less stringent standards, and to obtain "permanent" status by meeting the full array of Subtitle C regulation. In the 1984 HSWA, Congress set firm deadlines to retire all interim status facilities, the last of which fell due in 1992.

income stream available to meet expenses. Anticipating this situation, as part of licensure, a facility-specific closure plan is required and its cost is estimated using a sort of "worst case scenario." This figure is adjusted annually to reflect revisions (if any) in the plan itself, and changes in plan costs due to inflation or other factors. The law requires that the TSD operator give a financial assurance in that amount by establishing a closure trust fund during the operational life of the facility, obtaining a surety bond or irrevocable letter of credit, purchasing closure insurance, or, under certain corporate solvency conditions, giving a corporate guarantee. To alleviate problems of TSD operator insolvency that may occur before closure, a second prong of the financial responsibility regulation requires the purchase of liability insurance, or its equivalent, for both sudden and non-sudden accidental releases of hazardous materials.

## COMMENTARY AND QUESTIONS

1. **RCRA's regulatory scheme as a series of statutory types.** Recall the variety of statutory types studied in preceding chapters. As discussed so far, what kind of statute is RCRA? Although several facets of RCRA have been mentioned only briefly, or will be more fully described in the remainder of this chapter, RCRA can already be seen to be a composite statute that integrates many taxonomic regulatory mechanisms into a comprehensive, although not complete, hazardous waste management system:

- The manifest system is a form of mandatory disclosure;
- The hammer clauses (i.e., the "land ban", considered later in this chapter) are a form of roadblock statute;
- The TSD licensing procedure is, in part, a form of a traditional review and permit statute;
- The financial responsibility requirements are a form of control of market access;
- A number of the congressionally-fixed TSD facility design requirements are a form of specific, directly-legislated standards;
- The limitation on land-based disposal, making necessary the development of alternative disposal methods, is a form of technology-forcing;
- The Toxicity Characteristic Leaching Procedure test used to define some wastes as hazardous is a form of harm-based ambient standard;
- EPA's land disposal waste treatment regulations are, in part, based on BDAT (best demonstrated available technology, considered later in this chapter), a form of technology-based regulation;
- In an indirect way, due to the high cost of dealing with hazardous solid waste under Subtitle C, RCRA rewards and encourages waste reduction, thereby serving as a market incentives statute;
- The power of EPA to order corrective action is a form of cleanup statute;
- And, finally, the siting requirements for TSD facilities are a form of land-use control.

The wonder is that this spectrum of approaches appears to have evolved into a coherent overall program.

2. **RCRA's impact.** A 1982 EPA study found that there were in excess of 180,000 facilities at which hazardous waste disposal was occurring prior to RCRA's enactment.[17] By 1986, the number of sites at which legal (RCRA-permitted) disposal of hazardous waste was occurring had dropped below 2,000.[18] Estimates of the amount of hazardous waste generated in the United States vary considerably. EPA's estimate for 1985, based on a census of all waste management facilities, reported that RCRA-regulated hazardous waste totalled 247 million metric tons (MMT). The same EPA study found that 322 MMT of RCRA-exempt hazardous waste were generated in that same year. The reliability of this estimate and many others is open to question.[19]

What is so impressive about the reduction in the number of facilities at which hazardous waste disposal is occurring? Recalling the "if I know where it is, I know that it's not somewhere else that's worse" aspect of the RCRA system, it should be clear that herding a substantial portion of the nation's hazardous wastes into RCRA Subtitle C facilities is a vast improvement over past practices. Traditionally, most generators either kept hazardous waste on-site in slag piles, pits, ponds, and lagoons, or shipped it away for disposal at sites that employed the same unsophisticated disposal practices.

3. **The cost of RCRA disposal.** How expensive has RCRA made the lawful disposal of hazardous waste? Estimates of the cost of building a RCRA-compliant hazardous waste TSD facility range in the tens of millions of dollars for a moderate-to-large-sized facility. The process of obtaining a permit alone may cost in excess of $1,000,000.

These costs will, of course, be passed through to firms that send their wastes to TSD facilities. Nevertheless, by 1984 the total national cost for disposal of hazardous wastes was only $2.4 billion. When adjusted to constant dollars, this figure represented a 70 percent increase during the eight-year life span of RCRA. The 1984 cost of disposal represented .106 percent (just over one-tenth of one percent) of the total value of products shipped by the generators of that waste. For chemical and primary metals, the two most affected industries, the percentages were .255 percent and .237 percent, respectively. Even the advent of land disposal restrictions (LDR) in the 1984 amendments to RCRA were predicted to no more than double the cost of hazardous waste disposal.[20]

What will be the impact of these costs on waste handling practices in the United States? Despite the seemingly small aggregate impact of hazardous waste disposal cost as a percentage of the value of products produced, there appears to be general agreement that the high cost of RCRA disposal is simultaneously an incentive to

---

17 . See EPA, Surface Impoundment Assessment: National Report (Dec. 29, 1982).

18 . See United States General Accounting Office, Report to the Chairman, Subcommittee on Environment, Energy, and Natural Resources, Committee on Government Operations, House of Representatives, "Hazardous Waste — The Cost and Availability of Pollution Insurance" 12 (October, 1988).

19. See the GAO Report at 12.

20. See J. McCarthy & M. Reisch, Hazardous Waste Fact Book 5-19 (Congressional Research Service No. #87-56 ENR, Jan. 30, 1987).

both dangerous and disruptive illegal dumping and to beneficial waste reduction efforts as well. Firm RCRA disposal price data is hard to obtain, but analogies can be drawn from the CERCLA cleanup context where disposal costs are quite high. An EPA report found, for example, that the cost of depositing 1 cubic yard of gasoline-contaminated soil in a hazardous waste landfill (i.e., a RCRA Subtitle C permitted facility) ranged between $100–$200. A 1991 list of disposal costs provided to one of the authors by an industry source listed PCB-contaminated soil as the most expensive for land disposal, costing $470/ton for disposal.

4. **TSD industry characteristics.** One of the avowed aims of RCRA was to drive under-capitalized firms from the industry, and RCRA seems to have succeeded in this area. A 1988 GAO survey of all non-federal RCRA-permitted land disposal, land treatment, and surface impoundment facilities indicated that the industry had become the province of large firms.[21] Two-thirds of the 1200+ firms responding to the survey had sales in excess of $11 million per year, half had sales of over $50 million per year, one-third had sales of over $100 million per year, and over 20 percent had sales of over $500 million per year.[22]

5. **Criticizing RCRA: Under-regulation.** More than half of the nation's hazardous waste is outside of the RCRA system. The most significant legal reason for this under-regulation is that Congress and EPA have excluded whole categories of waste from regulation. Why should those categories be exempt from RCRA regulation? Although cost is alleged by some to be the answer, the cost of safe (or at least far safer) disposal is not large in comparison to the value of the finished products of which the wastes are a by-product.

The largest RCRA "loophole" involves industrial waste[23] not legally defined as hazardous:

> There exists a widespread perception that Subtitle D, or nonhazardous waste, is mostly municipal waste. This perception is reinforced by news reports highlighting disposal capacity, ash barges, recycling, and the anticipated publication of EPA's final municipal waste regulations. However, this perception is wrong. Between hazardous waste and municipal waste is a kind of waste that is generated in vastly greater volumes than the other two combined — nonhazardous industrial waste, or simply industrial waste.
>
> The magnitude of the industrial waste problem is overwhelming when it is stated in figures. Nationally, about 211 million tons of municipal waste and approximately 300 million tons of hazardous waste are generated annually.

21. United States General Accounting Office, Hazardous Waste: The Cost and Availability of Pollution Insurance 15 (October, 1989).

22. That same survey found that the purchase of pollution insurance is becoming less common and significantly more expensive for firms choosing that method of satisfying the financial responsibility requirements of RCRA. See Hazardous Waste: An Update on the Cost and Availability of Pollution Insurance (GAO/PEMD-94-161).

23. Industrial waste is not specifically defined by RCRA. The category includes more than 90 percent of the waste streams of factories, foundries, mills, processing plants, refineries and slaughterhouses. It also includes sludges and other by-products of in-plant waste treatment and those generated by water pollution control facilities. Many of the compounds that are included in this waste stream have chemical constituents similar to hazardous wastes. As an example, off-specification pesticides containing multiple active ingredients fall into the industrial waste category, as does waste containing concentrations of hazardous materials that fall below the EPA thresholds for hazardousness.

These numbers seem small compared with the 7,600 million tons of industrial waste that are generated and disposed of on-site annually....

Waste that does not meet the legal definition of "hazardous," however, is subject only to EPA's open dump criteria. These criteria apply to only a limited number of waste disposal problems, address many of these problems rather vaguely, and do not apply to treatment, storage, or transportation. [40 CFR §257.] RCRA does not expressly require that nonhazardous waste treatment, storage, and disposal facilities be permitted. Generally, Subtitle D treats all nonhazardous waste the same and only includes specific provisions for municipal waste, household hazardous waste, small-quantity generator hazardous waste, and recycled oil. Industrial waste is not given separate attention. The disparity in regulatory control between hazardous and nonhazardous waste is so great that delisting of a hazardous waste means virtual federal regulatory abandonment. John Dernbach, Industrial Waste: Saving the Worst for Last?, 20 ELR 10283, 10283–85 (1990).

Professor Dernbach explains in some detail how dangerous wastes can evade RCRA listing as hazardous and concludes that the sharp divergence in regulation is "inappropriate because of the environmental and public health risks posed by industrial waste." Id. at 10285–86.

6. **Criticizing RCRA: Over-regulation.** RCRA is, without question, a giant step forward from unregulated hazardous waste disposal practices, but RCRA inevitably overregulates in a way that has unintended results. Dr. Robert Powitz, the Director of Environmental Health and Safety at Wayne State University, posed the following examples in a lecture to law students:

Waste acids can often be combined in a chemical reaction with waste bases to form a salt and water. If performed, this reaction would eliminate the need for transport of two hazardous substances (the acid and the base), having changed them to non-hazardous materials. To do so, however, is to perform treatment under RCRA which requires the treater to obtain a TSD license that the University cannot afford to obtain. The University estimates that the cost of mere application for a license is in excess of $1 million. The University's annual disposal costs attributable to materials that could be treated safely on campus without major capital investments is in the $50,000 per year range. The alternative is to ship the hazardous material 80 miles through several heavily populated areas to a licensed TSD facility.

A major chemical facility in the suburbs of Detroit, Michigan produces isocyanate (of Bhopal infamy) as a by-product of plastics production. Isocyanates react readily with water to produce non-toxic by-products. Again, however, to combine them with the water is to engage in treatment and requires a TSD license that the chemical company does not wish to obtain. (Here the hesitancy to seek licensure is less the cost than the desire to avoid being a TSD facility with all of the regulatory burdens that entails.) The lawful disposal requires shipment of isocyanate through residential areas in the vicinity of the plant and highway travel to a facility some 60 miles away.

Do the examples demonstrate that RCRA thwarts its own objectives of increased safety and waste minimization? Should EPA write a blanket exception for safety-enhancing treatment at generators' sites, or promulgate certain categorical exceptions from TSD licensure requirements?

7. **Criticizing RCRA: definitional nightmares concerning "hazardous" wastes.** As the Dithiocarbamate case highlights, one of RCRA's most obvious problems lies in the complex set of definitions and rules that combine to identify what materials qualify as hazardous wastes subject to its stringent regulatory provisions. Some of the complexity is attributable to what wastes are "characteristic" or, as in Dithiocarbamate, what wastes are properly "listed" by EPA. Other cases construing RCRA's definition of "hazardous waste" include American Mining Congress v. EPA, 824 F.2d 1177 (D.C. Cir., 1987) (EPA is not authorized to regulate in-process recycled materials because they are not "discarded materials"), Horsehead Resource Development Co. v. Browner, 16 F.3d 1246 (D.C. Cir., 1994) (EPA can regulate cement kiln dust and combustion residues when they are produced by boilers and industrial furnaces that burn fuel containing hazardous waste), and NRDC v. Hazardous Waste Treatment Council, 25 F.3d 1063 (D.C. Cir., 1994) (used oil need not be listed as a hazardous waste in all circumstances).

Still greater complexity is added by the "mixture" and "derived from" rules. In 1991, a major blow to EPA's RCRA administration was struck when the D.C. Circuit vacated EPA's "mixture" and "derived-from" rules in Shell Oil Co. v. EPA, 950 F.2d 741 (D.C. Cir., 1991). The ground for vacating the rules was a failure by EPA properly to allow for notice and comment, a defect that could be overcome by repeating the process with adequate procedural steps. EPA then re-enacted the rules on an interim basis until new rules could be promulgated with full notice and comment. The interim rules were also challenged in the D.C. Circuit. In response to this challenge, Congress enacted legislation stating that the interim mixture and derived-from rules "shall not be terminated or withdrawn until revisions are promulgated and become effective." Congress also set a deadline of October 4, 1994 for promulgation of the new rules, but EPA missed the deadline. Faced with lawsuits over failing to meet the deadline, EPA signed a consent decree requiring it to propose a new Hazardous Waste Identification Rule (HWIR).

On December 21, 1995, EPA proposed a new HWIR (60 Fed. Reg. 66344) that would allow listed wastes, as well as wastes subject to the mixture and derived from rules, to avoid Subtitle C regulation when their specified hazardous constituents fall below certain levels. EPA proposed "exit levels" for 376 chemical constituents in listed hazardous wastes. Listed hazardous wastes (which, under the proposal, would include mixtures, treatment residues, and contaminated media from remediation sites) could be exempt from regulation if they do not contain one of the 376 contaminants above its exit level. The exit levels are based on a complex, risk-based system using "one in one million" (for cancer risks) and "no observable toxic effects" (for non-carcinogenic and ecological risks) as endpoints. The HWIR would be "self-executing" meaning that generators could exit subtitle C without advance approval. Does EPA's HWIR proposal signal a trend away from technology-based regulation of hazardous wastes under RCRA towards a harm-based regulatory approach? If so, will EPA's proposal cure the definitional nightmares that plague the mixture and derived-from rules? Will EPA's proposal address the under-regulation and over-regulation problems of RCRA? Will it reduce the costs of administering and complying with RCRA? After searching criticism of the Multipathway

Risk Assessment, on which the proposed HWIR was based, EPA withdrew the proposed rule and agreed to repropose it by October 31, 1999.

8. **Criticizing RCRA: definitional nightmares concerning recycling.** Another definitional quagmire arises in the determination of how to treat recycling. Under existing statutory definitions, most recycled materials are defined as solid wastes. Does subjecting recycled material (if it meets one of the definitions of "hazardous") to rigorous regulation encourage the reuse of those materials, or does it make the use of new raw materials more attractive? To put a damper on recycling would be inconsistent with RCRA's own materials conservation goals. EPA has sought to avoid that dilemma by making its definition of recycled material a term of art that defines some and not other processes as solid waste, and, hence, subject to RCRA Subtitle C if hazardous. For example, using scrap metal as fill material or adding used oil to boiler fuel are defined as recycling, and the material is therefore solid waste. The principle that places these examples on the regulated side of the solid waste line is that they all involve processes that tend to place material into the environment without treatment. By contrast, reclaimed material intended for reuse in the original primary production process in which it was generated is not solid waste. These distinctions reduce the deterrence to recycling, but do not eliminate it. Another EPA concern is that materials intended for recycling and reuse may not be so used. For example, what if waste oil intended to be resold as boiler fuel finds no buyers due to a dip in energy prices? If that material were not defined as solid waste, its disposal would not be regulated by RCRA. For a more thorough account of the intricacies that confound this area, see Johnson, Recyclable Materials and RCRA's Complicated, Conflicting, and Costly Definition of Solid Waste, 21 ELR 10357 (1991); Gaba, Solid Waste and Recycled Materials Under RCRA: Separating Chaff From Wheat, 16 Ecology L.Q. 623 (1989).

9. **When exempt household waste is incinerated, is its hazardous ash exempt too?** In 1994, the United States Supreme Court resolved a split between two of the nation's Circuit Courts of Appeal with regard to whether ash created by the incineration of municipal solid waste can be regulated as hazardous waste under RCRA Subtitle C. Items that would normally qualify as hazardous solid waste, such as discarded batteries, paint, garden care products, and many others, are mixed with other refuse in municipal garbage. Congress foresaw the burden municipalities would face if their entire waste streams had to be disposed of at Subtitle C facilities, and Congress therefore exempted municipal solid waste (MSW) from Subtitle C. However, when burned, as is common in trash-to-energy incinerators, the ash left after the combustion of MSW would often, depending on its characteristics, be considered a hazardous waste that required RCRA Subtitle C disposal. Perhaps displaying insufficient foresight, Congress did not specify if ash from incineration of MSW is also Subtitle C exempt. The Supreme Court held that the generation of toxic ash is not included within the activities covered by the exemption, and thus must be regulated under Subtitle C if the ash possesses the characteristics of hazardous waste. Chicago v. EDF, 511 U.S. 328 (1994). Congress is considering whether to amend RCRA in order to clarify that municipal incinerator ash is to be treated as a "special waste," not as hazardous waste.

10. **Rethinking RCRA.** In their Dialogue entitled Rethinking the Resource Conservation and Recovery Act for the 1990s, 21 ELR 10063 (1991), Marcia E. Williams and Jonathan Z. Cannon make a series of very technical, but very telling criticisms of RCRA as it has developed. One of their most fundamental attacks on RCRA can be stated in simplified form — RCRA makes a great deal turn on the division of wastes into the categories of hazardous and non-hazardous, and then draws that line in a fiendishly complicated way. This leads to a multitude of untoward results. First, because the cost of disposal of hazardous waste is vastly greater than the cost of disposal of non-hazardous waste, generators have immense incentives to contest the categorization decisions. In conjunction with the byzantine definitional rules that are currently in force, a disproportionate amount of both regulatory and enforcement effort is directed to issues of coverage that result in little or no environmental benefit. A related criticism is that the definitional distinctions drawn between hazardous and non-hazardous are too often irrational if one keeps in mind RCRA's goal of reducing the release of dangerous substances. Here, the principal examples are the listing of some compounds as hazardous and the non-listing of chemically similar compounds having much the same potential for damaging human health and the environment. Moving from the definitional into the regulatory sphere, Williams and Cannon accuse RCRA of severe under- and over-regulation. The under-regulation occurs in regard to the laxity with which non-hazardous wastes are treated. Their point is that many waste streams that are designated as non-hazardous contain substantial quantities of hazardous materials that find their way into the environment. The over-regulation occurs in practices that overestimate risks (such as assuming that all wastes will be totally mismanaged), or in the adoption of anti-dilution rules that are inflexibly applied as rigid "tracking" rules so that wastes remain legally hazardous, even after treatment that produces a by-product that is non-hazardous according to EPA standards.

A somewhat different perspective on RCRA's future focuses on the failure of Subtitle C to address the larger issues of the solid waste problem posed by the need to safely dispose of such vast quantities of material. Taken together, the severity of regulation under Subtitle C, the expense entailed by detoxification of materials under that portion of RCRA, and the laxity of regulation under Subtitle D, form an unsatisfactory whole. Too little waste is required to be treated, and the waste that is treated is treated in ways that are too expensive to be used for substantial additional quantities of waste. In the end, long-term land disposal of Subtitle D solid waste imposes risks of "creating new environmental problems in the distant future when and if containment breaks down." Pedersen, The Future of Federal Solid Waste Regulation, 16 Colum. J. Envtl L. 109, 110 (1991). Pedersen contends that "since our current approach to the solid waste problem has reached its natural limits, market-based approaches provide the best option to induce further reduction of the quantity and toxicity of wastes disposed on land." His article goes on to suggest such things as a deposit on automobiles and other large-item sources of waste (similar to deposits on beverage containers); taxes on disposal of toxic wastes that present major threats of future harm; and a waste disposal allowance system similar to the tradeable emissions credits of the 1990 Clean Air Act Amendments.

11. **International shipments.** RCRA is not limited merely to domestic hazardous wastes. RCRA directs exporters to notify the EPA of the nature of international shipments (e.g., dates quantity, and description of wastes) at least 4 weeks prior to shipment. Within 30 days of the receipt of the notification, the State Department, on behalf of the EPA Administrator, must inform the receiving country about the export. The importing country must, in turn, consent (in writing) to accept the waste, unless an existing international agreement provides otherwise.

The Clinton Administration has recommended a ban on exports of hazardous waste to nations other than Canada and Mexico. The three North American countries routinely ship waste across borders for cheaper and more convenient disposal. The United States has ratified the Basel Convention, which sharply limits international shipments of hazardous waste, but has not yet enacted legislation to put its provisions into effect. All told, the United States exports less than 1 percent of its hazardous wastes (approximately 145,000 tons per year).

12. **Underground storage tank regulation.** Subtitle I of RCRA, 42 U.S.C.A. §6991 et seq., establishes a comprehensive regulatory program for Underground Storage Tanks ("USTs").[24] RCRA defines an UST as:

> Any one or combination of tanks (including underground pipes connected thereto) which is used to contain an accumulation of regulated substances [hazardous substances and petroleum, except for RCRA Subtitle C hazardous wastes], and the volume of which (including the volume of underground pipes connected thereto) is 10 percent or more beneath the surface of the ground. 42 U.S.C.A. §6991(1).

The UST Program contains the following elements:

> Standards for design, construction, and installation of new tanks;
> Requirements for retrofitting existing tanks with anti-corrosion, overfill prevention, and release detection systems (existing tanks must upgrade by December 1998 or close down);
> Operation, maintenance, and inspection requirements;
> Release detection, investigation, and reporting requirements;
> Corrective action obligations;
> Tank closure procedures; and
> Financial responsibility requirements.
> A miniature Superfund (the Leaking Underground Storage Tank Trust Fund, financed by a tax on motor fuels) has been created to fund EPA or state cleanups of UST releases.

13. **Life cycle assessment in the private sector.** As the following excerpt indicates, life cycle assessment, which underlies RCRA's regulatory strategy, is becoming popular in the private sector:

> Life cycle assessment ("LCA") is intended to evaluate as comprehensively as possible "cradle-to-grave" environmental consequences of a product, package, process, or practice. It is supposed to account for energy and material inputs and outputs associated with making, using, and retiring a product, including the environmental risk associated with the life cycle of the product. It could

---

24. Now called the UST Program. It was originally referred to as the LUST (Leaking Underground Storage Tank) Program.

similarly be applied to evaluate processes and practices in manufacturing to account for every resource and environmental risk encountered in making, using, and disposing of a product. LCA is thus a tool for identifying material and energy use and the waste released during production, formulation, distribution, consumer use, recycling, and disposal....

The current technical framework for LCA consists of three distinct, but inter-related components:

*Life Cycle Inventory* — An objective, data-based process of quantifying energy and raw material requirements, air emissions, waterborne effluents, solid waste, and other environmental releases incurred throughout the life cycle of a product, process, or activity.

*Life Cycle Impact Analysis* — A technical, quantitative, or qualitative process to characterize and assess the effects of the environmental loadings identified in the inventory component. The assessment should address both ecological and human health considerations as well as other effects such as habitat modification and noise pollution.

*Life Cycle Improvement Analysis* — A systematic evaluation of the needs and opportunities to reduce the environmental burden associated with energy and raw materials use and waste emissions throughout the life cycle of a product, process, or activity. This analysis may include both quantitative and qualitative measures of improvements, such as changes in product design, raw materials use, industrial processing, consumer use, and waste management.

Environmental benefits can be realized at each step in the LCA process. For example, the inventory alone may be used to identify opportunities for reducing emissions, or the use of energy and materials. The impact analysis and improvement analysis tools meanwhile can help ensure optimization of potential reduction strategies and avoidance of unanticipated impacts in improvement programs. Denison, Evaluating Environmental Impacts, in National Academy of Engineering, Industrial Ecology: U.S.-Japan Perspectives, 29–30 (1993).

In the light of subsequent paradigm shifts in private-sector thinking, such as LCA, RCRA's life cycle approach was far ahead of its time. RCRA's conceptual framework may ultimately prove as important as its regulatory provisions in stimulating pollution prevention.

## B. THE "LAND BAN" AND THE USE OF "HAMMERS" TO CONTROL AGENCY ACTION

The Hazardous and Solid Waste Amendments of 1984 (HSWA)[25] made important changes that greatly expanded the reach of federal hazardous waste law. In what may be its most significant feature, the HSWA added stringent regulation of land disposal of hazardous wastes,[26] often referred to as the land ban. In Congress' own words —

25. Pub. L. No. 98-616 (1984). For a discussion of the amendments, see Rosbe & Gulley, The Hazardous and Solid Waste Amendments of 1984: A Dramatic Overhaul of the Way America Manages Its Hazardous Wastes, 14 ELR 10458, 10459 (1984)(hereinafter cited as Rosbe & Gulley).

26. The term "land disposal" as defined by RCRA includes, but is not limited to, "Any placement of...hazardous waste in a landfill, surface impoundment, waste pile, injection well, land treatment facility, salt dome formation, salt bed formation, or underground mine or cave." RCRA §3004(k), 42 U.S.C.A. §6924(k).

reliance on land disposal should be minimized or eliminated and land disposal, particularly landfill and surface impoundment, should be the least favored method for managing hazardous wastes.... 42 U.S.C.A. §6901(b)(7).

As the Florio article above points out in reviewing RCRA's history, Congress feared undue delay if the implementation of its objectives were left to EPA's discretion. Thus, Congress placed stringent time deadlines on EPA for the issuance of regulations. To make sure EPA acted promptly, Congress included "hammer clauses" that amounted to direct Congressional regulation if EPA failed to act in a timely fashion. Congress took a three-pronged approach to land disposal: (1) it made liquids, because of their role in facilitating the migration of hazardous wastes away from disposal sites, a particular focus of regulation;[27] (2) it overhauled the means by which solid wastes could be defined as hazardous for purposes of land disposal; and (3) it set specific standards for landfills and surface impoundments that stressed multiple leachate control mechanisms.[28]

To ensure that EPA did not dally in its assigned regulatory tasks, Congress used the threat of a total nationwide ban on land disposal of hazardous waste as a hammer — EPA could avoid the land ban only by promulgating rigorous disposal standards within the allotted time periods. The lists of hazardous wastes were in part developed by Congress and in part by EPA.[29] Before authorizing the land disposal of any listed waste, EPA had to first conclude that a ban on the land disposal of that particular hazardous waste was "not required...to protect human health and the environment for as long as the waste remains hazardous." In making that determination, EPA had to consider "(A) the long-term uncertainties associated with land disposal, (B) the goal of managing hazardous waste in an appropriate manner in the first instance, and (C) the persistence, toxicity, mobility, and propensity to bioaccumulate of such hazardous wastes and their hazardous constituents." 42 U.S.C.A. §6924(d). Congress also circumscribed EPA's discretion by stating that land disposal could not be allowed unless EPA found that wastes had been treated to levels that "substantially diminish the toxicity of the waste or substantially reduce the likelihood of migration of hazardous constituents from the waste so that short-term and long-term threats to human health and the environment are minimized." 42 U.S.C.A. §6924(m).

The land ban portended far-reaching changes. As one commentary indicated:

---

27. RCRA §3004(c), 42 U.S.C.A. §6924(c). Uncontainerized liquid hazardous waste was banned from landfills as of May, 1985; the placement of nonhazardous liquids in landfills containing hazardous waste was banned as of November, 1985; and containerized liquid hazardous waste and free liquid in containers containing other hazardous wastes were to be minimized as of February, 1986.

28. Congress required all systems to have at least two liners, a leachate collection system above and between liners in landfills, and groundwater monitoring. RCRA §3004(o)(1), 42 U.S.C.A. §6421(o)(1). EPA was also required to promulgate additional design standards that would require leak detection systems to be present in all types of new facilities.

29. Congress adopted the so-called "California list" that identified a number of specific materials at varying concentrations as hazardous. See RCRA §3004(d)(2), 42 U.S.C.A. §6924(d)(2). In addition, Congress required regulation of certain solvents and dioxins. See RCRA §3004(e), 42 U.S.C.A. §6924(e). Finally, EPA was to develop a schedule for reviewing all other hazardous wastes (see RCRA §3001, 42 U.S.C.A. §6921). EPA was given a triparte deadline for completing this process, which led to the description of the EPA regulations as being first third, second third, and third third. See RCRA §3004(g), 42 U.S.C.A. §6924(g).

By these Amendments, Congress effectively has required EPA to phase out most, if not all, methods of land disposal of hazardous wastes. To the extent that any method of land disposal might still be allowed, Congress has shifted the burden to EPA to take action before the statutory prohibitions take effect and to industry to urge that EPA act in time. It is doubtful that EPA is capable of meeting the statutory deadlines, even with prodding from industry, unless it can develop simple new procedures for evaluating land disposal methods' protection of health and the environment. Even if EPA develops such procedures, the burden placed on a company to demonstrate "to a reasonable degree of certainty" that there will be "no migration of hazardous constituents" from the unit "for as long as the waste remains hazardous" may be virtually insurmountable. Thus, industry may, instead, elect to invest in incineration and physical-chemical treatment as methods of managing the California list wastes, dioxin-containing wastes, and listed spent solvents rather than attempt to obtain an exception for a method of land disposal for these wastes. With regard to the other listed wastes, industry may decide to focus its efforts on urging EPA to promulgate reasonable treatment standards that would avoid the regulatory prohibitions rather than trying to overcome the burden necessary to obtain an exception. If this happens, Congress will have effectively achieved its goal of forcing the increased use of non-land disposal hazardous waste management methods and the development of new hazardous waste management technology. Whether the waste disposal industry can respond, within the time allowed, to this new technology-forcing imperative with enough effective treatment and incineration capacity to handle the growing hazardous waste load remains to be seen. Rosbe and Gulley at 10463.

To the surprise of many, EPA met many of the HSWA land ban deadlines.[30] What emerged, though, was not a set of substance-specific treatment standards. Instead, EPA relied on a general treatment standard for hazardous waste that requires treatment using the best demonstrated available technology (BDAT) prior to landfilling of the waste.[31]

The BDAT approach creates a problem of inadequate treatment capacity. Especially in the shorter term, there is insufficient capacity nationwide to treat all of the waste that is in need of land-based disposal. As a result, EPA has been forced to issue variances, because disposal of untreated hazardous wastes in permitted Subtitle C facilities is preferable to storing the materials in other locations until treatment capacity is increased. Over time the supply of BDAT treatment capacity will grow, although that growth has been severely inhibited by the NIMBY phenomenon and the obstacles it presents to siting hazardous waste treatment facilities (see Chapter 25).

EPA's move to select BDAT treatment as a precondition for land disposal provoked a legal challenge. Generators feared that they would now be faced with the

---

30. See generally Note, An Analysis of the Land Disposal Ban in the 1984 Amendments to the Resource Conservation and Recovery Act, 76 Geo. L.J. 1563 (1988); Williams & Cannon, Rethinking the Resource Recovery and Conservation Act for the 1990s, 21 ELR 10063 (1991).

31. EPA had initially proposed to set harm-based treatment standards with reference to limiting health effects to what EPA deemed acceptable levels. See Hazardous Waste Management System: Land Disposal Restriction, 51 Fed. Reg. 1602 (1986). Under the proposed methodology, EPA would make a comparative risk assessment that compared the risks of commercially available treatment technologies to the risks of land disposal. Only treatments that resulted in lower risk levels could be selected as treatment standards. This proposal generated substantial adverse comment. Ultimately, EPA adopted the far less problematic strategy for defining treatment standards by reference to BDAT.

costly prospect of incineration, even in circumstances where putting untreated waste in landfills would arguably provide adequate protection of human health and the environment.

### Hazardous Waste Treatment Council v. United States Environmental Protection Agency
United States Court of Appeals for the District of Columbia Circuit, 1989
886 F.2d 355

Before Wald, Chief Judge, Silberman and D.H. Ginsburg, Circuit Judges. Per Curiam:

RCRA requires EPA to implement the land disposal prohibition in three phases, addressing the most hazardous "listed" wastes first. In accordance with strict statutory deadlines, the Administrator is obligated to specify those methods of land disposal of each listed hazardous waste which "will be protective of human health and the environment." In addition, "[s]imultaneously with the promulgation of regulations...prohibiting...land disposal of a particular hazardous waste, the Administrator" is required to

> promulgate regulations specifying those levels or methods of treatment, if any, which substantially diminish the toxicity of the waste or substantially reduce the likelihood of migration of hazardous constituents from the waste so that short-term and long-term threats to human health and the environment are minimized. §6924(m).

SECTION 3004(M) TREATMENT STANDARDS... In the Proposed Rule, EPA announced its tentative support for a treatment regime embodying both risk-based and technology-based standards. The technology-based standards would be founded upon what EPA determined to be the Best Demonstrated Available Technology ("BDAT"); parallel risk-based or "screening" levels were to reflect "the maximum concentration [of a hazardous constituent] below which the Agency believes there is no regulatory concern for the land disposal program and which is protective of human health and the environment." The Proposed Rule provided that these two sets of standards would be melded in the following manner:

First, if BDAT standards were more rigorous than the relevant health-screening levels, the latter would be used to "cap the reductions in toxicity and/or mobility that otherwise would result from the application of BDAT treatment[.]" Thus, "treatment for treatment's sake" would be avoided. Second, if BDAT standards were less rigorous than health-screening levels, BDAT standards would govern and the screening level would be used as "a goal for future changes to the treatment standards as new and more efficient treatment technologies become available." Finally, when EPA determined that the use of BDAT would pose a greater risk to human health and the environment than land disposal, or would provide insufficient safeguards against the threats produced by land disposal, the screening level would actually become the 3004(m) treatment standard.

EPA invited public comment on alternative approaches as well. The first alternative identified in the Proposed Rule (and the one ultimately selected by EPA) was based purely on the capabilities of the "best demonstrated available technology."

The Agency received comments supporting both approaches, but ultimately settled on the pure-technology alternative. Of particular importance to EPA's decision were the comments filed by eleven members of Congress, all of whom served as conferees on the 1984 RCRA amendments. As EPA recorded in the preamble to the Finale Rule:

> [these] members of Congress argue strongly that [the health screening] approach did not fulfill the intent of the law. They asserted that because of the scientific uncertainty inherent in risk-based decisions, Congress expressly directed the Agency to set treatment standards based on the capabilities of existing technology.

The Agency believes that the technology-based approach adopted in [the] final rule, although not the only approach allowable under the law, best responds to the above stated comments.

EPA also relied on passages in the legislative history supporting an approach under which owners and operators of hazardous waste facilities would be required to use "the best [technology] that has been demonstrated to be achievable." And the agency reiterated that the chief advantage offered by the health-screening approach — avoiding "treatment for treatment's sake — could "be better addressed through changes in other aspects of its regulatory program." As an example of what parts of the program might be altered, EPA announced that it was "considering the use of its risk-based methodologies to characterize wastes as hazardous pursuant to section 3001 [of RCRA]...."[32]

CMA challenges EPA's adoption of BDAT treatment standards in preference to the approach it proposed initially primarily on the ground that the regulation is not a reasonable interpretation of the statute. CMA obliquely, and Intervenors Edison Electric and the American Petroleum Institute explicitly, argues in the alternative that the agency did not adequately explain its decision to take the course that it did. We conclude, as to CMA's primary challenge, that EPA's decision to reject the use of screening levels is a reasonable interpretation of the statute. We also find, however, that EPA's justification of its choice is so fatally flawed that we cannot, in conscience, affirm it. We therefore grant the petitions for review to the extent of remanding this issue to the agency for a fuller explanation.

CONSISTENCY OF EPA'S INTERPRETATION WITH RCRA... Our role in evaluating an agency's interpretation of its enabling statute is as strictly circumscribed as it is simply stated: We first examine the statute to ascertain whether it clearly forecloses the course that the agency has taken; if it is ambiguous with respect to that question, we go on to determine whether the agency's interpretation is a reasonable resolution of the ambiguity.

CHEVRON STEP I: IS THE STATUTE CLEAR?... CMA reads the statute as requiring EPA to determine the levels of concentration in waste at which the various solvents here at issue are "safe" and to use those "screening levels" as floors below which treatment would not be required. CMA supports its interpretation with the observation that the statute directs EPA to set standards only to the extent that "threats to human health and the environment are minimized." We are unpersuaded, however, that Congress intended to compel EPA to rely upon screening levels in preference to the levels achievable by BDAT.

The statute directs EPA to set treatment standards based upon either "levels or methods" of treatment. Such a mandate makes clear that the choice whether to use "levels" (screening levels) or "methods" (BDAT) lies within the informed

---

32. Eds.: EPA's announcement foreshadowed its subsequently proposed Hazardous Waste Identification Rule, discussed above.

discretion of the agency, as long as the result is "that short-term and long-term threats to human health and the environment are minimized." To "minimize" something is, to quote the Oxford English Dictionary, to "reduce [it] to the smallest possible amount, extent, or degree." But Congress recognized, in the very amendments here at issue, that there are "long-term uncertainties associated with land disposal," 42 U.S.C. §6924(d)(1)(A). In the face of such uncertainties, it cannot be said that a statute that requires that threats be minimized unambiguously requires EPA to set levels at which it is conclusively presumed that no threat to health or the environment exists.

This is not to say that EPA is free, under §3004(m), to require generators to treat their waste beyond the point at which there is no "threat" to human health or to the environment. That Congress's concern in adopting §3004(m) was with health and the environment would necessarily make it unreasonable for EPA to promulgate treatment standards wholly without regard to whether there might be a threat to man or nature. That concern is better dealt with, however, at *Chevron's* second step; for, having concluded that the statute does not unambiguously and in all circumstances foreclose EPA from adopting treatment levels based upon the levels achievable by BDAT, we must now explore whether the particular levels established by the regulations supply a reasonable resolution of the statutory ambiguity.

*CHEVRON* STEP II: IS EPA'S INTERPRETATION REASONABLE?... The screening levels that EPA initially proposed were not those at which the wastes were thought to be entirely safe. Rather, EPA set the levels to reduce risks from the solvents to an "acceptable" level, and it explored, at great length, the manifest (and manifold) uncertainties inherent in any attempt to specify "safe" concentration levels. The agency discussed, for example, the lack of any safe level of exposure to carcinogenic solvents, the extent to which reference dose levels (from which it derived its screening levels) understate the dangers that hazardous solvents pose to particularly sensitive members of the population, the necessarily artificial assumptions that accompany any attempt to model the migration of hazardous wastes from a disposal site, and the lack of dependable data on the effects that solvents have on the liners that bound disposal facilities for the purpose of ensuring that the wastes disposed in a facility stay there. Indeed, several parties made voluminous comments on the Proposed Rule to the effect that EPA's estimates of the various probabilities were far more problematic than even EPA recognized.

CMA suggests, despite these uncertainties, that the adoption of a BDAT treatment regime would result in treatment to "below established levels of hazard." It relies for this proposition almost entirely upon a chart in which it contrasts the BDAT levels with (1) levels EPA has defined as "Maximum Contaminant Levels" (MCLs) under the Safe Drinking Water Act; (2) EPA's proposed "Organic Toxicity Characteristics," threshold levels below which EPA will not list a waste as hazardous by reason of its having in it a particular toxin; and (3) levels at which EPA has recently granted petitions by waste generators to "delist" a particular waste, that is, to remove it from the list of wastes that are deemed hazardous. CMA points out that the BDAT standards would require treatment to levels that are, in many cases, significantly below these "established levels of hazard."

If indeed EPA had determined that wastes at any of the three levels pointed to by CMA posed no threat to human health or the environment, we would have little hesitation in concluding that it was unreasonable for EPA to mandate treatment to substantially lower levels. In fact, however, none of the levels to which CMA compares the BDAT standards purports to establish a level at which safety is assured or "threats to human health and the environment are minimized." Each is a level established for a different purpose and under a different set of statutory criteria than concern us here; each is therefore irrelevant to the inquiry we undertake today....

In sum, EPA's catalog of the uncertainties inherent in the alternative approach using screening levels supports the reasonableness of its reliance upon BDAT instead. Accordingly, finding no merit in CMA's contention that EPA has required treatment to "below established levels of hazard," we find that EPA's interpretation of §3004(m) is reasonable.

To summarize [EPA's explanation for abandoning the combination of using BDAT and screening levels in favor of BDAT alone]: after EPA issued the Proposed Rule, some commenters, including eleven members of Congress, chastised the agency on the ground that the use of screening levels was inconsistent with the intent of the statute. They stated that because of the uncertainties involved, Congress had mandated that BDAT alone be used to set treatment standards. EPA determined that the "best respon[se]" to those comments was to adopt a BDAT standard. It emphasized, however, that either course was consistent with the statute (and that it was therefore not required to use BDAT alone). Finally, it asserted, without explanation, that its major purpose in initially proposing screening levels "may be better addressed through changes in other aspects of its regulatory program," and gave an example of one such aspect that might be changed.

This explanation is inadequate. It should go without saying that members of Congress have no power, once a statute has been passed, to alter its interpretation by post-hoc "explanations" of what it means; there may be societies where "history" belongs to those in power, but ours is not among them. In our scheme of things, we consider legislative history because it is just that: history. It forms the background against which Congress adopted the relevant statute. Post-enactment statements are a different matter, and they are not to be considered by an agency or by a court as legislative history. An agency has an obligation to consider the comments of legislators, of course, but on the same footing as it would those of other commenters; such comments may have, as Justice Frankfurter said in a different context, "power to persuade, if lacking power to control."

It is unclear whether EPA recognized this fundamental point. On the one hand, it suggested that the adoption of a BDAT-only regime "best-respond[ed]" to the comments suggesting that the statute required such a rule. On the other hand, EPA went on at some length to establish that the comments were in error, in that screening levels are permissible under the statute. EPA's "rationale," in other words, is that several members of Congress (among others) urged upon it the claim that Proposition X ("Congress mandated BDAT") requires Result A ("EPA adopts BDAT"), and that although Proposition X is inaccurate, the best response to the commenters is to adopt Result A.

Nor is anything added by EPA's bald assertion that its reason for initially preferring Result B (screening levels) "may be" better served by other changes in the statutory scheme. In its Proposed Rule, EPA had, after extensive analysis of the various alternatives, come to the opposite conclusion. It is insufficient, in that context, for EPA to proceed in a different direction simply on the basis of an unexplained and unelaborated statement that it might have been wrong when it earlier concluded otherwise.... Accordingly, we grant the petitions for review in this respect.

COMMENTARY AND QUESTIONS

1. **Politics and judicial review.** In the *HWTC* case, we catch a rare glimpse of an administrative agency caught in the middle between a Congress and an Executive Branch with widely different political agendas. An agency must simultaneously attempt to placate both its titular "boss," the Chief Executive, who appoints its leaders and filters its requests for funding, legislative authority, and clearance of proposed regulations, and the legislature that provides its funding and legislative authority, in addition to holding potentially embarrassing oversight hearings. Faced with a Congress enthusiastic about RCRA and an Executive Branch intent upon turning the statute into symbolic assurance by non-enforcement, EPA, perhaps wisely, decided to procrastinate. The result was Congressional frustration and the legislative micromanagement encountered in the HSWA of 1984. EPA's delicate political position was exemplified by its painfully ambiguous and inconsistent explanation of its change in strategy from the Proposed to the Final §3004(m) rule. The court, although operating under a highly deferential standard of judicial review, forced EPA to take a definite stand on this issue by remanding for the production of a rational and consistent explanation of EPA's position. As in this case, the requirement that an agency produce an adequate record for judicial review (Chapter 7) raises the visibility of politicized issues and compels an agency to adopt clear, if not universally popular, positions.

2. **Legislative micromanagement, pro and con.** In this situation, legislative micromanagement appears to have been successful in breaking the political logjam and pushing a reluctant EPA to implement RCRA. But there are possible disadvantages to legislative control of agency regulatory agendas in highly technical areas such as hazardous waste management. In 1986, Congress attempted to goad the Reagan Administration into increasing its sluggish pace of CERCLA cleanups by enacting §116 of CERCLA, 42 U.S.C.A. §9616, which required EPA to commence specified numbers of remedial investigations/feasibility studies by definite dates, and also to begin remedial actions at the rate of 175 during the first three years after enactment and an additional 200 during the following two years. Given EPA's level of funding and the complexity of the cleanup determinations involved, these timetables proved to have been wildly unrealistic. A similar result occurred when Congress amended the Safe Drinking Water Act, in 1986, to place EPA on a mandatory timetable for promulgating maximum contaminant goals and maximum contaminant levels for toxic contaminants in drinking water. 42 U.S.C.A. §300g-1. It appears that legislative micromanagement works best where Congress resorts to a technically crude device such as a hammer clause.

3. **Hammer clauses.** The generally accepted explanation for the presence of hammer clauses in the HSWA (the 1984 amendments to RCRA) is congressional displeasure with the dilatory performance of EPA in the early years of RCRA. Have the hammer clauses proved effective? The short answer is that the hammer clauses and the threat of a true land ban[33] did force EPA into prompt action to provide an

---

33. See, e.g., RCRA §3004(g)(6)(C), 42 U.S.C.A. §6924(g)(6)(C) (total prohibition on land disposal unless EPA promulgates adequate standards).

alternative that was less disruptive of on-going economic activity. If the RCRA scenario is to serve as a basis for generalization, it seems that hammer clauses work well as long as the contingent legislative regulation (the hammer) is so stringent that the outcome of administrative process is likely to be more favorable to the regulated community.

**4. Is BDAT bad?** In opting for treatment standards founded on BDAT, EPA seems to be locking-in existing treatment methods as the future norm, thereby deterring, rather than spurring, advances in the field. A second major criticism of BDAT as the treatment standard is that it trades a land disposal problem for an air pollution problem. This criticism arises because incineration is the current BDAT for most types of hazardous waste, and even in the best incinerators many hazardous constituents are not fully destroyed. Beyond that, incineration is not a complete treatment insofar as the ash that remains is itself usually a hazardous material in need of subsequent disposal. Still, BDAT is not without some redeeming features, one of which is its clarity. Once a technology is determined to be the BDAT for the treatment of a hazardous substance, generators and TSD facilities alike know what they must do to comply with the law.

**5. The "no migration" variance.** RCRA authorizes variances to the land ban based on a harm-based review. In order to obtain a variance from BDAT standards, a petitioner must show "to a reasonable degree of certainty, that there will be no migration of hazardous constituents from the disposal unit or injection zone for as long as the wastes remain hazardous." EPA interprets this statutory language to mean that concentrations of hazardous constituents shall not exceed Agency-approved health-based or ecosystem-based levels, in any environmental medium, at the boundary of the unit or injection zone. EPA has set strict ambient standards for granting a "no migration" variance, and few variances have been granted thus far. See Proposed EPA Interpretation Of RCRA No Migration Variances, 57 FR 3590, August 11, 1992. The "no migration" variance is an interesting taxonomic device in that it places the burden of overcoming uncertainty on the applicant, who must show that the fundamental technology-based standard is unnecessary. This approach remedies one of the shortcomings of the pure harm-based approach — the heavy regulatory burden placed on a standard-setting agency to establish harm-based standards under conditions of pervasive scientific uncertainty and political rancor.

**6. Underground Injection.** The underground injection of hazardous waste through wells is a form of land disposal that is covered by RCRA and by the Underground Injection Control ("UIC") program under part C of the Safe Drinking Water Act, 42 U.S.C.A. §300 (h) *et. seq.* The UIC regulations (See 40 C.F.R. parts 144-148) are primarily concerned with the protection of underground sources of drinking water. The UIC program categorizes hazardous waste injection wells as Class I wells, which receive the highest level of UIC regulation. See 40 C.F.R. §146.61. Although the surface storage and management of hazardous wastes are still subject to RCRA, and although certain closure, corrective action, land disposal, and general RCRA requirements apply to Class I wells, generally the RCRA regulations defer to the UIC regulations for the actual injection process. 40 C.F.R. §264.1(d).

7. **Undersupply of TSD capacity.** Does the combination of a growing universe of generators and the comprehensive regulation of TSD facilities threaten a supply and demand imbalance in which more hazardous waste needs to be processed than can be handled by permitted facilities? In the short term, the problem has been finessed by allowing variances to TSD facilities by which they can obtain interim permits even though they are not yet employing BDAT treatment of waste prior to land disposal. Is the variance expedient likely to become a near-permanent fixture in the RCRA program? Another factor in the TSD supply equation is, of course, the NIMBY phenomenon.

Is there any guarantee that there will be adequate disposal capacity? The answer to that question may lie in CERCLA §104(c)(9), 42 U.S.C.A. §9604(c)(9), which threatens to withhold Superfund remedial actions in states that do not provide disposal capacity for wastes generated within their borders. Under that provision, every state was required to submit, by 1989, a capacity assurance plan (CAP) for EPA approval. These plans must:

> assure the availability of hazardous waste treatment or disposal facilities which — (A) have adequate capacity for the destruction, treatment, or secure disposal of all hazardous wastes that are reasonably expected to be generated within the State during the 20-year period following [the giving of the assurance].

These facilities need not be located in-state, but if a CAP calls for interstate shipment of the hazardous waste for treatment, storage, or disposal, the arrangement with the waste receiving state must be worked out in advance and be evidenced by a formal interstate agreement.

Notice how the CAP requirement is a partial protection for states having RCRA permitted facilities that do not wish to accept out-of-state hazardous wastes deposited in their facilities. Unless the prevailing view of the United States Supreme Court changes, the dormant commerce clause (see Chapter Six) will continue to require that out-of-state waste be accepted. But §104(c)(9) increases the likelihood that most states will develop in-state capacity (or agreements for out-of-state capacity) rather than risk the loss of Superfund money. In the belief that forcing other states to live up to the CAP requirements will slow the flow of hazardous waste into its RCRA permitted facilities, New York has challenged EPA approval of CAPs of other states in the region. New York's challenge attacks CAPs that either rely on New York facilities without having formal agreements with New York, or that rely on planned new sites that have not been constructed due to local opposition. See New York Announces Lawsuit Against EPA for Failure to Enforce Capacity Requirement, 22 BNA Envtl Rep. 1363 (Sept. 27, 1991). The CAP requirement loses force to the extent that the expenditure by EPA of CERCLA funds becomes a less significant item than it was in the 1980s heyday of CERCLA cleanups.

8. **The RCRA Subtitle C universe.** In a probing review, EPA identified many trends and problems with its RCRA program. See generally EPA, The Nation's Hazardous Waste Management Program at a Crossroads: The RCRA Implementation Study (July, 1990). EPA described the impact of the HSWA as follows:

HWSA GREATLY EXPANDED THE REGULATED UNIVERSE... To strengthen the nation's shield against hazardous wastes, HWSA established over 70 statutory requirements (often with very tight deadlines) for EPA's action. They can generally be summarized as follows:

- Move away from land disposal as the primary means of hazardous waste management by requiring the treatment of wastes before their final disposal.

- Reduce the environmental and health risks posed by hazardous waste still managed at land disposal facilities by establishing minimum technology requirements.

- Close down facilities that cannot safely manage wastes.

- Decrease and clean up releases to the environment from waste management units by requiring facilities to take corrective action.

- Issue permits for all treatment, storage, and disposal facilities within prescribed time frames.

- Close loopholes in the types of wastes and waste management facilities not covered under RCRA.

- Expand the universe of regulated sources by including generators of small quantities of hazardous wastes.

- Minimize the amount of wastes being produced.

With this comprehensive sweep of hazardous waste issues, HWSA greatly expanded the magnitude of waste types and waste management facilities requiring regulation. Today the RCRA regulated universe consists of 4,700 hazardous waste treatment, storage, and disposal facilities. Within these facilities are approximately 81,000 waste management units, most of which are units that have received hazardous waste and from which contamination may have spread to the soil and ground water. In addition to these 4,700 facilities are 211,000 facilities that generate hazardous waste. *Id.* at 7.

The same part of the report also predicted that the continuing expansion of the list of hazardous wastes due to the operation of the TCLP would lead to a further increase in the size of the Subtitle C universe. With more substances considered hazardous, some existing facilities that in the past were not considered to be within RCRA's reach will become covered. The growth in numbers of TSD facilities currently under RCRA regulation is a bit misleading in regard to the longer-term trend. Other data in the report indicate that many of the regulated facilities (almost 3,000) are closed (but still regulated) or in the process of closing rather than meeting RCRA's stringent technology-based standards. *Id.* at 42–43.

## C. RCRA CITIZEN SUITS TO OBTAIN CLEANUP AND POTENTIAL COST RECOVERY

CERCLA, studied in Chapter 18, is the traditional vehicle by which cleanups and cost recoveries are obtained. Historically, however, RCRA came first, having been enacted in 1976, followed by CERCLA in 1980. For a time, then, RCRA was the only federal law available for obtaining cleanups, and it was utilized, especially by the federal government, as the basis for seeking the cleanup of contaminated sites.[34]

With the passage of CERCLA in 1980, Congress made plain its intent that CERCLA, not RCRA, was the primary vehicle for not only the federal government but also for private parties to obtain cleanups and cost recoveries. RCRA §7002 (citizen suits) was amended to include provisions that forbade suit if CERCLA processes had been invoked. See 42 U.S.C.A. §6972(b)(2)(B). However, CERCLA processes cannot always be invoked. This is especially important with respect to releases of petroleum products. Petroleum products are not covered by CERCLA, having been specifically excluded by Congress from CERCLA's definition of "hazardous substances." See 42 U.S.C.A. §9601(14). RCRA does not have the same limitation, which has led to efforts by parties whose land was contaminated by petroleum releases to seek a remedy under RCRA utilizing RCRA's citizen suit provision.

For many years, it appeared that the citizen suit remedy provided by RCRA was limited to abatement of the contamination, not reimbursement for cleanup costs incurred by the RCRA plaintiff. In KFC Western, Inc. v. Meghrig, 49 F.3d 518 (9th Cir. 1995), a private cost recovery action against former service station operators was successfully maintained by a party who had cleaned up a petroleum release on that parcel. Other circuits, however, held that no such cause of action existed under RCRA. The Meghrig decision was reviewed and reversed by the Supreme Court in the opinion that follows.

### Meghrig v. KFC Western, Incorporated
516 U.S. 479
Supreme Court of the United States, 1996

O'CONNOR, J. We consider whether §7002 of the Resource Conservation and Recovery Act of 1976 (RCRA), 42 U.S.C. §6972, authorizes a private cause of action to recover the prior cost of cleaning up toxic waste that does not, at the time of suit, continue to pose an endangerment to health or environment. We conclude that it does not.

Respondent KFC Western, Inc. (KFC), owns and operates a "Kentucky Fried Chicken" restaurant on a parcel of property in Los Angeles. In 1988, KFC discovered during the course of a construction project that the property was contaminated with petroleum. The County of Los Angeles Department of Health Services ordered KFC to attend to the problem, and KFC spent $211,000 removing and disposing of the oil-tainted soil.

Three years later, KFC brought suit under the citizen suit provision of RCRA...seeking to recover these cleanup costs from petitioners Alan and Margaret Meghrig. KFC claimed that the contaminated soil was a "solid waste" covered by RCRA...that it had previously posed an "imminent and substantial endangerment to health or the environment,"...and that the Meghrigs were responsible for "equi-

---

34. An early example of the use of RCRA was United States v. Northeastern Pharmaceutical & Chemical Co. ("NEPACCO"), 810 F.2d 726 (1986)(see Chapter 18), initially filed by the federal government under RCRA § 7003 and then amended to include counts under the newly passed CERCLA legislation.

table restitution" of KFC's cleanup costs under [the citizen suit provision, 42 U.S.C.] §6972(a)] because, as prior owners of the property, they had contributed to the waste's "past or present handling, storage, treatment, transportation, or disposal."...

RCRA is a comprehensive environmental statute that governs the treatment, storage, and disposal of solid and hazardous waste. Unlike the Comprehensive Environmental Response, Compensation and Liability Act of 1980 (CERCLA), RCRA is not principally designed to effectuate the cleanup of toxic waste sites or to compensate those who have attended to the remediation of environmental hazards. RCRA's primary purpose, rather, is to reduce the generation of hazardous waste and to ensure the proper treatment, storage, and disposal of that waste which is nonetheless generated, "so as to minimize the present and future threat to human health and the environment." 42 U.S.C. §6902(b)....

Two requirements...defeat KFC's suit against the Meghrigs. The first concerns the necessary timing of a citizen suit brought under §6972(a)(1)(B): That section permits a private party to bring suit against certain responsible persons, including former owners, "who ha[ve] contributed or who [are] contributing to the past or present handling, storage, treatment, transportation, or disposal of any solid or hazardous waste which may present an *imminent* and substantial endangerment to health or the environment." (Emphasis added by Court.) The second defines the remedies a district court can award in a suit brought under §6972(a)(1)(B): Section 6972(a) authorizes district courts "to restrain any person who has contributed or who is contributing to the past or present handling, storage, treatment, transportation, or disposal of any solid or hazardous waste,...*to order such person to take such other action as may be necessary*, or both." (Emphasis added by the Court.)

It is apparent from the two remedies described in §6972(a) that RCRA's citizen suit provision is not directed at providing compensation for past cleanup efforts. Under a plain reading of this remedial scheme, a private citizen suing under §6972(a)(1)(B) could seek a mandatory injunction, i.e., one that orders a responsible party to "take action" by attending to the cleanup and proper disposal of toxic waste, or a prohibitory injunction, i.e., one that "restrains" a responsible party from further violating RCRA. Neither remedy, however, is susceptible of the interpretation adopted by the Ninth Circuit, as neither contemplates the award of past cleanup costs, whether these are denominated "damages" or "equitable restitution."

In this regard, a comparison between the relief available under RCRA's citizen suit provision and that which Congress has provided in the analogous, but not parallel, provisions of CERCLA is telling. CERCLA was passed several years after RCRA went into effect, and it is designed to address many of the same toxic waste problems that inspired the passage of RCRA. Compare 42 U.S.C. §6903(5).... (RCRA definition of "hazardous waste") and §6903(27) (RCRA definition of "solid waste") with §9601(14) (CERCLA provision incorporating certain "hazardous substance[s]," but not the hazardous and solid wastes defined in RCRA, and specifically not petroleum). CERCLA differs markedly from RCRA, however, in the remedies it provides. CERCLA's citizen suit provision mimics §6972(a) in providing district courts with the authority "to order such action as may be necessary to correct the violation" of any CERCLA standard of regulation. 42 U.S.C. §9659 (1988 ed.). But CERCLA expressly permits the Government to recover "all costs of removal or remedial action," §9607(a)(4)(A), and it expressly permits the recovery of any "necessary costs of response, incurred by any...person consistent with the national contingency plan," §9607(a)(4)(B). CERCLA also provides that "[a]ny person may seek contribution from any other person who is liable or potentially liable" for these responses costs. See §9613(f)(1). Congress thus demonstrated in CERCLA that it knew how to provide for the recovery of cleanup costs, and that the language used to define the remedies under RCRA does not provide that remedy.

That RCRA's citizen suit provision was not intended to provide a remedy for past cleanup costs is further apparent from the harm at which it is directed. Section 6972(a)(1)(B) permits a private party to bring suit only upon a showing that the solid or hazardous waste at issue "may present an imminent and substantial endangerment to health or the environment." The meaning of this timing restriction is plain: An endangerment can only be "imminent" if it "threaten[s] to occur immediately," Webster's New International Dictionary of English Language 1245 (2d ed. 1934), and the reference to waste which "may present" imminent harm quite clearly excludes waste that no longer presents such a danger. As the Ninth Circuit itself intimated in Price v. United States Navy, 39 F.3d 1011, 1019 (1994), this language "implies that there must be a threat which is present now, although the impact of the threat may not be felt until later." It follows that §6972(a) was designed to provide a remedy that ameliorates present or obviates the risk of future "imminent" harms, not a remedy that compensates for past cleanup efforts. Cf. §6902(b) (national policy behind RCRA is "to minimize the present and future threat to human health and the environment").

Other aspects of RCRA's enforcement scheme strongly support this conclusion. Unlike CERCLA, RCRA contains no statute of limitations, compare §9613(g)(2) (limitations period in suits under CERCLA §9607), and it does not require a showing that the response costs being sought are reasonable, compare §§9607(a)(4)(A) and (B) (costs recovered under CERCLA must be "consistent with the national contingency plan"). If Congress had intended §6972(a) to function as a cost-recovery mechanism, the absence of these provisions would be striking. Moreover, with one limited exception,...(noting exception to notice requirement "when there is a danger that hazardous waste will be discharged"), a private party may not bring suit under §6972(a)(1)(B) without first giving 90 days' notice to the Administrator of the EPA, to "the State in which the alleged endangerment may occur," and to potential defendants, see §6972(b)(2)(A)(I)-(iii). And no citizen suit can proceed if either the EPA or the State has commenced, and is diligently prosecuting, a separate enforcement action, see §6972(b)(2)(B) and (C). Therefore, if RCRA were designed to compensate private parties for their past cleanup efforts, it would be a wholly irrational mechanism for doing so. Those parties with insubstantial problems, problems that neither the State nor the Federal Government feel compelled to address, could recover their response costs, whereas those parties whose waste problems were sufficiently severe as to attract the attention of Government officials would be left without a recovery....

RCRA does not prevent a private party from recovering its cleanup costs under other federal or state laws, see §6972(f) (preserving remedies under statutory and common law), but the limited remedies described in §6972(a), along with the stark differences between the language of that section and the cost recovery provisions of CERCLA, amply demonstrate that Congress did not intend for a private citizen to be able to undertake a clean up and then proceed to recover its costs under RCRA....

Without considering whether a private party could seek to obtain an injunction requiring another party to pay cleanup costs which arise after a RCRA citizen suit has been properly commenced,...or otherwise recover cleanup costs paid out after the invocation of RCRA's statutory process, we agree with the Meghrigs that a private party cannot recover the cost of a past cleanup effort under RCRA, and that KFC's complaint is defective for the reasons stated by the District Court. Section 6972(a) does not contemplate the award of past cleanup costs, and §6972(a)(1)(B) permits a private party to bring suit only upon an allegation that the contaminated site presently poses an "imminent and substantial endangerment to health or the environment," and not upon an allegation that it posed such an endangerment at some time in the past. The judgment of the Ninth Circuit is reversed.

## COMMENTARY AND QUESTIONS

1. **Remaining questions regarding the scope of Section 7002.** Can a private party sue under §7002(a)(1)(B) while an imminent endangerment still exists and obtain restitution of response costs for work taken thereafter? *Meghrig* expressly avoids answering that question. Would the Court be reluctant to provide such a remedy given Congress' failure to do so expressly? How could such a remedy be implied, if, as Justice O'Connor concluded, "Congress thus demonstrated in CERCLA that it knew how to provide for the recovery of cleanup costs, and that the language used to define the remedies under RCRA does not provide that remedy?"

2. **The importance of *Meghrig*.** In advance of the Supreme Court decision in *Meghrig*, one commentator wrote, "The implications of the Ninth Circuit ruling in KFC Western are significant. Private parties can now obtain more complete relief under §7002(a)(1)(B) than they can obtain under [CERCLA]." J. Martin Robertson, Restitution Under RCRA §7002(a)(1)(B): The Courts Finally Grant What Congress Authorized, 25 ELR 10491 (1995). Does the *Meghrig* decision leave a "gap" in which no remedies are available to recover costs paid to remediate petroleum spills? Probably not. Up until the Ninth Circuit's *Meghrig* decision, RCRA had been on the books for almost fifteen years without great fanfare surrounding the lack of a restitutionary remedy. While CERCLA had lacked jurisdiction over petroleum releases and was far too cumbersome in many ways, state common law and statutory remedies for contamination were available, although sometimes open to criticism. See, Samuel P. Lopez, Cost Recovery for Petroleum Contamination: Will RCRA Citizen Plaintiffs be Cookin' with KFC or Relegated to a State Law Jungle? 10 Toxics Law Reporter 946 (1996).

3. **Strategic considerations after *Meghrig*.** After the Supreme Court's decision in *Meghrig*, does a party faced with petroleum contamination on its property have an incentive to sue those responsible for the contamination before undertaking the cleanup? If a party defers cleanup and instead seeks relief from those contributing to an imminent and substantial endangerment, that party may still seek an injunction to require those responsible to participate in the cleanup and may also seek to recover its prospective cleanup costs. Is the *Meghrig* decision, then, one which provides a strategic incentive to sue first and clean up later, in hopes of recouping cleanup costs? Could such an incentive — to defer cleanups rather than to expedite them — be one which Congress had intended?

# Chapter 18

# REMEDIAL LIABILITY STRATEGIES: CLEANUPS AND THEIR FUNDING UNDER CERCLA AND STATE PROGRAMS

A. *CERCLA's Liability Rules as Developed through the Judicial Process of Statutory Interpretation*

B. *EPA's Administrative Order Authority*

C. *Identifying Sites, Funding, and Setting the Standards for Cleanups*

D. *EPA's Strategy for Cost Recovery and Loss Allocation*

Few events have so galvanized public opinion as have high profile cases involving the release of hazardous substances into the environment and the resultant threats to public health caused by those releases. There are few symbols as potent as the homes and schools at Love Canal virtually afloat on a toxic stew, or the men in space suit-like outfits removing PCBs from the newly abandoned ghost town at Times Beach, Missouri. In the face of that degree of public outrage, an almost certain political reaction is to pass laws addressing the subject, not only laws that seek to avert repetition of the calamity, as with Subtitle C of RCRA (see Chapter 17), but also laws that seek to assuage public anger at the parties responsible for the events by making those parties accountable for the results of their actions.

Enacting into law the public desire for an accounting from responsible parties may be a natural enough sentiment, but to do so within the constraints imposed by the United States Constitution, and to do so effectively, is a more sophisticated proposition. Newly enacted laws that attempt to attach present consequences for actions that occurred in the past have some hurdles to overcome. Not only does Article I, section 9, clause 3 of the Constitution state that, "No bill of Attainder or ex post facto law shall be passed," that provision is complemented by the more general notion that constitutionally guaranteed due process of law requires fair advance notice of what the law requires before sanctions can be imposed for disobedience of the legal command. Beyond the retroactive application of law, crafting a law that holds the "right" actors accountable for acts that may have occurred at some distance in the past raises a host of additional complexities.

In enacting the Comprehensive Environmental Response, Compensation, and Liability Act (CERCLA, popularly named "Superfund"), Congress took on those challenges and more—it imposed retroactive liability on a broad group of actors whom it deemed to be the responsible parties, and it created a system that was intended to secure prompt environmental cleanups of releases of hazardous substances into the environment. At bedrock, CERCLA makes a very serious effort to effectuate the polluter-pays principle (PPP), i.e., re-internalizing the costs of environmental harm by imposing an accounting upon those whose actions caused the harm. Its principal method of doing so is to insist on cleanup of the environment in conjunction with a liability scheme that passes the costs of cleanup on to those responsible for the release of the hazardous material into the environment. In effectuating that scheme, CERCLA incorporates devices that ensure that most sites of contamination will be discovered and, thereafter, orchestrates their cleanup and the eventual shifting of the cost to the responsible parties.

CERCLA embodies a particular implementation strategy, that of remedial cost internalization. CERCLA seeks to remediate contamination and to establish liability for past contamination practices that have ongoing environmental consequences and effects. In reviewing CERCLA's remedial implementation strategy, several rather distinct features immediately stand out: (1) the extent to which traditional norms of tort liability are inadequate to obtain remedial cost internalization, (2) the difficulties in equitably applying the PPP to past occurrences that were not monitored with the PPP in mind, and (3) the whole panoply of powers that must be granted to the administering agency to allow for the development of a coherent implementation strategy. Beyond those implementation-based observations, CERCLA's operation and implementation also provide a most instructive case study of statutory evolution.

One of the key, and most well-known, statutory mechanisms created by Congress in CERCLA is the "Superfund" itself. Especially after the amendment and reauthorization of CERCLA in 1986,[1] the Superfund has operated as a mechanism to ensure that funding would be available to pay for cleanups at the most seriously contaminated sites. The need for the fund part of a Superfund law, however, may not be immediately obvious. After all, if state common law is inadequate to fix liability on the industries that generate, transport, and dispose of hazardous wastes, a federal law imposing liability on a somewhat broader range of potentially responsible parties would seem to be all that is needed. Under such a law, those responsible for hazardous releases could be ordered to undertake a cleanup and to compensate others damaged by their releases. This latter damage calculation would include any cleanup expenses incurred by third parties or government.

The major reasons for the fund component of Superfund are that the responsible parties cannot always be identified — as in the notorious practice of "midnight dumping"— and that responsible parties may be unable to pay the amount of the cleanup costs. The reason that the fund must be "super" is a function of cost. Purging a hazardous waste site of contaminants can be a multi-million dollar undertaking.

The principal statutory mechanisms of CERCLA were succinctly described at the time of its enactment:

> Essentially, CERCLA authorizes governmental responses to actual and threatened releases of a wide range of harmful substances. Parties causing releases of such substances may then be held liable without regard to fault for certain

---

1. Superfund Amendments and Reauthorization Act of 1986 (SARA), Pub. L. 99-499, 100 Stat. 1613.

damages resulting from the release, which primarily include government incurred costs for cleanup, removal, and resources restoration. To ensure that such injuries are redressed, the law establishes a $1.6 billion [$8.5 billion, after SARA in 1986] Hazardous Substances Response Fund, financed jointly by industry and the federal government over five years. When polluters are unknown, or are unable or unwilling to provide recompense, a claim for specified damages may be filed against the fund. Payment of claims by the fund then subrogates the fund to the rights of the claimant.[2]

Focusing on specific remedial provisions, CERCLA's provisions retrace the imminent hazard provisions of RCRA[3] and add provisions that relate to recoupment and allocation of cleanup costs already incurred in response to hazardous waste releases.[4]

Although CERCLA's remedial implementation strategy was designed to force cleanups of contaminated sites, that strategy has not always functioned as intended. Perhaps the best example of CERCLA's unintended consequences concerns sites known as "brownfields" — abandoned, idled, or underutilized industrial or commercial sites suffering from environmental contamination. Fearing the broad liability provisions of CERCLA, many prospective purchasers, developers, and lenders historically chose to avoid brownfields redevelopment altogether, with the result that brownfields sites have often become major community and taxpayer burdens. As Chapter 20 details, EPA and the states have recently come to recognize that CERCLA's remedial implementation strategy has, unfortunately, contributed to the perpetuation of brownfields rather than their remediation. As a result, EPA and the states have now sought to work more closely with the regulated community to develop new policies and programs seeking to encourage the redevelopment of brownfields. This shift in focus, towards a more flexible and cooperative approach, signals a new trend in environmental cleanup strategies.

## A. CERCLA'S LIABILITY RULES AS DEVELOPED THROUGH THE JUDICIAL PROCESS OF STATUTORY INTERPRETATION

Congress expended considerable effort filling in the details of the remedial side of CERCLA, but also left many areas in need of judicial interpretation and clarification. Consequently, CERCLA, like RCRA, has become one of the most actively litigated statutes in environmental law. Together, supplemented by state common law tort theories studied in Chapters Three and Four, they form the legal basis for determining who will bear the costs associated with the release of hazardous materials on land and into groundwater.[5]

---

2. Comment, Superfund at Square One: Promising Statutory Framework Requires Forceful EPA Implementation, 11 ELR 10101 (1981).

3. See CERCLA, §106, codified at 42 U.S.C.A. §9606.

4. See CERCLA, §107, codified at 42 U.S.C.A. §9607. The 1986 Amendments to §107, while adding some material, do not make major changes in the scope and coverage of §107. Its impact with regard to the liability of "innocent purchasers" of realty that is discovered to be contaminated is significantly affected by the amendments to §101(35), wherein the obligations of purchasers to use due diligence to discover the presence of contaminants are spelled out.

5. The release of hazardous materials into the navigable waters (i.e., surface waters) of the United States is governed by the Clean Water Act, 33 U.S.C.A. §§1251 et. seq., studied in Chapter 9.

### Section 1. THE BASICS OF STATUTORY REMEDIAL LIABILITY FOR CLEANUP OF HAZARDOUS MATERIALS

**42 U.S.C.A. §9607 [original Act's §107]. Liability... (a) Covered persons; scope; recoverable costs and damages; interest rate; "comparable maturity" date.**

Notwithstanding any other provision or rule of law, and subject only to the defenses set forth in subsection (b) of this section —

(1) the owner and operator of a vessel or a facility,

(2) any person who at the time of disposal of any hazardous substance owned or operated any facility at which such hazardous substances were disposed of,

(3) any person who by contract, agreement, or otherwise arranged for disposal or treatment, or arranged with a transporter for transport for disposal or treatment, of hazardous substances owned or possessed by such person, by any other party or entity, at any facility or incineration vessel owned or operated by another party or entity and containing such hazardous substances, and

(4) any person who accepts or accepted any hazardous substances for transport to disposal or treatment facilities, incineration vessels or sites selected by such person, from which there is a release, or a threatened release which causes the incurrence of response costs, of a hazardous substance, shall be liable for —

(A) all costs of removal or remedial action incurred by the United States Government or a State or an Indian tribe not inconsistent with the national contingency plan;

(B) any other necessary costs of response incurred by any other person consistent with the national contingency plan;

(C) damages for injury to, destruction of, or loss of natural resources, including the reasonable costs of assessing such injury, destruction, or loss resulting from such a release; and

(D) the costs of any health assessment or health effects study carried out under section 9604(i) of this title....

**(b) Defenses...** There shall be no liability under subsection (a) of this section for a person otherwise liable who can establish by a preponderance of the evidence that the release or threat of release of a hazardous substance and the damages resulting therefrom were caused solely by —

(1) an act of God;

(2) an act of war;

(3) an act or omission of a third party other than an employee or agent of the defendant, or than one whose act or omission occurs in connection with a contractual relationship, existing directly or indirectly, with the defendant (except where the sole contractual arrangement arises from a published tariff and acceptance for carriage by a common carrier by rail), if the defendant establishes by a preponderance of the evidence that (a) he exercised due care with respect to the hazardous substance concerned, taking into consideration the characteristics of such hazardous substance, in light of all relevant facts and circumstances, and (b) he took precautions against foreseeable acts or omissions of any such third party and the consequences that could foreseeable result from such acts or omissions; or

(4) any combination of the foregoing paragraphs....

**(f) Actions involving natural resources; maintenance, scope, etc...** (1) Natural resources liability — In the case of an injury to, destruction of, or loss of natural resources under subparagraph (C) of subsection (a) of this section liability shall be to the United States Government and to any State for natural resources within the State or belonging to, managed by, controlled by, or appertaining to such State and to any Indian tribe for natural resources belonging to, managed by, controlled by, or appertaining to such tribe....

A review of CERCLA's definition sections demonstrates that the universe of conduct that might fall within §107 is quite broad and does not clearly describe the standards of liability that determine what conduct is actionable and what is not. This void has been filled by the courts. The following excerpt provides a roadmap to some of the major rulings that have emerged in defining the operation of CERCLA.

### Rich, Personal Liability for Hazardous Waste Cleanup: An Examination of CERCLA §107

13 Boston College Environmental Affairs Law Review 643, 653–58 (1986)

Section 107 of CERCLA designates certain parties who may be liable for the cleanup costs of a hazardous waste site. Section 107 imposes liability for cleanup costs and damage to natural resources[6] on: (1) past and present owners and operators of hazardous waste facilities; (2) persons who arrange for disposal of hazardous substances to facilities (usually generators); and (3) persons who transport hazardous substances to facilities from which there is a release or a threatened release of toxic chemicals that results in response costs. These responsible parties are liable for three types of costs incurred as a result of a release or a threatened release of hazardous waste: (1) governmental response costs (costs incurred by the federal government to clean up hazardous waste sites); (2) private response costs (costs incurred by other parties consistent with the National Contingency Plan), and (3) damages to natural resources.

Section 107 provides limited defenses. Parties otherwise liable under §107 may escape liability if they can establish that the release or threat of release of hazardous substances and resulting damages were caused by an act of God, an act of war, or an act or omission of a third party other than an employee or agent of the defendants, or one whose act or omission occurs in connection with a contractual relationship with the defendants. The third party exception applies only if defendants both exercised due care with respect to the hazardous substance, and took necessary precautions against acts or omissions by the third party.

STRICT LIABILITY... In spite of the comprehensive nature of its hazardous waste cleanup provisions, CERCLA's standards of liability are vague. Congress removed references to strict liability and joint and several liability before the bill's final passage, leaving these matters for judicial interpretation.

The standard of liability under CERCLA is strict liability. Although it does not specifically mention strict liability, §101, CERCLA's definitional section, states that liability under CERCLA "shall be construed to be the standard of liability which obtains under §311 of the Federal Water Pollution Control Act." Although §311 of the Federal Water Pollution Control Act (FWCPA) does not explicitly mention strict liability, courts have inferred such liability from the language of that

---

6. "Natural resources" under CERCLA means "fish, wildlife, biota, air, water, groundwater, drinking water supplies, and other such resources belonging to, managed by, held in trust by, appertaining to, or otherwise controlled by the United States...any state or local government, or any foreign government." 42 U.S.C.A. §9601(16).

Act, which subjects certain parties to liability unless they can successfully assert one of the limited defenses specified. Congress' reference to FWCPA §311 in CERCLA is logical, because the same defenses to liability found in FWCPA §311 also appear in §107 of CERCLA. Courts construing CERCLA have therefore held parties strictly liable for statutory violations.

JOINT AND SEVERAL LIABILITY... Congress also deleted references to joint and several liability from the final version of CERCLA. The original Senate proposal specifically imposed joint and several liability, but this language was deleted from the final version of the bill as part of the "hastily drawn compromise which resulted in the enactment of CERCLA." Federal courts construing liability under CERCLA, however, uniformly have held that CERCLA permits, but does not mandate, joint and several liability. It is therefore within the discretion of the court to impose joint and several liability. Furthermore, some courts have held that joint and several liability should be imposed under CERCLA, unless the defendants can establish that a reasonable basis exists for apportioning the harm against them.[7]

CERCLA's standard of strict liability, coupled with the possibility of joint and several liability, places a heavy burden on defendants. CERCLA does, however, place some constraints on the amount of liability that courts may impose under §107. Section 107 liability is premised upon a governmental response pursuant to §104 and the National Contingency Plan, or a response by another party in accordance with the National Contingency Plan. Both §104 and the National Contingency Plan impose practical limitations on the extent and cost of hazardous waste cleanup operations....

The National Contingency Plan establishes procedures and standards for responding to releases of hazardous substances, pollutants, and contaminants. These procedures include methods for discovering and investigating hazardous substance disposal facilities, for determining the appropriate extent of removal of the substances, for assuring that remedial actions are cost-effective, and for determining priorities among releases or threatened releases. The statute and the National Contingency Plan thus limit the extent of liability under CERCLA §107.

PERSONAL LIABILITY UNDER CERCLA §107... As discussed earlier, CERCLA imposes liability on: (1) past and present owners and operators of hazardous waste facilities; (2) persons who arrange for the transport of hazardous waste; and (3) persons who transport hazardous waste. These parties include individuals as well as corporations. The federal government has sought to hold both corporations and their corporate officers and employees responsible for the costs of hazardous waste cleanup under CERCLA. Although individual defendants have argued that their actions were the actions of the corporation, thereby shielding them from liability under the doctrine of limited liability, this argument has not succeeded. The few district courts to consider this issue have uniformly held that the corporate form does not shield individuals from personal liability where such individuals have exercised personal control over, or have actually been involved in, the disposal of hazardous waste.

7. U.S. v. Northeastern Pharm. & Chem. Co. (NEPACCO), 579 F. Supp. 823, 844 (W.D. Mo. 1984).

## COMMENTARY AND QUESTIONS

1. **CERCLA and Section 311 of the Federal Water Pollution Control Act.** Although the Rich excerpt mentions no canons of construction contributing to the interpretation given to CERCLA §107, the "shall be liable" language and reference to §311 of the Federal Water Pollution Control Act (which became the Clean Water Act, [CWA] led courts to look to cases interpreting the CWA as precedents for the interpretation of §107. In §311, Congress imposed liability on owners and operators of the vessels or facilities causing spills of oil or hazardous substances on navigable waters, requiring owners and operators to pay the government's response costs. Congress also established a $35 million revolving fund, for use by EPA and the Coast Guard when responding to such spills. Section 311 thus provided a model for Congress in developing CERCLA. Following CWA §311, Congress created the Superfund to enable EPA to remediate contaminated sites using federal money and then, under §107, empowered EPA to recover its costs from persons responsible for the contamination.

2. **A common law substitute for Superfund?** What does CERCLA § 107 accomplish that the common law could not?[8] The common law can do some of the things that §107 provides for. It is quite possible that a common law court would be willing to hold defendants who release hazardous materials into the environment strictly, jointly and severally liable even in the absence of a statute allowing it. Perhaps the common law might also adopt a relaxed standard of proof of causation similar to that of CERCLA in cases involving concurrent actions of multiple tortfeasors. (In the CERCLA cases, however, the furtherance of legislative policy is a key element underlying judicial willingness to relax traditional tort law standards of proof.) Going further, §107 does things that it would be very difficult for common law to do. The damage assessment of §107(a)(4)(A) is not a traditional damage measure — it assesses the actual costs of environmental remediation, not the amount of a plaintiffs' loss. Compare, for example, the award of damages paid in *Boomer*. By providing damages for natural resources, §107(a)(4)(C) also moves a step beyond traditional tort law, and §107(a)(4)(D) makes clear that health studies are an item of recoverable damage, hardly a regular feature of damage awards under the common law.

3. **Joint and several liability in CERCLA cases.** Strategically, joint and several liability is the concept (imported from common law) that makes CERCLA so potent. Courts uniformly interpret CERCLA as manifesting an intent on the part of Congress to allow joint and several liability among potentially responsible parties (PRPs). The consequence of imposing joint and several liability is potentially to shift the entire burden of cleanup onto any identifiable PRP. In deciding whether to impose joint and several liability, the standard view taken by most courts is to decide, on a case-by-case basis, whether harm is sufficiently severable to apportion liability.

---

8. CERCLA as a whole does many things that are far beyond the realm of common law possibility. Most obviously, its creation of a national fund from which cleanup expenses can be paid is a mechanism that the common law does not provide. Similarly, the creation of a National Priorities List that identifies and ranks sites as to the need for cleanup action is unthinkable without the intervention of a public law mandate.

United States v. Monsanto, 858 F.2d 160 (4th Cir. 1988) is illustrative. In that case, the Fourth Circuit held that site-owners and generator defendants were jointly and severally liable under §107(a) of CERCLA for the response costs expended by the United States and by South Carolina, in removing hazardous wastes from a disposal facility. As to the site-owners' liability, the court found it sufficient that they owned the site at the time that the hazardous substances were deposited there. As to the generator defendants' liability, the court found them liable because it was undisputed that (1) they shipped hazardous substances to the facility, (2) hazardous substances "like" those present in the generation defendants' waste were found at the facility, and (3) there had been a release of hazardous substances at the site.

Turning next to the issue of apportionment of liability, the Fourth Circuit recognized that CERCLA permits the imposition of joint and several liability in cases of indivisible harm. The court clarified the applicable legal principles by referencing the common law (858 F.2d at 171–2.):

> Under common law rules, when two or more persons act independently to cause a single harm for which there is a reasonable basis of apportionment according to the contribution of each, each is held liable only for the portion of harm that he causes. When such persons cause a single and indivisible harm, however, they are held liable jointly and severally for the entire harm. We think these principles, as reflected in the Restatement (Second) of Torts, represent the correct and uniform federal rules applicable to CERCLA cases.

Applying these principles to the facts before it, the court rejected the generator defendants' argument that there was a reasonable basis for apportioning the harm. In particular, the court found that the generator defendants presented no evidence showing a relationship between waste volume, the release of hazardous substances, and the harm at the site. Because hazardous substances at the site were commingled, there could be no reasonable apportionment "without some evidence disclosing the individual and interactive qualities of the substances deposited there. Common sense counsels that a million gallons of certain substances could be mixed together without significant consequences, whereas a few pints of others improperly mixed could result in disastrous consequences". Id. at 172. Because volume could not establish the effective contribution of each waste generator to the harm at the site, the court affirmed the imposition of joint and several liability.

4. **The unfairness of joint and several liability.** Is it patently unfair to make a deep pocket responsible party, such as Monsanto, pay for an entire cleanup when it is demonstrable that they are but one of several causes of the problem? Is it fair to tap the assets of only one of the responsible parties for the entire cost of the cleanup? The Fourth Circuit in its Monsanto decision rationalized the initial imposition of potentially unfair allocations in reliance on the later ability of the unfairly burdened party to reallocate some part of the loss by obtaining contribution from fellow joint tortfeasors. Specifically, the court concluded that "the defendants still have the right to sue responsible parties for contribution, and in that action they may assert both legal and equitable theories of cost allocation." 858 F.2d at 173. Although the topic of contribution will be considered at length later in this Chapter, can you predict why it may prove difficult for parties who pay more

than their fair share in a government cleanup action to recover an appropriate amount via contribution?

**5. Divisibility of harm or of costs?** In cases like *Monsanto*, the indivisibility of the environmental harm is the predicate for application of joint and several liability. In United States v. Kramer, 757 F. Supp. 397 (D.N.J. 1991), the generator defendants at a landfill site argued as a defense that the bulk of the anticipated $60 million cleanup cost was attributable to the quantitatively large volume of municipal solid waste and sludge deposited at the site. More narrowly, the non-municipal generator defendants sought to limit their liability to an amount that could be calculated arithmetically as the difference between the cleanup cost with, and without, their waste being present at the site. Why might this approach prove less costly to the non-municipal defendants?

Given the limited ability of municipalities to raise large sums of money, an apportionment that left the lion's share of the liability with the municipalities could pose a collectability problem for EPA. To date, EPA has frequently limited its efforts to recover a "fair" share from municipalities at sites where other potentially responsible parties (PRPs) can be identified and pursued. As an example, at the Kramer site, EPA did not name the municipalities as defendants in its original complaint, but they remained vulnerable to contribution claims from the named defendants.

**6. Emerging cracks in EPA's joint and several armor.** In United States v. Alcan Aluminum Corp., 990 F.2d 711 (2d Cir. 1993) and a separate case also entitled United States v. Alcan Aluminum Corp., 964 F.2d 252 (3d Cir. 1992), some modest inroads were made in the unrelenting stream of decisions imposing strict joint and several liability on all of the PRPs involved in the litigation. More significantly of the two, the Third Circuit *Alcan* case ordered the lower court to hear evidence of divisibility of harm. Relying heavily on the Restatement (Second) of Torts 433A, the court set the test for divisibility as follows:

> In sum, on remand, the district court must permit Alcan to attempt to prove that the harm is divisible and that the damages are capable of some reasonable apportionment. We note that the Government need not prove that Alcan's emulsion caused the release or the response costs. On the other hand, if Alcan proves that the emulsion did not or could not, when mixed with other hazardous wastes, contribute to the release and the resultant response costs, then Alcan should not be responsible for any response costs. In this sense, our result thus injects causation into the equation but, as we have already pointed out, places the burden of proof on the defendant instead of the plaintiff. We think that this result is consistent with the statutory scheme and yet recognizes that there must be some reason for the imposition of CERCLA liability. Our result seems particularly appropriate in light of the expansive meaning of "hazardous substance." Of course, if Alcan cannot prove that it should not be liable for any response costs or cannot prove that the harm is divisible and that the damages are capable of some reasonable apportionment, it will be liable for the full claim...964 F.2d at 270–71

The Second Circuit took a similar tack, concluding that based on common law principles, "Alcan may escape any liability for response costs if it either succeeds in proving that its oil emulsion, when mixed with other hazardous wastes, did not contribute to the release and the clean-up costs that followed, or contributed at most to only a divisible portion of the harm." 990 F.2d at 722.

Is there now an *Alcan* defense? How many PRPs will be in a position to carry the burden of proof on divisibility and basis for apportionment? One commentary on these developments suggests that only deep pocket, technically sophisticated PRPs will benefit from *Alcan*. See Daniel P. Harris & David M. Milan, Avoiding Joint and Several Liability Under CERCLA, 23 BNA Environment Reporter 1726 (1992).

A subsequent case, *Bell Petroleum*, may go even further than the *Alcans* in supporting the belief of some defense counsel that their clients can escape CERCLA joint and several liability. In Bell Petroleum Services Inc. v. Sequa Corp., 3 F.3d 899 (5th Cir. 1993), Sequa, one of three successive operators of a chromium plating facility, offered evidence of comparative sales, chrome flake purchases, and electric utility bills, in an effort to show the relative contribution of the three PRPs. The records offered were incomplete and relied on a variety of assumptions in projecting the amount of contamination attributable to each PRP, and the trial court initially ruled that Sequa was jointly and severally liable with the other PRPs. Because the government had previously settled with the other PRPs for $1.1 million out of a total of $1.7 million spent cleaning the site, this left Sequa with a judgment that would require it to pay $600,000.

On appeal, the Fifth Circuit, engaging in *de novo* review of the lower court's divisibility ruling, found that Sequa's evidence provided a reasonable basis for apportionment, rendering the imposition of joint and several liability inappropriate, and remanded the case for a determination of Sequa's share of the liability. The trial court interpreted the remand order as requiring obedience not only to the divisibility ruling, but also to a particular apportionment of only 4%, entered judgment against Sequa for $68,000. The trial court expressed its view that it could not take into account the full gamut of what it felt were relevant considerations saying it was "convinced that further evidence ... would demonstrate Sequa's share of the contamination is much higher." United States v. Bell Petroleum Services Inc., MO-88-CA-005 (W.D.Tex. March 11, 1994), discussed at 8 Toxics Law Reporter 1191 (March 23, 1994).

**7. Administrative order powers.** CERCLA §106 and RCRA §7003 both grant EPA power to issue orders requiring cleanups that address imminent threats to health and the environment caused by the release of hazardous substances into the environment. In a sense, these sections are additional liability sections that complement §107. Parties subject to the orders are required to expend resources on the cleanups, sometimes with little hope of shifting the loss to other responsible parties. RCRA §7003 appears in, and is addressed in the *NEPACCO* case í below at page 815. The extraordinary nature of the CERCLA §106 administrative order power is addressed in Part B. of this chapter.

## Section 2. **THE GOVERNMENT'S RELAXED BURDEN OF PROOF OF CAUSATION IN CERCLA CASES**

You will recall from the earlier material on toxic tort litigation the difficulty that plaintiffs encounter in proving that the defendant's activities are the cause in fact of plaintiffs' injuries. Even in a strict liability regime, that same difficulty could scuttle much of CERCLA's effectiveness if the government in every case had to trace each facet of cleanup costs to the actions of a particular defendant. This is especially true in older sites or midnight dumping sites where the records of what wastes were deposited by whom are sketchy or non-existent. The courts confronted this problem within the first years following CERCLA's enactment.

### United States v. Wade (Wade II)
United States District Court, Eastern District of Pennsylvania
577 F. Supp. 1326 (1983)

[The Wade litigation involved a large disposal site in Chester, Pennsylvania. The site was an extraordinarily high visibility one, having been the scene of a major fire in 1978 which damaged many of the several thousand tank cars and drums stored on the property. After testing discovered the presence of more than fifty hazardous substances at the site, many of which were leaking into the groundwater and from there into the Delaware River, legal action was instituted.

The Wade site was among the first sites for which the United States EPA sought remedies under RCRA and CERCLA. The litigation began in 1979 with the filing of a RCRA §7003 complaint. Shortly after the enactment of CERCLA in 1980, an amended complaint added counts under CERCLA §§106 and 107. The United States sought both injunctive relief as to the cleanup of the site and monetary relief for the response costs incurred by the government and others who had already undertaken steps to begin to seal the site and remove additional wastes still stored there. The parties sued by the United States included the site's owner (Wade), several off-site generators and some of the transporters who had deposited materials at the site. Earlier litigation had focused on the scope and retroactivity of the major statutes; the excerpted portion of this decision addresses only the issue of proof of causation.]

NEWCOMER, J. This is a civil action brought by the United States against several parties allegedly responsible for the creation of a hazardous waste dump in Chester, Pennsylvania. The government seeks injunctive relief against Melvin R. Wade, the owner of the dump site, ABM Disposal Service, the company which transported the hazardous substances to the site, and Ellis Barnhouse and Franklin P. Tyson, the owners of ABM during the time period at issue ("non-generator defendants"). The government also seeks reimbursement of the costs incurred and to be incurred in cleaning up the site from the non-generator defendants as well as from Apollo Metals, Inc., Congoleum Corporation, Gould, Inc., and Sandvik, Inc. ("generator defendants").

The claims for injunctive relief are brought pursuant to §7003 of the Resource Conservation and Recovery Act of 1976 ("RCRA"), 42 U.S.C.A. §6973, and §106 of CERCLA, 42 U.S.C.A. §9606. The claims for monetary relief are based on §107(a) of CERCLA, 42 U.S.C.A. §9607(a), as well as a common law theory of restitution. Presently before the Court are the government's motions for partial summary judgment on the issue of joint and several liability under §107(a) against each of the defendants....

The generator defendants' motions for summary judgment on the CERCLA claims generally advance two arguments. First, they argue that the government has not and cannot establish the requisite causal relationship between their wastes and the costs incurred by the government in cleaning up the site....

THE CAUSATION ARGUMENT... Even assuming the government proves that a given defendant's waste was in fact disposed of at the Wade site, the generator defendants argue it must also prove that a particular defendant's actual waste is presently at the site and has been the subject of a removal or remedial measure before that defendant can be held liable. In the alternative, the generator defendants argue that at a minimum the government must link its costs incurred to waste of the sort created by a generator before that generator may be held liable....

Part of the generator defendants' argument revolves around the use of the word "such" in referring to the "hazardous substances" [in CERCLA §107(a)(3)] contained at the dump site or "facility." It could be read to require that the facility contain a particular defendant's waste. On the other hand it could be read merely to require that hazardous substances like those found in a defendant's waste must be present at the site. The legislative history provides no enlightenment on this point. I believe that the less stringent requirement was the one intended by Congress.

The government's experts have admitted that scientific technique has not advanced to a point that the identity of the generator of a specific quantity of waste can be stated with certainty. All that can be said is that a site contains the same kind of hazardous substances as are found in a generator's waste. Thus, to require a plaintiff under CERCLA to "fingerprint" wastes is to eviscerate the statute. Given two possible constructions of a statute, one which renders it useless should be rejected. Generators are adequately protected by requiring a plaintiff to prove that a defendant's waste was disposed of at a site and that the substances that make the defendant's waste hazardous are also present at the site....

I turn now to the generator defendants' contention that the government must link its costs incurred to wastes of the sort created by them.

A reading of the literal language of the statute suggests that the generator defendants read too much into this portion of its causation requirement. Stripping away the excess language, the statute appears to impose liability on a generator who has (1) disposed of its hazardous substances (2) at a facility which now contains hazardous substances of the sort disposed of by the generator (3) if there is a release of that or some other type of hazardous substance (4) which causes the incurrence of response costs. Thus, the release which results in the incurrence of response costs and liability need only be of "a" hazardous substance [the language of CERCLA §107(a)(4)] and not necessarily one contained in the defendant's waste. The only required nexus between the defendant and the site is that the defendant have dumped his waste there and that the hazardous substances found in the defendant's waste are also found at the site. I base my disagreement with defendants' reading in part on the Act's use of "such" to modify "hazardous substance" in paragraph three and the switch to "a" in paragraph four....

Deletion of the causation language contained in the House-passed bill and the Senate draft is not dispositive of the causation issue. Nevertheless, the substitution of the present language for the prior causation requirement evidences a legislative intent which is in accordance with my reading of the Act.

## COMMENTARY AND QUESTION

1. **Comparison to toxic tort cases.** How does the relaxation of the government's burdens in proving causation in CERCLA cases compare with handling of burden of proof issues in traditional and toxic tort cases that were studied in Chapters Three and Four?

### Section 3. THE INDIVIDUAL LIABILITY OF MANAGERIAL OFFICERS

The focus of the Rich excerpt is personal individual liability for §107 recoveries. The typical cases in which this issue arises are those in which a hazardous waste generator, transporter, or disposer is a corporation, and a §107 action seeks to hold individual corporate officers or employees liable (for fiscal or punitive reasons). Their classic defense is to argue limited liability for corporate acts, the protective doctrine that provides such an important incentive to corporate entrepreneurialism. But courts increasingly have allowed application of individual personal liability for corporate officers under CERCLA and other statutes.

Analytically the cases usually fall into three categories:

The first category, occurring most often in small, closely held corporations, involves piercing the corporate veil when corporate structure stands as an impediment to reaching the assets of individuals who have directly profited from the corporation's activities, even though they may not have been personally involved in day-to-day operations. These cases require the sorts of rigorous showings that are required in non-CERCLA veil-piercing cases.

The second class of cases is where officers are held liable for their own wrongful personal actions, for instance where they themselves personally dumped toxics or directly ordered the illegal act.

The third class of individual liability is where individuals are held liable because of their status as managerial officers, responsible for directing the corporate activity in which violations occurred. Several of these liability theories are explored further in the criminal law materials in Chapter 19, and in the following case arising under CERCLA and RCRA:

### United States v. Northeastern Pharmaceutical & Chemical Co. [NEPACCO]
United States Court of Appeals for the Eighth Circuit
810 F.2d 726 (1986)[9]

McMILLIAN, J. Northeastern Pharmaceutical & Chemical Co. (NEPACCO), Edwin Michaels, and John W. Lee appeal from a final judgment entered in the District Court for the Western District of Missouri finding them and Ronald Mills jointly and severally liable for response costs incurred by the government after December 11, 1980, and all future response costs relative to the cleanup of the Denney farm site that are not inconsistent with the national contingency plan (NCP) pursuant to §§104 and 107 of the Comprehensive Environmental Response, Compensation, and Liability Act of 1980 (CERCLA), 42 U.S.C.A. §§9604, 9607....

The following statement of facts is taken in large part from the district court's excellent memorandum opinion, 579 F. Supp. 823 (W.D. Mo. 1984). NEPACCO was incorporated in 1966.... Although NEPACCO's corporate charter was forfeited in

---

9. Cert. denied, 484 U.S. 848 (1988).

1976 for failure to maintain an agent for service of process, NEPACCO did not file a certificate of voluntary dissolution with the secretary of state of Delaware. In 1974 its corporate assets were liquidated, and the proceeds were used to pay corporate debts and then distributed to the shareholders. Michaels [had] formed NEPACCO, was a major shareholder, and was its president. Lee was NEPACCO's vice-president, the supervisor of its manufacturing plant located in Verona, Missouri, and also a shareholder. Mills was employed as shift supervisor at NEPACCO's Verona plant.

From April 1970 to January 1972, NEPACCO manufactured the disinfectant hexachlorophene at its Verona plant. NEPACCO leased the plant from Syntex Agribusiness, Inc. (Syntex).... Michaels and Lee knew that NEPACCO's manufacturing process produced various hazardous and toxic byproducts, including 2,4,5-trichlorophenol (TCP), 2,3,7,8-tetrachlorodibenzo-p-dioxin (TCDD or dioxin), and toluene. The waste byproducts were pumped into a holding tank which was periodically emptied by waste haulers. Occasionally, however, excess waste byproducts were sealed in 55-gallon drums and then stored at the plant.

In July 1971 Mills approached NEPACCO plant manager Bill Ray with a proposal to dispose of the waste-filled 55-gallon drums on a farm owned by James Denney located about seven miles south of Verona. Ray visited the Denney farm and discussed the proposal with Lee; Lee approved the use of Mills' services and the Denney farm as a disposal site. In mid-July 1971 Mills and Gerald Lechner dumped approximately 85 of the 55-gallon drums into a large trench on the Denney farm (Denney farm site) that had been excavated by Leon Vaughn. Vaughn then filled in the trench. Only NEPACCO drums were disposed of at the Denney farm site.

In October 1979 the Environmental Protection Agency (EPA) received an anonymous tip that hazardous wastes had been disposed of at the Denney farm. Subsequent EPA investigation confirmed that hazardous wastes had in fact been disposed of at the Denney farm and that the site was not geologically suitable for the disposal of hazardous wastes. Between January and April 1980 the EPA prepared a plan for the cleanup of the Denney farm site and constructed an access road and a security fence. During April 1980 the EPA conducted an on-site investigation, exposed and sampled 13 of the 55-gallon drums, which were found to be badly deteriorated, and took water and soil samples. The samples were found to contain "alarmingly" high concentrations of dioxin, TCP and toluene.

In July 1980 the EPA installed a temporary cap over the trench to prevent the run-off of surface water and to minimize contamination of the surrounding soil and groundwater.... The 55-gallon drums are now stored in a specially constructed concrete bunker on the Denney farm. The drums as stored do not present an imminent and substantial endangerment to health or the environment; however, no plan for permanent disposal has been developed, and the site will continue to require testing and monitoring in the future.

In August 1980 the government filed its initial complaint against NEPACCO, the generator of the hazardous substances; Michaels and Lee, the corporate officers responsible for arranging for the disposal of the hazardous substances; Mills, the transporter of the hazardous substances; and Syntex, the owner and lessor of the Verona plant, seeking injunctive relief and reimbursement of response costs pursuant to RCRA §7003. In August 1982 the government filed an amended complaint adding counts for relief pursuant to CERCLA [which] was enacted after the filing of the initial complaint....

CERCLA RETROACTIVITY: APPLICATION OF CERCLA TO PRE-1980 ACTS... Appellants first argue the district court erred in applying CERCLA retroactively, that is, to impose liability for acts committed before its effective date, December 11, 1980. CERCLA §302(a) provides that "[u]nless otherwise provided, all provisions of this chapter shall be effective on December 11, 1980." Appellants argue that CERCLA should not apply to pre-enactment conduct that was neither negligent nor unlawful when committed. Appellants argue that all the conduct at issue occurred in the early 1970s, well before CERCLA became effective. Appellants also argue that there is no language supporting retroactive application in CERCLA's liability section, or in the legislative history. Appellants further argue that because CERCLA imposes a new kind of liability, retroactive application of CERCLA violates due process and the taking clause. We disagree.

The district court correctly found Congress intended CERCLA to apply retroactively. We acknowledge there is a presumption against the retroactive application of statutes. We hold, however, that CERCLA §302(a) is "merely a standard 'effective date' provision that indicates the date when an action can first be brought and when the time begins to run for issuing regulations and doing other future acts mandated by the statute."

Although CERCLA does not expressly provide for retroactivity, it is manifestly clear that Congress intended CERCLA to have retroactive effect. The language used in the key liability provision, CERCLA §107 refers to actions and conditions in the past tense: "any person who at the time of disposal of any hazardous substances owned or operated," CERCLA §107(a)(2), "any person who...arranged with a transporter for transport for disposal," CERCLA §107(a)(3), and "any person who...accepted any hazardous substances for transport to...sites selected by such person," CERCLA §107(a)(4).[10]

Further, the statutory scheme itself is overwhelmingly remedial and retroactive. CERCLA authorizes the EPA to force responsible parties to clean up inactive or abandoned hazardous substance sites, CERCLA §106, and authorizes federal, state and local governments and private parties to clean up such sites and then seek recovery of their response costs from responsible parties, CERCLA §§104, 107. In order to be effective, CERCLA must reach past conduct. CERCLA's backward-looking focus is confirmed by the legislative history. See generally H.R.Rep. No. 1016, 96th Cong., 2d Sess., reprinted in 1980 U.S. Code Cong. & Ad. News 6119 (CERCLA House Report). Congress intended CERCLA "to initiate and establish a comprehensive response and financing mechanism to abate and control the vast problems associated with abandoned and inactive hazardous waste disposal sites."

The district court also correctly found that retroactive application of CERCLA does not violate due process... Appellants failed to show that Congress acted in an arbitrary and irrational manner. Cleaning up inactive and abandoned hazardous waste disposal sites is a legitimate legislative purpose, and Congress acted in a rational manner in imposing liability for the cost of cleaning up such sites upon those parties who created and profited from the sites and upon the chemical industry as a whole. We hold retroactive application of CERCLA to impose liability upon responsible parties for acts committed before the effective date of the statute does

---

10. The court in United States v. South Carolina Recycling & Disposal, Inc., 20 ERC (BNA) 1753, 1760 (D.S.C. 1984), noted that CERCLA does not apply "retroactively" because it does not impose liability for past conduct; rather, CERCLA imposes liability upon those parties responsible for causing certain conditions, that is, the release or threatened release of hazardous substances, that are the present or future results of their past actions.

not violate due process.

[The opinion went on to demonstrate at some length that pre-1980 cleanup expenditures, as well as pre-1980 acts of dumping, were covered by CERCLA.]

RCRA: STANDARD AND SCOPE OF §7003 LIABILITY... We have considered the 1984 amendments and the accompanying legislative history and, for the reasons discussed below, we believe the 1984 amendments support the government's arguments about RCRA's standard and scope of liability and retroactivity.

The critical issue is the meaning of the phrase "contributing to." Before its amendment in 1984, RCRA §7003(a), 42 U.S.C. §6973(a), imposed liability upon any person "contributing to" "the handling, storage, treatment, transportation or disposal of any solid or hazardous waste" that "may present an imminent and substantial endangerment to health or the environment." The district court did not find either the statutory language or the statutory framework helpful in determining whether past non-negligent off-site generators and transporters were liable under RCRA §7003(a)(prior to the 1984 amendments). The district court then considered the legislative history of the 1980 amendments because "[t]he legislative history of the [RCRA] as originally enacted contains no specific discussion of the reach of §7003 and no mention of the reasons for its insertion...."

Then, in November 1984, Congress passed and President Reagan signed the 1984 amendments which were described as "clarifying" amendments and specifically addressed the standard and scope of liability of §7003(a). As amended in 1984, RCRA §7003(a), 42 U.S.C.A. §6973(a)(West Supp. 1986)(new language italicized; deleted language in brackets), now provides in pertinent part:

> Notwithstanding any other provision of this chapter, upon receipt of evidence that the *past or present* handling, storage, treatment, transportation or disposal of any solid waste or hazardous waste may present an imminent and substantial endangerment to health or the environment, the Administrator may bring suit on behalf of the United States in the appropriate district court [to immediately restrain any person] *against any person (including any past or present generator, past or present transporter, or past or present owner or operator of a treatment, storage, or disposal facility) who has contributed or who is* contributing to such handling, storage, treatment, transportation or disposal [to stop] *to restrain such person from* such handling, storage, treatment, transportation, or disposal [or to take such other action as may be necessary], *to order such person to take such other action as may be necessary, or both.*

As amended, RCRA §7003(a) specifically applies to past generators and transporters. Congress' intent with respect to the standard of liability under RCRA §7003(a) as amended by the 1984 amendments, is clearly set forth in the accompanying House Conference Report. The House Conference Report also expressly disapproved of the *Wade* and *Waste Industries* cases, which were relied upon by the NEPACCO [trial] court, as well as the NEPACCO [trial court] decision itself. The House Conference Report stated:

> Section 7003 focuses on the abatement of conditions threatening health and the environment and not particularly human activity. Therefore, it has *always reached those persons who have contributed in the past or are presently contributing to the endangerment, including but not limited to generators, regardless of fault or negligence.* The amendment, by adding the words "have contributed" is merely intended to clarify the existing authority. Thus, for example, *non-negligent generators whose wastes are no longer being deposited or dumped at a particular site may be ordered to abate the hazard*

*to health or the environment posed by the leaking of the wastes they once generated and which have been deposited on the site.* The amendment reflects the long-standing view that generators and other persons involved in the handling, storage, treatment, transportation or disposal of hazardous wastes must share in the responsibility for the abatement of the hazards arising from their activities. The section was intended and is intended to abate conditions resulting from past activities. Hence, the district court decisions in United States v. Wade, 546 F. Supp. 785 (E.D. Pa. 1982), United States v. Waste Industries, Inc. 556 F. Supp. 1301 (E.D. N.C. 1983), and United States v. Northeastern Pharmaceutical & Chemical Co., 579 F. Supp. 823 (W.D. Mo. 1984), which restricted the application of section 7003, are inconsistent with the authority conferred by the section as initially enacted and with these clarifying amendments. H.R.Conf. Rep. No. 1133, 98th Cong., 2d Sess. 119 (1984) (emphasis added).

Thus, following the 1984 amendments, past off-site generators and transporters are within the scope of RCRA §7003(a). We reverse that part of the district court judgment holding that RCRA does not apply to past non-negligent off-site generators and transporters.

SCOPE OF LIABILITY... The district court found NEPACCO liable as the "owner or operator" of a "facility" (the NEPACCO plant) under CERCLA §107(a)(1) and as a "person" who arranged for the transportation and disposal of hazardous substances under CERCLA §107(a)(3). The district court found Lee liable as a "person" who arranged for the disposal of hazardous substances under CERCLA §107(a)(3) and as an "owner or operator" of the NEPACCO plant under CERCLA §107(a)(1) by "piercing the corporate veil." Id. at 848–49. The district court also found Michaels liable as an "owner or operator" of the NEPACCO plant under CERCLA §107(a)(1).

Appellants concede NEPACCO is liable under CERCLA §107(a)(3) for arranging for the transportation and disposal of hazardous substances at the Denney farm site. Because NEPACCO's assets have already been liquidated and distributed to its shareholders, however, it is unlikely that the government will be able to recover anything from NEPACCO.

Appellants argue (1) they cannot be held liable as "owners or operators" of a "facility" because "facility" refers to the place where hazardous substances are located and they did not own or operate the Denney farm site, (2) Lee cannot be held individually liable for arranging for the transportation and disposal of hazardous substances because he did not "own or possess" the hazardous substances and because he made those arrangements as a corporate officer or employee acting on behalf of NEPACCO, and (3) the district court erred in finding Lee and Michaels individually liable by "piercing the corporate veil." Appellants have not claimed that any of CERCLA's limited affirmative defenses apply to them.

The government argues Lee can be held individually liable without "piercing the corporate veil," under CERCLA §107(a)(3), and that Lee and Michaels can be held individually liable as "contributors" under RCRA §7003(a). For the reasons discussed below, we agree with the government's liability arguments.

LIABILITY UNDER CERCLA §107(A)(1)... First, appellants argue the district court erred in finding them liable under CERCLA §107(a)(1) as the "owners and operators" of a "facility" where hazardous substances are located. Appellants argue that, regardless of their relationship to the NEPACCO plant, they neither owned nor operated the Denney farm site, and that it is the Denney farm site, not the

NEPACCO plant, that is a "facility" for purposes of "owner and operator" liability under CERCLA §107(a)(1). We agree.

CERCLA defines the term "facility" in part as "any site or area where a hazardous substance has been deposited, stored, disposed of, or placed, or otherwise come to be located." CERCLA §101(9)(B); see New York v. Shore Realty Corp., 759 F.2d 1032, 1043 n.15 (2d Cir. 1985). The term "facility" should be construed very broadly to include "virtually any place at which hazardous wastes have been dumped, or otherwise disposed of." United States v. Ward, 618 F. Supp. at 895. In the present case, however, the place where the hazardous substances were disposed of and where the government has concentrated its cleanup efforts is the Denney farm site, not the NEPACCO plant. The Denney farm site is the "facility." Because NEPACCO, Lee and Michaels did not own or operate the Denney farm site, they cannot be held liable as the "owners or operators" of a "facility" where hazardous substances are located under CERCLA §107(a)(1).

INDIVIDUAL LIABILITY UNDER CERCLA §107(A)(3)... CERCLA §107(a)(3) imposes strict liability upon "any person" who arranged for the disposal or transportation for disposal of hazardous substances. As defined by statute, the term "person" includes both individuals and corporations and does not exclude corporate officers or employees. Congress could have limited the statutory definition of "person" but chose not to do so. Compare CERCLA §101(20)(A)(limiting definition of "owner or operator"). Moreover, construction of CERCLA to impose liability upon only the corporation and not the individual corporate officers and employees who are responsible for making corporate decisions about the handling and disposal of hazardous substances would open an enormous, and clearly unintended, loophole in the statutory scheme.

First, Lee argues he cannot be held individually liable for having arranged for the transportation and disposal of hazardous substances under CERCLA §107(a)(3) because he did not personally own or possess the hazardous substances. Lee argues NEPACCO owned or possessed the hazardous substances.

The government argues Lee "possessed" the hazardous substances within the meaning of CERCLA §107(a)(3) because, as NEPACCO's plant supervisor, Lee had actual "control" over the NEPACCO plant's hazardous substances. We agree. It is the authority to control the handling and disposal of hazardous substances that is critical under the statutory scheme. The district court found that Lee, as plant supervisor, actually knew about, had immediate supervision over, and was directly responsible for arranging for the transportation and disposal of the NEPACCO plant's hazardous substances at the Denney farm site. We believe requiring proof of personal ownership or actual physical possession of hazardous substances as a precondition for liability under CERCLA §107(a)(3) would be inconsistent with the broad remedial purposes of CERCLA.

Next, Lee argues that because he arranged for the transportation and disposal of the hazardous substances as a corporate officer or employee acting on behalf of NEPACCO, he cannot be held individually liable for NEPACCO's violations. Lee also argues the district court erred in disregarding the corporate entity by "piercing the corporate veil" because there was no evidence that NEPACCO was inadequately capitalized, the corporate formalities were not observed, individual and corporate interests were not separate, personal and corporate funds were commingled or corporate property was diverted, or the corporate form was used unjustly or fraudulently.

The government argues Lee can be held individually liable, without "piercing the corporate veil," because Lee personally arranged for the disposal of hazardous substances in violation of CERCLA §107(a)(3). We agree. As discussed below, Lee can be held individually liable because he personally participated in conduct that violated CERCLA; this personal liability is distinct from the derivative liability that results from "piercing the corporate veil." "The effect of piercing a corporate veil is to hold the owner [of the corporation] liable. The rationale for piercing the corporate veil is that the corporation is something less than a bona fide independent entity." Donsco, Inc. v. Casper Corp., 587 F.2d 602, 606 (3d Cir. 1978). Here, Lee is liable because he personally participated in the wrongful conduct and not because he is one of the owners of what may have been a less than bona fide corporation. For this reason, we need not decide whether the district court erred in piercing the corporate veil under these circumstances.

We now turn to Lee's basic argument. Lee argues that he cannot be held individually liable for NEPACCO's wrongful conduct because he acted solely as a corporate officer or employee on behalf of NEPACCO. The liability imposed upon Lee, however, was not derivative but personal. Liability was not premised solely upon Lee's status as a corporate officer or employee. Rather, Lee is individually liable under CERCLA §107(a)(3) because he personally arranged for the transportation and disposal of hazardous substances on behalf of NEPACCO and thus actually participated in NEPACCO's CERCLA violations.

> A corporate officer is individually liable for the torts he [or she] personally commits [on behalf of the corporation] and cannot shield himself [or herself] behind a corporation when he [or she] is an actual participant in the tort. The fact that an officer is acting for a corporation also may make the corporation vicariously or secondarily liable under the doctrine of respondeat superior; it does not however relieve the individual of his [or her] responsibility. Donsco, Inc. v. Casper Corp., 587 F.2d at 606.

Thus, Lee's personal involvement in NEPACCO's CERCLA violations made him individually liable.

INDIVIDUAL LIABILITY UNDER RCRA §7003(A).... The district court did not reach the question of individual liability under RCRA because it concluded that RCRA did not impose liability upon past non-negligent off-site generators like NEPACCO.... RCRA is applicable to past non-negligent off-site generators. The government argues Lee and Michaels are individually liable as "contributors" under RCRA §7003(a). We agree.

RCRA §7003(a) imposes strict liability upon "any person" who is contributing or who has contributed to the disposal of hazardous substances that may present an imminent and substantial endangerment to health or the environment. As defined by statute, the term "person" includes both individuals and corporations and does not exclude corporate officers and employees. As with the CERCLA definition of "person," Congress could have limited the RCRA definition of "person" but did not do so. [Again] compare CERCLA §101(20)(A)(limiting definition of "owner and operator"). More importantly, imposing liability upon only the corporation, but not those corporate officers and employees who actually make corporate decisions, would be inconsistent with Congress' intent to impose liability upon the persons who are involved in the handling and disposal of hazardous substances.

Our analysis of the scope of individual liability under the RCRA is similar to our analysis of the scope of individual liability under CERCLA. NEPACCO violated RCRA §7003(a) by "contributing to" the disposal of hazardous substances at the Denney farm site that presented an imminent and substantial endangerment to health and the environment. Thus, Lee and Michaels can be held individually liable if they were personally involved in or directly responsible for corporate acts in violation of RCRA.

We hold Lee and Michaels are individually liable as "contributors" under RCRA §7003(a). Lee actually participated in the conduct that violated RCRA; he personally arranged for the transportation and disposal of hazardous substances that presented an imminent and substantial endangerment to health and the environment. Unlike Lee, Michaels was not personally involved in the actual decision to transport and dispose of the hazardous substances. As NEPACCO's corporate president and as a major NEPACCO shareholder, however, Michaels was the individual in charge of and directly responsible for all of NEPACCO's operations, including those at the Verona plant, and he had the ultimate authority to control the disposal of NEPACCO's hazardous substances. Cf. New York v. Shore Realty Corp., 759 F.2d at 1052-53 (shareholder-manager held liable under CERCLA).

In summary, we hold Lee individually liable for arranging for the transportation and disposal of hazardous substances in violation of CERCLA §107(a)(3), and Lee and Michaels individually liable for contributing to an imminent and substantial endangerment to health and the environment in violation of RCRA §7003(a)....

BURDEN OF PROOF OF RESPONSE COSTS... The district court found appellants had the burden of proving the government's response costs were inconsistent with the NCP, and that response costs that are not inconsistent with the NCP are conclusively presumed to be reasonable and therefore recoverable.

We believe the district court's analysis is correct. CERCLA §107(a)(4)(A) states that the government may recover from responsible parties "all costs of removal or remedial action...not inconsistent with the [NCP]." The statutory language itself establishes an exception for costs that are inconsistent with the NCP, but appellants, as the parties claiming the benefit of the exception, have the burden of proving that certain costs are inconsistent with the NCP and, therefore, not recoverable.... Because determining the appropriate removal and remedial action involves specialized knowledge and expertise, the choice of a particular cleanup method is a matter within the discretion of the EPA. The applicable standard of review is whether the agency's choice is arbitrary and capricious .... Here, appellants failed to show that the government's response costs were inconsistent with the NCP. Appellants also failed to show that the EPA acted arbitrarily and capriciously in choosing the particular method it used to clean up the Denney farm site....

GIBSON, J. (concurring in part and dissenting in part) I concur with the court's opinion except for [those] parts holding that RCRA §7003(a) imposes liability on past off-site nonnegligent generators and transporters and determining that the government could recover its response costs from Lee and Michaels under §7003(a). I respectfully dissent from the court's opinion as to those points.

The majority's analysis of liability under the RCRA focuses exclusively on the legislative history of the 1984 amendments to the RCRA. The majority particularly rely on House Conference Report No. 1133, which singles out the district court's opinion and states that it is "inconsistent with the authority conferred by [§7003] as initially enacted and with these clarifying amendments." H.R.Conf.Rep. No. 1133, 98th Cong., 2d Sess. 119 (1984), reprinted in 1984 U.S. Code Cong. & Ad. News 5649, 5690. The Conference Report also states that §7003 "has always" reached nonnegligent generators and transporters. Id. From these statements, the majority conclude that "the 98th Congress made clear that the intention of the 94th Congress in enacting the RCRA in 1976 had been to impose liability upon past nonnegligent off-site generators and transporters of hazardous waste." Thus, the majority hold that the RCRA as it read prior to the 1984 amendments imposed strict liability upon past generators and transporters and that the district court erred in holding that proof of fault or negligence was necessary for the government to recover its response costs under the RCRA.

I think that the 1984 House Conference Report is nothing more than a blatant effort by members of a later Congress to graft their personal views of the scope of liability under the RCRA onto the original Act. It is bootstrapping, and the majority fail to recognize it as such. The Conference Report characterizes the 1984 amendments as "clarifying" the RCRA. The "clarifying" amendments to §7003, however, did not alter the crucial phrase "contributing to," the construction of which the majority acknowledge as "the critical issue," other than to cast it in both the present and the past tense: "has contributed to or... is contributing." 42 U.S.C.A. §6973(a). Nor do the amendments supply a definition for this phrase. The amendments to section 7003(a) are directed toward changing the scope of the section to reach past as well as present and future generators and transporters of hazardous waste. I believe this to be a substantive change, rather than a clarification. In any event, because the amendments did not relate to the "contributing to" language, the statements in the House Conference report regarding the standard of liability under §7003(a) — negligence versus strict liability — are wholly gratuitous.

### COMMENTARY AND QUESTIONS

1. **Private plaintiffs and cleanup legislation.** NEPACCO, like many other cases brought under RCRA and CERCLA, features the United States as plaintiff. Private plaintiffs may also sue to enforce those statutes. For example, a subsection of the citizen suit provision of RCRA, 42 U.S.C. §6972(a)(1), authorizes private suits to enforce violation of any of RCRA's regulatory mechanisms, or the imminent hazard provision (see Chapter 17). Still, even with the presence of a citizen suit provision allowing its enforcement, RCRA has been held to create no private cause of action for damages. See Walls v. Waste Resource Corp., 761 F.2d 311 (6th Cir. 1985). CERCLA does allow private recovery of response costs, a matter that is considered more fully later in this Chapter.

2. **Retroactivity.** The retroactive application of CERCLA continues to be quite perplexing to the courts, on both constitutional and statutory interpretation grounds. One federal court recently ruled that CERCLA could not be applied retroactively, only to have that decision reversed by the Eleventh Circuit in USA v. Olin Corp., 107 F.3d 1506 (11th Cir. 1997). The Eleventh Circuit concluded that an analysis of CERCLA's purpose, as evinced by its structure and legislative history, supported the view that Congress intended the statute to impose retroactive liability for clean-

up of hazardous waste. The court noted that an essential purpose of CERCLA is to place ultimate responsibility for the clean-up of hazardous waste on those persons responsible for the waste's disposal, finding that this goal could only be achieved through retroactive application of CERCLA's liability provisions. The court also rejected the district court's determination that Congress' passage of CERCLA was an invalid exercise of Congress' power under the Commerce clause. The court concluded that the regulation of intrastate, on-site waste disposal constituted an appropriate element of Congress' broader scheme to protect interstate commerce and industries from pollution.

3. **The strategy of avoiding §107 recoveries.** In *Wade I*, the government sought an injunctive order requiring the defendant generators to clean up the site under CERCLA §106. As noted previously, CERCLA provides for creation of a Superfund from which the government may draw to pay for the cleanup of hazardous waste contamination. The government, when it uses the fund to pay for cleanups, may then sue responsible parties to recoup sums spent and thereby replenish the fund. Given the existence of Superfund cleanup funding and recoupment provisions under §107, and state law damage remedies, is it clear to you why EPA might seek such an order? Few if any of the parties ordered to clean a site are in a position to do the work themselves. Viewed in this light, the order to clean a site looks like an order to pay a contractor to clean the site, which looks like a damage remedy. When first authorized, Superfund had only $1.6 billion available under §107, and the pace of efforts that would have replenished the fund was slow. By obtaining relief under the imminent hazard prongs of RCRA §7003 and CERCLA §106, EPA could bypass the potential cash flow problem facing Superfund cleanups. By 1986 EPA's position was validated by the fact that CERCLA reimbursement was very problematic: a study conducted by EPA's Inspector General revealed that only 1.1 percent of $1.3 billion expended on Superfund cleanups up to 1986 had been recovered and put back into the fund.

4. **The relevance of the views of a subsequent Congress.** Who gets the better of the debate between the majority and the dissent in NEPACCO about the relevance of 1984 legislative history to the interpretation of 1980 language? What should not be obscured is that the 1984 Congress is free to adopt prospectively whatever rule it wants; this is simply an exercise of its constitutional power to legislate granted by Article I. Whatever the state of prior legislation, a later Congress is not required to continue it unchanged. In contrast, what is involved here is the meaning of a provision that the 1980 Congress had enacted as law. Aren't questions of statutory interpretation to be decided by courts, not subsequent legislatures? What is the relevance of the views of members of a later Congress as evidence of what members of the 1980 Congress actually intended? Are they legislative history?

5. **Arranging for disposal under CERCLA §107(a)(3).** The most far-reaching development in the NEPACCO case is probably its ruling that holds Michaels personally liable under RCRA §7003 as a person who "contributed" to the disposal of hazardous waste, even though Michaels was not involved in the day-to-day operations of the plant in Verona, Missouri. The key phrases in the court's holding on this point cast a broad net — Michaels was "the individual in charge and directly

responsible...and he had ultimate authority to control the disposal of NEPACCO's hazardous substances." Doesn't that description fit almost all chief operating officers of corporations? Looking at CERCLA §107(a)(3), can the "arranging for disposal" language of that liability section be read as broadly? One court has proposed a liability standard based on ability to prevent improper disposal:

> This standard is different, but more stringent on the whole than traditional corporate liability, yet it requires more than mere status as a corporate officer or director.... The test — whether the individual in a close corporation could have prevented or significantly abated the release of hazardous substances — allows the fact-finder to impose liability on a case-by-case basis.... Michigan v. ARCO Industries Corp., 723 F. Supp. 1214, 1219 (W.D. Mich. 1989).

As discussed later in this Chapter, setting appropriate limits to the scope of liability in "ability to control" situations has become an even hotter issue in other contexts. The ARCO Industries standard applies to close corporations, i.e. corporations owned and controlled by just a few shareholders. Is there any reason why the same standard would not be equally well-suited to determining liability of corporate offers in large publicly-held corporations?

6. **Selling hazardous materials as a form of disposal.** Given the breadth of RCRA and CERCLA liability, is it possible that the sale of products that contain hazardous materials such as creosote (a wood preservative that is itself a hazardous substance) can be considered "arranging for disposal" of those materials under §107(a)(3) of CERCLA? Congress did not define the term "arranged" in the statute and courts have had to supply a definition. In general, the courts have been quick to reject liability, protecting the sellers of products containing hazardous substances from liability. See, e.g., Edward Hines Lumber Co. v. Vulcan Materials Co., 685 F. Supp. 651 (N.D. Ill. 1988), aff'd on other grounds, 861 F.2d 155 (7th Cir. 1988); Amcast Industries Corp. v. Detrex Corp., 2 F.3d 746 (7th Cir. 1993) (rejecting the assertion that any spillage constitutes disposal). See also Gaba, Interpreting Section 107 (a)(3) of CERCLA: When Has A Person "Arranged For Disposal"?, 44 Sw. L. J. 1313 (1991).

7. **Processing hazardous materials through third parties as a form of disposal.** Another important issue under §107(a)(3) of CERCLA is whether companies owning a particular substance may be liable for disposal that occurs when a third party is processing or refining that substance. The decision by the Eighth Circuit in United States v. Aceto Agricultural Chemicals Corp., 872 F.2d 1373 (8th Cir. 1989) is the leading case on this point. In Aceto, the court broadly construed the phase "arranged for disposal" in §107(a)(3) to include manufacturers who sent their pesticide ingredients to a formulator under a tolling agreement, where the formulation activities gave rise to contamination. The manufacturers argued that they could not be said to have "arranged for disposal" of any hazardous substances, because they only provided base materials that were to be processed into a valuable product. Nonetheless, in denying a motion to dismiss, the Court ruled the manufacturers were independently liable as "arrangers" for disposal (872 F.2d at 1381-2):

> Defendants nonetheless contend they should escape liability because they had no authority to control Aidex's operations, and our NEPACCO decision states "[i]t is the authority to control the handling and disposal of hazardous substances that is critical under the statutory scheme." ... In NEPACCO, we were

confronted with the argument that only individuals who owned or possessed hazardous substances could be liable under CERCLA. We rejected that notion and imposed liability, in addition, on those who had the authority to control the disposal, even without ownership or possession.... Defendants in this case, of course, actually owned the hazardous substances, as well as the work in process. NEPACCO does not mandate dismissal of plaintiffs' complaint under these circumstances.

*Aceto* has led to liability in subsequent cases. Of particular note, in FMC Corp. v. U.S. Dept. of Commerce, 786 F.Supp. 471 (E.D.Pa. 1992), the district court held that a party will be liable where it (1) supplied raw materials to another and (2) owned or controlled the work done at the site, where (3) the generation of the hazardous substances was inherent in the production process. The district court found those three elements satisfied and imposed liability on the federal government for its role in the production of rayon at the site. Subsequently, on appeal after rehearing, the Third Circuit found itself "equally divided" on the issue of the government's arranger liability and consequently affirmed by "holding the government liable as an arranger without discussion." FMC Corp. v. U.S. Dept. of Commerce, 29 F.3d 833, 846 (3d Cir. 1994). On somewhat similar facts, however, the federal government was not held liable for the contamination associated with the production of Agent Orange. See, United States v. Vertac Chemical Corp., 841 F.Supp. 884 (E.D. Ark. 1993).

8. **Recycling.** Where on the continuum between sale of a useful product and arranging for disposal does recycling fall? The short answer is that, in most cases, conventional recycling, even where the recycler pays for the used product, renders the seller of the used product liable as an arranger. The typical case of this sort might involve sellers of lead-acid batteries to lead reclaimers. See, e.g., Chesapeake and Potomac Telephone Co. of Va. v. Peck Iron & Metal Co., Inc., 814 F.Supp. 1269 (E.D. Va. 1992); but see Catellus Development Corp. v. United States, 828 F.Supp. 764 (N.D.Cal. 1993) (holding auto parts company not liable for sale of spent batteries to lead reclamation firm that caused release). Another case of this genre is California v. Summer Del Caribe, Inc., 821 F.Supp. 574 (N.D.Cal. 1993), where the sale to a recycler of solder dross left over after the defendant's manufacturing process resulted in liability when the solder dross was released into the environment at the recycling facility. Will the imposition of arranger liability in the recycling context work at cross purposes with the desirability of recycling when compared to the use of virgin raw materials?

### Section 4. THE CLASSES OF PARTIES WHO MAY BE HELD LIABLE UNDER CERCLA

CERCLA holds liable all persons or entities classified as owners or operators of treatment, storage, or disposal ("TSD") facilities, and generators[11] and transporters of hazardous waste. These terms are, in part, easily understood, especially in the

---

11. Generator liability is traceable to the previously reproduced provision in §107(a)(3) holding liable persons who arranged for disposal of hazardous materials that later are the subject of a removal or remedial action.

case of generators and transporters. Owners and operators is a more specialized term and is defined as follows by §101(20) of CERCLA:

> (A) The term "owner or operator" means (i) in the case of a vessel, any person owning, operating, or chartering by demise, such vessel, (ii) in the case of an onshore facility or an offshore facility, any person owning or operating such facility, and (iii) in the case of any facility, title or control of which was conveyed due to bankruptcy, foreclosure, tax delinquency, abandonment, or similar means to a unit of State or local government, any person who owned, operated or otherwise controlled activities at such facility immediately beforehand. Such term does not include a person, who, without participating in the management of a vessel or facility, holds indicia of ownership primarily to protect his security interest in the vessel or facility....

> (D) The term "owner or operator" does not include a unit of State or local government which acquired ownership or control involuntarily through bankruptcy, tax delinquency, abandonment, or other circumstances in which the government involuntarily acquires title by virtue of its function as sovereign. The exclusion provided under this paragraph shall not apply to any State or local government which has caused or contributed to the release or threatened release of a hazardous substance from the facility, and such a State or local government shall be subject to the provisions of this chapter in the same manner and to the same extent, both procedurally and substantively, as any nongovernmental entity, including liability under section 9607 of this title.

Despite the presence of explicit statutory definition, the scope of the owner and operator provisions of CERCLA has proved particularly troublesome. The courts have played an important role in delineating the contours of hazardous waste liability through case law interpreting the statutory terms. Three major areas of litigation have emerged.

The first line of cases focuses on attempts to expand the class of operators. Many of these cases concern the potential liability of lenders who make loans to operators of TSD facilities or to generators. Frequently, when the borrower encounters financial difficulty, the lender will try to salvage its loan by becoming involved in the operation of the debtor's business. Not surprisingly, the presence of a solvent entity (the lender) participating in the affairs of a financially troubled TSD facility or generator has typically made an inviting target for a CERCLA plaintiff. After years of litigation, as detailed below, EPA sought and obtained a "legislative fix", in the form of an amendment to CERCLA, that attempts to clarify the scope of lender liability under the secured creditor exemption of CERCLA, §101(20)(A).[12]

The second line of cases focuses less on expanding the class of operators and more on expanding the class of owners. For the most part, these cases involve pinning down who really owns the facility. Here the issues are ones of corporate structure, such as the relationship of a parent corporation to a subsidiary, or corporate succession, such as deciding whether a successor corporation is responsible for the liabilities of the entity it took over.[13] These cases have resulted in substantial dis-

---

12. That part of CERCLA §101(20)(A) known as the "secured creditor exemption" provides: ["Owner" or "operator"] does not include a person, who, without participating in the management of a vessel or facility, holds indicia of ownership primarily to protect his security interest in the vessel or facility.

13. These issues are not limited to the ownership of TSD facilities, but can also arise in the context of deciding who is a generator or transporter.

agreement among the federal circuit courts. In particular dispute are the circumstances under which a parent corporation will be found liable for environmental conditions caused by its subsidiary, a controversy which the Supreme Court has now chosen to resolve.

Finally, there is a great deal of legal uncertainty surrounding the statutory effort to exonerate innocent purchasers of contaminated parcels from liability. As previously noted, current owners of contaminated property are liable under §107(a) unless they can establish an affirmative defense under §107(b). The first two of these defenses apply only when either an act of God or an act of war is the sole cause of the release or threatened release and the resulting harm. See §107(b)(1) and (2). To date, these provisions have resulted in little case law and virtually no relief for CERCLA defendants.[14] The third affirmative defense, §107(b)(3), applies if a party not in contractual privity with the person asserting the defense was the sole cause of the relevant release or threatened release and the resulting harm. This defense protects property owners against unauthorized "midnight dumping" but it does not protect predecessors in the chain of title, with whom there will often be a contractual relationship. Congress, aware of this problem, tried to address it by amendments now codified in §101(35), as noted more fully below.

COMMENTARY AND QUESTIONS

1. **The Superfund Amendments and Reauthorization Act of 1986 (SARA).** In 1986, Congress revisited a number of areas of CERCLA in a far-reaching set of amendments that also reauthorized the continuing operation of the Superfund system. Pub. No. 99-499. SARA, as the 1986 legislation is known, spoke to a number of liability issues, usually in ways that confirmed broad judicial interpretations of the liability provisions. As in §101(35), Congress clarified a variety of questions about the scope of the statute. SARA did not cut back on the scope of CERCLA liability. To the contrary, the generally pro-liability posture of SARA led some experts in the field to suggest that its acronym ought to be changed to RACHEL, because the Reauthorization Act Confirms How Everyone's Liable. See, e.g., United States v. Kramer, 757 F. Supp. 397 (D.N.J. 1991); Glass, Superfund and SARA: Are There Any Defenses Left?, 12 Harv. Envtl L. Rev. 385 (1988). In the same vein, one commentator has written, "With only slight exaggeration, one government lawyer has described a [CERCLA] trial as requiring only that the Justice Department lawyer stand up and recite: 'May it please the Court, I represent the government and therefore I win.'" Marzulla, Superfund 1991: How Insurance Firms Can Help Clean Up the Nation's Hazardous Waste, 4 TXLR 685 (1989).

2. **Lender Liability and the 1996 Superfund Amendments.** Although CERCLA's secured creditor exemption, §101(20)(A), was designed to protect lenders from strict CERCLA liability, for years there was substantial confusion and litigation over the exemption's proper scope. The chief difficulty concerned the phrase "participating in the management." Some courts held that a lender does not participate

---

14. See, e.g., United States v. Stringfellow, 661 F. Supp. 1053, 1061 (C.D. Cal. 1987) (heavy but foreseeable rains do not constitute an act of God).

in management unless it actually managed the vessel's or facility's operations. See, e.g., In re Bergsoe Metal Corp., 910 F.2d 668 (9th Cir. 1990). In contrast, other courts found creditors liable based simply on their capacity to control a vessel or facility's operations. See, e.g., United States v. Fleet Factors Corp., 901 F.2d 1550 (11th Cir. 1990). In light of these conflicting judicial interpretations, lenders faced great uncertainty concerning their potential exposure.

To attempt to alleviate this confusion, EPA promulgated regulations to define the secured creditor exemption's scope. EPA's lender liability rule, which was issued in April 1992 and codified at 40 C.F.R. 300.1100(c), was short-lived. In response to industry challenges, the D.C. Circuit vacated the rule, holding its promulgation to be beyond EPA's statutory authority. Kelley v. E.P.A., 15F.3d 1100 (D.C. Cir. 1994), cert. denied sub nom., American Bankers Ass'n v. Kelley, 115 S. Ct 900 (1995). In response to the Kelley decision, and the continuing uncertainty surrounding the secured creditor exemption, Congress amended CERCLA in 1996 in the Asset Conservation, Lender Liability, and Deposit Insurance Act, P.L. No. 104-208 (the "Act").

The Act effectively overruled the Kelley decision by statutorily reinstating EPA's lender liability rule. The Act amended CERCLA's definition of "owner or operator" to clarify that most routine lending activities do not constitute "participating in the management" of a vessel or facility. Instead, CERCLA now provides that a lender cannot be liable as an owner or operator unless the lender "actually participates in the management or operational affairs of a vessel or facility." See §101(20)(E)-(G). In addition, the Act specified that the following activities, routinely performed by lenders in administering a loan, do not amount to "participating in the management" of a vessel or facility: holding, abandoning, or releasing a security interest; including a covenant or warranty of environmental compliance in a loan or security instrument; monitoring or enforcing the terms and conditions of a loan instrument; monitoring or inspecting a facility or vessel; requiring the borrower to address a release or threatened release of hazardous substances; providing financial advice to the borrower or otherwise taking steps to prevent diminution of value of collateral; restructuring or renegotiating the terms of a loan or security interest; exercising available remedies for breach of a condition of the loan; and conducting a response action under the direction of state or federal on-site officials. Id. Perhaps most significantly, the Act attempts to clarify when creditors may foreclose on property without risking liability. The Act allows a lender to foreclose and wind up operations as long as it subsequently divests the property at the "earliest practicable, commercially reasonable time, on commercially reasonable terms, taking into account market conditions and legal and regulatory requirements." See §101(20)(E)(ii)(II). For further details on the events leading to the promulgation of the Act, see EPA Policy on Interpreting CERCLA Provisions, Addressing Lenders and Involuntary Acquisitions by Government Entities, BNA Env. Rptr. 21:5981 (8/1/97).

3. **"The time has come," the walrus said, "to talk of many things...of 'subsids,' parents, shareholders, of cabbages and kings."** The courts consistently have construed CERCLA's scope of liability broadly in a variety of contexts that involve scrutiniz-

ing a corporation's form. At times this has gone beyond the traditional common law doctrine that allows for piercing the corporate veil when corporate form is being used as a sham to defraud creditors. To go beyond traditional rules of corporate law in imposing liability on owners of corporations is a very delicate matter because one of the principal assurances of corporate form is that only corporate assets are put at risk by corporate activities; personal assets of a corporation's owners are not supposed to be put at risk. As a matter of policy, adherence to this general principle is quite important. Limited liability invites the formation of new companies that may or may not survive, and is thus vital to economic innovation and dynamism. Shareholder immunity from liability is likewise a vital element in capital formation. Without it, shareholders would be inhibited from purchasing stock as a form of investment in corporations.

Despite all of these dangers, CERCLA liability has been extended in certain federal circuits beyond the normal limits of corporate law in a number of disparate settings.

*Corporate parent-subsidiary relationships...* It is not unusual for a corporate parent to create a number of subsidiary corporations that engage in different activities. In fact, the use of subsidiaries may be a legitimate attempt to protect the parent against claims for excess liabilities of a subsidiary that is going to enter a risk-laden field, such as hazardous materials operations in a post-CERCLA world. When the subsidiary is a mere sham, the common law has long disregarded the corporate form, usually looking to a series of factors to determine if the subsidiary was a bona fide separate entity. The factors include whether the subsidiary was adequately capitalized, the extent to which the parent retained direct control of the subsidiary's action, the presence of interlocking directorates and common corporate officers, etc. Many of the CERCLA cases, however, have included concepts of ability to control as a vital issue. In the parent-subsidiary context the parent, by virtue of its ownership of the subsidiary, always has a long-term power to control the subsidiary's actions. Thus far the cases have not been quick to disregard the corporate form, although a split in the circuits has developed. The leading cases that vindicate the usual principles of corporate law are Joslyn Manufacturing Co. v. T. L. James & Co., 893 F.2d 80 (5th Cir. 1990) and United States v. Cordova Chemical Co. of Michigan, 113 F.2d 572 (6th Cir. 1997). The leading case imposing liability on a corporate parent based on a showing that would not qualify for traditional common law veil-piercing is United States v. Kayser-Roth Corp., 910 F.2d 24 (1st Cir. 1990).

Addressing this split in the circuits, the Supreme Court granted certiorari on December 12, 1997 in *Cordova Chemical*. In that case, the Sixth Circuit concluded that "where a parent corporation is sought to be held liable as an operator [pursuant to CERCLA]...based upon the extent of its control of its subsidiary which owns the facility, the parent will be liable only when the requirements necessary to pierce the corporate veil are met." Id. at 580. With respect to the parent corporation, the Sixth Circuit held that its 100% ownership of the subsidiary, participation on the board of directors, active involvement in environmental matters, and control over budget and capital expenditures did not constitute the degree of control necessary to pierce the corporate veil under established Michigan law. 113 F.2d at 581. In reaching this result, the Sixth Circuit recognized that a number of federal circuit courts have concluded that parent corporations could become operators by virtue of involvement with a subsidiary, regardless of whether the corporate veil could be pierced. The Sixth Circuit concluded that had Congress wished to alter the protections provided by the corporate form, it could have done so explicitly.

*Corporate shareholders of dissolved corporations...* Corporations at times wind up their affairs and go out of existence through a state law dissolution process. Dissolution provides a period of time after a petition for dissolution is filed in which claims against the corporation may be brought and satisfied from corporate assets that would otherwise be distributed to the corporation's shareholders. Usually, in order to have a measure of finality in these matters, claims that are not filed during the designated period are thereafter barred. The issue in the CERCLA context is whether a post-dissolution suit can be brought against shareholders to whom corporate assets were distributed. Again, in the absence of fraud, the usual rule of corporation law is that such suits are barred. Leading federal cases on point include Onan Corp. v. Industrial Steel Container Co., 909 F.2d 511 (8th Cir. 1990); Louisiana-Pacific Corp. v. Asarco Inc., 5 F.3d 431 (9th Cir. 1993); but see United States v. Sharon Steel, 681 F. Supp. 1492, 1495–98 (D. Utah 1987) (construing CERCLA as pre-emptive of state dissolution law).

As a matter of policy, it is not fundamentally important that corporate assets distributed upon dissolution should be transferred to shareholders free of claims related to corporate wrongdoing. Stated differently, the policy favoring repose and finality that is behind the usual operation of dissolution proceedings is not as vital to the functioning of the corporate system as are the interests in protecting the limited liability aspects of corporate form. Indeed, there is a sense in which failure to seek recovery of the distributed corporate assets allows the shareholders to retain ill-gotten gains, especially if the corporation was actively engaged in environmental misdeeds during its existence.

*Successor corporations...* Often one corporation will purchase the productive assets of another, either via merger, through the purchase of stock, or through the purchase of the assets themselves. Corporate law has developed general principles that establish when successor corporations will be held to have purchased the liabilities of their predecessors. EPA has issued the following guidance document that sets forth its general approach to issues of corporate succession:

> In establishing successor liability under CERCLA, the Agency should initially utilize the "continuity of business operation" approach of federal law. However, to provide additional support or an alternative basis for successor corporation liability, the Agency should be prepared to apply the traditional exemptions to the general rule of non-liability in asset acquisitions. EPA Memorandum of Courtney Price, Liability of Corporate Shareholders and Successor Corporations For Abandoned Sites Under [CERCLA] at 15–16 (June 13, 1984).

At least one commentator has argued that this position marks a substantial expansion of successor liability because the continuation of the business entity test ignores the nuances of asset transfer that are often a key to determining successor liability under traditional state corporation law. See Wallace, Liability of Corporations and Corporate Officers, Directors, and Shareholders Under Superfund: Should Corporate and Agency Law Concepts Apply?, 14 J. Corp. L. 839, 879–884 (1989). The business continuation standard, instead, has its roots in the modern products liability revolution that has so greatly expanded liability in that realm.

In general, the courts have been receptive to imposing successor liability in CERCLA cases, particularly where the predecessor corporation would have been a PRP at the site. See, e.g., Smith Land & Improvement Corp. v. Celotex Corp., 851 F.2d 86 (3d Cir. 1988); Louisiana-Pacific Corp. v. Asarco, Inc., 909 F.2d 1260 (9th Cir. 1990); U.S. v. Mexico Feed and Seed Co., 980 F.2d 478 (8th Cir. 1992); City Environmental Inc. v. U.S. Chemical Co., 814 F. Supp. 624 (E.D. Mich. 1993). The traditional corporate law dividing line for liability in these cases is often linked to whether the entity is a mere asset purchaser (non-liability for the past actions of the seller) or a corporate successor (liability). CERCLA has pushed the precedents that are used to recognize corporate successorship to where liability can, at times, be found in cases where it would not have in the past. These areas are usually referred to as "continuing business enterprise" cases and "product line" cases. For a succinct summary of the developments in these areas, as well as a good overview of the general distinction between successorship and asset purchases, see Ronald Janke & Matthew Kuryla, Environmental Liability Risks for Asset Purchasers, 24 BNA Environment Reporter 2237 (1994).

**4. How the courts make CERCLA liability policy.** After reviewing the proceeding notes' forays into the nuts and bolts of CERCLA liability, the prominent role of courts in framing the contours of CERCLA as part of a case-by-case development should be apparent. What is less clear is whether the courts are interpreting statutes or making law. In any event, the courts are not merely engaged in a rote process of statutory interpretation that deduces the intent of Congress through a series of simple logical steps. The process of judicial interpretation frequently calls upon courts to weigh and balance competing policy concerns, giving the process of statutory interpretation much of the same dynamism as the common law. The Sixth Circuit, in a successor liability case, reflected on the role of courts in these terms:

> The Supreme Court has stated that "the authority to construe a statute is fundamentally different from the authority to fashion a new rule or to provide a new remedy which Congress has decided not to adopt." Northwest Airlines, Inc. v. Transport Workers Union of America, 451 U.S. 77, 97 (1981). As Justice Stevens wrote in Northwest Airlines, "Broadly worded constitutional and statutory provisions necessarily have been given concrete meaning and application by a process of case-by-case judicial decisions in the common-law tradition." Id. at 95.
>
> Of course, the line separating statutory interpretation and judicial lawmaking is not always clear and sharp. If a statute is found to be abundantly clear and well defined, a judicial decision that expands or contracts its reach or adds or deletes remedies fashions federal common law. On the other hand, if the court detects only gaps in definitions or descriptions, it may fill these interstices of

the statute by exercising its authority to interpret or construe the statute. As the Supreme Court has stated, these two exercises of judicial authority are fundamentally different, and they are subject to different standards. The authority to construe a statute lies at the very heart of judicial power and is not subject to rigorous scrutiny. The rule is otherwise with respect to outright judicial lawmaking, however. Before a federal court may fashion a body of federal common law, it must find either (1) that Congress painted with a broad brush and left it to the courts to "flesh out" the statute by fashioning a body of substantive federal law, or (2) that a federal rule of decision is necessary to protect uniquely federal interests. Anspec Company, Inc. v. Johnson Controls, Inc., 922 F.2d 1240, 1245 (6th Cir. 1991).

Which sort of exercise are the courts engaged in when they address issues such as successor liability? The court in *Anspec* held that CERCLA issues are matters of statutory construction and that CERCLA, properly construed, intended to impose liability on successor corporations.

**5. Would you buy this land?** Assume that you are a commercial investor and are aware of a contaminated parcel that is otherwise well suited for investment. Should you purchase the property? As is made plain by CERCLA §101(35), as a purchaser of the property with knowledge of its contamination, you would be liable for cleanup costs as a responsible party under CERCLA. If the sum of the purchase price plus the cost of cleanup is sufficiently low that the parcel freed of contamination is worth more than that sum, the purchase should be consummated. In the case of badly contaminated parcels, however, the cleanup costs alone often dwarf the "clean" market value of the parcel. Those are problem cases for society because one important goal of CERCLA is (or ought to be) the return of contaminated sites to productive use. Recently, there has been substantial legislative and regulatory action seeking to encourage the redevelopment of contaminated "brownfields" on both the federal and state levels. These developments, which signify a policy of greater flexibility and cooperation by EPA and the states in the enforcement of the environmental laws, are detailed in Chapter 20.

**6. The "act of a third party" defense.** CERCLA §107(b)(3), set forth in the first section of this Chapter, permits a defense when the hazardous release or threatened release is caused solely by the act of a third party with whom the defendant has little or no relation. Section 101(35) in relevant part reads as follows:

§101(35)(A) The term "contractual relationship," for the purpose of §9607(b)(3) of this title includes, but is not limited to, land contracts, deeds or other instruments transferring title or possession, unless the real property on which the facility concerned is located was acquired by the defendant after the disposal or placement of the hazardous substance on, in, or at the facility, and one or more of the circumstances described in clause (i), (ii), or (iii) is also established by the defendant by a preponderance of the evidence:

(i) At the time the defendant acquired the facility the defendant did not know and had no reason to know that any hazardous substance which is the subject of the release or threatened release was disposed of on, in, or at the facility.

(ii) The defendant is a government entity which acquired the facility by escheat, or through any other involuntary transfer or acquisition, or through the exercise of eminent domain authority by purchase or condemnation.

(iii) The defendant acquired the facility by inheritance or bequest. In addition to establishing the foregoing, the defendant must establish that he has satisfied the requirements of §9607(b)(3)(a) and (b) of this title.

(B) To establish that the defendant had no reason to know, as provided in clause (i) of subparagraph (A) of this paragraph, the defendant must have undertaken, at the time of acquisition, all appropriate inquiry into the previous ownership and uses of the property consistent with good commercial or customary practice in an effort to minimize liability. For purposes of the preceding sentence the court shall take into account any specialized knowledge or experience on the part of the defendant, the relationship of the purchase price to the value of the property if uncontaminated, commonly known or reasonably ascertainable information about the property, the obviousness of the presence or likely presence of contamination at the property, and the ability to detect such contamination by appropriate inspection....

Consider whether that defense is available in the following hypothetical situation: RHA is considering buying a piece of commercial property that shows no obvious signs of contamination. Under what circumstances, if any, will RHA be free from §107(a)(1) owners liability if in the future it is discovered that previously disposed of hazardous substances are buried under the surface and are releasing toxic contaminants into the groundwater?

7. **Insurance.** CERCLA has created a high-stakes specialized cottage industry in the litigation of defense against claims and the pollution exclusion clause sections of insurance policies. The most readily understood of these cases arise initially when a facility owner PRP receives a PRP letter and looks to its insurer to provide (and pay for) the costs of defending the claim. Later, after being held liable, the PRP seeks indemnification from the insurer. The cases, in the main, involve comprehensive general liability policies (CGL), most of which included a "pollution exclusion" clause that excepted ordinary pollution, but covered "sudden and accidental" events. See, e.g., Allstate Insurance Co. v. Klock Oil Co., 426 N.Y.S.2d 603, 604 (1980). Pollutants leaching into groundwater over many years, a typical CERCLA scenario, have proven hard to classify. Intra-insurer conflicts arise because of the durational aspect of the cases — CGL polices cover specific periods of time, but the leaking may have occurred over a period of years, implicating a whole series of insurance polices, which may have been issued by different insurers.

8. **Insolvency.** Insolvency issues have led the development of CERCLA into another area of law, that of bankruptcy. A fundamental tension exists between the remedial goals and aspirations of CERCLA and the objectives of bankruptcy law. One goal of bankruptcy law is to distribute the bankrupt's assets fairly among all of the creditors. A second objective is to provide the bankrupt with a fresh start, freed of the previous debts. In contrast, a central concern animating CERCLA is assuring the availability of sufficient resources for the cleanup of hazardous release sites. Accordingly, CERCLA has a strong interest in making all the bankrupt's assets, both present and future, available to remediate the hazards that the PRP bankrupt has helped to create. This CERCLA-based interest collides with bankruptcy law, when bankruptcy law seeks to protect co-creditors through a fair division of the available assets. Specifically, bankruptcy law gives preference to secured creditors over unsecured creditors such as the government would be in regard to a CERCLA

recovery. As a second matter, under normal bankruptcy law, the debtor can expect to be absolved from personal post-bankruptcy obligations relating to CERCLA liabilities. Congress did nothing to broker the competition between these two statutory children, CERCLA and the bankruptcy act, so that task has fallen to the courts. This seemingly narrow area of intersection has its own treatise. See, Kathryn R. Heidt, Environmental Obligations in Bankruptcy (1993).

### Section 5. PRIVATE LITIGATION UNDER CERCLA §107

Under §107(a)(2)(B), even non-governmental entities are accorded a remedy to recover for costs that are consistent with the National Contingency Plan (NCP).[15] In this way, CERCLA expressly authorizes private litigants to seek recoveries from PRPs. This cause of action is complementary to causes of action that may exist under the common law, for the allowable scope of recovery relates exclusively to costs that are incurred in the cleanup of a contaminated site. Items such as recovery for personal injuries, or loss of amenity value, remain the province of traditional actions in tort.

The typical scenarios of private §107 actions involve current owners of contaminated property as plaintiffs suing either former occupiers of the property, parties whose wastes were disposed of there, or parties whose wastes have migrated there.[16] In some cases, the current owner will already have been ordered to clean the site by the government; in other cases, the cleanup effort may have preceded governmental involvement. For some time there was ambiguity about whether costs could be incurred consistent with the NCP in advance of a governmentally-initiated investigation or cleanup order. That matter has been resolved by the courts in favor of broad recovery. See, e.g., Wickland Oil Terminals v. Asarco, Inc., 792 F.2d 887 (9th Cir. 1986).

The private cause of action under §107 has four basic elements: the plaintiff must prove that (1) the site in question is a "facility," (2) the defendant is a liable party under CERCLA §107(a), (3) a release or threatened release of a hazardous substance has occurred at the facility, and (4) the plaintiff has incurred response costs consistent with the NCP in responding to the release or threatened release. Given the broad readings given to CERCLA liability issues, the consistency (with the NCP) requirement has often been the most ardently litigated issue in private §107 suits.[17]

General Electric Co. v. Litton Industrial Automation Systems, Inc, 920 F.2d 1415 (1990), cert. denied, 111 S. Ct. 1390 (1991), a leading case on consistency with the NCP, concerned the merger by Litton with a former owner and occupant of land now owned by GE. From 1959 to 1962, during the occupancy of the company taken over by Litton, improper disposal of cyanide based electroplating wastes, sludges, and other pollutants had occurred on the parcel. In the early 1980s, GE and

---

15. The NCP is discussed more fully below. For present purposes, the NCP can be understood as a set of guidelines framed by the United States that delineate the proper procedures and actions that are to be taken in cleaning up a Superfund site.

16. Adversely affected adjacent landowners are also allowed to sue. See, e.g., Standard Equipment, Inc. v. The Boeing Co., No. C84-1129 (W.D. Wash. 1986).

17. See Steinway, Private Cost Recovery Actions Under CERCLA: The Impact of the Consistency Requirements, 4 TXLR 1364 (1990).

the Missouri Department of Natural Resources (MDNR) investigated the site and decided that no cleanup was necessary. In 1984, GE sold the site to a commercial real estate developer. Shortly thereafter, the MDNR changed its position on the need for a cleanup, at which point GE was threatened with CERCLA lawsuits by both its vendee and MDNR. Negotiations followed in which GE agreed to clean up the site and did so to the satisfaction of MDNR.

Thereafter GE sued Litton under §107. Litton's most vigorous defense was that the cleanup was not consistent with the NCP. The District Court ruled in favor of GE, awarding $940,000 as reimbursement for response costs and an additional $419,000 in attorneys' fees. See General Electric Co. v. Litton Business Systems, 715 F. Supp. 949 (W.D. Mo. 1989). In reviewing the critical finding that the costs incurred were consistent with the NCP despite having omitted some detailed requirements mentioned in the NCP, the court wrote:

> We are satisfied that the thorough evaluation that was performed here is consistent with the NCP, specifically with 40 CFR 300.65(b)(2). The site evaluation does not have to comply strictly with the letter of the NCP, but only must be consistent with its requirements. It is not necessary that every factor mentioned by the NCP be dealt with explicitly; thus, for instance, a failure to consider explicitly the weather conditions factor is not fatal to an evaluation's consistency with the NCP. 920 F.2d at 1420.

### COMMENTARY AND QUESTIONS

1. **The purpose of the consistency requirement.** Why must cleanups be consistent with the NCP to allow recovery in a §107 action? Why isn't the key issue whether the response action was effective? One answer was suggested by counsel for Litton in the oral argument in the Eighth Circuit when he indicated that defendants in private cost recovery suits need protection from parties that voluntarily perform "a Rolls-Royce cleanup when a Volkswagen one would do." See 5 TXLR 651 (1990). (The issue of "Cadillac cleanups" is discussed below.) On the other end of the scale, NCP-consistent cleanups are a means of guaranteeing that the effort is effective. Particularly under the new NCP, satisfying its requirements would help to ensure an effective cleanup and also involve community sentiment as a factor in the cleanup process.

2. **Standing in the shoes of the government.** In a private §107 action, should the plaintiff enjoy all of the same advantages (joint and several strict liability with a relaxed standard of causation) as the government does when it sues PRPs? In general, the cases seem to point in that direction. In Dedham Water Co. v. Cumberland Farms Dairy, Inc. 889 F.2d 1146 (1st Cir. 1989), for example, the appeals court reversed a ruling that had required the plaintiff to prove which of two possible sources had caused the contamination of its well that had given rise to CERCLA response costs. The court drew heavily on the liberal liability provisions of CERCLA to find that "a literal reading of the statute imposes liability if releases or threatened releases from defendant's facility cause the plaintiff to incur response costs; it does *not* say that liability is imposed only if the defendant causes actual contamination of the plaintiff's property." (Emphasis by the court.) Does it seem

odd to hold a party like Cumberland Farms liable when the facts as found by the trial court (and not overturned on appeal) were that two other nearby operations "were 'probable' causes" of the contamination of plaintiff's wells? Isn't this like the *Wade II* relaxed standard of causation that, in effect, treats all parties whose acts are potential causes of the pollution as being actual causes of the problem?

3. **Private CERCLA lawsuits seeking contribution.** Are all CERCLA §107 private actions in reality claims for contribution? The answer is clearly no because the plaintiff in a §107 suit will at times be a party who is not a PRP, such as an innocent neighbor like Dedham Water Company. Often, however, the plaintiff will be a PRP who has paid a disproportionate share and seeks to use a §107 action to vindicate the statutory right of contribution created by §113(f)(1). When the suit sounds in contribution, the issue of loss allocation includes assigning a share to the plaintiff, and the rote application of strict joint and several liability of defendants for the entire loss is no longer appropriate. In this context, the differences between private cost recovery and contribution have recently increased in importance. Case law has emerged that distinguishes private cost recovery suits filed under §107(a) and contribution actions filed under §113(f)(1). The principal reason to characterize a suit as one or the other is the posture of the party bringing the suit — are they an innocent victim of the contamination (§107 available) or a member of the PRP class (only §113 available). See, e.g., United Technologies Corp. v. Browning-Ferris Industries. 33 F.3d 96 (1st Cir. 1994); Akzo Coatings v. Aigner Corp., 30 F.3d 761 (7th Cir. 1994); In re Dant & Russell, 951 F.2d 246 (9th Cir. 1989). With the loss of cost recovery goes the loss of joint and several liability and a shift to an equitable contribution action in which the plaintiff (and all of the other parties) have to try to persuade the trier of fact of how responsibility ought to be apportioned. But there are other differences as well, including a different, and shorter (three years rather than six) statute of limitations.

4. **A reminder about state law remedies.** Even if it borders on redundancy, it is important to keep in mind the continuing availability of state statutory and common law remedies for environmental harms caused by hazardous materials. Despite the broad federal efforts to govern hazardous groundwater contamination, reflected in both RCRA and CERCLA, Congress was well aware that they were entering a field having a strong tradition of state regulatory and remedial primacy. Both RCRA and CERCLA contain provisions extending authority to states to enact additional more stringent measures.[18] Beyond that, §114(a) of CERCLA provides:

> Nothing in this chapter shall be construed or interpreted as pre-empting any State from imposing any additional liability or requirements with respect to the release of hazardous substances within such State.[19]

18. RCRA §3009, codified at 24 U.S.C.A. §6929; CERCLA §114(a), codified at 42 U.S.C.A. §9614(A).
19. Despite this expressly non-pre-emptive character, there are narrow areas of state legislative authority that are pre-empted by CERCLA and RCRA. These cases arise when states enact their own mini-Superfund laws and fund them via a tax like that used to fund CERCLA. See Exxon Corp. v. Hunt, 475 U.S. 355 (1986). There have also been cases pre-empting local regulation of RCRA-regulated waste handling facilities. See ENSCO Inc. v. Dumas, 807 F.2d 743 (8th Cir. 1986) (pre-empting local waste handling regulations that bar methods encouraged by RCRA). The pre-emption of common law by statutes is generally disfavored; the canon of statutory construction cautions that statutes in derogation of common law are to be narrowly construed.

5. **Attorney's fees awards in CERCLA cases.** As with so many CERCLA issues, the recoverability of attorney's fees as a part of 107(a)(4)(b) response costs is an issue not answered by the statute or its legislative history. The general argument in favor of allowing fee recovery looks at the statutory language as indicating a desire that all costs of remediation are covered, even those that are incurred in obtaining the remedy. At a policy level, the argument stresses that the remedial nature of the statute evidences congressional intent that plaintiffs who have incurred costs of any kind should be made whole. Standing in opposition to these arguments are more traditional notions grounded in the American rule against fee shifting. Eventually, this issue found its way to the United States Supreme Court. In Key Tronic Corp. v. United States, 511 U.S. 809 (1994), the Court ruled that CERCLA §107 does not provide for the award of private litigants' attorney's fees associated with bringing a cost recovery action.

## B. EPA'S ADMINISTRATIVE ORDER AUTHORITY

In creating CERCLA's liability rules, Congress empowered EPA to remediate contaminated sites itself, using federal money, and also allowed EPA to recover its expenditures from persons responsible for the contamination. In passing CERCLA, however, Congress also established another powerful mechanism for use by EPA in seeking to remediate contaminated sites. In CERCLA §106, Congress empowered EPA to bring administrative or judicial enforcement actions against responsible parties to force them to perform the remediation. EPA's administrative order authority provides EPA with perhaps its most potent enforcement tool (see Chapter 20). By its terms, §106 authorizes EPA to seek relief whenever it determines that a site "may" present "an imminent and substantial endangerment to public health or ...the environment." It authorizes EPA to issue "such orders as may be necessary to protect public health and welfare and the environment." The full text is as follows:

> **42 U.S.C.A. §9606 [original Act's §106]. Abatement actions... (a) Maintenance, jurisdiction, etc.** In addition to any other action taken by a State or local government, when the President determines that there may be an imminent and substantial endangerment to the public health or welfare or the environment because of an actual or threatened release of a hazardous substance from a facility, he may require the Attorney General of the United States to secure such relief as may be necessary to abate such danger or threat, and the district court of the United States in the district in which the threat occurs shall have jurisdiction to grant such relief as the public interest and the equities of the case may require. The President may also, after notice to the affected State, take other action under this section including, but not limited to, issuing such orders as may be necessary to protect public health and welfare and the environment....
>
> **(b) Fines; reimbursement.** (1) Any person who, without sufficient cause, willfully violates, or fails or refuses to comply with, any order of the President under subsection (a) of this section may...be fined not more than $25,000 for each day in which such violation occurs or such failure to comply continues....

Section 106 is often invoked by EPA to encourage PRPs to do more of the removal and remedial work at sites themselves. When a voluntary agreement to do so cannot be reached (or when a previous agreement is breached), EPA may require PRPs to respond. EPA states its policy as follows:

> EPA prefers to obtain private-party response action through the negotiation of settlement agreements with parties willing to do the work. When viable private parties exist and are not willing to reach a timely settlement to undertake work under a consent order or decree, or prior to settlement discussions in appropriate circumstances, the Agency typically will compel private-party response through unilateral orders. If PRPs do not comply with the order, EPA may fund the response or may refer the case for judicial action to compel performance and recover penalties. EPA, OSWER Directive No. 9833.0-1a at page 3 (March 7, 1990).

Section 106(a) administrative orders cannot be disobeyed without substantial risk. Section 106(b)(1) allows EPA to come to court and seek a fine of up to $25,000 per day against "[A]ny person who, without sufficient cause, willfully violates, or fails or refuses to comply with, any order...." Alternatively, pursuant to CERCLA §107(c)(3), EPA can undertake the action itself and then sue for reimbursement and statutory punitive damages *of up to three times the amount of the cost of the government action!* There is nothing in the statutory language to suggest that EPA cannot seek both the daily penalties and the punitive damages in cases where EPA eventually undertakes the work. See, e.g., U.S. v. Midwest Solvent Recovery, Inc., No. H-79-556 (N.D.Ind.), discussed at 5 Toxics L. Rep. 797 (Nov. 21, 1990).

Administrative orders are even more powerful because they are not subject to pre-enforcement review. CERCLA §113(h) explicitly provides that no federal court has jurisdiction "to review any challenges to...any order issued under §9606(a) [CERCLA §106(a)]...." The jurisdictional proviso lists a number of exceptions, only one of which can take place before the required action has been performed. That one exception is a suit brought by EPA to compel a remedial action. See CERCLA §113(h)(5). Courts interpret the law to prevent pre-enforcement review. In so doing, the courts have rejected constitutional attacks that challenge the Hobson's choice (take expensive action pursuant to an administrative order that you allege to be illegal, or risk a far more costly array of punitive sanctions if your post-cleanup attack on the order fails) as being a denial of due process. See, e.g., North Shore Gas Co. v. EPA, 753 F.Supp. 1413 (N.D.Ill. 1990), aff'd 930 F.2d 1239 (7th Cir. 1991); Aminoil, Inc. v. EPA, 599 F. Supp 69 (N.D.Cal 1984).

Defense of subsequent suits seeking sanctions for non-compliance with §106(a) orders is also difficult. The defendant-violator has the burden of proving that there was "sufficient cause" for non-compliance. This amounts to proving that either (1) the defendant was not a person to whom the order could have been issued (i.e., was not a PRP), or (2) the actions ordered were inconsistent with the NCP. Making the sufficient cause defense even harder to establish, at least one court has ruled that the defendant must, by objective evidence, prove that its belief in the invalidity of the order was held reasonably and in good faith. See Solid State Circuits, Inc. v. U.S., 812 F.2d 383 (8th Cir. 1987).

In connection with whether the defendant in a §106 Order is a proper PRP, most courts have concluded that §107 establishes the relevant liability principles both with respect to the identity of the parties and the applicable standard of liability. See, e.g., United States v. Price, 577 F. Supp. 1103, 1113 (D. N.J. 1983) (concluding that §106(a) is dependent upon the substantive liability provisions of §107).

### COMMENTARY AND QUESTIONS

1. **EPA's use of its §106 power.** Given the formidable §106 power, it might seem strange that EPA does not always make administrative cleanup orders its remedial method of choice. Walter Mugdan, EPA Deputy Regional Counsel for Region II, listed six reasons why EPA would still prefer to negotiate consent decrees for remedial (as opposed to removal) actions. These included setting the proper tone for the long-term relationship that is entailed in EPA supervision of a PRP conducted cleanup, rewarding volunteers (by working out fair agreements) and punishing recalcitrants, the Congressional policy favoring settlements, judicial supervision of court orders, the availability of CERCLA §122(l) civil penalties, and the availability of CERCLA §122(e)(3)(B) administrative subpoenas to compel testimony and the production of information. See, Mugdan, The Use of CERCLA Section 106 Administrative Orders To Secure Remedial Action, in ALI-ABA, Study Materials on Hazardous Wastes, Superfund, and Toxic Substances 601–03 (October 25–27, 1990).

2. **Punitive treble damages.** Despite its presence in CERCLA since original enactment in 1980, the treble damage remedy has not been frequently used. U.S. v. Parsons, 723 F. Supp. 757 (N.D. Ga. 1989), marked the first time that treble damages had been awarded for non-compliance with a CERCLA §106(a) order, although that remedy was being sought in 13 other pending cases.[20] After subsequent litigation over the issue of whether one of the Parsons defendants had made a good faith effort at compliance with the order, the court entered judgment for EPA in the amount of $2,260,173.72, based on proven EPA response costs of $753,391.24. EPA sought reconsideration of the award, arguing that it was entitled to both the response costs and the penalty. The District Court ruled against awarding EPA "quadruple" damages. U.S. v. Parsons, 738 F.Supp. 1436 (N.D. Ga. 1990), but was reversed on appeal, U.S. v. Parsons, 936 F.2d 336 (11th Cir. 1991).

3. **Agency leverage or abuse of power?** The power to seek treble damages for non-compliance with agency orders is, obviously, a powerful tool. How far can the agency go in threatening a treble damage claim as a means to obtain agreement on other matters? A case pending in New Jersey under its spill law raises this question. There the state Department of Environmental Protection (DEP) sought to have Mobil Oil Corp. sign an administrative consent order (ACO) that would govern Mobil's subsequent cleanup responsibilities at the site. Several of the provisions of the ACO were objectionable to Mobil, including limitations on judicial review and stipulated penalties for non-compliance with the order. When Mobil refused to sign the ACO the DEP threatened to interpret that refusal as a violation of a DEP "directive," the New Jersey spill act's equivalent to a §106 administrative order. See New Jersey v. Mobil Oil Corp., N. J. Sup. Ct., No. 33,408 (Mar. 20, 1991);

---

20. See "EPA Granted Damages for Company's Failure to Obey 106 Order To Perform Response Action," 4 Toxics L. Rep. 515 (Oct. 4, 1989).

the proceedings are described at 6 Toxics L. Rep. 1349-50 (Mar. 27, 1991). What is the gravamen of Mobil's legal claim? Being coerced to waive procedural rights certainly played a part.

4. **The common law, §106, and RCRA corrective action.** What does CERCLA §106 accomplish that the common law does not? Section 106 makes prospective relief routinely available. Under the common law, it is only the extraordinary case like *Wilsonville* that prevents a harm before it happens. Section 106 offers an extra-judicial remedy: EPA can go to court, but it can also issue its own administrative orders against polluters. RCRA §7003 also offers EPA an extra-judicial remedy. Under RCRA §7003, EPA can go to court (as in NEPACCO), but EPA can also issue "such orders as may be necessary to protect public health and the environment." However, RCRA corrective action is not governed by the same set of liability rules as CERCLA §106. For example, under RCRA, a party may, in connection with corrective action, move or excavate soil within a corrective action management unit (CAMU) without liability attaching. Movement of waste within a CAMU does not constitute treatment, storage, or disposal of hazardous waste under RCRA, does not constitute "land disposal" triggering RCRA hazardous waste disposal requirements, and does not "produce" hazardous waste implicating RCRA generator requirements. Under CERCLA, by contrast, a party which moves or excavates soils causing a release of hazardous substances, even if in connection with a required cleanup under §106, can nonetheless be held liable either as an operator (under CERCLA §107(a)(2)) or for accepting hazardous substances for transport to sites which it has selected (under CERCLA §107(a)(4)). See, e.g., Kaiser Aluminum & Chemical Corporation v. Ferry, 976 F.2d 1338 (9th Cir. 1992) (holding liable under CERCLA contractor hired to excavate land who spread contaminated soil over uncontaminated soil in the process).

## C. IDENTIFYING SITES, FUNDING, AND SETTING THE STANDARDS FOR CLEANUPS

CERCLA not only sets up liability rules enforceable under §106 and §107 but also creates an administrative system for environmental remediation — removing harmful materials improperly dumped into the environment over past years. In this context, what is important are matters of process and execution: identifying sites in need of environmental cleanups, setting priorities among the needed cleanup efforts, planning what actions are needed on a site-by-site basis, and ensuring that planned responses are properly executed. This process begins with a procedure for identifying and ranking the hazards posed by sites of hazardous materials contamination. On the basis of that hazard ranking system (HRS), CERCLA establishes a national priorities list (NPL) that then functions to ensure that the most dangerous sites are remediated first. CERCLA requires EPA to establish a National Contingency Plan, which is, in essence, a compendium of the standards and procedures for cleanups that will ensure an acceptable result. Cleanups are of two kinds: removals are short-term measures taken to minimize the dangers to health and the environment from emergency situations, whereas remedial actions are long-term efforts that attempt to rid the site of dangers on a permanent basis.

Generally, CERCLA's cleanup process has worked as expected.[21] The HRS has been used to identify sites and subsequently generate the NPL that serves as the principal means of dictating EPA's cleanup priorities. EPA, through a combination of Superfund money and PRP-funded response and remedial actions, has made progress in the remediation of numerous sites throughout the nation. Nevertheless, the cost and complexity of cleanups has made CERCLA an exciting and intensely fought aspect of hazardous materials regulation. There are literally billions of dollars to be paid by PRPs, as thousands of sites of hazardous material releases are remediated. For many lawyers representing PRPs, the problem is less one of environmental law than it is one of engaging in strategic behavior to minimize both the amount spent on cleanups and the share of the cleanup cost allocated to their clients. EPA, too, is engaged in a strategic process, whereby it seeks to accomplish as much of the massive cleanup job as it can with limited human and material resources.

Cleanup procedures are governed by the National Contingency Plan (NCP). According to CERCLA §105, in the NCP EPA is to "establish procedures and standards for responding to releases of hazardous substances, pollutants, and contaminants...." The statutorily mandated scope of the NCP includes methodologies that will identify sites in need of remediation, analyze the danger to health and the environment posed by releases and threatened releases, determine the scope and extent of needed remedial measures, and ensure that remedial actions are cost-effective.[22] The NCP must address such mundane matters as the procurement and maintenance of response equipment, and the qualifications of private cleanup firms that will be engaged to do the cleanup work on Superfund projects. More politically sensitive matters must also be covered by the NCP. These include the division of authority between the federal, state, and local governments in effectuating the plan, and the standards by which innovative cleanup technologies will be judged.[23]

The required priority ranking of sites in order of hazard (i.e., the HRS/NPL process) is also a part of the NCP. In this area, Congress has provided some general directions for EPA. EPA, for example, is required to revise the NPL to reflect new information about existing and additional sites.[24] Similarly, CERCLA specifies that the relative risk assessment under the HRS should include the extent of the population put at risk by the site, the hazard potential of the substances found at the site, the potential to contaminate groundwater or surface water that is used for

---

21. CERCLA's major miscalculation has been its gross underestimation of cleanup costs and recoupment rates. Estimates of the total cost for U.S. hazardous waste cleanup fall in the range of $300 to $700 billion. See Passell, Experts Question Staggering Costs of Toxic Cleanups, New York Times (national edition), Sept. 1, 1991, at page 1. Recoupment rates are not promising as a source of funding the program. For CERCLA's first decade of operation EPA had spent or obligated itself to expenditures totalling more than $4 billion, but had successfully recovered only $230 million from PRPs. See J. Acton, Understanding Superfund: A Progress Report 37, 46-47 (1989). In addition, EPA had either filed claims for, or sought prosecution by the Department of Justice for, recoveries that would total another $824 million.
22. CERCLA §105(a)(1)-(3), (7), 42 U.S.C.A. §9605(a)(1)-(3),(7).
23. CERCLA §105(a)(5)-(6), (9)-(10), 42 U.S.C.A. §9605(a)(5)-(6), (9)-(10).
24. CERCLA §105(a)(8), 42 U.S.C.A. §9605(a)(8).

either drinking water supply or recreation, the potential for direct human contact, the potential for the destruction of natural resources that affect the human food chain, state preparedness, and "other appropriate factors."[25]

Finally, the statute puts EPA in charge of obtaining the needed cleanups of sites on the NPL in ways that are consistent with the NCP. In this regard, EPA is empowered to (1) undertake cleanups itself, using Superfund monies, and to seek reimbursement from PRPs; (2) issue administrative orders to PRPs directing them to undertake cleanups; (3) seek court orders directing PRPs to undertake cleanups; or (4) use a combination of approaches.

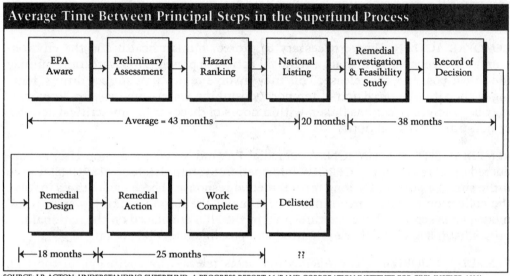

SOURCE: J.P. ACTON, UNDERSTANDING SUPERFUND: A PROGRESS REPORT 16 (RAND CORPORATION INSTITUTE FOR CIVIL JUSTICE, 1989).

After an uneven start,[26] EPA made extensive efforts to regularize Superfund procedures to ensure that all sites receive a thorough investigation and that decisions about remedial actions at each site are made by reference to consistent principles — focusing in each case on a site study document known as a Remedial Investigation/Feasibility Study (RI/FS). After the study and analysis is complete, EPA issues a record of decision (ROD) that selects the principal remedial actions to be taken. An even more detailed remedial design (RD) is prepared and, finally, remedial activity begins. The diagram above shows the major steps in the CERCLA process and the average duration of each of those steps.

25. CERCLA §105(a)(8)(A), (c)(2), 42 U.S.C.A. §(a)(8)(A), (c)(2).

26. During the Reagan presidency, when extensive government regulation and intervention was ideological anathema, EPA was not allowed to take an active role under Superfund. In fact, Superfund's misadministration by EPA in the early 1980s was a source of scandal, and several EPA officials were criminally prosecuted and convicted. This period in EPA's CERCLA history is recounted in detail in Mintz, Agencies, Congress, and Regulatory Enforcement: A Review of EPA Hazardous Waste Enforcement Effort, 1970–1987, 18 Envtl. Law 683, 715–43 (1988).

## Starfield, The 1990 National Contingency Plan — More Detail and More Structure, But Still a Balancing Act
### 20 Environmental Law Reporter 10222, 10228–10229, 10236–10241 (1990)

...A ROAD MAP TO THE CERCLA SITE RESPONSE PROCESS [SUBPART (E) OF THE NCP]: SITE DISCOVERY. The process begins with the discovery of a release by one of several possible mechanisms (e.g., notification requirements under CERCLA §103(a) or (b) under other laws, a petition from a citizen, etc.). In the case of an emergency (e.g., fire, explosion), a removal action will be taken to stabilize the site.

REMOVAL ASSESSMENT. In non-emergency situations, the release is evaluated to determine if a removal action is appropriate based on a removal preliminary assessment (PA) and, if appropriate, a removal site inspection (SI).

REMOVAL ACTION. Where necessary to protect human health and the environment, the Agency may initiate a removal action to prevent, mitigate, or minimize the threat posed by the release. This may involve removal of surface drums, fencing of the site, the provision of temporary drinking water supplies, etc. Removals may be emergency actions (taken within hours of discovery), time-critical actions, or non-time-critical actions.

REMEDIAL SITE EVALUATION. A remedial PA (and SI, where appropriate) is conducted on all sites in the CERCLA Information System database (CERCLIS), to see if the site is a priority for long-term remedial response. These evaluations involve the collection of data for scoring the site under the hazard ranking system (HRS) model; sites scoring above the threshold in the HRS are placed on the national priorities list (NPL) for further evaluation and possible remedial action.

REMEDIAL PRIORITIES. The Agency evaluates releases for inclusion on the NPL based on the HRS score or one of the other methods for listing outlined in the NCP. The Agency may spend Fund monies for remedial action only at those sites that are on the NPL. ("Fund-financed remedial action" does not include removal action or enforcement action.)

REMEDIAL INVESTIGATION/FEASIBILITY STUDY. The Agency will undertake a remedial investigation and feasibility study (RI/FS) at sites that are, or appear to be, priorities for action (i.e., that are on, or are proposed for listing on, the NPL). The RI/FS, like any other investigation conducted pursuant to CERCLA §104(b), is a removal action under CERCLA §101(23), despite the word remedial in its name.

During the RI, the nature and extent of the threat posed by the contamination is studied; concurrently, alternative approaches are developed as part of the FS for responding to and managing the site problem.

PRELIMINARY REMEDIATION GOAL. The first step in developing alternatives during the FS is the establishment of a preliminary goal for the remediation of the site. This goal is initially based on readily available information, such as chemical-specific applicable, relevant and appropriate requirements of other environmental laws (ARARs), or the "point of departure" in the range of acceptable risk. Alternatives are then developed that are capable of attaining the preliminary remediation goal. (The goal may be modified as additional information is developed.)

SCREENING OF REMEDIAL ALTERNATIVES. A broad list of alternatives is then reviewed and screened, with the more extreme, impracticable options being eliminated before the detailed analysis of alternatives begins. Alternatives may be eliminated during screening based on effectiveness, implementability, or "grossly excessive" cost.

ANALYSIS OF ALTERNATIVES USING THE NINE CRITERIA. The Agency then conducts a detailed analysis of the remaining alternatives (usually three to nine [of them], depending on the complexity of the problem). The advantages and disadvantages of the alternatives are studied and compared using the following nine remedy selection criteria:[27]

- Overall protection of human health and the environment,
- Compliance with (or waiver of) the ARARs of other laws,
- Long-term effectiveness and permanence,
- Reduction of toxicity, mobility, or volume through treatment,
- Short-term effectiveness,
- Implementability,
- Cost,
- State acceptance, and
- Community acceptance.

SELECTION OF REMEDY. The nine criteria are then used to select the remedy by evaluating them in three functional categories (threshold, balancing, and modifying criteria), in order to reflect the nature and/or timing of their application. The first two criteria — protectiveness and compliance with ARARs — are identified as threshold criteria; only the alternatives that meet those criteria may be carried forward.

Protective, ARAR-compliant alternatives are then "balanced" (i.e., used to evaluate tradeoffs) based on the middle five criteria (and the two modifying criteria, to the extent they are known). The Agency then attempts to select the remedial alternative that "utilizes permanent solutions and treatment...to the maximum extent practicable," and is "cost-effective" based on a comparison of the appropriate balancing or modifying criteria. Alternatives are judged cost-effective if their costs are "in proportion" to their overall effectiveness; an alternative is found to achieve the maximum permanence and treatment practicable based on a balancing of the seven nonthreshold criteria, with an emphasis on the factors of "long-term effectiveness and permanence" and "reduction in mobility, toxicity or volume through treatment."

EPA and the state then discuss the remedial options and issue a proposed plan, which sets out the lead agency's recommended alternative. Consistent with CERCLA §117, the public is afforded an opportunity to review and comment on the alternatives studied in the FS and the proposed plan. After review of and response to public comments, and formal consideration of the two modifying criteria (state and community acceptance), the final remedy selection is documented in a record of decision (ROD).

---

27. NCP §300.430(e)(9).

REMEDIAL DESIGN/REMEDIAL ACTION AND OPERATION AND MAINTENANCE. The lead agency then sets about designing, constructing, and implementing the selected remedy. Often, the remedial action plan set out in the ROD will need to be modified in light of information developed during the design phase (e.g., the Agency may learn that more soil is contaminated and needs to be excavated). If the remedial action to be taken differs "significantly" from the remedy selected in the ROD with respect to scope, performance, or cost, the lead agency will issue an explanation of significant differences (ESD). If the action to be taken "fundamentally alters" the basic features of the remedy selected in the ROD, the lead agency will propose and take comment on a ROD amendment.

Once the remedy is operational and functional (or later, for groundwater restoration remedies), the state undertakes responsibility for funding and carrying out operation and maintenance (O&M) of the remedy.

DELETION FROM THE NPL, FIVE-YEAR REVIEW. Once EPA has determined that no further response action is appropriate, the site may be proposed for deletion, or recategorized on the NPL, even where O&M is continuing. Sites at which hazardous substances remain above levels that allow for unlimited use and unrestricted exposure must be reviewed at least every five years after the initiation of the remedy (not merely after completion), consistent with CERCLA §121(c)....

RISK ASSESSMENT AND RISK RANGE... The NCP contemplates the use of risk assessments as an integral part of the process for developing remedial alternatives that are protective of human health and the environment.

Risk analysis begins during the early stages of the RI, when a "baseline risk assessment" is performed to evaluate the risk posed by a site in the absence of any remedial action. It is based on a comparison with this no-action risk level that the lead agency will target levels of risk that will be adequately protective of human health for a particular site. The baseline risk assessment also helps to provide justification for performing remedial action at the site.

Concurrently, the lead agency would begin to set a "preliminary remediation goal" as part of the FS. The preliminary remediation goal is an initial statement of the desired endpoint concentration or risk level, and alternatives are developed that are capable of meeting that goal. It is based on readily available information, such as chemical-specific ARARs (e.g., a drinking water standard), concentrations associated with the reference doses or cancer potency factors, or the point of departure for the Agency's acceptable risk range, discussed below....

Where environmental effects are observed, EPA sets remediation goals based on environmental ARARs (where they exist) and levels based on a site-specific assessment of what is protective of the environment.....

The use of a range of acceptable risk is general practice for most government programs. As discussed below in the section on role of cost, it affords the Agency the flexibility to take into account different situations, different kinds of threats, and different kinds of technical remedies. If a single risk level had been adopted (e.g., at the more stringent end of the risk range), fewer alternatives would be expected to pass the protectiveness threshold and qualify for consideration in the balancing phase of the remedy selection process....

ROLE OF COST. The role of cost in remedy selection has been one of the most hotly disputed issues in the Superfund program. Many PRP groups argue that cost must be a major factor in deciding on an appropriate remedy and note that the require-

STEVEN NOVICK

*An EPA aerial survey photograph of a New England toxic waste storage site. Many drums at this and similar sites are unmarked and leaking; some of the semi-trailers are filled with materials too unstable to be unloaded; site owners lack the resources required to maintain storage integrity or to clean up toxic contamination on the site.*

ment to select "cost-effective" remedies appears in CERCLA §121(a) and (b). Many environmentalists and some legislators have argued that cost is given too much emphasis in remedy selection and have posited that cost should be considered only in determining the cost-efficient method for implementing a selected remedy. In effect, they argue that the proper cleanup level for a site should be set, and then a remedy should be selected to attain that level, without consideration of cost....

Cost is specifically considered during the final balancing process, as the Agency attempts to satisfy two statutory mandates of CERCLA §121(b)(1) by identifying the remedial alternative that utilizes "permanent solutions and treatment ... to the maximum extent practicable" while being cost-effective. These determinations are intended to be made simultaneously; however, for ease of analysis, they are discussed separately in the NCP.

COST-EFFECTIVENESS. The determination whether a proposed remedial alternative is cost-effective is based on an evaluation of several of the nine criteria. First, overall effectiveness is assessed based on: long-term effectiveness and permanence; reduction of mobility, toxicity, or volume through treatment; and short-term effectiveness. The overall effectiveness is then compared to the cost of the alternative to determine if they are "in proportion" to one another (i.e., does the approach represent a reasonable value for the money?). In making this comparison, the decisionmaker is not directed by the NCP to place special emphasis on the factors of "reduction of toxicity, mobility or volume through treatment" and "long-term effectiveness and permanence," as is required during the assessment of permanence and treatment to the maximum extent practicable (as provided in NCP §300.430(f)(1)(ii)(E)). However, because "effectiveness" is measured based on those two factors (plus short-term effectiveness), an alternative that is high in treatment and permanence will be considered more effective and thus can justify a relatively higher cost (high effectiveness and high cost would be in proportion). The comparison of cost to effectiveness is performed for each alternative individually and for all the alternatives in relation to one another. This latter analysis allows the Agency to identify alternatives that produce an incremental increase in effectiveness for a reasonable increase in cost, based on a comparison of corresponding increases for other alternatives. Several alternatives may be found to be cost-effective....

COST AND PRACTICABILITY. The statutory requirement to select the alternative (there is only one) that utilizes permanence and treatment to the maximum extent practicable is fulfilled by selecting the protective, ARAR-compliant alternative that provides the best balance of tradeoffs among alternatives based on a review of all the balancing and modifying criteria (if the latter are known). It is a subjective judgment, but the NCP sets out some parameters to help assure consistency in its application. Specifically, the NCP requires that during the balancing process, the factors of long-term effectiveness and permanence and reduction in toxicity, mobility, or volume should be emphasized, and that the "preference for treatment as a principal element" and the "bias against off-site land disposal of untreated wastes" must be considered. This statutory determination is the final step in the process before a remedy is recommended in the proposed plan.

Although cost, as one of the nine criteria, is considered in making this determination, it is not expected to play a major role. The importance of almost every other criterion to this determination is emphasized by the NCP....

COST AS A SCREEN. Cost may also be considered during one other aspect of the remedy selection process: screening, when alternatives that are deemed not to be viable are eliminated from more thorough consideration. The use of cost at this early stage has also been the subject of considerable comment. Many were concerned that cost would be used to screen out appropriate remedial technologies early in the process before they were given a fair evaluation and without the benefit of public review and comment.

The final NCP has been revised to narrow the circumstances under which cost may be considered when screening alternatives at the start of the evaluation process. Specifically, the final rule provides that a given alternative may be eliminated during screening if it is determined that the cost of the alternative is "grossly excessive" compared with its effectiveness. This provision will allow the Agency to avoid the need to conduct resource-intensive analyses of extreme and unrealistic options, while at the same time not allowing cost to compromise consideration of viable options that may simply be more expensive than other alternatives....

### COMMENTARY AND QUESTIONS

1. **The slow pace of CERCLA remediation**. Are you surprised at the overall average of 10+ years of time elapsed between EPA's initial discovery of a potential site's existence and completion of cleanup? With the exception of the period of time needed to do the site remediation, all of the stages seem to be longer than necessary, especially the five years that go by at the front end of the process in which the only real activity is making preliminary assessments and obtaining a hazard ranking score. Acton's study suggests a number of factors that may combine to explain the slow pace. These include a lack of aggressiveness by EPA, the complexity of the Superfund program, delays caused while legal interpretations of various portions of the law are obtained, program rigidity, the litigious atmosphere surrounding the program, uncertainty about the efficacy of remedies, and shortages of critical personnel.

Would the pace of Superfund remediation be improved by EPA's adopting standardized procedures to be used at all of the sites? In an apparent effort in this direction, EPA promulgated model language in 1991 for use in all consent decrees that govern the RI/FS and the RD/RA processes, in an attempt to "reduce transaction time and costs." See 6 Toxics L. Rep. 151 (1991). How does standardized language improve the pace of negotiations? In theory, standardization reduces the number of items which are subject to bargaining and thereby makes it easier for parties to reach agreement. Lawyers for PRPs, however, were quick to criticize the proposals as too one-sided in favor of EPA. They felt that the new terms would deprive PRPs of so many of the benefits of settlement as to have the perverse effect of discouraging settlements.

2. **Lead agencies and PRP-led activities**. Part of the problem that EPA has faced in administering CERCLA is the burden of too much work to be done by too few people. The NCP addresses this problem by allowing EPA to delegate "lead agency" status to a state, political subdivision of a state, or Indian tribe that EPA finds to have adequate ability and enforcement authority (under state or tribal law) to carry

out a NCP-consistent removal or remedial action. EPA is also authorized to allow PRPs to conduct many of the phases of the CERCLA process, including, for example, performing the RI/FS,[28] or doing the actual site remediation work. In instances where PRPs take the lead role, EPA remains the official lead agency. The work is done by the PRPs pursuant to a court or administrative order, or in accordance with an express agreement with EPA.

3. **The vital points in the process.** While it is probably fair to say that all of the steps in the remediation process are important, the RI/FS and ROD stages stand out as the points at which the site-specific remedy is selected. Remedy selection determines many of the issues that people care most about. For the affected community, the remedy selection determines the extent to which the hazard will be eliminated. For the PRPs, the remedy selection commits the EPA to having a particular type and amount of work done, the cost of which will be borne by the PRPs. By statute, the RI/FS and ROD process is designed to allow input from states and affected communities as well as from PRPs and the EPA itself. Toward that end, the statute authorizes EPA to make grants of up to $50,000 to affected communities for hiring experts to make community participation in the RI/FS and ROD process more effectual.[29]

4. **The forces that govern EPA's NCP-based decisionmaking.** One commentator has suggested that EPA is driven by several factors in addition to the operating legal criteria of the NCP when it makes its decisions about site remediation. These factors include "(a) the large costs that must be borne by either the fund...or responsible parties if complete and thorough cleanups are to be implemented, (b) pressure from the Office of Management and Budget to minimize the costs to American industry, (c) the political need to proceed more quickly with cleanups at Superfund sites because of the perceived failures of the Reagan Administration, (d) the technical complexity of making decisions about health and environmental harm from contaminants that may be left at the site after cleanup, and, (e) the legal requirements of Superfund that structure how these cleanup standards shall be set." Brown, EPA's Resolution of the Conflict Between Cleanup Costs and the Law in Setting Cleanup Standards Under Superfund, 15 Colum. J. Envtl L. 241 (1990). Assuming that Brown has identified correctly the mix of pressures that govern EPA's decisionmaking, how would they affect remedy selection in a typical case? Using both historical and legal analysis, and an illuminating case study of ROD selection, Brown concludes that the complexity of the technical issues surrounding the postremedial effects of a remedial plan mask the selection of "remedies that only partially mitigate the impact of the site on the environment" despite legal requirements that the remedy selected must be fully protective of health and environment. Id. at 301. As a cure for this phenomenon, Brown suggests (1) clear congressional definition of "how clean is clean," and (2) allowing RODs that explicitly rely on excessive cost and engineering infeasibility as justifications for selecting a remedy that merely mitigates, but does not completely remediate, environmental harm at the site.

---

28. See CERCLA §104(a), 42 U.S.C.A. §9604(a).
29. See CERCLA §104(c)(2), §113(k)(2), §117, 121(f); 42 U.S.C.A. §9604(c)(2), §9613(k)(2), §9617, §9621(f).

5. **Challenging EPA's decisions**. Congress provided for judicial review of EPA's remedy selection process. The key provisos governing judicial review are a limitation on the scope of review to the administrative record,[30] and setting "arbitrary and capricious" as the standard of review.[31] Interested parties can participate in the building of the administrative record,[32] and EPA must give reasonable notice of the proceeding to identifiable interested parties, including PRPs and the affected community. Do these procedures give interested parties a meaningful opportunity to participate in the remedy selection process? See Friedman, Judicial Review Under the Superfund Amendments: Will Parties Have Meaningful Input to the Remedy Selection Process?, 14 Colum. J. Envtl L. 187 (1989).

6. **ARARs (applicable, relevant, and appropriate requirements) as cleanup standards**. ARARs function in a very real sense as cleanup standards, defining how thorough the remedial action must be in its efforts to eliminate environmental hazards at the site. Why does the NCP place so heavy a reliance on ARARs? At a minimum, the borrowing of environmental standards from other areas of the law relieves EPA and the NCP of redundant proceedings concerning contaminant issues that have already been fully determined in other environmental regulatory processes. Simultaneously, by employing the ARARs concept, issues of competing applicability of parallel standards do not arise because there is only one standard to apply.

One of the more perplexing ARARs problems has been whether the exceedingly stringent land disposal regulations of RCRA, the hazardous wastes management statute, are applicable as ARARs at CERCLA sites. Paradoxically, RCRA's treatment standards can, if applicable as ARARs, require EPA to elect a less complete remedial action due to the great cost associated with treatment in accordance with RCRA standards. See Chapter 17.

7. **The "Superfund syndrome."** In a congressionally mandated study of the Superfund process and experience, the Congressional Office of Technology Assessment (OTA) described what it called the "Superfund syndrome":

> Public fears of toxic waste and toxic chemicals set high expectations for Superfund; site communities perceive substantial risks to their health and environment and they want effective and stringent cleanups from EPA, regardless of cost; but communities have experienced slow, incomplete and uncertain cleanups. EPA tries to limit fund-financed cleanups by getting parties held liable for sites to voluntarily pay for cleanups. However, responsible parties often believe that their liabilities are largely unfair, that risks are not as bad as communities think they are, that cleanup objectives are unnecessarily stringent, and, therefore, that they must work hard to minimize their cleanup costs.[33]

Is this snapshot of differing perspectives and attitudes toward Superfund consistent with the picture of it that you have obtained from the materials and your own

---

30. CERCLA §113(j)(1), 42 U.S.C.A. §9613(j)(1).

31. CERCLA §113(j)(2), 42 U.S.C.A. §9613(j)(2).

32. CERCLA §113(k), 42 U.S.C.A. §9613(k).

33. Congressional Office of Technology Assessment, Coming Clean: Superfund Problems Can Be Solved... 3 (1984).

experience? Can the syndrome be eliminated by small changes at the margin of the Superfund program, or are major changes needed? OTA concluded that fundamental changes were needed in three broad areas: health and environmental protection priorities and goals; workers and technology; and government management.

8. **The staggering cost of "Cadillac" cleanups.** In a provocative article, Peter Passell quotes a noted economist as saying, in reference to how thorough hazardous waste cleanups should be, "Everybody wants a Cadillac as long as someone else is paying."[34] To illustrate the impact of that attitude on CERCLA cleanups, Passell gives the example of the options available for remediating one small (in area) Missouri Superfund site. An expenditure of $71,000 could permanently isolate the contaminants at the site and prevent any exposure from ever reaching the community; an expenditure of $3,600,000 could clean up virtually all hazardous material residues and bury any remaining traces under a blanket of clay; an expenditure of $41,500,000 could remove and incinerate the 14,000 tons of contaminated soil and building materials at the site. EPA selected a mix — incineration of the most severely contaminated materials, and clay-lined on-site disposal of the remainder, at a cost of $13,600,000.

Under the NCP, is each of these options sufficiently protective of health and environment? What are the advantages of the more expensive approaches? The most obvious difference between the low-end and high-end choices is that the high-end choices return the site to suitability for renewed use. As a matter of social policy, is spending $10 million to reclaim a few acres in Missouri a wise investment of resources? Can the predictable local opposition to anything less than a total cleanup (recall Professor Sandman's outrage factor in risk assessment, in Chapter Two) be ignored? Two possibilities raised by economists are to make local citizens help pay for "Cadillac" cleanups, or rebate to local communities a percentage of the difference between such a cleanup and a "merely" functional one.

9. **How much will this cost?** The Congressional Budget Office, in a February, 1994 report entitled, "The Total Cost of Cleaning Up Nonfederal Superfund Sites," offered a series of estimates of the total outlays likely to be spent at nonfederal Superfund sites. It made low-end, middle, and high-end projections as follows:

| PROJECTION | # OF NPL SITES | COST (IN 1992 $) | COMPLETED BY YEAR |
|---|---|---|---|
| Low-end | 2,300 | $ 42 billion | 2047 |
| Middle | 4,500 | $ 75 billion | 2060 |
| High-end | 7,800 | $120 billion | 2075 |

If these figures are not sufficiently disconcerting, remember that they do not include cleanups at federal sites, such as the Rocky Mountain Arsenal, which appear to be multi-billion dollar problems in their own right. Also remember that the calculation in 1992 dollars means that future expenditures are inflation-

---

34. See Passell, Experts Question Staggering Costs of Toxic Cleanups, New York Times (national edition), Sept. 1, 1991, p.1, at 28.

adjusted and discounted, so, for example, the $75B mid-range figure represents the present discounted value of actual future outlays of $230B (also in 1992 dollars). Perhaps in an effort to underscore the need for a change in Superfund policy, the report expressly states that it assumes no changes in present policy, and no limits on authorized spending. It also does not make any adjustment for technological changes that may improve cleanup efficiencies.

10. **And just who is paying?** The staggering amounts of money that are needed for CERCLA cleanups has to come from somewhere, but where? For almost a decade and a half, the answer was that the polluter-pays principle was going to be invoked with a vengeance. Given the way CERCLA's liability scheme works, especially with the almost inescapable imposition of joint and several liability on PRPs, PRPs appear likely to pay almost all of the costs. For the most part, the Superfund itself will pay only in those cases where no financially solvent, jointly and severally liable PRPs can be identified. Moreover, recall that the Superfund is funded primarily by a tax on chemical feedstocks, so the chemical industry takes a hit beyond its PRP, share and the public at large escapes the cost.

With a small administrative flick of the pen in June 1994, however, the public share has suddenly leaped to nearly one-third of the future expense. That major shift in financial burden occurred when the Internal Revenue Service (IRS) issued Revenue Ruling 94-38 concerning the deductibility of CERCLA cleanup costs. See Internal Revenue Bulletin 1994-25 (June 20, 1994). Up until that point, IRS had taken the position that cleanups were to be capitalized as part of the land — that is, the expense of cleanup was to be added to the taxpayer's basis in the asset, its cost of acquiring the land and maintaining its value for sale. Thus, under the previous IRS position, the only effect cleanup expenditures would have on the taxpayer's tax liability would come into play when the land was sold. The profit (if any) on the sale of the land would be less and therefore the tax liability then would be less. Under Revenue Ruling 94-38, however, cleanup costs, except those that are incurred for the construction of an ongoing treatment facility, are now fully deductible under §162 of the Internal Revenue Code as ordinary business expenses of the year in which the costs are incurred. This means that the immediate tax liability of the affected firm is greatly reduced. Consider this example: In 1994, profitable Major Corporation A spends $100,000 on CERCLA cleanup. The present level of the corporate tax is 35%. With the $100,000 now being deductible, A's 1994 net profit is now $100,000 less and its tax liability is $35,000 less. This is money that the federal treasury no longer receives for the benefit of the general public.

11. **CERCLA as the model for the Oil Pollution Act of 1990.** Galvanized into action by the Exxon Valdez oil spill in 1989, Congress enacted the Oil Pollution Act of 1990 (OPA '90),[35] which integrated and strengthened prior federal law covering liability for and cleanup of oil spills. Modelled on CERCLA, OPA '90 establishes a billion dollar Oil Spill Liability Trust Fund financed by the imposition of a five cents per barrel tax on oil delivered at the refinery. Owners and operators of vessels and onshore and offshore facilities are strictly liable for cleanup and natural resource

---

35. Pub. L. No. 101-380 (1990).

damages, subject to the defenses of (1) act of God, (2) act of war, or (3) negligence of a third party not associated with the owner or operator. Facilities must develop spill prevention, control, and countermeasure (SPCC) plans, have them approved by EPA or the Coast Guard, and implement them, or face heavy civil and criminal penalties. Single-hull tankers are to be phased out, and licensing and supervision of officers and seamen are strengthened. The OPA '90 explicitly does not preempt state oil spill laws.

**12. Superfund's more recent scorecard.** As part of recent congressional hearings, EPA Administrator Carol Browner was called upon to announce the Clinton Administration position on Superfund. Her statement of May 12, 1993 to a Senate subcommittee was not overly revealing, but did sound some new notes. She began with a barrage of statistics intended to demonstrate a pattern of increasing EPA activity and success in moving NPL sites through the several phases of the Superfund process. The roll call was impressive, including over 3000 removal actions at over 2600 sites including all 1200 currently on the NPL, RI/FSs "underway or completed at almost 1200 sites, remedies selected at 800 sites, remedial designs underway or completed at nearly 700 sites, and remedial actions underway or completed at nearly 500 sites." Beyond that, 54 sites had been delisted, that is, cleaned to the point that they merited removal from the Superfund system. On the money side, Browner emphasized EPA's recent success with what it euphemistically calls an "Enforcement First" policy. "Enforcement First," initiated in 1989, simply means that "EPA attempts to get responsible parties to perform cleanups before it uses taxpayer dollars to perform the cleanup itself." Over the life of Superfund, and especially in recent years, PRPs have committed to pay more than $7.4 billion. PRP-led work is now running at 72% of remedial action work, up from 32% in 1988. In somewhat less precise terms, Administrator Browner also explained that Superfund was influencing corporate and municipal behavior by inducing voluntary cleanup actions and waste minimization efforts. Further, she cited a significant degree of technological innovation in the cleanup industry as both improving the cost-effectiveness of cleanups and as a product that will be available for export to other nations.

Administrator Browner also identified areas in which the Clinton Administration is displeased with the Superfund program. Here she noted that:

> we are paying a high price in terms of administrative and cleanup costs incurred by EPA, and a high price in terms of the transaction and cleanup costs incurred by companies and state and local governments potentially liable for contamination. We are paying a high price in terms of uncertainty and wasted time. We are paying a high price in terms of basic fairness —or unfairness — of the program. Finally, we are paying a high price in terms of the anxiety and frustration of local communities concerned about delays in cleaning up contaminated sites.

In detailing the nature of the complaints about Superfund, Administrator Browner highlighted transaction costs, municipal liability fairness concerns, the possibility that cleanups in minority areas are being handled differently (and less advantageously for the residents than cleanups in majority areas), and the volatile question of "How clean is clean?"

13. **Documenting Superfund's inefficiency; a/k/a the high cost of lawyers.** A 1992 Rand Corporation study found very high transaction costs under Superfund. See Jean Paul Acton & Lloyd S. Dixon, Superfund and Transaction Costs (1992). For large private sector PRPs studied in their report, transaction costs during the 1984-89 period were 21% of their Superfund outlays, with the bulk of that money being spent on legal representation. Id. at 56. For insurance companies, many of whom seemed insistent on litigating every conceivable coverage issue to the death, transaction costs were astronomical. Of an estimated $470 million spent industrywide on claims related to inactive hazardous waste sites in 1989, Acton and Dixon found that 88% ($410 million) went to transaction costs, of which $200 million was expended on coverage disputes with policy holders and $175 million was spent on defending policy holders in litigation, with the remaining $35 million going to internal insurance company overhead. Id. at 24, 30-32.

How damning is this data? Is it simply an indication that insurance companies have made a living off of litigation in the past (i.e., reducing outlays by contesting them) and are doing so again in the hazardous waste liability area? The study offers some evidence of that. In other areas of general liability insurance, transaction costs tend to run high also, including areas having few coverage disputes. For example, Acton and Dixon note that a major insurance industry reporting service found industry wide transaction costs as high as 42% for medical malpractice liability claims and 32% for more general liability claims (such as homeowners). These costs occur in areas where there is seldom extended coverage litigation. This permits a comparison to hazardous waste claims. If the coverage dispute costs are deleted from the Superfund findings, they are still out of line: lawyers are still getting the lion's share of the money, by a ratio of almost 3:1 over indemnity payments actually made. The comparable ratios of transaction costs to indemnity payments are .7:1 and .5:1 for malpractice and general liability respectively.

14. **Natural resource damage.** CERCLA §107(a)(4)(C), provides for the recovery of natural resource damage caused by the release of hazardous materials. The federal government, the states (and their subdivisions), and Indian tribal governments are designated as trustees empowered to sue for those damages by §107(f). While natural resource damage claims have, to date, been secondary to those involving cost recovery, they represent a "sleeping giant," because the potential liability can be enormous.

Section 301(c) of CERCLA authorized the Department of Interior to promulgate regulations for the assessment of natural resource damages, although trustees may seek to establish an alternative measure of damages in any particular case. See, 43 C.F.R. §11.10.[36] However, a rebuttable presumption of validity attaches to those assessments conducted in accordance with Interior's regulations, and, accordingly, trustees have a significant incentive to conduct their assessments pursuant to Interior's rules.

---

36. Congress authorized recovery of natural resource damages under both CERCLA and the Oil Pollution Act, 42 U.S.C.A. §9651(c). Under the Oil Pollution Act (OPA), the National Oceanic and Atmospheric Administration ("NOAA") promulgates regulations for natural resource damage assessments.

The most significant issue in the natural resource damages context involves the appropriate measure of damages. In Ohio v. United States Department of Interior, 880 F.2d 432 (D.C. Cir. 1989), Ohio challenged Interior's regulation providing that natural resource damages shall be the "lesser of" (1) restoration or replacement costs, or (2) lost-use-value. The court invalidated the "lesser of" rule, holding that Congress established a distinct preference for restoration cost as the measure of recovery in natural resource damage cases. The court also concluded, however, that there might be some cases where other considerations — such as infeasibility of restoration or grossly disproportionate cost to use value — might warrant a different standard. Thereafter, in March, 1994, Interior issued revisions to its rules, eliminating the "lesser of" rule and replacing it with a requirement that the trustee consider a wide array of "restoration" alternatives and select the most appropriate one. See 43 C.F.R. §11.83. Interior stopped short of requiring significant active restoration in every case. The rule specifically contemplates that included among the "restoration" alternatives to be considered must be one that relies on "natural recovery with minimal management actions." 43 C.F.R. §11.83(c).

The rule lists ten factors to be considered in selecting from among restoration alternatives:

(1) Technical feasibility; (2) the relationship of the expected costs of the proposed actions to the expected benefits from the restoration, rehabilitation, replacement, and/or acquisition of equivalent resources; (3) cost-effectiveness; (4) the results of any actual or planned response actions; (5) the potential for additional injury resulting from the proposed actions, including long-term and indirect impacts, to the ... injured resource or other resources; (6) the natural recovery period; (7) the ability of the resource to recover with or without alternative actions; (8) any potential effects of the action on human health and safety; (9) consistency with applicable Federal and State and tribal policies; and (1) compliance with applicable Federal, State and tribal laws. 43 C.F.R. §11.83(d).

Recent decisions of the D.C. Circuit have now upheld most elements of Interior's regulations, specifying the procedures that are sufficiently "reliable and valid" for trustees to use in calculating their damage assessments. See Kennecott Utah Copper Corp. v. U.S. Department of the Interior, 88 F.3d 1191, 1217 (D.C. Cir. 1996) (upholding Interior's natural resource damage assessment regulations to allow public trustees to consider acquisition of equivalent resources equally with strategies for restoration or replacement of natural resources); General Electric Co. v. Department of Commerce, 128 F.3d 767 (D.C. Cir. 1997) (upholding NOAA final rule concerning liability for natural resource damages arising from oil spills under OPA.)

**15. The end of Superfund as we know it.** After almost two decades, Superfund has accomplished much of its primary business. The worst, most contaminated sites nationwide have been identified and cleanups are either completed or well underway at almost all of them. The remaining sites tend to be less contaminated, more localized in character, and are often located in urban areas. The extremely cumbersome CERCLA process ill fits many of these sites, and more and more of them are being remitted to state-run voluntary cleanup programs that operate with greater PRP input and under cleanup standards that often take planned future use of the parcel into account. This trend is more fully addressed in Chapter 20 in relation to brownfields redevelopment.

## D. EPA'S STRATEGY FOR COST RECOVERY AND LOSS ALLOCATION

EPA is charged with many responsibilities in the hazardous waste arena, including its responsibility not only to obtain cleanups at NPL sites, but also to ensure that the burden of paying for those cleanups falls on PRPs rather than the Superfund itself. Although it was understood that the Superfund would have to absorb the costs of cleanups of orphan sites where no solvent PRPs could be identified, the mandate to assign the cost of cleanups to the PRPs is a central feature in CERCLA's structure.

THE COSTS OF COST RECOVERY... The problems facing EPA in husbanding the monies of the Superfund and running the cost recovery program can be divided into three distinct categories. Perhaps the most rudimentary problem is cash flow. If the average cleanup spans a ten-year period, and EPA is expending funds at a large number of NPL sites from the investigatory stages onward, the fund may get depleted before §107 cost recovery actions can replenish it. Second, years of experience with the cost recovery program have revealed that the program has a surprisingly low rate of recovery. Finally, EPA has a severe staffing problem in both the site management and cost recovery aspects of its operations. The site management staffing problem is simply a lack of sufficient trained and experienced personnel to ensure that sites are cleaned up in the proper manner. The cost recovery staffing problem arises in large part as a result of the nature of CERCLA cases. In most instances, NPL sites involve numerous PRPs with substantial liabilities. The high stakes create a sufficient incentive for PRPs to fight hard to limit their losses on many fronts. They will also be inclined to challenge EPA decisions regarding selection of expensive cleanup measures. PRPs try to minimize EPA's assessment of their contribution to the site, contesting the accuracy of EPA's particular "Waste-In" lists,[37] and the identification of materials found at the site as belonging to them rather than some other PRP. Even though PRPs are almost always held to be jointly and severally liable for cost recoveries,[38] they are given a statutory right of contribution[39] and may join their cross-claims for contribution to EPA's cost recovery suit. The effort to sort out comparative responsibility has the potential to make each of the cost recovery suits a quagmire for all involved. Finally, even when the

---

37. A "Waste-In" list is a computer printout generated by EPA after extensive detective work on each site, collecting much data on who dumped what, based on identifiable barrels, trucking invoices, interviews with workers, corporate records, etc. Based on the list, EPA sends out PRP liability notices, sometimes to hundreds of potentially liable addressees.

38. Recall that courts have found that joint and several liability will not be applied in the event that the PRPs can show that the harm is divisible or that there is an appropriate basis on which to apportion liability.

39. CERCLA §113(f), 42 U.S.C.A. §9613(f).

cost allocation issue is absent, experience in all fields of law has shown that complex multiparty litigation invariably imposes massive burdens on all of the parties involved.

Lawsuits prosecuted under RCRA §7003 and CERCLA §§106 and 107 have proven particularly burdensome and expensive to litigate, to the extent that litigation at times proves to be counter productive. A great deal of money is spent that might otherwise be directed toward remediation of toxic contamination. For example, in United States v. Conservation Chemical Co., 628 F.Supp. 391 (W.D. Mo. 1985), the cost of continuing to litigate the case was estimated to exceed the cost of the proposed remediation at the site. On the basis of that letter, the court allowed time for settlement negotiations which eventually resulted in an agreement that was upheld over the objections of non-settling PRPs.

### COMMENTARY AND QUESTIONS

1. **The likelihood of settlement**. Assume that a site presents a complex groundwater remediation problem. How often will a settlement be achieved? The special facts of the *Conservation Chemical* case noted above and litigation costs substantially in excess of cleanup costs are the hallmarks of a case that should be settled, but how often will that happen? The key factors will include the cost of the cleanup, the sheer number of PRPs, their solvency, the accuracy of the "waste-in" list, and, perhaps, the negotiating strategy of the parties. The high costs of litigation can act as an inducement to settlement. Lowering the total cost, such as by obtaining EPA approval of a PRP-managed cleanup, can also improve the chances of settlement, as noted more fully below. Settling PRPs are protected against additional liability and may seek contribution from non-settling PRPs. See also Bernstein, The *Enviro-Chem* Settlement: Superfund Problem Solving, 13 ELR 10402 (1983).

2. **Settlements and administrative orders as cures for Superfund solvency issues and litigation burdens.** In order to preclude the cash flow and low recovery rate problems, EPA has tried to reduce outlays of monies from the Superfund by increasing the amount of the cleanup work done by the PRPs (or their contractors) rather than by contractors hired by EPA. One means for shifting the costs to PRPs has been to enter into settlements with PRPs in advance of cleanup that place the full anticipated present and future costs on the PRPs. This method of proceeding has the additional advantage of avoiding two types of staffing problems. PRP-led cleanups require EPA oversight, but that is a far more modest task than managing the cleanup. Similarly, by settling in advance of litigation, the burdens of complex litigation are greatly reduced.[40] A second avenue toward increasing the amount of cleanup work done by PRPs is to require that PRPs do the work pursuant to administrative order, a power expressly granted to EPA by Congress. This power is limited to cases where a release or threatened release of hazardous material poses "an

---

40. Litigation is not wholly avoided. At times, settlements will be reached after litigation is initiated but before it has matured. At other times, settlements will be reached with less than all of the PRPs, leaving EPA to litigate with the remaining PRPs. See, e.g., O'Neil v. Picillo, below.

imminent and substantial endangerment to public health or welfare or the environment...."[41] Given the nature of Superfund sites, few, if any, do not pose such a danger.

3. **Congressional guidelines for EPA settlements.** Owing to the abuses of the Superfund program in the early years of the Reagan administration, Congress, when it reauthorized CERCLA in 1986, added extremely detailed provisions that were intended to support EPA's pursuit of settlements while keeping a check on EPA to be sure that the settlement process was administered in an even-handed way. See CERCLA §122, 42 U.S.C.A. §9622. EPA has fully complied with the directive and has promulgated a whole series of guidance documents that announce EPA settlement policies and procedures, discussed below.

4. **PRP letters — the invitation to the dance.** One of the rituals of Superfund enforcement is the way in which many of EPA's actions are begun. After identifying a site and compiling a list of PRPs, EPA mails letters informing PRPs of their (unhappy) status and inviting them to a forthcoming meeting, usually at a large meeting hall or hotel ballroom near the site. At that meeting, EPA typically presents its waste-in list and a summary of what the agency knows about the site, and then tells the assemblage that they have a few hours to organize themselves into groups for the purpose of negotiating settlements with EPA. The EPA representatives then depart, returning after a few hours to begin discussions with the various newly-formed PRP groups. If settlements are not reached within sixty days, the period for negotiation (unless extended for an additional sixty days by EPA) is over and EPA will file suit or issue administrative orders. Is this reliance on PRPs to organize themselves on such short notice a good procedure to follow in complex Superfund cases? Are brutally short deadlines appropriate and necessary?

### O'Neil v. Picillo
United States Circuit Court of Appeals for the First Circuit, 1989
883 F.2d 176, cert. denied 110 S. Ct. 1115 (1990)

COFFIN, J. In July of 1977, the Picillos agreed to allow part of their pig farm in Coventry, Rhode Island to be used as a disposal site for drummed and bulk waste. That decision proved to be disastrous. Thousands of barrels of hazardous waste were dumped on the farm, culminating later that year in a monstrous fire ripping through the site. In 1979, the state and the Environmental Protection Agency (EPA) jointly undertook to clean up the area. What they found, in the words of the district court, were massive trenches and pits "filled with free-flowing, multi-colored, pungent liquid wastes" and thousands of "dented and corroded drums containing a veritable potpourri of toxic fluids." O'Neil v. Picillo, 682 F. Supp. 706, 709, 725 (D.R.I. 1988).

This case involves the State of Rhode Island's attempt to recover the clean-up costs it incurred between 1979 and 1982 and to hold responsible parties liable for all future costs associated with the site. The state's complaint originally named thirty-five defendants, all but five of whom eventually entered into settlements totalling $ 5.8 million, the money to be shared by the state and EPA. After a month-long bench trial, the district court, in a thorough and well reasoned opinion, found

---

41. See CERCLA §106(a), 42 U.S.C.A. §9606(a). That same subsection authorizes EPA to initiate litigation seeking injunctive relief to the same effect.

three of the remaining five companies jointly and severally liable under §107 of CERCLA for all of the State's past clean-up costs not covered by settlement agreements, as well as for all costs that may become necessary in the future. The other two defendants obtained judgments in their favor, the court concluding that the state had failed to prove that the waste attributed to those companies was "hazardous," as that term is defined under the Act.

Two of the three companies held liable at trial, American Cyanamid and Rohm & Haas, have taken this appeal. Both are so called "generators" of waste, as opposed to transporters or site owners. See §107(a)(3), 42 U.S.C. §9607. Neither takes issue with the district court's finding that some of their waste made its way to the Picillo site. Rather, they contend that their contribution to the disaster was insubstantial and that it was, therefore, unfair to hold them jointly and severally liable for all of the state's past expenses not covered by settlements....

JOINT AND SEVERAL LIABILITY: STATUTORY BACKGROUND... It is by now well settled that Congress intended the federal courts to develop a uniform approach governing the use of joint and several liability in CERCLA actions. The rule adopted by the majority of courts, and the one we adopt, is based on the Restatement 2d of Torts: damages should be apportioned only if the defendant can demonstrate that the harm is divisible.

The practical effect of placing the burden on defendants has been that responsible parties rarely escape joint and several liability, courts regularly finding that where wastes of varying (and unknown) degrees of toxicity and migratory potential commingle, it simply is impossible to determine the amount of environmental harm caused by each party. It has not gone unnoticed that holding defendants jointly and severally liable in such situations may often result in defendants paying for more than their share of the harm. Nevertheless, courts have continued to impose joint and several liability on a regular basis, reasoning that where all of the contributing causes cannot fairly be traced, Congress intended for those proven at least partially culpable to bear the cost of the uncertainty.

In enacting the Superfund Amendments and Reauthorization Act of 1986 (SARA), Congress had occasion to examine this case law. Rather than add a provision dealing explicitly with joint and several liability, it chose to leave the issue with the courts, to be resolved as it had been — on a case by case basis according to the predominant "divisibility" rule first enunciated by the *Chem-Dyne* court [572 F. Supp. 802 (S. D. Ohio 1983)]. Congress did, however, add two important provisions designed to mitigate the harshness of joint and several liability. First, the 1986 Amendments direct the EPA to offer early settlements to defendants who the Agency believes are responsible for only a small portion of the harm, so-called *de minimis* settlements. See §122(g). Second, the Amendments provide for a statutory cause of action in contribution, codifying what most courts had concluded was implicit in the 1980 Act. See §113(f)(1). Under this section, courts "may allocate response costs among liable parties using such equitable factors as the court determines are appropriate." We note that appellants already have initiated a contribution action against seven parties before the same district court judge who heard this case.

While a right of contribution undoubtedly softens the blow where parties cannot prove that the harm is divisible, it is not a complete panacea since it frequently will be difficult for defendants to locate a sufficient number of additional, solvent parties. Moreover, there are significant transaction costs involved in bringing other responsible parties to court. If it were possible to locate all responsible parties and to do so with little cost, the issue of joint and several liability obviously would be of only marginal significance. We, therefore, must examine carefully appellants' claim that they have met their burden of showing that the harm in this case is divisible....

REMOVAL COSTS... The state's removal efforts proceeded in four phases, each phase corresponding roughly to the cleanup of a different trench. The trenches were located in different areas of the site, but neither party has told us the distance between trenches. Appellants contend that it is possible to apportion the state's removal costs because there was evidence detailing (1) the total number of barrels excavated in each phase, (2) the number of barrels in each phase attributable to them, and (3) the total cost associated with each phase. In support of their argument, they point us to a few portions of the record, but for the most part are content to rest on statements in the district court's opinion. Specifically, appellants point to the following two sentences in the opinion: (1) "I find that [American Cyanamid] is responsible for ten drums of toxic hazardous material found at the site"; and (2) as to Rohm & Haas, "I accept the state's estimate [of 49 drums and 303 five-gallon pails]." Appellants then add, without opposition from the government, that the ten barrels of American Cyanamid waste discussed by the district court were found exclusively in Phase II, and that the 303 pails and 49 drums of Rohm & Haas waste mentioned by the court were found exclusively in Phase III. They conclude, therefore, that American Cyanamid should bear only a minute percentage of the $995,697.30 expended by the state during Phase II in excavating approximately 4,500 barrels and no share of the other phases, and that Rohm & Haas should be accountable for only a small portion of the $58,237 spent during Phase III in removing roughly 3,300 barrels and no share of the other phases. We disagree.

The district court's statements concerning the waste attributable to each appellant were based on the testimony of John Leo, an engineer hired by the state to oversee the cleanup. We have reviewed Mr. Leo's testimony carefully. Having done so, we think it inescapably clear that the district court did not mean to suggest that appellants had contributed only 49 and 10 barrels respectively, but rather that those amounts were all that could be positively attributed to appellants.

Mr. Leo testified that out of the approximately 10,000 barrels that were excavated during the four phases, only "three to four hundred of the drums contained markings which could potentially be traced." This is not surprising considering that there had been an enormous fire at the site, that the barrels had been exposed to the elements for a number of years, and that a substantial amount of liquid waste had leaked and eaten away at the outsides of the barrels. Mr. Leo also testified that it was not simply the absence of legible markings that prevented the state from identifying the overwhelming majority of barrels, but also the danger involved in handling the barrels. Ironically, it was appellants themselves who, in an effort to induce Mr. Leo to lower his estimate of the number of barrels attributable to each defendant, elicited much of the testimony concerning the impossibility of accurately identifying all of the waste.[42]

---

42. Appellants contend that the state's record keeping was subpar.... In the context of this case, the state's failure to document its work during Phase I was harmless error since Mr. Leo testified that even when the state made an effort to identify the barrels, it could rarely do so.

In light of the fact that most of the waste could not be identified, and that the appellants, and not the government, had the burden to account for all of this uncertainty, we think it plain that the district court did not err in holding them jointly and severally liable for the state's past removal costs. Perhaps in this situation the only way appellants could have demonstrated that they were limited contributors would have been to present specific evidence documenting the whereabouts of their waste at all times after it left their facilities. But far from doing so, appellants deny all knowledge of how their waste made its way to the site. Moreover, the government presented evidence that much of Rohm & Haas' waste found at the site came from its laboratory in Spring House, Pennsylvania and that during the relevant years, this lab generated over two thousand drums of waste, all of which were consigned to a single transporter. Under these circumstances, where Rohm & Haas was entrusting substantial amounts of waste to a single transporter who ultimately proved unreliable, we simply cannot conclude, absent evidence to the contrary, that only a handful of the 2,000 or more barrels reached the site.[43]

Appellants have argued ably that they should not have been held jointly and severally liable. In the end, however, we think they have not satisfied the stringent burden placed on them by Congress. As to all other issues, we affirm substantially for the reasons set out by the district court. Appellants should now move on to their contribution action where their burden will be reduced and the district court will be free to allocate responsibility according to any combination of equitable factors it deems appropriate. Indeed, there might be no reason for the district court to place any burden on appellants. If the defendants in that action also cannot demonstrate that they were limited contributors, it is not apparent why all of the parties could not be held jointly and severally liable. However, we leave this judgment to the district court. See, e.g., Developments, Toxic Waste Litigation, 99 Harv. L. Rev. 1458, 1535–43 (1986). Affirmed.

## COMMENTARY AND QUESTIONS

1. **The unfairness of joint and several liability**. Although the proofs in the case are riddled with uncertainty, assume for a moment that the amounts actually contributed to the Picillo site by Cyanamid and Rohm & Haas were little more than the 59 identifiable barrels, and that they were present in only one of the four trenches. Those companies are now liable for all past and future costs at the site not paid by other PRPs. Although the court does not make the point explicitly, the unpaid past costs plus all future costs could amount to millions of dollars beyond the $5.8 million already recovered through settlement with other PRPs. (In fact, Cyanamid and Rohm & Haas were subsequently found liable for $3.5 million in addition to $1.5 million they had already paid.[44]) Both Cyanamid and Rohm & Haas are large, well-financed companies and can pay the amount due. To whatever

---

43. Even if it were possible to determine how many barrels each appellant contributed to the site, we still would have difficulty concluding that the state's removal costs were capable of apportionment.... Appellants have proceeded on the assumption that the cost of removing barrels did not vary depending on their content. This assumption appears untenable given the fact that the state had to take added precautions in dealing with certain particularly dangerous substances.... Moreover... because there was substantial commingling of wastes, we think that any attempt to apportion the costs incurred by the state in removing the contaminated soil would necessarily be arbitrary.

44. The additional liability figure was reported at 5 Toxics L. Rep. 289 (Aug. 1, 1990). The attorney for the two firms, in a conversation with one of the editors, noted the prior payment as well.

extent that amount (under the present assumptions of limited contribution of materials to the site) is grossly disproportionate to their responsibility for causing the problems at the site, the operation of joint and several liability seems unfair.

The court refers on several occasions to the possibility that subsequent contribution actions by Cyanamid and Rohm & Haas will remedy the unfairness of being held liable for an overly large share of cleanup costs. This may be disingenuous on the part of the court. The possibility of obtaining contribution in this case was limited because the other parties whom EPA identified as PRPs had settled with the government, and these settlements act as a defense to contribution actions. Cyanamid and Rohm & Haas have filed a contribution action against an additional 17 parties, whom they allege should also be held to be PRPs.[45] The contribution case progressed slowly while O'Neil v. Picillo was still being fought.

2. **The unfairness of uncertainty.** The unfairness in this case appears to be exacerbated by the actions taken by Rhode Island in cleaning up the site in a way that leaves so much uncertainty about whose wastes were actually present at the site. The court, in essence, answers this complaint by claiming that Congress intended PRPs — as the ones who had benefitted from inadequate disposal practices — to bear the risk of occasionally unfair allocations rather than thrusting that risk onto the Superfund. Does the potential unfairness to PRPs of poorly managed cleanups help to explain why the NCP standards for cleanups are so elaborate?

3. **Seeking fairer alternatives.** Even if Cyanamid and Rohm & Haas can justly claim unfairness, are there better alternatives to arming EPA with joint and several liability and placing the burden on PRPs to show divisibility of harm? One family of alternatives, the insistence on the traditional rules of liability, seems to leave EPA and the Superfund without any means by which to shift the loss to PRPs. Forcing EPA to meet traditional cause-in-fact standards, for example, would result in minimal cost recoveries whenever a highly accurate "waste-in" list doesn't exist. In the Picillo pig farm case the cost recovery would have been only a small percentage of the total amount expended. In the end this burdens the taxpayers who, comparatively speaking, are surely more "innocent" than any of the PRPs. A more promising avenue is to consider ways in which costs that cannot be attributed to any particular PRP might be shared among the PRP group, rather than thrust upon a single PRP using joint and several liability. The law has generally made this attempt in regard to contribution actions, which are studied in the materials that follow.

4. **Contribution among PRPs.** In light of strict liability and the difficulty of proving that the toxic cleanup harm can be apportioned, PRPs increasingly are faced with the certainty that, if sued under CERCLA, they will lose and be held jointly and severally liable for all recoverable costs. In the event that a party pays the entire loss, the appropriate course of action is to seek to shift all or part of the loss to other PRPs via contribution.[46]

---

45. American Cyanamid Co. v. King Industries, No. 87-0110 (D. R.I. Feb. 27, 1990).

46. Indemnity may also be a possibility. CERCLA itself creates no general right of indemnification in favor of one responsible party against another. Indemnity is available under traditional common law doctrines, such as granting indemnity pursuant to contractual indemnity agreements, or permitting a party that is only passively responsible to seek indemnity from parties that are actively responsible for harm or loss.

Congress directs the courts to apply a federal law of contribution under §113(f)(1) of CERCLA "using such equitable factors as the court determines are appropriate." One of several commentators who have addressed this subject summarizes federal practice to date:

> Recent cases suggest that federal courts are creating a federal common law of contribution that follows the Restatement [Second of Torts], §886A, and apportions liability according to a modified comparative fault approach that incorporates equitable defenses as to mitigation of damages, and the multi-factor approach suggested by the [unenacted] Gore Amendment [to CERCLA].[47]

The Restatement (Second) of Torts §886A provides generally that in actions for contribution joint tortfeasors cannot be held liable for more than their equitable share. Its key language provides:

> (2) The right of contribution exists only in favor of a tortfeasor who has discharged the entire claim for the harm by paying more than his equitable share of the common liability, and is limited to the amount paid by him in excess of his share. No tortfeasor can be required to make contribution beyond his own equitable share of the liability.

In its commentary on the "method of apportionment," the Restatement identifies two approaches, either pro rata contribution or something along the lines of a comparative fault determination.

The pro rata (equal shares) approach has its roots in the equitable maxim that, "Equality is equity." A pro rata share, moreover, is easy to calculate. The total amount paid in the CERCLA case is divided by the number of parties who were found jointly and severally liable.[48] An equal sharing of costs may be fair in some cases, but the typical CERCLA case involves PRPs having markedly different degrees of responsibility for conditions at the site. Some may have minimal volumes of relatively benign wastes at the site while others have been major contributors to the problem. If the PRP selected by EPA to pay the judgment is in the former category, a pro rata recovery on the contribution claim is unsatisfactory.

To obtain a non-pro rata basis for contribution the party seeking that result has to provide the court with a reasonable alternative basis on which to apportion responsibility. Even using the Gore Amendment factors, that task has a Catch-22 quality about it. Recalling that joint and several liability was imposed initially because of the great difficulty of apportioning responsibility among PRPs, PRPs with only a

---

47. Comment, Contribution Under CERCLA: Judicial Treatment After SARA, 14 Colum. J. of Envtl. L. 267, 278 (1989). [The Gore Amendment, though never enacted, has nevertheless been applied as persuasive analysis by the courts. Eds.] The factors in the Gore Amendment that facilitate a comparative approach include (1) the extent to which the defendant's level of contribution to the problem can be distinguished, (2) the amount of hazardous waste involved, (3) the degree of toxicity of the hazardous waste involved, (4) the degree of involvement by the parties in the generation, transportation, treatment, storage or disposal of the hazardous waste, (5) the degree of care exercised, taking into account the characteristics of the hazardous materials involved, and (6) the degree of cooperation of the party with public officials in working to prevent harm to public health or the environment. See 126 Cong. Rec. 26,781 (1980). See also Garber, Federal Common Law of Contribution under the 1986 CERCLA Amendments, 14 Ecology L.J. 365 (1987); Dubuc & Evans, Recent Developments Under CERCLA: Toward a More Equitable Distribution of Liability, 17 Envtl. L. Rep. 10197 (1987).

48. If some of the jointly liable parties are unable to pay their shares due to insolvency, the usual rule is that the shares of all remaining parties are increased.

small share of the responsibility face an unpleasant paradox: they could get contribution (on other than a pro rata basis) if the harm could be apportioned, but they are being held jointly liable precisely because the harm cannot be apportioned.

The availability of contribution, even properly apportioned, is not a panacea for PRPs who have paid more than their "fair share." The PRP who pays the judgment to the government will find that co-PRPs who settled with EPA or the state are immune to suits for contribution. In 1986, Congress added §113(f)(2) to CERCLA establishing the effect of settlement on settling parties' subsequent liability for contribution:

> A person who has resolved its liability to the United States or a State in an administrative or judicially approved settlement shall not be liable for claims for contribution regarding matters addressed in the settlement. Such settlement does not discharge any of the other potentially liable persons unless its terms so provide, but it reduces the potential liability of the others by the amount of the settlement.

5. **Catch-22 revisited.** The seemingly empty promise of non-pro rata contribution described in the text overstates to some extent the problem of apportionment among the PRPs in contribution suits. The rationale for creating a de facto presumption that CERCLA site harms are not divisible in government suits for cost recovery is the congressional policy of imposing the cost of cleanups on PRPs rather than on the Superfund. In the contribution suit, no party comes to the court with a preferred position. All of the PRPs are partly responsible for the harm and none is entitled to preferential treatment as a matter of statutory policy; thus the court in the contribution suit will seek to do whatever is most equitable. In that apportionment setting, it is as if no party has the burden of proof on the apportionment issue.[49]

6. **Congressional intent on encouraging settlements.** Why did Congress grant contribution protection to settling PRPs? The answer has almost nothing to do with contribution and a great deal to do with encouraging settlement. In a settlement, a settling PRP pays only once, an amount that both the PRP and the government think fairly represents the settlor's liability. Absent contribution protection, the settling PRP is at risk of later being held liable for contribution in judgments arising in other subsequent cases, which would reduce the benefits of settling. Settlement without contribution protection would not fix for all time the amount of liability, would not preclude the expense of litigation (e.g., for defense on the merits in contribution actions), and it would not offer any respite from the possibility of greater liability that inheres in litigation.

7. **EPA's use of contribution protection as a sword.** Can EPA use §113(f)(2) to coerce parties into settlements? Settling PRPs are free of any contribution responsibility, so if EPA enters into "sweetheart" settlements (i.e., settlements that do not recover a fair proportion of the total liability in relation to the responsibility of settling

---

49. If this seems unclear, consider the following analogy of the burden of proof to elections. In the government's action, a PRP seeking to be held liable only on a several basis must, because of the Congressional policy favoring recoveries by the government, win by a clear majority. In the subsequent contest (the contribution lawsuit) among the PRPs, none of whom enjoy a congressionally-favored position, the contest can be won by a mere plurality.

PRPs for expenses at the site), non-settling PRPs will inevitably end up paying a disproportionate share. EPA generally does not want to act in ways that are arbitrary and unfair, but making strategic use of legal rules in furtherance of the legitimate policy of seeking to promote settlement is not arbitrary. As you will see in the next section, EPA has been able to make settlements attractive even without offering over-lenient terms.

8. **State law analogies, and pitfalls in obtaining contribution**. Although relatively little has been said in this chapter about parallel state cleanup laws — often called spill laws or polluter-pay laws — at times they impose even harsher consequences than CERCLA on parties who pay for cleanups. A recent New Jersey Supreme Court decision dismissed the appeal of the present owner of a parcel who had cleaned up a toluene contamination site under the New Jersey Environmental Cleanup Responsibility Act,[50] a strict liability statute that requires owners to remedy contamination before they can transfer the parcel. The present owner sought contribution from other parties, including the former owner of the parcel who had contributed to the toluene pollution. The owner was not able to invoke the benefits of strict and joint and several liability in its contribution suit against the past owner.[51] Instead, it had to carry the ordinary common law burdens of proof on the issues of causation and severability of harm in order to recover against the former owner. See Superior Air Products v. NL Industries, 522 A.2d 1025 (N.J.Super. Ct. App. Div. 1987), appeal dismissed, No. 32,106 (N.J.S.Ct. Apr. 4, 1991); see also 5 Toxics L. Rep. 1455 (1991).

9. **Strategic EPA behavior in seeking settlements**. EPA can do a great deal to encourage settlement. Consider its tool set: §106 orders, contribution protection, control of the remedy selection process, and, of course, the ability to use Superfund monies to remediate the site and seek to impose §107 liability. Are there policies EPA could adopt that would reward settling PRPs and punish "recalcitrants"? Could EPA manipulate the way it accounts for the possibility of undiscovered pollution, or cleanup cost overruns? The short answer to both of these questions is in the affirmative. In fact, EPA has developed explicit policies in this area. PRPs who find these policies unfair to them, are most often left with futile lawsuits in which they are challenging a consent decree being entered into by EPA and the settling PRPs. See, e.g., United States v. Cannons Engineering Corp., 720 F.Supp. 1027 (D. Mass. 1989).

---

*"If seven maids with seven mops,*
*"Swept it for half a year,*
*"Do you suppose," the Walrus said,*
*"That they could get it clear?"*
*"I doubt it," said the Carpenter,*
*And shed a bitter tear.*

— Lewis Carroll, Through the Looking Glass, 1871

---

50. N.J. Environmental Cleanup Responsibility Act (ECRA), 13 NJSA § 13:1K-6 (1983).

51. Had the state been prosecuting the cleanup action under the New Jersey Spill Compensation and Control Act, every "discharger" of contaminants would have been jointly and severally strictly liable. This would have included the former property owner.

# PART FIVE

# COMPLIANCE, ENFORCEMENT, AND
# DISPUTE RESOLUTION MECHANISMS

OUT-OF-DOORS, n. That part of one's environment upon which no government has been able to collect taxes. Chiefly useful to inspire poets....

— Ambrose Bierce, The Devil's Dictionary

# Chapter 19

# CRIMINAL PROSECUTION

A. *Tactical Rediscovery of Criminal Provisions: The 1899 Refuse Act*
B. *An Increasing Willingness to Prosecute Environmental Crimes*
C. *Criminal Liability: Problems of Knowledge and Intent*
D. *Problems Raised in Corporate and Executive Prosecutions*
E. *Regulatory Prosecutions and the Effect of Federal Sentencing Guidelines*

Criminal punishment is an ancient societal instinct, levying fines, imprisonment, and corporal punishments including death. In legal process terms the criminal law is often a crude blunt instrument, in comparison to civil remedies, yet even in highly developed modern regulatory systems the force of the criminal law remains an important functional component. In environmental law, despite its highly developed civil and administrative complexity and the growing culture of compliance within the industrial community, the importance of criminal law appears to be increasing rather than shrinking.

Prior to the 1960s, virtually no criminal law was applied to environmental cases. In the Allied Chemical Kepone disaster in the 1970s chronicled in Chapter One, the prospect of criminal fines was raised by the federal Refuse Act, and ultimately the company had to pay substantial fines under the newly-amended federal Clean Water Act, but no one went to jail. In the Woburn case in the late 1980s the federal government used evidence from the private lawsuit to hit one of the defendant companies with $10,000 in criminal fines for perjury in failing to report toxic discharges. In *Smithfield Packing* in the late 1990s, the Smithfield official who destroyed environmental records — not a life-threatening act — went to jail for 30 months on felony charges. Convicted environmental defendants today face actual personal time in jail as well as punitive fines that may be quite large and cannot be charged to insurance or deducted from income taxes as business expenses.

Criminal law seeks to punish bad actors in order to accomplish several different public policy objectives not so directly involved in civil law —

- incapacitation (the prevention of repeat offenses by holding perpetrators in prison or controlled probation),
- specific deterrence, by making the defendant apprehensive about future conduct,
- general deterrence, by showing other potential culprits that crime does not pay,

- revenge and retribution, through physical and fiscal punishment, for defendants' bad actions, and

- rehabilitation (although in some settings this is merely theoretical)

Regulatory enforcement attorneys consider the utility of potential criminal charges in designing their enforcement agendas, despite the increased difficulties of proof. All the listed rationales for criminal punishment can apply in environmental prosecutions, and to the list should be added the club-in-the-closet function: for environmental regulatory agencies, the background threat of criminal sanctions against violators strongly reinforces negotiations on administrative civil penalties, and compliance.

Criminal prosecutions, more than civil, reflect the governing moral climate of the moment. Criminal law was enlisted in legal efforts to protect the environment when a broadened environmental consciousness infiltrated the general public. Although for some Americans "Throw the bums in jail" was always at least as natural as "Sue the bastards" as a gut reaction to many pollution controversies, only since the 1980s have environmental prosecutions ceased being rare occurrences. They are and probably will remain a small proportion of the environmental litigation total, although the broad availability of criminal punishment remains important practically as well as conceptually. Often criminal proceedings proceed parallel to civil proceedings brought by citizen plaintiffs or the government, with obvious tactical consequences.

The initial rarity of criminal prosecutions for environmental violations was not based upon a lack of criminal law on the books. States have always had general crimes like battery and homicide that could have been applied, and most of the major federal environmental statutes contain criminal penalty provisions along with civil penalties. Many other state and federal penal laws with potential application to environmental cases, particularly those in the area of public health, still lie virtually unused. Nevertheless, criminal law prosecutions of environmental offenses play a special role in the legal system's response to problems of pollution and environmental quality. Whether that role is ultimately effective, or well-advised, however, is the subject of some continuing debate.

## A. TACTICAL REDISCOVERY OF CRIMINAL PROVISIONS: THE 1899 REFUSE ACT

Here is an illuminating example of how criminal laws lingering on the statute books can have dramatic application in the environmental setting.

In the 1960s, when environmental activists following the lead of Rep. Henry Reuss of Wisconsin discovered the 1899 Refuse Act (passed in 1899 as a part of the Federal Rivers and Harbors Appropriation Act of that year), they read its terms with pleased anticipation:

### §407 Deposit of Refuse in Navigable Waters Generally

It shall not be lawful to throw, discharge, or deposit or cause, suffer, or procure to be thrown, discharged, or deposited either from or out of any ship, barge, or

other floating craft of any kind, or from the shore, wharf, manufacturing establishment, or mill of any kind, any refuse matter of any kind or description whatever other than that flowing from streets and sewers and passing therefrom in a
liquid state, into any navigable water of the United States, or into any tributary of
any navigable water from which the same shall float or be washed into such navigable water, [or] on the bank of any navigable water, where the same shall be liable
to be washed into such navigable water...whereby navigation shall or may be
impeded or obstructed: *Provided*, That...the Secretary of the Army, whenever in
the judgment of the Chief of Engineers anchorage and navigation will not
be injured thereby, may permit the deposit of any material above mentioned in
navigable waters, within limits to be defined and under conditions to be prescribed
by him....

### §411. Penalty for Wrongful Deposit of Refuse: Use of or Injury to Harbor Improvements, and Obstruction of Navigable Waters Generally

Every person and every corporation that shall violate or that shall knowingly
aid, abet, authorize, or instigate a violation of the provisions of...this title shall be
guilty of a misdemeanor, and on conviction thereof shall be punished by a fine not
exceeding $2,500 nor less than $500, or by imprisonment (in the case of a natural
person) for not less than thirty days nor more than one year, or by both such fine
and imprisonment...one-half of said fine to be paid to the person or persons giving
information which shall lead to conviction.

### COMMENTARY AND QUESTIONS

1. **The Refuse Act in the 1960s.** Upon the discovery of the Refuse Act, a number
of prosecutions were begun across the country, as United States District Attorneys
responded to the 1960s explosion of environmental consciousness in the media
and the electorate. In part the Refuse Act's strategic novelty was due to the fact
that it even existed as an actionable pollution statute, not that it was criminal.
Most activists in the 1960s had presumed that there were no existing environmental laws with teeth in them, and that legal action would therefore have to
await further legislative action. Instead, prosecutors were able to go immediately
against a wide range of defendants, from small dumpers to major corporations,
obtaining convictions quickly and decisively, and levying substantial fines. The
American Chamber of Commerce and the National Association of Manufacturers
began to urge repeal of the drastic Refuse Act. The Comprehensive Federal Water
Pollution Control Act of 1972 took over most of the Refuse Act's pollution coverage. For a time, however, the Refuse Act was undoubtedly the nation's most direct
and effective environmental statute.

2. **Ease of prosecution.** If you were an environmentally-minded U.S. Attorney in
the 1960s, and the Refuse Act was brought to your attention along with bottles and
samples of muck from a particular water pollution outfall pipe, why would you
find your case against the suspect dumper so easy to prove? Note first of all the
geographical scope of the statute. To what geographical areas does it *not* apply? To
what polluting materials does it apply? Is it clear that it applies to liquid pollutants? All liquid pollutants? And what are the elements of the criminal offense?
Virtually no dischargers had obtained a permit from the U.S. Army Corps of

Engineers. Not much more had to be proved. The Supreme Court helped by holding, in U.S. v. Republic Steel, 362 U.S. 482, 491 (1960), that the Act meant what it said in plain words: pollution was "refuse," and where there were doubts, the Act should be read "charitably in light of the purpose to be served." (What *was* the 1899 Act's purpose?) What about the question of criminal "mens rea" or intent? Section 411 contains the requirement that defendants who aid and abet must be acting "knowingly," but that seems to apply only to aiding and abetting, not to direct violations of §407. To what extent can we punish persons who didn't know what they were doing was wrong? What does "knowing" mean? Does it mean that a person was not acting unconsciously? Does it mean that a defendant must know that she does not have a permit and that federal law requires one? These questions are considered later in this chapter.

3. **Citizen prosecution — qui tam?** If federal (and potentially state) prosecutors decline to prosecute a particular action, for whatever prosecutorial discretion reason, the violation is unlikely to be criminally prosecuted. In some circumstances citizens attempted to obtain prosecution of particularly egregious polluters by seeking to file qui tam actions themselves against polluters. The qui tam action is a traditional remedy by which a citizen can bring a law suit "in the name of the King," particularly where the citizen has a direct personal stake in the prosecution. The potential reward offered in §411 of the Refuse Act appears to be sufficient to establish a standing basis for citizen prosecutors. As it happened, the courts were generally inhospitable to citizen qui tam actions under the Refuse Act, so that initiation of prosecution depended upon political, social, and media pressures applied to prosecutorial authorities. Most qui tam suits have failed, but cf. Alameda Conservation Association v. California, 437 F.2d 1087 (9th Cir. 1971), cert. denied, 402 U.S. 908 (1971).

4. **Statutory interpretation issues.** What is "refuse"? If it includes pollution (which is indeed a leap of sorts), what about the argument that it does not include oil spills, because oil is a valuable commodity that is not being disposed of as waste, but rather was lost by accident? See U.S. v. Standard Oil Company, 384 U.S. 224 (1966). As the courts developed the doctrines of the Refuse Act, ultimately even temperature changes came to be regarded as "refuse" and thereby violations of the statute.

What does the Refuse Act teach you about the life history of statutory enactments? Industrial corporations were the primary targets of Refuse Act prosecutions in the 1960s. Is there any question in your mind what would have happened if someone had told the Congress in 1899 that the statute would be applied against manufacturers producing liquid pollution wastes?

A criminal statute is a potent piece of legislatively-created law. It is, however, both a crude blunt instrument and a relatively unguided missile. The words that it embodies continue to be law while surrounding circumstances may change. The legislators who write a statute do not thereafter act as judges determining how it should be applied; the separation of powers sees to that. If the words of the statute are perfectly clear, its application follows, even seventy years after the statute was written. If the citizen activists who pushed prosecutions of the Refuse Act knew that the legislature that had passed the law intended that it have no application to circumstances like pollution, were they being unethical in seeking prosecutions under the Act?

5. **Permits.** Even if prosecutions under the Refuse Act were not certain to follow, many polluters in the 1960s understandably wanted to avoid the possibility of being prosecuted, and started seeking permits from the Corps of Engineers to cover their effluent outfall pipes. Under the terms of the statute, can or must the Corps of Engineers' Chief of Engineers issue permits? Must a permit's issuance or denial be based solely on questions of anchorage and navigation, or can the Corps include other public concerns like pollution, especially after 1970, when NEPA became law? NEPA declared, in vague terms, the responsibility of all federal government agencies to improve environmental quality. See Zabel v. Tabb, 430 F.2d 199 (5th Cir. 1970). *Must* the Corps of Engineers base its permit issuance on considerations of public health and environmental quality?

6. **Implied civil remedies? Injunctions?** Why did the 1898 Congress make it a criminal offense rather than providing for civil penalties, damages, and injunctions? Can a court that finds a polluter in violation of the criminal offense tack on civil remedies like injunctions and damages as well, by "implying civil remedies" from the penal statute? Some 1960s Refuse Act cases did so. U.S. v. Jellico Industries, 3 ERC 1519 (M.D. Tenn. 1971). The Supreme Court, however, in Cort v. Ash, 422 U.S. 66 (1975), severely limited such civil remedy add-ons.

7. **Juries.** In virtually all environmental prosecutions, the defendants will have the right to a jury. How is that likely to affect the course and outcome of criminal proceedings? Is it any surprise that most of the reported appellate cases (i.e., where there is an appeal because defendants lost at trial and were convicted) are cases tried to a judge without a jury? In all probability, as in the *Kepone* case, why didn't they request juries in those cases?

Prophesying jury reactions and jury verdicts has become a major feature of the defense attorney's art. Besides the individual proclivities of each juror, there are situational differences that can have great bearing. How dramatic is the environmental consequence of the indicted offense? How readily can the jury see itself in the role of the defendant rather than the victims? What deference attaches to corporate white collar defendants? Is jury nullification — always a possibility in the Anglo-American jury system — a reasonable tactic, or is the jury's hyper-vindictiveness rather to be feared?

8. **The effectiveness of the Refuse Act.** The effectiveness of the Refuse Act was extraordinary in getting the attention of American polluters. Why does criminal law have this effect? In reality, not many executives can expect to go to jail, and their corporations certainly can be expected to pay any individual fines that corporate officers are assessed in criminal prosecutions. Conviction of a criminal offense, even a misdemeanor, seems to attach some special stigma to corporate officials, unlike civil penalties that are just a nominal cost of doing business. Even though the chance of being convicted may be small, the uncertain possibility is something that no executive lives with easily.

Some of the provisions of the Refuse Act were amended by the Clean Water Act, which established a more direct, comprehensive federal water pollution control system, albeit with less decisive teeth than the Refuse Act. Some of the provisions of the Refuse Act set out here are still in force. Ten to fifteen major Refuse Act prosecutions are initiated each year by the Department of Justice, mostly under §407. According to one federal prosecutor, the old statute has major advantages over comparable provisions of the modern Clean Water Act. Under the latter statute, for example, defendants can gain immunity from prosecution by self-reporting; the Refuse Act includes no such immunity. The Act continues to serve as an indication of the perils and potential of environmental criminal statutes.

9. **Questioning the effectiveness of criminal prosecutions.** What particular effectiveness does a criminal statute add to the system of pollution laws? Environmental criminal statutes are crude instruments. Often environmental crimes are "accidental." In such cases, is it clear that criminal penalties are appropriate? When criminal prosecutions are filed, they certainly pack a punch. But when do they constitute overkill? Criminal fines bear no necessary relationship to the amount of harm caused by pollution, and they are not paid into a pollution control fund. Jail sentences can vary widely from judge to judge, although now the federal sentencing guidelines have reduced the variations between sentences for similar offenses.

Even in the most dramatic cases, criminal prosecutions pose logistical and political problems. The Exxon-Valdez oil spill of March 24, 1989, for example, was the worst oil spill in the history of the United States, with environmental consequences that will to some extent be irreparable and in any event will require decades for Prince William Sound to return to an ecosystem roughly similar to that preceding the accident. Social and economic dislocations have likewise been drastic. It now appears probable that the Alaska spill was not caused only or even primarily by the known alcoholism of the tanker's captain. At least in part there also appears to have been a consistent course of corporate conduct shortcutting safety procedures, cutting back on necessary shipboard personnel to save on payrolls, and perhaps even using financial incentives to encourage ships to run at higher speeds regardless of weather and water conditions. If these and other assertions were proved true and causative, the corporation and its officers would face criminal charges under the Refuse Act §407 and other federal statutes, as well as state laws. But the wreck was not an intentional act; it was "accidental." What further purpose was served by criminal prosecution, especially in light of the civil costs and loss of good will that the corporation had already sustained? What does it say about environmental criminal prosecutions that both the federal and Alaska state governments strenuously avoided criminal trials against Exxon, Alyeska, and their executives?[1]

---

1. The federal government ultimately negotiated a criminal settlement out of court with Exxon, by which a fine of $100 million was remitted down to $25 million in light of the civil responsibility the defendant had taken on. Captain Hazelwood was not prosecuted under the federal water pollution act because the CWA provides immunity for self-reported acts, and Hazelwood had self-reported the spill when he had radioed the Coast Guard, "Uh... we seem to have got stuck on Bligh Reef, and are losing a little oil...."

## B. AN INCREASING WILLINGNESS TO PROSECUTE ENVIRONMENTAL CRIMES

### People of the State of Illinois v. Film Recovery Systems, Inc.; Metallic Marketing Systems, Charles Kirschbaum, Daniel Rodriguez, Steven O'Neil
Circuit Court, Cook County, Illinois, 4th Division

No. 83-11091 (involuntary manslaughter); No. 84-5064 (murder), June 14, 1985
Oral Verdict from the Bench

BANKS, J. This court is being reconvened this afternoon in order for me to render a decision in the case against Film Recovery Systems, Inc., Metallic Marketing Systems, Inc., Steven O'Neil, Charles Kirschbaum, and Daniel Rodriguez.

The record should be clear the defendants are charged with the following offenses: Steven O'Neil, Charles Kirschbaum, and Daniel Rodriguez are charged by way of indictment No. 84 C–5064 with murder as defined in Chapter 38 Section 9-1-a-2, that being "A person who kills an individual without lawful justification commits murder if, in performing the acts which cause the death, such person knows that such acts create a strong probability of death or great bodily harm to the individual or another." Also, the defendants Film Recovery Systems, and Metallic Marketing Systems, Inc. are charged by way of indictment No. 83 C–11091 with involuntary manslaughter and fourteen counts of reckless conduct. Also, Steven O'Neil, Daniel Rodriguez, and Charles Kirschbaum are charged in the same indictment with fourteen counts of reckless conduct.

Before I render a decision in this case, I would like to set forth some of the reasons for my decision. I would like to make it known and make it perfectly clear that the reasons I state are not the total basis for my decision in this case. My decision in this case is based on total review of all evidence presented in this case by both the State and Defense.... During my deliberations and evaluations of all the evidence, let it be known that I never forgot the most important concept in criminal law, that being the defendants are presumed innocent and that it is the burden of the State that they must prove guilt beyond a reasonable doubt.

I hereby make the following findings: No. 1: Stefan Golab died of acute cyanide toxicity. I arrived at that conclusion in the following way: many witnesses testified to the conditions of the air in the plant; not only workers, but independent witnesses as well, such as insurance inspectors, OSHA inspectors, Environmental Protection Agency inspectors, police officers and other service representatives. The testimony of the police investigators is the most important because although we do not know the actual amount of hydrogen cyanide gas in the air on February 10, 1983, the date of the death of Stefan Golab.... The symptoms were classical symptoms, which, according to the Material Safety Data Sheet, would occur if exposed to hydrogen cyanide gas at high levels — nausea, burning throat, burning eyes, difficulty breathing, plus others.

No. 2: I believe also the Medical Examiner, because in the Medical Examiner and toxicologist reports, the victim had a blood cyanide level of 3.45 micrograms per milliliter, which is a lethal dose and can be fatal. The manufacturer states that sodium cyanide...when mixed with a weak alkali, with water in this case, having a pH of approximately seven, will create hydrogen cyanide gas.

I find that the conditions under which the workers in the plant performed their duties was totally unsafe. There was an insufficient amount of safety equipment

SCOTT SANDERS/DAILY HERALD, ARLINGTON HEIGHTS, ILLINOIS

*Former president of Film Recovery Systems Inc., Steven O'Neil, being searched before being sentenced to 25 years in prison for the job-related death of an employee at his Elk Grove Village plant. Prosecutors said O'Neil and two other executives were "motivated by greed and greed alone." Convicted of murder, he theoretically could have faced execution.*

present on the premises. There were no safety instructions given to the workers. The workers were not properly warned of the hazards and dangers of working with cyanide. The warning signs were totally inadequate. The warning signs were written in Spanish and English. The warning signs stated the words "poison," or "veneno" meaning poison in Spanish. The problem with that is that...aside from the Spanish and American workers, there was Stefan Golab, plus other Polish workers. The evidence has shown that Stefan Golab did not speak English, could not read or write English, so a sign in Spanish had no benefit to that man at all.

The Cyanogran label...states that there are three ways in which cyanide can be fatal; one being inhalation of the gas hydrogen cyanide, one being ingestion of sodium cyanide, and third, the absorption into the skin of the sodium cyanide.... This was not told to the workers....

I also find the defendants were totally knowledgeable in the dangers which are associated with the use of cyanide.... The defendants knew that the workers were becoming nauseated and vomiting. The workers complained to all three of the defendants. Steven O'Neil knew hydrogen cyanide gas was present. He knew hydrogen cyanide gas, if inhaled, could be fatal. Charles Kirschbaum saw workers vomiting. He was given a Material Safety Data Sheet. He read the label, and he knew what it said. He said that he did not wear the same equipment the workers did because he did not do the same work as the workers, even though he testified to the contrary.... I also find that Steven O'Neil, who was the President of Film Recovery Systems and Metallic Marketing Systems, was in control and exercised control over both Film Recovery Systems and Metallic Marketing Systems before and after the death of Stefan Golab, which was on February 10, 1983.

Using all the facts stated above and all other evidence pertinent to this case, I find that the conditions present in the work place which caused sickness and injury to workers was reckless conduct. I also find that the death of Stefan Golab was not accidental but in fact murder. I also find that the defendants created the conditions present in the plant by their acts of omission and commission....

Therefore, it is the decision of this Court that the defendants Steven O'Neil, Charles Kirschbaum and Daniel Rodriguez are guilty of murder both as individuals and also as officers and high managerial personnel of Film Recovery Systems and Metallic Marketing Systems, Inc. I also find that they are guilty of murder and reckless conduct....

I also find that because of the negligence and reckless behavior of both Film Recovery Systems, Inc. and Metallic Marketing Systems...the corporations are guilty of involuntary manslaughter and fourteen counts of reckless conduct....

Finally, and this is the most important part and most difficult part for a Judge, I believe because the cloak of innocence has been removed from the accused and because the charge of murder, which the defendants have been found guilty of, does not carry probation and carries a minimum of twenty years in the penitentiary, it is my duty to revoke all bail and the defendants shall be remanded to the custody of the Sheriff's Office, awaiting sentencing, and it is the order of this Court that the bonds be revoked.

At this time, gentlemen, I am going to set a date for sentencing....

### Steven Ferrey, Hard Time: Criminal Prosecution for Polluters
10.4 Amicus Journal 11 (Fall 1988)

On the surface, it was a model company. It recycled valuable minerals from waste materials, and had a stellar record on hiring minorities. But beyond the facade lurked a darker, more ominous, and deadly story.

Film Recovery Systems...extracted trace amounts of silver from hospitals' discarded X-ray film by using sodium cyanide. In its heyday, the company employed eighty workers and earned about $18 million annually. But in its unventilated workroom, employees hunched over 140 bubbling, foaming cauldrons of sodium cyanide. They were issued no protective gear and were not instructed in safety measures. While manually stirring these vats, sodium cyanide slopped over the sides, soaking the workers' clothing and skin. The air was choked with the fumes of hydrogen cyanide gas.

Film Recovery employed illegal Mexican and Polish immigrant laborers almost exclusively in its silver-recovery process.... Few workers spoke English; even fewer could read. The common antidote for cyanide poisoning, amyl nitrite, was not available at the facility. Even the skull-and-crossbones warning labels on the drums of the cyanide were covered over or obscured by management. One day in February 1983, Stefan Golab, a Polish immigrant, stumbled into the lunchroom, fell to the floor with nausea, and died from acute cyanide poisoning. He was fifty-nine years old...

Jay Magnuson, of the Cook County State's Attorney's Office [who obtained the original indictments] prosecuted Film Recovery President Steven O'Neil, the plant manager, and the foreman, for murder. "Callously, they knowingly maintained an unsafe plant environment that was likely to cause death to workers,"

Magnuson remarks. "I never had a second thought that they should be convicted for murder."...

Investigators later discovered almost 15 million pounds of cyanide waste from Film Recovery that had been dumped illegally in rented truck trailers parked in other parts of Illinois. The EPA used $4.5 million of taxpayer's funds to clean up this toxic debris. Decontamination of the facility cost the building's landlord $250,000.

[Before *Film Recovery*,] jail sentences for polluters were unheard of. At worst, the penalty for violating environmental or workplace safety laws was a modest fine. On the remote chance of getting caught, the fines could be rationalized as just another cost of doing business.

But times are changing. Federal and state laws covering hazardous waste, clean air, clean water, and workplace safety impose stiff civil and criminal penalties of up to $25,000 per violation. Like expanding reflections in a carnival mirror, one transgression magnifies into multiple dimensions. A single polluting action can violate several laws simultaneously, and each day of violation is counted by the courts as if it were a new violation. A single act of pollution becomes a serious and compounded felony. "Corporate America will readily take notice of environmental statutes when they start going to jail for their violations," says Glenn Sechen, assistant prosecutor for Cook County. "It simply ceases to be a cost of doing business when it becomes their own necks."

The impact of environmental prosecution has been refocused on individuals. The protective wall between corporate actions and corporate executives is eroding.... The U.S. Department of Justice has brought criminal indictments against 328 individuals and 117 corporations for environmental pollution. The courts have imposed 203 years of jail time and collected $12 million in fines. Sixty-four years of those sentences already have been served. Of those sentenced, about one-third were corporate presidents, 12 percent were vice-presidents, an additional 5 percent were corporate officers, and 20 percent were managers or foremen. Less than 25 percent of those sentenced to jail were the workers who actually released the pollution.

How high in the corporate hierarchy prosecutions reach is a function of employee cooperation in providing evidence against co-workers. An emerging lesson is that the middle of a large corporate ladder can be a perilous place to perch in a company that ignores environmental requirements. At the lower end of the corporation, the "Nuremberg defense" can be an effective escape. Prosecutors are reticent to indict lower-level personnel who claim that they unknowingly were "just following orders" when breaking an environmental law.

Correspondingly, in large corporations, the top-level management may not have direct knowledge of polluting activities. The buck often stops on the desk of middle-level managers, identified by employees as the ones giving the orders to engage in polluting activities. Ironically, a large corporation, with a diffuse management structure and unclear lines of responsibility, may shield executives from potential criminal liability.

In a survey of environmental prosecutions on the East Coast...the typical company cited was small, employing less than fifty persons..... About a quarter are dismissed before a verdict, about half result in guilty pleas by defendants, and of the remaining cases that proceed through a trial, three quarters result in convictions while about a quarter result in acquittals.

Despite successful prosecutorial records in several states, most local prosecutors do not actively pursue criminal environmental polluters. The barriers can be daunting. "Judges understand a smoking gun and a bag of heroin as criminal. They do not understand environmental pollution," laments Lieutenant Gary Long of the Illinois State Police environmental unit — some prosecutors argue privately that criminal court judges, experienced in dealing with common criminals, are uncomfortable with prosecution of executives in Gucci loafers [and with] the very large penalties in environmental statutes ($25,000 per violation per day)....

Problems of proof can be substantial. Documenting the facts and dates of actual polluting activities can prove elusive without help from informants. Allegations against criminal defendants must be proved beyond reasonable doubt. Not all convictions result in jail sentences, and not all jail sentences actually are served. Liberal use of suspended sentences, immediate probation, sentences served on weekends only, and other "innovative" programs mitigate the service of "hard" time. A typical jail sentence is about sixty to ninety days.
Environmental criminals often qualify for treatment that Lynch describes as "commit a crime, go to your room." With jails overcrowded, convicted executives typically fit the profile for release programs: they have ties to the community, references from prominent persons, and are not violent or likely to flee. Consequently, some serve time by wearing an identification bracelet and confining their activities to their homes.

Despite practical problems, criminal prosecution has assumed center stage in environmental enforcement. For an executive, the prospect of incarceration with violent felons focuses the attention like few other sanctions. In return for no jail time, defendants often are willing to plead guilty to violations carrying very large fines.... Until the corporation also can serve time, criminal prosecution of individual corporate executives will remain the most potent weapon in the expanding arsenal of environmental enforcement.

### COMMENTARY AND QUESTIONS

1. **The aftermath of the *Film Recovery* convictions.** *Film Recovery* was a strategic environmental prosecution because of the dramatic way its precedent-setting homicide charge was covered by the press (the first time in living memory that a corporate executive had been prosecuted for murder in connection with environmental pollution). Less press attention was paid to the aftermath: Judge Banks sentenced Steven O'Neil to twenty-five years in jail for murder and reckless conduct, but after several appeals considering whether the state homicide statute was preempted by the federal OSHA statute (it wasn't) an Illinois appellate court overturned the convictions in 1991. The court held —

> Because the offenses of murder and reckless conduct require mutually exclusive mental states, and because we conclude [that the trial court used the] same evidence of the individual defendants' conduct...to support both offenses and does not establish, separately, each of the requisite mental states, we conclude that the convictions are legally inconsistent. People v. O'Neil, 550 N.E.2d 1090, 1098 (Ill.App. 1991).

Do you see the problem? In most states, murder in the first or second degree requires proof of an *intent* to kill, while negligent homicide (involuntary manslaughter) and the lesser charge of reckless conduct are based on *unintentional* harms. The trial judge may have based his verdicts on the wording of part of the Illinois murder statute which seems to allow a murder conviction without intent to kill, if a person "knows that such acts create a strong probability of death or great bodily harm to that individual or another," Chap. 720 ILCS 5/9-1, but the appeals court rejected that logic.

To avoid a re-trial, the Film Recovery executives cut a deal. On the factual record found in Judge Banks' opinion, in 1993 O'Neil, Kirschbaum, and Rodriguez pleaded guilty to involuntary manslaughter. O'Neil served three years in prison, Kirschbaum got two years in prison, and Rodriguez received two years' probation. Another executive, David McKay, pleaded down to one misdemeanor charge of reckless conduct, and got six months probation, 100 hours of community service, and a $1,000 fine. The new Cook County state's attorney apparently made the deals because he did not believe murder charges were warranted on these environmental facts. Given the murder count, it is not clear why the executives had not also initially been charged with involuntary manslaughter, instead of the lesser reckless conduct. (Note the remarkably different options available to prosecutors in environmental cases, in this case ranging from reckless conduct, with simple misdemeanor fines, up to first degree murder for which O'Neil could theoretically have been executed.) How would you have chosen among the relevant variables with regard to criminal intent, whether to charge murder, the range of appropriate penalties, and whether the fact that harm was caused by an indirect environmental exposure lessens the criminality of the act?

The media coverage of *Film Recovery's* original murder convictions appears to have encouraged prosecution throughout the country for environmental crimes. In Los Angeles, for instance, District Attorney Ira Reiner made a name for his department by setting up an environmental crime specialty division with 20 attorneys and investigators, prosecuting a wide range of offenses, and L.A. attorneys who specialize in environmental defense work are currently billing at $400 an hour with no market resistance from their frightened clientele. "Clients will say, 'If I'm being sued for dumping toxic wastes, I don't care what it costs to pay the lawyer. I just need to get out of this problem,'" L.A. Times, 18 Sept. 1989, 1.

2. *Film Recovery* **and pre-emption.** What is your assessment of the reliability of law enforcement efforts by the federal Occupational Safety and Health Administration (OSHA) in the *Film Recovery* case? Should the existence of OSHA preclude other remedies like the state's criminal charges? As Professor Ferrey notes, "The tragedy of Stefan Golab's death is compounded by the fact that OSHA had given the firm a clean bill of health only months before. In the fall of 1982 OSHA inspectors visited the plant, but they never got past the front office, where they saw nothing out of the ordinary in the company's paperwork. They did not walk the additional twenty-five feet beyond the office doors to observe Golab and others hunched over gurgling vats of cyanide. After Golab's death, OSHA inspectors descended on the plant, fining management the seemingly arbitrary and insignificant amount of $4,855. Film Recovery refused to pay, so OSHA reduced it by half, though to this day it has not collected."

Despite an agency's general recklessness, however, defendants are sometimes successful in persuading courts that the existence of federal statutory remedies precludes and preempts application of general state criminal statutes. See People v. Chicago Magnet Wire, 510 N.E.2d 1173 (Ill. App. 1987) (reversed in 1989 by the Illinois Supreme Court).

3. **Federal prosecutions.** Environmental prosecutions have been heating up at the federal level as well. During the 1970s, under avowed conservationist Jimmy Carter, only 25 federal environmental prosecutions were commenced. Between 1982 and 1989 under Ronald Reagan there were more than 450 indictments, more than 325 pleas or convictions, almost 100 of them against corporations, with assessed fines of over $13 million (although 20 percent or more of these appear to have been suspended) and jail terms of more than 200 years (mostly against non-corporate individual offenders), with nearly 65 years of jail time actually being served. Through the Clinton Administration years the rate of criminal prosecutions continued to rise. The majority of today's environmental prosecutions, however, unlike *Film Recovery*'s murder indictment, are straightforward *regulatory enforcement* actions brought by state and federal agencies based on alleged violations of permits and statutory requirements under the CWA, CAA, ESA, and the like, and their state equivalents. Criminal prosecutions are now a normal part of the administrative arsenal, considered as a necessary backup to regulatory compliance programs.

## C. CRIMINAL LIABILITY: PROBLEMS OF KNOWLEDGE AND INTENT

All the materials of this chapter contain the implicit question: how much "criminal intent," a.k.a. "*mens rea* knowledge" or "scienter," must be proved in order to convict a defendant of an environmental crime? Where a statute requires proof of a "knowing" or "willful" violation, how much knowledge does that mean, of what? (and where a statute contains *no* expressed requirement of knowledge or willfulness, like §411 of the Refuse Act, when can a defendant constitutionally be convicted without any proof of criminal intent?)

### United States v. Attique Ahmad
United States Court of Appeals for the Fifth Circuit, 1996
101 F.3d 386

Attique Ahmad appeals his conviction of, and sentence for, criminal violations of the Clean Water Act.... This case arises from the discharge of a large quantity of gasoline into the sewers of Conroe, Texas, in January 1994. In 1992, Ahmad purchased the "Spin-N-Market No. 12," a combination convenience store and gas station.... The Spin-N-Market has two gasoline pumps, each of which is fed by an 8000-gallon underground gasoline tank. Some time after Ahmad bought the station, he discovered that one of the tanks, which held high-octane gasoline, was leaking. This did not pose an immediate hazard, because the leak was at the top of the tank; gasoline could not seep out. The leak did, however, allow water to enter into the tank and contaminate the gas [and] Ahmad was unable to sell from it....

In October 1993, Ahmad hired CTT Environmental Services, a tank testing company, to examine the tank. CTT determined that it contained approximately 800 gallons of water, and the rest mostly gasoline. Jewel McCoy, a CTT employee, testified that she told Ahmad that the leak could not be repaired until the tank was completely emptied, which CTT offered to do for 65 cents per gallon plus $65 per hour of labor. After McCoy gave Ahmad this estimate, he inquired whether he could empty the tank himself. She replied that it would be dangerous and illegal to do so. On her testimony, he responded, "Well, if I don't get caught, what then?"...

On January 25, 1994, Ahmad rented a hand-held motorized water pump from a local hardware store, telling a hardware store employee that he was planning to use it to remove water from his backyard. Victor Fonseca, however, identified Ahmad and the pump, and testified that he had seen Ahmad pumping gasoline into the street. Oscar Alvarez stated that he had seen Ahmad and another person discharging gasoline into a manhole. Tereso Uribe testified that he had confronted Ahmad and asked him what was going on, to which Ahmad responded that he was simply removing the water from the tank.... In all, 5,220 gallons of fluid were pumped from the leaky tank, of which approximately 4,690 gallons were gasoline....

The gasoline discharged onto Lewis Street...entered a storm drain and...flowed through a pipe...into Possum Creek [which] feeds into the San Jacinto River, which eventually flows into Lake Houston. The gasoline that Ahmad discharged into the manhole...entered the city sewage treatment plant.... The plant supervisor ordered that non-essential personnel be evacuated from the plant and called firefighters and a hazardous materials crew to the scene. The Conroe fire department determined the gasoline was creating a risk of explosion and ordered that two nearby schools be evacuated. Although no one was injured as a result of the discharge, fire officials testified at trial that Ahmad had created a "tremendous explosion hazard" that could have led to "hundreds, if not thousands, of deaths and injuries" and millions of dollars of property damage. By 9:00 a.m. on January 26, investigators had traced the source of the gasoline back to the manhole directly in front of the Spin-N-Market.... The investigators questioned Ahmad, who at first denied having operated a pump.... Soon, however, his story changed: He admitted to having used a pump but denied having pumped anything from his tanks.

Ahmad was indicted for three violations of the CWA: knowingly discharging a pollutant from a point source into a navigable water of the United States without a permit, knowingly [discharging into a public sewage works] in violation of a pretreatment standard, and knowingly placing another person in imminent danger of death or serious bodily injury by discharging a pollutant.... 33 U.S.C.A. §1319 says that "any person...commits a felony...who knowingly violates" any of a number of other sections of the CWA [including sections 1311(a), 1317(d), and 1319(c)(3) which comprise the three charges].

At trial, Ahmad did not dispute that he had discharged gasoline from the tank or that eventually it had found its way to Possum Creek and the sewage treatment plant. Instead, he contended that his discharge of the gasoline was not "knowing," because he had believed he was discharging water....

The jury instruction on count one stated in relevant part: For you to find Mr. Ahmad guilty of this crime, you must be convinced that the government has proved each of the following beyond a reasonable doubt:

(1) That on or about the date set forth in the indictment,

(2) the defendant knowingly discharged

(3) a pollutant

(4) from a point source

(5) into the navigable waters of the United States

(6) without a permit to do so.

Ahmad contends that the jury should have been instructed that the statutory mens rea — knowledge — was required as to each element of the offenses, rather than only with regard to discharge. The principal issue is to which elements of the offense the modifier "knowingly" applies.... Ahmad argues that within this context, "knowingly violates" should be read to require him knowingly to have acted with regard to each element of the offenses. The government, in contrast, contends that "knowingly violates" requires it to prove only that Ahmad knew the nature of his acts and that he performed them intentionally. Particularly at issue is whether "knowingly" applies to the element of the discharge's being a pollutant, for Ahmad's main theory at trial was that he thought he was discharging water, not gasoline....

In Staples v. United States, 511 U.S. 600 (1994), the Court found that the statutes criminalizing knowing possession of a machinegun require that defendants know not only that they possess a firearm but that it actually is a machinegun.... Statutory crimes carrying severe penalties are presumed to require that a defendant know the facts that make his conduct illegal.... In United States v. Baytank (Houston), Inc., 934 F.2d 599, 613 (5th Cir. 1991), we concluded that a conviction for knowing and improper storage of hazardous wastes requires "that the defendant know...factually what he is doing: storing, what is being stored, and that what is being stored factually has the potential for harm to others or the environment, and that he has no permit...." This is directly analogous to the interpretation of the CWA that Ahmad urges upon us. Indeed, we find it eminently sensible that the phrase "knowingly violates" in §1319, when referring to...offenses, should uniformly require knowledge as to each of those elements rather than only one or two. To hold otherwise would require an explanation as to why some elements should be treated differently from others, which neither the parties nor the caselaw seems able to provide....

At best, the jury charge made it uncertain to which elements "knowingly" applied. At worst, and considerably more likely, it indicated that only the element of discharge need be knowing. The instructions listed each element on a separate line, with the word "knowingly" present only in the line corresponding to the element that something was discharged.... Knowledge was required only as to the fact that something was discharged, and not as to any other fact. In effect, with regard to the other elements of the crimes, the instructions implied that the requisite mens rea was strict liability rather than knowledge....

We conclude that the instructions...withdrew from the jury's consideration facts that it should have been permitted to find or not find.... The district court's instructions...indicate that it thought "knowingly" modified only the element that something was discharged.... Ahmad's defense...was built around the idea that he thought water, rather than gasoline, was being discharged. A rational jury could so have found....

We reverse Ahmad's convictions.

**United States v. Weitzenhoff et al.**
United States Court of Appeals for the Ninth Circuit, 1993
35 F.3d 1275, cert. denied, 115 S. Ct. 939 (1995)

Michael Weitzenhoff and Thomas Mariani...appeal their convictions for violations of the Clean Water Act...contending that the district court misconstrued the
word "knowingly" under §1319....

In 1988 and 1989 Weitzenhoff was the manager and Mariani the assistant
manager of the East Honolulu Community Services Sewage Treatment Plant
located not far from Sandy Beach, a popular swimming and surfing beach on
Oahu. The plant is designed to treat some 4 million gallons of residential wastewater each day....

Weitzenhoff and Mariani instructed two employees at the East Honolulu
sewage treatment plant to dispose of waste activated sludge on a regular basis by
pumping it from the storage tanks directly into the outfall, that is, directly into
the ocean. The sludge thereby bypassed the plant's effluent sampler so that the
samples taken and reported to Hawaii's Department of Health and the EPA did not
reflect...some 436,000 pounds of pollutant solids being discharged into the
ocean.... Most of the discharges occurred during the night.... Inspectors contacted
the plant on several occasions in 1988 in response to complaints by lifeguards at
Sandy Beach that sewage was being emitted from the outfall, but Weitzenhoff and
Mariani repeatedly denied that there was any problem at the plant.... One of the
plant employees who participated in the dumping operation testified that
Weitzenhoff instructed him not to say anything about the discharges, because if
they all stuck together and did not reveal anything, "they [couldn't] do anything
to us."...

The district court construed "knowingly" in §1319(c)(2) as requiring only that
Weitzenhoff and Mariani were aware that they were discharging the pollutants in
question, not that they knew they were violating the terms of the statute or
permit. According to appellants, the district court erred in its interpretation of the
CWA and in instructing the jury that "the government is not required to prove that
the defendant knew that his act or omissions were unlawful...."

As with certain other criminal statutes that employ the term "knowingly," it
is not apparent from the face of the statute whether "knowingly" means a knowing violation of the law or simply knowing conduct that is violative of the law....
Our conclusion that "knowingly" does not refer to the legal violation is fortified
by decisions interpreting analogous public welfare statutes. The leading case in
this area is United States v. International Minerals & Chem. Corp., 402 U.S. 558
(1971). In *International Minerals*, the Supreme Court construed a statute which
made it a crime to "knowingly violate any...regulation" promulgated by the
ICC...for the safe transport of corrosive liquids. The Court held that the term
"knowingly" referred to the *acts* made criminal rather than a violation of the regulation, and that "regulation" was a shorthand designation for the specific acts or
omissions contemplated by the Act. "Where...dangerous or deleterious devices or
products or obnoxious waste materials are involved, the probability of regulation
is so great that anyone who is aware that he is in possession of them or dealing
with them must be presumed to be aware of the regulation."...

Parties such as Weitzenhoff are closely regulated and are discharging waste
materials that affect public health. The *International Minerals* rationale requires

that we impute to these parties knowledge of their operating permit.[3] This was recognized by the Court in Staples v. United States, 511 U.S. 600 (1994)...holding... that the government is required to prove that a defendant charged with possession of a machinegun knew that the weapon he possessed had the characteristics that brought it within the statutory definition of a machinegun. But the Court...explicitly contrasted the mere possession of guns to public welfare offenses, which include statutes that regulate "dangerous or deleterious devices or products or obnoxious waste materials," and confirmed the continued vitality of statutes covering public welfare offenses, which "regulate potentially harmful or injurious items" and place a defendant on notice that he is dealing with a device or a substance "that places him in responsible relation to a public danger. In such cases Congress intended to place the burden on the defendant to ascertain at his peril whether [his conduct] comes within the inhibition of the statute."...

The dumping of sewage and other pollutants into our nation's waters is precisely the type of activity that puts the discharger on notice that his acts may pose a public danger. Like other public welfare offenses that regulate the discharge of pollutants into the air, the disposal of hazardous wastes, the undocumented shipping of acids, and the use of pesticides on our food, the improper and excessive discharge of sewage causes cholera, hepatitis, and other serious illnesses, and can have serious repercussions for public health and welfare.

The criminal provisions of the CWA are clearly designed to protect the public at large from the potentially dire consequences of water pollution, and as such fall within the category of public welfare legislation.... The government did not need to prove that Weitzenhoff and Mariani knew that their acts violated the permit or the CWA. We affirm both the convictions....

## COMMENTARY AND QUESTIONS

1. *Ahmad* and *Weitzenhoff.* Are these two cases inconsistent? The *Ahmad* court didn't think so, saying that *Weitzenhoff* "was concerned almost exclusively with whether the language of the CWA creates a mistake-of-law defense, [and didn't address the] mistake of fact or the statutory construction issues raised by Ahmad." *If* a jury decided that Mr. Ahmad truly did not realize that he was discharging gasoline, doesn't the *Ahmad* decision make sense on mistake of fact grounds? (You may suspect that Mr. Ahmad actually did know he was discharging gasoline, but the court reminds us that this issue was contested and had not yet been decided by a jury.) Or would it be enough that he knew he was discharging *something dangerous, or illegal* (which Ms. McCoy's evidence indicated) which would bring him closer to *Weitzenhoff?* The two cases also clearly reach contrary conclusions about whether CWA violations are "public welfare offenses."

2. [In] United States v. Speach, 968 F.2d 795, 796-97 (9th Cir. 1992)...we held that 42 U.S.C. §6928(d)(1), which imposes criminal liability on parties who "knowingly transport...hazardous waste...to a facility which does not have a permit," requires that the transporter know that he acted in violation of the statute.... Speach recognizes the general rule that public welfare offenses are not to be construed to require proof that the defendant knew he was violating the law in the absence of clear evidence of contrary congressional intent, and finds only a narrow exception to this general rule...that the defendant was not the permittee but simply the individual who transported waste to the permittee, and...was not...in the best position to know the facility's permit status.

2. **Degrees of knowledge and "intent."** There is a spectrum of interpretation of the different degrees of knowledge that may be applied in cases like this where a statute requires proof that defendants "knowingly" violate its provisions. The range analytically extends from defendants' mere consciousness of the fact of their physical action, to highly specific and willed violation of particular known laws. Here is a rough progression of possible interpretations of what amount of "knowledge" or "scienter" of defendents is required to be proved in order to convict —

(a) "Knowledge" only that they are doing a specific physical action,[3] while not realizing at all that the action happens to fit the description of a crime. (This is the lowest level of "knowledge," only requiring proof that they did the physical act consciously, rather than unconsciously while sleepwalking or the like, and amounts to liability with no proof of intent. Proof of at least this level of knowledge is probably necessary in every crime.)

(b) Knowledge of the identity of an instrument to some degree of specificity — e.g., knowing that a liquid being discharged is gasoline, or a toxic chemical, or a sludge — without knowing that dumping of such liquids is illegal.

(c) Knowledge of a specific necessary element of a particular violation, as for discharges under an invalid permit, where defendants say they did not know the permit wasn't valid.

(d) Knowledge, actual or constructive, that such an act *might* harm individuals or the public (with different degrees of probability ranging from trivial to high likelihood; this often constitutes a negligence-based rather than intent-based culpability).

(e) Knowledge that an act would harm individuals or the public, and specifically intending so to hurt them.

(f) Knowledge that an action is *probably illegal* because it may harm individuals or the public.

(g) Knowledge that an action is illegal, but not knowing what specific law is violated (this may also include different degrees of knowledge about degrees of seriousness of the offense, as in acting in the belief that a serious felony is just a trivial misdemeanor).

(h) Knowledge that what they are doing specifically violates a particular provision, e.g. "Hah, this will violate 40 C.F.R. §129.102(b)(3)(i) under 33 U.S.C.A. §1317(a)(2)!"

Isn't it likely that virtually no defendants will have this latter highest degree of specialized knowledge? The question is rather where a court will draw the line — based on statutory interpretation, the common law of a statute, and constitutional due process — defining the minimum necessary degree of proof of knowledge.

Courts tend to accept decreased degrees of knowledge when the offense is recognized as a "public welfare offense," and tend to require greater degrees of knowledge, or "specific intent," where penalties are severe and include incarceration.

---

3. Acts of omission add another level of subtlety: where defendants can violate a law by failing to act, how much in each case do they have to know of the duty to act and how it may be breached?

When a court says the prosecution must prove "specific intent," however, it is not necessarily clear which kind of specific intent is being required. Would the Ahmad court, after holding that Mr. Ahmad had to know his discharge was gasoline (on the "mistake-of-fact" defense), also require proof that he specifically knew Lake Houston was navigable, and Possum Creek flowed into it? or that his pump was legally a "point source" (on a mistake-of-law defense)? If not, the court implicitly concedes that not all the elements of a crime must be known by the defendant in order to convict. The Fourth Circuit, however, has implied that strict proof of knowledge of both law and fact elements is required. U.S. v. Wilson, _F.3d _; 45 ERC 1801 (1997).

3. **Syntax as part of deciding which elements must be "knowingly" violated.** In United States v. Hoflin, 880 F.2d 1033 (9th Cir. 1989), a city's Director of Public Works was convicted under RCRA §6928(d)(2)(A) of ordering his workers to take fourteen barrels filled with waste highway paint to the grounds of the sewage treatment plant, dig a hole, and dump the drums in. Some of the drums were rusted and leaking, and at least one burst open in the process. The hole was not deep enough, so the employees crushed the drums with a front-end loader to make them fit, and they were then covered with sand. Hoflin appealed on the grounds that the jury should have been required to find that he *knew* the city did not have a permit to dispose of the barrels. RCRA §6928(d)(2)(A) provides —

> (d) CRIMINAL PENALTIES... Any person who... (2) knowingly treats, stores or disposes of any hazardous waste identified or listed under this subchapter either — (A) without having obtained a permit...; or (B) in knowing violation of any material condition or requirement of such permit; ...shall, upon conviction, be subject to [fines, imprisonment, or both].

The Ninth Circuit interpreted this provision to require only proof that Hoflin knew the paint wastes were hazardous, not to require proof that he knew there wasn't any permit. The Third Circuit, in U.S. v. Johnson & Towers, Inc., 741 F.2d 662 (3d Cir. 1984) decided the other way — at least as regards prosecution of subordinate employees, the "knowingly" requirement pours over from the first clause of Subsection (d)(2) into (d)(2)(A). Which court has the better of the statutory interpretation, in terms of the provision's syntax? (The word "knowing" is left out of the middle clause.)

Do you see also that in cases like *Hoflin* ignorance of the law is no defense? The court did not require proof that Hoflin knew the hazardous dumping was illegal. It used the argument that for regulatory "public welfare" statutes involving grave issues of public health, there is no need to prove mens rea unless statutory terms require it. Does the public welfare offense argument presume that when something is so noxious, everyone must know it is likely to be illegal? Many other environmental statutes besides RCRA would seem to fit this category.

4. **Constitutional dimensions: "void for vagueness."** As in many criminal cases, Mr. Weitzenhoff argued that the statute as applied was void for vagueness because it didn't clearly give notice of what permit requirements would ground violations. In rejecting the vagueness defense, along with an entrapment claim, the court said, "A defendant is deemed to have fair notice of an offense if a reasonable person of

ordinary intelligence would understand that his or her conduct is prohibited by the law in question," and the standard is even easier if the defendants have specialized training —

> Weitzenhoff and Mariani were knowledgeable in the wastewater field and can be expected to have understood what the permit meant. In particular, they should have known that it did not give them license to dump thousands of gallons of partially treated sewage into the ocean on a regular basis. We are further persuaded that appellants had adequate notice of the illegality of their dumping by the considerable pains they took to conceal their activities."

The "void for vagueness" challenge is a serious due process argument, but generally "in the field of regulatory statutes governing business activities, where the acts limited are in a narrow category, greater leeway [in required specificity of notice] is allowed than in statutes applicable to the general public." People v. Martin, 259 Cal. Rptr. 770, 773 (1989) (a dumper of toxics disputed the specificity of "hazardous wastes"); U.S. v. Protex, 874 F.2d 740 (10th Cir. 1989) (a chemical company was convicted of "knowing endangerment" of workers who suffered solvent poisoning, under 42 U.S.C.A. §6928(e), of RCRA.)

**5. Constitutional dimensions: due process.** Does due process nevertheless require proof of criminal knowledge, intent, or negligent fault, in no-fault crimes where the legislature expressly excludes it?

Contrast two oil spill cases: The Exxon Corporation paid millions of dollars in criminal fines for the unintended Exxon-Valdez oil spill, but that penalty did not seem to shock fundamental fairness, perhaps because defendants' behavior showed elements of fault: Exxon should have known its operating practices were unsafe. On the other hand, in United States v. White Fuel Corp., 498 F.2d 619 (1st Cir. 1974), a company had to pay a $1000 fine for violating §407 of the Refuse Act, for oil seepage from a half a million gallon underground leakage under their tank farm abutting Boston Harbor. White Fuel had no warning of the leakage, worked diligently to drain the accumulation, and paid for the cleanup. The court upheld criminal liability because public welfare offenses "are in the nature of neglect where the law requires care, or inaction where it imposes a duty.... The accused, if he does not will the violation, usually is in a position to prevent it with no more care than society might reasonably expect and no more exertion than it might reasonably exact from one who assumed his responsibilities. Morissette v. U.S., 342 U.S. 246, 255-256 (1952)." Skepticism of this standard arises in cases like *White Fuel*, where *no such neglect and no prior duty were ever proved.* When there is truly "no fault" in such cases, isn't there a sense of violated due process? This sense of constitutional unfairness, however, may seem assuaged if (a) the criminal penalty is small, like *White Fuel*'s $1000 fine, and (b) it is a corporation, not a person, that faces criminalization.

Contrast two endangered wildlife cases raising the tougher problem — where individual persons faced no-fault jail time: In U.S. v. Wulff, 758 F.2d 1121 (6th. Cir. 1985) the defendant sold a necklace made of red-tailed hawk and great-horned owl talons to a special agent of the United States Fish and Wildlife Service. In U.S. v. Engler, 806 F.2d 425 (3d Cir. 1986) the defendant was convicted under the same Act for the innocent sale of a protected falcon in interstate commerce. The Migratory Bird Treaty Act (MBTA, 16 U.S.C.A. §701) provides strict liability for sale of raptors. Without proof of knowledge or intent, defendants "shall be guilty of a felony and fined not more than $2,000 or imprisoned not more than two years, or both...."

Both courts considered the crimes "public welfare offenses," so that proof of criminal intent was not necessarily required by the Constitution. The *Wulff* court, however, found that no-fault convictions violated due process unless "the penalty is relatively small, and conviction does not gravely besmirch" an individual's reputation, quoting a test from Judge Blackmun in Holdridge v. U.S., 282 F.2d 302 (8th Cir. 1960). But, they held, the MBTA's fines and two-year jail sentences "were not 'relatively small penalties.' A convicted felon loses his right to vote, his right to sit on a jury and his right to possess a gun, among other civil rights, for the rest of his life."

The *Engler* court, on the other hand, upheld the MBTA conviction, quoting the Supreme Court that "public policy may require in prohibition or punishment of particular acts...that he who shall do them shall do them at his peril and will not be heard to plead good faith or ignorance in defense.... This court cannot set aside legislation because it is harsh. Shevlin-Carpenter v. Minn., 218 U.S. 57, 70 (1910)." *Engler* held that "Due process is not violated by the imposition of strict liability as part of a regulatory measure in the interest of public safety, which may well be premised on the theory that one would hardly be surprised to learn that the prohibited conduct is not an innocent act." Does this imply constructive knowledge? Is the sale of endangered wildlife an act that is obviously not innocent, and an offense against public welfare? Does the prohibition of such sales, as the court said, serve "a national interest of very nearly the first magnitude"?

The *Engler* court ridiculed *Wulff*'s "besmirchment" line-drawing between felonies and misdemeanors, and went on to add a practical element to the due process balance: "Where the offenses prohibited and made punishable are capable of inflicting widespread injury, and where the requirement of proof of the offender's guilty knowledge and wrongful intent would render enforcement of the prohibition difficult if not impossible, the legislative intent to dispense with mens rea as an element of the offense has justifiable basis." (A practical argument in the other direction is that, insofar as a statute is designed to *deter* proscribed acts, proof of knowing, or at least careless, acts seems logically necessary.)

6. **A scienter requirement balance?** Are some public welfare offenses more dramatic than others, so "less" scienter is required, or in such cases does more "besmirchment" of individual reputation occur, thus requiring proof of "more" scienter? Should distinctions be drawn between protections of endangered birds and protections of human health against toxic pollution? In *Weitzenhoff* the court noted that in the *Staples* machinegun case the Supreme Court had acknowledged a changing balance: "The penalty attached to a violation of a criminal statute in the past has been a relevant factor in determining whether the statute defines a public welfare offense.... Public welfare offenses originally involved statutes that provided only light penalties such as fines or short jail sentences, *but modern*

*statutes now punish public welfare offenses with much more significant terms of imprisonment."*

7. **Strict liability and sentencing options.** In these strict liability crime cases would you feel differently about convictions that lead only to fines, and convictions that could lead to incarceration? Note also that, although fines and imprisonment are the standard criminal sanctions available to environmental prosecutors, *injunctions* are also available as remedies for many crimes. The field of criminal injunctions is little studied, but has particular utility in the field of environmental crimes. Where due process concerns are implicated in no-fault crimes, moreover, the prospective nature of a criminal injunction intrudes far less upon defendant's rights.

## D. PROBLEMS RAISED IN CORPORATE AND EXECUTIVE PROSECUTIONS

By the nature of the American economic system, much of the pollution dumped into the air and waters of the U.S. comes from corporate polluters, especially the most toxic of such waste streams. In *Film Recovery* the corporation had folded, but in many cases prosecutors target established ongoing corporate enterprises in their tactical gunsights. Successful prosecution of criminal environmental violations always faces an array of difficulties not encountered in civil lawsuits, notably in Fifth Amendment and other limitations on discovery, and the special burden of proof required to prove defendants guilty "beyond a reasonable doubt," not just liable by a simple preponderance of the evidence. These difficulties are particularly pronounced in the case of prosecutions of corporations and corporate executives.

### Section 1. THE FIFTH AMENDMENT AND THE CORPORATION

A corporation can claim Fifth Amendment protections against regulatory takings and violations of procedural due process. Can a corporation take the Fifth, refusing to produce documents that may tend to incriminate it, as a natural person can? The Supreme Court's answer apparently is "No." See Hale v. Henkel, 201 U.S. 43 (1906); U.S. v. Morton Salt, 338 U.S. 632 (1950); Bellis v. U.S., 417 U.S. 85 (1974). In some cases the corporation cannot even claim attorney-client privilege. People v. Keuffel & Esser Co., 181 Cal. App. 3d 785, 227 Cal. Reptr. 13 (1986)(zinc pollution). Not only can't the company claim Fifth Amendment privilege, but it also must deliver up documents in its possession even if they directly incriminate the individuals who make up the corporation. In such circumstances, by virtue of their corporate positions, corporate officers effectively lose the protections of the Fifth Amendment.

### Section 2. DIFFICULTIES IN PROVING COLLECTIVE ACTIVITY CRIMES

The narrative history of the Allied Chemical *Kepone* case was set out earlier in Chapter One. The following excerpt notes some of the interesting issues raised by the criminal indictments filed in the *Kepone* case....

## Goldfarb, Kepone: A Case Study
### 8 Environmental Law 645 (1978)

On May 7, 1976, the Federal grand jury in Richmond, Virginia, handed up two indictments charging Allied, LSP, the City of Hopewell, and six individuals with a total of 1,097 counts (separate offenses) relating to the Kepone incident at Hopewell. Then on July 28th, the grand jury was reconvened to hear further evidence, and the result was a third indictment issued on August 2, 1976.

Indictment #1 charged Allied with 940 alleged violations of the Refuse Act and FWPCA for discharging Kepone, TAIC, and THEIC from Allied's Semi-Works without permits; and one count for an alleged conspiracy to violate control laws among Allied and five of its employees. Each of the individual defendants was also charged with conspiracy to defraud the United States by providing false information regarding the Semi-Works effluent.

Indictment #2 charged Allied, LSP, Hundtofte, Moore, and the City of Hopewell with 153 counts apiece relating to the unlawful discharge of Kepone by LSP into the Hopewell sewer system. In addition, Hopewell was charged with three counts of failure to report the presence of Kepone in its municipal treatment works.

Indictment #3 contained only one count, charging Allied, LSP, Hundtofte, and Moore with conspiracy relating to LSP's discharge of Kepone.

None of the indictments related to conditions within the LSP plant, because no federal law provided for criminal sanctions for such occupational hazards.

The corporate and individual defendants were confronted by the prospect of heavy fines and jail terms if found guilty and accorded maximum sentences. Allied faced a maximum fine of more than $17 million; LSP and its co-owners $3.8 million each; the City of Hopewell $3.9 million; and the alleged co-conspirators $10,000 on each conspiracy count. The more serious potential penalty, however, was imprisonment. The counts for discharging without a permit — 940 counts in Indictment #1 and 153 in Indictment #2 — carried a maximum jail term of one year on each count. The possible penalty on the conspiracy counts was up to five years on each count....

The CWA goes beyond the Refuse Act by explicitly extending liability to a "responsible corporate officer" for the illegal acts of his corporation. LSP as discharger and Hundtofte and Moore as its only officers obviously contravened the CWA by discharging pollutants which interfered with the Hopewell treatment plant, and continuously violating pretreatment standards — all with the knowledge of Hundtofte and Moore. The City of Hopewell was clearly in violation of its own NPDES permit by discharging an unpermitted and unreported substance (Kepone) with knowledge of its presence in the system.

Given the clear-cut direct criminal liability in this case, it is not surprising that the defendants, after having made some unsuccessful preliminary motions, chose to change their pleas from "not guilty" to "nolo contendere" on the direct liability counts[4]....

---

4. There are two main reasons for entering a nolo plea. First, carrying less of a stigma than "guilty," it may be part of a plea bargaining process in which a prosecutor agrees that in return for avoiding the delay and expense of a trial he will accept a nolo plea and request the judge to impose a sentence which is lighter than the maximum. Second, the conviction of a defendant after a nolo plea cannot be used as evidence in another legal proceeding arising out of the same set of facts — for example, in a civil action for damages. Had the defendant pleaded or been found guilty, on the other hand, such a conviction would make a prima facie case for the plaintiffs in related civil cases.

Virgil Hundtofte was permitted to plead nolo on 79 of the 153 counts of Indictment #2 (the remaining 74 counts were dismissed), and to plead "guilty" to a reduced charge of conspiring to furnish false information to the Federal government. Hundtofte also pleaded nolo to the single conspiracy count of Indictment #3. Hundtofte also consented to appear as a witness for the United States against Allied.

Allied unexpectedly requested permission to plead nolo on 940 counts of Indictment #1. The prosecutor objected vehemently to Allied's request, but Judge Merhige accepted the nolo plea "in the interest of justice." Judge Merhige, in accepting Allied's nolo plea, afforded Allied a profound tactical advantage in subsequent civil suits.

As a result of plea bargaining, all relevant defendants had pleaded nolo to all outstanding counts charging direct violations of pollution control laws.... However, the ease with which the United States obtained convictions on the counts involving direct violations of law stands in stark contrast to its inability to establish any vicarious liability or conspiracy regarding Allied.

As to vicarious liability, by pretrial motion, Allied sought a ruling dismissing the "conspiracy to provide false information" count on the ground that, as a matter of law, a corporation cannot be in conspiracy with its own employees who are acting within the scope of their authority.... Allied was arguing that it could not be in conspiracy with itself. The court agreed, and dismissed the count as to Allied.

Although the 153 counts of Indictment #2 and the single conspiracy count of Indictment #3 represented less than ten percent of the total number of counts in the three indictments, they were undoubtedly the most controversial and significant from the standpoint of law and public policy since they held Allied responsible for the criminal acts of LSP....

In attempting to hold Allied criminally liable for LSP's discharges, the United States relied upon four legal theories: (1) that LSP was an *instrumentality* of Allied; (2) that LSP was an *agent* of Allied; (3) that Allied was an *accomplice* of LSP; and (4) that Allied and LSP were engaged in a *conspiracy* to violate pollution control laws.

Under the instrumentality theory, the United States was called upon to prove "actual domination" of LSP by Allied. Somewhat less was necessary to establish an agency relationship: a continuous right of control by Allied (rather than actual domination), along with a consent by LSP to produce Kepone primarily for the benefit of Allied, and at least a tacit acceptance by Allied, if not an explicit condonation, of LSP's unlawful acts. Imposing accomplice liability depended upon proving that Allied "aided and abetted" LSP's illegal discharges. Accomplice liability moves from the realm of control to that of association and assistance, preserving the autonomy of accomplice and perpetrator. It is a kind of vicarious liability that does not require the corporate veil to be pierced. Finally, a conspiracy is a formal or informal agreement to commit another crime. Under a conspiracy theory, Allied and LSP would also be treated as distinct entities.

At the trial, witnesses for the United States, including Hundtofte and Moore, emphasized Allied's close knowledge of Kepone production and toxicity; the relationship of Allied to Hundtofte and Moore; the onesideness of the tolling agreement; Allied's provision of services to LSP — including sampling its effluent on a regular basis, and tours of the LSP plant by Allied's employees and consultants; and Allied's constant urging of LSP to greater Kepone production....

The defense relied on letters from LSP to Allied, allegedly written over a period of years, reassuring Allied that LSP was not discharging in violation of the law. Allied's reasonable reliance on these letters, it was urged, refuted the "instrumentality" and "agency" theories and also precluded the requisite criminal intent to aid and abet LSP's illegal discharges and to agree upon an illegal course of conduct (conspire). Counsel for Allied also highlighted Allied's willingness to pay for LSP's pollution control equipment, claiming that Allied could not have intended to break the law when it was spending money to ensure LSP's compliance.

Without a formal opinion in the case, the court exonerated Allied on all counts involving vicarious liability for LSP. While Judge Merhige's remarks during and after the trial were cryptic, he did indicate that he was not convinced beyond a reasonable doubt of Allied's having possessed the necessary intent upon which to base a conviction, a holding which might encourage corporations to enter into tolling agreements in order to evade the costs of pollution control.

Much greater publicity was accorded to the imposition of the maximum fine on Allied for its own discharges. For its conviction on the 940 counts of Indictment #1 (to which it pleaded "nolo"), Allied was fined $13.2 million. However...Allied sought a reduction in sentence based on its having set aside $8 million to fund the Virginia Environmental Endowment, a nonprofit corporation which would perform research and implement programs to mitigate the environmental effects of Kepone. Judge Merhige then adjusted the fine down to $5 million....

Hundtofte and Moore were fined $25,000 each. LSP received a fine of close to $4 million, a meaningless gesture in light of LSP's lack of assets. The city of Hopewell was fined $10,000....

Did the Kepone sentences actually do justice? Did they achieve the retribution and deterrence (both for the defendants and prospective violators) for which the criminal law strives?... Was Allied's "corporate image" tarnished, as its attorneys claimed prior to sentencing? This argument would deserve greater credence if Allied's operations were more closely related to the general public; but in fact Allied sells almost all of its chemicals to other corporations.... Would it have better served the purposes of the criminal law to have imposed jail terms on some of Allied's executives, and perhaps Hundtofte and Moore? The American public does not look favorably upon the imprisonment of corporate officers for corporate crimes. This explains why jail terms were never a viable alternative in the Kepone case. (Judge Merhige commented early on that "nobody is going to jail in this case.") Moreover, the imprisonment of corporate officers frequently does more harm than good, fostering a "demonology myth" that a few greedy industrialists are responsible for the pollution problem, whereas pollution is a pervasive result of our economic system's "externalization" of certain costs of production. The light fines imposed upon Hundtofte and Moore typify the generous treatment which cooperating corporate officials can expect to receive at the hands of the law.

But is not the function of the criminal law in pollution cases really a symbolic one, to stigmatize an offender so as to achieve deterrence, and to effectuate a catharsis of public outrage?

## COMMENTARY AND QUESTIONS

1. **The judge, and the absence of a jury.** Where was the jury in this criminal prosecution? Obviously Allied and its indicted executives chose to waive their constitutional right to a jury. Was this a good move? Note the effect of Judge Merhige's

rulings on pleadings, on required elements of collective action crimes, and on sentencing, as well as his comments at the early stages of trial ("Nobody is going to jail..."). What effect did these have on the litigative parties? If there had been a jury, would there have been a different judicial posture?

2. **The perils of plea bargaining.** The negotiations between the U.S. Attorney's office and Hundtofte, Moore, and the City of Hopewell illustrate the potential benefits of plea bargaining to both prosecutor and defendants. Note, however, that bargains struck between the parties do not bind the judge. A tough judge could have refused to dismiss the original counts or to allow the lesser pleas, or could have ignored the prosecutors' recommendations for lighter sentences. Judges can go softer on defendants than the terms of a bargain, as well. Judge Merhige felt free to ignore the U.S. Attorney's opposition to Allied's nolo plea, even though it undermined the prosecutors' basis for the prior plea bargains. Can defendants or prosecutors whose plea bargains have not been followed by the trial judge get relief from an appellate court? Not likely. In environmental cases, where criminal liability is a relatively novel phenomenon for judges, the reliability of plea bargaining for both sides may be relatively unpredictable.

3. **Allied's vicarious liability.** It is not clear why Judge Merhige dismissed all the vicarious liability counts against Allied. Does it appear that Allied was a stranger to the sloppy operations at Life Science's plant? Did Allied not have the requisite knowledge of what was going on? Should "tolling" and "maquiladora" agreements legally insulate corporate principals from the pollution of their "independent" subcontractors? If the United States had appealed dismissal of the counts holding Allied vicariously liable for LSP's pollution, which argument on the Kepone facts — "instrumentality," "agency," "accomplice," or "conspiracy" — would have appeared strongest?

4. **The Kepone fines, and taxes.** Defendant industries that negotiate SEPs (supplemental environmental projects) as setoff alternatives to larger penalties, often do so in order to write the sums off on their income tax returns as business expenditures under §162 of the Internal Revenue Code, or as charitable deductions under §170. As noted, Allied agreed with the judge to set up an $8 million Virginia Environmental Endowment, and the fines were then reduced from $13.2 million down to $5 million. When Allied deducted the $8 million as a business expense, the IRS balked. When the tax case came to trial almost 20 years later, the court had to decide —

> Whether petitioner's payment of $8,000,000 in 1977 to the Virginia Environmental Endowment Fund is deductible under §162(a) as an "ordinary and necessary business expense" or whether such payment is a "fine or similar penalty" [like the $5 million] the deductibility of which is proscribed by §162(f)....

> We accept petitioner's characterization of a "fine or similar penalty" as an involuntary payment [but] in the present case, petitioner made the $8 million payment to the Endowment with the virtual guarantee that the sentencing judge would reduce the criminal fine by at least that amount. Petitioner's characterization of this payment as "voluntary" is simply not borne out by the record as a whole.... We hold that the payment by petitioner to the Endowment was in substance a "fine or similar penalty" within the meaning of §162(f). Allied-Signal, Inc. v. Commissioner, 63 T.C.M. (CCH) 2672 (1992), aff'd with-

out opinion, 54 F.3d 767 (3d Cir. 1995), (containing many details of the Kepone case never before published).

If prosecutors negotiating penalties wish to have penalty funds used for onsite remedies rather than merely pouring into the federal treasury, tax deductibility is a settlement incentive. Can such SEPs be made deductible? In Chapter One's *Smithfield Packing* that would probably have been possible if the remediation fund had been set up before the judge issued a penalty ruling, but not after. Is such tax deductibility a good idea?

## Section 3. EXECUTIVE LIABILITY FOR ACTS OR OMISSIONS BY SUBORDINATES

### United States v. Park
United States Supreme Court, 1975
421 U.S. 658, 95 S. Ct. 1903, 44 L.Ed.2d 489

BURGER, C.J. Acme Markets, Inc., is a national retail food chain with approximately 36,000 employees, 874 retail outlets, 12 general warehouses, and four special warehouses. Its headquarters, including the office of the president, respondent Park, who is chief executive officer of the corporation, are located in Philadelphia, Pa. In a five-count information filed in the United States District Court for the District of Maryland, the Government charged Acme and respondent with violations of the Federal Food, Drug and Cosmetic Act. Each count of the information alleged that the defendants had received food that had been shipped in interstate commerce and that, while the food was being held for sale in Acme's Baltimore warehouse following shipment in interstate commerce, they caused it to be held in a building accessible to rodents and to be exposed to contamination by rodents. These acts were alleged to have resulted in the food's being adulterated within the meaning of 21 U.S.C. §§342(a)(3) and (4), in violation of 21 U.S.C. §331(k).

Acme pleaded guilty to each count of the information. Respondent pleaded not guilty. The evidence at trial demonstrated that in April 1970 the Food and Drug Administration (FDA) advised respondent by letter of insanitary conditions in Acme's Philadelphia warehouse. In 1971 the FDA found that similar conditions existed in the firm's Baltimore warehouse. An FDA consumer safety officer testified concerning evidence of rodent infestation and other insanitary conditions discovered during a 12-day inspection of the Baltimore warehouse in November and December 1971. He also related that a second inspection of the warehouse had been conducted in March 1972. On that occasion the inspectors found that there had been improvement in the sanitary conditions, but that "there was still evidence of rodent activity in the building and in the warehouse and we found some rodent-contaminated lots of food items."

...The Government's final witness, Acme's vice president for legal affairs and assistant secretary, identified respondent as the president and chief executive officer of the company and read a bylaw prescribing the duties of the chief executive officer. He testified that respondent functioned by delegating "normal operating duties," including sanitation, but that he retained "certain things, which are the big, broad, principles of the operation of the company," and had "the responsibility of seeing that they all work together."

At the close of the Government's case in chief, respondent moved for a judgment of acquittal on the ground that "the evidence in chief has shown that Mr.

Park is not personally concerned in this Food and Drug violation." The trial judge denied the motion, stating that United States v. Dotterweich, 320 U.S. 277 (1943), was controlling.

Respondent was the only defense witness. He testified that, although all of Acme's employees were in a sense under his general direction, the company had an "organizational structure for responsibilities for certain functions" according to which different phases of its operation were "assigned to individuals who, in turn, have staff and departments under them." He identified those individuals responsible for sanitation, and related that upon receipt of the January 1972 FDA letter, he had conferred with the vice president for legal affairs, who informed him that the Baltimore division vice president "was investigating the situation immediately and would be taking corrective action and would be preparing a summary of the corrective action to reply to the letter." Respondent stated that he did not "believe there was anything [he] could have done more constructively than what [he] found was being done."

On cross-examination, respondent conceded that providing sanitary conditions for food offered for sale to the public was something that he was "responsible for in the entire operation of the company," and he stated that it was one of many phases of the company that he assigned to "dependable subordinates." Respondent was asked about and, over the objections of his counsel, admitted receiving, the April 1970 letter addressed to him from the FDA regarding insanitary conditions at Acme's Philadelphia warehouse.... Finally, in response to questions concerning the Philadelphia and Baltimore incidents, respondent admitted that the Baltimore problem indicated the system for handling sanitation "wasn't working perfectly" and that as Acme's chief executive officer he was responsible for "any result which occurs in our company."

...The jury found respondent guilty on all counts of the information, and he was subsequently sentenced to pay a fine of $50 on each count.

The Court of Appeals reversed [saying] as "a general proposition, some act of commission or omission is an essential element of every crime."... It reasoned that, although our decision in United States v. Dotterweich, 320 U.S. at 281, had construed the statutory provisions under which respondent was tried to dispense with the traditional element of "awareness of some wrongdoing," the Court had not construed them as dispensing with the element of "wrongful action." The Court of Appeals concluded that...proof of this element was required by due process.... We reverse.

In *Dotterweich* [on similar facts to *Park* concerning contaminated drugs] a jury...convicted Dotterweich, the corporation's president and general manager.... This Court...observed that the Act..."dispenses with the conventional requirement for criminal conduct — awareness of some wrongdoing. In the interest of the larger good it puts the burden of acting at hazard upon a person otherwise innocent but standing in responsible relation to a public danger."... The interpretation given the Act in *Dotterweich*, as holding criminally accountable the persons whose failure to exercise the authority and supervisory responsibility reposed in them by the business organization resulted in the violation complained of, has been confirmed in our subsequent cases.... "the public interest in the purity of its food is so great as to warrant the imposition of the highest standard of care on distributors." ... The Act punishes "neglect where the law requires care, or inaction where it imposes a duty." Morissette v. United States, at 255. "The accused, if he does not will the violation, usually is in a position to prevent it with no more care than society might reasonably expect and no more exertion than it might reasonably exact from one who assumed his responsibilities."...

Congress has seen fit to enforce the accountability of responsible corporate agents dealing with products which may affect the health of consumers by penal sanctions cast in rigorous terms, and the obligation of the courts is to give them effect so long as they do not violate the Constitution.

The concept of a "responsible relationship" to, or a "responsible share" in, a violation of the Act indeed imports some measure of blameworthiness; but it is equally clear that the Government establishes a prima facie case when it introduces evidence sufficient to warrant a finding by the trier of the facts that the defendant had, by reason of his position in the corporation, responsibility and authority either to prevent in the first instance, or promptly to correct, the violation complained of, and that he failed to do so.

## COMMENTARY AND QUESTIONS

1. **Fighting over principles?** Note that this case went up to the Supreme Court of the United States on appeal of a sentence of $50 for each of five counts. Why did Mr. Park bother? The corporation itself was also prosecuted, but did not attempt to fight the conviction.

2. **Who gets targeted? the "responsible corporate officer doctrine.** "The government, if it had wished, could have prosecuted the actual workers whose acts or omissions had caused the contamination. Many statutes can be so applied, but governmental prosecutors often understandably choose to prosecute higher up the corporate chain of command if they can. The U.S. Department of Justice's environmental crimes division has a policy of prosecuting in each case the highest-ranking corporate officer it can reach. See Starr, Countering Environmental Crimes, 13 B.C. Envtl. Aff. L. Rev. 379 (1986).

The last line in the *Park* excerpt seems to set out an extremely inclusive definition for "responsible corporate officer" liability. Is it really that broad? The presidents of auto companies, for example, clearly have authority to prevent or correct violations of a far-off subsidiary if they are brought to their attention; the question is the interpretation to be given to the word "responsibility." Two 1991 cases imposed much stricter requirements for the prosecution of corporate executives: In U.S. v. MacDonald & Watson Waste Oil Co., 933 F.2d 35 (1st Cir. 1991), and U.S. v. White, 766 F. Supp. 873 (E.D. Wash. 1991), the courts held that, at least for crimes for which knowledge is an element, a mere showing of official responsibility is not an adequate substitute for direct or circumstantial proof of actual knowledge. A recent analysis concluded that —

> No cases under the CWA have held a responsible corporate officer liable merely because of his or her position and it is unlikely that such a holding would occur for violations that require proof of some culpable knowledge. Such a decision may be possible, however, where the violation is based on strict liability or negligence, since there would be no scienter requirement and the conduct of the responsible corporate officer could be portrayed as deficient or negligent in some respect.... Courts have been extremely reticent to punish criminally those with only an attenuated relationship to wrongdoing.

Executives must remain wary, however because decisions offering broad definitions of the rule are still being developed, particularly where hazardous substances are involved. Carr et. al, Environmental Criminal Liability: Avoiding
and Defending Enforcement Actions, 1995.

The Department of Justice prosecutorial guidelines advise federal prosecutors to
make a particularized scienter showing (direct or circumstantial) even where a
statute does not require knowledge.

3. **Defensive organizational responses.** Aware of new liabilities as well as the growing public concern for the environment, many corporations are altering their internal structures to ensure environmental compliance. One common change is
creation of a centralized office charged with company-wide oversight, to try to
ensure that pollution standards are not compromised for the sake of production,
particularly given the pressures to cut corners common in times of recession. After
*Park*, would you accept appointment as a major corporation's vice president
responsible for pollution control?

4. **Executive liability, civil as well as criminal.** *Park* demonstrates judicial willingness to extend individual criminal liability far up the corporate executive ladder.
Although this chapter focuses on criminal liability, it is appropriate to note the
similarities to executive civil liability issues.

As with civil liability, corporate officers can be held criminally liable for their individual acts where they themselves dumped toxics or directly ordered employees to
do so (this is obvious, but is rarely easy to prove). They also can be held liable, both
civilly and criminally, for actions that take place within areas of their corporate
responsibility and authority.[5] In some cases, where a corporate officer is in active
daily managerial control of the area of corporate activity that caused a statutory
violation, liability may reflect an inference that the executive in fact personally
ordered, encouraged, or winked at the acts — where these facts cannot be directly
proved.[6] In other cases liability appears to be based on a more indirect nexus — the
officer's status and general authority over corporate matters. In *Dotterweich*,
Justice Frankfurter held that, at least with regard to public health crimes, it is permissible to place the burden on corporate individuals who are in a position to prevent the harm from occurring "rather than to throw the hazard on the innocent
public who are wholly helpless." 320 U.S. at 285. In a Vermont case, the court
based liability on a finding that "each individual defendant here was either personally involved in corporate acts of Staco, *or was in a position* as a corporate officer or majority stockholder *to have ultimate control.*" Vermont v. Staco Inc., 27
ERC 1084 (DC Vt. 1988) (emphasis added). See Seymour, Civil and Criminal
Liability of Corporate Officers under Federal Environmental Laws, 20 Env. Rptr.
337 (1989). Seymour notes that "even though...actual operating functions had been
delegated to subordinate employees who exercised responsibility over the everyday

---

5. The concept of piercing the corporate veil is rarely relevant to the question of officer liability in
the criminal setting, where proof of individual responsibility rather than availability of assets is the
issue.

6. This may explain the liability found against certain officers in the cases of U.S. v. Carolawn Co.,
21 ERC 2124 (D.C. S.C. 1984); U.S. v. Pollution Abatement Services, Inc. of Oswego, 763 F.2d 133
(2d Cir. 1985); and In re BED, EPA No. TSCA-IV-860001, 12/8/88.

operations of the company, the court...in *Park*...indicated that with the power to delegate comes a corresponding obligation on the part of high-level corporate officers to control the behavior of subordinates...." Failure to discover and correct violations, as well as failure to provide adequate supervision, can be the basis of criminal as well as civil liability. How far up the ladder does such responsibility go? Is the CEO of a Big Three automaker personally liable for an acid spill in one of the company's plating plants in Seattle? The latter, indirect theory of executive responsibility, which comes closest to executive strict liability, raises special problems in the criminal setting. What if the defendant has no specific knowledge of the illegal acts? The degree to which penal sanctions can then be applied is considered in the following section of this chapter: some statutes are written without a requirement of proof of knowledge, but constitutional questions arise whether knowledge is nevertheless required. Civil liability is freer of such constraints. Into which liability theory does *Park* fall, or defendant Michaels' circumstances in *NEPACCO* ?

The same defenses that may be available to executives in criminal actions — inability to prevent the violation, or ignorance of the violation — are sometimes available in the civil context as well. In any case, criminal sanctions, because of their stigma and potential severity, are generally more credible as deterrents than civil penalties.

5. **Corporate ignorance as a defense.** In *Park* the defendant admitted knowing fairly specifically that there was a violation of federal law that was not being corrected. What if, as in most cases, executives say they did not know that the criminal violation was occurring? How far does the criminal responsibility set out in *Park* and *Dotterweich* extend beyond the facts of those two cases? Could prosecutors — who are continually amazed by how little, according to litigation affidavits, corporate executives know about what really goes on in their factories — base executive criminal liability on a theory of "willful ignorance"? Some executives surely instruct their employees that they "don't want to know" how certain things get done, "just get it done."

In 1991, the "California Corporate Criminal Liability Act" went into effect, making it a crime whenever a corporation or manager has "actual knowledge" of a serious concealed danger associated with a product or business practice, and knowingly fails within 15 days (or immediately, if there is imminent risk of great bodily harm or death) to notify the state occupational safety and health agency and affected employees. Cal. Pen. Code §387. The statute provides that knowledge need not be actual awareness, but may simply be possession of facts that would lead a reasonable person to believe that a danger exists. Questions about how much knowledge or intent must be proved in criminal prosecutions continue in the following materials.

6. **Probation for corporations.** Note that probation is an available remedy in prosecutions against corporations as well as individuals. Probation can, of course, be used to blunt the force of other remedies, when used by sentencing judges to suspend fines and jail sentences so long as probation conditions are not violated. If, on the other hand, judges apply it as a *supplement* rather than as a substitute for fines

and imprisonment, probation allows a court to maintain a watchful eye and tough control over defendants who otherwise might cut corners in future environmental compliance. A court can set out very specific terms for probation, with particular action requirements and performance standards (not to mention community service penance obligations) monitored by a probation officer to whom the defendant corporation must report regularly "like a common criminal." If the terms of probation are violated, the corporate defendants know that further specified penalties will be directly forthcoming. See Gruner, To Let the Punishment Fit the Organization: Sanctioning Corporate Offenders through Corporate Probation, 16 Am. J. Crim. L. 1 (1988)

## E. REGULATORY PROSECUTIONS AND THE EFFECT OF FEDERAL SENTENCING GUIDELINES

The United States Sentencing Commission, originally set up by the Reagan Administration as part of its law and order policy, ended up establishing remarkably stringent Sentencing Guidelines applicable to all federal crimes including environmental crimes, as authorized by the Sentencing Reform Act of 1984, 28 U.S.C.A. Title 58. The following regulatory prosecution illustrates the modern process of applying a generic sentencing formula under the guidelines, in an area that always before had been in the realm of the trial judges' unfettered discretion.

### United States v. John W. Rutana
United States Court of Appeals for the Sixth Circuit, 1994
18 F.3d 363

KENNEDY, CIRCUIT JUDGE ...Defendant John W. Rutana pled guilty to eighteen counts of knowingly discharging pollutants into a public sewer system in violation of the Clean Water Act.... Defendant was part owner and chief executive officer of Finishing Corporation of America ("FCA"), a now-bankrupt corporation. In 1985, FCA opened a plant in Campbell, Ohio that anodized aluminum. This process produced large quantities of highly acidic and highly alkaline wastewater. FCA discharged these hazardous pollutants into a city sewer line that led directly to the Campbell Waste Water Treatment Plant ("CWWTP"). The CWWTP discharges its effluent into the Mahoning River, which supplies drinking water to some downstream communities. In January, February, March and April of 1987, four major bacteria kills occurred at the treatment plant. (The CWWTP uses bacteria to treat waste.)... FCA was notified after each kill of its involvement in the kills, but the company continued its discharges.... FCA failed to obtain any permit that would allow any discharges....

On April 9, 1988, a CWWTP employee was burned while attempting to sample FCA's discharges.... In July, 1988, after an investigation by the FBI, defendant agreed to voluntarily close the plant. However, FCA's discharges continued through 1988 and the treatment plant experienced additional bacteria kills. A second CWWTP employee was burned on December 16, 1988 while sampling a discharge from FCA.

Defendant was subsequently indicted for the following crimes: eighteen counts of knowingly discharging pollutants into a public sewer system, and thereby into the CWWTP in violation of national pretreatment standards, in viola-

# FEDERAL SENTENCING TABLE
(stated in months of imprisonment)

## Criminal History Category (Criminal History Points)

| | Offense Level | I (0 or 1) | II (2 or 3) | III (4,5,6) | IV (7,8,9) | V (10,11,12) | VI (13 or more) |
|---|---|---|---|---|---|---|---|
| | 1 | 0–6 | 0–6 | 0–6 | 0–6 | 0–6 | 0–6 |
| | 2 | 0–6 | 0–6 | 0–6 | 0–6 | 0–6 | 1–7 |
| | 3 | 0–6 | 0–6 | 0–6 | 0–6 | 2–8 | 3–9 |
| Zone A | 4 | 0–6 | 0–6 | 0–6 | 2–8 | 4–10 | 6–12 |
| | 5 | 0–6 | 0–6 | 1–7 | 4–10 | 6–12 | 9–15 |
| | 6 | 0–6 | 1–7 | 2–8 | 6–12 | 9–15 | 12–18 |
| | 7 | 0–6 | 2–8 | 4–10 | 8–14 | 12–18 | 15–21 |
| | 8 | 0–6 | 4–10 | 6–12 | 10–16 | 15–21 | 18–24 |
| | 9 | 4–10 | 6–12 | 8–14 | 12–18 | 18–24 | 21–27 |
| Zone B | 10 | 6–12 | 8–14 | 10–16 | 15–21 | 21–27 | 24–30 |
| Zone C | 11 | 8–14 | 10–16 | 12–18 | 18–24 | 24–30 | 27–33 |
| | 12 | 10–16 | 12–18 | 15–21 | 21–27 | 27–33 | 30–37 |
| | 13 | 12–18 | 15–21 | 18–24 | 24–30 | 30–37 | 33–41 |
| | 14 | 15–21 | 18–24 | 21–27 | 27–33 | 33–41 | 37–46 |
| | 15 | 18–24 | 21–27 | 24–30 | 30–37 | 37–46 | 41–51 |
| | 16 | 21–27 | 24–30 | 27–33 | 33–41 | 41–51 | 46–57 |
| | 17 | 24–30 | 27–33 | 30–37 | 37–46 | 46–57 | 51–63 |
| | 18 | 27–33 | 30–37 | 33–41 | 41–51 | 51–63 | 57–71 |
| | 19 | 30–37 | 33–41 | 37–46 | 46–57 | 57–71 | 63–78 |
| | 20 | 33–41 | 37–46 | 41–51 | 51–63 | 63–78 | 70–87 |
| | 21 | 37–46 | 41–51 | 46–57 | 57–71 | 70–87 | 77–96 |
| | 22 | 41–51 | 46–57 | 51–63 | 63–78 | 77–96 | 84–105 |
| | 23 | 46–57 | 51–63 | 57–71 | 70–87 | 84–105 | 92–115 |
| | 24 | 51–63 | 57–71 | 63–78 | 77–96 | 92–115 | 100–125 |
| Zone D | 25 | 57–71 | 63–78 | 70–87 | 84–105 | 100–125 | 110–137 |
| | 26 | 63–78 | 70–87 | 78–97 | 92–115 | 110–137 | 120–150 |
| | 27 | 70–87 | 78–97 | 87–108 | 100–125 | 120–150 | 130–162 |
| | 28 | 78–97 | 87–108 | 97–121 | 110–137 | 130–162 | 140–175 |
| | 29 | 87–108 | 97–121 | 108–135 | 121–151 | 140–175 | 151–188 |
| | 30 | 97–121 | 108–135 | 121–151 | 135–168 | 151–188 | 168–210 |
| | 31 | 108–135 | 121–151 | 135–168 | 151–188 | 168–210 | 188–235 |
| | 32 | 121–151 | 135–168 | 151–188 | 168–210 | 188–235 | 210–262 |
| | 33 | 135–168 | 151–188 | 168–210 | 188–235 | 210–262 | 235–293 |
| | 34 | 151–188 | 168–210 | 188–235 | 210–262 | 235–293 | 262–327 |
| | 35 | 168–210 | 188–235 | 210–262 | 235–293 | 262–327 | 292–365 |
| | 36 | 188–235 | 210–262 | 235–293 | 262–327 | 292–365 | 324–405 |
| | 37 | 210–262 | 235–293 | 262–327 | 292–365 | 324–405 | 360–life |
| | 38 | 235–293 | 262–327 | 292–365 | 324–405 | 360–life | 360–life |
| | 39 | 262–327 | 292–365 | 324–405 | 360–life | 360–life | 360–life |
| | 40 | 292–365 | 324–405 | 360–life | 360–life | 360–life | 360–life |
| | 41 | 324–405 | 360–life | 360–life | 360–life | 360–life | 360–life |
| | 42 | 360–life | 360–life | 360–life | 360–life | 360–life | 360–life |
| | 43 | life | life | life | life | life | life |

tion of 33 U.S.C. §§1317(d) and 1319(c)(2)(A); two counts of knowingly placing people in imminent danger of death or serious bodily injury, in violation of 33 U.S.C. §§1317(d) and 1319(c)(3); and two counts of making a false statement in violation of 18 U.S.C. §1001. Defendant pled guilty to the first eighteen counts of the indictment and the remaining counts were dismissed.

THE PRE-SENTENCE REPORT ["PSR"] calculated defendant's offense level of eighteen (18) as follows:

(1) Base offense level of eight (8) for mishandling of hazardous or toxic substances, under U.S.S.G. §2Q1.2(a).

(2) Increase of six (6) levels for repetitive discharge, under U.S.S.G. §2Q1.2(b)(1)(A). [NOTE 5: BASED ON HARMFULNESS OF CONTAMINATION CAN DEPART UP OR DOWNWARD BY 2]

(3) Increase of four (4) levels for disruption of a public utility, under U.S.S.G. §2Q1.2(b)(3). [NOTE 7: 2 UP OR DOWN]

(4) Increase of two (2) levels for playing a leadership role in the activity, under U.S.S.G. §3B1.1(c).

(5) Decrease of two (2) levels for acceptance of responsibility, under U.S.S.G. §3E1.1(a).

[i.e., 8+6+4+2-2=18; for this the guidelines indicate a term of imprisonment of 27 to 33 months, based upon an offense level of 18 and a criminal history category I (Rutana had no prior offenses). See Chart — eds.]

While the court accepted the facts and findings of [the PSR], it nevertheless departed downward from level 18 to level 6, and sentenced defendant to five years of probation, combined with 1,000 hours of community service. The court also imposed a $90,000 fine, which represented $5,000 per violation, and a special assessment of $950. In granting the departure, the District Court had relied upon defendant's ownership of another company, which might fail if defendant were incarcerated, which in turn would cause the loss of jobs, and upon its belief that the minimum fine, which it believed to be mandatory, was too harsh. On appeal, this Court reversed....

Upon remand, a different district judge ordered the preparation of a second pre-sentence report [but rejected its] recommended offense level of 17...and sentenced defendant to four months of home confinement without an electronic monitoring device, three years of probation, and imposed a fine of $30,000....[using an offense level of 8, and] refused to add four levels for defendant's disruption of a public utility under U.S.S.G. §2Q1.2(b)(3) which provides: "If the offense resulted in disruption of public utilities..., or if cleanup required a substantial expenditure, increase by 4 levels...." The court drew a distinction between a "disruption" and an "impact" and found that defendant's activities had *impacted* a public utility but had not *disrupted* it....

We find, however, that what occurred in this case was a disruption of a public utility. The undisputed evidence shows that defendant's discharges caused several bacteria kills at the CWWTP and burned two CWWTP employees.... Defendant's discharges caused the CWWTP to violate its clean water permit.... We hold that the District Court erred in failing to apply section 2Q1.2(b)(3).

[On sentencing remand, after a third PSR recommended a level of 17, the judge ultimately accepted a compromise deal in which John Rutana agreed to serve five months in jail and five months home detention, with a $16,700 fine, on a final adjusted offense level of 12.]

## COMMENTARY AND QUESTIONS

1. **The mechanics and strategics of a sentencing formula.** The sentencing history of *Rutana* gives a good idea of how the guidelines can work. PSRs are prepared by the office of the U.S. Probation Service assigned to that federal court. Normally the sentencing judge takes the PSR's offense level number, and simply cross-references that number with the defendant's criminal history category (see chart), which then indicates the range of possible sentences within which the trial judge has discretion. Sentencing judges may try to extend the range of their discretion further by pegging the offense level higher or lower than the PSR's recommendation. Under the U.S.S.G. Commentary, for example, a judge can adjust the offense levels for "repetitive discharges" (6) and "disrupting a public utility" (4) up or down by two, based on severity. (2Q1 Note 5; 2Q3 Note 7.) In *Rutana's* first sentencing, the judge apparently considered environmental offenses less important than maintaining an ongoing business. His downward revision of offense level to 6 was reversed and remanded as unjustified. On first remand, the second sentencing judge lowered the PSR level from 17 to 8 by ignoring the POTW disruption and using two downward adjustments from the Commentary, and then after reversal on the POTW issue, at the third sentencing, accepted a negotiated deal for penalties at level 12.

Why can the offense levels vary so dramatically in such a case? These discharges were apparently bad stuff, burning the skin of people who touched them.[7] The art of calculation is still being learned, however, and perhaps some unspoken mitigating features of the *Rutana* case justified a departure from the guidelines. Sometimes isn't it desirable for a judge to have the ability to tailor criminal remedies to the realities of the case? Such judicial balancing, however, (which is as old as Aristotle's *equitas*), led to such wild disparities between different courts that Congress decided to force uniformity upon federal sentencing. As *Rutana* demonstrates, judicial discretion did not disappear, although it may now be somewhat constrained. In *Rutana*, did the fact that the conviction involved an environmental violation and an entrepreneurial executive incline the judges to take it less seriously?

2. **An array of fudge factors in criminal sentencing.** Because of the Guidelines some further tailoring of remedies now occurs at the beginning of a case, in the prosecution's decisions and plea bargaining over what charges and level-enhancing factual allegations will be made. If you are an EPA or state enforcement attorney, note the range of options you can array against polluters in negotiations on consent agreements. If a defendant will not cut a deal on providing desired information, or a restoration remedy, or funding a SEP supplemental environmental project, filing a complaint for criminal violations poses the threat of locking-in a range of severe potential penalties.

The variability in sentencing options that remains available despite the federal guidelines was evident in the aftermath of the Exxon-Valdez oil spill. Exxon, as a

---

7. The prosecutor from the U.S. Attorney's office in Cleveland, Gregory Sassé, and the FBI agent assigned to the case both appear to have been motivated by the fact that Mr. Rutana reportedly lied during the investigation, minimized the importance of sewage disruptions, and tried to persuade the manager of the POTW to falsify discharge data to get them both off the hook.

corporation, could not be imprisoned, so the federal judge was able to take the federal fine of $100 million and remit it down to $25 million, apparently taking into consideration Exxon's acceptance of extensive civil liability. (Criminal fine remittitur is an important and little-studied judicial power.) The federal guidelines, of course, do not apply to state sentences. Captain Hazelwood was convicted by an Alaska state jury of negligent discharge of oil, a misdemeanor, and was sentenced to ninety days in jail and a $1000 fine, but the judge then issued an alternate conditional sentence: he suspended the fine and the jail sentence on condition that Hazelwood complete one year of probation, perform 1000 hours of community work, and pay $50,000 in restitution.

3. **A critique of criminalization for environmental injuries.** Professor Herbert Packer has criticized the vagaries of criminal penalties based on evolving concepts of "morality." As to punishment of executives for "economic crimes," he writes that "these are, generally speaking,...uniquely deterrent...sanctions addressed to the law-abiding.... Intimidation...incapacitation [and] rehabilitative effect [are not the reasons for] the imposition of criminal punishment on those pillars of the community who happen to get convicted of economic offenses." He concludes that "it takes a substantial enforcement effort, and the resources required to bring the threat up to its minimal level of credibility might be better expended in noncriminal modes of regulation." See Packer, The Limits of the Criminal Sanction, 249–259, 356–363 (1968).

> This perspective offers a reminder of the special nature of criminal punishment — its costs, consequences, and variable degrees of efficacy. How do you weigh, in each environmental setting, the aptness of criminal sanctions in terms of accomplishing the traditional objectives of penal law noted at the beginning of this chapter — societal revenge and retribution, general deterrence, incapacitation, specific deterrence, and rehabilitation — or is there more to it than that?

4. **Economics.** How about the overview economic analysis that underlies so much of modern environmental law? Environmentalists use legal remedies to make producers take full account of the environmental costs and values, tangible and intangible, imposed by their activities. When environmental prosecutions successfully skewer a polluting defendant and the sentencing guidelines prescribe a jail term, does that necessarily skew the economics of rational accounting, or can it make a nice fit with the rest of the common law and administrative civil remedies in modern environmental legal process?

5. **Ecoguerrillas and the criminal law? The Necessity Defense.** And for a completely different angle on enviro-criminal law, how should the legal system treat activists like EarthFirst! when they spike trees to frustrate legal redwood logging, or sabotage highway layouts and electric transmission lines? Is the societal-interest "necessity defense" available to override the letter of the law? See California v. McMillan, San Luis Obispo Mun. Ct. 87-D 00518 (1987)(necessity defense applied to defendants in a nuclear protest case), and E. Abbey, The Monkeywrench Gang (1975).

# Chapter 20

# EVOLVING PATTERNS OF ENFORCEMENT AND COMPLIANCE

A. *The Governmental Enforcement Process*

B. *Citizen Enforcement to Complement Governmental Efforts*

C. *The Impetus to Self-Generated Compliance*

---

Environmental enforcement in the United States is in transition. After the passage in the early 1970s of both the Clean Air Act (see Chapter Eight) and the Clean Water Act (see Chapter Nine), the EPA began to embrace an enforcement ideology based on the premise that deterrence is at the heart of an effective regulatory program. Driven by civil and criminal command-and-control requirements, EPA sought to maintain accountability for noncompliance by identifying, prosecuting, and penalizing wrongdoers.

As environmental enforcement continued through the 1980s, EPA maintained and honed its deterrence approach. EPA did not seek out partnerships with the regulated community to induce environmental compliance. Instead, EPA maintained an arms-length approach to enforcement, with an emphasis on sanctioning violators and deterring other parties from committing violations.

By 1990, as hundreds of thousands of regulated entities attempted to comply with an increasingly complex set of federal and state environmental statutes and regulations,[1] the nation had spent over $700 billion on environmental cleanup efforts. That same year, approximately 2 percent of the gross national product, or $86 billion, was spent on pollution control and regulation.[2] The magnitude of these expenditures reflected a major shift in American business priorities. Environmental issues had become a significant factor in virtually every major business decision or transaction. No sale of a business, transfer of real estate, or use of hazardous chemicals could proceed prudently, without consideration of the environmental risks, costs, or effects.

Under the traditional enforcement yardsticks employed by EPA — measured in the "bean counting" terms of number of cases brought and total dollar penalties

---

1. By the early 1990s, federal environmental statutes alone exceeded 1300 pages, and federal environmental regulations exceeded 12,000 pages. See West's Selected Environmental Law Statutes, and 40 C.F.R. pts. 1-1517 (1995).

2. J. Mintz, Enforcement at the EPA 1 (1995). These numbers have undoubtedly continued to grow. By 1995, it was estimated that approximately 2.5 percent of the gross national product, or about $93 billion, stems from environmental regulation. See Elliott, Morley, and Pitt, A Practical Guide to Writing Environmental Disclosures, 25 ELR 10237 (1995).

imposed[3] — EPA's deterrence strategy was a success. Nonetheless, there was a growing recognition at EPA, and elsewhere, that an enforcement strategy based on deterrence has important limitations. Critics of EPA argued that new approaches and attitudes were needed which recognized that it is more effective (1) to prevent pollution than to punish violations after they occur, (2) to harness market forces proactively (rather than relying on command-and-control), and (3) to seek partnerships with American business that advance environmental priorities rather than dealing with American business at arms-length.

With the reorganization of EPA in 1993 and 1994, the Agency began to assess whether its historic enforcement ideology should be modified or replaced by new initiatives emphasizing compliance assurance and noncompliance prevention. As the following article illustrates, while critics have praised EPA's new-found enforcement initiatives, they continue to criticize the pace of EPA's implementation of alternative enforcement methods, particularly in light of compliance efforts already underway in the American business community.

### Theodore L. Garrett, Reinventing EPA Enforcement
Natural Resources & Environment 180 (Winter, 1998)

...In the early 1970s, EPA was occupied primarily by the formidable task of adopting regulations implementing the new environmental laws such as the Clean Air Act...and the Clean Water Act...which were passed in 1970 and 1972 respectively. There was a good deal of confusion and lack of information concerning these new programs. EPA enforcement tended to focus on compliance and technical assistance. The objective was to ensure that the regulated community understood the law and developed plans and schedules to achieve compliance. If a company was found to be in violation, the emphasis was on arriving at specific plans to gain compliance. Penalties were usually negotiated as part of a settlement agreement, but the penalties were generally in the five figure range and were not a significant end in themselves or a significant focus of negotiations. Of course, a company knew that if it did not settle, it would be exposed to higher penalties in a government lawsuit seeking both injunction relief and fines.

The paradigm changed in the 1980s, the model became command-and-control. Congress and EPA develop strict laws and regulations, violations are detected through rigorous inspections and mandatory self-reporting, and EPA and, ... the Department of Justice (DOJ) file enforcement actions and collect fines and penalties. Under this deterrence approach, it is assumed that the more inspections are conducted and enforcement actions taken, the greater the deterrent effect and the higher level of compliance. The federal government significantly expanded its enforcement resources at both EPA and DOJ. EPA created a new office of criminal enforcement. There are now hundreds of enforcement lawyers, investigators and other support personnel at DOJ and EPA. United States' attorneys in the ninety-four

---

3. The enforcement "bean" has traditionally been a valuable commodity at EPA, dominating EPA's method of measuring national, regional, and individual enforcement performance. During fiscal year 1994, for example, EPA reported the initiation of 2,249 federal enforcement actions, including civil and criminal judicial referrals and administrative penalty orders. A total of 430 civil and 220 criminal cases were referred to the Justice Department for prosecution. Criminal charges were brought against 250 individuals and corporations. Over $165 million in penalties were collected, including $128.4 million in administrative and civil judicial penalties and $36.8 million in criminal fines. See New Records For Actions, Fines Set by EPA Despite Restructuring of Program, 25 Env. Rep. 1501 (1994).

separate judicial districts have their own independent environmental enforcement programs, drawing upon state and local resources. The mission of these programs is deterrence: to enforce and prosecute violations of environmental laws and regulations. These actions are then publicized in an effort to motivate similarly situated persons to achieve compliance.

This deterrent approach may have been justified in the late 1970s and early 1980s. The theory was that the new environmental regulations required a change in corporate culture to place environmental compliance high on the list of management priorities. Flash forward to the 1990s. That change has occurred because of and independent of government enforcement efforts. Environmental compliance is now a major priority of most companies. Billions of dollars are spent each year by corporations to improve the environment. The cost of making incremental improvements continues to rise. Companies are to a large extent driven by international standards such as ISO 14000 and have adopted "beyond compliance" programs such as the Chemical Manufacturers Association "Responsible Care" program, which calls for continual environmental improvement. The emphasis no longer is simply at the end of the (waste) pipe or the back end of the manufacturing process. Executives of major companies take as a given compliance with permits and standards for discharges and emissions. Their focus now is on management systems and sustainable development, reuse/recycling, and pollution prevention. The goals are to use fewer hazardous substances in the manufacturing process, reuse/recycle those that are used, and develop systems to prevent pollution.

Unfortunately, federal environmental enforcement has lagged behind these developments in the corporate community. Enforcement actions have become ends in themselves rather than a means of achieving compliance. At a time when corporations are reducing emissions and improving compliance, the government is somewhat perversely driven to bring an increasing number of lawsuits and to collect higher fines to justify their budgets and prove that they are performing. One has only to review EPA's annual enforcement report to Congress to observe the pressures that are self-imposed by the measure of success that EPA has selected.

This deterrence approach has a number of drawbacks. By focusing on "bean counting" the amount of penalties and number of lawsuits rather than environmental improvements or the overall state of compliance, this approach leads to confusion over ends and means. In a recent case in Utah, for example, EPA brought a complaint seeking additional penalties under RCRA in a case where the State of Utah had already sued and obtained penalties for the same violations. ...The deterrence approach focuses on punishing violations after they occur, rather than encouraging systems to prevent violations. It relies on governmental enforcement actions rather than enhancing or rewarding voluntary private-sector compliance. This approach will necessarily be strained by the limitations on enforcement budgets and capabilities. Finally, deterrence leads to aggressive enforcement actions in cases where the scope of the regulations is unclear.... Confrontation rather than cooperation all too often is the result of this approach toward enforcement....

---

The debate over enforcement strategies exemplified by the Garrett excerpt raises important issues pertaining to environmental enforcement, environmental compliance, and their interrelationship:
   • How does the existing governmental enforcement process work? What are the key steps in the enforcement process, and what enforcement tools are available and effective?

• What is the significance of citizen involvement in environmental enforcement? Do citizen suits prod government to act, or provide a credible enforcement alternative when government fails to act?

• If environmental compliance is now a major priority of most companies, what factors caused this shift in business goals? Are there major business events that trigger the need for environmental compliance? What compliance tools are available to American business, and how effective are they? Is American business engaged today in self-generated compliance independent of environmental enforcement, or because of the continuing enforcement paradigm?

• What is the future of enforcement and compliance? What patterns of enforcement and compliance exist, and what changes are likely to occur?

This chapter will explore the scope and effectiveness of environmental enforcement. Since the early, formative days of the 1970s, when EPA and the states began credibly enforcing the environmental laws, layers of new requirements have made the regulatory structure extremely complicated. Amidst these changes, however, there remains a key constant: for environmental regulation to achieve its goals, it must induce compliance. Thus, the interplay between environmental enforcement and compliance remains a central inquiry.

## A. THE GOVERNMENTAL ENFORCEMENT PROCESS

Governmental enforcement of the environmental laws cuts across all of the environmental statutes. Although the particular means of enforcement varies from statute to statute, or may be modified as a statute is amended or reauthorized,[4] the governmental enforcement process typically moves violators along towards an inevitable day of reckoning.

### Section 1. PHASES IN THE ENFORCEMENT PROCESS

#### Joel Mintz, Enforcement at the EPA
#### 13–16 (1995)

At EPA, enforcement cases typically go through three phases; inspection and information gathering, administrative case development, and (if the matter has not yet been resolved) formal litigation. In noncriminal cases, the agency has several primary sources of compliance information: self-monitoring, record keeping and reporting by individual sources of pollution, inspections by government personnel, and the specific complaints of concerned citizens.

Most EPA inspections are announced to the pollution source ahead of time to ensure the presence of vital plant personnel. Inspections may be either "for cause," that is, based on a reasonable suspicion that the inspected source is in violation, or

---

4. On a variety of occasions, Congress has revised federal statutory enforcement mechanisms. For example, when amending the Clean Air Act in 1990, Congress sought to improve the reporting of violations and compliance monitoring. In §113(f) of the Clean Air Act, Congress added a bounty provision authorizing EPA to pay up to $10,000 as a reward to anyone providing information leading to a civil penalty or criminal conviction under the Act. 42 U.S.C.A. §7413(f). To improve monitoring, Congress amended the Act to add the requirement that major sources of air pollution conduct "enhanced monitoring" of their emissions and their pollution control equipment (see CAA §114(a)(3), 42 U.S.C.A. §7414(a)), a phrase interpreted by EPA to require facilities to develop monitoring protocols that would be incorporated into their Title V permits.

else routinely conducted pursuant to a "neutral inspection scheme." Perhaps surprisingly, of the approximately 1,600 individuals who perform EPA inspections, more than 75 percent do so less than 20 percent of the time.

When the agency conducts an investigation on the basis of citizen information, that information may have come from a variety of individuals. Citizen informants often include, for example, disgruntled employees of suspected violators, neighbors, state or local inspectors, environmental citizens organizations, and suspected violators' economic competitors. In potential criminal matters, these sources of information may be replaced — or supplemented — by targeted inspections, conducted under color of search warrant, by EPA criminal investigators and/or special agents of the Federal Bureau of Investigation (FBI), as well as by grand jury proceedings under the auspices of the DOJ.

Once EPA (and/or DOJ) investigators have completed their information gathering, they must determine whether the source in question is in violation of applicable standards and, if so, what type of enforcement response the agency will make. Under most of the relevant federal environmental statutes, EPA has a range of options available to it. It may begin enforcement by issuing a notice of violation to the allegedly violating source, describing the violation and inviting the source to confer informally with agency enforcement personnel. Alternatively, EPA may issue the source an administrative order requiring compliance with applicable requirements and, in some cases, an assessed civil penalty. In addition, EPA is generally authorized to refer enforcement matters to the DOJ for civil action or criminal prosecution. If it deems the circumstances appropriate, the agency may defer to a planned or ongoing enforcement action by state or local environmental officials.

EPA decisions as to which of these various enforcement options to pursue are generally made at the regional level by technically trained personnel working in cooperation with enforcement attorneys. These determinations frequently take account of a number of factors. Regional officials typically consider, among other things, the degree to which the source's discharge or emission exceeds applicable legal requirements, the duration of the violation, the number of previous enforcement actions that have been taken successfully against the same source, any relevant national EPA enforcement policies, the potential deterrence value of the case, the resources available to the agency and DOJ at the time of the decision, EPA's working relationship with interested state and local officials, and the agency's estimation of the enforcement capability of those same officials. These calculations, which are usually made with little public knowledge or participation, have great administrative significance....

At EPA, as at many regulatory agencies and departments, enforcement work involves considerable bargaining. In most instances, bargaining serves the interests and goals of both the agency itself and the regulated enterprises that are subject to enforcement action. From EPA's point of view, the time and energy of its enforcement staff is limited. To accomplish its objectives, it is usually to the agency's advantage to resolve acceptably as many enforcement matters as possible, without resorting to expensive and resource-intensive litigation. Another consideration for agency officials is the bureaucratic wish to retain control over decisions within one's area of responsibility. When compromise is not possible and EPA refers a matter to the DOJ for litigation, some of that control is inevitably relinquished to judges and DOJ attorneys and managers.

Although a number of EPA enforcement cases implicate minor, routine violations that are amenable to prompt resolution, in other matters the enforcement process is laborious and time consuming. For all concerned, these more complex cases involve high stakes and hard choices.

For regulated enterprises, the risks of enforcement sanctions — including the possibility of monetary penalties, mandatory pollution control measures that may be expensive to install and maintain, and even, in some criminal cases, jail time for responsible corporate officials — are very great....

Beyond avoiding or minimizing sanctions, regulated industries have an interest in dispelling uncertainties about their future environmental responsibilities and the costs those responsibilities will entail. In many cases, they are also concerned with preserving (or repairing) their public image as responsible corporate citizens and in reassuring lenders, shareholders, and potential investors of their good faith and freedom from impending open-ended liability. At the same time, regulated enterprises must take care that any settlement they enter into with EPA enforcement officials not harm their firm's competitive standing within its industry. Monies expended on pollution control measures and environmental penalties will not be available for investment in productive manufacturing equipment that can increase corporate profits. As they negotiate with regulators, representatives of industrial firms are thus often mindful of individuals within their companies who focus mostly on the bottom line and see little need for or benefit from corporate environmental expenditure.

For EPA's representatives there are difficult choices as well in enforcement negotiations. Any attempt at standardized decision-making by EPA is confounded by the enormous variety of conditions and circumstances that individual cases involve. The agency's enforcement engineers and attorneys frequently face sensitive decisions with respect to the pollution control measures they will accept, the penalties they will assess, the amount of time they will allow a violator to come into compliance, the legal prerogatives and safeguards they will insist upon, and the appropriateness of avoiding, or terminating, negotiations and referring a matter to the Justice Department for civil or criminal action. These judgments are complex and demanding....

### Section 2. THE FLOW OF THE ENFORCEMENT PROCESS

Successful enforcement typically occurs in a setting that balances the formality of the enforcement bureaucracy with the informality that necessarily affects and informs the prosecutorial discretion of environmental authorities. Although a certain degree of flexibility is inherent in the governmental enforcement process, for the most part steps in the process reflect a particular order and manner.

As the flow chart below shows, the three phases of enforcement at EPA — (1) inspection and information gathering, (2) administrative case development, and (3) formal litigation — can be illustrated as a series of steps moving violators along a path that, if uninterrupted, will inevitably result in civil or criminal adjudication.

Inspection and information gathering, often triggered by a letter of inquiry from EPA, usually begins the enforcement process. As the flow chart illustrates, the goal of this first phase in the enforcement process is for EPA, as the prime enforcer of the federal environmental statutes, to make a decision concerning whether or not to proceed with enforcement. Typically, EPA's enforcement decision will be informed by the quality and quantity of information gathered by EPA investigators and technical personnel through site observations, sampling, lab analysis, and other investigative techniques. EPA's ability to gather the informa-

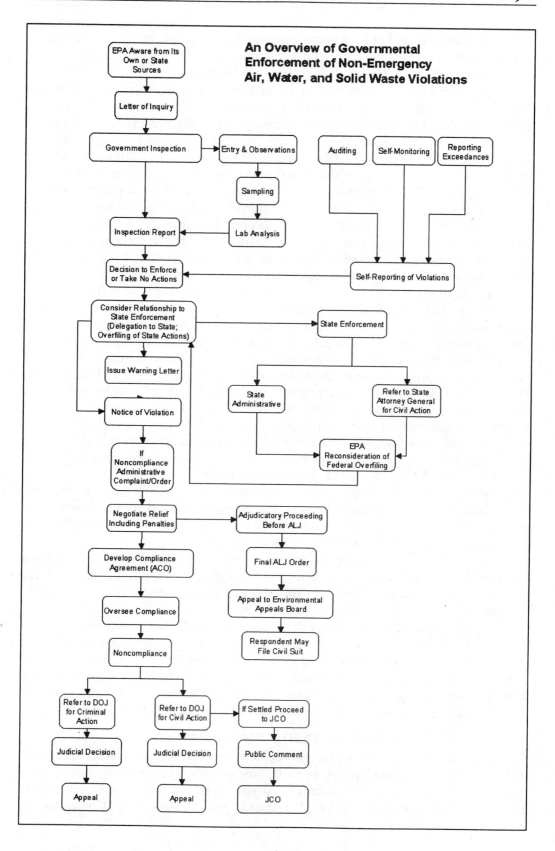

An Overview of Governmental Enforcement of Non-Emergency Air, Water, and Solid Waste Violations

tion essential to sound enforcement judgments, in part, relies on the mandatory self-monitoring, record keeping, and reporting requirements of various environmental statutes, that enable EPA to gather information on regulatory targets.

As part of its enforcement decision, EPA must consider whether EPA or the applicable state should take the enforcement lead. Under many federal environmental statutes, EPA may delegate implementation and enforcement authority to those states that demonstrate the capability to enforce adequate environmental programs. Generally, delegation under applicable statutes is only allowable when a state has developed a program that is substantially equivalent to, or no less stringent than, the federal program developed by EPA. Where a federal statute does not allow delegation to a state, EPA may alternatively enter into "cooperative agreements" allowing state involvement. EPA also retains authority to initiate enforcement actions concurrent with that of a state taking the enforcement lead (an enforcement technique known as "overfiling"). Even when a state has already taken the enforcement lead, EPA nevertheless retains authority to take its own enforcement action if EPA concludes that the state action is not timely or sufficient.

Phase two of the enforcement process, administrative case development, proceeds from the decision to enforce. If the state takes the enforcement lead, then the state may invoke its own administrative process, as the flow chart illustrates. Alternatively, if EPA takes the lead, then EPA will typically initiate an administrative process commencing with the issuance of a warning letter or notice of violation (NOV). This administrative process can result in administrative orders and penalties, negotiated penalties with non-complying entities or individuals, and compliance agreements with continuing EPA oversight and supervision. If EPA assesses administrative civil penalties that are contested, then an alleged violator can seek relief from an administrative law judge (ALJ), whose decisions are subject to judicial review based on the administrative record. Although ALJ's are EPA employees, they are full-time judges. Proceedings before an ALJ involve trial-type procedures, although typically they are less formal than civil trial proceedings in federal court. To hear appeals of administrative enforcement decisions, EPA has created a permanent Environmental Appeals Board.

If the EPA, or a state taking the enforcement lead, cannot or will not resolve a matter administratively, or if an action ordered by the EPA in an administrative proceeding is not obeyed, then the third phase of enforcement, namely formal litigation, can result. On the federal level, as the flow chart shows, EPA can refer cases to the Department of Justice (DOJ) and assist DOJ with civil and criminal environmental investigations and proceedings. On the state level, a state can refer cases to its attorney general or other enforcement arm for civil or criminal litigation if a matter cannot be resolved administratively. Because litigation is expensive and time-consuming, federal and state enforcement authorities typically reserve this third phase of enforcement for only the most significant violations.

## Section 3. ENFORCEMENT TOOLS

As a case moves along in the enforcement process, EPA utilizes an arsenal of enforcement tools to implement its goals, prerogatives, and strategies. Four sets of tools are most prominent: (1) administrative orders; (2) civil actions for injunctions, penalties, and other relief; (3) criminal prosecutions; and (4) suspension, debarment, and listing.

ADMINISTRATIVE ORDERS... EPA is increasingly utilizing administrative orders to achieve its enforcement agenda. Administrative orders typically require fewer resources than litigation, can be issued unilaterally, do not require the consent of the alleged violator, and allow EPA to control the direction and outcome of enforcement without DOJ involvement.

Administrative orders have a variety of purposes. They may be issued to gather information, to require compliance, to require remedial action, to suspend or revoke permits, or to assess penalties. Administrative orders also have significant force. Normally, such orders are not subject to pre-enforcement review and accordingly place considerable pressure on alleged violators to comply or suffer significant consequences. Only when EPA attempts to enforce administrative orders are they subject to judicial review.

By their terms, administrative orders can be elaborate and detailed. A typical §106 order issued under CERCLA, for example, may be lengthy and exacting in ordering remedial action activities at a facility to abate an alleged imminent and substantial endangerment presented by the release or threatened release of hazardous substances. Such an order may contain multiple parts and pages, including (I) identification of the parties bound; (II) detailed findings of fact and determinations by EPA pertaining to the conditions at the facility, the responsible parties, and the actions or factors resulting in liability; (III) ordering provisions specifying the work to be performed, requiring EPA approval of engineers and contractors,[5] and further requiring EPA approval of the remedial plan and design; (IV) requirements allowing further EPA periodic review; (V) quality assurance provisions imposed by EPA requiring that remedial action be performed to specified standards; (VI) provisions allowing EPA future facility access, sampling, and document availability; (VII) requirements for periodic progress reports to be made to EPA; and (VIII) notice outlining penalties for non-compliance.[6]

Violations of administrative orders may result in assessments of civil penalties, often of up to $25,000 for each day of non-compliance for each violation. In determining the amount of the penalty to be assessed, EPA is guided by civil penalty policies. Under its primary policy on civil penalties, EPA calculates the size

---

5. A §106 order requiring EPA approval of contractors and engineers typically provides:

All remedial work to be performed by the Respondents pursuant to this Administrative Order shall be under the direction and supervision of a qualified professional engineer. Prior to the initiation of remedial work at the Facility, the Respondents shall notify U.S. EPA and the State environmental agency, in writing, of the name, title and qualifications of any proposed engineer to be used in carrying out the remedial work to be performed pursuant to this Administrative Order. Selection of any such engineer shall be subject to approval by U.S. EPA, in consultation with the State environmental agency....

6. A §106 order carries substantial risks for non-compliance, including penalties of three times the amount expended by EPA from the Superfund as a result of a PRP's failure to comply, without sufficient cause, with the order. Thus, the notice of penalty provision of a §106 order typically provides:

The Respondents are advised, pursuant to §106(b) of CERCLA, 42 U.S.C. §9606(b), that willful violation or subsequent failure or refusal to comply with this Order, or any portion thereof, may subject the Respondents to a civil penalty of no more than $25,000 per day for each day in which such violation occurs, or such failure to comply continues. Failure to comply with this Administrative Order, or any portion thereof, without sufficient cause may also subject the Respondents to liability for punitive damages in an amount equal to three times the amount of any costs incurred by the U.S. EPA as a result of the Respondents' failure to take proper action, pursuant to §107(c) (3) of CERCLA, 42 U.S.C.A. §9607(c)(3).

of the penalty for which it will settle, by first considering the gravity of the violation and the economic benefit derived from the violation. Under the gravity component, EPA reviews the seriousness of the violation and the extent to which the
violation varies from specified requirements. Under the economic benefit component, EPA determines the gains derived from failure to comply. In calculating the
benefits received by the violator from non-compliance, EPA utilizes a computer
model known as the BEN model. EPA has encouraged state and local agencies to use
the BEN model as well, especially in cases where EPA has delegated federal enforcement responsibilities. After calculating the base penalty, EPA may make adjustments in light of willfulness, cooperation, history of non-compliance, and
mitigating factors demonstrated by the violator including the violator's ability to
pay (a factor in lowering penalties).

Another EPA civil penalty policy is its Supplemental Environmental Project
policy (SEP), pursuant to which EPA may mitigate a portion of the penalty as a quid
pro quo for the violator's undertaking an environmental improvement not otherwise required. SEPs typically are part of a negotiated settlement, utilized as partial
offsets to penalties. A SEP precludes the competitive advantage of noncompliance,
by causing the violator to expend funds on environmental improvements. In negotiating SEPs, EPA will consider whether a penalty should be mitigated by benefits
to the environment or the public from a supplemental project; innovation caused
by the project; risk reduction to minority or low income communities; multimedia impacts; and pollution prevention. By encouraging supplemental environmental projects, EPA seeks to produce more environmentally beneficial enforcement
settlements. However, qualifying SEPs must maintain a nexus between the original violation and the supplemental project and are not intended to reward the violator for undertaking activities obviously in its economic self-interest.

An additional enforcement mechanism closely related to SEPs are
Environmentally Beneficial Expenditures (EBEs). Enforcement actions frequently
result in pre-trial consent decrees, which can include polluter-financed EBEs, such
as donations to purchase critical lands in watersheds where violations have taken
place, or donations to universities to perform studies. After the Kepone disaster in
Chapter One, for instance, Allied Chemical gave $8 million to set up the Virginia
Environmental Endowment. See Sierra Club v. Electronic Controls Design, 909
F.2d 1350 (9th Cir. 1990) for further discussion of the legality of EBEs.

CIVIL ACTIONS FOR INJUNCTIONS, PENALTIES, AND OTHER RELIEF... In addition
to issuing administrative orders to achieve its enforcement goals, EPA can, alternatively, seek a judicial order by requesting DOJ to initiate a civil action in federal
court. Because this alternative requires coordination with DOJ, involves the commitment of resources in litigation, and does not allow the EPA directly to control
the outcome of enforcement, judicial enforcement is used less frequently than
administrative enforcement.

If EPA issues an administrative order that is not obeyed, EPA must proceed in
federal court to secure compliance. Of course, when EPA attempts to enforce
administrative orders, such orders are then subject to judicial review, and the
statutory provisions prohibiting pre-enforcement review are inapposite.

Once suit is filed in federal court, it may be resolved by settlement in lieu of trial. Normally, DOJ only files actions when DOJ believes, and when the likelihood is, that DOJ will prevail. Consequently, few enforcement cases are tried, because most defendants find it advantageous to settle such cases. Settlement often reflects the reality that violations may be straightforward or readily proved, using the violator's own discharge monitoring or other reports. Settlements are typically embodied in consent decrees, in which the parties agree on a penalty amount and a compliance schedule. DOJ policy requires that all proposed consent decrees be available for public comment prior to entry. In reviewing consent decrees or otherwise deciding whether to impose penalties, courts are not bound by EPA's penalty policies, although such policies may provide useful guidance and receive substantial deference in court. If a consent decree is approved, the court will enter it as an enforceable court order.

CRIMINAL PROSECUTIONS... Environmental criminal prosecution is increasing.[7] The federal environmental statutes provide for criminal liability for violators, even in certain cases without a requirement of knowledge or other evidence of criminal intent. (See Chapter 19.) When determining whether to proceed criminally against an individual or corporation, EPA will consider the degree of actual or threatened harm as well as the type and nature of the culpable conduct. On the basis of this review, EPA will decide whether to make a referral to DOJ for criminal prosecution. In deciding whether to proceed criminally, DOJ will consider, among other factors, voluntary compliance and voluntary disclosure of non-compliance to prosecuting authorities.[8]

Fines as well as incarceration for individuals are available to sanction criminal violators. Statutory provisions as well as United States Sentencing Commission Guidelines[9] establish the range of punishment generally available for criminal environmental violations. Although criminal sanctions do not include injunctive orders for compliance or to remedy environmental harm, such requirements may be imposed in connection with fashioning an appropriate penalty under the Sentencing Guidelines. To remedy environmental problems and punish violators, the government can also seek to pursue "parallel" civil and criminal proceedings at the same time, as long as doing so is consistent with due process and other constitutional and statutory protections.

SUSPENSION, DEBARMENT, AND LISTING... With the increase in civil and criminal enforcement, EPA is now making more use of its contractor listing program under §508 of the Clean Water Act and §306 of the Clean Air Act. Under these pro-

---

7. While the growing profile of EPA's criminal enforcement program provides important deterrence, civil enforcement remains much more pervasive at both the federal and state levels. Civil actions far outstrip criminal prosecutions, both in the numbers initiated and the fines levied. See J.T. Banks, EPA's New Enforcement Policy: At Last, A Reliable Roadmap to Civil Penalty Mitigation for Self-Disclosed Violations, 26 ELR 10227 (May, 1996).

8. See U.S. DOJ, Factors in Decisions on Criminal Prosecutions For Environmental Violations in the Context of Significant Voluntary Compliance or Disclosure Efforts by the Violator ( July 1, 1991).

9. United States Sentencing Guidelines provide guidance for fines and incarceration including appropriate prison terms for individuals including corporate officers. See U.S. Sentencing Commission Guidelines Manual, Ch. 2Q (guidelines for environmental violations for individuals) and Ch. 8 (guidelines for sentencing organizations).

grams, EPA may suspend (an interim period of probation), debar (a prohibition from contracting for a defined period), or list facilities that are guilty of criminal violations. The result of placement on the list is to disqualify the facility from receiving federal grants or contracts. Such action can be crippling to a violator heavily dependent on such contracts. Until recently, this enforcement power received little attention. Its use by EPA, however, is on the increase, and it provides an additional and important penalty.

### COMMENTARY AND QUESTIONS

1. **Congressional commitment (or lack thereof) to environmental enforcement.** In the 30 years since EPA first began to enforce the federal environmental laws, Congress has repeatedly expanded their scope and reach. At the same time, however, resources committed by Congress to EPA have not kept pace:

> In constant (1982) dollars, EPA's operating budget, which covers all its programs except for the Superfund cleanup program and construction grants for sewage treatment plants, went from $1.7 billion in 1979 down to $1.0 billion in 1983 and rose back up to $1.7 billion again in 1991.
>
> Yet during this same period, EPA's responsibilities grew enormously. The 1984 amendments to the Resource Conservation and Recovery Act, for example, known as the Hazardous and Solid Waste Amendments, significantly broadened EPA's responsibilities for regulating the generation, treatment, storage and disposal of hazardous waste. The amendments also directed EPA to issue regulations for underground storage tanks. In 1986, the Safe Drinking Water Act was amended, requiring EPA to regulate 83 specific drinking water contaminants. In the same year, the Asbestos Hazard Emergency Response Act was passed, requiring EPA to set standards for responding to the presence of asbestos in school buildings, and to study the problems of asbestos in other public buildings. The 1980s also saw significant new responsibilities for the EPA under amendments to the Clean Water Act, the Federal Insecticide, Fungicide and Rodenticide Act, and Superfund legislation (in Title III, the Emergency Planning and Community-Right-to-Know Act). Observations on the Environmental Protection Agency's Budget Request for Fiscal Year 1992, Hearing Before the U.S. Senate Comm. on Environment and Public Works, 102d Cong., 1st Sess. (1991) (Statement of Richard L. Hembra, Director, Environmental Protection Issues, Resource, Community, and Economic Development Division, U.S. General Accounting Office).

Since 1991, EPA's budgetary constraints have continued. In fiscal year 1996, for example, Congress appropriated $1.68 billion for EPA's environmental programs and management. See House Panel Reports Fiscal 1997 Funding of $3.55 billion for EPA, with No Riders, 27 Env't Rep. 399 (June 7, 1996).

Given these budgetary constraints on EPA's ability to implement the ambitious statutory agenda passed by Congress, does EPA have the resources and manpower to perform its workload effectively? The lack of resources inhibits enforcement in less dramatic ways as well. For example, low salaries have led experienced professional staff to leave EPA to pursue more lucrative employment opportunities in the private sector. One commentator has observed that "the very frequent replacement of EPA enforcement personnel has substantially denied the Agency a firm foundation of experienced professional staff, as well as a reliable 'institutional memory' that it can rely on as it pursues its enforcement work." J. Mintz, Rebuttal: EPA Enforcement and the Challenge of Change, 26 ELR 10538 (Oct. 1996).

2. **Enforcement "beans."** EPA has traditionally measured its enforcement success by bean counting — toting up, for each fiscal year, the number of enforcement cases initiated and resolved. Bean counting, as the measure of success, has serious implications for enforcement. Merely counting beans gives as much credit for enforcement based on mandatory self-reporting as for enforcement based on extensive investigation. Counting beans focuses on quantity, not quality, giving as much credit for initiating a case with little hope of improving environmental quality as one that seeks to redress serious environmental harm. Counting beans prefers actions yielding high penalties over actions yielding greater impact on environmental quality:

> Budgetary constraints encourage EPA to put resources into activities that have a measurable payoff. Since current measures of enforcement success place almost exclusive reliance on initiation (and, to a lesser extent, the resolution) of enforcement cases, funding tends to go to activities that will result in production of the much-craved, commodity — the enforcement 'bean'. B. Diamond, Confessions of an Environmental Enforcer, 26 ELR 10253 (1996).

Perversely, seen in this perspective, compliance "can become a hindrance to the bean harvest, rather than a welcome sign of progress. This doesn't mean that EPA officials encourage violations, but bean counting does tend to isolate enforcement personnel from larger issues of environmental progress." *Id.*

Is there any way to measure enforcement progress other than by utilizing "the enforcement bean"? Because EPA has for so many years reported its enforcement activity as an accomplishment, Congress has grown accustomed to measuring EPA's success by relying on the number of enforcement cases filed. Declining numbers are interpreted as evidence of a less vigilant EPA. When EPA's level of civil enforcement actions dropped in 1995, for example, EPA came under fire for reduced performance.

A related and equally important question is whether bean counting is a real measure of success. By relying for so long on the enforcement bean, EPA "has no comparative basis for evaluating whether this is the best approach to improving environmental protection. Indeed, the Agency cannot say with any level of precision what impact its enforcement cases have had, either on compliance with environmental requirements or on the environment itself. EPA has simply filed its cases, counted up its penalties, and assumed it was making progress." *Id.*

3. **Calculating civil penalties.** EPA's civil penalty policies, on their face, appear to provide a rational basis for establishing settlement amounts, by utilizing what EPA claims to be fair and equitable formulas. Those facing civil penalties, however, often encounter a world unto itself, consisting of statute-specific civil penalty policies, gravity (of environmental harm) calculation matrices, and computer models designed to determine the economic benefit of noncompliance (BEN), the present value of supplemental environmental projects (SEPs), and the ability to pay for both

pollution controls and civil penalties (ABEL). See R. Fuhrman, Almost Always ABEL: EPA Treatment of Ability-to-Pay Issues In Civil Penalty Cases, Toxics L. Rprt. 1125 (March 12, 1997).

As an example, consider the application of the Clean Water Act's civil penalty policy. That policy can be summarized in the following formula:

**Settlement Penalty = Economic Benefit + Gravity Component ± Adjustments.**

Although the policy provides the appearance of objectivity, consider the following commentary:

> Under the CWA civil penalty policy, a monetary value is placed on gravity through the use of a scoring system in which each point adds $1,000 to the penalty.... EPA personnel are instructed to assign points based on four criteria: the significance of the violation, harm to health and the environment, the number of violations, and the duration of non-compliance. Points are to be assigned for each month in which a violation occurred, and one additional point is to be added for each such month.

> The methodology for quantifying the "significance of the violation" is based on the most significant effluent violation in each month and appears quite quantitative. The CWA policy contains a table that translates the percentage of the exceedance over the allowable level of effluence into a number of points. The point system ranges from zero to 15 points for non-toxic and from zero to 20 for toxic pollutants. Harm to health and the environment is much more difficult to quantify. Nonetheless, the CWA policy allows the attribution of between 10 points and 25 points per month for violations that affect human health. Alternatively, between one point and 10 points may be assigned for impacts on the aquatic environment.

> This aspect of the methodology is highly arbitrary, overlaps with the significance of the violation criterion, and avoids the difficult task of identifying and quantifying the harm to human health and natural resources caused by a release of pollutants. It also provides EPA with great flexibility to increase or decrease the monetary value attributed to the gravity component, depending on the attitudes of the litigation team. The guidance for assessing the number of violations is vague. It allows for assigning between zero and five points based on the total number of violations each month, but provides very superficial guidance on how many points should be assigned in a given situation. The discussion of how to assign points for the duration of non-compliance is even more vague. This factor is intended to punish the violator of continuing, long-term violations of an effluent limitation or permit conditions, generally defined as violations continuing for three or more consecutive months. The plaintiffs may identify between zero and five points per month for this category. Given the subjective nature of some of these criteria, two entities in identical situations may receive quite different assessments.

> According to the CWA civil penalty policy, after calculating the initial penalty amount (i.e., after adding together the economic benefit and monthly gravity components), this total may be modified by three adjustment factors: the history of non-compliance (which can increase the penalty up to 1.5 times the initial amount), the violator's ability to pay (which may lead to a decrease in the penalty), and litigation considerations (which may also lead to a decrease)....

> The penalty policy's discussion of how to treat recalcitrance is so lacking in specifics that almost any outcome can be rationalized within its guidance. The discussion also tells the EPA staff that they may increase the recalcitrance

factor during the negotiations if the alleged violator continues to be recalcitrant "with the remedy or with settlement efforts." Clearly, the policy provides leverage for plaintiffs. While recognizing that recalcitrance is an explicit
consideration in assessing penalties under most environmental statutes, one
can easily criticize the amorphous nature of this part of the guidance.
Although it is unlikely that recalcitrance is a factor in all environmental violations, when EPA starts negotiating with an alleged CWA violator, it typically
increases the initial penalty at least 50 percent due to alleged recalcitrance.
The guidance provides no benchmark for analyzing the appropriate adjustment
factor for recalcitrance in a case with a given fact pattern. R. Fuhrman,
Improving EPA's Civil Penalty Policies — And Its Not-so-Gentle BEN Model,
23 Envt'l L. Rep. 874, 876–878 (1994).

In light of questions that can be raised about EPA's economic benefit methodology,
does it seem unfair to increase the recalcitrance factor when both parties are negotiating in good faith? The guidance about recalcitrance would be more useful to
EPA and the regulated community if it contained examples of situations where the
factor was set at specific levels. However, in many cases involving alleged CWA
violations, EPA has chosen not to share the basis for its gravity calculations with
defendants. This practice preserves the government's flexibility to raise or lower
the monetary amount attributed to this factor in settlement negotiations. Does the
failure to disclose fuel the perception that the government has not treated the
alleged violator objectively and even-handedly?

4. **EPA's use of enforcement powers: the "any credible evidence" rule.** Generally,
there are two types of evidence that can be used to prove Clean Air Act violations.
The first type, which parties currently use under EPA regulations, is commonly
known as the reference test method. In simple terms, this is a procedure that provides precise instructions to enforcement officials on how to measure whether a
source is exceeding established emission limits. The second type of evidence is
based on the words "any credible evidence" in §113(e) of the Clean Air Act, 42
U.S.C.A. §7413(e). Invoking that statutory language, EPA developed a final rule
(now under legal challenge) that would substantially expand the types of evidence
enforcement officials and citizen groups can use to prove violations of the statute.
This category includes all evidence that is deemed credible as defined by applicable rules of evidence. This evidence might include, for instance, monitoring data
that a source has collected for purposes other than enforcement. The key difference
between the two types of evidence comes down to whether a party must conduct
a specific test that is prescribed by the regulation being enforced, or whether that
party can use other available evidence to show a violation has occurred. EPA's any
credible evidence rule would codify the latter approach, expanding the type of evidence that can be used in enforcement actions.

In reviewing EPA's desire to utilize "any credible evidence," consider the following:

EPA first proposed its "any credible evidence" (ACE) rule as part of its
enhanced-monitoring rule proposal in October 1993. The ACE rule would
amend 40 C.F.R. Parts 51, 52, 60, and 61 to eliminate language that has been
read to provide for exclusive reliance on reference test methods as the means
of demonstrating compliance with emission limits under the Clean Air Act
("CAA"), and to clarify that credible evidence can be used for compliance
determinations.

The proposed ACE rule would permit a source to certify compliance by using a range of methods, including reference test methods and enhanced monitoring. The proposed ACE rule would require that SIPs promulgated under the CAA also allow the use of any credible evidence to establish a source's violations. The proposed ACE rule further provides that any "testing, monitoring, or information-gathering method[s]" that "produce[d] information comparable" to any of the methods approved for compliance certification by the source would be regarded as "presumptively credible" evidence. Thus, it appears that the drafters of the ACE rule intended that no one type of credible evidence (including reference test methods specified in applicable emissions tests or standards) would be given preferred status under the proposed rule.

To understand the issues surrounding the proposed ACE rule, it is necessary to understand the concept of a reference test method and its historic use in EPA and state enforcement under the CAA. Essentially, a reference test method is a specific test method used to determine compliance with a particular EPA emission standard or limitation. In many cases, EPA has specified the use of a particular reference test method in connection with the promulgation of a particular emission standard or limitation. According to EPA, many states and sources believed that the EPA-specified reference test method contained in SIPs was the exclusive method that could be used to determine compliance or non-compliance with the EPA standard.

In establishing a reference test method, EPA often specified: (1) training of test personnel; (2) how the test is to be conducted; (3) how test results are to be analyzed; (4) how often tests are to be conducted; and (5) how compliance with the standard is to be determined, using the test results. For example, in the case of certain opacity regulations, EPA has specified: how observers are to be trained to conduct opacity testing; how opacity tests are to be conducted; when opacity tests are to be conducted; and how test results are to be used to determine compliance with opacity regulations.

However, it is well known today that there are often alternative methods that could theoretically be used to determine compliance, with particular EPA air-quality regulations. For example, in the case of opacity, there are now continuous emission monitors (CEMs) that use lasers to measure the opacity of plumes coming out of a plant stack. The readings produced by these monitors are often more frequent, and in many cases more reliable, than the estimates prepared by even the best-trained human observers called for in the EPA opacity reference test. In addition to CEMs, there are often physical process parameters related to plant emission — such as the temperature, pressure, and speed of gas flows — that can be used to reliably estimate plant emissions of certain pollutants.

Under historic EPA practice, EPA used and strongly recommended (if it did not actually require) that states use the results of a reference test to determine compliance with the emissions standard for which the reference test was established. The ACE rule would significantly broaden EPA practice, and citizen-suit enforcement, by permitting compliance with EPA emission standards to be determined through use of "comparable" CEMs data and other measurements such as reliable indirect physical measurement or parametric data. G. Van Cleve and K. Holman, Promise and Reality in the Enforcement of the Amended Clean Air Act Part I: EPA's "Any Credible Evidence" and "Compliance Assurance Monitoring" Rules, 27 ELR 10097, 10099-100 (1997).

Has the EPA adopted an overly expansive view of the "any credible evidence" language, as industry contends? Or, does the rule simply clarify the existing law, as

EPA contends? In light of Congress' strengthening the enforcement capabilities of EPA, the states, and citizens in the 1990 CAA Amendments, did Congress intend that EPA base its broadened regulatory authority and strengthened enforcement program on the best possible data concerning the actual operations of air pollution sources?

### Section 4. BROWNFIELDS FEDERALISM AND ITS POLICY OF GREATER FLEXIBILITY AND COOPERATION

Changes in the patterns of environmental enforcement are occurring. The area in which the greatest strides have been made is in relation to regulatory developments pertaining to brownfields. As defined by EPA, brownfields are "abandoned, idled, or under used industrial and commercial sites where expansion or redevelopment is complicated by real or perceived environmental contamination that can add cost, time or uncertainty to a redevelopment project."[10]

In the past, redevelopment of brownfields was often avoided for fear of environmental liabilities arising primarily under CERCLA (See Chapter 18), its state equivalents, and the Resource Conservation and Recovery Act (See Chapter 17). The extensive jurisdictional reach of these statutes, their broad liability provisions, and the fear of federal and state enforcement were all blamed for impeding the redevelopment of many brownfield sites. Historically, prospective purchasers, who often desired to quantify cleanup costs before purchasing a contaminated site, found that governmental entities were unwilling or unable to provide assistance in determining what constitutes an acceptable cleanup. In large part, therefore, brownfields sites sat idle and undeveloped, even if such development were in the public interest. Potential investors, faced with uncertain costs and potential associated legal liabilities, sought development elsewhere, often at pristine rural sites (labeled "greenfields"). Brownfield sites, in turn, became major burdens on the community and taxpayers.

Commencing in the early 1990s, EPA and the states began to recognize that, rather than encouraging brownfield redevelopment, their deterrent enforcement strategies were actually having the opposite effect by discouraging prospective purchasers. In response, federal and state regulatory reforms were announced with the express purpose of spurring brownfields redevelopment. These reforms reflected (1) a shift from historical reliance on a deterrent and penalty-based enforcement ideology to more flexible initiatives, seeking to induce brownfields development through partnering with the regulated community; and (2) a shift towards increasing cooperation between federal and state enforcement authorities, seeking to harmonize enforcement priorities to allow brownfields development to move forward.

---

10. US EPA Region 5, Office of Pub. Affairs, Basic Brownfields Fact Sheet (1996). There are an estimated 130,000 to 450,000 contaminated brownfields sites around the country. U.S. Gov. Accounting Office, GAO/RCED-95-172, Community Development — Reuse of Urban Industrial Sites (1995). Current cleanup estimates range up to $650 billion. See Northeast-Midwest Inst., Coming Clean For Economic Development 1-2 (1996).

### United States Environmental Protection Agency, Brownfields Action Agenda
(1995)

[This agenda had six key reforms, each designed to deal with particular obstacles to brownfields redevelopment:]

1. Prospective purchaser agreements. This reform represents EPA's effort to provide a liability waiver to prospective buyers of brownfields sites. A prospective purchaser agreement is a binding contract entered into between EPA, the owner of a contaminated property, and a prospective purchaser, exonerating the purchaser from any future environmental liability at the site and obligating the EPA not to sue the purchaser for any existing contamination. Although EPA issued a policy guidance in 1989 setting forth criteria for such agreements (see 54 Fed. Reg. 34,235 (Aug. 18, 1989)), only 16 prospective purchaser agreements were made between 1989 and 1995. In response to pressure for a more flexible, compliance oriented policy, EPA revised its prospective purchaser guidelines in 1995, specifically clarifying and encouraging the use of prospective purchaser agreements. See EPA, Announcement and Publication of Guidance on Agreements With Prospective Purchasers of Contaminated Property and Model Prospective Purchaser Agreement, 60 Fed. Reg. 34,792–98 (1995).

2. Delisting sites from the CERCLIS database. To remove the stigma from listing a site on CERCLIS, a national list of CERCLA sites, EPA voluntarily delisted 25,000 (of a total of 38,000) sites for which it plans no further remediation. See CERCLIS Definition Change, 60 Fed. Reg. 16,053 (1995).

3. Other purchaser protections. EPA also issued a guidance document pledging not to pursue innocent landowners with contaminated acquifers and pledging to issue "comfort letters" to those engaged in voluntary cleanups. See U.S. EPA Policy Toward Owners of Property Containing Contaminated Acquifers (Nov. 1995); EPA Region I Announces Measure to Speed Cleanup of Wastes Sites, BNA Daily Rep. Executives, Feb. 22, 1995 at 35.

4. Land use policy. EPA also promulgated a directive allowing future land uses to be considered in selecting the appropriate remedial action at sites on the National Priorities List. See U.S. EPA, Land Use in the CERCLA Remedy Selection Process, OSWER Directive No. 9355.7-04 (May 25, 1995).

5. Pilot Project Grants. EPA agreed to fund economic redevelopment projects at brownfield sites, in an effort to develop new and more cost-effective cleanup standards. See Superfund: Reports Cite Savings in Remedy Selection Resulting from Superfund Reform at EPA, 27 Env't Rep. 1874 (1997); and

6. Memorandums of Agreement Regarding State Voluntary Cleanups. Certain EPA Regions entered into Memorandums of Agreement (MOAs) with state environmental agencies, providing that EPA will not take enforcement action at sites where private parties have conducted cleanups under the state's direction or under state voluntary cleanup statutes. See ABA, Brownfields Redevelopment: Cleaning Up The Urban Environment 117-25 (March 7, 1996).

### COMMENTARY AND QUESTIONS

1. **The old horrors of Superfund cleanups.** Chapter 18 gave a brief glimpse of how Superfund works, or in the eyes of many critics, how Superfund fails to work. Why was EPA so insistent on rigid, dictatorial cleanups, and harsh bargaining positions in Superfund's earlier years? Many somewhat speculative answers are possible.

Some relate to the backlash against the Gorsuch era non-enforcement of most of Superfund; others relate to the unthinking attitude of EPA as an overzealous agency taking itself too seriously in the exercise of the enormous powers granted by sections 106 and 107. There are more benign possibilities as well; for example, the change could have been part of a natural agency learning process, through which the agency was able to recognize that a different approach better served the public interest. Most flattering to EPA, it is also possible that the change in course coincided with a change in the nature of the underlying problem and the behavior of the regulated community that had been brought about by EPA's past practices. As to the problem itself, through 1995, EPA had listed the worst 1400 sites on the NPL and had cleanups well underway at most of them. Sites not on the NPL tend to pose less public health hazard, exhibiting problems of a more localized nature that do not waken the Love Canal and Times Beach hysteria. Remediation techniques and cleanup methods are better understood and somewhat more efficacious as a result of past experience. Moreover, the regulated entities understand the CERCLA liability scheme better. They are far more adept at estimating their own liabilities under the law, and far more wary of protracted litigation, or strategies of recalcitrance. The combination of less seriously polluted sites and regulated parties ready to negotiate allows EPA the leeway to adopt more flexible approaches.

2. **State law and policy changes affecting enforcement.** Along with federal policy changes, state agencies and state cleanup laws have also changed, perhaps to an even greater degree. Many state laws that mimicked CERCLA were at least as Draconian. See Elizabeth Geltman-Glass, Recycling Land: Encouraging the Redevelopment of Contaminated Property, 10 Nat. Res. & Envt. 3 (Spring 1996). In particular, at least 30 states implemented voluntary cleanup programs or enacted brownfields legislation, and up to six additional states announced plans to enact similar legislation. These state developments are illustrated in the pie chart set forth below in Figure 1.

## Figure 1: State Brownfield and Voluntary Cleanup Programs

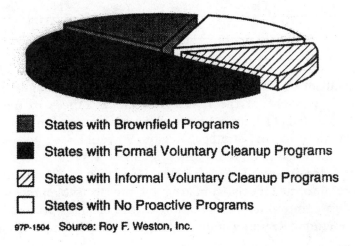

■ States with Brownfield Programs

■ States with Formal Voluntary Cleanup Programs

▨ States with Informal Voluntary Cleanup Programs

□ States with No Proactive Programs

97P-1504  Source: Roy F. Weston, Inc.

State brownfields legislation generally has four basic components: (1) risk-based, end-use cleanup standards and voluntary programs; (2) implementation of liability control, comfort, and protection through the use of covenants not to sue; (3) an accelerated program for cleaning up contaminated sites to standards pegged to future property use (so called "tiered action" objectives); and (4) economic and employment opportunities, particularly for disadvantaged areas, through the cleanup and redevelopment of contaminated sites. Many states have also added unique and potentially important components to their legislative efforts, including tax breaks or incentives for the cost of investigation and remediation associated with an individual site, and financial lender liability protection. This protection often provides for a definition of "owner" that eliminates the lender as a PRP.

Looking more closely at examples of how these individual states are tackling the Brownfield problem provides some insight into the impact of economic development on enforcement strategies. Figure 2 shows selected states and the legislative status and important features of their programs. An interesting aspect of many state initiatives is the impact of neighboring state legislation on their programs, and the "competing" economic development and environmental programs developed in efforts by certain states to become more "user friendly" to business.

## Figure 2: Status of Selected State Brownfield Programs

| STATE | BROWNFIELD LEGISLATION | END-USE VOLUNTARY PROGRAM | RISK BASED/ BUYER CLEANUP STANDARDS | LENDER LIABILITY PROTECTION | LIABILITY PROTECTION | TAX INCENTIVES |
|---|---|---|---|---|---|---|
| Pennsylvania | Yes | Yes | Yes | Yes | Yes | Yes |
| Delaware | Yes | Yes | Yes | Yes | No | Yes |
| New Jersey | Yes | Yes | Yes | Yes | No | No |
| Massachusetts | Yes | Yes | Yes | Yes | Yes | Yes |
| Georgia | Yes | Yes | Partial | No | No | No |
| Illinois | Yes | Yes | Yes | Yes | Yes | No |
| Minnesota | Yes | Yes | Yes | Yes | No | No |
| New York | Yes | Yes | Yes | Yes | No | No |
| Michigan | Yes | Yes | Yes | Yes | Yes | No |
| Ohio | Yes | Yes | Yes | Yes | No | No |

3. **Cooperative federalism in enforcement: federal and state memoranda of agreement.** EPA Region V was one of the first EPA regional offices to organize a Brownfields Task Force. This task force first issued a proposed enforcement strategy in 1993-4. According to this strategy, Region V would seek to encourage brownfield redevelopment based on four basic principles: (1) promote cleanups by encouraging participation in state voluntary cleanup programs; (2) provide information to promote informed decisionmaking by prospective purchasers and lenders; (3) encourage community participation in the cleanup process; and (4) develop partnerships among Region V states, local governments, and stakeholders.

The strategy also delineated specific initiatives, including issuing generic "comfort letters," developing site-specific covenants not to sue, and developing consensus on risk-based cleanup protocols linked to future land use scenarios.

To accomplish these goals, Region V developed a Memorandum of Agreement (MOA) with each of the Midwestern states to include language that releases sites remediated successfully under state authority from further attention by Region V. Region V's MOA with the State of Illinois, executed on April 6, 1995, is set forth below:

### Superfund Memorandum Of Agreement

### Illinois Environmental Protection Agency, United States Environmental Protection Agency, Region V
(1995)

I. BACKGROUND... The Illinois Environmental Protection Agency ("IEPA") and the United States Environmental Protection Agency, Region V ("Region V") entered a Superfund Memorandum of Agreement (SMOA) effective December 18, 1991. Among other things, the SMOA established operating procedures for general Superfund program coordination and communication between IEPA and Region V.

II. BROWNFIELDS... In 1993 IEPA and Region V began developing strategies to promote the remediation and redevelopment of "Brownfield" sites. Both agencies recognize that a key factor to the Brownfields program in Illinois is for both agencies to exercise their authorities and use their resources in ways that are mutually complementary and are not duplicative. Two operational factors are important in this regard. First, the IEPA has successfully operated a voluntary cleanup program since the late 1980s. This program, more formally known as the Pre-Notice Site Cleanup Program ("PNSCP"), provides guidance assistance and oversight by IEPA to owners and operators of sites in Illinois who perform site assessment and remediation in accordance with the practices, and under the approval, of the IEPA. In addition, IEPA has established a consistent cleanup objectives process across all its remediation programs (PWSCP, CERCLA, RCRA, and LUST) which is protective of human health and the environment. Second, USEPA has administered a national site assessment program to assess sites listed on the federal CERCLIS list. This assessment process identifies and prioritizes sites for remediation needs and also establishes a "no further remedial action planned" or NFRAP category of sites. As a result of the success of these two programs, IEPA and Region V have concluded that the principles and procedures set forth in this Addendum will meaningfully assist in the remediation and development of Brownfield sites.

III. PRINCIPLES... If a site in Illinois has been remediated or investigated under the practices and procedures of the Illinois PNSCP and IEPA has approved the remediation as complete or made a no-action determination upon review of an investigation, consistent with existing information the site will not be expected to require further response actions. Accordingly, Region 5 will not plan or anticipate any federal action under Superfund law unless, in exceptional circumstances, the site poses an imminent threat or emergency situation. Region 5 will also continue to work with Illinois to remove any concerns about federal activity under Superfund so as to encourage appropriate redevelopment.

This Principle does not apply to sites which have been listed on the National Priorities List or sites subject to an order or other enforcement action under Superfund law or sites imminently threatening public health or the environment. Future IEPA activities at the site will be based on the conditions of the remediation approval and whether any imminent threat subsequently arises.

IV. REPORTING... On an annual basis IEPA will report to Region V on the following:

1. number of sites in the PNSCP;

2. sites entering the PNSCP the previous year;

3. sites having received approvals by IEPA of full or partial completions in the previous year...

COMMENTARY & QUESTIONS

1. **How much assurance?** EPA has, on a case-by-case basis, negotiated agreements with PRPs that include express promises not to go to court and commence enforcement proceedings (covenants not to sue). The MOA does not rise to the level of a covenant not to sue. The MOA does provide prospective purchasers with assurance that, by participating in the Illinois Cleanup Program, they are unlikely to face federal enforcement action. Is that enough assurance to satisfy the PRPs desire to put an upper bound on liability? Also note that the MOA contains exceptions for sites listed on the National Priorities List, for sites already subject to enforcement action under Superfund, and for sites imminently threatening the public health or the environment. Why were these exceptions made? Do the exceptions create "pariah parcels," in the sense that no prospective purchasers will buy such a parcel when there are MOA-eligible parcels also available? At a minimum, Region V's MOA encourages prospective purchasers to work more closely with Illinois environmental officials to remediate properties under Illinois law. Does the MOA represent evidence that cooperative federalism is maturing, at least where brownfields are concerned?

2. **Enforcing promises of regulatory forbearance.** As suggested above, a covenant not to sue represents a form of promise by the regulator to exercise its authority in a particular fashion. It is akin to a contract, but is it (or any other promise of regulatory forbearance) enforceable against the government if the government changes its mind? Consent decrees that extinguish liabilities bind government to its promises because of their res judicata effect, but mere promises of the regulator are seldom enforceable. See David B. Toscanao, Note, Forbearance Agreements: Invalid Contracts for the Surrender of Sovereignty, 92 Colum. L. Rev. 426 (1992). See also, Robert Abrams, Binding Agreements With Governmental Entities, ABA Water Law Conference Proceedings, February 20, 1998. This landscape may be changing in the wake of United States v. Winstar Corp., 116 S.Ct. 2432 (1996), a case that upheld a governmental promise to bear the risk (i.e., the monetary loss) of a regulatory change it had promised not to make. The reasons that government is free to "change its regulatory mind," even after promising not to do so, have to do with the preservation of sovereignty. Is the enforceability of promises of regulatory forbearance critical to EPA's new policies of more cooperative relations with

the regulated community? The area in which this issue may come to a head is with negotiated Habitat Conservation Plans (HCPs) under the Endangered Species Act. See Chapter 14. Interior has announced a "No Surprises" policy, under which FWS agrees that it will seek no further concessions from private parties who enter into HCPs in relation to the effects of their development activities on critical habitat of listed species.

3. **EPA's Environmental Leadership Program, Common Sense Initiative, and Project XL.** In addition to its brownfields initiatives, EPA began to consider additional cooperative approaches to environmental enforcement after its reorganization in 1993-94. Traditional enforcement tools — monitoring, administrative actions, criminal sanctions, and monetary penalties — were not leading to "sustained compliance," according to EPA's Fiscal Year 1994 Enforcement and Compliance Assurance Accomplishment Report. To supplement its traditional enforcement strategies, EPA began to develop new compliance assistance programs, including the Environmental Leadership Program (ELP), the Common Sense Initiative (CSI), and Project XL.

The ELP recognizes facilities that develop and implement environmental management systems and "beyond compliance programs" and shares those innovative approaches with the regulated community. EPA selected 12 facilities to participate in the 1995 pilot program, designating these facilities to receive public recognition of their accomplishments, a grace period to correct violations, and fewer random inspections. In 1997, EPA launched a full-scale ELP program. Innovations encouraged by EPA under this program include developing: (1) the best methods to incorporate environmental management systems comparable to ISO 14000;[11] (2) the benefits of using third party auditors to verify compliance; (3) evaluation techniques for the public to analyze a company's compliance; and (4) procedures for multimedia (non-industry specific) compliance and community involvement.

To further enhance compliance efforts, EPA also developed its Common Sense Initiative, a sector-based approach that EPA designed to address compliance problems pervading certain industries. Six industrial sectors have been selected: iron and steel; electronics and computers; metal plating and finishing; auto assembly; petroleum refining; and printing. Under CSI, EPA is working with each sector to (1) promote pollution prevention programs; (2) conduct regulatory reviews; (3) develop innovative compliance assistance and enforcement mechanisms; (4) simplify reporting and record keeping; (5) streamline the permitting process; and (6) promote innovative environmental technologies.

Project XL was designed by EPA to allow flexibility in compliance for companies using innovative techniques achieving results greater than current federal

---

11. The International Organization for Standardization (ISO), an association of over 100 countries, has developed voluntary environmental management guides to assist regulated entities in developing their own management systems. A number of environmental guides have been published as part of the ISO 14000 series. For example, ISO 14001 guides the development of an Environmental Management System to develop an entity's environmental policy, including planning methods, procedures, and evaluations. Participating entities may receive ISO 14001 certification, which may provide competitive benefits in the global market, particularly to the extent companies require that their suppliers be certified.

standards. Participating facilities join with environmental agencies to make a Final Project Agreement, which, once made, is a final contract detailing the facility's plans to achieve compliance and the exemptions that the regulators will provide in exchange.

ELP, CSI, and Project XL, though innovative, have met with criticism and mixed reviews. Industry groups have criticized them as limited, ad hoc, and inflexible. In light of these reactions, are these types of EPA programs sufficiently bold and far-reaching? Does EPA cling to its historic enforcement ideology, even when seeking to develop incentive-based voluntary initiatives?

## B. CITIZEN ENFORCEMENT TO COMPLEMENT GOVERNMENTAL EFFORTS

In the early 1980s, a new development emerged in federal environmental law: private environmental organizations seized the opportunity to enforce the major environmental statutes against polluters by invoking the "citizen suit" provisions of the statutes. Beginning in 1970 with the Clean Air Act, Congress included citizen suit provisions in virtually all of the major environmental laws.[12] Although the use of citizen suit provisions in federal environmental statutes was new at the time, citizen enforcement was not a new concept. Stockholder derivative suits under the securities laws, various private rights of action via statutes like the civil rights acts, and statutory torts provided precedents for private enforcement of federal environmental statutes.

In enacting the citizen suit provisions of the environmental laws, Congress viewed the citizen suit as an efficient policy instrument and as a participatory mechanism, based on Athenian democratic ideals, allowing concerned citizens to redress environmental pollution.[13] From this perspective, citizen suits serve as adjuncts to federal, state, and local enforcement efforts. In a time of limited resources, when governmental enforcers cannot always seek compliance from polluters, citizen suits represent an enforcement safety valve. Congress also suspected that there would be occasions when the executive branch would not perform its responsibilities under the environmental laws. Thus, citizen suit provisions were also enacted to address the concern that citizen action might be necessary to force government agencies to perform their civic duties.

---

12. Citizen suit provisions, for example, appear in the Clean Air Act, CAA §304; the Clean Water Act, CWA §505; the Endangered Species Act, ESA §11(g); the Resource Conservation and Recovery Act, RCRA §7002; the Toxic Substances Control Act, TSCA §18, and the Comprehensive Environmental Response, Compensation, and Liability Act, CERCLA §310. There is no citizen suit provision in the Federal Insecticide, Fungicide, and Rodenticide Act (FIFRA) or in the Marine Mammal Protection Act (MMPA).

13. Although this assessment is shared by a large majority of legal scholars, not all agree. See M. Greve, The Private Enforcement of Environmental Law, 65 Tul. L. Rev. 339 (1990) (arguing that Congressional support for private environmental law enforcement is an outgrowth of interest group politics, and contending that citizen suit provisions are an off-budget entitlement program for the environmental movement).

### E. Guana, Federal Environmental Citizen Provisions: Obstacles and Incentives On The Road to Environmental Justice
22 Ecology Law Quarterly 1, 39–43 (1995)

EPA, charged with enforcement of most federal environmental laws, lacks the ability to enforce all environmental laws to the maximum extent possible. Understanding that there would be undesirable under-enforcement of environmental laws because of limited regulatory resources, Congress equipped many federal environmental laws with citizen suit provisions, which essentially confer "private attorney general status" on the citizenry. Under citizen suit provisions, private individuals have statutory authority to prosecute members of the regulated community for certain violations of requirements of some environmental laws. In addition to "enforcement" suits against violators, citizens also have the authority to undertake "action-forcing" suits against public officials such as the Administrator of EPA for alleged failure to perform nondiscretionary duties under the environmental law in question. Although private attorney general status is not without controversy, private enforcement remains an important part of environmental regulation.

---

Early legislative history reveals the practical and philosophical controversy behind the private attorney general concept of environmental citizen suit provisions. Some legislators viewed the private citizen action as a welcome supplement to regulatory agencies' inevitable under-enforcement due to lack of resources. Other lawmakers saw the provisions as imposing yet another burden on judicial resources. Commentators, as well, differ in their views on the value of the citizen as authority; others see private enforcement as a device that enhances public participation and ultimately legitimizes the regulatory state....

The final forms of citizen suit provisions in many statutes reflect the inevitable compromise in the debate about the wisdom of private enforcement in the environmental context. Before 1970, citizen suit provisions were common to some nonenvironmental laws, but generally only allowed actions by individuals injured by a violation of a federal law. Environmental citizen suit provisions are different in an important respect. They grant citizens the ability to act as real private attorneys general to sue on behalf of the community at large, rather than to vindicate individual rights resulting in economic loss. Thus, environmental citizen suit provisions typically provide a means to obtain injunctive relief and do not afford the citizen an avenue to recover damages resulting from violations of environmental laws. Logically, then, citizen suits are fueled by the altruism of the citizen enforcer. Although desirable as a philosophical matter, this might work systematically against the citizen enforcer who is hampered by lack of resources and has to decide whether litigation is worthwhile.

In addition, to limitations as to damages, environmental citizen suit provisions do not give private individuals carte blanche authority to sue polluters or government enforcers for any reason. From the perspective of the regulated and the regulators, substantive limitations and strict procedures on citizen suits are desirable and control private enforcement in a manner that complements rather than supplants public enforcement. Procedural and substantive limitations vary depending upon the statute at issue and whether the citizen suit is against a polluter (to force compliance requirements) or against a regulatory official (to perform a nondiscretionary duty)...

Neither governmental enforcement nor citizen enforcement of the environmental laws occurs in a vacuum. Citizen enforcement historically has acted as a check on government, provoking enforcement action or providing an alternative when government fails to act. When business fails to comply with environmental requirements, governmental and citizen enforcement together can create an impressive threat to business in the marketplace economy. The credibility of that enforcement threat, however, continues to depend on the relationships, attitudes, and perceptions of the principal actors, as the following discussion and case point out.

### B. Boyer and E. Meidinger, Privatizing Regulatory Enforcement: A Preliminary Assessment of Citizen Suits Under Federal Environmental Laws
33 Buffalo Law Review 833, 957–961 (1985)

Despite the fact that private enforcement has eroded administrative control over the enforcement process, the agencies still retain a dominant position in defining and implementing enforcement policy. At least at the federal level, the growth of private enforcement is acting as a competitive spur to government enforcers, prodding them to improve their management tools for measuring, securing, and overseeing compliance. This increased emphasis on compliance might well have evolved even without the consistent pressure of private enforcers...Still, there is no doubt that private enforcement helped to keep compliance issues high on the agendas of top agency officials and gave additional urgency to their attempts to abate the most serious violations.

While citizen suits are prodding the EPA and the state agencies to reassert their control over environmental enforcement, it seems unlikely that the government can wholly recapture its enforcement monopoly. In the short run, compliance rates are not likely to rise to such high levels that private enforcement becomes unnecessary, or unattractive to plaintiff organizations. The sweep of environmental regulations is too broad, the resources available to the agencies for enforcement too modest, and the difficulties of the regulated industries too severe to predict dramatic increases in the compliance rates...[P]rivate enforcement will probably continue to be a significant force in environmental regulation.

This private enforcement power is tempered by the fact that the agencies will retain the initiative in responding to private enforcers. By deciding how regulations will define compliance, what kinds of monitoring and reporting will be required, how compliance information will be gathered and disseminated, and what levels of noncompliance will be considered significant, the EPA and the state agencies will effectively determine what role private enforcement can play in particular regulatory programs...

The groups bringing the private enforcement actions must be concerned not only about the agencies' response to them, but also about...other potential problems. Most immediate is the need to...make private enforcement a legal and economic success.... Beyond the resource questions, however, is the more fundamental issue of whether private enforcement will be grudgingly accepted or bitterly resisted by the regulated industries and their representatives. Plainly, there is considerable resentment within the regulatory community at having the 'rules of the game' changed and at having established relationships and understandings undermined by private enforcement campaigns. There is also widespread skepticism about both the motivations of private enforcers and their legitimacy as surrogates for government...The direction of development seems to depend less on the inherent characteristics of the citizen suit than on the nature and quality of the relationships that evolve among the major parties....

Assessments of the impacts of third-party interventions like private enforcement depend heavily upon the observer's belief about the substantive desirability of the regulatory program and upon the program's compliance history. If one believes that third-party participation will disrupt the status quo, it then becomes necessary to ask whether that status quo is good or bad, and how and why it developed the way it did. In the case of environmental compliance, the argument that giving increased leverage to single-issue constituency groups might tilt agency policy unduly toward protectionist values implies that the existing system reflects a desirable — or at least acceptable — social equilibrium.... Opportunities for third party intervention might be better viewed as corrective devices to help keep the agency from straying too far outside the bounds of political consensus.

### Comfort Lake Association, Inc. v. Dresel Contracting, Inc.
United States Circuit Court of Appeals for the Eighth Circuit
1998 WL 92213

LOKEN, Circuit Judge. The timing of the various activities underlying this dispute is significant. In the Fall of 1994, MPCA issued Dresel and Fain a National Pollution Discharge Elimination System ("NPDES") permit for construction of a Wal-Mart store in Forest Lake, Minnesota. The permit required erosion and sediment control facilities because run-off of pollutants from the construction site threatened the water quality of nearby Comfort Lake and its tributaries. After investigating complaints, MPCA sent Dresel and Fain a warning letter on December 20, 1994, noting permit violations. Dresel and Fain responded in early January 1995, claiming to have properly addressed these problems.

On January 31, Comfort Lake, a non-profit association dedicated to protecting the lake and its tributaries, issued a notice of intent to sue Dresel and Fain over the same NPDES permit violations noted in MPCA's December 20 letter. Under the Clean Water Act, plaintiff must give such a notice of intent to sue to the Administrator of the Environmental Protection Agency, the affected state agency, and the alleged violator at least sixty days before commencing a citizen suit. On April 3, Comfort Lake filed this citizen suit.... Meanwhile, on February 13, MPCA again inspected the construction site, found continuing violations, and issued a Notice of Violation to Dresel and Fain. They responded that the violations were remedied, but after another inspection, MPCA issued a follow-up letter citing specific permit violations and demanding, within ten days, "a detailed schedule for correcting these deficiencies." MPCA issued a second Notice of Violation on May 10, advising Dresel and Fain that the MPCA Board would consider issuing an administrative cease and desist order at its May 23 meeting. On May 19, Dresel and Fain reported full compliance with the permit. MPCA promptly inspected, and a May 22 internal agency memorandum states that the violations had indeed been corrected.

Dresel and Fain completed store construction in November 1995 and applied for termination of the NPDES permit. MPCA terminated the permit on April 11, 1996. MPCA staff negotiated and then proposed to the agency Board a Stipulation Agreement requiring payment of $12,203 in civil penalties for all past violations of the permit, including $6,100 payable to the City of Forest Lake for "a diagnostic study of Comfort Lake." On May 21, 1996, MPCA issued its thirty-four page

Findings of Fact, Conclusions of Law and Order approving the Stipulation Agreement over Comfort Lake's opposition. The Stipulation Agreement recites that it...

> covers all alleged NPDES/SDS Permit violations that occurred at the Wal-Mart construction site and that were known by MPCA as of the effective date of this agreement. The alleged violations are considered past violations that have been satisfactorily resolved or corrected. This Agreement contains no remedial or corrective action requirements because construction at the Wal-Mart site has been completed. The NPDES/SDS Permit has been terminated; thus, there is no likelihood that the NPDES/SDS Permit violations will recur at the Wal-Mart site.

Dresel and Fain then renewed their motion for summary judgment. The district court granted that motion, and in a separate order denied Comfort Lake an award of costs and attorney's fees. These appeals followed. Broadly stated, the issues are whether MPCA's enforcement actions preclude Comfort Lake's claims for injunctive relief[14] and civil penalties, and whether the district court abused its discretion in denying an award of costs and attorney's fees.

IS THE CLAIM FOR CIVIL PENALTIES PRECLUDED?... Comfort Lake's complaint asked the court to impose civil penalties of $25,000 per day for each Clean Water Act violation. Contending that Dresel and Fain's payment of $12,203 in civil penalties under the MPCA Stipulation Agreement is an insufficient sanction for their permit violations, Comfort Lake argues that its claim for civil penalties should be allowed to proceed even if its claim for injunctive relief is moot. When a claim for injunctive relief becomes moot, a related claim for money relief is not mooted "as long as the parties have a concrete interest, however small, in the outcome of the litigation."

A Clean Water Act citizen suit, including any claim for civil penalties, must be based upon on-going violations, "that is, a reasonable likelihood that a past polluter will continue to pollute in the future." *Gwaltney*, 484 U.S. at 57. Despite this limitation, a number of circuits have concluded that, even if a polluter's *voluntary* permanent cessation of the alleged violations moots a citizen suit claim for injunctive relief, it does not moot a related claim for civil penalties.... We agree with these decisions. Congress has granted the citizen suit plaintiff standing to seek civil penalties as well as injunctive relief against on-going violations. Plaintiff retains "a concrete interest" in enforcing its penalties claim, even if any penalties recovered from the polluter go to the United States Treasury. When there is no agency enforcement action in the picture, a polluter should not be able to avoid otherwise appropriate civil penalties by dragging the citizen suit plaintiff into costly litigation and then coming into compliance before the lawsuit can be resolved.

However, this is not a case of voluntary compliance mooting the citizen suit's claim for injunctive relief. Here, the on-going violations alleged in Comfort Lake's complaint are moot because of subsequent MPCA enforcement actions that terminated the NPDES permit and assessed Dresel and Fain civil penalties for past violations. The Second Circuit addressed a similar situation in two cases. In *Eastman Kodak*, the state agency extracted $2,000,000 in criminal fines and civil penalties from the polluter. The Second Circuit held that the citizen suit "may not revisit the terms of a settlement reached by competent state authorities" absent proof of

---

14. Eds.: The court found these claims moot.

a realistic prospect that the alleged violations "will continue notwithstanding the settlement." 933 F.2d at 127 [excerpted in Chapter Nine]. But in Atlantic States Legal Found., Inc. v. Pan American Tanning Corp., 993 F.2d 1017, 1022 (2d Cir.1993), the court held that a citizen suit claim for civil penalties was neither moot nor precluded when the polluter's settlement with a local agency involved a fine of only $6,600 and "did not cover all of the violations plaintiffs allege."

These Second Circuit cases confirm that the problem here is not mootness. Because Comfort Lake satisfied *Gwaltney's* on-going violation test when its complaint was filed, there remains an actual controversy over its claim for civil penalties for these violations. Rather, the issue is what effect Dresel and Fain's settlement with MPCA has on that claim for civil penalties. Or, to state the question differently, may Comfort Lake collaterally attack MPCA's decision that civil penalties of $12,203 are appropriate *for the very same violations alleged in the citizen suit....*

An underlying principle of the Clean Water Act is that "the citizen suit is meant to supplement rather than to supplant" government enforcement action. For example, if EPA or MPCA commences a court enforcement action before or within sixty days after a citizen suit plaintiff's notice of intent to sue, the citizen suit is completely barred. Even when an agency enforcement action is not commenced until after the citizen suit, final judgment in the agency's court action will be a res judicata or collateral estoppel bar to the earlier citizen suit. See United States EPA v. City of Green Forest, 921 F.2d 1394, 1402-05 (8th Cir.1990), cert. denied, 502 U.S. 956 (1991).

In addition to court enforcement actions, EPA and many state agencies have statutory authority to proceed by formal administrative action. When EPA "has commenced and is diligently prosecuting" such an administrative action, or when MPCA has commenced and is diligently prosecuting "an action under a State law comparable to this subsection," a *subsequent* citizen suit for civil penalties is barred. 33 U.S.C.§1319(g)(6). In its initial ruling, the district court held that MPCA's December 1994 non-compliance letter and its February 1995 Notice of Violation did not "commence" an administrative enforcement action, and therefore Comfort Lake's citizen suit was not wholly barred by §1319(g)(6). The Stipulation Agreement between MPCA and Dresel and Fain is not a res judicata or collateral estoppel bar, like the judicially approved consent decree in *Green Forest.* But as a final agency enforcement action, that Agreement is entitled to considerable deference if we are to achieve the Clean Water Act's stated goal of preserving "the primary responsibilities and rights of States to prevent, reduce, and eliminate pollution." 33 U.S.C. §1251(b). Moreover, respondents like Dresel and Fain will be disinclined to resolve disputes by such relatively informal agreements if additional civil penalties may then be imposed in pending citizen suits, thereby depriving MPCA of this resource-conserving enforcement tool. For these reasons, we conclude that an administrative enforcement agreement between EPA or MPCA and the polluter will preclude a pending citizen suit claim for civil penalties if the agreement is the result of a diligently prosecuted enforcement process, however informal.

In this case, MPCA began informal action to enforce the NPDES permit in December 1994, before Comfort Lake issued its notice of intent to sue for the same violations. The agency diligently pursued Dresel and Fain to end permit violations until May 1995, when it concluded compliance had been achieved. After construction was complete, MPCA terminated the permit and negotiated stipulated penalties for past violations. As the district court noted, MPCA extracted a civil penalty that "exceeds penalties imposed in similar cases [and] was derived by looking at factors substantially similar to those which must be considered by a court imposing penalties under" the Clean Water Act. Because MPCA diligently prosecuted its enforcement demands, the civil penalties it elected to extract in settling those demands may not be reconsidered in this citizen suit. While Comfort Lake might have preferred more severe civil penalties, MPCA has the primary responsibility for enforcing the Clean Water Act.

SHOULD ATTORNEY'S FEES HAVE BEEN AWARDED?... Although Comfort Lake's claims for affirmative relief are foreclosed by the subsequent MPCA enforcement actions, Comfort Lake may still be entitled to an award of costs and a reasonable attorney's fee as a prevailing party under 33 U.S.C. §1365(d) if its citizen suit was the catalyst for agency enforcement action that resulted in the cessation of Clean Water Act violations. However, the district court determined that Comfort Lake was not a catalyst, both because MPCA began enforcing the permit before Comfort Lake's notice of intent to sue, and because Comfort Lake "actually impeded" agency enforcement by suing MPCA in state court and then actively opposing the proposed Stipulation Agreement. This finding of fact is not clearly erroneous. The finding is well supported by the affidavit of MPCA's supervisor in charge of enforcing the NPDES permit, who averred that Comfort Lake impeded and delayed the enforcement process and that "MPCA's enforcement actions would have been the same even in the absence of a citizen's suit by the Comfort Lake Association, except that the enforcement actions would have been completed sooner." Because Comfort Lake was not a prevailing party, the district court properly denied its request for costs and attorney's fees. The judgment of the district court is affirmed.

COMMENTARY & QUESTIONS

1. **Citizen suits and the command-and-control model.** Citizen suits typically do not interfere with the formal processes by which government sets enforcement priorities and balances costs and benefits. Instead, citizen suits implement those decisions by enforcing them. Generally, as in *Comfort Lake*, the government remains the party charged with the policy assessment. The citizen suit, in turn, concerns whether the alleged violator has met the governmental standards, or whether the governmental administrator has carried out the mandatory duties that Congress has prescribed. Nonetheless, citizen suits can affect the command-and-control model. By allowing private enforcement of the goals defined, citizen suits can affect enforcement priorities. Citizen suits can also have the beneficial effect of exposing those priorities to public scrutiny and comment. For example, in the early 1980s, when the EPA (under the Anne Gorsuch regime) virtually stopped enforcing the environmental laws, citizen groups filed hundreds of suits that not only enforced the environmental laws (primarily the Clean Water Act at the time) but also exposed the EPA's abdication of its enforcement responsibilities.

2. **EPA's inattention to enforcement.** One of the primary rationales for citizen enforcement of the environmental laws is that governmental enforcers do not always have the resources, interest, or will to enforce. Now, almost thirty years after the first citizen suit provisions were passed, is EPA paying more attention to

enforcement? A 1996 critique by the United States General Accounting Office (GAO) concludes that, at least where water pollution is concerned, EPA is still not paying attention.

Pursuant to a Congressional request, GAO reviewed the EPA's progress in ensuring that facilities comply with federal pollutant discharge requirements, focusing on: (1) the frequency of facilities' violations; (2) the limitations of EPA systems and the effects of these limitations; and (3) EPA plans to correct these violations. GAO found that: (1) EPA compliance data for Fiscal Year 1994 show that 1 in 6 of the nation's 7,053 major regulated facilities have significantly violated the discharge limits in their permits; (2) EPA considers facilities to be in significant noncompliance of their discharge levels when discharged pollutants exceed permit limits by 20 percent or more in a 2-to-6 month period; (3) EPA is unable to identify all of the facilities that violate their discharge limits because the criteria it uses to screen facilities have not remained consistent with the types of discharge limits used in permits; (4) EPA has expanded its criteria for identifying cases of significant noncompliance and assigning priorities of enforcement action in order to identify major facilities that have violated discharge levels in the past; and (5) EPA assessed penalties of about $25 million in 323 cases of Clean Water Act violations in 1994, and its studies indicate that very few penalties are assessed for significant violations of daily maximum discharge limits. See Water Pollution: Many Violations Have Not Received Appropriate Enforcement Attention (Letter Report, 03/20/96, GAO/RCED-96-23).[15]

3. **How much is accomplished by citizen suits?** Quantitatively, it is tempting to give a bean counter's answer based on the number of filings, but the more probing answer lies in estimating the impact of citizen suits and their availability on governmental enforcement performance and voluntary compliance by regulated entities. All such estimates agree that citizen suits have had an immense positive impact on both governmental and regulated entity performance. See, e.g., H. Maples, Reforming Judicial Interpretation of the Diligent Prosecution Bar: Ensuring An Effective Citizen Role In Achieving the Goals of the Clean Water Act, 16 Va. Envt'l. L.J. 195, 203–4 (1996) ("Citizen suits have become so effective that now industry fears them more than negotiation and settlement with the enforcing agency"); J. Miller, Private Enforcement of Federal Pollution Control Laws Part I, 13 Envt'l. L. Rep. 10309 (1983) (concluding that the most celebrated uses of citizen suits have been against EPA for its failures to implement environmental statutes in a timely and complete manner, and that the significance of citizen suits can hardly be doubted); Mann, Polluter-Financed Environmentally Beneficial Expenditures: Effective Use or Improper Abuse of Citizen Suits Under the Clean Water Act?, 20 Environmental Law 176, 182–185 (1990) (concluding that citizen suits seeking relief against EPA for failing to perform mandatory duties have had a major impact on shaping implementation of the environmental statutes).

---

15. See also H.R. Rep. 1086, 102nd Cong., 2d Sess. 1992 (Dec. 31, 1992) documenting the snail's pace of regulatory effort under FIFRA, which has no citizen suit provision. Despite a program budget of over $100 million, the EPA had, as of mid-1992, completed the final re-registrations for only 2 of the almost 20,000 registered pesticide and-use products.

4. **Forms of relief available in citizen suits.** Under the citizen suit provisions of the environmental laws, private citizens can enforce statutory, regulatory, or permit requirements through suits seeking compliance orders and penalties. In addition to this enforcement type of citizen suit, a mandamus type of action is also available for citizens seeking to require a regulator to comply with his duties under the environmental laws. For example, under the Clean Water Act, the EPA Administrator may be sued by citizens "where there is alleged a failure of the Administrator to perform any act or duty...which is not discretionary." CWA §505(a)(1)(2), 33 U.S.C.A. §1365(a)(1)(2). Significantly, mandamus is not available to require EPA to take enforcement action when a citizen provides EPA with notice of an alleged violation. This point had been the subject of a split in the early cases, particularly because CWA §309(a)(3) provides in pertinent part:

> Whenever on the basis of any information available to him, the Administrator finds that any person is in violation of §1311[relating to unpermitted discharges] ... he shall issue an order requiring such person to comply with such section ..., or he *shall* bring a civil action in accordance with subsection (b) of this section. [emphasis added.]

In what has become the leading case on the issue, Dubois v. Thomas (Administrator of EPA), 820 F.2d 943 (8th Cir. 1987), the court invoked *Chevron* and deferred to EPA's interpretation that claimed discretion not to enforce in spite of the presence of the usually obligatory word "shall." To buttress its position, the court relied on Heckler v. Chaney, 470 U.S. 821, 831 (1985), which said:

> An agency decision not to enforce often involves a complicated balancing of a number of factors which are peculiarly within its expertise. Thus, the agency must not only assess whether a violation has occurred, but whether agency resources are best spent on this violation or another, whether the agency is likely to succeed if it acts, whether the particular enforcement action requested best fits the agency's overall policies, and indeed, whether the agency has enough resources to undertake the action at all. An agency generally cannot act against each technical violation of the statute it is charged with enforcing.

5. **Prerequisites to citizen enforcement.** Before suit can proceed, however, several key statutory and jurisprudential hurdles must be overcome. This should be a familiar topic, having appeared at least twice before, in Chapter One's consideration of the *Gwaltney* case interpreting the CWA citizen suit provision as inapplicable to cases alleging wholly past violations, and in Chapter Seven's standing materials. Beyond those doctrines, there are additional barriers to citizen suits that seek to integrate citizen enforcement with the regulatory regime as administered by governmental officials. First, in order to initiate suit, the citizen must give notice to the EPA, the state where the violation occurred, and the alleged violator. Generally, sixty days notice is required, although the amount of notice can vary for certain kinds of violations. The purpose of notice is to allow the federal government the opportunity to initiate its own suit, precluding the citizen's suit, or to allow the violator to comply and correct its violation. Second, suit must be brought within the applicable statute of limitations, generally viewed, in most citizen suit actions, to be five years. See, e.g. Atlantic States Legal Found. v. Tyson Foods, Inc., 897 F.2d 1128 (11th Cir. 1990); Sierra Club v. Chevron U.S.A., Inc., 834

F.2d 1517 (9th Cir. 1987). Third, the citizen suit provisions generally specify that if federal or state authorities are diligently prosecuting an action to require compliance, filing of a citizen suit is barred, although citizens may still intervene in federal enforcement actions as of right. This hurdle is designed to prevent citizen suits from infringing on the exercise of enforcement discretion by federal and state authorities. Although a citizen suit is precluded if there is a pending *judicial* action by a regulatory authority that is being diligently prosecuted, does an administrative action by a regulatory authority also have a preclusive effect on a citizen suit? One court summarized the case law as follows:

> Four courts have interpreted the statutory language concerning citizen suits when the state has already begun an administrative action. In Baughman v. Bradford Coal Co., 592 F.2d 215 (3d Cir. 1979), the court first held that in certain circumstances an administrative hearing can be the equivalent of a court action. It then held that the court should measure the power of the administrative agency against that of the court to determine whether the administrative action was similar enough to a court action to fall within the statutory language. In Friends of the Earth v. Consolidated Rail Corp., 768 F.2d 57 (2d Cir. 1985), the Second Circuit rejected this rationale, stating it would be inappropriate to expand the statutory language to include administrative enforcement actions. The Ninth Circuit adopted the *Friends of the Earth* rationale, and held that the plain language of the statute provided that only an ongoing action in a court, rather than an administrative agency, would preclude a citizen suit. Sierra Club v. Chevron U.S.A., Inc., 834 F.2d 1517, 1525 (9th Cir. 1987). At least one District Court outside these circuits has followed the *Friends of the Earth* interpretation in Maryland Waste Coalition v. SCM Corp., 616 F.Supp. 1474, 1478-81 (D.Md. 1985). This Court also adopts the *Friends of the Earth* rationale. Lykins v. Westinghouse Electric Corp, 715 F. Supp. 1357, 1358–9 (1989). [But see CWA §309(g) (1987), discussed in the *Comfort Lake* case, which codified the *Baughman* rule.]

6. **Citizen suit notice.** One of the most frequently litigated issues under the citizen suit provisions of the environmental laws is whether to dismiss cases filed by plaintiffs who "jump the gun" and either file suit before passage of the requisite notice period or file a defective notice. In Hallstrom v. Tillamook County, 493 U.S. 20 (1989), the Supreme Court considered whether a case should be dismissed for the complete failure to give notice. Although affirming dismissal, the Court left open whether notice is a jurisdictional prerequisite to suit and how to treat issues of incomplete or defective notice. Should defects in the content and form of notice (as opposed to the timing) result in dismissal? In Dague v. City of Burlington, 935 F.2d 1343 (2d Cir. 1991), the Second Circuit addressed that question in reviewing the RCRA citizen suit requirements, finding that prior notice in suits involving hazardous wastes is of minimal value and that dismissal should not follow for failure to follow technical aspects of notice provisions.

7. **Cessation of violation in a post-*Gwaltney* world.** Gwaltney of Smithfield, Ltd. v. Chesapeake Bay Foundation, 484 U.S. 49 (1987), the case in which the Supreme Court held that citizen suits under the CWA would not lie for wholly past violations, has become standard fare in the interpretation of citizen suit provisions. As in *Comfort Lake*, courts now carefully inspect the language of the specific provision being considered to see if it refers to past or to current violations, and rule

accordingly. After *Gwaltney*, where the relevant citizen suit provision speaks of violation in the present tense, citizens must be prepared to prove at least the likelihood of ongoing violations in order to prevail. See, e.g., Coburn v. Sun Chemical Co., 1998 WL 120739 (construing "to be in violation" language of RCRA §7002(a)(1)(A) to prevent suit against past owners of parcel allegedly presenting an imminent endangerment while permitting suit against present owner).

The cases in this area tend to be somewhat technical and formalistic in deciding what suffices to constitute allegation of an ongoing violation. First, judgments concerning whether a violation is ongoing are to be made as of the time the complaint is filed. See Atlantic States Legal Found., Inc. v. Tyson Foods, Inc., 897 F.2d 1128 (11th Cir. 1990). Second, a violation will not be considered to be ongoing if remedial measures establish that there is no reasonable prospect for recurrence. See Chesapeake Bay Found. v. Gwaltney of Smithfield, Ltd., 844 F.2d 170 (4th Cir. 1988). Third, plaintiffs, as a pleading matter, need only make a good-faith allegation of an ongoing or repeat violation in order to be able to file suit, see Sierra Club v. Union Oil of California, 853 F.2d 667 (9th Cir. 1988), but plaintiffs must be able to prove an ongoing or repeat violation in order to prevail at trial. See Carr v. Alta Verde Indus., 924 F.2d 558 (5th Cir. 1991). Finally, ongoing violations can be established by showing that violations continued on or after the filing of a complaint or by producing evidence from which a reasonable trier of fact could find a continuing likelihood that intermittent or sporadic violations would occur. See Connecticut Coastal Fishermen's Assn. v. Remington Arms Co., 989 F.2d 1305 (2d Cir. 1993).

Of what significance are these technical post-*Gwaltney* decisions? In part, they reflect an attempt by the federal courts to avoid cluttering their dockets with citizen suits. Consider, for example, the following comment on the proliferation of citizen suits under §505 of the Clean Water Act:

> The primary reason for the predominance of citizen suits under §505 is the relative ease of uncovering and proving a violation under CWA §402's NPDES program.... [D]ischargers under the program must routinely file discharge monitoring reports [DMRs] with both state regulatory agencies and the EPA. The discharger must certify the accuracy of each DMR and the CWA imposes substantial penalties for false reports. Each DMR must list the actual quantity of waste discharged, as well as the permitted amount that may be discharged. As a consequence, in many instances spotting permit violations is as easy as comparing two numbers on a printout.... The majority of courts have held that DMRs are admissible as evidence of the violations, and have granted summary judgment to citizen plaintiffs based solely on DMRs.... Mann, Polluter-Financed Environmentally Beneficial Expenditures: Effective Use or Improper Abuse of Citizen Suits Under the Clean Water Act?, 20 Environmental Law 176, 183-4 (1990).

From this perspective, judicial reliance on jurisprudential mechanisms to limit the number and scope of citizen suits can be seen as a form of judicial administration, seeking to minimize litigation based on spotting permit violations simply by "comparing two numbers on a printout." Id.

8. **The *Steel Company* case.** Another post-*Gwaltney* question was resolved by the Supreme Court itself, in addressing whether a violator may escape liability by

completing remedial action after receiving notice of a citizens group's intent to file a suit but before the citizen suit is filed. In Steel Company v. Citizens For A Better Environment (CBE), 118 S.Ct. 1003 (1998), the Steel Company was charged by a citizens group with violating the Emergency Planning and Community Right to Know Act (EPCRA), 42 U.S.C.A. 11001, et seq., by failing to file timely toxic and hazardous chemical storage and emission reports for past years. By the time the complaint was filed, after the requisite statutory notice period, the Steel Company had brought its filings up to date. The Supreme Court held that because none of the relief sought would remedy the citizen group's alleged injury in fact, there was no standing to maintain the suit, and the complaint should be dismissed. In particular, the Supreme Court found that none of the specific items of relief sought — a declaratory judgment that the Steel Company violated EPCRA; injunctive relief authorizing CBE to make periodic inspections of the Steel Company's facility and records and requiring the Steel Company to give CBE copies of its compliance reports; and orders requiring the Steel Company to pay EPCRA civil penalties to the Treasury and to reimburse CBE's litigation expenses — and no conceivable relief under the complaint's final general request, would serve to reimburse CBE for losses caused by the Steel Company's late reporting, or to eliminate any effects of that late reporting upon CBE. (See Chapter Seven.)

Faced with the prospect of enforcement through citizen efforts, can a company, after the decision in *Steel Company*, target its compliance to eliminate identified sources prior to the filing of a citizen suit? If so, citizen enforcement efforts are thereby chilled; citizens, moreover, then get no reimbursement fees for performing this enforcement compliance function since the case cannot survive in court. There is a special sense in which this is a particular problem with EPCRA, where compliance can take the form of filing reports, rather than installing complex pollution control equipment that may or may not adequately reduce discharges or emissions. In the EPCRA context, as the Seventh Circuit noted below in *Steel Company*, to say that industries cannot be sued when they withhold information from the public about use and release of toxic chemicals until citizens file enforcement notices, if they just provide the overdue information prior to the lawsuit, raises important questions concerning the significance of citizen enforcement provisions. "If citizen suits could be fully prevented by 'completing and submitting' forms, however late, citizens would have no real incentive to incur the costs of learning about EPCRA, investigating suspected violators, and analyzing information." If "citizen suits could only proceed when a violator received notice of intent to sue and still fails to spend the minimal effort required to fill out the forms and turn them in,...private citizens would have to absorb much of the cost of [enforcement], with little or not hope of recovering those costs through awards of litigation expenses.... " 90 F.3d 1237, 1244–5 (7th Cir. 1996).

9. **Defining agency enforcement diligence.** Citizens affected by a polluter's actions often suffer real and immediate consequences as a result of the pollution. Governmental regulators have a different perspective that is shaped by their need to administer the program to achieve its regulatory ends within the constraints of a limited agency budget and under the realities of having to work with the regu-

lated entities on an on-going basis. Given these differences in perspective, cases like *Comfort Lake* arise in which the citizens assert that the governmental agency is not prosecuting diligently. Some of these citizen suits allege, or at least imply, that the governmental filing is collusive and is intended to shield the polluter from enforcement rather than to seek enforcement. Courts have already had to decide cases, for example, where defendants sought to ensure diligent prosecution for the sole purpose of avoiding a citizen suit. In Friends of the Earth, Inc. v. Laidlaw, 890 F. Supp. 470 (D.S.C. 1995), the defendant requested that its settlement with the state environmental agency and EPA be filed as a lawsuit, so as to avoid the looming citizen suit. The agencies accepted the request on the condition that the defendant cover the expenses. The defendant thereafter funded the filing of a complaint against itself on behalf of the state environmental agency. When the citizen suit was filed two days later, the defendant filed a motion to dismiss based on the diligent prosecution bar. Although the motion was denied, the case warns of the potential misuse of the diligent prosecution bar.

10. **Environmentally Beneficial Expenditures (EBEs).** Note that, in *Comfort Lake*, the negotiated civil penalty included $6,100 payable to the City of Forest Lake for a diagnostic study of Comfort Lake. This type of polluter-financed expenditure, frequently appearing in consent decrees in both governmental and citizen enforcement actions, is known as an Environmentally Beneficial Expenditure (EBE). Like SEPs, EBEs are a type of penalty, typically negotiated among the parties, designed to offset the benefits gained through polluting activity by requiring the polluter to expend funds in support of an environmentally beneficial study or activity.

11. **Attorneys' fees and costs under citizen suit provisions.** When citizens embark as "private attorneys-general" attempting to enforce existing law in agencies and courts, they often face substantial administrative and financial burdens, and opponents who are either public officials or well-financed corporate entities writing off expenses against revenues. Expert witnesses and attorneys cost money. For plaintiff groups like the citizens in Overton Park, this often means having to raise funds through bake sales, raffles, selling logo tee-shirts, or passing the hat. The larger national environmental groups have substantially greater resources, but are confronted with a proportionally broader range of advocacy commitments, and likewise depend upon volunteer contributions. Environmentalists have turned to both the courts and Congress in attempts to win financial recognition of the role played by private attorneys-general. In court, environmentalists face the "American Rule" of fee-shifting; unlike their counterparts under the English rule, prevailing plaintiffs in American courts generally are unable to recover the costs of litigation from defendants. (In part this explains why punitive damages are often sought in common law litigation.)

The opportunity to recover attorneys' fees and costs is often vital to citizen suit enforcement and, as in *Comfort Lake*, is often a vigorously contested issue. The citizen suit provisions of the Clean Air Act allow an award of attorney's fees and costs where appropriate. See CAA §304(d), 42 U.S.C.A. §7604(d). Citizen suit provisions of the Clean Water Act, RCRA, and CERCLA provide for an award of attorney's fees and costs to prevailing parties or substantially prevailing parties. See

CWA §505(d), 33 U.S.C.A. §1365(d); RCRA §7002(e), 42 U.S.C.A. §6972(e); CERCLA §310(f), 42 U.S.C.A. §9659(f).[16] Environmental "fee shifting" provisions are typically viewed as a necessary incentive to environmental enforcement, because few private plaintiffs can afford to finance expensive environmental litigation that typically results in nonmonetary benefits to the public at large (rather than damage awards to the individual plaintiffs). Congress accordingly included fee shifting incentives in various environmental statutes as an incentive to spur enforcement of meritorious claims. Once a plaintiff demonstrates to the court that an award is appropriate (when the plaintiff prevails in some respect or the lawsuit is a contributing factor to the defendant's ultimate actions), then the court may award reasonable attorneys' fees and costs. The appropriate amount of fees is typically calculated as the product of reasonable hours times a reasonable rate, also known as the "lodestar" amount.

Prevailing plaintiffs, however, have often found courts responsive to defendants' attempts to restrict such awards, finding that public interest plaintiffs — since they are supposed to be motivated by civic impulse rather than commercial incentive — should be given less than commercial fee rates. In City of Burlington v. Dague, 505 U.S. 557 (1992), the Supreme Court faced another situation: whether a citizen enforcement fee should be able to claim an enhancement over normal hourly rates to take account of the fact that attorneys take a gamble on a zero recovery when they represent citizen plaintiffs enforcing federal law. The Court held that the lodestar amount cannot be adjusted upward to account for the contingency nature of many environmental citizen suits. Citizen groups had fought for upward adjustments to allow the lodestar to be increased by a factor reflecting the contingent risks of bringing suit. Will the Supreme Court's opinion cripple citizen suit enforcement? Absent the right to seek increased fees for contingent risk, will there be an insufficient incentive to bring citizen suits? Some environmental organizations fund significant parts of their environmental public interest watchdog operations on citizen suits, using the lodestar to provide more than public interest salaries and their victories on the merits to pay experts who then work on additional issues. See Axline, Decreasing Incentives to Enforce Environmental Laws: City of Burlington v. Dague, 43 J. Urban & Contemporary L. 257 (1993).

Environmentalists can also win fees and costs under broad provisions of the Equal Access to Justice Act (EAJA), 28 U.S.C.A. §2412(d). Prevailing parties, in situations where the reviewing court considers the government agencies' position not "substantially justified," can claim expert witness and attorneys' fees. EAJA litigation extends the realm of fee-shifting even, as in NEPA, where enforced statutes do not specifically grant citizens standing. Where no statute provides for grants of fees, there are several nonstatutory avenues to funding public interest litigation. Under equity principles, American courts have evolved several exceptions to the

---

16. In a variety of federal statutes authorizing citizen suits, as in the Clean Water Act's §505, Congress consistently inserted a fee recovery provision in terms similar to the following:

§505(d) Litigation costs. The court, in issuing any final order in any action brought pursuant to this section, may award costs of litigation (including reasonable attorney and expert witness fees) to any prevailing or substantially prevailing party, whenever the court determines such award is appropriate. 33 U.S.A. §1365(d).

American Rule in addition to private attorney-general theories, including where defendants act in bad faith and where the defendants' actions have built up a "common fund" against which plaintiffs' costs can reasonably be assessed. Several state and federal courts initially expanded the private attorney-general approach by adding a right to recover attorneys and expert witness fees when citizen suits prevailed. The Supreme Court, however, in a case arising from environmental efforts to halt or improve the safety of the Trans-Alaska Oil Pipeline, held that federal courts would no longer be permitted to grant expert witness or counsel fees to environmental plaintiffs acting as private attorneys-general unless they could prove bad faith, a common fund, or specific statutory authorization for fee awards. Alyeska Pipeline Service Co. v. Wilderness Society, 421 U.S. 240 (1975). Although federal courts were thus halted in recognizing fee-shifting in most private attorney-general suits, state courts retain the authority to apply their own equity principles, awarding fees to citizens whose efforts enforce the law and defend a public good. See Troutwine, A Primer on Attorneys' Fees Award: Fee Computation under Federal and State Attorneys' Fees Statutes, in PLI, Court Awards of Attorneys' Fees 99–108 (1987); Robertson & Fowler, Recovering Attorneys' Fees From the Government Under The Equal Access to Justice Act, 56 Tul. L. Rev. 903, (1982).

## C. THE IMPETUS TO SELF-GENERATED CORPORATE COMPLIANCE

As reviewed in earlier parts of this chapter, a critical debate is ongoing concerning whether the deterrent enforcement strategies traditionally used to control pollution should continue to be the highly prescriptive ones inherited from the command-and-control realm or, alternatively, should be "kinder, gentler" ones emphasizing compliance assurance and noncompliance prevention. The appropriate role of citizen enforcement has added fuel to this debate.

In recent years, however, with the exponential growth in the scope and complexity of the environmental laws, the debate has entered a new phase. As even those long charged with environmental enforcement have come to recognize, a major shift has taken place in the attitudes and business priorities of American business:

> Even the most curmudgeonly old enforcer must recognize...that the general attitudes of the regulated sector have altered over time. Deliberate efforts to evade environmental controls have become rarer (although by no means unknown), the importance attached to compliance has increased, and the resources and management attention devoted to the environmental protection has greatly expanded. Environmental management was once commonly considered a nuisance activity to be conducted and supervised as a corporate backwater function. It has now taken a much more central role, becoming a core part of many companies' management structures. B. Diamond, Confessions of an Environmental Enforcer, 26 ELR 10252, 10254 (1996).

If environmental compliance has now made the transition from a corporate backwater function to a top business priority, what implications does this have for the future of environmental enforcement? If corporations are now reducing emissions and achieving compliance on their own initiative, will this self-generated compliance continue, or is the credible threat of continued governmental and citizen enforcement still required?

## Section 1. THE TRIGGERS FOR ENVIRONMENTAL COMPLIANCE

Today, buyers, sellers, borrowers, and lenders almost invariably confront environmental issues when engaging in their regular business activities. While the magnitude of potential liability, and the likelihood of its occurrence, may be greater in certain business sectors (e.g., chemical manufacturers) than in others, the scope of environmental regulation now covers almost every type of property or business. Environmental risks, costs, and benefits have become a factor in virtually every transaction.

Environmental issues typically arise in connection with five key types of business events that trigger attention to the need for environmental compliance in order to avoid environmental liabilities and risks. These five triggers are: (1) permitting and reporting; (2) Securities Exchange Commission (SEC) disclosure by public companies; (3) the satisfaction of corporate information needs; (4) borrowing for ongoing business needs; and (5) the purchase or sale of a business or property.

PERMITTING AND REPORTING... Hundreds of thousands of dischargers and waste management facilities are subject to the permit programs established under federal and state environmental laws.[17] Permits define and facilitate compliance and enforcement, by transforming generally applicable limitations promulgated by governmental enforcers (e.g., "discharges shall be treated in accordance with best available technology") into specific obligations, including a timetable for compliance for the individual discharger. Permits thus provide an effective means of assuring that the permittee is on notice of its obligations as spelled out in the permit, that regulators are notified of releases and discharges by permitters as required by the terms of the permit, and that the specific requirements applicable to a particular discharge or activity are identified and clarified.

By applying federal and state requirements to individual pollution sources and hazardous waste management activities, permits play a crucial role, and the inability or failure to obtain a necessary permit can be fatal to business operations. Thus, obtaining permits in the first instance, and then complying with their reporting and other standards, are key events triggering attention to environmental concerns. For these reasons, the need to obtain and comply with permits is taken as a given by business executives today.

SEC DISCLOSURE REQUIREMENTS FOR PUBLIC COMPANIES... There are two events that may trigger a company's duty to disclose certain of its environmental liabilities under the federal securities laws. First, disclosure may be required as part of a publicly held company's mandated securities filings. See Regulation S-K, 17 C.F.R. Part 229. Second, disclosure may be required when a company is subject

---

17. Federal statutes creating one or more permit systems include the CAA §110(a)(2), 42 U.S.C.A. §7410(a)(2); the CWA §412(b), 33 U.S.C.A. §1342(b); the SDWA §1422(b), 33 U.S.C.A. §300h-1(b); and RCRA §3006(b), 42 U.S.C.A. §6929(b). State agencies will issue the permits either when EPA has delegated its authority to implement a program to the state, or when the state has adopted an independent regulatory program.

to SEC Rule 10b-5, an anti-fraud rule that usually comes into play as a result of a company selling its securities, such as in a stock purchase agreement in which the company makes representations and warranties concerning its operations, its compliance with laws, and other material facts in the agreement. The importance of compliance with these disclosure obligations is detailed below.

## F. Friedman and D. Giannotti, Environmental Self Assessment, in Law of Environmental Protection, Environmental Law Institute, 7-28 to 7-33 (1998)

Publicly held companies must also identify environmental problems to ensure timely and accurate reports under the securities and exchange laws and SEC regulations. An SEC finding that a company failed to disclose environmentally related matters, thereby deceiving investors, could jeopardize the company's ability to raise capital through new stock offerings or debt instruments. It can also result in SEC initiation of costly and time-consuming administrative proceedings. Any such action by the SEC can give rise to shareholders' class actions and derivative suits. Thus, SEC enforcement of environmental laws and regulations, although indirect, is potentially more powerful than that of direct agency enforcement of environmental laws and regulations. Included within the scope of required SEC reporting are environmentally related matters, such as: (1) two-year estimates of capital expenditures for environmental compliance, or for a longer period if such estimates have been developed and a failure to disclose would be misleading; (2) particular types of environmental proceedings; and (3) circumstances under which companies must disclose their policies or approaches concerning environmental compliance.

With respect to proceedings, any governmental administrative or judicial proceedings arising or known to be contemplated under any federal, state, or local provisions regulating the discharge of materials into the environment or otherwise relating to the protection of the environment must be disclosed if any one of three conditions exist. Any private or governmental proceeding that is material to the business or financial condition of the corporation must be reported. Any private or governmental proceeding for damages, potential monetary sanctions, capital expenditures, deferred charges or charges to income is reportable if the amount involved (exclusive of interest and costs) exceeds 10 percent of the current assets of the corporation. And any governmental proceeding must be reported if monetary sanctions (exclusive of interest and costs) will or reasonably are expected to exceed $100,000....

The SEC's May 1989 interpretative release concerning the disclosure required in Management's Discussion and Analysis of Financial Condition and Results of Operations (MD&A) in SEC filings further details the scope of disclosure. The MD&A release states that "once management knows of a potentially material environmental problem, it must disclose it unless it can determine that the problem is not reasonably likely to cause a material effect, either because the event is not likely to happen or if it does happen, the effect is not likely to be material."[18] Thus, in preparing SEC filings, data developed during routine assessments and assessments made for acquisition and sale of properties becomes important....

The basis for measuring environmental liability is very important and is worth quoting in detail.

---

18. 54 Fed. Reg. at 22427.

In measuring its environmental liability, a registrant should consider available evidence including the registrant's prior experience in remediation of contaminated sites, other companies' cleanup experience, and data released by the Environmental Protection Agency or other organizations. Information necessary to support a reasonable estimate or range of loss may be available prior to the performance of any detailed remediation study. Even in situations in which the registrant has not determined the specific strategy for remediation, estimates of the costs associated with the various alternative remediation strategies considered for a site may be available or reasonably estimable. While the range of costs associated with the alternatives may be broad, the minimum clean-up cost is unlikely to be zero. SEC Staff Accounting Bulletin No. 92.

...[The] tightening interpretation of what financial information must be disclosed greatly increases the potential liability exposure for failure to disclose or properly accrue. Legal involvement is critical as these issues are examined....

CORPORATE MANAGEMENT INFORMATION NEEDS... Environmental considerations are also triggered by a company's corporate management information needs, which can include financial planning, risk management, the setting of appropriate accounting reserves, consideration of new product lines, and the acquisition of appropriate amounts and type of insurance coverage for environmental risk.

Assume, for example, that, in developing a new product line, a company will be developing a product utilizing a new chemical substance. Under ToSCA (see Chapter 15), a company would need to consider whether there may be limitations on the product's use or safety associated with the product's manufacture or processing. Such concerns obviously affect the cost of the product and the ability to market it. Alternatively, assume that a company seeks to establish, under RCRA (see Chapter 17), that it can provide the financial assurance necessary to operate a TSD facility. Evaluation of environmental risks may be essential to establishing that the company qualifies as financially responsible, including covering (through bonds, insurance, and the like) both closure and post closure costs. As another example, assume that a company is seeking to open another facility. Under the Clean Air Act (see Chapter Eight), the company must identify whether the new facility will be in an attainment or non-attainment area, a factor that can affect preconstruction review. Similarly, the company must evaluate whether, under CERCLA (see Chapter 18), the new facility may be near a waste disposal site requiring potential cost and expense of remediation.

As the article below concludes, sound corporate management especially requires gathering information to address the needs of company auditors. The reporting of environmental contingencies is now a permanent part of the financial landscape within which a business must operate.

### S. Frankel, Full Disclosure: Financial Statement Disclosures under CERCLA
3 Duke Environmental Law & Policy Forum 57, 65–67 (1993)

Companies typically prepare their financial statements in accordance with Generally Accepted Accounting Principles (GAAP). GAAP is a hierarchy of accounting standards promulgated by various professional accounting bodies, most notably the Financial Accounting Standards Board (FASB) and the American Institute of Certified Public Accountants (AICPA). SFAS-5 is the primary source of guidance available to companies for estimating and disclosing environmental liabilities in their financial statements.

SFAS-5 uses probabilities to determine the likelihood that a loss contingency will eventually be realized. There are three levels of probability at which a contingency may be classified by a business entity:

1. *Probable.* The future event or events are likely to occur.
2. *Reasonably possible.* The chance of future event or events occurring is more than remote but less than likely.
3. *Remote.* The chance of the future event or events occurring is slight.

SFAS-5 delineates appropriate treatment of financial statements based upon each contingency classification. If a loss contingency appears probable *and* the amount of the loss can be reasonably estimated, the contingency "shall be accrued by a charge to income." This means the estimated amount will be recognized as a loss as well as disclosed in the financial statement. If the loss cannot be estimated but the likelihood of it occurring is probable, the contingency should be disclosed with an explanation of why no estimate can be made. If the loss is reasonably possible, accrual of the expense is not required, but disclosure of the nature of the contingency and an estimate of the potential loss is necessary. Finally, if the contingency is classified as remote, there is generally no impact reflected in financial statements.

In Appendix A to SFAS-5, FASB gives several examples of the application of SFAS-5 to specific situations. With respect to Superfund disclosures, the most appropriate example is set out under the heading "Litigation, Claims, and Assessments". In the discussion, SFAS-5 indicates that the decision to accrue and/or disclose a loss that may result from pending and potential litigation should be based in large part on the "degree of probability of an unfavorable outcome." Several factors are listed that should be considered in assessing the probability of litigation outcome:

> The nature of the litigation, claim, or assessment, the progress of the case..., the opinions or views of legal counsel and other advisers, the experience of the enterprise in similar cases, the experience of other enterprises, and any decision of the enterprise's management as to how the enterprise intends to respond to the lawsuit, claim or assessment....

Once it is determined that an unfavorable litigation outcome is either probable or reasonably possible, the company must derive an estimate for disclosure. In the context of Superfund, that task is even more challenging. Factors such as the number of PRPs, their respective financial resources, joint and several liability, allocation of liability to each PRP, existence of insurance coverage, time frame of the investigation, and related litigation all make the estimation process very difficult and imprecise. Added to the obstacles posed by the estimation process is the fact that companies are generally loath to report information that may attract negative publicity, especially if it is not clear that the loss or other liability will materialize. Consequently, disclosure policies among companies regarding environmental contingencies vary greatly....

---

BORROWING FOR ON-GOING BUSINESS NEEDS... In order to continue existing operations, to expand to new operations, or to meet capital obligations, companies must consider borrowing to satisfy their on-going business needs. As a practical matter, without such financing, many private undertakings cannot be pursued.

Lenders typically seek information about environmental issues affecting the property or business that is the subject of the contemplated loan; it is extremely important for both credit worthiness considerations and assessment of potential collateral. Conducting a due diligence investigation, or requiring the borrower to conduct one as a condition precedent to the loan, is often a necessity for assessing, to the extent possible, the value of the property. Likewise, a borrower's ability to repay the loan may be impaired if the borrower must spend significant sums to comply with environmental laws or to clean up historic contamination.

Representations and warranties can be used by a lender to create a mechanism in the event of default should the representation turn out to be false; representations and warranties also can be used to cut off a borrower's ability to make further draws under a revolving credit facility, when something has happened during the term of the loan and the borrower is no longer able to reaffirm the validity of the representations as would be required at the time of the draw request. Also, representations can be used to elicit due diligence information on the target company. Lenders typically require the borrower to provide notice of certain events during the life of the loan (such as receipt of a notice of violation or an information request pertaining to off-site disposal of hazardous substances) to enable the lender to reevaluate its position in light of new events.

In lending for on-going business needs, lenders are also concerned about their own potential liabilities under the environmental laws. In 1996, after several years of lobbying by the financial services and real estate industries, Congress adopted significant amendments to CERCLA's security interest exemption, in an effort to limit the risks to lenders arising from the environmental liabilities of their borrowers.[19] Nonetheless, concerns about lender liability persist, adding additional motivation to lenders' desire to require their borrowers to engage in environmental compliance.

THE PURCHASE AND SALE OF A BUSINESS OR REAL ESTATE... Under CERCLA, and some analogous state laws, present owners of real property may be strictly liable for remediation of contamination that exists on or beneath, or that flows from, acquired property, despite their lack of participation in or knowledge of activities that caused the contamination. Common law damage actions by neighboring landowners based on common law trespass, nuisance, or negligence grounds may also be brought against the present owners on the theory that they are continuing the tortious interference (as noted in Chapters Three and Four). In addition, compliance deficiencies and enforcement actions that are directed at ongoing conduct may become the burden of new owners either of the property or of the operations that are maintained on the property. Thus, one who acquires a corporation that owns real property or an entity that merges or consolidates with a corporate property owner may, in appropriate circumstances, succeed to the liabilities of the predecessor. See Chapter 18.

---

19. These amendments were codified in The Asset Conservation, Lender Liability, and Deposit Insurance Protection Act of 1996 (Act), which essentially codified into law the EPA's Lender Liability Rule pertaining to the scope of the secured creditor exemption under CERCLA. See 57 Fed. Reg. 18344 (April 29, 1992). That rule had not enjoyed smooth going in the courts. In February, 1994, the D.C. Circuit struck down that rule, concluding that Congress made the federal courts, not EPA, the ultimate arbiter of CERCLA's liability provisions. See Kelley v. EPA, 15 F.3d 1100, (D.C. Cir.), reh'g denied, 25 F.3d 1088 (D.C. Cir. 1994). Thereafter, Congress passed the Act, which defines what is (and what is not) "participation in management" sufficient to subject a lender to CERCLA liability. See 42 U.S.C.A. §9601(20)(E)-(G).

Identifying, analyzing, and allocating the risks of these potential liabilities among the parties to the purchase or sale of a business or real estate brings environmental considerations into virtually every transaction. The assessment and allocation of the risks of a transaction requires an understanding of both the nature of the environmental liabilities and the types of contract provisions available for incorporation into an agreement as a mechanism for risk allocation among the parties to the transaction. Examples of the types of contract provisions available for allocation of financial responsibility and risk include (1) purchase price adjustments, (2) cost-sharing arrangements, (3) escrowed monies, (4) representations and warranties, (5) indemnification provisions, and (6) conditions precedent and subsequent to the transaction.

Increasingly, buyers are requiring, as a condition precedent to transactions, that environmental risks be identified and either eliminated or minimized before a transaction will close. This type of contractual provision implements the buyer's requirement that, before closing, a property or business come into compliance with the environmental laws, so that the buyer may avoid or limit environmental liability and risk. A typical example of such a condition precedent to closing, in a real estate transaction in Illinois, is set forth below:

ENVIRONMENTAL REMEDIATION... Seller has advised Purchaser that environmental remediation has commenced on the Property. Such remediation shall be subject to the following conditions:

(a) Seller has advised Purchaser that Seller is undertaking remediation of certain hazardous contamination on a portion of the Property, with the goal that, upon completion of such remediation, the Property will not pose a threat to Purchaser's intended use of the Property or to the environment. Seller shall seek to obtain a letter from the Illinois Environmental Protection Agency (IEPA) confirming that no further remediation of said contamination will be necessary with respect to the Property (the IEPA Letter).

(b) Seller shall pay all costs associated with the remediation of the Property. In the event that Seller cannot accomplish the site remediation (including the delivery to Purchaser of the IEPA Letter) by November 1, 1997, Purchaser may elect any of the following options: (i) to terminate the Contract, in which event the escrowee shall release the earnest money and all interest earned thereon to Purchaser immediately and neither party shall have any further obligations or liabilities to each other hereunder; (ii) to waive receipt of the IEPA Letter, provided all site remediation has otherwise been completed and Purchaser has given at least ten (10) business days advance written notice of such waiver; or (iii) to extend in writing the date by which the site remediation may be completed and the IEPA Letter obtained to February 1, 1998.

This contractual provision is a form of self-generated compliance. Buyers are increasingly insisting that businesses and properties that are the target of a transaction come into compliance with federal and state environmental laws before the transaction can proceed. From the buyer's perspective, achieving compliance beforehand is obviously preferable to participating in a transaction that exposes the buyer to potential governmental or citizen enforcement.

## COMMENTARY & QUESTIONS

1. **The cooperative agreement between EPA and the SEC.** EPA and the SEC have a cooperative agreement that allows the SEC access to EPA data to audit the adequacy of the data a company releases. Under the agreement, the SEC has offered to perform "full disclosures" of any corporation for EPA, and EPA allows the SEC access to various EPA files. EPA has agreed to provide the SEC with six categories of information on a quarterly basis. See Harrelson, EPA Agrees to Information Exchange With SEC, Inside EPA Superfund Rep., Mar. 28, 1990, at 2. The types of information to be provided are: (1) names of parties receiving Superfund notice letters identifying them as potentially liable for the cost of a Superfund cleanup; (2) lists of all filed (but not concluded) RCRA and CERCLA cases; (3) lists of all recently concluded civil cases under federal environmental laws; (4) lists of all filed criminal cases under federal environmental laws; (5) lists of all facilities barred from government contractors under the Clean Water Act; and (6) lists of all RCRA facilities subject to cleanup requirements.

What impact does this mutual exchange of information have on the regulated community? In light of the cooperation between EPA and the SEC, should a company take particular steps to ensure that its disclosures to EPA and to the SEC are consistent? What might be the consequences if there were inconsistency?

2. **The disparity between EPA reporting and SFAS-5 disclosures.** SEC reporting requirements are much more stringent than current Generally Accepted Accounting Principles. For an SEC registered company, there can be a significant disparity between information disclosed in its SEC filings and information disclosed under GAAP in the Notes to the Consolidated Financial Statements. For a company not subject to the SEC reporting requirements, this often means that environmental contingencies are either not disclosed or are underdisclosed in the financial statements. See S. Frankel, Full Disclosure: Financial Statement Disclosures Under CERCLA, 93 Duke Envir. Law & Policy Forum 57, 70–71 (1993).

3. **Private arrangements for loss allocation.** What is the relationship of private agreements that shift or allocate losses and the law's allocation of liability? For example, can a generator PRP escape liability through an indemnity agreement with a transporter or TSD operator, or could a seller, by agreement, agree to assume the CERCLA liability of the facility purchaser? CERCLA §107(e)(1), despite seeming ambiguity, gives a perfectly clear answer, "Yes and No." It states:

No indemnification, hold harmless, or similar agreement or conveyance shall be effective to transfer from [a PRP] to any other person the liability imposed under this section. Nothing in this subsection shall bar any agreement to insure, hold harmless, or indemnify a party to such agreement for liability under this section.

As the courts eventually realized, the statute does not allow private arrangements to limit the legal liability of the parties, which would plainly contravene the statute's policy, but the statute expressly allows the enforcement *inter sese* of the parties to those private agreements. In short, private arrangements for post-liability loss shifting are allowed and can be enforced. See, e.g., AM International v. International Forging Equip. Corp., 982 F.2d 989 (6th Cir. 1993); Jones-Hamilton v. Beazer Materials & Services, Inc., 973 F.2d 688 (9th Cir. 1992).

## Section 2. DUE DILIGENCE, AUDITS, AND OTHER AVENUES TOWARD VOLUNTARY COMPLIANCE

As business events trigger the need for environmental compliance, companies have increasingly relied on two key tools to evaluate such compliance: environmental due diligence, and environmental audits.

ENVIRONMENTAL DUE DILIGENCE... Due diligence has long been standard practice for companies considering the purchase of the stock, assets, or real estate of a target company. In the environmental context, due diligence essentially involves the examination of a company's compliance with environmental requirements and the assessment of the target's potential or contingent environmental liabilities. The information obtained from the due diligence investigation may be used for different purposes by the various parties to the transaction. For example, due diligence may reveal potential problems that will make a target unattractive to the buyer and suggest abandoning the transaction. Alternatively, it may allow the purchaser to negotiate adjustments to the price, to change the structure of the deal, or to redraft other important contractual provisions,[20] "appropriate inquiry" requirement of CERCLA's innocent purchaser defense. See CERCLA §101(35)(A), 42 U.S.C.A.§9601 (35)(A). ASTM has also produced a guide to due diligence inquiry, providing checklists for document reviews and questionnaires for use in environmental due diligence reviews.

Environmental due diligence also helps a potential lender determine whether to proceed with a loan. It permits a lender to assess whether contingent environmental liabilities may impair a borrower's ability to repay the loan or damage the borrower's credit rating, making it difficult or impossible for the lender to sell the loan. It also enables the lender to identify any environmental contamination that could affect the desirability of foreclosing on property or, securing the loan. Furthermore, an environmental due diligence investigation can serve to alert the purchaser or lender to present or future environmental problems that may require management or remedial action.

ENVIRONMENTAL AUDITS... Environmental audits are somewhat more formal and extended than due diligence inquiries. EPA defines an environmental audit as a "systematic, documented, periodic and objective review by regulated entities of facility operations and practices related to meeting environmental requirements."[21] An audit represents a "snapshot" of a company's environmental compliance at a moment in time, enabling a company to assess its state of environmental compliance and to identify what, if anything, is necessary to achieve full compliance. Audits generally involve a review of past and present operations; the history

---

20. In May 1993, the American Society for Testing and Materials (ASTM) promulgated standards for environmental site assessments, or environmental due diligence investigations. The first standard sets out a "Transaction Screen" process for commercial property transactions where environmental problems are unlikely to be of major concern. See ASTM, Standard Practice for Environmental Site Assessment, Transaction Screen Process; E1528-93. The second standard is designed for use in transactions where a more thorough inquiry into environmental issues is necessary. See ASTM, Standard Practice for Environmental Assessments; Phase I Environmental Site Assessment Process, E-527-93.

21. EPA Environmental Audit Policy Statement, 51 Fed. Reg. 25,004, 25,005 (July 9, 1986).

of compliance with federal, state, and local environmental laws; permits; waste practices; disclosure and reporting practices; operations and processes; budgets for environmental expenditures; and developing environmental strategies.

EPA generally considers the need for penalties in the context of a company's good faith efforts to comply with environmental laws and regulations. Although the existence of an audit program is not a mitigating factor, EPA may consider honest and genuine efforts of regulated entities to avoid and promptly correct violations discovered through audits when fashioning penalties for regulatory violations.

While the existence of an auditing program may have a mitigating effect in enforcement proceedings, there is also a risk that an audit report may be used against a company in administrative, civil or criminal enforcement actions. To date, both EPA and DOJ have been unwilling to provide explicit assurances that the results of any audits will not be used as the basis for criminal prosecution. Historically, EPA's position has been that it is free to seek disclosure of internal environmental audit reports on a case-by-case basis.

In July 1991, DOJ issued a long-awaited guidance document entitled "Factors in Decisions on Criminal Prosecutions for Environmental Violations in the Context of Significant Voluntary Disclosure of Compliance Efforts by the Violator." To promote self-auditing, self-policing, and voluntary disclosure of environmental regulation by the regulated community, the DOJ delineated several factors that it will review in considering whether, and to what extent, to prosecute criminally under the environmental laws.

In recent years, the EPA and DOJ policies have come under close scrutiny. There is great concern in the business community that the risk that environmental audit reports may be used against a company in enforcement proceedings is a disincentive to candid, self-evaluative environmental auditing. As a result, numerous states have enacted statutes establishing a privilege for environmental audit reports and granting immunity from prosecution for violations discovered by an environmental audit and then promptly fixed and reported to appropriate authorities. In general, three conditions must be met under most state audit-privilege laws in order to invoke the privilege or qualify for reduced penalties or immunity: (1) the regulated entity must conduct an audit that uncovers environmental violations; (2) the entity must voluntarily report the violations to authorities within a certain period of time; and (3) the entity must expeditiously correct the violation.

In December 1995, EPA responded to the concerns raised in the business community that environmental audit laws will be used on the federal level to assist in enforcement proceedings. EPA replaced its 1986 Environmental Audit Policy Statement with a new guidance document (effective January 22, 1996) entitled "Incentives for Self-Policing: Discovery, Disclosure, Correction and Prevention of Violations" (Incentives Policy).[22] The Incentives Policy does not provide absolute protection from discovery or an evidentiary privilege. Instead, the policy provides

---

22. 60 Fed. Reg. 66706 (Dec. 22, 1995); see also ELR Admin. Mat. I 35639. In addition, on June 3, 1996, EPA issued a policy designed to provide small businesses with an incentive to conduct environmental audits and engage in compliance activities. See 61 Fed. Reg. 27,984 (June 3, 1996).

that EPA will not request or use an environmental report to initiate a civil or criminal investigation, but if EPA has an independent reason to believe that a violation has occurred, EPA may seek any information relevant to identifying violations or determining liability or extent of harm. The Incentives Policy only provides that EPA will seek reduced civil fines if certain outcomes are met (e.g., the company discovers the violation through a self-audit, voluntarily discloses the violation within 10 days, corrects the violation promptly, and cooperates with EPA) and will not refer the matter for criminal enforcement if certain other criteria are met (e.g., EPA determines that the violation does not involve a corporate philosophy or practice, or does not involve higher level corporate involvement in, or willful blindness to, the violation).

Rather than aligning with the trend in the states towards developing audit privileges, however, EPA remains staunchly opposed to such privileges. In the Incentives Policy, EPA has stated its opposition to any state legislation that jeopardizes the fundamental national interest in assuring that violations of federal law do not threaten the public health, the environment or make it profitable not to comply. EPA has further stated that it reserves its right to bring independent action against regulated entities for violations of federal law that threaten human health, the environment, reflect criminal conduct, repeated noncompliance or allow one company to make a substantial profit at the expense of its law-abiding competitors. EPA has also requested that some states revise existing audit-privilege laws and has informed certain states that failure to amend privilege and immunity laws may jeopardize their federally delegated authority.

COMMENTARY AND QUESTIONS ·

1. **Marketplace induced compliance.** Simply doing business in America today involves engaging in activities that trigger material attention to environmental concerns. The development and increasing use of environmental due diligence and auditing, as tools to measure and enhance compliance efforts, reflect these realities. Marketplace priorities are changing. Industry is internalizing new environmental priorities, because the business risks and costs of environmental non-compliance are a fundamental factor in business planning. How likely is the prospect of voluntary compliance in the absence of credible threats of governmental or citizen enforcement? Even if more cooperative approaches are desirable, most agree that cooperation still needs to be tempered by the threat of credible environmental enforcement. Despite the professed desires of business to engage in self-generated compliance, altruism alone does not typically prompt American business to respond. Rather, the ultimate driving force remains the material cost of non-compliance and its adverse effect upon the bottom line. In the words of former EPA Administrator William D. Ruckelshaus, "environmentalism is here to stay" and "paying attention to the environmental impact of technology or processes benefits the bottom line." See W.D. Ruckelshaus, Stopping the Pendulum, Envt'l Forum, Nov./Dec. 1995 at 25–6.

2. **EPA and audit privileges.** Critics view EPA's recent actions limiting the scope of protection it will allow to information discovered through environmental audits as

an attempt to coerce states into rescinding, altering, or declining to enact audit-privilege legislation. One pair of commentators has referred to this type of opposition by EPA as "delegation blackmail" because EPA has threatened to rescind delegation of enforcement authority in states where audit privileges immunize many of the violations uncovered in the audit. See Timothy A. Wilkins & Cynthia A.M. Stroman, Delegation Blackmail: EPA's Use of Program Delegation to Combat State Audit Privilege Statutes 11, 16th Annual RCRA/CERCLA and Private Litigation Update, A.B.A. Sec. Nat. Resources, Energy & Envtl. L., 25th Annual Conference on Environmental Law (Dec. 12-13, 1996).

3. **The Congressional view of state environmental audit privileges.** In the absence of a federal statutory environmental audit privilege, what is the Congressional view of audit privileges? Following a series of hearings, members of a House Committee expressed disapproval of EPA's hostility to state audit-privilege laws:

The greatest burden of environmental enforcement rests in the states, yet testimony received by the Committee suggests that the states may be threatened with the loss of delegation of this responsibility if they do not conform their self-audit laws in ways to meet the specific approval of EPA. The Committee would take a very dim view of such a response on the part of EPA. States should be encouraged to create and implement new, non-adversarial and cost effective alternatives to the traditional "command-and-control" approach for environmental enforcement, such as the self-audit. The Committee strongly urges EPA to allow states — indeed, even assist the states — to go forward in implementing their self-audit laws, giving states the opportunity to demonstrate whether greater flexibility and cooperation will be in fact lead to lowering the overall cost of achieving a clean and healthy environment while assuring that legal action remains for those not willing to meet the law. Reprint of House Committee on Appropriations on H.R. 3666, Department of Veterans Affairs and Housing and Urban Development and Independent Agencies 1997 Appropriations Bill, June 18, 1996.

Are the tactics employed by EPA with the states impeding the development of innovative, progressive state programs that could help determine whether greater flexibility and cooperation with industry would lead to improved environmental compliance? Do these tactics represent an appropriate use of enforcement tools for federal management of state environmental agencies?

4. **Citizen groups and environmental audits.** The citizen's right of access to information is often forgotten in the debate over environmental audits. Local citizen groups have fought extensively for greater access to information about corporate environmental compliance, and these groups are reluctant to concede to businesses any additional control over information on corporate compliance with environmental regulations. Citizen groups view businesses' desire for self-regulation as a means to avoid environmental disclosure, on the ground that providing business with more secrecy for environmental audits is like the "fox guarding the hen house." Can the views of citizen groups be reconciled with the desire of business to monitor its own compliance with the environmental laws? Could an auditing

privilege be fashioned that excludes audits as admissible evidence in civil suits or government enforcement actions but still allows the results to be available to the public?

5. **Striking the right enforcement balance.** What is the future of enforcement and compliance? Undoubtedly, enforcement strategies are evolving. In the meantime, EPA must continue to search for the right enforcement balance, by punishing violators harshly while learning to work with, rather than against, responsible members of the regulated community. At the same time, the regulated community must not come to regard environmental protection as the responsibility of others, with unfortunate consequences for environmental quality.

There is a growing awareness within the federal government and the states that cooperative approaches are likely to be more effective in producing further gains in environmental compliance and improvements.... In recent years, EPA has given some consideration to new approaches to environmental enforcement. EPA launched a series of pilot projects in 1993 aimed at testing innovative compliance programs under the Environmental Leadership Program (ELP). Three other initiatives, the Common Sense Initiative (CSI), Project XL, and the ELP, focus on working with industries to develop alternative methods of complying with environmental laws and regulations. In late 1995, EPA issued its policy statement on incentives for voluntary audits... Last summer, EPA issued a policy intended to provide small businesses with incentives to participate in compliance assistance programs and to conduct environmental audits.... While these pilot programs are a step in the right direction, industry groups criticized them as too limited. The key question is whether EPA can build on these ad hoc efforts and develop permanent and meaningful changes.... Garrett, Reinventing EPA Enforcement, Natural Resources & Environment 180, 182 (1998)

### Section 3: A CORPORATE LAW RETROSPECTIVE — THE PACIFIC LUMBER CONTROVERSY

In evaluating further how to strike the right enforcement balance, consider the following retrospective on the Pacific Lumber controversy and, in particular, the extent to which the credible threat of environmental enforcement remains an essential impetus to self-generated compliance.

### Anderberg, Wall Street Sleaze: How the Hostile Takeover of Pacific Lumber Led to the Clear-Cutting of Coastal Redwoods
10 Amicus Journal No. 2, 8 (1988)

Debate has been vigorous over the effects of so-called junk-bond financing on American corporations and the United States economy in general, and whether it forces a healthy reassessment by managers and investors of a company's business or rather simply benefits the deal makers who undertake highly debt-leveraged corporate acquisitions.

But, many people on both sides of the debate agree, one junk bond-financed acquisition in northern California may result in a horror story in which mighty coastal redwoods are clear-cut in order to amortize junk debt incurred in the hostile takeover of a once venerated timber company.

©1990 DAVID J. CROSS

*Boundary line and clearcut area of Maxxam Corporation (Pacific Lumber Co.) redwood clearcutting operation, located above All Species Creek, southeast of Eureka, California. The trees in the distance are old-growth redwoods 3 to 6 feet in diameter, averaging more than 200 feet tall, as were the trees in the clearcut area.*

Prior to 1985, the family-run Pacific Lumber Company was widely respected as the most environmentally sensitive timber company in the industry. While other lumber companies often over harvested their inventory of redwoods and firs and depleted their long-term yield (scarring the landscape and wreaking havoc on the local economy), Pacific Lumber selectively cut old-growth redwoods under a sustained-yield policy that allowed new lumber to grow faster than old lumber was cut. For over forty years the company refused to clear-cut any of its forest holdings. The company was even known to have worked closely with the Save the Redwoods League, agreeing to preserve critical acreage until it could be incorporated into the national park system.... Even after the company went public in 1975 (with its stock trading on the New York Stock Exchange), the company was still considered by environmentalists and employees alike as a "bulwark of responsibility."

Pacific Lumber was also unique in one other respect. While its 189,000-acre holdings do not even make it the largest timber company in its area, Pacific Lumber owns by far the largest majority of the virgin old-growth redwoods (*Sequoia sempervirens*, or Coast redwoods) that are not already incorporated into federal, state, or regional park systems. A tall relic of a vast forest system that prior to the Ice Age covered millions of acres, virgin old-growth redwoods today occupy some 110,000 acres. The trees, some more than twenty centuries old, grow in magnificent and serene groves. About 70 percent of this acreage is protected as parkland, and the lion-sized share that is not (some 16,000 to 17,000 acres) is owned by Pacific Lumber and was thought to be relatively safe.

A certain Charles E. Hurwitz changed all this one early September morning in 1985. While denominating himself as a Texas farm boy, Hurwitz is, in fact, a corporate raider, who through his investment vehicle Maxxam Group, Inc. of New York (the former Simplicity Pattern Company) has built a large fortune by making heavily debt-financed acquisitions of companies whose assets (as measured by the price of their stock on an established stock exchange) are undervalued and thus can be purchased at a relative bargain.

The very factors that made Pacific Lumber so venerated among environmentalists and others may have made it a sitting duck for Hurwitz. Pacific Lumber in effect had stockpiled its inventory of redwoods, allowing trees to grow for decades before selectively cutting them in a manner designed to maintain consistent harvests. A corporate raider could obtain control of such vast timber reserves, radically increase harvests to increase cash flow and short-term profits, and subsequently sell the company. Augmenting the situation was Pacific Lumber's conservative management ("under-managed," according to Hurwitz) which resulted in the company's having a fairly low stock price (perhaps even significantly lower than the net asset value of its timber), flat earnings, and no significant debt load.

Beginning on that fateful September morning in 1985, Hurwitz moved to obtain control of Pacific Lumber, initially through a hostile tender offer (an offer to purchase on the open market approximately 22 million shares of Pacific Lumber that were traded on the New York Stock Exchange). By January, 1986, Hurwitz's Maxxam Group had completed its acquisition of the outstanding stock of Pacific Lumber, but at a cost: some $868 million, approximately $680.5 million of which was debt-financed by three issues of high-interest, low-grade investment (risky) "junk bonds," debt instruments that [were] the forte of Wall Street investment banking house Drexel Burnham Lambert. They are backed solely by the assets of Pacific Lumber, not by Maxxam. Perhaps more telling, the purchasers of the junk bonds (primarily large institutional investors) can look for repayment of interest and principal on such bonds *only* from the sale or other use of Pacific Lumber's assets.

After obtaining control of Pacific Lumber, and as is common in a highly debt-leveraged acquisition, Hurwitz first sold the company's non-timber assets (the corporate headquarters for $30 million and an unrelated cutting and welding operation for about $250 million). Hurwitz then turned his attention to the remaining large asset of Pacific Lumber: its inventory of coastal redwoods. In 1986, Hurwitz stepped up harvests from 137 million to 248 million board feet per year (including clear-cutting of selected tracts of up to 500 acres and the harvesting of virgin redwoods), conceding in testimony before the California legislature that the increase in harvest was primarily to pay off the massive debt load incurred in acquiring Pacific Lumber. Many have noted that the interest payments on the junk debt used to acquire Pacific Lumber [amount to] $83 million a year, more than Pacific Lumber's preacquisition cash flow.

Many environmentalists, residents, and even company loggers worry that not only is Pacific Lumber destroying a national treasure, but that the trees are being harvested at a rate that will ultimately jeopardize the sustained yield of the forests and the economy of the local region. Said one Pacific Lumber worker: "They're just leveling everything.... They're destroying the future, leaving nothing for the next generation." And Woody Murphy, a great-grandson of the Murphy that built Pacific Lumber into a venerated logging company, said, "And when they're through, it'll be a moonscape."

Pacific Lumber executives claim that if they reduce timber cutting after twenty years of intense harvesting to preacquisition harvest levels, Pacific Lumber's lands will still have a substantial inventory of redwoods and Douglas fir left for the future....

Meanwhile, Hurwitz claims he was victimized in the Pacific Lumber takeover by Drexel Burnham Lambert investment banker Dennis B. Levine, who allegedly leaked insider information concerning the prospective acquisition to arbitrageur (and convicted felon) Ivan Boesky, who used such information to quietly purchase large blocks of Pacific Lumber stock (thereby driving up its market price) shortly before Hurwitz's acquisition was announced. The Justice Department, Securities and Exchange Commission, and New York Stock Exchange are investigating the charges.

Ironically, Hurwitz may fail for economic reasons in his bid to use the coastal redwoods to pay off his junk bonds. John E. Mack, Jr., an analyst with Warberg, Rowe, and Pittman, Akroyd, Inc., states that Hurwitz may end up "flooding the market" with redwood, lowering prices, and destroying the company's ability to liquidate its inventory at a profit.

At the very least, Pacific Lumber is a vignette of what Representative John D. Dingell (D. Michigan) calls "the takeover and dismemberment of a good corporate citizen"; a hostile corporate acquisition that turned the most respected timber company in America into the least respected, while radically increasing the debt-load and jeopardizing the economic health of a soundly run company. "This case has enormous implications," warns Representative Ron Wyden (D. Oregon), a member of the House Banking, Finance and Urban Affairs Subcommittee that is investigating the Pacific Lumber acquisition. "I'm not convinced it's responsible for management to cut trees to pay debts to people who live thousands of miles away...."

Even more troubling is the question of whether other industries involved in the extraction of our nation's natural resources and whose operations have a critical effect on the overall quality of our environment could suffer the fate of the Pacific Lumber Company and the *Sequoia sempervirens*. Are we in danger of becoming a country in which our natural resources will be dismembered in transactions that benefit nobody but the deal makers?

### COMMENTARY AND QUESTIONS

1. **Corporate law and social responsibility.** Corporations are the fundamental building blocks of the American economy, and since economic decisions are so often the causes of long-term negative environmental effects, corporate law is an obvious candidate for environmental attorneys' attention. Corporate attorneys have learned to their dismay about dozens of statutory areas where they now must be sensitive to environmental concerns — in modern air, water, and chemical pollution regulations, in SEC reporting, lender liability, real estate transactions, tax treatment of pollution control, and so on. But getting legislatures to pass effective new statutes restricting corporate conduct is immensely difficult.

This section is not aimed at the depredations of junk bond raiders. Although leveraged buyouts still continue, junk bond financing is increasingly out of fashion. Rather, the *Pacific Lumber* case raises the larger question: Does corporate law contain any inherent principles of corporate responsibility that, in the absence of legislation, can be mobilized to induce corporations to take account of environmental harms?

It is difficult to intrude long-term public and intangible values into the corporate arena, unless they can be made to serve the interests of the corporation and its shareholders. In the recent past, the primary approach for insinuating environmental concerns into corporate practice has been through non-legal means, as environmentalists try through demonstrations, media, shareholder ballot questions, and boycotts to convince corporate officers and shareholders to make environmentally sensitive corporate policy. These efforts have been laudable but typically quite unsuccessful, as public interest environmental initiatives drown in a flood of institutional proxies, short-term profit maximization, and management indifference. A corporation is not in business to accomplish the public's good. Long-term problems, intangible costs, and any costs that can be externalized are not the concern of the corporate entity. Corporate managers, in fact, might be held liable if they expended corporate assets for purposes which cannot be justified in terms of protecting and enhancing the value of the corporation. It is this single mindedness that has helped to build the world's greatest national economy and underlies the problem of corporate social responsibility.[23]

---

23. The difference between the long-term and short-term corporate perspectives illustrates other problems in American corporate law. In Japan, for instance, corporate executives are evaluated based on their contribution to the corporation's long-term growth and strength. In American practice, however, executives are typically evaluated based upon net earnings performance per quarter. Money reinvested in the corporation – in research and development, energy conservation, or environmental planning – is regarded as a cost and weighed against earnings. If internal corporate reward systems are based on short-term gratification they tend to undermine long-term needs for productivity and competitiveness, not to mention environmental rationality.

2. **Valdez Principles.** More recently, especially under clouds of media coverage generated by dramatic chemical contaminations, oil spills, and other corporate disasters, many corporations, especially those vulnerable to public identification of names and trademarks, have taken hesitant steps toward internalizing some environmental sensitivity. In the wake of the Exxon-Valdez oil spill, for instance, a group of environmental organizations, the Coalition for Environmentally Responsible Economics (CERES), has had some success in persuading corporations to accept the "Valdez Principles," a statement of long-term corporate commitment to environmental values. The Valdez Principles urge companies to abide by the following code:

1. Protection of the biosphere. We will minimize and strive to eliminate the release of any pollutants that may cause environmental damage to the air, water, or earth or its inhabitants. We will safeguard habitats and rivers, lakes, wetlands, coastal zones and oceans, and will minimize contributing to the greenhouse effect, depletion of the ozone layer, acid rain, or smog.

2. Sustainable use of natural resources. We will make sustainable use of renewable resources such as water, soils and forests. We will conserve non-renewable natural resources through efficient use and careful planning. We will protect wildlife habitat, open spaces and wilderness while preserving biodiversity.

3. Reduction and disposal of waste. We will minimize the creation of waste, especially hazardous waste, and wherever possible recycle materials. We will dispose of all waste through safe and responsible methods.

4. Wise use of energy. We will make every effort to use environmentally safe and sustainable energy sources to meet our needs. We will invest in improved energy efficiency and conservation in our operations. We will maximize the energy efficiency of products we produce or sell.

5. Risk reduction. We will minimize the environmental, health and safety risks to our employees and the communities in which we operate by employing safe technologies and operating procedures and by being constantly prepared for emergencies.

6. Marketing of safe products and services. We will sell products or services that minimize adverse environmental impacts and that are safe as consumers commonly use them. We will inform consumers of the environmental impacts of our products and services.

7. Damage compensation. We will take responsibility for any harm we cause to the environment by making every effort to fully restore the environment and to compensate those persons who are adversely affected.

8. Disclosure. We will disclose to our employees and to the public incidents relating to our operations that cause environmental harm or pose safety or health hazards. We will disclose potential environmental, health, or safety hazards posed by our operations, and we will not take any action against employees who report any condition that creates a danger to the environment or poses health and safety hazards.

9. Environmental directors and managers. At least one member of the Board of Directors will be a person qualified to represent environmental interests. We will commit management resources to implement these Principles, including the funding of the office of Vice-President for Environmental Affairs or an equivalent executive position, reporting directly to the CEO, to monitor and report upon our implementation efforts.

10. Assessment and annual audit. We will conduct and make public an annual self-evaluation of our progress in implementing these Principles and in complying with all applicable laws and regulations throughout our worldwide operations. We will work towards the timely creation of independent environmental audit procedures which we will complete annually and make available to the public.

If adopted and implemented by all major corporations, the Valdez Principles could go far toward changing the current linkage between economic productivity and long-term ecological degradation. But is it realistic to think that corporate conscience and consumer awareness will attract sufficient adherence to the Principles to give them practical effect? Charles Hurwitz was reported to have defined his corporate Golden Rule as "He who has the gold, rules."[24]

3. **Exploring corporate law remedies.** The classic problem presented by the Pacific Lumber story is that there was no obvious feature of corporate law that could resist the logic of the raider who takes aim at a "sitting duck," a debt-free company with long-term environmentally-sensitive management policies, and replaces it with a drastic cut-and-run corporate regime. The standard answer is that as long as shareholders receive a fair price for their shares, corporate law has no complaints. Hurwitz purchased Pacific Lumber's shares at forty dollars, when previously they had been selling, albeit under-valued, for around thirty.

But are there doctrines of corporate law that could have been mobilized to attempt to rectify the Pacific Lumber problem in court actions seeking damages or injunctions? (Statutory efforts had failed in the state legislature.) The Murphy family originally tried unsuccessfully to halt the takeover with a shareholders' derivative suit arguing that the board had failed to exercise due care. But other approaches may deserve exploration.

Here is a brainstorming checklist for analyzing how corporate law might have been employed to take account of the Pacific Lumber problem:

**Timing:** Note that there are two different settings for legal action — preventive action before a takeover, and retrospective action afterward. The preventive action is tactically preferable.

**Remedies to be sought:** *Injunctions* — to block a takeover in advance, or, afterward, to reconvey back to the old corporation, refinance, slow down the cutting, replace various corporate directors and officers, etc.; and *Damages*, after the fact, to recapture windfalls, losses of asset values, potential bankruptcy losses, etc.

---

24. Los Angeles Times, 10 April 1987. See also Comment, The Valdez Principles: Is What's Good for America Good for General Motors?, 8 Yale L. & Pol'y Rev. 180 (1990).

**Players:** *Defendants* — the raiders, investment bankers, directors and officers charged with wrongful conduct; and *Plaintiffs* — minority shareholders, possibly labor representatives, anti-takeover directors and officers.[25]

Wrongful acts alleged

*Injury to the environment:* But in corporate lawsuits, judges are not interested in such claims.

*Injury to the region:* Likewise useless.

*Injury to the employee work force:* This claim has some slight chance of being heard under a few states' corporate law, as in New York.

*Violation of duty of due care:* An umbrella minimum standard applying to management practices before and after a takeover. But courts tend to defer to corporate decisions under the "business judgment" rule unless more specific violations are claimed. (Injury *to the corporation itself* is the major premise to be developed in this and subsequent inquiries.)

*Failure to supervise:* Where directors fail to take account of relevant issues and facts like the rate of cutting, they permit inaccurate asset inventories, etc.

*Self-dealing:* This gets around the business judgment rule, if officers and director shareholders stand to gain more than others if the takeover goes through.

*Breach of duty of loyalty:* Where a raider becomes chief executive officer of the captured company and presides over its cut-rate dismemberment, or where management officers go along with a takeover to save their own jobs, especially if the price is alleged to be too low.

*Duty of intrinsic fairness:* This largely replicates the preceding standard.

*Fair price:* If the management knows that the takeover price paid per share is an undervaluation, not a fair price, it breaches its duties by acquiescing.

*Loss of value of going concern:* Although some economic doctrines argue otherwise, the strip-and-sell tactic of junk-bond raiders may result in fire-sale prices and fail to capture the value of the assembled company as a going concern.

*Waste of assets:* If an accelerated cutting regime floods the market and depresses prices, the raider's exploitation policy results in a diminished return on corporate assets, the trees.

*Violation of long-term profit maximization:* This is a key novel claim. Most corporate law decisions ignore the long-term values that environmentalists want to stress, in favor of short-term, quarter-to-quarter profit maximization, reflected in maximum current share value. But it can be argued that the long-term values of the company are greater, even discounted into the future, than the short-term raider's price, if the sustained

---

25. Many of the following possible remedies are far easier to apply where the old management opposes the takeover bid, as in internal corporate maneuvers like "poison pills," and "asset lockups" selling prime assets via long-term contracts to a white knight or the employee pension plan.

managed harvest over time will maximize the company's market position, given foreseeable market price premiums for prime resources in the future. This is especially so with a timber company where the tree resource assets will grow each year that they aren't cut down. To the extent this is so, current market prices will be undervalued.

***Loss of corporate personality:*** This picks up from the preceding: if a corporation has established a "corporate personality" or "corporate culture" emphasizing long-term profit maximization (and especially if, like Pacific Lumber before and after takeover, it represented that policy to investors) a new theory allows a court to take account of the long-term. The *Time-Warner-Paramount* litigation, 571 A.2d 1140 (Del. 1989), accepted the directors' right (but not duty) "to follow a course designed to achieve long-term value even at the cost of immediate value maximization." If this is a right of directors, in appropriate cases it may become a duty.

***Loss of investment quality:*** Similar to the preceding, where a stable old blue chip company is turned into a junk-bond volatile issue.

***Risking bankruptcy:*** Where a company is bought out, but is maintained as a separate entity and stripped of assets, bankruptcy may well follow.

***Rule 10(b)(5) of the Securities and Exchange Act:*** This can effect liability for failure to disclose environmental violations to investors if shareholders might suffer under those violations.

***Other securities law violations:*** By studying a takeover's history, it may be possible to show that the raider's stock purchases were done improperly, as by hiding initial purchases in violation of federal disclosure laws, etc.

***Other violations of duty of care:*** There are other potential claims: increasing the likelihood of harmful police power regulation, risking eminent domain condemnation, loss of corporate reputation and good will, dislocating a skilled labor pool with attendant costs, and so on.

Ultimately, it is not clear which of these attempts, if any, would be likely to achieve some corporate law accounting of the Pacific Lumber cut-and-run problem. Given the ecological and economic dangers of corporate behavior, however, the corporate law theatre is worth the effort, as imaginative environmental attorneys attempt to save corporate America and the national economy from tunnel vision.

*This noblest patrimony ever yet inherited by any people must be husbanded and preserved with care in such manner that future generations shall not reproach us for having squandered what was justly theirs.*

— The Whig Almanac, 1843

# Chapter 21

# ALTERNATIVE DISPUTE RESOLUTION PROCESSES

A. *Why Alternative Dispute Resolution?*
B. *Environmental ADR*

## A. WHY ALTERNATIVE DISPUTE RESOLUTION?

Environmental law was born and raised in the arena of adversarial combat — the traditional litigation mode in court and agency proceedings. Few would argue, however, that the adversarial litigative process is ideal. Litigation often proves to be a crude mechanism for achieving resolutions, results in antagonistic relationships, and drains scarce resources in terms of time, money, and energy. Because of its obstacles and inefficiencies, ultimately, many disputes never get resolved within the formal mechanisms of the legal system. Because of its practical burdens, the traditional model is often unavailable to those who lack financial and political resources.

Even within traditional adversarial litigation, of course, most disputes are settled out of court through a process of negotiation prior to final judgment. But other options for conflict resolution are increasingly available. A growing movement both within and outside the legal profession has been calling for a shift to ADR — alternative dispute resolution mechanisms like mediation, arbitration, non-litigative negotiation, minitrials, and other procedures. Whether by statutory mandate or pragmatic decision of the parties, many issues that previously would have been handled by litigation or agency enforcement now have the possibility of being resolved through ADR. The trend reemphasizes that the practice of law need not be what many laypersons consider it — an unproductive, insulated mechanism for implementing the more negative elements of human nature — but rather a profession that ultimately tries to make social relationships and civic mechanisms work.

ADR has been increasingly visible in the environmental setting (where it is often referred to as "EDR") only since the late 1970s.[1] Unlike most litigation models, the ADR approach can be forward-looking — designed to anticipate future policy or practical conflicts[2] — as well as retrospective and reactive to existing disputes.

---

1. For an overview of major environmental disputes in which ADR methods were used, see Talbot, Settling Things (1983), and L. Susskind, L. Bacow and M. Wheeler, Resolving Environmental Regulatory Disputes (1983).
2. This mode has been called "front-loading" or anticipatory consensus-building.

The viability of ADR as an alternative to litigation has been the subject of fierce debate in both the academic and practice communities. Richard Mays, arguing for expanded environmental use of ADR, notes that in standard EPA enforcement cases "the average time between discovery of a violation and settlement might easily be three to five years or more. Even after this delay, [ultimately all but five] percent of EPA's judicial cases are settled rather than tried."[3] Enormous amounts of time and resources spent on such cases could be reduced dramatically if resolutions were reached through negotiation rather than the process or threat of litigation.

Not all cases can or should be settled through ADR. Even proponents like Mays agree that adversarial litigation is necessary and appropriate in some cases — for example if there are important precedential legal issues that need resolution, if injunctions or other court-supervised remedies are necessary and parties lack the time or interest required for negotiating settlements, or if, in light of a party's egregious conduct, the public interest requires an open public trial and punishment. These exceptional cases, they argue, however, make up only a small percentage of the total number of environmental suits filed each year.

Some opponents of alternative remedies claim that ADR's purported savings in time and expense are bought at the cost of accuracy, justice, and democratic process. Edward Brunet, a staunch opponent of ADR, claims that "only formal litigation and adjudication provide a mechanism for accurate determination of facts."[4] Brunet maintains that the informality of ADR procedures makes them "weak since they rely on voluntary party exchange of data and do not have an authority figure equivalent to a judge to prevent discovery abuse." In environmental disputes, Brunet claims, the informality of ADR is particularly dangerous. Given the complexity of environmental disputes, "the 'facts' produced in an environmental mediation are likely to be incomplete and inaccurate."

On the other hand, ADR sometimes presents clear advantages. It can, for example, promote effective joint factfinding techniques producing facts faster and with greater accuracy than traditional discovery. If parties can develop a mutually-acceptable factfinding agenda and methodology, then the traditional "battle of the experts" can be averted and questions shifted from a "position-based" to a broader "interest-based" resolution process on the merits, as noted in Chapter 11's rangeland advisory council innovations.[5]

### Sander, Alternative Methods of Dispute Resolution: An Overview
### 37 University of Florida Law Review 1 (1985)

Beginning in the late Sixties, American society witnessed an extraordinary flowering of interest in alternative forms of dispute settlement. This interest

---

3. Mays, Alternative Dispute Resolution and Environmental Enforcement: A Noble Experiment or a Lost Cause?, 18 ELR 10087, 10088 (1988).

4. Brunet, The Costs of Environmental Alternative Dispute Resolution, 18 ELR 10515, 10516 (December 1988). See also Fiss, Against Settlement, 93 Yale L.J. 1073 (1984), and Out of Eden, 94 Yale L.J. 1669 (1985), arguing that ADR undermines the important law-building, law-applying functions of judicial litigation, and finding other major shortcomings.

5. See L. Susskind and J. Cruikshank, Breaking the Impasse: Consensual Approaches to Resolving Public Disputes (1987); also R. Fisher and W. Ury, Getting to Yes (1981).

emanated from a wide variety of sources ranging from the Chief Justice of the United States Supreme Court to corporate general counsel, the organized Bar and various lay groups....

The Sixties were characterized by considerable strife and conflict, emanating in part from the civil rights struggles and the Vietnam War protests. An apparent legacy of those times was a lessened tolerance and a greater tendency to turn grievances into disputes. Also relevant was a significant increase in the statutory creation of new causes of action....

Courts found themselves inundated with new filings, triggering cries of alarm from the judicial administration establishment. This judicial congestion led to the claim that equal access to justice had been denied. Spurred in part by these conditions, parties attempted to resolve some of these disputes through alternative dispute resolution mechanisms.... The Ford Foundation established the National Center for Dispute Settlement and the Institute of Mediation and Conflict Resolution to study dispute resolution mechanisms....

Four goals of the alternatives movement emerged:

1. To relieve court congestion, as well as undue cost and delay.

2. To enhance community involvement in the dispute resolution process.

3. To facilitate access to justice.

4. To provide more "effective" dispute resolution.[6]

These goals might overlap and conflict. Consider, for example, the problem of "excessive" access. If society is too ready to provide access for all kinds of disputes, this will lengthen the queue and aggravate the congestion problem. Similarly, measures aimed at relieving court congestion would take a very different form from measures designed to enhance community control over dispute settlement. Hence, it is essential to think clearly and precisely about the reasons for pursuing ADRMs.

Considering the complex social conditions that have led to court congestion and concomitant delay...the notion that a pervasive use of arbitration and mediation will solve the "court crisis" seems misguided. The principal promise of alternatives stems from the third and fourth goals set forth above. Our primary efforts should be directed toward these two goals. And since the access goal can only be fulfilled by providing access to an ADRM that is appropriate for the particular dispute,[7] the third and fourth goals in effect coalesce....

One could posit a number of plausible criteria for determining the suitability of various dispute mechanisms.... Adjudication typically seeks to make a definitive determination with respect to past events, while mediation attempts to restructure the [present and future] relationship of the disputants.... The open-ended and non-coercive process of mediation is also more likely to teach the parties to recognize and resolve future controversies. Mediation thus gives maximum durability to the settlement....

---

6. Although no definitive work has been done with respect to how to measure "effectiveness," presumably to be taken into account are such factors as cost, speed, satisfaction (to the public and the parties) and compliance. At present, it is almost accidental if community members find their way to an appropriate forum other than regular courts.

7. Several other models of dispute resolution...are available in many communities [but] since they are operated by a hodge-podge of local government agencies, neighborhood organizations, and trade organizations, citizens must be very knowledgeable about community resources to locate the right forum for their particular dispute.

A significant qualification, however, is presented in the case where the two disputants have substantially disparate bargaining power. In such a case, mediation is either pointless, or worse yet, threatens to take undue advantage of the weaker party. ADRM specialists must learn far more about the optional combination of formal adjudicative and informal mediation processes for this type of case....

What is the proper role of attorneys in alternative dispute resolution mechanisms? First, ADRMs must distinguish between a lawyer's role as a representative of the disputants, and a lawyer's role as a dispute resolver.... Unfortunately, much of a law student's training is in adversary dispute settlement rather than accomodative problem-solving. This situation is rapidly changing, however. Increasingly, legal education encompasses mediation and other ADRM training....

## B.  ENVIRONMENTAL ADR

### Section 1. AN ARRAY OF ADR METHODS

**National Institute for Dispute Resolution, Paths to Justice:
Major Public Policy Issues of Dispute Resolution**
in Administrative Conference of the United States, Sourcebook: Federal Agency
Use of Alternative Means of Dispute Resolution 5–47 (1983, 1987)

Some conflict contributes to and, indeed, is essential to a healthy, functioning society. Social change occurs through dispute and controversy. Some observers attribute the long-term stability of the country to its ability to hear and reconcile the disagreements of its diverse population. Thus one should focus not only on avoiding disputes, but also on finding suitable ways of hearing and resolving those that inevitably arise....

Dispute resolution techniques can be arrayed along on a continuum ranging from the most rulebound and coercive to the most informal. Specific techniques differ in many significant ways, including:
  • whether participation is voluntary;
  • whether parties represent themselves or are represented by counsel;
  • whether decisions are made by the disputants or by a third party;
  • whether the procedure employed is formal or informal;
  • whether the basis for the decisions is law or some other criteria; and
  • whether the settlement is legally enforceable.

At one end of the continuum is adjudication (including both judicial and administrative hearings): parties can be compelled to participate; they are usually represented by counsel; the matter follows specified procedure; the case is decided by a judge in accordance with previously established rules; and the decisions are enforceable by law....

At the other end of the continuum are negotiations in which disputants represent and arrange settlements for themselves: participation is voluntary, and the disputants determine the process to be employed and criteria for making the decision. Somewhere in the middle of the continuum is mediation, in which an impartial party facilitates an exchange among disputants, suggests possible solutions, and otherwise assists the parties in reaching a voluntary agreement....

[Here follows a definitional survey of ADR forms:]

**Arbitration**...involves the submission of the dispute to a third party who renders a decision after hearing arguments and reviewing evidence. It is less formal and less complex and often can be concluded more quickly than court proceedings. In its most common form, binding arbitration, the parties select the arbitrator and are bound by the decision, either by prior agreement or by statute.[8] In last-offer arbitration, the arbitrator is required to choose between the final positions of the two parties....

**Court-annexed arbitration**, a newer development. Judges refer civil suits to arbitrators who render prompt, non-binding decisions. If a party does not accept an arbitrated award, some systems require they better their position at trial by some fixed percentage, or court costs are assessed against them. Even when these decisions are not accepted, they sometimes lead to further negotiations and pretrial settlement.

**Conciliation**, an informal process in which the third party tries to bring the parties to agreement by lowering tensions, improving communications, interpreting issues, providing technical assistance, exploring potential solutions and bringing about a negotiated settlement, either informally or, in a subsequent step, through formal mediation. Conciliation is frequently used in volatile conflicts and in disputes where the parties are unable, unwilling or unprepared to come to the table to negotiate their differences.

**Facilitation**, a collaborative process used to help a group of individuals or parties with divergent views reach a goal or complete a task to the mutual satisfaction of the participants. The facilitator functions as a neutral process expert and avoids making substantive contributions, [helping] bring the parties to consensus....

**Fact finding**, a process used from time to time primarily in public sector collective bargaining. The fact finder, drawing on information provided by the parties and additional research, recommends a resolution of each outstanding issue. It is typically non-binding and paves the way for further negotiations and mediation.

**Med-Arb**, an innovation in dispute resolution under which the med-arbiter is authorized by the parties to serve first as a mediator and, secondly, as an arbitrator empowered to decide any issues not resolved through mediation.

**Mediation**, a structured process in which the mediator assists the disputants to reach a negotiated settlement of their differences. Mediation is usually a voluntary process that results in a signed agreement which defines the future behavior of the parties. The mediator uses a variety of skills and techniques to help the parties reach a settlement but is not empowered to render a decision.[9]

**The Mini-trial**, a privately-developed method of helping to bring about a negotiated settlement in lieu of corporate litigation. A typical mini-trial might entail a period of limited discovery after which attorneys present their best case before managers with authority to settle and, most often, a neutral advisor who may be a retired

---

8. In a somewhat surprising 1990 case, representatives of a Phillips 66 petrochemical plant and citizens of a Texas Gulf Coast community agreed to arbitration to resolve a dispute over the company's discharge of polluted waste water into Linnville Bayou. Under the terms of the agreement assenting to arbitration, a panel of three scientists was given binding authority to determine the extent of pollution in the bayou and to set out the best clean-up method. The decision of the arbitration panel could be appealed only to a retired judge, and appeal was limited to the narrow issue of whether the decision was arbitrary.

9. Mediation has been a particularly successful method for reaching settlement and allocating responsibility among potentially responsible parties in dozens of EPA Superfund toxic waste clean-up cases.

judge or other lawyer. The managers then enter settlement negotiations. They may call on the neutral advisor if they wish to obtain an opinion on how a court might decide the matter.[10]

**The Multi-door center (or Multi-door courthouse)**, a proposal [by Professor Sander] to offer a variety of dispute resolution services in one place with a single intake desk which would screen clients. Under one model, a screening clerk would refer cases for mediation, arbitration, fact-finding, ombudsman or adjudication....

[**Negotiation** is the generic process that recurs in many of these ADR forms. In its simplest incarnation, however, negotiation constitutes discussions between the parties, with no formalized format, groundrules, or third party participation.]

**Neighborhood Justice Centers (NJCs)**, the title given to... about 180 local centers now operating through the country under the sponsorship of local or state governments, bar associations and foundations.... They are also known as Community Mediation Centers, Citizen Dispute Centers, etc.

**Ombudsman**, a third party [on the Scandanavian model] who receives and investigates complaints or grievances aimed at an institution by its constituents, clients or employees. The Ombudsman may take actions such as bringing an apparent injustice to the attention of high-level officials, advising the complainant of available options and recourses, proposing a settlement of the dispute or proposing systemic changes in the institution....

**Public policy dialogue and negotiation**, aimed at bringing together affected representatives of business, public interest groups and government to explore regulatory matters. The dialogue is intended to identify areas of agreement, narrow the areas of disagreement, and identify general areas and specific topics for negotiation. A facilitator guides the process.

[**Reg-neg** is the term given to a process of intensive multiparty negotiations leading to governmental issuance of regulatory rules.]

**Rent-a-judge**, the popular name given to a procedure, presently authorized by legislation in six states, in which the court, on stipulation of the parties, can refer a pending lawsuit to a private neutral party for trial with the same effect as though the case were tried in the courtroom before a judge. The verdict can be appealed through the regular court appellate system.

## Section 2. A CASE STUDY IN EDR

### Allan Talbot, The Hudson River Settlement
Settling Things: Six Case Studies in Environmental Mediation (1983)

Of all the natural resource disputes resolved in recent years through mediation, perhaps none was as complex or as significant as the so-called Hudson River settlement, the conclusion of a 17-year war between and among three environmental groups, four public agencies, and five electric utility companies over the use of the Hudson River for producing electric power.

Storm King Mountain...attracted national attention [with its conflict over] construction of a hydroelectric power facility at the mountain's base [see page 562 *supra*].... After the Federal Power Commission (FPC) granted the license, a U.S. Appeals Court ruled that the FPC must consider the preservation of scenic beauty

---

10. Since the mid-1980s, the Army Corps of Engineers has used the minitrial technique in resolving a number of regulatory environmental disputes.

in its licensing decisions. The court [held] that [Scenic Hudson Preservation Conference,] a citizens' group with no proprietary interest...nonetheless had the right to intervene in...licensing hearings....

In subsequent years, as the FPC reconsidered Consolidated Edison's licensing bid, the issues surrounding Storm King came to involve more than the scenic impact of an immense power station constructed at the base of the mountain. And, among all of the legal, economic, and environmental questions raised by opponents, none proved to be as complicated and as intriguing as the impact of the plant on the fish in the Hudson River....

An organization called the Hudson River Fishermen's Association (HRFA) pointed out, in November 1964, that the Hudson Highlands were a major spawning ground for anadromous fish, especially striped bass. In fact, the HRFA said, most of the striped bass caught in the Atlantic between Cape Code and the Jersey Shore were spawned in the vicinity of Storm King Mountain. Scenic Hudson, originally concerned merely with the aesthetic aspect of Consolidated Edison's project, quickly seized on the fish issue as well, claiming that the hydroelectric plant would have disastrous consequences for the river's striped bass population.

The question of harm to fish life was posed subsequently by HRFA concerning several other power stations along the river where water was used for cooling. The biggest of these power stations was the Indian Point nuclear complex located in Westchester County some 15 miles south of Storm King [using] river water to cool plant condensers. Water going back into the river was several degrees warmer than when it came out. Many fish are attracted to warm water, especially in the winter, and large numbers of fish were caught on the plant intake screens. The resulting kills were dramatic creating measurable evidence of the dangers to fish life posed by power production.

Less obvious, but in the view of many fish biologists far more serious, was the entrainment of young fish and fish eggs into plant cooling systems.... [A total of six existing power stations using] the waters of the Hudson, and several proposed new units,] each posed some danger to fish life, and the combined effect on the river and the fish was, at best, unclear and therefore in dispute.

Because of its size and involvement in all the proposed or recently built Hudson River plants, Consolidated Edison bore the brunt of the charges that the utilities were decimating the river's aquatic life. Its initial response at Storm King in FPC's 1964 hearings was to dismiss the issue as irrelevant, and then, in 1967 as the controversy spread to Indian Point, to minimize the problem. Finally, when the FPC held a new round of Storm King hearings in 1968...the utility sponsored some ambitious and expensive fish studies by a variety of consultants. During the 1970s, the utility claims, it spent about three million annually on research into the life cycles and spawning patterns of the Hudson's striped bass, shad, perch, tomcod, and anchovy populations. Consolidated Edison used these data to persuade such licensing agencies as the FPC and the Nuclear Regulatory Commission (NRC) that power production at Storm King and at Indian Point was compatible with survival of the river's fish. Experts retained by the environmental groups invariably disputed these claims. FPC and NRC hearing records contain 20,000 pages of disagreements over probability and acceptable rates of fish kills....

The regulatory agency hearings were a stage for what Ross Sandler, lawyer for the NRDC, a public interest law group, calls "the drama of advocacy science." His legal opponent, Peter Bergen, an attorney representing Con Edison, agrees that the

impact on fish life of any power plant "depended on whose experts you were prepared to believe."

Determining the adverse effects of any one power plant was a minor challenge
compared to that of assessing the combined effect of all the plants. This was the
job facing the EPA when, in 1972, it assumed responsibility for curbing pollution
in the Hudson River under the...Clean Water Act. Thermal discharges were among
the pollutants the act sought to eliminate or control....

In the spring of 1975, the EPA notified the utilities that the agency was prepared to issue conditional discharge permits requiring that thermal discharges
from the [steam] plants be reduced by 90 percent, meaning, for all practical purposes, that the utilities would have to construct cooling towers within five years.
The EPA gave the utilities 30 days to challenge its decision, and challenge it, of
course, they did.

After reviewing the existing fish studies and retaining its own experts, the EPA
staff concluded that cooling towers were the only way to assure that the plants
would not do irreparable damage to the Hudson River.... [EPA attorney] Jonathan
Strong says that "other industries would be watching to see if we were for real, and
we braced ourselves for a fight." This meant getting the necessary budget and
cooperation from the U.S. Fish and Wildlife Service to sustain EPA's decisions
through what promised to be a lengthy adjudication process.

The utilities' reaction to EPA's position was, predictably, one of dismay. The
permit conditions changed long-term operating and construction costs. "We estimated the total cost of the cooling towers to be as much as $350 million..." says
Joseph Block, executive vice-president and general counsel of Consolidated
Edison....

When the protagonists met, in February 1977, to schedule the presentation of
evidence and cross-examination before the hearing examiner, Con Edison attorney
Peter Bergen challenged EPA's jurisdiction. He argued, to everyone's surprise and
annoyance, that New York State's Department of Environmental Conservation
ought to take charge of the permit process [under NPDES]....

While the utilities challenged EPA's [permit] jurisdiction in the courts, EPA
attacked the utilities in its adjudication hearings, eventually amassing still another
20,000 pages of records....

"The permit question," Albert Butzel, Scenic Hudson's attorney, says, "could
have dragged on for years. And in the background, the FPC awaited the outcome
before proceeding with more hearings on the Storm King project."

"It was getting boring," admits Peter Bergen, whose legal involvement in the
Hudson River case, just as Butzel's, went back to the 1965 Scenic Hudson decision.
He and Butzel had been arguing the same issues for close to 14 years, and there was
no end in sight.

In March 1979, Butzel and Sandler met with Bergen to discuss the possibility
of some kind of negotiations. "No one would benefit by continuing what
amounted to a stalemate," says Butzel.... Bergen agreed that a negotiated settlement probably made sense, and said he would convey Butzel's and Sandler's over-
ture to the other utilities through Joseph Block.

Ending the legal wars on the Hudson River was also on the minds of several
utility company executives, especially at Consolidated Edison. Consolidated
Edison's readiness to negotiate was attributable, at least partly, to its chairman,
Charles Luce, who had come to the company from the U.S. Department of the
Interior in 1967, during one of the most difficult periods in Consolidated Edison's

history. It was a time of black-outs and shrinking profits. The company found strong opposition wherever it attempted to build new power-generating facilities including, of course, at Storm King. Through management changes, a major capital improvement program, and the establishment of better power interconnections with other utilities, Luce had gradually improved the reliability of Consolidated Edison's generating and distribution system, its financial position, and its corporate image.

"I was close to retirement in 1979," Luce said recently, "and I wanted to settle these outstanding Hudson River cases before I left. I went to the board [members] and asked them for permission to see if they would allow me to pursue some sort of settlement, and they said, 'Go ahead....'"

"Storm King was still an important long-range project for us," says Block, "but no longer a priority." Project costs had soared, and the supplementary power that Storm King was supposed to provide was now coming from gas turbines installed at most of Consolidated Edison's existing power stations during the late 1960s. "The big question," says Block, "was not so much what could be negotiated, but the process: who would be involved and who would mediate it." Block feels that the parties were too numerous and too locked into their positions to be able to stop battling and begin negotiating on their own. "This one needed a neutral third person," he says.

Luce's first choice for a mediator was Laurance S. Rockefeller, who directs the Rockefeller family's conservation interests. Rockefeller declined Luce's invitation, but suggested Russell Train, president of the World Wildlife Fund and a former administrator of the Environmental Protection Agency. Luce like that idea, and asked Rockefeller to approach Train.

Train remembers getting a call, early in April 1979, from George Lamb, an associate of Laurance Rockefeller's, about entering the case. He agreed to do so, Train says, and then he "oozed into the role of mediator." His first step was "to do some quiet checking with the parties involved."

He first contacted Luce, whom he knew personally and with whom he had served in the U.S. Department of the Interior and on the National Water Commission. Luce assured him that the utilities were serious about settling, and that he would be personally delighted if Train intervened. During this and subsequent conversations with Luce, Train became convinced that the Consolidated Edison chairman was committed to a settlement and that he was crucial in getting the participation and continuing cooperation from the other utilities....

Train, who had served on the NRDC board, then contacted John Adams, Ross Sandler's boss at NRDC. Adams told him that NRDC felt that a settlement was possible and that Train was just the person to pull it off.

Getting the EPA to participate was more difficult and time-consuming. EPA's primary activity in this dispute was its insistence on cooling towers [at the steam plants]. It was becoming clear to Train that cooling towers were only one issue to be mediated and might be compromised or traded off in favor of other issues, such as the abandonment of Storm King or the litigation fees of the environmental groups....

Train called Douglas Costle, the EPA administrator at that time, and the two talked about Train as a possible mediator. Costle indicated that mediation was a good idea, but he wanted to check with his staff before committing the agency. Train recalls that about three weeks later he received a call from EPA's general counsel, Joan Z. Bernstein. "She was positive," Train recalls, "but laid down three conditions. EPA's regional office would participate only if the adjudicatory hearings on the cooling towers continued, if the utilities would agree that the cooling towers would have to be considered in a settlement, and if I served as mediator."

The conditions cemented Train's mediator role while also blurring the importance of cooling towers in the discussions. By agreeing to the EPA condition that cooling towers would have to be "considered" in mediation, Train was committing himself to keeping the idea alive. "The essential ambiguity of the word 'considered' also gave us some leeway," Train says.

The formal mediation sessions began on August 28, 1979, at the American Bar Association headquarters on West Forty-fourth Street in New York City. The cast was impressive: 28 people representing 11 groups: Consolidated Edison, Central Hudson, Orange and Rockland Utilities, Niagara Mohawk, the New York State Power Authority, the regional office of the Environmental Protection Agency, the New York State Attorney General's Office, the New York State Department of Environmental Conservation, the Hudson River Fishermen's Association, the Natural Resources Defense Council, and Scenic Hudson.

While all of these organizations had a direct interest in the case, there were really three primary players. Among the public agencies, the EPA was the most critical, since its permit conditions were one of the issues on the bargaining table. Two of the state agencies — the New York State Attorney General's Office and the Department of Environmental Conservation (DEC) — had been involved in the Storm King litigation (by 1978, both had petitioned the Federal Energy Regulatory Commission [FERC] to terminate the license), and DEC was in the potential position of taking over the issuances of discharge permits for the disputed plants. But they didn't have as much at stake, directly, as the EPA.

Consolidated Edison was clearly the major participant among the utilities concerned.... It was generally, and correctly, assumed that other private utilities would follow Consolidated Edison's lead.... Sandler and Butzel, representing the environmental groups, were crucial participants. They saw themselves as the initiators of mediation and were individually committed to making it succeed. They felt they were freer to negotiate than all the other parties, which gave them greater flexibility, and eventually placed them in the role of intermediaries between those parties whose positions, and risks, were more sharply drawn.

The opening session in August was formal, and it was restricted to setting procedures. Train suggested that all press and other inquiries about the mediation effort to be directed to him, and that no participant talk publicly about what was happening. Everyone agreed. Interestingly enough, there never were press inquiries or coverage. It was also agreed that offers or proposals made in mediation would be off the record as far as the adjudicatory hearings or other litigation were concerned. Train also asked the participants to submit written proposals directly to him, which he would distribute to all the parties. He then set September 24 as the date for the next meeting.

Scheduling, always an important part of a mediator's role, was in Train's case especially so. "Russ proved to have a very busy schedule," says Ross Sandler, "and we just had to grab him when he was available." Joseph Block of Consolidated Edison agrees. "Everyone saw him as a busy and important person," says Block. "If he was willing to set a date, then the rest felt that they better go along." This readiness to follow Train's schedule eventually helped keep the mediation effort moving when, during the next 16 months, the parties became discouraged or there was no apparent progress. If Train was willing to press on, the rest of them felt they ought to do the same.

At the September 24 meeting, the environmental groups presented five proposals or issues for discussion. The first, and perhaps most significant, was their willingness to consider what they called a "non-hardware" solution to the fish problem [on the units other than Storm King]. While they wanted further consideration of cooling towers, they were also prepared to consider operational methods of reducing fish kills, for example plant...shutdowns during the spawning season.

Dropping the Storm King plant...was more a demand than a proposal. The three groups also insisted that the land purchased by Consolidated Edison for the project be placed in public ownership to provide permanent protection for Storm King Mountain. They also wanted a moratorium on future power plants in the lower Hudson River Valley. Finally, the environmental representatives asked the utilities to fund a research organization that would develop reliable, long-range information on the river's aquatic life. They also wanted to be reimbursed for their legal costs. This last item raised some eyebrows, and there was, in fact, some disagreement between Sandler and Butzel over whether and how hard they should push for such payment.

The utilities' proposal was some distance from that of the environmentalists. Charles Luce, who presented the utilities' proposal, rejected the idea of periodically closing down the plants. "It raises many practical problems," he said. Luce also ruled out cooling towers. He suggested instead that the utility companies might install elaborate "Ristroph screens," equipped with revolving troughs, that would collect fish impinged in cooling water intakes and deposit them back into the river.... If the cooling tower requirement were dropped and this screen arrangement substituted, Luce said, the utilities would fund a Hudson River fish hatchery, would conduct further research, and would agree to drop Storm King.

The EPA proposal dropped the cooling tower requirement at [one] plant, substituted a Ristroph screen solution in its place and called for periodic closings of the plant during times of heaviest fish entrainment....

While these written positions contained some compromises, they also aggravated suspicions. Some of the EPA representatives sensed that the environmental groups, for example, may have been more interested in killing the Storm King plant than in getting the utilities to construct cooling towers. The absence even of the possibility of cooling towers in the utilities' position seemed, to the EPA, to indicate a lack of good faith. Jonathan Strong, the EPA attorney, recalls that "their throwing Storm King on the table was no concession at all as far as we were concerned." Strong believed that Consolidated Edison really wanted to drop the project anyway, and it was simply looking for an excuse to do so.

Butzel and Sandler were surprised and bothered that Luce's formal statement had so quickly dismissed operating changes as a possible remedy. In fact, much of the September 24 meeting was devoted to persuading the utilities to think about changes in plant operation that might lessen the fish dangers. Luce said he would tell his staff to give it a try. "We then did a 180-degree turn," remembers Block of Consolidated Edison. "We began with hardware solutions, like screens, and in just a month or so we were working on...operating approaches."

During a third meeting, on November 2, 1979, the utilities submitted a significantly expanded proposal, which, in addition to the original offer, included [seasonal plant shutdowns and other operating approaches].... The utilities...outlined the favorable effects of these modifications for reducing fish impingement and entrainment. By the end of December, the utilities had made even further concessions, suggesting that they would reimburse the legal fees of the environmental groups and that they would provide $3 million for an independent research organization.

These offers represented major steps forward in the negotiations. They might even have led to an early agreement except for one major stumbling block. The claims made by the utilities for the reductions in fish mortality proved to be erroneous, or at least dubious....

In January 1980, the mediation effort took a new turn. Rather than continue to deal in claims or charges about fish mortality, the parties now decided to turn over the entire fish question to a smaller technical committee, composed of biologists and other experts retained by the EPA and the utility companies. The committee would devise an operating test [of effects on fish] that all sides could support....

The technical committee struggled valiantly during the winter of 1980 to resolve the complexities.... But, in the end, they could not even agree on how long a suitable test should take. Ross Sandler, who participated in the technical committee sessions, describes them as "confusing and frustrating." "Around April," he says, "I called Joe Block and told him that there was no way that the technical committee would come up with an acceptable testing program. If the negotiations were to succeed, the utilities or the EPA would have to change their positions."

The mediation effort was now in serious trouble. Neither the utilities nor the EPA seemed prepared to budge now that a testing program seemed out of the questions. Rather than dealing in possible solutions, their representatives began trading barbs and insults. As a New York State Power Authority representative put it at one angry meeting, "The whole effort is fruitless." In June, mediator Train asked whether members of the technical committee, together with Butzel and Sandler, might work on some new ideas, not being at all sure what those ideas might be. "My purpose at this point," says Train, "was just to keep the process moving."

The technical committee members included John Lawler and Tom Englert, who were the utilities' fish consultants; John Borman, a consultant to the U.S. Department of the Interior who was serving as the EPA expert; and Robert Henshaw and Edward Horn of the New York State Department of Environmental Conservation. During the summer of 1980, these five people, together with Butzel and Sandler, constituted the heart of the mediation effort. They seemed to perceive that at this stage success or failure depended very much on them. "This period in the mediation," says Butzel, "showed that mediation often requires that the parties involved be separated, including some insulation between the expert consultants and their clients. In this smaller setting, there was a new effort to work something out...."

In late August 1980, Butzel prepared a memorandum summarizing how [a] new combination of [abandoning Storm King and seasonal plant shutdown] outages, together with reduced water withdrawals, the installation of dual-speed pumps at Indian Point, and the construction of a fish hatchery, would substantially reduce fish dangers. The package offered more benefits than the original utility companies' offer, although not to the point of 50 percent of the protection of cooling towers — the minimum objective required by the EPA.

While the utilities seemed ready to back these new ideas, the EPA was not. They did not include cooling towers, nor did they meet the agency's 50 percent standard. While there were still numerous outstanding issues to be argued, such as the size of the research fund and the methods of enforcement, the utilities and the environmental groups now seemed to be moving toward an agreement and, in the process, isolating the EPA. "We were way out on a limb," remembers Jonathan Strong, "and everyone seemed to be sawing it off."

By September 1980, other factors also had undermined the EPA position. Its budget for the case was running low. The New York State Department of Environmental Conservation now indicated its readiness to take over the [NPDES] permit process for the power plants. Bergen, the utilities' lawyer, was back in court arguing that, since EPA's 1975 permits were about to expire, the state surely should assume jurisdiction. Charles Warren, EPA's regional administrator at the time...point[ed] out that the entire permit procedure was, by 1979, proving to be unworkable. "The jurisdictional problem with the state, and the utilities' readiness to appeal the permit conditions, meant that this dispute could have gone on for years. In my view, the striped bass would be better protected by the settlement at hand than they would have been by cooling towers that might never have been built, given the procedural and enforcement problems."

Nonetheless, EPA's enforcement division, and Jonathan Strong in particular, balked at any further mediation attempts. Strong felt that the agency had made concessions, but that there had been no real movement by the utilities....

Faced with this opposition to further mediation, including some obvious conflict within the EPA's regional office, Train called Jeffrey Miller, EPA's assistant administrator for enforcement in Washington, and proposed a meeting where he, Butzel and Sandler, and representatives from the regional office would make their respective cases for and against the EPA's continued participation in negotiations. Train argued in the meeting that an agreement seemed to be a month or so away, that it was an election year, and that a settlement would reflect well on the parties, including the EPA. Train was persuasive. Miller told the EPA regional staff to go back to the bargaining table.

With EPA back in the process, the warring parties now entered the most intensive bargaining period, stretching from late September to mid-December 1980. While the general principles of the potential agreement were by now emerging — the termination of the Storm King project, operating modifications for reduction of fish kills, development of a fish hatchery, establishment of some kind of research fund, and reimbursement of legal fees — there were many details still to be worked out.

Negotiations on such issues as the level of funding and the organization of the research fund, reimbursement of legal fees, and the implementation of the agreement proved to be difficult and often acrimonious. The environmental representatives and the New York State Attorney General's Office were suggesting some very large numbers. "They were taking large bites from the utilities, especially Con Edison," remembers Jonathan Strong of EPA. The utilities started with a $3 million offer for a research fund, but eventually went up to $12 million. They also settled on $500,000 as reimbursement for legal fees.

The utilities, especially the smaller ones, balked at such figures. Consolidated Edison, predictably, ended up paying the most. Block says that his company put up an amount of money roughly equivalent to its "cooling tower exposure": in other words, Consolidated Edison's share of the cooling towers' costs if they had been built.... The utilities also put up, or lost, money in other parts of the agreement. These included an estimated $36 million that Consolidated Edison had invested in Storm King....

While the utilities were concerned by the growing costs of the agreement, they rationalized the price tag as being substantially lower than the $350 million required to construct cooling towers and the $100 million needed annually to operate them. The utilities, of course, also planned to recover these costs through consumer rate increases.

Negotiations became tense indeed when the utilities raised the issue of getting the public service commissions of New York and New Jersey to approve the costs of the agreement before it was executed. Butzel and Sandler knew that the utilities would require legal assurances, such as curtailment of the adjudicatory hearing and the discharge permit conditions, approvals from a variety of environmental review agencies, and the promise from environmental organizations that they would drop their opposition to the plants. But they had not expected that the utilities would want advance approvals from rate regulators. To make matters more difficult, the utilities wanted the environmental organizations to support actively the utilities' bid to pass along the costs of the agreement to consumers.

By December, the parties developed a draft agreement that underwent daily changes. The haggling and bargaining was as intense as ever. Train now pushed everyone to agree on a date, December 18, 1980, on which the arguing would end and something would actually be signed.

Train conducted this formal signing session, attended by the press and representatives from the 11 participants, with a stern hand. There was nervous laughter when he insisted that no one but he would speak until everyone signed the agreement. He says today that he wasn't being funny. There was a real possibility that a fiery speech or an angry word in advance of the signing might have blown apart the whole agreement.

The war on the Hudson ended with Consolidated Edison's agreement to forfeit its Storm King license and to turn the site over to the Palisades Interstate Park Commission. Consolidated Edison and the other utilities promised that they would reduce their plants' water withdrawals through plant outages from May to July for a period of 10 years. They also promised a fish hatchery, new water intakes at Indian Point, a $12 million endowment for a research organization, the reimbursement of legal costs to the environmental groups, and a 25-year moratorium on any new power plants without cooling towers north of the George Washington Bridge. In return, the cooling tower requirements at Indian Point, Roseton, and Bowline were dropped; all litigation and administrative proceedings among the parties ceased; and the environmental groups actively supported the agreement, and its costs, before regulatory agencies.

On December 10, 1981, one year later, New York State issued the necessary [NPDES] discharge permits, which incorporated the terms of the mediated settlement, to the utilities. The research fund had been established, the environmental groups had been reimbursed for their legal fees, and everyone had done what they had agreed to do....

## COMMENTARY AND QUESTIONS

1. **The determinants of the Hudson River Settlement.** Note the ingredients of a successful ADR case, as they are illustrated in this narrative. The choice of method, for example, was apparently well done. Only mediation seems likely to have been viable — the parties would not have accepted binding arbitration, and negotiations without a third party overseer would clearly have come to chaos. Russell Train was

also clearly the right mediator for the job, not only as a matter of background skills and temperament, but also because he had ties to all the major players.

Other elements, not present in all disputes, were also crucial: all parties had a genuine interest in accurate factfinding; there was room to compromise in a major arena, power plant operations; a small group of representatives could cover the wider spectrum of interests and commit their respective sides in ongoing negotiations; there were split interests within the different groupings, no monolithic blocks; there was a governmental participant holding a potential hammer; the corporate parties were financially well-secured to fund a compromise; and all representatives had sufficient expertise to speak the same language.

2. **Was this one too easy?** Although the participants would recoil, could one say this mediation was uncharacteristically soluble? Scrapping Storm King was a ready bargaining chip for the utilities. But what if this case had dealt with Storm King alone? The case shows how ADR can reach out to encompass and resolve a range of somewhat related bargaining items in a way a court could never do. What about the fortuitous presence of Luce and Train, and their special fit with the utilities, environmental attorneys, and governmental reps? What if there had not been such an Ivy League buddy cohort?

3. **The role of citizen suit injunctions.** What does the Hudson River case have to say to ADR advocates who deplore those who run to court? What role would the citizen environmentalists have played in the negotiation process (would there have been any such process?) if they had not initially won an injunction in the *Storm King* case? Professor Sander wrote in note 59 of his article that initial adjudication may be required to "equalize the power relationship and bring the more powerful respondent to the bargaining table." Many environmental negotiations involving citizen initiatives therefore necessarily take place "in the shadow of the courts."

4. **The Upstate/Downstate New York water negotiation.** After determining that the safety of New York City's water supply was gravely at risk due to a variety of bacterial threats, in June 1993 EPA filed suit to force the City to clean up its water system, a project estimated to cost more than $6 billion for high-technology high-volume filters and filter stations throughout the upstate watershed region as well as at the terminus. The City proposed that, instead of a filtering system, it somehow negotiate an alternative regional management system to assure the intake of cleaner water entering the City's conduits upstate. The City's water supply comes primarily from areas around the Catskill Mountains and adjacent farming areas, a large land area with widely differing population groups. The EPA allowed the City time to prepare and submit a proposal.

The City set off in quest of a multi-party negotiation[11] with a variety of parties with which it clearly did not have good relations. Many of the important interests

---

11. See K.A. Stave, Resource Use Conflict in New York City's Catskill Watersheds: A Case for Expanding the Scope of Water Resource Management, in Austin, L.H., ed., Water in the 21st Century: Conservation, Demand, and Supply: Proceedings of the American Water Resources Association, at 61–68 (1995); and K.A. Stave, Describing the Elephant: Multiple Perspectives in New York City's Watershed Protection Conflict. Proceedings of the Water Environment Federation Watershed '96 Conference (1996); New York Times, April 25, 1997 at B4.

in the upstream water supply source areas resented the City, due to years of fractious relations over past apportionments of statewide power, conflicting regulatory spheres, politics, and feelings of mutual exploitation. It was clear to all, moreover, that thanks to the EPA the upstate interests largely had the City over a barrel (although the City had been given eminent domain powers in upstate watersheds that provided a messy ace in the hole). In a long process of negotiations with cities and towns, industries, farm groups, other land-owning entities and a number of important individuals, the City's negotiators attempted to identify mutually beneficial ways to clean up water supplies without adversely harming local interests, and were clearly willing to pay large sums of money to buy their way out from under the $6 billion EPA threat.

Ultimately a rough agreement package was put together in 1997, involving extensive purchases of fee titles and easements in areas adjoining water supply sites, design and financing of agricultural pollution control facilities in wide areas of the watersheds, subsidized infrastructure improvements for upstate communities, and individualized negotiated solutions with many players. Many of the upstate parties negotiated in ad hoc groups formed to pool their tactical and political efforts to equalize bargaining powers with the City. The City ultimately made very large financial concessions.

During the entire process, EPA was breathing down the City's neck, threatening to resume the lawsuit if the city water supply did not quickly move toward compliance. The agreement between the upstream interests, the City, and the EPA is more than a thousand pages long, and has not yet been released to the public.

The City's side of the bargain amounted to more than $1.5 billion. In terms of ADR, the cost of reaching a patchwork agreement with so many different communities and individuals, many of whom had extra-legal axes to grind with the City and would not be bought off at market value, was high. The City, however, was willing to pay a fair amount of minor extortion in order to avoid the looming EPA tab. No one is sure if the agreement will hold, as EPA has continued to criticize the City's performance.

5. **ADR and democracy.** ADR processes are frequently closed-door affairs, although citizens are often included as participants or even central players. But *which* citizens get to play, or even to observe? In practice the parties in an ADR case typically include everyone who can substantially shape, or disrupt, the Deal. Does ADR dilute the rights of minor players, interested nonplayers, or even of the participants themselves? Does a society have a duty to resolve its major public controversies in public?

## Section 3. NEGOTIATED RULEMAKING

### Susskind & McMahon, The Theory and Practice of Negotiated Rulemaking
### 3 Yale Journal on Regulation 133, 140–141, 142–146 (1985)[12]

Since the late 1970s, advocates of negotiated approaches to rulemaking have argued that the legitimacy of proposed rules could be restored — and time-consuming court challenges avoided — if informal, face-to-face negotiations were used to supplement the traditional review and comment process.Critics, however, have responded quite negatively to what they perceive as the dangers of "deal-making behind closed doors." Nevertheless, proponents of the innovation have persisted, and during the last few years several federal agencies have experimented with negotiated approaches to rulemaking....

Negotiated rulemaking will only be utilized more broadly if it achieves better results than the traditional rulemaking process.... Each party must feel that the negotiated rule serves its interest at least as well as the version of the rule most likely to be developed through conventional process.... A negotiation should yield real-istic commitments from all of those involved. A rule that satisfies everyone in principle but cannot be implemented is of little use. Not only is the support of the participants important, but so too is the support of any interested party.... The interests of the parties should be so well-reconciled that no possible joint gains are left unrealized. Changes which would help a party without harming another party should not be missed. If a more elegant method of reconciling conflicting interests of the parties is possible, it will probably emerge once the draft of the agreement is publicized.... The agency should be able to demonstrate that it has upheld its statutory mandate, and the public-at-large should feel satisfied that both the process and outcome were fair.... Relationships among the participants in the negotiations should improve, not deteriorate, as a result of their interactions. The parties should be in a better position to deal with their differences in the future.... The negotiated rule should take account of the best scientific and technological information available at the time of the negotiation.

EPA'S REGULATORY NEGOTIATION DEMONSTRATIONS... The notion of using a negotiated approach to rulemaking at EPA first emerged during the Carter Administration.... While the change of Administration slowed the momentum, appointment of Joseph Cannon as Acting Associate Administrator of EPA's Office of Planning and Resource Management in 1981 brought renewed interest.... In February 1983, EPA published a notice in the Federal Register indicating that it intended to pursue the idea of negotiated rulemaking and used solicitation letters to invite interested parties to suggest candidate rules....

In December 1983, David Doniger of the Natural Resources Defense Council (NRDC) formally proposed [rulemaking on CAA motor vehicle emissions] noncon-formance penalties [NCPs] as a candidate rule for negotiated rulemaking. Between December 1983 and March 1984, [EPA] found widespread support for negotiating the NCP rule among potential stakeholders. Charles Freed, Director of EPA's Manufacturers Operations Division, the program office responsible for the rule,

---

12. Copyright 1985 by Yale Journal on Regulation, Box 401A Yale Station, New Haven, CT 06520; reprinted from Volume 3:133 by permission. Other useful works on reg-neg include Philip Harter's Negotiated Regulations: A Cure for Malaise, 71 Georgetown L. Rev. 1 (1982) and Perritt, Negotiated Rulemaking Before Federal Agencies, 74 Georgetown L. Rev. 1625 (1986).] The Administrative Conference has published a useful collection: Negotiated Rulemaking Sourcebook (1990).

enthusiastically supported using a negotiated approach, as did the EPA Office of General Counsel and Office of Program Planning and Evaluation. Environmentalists were generally supportive, viewing NCPs as a means to accommodate temporary industry needs while holding industry to technology-forcing standards. Smaller manufacturers were somewhat wary of the costs of participating in a negotiated rulemaking and felt that any NCP rule had to preserve their competitiveness. Larger manufacturers generally supported the proposed process and felt that they had adequate staff to participate in the process. In general, all stakeholders felt that the rule was important enough to merit their involvement and that it did not involve the type of "life and death" value questions that would have made negotiation — an unfamiliar process at any rate — appear less workable.

In an April 1984 Federal Register notice, EPA announced its intention to develop an NCP rule using a regulatory negotiation. At an organizational meeting...some twenty participants met to learn more about the proposed process and to discuss how the negotiations would proceed. At that time, EPA announced the creation of a $50,000 resource pool — a fund that any or all of the participants would be able to draw upon to cover the costs of technical studies or other costs related to their participation.

Negotiations began June 14, 1984, and ended October 12, 1984. In order to develop some structure for the process, a negotiation facilitator opened the June session by asking participants to produce a statement of issues reflecting their interests. A final list of ten issues was synthesized to help organize the work of the negotiating committee. Three work groups were formed....

Five one-day negotiating sessions dealing with substantive aspects of the NCP rule and numerous work group sessions dealing with specific technical and administrative issues were held during a four month period. The NCP negotiating committee used over $10,000 to fund an independent study of a proposed engine testing plan. Other collaborative technical work was done by committee members who designed a micro-computer-based spreadsheet model to test the impacts of parameter changes in the penalty formula.

The negotiations were conducted under a Federal Advisory Committee Act (FACA) charter. Notice of the NCP negotiating committee sessions was given in the Federal Register, and meetings were open to the public. The committee eventually reached consensus on all of the issues it originally identified in the first meeting.

In reaching this consensus, EPA's choice of a facilitator was crucial. The ERM-McGlennon team, which had extensive mediation experience, took the lead in generating agreement on a detailed agenda and work schedule, organizing work group meetings at which components of the final version of the regulation were drafted, and convening the full group to review these work group drafts.... [T]he facilitation team initiated caucuses during and outside of meetings, maintained frequent contact with all participants, and intervened quite actively during several of the sessions.

After the last negotiation session on October 12, 1984, in which all the issues were resolved, a four-member subcommittee — consisting of EPA, state, environmental, and industry representatives — was given the responsibility of translating the tentative agreement into a consensus document. A first draft was circulated in mid-October, and comments were solicited. The subcommittee then used several conference calls to prepare the final draft that was signed by the entire committee in December 1984. With the consensus statement signed by all participants, EPA published its notice of proposed rulemaking on March 6, 1985. Only thirteen comments were received during the comment period, all in support of the committee's proposal. The final rule was promulgated without opposition on August 30, 1985....

## COMMENTARY AND QUESTIONS

1. **Statutory ADR and regneg.** In 1990, Congress formally recognized the utility of ADR and negotiated rulemaking, and made them federal policy. The 101st Congress passed the Administrative Dispute Resolution Act (P.L. 101–552) and the Negotiated Rulemaking Act (P.L. 101–648) as amendments to the adjudication section of the Administrative Procedure Act. Under the ADRA, agencies are required to appoint resolution specialists and to develop policy addressing the potential uses of ADR in that agency. The Act does not force agencies to use ADR mechanisms, but each agency must review its litigation and administrative disputes to determine where ADR techniques may be useful. The second statute explicitly establishes the authority of federal regulatory agencies to use negotiated rulemaking, and permits the use of federal funds to cover the expenses of private party participants. These policies may give ADR methods new legitimacy and force, although temperaments and practical constraints do not automatically change. FRCP Rules 16 and 68 also attempt to promote nonlitigative resolutions in cases filed in federal court.

2. **Technical details.** The EPA regneg illustrates several technical issues. It is always a question, for instance, who pays — especially where citizen groups are involved. How many participants are too many? Federal rules may well directly affect thousands. What about the records of an ADR process (this issue applies equally to non-regneg cases)? ADR specialists typically try to keep as few records as possible, and get the parties to contract to confidentiality, to avoid the disruptive possibility that information may be subpoenaed to be used in other more litigious forums. (In some jurisdictions a nascent "mediation privilege" is being recognized, analogous to an attorney-client privilege.)

And what about the administrative law consequences? Does regneg violate the delegation doctrine because non-officials effectively make the decision?[13] Do split caucuses in regneg violate the ban on ex parte contacts with agency decision-makers?[14] Will courts still feel obliged to scrutinize closely to assure that agencies gave a "hard look" to the facts and law?[15]

3. **Evaluating ADR.** Ultimately, evaluation of ADR depends not only on whether cases reach settlement, but also upon what it is intended to achieve. And different observers have very different views. Justice Burger wanted to unclog the courts.

---

13. Susskind argues that it doesn't, because agency officials have the last word. 3 Yale J. on Reg. at 158.

14. Perritt argues that it doesn't, 74 Georgetown L.Rev. 1625, 1697 (1986).

15. Susskind argues that the hard look will be satisfied if the regneg incorporates: notice; equal footing, including funding of citizens; reasonable record; round-robin review of the final draft; full discussion of comments; procedural equality; clear statement of agency negotiation positions; and an opportunity for all parties to sign off on the final rule. 3 Yale J. on Reg. at 164. Cf. Wald, Negotiation of Environmental Disputes: a New Role for the Courts?, 10 Colum. J. Envtl Law 1 (1985).

Professor Fiss discerns a questionable political goal "to insulate the status quo from the judiciary."[16] Professor Sander, in the excerpt quoted above, doubted whether comparative efficiency was the point, including "satisfaction" as part of the goal. McThenia & Shaffer likewise focus on more holistic goals, quoting Socrates: "Justice is what we discover — you and I — when we walk together, listen together, and even love one another, in our curiosity about what justice is and where justice comes from."[17] (Fiss says he's as much for love as anybody, but dispute resolution has broader goals and constraints.) Are a governing system's needs adequately fulfilled when the interests of all parties involved in a particular conflict are satisfied, or are there further systemic goals, like establishing precedent?

*We are confronted with insurmountable opportunities.*

— Pogo

---

16. Against Settlement, 94 Yale L.J. 1669, 1670 (1985).
17. For Reconciliation, 94 Yale L.J. 1660, 1665 (1985).

# PART SIX

# PRIVATE AND PUBLIC-SOCIETAL RIGHTS AND RESPONSIBILITIES

*As for me, I am establishing my covenant with you and your descendants after you, and with every living creature that is with you....*

— Genesis 9:9–10

# Chapter 22

# PUBLIC ENVIRONMENTAL RIGHTS AND DUTIES: THE PUBLIC TRUST DOCTRINE

A. *A Note on Federal Constitutional Environmental Rights*
B. *Modern Rediscovery of the Public Trust Doctrine*
C. *Applying the Modern Public Trust Doctrine*
D. *Similar Environmental Rights From Constitutions and Statutes*


*...So neither can the king intrude upon the common property, thus understood, and appropriate it to himself or to the fiscal purposes of the nation. [T]he enjoyment of it is a natural right which cannot be infringed or taken away, unless by arbitrary power, and that, in theory at least, [can]not exist in a free government....*
— Arnold v. Mundy, 6 N.J.L. 1, 87–88 (1821)

## A. A NOTE ON FEDERAL CONSTITUTIONAL ENVIRONMENTAL RIGHTS

Americans like to find vindication for any and all cherished principles within the text of the federal Constitution, particularly within the Bill of Rights. During the original debates on NEPA, several legislators asserted that a constitutional right to environmental quality already existed in the Constitution, but that claim was not widely accepted. Congr. Rec., Dec. 20, 1969, 40, 417. Beyond the difficulties involved in defining just exactly where such claims of right might come from and what exactly they would mean, the courts have appeared hesitant to adopt such constitutional assertions because of the way they would vastly complicate environmental litigation. Perhaps environmental cases are daunting enough without raising the ante to the level of a constitutional battle.

Public trust arguments, introduced in Chapter One and explored further in this chapter, offer a more particularized basis for the definition of public environmental rights and duties, for governments and citizens.

The following case demonstrates the dim prospects of broad, vague constitutional claims:

**Tanner et al. v. Armco Steel et al.**
United States District Court, Southern District of Texas, 1972
340 F. Supp. 532

[Plaintiffs lived along the Houston Ship Channel, near defendants' petroleum refineries and factories. Complaining of personal and property damages caused by air pollution, they sought to sue under a variety of constitutional theories.]

NOEL, J. Plaintiffs purport to construct a claim upon the following foundations: (1) the Constitution of the United States "in its entirety"; (2) the Due Process Clause of the Fifth Amendment; (3) the Ninth Amendment; (4) the Fourteenth Amendment in conjunction with the Civil Rights Act of 1871; 42 U.S.C.A. §1983, and its jurisdictional statute, 28 U.S.C.A. §1343; (5) the National Environmental Policy Act of 1969, 42 U.S.C.A. §§4321 et seq.; (6) and, finally, the general federal question jurisdictional statute, 28 U.S.C.A. §1331 (a)....

The allusion in the complaint to the Federal Constitution "in its entirety" is not a plain statement of the ground upon which the Court's jurisdiction depends, and is therefore insufficient pleading under FRCP Rule 8(a)(1).

The Due Process Clause of the Fifth Amendment to the Federal Constitution...operates only as a restraint upon the National Government and upon the States through the Fourteenth Amendment, but is not directed against the actions of private individuals such as...defendant private corporations....

The Ninth Amendment, through its "penumbra" or otherwise, embodies no legally assertable right to a healthful environment. EDF v. Corp of Engineers, 325 F. Supp. 728, 739 (E.D.Ark. 1971)....

[Claims under] the Fourteenth Amendment, in conjunction with the Civil Rights Act of 1871, 42 U.S.C.A. §1983...must embrace two elements properly alleged: (1) a constitutional deprivation, and (2) state action.... This Court is persuaded that plaintiffs have not alleged the quantum of state or municipal regulatory involvement necessary to clothe defendants with the mantle of the State [and] plaintiffs have failed to allege a violation by defendants of any judicially cognizable federal constitutional right.... Although there has been something of a boom recently in..."grandiose claims of the right of the general populace to enjoy a decent environment," 324 F. Supp. at 303, such claims "have been more successful in theory than in operation." Rheingold, A Primer on Environmental Litigation, 38 Brooklyn L.Rev. at 126 (1971). In view of the dearth of supportive authority, this Court must decline "to embrace the exhilarating opportunity of anticipating a doctrine which may be in the womb of time, but whose birth is distant...."

Such a task would be difficult enough with the guidance of a statute, but to undertake it in the complete absence of statutory standards would be simply to ignore the limitations of judicial decision-making.... From an institutional viewpoint, the judicial process, through constitutional litigation, is peculiarly ill-suited to solving problems of environmental control. Because such problems frequently call for the delicate balancing of competing social interests, as well as the application of specialized expertise, it would appear that their resolution is best consigned initially to the legislative and administrative processes. Furthermore, the inevitable trade-off between economic and ecological values presents a subject matter which is inherently political, and which is far too serious to relegate to the ad hoc process of "government by lawsuit" in the midst of a statutory vacuum....

To the extent that an environmental controversy such as this is presently justiciable, it is within the province of the law of torts....

As the United States Supreme Court recently observed in rejecting a similarly imaginative constitutional claim, "the Constitution does not provide judicial remedies for every social and economic ill."... Dismissed.

COMMENTARY AND QUESTIONS

1. **Why assert a *constitutional* right?** Efforts to make environmental quality a literal provision of the federal Constitution regularly recur. In the early '90s the National Wildlife Federation proposed an amendment stating —

> Each person has the right to clean air, pure water, productive soils and to the conservation of the natural, scenic, historic, recreational, aesthetic and economic values of America's natural resources. It is the responsibility of the United States and of the several States as public trustees to safeguard them for the present and for the benefit of posterity.

Professor Jim Krier proposed that such an amendment be added to the Constitution (albeit with a specific proviso that it be only aspirational, not enforceable in court). The Environment, the Constitution, and the Coupling Fallacy, 32 Michigan Law Quadrangle Notes 35 (1988). Why bother? Perhaps it is a legacy of the mid-20th century, when major advances in individual and pluralistic democratic rights were based on constitutional theories. Perhaps it is an American habit or instinct that important principles should be enshrined in our society's Supreme Law, or that, faced with corporate, bureaucratic, and legislative inertia, citizens feel impelled to seek the crude blunt instrument of rights talk to capture the political and legal processes' practical attention. Whatever the reason, note that the proposed constitutional amendment includes the public trust doctrine, which *already* exists within American law process with a known structure and a fairly extensive interpretive caselaw.

As noted later in this chapter, some states have provided a laboratory for testing the idea of environmental constitutional provisions, with variable but generally undramatic results.

2. **Why talk of *rights?*** Some legal thinkers have begun reconsidering the emphasis on rights, exploring the need to define complementary *duties* in order to balance the social contract. See Mary Ann Glendon, Rights Talk: The Impoverishment of Political Discourse (1991). This perspective is not a naïve call for law and order and citizens' respect for authority. Professor Glendon notes that corporations and public agencies also require lessons in civic responsibility, and implies recognition of the fact that citizens — some employing rights arguments — have often played an active role in trying to make civic governance work.

In some settings, a focus on rights may not be particularly useful. Professor Cass Sunstein, a supporter of many regulatory programs introduced through citizen clamor in the 1960s and 1970s (and the author of After the Rights Revolution: Reconceiving the Regulatory State (1990)), reviewing Professor Glendon's book, said:

> Efforts to think about social and economic problems in terms of rights can obscure those problems. A claimed right to clean air or water, or safe products or workplaces, makes little sense in light of the need for close assessment, in particular cases, of the advantages of greater environmental protection, or more safety, as compared with the (sometimes) accompanying disadvantages of higher prices, lower wages, less employment, and more poverty. To the extent that the regulatory programs of the 1970s were billed as vindications of "rights," they severely impaired political deliberation about their content....

Often, rights emerge precisely because of the refusal of private and public institutions to recognize and carry out their duties. When the environment is degraded, or when the vulnerable are simply left to fend for themselves, it should be unsurprising to find vigorous claims for "rights." The claims for a right to clean air and water, to food, to a decent place to live, to a safe workplace, or to "free reproductive choice" — all these must be understood in their context, as responses to failures of social responsibility. Sunstein, Rightalk, 205 The New Republic No. 10, 33, 34–36 (Sept. 2, 1991).

## B. THE MODERN REDISCOVERY OF THE PUBLIC TRUST DOCTRINE

### Joseph L. Sax, Defending The Environment: A Strategy for Citizen Action
#### 163–165 (1970)

Long ago there developed in the law of the Roman Empire a legal theory known as the "doctrine of the public trust." It was founded upon the very sensible idea that certain common properties, such as rivers, the seashore, and the air, were held by government in trusteeship for the free and unimpeded use of the general public. Our contemporary concerns about "the environment" bear a very close conceptual relationship to this venerable legal doctrine.

Under the Roman law, perpetual use of common properties "was dedicated to the public." As one scholar, R.W. Lee, noted: "In general the shore was not owned by individuals. One test suggests that it was the property of the Roman people. More often it is regarded as owned by no one, the public having undefined rights of use and enjoyment."[1] Similarly in England, according to R.S. Hall, the law developed that "the ownership of the shore, as between the public and the King, has been settled in favor of the King: but...this ownership is, and had been immemorially, liable to certain general rights of egress and regress, for fishing, trading, and other uses claimed and used by his subjects."

American law adopted the general idea of trusteeship but rarely applied it to any but a few sorts of public properties such as shorelands and parks. The content and purpose of the doctrine never received a careful explication, though occasionally a comment can be found in the cases to the effect that it is "inconceivable" that any person would claim a private-property interest in the navigable waters of the United States, assertable against the free and general use of the public at large. And from time to time provisions can be found, as in the Northwest Ordinance of 1787, which stated that "the navigable waters leading into the Mississippi...shall be common highways and forever free...to the citizens of the United States..."

The scattered evidence, taken together, suggests that the idea of a public trusteeship rests upon three related principles. First, that certain interests — like the air and the sea — have such importance to the citizenry as a whole that is

---

1. [The Latin concepts are *res communes* and *res nullius*. The former referred to such things which, while not susceptible to exclusive ownership, can be enjoyed and used by everyone (such as water, air, and light); the latter referred to things which belonged to no one, "either because they were unappropriated by anyone, such as unoccupied lands or wild animals, or things similar to *res sacrae* or *res religiosae* 'to which a religious character prevents any human right of property attaching.'" Coquillette, Mosses from an Old Manse: Another Look at Some Historic Property Cases about the Environment, 64 Cornell L. Rev. 761, 803 n. 196 (1979); Black's Law Dictionary 1304–1305, 1306 (6th ed. 1990). For more from Justinian's Institutes, see Jolowicz, Historical Introduction to the Study of Roman Law, 502–503 (2d ed. 1954).]

would be unwise to make them the subject of private ownership. Second, that they partake so much of the bounty of nature, rather than of individual enterprise, that they should be made freely available to the entire citizenry without regard to economic status. And, finally, that it is a principal purpose of government to promote the interests of the general public rather than to redistribute public goods from broad public uses to restricted private benefit....

### Sax, The Public Trust Doctrine in Natural Resource Law: Effective Judicial Intervention
#### 68 Michigan Law Rev. 471, 489-502 (1970)

The most celebrated public trust case in the American law is the decision of the United States Supreme Court in Illinois Central Railroad Company v. Illinois, 146 U.S. 387 (1892). In 1869 the Illinois legislature made an extensive grant of submerged lands, in fee simple, to the Illinois Central Railroad. That grant included all the land underlying Lake Michigan for one mile out from the shoreline and extending one mile in length along the central business district of Chicago — more than one thousand acres of incalculable value, comprising virtually the whole commercial waterfront of the city. By 1873 the legislature had repented of its excessive generosity, and it repealed the 1869 grant; it then brought an action to have the original grant declared invalid.

The Supreme Court upheld the state's claim and wrote one of the very few opinions in which an express conveyance of trust lands has been held to be beyond the power of a state legislature.... But the Court did not actually prohibit the disposition of trust lands to private parties; its holding was much more limited. What a state may not do, the Court said, is to divest itself of authority to govern the whole of an area in which it has responsibility to exercise its police power; to grant almost the entire waterfront of a major city to a private company is, in effect, to abdicate legislative authority over navigation.

But the mere granting of property to a private owner does not ipso facto prevent the exercise of the police power, for states routinely exercise a great deal of regulatory authority over privately owned land. The Court's decision makes sense only because the Court determined that the states have special regulatory obligations over shorelands, obligations which are inconsistent with large-scale private ownership. The Court stated that the title under which Illinois held the navigable waters of Lake Michigan is different in character from that which the state holds in lands intended for sale.... It is a title held in trust for the people of the state that they may enjoy the navigation of the waters, carry on commerce over them, and have liberty of fishing therein freed from the obstruction or interference of private parties.

With this language, the Court articulated a principle that has become the central substantive thought in public trust litigation. When a state holds a resource which is available for the free use of the general public, a court will look with considerable skepticism upon *any* governmental conduct which is calculated *either* to reallocate the resource to more restricted uses *or* to subject public uses to the self-interest of private parties.

The Court in *Illinois Central* did not specify its reasons for adopting the position which it took, but the attitude implicit in the decision is fairly obvious.... While there may be good reason to use governmental resources to benefit some group smaller than the whole citizenry, there is usually some relatively obvious reason for the subsidy, such as a need to assist the farmer or the urban poor. In addition, there is ordinarily some plainly rational basis for the reallocative structure of any such programs — whether it be taxing the more affluent to support the poor or using the tax base of a large community to sustain programs in a smaller unit of government. Although courts are disinclined to examine these issues through a rigorous economic analysis, it seems fair to say that the foregoing observations are consistent with a general view of the function of government. Accordingly, the court's suspicions are naturally aroused when they are faced with a program which seems quite at odds with such a view of government.

In *Illinois Central*, for example, everything seems to have been backwards. There appears to have been no good reason for taxing the general public in order to support a substantial private enterprise in obtaining control of the waterfront. There was no reason to believe that private ownership would have provided incentives for needed developments, as might have been the case with land grants in remote areas of the country; and if the resource was to be maintained for traditional uses, it was unlikely that private management would have produced more efficient or attractive services to the public. Indeed, the public benefits that could have been achieved by private ownership are not easy to identify.

Although the facts of *Illinois Central* were highly unusual — and the grant in that case was particularly egregious — the case remains an important precedent. The model for judicial skepticism it built poses a set of relevant standards for current, less dramatic instances of dubious governmental conduct. For instance, a court should look skeptically at programs which infringe broad public uses in favor of narrower ones. Similarly there should be a special burden of justification on government when such results are brought into question. But *Illinois Central* also raises more far-reaching issues. For example, what are the implications for the workings of the democratic process when such programs, although ultimately found to be unjustifiable, are nonetheless promulgated through democratic institutions? Furthermore, what does the existence of those seeming imperfections in the democratic process imply about the role of the courts, which, *Illinois Central* notwithstanding, are generally reluctant to hold invalid the acts of co-equal branches of government?

THE CONTEMPORARY DOCTRINE OF THE PUBLIC TRUST: AN INSTRUMENT FOR DEMOCRATIZATION... The *Illinois Central* problem has had its most significant modern exegesis in Massachusetts. In that state, the Supreme Judicial Court has shown a clear recognition of the potential for abuse which exists whenever power over lands is given to a body which is not directly responsive to the electorate. To counteract the influence which private interest groups may have with administrative agencies and to encourage policy decisions to be made openly at the legislative level, the Massachusetts court has developed a rule that a change in the use of public lands is impermissible without a clear showing of legislative approval.

In Gould v. Greylock Reservation Commission,[2] the Supreme Judicial Court of Massachusetts took the major step in developing the doctrine applicable to changes in the use of lands dedicated to the public interest....

Mount Greylock, about which the controversy centered, is the highest summit of an isolated range which is surrounded by lands of considerably lower elevation. In 1888 a group of citizens, interested in preserving the mountain as an unspoiled natural forest, promoted the creation of an association for the purpose of laying out

2. 350 Mass. 410, 215 N.E. 2d 114 (1966).

a public park on it. The state ultimately acquired about 9,000 acres, and the legislature enacted a statute creating the Greylock Reservation Commission and giving it certain of the powers of a park commission. By 1953 the reservation contained a camp ground, a few ski trails, a small lodge, a memorial tower, some TV and radio facilities, and a parking area and garage. In that year, the legislature enacted a statute creating an Authority to construct and operate on Mount Greylock an aerial tramway and certain other facilities, and it authorized the original commission to lease to the Authority "any portion of the Mount Greylock Reservation."

For some time the Authority was unable to obtain the financing necessary to go forward with its desire to build a ski development, but eventually it made an arrangement for the underwriting of revenue bonds. Under that arrangement the underwriters, organized as a joint venture corporation called American Resort Services, were to lease 4,000 acres of the reservation from the Commission. On that land, the management corporation was to build and manage an elaborate ski development, for which it was to receive forty percent of the net operations revenue of the enterprise....

After the arrangements had been made, but before the project went forward, five citizens of the county in which the reservation is located brought an action against both the Greylock Reservation Commission and the Tramway Authority. The plaintiffs brought the suit as beneficiaries of the public trust under which the reservation was said to be held, and they asked that the court declare invalid both the lease of the 4,000 acres of reservation land and the agreement between the Authority and the management corporation. They asked the court to examine the statutes authorizing the project, and to interpret them narrowly to prevent both the extensive development contemplated and the transfer of supervisory powers into the hands of a profit-making corporation. The case seemed an exceedingly difficult one for the plaintiffs, both because the statutes creating the Authority were phrased in extremely general terms, and because legislative grants of power to administrative agencies are usually read quite broadly. Certainly, in light of the statute, it could not be said that the legislature desired Mount Greylock to be preserved in its natural state, nor could the legislature be said to have prohibited leasing agreements with a management agency. Nonetheless, the court held both the lease and the management agreement invalid on the ground that they were in excess of the statutory grant of authority.

*Gould* cannot be considered merely a conventional exercise in legislative interpretation. It is, rather, a judicial response to a situation in which public powers were being used to achieve a most peculiar purpose.[3] Thus, the critical passage in the decision is that in which the court stated:

The profit sharing feature and some aspects of the project itself strongly suggest a commercial enterprise. In addition to the absence of any clear or express statutory authorization of as broad a delegation of responsibility by the Authority as is given by the management agreement, we find no express grant to the Authority of power to permit use of public lands and of the Authority's borrowed funds for what seems, in part at least, a commercial venture for private profit.

In coming to this recognition, the court took note of the unusual developments

3. For a confirmation that the "feel" of a case is critical to its decision, the *Gould* case should be compared with People ex rel. Kurcharski v. McGovern, 245 N.E. 2d 472 (Ill. 1969). In the latter case, the court upheld recreational developments in a forest preserve, despite a limited statute of authorization, apparently because the public action seemed reasonable and it was the posture of the objector which gave rise to suspicion.

which led to the project. What had begun as authorization to a public agency to construct a tramway had developed into a proposal for an elaborate ski area. Since ski resorts are popular and profitable private enterprises, it seems slightly odd in itself that a state would undertake such a development. Furthermore, the public authority had gradually turned over most of its supervisory powers to a private consortium and had been compelled by economic circumstances to agree to a bargain which heavily favored the private investment house.

It hardly seems surprising, then, that the court questioned why a state should subordinate a public park, serving a useful purpose as relatively undeveloped land, to the demands of private investors for building such a commercial facility. The court, faced with such a situation, could hardly have been expected to have treated the case as if it involved nothing but formal legal issues concerning the state's authority to change the use of a certain tract of land.

Yet the court was unwilling to invalidate an act of the legislature on the sole ground that it involved a modification of the use of public trust land. Instead, the court devised a legal rule which imposed a presumption that the state does not ordinarily intend to divert trust properties in such a manner as to lessen public uses. Such a rule would not require a court to perform the odious and judicially dangerous act of telling a legislature that it is not acting in the public interest, but rather would utilize the court's interpretive powers in accordance with an assumption that the legislature is acting to maintain broad public uses. Under the Massachusetts courts' rule, that assumption...is to be altered only if the legislature clearly indicates that it has a different view of the public interest....

Although such a rule may seem to be an elaborate example of judicial indirection, it is in fact directly responsive to the central problem of public trust controversies. There must be some means by which a court can keep a check on legislative grants of public lands while ensuring that historical uses may be modified to accommodate contemporary public needs and that the power to make such modifications resides in a branch of government which is responsive to public demands....

While it will seldom be true that a particular governmental act can be termed corrupt, it will often be the case that the whole of the public interest has not been adequately considered by the legislative or administrative officials whose conduct has been brought into question. In those cases, which are at the center of concern with the public trust, there is a strong, if not demonstrable, implication that the acts in question represent a response to limited and self-interested proponents of public action. It is not difficult to perceive the reason for the legislative and administrative actions which give rise to such cases, for public officials are frequently subjected to intensive representations on behalf of interests seeking official concessions to support proposed enterprises. The concessions desired by those interests are often of limited visibility to the general public so that public sentiment is not aroused; but the importance of the grants to those who seek them may lead to extraordinarily vigorous and persistent efforts. It is in these situations that public trust lands are likely to be put in jeopardy and that legislative watchfulness is likely to be at the lowest levels. To send such a case back for express legislative authority is to create through the courts an openness and visibility which is the public's principal protection against overreaching, but which is often absent in the routine political process. Thus, the courts should intervene to provide the most appropriate climate for democratic policy making.

*Gould*...provides a useful illustration that it is possible for rather dubious projects to clear all the legislative and administrative hurdles which have been set up to protect the public interest....[4] More significantly, the technique which the court used to confront the basic issues suggests a fruitful mode for carrying on such litigation.

### COMMENTARY AND QUESTIONS

1. **The history of the public trust doctrine in the United States.** Professor Sax's article can claim the majority of credit for the active presence of the public trust doctrine in American environmental law. (It has been so often cited as the seminal work in the field that Professor Sax was recently introduced at a conference on western public interest law as "Seminal Sax" and received a standing ovation on the point.) But the public trust doctrine did exist earlier in the case law of the United States, waiting to be re-discovered (somewhat like the Refuse Act of 1899). In 1810, in the Pennsylvania case of Carson v. Glazer, 2 Binn. 475, the Pennsylvania court asserted the public trust doctrine to affirm that no one could own the rights to fish in a Pennsylvania river, as against the public. That case is notable, moreover, not only for the fact that it used the term "trust" in the very modern sense that Sax uses it, but also that the court quite matter of factly extended the traditional trust from navigable waters and ocean waters to inland waterways with no suggestion of navigability. The New Jersey Supreme Court followed in Arnold v. Mundy, 6 N.J.L. 1 (1821), asserting that no one could own shellfishing beds as against the public. Other cases prior to *Illinois Central* had established the same principle. Martin v. Waddell, 41 U.S. 367 (1842). Accordingly, there does not seem to be much dispute about the existence of the public trust doctrine within the body of American law. The questions that have arisen about the public trust doctrine do not deny that fact; rather, they debate the terms upon which the trust exists and applies.

---

4. [Sax notes the common problem of agency insulation and the low visibility of official decisions]: After the massive oil leakage off the Santa Barbara coast...the governmental agency charged with protecting the public interest decided against holding public hearings prior to granting approval for a project because the agency "preferred not to stir the natives up any more than possible [sic]" Interoffice Memo from Eugene W. Standley, Staff Engineer, U.S. Dept. of the Interior, Feb. 15, 1968. When questions were raised, the agency publicly responded by saying, "we feel maximum provision has been made for the local environment and that further delay in the lease sale would not be consistent with the national interest." N.Y. Times, March 25, 1969, at 30, col. 6 (quoting from a letter from the Undersecretary of the Interior to the chairman of the board of supervisors of Santa Barbara County). But the agency privately indicated that "The 'heat' has not died down but we can keep trying to alleviate the fears of the people," *id.* at col 3, and noted that pressures were being applied by the oil company whose equipment worth "millions of dollars" was being held "in anticipation."

There are a variety of other ways in which agencies minimize public participation in their deliberations. For example, the duty to hold a public hearing may technically be satisfied by holding a hearing which is "announced" to the public by posting a notice on an obscure bulletin board in a post office. Nashville I-40 Steering Comm. v. Ellington, 387 F.2d 179, 183 (6th Cir. 1967), cert. denied, 390 U.S. 921 (1968). Alternatively, a statutory hearing requirement may simply be ignored, and the argument later made that despite the omission no citizen has legal standing to challenge the agency's action. See D.C. Fed'n. of Civic Ass'ns., Inc. v. Airis, 391 F. 2d 478 (D.C. Cir. 1968).

[Many courts do not recognize the role of citizens,] e.g., Harrison-Halsted Community Group v. Housing & Home Fin. Agency, 310 F.2d 99, 105 (7th Cir. 1962), cert. denied, 373 U.S. 914 (1963): "The legislature, through its lawfully created agencies, rather than 'interested' citizens, is the guardian of the public needs to be served by social legislation."

2. **The public trust as trust law.** The public trust doctrine is an equitable doctrine which shares its elements with the far more commonly litigated doctrine of private trusts. In both cases, what are the elements of a trust situation? First there must be the "thing" about which the trust is concerned: the "corpus" or "res," the defined bundle of assets owned and managed under the trust framework. Then there must be a trustee, a person or entity legally charged with responsibilities and rights. Trustees in Anglo-American law actually "own" the resources in terms of legal title. They accordingly have the right to manage, sell, lease, develop, etc., the assets, but only insofar as a careful fiduciary would and could so as to protect the existence of the assets and achieve the purposes of the trust. When trustees own a parcel of land in an urban area, as in the case of a number of private or charitable trusts, they may go to an equity court and request permission to sell, lease, or develop the trust property so as to maximize the economic benefits that typically constitute the trust terms in private trusts. The "terms" of a trust, however, differ from trust to trust and are critically important. When a trust has been set up by the "trustor" or "settlor," the trustees must follow the precise dictates and terms of the trust stipulations. If a trust is mandated to maximize the financial security of family members, then the management of the assets will be judged by the careful economic standards necessary to achieve that end. If the trust is set up to care for a park or an educational institution, then the primary trust standard is to maintain the character of the trust property.

While the legal title of a trust rests with the trustee, the real "equitable" or "beneficial" title to the property, enforceable in court, is held by the "beneficiaries." In most trusts the court's enforcement and oversight comes at the request of beneficiaries, any one of whom has standing to call for an accounting from the trustees, in court.

These then are the generic elements of a trust. Can you roughly identify how each of them is to be defined in the case of the public trust doctrine? In a public trust, who is the trustee, who are the beneficiaries, what is the corpus, and, perhaps most important, what are the terms? (The identity of the settlor probably depends upon your theological inclinations.)

3. **What is the public trust and where is it going?** There is little controversy about the existence of the public trust historically in the United States. But what, exactly, is it? Is it a common law doctrine? If so, how is it that it can overturn a *statutory* enactment, as in *Illinois Central*? Is it a federal or state doctrine? Note that in *Illinois Central* the doctrine was used by a federal court to overcome the action of a sovereign state. Does the doctrine apply to the federal government as well? In several cases, courts have asserted that the federal government is equally accountable and restricted under the terms of the public trust doctrine. See *Steuart Transportation* in Chapter One, and U.S. v. 1.8 Acres, 523 F. Supp. 120, 124 (D. Mass. 1981). The federal government is a creature of the states by delegation through the Act of Union and the federal Constitution. If the federal government is therefore exercising delegated powers, it would appear straightforward that it cannot have greater rights and fewer limitations than the entities that created it. Is the public trust then a principle of federal common law? A number of courts and commenta-

tors have indicated that neither the federal government nor the state governments can act to abolish the public trust doctrine. See Chapter One's Marks v. Whitney, 491 P. 2d at 380–81. As trustees, the state sovereignties and federal government are bound by the terms of the trust. Is it then a principle of federal constitutional law? If so, where does it lie?

Where is the public trust going? If it is clear that governments — state and perhaps federal — are the trustees, then what is the scope of the assets held in trust? Is it just tidal waters or navigation and fishing in tidal waters? The doctrine has already spread far beyond that locale, as we will see. It clearly applies on dry land as well, but the ultimate scope of the doctrine is not clearly delineated, at least not yet.[5]

What are the terms of the trust? As noted in Chapter One, it has been applied in three basic settings: resource-defense or "derogation" cases where trust assets are threatened with pollution or destruction,[6] the "alienation" situation restricting government attempts to sell public trust assets, and "diversion" cases limiting shifts of public trust assets from one public use like parkland to other more exploitive uses.[7]

But does the public trust require absolute protection of all trust resources? Like standard trust law, variations of the public trust are permissible through a careful fiduciary balancing process. This is more than merely a procedural requirement of specific statutory authorization described by Professor Sax. Simple legislative or referendum majorities are probably not enough to alter trust protections. A substantive trust balance seems necessary under traditional equity standards. After the *Illinois Central* case, the U.S. Supreme Court and state supreme courts have sometimes found that a conscientious substantive balancing of public trust interests permitted alteration of trust assets. In State v. Public Service Comm'n, 81 N.W.2d 71 (Wis. 1957), the issue was the proposed filling of a small percentage of Lake Wingra in the town of Madison, Wisconsin, for the purposes of making a park area more enjoyable and accessible. The court held, after a careful balancing of public trust considerations, that this action would not violate the trust. See also Milwaukee v. State, 214 N.W. 820 (Wis. 1927).

An interesting reprise to *Illinois Central* played out on the Lake Michigan shoreline only a few miles north of the site of the famous case. In Lake Michigan Federation v. Army Corps of Engineers, 742 F. Supp. 441 (N.D. Ill. 1990), Loyola University proposed an 18.5 acre lakefill project that would be owned by the University, with a 35-foot public promenade on the outer rim, and athletic fields on the interior likewise available to the public. The district court held that because

---

5. See Rieser, Ecological Preservation as a Public Property Right: an Emerging Doctrine in Search of a Theory, 15 HELR 393 (1991); Coastal States Org., Putting the Public Trust to Work (symposium proceedings, 1990) (including a 29-state survey); Symposium, 19 Envtl. Law 425 et seq. (1990).

6. See e.g., Tennessee Code Annotated §§70.324 et seq.; beyond water resources, see the redwood cases, invoking the trust to protect redwoods against erosion and destruction. 396 F. Supp. 90 (N.D. Cal. 1974), 398 F. Supp. 284 (N.D.Cal. 1975).

7. Lying in a grey area between the alienation and diversion categories are cases like Vermont v. Central Vt. Ry., 571 A.2d 1128 (1989), where the state supreme court held that a public utility railroad company's grant of lands on the shores of Lake Champlain would be restricted to public trust uses, where the company, which held title, wanted to undertake resort and commercial development of the lands.

the main purpose of the project was for a private interest, the trust land could not be alienated. The court looked solely to the original motivation of the project, rather than balancing the benefits of the public use of the project against the loss of trust land. The University abandoned the project without appealing the decision. Could a trust balancing process have been argued that would have validated the project? See People ex rel. Moloney v. Kirk, 45 N.E. 830 (Ill. 1896).

What are the standards of the trust? The following modern Illinois case, denying plaintiff's claims, echoes Sax's procedural authorization reasoning but also experiments with the process of defining substantive standards.

## C. APPLYING THE MODERN PUBLIC TRUST DOCTRINE

### Section 1. PUBLIC TRUST BALANCING

#### Paepke v. Building Commission
Supreme Court of Illinois, 1970
46 Ill. 2d 330, 263 N.E.2d 11

BURT, J. Plaintiffs, who are citizens, residents, taxpayers and property owners of the city of Chicago, appeal from an order of the circuit court of Cook County dismissing their complaint by which they sought to prevent defendants, the City of Chicago, the Board of Education of Chicago, and the Chicago Park District, from implementing plans to construct school and recreational facilities in Washington Park. This court has jurisdiction on direct appeal because of the constitutional questions involved....

The Public Building Commission of Chicago, at the request of the Board of Education of the City of Chicago, has undertaken a program involving the construction, alteration, repair, renovation, and rehabilitation of public schools in the city, together with park, recreational, playground, and other related public facilities which will be leased by the Building Commission to the Board of Education, the Chicago Park District, and other governmental agencies....

A site has been designated in Washington Park for the erection of a school-park facility. The Chicago Park District proposes to convey to the Public Building Commission of Chicago for such purposes a total of 3.839 acres located in the northwest portion of the park about 250 feet from the northern boundary. On 2.586 acres of this site the building commission proposes to construct a middle school for approximately 1500 students to be leased to the Board of Education of the City of Chicago. The remaining 1.253 acres would be utilized in the construction of a gymnasium and recreational facilities which will be leased to the Chicago Park District. Construction had started on this site at the time suit was filed but had not proceeded to a point where original use of the land would no longer be possible....

It is plaintiffs' theory that the parks in question are so dedicated that they are held in public trust for use only as park or recreational grounds and that those of them who are property owners adjacent to or in the vicinity of a park dedicated by the acts of 1869 have a private property right to the continuation of the park use of which even the legislature cannot deprive them. They further contend that all plaintiffs who are citizens and residents of any area of the city have a public property right to enforce the public trust existing by reason of the dedication of the parks as aforesaid and to require that no change of park use be permitted because the legislature has not explicitly and openly so provided by statute....

Such dedication having been made by the sovereign, the agencies created by it hold the properties in trust for the uses and purposes specified and for the benefit of the public. See Illinois Central Railroad Co. v. Illinois, 146 U.S. 387 (1892); Sax, The Public Trust Doctrine in Natural Resource Law: Effective Judicial Intervention, 68 Mich. L. Rev. 471–566. [extensive quotations from Professor Sax's article omitted.]

Have plaintiffs who are property owners adjacent to or in the vicinity of the parks...a *private* property right to continuation of the park use?... This question must be answered in the negative. The mere dedication by the sovereign of lands to public park uses does not give property owners adjoining or in the vicinity of the park the right to have the use continue unchanged even though, when the park was established, abutting or adjoining owners were assessed for special benefits conferred....

As to the interests of plaintiffs and their standing to bring the action, the trial judge found that they had no rights sufficient to enable them to maintain the action [holding they had no public nuisance or taxpayer standing]. If the public trust doctrine is to have any meaning or vitality at all, however, the members of the public, at least taxpayers who are the beneficiaries of that trust, must have the right and standing to enforce it. To tell them that they must wait upon governmental action is often an effectual denial of the right for all time. The conclusion we have reached is in accord with decisions in other jurisdictions...wherein plaintiffs' rights...in a trust of public lands were enforced without question.

As to...whether there has been a sufficient manifestation of legislative intent to permit the diversion and reallocation contemplated by the plan proposed by defendants, it...is our conclusion [that the] legislation is sufficiently broad, comprehensive and definite to allow the diversion in use involved here.

In passing we think it appropriate to refer to the [substantive balancing] approach developed by the courts of our sister state, Wisconsin, in dealing with diversion problems.... The Supreme Court of Wisconsin [has] approved proposed diversions in the use of public trust lands under conditions which demonstrate (1) that public bodies would control use of the area in question, (2) that the area would be devoted to public purposes and open to the public, (3) the diminution of the area of original use would be small compared with the entire area, (4) that none of the public uses of the original area would be destroyed or greatly impaired and (5) that the disappointment of those wanting to use the area of new use for former purposes is negligible when compared to the greater convenience to be afforded those members of the public using the new facility. We believe that the present plans for Washington Park meet all of these tests....

In conclusion, let it be said that this court is fully aware of the fact that the issues presented in this case illustrate the classic struggle between those members of the public who would preserve our parks and open lands in their pristine purity and those charged with administrative responsibilities who, under the pressures of the changing needs of an increasingly complex society, find it necessary, in good faith and for the public good, to encroach to some extent upon lands heretofore considered inviolate to change. The resolution of this conflict in any given case is for the legislature and not the courts....

COMMENTARY AND QUESTIONS

1. **The scope of the trust.** Note here in the *Paepke* case how matter-of-factly the court accepts the assumption that the public trust doctrine, developed in the oceans of the Roman Empire, applies to a public parkland, and that citizens have standing to sue. The public trust doctrine has three strategic advantages over common law remedies: (1) automatic standing (unlike public nuisance, which the lower court in *Paepke* relied on to deny standing); (2) a presumption in favor of public uses, transferring the burden of proof to the the public trustee to justify a diversion or alienation; and (3) an ability to avoid sovereign immunity (in this sense at least the public trust clearly acts like a constitutional provision). In fact there has been little serious argument in the public trust cases over the past two decades about whether the public trust doctrine can appropriately be applied to dedicated parklands. The fundamental idea of a park, it appears, is a long-term special management relationship between land, people, and government. (This may help to explain why Professor Sax's public trust scholarship moved quite naturally into an extensive study of the meaning of parks and wilderness in the 20th Century. See Sax, Mountains without Handrails (1981).) What is a "park"? The United States invented the idea of national parks, but there is a continuing debate about what they mean. If the public trust doctrine applies to "parks," does it apply to state or federal forests? Is the concept of "dedication," in some terms, implied or express, the distinguishing factor?

2. **The *Paepke* court's balancing process: a substantive, not merely procedural, standard?** Is the *Paepke* court's holding based on the Wisconsin (substantive) or the Massachusetts (procedural) trust analysis? If, based on Professor Sax's description of the Massachusetts cases, the public trust balance is merely procedural, all a development-minded legislature would have to do to override the trust would be to pass exceedingly specific authorization for a favored project. (In *Paepke*, unlike Sax's description, the court did not even require specific authorization: "the legislation is sufficiently broad, comprehensive and definite to allow the diversion.") The *Paepke* case implies, however, that governments also have substantive trusteeship duties as well as procedural requirements — if the court had found that the Wisconsin trust tests were violated, the construction would have been enjoined despite its statutory authorization.

Under the Wisconsin tests, proposed alterations of trust resources will apparently be tested by scrutiny of the actual balance struck between trust obligations and values on one hand and economic or other legislative development motives on the other. The public trust's long-term legacy value is presumed to be primary. Departures from the trust apparently bear the substantive burden of persuasion. When the government is acting as a trustee, it comes before the equity court as a fiduciary subject to special scrutiny.[8] Although courts review the acts of other

---

8. See People ex rel. Scott v. Chicago Park District, 360 N.E.2d 773 (Ill. 1977). The Illinois legislature wanted to convey 194.6 acres of submerged lands under Lake Michigan to United States Steel — remarkably like the circumstances of *Illinois Central*. Despite a legislative assertion in the bill that the conveyance would result in "the conversion of otherwise useless and unproductive submerged land into an important commercial development to the benefit of the people of the State of Illinois," the court wasn't biting. "The self-serving recitation of a public purpose within a legislative enactment is not conclusive of the existence of such purpose." 360 N.E.2d at 781.

branches of government deferentially, equity precedents for trust accountings from public officials, as in charitable trusts, argue for less deference.

The standards applied by the *Paepke* court, and the process by which it applied them, have the ring of good common sense. The court recognizes that parklands are important public trust resources, and takes seriously, it seems, its role of determining whether or not the diversion ordered by the governmental process will be permitted to chop a piece out of Washington Park. What do you think of the Wisconsin standards and the way the *Paepke* court applied them to the case? Take the five tests one by one and ask yourself whether they sufficiently capture the protective ideas of the public trust. Is there anything missing that could be added as a litigable standard in *Paepke*?

Why was the city of Chicago diverting this section of parkland to its school department's use? Is this the only place in this area of Chicago where the school board could build a new school and facilities? Or is it rather an economic trade-off? Presumably, since they have the power of eminent domain, the school board and city authorities could take 3.8 acres anywhere in this part of the city. The only problem is cost, because it would surely cost a great deal more to take private property than to grab public property for free. But that motive — saving cash — will in every case result in diversion or destruction of public trust resources. In the *Overton Park* case, analyzed in Chapter Seven, the Supreme Court of the United States interpreted a statutory formulation by which the Congress, faced with the same dilemma of automatic trade-offs, declared that no parkland shall be taken for a federal-aid highway unless there is "no feasible and prudent alternative." Professor Sax would clearly not object to that standard.

For another formulation of the balance, see Payne v. Kassab, 312 A.2d 86, 94-94 (Pa. App. 1973). The *Payne* court, citing no precedent, asserted that a change in use of public trust parkland must meet three standards: (1) compliance with applicable statutes and regulations; (2) a reasonable effort to minimize environmental "incursions" resulting from the change in use; and (3) benefits must outweigh any resulting harms. The third test is clearly the key to determining whether there will be a meaningful trust balance or a mere conclusory bureaucratic write-off: Will harms be weighed in terms of long-term intangible trust values, or market dollars? Will project benefits be accounted realistically, or in the promoters' hyperbolic terms? Will alternatives be scrupulously weighed against the proposal? Only with a balance weighing the full range of societal legacy values will the sensitive principles of the trust be honored.

And note that the terms of the trust balance, weighing how much if any modification is permissible, may be quite different in the three different trust settings of resource derogation, alienation, and diversion.

**3. A diversity of values: tradeoffs?** If the City of Chicago was merely trying to save a few dollars and could just as well have condemned private land near the park for its school, that surely should be weighed against the city's proposal. But should the court also consider whether particular proposed alternative locations would disrupt stable, low-income, minority neighborhoods?

Or what if protection of the public trust resource imposes heavy water conservation burdens and expenses on millions of citizens, rich and poor, in a major American city? —

### National Audubon Society v. Superior Court of Alpine County (*Mono Lake*)
Supreme Court of California, 1983
33 Cal.3d 419, 189 Cal.Reptr. 346, 658 P.2d 709

[The City of Los Angeles, located in its dry coastal enclave on the southern California coast, has 3 million inhabitants, and continues to grow by 5[+] percent each year. To assure that water supplies critical to its survival and growth would remain available, city officials thought that they had locked up sufficient appropriated/contract water rights in the Sierra Nevada Mountains[9] to last well into the 21st century. Then, using the public trust doctrine, plaintiff environmentalists filed a lawsuit against Los Angeles' water diversions. The case eventually came to the California Supreme Court on a federal trial judge's request for clarification of the state's public trust doctrine:]

BROUSSARD, J. ...Mono Lake, the second largest lake in California, sits at the base of the Sierra Nevada escarpment near the eastern entrance to Yosemite National Park. The lake is saline; it contains no fish but supports a large population of brine shrimp which feed vast numbers of nesting and migratory birds. Islands in the lake protect a large breeding colony of California gulls, and the lake itself serves as a haven on the migration route for thousands of Northern Phalarope, Wilson's Phalarope, and Eared Grebe. Towers and spires of tufa on the north and south shores are matters of geological interest and a tourist attraction.

Although Mono Lake receives some water from rain and snow on the lake surface, historically most of its supply came from snowmelt in the Sierra Nevada. Five freshwater streams — Mill, Lee Vining, Walker, Parker and Rush Creeks — arise near the crest of the range and carry the annual runoff to the west shore of the lake. In 1940, however, the state Division of Water Resources granted the Department of Water and Power of the City of Los Angeles (DWP) a permit to appropriate virtually the entire flow of four of the five streams flowing into the lake. DWP promptly constructed facilities to divert about half the flow of these streams into DWP's Owens Valley aqueduct. In 1970 DWP completed a second diversion tunnel, and since that time has taken virtually the entire flow of these streams....The ultimate effect of continued diversions is a matter of intense dispute, but there seems little doubt that both the scenic beauty and the ecological values of Mono Lake are imperiled....

The case brings together for the first time two systems of legal thought; the appropriative water rights system which since the days of the gold rush has dominated California water law, and the public trust doctrine which, after evolving as a shield for the protection of tidelands, now extends its protective scope to navigable lakes. Ever since we first recognized that the public trust protects environmental and recreational values (Marks v. Whitney, 491 P.2d 374 (1971)), the two systems of legal thought have been on a collision course. Johnson, Public Trust Protection for Stream Flows and Lake Levels, 14 U.C. Davis L.Rev. 233 (1980)). They meet in a unique and dramatic setting which highlights the clash of values.

---

9. The bitter battles over those water rights formed part of the political backdrop for Roman Polanski's movie "Chinatown."

*Views of Mono Lake; top photograph shows the setting and tufa spires rising from the lake bed. Bottom photograph shows land bridge to Negit Island created by falling water levels in 1979 — because of feeder stream diversions to Los Angeles — allowing invading predators to cross over and destroy the island's nesting population of 38,000 California gulls, three-fourths of the gull's total population in the state.*

Mono Lake is a scenic and ecological treasure of national significance, imperiled by continued diversions of water; yet, the need of Los Angeles for water is apparent, its reliance on rights granted by the board evident, the cost of curtailing diversions substantial.

Attempting to integrate the teachings and values of both the public trust and the appropriative water rights system, we have arrived at certain conclusions which we briefly summarize here. In our opinion, the core of the public trust doctrine is the state's authority as sovereign to exercise a continuous supervision and control over the navigable waters of the state and the lands underlying those waters. This authority applies to the waters tributary to Mono Lake and bars DWP or any other party from claiming a vested right to divert waters once it becomes clear that such diversions harm the interests protected by the public trust. The corollary rule which evolved in tideland and lakeshore cases barring conveyance of rights free of the trust except to serve trust purposes cannot, however, apply without modification to flowing waters. The prosperity and habitability of much of this state requires the diversion of great quantities of water from its streams for purposes unconnected to any navigation, commerce, fishing recreation, or ecological use relating to the source stream. The state must have the power to grant nonvested usufructuary rights to appropriate water even if diversions harm public trust uses. Approval of such diversion without considering public trust values, however, may result in needless destruction of those values. Accordingly, we believe that before state courts and agencies approve water diversions they should consider the effect of such diversions upon interests protected by the public trust, and attempt, so far as feasible, to avoid or minimize any harm to those interests....

DWP expects that its future diversions of about 100,000 acre-feet per year will lower the lake's surface level another 43 feet and reduce its surface area by about 22 square miles over the next 80 to 100 years, at which point the lake will gradually approach environmental equilibrium (the point at which inflow from precipitation, groundwater and nondiverted tributaries equals outflow by evaporation and other means). At this point, according to DWP, the lake will stabilize at a level 6,330 feet above the sea's, with a surface area of approximately 38 square miles. Thus, by DWP's own estimates, unabated diversions will ultimately produce a lake that is about 56 percent smaller on the surface and 42 percent shallower than its natural size.

Plaintiffs consider these projections unrealistically optimistic. They allege that, 50 years hence, the lake will be at least 50 feet shallower than it now is, and will hold less than 20 percent of its natural volume. Further, plaintiffs fear that "the lake will not stabilize at this level", but "may continue to reduce in size until it is dried up." Moreover, unlike DWP, plaintiffs believe that the lake's gradual recession indirectly causes a host of adverse environmental impacts. Many of these alleged impacts are related to an increase in the lake's salinity, caused by the decrease in its water volume.

As noted above, Mono Lake has no outlets. The lake loses water only by evaporation and seepage. Natural salts do not evaporate with water, but are left behind. Prior to commencement of the DWP diversions, this naturally rising salinity was balanced by a constant and substantial supply of fresh water from the tributaries. Now, however, DWP diverts most of the fresh water inflow. The resultant imbalance between inflow and outflow not only diminishes the lake's size, but also drastically increases its salinity....

Plaintiffs predict that the lake's steadily increasing salinity, if unchecked, will wreck havoc throughout the local food chain. They contend that the lake's algae, and the brine shrimp and brine flies that feed on it, cannot survive the projected salinity increase. To support this assertion, plaintiffs point to a 50 percent reduction in the shrimp hatch for the spring of 1980 and a startling 95 percent reduction for the spring of 1981. These reductions affirm experimental evidence indicating that brine shrimp populations diminish as the salinity of the water surrounding them increases. DWP admits these substantial reductions, but blames them on factors other than salinity.

DWP's diversions also present several threats to the millions of local and migratory birds using the lake. First, since many species of birds feed on the lake's brine shrimp, any reduction in shrimp population allegedly caused by rising salinity endangers a major avian food source. The Task Force Report considered it "unlikely that any of Mono Lake's major bird species...will persist at the lake if populations of invertebrates disappear."...

The California gull is especially endangered, both by the increase in salinity and by loss of nesting sites. Ninety-five percent of this state's gull population and 25 percent of the total species population nests at the lake. Most of the gulls nest on islands in the lake. As the lake recedes, land between the shore and some of the islands has been exposed, offering such predators as the coyote easy access to the gull nests and chicks. In 1979, coyotes reached Negit Island, once the most popular nesting site, and the number of gull nests at the lake declined sharply. In 1981, 95 percent of the hatched chicks did not survive to maturity. Plaintiffs blame this decline and alarming mortality rate on the predator access created by the land bridges; DWP suggest numerous other causes, such as increased ambient temperatures and human activities, and claims that the joining of some islands with the mainlands is offset by the emergence of new islands due to the lake's recession.

Plaintiffs allege that DWP's diversions adversely affect the human species and its activities as well. First, as the lake recedes, it has exposed more than 18,000 acres of lake bed composed of very fine silt which, once dry, easily becomes airborne in winds. This silt contains a high concentration of alkali and other minerals that irritate the mucous membranes and respiratory systems of humans and other animals. While the precise extent of this threat to the public health has yet to be determined, such threat as exists can be expected to increase with the exposure of additional lake bed. DWP, however, claims that its diversions neither affect the air quality in Mono Basin nor present a hazard to human health.

Furthermore, the lake's recession obviously diminishes its value as an economic, recreational, and scenic resource. Of course, there will be less lake to use and enjoy. The declining shrimp hatch depresses a local shrimping industry. The rings of dry lake bed are difficult to traverse on foot, and thus impair human access to the lake, and reduce the lake's substantial scenic value. Mono Lake has long been treasured as a unique scenic, recreational and scientific resource, but continued diversions threaten to turn it into a desert wasteland like the dry bed of Owens Lake.

[The federal court requested a ruling on an] important issue of California law: "What is the interrelationship of the public trust doctrine and the California water rights system, in the context of the right of the DPW to divert water from Mono Lake pursuant to permits and licenses issued under the California water rights system? In other words, is the public trust doctrine in this context subsumed in the California water rights system, or does it function independently of that system? Stated differently, can the plaintiffs challenge the Department's permits and licenses by arguing that those permits and licenses are limited by the public trust doctrine, or must the plaintiffs challenge the permits and licenses by arguing that the water diversions and uses authorized thereunder are not 'reasonable or beneficial' as required under the California water rights system?..."

[The State Superior] court entered summary judgment against plaintiffs. Its notice of intended ruling stated that "the California water rights system is a comprehensive and exclusive system for determining the legality of the diversions of the City of Los Angeles in the Mono Basin.... The Public Trust Doctrine does not function independently of that system. This Court concludes that as regards the right of the City of Los Angeles to divert waters in the Mono Basin that the Public Trust Doctrine is subsumed in the water rights system of the state." ... We set the case for argument....

THE PUBLIC TRUST DOCTRINE IN CALIFORNIA... "By the law of nature these things are common to mankind — the air, running water, the sea and consequently the shores of the sea." (Institutes of Justinian 2.1.1.) From this origin in Roman law, the English common law evolved the concept of the public trust, under which the sovereign owns "all of its navigable waterways and the lands lying beneath them 'as trustee of a public trust for the benefit of the people.'" The State of California acquired title as trustee to such lands and waterways upon its admission to the union (see City of Berkeley v. Superior Court (1980) 26 Cal. 3d at 521 and cases there cited). From the earliest days (see Eldridge v. Cowell (1854) 4 Cal. at 87) its judicial decisions have recognized and enforced the trust obligation.

Three aspects of the public trust doctrine require consideration in this opinion: the purpose of the trust; the scope of the trust, particularly as it applies to the non-navigable tributaries of a navigable lake; and the powers and duties of the state as trustee of the public trust....

THE PURPOSE OF THE PUBLIC TRUST... The objective of the public trust has evolved in tandem with the changing public perception of the values and uses of waterways. As we observed in Marks v. Whitney,

> public trust easements [were] traditionally defined in terms of navigation, commerce and fisheries. They have been held to include the right to fish, hunt, bathe, swim, to use for boating and general recreation purposes the navigable waters of the state, and to use the bottom of the navigable waters for anchoring, standing, or other purposes.

We went on, however, to hold that the traditional triad of uses — navigation, commerce and fishing — did not limit the public interest in the trust res. In language of special importance to the present setting, we stated that

> the public uses to which tidelands are subject are sufficiently flexible to encompass changing public needs.[10] In administering the trust the state is not burdened with an outmoded classification favoring one mode of utilization over another. There is a growing public recognition that one of the most important public uses of the tidelands—a use encompassed within the tidelands trust—is the preservation of those lands in their natural state, so that they may

---

10. "The public trust doctrine, like all common law principles, should not be considered fixed or static, but should be molded and extended to meet changing conditions and needs of the public it was created to benefit." Neptune City v. Avon-by-the-Sea, 294 A.2d 47, 54 (N.J. 1972).

serve as ecological units for scientific study, as open space, and as environments which provide food and habitat for birds and marine life, and which favorably affect the scenery and climate of the area.

Mono Lake is a navigable waterway. It supports a small local industry which harvests brine shrimp for sale as fish food, which endeavor probably qualifies the lake as a "fishery" under the traditional public trust cases. The principal values plaintiffs seek to protect, however, are recreational and ecological — the scenic views of the lake and its shore, the purity of the air, and the use of the lake for nesting and feeding by birds. Under Marks v. Whitney, *supra*, 6 Cal.3d 251, it is clear that protection of these values is among the purposes of the public trust.

THE SCOPE OF THE PUBLIC TRUST... Mono Lake is, as we have said, a navigable waterway. The beds, shores and waters of the lake are without question protected by the public trust. The streams diverted by DWP, however, are not themselves navigable. Accordingly, we must address in this case a question not discussed in any recent public trust case — whether the public trust limits conduct affecting nonnavigable tributaries to navigable waterways....

The principles recognized by [our early public trust dambuilding and streambed gold mining] decisions apply fully to a case in which diversions from a nonnavigable tributary impair the public trust in a downstream river or lake. "If the public trust doctrine applies to constrain fills which destroy navigation and other public trust uses in navigable waters, it should equally apply to constrain the extraction of water that destroys navigation and other public interests. Both actions result in the same damage to the public interest." Johnson, 14 U.C.Davis L.Rev. at 257–258.... We conclude that the public trust doctrine, as recognized and developed in California decisions, protects navigable waters from harm caused by diversion of nonnavigable tributaries.

DUTIES AND POWERS OF THE STATE AS TRUSTEE... In the following review of the authority and obligations of the state as administrator of the public trust, the dominant theme is the state's sovereign power and duty to exercise continued supervision over the trust. One consequence, of importance to this and many other cases, is that parties acquiring rights in trust property generally hold those rights subject to the trust, and can assert no vested right to use those rights in a manner harmful to the trust.

As we noted recently in City of Berkeley v. Superior Court, 26 Cal. 3d 515, the decision of the United States Supreme Court in *Illinois Central* "remains the primary authority even today, almost nine decades after it was decided." The legislature, it held, did not have the power to convey the entire city waterfront free of trust, thus barring all future legislatures from protecting the public interest. The opinion declares that:

> A grant of all the lands under the navigable waters of a State has never been adjudged to be within the legislative power; and any attempted grant of the kind would be held, if not absolutely void on its face, as subject to revocation. The State can no more abdicate its trust over property in which the whole people are interested, like navigable waters and soils under them...than it can abdicate its police powers in the administration of government and the preservation of the peace. In the administration of government the use of such powers may for a limited period be delegated to a municipality or other body, but there always remains with the State the right to revoke those powers and exercise them in a more direct manner, and one more conformable to its

wishes. So with trusts connected with public property, or property of a special character, like lands under navigable waterways, they cannot be placed entirely beyond the direction and control of the State." *Illinois Central*, 146 U.S. at 453–454.

In summary, the foregoing cases amply demonstrate the continuing power of the state as administrator of the public trust, a power which extends to the revocation of previously granted right or to the enforcement of the trust against lands long thought free of the trust. Except for those rare instances in which a grantee may acquire a right to use former trust property free of trust restrictions, the grantee holds subject to the trust, and while he may assert a vested right to the servient estate (the right of use subject to the trust) and to any improvements he erects, he can claim no vested right to bar recognition of the trust or state action to carry out its purposes.

Since the public trust doctrine does not prevent the state from choosing between trust uses, the Attorney General of California, seeking to maximize state power under the trust, argues for a broad concept of trust uses. In his view, "trust uses" encompass all public uses, so that in practical effect the doctrine would impose no restrictions on the state's ability to allocate trust property. We know of no authority which supports this view of the public trust, except perhaps the dissenting opinion in *Illinois Central*. Most decisions and commentators assume that "trust uses" relate to uses and activities in the vicinity of the lake, stream, or tidal reach at issue.... The tideland cases make this point clear: after *City of Berkeley*, no one could contend that the state could grant tidelands free of the trust merely because the grant served some public purpose, such as increasing tax revenues, or because the grantee might put the property to a commercial use....

Thus, the public trust is more than an affirmation of state power to use public property for public purposes. It is an affirmation of the duty of the state to protect the people's common heritage of streams, lakes, marshlands and tidelands, surrendering that right of protection only in rare cases when the abandonment of that right is consistent with the purposes of the trust....

THE RELATIONSHIP BETWEEN THE PUBLIC TRUST DOCTRINE AND THE CALIFORNIA WATER RIGHTS SYSTEM... As we have seen, the public trust doctrine and the appropriative water rights system administered by the Water Board developed independently of each other. Each developed comprehensive rules and principles which, if applied to the full extent of their scope, would occupy the field of allocation of stream waters to the exclusion of any competing system of legal thought. Plaintiffs, for example, argue that the public trust is antecedent to and thus limits all appropriative water rights, an argument which implies that most appropriative water rights in California were acquired and are presently being used unlawfully. Defendant DWP, on the other hand, argues that the public trust doctrine as to stream waters has been "subsumed" into the appropriative water rights system and, absorbed by that body of law, quietly disappeared: according to DWP, the recipient of a board license enjoys a vested right in perpetuity to take water without concern for the consequences to the trust.

We are unable to accept either position. In our opinion, both the public trust doctrine and the water rights system embody important precepts which make the law more responsive to the diverse needs and interests involved in the planning and allocation of water resources. To embrace one system of thought and reject the other would lead to an unbalanced structure, one which would either decry as a breach of trust appropriations essential to the economic development of this state, or deny any duty to protect or even consider the values promoted by the public trust. Therefore, seeking an accommodation which will make use of the pertinent principles of both the public trust doctrine and the appropriative water rights system, and drawing upon the history of the public trust and the water rights system, the body of judicial precedent, and the views of expert commentators, we reach the following conclusions:

a.   The state as sovereign retains continuing supervisory control over its navigable waters and the lands beneath those waters. This principle, fundamental to the concept of the public trust, applies to rights in flowing waters as well as to rights in tidelands and lakeshores; it prevents any party from acquiring a vested right to appropriate water in a manner harmful to the interests protected by the public trust.

b.   As a matter of current and historical necessity, the legislature, acting directly or through an authorized agency such as the Water Board, has the power to grant usufructuary licenses that will permit an appropriator to take water from flowing streams and use that water in a distant part of the state, even though this taking does not promote, and may unavoidably harm, the trust uses at the source stream. The population and economy of this state depend upon the appropriation of vast quantities of water for uses unrelated to in-stream trust values. California's constitution, its statutes, decisions, and commentators all emphasize the need to make efficient use of California's limited water resources: all recognize, at least implicitly, that efficient use requires diverting water from in-stream uses. Now that the economy and population centers of this state have developed in reliance upon appropriated water, it would be disingenuous to hold that such appropriations are and have always been improper to the extent that they harm public trust uses, and can be justified only upon theories of reliance or estoppel.

c.   The state has an affirmative duty to take the public trust into account in the planning and allocation of water resources, and to protect public trust uses whenever feasible. Just as the history of this state shows that appropriation may be necessary for efficient use of water despite unavoidable harm to public trust values, it demonstrates that an appropriative water rights system administered without consideration of the public trust may cause unnecessary and unjustified harm to trust interests. As a matter of practical necessity the state may have to approve appropriations despite foreseeable harm to public trust uses. In so doing, however, the state must bear in mind its duty as trustee to consider the effect of the taking on the public trust (see United Plainsmen v. State Water Cons. Comm'n, 247 N.W. 2d 457, 462-463 (N.D. 1976)), and to preserve, so far as consistent with the public interest, the uses protected by the trust.

Once the state has approved an appropriation, the public trust imposes a duty of continuing supervision over the taking and use of the appropriated water. In exercising its sovereign power to allocate water resources in the public interest, the state is not confined by past allocation decisions which may be incorrect in light of current knowledge or inconsistent with current needs.

The state accordingly has the power to reconsider allocation decisions even though those decisions were made after due consideration of their effect on the public trust. The case for reconsidering a particular decision, however, is even stronger when that decision failed to weigh and consider public trust uses. In the case before us, the salient fact is that no responsible body has ever determined the impact of diverting the entire flow of the Mono Lake tributaries into the Los Angeles Aqueduct. This is not a case in which the Legislature, the Water Board, or any judicial body has determined that the needs of Los Angeles outweigh the needs of the Mono Basin, that the benefit gained is worth the price. Neither has any responsible body determined whether some lesser taking would better balance the diverse interests. Instead DWP acquired rights to the entire flow in 1940 from a water board which believed it lacked both the power and the duty to protect the Mono Lake environment, and continues to exercise those rights in apparent disregard for the resulting damage to the scenery, ecology, and human uses of Mono Lake.

It is clear that some responsible body ought to reconsider the allocation of the waters of the Mono Basin. No vested rights bar such reconsideration. We recognize the substantial concerns voiced by Los Angeles — the city's need for water, its reliance upon the 1940 board decision, the cost both in terms of money and environmental impact of obtaining water elsewhere. Such concerns must enter into any allocation decision. We hold only that they do not preclude a reconsideration and reallocation which also takes into account the impact of water diversion on the Mono Lake environment....

The federal court inquired first of the interrelationship between the public trust doctrine and the California water rights system, asking whether the "public trust doctrine in this context [is] subsumed in the California water rights system, or...function[s] independently of that system?" Our answer is "neither." The public trust doctrine and the appropriative water rights system are parts of an integrated system of water law. The public trust doctrine serves the function in that integrated system of preserving the continuing sovereign power of the state to protect public trust uses, a power which precludes anyone from acquiring a vested right to harm the public trust, and imposes a continuing duty on the state to take such uses into account in allocating water resources.

Restating its question, the federal court asked: "Can the plaintiffs challenge the Department's permits and licenses by arguing that those permits and licenses are limited by the public trust doctrine, or must the plaintiffs [argue] that the water diversions and uses authorized thereunder are not 'reasonable or beneficial' as required under the California water rights system?" We reply that plaintiffs can rely on the public trust doctrine in seeking reconsideration of the allocation of the waters of the Mono Basin....

This opinion is but one step in the eventual resolution of the Mono Lake controversy. We do not dictate any particular allocation of water. Our objective is to resolve a legal conundrum in which two competing systems of thought — the public trust doctrine and the appropriative water rights system — existed independently of each other, espousing principles which seemingly suggested opposite results. We hope by integrating these two doctrines to clear away the legal barriers which have so far prevented either the Water Board or the courts from taking a new and objective look at the water resources of the Mono Basin. The human and environmental uses of Mono Lake — uses protected by the public trust doctrine — deserve to be taken into account. Such uses should not be destroyed because the state mistakenly thought itself powerless to protect them.

COMMENTARY AND QUESTIONS

1. **Scope of the public trust doctrine.** Just what is the public trust resource that is being protected in *Mono Lake*? It clearly has not much to do with navigability. Is it the lake itself that is the public trust asset? If so, is it the lake in its original form, as it is today, or at some intermediate point? Is it the economic use of the water, based on harvesting brine shrimp? Is it the brine shrimp themselves? The California gulls?

*Mono Lake* may stand for the proposition that the public trust doctrine is capable of reaching out and encompassing the ecological values of an entire functioning ecosystem. Does this mean all ecosystems, or just those ecosystems fortunate enough to inhabit a photogenic environment?

Note something else striking about *Mono Lake*. The decision apparently applies to *private* rights. True, the water rights to the various streams flowing into Mono Lake are owned by the government of Los Angeles, but it owns them by purchase water rights in the same way that those rights would be obtained and held by a private citizen. Does the public trust lie latent within private property rights? Chapter One's Marks v. Whitney, cited in the main opinion, held precisely that there was an inherent public right in privately-owned submerged lands, so that the private property owner was completely restricted unless the government gave permission to fill in the submerged lands and make them economically useful. What if you owned the oldest burr oak tree in Illinois, or the house in which Benjamin Franklin was born, or the land on which the state's oldest church was located, and in each case you wanted to bulldoze the property to make a profitable parking lot? Might the public trust doctrine apply with full force and litigibility to your case as well? What standards would apply?

2. **The terms of the trust balance.** Note that in this case, the state's Attorney-General argued against the applicability of the public trust doctrine. Why? Ultimately the court defined a public trust role for the state government that held it to a new and higher standard of decision-making. The state could no longer merely be a mechanism of majoritarian politics; it apparently now had enforceable long-term fiduciary obligations to an indefinite constituency including generations unborn.

After the decision in *Mono Lake*, what are the standards by which the public trust balance will be struck, to determine how much of Los Angeles' private water rights and how much of Mono Lake's public trust assets will be legally protected? There is a serious apples and oranges problem. How can two such disparate public interests be balanced? It is notable, however, that the courts have declared that the public trust doctrine cannot be abrogated, which apparently asserts that the trust obligations, whatever they are, must be substantively fulfilled. After *Mono Lake*, if you were an attorney for the Los Angeles Water Board, or on the other hand for the environmental coalition, how would you go about preparing for subsequent proceedings in state court to determine what actually would happen to Mono Lake? To what extent in that balance does the lack of prior notice of the trust's existence to owners of the water rights matter to you? Are public trust rights necessarily superior to private property rights, if indeed they conflict? If the trust balance results in a restriction of private water rights, do the losers have a right to compensation for an unconstitutional "taking"? See the next chapter on this.

**3. A reprise on *Mono Lake*.** What further developments in California public trust law followed the decision in *Mono Lake*? The destiny of Mono Lake remains in doubt. The years initially following the California Supreme Court decision were unusually wet and the level of Mono Lake actually rose.[11] Then there was an extended drought. The Court had sent the case back to the Water Board to determine whether and to what extent Los Angeles should cut back its diversions from the Mono Lake tributaries in order to protect public trust values. Even if that task had been undertaken with maximum dispatch, it would have taken years before any final order actually changing the flows into Mono Lake would have been forthcoming. In fact, seven years after the decision, the Water Board has still not completed its investigations and its environmental report. In 1989, officials for the city of Los Angeles and the Mono Lake Committee reached an agreement whereby Los Angeles would abide by a court-set lake level and would give up some of its water rights, in exchange for assistance from the state in finding alternate sources of water. But controversy has continually recurred. An entirely new suit to protect the lake was successfully brought under two obscure provisions of the Fish and Game Code requiring releases from dams sufficient to re-establish and maintain fish populations below the dams.

In the late 1990s rain levels were again high and the lake level gained. While awaiting the Water Board studies on Mono Lake, the trial court issued a preliminary injunction requiring that the lake be maintained at 6,377 feet above sea level, some two feet above its existing level but still more than forty feet below the level it had prior to L.A.'s diversion project. That case has now been expanded to encompass issues other than the balance between public trust and municipal supply needs (the plaintiffs have been concerned that their doctrinal public trust victory might be "balanced away"). One such issue is violation of air quality requirements resulting from blowing dust created by exposure of shoreland flats as the lake level declined. Another is a claim to lake level maintenance on behalf of the U.S. government. The interest of the federal government has come to the fore because in 1984 Congress established a Mono Basin National Forest Scenic Area in order to protect the geological, ecological, and cultural resources of Mono Basin. The Scenic Area statute provides, however, that "nothing in [this law] shall be construed to...affect the present (or prospective) water rights of any person...including the City of Los Angeles." 16 U.S.C.A. §543c(h). For its part, despite a 1989 negotiated agreement and three trial court rehearings on minimum lake levels, the city continues to oppose the restrictions on withdrawal.

On yet another front, the State of California enacted a statute that makes as much as $60 million available to mitigate the cost to Los Angeles of finding a substitute for the reductions it will eventually bear at Mono Lake. The law anticipates innovations such as conservation, waste water reclamation, conjunctive use, and

---

11. This update is adapted from Sax, Abrams, and Thompson, Legal Control of Water Resources 588–596 (2d ed. 1991).

groundwater recharge. The idea of the law presumably is that state-wide sharing of the costs of finding alternatives will smooth the way to an actual solution of the controversy, and keep the legal dispute from continuing indefinitely. To date the prospect of money has not generated a quick or clear solution.

How will Los Angeles ultimately deal with its loss at Mono Lake? No one knows, and no one yet knows the extent of the potential loss. In an ordinary year the 10,000 acre-foot per year diversion represents about 15 percent of the city's total water supply. What are the current alternatives facing Los Angeles and other South Coast cities? The adaptation that would produce the least reverberations elsewhere would be reduction of demand through conservation. Alternatively, Los Angeles might purchase the water from other rights owners, most likely agricultural users. The possibility remains, however, that Los Angeles may use its Mono Lake losses to press for new water mega-projects, in which case environmental concerns will simply have been shifted to a new arena.

The opinion in *Mono Lake* has spawned a number of interesting cases exploring the intersection of water rights and the public trust and further defining the balance between water needs and public trust interests that the *Mono Lake* court left for future determination. One case supported the state water board's requirement of upstream releases of water to protect the fish and wildlife of the Sacramento-San Joaquin River Delta against salt water intrusion.[12] A second significant case applied *Mono Lake* to an initial appropriation of water, permitting a requested diversion but imposing strict downstream flow maintenance requirements in order to protect public trust values below the point of diversion, primarily chinook salmon.[13]

The latter court's view of *Mono Lake* was that it —

> encourages and requires the trier of fact to balance and accommodate all legitimate competing interests in a body of water...rather than the "unbalanced structure" that would result from a flat preference for either instream or consumptive values.... Water quality [for municipal use] cannot be excluded from the analysis simply because it does not fit plaintiffs' and intervenors' conception of a public trust value. Neither, however, can the importance of the public trust be diluted by treating it as merely another beneficial use...co-equal with irrigation, power production, and municipal water supply.... Public trust doctrine occupies an exalted position in any judicial or administrative determination of water resource allocation....

The balance, in other words, still remains very unclear. In the arid West, water-fights tend to be long running battles.

## Section 2. HOW FAR DOES THE PUBLIC TRUST DOCTRINE GO?

The public trust doctrine asserts that certain special public rights and duties lie latent within various natural resources, whether publicly or privately owned, with consequences that can be dramatic. Once the public trust genie has been

---

12. [The "Delta" case, U.S. v. State Water Resources Control Board, 182 Cal. App. 3d 82, 227 Cal. Rptr. 161 (1986).]

13. [The "East Bay MUD" case, E.D.F. v. East Bay Munic. Util. Dist. (No. 425955, Superior Court, Alameda Co., California, Jan. 2, 1990).]

released from the bottle, moreover, it arguably can cast its shadow over situations previously unknown.

The following case unfolded in 1969, a short distance west of Colorado Springs, Colorado, where an accident of geology 10 million years ago had created a remarkably rich 6,000 acre area of fossil beds. The Florissant Fossil Beds, layer upon layer of paper-thin shales filled with biological artifacts, was a unique and nationally-famous archaeological site, featured in many junior high school textbooks. Congress, in desultory fashion, had been discussing whether to purchase the beds in order to create a national monument. Meanwhile, a group of private developers contracted to purchase the 6,000 acre tract. They had determined that in market-place terms the area's best commercial use lay in subdivision construction, and the bulldozers were poised, ready to roll, to carve roads, driveways, and split-level foundations into the fragile fossil beds....

## Defenders of Florissant v. Park Land Development Co. et. al.
(unreported) V. Yannacone, Environmental Law, 47–60 (1970)

IN THE UNITED STATES DISTRICT COURT FOR THE DISTRICT OF COLORADO

| | |
|---|---|
| DEFENDERS of FLORISSANT, Inc., individually and on behalf of all those entitled to the full benefit use and enjoyment of the national natural resource that is the proposed FLORISSANT FOSSIL BEDS NATIONAL MONUMENT, and all those similarly situated, <div style="text-align:center">Plaintiffs,</div> <div style="text-align:center">vs.</div> PARK LAND COMPANY, CENTRAL ENTERPRISES, INC., CLAUDE R. BLUE, KENNETH C. WOFFARD; J. R. FONTAN, M. L. BARNES; W. NATE SNARE, A. W. GREGG, R. MITSCHELE, MARILDA NELSON; DELBERT and EMMA WELLS; E. D. KELLY, JOHN BAKER, and their successors in interest, if any, as their interest may appear, <div style="text-align:center">Defendants.</div> | ) ) ) ) ) ) ) ) ) ) ) ) ) ) ) |

### NOTICE OF MOTION

PLEASE TAKE NOTICE that the Plaintiffs will move this Court at the United States District Court House, Denver, Colorado, on the 8th day of July, 1969, at half past nine o'clock in the forenoon of that day, or as soon thereafter as counsel can be heard, for an order:

RESTRAINING the Defendants from any actions which may cause serious permanent or irreparable damage to the national natural resource that is the area included within the proposed Florissant Fossil Beds National Monument; or in the alternative,

DIRECTING the immediate hearing on the merits of the Plaintiff's application for a temporary injunction,

TOGETHER with such other and further relief as to the Court shall seem just and proper under the circumstances.

Respectfully submitted,
Victor J. Yannacone, Jr., Attorney for Plaintiff

## VERIFIED COMPLAINT

The Plaintiffs, complaining of the Defendants by their attorney, Victor J. Yannacone, Jr., set forth and allege:

1. JURISDICTION: Jurisdiction of this Court is invoked under Title 28 U.S.C.A. §1331(a), "The district courts shall have original jurisdiction of all civil actions wherein the matter in controversy exceeds the sum or value of $10,000, exclusive of interest and costs, and arises under the Constitution, laws, or treaties of the United States."...

2. JURISDICTION: Jurisdiction of this Court is invoked under Title 28 U.S.C.A. §343(3): "To redress the deprivation, under color of any State law, statute, ordinance, regulation, custom or usage, of any right, privilege or immunity secured by the Constitution of the United States or by any Act of Congress providing for equal rights of citizens or of all persons within jurisdiction of the United States."...

3. JURISDICTION: This is also a proceeding for Declaratory Judgment under Title 28 U.S.C.A. §§2201, and 2202, declaring the rights and legal relations of the parties to the matter in controversy, specifically:

(a) That the proposed Florissant Fossil Beds National Monument is a national natural resource.

(b) The right of all the people of the United States in and to the full benefit, use and enjoyment of the unique values of the proposed Florissant Fossil Beds National Monument, without diminution or degradation resulting from any of the activities of the Defendants or their Successors in interest, sought to be restrained herein.

(c) That the degradation of the unique National Natural Resources of the proposed Florissant Fossil Beds National Monument by the Defendants or their Successors in interest violates the rights of the Plaintiffs, guaranteed under the Ninth Amendment of the Constitution of the United States and protected by the due process and equal protection clauses of the Fifth and Fourteenth Amendments of the Constitution of the United States.

4. CLASS ACTION: The Plaintiff is a non-profit, public-benefit corporation duly organized and existing under Colorado law. DEFENDERS OF FLORISSANT, INC. is made up of scientists and other citizens dedicated to the preservation of this natural treasure....

5. THE PROPOSED FLORISSANT FOSSIL BEDS NATIONAL MONUMENT: The proposed national monument comprises an area of 6,000 acres on the east slope of the Rocky Mountains. Located in a region of high recreation use and relatively close to a fast growing metropolitan complex, heavy visitation is expected.

The primary resources are the unique Oligocene lake beds with their plant and insect fossil-bearing layers and related geological features. These resources, combined with a scenic setting and secondary recreational and biological resources, constitute a relatively compact natural unit.

The ancient lake beds of Florissant preserve more species of terrestrial fossils than any other known site in the world. The insect fossils are of primary significance. They represent the evolution and modernization of insects better than any other known site in America. In addition, the fossil plants, emphasized dramatically by the petrified tree stumps and the great variety of leaf fossils, add greatly to the primary values. Fossils of spiders, other invertebrates, fish, and birds also have been found at Florissant.

The beds have been a famous collecting ground by numerous scientists for nearly a century and continue to be of great value for paleontological research.

The present-day vegetation is one of pine-covered hills and grassy meadows. In good years the wildflower display in June and July may be spectacular and is an acknowledged tourist attraction....

Geological History: Subsequent to the birth of the Rocky Mountains, 60 million years ago, a period of erosion ensued. By Oligocene time, 40 million years ago, the mountains in the Florissant region had been reduced generally to a broad, gently rolling hill land — a piedmont of low relief and moderate elevation.

Volcanic eruptions covered the region with pyroclastics to a depth of 40 to 60 feet or more, and the drainage of the area was blocked, thus forming the Florissant Lake. The rolling slopes and the lakeshore were mantled by many types of deciduous trees and immense Sequoia groves.

Explosive eruptions and mud flows eventually filled the lake. The mud flows engulfed and buried the lakeshore trees which were gradually petrified. Insects, leaves, and other forms of life were carried to the lake bottom and preserved between alternating layers of volcanic ash. The source of the volcanic material appears to have been the Guffey volcano, 15 miles southwest of Florissant....

A number of the tree stumps, including large Sequoias, are exposed at the two commercially operated petrified forest areas. Some of these have been exposed by excavating around them. Many other stumps could be exposed by removing a very shallow over-burden. Some of the exposed stumps have fallen apart as a result of exposure; some are wired together by steel cables.

In addition to the insect, leaf, and wood fossils, the beds contain numerous microfossils. These occur in light-colored diatomited and sapropel laminae which alternate with one another, and in some places with light-colored pumice and graded tuff laminae. Ranking below the fossil insects and leaves in numbers of specimens found here are thin-shelled mollusks, and fresh water fishes. Several bird feathers and a few bird carcasses have been found.

Significance of Geological Resources: These deposits represent a small chapter of the geological history of the earth, but one very closely related to the present. What happened here in Oligocene times — the environmental conditions that existed, the life forms that prevailed, the whole story — is written into the Florissant deposits. Scientists have revealed parts of this story; more remains to be told.

The rare quality of the Florissant site lies in the delicacy with which thousands of fragile insects, tree foliage, and other forms of life — completely absent, or extremely rare in most paleontological sites — have been preserved. There is no known locality in the world where so many terrestrial species of one time have been preserved. A total of 144 plant entities or species have been found there. Thirty of these are of uncertain affinity, but the remaining 114 are identifiable with modern species. Approximately 60,000 specimens of insect fossils have been collected here, the site having a world-ranking second only to the Baltic amber sites in Europe. Almost all the fossil butterflies of the new world have come from this site. Even the presence of fresh water diatoms in the Florissant beds is their earliest known occurrence.

COURTESY FLORISSANT FOSSIL BEDS
NATIONAL MONUMENT

*A view of today's Florissant Fossil Beds National Monument, showing an area in which ditch excavations have revealed rich layering of fossils going back 50 million years.*

The Florissant site has been visited by scientists for nearly a century, and almost all have expressed admiration for the quantity and remarkable perfection of the fossils discovered here. Textbooks of paleontology, historical geology, and entomology cite Florissant as an outstanding locality for fossil insects. Fossil leaves from here are noteworthy and have been described in paleontological and botanical literature. Probably no formation of such limited extent has ever been the subject of as large a body of literature as the Florissant lake beds (226 papers)....

In years of average or better rainfall, the wildflower display in June and July is truly spectacular; every open area is carpeted with paintedcup, many penstemon and crazyweed species, composites, mariposas, harebells, and other varieties. Under the aspens and in wet meadows may be found columbines, pedicularis, iris, shooting-stars, and many others. In August and early September, various sunflowers, groundsels, and fireweed take the place of the earlier flowers, and if there is a late summer rain, frequently this display is as spectacular as the earlier one.

There are many species of large and small mammals, including deer, antelope, elk, mountain lions, bobcats, coyotes, beaver, cottontail and jack rabbits, porcupines, one or more bat species, badgers, goldenmantled ground squirrels, chipmunks, Albert squirrels, white-tailed prairie dog, various mice species, and probably well over 100 bird species. In addition, there are numerous insect and butterfly species....

6. THE DEFENDANT: That upon information and belief, the defendants, individually and collectively, as their interests may appear, are the owners in fee of lands included within the proposed Florissant Fossil Beds National Monument.

Upon information and belief the defendants individually and collectively as their interests may appear are subject to the exercise of eminent domain by the United States of America upon final action by the Congress of the United States which, upon information and belief, should occur during the current session of the Congress.

7. DEFENDANTS' ACTIONS: That upon information and belief, unless restrained by order of this Court, the Defendants, individually, or their Successors in Interest, will develop the area to be included within the proposed Florissant Fossil Beds National Monument, in such a way as to cause serious, permanent and irreparable damage to the unique national natural resource that is the Florissant Fossil Beds.

That the development of the region of the Florissant Fossil Beds in any way which involves road building, excavation, or covering the fossil beds with permanent dwelling units or building structures, will cause serious permanent and irreparable damage to the unique paleontological resource that is the Florissant Fossil Beds....

That upon information and belief the operation of conventional building construction methods will cause serious permanent and irreparable damage to the unique national paleontological resource represented by the Florissant Fossil Beds.

That the development of the area encompassed within the proposed Florissant Fossil Beds National Monument by Defendants is not compatible with the maintenance of the unique national natural resources, that is the Florissant Fossil Beds.

Upon information and belief, the defendant Park Land Company, Claude R. Blue, Kenneth C. Woffard, J. R. Fontan, and M. L. Barnes, jointly or severally intend to commence construction operations immediately which will cause serious permanent and irreparable damage to the National Natural Resource which is the Florissant Fossil Beds....

8. EQUITABLE JURISDICTION: That this action is properly brought in equity before this court on the following grounds:

(a) The subject matter of the dispute is equitable in nature. This action is brought for the purpose of restraining the Defendants individually, and their Successors in Interest, from damaging or degrading the unique national natural resource that is the Florissant Fossil Beds, within the area proposed for inclusion in the Florissant Fossil Beds National Monument. The injury which may be inflicted by the Defendants individually or their successors in Interest, if they are permitted to develop the area without regard for the unique national natural resources represented thereby, will be irreparable, in that it cannot be adequately compensated in damages. The declaratory judgment demanded by the Plaintiffs, together with the equitable relief related thereto are equitable remedies in the substance of character of the rights sought to be enforced or historically, in the province of the Court of Chancery.

(b) There is no adequate remedy at law. The law does not afford any remedy for the contemplated wrong to the American people resulting from the degradation of the unique national natural resources represented by the Florissant Fossil Beds from the development thereof by the Defendants and/or their Successors in Interest, in a way inconsistent with the protection of the paleontological, paleobotanical and palynological resources represented thereby. There is no plain adequate and complete remedy at law as practicable and efficient as the equitable relief sought herein. Nor would the damages sustained by the people of the United States as a result of the improper development of the area by the Defendants or their Successors in Interest, be capable of measurement and determination in any action at law.

9. TRUST: That the Defendants individually and their Successors in Interest, hold the unique national natural resource of the Florissant Fossil Beds, with respect to its paleontological, paleobotanical and palynological values in trust for the full benefit, use and enjoyment of all the people of this generation, and those generations yet unborn.

That the maintenance of this trust is compatible with the proper efficient development of the resource represented by the area encompassed within the proposed Florissant Fossil Beds National Monument area.

That the administrative agencies of the Federal and State governments are incapable of preventing the irreparable damage which will result from the improper development of the region by the Defendants or their Successors in Interest without regard for the protection of the unique paleontological, paleobotanical and palynological values represented by the Florissant Fossil Beds.

That the maintenance of the trust is consistent with private ownership of the property and does not constitute any taking of the Defendant's property.

WHEREFORE, the plaintiffs individually and on behalf of all those entitled to the full benefit, use and enjoyment of the national resource that are the proposed Florissant Fossil Beds National Moment, respectfully pray:

That this Court take jurisdiction of the matter, and that a three judge court be convened to hear and determine this cause as provided by Title 28 U.S. Code, §2281, et seq. and upon such hearing:

(a) Grant judgment declaring the right of the Plaintiff and all others to the full benefit, use and enjoyment of the national natural resources that are the proposed Florissant Fossil Beds National Monument, without any degradation resulting from the improper development thereof by the Defendants and/or their Successors in Interest.

(b) That the Court issue such orders as will protect the unique paleontological, paleobotanical and palynological values encompassed within the Florissant Fossil Beds, pending the final hearing of determination of this action.

(c) That the Court issue such orders as will protect the unique paleontological and palynological values encompassed within the Florissant Fossil Beds.

(d) Together with all such other and further relief as to the Court may seem just, proper, and necessary under the circumstances to protect the unique national natural resources that are in the Florissant Fossil Beds.

(Signed) Victor Yannacone
*Attorney for Plaintiff*

## [AFFIDAVIT]

STATE OF COLORADO, CITY AND COUNTY OF DENVER

Estella B. Leopold, being duly sworn deposes and says:

1. That she is a Paleontologist presently employed by the United States Geological Survey, and is personally familiar as a research scientist with the area to be included within the proposed Florissant Fossil Beds National Monument, and in particular the land and area presently being threatened by the activities of the Defendants with respect to excavation and road building.... [Dr. Leopold's affidavit provided detailed description and analysis, and was the source of most of the material set out in the Complaint.][The District Court, however, dismissed the action for failure to state a claim upon which relief could be granted. The plaintiffs quickly appealed to the Tenth Circuit for temporary injunctive relief.]

UNITED STATES COURT OF APPEALS FOR THE TENTH CIRCUIT

| | |
|---|---|
| DEFENDERS OF FLORISSANT, INC., individually and on behalf of all those entitled to the full benefit, use and enjoyment of the national natural resource that is the proposed FLORISSANT FOSSIL BEDS NATIONAL MONUMENT, and all those similarly situated,<br>Plaintiffs,<br>vs.<br>PARK LAND COMPANY, et al.<br>Defendants. | No. 00341-69 |

### ORDER

Upon reading and filing the application of the plaintiffs herein for a temporary restraining order, together with the transcript of the hearing on the application of plaintiffs for similar relief before the United States District Court, District of Colorado on July 9, 1969, together with the oral application of counsel for the plaintiffs before this Court on this date, including a complete recital of all the efforts by counsel for the plaintiffs to secure the appearance of the defendants, Claude R. Blue and J. R. Thornton, individually and as partners of the Park Land Company, the principal defendant herein, including recital of the substance of the conference held among the parties in the United States District Courthouse...on July 10, 1969...and representations by counsel for the defendants, Robert Johnson of Colorado Springs, that he would not enter a formal appearance under any circumstances in this action at this time, together with telegraphic notice...to which no reply had been received.

AND IT APPEARING TO THE COURT from the representations of counsel and the information contained in the verified complaint and exhibits annexed thereto, the affidavits submitted therewith of Dr. Estella Leopold, Paleontologist for the United States Geological Survey, that the Florissant Fossil Beds represent a unique national natural resource, and that the excavation with road building or other construction equipment of these fossil beds will result in serious, permanent, irreparable damage and render the action for preliminary injunction pending for trial in the United States District Court on July 29, 1969, moot, and it appearing from the uncontradicted statements contained in the transcript of the hearing of July 9, 1969, conducted in the presence of defendants and their counsel and the similar representations of plaintiff's counsel before this Court, and that there will be no damage to the defendants by order of this Court restraining construction activities at the area of the Florissant Fossil Beds,

IT IS ORDERED that the defendants, jointly or severally, individually or collectively, or by their agents, servants or employees, their contract vendees or their successors in interest, be and are hereby restrained from disturbing the soil, or subsoil or geologic formations at the Florissant Fossil Beds by any physical or mechanical means including, but not limited to excavation, grading, roadbuilding activity or other construction practice until a hearing on the merits of the plaintiff's application for preliminary injunction to be heard in the United States District Court, District of Colorado, on July 29, 1969, at 9:30 A.M.

IT IS FURTHER ORDERED that service of this order shall be made by the United States Marshal on any workman engaged in construction activities at the Florissant Fossil Beds forthwith and that personal service shall also be made on each of the defendants subject to the jurisdiction of the Court.

It is ordered that the effectiveness of the temporary restraining order issued by this court this date is conditioned upon the filing by the plaintiff with the Clerk of the United States District Court for the District of Colorado a cash bond in the amount of $500.00 for the payment of such costs and damages as may be incurred or suffered by any party who is found to have been wrongfully restrained during the period of the temporary restraining order.

> ALFRED P. MURRAH, Chief Judge
> JEAN S. BREITENSTEIN, Judge
> JOHN J. HICKEY, Judge
> United States Court of Appeals
> Dated: July 10, 1969

[On remand, at the hearing for a preliminary injunction, the district court again dismissed the case. On appeal to the Tenth Circuit again, the appellate judges ordered that the above injunction be continued indefinitely, until further order of the Court of Appeals. The federal government authorized eminent domain purchase by a bill signed on August 14, 1969, P.L. 91-60, and the injunction remained in effect during the time that the federal government was acquiring the lands in question. The fossil beds are now a national monument.]

### COMMENTARY AND QUESTIONS

1. **The basis of the injunction?** The injunction issued in the Florissant fossil beds case (which, it should be noted, is hardly a typical run of the mill environmental case) froze the use of the private land pending possible governmental purchase. What was the basis of the injunction? The court never issued an opinion, so the precise rationale is not clear. An injunction, in modern legal practice, is not itself a cause of action. It requires a foundation tort or other cause of action in order to be issued. In the course of oral argument in the trial court, the attorney for the fossil beds was asked by the judge what his cause of action was, and he replied that he did not have a clear cause of action. He was dismissed. The Tenth Circuit Court of Appeals panel later asked the same question, and attorney Yannacone replied, more or less, "Your Honors, if I told you that the original U.S. Constitution somehow lay buried there in the fossil beds, would you let the bulldozers roll?" When the court said "Of course not, we'd issue an injunction," the attorney said, "Whatever you'd use there, I'm using here." Was it, in fact, the public trust?

The complaint uses the phrase "trust" in substantially the same manner as the public trust doctrine might be applied. Is that the basis of the case? Note that the "trustee" according to the plaintiffs' allegation was not the government, but the private owner, certainly a most disgruntled potential trustee.

2. **The balancing process in *Florissant*.** In *Florissant*, the environmentalists were attempting to hold up bulldozing of the fossil bed area until such time as the federal Congress would pony up the money to pay for purchasing it from the owners.

Bills were proceeding in both the House and the Senate to that end, but the private developer, with an instinct, perhaps, for playing the role of environmental defendant to the dastardly hilt, reportedly announced that it was going to bulldoze some of the fragile areas immediately. The defendant corporation's only concession to the existence of the fossil beds was to offer to sell them to the environmental coalition for a price double what it had itself paid for the property the week before. If the environmentalists would not pay the 100 percent mark-up, the defendants clearly wished to proceed quickly, because eminent domain proceedings for governmental purchase, as we will see in the next chapter, would only pay them fair market value, which was presumptively the amount that they themselves had just paid for the land. In *Florissant*, the trust balance might have been very different if plaintiffs had sought to freeze the fossil beds permanently from development, without the imminent likelihood of governmental purchase that in fact settled the case. The trust balance may in that case have been a process of weighing the strategic time values of maintaining the status quo, as well as public and private rights.

Does it shock you that these privately-owned fossil beds were protected by the court with an injunctive order, freezing them from development, for aesthetic public reasons with no compensation required by the injunction? The following chapter considers such constitutional takings issues at length.

**3. Governmental use of the trust.** Governments have often used the trust doctrine, most often to affirm the existence of their governmental powers to regulate, as in wildlife cases, where the state acts as trustee. In Chapter One's *Steuart Transportation* oil spill case, for example, countering defendant's argument that neither the federal nor the state government plaintiffs "owned" the birds and ducks destroyed by oil, both governments successfully argued the public trust doctrine to win standing for recovery of damages. The trust can aid in defending against regulatory takings challenges as well. When governments cite the trust in affirming their authority over a matter, however, they may concurrently also expand their active liabilities, opening themselves to trust suits by disgruntled environmentalist "beneficiaries." This scenario may help explain the California attorney-general's hesitation in *Mono Lake*, and why public trust law has generally been developed, like so many other areas of environmental law, through citizen rather than governmental efforts.

**4. Familiarizing the trust.** An initial obstacle to courts' active adoption of public trust theories, understandably, was the fact that many judges had never heard of the trust. Attorneys often faced the task of establishing the existence of the doctrine in their state's common law heritage. Consider the following on researching public trust caselaw—

> Courts may react hesitantly when faced with potent and unfamiliar legal doctrines introduced into litigation.... The holdings of Supreme Court decisions, especially *Illinois Central*, clearly establish the existence and applicability of the doctrine in all of the states of the Union, while leaving the detailed articulation of the doctrine, in great part, to subsequent state adjudication.

> Often public trust law lies latent in a state's case law. Experience in Tennessee, which is not a leading state in environmental protection, may be indicative: In 1970 the public trust was an unfamiliar principle in Tennessee practice. The

drafters of the 1972 water pollution act inserted the public trust concept into that statute (as to water quality only) but the effect of the trust language was not clear. When environmental law classes focused upon the public trust doctrine, however, they came up with a wealth of public trust law starting in the earliest days of statehood. More than 50 cases were found dealing with the trust (often in direct and express terms) in state parklands, lakes, and watercourses, wildlife, roads and streets, railroad rights of way, subterranean water, and school lands.

When the state's regional prison program subsequently proposed a diversion of state forest lands, cutting approximately 50 acres out of the center of a wild public preserve, the student researchers and local attorneys were able to marshal sufficient federal and state case law to convince the court that the trust existed, that citizens had standing as beneficiaries to enforce the trust, and that trust standards had to be complied with prior to any diversion of the resource.[14] Plater, The Non-Statutory Public Trust: Affirmative New Environmental Powers for Attorneys-General, Nat'l Assoc. of Attorneys-General Envntl. Control J., April 1976, 13–14.

5. **The public trust doctrine: is it amphibious?**[15] As the excerpt from Marks v. Whitney in *Mono Lake* demonstrates, the public trust in water resources has grown far beyond the traditional trust terms of Roman law. To what extent does it apply beyond water-based resources? Parklands are obviously included today, though unknown to Justinian. Why? What is it about parklands that makes them public trust resources? Is it an inherent premise of open, shared public use? During the Pigeon River Forest litigation on the state of Michigan's duty to keep oil wells out of a state forest preserve, West Mich. Env. Action Council v. NRC, 275 N.W.2d 538 (1978), the assistant attorney general, arguing for the oil companies, asked, "Is all publicly-owned land now invested with the public trust, even dumps and highway yards?" It's a good question. If they are not, where is the line to be drawn?

Above the water line, the trust doctrine has been applied, at various times, to parks (*Paepke*, etc.); wildlife and archaeological artifacts — In re Steuart Transp. Co., 495 F.Supp 38 (E.D. Va. 1980) and Wade v. Kramer, 459 N.E. 2d 1025 (Ill. 1984); beach access over uplands — Matthews v. Bay Head Imprvm't Assoc., 471 A.2d 355 (N.J. 1984);[16] stream access, including the right to portage around barriers by traversing adjacent private land — Montana Coalition for Stream Access v. Hildreth, 684 P.2d 1088 (Mont. 1984); critical upland areas surrounding a redwood forest—Sierra Club

---

14. Marion County v. Luttrell, No. A-3586 (Chancery Ct., Davidson Co., Tenn., June 28, 1974). The case was finally resolved extrajudicially, without a statement by higher courts, through local citizens' political pressuring and dynamite threats against development of the forest resource. Citizen standing was also upheld on trust beneficiary principles in State *ex rel.* SOCM v. Fowinkle, No. A-2914-A (Chancery Ct., Davidson Co., Tenn., Nov. 2, 1973).

15. See Scott Reed's article of the same name, 1 J. Envtl. Law & Litig. 107 (1986).

16. An active case law has developed around the question of public access to beaches, generally asserting the public's rights to use all beaches, sometimes including even the right to go over private land to reach the public beach area. See Matthews v. Bay Head Imprvm't Assoc., 471 A.2d 355 (N.J. 1984); Note, Public Trust Doctrine—Beach Access... 15 Seton Hall L.Rev. 344 (1985); D. Brower, Access to the Nation's Beaches: Legal and Planning Perspectives (1978). Massachusetts and Maine are anomalies, due to the courts' interpretation of a 1647 colonial ordinance issued under authority granted by the King purporting to convey private property grants down to the low water mark, subject only to a public easement for "fyshynge, fowleing, and navigation," but not for beach use. Opinion of the Justices, 313 N.E.2d 561 (Mass. 1974). There is some question whether the King himself possessed such authority.

v. Dept. of Interior, 396 F. Supp. 90, 398 F. Supp. 284 (N.D. Cal. 1974); trees threatened by resort developments — Irish v. Green, 4 ERC 1402 (Mich. Cir. Ct. 1972); trees damaged by oil spills — S.S. Zoe Colocotroni, 628 F. 2d 652 (1st Cir. 1980) (although these were water-based mangrove trees); perhaps fossil beds, as we have seen; and more.

Take this not-so-hypothetical: What if, after purchasing a painting by the renowned post-Impressionist Paul Cezanne for $800,000, two entrepreneurial MBAs announce that they have decided to cut it up into one-inch squares because their marketing analysis indicates they can sell off the tiny "authentic Cezannes" for more than $1.5 million? See J. Held, Alteration and Mutilation of Works of Art, 62 S.Atl. Quarterly 1, 19 (Winter 1963, noting commercial "butchery" chop-jobs on works of Van Eyck, VanderWeeden, and Jackson Pollock); The Case of the Dismembered Masterpieces, ARTnews, Sept. 1980 at 68; Cal. Civ. Code §987, Protection of fine art against alteration or destruction (1997). Could a public trust be argued here, or public nuisance? Who has standing to sue? What remedy — an injunction pending imminent public purchase, as in *Florissant*? Would the same kind of theory be applicable to the protection of ancient petroglyphs — prehistoric human rock paintings — from willful destruction?

Once started on this road, the trust's complications abound, but the doctrine's recognition of intangible public values undeniably captures a piece of reality, the legal significance of a society's common cultural heritage.

6. **The third category of public trust situations.** Whenever the trust is used to support antipollution efforts (see Tennessee Water Pollution Control Act, T.C.A. §§70.324 et seq., and State v. Amerada Hess, 350 F. Supp. 1060 [Md. 1972]), to prevent destruction of trust resources by public or private actors (see the redwood cases in the preceding note), or to recover damages for the destruction of trust assets (see In re Steuart Transp. Co., in the preceding note, or the state of Alaska's oil spill litigation), it is analytically focused on defense of the quality of the resource against derogation rather than protecting the character of ownership. Emperor Justinian, remember, began his list of public trust resources with *air*, for which issues of ownership are irrelevant, but issues of quality essential. In practice, however, the application of the trust analysis in this third, resource-defense, or "derogation" category parallels the alienation and diversion cases, and is the implicit basis for state pollution laws. The issue in each setting is to determine to what extent the qualities of the trust resources are to be preserved and stewarded against short-term exploitation.

7. **What *is* the public trust, and how will it evolve?** At this point, are we in any better position to figure out what exactly the public trust doctrine *is*? Is it constitutional? Is it federal common law? Is it a Rawlsian, Lockian, "pre-political" natural right? Is it Professor Krier's constitutional right? Is it intergenerational democracy, mediating resource legacies over the years? Is it enforceable? Is it merely an administrative law "hard look" doctrine applied to natural resources? Is it like Burke's tree: we honor it for its years of growth, but also because we don't understand exactly whence it comes?

As environmental consciousness grows, public conceptions of public rights inevitably expand, and public and private property expectations follow suit. The United States has been learning to accept the end of the myths of the frontier, of unlimited resources, of the ability to walk away from mistakes to fresh terrain. The public trust doctrine reflects societal realities long accepted in other modern nation states which have had to deal with problems of limited resources and high population densities. Does the public trust represent a tendency pushing government agencies into less political civic roles? Does it represent a tendency bringing American private property rights closer to those in other industrial nations' legal systems, where property owners generally have "privileges" to develop, rather than relatively unfettered "rights"? Does this prospect worry you? See the next chapter.

## D. SIMILAR ENVIRONMENTAL RIGHTS FROM CONSTITUTIONS AND STATUTES

The public trust doctrine currently is not the only evolving legal principle of environmental stewardship. In a number of states there have been constitutional or statutory attempts to establish environmental rights and duties, often expressly incorporating the public trust doctrine.

### Section 1. CONSTITUTIONAL ENVIRONMENTAL RIGHTS

A number of states have experimented with constitutional environmental provisions,[17] and there is significant diversity among their approaches to the declaration of constitutional rights. Some are clear, some unspecific. Some appear to be enforceable by courts and some appear to be mere political posturing. For more on state constitutional provisions, see Howard, State Constitutions and the Environment, 58 Va.L.Rev. 193 (1972).

But just because there is a constitutional right doesn't necessarily mean that one can do anything with it in a court of law. Is the constitutional provision self-enforcing or does it depend on subsequent legslative action? The following state constitutional provision[18] sets up the following case considering whether or not state constitutional provisions are self-executing and enforceable.

---

17. See, for example, Montana Const Art. IX; Illinois Const Art. 11, §1; Hawaii Const Art. 11, §9; Louisiana Const Art. 9, §1; Minnesota Const Art. 11, §14; New Mexico Const Art. 20, §21; California Const Art. 16, §14; Pennsylvania Const Art. 1, §27.

18. Contrast the Pennsylvania provision with the following:

The people shall have the right to clean air and water, freedom from excessive and unnecessary noise, and the natural, scenic, historic, and esthetic qualities of their environment; and the protection of the people in their right to the conservation, development and utilization of the agricultural, mineral, forest, water, air and other natural resources is hereby declared to be a public purpose. The general court [legislature] shall have the power to enact legislation necessary or expedient to protect such rights. Constitution of the Commonwealth of Massachusetts, Article 49.

The conservation and development of the natural resources of the state are hereby declared to be of paramount public concern in the interest of the health, safety and general welfare of the people. The legislature shall provide for the protection of the air, water and other natural resources of the state from pollution, impairment and destruction. Michigan Constitution, Article IV, §52.

**Constitution of the Commonwealth of Pennsylvania, Article 1, §27 (1971):**

The people have a right to clean air, pure water, and to the preservation of the natural, scenic, historic and esthetic values of the environment. Pennsylvania's public natural resources are the common property of all the people, including generations yet to come. As trustee of these resources, the Commonwealth shall conserve and maintain them for the benefit of all the people.

### Commonwealth v. National Gettysburg Tower, Inc.
Supreme Court of Pennsylvania, 1973
454 Pa. 193, 311 A.2d 588

[In this case the Commonwealth of Pennsylvania, acting through and by its Attorney General, sought to enjoin the defendant from erecting a steel tower more than 300 feet tall that would loom over a portion of the Gettysburg battlefield, based on Article I, §27, the state constitution's environmental amendment.]

O'BRIEN, J. (joined by Mr. Justice Pomeroy) ... The chancellor, after making detailed findings concerning the location and characteristics of the tower and the neighborhood of the park, concluded that the Commonwealth had failed to show by clear and convincing proof that the natural, scenic, historic or aesthetic values of the Gettysburg environment would be injured by the erection of the tower.... The chancellor first found to be without merit the defense interposed by appellees that Article 1, §27 of the Pennsylvania Constitution — upon which the Commonwealth relied for the authority of the Attorney General to bring this suit — was not self-executing and, therefore, legislative authority was required before the suit could be brought....

By familiar principles, the appellees, as the owners of the site, may use their property as they please, provided they do not interfere with their neighbors' reasonable enjoyment of their properties and subject to reasonable regulations for the public good imposed under the police power of the State, of which there are none here....

Similarly, there is no statute of the Pennsylvania Legislature, which would authorize the Governor and the Attorney General to initiate actions like the law suit in the instant case. Rather, authority for the Commonwealth's suit is allegedly based entirely upon Article 1, §27 of the State Constitution, ratified by the voters of Pennsylvania on May 18, 1971....

It is the Commonwealth's position that this amendment is self-executing; that the people have been given a right "to the preservation of the natural, scenic, historic and esthetic values of the environment," and "that no further legislation is necessary to vest these rights in the people."

The general principles of law involved in determining whether a particular provision of a constitution is self-executing....

A Constitution is primarily a declaration of principles of the fundamental law. Its provisions are usually only commands to the legislature to enact laws to carry out the purposes of the framers of the Constitution, or mere restrictions upon the power of the legislature to pass laws, yet it is entirely within the power of those who establish and adopt the Constitution to make any of its provisions self-executing....

Cooley's Constitutional Limitations (8th ed.), Vol. 1 p. 165 says: "But although none of the provisions of a constitution are to be looked upon as immaterial or merely advisory, there are some which, from the nature of the case, are as incapable of compulsory enforcement as are directory provisions in general. The reason is that, while the purpose may be to establish rights or to impose duties, they do not in and of themselves constitute a sufficient rule by means of which such right may be protected or such duty enforced. In such cases, before the constitutional provision can be made effectual, supplemental legislation must be had; and the provision may be in its nature mandatory to the legislature to enact the needful legislation, though back of it there lies no authority to enforce the command. Sometimes the constitution in terms requires the legislature to enact laws on a particular subject; and here it is obvious that the requirement has only a moral force: the legislature ought to obey it; but the right intended to be given is only assured when the legislation is voluntarily enacted."

In Davis v. Burke, 179 U.S. 399, 403, the United States Supreme Court said: "Where a constitutional provision is complete in itself it needs no further legislation to put it in force. When it lays down certain general principles, as to enact laws upon a certain subject...or for uniform laws upon the subject of taxation, it may need more specific legislation to make it operative. In other words, it is self-executing only so far as it is susceptible of execution." O'Neill v. White, 22 A.2d at 26-27 (Pa. 1941).

The Commonwealth makes two arguments in support of its contention that §27 of Article 1 is self-executing. We find neither of them persuasive.

First, the Commonwealth emphasizes that the provision in question is part of Article 1 and that no provision of Article 1 has ever been judicially declared to be nonself-executing. The Commonwealth places particular emphasis on the wording of §25 of Article 1. See Erdman v. Mitchell, 56 A. 327 (Pa. 1903). Section 25 of Article 1 reads as follows:

To guard against transgressions of the high powers which we have delegated, we declare that everything in this article is excepted out of the general powers of government and shall forever remain inviolate.

However, it should be noted that Article 1 is entitled "Declaration of Rights" and all of the first twenty-six sections of Article 1 which state those specific rights, must be read as limiting the powers of government to interfere with the rights provided therein.

Section 25 of Article 1 should be read as summarizing the philosophy of the first twenty-four sections of Article 1, particularly when it declares that "...everything in this article is *excepted out of the general powers of government* and shall remain forever inviolate." (emphasis supplied.)

Unlike the first twenty-six sections of Article 1, §27, the one which concerns us in the instant case, does not merely contain a limitation on the powers of government. True, the first sentence of §27, which states:

"The people have a right to clean air, pure water, and to the preservation of the natural, scenic, historic and esthetic values of the environment,"

can be read as limiting the right of government to interfere with the people's right to "clean air, pure water, and to the preservation of the natural, scenic, historic and aesthetic values of the environment." As such, the first part of §27, if read alone, could be read to be self-executing.

ᐟ But the remaining provisions of §27, rather than limiting the powers of government, expand those powers. These provisions declare that the Commonwealth is the "trustee" of Pennsylvania's "public natural resources" and they give the

Commonwealth the power to act "to conserve and maintain them for the benefit of all people." Insofar as the Commonwealth always had a recognized police power to regulate the use of land, and thus could establish standards for clean air and clean water consistent with the requirements of public health, §27 is merely a general reaffirmation of past law. It must be recognized, however, that up until now, aesthetic or historical considerations by themselves have not been considered sufficient to constitute a basis for the Commonwealth's exercise of its police power.

Now for the first time, at least insofar as the state constitution is concerned, the Commonwealth has been given power to act in areas of purely aesthetic or historic concern.

The Commonwealth has cited no example of a situation where a constitutional provision which expanded the powers of government to act against individuals was held to be self-executing... It should be noted that §27 does not give the powers of a trustee of public natural resources to the *Governor* or to the *Attorney General* but to the *Commonwealth.*

If we were to sustain the Commonwealth's position that the amendment was self-executing, a property owner would not know and would have no way, short of expensive litigation, of finding out what he could do with his property. The fact that the owner contemplated a use similar to

**NATIONAL TOWER**
Gettysburg, Pa.

GETTYSBURG
"Where history comes alive"
on top of the National Tower
Provisions for handicapped, deaf and blind
Foreign translations available of Sound Program

*A brochure showing the tower.*

others that had not been enjoined would be no guarantee that the Commonwealth would not seek to enjoin his use. Since no executive department has been given authority to determine when to [sue] to protect the environment, there would be no way of obtaining, with respect to a particular use contemplated, an indication of what action the Commonwealth might take before the owner expended what could be significant sums of money for the purchase or the development of the property. We do not believe that the framers of the environmental protection amendment could have intended such an unjust result...

To summarize, we believe that the provisions of §27 of Article 1 of the Constitution merely state the general principle of law that the Commonwealth is trustee of Pennsylvania's public natural resources with power to protect the "natural, scenic, historic and esthetic values" of its environment. If the amendment was self-executing, action taken under it would pose serious problems of constitutionality, under both the equal protection clause and the due process clause of the Fourteenth Amendment. Accordingly, before the environmental protection amendment can be made effective, supplemental legislation will be required to define the values which the amendment seeks to protect and to establish procedures by which the use of private property can be fairly regulated to protect those values....

ROBERTS, J. (concurring). I agree that the order of the Commonwealth Court should be affirmed; however my reasons for affirmance are entirely different from those expressed in the opinion by Mr. Justice O'Brien. I believe that the Commonwealth, even prior to the recent adoption of Article I, Section 27 possessed the inherent sovereign power to protect and preserve for its citizens the natural and historic resources now enumerated in Section 27. The express language of the constitutional amendment merely recites the "inherent and independent rights" of mankind relative to the environment which are "recognized and unalterably established" by Article I, Section 1 of the Pennsylvania Constitution.

Prior to the adoption of Article I, Section 27, it was clear that as sovereign "the state has an interest independent of and behind the titles of its citizens, in all the earth and air within its domain...." Georgia v. Tennessee Copper Co., 206 U.S. 230, 237 (1907). The proposition has long been firmly established that

> it is a fair and reasonable demand on the part of a sovereign that the air over its territory should not be polluted...that the forests on its mountains, be they better or worse, and whatever domestic destruction they have suffered, should not be further destroyed or threatened...that the crops and orchards on its hills should not be endangered.... 206 U.S. at 238.

Parklands and historical sites, as "natural resources," are subject to the same considerations.[19]

Moreover, "it must surely be conceded that, if the health and comfort of the inhabitants of a state are threatened, the state is the proper party to represent and defend them...." Missouri v. Illinois, 180 U.S. 208, 241 (1901). Since natural and historic resources are the common property of the citizens of a state, see McCready v. Virginia, 94 U.S. 391 (1876), the Commonwealth can — and always could — proceed as parens patriae acting on behalf of the citizens and in the interests of the community,[20] or as trustee of the state's public resources.[21]

However, in my view, the Commonwealth, on this record, has failed to establish its entitlement to the equitable relief it seeks, either on common law or constitutional (prior or subsequent to Section 27) theories.... Moreover, I entertain serious reservations as to the propriety of granting the requested relief in this case in the absence of appropriate and articulated substantive and procedural standards.

MANDERINO, J., joins in this opinion. NIX, J., concurs in the result.

---

19. See Snyder v. Bd. Park Comm'rs, 181 N.E. 483, 484 (Ohio 1932): "[W]e...are of the opinion that, to the extent to which a given area possesses elements or features which supply a human need and contribute to the health, welfare, and benefit of a community, and are essential for the well being of such a community and the proper enjoyment of its property devoted to park and recreational purposes, the same constitute natural resources."

20. See Georgia v. Pennsylvania R.R. Co., 324 U.S. 439 (1945); Sparhawk v. Union Passenger Ry. Co., 54 Pa. 401 (1867).

21. Illinois Central R.R. Co. v. Illinois, 146 U.S. 387 (1892); Sax, The Public Trust Doctrine in Natural Resource Law: Effective Judicial Intervention, 68 Mich.L.Rev. 471 (1970).

JONES, J., dissenting... This Court has been given the opportunity to affirm the mandate of the public empowering the Commonwealth to prevent environmental abuses; instead, the Court has chosen to emasculate a constitutional amendment by declaring it not to be self-executing. I am compelled to dissent....

If the amendment was intended only to espouse a policy undisposed to enforcement without supplementing legislation, it would surely have taken a different form. But the amendment is not addressed to the General Assembly. It does not require the legislative creation of remedial measures. Instead, the amendment creates a public trust. The "natural, scenic, historic and aesthetic values of the environment" are the trust *res*, the Commonwealth, through its executive branch, is the trustee; the *people of this Commonwealth* are the trust beneficiaries. The amendment thus installs the common law public trust doctrine *as a constitutional right to environmental protection* susceptible to enforcement by an action in equity.

Each of the equivalent [environmental protection] amendments [in Massachusetts, Illinois, New York and Virginia] purports to establish a policy of environmental protection, but either omits the mode of enforcement or explicitly delegates the responsibility for implementation to the legislative branch. The Pennsylvania amendment defines enumerated rights within the scope of existing remedies. It imposes a fiduciary duty upon the Commonwealth to protect the people's "rights to clean air, pure water and to the preservation of the natural, scenic, historical and aesthetic values of the environment." That the language of the amendment is subject to judicial interpretation does not mean that the enactment must remain *an ineffectual constitutional platitude* until such time as the legislature acts.

Because I believe Article 1 §7 is self-executing, I believe that our inquiry should have focused upon the ultimate issue of fact: does the proposed tower violate the rights of the people of the Commonwealth as secured by this amendment?...

The facts indicate that the proposed tower is a metal structure rising 310 feet above the ground. It is shaped like an hourglass; about 90 feet in diameter at the bottom, 30 feet in the middle and 70 feet at the top. The top level will include an observation deck, elevator housings, facilities for warning approaching aircraft and an illuminated American flag. The proposed site of the tower is an area around which the third day of the battle of Gettysburg was fought. It is located immediately south of the Gettysburg National Cemetery.

The Commonwealth presented compelling evidence that the proposed observation tower at Gettysburg would desecrate the natural, scenic, aesthetic and historic values of the Gettysburg environment. The director of the National Park Service, George Hartzog, appeared as a witness for the Commonwealth....

> I described it as a monstrosity. I advised Mr. Ottenstein that between all of the mistakes which I felt the federal government had made here, and all of the mistakes I felt the commercial interests had made here, nevertheless Gettysburg remained a very sacred symbol to the more than 200,000,000 people across the United States, and that an intrusion of this immensity would, in our judgment, be an absolute monstrosity in this kind of environment and I was very much opposed to it."

Mr. Hartzog offered eloquent testimony on the question of the tower's impact upon the Gettysburg environment....

Q.Would it, in your opinion, be possible to measure the damage that would occur to this historic site if that tower were erected?

A.Well, I don't think that you can measure these things in a normal system of values that we articulate in terms of dollars and cents. You measure them more in terms of matters of integrity and understanding and inspiration and involvement. And from this standpoint, I think a monstrous intrusion such as this tower is, into the historical, pastoral scene of the battlefield park and Eisenhower National Site and the National Cemetery and the place where Lincoln spoke, is just destructive of the integrity of its historical value.

Q.And you are saying you can't put a price tag on those values?

A.No, you can't. There is one Yorktown and there is one Gettysburg....

I would enjoin the construction of this tower by the authority of Article 1 §27 of the Pennsylvania Constitution. I dissent!!

EAGEN, J., joins in this opinion.

## COMMENTARY AND QUESTIONS

1. **A split decision on constitutional enforcement?** As you count the votes on the different merits of this case, how many justices of the state supreme court were of the opinion that the tower did not amount to a violation of law? Clearly the tower won. How many of them, on the other hand, actually held that the constitutional provision was not self-executing? It appears that only the first two justices were convinced that §27 needed further legislative action. This reading of the court is supported by the fact that, like a number of other state high courts, the Pennsylvania Supreme Court subsequently held that §27 of the state constitution is self-executing. Payne v. Kassab, 361 A.2d 263 (1976).

2. **The state constitution and the public trust.** Note how the constitutional provision here was intertwined with the public trust doctrine, especially in Justice Robert's concurrence. How many of the justices appeared to accept that public trust principles were at least theoretically applicable to the private lands surrounding the battlefield? Did §27 add anything to pre-existing trust law?

3. **Commercialization, and a parade of horribles.** In hindsight, could you have litigated this case differently so as to have achieved a different result? One way might have been to remind the state supreme court that its decision could well spawn a rash of other towers surrounding the Gettysburg battlefield. If the image of the arrival of a thicket of towers and other tourist attractions (shooting galleries, water slides, cemetery-view ferris wheel rides?) would move the court, could it not draw the line here, enjoining the first tower?

One of the classic problems of public parklands is the way they attract the crassest commercialization to their boundaries — Estes Park at the gateway to the Rockies; West Yellowstone, Montana; and Pigeon Forge at the gateway to the Smokies National Park, with its Dinosaurland, Waterslides, Spaceship rides, Ripley's Believe-It-Or-Not, the Tourist Gardens of Christ, and the only hula dance-porpoise show in the Appalachians. Can the public trust doctrine extend to the surroundings of parklands, to protect park resources from the depredations of the tourist marketplace carnival? How about public nuisance? How about legislation?

See (as usual) Sax, Helpless Giants: The National Parks and the Regulation of Private Lands, 74 Mich. L. Rev. 239–45 (1976). See also Chapter 24.

### Section 2. STATE STATUTORY ENVIRONMENTAL RIGHTS: THE MICHIGAN ENVIRONMENTAL PROTECTION ACT (MEPA)

The Michigan Environmental Protection Act (MEPA) is a rather unusual approach to environmental regulation. Drafted by Professor Sax, MEPA is grounded on the belief that insular decision making having adverse environmental impacts ought to be subject to judicial review and correction. Here are the central provisions of MEPA as recodified in 1995:[22]

§**1701**(1) The attorney general or any person may maintain an action in the circuit court having jurisdiction where the alleged violation occurred or is likely to occur for declaratory and equitable relief against any person for the protection of the air, water, and other natural resources and the public trust in these resources from pollution, impairment, or destruction.

(2) In granting relief provided by subsection (1), if there is a standard for pollution or for an antipollution device or procedure, fixed by rule or otherwise, by the state or an instrumentality, agency, or political subdivision of the state, the court may:

(a) Determine the validity, applicability, and reasonableness of the standard.

(b) If a court finds a standard to be deficient, direct the adoption of a standard approved and specified by the court....

§**1703**(1) When the plaintiff...has made a prima facie showing that the conduct of the defendant has polluted, impaired, or destroyed or is likely to pollute, impair, or destroy the air, water, or other natural resources or the public trust in these resources, the defendant may rebut the prima facie showing by the submission of evidence to the contrary [or] show, by way of an affirmative defense, that there is no feasible and prudent alternative to defendant's conduct and that his or her conduct is consistent with the promotion of the public health, safety, and welfare in light of the state's paramount concern for the protection of its natural resources from pollution, impairment, or destruction. Michigan Compiled Laws Annotated, Chapter 324[23]

After a showing that an action will "pollute, impair or destroy" natural resources or the public trust as it relates to those resources, the burden switches to the defendant to rebut the claim of resource harm or to prove an affirmative defense. The statute provides a defense if there is no "prudent and feasible alternative" to the action consistent "with the promotion of the public health, safety and welfare in

---

22. M.C.L.A. §324.1701 et seq.; See P.A. 1994, No. 451, §90101, eff., March 30, 1995.

23. Under §1705, if the Attorney-General or any citizen intervenes in any relevant agency proceeding, "alleged pollution, impairment, or destruction of the air, water, or other natural resources, or the public trust in these resources, shall be determined, and conduct shall not be authorized or approved that has or is likely to have such an effect if there is a feasible and prudent alternative consistent with the reasonable requirements of the public health, safety, and welfare."

light of the state's paramount concern for the protection of its natural resources from pollution, impairment or destruction." See §1703.

MEPA embodies an approach that encourages overall environmental assessment. It requires courts to consider wide-ranging environmental effects and alternatives that may ordinarily be downplayed as a matter of regulatory convenience, cost externalization, or simply unintended oversight. Courts are authorized to issue declaratory or injunctive relief and may review administrative standards, directing that different standards be adopted if needed to protect the environment as MEPA requires. Damage remedies are not provided by MEPA; this omission was a deliberate compromise made to obtain passage of the statute.

Important statutory terms, like "pollute, impair or destroy," and the term "natural resources" are not defined by the legislature. This requires the courts of Michigan to interpret the statute's broad language. In one of the first MEPA cases to reach the Michigan Supreme Court, Ray v. Mason Country Drain Commissioner, 224 N.W.2d 883 (Mich. 1975), the court found that MEPA charges the courts to create the equivalent of an environmental common law. In response to the defendant's claim that the statute was so broad as to be an unpermitted delegation of legislative authority to the courts, the opinion conceded that the legislature "paints the standard for environmental quality with a rather broad stroke of the brush, [but] the language used is neither elusive nor vague. 'Pollution,' 'impairment,' and 'destruction' are taken directly from the constitutional provision which sets forth this state's commitment to preserve the quality of our environment." 224 N.W.2d at 888.

Beyond the authorization to create a common law of environmental quality, another of MEPA's revolutionary features is the second portion of §1701 Here MEPA expressly rejects the administrative law norm that courts should defer to agency expertise in standard-setting matters. Although this power has seldom been exercised by the courts in MEPA cases, in one early case the judge literally rewrote the discharge permit of a small sewage treatment plant in order to reduce the noxious effects of its discharges on a downstream chain of lakes. See Lakeland Property Owners v. Township of Northfield, 3 ERC 1893, 2 ELR 20331 (Livingston Cty. Cir. Ct. 1972).

At least until the decision in Nemeth v. Abonmarche Development, Inc. 1998 WL 188049 (Mich.) the most consistently vexing question in MEPA cases is determining whether there is some minimum threshold of environmental harm that must be crossed before conduct is actionable under the statute.[24] Consider, for example, a case in which a road commission proposes to cut down a few trees at a forest's edge to widen a highway right-of-way to improve safety. How should this case be analyzed under MEPA? At some literal level, the tree cutting obviously involves the destruction of natural resources and, therefore, appears to establish a prima facie case. The situation can be analyzed two ways. Under one view, the mundane nature of the act and its lack of significance in maintenance of the larger forest resource make it seem unlikely that the legislature intended such a modest

---

24. See Abrams, Thresholds of Harm in Environmental Litigation: The Michigan Environmental Protection Act as a Model of a Minimal Requirement, 7 Harv. Envtl L. Rev. 107, 114 (1983).

showing of harm to constitute a prima facie case. One of the maxims of equity is that "the law does not concern itself with trifles."[25] In the road commission hypo it is impossible, if treecutting is a prima facie case of harm, those facts cannot be rebutted, so the defendant is left only with a chance to make the affirmative defense of no feasible and prudent alternative, which often is hard to establish. In the road commission hypothetical, for example, guard rails would provide similar safety benefits. Some defendants persuaded courts that the legislature did not intend small-scale cases to be subject to MEPA. See e.g. City of Portage v. Kalamazoo County Road Commission, 355 N.W.2d 913 (Mich. App. 1984). In an effort to give guidance to as to where the threshold was set, the *Portage* court offered a series of four factors: "In determining whether the impact of a proposed action on wildlife is so significant as to constitute an environmental risk and require judicial intervention, the court should evaluate the environmental situation prior to the proposed action and compare it with the probable condition of the particular environment afterwards. The factors the court should consider include: (1) whether the natural resource involved is rare, unique, endangered, or has historical significance, (2) whether the resource is easily replaceable (for example, by replanting trees or restocking fish), (3) whether the proposed action will have any significant consequential effect on other natural resources (for example, whether wildlife will be lost if its habitat is impaired or destroyed), and (4) whether the direct or consequential impact on animals or vegetation will affect a critical number, considering the nature and location of the wildlife affected. The magnitude of the harm likely to result from the proposed action will depend on the characteristics of the resources involved. Esthetic considerations alone are not determinative of significant environmental impact." *Portage* at 915–16.

In *Nemeth*, the Michigan Supreme Court rejected the *Portage* approach to thresholds without expressly overruling the decision. In *Nemeth*, the plaintiffs sought to enjoin a multimillion dollar marina project on the Lake Michigan waterfront in the City of Manistee. The project stripped 30 acres of barrier beach and involved moving thousands of cubic yards of sand. During the preliminary stages, a December storm wreaked havoc with the site, burying neighboring parcels in deep drifts of sand, snow, fly ash, and other sediments. Not long after that plaintiffs sued, on theories that included MEPA. The crux of the MEPA case turned on whether the defendants' violation of the Michigan Soil Erosion and Sediment Control Act (SESCA) constituted sufficient evidence that the defendants' activities violated MEPA "by either polluting, impairing,[or] destroying [the] air, water, or other natural resources, or were likely to do so." On that issue, the court in a mini-ecology lesson, explained the substantial adverse impact of sedimentation on water quality and other facets of environmental quality and concluded that the standards of protection set by the legislature in SESCA, when violated, constitute a prima facie MEPA case. The court dealt with the threshold of harm question by saying that each case requires a careful judicial evaluation, not a wooden standard or particular set of factors, saying, "The trial judge has a responsibility to independently determine the existence of actual or likely pollution, impairment or destruction."

25. De minimis non curat lex.

COMMENTARY & QUESTIONS

1. **MEPA as model legislation.** Within a few years following its enactment, MEPA served as a model for similar statutes in six additional states,[26] but thereafter the concept seems to have languished. The failure of MEPA to be more widely copied is attributable, in part, to the enormous expansion in other environmental legislation that took place in the early 1970s. To the extent that MEPA was designed to change the inertia of state environmental control agencies, some of that inertia was corrected by the federal air and water statutes that forced all states to control the most obvious sources of pollution.

2. **The underutilization of MEPA.** Despite its broad applicability and universal standing provisions, a longitudinal study of MEPA conducted by Professor Sax and a number of other researchers shows surprisingly small numbers of MEPA cases, with no more than a few dozen cases filed per year.[27] Those same studies reveal that the most frequent MEPA plaintiffs are governmental environmental enforcement agencies who use MEPA's injunctive remedies to supplement their other powers. Why are private suits uncommon? The evidence obtained from interviews with attorneys who have filed MEPA cases points toward the burdensome expenses of obtaining the expert testimony (often $10,000 to $15,000 even in relatively simple cases) needed to make out the credible prima facie showings. This also tends to explain the relative popularity of MEPA with pollution control agencies that have their own in-house expertise. Similarly, the absence of a damage remedy means that there is no potential fund of money available to help defray the cost of plaintiffs' attorneys' fees, making those fees a further disincentive to MEPA's use. The *Nemeth* court by narrow majority rejected an argument that the statutory statement that "costs may be apportioned to the parties if the interests of justice require," did not authorize the trial court's grant of attorneys' fees to the plaintiffs. In other settings, and perhaps in the future in Michigan, plaintiffs may be able to get expert witness and attorneys fees as a function of the traditional equitable power to grant fee-shifting upon a finding of "common fund" benefits (to be reallocated from defendants to the public), defendants' "bad faith," and private attorney-general theories. See Chapter 20 B.

3. **Assessing the Michigan experiment.** The Michigan statute was hailed as a breakthrough in citizen reform of the environmental protection process, cursed as a disruptive attack on the state's economic integrity, and belittled as a minor procedural change in standing law. What lessons emerge from the Michigan experience to inform the statutory and common law development of environmental law in other states?

---

26. Minn. Stat. Ann. §§116B.01-116B.13 (Supp. 1973); Mass. Ann. Laws, ch. 214, §10A (Supp. 1972); Conn. Gen. Stat. An. §§22a-20 (Supp. 1973); S. Dak. Comp. Laws. Ann. §§21-10A-1 to 21-10A-15 (Supp. 1973); Fla. Stat. Ann. §403.412; Ind. Ann. Stat. §§13-6-1-1 to 13-6-1-6 (1973); N.J. Stat. Anno. 2A: 35A-1 et seq. (Supp. 1970).

27. See generally Sax & Connor, Michigan's Environmental Protection Act of 1970: A Progress Report, 70 Mich. L. Rev. 1003 (1972); Sax & DiMento, Environmental Citizen Suits: Three Years' Experience Under the Michigan Environmental Protection Act, 4 Ecol. L.Q. 1 (1974); Haynes, Michigan's Environmental Protection Act in its Sixth Year: Substantive Environmental Law from Citizen Suits, 53 J. Urb. L. 589 (1976); Slone, The Michigan Environmental Protection Act: Bringing Citizen-Initiated Environmental Suits into the 1980s, 12 Ecol. L.Q. 271 (1985).

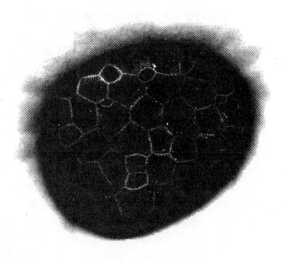

*The law locks up both man and woman*
*Who steals the goose from off the common,*
*But lets the greater felon loose*
*Who steals the common from the goose.*

— Old English quatrain

*We shall never achieve harmony with land, any more than we shall achieve jus-*
*tice and liberty for [all] people. In these higher aspirations, the important thing*
*is not to achieve, but to strive.*

— Aldo Leopold, Sand County Almanac at 72

# Chapter 23

# PUBLIC RIGHTS AND PRIVATE PROPERTY: CONSTITUTIONAL LIMITS ON PHYSICAL AND REGULATORY TAKINGS

A. *Eminent Domain Condemnations*

B. *Inverse Condemnation: a Constitutional Tort?*

C. *Challenges to Regulations as Unconstitutional "Takings"*

How far can government go in imposing public demands on private property rights? That intensely political question, a central issue of democratic governance, lies latent or explosively obvious within a vast number of environmental issues. Whether by physical appropriations or regulatory restrictions on individual and corporate behavior, the imposition of public values, needs, or whims upon private property and private actions sets up political confrontations, of constitutional proportions.

Consider, for instance, this statutory provision in several bills that marketplace forces almost succeeded in passing in the mid-1990s:

> §3(a) The Federal Government shall compensate an owner of property whose use of any portion of that property has been limited by an agency action, under a specified regulatory law, that diminishes the fair market value of that portion by 20 percent or more. The amount of the compensation shall equal the diminution in value that resulted from the agency action. If the diminution in value of a portion of that property is greater than 50 percent, at the option of the owner, the Federal Government shall buy that portion of the property for its fair market value.[1]

This piece of automatic-compensation legislation from the "Contract with America," which was disingenuously touted as "merely codifying existing constitutional rulings," would have had a sweeping effect on federal environmental regulation. The tension that motivated it, between the marketplace economy and the demands of the civic and natural economies, will always be a powerful presence in environmental policy.

Government is sometimes an environmental protector, and sometimes a destructive promoter. On one hand the power of the state can be a strong ally of

---

1. 104 H.R. 925, the "Private Property Protection Act," 104th Cong., 1st Sess. (passed by the House March 3, 1995); see also Senate "Omnibus Property Rights Act" bill sponsored by Senator Dole, 104 S. 605 §403. Similar marketplace-driven legislation has been introduced in several states; one such bill was signed into law by Gov. George M. Bush of Texas. Tex.Govt Code §2007.002, Title 10, subtitle A, Chap. 2007, subchap. A-C; see also Fla. Stat. Anno. Title VI, Chap. 70, §70.001.

environmentalists, since in most cases government actions are backed by substantial public resources and are presumed valid until proven to be unauthorized, arbitrary and capricious, or otherwise invalid. On the other hand, environmentalists who question governmental development programs, like marsh-draining and highway construction, try to override the government actions presumption of validity.

Local, state, and federal governments each functionally possess, as a basic attribute of sovereignty, the coercive "police power"[2] — the power of government to force anyone within its jurisdiction to do or not to do things that the government believes would affect the health, safety, or general welfare of its citizens. Thus government can prohibit you from dumping pollutants or filling a wetland, force you to sell your land for a public park or parking lot, or regulate your use of wilderness areas and wildlife. The police power includes, in other words, both physical appropriation and regulatory powers.

Physical appropriations by government — eminent domain condemnations — are difficult to defend against. Environmental cases have begun to develop substantive challenges to physical condemnations, scrutinizing eminent domain decisions (Subchapter A, where government accepts the necessity of paying compensation), and imposing liability on government for nuisance-like physical invasions (Subchapter B on inverse condemnation).[3]

Constitutional attacks against regulations, arguing that environmental restrictions are "invalid regulatory takings" of private property, are one of the most pervasive themes of environmental regulation and politics at all levels of government. Almost by definition, civic regulations trying to correct market failures arouse instinctive marketplace resistance.

The constitutional combats between public rights and private property are based on the language of the Fifth Amendment to the U.S. Constitution (as incorporated in the Fourteenth Amendment for state actions and substantially replicated in corresponding provisions in most state constitutions) —

> No person shall be...deprived of life, liberty, or property, without due process of law; nor shall private property be taken for public use, without just compensation.

Analytically, this language embodies two different constitutional rights applicable to private property: a right against deprivation without due process (substantive as well as procedural), and a protection against uncompensated "takings." Structurally these rights are virtually identical. Whether challenged physical

---

2. The police power resides in all state governments by definition, from which it is broadly delegated to local governments for various health, safety, and welfare purposes. The federal government does not possess a general police power, but the federal government exercises such a similar range of powers through its commerce, national defense, property, and other delegated authorities that its exercises of these powers are also at times referred to as "police power" actions.

3. Although the "inverse condemnation" rubric is now sometimes used in claims against regulations as well as against physical acts by government, its application in the regulatory setting follows the tests for regulatory takings rather than the inverse condemnation tests for governmental physical takings. Since governments have the choice, in the event a regulation is found to be a taking, whether to waive or buy, *First English*, 482 U.S. 304 (1987), it makes sense to use "inverse condemnation" as a particular cause of action in the physical appropriation context, not as a separate theory of regulatory taking.

actions or regulations are federal, state, or local, they are subjected to the same five basic categories of constitutional attack, one procedural and four substantive:

**THE FOUR BASIC INQUIRIES IN SUBSTANTIVE JUDICIAL REVIEW[4]...** Dividing the areas of substantive judicial scrutiny of governmental actions into four separate diagnostic inquiries can clarify many issues of judicial review. These four substantive inquiries are discernible throughout the case law, and appear to encompass all nonstatutory substantive questions typically raised in judicial review of governmental action. Zoning cases, which offer frequent and familiar (if homely) examples of constitutional challenges, provide an area of litigation that helps illustrate issues in all four substantive categories.

**1. AUTHORITY...** A challenger to a zoning decision can assert the government's lack of general or specific authority to act. Such a challenge presents an *ultra vires* question, which clearly is constitutional. Ultra vires challenges involve substantive inquiry because they dispositively review the foundation of the right by which the government constrains private interests in the possession, use, and enjoyment of an individual parcel of property.

In the zoning setting, a plaintiff may attack a municipality by alleging that it has no power to pass a particular zone regulation for lack of sufficient delegated power under the state enabling statute, by alleging pre-emption of local or state authority, or the like. The same inquiry, of course, can be found in other kinds of cases throughout the range of federal and state regulatory actions arising under the police power and correlative powers ceded to the federal government. This inquiry is analytically a threshold question, not a focus on the particular merits of the governmental act challenged.

**2. PROPER PUBLIC PURPOSE...** The second category of challenges addresses proper public purpose. Zoning laws, for example, were originally attacked as not fitting within the "general welfare" component of the police power's classic triad of basic regulatory purposes: health, safety, and welfare. Once Euclid v. Ambler, 272 U.S. 365 (1926) established that the harmony of planned development constituted a proper, generalized public-welfare purpose, the attacks shifted to attempts to define further, particularized, improper purposes. Such narrower "poison purpose" allegations have included, with varying degrees of success, claims that regulations were "purely aesthetic," were for "purely private purposes," were motivated by a desire to drive down land prices for future condemnation, were racially exclusionary or otherwise invidiously intended to discriminate, or, like some motorcycle helmet prohibitions, impermissibly protected individuals against their own rugged wills. Analogous attacks are regularly posed in other regulatory settings as well. This inquiry as to proper public purpose, too, is a form of threshold question, testing the propriety of the governmental objective rather than the nature of the actual decision itself.

---

4. The text here is developed at greater length in Plater and Norine, Through the Looking Glass of Eminent Domain: Exploring the "Arbitrary and Capricious" Test and Substantive Rationality Review of Governmental Decisions, 16 Envtl. Rev. L.Rev. 661, 707–12 (1989).

**3. MERITS REVIEW: MEANS RATIONALLY RELATED TO ENDS...** The third category of challenges involves attacking a governmental action on its merits for lack of *rational relationship of means to ends....* Where the purposes of challenged governmental actions are perfectly proper, the design of an ordinance or the factual reasoning supporting a decision may nevertheless be insufficiently, illogically or erroneously related to achieving the purposes. Thus zoning acts have been struck down, as applied to specific parcels, when the lines drawn are found to bear no rational nexus to purposes, or when the pattern of regulation has insufficient supporting data or planning. The floodplain safety zone, for example, cannot rationally be applied to hilltop land; a residential zone cannot be applied to land that could never be used for residences. Analytically, moreover, this third means-end inquiry may also incorporate "least drastic means" and equal protection review. Thus, when a zone discriminates against poor people or mobile homes, its distinctions and classifications can be challenged as not rationally related to the purposes of zoning. Beyond zoning, this third inquiry can be widely discerned in judicial declarations that governmental determinations and classifications must "have reasonable relation to a proper legislative purpose, and [be] neither arbitrary nor discriminatory [to satisfy] the requirements of due process," and must "rationally advance...a reasonable and identifiable governmental objective."

**4. PRIVATE BURDEN...** The fourth inquiry, the degree of burden imposed on the individual, is often the emotional heart of substantive review. Its most common manifestation is the allegation of "confiscatory" takings burdens in regulatory cases, asking a question basic to justice and democracy: how far can the collective power of the majority erode the property of the individual for the sake of public well-being? The usual answer in regulatory takings cases is what one of the authors has previously dubbed the "residuum" takings tests.[5] According to these tests, property owners must be left with a beneficial (or "profitable" or "reasonable") remaining use of their regulated property. These various versions of the diminution test require a fair amount of implicit balancing of potential public harms against private property losses, but, if such balancing is done, offer a workable and philosophically defensible test for application far beyond the field of land-use regulation. Of course, when physical appropriation of property is involved under eminent domain, the fourth inquiry is less a balancing than a straightforward measure of governmental payment at fair market value rates to compensate the burdened individual for property rights taken.

**5. PROCEDURAL DUE PROCESS...** Courts also apply procedural due process requirements. One form considers a contextual balance whether government has given enough process — questions of notice, opportunity to contest issues at a hearing, the quantity of hearing procedures available, the clarity of legal standards to be applied, and the opportunity to obtain review of the application of a law to a particular case. A second form of procedural requirements is owed to the courts themselves. As in *Overton Park*, in order for courts to fulfill their judicial review

---

5. Plater, The Takings Issue in a Natural Setting: Floodlines and the Police Power, 52 Texas L. Rev. 201 (1974).

functions government processes must produce a meaningful reviewable record, showing the basis of official actions and that officials have considered all relevant factors in reaching determinations.

These diagnostic categories are not carved in stone, but offer a useful analytical organization that can be applied to the often complex and confusing controversies surrounding the imposition of public power upon private property, as noted in the following materials of this chapter. Do you see why governmental actions that violate Inquiries Number 1, 2, or 3 usually would be declared "void on their face," while violations of the fourth and fifth are usually voided "as applied" to that particular land?

## A. EMINENT DOMAIN CONDEMNATIONS

Eminent domain is one important subcomponent of the police power. Governments occasionally use the eminent domain power in the service of environmental goals, for instance to condemn land for parks. More frequently, however, the condemnation power is used in operations that do not take sufficient account of environmental values — cutting highways through wilderness, building publicly owned office towers in low-income neighborhoods, siting regional trash dumps or power plants, creating development parks in bucolic areas to attract industry, or (through delegation of power to private companies), condemning rights-of-way for power lines, pipelines, ditches, and drains, or taking private lands so that mining companies can operate strip mines. In each case, environmentalists would like to raise some legal questions.

### Section 1. THE DOMAIN OF DEFERENCE

The power of the public to appropriate private property via condemnation is a universal attribute of sovereign governments, clearly necessary to the functioning of a modern state.[6] As a result, governmental eminent domain decisions in the United States have generally received a most respectful reception in courts, both state and federal. Given that the government concedes that it will pay just compensation for a taking, many courts in effect declare that they have no further questions.[7] The governmental agency's assertions of condemning authority, proper public purpose, and rational choice of means are, in practice, "well-nigh unassailable."[8]

6. Kohl v. United States, 91 U.S. 367, 371–372 (1875); the following text has been adapted from Plater and Norine, Through the Looking Glass of Eminent Domain: Exploring the "Arbitrary and Capricious" Test and Substantive Rationality Review of Governmental Decisions,"16 Envtl Aff. L. Rev. 661, 662-663 (1989).

7. The general invulnerability of eminent domain appears to exist irrespective of which level of condemning authority is involved — federal, state, local, or public utility corporation. Analytically, as well, there are no meaningful differences between these condemnors. Each must have a proper grant of authority and must satisfy the other three categories of police power tests. Judicial review of the rationality of the condemnor's site-selection choice is typically very deferential. In most cases, condemnees cannot require a specific showing why a particular site was not chosen. The Colorado Supreme Court, however, has suggested that public utility condemnations may deserve more scrutiny than governmental takings. Arizona-Colorado Land & Cattle Co. v. District Court, 511 P.2d 23, 24–25 (Colo. 1975).

8. Berman v. Parker, 348 U.S. 26, 35 (1954).

The usual eminent-domain case is cut and dried. The condemning entity files a complaint in court against a parcel of land; the "remedy" sought is a court order transferring title. For the condemnation to succeed, the court need only be convinced —

(1) that the condemning entity, which is normally either a unit of government or a public utility, has the power of eminent domain under the applicable statutes, and follows the necessary procedures for its exercise;

(2) that the condemnation is for a stated proper public purpose;

(3) that the condemnation decision is not "arbitrary and capricious," (or, in some states, whether the condemnation is "necessary," usually an inquiry at the level of "are highways necessary?" rather than "is this particular land essential if a highway is to be built?"); and

(4) that appropriate just compensation will be paid.

The location, amount of land to be taken, and ecological effects of condemnations are normally not open to question. Thus in the vast majority of cases the opponents of condemnation can only stand and fight on the amount of compensation trying to make the taking more expensive. This is often impossible for environmentalists, who do not own the subject property, and it is not very satisfying anyway, since money may be small comfort for the loss of a marsh or forest.

## Section 2. CHALLENGING AN EMINENT DOMAIN CONDEMNATION

The wonder is that eminent domain condemnation, a governmental power that is so drastic and has such wide-ranging consequences, has been subjected to so little active judicial scrutiny. There are a variety of legal avenues, however, that potentially may be used to open up governmental eminent domain decisions to substantive judicial review, giving challengers the opportunity to nullify condemnations on the merits.

The primary target of such substantive challenges is the question of rationality or arbitrariness. If a court allows propertyowners a serious hearing on their claim of irrationality, and weighs that defense according to the standard tests of arbitrariness applied in other administrative law settings, substantive challenges can be successful.

One approach is available where propertyowners can claim that their land serves quasi-public environmental purposes. When one government tries to condemn another governmental entity's property, courts determine the winner under the "paramount public use" balance. Several courts have extended this defense to private lands.[9]

More broadly, some state courts matter-of-factly allow defenses alleging that a particular taking is "unnecessary."[10] Viewed analytically, however, there seem to

---

9. See Texas Eastern Transm. Co. v. Wildlife Preserves, 225 A.2d 130 (N.J. 1966); Merrill v. City of Manchester, 499 A.2d 216 (N.H. 1985)(the court weighed the "recreational, scenic and ecological importance" of the private land dedicated to open space preservation, against a proposed town industrial park taking); Oxford County Agricultural Society v. School District, 211 A.2d 893 (Me. 1965), and Middlebury College v. Central Power Corporation 143 A. 384 (Vt. 1928).

10. See Plater and Norine, Looking Glass, 16 Envtl. Aff. L. Rev. 661, 689–693.

be compelling arguments for a lessening of deference in federal and state courts generally.

Two hypothetical cases[11] help to set out the legal basis for serious substantive review of condemnation decisions.

**A MEANS-ENDS FACTUAL IMPLAUSIBILITY CASE...** Assume that a federal agency with an express statutory mandate to "promote regional economic development" decided to condemn 38,000 acres of farm land to build a regional industrial park for future corporate tenants.[12] The 300+ farm families that owned the land would typically make a barrage of complaints — that this is a "land-grab," a taking of private land to be turned over to other private interests, a taking of "excess" land, a "socialistic" governmental land speculation, and so on. Defense attorneys in eminent domain cases turn these verbal complaints into defensive legal arguments, all focused on alleged improper public purposes and all dead losers.[13]

Assume, however, that the agency had previously used exactly the same rationale to condemn a total of more than 200 square miles of farmland for four other neighboring industrial parks, *and that virtually no industrial development occurred*. These condemnation defendants realistically cannot argue that industrial development is not a proper public policy or public purpose, but they have a further argument: they should now be allowed to try to prove that condemnation of their lands is not rationally related to the accomplishment of the agency's expressed public purpose. That is, whereas a court initially could well have deferred to the agency on its first industrial parks, now that the factual record clearly shows their implausibility, private property owners must be allowed at least a practical chance to challenge the rational basis of such condemnations in court.

The private property owners' defense straightforwardly questions the rational basis of the agency's condemnation: that based on the factual record no governmental official could reasonably believe that the governmental choice of means — condemnation of these lands — would achieve the avowed governmental ends of industrial development. The fundamental problem of modern eminent domain law, however, is that, at least in practical terms, under the deferential standard of review applied in condemnation takings the defendants in most federal courts today would not be allowed to take even this first step. The agency's discretion and the rationality of its decisions to condemn, short of lunacy, are supported in court by the strongest presumption of validity.[14]

**A RATIONAL ALTERNATIVES CASE...** The second paradigm requires the reviewing court to apply the rationality rule in a contextual setting, reviewing how an agency has chosen between several competing alternatives that admittedly would each achieve the public purpose but are irrational when viewed in context. Poletown

11. The text is adapted from 16 Envtl. Aff. L. Rev. 661, at 671–677.

12. This hypothetical is, in fact, the case of TVA's Columbia and Tellico Dam Projects. See Chapter Fourteen. By acquiring more than sixty square miles for the Tellico project, only 16,000 acres of which would be flooded, TVA projected that it could resell up to 35 square miles of condemned farmlands to a hypothetical industrial city to be called "Timberlake," theoretically to be built by the Boeing Corporation with congressional subsidies.

13. Since Berman v. Parker, 348 U.S. 26, 35 (1954), legislative purpose and means are perceived valid.

14. Some state courts allow review of the rationality of condemnation decisions, though most have followed the federal courts' extremely deferential example. Use of the federal Administrative Procedures Act §706 and its state corollaries could in the future help open up such judicial review.

*Detroit's Poletown area, before and after. General Motors and the city used eminent domain powers to eliminate everything standing on the 465 acres of this integrated low-income residential-commercial neighborhood — the homes of 4,200 people, 144 local businesses, 16 churches, two schools, and a hospital — in order to build a Cadillac assembly plant, despite the existence of alternative undeveloped industrial park sites in the area.*

Neighborhood Council v. City of Detroit illustrates this paradigm.[15]

Assume that a federal redevelopment agency, working through the auspices of a city government, decides to encourage the construction of a new job-creating, manufacturing plant within city limits. It decides to condemn and raze an urban neighborhood of fifty square blocks — containing 1,100 homes, 144 businesses, 16 churches including two cathedrals, two schools, and a hospital — causing a substantial amount of personal and commercial distress, in order to turn over the 500-acre parcel to a major automobile manufacturer for construction of a Cadillac assembly plant.

The property owners might, as usual, attack the taking as based on an improper public purpose — a "private use," for example — and, as usual, would lose. They might argue further that condemnation payments will never provide sufficient funds for replacement of their homes and businesses at relocated sites, but, in the absence of special statutory provisions, this argument also fails because just compensation is assessed according to the market value of what is taken with no guarantee of relocation or replacement costs.

Assume further, however, that at the time the officials decided to condemn and raze the neighborhood there were at least four other empty industrial sites of 500 acres each available within city limits with equivalent access to rail, highways, and utilities. The landowners may now make a further argument: that, given the drastic burden imposed upon them, and the available alternative sites that cannot be rationally distinguished from their neighborhood's site (except that they are *less* expensive to develop given the cost of condemnation to the city), no official could rationally have chosen to condemn their homes and businesses rather than go to one of the other four open sites.[16]

---

15. See 304 N.W.2d 455 (Mich. 1981)(per curiam); see also Crosby v. Young, 512 F. Supp. 1363, 1374 (E.D. Mich. 1981). For a factual chronicle of Poletown, see Poletown, 304 N.W.2d at 464–71 (Ryan, J., dissenting). See Jeanie Wylie, Poletown: Community Betrayed, Univ. of Illinois Press (1989); Bukowczyk, The Decline and Fall of a Detroit Neighborhood: Poletown vs. GM and the City of Detroit, 41 Wash. & Lee L. Rev. 49 (1984); Poletown Lives, (documentary film), Information Factory, 3512 Courville St., Detroit MI 48224. General Motors, despite the desperate efforts of property owners and Ralph Nader, successfully induced a federally-funded redevelopment condemnation project to give the corporation land in Poletown, a stable, mixed-race, low income neighborhood of Detroit, to build a Cadillac plant.

16. "The Poletown environmental impact statement identified nine potential sites for the Cadillac factory, but, from the beginning, General Motors' site criteria were so particular to the Poletown site that only it would fit. The company demanded 'an area of between 450 and 500 acres; a rectangular shape (3/4 mile by 1 mile); access to a long-haul railroad line; and access to the freeway system.'" 304 N.W.2d at 460 (Fitzgerald, J., dissenting).

Never clarified in the legal battle was the fact that others of the nine potential sites were basically "green field" sites fitting all but the rectangular criterion. In addition, they were also empty of houses, churches, and small businesses and thus available without the massive disruption of Poletown; but they all were rejected at GM's insistence, basically because they were not rectangular. Was shape a critical or a superficial requirement? When Detroit's planning office staffers inquired informally of GM, they were told that the corporation was insisting on a rectangle so that it could use the same blueprint layout of parking lots and assembly units as at an existing GM plant in Oklahoma. But could not the design of parking lots be shifted to fit the shape of the existing Detroit industrial sites? They could, the GM staff said, or a parking structure could be built instead of open lots to accommodate the plant worker's needs at the less disruptive sites. But GM adamantly refused to consider shifting the parking lot layout or building a parking structure. The latter could cause congestion, and either would require a modification of the Oklahoma blueprints, which the company simply declined to do. 'Once we had decided what we wanted, we would not retrench,' said one GM employee." Plater & Norine, Through the Looking Glass of Eminent Domain: Exploring the "Arbitrary and Capricious" Test and Substantive Rationality Review of Governmental Decisions, 16 Envtl. Aff. L. Rev. at 675, n. 37.

Such an argument is *not* a means-end argument that the condemnation of Parcel A will not in fact or logic serve the avowed public purpose of industrial development, but rather that, viewed in the factual context of drastic costs and available alternative sites at B, C, D, and E, no rational official could have picked A. This version of rationality review is analytically more complex and difficult, dealing not with basic factual implausibility but with a judicial cost-benefit-alternatives review. In effect, it involves judicial acknowledgment of a "less-drastic-means" inquiry in review of some governmental condemnation actions. Deference to governmental decisions is an even greater consideration here, but the fundamental question remains: if to serve the legitimate, expressed public purpose of industrial development a site must be chosen, but in light of the disproportionate private and public burdens no rational official could have thought that Parcel A was preferable for that legitimate purpose, doesn't a defendant have the right to ask a court to scrutinize the substance of the condemnation decision and rescind it if it fails the test?

These two paradigms present instances in which private property owners would want at least the opportunity to go forward with the burden of proving that a governmental decision is not rational, in terms showing that a rational official could not so have decided. In both these cases, however, the "arbitrary and capricious" standard would be honored in the breach. Federal courts currently do not take on a particularized rational basis scrutiny of governmental condemnation decisions, but instead defer in general terms to the exercise of official discretion, leaving condemnation defendants with no practical substantive review of takings decisions.

The paradigms are admittedly rather extreme examples of eminent domain condemnation, but such cases permit clearer insights into condemnation review. Lest they be thought hyperbolic, moreover, it should be remembered that both have actually occurred and may well occur again.

#### COMMENTARY AND QUESTIONS

1. **The legal basis for more active review.** In the *Poletown* case, the arguments actually made in court for the neighborhood were almost entirely based on challenges to the constitutionality of the public purpose in giving land to a private corporation, and predictably came to nought. The Supreme Court, however, implicitly accepted a substantive due process test for eminent domain decisions in upholding Hawaii's land reform act: in order to meet constitutional requirements it must be shown that "the Legislature *rationally could have believed* that the [Act] would promote its objective." Hawaii v. Midkiff, 467 U.S. 229, 242 (1984) (O'Connor, J., emphasis in original). Under administrative procedure acts, moreover, courts are directed to review and rescind government agency actions found to be "arbitrary and capricious." 5 U.S.C.A. §706(a)(2), Administrative law interprets that test far more rigorously than eminent domain case law does, so the door is open for administrative law challenges of agency condemnations, and, by natural extension, of public utility condemnations.

2. **Uncorking judicial review of condemnation.** Is this an area of practice that is about to awaken, after a century of torpor, under the pressures of environmental challenges to governmental condemnation decisions? Once judicial scrutiny is let loose in an area previously characterized by deference, do you realize how difficult it might be later to get the genie back into the bottle? In practical terms, how much would governments be burdened by the necessity of defending their condemnation decisions?

3. **The politics of eminent domain.** The political backdrop to environmentalists' efforts to open up judicial review of condemnation is interesting. On one hand, eminent domain is a longstanding rhetorical bugbear of "conservatives." On the other, those who get hit by government condemnations are rarely the wealthy and powerful, as in highway and porkbarrel water projects. Often, in fact, as in the *Poletown* case, private corporate interests stand foursquare with government in favor of condemnation, opposing private propertyowners. Indeed, as in *Poletown*, the business bloc may have initiated and controlled the government's exercise of eminent domain from the start. In *Poletown*, who were the conservatives and who the liberals? Does anyone still know, in the environmental era, what those labels mean?

## B. INVERSE CONDEMNATION: A CONSTITUTIONAL TORT?

At first glance, inverse condemnation scarcely resembles eminent domain. The facts in the following material resemble tort cases, not constitutional law. Governmental actions here result in noise, vibrations, smells, and general disruptions to the neighboring environs.

Why then make these into constitutional cases? The simple answer is: to get around sovereign immunity. If the federal, state, or local government performing a governmental function has not consented to be sued, the immunity doctrine is a defense to tort actions.[17] The right to challenge government action on *constitutional* grounds, however, remains available.

Why call it "inverse" condemnation? In an ordinary condemnation case, the government decides it wants someone's property, and sues to get it. As part of its suit, the government declares its willingness to pay the value of the property as set by the court. But what if, instead of suing to get the property, the government has in effect simply gone ahead and taken it physically? In that case, the victim of the taking may sue the government for compensation, and since the government becomes the defendant instead of the plaintiff, the proceeding is called inverse condemnation or "reverse condemnation." The plaintiff is effectively saying, "The government has in reality condemned my property by physically taking it, without admitting it, so I want to sue them in court, to make them pay me eminent domain compensation."

---

17. The availability and extent of governmental liability, short of constitutional claims, depends on the vagaries of statutory and common law exceptions to immunity.

Of course, it may be that the reason the government didn't offer compensation was that it didn't think what it was doing was condemnation. As in the following cases, the government may have done something, like running an airport, without considering significant effects on private property.

In the usual eminent domain case, the only issue is the amount of compensation. In inverse condemnation cases, however, there is a prior issue: was there a taking at all?

### Thornburg v. Port of Portland
Supreme Court of Oregon, 1962
233 Ore. 178, 376 P.2d 100

GOODWIN, J. The issues in their broadest sense concern rights of landowners adjacent to airports and the rights of the public in the airspace near the ground. Specifically, we must decide whether a noise-nuisance can amount to a taking.

The Port of Portland owns and operates the Portland International Airport. It has the power of eminent domain. It has used this power to surround itself with a substantial curtilage, but its formal acquisition stopped short of the land of the plaintiffs. For the purposes of this case, the parties have assumed that the Port is immune from ordinary tort liability....

The plaintiffs own and reside in a dwelling house located about 6,000 feet beyond the end of one runway and directly under the glide path of aircraft using it. Their land lies about 1,500 feet beyond the end of a second runway, but about 1,000 feet to one side of the glide path of aircraft using that runway. The plaintiffs contend that flights from both runways have resulted in a taking of their property. Their principal complaint is that the noise from jet aircraft makes their land unusable. The jets use a runway the center line of which, if extended, would pass about 1,000 feet to one side of the plaintiffs' land. Some planes pass directly over the plaintiffs' land, but these are not, for the most part, the civilian and military jets which cause the most noise.

The plaintiffs' case proceeded on two theories: (1) Systematic flights directly over their land cause a substantial interference with their use and enjoyment of that land. This interference constitutes a nuisance. Such a nuisance, if persisted in by a private party, could ripen into a prescription. Such a continuing nuisance, when maintained by government, amounts to the taking of an easement, or, more precisely, presents a jury question whether there is a taking. (2) Systematic flights which pass close to their land, even though not directly overhead, likewise constitute the taking of an easement, for the same reasons, and upon the same authority.

The Port of Portland contends that its activities do not constitute the taking of easements in the plaintiffs' land. The Port argues: (1) The plaintiffs have no right to exclude or protest flights directly over their land, if such flights are so high as to be in the public domain, i.e., within navigable airspace as defined by federal law.[18] (2) The plaintiffs have no right to protest flights which do not cross the airspace above their land, since these could commit no trespass in any event. Accordingly, the Port contends, there is no interference with any legally protected interest of the plaintiffs and thus no taking of any property for which the plaintiffs are enti-

18. See Civil Aeronautics Act, 49 U.S.C.A. §551(a)(7)(1952). One FAA rule fixed 500 feet as the minimum safe altitude over persons, vehicles, and structures. 14 CFR 60.107. Congress has, during all material times, denominated the airspace 500 feet above any person, vessel, vehicle or structure in other than congested areas as navigable airspace which is subject to a public right of transit.

tled to compensation. In short, the Port's theory is that the plaintiffs must endure the noise of the nearby airport with the same forbearance that is required of those who live near highways and railroads....

The trial court proceeded as if the rights of the plaintiffs were limited by the imaginary lines that would describe a cube of airspace exactly 500 feet high and bounded on four sides by perpendicular extensions of the surface boundaries of their land. The trial court thus in effect adapted the law of trespass to the issues presented in this case, and held that unless there was a continuing trespass within the described cube of space there could be no recovery. The trial court...adopted the view that even if there was a nuisance, a nuisance could not give rise to a taking....

Since United States v. Causby, 328 U.S. 256 (1946), and particularly since Griggs v. Allegheny County, 369 U.S. 84 (1962), we know that easements can be taken by repeated low-level flights over private land...[and] compensation must be paid to the owners of the lands thus burdened....

It is not so well settled, however, that the easements discussed in the *Causby* and *Griggs* cases are easements to impose upon lands near an airport a servitude of noise. Courts operating upon the theory that repeated trespasses form the basis of the easement have not found it necessary to decide whether a repeated nuisance, which may or may not have been an accompaniment of a trespass, could equally give rise to a servitude upon neighboring land. It must be remembered that in both the *Causby* and *Griggs* cases the flights were virtually at tree-top level. Accordingly, both decisions could perhaps be supported on trespass theories exclusively. Following the *Causby* case, several federal district courts held that while repeated flights at low levels directly over private land may amount to a taking for which compensation must be paid, repeated flights nearby but not directly overhead must be endured as mere "damages" which, for various reasons, may not be compensable....

The Tenth Circuit...held...that there must be a trespass before there can be a taking. Batten v. United States, 306 F.2d 580 (10th Cir. 1962). As pointed out in a dissent by Chief Judge Murrah, the interference proven was substantial enough to impose a servitude upon the lands of the plaintiffs, and under the *Causby* and *Griggs* cases equally could have constituted a taking.... We believe the dissenting view in the *Batten* case presents the better-reasoned analysis of the legal principles involved, and that if the majority view in the *Batten* case can be defended it must be defended frankly upon the ground that considerations of public policy justify the result: i.e., that private rights must yield to public convenience in this class of cases....

While not every wrong committed by government will amount to a taking of private property, there are some wrongs which do constitute a taking.... We must decide whether a nuisance can ever constitute a taking.... If the government substantially deprives the owner of the use of his land, such deprivation is a taking for which the government must pay. If, on the other hand, the government merely commits some tort which does not deprive the owner of the use of his land, then there is no taking.

Therefore, unless there is some reason of public policy which bars compensation in cases of governmental nuisance as a matter of law, there is a question, in each case, as a matter of fact, whether or not the governmental activity complained of has resulted in so substantial an interference with use and enjoyment of one's land as to amount to a taking of private property for public use. This factual question, again barring some rule which says we may not ask it, is equally relevant whether the taking is trespassory or by a nuisance. A nuisance can be such an invasion of the rights of a possessor as to amount to a taking, in theory at least, any time a possessor is in fact ousted from the enjoyment of his land....

The plaintiffs concede that single-instance torts, as torts, are not compensable. Inverse condemnation, however, provides the remedy where an injunction would not be in the public interest, and where the continued interference amounts to a taking for which the constitution demands a remedy. In summary, a taking occurs whenever government acts in such a way as substantially to deprive an owner of the useful possession of that which he owns, either by repeated trespasses or by repeated non-trespassory invasions called "nuisance."...

If we accept, as we must upon established principles of the law of servitudes, the validity of the propositions that a noise can be a nuisance; that a nuisance can give rise to an easement; and that a noise coming straight down from above one's land can ripen into a taking if it is persistent enough and aggravated enough, then logically the same kind and degree of interference with the use and enjoyment of one's land can also be a taking even though the noise vector may come from some direction other than the perpendicular.

If a landowner has a right to be free from unreasonable interference caused by noise, as we hold that he has, then when does the noise burden become so unreasonable that the government must pay for the privilege of being permitted to continue to make the noise? Logically, the answer has to be given by the trier of fact.... The balancing of private rights and public necessity is not a novel problem.

Whether expressed in so many words or not, the principle found in the *Causby* [and] *Griggs*...cases is that when the government conducts an activity upon its own land which, after balancing the question of reasonableness, is sufficiently disturbing to the use and enjoyment of neighboring lands to amount to a taking thereof, then the public, and not the subservient landowner, should bear the cost of such public benefit.... The real question was not one of perpendicular extension of surface boundaries into the airspace, but a question of reasonableness based upon nuisance theories. In effect, the inquiry should have been whether the government had undertaken a course of conduct on its own land which, in simple fairness to its neighbors, required it to obtain more land so that the substantial burdens of the activity would fall upon public land, rather than upon that of involuntary contributors who happen to lie in the path of progress....

Logically, it makes no difference to a plaintiff disturbed in the use of his property whether the disturbing flights pass 501 feet or 499 feet above his land. If he is in fact ousted from the legitimate enjoyment of his land, it is to him an academic matter that the planes which have ousted him did not fly below 500 feet. The rule adopted by the majority of the state and federal courts is, then, an arbitrary one. The barring of actions when the flights are above 500 feet is also difficult to reconcile with the theory that recovery should be based upon nuisance concepts rather than upon the trespass theory which we have rejected. Whether a plaintiff is entitled to recover should depend upon the fact of a taking, and not upon an arbitrary rule. The ultimate question is whether there was a sufficient interference with the landowner's use and enjoyment to be a taking.... Congress may very properly declare certain airspace to be in the public domain for navigational purposes, but it does not necessarily follow that rights of navigation may be exercised unreasonably.... There is a point beyond which such power may not be exercised without compensation. *Causby*. The same limitation applies to lesser governmental agencies....

PERRY, J., dissenting.... It should be noted that to reach a reversal of the judgment of the trial court, the majority rely upon the law of nuisance. The majority seem to admit that this has never been the law of this state, but argue that it should be.... Where a flight directly over the land, by reason of noise and vibration, can be said in fact to cause serious interference in the owner's use and enjoyment of the property, it is a trespass, which is a constitutional taking, and requires full compensation. In the matter before us, however, after searching the record, I am unable to find any evidence that would support a judgment of a taking, based on interference with the plaintiffs' use and enjoyment of the land by airplane flights above the 500-foot level....

That the definition of a constitutional taking has consistently been grounded in the appropriation of an interest in the realty itself has been a rule of law of long standing under the Constitution of the United States is shown by the case of Portsmouth Harbor Land & Hotel Co. v. United States, 260 U.S. 327 (1922). In this case damages were sought in inverse condemnation because of the establishment of a fort in which there were gun emplacements and shells were fired over and across the plaintiff's land. Mr. Justice Holmes, speaking for the court, said: "This is a claim in respect of land which, or an interest in which, is alleged to have been taken by the United States Government...."

A nuisance, although a tort, does not contemplate a physical invasion of the property of another, but the use of a person's own property in such a way as to interfere with another's free enjoyment of his property.... Practically all human activities engaged in carrying out a commercial enterprise may interfere with someone's enjoyment of his property. It is the right of an owner of land to use his land in any lawful manner, and it is only when the manner of use creates a grave interference with another's enjoyment of his property that the law will seek to redress this type of wrong. This is a natural requirement of organized society. There must be some give and take to promote the well-being of all. The underlying basis in nuisance law is the common-sense thought that in organized society there must be an adjustment between reasonable use and personal discomfort. No such consideration is involved in the law of trespass.

Trespass of property which, as has been pointed out, effects a taking in a constitutional sense, comprehends a physical invasion of the property either by the person or by causing a physical object to enter upon or over the property of another.... Therefore, it is the taking of an owner's possessory interest in land as compared with interfering with an owner's use and enjoyment of his land that distinguishes a trespass which is a "taking" from a nuisance, which is not....Nuisance [is based on] the balancing of the interests of owners.... Such considerations are foreign to the law of trespass.... Where a permanent trespass is committed by government, the constitution will not permit a balancing of the value of the taking for the benefit of the public against the interests of an owner. The owner must be fully compensated for his loss....

A nuisance takes none of the title in the property. The full legal title rests in the owner. If the nuisance is abated in any manner, the damage suffered has ended and the land is again restored to its full value to the owner. On the other hand, if there is a taking, the property right of ownership or some interest therein has been transferred from the owner to the sovereign, and does not again revert to the original owner even though the use to which the property has been put by the sovereign ceases....

COMMENTARY AND QUESTIONS

1. **Nuisance as a "servitude."** The majority and dissent agree that a plane's physical trespass will constitute the taking of a servitude (more properly labelled an "easement"). They split over the rather technical point of whether a nuisance can do likewise. The distinction echoes a principle of eminent domain compensation allowing extensive recovery for "consequential" damages if government has condemned any piece of your real property, however tiny, but none if no land is taken. Both opinions ignore a fairly well-established line of cases holding that nuisances can create prescriptive easements to pollute, and that government can take easements that are not permanent. Both recognize that nuisance law involves more balancing than trespass law, although neither is very clear about intentional nuisance doctrine. To what extent should airport inverse condemnation cases balance the noise and vibrations suffered by plaintiffs against the public's need for an airport? Or should any substantial burden on neighbors be compensated as a cost of doing business? Should it make any difference that government, rather than a private entity, operates the harmful airport?

2. **Extending physical inverse condemnation theories.** There has been some limited extension of the inverse condemnation remedy beyond airport cases. Compensation has been ordered for loss of access (where a public road was converted to a limited-access highway), and loss of light and air (where a bridge or overpass was built alongside a house), even though no part of the plaintiffs' land or airspace was physically invaded. The court notes "the forbearance that is required of those who live near highways and railroads," likewise facing dust, noise, vibrations, flashing lights, and severe losses in property value. Are these compensable now? If so, the costs could bankrupt public transit programs.

Inverse condemnation claims can also arise in the wild. Can't it be argued that the government takes an easement in my property without compensation when it forbids me from fencing out the antelope that want to eat my grass (giving the antelope an easement of access over my land), or when I am forbidden to shoot the endangered grey wolf that still thinks my property is her territory and eats one of my cows every week, or when the Forest Service adopts a "let-burn" policy for national forests so that my private trees and vacation cabin are destroyed by fire? See U.S. v. Lawrence, 848 F.2d 1502 (10th Cir. 1988) (antelope); Christy v. Hodel, 857 F.2d 1324 (9th Cir. 1988) (grizzlies); Wiener, Uncle Sam and Forest Fires, 15 Envtl. L. 623 (1985); Keiter and Holscher, Wolf Recovery under the Endangered Species Act: a Study in Contemporary Federalism, 11 Public Land L. Rev. 19 (1990). This kind of claim has played a major role in constitutional challenges to "regulatory takings" (see below).

Pushing the inverse condemnation doctrine further, consider the fact that many Americans are starting to worry about clusters of leukemia and other ailments that have been correlated in some cases with the presence of high-tension electrical transmission facilities. If clients are worried about high electro-magnetic fields (EMF) on their property caused by utility transmission lines, but cannot prove tort liability, can an attorney file an inverse condemnation claim for a "taking" by the public utility company (which has the power of eminent domain) of an "electromagnetic easement" of right of way over their property? See Brodeur, Annals of Radiation: Calamity on Meadow Street, July 9, 1990 New Yorker Magazine at 50. Or likewise against the federal government for low frequency radio transmissions? Wisconsin v. Weinberger, 745 F.2d 412 (7th Cir. 1984). Or even to use a physical taking argument to circumvent sovereign immunity in tort cases like Nevin v. U.S., 696 F.2d 1229 (9th Cir. 1987), where members of the public were injured by clandestine governmental testing of bacillary and chemical agents in urban public areas? (As to the latter, public notice is now required by law. 52 U.S.C.A. §1520.)

## C. CHALLENGES TO REGULATIONS AS "UNCONSTITUTIONAL TAKINGS"

### Section 1. REGULATORY TAKINGS AND WETLANDS

Determining how far the collective power of the majority can intrude upon individual rights has always been one of the classic problems of democracy. When government regulates private property under the police power, tensions tend to get particularly hot because it does not generally pay for the privilege. Few Americans actively welcome the state's directives about how they should use their land, especially when restrictions get in the way of private profits. In modern America, where rugged frontier individualism lives on in private property doctrines that built the world's greatest economy, environmental regulations may be particularly resented because they are relatively new to the scene, dealing with public "rights" and objectives that the market economy had never heard of before Silent Spring.

"Regulatory takings" attacks on environmental statutes and regulations are likely to occur wherever private property rights are impacted, which is to say they arise throughout the field. When a state prohibits development in wetlands, when the federal government prohibits billboards on interstate highways, when a local town council prohibits junkyards, or when a government entity proposes to restrict any of a host of other concerns — automobile pollution, trade in endangered species ivory, use of off-road vehicles on public lands, destruction of historic buildings, biogenetic experimentation and drug development, agricultural pesticides and herbicides, destruction of wildlife and its habitat, air and water pollution, stripmining, throwaway bottles, and so on — in each case the "invalid takings" argument will be heard loudly in the legislative and administrative process. These complaints about government high-handedness are sometimes coupled with a dire warning from lobbyists that if the restriction is passed, those who vote for it as well as the agency regulators may find themselves personally liable for damages for violating the regulatees' civil rights.

Often the mere threat of a lawsuit raising a takings challenge is enough to dissuade legislators and city councils from passing environmental measures, even where the proposed regulation clearly would comply with judicial takings tests. Often, however, the legal tests of validity and invalidity are indeed not clear. As Professor Sax has written, "the 'crazy-quilt pattern' of Supreme Court doctrine has effectively been acknowledged by the Court itself, which has developed the habit of introducing its uniformly unsatisfactory opinions in this area with the understatement that 'no rigid rules' or 'set formula' are available to determine where [valid] regulation ends and [invalid] taking begins."[19]

When a restriction is actually challenged in court, the argument typically begins with the allegation of economic loss. (The first three areas of police power tests — authority, proper public purpose, and the restriction's reasonable relationship of means to ends — are relevant but usually are in effect conceded.) The attack alleges that even though the restriction does not take physical possession of all or part of the private property (which in virtually all cases would clearly require eminent domain compensation), it so restricts property rights that it amounts to a taking under the due process clause and the eminent domain clause of the Fifth Amendment and their state corollaries. The test is the same under either clause, and usually turns in some manner on the amount of property loss, viewed in a vacuum. If a court finds a restriction excessive, or confiscatory, the government can accept an equitable remedy nullifying the law as applied to the subject property, or agree to pay damages for the invalid taking (which explains why these verdicts are often confusingly referred to as "inverse condemnation" or "eminent domain").[20]

Paradoxically, although courts go to extraordinary lengths to defer to and uphold eminent domain actions, as seen above in Subchapter A, the judicial approach to regulatory acts is discernibly more critical. Given a loss of property values — an inevitability in most police power settings — many courts in effect shift the burden to government, ignoring the usual presumption of validity for governmental acts. Takings challenges can be significant in all areas of government, but nowhere more pressingly and vividly than in the field of environmental protection.

Although an inquiry into regulatory takings could be based in any of dozens of environmental fields, wetlands protection regulations are chosen here as the vehicle for raising some of the tough questions presented — questions of property law, private rights, public rights, democracy, fairness, and justice.

### President's Council on Environmental Quality, Our Nation's Wetlands
#### 1–2, 19–28, 50 (1978)[21]

The early settlers on this continent found a land of extraordinary physical beauty and fertility. Sparkling wild rivers coursed through mature forests, the woods teemed with game, and fish thrived in estuaries and the pure waters of mountain lakes....

Today we know that the gifts of clean water, fertile land, and bountiful energy supplies are not inexhaustible.... There has grown an increasing awareness of the

---

19. Sax, Takings and the Police Power, 74 Yale L.J. 36, 37 (1964).

20. The *remedies* sought in regulatory challenges can be the same as in inverse condemnation and eminent domain cases: damages for the taking, or injunctions to block the government action. But the substantive elements of the claims are very different in the regulatory and the physical taking settings.

21. Perhaps because wetlands protection was identified as an area of marked controversy between developers and conservationists, this report — produced during the Carter years — was quickly recalled and sequestered in 1981 by the Reagan administration.

SOUTH FLORIDA WATER MANAGEMENT DISTRICT

*An extensive wetland area, all privately-owned lands, lying ready for draining and development. Limited to their natural state, the wetlands have low market value. If drained, they may increase from ten to a hundred times in value.*

*This wetland overview happens to be the Kissimmee River wetlands of south-central Florida shortly before they were channelized and drained at government expense in 1961 by the Army Corps of Engineers. The drainage project, which had been strongly opposed by environmentalists, created immensely valuable private lands. It also turned out to create a nightmare. The natural meandering streams and wetlands had served as a giant natural filter absorbing and cleaning the water of fertilizer runoffs, other nutrients, and pollution. Without the natural system, Lake Okechobee, a major water source for South Florida, immediately began to choke up with pollution, organic detritus, and eutrophication effects.*

*Now Corps and Florida officials are attempting to return much of the river system to its original state, hoping to save public water supplies. To restore the river, however, will require $343.6 million (the 1961 channelizing cost less than $30 million), much of the current cost is for governmental compensation payable to private landowners for loss of dryland market values initially created by the public drainage project itself.*

need for making conscious, informed choices about further modification of the natural environment. Inland and coastal wetlands — only yesterday considered useless — are now seen as valuable endangered natural resources. Estimates of irreversibly altered or destroyed wetlands in the 48 continental states have already reached 40 to 50 percent.... Of California's original 3.5 million wetland acres, in 1954 only 450,000 remained. In 1959 it was estimated that 45 percent of Connecticut's coastal marshes had been lost since a 1914 survey. At current rates of destruction, it was predicted that only 14 percent might remain by the year 2000. Surveys disclosed that the Rainwater Basin of south-central Nebraska had lost over 80 percent of its marshes by the 1960s. Southeastern Wisconsin had lost

61 percent by 1968. An estimated one-half the wetlands in the prairie pothole region of the United States had been drained by 1950. It is estimated that 35,000 acres of prime prairie wetlands are now being sacrificed each year. A survey conducted by the Fish and Wildlife Service in 1974 revealed that over 40 percent of the potholes existing in 1964 in western Minnesota had been destroyed in that 10-year period....

Many former marshes and swamps are [today] vacation homes and marinas. Other wetlands are used as dumping grounds.... With greater affluence and increased population, the pressures for development of wetlands — for agricultural production, for highways, for residential and commercial building sites, for ports, for marinas, for parking lots, for industries and power plants which require large quantities of cooling water — seem destined to increase....

Evaluating all these uses is not easy. Clearly it is blatantly wasteful to turn a productive wetland into a dump. But it is harder to assign relative values to leaving a wetland in its natural state or using it for luxurious waterfront dwellings. Still more difficult is balancing the values between natural wetland and highly productive cultivated farmland. The results of past practices, recent scientific discoveries, and our changing priorities must all weigh in decisions on how much to conserve of the remainder of our wetland heritage — for the benefit of society as a whole and for the use and enjoyment of future generations.

We do know that wetlands are vital fish and wildlife habitats. Two-thirds of the commercially important fish and shellfish harvested along the Atlantic and in the Gulf of Mexico depend on coastal estuaries and their wetlands for food sources, for spawning grounds, for nurseries for the young, or for all these critical purposes; for the Pacific coast, the figure is almost one-half. Wetlands provide essential resting, wintering, and nesting grounds for many species of migratory waterfowl, other waterbirds, and many songbirds. They are among the most productive ecosystems in the world. They are important in maintenance of ground water supplies and water purification. Marshes and swamps along coasts, rivers, and lakes protect shorelines and banks from erosion. Wetlands also have the capacity to store flood waters temporarily and in some instances to reduce the volume and severity of floods.

The less tangible values of wetlands may be classified as recreational, educational, scientific, and aesthetic. It is curious that the sight of tall marsh grasses dipping and bending with the wind and currents have been so little admired until recent years by any except a few naturalists and artists. The poets have offered us images with which we can readily express our wonder at the magnitude of the oceans and the mountains, but apparently they have been defeated by the fact that so few words rhyme with "swamp." Many of us who readily grasp the importance of preserving forests, sand dunes, and lakes for their aesthetic values alone remain blind to the less obvious charms of a healthy marsh bordered by deep yellow marsh marigolds or a swamp in which ospreys nest high in the cypresses....

WETLAND FUNCTIONS... An ecosystem is a unit of plants, animals, and their physical and chemical environment in which no one part exists independently of the others. The tidal wetlands and the estuary — where a stream's freshwater mixes with the saltwater of the sea — form a distinctive ecosystem in which plants and animals exist with each other and with the nonliving environment in a complex system of interdependencies.

THE FOOD WEB... The source of the energy needed by all plants and animals to sustain life is the sun, but only plants have the capacity to transform the sun's energy into food through photosynthesis. This energy, in the form of plant material, carbohydrates, fats, and proteins, then becomes available to the entire animal world, including people.... Energy continues to flow as creatures feed on each other. As detritus is carried through the marsh, it is consumed by microorganisms, by fiddler crabs, by the larvae of marsh insects, and by mussels, clams, and other creatures which are then ingested by even larger animals. The energy from the sun which was harnessed by marsh vegetation reaches people as we consume the oysters and fish which feed in the estuary — or their predators which live in the coastal waters.

The estuary offers a veritable smorgasbord for the fish which visit seasonally and for those which enter with the tides. Their prey includes the mud-dwelling insects, worms, mollusks, and crustaceans and the young of other species which use the estuary as a nursery because of the abundance of food and the shelter of shallow water and grasses. As fish and shellfish which feed in the estuary swim into deeper waters, larger predatory fish await them. Birds also find a variety of food in and near the marshes. Hawks sweep the area in search of smaller birds and mice. The clapper rail hunts small fish, fiddler crabs, insects, and snails in the vegetation along the edges of the marsh.

Inland marshes also teem with life. Red-winged blackbirds nest in cattails and shrubs and fly out, displaying their gaudy epaulets, to feed on grain, snails, beetles, and grubs. Foraging herons stretch their long necks to snatch fish, frogs, or small crustaceans swimming about in the shallow waters, and kingfishers watch at the water's edge. Raccoons, which like people will feast on either plant or animal matter, prowl the marsh at dusk. Newly hatched ducklings take to the water where they conceal themselves from predators among the bordering plants.

WETLAND PRODUCTIVITY... The estuary and tidal marshes are extraordinary natural systems in which tidal energy circulates nutrients, animals feed on plants and on each other, and excess nutrients are washed out to feed the organisms which live offshore. The crop is automatically cultivated and stored within the system, requiring neither human investment nor labor....

A primary measure of wetland productivity is fish yield. Of the 10 fish and shellfish most valuable commercially — shrimp, salmon, tuna, oysters, menhaden, crabs, lobsters, flounders, clams, and haddock — only tuna, lobsters, and haddock are not estuarine dependent. The highest-ranking commercial species in terms of quantity is menhaden, a wetland-dependent fish valued not for human consumption but for its oil, which is used in tanning leather, in paint and varnish, insect spray, and soap, and in fertilizer, animal feed, and fish food. The average annual harvest of menhaden for the 5 years 1969-73 was 1.9 billion pounds.

Figures on wetland-dependent fish yields have been the subject of numerous studies. The Georgia Game and Fish Commission estimated the per acre yield of freshwater wetland fish at 75 pounds. In Connecticut's marshy Niantic River, the annual scallop harvest is 15,000 bushels, amounting to 300 pounds per acre per year, which exceeds the beef yield on excellent grazing grounds. Wetland productivity also includes waterfowl....

POLLUTION CONTROL... There is general recognition of the fact that wetlands are vital to fish and wildlife. A subject of livelier debate and growing intensity is how wetlands function as pollution filtration systems and as natural flood control mechanisms. The implications of current scientific findings for these subjects are of great interest to ecologists, planners, and engineers.

The role of wetlands in reducing the pollution levels in water has recently become one of the most compelling arguments for their preservation. Because wetland ecosystems hold nutrients, they simultaneously act as a pollution filtration system. Water arriving from such "point" sources as waste water treatment plants and from such "nonpoint" sources as runoff from agricultural fields and city streets carries a high level of pollutants, particularly excess levels of nitrogen and phosphorous. As the water circulates through a wetland, the plants take up and use these pollutants as nutrients.

A study by the Georgia Water Quality Control Board of Mountain Creek, a tributary of the Alcovy River, showed that water heavily polluted with human sewage and chicken offal was designated clean after passing through 2.75 miles of swamp forest. A study of the Tinicum Marsh, located a few miles from the Philadelphia airport, measured pollutants in the broad tidal creek which transects the marshes and again when the water returned to the creek after draining for 2–5 hours. Chemical and bacteriological samplings indicated that the marshes significantly improved water quality by increasing the oxygen content and by reducing the nutrient load....

Interest currently centers on the role that river marshes play through their filtration function in protecting lakes from accelerated aging. In the natural and normally slow aging process, lakes accumulate nutrients and sediments and become so shallow that plants grow and emerge through the surface. When a lake accumulates excess quantities of nutrients through natural or manmade causes, the aging process is accelerated, as evidenced by increased turbidity and the growth of algae. Oxygen levels in the water drop and fish die....

FLOOD PROTECTION... One of the most innovative practical applications of current findings about wetland functions is the Charles River plan. Although some people still believe that engineers automatically insist on altering natural systems so that they can get on with their construction, the Corps of Engineers is responsible for devising the simplest yet the most innovative of plans for natural flood control in the Massachusetts Charles River watershed.

Within the Charles River watershed there are 20,000 acres of undeveloped wetland amounting to 10 percent of the entire drainage area. At times of high water, these wetlands absorb the water and release it slowly after the floodwaters recede.

"The logic of the scheme is compelling," said the Corps final report in 1972: Nature has already provided the least-cost solution to future flooding in the form of extensive wetlands which moderate extreme highs and lows in stream flow. Rather than attempt to improve on this natural protection mechanism, it is both prudent and economical to leave the hydrologic regime established over the millennia undisturbed. In the opinion of the study team, construction of any of the most likely alternatives, a 55,000 acre-foot reservoir, or extensive walls and dikes, can add nothing....

THE VALUE OF WETLANDS... In its study of the Charles River Basin, the Corps of Engineers tagged the annual flood control benefits of the Natural Valley Storage Plan at $1,203,000 — "The difference between annual flood losses based on present land use and conditions" of the 8,500 acres of wetlands and "those associated with projected 1990 loss of 30 percent of valley storage."

It is difficult to quantify the value of wetlands, and attempts to do so generate considerable disagreement, but because alternative approaches to engineering problems are often judged today by cost-benefit comparisons, such financial estimates are now common. Today a number of ecologists are attempting to apply accounting procedures to wetlands, making financial evaluations of the services which wetlands perform in their natural state and urging that the figures be seriously considered in decisions on uses of water resources.

Most quantifiers have concerned themselves solely with wetlands functions. Placing a dollar value on purely aesthetic delight may seem impossible to many scientists who feel on surer ground pricing wetlands in relation to damage projections or to the known commercial values of estuarine-dependent shellfish, for example....

**State of Maine v. Johnson**
Supreme Court of Maine, 1970
265 A.2d 711

MARDEN, J. On appeal from an injunction granted under the provisions of 12 M.R.S.A. §§4701-4709, the Wetlands Act, which places restrictions upon the alteration and use of wetlands, as therein defined, without permission from the municipal officers concerned and the State Wetlands Control Board. The Act is a conservation measure under the police power of the State to protect the ecology of areas bordering coastal waters.[22]

The appellants own a tract of land about 220 feet wide and 700 feet long extending across salt water marshes between Atlantic Avenue on the east and the Webhannet River on the west in the Town of Wells. Westerly of the lots fronting on Atlantic Avenue the strip has been subdivided into lots for sale. The easterly

---

22. Pertinent portions of the wetlands act are quoted:

§4701. No person, agency or municipality shall remove, fill, dredge or drain sanitary sewage into, or otherwise alter any coastal waters, as defined herein...without filing written notice of his intention to do so, including such plans as may be necessary to describe the proposed activity, with the municipal officers in the municipality affected and with the Wetlands Control Board.... The municipal officers shall hold a public hearing on the proposal.... For purposes of this chapter, coastal wetland is defined as any swamp, marsh, bog, beach, flat or other contiguous lowland above extreme low water which is subject to tidal action or normal storm flowage at any time excepting periods of maximum storm activity.

§4702. **Permits** Permits to undertake the proposed alteration shall be issued by the municipal officers within 7 days of such hearing providing the Wetlands Control Board approves. Such permit may be conditioned upon the applicant amending his proposal to take whatever measures are deemed necessary by either the municipality or the Wetlands Control Board to protect the public interest. Approval may be withheld by either the municipal officers or the board when in the opinion of either body the proposal would threaten the public safety, health or welfare, would adversely affect the value or enjoyment of the property of abutting owners, or would be damaging to the conservation of public or private water supplies or of wildlife or freshwater, estuarine or marine fisheries.

§4704. **Appeal** Appeal may be taken to the Superior Court within 30 days after the denial of a permit or the issuance of a conditional permit for the purpose of determining whether the action appealed from so restricts the use of the property as to deprive the owner of the reasonable use thereof, and is therefore an unreasonable exercise of police power, or which constitutes the equivalent of a taking without compensation. The court upon such a finding may set aside the action appealed from.

§4705. **Wetlands Control Board** The Wetlands Control Board shall be composed of the Commissioners of Sea and Shore Fisheries and of Inland Fisheries and Game, the Chairman of the Water and Air Environmental Improvement Commission, the Chairman of the State Highway Commission, the Forest Commissioner and the Commissioner of Health and Welfare or their delegates.

§4709. **Violations** Violators are subject to fine and/or injunctive process.

260 feet approximately of the strip has been filled and bears seasonal dwellings. Westerly of this 260 foot development is marsh-land flooded at high tide and drained, upon receding tide, into the River by a network of what our Maine historical novelist Kenneth E. Roberts called "eel runs," but referred to in the record as creeks. Similar marsh-land, undeveloped, lies to the north and south of appellants' strip and westerly of the River, all of which makes up a substantial acreage (the extent not given in testimony, but of which we take judicial notice) of marshland known as the Wells Marshes. Appellants' land, by raising the grade above high water by the addition of fill, is adaptable to development for building purposes.

Following the effective date of the Act, an application to the municipal officers, with notice to the Wetlands Control Board, for permission to fill a portion of this land was denied by Board.... [Subsequently,] fill was deposited on the land in question, as the result of which the State sought an injunction....

The record establishes that the land which the appellants propose to build up by fill and build upon for sale, or to be offered for sale to be built upon, are coastal wetlands within the definition of the Act and that the refusal by the Board to permit the deposit of such fill prevents the development as proposed. The single Justice found that the property is a portion of a salt marsh area, a valuable natural resource of the State, that the highest and best use for the land, so filled, is for housing, and that unfilled it has no commercial value.

The issue is...whether the [wetlands restrictions] so limit the use to plaintiffs of this land that such deprivation of use amounts to a taking of their property without constitutional due process and just compensation.[23]

Due process of law has a dual aspect, procedural and substantive. Procedurally, "notice and opportunity for hearing are of the essence."... The Act meets all requirements of procedural due process.

Substantively, [due process] is "the constitutional guaranty that no person shall be deprived of...property for arbitrary reasons, such a deprivation being constitutionally supportable only if the conduct from which the deprivation flows is proscribed by reasonable legislation (that is, legislation the enactment of which is within the scope of legislative authority) reasonably applied (that is, for a purpose consonant with the purpose of the legislation itself)." 16 Am. Jur. 2d, Constitutional Law §550.

It is this substantive due process which is challenged in the Act.... The constitutional aspect of the current problem is to be determined by consideration of the extent to which appellants are deprived of their usual incidents of ownership — for the conduct of the public authorities with relation to appellant's land is not a "taking" in the traditional sense. Our State has applied a strict construction of the constitutional provisions as to land.

We find no constitutional definition of the word "deprive," since the constitutionally protected right of property is not unlimited. It is subject to reasonable restraints and regulations in the public interest by means of the legitimate exercise of police power. The exercise of this police power may properly regulate the use of property and if the owner suffers injury "it is either damnum absque injuria, or, in the theory of law, he is compensated for it by sharing in the general benefits which

23. Maine Constitution Article I §6. "He shall not be...deprived of his...property...but by the law of the land."

"Section 21. Private property shall not be taken for public uses without just compensation...."

the regulations are intended...to secure." The determination of unconstitutional deprivation is difficult and judicial decisions are diverse.... A guiding principle appears in the frequently cited case of Pennsylvania Coal Company v. Mahon, 260 U.S. 393, 413 (1922), where Mr. Justice Holmes declared:

> Government hardly could go on if to some extent values incident to property could not be diminished without paying for every such change in the general law....But obviously the implied limitation must have its limits or the contract and due process clauses are gone....

Confrontation between public interests and private interests is common in the application of zoning laws, with which the Wetlands Act may be analogized, and the great majority of which, upon their facts, are held to be reasonable exercise of the police power. There are, however, zoning restrictions which have been recognized as equivalent to a taking of the property restricted....

Between the public interest in braking and eventually stopping the insidious despoliation of our natural resources which have for so long been taken for granted, on the one hand, and the protection of appellants' property rights on the other, the issue is cast.

Here the single Justice has found that the area of which appellants' land is a part "is a valuable natural resource of the State of Maine and plays an important role in the conservation and development of aquatic and marine life, game birds and waterfowl," which bespeaks the public interest involved and the protection of which is sought by §4702 of the Act. With relation to appellants' interest the single Justice found that appellants' land absent the addition of fill "has no commercial value whatever." These findings are supported by the evidence and are conclusive.

As distinguished from conventional zoning for town protection, the area of Wetlands representing a "valuable natural resource of the State," of which appellants' holdings are but a minute part, is of state-wide concern. The benefits from its preservation extend beyond town limits and are state-wide. The cost of its preservation should be publicly borne. To leave appellants with commercially valueless land in upholding the restriction presently imposed, is to charge them with more than their just share of the cost of this state-wide conservation program, granting fully its commendable purpose.... Their compensation by sharing in the benefits which this restriction is intended to secure is so disproportionate to their deprivation of reasonable use that such exercise of the State's police power is unreasonable.

The application of the Wetlands restriction in the terms of the denial of appellants' proposal to fill, and enjoining them from so doing deprives them of the reasonable use of their property and...is both an unreasonable exercise of police power and equivalent to a taking....

Holding, as we do, that the prohibition against the filling of appellants' land, upon the facts peculiar to the case, is an unreasonable exercise of police power, it does not follow that the restriction as to draining sanitary sewage into coastal wetlands is subject to the same infirmity. Additional considerations of health and pollution which are "separable from and independent of" the "fill" restriction may well support validity of the acts in those areas of concern....

### K & K CONSTRUCTION, INC, J.F.K. CO. et al. v. DEPARTMENT OF NATURAL RESOURCES
Supreme Court of Michigan, 1998
No. 106712, 1998 WL 130936

CAVANAGH, J. This case requires us to decide whether the denial of a permit to fill wetlands on the plaintiffs' property constitutes a regulatory taking of the property without just compensation. The trial court found that the permit denials effectively rendered part of the plaintiffs' land worthless; therefore, the DNR was required to compensate the plaintiffs.

Plaintiffs J.F.K. Company and Resorts and Company own eighty-two acres of property...in Waterford Township. J.F.K. is a Michigan limited partnership consisting of the five children of Joseph and Elaine Kosik.... Mr. Kosik and his son are the sole shareholders of K & K Construction [which] has contracted with the owners to build a C.J. Barrymore's restaurant and sports complex on the property.

The property consists of four defined parcels, all of which are contiguous. Parcel one consists of approximately fifty-five acres, twenty-seven acres of which are wetlands. It is zoned for commercial use. Parcel two (sixteen acres) is directly south of parcel one. It contains a small portion of the wetlands. Parcel three (9.34 acres) is directly south of parcel two, and does not contain any wetlands. Parcel four (3.4 acres) borders the south side of parcel one, and the east side of parcel two. It is also free of wetlands. Parcels two, three, and four are zoned for multiple family residential housing (R-2). Parcel three has already been developed; parcels two and four have not been developed....

Plaintiffs' original plan...was to build a restaurant and sports complex on forty-two acres of parcel one, and several multiple-family residential structures with a storm-water retention pond on parcels two and four. Pursuant to this plan, plaintiffs applied for a permit to fill part of parcel one in June 1988. The DNR denied the permit, finding that approximately twenty-eight acres of the property were protected wetlands [under the state Wetlands Act, M.C.L. §281.701].... The trial court held that parcel one was the only property relevant to the taking analysis, and that denial of the permit to construct the restaurant and sports complex effectively rendered plaintiffs' property commercially worthless. The DNR was required to compensate plaintiffs for the full value of their property....

Faced with a substantial adverse judgment, the DNR attempted to mitigate the loss in value of the property by allowing development to commence [on some of the wetlands]. Even so, the trial court held that the DNR owed plaintiffs damages both for a "temporary" taking of the land that could now be developed...and also for the full value of the [unpermitted parcel one] wetlands.... The trial court ultimately decided that the DNR was liable for approximately $3.5 million for the [unpermitted] wetlands, and approximately $500,000, plus interest for the temporary taking. The Court of Appeals affirmed....

As stated by Justice Holmes, "The general rule at least is, that while property may be regulated to a certain extent, if regulation goes too far it will be recognized as a taking." Pennsylvania Coal Co. v. Mahon, 260 U.S. 393, 415(1922)....

Regulations effectuate a taking in...two situations: (a) "categorical" taking, where the owner is deprived of "all economically beneficial or productive use of land," Lucas v. South Carolina Coastal Council, 505 U.S. 1003, 1015 (1992); or (b) a taking recognized on the basis of the application of the traditional "balancing test" established in Penn Central v. New York City, 438 U.S. 104 (1978)....

In the former situation...a reviewing court need not apply a case-specific analysis, and the owner should automatically recover for a taking of his property...in the case of a physical invasion of his property by the government (not at issue in this case), or where a regulation forces an owner to "sacrifice all economically beneficial uses [of land] in the name of the common good...." *Lucas.* at 1019.

In the latter situation, the balancing test, a reviewing court must engage in an "ad hoc, factual inquir[y]," centering on three factors: (1) the character of the government's action, (2) the economic effect of the regulation on the property, and (3) the extent by which the regulation has interfered with distinct, investment-backed expectations. *Penn Central*, 438 U.S. at 124.

The trial court found that the Wetlands Act had effectively eliminated the economically viable use of plaintiffs' land; therefore, plaintiffs were due compensation for a taking of their property. Significantly, the trial court only considered the effect of the regulations on parcel one of plaintiffs' property, finding that parcel one was the only relevant parcel for the taking analysis...which meant that plaintiffs could recover categorically for the taking under...*Lucas.*.

The first step in our analysis is to determine which parcel or parcels owned by plaintiffs are relevant for the taking inquiry. The determination of what is referred to as the "denominator parcel" is important because it often affects the analysis of what economically viable uses remain for a person's property after the regulations are imposed. Plaintiffs urge us to focus our analysis only on parcel one, while defendant argues that we must look at all four of plaintiffs' parcels as a single unit....

One of the fundamental principles of taking jurisprudence is the "nonsegmentation" principle. This principle holds that when evaluating the effect of a regulation on a parcel of property, the effect of the regulation must be viewed with respect to the parcel as a whole. *Keystone Bituminous*, 480 U.S. 498. Courts should not "divide a single parcel into discrete segments and attempt to determine whether rights in a particular segment have been entirely abrogated." *Penn Central*, 438 U.S. 130. Rather, we must examine the effect of the regulation on the entire parcel, not just the affected portion of that parcel....[24]

Both permit applications filed by plaintiffs with the DNR contemplated a comprehensive development using part of parcels one, two, and four. In a similar situation, the United States Court of Claims held that a plaintiff may not separate a certain lot of property from others that he owned with regard to his taking claim when he had previously treated them as "a single parcel for purposes of purchase and financing."... We can safely state that the denominator parcel includes parcels one, two, and four.... On remand, we instruct the trial court to determine... whether...all four parcels should be considered in the taking analysis....[25]

The case is remanded to the trial court. On remand, the trial court must determine —

---

24. "Clearly, the quantum of land to be considered is not each individual lot containing wetlands or even the combined area of wetlands. If that were true, the...protection of wetlands via a permit system would, ipso facto, constitute a taking in every case...." Tabb Lakes, Ltd. v. United States, 10 F.3d 796, 802 (C.A.Fed., 1993).

25. Parcel three was not included in plaintiffs' development plan; it had previously been developed.... However...the failure to include a parcel of land in a development plan should not, by itself, exclude that parcel from consideration as part of the denominator. To so conclude would encourage piecemeal development. Thus...we instruct the trial court to determine the extent of J.F.K.'s ownership interest in parcel three, and whether it is sufficiently connected to the other parcels....

(1) if parcel three of plaintiffs' property should be included in the denominator parcel, and

(2) whether the effect of the regulations on the entire denominator parcel resulted in a taking under the balancing test.

## COMMENTARY AND QUESTIONS

1. **Setting a baseline.** Most wetlands takings cases, like most takings cases generally, focus on the individual landowner's property value diminution, usually asking not how much was taken but how much remains. Note the games that can be played in determining the "baseline" against which to measure whether there is a reasonable remaining use. If you do a schematic diagram of the *Johnson* case, it rapidly becomes clear that Dr. Johnson made a tidy profit from the earlier sale of dry land portions of his property that were previously sold for cottages. The court in *Johnson* asked the question whether there was a reasonable remaining profitable use *only of the regulated portion of the property*, not looking at the entire parcel, at which point, since it looked like a total wipeout, it seemed no subtle constitutional balance was required.

The *K&K* court looked at the regulations' effect on the private profit from the plaintiffs' contiguous property as a whole, not merely at the regulated portion. Not coincidentally, a focus on the regulated portion alone in wetland cases (and many other environmental settings) typically reveals that the regulation has eliminated virtually all economic value, while focus on the property owner's parcel as a whole often reveals a substantial profit that has been made or may be made in the future on unregulated portions, rendering the regulation valid. This question of what to consider as the property baseline for judicial review of takings (or the "denominator" of the diminution fraction, as the *K&K* court called it[26]) is an important fundamental point, considered further in the next section.

2. **Balancing?** The majority of wetlands cases probably have resembled *Johnson* rather than *K&K* in terms of their judicial balancing test as well as their baseline definition. Judges in wetlands cases are not oblivious to wetlands' ecological values. In *Johnson*, for example, the Maine court noted arguments for protecting wetlands, but it did so only as a basis for establishing that the act served a proper public purpose. Having done so, the *Johnson* opinion focused exclusively on the private loss, without further consideration of the environmental context. Wetland regulations have a dramatic impact on market values, but shouldn't the constitutional balance on takings burdens have some place in it for weighted consideration of the public ecological harms which motivated the challenged regulation in the first place? Courts have found it easy to recognize the costs "externalized" onto *private* property by regulation, but less obvious that there should be a weighing of harms externalized onto the *public* by private action. Not knowing how to do so, most courts remain focused exclusively on *private* diminution of value, the market loss figure.

---

26. The phrase, as noted below, comes from Michelman, Property, Utility, and Fairness: Comments on the Ethical Foundations of Just Compensation Law, 80 Harv. L. Rev. 1165, 1192 (1967).

*K&K*, however, clarifies regulatory takings review on two levels. First, although the *K&K* plaintiffs suffered more than $3.5 million in market value diminution, the Michigan Supreme Court holds that the degree of individual private burden is to be measured relatively, against a broader baseline than viewing just the loss on the regulated wetlands alone. It is to include three or four parcels in the "denominator."

Even more important, the K&K court holds that the constitutional test must include a "balancing of interests." This constitutional balance is not clearly spelled out, but apparently includes public values. Wetlands cases are particularly difficult, even if a geographic baseline "denominator" can be agreed, because large amounts of money can be involved and it is not clear how the public and private interests in wetlands are to be weighed against one another. In a New Hampshire coastal wetlands case the court held that the regulation was "not an appropriation of the property to a public use, but the restraint of an injurious private use by the owner.... The validity of the state action is determined by balancing the importance of the public benefit which is sought to be promoted against the seriousness of the restriction of a private right sought to be imposed." Sibson v. State, 336 A.2d 239 (N.H. 1976) How are the public interests in wetlands, noted in the CEQ Report above, to be balanced? Are all "public benefits" to be balanced, or only "public harms"?

3. **The public-private property issue, in national politics.** The nation's largest wetlands protection program is the CWA §404 program. What would have been the effect on the federal wetlands regulation program of applying the regulatory takings compensation provision noted at the beginning of this chapter? What is the effect of narrowing the baseline to a property's "regulated portion"? (Note also that the compensation requirement could have been applied to all federal pollution regulations administered by the EPA.)

Antagonism to regulatory restrictions on uses of corporate and individual land in order to protect endangered species under ESA §9, in fact was one of the driving market forces behind the automatic-compensation provisions noted at the beginning of this chapter. Industries have invested a great deal of money and effort to characterize species protections as frivolous and insubstantial when weighed against profitmaking activities like clearcutting, calling for compensation for any regulated portion of property, and inserting amendments for negotiated erosions of species protections where they cause market value losses.[27]

Automatic-compensation regulatory takings bills pushed by industry lobbies continue to surface in the state and federal legislative process, with the potential for dramatic effects on environmental and other regulation. Note that the so-called "nuisance exception" in such bills is not much of a balance. As Professor Sax has noted about these bills, "A nuisance standard operates to restrict regulation to pre-existing covered areas, and to impose judicial standards of proof designed for private litigation, rather than for public standards which are often designed to deal with

---

27. See above, pages 703–708; see also The Embattled Social Utilities of the Endangered Species Act — a Noah Presumption, and a Caution Against Putting Gas Masks on the Canaries in the Coal Mine 27 Envtl Law 845 (1997); Oliver A. Houck, Why Do We Protect Endangered Species, and What Does That Say About Whether Restrictions on Private Property to Protect Them Constitute "Takings"?, 80 Iowa L. Rev. 297 (1995); and Professor Sax's article noted at the end of this comment.

risks to public health and welfare while proof is still uncertain." Sax, Using Property Rights to Attack Environmental Protection, 14 Pace Envtl. L. Rev. 1 (1996).

4. **The U.S. Supreme Court's classic takings cases.** *K&K* also introduces four of the most important regulatory takings cases,[28] all explored further in the next section —

• *Pennsylvania Coal*, in 1922, was the first case to hold a regulation invalid as a taking, based on a test of "diminution" of private property value caused by a state statute prohibiting the mining of coal pillars if surface streets and homes would thereby be destroyed. Justice Holmes said the virtual elimination of each pillar's value was constitutionally excessive.

• *Keystone Bituminous*, on virtually the same facts as *Pennsylvania Coal*, also focused on private diminution but effectively overruled the way *Pennsylvania Coal* had viewed the baseline denominator. Justice Stevens viewed the private loss in the context of the entire coalfield, not just the regulated pillars, and upheld the law. *Keystone Bituminous* also implied that takings review went beyond a focus on individual loss, incorporating a balancing of public interests through consideration of "noxiousness," a "nuisance exception," or the like.

• *Penn Central* likewise weighed the amount of private diminution loss by viewing plaintiffs' entire property (Grand Central Station, which the Landmark Commission had designated a historic landmark, prohibiting construction above it) and not just the regulated portion (the air space above the terminal).

• *Lucas* struck down the South Carolina coastal protection act's prohibition of building on barrier beach lots, under a "categorical rule" requiring compensation for regulatory wipeouts where no economic value remains, although the "categorical" rule as described also allowed consideration of nuisance-like public harms.

Section 2. **TWO PENNSYLVANIA COAL CASES, AND DIMINUTION BASELINES**

*Pennsylvania Coal* is the classic takings decision referred to in *Johnson, K&K*, and virtually every other takings case since 1922. It is the first case in which restricted property owners successfully persuaded the U.S. Supreme Court to expand the original constitutional prohibition on uncompensated physical takings to non-physical regulatory actions.[29] The *Pennsylvania Coal* opinion, like its author, was suitably both eminent and enigmatic:

**Pennsylvania Coal Co. v. Mahon**
Supreme Court of the United States, 1922
260 U.S. 393

HOLMES, J. This is a bill in equity brought by the defendants in error to prevent the Pennsylvania Coal Company from mining under their property in such way as to remove the supports and cause a subsidence of the surface and of their house. The bill sets out a deed executed by the Coal Company in 1878, under which the

---

28. Pennsylvania Coal Co. v. Mahon, 260 U.S. 393 (1922); Keystone Bituminous Coal Ass'n v. DeBenedictis, 480 U.S. 470 (1987); Penn Central Transportation Co. v. New York City, 438 U.S. 104 (1978); Lucas v. South Carolina Coastal Council, 505 U.S. 1003, 1015 (1992).

29. The Founding Fathers quite clearly did not intend that regulations could be takings (see Bosselman, Callies, and Banta, The Taking Issue (1973)) — a fact of constitutional history that gives pause to some who are otherwise strict-constructionists.

*Photographs from Scranton Pennsylvania showing mine subsidence cave-ins caused by removal of coal pillars beneath the city. The photo above, taken shortly before 1920, was presented to the legislature as part of the city's case for passage of the 1921 Kohler Act, which was declared unconstitutional in Pennsylvania Coal. The bottom left photograph was taken in the first decade of the century. The residents of the home, Mr. and Mrs. Buckley, escaped safely by ladder up to the surface from their attic window.*

plaintiffs claim. The deed conveys the surface but in express terms reserves the right to remove all the coal under the same and the grantee takes the premises with the risk and waives all claim for damages that may arise from mining out the coal. But the plaintiffs say that whatever may have been the Coal Company's rights, they were taken away by an Act of Pennsylvania, approved May 27, 1921 (P. L. 1198), commonly known there as the Kohler Act.... The statute forbids the mining of anthracite coal in such a way as to cause the subsidence of, among other things, any structure used as a human habitation [eds.- preventing coal companies nearing the end of mining in underground coal seams from quarrying away parts of the supportive "pillars" of coal that are kept in place to hold up the ceilings of working mines, if there are homes, public buildings, roads, lakes, or streams above].... As applied to this case the statute is admitted to destroy previously existing rights of property and contract. The question is whether the police power can be stretched so far.

Government hardly could go on if to some extent values incident to property could not be diminished without paying for every such change in the general law. As long recognized some values are enjoyed under an implied limitation and must yield to the police power. But obviously the implied limitation must have its limits or the contract and due process clauses are gone. One fact for consideration in determining such limits is the extent of the diminution. When it reaches a certain magnitude, in most if not in all cases there must be an exercise of eminent domain and compensation to sustain the act. So the question depends upon the particular facts. The greatest weight is given to the judgment of the legislature but it always is open to interested parties to contend that the legislature has gone beyond its constitutional power....

This is a case of a single private house. No doubt there is a public interest even in this, as there is in every purchase and sale and in all that happens within the commonwealth. But usually in ordinary private affairs the public interest does not warrant much of this kind of interference. A source of damage to such a house is not a public nuisance even if similar damage is inflicted on others in different places. The damage is not common or public. The extent of the public interest is shown by the statute to be limited, since the statute ordinarily does not apply to land when the surface is owned by the owner of the coal. Furthermore, it is not justified as a protection of personal safety. That could be provided for by notice. Indeed the very foundation of this bill is that the defendant gave timely notice of its intent to mine under the house. On the other hand the extent of the taking is great. It purports to abolish what is recognized in Pennsylvania as an estate in land — a very valuable estate — and what is declared by the Court below to be a contract hitherto binding the plaintiffs. If we were called upon to deal with the plaintiffs' position alone we should think it clear that the statute does not disclose a public interest sufficient to warrant so extensive a destruction of the defendant's constitutionally protected rights.

But the case has been treated as one in which the general validity of the act should be discussed. The Attorney General of the State, the City of Scranton, and the representatives of other extensive interests were allowed to take part in the argument below and have submitted their contentions here. It seems, therefore, to be our duty to go farther in the statement of our opinion, in order that it may be known at once, and that further suits should not be brought in vain. It is our opinion that the act cannot be sustained as an exercise of the police power, so far as it affects the mining of coal under streets or cities in places where the right to mine such coal has been reserved. As said in a Pennsylvania case, "For practical purposes, the right to coal consists in the right to mine it." What makes the right to mine coal valuable is that it can be exercised with profit. To make it commercially impracticable to mine certain coal has very nearly the same effect for constitutional purposes as appropriating or destroying it. This we think that we are warranted in assuming that the statute does.

The protection of private property in the Fifth Amendment presupposes that it is wanted for public use, but provides that it shall not be taken for such use without compensation. A similar assumption is made in the decisions upon the Fourteenth Amendment. When this seemingly absolute protection is found to be qualified by the police power, the natural tendency of human nature is to extend the qualification more and more until at last private property disappears. But that cannot be accomplished in this way under the Constitution of the United States.

The general rule at least is that while property may be regulated to a certain extent, if regulation goes too far it will be recognized as a taking. It may be doubted how far exceptional cases, like the blowing up of a house to stop a conflagration, go — and if they go beyond the general rule, whether they do not stand as much upon tradition as upon principle. In general it is not plain that a man's misfortunes or necessities will justify his shifting the damages to his neighbor's shoulders. We are in danger of forgetting that a strong public desire to improve the public condition is not enough to warrant achieving the desire by a shorter cut than the constitutional way of paying for the change. As we already have said this is a question of degree — and therefore cannot be disposed of by general propositions. But we regard this as going beyond any of the cases decided by this Court. We assume, of course, that the statute was passed upon the conviction that an exigency existed that would warrant it, and we assume that an exigency exists that would warrant the exercise of eminent domain. But the question at bottom is upon whom the loss of the changes desired should fall. So far as private persons or communities have seen fit to take the risk of acquiring only surface rights, we cannot see that the fact that their risk has become a danger warrants the giving to them greater rights than they bought. Decree reversed.

BRANDEIS, J., dissenting.... The right of the owner to use his land is not absolute. He may not so use it as to create a public nuisance, and uses once harmless may, owing to changed conditions, seriously threaten the public welfare. Whenever they do, the Legislature has power to prohibit such uses without paying compensation.... If by mining anthracite coal the owner would necessarily unloose poisonous gases, I suppose no one would doubt the power of the state to prevent the mining, without buying his coal fields. And why may not the state, likewise, without paying compensation, prohibit one from digging so deep or excavating so near the surface, as to expose the community to like dangers? In the latter case, as in the former, carrying on the business would be a public nuisance.

It is said that one fact for consideration in determining whether the limits of the police power have been exceeded is the extent of the resulting diminution in value, and that here the restriction destroys existing rights of property and contract. But values are relative. If we are to consider the value of the coal kept in place by the restriction, we should compare it with the value of all other parts of the land. That is, with the value not of the coal alone, but with the value of the whole property. The rights of an owner as against the public are not increased by dividing the interests in his property into surface and subsoil. The sum of the rights in the parts cannot be greater than the rights in the whole.... For aught that appears the value of the coal kept in place by the restriction may be negligible as compared with the value of the whole property, or even as compared with that part of it which is represented by the coal remaining in place and which may be extracted despite the statute.

COMMENTARY AND QUESTIONS

1. *Keystone Bituminous Coal* and the judges' baseline game. If private loss is to be a dominant factor (other factors are discussed below) the baseline question of what portion of property to view for the determination of diminution loss is key. If courts look just at the regulated portion of property, many environmental regulations will be struck down. Requiring catalytic converters on automobile engines would by this logic be held unconstitutional if automobile companies could not make a profit on that particular element of their automobiles.

In *Pennsylvania Coal* Holmes focused on the restricted pillar of coal, and Brandeis viewed the context of the entire coal field. Precisely the same arguments were repeated in the Supreme Court's 1987 opinion in Keystone Bituminous Coal Ass'n v. DeBenedictis, 480 U.S. 470 (1987) which remarkably also involved a Pennsylvania statute requiring coal companies to keep underground pillars to support the surface. After arguing (quite unconvincingly) that he was not overruling *Pennsylvania Coal*, Justice Stevens held that the takings test should be based on the entire coal field owned by the coal company petitioners, not just on the coal pillars that the companies were required to leave untouched.

> Petitioners...claimed that they have been required to leave a bit less than 27 million tons of coal in place.... The total coal in [their] thirteen mines amounts to over 1.46 billion tons. Thus [the Act] requires them to leave less than 2 percent of their coal in place.... Petitioners have sought to narrowly define certain segments of their property and assert that when so defined, the Subsidence Act denies economically viable use.... First, they focus on the specific tons of coal that they must leave in the ground under the Subsidence Act.... Second, they contend that the Commonwealth has taken a separate legal interest in property — the "support estate." The 27 million tons of coal do not constitute a separate segment of property for takings law purposes.... The Court of Appeals...concluded that as a practical matter the support estate is always owned by either the owner of the surface or the owner of the minerals.... Its value is merely a part of the entire bundle of rights possessed by the owner of either the coal or the surface. *Keystone Bituminous*, 480 U.S. at 496–501.

In vigorous dissent, Justice Rehnquist argued:

> In this case, enforcement of the Subsidence Act and its regulations will require Petitioners to leave approximately 27 million tons of coal in place. There is no question that this coal is an identifiable and separable property interest.... From the relevant perspective — that of the property owners — this interest has been destroyed every bit as much as if the government had proceeded to mine the coal for its own use.... Operation of this [Act] extinguishes the Petitioners' interests in their support estates, making worthless what they purchased as a separate right under Pennsylvania law. Like the restriction on mining particular coal, this complete interference with a property right extinguishes its value, and must be accompanied by just compensation. *Id.*

Who got the better of this crucial definitional debate? The "divide-and-conquer" antiregulatory strategy of defining narrower baselines, to increase the chances of findings of excessive loss, has been dubbed *"conceptual severance"* by Professor Margaret Radin.[30] The conceptual severance effort continues to the present. The Federal Circuit, created in the 1980s with a focus on compensation cases, has often followed the Rehnquist dissent rather than the *Keystone* majority, and Justice Scalia reopened the tactic in *Lucas*.[31]

In *Keystone Bituminous* Justice Rehnquist argued further that there should be no difference between physical takings tests, like those applied in the airplane inverse condemnation cases, and regulatory takings, citing *Causby*, the classic physical takings case, for the proposition that regulatory action might result in "as complete [a loss] as if the government had entered upon the surface of the land and taken exclusive possession of it." 480 U.S. at 516, citing *Causby*, 328 U.S. 256, 261 (1946). In the airport cases the taking of the easement, even though it amounted to a fraction of the property value, required compensation as a governmental appropriation. Is there a distinction between physical and regulatory takings? If there isn't, whatever regulated private interests can be defined in private easement form would immediately require compensation, wouldn't they? Does that argument prove too much?

What should be the baseline in the wetlands cases excerpted above? If the court in Maine v. Johnson looked at the full property owned by plaintiffs, including contiguous parcels previously developed, it would have faced a very different question. The *K&K* court defined the baseline to include possible weighing of all four parcels, including valuable portions of property beyond the regulated portions, changing the denominator, and virtually assuring the wetland prohibition's constitutional validity.

3. **Challengers' baseline games.** What if a property owner sells all the profitably developable portions of her property, and then goes to court claiming that the regulated leftover has no economic use? Presumably the court can take account of past profits as part of the balance. Does the timing of the regulation make any difference? What if a property owner consciously buys a heavily-regulated piece of land at a bargain price, and then goes to court claiming unconstitutional hardship? Some courts have held that property owners are estopped from attacking regulations that they knew about at the time of purchase. The majority of states, however, allow a person to buy land cheap, and then to argue that the regulation that had held down the purchase price was unconstitutional because it prevented profitable use. These states hold that one can never waive one's constitutional rights. The doctrine of "self-imposed hardship," however, developed in zoning law when

---

30. Radin, The Liberal Conception of Property: Cross Currents in the Jurisprudence of Takings, 88 Colum. L. Rev. 1667, 1676 (1988).

31. *Lucas*, 505 U.S. at fn. 7: "When, for example, a regulation requires a developer to leave 90% of a rural tract in its natural state, it is unclear whether we would analyze the situation as one in which the owner has been deprived of all economically beneficial use of the burdened portion of the tract, or as one in which the owner has suffered a mere diminution in value of the tract as a whole." [The footnote goes on to suggest adoption of conceptual severance definitions from Justice Rehnquist's *Keystone* dissent.]

challengers have consciously created sub-standard lots, argues that such diminution does not amount to a constitutional taking.

**4. Was there a balancing?** Beyond the arguments of setting baselines, was there any balance between the public's interests and the private losses in the two coal cases? In Pennsylvania Coal Holmes noted that there were public "exigencies," but that apparently was mentioned only for establishing a valid public purpose, and did not weigh into a balance. The poison gas hypothetical in Brandeis' dissent, which seemed to raise public harms in a balance, was ignored. *Keystone Bituminous* did more. Justice Stevens noted that

> Many cases before and since *Pennsylvania Coal* have recognized that the nature of the State's action is critical in takings analysis.... Just five years after the *Pennsylvania Coal* decision, Justice Holmes joined the Court's unanimous decision in Miller v. Schoene, 276 U.S. 272 (1928), holding that the Takings Clause did not require the State of Virginia to compensate the owners of cedar trees for the value of the trees that the State had ordered destroyed. The trees needed to be destroyed to prevent a disease from spreading to nearby apple orchards, which represented a far more valuable resource. In upholding the state action, the Court did not consider it necessary to "weigh with nicety the question whether the infected cedars constitute a nuisance according to common law; or whether they may be so declared by statute." Rather, it was clear that the State's exercise of its police power to prevent the impending danger was justified, and did not require compensation.... Although a comparison of values before and after a regulatory action is relevant, it is by no means conclusive.... The question whether a taking has occurred "necessarily requires a weighing of private and public interests." [citing Agins]...
>
> The Court's hesitance to find a taking when the State merely restrains uses of property that are tantamount to public nuisances...can also be understood on the simple theory that since no individual has a right to use his property so as to create a nuisance or otherwise harm others, the State has not "taken" anything when it asserts its power to enjoin the nuisance-like activity. *Keystone Bituminous*, 480 U.S. 470 at 491.

This introduces an active consideration of the public harms into a regulatory takings balance, although the terms remain unspecific.

## Section 3. PENN CENTRAL, "REASONABLE ECONOMIC USE," AND A BALANCING?

Given the many different ways and degrees in which modern government can directly or incidentally burden private property, there can be no bright line objective test for delineating the point at which regulations "go too far." In *Pennsylvania Coal* for the first time in the nation's history, the Court actually struck down a regulation on the strength of a takings argument. In doing so, it created the perplexing problem of developing a formula for defining just when invalid regulatory takings occur.

The takings analysis advanced by Holmes in *Pennsylvania Coal* was characteristically perceptive, common-sensical, and flawed. It was quickly seized upon by succeeding generations of grateful courts, especially those tending toward an antiregulatory stance, as a beacon providing a verbal formulation for guidance in handling the daunting takings issue when it arose in judicial reviews of police power actions. Holmes, although he himself expressly said that he was presenting a limited, partial analysis, in fact focused only on "diminution." Because he discussed no other factor, many courts following his lead have tended to do the same. Whether they uphold or strike down challenged regulations, most courts tend to avoid defining any direct conception of how public and private rights are to be balanced against one another. Typically, as Holmes did in *Pennsylvania Coal*, public rights elements are discussed only in the threshold due process inquiry: Is there a proper public purpose? Typically this is checked-off affirmatively.

A few courts, especially prior to the 1960s, deferred so much to governmental acts that they virtually ignored regulatory effects upon private property rights in takings challenges, satisfying themselves that full due process has been accorded when just the public power requisites of authority, proper purpose, and rationality were established.[32] At the opposite pole, many courts since then focus on private property diminution effects as the dominant factor, in effect in a constitutional vacuum, without expressly weighing any relativity or proportionality to public interests. Even where courts discuss both public and private elements to some extent, as Holmes did in *Pennsylvania Coal*, they don't weigh them directly against one another because no judicial test for doing so has been established. The U.S. Supreme Court for a long time ducked takings cases as much as it could, perhaps reflecting the Court's recognition that lack of an intelligible standard invites mere judicial gut reactions. Since the ascendancy of Justice Rehnquist, the Court has begun to show a heightened interest in taking on takings cases, often with the result of restricting police power regulation of economic interests.

*Penn Central* tested regulatory validity under a "reasonable economic use" test drawn from municipal zoning case law, widely followed by state and federal courts. In *Penn Central*, when the Court had to determine whether New York City's historic preservation ordinance could block the owners of Grand Central Station from raising a skyscraper over the old landmark, it used reasonable remaining use reasoning, on a full rather than narrowed baseline.[33] As articulated in *Penn Central* and a host of other cases, police power regulations are valid if they leave property owners with some reasonable residuum. The *Penn Central* Court concluded, however, that "if appellants can demonstrate at some point in the future that circumstances have changed such that the Terminal ceases to be...economically viable," appellants may obtain relief, and the majority opinion's final paragraph referred to the need for a remaining "reasonable beneficial use." 438 U.S. at 138, and fn 27.

---

32. These courts say that where authority, proper purpose, and rationality are established, regulations do not amount to a taking or violation of due process if they cause only "incidental" private property loss. See e.g. U.S. v. Central Eureka Mining Co., 357 U.S. 155, 165–169 (1958); Consolidated Rock Products v. Los Angeles, 370 P.2d 342, 346–347, 351–352 (Cal. 1962). By focusing on the first three tests, these courts disregard any question of the proportionality or fairness of the effect on individual private property. As to whether the private loss is "incidental," in point of fact property burdens are almost *always* incidental (if incidental means "not directly intended"), since imposing them is initially never the motivating public purpose.

33. In *Penn Central* the Court explained "takings jurisprudence does not divide a single parcel into discrete segments and attempt to determine whether rights in a particular segment have been entirely abrogated. In deciding whether a particular governmental action has effected a taking, this Court focuses rather both on the character of the action and on the nature of the interference with rights *in the parcel as a whole*...."

The "reasonable remaining use" test developed in the particular setting of zoning cases. Because the public "harms" that zoning addressed could not readily be quantified, like many environmental values including historic preservation, it was at least a practicable line to say that if too little was left over after zoning to provide an economically viable use, then zoning had probably gone too far as applied. Since 1926, the reasonable remaining use test has served as an accepted takings norm for zoning cases. Moreover, since zoning cases have provided the vast majority of takings challenges, it is no surprise that the takings standard used in zoning cases has been applied in other areas.

Did *Penn Central* also contain the elements of public-private balancing? In the reading of the *K&K* court, *Penn Central* contributed some new phrases for weighing regulatory takings, and incorporated a public-private balance. Picking up on *Keystone's* language on balancing of the character of state action, in *Penn Central* Justice Brennan had noted that —

> in engaging in these essentially ad hoc factual inquiries, the Court's decisions have identified several factors that have particular significance. The economic impact of the regulation on the claimant and, particularly, the extent to which the regulation has interfered with distinct investment-backed expectations are...relevant considerations. So too is the character of the governmental action. *Penn Central*, 438 U.S. at 124

In this triad, the "economic impact" element apparently means diminution; the "reasonable investment-backed expectations" clause emphasizes frustration of market investment judgments;[34] but the "character of the governmental action" element, which in part referred to whether a government act was physical or regulatory, may mean more. *Penn Central* is often considered, as in *K&K*, to imply a balancing of public and private interests as well. The "character of the governmental action" element invites judges to consider, as in *Keystone Bituminous*, whether or not the government is regulating nuisance-like public harms. This is a public-private balance.

Does the "reasonable remaining use" rubric likewise incorporate a balance? Its terms seem to focus on individual diminution, but implicitly it may import a weighing of relativity and proportionality. It is doubtful that a court would hold a regulation unconstitutional if a polluting factory proved that it would be put out of business if forced to clean up. Why? Probably because the court implicitly would consider public harms from pollution, and in that context a shutdown factory is a "reasonable use." If implicit balancing takes place, it is not yet clear and probably should be made explicit, an issue discussed further below.

---

34. Prof. Michelman invented the investment-backed expectations phrase in a book review, 80 Harv. L.Rev. 1165, 1192 (1967), intended not as a constitutional test but as a policy guide for voluntary compensations. Its utility to takings challengers is evident, and thanks to *Penn Central* it has crossed-over beyond its author's intent. Consider this test in the context of Brandeis' poison gas example in *Pennsylvania Coal*: if a landowner discovers, to her dismay, that her land contains poison gas deposits, so that it cannot safely be developed, her expectations clearly are frustrated; but is that constitutional injury, or merely bad luck? The legislature may well decide to reimburse her as charity, but must it? The expectations may be a factor, but not determinative of takings invalidity.

### COMMENTARY AND QUESTIONS

1. **Defining "reasonable remaining use."** If the courts are going to look only at whether there is a reasonable remaining use on whatever property baseline is defined, how does one determine what is a reasonable use? Compared to what? Presumably most land could be used to raise geraniums for sale, producing at least some small income. Is that enough? If the phrase means that the property owner must make a profit on the land, how much profit — 1 percent, 6 percent, 12 percent? And net profit based on what? If the landowner received the land free from her aunt, is that different from just having purchased it for a million dollars? The standard answer for *zoning* cases seems to be that the land must be able to produce a reasonable profitable return, based on its market value in comparison to similarly situated parcels. Thus the market value of private property (which ignores externalized harms in much the same way as the industrial marketplace does) becomes the foundation of the typical zoning constitutional takings equation.

2. **A time baseline in takings?** What about a *time* baseline on which to weigh "reasonable economic use?" In *Keystone Bituminous*, for example, assume the company had bought the land for $500,000 twenty years before the regulation, and made $200 million profit from the coal over that time, during which time most of the coal had been excavated except for the final "pillars," removal of which would destroy homes and resources on the surface: Is the constitutional "reasonable beneficial use" or "economically viable use" to be measured only by profits earnable *after* the regulation that is passed in order to prevent incipient harm? Does each parcel of property have a *perpetual* right to profit in the face of regulation? The concept of "investment-backed expectations," which often acts to strengthen private claims against regulations, in this case supports the validity of regulatory prohibitions by defining a time baseline in terms of economic return on the *original* investment, not post-regulation profits. Thus the *K&K* court allowed prior profits on developed land to weigh in the takings balance. Amortization cases, including billboard removal cases, also support that time baseline, holding removal ordinances valid if the original investment can be reasonably recouped, establishing a baseline that extends back as well as forward in time. See Venezia, Looking Back: a Full-Time Baseline in Regulatory Takings Analysis, 24 B.C. Envtl Aff. L.Rev. 199 (1996).

3. **Other takings tests.** Among a wide variety of competing alternative takings test proposals, here are some more: Professor Dunham proposed a shift away from consideration of private economic loss, instead basing a takings test on public purpose: if the public purpose is to prevent a harm, then the regulation is valid; if the public purpose is to obtain a free benefit without paying for it, then the regulation is a taking. In clear cases at either end of the spectrum, this test is obviously sensible, and was echoed in Professor Sax's first takings analysis.[35] Do you see, however, how its definition in the middle grey area is either subjective, or a tautological self-fulfilling prophecy? Dunham, A Legal & Economic Basis for City Planning, 58 Colum. L. Rev. 650 (1958); and Dunham, Flood Control Via the Police Power, 107 U. Pa. L. Rev. 1098 (1959).

---

35. Sax, Takings and the Police Power, 74 Yale L.J. 36 (1964) (government need not pay when it is acting to arbitrate harms, but must pay when it enhances its resources in an enterprise capacity).

Professor Sax subsequently argued that reviewing courts should look for "spillovers." Property owners have no right to impose spillover effects on surrounding parcels, and if spillovers exist the legislature can choose which activity to prohibit, without having to pay compensation. The problem here is that Professor Sax takes no account of spillovers' different magnitudes, qualities, or fairness expectations. He classes even visual effects as spillovers, so if house construction on my property would block public view of a beautiful landscape, the house could be prohibited without compensation. Sax's theory invites further balancing. Sax, Takings: Private Property & Public Rights, 81 Yale L.J. 149, 155–72 (1971).

"Reciprocity of advantage." Picking up on a comment by Justice Holmes in *Pennsylvania Coal*, Justice Rehnquist also advanced the argument in *Keystone Bituminous* that since the early regulatory cases established that restrictions on property were constitutional if they provided a "reciprocity of advantage" to the regulated land-owner who shared in the restrictions' public benefits, the obverse was also true: if a property owner did not receive an equal advantage from a regulation, then that established the restrictions' invalidity. The cases he cites, however, use reciprocity as a support for validity, but do not use lack of reciprocity as a test of invalidity. No other justices have yet followed him down the reciprocity of advantage path, requiring that police power regulations be struck down if they don't provide benefits equal to regulatees' costs, although there is a sly reciprocity side-comment in *Lucas*. What would happen if that test were adopted?

As a different form of test, Judge Lehman once proposed a rubric that has struck a responsive chord with dozens of courts since then: A regulation will be unconstitutional, he wrote in Arverne Bay Construction Co. v. Thatcher, 15 N.E.2d 587 (N.Y. 1938), if it removes all valuable incidents from the property owner "except the duty to continue paying property taxes on the land." This quip is probably wrong: if property as regulated has sharply reduced market values, landowners have a constitutional right to roll tax assessments back down to *market value as restricted*, eliminating most of the burden of property taxes thereon.

### Section 4. CONSTITUTIONAL BALANCING, AND *LUCAS'* CATEGORICAL ATTEMPT TO AVOID IT

#### a. Balancing

The limited logic of the diminution test, in focusing on private loss and not expressly balancing the public interests for which challenged regulations were passed, made sense in the zoning cases where public harms are indistinct. The "reasonable remaining use" approach became so familiar, however, that many courts used the zoning case law test to reach extreme conclusions even in cases where public harms were discrete and obvious — for instance striking down floodplain restrictions even where a developer planned to put 300 homes in coastal lowlands repeatedly hit by hurricane flooding. Dooley v. Fairfield, 226 A.2d 509 (Conn. 1967).[36] In First English Evangelical Lutheran Church v. Los Angeles, 482 U.S. 304

36. See The Takings Issue in a Natural Setting: Floodlines and the Police Power, 52 Texas L. Rev. 201, 244–252 (1974).

(1987), decided on other grounds, Justice Rehnquist even posited that a floodplain ordinance was an unconstitutional confiscation because it eliminated the economic value of a canyon floor parcel used as a camp for handicapped children. This amounted to saying that because the market value ignored the dangers, the propertyowner had a constitutional right to house 200 children in the path of recurring floods, or be compensated fully for the prohibition of that use.

The logic of incorporating a balance in regulatory takings challenges, however, has become increasingly clear. On remand of the *First English* case, the California appellate court undertook a refreshingly explicit balancing process, but also, in upholding the regulation, clarified the common sense assertion that different public purposes weigh differently in the takings balance —

> This property could be used for "agricultural and recreational uses," and under the permanent ordinance...appellants are specifically allowed to build swimming pools, parking lots, and accessory buildings within the flood zone portion of its property. What First English can no longer do is rebuild the bunkhouses and similar permanent living structures which might house the potential victims of a future flood or if carried away by that flood cause death, injury and property damage to other properties further downstream. We have no problem concluding these zoning restrictions represent a valid exercise of the police power and not an unconstitutional "taking without compensation." On balance, the public benefits this regulation confers far exceed the private costs it imposes on the individual property owner....

> If there is a hierarchy of interests the police power serves — and both logic and prior cases suggest there is — then the preservation of life must rank at the top. Zoning restrictions seldom serve public interests so far up on the scale. More often these laws guard against things like "premature urbanization," or "preserve open spaces," or contribute to orderly development and the mitigation of environmental impacts. When land use regulations seek to advance what are deemed lesser interests such as aesthetic values of the community they frequently are outweighed by constitutional property rights. Nonetheless, it should be noted even these lesser public interests have been deemed sufficient to justify zoning which diminishes — without compensation — the value of individual properties. The zoning regulation challenged in the instant case involves this highest of public interests — the prevention of death and injury. Its enactment was prompted by the loss of life in an earlier flood. And its avowed purpose is to prevent the loss of lives in future floods.... It would be extraordinary to construe the Constitution to require a government to compensate private landowners because it denied them the "right" to use property which cannot be used without risking injury and death. First English Lutheran Church v. Los Angeles, 210 Cal. App. 3d 1353 at 1366, 1370 (1989) (The Supreme Court denied certiorari in 1990. 110 S. Ct. 866).

The reasonable conclusion would seem to be that the constitutional balance of alleged environmental takings must be relative, not a simplistic all-or-nothing definition of whether or not something is a "nuisance" recognized by the courts. Otherwise the market value of private property losses will completely dominate the question. As in the floodplain setting, market values often ignore the potential for catastrophic impacts on the public and future inhabitants of regulated areas. Market values, after all, are set in such circumstances by the dumbest class of buyers — whoever will offer the highest price for a piece of residential riverfront land. To elevate such short-sighted market judgment to a constitutional determinant is not a compelling exercise of constitutional logic.

A discriminating balancing process requires some proportionality between the degrees of public need and private loss. As the California Supreme Court's *First English* remand indicated, minor threats to the public cannot justify devastating private losses, but they can justify minor erosions of private property values, and large personal losses may be supportable when great public interests are imperiled.

The essential proposition that distills from the confusion of the takings tests is that courts must explicitly recognize both the individual losses that government regulation causes and the costs that private uses potentially impose upon the public. This approach forces courts to consider complex physical and ecological resource relationships and to distinguish between the different effects of property use. Using this process, the courts are in a far better position to undertake the balancing task at the heart of judicial review. This balancing approach produces a de facto two-stage takings inquiry:

The first stage of this "diminution-balancing" approach draws upon the accepted diminution test: zoning cases make clear that the plaintiff must prove the inadequacy and "unreasonableness" of the property's beneficial use as regulated, viewed over the plaintiff's entire contiguous property, not just the regulated segment thereof. This threshold definition remains a subjective task .

The second stage of the takings balance follows the proposition that regulations must be deemed constitutionally valid if the costs that an unrestricted property use imposes upon the public would be greater than private diminution losses. Thus a plaintiff's prima facie case against a regulation should bear the burden of showing not only economic loss, but also that the private loss exceeds the public harms the regulation was reasonably designed to prevent. No private loss, in other words, can be constitutionally excessive if it is less than the harms it would impose on others.

Here too subjectivity remains. What is a public "harm," and what on the other hand is a public "benefit" for which government should compensate? The "nuisance exception" noted in *Keystone* and other cases has provided guidance to the courts substantively and procedurally: If regulations protect against actions that have been deemed public nuisances at common law, then they are harms. If they have not been so recognized (as many newly-recognized environmental harms have not), then the classic balancing process by which nuisances are defined at common law likewise provides a test for whether actions are "nuisance-like" harms to be balanced.

### b. *Lucas*

But what happens in cases — like marginally economic polluting factories, floodplain residential development projects, and the like — where protective regulations would reduce property values to a profitless level, but the properties cause great public harm? Does the constitution require governments either to pay off owners of such properties, or else allow them a constitutional right to harm the public? In his majority opinion in Lucas v. South Carolina Coastal Council, 505 U.S. 1003 (1992), Justice Scalia seizes upon a seemingly exceptional circumstance to try to carve out a "categorical rule" circumventing public-private takings balancing. *Lucas* may be narrow on its facts, but it invites antiregulatory arguments to come:

### David H. Lucas v. South Carolina Coastal Council
United States Supreme Court, 1992
505 U.S. 1003

[Petitioner Lucas is a contractor, manager, and part owner of the Wild Dune development on the Isle of Palms.[37] He has lived there since 1978. In December 1986, he purchased lots #22 and #24, two of the last four pieces of vacant property in the development.[38] The area is notoriously unstable. In roughly half of the last 40 years, all or part of petitioner's property was part of the beach or flooded twice daily by the ebb and flow of the tide. Between 1957 and 1963, petitioner's property was under water. Between 1963 and 1973 the shoreline was 100 to 150 feet onto petitioner's property. In 1973 the first line of stable vegetation was about halfway through the property. Between 1981 and 1983, the Isle of Palms issued 12 emergency orders for sandbagging to protect property in the Wild Dune development. At the time of the purchase, the state's coastal zone building permit line did not preclude Lucas's lots. In 1988, however, the state legislature enacted the Beachfront Management Act, which barred construction seaward of a coastal erosion line to be set after hydrological analysis of the barrier beach locations. The Council determined that Lucas's lots had been within the surf zone 50% of the time since 1949, and that they were well within the restricted 40-year erosion cycle area. Accordingly Lucas was prohibited from erecting any permanent habitable structures on his parcels.[39] He filed suit, arguing that the ban deprived him of all "economically viable use" of his property and therefore effected a "taking." The state trial court agreed, finding that the ban rendered Lucas's parcels "valueless," and entered an award exceeding $1.2 million. In reversing, the state supreme court accepted the legislature's "uncontested...findings" that new construction in the coastal zone threatened a valuable public resource, and that when a regulation is designed to prevent "harmful or noxious uses" of property, akin to public nuisances, no compensation is owed under the Takings Clause regardless of the regulation's effect on the property's value.]

SCALIA, J. ...The trial court found that the Beachfront Management Act decreed a permanent ban on construction [that] deprived Lucas of any reasonable economic use of the lots...eliminated the unrestricted right of use, and rendered them valueless.... Our decision in [Pennsylvania Coal v.] Mahon offered little insight into when, and under what circumstances, a given regulation would be seen as going "too far" for purposes of the Fifth Amendment. In 70-odd years of succeeding "regulatory takings" jurisprudence, we have generally eschewed any " 'set formula' for determining how far is too far, preferring to "engag[e] in...essentially ad hoc,

---

37. The background facts are drawn in part from the dissent of Blackmun, J.

38. The properties were sold frequently at rapidly escalating prices before Lucas purchased them. Lot 22 was first sold in 1979 for $96,660, sold in 1984 for $187,500, then in 1985 for $260,000, and, finally, to Lucas in 1986 for $475,000. He estimated its worth in 1991 at $650,000. Lot 24 had a similar past. The record does not indicate who purchased the properties prior to Lucas, or why none of the purchasers held on to the lots and built on them.

39. The Act did allow the construction of certain nonhabitable improvements, e.g., "wooden walkways no larger in width than six feet," and "small wooden decks no larger than one hundred forty-four square feet."

factual inquiries...." We have, however, described at least two discrete categories of regulatory action as compensable without case-specific inquiry into the public interest advanced in support of the restraint. The first encompasses regulations that compel the property owner to suffer a physical "invasion" of his property.... The second situation in which we have found categorical treatment appropriate is where regulation denies all economically beneficial or productive use of land....[40] As we have said on numerous occasions, the Fifth Amendment is violated when land-use regulation "does not substantially advance legitimate state interests *or denies an owner economically viable use of his land.*"[41]

We have never set forth the justification for this rule. Perhaps it is simply, as Justice Brennan suggested, that total deprivation of beneficial use is, from the landowner's point of view, the equivalent of a physical appropriation. See San Diego Gas & Electric Co. v. San Diego, 450 U.S., at 652 (Brennan, J., dissenting). "For what is the land but the profits thereof?" 1 E. Coke, Institutes ch. 1, §1 (1st Am. ed. 1812)....

Regulations that leave the owner of land without economically beneficial or productive options for its use — typically, as here, by requiring land to be left substantially in its natural state — carry with them a heightened risk that private property is being pressed into some form of public service under the guise of mitigating serious public harm....

It is correct that many of our prior opinions have suggested that "harmful or noxious uses" of property may be proscribed by government regulation without the requirement of compensation.... The "harmful or noxious uses" principle was the Court's early attempt to describe in theoretical terms why government may, consistent with the Takings Clause, affect property values by regulation without incurring an obligation to compensate.... The transition from our early focus on control of "noxious" uses to our contemporary understanding of the broad realm within which government may regulate without compensation was an easy one, since the distinction between "harm-preventing" and "benefit-conferring" regulation is often in the eye of the beholder. It is quite possible, for example, to describe in either fashion the ecological, economic, and aesthetic concerns that inspired the South Carolina legislature in the present case. One could say that imposing a servitude on Lucas's land is necessary in order to prevent his use of it from "harming" South Carolina's ecological resources; or, instead, in order to achieve the "benefits" of an ecological preserve.[42]... A given restraint will be seen as mitigating

---

40. [Original fn 7] Regrettably, the..."deprivation of all economically feasible use" rule...does not make clear the "property interest" against which the loss of value is to be measured. When, for example, a regulation requires a developer to leave 90% of a rural tract in its natural state, it is unclear whether we would analyze the situation as one in which the owner has been deprived of all economically beneficial use of the burdened portion of the tract, or as one in which the owner has suffered a mere diminution in value of the tract as a whole....

41. [Citing *Agins*. Eds.- Justice Scalia leaves off the modifier in the quote from *Agins* that applied this dictum only to zoning, where public harms are not measurable, rather than to land use regulations generally. Some physical invasions have been held noncompensable, U.S. v. Caltex, 344 U.S. 149, 155 (1994), and no prior case had held that denials of all economic value were categorically void. ]

42. [Original fn 10, 11] The legislature's express findings include the following: "The General Assembly finds that: "(1) The beach/dune system along the coast of South Carolina is extremely important to the people of this State and serves the following functions: "(a) protects life and property by serving as a storm barrier which dissipates wave energy and contributes to shoreline stability in an economical and effective manner; "(b) provides the basis for a tourism industry that generates approximately two-thirds of South Carolina's annual tourism industry revenue which constitutes a significant portion of the state's economy. The tourists who come to the South Carolina coast to enjoy the ocean and dry sand beach contribute significantly to state and local tax revenues; "(c) provides habitat

"harm" to the adjacent parcels or securing a "benefit" for them, depending upon the observer's evaluation of the relative importance of the use that the restraint favors.... None of [our decisions] that employed the logic of "harmful use" prevention to sustain a regulation involved an allegation that the regulation wholly eliminated the value of the claimant's land.

Where the State seeks to sustain regulation that deprives land of all economically beneficial use, we think it may resist compensation only if the logically antecedent inquiry into the nature of the owner's estate shows that the proscribed use interests were not part of his title to begin with....The notion pressed by the Council that title is somehow held subject to the "implied limitation" that the State may subsequently eliminate all economically valuable use is inconsistent with the historical compact recorded in the Takings Clause that has become part of our constitutional culture.

Where "permanent physical occupation" of land is concerned, we have refused to allow the government to decree it anew (without compensation), no matter how weighty the asserted "public interests" involved.... We believe similar treatment must be accorded confiscatory regulations, i.e., regulations that prohibit all economically beneficial use of land: Any limitation so severe cannot be newly legis-

---

for numerous species of plants and animals, several of which are threatened or endangered. Waters adjacent to the beach/dune system also provide habitat for many other marine species; "(d) provides a natural health environment for the citizens of South Carolina to spend leisure time which serves their physical and mental well-being. "(2) Beach/dune system vegetation is unique and extremely important to the vitality and preservation of the system. "(3) Many miles of South Carolina's beaches have been identified as critically eroding. " (4)...[D]evelopment unwisely has been sited too close to the [beach/dune] system. This type of development has jeopardized the stability of the beach/dune system, accelerated erosion, and endangered adjacent property. It is in both the public and private interests to protect the system from this unwise development. "(5) The use of armoring in the form of hard erosion control devices such as seawalls, bulkheads, and rip-rap to protect erosion-threatened structures adjacent to the beach has not proven effective. These armoring devices have given a false sense of security to beachfront property owners. In reality, these hard structures, in many instances, have increased the vulnerability of beachfront property to damage from wind and waves while contributing to the deterioration and loss of the dry sand beach which is so important to the tourism industry. "(6) Erosion is a natural process which becomes a significant problem for man only when structures are erected in close proximity to the beach/dune system. It is in both the public and private interests to afford the beach/dune system space to accrete and erode in its natural cycle. This space can be provided only by discouraging new construction in close proximity to the beach/dune system and encouraging those who have erected structures too close to the system to retreat from it.... "(8) It is in the state's best interest to protect and to promote increased public access to South Carolina's beaches for out-of-state tourists and South Carolina residents alike." S. C. Code §48-39-250 (Supp. 1991).

[11] In the present case, in fact, some of the "[South Carolina] legislature's 'findings'" to which the South Carolina Supreme Court purported to defer in characterizing the purpose of the Act as "harm-preventing," 304 S. C. 376, 385, 404 S. E. 2d 895, 900 (1991), seem to us phrased in "benefit-conferring" language instead. For example, they describe the importance of a construction ban in enhancing "South Carolina's annual tourism industry revenue," S. C. Code §48- 39250(1)(b) (Supp. 1991), in "provid[ing]" habitat for numerous species of plants and animals, several of which are threatened or endangered," §48- 39-250(1)(c), and in "provid[ing] a natural healthy environment for the citizens of South Carolina to spend leisure time which serves their physical and mental well-being." §48-39-250(1)(d). It would be pointless to make the outcome of this case hang upon this terminology, since the same interests could readily be described in "harm-preventing" fashion. Justice Blackmun, however, apparently insists that we must make the outcome hinge (exclusively) upon the South Carolina Legislature's other, "harm- preventing" characterizations, focusing on the declaration that "prohibitions on building in front of the setback line are necessary to protect people and property from storms, high tides, and beach erosion." He says "[n]othing in the record undermines [this] assessment," ibid., apparently seeing no significance in the fact that the statute permits owners of existing structures to remain (and even to rebuild if their structures are not "destroyed beyond repair," S. C. Code Ann. §48- 39-290(B)), and in the fact that the 1990 amendment authorizes the Council to issue permits for new construction in violation of the uniform prohibition.

lated or decreed (without compensation), but must inhere in the title itself, in the restrictions that background principles of the State's law of property and nuisance already place upon land ownership. A law or decree with such an effect must, in other words, do no more than duplicate the result that could have been achieved in the courts — by adjacent landowners (or other uniquely affected persons) under the State's law of private nuisance, or by the State under its complementary power to abate nuisances that affect the public generally, or otherwise.[43]

On this analysis, the owner of a lake bed, for example, would not be entitled to compensation when he is denied the requisite permit to engage in a landfilling operation that would have the effect of flooding others' land. Nor the corporate owner of a nuclear generating plant, when it is directed to remove all improvements from its land upon discovery that the plant sits astride an earthquake fault. Such regulatory action may well have the effect of eliminating the land's only economically productive use, but it does not proscribe a productive use that was previously permissible under relevant property and nuisance principles. The use of these properties for what are now expressly prohibited purposes was always unlawful, and (subject to other constitutional limitations) it was open to the State at any point to make the implication of those background principles of nuisance and property law explicit....When, however, a regulation that declares "off-limits" all economically productive or beneficial uses of land goes beyond what the relevant background principles would dictate, compensation must be paid to sustain it.[44]

The "total taking" inquiry we require today will ordinarily entail (as the application of state nuisance law ordinarily entails) analysis of, among other things, the degree of harm to public lands and resources, or adjacent private property, posed by the claimant's proposed activities, see, e.g., Restatement (2d) of Torts §§826, 827, the social value of the claimant's activities and their suitability to the locality in question, id., §§828, 831, and the relative ease with which the alleged harm can be avoided through measures taken by the claimant and the government (or adjacent private landowners) alike, id., §§827, 828, 830. The fact that a particular use has long been engaged in by similarly situated owners ordinarily imports a lack of any common-law prohibition (though changed circumstances or new knowledge may make what was previously permissible no longer so, see Restatement (Second) of Torts, supra, §827, comment g. So also does the fact that other landowners, similarly situated, are permitted to continue the use denied to the claimant.

It seems unlikely that common-law principles would have prevented the erection of any habitable or productive improvements on petitioner's land; they rarely support prohibition of the "essential use" of land. The question, however, is one of state law to be dealt with on remand.... To win its case, South Carolina must,...as it would be required to do if it sought to restrain Lucas in a common-law action for public nuisance, must identify background principles of nuisance and property law that prohibit the uses he now intends in the circumstances in which the prop-

43. [Original fn 16] The principal "otherwise" that we have in mind is litigation absolving the State (or private parties) of liability for the destruction of "real and personal property, in cases of actual necessity, to prevent the spreading of a fire" or to forestall other grave threats to the lives and property of others. Bowditch v. Boston, 101 U.S. 16, 18–19 (1880); see United States v. Pacific Railroad, 120 U.S. 227, 238–239 (1887).

44. [Original fn 17] Of course, the State may elect to rescind its regulation and thereby avoid having to pay compensation for a permanent deprivation. See First English Evangelical Lutheran Church, 482 U.S., at 321. But "where the [regulation has] already worked a taking of all use of property, no subsequent action by the government can relieve it of the duty to provide compensation for the period during which the taking was effective."

erty is presently found. Only on this showing can the State fairly claim that, in proscribing all such beneficial uses, the Beachfront Management Act is taking nothing.[45] The judgment is reversed and the cause remanded....

KENNEDY, J., concurring... The common law of nuisance is too narrow a confine for the exercise of regulatory power in a complex and interdependent society. The State should not be prevented from enacting new regulatory initiatives in response to changing conditions, and courts must consider all reasonable expectations whatever their source. The Takings Clause does not require a static body of state property law.... Coastal property may present such unique concerns for a fragile land system that the State can go further in regulating its development and use than the common law of nuisance might otherwise permit.... [South Carolina, however, failed to make a showing that coastal protections should have been part of the owner's investment-backed expectations.]

BLACKMUN, J., dissenting... Today the Court launches a missile to kill a mouse. The State of South Carolina prohibited petitioner Lucas from building a permanent structure on his property from 1988 to 1990. Relying on an unreviewed (and implausible) state trial court finding that this restriction left Lucas' property valueless, this Court granted review to determine whether compensation must be paid in cases where the State prohibits all economic use of real estate. According to the Court, such an occasion never has arisen in any of our prior cases, and the Court imagines that it will arise "relatively rarely" or only in "extraordinary circumstances." Almost certainly it did not happen in this case. Nonetheless, the Court presses on to decide the issue, and...creates simultaneously a new categorical rule and an exception (neither of which is rooted in our prior case law, common law, or common sense).... My fear is that the Court's new policies will spread beyond the narrow confines of the present case. For that reason, I, like the Court, will give far greater attention to this case than its narrow scope suggests — not because I can intercept the Court's missile, or save the targeted mouse, but because I hope perhaps to limit the collateral damage....

The Beachfront Management Act includes a finding by the South Carolina General Assembly that the beach/dune system serves the purpose of "protect[ing] life and property by serving as a storm barrier which dissipates wave energy and contributes to shoreline stability in an economical and effective manner." The General Assembly also found that "development unwisely has been sited too close to the [beach/dune] system, [and there is] need to "afford the beach/dune system space to accrete and erode." This type of development has jeopardized the stability of the beach/dune system, accelerated erosion, and endangered adjacent property." If the state legislature is correct that the prohibition on building in front of the setback line prevents serious harm, then, under this Court's prior cases, the Act is constitutional.... Nothing in the record undermines the General Assembly's assessment that prohibitions on building in front of the setback line are necessary

---

45. [Original fn 18] Justice Blackmun decries our reliance on background nuisance principles at least in part because he believes those principles to be as manipulable as we find the "harm prevention"/"benefit conferral" dichotomy. There is no doubt some leeway in a court's interpretation of what existing state law permits-but not remotely as much, we think, as in a legislative crafting of the reasons for its confiscatory regulation. We stress that an affirmative decree eliminating all economically beneficial uses may be defended only if an objectively reasonable application of relevant precedents would exclude those beneficial uses in the circumstances in which the land is presently found.

to protect people and property from storms, high tides, and beach erosion. Because that legislative determination cannot be disregarded in the absence of such evidence, and because its determination of harm to life and property from building is sufficient to prohibit that use under this Court's cases, the South Carolina Supreme Court correctly found no taking....

The trial court...found the property "valueless." The court accepted no evidence from the State on the property's value without a home, and petitioner's appraiser testified that he never had considered what the value would be absent a residence. The appraiser's value was based on the fact that the "highest and best use of these lots...[is] luxury single family detached dwellings." The trial court appeared to believe that the property could be considered "valueless" if it was not available for its most profitable use....

I first question the Court's rationale in creating a category that obviates a "case-specific inquiry into the public interest advanced," if all economic value has been lost. If one fact about the Court's taking jurisprudence can be stated without contradiction, it is that "the particular circumstances of each case" determine whether a specific restriction will be rendered invalid.... In none of the cases did the Court suggest that the right of a State to prohibit certain activities without paying compensation turned on the availability of some residual valuable use. Instead, the cases depended on whether the government interest was sufficient to prohibit the activity, given the significant private cost.

These cases rest on the principle that the State has full power to prohibit an owner's use of property if it is harmful to the public.... It would make no sense...to suggest that an owner has a constitutionally protected right to harm others, if only he makes the proper showing of economic loss.... Ultimately even the Court cannot embrace the full implications of its per se rule: it eventually agrees that there cannot be a categorical rule for a taking based on economic value that wholly disregards the public need asserted. Instead, the Court decides that it will permit a State to regulate all economic value only if the State prohibits uses that would not be permitted under "background principles of nuisance and property law."[46]

Until today, the Court explicitly had rejected the contention that the government's power to act without paying compensation turns on whether the prohibited activity is a common-law nuisance.[47] The brewery closed in *Mugler* was not a common-law nuisance.... In determining what is a nuisance at common law, state courts make exactly the decision that the Court finds so troubling when made by

---

46. Although it refers to state nuisance and property law, the Court apparently does not mean just any state nuisance and property law. Public nuisance was first a common-law creation, see Newark, The Boundaries of Nuisance, 65 L. Q. Rev. 480, 482 (1949) (attributing development of nuisance to 1535), but by the 1800s in both the United States and England, legislatures had the power to define what is a public nuisance, and particular uses often have been selectively targeted. See Prosser, Private Action for Public Nuisance, 52 Va. L. Rev. 997, 999–1000 (1966); J.F. Stephen, A General View of the Criminal Law of England 105–107 (2d ed. 1890). The Court's references to "common-law" background principles, however, indicate that legislative determinations do not constitute "state nuisance and property law" for the Court.

47. Also, until today the fact that the regulation prohibited uses that were lawful at the time the owner purchased did not determine the constitutional question. The brewery, the brickyard, the cedar trees, and the gravel pit were all perfectly legitimate uses prior to the passage of the regulation. See Mugler v. Kansas, 123 U.S. 623, 654 (1887); Hadacheck v. Los Angeles, 239 U.S. 394 (1915); Miller, 276 U.S., at 272; Goldblatt v. Hempstead, 369 U.S. 590 (1962). This Court explicitly acknowledged in Hadacheck that "a vested interest cannot be asserted against [the police power] because of conditions once obtaining. To so hold would preclude development and fix a city forever in its primitive conditions." 239 U.S. at 410.

the South Carolina General Assembly today: they determine whether the use is harmful....

Although, prior to the adoption of the Bill of Rights, America was replete with land use regulations,...the Fifth Amendment's Taking Clause originally did not extend to regulations of property, whatever the effect.[48] Most state courts agreed with this narrow interpretation of a taking. "Until the end of the nineteenth century...jurists held that the constitution protected possession only, and not value." Siegel, Understanding the Nineteenth Century Contract Clause: The Role of the Property-Privilege Distinction and "Takings" Clause Jurisprudence, 60 S. Cal. L. Rev. 1, 76 (1986); F. Bosselman, D. Callies & J. Banta, The Taking Issue 80–81, 106 (1973)....

In short, I find no clear and accepted "historical compact" or "understanding of our citizens" justifying the Court's new taking doctrine. Instead, the Court seems to treat history as a grab-bag of principles, to be adopted where they support the Court's theory, and ignored where they do not.... What makes the Court's analysis unworkable is its attempt to package the law of two incompatible eras and peddle it as historical fact.

The Court makes sweeping and, in my view, misguided and unsupported changes in our taking doctrine. While it limits these changes to the most narrow subset of government regulation — those that eliminate all economic value from land — these changes go far beyond what is necessary to secure petitioner Lucas' private benefit. One hopes they do not go beyond the narrow confines the Court assigns them to today. I dissent.

STEVENS, J., dissenting... In my opinion,...the categorical rule the Court establishes is an unsound and unwise addition to the law and the Court's formulation of the exception to that rule is too rigid and too narrow.... The categorical rule will likely have one of two effects: Either courts will alter the definition of the "denominator" in the takings "fraction," rendering the Court's categorical rule meaningless, or investors will manipulate the relevant property interests, giving the Court's rule sweeping effect. To my mind, neither of these results is desirable or appropriate, and both are distortions of our takings jurisprudence.... The Court's new rule is unsupported by prior decisions, arbitrary and unsound in practice, and theoretically unjustified. In my opinion, a categorical rule as important as the one established by the Court today should be supported by more history or more reason than has yet been provided....

The Court's holding today effectively freezes the State's common law, denying the legislature much of its traditional power to revise the law governing the rights and uses of property. Until today, I had thought that we had long abandoned this approach to constitutional law. More than a century ago we recognized that "the great office of statutes is to remedy defects in the common law as they are developed, and to adapt it to the changes of time and circumstances."... Arresting the development of the common law is not only a departure from our prior decisions;

---

48. James Madison, author of the Taking Clause, apparently intended it to apply only to direct, physical takings of property by the Federal Government. See Treanor, The Origins and Original Significance of the Just Compensation Clause of the Fifth Amendment, 94 Yale L.J., 694, 711 (1985). Professor Sax argues that although "contemporaneous commentary upon the meaning of the compensation clause is in very short supply," 74 Yale L.J., at 58, the "few authorities that are available" indicate that the clause was "designed to prevent arbitrary government action," not to protect economic value. Id., at 58–60.

it is also profoundly unwise. The human condition is one of constant learning and evolution — both moral and practical. Legislatures implement that new learning; in doing so they must often revise the definition of property and the rights of property owners. Thus, when the Nation came to understand that slavery was morally wrong and mandated the emancipation of all slaves, it, in effect, redefined "property." On a lesser scale, our ongoing self-education produces similar changes in the rights of property owners: New appreciation of the significance of endangered species, the importance of wetlands, and the vulnerability of coastal lands, shapes our evolving understandings of property rights.

Of course, some legislative redefinitions of property will effect a taking and must be compensated — but it certainly cannot be the case that every movement away from common law does so.... We live in a world in which changes in the economy and the environment occur with increasing frequency and importance.... The rule that should govern a decision in a case of this kind should focus on the future, not the past. The Court's categorical approach rule will, I fear, greatly hamper the efforts of local officials and planners who must deal with increasingly complex problems in land-use and environmental regulation. As this case...well demonstrates, these officials face both substantial uncertainty because of the ad hoc nature of takings law and unacceptable penalties if they guess incorrectly about that law....

The impact of the ban on developmental uses must also be viewed in light of the purposes of the Act.... The State, with much science on its side, believes that the "beach/dune system acts as a buffer from high tides, storm surge, and hurricanes." This is a traditional and important exercise of the State's police power, as demonstrated by Hurricane Hugo, which in 1989, caused 29 deaths and more than $6 billion in property damage in South Carolina alone.

In view of all of these factors, even assuming that petitioner's property was rendered valueless, the risk inherent in investments of the sort made by petitioner, the generality of the Act, and the compelling purpose motivating the South Carolina Legislature persuade me that the Act did not effect a taking of petitioner's property....

STATEMENT OF JUSTICE SOUTER. I would dismiss the writ of certiorari in this case as having been granted improvidently. After briefing and argument it is abundantly clear that an unreviewable assumption on which this case comes to us is both questionable as a conclusion of Fifth Amendment law and sufficient to frustrate the Court's ability to render certain the legal premises on which its holding rests.... The trial court's conclusion...that the state by regulation had deprived the owner of his entire economic interest in the subject property...is highly questionable.... Because the questionable conclusion of total deprivation cannot be reviewed, the Court is precluded from attempting to clarify the concept of total...taking on which it rests, a concept which the Court describes as so uncertain under existing law as to have fostered inconsistent pronouncements by the Court itself. Because that concept is left uncertain, so is the significance of the exceptions to the compensation requirement that the Court proceeds to recognize. This alone is enough to show that there is little utility in attempting to deal with this case on the merits....

COMMENTARY AND QUESTIONS

### 1. Environmental policy: back off from challenging the sea.

*Everyone who hears these words of mine and does not put them into practice is like a foolish man who builds his house on sand. The rains come down, the streams rise, and the winds blow, and it falls with a great crash.*

                                                                Matthew 7:26–27

The modern real estate market's drive to develop prime residential housing on the barrier beaches of the U.S. has led to a series of disasters but no diminution of the building boom. The rate of building on our coastal beaches is five times greater than on inland locations. The threat of hurricane wipeouts is blunted by federally-subsidized flood hazard insurance that provides a base for mortgage financing that otherwise would not exist. (The insurance requires that localities be zoned with storm and erosion setback regulations, but the model regulations provide for variances where enforcement would impose economic burdens.) The obvious wise policy in confronting the inevitable onslaughts of coastal storms is not to stake out private property development lines at the shifting fragile edge of the seacoast, but to manage a measured retreat from the confrontation with nature. See Hearings on H.R. 5981 to establish a Barrier Islands Protection System, 96th Cong. 2d Sess., March 1980.

And in eco-economic terms, what would the commercial market value of Mr. Lucas's million-dollar property be if it were not for the massive public subsidies that the real estate industry lobbied for and now takes for granted? Subtract from market value the amounts attributable to subsidized flood insurance; highway, causeway, and bridge construction and reconstruction; linear barrier beach extension of sewer and utilities; beach re-nourishment and beach protection; rescue operations; disaster aid; reconstruction financing; and the like, and the willingness of banks to finance and buyers to pay for risky barrier beach locations would drop to very little. See Siffin, Bureaucracy, Entrepreneurship, and Natural Resources: Witless Policy and the Barrier Islands, 1 Cato Journal (1981) (cataloguing the remarkable list of federal subsidies obtained by barrier beach developers). But the constitutional calculus apparently cannot offset public elements in private property value, and must use full market value as the constitutional starting point. The political process could cut the subsidies, or require that they be weighed in the procedures proposed in various Wise Use property rights bills, but the political forces involved in subsidies make this highly unlikely.

### 2. Reading *Lucas.*

The *Lucas* case is a vast, rich accumulation of takings debate. The full text of the five *Lucas* opinions totals 75 pages. Behind the pitched arguments about what substantive takings tests should apply to property value wipeouts — and questions whether this action was truly "ripe" for review, whether the land was truly valueless, and how much a federal court should defer to the findings of state legislatures and supreme courts — lie a concatenation of judicial politics. Has this majority overthrown the *Keystone Bituminous* majority? Why was certiorari granted in this case and not to the *First English* floodplain case after the California court had upheld that wipeout on remand? Does the majority decide this case as an extraordinary exception, where there is a total wipeout, or is it setting a test to encourage wider invalidations of regulatory restrictions? Would the votes have been quite different if it had not be such an extreme case?

Here is Professor Sax's read on *Lucas* –

> How is Justice Scalia's aggressive opinion in *Lucas* to be understood?... I believe Justice Scalia...had a clear message which he sought to convey: States may not regulate land use solely by requiring landowners to maintain their property in its natural state as part of a functioning ecosystem, even though those natural functions may be important to the ecosystem.... The target of *Lucas* is broader than its immediate concern of coastal dune maintenance. The opinion encompasses such matters as wetlands regulation, which recently has generated a great deal of controversial litigation [and] anticipates cases that will be brought under Section Nine of the Endangered Species Act, under which private landowners may be required to leave [part of] their land undisturbed as habitat. In general, *Lucas* addresses legislation imposed to maintain ecological services performed by land in its natural state.... If the South Carolina regulation had been sustained, the decision would have constitutionalized a broad panoply of laws requiring landowners to leave their property in its natural condition.... The Court correctly perceives that an ecological worldview presents a fundamental challenge to established property rights, but the Court incorrectly rejects that challenge [because, Sax says, the decision should have incorporated the "economy of nature" noted above in Chapter One]. Sax, Property Rights and the Economy of Nature: Understanding Lucas v. South Carolina Coastal Council, 45 Stanford Law Review 1433 (1993).

Sax further argues that the doctrinal distinctions that Justice Scalia attempts to establish — an inelastic nuisance definition, avoidance of harm/benefit analyses, and the inappositeness of personal property analogies — cannot practically be applied as categorical elements.

3. **Takings tests after *Lucas*.** What if anything has changed after *Lucas*? Is there now a categorical "bright line" test for regulatory takings, at least for wipeouts? "Categorical" means "admitting of no exceptions." A major exception was apparently built into the test by saying that restrictions must inhere in limits that "background principles of the State's law of property and nuisance already place upon land ownership." But what does this mean? Are the common law precedents existing as of the date of this opinion the limit? Or is there still a balance?

On remand, the South Carolina Supreme Court fulfilled the fears of Justices Blackmun and Stevens. The court's major inquiry of the Coastal Commission's attorney was simply whether any South Carolina nuisance case existed directly on point. Told there was no such case, the court said "We hold that the sole issue...is a determination of the actual damages Lucas has sustained as the result of his being temporarily deprived of the use of his property." 424 S.E.2d 484 (1992). There was no balancing of nuisance-like public harms.

Does the *Lucas* opinion really freeze the law by requiring a prior tort case on point? Justice Scalia offers an example of a valid wipeout regulation: "a nuclear generating plant...astride an earthquake fault." But why? There is no common law nuisance case in any state holding earthquake fault siting to be a tort, so even in the supposed categorical setting, Scalia must be adopting a flexible modern balancing view of what constitutes "nuisance-like" restraints. This re-imports judicial harm-weighing judgments into takings jurisprudence, and goes far beyond traditional common law, even in the wipeout setting. Many lower courts, however, will undoubtedly miss the subtlety and require a case on point, like the South Carolina *Lucas* court on remand.

Other issues likewise remain unclear....

### 4. Is the categorical rule only for wipeouts? What's a wipeout? Among the questions that *Lucas* stirs up but doesn't resolve is the question "when is property value wiped out?" In fact, although the Court chose to accept the trial judge's finding that the land was "valueless," it is almost impossible to believe that Lucas's seafront lots, and any other parcel in the land for that matter, had absolutely no market value remaining.[49]

If you accept the premise as the Court did that Lucas' lots were totally valueless, however, does that mean that the *Lucas* reasoning will virtually never be applied again, because probably no such exceptional findings of zero value, total wipeouts will ever occur, even on Footnote 7's re-narrowed baselines?

Not likely. The wording of the threshold definition of excessive private loss in *Lucas* may not require a total wipeout. Justice Scalia practically invites imprecise judicial interpretations of how much diminution is needed to trigger categorical invalidation of regulations. In places, the opinion says its rule applies to "total taking[s]" where regulations remove "*all* economically *beneficial* use of land." It's not clear what that means, though it sounds like a total wipeout. But in other places Justice Scalia casually mentions the "no economically viable use" of the old zoning cases. This can easily allow misinterpretation by the inexpert to apply the "categorical' rule — removing the need for any public-private balancing — even from cases where there is far less than a wipeout, whenever regulated economic uses are not "viable," or "profitable." Even the *K&K* court, for instance, implies that the "categorical" *Lucas* test applies where there is no "economically viable use" of land.[50] This phrasing likewise lies at the heart of the California case City of Monterey v. Del Monte Dunes Corp., 95 F.3d 1422 (9th Cir., 1997, cert. granted 1998), where the court gave the question of what was an economically viable use to a jury, under a categorical taking rule.[51] Justice Scalia has opened the door for

---

49. When Lucas' attorney began his argument by saying the regulated land was worthless, Justice Blackmun leaned over the bench and asked, "Then will he give it to me?" The attorney hesitated, then replied, "Yes, if you pay the taxes," missing the point that property taxes are assessed on value.

50. Even the Supreme Court Clerk's Syllabus, though unofficial, was thereby misled to summarize *Lucas'* holding as: "Regulations that deny the property owner all 'economically viable use of his lan'" constitute one of the discrete categories of regulatory deprivations that require compensation without the usual case-specific inquiry into the public interest," setting out the distinction dead wrong.

51. The *Del Monte Dunes* court remarkably gave three of the most subtle constitutional tests to a jury, to determine whether a temporary taking had occurred: whether the regulation was sufficiently "reasonably related" to legitimate public purposes, whether the land (which plaintiff who had later sold to the government for $800,000 more than it had paid) had been deprived of all "economically viable use" (interpreted in terms of loss of profit expectations, not valueless wipeouts), and whether the city had treated different properties differently in violation of the equal protection clause. "Whether the government's actions are 'reasonable' is often a jury issue. See, e.g., Chew v. Gates, 27 F.3d 1432, 1443 (9th Cir. 1994) (whether release of police dog on individual was reasonable)." The court seized upon some of the most expansive phrasings of the *Lucas* opinion, and added a "substantial proportionality" test from the *Dolan* physical exactions case at the end of this chapter.

By shifting takings tests to juries, this case's approach opens a strong new antiregulation tactic, to be considered by the Supreme Court on certiorari.

extensions of his automatic-compensation rule to restrictions far less pronounced than in *Lucas*, and invites judges to ignore the public-private rights balancing of modern takings cases, turning back to constitutional tests that look only at the impact on private property.

5. **Continued baseline games.** Does *Lucas* footnote 7 now re-open the baseline games? After *Lucas*, in Concrete Pipe & Products, Inc. v. Construction Laborers Pension Trust, 508 U. S.602 (1993) the Court including Justice Scalia used an aggregate baseline instead of conceptual severance, holding that "a claimant's parcel of property [cannot] first be divided into what was taken and what was left" in order to demonstrate a compensable taking. The Court of Claims and the Federal Circuit, however, often continue to apply the Rehnquist *Keystone* dissent's conceptual severance arguments. See Loveladies Harbor v. U.S., 28 F.3d 1171 (Fed. Cir. 1994). In *Loveladies*, the developer had sold off most of a parcel of more than 300 acres for a substantial profit in the years immediately prior to the regulation. The Federal Circuit decided that the baseline was the remaining 12-acre regulated wetland alone, weighted the balance heavily on the side of libertarian interests, and found the regulation an invalid taking.

6. **The story behind the story.** Do you detect an attempt by Justice Blackmun to raise skepticism about Mr. Lucas's bona fides? Lucas was portrayed in the media as just like any other private citizen who wanted to build a home for himself and his family and another for resale, and got steamrolled by government. Lucas plunked down almost a million bucks for the two lots. This apparently was the highest price ever paid for lots in the Beachwood subdivision of the Wild Dunes development. Yet Lucas had been intimately associated with that development since 1979, having served as a contractor, a realtor, and as a planning assistant to the Wild Dunes developer. (see trial transcript at 24, 33–34.) Is it likely that such insiders normally wait until the last, so as to be able to pay top dollar for a lot? And then for 19 months, from December 1986 until passage of the new act in June 1988, Lucas did nothing with the land, except, presumptively, paying approximately $10,000 a month in payments of interest charges and principal. (In media interviews, Lucas complained about his payments for taxes and insurance, but did not mention that he was paying any carrying charges on his property.) Was the case a put-up job, trying to create a good test case for the privateering "wise-use" movement? Does it matter?

7. **On the beach.** Almost immediately after the remand decision, David Lucas applied for permission to develop his lots under the amended act. The request was quickly granted by the Council, in effect acknowledging that although theoretically a whole new review was possible, this case had been won by Lucas. Shortly thereafter, on July 7, to forestall Lucas's claims for attorneys fees and temporary takings damages, the Council negotiated a lump sum settlement, including purchase of Lucas's two lots, for a total payout of $1.575 million, apportioned at $425 thousand per lot and $725 thousand for "interim interest, attorney's fees, and costs."

Adding to the intimations of disingenuity abounding in this case, it has been reported that the state, having been forced in effect to buy the two Lucas lots, has thereafter felt financially-impelled to re-sell them at market value, for residential construction.

8. **Can wetland regulations prevail under a reformed takings test?** The diminution-balancing test advocated in the preceding text would require a two-stage review, first to determine whether there is any reasonable remaining use, and second whether private losses exceed public harms. Won't wetland regulations fail both these tests, unless fortuitously the property owner's parcel contains buildable high ground outside of the wetlands area? The problem is that a wetlands parcel that is completely restricted typically has no appreciable commercial use. That leaves wetlands restrictions dependent upon the assertion that building on wetlands will potentially cause more harm than the private losses sustained. But are courts willing to count wetland losses as "harms" in the same league as floodplain property and safety hazards, earthquake and mudslide hazards, avalanche hazards, or the other hypotheticals discussed earlier? The loss of a 5-acre parcel of wetlands, as noted in the *Johnson* case, is the loss of "a valuable natural resource [that] plays an important role in the conservation and development of aquatic and marine life, gamebirds and waterfowl." Coastal wetlands are the spawning areas for millions of dollars worth of commercial fish caught in the open ocean, and all wetlands serve as natural sponges, buffering and holding high water conditions. But aren't the effects of wetlands losses rather abstract and remote, especially because they are based on cumulative losses of thousands of acres of wetlands? If water-based ecological resources of wetlands are identified as public property rights under the public trust, would that counterweigh private market losses?

9. **Can a court consider ecological cumulation?** What of the reality that environmental losses are cumulative? In coastal wetlands cases, for instance, it might be possible to show that if regulations are struck down unless compensated (a fiscal impossibility), the cumulative loss of spawning resources would eliminate 20 percent of commercial fish stocks supporting a $400 million fisheries industry. Would that catch a judge's eye and be legitimately factored into the constitutional balance? If a harms-based takings test is applied case by case, without regard to cumulation, it would result in the piecemeal cumulative destruction of a widespread wetland resource. If harms are cumulated, on the other hand, it might be virtually impossible for any private property owner to overturn wetlands regulations. If a court cumulates public harms, should it also cumulate all private market value losses in order to balance constitutional factors? These and other constitutional and ecological conundrums are presented with particular vividness by the wetlands situation, although *Florida Rock* and *Sibson* are the rare exceptions in taking on the question of the overall balance of public versus private rights in takings cases.

### Section 5. A TAKINGS ROLE FOR THE PUBLIC TRUST DOCTRINE?

In Lucas, Justice Scalia held that, at least where property values were wiped out —
> Any limitation so severe cannot be newly legislated or decreed (without compensation), but must inhere in the title itself, in the restrictions that background principles of the State's law of property and nuisance already place upon land ownership. *Lucas* at 505 U.S. at 1029.

Did this inadvertently open the door to an additional weighing of public rights (and perhaps even the "natural economy") against private marketplace rights, by incorporating the public trust doctrine into the takings balance?

### Hope Babcock, Has the U.S. Supreme Court Finally Drained the Swamp of Takings Jurisprudence? — The Impact of Lucas v. South Carolina Coastal Council on Wetlands and Coastal Barrier Beaches
19 Harvard Environmental Law Review 1 (1994)

Most of the *Lucas* majority opinion focuses on the uses proscribed by state nuisance law. Little attention has been paid to a further source of guidance: state property law [in the public trust doctrine, and custom].... As the essence of the...common law doctrine of custom... is the "understandings of our citizens," custom would appear to be one of the *Lucas* Court's "background principles of property" that "inhere[s] in the title itself." As such, it could be used where applicable to support "measures newly enacted by the state in legitimate exercise of its police powers on property impressed with a customary usufruct."...

The public trust doctrine...is considerably more versatile. Unlike custom, the doctrine of public trust has shown enormous vitality and flexibility in the modern era. The *Lucas* decision could give the doctrine even more prominence, as public trust principles may well be employed by government regulators in their attempts to justify their actions under the *Lucas* takings rule....

The relationship between the public trust doctrine and takings jurisprudence has been largely unexplored by the courts.... Courts have commonly given several reasons why exercises of public trust authority should bar a takings claim.... The land in question is not, like ordinary private land held in fee simple absolute, subject to development at the sole whim of the owner, but is impressed with a public trust, which gives the public's representatives an interest and responsibility in its development....

Another reason commonly given is that since private rights attached to the trust resources later than the public's rights, which originated with (or even prior to) sovereignty, private title does not include the right to affect trust resources adversely.... It is as though the private property owner of trust lands is merely a custodian of those lands for present and future generations, and the state has an easement over her lands that permanently burdens ownership of them....

Reliance on these doctrines by government regulators to defend against takings claims may...destabilize expectations about property.... Frustrating the expectations of landowners could lead to a backlash not only against the doctrines, but also against the environmental laws which protect wetlands and barrier beaches. The public trust doctrine [however] helps to harmonize the laws of nature and the law of property, bringing the expectations of landowners into harmony with the needs of nature by infusing an ecological perspective into property law. This is beneficial because the laws of nature are fundamental and irrefutable, unlike the laws of property, which can be changed by legislative or executive fiat.... The doctrines of custom and public trust could thwart the [*Lucas*] decision's preference for private property rights by underscoring the public's superior right to access and use certain resources, but this is not as destabilizing as it sounds because both common law doctrines are a reflection of public expectations....

COMMENTARY AND QUESTIONS

1. **The public trust and private property rights.** If public trust rights exist within particular private property, then regulations merely giving effect to a pre-existing potential limitation within the private title do not amount to an invalid regulatory taking. You cannot be deprived of what you never really had, and you may never have had an unfettered right to develop. Private property is always held under the risk that some pre-existing cloud may upset expectations. When a gravel company is suddenly told that it may not quarry its lands because they are public trust wetlands, as in Potomac Sand and Gravel Co. v. Maryland, 293 A.2d 241 (Md. 1972), the trust doctrine can create unexpected economic losses, anger, and political backlash.

2. **A society's underlying "expectations," in takings balances.** Expectations, both private "investment-backed expectations" and public expectations, play a role in the takings balance, as Professor Babcock notes. Professor Sax, who argued that the *Lucas* case should have considered public trust-like values of "the natural economy" in the takings balance,[52] has argued that the public trust is part of a society's expectations:

> The essence of property law is respect for reasonable expectations. The idea of justice at the root of private property protection calls for identification of those expectations which the legal system ought to recognize. We all appreciate the importance of expectations as an idea of justice, but our concern for expectations has traditionally been confined to private owners.... The central idea of the public trust is preventing the destabilizing disappointment of expectations held in common but without formal recognition such as title. The function of the public trust as a legal doctrine is to protect...public expectations against destabilizing changes, just as we protect conventional private property from such changes.[53]

Sax also argued that a society's expectations about what are and are not unfair impositions on private property change over time.[54] In Sanderson v. Penn Coal,[55] a coal company was mining and dumping its wastes in a river, and a downstream landowner objected, claiming traditional riparian rights and protections under nuisance law. The coal company urged that "the law should be adjusted to the exigencies of the great industrial interests of the Commonwealth and that the production of an indispensable mineral...should not be crippled and endangered by adopting a rule that would make colliers answerable in damages for corrupting a stream." The court held —

> We are of opinion that mere private personal inconvenience...must yield to the necessities of a great public industry, which...subserves a great public interest.

---

52. Sax, Property Rights and the Economy of Nature: Understanding Lucas v. South Carolina Coastal Counsel, 45 STANFORD LAW REV. 1433 (1993).

53. Sax, Liberating the Public Trust Doctrine from its Historical Shackles, 14 U. Cal. Davis L.Rev. 185, 186–194 (1980). A 1988 Supreme Court public trust case turned upon whether a state's assertion that it owned certain tidal wetlands upset "settled private expectations." Philips Petroleum Co. v. Mississippi, 484 U.S. 469 (1988) decided that it did not, in an opinion emphasizing the traditional role of the states in defining their public trust; see also e.g. Shively v. Bowlby, 152 U.S. 1, 26 [1894]).

54. Sax, The Limits of Private Rights in Public Waters, 19 Environmental Law 473 (1989).

55. 113 Pa. 126, 6 A. 453, (1886). See also Horwitz, The Transformation in the Conception of Property In American Law 1780–1860, 40 U. Chi. L. Rev. 248 (1973).

> To encourage the development of the great natural resources of a country, trifling inconveniences to particular persons must sometimes give way to the necessities of a great community. 6 A. 453, 459.

In 1886 this ascendancy of marketplace needs did not arouse a horrified reaction in defenders of private property rights. Sax posits that most people are implicitly on notice today that wetlands, beaches, and perhaps even privately-owned historic sites may be subjected to future regulation in the public interest.

3. **Are overrides of common law a regulatory taking?** The common law is traditionally aimed at particular localized conditions; police power regulatory permits are typically set with reference to generalized state-wide minimum standards in a hurly-burly administrative process, and do not purport to be affirmative authorizations of a right to pollute to such levels.

The industrial lobby in Alaska passed a bill in 1994 that effectively repealed the common law tort protections available to private propertyowners if a factory was in compliance with state permits. If a polluting papermill, for instance, complied with the statewide emission standards, it could not be sued for its particular local effects on the neighbors. Alaska Statutes §09.45.230. This raises the fascinating constitutional question whether private property due process rights are violated if landowners are stripped of their traditional tort protections. See Hasselman, Alaska's Nuisance Statute Revisited: Federal Substantive Due Process Limits to Common Law Abrogation," 24 B.C. Envtl Aff. L.Rev. 347 (1997) (concluding after extensive review that it probably does). The amendment also provided a fascinating takings fallback, requiring any industry that availed itself of the shield to cover the state's costs in defending the statute and paying the state's damages owed from any citizens' inverse condemnation challenge against the statute!

4. **Rethinking rights.** The beginning of this chapter noted that extremely rigorous defense of private property rights has been a special characteristic of American democracy, and one of the commonly-credited reasons (along with the nation's extraordinary natural wealth available for exploitation) for the American economy's world dominance. In other nations more densely populated and less richly endowed, property rights resemble privileges and are tempered by public rights. In many countries, for instance, landowners have only qualified rights to mineral resources beneath the surface, and are forced to share the authority to permit mining, and royalties, with their governments. In most modern nations it would be unthinkable for property owners to assert a right to destroy permanently the utility and value of their land, but environmental defendants in this country have recurrently made that fundamental claim, as in the coal stripmining controversies.

The awakening communitarian debate about civic responsibilities as counterweights to rights invites further questions about the absolutist nature of the private property assertions so regularly heard contesting regulatory actions by federal, state, and local governments:

> [When rights in general] have a strident and absolutist character, they impoverish political and judicial discourse. They do not admit of compromise. They do not allow room for competing considerations. They impair and even foreclose deliberation. Rooted in 19th century ideas of absolute [private]

sovereignty over property, they are ill-adapted to a long discussion of tradeoffs and competing needs. They are, moreover, overly individualistic [and focused on the short-term].... They miss the "dimension of sociality" and posit selfish, isolated individuals asserting what is theirs rather than participating in communal life. Sunstein, Rightalk, 205 The New Republic No. 10, 33 (Sept. 2, 1991).[56]

Although the rights-and-responsibilities theorists have sometimes been considered reactionaries, the more sophisticated civic debate they call for cannot be typecast. In the regulatory takings field, for instance, it could do much to temper the average court's preclusive focus on private effects to the exclusion of careful consideration of the public harms that motivate regulation.[57] Coupled with notions of the public trust — and modern acknowledgment of the loss of the mythical American frontier with its boundless resources and ability to absorb mistakes — might it mean that old conceptions of isolated private sovereign rights in land are changing?

### Section 6. OTHER TAKINGS ISSUES: REMEDIES, EXACTIONS, AND INNOCENT LANDOWNER WIPEOUTS

#### a. Takings remedies

The *First English* case, in which land use regulations were ultimately held valid without compensation, earlier had gone to the Supreme Court on the question of what remedies were theoretically available if a takings challenge succeeds. 482 U.S. 304 (1987). This remedies decision established that if a regulation is finally determined to be an invalid taking two remedy options are generally available: (1) an equitable injunction or declaration that the regulation is void on its face or as applied to that particular parcel, or (2) payment by the government for the taking under the rubric of "inverse condemnation" applied to regulatory takings. Governments have the choice whether to pay compensation and continue to apply a regulation that has been found to go too far, or to accept its nullification as to the challenger's property, thereby avoiding the need to pay (although temporary interim damages may be assessed).

Governments will only rarely choose to buy off a regulated property owner if regulation has been found to be a taking. If it does so choose, it is not clear how compensation should be measured. Take a zoning example, with regard to a parcel that would have a full fee simple market value of $100,000 if unregulated. Assume that a court is willing to make especially precise findings of fact, and determines that market value after zoning is $20,000 and that is too little, hence unconstitutional, but that a remaining value of $60,000 would have been constitutional. How much would government have to pay, if it is not taking possession but only maintaining the regulation? $80,000? $40,000?

---

56. (Professor Sunstein is describing Professor Glendon's analysis. Mary Ann Glendon, Rights Talk: The Impoverishment of Political Discourse (1991).) This dimension of communitarian sociability is fine, says the landowner, but why do *I* have to bear the brunt of your highminded civic protections?

57. After surveying the cases, Professor Sax observed that in most cases there apparently is "a hierarchy [of constitutional values] in which the right to profit stands first, with [only] a grudging exception for exigent public need." Sax, Takings, Private Property, and Public Rights, 81 Yale L.J. 149, at n. 7 (1971).

Even tougher is the question of valuing temporary takings, where the state decides to give up and suspend the regulation's application to the parcel, but the landowner, using the further element of *First English*'s remedy case, demands compensation for the "temporary" taking between the time the regulation was applied and the time that it is suspended. What should the measure of such temporary damages be? If it is the difference in market value, that will often have *increased* between the time of the initial regulation and the time the regulation is released. Some courts have argued that "rent" must be paid by government, or even "lost profits." These latter figures can become huge, thereby chilling the exercise of the police power from the start, which may be the point in the first place. What local government wants to undertake an environmental regulation when affected property owners can argue that it confiscates their property, and force payment of millions in lost profits if a court agrees with them? See Almota Farmer's Elevator & Warehouse Company v. U.S., 409 U.S. 470 (1973) (rental value was used as the measure of damages in a physical appropriation case).

### b. Amortization and offset alternatives?

One way government can attempt to secure their regulations against takings challenges is by providing a period of delay before enforcement, to allow the property-owner to "amortize" and recoup her investment before it is shut down. If state or local governments wish to ban billboards, for example, they may provide a four-year amortization period. The billboard industry, one of the strongest lobbies in the nation, is sure to challenge the ban as a regulatory taking. How is amortization, which has been upheld in a wide variety of other property land use regulations, likely to fare against billboards? See Mayor and Council of New Castle v. Rollins Outdoor Advertising, Inc., 459 A.2d 541 (Del. 1983) (three years insufficient); Village of Skokie v. Walton, 456 N.E.2d 293 (Ill. App. 1983) (seven years OK). Is it relevant that a billboard company has long since written off the billboard in depreciation credits on its tax books for the Internal Revenue Service? Nat'l Advertising Co. v. County of Monterey, 464 P.2d 33 (Cal. 1970) (tax depreciation can be considered); Art Neon v. Denver, 488 F.2d 118 (10th Cir. 1973) (amortization need not await depreciation); Modjeska Sign Studios, Inc. v. Berle, 373 N.E.2d 255 (N.Y. 1977) (ditto).

Another possibility is a takings compensation offset. If, for example, the state and federal governments created thousands of acres of private agricultural land out of Florida swamps by channelizing the Kissimmee River at public expense, must they now, 30 years later, pay full dry-land market value when they decide that groundwater levels must be raised, returning some of the lands to wetlands (because the loss of marshes turned out to cause massive pollution effects in downstream water supplies and Lake Okeechobee)? Can a state condemning a billboard agree to pay its fair market value *minus an offset amount attributable to public expenditures,* i.e., excluding all value attributable to the highway? See U.S. v. Cors, 337 U.S. 325 (1949) (government expropriating a vessel need not pay higher values attributable to demand caused by government program). U.S. v. Miller, 317 U.S. 369 (1943). Successful offset arguments, however, are rare.

### c. Exactions and the *Nollan* and *Dolan* cases

Physical appropriations by the public, as opposed to mere regulatory prohibitions, are virtually always a taking. See Loretto v. Teleprompter, 458 U.S. 419 (1982). In many so-called "exaction" cases, however, government regulations have been upheld when they required regulated landowners to provide free property for public parks, or public schools, or roadways, and the like, for public ownership and use, in return for getting development permits, as in subdivision regulation and urban "linkage" programs.

In Nollan v. California Coastal Comm'n, 483 U.S. 825 (1987), the California Coastal Commission had denied the owners of a 1/10th acre lot permission to expand their seashore cabin into a three-bedroom home unless they allowed members of the public using the beach to walk alongside the Nollan's' seawall. The Commission said it needed this right-of-way easement for pedestrian passage along the rocky coastline, because without it beachgoers would not have a "visual access" visibly linking public sandy beaches north and south of the Nollan's property.[58]

In *Nollan*, the Supreme Court struck down the exaction, but held that exactions in general are valid if they (a) occur in a case where the government could constitutionally have denied the entire permit application outright,[59] and (b) if there is a sufficient relationship between the exaction and the regulation — in effect to assure that the exaction is not arbitrary extortion. The definition of this latter "sufficient relationship" was and is the difficult part. Writing for the Court, Justice Scalia did not question the first step. The Commission apparently could validly have prohibited the application outright because the Nollans had a reasonable remaining use of the cabin as it was. But he rejected the second step:

> The evident constitutional propriety disappears...if the condition substituted for the prohibition utterly fails to further the end advanced as the justification for the prohibition. When that essential nexus is eliminated, [the exaction is void].... Unless the permit condition serves the same governmental purpose as the development ban, the building restriction is not a valid regulation of land use but "an out-and-out plan of extortion...." It is quite impossible to understand how a requirement that people already on public beaches be able to walk across the Nollans' property reduces any obstacles to viewing the beach created by the new house.... 483 U.S. at 837–38. [Police power restrictions on property rights must constitute] a "'substantial advanc[e]'of a legitimate state interest." 483 U.S. at 841, (emph. in original).

In *Nollan*, Scalia found there was not a sufficient relationship between the purpose of the regulation (regulation of coastal density, access to the ocean, etc.) and the required lateral easement. He indicated that if the exaction had been to require

---

58. This is as hard to visualize as it was to litigate. Apparently the state commission argued that, lacking a declared easement, beachgoers looking along the shore to the next beach would see only private cabins, seawalls, and rocks coming down to the edge of the sea, and would not realize that there was actually an existing narrow path through the rocks on public property (below the high water mark) along the shore linking the two beaches. By opening up a declared easement, the implied visual barrier would be eliminated.

59. "The Commission argues that a permit condition that serves the same legitimate police-power purpose as a refusal to issue the permit should not be found to be a taking if the refusal to issue the permit would not constitute a taking. We agree." 483 U.S. at 836.

an easement of visual access across Nollan's property *to* the beach from the shore road, that might well have been sufficiently related and OK. What is the "essential nexus"? The exaction apparently must have a nexus both to the *purpose* of the police power regulation, and to burdens that would be directly created and imposed upon the public by the proposed development.

In the case of Florence Dolan v. City of Tigard, 512 U.S. 374 (1994), the Supreme Court seized the opportunity to tighten the terms of how much nexus had to be shown in exactions. The city, acting through its Land Use Board of Appeals (LUBA), gave petitioners a discretionary permit to double the size of their electric and plumbing supply store and to expand their parking lot, but required as exaction conditions that they dedicate roughly 10% of their land within the 100-year floodplain for a recreational low-density "greenway" flood area and improvement of storm drainage and, further, that they dedicate an additional 15-foot strip of land adjacent to the floodplain as a pedestrian/bicycle pathway. LUBA found a reasonable relationship between (1) the development and the requirement to dedicate land for a greenway, since the larger building and paved lot would increase the impervious surfaces and thus the runoff into the creek, and (2) the impact of increased traffic from the development and facilitating a bikeway as an alternative means of transportation. The Oregon Supreme Court found that there was a sufficient "nexus." Writing for the majority, Justice Rehnquist disagreed:

> The question for us is whether these findings are constitutionally sufficient to justify the conditions imposed by the city on petitioner's building permit.... We think a term such as "rough proportionality" best encapsulates what we hold to be the requirement of the Fifth Amendment. No precise mathematical calculation is required, but the city must make some sort of individualized determination that the required dedication is related both in nature and extent to the impact of the proposed development....

> Keeping the floodplain open and free from development would likely confine the pressures on Fanno Creek created by petitioner's development.... But the city demanded more — it not only wanted petitioner not to build in the floodplain, but it also wanted petitioner's property along Fanno Creek for its Greenway system.... The difference to petitioner, of course, is the loss of her ability to exclude others. As we have noted, this right to exclude others is "one of the most essential sticks in the bundle of rights that are commonly characterized as property." Kaiser Aetna, 444 U. S. at 176. It is difficult to see why recreational visitors trampling along petitioner's floodplain easement are sufficiently related to the city's legitimate interest in reducing flooding problems along Fanno Creek, and the city has not attempted to make any individualized determination to support this part of its request.... We conclude that the findings upon which the city relies do not show the required reasonable relationship between the floodplain easement and the petitioner's proposed new building.

> With respect to the pedestrian/bicycle pathway, we have no doubt that the city was correct in finding that the larger retail sales facility proposed by petitioner will increase traffic on the streets of the Central Business District. The city estimates that the proposed development would generate roughly 435 additional trips per day.... But on the record before us, the city has not met its burden of demonstrating that the additional number of vehicle and bicycle trips generated by the petitioner's development reasonably relate to the city's

requirement for a dedication of the pedestrian/bicycle pathway easement.... The city must make some effort to quantify its findings in support of the dedication for the pedestrian/bicycle pathway beyond the conclusory statement that it could offset some of the traffic demand generated.

Cities have long engaged in the commendable task of land use planning, made necessary by increasing urbanization particularly in metropolitan areas such as Portland. The city's goals of reducing flooding hazards and traffic congestion, and providing for public greenways, are laudable, but there are outer limits to how this may be done. "A strong public desire to improve the public condition [will not] warrant achieving the desire by a shorter cut than the constitutional way of paying for the change." Pennsylvania Coal, 260 U. S. at 416. The judgment of the Supreme Court of Oregon is reversed....

### COMMENTARY AND QUESTIONS

1. **The battles of *Dolan*: a new essential nexus?** The shadow of the property rights movement loomed behind the pitched battles in the *Nollan* and *Dolan* opinions. Although all the justices in *Dolan* assumed the necessity of a nexus between the exaction and the *burdens imposed* by the proposed development (by no means previously a foregone conclusion), the strategic question was "*how much* nexus?" The Rehnquist opinion seemed to say "a lot, more than ever before," but as the four dissenters (Stevens, Souter, Ginsburg, and Blackmun) noted, the quantum required and the lack thereof were not defined.

"Rough proportionality" is a concept that will require a good deal of further judicial elaboration. If the floodplain portion of a proposed housing subdivision could be sold to buyers ignoring flood hazards for $200,000 a lot, would an exaction of a flowage easement preventing home construction have to demonstrate that each built lot would cause roughly $200,000 in discounted risk of death and destruction?

2. **Presumption of validity/burden of proof.** A strategic issue looming even larger than the heightened nexus requirement is who has the burden of proving their case. Previously the presumption of validity was presumed to cast the burden on the private party attacking government. The Rehnquist opinion attempted to shift the burden onto government to show the probability that there would be serious effects. While not directly saying they were doing so, the majority justified the shift by saying the city's decision was "adjudicative," for which more evidence was necessary. The vast majority of governmental regulatory actions, permits for example, are informal "adjudications." If indeed this case marked a shift toward putting the burden of proof of validity upon regulatory government, its consequences would change the administrative state as we know it. For political reasons, such a judicial shift in presumption is probably more likely to be applied against environmental regulations than generally, as against regulations managing securities markets, or ordinances regulating speech or demonstrations.

3. **Other worms in the can.** In initially presenting Ms. Dolan's case, Justice Rehnquist had noted that "the city has identified 'no special benefits' conferred on her." Was this a setup for future assertions of his dissenting argument in *Keystone Bituminous* that a regulation is void if it does not give the regulatees a "reciproc-

ity of advantage" roughly proportional to the burdens imposed (as opposed to precedents which used reciprocity only as an affirmance of validity)?

Will there be increasing judicial judgments about what regulations are " necessary"? The majority opinion used a quotation from *Penn Central* about the basic due process requirements of valid regulation: "a use restriction *may constitute a taking if not reasonably necessary* to the effectuation of a substantial government purpose" (emphasis added). In so doing, were they opening up a general inquiry by judges into the wisdom of legislative judgments about how social problems should best be addressed? The temptation toward an activist judiciary is not restricted to the progressive sector.

**4. Predicting the future.** What will be the future effect of *Dolan* on exactions? Faced with the difficulties of negotiating conditions that can be practically defended against *Dolan* challenges, will local governments just deny permits outright, forswearing the flexibility and adjustments previously available under prior exactions law? Will the rough proportionality concept be expanded further, so that local governments will have to bear the burden of convincing a judge that the private property burdens of regulatory decisions are justified in each case by public harms imposed, even where reasonable, economically viable uses remain? In Monterey v. Del Monte Dunes Corp., 95 F.3d 1422 (9th Cir., 1997, cert. granted 1998), one of the novel elements of the case was the extension of Justice Rehnquist's "rough proportionality" language to the rationality nexus of a regulatory takings case.[60] The politics and law of this debate will continue to be interesting.

### d. Due process and the innocent landowner

Here is a final, tough takings problem presented by environmental regulation: assume that your client has purchased a 3-acre piece of land for $20,000 in order to build a greenhouse. She begins digging foundations but suddenly hits fifty leaking unmarked barrels filled with toxic wastes. She notifies the appropriate government agencies, which congratulate her on her forthrightness, and then tell her that the bill for cleanup, for which she is responsible under state and federal statutes, will be $600,000! She turns to you and says, "This has got to be unconstitutional." That hypothetical situation was possible under the federal Superfund statute prior to SARA's 1986 "innocent landowner" exceptions, and is still possible under some state Superfund statutes and in other statutory settings.

Is there a viable constitutional argument against the validity of such heavy monetary burdens imposed by regulation, perhaps focusing on the innocent landowner's lack of fault, intent, or "nexus" to the causation of toxic leakage? The landowner is not, in any conventional sense, the cause of the problem. Would the legal challenges focus upon individual confiscatory effects, the fourth category of police power tests, or upon the third, "rational relationship," test?

---

60. "Even if the City had a legitimate interest in denying Del Monte's development application, its action must be 'roughly proportional' to furthering that interest. The City's denial [i.e. regulatory, not a physical exaction] must be related 'both in nature and extent to the impact of the proposed development.'" (citing *Dolan*.)

Most property owners would reasonably expect that when they buy land, they are taking some chances; *caveat emptor*, buyer beware. But the most one thinks is being risked is the amount of the purchase price of the land. Environmental cases have demonstrated that potential liability may be a hundred times the purchase price of the land. This is a setting in which "fairness expectations" are clearly upset. Does that mean the regulations are unconstitutional?

In an acid mine pollution case, Commonwealth v. Barnes & Tucker Company, 371 A.2d 461 (Pa. 1977), the court noted that the mining company had proved that virtually all of the acid mine water draining from its mine came from the past wrongful activities of neighboring coal mines now abandoned. The court nevertheless held the defendant liable to pay for the entire cleanup, perhaps under some sort of theory of "enterprise liability," an approach that has been followed by other courts. But what about innocent *non*industry landowners, especially if they have not been negligent in failing to discover the toxic materials prior to buying the land?[61] Professor Laitos has pioneered this inquiry into the constitutional invalidity of liability without fault. Laitos, Causation and the Unconstitutional Conditions Doctrine: Why the City of Tigard's Exaction Was a Taking, 72 U. Denver L.R. 893 (1995); the Supreme Court confronted this innocent liability issue in 1998 in Eastern Enterprises v. Appel, No. 97-42 (cert. granted 1997), involving liability for workplace environmental exposures.

The innocent propertyowner is constitutionally a tough problem. Clearly, the innocent owner's land still may be leaching poisonous materials into public groundwater. The landowner would seem to have some responsibility. To extend it, however, to the massive financial burden of cleaning up all toxic wastes on-site raises a difficult fairness problem that, given the heritage of the American bench and bar, is likely to be a serious and challenging constitutional question.

*As the man said, "Money can always wait."*
                                        — Joseph Sax, Defending the Environment, 51 (1970).

*Property is that which is peculiarly yours, whether it is your money, your wife, your children, your house, your car, or your real estate.*
                                        — Don Gerdts, founder, Property Rights Council of America (a Wise Use organization),
                                        in Albany Times-Union, April 11, 1992

---

61. One analogy is the constitutionality of forfeitures of private property used in crimes, even where the owner is totally innocent, Bennis v. Michigan, 116 S.Ct. 995 (1996), a result that many people consider grossly unfair.

*We don't want to be a regulatory agency. We want to be a development agency on our national lands.*

> Secretary of Interior Manuel Lujan,
> speaking to coal executives.
> N.Y. Times, 29 Nov. 1992 at 1, 30.

*It is vain to dream of a wilderness distant from ourselves.*

> — Henry David Thoreau

# Chapter 24

# PUBLIC RESOURCE MANAGEMENT STATUTES

Public resources, whether natural or man-made, are owned by, or held in trust for, all members of a broad community, some of whom actually use the resources and some of whom do not. Public libraries, beds and banks of navigable waterbodies, and public parks are examples of public resources. In order to prevent the tragedy of the commons that threatens resources to which the public has unlimited access, various governmental institutions frequently impose resource management controls, in Hardin's terms of "mutual coercion, mutually agreed upon." The primary source of such coercion in practice lies in public resource management statutes. Those statutes delegate responsibility, through enabling or organic legislation, to administrative agencies in order to regulate public access and use consistent with legislative goals and requirements.

In each case, subtle and contentious issues are woven into the legal management regime of public resources: Are the resources a legacy for the future or assets for maximization of current economic revenues? Are the resources appropriately consigned to one dominant use, or to be managed for a diversity of uses? Are local citizens specially privileged to use them, or are they for all Americans? What if the activity of one class of resource users interferes with the uses of others? Finally, how are these recurrent political and theoretical questions to be resolved?

This chapter focuses on the Federal Land Policy and Management Act ("FLPMA," pronounced "flipma"), 43 U.S.C.A. § 1701 et seq., and the federal Bureau of Land Management (BLM), an agency within the United States Department of the Interior. Part A of the chapter introduces the federal public lands. Part B presents a brief history of grazing on the public lands and a description and analysis of FLPMA. Part C examines a number of issues raised by one of the keystone public land law cases, Kleppe v. New Mexico, 426 U.S. 529 (1976), analyzing BLM's authority to regulate wild horses on federal land in New Mexico. Part D develops a case study of off-road vehicle use on BLM lands. The resource commons can be destroyed by unlimited recreational use, as well as by grazing and other consumptive uses, and the BLM and other federal land management agencies are increasingly called upon to allocate access to their lands among competing recreational groups.

As you read this chapter, consider its close relationship to Chapter 13 on NEPA and Chapter 14 on the Endangered Species Act. NEPA and ESA cases often concern activities planned by federal agencies or their private permittees on federally-owned lands. Moreover, land-use planning for federal lands, such as that required by FLPMA, is inextricably connected to the preparation of environmental impact documents and mandatory endangered species consultations. In most cases the land-use plan, the negative declaration or environmental impact statement, and the ESA biological assessment are contained in a single document.

## A. THE PUBLIC LANDS

The most extensive public resource in the United States is the federal public land system. Almost one-third of the nation's land (over 700 million acres, particularly in the West and Alaska) is owned by the federal government. The federal government owns roughly one-half of all the land in the eleven contiguous western states, including eighty-five percent of the State of Nevada and sixty-three percent of the State of Utah.[1] These massive federal landholdings persist despite the federal government's spirited attempts, during most of the nineteenth and twentieth centuries, to dispose of the lands obtained in treaties with Great Britain, France, Spain, Russia, and Indian tribes. Between 1781 and 1985, over one billion acres of federal public land were sold or granted to homesteaders (287 million acres), railroads (140 million acres), states (72 million acres in the western states), and other persons and entities. The remaining federal public lands are managed, more or less successfully, by numerous federal agencies, some located in different departments of the federal government, with different enabling acts, goals, management philosophies, levels of support and supervision from Congress, and political alliances.

The massive disposal of federal public lands — along with the water, timber, range, and mineral resources associated with them — was, for the most part, implemented in accordance with the "First in time is first in right" (i.e., "First come, first served") principle. The young United States was intent upon asserting its Manifest Destiny by stimulating settlement and economic development of the West's natural resources as expeditiously as possible. This public land policy engendered an "exploit and run," or "use it or lose it" mentality that was inimical to sustainable resource use, conservation, non-extractive uses such as recreation, and the interests of Native Americans and other indigenous minorities. Withdrawals and reservations for these purposes tended to be sporadic, limited and unpopular in the West.[2]

---

1. See Coggins, Wilkinson, and Leshy, Federal Public Land and Resources Law (3rd ed., 1993) (hereafter Coggins et al.), an invaluable reference work for the study of public land law.

2. The history and modern consequences of the "Disposal Era" have been wonderfully chronicled in Professor Charles Wilkinson's Crossing The Next Meridian (1992). Withdrawals of federal land are proscriptions of particular uses that would otherwise be permitted, such as mining or grazing. Reservations are designations of areas for certain uses, such as Native American reservations or military bases.

The BLM administers 170 million acres of arid or semiarid federal land in the eleven western states pursuant to the congressional directives included in FLPMA. There are several reasons for this chapter's concentration on FLPMA and the BLM:

- FLPMA is the most unified and comprehensive organic management legislation governing the activities of any federal resource management agency;

- the BLM range lands exhibit a classic tragedy of the commons (destructive overgrazing) caused by the "capture" of a regulatory agency by a single user group and its political allies; and

- FLPMA adopts a "multiple use-sustained yield" management standard, the standard that prevails with regard to most of the federal public lands, including the roughly 200 million acres administered by the U.S. Forest service, located in the Department of Agriculture, in addition to the BLM's own vast holdings...

The BLM lands have traditionally been managed for grazing of private livestock. In 1974, approximately 23,000 western ranches held BLM permits or leases to graze 3.5 million cattle and horses and 4.5 million sheep and goats on BLM lands.[3] This five percent of all American ranchers using approximately three percent of national livestock forage production has had an inordinately strong impact on congressional and BLM policy regarding BLM lands. Some of the reasons for the extraordinary political influence of this segment of the livestock industry are its entrenchment in American mythology, historic dominance over the BLM, consistent single-mindedness, abundant financial resources, and close proximity to information and the BLM field personnel who manage the resource. Locally prominent individuals and interest groups typically have supported the demands of the local livestock industry. Since grazing permits are comparatively permanent privileges, they add great economic value to the ranchers' private "base properties" contiguous to federal permit grazing lands. Consequently, local financial institutions that loan money to ranchers, with grazing permits as security, actively oppose proposals that might have negative effects on the short-term profit margins of local ranchers — such as cutbacks in grazing allotments in order to revive overgrazed range.

Western state governments also constitute a "public" deeply concerned about BLM management of federal public lands. States cannot impose property taxes on federal property. Instead, they have persuaded Congress to provide annual federal reimbursement payments in lieu of property taxes. These "in lieu payments" are themselves paid from funds generated by fees on private use of federal lands. Western states, for example, receive 12.5 percent of BLM income from grazing fees.[4] Thus, state officials also support continued heavy grazing on BLM lands out of their own institutional fiscal imperatives. Since the 1960s, however, public land law has been revolutionized by the emergence of powerful conservationist and preservationist organizations:

---

3. Coggins, Evans, and Lindeberg-Johnson, The law of Public Rangelend Management I: The Extent and Distribution of Federal Power, 12 Envt'l L. 536-621, 559 (1982) (hereafter cited as "Coggins I").

4. Coggins and Lindeberg-Johnson, The Law of Public Rangeland Management II: The Commons and Taylor Act, 13 Envt'l L. 1, 11 (1982) (hereafter cited as "Coggins II").

It is not possible to delineate precisely just who the new parties are or what they represent. In some cases, private landowners have rejected economic benefit to themselves by various forms of development on or adjacent to their property.... Allied to new landowner attitudes is a new aggressiveness on the part of non-consumptive economic users of public lands. Resorts, guides, river outfitters, backpacking equipment manufacturers, and so forth have resisted development of a resource valuable to them as primitive real estate....

Many of the largest changes have come about through institutional strategies and actions by established and new environmental organizations. Among the most active and effective organizations are the old-line Sierra Club and Wilderness Society, and three newcomers, the Environmental Defense Fund (EDF), the Natural Resources Defense Council (NRDC), and the National Wildlife Federation. Even the traditionally apolitical Audubon Society has found itself lobbying and litigating. These organizations alone — and there are dozens of similar if less visible groups — have wrought legislative change, pursued hundreds of lawsuits...and mobilized considerable public support. Coggins et al., 6–7.

This new "non-consumptive use" public, while generally sharing basic preservationist goals, is not monolithic. Local river rafting outfitters, for instance, have occasionally faced off against national kayaking groups over National Park Service allocations of permits for trips down the Colorado River.[5]

---

## B. THE BLM, FLPMA, AND GRAZING ON THE PUBLIC LANDS

During the years between 1789 and 1976, when the federal government pursued a policy of disposing of western public lands, a concurrent federal policy was to forestall monopolies by large landholders. Given the relatively unproductive character of the western range, the disposal and antimonopoly policies came into conflict, causing legendary fraud and corruption as well as overgrazing of small holdings.

Federal land was given to five distinct classes of beneficiaries, but in parcels too small or too scattered to overcome the inherent problems of low vegetative productivity in much of the West. States, railroads, miners, farmers, and ranchers received most of the federal largess.

The federal government gave an enormous amount of public land to the states...estimated to be 72 million acres in the eleven western states.... Those lands are often still arbitrarily interspersed among private and federal lands.... The railroad land grants continue to obstruct integrated management because they are frequently checkerboarded section-by-section with the public lands.[6] Mining claims are also interspersed, but more randomly. Prospectors who locate a valuable mineral discovery are allowed to take title to the land on which the mineral is found. Agrarian homesteaders claimed hundreds of millions of acres under the various disposition laws, all of which limited the

---

5. See Wilderness Public Rights Fund v. Kleppe, 608 F.2d 1250 (9th Cir. 1979), cert. denied, 446 U.S. 982 (1980).

6. Ed. Note: As an incentive to build the transcontinental railroads, railroad companies were given odd-numbered sections of land within 20 miles on both sides of their rights of-way. These odd-numbered sections were later sold to private parties, creating a "checkerboard pattern" of land ownership with the even-numbered federally-retained sections. See the map, infra.

number of acres that could be granted to one individual. Homesteading policy was liberalized many times to accommodate rancher desires for more land, but the effort proved futile in the end: profitable ranching in the Inter mountain West required more land per operation than Congress was willing to grant.[7]

The lands retained by the federal government were those that, as Professor Coggins puts it, "Nobody was willing to buy or steal." Nevertheless, these huge expanses of federal land became immensely valuable as supplementary grazing land to landholders who discovered that their arid lands were profitable only for grazing cattle, and that the relatively small size of their holdings precluded successful ranching operations.

Until 1934, the federal government maintained a laissez-faire attitude toward public lands, perpetuating an unregulated commons that deteriorated into a severely overgrazed range. (In terms of the "three economies," the marketplace economy dominated the range, largely ignoring the needs of the natural economy and the long term civic-societal interests it served.) A combination of drought and the New Deal prompted a reevaluation of federal range policy, resulting in the Taylor Grazing Act of 1934.[8] Congress had two avowed purposes in enacting the Taylor Act — to end overgrazing and to stabilize the livestock industry. Once again, federal policies that appeared laudable in theory were inconsistent in practice; the Taylor Act did stabilize the livestock industry, but did little to alleviate range deterioration.

The Taylor Act had three main components: (1) it authorized the Secretary of the Interior to withdraw the unappropriated public lands from homesteading and organize them into grazing districts; (2) it gave preference in obtaining and renewing grazing permits to adjacent landowners; and (3) it established district advisory boards, composed mainly of ranchers, that had to be consulted before management decisions were made. The unfortunate result was a "captured agency," in which large adjacent ranchers dominated an understaffed Grazing Division (the BLM's predecessor) through advisory boards, gaining for themselves excessive grazing allotments at fees far below market value:

> The first round of grazing permit decisions set a pattern for the next four decades. Adjacent ranchers first received temporary one-year permits. Later hearings to determine carrying capacity for purposes of permit adjustments were conducted by the ranchers through the advisory boards. Ten-year permits — the maximum allowed by statute — soon became the norm.

> By early 1936, board representatives and the Grazing Division (which had already issued thousands of permits) worked out rules for preference and fees.... The Division set grazing fees at five cents per month for cows and one cent for sheep. The permits were theoretically limited to "carrying capacity." That term, however, turned out to have a different meaning in practice than in science because capacity was determined (primarily by the stockmen) within the first year or two of Taylor Act administration without benefit of survey or biological opinion. In most districts permits had been issued for many more livestock than the range could properly support. When later scientific information,

---

7. Coggins II, 5-6.
8. 43 U.S.C.A. § 315 et seq.

however inadequate, indicated the need for downward revision, ranchers often effectively opposed cuts.[9]

Instead of affording security to the livestock industry in exchange for responsible grazing practices on public lands, the Taylor Act provided further subsidies to ranchers — primary access to the public lands, preferential permits, federal funds for "range improvements" (fencing, revegetation, etc.), and low grazing fees — to continue their traditional overuse of the federal range resource.

In 1946, the Grazing Division was merged with the General Land Office (an agency with strong disposal inclinations) to form the BLM. There was little change in BLM range policies until 1974, despite a 1970 report of the Public Land Law Review Commission recognizing the deteriorated condition of a substantial amount of BLM lands, implicitly criticizing BLM as a servant of grazing interests (and of the mining and timber industries), and recommending that grazing allotments should be consistent with the productivity of the land.[10] In 1974, a NEPA lawsuit, NRDC v. Morton, 388 F. Supp. 829 (D.C.D.C. 1974), transformed federal range management. BLM had prepared a programmatic environmental impact statement on its grazing program after the enactment of NEPA in 1970. The NRDC sued, alleging that the programmatic EIS was inadequate because it did not address the site-specific impacts of grazing. The federal district court sided with NRDC, ordering BLM to prepare EISs for each grazing district. Compelled to study rangeland conditions openly and "go public" with its findings, BLM "has had no choice but to reduce allotments down to carrying capacity."[11] NRDC v. Morton also alerted Congress to the deplorable condition of the BLM lands and the failure of the Taylor Act, leading directly to passage of the Federal Land Policy and Management Act of 1976.

### Coggins, The Law of Public Rangeland Management (IV): FLPMA, PRIA, and the Multiple Use Mandate
14 Environmental Law 1, 5–6 (1983)[12]

FLPMA does not repeal the major Taylor Act provisions. Instead, the 1976 Act superimposes a new management system, with more diverse goals and emphases. FLPMA requires the multiple use-sustained yield that the BLM has long claimed to practice. The 1976 Act mandates intensive planning; of equal importance, specific management decisions made after the land use plans are completed must accord with the plans. The Act also protects grazing permittees to a limited extent. On the whole, however, FLPMA represents a condemnation of past stewardship and requires that the BLM utilize a broader approach to public rangeland management....

FLPMA resolves two fundamental issues: Congress decided to retain the public lands in public ownership and to manage the lands in ways that avoid the "unnecessary or undue degradation" so common in the past.

The framework of FLPMA apparently originated in the 1970 report of the Public Land Law Review Commission (PLLRC). Senator Henry Jackson later claimed that

---

9. Coggins II, 58-59.

10. One-Third of the Nation's Land, 106–108.

11. Coggins I, 555.

12. Hereafter cited as "Coggins IV."

FLPMA embodies the enactment of over 100 PLLRC recommendations into law. In the area of range management, however, the dissimilarities between the report and the final legislation are at least as prominent. The PLLRC recommended that Congress authorize the sale to permittees of lands chiefly valuable for grazing, give ranchers greater security of tenure while requiring them to pay higher fees to use the retained lands, and make livestock grazing the "dominant use of retained lands where appropriate." FLMPA secures permittee tenure in some ways and holds down grazing fee increases, but Congress rejected the generous PLLRC attitude toward ranchers in those other respects. FLMPA adopts the PLLRC recommendations that sought consistency between grazing and land "productivity," that put "priority on the rehabilitation of deteriorated rangeland where possible," that required more administrative flexibility, and that paid more attention to public values, including wildlife. Congress arguably stopped short of adopting the PLLRC recommendation to exclude livestock from "frail lands" and did not make the permittee responsible for the frail condition of the land....

Section 1701(a) of FLPMA declares thirteen sweeping policies. Although it contains some apparent inconsistencies, the section is Congress' most thorough and unambiguous statement of public land policy. The statement is qualified by the proviso in §1701(b) that FLPMA policies are not "effective" until specifically enacted in the Act itself or elsewhere. The courts faced with questions involving §1701(a), however, have uniformly assumed that the policies are binding and effective in the absence of contrary provisions. Whatever their precise legal status, the congressional policies ought to serve as fundamental range management guidelines.

Congress first stated that the public lands will remain in federal ownership unless planning determines that the "national interest" requires disposal of "a particular parcel."... The second policy is that "the national interest will be best realized if the public lands and their resources are periodically and systematically inventoried and their present and future use is projected through a land use planning process coordinated with other Federal and State planning efforts."... [Policies Three to Six involve reviews of existing federal land classifications, restraints on executive withdrawals, encouragement of public participation in BLM decision-making, and judicial review of public land adjudications.]

The seventh congressional statement should be, but has not yet become, the touchstone of public rangeland management. Congress declared that "goals and objectives be established by law as guidelines for public land use planning, and that management be on the basis of multiple use and sustained yield unless otherwise specified by law." Congress specifically enacted these general requirements, but the BLM has neither understood nor carried out these commands.

The eighth statement of policy is a radical departure from all prior rangeland management understanding. Congress required that:

> the public lands be managed in a manner that will protect the quality of scientific, scenic, historical, ecological, environmental, air and atmospheric, water resource, and archeological values; that, where appropriate, will preserve and protect certain public lands in their natural condition; that will provide food and habitat for fish and wildlife and domestic animals; and that will provide for outdoor recreation and human occupancy and use.

Whether or to what extent Congress specifically enacted this goal is unclear. Some sections of FLPMA and other statutes support an argument that this policy binds public land managers, but all the statutory provisions are qualified in some way.

In its ninth policy, Congress sought "fair market value" for public land uses and resources "unless otherwise provided by statute." This policy is definitely not law; not only are grazing fees set at a fraction of market value, but the United States probably does not receive full value for any of the nation's resources.... Congress's tenth policy statement calls for uniform procedures for disposal, exchange, or acquisition of public lands. This policy was enacted in other FLPMA sections.... The eleventh policy seeks rapid protection of "areas of critical environmental concern"; the statute provides that protection.

The twelfth congressional policy balances or counteracts the eighth by emphasizing use instead of preservation. Congress required that "[t]he public lands be managed in a manner which recognizes the Nation's need for domestic sources of minerals, food, timber, and fiber from the public lands."... The thirteenth and final policy calls for equitable reimbursement to states for the local tax burden caused by federal immunity from taxation. This policy was enacted in the Payment in Lieu of Taxes Act of 1976....

For the first time, the BLM is forced by law to develop land use plans in fairly precise ways and, after the plans are promulgated, to act in accordance with the guidelines established in the plans. Section 1711 commands a detailed inventory of all public land resources, and §1712 requires preparation of land use plans for all public land areas.... Section 1732(a) negates any implication that the plans are to be just public relations make-work by making the plans binding on all subsequent multiple use decisions....

FLPMA emphatically rejects the grazing-as-dominant-use tradition in public rangeland management in favor of multiple use-sustained yield principles.... In theory, the standard requires the agency to give all listed resources roughly equal consideration and weight in all decisionmaking. Multiple use-sustained yield is basically a utilitarian principle requiring high-level annual production of all resources in combination.[13] Congress defined both multiple use and sustained yield in sweeping terms. Apparently, however, the legislature never debated precisely how those management concepts were to be applied. Congress assumed instead that the standard was a significant, environmentally-oriented advance over existing authorities. Contrary to the opinions of several commentators, and to BLM predilections, multiple use and sustained yield are more than idle slogans allowing the agency to do as it professionally pleases. If courts begin reviewing multiple use decisions with any depth or insight, the standard as applied through planning processes will reverse the course of public rangeland management....

Before investigating the limitations on management discretion inherent in the multiple use standard, the uses or resources themselves should be defined. In the Multiple Use-Sustained Yield Act (MUSY),[14] the "renewable surface resources" include only "outdoor recreation, range, timber, watershed, and wildlife and fish purposes." In 1976, Congress broadened the list of uses to "renewable and nonrenewable resources including, but not limited to, recreation, range, timber,

13. Ed. Note: Multiple use-sustained yield standards do not necessarily apply to each management unit where multiple use would be inconsistent with the nature of the resource base. In such cases, multiple use-sustained yield must be maintained on the level of some larger, more inclusive planning unit.

14. Ed. Note: The Multiple-Use, Sustained Yield act of 1960, 16 U.S.C.A. § 528 et seq., along with other statutes, governs the activities of the United States Forest Service.

minerals, watershed, wildlife and fish, and natural scenic, scientific, and historical values."...

Most of the listed resources are "renewable," meaning that they regenerate in some biological or climatological fashion. Although minerals are now included in the list, both hardrock mining and mineral leasing remain primarily governed by other statutes that have given mineral exploitation legal or de facto priority over other uses. Water itself, the key resource, was omitted,[15] probably because water allocation was seen as a state function. Wilderness, or "preservation," is not specifically listed, but is supplied in §1782....

The key to multiple use-sustained yield management as a land management system is in the statutory definition of the two phrases. FLPMA borrows heavily from the MUSY Act:

43 U.S.C.A. §§1702...(c) the term "multiple use" means the management of the public lands and their various resource values so that they are utilized in the combination that will best meet the present and future needs of the American people; making the most judicious use of the land for some or all of these resources or related services over areas large enough to provide sufficient latitude for periodic adjustments in use to conform to changing needs and conditions; the use of some land for less than all of the resources; a combination of balanced and diverse resource uses that takes into account the long-term needs of future generations for renewable and nonrenewable resources,...and harmonious and coordinated management of the various resources without permanent impairment of the productivity of the land and the quality of the environment with consideration being given to the relative values of the resources and not necessarily to the combination of uses that will give the greatest economic return or the greatest unit output....

(h) The term "sustained yield" means the achievement and maintenance in perpetuity of a high-level annual or regular periodic output of the various renewable resources of the public lands consistent with multiple use.

The main differences between the 1960 and 1976 definitions, apart from the inclusion of additional resources and values in 1976, are the congressional emphasis on intergenerational equity, the clear directive to achieve long-term conservation, and the requirement of environmental nonimpairment....

[After discussing the numerous discretionary aspects of these statutory definitions, Professor Coggins comments on what he considers to be their enforceable aspects: (1) avoiding impairment of productivity of land and the quality of the environment; and (2) managing for sustained yield.]... This [nonimpairment] standard is fairly precise, and it ought to be enforceable. In a sense, the limitation is a restatement of the watershed value because rangeland productivity requires both water to grow grass and grass to keep the soil in place. "Productivity" is the capacity of the land to support flora and fauna and to furnish "the various renewable resources" in the future. The two key elements in production are soil and water. Therefore, soil and water quality and quantity should be the central focus of public rangeland management attention, but that has not been the case so far.

If the manager were to allow a practice, such as prolonged overgrazing, that causes permanent reductions in future grass production, the nonimpairment limitation would make that action illegal as well as arbitrary. Moreover, when enjoyment of a listed use depends on a rare or unique attribute of an area, the manager

---

15. Ed. Note: Watershed protection, in multiple use legislation, means preservation of the soil and vegetation conditions necessary to provide adequate supplies of clean water.

must safeguard (or preserve) that attribute to ensure nonimpairment. For example, if a particular vista is especially attractive for hikers or tourists (the "outdoor recreation" resource), actions that seriously and permanently interfere with those scenic qualities arguably violate the nonimpairment standard... The nonimpairment standard is clear, mandatory and nondiscretionary....

The most significant management limitation in FLPMA is the definition of "sustained yield" in §1702(h). The phrase means *perpetual, high level* annual resource outputs of *all* renewable resources. Sustained yield is a separate, binding standard that makes continuing resource productivity the highest management criterion. The plain meaning of sustained yield...is that administrators may not sacrifice the future output of any renewable resource in present resource allocations. The "permanent" impairment provision qualifies the sustained yield limitation by ensuring that only serious, longlasting damage is prohibited.... In other words, the agency must plan to accommodate recreation, timber, watershed, wildlife, and natural values, as well as grazing, at high levels in perpetuity, and then act according to that plan....

The search for compatible use combinations at optimum production levels will encounter more conflict than harmony. The main point of multiple use decisionmaking is conflict resolution, with all of the political problems that phrase implies. The manager must try to accommodate all resource uses to the extent possible, giving priority to none — at least on the broad scale — and consideration to all. Sustained yield in compatible combinations does resolve conflicts by theoretically forbidding the optimization of one resource at the expense of others. Such optimization of one resource could leave multiple use decisions vulnerable to attack on sustained yield grounds....

Multiple use-sustained yield management was meant to be more than a "succotash syndrome." Inherent in the concept are detailed and comprehensive commands to force thinking before acting and to mold individual actions into a long-range scheme for the public benefit. FLPMA does not allow the manager to do whatever appears politic or expedient at the time....

### COMMENTARY AND QUESTIONS

1. **Public land management philosophies.** Multiple use-sustained yield is the management philosophy that applies to BLM lands and national forests managed by the Forest Service. Its major rival is "dominant use," a standard recommended by the Public Land Law Review Commission for BLM lands, but disavowed by Congress in FLPMA. In a dominant use management system, a primary use is selected for a portion of the public lands; after that, only those secondary uses that are compatible with the dominant use will be allowed there. Where grazing or mining are set as dominant uses, environmental values would be broadly precluded. Given BLM's historic capture by the grazing industry and its supporters, Congress' multiple use directive has, in practice, been superseded by a de facto dominant use system favoring grazing. Should Congress set grazing as the dominant use on BLM lands? What are the major advantages and disadvantages of multiple use-sustained yield versus dominant use as public land management philosophies?

2. **Multiple use-sustained yield reconsidered.** Despite his earlier enthusiasm for the concept, Professor Coggins has recently given up on multiple use-sustained yield:

> [Multiple use-sustained yield] is a product of history: it is the latter-day off-
> shoot of Gifford Pinchot's utilitarian maxim, the most benefits for the most
> people in the long run. Still, however, nobody knows what multiple use really
> means, but all have opinions. To the resource exploitation industries, multiple
> use means full speed ahead on the development of all surface and subsurface
> resources. To the managers on the ground, it means that they are free to decide
> every question according to their expert judgment without legal standards or
> judicial review. Neither ever mention sustained yield, except in the context of
> timber. This commentator once argued that multiple use laws actually meant
> something — not much, but something — but no court or agency has ever
> taken that argument seriously. Fortunately (from this perspective), multiple
> use as an operational standard is already dying a slow death, even without
> statutory repeal or revision.... Multiple use is obsolete.[16]

Professor Michael Blumm agrees that multiple use-sustained yield has failed. In
his view, it has meant "the adjacent allocation of dominant uses to fulfill the pre-
existing commitment to sustained commodity production."[17] Secretary of the
Interior Bruce Babbitt has advocated replacing the allegedly discredited multiple
use philosophy with a dominant "public use" system: "From this day on, we must
recognize the new reality that the highest and best, most productive use of western public land will usually be for public purposes — watershed, wildlife, and
recreation...."[18] It sounds like renewed recognition of the needs of the natural and
societal economies. Are these reports of multiple use's death premature? The
"New West" is an increasingly urbanized area where environmental interests are
attaining greater political influence. Additionally, public demand for beef has
shown a steady decline. Will changing demographics and public preferences bring
a trend toward real multiple use-sustained yield? Is a dominant "public use"
system capable of dealing with issues such as excessive recreational use of public
lands?

3. **Dominant use management on public lands: mining, logging, wilderness, ...**
National Wildlife Refuges are managed by the Fish and Wildlife Service, of the
Department of the Interior, primarily for the benefit of fish and wildlife conservation. A refuge manager may "permit the use of any area within the System for any
purpose, including but not limited to hunting, fishing, public recreation and
accommodations, and access whenever he determines that such uses are compatible with the major purposes for which such areas were established."[19] Is hunting
appropriate in a wildlife refuge? What about Off-Road Vehicle (ORV) or motorboat
use? Would dominant use justify opening a wildlife refuge for oil recovery operations that impinge on only a small part of the surface area, but drain a pool of oil
that underlies the entire refuge?

Perhaps the best known dominant use statute is the Wilderness Act of 1964, 16

---

16. Coggins, Commentary: Overcoming the Unfortunate Legacies of Western Public Land Law, 29
Land and Water Law Rev. 381, 389 (1994).

17. Blumm, Public Choice Theory And The Public Lands: Why "Multiple Use" Failed, 18 Harv. Env.
L. Rev. 405, 426 (1994).

18. Coggins et al., 1080-1081.

19. National Wildlife Refuge Administration Act, 16 U.S.C.A. §668dd(d)(1). This Act was amended by
Pub. L. 105–57 (1997), which strengthened the conservation mandate of the FWS in National Wildlife
Refuges.

U.S.C.A. §1131 et seq. Under the express terms of this statute, all commercial logging and permanent roads and most structures and installations, temporary roads, commercial enterprises, and motorized equipment and forms of transportation are prohibited, but the following secondary uses are explicitly permitted: mining claims; mineral leases, and grazing permits obtained before January 1, 1964; water resources projects approved by the President; commercial services provided by guides, packers, and river runners; and hunting and fishing. Are these secondary uses compatible with a wilderness area, which is defined by the Act as "an area where the earth and its community of life are untrammeled by man, where man is himself a visitor who does not remain." 16 U.S.C.A. §1131(c).

Hardrock mining on public lands represents an extreme form of dominant use. It is still substantially governed by the General Mining Law of 1872, which declares all unreserved public lands open to mineral exploration and extraction.[20] Under this statute, a prospector locating minimum amounts of valuable minerals on public lands can stake a mining claim, exclude other prospectors and interfering recreationists from it, build a house on the property, and use whatever timber exists there for mining purposes. After several years of negligible work, and payment of a modest fee, the locator can be granted a federal patent that will entitle her to outright ownership of the former mining claim. Once a claim has been patented, the owner can do whatever she wants with the property, including using it or selling it for non-mining purposes. At no time is a locator-patentee required to make rental or royalty payments to the United States. Environmental abuses on mining claims and patented lands have been frequent and serious, sometimes resulting in abandoned mines that pose threats to local water supplies.[21]

Although logging in National Forests is ostensibly regulated by the multiple use-sustained yield standard of the National Forest Management Act, 16 U.S.C.A. §1600 et seq., many would argue that, like the BLM lands, the National Forests have been managed according to a de facto dominant use for timber production.[22]

Water is the key to other land uses in the arid West, but water allocation is not listed as one of FLPMA's multiple uses because water diversion on federal land has traditionally been governed by state law. West of the Mississippi River, almost all state water allocation laws are based on the "prior appropriation" principle ("First in Time is First in Right"). Until comparatively recently, environmental protection has been difficult to achieve under Western state water allocation systems.[23]

4. **Unenforceable policies and mixed mandates.** FLPMA, like almost every other federal and state statute, has a section (§102) entitled "Declaration Of Policy."

---

20. 30 U.S.C.A. §22 et seq. In the Mineral Leasing Act of 1920, 30 U.S.C.A. §181 et seq., Congress removed fuel minerals from the ambit of the General Mining Law and established a leasing system, based on competitive bidding, including provisions that authorize the BLM (which also oversees mineral leases on federal lands) to insert environmentally protective provisions in mineral leases.

21. For a portrait and analysis of the General Mining Law in operation, see Wilkinson, Crossing The Next Meridian, ch. 2 (1992).

22. Wilkinson, Crossing The Next Meridian, ch. 4; Yaffee, The Wisdom Of The Spotted Owl (1994); see Part E, *infra*.

23. See generally J. Sax, R. Abrams, and B. Thompson, Legal Control Of Water Resources ch. 3 (2d. Edition, 1991).

Section 102(b) states that "[t]he policies of this Act shall become effective only as specific statutory authority for their implementation is enacted by this Act or by subsequent legislation...." As the above excerpt points out, some of FLPMA's policies have been enacted, some have been conditionally enacted, some have not been enacted, and some — e.g., the "fair market value" policy — are being ignored by the BLM. Moreover, FLPMA §102 contains policies encouraging both preservation and consumption. What are the functions of legislative policy statements such as these? Are they intended to mislead an unwary public? Are they media "sound bites"? Do they serve to mollify interest groups that have not received all they wanted? Or are they statements of long-term goals that may or may not now be practicable? In fact, all of these concerns, among others, motivate draftspersons when drafting statutory declarations of policy. Consequently, in reading statutes, one must be sensitive to the difference between hortatory, emotive, and political statements, on the one hand, and enforceable commands on the other.

5. **The public trust and the public lands.** Does the public trust doctrine (see Chapter 22) impose obligations on federal land managers supplementary to those found in their management statutes? Compare Sierra Club v. Department of the Interior, 376 F. Supp. 90 (D.N.D.Cal.1974) and Sierra Club v. Department of the Interior, 398 F. Supp. 284 (D.N.D.Cal.1975) (the public trust doctrine applies to the activities of the National Park Service with regard to the management of Redwood National Park), with Sierra Club v. Block, 622 F. Supp. 842 (D.Col.1985), vacated on other grounds *sub. nom.* Sierra Club v. Yeutter, 911 F. Supp.1405 (10th Cir. 1990) (where Congress has set out statutory duties, they comprise all the responsibilities of a federal land management agency). The public trust doctrine has, however, been applied to a state allocation of water rights that detrimentally affected federal public lands.

As a remarkable feature of federal public trust powers in public lands management, note the President's inherent stewardship power to withdraw lands into reserves. Teddy Roosevelt withdrew almost 130 million acres from the public domain between 1901–1908 to set up wildlife, forest, and oil reserves, a power validated in U.S. v. Midwest Oil Co., 236 US 459 (1915). The executive apparently has affirmative power to declare such protections, unless limited by congressional action (a political process that confronted the Clinton administration's unilateral extension of rangeland protections).

6. **"Cooperative Management" and the BLM.** In the Public Rangelands Improvement Act of 1978, 32 U.S.C.A. §1901 et seq., Congress found that "vast segments" of the public lands were in "unsatisfactory condition" because they were "producing less than their potential" for the multiple uses detailed in FLPMA. The Congressional prescription was improved management by the BLM, including discontinuance of grazing on stressed lands and "explor[ation of] innovative grazing management policies and systems which might provide incentives to improve range conditions." Relying on this language, BLM established a Cooperative Management Agreement (CMA) program authorizing BLM to enter into special permit arrangements with selected ranchers who had demonstrated "exemplary rangeland management practices." The purpose of the CMA program was to allow

these exemplary ranchers to "manage livestock on the allotment as they determine appropriate" for ten-year periods. "Exemplary practices" were not defined in
the regulation, nor were the agreements required to contain performance standards
or any other limiting terms or conditions. If a permittee did not comply with the
nebulous goals of the program, BLM's only remedy was to deny renewal of the
agreement after its ten-year term had elapsed. In NRDC v. Hodel, 618 F. Supp. 848
(D.E.D.Cal.1985), the court, finding that "the CMA program is *not* an experiment,
but is a permanent system of permit issuance aimed at a group of favored permittees," struck down the CMA regulations as inconsistent with BLM's statutory
obligation to "prescribe the manner in and the extent to which livestock practices
will be conducted on public lands."

7. **Grazing fees and other public land-use subsidies.** All attempts to raise the grazing fee to a figure approaching market value (the current federal grazing fee is less
than two dollars per cow, per month, in contrast with current forage market rates
of over ten dollars per cow, per month) have been unsuccessful. Other subsidies for
resource use on public lands include below-cost timber sales from the National
Forests,[24] federal payments to timber companies for logging road construction
when they buy timber in the national forests,[25] extraction of hard-rock minerals
from the public lands without paying royalties to the federal government, below-
cost sales of water from federally-constructed dams, cost-free water diversions
from federal lands, free access to off-road vehicles, and below-cost fees for public
access to National Parks.[26] Are there good reasons for subsidizing resource use on
public lands? Should the Forest Service sell timber below cost as benign support
for the economies of timber-dependent communities?[27] Should fees for National
Park access be kept low in order to attract low and middle-income visitors? Should
grazing fees remain low in order to preserve the economic viability of the small
rancher?[28]

8. **Recent grazing reform regulations.** On February 22, 1995, the BLM promulgated
a new set of grazing regulations (60 Fed. Reg. 9894–9971, 43 CFR Part 4, §§1780,
4100). Among other provisions, the regulations 1) replace the district advisory
boards composed of ranchers with multi-stakeholder Resource Advisory Councils;
and 2) require BLM to set statewide or regional standards to assure the ecological
health of grazing lands, and to take appropriate management action (e.g., reducing
stocking rates or adjusting periods of grazing) where the standards are not being

---

24. See Chapter 14.

25. In February, 1998, the Clinton Administration imposed an 18-month moratorium on logging road
construction in most national forests, even if timber companies are willing to build the roads without
federal subsidies.

26. See generally Wilkinson, Crossing The Next Meridian (1992) for a discussion of subsidies for
ranchers, miners, and water users.

27. See the discussion in Anderson, Below-Cost Timber Sales & Community Economic Subsidies: A
Conflict of Values," 5 Maryland Journal of Contemporary Legal Issues 129 (1995).

28. Only 12 percent of grazing permit holders are listed by the Interior Department as small operators. Ten percent of permit holders — including the Metropolitan Life Insurance Company (800,000
acres), the Mormon Church, a Japanese conglomerate, the Nature Conservancy, and some of the
wealthiest families in the nation — control about half of all public grazing land. Egan, "Wingtip
'Cowboys' in Last Stand to Hold on to Low Grazing Fees," N.Y. Times, October 29, 1993, p. 27.

met. Commentary on these regulations has run the gamut from quite favorable to substantially unfavorable.[29]

## C. FEDERAL-STATE AND PUBLIC-PRIVATE ISSUES ON THE PUBLIC LANDS

The following Supreme Court decision is the most significant development in over a century of vitriolic litigation regarding federal versus state power and public versus private rights on the public lands, and reflects a chapter in the anti-federal "Sagebrush Rebellion." As you read the opinion, consider which legal questions have been definitively settled and which are still open.

### Kleppe v. New Mexico
United States Supreme Court, 1976
426 U.S. 529, 96 S.Ct. 2285, 49 L.Ed. 2d 34

MARSHALL, J. At issue in this case is whether Congress exceeded its powers under the Constitution in enacting the Wild Free-Roaming Horses and Burros Act, 16 U.S.C.A. §§1331–1340,...in 1971 to protect "all unbranded and unclaimed horses and burros on public lands in the United States" from "capture, branding, harassment, or death." The Act provides that all such horses and burros on the public lands...are committed to the jurisdiction of the respective Secretaries, who are "directed to protect and manage [the animals] as components of the public lands...in a manner that is designed to achieve and maintain a thriving natural ecological balance on the public lands." If protected horses or burros "stray from public lands onto privately owned land, the owners of such land may inform the nearest Federal marshall or agency of the Secretary, who shall arrange to have the animals removed...."

On February 1, 1974, a New Mexico rancher, Kelley Stephenson, was informed by BLM that several unbranded burros had been seen near Taylor Well, where Stephenson watered his cattle. Taylor Well is on federal property, and Stephenson had access to it and some 8,000 surrounding acres only through a grazing permit.... After BLM made it clear to Stephenson that it would not remove the burros and after he personally inspected the Taylor Well area, Stephenson complained to the [New Mexico] Livestock Board that the burros were interfering with his livestock operation by molesting his cattle and eating their feed. Thereupon the Board rounded up and removed 19 unbranded and unclaimed burros pursuant to the New Mexico Estray Law. Each burro was seized on the public lands of the United States.... On February 18, 1974, the livestock Board, pursuant to its usual practice, sold the burros at public auction. After the sale, BLM asserted jurisdiction under

---

29. See, e.g., Feller,'Til The Cows Come Home: The Fatal Flaw in the Clinton Administration's Public Lands Grazing Policy, 25 Envt'l L. 703 (1995) (although these regulations are an improvement over the former situation, they reveal a "fatal flaw" in the Clinton Administration's grazing policy—"the failure to admit that substantial portions of the public lands are poorly suited to livestock production and therefore should be retired from grazing in favor of other resources and uses."; Arruda and Watson, The Rise and Fall of Grazing Reform, 32 Land & Water Law Rev. 423 (1997) ("The final regulations weaken the potential of the reforms to improve the range's condition, even though the extent of the regulatory changes has remained substantial."); Pendery, Reforming Livestock Grazing on the Public Domain: Ecosystem Management-Based Standards and Guidelines Blaze a New Path for Range Management, 27 Envt'l L. 513 (1997) ("[The standards] could lead to dramatic changes in livestock grazing over a vast portion of the West.").

the Act and demanded that the Board recover the animals and return them to the public lands.

On March 4, 1974, appellees [New Mexico public officials] filed a complaint...seeking a declaratory judgment that the [Act] is unconstitutional and an injunction against its enforcement.... [The District Court held the Act unconstitutional and granted the injunction; the Supreme Court reversed.]

The Property Clause of the Constitution provides that "Congress shall have Power to dispose of and make all needful Rules and Regulations respecting the Territory or other Property belonging to the United States." In passing the Wild Free-Roaming Horses and Burros Act, Congress deemed the regulated animals "an integral part of the natural system of the public lands" of the United States, and found that their management was necessary "for the achievement of an ecological balance on the public lands." According to Congress, these animals, if preserved in their native habitats, "contribute to the diversity of life forms within the Nation and enrich the lives of the American people." Indeed, Congress concluded, the wild free-roaming horses and burros "are living symbols of the historic and pioneer spirit of the West." Despite their importance, the Senate Committee found that these animals

> have been cruelly captured and slain and their carcasses used in the production of pet food and fertilizer. They have been used for target practice and harassed for "sport" and profit. In spite of public outrage, this bloody traffic continues unabated, and it is the firm belief of the committee that this senseless slaughter must be brought to an end.

For these reasons, Congress determined to preserve and protect the wild free-roaming horses and burros on the public lands of the United States. The question under the Property Clause is whether this determination can be sustained as a "needful" regulation "respecting" the public lands. In answering this question, we must remain mindful that, while courts must eventually pass upon them, determinations under the Property Clause are entrusted primarily to the judgment of Congress.

Appellees argue that the Act cannot be supported by the Property Clause. They contend that the Clause grants Congress essentially two kinds of power: (1) the power to dispose of and make incidental rules regarding the use of federal property; and (2) the power to protect federal property. According to appellees, the first power is not broad enough to support legislation protecting wild animals that live on federal property; and the second power is not implicated since the Act is designed to protect the animals, which are not themselves federal property, and not the public lands. As an initial matter, it is far from clear that the Act was not passed in part to protect the public lands of the United States[30] or that Congress cannot assert a property interest in the regulated horses and burros superior to that of the State.[31] But we need not consider whether the Act can be upheld on either of these grounds, for we reject appellees' narrow reading of the Property Clause....

In brief...appellees have presented no support for their position that the [Property] Clause grants Congress only the power to dispose of, to make incidental rules regarding the use of, and to protect federal property. This failure is hardly

---

30. Congress expressly ordered that the animals were to be menaged and protected in order to "achieve and maintain a thriving natural ecological balance on the public lands."

31. The Secretary makes no claim here, however, that the United States own the wild free roaming horses and burros found on public land.

surprising, for the Clause, in broad terms, gives Congress the power to determine what are "needful" rules "respecting" the public lands. And while the furthest reaches of the power granted by the Property Clause have not yet been definitively resolved, we have repeatedly observed that "the power over the public land thus entrusted to Congress is without limitations." United States v. San Francisco, 310 U.S. 16, 29 (1940).

The decided cases have supported this expansive reading. It is the Property Clause, for instance, that provides the basis for governing the territories of the United States. And even over public land within the States, "the general government doubtless has a power over its own property analogous to the police power of the several states, and the extent to which it may go in the exercise of such power is measured by the exigencies of the particular case." Camfield v. United States, 167 U.S. 518, 525 (1897). We have noted, for example, that the Property Clause gives Congress the power over the public lands "to control their occupancy and use, to protect them from trespass and injury, and to prescribe the conditions upon which others may obtain rights in them...." Utah Power & Light Co., v. United States, 243 U.S. 389, 405 (1917).... In short, Congress exercises the powers both of a proprietor and of a legislature over the public domain. Although the Property Clause does not authorize "an exercise of a general control over public policy in a State," it does permit "an exercise of the complete power which Congress has over particular public property entrusted to it." United States v. San Francisco, 310 U.S., at 30. In our view, the "complete power" that Congress has over public lands necessarily includes the power to protect the wildlife living there.

Appellees argue that if we approve the Wild Free-Roaming Horses and Burros Act as a valid exercise of Congress' power under the Property Clause, then we have sanctioned an impermissible intrusion on the sovereignty, legislative authority and police power of the State and have wrongfully infringed upon the State's traditional trustee powers over wild animals. The argument appears to be that Congress could obtain exclusive legislative jurisdiction over the public lands in the State only by state consent, and that in the absence of such consent Congress lacks the power to act contrary to state law. This argument is without merit....

While Congress can acquire exclusive or partial jurisdiction over lands within a State by the State's consent or cession [under the so-called Enclave Clause of the Constitution, Article I, §8, cl. 17], the presence or absence of such jurisdiction has nothing to do with Congress' powers under the Property Clause. Absent consent or cession a State undoubtedly retains jurisdiction over federal lands within its territory, but Congress equally surely retains the power to enact legislation respecting those lands pursuant to the Property Clause. And when Congress so acts, the federal legislation necessarily overrides conflicting state laws under the Supremacy Clause. As we said in Camfield v. United States, 167 U.S., at 526, in response to a somewhat different claim, "A different rule would place the public domain of the United States completely at the mercy of state legislation."...

Appellees' fear that the Secretary's position is that "the Property Clause totally exempts federal lands within state borders from state legislative powers, state police powers, and all rights and powers of local sovereignty and jurisdiction of the states," is totally unfounded. The Federal Government does not assert exclusive jurisdiction over the public lands in New Mexico, and the State is free to enforce its criminal and civil laws on those lands. But where those state laws conflict with the Wild Free-Roaming Horses and Burros Act, or with other legislation passed pursuant to the Property Clause, the law is clear: the State laws must recede....

Appellees are concerned that the Act's extension of protection to wild free-roaming horses and burros that stray from public land onto private land will be read to provide federal jurisdiction over every wild horse or burro that at any time sets foot upon federal land. While it is clear that regulations under the Property Clause may have some effect on private lands not otherwise under federal control, Camfield v. United States, 167 U.S. 518 (1897), we do not think it appropriate in this declaratory judgment proceeding to determine the extent, if any, to which the Property Clause empowers Congress to protect animals on private lands or the extent to which such regulation is attempted by the Act....

### COMMENTARY AND QUESTIONS

1. **The statutory policy.** The Wild Free-Roaming Horses and Burros Act is a statute that causes mixed feelings amongst both ranchers and environmentalists. On one hand these animals, brought from Europe by Spanish and English pioneers, are living symbols of the historic or mythical frontier West, and creatures that deserve humane treatment. On the other, they have multiplied so successfully in some niches of their transplanted habitat that they destroy the forage and threaten the survival of native species in the western ecosystem, like antelope and black-footed ferrets, as well as private livestock.

A vivid, highly-focused citizens' campaign — using video footage of dog food suppliers stampeding and butchering terrified wild horses — pushed the statute through Congress, and as law it must be enforced by federal land managers. But the statute does not confront the policy contradictions it presents, with endangered species laws for instance. Some environmentalists have suggested the compromise of inserting IUDs in wild horses and burros (as birth control-laced pigeon food has been advocated in somewhat analogous urban settings), but the issues are likely not to be so easily resolved.

2. **Public land and private land.** Consider a situation where a herd of free-roaming horses and burros strays from public land onto adjacent private land, the rancher informs the BLM, and the BLM fails to remove the animals. The Act specifies that the Secretary "shall arrange to have the animals removed," but it contains no time limitation for BLM action. If the animals injure the private range, can the rancher sue the federal government in inverse condemnation? In Mountain States Legal Foundation v. Hodel, 799 F.2d 1423 (10th Cir. 1986), cert. denied, 480 U.S. 951 (1987), the court rejected a takings claim by a grazing association in a similar situation on the grounds that:

From Camfield v. U.S., 167 U.S. 518 (1897) — Illustrates the checkerboard land ownership pattern the dotted lines show the fence-building tactic employed by Mr. Camfield.

1) wild horses are wild animals, not instrumentalities of the federal government; 2) "[o]f the courts that have considered whether damage to private property by protected wildlife constitutes a 'taking,' a clear majority have held that it does not and that the government does not owe compensation"; and 3) the plaintiffs had not shown a deprivation of substantially all economically viable uses of their lands.

3. **Helpless giants?** Does the Property Clause give the federal government the authority to regulate activities on state, local, or private lands within ("inholdings") or outside federal landholdings when those activities are interfering with the uses of the federal lands? For example, assume that the Fish and Wildlife Service seeks an injunction that forbids a promoter from holding rock concerts just outside a National Wildlife Refuge, or that the National Park Service wants to prevent the construction of a hideously ugly commercial structure adjacent to — and painfully visible from — a national battlefield.[32] Camfield v. United States, 167 U.S. 518 (1897), cited frequently in *Kleppe*, would appear to authorize the federal government to protect its property against external threats. In *Camfield*, an owner of alternate, odd-numbered sections (purchased from a railroad) effectively fenced off 20,000 acres of federal land by building a zigzag fence on his own property (see Figure 1). Declaring that the federal government, under the Property Clause, has the power to protect its land against nuisances, the Supreme Court held that the fence was a violation of a federal statute prohibiting enclosures of public lands. Since *Camfield*, federal circuit courts of appeals have consistently upheld federal regulation of external threats. See Stupak-Thrall v. U.S., 70 F.3d 881 (6th Cir. 1995) and cases cited. The federal land management agencies have been unenthusiastic about exercising these powers. See Sax, Helpless Giants: The National Parks and the Regulation of Private Lands, 75 Mich. L. Rev. 239 (1976). If the federal government has the power to regulate external activities, how far does it extend? Can the National Park Service promulgate a regulation requiring a large agricultural operation, fifty miles upriver of a national park, to cease discharging nutrients because these pollutants are causing the river in the park to become eutrophic (prematurely aged)?

4. **Access problems.** On checkerboard land grants, can private owners of alternate, odd-numbered sections deny access to recreationists traveling on a BLM-constructed road through sections 14, 22, and 16 (see Figure 1) in order to reach a federal reservoir, even though the public road only touches their sections 15, 21, and 23 at the corners? In Leo Sheep Company v. United States, 440 U.S. 668 (1979), the Supreme Court rejected express or implied easements across private lands, thus requiring the BLM to purchase or condemn road easements. Justice Rehnquist, writing for the majority, distinguished *Camfield* in unconvincing fashion. Isn't the Leo Sheep Company really enclosing public lands? In a condemnation proceeding, would the fair market value of Leo Sheep's land include its proximity to the water supply and recreation provided by the federally-funded reservoir?[33]

---

32. The latter example is, unfortunately, not a hypothetical one. See the discussion of the *Gettysburg Tower* case in Chapter 22.

33. For a case holding against the landowner on far more favorable facts, see Branch v. Oconto County, 13 Wis.2d 595, 109 N.W.2d 105 (1961).

5. **The "Sagebrush Rebellion" and the "Wise Use" Movement.** Problems caused by interspersed federal and private lands, exacerbated by FLPMA's declaration that the federal lands will generally remain in federal ownership and be managed for multiple use and sustained yield, generated a reaction known as the "Sagebrush Rebellion," one manifestation of which consisted of a number of Western states contesting the constitutionality of federal ownership of the public lands. In 1978, the State of Nevada sued the federal government, claiming that federal land ownership was a violation of both Nevada's Tenth Amendment rights and its right to be admitted on an "equal footing" with the original thirteen states, in which there is comparatively little federal land. While that case was pending, the Nevada legislature enacted a statute claiming title to most of the federal lands (excepting wildlife refuges and Native American reservations) in the state. The federal district court dismissed Nevada's claim on the merits, Nevada ex. rel. Nevada State Board of Agric. v. United States, 512 F.Supp. 166 (D.Nev.1981), aff'd for lack of justiciability, 699 F.2d 486 (9th Cir. 1983). Nye County, Nevada's attempt to assert county ownership of federal lands met the same fate. United States v. Nye County, Nevada, 920 F.Supp. 1108 (D.Nev.1996).[34] The Ninth Circuit Court of Appeals has recently reaffirmed federal ownership of federal public lands. United States v. Gardner, 107 F.3d 1314 (1996) (involving a defense to an enforcement action for unauthorized grazing on public lands). The "Wise Use" movement, the loosely-organized but high profile anti-environmental and anti-regulatory coalition of mostly Western populist groups, funded by industry, continued to pursue the Sagebrush Rebellion agenda of "Local Sovereignty," along with a focus on private property rights, through the media, the political process, and the courts.

6. **Public Land and ecosystem management.** The Wild Free-Roaming Horses and Burros Act, which deems the animals to be "an integral part of the natural system of the public lands," is Congress' clearest acceptance to date of Aldo Leopold's concept of land as an ecological community rather than a commodity. Increasingly, Americans are looking beyond preservation of particular species or resources (e.g., endangered species or wild and scenic rivers), which is based on a variety of "zoo" mentality, toward preservation of entire ecosystems and their biodiversity.[35] All four of the federal public land management agencies — the BLM, Forest Service, Fish and Wildlife Service, and the National Park Service — have announced that they will implement an ecosystem approach to managing their lands and natural resources. Apart from the primitive character of current ecological data, the most obvious impediment to ecosystem management on federal lands is that ecosystems transcend jurisdictional boundaries, not only those of any particular federal land management agency, but also those of the federal government itself:

> While ecosystem management will require unparalleled coordination among federal agencies, disparate missions and planning requirements set forth in federal land management statutes and regulations hamper such efforts. And

34. See also Boundary Backpackers v. Boundary County, 913 P.2d 1141 (Idaho 1996) (county ordinance that requires use of federal lands to be consistent with county land-use ordinance is preempted).

35. For a critique of the resource-by-resource preservation approach, in the context of the Endangered Species Act, and an examination of the potential legal means of protecting biodiversity, see Doremus, Patching the Ark: Improving Legal Protection of Biological Diversity, 18 Ecol. L. Q. 265 (1991).

although ecosystem management will require collaboration and consensus-building among federal and nonfederal parties within most ecosystems, incentives, authorities, interests and limitations embedded in the larger national land and natural resource use framework — many beyond the ability of the federal land management agencies individually or collectively to control and affect — constrain these parties' efforts to work together effectively. USGAO, Ecosystem Management: Additional Actions Needed to Adequately Test a Promising Approach (1994), p. 5.

Is ecosystem management consistent with a multiple-use, sustained yield statutory mandate? What about a dominant-use directive?

7. **Can states regulate resource extraction on federal lands?** In California Coastal Commission v. Granite Rock Co., 480 U.S. 572 (1987), the Supreme Court drew a distinction between land use planning and environmental regulation, holding that the National Forest Management Act preempts state land use planning in national forests, but not state environmental regulation.[36] Is there a discernible difference between land use planning and environmental regulation in the context of public lands management? States typically regulate hunting and fishing on federal lands unless the federal government has declared otherwise, as in the Wild Free-Roaming Horses and Burros Act.

## D. THE BLM AND OFF-ROAD VEHICLES: A CASE STUDY

The following case study involving BLM management of Off-Road Vehicles (ORVs) illustrates the BLM's political capture by a secondary clientele,[37] the ORV lobby, a powerful coalition of vehicle manufacturers, the petroleum industry, tire manufacturers, and ardent ORV recreationists. Note that excessive recreational use can be as damaging to public natural resources as insensitive extractive uses. It is often said that, as a nation, we are "loving our public lands to death."

### D. Sheridan, Off-Road Vehicles on Public Lands
### 7–12 (1979)

Off-road vehicles (ORVs) have damaged every kind of ecosystem found in the United States: sand dunes covered with American Beach grass on Cape Cod; pine and cypress woodlands in Florida; hardwood forests in Indiana; prairie grasslands in Montana; chaparral and sagebrush hills in Arizona; alpine meadows in Colorado; conifer forests in Washington; arctic tundra in Alaska. In some cases the wounds will heal naturally; in others they will not, at least for millennia....

Federal lands have borne a disproportionate share of the damage. State lands are far less extensive; in addition, some states have either prohibited ORV use on their lands (Indiana) or have restricted their use to designated trails (Massachusetts). And the federal government has been more willing to open the lands which it manages for the American public to ORVs than have private landowners....

The ready availability of federal land has profoundly shaped the ORV phenomenon. Per capita ownership of ORVs is significantly higher in areas that

---

36. See the discussion of *Granite Rock* in Chapter Six.
37. The BLM's primary "clientele," i.e., regulated industry, is the grazing industry.

possess a lot of public land. The reason is simple: a person is more likely to buy an ORV if he has some place to drive it.... Thus federal land policy has been an important stimulant to ORV growth. Because the federal government has allowed ORVers to consume public resources free of charge, the general public has in a sense subsidized the ORV phenomenon. A second consequence of federal land policy has been to discourage private enterprise from meeting ORVers demand for land. Commercially developed ORV areas are extremely rare....

First and foremost [among environmental costs of ORV use], ORVs eat land. It is because ORVs attack that relatively thin layer of disintegrated rock and organic material to which all earthly life clings — soil — that they can have such a devastating effect on natural resources....

There seem to be two basic soil responses to ORV use. One, sandy and gravelly soils are susceptible to direct quarrying by ORVs, and when stripped of vegetation they are susceptible to rapid erosion processes — usually by rill and gully erosion. Near Santa Cruz, California, for example, ORV trails used for about 6 years are now gullies 8 feet deep. Two, more clay-rich soils are less sensitive to direct mechanical displacement by ORVs, but the rates of erosion of stripped clay-rich soil are much higher under ORV use than under natural conditions. Furthermore, ORV pounding of clay-rich soil causes strong surface seals to form, thereby reducing the infiltration of water. This, in turn, leads to greater rainwater runoff, which causes gullying lower in the drainage.

Once massive soil erosion begins, it will stop only after ORV riding stops and the native vegetation has had a chance to reestablish itself and stabilize the soil. In arid and semiarid areas, recovery is very slow. The same holds true for hilly or mountainous areas which receive heavy rainfall, such as Appalachia or northern California.... In flat, dry areas ORVs expose the soil to another powerful erosional force — the wind. In damp flat areas such as wet prairies or meadows, ORV ruts can turn into drainage ditches — siphoning off water held in the surrounding area.... ORVs destabilize sand dunes, making them more vulnerable to wind erosion and, in the case of coastal dunes, to sea erosion....

A major difficulty with ORVs...is that the terrain which truly challenges the capability of these machines, and which is therefore most attractive to many ORV operators, is exactly that which is most highly sensitive to erosional degradation. This open contradiction between machine capability and land sensitivity is a key issue.

Aside from tearing up soils, ORVs also damage vegetation. They kill plants in several ways. By direct contact — the ORV runs over the plant or brushes against it, breaking off limbs or branches. Sometimes ORV use around a plant so badly erodes the soil that the plant simply collapses from lack of anything to hold onto. Also, ORV soil compaction injures root systems and larger perennials eventually die. In addition, ORVs crush seedlings beneath their wheels or treads as well as seeds germinating on or within the ground. Lastly, on slopes, soil eroded because of ORV use washes to the bottom where it smothers plants that are growing there.

ORVs also disrupt animal life.... They collide with animals, especially smaller mammals and reptiles. By destroying vegetation, they are also destroying animal food and shelter.

In addition, ORVs afford hunters and fishermen access to remote, heretofore untouched areas, thereby dramatically increasing the fish and game kills in those areas. The effects of ORV noise on animals, although imperfectly understood, is thought to be very damaging....

CONFLICTS WITH OTHER USERS... ORV and snowmobile use of the land conflicts with other human uses of the land [and] the conflicts engendered by these machines can be quite bitter.

Reports from public land managers in nine western states indicate that conflict occurs, upon occasion, between commercial users of the land, such as ranchers, and ORV recreationists. The conflict with grazing, in fact, seems to be more common than with logging or mining. For example, New Mexico BLM director Arthur W. Zimmerman notes that complaints from ranchers have been received concerning trespass, cut fences, broken gates, polluted livestock water, new jeep roads, noise, gully erosion caused by hill climbs, and interference with their livestock operations. The less frequent complaints received from loggers and miners usually concern vandalism of their equipment and property by ORVers.

The most serious conflict arises between ORV operators and nonmotorized picnickers or campers, hikers, backpackers, sightseers, and so on — or between ORVers and persons using the land for educational purposes — students, teachers, researchers. Nonmotorized recreationists do not enjoy their encounters with motorcycles, dune buggies, and four-wheel drive vehicles, numerous studies have shown. The ORV operator, on the other hand, is often quite tolerant, even oblivious, of the person on foot or on horseback.

ORVs, in other words, impair other people's enjoyment or understanding of the outdoors on public land. In terms of public policy, this is a problem equal in importance to ORV damage of the environment.

### COMMENTARY AND QUESTIONS

1. **Initial federal responses.** To the BLM's credit, it was the first federal agency that recognized the magnitude of the ORV problem on public lands and attempted to do something about it. In 1968, the California state office of the BLM and the Western Regional office of the National Park Service published a document detailing the damage caused by ORVs in the California Desert and recommending that BLM develop special ORV centers where environmental damage could be kept to a minimum. In 1969, the BLM in California convened an Off-Road Advisory Council composed of ORV organization representatives, environmentalists, ranchers, and businessmen. Despite heated internal disputes, the Council recommended that ORV use not be permitted on highly erodable lands; sites unique for historic, ecological, or archaeological value; or lands typically used for other kinds of public recreation. Apparently, these recommendations led the ORV organizations to withdraw their support for the Advisory Council Process and use their contacts in the Interior Department for their own self-interest. In 1971, the Secretary of the Interior formed an ORV task force that whitewashed the ORV problem, recommending further study, state regulation of ORV use, and the development of private ORV facilities (with no mention of increased federal regulation or subsidies to stimulate the private sector).

By 1972, however, environmental abuse of the public lands by the burgeoning ranks of ORV users was becoming so pronounced that President Nixon issued Executive Order 11644, calling for a unified federal policy toward ORVs on the public lands. E.O. 11644 established a presumption that public lands should be closed to ORV use unless specifically opened by agency regulation, after findings are made under the following criteria:

(1) Areas and trails shall be located to minimize damages to soil, watershed, vegetation, or other resources of the public lands.

(2) Areas and trails shall be located to minimize harassment of wildlife or significant disruption of wildlife habitats.

(3) Areas and trails shall be located to minimize conflicts between off-road vehicle use and other existing or proposed recreational uses of the same or neighboring public lands and to ensure the compatibility of such uses with existing conditions in populated areas, taking into account noise and other factors.

(4) Areas and trails shall not be located in officially designated Wilderness Areas or Primitive Areas. Areas and trails shall be located in areas of the National Park system, Natural Areas, or National Wildlife Refuges and Game Ranges only if the respective agency head determines that off-road vehicle use in such locations will not adversely affect their natural, aesthetic, or scenic values.

2. **BLM backslide.** The BLM regulations implementing E.O. 11644, however, established the opposite presumption, that public lands should be open to ORV use until closed by the management agency because of environmental damage or conflict with other users.[38]

In National Wildlife Federation v. Morton, 393 F. Supp. 1286 (D.D.C.1975), a federal district court overturned the BLM regulations as inconsistent with E.O. 11644, remarking that "BLM has significantly diluted the standards emphatically set forth in Executive Order 11644."

FLPMA, enacted in 1976, was primarily addressed to the grazing issue, and its treatment of ORV use was cursory. Section 601 of FLPMA established a planning process for the 12 million-acre California Desert Conservation Area, one objective of which was that —

§601(4)...the use of all California desert resources can and should be provided for in a multiple use and sustained yield management plan to conserve these resources for future generations, and to provide present and future use and enjoyment, particularly outdoor recreation uses, including the use, where appropriate, of off-road recreational vehicles.

In other words, ORVs were perceived by Congress as just another one of the multiple uses to be accommodated on public lands.

In response to the hesitancy of federal agencies to control ORV use and implement E.O. 11644, President Carter issued E.O. 11989 in 1977.[39] E.O. 11989 reiterated many of the provisions of E.O. 11644, but, in addition, ordered agency heads (1) "to develop and issue regulations [governing the] designation of the specific areas and trails on public lands on which the use of off-road vehicles may be permitted," and (2) to immediately ban ORVs where ORV use "will cause or is causing considerable

---

38. In other words, whereas E.O. 11644 minimized false negatives (was proactive), the BLM regulations minimized false positives (were reactive) (see Chapter Two).

39. See generally, Bleich, Chrome on the Range: Off-Road Vehicles on Public Lands, 15 Ecol. L. Q. 159, 166–67 (1988).

adverse effects." Nevertheless, two days after President Carter signed E.O. 11989, the Interior Department issued a press release interpreting the order as applying only to "fragile areas which are actually threatened with serious damage," disclaiming a general ban on ORV use on public lands, and stressing voluntary action on the part of ORV users. E.O. 11644 had declared that "areas and trails shall be located to minimize [environmental] damages," a highly protective standard; as for closure of existing trails, E.O. 11989 required the agency to prove "considerable adverse effects." The BLM, in its California Desert Conservation Area Plan, applied the latter order's looser closure standard, instead of the more protective minimization standard, in its designation of new trails, thus making it far easier to designate ORV routes. This aspect of the plan was struck down in American Motorcyclist Association v. Watt, 543 F. Supp. 789 (C.D.Cal. 1982). The following case involved an attempt by a citizens group to have a particular ORV trail closed.

**Sierra Club v. Clark**
United States Court of Appeals for the Ninth Circuit, 1985
756 F.2d 686

POOLE, J. Plaintiffs...filed this action seeking review under the APA §706(1), of the failure of the defendants Secretary of the Interior, Director of the BLM, and California State Director of BLM to close Dove Springs Canyon to ORV use. Sierra Club appeals from the district court's denial of their motion for summary judgment, and the grant of the Secretary's motion for summary judgment. We affirm.

Dove Springs Canyon is located in the California Desert Conservation Area.... The Desert Area covers approximately 25 million acres in southeastern California, approximately 12.1 million of which are administered by the BLM. Dove Springs Canyon is comprised of approximately 5500 acres; 3000 acres are designated "open" for unrestricted use of ORVs.

Dove Springs Canyon possesses abundant and diverse flora and fauna. Over 250 species of plants, 24 species of reptiles, and 30 species of birds are found there. It also offers good habitat for the Mojave ground squirrel, the desert kit fox, and the burrowing owl. Because the rich and varied biota is unusual for an area of such low elevation in the Mojave Desert, the canyon was once frequented by birdwatchers and naturalists, as well as hikers and fossil hunters.

Recreational ORV usage of Dove Springs Canyon began in 1965 and became progressively heavier in the ensuing years. By 1971, the Canyon was being used intensively by ORV enthusiasts. It became especially popular because the site's diverse terrain, coupled with relatively easy access, provides outstanding hill-climbing opportunities. By 1979, up to 200 vehicles used the Canyon on a typical weekend; over 500 vehicles used it on a holiday weekend. In 1973, the BLM adopted the Interim Critical Management Program for Recreational Vehicle Use on the California Desert ("Interim Program") which designated Dove Springs Canyon as an ORV Open Area, permitting recreational vehicle travel in the area without restriction.

Extensive ORV usage has been accompanied by severe environmental damage in the form of major surface erosion, soil compaction, and heavy loss of vegetation. The visual aesthetics have markedly declined. The character of the Canyon has been so severely altered that the Canyon is now used almost exclusively for ORV activities.

In July of 1980 Sierra Club petitioned the Secretary of the Interior to close Dove Springs Canyon to ORV use under the authority of Executive Order No. 11644 as amended by Executive Order No. 11989, because of "substantial adverse effects" on the vegetation, soil and wildlife in the Canyon. The Secretary responded that the matter would be addressed in the California Desert Conservation Plan and Final Environmental Impact Statement ("the Final Plan").

The Final Plan approved by the Secretary in December 1980 maintained unrestricted ORV use in Dove Springs of 3000 of the 5500 acres. Sierra Club filed this action on January 6, 1981, alleging that the Secretary's failure to close Dove Springs violated Executive Order No. 11644, as amended by Executive Order No. 11989, and FLPMA §1732(b), which requires the Secretary to prevent "unnecessary or undue degradation of the lands;" and §§1781(b) and (d), which require the Secretary to maintain and conserve resources of the Desert Area under principles of "multiple use and sustained yield."...

The Secretary interprets "considerable adverse effect" to require determining what is "considerable" in the context of the Desert Area as a whole, not merely on a parcel-by-parcel basis. The Secretary contends such a broad interpretation is necessary and is consistent with §1781(a)(4) which expresses a congressional judgment that ORV use is to be permitted "where appropriate."

Sierra Club argues against the Secretary's interpretation. Sierra Club contends that the interpretation of the Executive Orders set forth by the Council on Environmental Quality (CEQ) in its August 1, 1977 memorandum is entitled to great deference, and that the CEQ's interpretation requires the closure of the canyon. This argument fails on two grounds.

First, the CEQ's interpretation of the Executive Order does not directly conflict with the Secretary's interpretation of the regulation. While it states that "the term 'considerable' should be liberally construed to provide the broadest possible protection reasonably required by this standard," it does not purport to decide whether the term "considerable adverse effects" should be analyzed in the context of the entire Desert Area, or on a site-specific basis. Moreover, the memorandum acknowledges that the responsibility for closing particular areas rests with "responsible federal officials in the field" "[b]ased on their practical experience in the management of the public lands, and their first-hand knowledge of conditions 'on-the-ground.'"

Second, the authority of the CEQ is to maintain a continuing review of the implementation of the Executive Order. The authority of the Secretary, on the other hand, is to promulgate regulations to provide for "administrative designation of the specific areas and trails on public lands on which the use of off-road vehicles may be permitted, and areas in which the use of off-road vehicles may not be permitted." Discretion rests with the Secretary, therefore, to determine whether and to what extent specific areas should be closed to ORV use. Thus, it is the Secretary's interpretation which is entitled to our deference.

Sierra Club argues that even if the CEQ's interpretation of the closure standard is not controlling, the Secretary's interpretation should not be adopted because it is unreasonable. Sierra Club insists that the sacrifice of any area to permanent resource damage is not justified under the multiple use management mandate of §1702(c) that requires multiple use "without permanent impairment of the productivity of the land and the quality of the environment." In further support of its position Sierra Club adverts to the requirement in the Act that the Secretary prevent "unnecessary and undue degradation" of the public lands. In addition, Sierra

ORV use on public lands. this ridge in California's Jawbone Canyon has been stripped of vegetation by heavy ORV recreational use. The plume of dust marks the uphill run of an all-terrain motorcycle. In the desert, even in cases of low-volume ORV use, noise levels can be deafening, and the tire track ruts made by one machine in one 15-minute run through the fragile ecology of the desert floor may remain visible for more than 50 years.

© 1989 HOWARD WILSHIRE

Club contends, when Congress established the Desert Area it intended the Secretary to fashion a multiple use and sustained yield management plan "to conserve [the California Desert] resources for future generations, and to provide present and future use and enjoyment, particularly outdoor recreational uses, including the use, where appropriate, of off-road recreational vehicles." Sierra Club argues that it is unreasonable for the Secretary to find ORV use "appropriate" when that use violates principles of sustained yield, substantially impairs productivity of renewable resources and is inconsistent with maintenance of environmental quality.

We can appreciate the earnestness and force of Sierra Club's position, and if we could write on a clean slate, would prefer a view which would disallow the virtual sacrifice of a priceless natural area in order to accommodate a special recreational activity. But we are not free to ignore the mandate which Congress wrote into the Act. Sierra Club's interpretation of the regulation would inevitably result in the total prohibition of ORV use because it is doubtful that any discrete area could withstand unrestricted ORV use without considerable adverse effects. However appealing might be such a resolution of the environmental dilemma, Congress has found that ORV use, damaging as it may be, is to be provided "where appropriate." It left determination of appropriateness largely up to the Secretary in an area of sharp conflict. If there is to be a change it must come by way of Congressional reconsideration. The Secretary's interpretation that this legislative determination calls for accommodation of ORV usage in the administrative plan, we must conclude, is not unreasonable and we are constrained to let it stand....

Under the California Desert Conservation Area Plan, approximately 4 percent (485,000 acres) of the total acreage is now open to unrestricted ORV use. Dove Springs itself constitutes only 0.025 percent of BLM administered lands in the Desert Area. Although all parties recognize that the environmental impact of ORV use at Dove Springs is severe, the Secretary's determination that these effects were not "considerable" in the context of the Desert Area as a whole is not arbitrary, capricious, or an abuse of the broad discretion committed to him by an obliging Congress....

### COMMENTARY AND QUESTIONS

1. **Straw man in the desert.** Do you agree that application of the closure standard to specific portions of the desert, rather than the Desert Area as a whole, would inevitably result in the total prohibition of ORV use in violation of statute? Doesn't this argument assume that there are no qualitative differences among desert sections? Indeed, Sierra Club was arguing that Dove Springs had been a unique ecological resource. (Note the poignancy of the court's use of the past tense in "the Canyon was once frequented by birdwatchers, naturalists, hikers, and fossil hunters.") Do you think that the court might have been implicitly reacting to a perception that the Canyon was already too degraded to support its past natural uses?

2. **Another look at multiple use-sustained yield.** Is the *Dove Springs* case simply another indication that the ambiguous multiple use-sustained yield management standard, when added to the deferential "arbitrary and capricious" standard of judicial review (see Chapter Seven), places virtually no legal restrictions on federal land managers? Should courts begin to actively enforce FLPMA's "nonimpairment" and "prevention of unnecessary and undue degradation" criteria in allegedly clear cases such as *Dove Springs?* Of course, Congress can resolve the problem by clarifying preferable land uses in particular areas.

3. **The enforcement problem.** No public lands management directive can be meaningful if the management agency lacks the resources to enforce it:

> The BLM lacks sufficient personnel to police its domain in anything more than a cursory fashion. Some range managers, for instance, are individually responsible for overseeing activities on a million or more acres. The offenses by non-permittees — such as taking off-road vehicles into closed areas — are likely to go unpunished for that reason and because the relative triviality of the transgression will discourage use of the prosecutorial apparatus. Coggins, IV, 30.

Does the ORV lobby campaign for or against greater funding for BLM enforcement? Can the BLM plead lack of resources as a defense to an action to compel it to perform its FLPMA duties?[40]

---

40. See NRDC v. Morton, 388 F.Supp.829 (D.C.D.C.1974), where the court rejected BLM's pleas of poverty in a NEPA case.

4. **ORVs in the national parks.** The National Park Service (NPS) operates with a mixed mandate, to "promote and regulate the use of the Federal areas known as national parks, monuments, and reservations" in order to "conserve the scenery and the natural and historic objects and the wild life therein and to provide for the enjoyment of the same in such manner and by such means as will leave them unimpaired for the enjoyment of future generations." 16 U.S.C.A. §1. Although the NPS is considered to have a "single use" mission to administer the public lands under its jurisdiction for public recreation, the tension between "promotion" and "regulation" forces the NPS to choose or mediate between users contending for incompatible high and low-intensity recreational opportunities. This conflict is often reflected in lawsuits contesting "overcommercialization" of national parks.[41]

The NPS has also been involved in ORV litigation, particularly with regard to ORV use in the Cape Cod National Seashore in Massachusetts. In Conservation Law Foundation v. Secretary of the Interior, 864 F.2d.954 (1st Cir. 1989), the ORV component of the NPS' Management Plan for the seashore was upheld against claims that it violated the Cape Cod National Seashore Act and the ORV-related executive orders. Obviously impressed by the NPS' environmental research and consequent limitations on ORV routes, the court held that NPS' ORV policy was not arbitrary and capricious or a violation of the Act. The court noted that "the National Park Service has added a number of rangers to improve patrol of the seashore." In light of decisions like *Dove Canyon* and *Conservation Law Foundation,* are conservationist lawsuits that contest ORV components of public land-use management plans quixotic? If nothing more, they raise the visibility of certain issues so that federal agencies may be compelled to enlarge their perspectives and conduct further studies to examine potential environmental damage.

---

## E. PUBLIC LAND PLANNING

Increasingly, statutory planning processes are becoming the locus of public resources management on the federal lands. FLPMA and the National Forest Management Act (NFMA) require formal, participatory land-use planning, and the resulting plans are legally binding because on-the-ground-management decisions must be consistent with the adopted plans.[42] Under NFMA,[43] the Forest Service (FS) must prepare Land and Resource Management Plans (LRMPs) for all national forests:

> The LRMP defines the "management direction" for the forest. It constitutes a program for all natural resource management activities and establishes management requirements to be employed in implementing the plan. It identifies the resource management practices, the projected levels of production of goods

---

41. See, e.g., Friends of Yosemite v. Frizzel, 420 F.Supp.390 (D.N.D.Cal.1976)(plaintiffs' allegation that NPS was breaching the public trust by overcommercializing Yosemite National Park rejected because NPS had not violated a statutory duty).

42. See the discussions of the Coastal Zone Management Act and the Wild and Scenic Rivers Act in Chapter 25 for other examples of "consistency clauses."

43. NFMA planning will be primarily discussed in this section because it has evolved much further than FLPMA planning by the BLM; and see the discussion of NFMA in Chapter 11.

and services, and the location where various types of resource management may occur. Implementation of the LRMP is achieved through individual site-specific projects and all projects must be consistent with the LRMP. 16 U.S.C.A.§1604, 36 C.F.R. §219.

But, as the following case indicates, if natural resources planning is to be truly participatory and unbiased, it must not be a post hoc rationalization of previously determined agency policies:

## Sierra Club v. Thomas
United States Court of Appeals, Sixth Circuit, 1997
105 F.3d 248, cert. granted, 118 S.Ct. 334

BOYCE F. MARTIN, JR., Chief Judge... The Sierra Club and Citizens Council on Conservation and Environmental Control appeal the district court's order granting summary judgment to Jack Ward Thomas, Chief of the United States Forest Service, and officials of the United States Forest Service, pursuant to the district court's review of the Land and Resource Management Plan for the Wayne National Forest. For the reasons described below, we reverse and remand this matter to the district court for further proceedings consistent with this opinion.

In 1988, the regional forester for the Eastern Division of the United States Forest Service issued a decision, pursuant to the National Forest Management Act, adopting a ten-year plan for Ohio's Wayne National Forest. The plan designated 126,107 acres of the Wayne from which timber could be removed or cut. During the ten-year life of the plan, 7.5 million board feet of timber could be cut per year. The plan designated that eighty percent of all timbering techniques would be "even-aged" management, a harvest technique aimed at creating a regeneration of trees which are essentially the same age. In almost all cases, the even-aged management contemplated clearcutting of the timber. Clearcutting involves the removal of all trees within areas ranging in size from fifteen to thirty acres, and is thus a very sensitive public issue. The Sierra Club appealed the regional forester's decision to the chief of the Forest Service pursuant to the applicable regulations. In 1990, the chief of the Forest Service denied the Sierra Club's appeal and affirmed the plan....

The National Forest Management Act was enacted as a direct result of congressional concern for Forest Service clearcutting practices and the dominant role timber production has historically played in Forest Service policies. Congress was concerned that, if left to its own essentially unbridled devices, the Forest Service would manage the national forests as mere monocultural "tree farms." Procedurally, the Act requires the Forest Service to develop Land and Resource Management Plans for the national forests. This formal planning process was designed to curtail agency discretion and to ensure forest preservation and productivity. Substantively, the Act imposes extensive limitations on timber harvesting by restricting the use of clearcutting to situations in which clearcutting is the optimum method for harvesting....

The Sierra Club contends that the even-aged logging agenda is illegal in that the Forest Service has not complied with the constraints on its choice of even-aged management techniques contained in the National Forest Management Act [because the Forest Service is biased in favor of clearcutting]....

Although it would be impractical to set forth the details of the administrative record here, one example of bias [in favor of clearcutting] is particularly illustrative. The Forest Service argues that its even-aged management plan is based on evidence that timbering will provide new opportunities for recreation that will, in turn, preserve and enhance the diversity of plant and animal communities in the Wayne National Forest. Most recreation does not require timber harvesting, however. Further, as the Forest Service's own records reflect, the Wayne is surrounded by and intermingled with privately-held land which already contains an abundance of diverse plant and animal life. Timbering simply does not promote the kind of recreational activities that are in demand in the Wayne; in fact, recreation like fishing and hiking is harmed by clearcutting. The planners also failed to recognize that cutting is unlikely to stimulate new and valuable forms of recreation because much of the Wayne has already been cut or developed. In that particular environment, clearcutting loses its value.

The National Forest Management Act mandates that the Service ensure that even-aged management practices be used in the national forests only when "consistent with the protection of soil, watershed, fish, wildlife, recreation, and aesthetic resources, and the regeneration of the timber resource." 16 U.S.C. §1604(g)(3)(F)(v). The National Forest Management Act thus contemplates that even-aged management techniques will be used only in exceptional circumstances. Yet, the defendants would utilize even-aged management logging as if it were the statutory rule, rather than the exception. By arbitrarily undervaluing the recreational value of wilderness, the Forest Service created a very distorted picture of the Wayne National Forest. Based on false premises such as these, the Forest Service improperly concluded that clearcutting was necessary.

It is not surprising that the Forest Service came to this conclusion. Created, in part, to ensure a reliable timber supply, the Forest Service has a history of preferring timber production to other uses. Rather than being a neutral process which determines how the national forests can best meet the needs of the American people, forest planning, as practiced by the Forest Service, is a political process replete with opportunities for the intrusion of bias and abuse. Because national forests are located near rural communities, foresters make management decisions to support perceived needs in the communities. By sharing timber proceeds with those communities, the Forest Service strengthens the link between timber sales and the livelihoods of local constituencies. See, Office of Technology Assessment, Forest Service Planning: Accommodating Uses, Producing Outputs, and Sustaining Ecosystems 46 (1992). The resulting dependency of these communities on timber production causes over-harvesting and destructive harvesting methods. The relationship of the Forest Service to the timber industry also constrains the Forest Service's planning freedom. Rural constituencies reliant on timber sale revenues may provoke politicians to place pressure on the Forest Service to sustain that revenue. Consequently, the Forest Service becomes trapped: cutting off timber sales would cause loss of employment and revenue in local communities but continued timber sales risk over-harvesting and below-cost sales.

The Forest Service budgeting process, which allows the Forest Service to keep a percentage of the funds it realizes from timber sales, provides an incentive for the Forest Service to sell timber below cost or at a loss. See Randal O'Toole, Reforming the Forest Service 122 (1988). Also, to maximize its budget, the Forest Service uses expensive timber management and reforestation techniques, such as clearcutting. Again, conflicting interests lead to perverse results: clearcutting provides the Forest Service with a higher congressional subsidy because the Forest Service can request preparation and administrative costs. Consequently, decisions may be made, not because they are in the best interest of the American people but because they benefit the Forest Service's fiscal interest.

Each of these biases undermines even the facial neutrality of the National Forest Management Act. Even when there may be more valuable uses for the land, the above biases and constraints cause the Forest Service to manage primarily to maximize timber outputs....

BATCHELDER, Circuit Judge, concurring. ...I write separately because, while I, too, have serious questions and concerns about the management practices and policies of the Forest Service, I do not believe that the majority's largely undocumented broadside against the Forest Service is appropriate. The issue before us is simply whether the Plan was properly promulgated within the appropriate exercise of the agency's discretion and is therefore within the law. We conclude that it is not. Our speculation about the motives and biases of the Forest Service, even if accurate, is unnecessary, and therefore, ought not to be voiced in this opinion.

### COMMENTARY AND QUESTIONS

1. **"Garbage In — Garbage Out" planning.** In Citizens for Environmental Quality v. United States, 731 F.Supp. 970 (D.C.Col. 1989) the court threw out a LRMP based on a computer model ("FORPLAN") containing artificially limited alternatives:

> From the record, it appears that the Forest Service first established production goals, and then formulated alternatives which would reach those goals through employing data constraints.... We find that this result-based decision making process prevented the Forest Service from establishing a legitimately broad range of reasonable alternatives as required by the statutory and regulatory scheme.... Defendants' range of alternatives cannot be said to reflect a wide range of goals since the proposed alternatives each contemplate timber production at a highly unprofitable level. A broad range of alternatives must also include an alternative which contemplates timber harvesting at a profitable level even if that level requires reducing current timber production goals.... From its evaluation, it is clear that the Forest Service gave a "hard look" only to those alternatives which increased timber production. 731 F.Supp. at pages 989–990.

2. **The planning "shell game."** Professor Robert Feller, a keen observer of BLM grazing management practices, comments that

> concerned citizens and environmental organizations who urge BLM and the Forest Service to assess the appropriateness of grazing on particular parcels of public lands find themselves engaged in a bureaucratic shell game in which the agencies avoid the issue by sliding it back and forth between their land use planning processes and their decision making processes for individual grazing allotments. When citizens request that a land use plan include a review of the appropriateness of grazing on particular sites or allotments within a planning area, they are typically informed that the land use planning process is not designed to address such site-specific issues, and that they should raise the issue when allotment management plans (AMPs) are developed for the allotments in question. However, when the issue is raised during the development of an AMP or the issuance of a permit for an allotment, the agency responds that it is a land use planning issue that should have been raised during the development of the applicable land use plan. In fact, the issue is never addressed, and grazing continues without ever being seriously questioned.

Feller, 'Till The Cows Come Home: The Fatal Flaw in the Clinton Administration's Public Lands Grazing Policy, 25 Envt'l L. 703, 748 (1995).

At least one federal circuit court has made this shell game even more difficult to win by denying standing to environmental groups to contest an LRMP because the mere existence of an LRMP, as opposed to a proposal for a site-specific action, does not produce an imminent injury in fact. Sierra Club v. U.S. Forest Service, 28 F.3d 753 (8th Cir.1994). This harsh standing rule has been rejected by the Sixth, Seventh, and Ninth Circuits.[44]

3. **Planning and consensus management.** The Clinton Administration's policy for resolving natural resource disputes on public lands is to bring the stakeholders together and attempt to achieve consensus by suggesting "win-win" outcomes. See Chapter 11. A truly participatory, balanced planning process can facilitate consensus-building. One commentator has concluded that the Clinton Administration's attempt to build consensus on Western natural resource issues has thus far resulted in few successes. Melling, Bruce Babbitt's Use of Governmental Dispute Resolution: A Mid-Term Report Card, 30 Land and Water Law Rev. 57 (1995).[45]

4. **The aftermath of Sierra Club v. Thomas.** On certiorari the Supreme Court vacated the override of the Wayne Forest Plan on pure ripeness grounds. 118 S.Ct. 1665 (1998). In the Court's view, the LRMP was not ripe for review because it did not inflict present significant practical harm on the Sierra Club's interests. Before the Forest Service permits logging it must comply with NEPA and allow public participation, and a court can then review a more specific proposal; with more time, the Forest Service may correct its own mistakes in implementing the plan; and the Plan is still too abstract for judicial review. Does the Supreme Court ignore the tendency of Forest Service plans to become "self fulfilling prophecies" by concretizing agency attitudes and clientele expectations? If a plan is facially illegal, why should it not be immediately invalidated before it causes wasteful sunk costs?

The Sixth Circuit majority opinion in Sierra Club v. Thomas remains a probing criticism of Forest Service management of logging in national forests. It illuminates administrative realities that have long undercut the civic conservation mandate of government agencies trying to regulate natural resource industries, and underscores the need for rational reform of natural resource conservation programs. Only time will tell whether the new natural resource planning processes will bring modern resource management rationality to the public lands, or business-as-usual under a different guise.

5. **Theoretical dilemmas underlying public resource management.** This chapter does not provide clear answers to the generic questions with which it began: are

---

44.The court in the principal case above rejected this argument. See also Resources Ltd. v. Robertson, 8 F.3d 1394 (9th.Cir.1993), and Sierra Club v. Forest Service, 46 F.3d 606 (7th Cir.1995) ("if the Sierra Club had to wait until the project level to address general procedural injuries regarding a broad issue like biological diversity, implementation of the forest plan might have progressed too far to permit proper redress").

45. In Melling's estimation, Secretary Babbitt's failure to achieve consensus on grazing reform is attributable to the lack of "voluntariness" in the negotiation process. Melling believes that ranchers and environmentalists share important interests, which might result in a negotiated settlement in a less coercive and divisive atmosphere. One of these common interests is that "perhaps the biggest threat to the West in the 21st century is the explosion of condominiums and secondary homes." See also Ellickson, Order Without Law: How Neighbors Settle Disputes (1991).

public resources a continuing legacy or current profit-maximizers, assigned to single or multiple uses, to be used for local or nationwide benefit, precluding or harmonizing various competing interests? Statutes like the Wilderness Act and FLPMA attempt to establish long-term basic principles to guide resource management, which inevitably collide with the pressures of economic interests that focus, as we all do, on the short term specific.

It doesn't make much difference to the mayor of a small Northwest logging town whether the surrounding mountains are public or private; the old growth forests that remain there are a source for a half dozen more years of economic life for the community on the only terms that are available — clearcutting according to prevailing corporate practice. For as long as these last forests are allowed to be cut, by just so long will local citizens be able to pay their mortgages and taxes, and avoid having to go on welfare or move away. The practices of the timber industry, and its failures to implement successful long-term renewable, sustainable timber supply, are matters beyond the control of the community.

What is lost when an ancient forest is gone, beyond a localized depreciation of natural environment? Are there public losses other than those that occur in terms of recreation, tourism, water quality, etc.? What exactly was the value of the old Methusaleh tree, in Chapter One at 90–91? Such questions become even more abstract when it isn't the oldest single tree, or the last carrier pigeon, but thousands of acres comprising the last 5 per cent of our original natural forest — or when human actions do not destroy the resource, but change its setting. Joe Sax once was startled as he climbed up a tortuous ridge in Tennessee to look out over a sprawling, forested, mountain-girded gulf in the Great Smokies National Park, and saw a white high-rise Sheraton hotel thrusting up in the middle distance of the valley, built on an inholding within the Park. Sax, Mountains Without Handrails: Reflections on the National Parks (1980); Helpless Giants: The National Parks and the Regulation of Private Lands, 75 Mich. L.Rev. 239 (1976). Like the tower at the Gettysburg battlefield, what kind of experiential or aesthetic issues did this commercial intrusion raise? What is a "wilderness experience"?

Or, for another situation raising a composite of these issues, consider the re-introduction of wolves, grizzlies, and other endangered predator species to areas from which they had previously been exterminated. Montana, Wyoming, Minnesota, and other northern tier states have seen a number of attempts to restore large predators on public lands, especially national parks. For ranchers grazing cattle on nearby public and private rangelands, these ecological experiments represent the height of public policy folly. Keiter and Holscher, Wolf Recovery under the Endangered Species Act: a Study in Contemporary Federalism, 11 Public Land L. Rev. 19 (1990). Killing bears, mountain lions, and wolves seems to be an atavistic human instinct, coupled with a farmer's vivid sense of emotional and economic injury upon finding a calf slaughtered in an early morning meadow. Doesn't a policy to bring back the predators seem irrational? To shoot the animal that killed your calf, however, runs the risk of fine and imprisonment.

At the very least we owe future generations an attempt to clarify what our national public resources policies are.

# Chapter 25

# LAND USE-BASED ENVIRONMENTAL PROTECTION STATUTES

A. *The Federal Coastal Zone Management Act*

B. *State Hazardous Waste Facility Siting Statutes*

C. *Critical Area Protection Statutes*

D. *Comprehensive State and Regional Planning and Management*

E. *Traditional Land-Use Controls and the Environment: Zoning, Subdivision Regulation, et al.*

---

This chapter primarily deals with governmental environmental protection restrictions on private land. Every land-use decision has environmental consequences; most environmental protection measures have land-use consequences. In fact, it is probable that virtually all the environmental controversies reflected in this book are somehow based on land-use decisions. The interrelationships between land-use controls and environmental protection mechanisms are so strong that there can be no bright line between environmental law and land-use law. In fact, it is not even clear that the two are separate fields.[1]

Although there may be no clear logical or legal distinction between land-use and environmental regulation, there certainly is a palpable political distinction between the two. Poll after poll indicates that most people will accept painful sacrifices in the name of environmental protection while they passionately resist added restrictions on the use of their land. Apparently many Americans do not perceive an inevitable linkage of environmental protection and land-use regulation, and treat land purely as a commodity rather than as a natural economy as well.

The American attitude toward land-use is unique. In other parts of the world, land development is not a right but a privilege. Land-use decisions are often con-

---

1. In California Coastal Commission v. Granite Rock Co., 480 U.S. 572 (1987), the Supreme Court awkwardly tried to articulate a distinction between land-use regulation and environmental controls:

> The line between environmental regulation and land use planning will not always be bright.... Land use planning in essence chooses particular uses for the land; environmental regulation, at its core, does not mandate particular uses of the land but requires only that, however the land is used, damage to the environment is kept within prescribed limits.... Congress clearly envisioned that although environmental regulation and land use planning may hypothetically overlap in some instances, these two types of activity would in most cases be capable of differentiation. 480 U.S. at 587–88.

Justice Powell and Justice Stevens, however, found this distinction "unsupportable, either as an interpretation of the governing statutes or as a matter of logic...a distinction...without a rational difference." 480 U.S. at 601, 603.

strained by comprehensive land-use plans that represent the interests of all members of the community, including, in some areas, non-human members. In the United States, by contrast, comprehensive land-use planning, other than local zoning, is the exception rather than the rule. Governmental restrictions on the unfettered use of private land — especially federal restrictions — are strenuously resisted, and even command some degree of constitutional protection, as studied in Chapter 23. In order to avoid stigma, environmental protection agencies at all levels of government often feel compelled to repeat the mantra that they are not regulating land-use but protecting the environment. One challenge to 21st-century environmental law will be to implement fair and reasonable systems of land-use management without disrupting the powerful political consensus that has supported — against several strong political counterattacks — the manifold environmental improvements since 1970.

The more that environmental and natural resources management policy confronts the impacts of land-use on environmental change, the more the area of land-use becomes a necessary stage for future rational overview accounting of short- and long-term effects. For example, urban sprawl development takes a heavy toll on environmental quality, especially in coastal zones:

> A trend is emerging in both developed and developing countries: cities from Los Angeles to Jakarta, Indonesia, are rapidly expanding outward, consuming ever greater quantities of land. This urban sprawl, characterized by low-density development and vacant or derelict land, leads to the wasteful use of land resources, higher infrastructure costs, and excessive energy consumption and air pollution because of the greater use of motorized transport. Many criticize urban sprawl for aesthetic reasons as well.

> The United States provides an apt example. Urban population growth there has slowed to less than 1.3 percent per year, yet urban development continues to encroach on surrounding lands as residents abandon inner cities and move to the suburbs. The total amount of land dedicated to urban uses increased from 21 million hectares[2] in 1982 to 26 million hectares in 1992. In one decade, 2,085,945 hectares of forestland, 1,525,314 hectares of cultivated cropland, 943,598 hectares of pastureland, and 774,029 hectares of rangeland were converted to urban uses....

> Coastal ecosystems, including wetlands, tidal flats, salt-water marshes, mangrove swamps, and the flora and fauna that depend on them, are especially threatened by urban land conversion. Already, coastal urban centers are home to almost 1 billion people worldwide and are experiencing unprecedented growth. Much of this growth will take place in developing nations;...[but] even in developed countries such as the United States, some of the highest levels of urban growth are occurring in small coastal cities.[3] Accordingly, urban impacts along the coasts stand to increase markedly in the years ahead.

> In coastal cities, the higher value placed on shoreline locations increases the economic incentives to develop there. Thus, as coastal cities grow and expand, original coastal habitat is increasingly converted to other uses. Land conversion activities range from draining and filling of marshes and other wetlands to constructing homes or resorts on beaches or dunes, to building seawalls, to

---

2. A hectare is equal to 2,471 acres. [Eds.]

3. Roughly 75percent of the American population lives within 50 miles of an ocean or one of the Great Lakes. [Eds.]

undertaking large-scale reclamation projects that extend the shoreline into the sea.... Along the San Francisco Bay, the most highly urbanized estuary in the United States, filling has reduced the areal extent of the bay by one-third in the past 150 years. Of the estimated 80,940 hectares of coastal marshes that originally fringed San Francisco Bay, 80 percent have been lost to development. In addition to habitat loss, shoreline development can intensify coastal erosion, alter the hydrology of estuaries, and otherwise disrupt natural processes. The United Nations Environment Programme, World Resources at 59–62 (1996).

Many of these urban developments are relatively small and ostensibly insignificant from an environmental standpoint, but when viewed cumulatively and synergistically with similar developments they may have major regional environmental impacts.[4]

Land-use restrictions take a variety of forms, falling along a continuum — ranging from processes that raise a strong presumption of non-development to processes that raise a strong presumption of development, with various intermediate gradations. Siting statutes, for example, presume that certain facilities should be sited but in a process that keeps social costs to a minimum. At the other end of the continuum, critical area protection statutes presume that no development should take place in particularly valuable and vulnerable areas unless it is clearly innocuous or else necessary to satisfy a paramount public purpose. Zoning acts and "cooperation" statutes, such as the Coastal Zone Management Act (CZMA) of 1972, 16 U.S.C.A. §1451 et seq., fall somewhere between siting and critical area protection legislation on this continuum.

Local governments currently dominate the field of land-use controls, using subdivision regulations and zoning. If one pictures land use as a pyramid, local zoning is its broad base; going upward, state land-use laws are far fewer, and federal law governing private land-use is at the narrow apex. Because this book focuses on legal process techniques, however, this chapter proceeds in inverse order, with local land-use controls noted at the end of the chapter.

The CZMA is the first model analyzed, an interesting model of cooperative federalism that addresses both siting and critical area protection, but in a way that encourages state planning rather than imposing federal regulation of private land-use decisions. Next, state hazardous waste facility siting statutes are examined as examples of a type of siting process that has been popular, although fraught with major difficulties. Then several varieties of critical area protection statutes are presented: a site-specific permitting model (§404 of the Clean Water Act); a single-purpose regional model (the Federal Wild and Scenic Rivers Act); and a comprehensive regional model. Finally, local zoning is discussed as a means of achieving environmental protection.

## A. THE FEDERAL COASTAL ZONE MANAGEMENT ACT

Most federal environmental regulation affects the siting of new development and the protection of critical areas in some way. This influence is, for the most part, indirect and implicit. The "Nonattainment" and "PSD" (Prevention of

---

4. There is a "nibbling effect" when a series of small projects add up to large cumulative impacts.

Significant Deterioration) sections of the Clean Air Act, for example, provide general rules for attaining and maintaining federally-specified ambient air quality standards in particular areas. States then determine the mix of sources that will be permitted to use the available assimilative capacities of the relevant airsheds. (Chapter Eight.) Similarly, federal water pollution control law requires states to prevent degradation of high quality waterbodies, but a state may choose to allow lower water quality where "necessary to accomodate important economic or social development" unless Outstanding National Resource Waters are involved. States may also be required to restrict growth in heavily-polluted areas where water quality standards are being violated (Chapter Nine.) However, only rarely does the federal government directly control private land-use decisions, as in the Endangered Species Act (Chapter 14) and in §404 of the Clean Water Act (*infra*.). Significantly, it is these direct federal restrictions on private land-use that evoke the most highly-charged political reactions to federal protection of the environment.

Congress' reluctance to confront private land-use explicitly and directly is a function not only of the American public's apparent aversion to land-use control, but also of Congress' deference to the traditional state police power to regulate private land-use for the public health, safety, and welfare. Under the Tenth Amendment to the United States Constitution, all powers not specifically delegated to the federal government or denied to the states are reserved to the states. This fundamental principle of federalism incorporates the state police power over private land-use, and the federal government has always trod lightly in this area. Only when other public interests have become compelling has Congress enlisted constitutional powers, such as the Commerce Clause, in aid of regulating land-use, albeit indirectly most of the time.

The CZMA does not authorize federal land-use controls, but it is explicitly land-use legislation. It is fundamentally a planning statute, in that it authorizes federal matching grants for the purpose of assisting coastal states, including Great Lakes states, in the development of management programs for the land and water resources of their coastal zones. The CZMA attempts to assure implementation of state coastal management programs in two ways: (1) authorizing the suspension of federal funding if a coastal state fails to adhere to its management program; and (2) mandating that any federal activity within a state's coastal zone be consistent with that state's approved coastal management program. In the following excerpt, Professor J.B. Ruhl summarizes the CZMA and argues that it is an example of a "Cooperation" strategy that is preferable to both the "Coercion" approach (e.g., the ESA and §404) and the "Coordination" model (e.g., NEPA) for the conservation of biodiversity.

### J.B. Ruhl, Biodiversity Conservation and the Ever-Expanding Web of Federal Laws Regulating Nonfederal Lands: Time for Something Completely Different?
66 University of Colorado Law Review 555, 616–623 (1995)

The CZMA was enacted in 1972 to promote the "national interest in the effective management, beneficial use, protection, and development of the coastal zone." Ecological protection was paramount among the concerns Congress expressed as reason for addressing the "increasing and competing demands upon the lands and waters of our coastal zone."... Hence, Congress stated as its principal goal for the CZMA "to preserve, protect, develop, and where possible, to restore or enhance, the resources of the Nation's coastal zone for this and succeeding generations."

The approach Congress took in the CZMA, however, is decidedly different from the regulatory structures of the Endangered Species Act and §404 of the Clean Water Act. Congress was convinced that "[t]he key to more effective protection and use of the land and water resources of the coastal zone is to encourage the states to exercise their full authority over the lands and waters in the coastal zone." The CZMA does this by establishing a method by which the states, in cooperation with federal and local governments, can establish "unified policies, criteria, standards, methods, and processes for dealing with land- and water-use decisions of more than local significance." The two CZMA programs for carrying out that objective are the development and approval of coastal management plans ("CMP"s) and the review of federal actions for consistency with established CMPs.

Sections 305 and 306 of the CZMA provide federal grants to the...coastal states for developing and implementing their CMPs. A CMP must be consistent with guidelines established by the Secretary of Commerce, which must require "identification of the means by which the State proposes to exert control over the land uses and water uses" and the "priorities of uses in particular areas." A state's CMP development must be conducted "with the opportunity of full participation by relevant [governmental agencies and private persons]" and must provide "an effective mechanism for continuing consultation and coordination" between those entities. The CMP must define permissible land and water uses in the coastal zone and identify in that regard "areas of particular concern." The CMP also must demonstrate that land and water uses can be controlled and coordinated through either state establishment of standards for local implementation, direct state regulation, state review of all state, local, and private development proposals for consistency with the CMP, or a combination of those three general approaches.

The Secretary's CZMA regulations, promulgated through the National Oceanic and Atmospheric Administration ("NOAA"), elaborate on each of those key statutory elements for CMP development and approval. Significantly, NOAA's rules for special management areas address in detail the "areas of particular concern" feature of the CMP. NOAA's rules recognize that a state's set of controls for the coastal zone may vary throughout the zone in intensity, scope, and detail. NOAA requires that "[w]here these policies are limited and non-specific, greater emphasis should be placed on areas of particular concern [in the CMP] to assure effective management and an adequate degree of program specificity." ...

Once a state's CMP is in place, the CZMA requires that all actions carried out by federal agencies directly, or by nonfederal entities requiring some form of federal approval or funding, be concurred with by the state or its designated agency as consistent with the CMP. Significantly, the consistency review requirement applies not only to activities physically located within the CMP boundary, but also to activities outside the boundary which may affect the coastal zone. NOAA's regulations implement a detailed consistency review procedure....

The chief advantage the CZMA presents for promoting biodiversity protection is its flexibility, which operates on many levels. The CZMA allows a state flexibility to adopt the management approach...most consistent with that state's general style of land-use regulation and management....

The CZMA also exhibits flexibility in terms of geographic emphasis and intensity of the regulatory program. The program for areas of particular concern allows states to focus regulatory efforts on specified areas in need of close attention, such as those needing intense biodiversity protection. The CZMA also inherently recognizes that land and water uses will occur in the coastal zone and must be accommodated. Hence, rather than requiring a uniform level of regulation throughout the coastal zone ecosystem, the CZMA recognizes that some areas will require more development than others and some will require a greater degree of protection than others. Also, the CZMA recognizes that activities outside the coastal zone boundary may affect coastal resources and thus need to be addressed....

The CZMA's flexibility, however, also imposes burdens in terms of developing and implementing the CMP according to the loosely-stated federal guidelines. The danger exists that goals such as biodiversity protection will become diffusely enforced and thus ineffective as management tools. In that sense, then, if the detailed consistency review procedures are not closely followed, the CZMA could prove ineffective for biodiversity protection in the coastal zone....

The Cooperation model offers some measure of balance between Coercion and Coordination model statutes, holding traits of each. The essence of the Cooperation model is the expression of strong federal goals and policies in the context of a flexible partnership between federal, state, and local interests in seeing to it that the federal policies are implemented in the form of substantive legal requirements. Cooperation model statutes often hold out some form of regulatory carrot or stick, or blend of both, as an incentive for the partners to act together within the framework of the federal goals and policies, but substantive review criteria and outcomes generally are not prescribed. Rather, it is left to the cooperative process to formulate a regulatory response directed at the particular state or local planning area.

The Cooperation model statutes thus are expensive to operate. They involve substantial transaction costs and time as the cooperating partners forge consensus over the final substantive shape of the regulatory policy. But the final result offers promise of achieving the substantive outcome with greater impact than the Coordination model offers, and with greater consensus than the Coercion model offers....

[My] proposal calls for a unified federal biodiversity conservation statute [modelled on the CZMA], the Biological Resources Zone Management Act ("BRZMA"), centered around three stages of biodiversity conservation management: (1) state identification, inventory, and nomination of biological resource zones; (2) local and private development, and federal approval, of biological resource zone management plans; and (3) implementation of the management plan in lieu of the existing federal regulatory structure. The first stage allows states to identify areas of biological resources which are in need of protection and which may present controversial issues if those protective measures are carried out through the existing coercive federal regulations. The second stage allows the local and private entities potentially most at risk of bearing the brunt of federal regulation to develop a comprehensive management plan for the biological resources zone, knowing that it must not only meet their needs, but also the federal objectives of biodiversity conservation. The third stage provides the reward to the state, local, and private interests for their expenditure of time and effort and their commitment to the plan — complete relief from all the headaches of the existing federal structure, including the multiple permitting requirements, inflexible and overlapping regulatory standards, different agencies and policies, and never-ending litigation....

COMMENTARY AND QUESTIONS

1. **"Yes, but will they come?"** The linchpin of the BRZMA variation of the Cooperation model is the willingness of states to escape the "coercive" aspects of current regulation by themselves meaningfully regulating land-use or effectively directing local land-use approval processes. It is not clear that states will appreciate being placed in the potentially unpopular position of superseding closely-guarded local powers over land-use. In addition, states may also be unwilling to relinquish their politically convenient strategy of scapegoating "The Feds." Industrial and development interests, in general, possess proportionately greater political power at the state level than at the federal level. As a result, state governments frequently find it politically comfortable to satisfy one political constituency by protecting the environment, but simultaneously to placate economic interests by proclaiming that "The Feds made us do it." The BRZMA proposal may give states credit for more political fortitude than they can actually muster.

2. **Resolving interstate resource disputes.** How would the Cooperation model — based on discretionary state participation and individual state planning and management — resolve a dispute where an area of critical environmental concern (e.g., the critical habitat of an endangered species) transcends state lines and the affected states disagree about how the resource should be managed? Under the CZMA, a state may veto any proposed federal activity or permit that is inconsistent with the state's CMP. Since consistency review applies to activities outside the coastal zone boundary (and also, presumably, outside the state) that may affect the coastal zone, neighboring states with approved CMPs might hold conflicting views regarding a proposed federal activity that would impact both their coastal zones. The CZMA provides for override by the Secretary of Commerce of a state veto under certain circumstances. See North Carolina v. Commerce Department, 42 ERC 1254, 1995 WL 852123 (D.C.D.C.1995), where the court upheld the Secretary's override of North Carolina's veto of a federal §404 permit for a proposed project by Virginia Beach, Virginia, to withdraw 60 million gallons of drinking water per day from the bi-state Lake Gaston. Under the BRZMA concept, one participating state might be implementing an approved BRZMA management plan, while its neighbor, a non-participating state, would be operating under applicable federal law. What if these regulatory schemes produce different results with regard to management of a shared resource? Federal law would probably prevail in such a situation.

3. **Of time and money.** Professor Ruhl recognizes that the Cooperation approach will be expensive and time-consuming. Is such a system compatible with the conservation of endangered species and other unique environmental resources? To use NEPA terms, is it possible that procedural delays and funding shortages might cause "irretrievable commitments of resources"? A Cooperative approach could include exceptions where federal law might preempt the process in emergency situations. Where should the line be drawn between these emergency situations and ordinary situations where the operations of state law may continue unimpeded?

What about situations where ostensibly innocuous proposals, taken by themselves, might have extremely deleterious impacts when viewed cumulatively with other completed projects or pending development proposals?

4. **Mixed mandates and diffuse expectations.** Professor Ruhl also understands that the CZMA's guidelines are mainly aspirational, which might render them "diffusely enforced and thus ineffective as management tools." In fact, the CZMA involves a balancing of environmental and economic factors: state coastal management planning must give "full consideration to ecological, cultural, historic, and esthetic values as well as to needs for compatible economic development." 16 U.S.C.A. §1452(2). Given the equal vagueness of concepts such as "biodiversity," environmentally conscious states might, as Professor Ruhl anticipates, identify and nominate biological resource zones ("BRZ"s) "corresponding to local and regional ecosystems requiring the greatest levels of protection because they are unique, sensitive, or threatened." Other participating states, however, might choose to maximize economic opportunities by nominating few, if any, BRZs. Such interstate economic competition might encourage the "race to the bottom" that provoked the federalization of much of environmental law in the first place (Chapter Six). Thus, a substantial federal presence would still be necessary to administer this system. Existing federal law would continue to apply in nonparticipating states. Strong federal oversight would also be necessary to deter participating states from adopting "minimal protection" strategies, and the federal government would have to step in and rescind plan approval in states that are not adequately enforcing their plans. Strong federal oversight is potentially inconsistent with the attempt to provide states with "complete relief from all the headaches of the existing federal structure." Quite the contrary, the BRZMA might simply add another unwelcome layer of bureaucracy to what is already a complex regulatory process, or else operate as a Trojan Horse to undercut effective regulation.

5. **Has the CZMA worked?** "As a vehicle for promoting state and local land use planning along coastal America, the CZMA has largely succeeded."[5]

> As for the tough, nasty business of land use regulation, there is evidence that difficult decisions are being made and, at times, against economic and development interests. Spurred forward by CZMA grants of money and authority, some states have passed highly-controversial set-back ordinances, made generous provisions for public access to coastal resources, and banned certain development altogether. On the other hand, states have been almost equally free to look the other way. *Id.*, Houck and Rolland, at 1297–1298.

Nevertheless, this statute has been unsuccessful in curbing what Professor Oliver Houck calls "America"s Mad Dash to the Sea." Houck, America's Mad Dash to the Sea, Amicus Journal, 21–36 (Summer 1988). According to Professor Houck, "we are expecting state regulation, under the Coastal Zone Management Act, to overcome formidable economic and political pressures without the safeguard of a clear, national mandate." Will the additional "carrot" of a dispensation from existing

---

5. Houck and Rolland, Federalism in Wetlands Regulation: A Consideration of Delegation of Clean Water Act Section 404 and Related Programs to the States, 54 Md. L. Rev. 1242, 1297 (1995).

federal regulations, as advocated by Professor Ruhl, be sufficient to overcome traditional state reluctance to constrain development in coastal zones? When dealing with biodiversity preservation, can we afford to adopt a system in which states are, to a great extent, "free to look the other way?"

**6. ISTEA, a "Cooperation statute."** America's dependence on the automobile, facilitated by massive governmental investments in roads (3 million miles) and interstate highways (45,000 miles), has fostered urban sprawl development, which, in addition to the impacts outlined above, has also led to a lack of affordable housing and the decline of our central cities and their systems of mass transit. In 1991, Congress tentatively responded to this phenomenon by enacting the Intermodal Surface Transportation Efficiency Act, 23 U.S.C.A. §134 et seq. ("ISTEA" — commonly pronounced "Ice-Tea").

Perhaps the most important aspect of ISTEA was its funding flexibility.[6] Whereas federal transportation funding had traditionally been restricted to highway projects, ISTEA made over half of its $155 billion authorization available for any surface transport mode, including construction and maintenance of intracity mass transit systems, bikeways, and pedestrian systems. Second, ISTEA invigorated regional transportation planning by requiring states to develop statewide "Transportation Improvement Programs" ("TIPs") that must be consistent with transportation plans formulated by metropolitan planning organizations ("MPOs"), with participation by all affected stakeholders. The purpose of this planning process was to promote the development of intermodal transportation systems "which will efficiently maximize mobility of people and goods within and through urbanized areas and minimize transportation-related fuel consumption and air pollution." Planners were required to consider the "overall social, economic, energy, and environmental effects of transportation decisions." Third, TIPs had to be consistent with State Implementation Plans ("SIPs") under the Clean Air Act (Chapter Eight) in order for transportation projects included in TIPs to be eligible for federal funding. The Clean Air Act itself bars federal licenses or permits for activities that are inconsistent with SIPs.[7]

## B.  STATE HAZARDOUS WASTE FACILITY SITING STATUTES

All siting statutes presume, to one degree or another, that the facilities involved in the siting process are necessary to society. The purpose of siting statutes is to site these facilities with as little social cost (including environmental cost) and disruption as possible.

Siting facilities for disposal of solid waste, hazardous waste, and nuclear waste has become extraordinarily difficult because of the way that "LULUs" (Locally Undesirable Land Uses) trigger the "NIMBY" (Not In My Back Yard) Syndrome

---

6. The following summary of ISTEA is, in part, based on Pelham, Innovative Growth Control Measures: The Potential Impacts of Recent Federal Legislation and the Lucas Decision, 25 Urb. Law. 881 (1993).

7. 45 U.S.C.A. §7506(c).

local reaction.[8] Waste management tragedies like Love Canal, New York, and Times Beach, Missouri — along with the close participation of state and federal government officials in the siting and permitting of some of these misplaced and mismanaged facilities (as in the *Wilsonville* case in Chapter Two) — have created a mood of deep public skepticism about whether waste disposal can be safely performed, and cynicism about whether state or federal governments are sufficiently competent and objective to protect the health and safety of host communities. In addition, local residents harbor reasonable fears that a waste disposal facility will create few jobs, produce little additional tax revenue, overburden local services (e.g., fire, police) and infrastructure (e.g., roads, sewerage facilities), and negatively affect property values. Any proposal to site a waste disposal facility is met by a generally effective combination of zoning prohibitions, political opposition, media denunciation, lawsuits, and civil disobedience.

Unlike states, municipalities possess no inherent powers. They are capable of exercising only those powers delegated to them by the state governments that created them. Thus even where a state constitution contains a Home Rule provision to the effect that municipalities are responsible for control of land-use within their boundaries, the state can legally override municipal decisions to "zone out" particular waste disposal facilities.

A number of states have enacted hazardous waste disposal facility siting statutes relying on Alternative Dispute Resolution ("ADR") ( Chapter 21), with regard to providing compensation for host communities and allaying their safety concerns by establishing environmental monitoring and response mechanisms in addition to those required by federal and state laws. Four state hazardous waste facility siting statutes stand out as contrasting types.

Minnesota law gives the community — broadly defined as the county — control over final siting decisions. Minn. Stat. §115A.191. Counties volunteer sites by passing non-binding Resolutions of Interest, which may be withdrawn at any time before binding site contracts have been signed. Once a county volunteers an environmentally acceptable site, the Minnesota Waste Management Board simultaneously negotiates a siting contract with the county and searches for a private developer to build and operate a facility on the site. During its negotiations with the Board, the county receives up to $4,000 per month in local government aid. If a siting contract is ultimately signed, the county receives an additional $150,000 per year for two years. These incentives are in addition to any other payments the county may negotiate with the Board, including tax breaks and other forms of state assistance. Additional compensation mechanisms, however, may require legislative approval.

New Jersey law gives the state Hazardous Waste Facility Siting Commission the power to obtain a site by eminent domain and override local zoning where necessary to site a facility. N.J. Rev. Stat. §13.1E-52-59. After preparing siting criteria,

---

8. Some other common acronyms inspired by LULU and NIMBY are "OOMBY" (Out Of My BackYard), "NIFYE" (Not In My Front Yard Either), "NIMTOO" (Not In My Term Of Office), "NOPE" (Not On Planet Earth), and "BANANA" (Build Absoulutely Nothing Anywhere Near Anything).

the Commission searches for the most environmentally acceptable sites. During the latter phases of the siting process, potential host communities are given grant funds to perform their own site suitability studies. Once the site has been chosen, a qualified developer is expected to enter into negotiations with the host community for compensation and safety measures. The host community is entitled to at least five percent of the gross receipts of any facility constructed within its boundaries in order to mitigate the effects of the facility.

In Wisconsin, the developer chooses the site and requests each affected municipality to identify relevant local regulations. Wis. Stat. §144.44. The municipality has the choice of whether or not to negotiate with the developer. If the municipality chooses not to negotiate, all applicable local regulations enacted within 15 months of the developer's submission of a site feasibility report are pre-empted. If an affected municipality chooses to negotiate, it must enact a formal siting resolution stating its intent to negotiate and, if necessary, submit to binding arbitration. Arbitrable issues are severely circumscribed. Reimbursement of a community's costs of evaluating a site and participating in the negotiation and arbitration process are limited to $2,500. In the arbitration process, each party immediately submits its final offer, and the arbitrator must choose one of these without modification.

In Massachusetts, all post-siting statutes, local permits, and zoning changes promulgated to exclude particular facilities are preempted. Mass. Gen. L. 21D §3-15.The developer initiates the siting process by filing a notice of intent with the state Hazardous Waste Facility Siting Council. The Council may then issue a finding that the proposal is "feasible and deserving" in terms of the developer's financial capability and past management practices, technical feasibility of the proposal, need for the facility, and compliance with state and federal laws. If a feasible and deserving determination is issued, the community, aided by state technical assistance grants, is required to negotiate with the developer and the state. The State is a party to the negotiations because the outcome may include state incentives to a host community. If the negotiations result in impasse, an arbitrator prepares a draft settlement for public comment. The final settlement is submitted to the Council and is subject to judicial review.

### COMMENTARY AND QUESTIONS

1. **The track record of siting statutes.** In spite of these sophisticated statutes, in fact no major hazardous waste disposal facility has been sited, using the new procedures, in any of these four states or in any of the other approximately eight states that have enacted similar hazardous waste facility siting statutes. Ironically, the two most recently constructed hazardous waste incinerators have been located in states without ADR-type siting statutes. See Polumbo v. Waste Technologies, 989 F.2d 156 (4th Cir. 1993), and Coalition For Health Concern v. LWD, Inc., 60 F.3d 1188 (6th Cir. 1995) (hazardous waste incinerator sitings in Ohio and Kentucky upheld over public opposition). Professor Barry Rabe and his colleagues describe successful efforts to site hazardous waste disposal facilities in the Canadian

provinces of Alberta and Manitoba.[9] First, a moratorium on siting proposals was accompanied by extensive public education as to the problems of hazardous waste management and the potential economic benefits for a host community. Those communities expressing interest were informed that they were free to opt out of the siting process at any time. Those that continued were encouraged to negotiate such factors as site selection and design (within broad site elimination guidelines), type of disposal technology, and impact management (mitigation, compensation, and contingency measures). It is not clear whether participating communities received grants to employ independent experts with regard to these issues. Although negotiations were conducted by local governments, final plebiscites were held to determine community acceptance. Agreements were made with host communities that committed the federal government to (1) restrict out-of-province waste imports to the new facilities, (2) develop transfer and disposal facilities in other provinces, and (3) reduce the volume of wastes being generated and requiring disposal. Responding to fears that private contractors operating these facilities would be unreliable, a "crown corporation" was established to share facility management with private companies, with the entire operation to be overseen by provincial regulatory authorities. Would such a siting system — emphasizing public education and participation, burden sharing, and a substantial federal role in facility management — be successful in the United States? For one thing, restrictions on waste imports from other states would probably be unconstitutional unless specifically approved by Congress (Chapter Six).

2. **Community veto?** The Minnesota siting act gives communities ultimate power to accept or reject hazardous waste disposal facilities. Some commentators believe that given the current NIMBY climate and the probable success of communities that oppose LULUs, this is the most viable way to site hazardous waste disposal facilities:

> A community that feels coerced into having a facility is likely to experience too much anger, fear, and outrage about the siting process itself to be concerned about examining the content of the proposal. Guaranteeing a community the right to say no to any proposal it found unacceptable would, by freeing it from the threat of coercion, allow it to explore whether having a facility would be a better option than having none. Given the right to say no, a community might weigh the costs, risks, and benefits of hosting a facility and try to negotiate a package that would be more attractive than maintaining the status quo. E. Schmeidler and P. Sandman, Getting To Maybe, 48 (1988).

On the other hand, one could argue that (1) a community possessing a veto will almost certainly exercise it, (2) a developer will not negotiate with a community possessing a veto, (3) local politicians will never take anything but a "hard line" and then complain that "they made us accept the facility," (4) a community will only negotiate if it believes that the facility is inevitable because the state will override its objections, and (5) a community, which bears the concentrated costs of a facility, will be incapable of recognizing the facility's dispersed, statewide benefits.

9. Rabe et al., NIMBY and Maybe: Conflict and Cooperation in the Siting of Low-Level Radioative Waste Disposal Facilities in the United States and Canada, 24 Envtl. L. 67 (1994).

The New Jersey statute assumes that communities will not negotiate about compensation and mitigation until after the siting decision has been made. How much leverage does a community possess at that point? Has a community by then become so alienated and defensive that it will only dig in its heels and fight? Professor Kent Portney has concluded that political factors militate against state or siting board preemption of local land-use authority, even where, as in New Jersey, a siting statute authorizes preemption. Portney, Siting Hazardous Waste Treatment Facilities, 9, 50–51 (1991).

3. **Choosing the site.** There is general agreement that decisions about the need for hazardous waste disposal facilities and appropriate technologies for these facilities are best made at the state level before making site-specific decisions. But states differ in their approaches to choosing sites. In Minnesota, counties volunteer sites and the state determines the best disposal site from among those volunteered. In New Jersey, the state selects the best sites based on predetermined siting criteria adopted with public participation. In Wisconsin, the developer chooses the site and initiates the siting process by notifying affected municipalities. The State then judges each application against minimum state siting criteria, without comparing other potential sites or determining whether better sites exist. Massachusetts follows a similar procedure, except that the developer first notifies the Council by filing a notice of intent.

Should a developer be permitted to choose a site? Hazardous waste disposal facilities have been disproportionately sited in low-income and minority communities. (See Cole, Empowerment As The Key To Environmental Protection: The Need For Environmental Poverty Law, 19 Ecology L.Q. 619, 622 (1992). Would a developer most likely select a disadvantaged community that is poorly organized and desperate for development? Is it necessarily inequitable to locate LULUs in disadvantaged communities, or is the problem one of unequal access to information and political power? As for information, in New Jersey and Massachusetts state grants are available to communities to assist them in collecting information relative to siting. In Wisconsin, however, the municipality must utilize its own resources to evaluate the proposal, and in arbitration can only recover a maximum of $2,500 to cover all costs of negotiation and arbitration. This system would appear to be unfair to a Wisconsin community that bears the burden of showing, among other things, that there are better sites. In this regard, a state might adopt a "best site" or an "available site" strategy. If an available site strategy is chosen, will a state cast its net so wide, in order to assure that a facility will be sited, that its catch will include sites having *Wilsonville*-like problems?

4. **Negotiations: who, what, and when?** In Minnesota, the county proposes a site and negotiates with the State; the developer is not involved in the negotiations. Is the county the proper institution to represent a host municipality? There is a danger here that the State will "give away the store" in its negotiations with local communities and discourage potential developers. Will other municipalities — especially those whose applications have been rejected — resist the authorization of extraordinary incentives for host communities by opposing the special legislation necessary to enact them?

Negotiation is mandatory in Massachusetts. The State will be part of the negotiations because enhanced state services and benefits are factors that the community and developer may consider. In Wisconsin, an affected municipality is not required to negotiate, but if it does not quickly resolve to negotiate and be subject to arbitration, it loses its power to influence the facility because it cannot "zone out" the facility. (If you were a Wisconsin community, would you swiftly pass a restrictive zoning ordinance and hope that no developer would contact you during the next 15 months?) The developer must negotiate if the municipality resolves to participate in the siting process. Is negotiation that is mandatory (or virtually so as in Wisconsin) a contradiction in terms? Will a party bargain in good faith if it cannot say "no"? The spectre of binding arbitration if a siting agreement is not reached — as is the case in both Massachusetts and Wisconsin — will often spur the parties to negotiate in good faith. As a community or a developer, what would your strategy be in Wisconsin, where the arbitrable issues and judicial review are limited, and the arbitrator must accept, as a total package, the "last best offer" of one side or the other? How would that strategy differ in Massachusetts, where the arbitration is wide-ranging and the arbitrator can draft a compromise settlement that is open for public comment and must be approved by the Council, with broad judicial review available?

In Wisconsin, when a community opposes a facility, it passes a siting resolution in order to keep the negotiation option open, but agrees with the developer to hold negotiations in abeyance while the community fights the site on technical and environmental grounds in separate State licensing proceedings. More tractable communities tend to negotiate and participate in the licensing proceeding simultaneously. The Wisconsin process has resulted in numerous completed siting agreements for projects such as solid waste landfills. None, however, has involved a major offsite hazardous waste disposal facility. Can the success of the Wisconsin siting statute be explained by the fact that its coverage is so inclusive, covering solid waste facilities, on-site facilities, and expansions, as well as new, off-site hazardous waste disposal facilities? Does the expansion of the existing facility paradigm overcome the potential stigma of having a facility sited in a community? Or does the community accept the facility because it hasn't the resources to fight the developer, and the arbitrable issues are so circumscribed? Or is it something about the political culture of Wisconsin? Whatever the reason, Wisconsin communities have accepted waste disposal facilities, negotiating for direct payments, property value protection, disposal privileges, extra monitoring, infrastructure subsidies, and public access for surveillance.

The Massachusetts siting act places extensive technical evaluation of the site and the developer's waste disposal technology at the end of the process, rather than at the beginning or concurrent with negotiations, as in Wisconsin. The belated occurrence of technical review has been given as one reason for the failure of the Massachusetts siting act. A different drawback of the Massachsetts process is its excessive complexity. At least five State agencies are closely involved; draft and final reports, public briefings, comment periods, and hearings abound. Negotiations are tripartite, rather than bipartite. Professor Wheeler identifies other

flaws in the Massachusetts system as (1) the requirement that communities negotiate, (2) the adversarial nature of the bargaining process — potentially resulting in
impasse arbitration — which polarizes the issue and leads to "gunpoint negotiation," and (3) an insufficiently neutral state role in mediation and facilitation, leading to suspicion of the entire process. Wheeler, Negotiating NIMBYs: Learning from
the Failure of the Massachusetts Siting Law, 11 Yale J. Reg. 241, 244 (1994).

5. **Other siting recommendations.** Professor Frank B.Cross believes that

> ...one promising approach to public participation in the risk regulation [and
> facility siting] process is the "citizen panel." Citizen panels are groups of indi-
> viduals who hear the evidence on the full scope of risk controversies and pro-
> vide input to decision makers. These panels could be selected randomly almost
> like a jury panel. After selection, the panels would hear witnesses and evidence
> to inform themselves about a risk controversy. The panel could then provide
> input into the government's decision. Cross, The Public Role in Risk Control,
> 24 Envtl. L. 887, 956 (1994).

Would citizen panels possess the political credibility to overcome intransigent
NIMBY reactions? Michael Gerrard implicitly answers "No" when he concludes
that the facility siting problem is so intractable that federal intervention is necessary. In his view, potential volunteer host communities do exist, but "single waste
myopia," fostered by the fragmentation of hazardous waste regulatory statutes,
inhibits a comprehensive approach to hazardous waste disposal. Gerrard recommends that a limited number of centralized treatment and disposal facilities for all
non-radioactive hazardous wastes be constructed on already contaminated land,
such as Superfund sites and contaminated military bases. Following a federally-
conducted hazardous waste disposal needs assessment, a Federal Waste Disposal
Commission (modeled on the Defense Base Closure and Realignment
Commission) would allocate sites to States — based on equity and environmental
factors — subject to Congressional approval or rejection. Each state would be
responsible for developing incentives to attract volunteer communities to accept
the allocated sites. If a state fails to site its allocated facilities, the Commission
would be authorized to conduct its own preemptive siting process.[10] Would a
system such as this be acceptable to the American public, which is cynical about
federal policy initiatives? Would it instead be preferable for the federal government
to build hazardous waste facilities on federal land, or to lease federal land for private disposal operations? Would Gerrard's proposal only exacerbate environmental
injustice, in that only low-income or minority communities would feel compelled
to bid for these LULUs? Why not open the regional LULU allocation process to all
LULUs, including prisons, drug treatment facilities, etc.?

6. **Environmental Justice siting debates.** From the beginning, toxic siting has provided the most dramatic focus for the the environmental justice movement which
criticizes the disproportionate cumulative impacts suffered by low income communities and communities of color. Charles Lee's "Toxic Wastes and Race in the
United States" (1987) written for the United Church of Christ Commission for

---

10. Gerrard, Turning NIMBY on its Head: A Siting Solution Based on Federal Allocation, State
Responsibility, and Local Control, 1995 BNA Env. Rptr. Curr. Dev., 2257.

Racial Justice, and Dr. Robert Bullard's Dumping in Dixie: Race, Class & Environmental Quality (1990) presented data showing that risk of exposure to toxic waste hazards appeared to be both quantitatively and qualitatively greater for communities of color and low income than than for the general public, a conclusion backed by much subsequent research. Some scholars, however, have criticized the studies' accuracy and argue that even if LULUs disproportionately affect minorities, that is not necessarily the result of racism.[11]

Legal attempts to prove intentional discrimination on the basis of race and poverty in toxics siting decisions have not been very successful in court.[12] Courts (unlike EPA, which has issued "discriminatory effect" regulations under Title VI of the 1964 Civil Rights Act[13]) generally require a showing of "discriminatory *intent*" which is most difficult to prove. Arlington Heights v. Metro. Housing Dev't, 429 U.S. 252, 265 (1977). As noted in Chapter One, is it racism for corporate managers to seek out (1) the most inexpensive land and (2) areas where they will face the least effective political opposition and the most desperate welcome for jobs and economic activity? The correlation of toxic sitings with race and low income thus may well derive from cold marketplace logic rather than discriminatory bias. Likewise Professor Been notes the sad likelihood that even if the community surrounding a toxic site is not initially low income or of color, market conditions will soon make it so.[14]

---

11. Prof. Vicki Been, Analyzing Evidence of Environmental Justice, 1995 Journal of Land Use & Environmental Law 1 (noting e.g., that Lee used zipcode area correlations rather than the more difficult but more accurate census tracts or radial distances from toxic sites); D. Kevin, A Critique of Environmental Justice Theories and Remedies, 8 Vill. Envtl. L.J. 121 (1996).

Proving discriminatory intent is almost impossible; even proving disparate effect is not easy. As in regulatory takings, the choice of a baseline determines the scope of the examination, and has a huge impact on the determination of whether or not there is an excessive burden on a low-income or racial minority neighborhood. In making its determination of racial or low-income bias, should a court examine only the past siting decisions of the particular agency involved, or the actions of the municipal government as a whole? How far back in time should a court look — 5 years, 20 years, or 100 years? How should it define the membership boundary of the group alleging the discrimination? Which individuals should be included in a "minority" classification? Which minorities are most likely to be discriminated against, and most in need of heightened judicial scrutiny? What dollar amount defines "low-income"? What percentage of the families on a block must be below this amount for the block to be included within the class requesting heightened judicial scrutiny? Finally, what should the baseline geographic unit be? City blocks? Neighborhoods? Census tracts? City quadrants? County lines? The most appropriate basis for ascertaining the degree of disparate impact upon populations probably is to assess demographics within a given radius distance from the challenged sites, but that is expensive and difficult.

12. See East Bibb Twiggs Nbhd. Assoc. v. Macon-Bibb County Planning & Zoning Comm., 706 F.Supp. 880 (M.D. Ga. 1989); Bean v. Southwestern Waste Management Corp., 482 F. Supp. 673 (S.D. Tex. 1979).

13. Title VI of the 1964 federal Civil Rights Act, 42 U.S.C.A. §2000d, reads—

No person in the United States shall, on the ground of race, color, or national origin, be excluded from participation in, be denied the benefits of, or be subjected to discrimination under any program or activity receiving Federal financial assistance.

Title VI was long thought not to offer serious remedies for the kinds of problems involved in environmental justice. Since 1993, however, the EPA's Office of Civil Rights has reversed that position and opened investigatory files on more than a dozen major cases alleging violations of Title VI, and EPA regulations, 40 C.F.R. §7.35, and the Browner Guidance, have strengthened internal consideration of environmental justice issues.

14. Been, Locally Undesirable Land Uses in Minority Neighborhoods: Disproportionate Siting or Market Dynamics? 103 Yale L.J. 1383 (1994)

Faced with the logic of distributional inequity in exposure to toxics, how can siting processes escape this Catch-22? One approach that might be implemented in the state siting processes noted in text above is what Professors Schmeidler and Sandman advocated in Getting to Maybe: communal bribery, the ability of poor communities to extort large economic premiums (and hopefully large safety infrastructures) in return for accepting such hazardous land uses. Government could play a direct role, itself taking over toxic disposal functions, or, failing this, require race and income-conscious protections in licensing the immensely lucrative hazardous waste facilities studied in Chapter 17.

The Clinton Administration's Executive Order, E.O. 12898 called upon all federal agencies to integrate active consideration of environmental justice issues in their administration of federal laws. Subsequently the EPA under Administrator Carol Browner substantially increased programmatic attention to the issue, and the federal Civil Rights Commission has opened investigations of state siting laws accused of disproportionate impacts. The seriousness with which EPA and other agencies seem to be taking the issue and the Executive Order may well change the balance of power in environmental cases, making it easier for citizens to enlist agency regulatory leverage in resistance to cumulative environmental impacts. Citizens in the poor, predominantly African-American community of Chester Pennsylvania, for example, were able to convince a circuit court to recognize a private cause of action to enforce Title VI, with support from EPA's "discriminatory effect" regulations, challenging state permits for a solid waste disposal facility.[15]

7. **The nuclear waste disposal dilemma.** Disposal of high-level nuclear wastes, primarily produced by commercial nuclear power plants and government defense-related activities, presents an especially complex and contentious siting dilemma. Despite the enactment of a federal siting statute, the Nuclear Waste Policy Act, 42 U.S.C.A., §§10101 et seq., there is currently no ultimate disposal facility for high-level nuclear wastes. See USGAO, Nuclear Waste: Yucca Mountain Project Behind Schedule and Facing Major Uncertainties (1993), and Indiana Michigan Power Co. v. Energy Department, 88 F.3d 1272 (DC Cir. 1996) (Energy Department was told to provide for disposal of high-level nuclear waste by January 31, 1998; it didn't happen). As plans for siting temporary and permanent high-level nuclear waste disposal facilities in the Southwest have become bogged down by NIMBY-type, as well as national environmental group opposition, the Mescalero Apache Tribe of New Mexico and the Goshute Tribe of Central Utah have proposed the construction of interim hazardous waste storage facilities on their lands. See Leonard, Sovereignty, Self-Determination, and Environmental Justice in the Mescalero Apache's Decision to Store Nuclear Waste, 24 B.C. Env. Aff. L. Rev. 651 (1997). Leonard sees no easy answer to the question, "Is this an example of large corporations practicing environmental racism or tribes asserting long sought-after autonomy in order to provide schools and services for their people?" The siting outlook is no brighter with regard to disposal of low-level radioactive wastes produced by, for example, hospitals and research laboratories. Under the Low-Level Radioactive Waste Policy

---

15. See Chester Residents v. Pennsylvania DEP, 132 F.3d 925 (3rd. Cir. 1997).

Act, 42 U.S.C.A. §§2021(b) et seq., states are required to dispose of their own commercially generated waste, either individually or in interstate compacts. Since the statute was enacted in 1980, nine regional low-level nuclear waste compacts, covering 38 states, have been approved by Congress, but no new disposal facilities have been constructed under any of these compacts. See USGAO, Radioactive Waste: Status Of Commercial Low-Level Facilities (1995), McGinnis, Collective Bads: The Case of Low-Level Radioactive Waste Compacts, 34 Nat. Res. J. 563 (1994), and New York v. United States, 112 S.Ct. 2408 (1992) (striking down, on Tenth Amendment grounds, portions of the Low-Level Radioactive Waste Policy Act). Disposal of government-generated low-level nuclear waste in the Waste Isolation Pilot Project ("WIPP"), in southeastern New Mexico, has also been delayed by environmental considerations.

## C. CRITICAL AREA PROTECTION STATUTES

### Section 1. SITE-BY-SITE PERMITTING: §404 OF THE CLEAN WATER ACT

Section 404 of the Clean Water Act, 33 U.S.C.A. §1344 et seq., governs the discharge of dredged or fill material into waters of the United States. The most environmentally significant and politically controversial use of §404 involves wetlands protection. Wetlands are critically important and exceptionally vulnerable environmental resources:

> Unlike in the past, when wetlands were considered unimportant areas to be filled or drained for various uses, the many important roles that wetlands play are now recognized. Wetlands — which generally include swamps, marshes, bogs, and similar areas — provide vital habitat for fish, waterfowl, and other birds and wildlife. They are also important to commercially valuable fish and shellfish enterprises. In addition, wetlands help maintain water quality and acquatic productivity, aid flood control and erosion control, and provide recreation sites and aesthetically pleasing landscapes.

> However, according to estimates, the contiguous 48 states lost approximately 53 percent of their original 221 million acres of wetlands over the 200-year period from the 1780s to the 1980s. [The U.S. Fish and Wildlife Service] estimated that wetlands losses during the period from the mid-1950s to the mid-1970s were about 458,000 acres per year. FWS' most recent estimates covering the years 1974 through 1983 suggest that about 290,000 acres were being lost each year. The Soil Conservation Service [now the Natural Resources Conservation Service] reported that losses of wetlands on nonfederal rural areas in the period from 1982 to 1991 totaled about 120,000 acres per year. USGAO, Wetlands Protection: The Scope of the §404 Program Remains Uncertain, 8 (1993).

The USEPA has recently estimated that, through the early 1990s, wetlands losses have declined to approximately 90,000 acres per year. EPA, Environmental Indicators Of Water Quality In The United States, 11 (1996).[16] This decline is due

---

16. The Fish and Wildlife Service estimates are slightly higher: 117,000 acres of wetlands lost per year between 1985 and 1995. The FWS credits Section 404, among other changes in federal law, for the reduction of wetlands losses.

mostly to the fact that prices for agricultural land have decreased so sharply that it is now cheaper for farmers to buy uplands than to convert wetlands to farmland by ditching and diking. Nevertheless, any further loss of wetlands is clearly excessive in light of our explicit national policy of "no net loss" of remaining wetlands.[17]

As the following case indicates, §404 process has profound land-use implications.

### Bersani v. Environmental Protection Agency
United States Circuit Court for the Second Circuit, 1988
850 F.2d 36, *Cert. Denied*, 489 U.S. 1089 (1989)

TIMBERS, J. Appellants ("Pyramid")...appeal from a judgment entered...granting summary judgment in favor of appellees, the EPA and the United States Army Corps of Engineers, and denying Pyramid's motion for summary judgment.

This case arises out of Pyramid [development company's] attempt to build a shopping mall on certain wetlands in Massachusetts known as Sweeden's Swamp. Acting under the Clean Water Act, EPA vetoed the approval by the Corps of a permit to build the mall because EPA found that an alternative site had been available to Pyramid at the time it entered the market to search for a site for the mall. The alternative site was purchased later by another developer and arguably became unavailable by the time Pyramid applied for a permit to build the mall....

Sweeden's Swamp is a 49.5 acre wetland which is part of an 89 acre site near Interstate 95 in South Attleboro, Massachusetts. Although some illegal dumping and motorbike intrusions have occurred, these activities have been found to have had little impact on the site, which remains a "high-quality red maple swamp" providing wildlife habitat and protecting the area from flooding and pollution.

One of the sections of the Clean Water Act relevant to the instant case is §301(a), which prohibits the discharge of any pollutant, including dredge or fill materials, into the nation's navigable waters, except in compliance with the Act's provisions, including §404. It is undisputed that Sweeden's Swamp is a "navigable water"...and that Pyramid's shopping center proposal will involve the discharge of dredged or fill materials.

Section 404 of the Act, focusing on dredge or fill materials, provides that the United States Army and EPA will share responsibility for implementation of its provisions. EPA and the Corps also share responsibility for enforcing the Act.

As with virtually all critical areas regulatory programs, applicants seeking permit approval to build a development in the regulated area must submit site plans, various traffic, economic, and environmental analyses, and propose mitigation measures as necessary.

Section 404(a) authorizes the Secretary of the Army, acting through the Corps, to issue permits for the discharge of dredged or fill materials at particular sites. Section 404(b) provides that, subject to §404(c), the Corps must base its decisions regarding permits on guidelines (the "§404(b)(1) guidelines") developed by EPA in conjunction with the Secretary of the Army.

The §404(b)(1) guidelines, published at 40 CFR §230 (1987), are regulations containing the requirements for issuing a permit for discharge of dredged or fill materials. 40 CFR §230.10(a) covers "non-water dependent activities" (i.e., activities that could be performed on non-wetland sites such as building a mall) and provides

---
17. The Clinton Administration has announced an initiative to achieve a net gain of 100,000 acres of wetlands by the year 2005.

essentially that the Corps must determine whether an alternative site is available that would cause less harm to the wetlands. Specifically, it provides that "no discharge of dredged or fill material shall be permitted if there is a practicable alternative" to the proposal that would have a "less adverse impact" on the "aquatic ecosystem." It also provides that a practicable alternative may include "an area not presently owned by the applicant which could reasonably be obtained, utilized, expanded, or managed in order to fulfill the basic purpose of the proposed activity." It further provides that "unless clearly demonstrated otherwise," practicable alternatives are (1) "presumed to be available," and (2) "presumed to have less impact on the aquatic ecosystem." Thus, an applicant such as Pyramid must rebut both of these presumptions in order to obtain a permit. Sections 230.10 (c) and (d) require that the Corps not permit any discharge that would contribute to significant degradation of the nation's wetlands and that any adverse impacts must be mitigated through practicable measures.

In addition to following the §404(b)(1) guidelines, the Corps may conduct a "public interest review." 33 CFR §320.4 (1987). This public interest review is not mandatory under §404, unlike consideration of the §404(b) guidelines. In a public interest review, the Corps decision must reflect the "national concern" for protection and use of resources but must also consider the "needs and welfare of the people."

Under §404 of the Act, EPA has veto power over any decision of the Corps to issue a permit. It is this provision that is at the heart of the instant case.

Specifically, §404(c) provides that the Administrator of EPA may prohibit the specification of a disposal site "whenever he determines, after notice and opportunity for public hearings, that the discharge of materials into such area will have an unacceptable adverse effect" on, among other things, wildlife. An "unacceptable adverse effect" is defined in 40 CFR §231.2(e) as an effect that is likely to result in, among other things, "significant loss of or damage to...wildlife habitat...." The burden of proving that the discharge will have an "unacceptable adverse effect" is on EPA.

In short, both EPA and the Corps are responsible for administering the program for granting permits for discharges of pollutants into wetlands under §404. The Corps has the authority to issue permits following the §404(b)(1) guidelines developed by it and EPA; EPA has the authority under §404(c) to veto any permit granted by the Corps. The Corps processes about 11,000 permit applications each year. EPA has vetoed five decisions by the Corps to grant permits....

On appeal, the thrust of Pyramid's argument is a challenge to what it calls EPA's "market entry" theory, i.e., the interpretation by EPA of the relevant regulation, which led EPA to consider the availability of alternative sites at the time Pyramid entered the market for a site, instead of at the time it applied for a permit....

We hold (1) that the market entry theory is consistent with both the regulatory language and past practice; (2) that EPA's interpretation, while not necessarily entitled to deference [because the other federal agency administering §404, the Corps, disagreed with EPA's interpretation], is reasonable; and (3) that EPA's application of the regulation is supported by the administrative record....

The effort to build a mall on Sweeden's Swamp was initiated by Pyramid's predecessor, the Edward J. DeBartolo Corporation. DeBartolo purchased the Swamp some time before April 1982. At the time of this purchase an alternative site was available in North Attleboro (the "North Attleboro site"). Since Massachusetts requires state approval (in addition to federal approval) for projects that would fill wetlands, DeBartolo applied to the Massachusetts Department of Environmental Quality Engineering ("DEQE") for permission to build on Sweeden's Swamp. DEQE denied the application in April, 1982.

Pyramid took over the project in 1983 while the appeal of the DEQE denial was pending. In April 1983, Massachusetts adopted more rigorous standards for approval of permits. The new standards added wildlife habitat as a value of wetlands to be protected and required the absence of a "practicable alternative."...

One of the key issues in dispute in the instant case is just when did Pyramid begin searching for a suitable site for its mall. EPA asserts that Pyramid began to search in the Spring of 1983. Pyramid asserts that it began to search several months later, in September 1983. The difference is crucial because on July 1, 1983 — a date between the starting dates claimed by EPA and Pyramid — a competitor of Pyramid, the New England Development Co. ("NED"), purchased options to buy the North Attleboro site. The site was located upland and could have served as a "practicable alternative" to Sweeden's Swamp, if it had been "available" at the relevant time. Thus, if the relevant time to determine whether an alternative is "available" is the time the applicant is searching for a site (an issue that is hotly disputed), and if Pyramid began to search at a time before NED acquired options on the North Attleboro site, there definitely would have been a "practicable alternative" to Sweeden's Swamp, and the Pyramid application should have been denied. On the other hand, if Pyramid did not begin its search until after NED acquired options on the North Attleboro site, then the site arguably was not "available" and the permit should have been granted....

In August 1984, Pyramid applied under §404(a) to the New England regional division of the Corps (the "NE Corps") for a permit. It sought to fill or alter 32 of the 49.6 acres of the Swamp; to excavate nine acres of uplands to create artificial wetlands; and to alter 13.3 acres of existing wetlands to improve its environmental quality. Later Pyramid proposed to mitigate the adverse impact on the wetlands by creating 36 acres of replacement wetlands in an off-site gravel pit....

In November, 1984, EPA and FWS submitted official comments to the NE Corps recommending denial of the application because Pyramid's proposal was inconsistent with the the §404(b)(1) guidelines. Pyramid had failed (1) to overcome the presumption of the availability of alternatives and (2) to mitigate adequately the adverse impact on wildlife. EPA threatened a §404(c) review. Pyramid then proposed to create additional artificial wetlands at a nearby upland site, a proposal it eventually abandoned.

In January 1985, the NE Corps hired a consultant to investigate the feasibility of Sweeden's Swamp and the North Attleboro site. The consultant reported that either site was feasible but that from a commercial standpoint only one mall could survive in the area. On February 19, 1985, the NE Corps advised Pyramid that denial of its permit was imminent. On May 2, 1985, the NE Corps sent its recommendation to deny the permit to the national headquarters of the Corps. Although the NE Corps ordinarily makes the final decision on whether to grant a permit, see 33 CFR §325.8 (1982), in the instant case, because of the widespread publicity, General John F. Wall, the Director of Civil Works at the national headquarters of the Corps, decided to review the NE Corps' decision. Wall reached a different conclusion. He decided to grant the permit after finding that Pyramid's offsite mitigation proposal would reduce the adverse impacts sufficiently to allow the "practicable alternative" test to be deemed satisfied. He stated:

In a proper case, mitigation measures can be said to reduce adverse impacts of a proposed activity to the point where there is no "easily identifiable difference in impact" between the proposed activity (including mitigation) versus the alternatives to that activity.

On May 31, 1985, Wall ordered the NE Corps to send Pyramid, EPA and FWS a notice of its intent to grant the permit. The NE Corps complied on June 28, 1985.

On July 23, 1985, EPA's RA [Regional Administrator] initiated a §404(c) review of the Corps decision....

On May 13, 1986, EPA issued its final determination, which prohibited Pyramid from using Sweeden's Swamp. It found (1) that the filling of the Swamp would adversely affect wildlife; (2) that the North Attleboro site could have been available to Pyramid at the time Pyramid investigated the area to search for a site; (3) that considering Pyramid's failure or unwillingness to provide further materials about its investigation of alternative sites, it was uncontested that, at best, Pyramid never checked the availability of the North Attleboro site as an alternative; (4) that the North Attleboro site was feasible and would have a less adverse impact on the wetland environment; and (5) that the mitigation proposal did not make the project preferable to other alternatives because of scientific uncertainty of success....

As EPA has pointed out, the preamble to the §404(b)(1) guidelines states that the purpose of the "practicable alternatives" analysis is "to recognize the specific value of wetlands and to avoid their unnecessary destruction, particularly where practicable alternatives *were* available in non-aquatic areas to achieve the basic purpose of the proposal." 45 Fed. Reg. 85,338 (1980) (emphasis added). In other words, the purpose is to create an incentive for developers to avoid choosing wetlands when they could choose an alternative upland site. Pyramid's reading of the regulations would thwart this purpose because it would remove the incentive for a developer to search for an alternative site at the time such an incentive is needed, i.e., at the time it is making a decision to select a particular site. If the practicable alternatives analysis were applied to the time of the application for a permit, the developer would have little incentive to search for alternatives, especially if it were confident that alternatives soon would disappear. Conversely, in a case in which alternatives were not available at the time the developer made its selection, but became available by the time of application, the developer's application would be denied even though it could not have explored the alternative site at the time of its decision....

PRATT, Circuit Judge, dissenting: ... This market entry theory approaches a sensitive environmental problem through a time warp; it ignores the statute's basic purpose and it creates unfair and anomolous results...ignoring the crucial question of whether the site itself should be preserved. Under the market entry theory, developer A would be denied a permit on a specific site because when he entered the market alternatives were available, but latecomer developer B, who entered the market after those alternatives had become unavailable, would be entitled to a permit for developing the same site. In such a case, the theory no longer protects the land but instead becomes a distorted punitive device: it punishes developer A by denying him a permit, but grants developer B a permit for the same property — and the only difference between them is when they "entered the market."

The market entry theory has further problems. In this case, for example, if a Donald Trump had "entered the market" after NED took the option on the North

Attleboro site and made it unavailable, under EPA's approach he apparently would have been entitled to a permit to develop Sweeden's Swamp. But after obtaining the permit and the land, could Trump then sell the package to Pyramid to develop? Or could he build the mall and sell the developed site to Pyramid?...

Furthermore, in a business that needs as much predictability as possible, the market entry theory will regrettably inject exquisite vagueness. When does a developer enter the market? When he first contemplates a development in the area? If so, in what area — the neighborhood, the village, the town, the state or the region? Does he enter the market when he first takes some affirmative action? If so, is that when he instructs his staff to research possible sites, when he commits money for more intensive study of those sites, when he contacts a real estate broker, when he first visits a site, or when he makes his first offer to purchase? Without answers to these questions a developer can never know whether to proceed through the expense of contracts, zoning proceedings, and EPA applications....

Since Congress delegated to EPA the responsibility for striking a difficult and sensitive balance among economic and ecological concerns, EPA should do so only after considering the circumstances which exist, not when the developer first conceived of his idea, nor when he entered the market, nor even when he submitted his application; rather, EPA, like a court of equity, should have the full benefit of, and should be required to consider, the circumstances which exist at the time it makes its decision. This is the only method which would allow EPA to make a fully informed decision — as Congress intended — based on whether, at the moment, there is available a site which can provide needed economic and social benefits to the public, without unnecessarily disturbing valuable wetlands.

## COMMENTARY AND QUESTIONS

1. **Timing theories in *Bersani*.** Should the "practicable alternative" test be applied at the time of "market entry," permit application, or "time of decision"? There are several problems with Judge Pratt's dissenting "time of decision" test. First, there is the question of which of many decision points is applicable. In this case is it Massachusetts DEQE's original rejection, its subsequent approval, the Corps' original rejection, its subsequent approval, the EPA decision, or the decisions of the two state or two federal courts that considered this matter on judicial review? Second, since the "time of decision" comes rather late in the process, it is doubtful that a developer would take a substantial financial risk in the face of possible permit denial based on distant events that it can neither control nor predict. Third, the developer will have invested so much in project preparation by the time of decision that agencies will be reluctant to deny it a permit based on the availability of a site that has only recently come on the market. But if, as a general matter, the "time of decision" test is problematic, does that mean that the "time of entry" test is necessarily the proper one to apply in all cases? The real issue here is whether the developer, in good faith, considered non-wetland sites. Would it perhaps be better not to adopt a formal timing rule, but to encourage the agencies to determine the matter of good faith consideration of alternatives on a case-by-case basis?

2. **The "practicable alternative" test.** Is the §404 "practicable alternative" test a good one? As the dissent points out, this test has nothing to do with the desirabil-

ity of building in a wetland. Developers are, unfortunately, drawn to wetlands because they are conveniently located, available, and relatively inexpensive. Professor Oliver A. Houck explains that an applicant can manipulate the "practicable alternative" test by defining the project so narrowly that only the proposed site will accomodate it. Houck, Hard Choices: The Analysis of Alternatives under §404 of the Clean Water Act and Similar Environmental Laws, 60 U. Colo. L. Rev. 773, 788–789, 832–836 (1989). What if Pyramid had proposed a "unique shopping experience in a magnificent aquatic setting"? Since 1989, the Corps has somewhat modified its previous position of deferring to the applicant's statement of purpose and need. Professor Houck considers the *Bersani* decision to be "the most tough-minded [judicial] interpretation of alternatives analysis under §404":

> To the *Bersani* court, then, an alternative to a large commercial development was feasible although it was neither the developer's choice nor the developer's most profitable option; the availability of this alternative would be measured at the time the developer's own, internal choice is being made; and offers of mitigation would not finesse this alternatives analysis but, rather, would follow it to offset losses that could not otherwise be avoided.... The *Bersani* dissent, however, found this result more than remarkable. In its view, the majority mistook §404's "basic purpose," which is not to provide an incentive for developers to avoid choosing wetlands but, rather, to provide a balancing analysis between the "biological integrity" of a wetland area and "commerce and other economic advantages." Alternatives are but a "factor" in this determination. This relatively free-wheeling balancing approach is, of course, reminiscent of the Corps public interest review regulations and has found a secure home in a second line of cases interpreting the alternatives requirement of §404[18] (Houck, *supra.*, pp.806–807).

Professor Houck concludes that, because the "practicable alternative" test is fatally flawed, §404 should be amended to "make the water dependency test dispositive.... Unless this type of activity needs to be located in waters of the United States, it will not be." (Houck, *supra.*, p.830.)

3. **An uncomfortable partnership.** The sharing of §404 implementation responsibility between the Corps and EPA has been cumbersome and contentious, and the effectiveness of §404 has suffered as a result. The Corps is responsible for permit issuance and initial enforcement; while EPA is authorized to (1) develop the environmental guidelines used to evaluate permit applications, (2) veto proposed permits with unacceptable environmental impacts, (3) oversee state assumption of the §404 program, (4) interpret statutory exemptions, (5) determine the jurisdictional reach of the program, (6) set aside areas where no disposal of fill will be permitted, and (7) enforce in cases where the Corps has not adequately done so. As a primarily construction agency, the Corps has not always been a zealous defender of wetlands:

> The Corps receives about 15,000 individual permit applications annually. Of these 15,000 applications, the Corps issues approximately 10,000 individual permits (67 percent). The Corps denies approximately 500 individual permit

---

18. See Louisiana Wildlife Fed'n v. York, 761 F.2d 1044 (5th Cir. 1985), and Fund For Animals v. Army Department, 85 F.3d 535, 543 (11th Cir. 1996)("...the Corps'...practicable alternatives analysis is not subject to numerical precision, but instead requires a balancing of the applicant's needs and environmental concerns").

applications, or about 3 percent of the applications it receives. The remaining 30 percent, about 4,500 applications, are either withdrawn or qualify for letters of permission or general permits. In addition, the Corps authorizes about 40,000 activities under regional or nationwide general permits each year. (USGAO Report, *supra.*, p. 12.)

The USGAO also found that Corps enforcement of §404 has been sporadic. EPA, on the other hand, does not possess the resources to adequately supervise the Corps' performance. As of 1993, EPA had used its §404(c) veto power only eleven times since 1979. Only two states, Michigan and New Jersey, have received delegation from EPA to administer the §404 program.[19]

4. **The coverage of §404.** EPA regulations define *wetlands* as

...those areas that are inundated or saturated by surface or ground water at a frequency and duration sufficient to support, and that under normal circumstances do support, a prevalence of vegatation typically adapted for life in saturated soil conditions. 40 C.F.R. §230(t).

Thus, a wetland is an area, including an area constructed by human beings, that exhibits some combination of hydric soils, wetland vegetation, and wetland hydrology. This leaves a great deal of vagueness in the regulatory definition, and the precise identification of individual wetlands depends on interpretive manuals and on-the-ground judgment by Corps and EPA officials. Needless to say, the specific criteria to be used in wetlands identification have been the subject of heated political controversy. For example, in 1991 the Corps proposed regulations to replace the existing requirement of inundation by surface water or saturation by groundwater to at least 18 inches of the surface for one week or more during the growing season, by a more demanding one requiring inundation for 15 or more consecutive days, or saturation to the surface for 21 or more consecutive days during the growing season. With the advent of the Clinton Administration in 1992, the proposed regulations were withdrawn, but bills are frequently introduced in Congress to limit the coverage of §404.

Most federal courts have broadly construed the geohydrological coverage of §404. In U.S. v. Riverside Bayview Homes Inc., 106 S.Ct. 455 (1985), the Supreme Court upheld Corps regulations including wetlands that were adjacent to navigable waters within the ambit of §404, even though, in that case, there was no evidence that those wetlands were periodically inundated by flooding of the neighboring waterbody. Other courts have held that isolated wetlands can be regulated under §404 if migratory birds have been shown to frequent them. See Hoffman Homes, Inc., v. EPA, 999 F.2d 256 (7th Cir. 1993) (remanded because of lack of evidence that migratory birds actually used the subject wetlands), and Leslie Salt Co. v. U.S., 55 F.3d 1388 (9th Cir. 1995), *cert. denied sub. nom.* Cargill Inc., v. U.S., 111 S.Ct. 1089 (1995)(isolated, man-made wetlands that are dry much of the year may be regulated under §404). In U.S. v. Banks, 115 F.3d 916 (11th Cir. 1997), *cert. denied* 118 S.Ct. 852 (1998), the court held a parcel of land connected to navigable waters primarily

19. For an analysis of existing delegation programs under §404, see Houck and Rolland, Federalism in Wetlands Regulation: A Consideration of Delegation of Clean Water Act Section 404 and Related Programs to the States, 54 Md. L. Rev. 1242 (1995). The authors argue that if delegation "is done carefully and with the proper mix of federal inducements and safeguards, it could succeed"(p. 1314).

by groundwater to be within the coverage of §404. However, in U.S. v. Wilson, 133 F.3d 251 (4th Cir. 1997), the court, in reversing a criminal conviction for illegally filling a wetland for residential development, held it erroneous for the trial judge to have instructed the jury to extend the jurisdiction of §404 to waters that lack a direct or indirect surface connection to interstate or navigable waters. In a concurring opinion, Judge Payne criticized, as inconsistent with *Riverside Bayview*, the portion of the majority opinion that required a surface connection between a water of the United States and a wetland in order for the wetland to be considered "adjacent" to a navigable waterway.

The *Wilson* decision also narrowly construed the activities that may be regulated under §404, holding that "sidecasting" — digging ditches with heavy construction equipment in order to drain a wetland, and depositing the excavated dirt next to the ditches — was not an *addition* of a pollutant so as to constitute a "discharge" under §502(12) of the Clean Water Act. Most other federal courts have held that "redeposit" of dredged material is a "discharge" under §404.[20]

5. **Mitigation of environmental damage.** Typical of §404's administration, Pyramid's mitigation proposals played an important part in the *Bersani* decision. Mitigation, however, continues to be a highly controversial device:

> In the context of existing wetland regulation, mitigation generally refers to avoidance, minimization, and compensation. These steps are frequently applied in a sequential manner. First, a party seeking a permit for a project that affects wetlands must demonstrate that the least environmentally damaging alternative will be used. Second, the permit applicant must develop a plan to minimize the environmental harm from any unavoidable impacts. Finally, the applicant must compensate for or offset any harm done to wetland functions and values which is not avoided or minimized. The applicant satisfies the compensation requirement by enhancing, restoring, creating, or preserving other wetlands that may be located on or off the project site. [There is a] preference for on-site mitigation and for in-kind [restoring the type of wetland function that a development project affects] mitigation, [as well as a preference for] restoration and enhancement, rather than creation or preservation.... Mitigation banking involves mitigating for wetland impacts before an activity causes environmental harm. Mitigation banking occurs when one restores, enhances, creates, or preserves wetlands, thereby generating mitigation credits. A regulatory agency determines the amount and value of the mitigation credits which the credit generator may use to offset the adverse wetland impacts of its own development projects, [or] in a more complex scenario,...a private entity generates credits, which a third party purchases to meet its own unrelated mitigation requirements.

---

20. See, e.g., Avoyelles Sportsmen's League v. Marsh, 715 F.2d 897 (5th Cir. 1983)(redeposit of material dredged from a wetland by heavy equipment is covered by §404); United States v. M.C.C. of Florida, 772 F.2d 1501 (11th Cir. 1985), *vacated and remanded on other grounds*, 481 U.S. 1034 (1987), *readopted in part and remanded on other grounds*, 848 F.2d 1033 (11th Cir. 1988)(redeposit of spoil dredged by the propellers of defendant's tug boats constituted a "discharge"); and Rybachek v. E.P.A., 904 F.2d 1276 (9th Cir. 1990)(dirt and gravel waste from placer gold mining in a stream is an addition of a pollutant). (The *Rybachek* case is extensively discussed in Chapter Nine.) But see American Mining Congress v. Army Department, 951 F.Supp. 265 (D.C.D.C.1997)(striking down the Corps' "Tulloch Rule" regulations requiring permits where wetlands development caused "incidental fallback" of fill). Judge Payne's concurring opinion in *Wilson* also criticized the majority's holding that sidecasting in not covered by §404.

Gardner, Banking on Entrepreneurs: Wetlands, Mitigation Banking, and Takings, 81 Iowa L. Rev. 531–537 (1996).

According to Professor Gardner, "[t]he failure of compensatory mitigation is wetland regulation's dirty little secret" (p. 540). Parties agreeing to perform mitigation often lack the technical or economic resources to fulfill their obligations. Noncompliance is common, and enforcement is sporadic. Moreover, scientific uncertainties regarding wetlands ecology militate against the success of mitigation through creation or preservation. Environmentalists also complain that mitigation sends the wrong message to the American public, and glosses over the need for humility and restraint with the natural world.

**6. Evaluation of §404 as an example of site-by-site permitting.** Section 404 has undoubtedly been successful in preserving some wetlands from development, but the site-by-site approach, as illustrated by §404, nevertheless has significant disadvantages as a critical area protection mechanism. To reiterate a point made above, §404 only applies to the deposit of dredged or fill material in wetlands; it does not apply to all wetland development activities. See, e.g., Save Our Community v. EPA, 971 F.2d 1155 (5th Cir. 1992) where a permit was not required for draining a wetland. Neither does §404 apply to activities on neighboring non-wetland areas that lead to impairment of wetlands functions. Second, §404 administration is replete with statutory exemptions (e.g., for many agricultural activities) and general permits (both nationwide and regional) that limit the scope of the program. See 40 C.F.R. §323.3 ("Activities Not Requiring Permits"), and 33 C.F.R. §330 ("Corps of Engineers Nationwide Permit Program Regulations"). Of the approximately 50,000 projects that are currently covered by §404 permits, roughly 35,000 are operating under either nationwide or regional permits, which entail a minimum of paperwork and are desultorily enforced. Nationwide permits involving discharge of dredged or fill material into isolated and headwaters wetlands and construction of single-family homes in wetlands have been especially controversial. Third, cumulative impacts of past, proposed, and potential projects are also systematically neglected in the §404 permitting process. The USGAO Report commented, "case files we reviewed indicated that Corps districts generally considered the impacts of projects on a case-by-case basis, and that cumulative impacts were sporadically addressed...." This is plainly a matter of Corps choice, for Buttrey v. U.S., 690 F.2d 1170 (5th Cir. 1982) indicates that the Corps is authorized to, and sometimes does, consider cumulative impacts in making §404 permitting decisions. Thorough critical area protection can only be assured through a preventive land-use planning and management program administered by an institution that possesses jurisdiction over an area that includes the entire resource to be protected. In the wetlands context, one commentator has suggested that EPA could achieve biodiversity protection through the §404 process by "exercis[ing] its *advance* veto authority, which can be used to protect relatively intact ecosystems in advance of a 404 permit application." Fischman, Biological Diversity and Environmental Protection: Authorities to Reduce Risk, 22 Env. L. 435, 496 (1992). Whether EPA will have the political leverage to exercise this authority is another matter entirely.

## Section 2. SINGLE-PURPOSE REGIONAL CRITICAL AREA PROTECTION: THE FEDERAL WILD AND SCIENIC RIVERS ACT

The Federal Wild and Scienic Rivers Act of 1968 ("WSRA"), 16 U.S.C.A. §1271 et seq., is a prime example of Congressional cynicism toward federal control over private lands. This statute has been somewhat effective in protecting certain values on segments of designated rivers on federal lands. It has done little, however, to protect rivers and riverine ecosystems from incompatible private development. See generally Raffensperger and Tarlock, The Wild And Scenic Rivers Act At 25: The Need For A New Focus, 4 Rivers 81 (1993).

The scope of the WSRA is limited to designated "Wild," "Scenic," and "Recreational" Rivers, with their "immediate environments," defined as narrow corridors extending approximately one-quarter mile from the ordinary high water mark on both sides of the rivers. Wider watershed impacts of development on private lands outside the management corridors, such as polluted runoff caused by residential development or agricultural operations, are beyond the WSRA's scope. The alternative designation processes of the WSRA, one initiated by Congress and the other by host states, are so cumbersome that they actually discourage the addition of any but the least controversial rivers to the system. Nevertheless, once a river is admitted to the system, certain tangible protections do follow. Most important, a "roadblock" (Chapter 14) is placed in the way not only of Federal Energy Regulatory Commission licensing of any dam "on or directly affecting" a designated river, but also in the way of any other federal agency that proposes to assist — by loan, license, permit, or otherwise — "in the construction of any water resources project that would have a direct and adverse effect on the values for which such river was established...." 16 U.S.C.A. §1278. Rivers that flow through federal land receive special protection under the WSRA. Federal agencies that manage lands "which include, border upon, or are adjacent to" any designated river — including lands outside the management corridor — "shall take such action respecting management policies, regulations, contracts, [and] plans, affecting such lands...as may be necessary to protect such rivers...." 16 U.S.C.A. §1283.

In the unlikely situation that the prevailing political climate would permit the designation of a segment containing sizeable tracts of private land, the WSRA, in practice, is ineffectual with regard to restraining private development within the management corridor that is inconsistent with wild and scenic river values. The WSRA provides no federal regulatory authority in the narrow corridors of designated rivers. In addition, federal land aquisition power within the corridors is sharply limited. For example, the federal government is barred from aquiring, by any means, more than approximately fifty percent of land within a particular corridor, and lands owned by a State may be aquired only by donation. As supplements to the WSRA, many states and local governments also administer programs to protect wild and scenic rivers. However, these programs, like the WSRA, have also been strongly influenced by the pervasive fear of governmental interference with private land-use decisions.

## D. COMPREHENSIVE STATE AND REGIONAL PLANNING AND MANAGEMENT

Comprehensive state and regional planning and management systems, including protections of environmentally critical areas, have only emerged sporadically across the United States, except for federal lands as noted in the preceding chapter. Regional land-use planning and management is clearly the exception to the American rule of local control over land-use decisions. Bi-state land-use commissions have been established for Lake Tahoe and the Columbia River Gorge.[21] Other states have established substate regional land-use planning and permitting agencies to supervise development along the California Coast, in the Hackensack Meadowlands and Pinelands of New Jersey, and in the Adirondack Mountains of New York State.[22] Additionally, some established regional institutions, such as the Delaware River Basin Commission and the South Florida Water Management District, perform land-use planning and management functions with conservation as one of their goals.

In practice, regional planning and management are often necessary for rational resolution of problems that extend beyond village limits, but regional coordination (if it has any teeth) threatens both existing governmental institutions and development interests.[23] There is, moreover, a justifiable fear that new regional institutions and regional planning by existing institutions will be expensive and cumbersome. Local "Home Rule" land-use powers are closely guarded perquisites. It will be interesting to see what coordination mechanisms will be adopted in the future to reconcile local land-use control with the necessity to protect regional environmental values.

Nine states — Florida, Vermont, Oregon, Georgia, Maine, Maryland, New Jersey, Rhode Island, and Washington — have enacted comprehensive growth management statutes that require local master plans and zoning ordinances to be consistent with state plans that emphasize protection of natural resources.[24] See F. Bosselman, The Quiet Revolution in Land Use Control (1972).

Oregon has implemented one of the most interesting state-level land-use systems. The Comprehensive Land Use Planning Coordination Act, Ore. Rev. Stat., Title 19, Chap. 197 (1973), sets up a state Land Conservation and Development Commission (LCDC) with authority to establish state-wide land-use planning goals. The LCDC adopted nineteen statewide goals categorized into four broad areas: (1) goals related to planning procedures; (2) conservation goals related to farm lands, forest lands, and natural resources; (3) development goals related to

---

21. Pub. L. No. 91-148, and 16 U.S.C.A. §544 et seq.

22. Cal. Pub. Res. Code §30601; N.J. Stat. Ann. §13:17-6; and N..Y. Exec. Law §800; N.Y. Const. Art. 14 §1.

23. The 1970s campaigns to create regional "councils of governments" (COGs) appear to have foundered on these twin shoals.

24. For a useful review of these statutes, see Wickersham, The Quiet Revolution Continues: the Emerging New Model for State Growth Management Statutes, 18 Harv. Env. L. Rev. 489, 524–529 (1994). On Vermont's elaborate state-wide land use review and permit legislation, Act 250 [10 VSA §6086(a)(1-10)], see the two-volume treatise edited by Richard Brooks, Toward Community Sustainability: Vermont's Act 250 (1997).

housing, transportation, and public facilities and services; and (4) coastal resource goals. These guidelines are not law, but each local entity must adopt a comprehensive plan and land-use regulations implementing the goals, and they must be approved ("acknowledged") by the LCDC. Any "land conservation and development action" must be consistent with the plans and local regulations. If there is no approved plan or regulations, the state guidelines can be applied directly. See Note, 31 Willamette L. Rev. 449. Oregon's land-use planning system combines statewide standards with implementation by local agencies in local regulatory programs that are initially approved and subsequently monitored by the state agency — in a process remarkably like the federal EPA's relationship to state SIPs under the CAA.

## E.  TRADITIONAL LAND-USE CONTROLS AND THE ENVIRONMENT: ZONING, SUBDIVISION REGULATION, ET AL.

In day-to-day practice, the overwhelming majority of land-use management occurs at the local level, predominantly through local government regulation (the focus of this part of the chapter) counterbalanced by the constitutional protection afforded to landowners to protect their property rights from unreasonable governmental interference (Chapter 23). Local land-use law is quite variable from jurisdiction to jurisdiction, and thus cannot be treated in more than cursory fashion in this textbook.

### Section 1. SUBDIVISION REGULATIONS

There are a variety of environmental problems that commonly arise throughout the United States when subdividers take large parcels of land (often farms or ranches purchased in large blocks) and divide them up legally into many small lots (often a quarter of an acre or less) to be resold subject to a master recorded deed ("plat"). The problems posed by subdivisions can be severe. Developers too often lack design sophistication, ignoring topography so that various roads and lots lie at steep angles. Physical site disruption and other problems can occur: for example, erosion and septic overflows from high-density uses frequently cause degradation of lakes and rivers.

Subdivision regulations work by focusing on the registration of the master deed plat: before a master plat subdividing a parcel into lots can be recorded, the ordinance requires that it meet a variety of legal requirements — e.g., sewerage, utilities, and road criteria — often expressed in the form of certificates annexed to the master plat itself.

To these basic requirements, which have obvious environmental consequences, communities have started adding more sophisticated subdivision requirements: e.g., erosion and sedimentation control standards; dedication of park land and other "exactions" offsetting burdens imposed on the community;[25] certified landscape architects' plans with analyses of groundwater flows and slope

---

25. Exactions may have takings implications. See Chapter 23.

*A standard design subdivision, laid out with little regard to pre-existing topographical and ecological conditions, causing the maximum amount of site usage with no open or common areas or clustering of residential sites.*

configurations; and the like.[26] Subdivision regulations can also require that developers put enforceable restrictive covenants and other private law devices on the master deed, like requirements for open space protection, density controls, and other use restrictions, which are specifically enforceable both by the local government, as third party beneficiary, and also by other lot owners. The more carefully such ordinances are drafted, the more they assure that developments will be harmonious with their surrounding environment. These ordinances frequently enhance the profitability of developments. They may be more acceptable to the developer than other forms of land-use regulaton because they bear a clear relationship to the value of parcels in the subdivision.

### COMMENTARY AND QUESTION

1. **Capturing amenity value in the marketplace**. Subdivision requirements arguably "create" value. How does this happen? Each buyer of a parcel in the subdivision is assured of certain amenity values, which are reflected in the buyer's willingness to pay more for the parcel than for comparable properties. In economic terms, this is an instance in which the developer is able to capture what might otherwise be a positive externality.

---

26. Design standards can encourage site plans that "cluster" residential structures to preserve the maximum amount of amenities and useful space for the inhabitants of the subdivision, rather than cutting up the parcel into the allowable number of standardized front, back, and side lots covering the site like a checkerboard.

## Section 2. **ZONING**

By far the most common land-use control device in the United States is local zoning, which is quite different from subdivision and site-plan review because zones, included in a Master Plan, apply to every square inch of the jurisdiction, and set out a comprehensive set of land-use district designations specifying, before the fact, which uses will automatically be allowed and which excluded. The most common form of zone ordinance is the "Euclidean" model, named for Village of Euclid v. Ambler Realty Co., 272 U.S. 365 (1926), the case that established zoning's general validity.[27]

Zoning directly affects private property decisions, which explains why, from its inception, it has stirred up a hornet's nest of opposition. Nevertheless, because the land-use problems of American communities have become so much more complex and pressing since World War II, zoning has become an unloved but widespread phenomenon. Of major American cities, only Houston has refused to employ zoning, and has apparently paid the price in chaotic land-development patterns.

Zoning implicitly incorporates some environmental values. If a zone planning agency knows which way the political wind is blowing, it will not locate residential areas downwind from its industrial zone districts. "Densities" (concentrations of permitted structures) designated for various districts may have direct consequences for local quality of life. The districting process, however, must build upon existing political systems, and in many cases "Home Rule" laws induce each community to perceive itself as a separate little city-state, with prime residential areas, industrial zones to capture tax base, no waste-disposal sites, and no coordination on a county or regional basis to determine how and where larger settlement and economic development patterns should be located.

Over the years, a variety of other environmental regulations have often been grafted as overlays to basic zoning ordinances, capitalizing upon zoning's established political and legal acceptability. Thus, when some communities wanted to protect wetlands or flood plains, they added overlay categories to their zone maps; land in any district that had the characteristics of flood plain or wetland had to comply with the added requirements. Some communities have added "open space" overlays or green belt requirements, erosion and sedimentation restrictions, historic preservation controls, and similar modern environmental resource protections to the basic zone ordinance and map.

Over time, as local zoning increasingly reflects the growing sophistication of the land-use planning and landscape architecture specialties, more and more environmentally-oriented elements will be incorporated in the initial planning and the subsequent implementation of zone ordinances.

---

27. The Euclidean model requires: (1) a comprehensive Plan, adopted by the community, analyzing existing land uses and specifying future community development desires; (2) a separate zone ordinance creating a catalogue of zone district categories, defining the range of permitted uses, densities, and structural characteristics in each category; (3) an official zone map, incorporated as part of the ordinance, mapping out the districts on the ground; and, finally, (4) a zone enforcement agency, acting to interpret and apply the zone requirements throughout the community, and reviewing and determining enforcement issues, special exceptions, and variances as required.

## COMMENTARY AND QUESTIONS

1. **The local basis of zoning.** The federal government, as noted earlier, generally stays far away from regulating land use. State governments also typically avoid direct land-use regulation, leaving it up to the lowest level of government — local government — with a few exceptions.[28] Efforts to set up regional land-use controls have largely failed, due to the balkanized nature of intergovernmental relations and the traditional norms of local government home rule.

Consider the range of legal problems and political turmoil that would be engendered by shifting particularized land-use control decisions to the state or regional levels. How would one draw rational jurisdictional lines? According to river drainage watersheds? Airsheds? Metropolitan-based market areas? Zoning replays a traditional question of democracy: To what extent should single communities be able to operate as isolated units?

Along with the drawbacks of fracturing land-use controls into tens of thousands of small, uncoordinated jurisdictions, there are corresponding advantages. In addition to its widespread acceptance, zoning reflects local knowledge of the community and landscape in which it applies. It can often serve as a useful vehicle for carrying modern environmental ideas into practical land-development practice.

2. **TDRs.** A number of local governments have set up creative systems of "TDRs," transferable development rights, to give developers and the public a measure of design flexibility. Much like the markets in tradeable pollution credits noted in Chapter 16, TDRs represent unused development density at one site that can be transferred and sold to other sites that wish to build beyond standard regulatory limits.

> TDR programs aim to direct development away from environmentally sensitive land to land more suitable for development by creating a market for development rights. Logistically, TDR programs achieve this result by quantifying the development potential of sensitive properties ("sending sites"), and providing that this development potential may be sold to landowners to increase building density in areas suitable for development ("receiving sites"). Good v. U.S., 39 Fed. Cl. 81, 107 (1997)

New York City has a complex system of TDRs, featured in the *Penn Central* case, 438 U.S. 104 (1978), where the Supreme Court held that the value of TDRs is relevantly weighed in regulatory takings challenges. The technique has state and federal-level corollaries, notably the CAA's sale of sulfur oxides credits, and notable potential for further applications. The theory was charted out in Professor John Costonis' Development Rights Transfers: an Exploratory Essay, 83 Yale L.J. 75 (1973); for a current environmental TDR primer, see McEleney, Using Transferable Development Rights to Preserve Vanishing Landscapes and Landmarks, 1995 Illinois Bar Journal 634.

A particularly interesting environmental application of TDRs has been implemented in the Lake Tahoe Basin. The Tahoe Regional Planning Agency, created through a bi-state compact between Nevada and California, seeks to prevent

---

28. Hawaii and the state of Maine have state-based land-use regulatory systems that, at least in theory, cover the entire state.

overdevelopment of the watershed in order to reduce erosion and sewerage discharges into the lake. Under the terms of its integrated Basin management plan, designed to protect the lake's remarkably pure waters, owners of restricted parcels may sell TDRs within the Basin, even across the state line. *See* Richard Fink, Structuring a Program for the Lake Tahoe Basin, 18 Ecology L.Q. 485 (1991); Suitum v. Tahoe Regional Planning Agency, 117 S.Ct. 1659 (1997); Richard Lazarus, Litigating *Suitum...*, 12 J. Land Use & Envtl. L. 179 (1995). One challenge, in both constitutional and planning terms, is to assure a sufficient array of transfer-importing sites to maintain a market, while assuring that the TDR transfers serve and not undermine the public values sought to be protected in the base regulation.

3. **Impact Fees.** This evolving device resembles subdivision exactions. Impact fees respond to the problem that developers often locate high-density developments without sufficient regard to the public's costs of providing utilities and amenities. Impact fees are a self-defense mechanism, analyzing the imposed costs and requiring that they be paid in advance. Impact fees can defray costs of added parks and recreation facilities, schools, drainage and sewer construction, roads and other transportation infrastructure, groundwater recharge facilities, and an infinitely expandable range of other imposed costs.[29] In economic terms, what role do impact fees play? Do they force the project proponent to internalize costs, or are they instead merely a form of governmental extortion? Like other land-use devices currently applied at the local level, impact fees can mobilize the expertise and defensive instincts of local communities. They hold larger intercommunity and regional potential as well.

*Regulations, the wisdom, necessity, and validity of which, as applied to existing conditions, are...apparent...a century ago, or even a half a century ago, probably would have been rejected as arbitrary and oppressive.... While the meaning of the constitutional guaranties never varies, the scope of their application must expand or contract to meet the new and different conditions which are constantly coming within the field of their operation. In a changing world it is impossible that it should be otherwise.*

— Sutherland, J., in Euclid v. Ambler, 272 U.S. 365 at 387 (1926)

*The compact neighborhood is the true architecture of nature.... The loss of a forest or a farm is justified only if it is replaced by a village. A subdivision and a shopping center is not an even trade.*

— Andres Duany

---

29. See Blasser & Kentopp, Impact Fees: The Second Generation, 38 J. Urban & Contemp. Law 55 (1990).

# PART SEVEN

# GLOBALIZATION
# AND CONVERGENCE

*The Grinnell Glacier in Glacier National Park, photographed from the same vantage point in 1910, 1931, and 1997 (top to bottom at left), as average temperatures around the globe continue to rise by small increments over the decades. Having receded 3,100 feet in a century, the glacier is expected to disappear within 30 years.*

GLACIER NATIONAL PARK ARCHIVE

"Earth averaged 57.9 degrees, or 1.6 degrees hotter, in the 1990s than in 1860. Atmospheric carbon dioxide now measures 360 ppm; that's 30 percent higher than at the start of the industrial era, higher, in fact, than in the past 160,000 years. In half a century, that could double.... Atmospheric layers of gases (water vapor, methane, nitrous oxide and carbon dioxide) let in sunlight, then trap heat.... Trouble comes when humans artificially pump up the volume to unnatural levels. Concentrating carbon dioxide...trap[s] more heat. Can we 'think global, act local' regarding climate change? No. But we can invert the slogan to think about what we may lose locally, then act at a global forum." Bruce Babbitt, Park's Retreating Glaciers Signal a Climate Warning, Denver Post, November 16, 1997, at H-08. Cf. T.M. Moore, Climate of Fear: Why We Shouldn't Worry about Global Warming (1997).

# Chapter 26

# GLOBAL ENVIRONMENTAL LAW: INTERNATIONAL AND COMPARATIVE

A. *Comparative Environmental Law — Legal Analysis and Cultural Relativism*

B. *International Transboundary Pollution Law*

C. *International Law of the Global Commons*

D. *Evolving International Principles and Strategies*

---

This coursebook began with the metaphor of Spaceship Earth, emphasizing the interconnectedness of the planet's geophysical, ecological, and human components, and the law. Slowly circling the globe, an observing eye could catalog a depressingly long list of planetary environmental threats,[1] more daunting than the problems encountered in any single nation. This chapter can properly be called "global environmental law" because environmental law cannot realistically be limited to any set of national boundaries. Its challenge is inevitably international in scope.

Global environmental law, however, is not just international law on the level of relations between nation-states and within international organizations. Just as global environmental problems are built by an aggregation of dozens or billions of individual actions, the legal responses to global problems must inevitably draw upon multiple levels of law and governance — national, subnational, and supranational forces intersecting with the marketplace, governments and "transgovernmental" linkages, and citizen non-governmental organizations (NGOs).[2]

International law and comparative law are two very different enterprises, although many internationally-focused jurists concern themselves with both. International law concerns itself with law at the level of nation-states and international bodies like the United Nations and its commissions. Comparative law considers what goes on within regional alliances and nation-states.

In terms of environmental policy principles, there is a growing international consensus about what problems exist and what solutions are available. The global

---

1. A superb source for statistics and detailed analysis of global ecological conditions is the World Resources Institute's bi-annual deskbook, World Resources.

2. Dean Joseph Nye of the Kennedy School of Government has launched a project called "Visions of Governance for the 21st Century" offering a nine-cell matrix to describe these factors and their interactions. Professor Anne-Marie Slaughter has noted shifts from old international law models, and modern "transgovernmentalism," in her article The Real New World Order, 76 Foreign Affairs #5, Sep/Oct at 183 (1976) (1997). See Sciolino, It Turns Out That All Global Politics is Local, New York Times, Dec. 7, 1997 at WK 3.

setting presents the same tensions and interconnections between the dominant marketplace economy, the economy of Nature, and civic-societal imperatives for sustainability. Strategies for the global environmental future often build upon the remarkable accomplishments of the United States as a pioneer of environmental science, law, and policy.[3] There is a convergence here. Sustainable development, one of the most important "emerging principles" of international environmental law, is becoming a dominant focusing concept for law and policy-making at national, regional, and local levels as well. As the First Law of Ecology says, everything is connected to everything else.

## A. COMPARATIVE ENVIRONMENTAL LAW — LEGAL ANALYSIS AND CULTURAL RELATIVISM

Comparative law is to some extent a latent part of all competent modern legal practice: the process by which attorneys analyze and try to predict how a particular problem or case is likely to be handled in different legal settings. Competent environmental lawyers understand that very different legal processes and outcomes will occur when, say, factories in different places discharge the same large jolt of benzene air pollution — it makes a great difference whether it is in Mississippi, California, India, Germany, Japan, Great Britain, or wherever. Comparative law — studying the domestic law of different places — is typically more like "*intra-national*" law, looking into the domestic system of law within a specific regional , national, or subnational jurisdiction as it applies to a particular issue.

Cultural relativism — understanding and dealing effectively with the fact that the meaning and working of things differs from place to place and culture to culture — is a deeply relevant skill for modern attorneys, both internationally and domestically. The answers to a particular environmental problem in a modern suburban setting in the U.S. may bear no resemblance to the needs and available resolutions for another place and culture. Unlike international law, which deals with legal principles *between* nations, comparative law examines the law *within* a nation or several different nations. Learning to be a "quick study" in different jurisdictions' legal systems may often be of great importance in coping with environmental issues nationally and internationally. Comparative law, moreover, is often critically important in determining the possibilities for designing international legal programs for management of global environmental problems. As Professor Dernbach notes in subchapter D below, it may well be that governing systems at the level of nation-states, not the United Nations or other international forums, will be most important in achieving legal frameworks for long term global sustainability.

This subchapter merely opens the door to an inquiry into the processes of comparative law, an area that, like so many other components of the field, deserves its own course of study. As the practice of law becomes ever more globalized in its

---

3. Through an accident of socio-political, economic, and legal history (pushed largely by the efforts of NGOs), the United States took an early lead role in the development of environmental law. In the past decade the rest of the world has begun to take account of the need for such legal protections, often using models drawn from American law, while beginning in 1980 the U.S. has fallen behind under the political suasions of its marketplace economy.

interconnections, there is increasing likelihood that today's attorneys on occasion will have to understand how a legal issue might play out in a different legal system. Those who only know how to think within one familiar domestic legal system will be less competent. In addition, one never understands one's own home territory so well as when one sees it from somewhere else.

Examining the environmental law characteristics of other places often reveals strikingly different and perplexing rules and assumptions.[4] Imagine that you were invited to consult on an important environmental controversy in Japan that appeared to be quite deserving of legal process, only to find that many of the basic elements of environmental law that American lawyers take for granted were totally missing. Lake Biwa in Shiga Prefecture is a large, pristine, jewel-like mountain lake, much like Lake Tahoe. Lake Biwa was a national icon, beloved by Japanese honeymooners, the source of Biwa freshwater pearls, and familiar to many westerners through dozens of Japanese forest and lake landscape paintings over the centuries. In a noted legal controversy, the Japanese economic development ministry and the local government of Shiga Prefecture decided to build a chemical factory on an artificial island to be constructed in the lake near the town of Otsu. The development agencies also decided to concretize the entire lakeshore, eliminating the shoreline wetlands that had always served the lake as a protective filter, in order to create more farmland.[5]

To an American lawyer, on the merits such a development project would seem a no-brainer for judicial review. In Japan, however, for cultural and legal reasons, initiatives to question the Lake Biwa plan were matter-of-factly marginalized and dismissed. All planning and authorizations for the project took place in closed proceedings within the relevant ministries and corporate offices. When fishermen and local citizens tried to sue to halt or modify the project, they were forced to file more than 300 individual suits — there was no ability to join multiple suits, not to mention to file a class action. Japan, moreover, does not permit discovery in such cases. The plaintiffs, for example, were not allowed to ask the project developers what chemicals would be made on the island or discharged into the lake or what structures and processes they were building. For want of just such information, however, the citizens' suits were dismissed. Catch 22. For their part, the governmental environmental protection agencies had no interest in reviewing or questioning the industrial development agencies' project, and neither the national nor local press was of any help. The Japanese press lacks the ability and will to report inquiringly into controversies, even dramatically destructive official projects. And even if the citizens had been able to prove imminent degradation of the lake and public drinking water in court, they could not hope to get an injunction. The only remedy practically available in the Japanese legal system is individual

---

4. See Nicholas Robinson, ed., Comparative Environmental Law and Regulation (treatise with updates, 1996); Gerd Winter, ed., European Environmental Law: A Comparative Perspective (1996); Environmental Law Network, International Environmental Impact Assessment: European and Comparative Law and Practical Experience (1997); Ronald Brickman et al., Controlling Chemicals: The Politics of Regulation in Europe and the United States (1985); and Martin Fuehr & Gerhard Roller, eds., Participation and Litigation Rights of Environmental Associations in Europe (1991).

5. See Frank Upham, The Place of Japanese Legal Studies in American Comparative Law, 1997 Utah L.Rev. 639; Julian Gresser, Understanding the Japanese NegotiatiION g Code, Problems and Solutions in Int'l Business, 1995 Annual, Chapter 25.

damages, which would of course largely miss the point. Because of the lack, in court or agency, of a democratic ability to examine the details of the Biwa project's environmental threats, Lake Biwa today, an international treasure, has begun to move toward serious systemic degradation.

Comparative law analysis thus often turns on varying contextual cultural patterns — whether or not it is culturally unthinkable to question official decisions, whether or not much of what happens is ascribed to inexorable Fate, whether or not the individual is expected not to stand out from the collective citizenry, whether or not the future is intangible and scientific prognosis quixotic, and so on — as well as the structures, rules, and remedies of legal process, and the mechanisms of agencies and the press in different industrial democracies.

Even within the most familiar national and foreign settings — England, Canada, Mexico ... and New York, California, Iowa, Florida, Texas, Alaska — there are fundamental differences between legal systems.[6] When one moves into issues and controversies in the less-developed nations of the world, the analysis becomes even more complex, challenging, and idiosyncratic:

## Section 1. THE BHOPAL DISASTER

In the early morning hours of December 3, 1984 a highly toxic cloud of methyl isocyanate (MIC) was released from a leaky tank in Union Carbide's pesticide-producing factory at Bhopal, Madhya Pradesh, India.[7] The leak was caused by a series of mechanical and human errors; a portion of the safety equipment at the plant had been nonoperational for four months and the rest failed. MIC (CH3NCO) has an extremely corrosive effect on mucous membranes in lungs and gastrointestinal systems, and has high acute human toxicity when inhaled. The toxic cloud, because of wind and temperature conditions, travelled close to ground level, spreading out over the surrounding neighborhood where hundreds of Muslim economic migrant families lay sleeping in humble shelters or on the ground. When the plant finally sounded an alarm — an hour after the gas had escaped — 20 tons of MIC had been discharged and much of the harm had already been done. The city health officials had not been informed of the toxicity of the chemicals used at the Union Carbide factory. There were no emergency plans or procedures in place and no knowledge of how to deal with the poisonous cloud. The accident was the largest industrial disaster ever. 2,000 people living within two miles of the plant died immediately; eight thousand more exposed persons have died since then. 300,000 were injured, with 50,000 requiring serious hospitalization. In the 1990s many of the survivors were still suffering from partial or complete blindness, gastrointestinal injuries, impaired immune systems, reproductive disorders, and post traumatic stress.

6. See, for example, Coal Law from the Old World: 64 Kentucky L.R. 473 (1976)(analyzing the widely differing central review processes, citizen participation, and operational administrative controls in the development of coal mining projects in several European states and the United States.
7. Union Carbide of India Limited was a subsidiary of the multinational Union Carbide Corporation (UCC), which has its world headquarters head office in Greenwich, Connecticut. Since the arrival of a competing plant, Union Carbide-India had been losing $4 million a year. Local authorities urged against closing the plant, so a compromise was reached: production would continue but only by taking drastic cost-saving measures. Cut-backs were made in training, staff qualifications, and maintenance.

### C.M. Abraham and Sushila Abraham, The Bhopal Case and the Development of Environmental Law in India
40 International and Comparative Law Quarterly 334 (1991)

Law for environmental protection is not a new phenomenon in India.... *Dharma*, the fundamental Indian concept of law, is itself based on a recognition of the importance of harmonising human activities with Nature in order to maintain a universal order. The duty to maintain a clean environment can be found in various provisions in the ancient laws of India....

The doctrinal tools of modern environmental law could be based on the law of nuisance: nuisance actions could challenge every major industrial and municipal activity which is today a subject of comprehensive environmental legislation.... In India the offence of public nuisance is contained in Chapter 14 of the Indian Penal Code of 1860. Specific provisions prescribing punishment for fouling water and air are contained in sections 277 and 278. The Code of Criminal Procedure of 1973, which is based on several earlier codes since 1861, contains in section 133 specific provisions empowering a magistrate to make orders to abate public nuisance.... The 1976 amendment to the 1902 Code of Civil Procedure, section 91,...facilitated easier access to courts in lawsuits for public nuisance.... (The Code...of 1908 allowed suits against public nuisance only by or with the sanction of the Advocate General. The 1976 amendment...made it easier for the general public to sue "with the leave of the court" in cases of public nuisance and other wrongful acts affecting the public)....

In 1976...the 42nd Amendment of the Constitution of India incorporated a new Article 48A as a Directive Principle of State Policy... "The State shall endeavor to protect and improve the environment and to safeguard the forest and wildlife of the country... " So also Article 51A(g), incorporating Fundamental Duties... "It shall be the duty of every citizen of India...to protect and improve the natural environment including forests, lakes, rivers and wildlife and to have compassion for living creatures."...

The Stockholm Conference of 1972...prompted India to initiate legislation in line with developed countries to deal specifically with environmental pollution caused by industries. The Water (Prevention and Control of Pollution) Act 1974 was India's pioneer legislation to deal with industrial pollution...containing elaborate provisions for the constitution of administrative agencies both at the national and State level.... The control of water pollution was sought to be achieved through a "consent" system of administration. The Act did not initially bring about any changes in the state of the environment....[8] A separate Department of Environment under the new Ministry of Environment was set up as a focal administrative agency to plan, promote, and coordinate environmental programmes.

In 1981 the Air (Prevention and Control of Pollution) Act was enacted to combat air pollution...corresponding to the Water Act passed earlier..... The administrative agencies established under the Air Act merged with the functionaries established under the Water Act to form the Pollution Control Boards at the central and State levels..... The Water and Air Acts...were in fact neither readily enforceable nor effectively implemented....

---

8. For critical analyses of Indian environmental law, see Armin Rosenkranz and Shyam Divan, Environmental Law and Policy in India (1991, 2d ed. 1999); C.M. Abraham and Armin Rosenkranz, "An Evaluation of Pollution Control Legislation in India," 11 Colum. J. Env. L. 101 (1986).

The world's worst industrial disaster led to the biggest ever resort to litigation for damages. Immediately after the disaster more than 145 cases were brought against Union Carbide Corporation (UCC) by American lawyers in different courts in the United States on behalf of thousands of victims.[9] These cases were joined and assigned to the District Court for the Southern District of New York.... The Union of India filed a separate complaint before that court on 29 June 1985 pursuant to the Bhopal Gas Leak Disaster (Processing of Claims) Act which provided it with the right to represent the Indian plaintiffs. On 12 May 1986 United States District Judge John F. Keenan dismissed the American actions on the ground that a United States court was not an appropriate forum ["*forum non conveniens*"].[10]

After this the lethal drama moved back to India. The Union of India brought the case before the Madhya Pradesh District Court in Bhopal, [taking over] about 800 separate cases which had already been filed,...pursuant to the Bhopal Act, which gave exclusive rights to the Union to represent all claims against UCC.... [The applicable tort rule was strict liability.[11]] The District Judge of Bhopal, M.W. Deo, introduced an unprecedented legal development when he made an order for interim relief of 3,500 million rupees (equivalent to US$270 million)....[12] While the matter was before the Supreme Court of India, UCC and the Union of India agreed a settlement figure of US$470 million by way of full compensation...of all claims past, present and future for civil and criminal proceedings against UCC.[13]

Within days of the Bhopal disaster and immediately after the first few cases were filed in the United States courts, a Wall Street Journal editorial...commented on the Indian legal system: "Justice can be done in Indian courts. India is not Ruritania. The British left behind a perfectly good legal system — better in fact than the U.S. system.... Indian courts will make sure the company compensates the victims."

Although it is generally assumed that India is a common law country, the elements of its legal system are blended with its own traditional notions of law.... One [can] perceive the system as an incomprehensibly complex one, or perceive it as an open system taking in everything which is most suitable to its needs.... The early charters, which established the courts in India under the British rule, required the judges to act according to "Justice, Equity, and Good Conscience" in deciding civil disputes if no source of law was identifiable.... This formula was adopted in India to smooth out discrepancies between the two systems of law.... The law of torts in India, which remained uncodified, followed the English law in almost all aspects....

In its operation the Indian legal system is criticised generally for the massive backlog of cases causing enormous delays in the resolution of civil disputes. The problem of the law's delays has been a perennial one.... An appalling backlog of cases has unfortunately become the normal feature of all courts in the country...

---

9. Melvin Belli, a top United State personal injury lawyer, filed a US$15 billion class action for compensation against UCC on behalf of two families. [F. Lee Bailey Leonard Ring, Michael Ciresi, and Stanley Chesley were among the lead plaintiffs' attorneys.] Soon 145 cases had been brought against UCC in different United States federal courts on behalf of thousands of Indians, most class actions.... The damages sought in these cases varied from US $5–$50 billion, in addition to punitive damages and costs.

10. In Re: Union Carbide Corp. Gas Plant Disaster at Bhopal, India, aff'd 809 F.2d 195 (2d Cir. 1987).

11. The Supreme Court had held in M.C. Mehta v. Union of India (1987) 1 SCC 395 that: "where an enterprise is engaged in a hazardous or inherently dangerous activity and harm results to anyone...the enterprise is strictly and absolutely liable ." (citing Rylands v. Fletcher).

12. Union of India v. UCC, in the court of the district judge, Bhopal Gas Claims Case No. 113 of 1986.

13. Confirmed by Supreme Court, Union Carbide Corp. v. Union of India, 1 SCC 674 (1989).

The problem has persisted and has attained gigantic proportions. The system...to a great extent exists even today in a manner unsuitable to meet the needs of the Indian people, most of whom are economically very poor, apathetic to their own lot, and quite uninformed of the intricacies of the system....

The situation in India today is such that there is a great paucity of tort litigation, which makes the ideological credibility of Indian tort law a debatable issue. Several reasons could be given for the scanty litigation in India in this field:

(1) the institutional character of the legal system fails to encourage the pursuit of remedies of a civil nature for reducing interpersonal tensions in the community;

(2) the very technical approach adopted by judges and lawyers without taking into account the growing needs of Indian society;

(3) the tendency, noticed in most eastern societies in general, to prefer the process of mediation to that of the judicial process;

(4) the prohibitive cost of a lawsuit, the time, labour, and money expended ate very stage of litigation;

(5) the delays attendant on litigation;

(6) the unsatisfactory condition of the substantive law on certain topics, forexample the liability of the State for torts of its servants;

(7) the anomalies created in the minds of litigants by the coexistence of several statutory provisions;

(8) the low level of legal awareness among the general public;

(9) the difficulty of gaining access to law, because a large portion of the tort law remains uncodified;

(10) the bureaucratic attitude of government officers dissuading legitimate claims of citizens even though they are legally enforceable.

In the light of such hurdles, which obstruct the natural growth of tort law in India, the recent development in combining tort law with the constitutional right to personal liberty and its remedy through compensation has only to be welcomed....

A major legislative breakthrough was achieved through the Bhopal Gas Leak Disaster (Processing of Claims) Act of 1985. The Bhopal Act was an immediate legislative reaction to the disaster.... Under the Bhopal Act the government of India assumed the role of *parens patriae*, which gave to the Union government considerable powers to deal with the legal and administrative problems created by the disaster. The Bhopal Act was initially assessed by many as an executive manoeuvre that not only enabled the government to participate in the United States litigation but also avoided any litigation in India. It empowers the government to interpose an administrative compensation process as the exclusive primary resort of victims. The Act gives exclusive rights of representation to the central government in all claims arising out of the disaster as well as powers of review and investigation and the framing of a scheme for the registration, processing, and enforcement of claims.... The Act has been considered as the only realistic method of protecting the victims' rights of action. When a large number of claims cannot be handled effectively by what is generally acknowledged to be a slow legal system, a statutory claim and compensation system scheme may provide a faster remedy....

After the accident at Bhopal, the Department of Environment came under considerable pressure from both the Prime Minister's office and the general public to decide on "comprehensive legislation for controlling toxic and hazardous substances." A new umbrella statute, the Environment (Protection) Act, was enacted in May 1986.... The basic thrust of the Act is to empower the central government to correct deficiencies of policy-making and enforcement in the States.... New powers were conferred on the central government to set standards for pollution discharged or emitted into the environment and also to regulate the handling of hazardous substances. The Act established environmental laboratories responsible for analysing air sand water samples collected by the enforcement authorities, and substantially strengthened the government's capacity to penalise polluters. Even though the Act has closed some of the loopholes in the earlier laws, it is too early to say how effectively the environmental policies will be implemented through this legislation.

COMMENTARY AND QUESTIONS

1. **Aftermath in Bhopal.** The Indian Government initially had asked Union Carbide for $3 billion in total compensation, but settled for $470 million in 1989 over the opposition of groups representing victims. The funds were frozen for several years by legal challenges from people who wanted a larger settlement. Some gas victims got interim payments, which averaged about seven dollars a month, but the Government did not begin to pay formal compensation until eight years after the disaster through a claims registry that soon became a bureaucratic logjam charged with inefficiency and corruption. In 1997 the Indian Government reported it had given out about $300 million to 380,000 people, which is about two-thirds of the claimants, but the disbursement process has been secret. Union Carbide sold its shares in its Indian subsidiary to the Government of India for $90 million in 1989. The company and the Indian Government agreed to spend the proceeds on research and health care in Bhopal. A modern new hospital is under construction. The Bhopal Medical Commission says that more than one more hospital, Bhopal needs clinics where health workers can monitor outpatients and provide help such as classes in breathing exercises. Victims also need sheltered workshops where sick people can earn salaries. Union Carbide officials say they are planning to use part of the money to build 10 such clinics and possibly some workshops.

2. **Familiar and different.** Reading the Abraham article for a comparative law analysis of the Bhopal case, some elements seem quite familiar — the common law inherited from England at Independence, public nuisance as derived from criminal law but litigable by citizens as well as government officials, agency enforcement staff that appear more numerous than they are vigilant, a trend to broaden citizen standing, constitutional measures specifically mentioning environment like some American states' constitutions, state and national specialty statutes created to address different pollution media, the environmental justice issue of poor people living in hazardous locations, and the catalytic effect of public disaster on the formation of law. There is even a pioneering environmental citizen attorney-plaintiff, M.C. Mehta of New Delhi, who single-handedly has established more than a half-dozen major environmental precedents in the Indian Supreme Court, including the cited rule for toxic strict liability.

But note the differences as well. The constitutional provisions are worded in terms of duties and compassion; the constitutional provisions seem to be symbolic rather than litigable. Citations and codifications for statutes and cases seem low-tech and hard to manage — no West Publishing system. Government agencies appear to have proliferated at the various levels, but have done virtually nothing to change industrial practices, in part because of their "consent" orientation. Tort litigiousness was apparently uncommon before Bhopal. Once stung by the gas disaster a litigation flood did arise, but it was quickly taken over by the government as sole plaintiff, apparently for good reason. The Indian judge, reflecting the revulsion against the disaster, ordered the payment of interim damages before a verdict of liability had been reached, and did so in terms that no American judge would dare.[14] The claims settlement amount seems incomprehensibly small, and the public nonreviewability of the disbursement process surprising.

To understand the legal context of the Bhopal disaster fully, one would have to review the tort liability provisions of Indian common law, and relevant statutes including the Bhopal Gas Leak Disaster (Processing of Claims) Act, passed by the Ragta Sabha on March 18, 1985, Bill No. V-C/1985, as well as the interesting Bhopal litigation filed in the United States, where the government of India itself tried to assert that American jurisdiction was more appropriate for adjudicating liability and damages against the multinational corporate defendant. In re Union Carbide Corp., 809 F.2d 195 (2d Cir. 1987). See Gladwin, A Case Study of the Bhopal Tragedy, in Pearson, Multinational Corporations, Environment, and the Third World (1987).

By immersing oneself in the details of the Bhopal story it is possible to begin to get a feel for the special personality and flavor of the law and culture of the subcontinent. (Also, as so often happens in comparative law, immersion in the intricacies of cases in a foreign legal system gives one a clearer and more nuanced sense of one's own home system.)

Comparative law analysis comes with caveats, however:

Observers from other systems can sometimes perceive more about the legal context they survey than the locals who are there, but usually less, and always differently.

If one is able to build an informed sense of how the legal culture of India worked in the Bhopal case, this will nevertheless provide only a suggestion of how an identical case would be handled in Madhya Pradesh today.

---

14. Responding to the arguments of UCC's counsel F.S. Nariman that the legislature had not given courts the power to order pre-verdict interim damages, Judge Deo stated:

Can the gas victims survive until the tangible data with meticulous exactitude is collected and proved...? Will it not be prudent to order payment of a relative sum bearing in mind...the facts and figures (though not undisputed)....

It is a power inherent in the court by virtue of its duty to do justice between the parties before it.... Inherent powers are born with the creation of the court, like the pulsating life coming with a child born into the world.... The powers [delegated to] the court after its creation are like many other acquisitions of faculties which the child acquires after birth during its life. Thus inherent powers are of primordial nature. They are almost plenary except for the restriction that they shall not be exercised in conflict with any express provision to the contrary....

"What is the argument on the other side? Only this, that no case has been found in which it has been done before.... If we never do anything which has not been done before, we shall never get anywhere. The law will stand still whilst the rest of the world goes on , and that will be bad for both." [The quote is from Lord Denning.]

The ruling echoes the colonial background principles of "Justice, Equity and Good Conscience."

Perceptions of the legal process of this case would be of little use in understanding and predicting environmental law outcomes in the legal systems that most closely neighbor India — Bengla Desh, Sri Lanka, Pakistan, Nepal, [Tibet], Bhutan, China.

Likewise, in studying the very similar pesticide-factory gas cloud poisoning at Seveso, Italy in 1976[15] it is the skill of comparative law analysis rather than doctrinal conclusions from Bhopal that would be most useful.

The essence of comparative law is *not* that one tries to build a corpus of common doctrinal principles that can be expected to apply generally. Rather one seeks a knowledge and instinct for how different legal systems handle similar environmental problems, including predictions of how they can address future challenges, and an ability to sense deeply and celebrate the infinite variety of cultures' differences.

3. **The legal aftermath of Bhopal.** In legal terms the environmental law agencies of India received more regulatory legal authority and political stature in the aftermath of Bhopal, although most observers report that public administration in India continues to be a quite torpid overbuilt structure with limited functionality. Increasingly, sophisticated citizen litigation reportedly continues to play David to India's corporate-governmental marketplace establishments. An important innovation arose from the Supreme Court holdings on citizen litigation:

> In the 1980s, two remarkable developments in the Indian legal system have taken place. One concerns the broadening of the application of existing environmental laws in the country and the other relates to a type of judicial activity known as Public Interest Litigation ("PIL"). These two developments have given more scope to citizens and public interest groups to prosecute a public authority or corporation which violates basic human rights of citizens as well as government rules and policies generally....

> Until the enactment of the Environment (Protection) Act of 1986, the power to prosecute under Indian environmental laws belonged exclusively to the Government. Citizens had no direct statutory remedy against a polluter who, say, discharged an effluent beyond the permissible limit. But under Section 19 of the Environment Act [and Air Act 43 and Water Act 49], a citizen may prosecute an offender by a complaint to a magistrate. Prior to complaining, s/he must give the Government 60 days notice of her/his intention to complain.... Significantly... these sections require the Pollution Control Board to disclose relevant internal reports to a citizen seeking to prosecute a polluter. Thus, the activist can use the provisions in these laws to prosecute companies violating the environmental policies and regulations of India.

> Similarly, there has been an expansion of citizens' participatory rights in public interest litigation. Traditionally, only an individual who had her or his rights violated was entitled to seek remedy under PIL. In public actions, this meant that a person asserting a public right or interest had to show that s/he

15. Nanda, Ved, & Bruce Bailey, Export of Hazardous Waste..., 17 Denv. J. Int'l L. & Pol'y 154, 163–67 (1988). The July 10, 1976 explosion at the Icmesa Chemical plant owned by Givaudan, a subsidiary of the Swiss-controlled Hoffman-LaRoche chemical combine, emitted a cloud of wet dioxin gas that spread over the town of Seveso, causing burns or long term skin disease to more than 600 people, soil contamination, but no human deaths; costs were recouped by the state.

had suffered some special injury over and above what members of the public had generally suffered. However, cases such as air pollution caused by a particular corporation were difficult to redress. This led to a modification of the traditional rule which now permits a citizen to challenge harmful actions in the public interest even though that citizen has not suffered any harm personally.16 This has encouraged many lawyers, non-governmental organizations, environmental, and human right groups to take legal actions. The closure of limestone quarries in the Dehradun region as well as of polluting tanneries along the Ganges are examples of environmental cases taken up by public interest lawyers and environmental groups under PIL. Rosenkranz, Armin, and Kathleen Yurchak, Progress on the Environmental Front: the Regulation of Industry & Dev't in India, 19 Hastings Int'l & Comp. L. Rev. 489 (1996).

4. **America, Melvin Belli, F. Lee Bailey, and** *forum non conveniens.* Note some of the American legal culture in this case, playing an extraterritorial role in shaping events in India — the U.S.-led IMF pushing countries to increase their foreign currency earnings in order to become part of the competitive structure of the global marketplace, the Connecticut-based multinational corporation setting up an allegedly slipshod subsidiary in the Third World, conscious cost-cutting maintenance and safety compromises made as part of transnational business decisions, the avalanche of American tort lawyers coming to India to sign up victims for lawsuits to be filed in the Southern District of New York (which has jurisdiction over UCC's hometown of Greenwich), and the relevance of the U.S. administration's foreign policy stance toward India.

Why did the Wall Street Journal editorialize that India's law was just fine? This was also a time when UCC was starting to worry about whether it would get due process in Indian courts. (That question remained interesting, raised again when criminal warrants were issued to haul Union Carbide's CEO into the Madhya Pradesh jail.)

The doctrine of *forum non conveniens* — a ruling that it is more convenient for all concerned to have a case litigated in the country in which the incident occurred rather than where the plaintiffs filed it — was instrumental in the Bhopal case. Normally plaintiffs have the choice of where to file so long as they can get jurisdiction over the defendant. When defendants argue, often disingenuously, for *forum non conveniens* removal to other jurisdictions they often are forum-shopping for a better deal. If the Bhopal case had gone to trial in New York, Judge Keenan may well have applied Indian tort law, which on the books looked as if it would closely resemble New York tort law. But what kind of damage verdicts were likely to have come from the New York jury?

Convenience to the plaintiffs was not the problem. The Indian victims were quite ready to appear in the New York court. As the Abrahams note, the Government of India itself appeared in the New York court, under the specific auspices of the Bhopal Act, arguing that its own courts and legal system were insufficient to the task of processing the gas disaster claims. UCC argued that physical factfinding and

---

16. Cf. Justice Scalia's decision in Chapter Seven's *Lujan II* restricting citizen suits under remarkably similar provisions. Why might India's legal system be more able to handle pluralistic citizen participation in regulatory enforcement?

access to witnesses made a transfer to the Indian courts necessary. Judge Keenan made a typical balance, deciding that India's laws were capable, sending the case back to Madhya Pradesh with three conditions.[17] In re: Union Carbide Corporation Gas Disaster at Bhopal, Misc. No. 21-38, 1989 WL 66673 (S.D.N.Y., June 14, 1989).

5. **An Indian environmental case note**:

> GANGA POLLUTION: CLOSURE OF 190 UNITS ORDERED... The Supreme Court today ordered immediate closure of 190 industrial units situated on the banks of river Ganga in Uttar Pradesh for their failure to install effluent treatment plants to check pollution in the holy river. The direction was given by the Court during the resumed hearing of a public interest petition by Mr M. C. Mehta [eds. — a remarkable volunteer environmental lawyer] seeking directions to the Union Government and State Governments of Uttar Pradesh, Bihar and West Bengal to ensure that industries in the Ganga basin stop polluting the river by discharging untreated effluent. A division bench comprising Justice Kuldip Singh and Justice S. C. Agarwal passed the order on being informed by the counsel of the Uttar Pradesh Pollution Control Board, Mr P. Mishra that these industrial units have not complied with the direction of the board regarding setting up of effluent treatment plants and have not responded to the notices, public and individual, given to them by the board. All along, the Environment Ministry has remained conspicuous by its lackadaisical approach. This, despite the fact that under the Environment Protection Act (EPA), 1986, the Central/State Pollution Boards can order the closure of polluting units and can levy fines up to Rs 100,000 and imprisonment for 5 years in case of wilful default. Hindustan Times, 18 September 1993.

6. **Cultural and ideological divides.** There are quantum differences between societies, in culture and ideology, that dictate very different approaches and expectations for the capacities of law to make changes. There are, for instance, very different fundamental ideologies for the organization of social life. "A holistic ideology, of the sort found in Hindu India, subordinates the individual to society. An individualist ideology, of the sort that organizes the Christian West, subordinates society to the individual, whom it understands to be prior to, and independent of, the social whole." Berkowitz, The Idea to Which We Owe Everything: Liberalism Strikes Back, The New Republic, Dec. 15, 1997 at 36. Sweden reportedly straddles both sides of this divide, enjoying more efficient, non-adversarial regulatory compliance compared to the U.S., but retaining an active entrepreneurialism. James Q. Wilson, Bureaucracy: What Government Agencies Do..., Public Admin. Review, July 1992, at 406–407.

7. **Comparative law of regional systems.** The European Community, as the most elaborate regional legal system, has produced a trove of opportunities for comparative law development. See, for instance, Damien Geradin, Trade and the Environment: A Comparative Study of EC and US Law (1997). EC environmental

---

17. (1) UCC must submit to the Indian jurisdiction with no statute of limitations defenses; (2) UCC must agree to pay any Indian judgment that conforms with "minimal requirements of due process"; and (3) UCC must allow full discovery on the same terms as the U.S. Federal Rules of Civil Procedure. Rosenkranz, A., The Twists and Turns of the Bhopal Lawsuits, 18 Env. Policy & Law #3 (June 1998).

Courts in other states, including Florida and Texas, have begun to apply more lenient plaintiff-oriented tests of *forum non conveniens*, seeking, according to defendant cynics, to bring more litigation business to their states.

law has many different levels, from the quasi-constitutional down to the level of technical regulations. It also has relevant applications outside the Community's avowedly environmental structures. The European Court of Human Rights, for example, has held that a homeowner subjected to continuing air pollution from a non-permitted municipal waste treatment plant near her home, in a town with a heavy concentration of leather industries discharging into the system, could recover 5.5 million pesetas against the government of Spain for nonenforcement of Spanish laws. The Court broadly applied Article 8 of the European Convention on Human Rights: "1. Everyone has the right to respect for his private and family life, his home and correspondence. 2. There shall be no interference by a public authority with the exercise of this right except in accordance with the law...." Lopez-Ostra v. Spain, 20 EHRR 277 (1995).

## B. INTERNATIONAL TRANSBOUNDARY POLLUTION LAW

Though most international environmental dilemmas are caused by humans, and virtually all humans act within the jurisdiction of nation-states, ecological effects know no boundaries, spilling across political frontiers and causing cumulative effects throughout the global system. The fundamental challenge for international law is to handle problems which exist irrespective of frontiers, in a system of nation states that takes territorial sovereignty as one of its most sacred legal tenets.

This subchapter offers only a glimpse at the field of international environmental law. For a field so large and fast-growing, it is nevertheless possible to choose two paradigms that introduce most of the areas of international environmental law activity — Transboundary Pollution, and issues of the Global Commons.

First, in terms of historical development, is the issue of transboundary pollution. Over the years a number of international controversies have arisen from injury spilling over from one state's territory into another. Some resemble garden-variety domestic pollution cases, like the classic *Trail Smelter* case noted below, where air pollution fumes and particles happened to cross the international boundary between Canada and the United States. Transboundary pollution has since become more dramatic. One small but vivid example exists because many Nordic women have blond hair: acid rain from England falls on the Scandinavian coast, leaching copper oxides from residential plumbing systems into the drinking water, turning the blonde hair of some Norwegian women a pale shade of green. Beyond acid rain, Europe has witnessed the explosion of the Chernobyl nuclear reactor and the Sandoz chemical spill in the Swiss headwaters of the Rhine, both ecological disasters causing great human and economic suffering. Transboundary pollution is often incident- or locality-specific.

The second sector noted in the following section is more straightforwardly planetary: environmental problems imposed on the global commons. Sometimes this means global pollution; at other times, a global perspective on resource depletion. The global commons has suffered a wide variety of impacts — massive extinction of species; global warming and the $CO_2$ greenhouse effect caused in part by woodburning and fossil fuels; CFC-induced holes in the stratospheric ozone layer; desertification; disruption of traditional peoples and cultures; a distressing lack of nutrition and the spread of disease, especially in over-populated, high density areas; destruction and vandalization of archaeological sites; destruction of ancient forests; erosion and sedimentation; ocean pollution; toxic contamination of air, water and other resources; international dumping of toxic wastes, contaminated pharmaceuticals and other manufactures (most often in the third world); DDT in the tissues of living organisms, even in the Arctic and Antarctic; the fundamental stress of overpopulation; a decline in many societies' quality of life — all these and more are problems of global commons, and are not so susceptible as transboundary pollution to discrete limited international law remedies.

## THE PLAYERS

As with domestic environmental law, international environmental law involves a variety of players. The actors who cause environmental problems are often private parties — multinational corporations, smaller businesses, and private citizens — or quasi-private actors, governmental agencies acting in a corporate proprietary fashion or acting as development agencies. Beyond these, official actors in international environmental law are generally limited to nation states and the international organizations they form. But lurking significantly in the background, as in the domestic American process, are NGOs, the non-governmental organizations that create and advance the political context of "the environmental movement."

### Section 1. THE RHINE RIVER SPILL

A classic transboundary pollution case: at nineteen minutes after midnight, November 1, 1986, a traffic patrol of the cantonal police saw fire shooting from the roof of Warehouse 956 in the Sandoz Chemical Company's industrial compound near Basel, Switzerland, on the banks of the River Rhine. Within a few minutes, fire brigades began pouring tons of water into the warehouse and extinguished the blaze five hours later. The volume of water greatly exceeded the company's minimal catchbasin capacity around the warehouse. Between 10,000–15,000 cubic meters of water laced with chemicals poured into the Rhine — 11 metric tons of organic mercury compounds and more than 100 tons of insecticides, fungicides, herbicides and other agricultural chemicals.[18] A red toxic tide ultimately coursed 900 kilometers down the Rhine into the North Sea. The Sandoz spill was an ecological catastrophe. Hundreds of thousands of fish and waterfowl were killed; the extinction of living organisms extended to the base of the food chain, eliminating micro-organisms down to the microbe level. While no humans died (though a flock of sheep was lost near Strasbourg, France, when a farmer unwisely led them to drink at the river), the economic and ecological devastation was otherwise extraordinary. Citizen protests took place along the length of the Rhine, 10,000 people marching through the streets of Basel to protest the spill and demonstrating downstream in Germany, France, and the Netherlands. Estimates of the direct damages

18. Coincidentally, a spill from a nearby Ciba-Geigy chemical plant occurred the day before, and had not been reported; it was detected in the extensive water-testing following the Sandoz spill.

to property downstream from the Sandoz spill exceeded 100 million Swiss francs.

The following text focuses on two sources of international law — customary law and treaties — and their limitations in achieving practical remedies for transboundary pollution.

### Aaron Schwabach, The Sandoz Spill: The Failure of International Law to Protect the Rhine from Pollution
16 Ecology Law Quarterly 443, 454–471 (1989)

INTERNATIONAL LAW RELATING TO THE SANDOZ SPILL... Both customary international law and a treaty regime govern accidents such as that at the Sandoz plant. Unfortunately, customary international law in this area is informed by conflicting theories and approaches. Further, the treaty regime, while apparently solid, is plagued by structural and substantive weakness.

CUSTOMARY INTERNATIONAL LAW OF TRANSBOUNDARY RIVER POLLUTION... Customary international law has its sources in state practice, in the general principles of law that are recognized by civilized nations, and in judicial decisions and the teachings of respected jurists.[19] Examination of the relevant materials from each of these sources reveals a lack of consensus on the law governing pollution of transboundary rivers. There are four major legal approaches to transboundary river pollution, each of which depends on a different conception of sovereignty....

*1. Absolute Territorial Sovereignty: The Harmon Doctrine*
The absolute territorial sovereignty theory holds that a riparian state is free to do as it chooses with the water within its territory, without regard for the effects on the downstream or co-riparian states. Grotius expressed the theory of absolute territorial sovereignty more than three centuries ago when he stated, "a river, viewed as a stream, is the property of the people through whose territory it flows, or the ruler under whose sway that people is...to them all things produced in the river belong."[20]

A more recent manifestation of this theory is the Harmon Doctrine. In 1895, in response to Mexico's protest of the United States' diversion of water from the Rio Grande, then-Attorney General Judson Harmon stated that "the rules, principles, and precedents of international law impose no liability or obligation upon the United States."[21] The Harmon Doctrine has since become synonymous with the theory of absolute territorial sovereignty.

The absolute territorial sovereignty theory is naturally more appealing to upstream states than to downstream states. The appeal of the theory is somewhat diminished, however, by the fact that most countries are both upper and lower riparians....

The Harmon Doctrine has been almost universally denounced. Although no state formally adheres to the theory of absolute territorial sovereignty with regard to transboundary rivers, an argument can be made that many states continue to base their practice on such a theory, dumping wastes without regard for the welfare of downstream states.

*2. Absolute Territorial Integrity*
The absolute territorial integrity theory holds that a downstream riparian state

---

19. Statute of the International Court of Justice, Art. 38.
20. 2 H. Grotius, De Jure Belli et Pacis, ch. 2 §12 (Kelsey trans. 1925) (7th ed. 1646).
21. Re: Treaty of Guadalupe Hidalgo, 21 Op. Att'y Gen. 274, 283 (1895).

may demand the continuation of the full flow of the river from an upper riparian state, free from any diminution in quantity or quality. The theory is the inverse of the absolute territorial sovereignty theory and, as such, appeals to downstream states. The same weakness that plagues the first theory, though, also applies to the second — namely, most states are both upstream and downstream states.

### 3. Limited Territorial Sovereignty

The limited territorial sovereignty theory holds that a state may make use of the waters flowing through its territory to the extent that such use does not interfere with reasonable use of waters by the downstream states. Decisions of international and domestic tribunals, as well as pronouncements of private and public international bodies, support this approach to transboundary river pollution.

The *Trail Smelter* arbitration expresses the principle that a state has responsibility for environmental damage extending beyond its territorial limits. The arbitral tribunal stated that, under principles of international law,

> no State has the right to use or permit the use of its territory in such a manner as to cause injury by fumes in or to the territory of another or the properties or person therein, when the case is of serious consequence and the injury is established by clear and convincing evidence.[22]

The *Corfu Channel* case, although it did not concern pollution, also supports the general principle of limited territorial sovereignty.[23] The International Court of Justice held in that case that it is "every State's obligation not to allow knowingly its territory to be used for acts contrary to the rights of other States."

The *Lac Lanoux* arbitration[24] also applied this principle [of state responsibility, and extended it explicitly to pollution, although liability was not found]. In that case Spain objected to French hydroelectric plants on the Carol River. France proposed to divert the waters of the Carol, which flows across the border into Spain, in order to generate electricity. Water equal in quantity and quality would be returned to the Carol before it entered Spain. The arbitral tribunal stated:

> When one examines whether France, either during the discussion or in her proposals, has given sufficient consideration to Spanish interests, it must be stressed how closely linked together are the obligation to take into consideration, in the course of negotiations, adverse interests and the obligation to give a reasonable place to these interests in the solution finally adopted.[25]

In other words, the upstream state has an obligation to take into account, in good faith, the interests of the downstream riparians as well as its own interests....

National and international tribunals have also applied the concept of limited territorial sovereignty. In 1938, the Italian Corte de Cassazione asserted in dicta that:

> international law recognizes the right of every riparian state to enjoy, as a participant of a kind of partnership created by the river, all the advantages deriv-

---

22. Trail Smelter Case (U.S. v. Can.), 3 R. Int'l Arb. Awards 1905, 1965 (1941), reprinted in 35 Am. J. Int'l 684, 716 (1941); see Read, The Trail Smelter Dispute, 1 Can. Y.B. Int'l L. 213, 215–29 (1963). [Ed. note: Actually this is pure dicta. The tribunal had authority only to determine the extent of damages, and causation. Trail Smelter Arbitration, 9 Ann. Dig. & Rep. Rub. Int'l Cases 315-316 (1941). *Trail Smelter* is often cited for the customary law principle of state responsibility for pollution, but that proposition requires the application of the two cases following in the text.]

23. Corfu Channel Case (U.K. v. Alb.), 1949 IJ. 4, 21 (Apr. 9, 1949).[

24. Affaire du Lac Lanoux (Spain v. Fr.), 12 R. Int'l Arb. Awards 281 (1957), digested in 53 Am. J. Int'l L. 156 (1959).

25. Id. at 317.

ing from it. A State cannot disregard the international duty not to impede or to destroy the opportunity of the other States to avail themselves of the flow of water for their own national needs.[26]

Public and private international organizations have also embraced the limited territorial sovereignty approach. Principle 21 of the United Nations' Stockholm Declaration on the Human Environment provides that states have the "sovereign right to exploit their own resources pursuant to their own environmental policies," but along with this right comes the "responsibility to ensure that activities within their jurisdiction or control do not cause damage to the environment of other States or areas beyond the limit of national jurisdiction."[27]

The Helsinki Rules promulgated by the International Law Association also assume limited territorial sovereignty. Article IV of the Helsinki Rules states that "each basin State is entitled, within its territory, to a reasonable and equitable share in the beneficial uses of the waters of an international drainage basin."[28]

Articles X and XI of the Helsinki Rules specifically address transboundary river pollution. Article X prohibits "any new form of water pollution or any increase in the degree of existing water pollution in an international drainage basin which would cause substantial injury in the territory of a co-basin State." Article XI provides that a polluting state shall not only be required to cease the polluting activity but must also compensate the injured state.

The limited territorial sovereignty theory is thus the basis for the rules of international law most frequently applied to the pollution of transboundary rivers.

### 4. The Community Theory

The community theory holds that the water of a drainage basin should be managed as a unit, without regard to national territorial boundaries. The various co-riparians should manage and develop the drainage basin jointly, and share the benefits derived therefrom.

In its judgment with respect to the territorial jurisdiction of the International Commission of the River Oder, the Permanent Court of International Justice went beyond the limited territorial sovereignty theory and expressed some elements of the community theory, stating that —

> the community of interest in a navigable international river becomes the basis of a common legal right, the essential features of which are the perfect equality of all riparian States in the use of the whole course of the river and the exclusion of any preferential privilege of any one riparian State in relation to the others.[29]

Although the community theory is a favorite of legal theorists, it does not yet enjoy widespread acceptance in the practice of states. The community theory is perhaps better thought of as a goal or an ideal toward which international law strives rather than as a rule of practice.

TREATIES GOVERNING POLLUTION OF THE RHINE... In addition to customary international law, several treaties govern the pollution of the Rhine. Some of these

---

26. Judgment of Feb. 13, 1939, Corte Cass., Italy, 64 Foro It. I 1036, 1046, digested in 3 Dig. of Int'l L. 1050—51 (1938—39).

27. Report of the United Nations Conference on the Human Environment, Principle 21, U.N. Doc. A/CONF.48/14/Rev. 1 (1972).

28. ILA, Helsinki Rules on the Uses of the Waters of International Rivers (1966) at 163–71.

29. 1929 PI.J. (ser. A) No. 23, at 27 (Sept. 10, 1929).

date back to the last century, but the most important are two modern treaties: the Berne Convention and the Rhine Chemical Convention.

### 1. Historical Treaties

The Rhine's problems did not begin with the Sandoz accident. Rhine pollution has been a problem at least since 1834, when Coleridge first asked, "what power divine/Shall henceforth wash the river Rhine?" As early as 1868, the various riparian states of the Rhine agreed by treaty to certain restrictions on the transport of toxic substances on the river. Packages containing arsenic and other toxic materials were required to bear the warning "poison" in French and German, in clearly legible black oil paint....

Prohibition of pollution of the Rhine from land-based sources dates back at least 120 years to an 1869 fisheries treaty between Switzerland and the Grand Duchy of Baden, which forbade the discharge of industrial wastes into the Rhine or its tributaries between Konstanz and Basel. Despite these early efforts, however, the condition of the Rhine continued to worsen.

### 2. The Berne Convention

In 1946, the Netherlands delegation to the Central Commission for the Navigation of the Rhine drew attention to the serious problems resulting from the growing pollution of the waters of the Rhine and suggested that the matter be examined at an international conference.

A conference was held, as a result of which the Convention concerning the Commission for the Protection of the Rhine Against Pollution (the Berne Convention) was signed in Berne on April 29, 1963, by Switzerland, West Germany, the Netherlands, France, and Luxembourg and entered into force in 1965. The Convention set up the International Commission for the Protection of the Rhine Against Pollution (International Commission) and gave the Commission three tasks, [to identify pollution sources, identify protective measures, and propose international agreements thereon]....

The rulemaking procedures of the Berne Convention are hardly conducive to decisive action. Decisions under the Berne Convention require unanimity among the Contracting Parties. Each delegation has one vote, with the provision that the European Community can cast a number of votes equal to the number of European Community members who are Contracting Parties; the European Community may not vote in cases where its member states vote, and vice versa. In other words, the European Community may vote, as a bloc, with Switzerland the only country outside that bloc.

A single negative vote, or the abstention of more than one party, negates unanimity and thus prevents the adoption of a resolution. Switzerland, therefore, has effective veto power over any European Community proposal....

### 3. The Rhine Chemical Convention...

In the summer of 1971, the middle course of the Rhine was entirely without oxygen in an area over 100 kilometers long, a situation that ultimately prompted European governments to take action. On March 22, 1972, the European Community requested that the parties to the Berne Convention design an emergency program for decontaminating the Rhine. On June 20, 1975, the European Parliament passed a resolution calling on those countries that were both parties to the Berne Convention and members of the European Community to agree on "immediate, practical and coordinated measures to avoid the impending disaster." Finally, a conference called by the Netherlands between ministers of parties to the

Berne Convention led to the adoption of the Convention on The Protection of the Rhine Against Chemical Pollution (Rhine Chemical Convention).[30]

### a. General Provisions of the Rhine Chemical Convention

The Rhine Chemical Convention amends and modifies the Berne Convention by placing additional responsibilities on the International Commission and the Contracting Parties. Article I of the Convention sets two goals for improving the water quality of the Rhine: elimination of pollution of the Rhine by certain highly dangerous substances, enumerated in the "black list" of Annex I, and reduction of pollution of the Rhine by substances listed in the "grey list" of Annex II. Among the chemicals listed in Annex I are "organophosphoric compounds" and "mercury and mercury compounds." Chemicals in both of these categories were released into the Rhine by the Sandoz accident. Annex II contains a general category of "Biocides and their derivatives not appearing in Annex 1." This latter category includes most of the other chemicals released into the Rhine by the Sandoz fire....

The bulk of the Convention's provisions deal with deliberate discharges of pollutants.... The limits for discharges of Annex I substances are set by an international body, rather than a national one, albeit by the unanimous agreement of the Contracting Parties.... In contrast, national authorities set the limits for discharges of Annex II substances after mutual consultation within the International Commission....

The Convention contains only minimal provisions regulating accidental discharges, although such discharges are a major source of harm to the Rhine. To prevent accidental discharges, Article 7 of the Convention provides that "The Contracting Parties will take all the legislative and regulatory measures guaranteeing that the storage of Annex I and II substances shall be done in such a way that there is no danger of pollution for the waters of the Rhine...."

### b. International Alarm Plan Rhine

Article 11 of the Rhine Chemical Convention also provides for the establishment of an international warning system to handle pollution emergencies.... To implement Article 11 the International Commission set up a network of warning stations known as the International Alarm Plan Rhine....

### c. Rulemaking Powers

Under both the Berne Convention and the Rhine Chemical Convention, the International Commission's rulemaking function is purely advisory. The Commission may make recommendations and suggestions but may not make binding substantive rules, with the exception of setting limit values for the discharge of Annex I substances. Any decisions must be made by unanimous consent of the Contracting Parties.

The Convention does, however, place certain binding obligations on the Contracting Parties. It requires them to monitor discharges and to set up water quality testing stations. Of greater significance in the context of the Sandoz spill is the obligation to inform the International Commission and the Contracting Parties, without delay, of any accident which could seriously threaten the quality of Rhine water.[In the Sandoz incident] Switzerland delayed more than twenty-four hours before notifying the downstream states of the danger to the Rhine.

---

30. Convention on the Protection of the Rhine Against Chemical Pollution, Dec. 3, 1976, I.L.M. 242 (1977).

*d. Dispute Resolution*

Article 15 of the Rhine Chemical Convention provides that any dispute between the Contracting Parties concerning the interpretation or implementation of the Convention that cannot be settled by negotiation shall be submitted to arbitration....

THE FAILURE OF THE RHINE TREATY REGIME... The ways in which existing law failed to protect the Rhine...illustrate the need for new mechanisms to prevent these disasters in the future.

*1. Failure of the International Warning and Alarm Plan Rhine*

Although the downstream states accused Switzerland of deliberately concealing information, Switzerland's delay of more than twenty-four hours before notifying the downstream states resulted as much from poor planning as from deliberate secretiveness. Incompatibility between the various alarm systems delayed the response to the crisis.... Although some of the environmental damage caused by the Sandoz spill might not have occurred had adequate warnings been given, the greater part of the damage was inevitable once the chemicals had entered the river....

*2. Violation of the Rhine Chemical Convention*

The greater part of the environmental damage resulting from the Sandoz spill was caused not by the delay in warning downstream states but by the failure of various safety systems designed to prevent the entry of chemicals into the river in the event of a fire. But for the lack of adequate catchbasins for runoff water from firefighting, the absence of a fire alarm and sprinkler system at Warehouse 956, and the faulty installation of a drainage seal, the catastrophe might have been averted.

Sandoz insists that it broke no laws in storing the chemicals in Warehouse 956, despite the absence of catch basins for runoff water. This assertion appears to be true. If so Switzerland, which otherwise has an excellent record in the area of environmental legislation, failed to fulfill its obligation under Article 7 of the Rhine Chemical Convention to ensure by all necessary legislative and administrative measures that the storage of hazardous substances did not endanger the Rhine.... If Article 7 is given its broadest construction, it creates an affirmative duty on the part of the Swiss administrative authorities to carry out inspections and otherwise police waterfront warehouses to ensure that no danger to the Rhine exists.[31] Under this interpretation of the Convention, Switzerland's failure to fulfill its administrative obligations under Article 7 was extended from the time the permit was granted, in 1979, to the time of the fire.[32]

---

31. See Rhine Chemical Convention, Art. 7: "The Contracting Parties will take all the legislative and regulatory measures guaranteeing that the storage of Annex I and II substances shall be done in such a way that there is no danger of pollution."

Although neither the Swiss government nor the governments of the downstream states have taken any legal actions against Sandoz, private individuals have brought a criminal charge against an unknown party or parties and the public prosecutor has commenced an investigation.

32. An alternative approach is that the Swiss probably violated customary international law. Under the limited territorial sovereignty approach to transboundary pollution, Switzerland violated its duty not to interfere with the reasonable use of the waters of the Rhine by the lower riparians. The same is true under either the community theory or the absolute territorial integrity theory. The lower riparians suffered significant harm as a result of Switzerland's violation of its duty. The fishing industry was virtually wiped out. Alternative sources of drinking water had to be obtained, and the value of the river for recreational use and as a magnet for tourism was decreased.

WHY THE TREATIES FAILED... The Berne convention is purely institutional in nature; it lacks rulemaking powers and enforcement mechanisms.... The three tasks that the Convention sets for the International Commission are investigative rather than preventive in nature. The findings and proclamations of the International Commission are not binding. Switzerland's [possible] violation of Articles 7 and 11 of the Rhine Chemical Convention...is of little import...when one considers that the Convention provides neither incentives for compliance nor sanctions for noncompliance. Without either a carrot or a stick with which to induce the Contracting Parties to comply, the Convention is little more than a "feel-good" document that allows the Contracting Parties to voice concern over the deteriorating state of the Rhine without having to face the domestic economic and political sacrifices that a genuine commitment to cleaning up the Rhine would require....

## COMMENTARY AND QUESTIONS

1. **The problem of sovereignty.** One of the River Rhine's fundamental problems is that it flows through six sovereign nations. There is no one government which has responsibility for the river system, and many diverse reasons why no national government along the Rhine wishes to concede any superior position to the others. No country wants to yield a superior legislative, judicial, administrative, or enforcement power to any supra-national river authority. In the River Rhine conventions, for example, note the frequently-encountered requirement that provisions be adopted by unanimous consent, and the further fact that even those provisions typically lack specific mandatory requirements. The understandable perquisites of sovereignty form a fundamental constraint on the growth and application of international environmental law.

What it comes down to in the eyes of skeptics is a catch-22: Because of the jealousies of sovereignty, treaties with sufficient teeth to be worth the effort will not get ratified; and treaties with sufficient vagueness and nonmandatory generality that it can be ratified is probably not worth the effort. Or treaties are written with strong provisions, juxtaposed in contradiction so as to invite interest-based subjective interpretation.[33]

2. **The international litigation approach.** It would seem in many of these transboundary cases that liability is obvious. The corporations or individuals that cause pollution typically do so knowing that it can be transported over long distances by

---

33. As an example, compare two companion articles from the United Nations Convention on the Law of the Sea (UNCLOS) accords:

> **Art. 192.** ...States shall take all measures necessary to ensure that activities under their jurisdiction or control are so conducted as not to cause damage by pollution to other States and their environment, and that pollution arising from incidents or activities under their jurisdiction or control does not spread beyond the areas where they exercise sovereign rights in accordance with this Convention....
>
> **Art. 193.** ...States have the sovereign right to exploit their natural resources pursuant to their environmental policies and in accordance with their duty to protect and preserve the marine environment."

If exploitation is a right, and unavoidably pollutes, a coastal state can define its own "environmental policies" and "duty to protect" so as to provide a broad scope of relative slack for disruptive activity undercutting Article 192.

air or water to places where it may cause injury. The fact that the victims are outside the borders of the actor's nation, however, tends to externalize those costs. To what extent is litigation, the first instinct of American environmentalists, a practical possibility in the international realm?

Two threshold questions: what litigation forum could the injury be brought to, and what law applies? The Schwabach essay focuses on sources of law that could be a basis for international litigation on the Rhine spill, drawn from customary law and treaties. As to forum, there is no supra-national court that automatically has jurisdiction over controversies between two nation states. States must themselves decide to be subject to a higher level court, and, even if they do open themselves to adjudication, they typically retain loophole escape clauses for avoiding such jurisdiction.

3. **What forum for an accounting of the Rhine pollution damages?** What forums exist for after-the-fact resolution of liability issues arising from the Sandoz spill? Ideally, international lawyers instinctively would prefer to turn to a pre-existing supra-national mechanism created by agreement of the different national parties. As Schwabach's article illustrates, however, there usually is no such convention capable of enforcing standards and assigning liability for their breach. Since the Sandoz spill there have been few serious moves in the direction of creating such a mechanism. In 1987, the EC states updated the "Seveso Directive," a Community declaration that was originally issued in 1982 following the Seveso, Italy, chemical poisoning incident.[34] But even with the Sandoz spill fresh in mind, the parties could only agree to establish a better alarm and notification system, a pool of experts to study the problem, improved industrial safety goals, and standards for moving toward a uniform system of transporting and storing hazardous waste.

The absence of liability-assigning mechanisms is again apparent, mitigated in the Sandoz case by the industry's energetic attempts to offer generous private compensation settlements to all potential claimants.

For observers trained in the Anglo-American legal mold, international environmental incidents like the Sandoz spill cry out for some kind of adjudicative mechanism that permits economic accounting to proceed without relying on voluntary compensation or the glacial processes of international diplomacy. Several international adjudicative forums do exist: the International Court of Justice (ICJ) in The Hague, various regional tribunals that may exist by treaty, consensual arbitration panels, and the "municipal" (i.e., national domestic) courts in the various nation states.[35]

In the *Trail Smelter* case, Canada and the United States, after much diplomatic fencing, agreed that it was in their mutual interest to have the matter resolved by a higher authority, and appointed the International Joint Commission (IJC), a treaty body that had been set up to study and advise on transboundary issues, to act as an

---

34. Directive 82/501, 25 O.J. Eur. Comm. (No. L 230) 1 (1982), as modified by 30 Eur. Comm. (No. L 85) 36 (1987).

35. "Municipal" as used in international law refers to the domestic law of a nation, as opposed to international principals and international legal forms such as the ICJ.

arbitral tribunal to settle the case. The existence of this kind of forum depends on case by case happenstance, and is quite exceptional.

Many nation-states, on the other hand, have accepted the jurisdiction of the ICJ. The ICJ has the advantage that it operates at a supra-national level; it treats a pollution incident like the Sandoz spill at the international level best suited to resolution of transnational issues. But the ICJ jurisdiction has its limitations as well. Many member states have not agreed to full automatic ICJ jurisdiction. Some have agreed to only limited jurisdiction, and some, like the United States in the famous *Nicaragua* case,[36] have asserted their sovereign right to withdraw from their acquiescence to jurisdiction when unwelcome litigation is filed (despite original agreement that jurisdiction required six months notice to withdraw). In such circumstances, it is painfully evident that nation states will not usually be brought into ICJ adjudications when they strenuously do not want to participate, and no judicial enforcement remedy is available. Some limited exceptions exist: the European Court of Justice (ECJ) established in Luxembourg by the European Community (EC) has been granted supra-national adjudicative power within the Community and offers a fascinating potential regional forum, based on treaties between EC member states, although the scope of matters within that jurisdiction is limited and growing only slowly.[37] Switzerland is not a member of the EC.

As in transboundary suits within the United States, courts in one nation state can often exercise jurisdiction over defendants in other countries through a form of long-arm jurisdictional claim. In some acid rain and transboundary air pollution cases between the United States and Canada, litigants have found practical damage remedies in the municipal courts. Michie v. Great Lakes Steel, 495 F.2d 213 (6th Cir. 1974).

**4. Official state or private litigants?** There is a further issue whether litigants would be national governments representing their citizens on a parens patriae basis, or injured private parties themselves. A number of commentators have noted the inertia of governmental involvement except in the most dramatic cases. As one commentator[38] said —

> As evidenced by its role in the Basel accident, public international environmental law is nearly impotent, and will probably remain so barring a revolutionary change in the values underlying the distribution of authority in goals of the international system. Private international remedies may offer more effective legal solutions to environmental problems. The basic policy orientation parallels that of public law: the principal questions to be resolved are those of compensation for injury, rather than prevention of pollution. Theoretically, strengthening private remedies could lead to incentives for reduction of injury-creating pollution. If private remedies are frequently used, the cost of pollution will be internalized by the polluter, who may then take greater precautions for future accidents.... Proponents of the use of private rather than public remedies back the approach favored by the Organization for

---

36. Nicaragua v. U.S., Merits and Judgment, ICJ Reports 1986 at 14 et seq.

37. See, however, Phillippe Sands, European Community Environmental Law: Legislation and the European Court of Justice, Centre for International Environmental Law Monograph (1991), noting several recent cases strongly affirming environmental principles in interpretations of EC legislation.

38. Darrell, Killing the Rhine: Immoral, But is it Legal?, 29 Virginia J. Int'l L. 421, 454 (1989).

Economic Cooperation and Development (OECD)[39] in its recommendation "Principles Concerning Transfrontier Pollution," and the Scandinavians in their Nordic Convention.[40]

These latter efforts have sought the lowering of barriers for transborder private suits, advocating "equal right of access" and "non-discrimination" in cases of pollution litigation. Agreements for the mutual enforcement of civil judgments in Europe already exist.

Where the transborder polluter is a government agency, however, as in the Chernobyl nuclear disaster, it may be far more difficult to bring effective litigation in the municipal courts of either state. In the Rhine spill example, the transboundary pollution was not caused by governmental action, but nevertheless it was clear that governmental parties would be deeply involved in the legal discussions that followed.[41] When a pollution incident or a course of conduct has become so offensive that the affected state decides to take on the controversy (by no means a foregone conclusion), the first official stage of international law is typically diplomatic negotiation, which can be a slowmoving morass. As the acid rain experience in northern Europe and North America indicates, nations that produce power plant pollution can be quite unenthusiastic about assuming responsibility for the widespread costs caused by themselves and their citizens, dragging out negotiations and attempted mediations for decades.

5. **What law applies?** Even if a pollution question can be brought to a judicial or quasi-judicial forum, the question remains, what law applies? Within Europe, for instance, it may be quite difficult to apply a downstream nation's law against an upstream defendant; conflicts of law questions abound in any municipal forum. The European Community, with its legislature in Brussels, represents an ongoing (and atypical) experiment in supra-national jurisdiction and the creation of regional law, but the role of the European Court of Justice in pollution matters is just now beginning to develop. To the extent that the EC has established a supranational adjudicatory ability, the law of the Community may be applied, but that law is in its infancy as a set of principles governing transboundary pollution. The fascinating feature of EC law is that principles derived from European conventions can be applied in the municipal courts of member nations as well as in the European Court of Justice itself. Most areas of the world, lacking any entity like the European Community, have no such supra-national option available.

If a matter is brought to adjudication between nation states, upon what "law" will it be decided? The ICJ is rigorously limited in the "law" it can apply. The ICJ Statute states —

---

39. OECD Doc. (74) 224, in 114 I.L.M. 242 (1975).

40. Convention on the Protection of the Environment, February 19, 1974, Denmark-Finland-Norway-Sweden, in 13 I.L.M. 591 (1974).

41. In only a few cases are citizens of one country able to go directly into the courts of another country to litigate a case of transboundary pollution. Between the United States and Canada, for instance, it has been important that the courts of each are open to citizens of the other filing tort suits. See Michie v. Great Lakes Steel Co., 495 F.2d 213 (6th Cir. 1974). See also §115 of the Clean Air Act Amendments of 1970, and EPA findings thereunder, in N.Y. v. Thomas, 613 F.Supp. 1472 (D>D>C> 1985), rev'd 802 F.2d 1443 (D.C. Cir. 1986).

**Article 38:** (1) The Court, whose function is to decide in accordance with international law such disputes as are submitted to it, shall apply:

a. international conventions whether general or particular, establishing rules expressly recognized by the contesting states;

b. international custom, as evidence of a general practice accepted as law;

c. the general principles of law recognized by civilized nations ["jus cogens"];

d. subject to the provisions of Article 59, judicial decisions and the teachings of the most highly qualified publicists of the various nations, as subsidiary means for the determination of rules of law.

(2) This provision shall not prejudice the power of the court to decide a case ex aequo et bono, if the parties agree thereto....

**Article 59:** The decision of the Court has no binding force except between the parties and in respect of that particular case.

Article 38 apparently creates a hierarchy of authorities to be applied as law in international disputes. Needless to say, the easiest of these sources of law to apply is the first, because states have conceded the applicability of terms and standards of treaties and conventions which can then be applied to particular controversies. This source of law, however, depends first upon the accidental coincidence of the petitioning and responding states having ratified a common instrument, and also that the treaty or convention have terms which are crisp and clear enough to imply specific mandatory responsibilities, by no means a sure thing. The treaty texts that get ratified tend not to be very crisp, clear, or mandatory. As noted, both of the Rhine conventions included loopholes and exceptions which frustrated their direct application.

In transboundary cases, if there is no treaty or convention in force, by what combination of other international law principles can the rules of liability and remedy be determined?

Custom? The most frequent attempts by international environmental lawyers to define legal responsibilities for transboundary pollution are based on arguments of alleged custom. The trouble is that there is no generally agreed upon set of customary principles of international environmental law. As the Schwabach text indicates, there are a variety of competing theories. Publicists (eminent legal scholars working privately or for international governing organizations) either arrive at such vague generalities as to be meaningless, in protecting each nation's jealous sense of sovereignty, or attempt to assert specific mandates in a form that deters sovereign nations from wanting to acquiesce to these principles.

What is a principle of international custom to be based upon? It cannot be based upon the myriad Declarations, Resolutions, Protocols and other non-binding statements produced in a succession of wishful conferences held by various scholarly groups and IGOs (intergovernmental organizations). The dramatic 1972 Stockholm Declaration, for instance, produced at a conference held under the aegis of the United Nations, declared a series of fairly strong environmental principles.[42] Principles 21 and 22 stated —

---

42. The Declaration included much ambiguity and many potential escape clauses. Stockholm Declaration on the Human Environment, U.N. Doc. A/Conf. 4/8/14, in 11 I.L.M. 1416 (1972).

21. States have, in accordance with the Charter of the United Nations and the principles of international law, the sovereign right to exploit their own resources pursuant to their own environmental policies, and the responsibility to ensure that activities within their jurisdiction or control do not cause damage to the environment of other States or of areas beyond the limits of national jurisdiction. [Note the ambivalent mandates — Eds.]

22. States shall cooperate to develop further the international law regarding liability and compensation for the victims of pollution and other environmental damage caused by activities within the jurisdiction or control of such States to areas beyond their jurisdiction.

Virtually nothing official, however, has been done since 1972 to develop an international law of liability and compensation.[43]

One common line of argument for a customary rule of liability is the "due diligence" doctrine, which holds that there is "a custom-based rule of due diligence imposed on all States in order that activities carried out within their jurisdiction do not cause damage to the environment of other states." OECD, Report by the Environment Committee: Responsibility and Liability of States in Relation to Transfrontier Pollution (1984).

But what is due diligence? Many commentators try to define due diligence by reference to the familiar old common law nuisance principle sic utere tuo ut alienum non laedas.[44] This principle can be discerned in the *Corfu Channel* case and *Lac Lanoux*, but the fundamental problem is that its meaning is not clear, even in domestic American law. "The dearth of [international] caselaw deprives the principle of sic utere of the specificity that applications to particular instances of transboundary pollution would arguably furnish it. Instead, sic utere remains an abstraction, an empty concept that commentators hope to fill with substantive content...."[45] At what level does environmental injury reach the level of "significance" or "unacceptable damage" in transboundary situations? Is *any* injury compensable, thereby bringing into international law a straightforward "polluter-pays" liability as a cost-of-doing-business rule? Or does it import some theory of fault and negligence? Must a state act to prevent normal production-based pollution, or is due diligence focused on accidental catastrophes? Does due diligence imply a strict liability standard, or a negligence, or intentional tort type standard? The closer the definitions move toward strict liability,[46] the more resistance will be raised by both industrial states and LDCs[47] that want to get in on the money of industrial production.

The ambiguities of defining customary law are further increased by some commentators' assertion that a rule can be regarded as "customary" between two party litigants based on their own prior practice, even though it is not customary

---

43. Phillippe Sands, Chernobyl: Law and Communication 23 (1988).

44. "One should use one's own property in such a manner as not to injure that of another."

45. Developments in the Law — International Environmental Law, 104 Harv. L. Rev. 1484, 1501 (1991).

46. Some commentators hopefully assert that strict liability is already the customary standard. See Goldie, Transfrontier Pollution, 12 Syracuse J. Int'l L. and Commerce 185 (1985).

47. "Less developed country" is the current euphemism for Third World states.

between any other nation-states. This makes a distinction between duties based on a framework of general custom, and the "specific custom" of the disputing states as it lends content to that framework. Further, to assert that a rule is "customary" to a state, must it be shown to be applied in its domestic law, or is it to be based on the state's customary behavior in the international arena? In either event, much definition has to be done before a rule of law ready for ICJ jurisdiction is presented.

As to the *jus cogens*, the "general principles of law recognized by civilized nations" in Article 38, these focus almost exclusively on procedural rules, such as res judicata, and have never been the sole foundation of an ICJ decision.[48] As to the use of "judicial decisions and the teachings of publicists," this basis for ICJ doctrine is traditionally regarded as highly subordinate, not sufficient in itself to base a decision, and merely a source of definition for Article 38's first three bases of legal responsibility.

6. **State responsibility for nonaccidental pollution, before the fact as well as after the fact?** Does it make a difference whether transboundary environmental damages are caused by a one-shot disaster, or by the normal course of business pollution created by industrial technologies? The focus of transboundary pollution cases has most often been on "one-shot" occurrences, which are universally identified as disasters. Arguably, however, international liability applies equally to normal pollution, analogous to American intentional tort doctrines. Under this reasoning, a "due diligence" formula addresses a state's duty to insure the environmental safety of behavior within its borders in both accidental and non-accidental settings; it would apply both before the fact, in prevention, as well as after the fact in terms of response to transboundary pollution. In the Sandoz spill, Switzerland could be accused of violating a duty to monitor, investigate, and prevent dangerous instrumentalities from injuring the environment, as well as duties arising after the fact to warn downstream states that a pollution incident had occurred, facilitating rescue and response efforts to mitigate harms. The fact that Switzerland did neither, despite the fact that there were Rhine treaties as well as arguable customary law, emphasizes the shaky standing of such international environmental principles.

7. **Is international law really law?** The tools of international environmental law raise a fundamental riddle, especially for American observers. Is international law really "law" if it fundamentally does not have to be obeyed? Americans with their Wild West background tend to think that law isn't law unless it is directly enforceable. Because jealous guarding of sovereignty is such a fundamental principle of international legal policy, each state hesitates to the point of stalemate in yielding authority to higher levels of international authority. Accordingly a number of environmental activists have concluded that the most powerful tools for applying international principles are consumer boycotts in developed Northern industrial societies and the media. International sanctions are a tangible mechanism of international suasion, but often seem to become studies in circumvention. United Nations police actions, which theoretically could be the enforcement mechanism

---

48. H. Lauterpacht, Private Law Sources and Analogies of International Law 215–217 (1970).

of international law, are twice limited. First, they are extremely difficult to mobilize, requiring a resolution of the Security Council where one veto can block an initiative, even if the fundamental principle being enforced is clearly a violation of the U.N. Charter or international law. Second, police actions by the U.N. are at best crude blunt instruments, as unwieldly as they are rare. For the most part, international environmental law will never be able to rely upon U.N. direct enforcement efforts, and will have to be based on less assertive principles.

8. **Overview.** Looking back at the Sandoz Spill and the transboundary pollution issues it raises, what strength do you discern in the potential legal devices for responding to transboundary pollution? After the Chernobyl disaster, two international conventions dealing with future nuclear catastrophes were quickly promulgated and ratified by many states including the Soviet Union, but like the post-Sandoz Seveso Directive they dealt primarily with notification and emergency assistance.[49] Both conventions, moreover, provide specifically that states may ratify these conventions provisionally, opt out from particular paragraphs imposing mandatory duties, or "denounce" the treaty at any point and thereby de-ratify it. No legal actions for determining liability or damages have been filed, despite the drastic radioactive pollution consequences of the Chernobyl meltdown.[50]

---

## C. INTERNATIONAL LAW OF THE GLOBAL COMMONS

There have been a number of important international legal initiatives attempting to deal with problems of the global commons. The Montreal Convention on Protection of the Ozone Layer, for example, provides a fascinating example of the interplay between international concerns and domestic constraints in its moves to limit the production of chlorofluorocarbons (CFCs) that destroy stratospheric ozone.[51] The Law of the Sea conferences produced conventions that established common principles for the oceans even though the U.S. never ratified it.[52] Global warming, endangered species, population management, preservation of antiquities, Antarctica — all these and more could be the basis of extended international case studies.

---

49. Vienna Convention on Early Notification of a Nuclear Accident, 25 I.L.M. 1370 (1986), and Vienna Convention on Assistance in the Case of a Nuclear Accident or Radiological Emergency, 25 I.L.M. 1377 (1986).

50. For coverage of the Chernobyl issue generally, see Phillippe Sands, Chernobyl: Law and Communication (1988).

51. See the Vienna Convention for the Protection of the Ozone Layer, 26 I.L.M. 1516 (1987)(defining obligations of participating nations with regard to CFCs); Protocol on Chlorofluorocarbons (the "Montreal Protocol"), 26 I.L.M. 1541 (1987)(mandating reductions in CFC use pursuant to the Vienna Convention). Other important examples are the Basel Convention on the Control of Transboundary Movements of Hazardous Wastes and Their Disposal, 28 I.L.M. 657 (1989)(governing international restrictions on hazardous waste import and export); the Convention on the Regulation of Antarctic Mineral Resource Activities (the Wellington Agreement), 27 I.L.M. 859 (1988)(protecting the Antarctic environment from military and mining activity); and the Third United Nations Conference on the Law of the Sea (UNCLOS III), 21 I.L.M. 1261 (1982)(an attempt to govern the use and protection of the world's ocean resources).

52. U.N. Doc. A/CONF./62/122 (1982), 21 I.L.M. 1261, 1308 (1982).

This chapter part, however, chooses the more prosaic issue of whaling and its effects on the world's whale populations as its relatively clear and instructive example of international responses to problems of the global commons.

## Section 1. WHALING, A CLASSIC RESOURCE DEPLETION DILEMMA

### Patricia Birnie, Whaling: End of an Era
(1985)

Herman Melville shipped out on the whaling vessel Acushnet early in 1841 from New Bedford, Massachusetts, bound for Cape Horn and the South Pacific. The 22-year-old was between jobs during a period of hard times. But it was a boom time for the New England whaling industry. More than 700 American ships prowled the seas in search of whales during the 1840s. New Bedford was the busiest whaling port in the world. Crewing on a whaler was difficult and dangerous, and Melville left his ship in mid-voyage after 18 months. But his adventures were the fodder for *Moby Dick*, which many believe is the quintessential American novel.

Commercial whaling changed radically just a few years after the 1851 publication of *Moby Dick*. By the late 1860s the explosive harpoon had replaced the hand-thrown weapon used in Melville's day, and steam-powered catcher boats allowed whalers to hunt faster-swimming whales and to range farther in search of them. By the end of the 1930s whaling fleets from around the world had drastically depleted the numbers of eight of the nine largest species of whales, a group of mammals known as the great whales.

World War II interrupted nearly all commercial whaling, but in the late 1940s a handful of nations resumed operations. At the same time several nations with whaling industries took steps to ensure a continuous supply of whales, an effort that until recently was characterized more by political dissension than success. However, all but a handful of countries — notably the Soviet Union and Japan...agreed to end commercial whaling in 1986, and those two countries...indicated they will end their operations in 1988.

Some conservationists believe that may be too late for some species. Whalers were prohibited from hunting the slow-swimming right whale in 1936. But it is estimated that fewer than 4,000 right whales live today. "The population is at best stabilized, or at worst continuing to decline," said Peter Dykstra, a spokesman for Greenpeace, the environmental action group. Bowhead whales, which swim in extreme northern waters, also were decimated in the late 19th century. Although bowheads have not been hunted commercially since 1935, there are believed to be fewer than 5,000 alive today. Six other great whales — the gray, blue, fin, sei, humpback, and sperm — are considered endangered due to overharvesting.

Concerned by a decline in whale stocks...during the 1930s the antarctic whaling nations entered into several voluntary agreements designed to protect whales. Some of them — including the Geneva Convention of 1931, the eight-nation London Agreement of 1937 and a British-German-Norwegian agreement signed the following year — succeeded in reducing the number of whale catchers and limiting the time periods for hunting some species. But none of those agreements stopped the whales' decline. Several whaling nations set up the International

Whaling Commission (IWC) in 1946 to try to safeguard the whales and keep the industry alive.... [The IWC] was the first international body given the power to grant complete protection to endangered species and set up yearly hunting quotas for the other species. In addition, the IWC could limit whaling to specific seasons and ban the taking of nursing whales, whale calves, and adults under certain sizes. The commission also carries on regular inspections of whaling operations.... Nearly everyone agrees that the IWC has failed to achieve either goal. "It is widely known that the International Whaling Commission...presided during the first 20 years of its existence over the depletion of nearly all the world's whale populations," British biologist Sidney Holt, a longtime international fisheries expert, asserted. "And the whaling industry, instead of enjoying an orderly development, experienced a disorderly, though long drawn-out collapse."

A resurgence of whaling followed World War II, but by the early 1960s only the Soviet Union and Japan maintained extensive whaling operations. Those two nations, along with Norway, Iceland, Brazil, South Korea, Denmark, Peru, Spain, and the Philippines, are the only countries with commercial whaling industries today. A drop in whale oil prices during the worldwide Depression of the 1930s accounted for some of the decline. But the more important factor by far was the decimation of virtually every species of antarctic whale. The relatively slow-swimming humpback was the first to be hunted — and the first to be overharvested. Antarctic whalers killed so many humpbacks beginning in 1904 that they all but disappeared by 1916. Then the blue whale was hunted practically to extinction. "When there were too few blue whales to hunt, the whalers turned to the next largest species, the fin whale, then to the sei [in the mid-1960s], and finally to the little minke [in the mid-1970s]," Richard Ellis noted....

The discovery in the 1960s that the blue whale, the largest creature that has ever lived on earth, was in danger of extinction sparked an international "Save the Whales" campaign. Wildlife, environmental, animal-welfare, and conservation groups lobbied heavily to get nations to stop commercial whaling. The IWC first discussed a ban in 1972. But 10 years passed before the commission in 1982 voted to phase out all commercial whaling by 1986.

Under the terms of the IWC charter, nations that file formal objections to commission rulings do not have to abide by them. Japan, Norway and the Soviet Union — the nations with the largest commercial whaling operations — promptly filed the requisite formal complaints. Japan and Norway claimed that the ban was not based on scientific evidence and would wipe out profitable domestic whaling industries. The Soviet Union said that "political considerations," not scientific information, motivated the whaling ban. Japan, Norway, and the Soviet Union, however, indicated they would end their commercial ocean whaling operations by 1988.... "The handwriting is on the wall for commercial whaling," Patricia Forkan of the Humane Society of the United States commented....

It is generally conceded that, despite its unprecedented powers, the IWC did little to safeguard diminishing whale species until the 1970s. Still, unlike its predecessors, the commission continued to operate. The IWC "is really a remarkable organization in that it's managed to hold together through all these years and still has a certain amount of legitimacy. It actually seems to function," biologist Scott Krauss of the New England Aquarium in Boston said. "It may not function to my liking, but it does still function." Under increasing pressure from conservationists, the IWC in the late 1970s began cutting quotas and working toward implementing a total moratorium on commercial whaling. This led to the total ban that the commission adopted at its 1982 meeting.

The first unilateral U.S. restrictions on commercial whaling came with passage of the Endangered Species Act in 1969, which placed eight of the nine great whales on the U.S. endangered list and barred the granting of whaling licenses for those species. At the time there were only two small commercial whaling operations in this country, the Del Monte and Golden Gate Fishing companies in Richmond, California. The Marine Mammal Protection Act of 1972, which put a permanent moratorium on most killing of ocean mammals within the U.S. fishing zone and on importation of their products, "was the nail in the coffin for any commercial whaling in the United States," said Tom McIntyre, marine resources management specialist with the National Marine Fisheries Service.

CHANCES FOR SURVIVAL... Commercial whaling almost certainly will end within the next few years. But that does not mean that all other types of whaling also will cease. Article VII of the 1946 International Convention for the Regulation of Whaling gives countries the right to kill whales "for the purposes of scientific research." Thus far Iceland and South Korea have officially notified the IWC that they intend to carry out comparatively widescale whaling for scientific purposes.... Whalers in Japan and Brazil reportedly are pushing for those nations to undertake scientific whaling as well. Iceland planned to kill 80 fin whales, 80 minke whales ,and 40 sei whales annually from 1986 to 1989. South Korea said it would take 200 minkes a year.

Icelandic and South Korean officials maintain that the whales will be taken solely for research studies. But conservationists say those nations are actually trying to circumvent the IWC ban on commercial whaling. Conservationists point out that Iceland plans to export the meat from its whales to Japan. "Iceland has made no bones about the fact that they intend to sell [the whale meat] to Japan," Forkan said. "What we are looking at is the potential to make $30 million or so over the four years for a million and a half dollars' worth of research. We think that's commercial whaling."

The IWC allows another exception to its whaling bans, including those on catching totally protected species. IWC regulations permit the taking of whales so long as "the meat and products are to be used exclusively for local consumption by the aborigines." Aboriginal whaling has been permitted in recent years in Greenland where the Eskimos kill fin and humpback whales, in the Soviet Union where Siberian Eskimos take gray whales, and in the United States where Alaskan Eskimos kill bowheads. Conservationists have strenuously objected to these aboriginal whaling activities, alleging that the meat of the gray whales killed in Siberia is used illegally to feed animals on fur farms and that the Eskimos in Greenland and Alaska are killing too many of the rare humpbacks and bowheads.

"U.S. Eskimos are wreaking havoc on the bowhead stocks," Potter said. The problem is not so much the number of whales killed, but the much larger number of those struck and not killed, nearly 90 percent of which die. "The number of whales struck and not landed skyrocketed in the late '70s, early '80s," Potter said.

"Given the very low population estimates of these bowhead whales, there is great concern that [the Eskimos] are clearly taking more animals than are being reproduced each year. If you've only got a couple of thousand, it doesn't take long to extinct the species." Some IWC scientists have pushed to end Alaskan bowhead aboriginal whaling. The U.S. government, under pressure from the Alaska Eskimo whaling commission, requested that the IWC allocate 35 bowhead strikes for 1985. The commission eventually allocated the Eskimos 26 strikes a year for 1985, 1986, and 1987.

Then there is the issue of coastal whaling. At the 1985 IWC meeting, Japan asked the commission to give "special consideration" to whaling that takes place solely within 200 miles of a nation's coastline. It would be "totally improper," the Japanese said, for the IWC to have jurisdiction over "any additional species whose utilization is confined exclusively to the 200-mile zone." This was the start, conservationists say, of a Japanese lobbying campaign to reclassify coastal whaling as subsistence whaling, which would be exempt from IWC jurisdiction. Norway and other nations are expected to join Japan in seeking unrestricted coastal subsistence whaling.

THE CONTROVERSY OVER COUNTING POPULATIONS... What continued hunting means for the various whale populations is unclear. The International Whaling Commission has been setting quotas based on whale populations for decades. Yet the process of counting whales is an inexact science at best. This has led to charges by conservation groups that the IWC, bowing to pressure from whaling nations, continually overestimates whale populations. Whaling nations and IWC officials, for their part, claim that conservation groups deliberately understate their figures. "We tend on a worldwide basis to set quotas for the numbers of whales that can be killed without any firm idea of how many there are and whether or not those numbers may be harmful," said Dykstra of Greenpeace. "If you were to talk to a scientist who works for the Japanese government...[and] a scientist who works for a country that may tend towards conservation, you might find as much as a 5,000 percent difference in the estimate of a certain stock."

### COMMENTARY AND QUESTIONS

1. **Whales as a global commons.** "The oceans of the world continue to suffer from the survival of the philosophy of the commons. Maritime nations still respond automatically to the shibboleth of the 'freedom of the seas.' Professing to believe in the 'inexhaustible resources of the oceans,' they bring species after species of fish and whales closer to extinction." So wrote Garret Hardin.[53] To what extent does the imperiling of the whales reflect a global commons, and to what extent is it susceptible to the legal strategies that Hardin proposed in his famous article?

2. **Whales, extinction, the public trust doctrine, and other general principles of international environmental law.** It is ultimately probably in the best interests of all to prevent the extinction of whales, but because every market participant can

---

53. Hardin, The Tragedy of the Commons, 162 Science, 1243, 1245, Dec. 13, 1968.

make short-term profit by ignoring long-term resource destruction, and none trusts the others to forebear, the whales as a resource base are exploited into a downward spiral. In the case of many endangered species, moreover, the rarer the remaining individuals, the higher the unit price that is likely to be offered for them, which only accelerates the extinction.

Could this international environmental law problem find legal resolution in the absence of directly actionable legal mechanisms? Could it be litigated? There would of course be all the problems noted earlier as to transboundary pollution of finding a supra-national tribunal capable of wrestling with the actions of several independent sovereigns, especially where the actions and injuries took place on the high seas or other nonterritorial locations.[54]

Assuming jurisdiction in some tribunal, what "general principles" or "custom" or "jurisprudence of civilized nations" would permit the tribunal to take account of extinction of such a valuable and beautiful global resource? Granted, a few nations have passed relevant endangered species protections, but these municipal laws do not rise to the level of general principles. Is the public trust doctrine capable of supplying such a general principle? Although analytically the public trust doctrine, deriving from the ancient code of Justinian, offers some customary basis for argument,[55] its subsequent development in Anglo-American jurisdictions would only coincidentally make it a global legal doctrine. For the same reason the public trust doctrine in general, and a prohibition of extinctions in particular, is hardly likely to be classed as customary in general or between the contending parties. Nor would prior caselaw and the comments of scholars be likely to create principles rising to the level of international law.

3. **A first treaty on ocean fishing.** Delegates from 100 nations adopted and opened for ratification a U.N. Convention on Straddling Fish Stocks and Highly Migratory Fish in 1996, U.N. GAOR, 6th Sess., Pt. X. Art. 34 U.N. Doc. A/CONF. 164/37 (1995). This convention takes a step toward correcting unsustainable global fish harvesting practices by adopting a precautionary approach. Uncertainties about the ability of a fish stock to sustain a harvest level are resolved in favor of the fish with the imposition of precautionary conservation quotas. The treaty also contains a provision to minimize "bycatching" (unwanted species caught incidentally and dumped at sea). Since the majority of the world's fish are harvested within a country's coastal waters, however, the U.N. convention only pertains to 20% of the world's fish. The treaty also fails to address the over-capitalization of the world's fishing fleets, a major cause of over-fishing.

4. **Of sovereignty and enforceability.** As already discovered in the transboundary example, one of the classic problems of international environmental law is that there is no supra-national sovereign authority to play the role of Hardin's unitary owner who would incorporate and rationalize all costs and benefits of resource exploitation. The dilemma of the whales is a small example of dozens of major

54. Anthony D'Amato and Sudhir K. Chopra, in Whales: Their Emerging Right to Life, 85 AM. J. INT'L L. 21 (1991), present a comprehensive review of 100 years of whaling law.
55. See Nanda and Ris, The Public Trust Doctrine: A Viable Approach to International Environmental Protection, 5 Ecol. L.Q. 291 (1976).

issues of the global environmental commons which lead many wistful observers like ex-U.N. Secretary General U Thant to urge the creation of a new "global authority...a governing body capable of establishing binding standards...and an enforcement authority with power to make conclusive determinations as to compliance."[56] The United Nations is obviously not such an entity. Despite the fact that most lawyers in developed countries presume the necessity of a superior enforcement entity, the international community flees from such proposals. The wonder is that the International Whaling Commission has any mandatory powers at all. Article 1 of the International Agreement for the Regulation of Whaling provides that "the contracting Governments will take appropriate measures to ensure the application of the provisions of the present Agreement and the punishment of infractions," but it is far from clear what this means beyond providing inspectors on whaling factory ships. Article V, paragraph 3, as in many treaties, provides for a one-nation veto of IWC decisions by the filing of an "objection" to IWC quotas or regulations. In 1971 when the IWC voted 25 to 1 for a zero quota on North Pacific male sperm whales, Japan dissented, lodged an objection, and continued whaling with impunity.

Reading through any major multilateral treaty or convention collected in the International Environment Reporter, for example, one is repeatedly struck by the typical legal minuet between attempts to pin down meaningful standards, which may deter nation states from agreeing to them, and the creeping vacuity and loopholes that make a document agreeable to general consensus and ratification. The more meaningful provisions tend to be drafted and accepted after disasters occur, but even then, as in the Chernobyl example, states are hesitant to erode their hermetic sovereignty. Is protective international action therefore more likely to come from politics and media than from the evolution of law?

5. **IGOs and their actions.** The IWC is an example of an IGO, an inter-governmental organization. There are literally dozens of IGOs that have direct or indirect jurisdiction over international environmental problems. The United Nations is the premier IGO, and has gathered under its aegis most other IGOs through a process of coordination managed by the U.N. Economic and Social Council (ECOSOC). After the Stockholm conference, the general assembly created the United Nations Environment Programme (UNEP), now based in Nairobi. The UNEP, however, because it was created merely by an Assembly resolution and not by ratification by the states, has an uncertain legal status and no enforcement authority whatever, serving explicitly as a "coordinating body" to lead the environmental activities of other IGOs. The IWC, which predates the United Nations, coordinates with UNEP and ECOSOC, but analytically has separate legal status based on the treaty ratifications that created it.

What can IGOs do? Basically they can talk, formulate aspirational declarations, gather information in compendious detail, and enforce little or nothing. Yet through them one can understand some of the ultimate suasions of international

---

56. Public Papers of the Secretaries-General of the United Nations, Volume 8, 350 (1977); see Chayes, International Institutions for the Environment, in Law, Institutions, and the Global Environment at 2 (1972).

law. In 1985, a group representing displaced indigenous plantation workers petitioned the International Labor Organization (ILO)[57] to investigate the Indian Sardar Sarovar and Narmada dam-building programs. These projects were systematically causing serious environmental destruction, and displacing tens of thousands of rural workers in violation of ILO Convention Article 107. The resulting ILO investigation received immediate attention from the Indian government, even though the ILO had no enforcement powers.[58] The prospect of being censured or suspended by the ILO and made to look delinquent in the eyes of the world community — the potential "mobilization of shame" that gives impact to so much of international law's unenforceable mandates — prompted India to take the ILO's investigation extremely seriously. (The fact that subsequent pressure from India forced the ILO to suspend its investigation in spite of clear cut violations of the ILO Convention is a further realistic example of how the game of international law plays out.)

6. NGOs. An important and understated feature of many international environmental law issues like the IWC whaling story is the critical role played by intense pressure from non-governmental organizations (NGOs) in the evolution of conservation-oriented legal principles. Like many IGOs, the IWC was from the beginning susceptible to "capture" by industrial groups and the dozen whaling nations. (Indeed it was they who made up the IWC, and they held the predictable power and perspective of market participants who stand to make greater short-term revenues when conservation restrictions are minimal.) Even when IGOs are made up of broader, or even universal, state membership, they are unlikely to be rigorous in conservation measures due to constraints of inertia and diplomatic compromise. As one scholar has noted, IGOs and the development of international legal principles are often limited by the phenomenon of the "slowest boat" as well as the "freerider" problem.[59] The slowest boat phenomenon means that agreements tend to be drafted initially to attract maximum numbers of ratifying states, and therefore tend to have the loosest possible mandatory controls. After ratification, moreover, whatever mandatory provisions that exist tend to be designed to be least burdensome on out-voted minority members, thus reflecting a further lowest common denominator "bottom line."

The history of whaling and the IWC, however, was dramatically changed in the early 1960s by NGO pressure groups, based primarily in the United States. Judy Collins recorded a bestselling record album using hydrophone recordings of humpback whale songs as accompaniment to her plaintive ballads. Greenpeace and

---

57. See Matthew Tuchow, Tribal Land Protection: Lessons from the Sardar Sarovar Conflict (student paper, Harvard Law School, 1987), as reported (with dropped citation) in Plater, Multilateral Development Banks, Environmental Diseconomies, and International Reform Pressures on the Lending Process: the Example of Third World Dam-Building Projects, 9 Third World L.J. 169, 201–202 (1989).

58. Some observers see the ILO as an interesting model for improving the post-Rio Conference United Nations Environment Programme (UNEP). State delegations to the ILO contain two nongovernmental members (one labor, one employer-based) as well as two government officials. Under Article 26, *any* delegate may petition for adjudication of a matter by the ILO Committee of Experts. ILO thus offers an interesting combination of deliberative functions (its annual Council meetings) and adjudicative, both giving a significant institutionalized role to nongovernmental players.

59. Peter Sand, Lessons Learned in Global Environmental Governance, 18 Envtl Aff. L. Rev. 213, 220 et seq. (1991).

other citizen groups began a domestic and international program of media intervention and direct action (consumer boycotts; disrupting whale harpooners with little zodiac boats; ramming whaler ships with derelict old scows) designed to show the public the cruelties and needlessness of whale slaughter. More established environmental groups, working out of Washington, San Francisco, and New York, brought pressure to bear upon the federal government to pass tough domestic legislation noted in the next section and to impel active U.S. participation in the IWC. Pressure upon the State Department in turn produced U.S. diplomatic pressures on a number of nonwhaling states to join the IWC, thereby outnumbering the whaling nations that previously had controlled it.

As their political force grew in the United States, Canada, and several Western European nations, NGOs became regular observer participants at IWC annual meetings, completely changing the nature of scientific debate and political compromise. NGOs hired scientists who were not in thrall to the whaling industry, hired cameramen for the production of beautiful books, calendars, and horrifying videos of whaling, and prepared press kits and educational materials for schools all over the United States and Europe, to focus aroused environmental consciousness upon the problem of whale killing.

As the success of Western NGOs became evident, citizens groups were formed in a variety of other countries, including LDCs, broadening and focusing the political pressures.

At first most official IGOs, like the IWC, took the position that "the organization will speak only with nation states." After repeated political torture at the hands of NGOs (and reminders that the IGOs had always been quite happy to talk with nongovernmental industrial corporations and market organizations), the international community has now been largely pried open to the insistent and integrated participation of NGOs.[60] In this way too the lessons of environmentalism in the United States have become a matrix for the evolution of international environmental law. Without the pluralistic intervention of citizen NGOs, what level of response would have come from the international legal community to the environmental challenges of the past two decades?

---

60. The World Bank, the International Marine Organization, and other IGOs with establishment perspectives long held such exclusionary policies. Now the picture has changed, for functional as well as political reasons. As Mooen Quereschi, Senior Vice President of the World Bank in Washington has said, "As late as ten years ago what we knew about [our own] World Bank operations in many countries depended mainly on bureaucratic lines of information and supervision.... In today's global village, NGO networks can report a problem in rural northeast Brazil...within a week. Where [our own] bureaucratic eyes are astigmatic, NGOs provide vivid images of what is really happening at the grass roots." Speech to Society for International Development (Washington, April 22, 1988).

## D. EVOLVING INTERNATIONAL PRINCIPLES AND STRATEGIES

There is a growing mass of new and old law evolving to meet the newly-developing international consensus that environmental problems are ultimately important to the fate of all nations. The following collection of some of these principles and strategies emphasizes some of the fascinating legal process challenges they pose.

### Section 1. SUSTAINABLE DEVELOPMENT AND THE PATH TO AND FROM RIO

Beginning with the United Nations Stockholm Conference on the Human Environment in 1972, most countries of the world have awakened to the fact that environment will be a central determinant of human quality of life and national survival for the future. From the Brundtland Commission to UNCED — the United Nations Conference on Environment and Development at Rio de Janeiro, in 1992 — a developing collection of important new principles is being taken increasingly seriously in discussions of transnational governance.[61] Sustainable Development, encountered from the beginning of this coursebook, is the single principle that probably best captures the human, ecological, and governance imperatives that will guide the new millenium.

In his extensive article from which brief portions are excerpted below, Professor Dernbach surveys the emergence of sustainable development as an international environmental principle, and analyzes the organic requirements it places upon legal and government frameworks (and not just internationally). One of Professor Dernbach's underlying insights is that after 50 years of the United Nations it should be clear to all that implementation of critical global principles is as much or more the job of component regional, national, and subnational legal systems, than of some wistfully-anticipated world order.

### John Dernbach, Sustainable Development as a Framework for National Governance
#### 49 Case Western Reserve Law Review (1998)

The world's economy "has grown with unprecedented speed" since World War II, and most people have experienced a rise in their standard of living. Yet the traditional development model has foundered for two related reasons — growing poverty and a deteriorating global environment. A growing number of people live in hunger and poverty, and the gap between rich and poor continues to widen. More than a third of the word's population lacks access to a safe water supply. Health risks from the degradation of natural resources and the improper use of chemicals are also increasing. At the beginning of the next century, more than half of the world's population will live in urban areas, and mostly without adequate housing and sanitation....

---

61. See Jeffrey L. Dunoff, From Green to Global: Toward the Transformation of International Environmental Law, 19 Harv. Envtl. L. Rev. 241 (1995), for a review of current trends in international environmental law (IEL) and for insight into current and future debates that will shape the future of IEL. Dunoff discusses the tools and techniques that have aided in the development of IEL and the conflict between liberalized international trade and international environmental protection. He proposes several new directions which will further the "globalization" of IEL. Dunoff argues that "globalization" of IEL will address the ability of a small minority of nations to set the international environmental agenda and to determine the success or failure of multilateral environmental initiatives.

By a great many measures, the condition of the global environment is deteriorating. Among other things, we face widespread and even accelerating extinction of plant and animal species, growing emission of greenhouse gases into the atmosphere, the depletion of fish stocks in oceans throughout the world, loss of farmland and grazing land through overuse and poor practices, and growing and improper use of chemicals. In every region in the world, these conditions are growing worse....

The first major global conference on the environment, the United Nations Conference on the Human Environment in 1972, grew out of concern for growing environmental degradation around the world. The Stockholm conference, and the preparatory meetings that led to it, produced "a worldwide raising of consciousness" about the environment "for which there appears to be no precedent," reinforced national responsibility for environmental protection, officially recognized the need for cooperative international action, and began to bring the environment into the discussion of what development means. The conference also led to adoption and implementation of environmental laws in many countries, and to a rapid increase in the number and variety of treaties concerning protection of the environment. It did not, however, suggest a way to reconcile development and environment.

The conference produced a declaration of twenty-six principles, known as the Stockholm Declaration,[62] "to inspire and guide the peoples of the world in the preservation and enhancement of the human environment." Perhaps the single most important principle couples the sovereign right of nations to exploit their own resources with responsibility "to ensure that activities within their jurisdiction or control do not cause damage to the environment of other States or of areas beyond the limits of national jurisdiction."[63] This principle asserts both the need for environmentally protective economic development and the interdependence of nations. The Stockholm Declaration also recognizes the relationship between development and environment by stating, among other things, that "economic and social development is essential for ensuring a favorable living and working environment for man," and that the "environmental policies of all States should enhance and not adversely affect the present or future development potential of developing countries." The Stockholm conference also created a relatively brief action plan. Although the plan contained a section on "development and environment," it contained no comprehensive approach to reconciling the two concepts.

During the 1980s, it became more evident that development was imposing massive economic, human, and environmental costs. The General Assembly formed the World Commission on Environment and Development, headed by Norwegian Prime Minister Gro Harlem Brundtland, to examine the relationship between the development and environment. The Commission...issued its report, Our Common Future, in 1987[64] — although the "satisfaction of human needs and aspirations is the major objective of development," the Commission concluded, developmental inequity and environmental degradation are "inexorably linked." Peace and security, economic development, social development, and proper governance are all inextricably related to environmental protection.... Quite simply, effective governance requires a nation to consider and protect the environ-

---

62. U.N. Doc. A/CONF.48/14/Rev. 1 (1972)

63. Stockholm Declaration, Principle 21.

64. World Commission on Environment and Development [the Brundtland Commission], Our Common Future (1987).

ment and natural resources on which its current and future development depend. Any other approach is self-defeating. The connections between the environment and development thus provide a provide a powerful premise for environmental protection: enlightened self-interest.

No nation faces these challenges alone. Environmental problems and poverty occur in all states. Pollution also crosses national lines.... Each country's interests are bound up with those of the rest of the world, and each country is more likely to resolve its problems if it works cooperatively with other countries toward their resolution....

In June 1992, at the United Nations Conference on Environment and Development in Rio de Janeiro, the nations of the world agreed to an ambitious and unprecedented global plan of action for addressing the related and growing problems of environmental degradation and poverty. "Humanity stands at a defining moment in history."... The delegates to UNCED approved the Rio Declaration on Environment and Development,[65] a statement of twenty-seven principles for sustainable development.... More important than the Rio Declaration, however, is Agenda 21,[66] a comprehensive international "plan of action" or blueprint for sustainable development. It represents a broad and detailed commitment by nations around the world to take actions to further sustainable development...divided into four sections and a total of forty chapters,...[including chapters on] poverty, production and consumption patterns, combating deforestation, management of sewage and solid wastes, the role of nongovernmental organizations, the role of business and industry, science for sustainable development, and information for decision-making. Each chapter describes...a comprehensive inventory of activities necessary for sustainable development — ...the factual basis for recommended actions, the objective of those actions, the particular activities that governments and others should take, and the entities that need to support and fund these activities.... Agenda 21...established a process for reviewing the progress of individual nations in achieving sustainable development,...the Commission on Sustainable Development (CSD), a newly created U.N. entity...to review overall implementation of Agenda 21....

Agenda 21 and the Rio Declaration are based on sustainable development as a conceptual framework for achieving economic development that is socially equitable and protective of the natural resource base on which human activity depends. As important as these agreements are, the synthesis they contain is a fragile one. The power and the continuing independence of development are manifest in several ways. The right to development was reaffirmed at UNCED, for example, with no corresponding claim about a right to a decent environment....

Five years later, in June 1997, the United Nations General Assembly concluded a comprehensive review of progress since UNCED by stating that "overall trends for sustainable development are worse today than they were in 1992."[67]

---

65. Rio Declaration on Environment and Development, adopted June 14, 1992, U.N. Doc. A/CONF.151/5/Rev. 1 (1992)

66. United Nations Conference on Environment and Development, Agenda 21, U.N. Doc. A/CONF.151.26 (3 vols. 1992).

67. Programme for the Further Implementation of Agenda 21, U.N. GAOR, 19th Special Sess., ¶ 4 (advance unedited text, July 1, 1997). With the principal exception of population growth, which appears to be headed toward stabilization in 2050, virtually every negative trend identified in Rio remained unchanged after five years. See generally United Nations Environment Programme, Global Environmental Outlook (1997) (describing regional trends and concluding that environmental degradation is occurring in all regions).

Most countries were able to identify some domestic achievements, and there appeared to be a higher level of public support for sustainable development. In that five year period, however, few countries adopted or modified laws or policies to change the overall trajectory of their unsustainable development patterns.[68] In addition, their modest actions were dwarfed by growth in the number of people living in poverty around the world and the further deterioration of the global environment. Nations nonetheless reaffirmed their commitment to Agenda 21 and pledged "greater measurable progress in achieving sustainable development" by 2002, when the next comprehensive review was scheduled.[69]...

The literature tends to see sustainable development primarily in terms of its implications for international law and international institutions.... UNCED [however, also] created a coherent conceptual framework for domestic governance.... Sustainable development is a pragmatic, coherent, and positive response to deteriorating global conditions. It would make governance more economically efficient, more socially productive, and more environmentally protective. As a framework for governance, sustainable development also provides a response to many current trends that undermine the legitimacy and effectiveness of national governments in general, particularly globalization of the economy and the free market ideology that has become more prevalent since the collapse of the Soviet Union in 1989. Indeed, sustainable development provides an alternative to that ideology....

Because of UNCED, sustainable development is also an internationally recognized normative framework for guiding and evaluating the behavior of national governments and other actors.... National governments need to foster sustainable development by energizing all parts of society towards that end. All countries should ensure that environmental, social, and economic goals are harmonized, that polluters bear the environmental costs of their activities, and that natural features and human health are protected even where the scientific evidence for adverse effects is uncertain. Developed countries are expected to play a leadership role, not only in implementing national sustainable development policies, but also in providing financial and other assistance to developing nations.... Governments...need to repeal or modify subsidies and other laws that encourage or allow unsustainable development,...[and] use a variety of instruments to harness market forces and individual behavior on behalf of sustainable development.... Implementation requires the adaptation of sustainable development norms to local cultures, natural systems, and economies....

Unresolved issues in the sustainable development framework...include the comparative responsibilities of developed and developing countries, high consumption of materials and energy by developed countries, the role of international trade, and the substantial commitment most governments have already made to unsustainable economic activities....

---

68. U.N. Doc. E/CN/.17/1997/5 (1997) (noting progress in some areas but concluding that the primary challenge is "in moving from the policy development phase to implementation"); see also Dernbach et al., U.S. Adherence to its Agenda 21 Commitments, 27 E.L.R. 10,504 (1997) (little evidence that UNCED affected U.S. law or policy).

69. ...Two treaties...were opened for signature in Rio. Framework Convention on Climate Change, U.N. Doc. A/AC.237/18 (1992), reprinted in 31 I.L.M. 849 (1992); Convention on Biological Diversity, U.N. Doc. DPI/1307 (1992), reprinted in 31 I.L.M. 818 (1992). The meeting on the Climate-Change treaty, which was held at the end of 1997 in Kyoto, Japan, resulted in a protocol limiting emissions of greenhouse gases—so called because they are warming the earth's atmosphere. Kyoto Protocol, U.N. Doc. FCCC/CP/197/L.7/Add. 1.

Two substantial and related objections to implementation of sustainable development norms are —

(1) that Agenda 21, the Rio Declaration, and similar texts are not binding in international law. As a result, they may be trumped by trade and other treaties, which are legally binding, or simply ignored. (2) that it may not be possible to reverse a well-established pattern of national governance supported by economic interests in unsustainable development.

The basic means of overcoming these objections, however, are explicit or implicit in the instruments themselves. The most significant of these are probably public participation and information, although it is by no means clear that they will be effective. Perhaps, if we understand sustainable development as a framework for national governance, we may increase our chances of overcoming these obstacles....

The Rio Declaration affirms the premise of development that every human being is "entitled to a healthy and productive life," but it adds "in harmony with nature." To ensure that, nations must make simultaneous progress toward three related and equally important goals.... "Economic development, social development, and environmental protection are interdependent and mutually reinforcing components of sustainable development."... Sustainable development offers an alternative path that is difficult and challenging, but which provides hope for a better world for ourselves and future generations. We cannot take the latter path, however, unless we first recognize that we have a choice.

### COMMENTARY AND QUESTIONS

1. **Sustainable development and convergence.** Professor Dernbach, in examining the dominating logic of the sustainable development principle, does not despair of the possibilities for international-level solutions, noting the significant legal infrastructure that has been built over the past several decades, while emphasizing an important need for national and subnational legal structuring. Some observers reflect dismay that the momentum of international and municipal implementation of the sustainability principle has proceeded at an erratic pace, but the process of building law and practice across sovereignties has always been a process of accretion over time. If the fundamental logic is sound, then it will continually present itself through experiential imperatives. The progress of law at the global level— like law anywhere — may sometimes require disasters, hopefully small but vivid, to push it forward.

2. **UNCED, the Rio Conference.** The United Nations Conference on Environment and Development took years of preparation, attracted worldwide attention, and generated controversy, hope, and a tremendous amount of paperwork. 178 countries participated in the conference, which was attended by 140 heads of state, the largest gathering of national chiefs of state in the history of the world. The Earth Summit produced five international law documents for signature by the official delegates:[70]

---

70. This text draws in part upon Nick Yost's "Rio and the Road Beyond," 11 Envt'l L.Q. (ABA, 1992). For further brief descriptions of these documents, see generally Edith Brown Weiss, Introductory Note, 31 I.L.M. 814–17 (1992).

• The Rio Declaration on Environment and Development, U.N. Doc. A/CONF. 151/5, reprinted in 31 I.L.M. 874, 877 (1992) — A statement of 27 principles underlying the "Earth Summit," which was approved by all of the nations attending UNCED. It reaffirms the 1972 Stockholm Declaration on Human Environment, and proclaims the goal of UNCED to be the establishment of "a new and equitable global partnership." Principle 1 declares that "Human beings are at the center of concerns for sustainable development. They are entitled to a healthy and productive life in harmony with nature." The Declaration goes on to affirm "the right to development," and states that "eradicating poverty" is an "indispensable requirement for sustainable development." It goes on to encourage elimination of "unsustainable patterns of production and consumption," "right-to-know" provisions, and the development of environmental laws. It stresses the importance of internalizing the environmental costs of production, and concludes with a call for the "further development of international law in the field of sustainable development."

• Convention on Biological Diversity, June 5, 1992, reprinted in 31 I.L.M. 818 (1992) — This convention aims to lower the rate of global plant and animal extinction by establishing national conservation management systems. It also seeks to establish international standards for the biotechnology industry, including rules governing the commercial use of genetic resources. Under the terms of the convention, nations with natural resources valued by the biotechnology industry have an interest in both the direct sale of the natural resource, and in any patent or royalty arising from biotechnology derived from that resource. The accord between Merck Pharmaceutical and the government of Costa Rica is often used as an example. Signatories also agree to establish ecosystem inventories, and to develop national strategies and programs to implement the principles of the Biodiversity Convention. It was signed by 153 nations. The only delegation refusing to sign was that of the United States, citing concerns over "financing and protection of intellectual property rights." Thirty nations must ratify this convention for it to become a part of international law.

• The Framework Convention on Climate Change, U.N. Doc. A/AC. 237/18, reprinted in 31 I.L.M. 849 (1992) — Anthropogenic emission of greenhouse gases is the focus of this framework convention, specifically: how to stabilize global emissions of carbon dioxide, methane, and chlorofluorocarbons while achieving "sustainable social and economic growth." Article 3 sets forth the principles that should guide this endeavor, urging the parties to "protect the climate system for the benefit of present and future generations," and to "take precautionary measures to anticipate, prevent or minimize...climate change." Article 4 outlines the commitments of the signatories, including the sponsorship and exchange of research findings, and the development of national programs designed to mitigate climate change. References to specific timetables and precise emission levels were deleted in order to gain the endorsement of the U.S. delegation. All attending nations signed this convention. It must be ratified by fifty nations to become international law.

• Non-legally Binding Authoritative Statement of Principles for a Global Consensus of the Management, Conservation and Sustainable Development of all Types of Forests, U.N. Doc. A/CONF. 151/6, reprinted in 31 I.L.M. 881 (1992) — This statement sets worldwide standards for good forestry practices, stressing the importance of "sustainable use" in developing management regimes. It also addresses the financial and ecological relationships between timber-importing and timber-exporting countries. It urges that total global forest cover be increased, but puts no special emphasis on old growth forests.

Though it was finished during UNCED, the final wording is considerably weaker than the original version, a result of pronounced disagreements in point of view between "developed" and "developing" nations. The developed nations persisted in characterizing tropical forests as the world's "carbon sinks" or "carbon sponges," while the developing nations who control these forests saw them as sovereign national resources, to be dealt with as they saw fit. From this "Southern" perspective, the "Northern" countries were trying to buy the "right to pollute"; first generating the vast majority of the world's anthropogenic greenhouse gases, and then telling the South not to cut its forests so as to help soak up the excess carbon dioxide the Northern lifestyle required. This convention could lead to a binding treaty someday.

• Agenda 21, U.N. Doc. A/CONF. 15 1/4, reprinted in Agenda 21 & The UNCED Proceedings 47-1057 (Nicholas A. Robinson ed. 1992) – This is an 800-page, 120-chapter guide to the implementation of the Conventions on Climate Change and Biodiversity, and of the "sustainable development" principles contained within the Rio Declaration. It is designed to serve as the foundation for international environmental law and cooperation into the next century. It addresses everything from marine pollution to desertification to population dynamics to patterns of consumption. There are chapters on management of resources, the roles of "subgroups" (women, children, indigenous peoples, NGO's, etc.) within the environmental context, the development of a body of environmental laws within existing legal systems, and the actual "Means of Implementation" required to achieve these goals. Agenda 21 creates a permanent United Nations Commission on Sustainable Development, which will oversee compliance with the provisions of the Conventions on Climate Change and Biodiversity by their signatories. It also establishes a Global Environmental Facility to work with the World Bank on coordinating aid transfers from richer to poorer countries.

3. **Rio: Was it worth the effort?** Given the labor and high hopes poured into the Rio UNCED conference, the predictable inertia and marketplace resistance that followed the euphoria have been sobering. In hindsight, some observers have deemed the Rio "Earth Summit" a practical failure. Despite the biodiversity pact, 100,000 species may have become extinct between the 1992 Rio summit and the end of the decade. In addition most developed countries, including the United States, are expected to fail to reduce carbon dioxide emissions to 1990 levels, which the treaties at Rio committed them (at least in theory) to do. Developed countries have actually cut back on foreign aid expenditures since Rio while official development aid (ODA) levels were supposed to increase eventually from 0.34 percent of GDP (the 1992 average for developed nations) to 0.7 percent of GDP, ODA levels actually have fallen in the past five years, to 0.25 percent of GDP. A State Department official says the U.S. is unlikely to meet Rio's goals for foreign aid anytime soon, explaining that, "It is the Congress that controls the purse. And every year we fight with the Congress about how much money we put into all of those kinds of things." The United States is hardly alone in its failure to make strides toward the goals which were set at Rio. Most industrialized nations are unlikely to meet the aspirational cap on emissions, and only Japan has met the targets which were set at Rio for foreign aid to developing nations.

There is little evidence that the Rio Earth Summit had much effect on U.S. law or policy in the 1990s. The federal government established the President's Council on

Sustainable Development (PCSD), but made no coherent overall commitments to sustainable development analysis or implementation by government agencies. The PCSD is a 25-member board comprised of leaders from government and the private sector, addressing "development that meets the needs of the present without compromising the ability of future generations to meet their own needs."[71] No particular management or regulatory changes came from the effort. Few governmental or NGO initiatives occurred to inform the public and encourage public policy debate about the need for sustainable development and its implications. There was relatively little movement on issues of energy and resource consumption, or global warming, as political attention on these issues has come primarily in negative terms, from the marketplace interests that would be most required to adjust to sustainability principles. See Dernbach and Widener Seminar on Law and Sustainability, U.S. Adherence to Its Agenda 21 Commitments: A Five-Year Review, 27 E.L.R. 10,504 (1997).

Rio's legal developments, noted above, may be seen as slightly more tangible than the physical progress to date. Some observers have indeed been upbeat about UNCED's accords.[72] Professor David Wirth's measured assessment, based on close textual comparisons, concludes that Rio was a tango, two steps forward and one back in some directions, and vice versa in others:

> Different components of the Rio Declaration fall on a variety of points along the spectrum of the development of international environmental law. Some, such as Principle 10 on public participation, are substantial innovations.... Others, such as Principle 12 on the Polluter-Pays Principle, Principle 15 on the precautionary approach, and Principle 17 on environmental impact assessment, reinforce and codify at the universal level a consensus that had been building in more or less linear fashion since Stockholm. But in the implied rejection of an individual right to a minimally acceptable environment, in Principle 2 on transboundary pollution, and in the treatment of intergenerational equity, some elements of the Rio Declaration amount to outright backtracking. In many aspects, the Rio Declaration falls short of the highest standards set by predecessor instruments, and a number of well-accepted doctrines were lost or watered down. And in some cases, such as Principle 12 on the Polluter-Pays Principle, the particular formulations chosen by the drafters of the Declaration contain provisions that border on incoherence.
>
> If the history of the Stockholm Declaration teaches anything, it is that the long-term significance of a nonbinding, aspirational statement of purpose such as the Rio Declaration...cannot be predicted with certainty. The trajectory of discrete components of such an instrument may vary considerably as states make selective use of individual principles. A number of areas in which the Rio Declaration articulates more rigorous requirements than previously acknowledged on the global level, such as environmental impact assessment, the Polluter-Pays Principle, public participation, and even precautionary

---

71. Executive Order No. 12,852 , June 29, 1993. The PCSD has task forces on Eco-Efficiency, Energy and Transportation, Natural Resources Management and Protection, Principles and Goals, Population, Education, Sustainable Agriculture, and Sustainable Communities. The PCSD produced an anecdotal report in March, 1996, offering general recommendations. The PCSD also recognizes companies which have implemented environmentally responsible programs which provide for sustainable development.

72. See Symposium, 8 J. NAT. RES. & ENVTL LAW Number 2 (1993)(several assessments written by UNCED participants).

approaches, have operative significance in the day-to-day formulation of environmental policy [and in practice states may strengthen these] from both the policy and legal points of view. By contrast, over time the portions of the Rio Declaration that most obviously represent a retreat from more demanding international precedents—most notably the portions [diluting] a right to environment, intergenerational equity, and the reformulation of states' obligations to refrain from transboundary pollution—may appear to be anachronistic assertions of territorial sovereignty that later are overwhelmed by the irresistible momentum of global interdependence in environmental matters. Wirth, The Rio Declaration on Environment and Development: Two Steps Forward and One Back, or Vice Versa?, 29 GA. L. Rev. 599 (1995).

3. **Multi-lateral conventions before and after Rio.** Perhaps the two most successful examples of international environmental restrictions are the Convention on International Trade in Endangered Species (CITES)[73] which has imposed effective import controls in signatory countries, and the 1987 Montreal Protocol on Substances that Deplete the Ozone Layer.[74] Faced with threats of increasing ultraviolet exposures because of stratospheric ozone depletion, the Montreal Protocol began a process for reducing or phasing out the production of chlorofluorocarbons, halons, and other chemicals known to damage stratospheric ozone. Because developing countries threatened nonparticipation in this legal system, developed country parties agreed to give them an additional ten years to comply with the reduction requirements and to provide them financial assistance for compliance. Although it is too early to say that the stratospheric ozone layer is no longer in danger, virtually all countries are honoring the protocol's requirements. One of the most inspiring scientific charts an international lawyer can ever see is the plotted curve of stratospheric ozone, showing a clear decrease in the rate of depletion beginning one year after the European Community brought its Montreal compliance rules into effect, showing that nations can sometimes act in their mutual self-interest on a global scale.

4. **The Rio Declaration.** For reference — and as an exercise in observing the tone and method of international accords — here are the 27 Principles of the Rio Declaration:

The United Nations Conference on Environment and Development, Having met at Rio de Janeiro from 3 to 14 June 1992, Reaffirming the Declaration of the United Nations Conference on the Human Environment, adopted at Stockholm on 16 June 1972, and seeking to build upon it, With the goal of establishing a new and equitable global partnership through the creation of new levels of cooperation among States, key sectors of societies and people, Working towards international agreements which respect the interests of all and protect the integrity of the global environmental and developmental system, Recognizing the integral and interdependent nature of the Earth, our home, *Proclaims* that:

---

73. Convention on International Trade in Endangered Species of Wild Fauna and Flora, Mar. 3, 1973, 27 UST 1087, TIAS No. 8249, 993 UNTS 243, the stimulus to passage of Chapter 14's Endangered Species Act of 1973. The trade bans of the Convention have been enforced under importation restrictions of the U.S. Customs Service at ports of entry. Under Article VI §2 of the U.S. Constitution, of course, ratified treaties become part of the "Supreme Law of the Land."

74. S. Treaty Doc. No. 100-10 (Sept. 16, 1987), reprinted in 26 I.L.M. 1550 (1987). The protocol has been amended and adjusted by the conference of the parties on a regular basis since then, including amendments made in London in 1990 to ban production of CFCs and most uses of halons.

**PRINCIPLE 1** Human beings are at the center of concerns for sustainable development. They are entitled to a healthy and productive life in harmony with nature.

**PRINCIPLE 2** States have, in accordance with the Charter of the United Nations and the principles of international law, the sovereign right to exploit their own resources pursuant to their own environmental and developmental policies, and the responsibility to ensure that activities within their jurisdiction or control do not cause damage to the environment of other States or of areas beyond the limits of national jurisdiction.

**PRINCIPLE 3** The right to development must be fulfilled so as to equitably meet developmental and environmental needs of present and future generations.

**PRINCIPLE 4** In order to achieve sustainable development, environmental protection shall constitute an integral part of the development process and cannot be considered in isolation from it.

**PRINCIPLE 5** All States and all people shall cooperate in the essential task of eradicating poverty as an indispensable requirement for sustainable development, in order to decrease the disparities in standards of living and better meet the needs of the majority of the people of the world.

**PRINCIPLE 6** The special situation and needs of developing countries, particularly the least developed and those most environmentally vulnerable, shall be given special priority. International actions in the field of environment and development should also address the interests and needs of all countries.

**PRINCIPLE 7** States shall cooperate in a spirit of global partnership to conserve, protect, and restore the health and integrity of the Earth's ecosystem. In view of the different contributions to global environmental degradation, States have common but differentiated responsibilities. The developed countries acknowledge the responsibility that they bear in the international pursuit of sustainable development in view of the pressures their societies place on the global environment and the technologies and financial resources they command.

**PRINCIPLE 8** To achieve sustainable development and a higher quality of life for all people, States should reduce and eliminate unsustainable patterns of production and consumption and promote appropriate demographic policies.

**PRINCIPLE 9** States should cooperate to strengthen endogenous capacity-building for sustainable development by improving scientific understanding through exchanges of scientific and technological knowledge, and by enhancing the development, adaptation, diffusion, and transfer of technologies, including new and innovative technologies.

**PRINCIPLE 10** Environmental issues are best handled with the participation of all concerned citizens, at the relevant level. At the national level, each individual shall have appropriate access to information concerning the environment that is held by public authorities, including information on hazardous materials and activities in their communities, and the opportunity to participate in decision-making processes. States shall facilitate and encourage public awareness and participation by making information widely available. Effective access to judicial and administrative proceedings, including redress and remedy, shall be provided.

**PRINCIPLE 11** States shall enact effective environmental legislation. Environmental standards, management objective and priorities should reflect the environmental and developmental context to which they apply. Standards applied by some countries may be inappropriate and of unwarranted economic and social cost to other countries, in particular developing countries.

**PRINCIPLE 12** States should cooperate to promote a supportive and open international economic system that would lead to economic growth and sustainable development in all countries, to better address the problems of environmental degradation. Trade policy measures for environmental purposes should not constitute a means of arbitrary or unjustifiable discrimination or a disguised restriction on international trade. Unilateral actions to deal with environmental challenges outside the jurisdiction of the importing country should be avoided. Environmental measures addressing transboundary or global environmental problems should, as far as possible, be based on an international consensus.

**PRINCIPLE 13** States shall develop national law regarding liability and compensation for the victims of pollution and other environmental damage. States shall also cooperate in an expeditious and more determined manner to develop further international law regarding liability and compensation for adverse effects of environmental damage caused by activities within their jurisdiction or control to areas beyond their jurisdiction.

**PRINCIPLE 14** States should effectively cooperate to discourage or prevent the relocation and transfer to other States of any activities and substances that cause severe environmental degradation or are found to be harmful to human health.

**PRINCIPLE 15** In order to protect the environment, the precautionary approach shall be widely applied by States according to their capabilities. Where there are threats of serious or irreversible damage, lack of full scientific certainty shall not be used as a reason for postponing cost-effective measures to prevent environmental degradation.

**PRINCIPLE 16** National authorities should endeavor to promote the internalization of environmental costs and the use of economic instruments, taking into account the approach that the polluter should, in principle, bear the cost of pollution, with due regard to the public interest and without distorting international trade and investment.

**PRINCIPLE 17** Environmental impact assessment, as a national instrument, shall be undertaken for proposed activities that are likely to have a significant adverse impact on the environment and are subject to a decision of a competent national authority.

**PRINCIPLE 18** States shall immediately notify other States of any natural disasters or other emergencies that are likely to produce sudden harmful effects on the environment of those States. Every effort shall be made by the international community to help States so afflicted.

**PRINCIPLE 19** States shall provide prior and timely notification and relevant information to potentially affected States on activities that may have a significant adverse transboundary environmental effect and shall consult with those States at an early stage and in good faith.

**PRINCIPLE 20** Women have a vital role in environmental management and development. Their full participation is therefore essential to achieve sustainable development.

**PRINCIPLE 21** The creativity, ideals, and courage of the youth of the world should be mobilized to forge a global partnership in order to achieve sustainable development and ensure a better future for all.

**PRINCIPLE 22** Indigenous people and their communities, and other local communities, have a vital role in environmental management and development because of their knowledge and traditional practices. States should recognize and duly support their identity, culture, and interests and enable their effective participation in the achievement of sustainable development.

**PRINCIPLE 23** The environment and natural resources of people under oppression, domination, and occupation shall be protected.

**PRINCIPLE 24** Warfare is inherently destructive of sustainable development. States shall therefore respect international law providing protection for the environment in times of armed conflict and cooperate in its further development, as necessary.

**PRINCIPLE 25** Peace, development, and environmental protection are interdependent and indivisible.

**PRINCIPLE 26** States shall resolve all their environmental disputes peacefully and by appropriate means in accordance with the Charter of the United Nations.

**PRINCIPLE 27** States and people shall cooperate in good faith and in a spirit of partnership in the fulfillment of the principles embodied in this Declaration and in the further development of international law in the field of sustainable development.

## Section 2. MUNICIPAL LEVERAGE AND EXTRATERRITORIAL LAW?

As the whaling example illustrates, the development of international law ultimately can build upon the actions of domestic law as well as the action of international organizations or treaties. Without NGO pressures applied through the U.S. and a few Western governments, efforts to apply IWC conservation restrictions would probably still be stalled. International environmental law must increasingly internalize the stalemate-breaking pressure mechanisms available through well-targeted municipal law.

Many treaties, of course, foresee local enforcement by domestic law. In this regard, the Convention on International Trade in Endangered Species led to enforcement actions by federal agencies in the United States, to federal statutes like the Endangered Species and Marine Mammal Protection Acts, and to legislation by states of the union. Trade in endangered species depends on markets in developed nations; to the extent that these markets (for furs, whale oil products, etc.) can be closed off, the incentive for killing is diminished. Local market restrictions are thus a practical avenue for enforcing the mandates of conventions without going through the burdensome process of hauling states to the ICJ, even where that is jurisdictionally possible. Similar domestic enforcement can usefully be applied in the settings of other international agreements.

**INTERNATIONAL ISSUES IN DOMESTIC COURTS...** Another way the courts of one nation may have international environmental impact is by extending their reach to include jurisdiction over incidents occurring abroad. When a U.S. company ships defective pharmaceuticals overseas to sell them in a Third World country, or designs its overseas chemical plants so as to invite subsequent disasters, the victims of these instrumentalities may be well advised to try to sue the defendants in a U.S. courtroom. Lawsuits filed in Bolivia, Nigeria, Indonesia, or India, for example, are less likely to draw upon the heightened tort law awareness of American common law and juries, as Bhopal revealed. (The doctrine of *forum non conveniens*, however, is often a bar to such actions.) Extended application of domestic jurisdiction can be quite dramatic. In Filartiga v. Pena-Irala, 630 F.2d 876 (2d Cir. 1980), 577 F. Supp. 860 (E.D.N.Y. 1984), a human rights case arising from the torture killing of a Paraguayan by a Paraguayan official in Paraguay, a U.S. district court nevertheless allowed a civil lawsuit to be brought in the United States when the plaintiff family was able to serve a complaint on defendant when he happened to be visiting Disney World. Could a village of Indonesian forest-dwellers bring suit in the U.S. against a Japanese timber corporation doing business in the U.S. for its environmental or "genocidal" depredations in mountainous areas of Borneo?

**DOMESTIC LEGISLATION WITH INTERNATIONAL EFFECTS...** At another level, there has been an insistent argument that domestic legislation like NEPA and the Endangered Species Act can have a beneficial effect on the world environment, by forcing American agencies that are involved with development projects abroad to comply with American environmental standards. One of the principles of the legal advisory group to the World Commission on Environment and Development was that states shall apply, as a minimum, at least the same standards for environmental conduct and impacts regarding transboundary resources and environmental interferences as are applied domestically — paraphrased officially as "Do not do to others what you would not do to your own citizens."[75] If the Federal Highway Administration is building a highway through virgin jungle in Panama, does NEPA apply? See Sierra Club v. Adams, 578 F.2d 389, 392 n.14 (D.C. Cir. 1978) (assuming that it does); and see also President Jimmy Carter's Executive Order 12, 114 (44 Fed. Reg. 1,957 (1979)), accepting the application of NEPA, though modifying some of its requirements in international projects by requiring only an EA. Does the Endangered Species Act apply when the United States Agency For International Development (AID) finances a development scheme that would destroy the jungle habitat of Sri Lankan elephants, or other such international projects? Lujan v. Defenders of Wildlife, 112 S.Ct. 2130 (1992) (decided, as noted in Chapter Seven, on grounds of standing) produced a concurring opinion from Justice Stevens concluding that the constraints of the Endangered Species Act do *not* apply to federal agency actions overseas. The D.C. Circuit, on the other hand, has applied NEPA to agency actions in Antarctica. EDF v. Massey, 986 F.2d 528 (1993). The environmental applications of extraterritorial jurisdiction are obvious, and still very much in evolution.

But is it proper for environmental law to use the legal pressure of a major state's legislation to force the adoption of international environmental conservation practices? Several examples of such "altruistic bullying" raise the issue.

In the international whaling controversy, a critical moment occurred when NGOs successfully pressured the U.S. Congress to pass the Pelly Amendment to the Fishermen's Protective Act.[76] Under this provision, upon certification by the Secretary of Commerce that any nation's actions "diminish the effectiveness of an international fishery conservation program," the President is empowered to bar all or a portion of the offending nation's fish products from the U.S. market. When presidential enforcement lagged, Congress in 1979 added the Packwood-Magnuson Amendment to the Fisheries Conservation and Management Act, requiring mandatory cuts in foreign fishing quotas within the 200-mile U.S. fishery conservation zone.[77] Backed by this unilateral market blackmail, U.S. negotiators

---

75. World Commission on Environment and Development (Brundtland Commission), Our Common Future, Annexe One, Principle 13 (1987).
76. Pub.L 92–219, 22 U.S.A. §1978 (1971).
77. Pub.L. 96–61, 16 U.S.C.A. §1821(e)(2).

persuaded Japan and Russia to abide by minke whale quotas, pushed Peru, Chile, and South Korea to join the IWC, and pressured Iceland and Japan to curtail "scientific" whaling.[78] Even though the Reagan administration persuaded its Supreme Court in the *Japan Whaling* case to enlarge the role of executive enforcement discretion,[79] the threat of unilateral statutory sanction exerted useful pressure and established a useful precedent for application in other areas of global concern.

**THE WORLD TRADE ORGANIZATION AND DOMESTIC LAWS...** Under the international General Agreement on Tariffs and Trade (GATT), conflicts between free-trade principles and environmental concerns have repeatedly surfaced. There have been several interesting backlashes against American legislative attempts to reinforce the IWC and other marine mammal conservation efforts. In 1991 Mexico (reportedly pushed by marketplace prompting from the U.S.[80]) won a provisional decision from a trade tribunal panel under the GATT that U.S. restrictions on tuna imports violated free trade principles. Mexican fishermen set nets around dolphins in order to capture the tuna swimming below, in a process that ends up slaughtering thousands of dolphins. Under the Pelly-Packwood legislation, these actions raise barriers to seafood imports from Mexico. Under Articles 11 and 20 of GATT, the panel held that the U.S. legislation could not be applied to have extraterritorial effect on production methods in the Mexican fleet because it was not "necessary" to prevent domestic human or ecological effects.[81] Fearful that the panel decision would sour congressional support for NAFTA, however, Mexico "deferred indefinitely" the referral of the panel's decision to the GATT Council. Because panel decisions at that time had no effect until referred and ratified at a council meeting, the issue died. A second almost identical tuna-dolphin complaint was brought by the European Community in 1994, and the same thing happened: the U.S. lost, but the panel decision was not referred to council.

Since then there has been little progress in integrating environmental values into the world of free trade. In 1994 the Uruguay Round of free trade negotiations concluded with the execution of a series of treaties and the establishment of the World Trade Organization (WTO). One of the major changes of the Uruguay Round was to amend the dispute resolution procedures: (1) to provide that dispute resolution panel reports would automatically be adopted and given legal effect unless there was council consensus that they should *not* be adopted (the reverse of the prior rule), and (2) to provide for an appellate process complete with a "standing appellate body."[82]

78. For an excellent though dispirited analysis see Wilkinson, The Use of Domestic Measures to Enforce International Whaling Agreements, 17 Denv. J. Int'l L. & Pol'y 2 (1989).

79. Japan Whaling Assoc. v. American Cetacean Society, 478 U.S. 221 (1986).

80. Divine Porpoise, World Politics & Current Affairs, The Economist, American Survey 31 (Oct. 5, 1991).

81. GATT Panel — U.S.: Restrictions on Imports of Tuna (September 3, 1991).

82. See the WTO website for information about its formation, purpose and institutions, as well as for the texts of all of the dispute resolution reports referenced below. http://www.wto.org. There have been three dispute resolution proceedings on environmental protection under the new process: (1)the U.S. Standards for Reformulated and Conventional Gasoline under the CAA, challenged by Brazil and Venezuela, was struck down; (2) the European Community Measures Affecting Meat and Meat Products (Hormones), a challenge brought by the U.S., struck down for insufficient scientific evidence; and (3) the U.S. Import Prohibition of Certain Shrimp and Shrimp Products challenged by India, Malaysia, Pakistan and Thailand, was struck down in 1998.

New conflicts — including a dramatic 1998 shrimp-turtle controversy — will not be so avoided in the future. Under the 1994 GATT the presumption is reversed, and all panel decisions are automatically referred for ratification unless there is a unanimous vote not to do so. In the shrimp-turtle case (where the netting of shrimp with low-tech netting procedures drowns hundreds of endangered sea turtles each year) the panel decided the case based on the preamble to Article 20, holding that the U.S. measure was "unjustifiable discrimination" on its face because only environmental reasons had been given for the trade embargo. The shrimp-turtle case is a clear example of the narrow horizons of the trade panels, and perhaps will operate as a catalyst to force a general re-appraisal in the course of the U.S. appeal of the panel decision.

The future course of such confrontations between international trade policy and international conservation policy is unclear. Stimulated by the tuna-dolphin controversy, the GATT Committee on Trade and Environment — which in its first 20 years of existence had never held a meeting — produced a report in 1995 calling for integration between environmental concerns and trade issues, though no formal policy or guideline has yet emerged.[83]

**DOMESTIC LEGISLATION AND MULTILATERAL LENDING INSTITUTIONS...** In the case of the World Bank and other multi-lateral development banks (MDBs), a coalition of NGOs applied the same kind of domestic legislative pressures to force international lenders to consider the negative effects of their development projects upon environmental quality and the rights of indigenous people. MDB projects had provided textbook examples of how development planners can disastrously ignore the predictable physical, environmental, and human consequences of their projects.[84] The NGOs persuaded a powerful member of the U.S. Senate to attach a rider to annual appropriations bills for funding the World Bank, instructing the U.S. Executive Director of the Bank not to vote for any project which violated these criteria. The effect of such pressure can be extraordinarily practical in achieving environmental quality improvements internationally. The fact remains that it was produced by a unilateral decision by one country to force its will on the community of nations or upon an IGO, and what works benignly in one case may be malign in another.

What is the international legal propriety of donor nation pressure on MDBs? Even if one assumes that quite salutary environmental reforms have been so instigated, the use of direct pressure on an international compact entity raises worrisome concerns in some observers' minds. No matter how altruistic, the fact remains that certain nations are able to have this effect upon the MDBs in part because they possess financial leverage on the Bank board. For constructive reforms on the international stage to rely upon altruistic bullying is a troubling concept indeed.

---

83. On Oct. 7, when it withdrew the matter on the day before the Council meeting, Mexico also announced its own domestic dolphin conservation program.

84. See Plater, Multi-lateral Lending Banks, Environmental Diseconomies, and the International Lending Process: The Example of Third World Dams, 9 Third World L.J. 169, 208–212 (1989) (on the problems and the legal propriety of such long-arm pressures).

The question is presented with particular clarity in the World Bank initiatives because there the Congress applied its pressure via direct statutory enactment. A spectrum of arguments may be applied to such situations. At one end of the spectrum is the opinion of those members of Congress who have attached or attempted to attach policy conditions to appropriations bills for funding international lending organizations. As one senator said, it is always the right of a sovereign people to determine how their taxpayer dollars are going to be spent; if legislators attach directive conditions to their funding bills, or threaten a cut-off of their taxpayers' contributions based on particular policy positions, that is no more than one would expect and demand as a right of a democratic people.

At the other end of the spectrum is the quite skeptical position taken by Dr. Ibrahim Shihata, Vice-President and General Counsel of the World Bank, arguing that all such unilateral threats or suasions applied by donor nations are improper and even *contra legem* under international agreements, unless the policy conditions are directly related to the economic integrity of the Bank and its loans to member states.

Somewhere in the middle between the two polar positions is the opinion of several MDB legal counselors who informally expressed a fundamental pragmatism about such donor-nation pressures on international lending. Indeed, political reality indicates that some unilateral pressure on MDBs is completely inevitable and will take place regardless of whether or not it is formal or informal, direct or indirect, linked to economic concerns or not. From this middle perspective, the application of pressure to the appointees of member states, or to the elected representatives of blocks of member states, is perhaps best regarded with a shrug. In any event, the compromise position would note, the directives are typically not an attempt to *bind* the MDB organization as such.

According to the middle position, then, the only case where donor nations' political interference with lending decisions becomes *contra legem* is the case where political considerations lead to rescission in whole or part of a member state's prior commitment to contribute a specified amount of funding. In such cases a prior binding international agreement is being unilaterally abrogated. In other situations, including conditional refusals to commit further supplementary contributions, a member state is merely exercising its right to contract or to decline to do so.

**NAFTA, AND MORE TRADE vs. ENVIRONMENT QUESTIONS...** As the clashes between the WTO and U.S. tuna and sea turtle regulations illustrated, there is a sharp tension between protection of environmental values and today's energetic free-trade doctrines. The international marketplace economy, speaking through the GATT panels, strenuously resists acknowledging the civic-societal economics of the global commons. Regulation is deemed legitimate only when it is motivated by needs within the regulating sovereignty.

NAFTA, the 1994 North American Free Trade Agreement, illustrates the tension in two directions. Most environmental citizen groups were skeptical of the NAFTA proposal, fearing that it would make production and trade mechanisms dominant over environmental concerns in the Mexico, the U.S., and Canada, encouraging more of the rampant pollution and cynicism of the "maquiladora" factory system where companies put subsidiaries on the Mexican side of the border to take advantage of lax environmental controls and low labor costs. To persuade some groups to back the pact, terms were added to NAFTA discouraging each country from lowering its own environmental standards in efforts to encourage investment (NAFTA Chapter 11), and tacking on some environmental Side Agreement provisions — a Commission on Environmental Cooperation (CEC) to promote joint environmental efforts and hear complaints about failures to enforce environmental laws; a Border Environmental Cooperation Commission (BECC) to develop clean-up projects and certify projects for financing; and a North American Development Bank (NADBank) to arrange financing for BECC projects, with a promised $2 billion in funding.

One tension comes from GATT: complaints that NAFTA's Chapter 11 and Side Bar accords violate international free trade principles. The other comes from within NAFTA: resistance from its trade mechanisms to the application of environmental concerns. In a leaked internal report, Victor Lichtinger, the CEC's executive director, complained about the domination of CEC efforts by trade ministries in each of the three countries of NAFTA's implementation. The CEC itself has failed to issue enforcement orders in response to citizen complaints. Corporate flight to cross-border maquiladoras has increased rather than decreased — 300 in 1995 alone — and virtually no money was has been spent to cleanse the border pollution havens or enforce the laws Mexico has on its books. Thus when attempts were made to add Chile to NAFTA on a fast track, virtually all environmental and labor groups joined to defeat the bill. Free traders and environmental concerns don't seem to mix.[85]

### Section 3. PROCEDURAL REFORMS

Faced with the difficulty of defining substantive standards for environmental protection, another interesting trend can be discerned in concerned jurists' exploration of the efficacy of procedural approaches to international environmental quality. Broad scale requirements for environmental impact statement procedures are an obvious example. More than 20 countries have adopted some form of environment assessment requirement, as well as a number of IGOs, including lending institutions, in order to implement the common sense rationality of looking broadly and carefully before you leap. The problem, of course, is that, as the NEPA experience reveals in the United States, the pressures of short-term economic profit making and political momentum tend to undercut the broad principles represented by environmental impact assessment. Nations as well as federal agencies play with the definition of what is a "significant" project affecting the environment, and with the specificity required in the statements themselves.

---

85. See Atick, Environmental Standards Within NAFTA: Difference By Design and the Retreat from Harmonization, 3 Ind. J. of Global Legal Studies, 81, 89 (1995); Magraw, NAFTA's Repercussions: Is Green Trade Possible? Environment, Mar. 1994 at 14, 40; Wirth, Internat'l Trade Agreements: Vehicles for Reform? 1997 U. Chi. Leg. Forum 331; Garvey, Trade Law and Quality of Life: Dispute Resolution under the NAFTA Side Accords on Labor and the Environment, 89 Am. J. Int'l L. 439 (1995); Public Citizen's Global Trade Watch, the Institute for Policy Studies, and the Sierra Club, The Failed Experiment: NAFTA at Three Years (1997).

Other commentators have focused on a specific express or implied "duty to inform or disclose," the kind of requirement that was expressly included in the post-Chernobyl nuclear notification convention. Such a duty encounters similar problems in defining what relevant and available information must be disclosed and how quickly and how specifically it must be revealed. Because states perceive the specific obligation of prior disclosure as contrary to their interests, the duty is abstracted to such a level of generality that states may plausibly construe a wide range of conduct to satisfy the obligation.[86]

Yet another procedural approach is to add periodic official review and report procedures to international conventions. Thus in the 1987 Montreal Protocol on ozone depletion, the 1988 Sofia Protocol on long range air pollution, and the 1989 Basel Convention on the Control of Transboundary Movements of Hazardous Wastes and Their Disposal, each of the agreements was limited in the stringency of substantive requirements for which it could achieve ratification, but provided for subsequent high-level investigation and regular reporting. It is a technique that forces nation states to remain sensitive to the factual realities of an issue and to world opinion, and may thereby promote compliance with standards higher than the lowest common denominator.

## Section 4. NGOs

Clearly, the legitimacy of NGOs on the world stage has evolved over the last 20 years, with major legal consequences. With the ongoing delegitimation of authoritarian states, there is the prospect that lessons of pluralism developed in the American environmental movement will be echoed by enfranchising the voices of concerned citizens in states throughout the world community. The role of NGOs continues to have special impact in the environmental area, as NGOs participate actively in the councils of IGOs and international law. If the ILO model noted above is applied to international environmental organizations like UNEP, nongovernmental voices will be straightforwardly incorporated into official international discourse.

Pending such official incorporation of NGOs, the current confrontational adversarial/negotiation model of interaction between NGOs and IGOs is likely to continue. The role of indigenous Third World NGOs is growing, owing not only to philosophical principle but also to the fact that local NGOs are often the only accurate source of information on projects and their consequences.

Where indigenous NGOs lack the resources and sophistication to mount campaigns in international capitals, there is also a growing tendency for developed nations' NGOs to set up "partnerships" with Third World groups, to their mutual benefit.

Until the international community creates adjudicatory mechanisms to give aggrieved members of the public in developing countries direct access to the foreign aid decision-making process, the partnership model of public policy advocacy is the best prospect for improving the environmental quality of development assistance.... Partnerships with overseas counterparts enhance the legitimacy, efficacy, and accuracy of American environmental activism on

---

86. Developments — International Environmental Law, 104 Harv. L Rev. 1484, 1518 (1991).

these issues. Over time, and with continued successes, such partnerships may pave the way for greater accountability in development assistance and, ultimately, international legal processes generally. Wirth, Legitimacy, Accountability, and Partnership: A Model for Advocacy on Third World Environmental Issues, 101 Yale L.J. 2645 (1991).

### Section 5. MORE INTERNATIONAL TRADE MECHANISMS: ISO 14000

The International Standards Organization (ISO) has begun to adopt ISO 14000-series voluntary uniform standards to integrate environmental responsibility into corporate management practices. Companies adopt such management standards in order to be awarded ISO certification, which because of wide voluntary adherence facilitates their ability to do business throughout the world. In essence, ISO 14000 represents a market-driven privatizing approach to environmental protection that is potentially more effective in achieving significant environmental improvements than traditional "command and control" regulatory methods, especially regulation on the international level.

ISO 14001 is entitled "Environmental Management Systems — Specification." Other elements of ISO 14000 (such as labeling, environmental auditing and life cycle analysis) will be considered only guidelines for the present. A central element of the ISO 14001 standard is the "Environmental Policy" defined by an organization's top management, implemented by a formal internal oversight system to ensure that the environmental policy is carried out by the organization. This involves planning, implementation and operations, checking and corrective action, and management review. To gain ISO 14000 certification companies have to establish procedures to identify environmental aspects of all their activities in order to determine which have significant impacts, documenting environmental objectives and targets and include a commitment to the prevention of pollution. In addition, they have to train all personnel whose work may significantly affect the environment and create auditing systems to ensure that the program is properly implemented and maintained.

The ISO system is a fascinating study: an unprecedented marketplace initiative aiming to internalize civic-societal standards into private sector actions globally. It has already begun to produce significant market effects, especially for corporations seeking to do business with the European Union, where consumers and the civic cultures attach a premium to environmentally rational practices. In other sectors of the marketplace — like the billion-consumer market of China, whose environmental practices are grossly lax — ISO initiatives are likely to be ineffective.

### Section 6. INTERGENERATIONAL EQUITY

In ongoing discussions of international environmental policy, increasing prominence is being found for a principle that echoes the public trust doctrine in environmental law. Called variously the theory of "intergenerational equity" or the principle of "common heritage of human kind," its message is that in fundamental ethical terms no present generation has the right to consider itself the ultimate decisionmaker for global ecological changes. The doctrine is presented in the following excerpt from the work of Professor Edith Brown Weiss.

### Edith Brown Weiss, Our Rights and Obligations
### to Future Generations for the Environment
### 84 American Journal of International Law 198 (1990)

We, the human species, hold the natural environment of our planet in common with all members of our species: past generations, the present generation, and future generations.[87] As members of the present generation, we hold the earth in trust for future generations. At the same time, we are beneficiaries entitled to use and benefit from it.

There are two relationships that must shape any theory of intergenerational equity in the context of our natural environment: our relationship to other generations of our own species and our relationship to the natural system of which we are a part.

The human species is integrally linked with other parts of the natural system; we both affect and are affected by what happens in the system. The natural system, contrary to popular belief, is in many ways a hostile one. Deserts, glaciers, volcanoes, tsunamis can bring havoc to our species. Moreover, the natural environment can be toxic to our species, as through the natural toxicity of some plants and animals or the dramatic release of toxic clouds of carbon dioxide from Lake Nyos in the Cameroon, which killed 1,700 people. On the other hand, the natural system makes life possible for us. It gives us the resources with which to survive and to improve human welfare.

Our actions affect the natural system. We alone among all living creatures have the capacity to shape significantly our relationship to the environment. We can use it on a sustainable basis or we can degrade environmental quality and the natural resource base. As part of the natural system, we have no right to destroy its integrity; nor is it in our interest to do so. Rather, as the most sentient of living creatures, we have a special responsibility to care for the planet.

The second fundamental relationship is that between different generations of the human species. All generations are inherently linked to other generations, past and future, in using the common patrimony of earth.

To define intergenerational equity, it is useful to view the human community as a partnership among all generations. In describing a state as a partnership, Edmund Burke observed that "as the ends of such a partnership cannot be obtained in many generations, it becomes a partnership not only between those who are living but between those who are living, those who are dead, and those who are to be born."[88] The purpose of human society must be to realize and protect the welfare and well-being of every generation. This requires sustaining the life-support systems of the planet, the ecological processes and the environmental conditions necessary for a healthy and decent human environment.

In this partnership, no generation knows beforehand when it will be the living generation, how many members it will have, or even how many generations there will ultimately be. It is useful, then, to take the perspective of a generation that is placed somewhere along the spectrum of time, but does not know in advance where it will be located.[89] Such a generation would want to inherit the earth in at

---

87. See E. Brown Weiss, In Fairness to Future Generations: International Law, Common Patrimony and Intergenerational Equity (1989).

88. E. Burke, Reflections on the Revolution in France 139-40 (1790), in 2 Works of Edmund Burke 368 (London 1854).

89. See J. Rawls, A Theory of Justice (1971).

least as good condition as it has been in for any previous generation and to have as good access to it as previous generations. This requires each generation to pass the planet on in no worse condition than it received it in and to provide equitable access to its resources and benefits. Each generation is thus both a trustee for the planet with obligations to care for it and a beneficiary with rights to use it.

Intergenerational equity calls for equality among generations in the sense that each generation is entitled to inherit a robust planet that on balance is at least as good as that of previous generations. This means that all generations are entitled to at least the planetary health that the first generation had. In practice, some generations may improve the environment, with the result that later generations will inherit a richer and more diverse natural resource base. In this case, they would be treated better than previous generations. But this extra benefit would be consistent with intergenerational equity, because the minimum level of planetary robustness would be sustained and later generations would not be worse off than previous generations. The converse is also possible, that later generations would receive a badly degraded environment with major loss of species diversity, in which case they would be treated worse than previous generations. This latter case would be contrary to principles of intergenerational equity. Equity among generations provides for a minimum floor for all generations and ensures that each generation has at least that level of planetary resource base as its ancestors. This concept is consistent with the implicit premises of trusteeship, stewardship and tenancy, in which the assets must be conserved, not dissipated, so that they are equally available to those who come after....

I have proposed three basic principles of intergenerational equity. First, each generation should be required to conserve the diversity of the natural and cultural resource base, so that it does not unduly restrict the options available to future generations in solving their problems and satisfying their own values, and should also be entitled to diversity comparable to that enjoyed by previous generations. This principle is called "conservation of options." Second, each generation should be required to maintain the quality of the planet so that it is passed on in no worse condition than that in which it was received, and should also be entitled to planetary quality comparable to that enjoyed by previous generations. This is the principle of "conservation of quality." Third, each generation should provide its members with equitable rights of access to the legacy of past generations and should conserve this access for future generations. This is the principle of "conservation of access."

Planetary rights and obligations coexist in each generation. In the intergenerational dimension, the generations to which the obligations are owed are future generations, while the generations with which the rights are linked are past generations. Thus, the rights of future generations are linked to the obligations of the present generation. In the intergenerational context, planetary obligations and rights exist between members of the present generation. They derive from the intergenerational relationship that each generation shares with those who have come before and those yet to come. Thus intergenerational obligations to conserve the planet flow from the present generation both to future generations as generations and to members of the present generation, who have the right to use and enjoy the planetary legacy.

## Section 7. "SOFT LAW"

In a fascinating article surveying innovative approaches to practical environmental protection through international law, Peter Sand explores a variety of tacks for circumventing constraints imposed by 170+ jealous national sovereignties.[90] One of his interesting inquiries focuses on "soft law" —

> States may decide to forgo treaty-making altogether and to recommend common rules of conduct by joint declarations — usually referred to as "soft law" to distinguish them from the "hard law" of formal legal agreements. Environmental diplomacy has produced a wide variety of such declaratory instruments and resolutions. Their recognized practical advantage is that since they are not subject to national ratification, they can take instant effect. Their inherent risk, however, is precisely that lack of formality that makes them attractive as a shortcut....

> One of the most prolific makers of soft law has been the UNEP Governing Council. Since 1978, the UNEP has addressed a whole series of "environmental law guidelines and principles" to states, drafted in typical treaty language except for the copious use of "should" in the place of "shall." Once adopted by ad hoc groups of experts nominated by governments, these provisions normally are approved by the UNEP Governing Council for submission to the UN General Assembly, which either incorporates them in resolution (as in the case of the 1982 World Charter for Nature) or, less solemnly, recommends them to states for use in the formulation of international agreements or national legislation (as in the case of the 1982 Conclusions of the Study of Legal Aspects Concerning the Environment Related to Offshore Mining and Drilling Within the Limits of National Jurisdiction). In a number of cases, however, promulgation did not go beyond the level of a UNEP Governing Council decision (e.g., the 1980 Provisions for Co-operation Between States on Weather Modification).

> Soft law may be "hardened" by later international practice. When the government of Uganda, under gentle World Bank pressure, had to consult other Nile Basin countries on a proposed water use project for Lake Victoria in December 1983, it did so by way of reference to, among other documents, the 1978 UNEP Principles of Conduct in the Field of the Environment for the Guidance of States in the Conservation and Harmonious Utilization of Natural Resources Shared by Two or More States. Three months later, the governments of Egypt and Sudan in their replies in turn referred to the guidelines as "jointly honored principles of cooperation," thereby quietly promoting them to the status of common regional standards. UNEP soft law instruments have also served [in the area of hazardous wastes and chemical notification compacts] as forerunners of treaty law.... Sand, Lessons Learned in Global Environmental Governance, 18 Envtl Aff. L. Rev. 213, 239–240 (1991).

Professor Sand's pragmatic patience for non-mandatory soft law declarations, when no hard law document is feasible, may explain why the UNCED's "Non-Legally Binding Authoritative Statement of Principles for a Global Consensus on the Management, Conservation and Sustainable Development of All Types of Forests"[91] is not an oxymoron.

---

90. Sand, Lessons Learned in Global and Environmental Governance, 18 Envtl Aff. L. Rev. 213 (1991).
91. U.N. Doc. A/CONF.151/6/Rev. 1 (1992), reprinted in 31 I.L.M. 881 (1992).

## Section 8. **THE NORTH-SOUTH SPLIT**

A fundamental fact of international environmental law is the great difference between the "North," the developed world, and the "South," the less-developed world. Developed countries are pleased to urge less developed countries to conserve their forests, mountains and wilderness, to halt destructive burning, and the like. LDCs resent any limitations on their efforts to follow industrial societies into greater economic productivity. They point the finger at developed countries for generating the vast amount of past pollution, and the majority of present carbon dioxide and CFCs plaguing the global environment. The debate has led to calls for global redistribution of economic resources and a constraint on self-righteous preaching by developed countries to forbid the kind of environmental despoliation that accompanied their own economic industrial development. The issue led to acrimonious controversy over equitable distribution of benefits among developing and developed countries in the context of deep seabed mining in the Law of the Sea (LOS) treaties. Mzee Jomo Kenyatta, the first president of Kenya, argued in his Arusha Principle that if the North wishes LDCs to take care of the world environment, the North should help pay for it. The Montreal ozone protocol actually put money where that message was, providing for a $240 million CFC "transition fund" to help pay for the cost of converting LDCs to less ozone-destructive chemical materials. Given the votes possessed by each state in IGOs and the United Nations, irrespective of economic strength or population, it is evident that some form of accommodation between rich and poor nations will increasingly be a part of international agreements for environmental protection. "The primary goal of the Earth Summit was to lay the foundation for a global partnership between developing and more industrialized countries based on mutual need and common interests to ensure the future of the planet," declared Maurice Strong, Secretary General of the United Nations' Rio Conference.

## Section 9. **ONE WORLD, ONE TRIBE?**[92]

The global reality of environmental law is the indivisibility of environmental causes and effects. Over the past decades many jurists have wistfully hoped for the emergence and growth of legal mechanisms of international cooperation and coordination to cope with the environmental and economic realities of global interconnectedness. Some have hoped for some form of One World government. Many have watched the development of the European Community as an extraordinarily important experiment in supra-national law. In the 1980s, the European Community began moving toward integration of legal systems and affirmation of continental environmental norms.

There is a corresponding centrifugal tendency, however, that has lately been painfully evident around the world, with corollaries in environmental law .

A fundamental stumbling block in international law noted throughout this chapter has been the jealously-held sovereignties of 170[+] independent nation-states, states that often were created — and behave — without regard to the

---

92. The text of this section is adapted from Plater, A Modern Political Tribalism in Natural Resources Management, 11 Public Land L. Rev. 1 (1990).

common setting in which they exist. In the past several years, the pressures of divisive fractionalizing have dramatically expanded rather than diminished. Hungarians and Romanians, Serbs and Croats, Uzbeks and Kirghiz, Armenians and Azerbaijanis, Russians and Chechen-Ingushis, Hmung and Vietnamese — these insular allegiances represent a powerful human tendency to seek communal identity in narrowed terms.[93]

These insularizing tendencies can be seen within the domestic legal realm as well, including environmental law. Modern politics is characterized in many theaters, including environmental protection and natural resources management, by battlelines of narrow single-issue combatants and factional allegiances.

In fact, under the pressures of modern circumstances the governing metaphor for human relationships — local, regional, national, and international — may be atavistic tribalism.

TRIBALISM... Viewing the narrowed perspectives and localized interests of contemporary natural resources decisionmaking as "tribalism" offers a useful analytical perspective on its symptoms and consequences. Tribalism, as the anthropologists describe it, denotes the way groups of people live in a form of cohesive affiliation and narrowed community of interest, systematically including all members of that community, and deprecating or excluding all others as "outsiders."[94]

Tribalism has both positive and negative attributes. Both are periodically revealed in international and domestic legal systems,[95] and environmental conflicts often reflect the tensions of such latter-day tribalism. In an unfortunate paradox, moreover, preclusive local, national, and international tribalisms seem to increase the more that there are strains and limitations upon resource systems and the global commons, and in precisely those circumstances where increased integration and cooperation would seem to be most necessary.

In some circumstances it is drastically important that narrowed, localized "tribal" interests be represented at the heart of complex management decisions. It appears to be a completely functional instinct on the part of many of us, when faced with the complexity and stresses of modern politics and economics, to seek out a narrower affinity rather than to trust to some broader community. Even today, tribalism functions as a utilitarian phenomenon rather than a mere atavistic

---

93. Germany's reunification marked a reinvigoration of nationalism rather than the contrary international tendency. It is not at all clear that the European Community's supra-national experiments for resolving shared problems can survive the nationalistic fervors unleashed in Eastern Europe and the resurrection of the German nation. The trend previously was clear: the European Community's environmental policies were going to act as a matrix model for the rest of the world. Now the passions of that process may be going in the opposite direction.

94. A characteristic of tribalism that separates it from mere civic groupings within the body politic is its members' intense sense of internal identification and loyalty, one with the other, amounting to a broad and cohesive extended familyhood, with, moreover, a sense of focus that all share as a common mission the advancement of tribal interests as a top priority.

95. In the international realm, besides the diverse sovereignties, there are religious tribes, North-South tribes, haves and have-nots.... In Washington, D.C. it would seem quite realistic for a political anthropologist to discern the existence of a Sun Belt tribe and a Rust Belt tribe, an Urban tribe and a Farm Country tribe, a Pork-barrel public works subsidy tribe and an Environmental tribe, a Pro-life tribe and a Pro-choice tribe, and perhaps others — a Black tribe and a White tribe and so on.

throwback. If we wish to be heard, and to have our interests reflected in governmental decisions, we trust more to the focused pressures of our affiliated tribe than
to our marginal individual weight in governmental processes.

There is, however, a countervailing peril in tribalism. One of the fundamental
tragedies of many Third-World societies is that the nature of tribalism, by definition a narrowed, non-comprehensive, preclusive affiliation, seeks to dominate and
pre-empt all other interests. A tribalism may bring important information and
policy considerations into a decision, but if it completely dominates the decision,
its effects will only be rational in terms of the interests it represents. Tribal
localisms have a valid place in the consideration of resource decisionmaking; the
problem is to what extent a tribal localism should be accorded dominating or determinative weight in a decisional system.

Ultimately the balance comes down to a perplex of pluralistic democracy. A
diversity of tribal voices is critically important to coping with the breadth and
depth of complex realities we face on the planet. But tribal voices are inherently
unreliable, unless they can cultivate an instinct for the integration of external
views. We may aspire as a goal to rise above tribalism: a triumphal process of
research, intellectual analysis, and forward-looking coordination of human activities, necessarily encompassing an overarching comprehensive rationality, is certainly one of the implicit objectives of futurists, academics, political philosophers,
and our own profession. But perhaps that asks too much of human nature and the
human intellect.[96] If the future of the planet is to be a long-term proposition in
which humans continue to play a part, however, we should strive to play the role
of shepherds, acting in a cohesive, integrated, planet-wide systematic perspective.
Decisions affecting the equilibrium and natural balance of this fragile place
increasingly require comprehensive thought and cooperation.

Faced with the problems posed by contentious sovereignties and a human tendency in the face of adversity to move toward tribalism, perhaps we will find international law moving toward a single tribalism, a global tribalism, as ironically
predicted a generation ago by Aldous Huxley.[97] In the end it may be politics and
social evolution, not law, that build the requisite foundations for international
environmental protection.

---

96. As Shaw said, socialism doesn't work because it takes too many evenings.

97. "I don't see that it's in the least likely that we shall be able to breed a race of beings, at any rate
within the next few thousand years, sufficiently intelligent to be able to form a stable non-tribal
society.... In a few generations it may be that the whole planet will be covered by one vast American
tribe." Chelifer and Cardan in A. Huxley, Those Barren Leaves (1925). Tribalism, if we all feel ourselves part of the same tribe, would get us to the same destination of an integrated organic planetary
rationality.

# Afterword:

# FACING THE FUTURE

*For two reasons, our generation will bear a heavier responsibility for the future of planet Earth than any generation before it has. First, we know better — having gained access to an unprecedented wealth of new scientific information and a vastly improved capacity for analysis and prediction. Second, we can do better — having accumulated enough experience, technological and institutional, to take the necessary...action.*[1]

Predicting the future of environmental law — a field characterized by diverse legal approaches to scientific uncertainty — is itself a risky venture. Environmental law has evolved in response to unexpected and unsettling discoveries and events. Rachel Carson's identification of the pernicious effects of DDT chains in natural systems led directly to major revisions of the Federal Insecticide, Fungicide, and Rodenticide Act; the Environmental Defense Fund's discovery of toxic chemicals in the lower Mississippi River, which serves as the potable water supply for New Orleans, was instrumental in the enactment of the Safe Drinking Water Act; the Kepone debacle resulted in developments in common law and criminal law, and was partially responsible for the passage of the Resource Conservation and Recovery Act; and the Exxon-Valdez disaster has already stimulated the passage of a new Oil Pollution Act (OPA '90), and is initiating innovations in other areas of law as well. Why should the future of environmental law be any more predictable than its first decades?

Nevertheless, we can discern comparatively recent but established legal trends that are likely to continue into the foreseeable future. Some of these developments have been discussed in previous chapters: the dynamic growth of toxic tort law; the application of corporate, contract, and property law concepts to environmental issues; the increasing interactions between common law and statutes; the evolution of environmental criminal law; the unfolding of the public trust doctrine; the tension and competition between federal and state governments; the wrangling over competing uses of public lands; the increasingly sophisticated implementation of market incentives for pollution control; new types of environmental land-use mechanisms; the increased use of alternative dispute resolution; and the emergence of international environmental law.

There will be further amendments, extensions, applications, administrative and judicial interpretations, and enforcement (and nonenforcement) of existing environmental statutes. Congress may enact a limited number of new federal statutes — which may appear as amendments to existing acts — covering areas

---

1. Peter Sand, Lessons Learned in Global Environmental Governance, 18 Envtl. Aff. L. Rev. 1 (1990).

ignored or inadequately addressed by prior federal legislation, like groundwater pollution, indoor air pollution, and protection of biodiversity. Even though the emphasis during the next twenty years of environmental law will probably be on the implementation, fine-tuning, and interpretation of existing federal statutes, we must always be prepared for the revelations or catastrophes that galvanize the creation of new environmental law. And if the federal government shows increasing laxity in its approach to environmental protection, then — as in the field of civil rights — the cutting edge of the law will move to state legislatures and courts, and to the international realm.

**A TRIAD OF ENVIRONMENTAL CHALLENGES...** Professor Arnold Rietze pointed out that global environmental degradation can be attributed to three categories of human activity — population, consumption, and pollution — and of the three only the last (which is perhaps least important) has received major attention.[2]

**POPULATION...** There are currently between 5 and 6 billion people on earth. Because population grows exponentially, unless we have a global nuclear war or widespread famine and disease, by 2100 the earth's population will be 10.4 billion — more than twice that in 1988. Most of the increase will take place in the impoverished Third World.

Lester R. Brown of the Worldwatch Institute describes the environmental consequences of what has been called the Population Bomb:

> Ecologists looking at biological indicators ... see rising human demand, driven by population growth and rising affluence, surpassing the carrying capacity of local forests, grasslands, and soils in country after country. They see sustainable yield thresholds of the economy's natural support systems being breached throughout the Third World. And as a result, they see the natural resource base diminishing even as population growth is expanding.... Continuing rapid population growth and spreading environmental degradation have trapped hundreds of millions in a downward spiral of falling incomes and growing hunger. With the number of people caught in this life-threatening cycle increasing each year, the world may soon be forced to reckon with the consequence of years of population policy neglect.[3]

But population control runs afoul of deep-seated moral and religious convictions and human instincts, and comes close to being an intractable challenge.

**CONSUMPTION...** Critics of our inefficient, wasteful, consumption-oriented "throwaway" society advocate modes of sustainable economic activity that maintain a long-term equilibrium between production and ecological integrity.

William Ruckelshaus, a former EPA Administrator and now the Chief Executive Officer of the world's largest waste handling firm, notes the shift toward concepts of sustainability:

> Sustainability is a nascent doctrine that economic growth and development must take place, and be maintained over time, within limits set by ecology in the broadest sense — by the interrelations of human beings and their works, the biosphere, and the physical and chemical laws that govern it. The doctrine

---

2. Reitze, Environmental Policy — It Is Time for a New Beginning, 14 Colum. J. Envtl. L. 111 (1989).
3. In Population: The Neglected Issue, Worldwatch Institute, State of the World 1991, 15–18.

of sustainability holds to that the spread of a reasonable level of prosperity and security to the less developed nations is essential to protecting ecological balance and hence essential to the continued prosperity of the wealthy nations. It follows that environmental protection and economic development are complementary rather than antagonistic processes....[4]

For Ruckelshaus, the fundamental principles of a sustainable economy would be to recognize that:

- The human species is part of nature. Its existence depends on its ability to draw sustenance from a finite world; its continuance depends on its ability to abstain from destroying the natural systems that regenerate this world....

- Economic activity must account for the [full] environmental costs of production....

- The maintenance of a liveable global environment depends on the sustainable development of the entire human family.

Globally, as the Brundtland Commission declared, the concept of Sustainable Development is not just an aesthetic good; it is a necessary principle for long-term survivability. It involves not only the prevention of global threats such as global warming and ozone depletion, but also the assurance that citizens of less developed nations will receive equitable material treatment.[5]

Sustainability also means a commitment to maximizing biodiversity, both because other species may be necessary for human well-being, and also because all species are essential participants in ecological integrity. Sustainability cannot be achieved without conservation — of resources, of energy, and of a quality existence for all species on earth. Reaching a state of sustainability will certainly require the moderation of the wasteful modes of life that have become instinctive in some affluent nations.

**POLLUTION...** Pollution control efforts will become increasingly proactive, emphasizing pollution prevention rather than the infernal complexities of end-of-pipe command and control systems and cleanup liability.

The Pollution Prevention Act of 1990[6] illustrates that trend. Its basic premise is that source reduction "is fundamentally different and more desirable than waste management and pollution control." It envisions source reduction as a win/win opportunity for EPA and the regulated community because of "significant opportunities for industry to reduce or prevent pollution at the source through cost-effective changes in production, operation, and raw material use." These changes, in turn, ensure "reduced raw material, pollution control, and liability costs as well as help to protect the environment and reduce risks to worker health and safety."

---

4. Toward a Sustainable World, 261 Scientific American (No. 1) 166,167-68 (Sept. 1989).
5. Adlai Stevenson, who supplied the image of Spaceship Earth with which the Introduction to this casebook began more than a thousand pages ago, continued by saying that —

> We cannot maintain it half fortunate, half miserable, half confident, half dispairing, half slave to the ancient enemies of mankind, half free in a liberation of resources undreamed of until this day. No craft, no crew, can travel safely with such vast contradictions. On their resolution depends the survival of us all.

6. Pub. L. 101-508, Title VI, §§6601-6610, 42 U.S.C.A. §§13101–13119.

The most forceful language in the statute is its unequivocal declaration of policy:

> The Congress hereby declares it to be the national policy of the United States
> that pollution should be prevented or reduced at the source whenever feasible;
> pollution that cannot be prevented should be recycled and should be treated in
> an environmentally safe manner whenever feasible; and disposal or other
> release into the environment should be employed only as a last resort and
> should be conducted in an environmentally safe manner.

Thus far, pollution prevention has been hortatory rather than mandatory, but
EPA possesses the legal authority to include pollution prevention requirements in
permits and enforcement settlements; agencies in other nations are already far
along that trail.

### EVOLVING PRINCIPLES AND PROCESSES:

**SUSTAINABILITY...** "Sustainable development" is a powerful guiding concept carried into the new millenium. It is both a progressive and a conservative principle,
compelling to any human analysis concerned beyond the shortest short term. We
owe it to ourselves and our posterity to improve the quality of life on earth, stew-
arding the legacy of the resources we inherited, and not destroying the environmental birthright of future generations for the needs and profits of today. Healthy
societal economic systems are founded upon healthy and sustainable ecological
system cycles of soil, water, air, and living communities, human and all the others.
Development must not be based upon an erosive diminution of global assets, but
rather on governance systems of indefinitely extendable human sustenance and
life quality, in balance with the resource capacity of the planet's environments.

**INTEGRATED ENVIRONMENTAL PLANNING AND MANAGEMENT...** Throughout
this book we have provided examples of the traditional, incremental, medium-spe-
cific and site-specific approach to environmental protection. We can no longer
afford, however — either in an economic or an environmental sense — to hold to
this narrow and reactive style of environmental management. The resulting array
of laws is in too many ways an uncoordinated, unruly mess that is ineffective, or,
even worse, counter-productive.

A more integrated approach is inevitably necessary. An integrated overview
would consider the cumulative impacts and multi-media exposures threatened by
a potential polluting or resource-depleting activity or series of activities, facilitating more accurate assessments of risk, with attendant improvements in setting
environmental protection priorities and issuing permits. The most salient problem
with integrated environmental control is implementation. Institutions capable of
making the necessary holistic assessments are not yet in existence, and the track
record of governmental central management systems does not inspire confidence.
The inertia and institutional investments of the present fragmented systems
assure that any fundamental reorienting will meet with specific resistance. But
principles of integrated overview are ultimately unavoidable, and must eventually
be built into the diverse mechanisms that drive our societies.

**INSTITUTIONALIZED CAUTION...** Institutionalized caution — a principle enunciated in the Endangered Species Act that also serves more broadly as a general reminder of the importance of looking before we leap — implies a functional and effective planning process. The National Environmental Policy Act prescribes a basic form of that rational process, although most of the inside players still resist taking the medicine.

Meaningful environmental planning systems must be established in both the public and private sectors, and at all levels of government — local, state, interstate, national, regional, and international. The design and implementation of these innovative modes of environmental planning will constitute one of the profound and difficult challenges facing humankind during the 21st century.

**CITIZEN ACTION...** Citizen environmentalists over the years have all too often felt like Cassandra. The daughter of King Priam of Troy rejected the seductive blandishments of Apollo, and in retaliation the god burdened her with a terrible curse: she would accurately see the future — the impending onslaughts of storms, droughts, death lurking in the belly of the Trojan horse — but she would not be heeded.

Modern environmentalists' warnings about ecological dangers — acid rain, leukemia from hazardous wastes, the diminishing legacy of natural resources, pollution-caused health and welfare costs — have been important, as are environmentalism's systemic process warnings about narrow-minded decisionmaking, inattention to non-economic values, erosions of civic responsibility and governmental integrity, regressions in the state of the federal courts, the low level of the national information process, and many more. Despite chronic inertia and resistance within corporate and governmental establishments, there has been a significant increase in popular dismay about systemic environmental problems. Environmental concerns can no longer be dismissively caricatured as just a whimsical aesthetic fad, and the minions of the media, though typically superficial and erratic, know that it is important to try to tell the story.

Environmental law, which was built by citizen efforts in legislatures, courts, and agencies, will continue to assure that citizens play a fundamental role in the governance of our society. Because environmental law has become such a major presence in the law books and in public awareness, environmentalism is not likely ever to go away, nor ever again to be the lonely domain of a tiny group of unheard seers.

**THE COMMON HERITAGE OF HUMANKIND...** Our environment is indeed a global public trust. We have inherited from predecessor generations the responsibility for managing and shepherding it for our descendants and all other life forms. The principles of intergenerational equity advanced by Edith Brown Weiss suggest that rights and responsibilities of time, ultimately as a matter of law as well as ethics. If we are to fulfill this fiduciary responsibility successfully, we must overcome what one of the authors of this book has referred to as a modern form of divisive tribalism:

> As the problems of managing the economy and ecology...become ever more complex, subtly-interrelated, pressured and demanding, our processes of legal

and political governance might be expected to become more integrative and comprehensive in scope. Instead, however, there often appears to be a contrary dysfunctional tendency. The more complex and stressed an issue becomes, the more its political actors retreat into a narrow, insulated factionalism that can be viewed as a form of latter-day tribalism.

In framing environmental problems, it helps to conceive of humans and all other forms of life as members of a global tribe, a comprehensive and integrated social unit that transcends the incessant territorial skirmishing of fragmented factions.

The ancient Greeks understood that the core philosophical problem is how to maintain a balance between the individual and the community, between unity and diversity. We must learn to retain the energy and richness of our disparate individual diversities, while creating the national, international, and intergenerational cooperation necessary for ten billion human beings to live in relative harmony, managing a sustainable future for the planet and its natural systems. Facing the future it seems that, fundamentally, we're all in this together.

# REFERENCE MATERIALS

ACKNOWLEDGMENTS OF PERMISSION
TO REPRINT

GLOSSARY OF ACRONYMS

TABLE OF CASES

TABLE OF AUTHORITIES — BOOKS, ARTICLES,
MONOGRAPHS, ETC.

TABLE OF AUTHORITIES — STATUTES, REGULATIONS,
CONVENTIONS, ETC.

STATUTORY CAPSULE APPENDIX

GENERAL INDEX

# ACKNOWLEDGMENTS OF PERMISSION TO REPRINT

*The authors gratefully acknowledge the cooperation and generosity of many authors and publishers who consented to have portions of their works excerpted and reprinted in this book. The works are listed here in alphabetical order by last name of first author. Photographs and charts are acknowledged where they appear in the text.*

C. M. Abraham & Sushila Abraham, The Bhopal Case and the Development of Environmental Law in India, 40 International and Comparative Law Quarterly 334 (1991).

Bruce A. Ackerman and Richard B. Stewart, Comment: Reforming Environmental Law, 37 Stanford Law Review 1333. Reprinted material first appeared in 37 Stanford Law Review at page 1333. Copyright ©1985 by the Board of Trustee of Leland Stanford Junior University. Reprinted by permission of the copyright holder, the authors, and Fred B. Rothman Company.

Robert K. Anderberg, Wall Street Sleaze: How the Hostile Takeover of Pacific Lumber Led to the Clear-Cutting of Coastal Redwoods, 10 Amicus Journal 8. ©1988, The Amicus Journal, a publication of the Natural Resources Defense Council, reprinted with permission.

Hope Babcock, Has the U.S. Supreme Court Finally Drained the Swamp of Takings Jurisprudence? — The Impact of Lucas v. South Carolina Coastal Commission on Wetlands and Coastal Barrier Beaches, 19 Harvard Environmental Law Review 1 (1994).

Patricia Birnie, Whaling: End of an Era, International Whaling Regulation, 1985. Copyright 1985, Oceana Publications, reprinted with permission.

B. Boyer and E. Meidinger, Privatizing Regulatory Enforcement: A Preliminary Assessment of Citizen Suits Under Federal Environmental Laws, 33 Buffalo Law Review 833, 957-961 (1985). Reprinted by permission.

Rachel Carson, Silent Spring (1962). Copyright © 1962 by Rachel L. Carson. Reprinted by permission of Houghton Mifflin Company. All rights reserved.

Coggins, Charles, The Law of Public Rangeland Management IV: FLPMA, PRIA, and the Multiple Use Mandate, 14 Environmental Law 1 (1983). Reprinted by permission of Environmental Law.

John Dernbach, Sustainable Development as a Framework for National Governance (49 Case Western Reserve L.Rev.__ 1998).

Bruce Diamond, Confessions of an Environmental Enforcer, 26 ELR 10253–10254 (1996). Reprinted by permission.

Ray Druley & Girard Ordway, The Toxic Substance Control Act, pages 1–4 (1977). ©1977 by the Bureau of National Affairs, Inc., Washington, D.C. 20037. Reprinted by permission.

John P. Dwyer, The Pathology of Symbolic Legislation, 17 Ecology Law Quarterly 233 (1990). Reprinted by permission.

A. Denny Ellerman, Richard Schmalensee, Paul L. Joskow, Jaun Pablo Montero, Elizabeth M. Bailey, Emissions Trading Under the U.S. Acid Rain Program: Evaluation of Compliance Costs and Allowance Market Performance (MIT, 1997). Reprinted by permission.

Steven Ferrey, Hard Time Criminal Prosecution For Polluters. ©1988, The Amicus Journal, a publication of the Natural Resources Defense Council, reprinted with permission.

James Florio, Congress as Reluctant Regulator: Hazardous Waste Policy in the 1980's; 3 Yale J. on Reg. 351, 353-376 (1986). Reprinted by permission.

S. Frankel, Full Disclosure: Financial Statement Disclosures under CERCLA; 3 Duke Environmental Law 7 Policy Forum 57, 65–67 (1993). Reprinted by permission.

F. Friedman and D. Giannotti, Environmental Self Assessment, in Law of Environmental Protection; Environmental Law Institute, 7-28 to 7-33 (1998). Reprinted by permission.

Theodore L. Garrett, Reinventing EPA Enforcement Natural Resources & Environment 180–182 (Winter, 1998). Reprinted by permission.

William Goldfarb, Health Hazards in The Environment: The Interface of Science and Law, 8 Environmental Law 645. Reprinted by permission of Environmental Law.

Robert W. Hahn and Gordon L. Hester, Marketable Permits: Lessons for Theory and Practice, 16 Ecology L.Q. 361. © 1989 by Ecology Law Quarterly. Reprinted from Ecology Law Quarterly, Vol. 16, No. 2, pp. 361–406 by permission.

G. Hardin, The Tragedy of the Commons, 162 Science 1243–48 (12-13-68). Reprinted by permission of Science magazine.

Samuel Hays, Clean Air: From the 1970 Act to the 1977 Amendments, 17 Duq. L. Rev. 33. Reprinted by permission of the Duquesne Law Review.

Peter Huber, Safety and the Second Best: The Hazards of Public Risk Management in the Courts, 85 Columbia Law Review 277. Copyright ©1985 by the Directors of the Columbia Law Review Association, Inc. All Rights Reserved. This article originally appeared at 85 Colum. L. Rev. 277 (1985) Reprinted by permission.

Victor J. Kimm, The Delaney Clause Dilemma, EPA Journal 39–41 (January 1993).

Jan Laitos, Legal Institutions and Pollution: Some Intersections Between Law and History, 15 Natural Resources Law Journal 423 (1975). Reprinted by permission.

Howard Latin, Ideal versus Real Regulatory Efficiency: Implementation of Uniform Standards and "Fine-Tuning" Regulatory Reforms, 37 Stanford Law Review 1267. Reprinted material first appeared in 37 Stanford Law Review at page 1267. Copyright ©1985 by the Board of Trustee of Leland Stanford Junior University. Reprinted by permission of the copyright holder, the author and Fred B. Rothman Company.

Aldo Leopold, A Sand County Almanac. Copyright © 1949, 1977 by Oxford University Press, Inc. Reprinted with permission.

Michael McElroy, Clean Machines, The New Republic, May 4, 1998 at 24.

Al Meyerhoff, Let's Reform a Failed Food Safety Regime, EPA Journal 42–43 (January 1993).

Marshall Miller, Federal Regulation of Pesticides, in Environmental Law Handbook, 14th Edition pp. 284–301 (1997) Reproduced with permission. The entire publication, Environmental Law Handbook, is available from Government Institutes, Inc., 4 Research Place, suite 200, Rockville, Maryland 20850.

Joel Mintz, Enforcement at the EPA; 13–16 (1995). Reprinted by permission.

Talbot Page, A Generic View of Toxic Chemical and Similar Risks, 7 Ecology Law Quarterly 207 (1978). Reprinted by permission.

Peter Passel, Rebel Economists Add Ecological Cost to Price of Progress, 27 Nov. 1990, C1. Copyright © 1978 by the New York Times Company. Reprinted by permission.

Zygmunt J. B. Plater and William Lund Norine, Through the Looking Glass of Eminent Domain: Exploring the "Arbitrary and Capricious" Test and substantive Rationality Review of Governmental Decisions, 16 B. C. Envtl. Aff. L. Rev. 661. Reprinted by permission of the Boston College Environmental Affairs Law Review.

Zygmunt J. B. Plater, Statutory Violations and Equitable Discretion, 70 Cal. L. Rev. 524. Reprinted by permission of the California Law Review.

David A. Rich, Personal Liability for Hazardous Waste Cleanup: An Examination of CERCLA Section 107, 13 B.C.Env.Aff.L.R. 643. Reprinted by permission of the Boston College Environmental Affairs Law Review.

Mike Royko, A Road. Reprinted by permission of Mike Royko.

J. B. Ruhl, Biodiversity Conservation and the Ever-Expanding Web of Federal Laws Regulating Nonfederal Lands, 66 University of Colorado Law Review 555, 616–623 (1995). Reprinted by permission.

Thomas A. Sancton, What on Earth Are We Doing?, TIME, January 2, 1989. Copyright 1989 The Time Inc. Magazine Company. Reprinted by permission.

# A GLOSSARY OF ACRONYMS AND ABBREVIATIONS IN ENVIRONMENTAL PRACTICE

*Page numbers, where they appear, are references to a description of that term in the text.*

*For further references, see the Tables of Authorities and Index.*

| | | | | |
|---|---|---|---|---|
| AAIA | Airport & Aviation Import Act, 646 | | ASTM | American Society for Testing and Materials, 951 |
| ABEL | Ability to pay for environmental liability, both pollution controls and civil penalties, 917 | | BACT | Best Available Control Technology, 490 |
| ACE | Any Credible Evidence rule (CAA), 918 | | BADT | Best Adequately Demonstrated Pollution Control Technology (CWA), 490 |
| ACO | Administrative Consent Order, 840 | | BANANA | Build Absolutely Nothing Anywhere Near Anybody (see NIMBY), 1144 |
| ACRS | Advisory Committee on Reactor Safe-guards, 419 | | | |
| ADR | Alternate Dispute Resolution, 1144 | | BAT | Best Available Technology, 484, **or**, Best Available Technology Economically Achievable (CWA), 593 |
| AEC | Atomic Energy Commission (now NRC), 335 | | | |
| AICPA | American Institute of Certified Public Accountants, 945 | | BCT | Best Conventional Control Technology (CWA), 501 |
| AID | U.S. Agency for International Development, 1219 | | BDAT | Best Demonstrated Available Technology (RCRA), 790 |
| AMPs | Allotment management plans (grazing), 1132 | | BECC | Border Envtl Coop Comm., (NAFTA), 1223 |
| ANPR | Advanced Notice of Proposed Rulemaking, 667 | | BEN | EPA computer modelled value to determine the economic benefit of noncompliance, 917 |
| APA | Administrative Procedures Act, 376 | | | |
| AQCR | Air Quality Control Regions (CAA), 445 | | BLM | Bureau of Land Management (DoI), 581 |
| AR | Attributable Risk, 262 | | BMP | Best Management Practices, 513 |
| ARARs | Applicable, Relevant, Appropriate Requirements (CERCLA), 844 | | BNA | Bureau of National Affairs |
| | | | BOD | Biological Oxygen Demand (CWA), 503 |
| | | | BPJ | Best Professional Judgment (CWA), 522 |

| | | | | |
|---|---|---|---|---|
| BPT | Best Practicable Control Technology Currently Available (CWA), 517 | | CERCLA | Comprehensive Environmental Response, Compensation, and Liability Act (Superfund), 75, 803 |
| BRZ | Biological Resource Zones (BRZMA), 1142 | | CERCLIS | CERCLA Information System, 886 |
| BRZMA | Biological Resources Zone Management Act, 1140 | | CERES | Coalition for Environmentally Responsible Economics, 959 |
| | | | CFCs | Chlorofluorocarbons, 561, 1198 |
| CAA | Clean Air Act, 75, 441 | | CFR | Code of Federal Regulations |
| CAFO | Concentrated Animal Feeding Operation, 514 | | CGL | Comprehensive General Liability insurance, 834 |
| CAL-LEVs | California-Low-Emission Vehicle, 559 | | CITES | Convention on International Trade in Endangered Species, 1215 |
| CAM | Compliance Assurance Monitoring (CAA), 476 | | CMA | Calcium Magnesium Acetate (road salt substitute), 26, **or**, Cooperative Management Agreement (PRIA), 1113 |
| CAMU | Corrective Action Management Unit (CERCLA), 841 | | | |
| CAP | Capacity Assurance Plan (RCRA), 797 | | CMP | Coastal Management Plan (CZMA) |
| CARB | California Air Resources Board, 559 | | COD | Chemical Oxygen Demand, 504 |
| CBE | Citizens for a Better Environment (*Steel Company*), 939 | | COE, or Corps | U.S. Army Corps of Engineers, 476 |
| CBF | Chesapeake Bay Foundation (*Smithfields*), 61 | | COG | Council of Governments (regional planning), 1163 |
| CBO | Congressional Budget Office, 379 | | Corps | U.S. Army Corps of Engineers, 476 |
| CCC | California Coastal Commission, 339 | | CSD | Commission on Sustainable Development, 1209 |
| CDC | Center for Disease Control, 236 | | CSI | Common Sense Initiative (EPA compliance-assistance program), 927 |
| CEC | Comm. on Envtl Coop, (NAFTA), 1223 | | CSO | Combined Sewer Overflows (CWA), 524 |
| CEM | Continuous Emission Monitors, 920 | | CWA | Clean Water Act (FWPCA), 75, Chap. 9, 501 |
| CEQ | Council on Environmental Quality (Executive Office of the President), 616 | | CZMA | Coastal Zone Management Act, 75, 545 |
| CEQA | California Environmental Quality Act, 663 | | | |

| | |
|---|---|
| DEC | Department of Environmental Conservation (various states), 179 |
| DEIS | Draft Environmental Impact Statement (NEPA), 651 |
| DEQ | Department of Environmental Quality (various states), 1155 |
| DMRs | Discharge Monitoring Reports (CWA), 62, 938 |
| DNR | Department of Natural Resources, 309 |
| DoA | U.S. Department of Agriculture |
| DoI | U.S. Department of Interior |
| DoJ | U.S. Department of Justice |
| DoT | U.S. Department of Transportation, 384 |
| DWP | Department of Water and Power (state-level), 1000 |
| EA | Environmental Assessment (NEPA), 1219 |
| EAJA | Equal Access to Justice Act, 941 |
| EBEs | Environmentally Beneficial Expenditures (CWA), 914 |
| EC | European Community, 1193 |
| ECJ | European Court of Justice, 1193 |
| EDF | Environmental Defense Fund |
| EIS | Environmental Impact Statement (NEPA), 611 |
| ELP | Environmental Leadership Program, 927 |
| ELR | Environmental Law Reporter (by Environmental Law Institute) |
| EO | Executive Order |
| EPA | U.S. Environmental Protection Agency |
| EPCRA | Emergency Planning and Community Right-to-Know Act, 75, 939 |

| | |
|---|---|
| EPCRTKA | EPCRA |
| ERC | Emission Reduction Credits (CAA), 747, **or** BNA Environmental Reporter — Cases |
| ERDA | Energy Research and Development Commission |
| ESA | Endangered Species Act, 75, 927 |
| ESD | Explanation of significant differences (CERCLA), 846 |
| FACA | Federal Advisory Committee Act |
| FACE | For a Cleaner Environment (Woburn citizen group), 236 |
| FASB | Financial Accounting Standards Board, 945 |
| FDA | U.S. Food and Drug Administration, 715 |
| FDF | Fundamentally Different Factors (FDF) (CWA), 520 |
| FEIS | Final Environmental Impact Statement (NEPA), 651 |
| FELA | Federal Employers' Liability Act, 249 |
| FEPCA | Federal Environmental Pesticide Control Act, 248 |
| FERC | Federal Energy Regulatory Commission, 329 |
| FFDCA | Federal Food, Drug, and Cosmetics Act, 75, 716 |
| FHWA | Federal Highway Administration |
| FIFRA | Federal Insecticide, Fungicide, Rodenticide Act, 75, 319 |
| FIP | Federal Implementation Plan (CAA), as in "the state's SIP got shot down, and the state got FIPped," 444 |
| FLPMA | Federal Land Policy and Management Act, 581 |
| FOE | Friends of the Earth, 940 |

| | |
|---|---|
| FOIA | Freedom of Information Act, 414 |
| FONSI | Finding of No Significant Impact (NEPA), 632 |
| Form R | A toxic chemical Release Inventory Reporting Form (EPCRA); TRI information must be filed on a "Form R," 666 |
| FORPLAN | A computerized model to determine LRMPs, 1132 |
| FPC | Federal Power Commission, 399 |
| FQPA | Food Quality Protection Act of 1966      713 |
| FR | Federal Register |
| FRCP | Federal Rules of Civil Procedure |
| FS | U.S. Forest Service (DoA), 1129 |
| FSEIS (or FEISS) | Final Supplemental EIS, 659 |
| FWPCA | Federal Water Pollution Control Act (CWA), 310 |
| FWS | U.S. Fish and Wildlife Service (DoI) |
| GAAP | Generally Accepted Accounting Principles, 945 |
| GAO | General Accounting Office (Comptroller-General, congressional), 379 |
| GATT | General Agreement on Tariffs and Trade, 658, 1220 |
| GDP | Gross Domestic Product, 97 |
| GI-GO | Garbage In-Garbage Out, as in cooking the data in USFS planning documents |
| GNP | Gross National Product, 121 |
| HCFCs | Hydrochlorofluorocarbons |

| | |
|---|---|
| HCPs | Habitat Conservation Plans, 927 |
| HCs | Hydrocarbons, 553 |
| HEW | U.S. Department of Health, Education, and Welfare, 310 |
| HMTA | Hazardous Materials Transportation Act, 77 |
| HREC | Hampton Roads Energy Company (*CARE*), 485 |
| HRS | Hazard Ranking System (CERCLA), 841 |
| HRSD | Hampton Roads Sanit. District, a regional sewerage facility in Virginia, 60 |
| HSWA | Hazardous and Solid Waste Amendments (of 1984), 765 |
| HWIR | Hazardous Waste Identification Rule, 784 |
| I & M | Inspection and Maintenance (CAA auto & truck emissions), 445 |
| ICJ | International Court of Justice (The Hague), 1192 |
| ICOLP | International Cooperative for Ozone Layer Protection, 568 |
| ICS | Individual Control Strategy (CWA), 540; **or** |
| IEL | International Environmental Law, 1207 |
| IGO | Intergovernmental organization |
| IJC | International Joint Commission (US-Canada), 1192 |
| ILM | International Legal Materials document series |
| ILO | International Labor Organization, 1205 |
| Industrial Chemical Survey | (ToSCA), 529 |
| IPM | Integrated Pest Management, 748 |

ISC Interagency Scientific Committee (ESA), 675

ISO International Standards Organization, 927, 1225

ISTEA Intermodal Surface Transportation Efficiency Act, 1143

ITC Interagency Test Committee (ToSCA), 755

ITC Interagency Testing Committee, 737

IWC International Whaling Commission, 1199


LAER Lowest Achievable Emissions Rate (CAA), 445

LAs Load Allocations (CWA), 534

LCA Life Cycle Assessment, 787

LCCA Lead Contamination Control Act (SDWA), 361

LCDC Land Conservation and Development Commission (Ore.), 1163

LDCs Less-Developed Countries, 1196

LDRs Land Disposal Restrictions (CERCLA), 781

LEVs Low Emission Vehicles

LG&E Louisville Gas & Electric, 496

LI Environmental Law Institute

LOS Law of the Sea (treaties), also UNCLOS, 1229

LRMPs Land and Resource Management Plans (NFMA), 1129

LUBA Land Use Board of Appeals, 1096

LULU Locally Undesirable Land Use (see NIMBY), 1143

LUST Leaking Underground Storage Tank, 787

MA Materials Accounting, 667

MACT Maximum Available Control Technology, 446

MBTA Migratory Bird Treaty Act,

MCL Maximum Contaminant Level (CWA), 527

MCLG Maximum Contaminant Level Goals (CWA), 527

MD&A Management's Discussion and Analysis, 944

MDA Medical Device Amendments (*Talbott*), 343

MDB Multilateral Development Bank, 1221

MEPA Michigan Environmental Protection Act, 421

MMT Million Metric Tons, 781

MoA Memorandum of Agreement, 922

MoU Memorandum of Understanding

MPCA Minnesota Pollution Control Agency, 546

MPO Metropolitan Planning Organization (ISTEA), 1143

MSW Municipal Solid Waste, 785

MUSY Multiple Use-Sustained Yield Act, 1108


NAAQS National Ambient Air Quality Standards, 441

NACEPT National Advisory Council for Environmental Policy and Technology, 433

NADBank N. American Dev't Bank (NAFTA), 1223

NAFTA North American Free Trade Agreement, 658

NAM National Association of Manufacturers

| | | | |
|---|---|---|---|
| OSWER | Office of Solid Waste and Energy Response, 918 | RAC | Resource Advisory Council, 581 |
| OTA | Office of Technology Assessment (congressional), 851 | RACHEL | Reauthorization Act Confirms How Everyone's Liable (SARA's unofficial alternate name), 828 |
| OTAG | Ozone Transport Assessment Group, 499 | RACM | Reasonably Available Control Measurements (CAA), 581 |
| OTC | Ozone Transport Commission (mobile sources), 499 | RACT | Reasonably Available Control Technology (CAA), 445 |
| | | RAM | Real-time Air-quality-simulator Model, 465 |
| PCBs | Polychlorinated biphenyls, 128 | RAP | Refuse Act Program permit, 43 |
| PCSD | President's Council on Sustainable Development, 1213 | RARE I, II, III | Roadless Areas Review and Evaluation (Wilderness Act) |
| PIL | Public Interest Litigation | RCRA | Resource Conservation and Recovery Act, Chap. 17, 763 |
| PLLRC | Public Land Law Review Commission, 690 | RD | Remedial Design (CERCLA), 843 |
| PMNs | Pre-marketing Notifications (ToSCA), 756 | RECLAIM | Regional Clean Air Incentives Market, 759 |
| PMNs | Premarket Notifications (ToSCA), 737 | RI/FS | Remedial Investing/Feasibility Study (CERCLA), 843 |
| PNSCP | Pre-Notice Site Cleanup Program (CERCLA), 925 | ROD | Record of Decision, 843 |
| PNSCP | Pre-Notice Site Cleanup Program (Illinois EPA), 925 | RPAR | Rebuttable Presumption Against Registration (ToSCA), 724 |
| POCLAD | Program on Corporations, Law, and Democracy | RR | Relative Risk, 262 |
| POTW | Publicly Owned Treatment Works (CWA), 310 | RRA | Resource Recovery Act, 251 |
| PPA | Pollution Prevention Act, 76 | RRRSC | Relative Risk Reduction Strategies Committee, 151 |
| PRIA | Public Rangelands Improvement Act, 690 | | |
| PRP | Potentially Responsible Party (Superfund), Chap. 18 | SAE | Society of Automotive Engineers, 583 |
| PSD | Prevention of Significant Deterioration, 445 | SARA | Superfund Amendment and Reauthorization Act, 430 |
| | | SAV | Submerged Aquatic Vegetation, 70 |
| QNCR | EPA's Quarterly Noncompliance Reports, e.g. on water pollution permit violations, 69 | SCLDF | Sierra Club Legal Defense Fund, now Earth Justice |
| | | SCS | U. S. Soil Conservation Service (DoA), 621 |

SCS — U.S. Soil Conservation Service

SDWA — Safe Drinking Water Act, 75

SEIS — Supplementary Environmental Impact Statement (NEPA), 648

SEP — Supplemental Environmental Project, 895, 914

SESCA — Michigan Soil Erosion and Sediment Control Act, 1032

SFAS-5 — A Standard of Financial Accounting, incorporating envt'l liabilities, 945–46

SIC — Standard Industrial Classification, 666

SIP — State Implementation Plan (CAA), 444

SIR — Supplemental Information Report (NEPA), 648

SIU — Significant Industrial Users (CWA), 525

SLAPP — Strategic Lawsuits Against Public Policy, 176

SMCRA — Surface Mining Control and Reclamation Act, 236

SMOA — Superfund Memorandum of Agreement, 925

SMP — Supplemental Mitigation Projects (CWA), 481

SO$_2$ — Sulfur Dioxide

SPCC — Spill Prevention, Control, and Countermeasure (CERCLA), 854

SPDES — State Pollutant Discharge Elimination System (CWA), 528

SPP — Stormwater Prevention Plans (CWA), 524

SRF — State Revolving Loan Funds (CWA), 524

Superfund — CERCLA

SWDA — Solid Waste Disposal Act, 75

SWRCB — State Water Resources Control Board, a division of a state DEQ (Cal.), 339

TCE — Trichloroethylene, 236

TCLP — Toxicity Characteristic Leaching Procedure, 770

TCMs — Transportation Control Measures (CAA), 488

TCP — Trichlorophenol, 816

TDRs — Transferable Development Rights, 1167

TIP — Transportation Improvement Plan (ISTEA), 1143

TOC — Total Organic Carbon, 409

ToSCA — Toxic Substance Control Act, 593

TRE — Toxicity Reduction Evaluation (CWA), 540

TRI — Toxics Release Inventory, 666

TRO — Temporary Restraining Order

TSCA — ToSCA

TSD — Treatment, Storage, and Disposal (CERCLA), 764

TSS — Total Suspended Solids; Submerged aquatic vegetation (SAV); Smithfield

TTP — Trial Type Process (APA), 541

TVA — Tennessee Valley Authority, 623

U.S.S.G. — U.S. Sentencing Guidelines, 901

UAA — Use Attainability Analysis (CWA)

UCATA — Uniform Contribution Among Tortfeasors Act, 270

UCFA — Uniform Comparative Fault Act, 270

UIC — Underground Injection Control, 796

UNCED — United Nations Conference on Environment and Development, 1207

UNCLOS — United Nations Law of the Sea (treaties), 1229

UNEP       United Nations Environment
           Programme, 1204

USDA       U.S. Department of
           Agriculture

USFS       U.S. Forest Service (DoA),
           1129

USFS       United States Forest Service
           (see FS), 1129

USGAO      United States General
           Accounting Office (see GAO),
           379

UST        Underground Storage Tank,
           787

VOC        Volatile Organic Compounds,
           558

WET        Whole Effluent Testing
           (CWA), 540

WIPP       Waste Isolation Pilot Project,
           1152

WLA        Wasteload Allocation, 534

WQBEL      Water Quality Based Effluent
           Standards (CWA), 502

WQS        Water Quality Standards
           (CWA), 540

WRC        Water Resources Commission
           (Michigan)

WRP        Wetlands Reserve Program
           (CWA), 546

WSRA       Federal Wild and Scenic
           Rivers Act, 1152

WTO        World Trade Organization

ZEV        Zero Emission Vehicles (auto-
           mobiles), 559

ZID        Zones of Initial Dilution, 539

# TABLE OF CASES

*Cases which are the subject of major excerpts appear in italics, along with the specific page numbers for the excerpted text.*

# Table of Authorities — Books, Articles, Monographs, &c.

# Table of Authorities — Statutes, Regulations, Treaties, Constitutional Articles, &c.

# Capsule Summaries of Major Federal and State Environmental Statutes
## and citations to major international accords

*[Dates first given are dates of first significant enactment. Later significant amendments may be noted. Statutory section references may use the familiarly-used original act numbers, as noted in West's annual Selected Environmental Law Statutes. State statutes are alphabetized by State; citations to treaties and conventions are listed in a separate section below. For many statutes and treaties, page references to coursebook text are in the Glossary of Acronyms reference pages.]*

## INDEX — STATE & FEDERAL STATUTES — U.S. (STATUTORY CAPSULES BELOW)

- APA, Administrative Procedures Act, 5 U.S.C.A. §501 et seq.
- CAA, Clean Air Act
- California — Proposition 65
- CERCLA, (Superfund), Comprehensive Environmental Response, Compensation, and Liability Act
- CWA, Clean Water Act
- CZMA, Coastal Zone Management Act of 1972
- EPCRA, Emergency Planning and Community Right to Know Act
- ESA, Endangered Species Act
- FEPCA, Federal Environmental Pesticide Control Act of 1972, see FIFRA
- FFDCA, Federal Food, Drug, and Cosmetics Act
- FIFRA, Federal Insecticide, Fungicide, Rodenticide Act
- Florida — Critical Areas Act
- FLPMA, Federal Land Policy and Management Act
- FOIA, Freedom of Information Act
- FQPA, Food Quality Protection Act of 1996

- FWPCA, Federal Water Pollution Control Act, see CWA
- Hazardous Substance Act, 15 U.S.C.A. §1261; see RCRA
- HAZMATTranport, Hazardous Materials Transportation Act
- Michigan — MEPA, Michigan Environmental Protection Act
- MMPA, Marine Mammal Protection Act
- Mining Act of 1872
- Mineral Leasing Act of 1920
- NEPA, National Environmental Policy Act
- NFMA, National Forest Management Act
- New Jersey – ECRA,
- New York – Forever Wild provision
- OPA '90, Oil Pollution Act of 1990
- Oregon – LCDC Act
- OSHA, Occupational Health and Safety Administration
- RCRA, Resource Conservation and Recovery Act
- Refuse Act/Rivers and Harbors Appropriations Act of 1899

- RRA, Resource Recovery Act of 1970, see RCRA

- SDWA, Safe Drinking Water Act

- SMCRA, Surface Mining Control and Reclamation Act

- SWDA, Solid Waste Disposal Act of 1965; see RCRA

- ToSCA, Toxic Substance Control Act

- Vermont — Act 250

- Watershed Protection and Flood Prevention Act

- Wild and Scenic Rivers Act

- Wilderness Act of 1964

## INDEX — SOME INTERNATIONAL TREATIES, CONVENTIONS, AND RESOLUTIONS

(Access citations below)

- Agenda 21, and see Rio
- Basel Convention on the Control of Transboundary Movements of Hazardous Wastes and Their Disposal.
- Convention on Biological Diversity.
- Convention on International Trade in Endangered Species of Wild Fauna and Flora (CITES).
- Desertification Convention.
- European Community Directive on the Assessment on the Effects of Certain Public and Private Projects on the Environment.
- General Agreement on Tariffs and Trade (GATT).
- Kyoto Protocol on Global Warming .
- (internat'l) – Montreal Protocol (on Stratospheric Ozone, pursuant to Vienna Convention for the Protection of the Ozone Layer).

- OECD Polluter-Pays Principle.
- Resolution on Large-Scale Pelagic Driftnet Fishing and Its Impact on the Living Marine Resources of the World's Oceans and Seas.
- Rio Declaration on Environment and Development.
- Stockholm Declaration of 1972.
- Straddling Fish Stocks Convention.
- Treaty on the Non-Proliferation of Nuclear Weapons.
- UNCLOS, United Nations Convention on the Law of the Sea.

## STATE AND FEDERAL STATUTORY CAPSULES

### APA

**Administrative Procedures Act, 5 U.S.C.A. §501 et seq. (1946).** Passed virtually unanimously in 1946, the APA is the basic format statute for federal agencies' procedures for making law that affects persons outside the agencies (Title 5), and judicial review thereof (Title 7). It is binding on all federal agencies, and used as a model by most state administrative procedure codes and state courts' review thereof. Title 5 sets out some of the minimum procedural structures for rulemaking and adjudication (both can be done formally, with full TTP, trial-type-process, or informally), and the implicit basis for citizen participation therein. Informal rulemaking under §553 can be requested by any individual under §553(e). Agencies promulgate rules informally by notice-and-comment, with a Fed.Register Notice of Proposed Rulemaking, receipt and processing of written comments, and subsequent publication of a Notice of Final Rulemaking. Further formalization of rulemaking processes occurs with the voluntary or mandatory addition of hearings and other TTP. Title 7 creates a "generous review provisions" that should be given "a hospitable reception" in the reviewing courts. Abbott Labs, See Chapter Seven, 377–383. A valuable authoritative contemporaneous legal interpretation of all provisions of the APA is the U.S. Dep't of Justice, Attorney General's Manual on the APA (1946, reissued 1979). Amendments in the 1960s and '70s added the Freedom of Information Act (§552) and the [less effective] Government-in-the-Sunshine Open Meetings Act (§552a).

### CAA

**Clean Air Act, 42 U.S.C.A. §§7521 et seq. (1970).** Originally passed as 1970 Amendments to a weak prior federal law, the Clean Air Act (CAA) is the leading example of a modern federal regulatory statute governing an environmental medium. Extensively amended in 1977 and 1990, it comprises several coordinated programs that address the major sources of air pollution in the United States. More specifically, it has programs that separately address stationary sources (Title I) and mobile sources of air pollution (Title II); it also has a separate program that addresses the control of hazardous air pollutants (§112). As the first statute of its kind it was and remains the principal model of what is usually referred to as a "command and control" statute. Title II controls mobile source pollution by setting maximum allowable tailpipe emissions for each type of vehicle (autos, light duty trucks, etc.), on a pollutant-by-pollutant basis as a function of the number of miles driven. For stationary sources, the CAA sets standards for emitters on a source-by-source basis, reverse engineered from a planning process that begins with National Ambient Air Quality Standards (NAAQSs)(health-based primary standards, and welfare [property and environment]-based secondary standards) that must be attained for the most common air pollutants. CAA, as a cooperative federalism statute, offers states the leading regulatory role so long as they enact and enforce programs that meet the federally mandated quality standards, under State Implementation Plans (SIPs) that prescribe the allowable emissions from stationary sources that will insure NAAQS attainment. Special sub-programs govern SIPs in areas of "nonattainment" of NAAQS quality levels, and areas to be regulated to prevent significant deterioration (PSD). As of 1990 the CAA implements a large scale emissions trading program for sulfur dioxide emissions as part of the effort to combat acid deposition from long range transport of that pollutant. A second major trading program to combat the effects of NOx pollution is in its formative stages.

## Prop. 65

California "Proposition 65," Safe Drinking Water and Toxic Enforcement Act of 1986, Cal. Health & Safety Code §§25249 ff. (1990). All private businesses with more than ten employees must provide warnings with regard to consumer product exposures, occupational exposures, and environmental exposures to over 650 listed carcinogenic, mutagenic, and teratogenic substances. Carcinogens that pose "no significant risk" of contracting cancer and reproductive toxicants below a maximum risk level are exempted from the warning requirements. Warnings are required to be "clear and reasonble." Although Proposition 65 warnings have, in general, been inconspicuous and uninformative, the statute has been successful in achieving significant product reformulation and pollution prevention because of industry concerns about tort liability and consumer reactions to warnings.

## CERCLA, (Superfund)

Comprehensive Environmental Response, Compensation, and Liability Act, 42 U.S.C.A. §9601 et seq. (1980). Major amendment and reauthorization in 1986 known as the Superfund Amendments and Reauthorization Act (SARA). CERCLA is administered by EPA. Under CERCLA, Congress established the authority to remediate contamination from past waste disposal practices that now endanger, or threaten to endanger, public health or the environment. CERCLA does so primarily (1) by imposing strict liability on those parties responsible for the release of hazardous substances (§107); (2) by creating a "Superfund" to finance actions to clean up such releases (§111); and (3) by imposing the cleanup costs upon the parties who generated and handled hazardous substances. (§§107, 113.) CERCLA also empowers EPA to bring administrative or judicial enforcement actions against responsible parties to force them to perform site remediation. (§106.) In addition to establishing liability rules, CERCLA creates an administrative system to identify sites in need of environmental cleanups, to set priorities among cleanup efforts, to ensure that actions are taken on a site-by-site basis, and to require that planned responses are properly executed. (§105, 121.) CERCLA provides for civil and criminal penalties (CERCLA §103(b), (c), and (d)(2)), natural resource damages (§107(a)(4)(c)), and citizen enforceability (§310).

## CWA

Clean Water Act, 33 U.S.C.A. §1251 et seq. (1972). Originally passed as 1972 Amendments to a weak prior federal law (FWPCA: the Federal Water Pollution Control Act), significantly amended in 1977 and 1987. Authorizes EPA to establish national, uniform technology-based effluent limitations for point sources of pollution (e.g., factories and sewage treatment plants) discharging to waters of the United States, broadly defined to include wetlands. On waterways where technology-based limitations do not meet water quality standards based on fishable-swimmable quality, more stringent water quality-based effluent limitations must be imposed. Effluent limitations are enforced through the National Pollutant Discharge Eliminations System permit program, which has been delegated to 39 states. CWA §404 of the establishes another major permit program governing discharge of dredged and fill material into wetlands and other waters. The CWA does not apply to agricultural nonpoint source pollution (runoff), which accounts for approximately half of the water pollution in the United States. CWA §309 includes a wide range of civil and criminal enforcement mechanisms; and §505 contains a frequently-used citizen suit provision.

## CZMA

**Costal Zone Management Act of 1972, 16 U.S.C.A. §1451 et seq. (1972).** A federal land-use planning statute that authorizes federal matching grants for assisting coastal states, including Great Lakes states, in the development of management programs for the land and water resources of their coastal zones. Once NOAA has approved a state's coastal management program as complying with minimum federal standards, additional federal matching funds become available for administering the program. CZMA contains a "consistency clause" mandating that any federal activity within a state's coastal zone be consistent with that state's approved coastal management program. CZMA §1455b, added in 1990, requires a state with an approved coastal management program to submit a Coastal Nonpoint Pollution Control Program for developing and implementing management measures to control coastal nonpoint source pollution.

## EPCRA

**Emergency Planning and Community Right to Know Act, 42 U.S.C.A. §1100 et seq. (1986).** Establishes the Toxic Release Inventory ("TRI"), which requires certain manufacturing facilities to file annual reports with EPA that identify their use and release of one or more of 650 listed toxic chemicals above yearly threshold amounts. Results of this reporting are available on the Internet ("TOXNET"). Provides for a network of state and local emergency planning committees to facilitate preparation and implementation of emergency response plans.

## ESA

**Endangered Species Act, 16 U.S.C.A. §1531 et seq. (1973).** Legislated in furtherance of C.I.T.E.S., the Convention on International Trade in Endangered Species. ESA is administered by DoI's Fish & Wildlife Service and Commerce's National Marine Fisheries Service. Under ESA§4 the Services place endangered and threatened species on the federal endangered species list, and prepare recovery plans. Under ESA§7 all federal agencies are forbidden to "jeopardize the existence" or destroy "critical habitat" of listed species, and must enter "consultation" with the Services when a Service's Biological Assessment shows that conflicts exist. Agencies can try to get "incidental take" exemptions from the Secretaries. By 1978 amendment a Cabinet-level "God Committee" is given power to issue exemptions after stringent findings of necessity and lack of alternatives. ESA§9 prohibits the "taking" of species by anyone, interpreted to include habitat destruction, thus reaching onto private property interests. By 1982 amendment ESA§10 allows petitioners to get exemptions via "incidental take" permits from the Secretaries, after going through procedures, including HCPs (habitat conservation plans), that can attach strict controls to private project actions if the Secretary so desires. ESA§11 provides severe criminal and civil penalties, and citizen enforceability.

## FDCA

**Federal Food, Drug, and Cosmetics Act, 21 U.S.C.A. §301 et seq. (1938).** The FFDCA is administered by the Food and Drug Administration (FDA, in the Dep't of Health and Human Services). The FFDCA prohibits the introduction or delivery into interstate commerce of any food, drug, device, or cosmetic that is adulterated or misbranded. The FFDCA regulates the occurrence of pesticide residues on raw agricultural commodities. The Delaney Clause §409 prohibits additives that cause cancer when ingested by humans or animals, and until the FQPA of 1996 this was interpreted to include slightly carcinogenic pesticide residues in processed food as well. FFDCA violators face civil and criminal penalties.

## FIFRA

**Federal Insecticide, Fungicide, Rodenticide Act, 7 U.S.C.A. §135 et seq. (1972).** In 1972, Congress passed the Federal Environmental Pesticide Control Act, which amended the first version of FIFRA passed in 1947 by establishing the basic framework for pesticide regulation. FIFRA is administered by EPA. FIFRA requires any person distributing, selling, offering, or receiving any pesticide to register with EPA (§3). EPA will grant registration upon the determination that (i) the pesticide is effective as claimed, (ii) the labeling and other data supplied by the manufacturer meet federal standards, and (iii) the pesticide will not cause unreasonable risks to humans or the environment, taking into account the economic, social, and environmental costs and benefits of intended use. Registrations must also be followed by establishing official tolerance levels that set the maximum permissible exposure for each chemical. Once granted, registrations act as perpetual licenses to market, although they can be cancelled or suspended upon an appropriate showing that a pesticide poses a substantial risk of safety or imminent hazard to man or the environment (§6). Other major amendments to FIFRA were passed in 1975, 1978, 1980, 1988, and 1996, which, in substance, shifted the statutory emphasis from labeling and efficacy to health and the environment and provided EPA with greater flexibility in controlling dangerous chemicals. FIFRA provides civil and criminal penalties (§14) but has no citizen enforceability provision.

## Florida "Critical Areas" Act

**Florida Environmental Land and Water Management Act of 1972, Fla. Stat. Ch. 380.06 (1972).** The state legislature may designate certain environmental resources as "areas of critical concern." After designation, local development plans and regulations must be consistent with development principles established by the State Planning Agency. If local plans or regulations are not consistent with these principles, the State Administration Commission can override local authority and promulgate binding land-use plans and regulations for the area. Four areas, including the Big Cypress Swamp and the Florida Keys, have been designated to date. "Developments of regional impact" must be reviewed by Regional Planning Agencies if the relevant municipal plans and regulations have not been declared to be consistent with statewide planning goals.

## FLPMA

**Federal Land Policy and Management Act, 43 U.S.C.A. §1701 et seq. (1976).** The current organic act for the Bureau of Land Management (BLM) in the Department of the Interior. Applies a multiple use, sustained yield management standard — including scenic, historic, ecological, and environmental uses — to a land-use planning process for allocating private access to the public lands, especially for grazing. Declares that the public lands will remain in public ownership, except where the national interest requires disposal or exchange. FLPMA establishes uniform disposal and exchange procedures. Although declaring that "fair market value" will be charged for private use of public lands, FLPMA, in practice, continues the preferential system of grazing permits and low grazing fees included in the Taylor Grazing Act of 1936.

**FWPCA**

**Federal Water Pollution Control Act, see CWA**

**FOIA**

**Freedom of Information Act, 5 U.S.C.A. §552 (1966).** Provides that each agency state and publish in the Federal Register descriptions of its organization; location where the public may obtain information, make requests, or obtain decisions; nature of all formal and informal procedures; rules of procedure; statements of general policy adopted by the agency; and each amendment, revision, or repeal of the foregoing. Each agency shall make available for public inspection and duplication final opinions and orders made in the adjudication of cases; statements of policy not published in the Federal Register; and adminstrative staff manuals and instructions to staff that affect a member of the public. Fees for the furnishment of documents are limited to reasonable standard charges. Upon any request for records, each agency has ten days after the receipt of any request to determine whether to comply. Each agency has twenty days to determine whether to grant judicial review. Time limits may be extended only under "unusual circumstances." A request for records cannot be extended to matters (1) kept secret in the interest of national defense or foreign policy; (2) related solely to the internal personnel rules and practices of an agency; (3) specifically exempted from disclosure by statute; (4) trade secrets and commercial or financial information obtained from a person; (5) inter-agency or intra-agency memorandums or letters not generally available to the public; (6) disclosure of files which would constitute an unwarranted invasion of personal privacy; (7) records or information compiled for law enforcement purposes to the extent that the production of those records would interfere with an investigation or proceedings of law; (8) contained in or related to examination, operating, or condition reports prepared by or for the use of an agency responsible for the regulation or supervision of financial institutions; or (9) geological and geophysical information and data concerning wells.

**FQPA**

**Food Quality Protection Act of 1996, Pub. L. No. 104-170, 110 Stat. 1489 (1996).** Administered by EPA.Significantly amended both FIFRA and the Federal Food, Drug, and Cosmetic Act ("FFDCA"). Under FQPA, Congress did not comprehensively repeal the Delaney Clause, but did remove pesticide residues from its ambit by amending the FFDCA's definition of "food additive" (the Delaney Clause applies only to food additives) to exclude pesticide residues on raw or processed foods. In particular, Congress determined that a pesticide residue on such food is only to be considered unsafe if EPA has set a tolerance level for the substance and the residue fails to satisfy that level. The EPA is now allowed to grant a tolerance and register a pesticide upon a finding of safety (FQPA §405). Liberalized appeal rights for citizens is part of the compromise struck in eliminating the food additive ban.

**HMTA**

**Hazardous Materials Transportation Act, 49 U.S.C.A. §§5101 et seq. (1976).** HMTA is administered by the Department of Transportation. HMTA covers the transportation of all types of hazardous materials, regardless of whether they are raw materials, chemical intermediates, finished products or wastes. In particular, HMTA governs the safety aspects of transportation, and requires the specification of containers, warning signs, and the like, complementing RCRA. §3003(b) provides that RCRA transporter regulations are to be consistent with DOT regulations under HMTA when the transportation of hazardous waste is subject to both Acts.

**Hazardous Substances Act, see RCRA**

## MMPA

**Marine Mammal Protection Act of 1972, 13 U.S.C.A. § 1361 et seq. (1972).** Devised in response to a Congressional finding that some marine mammals were in danger of depletion or extinction. These mammals were found important to the ecosystem and warranted protection for the health and stability of the marine ecosystem rather than for commercial exploitation. The Secretaries of Commerce and of the Interior bear the responsibilities of this Act for their respective groups of mammals. Title I declares a permanent moratorium on the "taking" and importation of marine mammals or their products. Exceptions to this moratorium include (1) the "taking" of marine mammals for subsistence or for the manufacture of native clothing or crafts by Alaskan natives; (2) the "taking" of marine mammals for scientific research; and (3) additional one-year exceptions for those who might otherwise suffer undue economic hardship. Before the imposition of regulations, public hearings and publications of information are required. This Act directs the Secretary of Treasury to ban the importation of fish or products caught in a manner that causes death or injury in excess of federal standards. Regulations are issued with regard to the "taking" and importation of marine mammals. Violation of regulations and provisions of this Act results in either civil penalties, criminal penalties, or both, but the Act provides no citizen enforcement provision. Commerce and Interior Secretaries are responsible for enforcement, with assistance from the Coast Guard and state officers.

## MEPA

**Michigan Environmental Protection Act, M.C.L.A. §§1701 et seq. (1970).** MEPA represented the legislative embodiment of Professor Joseph Sax' efforts to open up the process of environmental regulation and law to citizen initiatives. In 1994, the law was recodified in a process that intended no substantive changes, but which removed some of MEPA's broad language of citizen enforcement. Along with broad citizen standing provisions, MEPA has two extraordinary substantive aspects: it invites the courts of Michigan to create a common law of environmental quality under the aegis of the statute (which has been done), and it grants courts the authority to ignore or revise administrative standards that the court finds inadequately protective of the public trust in the state's air, water, and natural resources. The limitation of relief to injunctive relief and not awarding attorney's fees to successful plaintiffs are the most probable explanations of why the statute has not been used in large numbers of cases.

## Mining Act of 1872

**General Mining Law of 1872, 30 U.S.C.A. §22 ff. (1872).** Governs hardrock mining on federal land. Declared all non-withdrawn federal land open to hardrock mineral exploration and extraction, without requiring payment of a fee to the United States. Established the system of "discovery – location – patent": (1) staking a mining claim entitles the claimant to an exclusive property right against all but the United States; (2) once a valuable mineral is located in a barely profitable quantity, the property right can be excercised even against the United States; and (3) after several years of negligible work and payment of a modest fee, the claimant can be granted a federal patent that gives her outright ownership of the former claim. Until fairly recently, federal land management agencies claimed to possess no statutory authority to regulate the environmental abuses caused by hardrock mining. Thus, abandoned and polluting mines are frequently encountered in the West.

### Mineral Leasing Act of 1920

**30 U.S.C.A. §181 ff. (1920).** One of several federal statutes – including the Federal Coal Leasing Amendments of 1975, 30 U.S.C.A. §1201 et seq. – that removed fuel minerals from the ambit of the General Mining Law, and established a leasing system administered by the BLM. This statute required competitive bidding for oil leases on federal lands, including the outer continental shelf, and reasonable royalty payments to the federal government. The BLM is authorized to include lease provisions protecting the environment against potential damage caused by extraction and road-construction.

### NEPA

**National Environmental Policy Act of 1969, 42 U.S.C.A. §4321 et seq. (1970).** NEPA §102(2)(c) requires all federal agencies proposing to undertake major actions that might significantly affect the human environment to prepare and circulate Environmental Impact Statements ("EISs"). Under CEQ's NEPA regulations, Draft EISs ("DEISs") must be made available to the public and other federal agencies possessing expertise regarding the proposal. The proposing ("lead") agency may not make irretrievable commitments of resources during the comment period and for 90 days after the publication of the Final Environmental Impact Statement ("FEIS"). NEPA does not contain a citizen suit provision, but the courts have recognized a lawsuit for violation of NEPA's "procedural" obligations — i.e., the responsibility of the lead agency to make full disclosure of the proposal's alternatives and environmental impacts, as well as the agency's balancing process between environmental protection and economic development. Once full disclosure has been made, an agency decision to implement a proposal cannot be overturned in court unless it is found to be arbitrary and capricious.

### NFMA

**National Forest Management Act, 16 U.S.C.A. 1600 et seq. (1976).** Applies a multiple use, sustained yield standard to management of the National Forests by the Forest Service (in the Department of Agriculture). Establishes a planning program requiring the development of Land and Resource Management Plans ("LRMPs"), with which site-specific activities, such as timber sales, must be consistent. NFMA sets vague guidelines, replete with exceptions, for timber harvesting in general, and clearcutting in particular.

### New Jersey ECRA

**Environmental Cleanup Responsibility Act, N.J.S.A. 13: 1K-6 ff. (1983).** This statute administered by the New Jersey Department of Environmental Protection ("DEP") ensures that when industrial properties are sold, any contamination will be discovered and remediated. ECRA applies only to industrial establishments with SIC Code numbers from 22 to 39 (industrial manufacturing), 46-49 (utilities), 51 (nondurable goods wholesaling), and 76 (miscellaneous repair services). ECRA is triggered by transactions such as sale, long-term lease, merger, bankruptcy, or closure. Prior to completing the transaction, the owner or operator must notify DEP, which determines the nature of site sampling that must take place before the transaction may be closed. The owner/operator must submit to DEP the sampling results, along with data regarding the history of the site, environmental permits and violations since 1960, hazardous materials stored onsite, etc. Depending on the condition of the site, the owner/operator must then submit a Negative Declaration or Cleanup (Closure) Plan to DEP for approval. If cleanup is necessary, DEP enters into an Administrative Consent Order with the owner/operator that sets cleanup schedules and ensures that financing (e.g., surety bonds) will be available for the cleanup. Owners and operators are strictly and jointly and severally liable for ECRA compliance. If ECRA is violated, DEP may void the transaction. However, ECRA has proven to be virtually self-executing in that financial institutions will not become involved in transactions that are not ECRA-compliant.

### New York: Forever Wild provision

**Forever Wild provision, McKinney's N.Y. Const. Art 14, § 1, (1894, amended 1995).** This provision dictates that the lands of the state, now owned or later acquired, constituting the Adirondack Park forest preserve as now fixed by law, shall be forever kept as wild forest lands. These lands will not be leased, sold or exchanged, or be taken by any corporation, public or private, nor shall the timber be sold, removed or destroyed. A citizen may bring a suit alleging a violation of this provision pursuant to Article 14 §5.

### OPA '90

**Oil Pollution Act of 1990, 33 U.S.C.A. §§ 2701 et seq. (1990).** First passed in 1990. Modelled on CERCLA, OPA is administered by EPA, in conjunction with the U.S. Coast Guard and the National Oceanic and Atmospheric Administration. Under OPA, Congress imposed strict liability upon owners or operators of vessels or facilities that discharge oil upon waters subject to United States jurisdiction, for cleanup costs and damages caused by such discharges (OPA §1002). However, Congress exempted cargo owners from such liability (OPA §1002). Facilities must develop spill prevention, control, and countermeasure ("SPCC") plans, have them approved by EPA or the Coast Guard, and implement them, or face heavy civil and criminal penalties. OPA '90 explicitly does not preempt state oil spill cleanup laws. Congress also placed limitations on the extent of liability. Under OPA §1004, Congress increased the federal liability limit eight-fold (to $1,200 per gross ton) over the cap previously provided in §311 of the Clean Water Act. Congress also created a $1 billion Oil Spill Liability Trust Fund to pay for cleanup costs in excess of the liability limit, with up to $500 million available for payments for damages to natural resources (OPA §1012). Congress further disavowed any intent to preempt state liability requirements with respect to oil spill and removal activities (OPA §1018). OPA provides for civil and criminal penalties (OPA §§4301-4303) for natural resource damages (OPA §1006).

### Oregon LCDC Act

**Oregon State Land Use Act of 1973, Or Rev. Stat. §197 (1973).** Established a seven member Land Conservation and Development Commission ("LCDC"). All municipalities and counties must prepare comprehensive land-use plans, and adopt and enforce zoning ordinances that are consistent with the statewide planning principles set by the LCDC. Nonconforming local plans or regulations may be rejected by the LCDC.

## OSHA

**Occupational Health and Safety Administration, 29 U.S.C.A. §651 et seq. (1970).** Under OSHA, employers are required to furnish a workplace free from recognized hazards that cause or are likely to cause death or serious physical harm to employees (§5). This act charged the Secretary of Labor with the responsibility of promulgating national consensus safety standards and established federal safety standards (§6). An employer may apply to the Secretary of Labor for a "temporary order" granting a variance from a standard or any provision under this section, establishing that (1) he is unable to comply with a standard because of an unavailability of professional or technical personnel, materials and equipment needed to come into compliance with the standard, or because necessary construction or alteration of facilities cannot be completed by the effective date, (2) he is taking all available steps to safeguard his employees against the hazards covered by the standard, and (3) he has an effective program for coming into compliance with the standard as quickly as practicable. The Secretary of Labor can establish emergency standards when employees are exposed to grave dangers from toxic materials or new hazards. Under §8, federal inspections and investigations of working conditions are authorized. Employees can request an inspection if they believe a safety or health violation exists in the workplace. If an employer is in violation of a standard, a federal inspector is authorized to issue a citation (§9). Section 17 outlines civil penalties for serious violations and willful or repeated violations. The Secretary of Labor can approve a state plan to develop and enforce standards if the plan is found in compliance with OSHA (§18).

## RCRA

**Resource Conservation and Recovery Act of 1976, 42 U.S.C.A. §6901-6992(k) (1976).** RCRA is administered by EPA. RCRA Subtitle C directs EPA to establish regulations ensuring the safe management of hazardous waste from "cradle to grave," in order to eliminate endangerment from present and future waste disposal (§3001)("non-hazardous" waste is much less regulated, under Subtitle D). RCRA was reauthorized and substantially amended by the Hazardous and Solid Waste Amendments of 1984 (HWSA), which imposed new technology-based standards on landfills handling hazardous wastes, required the phaseout of land disposal for certain untreated wastes, and increased federal authority over disposal of nonhazardous solid wastes. In creating "cradle to grave" regulation over hazardous waste, RCRA attempts to regulate all aspects of the life cycle of hazardous waste. RCRA does so by creating a tracking system that follows hazardous waste from the time of generation through treatment, storage, and disposal(§3002-4). RCRA also authorizes EPA to engage in corrective action that can prevent or remedy the release of hazardous wastes (§7003). EPA is authorized to seek significant civil and criminal penalties (§3008). RCRA also provides for citizen enforceability (§7002).

## Refuse Act

**Refuse Act/Rivers and Harbors Appropriations Act of 1899, Pub. L. 97–322, 33 U.S.C.A. §40ff (1899).** A statute passed at the end of the 19th century to facilitate the Corps of Engineers' mission to keep navigation channels free of obstruction. §407 forbade deposit without a permit of refuse in (or on the banks of so as to be washed into) any navigable river or any tributary thereto, which covers virtually the entire U.S. Other sections required permits for physical alterations to watercourses. §411 sets criminal penalties, and a reward for informants who report violations. When in the 20th century the word "refuse" came to be commonly defined to include pollution, the Act became the first effective public law weapon against pollution. Its enforcement federalized the field and changed the way industry regarded pollution. To moderate some of the harshness of the Refuse Act, Congress passed the Clean Water Act of 1972 with far tougher standards than otherwise would have been likely, repalcing some but not all of the Refuse Act's authority in the field. Federal prosecutors use the Act in cases of grave intentional discharges into water bodies.

## SDWA

**Safe Drinking Water Act, 42 U.S.C.A. §3007 et seq. (1974).** The SDWA regulates purveyors of potable water. It authorizes EPA to promulgate technology-based primary and secondary drinking water regulations, containing maximum contaminant levels ("MCLs"), applicable to public water systems, defined as systems that provide water to at least 25 individuals. Primary enforcement responsibility under the SDWA is delegated to states. The SDWA bans new installations of lead drinking water pipes, protects "sole source aquifers" from inconsistent federal actions, and contains a major regulatory program applicable to underground injection of hazardous wastes. With regard to funding, the SDWA authorizes federal grants to states for (1) improving state drinking water regulation, (2) establishing revolving loan funding mechanisms for low-interest loans to upgrade public water systems, and (3) facilitating state planning for the protection of wellhead areas.

## SMCRA

**Surface Mining Control and Reclamation Act, 30 U.S.C.A. §1201 et seq. (1977).** SMCRA established the Office of Surface Mining Reclamation and Enforcement in the Department of Interior, charged with administering the Act's regulatory and reclamation programs, and providing grants and technical assistance to the states. Title IV establishes a self-supporting Abandoned Mine Reclamation Fund to restore land adversely affected by past uncontrolled mining operations. Titles IV and V provide that the state and federal governments are jointly responsibile for acquiring lands and enforcing environmental protection regulations required by the Act. Under Title V, performance standards are set for environmental protection to be met by all major surface mining operations for coal. Title VI protects certain lands regarded as unsuitable for suface mining.

## SWDA

**Solid Waste Disposal Act of 1965, 42 U.S.C.A. §6901 et seq., see RCRA**

## ToSCA

**Toxic Substance Control Act, 15 U.S.C.A. §2601 et seq. (1976).** ToSCA is administered by EPA, and places on manufacturers the responsibility to provide data on the health and environmental effects of chemical substances, and provides EPA with comprehensive authority to prohibit the manufacture, distribution, or use of chemical substances that pose unreasonable risks. ToSCA also requires premanufacture notification of EPA for new chemicals or significant new uses of chemicals. To implement these goals, EPA has the authority (1) to require the testing of chemicals (ToSCA §4), (2) to require the premanufacture review of new chemical substances (ToSCA §5), (3) to limit or prohibit manufacture, use, distribution, and disposal of chemicals (ToSCA §6), and (4) to require recordkeeping and reporting (ToSCA §8). ToSCA provides for civil and criminal penalties (ToSCA §16) as well as citizen enforceability (ToSCA §20.)

### Vermont Act 250

**Vermont State Land Use and Development Act of 1970, Vt. Stat. Ann. Tit. 10 §6001 et seq. (1970).** All developers of public or private construction projects of more than ten acres, and residential units of more than ten units, must obtain a project permit from one of nine regional Environmental District Commissions ("EDCs"). A permit may be denied if it is "detrimental to the public health, safety, or general welfare." The burden is on the applicant to prove that the project will not cause undue environmental degradation. Project opponents bear the burden of proving unreasonable burden on infrastructure or damage to aesthetic or historic sites. A developer must obtain an EDC permit before applying for other necessary local development permits. See Richard Brooks' two-volume treatise, Toward Community Sustainability: Vermont's Act 250 (1997).

### Watershed Act

**Watershed Protection and Flood Prevention Act, 16 U.S.C.A. §1001 et seq. (1954).** The Act initiates a program where the Secretary of Agriculture cooperates with States and local agencies in the construction and financing of comprehensive soil conservation, flood-prevention and water control projects for small watersheds (§3). Under §4, the Secretary of Agriculture is permitted to determine the "proportionate share" of federal assistance that local organizations would receive for such projects. Under §5, the President issues rules and regulations necessary to carry out the purposes of the Act, and coordinates the projects under this Act with existing programs.

### WSRA

**Wild and Scenic Rivers Act, 16 U.S.C.A. 1271 et seq. (1968).** The WSRA establishes the Dep't of Interior's Federal Wild and Scenic Rivers System, including approximately 10,000 miles of designated wild, scenic, and recreational rivers and their corridors within one-quarter mile of each river bank. Dams are prohibited on designated rivers and their tributaries, and all federal activities must be consistent with the river's wild and scenic character. Federal lands abutting designated rivers must also be managed in a consistent manner. The WSRA contains no authority for federal regulation of private activities within the corridor of a designated river, and federal condemnation powers within the corridor are severely limited.

### Wilderness Act of 1964

**16 U.S.C.A. §1131 et seq. (1964).** Establishes the Wilderness System, including extensive Wilderness Areas where all commercial logging and permanent roads and most structures and installations, temporary roads, commercial enterprises, mining, grazing, and use of motorized equipment are prohibited. The following secondary uses are permitted: logging to control insect infestations and fires; mineral exploration; mining claims, mineral leases, and grazing permits obtained before January 1, 1964; commercial services provided by guides, packers, and river runners; and hunting and fishing. The Departments of Interior and Agriculture are the primary agencies. Each addition to the Wilderness System must be made by specific congressional enactment.

## SOME INTERNATIONAL TREATIES, CONVENTIONS, AND RESOLUTIONS — CITATIONS

**Agenda 21, see Report of the UNCED at Rio de Janeiro, June 3-14, 1992.**
United Nations Conference on Environment and Development, Agenda 21, U.N. Doc.
A/CONF. 151/26 (1992); reprinted in The Earth Summit: The United Nations Conference
on Environment and Development (UNCED) 125-508 (Stanley P. Johnson ed. 1993). See
also for annotations, Agenda 21: Earth's Action Plan Annotated (Nicholas A. Robinson
ed. 1993)

**Basel Convention on the Control of Transboundary Movements of Hazardous Wastes
and Their Disposal, Mar. 22, 1989.**
United Nations Environment Programme, UNEP/IG.80/3, March 22, 1989; reprinted in
28 I.L.M. 657 (1989).

**Convention on Biological Diversity, see Report of the UNCED at Rio de Janeiro,
June 3–14, 1992.**
United Nations Convention on Biological Diversity, June 5, 1992, S. Treaty Doc. 20
(1993); reprinted in 31 I.L.M. 818 (1992).

**Convention on International Trade in Endangered Species of Wild Fauna and Flora
(CITES), March 3, 1973.** 27 U.S.T. 1087, 999 U.N.T.S. 243; reprinted in 12 I.L.M. 1085
(1973).

**Desertification Convention**
International Convention to Combat Desertification in Those Countries Experiencing
Serious Drought and/or Desertification, Particularly in Africa, June, 17, 1994, U.N.
General Assembly Doc. A/AC. 241/15/Rev. 7 (1994); reprinted in 33 I.L.M. 1328 (1994).

**European Community Directive on the Assessment on the Effects of Certain Public and
Private Projects on the Environment**
Directive on the Assessment on the Effects of Certain Public and Private Projects on the
Environment, Council Directive 85/337/EEC, 1985 O.J. (L 175/40); 28 Official Journal of
E.C. 40 (1985) L-175.

**General Agreement on Tariffs and Trade (GATT), Oct. 30, 1947.**
T.I.A.S. No. 1700, 61-V Stat. All, 4 Bevans 639, 55 U.N.T.S. 18: Arts. I, III, IX, XI, XX.

**Kyoto Protocol on Global Warming**
Kyoto Protocol to the FCCC, FCCC Conference of the Parties, 3d Sess., UN Doc.
FCCC/CP/1997/L.7/
Add.1 (Dec. 10, 1997); reprinted in 37 I.L.M. 22 (1998). Final version was issued as part of
the Third Conference of the Parties Report, UN Doc. FCCC/CP/1997/7/Add.2.

**Montreal Protocol**
Montreal Protocol on Substances That Deplete the Ozone Layer, Sept. 16, 1987, S. Treaty
Doc. No. 100-10 (1987); reprinted in 26 I.L.M. 1550.

**Pursuant to Vienna Convention for the Protection of the Ozone Layer**
Vienna Convention for the Protection of the Ozone Layer, Mar. 22, 1985, U.N. Doc.
UNEP/Ig.53/Rev.1, S.Treaty Doc. No. 99-9, 99th Cong., 1st Sess. (1985), T.I.A.S. 11097;
reprinted in 26 I.L.M. 1529.

**OECD Polluter-Pays OECD Doc. C(72) 128**
OECD Council Recommendations on Guiding Principles Concerning International
Economic Aspects of Environmental Policies, adopted May 26, 1972, OECD Doc.
C(72)128, Annex A(a) in Organisation For Economic Co-operation and Development,
OECD and the Environment 24 (1986). Also available at 1972 WL 24710 (Int'l Envtl L.
Library).

**Resolution on Large-Scale Pelagic Driftnet Fishing and Its Impact on the Living Marine
Resources of the World's Oceans and Seas**
G.A. Res. 46/215, U.N. GAOR, 46th Sess., U.N. Doc. A/RES/46/215 (1992), Dec. 20,
1991; reprinted in 31 I.L.M. 241 (1992).

**Rio Declaration on Environment and Development, June 13, 1992.**
UNCED Doc. A/CONF.151/5/Rev. 1, June 13, 1992; reprinted in 31 I.L.M. 874 (1992); and
Agenda 21.

**Stockholm Declaration of 1972**
Stockholm Declaration of the United Nations Conference on the Human Environment,
June 16, 1972, Principle 21, U.N. Doc. A/Conf. 48/14 (1972), 11 I.L.M. 1416 (1972).

**Straddling Fish Stocks Convention**
Agreement for the Implementation of the United Nations Convention of the Law of the
Sea of 10 December 1988, Relating to the Conservation and Management of Straddling
Fish Stocks and Highly Migratory Fish Stocks, U.N. GAOR, 6th Sess., pt. x, art. 34, U.N.
Doc. A/CONF.164/37 (1995), reprinted in 34 I.L.M. 1542 (1995).

**Treaty on the Non-Proliferation of Nuclear Weapons, July 1, 1968.**
21 U.S.T. 483, 729 U.N.T.S. 161; reprinted in 7 I.L.M. 811 (1968): Art. III.

**UNCLOS, United Nations Convention on the Law of the Sea, Oct. 7, 1982.**
United Nations, Official Text of the United Nations Convention on the Law of the Sea
with Annexes and Index, U.N. Sales No. E83.v.5 (1983); see also U.N. Doc.
A/Conf.62/122; reprinted in 21 I.L.M. 1261 (1982).

# General Index

*See separate Tables for cases, statutes, books, articles, and authors. [Index is in part computer-generated, and thus errs on the side over over-inclusiveness.]*

ISBN 0–314–21135–7